KEY TO PRONUNCIATIONS

s	see, miss	z	zeal, lazy, those
sh	shoe, push	zh	vision, measure
t	ten, bit		
th	thin, path	ə	occurs only in unaccented syllables and indicates the sound of
th̶	that, other		
ŭ	up, love		
ū	use, cute		
û	urge, burn		a *in* alone
			e *in* system
v	voice, live		i *in* easily
w	west, away		o *in* gallop
y	yes, young		u *in* circus

600 B.C.–A.D. 125

B.C.

600
- Ezekiel
- Babylonians sack Jerusalem
- Exile in Babylon
- Second Isaiah
- Cyrus begins Persian Empire
- Haggai and Zechariah
- Second temple built

500
- Nehemiah rebuilds Jerusalem

400
- The Pentateuch accepted as Scripture (or 550?)
- Alexander conquers East

300
- Egypt rules Palestine
- The Prophets accepted as Scripture

200
- Syria rules Palestine
- Maccabees
- Hasmonean rulers

100
- Romans conquer Palestine
- Herod the Great
- Third temple built

A.D.
- Jesus' ministry
- Paul's ministry, letters
- Romans destroy Jerusalem

100
- The Writings close OT Canon
- Last NT books written

Dear Pastor Temme

I hope this will show in a small way my appreciation for your loving ministry to George and me and all our family.

Pauline Geiger

THE INTERPRETER'S DICTIONARY OF THE BIBLE

EDITORIAL BOARD

THE INTERPRETER'S DICTIONARY OF THE BIBLE

An Illustrated Encyclopedia

IDENTIFYING AND EXPLAINING ALL PROPER NAMES AND
SIGNIFICANT TERMS AND SUBJECTS IN
THE HOLY SCRIPTURES, INCLUDING THE APOCRYPHA
With Attention to Archaeological Discoveries and
Researches into the Life and Faith of Ancient Times

Supplementary Volume

מלאה הארץ דעה את־יהוה

The earth shall be full of the knowledge of the Lord—ISAIAH 11:9*c*

Abingdon
NASHVILLE

Library of Congress Catalog Card Number 62-9387

ISBN 0-687-19269-2

MANUFACTURED BY THE PARTHENON PRESS, AT NASHVILLE, TENNESSEE, UNITED STATES OF AMERICA

CONTRIBUTORS

MOSES ABERBACH, Professor of Hebrew Literature and Jewish History, Baltimore Hebrew College: *Calf, golden; Jeroboam I*

ELIZABETH ACHTEMEIER, Visiting Professor of Homiletics, Union Theological Seminary in Virginia: *Interpretation, history of, nineteenth and twentieth century Christian; Typology*

PETER R. ACKROYD, Samuel Davidson Professor of Old Testament Studies, University of London, King's College: *Chronicles I and II; Kings I and II*

YOHANAN AHARONI, Late Professor of Archaeology, University of Tel Aviv: *Arad; Beth-haccherem; Temples, Semitic*

RAINER ALBERTZ, Research Assistant, University of Heidelberg: *Genesis*

JOHN E. ALSUP, Assistant Professor of New Testament, Austin Presbyterian Theological Seminary: *Theophany in the NT*

RUTH AMIRAN, Field Archaeologist, The Israel Museum, Jerusalem: *Jerusalem*

MICHAEL C. ASTOUR, Professor of Ancient History, Southern Illinois University at Edwardsville: *Amphictyony; Androgyny; Arpad; Calneh; Canneh; Carmel, Mount; Chilmad; Dedan; Eden; Habiru; Hadrach; Hittites; Japheth; Joash; Kir; Kue; La'ir; Mitanni; Sepharad; Sepharvaim; Shalman; Sinites; Succoth-Benoth; Telassar; Yahwe; Ya'udi*

WILLIAM S. BABCOCK, Assistant Professor of Church History, Perkins School of Theology, Southern Methodist University: *Hadrian; Trajan*

LLOYD RICHARD BAILEY, SR., Associate Professor of Old Testament, Duke University Divinity School: *Dor; Gaza; Gehenna; Hebron; Horns of Moses; Pentateuch; Provincial systems in the ancient Near East; Tell; Table of archaeological sites*

WILLIAM BAIRD, Professor of New Testament, Brite Divinity School, Texas Christian University: *Knowledge in the NT; Myth in the NT*

DENIS BALY, Professor, Department of Religion, Kenyon College: *Forest*

JAMES BARR, Professor of Semitic Languages and Literature, University of Manchester: *Biblical theology; Revelation in history; Scripture, authority of*

LEWIS M. BARTH, Dean and Associate Professor of Midrash, Hebrew Union College–Jewish Institute of Religion, Los Angeles: *Synagogue, the Great; Head covering*

MARKUS BARTH, Professor of New Testament, University of Basel: *Baptism*

DOMINIQUE BARTHÉLEMY, O.P., Professor of Old Testament Exegesis, University of Fribourg: *Text, Hebrew, history of*

MEIR BEN-DOV, Deputy Director and Field Director, Jerusalem Archaeological Excavations at the Temple Mount: *Temple of Herod*

CRYSTAL-MARGARET BENNETT, Director, British School of Archaeology in Jerusalem: *Edom; Moab*

HANS DIETER BETZ, Professor of New Testament, School of Theology at Claremont and Claremont Graduate School: *Galatians, Letter to the*

OTTO WILHELM BETZ, Professor of New Testament and Jewish Studies, University of Tübingen: *Essenes*

AVRAHAM BIRAN, Director, Nelson Glueck School of Biblical Archaeology, Hebrew Union College–Jewish Institute of Religion, Jerusalem: *Dan (city)*

KALMAN P. BLAND, Assistant Professor of Religion, Duke University: *Interpretation, history of, early rabbinic; Lectionary cycle, rabbinic*

BERNARD BOYD, Late James A. Gray Professor of Biblical Literature, University of North Carolina: *Beer-sheba; Lachish*

DANIEL A. BOYD, McConnell Fellow, Institute of Islamic Studies, McGill University: *Cnidus; Ephesus; Hierapolis; Laodicea; Miletus; Perga; Pergamum; Phrygia*

ROBERT G. BRATCHER, Research Associate, Translations Department, American Bible Society: *Versions, modern (non-English)*

BEAT BRENK, Professor of History of Art, University of Basel: *Art, early Christian*

HERBERT CHANAN BRICHTO, Professor of Bible, Hebrew Union College, Cincinnati: *Cain and Abel*

RAYMOND E. BROWN, S.S., Auburn Professor of Biblical Studies, Union Theological Seminary, New York: *Genealogy (Christ); Peter; Virgin birth*

FREDERICK FYVIE BRUCE, Rylands Professor of Biblical Criticism and Exegesis, University of Manchester: *Altar, NT; Election, NT; Hebrews, Letter to the*

WALTER BRUEGGEMANN, Professor of Old Testament and Dean of Academic Affairs, Eden Theological Seminary: *Death, theology of; Presence of God, cultic; Yahwist*

ROBERT JEHU BULL, Professor of Church History and Director, Institute for Archaeological Research, Drew University: *Caesarea; Gerizim, Mount*

FREDERICK WM. BUSH, Assistant Professor of Old Testament, Fuller Theological Seminary: *Hurrians*

MARTIN J. BUSS, Associate Professor of Religion, Emory University: *Prophecy in Ancient Israel*

JOSEPH A. CALLAWAY, Professor of Old Testament Archaeology, Southern Baptist Theological Seminary: *Ai*

EDWARD F. CAMPBELL, JR., Francis A. McGaw Professor of Old Testament, McCormick Theological Seminary: *Shechem*

CHARLES E. CARLSTON, Norris Professor of New Testament Interpretation, Andover Newton Theological School: *Form criticism, NT; Parable*

LIONEL CASSON, Professor of Classics, New York University: *Ships and shipping*

DAVID R. CATCHPOLE, Senior Lecturer in Religious Studies, University of Lancaster: *Trial of Jesus*

HENRI CAZELLES, S.S., Professor of Exegesis, Catholic Institute of Paris, and Director of West Semitic Studies, the Practical School of Higher Studies, Sorbonne: *Biblical criticism, OT; Ten Commandments*

CONTRIBUTORS

JAMES HAMILTON CHARLESWORTH, Associate Professor of Religion, Duke University: *Odes of Solomon*

GLENN F. CHESNUT, Associate Professor of Ancient and Medieval History, Indiana University, South Bend: *Eusebius of Caesarea*

RONALD ERNEST CLEMENTS, Lecturer in Divinity, the University of Cambridge: *Exodus, book of*

DAVID J. A. CLINES, Senior Lecturer in Biblical Studies, Department of Biblical Studies, University of Sheffield: *New Year*

GEORGE W. COATS, Professor of Old Testament, Lexington Theological Seminary: *Tradition criticism, OT*

MARTIN A. COHEN, Professor of Jewish History, Hebrew Union College–Jewish Institute of Religion, New York: *Ahijah (prophet); Judah, formation of*

HANS G. CONZELMANN, Professor of New Testament, University of Göttingen: *Wisdom in the NT*

MICHAEL J. COOK, Assistant Professor of Hellenistic and Early Christian Literature, Hebrew Union College–Jewish Institute of Religion, Cincinnati: *Judaism, early rabbinic; Judaism, Hellenistic*

ROBERT B. COOTE, Assistant Professor of Old Testament, San Francisco Theological Seminary: *Tradition, oral*

JAMES L. CRENSHAW, Professor of Old Testament, Vanderbilt University Divinity School: *Prophecy, false; Riddle; Theodicy; Wisdom in the OT*

KEITH CRIM, Professor of Philosophy and Religious Studies, Virginia Commonwealth University: *Anathoth; Arioch; Bebai; Goliath; Versions, English; Virginity, tokens of*

ROBERT E. CROMACK, Professor of English and Director, Program in English Sociolinguistics, State University of New York at Cortland: *Discourse, direct and indirect*

JOHN BRIGGS CURTIS, Lecturer in Physics, Ohio State University: *Corruption, Mount of*

NILS ALSTRUP DAHL, Buckingham Professor of New Testament Criticism and Interpretation, Yale University Divinity School; *Ephesians, Letter to the; Letter*

MITCHELL JOSEPH DAHOOD, S.J., Professor of Ugaritic Language and Literature, Pontifical Biblical Institute, Rome: *Chiasmus; Poetry, Hebrew*

JOHANNES C. DE MOOR, Professor of Semitic Languages and Cultural History of the Ancient Near East, Theological Seminary, Kampen, The Netherlands: *Cloud; Diviner's oak; Ugarit*

WILLIAM G. DEVER, Professor of Near Eastern Archaeology, University of Arizona: *Archaeology; Aroer; Gezer*

CARL E. DEVRIES, Research Associate, The Oriental Institute, University of Chicago: *Egypt, chronology of*

SIMON JOHN DE VRIES, Professor of Old Testament, The Methodist Theological School in Ohio: *Chronology, OT*

ALEXANDER A. DI LELLA, O.F.M., Associate Professor of Semitic Languages, The Catholic University of America: *Daniel*

JOHN R. DONAHUE, S.J., Associate Professor of New Testament, Vanderbilt University Divinity School: *Passion narrative; Pilate, Pontius*

GLANVILLE DOWNEY, Distinguished Professor of History and of Classical Studies, Indiana University: *Antioch (Syrian); Cities, Greco-Roman*

JOHN I. DURHAM, Professor of Hebrew and Old Testament, Southeastern Baptist Theological Seminary: *Credo, ancient Israelite*

BARRY L. EICHLER, Associate Professor of Assyriology, University of Pennsylvania: *Bestiality; Nuzi*

E. EARLE ELLIS, Professor of Biblical Studies, New Brunswick Theological Seminary: *Prophecy in the early church; Spiritual gifts; Tongues, gift of*

ELDON JAY EPP, Harkness Professor of Biblical Literature, Case Western Reserve University: *Textual criticism, NT*

CLAIRE EPSTEIN, Department of Antiquities and Museums, Israel: *Dolmens*

A. JOSEPH EVERSON, Associate Professor of Religion, Luther College, Decorah, Iowa: *Day of the Lord*

WILLIAM R. FARMER, Professor of New Testament, Perkins School of Theology, Southern Methodist University: *Abba; Chreia; Teaching of Jesus*

FRANK CHARLES FENSHAM, Professor in Semitic Languages and Head of the Department, University of Stellenbosch, South Africa: *Zephaniah, book of*

ELISABETH SCHÜSSLER FIORENZA, Associate Professor, New Testament Studies, Notre Dame University: *Eschatology of the NT; First fruits, NT; Revelation, book of*

MICHAEL FISHBANE, Associate Professor of Biblical Studies, Brandeis University: *Abbreviations, Hebrew texts*

RICHARD L. FOLEY, Professor of Theological Studies and Chairman of the Department of Theological Studies, Saint Louis University: *Rome, Christian Monuments*

ROBERT TOMSON FORTNA, Professor of Religion, Vassar College: *Redaction criticism, NT*

FRED O. FRANCIS, Associate Professor of Religion and Head of the Department of Religion, Chapman College: *Colossians, Letter to the*

HARRY THOMAS FRANK, Professor of Religion, Oberlin College: *Herodian fortresses*

DAVID NOEL FREEDMAN, Professor of Biblical Studies, University of Michigan: *Ashdod; Bastard; Canon of the OT; Deuteronomic History, the*

TERENCE E. FRETHEIM, Associate Professor of Old Testament, Luther Theological Seminary, St. Paul: *Elohist; Source criticism, OT*

FRANK S. FRICK, Assistant Professor of Religious Studies, Albion College: *Rechabites*

TIKVA SIMONE FRYMER, Assistant Professor of Near Eastern Studies, Wayne State University: *Ordeal, judicial*

VICTOR PAUL FURNISH, Professor of New Testament, Perkins School of Theology, Southern Methodist University: *Festivals, Greco-Roman; Griesbach hypothesis; Guest room; Interpretation, history of, early Christian, Reformation and Enlightenment; Mark, Secret Gospel of*

W. WARD GASQUE, Associate Professor of New Testament Studies, Regent College, Vancouver: *Boldness; Courage*

DIETER GEORGI, Frothingham Professor of Biblical Studies, Harvard University: *Corinthians, First Letter to the; Corinthians, Second Letter to the; Folly*

JOHN CLARK LOVE GIBSON, Reader in Hebrew and Semitic Languages, University of Edinburgh: *Inscriptions, Semitic*

ALBERT GLOCK, Professor of Archaeology, Birzeit University, West Bank, Occupied Jordan, and Research Professor, Albright Institute of Archaeological Research, Jerusalem: *Taanach*

CYRUS HERZL GORDON, Gottesman Professor of Hebrew, New York University: *Hebrew language*

NORMAN K. GOTTWALD, Professor of Old Testament and of Biblical Theology and Ethics, Graduate Theological Union, Berkeley: *Israel, social and economic development; Nomadism; War, holy*

CARL GRAESSER, JR., Associate Professor of Exegetical Theology, Old Testament, Concordia Seminary in Exile: *Gibeah; Pillar*

JONAS CARL GREENFIELD, Professor of Ancient Semitic Languages, The Hebrew University of Jerusalem: *Aramaic; Philistines*

SAMUEL GREENGUS, Professor of Semitic Languages, Hebrew Union College, Cincinnati: *Law in the OT*

JEAN GRIBOMONT, O.S.B., Professor of Eastern Theology, Pontifical Atheneaum of St. Anselm, Pontifical Urbanian University, and Augustinian Institute, Rome: *Latin versions*

JOSEPH GUTMANN, Professor of Art and Art History, Wayne State University: *Art, early Jewish*

W. C. GWALTNEY, JR., Associate Professor and Chairman of Humane Learning, Milligan College: *Hair; Ishbosheth*

GERRY ALETTA CLARA HADFIELD, Research Scholar, Oundle, England: *Interpretation, history of, medieval Christian*

THOMAS O. HALL, JR., Chairman, Department of Philosophy and Religious Studies, Virginia Commonwealth University: *Army; Herodium; Mareshah*

RONALD M. HALS, Professor of Biblical Theology, Lutheran Theological Seminary, Columbus: *Ruth, book of*

R. G. HAMERTON-KELLY, Dean of the Chapel and Lecturer in Religious Studies and Classics, Stanford University: *Golden Rule; Matthew, Gospel of; Sermon on the Mount*

PAUL L. HAMMER, Professor of New Testament Interpretation, Colgate Rochester/Bexley Hall/Crozer Divinity School: *Inheritance in the NT*

PAUL D. HANSON, Professor of Old Testament, Harvard University: *Apocalypse, genre; Apocalypticism; Zechariah, book of*

MENAHEM HARAN, Y. Kaufmann Professor of Bible Studies, The Hebrew University of Jerusalem: *Exodus, the*

RIVKAH HARRIS, Associate Professor, Department of Religion, Northwestern University: *Woman in the ancient Near East*

GERHARD FRANZ HASEL, Professor of Old Testament and Biblical Theology, Chairman, Department of Old Testament, Andrews University: *Remnant*

DAVID M. HAY, Associate Professor of Religion and Chaplain, Coe College: *Interpretation, history of, NT interpretation of the OT*

JOHN BASIL HENNESSY, Edwin Cuthbert Hall Professor of Middle Eastern Archaeology, University of Sidney: *Bethlehem; Bozrah; Samaria*

RICHARD HYDE HIERS, Professor of Religion, University of Florida: *Kingdom of God*

SIDNEY B. HOENIG, Professor of Jewish History, Yeshiva University: *Interpretation, history of, medieval Jewish*

WILLIAM L. HOLLADAY, Lowry Professor of Old Testament, Andover Newton Theological School: *Grace in the OT; Jeremiah the prophet; New covenant*

SVEND HOLM-NIELSEN, Professor of Old Testament Exegesis, University of Copenhagen: *Shiloh*

SIEGFRIED H. HORN, Professor of Archaeology and History of Antiquity and Dean of the Theological Seminary, Andrews University: *Ammon, Ammonites; Heshbon*

HERBERT BARDWELL HUFFMON, Associate Professor of Old Testament, Drew University: *Amorites; Benjamin; Names, religious significance of; Prophecy in the ancient Near East*

JOHN MARTIN HULL, Lecturer in Education (Theology), University of Birmingham School of Education: *Demons in the NT; Exorcism in the NT*

W. LEE HUMPHREYS, Associate Professor of Religious Studies, University of Tennessee: *Esther, book of; Joseph story, the*

JOHN COOLIDGE HURD, JR., Professor of New Testament, Faculty of Divinity, Trinity College, Toronto: *Chronology, Pauline; Offering for the saints; Paul, the apostle; Thessalonians, First Letter to the; Thessalonians, Second Letter to the*

YAEL ISRAELI, Curator, Department of Hellenistic, Roman, and Byzantine Periods, The Israel Museum, Jerusalem: *Jerusalem*

HOWARD M. JAMIESON, Senior Minister, Tustin Presbyterian Church, Tustin, California: *Ramoth-gilead*

ARTHUR J. JELINEK, Professor of Anthropology, University of Arizona: *Prehistory in the ancient Near East*

GERT JEREMIAS, Professor of New Testament Interpretation, University of Marburg: *Teacher of Righteousness*

JÖRG JEREMIAS, Professor of Old Testament, University of Munich: *Theophany in the OT*

ROBERT JEWETT, Professor of Religious Studies, Morningside College: *Body; Conscience; Flesh in the NT; Man, nature of, in the NT; Spirit*

DAVID JOBLING, Associate Professor of Interpretation, Louisville Presbyterian Theological Seminary: *Ark of Noah; Dominion over creation*

ZECHARIA KALLAI, Associate Professor of Historical Geography of Palestine, The Hebrew University of Jerusalem: *Tribes, territories of*

LEANDER E. KECK, Professor of New Testament, Candler School of Theology and Chairman of the Division of Religion, the Graduate School, Emory University: *Exegesis; Higher criticism; Literary criticism; Lower criticism; Poor*

HOWARD CLARK KEE, Rufus Jones Professor of History of Religion and Department Chairman, Bryn Mawr College: *Aretalogy; Biblical criticism, NT; Divine man; Miracle stories, NT; Miracle workers*

CONTRIBUTORS

KATHLEEN M. KENYON, Sometime Director, British School of Archaeology in Jerusalem: *David, City of*

ANNE DRAFFKORN KILMER, Professor of Assyriology and Dean of Humanities, University of California, Berkeley: *Music*

WILLIAM KLASSEN, Professor of Religion and Head of the Department of Religion, University of Manitoba: *Friend, friendship in the NT; Humility in the NT; Love in the NT*

GÜNTER KLEIN, Professor of New Testament and Director of New Testament Studies, University of Münster: *Righteousness in the NT; Romans, Letter to the*

RALPH W. KLEIN, Associate Professor of the Old Testament, Concordia Seminary in Exile: *Samaria Papyri; Sanballat*

KLAUS KOCH, Professor of Old Testament and History of Ancient Near Eastern Religions, University of Hamburg: *Pseudonymous writing*

MOSHE KOCHAVI, Senior Lecturer in Archaeology, University of Tel Aviv: *Debir*

HELMUT KOESTER, John H. Morison Professor of New Testament Studies and Winn Professor of Ecclesiastical History, Harvard University: *Literature, early Christian; Philippians, Letter to the*

ROBERT A. KRAFT, Associate Professor of Religious Thought, University of Pennsylvania: *Apostolic Fathers; Septuagint § B*

GERHARD KRODEL, Professor of New Testament, Lutheran Theological Seminary, Philadelphia: *Rome, early Christian attitudes toward*

GEORGE M. LANDES, Baldwin Professor of Sacred Literature, Union Theological Seminary, New York: *Jericho; Jonah, book of; Rabbah*

NANCY L. LAPP, Museum Curator and Adjunct Professor, Pittsburgh Theological Seminary: *Pottery*

BENTLEY LAYTON, Visiting Professor of Early Christian Literature, French Biblical and Archaeological School, Jerusalem: *Coptic language*

BARUCH A. LEVINE, Professor of Hebrew, Department of Near Eastern Languages and Literatures, New York University: *Numbers, book of; Priestly writers; Priests*

HAROLD ALTER LIEBOWITZ, Assistant Professor, University of Texas: *Art, ancient Near Eastern*

JAMES E. LINDSEY, JR., Assistant Professor of Philosophy and Religious Studies, Virginia Commonwealth University: *Vengeance*

NORBERT LOHFINK, S.J., Professor of Old Testament Exegesis, St. George Seminary, Frankfort on the Main: *Deuteronomy*

BURKE O. LONG, Associate Professor of Religion, Bowdoin College: *Astrology; Divination in the ancient Near East*

DIETER LÜHRMANN, Professor of New Testament, Theological Seminary, Bethel, Germany: *Sayings of Jesus, form of*

ULRICH LUZ, Professor of New Testament, University of Göttingen: *Discipleship*

P. KYLE MCCARTER, JR., Assistant Professor of Religious Studies, University of Virginia: *Alphabet*

CARMEL MCCARTHY, Lecturer in Semitic Languages, University College, Belfield, Dublin, and in Religious Studies, Carysfort College of Education, Blackrock: *Emendations of the scribes*

DENNIS J. MCCARTHY, S.J., Professor of Old Testament Exegesis, Pontifical Biblical Institute, Rome: *Blood*

THOMAS L. MCCLELLAN, Assistant Professor of History, Bowie State College: *Zarephath; Zarethan*

MARTIN JOSEPH MCNAMARA, M.S.C., Dean of the Faculty of Theology and Professor of Sacred Scripture, Milltown Institute of Philosophy and Theology, Dublin: *Targums*

GEORGE W. MACRAE, S.J., Stillman Professor of Roman Catholic Theological Studies, Harvard University: *Adam, Apocalypse of; Nag Hammadi; Truth, Gospel of*

ABRAHAM J. MALHERBE, Associate Professor of New Testament, Yale University Divinity School: *Cynics; Epictetus*

MAX MALLOWAN, Professor Emeritus of Western Asiatic Archaeology, University of London: *Flood (Genesis)*

HUGO MANTEL, Professor, Department of Jewish History, Bar-Ilan University, Israel: *Sanhedrin*

ELBERT GARRETT MARTIN, Teaching Assistant, Duke University: *Rechabites*

RALPH P. MARTIN, Professor of New Testament, Fuller Theological Seminary: *Liturgical materials, NT*

CARLO MARIA MARTINI, Professor of Introduction to the New Testament, Pontifical Biblical Institute, Rome: *Text, NT*

WILLI MARXSEN, Professor of New Testament, University of Münster: *Christology in the NT*

HERBERT GORDON MAY, Vice-Chairman, RSV Bible Committee: *Authorized versions*

WAYNE A. MEEKS, Professor of Religious Studies, Yale University: *Moses in the NT*

JACQUES-E. MÉNARD, Professor of History of Religions, Catholic Faculty of Theology, University of Strasbourg: *Thomas, Gospel of*

GEORGE EMERY MENDENHALL, Professor of Ancient and Biblical Studies, University of Michigan: *Government, Israelite; Tribe*

HELMUT MERKEL, Lecturer, University of Erlangen: *Zealot*

CAROL L. MEYERS, Thayer Fellow, Albright Institute of Archaeological Research, Jerusalem: *Menorah*

ERIC M. MEYERS, Associate Professor of Religion, Duke University: *Synagogue, architecture; Tomb*

J. MILGROM, Professor of Bible and Near Eastern Studies, University of California, Berkeley: *Atonement in the OT; Atonement, Day of; Encroachment; First fruits, OT; First-born; Heave offering; Leviticus; Repentance in the OT; Sacrifices and Offerings, OT; Sanctification; Wave offering*

JAMES MAXWELL MILLER, Associate Professor of Old Testament Studies, Candler School of Theology, Emory University: *Joshua, book of*

MERRILL P. MILLER, Assistant Professor of Religion, Wesleyan University: *Midrash*

ROLAND E. MURPHY, O. Carm., Professor of Old Testament, Duke University Divinity School: *Song of Songs*

DAVID NEIMAN, Associate Professor, Department of Theology, Boston College: *Council, heavenly; Wind*

F. NEIRYNCK, Professor of New Testament, University of Louvain: *Q; Synoptic problem*

BARCLAY M. NEWMAN, JR., Translations Consultant, United Bible Societies: *Discourse structure*

MURRAY L. NEWMAN, JR., Professor of Old Testament, the Protestant Episcopal Theological Seminary in Virginia: *Moses*

GEORGE W. E. NICKELSBURG, JR., Associate Professor, School of Religion, University of Iowa: *Enoch, book of; Future life in intertestamental literature*

RICHARD A. NORRIS, JR., Professor of Dogmatic Theology, General Theological Seminary: *Immortality*

KEVIN G. O'CONNELL, S.J., Assistant Professor of Old Testament, Weston School of Theology: *Greek versions (minor)*

HARRY M. ORLINSKY, Effie Wise Ochs Professor of Bible, Hebrew Union College–Jewish Institute of Religion, New York: *Virgin*

JEAN OUELLETTE, Associate Professor of Jewish Studies, University of Montreal: *Jacin and Boaz; Sea, molten; Temple of Solomon*

ELAINE HIESEY PAGELS, Associate Professor and Chairman, Department of Religion, Barnard College, Columbia University: *Gnosticism*

SIMON B. PARKER: *Deities, underworld; Familiar spirit; Rephaim*

SHALOM M. PAUL, Senior Lecturer in Bible, The Hebrew University of Jerusalem and University of Tel Aviv: *Mnemonic devices*

MALCOLM L. PEEL, Associate Professor and Chairman, Department of Philosophy and Religion, Coe College: *Resurrection, the Treatise on*

NORMAN PERRIN, Professor of New Testament, University of Chicago: *Mark, Gospel of; Secret, messianic; Son of man*

FRANCIS EDWARD PETERS, Professor of History and Near Eastern Studies, Near East Center, New York University: *Hellenism*

WILLIAM G. POLLARD, Staff Member, Institute for Energy Analysis, Oak Ridge, Tennessee: *Science and the Bible*

MARVIN H. POPE, Professor of Northwest Semitic Languages, Yale University: *Homosexuality; Mot (deity); Rainbow*

KAY PRAG, Honorary Secretary, British School of Archaeology in Jerusalem: *Haran*

M. W. PRAUSNITZ, Archaeologist, Department of Antiquities and Museums, Jerusalem: *Acco; Achzib; Aphek; Beth-shan*

JOHN F. PRIEST, Professor of Religion and Director of Graduate Humanities, Florida State University: *Ecclesiastes; Etiology; Messianic banquet*

JAMES D. PURVIS, Professor of Religion, Boston University: *Samaritan Pentateuch; Samaritans*

ANSON FRANK RAINEY, Associate Professor of Ancient Near Eastern Cultures, University of Tel Aviv, and Associate Professor of Historical Geography, American Institute for Holy Land Studies, Jerusalem: *Anab; Aphekah;*

Beeroth; Dumah (city); Eglon §1; Ekron; Gath; Libnah (city); Madmannah; Rabbah (of Judah); Sela (of Edom); Sites, ancient, identification of; Tell el-Amarna; Ziklag

MERLIN D. REHM, Associate Professor of Semitic Languages, Concordia Senior College, Fort Wayne: *Zadok the priest*

JOHANNES M. RENGER, Oriental Institute Associate Professor of Assyriology, The Oriental Institute, University of Chicago: *Lex talionis*

JOHN REUMANN, Professor of New Testament and Greek and Acting President, Lutheran Theological Seminary, Philadelphia: *Faith, faithfulness in the NT; Reconciliation*

WILLIAM REYBURN, Translations Consultant for the Middle East, United Bible Societies: *Totemism*

H. NEIL RICHARDSON, Professor of Old Testament, Boston University School of Theology and Graduate School: *Cyprus*

PAUL A. RIEMANN, Associate Professor of Old Testament, Drew University Theological School: *Covenant, Mosaic*

HELMER RINGGREN, Professor of Old Testament Exegesis, University of Uppsala: *Monotheism*

ELLIS RIVKIN, Adolph S. Ochs Professor of Jewish History, Hebrew Union College–Jewish Institute of Religion, Cincinnati: *Aaron, Aaronides; Messiah, Jewish; Pharisees*

J. J. M. ROBERTS, Associate Professor, Department of Near Eastern Studies, The Johns Hopkins University: *El (deity); Zaphon, Mount; Zion tradition*

DAVID ROBERTSON, Assistant Professor of English, University of California, Davis: *Literature, Bible as*

WILLIAM CHILDS ROBINSON, JR., Taylor Professor of Biblical Theology and History, Andover Newton Theological School: *Acts, genre; Acts of the Apostles; Luke, Gospel of*

MAX GRAY ROGERS, Professor of Old Testament, Southeastern Baptist Theological Seminary: *Judges, book of*

WAYNE GILBERT ROLLINS, Visiting Professor of Religious Studies, Assumption College: *Philemon, Letter to; Slavery in the NT*

D. GLENN ROSE, Professor of Old Testament, the Graduate Seminary, Phillips University: *Eglon §2*

ROY A. ROSENBERG, Rabbi, Temple of Universal Judaism, New York: *Meteorites; Sedeq (god); Shalem (god); Star of Bethlehem*

JAMES F. ROSS, Professor of Old Testament, the Protestant Episcopal Theological Seminary in Virginia: *Israel, history of*

JAMES A. SANDERS, Auburn Professor of Biblical Studies, Union Theological Seminary, New York: *Hermeneutics; Torah*

SAMUEL SANDMEL, Distinguished Service Professor of Bible and Hellenistic Literature, Hebrew Union College—Jewish Institute of Religion, Cincinnati: *Israel, conceptions of; Jews, NT attitudes toward*

JACK M. SASSON, Associate Professor of Religion, University of North Carolina: *Ass; Generation, seventh; Mari; Twins; Wordplay in the OT*

ERNEST W. SAUNDERS, Professor of New Testament Interpretation, Garrett-Evangelical Theological Seminary: *Resurrection in the NT*

WOLFGANG SCHRAGE, Professor of New Testament, University of Bonn: *Ethics in the NT*

DAVID SCHROEDER, Professor of Bible, Canadian Mennonite Bible College: *Exhortation in the NT; Haustafel; Lists, ethical; Parenesis*

JOHN HOWARD SCHÜTZ, Professor of Religion, University of North Carolina: *Ethos of early Christianity*

JANE AYER SCOTT, Research Associate, Fogg Art Museum, Harvard University: *Sardis*

ROBIN SCROGGS, Professor of New Testament, Chicago Theological Seminary: *Marriage in the NT; Woman in the NT*

BYRON E. SHAFER, Associate Professor of Religious Studies, Fordham University at Lincoln Center: *Sabbath; Week*

PATRICK WM. SKEHAN, Professor of Semitic Languages and Literature, The Catholic University of America: *Ecclesiasticus*

D. MOODY SMITH, JR., Professor of New Testament Interpretation, Duke University Divinity School: *Beloved disciple; John, Gospel of; John, Letters of; Paraclete; Sign in the NT*

ROBERT HOUSTON SMITH, Fox Professor of Religion, The College of Wooster: *Cartography of Palestine; Holy Sepulchre, Church of the; Pella of the Decapolis*

LEIVY SMOLAR, President and Professor of History, Baltimore Hebrew College: *Calf, golden; Jeroboam I*

FRANK M. SNOWDEN, JR., Professor and Chairman, Department of Classics, Howard University: *Blacks, early Christianity and*

GRAYDON F. SNYDER, Dean and Professor of Biblical Studies, Bethany Theological Seminary: *Repentance in the NT*

S. DAVID SPERLING, Associate Professor of Religion, Barnard College, Columbia University: *Mount, mountain; Navel of the earth*

LAWRENCE E. STAGER, Assistant Professor of Syro-Palestinian Archaeology, The Oriental Institute, University of Chicago: *Achor; Agriculture*

WILLIAM FRANKLIN STINESPRING, Professor Emeritus of Old Testament and Semitics, Duke University Divinity School: *Zion, daughter of*

MICHAEL E. STONE, Senior Lecturer in Jewish Hellenism, The Hebrew University of Jerusalem: *Pseudepigrapha; Testaments of the Twelve Patriarchs*

MARGARET E. STOUT, Ph.D. Candidate, Institute of Archaeology, University of London: *Calah*

JAMES F. STRANGE, Associate Professor of Religious Studies, University of South Florida: *Capernaum; Crucifixion, methods of; Magdala*

M. JACK SUGGS, Professor of New Testament, Brite Divinity School, Texas Christian University: *Gospel, genre*

ALBERT C. SUNDBERG, Professor of New Testament Interpretation, Garrett-Evangelical Theological Seminary: *Canon of the NT; Muratorian Fragment*

CHARLES R. TABER, Associate Professor of World Mission and Anthropology, Milligan College: *Divorce; Kinship and family; Marriage; Semantics; Sex, sexual behavior*

ROBERT M. TALBERT, Assistant Professor of History, Philosophy, and Religious Studies, Virginia Commonwealth University: *Assyria and Babylonia; Ben-hadad*

SHEMARYAHU TALMON, Professor of Bible Studies and Dean, Faculty of Humanities, The Hebrew University of Jerusalem: *Conflate readings (OT); Ezra and Nehemiah; Wilderness*

CYNTHIA L. THOMPSON, Assistant Professor of Religion and Classics, Denison University: *Cenchreae; Corinth; Macedonia; Philippi; Thessalonica*

JOHN ALEXANDER THOMPSON, Research Consultant, Translations Department, American Bible Society: *Textual criticism, OT*

RAYMOND D. TINDEL, Oriental Institute Staff, University of Chicago: *Chronology, Mesopotamian (method)*

EMANUEL TOV, Senior Lecturer, Department of Bible, The Hebrew University of Jerusalem: *Septuagint §A*

W. SIBLEY TOWNER, Professor of Old Testament, Union Theological Seminary in Virginia: *Retribution*

PHYLLIS TRIBLE, Hitchcock Professor of the Hebrew Language and Literature, Andover Newton Theological School: *God, nature of, in the OT; Woman in the OT*

MATITIAHU TSEVAT, Professor of Bible, Hebrew Union College, Cincinnati: *King, God as; Rachel's tomb; Shalah (god); Samuel, I and II*

GENE M. TUCKER, Associate Professor of Old Testament, Candler School of Theology, Emory University: *Exegesis; Form criticism, OT*

COLIN M. TURNBULL, Professor of Sociology and Anthropology, Virginia Commonwealth University: *Aging, attitudes toward*

RICHARD PAUL VAGGIONE, Denyer and Johnson Research Student, University of Oxford: *Scythians*

ADAM SIMON VAN DER WOUDE, Professor of Old Testament and Intertestamental Literature, the State University of Groningen: *Melchizedek*

ADRIANUS VAN SELMS, Professor of Semitic Languages, Pretoria University, South Africa: *Jubilee, year of*

JOHN VAN SETERS, Associate Professor in Near Eastern Studies, University of Toronto: *Hyksos; Patriarchs*

EUGENE VANDERPOOL, Professor of Archaeology, Emeritus, American School of Classical Studies at Athens: *Areopagus; Athens*

RONALD A. VEENKER, Associate Professor of Religious Studies, Western Kentucky University: *Hem*

GEZA VERMES, Reader in Jewish Studies and Professorial Fellow of Wolfson College, University of Oxford: *Dead Sea Scrolls; Interpretation, history of, at Qumran and in the Targums; Manuscripts from the Judean desert*

ELEANOR K. VOGEL, Archaeological Researcher and Writer: *Elath; Ezion-geber; Tell el-Kheleifeh*

ARTHUR VÖÖBUS, Professor of Primitive Christianity and Ancient Church History, Lutheran School of Theology at Chicago, and Visiting Professor, Department of Near Eastern Languages and Civilizations, University of Chicago: *Syriac versions*

Ben Zion Wacholder, Professor of Talmud and Rabbinics, Hebrew Union College–Jewish Institute of Religion, Cincinnati: *Sabbatical year*

Mary Katharine Wakeman, Assistant Professor, Department of Religious Studies, University of North Carolina at Greensboro: *Chaos*

James M. Ward, Professor of Old Testament, Perkins School of Theology, Southern Methodist University: *Amos; Discipline, divine; Faith, faithfulness in the OT; Hosea; Isaiah; Micah the Prophet*

Roy Bowen Ward, Chairman and Associate Professor, Department of Religion, Miami University: *James, Letter of*

Gérard E. Weil, Director of the Institute of Hebrew and Cognate Languages and Head of the Biblical and Masoretic Department, Institute for Research and History of Texts, University of Nancy: *Omissions of the scribes; Qere-kethibh*

Moshe Weinfeld, Associate Professor of Bible, The Hebrew University of Jerusalem: *Covenant, Davidic*

Jacob Weingreen, Professor of Hebrew, University of Dublin, and Fellow of Trinity College, Dublin: *Interpretation, history of, within the OT*

Manfred Weippert, Lecturer in Old Testament Studies, University of Tübingen: *Canaan, conquest and settlement of*

Claus Westermann, Professor of Old Testament, University of Heidelberg: *Genesis; Promises to the patriarchs; Psalms, book of*

James Wharton, Pastor, Memorial Drive Presbyterian Church, Houston, Texas: *Redaction criticism, OT*

Roger Norman Whybray, Reader in Theology, University of Hull: *Proverbs, book of*

Ronald J. Williams, Professor of Near Eastern Studies, University of Toronto: *Wisdom in the ancient Near East*

Robert McLachlan Wilson, Professor of New Testament Language and Literature, St. Mary's College, University of St. Andrews: *Apocrypha, NT; Philip, Gospel of*

Walter Wink, Associate Professor of New Testament, Union Theological Seminary, New York: *John the Baptist*

Orval S. Wintermute, Associate Professor, Department of Religion, Duke University: *Cotton; Cush; Fear of Isaac; Serpent; Sites, sacred; Threshold*

Donald J. Wiseman, Professor of Assyriology, University of London: *Alalakh texts*

Frederik Wisse, Research Associate with Teaching Privileges, University of Tübingen: *John, Apocryphon of*

Wilhelm H. Wuellner, Professor of New Testament, Pacific School of Religion and the Graduate Theological Union, Berkeley: *Fishermen (NT)*

Yigael Yadin, Head, Institute of Archaeology, the Hebrew University of Jerusalem: *Bar Kochba; Hazor; Masada; Megiddo*

Edwin M. Yamauchi, Professor of History, Miami University: *Hermetic literature; Mandaeism*

WALTHER THEODOR ZIMMERLI, Professor Emeritus of Old Testament, University of Göttingen: *Ezekiel; Hope in the OT; Slavery in the OT*

BRUCE ZUCHERMAN, Ph.D. Candidate, Department of Near Eastern Languages and Literature, Yale University: *Job, book of*

TRANSLATORS

JOHN E. ALSUP, Assistant Professor of New Testament, Austin Presbyterian Theological Seminary: *Theophany in the OT*

KEITH CRIM, Professor of Philosophy and Religious Studies, Virginia Commonwealth University: *Canaan, conquest and settlement of; Promises to the patriarchs; Psalms, book of; Ten Commandments*

CHARLES C. DICKINSON, Visiting Assistant Professor of Religion and Philosophy, Morris Harvey College: *Art, early Christian; Melchizedek*

PAUL F. DVORAK, Assistant Professor of German, Virginia Commonwealth University: *Ezekiel; Hope in the OT; Romans, Letter to the; Slavery in the OT*

GEOFFREY GRAYSTONE, S. M., Professor of New Testament, Notre Dame Seminary School of Theology, New Orleans: *Latin versions; Qere-kethibh; Text, Hebrew, history of*

BARBARA GRAHAM GREEN, student, Yale Divinity School: *Deuteronomy; Genesis; Pseudonymous writing; Wisdom in the NT; Zealots*

EUGENE A. LAVERDIERE, Assistant Professor, Religious Studies Department, John Carroll University: *Biblical criticism, OT*

REINHOLD MIESSLER, Doctoral Candidate, Theological Seminary, Bethel, Germany: *Sayings of Jesus, form of*

PETER H. NICKELS, O.F.M. Conv., Professor of Sacred Scripture, St. Paul Seminary: *Text, NT*

JOHN E. STEELY, Professor of Historical Theology, Southeastern Baptist Theological Seminary: *Christology in the NT; Discipleship; Ethics in the NT; Righteousness in the NT; Teacher of Righteousness*

WILLIAM FRANKLIN STINESPRING, Professor Emeritus of Old Testament and Semitics, Duke University Divinity School: *Exodus, the*

EDITOR'S PREFACE

Since its publication in 1962, *The Interpreter's Dictionary of the Bible* has established itself as an indispensable reference work. Year after year it has been purchased and used by pastors, priests, rabbis, students, teachers of religion, and, indeed, by persons in many walks of life who are interested in understanding the Bible in its cultural and historical setting.

The Need for a Supplement

During these years, however, scholarly work in all areas of biblical knowledge has moved forward. The publishers of IDB, recognizing the need for keeping the work as nearly up-to-date as possible, decided in 1973 to prepare a supplementary volume that would make necessary additions to articles in areas where new knowledge had been gained and that would present new articles on topics not treated in the original four volumes.

Every effort has been made to preserve the positive values of the project as it was originally planned. The Supplement is directed to the same diverse audience, and consequently the articles range from those of wide general interest to those that are rather technical in nature and will be of major interest to persons who are able to use the ancient languages. The editors have sought to stimulate the interpretation of the Bible through articles on exegesis and hermeneutics and an extended series on the history of interpretation. At the same time they have sought to promote greater understanding of the ancient languages and the history of the transmission of the text.

In recent years there have been many changes in the way the belief structures that are reflected in the Bible are understood. The presuppositions and conclusions of biblical theology have been questioned in the light of a deeper understanding of the Bible, as has our understanding of the relationship of history and revelation. Contemporary discussions of Christology, the wisdom movement, and the role of sacrifice in the OT are also included in the Supplement, to mention only a few areas.

A primary area in which knowledge has increased is archaeology, including the new discipline of underwater archaeology. The supplement contains an article on methods and techniques and a number of articles on specific sites. There is also a major article, SITES, ANCIENT, IDENTIFICATION OF, a complex issue where new data may lead to the modification of long-accepted views.

Inscriptions and written manuscripts in a variety of languages have continued to come to light, and as newly discovered texts are published, scholarly research becomes possible in wider circles. There continues to be great interest in the Dead Sea Scrolls, and intensive study of the Gnostic documents from Nag Hammadi in Egypt has cast new light on the origins and development of Gnosticism. This latter collection of writings had only begun to be available to the scholarly world when IDB was published.

The Contributors

In order to present such a large and varied amount of information, the editors of the Supplement have called on some 271 writers, resident in many parts of the world. Some had contributed to the original four volumes, but many others are younger scholars who have established themselves in recent years. The original work was broadly based and brought together Jewish and Protestant scholars in a fruitful collaboration. In the Supplement many Roman Catholic writers are to be found. A measure of the progress in ecumenical co-operation may be seen in the fact that it now seems surprising that there were no Catholics involved in the preparation of the first four volumes. In addition, many more Israeli writers have contributed to the Supplement than to the original work. Many articles have been written by persons at the forefront of their particular area of research. Others have been prepared by scholars with a broad command of the discipline and wide knowledge beyond their fields.

The Nature of the Supplement

The format is the same as that of IDB, so that the set now consists of five volumes, rather than four. The editors have continued to use the Revised Standard Version as the basis for all citations of scripture, although renderings of more recent translations have been taken into account. The general style of language is the same. Authors and editors have endeavored to achieve a clear, forceful, and contemporary English style, especially where the difficulty of the content makes readability even more desirable. Often this has involved hard decisions as to where technical language ends and jargon begins.

A particularly valuable feature of the original is the presence of a large number of photographs. The Supplement contains eight pages of color photographs, particularly related to the articles on art. Color maps provide cartographic information not found in the first four volumes. In addition, there are a number of black-and-white maps, sketch maps of sites, and a wide selection of black-and-white photographs.

In the bibliographies to the articles, titles of works that have been translated from foreign languages are given in English. The date of publication, however, is that of the original work. If a number of years elapsed before the translation was published, this date is given in brackets, e.g. [ET 1975].

One measure of the Bible's impact on culture is its ability to speak to changing concerns of society. Accordingly, articles deal with the role of Blacks in antiquity, the status of women, attitudes toward various aspects of human sexuality, and the relation of the Bible to modern science. Secular disciplines have been drawn on for new insights from linguistics and anthropology in an attempt to promote interdisciplinary study and co-operation. Questions of the nature of language and of the way linguistic forms and semantic structures change and evolve are vitally important to the study of any ancient document. And just as the men and women of the Bible can be better understood in the light of their contemporary cultures, so too they can be better understood in the light of cultural anthropology and knowledge of the way all human cultures function.

Cross References

In the Supplement an asterisk appears in front of certain entries. This indicates that the article supplements an article of the same or similar title in the first four volumes. For example, the asterisk at CRUCIFIXION, METHOD OF will take you to the original article on CRUCIFIXION, and the one at DEATH, THEOLOGY OF to DEATH.

Similarly, an asterisk before an article in recent printings of the original four volumes will lead to a new article with the same title or a similar one, or to a dummy entry that refers you to one or more articles in the Supplement. In addition there are numerous cross references in the supplementary articles to the original work, e.g., *see* PHILIPPI, or to the supplement, e.g., *see* PHILIPPI[S]. Occasionally a reference to the Supplement takes the form "see supplementary article." Titles of articles found in small capitals in the body of an article may refer to both the original article and the supplementary one.

Procedures

The Editorial Board held its first meeting in the fall of 1973. The first task was to determine the nature and extent of the Supplement within the limits of one volume. Reviews of IDB had pointed out various omissions and occasionally an area where a writer had failed to take into account the full range of scholarly debate. In addition, many users of the encyclopedia had written the publisher and made suggestions. And the editors themselves had particular interests and concerns. We were all mindful of the thorough job that our predecessors, the editors of the first four volumes, had done, and we are grateful for the personal encouragement they gave us as we started to work.

The staff of Abingdon Press gave expert guidance and assistance at every stage. Jean Hager, special projects editor, Jeannie Crawford, editorial assistant for the Supplement, and David Wilson, book design supervisor, deserve particular recognition. Emory Bucke, senior editor of Abingdon Press, provided continuity with the original work, supporting us with encouragement, advice, and a never-failing sense of humor.

A particular source of satisfaction in a work of this sort is being able to draw upon the specialized knowledge and skills of colleagues. Lloyd Bailey, Associate Editor for OT, and Victor Furnish, Associate Editor for NT, brought to the project not only their own experience but the benefits of their wide contacts in the scholarly world.

In Conclusion

In preparing a work of this nature it is easy to become preoccupied with the details of scholarship and to see that scholarship as an end in itself. But the example of our predecessors and the expressions of appreciation from users of the first four volumes led us to see this supplementary work in a larger light, as an aid to the understanding of the Bible, designed to inspire those who use it and to strengthen and deepen their faith. May the joy of study and the delight which knowledge brings lift our eyes to the One who is in every age his people's constant help.

KEITH CRIM

ABBREVIATIONS

(Supplementary)

AAS — *Les annales archéologiques de Syrie*
AB. — Aboth
ABi — Anchor Bible
Acts Pil — Acts of Pilate
ACW — Ancient Christian Writers
AD — *'Αρχαιολογικὸν Δελτίον*
ADAJ — *Annual of the Department of Antiquities of Jordan*
AGJU — Arbeiten zur Geschichte des antiken Judentums und Urchristentums
AHW — W. von Soden, *Akkadisches Handwörterbuch*
AION — *Annali dell'istituto orientale di Napoli*
AJBA — *Australian Journal of Biblical Archaeology*
ALBO — Analecta lovaniensia biblica et orientalia
ALUOS — *Annual of Leeds University Oriental Society*
AnBib — Analecta biblica
ANE — Ancient Near East
ANESTP — J. B. Pritchard, ed., *Ancient Near East Supplementary Texts and Pictures*
Ang — *Angelicum*
ANQ — *Andover Newton Quarterly*
AnSt — *Anatolian Studies*
ANT — Arbeiten zur Neutestamentlichen Textforschung
AOAT — *Alter Orient und Altes Testament*
AOS — American Oriental Series
2-3 ApocBar — Syriac and Greek Apocalypse of Baruch
ApocMos — Apocalypse of Moses
ApocPet — Apocalypse of Peter
APOT — R. H. Charles, ed., *Apocrypha and Pseudepigrapha of the Old Testament*
AR — *Archaeological Reports*
ARM — Archives royales de Mari
ArOr — *Archiv orientální*
AS — Assyrological Studies, University of Chicago
ASNU — Acta seminarii neotestamentici upsaliensis
ASOR Newsletter — *American Schools of Oriental Research Newsletter*
ATANT — Abhandlungen zur Theologie des Alten und Neuen Testaments
ATD — Das Alte Testament Deutsch
AUSS — *Andrews University Seminary Studies*

BAR — *Biblical Archaeologist Reader*
BBB — Bonner biblische Beiträge
BCH — *Bulletin de correspondence hellénique*
BeO — *Bibbia e oriente*
BETL — Bibliotheca Ephemeridum Theologicarum Lovaniensium
BEvT — Beiträge zur evangelischen Theologie
BHTh — Beiträge zur historischen Theologie
BibOr — Biblica et orientalia
BIFAO — *Bulletin de l'institut français d'archéologie orientale*
BIJS — *Bulletin of the Institute of Jewish Studies*
BJRL — *Bulletin of the John Rylands Library*
BJRUL — *Bulletin of the John Rylands University Library*
BKAT — Biblischer Kommentar: Altes Testament
BMB — Bulletin du Musée de Beyrouth
BO — *Bibliotheca orientalis*
BR — *Biblical Research*
BThB — *Biblical Theology Bulletin*
BZNW — Beihefte zur ZNW

CAD — *The Assyrian Dictionary of the Oriental Institute of the University of Chicago*
CAH — *Cambridge Ancient History*
CAT — Commentaire de l'Ancien Testament
CBC — Cambridge Bible Commentary
CBQ — *Catholic Biblical Quarterly*
CBQMS — Catholic Biblical Quarterly Monograph Series
CD or CDC — Cairo Genizah Document of the Damascus Covenanters (The Zadokite Documents)
CHB — *Cambridge History of the Bible*
CJT — *Canadian Journal of Theology*
CNT — Commentaire du Nouveau Testament
CRAI — Comptes Rendus de l'Académie des Inscriptions et Belles-Lettres
CSCO — *Corpus scriptorum christianorum orientalium*
CT — *Cuneiform Texts . . . in the British Museum*
CTA — A. Herdner, *Corpus des tablettes en cuneiformes alphabétiques decovertes à Ras Shamra—Ugarit*
CTM — *Concordia Theological Monthly*

DACL — *Dictionnaire d'archéologie chrétienne et de liturgie*
DBSup — *Dictionnaire de la Bible, Supplément*
DISO — C. F. Jean and J. Hoftijzer, *Dictionnaire des inscriptions sémitiques de l'ouest*
DJD — *Discoveries in the Judean Desert*
DPaR — E. Forrer, *Die Provinzeinteilung des assyrischen Reiches*

EA — Knudtzon and Weber, *Die El-Amarna-Tafeln*
EKL — *Evangelisches Kirchenlexikon*
Ep Aris — Epistle of Aristeas
ETL — *Ephemerides theologicae lovanienses*
EvQ — *Evangelical Quarterly*
EvT — *Evangelische Theologie*

FBBS — Facet Books, Biblical Series
FGH — *Die Fragmente der griechischen Historiker*
FGLP — Forschungen zur Ge-

schichte und Lehre des Protestantismus

GCS — Grieschische christliche Schriftsteller

HALAT — W. Baumgartner *et al., Hebräisches und aramäisches Lexikon zum Alten Testament*
HDSB — *Harvard Divinity School Bulletin*
Hermeneia — Hermeneia, a Critical and Historical Commentary on the Bible
HeyJ — *Heythrop Journal*
HNT — Handbuch zum Neuen Testament
HNTC — Harper's New Testament Commentaries
HTKNT — Herders theologischer Kommentar zum Neuen Testament
HTS — Harvard Theological Studies

IB — *Interpreter's Bible*
IDB — *Interpreter's Dictionary of the Bible*
IG — *Inscriptiones Graecae*
ILN — *Illustrated London News*
Int. — *Interpretation*
IOVC — *The Interpreter's One-Volume Commentary on the Bible*

JAAR — *Journal of the American Academy of Religion*
JANES — *Journal of the Ancient Near East Society*
JB — Jerusalem Bible
JBC — R. E. Brown *et al.* (eds.), *The Jerome Biblical Commentary*
JCS — *Journal of Cuneiform Studies*
JEOL — *Jaarbericht . . . ex oriente lux*
JES — *Journal of Ecumenical Studies*
JESHO — *Journal of the Economic and Social History of the Orient*
JHS — *Journal of Hellenic Studies*
JJPES — *Journal of the Jewish Palestine Exploration Society*
JJS — *Journal of Jewish Studies*
JRS — *Journal of Roman Studies*
JSJ — *Journal for the Study of Judaism*
JSS — *Journal of Semitic Studies*
JSSR — *Journal for the Scientific Study of Religion*
JTC — *Journal for Theology and the Church*
Jud — *Judaica*

K. — Cuneiform Tablets of the Küyünjik Collection, British Museum
KAI — H. Donner and W. Röllig, *Kanaanäische und aramäische Inschriften*

LAB — *Liber Antiquitatum Biblicarum*
LCL — Loeb Classical Library
Leš — *Lešonénu*
LD — Lectio divina
LThQ — *Lexington Theological Quarterly*
LTK — *Lexikon für Theologie und Kirche*
LUA — Lunds universitets årsskrift

MAC — Monumenti di antichità christiana
McCQ — *McCormick Quarterly*
MDOG — Mitteilungen der deutschen Orient-Gesellschaft
MUSJ — *Mélanges de l'université Saint-Joseph*

NAB — New American Bible
NCCHS — R. D. Fuller *et al.* (eds.), *New Catholic Commentary on Holy Scripture*
NCB — New Century Bible
NEB — New English Bible
NICNT — New International Commentary on the New Testament
NovT — *Novum Testamentum*
NovTSup — Novum Testamentum, Supplements
NTAbh — Neutestamentliche Abhandlungen
NTD — Das Neue Testament Deutsch
NTL — The New Testament Library
NTSMS — New Testament Studies Monograph Series
NTTS — New Testament Tools and Studies

Odes Sol. — Odes of Solomon
Or — *Orientalia*
OrAnt — *Oriens antiquus*
OTL — Old Testament Library
OTS — *Oudtestamentische Studiën*

P — Pesher (commentary)
PAPS — *Proceedings of the American Philosophical Society*
PCB — M. Black and H. H. Rowley (eds.), *Peake's Commentary on the Bible*
PEF Annual — *Palestine Exploration Fund, Annual*
PEFQS — *Palestine Exploration Fund, Quarterly Statement*
PG — J. Migne, *Patrologia graeca*
PL — J. Migne, *Patrologia latina*
Prot. Jas. — Protevangelium of James
PRV — *Le Palais Royale d'Ugarit*
PSTJ — *Perkins School of Theology Journal*
P.T. — Palestine Talmud
PW — Pauly-Wissowa, *Realencyclopädie der classischen Altertumswissenschaft*
PWSup — Supplement to PW

1QapGen — Genesis Apocryphon from Qumran Cave I
4QCatena[a] — Nonbiblical MS fragment from Qumran Cave IV
QDAP — *Quarterly of the Department of Antiquities in Palestine*
4QFlor — Florilegium (or Eschatological Midrashim) from Qumran Cave IV
3Q15 — Copper Scroll from Qumran Cave III
4Q181 — A nonbiblical MS fragment from Qumran Cave IV
11QMelch — Melchizedek text from Qumran Cave XI
4QMess ar. — Aramaic "Messianic" text from Qumran Cave IV
4QPhyl — Phylacteries from Qumran Cave IV
4QPrNab — Prayer of Nabonidus from Qumran Cave IV
1QPs — Commentary on Psalms from Qumran Cave I
4QPs — Commentary on Psalms from Qumran Cave IV
11QPs[a] — Psalms scroll from Qumran Cave XI
4Qps-Dan — Fragment of pseudo-Daniel from Qumran Cave IV
4QSam[b] — The second scroll of Samuel from Qumran Cave IV
1QSb — Appendix B (Blessings) to 1QS
4QTest — Testimonia text from Qumran Cave 4
4QTLevi — Testament of Levi from Qumran Cave 4
11QtgJob — Targum of Job from Qumran Cave 11

R — Rawlinson, *Cuneiform Inscriptions of Western Asia*
R. — rabbi

RA — *Revue d'assyriologie et d'archéologie orientale*
RAC — *Reallexikon für Antike und Christentum*
RevExp — *Review and Expositor*
RevScRel — *Revue des sciences religieuses*
RGG — *Religion in Geschichte und Gegenwart*
RGVV — *Religionsgeschichtliche Versuche und Vorarbeiten*
RLA — *Reallexikon der Assyriologie*
RQ — *Revue de Qumran*
RS — Ras Shamra texts
RSO — *Rivista degli studi orientali*

SB — Sources bibliques
SBLDS — Society of Biblical Literature Dissertation Series
SBFLA — *Studii biblici franciscani liber annuus*
SBLMS — Society of Biblical Literature Monograph Series
SBS — Stuttgarter Bibelstudien
SBT — Studies in Biblical Theology
SBU — *Symbolae biblicae upsalienses*
SE — *Studia evangelica I, II, III* (=*TU* 73 [1959], 87 [1964], 88 [1964])
SEÅ — *Svensk exegetisk årsbok*
Sib. Or. — Sibylline Oracles
SJT — *Scottish Journal of Theology*
SPB — Studia postbiblica
SSK — Studien zur spätantiken Kunstgeschichte
ST — *Studia theologica*
StANT — Studien zum Alten und Neuen Testament
StNT — Studien zum Neuen Testament
Str-B — H. Strack and P. Billerbeck, *Kommentar zum Neuen Testament*
StudNeot — Studia neotestamentica
SUNT — Studien zur Umwelt des NT

TBTr — *The Bible Translator*
TCL — *Musée du Louvre . . . Textes cunéiformes*
TDNT — G. Kittel and G. Friedrich (eds.), *Theological Dictionary of the New Testament*
ThRev — *Theologische Revue*
TP — *Theologie und Philosophie*
TS — *Theological Studies*
TsT — *Tijdschrift voor Theologie*
TWAT — G. J. Botterweck and H. Ringgren (eds.), *Theologisches Wörterbuch zum Alten Testament*
TZ — *Theologische Zeitschrift*

UF — *Ugaritische Forschungen*
USQR — *Union Seminary Quarterly Review*
UT — C. H. Gordon, *Ugaritic Textbook*
UUA — *Uppsala universitetsårsskrift*

VAB — Vorderasiatische Bibliothek
VAT — Tablets in the Collections of the Staatliches Museum, Berlin
VC — *Vigiliae christianae*
VD — *Verbum domini*
VTSup — Vetus Testamentum, Supplements

WMANT — Wissenschaftliche Monographien zum Alten und Neuen Testament
WO — *Die Welt des Orients*
WUNT — *Wissenschaftliche Untersuchungen zum Neuen Testament*

YOS — Yale Oriental Series

ZRGG — *Zeitschrift für Religions- und Geistesgeschichte*

A

***AARON, AARONIDES.** The Bible reveals two Aarons: one is the brother and partner of Moses, leading Israel out of Egypt and through the wilderness; the other is a priest and the progenitor of an exclusive priestly class, the "sons of Aaron," or the Aaronides. The prophets and the writers of Samuel and Kings know only the first Aaron, while the second Aaron (and the Aaronides) co-exists with the first Aaron in the Pentateuch, Joshua, and Judges. Scholars have consistently demonstrated that the Aaron who sires a priesthood is to be found exclusively in the so-called P source (*see* Documents; Priestly Writers[S]). Since scripture attests to two Aarons, and since the two Aarons co-exist only in those composite books in which the work of P is evident, it is essential that we first turn to the prophets and those historical books of the Bible which seem to be free of P's handiwork.

It is striking that in the prophets, Aaron, like Moses, is rarely mentioned. Indeed, only Micah 6:4 mentions Aaron as having, along with Moses and Miriam, led Israel out of Egypt. All that we can deduce from this single reference is the fact that Aaron was known to have been a co-leader with Moses and Miriam, and that this co-leadership did not involve either Aaron's being a priest himself or the father of the Aaronides.

When we turn to the book of Kings, we do not learn even this much. Neither Aaron nor the Aaronides is mentioned.

If, then, we extrapolate from the one verse in Micah, our only source predating the promulgation of the Pentateuch (*ca.* 445/*ca.* 397 B.C.; *see* Canon of the OT §2; Canon of the OT[S] §§1, 4*a*), we may give credence to those Pentateuchal texts which picture Aaron as the co-leader with Moses in Egypt and in the wilderness. A similar credence may be given to equivalent texts in Joshua (21:19), I Samuel (12:6, 8), and Psalms (77:20 [H 21]; 105:26).

1. Aaron as brother of Moses and as co-leader. Aaron emerges as a co-leader with Moses when Moses is reluctant to speak because he was "slow of speech and of tongue" (Exod. 4:10). From then on, Aaron not only serves as Moses' spokesman, but plays an active role in his own right (4:27-31; 7:9-10, 19; 8:5-7, 16-17; 9:27-28; 10:3-6). His partnership with Moses is summed up in Exod. 11:10: "Moses and Aaron did all these wonders before Pharaoh; and the Lord hardened Pharaoh's heart."

Following the exodus from Egypt, however, the role of Aaron as Moses' partner diminishes. To be sure, Aaron experiences along with Moses the hostility of the Israelites in the wilderness (Exod. 16:1-3). So, too, it is Aaron whom Moses assigns to tell the people that Yahweh will provide them with food (Exod. 16:9-12). Aaron, like Moses, Nadab, Abihu, and the seventy elders, sees the God of Israel, but is not stricken (24:9-11). Similarly, Aaron, no less than Moses, angers Yahweh by striking the rock (Num. 20:1-13). He is alongside Moses when the spies return with their report (Num. 13:25-29). Indeed, Yahweh commands Aaron, no less than Moses, to communicate to the people Yahweh's curse on the generation of the wilderness (Num. 14:26-38). As punishment, Aaron, along with Moses, is denied the right to lead the people into the Promised Land (Num. 20:12). Yet, aside from these instances, Aaron's role is diminished, giving way to Joshua as the emergent leader. In Exod. 33:7-11 Joshua is Moses' understudy and looks after the tent of meeting; and in Exod. 17:8-16 Joshua leads the people in battle while Aaron and Hur merely hold up Moses' hands. Aaron ascends the mountain with Moses but must stand at a distance with Nadab and Abihu as Moses alone speaks with Yahweh (Exod. 24:1-2). Even more corrosive of Aaron's leadership was his building of the golden calf, which angered Yahweh and Moses (Exod. 32:1-35), and his joining with his sister Miriam in stirring discontent with Moses' leadership—an act of disloyalty which so provoked Yahweh that he struck them both with leprosy for seven days (Num. 12:1-16).

According to Num. 20:22-24, 29, Aaron died on Mount Hor, outside the Promised Land, because he had rebelled against the command of Yahweh. According to Deuteronomy, however, Aaron died either on Mount Hor (Deut. 32:50) or at Moserah (Deut. 10:6).

Aaron figures in Deuteronomy only as the builder of the golden calf, who so roused Yahweh to anger that only the prayerful intercession of Moses spared him (9:20). Otherwise we have only the brief notice of his death.

2. Aaron as progenitor of an exclusive priestly class. A radically different Aaron, however, appears alongside Aaron the co-leader of Moses in the Pentateuch and in Joshua. This Aaron, though still the brother of Moses, is pre-eminently a priest and the progenitor of a priestly family, "the sons of Aaron." It is to this priestly Aaron that much of Exodus (25–31; 35–40), all of Leviticus, and most of Numbers (1–10:25; 15–19; 25–35) are dedicated. Indeed, anyone who reads without interruption the books of Exodus, Leviticus, and Numbers will be struck by the overwhelming focus on Aaron, his sons, the cultus, and the tabernacle. Although Yahweh reveals his will and his teaching through Moses, it is Aaron and the Aaronides who are his prime concern, and the objects of his loving care. Moses pales before Aaron. *See, however,* Leviticus[S] §2.

Thus, whereas Moses was to transmit none of his authority to his sons, Aaron was to transmit his authority to his sons, and his sons only. Whereas God might from time to time speak to Moses face to face, the rules mandating the hegemony of Aaron and his sons over the cultus were proclaimed by Yahweh himself as eternal laws, unto all generations. Whereas Moses was here today, but gone tomorrow, the Aaronides are to enjoy their exclusive prerogatives of priests forever.

Aaron's authority and prestige—as well as that of his sons—are strongly underwritten. It is Yahweh himself who commands Moses, on Sinai, to establish a priestly system under Aaron's exclusive control (Exod. 28:1-2). Aaron and his sons alone are to offer the sacrifices (Num. 18:1-7); and they are to bless the people (Num. 6:22-27). When Korah and his fellow Levites challenge Aaron's supremacy, Yahweh buries Korah and the other rebels alive, and lashes out against Korah's sympathizers with fire and plague which only the firepans of Aaron can halt (Num. 16:1-50 [H 16:1–17:15]). The Levites are to function as Aaron's servants and under penalty of death are prohibited from burning sacrifices on the altar (Num. 18:2-7).

Aaron and his sons are charged with distinguishing between the holy and the profane and with teaching the children of Israel all the statutes which the Lord spoke to them by the hand of Moses (Lev. 10:10-11)—in contrast to Deuteronomy, where the entire tribe of Levi is charged with this authority (Deut. 17:8-11; 18:1-5; 33:10); and in contrast to Ezekiel (44:15-24) where the "sons of Zadok" are to do the distinguishing and the teaching.

Aaron's pre-eminence as the grand expiator is highlighted when Yahweh commands Moses that Aaron alone is to enter the holy of holies on the Day of Atonement (*see* ATONEMENT, DAY OF[S]) to make expiation for the entire people (Lev. 16:1-34). This procedure is to be followed, year in and year out, by Aaron during his lifetime and by his legitimate successor as an everlasting statute (Lev. 16:32-34).

Great care is taken to make certain that Aaron's authority will not be interred with his bones. Yahweh commands Moses and Aaron to ascend the mountain with Eleazar, Aaron's son, and strip Aaron of his garments and put them on Eleazar. Only then is Aaron "gathered to his people" (Num. 20:22-29). Most importantly, Moses turns over the mantle of his leadership to Joshua in the presence of Eleazar and bids Joshua to heed Eleazar the priest—"at his word they shall go out, and at his word they shall come in" (Num. 27:12-23).

The Aaronide texts of the Pentateuch reveal a stage in the religion of Israel that contrasts sharply with other stages. Thus, the tent of meeting of Exod. 33:7-11 bears only a nominal resemblance to the tent of meeting/tabernacle of the Aaronide texts. The former, unlike the latter, is a simple tent without altars or other cultic appurtenances, and the caretaker of the tent is Joshua, not Aaron. Indeed, this tent is set aside for God's revelations to Moses, face to face (Exod. 33:11). Likewise, the cultus envisaged in Exodus (20:24-26) provides for an altar wherever Yahweh causes his name to be mentioned, but makes no provision that this altar be set up either in the tent of meeting or in the tabernacle. No priestly class is endowed with exclusive altar prerogatives, nor is Aaron linked to such an altar in any way. Indeed, Aaron does not participate in the sacrifices following the theophany, even though Moses does (Exod. 24:1-8).

If, then, we set the two Aarons alongside each other, and if we compare the systems with which each is associated, we are struck by their incongruence. Aaron as co-leader never serves in a priestly role, even when Moses on one occasion builds an altar and dashes blood upon it (Exod. 24:3-8). The only cultic act ascribed to this Aaron —the building of the golden calf (Exod. 32)— scarcely commended him for an eternal priesthood! And as for the system which functions alongside this Aaron, it is one which makes no provision for a differentiated priesthood, or an elaborate cultus, or a resplendent tabernacle.

By contrast, the second Aaron is pre-eminently *the* priest, and he functions within a system which is pre-eminently cultic and which focuses on the expiatory role of the altar and the priesthood. It is a system in which the simple tent of meeting where Yahweh spoke to Moses face to face has been transformed into a magnificent tabernacle which Moses is unable to enter (Exod. 40:34-35). It is a system in which not only the three festivals —Passover, Pentecost, and Tabernacles—have become the occasion for massive sacrifices (Lev. 23:4-21, 33-43; Num. 28:16-31; 29:12-40), but each day there is to be a continual offering morning and evening (Num. 28:1-8). It is a system which even operates with a ritual calendar uniquely its own. Unlike Exod. 23:14-17 and Deut. 16:1-17, where no festival has a specified calendar date, and where numbered months are not used, it has fixed dates for Passover and for Tabernacles—not to speak of the first day and tenth day of the seventh month (Lev. 23:23-32; Num. 29:1-11)—and adheres meticulously to a calendar of numbered months. A sacred calendar so radically different from that attested to in the non-Aaronide levels of Exodus and Numbers and in Deuteronomy is a matter of no little significance. Indeed, could a more firm foundation for hegemony in Israel be envisaged than a calendar that bound the people, day in and day out, to the horns of the altar and to the priests who burnt the offerings to Yahweh upon it?

The Aaronide system is thus unique. Yet it is this "new creation" and none of the other systems that was functioning when the books of Chronicles and Ezra were published and when Ben Sirach penned his Ecclesiasticus. Indeed, the author of Chronicles so takes for granted that Yahweh revealed Aaronidism in the wilderness that he does not hesitate to rewrite the history of the monarchical period in such a way that its leitmotiv is the Aaronide priesthood, ministering at the altar in Jerusalem. No less striking is the testimony of Ben Sirach (*ca.* 280 or 180 B.C.). He describes the Aaronide system as a functioning reality which arouses within him exultant joy (Ecclus. 50:1-21).

He not only glorifies Aaron even more than Moses (45:1-22), but he also affirms that Aaron is to have authority over the commandments, statutes, and judgments, and to teach the testimonies and the Law (45:17). And, finally, there is the Samaritan schism (*ca.* 350 B.C.). So firmly established was Aaronidism that when the Samaritans broke away they took Aaronidism along with them. *See* SAMARITANS; SAMARITANS[S].

So effective, in fact, was the Aaronide system that it flourished until the eve of the Hasmonean Revolt, when the legitimate high priest, Onias III (*ca.* 180 B.C.), was ousted by his brother Jason, who bought the office from Antiochus. Although the priestly system was revived following the successful revolt, it no longer enjoyed the hegemony of years gone by. Simon the Hasmonean was elevated to the high priesthood by a great synagogue (I Macc. 14:41), even though he was not of the Aaron, Eleazar, Phineas, Zadok line, and a revolutionary scholar class, the Pharisees, arrogated to themselves the authority over the Law and over the Aaronides (*see* PHARISEES[S]). So long as the temple stood, the sons of Aaron continued to enjoy their exclusive right to offer the sacrifices, but once the second temple was destroyed by the Romans, the Aaronides faded out except for such vestigial honors as having the right to be called first for the reading of the Torah, to bless the congregation on the holidays, and to receive the five shekels on the occasion of the redemption of the first-born son.

Since the triumph of Aaronidism is thus more than amply attested, we are confronted with the problem of how so remarkable a system could have emerged. Unfortunately, the Bible, our only source, is not explicit. All that we can do is to point out that sometime after 445 B.C. (or 397 B.C.) the finalized Pentateuch with its focus on Aaron and the Aaronides became operative and the Aaronides were flourishing, whereas by contrast, as late as Malachi (*ca.* 450 B.C.) neither Aaron as priest or Aaronides as priesthood is anywhere attested to, not even in Ezekiel. We must, therefore, conclude that the Aaronides come to power with the finalized Pentateuch and, as such, are their own creation (*see, however,* ZADOK THE PRIEST[S]). The problem of how the Aaronides coalesced into a class; how they canonized the Pentateuch and promulgated it as the immutable revelation of Moses; and how they convinced the restored community to adopt the Pentateuch as the final and ultimate revelation so that they no longer looked to prophets as the articulators of Yahweh's will, we know not.

Yet we may guardedly speculate on the basis of the Aaronide data in the Pentateuch and on the basis of the operational Aaronidism described by Ben Sirach that a class of priests, denominating themselves the sons of Aaron, emerged to solve a series of problems: (1) the failure of Deuteronomy to serve as a viable blueprint for the restored community; (2) the failure to eliminate prophecy despite the cacophany of prophetic voices urging mutually exclusive plans of action; (3) the need to work out a *modus vivendi* with the Persian rulers that would, in return for Aaronide hegemony, assure them the loyalty of the restored community in a way that neither prophets nor Davidic kings possibly could. And since the historical record leaves no doubt that after a certain date, whether 445 or 397 B.C., the canonized Pentateuch was accepted by Jews everywhere; that the Aaronide priests were exercising hegemony over the Law and the cultus; that scions of David were neither sitting on the throne nor aspiring to it; and that the voice of the prophet was no longer heard in the land; we must conclude that our ignorance of the how, the why, and the when of the triumph of the Aaronides and the canonization of the Pentateuch cannot erase the fact that the Aaronides did indeed do what they did and their stunning success attests that they did it remarkably well.

Bibliography. A. Cody, *A History of OT Priesthood* (1969); Y. Kaufmann, *The Religion of Israel from Its Beginnings to the Babylonian Exile* (1960); E. Rivkin, "Ben Sira—The Bridge Between the Aaronide and Pharisaic Revolutions," *Eretz Israel,* XII (1975), 60-68, and *The Shaping of Jewish History: A Radical New Interpretation* (1971), pp. 3-83; J. Wellhausen, *Prolegomena to The History of Ancient Israel* (repr., 1965).

E. RIVKIN

***ABBA.** J. Jeremias, in his essay "Abba," first published in 1966 and subsequently included in *The Prayers of Jesus,* SBT, 2nd ser., VI (1967), 11-65, concludes that there is no evidence of "my Father" having been used as a personal address to God in early Palestinian Judaism. He argues further that the primitive church's use of the simple "Abba!" (Gal. 4:6; Rom. 8:15*b*-16) in addressing God goes back to Jesus himself, is representative of Jesus' own unique personal piety, and constitutes a central element of his faith in God. Jeremias holds, moreover, that Jesus' private teaching to his disciples included the instruction to address God in this intimate way, especially in prayer. For briefer presentations of Jeremias' views: *The Central Message of the NT* (1965), pp. 9-30, and *NT Theology: The Proclamation of Jesus* (1971), pp. 61-68.

W. R. FARMER

ABBREVIATIONS, HEBREW TEXTS. Abbreviations (abbr.) originated in the desire to conserve space, especially in the use of common words, or in marginal notations (which often were subsequently transferred to the text). When not recognized, they were often subsequently falsely rewritten or misvocalized. Thus numerous textual difficulties have entered the MT.

1. Nonbiblical examples. Simple abbr. are known in Akkad., e.g., *ku* for *kusarikku,* "ram." In a more complex example, Marduk is called ^{d}IM.KU.GAR.RA, an anagram (of Sumerograms) which provides a sentence description of the god's characteristics. This latter type is well attested in Enuma elish VII.

Examples in alphabetic script come from Ugarit and Phoenicia. In the names *b Plṣb l* and ביחמלך the b/ב is an abbr. for *ben,* "son of." In the Lachish inscriptions, ב is an abbr. for בקע, a weight. The Elephantine papyri often have ש for שקל (*shekel*) and ב for בית ("house"). Aramaic endorsements on cuneiform contracts include סראש for Šarrat-Ištar and ארבלסר for 'Arbel-Šarrat. In the DSS (CD

XV.1) אל is an abbr. for אלהים (Elohim) and אד for אדני (Adonay). In coins of John Hyrcanus I and II and Alexander Jannaeus חב is an abbr. for חבר ("community") and היה for היהודים ("the Jews").

2. The MT: method. We may be alerted to a possible abbr. by difficulties of grammar, formulation, or syntax, but authentication must be based upon sound comparative method, sane contextual judgment, and intrinsic probability. Of special importance are variants between the MT and the ancient versions or between parallel or synonymous passages. Although such variants provide material for sound comparative judgment, it is not always possible to decide whether the abbr. is original or merely has been assumed by a translator or copyist. In such cases, intrinsic probability is the only evaluative guide.

3. The MT: classification and examples. ***a. MT vs. the versions.*** i. *Omission of plural termination.* MT I Sam. 28:9 ידעני ("wizard") is likely an abbr. for ידענים (so LXX, Syr., Vulg.; cf. vs. 3; Lev. 19:31; 20:6). An alternative explanation would be error through haplography. *See also* II Sam. 22:44=Ps. 18:44 עם/עמי ("my people"/"people")—cf. עמים in the versions.

ii. *Abbr. of the divine name.* The assumption that י and ה are abbr. for יהוה (YHWH) explains MT Lev. 6:17 [H 10] מאשי ("my offering by fire")—cf. the versions and vs. 18 [H 11] מאשי י(הוה) ("from the Lord's offering by fire"); MT Jer. 6:11 חמת י—cf. LXX המתי; MT Jonah 1:9 עברי אנכי—cf. LXX עבד י אנכי; MT Jer. 25:33 ביום ההוא ("on that day")—cf. LXX 32:33 ביום ה ("on the day of the Lord"); MT Prov. 24:7 פיהו—cf. LXX פי ה.

iii. *Similarity of initial letter(s).* Hence LXX assumes י (עקב) for MT י (שראל) ("Israel") on eleven occasions and ישראל six times for MT יעקב. Note MT Jer. 32:26 אל ירמיהו ("to Jeremiah")—cf. LXX אלי ("to me"); 33:7 MT ישראל—cf. LXX ירושלים; MT Judg. 1:16 העם—cf. LXX העמלקי; MT Isa. 53:8 למו—cf. LXX למות, note the parallelism.

b. Parallel or synonymous MT passages. i. Omission of plural termination. *See* I Sam. 28:9 (§*ai above*).

ii. *Abbr. of the divine name.* Note Ezra 1:3 יהי אלהיו עמו ("may his God be with him")—cf. II Chr. 36:23 יהוה אלהיו עמו ("the Lord his God be with him!"); Josh. 22:16 עדת יהוה—cf. 22:18 עדת ישראל.

iii. *Similarity of initial letter(s).* ליהוה שמרים ("watching kept to the Lord") in Exod. 12:42*b* is difficult, but a parallel is restored if the original was לי(ל) שמרים ("a night of watching") as in vs. 42*a*. ביום in Lev. 14:57 may be a mistaken expansion of בי (for בין) as suggested by 10:10, 11:47, and the versions. Note also II Sam. 24:13 (שבע שנים)—cf. I Chr. 21:12 (שלוש שנים); Jer. 39:5 (אחריהם)—cf. 52:8 (אחרי המלך); Isa. 37:9 (וישמע)—cf. II Kings 19:9 (וישב).

c. Abbr. suggested by MT error or difficulty. i. *Omission of termination.* I Kings 19:11 has the masc. חזק ("strong"), possibly a shortened form of the fem. necessary for agreement with רוח ("wind"). In Prov. 3:18 מאשר may represent a masc. plural.

ii. *The divine name.* The object denoted by לי ("to me") in Exod. 4:25 is obscure. May it be an abbr. for ליהוה? In Num. 16:11 the context requires that Moses say, "against me (עלי) and Aaron" (cf. vs. 3), which likely has been expanded erroneously into the present "against the Lord (על יהוה) and Aaron."

iii. *Initial letters.* Neither Jehoshaphat nor Ahaz was king of Israel, and thus מלך ישראל in II Chr. 21:2 and 28:19 is an error for מלך י(הודה).

d. Abbr. which are notrikons and/or glosses. i. *Notrikon* is a rabbinic term for an anagram or acronym. They may be suggested by the versions: 85 (שמנים וחמשה) in MT I Sam. 22:18—cf. 305 (שלש מאות וחמשה) in LXX; an original שה was read by the former as an abbr., but by the latter as a notrikon. By parallel MT passages: Jer. 7:4 המה ["these"] stands for המקום הזה ["this place"] as is clear from vs. 3; cf. II Chr. 8:11. And by difficulties in the MT: we expect the name Achish son of Maoch [אכיש בן-מעוך] in Ps. 34:1, based upon I Sam. 21:13-15 [H 14-16]; 27:2; the notrikon אבמ has been misunderstood as an abbr. for Abimelech [אבימלך]) based upon 21:1 [H 2]. *See* WORDPLAY IN THE OT[S] §1*b*.

ii. *Glosses,* once marginal or supralinear, are compact lexical, grammatical, and theological notations. Hence in Ps. 61:7 [H 8] the problematic מן (RSV "bid") may have been a marginal notrikon for מלא נון (i.e., the letter *nûn,* in the following verb, is unexpectedly preserved). In Job 34:36 the superfluous אבי may have been a marginal rebuttal in notrikon of vs. 35 ("Job speaks without knowledge"): איוב בדעת ידבר ("Job does speak with knowledge!"). *See* INTERPRETATION, HISTORY OF[S] §A1*b, c.*

e. Abbr. suggested by Masoretic features. i. QERE-KETHIBH. In I Sam. 20:38 החצי ("the arrow") may be an abbr. for the plural found in the marginal *qere.*

ii. *Maqqeph.* When it has neither grammatical nor syntactical function, it may indicate an abbr. (so Perles). In II Kings 2:14 | אף-הוא may indicate איפה הוא ("Where is He?"), parallel to איפה יהוה ("Where is the Lord?").

iii. *Paseq.* In addition to II Kings 2:14 (above), see I Sam. 9:12 | לפניך מהר (". . . just ahead of you. Make haste"), possibly indicating לפניכם הראה ("The Seer is just ahead of you").

Bibliography. B. Kennicott, *Dissertatie* (1783), pp. 49-55; S. Frensdorf, *Ochlah we Ochlah* (1864), sec. 111, 113-15, 119, 126, 154; F. Madden, *Coins of the Jews* (1881), pp. 78-80, 89, 93, 98, 233-45; F. Perles, *Analekten zur Textkritik* (1895), pp. 4-35, and *Analekten* (NF 1922), pp. 1-10; G. R. Driver, "Abbr. in the MT," *Textus,* I (1960), 112-31, and "Once Again Abbr.," *Textus,* IV (1964), 76-94; S. Liberman, *Hellenism in Jewish Palestine* (1962), pp. 68-82. M. FISHBANE

***ACCO.** From 1950 onward excavations were undertaken by the Israel Department of Antiquities, and from 1973 on, by Haifa University and the Department of Antiquities, headed by Dothan and Lindner.

As attested by archaeological remains, Acco (Tell el-Fukhkhar, now called Tel Acco) was founded in the Middle Bronze Age (MB II), probably as early as the nineteenth century B.C. It immediately became one of the greatest coastal cities of the Levant, covering over forty-five acres. Surrounded by an immense earth wall, the city towered above the estuary of the Belus River, which provided a large outer and inner anchorage. Far-flung maritime and commercial connections during the Late Bronze Age are illustrated by the contents of tombs just N of the gates: a scarab and seal of Amen-ophis III (1412-1375 B.C.), as well as a Mitanni cylinder seal. Other finds included a gold diadem of Mycenaean inspiration; Mycenaean pottery; and, most remarkable for the archaeological student, a few Late Minoan IIIB sherds. Pottery of the twelfth to eleventh centuries proves that after the devastations by the Sea Peoples (*see* PHILISTINES), Acco retained its significance. This is also shown by the inability of the tribe of Asher to take Acco or any other maritime city (Judg. 1:31). Except for a short period at the time of David, Acco and Tyre were in possession of the coastal strip until the Assyrian conquest. Hundreds of seals, scarabs, and a few bullae show that Acco, under Assyrian and Babylonian suzerainty, recovered many of its connections overseas.

By the fourth century B.C., a colony of Athenian merchants lived in Acco. The city continued to expand rapidly at the beginning of the Hellenistic age after Tyre had been destroyed by Alexander the Great. In the third century B.C., Acco (now called Ptolemais after Ptolemy II of Egypt, who had seized it in 281 B.C.) had grown to at least twice its former size, stretching W to the coastline. In the Hellenistic age a new harbor was built, and the site became the chief arsenal between Egypt and Syria. Probably as a result of the wars between these two powers over Phoenicia, Acco ceased to be occupied. New city walls were built in the second century B.C., apparently enclosing the peninsula at the tip of the bay and leaving the tell outside.

After the Arab conquest (A.D. 636), Acco dwindled in size. During Crusader times, particularly in the thirteenth century, it regained magnificence, size, and splendor, since it became the major port of entry into the Holy Land.

Bibliography. N. Makhouly and C. N. Johns, *Guide to Acre* (rev. ed., 1946); L. Kadmann, *The Coins of Akko Ptolemais* (1961); M. Dothan, "Accho," *IEJ,* XXIII (1973), 257-58; G. Edelstein, "Tombes de Marchands Guerriers au Nord d'Acre," *Archeologia,* LX (1973), 57-66. M. W. PRAUSNITZ

***ACHOR.** In the Iron Age the Valley of Achor probably designated that desert region some three miles W of the Dead Sea, known today as the Buqe'ah (little valley). It is bounded on the N by the Wadi Dabr-Mukellik system and on the S by the Wadi en-Nar.

The key to this identification is the list of place names and landmarks running from Jerusalem (Jebus) to the Jordan River, delineating the boundary line between the tribal claims of Benjamin to the N and Judah to the S. The southern boundary of Benjamin is defined moving downhill, W to E (Josh. 18:16-19), passing from Jebus to En-rogel in the Kidron Valley, En-shemesh ('En Ḥoḍ), Geliloth, the Stone of Bohan (Ḥajar el-'Eṣba'), Beth-arabah (following Josh. 15:6), and Beth-hoglah (by 'Ain Ḥajla). The northern boundary of Judah is defined moving uphill, E to W (Josh. 15:6-8). These two lists are virtually identical except for one critical difference: the insertion between "Gilgal" (read Geliloth) and the Stone of Bohan in Josh. 15:7 that the boundary of Judah "goes up to Debir (a site on the Wadi Dabr?) from the Valley of Achor." If Wolff were correct in locating Achor N of Jericho near the Wadi en-Nu'eima (surely in Benjaminite territory), it would be most surprising to find the Valley of Achor used as a geographical referent in the description of the boundary line of Judah but not of Benjamin.

When Hosea, in an eschatological motif concerning a second Exodus-Conquest, refers to the Valley of Achor as the "door of hope" (Hos. 2:14-15 [H 16-17]), he may be making an ironic reference to this wilderness area, which served as an important but troublesome thoroughfare leading from Moab to Jerusalem in the Iron Age.

It takes about six hours to ride on horseback from Jerusalem down the Kidron Valley into the Buqe'ah, along the Wadi Dabr to Khirbet Qumran, up to Ḥajla Ford, and across the Jordan River. Before the Roman road was built along the Wadi Qelt from Jerusalem to Jericho, this was the main route between Judah and Moab.

The three rectangular compounds which form a N-S line of paramilitary settlements in the Buqe'ah may be mentioned in the list of six "cities" included in the desert province of Judah (Josh. 15:61-62). Only the southernmost, En-gedi (Tell ej-Jurn), can be identified with certainty. Archaeological evidence from the founding levels of these sites indicates that the desert province list could not have been compiled before the latter half of the seventh century B.C.

It was probably during the expansionist policies of King Josiah that frontiersmen and their families, never numbering more than one hundred settlers at most, established these permanent forts and farms in the Buqe'ah, an important link between Jerusalem and newly founded oasis settlements on the western shore of the Dead Sea. The soldier-farmers were able to maintain their paramilitary posts by building terrace dams and sluice gates for harnessing the flood waters which coursed down from the Judean Mountains to the W. In addition to the cultivation of wheat and barley, there is also archaeological evidence that they raised sheep and possibly goats. Two *lam-melekh* (belonging to the king) stamped handles discovered at Samrah suggest wine imports from the hill country.

When Jerusalem fell to the Babylonians under King Nebuchadrezzar, the Buqe'ah was once again abandoned to become the camping grounds of seasonal pastoralists, the hiding place of fugitives, and the haunt of brigands.

Bibliography. H. W. Wolff, "Die Ebene Achor," *ZDPV,* LXX (1954), 76-81; M. Noth, "Lehrkursus 1954," *ZDPV,* LXXI (1955), at 42-55; F. M. Cross, *Canaanite Myth and Hebrew Epic* (1973), pp. 109-10; L. Stager, "Ancient Irrigation Agriculture in the Buqei'ah Valley," *American Schools of Oriental Research Newsletter* 2 (1972-73), 1-4, and "El-Bouqei'ah," *RB,* LXXXI (1974), 94-96. L. E. STAGER

***ACHZIB (IN GALILEE).** Surveys and excavations were made by Prausnitz in 1958, 1960, and 1963-64 on behalf of the University of Rome and the Israel Department of Antiquities. Surrounded like an island by bays and river beds, Achzib was fortified by an earthen rampart in the Middle Bronze Age (MB II), near the end of the nineteenth century B.C. From the end of the eleventh century to the sixth century, the city prospered greatly and spread E to the mainland to which it has been linked ever since.

Two cemeteries of Achzib were excavated in continuation of work undertaken in 1941-42 by the Palestine Department of Antiquities. A new cemetery, situated beneath the walls of the city, was discovered and revealed well-built megalithic cists. One cist tomb contained the skeleton of a warrior and, apparently, his wife. The male had a bronze ritual double axe and a lance, as well as an iron dagger with bronze rivets and a copper bowl. The female's garment was closed by a fibula. The finds date the cists to the eleventh century and indicate that some of the tombs belonged to Sea Peoples other than the PHILISTINES.

Excavations in the E cemetery, er-Ras, and the S cemetery, Minat ez-Zib, made it possible to distinguish four different types of Iron Age burials:

(1) Inhumations of individuals in cists or in elongated pits, sometimes walled, as was common along the Palestinian coast at the end of the Late Bronze Age.

(2) Cremation-urn burials similar to those found in Neo-Hittite cemeteries in Syria.

(3) Rock-cut family tombs consisting of a shaft leading into the burial chamber with benches alongside three walls. The entrance was carefully sealed by a door slab. This type of burial is akin to the Israelite graves of the Iron Age.

(4) Rock-cut family tombs, shaft and chamber, with a *bemah* built above and into the ceiling of the chamber. On the *bemah* were found a table altar for offerings, stands, and libation vessels. This indicates traditional Canaanite practices.

The rock-cut family tombs were found to contain four hundred or more skeletons, which apparently belonged to the great families of Achzib. The tombs are believed to have been used for generations from the tenth century to the eighth century B.C., when the elite of Achzib, like that of Tyre, fled overseas before the city was captured by the Assyrians in 701. *See* TOMB[S].

M. W. PRAUSNITZ

ACROSTIC. *See* MNEMONIC DEVICES[S] §1.

ACTS, GENRE. Since the canonical book of Acts was written as a sequel to the Gospel of Luke (*see* LUKE, GOSPEL OF §2; ACTS OF THE APOSTLES §8 and supplementary articles), the question of the literary genre of Acts is bound up closely with the question of the gospel genre (*see* GOSPEL, GENRE[S]). The classification of Luke as more "biographical" and Acts as more "historical" is not fully satisfactory. The general caveat against such classifications expressed by Overbeck, K. L. Schmidt, and others (*see bibliog.*) still holds, especially with regard to the gospels. The primitive literature of Christianity was the product of eschatologically oriented communities which, for sociological and ideological reasons, did not aspire to the forms of worldly literature.

1. Cadbury's view. There are no recently recovered texts which throw much additional light on the genre of Acts, and Cadbury's summary of the data and the issues remains the most balanced and helpful (*see bibliog.*). Like Overbeck and Schmidt, Cadbury cautioned against fitting the gospels and Acts into formal literary categories, even though like them he regarded Luke, of all the evangelists, as coming closest to literary ambitions, especially in Acts (*see* ACTS OF THE APOSTLES §10*b*). Cadbury remained committed to seeking a genre for Luke's work as a whole, but he did not find it. He concluded that, in spite of Luke's attempt to give literary form and structure to essentially preliterary materials, the separate histories and forms of the traditional units he employed are still apparent: "[Luke's] efforts at literary form only bring into sharper outline the incurably unliterary character of his materials." In Cadbury's view, therefore, Luke's work as a whole has no full analogy in the literary types of his day, even though comparisons can be drawn between them and certain aspects of Luke-Acts.

2. The recent discussion. When comparisons are made between the parts of Luke's work and other literary works, differences as well as similarities become apparent. This has been demonstrated by several recent investigators. For example, Luke gave attention to the typical function accorded by Hellenistic writers to speeches set within a narrative (Plümacher). But the missionary speeches he composed for Acts were constructed according to his own theological intention (Conzelmann; cf. Beardslee) and did not follow the model of profane historiography. Moreover, whereas profane writers of the Hellenistic period imitated classical Greek literature, the missionary speeches in Acts imitated the LXX (Plümacher).

The narrative materials in Acts have been compared with Hellenistic romances (Pokorný), and such a comparison is especially important because of the prominence of the travel motif in Luke's work (*see* LITERATURE, EARLY CHRISTIAN[S] §7). But here again significant differences in Acts must be recognized. While Acts places Paul in the classic romance setting, notes numerous narrow escapes, and gives an extended account of the shipwreck (Beardslee), it does not dwell on scenes portraying high adventure, and it lacks such staples of the typical Hellenistic romance as the recognition scene and the erotic motif (Conzelmann, Pokorný). Cadbury noted the dramatic quality of Luke's work, and more recently Haenchen has shown that the dramatic episode is characteristic of Acts (telling history in stories). Plümacher has compared this with numerous instances of episodic style in Hellenistic historiography (e.g., Livy, Curtius Rufus).

It is still debated whether any single genre classification for Acts or (Cadbury's desideratum) Luke-Acts is possible. Conzelmann prefers to describe Acts by the general term "historical monograph" (with examples in Greek and Roman as well as in Jewish literature, e.g., I, II, III Maccabees). For Luke-Acts as a whole, Talbert has suggested a comparison with those lives of the philosophers which were followed by lists, and sometimes by accounts of members of the school (e.g., Diogenes Laertius). However, Conzelmann is probably right (like Cadbury before him) in concluding that broad, general comparisons of genre are relatively inconsequential, and that those literary similarities which are apparent are with parts rather than with the whole.

Bibliography. W. A. Beardslee, *Literary Criticism of the NT* (1970); H. J. Cadbury, *The Making of Luke-Acts* (1927 [2nd ed., 1958]), esp. pp. 127-39; H. Conzelmann, *Die Apostelgeschichte,* HNT, VII (1963); E. Haenchen, *The Acts of the Apostles: A Commentary* (rev. ed., 1965); E. Plümacher, *Lukas als hellenistischer Schriftsteller: Studien zur Apostelgeschichte,* SUNT, IX (1972); P. Pokorný, "Die Romfahrt des Paulus und der antike Roman," *ZNW,* LXIV (1973), 233-44; K. L. Schmidt, "Die Stellung der Evangelien in der allgemeinen Literaturgeschichte," in ΕΥΧΑΡΙΣΤΗΡΙΟΝ, ed. H. Schmidt, II, *FRLANT,* XXXVI (1923), 50-134; C. H. Talbert, *Literary Patterns, Theological Themes and the Genre of Luke-Acts,* SBLMS, XX (1975); A. Wikenhauser, *Die Apostelgeschichte und ihr Geschichtswert,* NTAbh, VIII (1921); F. Overbeck, "Über die Anfänge der patristischen Literatur," *Historische Zeitschrift,* XLVIII (1882), 417-72. W. C. Robinson, Jr.

***ACTS OF THE APOSTLES. 1. The theology of Acts.** In 1950 Vielhauer published what was destined to become the programmatic statement for a new wave of Lukan studies. Taken by itself it might fairly well be classed under Cadbury's statement of intention, "description not argument." But Vielhauer's was not the only, or even the first, attempt at a fresh assessment of Luke-Acts. The clouds of what van Unnik would later call "a storm center in contemporary scholarship" had been gathering even before 1950.

a. Käsemann, Bultmann, Cullmann. New perspectives on Acts first appeared in print in the November, 1948 issue of *Theologische Literaturzeitung* in a book review by Käsemann, where the subject of apostleship in Acts was treated in some detail. The preceding summer Käsemann had lectured on Acts 1–20 in Mainz; his notes were used by Haenchen as he reworked the first draft (1946) of his commentary on Acts. In his *TLZ* review Käsemann labeled as Lukan the view that an apostle can proclaim "historically verified truth" only because he has witnessed the actual events, and he referred at the same time to the "early catholic concept of the church in Acts, with its theory of tradition and succession." Although the notes of Käsemann's 1948 lectures are not available, his comments in the review can be augmented from the conclusion of an address delivered in 1949, "Ministry and Community in the NT." After noting that the NT lacked those terms for ministerial office which would imply official domination and subjection to it, he analyzed Paul's use of *charisma* as the concept of ministry, and concluded by contrasting the views in Acts with those held by Paul: In Acts, the concept of *charisma* is gone, and Paul himself is portrayed as upholding the "principle of tradition and legitimate succession." In Acts, the only valid witness is one who was a companion of the historical Jesus from the first (1:21; 10:39) and could thus guarantee the gospel tradition. Käsemann offered several examples from Acts of apostolic authority (e.g., the laying on of hands by Peter in Samaria, and the consequent receipt of the Spirit, 8:14-17) and concluded that the beneficiary of this portrayal is a church having to assert its legitimacy against heresy. It does this by claiming that its position rests on continuity with the original apostolate; outside the church there is no possession of the Spirit and no salvation. In Acts, Käsemann held, a "theology of glory" is in the process of replacing Paul's "theology of the cross."

Coincidentally, the same issue of *TLZ* which contained Käsemann's comments on apostleship in Acts carried a brief paragraph reporting the discovery of some MSS near the Dead Sea (later to figure significantly in the discussion of earliest Christianity, including Acts; *see* Dead Sea Scrolls[S] §§7, 8, 9), a lead article by Schlink reporting the First Assembly of the World Council of Churches, and Bultmann's review of Cullmann's *Christ and Time.* The title of Schlink's article, "The Church in God's Redemptive Plan," implied just the kind of redemptive-historical view of the church which Harbsmeier would later find in Luke-Acts and reject (*see* §1c *below*). Bultmann's review began by epitomizing Cullmann's position in a phrase which later furnished Conzelmann the title for a book on Luke: "Christ as the middle of time." Moreover, Käsemann's theological charge against Luke was in accord with Bultmann's assertion that Cullmann's concept of salvation history was a "wisdom" for the "mature" that "stands beyond the 'foolishness' of the 'word of the cross' which is the real ground of faith." Bultmann's claim was that, in earliest Christian faith, Christ was regarded as the end and goal of history (and of salvation history), not its center. The association of Cullmann's views with Luke and Bultmann's with Paul and John made Luke-Acts the field of conflict between the two theological forces.

b. Vielhauer broke away from the earlier preoccupation with Luke as a historian, by emphasizing the importance of an analysis of the theology in the speeches attributed to Paul in Acts. He thereby posed the question of whether there is a specifically Lukan theology.

Taking his start from Dibelius' study of the Areopagus sermon (Acts 17:22-31: "a Hellenistic speech about the true knowledge of God which becomes a Christian speech only at its conclusion"), Vielhauer went on to offer evidence of a "natural theology" proclaimed by Luke's "Paul." Luke's affinities with the later apologists and his distance from the real Paul were emphasized. The decisive difference between Acts and Paul, according to Vielhauer, is the understanding of the Crucifixion. Paul regarded Christ's death as a judgment on all humanity and also as reconciliation: with Christ's death and resurrection came the turn of the ages, the eschaton. The believer is "in Christ," belongs to the new world, and is thereby a "new creation." Salvation is wholly realized in the Cross of Christ, and is received by believers as they participate in Christ's body. In Acts, on the other hand, Jesus' crucifixion is viewed as "an error of justice and a sin of the Jews," and no saving significance is ascribed to the Cross. Vielhauer claimed that this is why Acts is silent about the reality of being "in Christ" and has removed eschatology from the center of faith to be a "section on the last things" (Dibelius).

Although, like Paul (and unlike the earliest believers), Luke held that the new age had broken in (Acts 2:16-35; cf. Luke 16:16), he differed from Paul in his belief that the decisive act of salvation would occur only at the PAROUSIA (Acts 3:19 ff.). Thus, Vielhauer emphasized the importance in Luke-Acts of a temporal dualism which is resolved only by means of a "continuous redemptive historical process." Luke relates the old and new aeons in his "redemptive historical pattern of promise and fulfillment," and this Lukan theology of history combines the OT belief in God's action on the historical plane with the Hellenistic idea of the kinship between the human race and God. Vielhauer's provocative conclusion was that Luke "no longer stands within earliest Christianity, but in the nascent early catholic church. His concept of history and his view of earliest Christianity are the same as theirs."

c. The discussion since Vielhauer. An almost immediate response to Vielhauer's essay came from Harbsmeier, who insisted that Christianity must always make a canonical choice between Luke and Paul, and that it should be a choice *for* Paul and thereby *against* illegitimate (Lukan) claims of authority by the church hierarchy. Wilder expressed some reserve toward this sort of thinking, noting that in America (as in Greek Orthodoxy) "the category of justification by faith is not emphasized as a hermeneutical key to the NT canon." But Harbsmeier's principle has been reaffirmed, though differently directed, by Kümmel. If the concept of a canon is to be retained (*see* CANON, NT; CANON, NT[S] §§1-3) at the same time that contradictions within it are recognized, then the "center" of the NT must be defined. In Kümmel's view, this center is to be found by appeal to those chronologically nearest Christianity's origin—Jesus, Paul, and John. Because, he believes, these three are in agreement in a theology of salvation history, Luke's position has been legitimated. Wilckens has also defended the legitimacy of Luke's theology. After analyzing the historical setting of the early discussion (*see* §1*a above*), he concluded that Käsemann's criticism of Luke's salvation history merely echoed what dialectical theology had said about liberalism in the 1920s. It is the existentially interpreted Paul, Wilckens contends, not the historical Paul, "who is so sharply set against Luke as the great but dangerous corruptor of the Pauline gospel."

Conzelmann, Haenchen, and others have objected to the imprecise use of such terms as "early catholicism" (*Frühkatholizismus*) which have often been used to describe Lukan theology: certain definite marks of early catholicism (the church, its offices and sacraments as an institution of salvation; the institutionalizing of the Spirit; apostolic succession) are almost completely lacking. Dahl, Borgen, and Jervell have argued that the differences between Luke and Paul have been overdrawn, and Wilckens has questioned whether, in any case, the one should be compared to the other. The lack of Jesus tradition in Paul (and Hellenistic Christianity) sets him apart from the gospels and shows us "two different realms of tradition." According to Wilckens, neither Luke nor Paul could have built on the theology of the other.

2. The historicity of Acts. Implicit in Dibelius' move from a source-critical understanding of the composition of Acts (by joining extended sources) to a more form-critically oriented view (in which the traditional materials existed in smaller separate units) was a reduction of confidence in the historical reliability of the Acts account (*see* Haenchen). Nor are the difficulties in defending Acts' historicity due simply to form-critical assumptions (*see* Hurd). Burchard and Löning hold that some historical information on Paul's Christian beginnings was available to Luke—a minimal assumption, since our primary sources (Paul's letters) establish that he had been a persecutor and was a convert—that Paul also knew of traditions about himself (Gal. 1:13-14, 23-24—"you/they heard"—cf. I Cor. 15:9; Phil. 3:6), that Luke had some tradition about Paul in fixed form (e.g., Acts 9:1-19*a*), and further that he had traditions on matters other than just Paul's beginnings as a Christian (Burchard, e.g., holding that the speeches by Peter and Paul, Acts 10 and 17, while thoroughly Lukan, were formed on the basis of traditions). Yet despite a critical attitude toward Haenchen's general rejection of historical reliability in Acts (*see esp.* Burchard's circumspect and sensible discussion of the existence, accessibility, and use of historical traditions in Acts), their conclusions put them much closer to Haenchen than to the anxious English (*see* Gasque and Marshall). While it is true that J. B. Lightfoot and William Ramsey showed Acts to be generally accurate in geographical and political matters (Gasque), it is not persuasive to compare Acts and Judith in this respect. Nor is it convincing, without taking into account that one writer lived centuries after the time setting of his story while the other lived during the conditions referred to, to conclude that one (i.e., Luke) was "careful to get the background right" and therefore "may be expected to tell a reliable story as well" (Marshall). Even if we grant that the author of Acts may have known his setting well and was careful to get it right, we have not thereby established a "reliable story"; correct local color cannot guarantee over-all historical reliability. The evidence so far adduced for the historical reliability of Acts is not persuasive, but the discussion of the matter continues.

3. Portrayal of Paul. Löning's detailed analysis shows a pre-Lukan genre shift in the tradition of Paul's conversion: from a novelistic, incredible event to a legend showing divine intervention to protect the worshiping community from persecution (cf. protection of the temple, II Macc. 3). This means, in Paul's case, that the emphasis is moved from the sanctity of the holy place to a missionary interest in converting the persecutor, an example of gracious election. Luke then moved the emphasis from divine power and gracious election to the "Damascus road experience." Paul saw the error of his ways when he recognized that Jesus was the Messiah, and at the same time he received his call to mission. Thereby Luke makes Paul the embodiment of what is, from the Christian point of view, the continuity of promise and fulfillment. This is what was at issue in the confrontation of the Jewish and the Christian hope. The prominence given promise and fulfillment in Luke's thought (by Burchard as well as Löning) is a return to Kümmel and Schubert and a repudiation of a threefold salvation history as Luke's organizing principle. Luke does not have Paul defending himself in Acts. Divinely commissioned, Paul needs no defense. His speeches are rather polemic against challenges to the legitimacy of the church, wherein Christianity's claim to the promises of Israel is asserted. Luke's concern was the legitimacy of the church at the close of the first century, and he made Paul the advocate of that concern.

Bibliography. Commentaries: H. Conzelmann, *Die Apostelgeschichte,* HNT, VII (1963); E. Haenchen, *The Acts of the Apostles: A Commentary* (rev. ed., 1965).

Studies: P. Borgen, "From Paul to Luke: Observations toward Clarification of the Theology of Luke-Acts," *CBQ,* XXXI (1969), 168-82; R. Bultmann, "Heilsgeschichte und Geschichte," *TLZ,* LXXIII (1948), cols. 659-66; C. Burchard, *Der dreizehnte Zeuge, FRLANT,* CIII (1970); H. Conzelmann, "Zur Lukasanalyse," *ZThK,* XLIX (1952), 16-33, and "Luke's Place in the Development of Early Christianity," *Studies in Luke-Acts,* ed. L. E. Keck and J. L. Martyn (1966), pp. 298-316; W. Gasque, "The Historical Value of the Book of Acts: The Perspective of British Scholarship," *TZ,* XXVIII (1972), 177-96, and *A History of the Criticism of the Acts of the Apostles,* Beiträge zur Geschichte der biblischen Exegese, XVII (1975); G. Harbsmeier, "Unsere Predigt im Spiegel der Apostelgeschichte," *EvT,* X (1950-51), 352-68; J. C. Hurd, *The Origin of I Corinthians* (1965), pp. 12-42; J. Jervell, "The Problem of Traditions in Acts," *Luke and the People of God* (1972), pp. 19-39; E. Käsemann, "Ministry and Community in the NT," *Essays on NT Themes,* SBT, XLI (1964), 63-94, and his review of M. Barth, *Der Augenzeuge, TLZ,* LXXIII (1948), cols. 665-70; W. G. Kümmel, "Current Theological Accusations against Luke," *ANQ,* XVI (1975-76), 131-45; K. Löning, *Die Saulustradition in der Apostelgeschichte,* NTAbh, IX (1973); I. H. Marshall, *Luke: Historian and Theologian* (1971); P. Schubert, "The Structure and Significance of Luke 24," *Neutestamentliche Studien für Rudolf Bultmann,* BZNW, XXI (1954), 165-86; P. Vielhauer, "On the 'Paulinism' of Acts," *Studies in Luke-Acts,* pp. 33-50; U. Wilckens, "Interpreting Luke-Acts in a Period of Existentialist Theology," *Studies in Luke-Acts,* pp. 60-83; A. Wilder, "Biblical Hermeneutic and American Scholarship," *Neutestamentliche Studien für Rudolf Bultmann,* pp. 24-32.

W. C. Robinson, Jr.

ADAM, APOCALYPSE OF. A Gnostic secret revelation preserved in Coptic and containing a prediction of future salvation history revealed to Adam. The Apocalypse of Adam is the concluding work in a collection of apocalypses (*see* Apocalypse, Genre[S]) in Codex V from the Coptic Gnostic library of Nag Hammadi, designated as V, *5*:64,1–85,32. Until it was first described by Doresse in 1958, the work was completely unknown. The fourth-century heresiologist Epiphanius speaks of "apocalypses of Adam" in use among the adherents of a Gnostic sect called the "Gnostikoi" (*Panarion* XXVI.viii.1), but it is not possible to identify the Coptic work with any of them. A host of pseudepigraphic works under the names of Adam and his son Seth circulated in antiquity among both Jews and Christians, but these works are generally not Gnostic in content. Many of them are preserved in Armenian (*see* Adam, Books of). Like other documents in the Nag Hammadi library, the ApocAd shares a number of features, such as the names of angelic beings, with other Gnostic writings. Most notably, the Gnostic Gospel of the Egyptians apparently presupposes a version of the same mythical narrative.

1. Origin. Of the origin of the work, very little can be said. Like most Gnostic literature surviving in Coptic, it was undoubtedly first written in Greek. The extant copy may be dated in the middle of the fourth century, but the original work is perhaps much older. On the basis of its contents, some scholars speak of a first- or second-century date. The place of writing is unknown, and the author has chosen to conceal his identity behind that of Adam, or of Seth. The title, which appears at both beginning and end, may or may not be original. There is also an *incipit* that serves as a subtitle: "The revelation (apocalypse) which Adam taught his son Seth in the seven hundredth year."

2. Contents. The apocalyptic character of the narrative is established by a series of literary devices in addition to the use of the word "apocalypse" and the assertion at the end that "this is the hidden gnosis (knowledge) of Adam which he gave to Seth." The reference to the "seven hundredth year," which is the length of Adam's life after the birth of Seth according to the LXX version of Gen. 5:4, implies that the book is a deathbed "testament" of Adam to his son. The bulk of what Adam reveals, he learned in a dream vision in which three heavenly men instructed him. And the message itself, transmitted by Seth to his Gnostic descendants, is described as not written in a book but delivered by angelic beings from its hiding place "on a high mountain, upon a rock of truth." The basis for the narrative is the Genesis story, but unlike many Gnostic retellings of it, the ApocAd never actually cites Genesis and seems indeed to depend on midrashic legend. A series of abrupt transitions and minor inconsistencies suggests that the book had undergone revisions before its translation into Coptic.

Adam first briefly recapitulates to his son the story of the Fall of himself and Eve and its consequences. The Gnostic theology of the work is immediately evident both in the prominence of the theme of the transmission and loss of gnosis and in the sharp distinction between the creator-god, "the ruler of the aeons and the powers," and the God of truth (*see* Gnosticism[S] §4). Because of the jealousy of the creator-god, Adam lives in ignorance, serving his maker "in fear and slavery," until the heavenly visitors reveal to him the future course of history, which forms the revelation proper in the narrative.

Adam then prophesies the repeated attempts of the creator-god to destroy the descendants of Seth, the Gnostics, by wiping out mankind, first by flood (the Noah story), then by fire (the Sodom and Gomorrah story). At each stage the Gnostics are to be saved by the intervention of angels, and will be placed on the earth again to provide continuity for the seed of Seth and to thwart the evil creator. The third stage in this apocalyptic schematization of history, familiar in Jewish apocalypses, is the coming of a heavenly savior figure, called the "Illuminator of Gnosis," who is to "redeem their souls from the day of death. The whole creation, which came from the dead earth will be under the authority of death; but those who reflect in their hearts on the gnosis of the eternal god will not perish, for they have received spirit, not from this kingdom alone, but from one of the eternal angels." In anger and rage "the powers and their ruler" will attempt to persecute the Illuminator but can harm only his human flesh. Eventually the Gnostics will prevail, and the other peoples will repent of their service to the creator-god.

At the point of the Illuminator's entrance into the story there is a remarkable syncretistic passage in which the powers speculate about the origin of this figure whom they do not know. Thirteen explanations are recounted as the apparently erroneous opinions of thirteen "kingdoms." These are written in a schematized poetic style and draw upon a wide variety of myths, known and unknown. The following example is typical:

The third kingdom says of him
that he came from a virgin womb.
He was cast out of his city, he and his mother;
he was brought to a desert place.
He was nourished there.
He received glory and power.
And thus he came to the water.

To these explanations the document contrasts the view of "the generation without a king," a common self-designation of Gnostics: the Illuminator comes from the alien world of God with knowledge of him.

3. Importance. The significance of the ApocAd lies, not only in the fact that it is an original work of Sethian Gnostics, but also in the possibility that it is a non-Christian document with a full-blown Gnostic redeemer myth, perhaps reflecting the transition between Jewish apocalyptic thought, infused with a dualism from outside Jewish circles, and the Christian Gnosticism of the second-century sects. It is possible to read the prediction of the Illuminator as a veiled reference to Jesus Christ as redeemer, but the fact that the whole work shows no clear dependence on any NT passage or idea has led many of its interpreters to view it as evidence for non-Christian Gnosticism, and thus as an early product of Gnosticism, though not necessarily chronologically pre-Christian. Its dependence on Jewish traditions highlights the essential Jewish element in the origins of Gnosticism. Finally, references to baptism in the closing pages suggest an origin in Jewish baptist circles, but the practice of baptism has given way to a spiritualized concept of baptism as the reception of gnosis. Numerous details in the work can be paralleled in both Mandaean and Manichean literature. *See* MANDAEISM[S]; MANICHEISM.

Bibliography. Text: A Böhlig and P. Labib, *Koptisch-gnostische Apokalypsen aus Codex V von Nag Hammadi* (1963). English trans.: W. Foerster, ed., *Gnosis: A Selection of Gnostic Texts,* II (1971), 13-23. Discussion: J. Doresse, *The Secret Books of the Egyptian Gnostics* (1958), pp. 182-87; G. MacRae, "The Coptic Gnostic Apocalypse of Adam," *HeyJ,* VI (1965), 27-35; K. Rudolph, "Gnosis und Gnostizismus, ein Forschungsbericht," *Theol. Rundschau,* XXXIV (1969), 160-69.

G. MACRAE

***AGING, ATTITUDES TOWARD.** In most, if not all, small-scale societies, age is a vital principle of social organization, and it may even surpass biological kinship in structural importance. This is perhaps because it is every bit as inevitable as kinship, but rather less questionable. The process of aging is seen as a corollary of life itself, and its inevitability and predictability fit it for the structural role it plays. That is perhaps why death, of all the life-cycle crises, usually calls for the greatest social comment, with the possible exception of puberty, and even this is often interpreted ritually as the death of childhood. Birth starts the process of aging, and in an age-structured society a series of rites of passage from birth onward divide life into stages, marking entry into each stage by a ritual that may be as informal as the giving of a new name, or as formal as an elaborate initiation (usually at puberty or adulthood) or ceremony (as for marriage). These stages are frequently correlated with a division of labor, giving the process of aging a prime economic function. When age is institutionalized into an age-set system, the whole society may be regarded in a sense as being in a permanent rite of passage. It is also noteworthy that in certain cases children are given a role which is considered vital to the survival of the society, so that every age level calls for respect, be it the level of childhood, youth, adulthood, or old age. These two factors, the allocation of vital role and the respect due because of that role, do much to lessen the friction that almost invariably builds up between adjacent generations as the younger generation challenges the position, wealth, and power of the older, simply by the process of itself growing older.

The division of labor according to age reveals the basis for some of the attitudes toward the aged. The division is not made exclusively on the grounds of physical or mental ability, though these are certainly major considerations. Plainly, whether the economy is that of hunting, gathering, herding, or cultivation, the major economic tasks can only be performed by adults. It is also easily understandable that the increased span of experience of the aged, which may be translated into wisdom, should be utilized in allocating them a specific role when they are no longer physically able to participate actively in the daily subsistence economy. But we do such societies a serious injustice if we relegate their utilitarian, structural approach to age to the mundane. Of equal importance is the area of spirit. Spirit is power, but unlike physical power, cannot be as readily controlled or utilized. Where is such power located? Plainly not in the physical, material world around us; it is invisible, intangible, but nonetheless real. Some see the breath of life in the wind, or in the flowing water, but always it is an unknown, and the greatest unknown of all is death. Here then, beyond death, may be the locus of spirit and spiritual power. It is because of this belief that so much importance is often placed on the ancestors or even the more recently departed (who may be considered to be more easily accessible). It is also for this reason that, in the structural utilization of the process of aging, such central and vital roles as are associated with spirit are allocated to the very young or the very old, for the very young have just come from that vast source of power, and the very old are on the verge of entering it, and are consequently seen as being closer and more accessible to the ancestors. It is those in the middle, the youths and adults, who are furthest removed from "spirit power." Their compensation and their sources of respect are their primarily economic and political roles.

In small-scale societies it is recognized that while one is born "pure," close to the source of spiritual power, the process of living contaminates and the process of aging removes one further and further from that source. But children, as a result of their physical and intellectual immaturity, are unable to wield this power to the advantage of society. They can, however, be made use of in rituals where spirit must be invoked. Thus among the Mbuti hunters of the African rain forest, it is only the young children who can light the propitiatory fires and alert the supreme spirit (the forest itself?) to the fact that its "children" are setting off to hunt, asking for its forgiveness for this act of violence. This even gives the young children a measure of social control, for such is the strength of the belief of the Mbuti that they will not set out on the hunt if the fire is not lit, as without the blessing of the forest the hunt will either be fruitless or disastrous.

As children move further away from the source of spirit at puberty, they assume a different, less spiritual and more political role. It is not until they enter old age and again approach that ultimate unknown that they are once more associated with spirit and engage again in what is essentially a religious role. They are beyond childbearing, their physical strength and senses no longer fit them for the strenuous and demanding economic role of adulthood, but as much as they are likely to resent being pushed into old age by the oncoming generation, they have the satisfaction of knowing that they will, by their very age, be moving into a position of power derived from their proximity to spirit. There may well be an intermediate step that overlaps, when their intellect is still undimmed and they are able to draw on their years of experience and act as counselors. But already anything they say is tinged with spirit and is respected for that reason rather than because of a mere accumulation of experience. The spiritually powerful elder is indeed a powerful social force, but his is only one of several vital roles and he can never become a despot; he needs the others as much as they need him. The strength of the structure lies in its built-in system of checks and balances, spiritual power frequently being balanced against material power. And whereas the child is primarily used as a ritual instrument, the elder is able to combine both belief and practice, spirit and ritual, to communicate with the beyond, and to invoke its spirit power to the aid of society.

However, the respect that in such societies is almost universally accorded the old is not always one of reverence, for power may be as easily abused as used for the social good. And the power that comes with growing old may produce either good or evil. Hence the ready association of the aged with witchcraft and sorcery (which terms I use to connote the unconscious and conscious manipulation of spiritual power for nonsocial or antisocial ends, respectively).

Age then, and the process of aging, is given good utilitarian usage in small-scale societies, and one of its most important structural functions was, and is, to link man with spirit, to provide limited access to the ultimate source of power.

Bibliography. N. Dyson-Hudson, "The Karimojong Age System," *Ethnology,* II (1963), 353-401; S. N. Eisenstadt, *From Generation to Generation; Age Groups and Social Structure* (1956); P. H. Gulliver, "Age Differentiation," *International Encyclopedia of the Social Sciences,* I (1968), pp. 157-61; A. H. J. Prins, *East African Age Class Systems* (1953); M. H. Wilson, "Nyakyusa Age Villages," *Journal of the Royal Anthropological Institute,* LXXIX (1949), 21-25.
C. M. TURNBULL

***AGRICULTURE. 1. Intensive hunting and food-collecting (Epi-Paleolithic).** Toward the end of the Paleolithic period in Palestine (*ca.* 9000 B.C.) hunters and gatherers established one of the earliest villages in the Near East—'Ain Mallaha in the Upper Jordan Valley. There are no signs that these villagers had begun to domesticate animals or cultivate plants. Apparently they were able to exploit enough wild game and cereals in one region to warrant an investment in permanent housing and storage facilities. Ninety per cent of their meat came from hunting gazelles, cervids, and pigs. In the spring they harvested rich stands of wild wheat (emmer) and barley.

Unlike domestic cereals, these wild types have a brittle rachis, which shatters when the ears ripen and disperses the grain. The harvesting season is thus as short as a week when hot dry winds blow in from the desert. However, the harvest time could be extended to a month if the reapers worked up from the Jordan Valley to the surrounding hills, where wild cereals matured later. In the Neolithic period and after, this problem disappeared, because the tough rachis of domesticated cereals must be separated by threshing. Propagation of these cereals depends upon sowing by humans.

2. Incipient agriculture and husbandry (Prepottery Neolithic). About 7000 B.C. (Prepottery

Neolithic B in Palestine) permanent agricultural villages sprang up in many parts of the Near East. Prehistoric farmers raised sheep and goats and grew domesticated varieties of wheat and barley. But Natufian settlements such as 'Ain Mallaha and even later Prepottery Neolithic A JERICHO should caution us against taking this "Neolithic Revolution" too literally. The earliest Neolithic inhabitants of Jericho, who built the defense wall and tower (s) around their ten-acre oasis settlement, still relied primarily on hunting rather than herding for their meat. In the next phase at Jericho (PPNB) hunting gazelle and other game was still important but was being replaced by a greater reliance on the large caprines (certainly goats and possibly sheep) for meat. Some of these goats were probably domesticated, although they would have differed little in appearance from their wild counterparts. An unusually high percentage of young goats found slaughtered at Beidha indicates unmistakably that Neolithic people brought these animals under their control.

The earliest plants cultivated in Palestine were the cereals: wheat and barley. Perhaps limited cultivation had begun as early as PPNA Jericho, where six grains of hulled two-row barley (*H. distichum*) and two grains of emmer (*T. dicoccum*) were found. But the sample is too small for grand inferences. In PPNB the plant record is more helpful. In addition to a greater abundance of emmer and barley, einkorn (*T. monococcum*), which has no wild progenitor in Palestine, appeared at Jericho. Farmers at Beidha were growing hulled barley—their main crop—and emmer. These plants were not far removed morphologically from their wild ancestors. Wild pistachio nuts, caloric and rich in protein, were significant in the diet of the Beidha villagers.

Wild lentils do not grow in the Jordan Valley, yet at both Jericho and Beidha these legumes appeared along with the earliest cultivated cereals. Other pulses—peas, horse beans, and possibly chick-peas—were discovered in the same context. If rotated, the cereals and legumes might have prevented soil exhaustion. These complementary cultigens dominated Palestinian agriculture for the next 4,000 years.

3. Established grain farming and pastoralism (Pottery Neolithic and Chalcolithic). Archaeologically the sixth millennium in Palestine has left few remains. This period was probably a pastoral interlude during which the herdsmen left only elusive evidence of their seasonal occupation.

Domestication seems well under way by the time pottery first appears in the fifth millennium. In the Upper Jordan Valley at Munhata (stratum 2), settlement resumed after a hiatus. Although the flocks were still dominated by large caprines, smaller goats and sheep (typical of the Chalcolithic period) began to appear. Swine (at Munhata) and cattle (at ha-Goshrim) were added to the domesticated stock of the Neolithic farmers. The faunal and botanical remains from Pottery Neolithic Jericho were meager but sufficient to show that for the first time sheep and goats had replaced gazelle as the primary source of meat, and that wheat (emmer and einkorn) as well as barley continued to be grown.

By the fourth millennium large caprines had practically disappeared from the flocks; most of the sheep and goats approximated modern species in size. (Animals are dwarfed by domestication.) For the first time wool rather than mutton prompted much of the sheep husbandry.

Most of the agricultural villages of the late Chalcolithic were located in the semiarid zone (e.g., near Beer-sheba and at Teleilat Ghassul). Barley (followed by wheat) was the most widely cultivated cereal in this zone, probably because of its resistance to aridity. Lentils were also grown. The mixed economy of cereal and legume cultivation and sheep-goat pastoralism gave a certain flexibility during the lean years.

The settlers near Tel Aviv and in the Wadi Gazzeh relied less on sheep and goats than on hogs and cattle. Perhaps the widespread appearance of oxen in the late Chalcolithic signals the introduction of the plow in Palestine. About this time in Mesopotamia (Warka IV) reliefs depict an ox pulling the scratch-plow, or ard. Of the animals controlled by man up to this time, oxen alone had the strength and endurance for pulling the plow.

Long after cereals and legumes had been established, olive and date cultivation began in Palestine. Today wild olives do not grow in the Jordan Valley; it is too dry. The olives found at Ghassul were probably from domesticated trees, hand-irrigated from nearby springs. Wild dates grow along the SE fringes of the Dead Sea, but their fruits are small and unpalatable. Probably the large date stones discovered at Ghassul came from domesticated trees in the vicinity.

4. Mediterranean economy (Early Bronze Age–Iron Age). Shortly after 3000 B.C. the sedentary population of Palestine increased considerably. For the first time the major valleys and foothills of the Mediterranean zone were being cultivated. Much of the population lived in walled settlements, frequently more than twenty-five acres in size, and accommodating 1,000-1,500 inhabitants. To support these larger concentrations of people with their growing number of craftsmen, bureaucrats, and religious functionaries, extensive tracts of land had to be cultivated. With the growth of more complex societies in the EB Age, the stability of these settlements depended more on the successful cultivation of the soils around them.

With the development of horticulture in the Early Bronze Age, the economy of Palestine acquired its distinctively Mediterranean character, which it retains to this day. Pomegranates, dates, and olives were grown, and grapes were cultivated for the first time.

By EB II potters in Syria and Palestine had developed a narrow-neck pitcher which could be sealed with a clay stopper. Its tapered base would have made "nesting" aboard ship possible. A type of "Abydos" ware, these vessels reached Egypt as early as the Proto-Dynastic period. The Syro-Palestinian potters had obviously designed these vessels to transport liquid commodities, probably wine and olive oil.

Only five fruit trees were domesticated, the ones that were easiest to propagate. Grapes, figs, and pomegranates were first domesticated by cuttings; olives, by basal knobs; dates, by transplanted offshoots. Fruit trees, such as apple, pear, and cherry, required grafting for their domestication, a technique not known until much later.

In the third millennium agriculture had the classical Mediterranean components: grain farming, horticulture, and sheep-goat pastoralism. The potential for an integrated agrarian economy, with each zone specializing in the products best adapted to it, was present for the first time. Whether such a scheme was realized during and after the Bronze Age is difficult to demonstrate until seeds, charcoal, and pollen samples have been systematically, rather than fortuitously, collected from sites in the various zones.

Although information is scanty, it seems that the second-first millennia B.C. registered no new additions to the plant and animal record. However, some technological innovations did occur which extended Mediterranean-type field crops and horticulture into the mountains and deserts.

5. Mountain agriculture (Iron Age). About 1200 B.C. there was a striking increase in the number of settlements straddling the highland ridge from Hebron to Shechem. Most of these were small hilltop villages, five acres or less, without fortifications.

Once the forests were decimated by man, the remaining soil cover was quickly stripped away by nature (*see* FOREST[S]). That population pressure had something to do with this deforestation seems clear (Josh. 17:17-18).

In order to make the denuded hills suitable for dry farming, the inhabitants transformed the slopes into a staircase of terraces. These were best suited to vine, olive, and nut cultivation. But the earliest terrace-farmers at AI and Khirbet Raddana grew cereals. This inefficient use of terraces suggests an attempt by the highlanders (probably "Israelites" during the period of the Judges) to maintain a subsistence cereal agriculture free from the Canaanite and Philistine spheres, where the primary "bread baskets" were located. By the time of the united monarchy, much of this cereal-producing area had been brought under Israelite control. Once again, the geopolitical conditions resulted in the integration of agriculture throughout the region. During Iron Age II terracing was further extended to areas with modest amounts of bottom land; there the slopes could be planted with trees and vines, and the valleys sown with cereals.

The transformation of the hill country was a gradual one, culminating in the Roman-Byzantine period, when the population was greatest and as much as fifty per cent of the region evidenced terrace agriculture.

6. Desert farming (Iron Age). Farmers must have confronted two basic problems when they attempted to make the desert bloom: where to find suitable soils—deep, permeable, and salt-free, and how to increase the water yield, three- or fourfold, to grow cereals and legumes. To cope with these problems desert farmers laid out a parallel series of stone walls laterally across tributary wadis whose floors nature had already covered with alluvium. The rectangular terraces between the stone walls formed fields that were planted during the rainy season when floodwaters and hillside runoff had collected in the wadi basin. Terrace dams retarded the velocity of the floods, spread the flow over a large surface, and allowed time for ponding in the fields behind the dams. In this way enough water was harnessed to grow wheat, barley, and other field crops. Usually a heavy stone wall, or "fence," encircled the fields and sometimes the farmer's house.

There is no conclusive evidence that desert farming was practiced before the Iron Age. The earliest farms were developed at Ramat Maṭred (late tenth-early ninth century B.C.) in the Negeb. The technological know-how was kept alive until the end of Iron II, when desert farmers were growing crops in the Judean Desert (the Buqe'ah Valley, *see* ACHOR[S]) and in the Negeb (Mishor ha-Ruaḥ). During Nabatean-Roman-Byzantine times desert farming in the Negeb flourished as never before.

See also PREHISTORY IN THE ANE[S].

Bibliography. Plants: H. Helback, "Pre-Pottery Neolithic Farming at Beidha," *PEQ* (1966), 61-66; D. Zohary, "The Progenitors of Wheat and Barley in Relation to Domestication and Agricultural Dispersal in the Old World," in *The Domestication and Exploitation of Plants and Animals,* ed. P. J. Ucko and G. W. Dimbleby (1969), pp. 47-66; M. Hopf, "Plant Remains and Early Farming in Jericho," *ibid.,* pp. 355-59; D. Zohary and M. Hopf, "Domestication of Pulses in the Old World," *Science,* CLXXXII (1973), 887-94; D. Zohary and P. Spiegel-Roy, "Beginnings of Fruit Growing in the Old World," *Science,* CLXXXVII, (1975), 319-27; L. Stager, "Ancient Agriculture in the Judaean Desert: A Case Study of the Buqê'ah Valley in the Iron Age" (diss., Harvard, 1975).

Animals: D. Perkins, Jr., "The Fauna from Madamagh and Beidha," *PEQ* (1966), 66-67; P. Ducos, "Les Débuts de l'Élevage en Palestine," *Syria,* XLIV (1967), 375-400, and "Methodology and Results of the Study of the Earliest Domesticated Animals in the Near East (Palestine)," in *The Domestication and Exploitation of Plants and Animals,* ed., P. J. Ucko and G. W. Dimbleby (1969), pp. 265-75; J. Clutton-Brock, "The Primary Food Animals of the Jericho Tell from the Proto-Neolithic to the Byzantine Period," *Levant,* III (1971), 41-55.

L. E. STAGER

***AHIJAH THE PROPHET.** An Israelite and scion of the priestly dynasty of Shiloh, he served as a rallying point for the Israelite interests opposed to the Judah-oriented united monarchy of David and Solomon. On the basis of this underlying opposition and an ideology that inveighed against alleged syncretism on Solomon's part, Ahijah symbolically kindled the spark of revolution in a meeting with JEROBOAM, son of Nebat, one of Solomon's officers in charge of forced labor. Ahijah tore Jeroboam's garment (or perhaps his own, since the text is not clear) into twelve parts, corresponding to the tribes, and gave Jeroboam ten; only two tribes, Benjamin and Judah, would remain with the Davidic dynasty (I Kings 11:26-40). (*See* HEM[S].) It is likely that Ahijah's faction expected Jeroboam to restore Shiloh and the decentralized political life characteristic of the days before the united monarchy. Though he established two royal sanctuaries, at BETHEL and DAN, Jeroboam was essentially a centralizer, and, according to some, no less a syncretist than Solomon. In actuality, the golden calves may represent a reversion to an older Israelite tradition, rather than the adoption of foreign cultic forms (*see* CALF, GOLDEN; CALF, GOLDEN[S]). Jeroboam's policies created such tensions with Ahijah's old guard that when Jeroboam's son, Abijah, became ill, the king sent his wife to Ahijah to learn the prince's fate instead of going himself. Ahijah predicted the death of the prince and the end of Jeroboam's short-lived dynasty.

The "prophecy of Ahijah the Shilonite," very likely identical with I Kings 11:26 ff., is cited in II Chr. 9:29 as a source for the history of Solomon.

Bibliography. M. A. Cohen, "The Rebellions During the Reign of David: An Inquiry into Social Dynamics in Ancient Israel," *Studies in Jewish Bibliography, History and Literature in Honor of I. Edward Kiev* (1971), pp. 91-112, and "The Role of the Shilonite Priesthood in the United Monarchy of Ancient Israel," *HUCA*, XXXVI (1965), 59-98. M. A. COHEN

*__AI. 1. Biblical data.__ *See* AI §1.

2. Location and excavation. Several sites E of Bethel have been proposed: Khirbet Hai, a small unfortified ruin SE of Mukhmas; Khirbet Khudriya, *ca.* 1¼ miles E of et-Tell; et-Tell; and, identifying Ai with Beth-aven, Khirbet Haiyan in the S edge of modern Deir Dibwan has been proposed.

Excavations at Haiyan in 1964 and 1969 and at Khudriya in 1966 and 1968 yielded no evidence earlier than the late Hellenistic period, and a surface survey of Khirbet Hai in 1966 discovered nothing earlier than the Byzantine period. Of the sites proposed, therefore, et-Tell with its Iron Age I village remains the only viable location.

Garstang conducted a series of soundings in 1928. The results of his work were negligible and never published. He did mention later the discovery of a Late Bronze Cypriot sherd, but it has never been published.

Marquet-Krause headed three major campaigns during 1933-35 and established that the site was occupied only in the Early Bronze Age and Iron Age I. The absence of LB evidence occasioned the questions regarding the conquest discussed in §5 below. The Joint Expedition to Ai led by the writer from 1964 to 1972 included excavations at Khudriya and Haiyan. In general, the conclusions of Marquet-Krause were sustained, although major revisions in phasing, chronology, and the cultures of the people represented must be made. The following chart reflects the conclusions of the writer:

Stratum	Description	Period	Chronology
Pre-Urban	Unwalled village	EB IB	*ca.* 3100-3000 B.C.
Urban C	First walled city; built by newcomers from Syria	EB IC	*ca.* 3000-2860 B.C.
Urban B	Second city; Urban C walls widened	EB II	*ca.* 2860-2700 B.C.
Urban A	Third city; Egyptian influence	EB IIIA	*ca.* 2700-2550 B.C.
Urban A′	Fourth city; Khirbet Kerak influence	EB IIIB	*ca.* 2550-2350 B.C.
Cobbled Street	Unwalled agricultural village	Iron Age IA	*ca.* 1220-1125 B.C.
Silo Granary	Same village, remodeled and expanded	Iron Age IB	*ca.* 1125-1050 B.C.

3. The EB city. People with origins traceable to N Syria and Anatolia seized the initial EB IB village settlement and transformed it into the well-planned urban C city. A temple and royal quarter complex was constructed at site D, and houses averaging about 13x29½ feet in size were built over the scanty remains of the village huts. The economy was supported by farming, sheep herding, and trade. This phase was the most formative in the history of the EB city and was probably the age of greatest achievement and power.

Internal conflict in Canaan apparently led to the overthrow of urban C and a new regime at the beginning of EB II. Emphasis was upon strengthening of defenses and functional modifying of houses. A general lack of initiative was apparently exploited by aggressive Second-Dynasty rulers of Egypt whose artifacts are found in the ruins of the urban B city.

Destruction by earthquake or a determined enemy led to a new era in EB IIIA. An Egyptianized temple at site D was prominent in the rebuilt city, and a unique stone-lined reservoir with a capacity of over 63,000 cubic feet was constructed at site K. This evidence of outside influence was concentrated in public buildings and installations, suggesting an Egyptian-oriented local regime.

An Egyptian outpost at Ai would have guarded a major point of entry to the hill country from the E against newcomers in the N who had settled at Khirbet Kerak and Beth-shan. The urban A city fell to Khirbet Kerak–oriented aggressors at the end of EB IIIA.

The new ruler seems to have converted the temple at site D into a citadel-like residence, and sanctuary A was established in a remodeled domestic house. A long period lacking in new developments ensued until the urban A′ city was sacked and burned *ca.* 2350 B.C., and the site was left in ruins.

Nomadic infiltrators in the period now usually designated EB IV have been credited with the final destruction of Ai, but there is evidence suggesting that aggressive pharaohs of the Fifth Dynasty may have destroyed the city.

4. The Iron Age I village. At least 1100 years elapsed between the destruction and abandonment

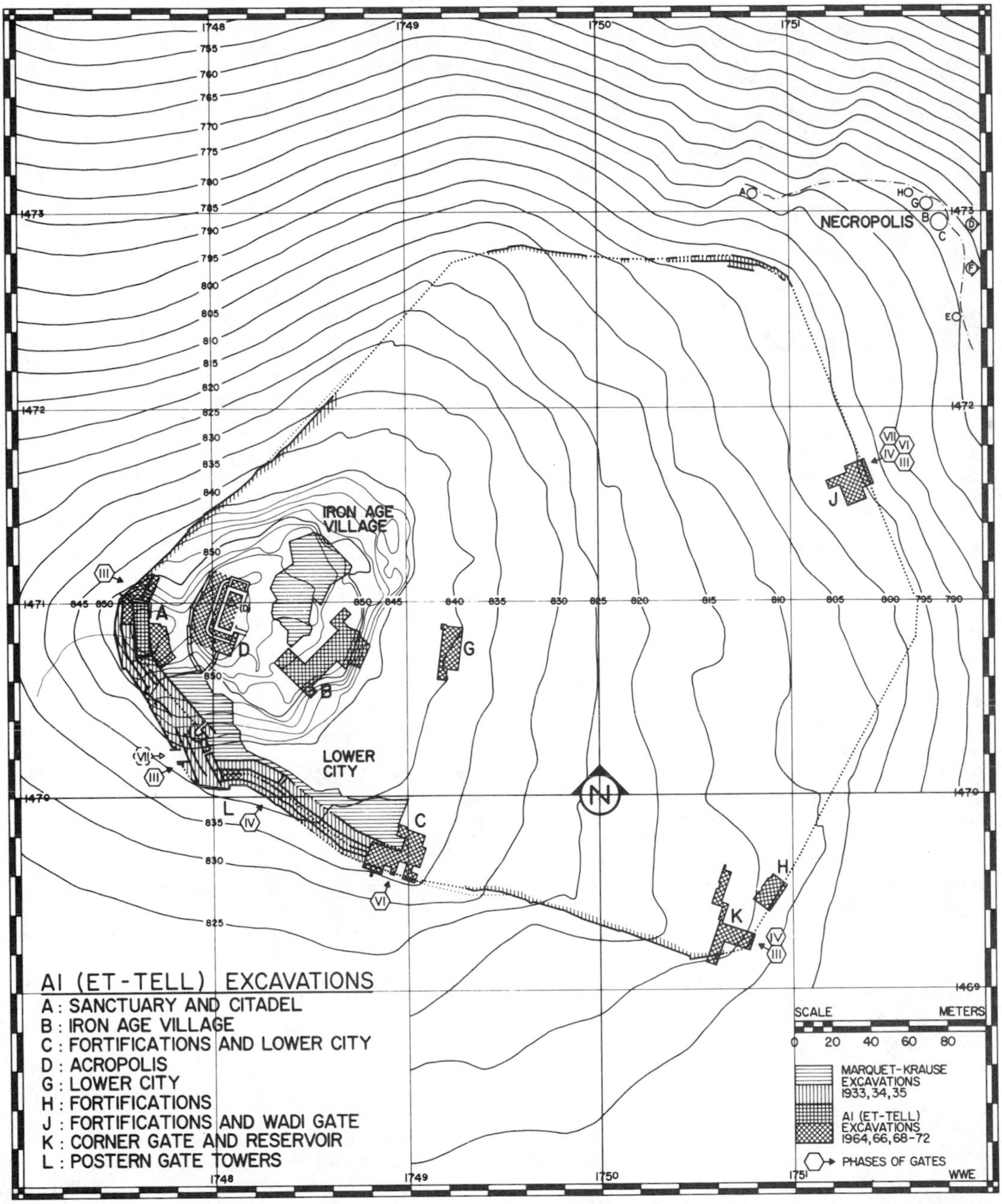

1. Plan of the Ai (et-Tell) excavations

of the last EB city and the arrival of newcomers (*ca.* 1220 B.C.) whose village covered only one tenth of the EB city mound.

The initial settlement was characterized by cobbled streets and a pier technique of house construction reflecting a high degree of prior development elsewhere. That the settlers came from a background of hill-country farming is evident from terracing on the E slope of the tell, a water supply utilizing rock-cut cisterns in individual houses, and tools used to process cereals.

An interruption of village life occurred *ca.* 1125 B.C. Numerous silo granaries were built over the cobblestone streets and in open places near houses, apparently by new population elements. One granary is shown in Fig. A2. Large round silo granaries were built in the corners of the ruined EB temple building at site D.

During the cobbled street phase, large jars were used for storage of grain, oil, and other foods and continued in use during the second phase. The introduction of dry silo structures in phase II brought a sudden transition in the method of storing grain and indicates an infusion of people

Courtesy J. A. Callaway
2. Phase I Iron Age village cobbled street partially blocked by a Phase II silo granary

who brought the custom with them. The manner in which the streets, court areas, and temple enclosure were converted by the newcomers into *ad hoc* granaries and shelter type living quarters suggests that they lacked the orderliness and experience in village life of their predecessors.

5. The problem of the conquest of Ai. Reconstruction of the capture of Ai by Joshua (Josh. 8:1-29) is difficult because the chronology of the village phases cannot be reconciled with prevailing views of the conquest. The older view of a 1400 B.C. conquest based upon I Kings 6:1, espoused by Garstang, is unsupported by the evidence, as is Albright's date of *ca.* 1250-1230 B.C. Because there is LB destruction of nearby Bethel, Albright ascribed the conquest related in Josh. 8 to Bethel instead of Ai and conjectured that later tradition had confused the accounts by attributing the event to Ai. This view is weakened by the LXX omission of a reference to men of Bethel participating in the defense of Ai in Josh. 8:17. A fragmentary Qumran text of Josh. 8:3-18 is also a shortened version like that of the LXX. The mention of Bethel may be secondary rather than the reverse. Noth held that Josh. 8 is legendary and etiological and therefore unhistorical. Marquet-Krause, and recently de Vaux, subscribed to this view also.

We seem to be left with the options of discounting the essential historicity of the events associated with Ai or of modifying the reconstruction of the conquest. The latter seems preferable for three reasons.

First, Josh. 7–10 relates the village of Ai rather technically to the geography of the region and to neighboring sites. Ai was small (Josh. 7:3), even smaller than Gibeon (Josh. 10:2), and this description could have originated only in Iron Age I. At any time after 1050 B.C., the obvious ruin of Ai was larger than Gibeon, covering 27½ acres.

Second, the association of the Israelites with Gibeon (el-Jib) as related in Josh. 9:17 and 10:6 would have occurred in Iron Age I when there was a village on the site with pillar type houses like those at Ai, instead of a time in the LB period when there is no evidence of a city or village apart from one tomb, no. 10 A-B.

Third, the two phases at Ai suggest that the cobbled street village people, called Israelites by Albright, came from a hill-country agricultural background and would not appear to be recent immigrants from either the Egyptian delta or the desert. However, the people of the silo granary phase could have come from this background. The capture of Ai, therefore, could have occurred *ca.* 1125 B.C. and given rise to the embellished account that we now have in Josh. 7–8.

Bibliography. W. F. Albright, "Ai and Beth-aven," *AASOR,* IV (1924), 141-49; J. Garstang, "The Destruction of Ai," *The Foundations of Bible History: Joshua, Judges* (1931), pp. 149-61, 355-56; J. Marquet-Krause, "La deuxième campagne de fouilles à Ay (1934), rapport sommaire," *Syria,* XVI (1935), 325-45; M. Noth, "Bethel und Ai," *PJ,* XXXI (1935), 7-29; L.-H. Vincent, "Les fouilles d'et-Tell-ʿAi," *RB,* XLVI, (1937), 231-66; J. M. Grintz, " ʿAi Which is Beside Beth-aven," *Bibl.,* XLII (1961), 201-16; J. A. Callaway, *Pottery from the Tombs at ʿAi* (1964), "New Evidence on the Conquest of ʿAi," *JBL,* LXXXVII (1968), 312-20; Callaway with M. Nicol, "A Sounding at Khirbet Ḥaiyân," *BASOR,* 183 (1966), 12-19; G. E. Wright, "The Significance of Ai in the Third Millennium B.C.," A. Kuschke, E. Kutsch, eds., *Archäologie und Altes Testament* (1970), pp. 299-319; R. Amiran, "The Egyptian Alabaster Vessels from Ai," *IEJ,* XX (1970), 170-79; J. A. Callaway, *The Early Bronze Age Sanctuary at Ai (et-Tell)* (1972).

J. A. CALLAWAY

ALALAKH TEXTS ă lä läh′ [Akkad. *a-la-la-aḫ;* possibly Hurrian, etymology unknown; cf. Egyp. *'irrh*]. A group of 466 Akkad. texts, giving information on the language, literature, culture, and religious life of the city of Alalakh in the seventeenth and fifteenth centuries B.C. Alalakh was the "special possession" *(sikultu)* of the god Addu (Hadad) to whom, with the goddess Ishtar (Hepat), sacrifices were offered.

1. Location. The site (Tell ʿAṭsānah) is in Turkey, near the pass leading from Antioch to Aleppo, by the Orontes River.

2. Excavations. Woolley, seeking to demonstrate the connection between E Mediterranean and Mesopotamian civilizations, excavated the site in 1937-39 and 1946-49. He uncovered seventeen strata dating from *ca.* 3100 B.C. (level XVI) to *ca.* 1200 B.C. (I). Early levels suggest comparisons with Palestine or with Nineveh and Ur (XIV). The primary occupation occurred in level VII (*ca.* 1720-1650 ["low" CHRONOLOGY]) when King Iarim-Lim built a fine palace with frescoed walls and strong defenses. One hundred and seventy-one tablets in the Old Babylonian script were found; half were contracts and half were ration lists.

The palace and town were rebuilt in level IV (*ca.* 1550-1473). From this period come 295 texts: letters, legal cases, marriage contracts, and many census lists. There were at least five scribes and a population of three thousand.

3. History. Prior to the discovery of these texts (hereafter AT) little was known of Syria in the mid-second millennium B.C. Abba'el (or Abban), a son of Hammurabi of Iamhad (Aleppo), obtained the town from a brother (*ca.* 1720) in exchange for Irrid near Carchemish. This new ownership is confirmed in one of the earliest treaty-texts so far known (AT 1), which summarizes the historical situation and lists stipulations, witnesses, and curses on any transgressor. This genre was used by the Mesopotamians, Hittites, and Hebrews for two millennia (*see* COVENANT; COVENANT, MOSAIC[S]). Exchanges or sales of towns or villages were common (AT 52-58), and this may indicate that the arrangements which Solomon entered into with Hiram (I Kings 9:11) were similar.

Abba'el's grandson Ammitaku left the city to a son in a will witnessed by senior state officials and the royal scribe (AT 6). He may have done this in order to avoid public rivalry among his sons, as David did (I Kings 1:17-36). Despite this, another son, Irkabtum, soon took over the throne and made peace with the troublesome, seminomadic HABIRU who were raiding in the neighborhood (AT 58; 161; 183). The city was probably destroyed by the Hittite Mursilis I who also captured Aleppo and Babylon.

After an unexplained interval (levels VI-V) the subsequent history can be read on the statue of Idrimi, inscribed with a speech recounting his adventures (*ca.* 1490). As the youngest son of Ilimilimma I of Aleppo, Idrimi went into exile after a popular revolt. After some time he crossed the desert with his maternal relations to Canaan (*kina'nim*) and joined other refugees from Syria to live among the Habiru. Seven years later he mounted an expedition by ship and regained the district of Mukish and its capital (Alalakh), where he was acclaimed king. There he built a new palace and temple with the spoils he won as he extended his kingdom. This has obvious parallels with parts of Genesis and especially with the Davidic narrative. David too fled to his mother's relatives in Moab (I Sam. 22:3) and, like Idrimi, consulted the divine will before his return (II Sam. 2:1-4; cf. 5:1-3).

An extract from a larger treaty tablet shows that Idrimi strengthened his position by making parity treaties with adjacent city-states, which included the right of extradition of fugitives (AT 3). The action of Shimei in I Kings 2:39-42 implies a similar agreement between Solomon and Achish of Gath, perhaps made in the light of David's own exile there (I Sam. 27:2-7). Other texts show that the elders of a city were responsible for seizing such persons (AT 2) and returning them (AT 101). After a period under Hittite control (III), Alalakh was destroyed by the "Sea Peoples" (*see* PHILISTINES §1) and thereafter ceased to be significant.

4. Social conditions. These texts supplement the information to be gained from the MARI texts and the Akkad. texts from UGARIT.

a. Administration. The king in both periods ruled as an autocrat, sitting as judge in any case brought before him. Many cases relate to the status of a citizen and of his land (AT 8; 79). By advancing loans and paying off his subjects' debts, the king soon won control of many individuals or families. They were forced to "dwell in the house of the king" to work off their debt (AT 18–27; 32), a phrase which may illumine Ps. 23:6. Slaves, recruited from prisoners of war as well as defaulting debtors, played an important role in the palace and were given as gifts between kings (AT 224). The average cost was 25 silver shekels or 5½ talents of copper, with the female worth double, compared with *ca.* 40 shekels at Ugarit and 30 in Israel. Some contracts include a clause preventing a slave's release under any royal proclamation of general amnesty (AT 65). Such practices should have been adequate warning to the later Israelites seeking a similar form of monarchy (I Sam. 8).

b. Classes. Many census and name lists show that the population was Semitic and Hurrian. Under the king were the higher officials, mostly chariot-owners, whose status was as much a result of their position as of their privileged class. Very few, if any, bear undoubtedly Indo-Aryan names. Their position could be inherited and carry religious obligations (AT 15). Below them were freedmen (Akkad. *šūzubu*, Hurrian *ehele*) while the majority of the population were semifree "rural retainers" (listed as "Haneans" or *ḫupšu* [comparable with the Heb. חפשי, Deut. 15:12-18]) who, as royal tenants, could also own private property. All these classes included craftsmen of various professions. Names also found in the OT include: Abinahmi (Abinoam), Ayabi (Job), Minuhham (Menahem), and Sisura (Sisera).

c. Customs. In marriage contracts (AT 91–94) we learn that the bridegroom "asked" his future father-in-law for the bride (cf. Gen. 29:18) and that betrothal gifts were customary (AT 17). Some state that if a wife failed to give birth to a son within seven years her husband could remarry (cf. Gen. 29:18-21). The position of "first-born son" was granted only to the first wife's son, rather than to the son of a concubine (cf. Gen. 21:10) (*see* FIRST-BORN[S]). Clothes were given as "additional payments" in some transactions (cf. II Kings 5:5-27).

Bibliography. Archaeology: C. L. Woolley, *Alalakh* (1955), *A Forgotten Kingdom* (1953).

Idrimi: S. Smith, *The Statue of Idri-mi* (1949), *ANET* (2nd ed., 1969), pp. 557-58.

Texts: D. J. Wiseman, *The Alalakh Tablets* (1953), and "Alalakh" in D. Winston Thomas, ed., *Archaeology and OT Study* (1967), pp. 119-35 (for relation to OT).

I. Mendelsohn, "On slavery in Alalakh," *IEJ*, V (1955), 65-72, and "On Marriage at Alalakh," *Essays on Jewish Life and Thought* (1959), pp. 351-57; M. Dietrich and O. Loretz, "Die soziale Struktur von Alalaḫ und Ugarit," *WO*, III (1966), 188-205, V (1969), 57-93.

D. J. WISEMAN

ALEXANDRIUM. *See* HERODIAN FORTRESSES[S].

***ALPHABET.** Recent advances in our understanding of the origin and early diffusion of the alphabet have come less often from newly discovered inscriptions than from improvements in epigraphic method (*see* ALPHABET §E). In particular, the development of the forms of the letters throughout the history of their use is becoming better known. As a result, the trained epigraphist can often identify the date and provenance of an inscription on the sole basis of the forms of the letters. It is now possible to trace the early history of the alphabet, observing with an increasing degree of understanding its emergence as a semipictographic system of signs in very ancient times, its gradual systematization in the Late Bronze Age, its differentiation into the various national scripts of the Iron Age, and finally its adoption by the Greeks and modification for use in writing non-Semitic languages.

1. The old Canaanite alphabet. The origin of the alphabet remains imperfectly understood and in dispute (*see* ALPHABET §D). A few archaic inscriptions of unusual appearance suggest that the earliest history of alphabetic writing may have been quite complicated. Experimental alphabets may have flourished briefly and died out. Yet the main line of descent can be traced from at least the end of the Middle Bronze Age to the early Phoenician script of the Iron Age and beyond. The so-called Proto-Sinaitic inscriptions, though still incompletely understood, certainly belong to the direct ancestry of the alphabet, as does LB material from such Canaanite city-states as Lachish, Megiddo, Hazor, and Beth-shemesh, as well as numerous lesser localities. In general, recent discoveries have confirmed the description by Cross of the main lines of alphabetic development in that period (*see* ALPHABET §B). The early predominance of vertical writing gave way in the Late Bronze Age to a preference for horizontal lines written in either direction. The transition to an exclusively right-to-left writing system was complete before the emergence early in the Iron Age of the Northwest Semitic national scripts, none of which was written vertically or from left to right. This development is suggestive for the early history of the South Semitic scripts, which, since they continued to employ columnar and multidirectional writing, must have descended from a parent tradition which had diverged from the northern line of alphabetic development before the demise of vertical writing. On the basis of this and other evidence, the origin of the Proto-Arabic script may be dated to about 1400 B.C.

2. The national scripts of the Iron Age. The decline of the Canaanite city-state system at the end of the Late Bronze Age prepared the way for larger, national communities (*see* CANAANITES §4; HABIRU; HABIRU[S] §2). Accompanying this development was the differentiation of the old Canaanite alphabet into a variety of national script traditions. Canaanite culture survived with least interruption in the new Sidonian state ruled by Tyre, and the early Phoenician script is best understood as a direct continuation of the old Canaanite alphabet. Not long after the traditional date of the refounding of Tyre in the twelfth century, the Phoenician alphabet had begun to acquire the distinctive features which would distinguish it from the older system. In particular, the forms of the letters were becoming fixed in what were to be their traditional stances, and the direction of right to left was beginning to dominate.

Among the first to develop a distinctive national script were the Israelites. Formal features of the Hebrew script suggest that it may have diverged from the main Canaanite-Phoenician line as early as the tenth century, i.e., roughly contemporary with the unification of monarchic Israel. Subsequently, the national script of Israel developed independently until its displacement by the Aramaic script as the imperial hand of the Persian period. The old tradition then became dormant for centuries, until it was revived amid the new nationalism of the Maccabean era as the archaizing Paleo-Hebrew script. *See* INSCRIPTIONS, SEMITIC[S] §2*a*.

Aramaic inscriptions from the ninth century B.C. exhibit distinctive formal features indicating that by that time the Aramaic script had diverged as another independent tradition. Again we note a correspondence to an important rise of national spirit, in this case accompanying the consolidation of the Aramean states under BEN-HADAD I of Damascus and his successors. *See* INSCRIPTIONS, SEMITIC[S] §3*d;* ARAMAIC; ARAMAIC[S] §E.

Evidence for the appropriation of the alphabet by the Transjordanian states has accumulated rapidly in recent years. In these instances, we ought to think not of branches of the old Canaanite alphabet itself, but of sub-branches of the Hebrew and Aramaic traditions. The Moabite and Edomite scripts remain incompletely understood. At least the former, as is clear from the famous Mesha stele (*see* MOABITE STONE), began its history within the Hebrew tradition; but both Moabite and Edomite exhibit traits divergent from Hebrew in later inscriptions, possibly under the influence of the internationalized Aramaic script. In happy contrast, the Ammonite national script is now broadly understood. The ninth-century Ammonite hand was still formally indistinguishable from contemporary Aramaic, but a distinctively Ammonite script emerged sometime in the middle of the eighth century, a period of material prosperity and considerable political autonomy (*see* AMMON[S]). This script later went the way of the Hebrew and was displaced by the common Aramaic hand of the Persian Empire. *See* INSCRIPTIONS, SEMITIC[S] §3*c*.

3. The transmission to Greece. Phoenician inscriptions have been recovered from maritime sites in Anatolia, Italy (Ischia), Malta, North Africa, and Spain, dating to the eighth century, and from Cyprus and Sardinia, dating to the ninth century or even earlier. Recent research confirms that the forms of the earliest Greek letters resemble most closely the corresponding Phoenician forms of the late ninth and early eighth centuries (*see* ALPHABET §A2). Thus the date of the borrowing of the alphabet must be assigned to this period. Nevertheless, certain archaic features in the early Greek scripts suggest some prehistory of experimentation with the Phoenician alphabet. Not only are individual, archaic letter-forms found, but there was no fixed direction of writing, and certain letter-forms regularly occurred in stances differing from those of the corresponding Phoenician forms of the ninth and eighth centuries. These data point to a prehistory of Greek experimentation with the alphabet, beginning perhaps as early as the end of the twelfth century, when the convention of writing from right to left was not yet firmly established in Phoenicia and when individual letter forms frequently occurred out of stance.

For further information, *see,* in addition to the bibliography cited below, WRITING AND WRITING MATERIALS §§A4, 5.

Bibliography. W. F. Albright, *The Proto-Sinaitic Inscriptions and Their Decipherment* (1966); F. M. Cross,

"Notes on the Ammonite Inscription from Tell Sīrān," *BASOR*, 212 (1973), 12-14, "Epigraphic Notes on the Ammān Citadel Inscription," *BASOR*, 193 (1969), 13-19, and "The Origin and Early Evolution of the Alphabet," *Eretz Israel*, VIII (1967), *8-*24; F. M. Cross and T. O. Lambdin, "A Ugaritic Abecedary and the Origins of the Proto-Canaanite Alphabet," *BASOR*, 160 (1960), 21-26; L. H. Jeffery, *The Local Scripts of Archaic Greece* (1961); P. K. McCarter, *The Antiquity of the Greek Alphabet and the Early Phoenician Scripts* (1975), and "The Early Diffusion of the Alphabet," *BA*, XXXVII (1974), 54-68; J. Naveh, *The Development of the Aramaic Script* (1970), and "Some Semitic Epigraphical Considerations on the Antiquity of the Greek Alphabet," *AJA*, LXXVII (1973), 1-8; J. B. Peckham, *The Development of the Late Phoenician Scripts* (1968).

P. K. McCarter

***ALTAR, OT.** *See* Beer-sheba[S]; Arad[S].

***ALTAR, NT.** The word "altar" in English versions of the NT represents three Greek words:

1. βωμός. Probably cognate with Greek βῆμα, "platform." This is the regular classical Greek word for "altar." It is used normally of a pagan altar, and this is its usual, but not invariable, meaning in the LXX. It occurs in the one place in the NT where a pagan altar is expressly mentioned —the Athenian altar inscribed "to an unknown god" (Acts 17:23), which supplied the text for Paul's Areopagus address. While an altar bearing this precise inscription (with the singular "unknown god") is not otherwise attested, we have the statement of Pausanias (*Description of Greece*, I.i.4) that in Athens there are "altars of gods called unknown" [βωμοὶ θεῶν ὀνομαζομένων ἀγνώστων]. This may be compared with his account (V.xiv.8) of "an altar to unknown gods" [ἀγνώστων θεῶν βωμός] beside the great altar of Zeus at Olympia. Philostratus (*Life of Apollonius*, VI.iii.5) says that in Athens there are erected "altars of unknown divinities" [ἀγνώστων δαιμόνων βωμοί], and it is probably the same kind of installation that Diogenes Laërtius has in mind when he mentions (*Lives of Philosophers*, I.cx) the "anonymous altars" [βωμοὶ ἀνώνυμοι] which were to be seen throughout Attica in his day (second-third century A.D.). The one surviving altar inscription of this kind is a defective one from the temple of Demeter in Pergamum (*ca.* 2nd century A.D.), which is most probably to be restored "to unknown gods" [θεοῖς ἀγνώστοις].

2. θυμιατήριον, place for incense [θυμίαμα]. This word appears once in the NT—in Heb. 9:4, where KJV and other older English versions render it "censer," because that is the sense which it bears in its three LXX occurrences (II Chr. 26:19; Ezek. 8:11; IV Macc. 7:11). When a censer is mentioned elsewhere in the NT, the Greek word is λιβανωτός (Rev. 8:3, 5). Theodotion and Symmachus use θυμιατήριον at Exod. 30:1 with the meaning "incense altar." So in Heb. 9:4 "altar of incense" is the more probable rendering (ASV, RSV, NEB, etc.), because the writer is enumerating pieces of furniture in the wilderness tabernacle. If he means "censer," it is doubly strange: first, because no emphasis is laid on one golden censer in the Pentateuchal description of the tabernacle, and second, because he then makes no reference to the incense altar, which was one of the principal pieces of furniture in the tabernacle. True, Heb. 9:4 assigns it to the holy of holies (so also I Kings 6:22; II Bar. 6:7), not to the holy place (as is implied in the Pentateuchal description). But even if it stood on the outer side of the curtain separating these two compartments, the incense altar played a significant part on the Day of Atonement, the one occasion in the year when the holy of holies was entered (Lev. 16:12, 13; cf. Exod. 30:10).

3. θυσιαστήριον, place of sacrifice [θυσία]. This is the word regularly used in the LXX to denote Israelite altars; it was free from the pagan associations of βωμός. In the NT it is the commonest word for "altar" and designates several different types of altar.

a) OT altars: that on which Abraham offered up Isaac (Jas. 2:21); the altar of burnt offering in Solomon's temple (Matt. 23:35; Luke 11:51); the altars of Yahweh which were demolished during the Baal apostasy under Ahab (Rom. 11:3).

b) The altar of burnt offering in Herod's temple: the place where gifts are offered (Matt. 5:23, 24); by which men swear light oaths (Matt. 23:18, 19, 20); at which only Levitical priests minister (Heb. 7:13), receiving the sacrificial flesh as their perquisite (I Cor. 9:13) and so becoming "partners in the altar" (I Cor. 10:18).

c) The incense altar in Herod's temple: where Zechariah, father of John the Baptist, was officiating as a member of the priestly division of Abijah when Gabriel announced to him the birth of his son (Luke 1:11).

d) The incense altar in the heavenly sanctuary: beneath which the souls of the martyrs await their vindication (Rev. 6:9); at which the prayers of the saints, mixed with incense, are presented on a golden censer by an angel to God (Rev. 8:3,4; cf. Tob. 12:15); and from which fire is then thrown on the earth, probably in response to the martyrs' prayer for vengeance on their persecutors (Rev. 8:5).

e) A Christian altar in Heb. 13:10: "We have an altar from which those who serve the tent (i.e. the Jewish sanctuary) have no right to eat." The significance of this altar is disputed, but the context helps us to understand it. The recipients of this letter (probably a household church of Jewish Christians) were reproached by their former co-religionists because they had no visible altar or sacrificial ritual. "We *have* an altar," is the reply, and a more adequate one than the altar of burnt offering in the Jewish sanctuary. Earlier in the letter the sacrifice of Jesus has been portrayed in terms of the sin offering on the Day of Atonement: his offering, by contrast with that earlier one, is permanently efficacious. There was no literal altar in his case; the term "altar" is used here by metonymy for his self-oblation and the benefits which it secures to believers. The flesh of the animal presented as a sin offering on the Day of Atonement was not eaten by the worshipers; it was incinerated "outside the camp" (Heb. 13:11). The fact that Jesus suffered death outside the gate of Jerusalem is taken to symbolize his rejection from the "camp" of the old religion. But he is permanently available for the spiritual food or sustenance of his people. (Some controversy about "food" is implied in vs. 9.) Whether or not the Eucharist is referred to is doubtful: elsewhere the writer to the Hebrews seems deliberately to avoid mentioning the Eucharist even when the opportunity to introduce it is wide open (e.g. in Heb. 7:1-10 the one feature in the Melchizedek narrative of Gen. 14:18-20 which he passes over in silence is Melchizedek's bringing bread and wine to Abraham). *See also* HEBREWS, LETTER TO THE[S].

Bibliography. E. Norden, *Agnostos Theos* (1913); P. Corssen, "Der Altar des unbekannten Gottes," *ZNW,* XIV (1913), 309-23; E. Meyer, *Ursprung und Anfänge des Christentums,* III (1923), 95-98; A. Deissmann, *Paul* (1927), pp. 287-91, pls. V, VI; H. Koester, "'Outside the camp': Hebrews 13.9-14," *HTR,* LV (1962), 299-315.

F. F. BRUCE

***AMMON, AMMONITES.** Numerous recent discoveries have provided additional information with regard to the Ammonite culture, history, and language.

1. Name. In 1961 a fragment of an inscription of *ca.* 600 B.C. was found at the Amman Theater, of which the second line reads *bn* ᶜ*m*[*n*]. The name is spelled in the same way as the name of the Ammonites in the Hebrew Bible. This same spelling occurs three times in the inscription from Tell Sīrān (*ca.* 600 B.C.).

2. The early Ammonite state. A Late Bronze Age temple at Amman seems to indicate that some kind of sedentary people lived there before the twelfth century B.C. This temple, first discovered in 1955, was excavated in 1966. Hundreds of imported objects point to a sophisticated civilization with international relations. Hence, it is probable that some form of an Ammonite state existed during the Late Bronze Age, from 1600-1200 B.C. In fact, the discovery of Middle Bronze Age tombs at Naur and Amman makes it possible to assume that a sedentary population existed from 1800-1600 B.C. in the area which the historical Ammonites later occupied. *See* EDOM[S].

3. Beginning of Ammonite expansion. The megalithic border fortresses, of which nineteen are so far known to have shielded Amman, have generally been dated to the Iron Age on the basis of ceramic surface finds. Recently, two of these structures have been excavated. Rujm el-Malfuf, to everyone's surprise, has proved to be of Roman origin. On the other hand Khirbet al-Hajjar must have been built first during the twelfth and eleventh centuries B.C. Later it was abandoned, but was rebuilt in the seventh and sixth centuries B.C. Only further excavations will provide a clear picture of the development of the defensive system of the Ammonite state.

4. Israelite conquest of Amman. When David conquered RABBAH, the crown of the Ammonite king fell into his hands. Containing a precious stone, it seems to have been of such an extraordinary value that David used it as his own crown (II Sam. 12:30; I Chr. 20:2). It is therefore of interest that nine stone statues found in and around Amman, all dated to the Iron Age, represent males wearing a headgear that resembles the Egyptian *atef*-crown, perhaps similar to the one captured by King David.

5. Kings. Thanks to the new Tell Sīrān inscription it is now possible to present an almost complete list of the Ammonite kings from Bod'el to Baalis (Jer. 40:14): Bod'el; 'Ammi-nadab I, *ca.* 667, known from the records of Ashurbanipal's first campaign; his son, *ca.* 650, whose name is not yet attested (Cross suggests that his name according to the practice of papponymy may have been Bod'el, or Hiṣṣal-'el); 'Ammi-nadab II, *ca.* 635; Hiṣṣal-'el (II?), his son, perhaps by 620; by 600 B.C., 'Ammi-nadab III; probably followed by Baalis, *ca.* 580.

6. Culture. The typical Ammonite pottery known until 1968 almost exclusively from tombs discovered at and near Amman has now come to light in large amounts during the excavations of Tell Ḥesbân (*see* HESHBON[S]). This pottery is indigenous to Transjordan and attests to a high cultural level.

An Iron Age tomb discovered in June 1966 on Jebel el-Qusur, Amman, has produced four anthropoid sarcophagi (*see* BETH-SHAN Fig. 38), and parts of a fifth one. It is possible that they were used by foreigners, descendants of the Sea Peoples (*see* PHILISTINES; PHILISTINES[S]) who may have served the Ammonite kings as mercenaries.

There is still very little known of the Ammonite religion. However, the name of the chief Ammonite god, known from the Bible as Milcom, has come to light in the Amman Citadel Inscription (spelled [*m*]*lkm*) and also on two Ammonite seals.

The discovery of several Ammonite inscriptions and ostraca has given us a much clearer picture of the Ammonite language and the use of writing among the Ammonite population. See INSCRIPTIONS, SEMITIC[S] §3*c*; ALPHABET[S] §2.

Bibliography. G. L. Harding, "A Middle Bronze Age Tomb at Amman," *PEF Annual,* VI (1953), 14-18; N. Avigad, "Seals of Exiles," *IEJ,* XV (1965), 223-28; R. W. Dajani, "The Amman Theatre Fragment," *ADAJ,* XII-XIII (1967-1968), 65-67; J. Naveh and H. Tadmor, "Some Doubtful Aramaic Seals," *Annali dell' Istituto Orientale di Napoli,* XXVIII (1968), 448-52 (also pp. 453-54); S. H. Horn, "The Ammān Citadel Inscription," *BASOR,* 193 (1969), 2-13; R. S. Boraas, "A Preliminary Sounding at Rujm el-Malfuf, 1969," *ADAJ,* XVI (1971), 31-46; H. O. Thompson, "The 1972 Excavation of Kihirbet al-Hajjar," *ADAJ,* XVII (1972), 47-72; E. N. Lugenbeal and J. A. Sauer, "Seventh-sixth century B.C. Pottery from Area B at Heshbon," *AUSS,* X (1972), 21-69; H. O. Thompson and F. Zayadine, "The Tell Siran Inscription," *BASOR,* 212 (1973), 5-11; S. H. Horn, "The Crown of the King of the Ammonites," *AUSS,* XI (1973), 170-80; F. M. Cross, "Notes on the Ammonite Inscription from Tell Sīrān," *BASOR,* 212 (1973), 12-15; V. Hankey, "A Late Bronze Age Temple at Amman," *Levant,* VI (1974), 131-78.

S. H. HORN

***AMORITES. 1. Amorites and Amurru.** The term "Amorite," in the older Akkadian form, "Amurru," is first attested in cuneiform sources from Mesopotamia dating to the latter half of the third millennium B.C. "Amurru" is used in these sources to designate both a group of Northwest Semitic-speaking people (described as stock raisers and as somewhat barbaric) and also the territory occupied by them. In the earliest sources the territory of Amurru is located in the Syrian steppe, W of the Middle Euphrates. (Akkad. *amurru* means "west.")

The label "Amorite" ("Amurrite") apparently derives from a self-designation, perhaps by one of the "tribes" of that area—note that Amurru is the name of a Hanaean "clan" in the MARI texts—which came to represent the whole people and the western territory generally. This designation is continued by Ammi-ṣaduqa of Babylon, who sums up the local population as "Akkadians and Amorites." At Mari, however, the people are summarized as "Akkadians and Hanaeans."

In Egyptian and cuneiform sources from the fourteenth and thirteenth centuries Amurru is a territory and a kingdom in central Syria, extending from the Mediterranean coast to the vicinity of the Orontes River. For a period Amurru was the northernmost Egyptian administrative district in Syria, bordering on Canaan to the S. Subsequently Amurru became a Hittite dependency and is known from its exchanges with the kingdom of UGARIT to the N as well as from Hittite sources (*see* HITTITES; HITTITES[S]). In the earlier Mari texts (eighteenth century) Amurru is a territory somewhere in central Syria, with several kings.

2. OT usage. The OT uses "Amorite" only as an ethnic label and does not mention the Syrian kingdom of Amurru, which came to an end *ca.* 1200 B.C. The Amorites are listed as one of the ethnic groups already in Palestine and Transjordan at the time following the Exodus. In a general sense the basic population of the whole area could be called Amorite (e.g., Gen. 15:16; Deut. 1:7; Josh. 10:5; 24:15; II Sam. 21:2), thereby apparently using a self-designation in an expanded sense, analogous to the Mesopotamian sources. (In a similar way, the term "Canaanite" can be used to designate the whole pre-Israelite population of the area W of the Jordan; *see* CANAANITES §2.) This wider use of Amorite is especially characteristic of the E and D traditions (*see* DOCUMENTS), but it is not limited to them. In the various lists of pre-Israelite population groups, the Amorites, together with the Canaanites and the Hittites, are very prominent. In the "standard" list there are seven great and mighty "nations": Hittites, Girgashites, Amorites, Canaanites, Perizzites, Hivites, and Jebusites (e.g., Deut. 7:1).

More specifically, Amorites are associated with Transjordan and with Sihon, king of the Amorites, and Og, king of the territory of Bashan, with its chief cities of Ashtaroth and Edrei. According to later tradition these are "the two kings of the Amorites" (e.g., Deut. 3:8; Josh 2:10) who opposed the Israelites after the Exodus. Og, who is also celebrated in tradition as the last of the legendary giant REPHAIM and the possessor of a famous iron bedstead (Deut. 3:11), seems, however, to be only secondarily associated with the Amorites. The history of Sihon reflects an ancient tradition identifying the Amorites—and the king of the Amorites, Sihon—as a major ethnic group in the Transjordanian area subsequently claimed or occupied by some of the Israelites. Sihon is honored in the old song cited in Num. 21:27-30. *See* HESHBON; HESHBON[S].

One of the primary characteristics of the Amorites as seen by Israelite tradition was that they went after other gods, after idols, and were accordingly associated with iniquity (e.g., Gen. 15:16; Josh. 24:15; Judg. 6:10; cf. Lev. 18:28; 20:22-23). For that reason God drove them out of the land.

3. The Amorites in Palestine and Transjordan. The antiquity of the Amorite occupation of the territory later occupied by Israel is a difficult question. The Egyptian execration texts attest to a group of princes in Palestine and Transjordan by *ca.* 1900 B.C. whose personal names are consistent in language and type with Amorite names of the same general period in Mesopotamia. However, for this period it is difficult to separate Amorite from (Proto-) Canaanite on linguistic grounds. Given the complex ethnic character of Syria-Palestine in general, terms may vary greatly regarding referents; note the long lists in the OT (e.g., Gen. 10:15-18), as well as the short lists (e.g., Exod. 23:28). This factor and the absence of written materials make it hard to correlate archaeological discoveries with specific ethnic groups. The Taanach tablets indicate an ethnic picture not hinted at by the archaeological remains; *see* TAANACH[S]. *See also* HURRIANS[S].

The evidence from personal names in Akkadian and Egyptian texts of the early second millennium indicates a modest dialectal differentiation into coastal-southern and inland linguistic areas, a differentiation that correlates to some extent with the archaeological evidence. The archaeologists themselves associate the coming of the Amorites with the new archaeological picture at the end of Early Bronze III, *ca.* 2300 B.C., or the beginning of Middle Bronze II (MB I), *ca.* 1900 B.C., although the discontinuities may have been over-emphasized. It is, moreover, now questioned that the Amorites can be described as nomads, which further complicates the task of correlation. The complex ethnic picture reflected in the literary sources (mostly later) and the patterns of population shifting in the area suggest that precise correlations should not be pressed at this time. The antiquity of the Amorites in Palestine and Transjordan is unclear, but Amorite elements must have been there at least by 1900 B.C., when they are clearly present in central and northern Syria, and perhaps were there much earlier.

Bibliography. G. Buccellati, *The Amorites of the Ur III Period* (1966); A. Haldar, *Who Were the Amorites?* (1971); H. B. Huffmon, *Amorite Personal Names in the Mari Texts* (1965); H. Klengel, *Geschichte Syriens im 2. Jahrtausend v.u.z.*, II (1969), 178-299; K. M. Kenyon, *Amorites and Canaanites* (1966); P. W. Lapp, *The Dhahr Mirzbâneh Tombs* (1966), pp. 86-116; K. Prag, "The Intermediate Early Bronze-Middle Bronze Age," *Levant*, VI (1974), 69-116. H. B. HUFFMON

***AMOS.** No fundamental changes have occurred recently in the scholarly consensus regarding the date and historical setting of the primary group of his oracles, or their main ethical and religious content. Recent discussion has focused upon the question of the cultic and literary origins of the traditions upon which the book draws, and the related question concerning the extent of Amos' association with the official Israelite cult. Decisions regarding the origin of the disputed parts of the book, notably the oracles against Tyre, Edom, and Judah (1:9-12; 2:4-5), the doxologies (4:13; 5:8-9; 9:5-6), and the closing promise of salvation (9:8*b*-15), have tended to hinge upon the answers given to these questions.

1. Liturgical forms in the book. Amos 1:3–2:16 may reflect a ritual of cursing directed against the enemies of Israel. Such rituals were conducted in ancient Egypt, using brief curses, proclaimed in a series according to a geographical pattern similar to the one found in Amos. The enemy nations round about are cursed first, and then the individual enemies within Egypt itself. The series in Amos proclaims impending divine judgment upon neighboring states, and then upon Israel itself (though here it is the nation as a whole). The geographical pattern breaks down, however, if the oracles against Tyre and Edom (1:9-12) are removed as secondary additions, as many scholars have done. The Judah oracle (2:4-5) is also widely deemed to be late, because of its vague, Deuteronomic language (as contrasted with the historical concreteness of the other oracles in the series) and its difference in form (along with the oracles on Tyre and Edom) from the remaining four. However, the formal unity of the entire pericope, 1:3–2:16, may be defended as the carefully articulated alternation of two related but slightly differing forms, in the pattern A, A, B, B, A, A, B, B^1. The concluding oracle against Israel is an expanded version of type B. An equally coherent pattern remains if the Judah oracle, whose authenticity is most doubtful, is removed. In this case the Israel oracle can be taken as applying to all Israel and not merely to the northern kingdom. Many critics believe that Amos himself used the name Israel in reference to the whole people of God, and that the separate references to Judah in the book are the result of the reapplication of his oracles to the kingdom of Judah after the fall of the northern Israelite kingdom in 721 B.C.

The historical allusions in the oracles against the nations have been scrutinized repeatedly, but the scanty information they provide makes it impossible to know whether they refer to events reported in the extant historical records, which are themselves highly fragmentary, or to otherwise unknown events. In the case of the oracles against Philistia (Gaza), Tyre, and Edom (1:6-12), we are not even told who are the victims of the crimes which are denounced. If the Egyptian cursing ritual was the ultimate model, then the Israelite ritual which Amos imitated would have dealt largely with crimes against Israel. But this would not mean that Amos himself referred only to crimes against Israel. There is a universality in his perspective that suggests otherwise.

Amos 4:6-11 (or 4:4-13) has been regarded by some as an adaptation of a ritual of cursing or, by others, of a liturgy from the supposed covenant-renewal ceremony of Israel (*see* COVENANT, MOSAIC [S]). Still others discern the pattern of a covenant lawsuit here, or in the larger complex, 3:1–4:13. (*See* LAW IN THE OT[S] §13.) These interpretations are not mutually exclusive, since curses have a prominent place in covenantal texts in the OT (e.g., Deut. 28 and Lev. 26) and in the formally related vassal treaties of the Hittites and Assyrians. Whether or not 4:4-13 reflects actual cultic practice, this passage and the oracles of Amos generally share the terminology of malediction standardized in a variety of liturgical and quasi-liturgical settings in the ancient world.

The doxologies (4:13; 5:8-9; 9:5-6) are widely believed to be derived from a hymn used in Israelite worship, but some scholars attribute to Amos their incorporation into the book, while others credit it to a redactor. On the grounds of the novel conclusion that II Kings 23:16-18 deals with Amos' denunciation of Bethel (cf. 4:4; 5:5-6; 9:1), Wolff theorizes that the doxologies were added to the book of Amos at the time of King Josiah's reform (621 B.C.), as part of a liturgical act of justification for the Judean king's destruction of the sanctuary of Bethel, the principal shrine of the northern Israelite kingdom. In any case, the doxologies do serve as climaxes to the three oracles in 4:4-13; 5:1-9; and 9:1-6, and these oracles form a logical series. Together they assert that instead of the comforting encounter with God which the Israelites have expected routinely in their rituals, there will actually be a nonroutine, disastrous encounter with God, ending in national destruction.

2. Amos' vocation. A few scholars have argued that Amos was actually a cultic prophet and that his oracles were proclaimed in a ritual setting. According to this theory the oracle of salvation which concludes the book (9:8*b*-15) is a word of Amos, uttered in the liturgy as the divine promise which balances the oracles of judgment, which were supposedly used in an earlier part of the ritual. However, most critics reject this theory and hold that 9:8*b*-15 is largely or wholly a postexilic addition reflecting religious aspirations of Jews in a later generation. Furthermore, they deny that the pre-exilic rituals of Israel were so rich in prophetic proclamation as the advocates of the former theory suppose. Surely the condemnations of the Israelite rituals themselves which are contained in the oracles of Amos and his prophetic contemporaries strongly suggest the opposite (cf., e.g., Amos 3:13-15; 4:4-5; 5:4-6, 21-27; Hos. 4:4-19; 5:1-2; 8:11-14; Isa. 1:10-15).

Explicit evidence concerning Amos' vocational associations is confined to the disputed statement in 7:14-15. Although many scholars continue to translate the verbless Hebrew clause in vs. 14 in the present tense ("I *am* no prophet . . . , but Yahweh called me. . . ."), and interpret the line as a denial by Amos of any association with the professional prophets of Israel, a growing number prefer the past tense ("I *was* no prophet . . . , but Yahweh called me. . . ."), and take the statement as an assertion of divine authority for his mission, rather than a denial of his role as a prophet.

3. Amos and wisdom. There are terms and literary forms in the book which are characteristic of, or at least common in, the wisdom traditions of the OT. These suggest to some scholars that

Amos' perspective was shaped by these traditions rather than, or in addition to, those of the cult (covenantal or otherwise). Among the features which are thought to show wisdom influence are the use of a series of rhetorical questions in 3:3-6; the repeated use of a numerical sequence of the type x/x+1 in 1:3–2:6; the presence of woe oracles in 5:18; 6:1, 4; the use of the formal admonition (as contrasted with the unconditional prophetic oracle of doom) in 4:4-5; 5:4-6, 14-15; the doxologies (4:13; 5:8-9; 9:5-6); and several individual terms and references that are distinctive in Amos, among the prophets. *See* WISDOM IN THE OT[S].

As in the case of the alleged cultic affinities of the book, it is debated whether these other features are distinctive of the wisdom tradition, or even at home in it. However, some of the evidence does appear to show that Amos' language and his forms of utterance were partly shaped by the special interests and habits of either the professional wise men or the elders of the Israelite clans. Unfortunately, too little is known about either for us to pinpoint the source of this influence upon Amos.

4. The message of Amos. Recent research tends to confirm the opinion that the forms and substance of Amos' message were deeply rooted in the religious traditions of Yahwism and were not merely the unprecedented innovations of a creative mind. Thus he can be seen more clearly than before as the representative of a dynamic community of faith which spanned the generations of Israel. And yet Amos' great originality, which is manifest above all in the unique configuration of his oracles, must be emphasized. Whatever traditional forms he may have used he invested with new meaning and power.

Bibliography. Commentaries and general works: S. Amsler, CAT, XIa (1965), 159-247; R. S. Cripps, *A Critical and Exegetical Commentary on the Book of Amos* (2nd ed., 1955); R. Fey, *Amos und Jesaja*, WMANT, XII (1963); H. E. W. Fosbroke, IB, VI (1956), 763-853; E. Hammershaimb, *The Book of Amos, a Commentary* (1970); R. L. Honeycutt, *Amos and His Message* (1963); V. Maag, *Text, Wortschatz und Begriffswelt des Buches Amos* (1951); J. L. Mays, *Amos, a Commentary* (1969); *RevExp*, LXIV (1966) and *Southwestern Journal of Theology*, IX (1966) are both devoted entirely to the book of Amos; J. M. Ward, *Amos and Isaiah* (1969); H. W. Wolff, BKAT, XIV (1969).

Special Studies: A. Bentzen, "The Ritual Background of Amos I.2–II.16," *OTS,* VIII (1950), 85-99; G. J. Botterweck, "Zur Authentizität des Buches Amos," *BZ* (NS), II (1958), 176-89; M. O'R. Boyle, "The Covenant Lawsuit of the Prophet Amos: III 1–IV 13," *VT,* XXI (1971), 338-62; W. Brueggemann, "Amos IV 4-13 and Israel's Covenant Worship," *VT,* XV (1965), 1-15; J. F. Craghan, "The Prophet Amos in Recent Literature," BThB, II (1972), 242-61; J. L. Crenshaw, "The Influence of the Wise upon Amos," *ZAW,* LXXIX (1967), 42-52, "Amos and the Theophanic Tradition," *ZAW,* LXXX (1968), 203-15, and "A Liturgy of Wasted Opportunity (Amos 4:6-12; Isa. 9:7–10:4)," *Semitics,* I (1970), 27-38; G. Farr, "The Language of Amos, Popular or Cultic?" *VT,* XVI (1966), 312-24; F. C. Fensham, "Common Trends in Curses of the Near Eastern Treaties and *kudurru*-Inscriptions Compared with the Maledictions of Amos and Isaiah," *ZAW,* LXXV (1963), 155-75; D. R. Hillers, *Treaty Curses and the Old Testament Prophets* (1964); W. E. March, "Prophecy," *Old Testament Form Criticism,* ed. J. H. Hayes (1974), 141-77; J. Muilenburg, "The 'Office' of the Prophet in Ancient Israel," *The Bible in Modern Scholarship,* ed. J. P. Hyatt (1965), pp. 74-97; S. M. Paul, "Amos 1,3-2,3," *JBL,* XC (1971), 397-403; H. Reventlow, *FRLANT,* LXXX (1962); W. H. Schmidt, "Die deuteronomistische Redaktion des Amosbuches," *ZAW,* LXXVII (1965), 168-93; W. E. Staples, "Epic Motifs in Amos," *JNES,* XXV (1966), 106-12; S. Terrien, "Amos and Wisdom," *Israel's Prophetic Heritage,* ed. B. W. Anderson and W. Harrelson (1962), pp. 108-15; M. Weiss, "The Pattern of the 'Execration Texts' in the Prophetic Literature," *IEJ,* XIX (1969), 150-57; H. W. Wolff, *Amos the Prophet, the Man and His Background* (1973).

J. M. WARD

AMPHICTYONY ăm fĭk' tē ə nē [Gr. ἀμφικτυονία from ἀμφικτύονες, var. of ἀμφικτίονες, "dwellers around"]. In Greece, the name for a specific form of league organized around a temple for its protection and maintenance. Certain scholars apply this term to a supposedly analogous organization of early Israel.

1. The Pylaean-Delphic amphictyony. A consideration of the hypothetical Israelite amphictyony must start from a brief outline of its alleged Greek counterparts. Among those, the Pylaean-Delphic amphictyony was the most important. It started as a league of a few small tribes on both sides of the vital Thermopylae Pass for protecting their security and exploiting in common the traffic through the pass. Delegates from member tribes met every autumn in the shrine of Demeter at Anthella, near the southern end of the "Gates" (*pylai*); hence *pylaia* for the assemblies, and *pylagorai* (or *pylagoroi*) for the delegates. The members of the amphictyony pledged, in case of war, not to cut off water from each other and not to destroy one another's towns. *Ca.* 600 B.C., the powerful Thessalians, followed by Euboea and Boeotia, joined the amphictyony. The expanded league now counted twelve member "peoples" (*ethnê*). The temple of Delphi was later placed under the protectorate and administration of the amphictyony, and members pledged sacred war against any state that would encroach on the domain of the temple. The amphictyonic council now met four times a year: twice at Anthella, twice at Delphi. Beside the *pylagorai,* who decided all legal questions relating to the amphictyony, there was established a board of *hieromnêmones* for administering the finances and construction works of the temple.

Very little is known of other Greek amphictyonies: around the temple of Poseidon at Calauria (with seven members); around the temple of Poseidon at Onchestus (number of members unknown); around the temple of Apollo at Delos (membership open to all states of Ionian origin). Outside the Greek world, the closest parallel is provided by the league of Etruscan cities, which always counted twelve members, though their names vary in different transmissions. Their representatives went every spring to a festival at a temple of Voltumna and elected the supreme priest of the league.

2. Noth's thesis. Occasional comparisons between the twelve tribes of Israel and Greek or Italian leagues with the same number of members were made since mid-nineteenth century, but it was Noth who first presented a systematic exposition of the hypothesis of an Israelite amphictyony. His thesis can be summarized as follows. The six tribes of the "Leah group" were the first to settle in Canaan. They established the "first amphictyony," under the name Israel, with the amphictyonic center just W of Shechem. The tribe of Benjamin arrived somewhat later, and the tribes of the house of Joseph came last, at the time of Pharaoh Mer-ne-Ptah, from the confines of the Egyptian Delta and the area of Kadesh. The remaining tribes had dwelt in Canaan along with the "Leah group," but could not join the amphictyony because its membership could only be doubled from six to twelve. The arrival of the Joseph tribes provided the missing two units, so that each tribe could maintain the amphictyonic shrine for one month of each year. It was only then that Yahweh, brought by the Joseph tribes and represented by the ark, became the common deity of the amphictyony. After the destruction of Shechem by Abimelech, the ark was transferred to Shiloh. The amphictyony celebrated common festivals. The member tribes were represented by their *n^e^śî'îm,* who corresponded to the Delphic *hieromnêmones.* There was an amphictyonic law (the Book of the Covenant or parts thereof), and there were amphictyonic wars (e.g., against Gibeah of Benjamin, Judg. 19–21). When Judah temporarily seceded after Saul's death, Hebron with its Abrahamic shrine at Mamre became the center of a six-member amphictyony composed of Judah, Simeon, Caleb, Othniel, Jerachmeel, and Cain. This "greater Judahite" amphictyony was perhaps even older than the twelve-tribe one. David transferred the ark to Jerusalem so that this neutral city could become the center of the restored Israelite amphictyony, which had by then evolved into a national monarchy.

3. Objections to the thesis. The principal objection to the thesis is its purely speculative character. Nowhere in the books of Judges and Samuel is there a reference to such an organization. Judg. 1 emphasizes that each tribe conquered its territory by its own efforts. Tales about the premonarchic period stress the absence of any common authority and extol the feats of individual clan chieftains, freebooters, single tribes, or, in rare cases, *ad hoc* coalitions of two or more tribes. No central shrine comparable to Delphi existed in Palestine. Sanctuaries were numerous and strictly local. Nowhere in the book of Judges is it said that Shechem played a central religious role for all or most of the tribes of Israel; nor is there a word in the whole OT that the ark was ever stationed at, or near, SHECHEM (*see* JOSHUA, BOOK OF[S] §5*d*). The ark is not mentioned anywhere in Judges, except Judg. 20:27, which places it at Bethel; but the verse is an obvious interpolation. According to another view (Albright), the central sanctuary remained at Shiloh from the conquest of Canaan to the eve of the royal period. However, the statements that Shiloh was the place where Joshua set up the tabernacle and allotted the land to the tribes (Josh. 18:1, 8-10; 19:51; 21:1-8; 22:9, 12) all belong to the postexilic Priestly Code (*see* PRIESTLY WRITERS[S]). Judg. 21:19-21 speaks of a yearly feast of Yahweh at Shiloh, but since only "the daughters of Shiloh" are said to have performed ritual dances in its vineyards, it must have been a local affair. In I Sam. 3:3; 4:3-4 the ark is stationed in the temple (*hêkāl*) of Shiloh, but nothing is said of intertribal assemblies there, and Eli is described only as the priest of the temple, not as the incumbent of "the chief magistracy of Israel." When the Philistines returned the ark to the Israelites, it remained for "some twenty years" forgotten in a private house at Kiriath-jearim (I Sam. 7:1-2), and somehow the unification of Israel under Saul proceeded at that very time without this alleged symbol of amphictyonic unity. The *n^e^śî'îm,* supposedly the administrators of the central shrine, are never mentioned in the historical books of the OT.

There is no trace of evidence of a six-tribe amphictyony at the time of the Egyptain rule in Palestine. Noth deduced the figure six, to which he attached much importance, from the patriarchal tale of Jacob's children by Leah; but the actual figure is seven—six sons and one daughter, derived from the popular motif of the seven planetary deities, six of them male and one (Venus) female. The case for the six-tribe "Greater Judahite amphictyony" is no stronger. The "Abrahamic shrine at Mamre" is not mentioned at all in the stories of David's enthronement at Hebron, first over Judah (II Sam. 2:1-4), later over Israel (5:1-5). The figure twelve, derived from the number of months in a year, was fixed as the number of Jacob's sons, but it plays no role in historical narratives which speak of "all Israel," "Israel and Judah," or "all tribes of Israel" (I Sam. 10:20; II Sam. 5:1; 15:10) without specifying their number. The Song of Deborah (Judg. 5) lists ten tribes, with Simeon, Levi, Judah, and Gad missing altogether. A classical presentation of the twelve-tribe scheme is found in the utopian vision in Ezek. 48, written long after the breakup of the tribal order. In it, the twelve tribes occupy equal shares of the land of Israel, seven N of the holy temple district, five S of it, with the *nāśî',* the priests, and the Levites installed in the holy district itself. This vision was taken over by the authors of the Priestly Code. They retrojected it into the remote past of the desert wandering, replacing the temple by a half-scale, movable tabernacle, the N-S sequence of the tribal portions by a circular camp with the tabernacle in its center, and Ezekiel's single *nāśî'* by twelve tribal *n^e^śî'îm.*

But even the imaginary desert congregation of the Priestly Code bears no resemblance to the Delphic amphictyony. In Delphi, an elected representative council of the *pylagorai* regularly met in set places and decided questions of common concern by a majority of votes; a similarly elected board of *hieromnêmones* controlled the finances and property of the temple. In Etruria, delegates of allied cities elected the chief priest of the league. In the Priestly Code, the congregation is a rigid theocracy under the strict personal rule of Moses whose orders come from Yahweh and are obeyed without discussion. The *n^e^śî'îm,* far from being the elected representatives of their tribes to a governing council, are Moses' appointees, responsible for the implementation of his decrees (Num. 1:2-17).

4. Near Eastern parallels. It is futile to seek confirmation of the twelve-tribe system in other genealogical charts of the Priestly Code which contain twelve members: Gen. 22:20-24; 25:12-17; and 36:9-19, if Amalek is not counted. These groupings are artificial and only reflect the Priestly compiler's predilection for duodecimal classification. It has been asserted that an amphictyony, similar to that of Delphi, existed in Sumer. At the time of the Third Dynasty of Ur, city governors had to deliver periodic contributions for the temple of Nippur. Most cities supplied the temple for one month, some for two to four months, sometimes three towns combined for a monthly tribute. The rotation was not on an annual basis (every year another group of cities was assigned), and no difference was made between cities of Sumer proper and newly conquered Hurrian and Elamite cities. To speak of an amphictyony in the authoritarian, hypercentralized Ur III Empire contradicts the basic meaning of the term, and to postulate on the ground of the quoted facts a "prehistoric Sumerian amphictyony" is unwarranted.

There are, however, much closer Near Eastern analogues to the premonarchic Israelite tribal order. Tribal associations, or confederations, are characteristic of nomadic tribes, both in their original conditions and in the process of their becoming sedentary. The MARI texts, which shed much light on nomadic tribes of N Mesopotamia, tell, e.g., of a "confederation (*ummātum,* cf. Heb. *'ummâ*) of all the 'fathers' (sheiks) of Ḫana," and of a confederation of three tribal kingdoms: Ubrabûm, Amnānûm, and Rabbûm. The former two tribes, along with two more, Yaḫrurûm and Yariḫûm, were collectively known as "sons of Yamina" (Benjaminites). They were linked to each other by a common way of life and a consciousness of kinship; intertribal alliances were expressed in terms of brotherhood. Tribes easily moved from one confederation to another: we hear, e.g., of "Benjaminite Ḫaneans." Treaties between Benjaminite chieftains and kings of city-states were accompanied by sacrifices, and could be concluded in a temple of one of the cities involved, but nothing points to the existence of a common shrine. The same pattern of tribal areas and intertribal confederations was later followed by Arameans, Chaldeans, and Arabs.

5. Conclusion. A loose confederation of an unstable number of tribes is all that emerges from the biblical traditions about premonarchic Israel. The balance of evidence favors the conclusion made by de Vaux: "The proposed rapprochement between the grouping of the tribes of Israel and the Greek amphictyonies is not justified."

Bibliography. H. Bürgel, *Die Pylaeisch-delphische Amphiktyonie* (1877); F. Cauer, "Amphiktyonia," PW, I (1894), cols. 1904-35; G. Busolt and H. Swoboda, *Griechische Staatskunde* (1925), pp. 1280-309; M. Noth, *Das System der zwölf Stämme Israels* (1930), and *The History of Israel* (2nd ed., 1960), pp. 85-109, W. F. Albright, *Archaeology and the Religion of Israel* (1942 [4th ed., 1956]), pp. 102-4; H. M. Orlinsky, "The Tribal System of Israel and Related Groups in the Period of the Judges," *OrAnt,* I (1962), 11-20; R. de Vaux, "La thèse de l'amphictyonie israélite,'" *HTR,* LXIV (1971), 415-36 (with exhaustive bibliog.); W. W. Hallo, "A Sumerian Amphictyony," *JCS,* XIV (1960), 88-114; J.-R. Kupper, *Les nomades en Mésopotamie au temps des rois de Mari* (1957); A. Malamat, "Mari and the Bible: Some Patterns of Tribal Organization and Institutions," *JAOS,* LXXXII (1962), 143-50.

M. C. ASTOUR

***ANAB.** Recent archaeological survey has shown that the Iron Age site is located at Khirbet 'Unnâb eṣ-Ṣaghîr, ¾ mile W of eẓ-Ẓāherîyeh, rather than at Khirbet 'Unnâb el-Kabîrah, two miles farther SW, which has only Roman, Byzantine, and later materials.

Bibliography. M. Kochavi, "The Land of Judah," *Judaea, Samaria and the Golan, Archaeological Survey 1967-1968* (1972), pp. 21, 76, 78, Hebrew.

A. F. RAINEY

ANATHOTH. 2. One of the "chiefs of the people" who joined Nehemiah in setting their seal to the covenant which the Judean community made with God (Neh. 10:19 [H 20]).

***ANDREW, ACTS OF.** *See* APOCRYPHA, NT[S].

ANDROGYNY ăn drŏj' ĭ nĭ [Gr., from ἀνήρ, ἀνδρός, "man" and γυνή, "woman"]. A belief in sexual ambivalence or change of sex in gods, mythical heroes, or human beings. Vestigial reminiscences of it can be discerned in the OT.

1. Sexual attributes. Since the earliest times, mankind has been fascinated by the male-female dichotomy. Masculinity and femininity were regarded as primordial essences. Each sex had its own set of characteristics and virtues, to be kept strictly apart. In the Near East, the standard emblem of masculinity was the bow (both as a weapon and as a symbol of male potency); of femininity, the spindle. Normally, each sex avoided the attributes of the opposite sex. It was feared that wearing a woman's attire by a man would contaminate him with feminine weakness, while the use of a man's garb and arms by a woman was considered presumptuous. But precisely because transvestism was not approved in everyday life, it could be practiced—as this was true for many other taboos—in special circumstances, such as religious ceremonies and marriage. On the other hand, somatic hermaphroditism, psychological transsexualism, and rare cases of apparent sex change at puberty, were no doubt observed in real life. But more than from such observations, the idea of androgyny arose from the inclination of human fantasy to create imaginary composite beings.

2. In Mesopotamia. Opposite sexual characteristics were combined in the image of the goddess Ishtar. On the one hand, she was the quintessence of voluptuous, seductive femininity (but, significantly, she had no children); on the other hand, she was a war-goddess, depicted with a bow and quivers, who led armies into battles, scattered and destroyed the enemy. Her planet, Dilbat (Venus), was "female as the evening star, male as the morning star." In pre-Sargonic Mari, a temple was built to Ishtar-NITA, "the male Ishtar." In a hymn of Nanâ (a manifestation of Ishtar), the goddess declares: "I am a hierodule in Uruk, I have heavy breasts in Daduni, I have a beard in Babylon, still I am Nanâ." In Assyria, Ishtar was represented "with a beard like Aššur." Conversely, her consort Dumuzi (Heb. Tammuz) shows vestiges of femininity. In his hymns, he is addressed as Damu, but elsewhere Damu appears as a goddess.

"It is within thy power, Ishtar, to change men into women and women into men," says an Old Babylonian invocation. The Hittites asked Ishtar of Nineveh to take away from the enemies their masculinity, prowess, and arms, and instead to "place in their hands the spindle and mirror of a woman" and to "dress them as women."

A ritual "change of sex" was achieved by change of clothing. The Old Babylonian expression formerly read as SAL*zi-ik-rum,* literally "a woman who is a man," is now properly to be read as SAL*se-ekrum,* "harem woman," and thus is not relevant here. Conversely, Ishtar's sacred personnel included singers and dancers called *kurgarrû* and *assinnu* (also *kulu'u*), of whom the Erra epic says that "Ishtar has changed them from men into women to teach the people piety." The Descent of Ishtar epic states that the *kurgarrû* were neither male nor female; they may have been eunuchs. The two categories performed dances "girt with the vestments of the goddess Narudu." It follows from certain contexts that they also served as male prostitutes.

3. In Syria. In Canaanite lands, Ishtar was parallelled by two almost identical goddesses, Astarte and Anath. They were hunters, warriors, and redoubtable killers, but at the same time full of beauty and charm. The strange epithet of the Carthaginian goddess, *Tnt pn B'l* is perhaps best translated "Tinnit with the face of Baal," i.e., with a bearded face. Astarte was depicted in Egypt with a shield and a spear, and a mythological text speaks of "Anath, the goddess, the victorious, a woman acting as a man, clad as a male and girt as a female." In the second century A.D., the sacred personnel of Atargatis (whom Lucian equated with Hera) included the self-castrated *galli* who wore women's dresses and did feminine work. Lucian's *De Dea Syra* may be late, but the rites described in it are extremely archaic.

4. In Cyprus and Greece. In Amathus, an ancient non-Greek city of Cyprus, a bearded androgynous Aphrodite was worshiped by men dressed as women and women dressed as men. The same ritual was observed in Argos at the festival of Hybristica. In several areas of Greece, the bridegroom wore a feminine dress; or the bride was dressed as a man, or wore a beard; or the newly wed exchanged their clothes and consummated the marriage in the presence of an androgynous divine image, or an ithyphallic statue in feminine garb. This strange custom, no doubt, aimed at assuring a perfect union of the sexes, so that they "become one flesh." Strong motifs of androgyny existed in the myth and cult of Dionysus. The god was visualized as an effeminate youth with quasi-feminine attire and hairdo. It was said that in his childhood he was raised as a girl. He was called *arsenothelys,* "male-female," and *pseudanôr,* "sham man." The ritual of Dionysus Pseudanôr was performed by *mimallones,* girls who imitated men. The heroes Leucippus, Iphis, and Caeneus were born as girls and were changed into men. The Theban soothsayer Tiresias was transformed into a woman and became a celebrated harlot, but after seven years he returned to his original sex. This myth reflects the Near Eastern institution of male prostitutes in feminine attire.

5. In the OT. Only traces of beliefs and practices of androgyny survive in the OT. The dirge for the deceased kings of Judah as cited in Jer. 22:18: "Alas my brother and alas sister! Alas lord and alas his majesty!" (author's trans.) perhaps goes back to the posthumous deification of Canaanite kings and their assimilation to the lamented god Adonis who, like Dumuzi and Dionysus, may have been imagined as sexually ambivalent. The persuasion that a man can lose his virility and become womanlike underlies David's curse (II Sam. 3:29) that the house of Joab, beside other afflictions, may never be without one "who holds the spindle." The prohibition of Deut. 22:5, "A woman shall not wear anything that pertains to a man, nor shall a man put on a woman's garment; for whoever does these things is an abomination to the Lord your God," must be understood, as W. Robertson Smith saw long ago, in the sense that "this is not a mere rule of conventional property but is directed against those simulated changes of sex which occur in Canaanite and Syrian heathenism."

6. In Talmud and Midrash. The Talmud uses the Greek loanword אנדרוגינוס in the physiological meaning "hermaphrodite" (so as not to use a term composed of two names of heathen deities). The only allusion to the motif is found in the midrash Berēshîth Rabbâ 8:1, in which the words of Gen. 1:27, "male and female he created them," are understood as the creation of a single individual, and Rabbi Jeremiah b. Elazar (second century A.D.) is quoted as explaining that this meant an *androgynos.* It is questionable whether this idea goes back to any ancient traditions (according to Babylonian beliefs, the first human beings created by the gods were already divided into males and females). Perhaps the opinion of Rabbi Jeremiah is an echo of Plato's parable in the Symposium about an early race of androgynous human beings whom Zeus sliced in two and so separated the sexes.

Bibliography. W. Robertson Smith, *The OT in the Jewish Church* (1892), p. 365, and *The Religion of the Semites* (1894), p. 478; Jessen, "Hermaphroditus," PW, VIII (1913), cols. 714-21; C. Virolleaud, *L'astrologie chaldéenne,* VIII (1905-12), 8 ff.; B. Meissner, *Babylonien u. Assyrien,* II (1925), 27-28; G. R. Driver and J. C. Miles, "The *SAL-ZIKRUM* 'Woman-Man' in Old-Babylonian Texts," *Iraq,* VI (1939), 66-70; L. Ginzberg, *The Legends of the Jews,* V (1947), 88-89; E. Dhorme, *Les religions de Babylonie et d'Assyrie* (1949), pp. 67-78, 89-93, 211-13; M. C. Astour, *Hellenosemitica* (2nd ed., 1967), pp. 153, 161-63, 188; H. A. Hoffner, "Symbols for Masculinity and Femininity," *JBL,* LXXXV (1966), 326-34; E. Reiner, "A Sumero-Akkadian Hymn of Nanâ," *JNES,* XXXIII (1974), p. 233; W. Meeks, "The Image of the Androgyne: Some Uses of Symbols in Earliest Christianity," *History of Religions,* XIII (1974), 165-208.

M. C. ASTOUR

***ANTIOCH (SYRIAN).** Recent literature on Antioch includes Glanville Downey, *A History of Antioch in Syria from Seleucus to the Arab Conquest* (1961), and *Ancient Antioch* (1963), condensed from the larger history, for the nonprofessional reader, but with added chs. on pagan and Christian society and culture, and greater illustrative material; Jean Lassus, *Les portiques d'Antioche,* Antioch-on-the-Orontes, V (1972); A. D. Nock, "*Isopoliteia* and the Jews," *Essays on Religion and the Ancient World,* ed. Z. Stewart (1972), II, 960-62, important for the Jewish community at Antioch.

G. DOWNEY

ANTIPATRIS. *See* APHEK[S].

***APHEK (IN THE SHARON).** Archaeological work by the Palestine (1934-36) and Israel (1958, 1961) Departments of Antiquities at Ras el-ʿAin has proven the occupation of the site in the Early Bronze Age, i.e., the first half of the third millennium B.C. After the site had apparently been deserted for over five hundred years, a city grew up covering an area of about thirty acres. It is probably the Aphek of the Egyptian execration texts, whose prince, Yanakilu, has a West Semitic (Amorite) name. Archaeological evidence continues to the Early Iron Age, thus reaffirming the identification of the site (questioned by some scholars) with the Aphek of the Philistines. Renamed Antipatris by Herod in honor of his father, it is mentioned in Acts 23:31: "The soldiers . . . took Paul and brought him by night to Antipatris."

Since 1972 an archaeological expedition by Tel Aviv University and the Baptist Theological Seminary of New Orleans, led by Kochavi and Kelm, has been conducted at Aphek. The main areas of excavation turned out to be outside the limits of the city of Bible times. Finds from tombs and pits include both LB and Iron Age pottery, such as Mycenaean, imported Cypriote, Philistine, and Samaria wares. Fragments of trilingual tablets inscribed in Sumerian, Babylonian, and Canaanite were discovered in what has been described as a "library-study" of the final LB Age town. The fragments were part of a revolving prism which, the excavators believe, served as a dictionary.

Bibliography. A. Eitan, "Excavations at the foot of Tel Rosh Haʿayin," *ʿAtiqot,* V (1969), 49-68, Hebrew M. Kochavi, "Tel Aphek," *IEJ,* XXIII (1973), 245-46.

M. W. PRAUSNITZ

***APHEKAH.** The identification of this site with el-Ḥadab, on the E side of the Seil ed-Dilbeh, has now been proposed. This is a prominent tell, having two major water sources at its foot, ʿAin ed-Dilbeh and ʿAin el-Fawâr. In addition to Hellenistic and Byzantine sherds, there was an abundance of Israelite materials.

Bibliography. M. Kochavi, "The Land of Judah," *Judaea, Samaria and the Golan, Archaeological Survey 1967-1968* (1972), pp. 21, 68, Hebrew.

A. F. RAINEY

APOCALYPSE, GENRE. 1. Genres in the postexilic period. While the influence of conventional forms never disappeared in ancient Jewish and Christian literature, later writers utilizing the genre of the apocalypse exercised considerable freedom in adapting it to their purposes, often fusing it with other genres. Since this resulted in wide diversity in expression, definitions must be flexible. Rather than describing an ideal type, therefore, it is preferable to sketch the typical features of the work originally designated "apocalypse" in antiquity, the book of Revelation, and then to consider which other compositions of the same era show sufficient similarity to justify extension of the term to them as well.

2. The apocalypse genre in the book of Revelation. *a. Structure and typical features.* These are expressed succinctly in Rev. 1:1-2: (1) a *revelation* is given by God, (2) through a *mediator* (here Jesus Christ or an angel), (3) to a *seer* concerning (4) *future events.* This basic structure is amplified through a number of recurring features. In 1:9-20 and *passim,* the revelation occurs in a vision in which the seer is allowed to peer into the heavens (cf. 4:1) to witness happenings which are determinative for future events on earth. The phrase "in the Spirit" (1:10; 4:2) indicates an ecstatic state. In 1:17-20 the Lord addresses the seer directly; elsewhere, the interpretation of the vision is conveyed by an angelic interpreter (1:1; 17:1-18; 22:6). In 21:9–22:5, the angel becomes a guide through heavenly places as the vision is transformed into a rapture. As for the seer, his response is one of awe (1:17; cf. 22:8), commonly followed by a word of comfort or admonition from the Lord or the angel (1:17; 22:9). Finally, though the vision can be expressed either as cosmic drama or in the form of elaborate symbolism, it always has bearing on "what is and what is to take place hereafter" (1:19; cf. 1:1; 4:1).

b. Setting and function. 1:9 gives the general setting of this genre ("I, John, . . . who share with you in Jesus the tribulation and the kingdom and the patient endurance"), and 1:19 indicates that the primary function is to disclose to the elect the secret of "what is and what is to take place," thereby serving to comfort the oppressed and encourage them to remain faithful to their beliefs. *See also* REVELATION, BOOK OF and supplementary article.

3. Other apocalypses. Many variations of these features are found in other apocalypses. Even Revelation suggests some of the possible variations. The apocalypse may comprise a single vision (1:9-20) or a collection of visions (the final form of the book); it may incorporate various other genres (examples in Revelation are the epistle and the hymn; in other apocalypses we commonly find the historical résumé, the prayer, and the testament); not only is there latitude for either "direct" description of heavenly events or symbolic description, but the disclosure can occur in a vision or in rapture (or in other books in a dream). Yet within this latitude enough conformity to the features of Revelation is found in some other compositions from the period 200 B.C.–A.D. 200 to justify extension of the term "apocalypse" to them as well.

a. Daniel 7–12 is a collection of apocalypses. The first, ch. 7, is a dream (or vision) referring to successive world kingdoms. The seer responds in alarm (vs. 15); the meaning of the vision, supplied by an angelic interpreter (vss. 16-27), concerns the imminent destruction of the oppressors and the granting of the kingdom to the saints. Similarly, Dan. 8: revelation, 1-14; mediator, 15-26; seer, 17-18, 27; future events, 19, 26; and Dan. 10–12: revelation, 10:5–11:1; seer, 10:8-10, 15-17; mediator, 11:2–12:4; future events, 10:14.

b. I Enoch contains an apocalypse in chs. 14–15. Seen in sleep, and called a vision, it is actually a rapture producing a direct description of heavenly things, especially the divine throne. It is not mediated by an angelic guide, but the seer responds with the usual dread (14:13-14). Its aim is to explain the corruption which will continue on the earth until the consummation.

c. IV Ezra gathers together a number of apocalypses. One type is found in chs. 11–12 (ch. 13 is very similar). In the form of a dream, it develops the zoomorphic symbolism of Dan. 7. The seer responds with perplexity and fear (12:3-4). There is no mediation of the interpretation, which is given directly by the Most High. The whole unit deals with imminent events of salvation and judgment. A related type is found in 9:26–10:59.

d. II Baruch 53–74 describes a vision seen in sleep. The seer responds in fear and awakes (54), and in answer to his prayer, an angel comes to explain (54-74) that the vision concerns the twelve ages of the world climaxing in woes, conflict, victory of the Messiah, and the reign of Peace.

e. Variations. In the majority of examples above, the apocalypse develops a historical résumé (using the technique of *vaticinia ex eventu*) which lends credibility to the seer's vision of the eschaton. That another emphasis is possible is indicated by I Enoch 14–15, where the major concern is with heavenly realities. This leads to the special apocalypse of the rapture elaborated in I Enoch 17–36, III Baruch, and II Enoch. In the last of these, two heavenly beings appear to the seer in sleep. They take him to the heavens, lead him from one level to the next, and show their respective secrets until finally he gazes at the Lord's face. Then he falls prone in fear (22:4). The rapture relates to "all that is and was and all that is now, and all that will be till judgement-day" (39:2).

f. Setting and function. Most of the apocalypses mentioned above seem to stem from settings of persecution within which they reveal to the faithful a vision of reversal and glorification (e.g., Dan. 12:1). This is made possible by concentration on heavenly realities, whether given in the form of symbols or in purported direct description. Earth's woes are seen as the shadows of a passing epoch. Though it is likely that ecstatic experience played a part in the apocalypses, there is also evidence of studied application of conventional devices.

Test. Levi 2–7 shows that the apocalypse genre could also be used to serve other functions. After an introduction in testamental form, a visionary rapture is described which serves to legitimate the Hasmonean royal priesthood.

4. Antecedents of the genre. (*See also* Apocalypticism[S] §3; Zechariah, Book of[S] §2.) A strong argument can be made in favor of designating the night visions of Zechariah as early apocalypses (though the fourth vision has peculiarities of its own). In them the seer is granted a vision, which is explained by an angelic interpreter who relates it to imminent events. There is a functional difference, however, which sets the Zechariah visions apart from most of the later apocalypses; they serve less to comfort the oppressed than to legitimate the hierocratic structures of the Zadokites (in this respect, the function approximates that of Test. Levi 2–7). Functionally, certain visionary units in Third Isaiah betray closer affinities to the later apocalypses (e.g., 59:15*b*-20) than do the apocalypses of Zechariah.

Though in terms of the typical features found in Revelation it is difficult to designate the visions of Ezekiel as apocalypses, individual motifs from his visions had profound influence on the development of the genre. And behind Ezekiel the line of influence can be traced to the visions of Jeremiah (e.g., 1:11-16), Isaiah (e.g., 6:1-13), Amos (7:1-9; 8:1-3), Michaiah ben Imlah (I Kings 22:19-23), and perhaps even to an ancient Canaanite genre reflected in *krt's* vision of *'el* (*CTA* 14[1K]); cf., also, the *aqht* legend. Another line of influence can be traced to dream accounts, especially those found in Genesis. A full investigation of antecedents should perhaps order these diverse visionary materials under the major rubric vision reports, under which such specific genres as *call vision, salvation vision, judgment vision, apocalypse,* and *revelation discourse* (a favorite genre in Gnostic writings) could be described and contrasted.

Bibliography. H. Gese, "Anfang und Ende der Apokalyptik, dargestellt am Sacharjabuch," *ZThK,* LXX (1973), 20-49; E. Hennecke and W. Schneemelcher, *NT Apocrypha,* II (1964), 582-87; K. Koch, *The Rediscovery of Apocalyptic,* SBT, 2nd ser., XXII (1970), 23-28.

P. D. Hanson

***APOCALYPTICISM.** A system of thought produced by visionary movements; builds upon a specific eschatological perspective in generating a symbolic universe opposed to that of the dominant society. This symbolic universe serves to establish the identity of the visionary community in relation to rival groups and to the deity, and to resolve contradictions between religious hopes and the experience of alienation (*see* §3*c below*) by according ultimate meaning solely to the cosmic realm, from which imminent deliverance is awaited.

1. NT usage
2. Definitions
   - *a.* Apocalypse
   - *b.* Apocalyptic eschatology
   - *c.* Apocalypticism
3. Historical-sociological sketch of apocalypticism
   - *a.* Ancient myth and the rise of prophetic eschatology
   - *b.* Transition to apocalyptic eschatology
   - *c.* Birth of the first apocalyptic movements

d. Apocalypticism in the second century B.C.
e. Apocalypticism in the first centuries A.D.
4. Theological significance
Bibliography

1. NT usage. "Apocalyptic" and related terms are derived from the Greek (ἀποκαλύπτειν [to reveal] and ἀποκάλυψις [revelation]). This terminology entered the realm of biblical scholarship by the extension to other writings of the word ἀποκάλυψις from the book of Revelation. But this extension invited confusion from the start by virtue of its arbitrariness, as connections were made first on the basis of various literary features, then on the basis of diverse doctrines or concepts. In Rev. 1:1 ἀποκάλυψις is used by the writer to designate this book, that is, to designate its literary genre. In vss. 1-2 the bare essentials of the genre are described; it involves a revelation of future events disclosed through the agency of an angel by God to his human servant, who bore witness "to all that he saw." The significance of this use of ἀποκάλυψις applies in the first instance to the definition of the literary genre apocalypse, rather than to the definition of the phenomenon of apocalypticism. The book of Revelation will help to clarify the latter, not by analysis of literary genre, but by a study of its position in the history of the socioreligious phenomenon of apocalyptic movements.

Apart from the use of ἀποκάλυψις as a literary designation in Rev. 1:1, this root (including its verbal forms) is used in the NT primarily in connection with the divine disclosure of saving plans which hitherto had been hidden. Such revelation draws attention to the saving significance of the events of Jesus' life (Matt. 16:17; Eph. 3:1-5) and looks forward to the consummation of those events in the PAROUSIA (Luke 17:30; Rom. 2:5; II Thess. 1:7; I Pet. 4:13). Paul emphasizes that he received this gospel not by consulting with the apostles, but through a "revelation" (Gal. 1:11-17).

The NT usage thus establishes this root's primary meaning as involving the unveiling of divine plans as salvation history unfolds, but it does not clarify the distinction between apocalyptic and eschatology, nor does it address the problem of OT and intertestamental antecedents. Such questions require a broadening of the inquiry into other linguistic horizons. The NT speaks of a series of events which inaugurated a new aeon, events belonging to a cosmic drama of salvation that is dependent upon no human powers or agents. This places the NT within an ancient stream of tradition which incorporates the perspective of apocalyptic eschatology.

2. Definitions. The technique of using formal lists (including everything from religious concepts to literary and psychological characteristics) in defining apocalypticism seems inadequate both in the analysis of individual compositions and in the attempt to establish the limits of the "apocalyptic corpus." Are we to include only apocalypses? This would exclude the bulk of the material in some of the works generally considered apocalyptic, such as DANIEL, I ENOCH, the Testament of Moses and the TESTAMENTS OF THE TWELVE PATRIARCHS. Then are we to include all works which incorporate apocalyptic eschatology? To do so empties the term of specific meaning by broadening it to embrace nearly all the postexilic writings of the Jewish canon, the NT, the APOSTOLIC FATHERS, and many of the rabbinic treatises. It seems advisable to replace the formal cognitive definition with a system that identifies three distinct levels which, while interrelated, betray individual peculiarities which should not be blurred. Moreover, the symbolic universe of an individual apocalyptic movement is not handed down to it ready-made by an authoritative antecedent tradition, but is formed within a specific historical-sociological matrix, and therefore this system of definitions must be characterized by flexibility. We are defining not a static system, but a phenomenon characterized by movement on several levels.

a. Apocalypse. This term designates a literary genre which is one of the favored media used by apocalyptic writers to communicate their messages. It is by no means the exclusive, or even the dominant, genre in most apocalyptic writings, but is found alongside many others, including the testament, the salvation-judgment oracle, and the PARABLE. The socioreligious phenomenon of apocalypticism, therefore, must not be uncritically identified with the literary form of the apocalypse (*see* APOCALYPSE, GENRE[S]).

b. Apocalyptic eschatology. The connections between the prophetic literature of the first temple period and the so-called apocalyptic writings are too numerous to be denied. Nevertheless, the obvious instances of not only sapiential material, but of materials deriving from Greek, Hellenistic, and various Eastern sources disallow the identification of apocalypticism as a simple rectilinear development out of prophecy. Prophecy is *one* current (even if the central one) alongside others. Moreover, the presence of scattered apocalyptic notions in works dominated by another perspective must be accounted for without carelessly gathering virtually all Jewish and Christian religious writings under the category of apocalypticism. These considerations call for a distinction between apocalyptic ESCHATOLOGY and the more restricted phenomenon of apocalypticism.

Apocalyptic eschatology, then, is neither a genre, nor a socioreligious movement, nor a system of thought, but rather a religious perspective, a way of viewing divine plans in relation to mundane realities. It is a perspective which is the exclusive property of no single religious or political party or group, though in certain periods it may be more characteristic of members of one party, sect, or social class than of others. Nor does it designate an absolute posture which an individual or a group either adopts exclusively or rejects completely, but it is a perspective which individuals or groups can embrace in varying degrees at different times, even as the modern person or community can vacillate between religious, superstitious, and scientific perspectives. Thus it is not surprising to find the perspective of apocalyptic eschatology in works as divergent as the sectarian writings of Qumran (*see* DEAD SEA SCROLLS[S]) and the rabbinical commentaries.

In its view toward the future as the context of divine saving and judging activity, apocalyptic eschatology can be seen as a continuation of prophetic eschatology. The difference involves the degree to which divine plans and acts are interpreted as being effected within the structures of mundane reality and through the agency of human persons. In prophetic eschatology the tendency was toward integration, that is, the recognition of divine action within events and persons of the political and historical realm (e.g., Isa. 7). As historical and sociological conditions made it increasingly difficult to identify contemporary individuals and structures with divine agents and end-time realities, as the elect increasingly were deprived of power within social and religious institutions, and as the vision of ancient myth began to offer world-weary individuals a means of resolving the tension between brilliant hopes and bleak realities, the perspective of prophetic eschatology yielded to that of apocalyptic eschatology. Gradually God's final saving acts came to be conceived of not as the fulfillment of promises within political structures and historical events, but as deliverance out of the present order into a new transformed order: "For behold, I create new heavens and a new earth; and the former things shall not be remembered or come into mind" (Isa. 65:17).

While apocalypticism cannot be identified with the perspective of apocalyptic eschatology, a relationship does exist: apocalypticism is latent in apocalyptic eschatology, and can grow out of the perspective it provides. Historical and social conditions may lead a group to elevate that perspective to an ideology which resolves contradictions between hopes and historical realities and provides the group with an identity in relation to other social and political groups and to the deity. When this happens, we witness the birth of an apocalyptic movement.

c. Apocalypticism. Apocalypticism refers to the symbolic universe in which an apocalyptic movement codifies its identity and interpretation of reality. This symbolic universe crystallizes around the perspective of apocalyptic eschatology which the movement adopts. Since the symbolic universes generated by different apocalyptic movements will differ from one another as a result of conditions surrounding the organic growth of the individual symbol systems, it is not possible to give one formal cognitive definition of apocalypticism. Indeed, since the typical apocalyptic universe develops as a protest of the apocalyptic community against the dominant society, it is concerned less with systemic consistency than with the demands of the immediate crisis, especially those of defining identity within a hostile world, and of sustaining hope for deliverance. While certain popular themes, traditions, and genres recur in apocalyptic compositions widely separated by time, other elements tend to be unique to individual works. The latter are drawn from broadly diverse quarters, including biblical traditions, ancient Canaanite myth, Zoroastrianism, neo-Babylonian astronomy, Greek myth, Hellenistic historiography, Jewish and foreign wisdom, and perhaps from "whatever the author happened to have heard yesterday." The result is often a collection of concepts and motifs which is highly eclectic in nature and characterized by the esoteric, the bizarre, and the arcane.

In the critical investigation of compositions to discern whether they betray an origin within an apocalyptic movement, the critic is aided by the fact that all ancient apocalyptic movements are characterized by (*a*) a particular type of social setting, and (*b*) a related group response. The *social setting* common to all ancient apocalyptic movements can be designated the group experience of alienation. This is the disintegration of the life-sustaining socioreligious structures and their supporting myths. The viability of life itself is called into question. Alienation can be the result of actual physical destruction of institutional structures, or it can arise as a community finds itself excluded from the dominant society and its symbolic universe, due either to choice or to ostracism. The result is a cultural vacuum which threatens life with chaos, a condition graphically described in Isa. 24, both in relation to the social fabric of society (vss. 1-13) and to the cosmic structure of reality (vss. 17-23). The strain becomes intolerable as members of the community are disenfranchised from institutional structures and reduced to powerlessness. Their existence becomes marginal, their orientation confused (cf. Isa. 66:5).

This social setting of apocalyptic movements leads to the second feature common to them, the *response* of the community to alienation. If the life of a community is to be sustained, a new symbolic universe must replace that which was dominant in the social system responsible for the experience of alienation. What makes the response of a particular group apocalyptic is its recourse to apocalyptic eschatology as the perspective from within which it constructs an alternative universe of meaning. Apocalyptic eschatology allows a community to maintain a sense of identity and a vision of its ultimate vindication in the face of social structures and historical events which deny both that identity and the plausibility of the vision. From this point of view it becomes possible to claim that true identity is derived, not from the structures and institutions of the society, but from a vision of what God is doing on the cosmic level to effect deliverance and salvation: "For behold, the Lord will come in fire, and his chariots like the stormwind, to render his anger in fury, and his rebuke with flames of fire" (Isa. 66:15). The significance and power of mundane structures are reduced to nothingness. "The kingdom of the world has become the kingdom of our Lord and of his Christ, and he shall reign for ever and ever" (Rev. 11:15). The creation of a new symbolic universe thus begins by denial of the ultimate significance of this world's structures and by a retreat into a vision of the "higher" reality and of what that reality implies for the future.

The different apocalyptic movements tend to fall into one of two basic types vis-à-vis the dominant social system. One type is composed of marginal persons within a nation who feel alienated from the symbol system of the dominant society and respond by giving expression to their group identity and vision of the future by constructing an apocalyptic symbolic universe. Such was the type found among the followers of Second Isaiah in the period after 520 B.C. In other cases an apocalyptic movement can consist of a broad cross section of a nation protesting against a symbolic universe which has been imposed upon them by a foreign power. Such was the case in the early stages of the Maccabean struggle against the Seleucids (Dan. 7–12).

A further set of distinctions must be made with regard to the function of apocalyptic works. While apocalyptic movements always generate their symbolic universes in opposition to the symbolic universe of the dominant society, the form of that opposition varies, depending upon the status of those involved, the intensity of the conflict, and the goals envisioned by the leaders. In early stages opposition is often channeled into social protest aimed at reform of the dominant society, in which case we can speak of an *alternative symbolic universe.* Oppression and disenfranchisement can lead to one of three responses: (1) the community can withdraw and establish a new society based upon a *symbolic utopian universe;* (2) it can yield in the face of opposition and go underground, leading to a subsociety expressing its identity in a *symbolic subuniverse;* (3) in the face of persecution, it may choose to reply with violence, becoming a revolutionary community constructing a *symbolic counter-universe.* These categories are of course ideal, and while examples can be suggested (e.g., Qumran, the early *hasidim,* the Zealots), usually a combination of goals will be found; for example, the members of the apocalyptic community at Qumran could withdraw, but then devise detailed plans for the day when God would lead them back to destroy and supplant the socioreligious system of the Hasmoneans.

A strict, inductive approach to the study of apocalypticism may seem to rule out any description of the typical features of the diverse apocalyptic symbolic universes. Strictly speaking, this is true. Nevertheless, they do develop from a shared matrix (alienation) and perspective (apocalyptic eschatology). Hence, many different apocalyptic universes share a common core. Typically, the group experience of alienation and the political function of the resulting symbolic universe leads to a sharp distinction between the elect and the wicked (I Enoch 5:6-7). Denigration of mundane structures in favor of the vision of what God is doing on the cosmic level to effect deliverance of the elect leads to a heaven/earth dichotomy: "Rejoice then, O heaven and you that dwell therein! But woe to you, O earth and sea, for the devil has come down to you" (Rev. 12:12). Events on earth are mere shadows of the decisive cosmic events (Dan. 10:12-21). Within a perspective from which heavenly realities alone are ascribed enduring validity, time is divided between the era before the inbreaking of the cosmic reality, and the aeon which follows: "the Most High has made not one Age, but two" (IV Ezra 7:50). Since the former era, that is, all previous history, is seen as a totality, it can be conceptualized schematically in various ways: as divided into periods (e.g., the four-kingdom notion), as degenerating into greater and greater decay, or as being determined from the beginning and thus amenable to summary in sweeping historical résumés.

The influence of MYTH on many apocalyptic symbol systems was profound, as seen for example in numerous traces of the notion that the end time will be like the time of primeval beginnings (*Endzeit wird Urzeit*). While it is undeniable that the historical orientation of earlier Israelite religion left its imprint on subsequent apocalyptic movements, the cosmic orientation emerging from apocalyptic eschatology and the added influence of myth combined as a powerful incentive toward radical experimentation with temporal and spatial categories within the various apocalyptic symbolic universes. Thus it is unsatisfactory to emphasize only the focus on the future. Rather, the past (whether captured in the résumés, in various schemata, or in the pseudonymous use of ancient heroes), the present (whether conceptualized in terms of cosmic woes, deadly dualistic struggles, or universal disintegration), and the future (whether perceived as reversion to the events of *Urzeit,* as the death of the old and the birth of a new order, or as the intervention of Israel's God "on that day") are all caught up in a cosmic context which opens up new dimensions of meaning. These dimensions (largely excluded by the closed system of the dominant society) include a new eternal (e.g., messianic) kingdom (*see* MESSIAH, JEWISH[S]), unlimited prosperity and glory, the transcendence of death, and transformation into new forms of existence (Dan. 12:3). (*See* FUTURE LIFE IN INTERTESTAMENTAL LITERATURE[S]; IMMORTALITY[S]; RESURRECTION.) Moreover, the partial suspension of spatial and temporal categories enabled the apocalyptic communities to celebrate proleptically these new possibilities in their communal life. The close bond between the apocalyptic literature of Qumran and that community's life of celebration serves as a reminder of the living character of the symbolic universes of apocalypticism. While such experimentation led to significant modifications in the earlier historical orientation of Hebrew prophecy, it did not reach the level of abstraction upon which the mundane concepts of space and time are abandoned entirely. Where the latter occurs we no longer speak of the symbolic universe of apocalypticism, but of Gnosticism (*see* GNOSTICISM [S]).

3. Historical-sociological sketch of apocalypticism. Whereas it is impossible to devise one list which includes all the important characteristics of apocalypticism, the preceding general picture suggests that a certain continuity characterizes the core of the major apocalyptic movements. The primary line of continuity is represented by the perspective of apocalyptic eschatology, which can be traced from the sixth century B.C. on. In periods of calm this eschatological perspective co-exists alongside other perspectives (e.g., pragmatic, scientific, etc.). In periods of alienation it is seized upon by groups which feel their life is marginal and confused, and which find its ideology useful in their efforts to reconstruct a universe of meaning. The result is the emergence of apocalypticism.

Either through eradication or through conversion back into the dominant system such movements dissipate in time, with the result that the perspective of apocalyptic eschatology is drawn back into the society, where it reassumes its position as a potentiality awaiting new crises, new polarizations, and new births of apocalyptic subuniverses. The importance of historical and sociological factors in this process of movement from potential to apocalyptic birth becomes apparent in the following tentative sketch.

a. Ancient myth and the rise of prophetic eschatology. Because apocalypticism in its many forms draws so heavily upon concepts and motifs of ancient myth, its roots must be traced to the great cosmogonic myths of the second millennium B.C. (*see* MYTH, MYTHOLOGY §A). But the attenuated form in which such concepts and motifs reached the apocalyptic movements cannot be understood apart from the intervening history of the Israelite tribal league, prophetism, and the royal cult. In that history, mythopoeic materials were recast, leading to the emergence of a perspective in many respects unique to the ancient world, that of prophetic eschatology (e.g., Isa. 29:5-7). Prophetic eschatology was born of the alienation experienced by a mixed group of tribes in the early Iron Age who experienced the collapse of a mythopoeic symbolic universe. The perspective which then emerged was subsequently hammered into shape within the ideological tensions between royal cult and prophetic and priestly circles in the period of the monarchy.

b. Transition to apocalyptic eschatology. The transformation of prophetic eschatology into apocalyptic eschatology was the gradual result of community crisis and national disintegration, circumstances which led prophets like Jeremiah and Ezekiel to envision redemption increasingly on a cosmic level through the use of motifs drawn from myth (Jer. 4:23-28; Ezek. 47). The full force of the alienation resulting from the disintegration of the pre-exilic social system and its supporting symbolic universe was experienced by Second Isaiah, in whose writings we witness an early, vivid expression of apocalyptic eschatology (*passim*). The bold application of myth (e.g., 51:9-11) led to a full description of the cosmic drama of salvation and introduced the heaven/earth and the past aeon/future aeon dichotomies (43:18-19) which became central to later apocalyptic subuniverses. Nevertheless, the integration of the cosmic vision into historical realities was kept alive by Second Isaiah's optimistic sense of nationhood (45:1-7).

c. Birth of the first apocalyptic movements. By introducing daring modifications into the symbolic universe of their antecedent traditions, Ezekiel and Second Isaiah both were able to bequeath to their followers programs of restoration written from perspectives quite advanced along the continuum from prophetic to apocalyptic eschatology (Ezek. 40–48 and Isa. 60–62). In the period of restoration following the return from exile, the two groups embracing these reform programs developed into rival parties. *See* PRESENCE OF GOD, CULTIC[S] esp. §5.

The Ezekiel program was adopted by the group under Zadokite leadership which returned from exile in the years following the Edict of Cyrus (538). After their return, the alienation caused by the catastrophic disintegration of nation and cult in 587 was exacerbated by hostility and economic hardship in Palestine. The situation was conducive to an apocalyptic movement, which in fact arose when the prophets Haggai and Zechariah seized upon the apocalyptic eschatology in Ezekiel's restoration program and transformed it into an apocalyptic symbolic universe (Hag. 2:6-9; Zech. 1–6), which functioned as a counteruniverse to that of the Persian overlords. It envisioned a magnificent intervention of Yahweh and the establishment of a messianic kingdom under a Davidide (*see* COVENANT, DAVIDIC[S]) and a Zadokite high priest (*see* ZADOK THE PRIEST[S] §2), events pictured vividly by Zechariah in the earliest apocalypses. This particular apocalyptic movement was short-lived, apparently being extirpated by the Persians, who removed its revolutionary leaders and co-operated with its more pragmatic members in constructing a hierocratic program in which the perspective of apocalyptic eschatology was abandoned in favor of a pragmatic social system enjoying Persian support (*see* AARON, AARONIDES[S]; PRIESTLY WRITERS[S] §4). From this pragmatic standpoint the apocalypses of Zechariah were re-edited and given a new function as propaganda for the hierocracy and its Zadokite leaders.

The second apocalyptic movement arising in the early postexilic period was not so easily assimilated into the dominant social system. From the early years of the return its adherents resisted the restoration efforts of the Zadokite group in the name of an even loftier vision of cosmic intervention and deliverance. For them the alienation arising from the Babylonian destruction and the chaotic conditions of the land was not resolved through collaboration with the Persians, but was increasingly aggravated by the oppression to which they were subjected by the Zadokite leaders (Isa. 66:1-5). Oppression was followed by excommunication, and thus the symbolic universe which these visionaries built around the apocalyptic eschatology of Second Isaiah broke increasingly with the restraints of the historical realm. The situation of "truth . . . fallen in the public squares" (Isa. 59:14) was addressed not with efforts to reform the social system, but with a THEOPHANY of Yahweh coming "like a rushing stream" to "repay, wrath to his adversaries, requital to his enemies" (59:18*b*-19). These bleak conditions and the sectarian response of the visionaries set in motion a powerful apocalyptic movement which increased in intensity in the last years of the sixth century and through most of the fifth century as well (cf. Zech. 12 and 14).

The latter apocalyptic movement persisted because the sociohistorical realm and its dominant social system continued to create feelings of alienation; it was a defiled realm in which they could not participate. Thus the apocalypticism of their symbolic universe was predicated upon the disintegration of the present order and the creation of a new cosmic order of blessedness for the elect. Responsibility to the political order which was a central characteristic of prophetic eschatology was abandoned in favor of a new supermundane universe of meaning. The result was the bipartite division of reality along several axes: past history as the epoch of evil/the coming epoch as glorious salvation; the enemy as wicked/the elect as righteous; the earthly order as decay/the heavenly order as life.

The writings which seem related to this apocalyptic movement (Isa. 34–35; 24–27; 56–66; Malachi; Zech. 9–14; Joel [?]) span the period from the Exile to the latter half of the fifth century. There seem to be no apocalyptic writings from the fourth century. The reason for this resides in the Chronicler's work. Ezra came to restore order in the Jewish community "according to the law of your God, which is in your hand" (Ezra 7:14). The spirit of the program of reform which he based on the law of Moses seems to be continued in the Chronicler's history. It was a latitudinarian work, integrating into one social system diverse elements which in the previous century and a half had become disenfranchised: Levites and prophets, for example, are brought back into the system, together with their archaic traditions (e.g., holy war). Though details are lacking, it seems that Ezra introduced a period of reconciliation in which the subuniverse of the second apocalyptic movement of the sixth-fifth centuries was absorbed into the symbol system of the dominant hierocracy. *See* CHRONICLES, I AND II and supplementary article; EZRA AND NEHEMIAH[S].

d. Apocalypticism in the second century B.C. In the second century B.C. we find the Jewish community engulfed by shattering events of a magnitude matched previously only by the Babylonian decimation of the sixth century. Political intrigue, military destruction, and the imposition of the symbolic universe of HELLENISM created an overwhelming sense of alienation which called into question the viability of the dominant social and religious structures. Circles like the early HASIDIM, who had preserved a strong eschatological perspective, responded to this situation in the manner of the earlier apocalyptic movements. The struggles of this earth were only shadows of battles occurring between the princes of heaven, and the outcome was certain to favor the elect (Dan. 10:10-21).

Resistance to the Seleucids (*see* SELEUCUS) was first unified under a broadly popular apocalyptic movement. But the military successes of the MACCABEES led to division, as some groups translated their energy into political reconstruction from a pragmatic standpoint which did not exclude cooperation with foreign powers like the Romans, whereas other groups withdrew further into the symbolic universe of apocalypticism. The sectarian writings from Qumran give us a vivid example of one group which responded by withdrawal and the creation of an elaborate symbolic utopian universe, which actually became the basis of a new social system. The writings of the period, including some of the PSEUDEPIGRAPHA, are replete with hints of other apocalyptic movements. But much detailed analysis is necessary before the rival symbolic universes of the period come into focus.

e. Apocalypticism in the first centuries A.D. The perspective of apocalyptic eschatology was carried into the first centuries A.D. by the PHARISEES, the ESSENES, and various other sectarian groups. It was the point of view from which JOHN THE BAPTIST preached REPENTANCE and Jesus announced the KINGDOM OF GOD. Because the NT writings reflect sources of influence as diverse as biblical prophecy, Jewish apocalypticism, Gnosticism, and Hellenism, it is impossible to give a single answer to the relation of its various parts to prophetic and apocalyptic eschatology. These perspectives stand in tension here as they did in all periods of biblical tradition (e.g., the juxtaposition of present reality and future kingdom in Jesus' preaching), and again the perspective of apocalyptic eschatology bore with it the possibility of apocalypticism (cf. Mark 13 and II Thess. 2:1-12). In new periods of alienation, certain Christian and Jewish communities responded to crises like the destruction of the temple and Roman persecution by seizing the perspective of apocalyptic eschatology and building new apocalyptic movements. The most noteworthy example of NT apocalypticism is the book of Revelation (*see* REVELATION, BOOK OF and supplementary article).

4. Theological significance. The prophets subjected all institutions and structures to their vision of a cosmic order of justice toward which all history was striving. In maintaining a field of tension between vision and mundane reality, they fought against the alternative religious postures: (1) abdication of social and political responsibility through escape into the timeless security of mythic reality; (2) reification of existing institutions and structures into a system accorded external validity. This tension threatened to dissolve during certain periods of biblical history: the early monarchy, the Exile, and various apocalyptic movements.

In an age witnessing the recrudescence of apocalypticism, how can ancient apocalypticism be evaluated? How can that evaluation be related to contemporary apocalyptic systems such as dispensationalism? Genuine apocalypticism arose within a setting of alienation, and was never a theological program self-consciously constructed in security and repose. Apocalyptic movements generated their alternative symbolic universes in periods within which the community of faith could be maintained only by retreat from the system of an oppressive society. Where such movements did not degenerate into sectarian dogmatism, the retreat was tactical, followed by re-entry and reapplication of the prophetic perspective to the social order. Historical studies, especially of the medieval period, also bear witness to pseudoapocalyptic movements which do not generate alternative universes of meaning in response to alienation, but which take the symbolic universe of an earlier movement and exploit it programmatically, often for nationalistic, racist, or dogmatic purposes. This phenomenon does not represent genuine apocalypticism, but is blind imitation bereft of the pain and struggle of attempting to relate faith to the experience of a disintegrating social and cosmic universe.

Myths of salvation are abundant in contemporary society, ranging from reification of political, economic, social, and psychological systems, to escapism into mythic consciousness, whether of Eastern or Judeo-Christian inspiration. Critical theology must subject all myths to evaluation from a prophetic point of view. Vis-à-vis contemporary dispensationalist movements, the question must be posed which was asked of ancient movements: Do they arise from the struggle to relate the dynamic of prophetic religion to contemporary social and political realities in a creative, compassionate and redemptive manner, or do they mechanically lift an ancient apocalyptic system out of its original setting and apply it programmatically in service of a lust for heroism, deification, and self-aggrandizement and in expression of a contemptuous death wish for the mass of humanity and the entire created order?

Biblical theology must deal with the riddles of ancient apocalypticism, such as its sectarian myopia and its disparagement of mundane realities, but it must always do so from within specific apocalyptic movements and with utmost care to grasp the concrete circumstances which gave rise to the symbolic universe in question. Contemporary theology must deal with the riddles of modern apocalypticism by distinguishing between the universe of meaning born of the horrors of the concentration camp or the persistent oppression of a totalitarian system, and the programmatic exploitation of an earlier apocalyptic universe. The often unpopular tasks of both disciplines will be carried out most responsibly in concert, with biblical theologians offering the perspective of the millennia, and the contemporary theologian transforming antiquarian concerns into life and death issues. *See also* ESCHATOLOGY OF THE OT; ESCHATOLOGY OF THE NT and supplementary article; ZECHARIAH, BOOK OF[S].

Bibliography. E. Hennecke and W. Schneemelcher, *NT Apocrypha,* II (1964); D. S. Russell, *The Method and Message of Jewish Apocalyptic* (1964); J. M. Schmidt, *Die jüdische Apokalyptik: Die Geschichte ihrer Erforschung von den Anfangen bis zu den Textfunden von Qumran* (1969); K. Koch, *The Rediscovery of Apocalyptic,* SBT, 2nd ser., XXII (1970); P. D. Hanson, *The Dawn of Apocalyptic* (1975), and "Prolegomenon to the Study of Jewish Apocalyptic," *Magnalia Dei,* ed. F. M. Cross, W. E. Lemke, P. D. Miller (1976), for previous scholarship and further bibliog; W. Schmithals, *The Apocalyptic Movement: Introduction and Interpretation* (1975).

P. D. HANSON

***APOCRYPHA, NT. 1. New material.** The Gnostic library of NAG HAMMADI has afforded a rich source of new material for evaluation. This library is not, however, the only source of new material. The PROTEVANGELIUM OF JAMES is contained in the Bodmer Papyrus V, the apocryphal Third Letter to the Corinthians in Bodmer Papyrus X; fragments of the Acts of Andrew have been found in papyri in Oxford and Utrecht and a fragment of the Acts of Paul in the Bodmer collection. *See* ANDREW, ACTS OF; PAUL, ACTS OF.

2. The term "apocrypha." The new Gnostic material shows that Gnostic writers often represented their teaching as secret doctrine to be kept confidential. Since the word "apocrypha" refers properly to esoteric writings, it is appropriately applied to these particular works. One document bears the title Apocryphon of John, while the Jung Codex Letter of James twice speaks of secret writings (p. 1.10,30-31). ApocryJn and the Books of Jeu (*see* PISTIS SOPHIA) contain stern warnings against divulging their contents to any unauthorized person. Since the Gnostic literature was judged heretical, the term naturally acquired the pejorative sense of "false" or "spurious." This does not apply, however, to all the works classed as apocrypha, some of which are comparatively "orthodox," even if they may appear rather eccentric.

The term is thus employed in several different, though related, senses: (*a*) in its original sense of "hidden" or "secret," particularly with reference to Gnostic documents; (*b*) as a description of books which were not accepted into the canon, although they might be accorded a limited recognition as suitable for private use (cf. the MURATORIAN FRAGMENT on Hermas); (*c*) as deriving from its application to Gnostic works the pejorative sense of "false" or "spurious." It should be emphasized that the OT Apocrypha (*see* APOCRYPHA §2) are in quite another category. Deriving from the intertestamental period and included in the LXX, the OT Apocrypha are accepted by some branches of the church. This has never been the case with the NT Apocrypha, apart from the sects which gave them birth.

3. Delimitation of the material. Early collections sometimes included the APOSTOLIC FATHERS among the apocrypha, but it is now recognized that these do not belong here. There still remains, however, the problem of framing a definition sufficiently comprehensive to include all the relevant material yet at the same time to exclude what does not belong in this category. The Nag Hammadi library, for instance, includes a defective translation of part of Plato's *Republic,* the collection of ethical aphorisms already known as the Sentences of Sextus, and parts of the Corpus Hermeticum (*see* HERMETIC LITERATURE[S]), none of which should be considered as NT Apocrypha. The same applies on a wider survey to the Christian Sibyllines (*see* SIBYLLINE ORACLES) and the ODES OF SOLOMON.

The most obvious solution would be to include those works which by their character or titles seem intended to be counterparts or rivals of the canonical books. However, the titles are often no clear indication of the contents. None of the Nag Hammadi "gospels" is a gospel in the canonical sense, for they provide no account of the life and ministry of Jesus, or of his death and resurrection (*see* GOSPEL, GENRE[S]). Only the Gospel of Thomas contains "sayings" of Jesus, and here sayings familiar from the canonical tradition are combined with other material of a different character. The Gospel of Truth is rather a meditation on the theme of the gospel as "good news," the Gospel of Philip a rambling didactic and hortatory discourse, and the Gospel of the Egyptians a Gnostic text presenting a system akin to that of ApocryJn but with elements derived from magic. Many of the other Gnostic "gospels" take the form of conversations between the risen Jesus and his disciples in the period between the Resurrection and the Ascension, which the Gnostics extended from forty days to eighteen months. Here we have an "orthodox" parallel in the EPISTLE OF THE

APOSTLES and a Gnostic in the Apocryphon of James, neither of which bears the title of gospel. *See* THOMAS, GOSPEL OF[S]; TRUTH, GOSPEL OF[S]; PHILIP, GOSPEL OF[S].

The situation is generally simpler with the apocryphal Acts (*see* ACTS, GENRE[S]), most of which were fairly obviously designed to fill in the gaps and provide "information" about the apostles, but the problem arises again with the apocalypses. Some of these follow the pattern of some works of Jewish apocalyptic by providing surveys of history under the guise of prophecy (e.g., the APOCALYPSE OF ADAM), others describe an ascent through the heavens (the Nag Hammadi ApocPaul), while a more common type of the "ordinary" apocryphal apocalypse presents a revelation of the terrors of hell (APOCALYPSE OF PETER, APOCALYPSE OF PAUL; but cf. the GOSPEL OF BARTHOLOMEW). Here again the title of a document may be no clue to its contents: works with the title "Apocalypse" or "Revelation" may be cosmological and soteriological rather than apocalyptic or eschatological, while apocalyptic material appears in works with other labels. *See* APOCALYPSE, GENRE[S].

Schneemelcher includes among the NT Apoc. noncanonical materials which, according to form-critical criteria, can be said to have developed forms and types present already in the NT, or which have taken over pre-Christian literary forms and types into the service of the gospel, or which have used literary fiction in the service of propaganda to produce a "tendency literature" in support of the views of a particular group.

Such a definition may be open to objection, but it is at least serviceable. It does, however, raise the question of the extent to which the Nag Hammadi library should be included with the apocrypha. It has already been noted that some texts definitely do not belong in this context, and there may be others. The problem is complicated by the fact that, for example, Eugnostos the Blessed (claimed by several scholars to be non-Christian) has been Christianized in the Sophia of Jesus Christ into the form of a Gnostic gospel. The solution may be either to include the whole library, with such exceptions as those already noted, in a separate category as "Gnostic apocrypha," distinct from the apocrypha proper; or to include with the apocrypha those documents which present a resemblance in type and form, and classify the rest apart as "tendency literature."

4. Duplication of titles. Earlier studies, when only the Nag Hammadi titles were known, frequently raised the question whether a document might be one quoted by the early Fathers. Publication of the text soon showed that it was not: GTh has no relation to the Infancy Gospel of Thomas, nor GPh to the work cited by Epiphanius; GEgypt is not the GOSPEL ACCORDING TO THE EGYPTIANS known to Clement of Alexandria, while ApocPaul is almost completely different from the apocalypse already known. In addition, there are in the same codex (Codex V) two quite different Apocalypses of James. We must avoid the natural but dangerous assumption that identity of title means the same book. A similar warning should perhaps be given against hasty ascriptions of authorship. When little more than fragments are available, it is dangerous to assume that the work is the one mentioned by the Fathers as written by Valentinus or Heracleon, and on the strength of this to ascribe other works to the same author. In the nature of the case, any such ascription can be no more than a possibility.

5. Redaction of Gnostic texts. Reference has already been made to the relation between Eug and SJC, perhaps not yet finally settled. There is also the question of possible connections between ApocAd and GEgypt, while we now have four copies of ApocryJn from two different recensions. Other works, like the Gospel of Mary, appear to be composite, with Christian elements superimposed on originally non-Christian material. Study and analysis of such questions, as the Nag Hammadi library becomes more fully available, may have much to teach us about the processes of development and elaboration within the Gnostic literature. Here again, however, a word of warning is in place: the current trend is to regard the Gnostic as primary, the Christianization as secondary. But if a text was *de*-Christianized, how could the Christian original be *proved* original?

6. Classification of the material. Reverting to the apocrypha proper, it is now possible to introduce some refinement of classification into the study of the apocryphal gospels. Reference should be made in the first place to the AGRAPHA, sayings of Jesus not recorded in the canonical gospels but preserved elsewhere in the NT, in the writings of early Fathers, or in other sources. Rigorous criticism has reduced the number regarded as possibly authentic to a handful, but some of them are still interesting in themselves. GTh is a collection of sayings, including some known from the canonical gospels and incorporating all those found in the famous OXYRHYNCHUS SAYINGS. Secondly there are some early gospel fragments (POx. 840, PEgerton 2), and others which may be from gospels although the extant remains are not enough for any final judgment (POx. 1224, PCair. 10 735, the Fayyum Fragment). The Jewish-Christian gospels present special problems, since three different titles have been handed down by the Fathers and it is not clear whether all refer to the same work, or two, or three. Finally there are the Gnostic gospels and related works. Authentic early material about Jesus may be preserved at most in a few of the Agrapha and in the early gospel fragments, with the possible addition of the GOSPEL ACCORDING TO THE HEBREWS. With regard to other material—the infancy gospels, the apocryphal Acts, and the apocalypses—there is but little to add. Where they were not written to serve a tendentious purpose, they are clearly the products of imagination, designed to supply edifying information, in accordance with the tastes of the time, to make good what appeared to be deficiencies in the canonical literature.

Not the least part of the significance of this literature is that it provides a standard of comparison and shows how NT types and forms, motifs and concepts, were developed and elaborated in the centuries following the NT period. *See also* GNOSTICISM, GNOSTICISM[S]; LITERATURE, EARLY CHRISTIAN[S].

Bibliography. The work of M. R. James (*see* APOCRYPHA, NT, bibliog.) is still a convenient collection of the more important texts, but includes little in the way of introduction and of course nothing about subsequent discoveries. Both these deficiencies are made good by E. Hennecke and W. Schneemelcher, *NT Apocrypha,* I (1959; rev. ed., 1968); II (1964). See also W. Foerster, *Gnosis,* I (1969); II (1971); R. Haardt, *Gnosis: Character and Testimony* (1967), although the English trans. is not always satisfactory; D. M. Scholer, *Nag Hammadi Bibliography 1948-1969* (1971), with supplements in *NovT,* (1971 ff.).

Protevangelium of James: M. Testuz, *Papyrus Bodmer V* (1958); E. de Strycker, *La forme la plus ancienne du Protévangile de Jacques,* Subsidia Hagiographica, XXXIII (1961).

III Corinthians: M. Testuz, *Papyrus Bodmer X-XII* (1959).

Epistle of the Apostles: M. Hornschuh, *Studien zur Epistula Apostolorum,* Patristische Texte und Studien, V (1965).

Agrapha: J. Jeremias, *Unknown Sayings of Jesus* (2nd ed., 1963). R. McL. WILSON

APODICTIC LAW. *See* LAW IN THE OT §3; LAW IN THE OT[S] §5.

APOPHTHEGM. *See* SAYINGS OF JESUS, FORM OF[S] §5.

***APOSTOLIC FATHERS.** (*See bibliog.* for all references to modern authors.) Recent attempts to restrict this term to a more homogeneous group of writings include: (1) Fischer and Altaner: noncanonical early literature continuing the tradition of the apostles and Paul (thus, only I CLEMENT, letters of IGNATIUS and POLYCARP, and Quadratus); (2) Grant (1964): early noncanonical authors of a practical (rather than theological or cultural) and traditional orientation writing for Christians (thus excluding apologies of DIOGNETUS and Quadratus). Strict attention to questions of literary form also encourage reclassification within more coherent larger groupings such as personal and community letters (I Clement, Ignatius, Polycarp); epistolary treatises, addresses, and martyrdoms (BARNABAS, II CLEMENT, Martyrdom of Polycarp [*see* POLYCARP, MARTYRDOM OF]); extended treatises (PAPIAS); community manuals (DIDACHE); apocalypses (HERMAS); apologies (Diognetus, Quadratus).

Study of early Christian literature has been spurred by such discoveries as the DEAD SEA SCROLLS and NAG HAMMADI MSS, and frequently has focused on questions such as the relation to Judaism and "Jewish Christianity" (esp. Barnabas, Didache, Hermas; also I Clement), or the conflicts of emerging "orthodoxy" with "heterodox" tendencies such as GNOSTICISM (esp. Barnabas, II Clement, Ignatius, Polycarp). Attention has focused on problems of sources (oral and written) and composition—e.g., "two ways" material in Barnabas, Didache, Hermas; use of "testimonia" collections behind Barnabas and I Clement; identification and use of "scripture" in Barnabas, I Clement, Didache, Ignatius; Jewish homiletic material in I Clement; a hymnic confession behind II Clement; gospel materials in Didache, Ignatius, Papias; interpolations in Ignatius; literary evolution of Barnabas, Didache, Hermas; integrity of Diognetus and of Polycarp's letter. Christian liturgical and institutional developments (esp. in I Clement, Didache, Ignatius) also receive continued attention along with conceptual issues such as eschatology and Christology/angelology (esp. in I Clement, Hermas), and moral/ethical attitudes. A healthy concern has developed for understanding these writings in their own right, rather than primarily as supports for earlier (NT) or later (orthodox) forms of Christianity.

1. Barnabas, "Epistle" of. Attempts to identify the source materials and stages of development behind this "catholic epistle" (so Clement of Alexandria) continue, with reference not only to the much discussed "two ways" materials but also to collections of scriptural testimonies and other midrashic and apocalyptic sources or traditions. The author may represent an early Christian school tradition employing respected exegetical and ethical approaches of that time (early second century). The epistle's strong Jewish connections and anticultic (not anti-Jewish) attitudes are noteworthy, while its proposed baptismal catechesis setting (*see,* e.g., Barnard) remains open to dispute. Debate over the epistle's precise place of origin continues: Syria (Prigent), Asia Minor (Wengst), and the Alexandrian region (Barnard, Kraft) all receive support.

2. I Clement, Epistle of. This writing is known already to Hegesippus (in Euseb. Hist. IV.xxii.1) and Irenaeus (Her. III.iii.2[3]). Its author may have made use of collections of Jewish scriptural texts arranged topically (testimonia in a loose sense). The exact nature of the problem addressed is disputed—was theological "heresy" being opposed as well as (or rather than) ecclesiastical insubordination? And if so, what sort of heresy? Bauer suggests Gnostic opponents. Beyschlag's claim that I Clement faithfully represents the "nascent catholicism" of a generation earlier is open to dispute; Knoch's argument that eschatology plays no vital role, but is accepted as part of the author's received tradition, has found more favorable reception.

3. II Clement. There has been relatively little recent study of this writing. Donfried describes it as a hortatory address (rather than homily) that originated from Corinth in the early second century, based on an earlier hymnic confession. Grant (1965) argues for Roman origin of this "appeal." II Clement may reflect a mildly Gnostic setting, which it opposes by means of futuristic eschatology and ethical exhortation.

4. Didache. The presence of various stages of development behind the present form is widely acknowledged. Continued attention has been lavished on the "two ways" material shared with Barnabas (also Hermas), especially in relation to the "two spirits" doctrine of the Dead Sea Scrolls. The case for dependence on a Jewish two ways tradition has been strengthened and Christian developments have been traced with greater precision (*see,* e.g., Giet, Layton). Audet's attempt to date the bulk of the Didache before 70 (similarly Giet) has received mixed reactions, although his identification of Syria as the place of origin finds many supporters (e.g., Giet; Kraft thinks Egypt more likely).

5. Diognetus, "Letter" to. The date and authorship of this apology remain disputed, although there is some tendency toward a second rather than third-century date. Andriessen argues that this is the lost apology of Quadratus (*see* §10 *below*), while Marrou attributes it to Pantaenus later in the second century. The last two chapters probably derive from a work (perhaps by Hippolytus) different from the preceding material.

6. Hermas, Shepherd of. In form, this is an apocalypse (*see* APOCALYPSE, GENRE[S]), but its ethical-hortatory content regarding REPENTANCE is not typical of other Jewish and Christian apocalypses. The widespread circulation of Hermas during the second through seventh centuries in Egypt continues to be attested by discoveries of Greek and Coptic papyrus and parchment fragments (*see* Whittaker, Treu) which, together with the Athos (not Athens) codex and Sinaiticus, supply a Greek text for all but the last eight sections (107-114= Sim. IX.30-X.4; Whittaker's ed. has replaced the older tripartite division with sequential section numbers). Early Christian attitudes to Hermas vary from referring to it as "scripture" or very useful (e.g., Irenaeus, Origen, Athanasius; see also the MURATORIAN FRAGMENT) to its caustic condemnation as a "shepherd of adulterers" by Montanist Tertullian (*Modesty* 10; but see his pre-Montanist use in *Prayer* 16). Recent studies have tended to focus on such issues as the stages of development behind the preserved form of Hermas (e.g., Giet, Snyder), and the relation of Hermas to Jewish (e.g., Qumran), Jewish-Christian (*see*, e.g., Daniélou), and emerging "orthodox" Christian attitudes and practices.

7. Ignatius, Epistles of. The question of the relationship between the three recensions of Ignatian letters has received close attention, especially from Brown and Weijenborg. Indeed, the latter argues that the short and middle recensions derive from the fourth-century "long recension," but reviewers have not found his evidence persuasive. Attention also has been given to Ignatius' ecclesiastical and theological outlook and setting, especially in relation to early second-century concepts of "heresy."

8. Papias. Schoedel dates Papias' lost *Expositions of the Dominical Logia* around 110 (under TRAJAN; *see* Euseb. Hist. III.xxxvi.2), while Grant (in his revision of Goodspeed) opts for *ca.* 120. Earlier attempts to see this as a work that interpreted Jewish scriptural testimonies or prophecies of Christ have not met wide acceptance, although the precise form and nature of the "dominical logia," as well as Papias' interpretation, remain problematic.

9. Polycarp, Epistle of and Martyrdom of. Harrison's hypothesis that the extant letter of Polycarp actually contains an earlier (chs. 13-14) and a later (chs. 1-12, *ca.* 135) letter is adopted in Fischer's edition (*see also* Quasten, Altaner) but rejected by Schoedel, who dates the entire work to the time of Trajan. The date of Polycarp's death remains disputed. Eusebius placed it *ca.* 166/67, but the "appendix" (regarded as an addition by many) to the Martyrdom has been used to argue for *ca.* 155/56; Schoedel opts for 155-60, while even a date as late as 177 has been proposed. Six Greek MSS of the Martyrdom are known, plus quotations and paraphrases in Eusebius and elsewhere, a Latin version, and various derivative materials in Armenian, Syriac, and Coptic.

10. Quadratus, Apology of. A fragment from a defense of Christianity addressed to HADRIAN (117-38) is preserved by Euseb. Hist. IV.iii. It refers to the survival "to our own day" of some persons who had been healed or raised by "the savior" when he was on earth. *See also* §5 *above*.

See LITERATURE, EARLY CHRISTIAN[S].

Bibliography. In general, see the relevant sections in *Elenchus Bibliographicus* (*Biblica*), *NT Abstracts*, and *Bibliographica Patristica*, ed. W. Schneemelcher (1956 ff.).

Text editions, discoveries, tools: The single most comprehensive older ed. (lacking Didache) remains that of O. Gebhart, A. von Harnack, T. Zahn, *Patrum apostolicorum opera* (1875-78). New minor critical eds. (with Fr. trans. and commentary) are appearing in the series Sources chrétiennes: X, Ignatius, Polycarp, Martyrdom of Polycarp, ed. P.-T. Camelot (4th ed., 1969); XXXIII, Diognetus, ed. H. I. Marrou (2nd ed., 1965); LIII, Hermas, ed. R. Joly (2nd ed., 1968); CLXVII, I Clement, ed. A. Jaubert (1971); CLXXII, Barnabas, ed. R. A. Kraft (text) and P. Prigent (1971). *Die apostolischen Väter*, ed. J. A. Fischer, I (1956), contains new eds. (with Ger. trans.) of I Clement, Ignatius, Polycarp, and Quadratus. M. Whittaker's major ed. of Hermas, GCS, XLVIII has been reissued with corrections and additions (2nd ed., 1967; add now the fifth-century papyrus fragment of Mand. IV, V, ed. K. Treu, "Ein neuer Hermas-Papyrus," *Vigiliae Christianae*, XXIV [1970], 34-39), and J.-P. Audet's ed. of Didache, *La Didachè* (1958; with extensive commentary and notes) remains standard. A new concordance, ed. H. Kraft, *Clavis Patrum Apostolicorum* (1963), includes variant readings and semantic contexts (does not cover Martyrdom of Polycarp, Diognetus, Quadratus). Vocabulary of the Apostolic Fathers (including Diognetus but not Quadratus) is covered by the Bauer-Arndt-Gingrich *Greek-English Lexicon of the NT and other Early Christian Literature* (4th ed., 1952) and by G. W. H. Lampe, ed., *A Patristic Greek Lexicon* (1961).

English translations, commentaries, introductions: *The Apostolic Fathers: A New Translation and Commentary*, ed. R. M. Grant: I, *Introduction* by Grant (1964); II, *I and II Clement* by Grant and H. H. Graham (1965); III, *Barnabas and Didache* by R. A. Kraft (1965); IV, *Ignatius of Antioch* by Grant (1966); V, *Polycarp, Martyrdom of Polycarp, Fragments of Papias* by W. R. Schoedel (1967); VI, *The Shepherd of Hermas* by G. F. Snyder (1968). M. Staniforth, *Early Christian Writings: The Apostolic Fathers* (1968, trans. only, lacking Hermas, Papias, Quadratus); Altaner, *Patrology* (5th ed., 1958; 6th Ger. ed., rev. A. Stuiber, 1966).

Special studies: P. Nautin, *Lettres et écrivains chrétiens des IIe et IIIe siècles* (1961); S. Laeuchli, *The Language of Faith: An Introduction to the Semantic Dilemma of the Early Church* (1962); J. Daniélou, *Theology of Jewish Christianity* (1958 [ET 1964]); R. M. Grant rev. ed. of E. J. Goodspeed, *A History of Early Christian Literature* (1966); J. de Watteville, *Le sacrifice dans les textes eucharistiques des premiers siècles* (1966); M. Lods, *Précis d'histoire de la théologie chrétienne du 2e au début du 4e siècle* (1966); C. Vogel, *Le Pecheur et la pénitence dans l'Église ancienne* (1966); A. P. O'Hagan, *Material Re-creation in the Apostolic Fathers*, TU, C (1968); L. Goppelt, *Apostolic and Post-Apostolic Times* (1962); H. von Campenhausen, *Ecclesiastical Authority and Spiritual Power in the Church of the First Three Centuries* (1952 [ET 1969]); J. Liebaert,

Les enseignments moraux des pères apostoliques (1970); W. Bauer and G. Strecker, *Orthodoxy and Heresy in Earliest Christianity* (2nd ed., 1964); F. Blanchetiere, "Aux sources de l'anti-judaisme chretien," *RHPR,* LIII (1973) 353-98; W. G. Doty, *Letters in Primitive Christianity* (1973); T. H. C. van Eijk, *La résurrection des morts chez les pères apostoliques* (1974).

Select studies of particular fathers or writings (see also the collections of articles by E. Peterson, *Frühkirche, Judentum und Gnosis* [1959] and L. W. Barnard, *Studies in the Apostolic Fathers and their Background* [1966]):

Barnabas: P. Prigent, *Les Testimonia dans le christianisme primitif: L'Épître de Barnabe I-XVI et ses sources* (1961); K. Wengst, *Tradition und Theologie des Barnabasbriefes,* Arbeiten zur Kirchengeschichte, XLII (1971); E. Robillard, "L'Épître de Barnabe: trois époques, trois théologies, trois rédacteurs," *RB,* LXXVIII (1971), 184-209.

I Clement: C. Eggenberger, *Die Quellen der politischen Ethik des 1. Klemensbriefes* (1951); O. Knoch, *Eigenart und Bedeutung der Eschatologie im theologischen Aufriss des ersten Clemensbriefes,* Theophaneia, XVII (1964); K. Beyschlag, *Clemens Romanus und der Frühkatholizismus: Untersuchungen zu I Clemens 1–7,* BHTh, XXXV (1966); P. Mikat, *Die Bedeutung der Begriffe Stasis und Aponoia für das Verständnis des I Clemensbriefes* (1969); R. Meneghelli, *Fede cristiana e potere politico in Clemente romano,* Scienze filosofiche, XV (1970); H. B. Bumpus, *The Christological Awareness of Clement of Rome and its Sources* (1972); G. Brunner, *Die theologische Mitte des Ersten Klemensbriefes,* Frankfurter theologische Studien, XI (1972); D. A. Hagner, *The Use of the Old and New Testaments in Clement of Rome,* NovTSup, XXXIV (1973).

II Clement: K. P. Donfried, *The Setting of Second Clement in Early Christianity,* NovTSup, XXXVIII (1974).

Didache: L. Clerici, *Einsammlung der Zerstreuten: Liturgiegeschichtliche Untersuchung zu Vor- und Nachgeschichte der Fürbitte für die Kirche in Didache 9,4 und 10,5* (1966); B. Layton, "The Sources, Date and Transmission of Didache 1.3b-2.1," *HTR,* LXI (1968), 343-83; S. Giet, *L'énigme de la Didachè* (1970); W. Rordorf, "Un chapitre d'éthique judéo-chrétienne: les deux voies," *RSR,* LX (1972), 109-28

Diognetus: P. Andriessen, "The Authorship of the Epistula ad Diognetum," *VC,* I (1947) 129-36; B. Billet, "Les lacunes de l' 'a Diognete': Essai de solution," *RSR,* XLV (1957), 409-18; R. Brändle, *Die Ethik der "Schrift an Diognet": Eine Wiederaufnahme paulinischer und johanneischer Theologie am Ausgang des zweiten Jahrhunderts,* ATANT, LXIV (1975).

Hermas: S. Giet, *Hermas et les Pasteurs: les trois auteurs du Pasteur d'Hermas* (1963); L. Pernveden, *The Concept of the Church in the Shepherd of Hermas,* Studia Theologica Lundensia, XXVII (1966); J. Reiling, *Hermas and Christian Prophecy: a Study of the Eleventh Mandate,* NovTSup, XXXVII (1973).

Ignatius: V. Corwin, *St. Ignatius and Christianity in Antioch,* Yale Publications in Religion, I (1960); M. P. Brown, *The Authentic Writings of Ignatius: A Study of Linguistic Criteria,* Duke Studies in Religion, XLII (1963); H. Rathke, *Ignatius von Antiochien und die Paulusbriefe* (1967); R. Weijenborg, *Les lettres d'Ignace d'Antioche: étude de critique littéraire et de théologie* (1969).

Polycarp: A. Bovon-Thurneysen, "Ethik und Eschatologie im Philipperbrief des Polycarp von Smyrna," *TZ,* XXIX (1973), 241-56.

Martyrdom of Polycarp: T. D. Barnes, "A Note on Polycarp" (date of death), *JTS,* XVIII (1967), 433-37; W. Rordorf, "Aux origines du culte des Martyrs," *Irenikon,* XLV (1972), 315-31. R. A. KRAFT

***ARAD.** An important city in the eastern Negeb, situated on the main road to Edom. "The Canaanite, the king of Arad, who dwelt in the Negeb" withstood the assault of the Israelite tribes (Num. 21:1; 33:40), defeating them at neighboring Hormah (Num. 14:44-45; Deut. 1:44). However there is the divergent tradition of the defeat of the king of Arad at Hormah in a second Israelite assault (Num. 21:2-3). Both cities are mentioned in the list of the defeated Canaanite kings (Josh. 12:14). According to Judg. 1:16 the Negeb near Arad was settled by Kenites related to the family of Moses. Pharaoh Shishak, in his list of conquered cities (*ca.* 920 B.C.), mentions the following names: *ḥqrm. ʿrd. rbt. ʿrd. nbt. yrḥm.* (nos. 107-12). i.e., the fortresses Arad the Great and Arad of the House of *Yrḥm* (=Jerahmeel? cf. I Sam. 27:10; 30:29). The last biblical reference to Arad lists the city in the Negeb district of Judah (Josh. 15:21, corrupted to עדר, Eder). Eusebius (Onom. 14:2) still knew a village called Arad, twenty Roman miles from Hebron and four from Malaatha (Moleatha), distances which fit exactly modern Tell ʿArad, situated *ca.* twenty miles ENE from Beer-sheba.

In excavations carried out during 1962-67, two different settlements were discovered at the site: (*a*) a large city of the third millennium B.C. and (*b*) a fortress of the Israelite and later periods.

1. The Early Bronze Age city. A large fortified city existed at the place during EB II (*ca.* 2900-2700 B.C.) preceded by an open settlement of the Late Chalcolithic period. The city was divided into quarters and the houses were built according to a fixed architectural concept, a distinct "broad house" with an entrance at one of the longer sides. Finds included a clay model of one of the houses, a cult stele apparently depicting the Mesopotamian grain god Dumuzi, vessels imported from Egypt, and an abundance of local pottery known hitherto mainly from Egyptian First-Dynasty tombs (Abydos ware), which gives evidence of intense trade with Egypt. After a last unfortified level, the city was destroyed and deserted before the end of EB II, i.e., not later than 2700 B.C.

2. The Iron Age fortress. A new settlement was founded on the SE ridge of the ancient city during the twelfth/eleventh century B.C. It was a small open village and in its center was a paved temenos with a crescent shaped *bamah* and a square altar. We may suppose that the venerated Kenite family, the descendants of HOBAB (Judg. 1:16 LXXA; cf. 4:11), served at this high place. On its place a temple was erected in the days of David or Solomon, which then became part of a strongly fortified royal citadel about sixty yards square. The citadel served as the royal military and administrative center of the border area until the end of the first temple. During that period it was destroyed and burnt six times (the first time evidently by Shishak), but always was quickly rebuilt (strata XI-VI). Later fortresses in the Persian, Hellenistic, Roman, and early Arab periods stood on the same site.

3. The temple. *See* TEMPLES, SEMITIC[S] §2*a*; for the ground plan of the temple *see* TEMPLE OF SOLOMON[S] Fig. T7.

4. The ostraca. About two hundred inscribed potsherds (ostraca) were found, half in Aramaic (*ca.* 400 B.C.) and the rest in Hebrew. The Aramaic ostraca are mainly dockets of the Persian garrison, containing lists of names, troops, and quantities of various commodities. The Hebrew ostraca derive from different Iron Age strata (a fact which increases their palaeographic importance), and most are letters and dockets from the royal archives. Letters from Eliashib son of Eshyahu, commander of the last two citadels (strata VII-VI), mention the Kittim (*ktym*), probably mercenaries of Aegean stock in the service of Judah. The end of both strata may be dated by the ostraca. Stratum VII was destroyed in 609 B.C. by the Egyptians. One ostracon contains an inventory by an Egyptian scribe in Hieratic; another is a letter by the king of Judah (probably Jehoahaz) mentioning his ascendance to the throne and calling for urgent preparations, mentioning the king of Egypt. Stratum VI was destroyed in 595 B.C. by the Edomites; a date formula (*bšlšt:* "in the third [year]") apparently refers to the third year of Zedekiah, and a letter from the same period contains an urgent order to dispatch reinforcements to Ramah of the Negeb (Josh. 19:8; I Sam. 30:27) against a threatening Edomite attack.

5. The identification. The excavations and the appearance of the name Arad in two Hebrew ostraca strengthen the identification of Tell ʿArad with the Israelite city. But the absence of remains of the Middle and Late Bronze Ages contradicts the biblical traditions regarding the Canaanite city. No LB sites have been discovered in the eastern Negeb, and the only two MB sites with typical Hyksos ramparts are at Tel Malḥata (Tell el-Milḥ) and at Tel Masos (Khirbet Meshâsh) eight to ten miles SW from Tell ʿArad. Two solutions have been suggested: *a*) In the Canaanite period no city of Arad existed, but this was the name of the whole region, the Negeb of Arad. *b*) Canaanite Arad was located at Tel Malḥata, and Hormah at Tel Masos. This suggestion is strengthened by the double appearance of Arad in the Shishak list. We may assume that "Arad of the House of Yrḥm" is the city which was settled by Jerahmeelite families (Tel Malḥata); "Great Arad" is then the citadel at Tell ʿArad, founded by David or Solomon on the site of the Kenite high place.

Bibliography. N. Glueck, *Rivers in the Desert* (1959), *passim;* B. Mazar, "The Sanctuary of Arad and the Family of Hobab the Kenite," *JNES,* XXIV (1965), 297-303; V. Fritz, "Arad in der biblischen Überlieferung und in der Liste Schoschenk I," *ZDPV,* LXXXII (1966), 331-42; Y. Aharoni, "The Negeb," in *Archaeology and Old Testament Studies,* ed. D. W. Thomas (1967), pp. 391-401, and "The Solomonic Temple, the Tabernacle and the Arad Sanctuary," *AOAT,* XXII (1973), 1-8.

Excavation Reports: Y. Aharoni and R. Amiran, "Excavations at Tel Arad . . . 1962," *IEJ,* XIV (1964), 131-47, "Arad: A Biblical City in Southern Palestine," *Archaeology,* XVII (1964), 43-53, "Excavations at Tel Arad . . . 1963," *IEJ,* XVII (1967), 233-49, and "Arad: Its Inscriptions and Temple," *BA,* XXXI (1968), 1-32; R. Amiran, *Ancient Arad* (forthcoming).

Ostraca: Y. Aharoni, "Hebrew Ostraca From Tel Arad," *IEJ,* XVI (1966), 1-7; S. Yeivin, "A Hieratic Ostracon From Tel Arad," *IEJ,* XVI (1966), 153-59; Y. Aharoni, "The Use of Hieratic Numerals in Hebrew Ostraca and the Shekel Weights," *BASOR,* 184 (1966), 13-16; S. Yeivin, "An Ostracon From Tel Arad Exhibiting a Combination of Two Scripts," *JEA,* LV (1969), 98-102; Y. Aharoni, "Three Hebrew Ostraca From Arad," *BASOR,* 197 (1970), 16-42; A. Rainey, "A Hebrew 'Receipt' From Arad," *BASOR,* 202 (1971), 23-29; Y. Aharoni, *The Arad Inscriptions* (forthcoming), Hebrew.

Y. AHARONI

***ARAMAIC.** The Arameans at first wrote, not in their own language, but in Canaanite dialects, and our earliest Aramaic inscriptions come from the ninth century.

The revised classification scheme for the Aramaic dialects, accepted by many scholars in recent years, is used here with some modifications.

A. Early Aramaic
1. Old Aramaic
2. Official (Royal) Aramaic

B. Middle Aramaic
1. Continuation of Official Aramaic
2. Western Aramaic
3. Eastern Aramaic

C. Late Aramaic
1. Western Aramaic
2. Eastern Aramaic

D. Modern Aramaic
1. Western Aramaic
2. Eastern Aramaic

E. Aramaic script

F. Aramaic influence on other Semitic languages

Bibliography

A. EARLY ARAMAIC. The various types of Aramaic from the early ninth century through the late fourth century B.C.

1. Old Aramaic. The language of the Aramaic inscriptions from Syria and Palestine from the early ninth century to the late eighth. Aramaic scribes adopted the Phoenician alphabet and scribal techniques, but a clearly definable Aramaic script with both monumental and cursive forms emerged (*see* ALPHABET[S] §2). The gradual introduction of the *matres lectionis* was a contribution of the Aramaic scribes. The Zakir inscription (*ca.* 800) used language reminiscent of biblical Hebrew; the Sefire inscriptions (*ca.* 740) have added to our knowledge of Aramaic and contain many idioms shared with biblical Hebrew. Inscribed sherds were found at Tel Dan, Hazor, and Ein Gev in the northern Galilee. Three inscriptions from Zinjirli (Sam'al; *see* YA'UDI[S]) are written in an archaic Aramaic dialect with Western traits (*see* INSCRIPTIONS, SEMITIC[S] §3*d*). In Old Aramaic the Proto-Semitic consonants are graphically expressed in the following manner: **ḏ*=ז (זנה, "this"); **ṯ*=ש (שלש, "three"); **ẓ*=צ (חץ, "arrow"), as in Canaanite, but **ḍ*=ק (ארק, "land").

2. Official (Royal) Aramaic. By the second half of the ninth century there is mention of an "Aramaic letter" by an Assyrian official; references to Aramaic documents and Aramaic scribes increase as Assyria conquered the Aramaic states to the W and absorbed their populations (*see* ARAMEANS). Aramaic and Assyrian scribes are depicted together on reliefs and wall paintings from the time of Tiglath-pileser III onward. The Aramaic used by the tribes within Assyria became the lingua franca of the Assyrian empire (*see* ARAMAIC §2). The spread of this dialect to Syria is attested at Zinjirli by Bir Rakkib (Bar Rekub) and by the Nerab inscriptions. A salient linguistic feature of this dialect is the dissimilation of emphatics: *kyṣ'* for *qyṣ'* (summer) and *kṭl* for *qṭl* (to kill).

The Neo-Babylonian Empire (625-539) succeeded Assyria and expanded its holdings. The role of Aramaic, the spoken language in Babylonia at this time, grew, and Aramaic scribes using Eastern Aramaic replaced those using the Assyrian dialect. With the Persian conquests under Cyrus and Cambyses, the Achaemenian empire reached from India to Egypt, encompassing Bactria, Sogdiana, and Choresmia (in present-day Soviet Union) and Asia Minor. Aramaic became the language of the Persian chanceries and served to unite the far-flung empire. Although the majority of the documents are in a relatively uniform Official Aramaic, some documents such as the AHIKAR proverbs (in which the dissimilation of emphatics is prominent) and the Hermopolis papyri use the Assyrian/North Syrian dialect. Elements of a literary Aramaic emerge in these texts. From Israel and Jordan there are an increasing number of ostraca, e.g., from *ca.* 350 the as-yet-unpublished Wadi Daliyeh papyri (*see* SAMARIA PAPYRI[S]); from Iraq there are dockets on Neo-Babylonian tablets; from Iran, dockets, graffiti, inscribed mortars and seals; from Turkey, inscriptions and bullae; and from North Arabia, inscriptions. The documents preserved in the Aramaic portion of Ezra (4:8–6:18; 7:12-26) are written in Official Aramaic (but the orthography has been modernized). They mirror the language and phraseology of official letters and decrees. In its early stages Official Aramaic borrowed from both the Assyrian and Babylonian dialects of Akkadian and in turn influenced them; in the Persian period many Iranian loanwords and phrases in the fields of administration, communications, dress, crafts, artisanry, and religion entered Aramaic.

In Official Aramaic we can trace the gradual transitions to normal Aramaic phonology: ḍ=ע (ארע, "land"); *ḏ*=ד (דנה, "this"); *ṯ*=ת (תלת, "three"); *ẓ*=ט (חטיא, "arrows"). Cf. Jer. 10:11, where both spellings for earth ארקא and ארעא are found. Some ELEPHANTINE PAPYRI display the same scribal confusion.

B. MIDDLE ARAMAIC. With the breakup of the Achaemenian Empire because of Alexander's conquests, Official Aramaic was replaced as the lingua franca by Greek and was gradually succeeded by local dialects of Aramaic. Nevertheless, the unifying effects of Official Aramaic remained important. This period is reckoned from 300 B.C. to A.D. 200, when Western and Eastern clearly emerged.

1. Continuation of Official Aramaic. A type of Official Aramaic became a standard dialect and could be read and understood throughout the former Persian Empire. Official decrees and documents were drawn up in this dialect, since legal documents are usually conservative in language and phraseology.

a. Standard Literary Aramaic continued the basic linguistic forms (primarily Eastern) of the earlier period and maintained in its vocabulary many Akkadian and Iranian elements, with local (Western) dialect features inevitably making themselves felt. The Aramaic portions of Daniel fit well into this dialect, containing tales recorded at an earlier date and reworked around 168 B.C. The Aramaic texts found in the Qumran caves are also written in Standard Literary Aramaic, with Tobit and the Dream of Nabonidus being perhaps the earliest, followed by Enoch and Melchizedek material, then by the Genesis Apocryphon, the Testament of Levi, and the Targ. of Job. It is only by extrapolation from the later Palestinian dialects that some Western features can be detected in these texts.

The Targs., Onkelos for the Pentateuch and Jonathan for the Prophets, were written in Palestine in this same dialect. The cultivation of these texts in the Babylonian academies led to the later introduction of some particularly Eastern forms and vocalizations. Two other texts written in this dialect are the *Meghillath Ta'anith* (Fasts Scroll) and the later *Meghillath Antiyochos* (the Scroll of the Hasmoneans).

b. Legal documents. The language of deeds and legal formulas is conservative; the formulas quoted in the MISHNA and in both TALMUDS have been recognized as a continuation of those known from the previous period. The Aramaic documents found in the Bar Kochba caves (*see* BAR KOCHBA [S]) date from the period A.D. 65-135 and reflect this tendency.

c. Epigraphic material. Aramaic maintained its importance as a means of public communication alongside Greek in many peripheral areas of the ancient Near East. Because of the perishability of most materials, it is primarily inscriptions on stone that have survived, but recent finds include papyri, ostraca, etc.

i. *Nabatean.* The NABATEANS used a form of Official Aramaic as their written dialect. Discoveries include dedicatory, religious, and burial inscriptions, ostraca, coins, and papyri. The legal documents in Nabatean found in the Bar Kochba cave at Naḥal Ḥever and the sepulchral inscriptions from El-Hejra share the legal tradition noted above. Nabatean texts have been found at Halutsa, Avdat and Nitṣanah in the Negeb as well as at Petra, Bozrah, etc. There is Arabic influence on the vocabulary and syntax of Nabatean.

ii. *Palmyrene.* Ancient TADMOR, Hellenistic Palmyra, and its environs in the Syrian desert have produced a great many texts—primarily dedicatory, funerary and religious—in Palmyrene (from *ca.* 50 B.C.–A.D. 250). A fragment of papyrus in Palmyrene was found at Dura-Europos. The language is a development of Official Aramaic; in later texts some Eastern forms are found. There are some traces of Arabic influence, since part of the population was Arabic-speaking. Palmyrene texts have been found in N Arabia, in Europe, and in the Merv oasis in Central Asia, witnessing the spread of Palmyrene merchants and mercenaries.

iii. *Other material.* Inscriptions in Aramaic have

been found in Afghanistan, Georgia, Soviet Armenia, and Turkey; some papyri have been found in Egypt, and a large group of ostraca have been found at Nisa in Turkmenistan from the Parthian period.

d. Aramaic ideograms in the Middle Iranian dialects. An important result of the use of Aramaic in the chanceries of the Persian Empire was the adoption of Aramaic script for the Iranian languages. Both Middle Persian (Pahlavi) and Parthian inscriptions use Aramaic ideograms for many nouns, verbal roots, and particles; in Book Pahlavi great confusion because of scribal error has developed. In Sogdian fewer ideograms were used, but continuity can be traced through the eighth century A.D. Such ideograms, especially in the Pahlavi text *Frahang i Pahlavik,* remain a source for Official Aramaic.

2. Western Aramaic. During the Middle Aramaic period, the first indisputable traces of Western Aramaic are discernible, especially in the growing number of inscriptions from the Jerusalem area. These consist of tomb inscriptions (e.g., Jason's tomb; the Ussiah tomb plaque, the Giv'at ha-Mivtar cave inscription in Paleo-Hebrew script; *see* JERUSALEM[S] §6); sarcophagi lids (e.g., from Bethphage), ossuaries, weights, and other items. From the NT such phrases as *talitha cumi; marana tha; ephphatha; eloi, eloi, lama sabachthani;* and *rabbouni* are easily recognizable as Aramaic. The same may be said for various personal names recorded therein and for such place names in the immediate vicinity of Jerusalem as AKELDAMA, GOLGOTHA, GETHSEMANE, and BETHESDA. The dialect spoken by Jesus and his disciples was Galilean, and was clearly distinguishable from that spoken in Jerusalem (cf. Matt. 26:73), but the Aramaic words quoted in the NT cannot be identified as to dialect. Josephus also recorded Aramaic words, but referred to them as "Hebrew" (in all likelihood an ethnic rather than a linguistic discription); he claims to have written the first draft of his *Wars* in Aramaic.

The BAR KOCHBA letters (A.D. 132-35) are a source for the colloquial Aramaic of Judah. In both the Hebrew and Aramaic letters Greek loanwords are found.

3. Eastern Aramaic. There are no extended texts for this period, but two finds, separated by time and place, are important. The first is an incantation text from Uruk in S Mesopotamia written in cuneiform syllabic writing from the second century B.C.; beside Eastern Aramaic vocabulary, it already witnesses the ending *-ē* as the masculine determined plural. From Northern Iraq of the Parthian period (second century A.D.) a large number of inscriptions and graffiti have been found at Asshur and Hatra. These have features of Eastern Aramaic. The same is true for the inscriptions from the Elymais in Iran.

C. LATE ARAMAIC. In this period (A.D. 200-900) which reached beyond the Arab conquest in both the W and the E, the dialect distinctions are clear. For the present our documentation for Western Aramaic is limited to the three Palestinian literary dialects—Jewish (Galilean) Aramaic, Christian Palestinian Aramaic, and Samaritan Aramaic, and to epigraphic material from Palestine. Syriac, Jewish Babylonian Aramaic, and Mandaic are usually considered the components of Eastern Aramaic. This scheme is followed here, but with the caveat that for reasons of vocabulary, morphology, and geography, Syriac may be seen as occupying a median position in this scheme. Some common features of Western and Eastern Aramaic should be noted here: (1) the prefix *he-* of the causative and passive-reflexive has been fully replaced by *'aleph,* e.g., *'ašlēm* for *hašlēm;* (ii) a new conjugation *'ittaph'al* (a passive of the causative) has developed; (iii) enclitic *d* replaces the relative pronoun *dī;* (iv) the passive participle *qĕtîl* is employed in certain verbs with active meaning; (v) there is a reordering of the tenses. The major differences between Eastern and Western Aramaic are: (i) *ē-* is used as the determined masculine plural; (ii) *l* or *n* is used as the prefix of the third-person imperfect instead of *y;* (iii) the determinative loses its force in Eastern Aramaic and replaces on the whole the absolute forms; (iv) the passive participle plus *l* with suffixes often serves to express the perfect in the Eastern; (v) the word order of Eastern Aramaic is looser than that of Western Aramaic; (vi) in Western Aramaic the infinitive of all verbal forms have a *mem* prefix.

1. Western Aramaic. The three known dialects of Western Aramaic share many distinctive features of vocabulary, morphology, and syntax. Although distinct scripts were used, the dialects were mutually comprehensible. Because of the widespread use of Greek in Syria, no records of the Aramaic used there have reached us.

a. Jewish Aramaic. This is the language of the Palestinian TALMUD (as best known from the Leiden MS and Genizah texts), the Palestinian Midrashim (Genesis Rabbah and Leviticus Rabbah as preserved in the better MSS and Genizah texts), and the Palestinian Targs. (*see* TARGUMS[S]). The latter group includes the Neofiti targ. text, the Yerushalmi "Fragment Targs.," and the Genizah fragments published by Kahle and others, and the Targ. to the *Kᵉthubhim.* Pseudo-Jonathan, representing a mixed-text type, must be used with caution for Western Aramaic studies. Written materials include: funeral inscriptions from Joppa (second-third centuries), Beth-shearim (third-fourth centuries), and Zoar on the Dead Sea (fifth century), synagogue inscriptions from Eshtemoa, Susya, the Hebron area, Beth Guvrin, En-gedi, Jericho, Naarah, Maon, Beth-shan, Hamath Gader, Hamat Tiberias, Capernaum, Umm el-'Amad and sites on the Golan Heights, etc. These range from the third to the sixth century. The language of these inscriptions is similar to that of the texts noted above. Interesting details as to the loss of laryngeals in the speech of certain parts of Galilee, as noted in the Talmud, is confirmed in the inscriptions from Beth-shan and Umm el-'Amad. Deeds and documents in this dialect from as late as the eleventh century have been found in the Cairo Genizah.

b. Christian Palestinian Aramaic was used in Judea, in all likelihood by Jews converted to Christianity. It is written in a type of Syriac script and contains morphological and vocabulary traits that point to Mishnaic Hebrew influence. *See* HEBREW LANGUAGE[S] §2*b*; ARAMAIC §3*c*.

c. Samaritan Aramaic was used by the SAMARITANS settled in the Shechem area and in the central highlands. A reliable reading tradition has been preserved. The laryngeals were lost in antiquity and have also been confused in writing; both *beth* and *waw* were pronounced "v" and are also confused in writing. The vocabulary has preserved many items not found in the other dialects. *See* ARAMAIC §3*b*.

2. Eastern Aramaic. Religious and cultural differences mark the literature of the three dialects that are representative of Eastern Aramaic; they are also written in different scripts. They are the remnants of a dialect group that once encompassed a good part of the Near East.

a. Syriac. The best documented of all the Aramaic dialects, with stable orthography, standardized vocalizations (*see below*), a large literature encompassing many genres of prose and poetry, and schools of native grammarians and lexicographers. From the early centuries of our era, we have only some inscriptions on stone, in caves, or on mosaics, primarily from Edessa, which was to emerge as one of the main cultural centers of Syriac-speaking Christianity. From the pagan period very little, beyond the works of Bar Daisan and the story of AHIKAR, has reached us. A Syriac slave-sale document drawn up at Edessa (A.D. 243) was found at Dura-Europos. This shows clearly that Syriac was by this time fully developed as a written language. With the translation of the OT (the Peshitta; *see* SYRIAC VERSIONS[S]) and the NT and the spread of Christianity among Aramaic speakers, Syriac became an important vehicle of literature and culture. Philosophical and scientific works and literature were translated from Greek in the West and from Middle Persian in the East. The literature that has reached us is, on the whole, religious in nature, but there are also some chronicles and historical works. A Western and an Eastern dialect emerged with distinct but related scripts and slightly divergent vocalization systems and pronunciation. Greek loanwords abound in the West, while Iranian ones occur in large numbers in the East. Syriac was the means of preaching Christianity in Persia, Turkestan, India, and China to the E, and was used for communication with S Arabia (the Christians of Najran in the sixth century), Egypt, and Ethiopia. There was a Gnostic literature in Syriac of which very little besides "The Hymn of the Pearl" has reached us. Syriac was spoken by MANI; his apostles in the third century used Syriac to spread his gospel. Syriac words were borrowed by various languages, especially in the ecclesiastical field. The script was used for various Middle Iranian languages, e.g., Christian Sogdian. Syriac continued to be used for literary purposes until the fifteenth century, and remains in use as the liturgical language in the various Syrian churches in the Near East and in their Western diasporas.

Although Syriac is classified as an Eastern dialect and does partake on the whole of the traits typical of those dialects, nevertheless in its earlier stages, especially in the inscriptions and the early gospel translations, it exhibits morphologic traits—the use of *y* prefix in the third-person imperfect, determination, sentence structure—that align it with the West. It is clear that early Syriac inherited from Standard Literary Aramaic a stable orthography which was only slightly modified in time, and that literary Syriac was a compromise between various dialects based on the one spoken in Edessa.

b. Jewish Babylonian Aramaic is represented primarily by the language of the Babylonian Talmud. This source is not monolithic, for the language of the tractates Nedarim, Nazir, Me'ilah, Kerithoth, and Tamid represent an earlier stage, and some MSS and Genizah texts show variant morphologic and lexicographic forms. Aramaic incantation bowls in Jewish and pagan scripts, and the writings of Anan, the Karaite leader, and of the Gaonim (heads of the academies in Babylon) are written in related dialects. Documentation extends from the third through the eleventh century until Aramaic was replaced by Arabic.

This dialect is marked by the weakening of the laryngeals; the frequent dropping of final consonants *l, b, d, m, n, r,* and the frequent replacement of *l* by *n,* e.g., *nhm* (*lḥm*), "bread," *nqṭ* (*lqṭ*), "he took"; the development of new forms in the morphology of the pronouns, the verb and the infinitive, e.g., (pael) *kattōbē* as compared to biblical Aramaic/Official Aramaic *kattābā;* ('aphel) *'aktōbē-haktābā.*

Jewish Babylonian Aramaic is replete with Akkadian loanwords, many already known from earlier dialects of Aramiac, but others, from the agricultural sphere, occur here for the first time. There are also many Iranian loanwords, some from an earlier period, others clearly from the Parthian and Sassanian periods. These are shared with Eastern Syriac and Mandaic.

c. Mandaic. The language of the Mandaeans, a non-Christian, Gnostic sect whose origins remain unclear, and whose remnants now dwell in S Iraq and Iran (*see* ARAMAIC §4*b*; MANDAEISM[S]). The earliest datable material in Mandaic are amulets on lead from the fourth century A.D. and clay incantation bowls (*ca.* sixth-seventh century). The two major literary works—the Ginza Rba and the Draša dYahya are probably from the same period, as is the Mandaic prayer book, but later copyists have left an impress of the Islamic period. Because of its composite nature, it is difficult to date much of Mandaic literature. A form of "colloquial modern" Mandaic has persisted to our times, although most Mandaeans speak Arabic or Farsi.

Mandaic is very close to Jewish Babylonian Aramaic. It has also lost the laryngeals and shares many of the morphologic innovations of Jewish Babylonian Aramaic. Certain features that go back to the Akkadian substrate are more prominent in Mandaic—the dissimilation of emphatics, e.g., *kušṭa* for *qušṭa;* dissimilation of gemination, e.g., *manda* for *madda'*. The *matres lectionis* ', ', *h, w, y* are widely used; this has been of great use in establishing the vocalization of Babylonian Aramaic. A possible archaic orthographic feature is the spelling *zahbā,* "gold," for usual Aramaic *dahbā; 'arqā,* "land," for *'ar'ā,* etc. At times the scribes were hypercorrect in their spelling, e.g., *qaprā* for *'aprā*, "earth," *zmā* for *dmā*, "blood." Mandaic writers continued the use of various poetic and rhetorical devices known from the ancient Near East. The syntax and vocabulary of Mandaic is similar to Babylonian Aramaic. There are many loanwords from Akkadian, particularly in the field of religion and astrology, and also from Iranian.

D. MODERN ARAMAIC. The dialects of Aramaic still spoken by Christians and Jews in the Near East.

1. Western Aramaic. A dialect of Western Aramaic is still spoken by Christian villagers in the Anti-Lebanon, particularly in Ma'lūla and Jubb-'adin, although these villagers speak Arabic with their Moslem neighbors. The language has undergone considerable change, and has been influenced in both vocabulary and syntax by Arabic, but the Western features are clearly distinguishable.

2. Eastern Aramaic. This is usually called Modern Syriac, but it is not a single dialect, and in all likelihood is not derived from classical Syriac. These dialects are spoken by Christians, descendants of the Aramaic speakers of an earlier age, in an area which extends from the Jezira in N Syria through E Turkey (the Lake Van area), Soviet Azerbaijan, N Iraq, and N Iran. Many speakers of these dialects have emigrated to the United States. Similar dialects were spoken by Jews in the mountains of Kurdistan, all of whom have emigrated to Israel. In the nineteenth century, Protestant missionaries developed a literary language using the dialect of Urmia as the base; many devotional and scholastic texts were translated and written in it, and the Bible was also translated into Modern Syriac. This group is called the Assyrians. Father P. Bedjan and others undertook a similar revival for the Catholics of the Mosul area, writing devotional works and biblical histories. This group is called the Chaldeans. Both groups used the Nestorian script. There has been a literary revival among the Assyrians of Iran. The Jews had an extended oral literature consisting of liturgy and tales and a traditional translation of biblical and other texts. They developed a literature using Hebrew script. The Jewish dialects reveal the influence of Hebrew and Jewish Aramaic in their vocabulary. The influence of Turkish, Kurdish, Persian, and Arabic, the contact languages, can be seen in the phonology, vocabulary, and syntax of these dialects. The morphology exhibits traits whose origins can be traced back to the Aramaic dialects spoken in these areas at an earlier date.

E. ARAMAIC SCRIPT. The Aramaic script developed from the Phoenician script, and by the late ninth century had its own recognizable form. In turn it was adopted by the Ammonites and Edomites. With the spread of Official Aramaic under the Achaemenian Empire, this script, especially in its cursive form, was widely used. It was called the "Assyrian script" (*see* ALPHABET; ALPHABET[S]). Although paleographic development can be traced, it showed no regional variations during this period. With the breakup of the Achaemenian Empire, various local script types emerged. Best known is the Hebrew square script, whose development can now be studied with the aid of the Qumran texts and other finds. In the West there is also the Nabatean script, long since known in monumental form, but now also known on documents (from this cursive writing the Arabic script developed), the Palmyrene script, and the Syriac scripts: Estrangela, Serto, and the Nestorian variety (in which Iranian languages were written by Christians). In the East the Aramaic script was particularly fruitful, since most Asiatic alphabets can be traced back to it. One branch developed into the East Aramaic type from which the scripts of Asshur, Hatra, the Elymais region, the Mandeans, and the Manicheans developed; the script of the Achaemenian chancery gave rise to the Pahlavi, Parthian, and Sogdian hands, and from the latter came the Uigur, Mongol, Manchu, Kalmuk, and Buriat scripts; still another form gave rise to the Karoshthi and Brahmi script of India, and through them the various scripts used throughout India, Tibet, Southeast Asia, and Indonesia. The Arabic script (cf. *above*) underwent minor modifications for Persian, Turkish, Urdu, and Malay use.

F. ARAMAIC INFLUENCE ON OTHER SEMITIC LANGUAGES. Aramaic in the West was, in the early period, under the strong influence of Canaanite language and scribal traditions; in the E there was the Akkadian influence. With the growing power of the Aramaic-speaking kingdoms and tribes, Aramaic in turn became quite important in the West. This may best be seen in biblical Hebrew. In the early biblical books certain words and forms that appear to resemble Aramaic are in reality survivals of an early poetic diction. In certain books an Aramaic word or form is used to give an exotic flavor to dialogue (Isa. 21:11-14), or perhaps to indicate the country of origin of one spoken to (Job, in the Dialogues); in other books one is dealing with northern or Israelite diction which was often closer to Aramaic than that of Judah (Judg. 5; or the Elijah/Elisha narratives), or with Israelite material which has been reworked in the South (parts of Deuteronomy, Proverbs). But real Aramaic influence may be seen in late books such as Ezekiel, the late Psalms, Esther, Song of Songs, Ezra, Nehemiah, the framework story of Job, and Chronicles. Other books—Ecclesiastes and the Hebrew portions of Daniel—may have been translated in whole or part from Aramaic. The growing influence of Aramaic on Hebrew may be traced in Ben Sirach and in some of the Qumran texts. Aramaic influence on the morphology, vocabulary, and syntax of Mishnaic Hebrew has been pointed out in recent studies. It is one of the main reasons for the profound distinction between the two stages of the language, comparable to the influence of Norman French on the development of English.

Aramaic played a role in the demise of Akkadian. A good part of the population of the Neo-Assyrian Empire spoke Aramaic while many of the speakers of Neo-Assyrian were ethnic Arameans. Neo-Babylonian, from the time of Nabopolassar on, was surely only a written language, while Aramaic was the spoken one. The full impact of Aramaic on Akkadian has still to be properly assessed.

Arabic religious terminology absorbed many terms

from Aramaic: *ṣalāt* (prayer), *zakāt* (charity), *raḥmān* (merciful one), *masjid* (mosque), etc., through the influence of both Judaism and Christianity. Words in the commercial and juridical sphere entered through Nabatean mediation. Aramaic served as the substrate language for the spoken Arabic of Palestine, Syria, and Iraq; the rural populations were often tenacious in their attitude toward Aramaic, and it served as the channel by which Hebrew and Canaanite elements in the spheres of agriculture, architecture, and artisanry were passed on to Arabic. Aramaic continues in use in the Jewish liturgy both in the home and the synagogue; it is used in the Syriac churches in Palestine, Lebanon, Syria, Iraq, and Iran.

Bibliography. Although some items in the bibliog. to ARAMAIC are outdated, it remains as a whole useful; E. Y. Kutscher, "Aramaic" in *Encyclopaedia Judaica,* III (1971), cols. 259-87, contains important bibliog. material.

J. GREENFIELD

***ARCHAEOLOGY.** The present article attempts to update the original essay with particular emphasis on recent trends in the general discipline in relation to the study of the Bible. This survey is largely limited to the historical period after *ca.* 3000 B.C. and to ancient Palestine, i.e., principally modern Jordan and Israel.

1. Excavations *ca.* 1955-1975
   a. Jordan and Israel to 1967
      i. Jordan
      ii. Israel
   b. Since the 1967 war
      i. Jordan
      ii. The West Bank
      iii. Jerusalem
      iv. Israel
2. Some contributions of recent archaeology
   a. Chronological periods and subdisciplines
      i. Prehistory
      ii. The Early Bronze Age
      iii. Canaan in the patriarchal age
      iv. The period of Philistine and Israelite incursions
      v. The Israelite and Judean monarchies
      vi. Exile and return
      vii. The Samaritan era
      viii. The Roman-Byzantine periods
   b. Over-all trends in the contribution of archaeology to the study of the Bible.
3. Method: the expanding scope of fieldwork
   a. Broader chronological, geographical, and cultural horizons
   b. Recent improvements in methodology
      i. Excavation
      ii. Other aspects of fieldwork
      iii. Volunteers
      iv. Recording
      v. Processing of materials and preparation for publication
   c. New analytical tools
      i. Refinement of current techniques
      ii. Newer experimental techniques
4. Theory: changing conceptions of archaeology
   a. Recent trends in American archaeology
   b. New approaches to Palestinian archaeology
   c. The future of "biblical archaeology"
Bibliography

1. Excavations *ca.* 1955-1975. The pace of excavation has quickened so greatly that we can note only a few of the more than two hundred sites dug in this period, and even then must restrict ourselves to Jordan and Israel.

a. Jordan and Israel to 1967. i. *Jordan.* The principal British excavations were those of Kenyon at Jericho from 1952 to 1958 and in Jerusalem from 1961 to 1967; of Parr, Kirkbride, Bennett, and others at Petra from 1955 on; and of Hennessy at the Damascus Gate from 1964 to 1966 and at Teleilat el-Ghassul in 1967. The French worked under de Vaux at Tell el-Far'ah (TIRZAH) from 1946 to 1960 and at Qumran and 'Ain Feshkha from 1949 to 1956. The Dutch excavated at Tell Deir'alla under Franken from 1960 to 1964. American excavations included those of Wright, Toombs, Campbell, and others at Shechem from 1956 to 1969; of Pritchard at Gibeon from 1956 to 1962; of Lapp at Taanach from 1963 to 1968; of Bull in the Samaritan sanctuary on Gerizim from 1964 to 1968; of Callaway at Ai from 1964 to 1969; and of Lapp at Bâb edh-Dhrâ' from 1965 to 1967. Dajani and other Jordanian excavators excavated Late Bronze and Iron Age tombs near Irbid and Amman and began clearance in the Amman Citadel from 1957 on.

ii. *Israel.* The Israeli "school" first came to international prominence with the large and superbly organized excavations of Yadin and others at Hazor from 1955 to 1958. Aharoni also excavated at Ramat Raḥel (*see* BETH-HACCHEREM[S]) from 1954 to 1962, and Yeivin at Tell Sheikh Aḥmed el-'Areinī (mistakenly called "Gath"; *see* GATH[S]) from 1956 to 1961. The 1960s saw the flourishing of this school, with large and significant excavations in the caves between Qumran and En-gedi under Bar-Adon, Aharoni, Avigad, Yadin, and others in 1960-61; at the Lower Pleistocene site of Ubeidiya under Stekelis from 1960 to 1963; of B. Mazar and T. Dothan at En-gedi from 1962 to 1965; of M. Dothan and others as Ashdod and Tell Mor from 1962 to 1972; of Aharoni and Amiran at Arad from 1962

H. T. Frank

3. Cleaning a grave. Small tools, often dental picks, must be used.

to 1975; of Yadin at Masada from 1963 to 1965; and of Biran at Dan beginning in 1966.

American scholars participated in several Israeli excavations but did not sponsor and direct their own projects until the Gezer excavations were launched in 1964 by Wright. Annual seasons were directed initially by Wright and thereafter by Dever, with Lance and Seger. This was the largest and longest running foreign excavation in Israel and had considerable impact on methodology (*see* §3*b below*).

b. Since the 1967 war. The brief interruption caused by the 1967 war was soon followed by a burst of archaeological activity on all sides.

i. *Jordan.* British excavations were conducted from 1968 onward at Tawilan and Buseira (*see* BOZRAH[S]) by Bennett. German scholars investigated the Madeba (MEDEBA) mosaics under Lux from 1964 to 1975 and began excavations at Umm Qeis under Lux and Kruger in 1974. American excavations were undertaken by the newly opened American Center of Oriental Research in Amman, first at Heshbon under Horn, Boraas, Sauer, and Geraty from 1968 to 1975; in Byzantine churches in Transjordan under Van Eldern from 1972 to 1974; and at Tell el-Husn under Boraas beginning in 1975. Hadidi, Zayadine and other Jordanian excavators continued work in the Amman citadel.

ii. *The West Bank.* Although all foreign excavations came to a halt after the war, some salvage operations continued. American-sponsored work was directed by Dever at the Middle Bronze I and Iron Age sites of Jebel Qa'aqir and Khirbet el-Kom (Shaphir?) W of Hebron from 1967 to 1971, and at Shechem in 1972-73. Callaway cleared an early Iron Age village at Radannah from 1969 to 1972. Survey work was also undertaken, notably the Israel Department of Antiquities survey of the Golan, Judea, and Samaria districts, extended later into Gaza and the Sinai. The information derived by Epstein and others from the Golan was especially significant, as this had been virtual *terra incognita* previously. *See* DOLMENS[S].

iii. *Jerusalem.* In the Old City of Jerusalem, a spate of excavations soon revealed more about the city's history than had been gleaned in a century of work. Paramount was the large-scale clearance of the area around the Western Wall by B. Mazar, commencing in 1967 and bringing to light monumental Herodian and later remains (*see* TEMPLE OF HEROD[S]). More modest but equally revealing were the soundings of N. Avigad during reconstruction work in the Jewish Quarter from 1968 on. Other projects were the work of Amiran and Eitan in the Citadel (Jaffa Gate) in 1968-69; that of Broshi in the Armenian quarter and elsewhere from 1970 on; of Lux and Kruger under the German Evangelical Church in the Muristan in 1970-71; of Beit-Arieh and Netzer along the Third Wall from 1972 to 1974; and of many Israeli and other archaeologists in Herodian tombs brought to light all around Jerusalem in construction work from 1967 on. *See* JERUSALEM[S].

iv. *Israel.* New excavations fielded outside Jerusalem in the post-1967 period included principally those of Aharoni at Tell Sheva (Iron Age Beersheba) from 1969 to 1975 (*see* BEER-SHEBA[S]); of A. Mazar at Tell Qasile from 1971 on; of Ussishkin at Lachish from 1972 on; of Kochavi at Ras el-'Ain (Aphek?) from 1972 on (*see* APHEK[S]); of Oren at Tell esh-Sherî'ah (Gath or Ziklag?) from 1972 on; and of M. Dothan at Acco from 1973 on. A number of the older excavations also continued, among them Ashdod, Arad, and Dan.

Among American excavations, Gezer continued through 1974. A number of other American excavations were launched by the W. F. Albright Institute and a consortium of American schools:

H. T. Frank

4. The geologist, having sought out field samples on the sites and in the general area, seeks to recover the geological history of the area. Here he works with a microscope in the geology tent.

H. T. Frank

5. The flotation tank crew. Second from left is the paleo-ethno botanist. By "floating" soil, seeds and fruit pits are recovered and ancient diets partially reconstructed.

Tell el-Hesī under Worrell and Toombs from 1970 to 1975 (*see* EGLON[S]); excavations in the synagogues at Khirbet Shema and Meiron under Meyers, Kraabel, and Strange; and a long-running project at Caesarea begun in 1971 by Bull. Other American excavations were those of Weinberg at Tell Anafa from 1968 to 1973; and Van Beek at Tell Jemmeh from 1970 on.

2. Some contributions of recent archaeology. So much information has accumulated in the last twenty years that we can only group the more significant contributions according to general areas, with major emphasis upon the illumination of biblical backgrounds.

a. Chronological periods and subdisciplines. i. *Prehistory*. The period before the advent of written records (about 3000 B.C.) is sufficiently important that it has usually been considered a separate discipline. Discoveries at Ubeidiya and Hazorea have produced human remains that are perhaps three million years old and rival those of Leakey's Olduvai Gorge materials for the earliest evidence of the emergence of *Homo sapiens* in the Lower Pleistocene Age. The Paleolithic and Neolithic periods in the tenth-fifth millennia B.C. also continue to be illuminated by the finds in the Nahal Oren, the Carmel Caves, the Wadi el-ʿAmud, and elsewhere. *See* PREHISTORY IN THE ANCIENT NEAR EAST[S].

ii. *The Early Bronze Age*. This period, Kenyon's "Proto Urban" period, spanning the third millennium B.C., has recently been brought into sharper focus by vast new evidence, especially from Tell el-Farʿah, Jericho, Meser, Arad, Bâb edh-Dhrâʿ, and Gezer. However, this period predates the beginning of written history in Palestine and the biblical era per se and thus falls largely outside the limitations of our survey. *See* JERICHO[S]; ARAD [S] §1; GEZER[S] §2.

iii. *Canaan in the patriarchal age*. The MB I and II periods (*ca*. 2200-2000 and 2000-1500 B.C., respectively) have been particularly well illuminated by recent discoveries. The first period is a nonurban interlude between the EB and MB cultures, now designated by Kenyon and others as the "Intermediate EB-MB" or simply the "Intermediate" period. It is characterized in Palestine by a seminomadic material culture which seems to have diffused from Syria and Mesopotamia with the early expansion of the AMORITES. For this reason Albright, Glueck, de Vaux, and many other scholars considered it to be the period of the biblical patriarchs. However, the conspicuous lack of MB I remains at such patriarchal centers as Shechem and Beer-sheba calls this association into question (*see* PATRIARCHS §3*a*; PATRIARCHS[S]; SHECHEM[S]).

The period itself has ceased to be one of Palestine's deepest "Dark Ages" and has emerged as the last phase of the long Early Bronze Age, and thus following a suggestion of Wright's has been called by Dever and Oren the "Early Bronze IV" period. Isolated cemeteries were previously known and others continue to come to light, but the discovery of the first substantial settlements has finally enabled us to draw a fuller picture of this culture. The evidence has come largely from Iktanu, Aroer and elsewhere in Tranjordan, Jebel Qaʿaqir, Yeruham, and from surface surveys across the Negeb into Sinai. The tendency is now to raise the dates for MB I by about a century, to *ca*. 2200-2000 B.C., in spite of Albright's attempt to lower them.

The MB II period (*ca*. 2000-1500 B.C., often divided into MB IIA, B, and C) represents the zenith of power and prosperity in the Canaanite city-states of Syria-Palestine. Massive fortifications have been uncovered at Dan, Hazor, Taanach, Tell el-Farʿah, Shechem, Gezer, Hebron, Ras el-ʿAin and elsewhere in Palestine, as well as at Tell Mardikh in Syria. At Shechem, Wright has connected an early open-air shrine (*ca*. 1800 B.C.) with the biblical traditions concerning patriarchal worship there (Gen. 33:18-20). An eighteenth-seventeenth-century B.C. unwalled village some distance from Beth-shemesh reveals a nonnucleated population, which may provide a suitable setting for the biblical patriarchs if we are to place them later than the MB I period.

Every MB II site excavated thus far shows a massive destruction around 1500 B.C., in many cases followed by a long gap in occupation. The latter part of the period is characterized as the "MB IIC" period, *ca*. 1650-1550/1500 B.C., especially by American scholars basing themselves on Shechem and Gezer. In general, there is today a tendency in the direction of the "middle chronology" (Hammurabi ± 1792-1750 B.C.), with a consequent raising of dates for the earlier MB phases by as

H. T. Frank
6. Pottery drawing

H. T. Frank
7. Survey architect at work in the field, taking levels, drawing, plotting

much as fifty to one hundred years. *See* CHRONOLOGY, MESOPOTAMIAN[S].

iv. *The period of Philistine and Israelite incursions.* The twilight of Canaanite culture at the end of the LB Age, *ca.* 1200 B.C., coincides with major movements of peoples, principally the "Sea Peoples" or PHILISTINES and the Israelites. The exotic and heretofore enigmatic material culture of the Philistines has been brilliantly illuminated by the finds at Ashdod (*see* ASHDOD[S]) ; the twelfth-eleventh-century occupation levels at Gezer (*see* GEZER[S] §5) ; the anthropoid coffins of Egyptian mercenaries at Deir al-Balah (*see also* ZARETHAN [S]) ; and especially by the temple at Tell Qasile, with its nearly intact paraphernalia. Destruction levels probably attributable to the incoming Israelites have been found at Dan, Hazor, Bethel, and other sites claimed by the Bible to have been destroyed; while at Shechem and Gezer the continuity of LB–early Iron I cultures further confirms the biblical tradition (*see* JOSHUA, BOOK OF[S] §5*c*) . However, Jericho, Ai, and Gibeon remain more a problem than ever, as the archaeological evidence does not indicate a destruction, or for that matter any settlement at all, in the period of the Conquest. Israelite occupation following a destruction seems witnessed at Hazor, Bethel, and Lachish; while distinctive settlements first founded in the twelfth century B.C. and representing early Israelite culture have been found at Raddanah and at Tel Masos, as well as in surveys by Aharoni in Upper Galilee. *See* CANAAN, CONQUEST AND SETTLEMENT OF[S].

v. *The Israelite and Judean monarchies.* The splendid reign attributed to Solomon has been glimpsed in the nearly identical casemate (or double) walls and city gates with four entryways at Hazor, Megiddo, and Gezer (cf. I Kings 9:15-17) ; the prototype of these gates has turned up at Ashdod. The era of Jeroboam I and Ahab in the ninth century takes almost equal place, with the discovery of the sanctuary and city gate at Dan (*see* DAN[S]) and the magnificently engineered water tunnels at Hazor and Megiddo.

The prosperous and generally homogeneous material culture of the monarchical period has been demonstrated in the domestic architecture, in our growing corpus of pottery, and in small finds of all sorts from everyday life. Numerous weights, measures, and silver hordes contribute to our understanding of commerce and trade. Local sanctuaries at Dan, Lachish, Arad, and possibly Beer-sheba (with "horned altars," cf. I Kings 1:50, at Dan and Beer-sheba) reflect the diversity of Israelite religion, despite the centralization of the cult in Jerusalem and the protests of the prophets against syncretism (*see* TEMPLES, SEMITIC[S] §2) . Vast numbers of recently discovered tombs (*see* TOMB; TOMB[S]) illustrate burial practice and belief. Our fund of epigraphic materials has multiplied several times (*see* INSCRIPTIONS, SEMITIC[S] §3) . Finally, both the Assyrian destructions in the late eighth century and the Babylonian destructions in the early sixth century B.C. have produced eloquent testimony at nearly every site investigated.

vi. *Exile and return.* The postdestruction, Persian, and Hellenistic periods in Palestine still remain insufficiently known, but the first attempts at synthesis can now be made. Light is gradually being shed by the excavations at Anafa, Shiqmona, Tell Megadim, SAMARIA, Shechem, En-gedi, Tell Jemmeh, Ashdod (Tel Mor) , Gezer, and in Jeru-

H. T. Frank

8. Bones are carefully studied in situ and then removed to the anthropologists' area for further examination and study, as shown here.

© Y. Yadin

9. Basket found in the Cave of Letters. *See* Bar Kochba[S]

salem itself. The evidence indicates a slow and painful local recovery, finally swept up in the advance of the classical Hellenistic cultures in the late third century B.C.

vii. *The Samaritan era.* This period has been relatively obscure until recently, but has now been illuminated by domestic levels at Shechem, as well as by the discovery of the dated SAMARIA PAPYRI. The probable Samaritan sanctuary on Mount Gerizim has been located and partially cleared.

viii. *The Roman-Byzantine periods.* Until recently "New Testament archaeology" has been an armchair discipline, dealing largely with classical texts, while the study of Jewish remains of the period has languished. Now, however, a series of discoveries has galvanized attention on the Roman and Byzantine periods. The Herodian era and the first century A.D. are perhaps the best known at present, thanks to the well-dated destruction levels of A.D. 70 being uncovered in Jerusalem, along with the monumental Herodian structures at the Western Wall. The excavation of MASADA, Herodian Jericho, and the HERODIUM have also contributed greatly.

Qumran and its scrolls have been less revolutionary than first expected but no less important (*see* DEAD SEA SCROLLS and supplementary article). The En-gedi caves and the excavations of Masada have yielded spectacular supplementary evidence of Jewish sects of the period. Many new synagogues have been located and ones already known have been re-excavated, including those at Meiron, Khirbet Shema, Chorazin, CAPERNAUM, Tiberias, Beth-shan, Ma'on, En-gedi, Masada, Samu', and Sussiyeh. The Galilean synagogues, formerly dated to the second-third century A.D., are now thought by some scholars to be mostly fourth- or fifth-century A.D. (*see* SYNAGOGUE, ARCHITECTURE[S]). Finally, Jewish ceremonial art has been greatly clarified by the increasing evidence of pagan motifs transformed and utilized in these synagogues. *See* ART, EARLY JEWISH[S].

Early Christian sites are still neglected, but a recent catalogue listed nearly two hundred known Byzantine churches in Palestine. The number is currently being swelled by the more intensive exploration and excavation of Transjordan. Recent discoveries on both banks of the Jordan would include churches at Khirbet Kerak, el-Koursi, Shavei Zion, Beit Sahur, PELLA, and several in the vicinity at Madeba (Medeba) in Transjordan.

Due to the political situation in the Middle East, the exploration of the areas more peripheral to the lands of the Bible has slowed in pace. Nevertheless, Transjordan is rapidly opening up. Parts of the gap in occupation postulated by Glueck between *ca.* 1900 and 1200 B.C. are slowly being filled. In the Iron Age, the Ammonite and Edomite cultures are emerging in greater clarity through excavations at Amman, Heshbon, Buseira, and elsewhere (*see* AMMON, AMMONITES[S] §2; HESHBON[S]). For the later periods, Petra has thrown great light on the Nabatean civilization. *See* EDOM[S].

Ancient Syria is less well known, despite its demonstrable archaeological riches, and we still need controlled excavation with modern stratigraphic methods. Older sites like Ras Shamra (*see* UGARIT[S]) continue to produce monumental architecture and written documents, but we lack reliable stratigraphic sequences or an adequate knowledge of the material culture as a whole. The same is true for ancient Phoenicia and the Lebanese coast. In Egypt and Iraq (Mesopotamia), foreign excavations have nearly halted, and the national departments of antiquities have not yet developed adequate personnel or resources. Turkey could yield enormous information, but its scientific investigation has hardly commenced, nor is it generally open at the moment to Western scholars.

b. Over-all trends in the contribution of archaeology to the study of the Bible. Archaeology in its broadest sense is the *only* possible source of material evidence for additional illumination of the biblical text. For that reason Albright long ago described an "archaeological revolution" in the twentieth-century study of the Bible, a phrase not at all exaggerated. Albright suggested that the cumulative result of the first generation of exploration and excavation was that the Bible no longer projected from antiquity like a "lone fossil." It can now be seen in its original setting, lost for centuries but increasingly reconstructed in detail through the evidence supplied by archaeology. There is no reason to believe that this revolution is exhausted; on the contrary, it has scarcely begun. With its growing precision in retrieving the empirical data and its increasing sophistication in interpreting it, modern archaeology has the potential for even greater illumination of the Bible.

3. Method: the expanding scope of fieldwork. ***a. Broader chronological, geographical, and cultural horizons.*** Recent finds have pushed back our time span in archaeology to three million years ago. For neglected or poorly perceived periods, they have refined chronology and suggested more accurate terminology. More important, they have filled out what was heretofore only a tantalizing outline of the successive material cultures of the ancient Near East. With the gradual extension of excavation into more peripheral areas—from Cyprus to Iran and from the Caucasus to Nubia—the "lands of the Bible" have come to include a vast geographical area. The result is that Near Eastern archaeologists, even those concentrating in the biblical period, are now confronted with a bewildering variety of peoples, places, and events nowhere equaled in the world.

b. Recent improvements in methodology. Much of the recent increase in material evidence from the past is due to more sophisticated and precise methods of retrieval, recording, and processing of data. In methodology Near Eastern archaeology has lagged behind until the last two decades but now is in the forefront of developments.

i. *Excavation.* Modern stratigraphic methods popularized by Kenyon at Jericho from 1952 to 1958 (discussed in ARCHAEOLOGY §B) have become standard procedure on nearly all British and American excavations. "Wheeler-Kenyon" technique, or more properly the "baulk/debris layer" method, goes back in principle to Reisner's excavations from 1908 to 1910 at Samaria. The more recent application introduces automatic, three-dimensional analysis and recording, making possible far greater precision in separating debris layers (*see* TELL[S]). It enables us to associate datable pottery and objects more confidently with architectural remains and thus to define building periods or strata more accurately. These drawn sections then serve as the basis for the publication, relating everything graphically and three-dimensionally for the reader.

American adaptations of British methods were first successfully employed at Shechem by Wright from 1956 on, then later at Taanach, Ai, and elsewhere. The essential modification was the use of detailed, daily ceramic analysis in the Albright tradition to complement the stratigraphic work in the field. Further advances were made in the application of these methods to larger architectural units when they were introduced in Israel on the Gezer excavations in the 1960s. Now such methods are routinely employed on all American excavations, especially in Jordan and in Israel.

Israeli excavators generally use more traditional methods, clearing larger architectural complexes and depending upon quantities of restorable pottery found *in situ* on living surfaces. Whereas British and American excavators with their more minute methods have tended to re-excavate older sites where a minimum of material remains, Israelis prefer virgin sites. Their approach has given us an impressive exposure at a wide range of sites, though details often seem lacking and interpretations remain needlessly controversial. The fieldwork is backed up by an excellent network of technical facilities in museums and laboratories, as well as by modern conservation and reconstruction at the sites. Despite differences in method, both "schools" have produced significant results. Moreover, a consensus is slowly developing on the crucial points, such as the need to utilize sections extensively and to record them for publication.

Whatever method is employed, growing recognition of the potential archaeological evidence available and the recent trend toward multidisciplinary staffs (*see* §4*b below*) have resulted in the recovery of data from remains that were formerly overlooked or discarded. This includes floral and faunal remains, industrial wastes, occupational residue on living surfaces, sediments accumulating through natural processes, and the like. Improved excavation methods per se are sufficient to recover some of these remains, but specific techniques may also be employed. As a single example, on modern excavations all debris from living surfaces, plus a routine percentage of other debris (perhaps 20%), may be sieved and then put through flotation equipment designed to ensure near total retrieval of organic materials. Cores of the debris layers may also be taken for pollen analysis (palynology).

ii. *Other aspects of fieldwork.* In prospecting for sites or choosing areas for excavation, proton magnetometers and electrical resistivity surveying sometimes enable large structures such as city walls to be traced underground without actual excavation (though these techniques are less useful in the deep, multilayered mounds of Palestine than elsewhere). Aerial photography and photogrammetric mapping also aid increasingly in locating new sites and in developing field strategy. In the case of coastal sites, underwater archaeology, a relatively new subdiscipline, will aid in planning the harbor and may also produce additional evidence from shipwrecks or from the bottom of the sea (*see* SHIPS AND SHIPPING[S]). Finally, surface surveying of large regions before selected sites are excavated has come a long way from the random sherd sampling of the past, and, if sufficiently systematic, may indicate settlement patterns and even the character of individual sites with surprising accuracy. (Again, this technique is more applicable to areas with one-period sites than it is to Palestine.)

iii. *Volunteers.* A new feature of Palestinian archaeology in the 1960s was the replacement of hired native labor by volunteers, usually brought from abroad. Yadin pioneered the use of volunteers on a large scale at Masada in 1963; but the Gezer excavations beginning in 1964 were the first to structure an archaeological project around an academic program designed for students and coupled with fieldwork. In addition to producing a new generation of highly trained professional archaeologists, we have recruited a large and enthusiastic corps of amateurs who are conversant with modern field archaeology and are capable of following the literature critically.

iv. *Recording.* The diary of the field or area supervisors is still basic, but now it is likely to include a daily top plan, detailed locus-by-locus descriptions, frequent sketches of sections and photographs, field readings of pottery, etc. In addition, specialists on the staff (*see* §v *below*) will have supplied geological analyses of soil layers, notes on various categories of material remains, and other technical data. Many excavation projects now have their own field manuals, describing in detail the digging and recording methods to be used, ensuring uniformity in the field reports which become the basis for the final publication.

v. *Processing of materials and preparation for publication.* Modern field archaeology amasses more data than can readily be assimilated. The routine processing of materials—i.e., selecting, cataloguing according to types, drawing and describing—is crucial. Two techniques have improved efficiency. One is a matter of practical ingenuity and consists of sectioning the sherd with a thin carborundum-bladed saw and drawing it 1:1. An additional benefit is that this aids with description and photography of ware, temper, manufacturing technique, and firing.

The second process is computer programming, still highly experimental but promising a breakthrough. Coding all classes of archaeological artifacts into computers speeds conventional sorting and cataloguing immensely and at the same time makes possible exhaustive analyses of comparative types which would otherwise be unfeasible. The first attempts to code all excavated materials from a site have already been undertaken, but apart from coins and other easily classified artifacts, there is not yet sufficient agreement on typological criteria to permit full computerization, especially with pottery.

The multidisciplinary approach to archaeology

today has made fieldwork more sophisticated, but also more difficult to work up for publication. It is no longer sufficient to send samples to consultants who will render an opinion. The ideal (not often attained) is to recruit specialists in allied disciplines who collaborate in the project design itself, supervise the excavation and recording of the material, provide on-the-spot and laboratory analyses, and finally incorporate their reports into the over-all synthesis of the history and culture of the site (*see* §4 *below*).

The problems which plague fieldwork seem more manageable than those faced in publication. The unfortunate result is that many excavations, even those well organized in the field, never produce a final report.

c. New analytical tools. Here we can deal only with additional techniques which are directly applicable to Palestinian archaeology in its present state (*see bibliog. for wider orientation*).

i. *Refinement of current techniques.* Perhaps the most significant breakthrough in the application of science to archaeology is radiocarbon-14 dating. This is not new, having been in use since the early 1950s, but its application in establishing absolute chronology is still debated. The original half-life figure of 5568±30 (the rate of decay of C^{14} in formerly living organisms) has now been raised by general agreement to 5730±40, but there are indications that further adjustments may be necessary. These changes would have the effect of raising dates in the ancient Near East by as much as three to five centuries by the time we reach back to the third and fourth millennia B.C. To illustrate the dilemma, in Egypt, for instance, this would wreak havoc with our present system of chronology, which is based on astronomical observations preserved in the literary sources and seems to provide satisfactory international synchronisms. Until greater precision and agreement can be obtained in radiocarbon dates, it may be better to continue to depend upon traditional chronological methods. *See* CHRONOLOGY, MESOPOTAMIAN[S]; EGYPT, CHRONOLOGY OF[S].

Neutron activation analysis of pottery, in which samples of sherds are irradiated and the gamma-ray spectra are used to measure the elements present, is capable of "finger printing" the clays used in pottery with considerable accuracy. As the corpus of analyzed samples from ancient clay beds grows, this method should be able to trace the manufacture of both local and imported pottery to their source, which would yield valuable information on commerce and trade. Already neutron activation has shown that most of the Late Bronze "bichrome ware" is not Palestinian but Cypriot; and studies under way on the Middle Bronze "Tell el-Yehudiyeh" and other wares may reveal similar surprises.

Less publicized but still useful is petrographic analysis of thin sections of sherds, in which the source of inclusions for tempering clays can often be localized.

ii. *Newer experimental techniques.* There are still newer laboratory techniques, potentially informative but not yet perfected or fully adapted for use on archaeological materials. Among those already being employed in some branches of archaeology are: potassium argon dating of geological samples; archaeomagnetic analysis of terra cotta and ceramic remains; hydration dating of obsidian implements; spectographic analysis of metals; and thermoluminescent dating of pottery.

4. Theory: changing conceptions of archaeology. Archaeology is more than a set of techniques in digging, recording, and manipulating data. It is an intellectual exercise in penetrating the past. The conceptual models on which this aspect of archaeology is based have undergone sweeping changes in the last decade. The vigorous debate generated by the discussion, particularly in America, is gradually making an impact on excavators working in the Middle East.

a. Recent trends in American archaeology. American (or "New World") archaeology has always been oriented more to anthropology than to history, in part because it deals largely with prehistory, i.e., with peoples who have not left written records. Ethnographic data from living primitive societies therefore is utilized alongside studies of the physical remains of extinct societies. The objective is usually not necessarily the history of a site but the elucidation of the cultural process itself. The attempt to understand past cultures in their total relation to their environment, and the effort to show the relevance of such research for humanistic studies in general, have led American archaeologists more recently to collaborate with social scientists, ecologists, and general systems theorists.

The latest innovation in America is the "new archeology" (usually so spelled), which has gone further in rejecting the "idiographic" or historical approach in favor of "nomothetic" or generalizing archaeology. Influenced heavily by scientific method and modern philosophy of science (J. Hempel and others), this school conceives its task as that of "explanation," i.e., of formulating and testing general covering laws which will satisfactorily account for cultural diversity and change.

These and other recent developments point to a concern to frame a general theory of what archaeology is and what it should do, at the same time emphasizing its still unfulfilled potential for understanding human behavior in the larger perspective of the past.

b. New approaches to Palestinian archaeology. The changes we have noted in the general conception of archaeology elsewhere have only recently affected American excavations in the Middle East. This is particularly true in Palestine, where American archaeology has traditionally been considered a branch of biblical studies. A typical American project in Jordan in the 1950s and early 1960s would have been digging at a biblical site, supported primarily by theological schools. The staff members were mostly seminary professors or theological students whose orientation was biblical history. Although they would have picked up considerable skills in the use of the traditional tools, stratigraphy and ceramic typology, only the director, if anyone, would have been a professional archaeologist. The objective of such a project was usually to recover a ceramic sequence and an outline of the "political history" (the major destructions) of the site—an objective which was quite narrow by the criteria outlined above.

As wider objectives were formulated, large multidisciplinary staffs began to be employed at Gezer and other American excavations in Israel in the late 1960s. By the early 1970s most excavation staffs included the traditional personnel, but also various combinations of geologists, geographers, physical and cultural anthropologists, paleo-ethnobotanists and zoologists, experts on the history of technology, professional ceramicists, computer programmers, and many other consultants. The basic orientation toward history, including that of the biblical period, was still dominant, but the presence of so many specialists in other areas inevitably expanded the scope of the project. Furthermore, financial support for such excavations came less from theological circles than from universities, private foundations, and U.S. government agencies, to whom the research had to be justified in terms of broad scholarship and humanistic values.

It must be acknowledged that the "new look" of these projects was sometimes superficial, the result more of pragmatic adaptation than of any revolutionary change in theory. There was often little rigorous examination of the underlying assumptions of the "new archeology," and some of its methods were uncritically applied to the unique stratified mounds of Palestine. Finally, these projects have not yet co-ordinated and published their results, so the alleged superiority of their methodology remains undemonstrated.

Two cautionary notes seem in order. Enthusiasm for newer experimental approaches is no substitute for competence in more traditional, proven methods, such as stratigraphy and ceramic typology, which remain basic in Palestine. Secondly, because we have a long sweep of written history, our essential orientation must be historical, and command of the languages and literatures, including those of the Bible, is fundamental.

c. The future of "biblical archaeology." The recent trends we have noted suggest to some scholars that American Palestinian archaeology in the near future may cease to be an adjunct to biblical studies and may become an autonomous discipline alongside the other brands of archaeology. These scholars have even abandoned the term "biblical archaeology" in favor of "Palestinian archaeology." This is not merely a matter of semantics. It represents a different conception of Palestinian archaeology, a determination to establish it as an academic field on its own merit and then to work out a new and more constructive relationship with biblical studies. This position still represents a minority view, but its main arguments may be worth noting. (1) There is a discipline properly called "Palestinian archaeology," or more accurately "Syro-Palestinian archaeology," i.e., a branch of general archaeology which deals with one specific geographical, cultural, and chronological entity. By consensus, this embraces the distinctive land bridge between Egypt and Mesopotamia, with its succession of cultures in the historical periods. (The study of the period before *ca.* 3500 B.C. belongs properly to Old World prehistory, and the study of later Jewish and Christian antiquities may better be considered a subdiscipline of Greco-Roman and Byzantine archaeology.) Obviously Palestinian archaeology extends far beyond the time period and the subject matter of the Bible. It is, therefore, a secular discipline whose canons are determined by archaeology and not by the special concerns of biblical scholarship. (2) This secular tradition of archaeology is a viable option. It has a long history in American scholarship, going back to Reisner's Harvard excavations at Samaria from 1908 to 1910, and continuing in the excavations of Chicago, Pennsylvania, and Yale at Megiddo, Beth-shan, and Jerash in the 1920s and 1930s. It has characterized nearly all British work in Palestine and is now dominant in the well-established "Israeli school," which uses the Bible not as a theological statement but as a document of national history. (3) It is granted that a secular approach to archaeology also has its bias, but removing the dialogue from "biblical" to "Palestinian" archaeology defines the issue as one not of faith but of scholarly method, which is appropriate to archaeology as an academic inquiry. (4) These interrelated trends in Palestinian archaeology are rapidly making the field a scholarly discipline in its own right, no longer subservient to biblical studies in America—a development which as we have seen already had taken place elsewhere. The recent declaration of independence is partly a matter of necessity, as Palestinian archaeology outgrows the ability of biblical circles to support it or even to be *au courant* regarding its results. It is also partly out of the conviction that allowing them their separate courses of development may foster the growth of both disciplines.

The real question is not whether Palestinian archaeology can survive, but whether parallel to it something called "biblical archaeology" can persist or can hope to become an academic discipline. As Palestinian archaeology and biblical studies are currently evolving, the only possibilities for "biblical archaeology" would seem to be as an interdisciplinary study. It could be pursued either by archaeologists specializing in the biblical period, or by biblical scholars utilizing selected discoveries of professional archaeologists and seeking to relate these to problems of biblical interpretation.

Two qualifications are necessary. The enterprise we have just described is legitimate and at its best may indeed be academically respectable; but it does not constitute an independent discipline. It can flourish only when both Palestinian archaeology and biblical studies are allowed sufficient integrity to carry out their respective tasks. Secondly, although it may seem a minor consideration, the term "biblical archaeology" should be avoided, at least in academic circles; the use of the word "biblical" as a qualifying adjective suggests a special kind of "holy archaeology." A more accurate and useful name for the interdisciplinary study we have been describing would be "the archaeology of Palestine in the biblical period," or simply "archaeology and the Bible."

Bibliography. Historical and archaeological syntheses: W. F. Albright, *The Archaeology of Palestine* (1956;

new Penguin ed. by W. G. Dever, 1976); K. Kenyon, *Archaeology in the Holy Land* (1960); Y. Aharoni, *The Land of the Bible* (1962).

Surveys of recent excavation: D. W. Thomas, ed., *Archaeology and OT Study* (1967); B. Mazar, ed., *Encyclopedia of Archaeological Excavations in the Holy Land,* 2 vols. (1970, Hebrew; a revised Eng. version in 4 vols. will appear in 1975-76); L. T. Geraty, "The Archaeology of Jordan—A History of Research" and J. A. Sauer, "The Archaeology of Jordan—The Results of Research," in *The Archaeology of Jordan and Other Studies,* ed. L. T. Geraty (1976); for full bibliog. to 1970, see E. Vogel, "Bibliography of Holy Land Sites," *HUCA,* XLII (1971), 1-96 (repr. by American Schools of Oriental Research); for current reports, see "Notes and News," in *IEJ* and "Chronique Archéologique," in *RB*.

History of American Palestinian archaeology: G. E. Wright, "The Phenomenon of American Archaeology in the Near East," in *Near Eastern Archaeology in the Twentieth Century,* ed. J. A. Sanders (1970), pp. 3-40.

Theory and method in Palestinian archaeology: G. E. Wright, "Archaeological Method in Palestine—An American Interpretation," *Eretz Israel,* IX (1969), 120-33; W. G. Dever, "Two Approaches to Archaeological Method—The Architectural and the Stratigraphic," *Eretz Israel,* XI (1973), 1-8; P. W. Lapp, *Biblical Archaeology and History* (1969); W. G. Dever, H. D. Lance, eds., *Gezer Excavation Manual* (1976).

Biblical archaeology: W. F. Albright, "The Impact of Archaeology on Biblical Research—1966" and G. E. Wright, "Biblical Archaeology Today," in *New Directions in Biblical Archaeology,* ed. D. N. Freedman, J. C. Greenfield (1969), pp. 1-14, 149-65, respectively; W. G. Dever, *Archaeology and Biblical Studies: Retrospects and Prospects* (1974); A. E. Glock, "Biblical Archaeology, An Emerging Discipline," in *The Archaeology of Jordan and other Studies,* ed. L. T. Geraty (1976).

New trends in general archaeology: D. Brothwell and E. S. Higgs, eds., *Science in Archaeology* (1969); P. J. Watson, S. A. LeBlanc, C. L. Redman, *Explanation in Archeology: An Explicitly Scientific Approach* (1971); C. L. Redman, ed., *Research and Theory in Current Archeology* (1973); F. Hole and R. F. Heizer, *An Introduction to Prehistoric Archeology* (3rd ed., 1973).

W. G. DEVER

***AREOPAGUS.** Investigations on the Areopagus have clarified the history of the site. The church whose ruins stand on the terrace below the summit of the hill on the N side has been shown to date from the sixteenth century. Evidence for an earlier church is provided by some architectural marbles found on the site and by a cemetery with at least thirty-five graves of early Christian times, the earliest being of the late sixth or seventh century. No foundations of this earlier church have been found. Pre-Christian remains on the terrace consist of a few scraps of house walls and some cisterns of Hellenistic and Roman times. No trace was found of the court of the Areopagus or of any of the pagan sanctuaries ascribed to the area. This led the excavators to conclude that we must look elsewhere on the hill. The present writer believes that the court, the pagan sanctuaries, and also the early Christian church probably lie hidden at the E end of the terrace just described, underneath the mass of rock that has fallen from the upper part of the Areopagus hill. This rock covers a considerable area and is too large to be moved.

A limestone fragment found *ca.* 220 yards NE of the hill may have some connection with the Areopagus court. On one smooth, natural rock surface it bears the word "lithos," i.e., "stone," written in Greek characters of Imperial Roman date. A stone which has the word "stone" on it must be special and could perhaps be one of those on which the accused and the accuser stood in the Areopagus court. *See also* ATHENS[S].

Bibliography. John Travlos and Alison Frantz, "The Church of St. Dionysios the Areopagite and the Palace of the Archbishop of Athens in the 16th Century," *Hesperia,* XXXIV (1965), 157-202; E. Vanderpool, "Lithos," *Hesperia,* XXXV (1966), 275-76.

E. VANDERPOOL

ARETALOGY ăr ə täl′ ə jē [ἀρεταλογία, ἀρετή virtue + λόγος, report]. Inscriptional evidence shows that the term was used in the period 300 B.C.–A.D. 300 to mean a report or celebration of the marvelous deeds of a deity. The word appears in the LXX in Sirach 36:13 (RSV 36:14) where God is urged to "fill Zion with the *celebration of* [his] *wondrous deeds,*" and is used similarly in Strabo's *Geography* (XVII.i.17).

The single common purpose of the aretalogies was to praise the miracle-working deity. Scholars disagree, however, on whether they also manifest a common form and style. Some biblical scholars believe that the aretalogy is a biographical, literary genre (*see* GOSPEL, GENRE[S] §3). Its more-or-less stylized framework, they argue, depicts the miraculous birth of a wise MIRACLE WORKER, his struggles with his opponents, his martyrdom, and his apotheosis. Others contend, more modestly, that the aretalogy simply recounted the miracles of a charismatic figure in order to demonstrate his status as a DIVINE MAN. It is questionable, however, whether the evidence adduced for these hypotheses really supports them. Down into the first century A.D. the term "divine man" (θεῖος ἀνήρ) was used of men of superior wisdom specially favored by the gods or in special communion with them. Only later in the second and third centuries was a synthesis of this figure with that of the miracle worker attempted. Even Philostratus' *Life of Apollonius of Tyana* follows no strict biographical pattern and leads to no martyrdom.

There are formal similarities between the individual stories of miracles attributed to Jesus in the gospels and those reported of supernaturally endowed men in the late Hellenistic world as well as in rabbinic miracle anecdotes. But the over-all framework of the NT narratives and their underlying aim are distinctive. Therefore, to refer to the "aretalogy" as though it were a fixed literary form (whether the biography of a wonder-working martyr or the report of a divinized miracle worker) is to distort the meaning the term had in antiquity and to obscure important literary and theological distinctions in present-day biblical interpretation. While pagan aretalogies report acts of the deities in the past, biblical writers from the sixth century B.C. down into the first century A.D. celebrate in advance the deeds which God is yet to perform (e.g., Sirach 36:6 ff.; Dan. 4:34-35; 6:26-27).

See also MIRACLE STORIES, NT[S]; THEOPHANY IN

THE NT[S] §§2, 3*a*; LITERATURE, EARLY CHRISTIAN [S] §7; SIGN IN THE NT[S].

Bibliography. For the older aretalogical texts: S. Reinach, "Les aretalogues dans l'antiquite," *BCH,* IX (1885), 257; A. Deissmann, *Bible Studies* (2nd ed., 1903), pp. 93-95. For the more recent texts: V. Longo, *Aretalogie nel Mondo Greco,* Pubblicazioni dell'Istituto di filologia classica dell'Universita de Genova, XXIX (1969); R. Merkelbach in *Zeitschrift für Papyrologie und Epigraphik,* X (1973), 45-54.

Aretalogy is treated as a fixed literary form in M. Hadas and M. Smith, *Heroes and Gods: Spiritual Biographies in Antiquity,* Religious Perspectives, XIII (1965) and by H. Koester, "One Jesus and Four Gospels," *HTR,* LXI (1968), 230-36. For a detailed critique of this position and a careful analysis of the texts: D. L. Tiede, *The Charismatic Figure as Miracle Worker,* SBLDS, I (1972); also H. C. Kee, "Aretalogy and Gospel," *JBL,* XCII (1973), 402-22.

H. C. KEE

ARIOCH. Commander of King Nebuchadnezzar's bodyguard (Dan. 2:14-15). He was given the responsibility for executing the "wise men" of Babylon, but became the intermediary through whom Daniel was admitted to the king's presence (Dan. 2:24-25).

***ARK OF NOAH.** Attempts to test archaeologically the historicity of the flood narrative (Gen. 6–8) have been of two kinds. First, evidence of alluvial layers in the remains of Mesopotamian cities has been assessed. It has failed to indicate any single widespread deluge. There is no such evidence at all from Palestine (*see* FLOOD [GENESIS] §4). Second, it has been claimed that there exist remains of the ark of Noah itself on "Mount Ararat."

According to Gen. 8:4, after the recession of the waters, "the ark came to rest upon the mountains of Ararat." Ararat is the Hebrew form of Urarṭu, an extensive country which covered parts of modern Turkey, Iran, and the Soviet Union (*see* ARARAT). The fabulous height of its peaks was clearly known as far away as Palestine. Genesis refers to no specific mountain, but later Christian tradition chose the southernmost of the great peaks of the area, Agri Dag in NE Turkey, as "Mount Ararat." At its foot was built in the Middle Ages the Monastery of St. James, whose monks satisfied pilgrims by showing relics of Noah and his family. The monastery was destroyed in 1840.

In this century a story has been current of a Russian aviator who, before the revolution of 1917, saw Noah's Ark from the air, resting on Mount Ararat, and of a subsequent investigation ordered by the Czar. The truth of no part of this story can be tested, since any records there may have been were destroyed in the revolution. But, partly on the basis of this story, a number of American expeditions have been organized since the 1950s. At a height of some 14,000 feet on the mountain, a large wooden structure has been found. A complete examination has been impossible up to the time of recent reports, since it is largely encased in ice. However, in 1970 the age of small fragments of the wood was estimated by the carbon-14 technique to be not more than 1200 years. It seems likely that monks of the Monastery of St. James, sparing no effort to provide appropriate relics, may have built something to pass for the ark high up on the mountain. However that may be, nothing found on the latter-day "Mount Ararat" has any relevance to the historicity of the biblical narrative.

Bibliography. F. Parrot, *Journey to Ararat* (1859) for accounts of the Monastery of St. James before its destruction; J. Bright, "Has Archaeology Found Evidence of the Flood?" *BA,* V (1942), 55-62; A. Parrot, *The Flood and Noah's Ark* (1955); G. E. Wright, "The Ark Again?" *ASOR,* No. 3 (1970-71); for a full account of the search for the ark by one who believes the biblical account literally to be true, see J. W. Montgomery, *The Quest for Noah's Ark* (1972).

D. JOBLING

***ARMY.** Knowledge of this subject is limited by three factors: (1) There is a scarcity of extant reliefs and drawings depicting Israelite military affairs. Only tentative conclusions should be drawn from material from other countries in Israel's cultural milieu. (2) Many OT military narratives are found in late literary sources, sometimes hundreds of years removed from the events described. (3) Because of the religious nature of the biblical narratives, military details, such as army organization, supply, and strategy may have been omitted as irrelevant.

1. A people's army. Until the rise of the monarchy, Israel's army was a people's force recruited in emergencies by clan or tribal leaders. Sometimes charismatic leaders enlisted warriors from several tribes. Prior to Saul, however, these leaders never commanded the entire tribal confederation (I Sam. 11:1-11). All Israel was involved in a war only once, and this was an internecine conflict, with the other tribes pitted against Benjamin (Judg. 20).

2. A professional army. The first truly professional army was organized by Saul, whose reign was a transition from the tribal league to the monarchy (I Sam. 13:2). His army included both native and foreign mercenaries, e.g., the Edomite, Doeg (I Sam. 21:7 [H 8]). The Davidic dynasty maintained a permanent mercenary army until 701, after which it was probably considered too costly. Sometimes these mercenaries are called נערים (RSV "young men"), but the context shows that they were professional soldiers, probably select troops (II Sam. 2:12-17; 16:2). In addition to purely military tasks the professionals served as royal bodyguards. At least one such group was the רצים (runners), whose guardroom was at the entrance to the palace (II Sam. 15:1; I Kings 14:27, 28; II Kings 10:25; 11:4). Perhaps, as is generally held, the kingdom of Israel did not employ a professional army, but it should at least be noted that Ahab used נערים against Ben-hadad of Syria (I Kings 20:15-20).

Pay for professionals, who apparently were not regarded as free men, was sometimes in the form of land grants (I Sam. 8:14) or a share of the booty (I Sam. 30:21-25). Simon Maccabeus made regular payments to mercenaries, probably in money (I Macc. 14:32), and this practice was continued by John Hyrcanus (Jos. War. I.ii.5).

3. A citizens' militia. As early as the latter part of David's reign a conscript army existed alongside the professional troops. A stage of this development is perhaps seen in the account of a census which David ordered Joab to take throughout all the tribes of Israel. As a professional soldier Joab felt it necessary to voice his objection (II Sam. 24:2-9); relationships between mercenaries and militiamen were not always amicable, and friction between these two segments of the army probably explains Joab's murder of Amasa (II Sam. 20:8-10). The militia was called annually for a period of service, and also in emergencies (I Chr. 27:1-22). In peacetime the reserve service was probably spent in the soldier's home district. After Sennacherib's invasion in 701, Judah depended entirely on the conscript militia.

4. Chariotry. The commonly held view that the chariot did not become an important part of Hebrew armies until Solomon is probably in error (cf. ARMY §3*d*). That a chariot corps is never mentioned in any of David's campaigns could indicate that chariots were only of minor importance compared to his infantry. After David captured a thousand chariots from Hadadezer, king of Zobah, he reserved a hundred, destroying the remainder (II Sam. 8:4, 5). This is usually interpreted to mean that to David the chariot was unimportant militarily, but it seems more reasonable to conjecture that his chariot corps, although perhaps not large, was already near full strength. Solomon emphasized the chariot and assigned the infantry to a subordinate position. The exact size of his chariot corps is difficult to determine. According to I Kings 4:26 he "had forty thousand stalls of horses for his chariots," but the Chronicler reduces this number to four thousand (II Chr. 9:25). If the former number is correct, his chariot corps was immense, numbering over thirteen thousand. The latter figure is more in harmony with I Kings 10:26-29, which records that Solomon, who purchased horses from Cilicia and chariots from Egypt, had fourteen hundred chariots. If however רכב (here translated "chariot") should mean chariot horse as it sometimes does (II Sam. 8:4), this would further reduce the number to around 475. This calculation is based on reliefs from contemporary countries showing the chariot being drawn by two horses, with a third held in reserve.

A high point in chariotry was reached during the reign of Ahab, who committed two thousand chariots to the battle against the Assyrians at Qarqar. Slightly later, Jehoshaphat of Judah willingly co-operated with Ahab in a campaign against Syria. This suggested the possibility that Ahab's large contribution to the anti-Assyrian coalition might have included chariots from Judah. Although MEGIDDO was one of Solomon's chariot cities (I Kings 9:15-19), the celebrated horse stalls discovered there did not belong to him but to Ahab. Approximately 450 stalls are identifiable, indicating that the location accommodated 150 chariots. Ahab's successors were unable to maintain his level, and when Samaria fell, the enemy captured only fifty chariots. In the late eighth century the Assyrians introduced chariots drawn by four horses, a practice Judah apparently adopted. SENNACHERIB's reliefs showing scenes from his destruction of LACHISH depict a Judean chariot, which appears essentially like those used by the Assyrians. This evidence would be more conclusive had these reliefs been carved by Judeans.

5. Cavalry. Israelite cavalry made its modest appearance as early as the reign of David, employing mules rather than horses (II Sam. 13:29; 18:9). However, horses were used as mounts for military scouts (II Kings 9:17-19). Development of cavalry is difficult to trace because פרשים (RSV "horsemen") could also refer to members of the chariot corps (I Kings 1:5; 4:26). At the end of the eighth century Judah possessed no mounted soldiers (II Kings 18:23). In the Hasmonean period cavalry was organized by Simon (I Macc. 16:4), and in the first century B.C. Herod the Great also recruited cavalry. The scroll of the WAR OF THE SONS OF LIGHT AND THE SONS OF DARKNESS, probably to be dated in the first half of the first century A.D., envisioned the use of cavalry resembling contemporary Roman army usage. *See* DEAD SEA SCROLLS §5*c*.

6. Military organization. Little is known about the organization of Israelite armies prior to the monarchy. During the days of the people's army, the clan formed the basic unit, and the recruits were probably commanded by their own leaders (I Sam. 17:18; 18:13). In this period אלף clearly denoted a subdivision of the tribe and not a unit of one thousand fighting men as it did later. In the predynastic period there seems to have been no pre-established command or military organization. Nor was there an intertribal system for enlisting troops, or anything more than verbal censure for failure to heed the call to arms. It is conceivable that there was intratribal military organization. On some occasions multitribal armies may have been organized into units according to their specialized weaponry (I Chr. 12:24-38). Numerous references to the threefold division of an army for attack bear witness to an elementary organization where two lieutenants served under a charismatic leader such as Gideon (Judg. 7:16). Even after the monarchy was established, Israelite armies often employed a tripartite division in battle (I Sam. 13:2; II Sam. 18:2). During the reign of David there developed a divided command, Joab over the professional army and Amasa over the militia. David and subsequent kings, however, remained head of the military organization. The militia, and presumably the professional army as well, was organized into units of one thousand, one hundred, fifty, and ten soldiers. In the Hasmonean period, Judas Maccabeus similarly divided his army (I Macc. 3:55), as did the Qumran sect. When militiamen were conscripted they were placed under the command of officers who were heads of clans; however, the use of a conscript army made essential a standing corps of professional officers (II Kings 25:19). An important figure was the scribe, who had the responsibility of enlisting recruits and deciding who would be exempt from military service (Deut. 20:5-9; II Kings 25:19). In I Chr. 27:1-15 David is credited with organizing twelve nontribal divisions, each of which was to provide 24,000 soldiers on a monthly rotating basis. Although the early date of such a highly sophisticated militia organization and the accuracy of such a large number of militia are subject to question, this indicates that the Chronicler was familiar with such a levy.

In the first century A.D., Jewish armies were generally organized according to the Roman model. The Roman Empire maintained twenty-five legions supported by various auxiliary forces. A legion consisted of six thousand men and was divided into ten cohorts, each of which consisted of six centuries. Each century was commanded by a centurion. A cavalry unit was attached to each legion.

See also WEAPONS AND IMPLEMENTS OF WAR §2; WAR, METHODS OF; DEVOTED.

Bibliography. G. E. Mendenhall, "The Census Lists of Numbers 1 and 26," *JBL,* LXXVII (1958), 52-66; R. de Vaux, *Ancient Israel,* I (1965), 213-67; Y. Yadin, *The Art of Warfare in Biblical Lands,* II (1963), 253-312, and *The Scroll of the War of The Sons of Light Against The Sons of Darkness* (1962), pp. 1-252.

T. O. HALL, JR.

***AROER.** **1.** A Transjordanian town on the N rim of the Wadi Mojib (Arnon Gorge; Josh. 13:16), to be identified with Khirbet ʿAraʿir three miles SE of Dhiban (*see* DIBON).

Excavations in 1964-66 revealed that the heavy walls visible on the surface belong to an Iron Age fortress, as N. Glueck had already surmised in the 1930s. The area defined by these walls is no less than fifty yards square. The roughly hewn rectangular masonry is laid in the header-stretcher style characteristic of tenth- and ninth-century B.C. Israelite sites. The main structure is a double-walled building of excellent proportions (Walls I-IV and V-VII), possibly the E tower of the city gate.

The published pottery associated with these buildings is from the ninth-eighth century B.C. Some forms are typical of Israelite sites of the period, but most of the pottery is in a local ceramic tradition closer to Deirʿalla, particularly in the white-slipped unburnished wares. The main buildings may be attributed to Mesha, who claims on the famous MOABITE STONE of the mid-ninth century B.C. to have fortified Aroer after his defeat of Israel. The lack of any pottery from the sixth century B.C. to the Nabatean period beginning in the early second century B.C. confirms that Aroer was abandoned after the Babylonian destruction (Jer. 48:18-20).

Fills and levels below the Iron Age fortress have produced Late Bronze II through Iron I pottery, *ca.* thirteenth-tenth centuries B.C., thus providing a context for the biblical account of the conquest by the tribe of Reuben (Josh. 13:15-23), its later restoration by Jephthah the Gileadite (Judg. 11:12-33), and its incorporation into the kingdom of David (II Sam. 24:1-5).

The preliminary reports do not mention any Middle Bronze II strata. Level VIb represents the earliest occupation, just above virgin soil. Together with VIa it spans the Early Bronze IV–Middle Bronze I periods, *ca.* 2400-2000 B.C. (the excavators' "Intermediate Bronze I-II," *ca.* 2250-1900 B.C.). No structures are reported, only a few pits. However, clear stratification was present, consisting of layers of ash, bone, and domestic debris, alternating with wind- and water-deposited soil. The pottery is a "hybrid," mostly in decadent local EB style, but showing some influence from the Syrian "caliciform" repertoire of the last quarter of the third millennium B.C.

The evidence from Aroer VIb-a suggests a fairly long span of semisedentary occupation, perhaps seasonal. Elsewhere in Transjordan many similar sites have been discovered by Glueck. Those which have been excavated also show two phases of occupation, with nearly identical pottery: Ader, C-A; Bâb edh-Dhrâʿ, EB IV–MB I; Iktanu, I-II; and Iskander, 3ii-i. The picture is one of a sizable though nonnucleated population. These peoples were probably displaced from central Palestine during the destruction or abandonment of the major urban centers there toward the last quarter of the third millennium B.C. It is striking that this is one of the few periods during the Bronze Age when Transjordan was extensively occupied.

2. A town in S Judah, on the border of the Negeb (I Sam. 30:28; "ADADAH" in Josh. 15:22). It is to be identified with modern Khirbet ʿArʿarah, twelve miles SE of Beer-sheba. In the marginal four- to eight-inch annual rainfall zone, it was apparently the southernmost Judean town that was permanently settled. Soundings by A. Biran in 1975 revealed heavy walls and concentrated pottery of the tenth, ninth, and especially the eighth-seventh centuries B.C.

Bibliography. E. Olávarri, "Sondages à ʿArôʿer sur l'Arnon," *RB,* LXXII (1965), 77-94, and "Fouilles à ʿArôʿer sur l'Arnon," *RB,* LXXVI (1969), 230-59; W. G. Dever, "The EB IV–MB I Horizon in Transjordan and Southern Palestine," *BASOR,* 210 (1973), 37-63.

W. G. DEVER

***ARPAD** [Heb. and Old Aram. ארפד, Assyrian *Arpadda* (once *Arpaddu*), medieval Arab. *Arfād*]. A city in northern Syria, now Tell Rifʿat, village and mound *ca.* 19 miles N of Aleppo. It was the capital of the Aramean kingdom of Arpad (since *ca.* 1000 B.C.), also known to the Assyrians under the tribal name of Bīt-Yaḫan and the dynastic name of Bīt-Agusi (Old Aram. בית גש). *See* HITTITES[S] and map.

It frequently opposed Assyria in the ninth and eighth centuries, was often allied with Damascus, and in 743 with Urartu (*see* ARARAT §2). It was conquered and annexed by Tiglath-pileser III in 740, revolted along with Hamath, Simirra, Damascus, and Samaria in 720, but was subdued by Sargon II. These events are referred to in Isa. 10:9; 36:19 (=II Kings 18:34); 37:13 (=II Kings 19:13); Jer. 49:23. The last king of Arpad, Mati'ilu, son of ʿAtar-sumki, concluded in 754 a vassal treaty with Ashur-nirari V of Assyria, preserved on an Akkadian tablet from Asshur and, in a different version, on three stelae inscribed in Old Aramaic and found at Sefire. In the latter, Ashur-nirari V appears as *Br-G'yh,* king of *Ktk.* Both versions are very important as parallels to OT treaties, treaty courses, and prophecies of doom.

Bibliography. V. M. S. Williams, "Preliminary Report on the Excavations at Tell Rifʿat," *Iraq,* XXIII (1961), 68-87, and "The Excavations at Tell Rifʿat, 1964 . . . ," *AAS,* XVII (1967), 69-84; *ARAB,* I, §§749-60; E. Weidner, "Der Staatsvertrag Aššurnirâris VI. von Assyrien mit Mati'ilu von Bît-Agusi," *AFO,* VIII (1932-33), 17-34; *ANET* (3rd ed.), pp. 532-33, 659-61; J. A. Fitzmyer, *The Aramaic Inscriptions of Sefire* (1967); *KAI,* nos. 222-24; J. Cantineau, "Remarques sur le stèle araméenne de Sefiré-Soudjin," *RA,* XXVIII (1931), 167-78.

M. C. Astour

ART, ANCIENT NEAR EASTERN.

1. General characteristics
2. The distinctions between Egyptian and Mesopotamian art
3. Developments in Egyptian and Mesopotamian art
4. The art of Palestine and Syria
Bibliography

1. General characteristics. The characteristics of ancient Near Eastern art are best illustrated by reliefs and paintings. The subject matter was usually taken from the natural world and is man-centered even when depicting the realm of the gods. Abstract designs are only sparingly employed. Symbols and signs exist, but colors are normally not used symbolically.

The reliefs and paintings are characterized by the absence of space, perspective, and environment. Figures and objects are rendered on a single spatial plane parallel to the picture surface. Adherence to the frontal plane is emphasized by the placement of figures on a horizontal ground line, and by rendering the head, hips, and legs in profile, but the eyes and shoulders frontally. While this convention is most commonly identified with Egyptian art, it is characteristic of Near Eastern art in general. Only with rare exception is the entire figure seen frontally.

While in Egyptian art figures overlap (e.g., in groups of soldiers or cattle), the conventional means of overlapping through closely placed concentric lines merely reinforces the single plane quality of the composition. The surface is divided into a series of registers, an organizing principle which accords with this single spatial vision. Scenes occupying deeper space are placed on the register above, so that each register retains the integrity of its spatial plane.

Adherence to a single spatial plane accords with the absence of the indications of perspective which were employed in Western art from the Hellenistic period onward: diminution, convergence, foreshortening, shade-and-shadow, and a real perspective, i.e., the dilution of the hue and the lightening of the value as objects recede into the distance. Figures within a given register vary in size to show status and relationship, rather than to indicate their relative spatial planes. Husbands are taller than wives; fathers are taller than sons; and kings taller than commoners. Individual figures and objects are flattened and reduced to two-dimensional illustrations by the elimination of shading. The masterful Middle Kingdom Bersheh coffin is a rare exception (*see* §3*a*).

Environment is also generally not depicted. There are few true landscapes, interior scenes, or architectural backgrounds except where essential for the theme. The artist manages to convey the environment through the introduction of props such as trees, thrones, etc., but these are merely signs. Behind these objects one sees the ubiquitous flat background. As in Byzantine and early Medieval painting, there are no clouds or sky.

2. The distinctions between Egyptian and Mesopotamian art. There are distinct differences between the art of Egypt and Mesopotamia, largely attributable to religious beliefs and practices. Motifs found in Egyptian tombs are reflexes of notions associated with the afterlife. Scenes of mummification, wailing women, the weighing of the heart, and the provision of food and other essentials, find no counterpart in Mesopotamian art. Composite human and animal figures populate the Egyptian pantheon, but are alien to Mesopotamia, where gods are anthropomorphic. Theological conceptions also govern the basically different manners of depicting the relationship of the king to the gods. The pharaohs, who are gods in their own right, walk hand in hand with them. Mesopotamian gods are more awesome and transcendent in spite of their consistent anthropomorphism. Kings, no less than commoners, stand reverently before them in one of two traditional poses: either with clasped hands, or with one hand brought across the chest while the other is raised in front of the face (perhaps to avoid gazing on the deity). In other scenes, a minor god leads the king by the hand into the presence of a major one. While seated Mesopotamian figures normally clasp their hands in a pious gesture, seated Egyptian figures normally place their hands on their knees in a secular pose.

Cylinder seals, characteristic of Mesopotamia, are alien to Egypt, where stamp seals and scarabs predominate. The cylinder seal motifs include combat between lions and bulls or lions and naked heroes, but these are not found on Egyptian seals. While the compositions on the stamp seals are limited to simple elements, those on the cylinder seals are more complex, continuous, and monumental.

Distinct differences occur also in the repertoire of poses, clothing, and hair styles. These differences alone enable the viewer to identify a work as either Egyptian or Mesopotamian.

Stylistically, Egyptian art minimized the use of curved forms and emphasized angularity. The seated figure is a congruent extension of the cubical stone seat which it occupies, and the standing figure is perpendicular to the ground. Mesopotamian art emphasized rounder forms, and there is a greater sense of movement. Egyptian art is generally more expressive; the full range of ages and emotions is rendered. Individual features characterize at least one school of Old Kingdom art; a haggard, worn look is characteristic of most Middle Kingdom rulers; brutal honesty is the hallmark of the representations of Akh-en-Aton; and finally, portraiture reaches its zenith of artistic accomplishment in the Egyptian Late period. In Mesopotamia, an excellent Old Babylonian head, identified as Hammurabi, parallels some of the finer Middle Kingdom portraits, but remains an isolated example.

Stylistic differences are evident also in details. While the eyes of Egyptian figures are decorated with eye liner (drawn out from the eyebrow and the outer corner of the eye to the center of the temple), the eyebrows of Mesopotamian figures are characteristically rendered as two arcs which converge above the bridge of the nose. Egyptian sculptors, who focused primarily on the human head, rendered the lips with finely raised lines at their outer edges. Though Mesopotamian sculptors of the Ur III period rendered the lips with sensitivity, they omit this stylistic feature.

Another Egyptian stylistic peculiarity is the amalgamation of perspectives when rendering scenes with ponds. While figures in the vicinity are rendered at eye level, the pond is seen from above.

Finally, there are obvious differences in technique: Egyptian standing figures characteristically have back pillars but Mesopotamian figures do not; sunk relief was frequently used in Egyptian art but not in Mesopotamian; wood was an accepted medium for sculpture in Egypt but was not used in Mesopotamia.

3. Developments in Egyptian and Mesopotamian art. ***a. Egypt.*** The Nar-mer Palette of the First Dynasty (*see* EGYPT Fig. 10) is the earliest work with characteristic Egyptian motifs and style. The king wears the crown of Upper Egypt on one side of the palette, the crown of Lower Egypt on the other. He wears a chin beard and strikes poses typical of subsequent periods. The art of the Old Kingdom (Third-Eighth Dynasties) is characterized by an interplay of experimentation and maturity. The expanded repertoire includes seated and standing rulers and nobles, group statues, seated scribes, separate portrait heads, and statues of servants at various chores. The tomb reliefs contain ritual scenes and scenes of nobles receiving offerings from their estates. Men normally wear short kilts, while women wear tight-fitting garments that reach almost to the ankles. One school produced idealized heads while the other produced individual features and more naturalistic modeling such as the bust of prince Ankh-haf (*see* Fig. A10).

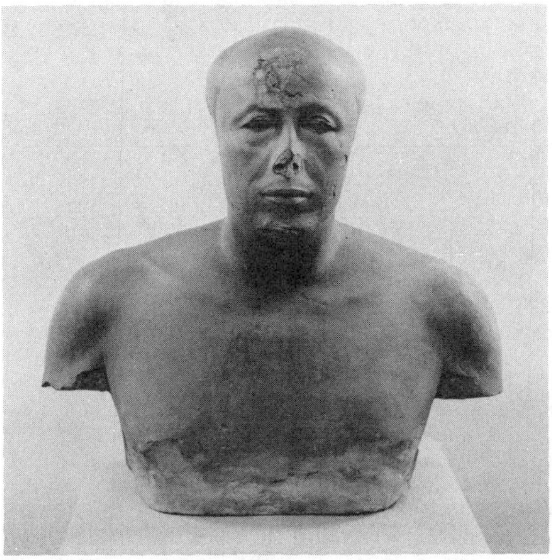

Courtesy Museum of Fine Arts, Boston

10. Bust of Ankh-haf

The art of the Middle Kingdom (Eleventh-Seventeenth Dynasties) betrays a general lack of national self-esteem. The seminudity of Old Kingdom statuary is abandoned, and the figures, wrapping themselves tightly in their cloaks, wear voluminous wigs. The confident, striding figures of Old Kingdom rulers and nobles are replaced by seated, immobile figures, and the serene look of the Old Kingdom god-kings is replaced by the lined faces of worn, harried men. Indeed, the quality of uncertainty and withdrawal is emphasized by the introduction (in the reign of Amen-em-het II and Sesostris II) of the block statue, a block of stone from which emerge a head, hands, and feet.

This introspective tendency translated itself into attempts at true portraiture. Royal statues are endowed with individual physical characteristics and reflect personality traits (*see* Fig. A11). Some statues are harsh, others sad, others introspective. By contrast, private statuary is rarely of outstanding merit. The rigidly posed figures upon their plain block bases display little individuality, vitality, or inspiration.

The Metropolitan Museum of Art, Carnarvon Collection, gift of Edward S. Harkness, 1926

11. Fragment of quartzite head of King Sesostris III, *ca.* 1850 B.C.

New motifs include the king with his hands placed on his ceremonial apron, a pet dog placed beneath its mistress' chair, and the sphinx, rendered as a lion with the mask of a woman. Substitute art forms which had developed during the First Intermediate period (Ninth-Tenth Dynasties) continue into the Middle Kingdom: the Old Kingdom stone servant statues are replaced by wooden models, and paintings on the interior of large wooden coffins contrast with the reliefs on stone coffins of the Old Kingdom. Painting comes into its own as an independent art form. The painted coffin of Twelfth-Dynasty nobleman Djehuty-nekht

Courtesy Museum of Fine Arts, Boston

12. Painted panel of the Bersheh coffin

The Egyptian Museum, Cairo

13. Seated pharaoh and wife; backrest of the throne of Tut-ankh-Amon

from Bersheh (*see* Fig. A12) is one of the finest examples.

Middle Kingdom archetypes are evident in the freestanding statues of the New Kingdom (Eighteenth-Twentieth Dynasties) mortuary temple of Hat-shepsut at Deir el-Bahri, but the forms are rounder and less muscular, and the proportions are more elegant. The sculpture of Thut-mose III evidences an even greater tendency toward elegance and delicacy at the expense of vitality. Indeed, elegance is a hallmark of mid-Eighteenth-Dynasty art. Following the conquest of Western Asia by Thut-mose III, Egypt began to import goods and ideas from Western Asia, and a demand arose for luxury items. The concern for elegance reached new heights during the reign of Amen-hotep III.

The art of the early part of the reign of Akh-en-Aton represents a radical departure from the elegant and the fashionable. The unusual physiognomy of the king is exaggerated and becomes a "fashionable distortion" (*see* AKH-EN-ATON Figs. 8, 9, 10). He is depicted with large ears, a jutting chin, narrow shoulders, broad hips, and heavy thighs. There is intimate portrayal of the private life of the king and a marked interest in landscape. Toward the end of his reign the harsh realism is softened. In spite of the subsequent return to Amon worship and the aesthetic values of the age of Amen-hotep III, the values of the Amarna Age continue to manifest themselves. They are seen, for example, in a casual pose of the king and queen on the back of Tut-ankh-Amon's golden throne (*see* Fig. A13).

Disregarding the numerous works which Ramses II re-used, the art of his reign emphasizes monumentality but lacks grandeur and inspiration. The last flowering of New Kingdom art can be seen in the works executed for Ramses III.

While in various periods there was an emerging naturalism and incipient portraiture, this tendency reaches its apogee in the Late period which produced such outstanding portraits as the Boston Green head and the Berlin Green head.

Egyptian art of the Hellenistic period manifests obvious Hellenizing features, but the knell was rung for Egyptian art following the Roman conquest. While some mummy portraits of the Roman period are of exceptional quality, they are Western in style and inspiration.

b. Mesopotamia. In spite of the lack of local stone, Mesopotamian art of the Early Dynastic period is noted for monumental sculpture. The Mesopotamian repertoire is more limited than the Egyptian. The limbs of statues are rendered as cylindrical forms with minimal modeling and no true attempt at musculature. Only the pectoral muscles of the male figures are rendered prominently.

Wall reliefs, popular in Egypt, are absent. Yet, there are a number of plaques in bold relief employing the register system. The fragmentary victory stele of Eannatum from Telloh (*see* NET Fig. 15) is a masterpiece; though the forms are simplified, there is a wealth of finely carved surface detail.

The Sumerians were master metalworkers, as evidenced by the large copper relief from Al-Ubaid of the Im-dugud or lion-headed bird and the two back-to-back stags with bodies in profile and frontal heads (*see* Fig. A14). Among the noteworthy small works in solid cast metal are: a rein ring with a lively onager from Ur; a copper model of a chariot team from Tell Aqrab (*see* CHARIOT Fig. 23); and the copper offering stand from Tell Aqrab featuring naked wrestlers.

Two harps were recovered from the Royal Cemetery at Ur. Each features the head of a sensitively rendered, bearded bull with inlaid lapiz lazuli

The British Museum

14. Copper relief from Tell Al-Ubaid, showing Imdugud and two stags, *ca.* 2900-2460 B.C.

eyes and elegantly curved horns (*see* UR Fig. 17). Careful observation of fauna is evident not only in the treatment of the bulls' heads, but also in an offering stand from Ur featuring a ram, in the head of a goat from Nippur, in the frog-shaped base of a stand from Kish, and on the inlaid front panel of the sound box on one of the harps from Ur.

Naturalistic scenes were introduced on cylinder seals following the style of the Early Dynastic I period. Scenes of individual combat between lions and bulls, naked heroes and lions, etc., replace the ritual scenes characteristic of the Uruk period. However, the motif of a file of animals, characteristic of the Uruk-Proto-literate period, was reintroduced.

Stylistic developments in the Akkadian period (2334-2154 B.C. ["middle" chronology]) are most evident in the cylinder seals. Individual figures stand out since they are surrounded by more space and since their musculature is painstakingly rendered. There is also an expansion of the repertoire of motifs.

Both the cylinder seals and the celebrated stele of Narām-Sin (2254-2218 B.C.) show concern for landscape (*see* ASSYRIA AND BABYLONIA Fig. 96). The register system is abandoned and man and beast walk along the undulating contours of a natural setting.

The heightened interest in musculature and precision of detail coalesce to produce the masterful bronze head from Quyunjiq identified as the head of Sargon (*see* Fig. A15).

In the Neo-Sumerian (Ur III) period (2112-2095 B.C.), there is a resurgence of piety. The standing and seated statues of Gudea depict the king as a benign, humble servant of the gods (*see* SUMER Fig. 87). The musculature of these figures betrays an Akkadian heritage.

Seals lack the repertoire of the Akkadian period and are primarily limited to presentation scenes in which the interceding goddess is frequently absent.

Statues found in the private homes of the Isin-Larsa period (2017-1763 B.C.) are basically crude. Yet a masterpiece like the statue of the goddess Ningal dates to this period (*see* Fig. A 16), as does the terra-cotta relief of the winged goddess Lilith with prominent talons. Statues of local rulers, particularly those of Mari, have long, stylized beards and emphasize surface detail (*see* MARI Figs. 12-14.) Seals of the Isin-Larsa period

Scala

15. Bronze head from Nineveh, *ca.* 2415-2290 B.C.

Courtesy the University Museum

16. Statuette of the goddess Ningal

are no more varied than those of the Neo-Sumerian period and display a decrease in quality.

The head from the First Dynasty of Babylon, identified as that of HAMMURABI (*see* Fig. A17), has aspects of true portraiture. In many ways it recalls some of the finest Egyptian Middle Kingdom royal portraits.

Some of the wall paintings from the palace at

The Louvre; Sculptures of the National Museums

17. Diorite head of a bearded prince, *ca.* 2255-2024 B.C.

Mari date to the age of Hammurabi and provide us with a glimpse of an art form which must have been widespread in Syria and Mesopotamia. The paintings include mythological, cultic, and military scenes in addition to more conventional scenes found on seals. The seals of the First Dynasty of Babylon combine the presentation scene with a number of subsidiary motifs. Toward the end of the dynasty there is a reduction in the number of figures and the inscription is emphasized once again. The period has also yielded several fine stone vessels decorated with animals.

The art of the Kassite period (1600-1100 B.C.) is hybrid, revealing Mesopotamian, Syrian, Aegean, and Egyptian elements. The Kassites introduced a wall relief composed of molded bricks. Several small-scale, painted terra-cotta works are highly successful. The only stonework of the age consists of numerous sculptured boundary stones covered either with symbols of the gods or figures of the kings. *See* Fig. A18.

The Middle Assyrian period displays features which characterize late Assyrian art. These features are most dramatically illustrated on seals, in which there is an expanded repertoire of motifs. The figures are well carved and are surrounded by ample space, recalling seals of the Akkadian period. Depiction of sequence is evident on the "White Obelisk" of Ashurnasirpal.

The palaces of the kings of the Late Assyrian period were covered with reliefs and paintings rich in detail, designed to overwhelm the visitor with the power of the ruler. Warfare is the most consistent motif: details of the army's march, the attack, the destruction and looting of cities, and the slaughter of the inhabitants. Figure style emphasizes musculature and physical prowess. Even hunting scenes, which show the king at leisure, are

The British Museum

18. Boundary stone of Marduknadinahhe, late 13th-10th century B.C.

designed to portray the power of the king, since his quarry is the mighty lion (*see* HUNTING Fig. 36). Motion is depicted on reliefs by multiple images of the same object. *See* ASSYRIA AND BABYLONIA Fig. 102, which shows three consecutive poses of one lion.

The scale of the figures in Neo-Babylonian art is smaller than that of contemporary Assyrian examples, and there is an elegance totally lacking in Assyrian art. In terms of innovation, the age provides us with figures in true profile, as seen on the boundary stone of Marduk-apla-iddina (714 B.C.). Palaces were decorated with glazed brick and featured volute and palmette capitals with connecting flower designs. Lions appear, but instead of threatening the visitor as they do in Assyrian reliefs, they form friezes, thus harking back to one of the most abiding motifs in the Mesopotamian repertoire. *See* LION Fig. 31.

4. The art of Palestine and Syria. The influence of Egypt and Mesopotamia on the art of Palestine and Syria can be traced from the Early Bronze Age through the close of the Persian period. Carved ivory bulls' heads (EB III) and the recently discovered silver cup from Ain Samiyeh (*see* Fig. A19) reflect Mesopotamian influence. Ivory inlay strips and silhouettes from an MB II tomb near el-Jisr and incised bone strips with figurative designs from Tell el-Ajjul and Tell Beit Mirsim reflect Egyptian influence, as do the poses of gods on Middle Bronze Age stelae from Ugarit (*see* UGARIT Fig. 7) and the numerous Middle Bronze Age metal figurines from Byblos. Egyptian influence becomes increasingly prominent through the course of the Late Bronze Age, as evidenced by the sophisticated ivories from Megiddo (*see* ART Figs. 70, 71), Tell el-Far'ah (*see* ART Figs. 68-69), and Ugarit (*see* ART Fig. 67). Mesopotamian influence is reflected in the file of animals decorating an incised ivory from Lachish. Egyptian influence retains its dominant, yet not exclusive, hold on the ivory carvers of the Iron Ages, as evidenced by the ivory hoards from Samaria, Arlsan Tash, and Nimrud. Even in the Iron Age, Mesopotamian motifs such as lions, files of animals, and combat scenes between lions and bulls occur. The Persian period has yielded a hoard of bronzes from Ashkelon and an Osiris figure from Gibeon with obvious Egyptian affinities.

Often, more than one foreign influence can be seen in a specific work. For example, a statue from Tell Mardikh combines Egyptian and Mesopotamian features. However, the artisans feel no constraint to adhere closely to their sources of inspiration. Enthroned figures hold palm fronds in their left hands as on Egyptian prototypes, but uncharacteristically they also hold cups in their right hands. Unfettered by weighty traditions, Palestinian and Syrian art allowed for greater experimentation. Shoulders are rendered frontally, but are narrower than those of Egyptian figurines. Moreover, Palestinian and Syrian figures are less substantial. This quality is carried over into three-dimensional sculpture, where figures are slight and lack articulation. The three-dimensional qualities are normally restricted to the heads, while the torsos are flat.

The frequently used term "Syro-Palestinian art" is a misnomer. In the Middle Bronze Age, four distinct regional schools have been isolated: Palestine, coastal Syria, the Orontes Valley, and the Upper Euphrates Valley. Further study will probably support the existence of regional differences in subsequent periods as well. The differences include greater interest in one genre or technique, a greater degree of naturalism, and differing sources of foreign influence. Incised bone inlay is characteristic of Palestine and, to a lesser extent, of coastal Syria during the Middle Bronze Age, but it is absent in the Orontes Valley and the Upper Euphrates Valley. While bronze sculpture is prevalent in northern Palestine and coastal Syria, it is absent from inland Syria. Terra-cotta sculpture is characteristic of inland Syria, but is absent from coastal Syria. During the Late Bronze Age, ivory replaced bone, and the technique of incised figurative drawing was almost entirely replaced by relief carving. Ivory carving remains the mainstay of Palestinian and Syrian art in the Iron Age, which is also the period of the great flowering of scarab-shaped seals.

In the MB II period Egyptian features manifest themselves in Palestine and at sites in coastal Syria. A mixture of Egyptian and Mesopotamian elements is evident at several Orontes Valley sites, with the Mesopotamian dominant. Cappadocian affinites are seen in the use of the file of four identical figures on cylinder seals from Alalakh

After the *Israel Exploration Journal,* XXI

19. Frieze on a silver cup from tomb 204a, Ain Samiyeh

and Tell Mardikh, and in the patterning of the body on basins from the latter site.

The opportunities that these foreign parallels provide for dating purposes have not been fully exploited. For example, it is possible to date the Megiddo VIIA plaque (*see* ART Fig. 70) to the early Ramside period on the basis of similarity with Ramside depiction of horses' legs. The same criteria enable us to date four ivory bars from Megiddo VIIA to the reign of Ramses III. An ivory box from Tell el-Far'ah (*see* ART Fig. 69) can be securely dated to the reign of Hor-em-heb (1342-1314 B.C.) by comparison of the flounced sleeves with dress on the reliefs from Hor-em-heb's tomb.

It had formerly been assumed that stone sculpture was not characteristic of Bronze Age Palestinian and Syrian art. Only the stone sculpture from Alalakh and a fine stone head of a god from the area of Djaboul were known. Recent excavations necessitate a revision of this view. Stone basins with remarkable carved sides, stelae, and statues have been found at Tell Mardikh. Stone carving of excellent quality and some fine enthroned figures were found in the Late Bronze Age temple at HAZOR. Also of note is the discovery of a fine stone statue of an enthroned king at Tell Sippor.

Bibliography. C. Aldred, *The Development of Ancient Egyptian Art* (1952); H. Frankfort, *The Art and Architecture of the Ancient Orient* (3rd ed., 1963); H. A. Groenegegen-Frankfort, *Arrest and Movement* (1951); H. Liebowitz, "Horses in New Kingdom Art and the Date of an Ivory from Megiddo," *Journal of the American Research Center in Egypt,* VI (1967), 129-34, "Regional Differences in the Art of Syria and Palestine in the Middle Bronze Age" (diss., Ann Arbor, 1972); A. Moortgat, *The Art of Ancient Mesopotamia* (1969); R. L. Scranton, *Aesthetic Aspects of Ancient Art* (1964); W. S. Smith, *The Art and Architecture of Ancient Egypt* (1958).

H. A. LIEBOWITZ

ART, EARLY CHRISTIAN. Stylistically, early Christian art belongs to the ancient Greco-Roman tradition. Its subject matter was drawn from the OT, NT, and Apoc., the church Fathers, Conciliar decrees, and the liturgy.

1. The periods of early Christian art
2. The Christian doctrine of images
3. The pre-Constantinian period
   a. Architecture
   b. Graphic and plastic art
4. The Constantinian period
   a. Architecture
   b. Graphic art
      i. Churches
      ii. Catacombs
   c. Plastic art
5. The Theodosian period
   a. Architecture
   b. Graphic art
   c. Plastic art
   d. Iconography

Bibliography

1. The periods of early Christian art. The first definitely Christian monuments date from the early third century. The second half of the sixth century signals the end of early Christian art and of the unified culture of the Mediterranean world as well. In the third through the sixth centuries there were pagan works of art on as high a level as Christian ones. The term "early Christian" should therefore not be used to designate an epoch (third to sixth centuries), but should be reserved for art with Christian subject matter. Indeed there are also works of art without Christian content which were commissioned by Christians.

There is no theory of pictures or images in the OT or NT. A theory of images is first found in the Apologists and is primarily directed against the heathen rather than being a positive Christian theory. Christian art was created in controversy with paganism and in defiance of the civil prohibition of Christianity during the period from *ca.* 220 to Constantine's Edict of Toleration in 313.

In the second period, after 313, Christian art was permitted by the state, and encouraged by the Emperor Constantine and the Constantinian imperial house. Constantine himself was the first great sponsor of Christian architecture, and with imperial support Christian artists developed their new styles and forms, primarily in church architecture.

The year 380 is a turning point: Theodosius I recognized Roman Christianity as the state religion (Theodosian Code XVI.i.2). Under Theodosius, Christian art was combined with Roman state art, and the state became a decisive force in the further development of Christian art. Shortly before Theodosius, the church, having gained considerable strength, began under Pope Damasus to express its dogmatic and religious concerns in pictorial art; now the papacy and the Empire were the most powerful patrons of art.

The third period lasted from 380 to the close of the sixth century. In the course of the sixth century, the ancient unified culture collapsed in most of the Mediterranean lands, with the exception of Constantinople. In Italy, France, N of the Alps, in Dalmatia, Illyria, Dacia, Moesia, and Pannonia, in Greece, Asia Minor, and North Africa artistic production decreased, and, in some places, stopped altogether. In the course of the seventh century in Syria, Palestine, and Egypt there arose a new art inspired by Islam. In Spain the Visigothic style was formed. In place of the former unity there now appeared a variety of styles and religious worlds.

2. The Christian doctrine of images. The Christian attitude toward images in the first three centuries A.D. was ambivalent, as was that of the Jews (*see* ART, EARLY JEWISH[S]). For Jews and Christians the prohibition of images in Exod. 20:4 was normative, but in late antiquity, both Jews and Christians evaded this prohibition.

Despite Exod. 20:4, even the OT mentions images: Num. 21:8-9 (the bronze serpent); Exod. 25:18-20 (two golden cherubim on the ark of the covenant); Exod. 37:7-9; Num. 7:89; I Sam. 4:4; I Kings 6:23-28; 8:6-7. The cherubim could be given a non-religious interpretation (Tert. Marcion II.xxii) and were thus legitimized. But pagan images of gods were rejected by both Jews and Christians (Ps.

135:15; Acts 19:26). Although pagan statues of gods were the principal object of Christian derision (Origen, *Against Celsus* VII.xxxvi, lxii; VIII.xxxv, xxxviii, xli), Christian art also introduced representations of God. But, unlike the pagans, the Christians did not venerate these representations. The idolatrous element in representations was heretical, but the representations themselves were not. In all events, the church Fathers were of differing opinions on this subject.

On the grounds that worship and veneration belong not to the image, but only to God the Father himself, the Synod of Elvira in 303 (Canon 36: Mansi II.xi) forbade paintings in churches: *picturas in ecclesia esse non debere, ne quod colitur et adoratur in parietibus depingatur* (there should be no pictures in churches, lest that which is worshiped and adored be depicted on the walls). The fact that, in the course of early Christianity, images nevertheless came to be worshiped, rests finally on a Platonic conception formulated by Basil the Great: "The honor given to the image [the icon] passes over to that which it represents [the prototype]" (ἡ τῆς εἰκόνος τιμὴ ἐπὶ τὸ πρωτότυπον διαβαίνει: *PG* XXXII, 149C).

In the first phase of the development of Christian art many writers recommended images that conveyed religious meaning on more than one level. Such were the signet images proposed by Clement of Alexandria (*The Instructor* III.xi). He recommended the following motifs: dove, fish, ship, lyre, anchor. When Clement wrote, these motifs had as yet no generally acknowledged Christian content, but were religiously neutral.

According to Ladner, it is the idea of the Incarnation which legitimated Christian art. He bases his opinion on Iren. Her. V.xvi.2 and speaks of an "incarnational conception" of the art of early Christianity.

From the time of Theodosius (d. 395) the advocates of Christian images increased in number, yet voices opposing images (e.g., Epiphanius) continued to be heard as late as the ninth century. Characteristic is the testimony of St. Nilus (d. 430), who counseled the Eparch Olympiodorus to depict scenes from the Bible on church walls instead of hunting scenes in order to enable the uneducated to learn holy history (*PG* LXXIX 578D-579A). And *ca.* 400 St. Paulinus of Nola described a complete program for the painting of a church (Epistles 32). From the fifth century onward, the catechetical function of pictures increased.

From the texts of the church Fathers we can draw only limited conclusions about visual art, since they do not describe what is usually portrayed in the catacombs and on sarcophagi. From them we learn more about the legitimization of art and the construction of Christian monumental architecture.

3. The pre-Constantinian period. ***a. Architecture.*** The catacombs were created by the Roman Christians of the third century to provide for the burial of the Christian masses. The straight subterranean passageways in soft tufa offered ample burial space in the walls. If more space was needed, the floor of the passageways was simply dug deeper, so that more wall space was obtained; or parallel and transverse passageways were dug. Individual wall graves (*loculi*) were closed with a tile or marble plaque on which was inscribed the name of the deceased. Larger grave chambers (*cubicula*) served as family crypts. Most have three *arcosolia;* a very few are decoratively painted. The earliest datable Christian inscriptions are from St. Callistus (*ca.* 220/30).

Of pre-Constantinian architecture, almost nothing remains. Christians gathered for worship in private houses (house churches), called *domus Dei, domus ecclesiae,* οἶκος τοῦ θεοῦ, *dominicum,* or κυριακόν from which come the words *Kirche, kerk,* kirk, church. Ἐκκλησία (the congregation of the faithful) is only later (fourth/fifth century) used for the church *building.* House churches are presupposed in Acts 2:42; 20:7-9; and actually mentioned in Rom. 16:5; I Cor. 16:19; Col. 4:15. Some buildings are called ἐκκλησίαι (Tert. *On Idolatry* vii; Lactantius, *Deaths of the Persecuted* xv; Euseb. Hist. VIII.i.5; VII.xxx.18). In Dura-Europos a house church dating from 232 is extant. It consists of an inner court with two inserted columns, around which are grouped six rooms. A stairway leads to the upper story. One room is painted with Christian pictures and a narrow side of the room has a rectangular basin, over which arches a *ciborium* on two pillars (*see* Fig. A20). The interpretation of the basin as a baptismal font is not certain.

Other buildings are known to us from written

Courtesy Mrs. George Ellis

20. The baptistery, the house church at Duro-Europos

sources. There appear to have been buildings which were built expressly as assembly rooms for Christian worship (cf. Apostolic Constitutions II.lvii.3).

b. Graphic and plastic art. Christian art seems to have developed almost simultaneously in the E and W of the ROMAN EMPIRE. Rome is the only center of such activity whose art has survived; that of other centers such as Alexandria is unknown.

Remarkably, almost identical Christian themes appear in the East in a house church, and in the West in catacombs and on sarcophagi. The house church of Dura-Europos has the following scenes: the Samaritan woman at the well, the healing of the paralytic, the shepherd (*kriophoros*), the women at the empty tomb of Christ, Christ walking on the water, the fall of Adam and Eve, David and Goliath (*see* Pls. XXXIII*b,* XXXVII*b*). In Asia Minor, the Jonah story was represented on small statuettes. In the Roman catacombs, the following rooms date from the earliest time: (1) the so-called sacrament chapels in St. Callistus, with the Jonah story, the meal of bread and fish, the fisherman, funeral feast, Moses' miracle of water from the rock, baptism, the healing of the lame man, Christ and the Samaritan woman, the raising of Lazarus, Abraham and Isaac praying before the sacrifice; (2) the Cappella Greca in the Priscilla Catacomb, with the three young men in the fiery furnace, Moses' miracle of water from the rock, funeral feast, Noah's ark, *kriophoros,* Isaiah and Mary with child (Isa. 7:14), Abraham's sacrifice; (3) the double chamber XY in Lucina.

The earliest indisputably Christian sarcophagi in Rome are the tub sarcophagus (ληνός) of Sta. Maria Antiqua (*ca.* 270), the sarcophagus of Velletri (*see* Fig. A21), and the sarcophagus of the Via Lungara. The following scenes and figures appear: the Jonah story, baptism, female *orans* (praying figure), philosopher with scroll (reading scene), *kriophoros,* the fisherman, Daniel in the lions' den, Noah in the ark, the Fall, the multiplication of loaves.

The female *orans,* the reading scene, the *kriophoros,* and the fisherman appear on pagan *and* Christian monuments. They are religiously neutral. The female *orans* means "piety toward God or the gods" (*pietas*); the reading scene illustrates the deceased's striving after virtue through popular philosophy. The shepherd symbolizes, according to Klauser, the human virtue of goodness or friendliness (*humanitas,* φιλανθρωπία). The interpretation of these motifs remains open to discussion; it depends on the accompanying scenes. If no unequivocally Christian scenes are present (e.g., on the sarcophagus of the Via Salaria, or the sarcophagus from La Gayolle), a Christian interpretation can be neither proved nor excluded.

Christian motifs come from both OT and NT, but OT scenes predominate. Jonah and Daniel typify salvation from peril, although it is not certain whether peril of the soul or the peril of death is meant. The Jonah story illustrates the idea of the Resurrection, for which it is certainly the most typical Christian paradigm. Along with salvation paradigms appear scenes of conversion to the Christian faith. A baptism scene was proof that one was a Christian. In addition, some of the earliest scenes are of Christ's miracles.

These four categories of pictures—religiously neutral pictures, salvation paradigms, proof of Christian faith, and Christ as miracle worker—are not limited to use as funeral art.

Christian scenes apparently come into use on sarcophagi later than they did in catacombs. From *ca.* 270 onward, the repertory of Christian themes expands to include such themes as the raising of Lazarus, the Sermon on the Mount, and additional miracles of Christ.

Not until Constantinian times are there whole groups of sarcophagi of similar pattern and with the same choice of scenes. This is because Christianity was until then a suppressed religion, and sarcophagus workshops could not undertake mass production. Every pre-Constantinian sarcophagus is a unique product.

4. The Constantinian period. By far the largest number of monuments extant from this period are in Rome. Other centers of Christian artistic activity are S Gaul (Arles, Marseille), Tarragona in N Spain, Cimitile and Aquileia in Italy, Constantinople, Asia Minor, northern Syria, and Palestine (Jerusalem). We know of no Christian works from

21. Figures from the sarcophagus at Velletri

Antioch or Alexandria which can be dated with certainty before 380. In North Africa, Syria (Antioch-Kaoussié), and Asia Minor several Christian buildings from this period have survived.

a. Architecture. The Christian basilica arose at the height of late Roman pagan architecture. It borrowed its form, except for the transept, from the Roman secular basilica. The Christian basilica was used as a church for assemblies and Christian worship. The apse (*presbyterium*) opposite the entrance was reserved as the place where the officiants performed their rites; the nave was for the congregation. In North Africa the nave was often used for the service, the aisles for the congregation. The transept is a Christian invention (Lateran: low wings; St. Peter's: continuous transept). It was reserved for the use of the clergy, as a place of prayer, and as a place for various liturgical acts (e.g., baptism).

The Emperor Constantine played a decisive role in the rise of Christian church architecture. In Rome he built the Lateran Basilica (313-*ca.* 320); St. Peter's over the tomb of the apostle Peter (324; *see* ROME, CHRISTIAN MONUMENTS[S] §2), Sts. Marcellinus and Peter (312-320) and St. Sebastian; in Jerusalem the Church of the Holy Sepulchre over the tomb of Christ (*see* HOLY SEPULCHRE, CHURCH OF THE[S]); in Bethlehem the Church of the Nativity over the Grotto of the Nativity; in Constantinople the Church of the Holy Apostles.

In Aquileia (*ca.* 313), Parenzo, and Trier (*ca.* 325) arose so-called double basilicas, two rectangular three-aisled buildings standing parallel to each other from 65 to 130 feet apart.

A special type of building is represented by the three-aisled basilicas with exedra opposite the entrance: Sts. Marcellinus and Peter, St. Lawrence Outside the Walls, St. Sebastian, St. Agnes Outside the Walls (338-350) in Rome. They are all near catacombs, but are not directly connected to them. To the basilica of Sts. Marcellinus and Peter was added later the mausoleum of the Empress Helena; to the basilica of St. Agnes the mausoleum of Constantina, a daughter of Constantine.

The most important Christian circular building is the rotunda over the tomb of Christ. In the history of architecture it was the first building with an inner circle of supporting columns and ambulatory. E of the rotunda, the so-called Anastasis, stood a five-aisled basilica.

As early as the time of Constantine there arose, along with the Christian basilica and circular building, the free-standing baptistery (Lateran). But such baptisteries become widespread only after the time of Theodosius. (*See* Pl. XL*b*.)

The transeptal basilica was not the only form for Christian churches. Also widespread were the three-aisled basilicas without transept and longitudinal rooms with a single nave (Gaul, Germany).

b. Graphic art. i. *Churches.* Little is known of the decoration of churches from 313 to 380. The apse of St. Peter's seems to have been decorated *ca.* 360/70 with the picture of the giving of the Law. The mosaic decoration of the mausoleum of Sta. Constanza (*ca.* 350; *see* Pl. XXXV *b*) is a fully developed program. In the cupola, twelve OT and twelve NT scenes are represented, and in the ambulatory apses there are two pictures of Christ enthroned. In the floor mosaics of the S church of Aquileia (*ca.* 320) are represented the Jonah story, cupids fishing, personified seasons, decorative busts, *kriophoros* with Syrinx and various animals (Pl. XL*a*). Of considerable importance is the mosaic-decorated cupola of the mausoleum (?) of Centcelles in N Spain, *ca.* 360, where a hunting frieze, the Fall, Daniel in the lions' den, the Jonah cycle, Noah's ark, the raising of Lazarus, the three young men in the fiery furnace, and the four seasons are depicted.

ii. *Catacombs.* The most important catacomb paintings of the fourth century are in Sts. Marcellinus and Peter, Praetextatus, Domitilla, and Callistus in Rome. The most common scenes are the raising of Lazarus, the multiplication of loaves, the Jonah story, Moses' miracle of water from the rock, the wedding at Cana, the adoration of the Magi, female and male *orantes* (praying figures), *kriophori,* Daniel in the lions' den, funeral feast, reading scene, Daniel condemning the two elders, the Fall, Christ teaching before the apostles, the seasons, the young men in the fiery furnace, shepherds, healing the blind or the lame, the personification of the sun, Tobias with the fish, and Job. In the new catacomb on the Via Latina in Rome, many OT scenes are depicted: Noah's drunkenness, Isaac blessing Jacob, the Samson cycle, the assumption of Elijah, Abraham's hospitality to the strangers, Jacob blessing Ephraim and Manasseh, the passage through the Red Sea, Rahab lowering Joshua's spies from the wall, and Jacob's Ladder. In the catacomb on the Via Latina some chambers, decorated with mythological figures, are most likely burial places of non-Christians.

c. Plastic art (sarcophagi). With the imperial toleration of Christianity, the making of sarcophagi increased rapidly. There was mass production of both single-zoned and double-zoned frieze sarcophagi, and the tub sarcophagus disappeared. A new type is the columnar sarcophagus (Junius Bassus, *ca.* 359). Pagan themes gradually receded but never entirely disappeared. New themes of sarcophagus sculpture were: the arrest of Paul, miracle scenes, resurrection scenes, the birth of Christ, Jesus before Pilate, assignment of work to Adam and Eve after the Fall, entry into Jerusalem, raising the dry bones (Ezek. 37), prediction of Peter's denial, Pilate washing his hands, the giving of the Law to Moses, and the giving of the keys to Peter.

In the Roman East very little Christian graphic and plastic art has survived from the time between 313 and 380. Perhaps the royal sarcophagus in Istanbul belongs to this period (*ca.* 360/70). Two angels are holding the *chrismon* ("Christ-monogram"; i.e., Chi-Rho), and two apostles flank the cross. The painted tomb in Nicomedia, with two peacocks flanking a *chrismon,* could date from before 380. From the late Constantinian period onward, the chi-rho monogram (Lactantius, *Deaths of the Persecuted* xliv; Eusebius, *Life of Constantine* I.xxviii-xxxi) was depicted and occasionally the cross as well. Frequent depiction of the cross began in the second half of the fourth century.

5. The Theodosian period. The third phase of early Christian art is the richest in monuments. This is the period of the full development of Christian art and its spread throughout the Roman Empire. Again, Rome has the most monuments, but in Italy there are three other centers as well: Naples, Milan, and Ravenna. Other important centers are S Gaul, Thessalonica, Constantinople, Ephesus, Cilicia, N Syria, Armenia, central Egypt, and North Africa. Each of these regions had its own distinct building forms. The leaders were Constantinople in the East and Rome and Ravenna in the West. Constantinopolitan art influenced all the Mediterranean provinces to some degree.

a. Architecture. Unlike the West, the East favored buildings with galleries above the aisles (three- and five-aisled, Thessalonica), the domed cross (Ephesus), the three-aisled transept (Menas Basilica), the triconch choir (Bethlehem), the tetraconch building with ambulatory (Seleucia Pieria; also St. Lawrence in Milan), pillar basilicas with piers (Syria), and finally the domed double-shell building (Hagia Sophia in Istanbul).

In the East and in North Africa both hewn stone technique and tile or brick technique (Constantinople) are used; in the West, the latter predominates.

In the East, the polygonal apses are usually flanked by so-called *pastophoria* (*prothesis* and *diakonikon*), i.e., side-rooms for liturgical use. Eastern architecture demonstrates a much greater richness of forms than does Western. The high point of Eastern architecture is Istanbul's Hagia Sophia (532-37), spatially the greatest creation of antiquity. Beginning in the fifth century, Eastern architecture also developed a new ornamental style, finely dentellated acanthus, wind-blown capitals; from the sixth century on, folded capitals and two-zoned capitals with animal protomas.

In the West the archivolt basilica predominated with or without transept. Baptisteries underwent an especially monumental development in Italy, where they were often octagonal or domed with semicircular and rectangular niches.

b. Graphic art. In the Roman West, catacomb painting decreased sharply after *ca.* 400. In the East, only a few small mausoleums are painted (Niš, Pécs, Thessalonica, el Bagawat). but there was a great increase in the number of large mosaics in churches (first known example: Paulinus of Nola, *Epistles* 32). Baptisteries, too, are decorated with mosaics (Naples, S. Giovanni in Fonte), and so were imperial mausoleums (Milan, S. Aquilino; Ravenna, the so-called Mausoleum of Galla Placidia, Pl. XXXVII*a*). Sta. Maria Maggiore in Rome, *ca.* 432, is the oldest extant church fully decorated with mosaics (Pl. XXXVI*b*). NT scenes decorated the triumphal arch; OT scenes (to be understood as pointing to Christ and the preexisting church) adorn the nave. The nave of S. Apollinare Nuovo in Ravenna (sixth century) has NT scenes and processions of saints before Christ and the Mother of God. A theophany (Christ and the twelve apostles; Christ with saints and the founder; Christ with angels; transfiguration of Christ) is usually depicted in the dome of the apse. The triumphal arch is decorated with scenes from the NT (Rome, Sta. Maria Maggiore) and the Apocalypse (Ravenna, S. Michele in Affricisco; Rome, SS. Cosma e Damiano). A picture of Christ is sometimes on the W entrance wall. In Parenzo (sixth century) the earliest picture of the Mother of God that has been preserved is found in the apse.

In the East, along with narrative cycles, aniconic decorations were popular (Thessalonica, Paraskevi; Istanbul, Hagia Sophia).

In the fifth and sixth centuries, especially in the East and in the Aegean, numerous churches were decorated with floor mosaics, usually with ornamental patterns (Bethlehem), but sometimes also with OT scenes (Misis-Mopsuestia) or with motifs that are not specifically religious (et-Tabgha). In Palestine the same forms of decoration appear in churches and synagogues (sixth century).

In the East, from the sixth century on, Byzantine icons (Sinai) are extant which were probably produced in Constantinople.

In both East and West book illuminators illustrated the OT (Quedlinburg Itala, *ca.* 400; Vienna Genesis, sixth century) and the NT (Sinope Fragment, Rossano Codex, both sixth century).

c. Plastic art. Roman production of sarcophagi increased *ca.* 370. There arose new "series" with depictions of the passage through the Red Sea, and columnar sarcophagi with Passion scenes and the giving of the Law. Roman sarcophagus production came to an end in the early fifth century, but in Gaul sarcophagus workshops still existed in the fifth and, in isolated cases, in the sixth century. The first sarcophagi with biblical scenes from the Greek East date from *ca.* 400; iconographically these are not fundamentally different from the work done in Rome. Other individual pieces date from the fifth and sixth centuries. Most of the Eastern sarcophagi known to us today are adorned with the *chrismon* or the cross.

From the late fourth century on, liturgical furniture such as ambos, chancel screens, and altars were exported from Constantinople (Proconnesian marble) to the entire Mediterranean world. In addition, such decorative pieces as capitals, columns, pedestals, and entablatures for church buildings were exported from Proconnesian workshops. These exports served as models for local production in Palestine, Syria, and North Africa.

Under Constantinopolitan influence, a rich local sarcophagus production began in Ravenna *ca.* 400 and lasted into the sixth century (columnar sarcophagi).

The ambos and chancel screens from Proconnesian workshops, like the Eastern sarcophagi, were usually adorned with crosses, but various scenes appear as well.

From 400 onward artists began to decorate wooden doors (Milan, S. Ambrogio; Rome, Sta. Sabina). In the East, these doors (Sinai; Sitt Barbara in Cairo) are predominantly but not exclusively ornamental; in the West, by contrast, they are rich in OT and NT scenes (Sta. Sabina).

From the time of Theodosius on, ivory was often used for liturgical objects. The Lipsanotheca of Brescia (*ca.* 380) is decorated with OT and NT scenes. Numerous pyxides for relics and diptychs from the fifth and sixth centuries are extant. The masterpiece of ivory carving is the episcopal throne of Maximian of Ravenna (sixth century). Bindings of books for liturgical use were adorned with ivory plaques. Relics were often kept in silver or simple metal caskets decorated with crosses, single figures, medallions with busts, or scenes from the OT and NT. Silverware for liturgical use (spoons, sieves, chalices, patens, censers, candlesticks, oil lamps, candelabra) has been preserved, particularly from the sixth century. *See also* Fig. A22.

Finally, Christian themes were depicted on ceramic objects such as clay lamps, vessels, dishes, and oil flasks.

d. Iconography. The third century gave us images from funerary art (*see* §3*b above*). From the late fourth, the fifth, and the sixth centuries there remain more images from a nonfunerary context. This situation reflects the accidental nature of the process by which ancient art objects survived. Questions of the origin of individual types of images are therefore insoluble.

In the third century individual images seem to have predominated; the earliest cycle is preserved in the four-phase Jonah story (sarcophagi, catacombs). Juxtaposed OT and NT scenes appear from the Constantinian frieze sarcophagi onward. In mixed OT-NT cycles, typology and salvation history play the leading role (Bassus sarcophagus, Sta. Constanza cupola, Sta. Maria Maggiore).

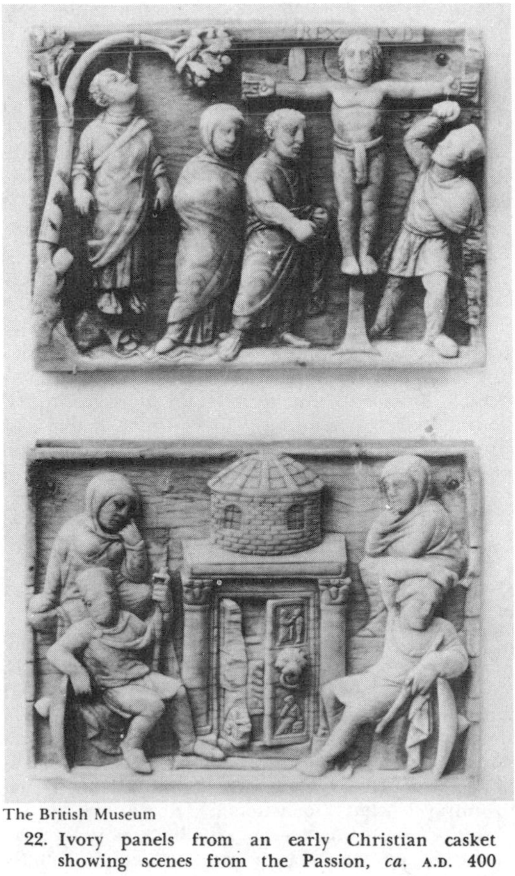

The British Museum

22. Ivory panels from an early Christian casket showing scenes from the Passion, *ca.* A.D. 400

Christ is seen in the third century as a Cynic philosopher with unkempt hair and beard, and in the time of Constantine as a fair Attis-like youth with curly hair (cf. Ps. 45:2; II Esdras 2:42-43). The time of Theodosius portrayed a dignified royal Christ with beard and with long hair falling over his shoulders. This Christ-type remained normative for the following centuries. From the time of Theodosius on, imperial attributes are transferred to Christ (purple and gold raiment, gemmed throne, scepter), and Christian scenes are portrayed with the devices of Roman imperial art.

Whereas in the time of Constantine the main sarcophagal themes were the youth of Christ and his miracles, in the second half of the fourth century they were the themes of Christ's passion. After 380, motifs from Revelation appear: the empty throne, the Lamb on the throne, the seven lampstands, and symbols of the apostles.

This development is observable only in Rome, but certain phases of the Roman development had parallels in the East.

Bibliography. Reference works: *Lexikon der christlichen Ikonographie,* several vols. (1968 ff.); *Reallexikon zur byzantinischen Kunst,* several vols. (1966 ff.); *RAC,* several vols. (1950 ff.); *DACL,* 15 vols. (1913-53).

General works: P. Testini, *Archeologia cristiana* (1958); W. F. Volbach and M. Hirmer, *Early Christian Art* (1958); W. F. Volbach and J. Lafontaine-Dosogne, *Byzanz und der christliche Osten,* Propyläen-Kunstgeschichte (1968); F. W. Deichmann, *Ravenna: Hauptstadt des spätantiken Abendlandes,* several vols. (1958 ff.); proceedings of the *Congresso internazionale di archeologia cristiana* have been published 1900 ff., since 1932 in the series, Studi di antichità christiana; P. Styger, *Römische Märtyrergrüfte* (1935); A. M. Schneider, "Die ältesten Denkmäler der römischen Kirche," *Festschrift zur Feier des 200-jährigen Bestehens der Akademie der Wissenschaften in Göttingen,* II (1951), 166-98; A. Grabar, *Early Christian Art,* The Arts of Mankind, IX (1969); C. R. Morey, *Early Christian Art* (2nd ed., 1953); E. Dinkler, "Älteste christliche Denkmäler—Bestand und Chronologie," *Signum Crucis* (1967), pp. 134-78.

Iconography: T. Klauser, "Studien zur Entstehungsgeschichte der christlichen Kunst," *Jahrbuch für Antike und Christentum,* 4 vols. (1958-61); C. Ihm, *Die Programme der christlichen Apsismalerei vom 4. bis zur Mitte des 8. Jahrhunderts* (1960); A. Grabar, *Christian Iconography: A Study of Its Origins,* Bollingen Series, XXXV (1968); G. B. Ladner, *Ad Imaginem Dei: The Image of Man in Medieval Art* (1965).

Architecture: R. Krautheimer, *Early Christian and Byzantine Architecture* (1965), and *Corpus Basilicarum Christianarum Romae,* MAC, several vols. (1937 ff.); A. Katchatrian, *Les baptistères paléochrétiens* (1962); A. Grabar, *Martyrium: Recherches sur le culte des reliques et l'art chrétien antique,* 2 vols. (1943-46); J. Lassus, *Sanctuaires chrétiennes de Syrie* (1947).

Plastic art: F. Gerke, *Die christlichen Sarkophage der vorkonstantinischen Zeit,* SSK, XI (1940); F. W. Deichmann, ed., and G. Bovini, H. Brandenburg, *Repertorium der christlich-antiken Sarkophage,* I (1967); J. Wilpert, *I sarcofagi cristiani antichi,* 5 vols. (1929-36); W. F. Volbach, *Elfenbeinarbeiten der Spätantike und des frühen Mittelalters* (2nd ed., 1952); R. Delbrück, *Die Consulardiptychen und verwandte Denkmäler,* SSK, II (1929); J. Kollwitz, *Die oströmische Plastik der theodosianischen Zeit,* SSK, XII (1941).

Graphic Art: J. Wilpert, *Die Malereien der Katakomben Roms,* 2 vols. (1903), and *Die römischen Mosaiken und Malereien der kirchlichen Bauten vom IV bis XIII*

Jahrhundert (1916); A. Ferrua, *Le pitture della nuova catacomba di Via Latina,* MAC, 2nd ser., VIII (1960); V. Lazarev, *Storia della pittura bizantina,* Biblioteca di storia dell'arte, VII (1967); G. Matthiae, *Mosaici medioevali delle chiese di Roma,* 2 vols. (1967); G. Forsyth and K. Weitzmann, *The Monastery of Saint Catherine at Mount Sinai* (1973). B. BRENK

*ART, EARLY JEWISH.

1. Art and Jewish law
2. The synagogue of Dura-Europos
   a. Meaning of painted cycle
   b. Relation to Christian art
3. Synagogue mosaics
4. Catacomb art

Bibliography

1. Art and Jewish law. Recent archaeological discoveries have occasioned no little surprise among scholars who had assumed that a rigid iconoclasm was normative for rabbinic Judaism during the early Christian period. In reality, no uniform, unchanging attitude toward images has prevailed throughout Jewish history. Rather, divergent positions toward and varying interpretations of the permissibility of images have been expressed by religious authorities in every age. First-century Palestinian Jewry, for example, frequently cited the anti-iconic proscription of the second commandment and objected violently to the contemplated placement of a statue of the Roman emperor Caius (Caligula) within the Jerusalem temple (Jos. Antiq. XVIII.viii.2; Wars II.x.1). In third-century Babylonia, however, no such objection seems to have been raised against the statue of a king in the synagogue of Nehardea, where the prominent talmudic sages worshiped (T.B. 'A.Z. 43b; R.H. 24b).

During the third and early fourth centuries A.D., when church Fathers unanimously rejected and forbade images in churches, Rabbi Johanan voiced no disapproval to paintings on synagogue walls; neither did Rabbi Abun censure his contemporaries who used figural mosaic decoration on synagogue floors in Palestine (J.T. 'A.Z. III.3). It should be noted that dogmatic strictures against images by religious leaders may not necessarily be in consonance with the prevailing practices. Moreover, they sometimes merely express personal philosophic commitments rather than reflect institutional policies.

2. The synagogue of Dura-Europos. Without doubt the most exciting and revolutionary discovery of early Jewish art is the series of paintings on the walls of this synagogue in Syria. Their excavation has already called into question the accepted historiography of that period. In particular, they have demanded critical re-evaluation of the supposed "normative rabbinic Judaism," which historians of Judaism have theorized had existed at that time. They have also reopened an older debate—whether indeed the origins of Christian art may be rooted in an antecedent, but now lost, Jewish art. *See* Pls. XXXIII*a*; XXXVI*a*; XXXVIII *a*.

The synagogue paintings are dated by inscriptions to A.D. 244-45 and owe their preservation to Roman military operations. Since the synagogue complex stood close to the western city gate, it was filled with earth as part of the fortifications to protect the city's wall against Sasanian siege operations in A.D. 256.

The four sides of the synagogue's walls were completely covered with five horizontal bands of painting. The lowest and uppermost bands were decorative. The three middle bands contain about fifty-eight biblical episodes in about twenty-eight preserved panels (roughly 60 per cent of the original decorations). All the horizontal bands converge on and are interrupted by the Torah shrine on the western wall, above which are two large panels, flanked in turn by two vertical wing panels on each side. The paintings at Dura are not frescoes, but executed in tempera with the paint applied to the plaster by the *al secco* method. They were probably made by local artists of modest ability familiar with the pictorial idioms of the area. Their style is ultimately dependent on the hybrid traditions of the Hellenized Orient that existed on the western edge of Parthia. They do not seem to be an example of Roman provincial art. What Greco-Roman features they share with Roman imperial art are perhaps more due to the preexisting hybrid style of the region than to direct borrowing. Little agreement exists among scholars as to the sequence of the synagogue paintings—whether they are to be read clockwise or counterclockwise, radiating toward or away from the Torah shrine, from the lower to the upper register, or vice versa. Neither does agreement exist as to the identification of all the individual panels, although they deal with such well-known biblical personages as Abraham, Isaac, Jacob, Moses, Aaron, Samuel, Elijah, Ezekiel, David, Solomon, Mordecai, and Esther. Moreover, scholars have noted details in many scenes that can only be understood by recourse to the vast contemporary haggadic and midrashic literature. *See* TALMUD §3; JUDAISM, EARLY RABBINIC[S] §2.

a. Meaning of painted cycle. Most studies on the Dura paintings have focused on interpreting the meaning of the entire cycle. Basically scholars have taken one of three positions: (1) no unifying idea can be discerned; (2) a single governing theme exists; (3) several diverse religious messages underlie the cycle of paintings.

Although differing widely in their interpretation of the paintings, scholars, with the exception of Goodenough, have generally agreed that any explanation of the paintings must be rooted in contemporary rabbinic Judaism. Goodenough maintains that the paintings can only be understood in terms of a mystic Hellenistic Judaism. "Normative rabbinic Judaism," according to Goodenough, was at best a minor sect—the religion of an intellectual minority who compiled the Talmuds. Rabbis, Goodenough asserts, with their anti-iconic and anti-mystical attitudes, would have been utterly shocked by the Dura synagogue's artistic representations and would have rejected them. Rabbinic literature is, therefore, an unreliable guide to unravel what Goodenough termed the "interpretation" of symbols—the articulate, objective explanation or meaning of symbols which usually changes in each culture—or the "value" of symbols—the emotional, subjective response to a "live" symbol, which remains essentially the same in differing cultures. When Judaism took over "live" symbols from the Greco-Roman world, the "interpretation" of the symbols changed, while their "value" remained relatively the same. Thus the masses, Goodenough believes, who worshiped in synagogues such as Dura, with "live" pagan symbols, were divorced from rabbinic jurisdiction and influence and subscribed to a popular "mystical" Judaism whose chief literary remains can best be discovered in the writings of the Hellenistic Jewish philosopher PHILO.

I have recently proposed that the Dura synagogue program reflects a regional expression of rabbinic Judaism that is unrecoverable from existing texts. Rabbinic Judaism had substituted prayers within synagogues for sacrifices at the Jerusalem temple. It had elevated the scholar-rabbi and done away with priestly intermediaries. It offered eternal life through personal salvation of the soul and bodily resurrection, rather than promising fertility of the land. Its authority was based on a revealed, twofold law—the written and the oral—in preference to the Pentateuch, the authoritative text of the priestly Judaism whose center was the temple. *See* PHARISEES[S].

The oral law, unlike the Bible, contains no connected historical narrative or biography. Biblical verses and stories, drawn from different biblical books and frequently embroidered with *haggadoth,* are simply used as proof texts to illumine non-biblical concepts. This mode of employing the Bible with haggadic additions, and without regard to the original biblical sequence, is the very method used in the Dura paintings. The second band of murals, for instance, used such biblical stories as the history and miracles of the ark as proofs to demonstrate non-biblical ideas—the continued function of the synagogue ark and its power to bring salvation. The congregation recounted through song—in an actual liturgical ark procession—what is depicted on the synagogue wall. The Dura paintings appear to represent an adaptation of a late pagan practice—the use of Greek mythological stories without regard to their original narrative sequence—as proofs for an entirely new liturgical-theological context. Moreover, the Dura murals may be the earliest forerunners of the great programmatic painting cycles, based on the Bible, which appear about two hundred years later in Christian art.

b. Relation to Christian art. Scholars are convinced that the origins of Christian art (*see* ART, EARLY CHRISTIAN[S] §1) are rooted in an antecedent Jewish art. They base their theories on the premise that illustrated Jewish MSS served as possible guides for the Dura artists. This hypothesis is questionable since no such MSS have been found, and the earliest illustrated Jewish MSS date only from the late ninth century A.D. Attempts to link iconographic elements in Dura scenes with later Byzantine and Jewish art have not been convincing. Recent investigations have revealed that many haggadic motifs appear not only in the Dura synagogue paintings, but also in the illuminations of Christian OT MSS, such as the sixth-century Vienna Genesis, the seventh-century Ashburnham Pentateuch, and the eleventh- and twelfth-century Byzantine Octateuchs. All these MSS are assumed to be based on lost earlier models. The fact that haggadic motifs, such as the serpent walking upright in the Garden of Eden, Noah's raven feeding on a human carcass, and God himself intervening in Abraham's sacrifice, are found in these MSS has led scholars to posit an ancient Jewish illustrated MS tradition, which served the Christian MSS as models. This theory is inconclusive, since our knowledge of early Christian illustrated biblical MSS is very limited. Moreover, since the church Fathers incorporated many haggadic passages in their writings and sermons, these may have inspired the Christian haggadic illustrations.

The Dura paintings are the earliest Jewish biblical scenes we possess; no similar Jewish cycle has yet been unearthed. The so-called "Judgment of Solomon" fresco from first-century Pompeii may not be biblical at all and may have nothing to do with Judaism; the recently found third-century Roman marble plate depicting King David dancing is probably a modern forgery.

3. Synagogue mosaics. The continuation of the tradition established at Dura can be observed in mosaic pavements from the fourth century and later which are found in various synagogues in Palestine and one in North Africa. *See* Pls. XXXIV *a*; XXXV*a*; Fig. A23.

The fifth-century mosaic pavement from Hammam Lif (Naro), Tunisia, has a series of symbolic representations whose meaning is uncertain (parts of the pavement are in the Brooklyn Museum). A cantharus with fountain is flanked by peacocks and palm trees; vine-trellises enclose a lion, birds, and baskets of fruit. Above the Latin inscription of Juliana, the donor, are two large fish and two ducks. In Palestine a well-defined program of decoration developed from the fourth century on. The synagogue mosaic pavements usually contain three main elements: (1) A biblical scene, frequently dealing with a theme of salvation, such as at Jerash (Gerasa), Transjordan, where a fifth-century mosaic floor features the animals of Noah's ark. At Naaran ('Ain Duq) near Jericho, the sixth-century synagogue floor has the story of Daniel and the lions, and the Beth Alpha mosaic depicts Abraham's sacrifice of Isaac. (2) A zodiacal circle which encloses the sun-god Helios riding his chariot and has four female seasons of the year in the corners, as in the synagogues of Hammath-Tiberias, Isfiya, Naaran, and Beth Alpha. (3) A representation of the Torah ark-chest, flanked by two seven-branched lampstands and such ceremonial objects as the shophar, lulab (sprigs), ethrog (citrus fruit), and so-called "snuff shovel." Torah curtains are sometimes suspended from the Torah ark, as at Hammath-Tiberias and BETH-SHAN. The stylistic quality of the mosaics varies considerably, depending on the ability of the artists employed and the wealth of the Jewish community. Some of the mosaics, like those at Jerash and Hammath-Tiberias, compare favorably with the mosaic work of provincial Byzantine artists; others have a rustic quality—the products of gifted folk artists, such as Marianos and his son Aninas, who proudly signed their work at Beth Alpha.

Just as Helios and his chariot echo pagan cosmological models, so King David, in the recently excavated Gaza synagogue mosaic, dated A.D. 508-9, reveals an adaptation from a model of a classical Orpheus taming the wild beasts. Artists may have employed standard motifs from no longer extant workshop pattern books and interchangeably used the same motifs in Christian, Jewish, and pagan mosaics, as can be seen in the sixth-century synagogue mosaic from Maon (Nirim) which closely resembles the church mosaic of 562 from Shellal in the Gaza region.

See also SYNAGOGUE, ARCHITECTURE[S].

4. Catacomb art. Of the six known Jewish catacombs in Rome, the catacomb of Vigna Randanini on Via Appia and that of Villa Torlonia on Via Nomentana are significant for Jewish art. None of the Roman Jewish catacombs are dated, but the red-green linear style which is also used in contemporary pagan and Christian catacombs points to the mid-third and the fourth centuries. On walls and vaults of cubicula we find, enclosed within an ornamental framework, such common pagan figures and motifs as Victory crowning a young man, Fortuna with a horn of plenty, naked *putti,* pheasants, and garlands. Interspersed with these pagan symbols are such typical Jewish symbols as the MENORAH, Torah ark, lulab, ethrog, and shophar. The name of Eudoxios, a Jewish painter, was found in the Via Appia catacomb. Whether the important Via Latina catacomb in Rome, with its forty-one OT images, was inspired by rabbinic exegesis or earlier Jewish art is still an open question.

About fourteen Jewish gold-leaf glasses, whose precise function is unknown, have been found in catacombs. Most come from Rome and date from the fourth century. They depict the Torah ark in the center, usually open to reveal the Torah scrolls within, flanked by two lampstands, shophar, lulab, ethrog, birds, and lions.

A parallel development to the Jewish catacombs in the West are the catacombs in the East, at Beth-shearim, Galilee. No direct artistic relationship or influence can be established. This significant catacomb complex dates from the late second century to the fourth and has buried within it such important people as the patriarch Judah I. Geometric and vegetative ornamentation is painted, incised, or sculpted in low relief on the walls, along with such Jewish symbols as the menorah and Torah ark, as well as figures of gladiators, horsemen, and ships. Catacomb Number 20 contained over one hundred sarcophagi. Their decoration includes a bearded human face, lions attacking a gazelle, eagles, and rosettes. Some marble sarcophagi even have figures from Greek mythology, such as Leda and the swan.

Bibliography. Art and Jewish law: J. Gutmann, ed., *No Graven Images* (1971), and *The Synagogue* (1974).

The Dura-Europos Synagogue: E. R. Goodenough, *Jewish Symbols in the Greco-Roman Period* (1953-68); C. H. Kraeling, *The Synagogue: Excavations at Dura-Europos,* Final Report VIII/1 (1956); J. Gutmann, ed., *The Dura-Europos Synagogue: A Re-Evaluation* (1973); "Was there biblical art at Pompeii?" *Antike Kunst,* XV (1972), 122-24; L. Castiglione, "Review of B. Thomas,

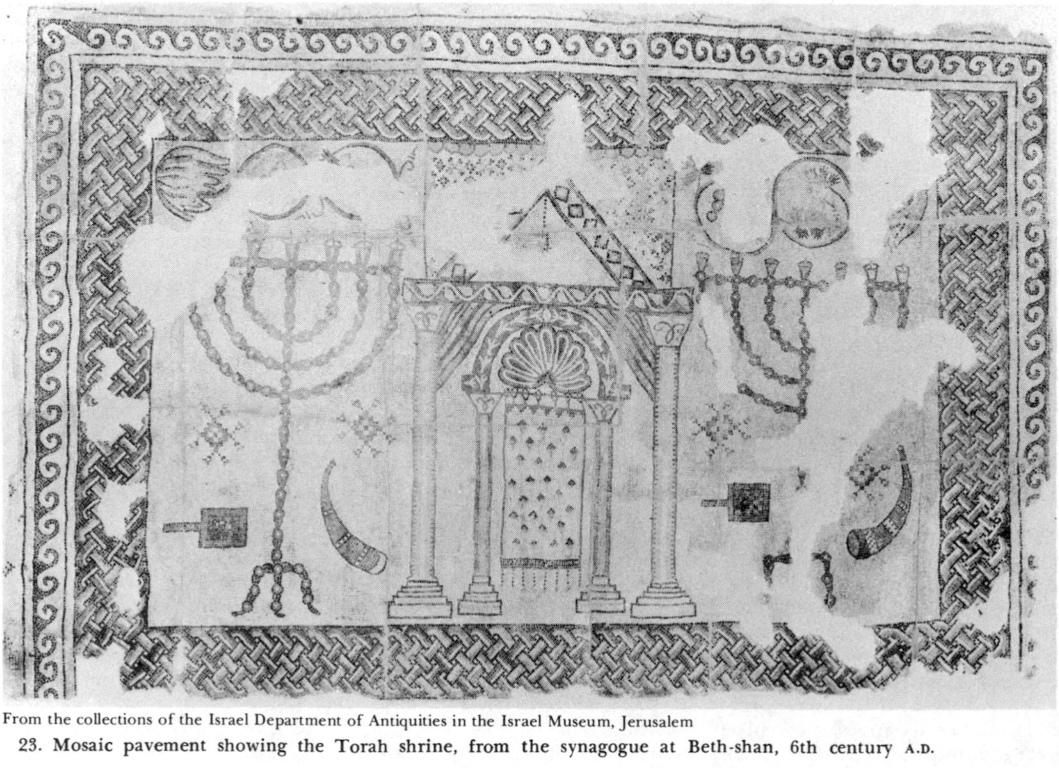

From the collections of the Israel Department of Antiquities in the Israel Museum, Jerusalem

23. Mosaic pavement showing the Torah shrine, from the synagogue at Beth-shan, 6th century A.D.

King David Leaping and Dancing: A Jewish Marble from the Roman Imperial Period," *Acta Archaeologica Hungaricae,* XXIII (1971), 231-45.

Synagogue mosaics: E. Kitzinger, *Israeli Mosaics of the Byzantine Period* (1965); B. Goldman, *The Sacred Portal* (1966).

Catacomb art: H. L. Hempel, "Die Bedeutung des Alten Testamentes für die Programme der frühchristlichen Grabmalerei" (Ph.D. diss., University of Mainz, 1956); U. Schubert, *Spätantikes Judentum und frühchristliche Kunst. Studia Judaica Austriaca,* II (1974); I. Schüler, "A Note on Jewish Gold Glasses," *Journal of Glass Studies,* VIII (1966), 48-61; B. Mazar, *Beth She'arim* (1973).

J. Gutmann

*__ASHDOD.__ A major city near the Palestinian coast (*see* Ashdod). Tell Ashdod, located *ca.* 2½ miles from the Mediterranean coast, is generally recognized as the site of ancient Ashdod, which is best known as a city of the Philistine pentapolis, although it was distinctively Philistine for little more than 175 years (*ca.* 1175-1000 B.C.). The site has been excavated in recent years by Moshe Dothan in a series of eight campaigns (1962, 1963, 1965, and annually in the years 1968-72). During the same general period, the three ancient ports near Ashdod, Ashdod-Yam (i.e., Ashdod-by-the-Sea), Tel Mor (Arab. Tell Kheidar), and Miṣpe Yonah (Arab. Nebi Yunis), have also been the subject of archaeological exploration. Only the highest part of the tell, the so-called acropolis, which is seventeen acres in size, was continuously occupied from the Bronze to the Byzantine Ages; various expansions of the site, S, W, and E, which reached their greatest extent in the Iron Age, covered between fifty and eighty acres.

1. **Bronze Age.** Ashdod was founded in the Middle Bronze period (MB IIA); the earliest city gate (similar to the east gate at Shechem) is dated somewhat later (MB IIC), *ca.* 1550, and associated with Egyptian activity in Syria-Palestine. Ashdod's principal second-millennium port, Tel Mor, was founded only a little later. Some Early Bronze Age (EB II) artifacts were found near bedrock, but these do not reflect any permanent settlement.

The commercial nature of the life of Ashdod in the Late Bronze Age is clear: pottery from the Mycenean-Cypriote sphere, notably Cypriote monochrome ware, is found, along with Palestinian bichrome ware. Ugaritic texts suggest that Ashdod was a center for processing, or at least shipping, textiles.

In the period around 1250-1200, Ashdod, like so many Syro-Palestinian and Anatolian sites, was overrun, possibly by the Sea Peoples (*see* Philistines §1). The destruction was not complete, however, and the unified cultural assemblage which followed spread itself over both ashes and unharmed Late Bronze Age structures. This transitional stratum may also belong to the Sea Peoples.

2. **Iron Age.** The Philistine occupation (i.e., a level characterized by certain distinctively Palestinian ceramics which show Aegean influence) followed shortly; its beginnings may be dated around 1175. The population of Ashdod increased greatly during Iron I, and new settlements were established in the areas S, W, and (briefly) E of the acropolis; the southern extension (or "lower city") was the most important and long-lived of these growth movements, lasting until the end of the seventh or the beginning of the sixth century. The Iron I expansion made Ashdod one of the largest cities in Palestine. Along with this growth came the need for new fortifications, and around the beginning of the eleventh century the upper city was fortified with walls that lasted about a century. The cultural horizons of Iron I Ashdod were not exclusively Philistine; Cypriote-Mycenean wares were found (*see* Philistines §3*d*), along with East Mediterranean-style gold discs and cylinder- and stamp-seals (*see* Seals and Scarabs).

The most striking finds of Philistine material culture were a small clay figurine and some seals. The figurine represents a goddess, the bottom half of whose body has been merged into the throne on which she sits, thus forming an offering table. It is Mycenean in conception and Philistine in decoration (*see* Fig. A24). The three seals bear signs similar to the Cypro-Minoan script which may represent the Philistine language (*see* Philistines[S]); two also show animals engraved in an Aegean mode.

Ashdod was destroyed early in the tenth century

From the collections of the Israel Department of Antiquities in the Israel Museum, Jerusalem

24. The "mother goddess table"

and remained unfortified, though not uninhabited, for a short period of time. Philistine pottery is not common after this destruction, though there are signs of its lingering influence, notably in an ornamental incense burner of Philistine shape and Canaanite decoration. The return of Ashdod to the common Palestinian heritage of material culture is signaled by its Iron II gate and gate tower which are similar to those of Gezer, Megiddo (*see* MEGIDDO §3*d*), and Hazor, and different from those of Iron I Ashdod. Four Iron II destruction layers have been recognized, and the excavator has linked these with four known attacks on the city: those of Uzziah (before 750), Sargon II (in 712), Psammetichos (seventh century), and Nebuchadrezzar (at the beginning of the sixth century).

From the collections of the Israel Department of Antiquities in the Israel Museum, Jerusalem

25. Incense burner with figures of musicians, found at Ashdod

The inscriptional material from Iron II Ashdod is meager but interesting. Three small fragments of a Sargon II victory stele confirm the association of that monarch with a destruction layer. A broken Hebrew sherd, probably from the eighth century, proves that Ashdod belonged to the linguistic continuum which included Phoenicia, Israel, and their neighbors.

See also POTTERY[S].

3. Later history. Ashdod remained a provincial capital throughout the Persian period. An ostracon in fifth-century Aramaic script is the only significant inscriptional find. Since Ashdod plays such a colorful role in Hasmonean history, it is difficult to say who was directly responsible for its final Maccabean leveling, but the best candidate is John Hyrcanus (after 114 B.C.). In the Roman period, Ashdod (Gr. Azotos Mesōgeios) declined in importance and by the sixth century of our era, it had been eclipsed by its daughter, Ashdod-Yam (Gr. Azotos Páralios). Ashdod (Arab. Isdûd) remained a good-sized village until A.D. 1948, when, during the Israel War of Independence, the Arabic-speaking population abandoned the site.

See also INSCRIPTIONS, SEMITIC[S] §3*d*.

Bibliography. Final Reports: M. Dothan and D. N. Freedman, *Ashdod I: The First Season . . . 1962*, 'Atiqôt English Series, VII (1967); M. Dothan, *Ashdod II-III: The Second and Third Seasons . . . 1963 1965, Soundings in 1967*, 'Atiqôt English Series, IX-X (1971).

Short Reports: M. Dothan, *IEJ*, XVIII (1968), 253-54; XIX (1969), 243 ff.; XX (1970), 119-20; XXI (1971), 175; XXII (1972), 166-67, 243-44.

Popular Accounts: M. Dothan, "Ashdod," *Archaeology*, XX (1967), 178-86; "Ashdod of the Philistines," *New Directions in Biblical Archaeology* (1971), 17-26.

Other studies: J. Kaplan, "Ashdod-Yam," *IEJ*, XVIII (1968), 137-49; M. Dothan, "The Foundation of Tel Mor and of Ashdod," *IEJ*, XXIII (1973), 1-17; F. M. Cross and D. N. Freeman, "The Name of Ashdod," *BASOR*, 175 (1964), 48-49.

D. N. FREEDMAN

***ASS. 1. As a riding animal.** "King Shapur said to (Rabbi) Samuel: 'Ye maintain that the Messiah will come upon an ass: I will rather send him a white horse of mine'" (T.B. Sanh. 98a). This talmudic anecdote reflects Rabbi Samuel's understanding of a tradition that kings and prophets rode asses. When Mohammed began his voyage to Jerusalem and his ascent to heaven, Gabriel presented him with Burāq, "a white animal half-mule, half-donkey, with wings on its sides, with which it propelled its feet." It was said that Mohammed's predecessors, Abraham, Moses, and Jesus, rode the same animal. Brockelmann speaks of a number of "prophets" and other leaders who were given the epithet "donkey-riders."

Our first evidence for donkey-riding as a royal tradition comes from a Sumerian text. In "Gilgamesh and Agga" (*ANET* [2nd ed.], pp. 44-47), the assembly of Uruk answers Gilgamesh: "O *ye* who are raised with the sons of the king; O *ye* who *press* the donkey's thigh (i.e., who ride donkeys). . . ." That children of urban dynasts of such an early period (*ca.* 2500 B.C.) rode donkeys should not be surprising, since the horse was apparently untamed before 2100. The famous royal tombs of Ur (*ca.* 2600) contain the remains of onagers hitched to the royal chariot. Gudea, the *ensi* (governor) of Lagash, who saw himself in a dream as a "donkey" (cf. Gen. 16:12), harnessed asses to the divine chariot (*ca.* 2100).

At around 1765 B.C., Baḫdi-Lim, a high official in Mari's palace, writes to remind his king of his (cultic?) duties and to request his return home. He adds: "May my Lord honor his kingship. You may be the king of the Haneans, but you are also the king of the Akkadians. May my Lord not ride horses; (instead) let him ride either a chariot or *kūdanū*-mules so that he would honor his kingship" (ARM VI:76:19-25). In this letter, the contrast is made between horses and *kūdanū*-mules; between Akkadians and Haneans. During the Old Babylonian period, the term "Akkadian" was applied to city-dwellers. The "Haneans," on the other hand, were members of tribal groups whose nomadic practices had become limited in scope and duration by Mari's rulers. Baḫdi-Lim was therefore urging his king to behave as would an urban ruler, heir to a Sumerian tradition.

Ugarit has produced no text that would document the existence of royal donkey-riding. However, its mythological texts, which probably reflect human behavior, record that donkeys were bearers of journeying deities.

Feigin has collected cuneiform omens of the first millennium B.C. which, he maintains, paralleled the prophecy of Zech. 9:9. They show that Babylonian diviners connected the appearance of one riding a donkey with events of importance to cities and kings. Some scholars reject the rendering "humble" (Zech. 9:9). Lipiński revocalizes the Hebrew עני and translates "praise him who rides an ass." Köhler has "triumphant and riding on an ass."

The Bible confirms that nobility rode donkeys and mules (Judg. 5:10; 10:4; 12:14). Saul's grandson rode a donkey (II Sam. 19:26). Solomon traveled to be anointed upon his father's mule (I Kings 1:38). The two following speculations draw their inspirations from this tradition.

a) Although Gen. 47:17 states that the patriarchs possessed horses, there are no references to their use as riding animals. Our sources are unanimous in referring to the donkey as the preferred beast of burden (Gen. 22:3, 5; 42:26-27; 43:18, 24; 44:3, 13; 45:23). Women usually rode camels (Gen. 24:61; 31:17, 34). It has been observed that the Genesis account predicted royal descendants for the Hebrew ancestors. Viewed in this light, the frequent reference to donkeys is to be construed less as evidence for "donkey-caravanning" (Albright) than as yet one more link to a continuing tradition of royal donkey-riding.

b) The entrance of Jesus into Jerusalem is a conscious effort to claim power rather than an act of humility, in fulfillment of Zechariah's prophecy. This episode cannot be divorced from the one which directly follows. If riding a donkey was the method by which Jesus chose to proceed into Jerusalem and by which he intended to accentuate his desire to be taken as a royal figure, his act of cleansing the temple was very likely meant to underscore his claim of priestly, if not prophetic, authority (cf. Pss. Sol. 17:32-33 [30]; Mark 11:16). Taken as a whole, the two acts offered proof that Jesus indeed was the Messiah.

2. In Israel's religious tradition. ARM II:37 is a letter sent around 1765 by Ibal-El, a Mari diplomat, to his king, Zimri-Lim: "The message of Ibal-Addu has reached me from Ashlakka, so I went to Ashlakka. They brought to me a puppy-[dog] and a goat in order to sacrifice a donkey-foal between the Haneans and the land of Idamaraṣ. But I did fear my lord! [So] I would not allow [the use of] a puppy and a goat. Instead, I [myself] sacrificed a donkey-foal, the young of a she-ass and [thus] established conciliation between the Haneans and the land of Idamaraṣ."

The W Semitic idiom *hayaram qatālum,* "to sacrifice a donkey-foal," occurs four more times in the Mari archives. All the attestations refer to a covenant-making procedure which initiated a peace agreement between a king of urban centers and leaders of nomadic groups. This Mari idiom has led scholars to assess the Shechem tradition (Gen. 34). Albright believes that Shechem's inhabitants "carried on the tradition of an early Amorite tribal confederacy, since their principal deity was called 'Baal-berith,' literally 'Lord of the Treaty (Covenant),' and since they traced their origins back to Hamor, literally 'Ass.'"

Held has shown that the expression *hayarum mār atānim,* "donkey-foal of a she-ass," of the Mari letter, is a hendiadys, exactly equivalent to עיר בן אתנות of Zech. 9:9. The latter is formed from the synonymously paralleled pair of words עיר ("colt") = בן־אתון ("young of a she-ass"), as in Gen. 49:11.

Still to be assessed is the unusual law of Exod. 13:13 (and 34:20): "Every first-born male ass you may redeem with a kid or lamb, but if you do not redeem it, you must break its neck" (NEB). The ass is the only unclean animal about whom a procedure for redemption is specifically outlined.

Bibliography. On §1: S. Feigin, "Babylonian Parallels to the Hebrew Phrase, 'Lowly and Riding on an Ass,'" *Studies in Memory of Moses Schorr,* ed. L. Ginzberg and A. Weiss (1944), pp. 227-40, Hebrew; C. Brockelmann, *History of the Islamic Peoples* (1947), p. 49; J. R. Kupper, ARM, VI (1954), text no. 76; E. Lipiński, "Recherches sur le livre de Zacharie," *VT,* XX (1970), 50-53; B. Köhler, "Sacharja IX.9. Ein neuer Übersetzungsvorschlag," *VT,* XXI (1971), 370.

On §2: W. F. Albright, *Archaeology and the Religion of Israel* (4th ed., 1956), p. 113; M. Höfner, *WZKM,* LIV (1957), 80 (on donkey sacrifice in South Arabia); M. Held, "Philological Notes on the Mari Covenant Rituals," *BASOR,* 200 (1970), 32-40 (with bibliog.).

J. M. SASSON

***ASSYRIA AND BABYLONIA. 1. New methodologies and trends.** Assyriology is the study of the history, languages, and literature of ancient Assyria and Babylonia (Assyrian was the earliest dialect of the Akkadian language to be deciphered). In a wider sense, Assyriology has become the study of all civilizations which used cuneiform scripts. Progress in Assyriological studies is measured not only by the increase in the amount of evidence, but also by the insight into the old evidence which new methodologies allow. Since there have been no new archival discoveries recently, current research deals primarily with problems of analysis and re-evaluation.

In field work today, there are several new methods for locating materials. These include portable X-ray machines, ground radar, and cesium magnetometers which detect variations in magnetism caused by objects as far as twenty feet beneath the surface. Aerial photography has also become a scientific method for locating sites and determining their dimensions.

Organic materials have been dated by carbon-14 techniques since the late 1940s, but recent correlations of these dates with tree-ring dating from bristle-cone pine trees have reduced the margin of error to around a century. Extremely ancient materials (40,000 years or more) can be dated by potassium-argon techniques; e.g., the use of potassium-argon dating has placed artifacts and other remains of early man in East Africa to at least 2,000,000 years ago.

Until recently, inorganic material such as fired clay could not be scientifically dated; however, the development of thermoluminescence now enables archaeologists to date such materials. Energy stored in inorganic matter is stimulated by heat and released as light, which can then be carefully measured. Two major laboratories using these new dating techniques have been established: one in Oxford, England, and the other in Philadelphia at the Museum of Applied Science Center for Archaeology (MASCA).

Computers are employed primarily as storage and retrieval systems for linguistic research and information on archaeological sites. For example, by using computers, University of Pennsylvania researchers have been able to reconstruct the Akh-en-Aton temple, using the original stones both as clues and as building materials.

Psychohistory, an emerging interdisciplinary technique, is beginning to establish itself in Assyriology. This application of psychological and psychoanalytic theories to historical analysis promises to yield interesting results.

The integration of Assyriology with other disciplines is advancing rapidly; collaborative efforts have already yielded a considerable number of works. Biblical studies and Assyriology are moving from previous conflict toward greater co-operation, which should enrich both fields.

2. **History.** ***a. Old Assyrian period*** (*ca.* 1900-1650 [middle chronology]). The Assyrians first asserted themselves as an independent power upon the collapse of the Third Dynasty of UR (*ca.* 2000). Their rulers used Akkadian names to assert direct succession from Sargon's dynasty at Akkad (*ca.* 2300).

The Cappadocian Tablets found at Kanish (modern Kültepe) show that the Assyrians were engaged in sophisticated trading operations in Anatolia (modern Turkey) during the nineteenth century. Some three thousand of the more than fifteen thousand texts have been published. Recent studies have shown that Assyria's penetration into Anatolia was commercial rather than military and that the Assyrians at Asshur were importing tin for the production of bronze rather than lead for the extraction of silver. Trade was organized by a number of large kinship-based groups called "houses" or "firms," and the Old Assyrian economic structure was comparable to the medieval Italian city-state. However, no definitive study of the trading firms exists as yet, and it is not clear that Kanish was typical of the entire area.

The period of Shamshi-Adad I (1813-1781) that followed has often been described as the "first Assyrian Empire," but the relationship of Shamshi-Adad I with the Assyrians at Asshur in the eighteenth century remains uncertain. He ruled from Shubat-Enlil, not Asshur, and the petty kingdom that survived his death was not a true empire. The texts indicate that his kingdom disintegrated rapidly as his sons lost their assigned cities to Zimri-Lim of MARI and HAMMURABI of Babylon. A major work is needed to trace the development and cultural continuity of the Old Assyrian period to Assyria's military thrust beginning in the tenth century.

b. Middle Assyrian period (*ca.* 1360-1075). Most of the evidence on the Middle Assyrian period comes from excavations at Asshur, Billa, Fekhariyeh, Kar-Tukulti-Ninurta, Nineveh, and Tell er-Rimaḥ. For over three centuries after Shamshi-Adad I, Assyria remained weak, a vassal first to Babylonia and then to MITANNI. But in the early fourteenth century when Mitanni strength began to wane because of increased pressure from the HITTITES, Assyria under Asshur-uballit I (1364-1329) began to move toward independence. The Assyrian kings began to use more monarchical titles such as "Mighty King," "King of the World/Universe," and "King of Assyria," and these became standard until the fall of the Neo-Assyrian Empire (end of seventh century).

Assyria's three great kings of the thirteenth century, Adad-nirari I (1306-1274), Shalmaneser I (1273-1244), and Tukulti-Ninurta I (1243-1207) restored the Asshur temple. A recent study which deals with the history of the temple and of the ceremonies and personnel connected with the cult concluded that Babylonia influenced Assyrian religion in the Middle Assyrian period. The Marduk statue was held in high esteem during its exile in Assyria and Ninlil was introduced as the spouse of Asshur. The popularity of Marduk in Assyria antedated Asshur-uballit's reign by only a few years. However, the cultural impact of Babylonia on Assyria during this period has not yet been fully assessed.

Neither Babylonia nor Assyria asserted hegemony over the other until the reign of Tukulti-Ninurta I in the thirteenth century. During his reign Assyrian strength reached its apogee. His list of victories was exceeded only by his list of new royal titles. The greatest of his exploits was the conquest of Babylonia and victory over Kashtiliashu IV (1235). Royal inscriptions and the famous epic which bears his name celebrate this feat. But Tukulti-Ninurta overextended his resources—Assyria could hold her gains only a few years. It was not until the final years of the Kassite dynasty that Assyria again intruded into Babylonian territory.

c. Neo-Assyrian period (930-612). After Tiglath-pileser I (1114-1076) re-established Assyria's military strength in the E and N and laid the foundation for growth in the W, Assyrian power waned once more until the late tenth century. The first Neo-Assyrian kings, Asshur-dan II (934-912) and Adad-nirari II (911-891), began the countless military campaigns in which the king, to do honor to the god Asshur, personally commanded the army and dedicated captives to Asshur. The Arameans between the Tigris and Euphrates were completely subjugated. Shalmaneser III (858-824) inherited a kingdom on the ascent, but when he attempted to consolidate Assyrian control across the Euphrates he encountered strong opposition. The encounter at Qarqar (853) provides biblical scholars with the first direct link between Assyria and Israel (*see* AHAB 1). The last confrontation (841) provides the only contemporary pictorial representation of an Israelite mentioned in the Bible (JEHU on the Black Obelisk). (*See also* ARMY[S] §4.) Assyrian scribes have provided the base from which the chronology in the OT has been established.

Both Babylon and the West felt the impact of the Assyrian army during the reign of Adad-nirari III (810-783). The stele found at Tell er-Rimaḥ in 1967 (*see* JOASH, KING OF ISRAEL[S]) refers to tribute received from Joash (Jehoash) of Israel. The correlation between Assyrian and Babylonian sources and the OT appear below.

ANCIENT NEAR EASTERN SYNCHRONISMS WITH THE OLD TESTAMENT

King	Regnal year	Event/Monarch	Julian Year B.C.	Source
Shalmaneser III	6th	Qarqar/Ahab	853	Annal
Shalmaneser III	18th	Tribute/Jehu	841	Annal
Adad-nirari III	1st	Tribute/Joash (Jehoash)	806	Rimaḥ stele
Tiglath-pileser III	3rd	Tribute/Azariah	742	Annal
Tiglath-pileser III	8th (?)	Tribute/Menahem	738?	Annal
Tiglath-pileser III	Unknown	Tribute/Pekah	744–727	Annal
Tiglath-pileser III	Unknown	Tribute/Ahaz	744–727	Annal
Tiglath-pileser III	Unknown	Hoshea	744–727	Annal
Shalmaneser V	5th	Fall of Samaria	722	Chronicle
Sargon II	1st	Fall of Samaria (claimed)	721	Annal
Sennacherib	3rd	Hezekiah	701	Annal
Esarhaddon	Unknown	Tribute/Manasseh	680–669	Annal
Ashurbanipal	Unknown	Tribute/Manasseh	668–627	Annal
Nabopolassar	14th	Fall of Nineveh	Ab/612	Chronicle
Nabopolassar	17th	Egyptians to Harran	Tammuz/609	Chronicle
Nabopolassar	21st	Battle of Carchemish	Nisan-Ab/605	Chronicle
Nebuchadrezzar II	7th	Siege of Jerusalem	Kislev/598	Chronicle
Nebuchadrezzar II	7th	Fall of Jerusalem	Adar/597	Chronicle

After a period of domestic strife, TIGLATH-PILESER III (744-727) inaugurated a century of imperial rule. He "seized the hands of Bel (Marduk)" in Babylon and became the first Assyrian since Tukulti-Ninurta I (1235) to claim the title "King of Babylon." Much later sources—Babylonian King List A, OT (II Kings 15:19; I Chr. 5:26), and Josephus —refer to him as Pūlu (Pul). Tiglath-pileser also revived the technique of wholesale relocation of populations in order to break down national loyalties, a policy continued by his successor, SHALMANESER V (726-722), who captured Samaria, capital of Israel's northern state, and exiled its inhabitants in 722. SARGON II (721-705) has traditionally been credited with this feat, but re-evaluation of the evidence indicates that his scribes altered the historical record. Sargon founded the last royal house of Assyria, called Sargonid after him. Stelae, found as far W as Ashdod and as far E as Godin Tepe in Iran, indicate that he was the most militarily active of the Neo-Assyrian rulers.

With the accession of SENNACHERIB (704-681), the traditional annual march of the Assyrian army was discontinued. Less than half of his twenty-four-year reign was spent on campaign duty. Although he is best known for his siege of Jerusalem in the time of Hezekiah (II Kings 18:13–19:37; Isa. 36–37) and the destruction of the city of Babylon, the true spirit of his age seems to be one of cultural pursuits. Esarhaddon (680-669) atoned for his father's act of sacrilege by restoring the city of Babylon and rebuilding the temple of Marduk (Esagila). The early years of Ashurbanipal's reign (668-627) marked the height of Assyrian culture. But the war which began in 652 between the king and his brother in Babylon extracted a high price from the participants and undermined the political and cultural structure of Assyria; Ashurbanipal's victory was an empty one. Within a short period, the weakened army was unable to protect the Assyrian heartland from the rising Medes. The last forty years of Assyrian history are somewhat obscure, but Assyria was no longer the aggressive force she had been.

NABOPOLASSAR seized the Babylonian throne in 625 and founded the new Chaldean or Neo-Babylonian dynasty. The old Assyrian capitals fell, Asshur in 614 and Nineveh in 612. Confusion still persists in the order and names of the Assyrian monarchs following Ashurbanipal. There was a brief effort to revive the failing empire from the city of HARAN, but when the Egyptian reconnaissance action was thwarted by the Babylonians at Carchemish (605), Assyrian hopes for a return to imperial grandeur were shattered.

d. Old Babylonian period (*ca.* 1850-1600). Hammurabi's archives remain the chief source for the social history of the period, and the Mari correspondence the best, though indirect, source on the political history. Although the volumes from Mari contain no mention of Egypt, there is evidence linking Mari with the West. Place names have become more firmly established through itinerary lists, e.g., Ekallâtum has been identified with modern Haikal and is now placed N of Asshur.

Recent works have shown that, during this time, private ownership of land became accepted and new marriage and family customs emerged. In addition, Akkadian replaced Sumerian as the literary language, new syllabaries appeared, personal name styles changed, and national epics were created.

*e. **Middle Babylonian period*** (*ca.* 1600-1160). Following Hammurabi's reign, several non-Semitic royal houses rose to power in the Mesopotamian area. The MITANNI kingdom was directed by a small ruling class, whose Indo-European names identify them as coming from the E. The kingdom over which they ruled was composed of a Hurrian population, and the two together formed a symbiotic relationship. *See* HURRIANS; HURRIANS[S].

To the S, the Kassites ruled Babylon for more than half a millennium (Babylonian King List A). (*See* CUSH[S].) However, serious problems exist at both ends of their dynastic rule and have left Kassite chronology in an unsettled state. The Kassite kings bore strange names (e.g., Burna-buriash, Kadashman-Enlil, Kurigalzu) and referred to Babylonia as Kar-Duniash. In the fifteenth century under Kurigalzu I they built a new administrative capital, Dûr Kurigalzu (modern 'Aqarquf), about fifteen miles W of modern Baghdad. The Kassite rulers of Babylon apparently had several border clashes with the Assyrians as well as some contact with Egypt. Evidence from the Amarna Age (fourteenth century) provides a clear picture of both Assyria and Babylonia (*see* TELL EL-AMARNA §2; TELL EL-AMARNA[S]). During this time, Babylonian strength increased with the intermarriage of its royal house with those of Egypt, Hatti, and Assyria; Babylonia was now ready to participate in power politics.

The political history of Babylonia between the middle of the fourteenth century and the middle of the twelfth (i.e., between Burna-buriash II and Enlil-nadin-aḫi) is not known, except in relation to Assyria. The lack of border shifting in this period indicates a stable balance of power, with neither Babylonia nor Assyria enjoying more than temporary success. Although Assyria overran Babylonia in 1235 B.C., her success was shortlived, as Assyrian military strength disintegrated. The question of Babylonian influence on Assyria during the late second millennium needs further analysis. Elamite invaders ended the Kassite dynasty in the mid-twelfth century.

There seems little dispute that the Kassites preserved Babylonian culture. Re-evaluation of evidence has destroyed the traditional picture of the Kassite era as a "dark age." The great scribal families of late Babylonian times traced their ancestry to the Kassite period; Kassite scribes edited many of the classics in the cuneiform libraries; and regnal-year dating came into vogue. Nebuchadrezzar I (1123-1102) of the Second Isin Dynasty later restored the lost Babylonian prestige, by retrieving the Marduk statue and elevating the god to the supreme position within the Babylonian pantheon.

f. Neo-Babylonian period (625-539). Not until the tenth century did Assyria dispel the Aramean threat to Mesopotamia. From then until the late seventh century Assyria dominated the Tigris and Euphrates region. The Neo-Babylonian or Chaldean period began with the reign of Nabopolassar (625-605); allying himself with the Medes, he ultimately conquered NINEVEH (612) and eliminated the Assyrian Empire. Seven years later, the Babylonian crown prince NEBUCHADREZZAR II (604-562) consolidated their success in the battle of Carchemish (605).

NABONIDUS (555-539) was the last Babylonian monarch. His attempt to supplant Marduk with the moon-god Sin led to his fall and that of the city itself. Dissatisfied priests of Marduk apparently aided CYRUS of Persia in his conquest of Babylon (539); the imperial capital was reduced to an administrative center in the Achaemenid Empire. When Seleucia-Ctesiphon was founded in the Hellenistic period, Babylon's importance decreased even further. The Parthian sack of Babylon in the second century B.C. left behind only ruins and memories.

See also CHRONOLOGY, MESOPOTAMIAN, METHOD[S].

Bibliography. Major works: *CAH* (3rd ed.), vols. I-II; J. A. Brinkman, *A Political History of Post-Kassite Babylonia* (1968); P. Garelli, *Les Assyriens en Cappadoce* (1963); W. W. Hallo and W. K. Simpson, *The Ancient Near East* (1971); T. Jacobsen, collected essays in W. L. Moran, ed., *Toward the Image of Tammuz and other Essays on Mesopotamian History and Culture* (1970), pp. 1-131, 319-65; A. L. Oppenheim, *Ancient Mesopotamia* (1968); G. van Driel, *The Cult of Aššur* (1969); D. J. Wiseman, ed., *Peoples of OT Times* (1973).

Sources: M. B. Rowton, "Ancient Western Asia," *CAH,* I/1 (1970), 193-239.

Methodologies: G. Buccellati, "Methodological Concerns and the Progress of Ancient Near Eastern Studies," *Or,* XLII (1973), 9-20.

Sources in translation: A. K. Grayson, *Assyrian Royal Inscriptions* (1972); J. B. Pritchard, ed., *ANET* (1969); R. Borger, *Handbuch der Keilschriftliteratur* (1967).

Review articles: M. T. Larsen, "The Old Assyrian Colonies in Anatolia," *JAOS,* XCIV (1974), 468-75; J. A. Brinkman, "Notes on Mesopotamian History in the Thirteenth Century B.C.," *BO,* XXVII (1970), 301-14; W. W. Hallo, "The Rise and Fall of Kalah," *JAOS,* LXXXVIII (1968), 772-75.

Encyclopedia article: W. von Soden *et al.,* "Mesopotamia and Iraq, History of," *Encyclopaedia Britannica,* XI (1974), 963-89, 1001-12.

R. M. TALBERT

ASTROLOGY. The art of foretelling the future by charting and studying the relative positions of the moon, sun, stars, and planets. In the sense of reading omens from celestial phenomena (*see* DIVINATION[S]), astrology originated in Babylon and went hand in hand with the development of precise mathematical astronomy (*see* SCIENCE §B2). Under the Assyrians, astronomical omens were systematically sought and regularly reported to the reigning monarch. The horoscope, however, appeared only in the Hellenistic period, after the invention of the zodiac, attested at the earliest around 700 B.C.

From Babylon the astrological arts spread into Egypt, and survived in Arabic culture of late antiquity. It is important to realize that the numbers of astrological texts, almost all of which derive from Hellenistic and Roman times, are very small relative to the extant astronomical records of the time.

Astrology at its core is a religious phenomenon. At the same time, its practice and theory relate to the growth of Western science. The early history is quite obscure. Its roots embrace the notion that heaven and earth were linked together and that astral bodies were gods. A Sumerian literary text mentions a dream in which King Gudea saw a woman (a goddess) studying a tablet on which the starry heaven was depicted. This is interpreted as meaning that Gudea is to build a temple: "the pure star (which determines) the building of the temple she has announced to you" (Falkenstein, p. 65). Similarly, a Canaanite goddess was associated with the astrological arts. *Pǵt,* sister of Aqhat, is said to be one who "knows the courses of the stars" (*ANET,* p. 153).

Astral omens, known from the beginning of the second millennium, were grouped in "series." The most important text, *Enūma Anu Enlil, ca.* 1000 B.C., links celestial events to future occurrences on earth: "If an eclipse occurs in the month of Siwan on the fourteenth day, and the (moon) god in his darkening darkens at the east side above and brightens on the west side below, a north wind gets up in the first night watch and abates (?) in the middle night watch, the (moon) god . . . will give therein a decision for Ur and the king of Ur: the king of Ur will see famine, the dead will be numerous" (Saggs, pp. 455-56). Much more elaborate are the reports sent by astrologers to the Assyrian kings, *ca.* 700 B.C. Some seventy tablets in the library of Ashurbanipal treat the moon, sun, stars, and planets, along with meteorological phenomena. The continuity with earlier omen series is obvious: "When Mars is visible in Tammuz, the bed of warriors will be wide. When Mercury stands in the north, there will be corpses, there will be an invasion of the King of Akkad against a foreign land" (Thompson, 231).

When the basic interest shifts to the individual and the circumstances surrounding his birth, the horoscope as the modern world understands it appears. The earliest example can be dated to April 29, 410 B.C., although a more primitive form is known from Hurro-Hittite culture. A text from 263 B.C. reads: "(In the) year 48 (of the Seleucid era, month) Adar, night of the twenty-third (?), the child was born. At that time the sun was in 13:30° Aries, the moon in 10° Aquarius, Jupiter at the beginning of Leo, Venus with the sun, Mercury with the sun, Saturn in Cancer, Mars at the end of Cancer. . . . He will be lacking in wealth. . . . His food will not satisfy his hunger" (Sachs, p. 57).

In Egypt, astrological texts date only from the Seleucid period and are clearly of the Babylonian type. The zodiac appeared *ca.* 250 B.C., and in general was a mixture of Greek imagery and Babylonian originals. The six known Greek horoscopes are later, dating from the reign of Augustus. Overall, Egyptian astronomical data seem to be connected with time divisions and the calendar, important for regulating religious observances, and lack the mathematical base so important to the late Babylonian texts. Thus, horoscopic applications appear to be a late, indigenous development in Mesopotamia, and were not due to Greek influence. Horoscopic astrology was exported to Hellenistic Egypt and lived on well into Roman times. The zodiacal signs even appear in synagogue mosaics of late antiquity. *See* SYNAGOGUE Fig. 100.

To judge from the OT, astrology was never assimilated into Israelite culture. It was recognized as Babylonian and was ridiculed (Isa. 47:13; cf. Dan. 2:27; 4:7 [H 4]; 5:7, 11). Prohibited as early as Deut. 4:19, it aroused hostility that continued well into Roman times, and even intensified. The Jews were praised for refusing to take up astral arts (Sib. Or. 218-30); Abraham was said to have studied the stars for an omen and realized his folly (Jub. 12:16-18); astrology was a monstrous sin let loose in the world by primordial giants (I Enoch 8:3). Two biblical passages which deal with diviners and soothsayers (Lev. 19:26; Deut. 18:10) were interpreted by the rabbis as having to do with astrologers (Sanh. 65b-66a). In the NT, astrology was felt to be a foreign element, associated with the three wise men from the east (Matt. 2).

Yet one can wonder to what extent astrological beliefs were a part of the earlier popular milieu. Certainly the climate was favorable. Use of a solar-lunar calendar in Israel necessitated fairly precise astronomical data (*see* CALENDAR §§1, 2). In accord with this are the references to the fixed orders of stars (Amos 5:8; Job 9:9; 38:31-32) and to the movements of celestial bodies (Pss. 19:5-6; 104:19; Job 31:26; Eccl. 1:5, cf. Ecclus. 43:1-12; I Enoch 72–82). Besides such elementary astronomy, astral religion—widespread in the ancient Near East—survived into Israelite times. Traces adhere to place names, such as Beth-shemesh (shrine of the sun) or Beth-yerah (shrine of the moon). Later prophetic invective shows the extent to which astral worship was really a part of everyday Israelite religion. It is linked to Hoshea (II Kings 17:16), Manasseh (II Kings 21:3, 5), and probably Ahaz (II Kings 23:12). Josiah purged the land (II Kings 23:4, 5, 11-12), but solar-lunar worship was still a problem for Jeremiah and Ezekiel (Jer. 8:2; 19:13; Ezek. 8:16, cf. Job 31:26-28). Archaeological remains tend to support the OT picture. A terra-cotta bull from ninth-century Hazor carries a solar emblem on its forehead; an incised star found on a temple wall at Megiddo is matched by another inscribed on a potsherd in Israelite Gibeon; a votive altar from Gezer shows a lion along with a star symbol. The picture, then, is of a rather widespread, indigenous astral religion, undoubtedly supported at times by the monarchs, especially during the period of Assyrian domination. Nevertheless, its popularity was probably confined to the masses.

Yet with all this hospitable milieu, the available evidence suggests that the Israelites did not develop a system of astrology. Joel 2:30-31 [H 3:3-4] possibly refers to astronomical omens, but more likely the verses involve traditional metaphorical language associated with the notion of Yahweh's coming in judgment (*see* Joel 2:10; 3:15; Zeph. 1:14-15; Isa. 13:10; Amos 8:9). Jer. 10:2 may imply that astrology was practiced in Israel, but this is not a necessary conclusion. Finally, Josh. 19:12*c*-13*b* could be interpreted as an incantation prayer uttered in the context of astrological speculation. It seems probable that if astrology were practiced in early Israel, it remained at a primitive level and never achieved the official standing given it in Mesopotamia.

Bibliography. For general treatments, see Wilhelm Knappich, *Geschichte der Astrologie* (1967); Jack Lindsay, *Origins of Astrology* (1971); P. I. Naylor, *Astrology: An Historical Examination* (1967); O. Neugebauer, *The Exact Sciences in Antiquity* (2nd ed., 1957); Will E. Peuckert, *Astrologie* (1960).

For astrology in Mesopotamia, see A. Falkenstein "Die Sumerische Überlieferung"; Recontre assyriologique internationale, XIV, *La Divination en Mésopotamie ancienne et dans les régions voisines* (1968); A. L. Oppenheim, *Ancient Mesopotamia* (1964), pp. 224-25, and "Divination and Celestial Observation in the last Assyrian Empire," *Centaurus*, XIV (1969), 97-135; A. J. Sachs, "Babylonian Horoscopes," *JCS*, VI (1952), 49-75; R. Campbell Thompson, *The Reports of the Magicians and Astrologers of Nineveh and Babylon*, 2 vols. (1900); H. F. W. Saggs, *The Greatness That Was Babylon* (1962).

For astrology in Hellenistic civilization, see F. H. Cramer, *Astrology in Roman Law and Politics* (1954); H. G. Gundel, *Weltbild und Astrologie in den griechischen Zauberpapyri* (1968); O. Neugebauer and H. B. van Hoesen, *Greek Horoscopes* (1959).

On astrology in ancient Israel, see J. S. Holladay, "The Day(s) the Moon Stood Still," *JBL*, LXXXVII (1968), 166-78; John McKay, *Religion in Judah Under the Assyrians* (1973); E. W. Maunder, *The Astronomy of the Bible* (1909); J. F. A. Sawyer, "Josh. 10:12-14 and the Solar Eclipse of 30 September 1131 B.C.," *PEQ*, CIV (1972), 139-46; G. Schiaparelli, *Astronomy in the Old Testament* (1905); E. J. Wiesenberg, *Astronomy and the Bible* (1974).

B. O. LONG

***ATHENS.** The discovery of the Royal Stoa in 1970 helps to clarify the topography of the Agora. The Basileios or Royal Stoa was a famous building often mentioned in ancient literature. It was the seat of the king archon, one of the principal magistrates of ancient Athens with jurisdiction over religious matters. Preliminary hearings for certain trials were sometimes held here, the most famous being that of Socrates. The Areopagus court occasionally met here, and some scholars think that the apostle Paul was arraigned here rather than on the AREOPAGUS itself. The stoa was very small, with only eight columns across its façade. A bench ran along the back and end walls. At either end of the façade a small projecting wing was added later for the display of inscribed stelai. Directly in front of the stoa is a large, smooth, flat stone, evidently the famous stone on which the archons stood to take their oath of office. The identification of the stoa is assured by its position, first on the right as one entered the Agora coming from the gates (Pausanias I.iii.1), by its relationship with the Stoa of Zeus directly S, and by the numerous herms and their bases found in the area, some inscribed as dedications by the king archon. This venerable building was originally built about the middle of the sixth century B.C. and remained in use throughout classical antiquity.

See Fig. A26.

Bibliography. John Travlos, *Pictorial Dictionary of Ancient Athens* (1971), an authoritative, beautifully illustrated work; H. A. Thompson and R. E. Wycherley, *The Agora of Athens* (1972), a full general account of the results of the excavations.

E. VANDERPOOL

ATHLETES, ATHLETICS. *See* FESTIVALS, GRECO-ROMAN[S].

***ATONEMENT IN THE OT** [כפר, *kippēr*].

1. Etymology
2. Ritual *kippēr*
   - *a*. *Kippēr* as "purge"
   - *b*. *Kippēr* as "cover"
   - *c*. *Kippēr* as "ransom/substitute"
   - *d*. *Kippēr* as "expiate"
   - *e*. Ritual atonement without *kippēr*
3. Nonritual *kippēr*
   - *a*. For sin
   - *b*. For the land
   - *c*. By intercession

1. Etymology. "Atone" or "expiate" is the customary translation for *kippēr*, but in most cases this is incorrect. In biblical poetry, its parallel synonym is usually *māḥâ* ("wipe"—RSV "blot out"—Jer. 18:23) or *hēsîr* ("remove," Isa. 27:9), suggesting that *kippēr* means "purge." Ritual texts also support this meaning since they regularly couple *kippēr* with *ṭihar* ("purify"—RSV "pronounce . . . clean") and *ḥiṭṭē'* ("decontaminate"—RSV, "cleanse" —Lev. 14:48, 52, 53). However, other poetic passages will use in parallel *kissâ* ("to cover"; Neh. 4:5 [H 3:37]), giving the contrary notion that *kippēr* connotes smearing on a new substance rather than effacing an existent one. Philologists have been divided on the etymology, since evidence from Semitic cognates can be cited in support of both, mainly from Arabic ("cover") and Akkadian ("wipe"). However, both meanings may go back to a common notion: "rub." Since a substance may either be "rubbed on" or "rubbed off," the derived meanings "wipe" and "cover" may be complementary and not contradictory. This is shown especially in Akkadian, where both usages are attested in medical/magical texts and where "the step between 'rubbing off' and 'rubbing on' is so short we cannot distinguish between cleaning and treatment" (Landsberger).

2. Ritual *kippēr*. *a*. Kippēr *as "purge."* In Israel the meaning "rub off" predominates in ritual texts, whereas "cover" probably never occurs. This is best illustrated by the blood of the *ḥaṭṭā'th*, the purgation offering (*see* SACRIFICES AND OFFERINGS, OT[S] §2*ai*). Its use is restricted to the sanctuary: it is never used on a person. (The rites for the healed leper and the consecration of the priest call for a *ḥaṭṭā'th*, but the blood with

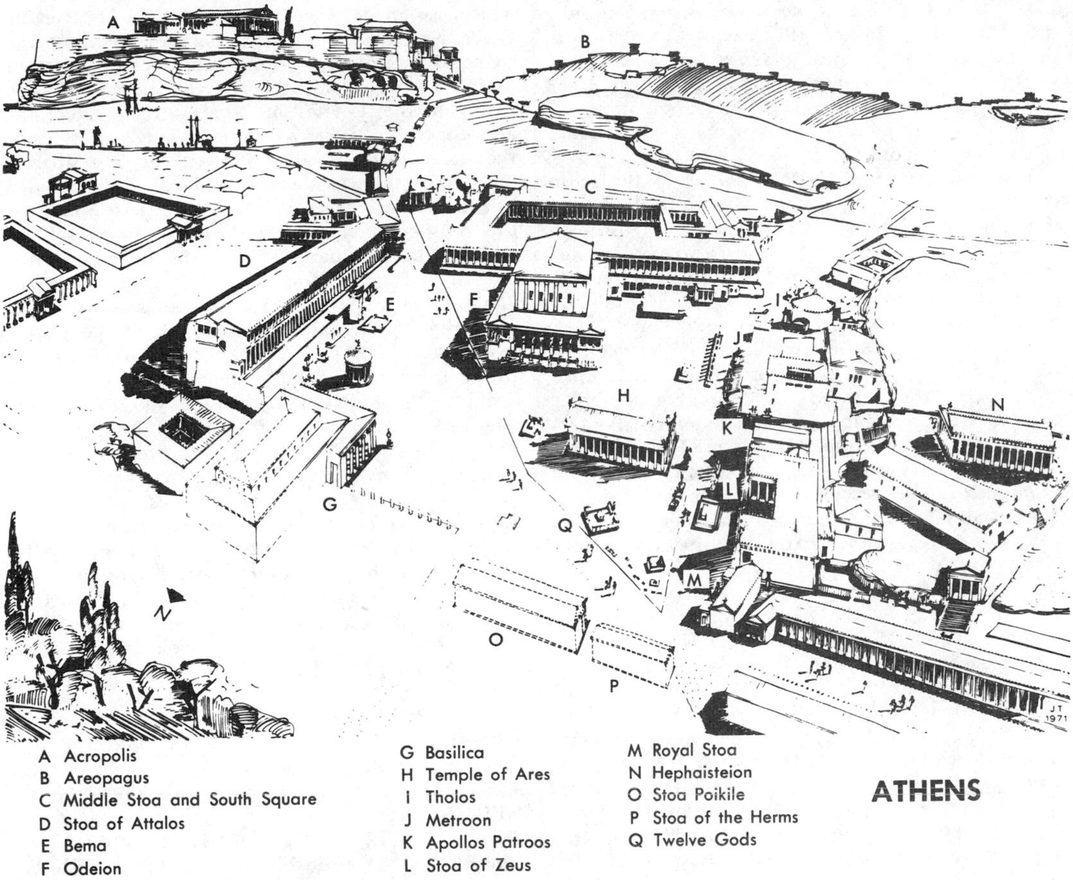
A
B
C
D
E
F
G
H
I
J
K
L
M
N
O
P
Q
N
JT 1971
A Acropolis
B Areopagus
C Middle Stoa and South Square
D Stoa of Attalos
E Bema
F Odeion
G Basilica
H Temple of Ares
I Tholos
J Metroon
K Apollos Patroos
L Stoa of Zeus
M Royal Stoa
N Hephaisteion
O Stoa Poikile
P Stoa of the Herms
Q Twelve Gods
ATHENS

American School of Classical Studies, Athens

26. The Agora, Athens, 2nd century A.D.

which they are daubed comes from other animal sacrifices.) This means that a person never is the object of the *kippēr* rite but only the beneficiary. The purpose of the *ḥaṭṭā'th* blood is not to purge the worshiper of alleged sin, as heretofore assumed, but to purge that to which it is applied, i.e., the sanctuary and its sanctums. By placing the blood upon the altar horns or bringing it inside the sanctuary (e.g., Lev. 16:14-19), the priest thereby purges the most-sacred areas on behalf of the person[s] who caused them to be contaminated, either by physical impurity (Lev. 12–15) or by inadvertent misdemeanor against God (Lev. 4). Presumptuous sins and impurities, however, cannot be purged by the offender's own *ḥaṭṭā'th* (Num. 15:30-31), but must await the annual rite of purgation for the sanctuary and the nation. *Kippēr* undergoes further qualification in the context of the sacrificial system, and it can be shown that expiatory sacrifices deal only with offenses committed against the Deity; they do not redress wrongs against human beings. *See* ATONEMENT, DAY OF[S] §§1, 2.

The net result of these deductions from the function of sacrificial *kippēr* is that we can reconstruct the heretofore missing priestly doctrine of THEODICY. It presumes that sin is a miasma that, wherever committed, is attracted magnet-like to the sanctuary. There it adheres and amasses until God will no longer abide in the sanctuary. Hence, it is forever incumbent upon Israel, through the indispensable medium of its priesthood, to purge the sanctuary regularly of its impurities, or else God will abandon it and the people to their doom. Thus, evil is never unheeded by God, even when the individual evildoer is not immediately punished, but it accumulates in the sanctuary until the point of no return is reached; the sum of individual sin leads inexorably to the destruction of the community.

This priestly theology of *kippēr* is easily traceable to pre-Israelite analogues, for the ancient Near East shared a common obsession with temple purification. In outward form, biblical religion here comes close to its antecedents. In content, however, the gap is never wider, for it bears all the hallmarks of Israel's monotheistic revolution. Thus the *kippēr* rite is not inherently efficacious. Since persons are never the direct object of *kippēr* (*see above*), the rite is not a device to counter the effects of magic or to cure disease. Moreover, God's forgiveness is always phrased as a passive, *wenislaḥ,* "that [he] may be (RSV "shall be") forgiven" (Lev. 4:20, 26, 31, 35; 5:10, 13, 16, 18; Num. 15:25-26, 28); it is not the automatic consequence of the priestly rite. Above all, the pagan was obsessed by the fear that demonic intruders would drive the deity out of his earthly abode; thus purifications are magical defense weapons. Israel, to the contrary, demythologized and devitalized cosmic evil. Only the physical and moral impurity of persons can pollute the sanctuary; they alone can drive God out.

b.* Kippēr *as "cover." Does *kippēr* in the sense of "rub on" occur in the Israelite cult? It might, if it could be shown that blood was an apotropaic as well as a cathartic. There are two possible instances. The first is the paschal blood upon the doorposts. Indeed, the term *pesaḥ* itself probably means "protection" (cf. Exod. 12:27 with Isa. 31:5), and the rite is paralleled in Babylonian rituals (e.g., Namburbi) where blood and other apotropaics are smeared on doors and keyholes that the "evil [plague] shall not enter the house." However, the root *kippēr* is not used in the texts on the paschal observance, and its sacrifice is not a *ḥaṭṭā'th.* The second possible instance is the blood-and-oil rite for the purified leper (Lev. 14) and consecrated priest (Exod. 29) and the double blood rite for the purged altar (Lev. 16:18, 20), where the term *kippēr* indeed occurs. A possibly related instance is the use of incense to stop a plague (Num. 16:46-47 [H 17:11-12]), but the precise meaning of *kippēr* is not certain.

The agents of ritual *kippēr,* exclusive of the *ḥaṭṭā'th* blood, not yet discussed are: the scapegoat (Lev. 16:10, 21-22), the heifer whose neck is broken (Deut. 21:1-9), the money for the military census (Exod. 30:16), the Levites (Num. 8:19), the human deaths in cases of idolatry (Num. 25:1-15) and homicide (Num. 35:32-33), and, finally, the blood of sacrifices other than the *ḥaṭṭā'th.*

c.* Kippēr *as "ransom/substitute." It has been noticed in Mesopotamian magic that "the dirt called *kupirtu* or *takpirtu* is absorbed by a medium, mostly dough, which is thrown away, buried or carried away" (Landsberger). This leads to the phenomenon of the "ransom/substitute," the substance to which the evil is transferred and thereupon eliminated. This notion of the *kippēr* carrier is clearly represented in the Bible in the cases of the scapegoat (*see* AZAZEL) and the heifer whose neck is broken, as shown by extrabiblical parallels. Though such evidence is not available for the remaining cases, the ransom principle is nonetheless operative. The common denominator of all these cases is their avowed goal: to siphon off the wrath of God from the entire community. This *kippēr* must be sharply distinguished from that of the sanctuary. In the latter case, the impurities are purged to keep them from causing the indwelling God to leave. However, in the present case, *kippēr* has the immediate goal of preventing the divine anger from incinerating innocent and guilty alike. Furthermore, in the case of the census money (Exod. 30:16), *lᵉkhappēr 'al naphšōthēkhem* is related to *kōpher naphšô* (Exod. 30:12); the same combination is again found in the homicide law (Num. 35:31-33). The verb *kippēr* is thus a denominative from *kōpher,* whose meaning is undisputed, i.e., ransom (Exod. 21:30). Therefore, there exists a strong possibility that all texts which assign to *kippēr* the function of averting God's wrath have *kōpher* in mind: innocent life spared by substituting for it the guilty parties or their ransom/substitute (already noted by Ibn Ezra for the Levites of Num. 8:19). Thus, the above-mentioned cases are elucidated as follows: though no substitute is allowed for a deliberate murderer, the accidental homicide is ransomed by the natural death of the high priest. Similarly, the census money ransoms each counted soldier, and the Levite guards replace the Israelites when one of the latter encroaches upon the sanctums (Num. 1:53; 8:19; 18:22-23). *See* ENCROACHMENT[S].

Finally, the remaining occurrence of the phrase "to ransom (*kpr*) your lives" occurs in Lev. 17:11, where the blood of the *šᵉlāmîm* sacrifice must be drained on the altar to ransom the life of the offerer for slaughtering the animal for food. *See* SACRIFICES AND OFFERINGS, OT[S] §3*b*.

d.* Kippēr *as "expiate." The final stage in the evolution of the root *kippēr* yields the abstract, figurative notion "expiate." Having begun as an action which eliminates dangerous impurity by absorbing it through direct contact (rubbing off) or indirectly (as a ransom/substitute), it eventuates into the process of expiation in general. Thus, the *kippēr* role of all other sacrifices whose blood is not daubed on the altar's horns like the *ḥaṭṭā'th* but is dashed on its sides is to expiate sin. This is one of the functions of the *'ōlâ* (Lev. 1:4) and the *minḥâ* (Lev. 14:20), and the sole function of the *'āšām* (Lev. 5:16, 18; 6:7 [H 5:26]). As for the *kappōreth* (RSV "mercy seat"; NEB "cover") placed over the tabernacle ark (Exod. 25:17-22), being a feminine abstract noun from *kippēr,* it probably means "that which expiates." And since it also designates the place where Moses "would hear the voice addressing him" (Num. 7:89), it is the source of expiation, par excellence.

***e. Ritual atonement without* kippēr.** Whenever a sacrifice concludes the purification ritual for physical impurity, it is always a *ḥaṭṭā'th,* and its purpose is to *kippēr* or purge the contaminated sanctuary. In this context the term "atonement" is meaningless, for the impure individual has done nothing sinful. For his own person, all he needs is to be cleansed, and for this the rite of ablution suffices. Indeed, it is striking that when prophet or psalmist resorts to a ritualistic metaphor in his call for moral purification, he never uses the term *kippēr,* but he uses one which signifies lustration with water (e.g., Isa. 1:16; Ezek. 36:23; Zech. 13:1; Ps. 51:2, 7 [H 4, 9]).

It is well-established that the nonritual texts of the Bible demand repentance as the proper atonement for moral wrongdoing (*see* §3 *below;* REPENTANCE IN THE OT[S]); it is not widely known, however, that the indispensability of repentance is stipulated by the ritual texts as well. To begin with, the possibility of sacrificial atonement is explicitly denied to the individual who brazenly violates God's law (Num. 15: 30-31). This, however, does not mean, as many scholars propose, that sacrificial atonement is possible only for involuntary wrongdoers. To cite but one exception, the *'āšām* offering is prescribed for premeditated crime (Lev. 6:1-7 [H 5:20-27]; Num. 5:5-8). A more correct assertion would be that the priestly system prohibits sacrificial atonement to the unrepentant sinner, to the one who "acts defiantly (RSV "with a high hand"), . . . it is the Lord he reviles" (Num. 15:30). Furthermore, it is precisely when the sin is deliberate, not accidental, that another penitential requirement is added, namely, that the contrition must be openly declared; it must be supplemented by confession (*wᵉhithwaddâ,* Lev. 5:5; Num. 5:7; cf. Lev. 16:21; 26:40). Indeed, the prophetic insistence that repentance is not an end in itself but must lead to rectification of the wrongdoing (e.g., Isa. 1:13-17; 58:6-12; Mic. 6:6-8) is only the articulation of a basic postulate of the sacrificial system.

3. Nonritual *kippēr*. *a. For sin.* Outside the sanctuary, *kippēr* undergoes a vast change that is at once made apparent by its new grammatical syntax. Whereas in ritual the subject of *kippēr* is invariably a priest and the direct object is a contaminated thing, in the nonritual literature usually the subject is the Deity and the direct object is a sin (e.g., Jer. 18:23; Ezek. 16:63 [RSV "forgive"]; Ps. 78:38). Actually, this represents no rupture with ritual *kippēr;* on the contrary, it gives voice to its implicit meaning. As for the object, though the cult concentrates mainly on the purging of sanctuary impurity, it too recognizes that its source is human sin. The subject implies even less change: though the priest performs the rituals, it is only due to the grace of God that the ritual is efficacious. Thus, nonritual exhortations, requiring no priestly mediation, uncompromisingly turn to God, the sole dispenser of expiation. True, there are a few *kippēr* passages with man as subject (e.g., II Sam. 21:3; Isa. 47:11), but all these exceptions are explicable by the substitutionary *kippēr;* i.e., man is required to provide the necessary ransom. The enigmatic *ʾᵃkhappᵉrâ pānâw* (Gen. 32:20 [H 21]; RSV "I may appease him") may be similarly interpreted, but the unique object "face" may go back to the Akkadian cognate, *kuppuru panê,* "wipe the face," hence "wipe [the anger from] the face" (Prov. 16:14). If rituals stipulate repentance as a precondition for atonement, moral exhortation will place a greater value upon repentance—and its vehicle prayer—than upon ritual and sacrifice (e.g., Lev. 26:40-42; Deut. 4:29; I Kings 8:28-30, 33, 35, 47-48; Pss. 51:17 [H 19]; 141:2).

In recent years it has been increasingly maintained that early Israel knew no forgiveness of sin because *kippēr* and *sālaḥ,* "forgive," are mainly found in postexilic texts, and because the preexilic literature speaks exclusively of *wᵉniḥām ʿal hārāʿâ* ("to repent of the threatened evil," Exod. 32:14) and *ʿabhar lᵉ,* implying that "God overlooks mild sins but does not obliterate them" (Koch). At once, a methodological objection should be raised against the arbitrary assignment of all cultic passages (where *kippēr* would chiefly occur) and all consolatory prophetic passages (where *sālaḥ* would predominate) to the postexilic period. Moreover, this view suffers from a more serious fault: it blurs the distinction between two stages in the process of divine pardoning common to all the biblical sources. The first, involving the abovementioned idioms, never occurs when God is contemplating punishment, but only when he has actually decided upon it. The consequence is that, before the guilty can implore God for forgiveness, they must prevail on him to revoke his decree. This is evident in the story of Moses' intercession for Israel on the occasion of their sin with the golden calf (Exod. 32–34). His initial plea (32:11-13) accomplishes the first stage: God renounced the punishment he had declared he would bring upon his people (32:14). Moses, however, is not content with the cancellation of the divine decree. After slaying many, presumably the most guilty, he presses for the complete obliteration of Israel's sin (32:30-32). This God does not grant (32:33-34), but, when he reveals to Moses that his mercy can supersede his justice (34:6-7*a*) whenever he desires (33:19*b*), an opening is provided Moses whereby he can explicitly ask for forgiveness (*sālaḥ,* 34:9).

That the renunciation of punishment must be distinguished from forgiveness of sin is also clear from another instance of prophetic intercession (Amos 7:1-8; 8:1-2). Amos wants forgiveness (7:2); God only concedes the cancellation of punishment (7:3, 6). Even this he will not do more than twice (7:8), and, finally, Israel's sins drive him to declare, "the end has come" (8:2). With Amos as with Moses, the language is crucial: God concedes partially to the prophet's plea; he suspends punishment but does not grant the complete remission of sin.

Finally, it should be noted that the idiom *nāśâ hēṭʾ/ʿāwôn/pešaʿ* can have the meaning "remove sin," implying forgiveness. Moreover, it is used synonymously with *māḥâ* and *kippēr* (note the occurrence of all three in Moses' plea, Exod. 32:30-32), *heʿᵉbhîr ʿāwôn* (Job 7:21), and *sālaḥ* itself (Num. 14:18-19). So many early sources illustrate this usage (e.g., Exod. 34:7; I Sam. 15:25; Hos. 14:2 [H 3]; Mic. 7:18) that it cannot be denied that the consciousness and absolution of sin were moral realities in all periods of Israel's history.

b. For the land. The holiness of the sanctuary is complemented in the Priestly source by the notion of the holiness of the land of Israel. Correspondingly, the land too is capable of defilement (e.g., Lev. 18:25, 28, for sexual immorality; Num. 35:33-34, for murder; cf. also Ezek. 36:17; Deut. 21:23), and just as the sanctuary needs *kippēr,* so does the land (expressly, Num. 35:33). Furthermore, the implications are likewise identical: defilement of the land will result in the destruction of Israel just as it did for the previous inhabitants (Lev. 18:28; 20:22), because God can no longer abide in it (Sifre Num. 161). Here, however, the parallels end; there is no ceremony by which the land is purged, and *kippēr,* therefore, is not used ritually but refers to general moral expiation. Atonement for the land becomes a more important concept in postbiblical times (e.g., Deut. 32:43 [LXX] and Jub. 6:22, where it is sacrificial!). The Dead Sea sectarians believed that their consecrated life was an atonement not just for themselves but for the entire land (1QS 8.6, 10; 9.4).

c. By intercession. Another postulate of the biblical doctrine of atonement is that God will spare the community by virtue of the merit of the just people in it, e.g., Abraham's intervention on behalf of Sodom and Gomorrah (Gen. 18:16-33). However, intercession is chiefly the vocation of the prophet. The psalmist eulogizes Moses for interceding on behalf of the worshipers of the golden calf (see Exod. 32:11 ff.) in these words: "He said he would destroy them—had not Moses, his chosen one, stood in the breach before him" (Ps. 106:23). To intercede at the risk of one's life is to "stand in the breach."

It has been thought that Ezekiel refutes this doctrine of the atonement by the righteous, because he says repeatedly and forcefully that the righteous will not save their generation, but that each person will be judged according to his sins (Ezek. 18). This is not the case. Ezekiel, a priest as well as a prophet, is enlarging upon a corollary of the priestly doctrine of the temple (*see* §2*a above*). The reason why God abandons his sanctuary is that the level of impurity rises to a point beyond toleration. After this point, God will neither seek man's repentance nor allow the prophet to intercede for him: the decree of doom becomes irrevocable. This postulate is found beyond the confines of the Priestly source; it informs all biblical teaching on evil, e.g., the hardening of Pharaoh's heart (Exod. 7:3, 14; etc.), Isaiah's harsh commission (Isa. 6:10), and the prohibition placed on the prophet to intercede (Jer. 15:1-2). This Jeremiah passage illuminates Ezekiel's message as well; both prophets experienced the destruction of Judah, and both had taught that their generation was doomed. However, Ezekiel never abandoned his belief in the efficacy of prophetic intercession, as demonstrated by his wistful comment on the psalmist's allusion to Moses' self-sacrifice: "I sought a man who would plug up the wall and stand in the breach before me on behalf of the land, that I should not destroy it; but I found none" (22:30).

The concept of atonement developed among the Dead Sea sectarians took a unique turn. Without the temple, they were forced to concentrate on nonsacrificial expiation (e.g., 1QS 9.4-5), and they developed a lofty spiritual doctrine which taught that purity of thought and deed were necessary preconditions of all ritual acts, and that the virtuous life of the individual effects atonement for others. However, the circle of the latter was restricted to members of the sect (perhaps also the like-minded, 1QS 5.5-7), and the rest of Israel was uniformly excluded. This insularity is not surprising in view of the teaching of Jeremiah and Ezekiel. Like these prophets, the sect also felt that universal doom was at hand, from which the righteous would save only themselves. This helps to explain the sectarians' insistence that their atonement also extended to the land (*see* §3*b above*): it was in need of atonement so that the righteous survivors of the impending cataclysm could settle on it immediately (1QSa 1.3).

The atoning power of the righteous reaches out not only horizontally to the community but vertically to posterity. This principle undergirds all of God's covenants with Israel: with the patriarchs for offspring and soil (Gen. 15; 17:1-8; 22:17-18; 25:23; 35:9-12; Exod. 32:13), with Phineas for a priestly line (Num. 25:12-13), and with David for a royal dynasty (II Sam. 7:12-16).

In the wisdom literature the suffering of the righteous is rationalized into a theological postulate: suffering is a test whereby God enables the righteous to merit an even greater reward (e.g., Ps. 66:9-12; Job 5:17-26; 36:8-10). This idea also informs the narratives of the wilderness (Exod. 16:4; Deut. 8:2, 16) and of the patriarchs (e.g., Gen. 22:1, 16-18). A logical extension of this theodicy is that suffering can serve as an atonement for society. However, it is not an explicit OT doctrine, because nowhere do the innocent suffer for the sake of the guilty. It may be adumbrated by the final Servant poems (Isa. 52:13–53:12), but its unfolding is realized in later times.

Bibliography. General: A Médebielle, "Expiation," in *DBSup,* III (1938), cols. 48-112; H. H. Rowley, *Worship in Ancient Israel* (1967).

Etymology: B. Landsberger, *The Date Palm and Its By-Products According to the Cuneiform Sources,* Archiv für Orientforschung, Beiheft 17 (1967), pp. 30-34; B. A. Levine, *In the Presence of the Lord* (1974), pp. 55-77.

Ritual: L. Moraldi, *Espiazione sacrificiale e riti espiatori nell' ambiente biblico e nell' Antico Testamento* (1956), pp. 109-81; R. de Vaux, *Studies in OT Sacrifice* (1964), pp. 91-112; J. Milgrom, *Studies in Levitical Terminology,* I (1970), 28-31, and "The Cultic *šᵉgāgâ* and Its Influence in Psalms and Job," *JQR,* LVIII (1967), 115-25.

Nonritual: Extreme opposing positions are taken by A. Buechler, *Studies in Sin and Atonement* (1928), and K. Koch, "Sühne und Sündenvergebung um die Wende von der exilischen zur nachexilischen Zeit," *EvT,* XXVI (1966), 217-39.

J. Milgrom

***ATONEMENT, DAY OF.** The Day of Atonement (*yôm hakkippurîm*) was the annual "day of purgation" for the temple and the people. This follows from the facts that its sacrifices are of one type, the *ḥaṭṭā'th* ("purgation offering"; *see* Sacrifices and Offerings, OT[S] §2*a*; cf. *ḥaṭṭā'th hakkippurîm* [RSV "sin offering of atonement"], Exod. 30:10; Num. 29:11), and that the three *ḥaṭṭā'th* animals are offered in behalf of the priesthood (Lev. 16:6, 11) and the people (16:5, 15).

According to the rabbis: "All the goats make atonement for the pollution of the temple and its sanctums. . . . For pollution that befalls the temple and its sanctums through wantonness, atonement is made by the goat whose blood is spilled within [the shrine] and by the Day of Atonement; for all other transgressions specified in the Torah—minor or grave, wanton or inadvertent, conscious or unconscious, through commission or omission . . . the scapegoat makes atonement" (M. Shebu. 1.4-7). The Mishna shows that the function of the slain *ḥaṭṭā'th* was to purge the temple of its pollution, and the function of the live *ḥaṭṭā'th,* the one dispatched to Azazel (Lev. 16:26), was to purge the people of their sins. This distinction is corroborated by the biblical text, which expressly declares that the slain bull and goat purge the shrine of the (physical) pollution, טמאות, of the Israelites and their brazen sins, פשעיהם (Lev. 16:16; cf. 16:19), and the scapegoat carries off their iniquities, עונתם (16:22).

1. Purging the temple. The purgation of the sanctuary rests on two complementary postulates: (*a*) The brazen defier of God's commandments is ineligible for sacrificial expiation (Num. 15:30-31), but the temple must be purged of his sins and impurities, and (*b*) since brazen sins possess the power not only to pollute the outer altar but to penetrate into the shrine, reaching even the holy ark, the entire temple complex must be purged on the Day of Atonement. *See* ATONEMENT IN THE OT[S] §2*a*.

Temple purifications dominate the cultic landscape of the Near East. Impurity was feared because of its demonic power. It threatened the gods themselves and especially their temples. Protector gods were erected before the entrances of temples and palaces (*šêdu* and *lamassu* in Mesopotamia and lion gargoyles in Egypt), and elaborate rituals were employed to rid these buildings of demons and prevent their return (e.g., *ANET* [2nd ed.], pp. 6-7, Egyptian; 346, Hittite; 333-34, esp. line 381; 334-38, esp. text C, lines 14-16, Mesopotamian). The antiquity and ubiquity of the Azazel rite are striking. Purgation and elimination rites go together in the ancient world. Exorcism of impurity is not enough; its power must be removed. This was accomplished in one of three ways: curse, destruction, or banishment. The last was often used; evil was banished to its place of origin (e.g., netherworld, wilderness) or to some place where either its malefic powers could work in the interest of the sender (e.g., enemy territory) or where it could do no harm at all (e.g., mountains, wilderness). Thus the scapegoat was sent to the wilderness, which was considered inhabited by the satyr-demon Azazel. In these cases, there is an integral connection between the actual purging (by aspersions, smearing, or incense) and the transfer of the released impurity onto a decapitated ram and its banishment via the river (e.g., *ANET,* pp. 333, lines 345-61; cf. Deut. 21:1-9). *See* SHALAH[S].

2. Purging the people. The purgation-expulsion nexus essential to pagan magic survived in Israel's cult, but its meaning underwent a revolution. As scholars have noted, the purgation and Azazel rites on the Day of Atonement are distinct: the slain *ḥaṭṭā'th* purges the tabernacle, but the live *ḥaṭṭā'th* carries off the people's sins. The reasons are clear: Israel, the holy people (Lev. 11:44; 19:2; 20:26), needs the same purification as the holy place, so that "they shall not pollute their camp in whose midst I dwell" (Num. 5:3*b*; *see* LEVITICUS[S] §1*e*). Moreover, the monotheistic dynamic is at work here: since the world of demons is nonexistent, the only source of rebellion against God is in the heart of man, and it is there that cathartic renewal must periodically take place.

Ordinarily, the hand-laying and confession must be performed by the offerer himself, but presumptuous, rebellious sin (פשע) bars its perpetuators from the sanctuary, and they must be represented by the high priest. The latter's officiation, however, is not inherently efficacious. The people, though excluded from the rites, must submit to fasting and other acts of self-denial (Lev. 16:29; 23:27-32; Num. 29:7). Thus repentance purges man as the *ḥaṭṭā'th* blood does the sanctuary. This ethical achievement is unmatched in the ancient world. True, the Babylonian new year calls for a ritual of humiliation for the king, followed by his prayer of confession. But in contrast to Israel's high priest, whose confessional specifies where he and his people have failed, the Babylonian king appears arrogant and self-righteous.

Finally, atonement by sacrifice is efficacious only for sins against God. The Mishna again has captured the ethical import: "For the sins between man and God, the Day of Atonement effects atonement; but for the sins between man and his fellow, the Day of Atonement will effect atonement only if he has appeased his fellows" (M. Yom. 8.9). That this spiritual principle is not an innovation of the rabbis, but constitutes this legacy from biblical times, is shown by its explicit presence in the אשם offering, where restitution to man must precede sacrificial expiation from God (Lev. 6:1-7 [H 5:20 ff.]).

3. The emergence of the day. The Day of Atonement itself may not be as old as its ceremonial. For example, in distinction from all other festival prescriptions which give the date before the ritual (e.g., Lev. 23), here alone the date is not specified until the end (Lev. 16:29). Moreover, it is part of an appendix (16:29-34) which uses a different technical terminology than the main text—e.g., מקדש הקדש, vs. 33 (RSV "sanctuary"), for the adytum. Evidence also points to the conclusion that originally this day was an emergency rite for purging the sanctuary (e.g., 16:1-2). However, it seems likely that it was fixed as a regular purgation ritual for the temple and nation on the tenth of Tishri—the seventh month—in pre-exilic times. The requirement that the people fast and abstain from work—contained in the appendix—may have been added later, especially since Nehemiah institutes a fast on the twenty-fourth of Tishri without even mentioning the Day of Atonement (Neh. 8–9). Nevertheless, it is possible that Nehemiah omitted the Day of Atonement from his instructions, since its observance is the concern of the temple and its priests and not the people; furthermore the writing, signing, and affirmation of the pact (Neh. 9:38 [H 10:1]) would have been inappropriate on the Day of Atonement.

In conclusion: an ancient ritual for the occasional purging of the sanctuary was restructured by Israel to include the purging of the nation's sins, which then was fixed as an annual observance on the tenth of Tishri.

Bibliography. Y. Kaufmann, *The Religion of Israel* (1960), pp. 302-9; M. Noth, *Leviticus* (1965), pp. 115-22; K. Elliger, *Leviticus* (1966), pp. 200-217; J. Milgrom, "The Function of the *Ḥaṭṭa'ṯ* Sacrifice," *Tarbiz,* XL (1970), 1-8, Hebrew, and *Cult and Conscience* (1976), pp. 127-28; B. A. Levine, *In the Presence of the Lord* (1974), pp. 53-114.

J. MILGROM

AUTHORITY, BIBLICAL. *See* SCRIPTURE, AUTHORITY OF[S].

***AUTHORIZED VERSIONS.** There are various kinds and degrees of authorization, e.g., by individual denominations, by church associations, by ecclesiastics or rulers who have authority to speak for such bodies; authorization to make or revise a translation; authorization for general use such as ecumenical or private reading, study, and devotions; or authorization for official liturgical usage.

Although there is no record of the authorization of the KJV (usually designated in Britain the "Authorized Version" or "AV"), the words "Appointed to be read in Churches" could hardly have been printed on the title page without good authority. The relevant Order in Council possibly was destroyed by fire at Whitehall in 1618 (?). A resolution of Canterbury Convocation in 1899 settled any doubts about the legality of its revision, the ERV.

The RSV (1946, 1952) is a revision of the ASV, authorized by the International Council of Religious Education, in which the educational boards of forty Protestant denominations of the U.S. and Canada were associated. Publication of the RSV was authorized in 1951 by the newly formed National Council of the Churches of Christ (NCCC). Its Division of Christian Education (DCE), successor to the ICRE, holds the copyright. The RSV Apocrypha was made at the request of the General Convention of the Protestant Episcopal Church. In 1965-66 the RSV Catholic edition was published, prepared by the Catholic Biblical Association (CBA) of Great Britain, the U.S. edition carrying both a British and a U.S. imprimatur. The national episcopal conferences of Great Britain and the U.S. authorized it for liturgical use, and their actions were confirmed by the Apostolic See. In 1965 Richard Cardinal Cushing gave the imprimatur to the Oxford Annotated Bible with the Apocrypha, the first time an English translation of the Bible received both Protestant and Catholic approval for general use. Approval of the original edition of the RSV was also given by the Roman Catholic bishops of Kenya and Tanzania.

The RSV Common (Ecumenical) Bible, 1973, with an arrangement of the deuterocanonical and other apocryphal books which recognizes the variant Protestant, Catholic, and Orthodox views of the canon, was approved by the DCE of the NCCC, not to pre-empt the title, but in recognition of our common biblical heritage. It is the hope of the DCE that this may establish a pattern for other ecumenical editions. The edition was endorsed by Cardinal Koenig, Archbishop of Vienna, as President of the World Catholic Federation for the Biblical Apostolate, by the Greek Orthodox Archbishop Athenagoras II of Thyateira and all Great Britain and Exarch of the Ecumenical Patriarchate of Constantinople, by the Rev. Gerald E. Knoff, Associate General Secretary for Christian Education of the NCCC, by the Greek Orthodox Archbishop Iakovos of North and South America, and by many others.

A revision of the Challoner-Rheims New Testament (1749-63) under the patronage of the Episcopal Committee for the Confraternity of Christian Doctrine (CCD) was published in 1941. After the promulgation of the encyclical *Divino Afflante Spiritu* by Pope Pius XII in 1943, the CCD requested the CBA of America to prepare a translation from the original languages. With the collaboration of four Protestant biblical scholars, the New American Bible appeared in 1970. In 1966 the Jerusalem Bible, an English edition of La Bible de Jérusalem (1956 in one vol.), was published in Great Britain, bearing the imprimatur of John Cardinal Heenan of Westminster; it is among the versions approved for church use by the Anglican and Episcopal churches.

In 1947 a Joint Committee on the New Translation of the Bible was formed in Great Britain (*see* VERSIONS, ENGLISH[S] §1). It appointed the three panels of biblical scholars and a literary panel, which produced the NEB. The NT was published in 1961 and the complete Bible with the Apocrypha in 1970. In 1965 the Church of England officially authorized the NEB NT along with the RSV as permissible alternatives for the epistles and gospels at Holy Communion, where hitherto the AV had been prescribed. It is assumed this covers the RSV CB. The Church of England authorized the NEB NT for use in church services in 1966 and the OT and Apoc. in 1971.

The NT (2nd ed.) of Today's English Version (TEV), sponsored and published by the American Bible Society, was granted the imprimatur by Cardinal Cushing (3rd ed. granted imprimatur by the Archbishop of Hartford). The General Convention of the Protestant Episcopal Church has authorized for church use the KJV, ERV, ASV, RSV, RSV CB, JB, NAB, and TEV NT.

The story of authorized versions and authorization involves ecumenical co-operation between the Secretariat for Promoting Christian Unity and the United Bible Societies; it involves ecumenism in devotional materials; and it involves Protestants, Catholics, and Orthodox.

It has been suggested that because of the special relationship of the Jewish Publication Society to contemporary Judaism, the New Jewish Version might well be characterized as an authorized version.

See also VERSIONS, ENGLISH and VERSIONS, ENGLISH[S].

Bibliography. O. Beguin and W. M. Abbott, S. J., *Roman Catholics and the Bible* (1968); W. M. Abbott, S. J., *Roman Catholics and the Bible Societies* (1970); W. M. Abbott, "Easy Access to Sacred Scripture for All," *CBQ* (Jan. 1968), pp. 69-75; P. R. Ackroyd, "An Authoritative Version of the Bible," *ET*, LXXXIV (1974), 374-77; UBS and SPCU, *Guiding Principles for Interconfessional Cooperation in Translating the Bible* (1968); Pope Paul VI, *Dogmatic Constitution on Divine Revelation* (1968).

H. G. MAY

***AZMAVETH.** For etymology *see* DEITIES, UNDERWORLD §2*b*ii.

***BAAL (DEITY).** *See* MOT[S]; NEW YEAR[S] §1*d*; UGARIT[S] §§2, 4; ZAPHON, MOUNT[S].

***BAPTISM.** Together with SACRIFICES, water rituals are among the most widespread features of religion. The essence and function of NT baptism, as well as the problems of how it is to be properly understood and administered, are summed up in the statement "baptism . . . saves" (I Pet. 3:21; cf. Mark 16:16; Tit. 3:5; *see* SALVATION §5). How is the baptism that was practiced in the early church related to the purification and initiation rites of the NT environment, to the death and resurrection of Jesus Christ, and to the ethics, organization, and mission of the Christian community?

1. The history of baptism
   - *a.* Religious morphology
   - *b.* The OT and Judaism
   - *c.* Greek terminology
   - *d.* Descriptions and forms in the NT
2. The baptism texts of the NT
   - *a.* John's baptism
   - *b.* The baptism of Jesus
   - *c.* Baptism in Acts
   - *d.* Baptism in Pauline and Deutero-Pauline letters
   - *e.* Baptism in Hebrews and in the Johannine literature
   - *f.* Baptism in I Peter

Bibliography

1. The history of baptism. Polemical NT references to diverse "washings" (*see* BATHING) and interpretations of baptism are found in I Cor. 1:13-17; 10:2; Rom. 6:1-4; Luke 11:38-41; Matt. 3:11; 28:19; Heb. 6:2; 9:13-22; John 1:19-34, esp. vs. 25; 3:5-8, 22-26; 4:1-3; Acts 18:24–19:6.

a. Religious morphology. Ritual use of blood, fire, or water is widespread. These elements serve to consecrate things, animals, and persons. Forms of the rituals are sprinkling or pouring water on a person or object, washing, drinking, and immersing in or passing through water. In extremely dry regions the application of drops of water has highest significance. At other places springs, rivers (such as the Nile, Euphrates, Ganges, JORDAN), fountains, lakes, the sea, or specifically prepared WATER FOR IMPURITY contribute to salvation. The contact with water signifies a specific relationship to nature, history, a special community or a deity. Water ceremonies contain all features of mimetic magic. By the grace of the deity invoked, through the knowledge and administration of the ministrant, and according to the faith of those initiated, the water rites bring into effect what they symbolize, and they demonstrate what they effect. Mythical tales or songs, legends narrating the origin of the ceremony, cultic formulas, and casuistic prescriptions guard the mystery performed. Among the various significations of Near Eastern water rituals, three may have influenced early Christian baptism.

(1) Baptism is an act of purification by which trespassers against hygienic, moral, and social taboos are restored or initiated to full membership in the community and to the service of the deity.

(2) Baptism is birth out of chaos, or LIFE out of DEATH. It conveys, strengthens, or saves life by mediating wondersome participation in the life (and death) of a deity. This can be achieved and revealed by a sprinkling of drops of water (semen of a god), or by lifting out of the water (womb of a goddess).

(3) Baptism is a transition (rite of passage) from one power sphere into another. By a ritual which sometimes includes extreme dangers and rigorous tests, events such as birth, name-giving, attainment of puberty, marriage, recovered health, warfare, victory, and death are shown to be more than mere natural, secular, incidental occurrences. The ritual reveals that they stem from, and lead into, a supratemporal realm. Swallowed up by the superior order, the temporal is sacralized, made bearable, and glorified.

Beginning in the third century B.C. several Oriental mystery religions began to penetrate the Greco-Roman domain (*see* GREEK RELIGION AND PHILOSOPHY §§4, 5). In their quest for salvation the mystery communities selected or combined the elements of purification, rebirth, and deification. Their forms of initiation ranged from bloody baths to solely oral communication of secret truth. While the mystery originally consisted of the life and death of the deity itself, the emphasis eventually shifted toward personally experienced conversion. In Greek, the name of the saving ceremony was "mystery," "symbol," "tradition," "consecration," "perfection," "seal," or "enlightenment," but never "baptism." Occasionally, vicarious initiation was permitted.

From *ca.* A.D. 90, the church's liturgical and doctrinal descriptions of Christian baptism increasingly used formulas and vocabulary derived from the mysteries. But it cannot be proven that the meaning of the activity of JOHN THE BAPTIST (esp. Mark 1:4-8; Matt. 3:1-11; Luke 3:1-16; John 1:19-27) or of the Pauline, Deutero-Pauline, and Johannine utterances on baptism and rebirth (e.g., I Cor. 12:13; 15:29; John 3:5; Tit. 3:5) were determined by them.

b. The OT and Judaism. Explicit and implicit NT references to Jewish temple, synagogue, and house rituals connected with water call for a sketch of the prototypes of NT baptism in the OT, intertestamental and later Jewish literature.

i. Water is employed for purification and consecration of the priest (Exod. 29:4; 40:32; Lev. 16:4), the (priestly!) people (Exod. 19:6, 10, 14, 22; Ezek. 16:4, 9), and of individuals who have become unclean (Lev. 12–15, etc.). The water for impurity was mixed with dust and ashes (Num. 5:17-28; 19:9, 13; cf. II Kings 5:10-14). While the OT temple ceremonies are connected with the history of God and his people, they do not have the character of sacramental representation or actualization. Prophetic promises and eschatological hopes oppose or surpass the priestly practices by referring to God: *he* will cause healing and purifying water to bubble; *he* will pour it out or sprinkle with it (Isa. 1:16-18; 44:3-4; Ezek. 36:25-29; 47:1-12; Zech. 13:1; Ps. 51:7-12; cf. Isa. 52:15 [KJV]). The "clean water" to be employed by God is identified in Ezek. 36; Ps. 51 (cf. Zech. 12:10; Joel 2:28-29 [H 3:1-2]) with "a new SPIRIT," the "spirit of God," or the "HOLY SPIRIT." The NT utterances on "baptism with the (Holy) Spirit" (I Cor. 12:13; Mark 1:8; Matt. 3:11; Luke 3:16; John 1:33; Acts 1:5; 11:16; cf. John 3:5-8; 4:14; 7:37-39; 19:34; 20:22; Acts 1:5; 2:16-21, 33; 10:45; Tit. 3:5) allude to these expectations: God's promise is carried out through Jesus the Messiah. However, neither in the OT nor in the NT does purification by clean water abolish or supersede sanctification by sacrifice.

ii. Water is the symbol and instrument of death when reference is made to the DEEP, the sea, or the FLOOD. It represents life when DEW, rain, springs, or RIVERS are mentioned. In both cases the element is subjected to God's power (Ps. 74:13-15; Job 38:8-11; Gen. 1:2–2:3; 2:4-14). The creation and prehistory of all mankind, Israel's special history including its destiny to be the mediator of a covenant with the Gentiles, and the experience of the infant Moses and of Jonah all reflect in various ways salvation, despite, or through, water. Unlike second-century and later Christian liturgies and literature, the NT is reticent in referring to such stories. Only the passing through the Sea of Reeds and Noah's salvation "through water" are called "types" of baptism (I Cor. 10:2, 11; I Pet. 3:19-21). No connection is made between John's baptism and the crossing of the Jordan (Josh. 3). It is not the power inherent in water, but the coming, presence, and action of God and his Anointed which procure liberation from slavery and sin.

iii. Heterodox Jewish groups listened to the prophetic voices declaring "to obey is better than sacrifice" (I Sam. 15:22) and criticized a mechanical understanding of sacrificial cultus. In opposition to wicked priests in Jerusalem, baptismal movements originated and flourished in the Jordan valley between 200 B.C. and A.D. 300. Best known among them are the Qumran community (=the Essenes?), Josephus' teacher Bannus, John the Baptist, the Ebionites, the Elchasaites, and the Mandaeans (*see* MANDAEISM[S]). Non-Jewish, especially Persian and Gnosticizing ideas, and finally, fully developed GNOSTICISM increasingly influenced these groups. Water appeared to them cleaner than blood—a symbol more directly related to the purification of the heart. Though several baptismal groups shared ethical, eschatological, and apocalyptic traits with the PHARISEES, the orthodox rabbinate considered them heretics (*see* HERESY). Among the (Christian) Ebionites, baptism was the sacrament of forgiveness, because it quenched the fires of the idol-makers, of the sacrifices, and of God's wrath (Pseudo Clement Recognitions I, 36-39, 48; VI, 6-9; Homilies III, 19-20; XI, 21-24). Only the Mandaeans surpassed them in their enthusiastic descriptions of the effect of baptism. For most other groups, baptism was not a sacrament; it did not in and of itself save, convey the spirit, or wash away sins (Sib. Or. IV, 162-69; VIII, 315-16; IQS 3.4-12; Philo, *On Husbandry* 162, etc.; Jos. Antiq. XVIII.v.2). The dispute "over purifying" (John 3:25) and the emphasis placed in I John 5:6-8 on Jesus Christ's coming "by water and blood," not with water alone, may reflect tensions existing among baptismal doctrines of salvation. For all concerned, however, baptism signaled a way of life and meant admission to a closely knit community.

iv. The same is true of PROSELYTE baptism (*see* BAPTISM §1*a*), an official ritual with legal character established for Gentiles who, after a period of preparation, joined the Jewish faith and people. This baptism is certainly attested by the end of the first century A.D. If it existed as early as John the Baptist's public activity (*ca.* A.D. 28) and was known to him, then John's baptism of Jews (John 1:31; Acts 13:24) was an affront to Jewish self-consciousness. More likely, proselyte baptism spread only after the success of the Christian mission. Eventually, effects similar to those attributed by Gentiles to mystery cults were ascribed to proselyte baptism by rabbinic teachers. But the legal character remained paramount.

c. Greek terminology. The verb used in the NT for the act of baptizing (βαπτίζω) was well known in the literature of the period. It denoted an intensive or repeated immersion and had in most cases a metaphorical sense. A person was "baptized" with wine, sleep, or debts; also "with misery" (Isa. 21:4 LXX). Those NT passages that call the death of Jesus Christ "a baptism to be baptized with," and the pouring-out of the Spirit a "baptizing with Spirit" (Luke 12:50; Mark 10:38-39; *see* §1*bi above* for references on Spirit baptism) were self-explanatory to Greek readers, without reference to the ritual performed by John the Baptist or the church. However, three times in the LXX (IV [RSV:II] Kings 5:14; Jth. 12:7; Ecclus. 34:25) a ceremonial act of washing is denoted by the verb, and the NT builds upon these rare precedents.

The noun βάπτισμα, unlike its cognates βαπτισμός and βάπτισις, has not yet been found in pre-NT literature. Most likely the NT authors, or the traditions upon which they depended, used the uncommon term in order to distinguish the church's baptism from Greek mysteries and Jewish purifications (*see*, e.g., I Pet. 3:21 and Heb. 6:2).

d. Descriptions and forms in the NT. Speculation that the early church knew of no baptism for converted Jews or Gentiles has not proved tenable. The reconstructed sources of the Synoptic gospels, Q, and UR-MARKUS (*see* SYNOPTIC PROBLEM), as well as Paul and the diverse traditions gathered by Luke in Acts, demonstrate that baptism was practiced from the earliest days of Christianity. It must be acknowledged, however, that baptism is mentioned rather infrequently in the NT. This suggests that it did not have originally that key position in the doctrine of salvation which it later acquired when church and sacraments began to overshadow the centrality of Christ's cross and resurrection. Some scholars dispute this conclusion on the following grounds: (1) that all NT passages which speak of washing, sealing, baptism with the Spirit, circumcision of Christ, enlightenment, rebirth, blessing of children, and anointment are baptismal texts; (2) that whatever the NT says of Jesus Christ, his cross, his resurrection, justification, the Spirit, or sanctification is by implication ascribed to baptism, which then assumes the role of mediation to the mediator; (3) that every time water is mentioned, especially in the Fourth Gospel, an allusion to baptism or an interpretation of its effect is present in the text; (4) that FORM CRITICISM (of the NT) and the study of cultic traditions can uncover a large number of NT verses, sentences, pericopes or books (e.g., Rom. 10:9-10; Col. 1:12 [or 15]-20; Ephesians and I Peter as wholes) containing baptismal formulas, confessions, hymns, sermons, or exhortations (*see* LITURGICAL MATERIALS, NT[S]). However, it is safer to rely only on those NT texts that speak explicitly of "baptism" and "baptizing" in the sense of a ritual act.

The forms of baptism have probably been manifold from the start. Immersion is suggested by the literal and metaphorical meaning of the Greek verb, the formula, baptize "into" the Jordan (Mark 1:9, Gr.), the reference to "much water" (John 3:23), and the mention of "descending" and "ascending" (Acts 8:38; Mark 1:9-10; Matt. 3:13-16; Luke 3:21-22). But it is unlikely that in Jerusalem, Samaria, Damascus, Philippi, Corinth, Rome, or Asia Minor enough water was always available for a full bath. The use of the formula "buried . . . with [Christ] by [*or* in] baptism" (Rom. 6:4; Col. 2:12) does not describe the form but the meaning of the rite, because Christ was not buried in water. On the other hand, the sprinkling of our hearts and the washing of our bodies "with pure water" (Heb. 10:22) contains an allegorical interpretation of an OT ritual, not a prescription for the modality of baptism. The DIDACHE (7:1-4; *ca.* A.D. 75) grants freedom to use cold or warm, also poured-out water whenever running water is not available. What is indispensable, however, at the administration of baptism, is some clear reference to its special cause and purpose. This may be either to Jesus Christ, or to the Father, Son, and Holy Spirit. The NT speaks of baptism "into," "upon," or "in the name of." Though reference to God's "name" can mean authorization (e.g., of healing, Acts 3:6) or appropriation (Isa. 43:1; Jas. 2:7), in baptismal texts it does not mean a transfer into the possession of the Lord, an insertion into salvation history, a magical transformation, or a mystical unification with the deity. It is rather—in analogy to the Hebrew formula *qârâ beshem* (calling on the name [of the Lord]: Gen. 4:26; 12:8; 13:4, etc.)—a proclamation and invocation (cf. Acts 4:12, 17-20; 2:21). Thereby the action performed is distinguished from seemingly similar Jewish or pagan rituals.

2. The baptism texts of the NT. In the NT the meaning, nature, and effect of baptism are neither discussed (except in John 3:25) nor defined (except in I Pet. 3:21). But baptism is preached in narrative, confessional, and hortatory forms that reveal both the diversity and the unity of faith.

a. John's baptism. (*See* BAPTISM §1*b*.) The Synoptic gospels present John as a man who "preached baptism" (cf. Acts 10:37). At the "beginning of the gospel of Jesus Christ" (Mark 1:1), the "Baptist's" baptism has found an honorable place in all canonical gospels. In referring especially to Second Isaiah and apocalyptic hopes, John announced the imminent arrival of "Him who comes" to establish by judgment the kingship of God on earth. John's baptism is far from providing an asbestos suit against the threatening torrents of fire; nobody can flee from the wrath to come (Matt. 3:7; Luke 3:7). The "way of righteousness" which must be "prepared" (Matt. 3:3; 21:32) consists of people who "justify God," i.e., who confess that God is right even in his judgment (Luke 7:29; cf. Rom. 3:4). In baptism people confess their sins, hoping that God may perhaps grant them forgiveness. In Matthew's account the words "for the forgiveness of sins" are absent after the mention of repentance (Matt. 3:2; contrast Mark 1:4), but occur in the report of the Last Supper. Thus, Matthew emphasizes as much as the Fourth Gospel that the blood of Christ (Matt. 26:28), viz. the "Lamb of God" (John 1:29), takes away sin. While all synoptic descriptions of the Baptist's disciples show that a life of prayer and fasting belonged to repentance and baptism, Luke places a special accent on the new conduct of those baptized (3:10-14). Josephus (Antiq. XVIII.v.2) suppresses John's announcement of the coming Messiah; thus the Baptist becomes a superior moralist. The opposite view is offered in the Fourth Gospel; there the Baptist speaks only of the coming Messiah, and baptism "with water" offers merely the occasion for the revelation of the Messiah to Israel (1:31).

The messianic hope, the expectation of judgment by fire, the reference to a purifying spirit, the formation of a community of penitents representing the rest of Israel, the absence of a sacramentalistic understanding of the water rite, and ascetic living are among the elements which indicate an indirect rather than immediate connection between John the Baptist and the Qumran community (*see* DEAD SEA SCROLLS §5*b*; DEAD SEA SCROLLS[S] §8). But the refusal of the Baptist to receive honors as a (priestly) Messiah, the absence of legalistic traits, and the reference to the Spirit which will be poured out by the Messiah, distinguish his message from the Qumran doctrine about two (or three) messianic figures, two basic and conflicting spirits, daily baptism, and a rigorous monastic discipline. For the evangelists, the Baptist and his baptism were a preparation for the Messiah and for baptism in the name of Jesus. They were not a halfway house between OT and NT.

b. The baptism of Jesus. (*See* BAPTISM §1*c*.) In narrating Jesus' baptism, the gospels emphasize different things. In John 1:19-34; 3:22–4:3, the revelation of Jesus' identity as the Anointed One and the Lamb receives the emphasis; Jesus' baptism by John is presupposed but not mentioned. Luke (3:21-22) mentions Jesus' baptism in passing, together with his prayer. These two gospels probably combat an overestimation (proto-Ebionite or proto-Gnosticizing?) of baptism in water (cf. I John 5:6-8). In Matthew (3:13-17) a sharp dialogue between the Baptist and Jesus explains why the water rite is "fitting"; it is the first step on the way to the Cross. Being tempted by the devil is a necessary consequence of Jesus' baptism, according to the Synoptic gospels; God tests and chastizes those whom he loves. The Father, the coming Messiah (or Son), and the Spirit mentioned in the Baptist's preaching became manifest in connection with Jesus' baptism. The shorter and the longer post-Easter baptismal formulas, "in the name of Jesus Christ" and "in the name of the Father and of the Son and of the Holy Spirit" (Acts 2:38; Matt. 28:19), include an implicit reference to Jesus' baptism by John, and in I John 5:6-8 the baptism of Jesus and that performed by the church are described by the same words.

Writers in the early church, Luther, and modern form-critical experts agree in considering Jesus' baptism as the institution of the church's baptism (cf. the LORD'S SUPPER §5). Jesus' descent into the water served to publicize his identity and mission, to establish his solidarity with sinners and to manifest the freedom in which he chose obedience, that is, the way to suffering and death. The declaration of the heavenly voice and the descent of the Spirit (Mark 1:9-11; Matt. 3:13-17; Luke 3:21-22) correspond to the "justification" of the crucified one by his resurrection (cf. I Tim. 3:16). Thus Jesus' baptism can be called his ordination and Christian baptism is in substance the ordination of each Christian.

c. Baptism in Acts. In the form of narrative theology Luke presents a collection of examples illustrating the meaning and function of baptism in the early church. Presuppositions of the administration of the rite are the following: the proclamation of and faith in Jesus the Messiah, the presence and manifestation of the Spirit, the gift of repentance and forgiveness, and the gathering and confirmation of one world-wide people of God. By baptism the church acknowledges the fact that God adds members to its body. Throughout Acts opposing views and practices are faced: a learned Alexandrian Jew who was in need of "more accurate" instruction from the Bible than John the Baptist had given when he announced the "coming" Messiah (18:24-28); disciples of the Baptist who did not know of the Spirit and had not realized that implicitly the Baptist had preached the coming Jesus and had baptized in his name (19:1-6); Samaritans who believed in Jesus and were baptized in his name but had not received the Spirit (8:12-17); a Samaritan magician (SIMON MAGUS, since the second century hailed or condemned as the father of Gnosticism) who considered the laying on of hands a (sacramental) means by which the Spirit was communicated (8:9-10, 18-24); and above all, Jewish Christians, including Peter and Philip, who needed special persuasion to prevent them from hindering the admission of Gentiles to baptism (8:36; 10:1–11:18).

According to Luke, the church learns step by step and from place to place what baptism is. The Spirit is a free gift of God which now precedes, now follows, the performance of the rite. A person who asks for and accepts baptism joins in the missionary proclamation of the name of Jesus Christ, expects or acknowledges the manifest power of the Spirit, seizes the chance to repent of his sins, begs with Jewish and Gentile fellow beggars for forgiveness, and rejoices in their company. While the mention of the baptism of "households" neither proves nor disproves infant baptism, the missionary and confessional setting of the baptism stories in Acts speaks against Origen's belief that this form of baptism reaches back to the age of the apostles.

d. Baptism in the Pauline and Deutero-Pauline letters. Unlike the Baptist of the Synoptic gospels and Acts, but in agreement with the image of John presented in the Fourth Gospel, Paul does not "preach baptism." Rather, he proclaims Jesus Christ as the Lord, crucified and risen for the justification of sinners. Most of the Pauline statements on grace and justification, and also those on communion (i.e., on dying, rising, and living with Christ), contain no mention of baptism (Gal. 2:15-21; II Cor. 4–5; Rom. 1–5; 9–10). Despite certain terminological parallels, the contents of Paul's sparse references to baptism cannot compete with the promises made by mystery religions concerning unity with a deity and a guaranteed transition from mortality into new or eternal life.

In the Pauline letters intimations regarding baptism occur only in ethical contexts. Decisive elements of the life and conduct in faith are structured after the model of baptism. I Cor. 1:13-17; 10:1-13; Gal. 3:26-28; Rom. 6:1-23; Col. 2:6-15; and Eph. 4:1-6 speak of the unity of the congregation as opposed to personality cult and party strife; oppose an inflated security which builds on baptism with the Spirit and with water (I Cor. 10:2); and witness to the equal dignity of all persons in Christ, to the old Adam's condemnation and the exclusion of immoral libertinism, to liberation from cultic and ascetic legalism, and to the high calling of all Christians as expressed by their confession. According to Gal. 3:27 baptism means taking up an office —much as a high priest or a Roman official took up an official function by donning a robe. The reference to the "confession" of Timothy may contain an appeal to his baptism (I Tim. 6:12). In each case, Christians are reminded of their baptism because it is a first step on a road still to be followed, an ordination, not a "mystery" that effects and guarantees righteousness. The one mystery, wisdom, and tradition, which the apostle serves and to which he bears testimony, is Jesus Christ, i.e., his sacrifice which is accepted by God. It is the gift of the Spirit rather than baptism that evokes that faith which corresponds to God's faithfulness.

According to Paul, neither death nor resurrection with Christ occur in baptism, but we are *buried* with Christ through baptism (Rom. 6:4; Col. 2:12). The striking description of baptism as a burial seems to offer less than the mystery religions, but it reveals that in baptism God's judgment is accepted (cf. Luke 7:29); i.e., in baptism the sinner accepts execution with Christ on the cross. Baptism is, at the same time, the confession of one's hope and confidence in resurrection with Christ—hope for the resurrection on the last day as well as the confident anticipation of it in the present work of the Spirit. Paul attributes the believer's incorporation into Christ's body and the sealing for the final liberation to the Spirit's baptism and sealing (e.g., I Cor. 12:13; II Cor. 1:22; 5:5) not to the water rite. The "washing of regeneration and renewal of the Holy Spirit" through which God "saved us" (Tit. 3:5) is most likely the shedding of Christ's blood and the work of the Spirit. Similarly in John 3:3-8; 4:14; 7:37-39; 20:22, the promised water out of which one is reborn and which provides eternal life is identified only with the Spirit.

No satisfactory interpretation of I Cor. 15:29 has yet been found. In analogy to Rom. 6:1-4 this text may refer to those who with Christ have died to sin.

Col. 2:11 (cf. Eph. 2:11-16) describes Christ's death on the cross as the one, mysterious, and perfect CIRCUMCISION (of the human race), which defies representations, re-enactments, or competition by any ritual. Because the context combats a worship which extols cultic practices at the expense of faith and love, a replacement of (Jewish) circumcision by baptism cannot be intended.

e. Baptism in Hebrews and in the Johannine literature. From *ca.* A.D. 250 the exclusion of a second repentance in Heb. 6:4; 10:26; 12:17 was understood as a prohibition of a repetition of baptism. The fierce persecution of Anabaptists in the sixteenth century resulted from this interpretation of texts that do not even mention baptism. *See also* §§1*bi*, 2*b*, *d above*.

f. Baptism in I Peter. In the framework of an exhortation to bear fearless testimony to Christ in a hostile, pagan environment, I Pet. 3:21 offers a definition of baptism. "Baptism . . . now saves you, not as a removal of the filth of the flesh, but as a prayer to God for a good conscience through the resurrection of Jesus Christ" (author's trans.). The polemic strikes out against a confusion of baptism with mystery cults and, perhaps, Jewish purifications as well. Baptism is neither just an external bath nor the mysterious death of the sinner. It "saves" the way faith, confession of Christ, and prayer do—not as a magic work but as a sign of liberation and gratitude. Redemption and healing are something else; they are effected by the blood and the wounds of Christ (I Pet. 1:18-19; 2:24). Just as confession of sin (Mark 1:5; Matt. 3:6; Luke 7:29) and prayer (Luke 3:21) belonged to baptism and were its very substance, so in the spurious ending of Mark (16:16), faith and baptism are linked together. According to I Pet. 3:18-22, a confident public prayer directed to God in the name of the risen Lord corresponds to Christ's death and resurrection and with Noah's public testimony to salvation. Here baptism is explained as a petition for purification of the conscience by forgiveness and a pledge of faithful witness to God. I Pet. 3:21 offers a summary of the NT teaching on baptism and a criterion for the understanding and administration of the rite which as much as the Lord's Supper forever connects the congregation of Christians with the history, worship, and mission of the people of Israel.

See also REPENTANCE IN THE NT[S].

Bibliography. Among more general works: E. Barnikol, "Das Fehlen der Taufe in den Quellenschriften," *Wissenschaftliche Zeitschrift der Univ. Halle,* VI (1956/57), 1-18; G. R. Beasley-Murray, *Baptism in the NT* (1962); A. D. Nock, *Conversion* (1933); H. J. Schoeps, *Theologie und Geschichte des Judenchristentums* (1949); J. Thomas, *Le mouvement baptiste en Paléstine et Syrie* (1935).

Among special studies of the Qumran materials: O. Betz, "Die Proselytentaufe der Qumransekte und die Taufe im NT," *RQ,* I (1959), 213-34; H. Braun, *Qumran und das NT,* II (1966), 1-29; W. H. Brownlee, *The Meaning of the Qumran Scrolls for the Bible* (1964); M. Burrows, *More Light on the Dead Sea Scrolls* (1958).

On the Pauline texts: R. Schnackenburg, *Baptism in the Thought of St. Paul* (1950 [ET 1964]); R. C. Tannehill, *Dying and Rising with Christ,* BZNW, XXXII (1967); G. Wagner, *Pauline Baptism and Pagan Mysteries* (1962).

Other special studies: K. Aland, *Taufe und Kindertaufe* (1971); C.-M. Edsman, *Le baptême de feu,* ASNU, IX (1940); M. Eliade, *Birth and Rebirth* (1958); N. Gäumann, *Taufe und Ethik,* BEvT, XLVII (1967); O. Heggelbacher, *Die christliche Taufe als Rechtsakt nach dem Zeugnis der frühen Christenheit* (1953); J. C. Kirby, *Ephesians, Baptism and Pentecost* (1968); P. I. Lundberg, *La typologie baptismale dans l'ancienne église* (1942); W. E. Moore, "One Baptism," *NTS,* X (1964), 504-16; J. A. T. Robinson, "The One Baptism as a Category of NT Soteriology," *Twelve NT Studies,* SBT, XXXIV, 158-75.

M. BARTH

BAR KOCHBA băr kōk'bä. The leader of the Second Revolt against Rome (A.D. 132-135). Until the discovery of his letters, even his exact name was unknown to scholars. The name "Bar Kochba" (son of the star), indicating a messianic belief, has been preserved only by the church Fathers (Euseb. Hist. 4:6, 2). In Jewish sources he is called Bar (or Ben) Koziba, which may be interpreted as alluding to the word *kāzāv,* a lie. (Sanh. 93b; B.K. 97b; J.T. Ta'an. 4:8, 68d). In his personal letters discovered in the Judean Desert caves he is called "Simeon bar/ben Kosiba (h)," and it has now been confirmed that the name Simeon which appears on coins from the time of the revolt, together with the addition of the title *nasi* (head of government) of Israel, refers to Bar Kochba himself.

1. The man and the leader. Both the Christian and the Jewish sources mention that he was an aggressive, powerful, and even cruel man, who enjoyed wide support among the people and the rabbis. Many looked upon him as the Messiah of Israel. Talmudic sources record R. Akiba as having said of Bar Kochba, "This is the King Messiah" (J.T. Ta'an. 4:8; Lam. R.2:2). One well-known haggadah relates that Bar Kochba's men were initiated by having one of their fingers cut off. He was also known for his self-confidence. It is clear that some of these descriptions came from his opponents and those who were disappointed over the failure of the revolt. Some saw him as a Messiah who had failed them, while others saw him as a courageous military hero. The haggadah relates how even Hadrian admired his bravery and leadership powers: "Bar Koziba was slain and his head taken to Hadrian. 'Who killed him?' asked Hadrian. A Samaritan said: 'I killed him.' 'Bring his body to me,' he ordered. He went and found a snake encircling its neck, so he exclaimed: 'If his God had not slain him, who could have overcome him?' " (J.T. Ta'an. 4:68, 74). Christian sources tell how Bar Kochba dealt harshly with Christian Jews who did not take part in the battle against Rome.

The title *nasi* of Israel found on the coins gives us no information about Bar Kochba's administrative powers, methods of organization, or the subdivision of those territories freed from the Romans.

The discovery of documents from this period in the Judean Desert caves (*see* §4*b below*) threw much light upon the questions relating to Bar Kochba's character, and also upon the socio-economic situation in Palestine during this period. *See also* MANUSCRIPTS FROM THE JUDEAN DESERT[S] §6.

2. The historical events prior to the outbreak of the revolt. The rise of Hadrian to power in A.D. 117 brought an atmosphere of calm to the Eastern Roman Empire, for the provinces were permitted to develop according to their national desires (*see* HADRIAN[S]). As part of his plan to bring civilization to the East, Hadrian promised the Jews that Jerusalem would be returned to them, and this in turn would allow them to rebuild the temple. But as time progressed Hadrian went back on his word and decided instead to develop Jerusalem as a pagan town for reasons that may either have been purely political or were connected to his firm desire to revitalize the Hellenistic world which he so greatly admired. In frustration and disappointment, the Jewish population began to prepare for war against Rome. Secretly they built fortifications and hoarded large amounts of weapons. Dio Cassius tells how the Jews would purposely damage the weapons given to them by the Romans for mending, so that they would not be acceptable and would therefore be abandoned to the Jews. In this way they accumulated weapons without arousing the suspicion of the Emperor. After Hadrian left Palestine (A.D. 128-132) the tension grew, and the Romans were forced to bring in another legion (VIth Ferrata) and to strengthen the Xth legion with auxiliary troops from neighboring countries. When he left the East the rebellion broke out in full force and, as Dio Cassius tells us, was simultaneously accompanied by the uprisings of Jews in the eastern Diaspora. It also appears that non-Jews took part in the battle, including some of the Samaritans who previously had treated the Jews badly.

Some historians claim that, as in the days of the Great Revolt (A.D. 66-73), so now too, local rulers and even "messiahs" gained power during the initial stages of the battles, but with the continuation of the revolt the messianic image of Simeon bar Kochba rose above all others, and he was proclaimed leader. Others, however, accept the historical sources which claim that Bar Kochba stood at the head of the rebellion from the beginning. His preparations for this included the establishment of fortifications, the preparation of approach roads, the accumulation of arms, and the training of men. Messengers were also sent to encourage the Jewish communities of the Diaspora to send monetary contributions and volunteers to fight. Unlike the First Revolt, there are no signs of internal conflicts among the people, and it seems that it was this united front that allowed the rebels to put up such a fierce and stubborn fight against the Romans.

3. The revolt. The revolt began with great momentum in A.D. 132. Military service was made compulsory. Bar Kochba gained control over all Judah, including Jerusalem, and also over large sections of the rest of the country. Independent government was established in the regained territory, and Hebrew coins were minted, dated in the year of "*geulat* (the Redemption) of Israel," "*herut* (the freedom) of Israel" or "*herut* Jerusalem." Lands that had belonged to Caesar now passed into the hands of the Jewish government and were leased on Bar Kochba's behalf. Among the documents found in the Judean Desert caves that pertained to the lease of land are some that have been dated to the first year of the revolt. The Jewish authorities appear to have organized themselves with incredible speed.

The second stage of the war began with the arrival of Publius Marcellus, the governor of Syria, in command of the legions stationed there and auxiliary troops from Egypt and Arabia. The Jews had the upper hand even against such formidable forces, and the XXII Legion (Diotrajana) that came from Egypt was totally destroyed, never to be mentioned again. During this stage the rebels extended their borders to the coast.

The third, decisive, stage began with the arrival of Julius Severus, the governor of Britain, together with his troops and other legions from the area around the Danube. Twelve Roman legions took part in this stage of the war—some in their entirety and others represented only by certain detachments. In addition, many auxiliary troops were sent to back them up. The legions that fought included the Xth, VIth, XXIInd (mentioned above), the IIIrd (Cyrenaica), the IVth (Scythica), the IInd (Trajana), the Vth (Macedonica), and the XIth Legion (Claudia).

During the early stages of the battle Galilee was taken from the Jews, and the full force of the war, with all its destructiveness, moved to the Judean Hills. Slowly but surely the Jews were forced into their last stronghold, Bether, SW of Jerusalem, commanding a strategic position at the edge of a mountain range.

The war lasted three and a half years and ended with the fall of Bether in A.D. 135, after a longe siege. According to Jewish tradition, Bether was captured on the ninth of Av, the same day that both the first and second temples were destroyed. Although the revolt officially ended with the conquest of Bether and the death of Bar Kochba, the last of the rebels fled to the caves of the Judean Desert, where they continued their desperate struggle against the Romans until they too were eventually destroyed.

Dio Cassius has recorded that when addressing the Roman Senate, Hadrian did not begin with the usual phrase: "I and my army are well," a sure sign that for the Romans too this was a fierce and difficult war. Dio Cassius writes of 50 fortresses and 985 villages that were destroyed in Judah, while 580,000 people were killed. Even if these numbers are somewhat exaggerated, they still impress upon us the extent of the damage in Judah.

4. Archaeological discoveries. ***a. Coins.*** Until the 1950s the thousands of Bar Kochba coins that were uncovered provided archaeologists with the sole proof of the existence of the Second Revolt. All these coins, whether silver or copper, were struck upon originally Roman coins, and on some of them Roman heads and letters can still be seen beneath the Hebrew lettering. Chronologically the coins may be grouped into 3 types by their inscriptions: (1) "Year One of the Redemption of Israel"; (2) "Year Two of the Freedom of Israel"; (3) "The Freedom of Jerusalem" or merely "Jerusalem." It is uncertain whether this latter type was struck in Year Three, or at the beginning of the revolt. One of the letters from the Judean Desert caves, dated "The Third Year of the Freedom of Jerusalem," may possibly be proof that the rebels held Jerusalem until the third year of the revolt. Many of the coins are stamped with Bar Kochba's first name, Simeon, sometimes accompanied by his title "*nasi* of Israel." Others also bear the name "Elazar the Priest," while the symbols on the coins signify the messianic nature of the revolt and the longing for the return of a Jewish government, particularly in Jerusalem. These symbols include the façade of the temple, palm branch and citron, an oil-libation jug, a bunch of grapes, a palm tree, a vine leaf, and a holy instrument from the temple.

b. The Bar Kochba documents. At the end of 1951 some Bedouin offered to sell to an antique dealer in Jerusalem a few pieces of papyrus with Hebrew and Greek lettering. The source of these papyri was the Wadi Murabba'at in the Judean Desert about 11 miles S of Qumran. During the course of 1952 similar papyri were bought from the Bedouin, among them a letter which opened with the words "From Simeon ben Kosiba to Joshua ben Galgula and the men of the fort, Shalom!" Here for the first time the true name of Bar Kosiba was revealed, and the riddle concerning his various names was solved. It appears that his admirers such as R. Akiba called him Bar Kochba, while his opponents, particularly after his failure, changed his name to Bar Koziba.

As a result of these discoveries Israeli archaeological expeditions were organized in 1953 and 1955 to survey the caves in Naḥal Ḥever, but returned with nothing of particular interest. In 1960/61 another expedition set out to survey a row of caves in Naḥal Ḥever, Naḥal Ze'elim, and Naḥal Mishmar. In the caves of Naḥal Ḥever dozens of documents and other finds from the Bar Kochba period were discovered. Above Naḥal Ḥever the remains of two Roman camps were found, proving that even after the fall of Bether the Romans continued to pursue the Jewish rebels now hiding out in the Judean Desert. *See also* MANUSCRIPTS FROM THE JUDEAN DESERT[S] §§2*a*, *b*, 6.

c. Caves in Naḥal Ze'elim. Here too articles from the time of Bar Kochba were uncovered, including the skeletons of men, women, and children, weapons (arrows), parts of phylacteries, and papyri written in Aramaic and Greek.

d. The caves of Naḥal Ḥever—the Cave of Horrors. The name is derived from the fact that forty skeletons were found there. In addition, coins from the time of the revolt were discovered, as well as pottery, glassware, tools, and some ostraca and papyri written in Hebrew.

e. The caves of Naḥal Ḥever—the Cave of the Letters. This cave was excavated under the supervision of Yadin in 1960-61 and is particularly famous for the rich treasure of documents belonging to the Bar Kochba period. Also discovered there was bronze ware obviously taken from the Romans as booty. The human figures or images on these vessels were totally or partially defaced, thus permitting the Jews to use the ware. Glass, wooden vessels, and many household utensils were discovered, and even cloth had remained in good condition as a result of the dry climate (*see* Fig. B1). Several groups of documents were also found in this cave:

i. *The archives of Babata.* The largest collection of documents found here constituted the archives of Babata, daughter of Simeon son of Menahem. There are thirty-five documents covering the years A.D. 93-132, written in Nabatean, Aramaic, or Greek. They deal with the events in the day-to-day life of Babata and her family, and thus throw light on the socioeconomic situation in Judah and the province of Arabia at this period.

ii. *The archives of the inhabitants of En-gedi.* This is a group of six documents written mainly in Hebrew with only a few in Aramaic. Some are dated "On the 28th of Marheshvan the Third Year of Simeon ben Kosiba *nasi* of Israel" and were actually written in En-gedi. All these documents deal with administrative matters concerning various land transactions between the official administrators of Bar Kochba in En-gedi and private individuals. Through them we learn much about the organization of government in Israel during this period and now know, for example, that the lands of En-gedi were leased by Jonathan Ben *Mhnym,* the administrator of Simeon ben Kosiba, *nasi* of Israel.

f. The Bar Kochba letters. These consist of fifteen documents in Hebrew, Aramaic, and Greek; fourteen were written on papyrus and one on a wooden board. The two Greek letters were written by Bar Kochba's officials. They are all in the first person, although they were clearly written by different scribes. Most of the letters begin, "Simeon bar Kosiba to Jonathan bar Ba'ayan and Masabala bar Simeon . . ." These two men were military commanders at En-gedi. The letters deal mainly with matters concerning the supply of grain, salt, *lulab* (palm branch), *ethrog* (citron), *hadas* (myrtles), and *arava* (willow). It appears from one of the Hebrew letters that the supply situation in Bar Kochba's army was bad and that his many requests were not fulfilled by the com-

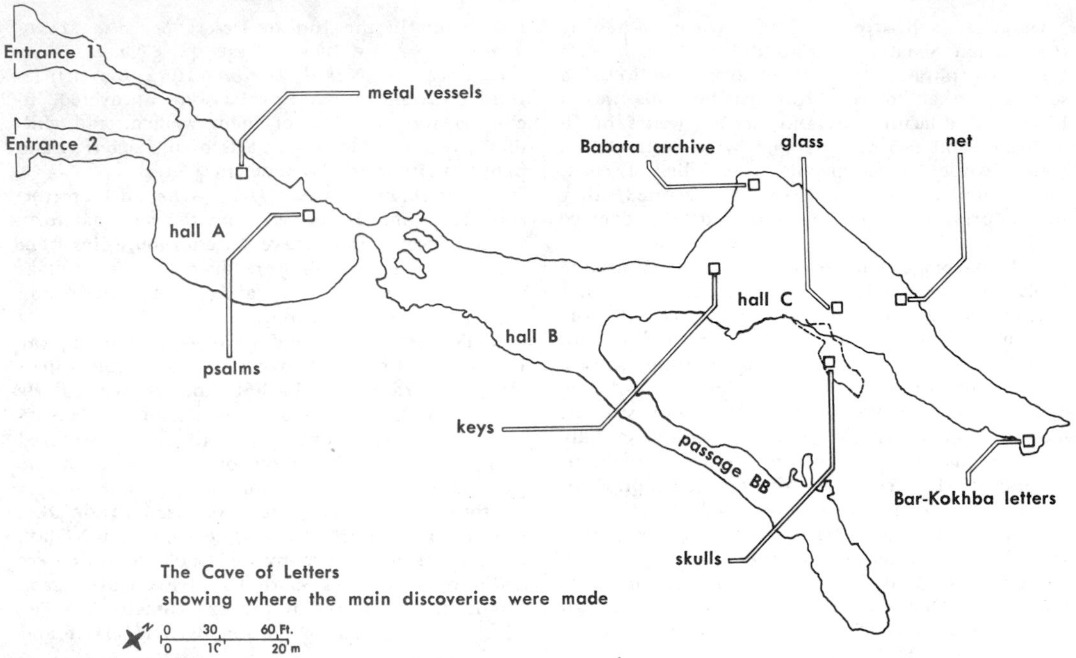

After Y. Yadin, *Bar-Kokhba*

1. The Cave of Letters, showing finds from the 1960 excavation

manders of this front: "From Simeon bar Kochba to the men of En-gedi, to Masabala and Jonathan bar Ba'ayan, peace! In comfort you sit, eat and drink from the property of the House of Israel, and care nothing for your brothers" (*see* INSCRIPTIONS, SEMITIC[S] Fig. 1). In a few letters Bar Kochba even demands the arrest of some inhabitants of En-gedi for not having fulfilled his orders.

From a document written in Greek we learn that non-Jews also served in Bar Kochba's army. This agrees with Dio Cassius, who wrote that other nations aided the Jews in their wars against Rome. A letter which is addressed to Jonathan bar Ba'ayan and Masabala informs the commanders that a man named Agrippas will be sent to them to collect the palm branches and citrons and to take them to the "camp of the Jews." Even in time of war these orthodox Jews still went out of their way to fulfill all the laws and customs of their religion (*see* MANUSCRIPTS FROM THE JUDEAN DESERT[S] §6). The letters also tell us that the men called each other "brother."

*g. **Sites connected with the revolt.*** i. *Bether* is today the Arab village *Bittir*. The hill upon which the fortress was built was naturally defendable, as it rises about 2,300 feet above sea level, is bounded on the NE and W by a deep canyon and on the S by a moat about 16 feet deep, 50 feet wide, and about 262 feet long. The fortified core spread out over 25 acres of land, but few remains can be seen on the surface today, and the site has not yet been excavated. The wall has semicircular towers. Its remains show that parts of it were built in a hurry. From aerial photographs taken of the area one can pick out a Roman wall ("circumvallatio") surrounding Bether, and Roman military camps established during the siege. The wall has a circumference of about 13,000 feet. The assault ramp that the Romans constructed to cross the moat is also clearly visible.

We learn from an inscription found near Bether that it was the Vth and the XIth Legions that camped there against the Jewish rebels.

ii. *Herodium. See* HERODIUM[S].

iii. *Qumran.* It was destroyed after the First Revolt, but finds at the site prove that even these ruins were inhabited by Bar Kochba's rebels. Many coins from this period were discovered here.

Bibliography. For detailed bibliography *see* Y. Yadin, *Bar-Kokhba* (1971).

Y. YADIN

***BARNABAS, EPISTLE OF.** *See* APOSTOLIC FATHERS [S] §1.

BASILIDES. *See* GNOSTICISM §2*d*; GNOSTICISM[S] §4*c*.

***BASTARD.** There is no clear evidence that scripture possesses any strict equivalent to this technical term.

1. New Testament. νόθος (Heb. 12:8), rendered bastard in KJV and illegitimate child in RSV, is used in contrast to the word for son. The general sense of the word is baseborn, spurious; it was used in Athenian law to designate the child of a citizen father and an alien mother, and in papyrus records to indicate half-breed animals. The latter senses of the term (or something like them) may have been intended by the author of Hebrews, especially if, as recent research has suggested, he was addressing the Samaritan community. The author's line of argument in the passage would be roughly the following: although the Samaritans are heirs to the promise made to Abraham (cf. Heb.

6: 13-20), to receive that promise they must accept suffering; if they fail to do so, they are only proving the correctness of Judahite anti-Samaritan propaganda, which insists that they are half-breeds. The Hebrew term *mamzēr* was used in the Mishnaic-Talmudic period to designate, among other things, the offspring of a Judahite mixed marriage. It is specifically said to include the offspring of unions between members of the ten tribes and the heathen nations (J.T. Yeb. 16b), and Cutheans (the Judahite term for Samaritans) are listed with *mamzērîm* in various Talmudic dicta (e.g., in J.T. Yeb. 68a).

2. Old Testament. ממזר [*mamzēr*] (Deut. 23:2 [H 23:3] and Zech. 9:6; bastard both times in KJV; so for the first in RSV, mongrel people for the second) is a term of uncertain meaning in biblical Hebrew. In the Mishnaic-Talmudic period, it meant the offspring of a forbidden union; one major tradition specified the offspring of a union punishable, according to Pentateuchal law, by death (lit. "cutting off," whence Jerome's translation of *mamzēr* as *separator*). Virtually all modern scholars, wisely refraining from too precise definition, accept some form of the Mishnaic-Talmudic understanding of the term. The rabbinic discussions of *mamzēr* are not characterized by consistency, and it is evident that the rabbis had no clear-cut traditions regarding the term (see T.B. Yeb. 49a, 44a-45a, 14a, 16a-b, 37b, 66a, 68a, 69b, 78b; T.B. Ḥor. 13a; T.B. Kid. 69a, 71a). In fact, it is possible that the term does not refer to blood descent at all. In the rabbinic discussions, attention is focused on a presumed semantic field or general area of meaning (irregular descent) and on the context of the Deuteronomic usage. Most rabbinic attempts to specify the meaning of *mamzēr* rely on exegeses of Deut. 22:30 [H 23:1], which in turn depend on attempts to harmonize that prohibition with the rest of the Pentateuchal incest laws. Now, it seems likely that a similar procedure was used to determine the presumed semantic field of *mamzēr* in prerabbinic times. Deut. 23:3 [H 23:4] refers to Ammonites and Moabites, cultural entities supposed in the Genesis narratives to be products of an incestuous union between Lot and his daughters (Gen. 19:30-38). Prerabbinic readings of the passage may well have assumed that the text of Deut. 23:2-3 [H 23:3-4] was arranged from the greater to the lesser, that is, that the prohibition of Ammonites and Moabites was only a special case of the *mamzēr* prohibition, and thus what was wrong with Ammon and Moab was wrong with *mamzērîm* in general.

Even if it is correct to reject the traditional association of biblical *mamzēr* with irregularity of descent, it is not easy to deduce the original sense of the term. The rabbis offer a clue by way of indirection: Deut. 23:1 [H 23:2] is almost never associated with Deut. 23:2 [H 23:3] in their debates (cf., however, T.B. Yeb. 75b). The parallelism of the verses may suggest, however, that they do belong together and that *mamzēr* originally designated a person with physically defective sex organs. In fact, the contrast of the two verses may suggest that Deut. 23:1 [H 23:2] refers to mutilated men unable to beget children and 23:2 [H 23:3] to those who, though mutilated, still could be fathers. The exact constitution of this group is hard to specify, but the threat of non-viral venereal and venereally transmitted diseases, some readily transmissible at birth, may be relevant.

The term is used in Zech. 9:6, but that entire oracle (vss. 1-8) is obscure and contributes little to the elucidation of the problem. It may refer to the reign of a half-breed king in Ashdod (cf. Neh. 13:23 ff. and possibly Josh. 11:22).

3. Jesus as *mamzēr*. One of the standard Jewish anti-Christian polemics of the Middle Ages, the *Toledot Ješu*, regards Jesus as a *mamzēr*. Cognate traditions specify that he was the son of a Roman soldier named Panthera, whose foreign origin made Jesus the child of a mixed marriage and thus a *mamzēr*. This tradition has roots in late antiquity. It first appears in Origen's *Contra Celsum* 1.32, in a passage containing information provided by Celsus' Jewish informant. The story is alluded to several times in the Mishnaic-Talmudic materials (T.B. Yeb. 49a-b; possibly T.B. Yom. 66d and T.B. Kallah 51a). The story was never dominant in Jewish polemic and is interesting only as a demonstration of how seriously Jews took the gospel narratives of Jesus' irregular birth.

Bibliography. §3: R. Travers Herford, *Christianity in Talmud and Midrash* (1903), pp. 43-50 and refs.

D. N. Freedman
M. P. O'Connor

***BEARD.** *See* Hair[s].

BEBAI. One of the "chiefs of the people" who joined Nehemiah in setting their seal to the covenant which the Judean people made with God (Neh. 10:15 [H 16]).

***BEEROTH.** This town could hardly have been in the N part of Benjamin's official territory since other clans, viz., Zuph, the Archites, and the Japhletites (from E to W) were there from very early times; Zuph must have included modern el-Bîreh since Ramah (Ramath-zophim) belonged to it (I Sam. 1:1, 19; 7:17; 9:5). The original Gibeonite territory must be sought in the S part of Benjamin where three of the four cities are positively identified: Gibeon, Chephirah, and Kiriath-jearim. The ancient name has been preserved at Khirbet el-Biyâr, a Roman-Byzantine ruin beside the wadi between Beit Ḥannînā and Nebī Samwîl, but the Gibeonite Beeroth was probably located on the ridge above at Khirbet el-Burj. Euseb. Onom. 48:9-10 means that the turnoff to Beeroth was seven miles from Jerusalem on the road to Nicopolis.

Bibliography. Z. Kallai-Kleinmann, "An Attempt to Determine the Location of Beeroth," *Eretz-Israel*, III (1954), 111-15, Hebrew; S. Yeivin, "The Benjaminite Settlement in the Western Part of their Territory," *IEJ*, XXI (1971), 142-44. A. F. Rainey

***BEER-SHEBA. 1. The site.** Tel Beer-sheba (Arab. Tell es-Sa ba') is situated *ca.* four miles E of the modern city of Beer-sheba. Excavations which began in 1969 have uncovered a well-planned city of the period of the united monarchy, apparently the administrative center of the Negeb. The city was built upon an artificial rampart, approximately nineteen or twenty feet high, affording both better security and an imposing view of the entire region. Although the city was quite small, no more than three acres, its defenses were of unusual strength. Two successive walls have been excavated, both of sun-dried brick with stone foundations. The earlier is a massive solid wall reinforced by a glacis; at the foot of the slope there was a deeply cut fosse. This wall, which existed throughout the tenth century (strata VI-V), was destroyed early in the ninth century and replaced by a casemate built upon the foundation of the solid wall. It was surrounded by a new and higher glacis resting on limestone revetments. The casemate existed almost two hundred years (strata III-II) and was destroyed in the eighth century.

2. The city. Beer-sheba was a well-planned city from the time of its inception. The salient feature was a street encircling the city, always equidistant from the casemate, with rows of buildings on either side. The architecture is consistently the typical "four-room house," with one broad and three long rooms divided by a row of pillars. On the SE side of the tell, two superimposed gates were discovered, belonging to the two successive walls, each containing a broad gateway flanked on either side by two gate rooms. Immediately to the right of the gate a complex of large, identical buildings was discovered, each with three long halls divided by two rows of pillars, with shelves in-between. Their contents clearly show that they were storehouses of the royal city, and strongly strengthen recent suggestions that the "Megiddo stables" were storehouses as well. The water system has been discovered in the NE section of the city, but has not been excavated. *See* MEGIDDO[S].

The Israelite city lasted only about 250 years and virtually came to an end when it was destroyed, probably by Sennacherib in 701. In the seventh century (stratum I) a retaining wall was built against the remains of the ruined casemate, but no floor levels or evidences of construction have been found. During the Persian, Hellenistic, and Roman periods the tell was the site of fortresses.

3. The altar. References by Amos (5:5; 8:14) led the excavators to assume the existence of a significant cult place in the city. But in view of Hezekiah's efforts at centralization of worship (II Kings 18:22), a cult site at Beer-sheba would probably have been destroyed. During excavation of the storehouse walls, there appeared, in a restored section of the walls, some smoothed ashlar blocks of calcareous sandstone. When removed and reassembled they were revealed to be a large horned altar (Exod. 27:2; 38:2; Amos 3:14; I Kings 1:50; 2:28). *See* ALTAR §2; Fig. B2.

4. The temples. Opposite the gate was a unique building with basements extending to bedrock and all previous strata completely absent. This suggests that this was the site of a temple which had been totally destroyed in the cultic reform of Hezekiah. The memory that the site was sacred may account for the construction of a Hellenistic temple nearby (third and second centuries B.C.).

Courtesy B. Boyd

2. Horned altar of burnt offerings from Beer-sheba, found in the 1973 season

5. The well. In front of the city gate there is a well which has already been excavated to more than sixty-five feet. Archaeologists suggest the intriguing possibility that this is the well of the partriarchal tradition. *See* PATRIARCHS[S] §1*d*.

Excavation at Tel Beer-sheba continues.

See also TEMPLES, SEMITIC[S].

Bibliography. Y. Aharoni, "Excavations at Tel Beer-sheba," *BA,* XXXV (1972), 111-27, "The Horned Altar of Beer-sheba," *BA,* XXXVII (1974), 2-6; Y. Aharoni *et al., Beer-sheba I* (1973). B. BOYD

***BELOVED DISCIPLE.** This unnamed disciple of Jesus who figures prominently in chs. 13–21 of the GOSPEL OF JOHN is identified as the author of the gospel in 21:20-24. These verses, as well as the rest of ch. 21, are almost certainly secondary in their present context, if not the product of a later hand. Other possible references to this same figure occur in 18:15 and 19:35. While 19:35-36 has been regarded as a redactional gloss, it may be a note from the evangelist referring to the authority standing behind his tradition. The other passages in which the beloved disciple figures are more integral to the gospel.

The numerous efforts to identify the beloved disciple with some historical figure began with the tradition of the early church, according to which he was John the son of Zebedee. Quite apart from the fact that no such explicit identification is made in the gospel, that tradition presents difficulties. It cannot be traced into the early part of the second century; none of the synoptic episodes involving John the son of Zebedee are found in John; and none of the specific incidents involving the beloved disciple are found in the Synoptics. Since no other identification of the beloved disciple with a single historical figure has gained wide acceptance, it has been maintained that he represents no historical personage at all, but is a purely symbolic figure. Clearly he is an idealized figure. For example, in his rivalry with Peter he seems always to have the edge. But just this depiction suggests that he was a person of some importance for the Johannine churches. Probably he was a historical figure, even though the gospel accounts of him may be largely legendary. Certainly 19:35 and 21:24 presume his actual existence. If his historicity is denied, such passages must be construed as the product either of ignorance or of intentional fabrication, and neither of these alternatives is satisfactory.

Bibliography. A. Kragerud, *Der Lieblingsjünger im Johannesevangelium* (1959); J. Roloff, "Der johanneische 'Lieblingsjünger' und der Lehrer der Gerechtigkeit," *NTS,* XV (1968/69), 129-51; R. Schnackenburg, "On the Origin of the Fourth Gospel," *Jesus and Man's Hope,* I (1970), pp. 223-46, esp. 233-43; T. Lorenzen, *Der Leiblingsjünger im Johannesevangelium,* SBS, LV (1971). D. M. SMITH

***BEN-HADAD.** At the heart of the "Ben-hadad controversy" has been the translation and meaning of the inscription on a votive stele found near Aleppo (*see* BEN-HADAD Fig. 28). It was dedicated to the Phoenician god Melqart (Milqart or Melcarth) by a certain Ben-hadad of Damascus.

H. Winckler and E. Meyer, followed by Albright, maintained that there were only two kings of Aram by the name of Ben-hadad. Scholars have recently proposed as many as four, each with different contemporaries from those Albright proposed. *See* DAMASCUS.

Using new photographs of the stele in various lightings, Cross has proposed the following reading: "The Stele which Bir-hadad, son of 'Ezer ('Iḏr) the Damascene, son of the king of Aram, set up to his lord Milqart to whom he made a vow and who heard his voice." On paleographical grounds, Cross dates the stele to the mid-ninth century B.C.; he then proposes the following chronology for the Damascus kings: Ben-hadad I (son of Ṭabrammān, *ca.* 885-870; Ben-hadad II (Hadad-'iḏr, *ca.* 870-842); Ben-hadad III (son of 'Iḏr, *ca.* 845-842—possibly co-regent ?); Hazael ("son of nobody," *ca.* 841-806); and Ben-hadad IV (Mar'ī, *ca.* 806-[?]).

If this dating is accurate, it identifies Ben-hadad II with the Adad-'idri (Hadad-'ezer) of the Assyrian annals and makes him a contemporary of King Ahab of Israel.

Bibliography. W. F. Albright, "A Votive Stele Erected by Ben-Hadad I at Damascus to the god Melcarth," *BASOR,* 87 (1942), 23-39; 90 (1943), 32-34, and "The Chronology of the Divided Monarchy of Israel," *BASOR,* 100 (1945), 16-22; B. Mazar, "The Aramean Empire and its Relations with Israel," *BA,* XXIV (1962), 98-120; H. L. Ginsberg, "Ben-Hadad," *Encyclopaedia Judaica,* IV (1971), 515-17; F. M. Cross, "The Stele Dedicated to Melcarth by Ben-Hadad of Damascus," *BASOR,* 205 (1972), 36-42. R. M. TALBERT

***BENJAMIN, BENJAMINITES. 1. The name.** Benjamin properly means "son of the South, Southerner," and seems to be a secondary formation. The gentilic forms, such as בן (ה)ימיני or בן איש ימיני (son of a man of Yamin), singular, or בני ימיני (sons of Yamin), plural, indicate an original tribal designation בני ימין (not attested). Such an analysis is supported by forms such as איש ימיני, "Yamini man, Benjaminite" (II Sam. 20:1), and ארץ ימיני, "Yamini land, land of Benjamin" (I Sam. 9:4). The name of the eponymous ancestor, Benjamin, would then be a secondary formation from an original group name, leading to the plural form בני בנימין, "Benjaminites."

2. Benjaminites and the Mari texts. The discovery in the MARI texts of a tribal confederation known as DUMU.(MEŠ)*-ya-mi-na* (and variants), "son(s) of the South, Southerners," whose members played an important role in the early second millennium, raised new questions. (The name of another confederation, the DUMU. [MEŠ]*-si-im-a-al,* "son[s] of the North, Northerners," removed any doubt about the interpretation of the name.) Initially this confederation's name was interpreted as West Semitic, viz., Benê-yamīna or Bin/Banū-yamīna, which is virtually identical with Benjamin. Some scholars saw a relationship in name only—"Southerners" being a tribal designation that could develop independently—while others, buttressed by the many parallels between Mari society and early Israel, saw the Israelite group as historically derived from the Mari confederation of the eighteenth century B.C. Further support for the derivation has been found in the Mari clan (?) name, Yariḫ (ū), associated at times with clans of the DUMU.MEŠ-yamina, which has been identified with the name of the Benjaminite city Jericho. (*See, however,* JERICHO[S] §1.) Also, of the three well-attested clans of the DUMU.MEŠ-yamina—individuals within the confederation were identified by their clan or town—*Ub/prab/p(iy)u* has been connected with RAPHA, Benjamin's fifth clan or "son"; *Yaḫurru/Yaḫruru*—probably to be identified with later *Ya'ur(r)i*—has been connected with the name of Judah's first-born "son," ER, and *Aw/mnanu* has been connected with the name of Judah's second-born "son," ONAN. But these identifications are only possibilities at best.

It now seems clear that the Mari scribes interpreted the confederation's name as either *Mār(ū)-yamīna*—reading the logogram as Akkadian, not as West Semitic—or merely Yaminites, which lessens the parallel. It is still possible that there was a relationship in more than name between the "Southerners" of Mari and Israel, but it cannot now be proven.

Bibliography. W. F. Albright, *Yahweh and the Gods of Canaan* (1968), pp. 79-80, 270; M. Astour, "Benê-Iamina et Jéricho," *Semitica,* IX (1959), 5-20; G. Dossin, "A propos du nom des Benjaminites dans les 'Archives de Mari'," *RA,* LII (1958), 60-62; J.-R. Kupper, *Les nomades en Mésopotamie au temps des rois de Mari* (1957), pp. 47-81; K.-D. Schunck, *Benjamin: Untersuchungen zur Entstehung und Geschichte eines israelitischen stammes* (1963). H. B. HUFFMON

***BESTIALITY. 1. In the Bible.** The practice of bestiality is implicitly rejected in the biblical account of the creation of Eve (Gen. 2:18-24), according to which the futile search for a fitting partner for man from among the animals, wild beasts, and birds necessitated God's creation of woman. The explicit prohibition against the copulation of human beings with any animal appears in the Covenant Code (Exod. 22:19 [H 18]), the Holiness Code (Lev. 18:23; 20:15-16) and the Deuteronomic ban (Deut. 27:21). Biblical legislation considers such unnatural couplings to be capital crimes, in which both the human being and animal are put to death. Bestiality is listed, together with incest and sodomy, among those crimes which pollute the land, causing the expulsion of its inhabitants.

2. In the ancient Near East. Aside from the biblical law corpora the only other ancient Near Eastern legal literature which deals with bestiality is that of the Hittites. The Hittite Laws distinguish between forbidden and permitted forms of bestiality. Sexual relations between a man and a cow, sheep, pig, or dog were categorized as *ḫurkel* and punishable by death (§§187, 188, 199—*ANET* [2nd ed], pp. 196-97). The Hittite term *ḫurkel,* which also designates incestuous offenses, is interpreted generally as "abomination; detestable act" (cf. Heb. *tô'ēbhâ*). Hoffner, however, cogently argues for the more restrictive meaning of "forbidden sexual combination" (cf. Heb. *tebhel*). Both the human and animal offenders were executed unless spared by the king. From the Hittite Instructions it is clear that the spared offender would nevertheless be subject to banishment. The execution of the animal alone is specified only when the act was initiated by a sexually aroused animal, in which case the human is absolved from blame. There is no indication, however, that the animal was ever spared in cases where the human offender was put to death. Sexual relations between a man and a horse or a mule were deemed permissible, entailing no punishment (§200A). The act, however, seems to have rendered the man defiled like one who had coupled with forbidden animals since both were not allowed to appear in the presence of the king. The impurity of bestiality also polluted the town of the offender so that after his death or banishment, purification rituals were performed to ensure the well-being of the community. Other Hittite rituals indicate that at a later period (fourteenth and thirteenth centuries) the human offender need not be killed or banished. By the performance of rituals in which the animal is sent forth from the town laden with the impurity of the act, the human offender could remain in his town without incurring divine wrath.

Mesopotamian references to bestiality are found in scholastic and literary texts. According to the dream omens from Susa, a man's dream of sexual relations with a bull or wild beast is interpreted as a propitious sign that his house will prosper. However, according to the omen series *shumma ālu,* the sexual advances of a dog or pig upon a woman bode ill for the land. Mesopotamian literary texts ascribe acts of bestiality to the goddess Ishtar-Inanna. The Sumerian hymn Ninegala refers to Inanna's copulation with horses. This motif is also reflected in the sixth tablet of the Gilgamesh Epic where the spurned goddess Ishtar is depicted as the wanton lover of a bird, lion, and stallion (lines 48-56; *ANET* [2nd ed.], p. 84). The assertion that the Gilgamesh Epic also refers to Enkidu's practice of bestiality before his encounter with the courtesan (tablet one) is only an assumption without explicit textual support.

Like the Mesopotamian literary references, Canaanite references to bestiality are limited to the mythological plane. The only attestations to this practice in Ugaritic literature are found in the Baal and Anath cycle describing Baal's copulation with a heifer and his fathering of a bull-calf. Such mythological references cannot be viewed as corroborating evidence for the biblical indictment against such Canaanite practice (Lev. 18:27), since mythology is not a direct reflection of human behavior. In myth, gods act at times in a manner considered criminal or immoral in human society. Furthermore, ancient conceptions of deities often blur distinctions between human and animal forms, and animals often appear in religious literature as poetic metaphors for gods. Thus the Egyptian text which describes the rape of Anath by Seth in the form of a sacred ram cannot be considered evidence for the Egyptian practice of bestiality.

3. In the Greco-Roman period. Both Christian and Jewish sources paint a dark picture of pagan morality in the Greco-Roman world. Paul's description of pagan sexual depravity (Rom. 1:24-27)

may allude to bestiality. Explicit reference is found in the Mishnaic prohibition against placing animals in inns kept by the heathen since they are suspected of intercourse with them ('A.Z. 2.1). It seems, however, that the only classic reference to the actual practice of bestiality is found in Herodotus (II.46), who, in relating that a woman from the Mendesian province had public intercourse with a he-goat, described the affair as "a monstrous thing." Other references in classic literature mention bestiality only in myths, fables, and romances. Zeus approached Leda as a swan and Persephone as a snake. Pasiphaë, wife of Minos of Crete, is said to have coupled with a bull, giving birth to Minotaur. Love scenes with animals were also represented in Greek theater, as in the pantomimus of *Pasiphaë* and Lucian's *Lucius or the Ass.* These references, however, do not attest to the common practice of bestiality among the Greeks or Romans.

Bibliography. H. A. Hoffner, "Incest, Sodomy, and Bestiality in the Ancient Near East," in *Orient and Occident,* ed. H. A. Hoffner, *AOAT,* XXII (1973), 81-90; D. Nussbaum, "The Priestly Explanation of Exile and its Bearing upon the Portrayal of the Canaanites in the Bible" (M.A. thesis, U. of Pa., 1974), pp. 35 ff.; W. A. L. Elmslie, *The Mishna on Idolatry* (1911); P. Brandt, *Sexual Life in Ancient Greece* (1953), pp. 157 ff., 504.

B. L. Eichler

BETH-EDEN. *See* Eden[S].

BETHEL-SHAREZER bĕth'əl shär ĕ'zĕr [בית-אל-שר-אצר, "May (the god) Bethel preserve the king!"]. A proper name, according to NEB Zech. 7:2. It would thus reflect a name-type common in Akkadian: (divine name)*-šar-uṣur,* e.g., Nergal-sharezer (Jer. 39:3), "May (the god) Nergal protect the king!" (*see* Bethel [Deity]). Other translations understand Bethel to be a place name: "[the people of] Bethel sent Sharezer . . ." (RSV), in which case Sharezer would be a shortened (or familiar) name (i.e., with the god name dropped), as in II Kings 19:37.

***BETH-HACCHEREM.** The site (in the abbreviated form כרם[καρεμ=vineyard]) is included in the Bethlehem district in a list of cities preserved in the LXX (Josh. 15:59). Jer. 6:1 mentions it as a stronghold S of Jerusalem. In the postexilic period it was a district capital. According to the Mishna (Midoth 3:4), the stones of the altar were brought from the Valley of Beth-haccherem. In 1QapGen. (22.13-14) the King's Valley near Jerusalem is identified with the Valley of Beth Karma (בית כרמא, the Aramaic form of Beth-haccherem). In 3Q15 Beth-haccherem is mentioned among the hiding places of treasures between "the great Naḥal" and the Pillar of Absalom near Jerusalem.

The sources define its location on a high point S of Jerusalem and in its immediate vicinity. This does not fit the commonly accepted identification with 'Ein Karem, located at a low spot W of Jerusalem. A much better suggestion is the identification with Tel Ramat Raḥel, situated on a hill between Jerusalem and Bethlehem. Five seasons of excavations there were carried out (1954, 1959-62) by a joint Israeli-Italian expedition.

Occupation commenced in the late ninth or eighth century B.C. (stratum VB) when a royal fortress was built, surrounded by private dwellings. This was probably the "House of the Vineyard" from which the name of the settlement stems. In the following level (stratum VA) one of the last kings of Judah erected an imposing palace surrounded by a lower citadel covering about five acres. Special finds included a seal impression of "Eliakim, steward of Yokhin (=Jehoiachin)." It seems probable that the palace was built by his father Jehoiakim, since it fits admirably the description in Jer. 22:13-19.

In the next settlement (stratum IVB) many seal impressions from the Persian period were found, which fits well the status of a district capital. In addition to numerous seal impressions inscribed "Yehud" (Judah) and "Jerusalem," others were stamped with the names Yehoezer and Ahzai, who were governors (and high priests?) during the fourth century B.C. After the destruction of this citadel an unwalled settlement (stratum IVA) took its place until the end of the second temple period. Later, buildings of the Xth Roman Legion were erected on the hill (stratum III), replaced in the fifth century A.D. by a church and monastery (stratum II). This is evidently the "Kathisma" church (mentioned in Byzantine sources) on the traditional resting place of Mary on her way to Bethlehem. The last occupation phase (stratum I) belongs to the early Arab period (seventh century).

Bibliography. B. Maisler, "Ramat Rahel and Khirbet Salih," *JJPES,* III (1934-35), 4-18, Hebrew; M. Stekelis, "A Jewish Tomb-Cave at Ramat Rahel," *JJPES,* III (1934-35), 19-40, Hebrew; Y. Aharoni, "Excavations at Ramath Raḥel, 1954," *IEJ,* VI (1956), 102-11, 137-57, and *Excavations at Ramat Raḥel, Seasons 1959 and 1960* (1962); *Seasons 1961 and 1962* (1964).

Y. Aharoni

***BETHLEHEM.** Minor excavations by the Franciscan Fathers in the grottoes beneath the basilica have produced evidence of Iron Age and first-century A.D. occupation, while E of the church of St. Joseph excavation has produced several deposits of Iron Age pottery. Perhaps most important has been the isolation, in 1969, of the Iron Age tell. The limits of the Iron Age occupation, while not entirely clear, appear to be on the flat surface and the slopes immediately beneath the basilica and to the E. The work was carried out by the Israel Archaeological Society.

Bethlehem appears to have been a major area of occupation from the Paleolithic period. The most recent survey is that of Stockton in 1964.

Bibliography. R. P. B. Bagatti, "Bethléem," *RB,* LXXII (1965), 270-72; S. Gutman and A. Berman, "Bethléem," *RB,* LXXVII (1970), 583-85; E. Stockton, "The Stone Age of Bethlehem," *SBFLA,* XVII (1967), 129-48.

J. B. Hennessy

***BETH-SHAN. 1. The tell.** Publications forty years after the excavations (1921-33) at Tell el-Husn, biblical Beth-shan, have elucidated important details concerning the site. Archaeological finds from the tell and from the Northern (so-called Philistine) Cemetery show that the coffin burials belong to mercenaries and dignitaries, including some Aegean or Sea Peoples in the service of Egypt (*see* BETH-SHAN Fig. 38; PHILISTINES). The pottery associated with the coffin burials can be related to the Iron I Age (level VI, which was subdivided into early and later). The early level VI was reckoned to have begun with the campaign of Ramses III into Palestine (1176 B.C.). Late level VI was considered the age of the Canaanite kings, including the time of Sea Peoples, at Beth-shan, Taanach, Megiddo, and Dor (Josh. 17:11-12). Level V was also divided into an upper and lower. Ceramic and historical research suggest that the transition from the Canaanite city (lower V) to the Israelite city (upper V) came after Shishak I (the last quarter of the tenth century B.C.). Upper level V continues to the end of the eighth century, the time of the Assyrian conquest, when biblical Beth-shan ceases to exist as an important city.

2. The outskirts. Widespread Chalcolithic settlements contemporary with basal levels XVIII-XVI of the tell have been discovered near the water sources of Beth-shan. On the strength of carbon-14 examinations these settlements are to be dated to the middle of the fourth millennium B.C.

Burials from the early sixth century B.C. add much-needed information about Beth-shan during the late Iron Age and the Persian period. These burials were found by Zori of the Department of Antiquities in 1951 inside rock-cut tombs to the E of the tell. They may possibly be related to a place of worship on top of the abandoned biblical city.

The Roman theater, which was cleared in 1961-63 by the Landscaping Commission of the Israeli Government, was erected in the time of Emperor Severus to seat eight thousand spectators. Julian the Apostate enlarged it about A.D. 360, but it went out of use in the middle of the fifth century.

Numerous fine mosaic floors of villas and monasteries attest to the prosperity of Christian Beth-shan in the fifth and sixth centuries.

In the Beth-shan area four synagogues were excavated by the Israel Department of Antiquities. Outstanding for its mosaic floor is the Judeo-Samaritan synagogue just outside Beth-shan's Byzantine city wall and adjacent to the Monastery of Holy Mary. The synagogue stood for two hundred years, but was burned down by the Byzantines after the Persian invasion, *ca.* 624. The mosaic floor depicted a complete Torah shrine flanked by Jewish ritual vessels, fruits, and the seven-branched candelabra (*see* ART, EARLY JEWISH [S] §3 and Fig. A23). In a neighboring room a Samaritan inscription which was set into the floor mentions a rural court which met there. Of great historical interest is another synagogue cleared in 1974 at Farwana just S of Beth-shan. The mosaic floor of the narthex contained the largest Hebrew inscription ever found on a mosaic, containing 29 lines, about 365 words. The inscription states halachic laws pertaining to the sabbatical year and the laws of tithing as they apply to those border areas "occupied by the returned exiles from Babylonia," which included the Beth-shan district. The site, Farwana, is believed to be the Byzantine 'Ροώβ (Rehov). The synagogue was in use during the fifth to seventh centuries and is believed to have collapsed after an earthquake. The mosaic inscriptions are partly known from the Jerusalem Talmud.

Bibliography. F. James, *The Iron Age at Beth Shan* (1966); E. Oren, *The Northern Cemetery at Beth Shan* (1973); I. Ben-Dor, *Guide to Beisan* (1943); N. Zori, "The Ancient Synagogue at Beth-Shan," *Eretz Israel,* VIII (1967), 149-67, Hebrew; F. Vitto, "Ancient Synagogue at Rehov," *'Atiqot,* VII (1974), Hebrew; F. M. Abel, *Géographie de la Palestine,* II (1938), pp. 433-44.

M. W. PRAUSNITZ

***BIBLICAL CRITICISM, OT.** During the first half of the twentieth century, the problem in biblical criticism was whether a rational textual examination such as was carried out in the areas of secular literature and history was compatible with the divine authority accorded the biblical text. The results obtained through methods called historical-critical (or philological) were such that universities in general and a great majority of the churches recognized their value. The Roman Catholic Church granted biblical criticism official status in the encyclical *Divino Afflante Spiritu* (1943). Such critical efforts illuminated the meaning of words, figures of speech, and entire books in the attempt to discover the true thought of the text and thus to resolve scholarly and confessional conflicts of interpretation. Surprisingly, however, the success of these methods did not lead to unanimously accepted conclusions.

A fundamentalist current, which still persists in diverse forms, attempts a direct encounter with God and his Word by viewing the text as an absolute *prout sonat* (exactly as it reads) without raising scholarly questions about literary genres or the history of the text and its composition.

The tentative results of biblical criticism have led to the publication of a series of nonconfessional theologies of the OT. Procksch initiated this trend, but it was the work of Eichrodt that was truly epoch-making. Like that of van Imschoot, his presentation remained rather systematic; those of Jacob and Vriezen are more thematic (*see* BIBLICAL THEOLOGY[S] §2). It is, however, the work of von Rad which paid the closest attention to historical analysis. Laurin has edited a collection of criticisms and summaries of each of these authors. Grelot and Knight preferred to deal with the OT in the light of the Christian affirmation, and indeed one may ask whether a Bible which ends with the OT provides full knowledge of a God who reveals himself in history. This issue underscores the importance of new research on the date of the closing of the canon (Sanders).

The *Theologisches Wörterbuch zum AT* follows its NT counterpart. It is a study of selected biblical terms and the evolution of their meaning from the prebiblical milieu through the time of the LXX and of the texts from Qumran. This publication has made it possible to update older typological studies by carefully avoiding any imposition of Christian notions onto the OT, a tendency for which Vischer has been criticized.

Understood in this way, the above research did not question the methods of biblical criticism. The development of the new social sciences, however, has proven more challenging, bringing their efforts to bear on language, society, and even the processes of understanding.

1. The challenge to previous biblical criticism
2. The possibility of a positive biblical criticism
3. The significance of history
4. The history of the text
Bibliography

1. The challenge to previous biblical criticism. *a*) Archaeology, without eliminating the value and necessity of literary criticism, nevertheless challenged its primacy. Biblical texts can no longer be considered as primitive forerunners of Greek culture. Rather, they must be placed in the context of the great cultures of the ancient Near East, in which WRITING had appeared at the beginning of the third millennium (Mesopotamia, Egypt, the Aegean) and which had a "classical" literature as early as the first half of the second millennium (Babylonia, Egypt, and the Hittites). Rather than developing in isolation, many of the institutions which might have been regarded as unique to Israelite civilization were thus shown to be common to the ancient Near East in the second millennium. Three major currents of OT criticism have sprung from these discoveries. One school, represented especially by Jewish authors (e.g., Kaufmann), accepted as belonging to the Mosaic age a goodly portion of the legislation which Wellhausen had attributed to the Exile or to the postexilic period. Such an early date did not necessarily include a denial of the distinctions among the DOCUMENTS J, E, D, and P. A second current, following the lead of Albright, maintains that, even while accepting the results of literary criticism and a progressive development of the Mosaic laws, the chronological sequence of the events given in the Bible retains great historical value. Finally, a third group, represented initially by Noth, remains skeptical about establishing contacts between biblical history and archaeology. De Vaux has proposed a synthesizing middle way. This has not achieved a scholarly consensus (cf. the response of Thompson).

b) Sociological analysis has proved to be a necessary supplement to research on the history of Israel. Indeed, many biblical texts cannot be understood apart from an analysis of the social situation in which they arose. *See* ISRAEL, SOCIAL AND ECONOMIC DEVELOPMENT[S].

It is possible to analyze the social structure in terms of Marxist outlines of the class struggle (cf. the notion of *'am ha'areṣ* advanced by Amusin). Attention is then focused on the polemic of preexilic prophets against the abuse of power and monopolies. Such analysis may also focus on legal texts to see if they are expressions of the ascendancy of the property owner, of a royal administration, or of a theocratic priestly power.

A more generalized sociological analysis would seek to detect the over-all structures of the society in which the people of the Bible lived. E.g., it might point out that the privileged position of men over women as found in the OT is a literary reflex of a patriarchal society. It might also study the modes of ownership and the commercial system (studies in *JESHO*). However, data with regard to ancient Palestine remain meager (cf. Baron's history).

Finally, sociological analysis may bear on the evolution of individual juridical cases, and thus show that the Torah cannot be understood as a static collection of regulations but rather reflects dynamic adaptations to new circumstances. In this case, sociological analysis complements antecedent literary analysis.

c) Since social interaction presupposes language and gives shape to speech forms, social structures and linguistic structures parallel one another (as Levy-Strauss in particular has shown for primitive societies). Structuralism first developed in linguistics, where it created a new vocabulary which literary criticism could not ignore. Rather than stressing evolution and history, structural research stresses the synchronic approach to the study of a linguistic system of phonemes, morphemes, and syntagmas. The text itself, as it stands, provides the point of departure. Greimas and Güttgemanns thus study the *semas,* or elements which make up the narrative, without reference to the author or the life situation.

It was in this manner that Leach studied Genesis as myth and that Lack studied the symbolism of the book of Isaiah (*see also* R. Barthes *et al.*). Here again, methods and analyses may differ. Lack states: "The ultimate aim of criticism is no longer to recover the intention of the author or to clarify a work through the study of its author or its milieu. . . . The functions of the imagination are governed by anthropological structures, . . . there is reason to ask whether the development of certain parts of the book of Isaiah did not proceed by following the patterns of human imagination" rather than through a historical development "that traced the object or event that is described." Others ascribe more importance to the historical process, the diachronic approach, by stressing the subsequent use of the biblical text as it grew through the redactional process in the course of Israel's history. They maintain that the patterns of the human imagination, even when they are concretely expressed in the structures and hymns of the Psalter, never account for the details of the text and provide only an initial approach to understanding it.

d) Research on the imaginative or poetic schemas (Lack, Alonso-Schökel), and on the *semas* which constitute a narrative, issues in a type of psychology. No longer is the mentality of the author at issue, but the deeper movements, which, beyond his consciousness and will, are at the source of his "statements." Understanding the Bible is viewed as dependent more on the subconscious than on the conscious reflection of the author or the reader. The name of Freud is attached to this kind of depth psychology and Freud himself produced such a study in his *Moses and Monotheism.* Others are more interested in the archetypes which underlie redaction of the texts that can be considered as myths or legends. Finally, the prophetic phenomenon can be analyzed both from a sociological and from a psychoanalytic point of view. Since not only in the Bible but also in other religions, the prophet, ecstatic or not, speaks in the name of the divine Absolute, that very notion is at stake if aspects of it spring from the unconscious. Alongside the analyses which Marx, Nietzsche, and Freud made of the notion of God, and which constitute a "hermeneutic of contestation" (Ricoeur), there is also room for philosophical analysis.

e) Philosophical problems have once again been introduced into biblical criticism. Criticism has sought to discover the meaning of texts. But what is meaning? Is it merely the relationship which exists among the elements of a discourse or does it necessarily refer to the historical life situations of the speaker or writer and of the reader or hearer? Hence the discussion of "the articulation of meaning" (Ladrière), the "parameters" of hermeneutics (Lapointe).

A second important question also arises. What is the relationship between spoken discourse and written discourse? Is writing only the fixing of the exchange of language among people, or is it programmatic, not only as an affirmation of reality, but an invitation to action? This is a fundamental question in the interpretation of juridical narratives and texts.

Does the written text possess an objectivity which can be discovered by the human mind? Or must we renounce any effort to find anything objective in history, human beings having become enclosed in their subjectivity and the historical process having brought us to the point where every text from the past is thereafter dead? Many hold the latter view. They speak of "doing history" and not of recreating historical events and personages. Nevertheless, Dilthey and Gadamer have made a major contribution which is of interest to biblical scholars because of its analysis of the subjective and objective data which have conditioned both the redaction and the reading of the text. Although every person and every text is historically conditioned, it is nevertheless possible to find some truth in spite of these contingencies. The work of Whitehead has also dealt with this problem.

Two great metaphysical problems remain, which concern the ministry more than they concern biblical exegesis. Can a book which depends upon culture or upon the culture of the time in which it was written contain eternal truth? Is it possible for us who live in time and contingency to comprehend the absolute God, who moves the world and gives it intelligibility? Criticism, for its part, may contribute to a solution of the problem by proper use of the comparative method, which, without detracting from the Bible's originality, situates it in the midst of the cultures and the human problems which it tries to express. It is along these lines that work continues on the primeval history in Genesis (Lambert and Millard), on the historical literary genres (Moscati), on prophecy (Moran, Ramlot), and especially on wisdom (Schmid).

2. The possibility of a positive biblical criticism. In spite of the chaos occasioned by previous studies which often prove contradictory (e.g., the extent of our knowledge about Moses), and despite the negativism asserted by certain methods with regard to the results of biblical criticism, it still appears possible to turn to anthropological research and thereby avoid what has been called historicism. Such historicism has given up all hope of finding in the Bible the revelatory message which Christians and Jews, and to a certain degree even Moslems, had found. Cazelles has tried to organize these methods in the third part of his *Écriture, Parole et Esprit* by dealing with the methodological "exigencies" and the "possibilities" of biblical criticism. The path has been traced with greater detail and precision by Richter. The problem is no longer to place "theology" in opposition to "criticism" but to pursue methodologically the critical operations which disengage the content from the forms in which it is expressed.

From the start, science presupposes textual criticism, whose function is not only to examine all the MS witnesses but also to explain their differences in terms of the social, historical, and psychological conditions which influenced the work of the scribes and their procedures. *See* TEXTUAL CRITICISM, OT[S].

Once the text can be viewed as established and intelligible, the literary-critical work proposed by Richter may begin. First it must be emphasized that the "literary units" are not easily perceptible to the modern reader, who is not a part of the literary world that produced the text. This point is frequently a source of misunderstanding between biblical scholars and structuralist literary critics. There is debate over the implications of doublets, repetitions, or contradictions in the narrative, and modifications in the lexemes. Some find harmony and fine writing where others discover incompatibilities and contradictions. Only by a thorough acquaintance with the vocabulary of the time and with the nuances and morphology of Hebrew syntax at different periods can the specialist discern those stylistic details which are indeed indicative of composite texts.

Once the basic unit has been established, its form must be determined. Such an analysis is of the greatest importance in order to avoid reading an ancient text with our own categories drawn from an altogether different civilization (*see* FORM CRITICISM; FORM CRITICISM[S]). Once the genre has been determined, the scope of criticism must be broadened. By comparing similar texts, it is possible to discern those elements which they have in common. Accordingly, we come to find the major literary categories in which biblical authors expressed themselves. Formerly it was customary to speak of such categories as laws, history, lyric poetry, but this classification was far too broad and did not correspond to the thought structures and to the social life of the time.

A literary genre is a function of a social relationship. Just as the structures of a society are given linguistic expression, and this expression evolves along with the structures, so the literary genres of a society depend on the functions of a group which makes use of them. The *Sitz im Leben* conditions both the communication of thought and the social life of the group. With the notion of literary genre we thus enter into the area of relationships between literature and real life, that is, the area of history. As is well known, a literary genre evolves and may lose or modify one element or another in its structure. E.g., the historical prologue in treaties of the second millennium practically disappears in the first, and the prophetic visions of an Amos are transformed into apocalyptic visions at the end of the prophetic period.

Following such a study of genres and their implications, Richter believes we can move to the study of traditions and of tradition history, while recognizing that each text does not necessarily imply the existence of a tradition (*see* TRADITION CRITICISM[S]). An anomaly in the use of a genre in a text may indicate that an extraneous element has been incorporated into the text at the time of its fixation in writing. When we are concerned with the evolution of the literary genre, it is sufficient to rely on literary data, but when we try to disengage a tradition present in a text, some nonliterary considerations are necessary, such as those drawn from geography, sociology, and general history.

The development of a legal tradition is the easiest example to grasp. With the limited means available to nineteenth-century criticism, it was possible to discern the four documents on the basis of laws relative to the sanctuary, to the clergy, and to tithes. But the evolution of a tradition (and consequently the fixing of its origin) or the additions to a text (for example, a ritual in Leviticus; cf. Koch and Elliger) cannot be objectively specified except by recourse to the social transformations which Israel underwent. On this basis it can be determined whether a law concerning the sabbath is Mosaic or whether it reflects the problems of postexilic theocracy.

3. The significance of history. Not all biblical texts are historical in the above sense, but all have a historical "coefficient," even if it is only the date of composition (or adaptation). Failure to grasp this could well falsify their interpretation; historical research is an extremely delicate task.

a) First there is the history of spectacular events, such as the fall of Jerusalem and of David's royal house. The importance of dating a text before or after the Exile has long been accepted. It is not so much a matter of knowing whether Jerusalem fell in 587 or in 586 (although even this can facilitate criticism, e.g., in the book of Jeremiah), but of knowing whether a text still presupposes a monarchic ideology.

Recent research has concentrated on the events surrounding the fall of Samaria. It seems that the fall of the kingdom of Israel, which represents the tradition of ten or eleven out of the twelve tribes, was a major event in the development of Israel's faith. The redaction of four prophetic books (Amos, Hosea, Micah, and Isaiah), some of the redactions of the Law (the Elohist text and Deuteronomy), and even redactions of the books called historical and of collections of Proverbs may well have been influenced by this major crisis. The events are numerous and critics also have at their disposal abundant extrabiblical material. This is a field of work which is developing and which allows us to discuss more precisely politics, biblical religion, and the interplay among the various parties.

b) The prophets and the authors of the Writings were not interested in events except in relation to their reverberations in the life of the people. In addition to the history of the events there must be research on the history of institutions (de Vaux) and, through them, of the social structures of Israel. Why does Deuteronomy grant a special status to judges, priest-Levites, and prophets in relation to the monarchy? Why does the Torah of Ezekiel retain only the priest and the *nāśî'*, who replaces the king of Israel? What elements of the Priestly code have survived in the texts? What is the position of the sages (*ḥᵃkhāmîm*) before and after the Exile? What is the *'am-ha'areṣ* and its relation to the court or to the sages? Does the study of the functions exercised by these public figures shed any new light on the early patristic notions of TYPOLOGY?

c) Finally, there is a third stage in historical research, which depends on the first two but is even more difficult: the investigation of the problems raised by various modes of thought in Israel. It is extremely important to distinguish between that in the Bible which springs from a transitory mentality and that which looks beyond the particular mentalities to the constants in the life of the people of God. The redaction of the Bible resulted from a dynamism which situated this book between the mentality termed "mythopoeic" (Frankfort, Jacobsen, and Irwin) and the Greco-Latin world, based on reason and law. If the redaction of the family histories of Genesis took place in a society in which dynastic legitimacy is a decisive factor in the salvation of the people, they cannot be perceived as they would be if the redaction took place in a postexilic society where the family problems of an Ezra or a Tobit have become essentially problems of fidelity to the faith of Abraham and of providing an education in this faith for an Israel which no longer enjoys political independence.

4. The history of the text. Thanks to the analysis of its literary formation, this is a primary factor in biblical criticism. Biblical criticism does not aim at identifying primitive texts by considering as secondary whatever has been added. The "secondary" is not really secondary; it constitutes the manner in which a prior stage of the biblical text has been preserved in new situations that have called forth a new stage in biblical revelation. It is the book in its completed state which can answer questions about the God of the universe, questions raised by the reader's expectations with regard to the biblical text. It is striking that what is new in the Bible does not suppress the old, even when its various redactions dissolve contradictions in terms. The beginnings of biblical criticism were disconcerting because they brought out the harshness of the text. Better knowledge of history and of the laws of language allows us to uncover the deeper meaning of the text and to rediscover all the human dimensions of the Bible. This book is composed of books written over a period of more than a millennium, in the midst of cultural transformations and the succession of empires. Each culture and empire influenced the destinies of this small people, which finally expanded into the universal church, at least for those who see in the new the fulfillment of the old. The Bible witnesses to an experience of fidelity in the midst of successive crises.

Bibliography. W. F. Albright, *From Stone Age to Christianity* (1940); L. Alonso-Schökel, *Estudios de poética hebrea* (1963); I. D. Amusin, "Narod zemli," *Vestnik Drevnei Istorii,* II[LII] (1955), pp. 14-36; S. W. Baron, *A Social and Religious History of the Jews,* 14 vols. (2nd ed., 1952); R. Barthes *et al., Structural Analysis and Biblical Exegesis* (1974); G. H. Botterweck and H. Ringgren, eds., *Theologisches Wörterbuch zum Alten Testament* (1970); W. Dilthey, *Gesammelte Schriften,* 14 vols. (1913-67); W. Eichrodt, *Theology of the OT,* 2 vols, (1961, 1967); K. Elliger, *Leviticus,* in *Handbuch zum AT,* IV (1966), 5-402; H. Frankfort *et al., The Intellectual Adventure of Ancient Man* (1946); S. Freud, *Moses and Monotheism* (1949); H. G. Gadamer, *Wahrheit und Methode* (1060); P. Grelot, *Sens chrétien de l'Ancien Testament* (1962); A. J. Greimas, *Sémantique structurale* (1966); E. Güttgemanns, *Offene Fragen zur Formgeschichte des Evangeliums* (2nd ed., 1971); P. van Imschoot, *Theology of the OT,* I (1965); E. Jacob, *Theology of the OT* (1958); Y. Kaufmann, *The Religion of Israel* (1960); G. A. F. Knight, *A Christian Theology of the OT* (1959); K. Koch, *Die Priesterschrift von Exodus 26 bis Leviticus 16* (1959); J. Ladière, *Language and Belief* (1972); R. Lack, *La symbolique du livre d'Isaïe* (1973); W. G. Lambert and A. R. Millard, *Atra-Ḫasis: The Babylonian Story of the Flood* (1969); R. Lapointe, *Les trois dimensions de l'herméneutique* (1967); R. B. Laurin, *Contemporary OT Theologians* (1970); E. Leach, *Genesis as Myth & Other Essays* (1969); C. Levy-Strauss, *Structural Anthropology* (1963); W. L. Moran, "New Evidence from Mari on the History of Prophecy," *Bibl.,* L (1969) 15-56; M. Noth, *The History of Israel* (2nd ed., 1960); Pius XII, *Divino Afflante Spiritu* (1943); O. Procksch, *Theology of the OT* (1949); G. von Rad, *OT Theology,* 2 vols. (1962, 1965); W. Richter, *Exegese als Literatur Wissenschaft* (1971); P. Ricoeur, *The Conflict of Interpretations* (1974); J. C. Rylaarsdam, ed., *Transitions in Biblical Scholarship* (1968); J. A. Sanders, "Cave 11 Surprises and the Question of Canon," *McCormick Quarterly,* XXI (1969), 284-98; T. L. Thompson, *The Historicity of the Patriachal Narratives* (1974); R. de Vaux, *Histoire ancienne d'Israël* (1972), "Method in the Study of Early Hebrew History," in *The Bible in Modern Scholarship,* ed. J. P. Hyatt (1965); W. Vischer, *The Witness of the OT to Christ* (1949); T. Vriezen, *Outline of OT Theology* (1958); J. M. Robinson and J. E. Cobb, eds., *New Frontiers in Theology* (1963). H. CAZELLES

***BIBLICAL CRITICISM, NT. 1. Text of the NT.** For a discussion of the methodological problems *see* TEXTUAL CRITICISM, NT[S], and for recent developments in the establishing of an actual critical text of the NT *see* TEXT, NT[S].

2. Literary criticism. For nearly a century LITERARY CRITICISM was employed primarily in the attempt to uncover the literary relationships among the Synoptic gospels. Recently, NT criticism has begun to raise broad literary questions concerning the NT writings. Pre-eminent among these is the question of literary genre (*see* §2*a below*). In this and other respects the literary criticism of the NT has been influenced by techniques employed in the study of other kinds of literature (*see* LITERATURE, BIBLE AS[S]). Moreover, continuing efforts toward identification of poetic and especially hymnic fragments have opened up new perspectives on the cultic and confessional aspects of early Christian faith and life (*see* LITURGICAL MATERIALS, NT[S]).

Among those engaged in literary criticism of the NT, there is a wide difference of opinion concerning the relationship of that enterprise to historical criticism. For some, literary analysis and interpretation can be carried on only in conjunction with historical criticism, which seeks to recover the life-situation, in its social, political, economic, and cultural dimensions, in which the writing was produced. Only then, it is maintained, can the intention of the author be discerned and a valid interpretation be achieved (Hirsch). Others, influenced by structuralism, assert that historical development cannot be traced in literature, that the deep structure in the mind of the author, which, consciously or unconsciously, shaped his writing, may be discovered by a method which examines the work with a view simultaneously to literary paradigms and to the sequential development of the plot or narrative. Analyses carried out along structuralist lines run the danger of highly subjective, generalized interpretive results, and the antihistorical bias implied in this approach runs counter to the NT emphasis on the incarnational, once-for-all quality of revelation.

a. The gospel as a genre. The genre question involves the study of the NT against the background of other literature—pagan and Jewish, Hellenistic and rabbinic, sophisticated and unpretentious. While it has been raised with respect to various literary types (*see* ACTS, GENRE[S]; APOCALYPSE, GENRE[S]) it has been debated most of all with relation to the NT gospels (*see* GOSPEL, GENRE[S]). The later development of the gospel tradition both in its narrative and sayings aspects is also being given more attention, due in part to newly discovered writings (*see* §3 *below*) that belong to what is loosely called the NT APOCRYPHA. The study of this literature has raised anew the issue of the NT canon: Which of the variety of viewpoints contained in the NT and the noncanonical Christian literature of the first several centuries have theological validity for the church? The effective extension of the literature of the early church has theological implications for the subject of Christian origins. *See* LITERATURE, EARLY CHRISTIAN[S].

b. Letters. A lively interest has also been shown in the structural and formal characteristics of the NT (especially Pauline) letters, and the relation of these to other types of ancient letters (*see* LETTER[S]). Special attention has also been given to allegedly Gnostic and "early catholic" elements in the Pauline letters, as well as to certain false Christologies which are seen by some to have set the Pauline Spirit-led community of grace over against the more rigid doctrinal structures of Paul's alleged opponents. While some attempts to identify Paul's opponents or the false Christologies are more ingenious than convincing, the availability of previously unknown Gnostic documents from the second and third centuries brings some control over the reconstruction of the evolution of GNOSTICISM and the assessment of its probable relation to Pauline thought. *See* PAUL THE APOSTLE[S] §1*b*, *d*.

c. The evangelists as authors and theologians. The older form-critical view of the gospel writers as editors has been largely and rightly discredited in favor of a recognition of the creative ways in which each of them has adapted and shaped his material to meet the special needs of his own community (*see* REDACTION CRITICISM, NT[S]; supplementary articles on each of the gospels and the book of Acts). The Q document (*see* Q and Q[S]) has also been given special analysis, theologically and in terms of its community setting, although some have questioned not only the existence of this hypothetical source for the gospels, but also the priority of Mark (*see* SYNOPTIC PROBLEM[S]). The "two-source hypothesis" prevails nevertheless and has served as a basis for the literary, form-critical, and theological analyses of the Synoptic gospels.

3. New sources from the NT period. Over the years since their discovery it has become increasingly apparent that the DEAD SEA SCROLLS will require the rewriting of the history of Palestinian Judaism in the post-Maccabean period. These sources provide many details about the interpretation of scripture, the range and types of biblical text then in use, the nature of the eschatological expectations, and the diversity of redemptive figures awaited by Jews in that epoch.

The Coptic Gnostic Library found in Egypt at NAG HAMMADI has provided other important new sources. These are valuable for documenting the range and development of Gnosticism, which became a parasite upon and a threat to the early church. Still unanswered is the question about the origins of Gnosticism; that Gnosticism was a pathological growth on a Christianity whose expectations of an imminent eschaton had been frustrated is called into question by the presence in these new documents of elements which seem to have roots in neither Judaism nor earliest Christianity.

Finally, excavation at several Palestinian sites—especially in Galilee (*see* CAPERNAUM[S]), Samaria (*see* GERIZIM, MOUNT[S]), in the Decapolis (*see* PELLA OF THE DECAPOLIS[S]) and at Caesarea (*see* CAESAREA[S])—is requiring a basic reconsideration of the extent of penetration of Hellenistic culture into these regions by the NT period. The use of Greek inscriptions and Hellenistic symbols and decorative modes in synagogues there, as well as the many Hellenistic artifacts discovered at Palestinian sites from the early imperial times (*see* ART, EARLY JEWISH[S] esp. §§1, 4), show that Galilee was by no means the backwash of pure Jewishness that has often been pictured (*see* HELLENISM[S] §2). The discovery of a letter by the supernationalist Bar Kochba (*see* BAR KOCHBA[S] §4*b*), written in Greek, offers dramatic evidence of the impact of Hellenistic culture on the most ardent defenders of Jewish separateness.

4. The history of primitive Christianity. *a. Diversity within early Christianity.* The newly discovered documents and archaeological remains require a reconsideration of the classic scholarly reconstructions of the Greco-Roman world in the NT period, and hence of the cultural and conceptual influences which helped to shape early Christianity. Rabbinic scholars have cautioned against reading the post–A.D. 70 conditions back into the prior period: after the triumph of the predominantly Pharisaic point of view, following the destruction of the temple and the stamping out of the revolutionary nationalist movement, the traditions preserved by the rabbis largely reflect their own point of view, and are therefore a precarious base for reconstructing the religious situation in Palestine in the time of Jesus (*see* PHARISEES [S]). Similarly, the pro-Pauline bias of much nineteenth-century Protestant critical scholarship led to an unduly unified and one-sided picture of early Christianity. And the drive to discover unity lying behind the diversities of the NT, as symbolized by the popularity of the concept of *kerygma* in the middle decades of the present century, has rightly given way to a recognition of the local, and in some instances, fundamental differences in outlook that characterized the early church virtually from the outset. The very fact that the later writings of the NT, especially Acts and the Pastorals, are seeking to impose a unity or to depict one as operative since the days of the apostles—in spite of evident sharp divergences of viewpoints—implies that the concept of common authority was being fostered in the attempt to bring theological and organizational unity into a thoroughly diverse situation. "Early catholicism" may be anathema to a modern devotee of the Pauline Spirit-led, law-free gospel, but it was likely a practical necessity if the ancient church was to survive. As it moved into a new era of visibility and of cultural and geographical penetration, it could not survive hostility from Jewish opponents and from the secular authorities without some functional unity as a common front against its enemies.

The praise of and regulations for itinerant, charismatic leaders of the church in Mark and Q are a far cry from the appeals for unity and order or for recognition of established authorities that are represented in Acts and Ephesians.

b. Christology. The question of the origin of the SON OF MAN concept has remained unresolved. Discovery of portions of the book of Enoch (*see* ENOCH, BOOK OF; ENOCH, BOOK OF[S]) at Qumran raised hopes that at least fragments of that section known as the Similitudes would be found, thus demonstrating the pre-Christian, Palestinian origin of the Son of man concept. But since parts of all sections of the Ethiopic Enoch literature have been found there except the Similitudes, there is only negative evidence, and that is not decisive. Sections of the TESTAMENTS OF THE TWELVE PATRIARCHS and the book of Jubilees (*see* JUBILEES, BOOK OF) have been recovered from Qumran, so that their origin or at least use within sectarian Judaism in the time of Jesus is now confirmed, and thus their christological views may be presupposed for the early understanding of Jesus' eschatological-redemptive role. *See* CHRISTOLOGY IN THE NT[S].

c. The historical Jesus question. The failure to achieve clear results in the so-called new quest of the historical Jesus has resulted in a scaling down of critical expectations. While there are those who think that by the principle of discontinuity (whatever cannot be attributed to his Jewish contemporaries or assigned to the early church may be assumed to go back to Jesus himself) the authenticity of some of the sayings material can be established, much of the recent work on the gospels is concerned rather with seeking to trace the tradition's development: from oral or earlier written forms (such as miracle cycles), through the stages of combination to the present diverse forms of the gospels as we have them. The continuum is the dynamic of the tradition; the variables are the aims and needs of the communities in whose interests the gospels were composed.

While the principle of discontinuity seeks to justify itself on the ground of objectivity, its result is to detach Jesus from his historical context by making him less of a Jew than we have any evidence to suspect that he was. Recent studies, such as that by Hengel (*see bibliog.*), have shown how much more diverse Judaism was in the time of Jesus than the handbooks on the Jews in NT times have indicated. The diversity and vitality of sectarian Judaism in the period offers new possibilities for viewing Jesus and the early Christians as they identified with and distanced themselves from various aspects of the Jewish tradition in their time.

In this connection, increasing attention is being given to the social setting of early Christianity, to the differences in the shaping of the early Christian ethical, narrative, cultic, and organizational traditions. FORM CRITICISM has made an enduring contribution to NT interpretation by its focus on the forms in which oral tradition is transmitted and the stages by which it is fixed in written form. Perhaps NT criticism will now come around to fulfilling the other half of the task set by the form critics: analyzing the dynamics of the societies, primitive and relatively sophisticated, in which the traditions were preserved and adapted. *See* ETHOS OF EARLY CHRISTIANITY[S] esp. §2; JUDAISM, EARLY RABBINIC[S]; JUDAISM, HELLENISTIC[S].

Bibliography. W. G. Kümmel, *The NT: The History of the Investigation of its Problems* (2nd ed., 1970), traces the historical development of NT criticism; and his *Introduction to the NT* (17th ed., 1975) provides extensive bibliog. on specific subjects. See also the bibliographies for articles which have been cross-referenced.

Studies: E. Käsemann, *NT Questions of Today* (3rd ed., 1965); D. O. Via, *Kerygma and Comedy in the NT* (1975); E. D. Hirsch, *Validity in Interpretation* (1967); M. Hengel, *Judaism and Hellenism,* 2 vols. (2nd ed., 1973); H. Koester, "NT Introduction: A Critique of a Discipline," in *Christianity, Judaism and Other Greco-Roman Cults,* ed. J. Neusner (1975), pp. 1-20.

H. C. KEE

***BIBLICAL THEOLOGY.** In the years since the original edition of this dictionary no subject has undergone greater convulsions or suffered greater changes in its status than biblical theology. When the articles by Stendahl and Betz in that edition were being written, biblical theology stood at its highest point of prestige and influence. Many expected that it would be an immensely reintegrating factor in the total theological enterprise; and in ecumenical study it was supposed that biblical theology could overcome the divisions between the churches, divisions caused by the nonbiblical elements in the tradition of each. There was indeed doubt and disagreement about the way in which biblical theology might be carried on, and this is evident in these articles themselves; but they betray no awareness of the massive criticisms that were soon to fall upon the entire subject as it then stood. For, by the time these articles were published, the tide was already turning; as Childs puts it (p. 87): "The Biblical Theology movement underwent a period of slow dissolution beginning in the late fifties. The breakdown resulted from pressure from inside and outside the movement that brought it to a virtual end as a major force in American theology in the early sixties."

However, we must also distinguish between two senses of the term "biblical theology." In the first sense, as quoted above, it designates a movement, a movement which for a time held considerable sway in theological thinking and in the life of the churches. But it is possible, and even necessary, to think not of a movement but rather of the wealth of individual studies that were produced, such as theologies of the OT and NT and depth studies of particular strata and concepts. The two senses cannot be strictly separated, but some such rough distinction seems necessary: (a) in some languages, such as German, the term "biblical theology" was used in the latter sense rather than the former, and this has caused some terminological misunderstandings; (b) the collapse which in the end overtook the movement of biblical theology did not in the same way affect all the work done in a host of individual studies; (c) just because these individual studies often differed from, or even questioned, the emphases which were characteristic of biblical theology as a movement, the resulting tensions may have been a factor in bringing about that collapse.

This article will look first at biblical theology as a movement in the postwar era and consider its decline; it will then go on to look at the individual studies and themes which were associated with it, and to consider some recent developments.

1. Biblical theology as a movement
   a. Characteristics
   b. Assessment
   c. Decline
2. Theologies of the OT and the NT
3. Bultmann
4. Stendahl
5. Language and semantics
6. Hermeneutics and presuppositions
7. Von Rad
8. Revelation in history
9. The unity and distinctiveness of the Bible; its "center"
10. OT and NT
11. The late OT period and postbiblical Judaism
12. The history of religion
13. Biblical theology and the canon of scripture
14. Conclusion

Bibliography

1. Biblical theology as a movement. ***a. Characteristics.*** The rise, the character, and the eventual decline of the biblical theology movement on the American scene has been vividly and accurately described by Childs in his first four chapters. He exaggerates, however, the degree to which the movement was distinctively American: in Great Britain and on the Continent the same broad tendencies existed, although the setting was different. The movement can be well seen in the organized study programs of the international ecumenical movement. The term "biblical theology" was not one invented afterward, or one used against the movement by its critics; it was so called by its practitioners at the time, at least in the English-speaking world.

Common to the entire movement was a strong reaction against the way in which the Bible had been studied under the "liberal" theology, with its dry historical exegesis, its analytic tendency and dependence on source criticism, its tendency to understand biblical material in terms drawn from the environing culture, its evolutionism, its complacently universal theological positions, and its lack of theological concern and existential fervor. Thus the positive position of the biblical theology movement included the following characteristic features:

i. An opposition to the influence of philosophy and philosophical theology. Biblical thought was constantly contrasted with philosophical modes of thinking.

ii. An opposition to what was understood to be the systematizing tendency of dogmatic theology. Biblical thought, it was said, was a living organism which could not be reduced to a system.

iii. A contrast between Hebrew and Greek thought. The Bible was animated by the distinctively Hebrew way of thinking, which had been distorted in much later theology through its adoption of Greek categories.

iv. An emphasis on the unity of the Bible, and in particular the belonging together of OT and NT. It was essential that the NT be interpreted in the Hebrew categories deriving from the OT, and not in the Greek categories of its own environment.

v. An approach to biblical language in which word studies were much emphasized. It was hoped to see the outlines of Hebrew thought reflected in the words of the Hebrew language, while Greek words also, when they came to be used in Christian writing, were thought to take on Hebraic content and to mirror the Jewish-Christian thought patterns.

vi. An emphasis on the distinctiveness of the Bible as against its environment. This was correlative with the unity of the Bible: as the Bible was seen to be an essential unity, so its complete distinctiveness in comparison with other cultures and their religions became clear. Such similarities and parallels as existed were only isolated and partial phenomena. When seen as wholes, the Bible (whether in OT or NT) and its environing cultures were almost totally different.

vii. An emphasis on revelation in history, which fits in with and embodies all of the above. Revelation through history was thought to be characteristic of Hebrew thought, unknown to the Greeks and to the extrabiblical world, common to the entire Bible and the basis of its inner unity, unintelligible to philosophy, and poorly appreciated by dogmatics.

viii. The interpenetration of biblical study and theological concern. As the work of the biblical scholar was to be informed at all stages by a theological consciousness, so the work of theology was to be informed by a biblical consciousness. This biblical-theological concern should have an existential care for the life of the churches and should express itself naturally in an interest in preaching.

b. Assessment. It is thus proper to see the biblical theology movement (in the period, say, 1945-60) as the biblical companion and parallel to the neo-orthodox movement in general theology. This does not mean that the biblical theologians shared the precise opinions of the neo-orthodox dogmaticians; for the most part the overlap was only partial. Biblical theologians in general did not have the massive understanding of theological and philosophical problems found in a man like Barth, nor did they share his deep concern for the whole tradition of theology. Nevertheless, their work, though carried out with different materials and on another level, represented a pressure in the same general direction as neo-orthodox theology.

Biblical theology in this sense was the intellectual side of a more general religious reaction. Its strength and its (temporary) success came from a grassroots reaction against the liberal theology and its use of the Bible; but this converged with factors that belonged to the occupational specialization of biblical scholars and ministers. Thus the suspicion of philosophy, though formally shared with Barth, came also in part from a certain Philistinism, compounded at a higher level with the wish of the technical biblical scholar to control his own material without interference from other disciplines. The hostility to Greek thought arose in part from ignorance of it: biblical theology made little deep analysis of Greek thought and worked mostly with cheap stereotypes of it. The suspicion of system and of systematic theology was on one side a typical pietistic reaction; on the other it was an amusing illusion, for opposition to system, far from being a mark of difference from dogmatic theology, was a mark of convergence with it, since dogmaticians were saying the same thing. There was a practical side also to the word-study method in biblical language, for it seemed to provide a way in which Hebrew and Greek words could be used in sermons and arguments by ministers and theologians whose ability to handle actual texts in these languages was exiguous. Some other supporting factors were not in fact religious: for instance, the opposition to evolutionism and the emphasis on seeing cultures and religions as wholes had been operative in social studies for some time.

c. Decline. The causes of the decline of the movement in this form are complex; some of them will be mentioned in the following sections. In many of its aims biblical theology seemed in the end to have failed. Both philosophical theology and the history of religions, which the movement had sought to make peripheral, emerged stronger than they had been before. The authority and relevance of scripture (*see* SCRIPTURE, AUTHORITY OF[S]) came under more radical attack than before, and the younger generation seemed unmoved by the typical biblical theology arguments. The end of the biblical theology movement seemed to leave many with the opinion that the Bible was just not very important, and a feeling of apathy about biblical study was widely observed. This was worse than things had been under the liberal theology. Paradoxically, it was liberalism that had handed to biblical theology much of its necessary equipment: knowledge of languages, thorough commentaries, historical analysis, an apparatus for understanding the environment of the Bible. It seemed doubtful whether biblical theology would leave so solid a legacy to the next stage of study.

2. Theologies of the OT and the NT. The actual theologies of OT and NT took a line somewhat different from that of the biblical theology movement as outlined above. In a very general sense they might lead in the same direction but they did not press the same arguments and methods so hard. The opposition to philosophy, to system, to Greek thought, might come in occasionally, but was not the stuff of which an entire theology of OT or NT could be built. OT theologies often professed an aim of building a connection with the NT and thus saying something about the unity of the Bible, but in fact this did not occupy the main effort of any of them; and most NT theologies paid even less attention to the OT.

Among the theologies written, those which most expressed the ethos of the biblical theology movement were those of Knight for OT and of Richardson for NT, and neither of these counted among the strongest of the theologies. Of those published, some took up a position of more straightforward historical (Jeremias) or phenomenological (Eichrodt, Jacob) character, which fitted ill with the prevailing anti-objectivist and commitment-oriented mood of the movement. Von Rad's theology denied that there was one single theology of the OT and maintained that it contained a number of quite different theologies. These massive works, many of which displayed scholarly grasp and comprehension much superior to the thinking of the biblical theology movement in the more general sense, fitted only in part with its ethos; this discrepancy was a factor in its decline.

3. Bultmann. Although he belonged to an older theological generation, Bultmann had much effect on biblical theology during our period. It is clear that he did not fit with the pattern of the biblical theology movement. Only certain elements of his thinking—e.g., his antiliberal position, his existential fervor, his avoidance of system and dislike of objectivization—were congenial to it; in other respects the movement could hardly claim his adherence. Bultmann was deeply anchored in the history-of-religions approach; his exegesis remained finely analytic; his view of the importance of the OT, though not as negative as has sometimes been alleged, was distinctly cool, and thus neither Hebrew thought nor the unity of the Bible was important to him. Nor was revelation in history, in the sense dear to the biblical theology movement, essential to his thought. To him the "historical" events of the biblical story, being miraculous, were largely myth, and the true emphasis lay on the historical "existence" of the believer. Biblical theologians mostly agreed that some kind of reinterpretation of the Bible was necessary in order to communicate with modern man, but not many accepted Bultmann's full demythologization program or his confidence in Heidegger's philosophy as the vehicle for the understanding of the gospel. Thus, though Bultmann had always been mentioned in connection with biblical theology, as the impact of his thinking became clearer it created increasing difficulties for the latter in its current form, and many biblical theologians became strong opponents of his position. In ecumenical study the voice of the Bultmannians had at first not been much heard, but after 1960 their increasing influence in that quarter tended to break down the dominance of biblical theology.

4. Stendahl. We can now better understand Stendahl's article in the first edition of this dictionary, which achieved just renown. Biblical theology, as he conceived it, had two great stages. The first was a descriptive task: to carry out an objective, historical description of the theology which lay within the Bible itself. The second was a hermeneutic task, through which a "translation" of the biblical thoughts into the modern situation was to be attempted. It was essential to keep the two apart, to distinguish between "what it meant" and "what it means." Again, the descriptive task and the work of systematic theology were clearly distinct operations. The Bible, as the "original," cannot act creatively upon the theologian unless its meaning in its own setting is strictly held apart from later problems and later interpretations.

Stendahl's article was thus quite unrepresentative of what was then generally going on under the name of biblical theology: it was a program of what he would have liked to have been done, rather than a statement of what was being done. The high value attached to objectivity in description, the strict separation between description and systematic theology, and the critical attitude toward dumping Semitic or Hebrew categories in the lap of the twentieth century—all these were quite the reverse of the positions then generally esteemed as biblical theology. It is not so clear, however, that the article was deliberately *intended* as an attack on the contemporary movement: there is little sign of this in the wording, and many aspects of that movement—the unity of the Bible, revelation in history, the importance of using only biblical categories—are still represented within it. Only with hindsight may we suppose that it "struck a blow at the very heart of the movement, as it was originally conceived" (Childs, p. 79, cf. p. 26).

Thus, paradoxically, in our original edition the flavor of biblical theology as it then was is exhibited less by Stendahl than by Betz (*see* BIBLICAL THEOLOGY, HISTORY OF, esp. §5).

5. Language and semantics. The status of biblical theology was deeply affected by criticism of its use of linguistic evidence. Barr's critique of the use of Hebrew and Greek words (1961-62) was not an attack on biblical theology in itself; he maintained that biblical theology had encouraged the misuse of linguistic evidence, but not that it necessarily depended on such misuse. It was possible that the positions criticized might have been supported on other grounds, even if the linguistic arguments used in their favor were faulty. But the question remained: would they ever have been believed, if the linguistic arguments had not been there? As we see it now, the situation was something like this: biblical theology had a point of view, but did it have a *method,* a scientific method of its own in handling the detailed facts of the Bible, a method which would be as characteristic of it as source analysis had been characteristic of the liberal approach and which would produce equally stable results? Its word studies and linguistic arguments were the nearest that the biblical theology movement came to possessing a scientific method of its own; and with the sudden sharp loss of this method the power and viability of biblical theology were greatly reduced.

The critique certainly had great effect. The production of word studies abruptly dropped. Though new theological dictionaries have been started (two in the OT field), these, far from reiterating the philosophy on which the Kittel *TWNT* was based, have made clear this determination to avoid misuses of linguistic evidence. The Kittel dictionary has continued to its completion, but few will now use it with the same expectations in mind that were common, and were encouraged, before 1961. Attempts to defend the dictionary by saying that the critique affected only some of the weaker articles cannot be accepted; on the contrary, it aimed squarely at the basic philosophy of the work and drew illustrations from many parts. There would have been no difficulty in extending it to cover later and major articles, except insofar as the later articles had themselves come to ignore the express philosophy of the work. It was with this philosophy that the biblical theology movement largely aligned itself. Not all Kittel's articles themselves took the position typical of biblical theology, as the term has been used here; but it was in biblical theology, as here described, that the work came to be idolized. On the other hand, the critique of the dictionary was a limited one, restricted to its semantic principles and procedures. Far from being an excessively severe attack, it left unsaid many of the criticisms which on quite other grounds deserved to be made, such as distortion of the evidence from later Judaism and apocalyptic.

Nevertheless, elements of that older general conception of language, which was picked up and used by biblical theology, continue to exist and will doubtless be slow to disappear. But the general situation in the understanding of language has rapidly altered. In Germany, which was the center of the more "idealistic" approach to language against which Barr's *Semantics* was directed, and where modern developments like structuralism had been relatively unknown, there has been since 1960 a vivid upsurge of interest in modern general linguistics. This is making a great impact on discussion, but the effect falls more on form criticism and the study of literature than on biblical theology. In French culture, structuralism both in language study and in the study of literature, religion, and society is much more strongly established. Again, still newer approaches to language have come into view, and the effects of Chomsky's ideas on biblical study have still to be explored. Chomsky's thought might bring us back to a relation between language structures and mental structures, but it would do so in a form which would have been useless to the older biblical theology, for it might suggest that the differences between languages belonged to surface structure, while in deep structure they were alike, and it would find ridiculous the supposition that Hebrew and Greek are polar opposites in structure. It would give no linguistic reason why biblical thinking should be radically different from any other kind of thinking.

6. Hermeneutics and presuppositions. An emphasis on hermeneutics was not strange to the biblical theology movement; in contrast to the approach under liberal theology, it had insisted that the Bible should be interpreted for today, and not simply explained with a dry historical statement about the past. Conversely, however, it thought that modern theology must not work simply with the ideas and categories of modern man, but must submit itself to those of the Bible and of Hebrew thought. As Bultmann came to be more fully understood, and as the impact of his successors continued, in America especially through the work of Robinson, it slowly became clear that the discussion must lead into fresh areas and could not be handled with the concepts familiar in current biblical theology. The philosophical basis of the discussion, derived from Heidegger and dreadful in its incoherence in English, though supposedly intended to assist in the understanding of the Bible, had rather the effect of driving Bible and theology apart (cf. Childs, pp. 80-81). At its religious roots the biblical theology movement had believed that the language of the Bible, if freed from certain dogmatic, Hellenic, philosophical, and historicist fetters, could speak clearly to the average person, or at least the average church member. The esoteric language and frenetic air of the hermeneutical discussion displayed that many minds were no longer attuned to the basic concerns and convictions of biblical theology.

Moreover, the hermeneutical discussion affected ideas of the authority of scripture. If the Bible as interpreted by one method meant something different from the Bible as interpreted by another method, could the Bible really be authoritative, and was it not the hermeneutical method that had final authority? How far could a biblical theology, even if true for the texts themselves, be decisive for the final interpretation of them? And if there was a difference between "what it meant" and "what it means," how could modern questions be settled by insisting on ancient concepts such as Hebrew thought or revelation in history, unless all biblical ideas were to be forced without alteration upon modern man?

It was especially over the matter of presuppositions in interpretation that biblical theology tied itself in knots. In its zeal against a purely historical reading of the Bible and against the supposed illusion of objectivity, it mostly insisted that objectivity and neutrality were impossible and that all interpretation involved presuppositions. Here was a deep inconsistency. If the presuppositions come from the Bible itself, i.e., from the study of the text, then they must be visible to, or verifiable by, any competent person studying the text. If they are derived from some prior position, logically anterior to the study of the Bible, then clearly biblical theology is not an independent discipline but is one subject to architectonic presuppositions derived from some other discipline, let us say from neo-orthodox dogmatic theology or from Heideggerian existentialism. Either horn of the dilemma was equally uncomfortable for biblical theology. An escape could be had through Stendahl's position, namely that biblical theology was an objective work of historical description, but this was unwelcome to most of those in the movement, and was destructive of other principles which it maintained.

7. Von Rad. The most important and fruitful single theology to appear in the late 50s and early 60s was von Rad's of the OT. The earlier stage of OT theology, best exemplified by Eichrodt, had sought, as against the analytic approach of historical exegesis and comparative religious study, to bring together a synthetic picture of the "world of faith" of the OT. Von Rad repudiated this method. He was concerned, not with the "world of faith," but with that to which Israel itself had witnessed, its "kerygma" or "confession." The content of this had always been the acts of God, and not Israel's own world of faith. There was no unified OT theology; on the contrary, there was a multiplicity of different traditions, and, for each of these, one had to ask what its essential kerygma was. Von Rad's work therefore separated out the different groups of traditions, distinguishing particularly the historical and the prophetic. The whole is preceded by a history of Yahwistic faith and followed by a section on hermeneutical problems, and especially on the "actualizing" or "re-presentation" of older traditions by later ones; this last works out into a typological principle of exegesis, which according to von Rad is essential for the connecting of OT and NT.

Of the various OT theologies, this is the one which had the greatest influence in stimulating fresh thought and research throughout the world of theology. Its richness is such that no full discussion can be attempted here. Its strength lay, perhaps, in its text-relatedness: it worked theologically with the various currents of tradition, just as these are read by the exegete. It thus came closer to exegesis than did the more systematic and structural kind of OT theology. It agreed with general opinion in laying heavy emphasis on history: Israel's confession was to events in history, and the OT was above all a book of history. But there was a marked difference of emphasis from the "God who acts" type of theology, made influential in the English-speaking world by Wright and others. Von Rad's emphasis was much more on the Israelite tradition, the growth and change in the tradition in which the OT expressed its confession; this corresponded to a literary and traditio-historical approach to texts. An approach like Wright's was more interested in the bare fact that God had acted in history, and its scholarly correlate was archaeology and the cultural history of the ancient world, rather than literary analysis; exegetically it was not very productive.

Nevertheless, von Rad's work, with its emphasis on the historical nature of the basic Israelite confession, fitted in a general sense with the sentiments of the biblical theology movement. If Eichrodt's OT theology had a certain rationalistic air about it, von Rad's style was more romantic; its expressions are often poetical and cloudy, and its definitions and distinctions often seem artificial.

8. Revelation in history (*see* REVELATION IN HISTORY[S]). This theme, basic to the biblical theology movement, fell under criticism from several directions after about 1960. Already in 1951 Minear had rightly discerned that history as a category had distinct advantages when used negatively, but that positively it was much less helpful. Among difficulties raised in later discussion we may mention: criticism of equivocation in a position like that of Wright (Gilkey); difficulties with the two histories, one critical and one confessional, in the work of von Rad (Hesse); the argument that the OT material is not generated out of an antecedent "history," but is rather a cumulative story into which later events are fitted (Barr); arguments that revelation through history, far from being unique to Israel, was common ground with its environment (Albrektson). By the late 1960s the formula "revelation in history" had clearly lost its magic and even those who tried to defend the position typical of biblical theology, like Wright, had greatly changed their emphasis.

9. The unity and distinctiveness of the Bible; its "center." From about 1960 on, less emphasis has been laid on the unity of the Bible; in different ways, Bultmann and von Rad were influences in favor of a greater recognition of diversity. An important shift was that from form criticism to redaction criticism. Early form criticism had sought to uncover the primitive kerygma, which could be supposed to have been unitary; but redaction criticism studied the differences between final units, like different gospels, which had used the same material. The insistence on the unity of the Bible, which had been directed so much against the liberal theology, could not deal with this newer development. Cullmann, for instance, had identified a view of time and salvation history as the basis for the unity of the NT; but Conzelmann argued that this view was peculiar to Luke and in contrast with Matthew and Mark. Examples like this brought into the limelight something that had always been known in critical scholarship: the relations of tension and polemic between one biblical writer and another. These were a vital clue used by scholars; was not the diversity of the Bible a more interesting and significant thing than its unity? At least it is premature to look for unity until the diversities have been fully explored. Käsemann typifies this trend: "The NT as we have it is a fragmentary collection of documents from the earliest period, while the bulk of the material has vanished for ever. By and large there is no internal coherence. The tensions everywhere evident amount at times to contradictions."

Similarly, the near-absolute distinctiveness once asserted of the Bible tended to pass into a more relative distinctiveness. The interest of many OT scholars in archaeology, Ugaritic, and Canaanite relations gradually led them to de-emphasize the separateness of Israel. The covenant functioned in the older biblical theology as a main symbol of the unity of the Bible and the separateness of its people from the environing culture; but later more interest was given to the Near Eastern setting and origins of the covenant concept, so that it came imperceptibly to function as a symbol of exactly the opposite relation. Bultmann and his school had always emphasized the Hellenistic origins of the NT, and we find a positive interest in Gnosticism as an integral element within the NT, and, again, the view that Christianity was a syncretistic religion from the beginning. For those holding such views, the absolute contrast of Hebrew and Greek thought could have no theological value. A recent theology like Pannenberg's finds certain common elements between the two and ascribes positive theological value to the part played by Hellenism in the Jewish-Christian tradition.

After von Rad no new OT theologies appeared for a decade or so, and one could wonder whether he had brought the series to an end; but now it has begun again with the contributions of Fohrer and Zimmerli. One major question is the identification of a "center" which can be held to have been the kernel of OT theology and round which such a book can be organized. Von Rad thought that the OT, unlike the NT, had no such center. But Smend argues that the search for a valid center was too easily given up and, following lines of Wellhausen's thinking, would orientate a theology upon the formula "Yahweh the God of Israel, Israel the people of Yahweh." Fohrer takes two points which form the focuses of an ellipse: the lordship of God, and community between God and man. Zimmerli's theology is built around the name of God, and especially the formula "I am that I am," with its implication of the freedom of God to do as he wills. Thus it seems likely that scholars will continue to operate with some idea of a center for theologies of OT or NT. Even where they accept a plurality of theologies and viewpoints within the Bible they mostly still find some principle of unity that gives coherence to their work. Von Rad found such a principle in the way in which Israel was able "to incorporate and absorb the experience of any one of its members into the design of the great history-picture of Israel"; and Käsemann also, after emphasizing diversity in the NT, can end up with the Lordship of Christ, "the revelation of Christ in its progress and varied interpretation," as a "real clue."

10. OT and NT. One mode of conjunction between the Testaments that was much discussed for a time was TYPOLOGY. The attempt to use typology as an exegetical principle in modern times depended on the primacy of revelation in history: typology, if it was to be used responsibly, must be of historical events and not of peripheral scenery, casual objects, or particular words. The subject was pursued in two main traditions, an English (Lampe and Woollcombe) and a German (von Rad). Von Rad thought that the same ability to reactualize traditions in a new situation, which for him was central to the OT, applied also to the relation between OT and NT. But this typological approach was criticized by Eichrodt, Pannenberg, and others, and today there seems to be much less interest in it. Barr has argued that (*a*) the typological exegesis of the OT within the NT was an element in the situation of that time, which cannot necessarily be appropriated by us in our time; (*b*) within the NT itself it is not possible to separate out a typology, based uniquely on historical events, from all sorts of other relations, including allegory.

A perspective from within the NT is offered by Hahn. For the men of the NT the OT remains as the given expression of the will of God; but the NT's attitude to the OT is a critical one. "The OT is for them no longer the way to salvation; rather it points forward to the final events of salvation and from there alone receives a light which is indispensable for the right understanding of the OT."

11. The late OT period and postbiblical Judaism. One of the great weaknesses in much biblical theology has been its inability to do justice to the postexilic period within the OT and the Judaism which grew out of the OT. OT theologies tend to represent the late period as a degeneration and to accord it little positive value. Yet this is both the period in which the final shape of the OT was reached and also the time during which it was historically transmitted to the NT. The facts of the "intertestamental" period are known and are studied, but means of giving them full theological recognition have as yet been lacking. The fault may lie with the concepts upon which the OT theologies have been built: for instance, the late OT period displays an increased concentration upon the Law and a reduced sense of revelation through history; historiography on Hebrew soil becomes rarer and the historical sense becomes attenuated. Within the categories of most OT theologies this can count only as a deterioration, and notably so with von Rad. His theology, predicated largely upon the Deuteronomic theology of history, cannot give positive value to later developments; and his typology, as a linkage of interpretations of historical events running between OT and NT, simply oversteps the intervening Judaism as if it did not exist for theology. Similarly, theologies which value the structural similarity of OT faith and NT faith may, and often do, ignore the function of the Jewish tradition of interpretation which lies between the two.

Some writers have begun to pay great attention to apocalyptic as the mental world within which

Christianity was born (so Pannenberg). But, as Koch points out, this cannot be realized as long as OT theologies themselves neglect the late period and leave its developments, including apocalyptic, on the margin. Von Rad strongly insists on separating apocalyptic from prophecy and connecting it with the wisdom tradition. This rather esoteric and improbable judgment is a consequence of the general conceptual design of the von Rad theology. Attention is directed almost solely to the canonical books of the two Testaments and to the finding of a center of gravity within OT and NT. Materials like apocalyptic which lie on the edge of the canon are thus almost necessarily distorted; and the historical tradition of religion and interpretation, which was the factual means of transmission of ideas from the OT into the NT period, is neglected.

If this position is to be repaired, we have to consider the paradoxical view that a theology of the Bible, i.e., of the canonical books, will not be possible without the inclusion of a theology of the noncanonical books and the intertestamental tradition generally. The biblical theology movement, for all its idolization of Hebrew thought as the background for the NT, never gave proper attention to Judaism as it really was (often substantially Hellenized!), and for this reason its treatment of Hebrew thought was abstract and unhistorical.

12. The history of religion. The biblical theology movement began with the intention, among other things, of producing "theologies" of OT and NT instead of the historical approach to the religions of the two which had been prevalent; and for a time this seemed to have taken place. Few books on the religion of Israel were written. But in NT studies more interest in the Hellenistic religious background continued, in the Bultmannian tradition in Germany and in work like that of Dodd in English. On the OT side, the study of Hebrew religion revived. Several works were written by authors who had also written an OT theology (Eichrodt, Vriezen, Fohrer), and another (Ringgren) makes it clear that at least some kinds of OT theology could not easily be distinguished from a study of Israelite religion. Even von Rad's theology included within itself a "history of Yahwistic faith," and a critic like Hesse argued that, in spite of von Rad's drastic contrast between his own theology and the religion of the Israelites, his work was in fact an elucidation of the history of Israelite religion. Thus, of all the "theological" research done in our period, a great deal can stand without change as valid history-of-religions material and is valid as theology only if it is valid on this other plane. The whole drastic effort to set up a theological approach to the Bible which would be sharply distinct from a study of biblical religion has been shown not only to have been a failure but to have been unnecessary and misguided in the first place. The future may well require a new direction of research which will amalgamate both these interests.

History of religions implies not only the history of Jewish and Christian religion but the relations of these with the surrounding world of religion. For all the distinctiveness of the Bible as a finished product, it can be seen in its beginnings to have emerged from the world of Near Eastern religions and to have received important stimuli from that world at later stages. It is increasingly seen that the significance of the Bible is not damaged if the effect of these stimuli is admitted and given positive valuation.

But this means that the opposition between revelation and religion—an opposition which was one of the main functions of the word "revelation"—is of doubtful value. It seems impossible within the biblical material to separate what is revelation from what is the religion of the biblical writers and the particular currents of tradition from which they came. Curiously, "revelation" was valued in the first place because it seemed to make room for a more biblical kind of theology; in the end it is biblical study itself that is cramped by the domination of this concept and would be freer without it.

13. Biblical theology and the canon of scripture. A rather different program for future biblical theology is set out by Childs. The canon is the context within which and from which biblical theology can rightly work. The older biblical theology having collapsed, this is a basis on which a new one can be constructed. The older movement, according to Childs, underestimated the importance of the canon; it "accepted uncritically the liberal hermeneutic presupposition that one came to the Biblical text from a vantage point outside the text" (p. 102). Thus the context of the canon is the normative and factual context for interpretation within the church. There are indeed other contexts within which one can work, e.g., the context of modern historical scholarship; the context of the canon is not a better one or a higher one, but simply a different one. The task of biblical theology is therefore to interpret the material as part of canonical scripture; the emphasis thus lies not on the historical reconstruction of earlier stages, or of what "lay behind" the text, but on the text as it stands in its final canonical form.

Childs' proposals fit well with the modern interest in canon as a feature of scripture; they also fit with the emphasis in modern linguistic and literary theory on the form of the final text as the essential material to be interpreted. It remains to be seen, however, whether this emphasis on canon can prove itself, and whether it can in fact lead to any "biblical theology" in a sense meaningfully connected with what has been previously done under that name. Contrary to Childs' position, this article has rather emphasized the fluidity of the lines marked by canonical and noncanonical, biblical and environmental, theological and religious. The universe of meaning, within which the language of the biblical books operated, was never one circumscribed by the canon of scripture, which did not then exist. An exegesis which would work strictly within the confines of the canon is certainly a possibility that could be added to other forms of exegesis, but it is doubtful how it could be the basic theological form of exegesis. And Childs' argument in favor of the final text, while an important consideration for the interpretation of individual books, like Genesis, or even the Pentateuch, or Matthew, does not thereby validate an extension to the point where the canon of the entire Scripture would define it as if it was a single text. Again, in spite of the decline of the older biblical theology, we have seen that particular enterprises like the writing of theologies of OT and NT have continued to prosper; it is not clear therefore that that kind of enterprise needs to be replaced by the kind of biblical theology that Childs has in mind, nor that his kind of biblical theology could perform these functions.

14. Conclusion. The biblical theology movement, as it was, now belongs to the past history of biblical studies; as we now see it, it was far too much determined by its negativity toward the liberal position. The most useful survival of elements of the movement may lie in the world of Roman Catholic theology; in that different setting its emphases may be more needed, may be understood in a less absolute sense, and may work more wholesomely and less frenetically than they did in Protestantism.

At least in some circles, the term "biblical theology" implied a certain claim to authority, a certain assumption to an unarguable normative status. But biblical theology has never in fact found itself able to exercise final authority or to work in isolation. All that it does differs only in level from various kinds of historical, linguistic, and religious study; and on the other hand, insofar as it seeks to exercise a truly theological function, its work is linked with logical, philosophical, and systematic-theological judgments also. It will do its best service and understand its own function best if it is aware that it is only one part in the total functioning unity of religious and theological study.

Bibliography. General: B. S. Childs, *Biblical Theology in Crisis* (1970); H.-J. Kraus, *Die biblische Theologie, ihre Geschichte und Problematik* (1970).

Recent theologies of OT: W. Eichrodt, *Theology of the OT* (2 vols., 1961, 1967); G. Fohrer, *Theologische Grundstrukturen des AT* (1972); E. Jacob, *Theology of the OT* (1958, newer Fr. ed., 1968); G. A. F. Knight, *A Christian Theology of the OT* (1959); G. von Rad, *OT Theology* (2 vols., 1962, 1965; later Ger. editions have significant modifications); Th. C. Vriezen, *An Outline of OT Theology* (1958); W. Zimmerli, *Grundriss der alttestamentlichen Theologie* (1972). Cf. also major studies such as G. von Rad, *Wisdom in Israel* (1972); H. W. Wolff, *Anthropology of the OT* (1974).

Of NT: H. Conzelmann, *An Outline of the Theology of the NT* (1969); J. Jeremias, *New Testament Theology*, I (1971); W. G. Kümmel, *The Theology of the NT* (1969); A. Richardson, *Introduction to the Theology of the NT* (1958); cf. O. Cullmann, *Christology of the NT* (1959) and *Salvation in History* (1967).

Semantics: J. Barr, *Semantics of Biblical Language* (1961); *Biblical Words for Time* (2nd ed., 1969, with survey of discussion since 1961); K. Koch, *Was ist Formgeschichte?* (3rd ed., 1974, with supplement on modern linguistics).

Hermeneutics: C. Westermann, ed., *Essays on OT Hermeneutics* (1963); J. M. Robinson and J. B. Cobb, *The New Hermeneutic* (1964).

Revelation in history: B. Albrektson, *History and the Gods* (1967); L. Gilkey, "Cosmology, Ontology and the Travail of Biblical Language," *JR*, LXI (1961), 194-205, and *Naming the Whirlwind* (1969): F. Hesse, "Kerygma oder geschichtliche Wirklichkeit?" *ZThK*, LVII (1960), 17-26; P. S. Minear, "Between Two Worlds: Eschatology and History," *Int.*, V (1951), 27-39; G. E. Wright, *God Who Acts* (1952), *The OT and Theology* (1969).

The "center": R. Smend, *Die Mitte des ATs* (1970); E. Käsemann, "The Problem of a NT Theology," *NTS*, XIX (1972-73), 235-45.

OT and NT: G. W. H. Lampe and K. J. Woollcombe, *Essays on Typology* (1957); W. Eichrodt in Westermann, ed., *Essays*, pp. 224-45; J. Barr, *Old and New in Interpretation* (1966); F. Hahn, "Das Problem 'Schrift und Tradition' im Urchristentum," *Evangelische Theologie*, XXX (1970), 449-68.

Late OT and Judaism: J. Barr, "Le judaïsme postbiblique et la théologie de l'AT," *RTP* (1968), pp. 209-17; K. Koch, *The Rediscovery of Apocalyptic* (1972); W. Pannenberg, ed., *Offenbarung als Geschichte* (1961).

Histories of Israelite religion: W. Eichrodt in *Historia Mundi*, II (1953) 377-448; G. Fohrer, *History of Israelite Religion* (1972); H. Ringgren, *Israelite Religion* (1966); Th. C. Vriezen, *The Religion of Ancient Israel* (1967).

The canon: Childs, *Biblical Theology in Crisis* (1970); E. Käsemann, ed., *Das NT als Kanon* (1970).

J. Barr

BLACKS, EARLY CHRISTIANITY AND. Biblical commentators of the first centuries after Christ frequently employed an "Ethiopian" symbolism in their statements of the catholic character and mission of Christianity. Among these writers the Greco-Roman image of the Ethiopian (as the Hebrew "Cushite" was known in the classical world) was a significant factor in the formation of a black-white imagery and in interpretations of the spiritual meaning of biblical Cushites. For an understanding of these developments the lineaments of the biblical and classical images of blacks, especially common elements, are a *sine qua non*.

1. Biblical and classical images of blacks. The OT mentions a Cush around the Tigris and Euphrates valleys (Gen. 2:13), but in the majority of OT texts Cush was an independent country below Egypt extending S from Syene (Ezek. 29:10, cf. Ezek. 30:4, 8-9; Isa. 11:11; 20:3). The blackness of the inhabitants was proverbial (Jer. 13:23; *see* Isa. 18:2 for their height). OT Cushites had great wealth (Job 28:19; Isa. 45:14), were remote (Ezek. 29:10; Esth. 1:1; 8:9), dwelling at the ends of the earth (cf. Ps. 72:8-9). They were "a people dreaded near and far, a nation strong and proud" (Isa. 18:2 NEB; cf. II Chr. 14:9-13), rulers of Egypt under Tirhakah (Isa. 37:9; II Kings 19:9), and at times mercenaries in Egypt (Jer. 46:9; II Chr. 12:3). Like other nations they were to be subject to God's judgment (Isa. 20; Ezek. 30:1-5; Zeph. 2:12). Their conversion was prefigured (Isa. 18:7; Zeph. 3:10; Ps. 68:31), and they were among those who acknowledged Zion as spiritual mother (Ps. 87:4).

Classical literature and later historical events preserved much of the Hebrew image of the Cushites, at times a successful and triumphant people. Greco-Roman accounts, however, added new elements to the Hebrew picture and gave rise to fresh perspectives relating to blacks. For the Greeks and Romans, Ethiopians, "burnt-faced men," were primarily dark-skinned peoples S of Egypt, and Cushites were so identified in Greek and Latin translations of the Bible. The term Ethiopians embraced

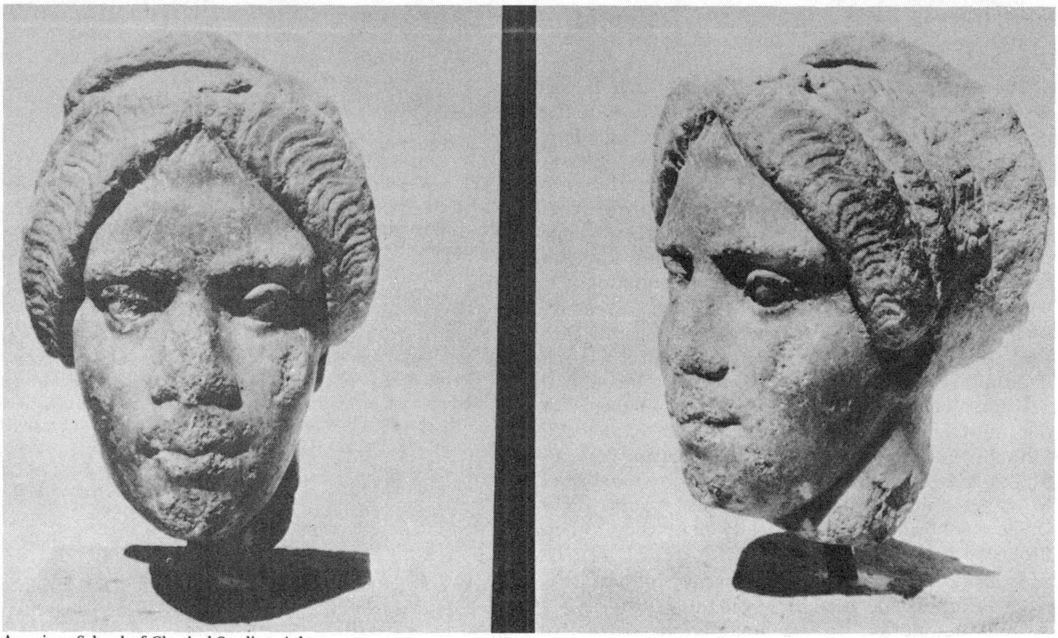

American School of Classical Studies, Athens

3. Head of a Negro, from the Roman cemetery in Athens

a variety of peoples, including the so-called true or pure Negro, a type with less pronounced Negroid characteristics, sometimes called Nilotic, and various mixed black-white types. Though their numbers, slave or free, cannot be precisely estimated, black, woolly-haired, thick-lipped Negroes and blacks of less pronounced Negroid features were far from rare sights in the predominantly white classical world, especially in Egypt, and were popular subjects for artists of all periods. Mentioned by Homer, Hesiod, and Xenophanes, Ethiopians—their country, physical traits, customs, military capability—became increasingly familiar from Herodotus onward. Their position was not affected by the existence, or memory, of vast numbers of black slaves, because by far the majority of slaves were white, not black (*see* SLAVERY IN THE NT[S] §2). Classical "anthropologists" attributed the physical differences of all men—black and white alike—to natural environment; social differences, to both the natural and social environment. Pale Scythians and Ethiopians burnt by the sun were frequently contrasted as anthropological and geographical extremes unlike the Greeks. The color of the Ethiopian's skin, the blackest of all men, was a mere geographical accident and resulted in no special racial theory about white superiority or black inferiority. The un-Mediterranean blackness of the Ethiopian was obviously different; its significance, however, was only skin-deep. Excellence, not color, was important, whether on the battlefield or in the amphitheater. A black person could have a soul as "white" as the whitest of whites. A Scythian-Ethiopian antithesis appeared in Menander's rejection of a common Hellenic criterion—birth—for determining a person's worth. It makes no difference, according to Menander, whether one is as physically different from a Greek as the Ethiopian or Scythian; it is individual merit, rather than blood, by which men should be evaluated.

2. Early Christian "Ethiopian" symbolism. Early exegetes realized that they could explicate their message more convincingly and scriptural references more effectively if they used a pattern of thought and a language familiar to their readers. Paul, for example, in his pronouncement on oneness in Christ (Col. 3:11) echoed traditional attacks upon distinctions between Greeks and barbarians and was perhaps adapting Menander's statement on the inconsequence of race. In this instance Paul used only "Scythian," but later, Origen reverted to the usual Scythian-Ethiopian formula, and enlarged it by the addition of other peoples. According to Origen, one may be born among the Hebrews, Greeks, Ethiopians, Scythians, or Taurians, yet God created them all equal and alike. By adopting a formula deeply rooted in Greco-Roman thought Origen left no doubt as to the meaning and comprehensiveness of his language.

The Greek proverb about washing an Ethiopian white and the Aesopian fable of the Ethiopian who was vigorously scrubbed and washed to no avail provided a meaningful imagery for the expression of a view that skin color was to be no more significant in the Christian than it had been in the classical view of man. Christ came into the world, according to Gregory of Nyssa, to make blacks white, and in the kingdom of heaven Ethiopians become white. The ETHIOPIAN EUNUCH, prepared for baptism by the reading of the prophet, prefigured the peoples of the Gentiles, changed his skin (Jerome, *Epistulae* CVIII.11 [*CSEL*]), and provided, in the opinion of St. Jerome, an answer to Jeremiah's question, "Can the Ethiopian change his skin or the leopard his spots?" (Jer. 13:23).

a. Origen on the Song of Songs. Origen's commentary on the Song of Songs is the source of a later "Ethiopian exegesis" (*see bibliog.*). The superficial meaning of the bride's words, "I am black and beautiful" (1:5 LXX), according to Origen is that the bride is black in complexion but, lacking neither natural beauty nor an inward beauty acquired by practice, she should not be reproached. Statements of preference as to physical beauty were not uncommon in classical literature. Persians, said Sextus Empiricus, prefer the whitest and the most hook-nosed, and Ethiopians, the blackest and the most flat-nosed. In the predominantly white Greco-Roman world there were also those who described Ethiopians as beautiful and stated their preference for blacks. Origen's observations on "black and beautiful" were similar to that classical view which rejected the ethnocentric yardstick of a majority, as expressed, for example, by Sextus Empiricus, and considered blacks naturally beautiful. Further, Origen's imagery of an "inward beauty" resembled that of a third-century A.D. epitaph, found in Egypt, contrasting the black skin of a humble slave darkened by the rays of the sun and his soul blooming with white flowers.

The bride's words, Origen explains, also have a mystical meaning. Representing the church gathered from among the Gentiles, the bride is replying to the daughters of an earthly Jerusalem who vilify her because of her ignoble birth. Though not descended from famous men, the bride has, she says, a beauty deriving from the Image and Word of God. This is similar to the position of the Sophist Antiphon (fifth century B.C.). Arguing that "we are all by nature born the same in every way, both barbarians and Greeks," he had attacked the practice of revering those born of noble fathers and of failing to honor those not descended from noble houses.

The mystery of the church coming out of the Gentiles and calling itself black and beautiful, Origen points out, is foreshadowed elsewhere in the Scriptures. The marriage of Moses to the Ethiopian woman is interpreted as a symbolic union of the spiritual law (Moses) and the church (the Ethiopian woman) gathered together from among the Gentiles. Origen recalls the suffering of Aaron and Miriam when they spoke against Moses, and he emphasizes that God never praised Moses, in spite of all his other great achievements, so highly as when he married the Ethiopian woman, whom he described as a "black Ethiopian." This phrase, as used by a person born in Egypt in the second or third century A.D., meant clearly an African and in most instances a Negro. Another adumbration of this mystery of the church was the visit of the Queen of Sheba to Solomon. In fulfillment of her type, the queen who came from the S, Ethiopia, the church comes from the Gentiles to hear the wisdom of the true Solomon, and true peace-lover, Jesus Christ. By saying that the queen came from the ends of the earth, and that she was called the queen of the S because Ethiopia lies in the southern regions, in the farthest place, Origen evoked Homer's Ethiopians, the most distant of peoples. In the same context, by citing Josephus, mentioning Meroe, and saying that the queen ruled not only over Ethiopia but also over Egypt, Origen reminded his readers of many familiar classical references to Ethiopians.

Additional passages were cited by Origen in support of his view that scriptural Ethiopians represented the church gathered from among the Gentiles: (1) a line from a hymn of praise, "Ethiopia shall stretch out her hand first to God" (Ps. 67:31 LXX, as cited by Origen [RSV 68:31]); (2) Zephaniah's prophecy that "from beyond the rivers of Ethiopia . . . they shall offer sacrifices to me" (Zeph. 3:10 LXX, as cited by Origen); and (3) the account of the Ethiopian eunuch Ebed-melech, who when he rescued Jeremiah from the pit (Jer. 38:7-13), by faith in the resurrection of Christ, drew Christ from the pit. All three references emphasized the precedence of Ethiopia, the people of the Gentiles, in approaching God. An Ethiopian "priority," however, with respect to the divine was not at all a new concept in the Greco-Roman world. In fact, "blameless" favorites of the gods as early as Homer, Ethiopians continued to be depicted as pious and just throughout classical literature. And as late as the first century B.C. Diodorus Siculus emphasized that Ethiopians were the first taught to honor the gods and enjoyed divine favor because of their well-known piety.

The classical image of outer blackness and inner whiteness appears in modified form in Origen's commentary on another verse from the Song of Songs: "Look not upon me, because I am dark, because the sun has looked down upon me" (1:6 LXX, as cited by Origen). Recalling the classical environment theory, Origen contrasts the natural blackness of Ethiopians, caused by the sun, with the blackness of the soul, which, unlike the Ethiopian's color appearing at birth, is acquired through neglect. In the tradition of the Ethiopian-Scythian antithesis, he notes that the visible sun darkens those to whom it comes close but does not burn those who are distant. The spiritual Sun of Justice, however, illuminates and brightens the upright in heart but looks askance at and blackens those who disobey him. A similar symbolism, emphasizing "Ethiopian beauty," is found elsewhere in Origen: "We ask in what way is she black and in what way fair without whiteness. She has repented of her sins; conversion has bestowed beauty upon her and she is sung as 'beautiful' . . . if you repent, your soul will be 'black' because of your former sins, but because of your penitence your soul will have something of what I may call an Ethiopian beauty." Origen's contribution to the language of spiritual blackness and whiteness is clear, but equally apparent is the similarity of his imagery to classical themes of black-white contrasts.

b. "Ethiopian" symbolism in other writers. An "Ethiopian" symbolism in the spirit of Origen's is used by other early Christian writers. In Alexandria, Origen had seen many Ethiopians, whose presence was a daily reminder of black countries to the S and may have influenced his choice of an "Ethiopian" symbolism. Similarly, Augustine's black-white imagery may have reflected a first-hand acquaintance with blacks in northwestern Africa. Augustine stated that under the name "Ethiopia" all nations were signified, a part representing the whole. "And" says Augustine, "properly by black men (for Ethiopians are black). Those are called to the faith who were before black, just they, so that it may be said to them 'Ye were sometimes darkness but now are ye light in the Lord.' [Eph. 5:8]. They are indeed called black but let them not remain black, for out of these is made the Church to whom it is said: 'who is she that cometh up having been made white?' [Song of S. 8:5 LXX]. For what has been made out of the black maiden but what is said in 'I am black and beautiful'?" (*Enarrationes in Psalmos* LXXIII.16 [*Corpus Christianorum, Series Latina*]). Augustine also declared that the catholic church was not to be limited to a particular region of the earth but would extend throughout the entire universe, reaching even the Ethiopians, the remotest and blackest of men. Much more than a mere literary device to explain Christianity, this "Ethiopian" symbolism was deeply rooted in the experience of early Christians in Africa.

The application of such an imagery to a North African black is vividly attested by a correspondence between Ferrandus, deacon of the church of Carthage from 520 to 547, and Fulgentius, Bishop of Ruspe (i.e., southern Tunisia), concerning the spiritual welfare of a black catechumen, Ethiopian in color, not yet whitened by the shining grace of Christ, from the most distant parts of a barbarous region where men are darkened by the dry heat of the fiery sun (Fulgentius, *Epistulae* XI–XII [*PL*]). The language of this correspondence, like Augustine's expression of faith in the spread of Christianity among the most distant Ethiopians, provides dramatic evidence of a North African effort to make Augustine's vision—"Aethiopia credet Deo"—a reality.

The meeting of Philip and the Ethiopian eunuch, the only NT reference to an Ethiopian (Acts 8:26-40), figures prominently in early commentaries. The high official of the CANDACE, the queen of Ethiopia, was said to have been the first Gentile to receive from Philip the mystery of the divine word, and to have returned to preach the gospel in his native land. It is not certain whether the episode was a straightforward record of actual events, suggested by hints in the OT, or included to illustrate the fulfillment of the promise of bearing witness "to the end of the earth" (Acts 1:8). Opinions vary as to whether the Ethiopian or the centurion Cornelius was the first Gentile Christian. It is clear, however, that for a reader of Acts, "Ethiopian" (ἀνὴρ Αἰθίοψ, Acts 8:27), as the eunuch was described, meant a black man, and doubtlessly a Negro from S of Egypt.

Readers of the first centuries after Christ would not have failed to associate the Ethiopian and the Candace of Acts with the campaigns of Augustus' general, Gaius Petronius, in Egypt in 24 and 22 B.C., the Ethiopian queen's encounter with Roman soldiers, and the treaty in which Augustus granted the Candace everything her ambassadors requested. The *Monumentum Ancyranum,* copies of which were set up in some, if not all, of the provinces, was also a constant reminder of Augustus' activity in Ethiopia. As late as the sixth century A.D., Philip's baptism of the eunuch was the subject of verses in which the Christian poet Arator emphasized the salient components of an imagery seen first in Origen's commentary on the Song of Songs—the symbolic marriage of Moses to the Ethiopian woman, the eternal bride, the church, which came, like the dark and beautiful maiden, from the burnt regions of Ethiopia. The eunuch was still for Arator, as for the reader of Acts, a black man, and he continued to be a dramatic symbol of Christianity's catholic mission, as he had been for the African Origen.

Bibliography. H. C. Baldry, *The Unity of Mankind in Greek Thought* (1965); F. M. Snowden, Jr., *Blacks in Antiquity: Ethiopians in the Greco-Roman Experience* (1970), esp. pp. 169-218 and Index of Sources, pp. 353-64 for other classical and biblical sources, "Ethiopians in the Graeco-Roman World," in *The African Diaspora: Interpretive Essays,* ed. R. I. Rotberg and M. L. Kilson (1976), and "Témoignages iconographiques sur les populations noires dans l'Antiquité gréco-romaine," in *L'Iconographie des Noirs dans l'Art Occidental,* ed. L. Bugner, I (1976); R. P. Lawson, *Origen: The Song of Songs, Commentary and Homilies,* ACW, XXVI (1957) provides an English trans. F. M. SNOWDEN, JR.

***BLOOD.** In the OT, blood has religious significance, that is, it is especially related to the divine, in two ways. (1) In accord with widespread belief, blood when shed had uncanny power. It called down vengeance which was assured by God. (2) It had a central role in ritual. In sacrifices it was set apart and applied to sacred objects, symbols of the divine presence and power. The explanation given is that it has power to atone because it is life and therefore stands in close relation to the living God. At the first Passover the blood of the lamb warded off death. In covenant ceremonial it seems to have symbolized sharing.

The NT applies the second group of concepts to the blood of Christ shed in the Passion. Christ's blood makes final, perfect atonement and so makes a pure, holy people of the new covenant. The NT goes beyond Hebrew thought in its emphasis on the redeeming power of this blood and in its insistance that it must be drunk, shared in a realistic way.

1. Ordinary meanings of the word. Most commonly it is used in the primary, concrete sense: the blood of men and animals. It can be a metaphor, e.g., "the blood of grapes" (Gen. 49:11; Ecclus. 39:26), or a description of a color (II Kings 3:22). Joined in the phrase "flesh and blood" it connotes frail human nature (Ecclus. 14:18; Matt. 16:17; I Cor. 15:50). It can also stand for bloodshed (in the OT usually in the plural, *dāmîm*) or for the guilt of murder in the formula of condemnation: "his blood is on his head" (Josh. 2:19; I Kings 2:32; Ezek. 33:4).

2. Religious connotations in the OT. ***a. Yahweh the avenger of blood.*** Quite generally the shedding of human blood has been regarded as a crime of particular significance, not merely because it destroys life, but because blood itself is uncanny. Of itself it arouses mysterious powers which demand compensation, blood for blood. So also in Israel (Num. 35:32-34), but there it was not the unreasoning furies attached to blood in itself (cf. Aeschylus, *Oresteia*) who protected blood. Because

Yahweh is the God of life and the guardian of the innocent (Gen. 9:4; Ps. 9:13), it is he who brings the shedder of blood to justice.

b. Use in ritual. The developed code for priests (Lev. 1–7) demands various dispositions as an intrinsic part of the sacrificial rituals. In the burnt offering (1:5 ff.), the peace offering (3:2 ff.), and the guilt offering (7:2), it was splashed against the sides of the altar. In the sin offering the priest was required to dip his finger in the blood, sprinkle some before the sanctuary veil seven times, and then anoint the altar horns (Lev. 4:5-7). The rest of the blood was poured out at the base of the altar.

In addition to these uses intrinsic to the sacrificial rite, the blood of the offerings was used to purify and sanctify. When consecrating the high priest, the officiant rubbed blood on the right eartip, thumb, and toe of the priest and sprinkled him with blood and oil from the altar. This made him and his vestments holy (Exod. 29:19-21; Lev. 8:22-30), set them apart (*see* HOLINESS §§A2*e*, 3*e*). A similar ceremony cleanses and atones for leprosy (Lev. 14:12-18). Anointing the altar with blood is a cleansing (literally, "removing of sin") and an atoning which creates or renews its holiness (Exod. 29:12-14, 36*b*-37; Lev. 8:15). *See* SACRIFICES AND OFFERINGS, OT[S] §§1*f*; 2*a*; 3*b*.

The accounts of the Exodus and of the theophany at Sinai are marked by rites in which blood plays a part. The blood of the paschal lamb identifies the dwellings of the Israelites so that the destruction visited on Egypt passes them by (Exod. 12:7, 13, 21-22). At Sinai the people affirm their allegiance to Yahweh by acclamation, and a part of the blood of the sacrifices is sprinkled on the altar and part, "the blood of the covenant," on the people (Exod. 24:6-8; cf. Ps. 50:5; Zech. 9:11).

c. Meaning assigned to blood. Lev. 17:11 is explicit about atonement: blood atones "by reason of the life." In fact, blood is life (Gen. 9:4; Lev. 17:14; Deut. 12:23) and life is characteristic of God (cf. Hos. 1:10 [MT 2:1]). Being so near the divine, blood is holy and efficacious. It removes sin and consecrates (Exod. 29:36*b*-37). Note that blood thus effects purification solely by application to the person or thing needing it. Blood is not given to God as atonement. Indeed, God is never the direct object of the verb "atone" as though the sacrificial offering must somehow affect him.

All these ideas are part of a system which sought to normalize and unify sacrificial practice. Because this system emphasized the expiatory role of sacrifice in general (e.g., Lev. 1:4 attaches expiation even to the burnt offering), the connection between the power of expiation and the divine element of life in the blood is practically a general theory of sacrifice. When one used blood properly in sacrifice, he dealt with something which was close to God and so, presumably, pleasing to him, and which sanctified whatever it touched. The expression of such explicit ideas about the meaning and power of blood is, of course, rather late and sophisticated—the sacrificial code belongs to P. However, it has its roots in feelings which are old and widespread in Israel. Blood was to be respected (cf. I Sam. 14:33; Deut. 12:24; both pre-P).

Even apart from the question of the antiquity of the belief that life is in the blood, this meaning of blood is normative for the OT in the form in which it has come to us. Thus the paschal blood on the Israelite doors seems originally to have been a signal, based on apotropaic magic, warning away the destroyer because he already had his portion. In the actual context of the over-all OT attitude toward blood and rite, it must be seen as marking off the chosen people, signifying their holiness in the basic sense of separation for the divine. So also the "blood of the covenant" (Exod. 24:8). Its origins must be connected with the universal conviction that the ritual sharing of blood creates a quasi-familial relationship. However, there is an inevitable shift in meaning toward the purification and consecration proper to sacrifice from the more primitive idea of blood brotherhood. Indeed, the solemn but festive atmosphere implied by the peace offerings in Exodus is a striking example of the special view of blood sacrifice in Israel. The ancients knew analogous blood covenant rites (Aeschylus, *Septem contra Thebas* 42-48; Xenophon, *Anabasis* II.ii.9), but they were dark ceremonies of cursing, because blood belonged to the drear gods of the underworld. In Israel it was life because it belonged to Yahweh.

The peculiar rite for purifying the leprous is a special case. No doubt something of the mystery of blood was felt, but in fact the rite is carefully separated from the properly religious, sacrificial purification. It is a relic of the widespread ancient practices for frightening away disease demons, and like them it is concerned to multiply efficacious agents. Unlike the blood of sacrifice, the blood needs to be augmented. It is merely one part of the paraphernalia along with the water, the red cloth, and the rest.

d. Background of the OT interpretation of blood. That there were so many different usages from different sources points to the antiquity and wide diffusion of a conviction that blood had a cardinal role in efficacious sacrifice. Further, the developing systematization of these usages increased the emphasis on blood. The conviction of its importance grew rather than diminished as theological reflection developed.

The data of comparative religion must be used with care, avoiding easy but inaccurate commonplaces such as the universality of beliefs about blood as life or the nature of the food of the gods. In fact, it is striking that the civilizations of the ancient world from which Israel drew its sacrificial practices show no sign of a belief in the importance of blood as such in sacrifice, much less of an idea that blood is life.

The other claim, that blood is a special divine food, even conflicts with the evidence for ancient concepts outside Israel. Sacrifices were widely considered the food of the gods. However, in one form coming from both Egypt and Mesopotamia this was expressed by making the offering a regular meal, in which blood had no special part (cf. the Israelite imitation of the usage, the shewbread). In another form in Greece, part of the meat and especially the fat belonged to the gods; the blood belonged to men and ghosts.

Ideas about blood as divine food, then, were superstitions and were firmly rejected by the central tradition (Ps. 50:13). So far was the idea from having any real force that Ezek. 44:7 can speak of fat and blood as divine food. Ezekiel is so secure in the spiritualization of sacrifice (contrast 43:25-26 with the related text, Exod. 29:36*b*-37) that he can use the food metaphor without any fear of misunderstanding.

In general, rite precedes interpretation. Usages were instituted first; then the principle, such as that blood is life or blood is divine food, was formulated. The visual impact of the manipulation of the sacrificial blood must have been strong, and it was this which stimulated the desire for an explanation, not the explanation which sought expression in a rite.

Given this fact, we may look for attested ideas about blood or reactions to it which could have been at hand to satisfy the urge to explain. Now, while blood may not always be *identified* with life and tied to the divine, clearly blood is often *associated* with life. Menstrual blood links it with life's origins, and losing blood means losing life. But equally, blood arouses aversion and has power to frighten. In the OT the story of the "bridegroom of blood" (Exod. 4:24-26) probably expresses most vividly this tie between blood and the irrational, the uncanny. It appears too in the widespread belief shared by Israel that blood by its own force summoned a venging power (Gen. 4:10) and must be requited to exorcise pollution (Num. 35:33). Blood is so powerful in a negative sense that even when bloodshed was justified in the wars of a hero it left its mark. David was marked in this way and consequently he could not build the temple (I Chr. 22:8; 28:3). It is not, then, an accident that the Nile was turned into blood (Exod. 7:14-24) and that this plague of blood became a sign of apocalyptic troubles (Rev. 8:9; 16:3-4). Blood can mean terror (cf. Joel 2:30-31 [MT 3:3-4]; Rev. 6:12).

Blood thus has more than one powerful connotation, and its relation to life need not have been seized upon to explain its religious symbolism. In the ancient Middle East, blood had its role in fearsome rites associated with death, and in Greece, which shared ritual practices with the Levant, blood was proper only to sacrifices to the underworld powers, to rites of cursing and death. There may be traces of this attitude in Israel. The blood of the Passover, as we have seen, may have been a sign that the dread destroyer—in Exod. 12:23 he is separate from Yahweh—had his due from the household. And Ps. 16:4*a*α, which may be translated: "Those who pursue another god multiply their pains," probably refers to idolatrous blood rites, i.e., those rejected in 4*a*β, to a god of disease and death.

But these are all traditions of settled peoples, and Israel had another strong tradition, the nomadic. Among the nomads of Asia the tradition of blood as a sign of brotherhood seems to have been particularly strong, and it kept this significance in religious ritual. Calling attention to the blood in rites emphasized a connection between blood and the forming of relationships. This is not yet a generalization equating blood to life, but at least it is a positive symbol, not a frightening one. The step from the idea of family to that of life is not a long one.

This tradition was combined with the ritual borrowed from Canaan, which stressed the role of sacrifice in forging unity between the community and the divine. Without forcing any change in the rubrics, this combination would put the ritual action in a new light and induce new attitudes. It offered the basis for differentiating the borrowed rites, something Israel did readily: witness the historicization of the seasonal agricultural festivals of Canaan, turning them into celebrations of single past events. It would draw attention to the use of blood and give it a meaning which set the rite apart from the Canaanite rite, where blood as such was not significant in sacrifice and where its symbolism was negative, tied to war and death. Combine all this with the fact that the God of Israel was pre-eminently the living God, and the possibilities of development were great. Sacrifice meant unity. So did blood. The blood of sacrifice could become the symbol of unity with divine life so that it was capable of expiating, purifying, and so bringing man into the divine sphere of life and holiness.

3. Religious connotations in the NT. ***a. Application of OT concepts.*** According to the NT, the blood of Christ offered in the Passion achieves once and for all the whole aim of rites prescribed by the Law: purity and unity (covenant: Heb: 9:14-22; 13:12, 20). This appears already in the Markan form of the eucharistic words (Mark 14:24): the blood which institutes the new covenant is "poured out for many." This recalls Isa. 53:10-13 which, especially in the LXX form, emphasizes that remission comes because the Servant bears the sins of the many, as Matt. 26:28 makes explicit. The blood of Christ, then, does not simply establish a covenant; it does this by remitting sins.

Further texts use the OT terms of expiation and sanctification in developing the significance of the blood. According to Rom. 3:24-25 expiation has been made by the blood so that redemption from sin has finally been effected. A new gift of God accomplishes what the blood of sacrifices had been designed to do (cf. the formulation of Rom 3:25 with Lev. 17:11, and see Rom. 3:20 and 5:9). I John 1:7 adopts the Greek verb for cleanse, καθαρίζειν, used in sacrificial contexts in the LXX for the Hebrew words meaning "atone" and "remove sin," to say that the blood of Christ cleanses from sin.

The Epistle to the Hebrews is explicitly concerned with the continuity and the contrast between old and new. The two have the common aim of purification and access to God, but it is only the new that effects what the old symbolized (cf. 9:22; 10:4, 19-22). This new reality is accomplished because the blood of Christ cleanses the conscience from dead works for the service of the living God (9:13-14). This is precisely the goal of the atoning blood of the OT—restoration and increase of life. By its cleansing effect, the blood of Christ's sacrifice creates a truly holy people (10:29; 9:14; 13:12) and produces the eternal covenant (13:20).

b. New developments. The NT extends the limits of this covenant achieved by Christ's blood. It has broken the barriers so that all humankind may be united in God (Eph. 2:13). Indeed, through it all heaven and earth are reconciled (Col. 1:20).

The NT, then, emphasizes that the blood of Christ redeems. The idea is not characteristic of the OT. There, blood has its effect entirely from being applied to the object of purification *(see* §1c *above)*. But the NT as early as Rom. 3:24-25 says that the blood redeems, that is, pays a debt. In Romans the idea is coupled with atonement. It stands by itself, apart from any other sacrificial concepts, in Eph. 1:7 and Rev. 5:9. The metaphor is carried to the full in I Pet. 1:18-19 where the blood is explicitly the ransom price.

Finally, the NT insists that the blood of Christ is actual drink. It is efficacious where the blood of the old sacrifices was only a sign, but to share in its power one must partake of it (John 6:53-56; cf. I Cor. 11:27). Such sacramental realism has gone far beyond Hebrew thought. *See* ATONEMENT §C6.

Bibliography. R. De Vaux, *Ancient Israel* (1961); D. McCarthy, "Further Notes on the Symbolism of Blood and Sacrifice," *JBL,* XCII (1973), 205-10, "The Symbolism of Blood and Sacrifice," *JBL,* LXXXVIII (1969), 166-76; R. Rendtorff, *Studien zur Geschichte des Opfers im Alten Israel* (1967), but see the critical review by S. McEvenue, *Biblica,* L (1969), 115-21; W. R. Smith, *The Religion of the Semites* (1889).

D. J. McCARTHY

***BODY. 1. In the LXX and the gospels.** The distinction between true self and flesh, or body, so natural for Greek and modern thought, is absent from the OT, where the physical body is not abstracted from the living reality and where human beings are defined in terms of their relationship to God, their creator. In the LXX the term σῶμα appears as a translation for (*a*) corpses, human or animal; (*b*) living physical bodies; (*c*) slaves, and (*d*) occasionally as a synonym for the self. The same general usage is found in the gospels, except for the innovative saying of Jesus, "This is my body" (Mark 14:22). Since neither σῶμα nor its Aramaic equivalent were used in connection with the making of an offering, the word here probably denotes the whole self of Jesus given for his disciples.

2. In the Pauline letters. Paul's use of σῶμα is so varied and original that it has been variously appraised. The several ways in which he uses the term can be understood best when one takes into consideration the historical context of his dealing with specific issues and with specific Christian congregations.

a. I Corinthians. Paul uses σῶμα in I Thessalonians, Galatians, and Philemon in a nontechnical sense, to mean the physical totality of a person. But then the same word suddenly appears in I Cor. 6:12-20 to designate that aspect of one's personhood through which one may relate to other persons and to God. This new use of the term by Paul was evidently prompted by a Gnostic slogan which must have run something like, "Food is to the stomach as fornication is to the body" (cf. I Cor. 6:12-13). In rebuttal Paul insists that the relation God establishes with the Christian's σῶμα precludes becoming "one body" with a prostitute. Σῶμα here means the whole person entering into both spiritual and sexual relations. The combination is extraordinary in a Hellenistic environment which downgraded the body, and there is a mystical exclusivity in Paul's usage which is profound and unique. The argument is climaxed by the unusual claim that the σῶμα is the temple of the Holy Spirit (6:19-20).

In the context of marriage this idea manifests itself in an egalitarian rule of conjugal obligation (I Cor. 7:4) whereby σῶμα denotes the basis of sexual relations. This sets the framework for interpreting I Cor. 7:34: the unmarried seeks "to be holy in body and spirit" by devotion to church work, but this does not imply the married achieve lesser holiness because of sexual relations. The fault in 7:32-35 relates to worldly distractions, not marital relations. *See* MARRIAGE IN THE NT[S].

In I Cor. 10:16-17 sacramental participation establishes a bond of "one body" between believers, excluding Gnostic participation in pagan meals and prostitution. I Cor. 11:17-34 deals with disorderly celebrations of the Lord's Supper caused by Gnostic disrespect. Paul insists upon the validity of the formula, "This is my body," and argues that the presence of Christ in the sacrament establishes a sphere of divine law which wreaks vengeance on violators. To eat "without discerning the body" (11:29) is to disregard the personal presence of the Lord whose sovereign grace and power claim the believers' lives totally and exclusively.

The most widely debated reference to σῶμα is I Cor. 12:12-13 where Paul inserts the realistic claim, "so it is with Christ" into a traditional metaphor of the body politic. To break from metaphor into realism and to identify a person with the σῶμα of the community were unparalleled in the Hellenistic world. Paul may have patterned this concept after the rabbinic idea of the gigantic body of ADAM which contained the souls of all mankind. The elaboration of the concept in 12:14-30 stresses mutual submission and interdependence, ideas directly opposed to Gnostic individualism.

I Cor. 15 answers a scornful question about the resurrection body (15:35) raised by Gnostics who assumed they had already transcended bodily existence. Paul accepts the premise that "flesh and blood cannot inherit the kingdom of God" (15:50), but he develops an unparalleled distinction between flesh and σῶμα, creating in the process the expression "spiritual body" (15:44). Though he is not following Hebraic terminology—the term "resurrection of the body" being unknown in ancient Judaism—Paul expresses a common thought that God alone provides the continuity between this life and the next (15:38-44). Such continuity includes the provision of a σῶμα, spiritually transformed but still bearing a distinctive personality and relational possibilities.

b. The later letters. In the later letters Paul's employment of σῶμα as a relation term recedes in favor of more traditional usage (II Cor. 4:10; 5:10; 10:10; 12:2-3). The adoption of a Gnostic idea in II Cor. 5:6-8, where the σῶμα is the prison of the true inner person, indicates a shift in argumentative strategy. The complex use of σῶμα in Romans also indicates sustained controversy. Only in Rom. 12:4-5 is it used in the technical sense of the basis of unity and relationship, but even here the realistic identification of the church with Christ is avoided. Otherwise σῶμα in Romans depicts the basis of selfhood in the old aeon (1:24; 4:19) and the new (Rom. 8:11, 23; 12:1). In Rom. 7:24; 8:10-11 Paul uses σῶμα where one would expect σάρξ ("flesh," cf. Rom. 7:25; 8:9, 12-13) because the former expresses the whole person more adequately. Elsewhere in Romans several unique combinations bear polemical implications: the "body of sin" (author's trans.) in 6:6 appears to correct the Gnostic idea of baptism as destruction of the material body; "body of death" in 7:24 appears in a slightly altered citation of a Gnostic lamentation about the deadly curse of a material body; "mortal body" in 6:12 (NEB; "mortal bodies," 8:11 RSV) counters enthusiastic claims to possess immortal life, while "dead body" (author's trans.) in 8:10 is correlated in a baptismal context with the phrase "because of sin" to avoid the Gnostic assumption that doom is due to materiality.

3. Other NT writings. Intensive debate and development of Pauline doctrine is reflected in later writings. By citing an enthusiastic hymn celebrating Christ as the head of the σῶμα of the universe and by adding the phrase "[of] the church," the author of Colossians counters the tendency to expand the "body of Christ" concept into universal triumphalism (1:18; cf. Eph. 1:23). The body of Christ is still only the church (Col. 1:24; Eph. 5:23), but its growth through the mission to the Gentiles will one day permeate the cosmos (Col. 2:19; Eph. 1:23; 3:8-10). In an adaptation of the Hellenistic concept of shadow versus reality, Col. 2:17 designates the "body of Christ" (author's trans.) as the reality toward which the universe is moving. This reality is not attained through ascetic rules for the body (Col. 2:23) but through the reconciliation effected in the crucifixion of Christ's "body of flesh" (Col. 1:22; 2:11; Eph. 2:15-16; cf. Heb. 10:10; I Pet. 2:24). The church becomes the "body" of the reconciled, bound together in mutual love (Eph. 4:4, 12, 16; Col. 3:15). The parallel between sexual and spiritual relations in the σῶμα is maintained as the supreme "mystery" (Eph. 5:28-33). The powerful sense of somatic solidarity is conveyed by a new term, σύσσωμος—"co-bodied," or belonging to the same body (Eph. 3:6; RSV "members of the same body"). A similarly affirmative view of bodily relations is found in Heb. 13:3.

See also FLESH IN THE NT; FLESH IN THE NT[S]; SPIRIT; SPIRIT[S]; MAN, NATURE OF, IN THE NT §B and supplementary article.

Bibliography. A. Schweitzer, *The Mysticism of Paul the Apostle* (1929); E. Käsemann, *Leib und Leib Christi* (1933), *Essays on NT Themes* (1960), and *Perspectives on Paul* (1969); K. Grobel, "Σῶμα as 'Self, Person' in the LXX," *Neutestamentliche Studien für R. Bultmann,* BZNW, XXI (1954), pp. 52-59; R. Bultmann, *Theology of the NT,* 2 vols. (1948-53); E. Schweizer, "Die Leiblichkeit des Menschen," *EvT,* XXIX (1969), 40-55, and "σῶμα," *TDNT,* VII (1964), 1024-94; C. Westermann, "Leib und Seele in der Bibel," *Zeichen der Zeit,* XXIV (1970), 41-46; R. Jewett, *Paul's Anthropological Terms,* AGJU, X (1971), includes a complete history of research; K. A. Bauer, *Leiblichkeit,* StNT, IV (1971).

R. JEWETT

***BOLDNESS.** Of the various words in the NT which refer to boldness or confidence, παρρησία is the most important theologically. In the LXX (where no special Hebrew word lies behind the concept) it is the gift of God to his people (Lev. 26:13) and is ascribed to the divine wisdom (Prov. 1:20-21). It is used in the LXX also in the sense of "freedom" or "free and joyful standing before God" (Job 27:9-10; 22:23-27; cf. Wisd. Sol. 5.1-2).

In secular Greek, παρρησία is used with reference to the free citizen of a city-state who could say anything publicly in the assembly. Aliens and slaves did not have this right. In the private sphere it represents freedom of friends who are unafraid to speak the whole truth to one another, even if this demands censure. In the NT period the word loses its original political associations and becomes simply the moral freedom to speak the truth (as one sees it) publicly. As such, it was one of the highest ideals of the Cynic philosophers. *See* CYNICS[S].

In the NT παρρησία and παρρησιάζομαι are used most in John, Acts, and the Pauline letters, but also in Hebrews and I John as well as in Mark 8:32. In the Pauline texts it combines the elements of courage and plainness of speech and is closely linked with the fearless proclamation of the gospel which characterized Paul and the entire early Christian community (cf. I Thess. 2:2; II Cor. 3:12; Phil. 1:20). In Acts it is a characteristic term for the missionary witness of the apostles, which again combines fearlessness and plainness in speaking (2:29; 4:13, 31; 9:27-28; 13:46; 14:3; 18:26; 19:8; 26:26). Indeed, Acts ends with Paul in Rome, "preaching the kingdom of God and teaching about the Lord Jesus Christ quite openly [lit. with all freedom of speech] and unhindered" (28:31).

In John παρρησία is used to indicate the revelatory nature of the words and deeds of Jesus, the openness of his sonship and messiahship (cf. 18:20). In I John it represents that free relationship with God which believers will experience in the day of judgment (2:28; 4:17) and which, in fact, is already realized in prayer (3:21; 5:14). Hebrews combines uses of the word for both the freedom of direct access to God, made possible by the sacrifice of Christ, and the open confession of faith in the midst of opposition. The use of παρρησία in I John and Hebrews paves the way for its use by the early Fathers.

Πεποίθησις is used six times in the NT, always by Paul, meaning "trust" or "confidence." It can be trust in God (Eph. 3:12) or in men (II Cor. 1:15). Paul has self-confidence in his calling as an apostle (10:2), a confidence which comes through Christ (3:4). *See also* COURAGE §4 and COURAGE[S].

Bibliography. H. Schlier, "παρρησία," *TDNT*, V (1954 [ET 1968]), 871-86; W. C. van Unnik, "The Christian's Freedom of Speech in the NT," *BJRL*, XLIV (1961-62), 466-88. W. W. GASQUE

***BOW.** *See* RAINBOW[S].

***BOZRAH (IN EDOM).** Excavations by the British School of Archaeology in Jerusalem commenced in 1971 and have continued each season since then.

The site covers some nineteen acres and is surrounded by a wall up to about thirteen feet in width. The wall is built entirely of dry stone, and part of it appears to be of casemate construction. The plaster surface on the slopes of the mound appears to be associated with the town wall.

The natural defenses of the site are well illustrated in the original article. The only reasonable access to the site is at the southern end, where the excavations have laid bare evidence of a massive system of fortifications. Immediately inside this, on the highest point of the settlement, remains of several monumental and important buildings are coming to light. It is not yet possible to determine whether these are administrative palaces or temple structures.

By the end of the 1972 season, three main phases of occupation had been isolated. The major period appears to belong to the eighth century B.C. Houses and public buildings are easily distinguished by the widespread use of both floor and wall plaster; there is evidence of several stages of rebuilding. Some of the pottery of this period, including a very fine polychrome ware, appears to be new in the Palestinian and Jordanian ceramic sequence.

Probably the town depended for its water on internal catchment and storage. The nearest fresh water source at present is situated approximately 1¼ miles from the site. There is evidence of a postern gate in the eastern wall of the city giving access to more monumental buildings on the slope beneath the acropolis.

Beneath the plastered floor and wall occupation there is evidence, in some trenches, of earlier occupations: a mud brick phase and, below that, flimsy constructions of dry-stone walling. It is not yet possible to give a final verdict on the date of these earlier occupations. The evidence suggests at present that it is unlikely to have been before the ninth century B.C.

The latest period of occupation, marked by a widespread use of fine ashlar masonry, could possibly be of the Assyrian period, and the plans of some of the buildings bear strong resemblances to those of Assyrian open-court buildings. Here, however, the excavators have been less fortunate, since most of the evidence has been removed by later stone robbing.

Bibliography. C.-M. Bennett, "Excavations at Buseirah, Southern Jordan," *Levant*, V (1973), 1-11; VI (1974), 1-24. J. B. HENNESSY

***BURIAL.** *See* TOMB[S].

C

***CAESAREA.** Caesarea Maritima lies destroyed under broad sand dunes. Literature about the city is plentiful, but its archaeological history is meager. Recent excavations, however, have enhanced our knowledge of the ancient city.

1. The harbor area. From the air the outline of the destroyed and submerged harbor can be seen extending a quarter of a mile out from shore. Limestone blocks fifty feet long and eighteen feet wide, mentioned by Josephus (Antiq. XV.ix.6) as part of the breakwater, have been found. In a wide semicircle around the harbor front some of the remains of the Roman city are visible: two aqueducts, an amphitheater, a hippodrome, and a theater. The high aqueduct conducted pure water from the limestone foothills through a rock-hewn tunnel 2½ feet wide by 3 feet high by 6 miles long and then on arches for another 6 miles to the city. The amphitheater, which has an arena larger than that of the Colosseum in Rome, was the probable site of the death of AGRIPPA I, also known as Herod Agrippa (Jos. Antiq. XIX.viii.2; Acts 12:21-23). The hippodrome, founded in the second century A.D., is more than a quarter of a mile long and one hundred yards wide. It is one of the larger hippodromes of the Roman world and seated over 30,000 people while the theater, located on the coast, seated 4,500 people.

On the sea front a long series of recently uncovered vaulted warehouses each ninety feet long give indication of the size of the port which Josephus in one place (War I.xxi.5) says was larger than Piraeus (but see Antiq. XV.ix.6). Beneath the city HEROD the Great built an extensive sewer system which, according to Josephus (Antiq. XV.ix.6), was cleaned out by the surge of the sea. One of these sewers, 10½ feet in height, has been found and is serving as one means of determining the plan of the buried city.

2. Other finds. Ten years after the death of Herod, Caesarea came under direct Roman rule (A.D. 6) and, apart from the reign of Agrippa I (A.D. 37-44), remained under that rule for over six hundred years. During this period it was the administrative and military center of Palestine. The residence of the procurators was there, and a lithic inscription referring to Pontius PILATE has been found. Public buildings including a forum, baths, columnated streets, and tetrapylons were built. Near the harbor a temple to Augustus and Roma contained two colossal statues. A white marble foot from one of these, three feet long, has been found. A second temple to Tyche-ASTARTE is pictured on coins from Caesarea, and a large marble Tyche figure has recently been recovered. A third-century Mithraeum (*see* Fig. C1), the first found in Palestine, was discovered in 1973.

George Whipple

1. The interior of the Mithraeum, showing the altar stone on the floor in the center

The population of Caesarea was always mixed. In addition to pagan temples, a Jewish synagogue and many Jewish tombstones from the Roman and Byzantine periods have been recovered. Samaritan lamps are frequently found, and two Christian churches and many Christian inscriptions from the Byzantine period are known.

By the Byzantine period the city was walled and had been substantially rebuilt. A large hexastyle public archive with mosaic inscriptions from Rom. 13:3 and industrial installations from this period have now been excavated. Caesarea flourished until it was captured by the Persians in A.D. 614 and destroyed by the Arabs in A.D. 639. Debris left from the Arab destruction has been found over the entire Byzantine city.

Bibliography. A. Reifenberg, "Caesarea, A Study in the Decline of a Town," *IEJ*, I (1950-51), 20-32; L. Kadman, *The Coins of Caesarea Maritima* (1957); A. Frova *et al., Scavi di Caesarea Maritima* (1965); J. Humphrey, "Prolegomena to the Study of the Hippodrome at Caesarea Maritima", *BASOR*, 213 (1974), 2-45; L. Levine, *Caesarea Under Roman Rule, Studies in Judaism in Late Antiquity,* VII (1975); L. N. Hopfe and G. Lease, "The Caesarea Mithraeum: A Preliminary Announcement," *BA*, XXXVIII (1975), 2-10; R. Bull, L. Holland, and C. Fritsch, eds., *The Joint Expedition to Caesarea Maritima: Studies in the History of Caesarea Maritima, I, BASOR* Supplementary Studies, 19 (1975); R. Bull, "A Mithraic Medallion from Caesarea," *IEJ*, XXIV (1974), 187-90.

R. J. BULL

***CAIN AND ABEL.** This narrative has lent itself to a wide range of interpretations, depending on varying assumptions as to the intention of the biblical author. Was that intention literal or symbolic (allegorical)? Or, would even a literal intention have assured the preservation of the narrative, were it not for the power of its symbolism?

Assuming a symbolic or didactic value, what is the basic lesson intended by the narrative? Is it, for example, an anthropological speculation on the conflict between two ways of life—the pastoral and the agricultural? Against this modern and widely held interpretation are the following considerations:

a) The witness of history in the early Near East is that clashes between communities resting on different economic bases were not between pastoral and agricultural peoples, but rather between sedentary, urban-agricultural societies on the one hand and less "civilized" hill peoples or steppe nomads on the other. (Even the urban-agricultural economies included substantial elements of wealth in the form of livestock.)

b) To root the story in such a conflict is to impute to the biblical author the assumption that the Deity favored either the pastoral way of life over the agricultural or vegetable offerings over animal sacrifice, in which case one is left with the anomaly that God tolerates the annihilation of the favored shepherd at the hands of the aggressor agriculturalist, who, in turn, is apparently driven to nomadism—with the result that both ways of life are destroyed. That the husbandman turned nomad-outcast then becomes the city-founder culture hero (Gen. 4:17) is an incongruity hardly eased by such an interpretation.

c) If source analysis is to be credited (*see* DOCUMENTS; SOURCE CRITICISM, OT[S]), the author of the Cain and Abel narrative (J) views Cain as propagator and representative of all mankind, not of a single branch. The P genealogy of antediluvians in Gen. 5 descends from Adam through Seth and his son Enosh and does not include Cain. The J genealogy in ch. 4 descends through Cain to the three sons of Lamech and knows no Seth. Hence 4:25-26*a* must be viewed as an editor's attempt to bridge the gap between the two differing genealogies.

Other problematical features in this narrative may offer clues as to its genre and to its basic motif. If, other than Cain and his parents, there was no society, what is the meaning of banishment? Who is the candidate ("whoever finds me," Gen. 4:14) who may feel free to kill Cain? And, assuming other men to exist, why should they desire Cain's death?

Unless J is to be written off as inept both as thinker and artist, the Cain and Abel episode must be seen as the culmination of the Eden story in chs. 2 and 3, a single composition, allegory or fable, articulating J's anthropology and theology. Since the characters are symbolic and prototypical, the tale is timeless; the conventions of life, however, are those of ancient Israel.

Two brothers are rivals for the favor of a divine monarch. The one offers the finest gift he can make; the other's gift is of middling quality. When the king makes known his displeasure with the latter, he also informs him that he is free to make amends and achieve restoration to favor; he warns him, however, that freedom of will makes him vulnerable to the demonic temptation of wrongdoing. The admonition is all too prophetic: the offender who began with niggardliness to this master now moves from petulance to murder. In the murderer's response to the question as to his brother's whereabouts, the author provides an exquisite insight into the psychology of the immoralist: he is one who rejects responsibility for his fellow.

Elsewhere in the Bible crimes against one's neighbor are pictured as polluting the earth upon which one lives and from which one draws sustenance. Here the decreed punishment is the earth's rejection of the killer who has forced upon her a diet of human blood. As in 3:17-19 (by the same hand) the penalty is a debarring from the soil's natural fertility; it will not even respond to cultivation. The result (as in 3:18) is a forced reversion from the life of the settled farmer to that of ranging wide to gather wild grains and fruits. (The expression *nā' wānādh*, "fugitive and wanderer" [4:12], has overtones of neither fugitivism nor nomadism; it is a hendiadys denoting one who is endlessly on the move.) The condemned one's response is that the decree is equivalent to a death sentence. In the context of ancient Israel's regulation governing homicide, the obligation of kinsmen to exact vengeance (cf. also vs. 24) is the deterrent which protects members of a society; the outcast is deprived of this protection. Being "hidden" from God (vs. 14) is common to court imagery, an expression for the denial of God's favor and protection. Yet, because Cain, in this account of J's, is the sole remaining progeny of the first couple, the Deity preserves him (and through him the human race) by taking him under his own protection, imprinting upon him an apotropaic mark, a warning to all and sundry that God himself will exact sevenfold vengeance for harm done to Cain.

A synopsis of the events in Eden is required to put the Cain and Abel denouement in proper perspective. In chs. 2 and 3, J addresses himself to the perplexing problem of how a Deity who is both just and benevolent could have destined human beings for death, the ultimate evil. The mythos he formulates envisions two alternative worlds: (1) the Age of Innocence (Eden), in which there is no death, where human beings live forever in the persons of the first couple, archetypes of the species, with no needs unfulfilled, and ignorant of sexuality, the instrument of procreation; and (2) the Age of Experience, featuring knowledge, sexuality, procreation—and death. Death is necessary because the limitations of space preclude the coexistence of procreation and deathlessness. It was by human choice that death came into the world—death and time and history with all their evils. For without the possibility of evil, without the *problemata* which are the stuff of history, there is no history. The choice of first man and woman in tasting the fruit of experience eventuated in the birth of Cain and Abel, in the possibility of history. And the first event in history is man's murder of his brother; Cain here represents all mankind, and all are members of one family. History is atrocity, not because human beings are ignorant, but because they have freedom of will and, despite instruction and admonition, exercise it in defiance of their Creator.

Bibliography. Cf. the standard Bible commentaries with special reference to E. A. Speiser, *Genesis*, ABi (1964). For rabbinic homilies cf. L. Ginzberg, *The Legends of the Jews*, 7 vols. (1909-38); Midrash Rabbah, *ad loc.*

H. C. BRICHTO

***CALAH. 1. Location.** Calah, today's Nimrud, is located on the E bank of the Tigris five miles N of its junction with the Zab. The Tigris once ran at the base of the walls on the W side, but has slowly moved westward to its present position about two miles away.

2. History of excavations. Between 1845 and 1851 Layard carried out a series of excavations. He discovered the Northwest Palace of Ashurnasirpal II and uncovered innumerable sculptures, reliefs, and small objects which are now in the British Museum. In 1949 the British School of Archaeology in Iraq began fourteen successful seasons of excavation which ended in 1963.

3. History of Calah. Although excavations have shown that Calah was inhabited as early as 2500 B.C., the city does not appear in historical accounts until *ca.* 1250 B.C. when it was founded as a town by Shalmaneser I of Assyria. Ashurnasirpal II (884-859 B.C.) enlarged Calah and made it his capital. He and his successors ruled Assyria from Calah until the late eighth century, when the capital was transferred to Khorsabad and soon after to NINEVEH. Ashurnasirpal set himself an ambitious plan for his new city. In five years he had completed most of the circuit wall, nearly five miles of solid mud-brick. This outer city wall enclosed an area of nine hundred acres. A stele commemorates the completion of the palace in the fifth year of his reign and mentions the feast given for the 63,000 citizens of Calah, including 47,000 workmen transported from conquered parts of the Empire. To help feed the expanded population, Ashurnasirpal built a canal which brought the fresh waters of the Greater Zab a distance of six miles to irrigate land and exotic ornamental gardens near the city. The canal is easily traceable over much of its course today and the Negub, the rock-cut tunnel which carried the water through a large conglomerate bluff, can be seen opposite the modern village of Quwair. Ashurnasirpal also built the temple of Ninurta, god of war and patron of Calah, and began work on the ziggurat adjoining the temple. The ziggurat, standing at a present height of over 141 feet, was completed by Ashurnasirpal's son Shalmaneser III (859-824 B.C.).

Nimrud (Calah's later and present name) continued as a provincial capital after its abandonment as capital of the Empire. It was destroyed during the Median invasions in 614-612 B.C. There were a few survivors who lingered, but the city was deserted by the time that Xenophon and his troops passed by in 401 B.C.

4. Major buildings. The temple of Ninurta, completed in the eighteenth year of Ashurnasirpal's reign, stood at the foot of the ziggurat in the NW corner of the citadel. Layard discovered the principal sanctuary and a subsidiary one, the latter decorated with reliefs of magical figures. In the storage magazines of the temple many valuable small objects were found in the debris, dropped by the looters when the city was sacked—small testimonials from what must have been the richest temple in the city.

The Northwest Palace was divided into two main sectors; the *babanu* (derived from Akkad. *babu*, "gate") around the outer courtyard where business was transacted and the public had access, and the *bitanu* (derived from Akkad. *bitu*, "house") around the inner courtyard with its reception rooms and residential quarters reserved for the private life of the king and his family. The two sectors were connected by the largest and most important room in the palace—the throne room. This plan, without precedent in the Middle-Assyrian period, became standard for Late Assyrian palaces. The S façade, now restored, is decorated with reliefs cut in the local gypsum (or "Mosul marble") depicting tribute-bearers. Two doorways flanked by winged bulls and lions lead into the throne room. The throne was placed before a relief showing the king twice, standing on either side of the "Sacred Tree" between winged genii who anoint him. On the S wall of the room ran double sculptured bands showing the king hunting lions and bulls and also engaging in warfare.

In the SE corner of the citadel were located the Nabu temple and the Burnt Palace. These are ascribed to the period of Adad-nirari III (808-782 B.C.). The Nabu temple, dedicated to the god of writing and his consort Tashmetum, has twin sanctuaries: stone-paved rectangular rooms with raised platforms for the statues of the deities. The shrines were surrounded by chambers housing the business and domestic activities of the temple.

To the N of the Nabu temple, a road passes through the original gate where the citadel wall is 122 feet thick and still stands to a height of 43 feet, and proceeds through the outer city to the arsenal built by Shalmaneser III in the southeasternmost corner of the city. This arsenal (Akkad. *ekal-masharti*) housed barracks, storage rooms, workshops, and a royal palace. Although the plan has similarities with the Northwest Palace, such as the throne room used as a division between the two sectors, the *ekal-masharti* is much more military in character. There is an extra throne dais in the great courtyard to facilitate the king's review of his troops. Among the important finds made in the arsenal was the throne base of Shalmaneser III and many of the ivories for which Calah is renowned: plaques, figurines, inlays for furniture, and pieces of furniture.

Bibliography. A. H. Layard, *Nineveh and its Remains* (1852); M. E. L. Mallowan, *Nimrud and its Remains* (1966); D. Oates, *Studies in the Ancient History of Northern Iraq* (1968). For further details see Mallowan's and Oates' preliminary reports published regularly in *Iraq* during the years the expedition was in the field.

M. E. STOUT

***CALF, GOLDEN.** A bull image, probably made of wood and overlaid with gold, which was worshiped in the wilderness and later in the northern kingdom of Israel. The image may have represented the god Yahweh or, like the ark and cherubim in the Jerusalem temple, an enthronement seat or pedestal for Yahweh.

Scholars disagree on the origin and function of the calf image. Eissfeldt suggests that the bull—and the ark—were genuine Israelite cultic symbols prior to the return of the Israelites to Canaan; while Bailey argues that the bull image represented the Mesopotamian moon-god Sîn, whose cult survived the patriarchal age as an acceptable form of Israelite religion. This contention, if correct, would render unnecessary the opinions that the calf was only a pedestal and did not interfere with exclusive Yahweh worship.

There are two different yet similar accounts of the introduction of the calf cult in Israel. The first, in Exod. 32, relates that the people became impatient during Moses' prolonged absence on Mount Sinai and demanded that Aaron make a god to lead them. This does not prove (as has been suggested) that the Israelites merely wanted a divine desert guide. The sequel indicates that fertility rites, which would be quite inappropriate in the case of a desert guide, were associated with the new cult. Having collected golden ornaments from the people, Aaron shaped them into the form of a bull, which was then proclaimed to be a representation of the god who had brought Israel out of Egypt.

Subsequently, Aaron built an altar and proclaimed "a festival unto Yahweh." The festival degenerated into a cultic orgy. Yahweh's wrath was aroused against the "stiff-necked" people, and he proposed to Moses that they be destroyed and replaced as God's chosen people by Moses' own clan, presumably the Levites who did not participate in the cultic ceremonies. Moses' supplication saved the people from wholesale destruction, but it was not enough to prevent the punishment of those who were prominently associated with the new cult.

On descending from the mountain, Moses pulverized the calf image, and mixing the powder with water, submitted the people to the "bitter water" ordeal normally reserved for a woman suspected of adultery (cf. Num. 5:11-28). A plague subsequently sent by Yahweh (Exod. 32:35) was, it may be assumed, Yahweh's way of weeding out the guilty from the innocent. *See* ORDEAL, JUDICIAL[S].

Another account, however, depicts Moses as ordering the Levites to kill even their closest relatives if they were involved in the worship of the calf. Some three thousand Israelites were thus put to death (Exod. 32:28). The Levites were henceforth consecrated as Yahweh's servants.

The role of Aaron in this episode is thoroughly condemned—not only in Exod. 32, where Moses places the entire blame on Aaron's shoulders, but also in Deut. 9:20, where we are told that Yahweh would have slain Aaron except for Moses' intercession.

Most scholars agree that there is a connection between the story of the golden calf made by Aaron and the account, in I Kings 12:26-33, of the two golden calves made by JEROBOAM and set up at the sanctuaries of Bethel and Dan. There are so many similarities between the two accounts that the dependence of one upon the other can hardly be doubted. In the formation of the calf cult, the building of the altar, the offering of the sacrifices, the role of the Levites, the description of the new cult as the sin par excellence, and the resultant divine displeasure leading to national disaster, the two accounts are remarkably similar in tendency, language, and style. Hence, conservative scholars assume that Jeroboam revived an ancient cult harking back to Aaron, whom he took as his model in all his cultic activities, even going so far as to name his two sons, Nadab and Abijah (=Abijahu=Abihu), after Aaron's eldest sons.

Most critics regard Exod. 32 as a thinly veiled attack on Jeroboam and his calf cult. The plural form "your gods" in both versions (Exod. 32:4; I Kings 12:28) lends support to this theory. Whatever the original story of the golden calf in the wilderness may have been (and one may concede that Jeroboam did not invent a new cult but restored an ancient one), its present form appears to denigrate Jeroboam who is, to all intents and purposes, identical with Aaron and to denounce the bull cult in the northern kingdom. In this account, Aaron is no saintly high priest serving as Moses' closest collaborator and spokesman, but is one who causes Israel to sin and is actually marked for death by Yahweh (Deut. 9:20). The detailed description of the violent reaction of Moses and the Levites was calculated to counteract the establishment of the calf cult at Bethel, where the priesthood traced its descent from Aaron (Judg. 20:26-28) and at Dan, which was served by a Levitical priesthood claiming Mosaic origin (cf. Judg. 17:7–18:31).

It appears, therefore, that Exod. 32 represents the attitude of the Zadokite priests of Jerusalem, who evidently did not identify with the Aaronite priesthood until after the Exile. In view of the prestige attached to Bethel and Dan, Jeroboam's separatist religious policy was as dangerous to the recently built Jerusalem temple as was his political separatism to the Davidic dynasty. The calf cult threatened to undermine the primacy of Solomon's temple and its newly risen priesthood. Whoever was associated with it was therefore a mortal enemy deserving the ultimate penalty. *See* ZADOK THE PRIEST[S].

It was only in the postexilic era that the Zadokite priesthood, anxious to be recognized as the sole legitimate priesthood (cf. Ezek. 44:15-31), endowed itself with Aaronite descent (I Chr. 6:3-15 [H 5:29-41]) as part of the fulfillment of the prophetic dream of unification of the northern and southern tribes. The elevation of Aaron in so many Pentateuchal passages and the partial mitigation of his culpability (e.g., Exod. 32:4, MT "they said" instead of "he said" as required by the context) evidently derives from the need to present Aaron, now considered *the* progenitor of the entire priesthood, in a more favorable light. *See* AARON, AARONIDES[S].

In postbiblical times the entire episode became

highly embarrassing and a source of much anxiety. It was probably to avoid exploitation by Alexandrian anti-Semites, who asserted that the Jews worshiped an ass in the temple (cf. Jos. Apion II.vii.10; Tacitus, *Histories* V.iii-iv), that Josephus omitted the golden calf story in his account of Moses' descent from Mount Sinai. Accordingly, the Israelites, dejected by anxiety because of Moses' prolonged absence, rejoiced when he came down at last and showed them the tablets of the law (Jos. Antiq. III.v.7-8; vi.1).

There was also some concern about Aaron's role in making the calf. Philo, who did not entirely suppress the narrative, nevertheless kept Aaron out of it (*Moses* II.161-74, 271). The rabbis likewise did their best to exonerate Aaron in view of his idealization (or that of his priestly successors) in biblical and rabbinic literature (e.g., M. AB. 1.12; ARN, ed. Schechter, *Version* A, 12; *Version* B, 24, pp. 24b-26a). In the final form of the Torah, Aaron is Moses' most trusted lieutenant. The rabbinic apology maintained that since he had been chosen to become high priest, it followed that he had not been really guilty of willful idolatry. He had been forced to make the calf by threats to his life, which he would have willingly sacrificed but for his wish to spare the people an additional burden of guilt. He tried to make the people change their mind by demanding the surrender of their precious ornaments and by procrastinating as long as possible. While he reluctantly gave his consent to the proceedings, the actual production of the calf was the work of two foreign-born magicians. In the Middle Ages, Saadia Gaon and Judah Halevi maintained that Aaron's sole purpose in yielding had been to entrap the idolators and rid the community of them.

In Christian polemic literature, the sin of the golden calf was the original source of the crime of the crucifixion and of Israel's general sinfulness and stiff-necked refusal to acknowledge Jesus (cf. Stephen's speech in Acts 7:41-53). The church Fathers frequently denounced the Jews for having worshiped the golden calf. The Jews had thus revealed their impatience and ingratitude as well as their foolish, immoral, stubborn, unrepentant, unbelieving, and murderous character. They had thereby nullified the Sinaitic covenant which had in fact never come into effect. Furthermore, by this act the Jews had abandoned God who, in turn, had repudiated them. The crime of the golden calf could never be erased and the Jews were therefore eternally damned; unless of course, they entered into the bosom of the church. In Augustine's interpretation, the powder of the calf's head, cast into water and given to the people to drink, represented a sacrament, so that the worshipers of the devil-calf became the body of the devil (*Expositions on the Book of Psalms* 62:5; 74:13). This may well have been the origin of the medieval identification of the Jew with the devil.

The rabbinic reaction to such attacks was ambivalent and seemingly inconsistent. On the one hand, there was full admission of the gravity of the sin of the golden calf. Thus, Israel was compared to "a shameless bride who plays the harlot within her bridal canopy" (T.B. Shab. 88b; Git. 36b). There were no mitigating factors. The rabbis conceded that all the calamities that had ever befallen Israel originated with the golden calf, which had been the worst calamity of all.

On the other hand, national pride and the need to maintain morale during centuries of humiliation and persecution necessitated a resolute defense of Israel vis-à-vis the church. The concessions were meant strictly for internal consumption. Toward the outside world the rabbis assumed a militant, uncompromising attitude. Far from forsaking Israel, God had forgiven their sin and continued to love them as his chosen people. In any case, only a small minority had been involved in the calf cult, and they were not even genuine Israelities but members of the Egyptian "mixed multitude" who had joined the Israelites at the Exodus (cf. Exod. 12:38).

Other lines of defense stressed that the covenantal relationship with God had not yet come into effect when the golden calf was made. Israel was therefore in a state of precovenantal innocence. Moreover, God himself was to blame for Israel's sin, and Moses rebuked the Almighty for having brought them to Egypt, where they learned idolatry, and for bestowing upon them excessive amounts of gold and silver which they used for making idols. Akiba, the foremost exponent of rabbinic Judaism, even made God himself admit that he rather than Israel was responsible for the golden calf, and that he would therefore cleanse Israel of this sin.

This daring line of defense—hardly to be taken literally—was not meant to be theologically tenable or to provide any consistent interpretation of the golden calf story. It was rather meant as a counterattack and as a morale booster in times of great physical distress and mental anguish. Preaching to synagogue audiences, the rabbis succeeded in renewing hope and restoring self-respect by assuring them of God's continued love which would culminate in Israel's restoration.

Bibliography. L. R. Bailey, "The Golden Calf," *HUCA,* XLII (1971), 97-115; M. Aberbach and L. Smolar, "Aaron, Jeroboam, and the Golden Calves," *JBL,* LXXXVI (1967), 129-40; M. Noth, *Exodus* (1962); J. Gray, *I and II Kings* (1963); W. Beyerlin, *Origins and History of the Oldest Sinaitic Traditions* (1965); H. Obbink, "Jahwebilder," *ZAW,* XLVII (1929), 264-74; O. Eissfeldt, "Lade und Stierbild," *ZAW,* LVIII (1940-41), 190-215; A. F. Key, "Traces of the Worship of the Moon God Sîn among the Early Israelites," *JBL,* LXXXIV (1965), 20-26; L. Smolar and M. Aberbach, "The Golden Calf Episode in Postbiblical Literature," *HUCA,* XXXIX (1968), 91-116.

L. SMOLAR
M. ABERBACH

***CALNEH (CALNO)** [כלנה Amos 6:2; כלנו Isa. 10:9; LXX Χαλαννη; Assyr. *Kullani, Kullania,* or *Kulnia*]. Capital city of the N Syrian kingdom of Patinu or Unqi (*see* HITTITES[S] §2 and map); it also appears in Assyrian records as Kinalia, Kinalua, Kunalia, Kunulua, and <Ku>nulia. Of the two names, *Kullani* was the Semitic name of the city (attested in Thut-mose III's list and Alalakh tablets), and *Kinalia* its Neo-Hittite name, perhaps derived from a Hittite divine name. Conquered by Tiglath-pileser III in 738 B.C., it became the center of the Assyrian province of Kullani. It is identifiable with the large mound of Tell Ta'yinat in the 'Amūq Plain. Excavations revealed a royal palace complex, including a temple (*ca.* 800), a palace of the Assyrian governor, and several Neo-Hittite and Assyrian works of art. The temple presents architectural parallels to the TEMPLE OF SOLOMON. As for the alleged Calneh in Shinar, Gen. 10:10, read *w^{e}kullānâ*, "all of them."

Bibliography. S. Parpola, "Kinalua" and "Kullani" in *Neo-Assyrian Toponyms* (1970), for Assyrian occurrences; R. J. Braidwood, *Mounds of the Plain of Antioch* (1937), pp. 6, 18, 32 (fig. 6), 33 (no. 126); C. W. McEwan, "The Syrian Expedition of the Oriental Institute. . . ," *AJA,* XLI (1937), 8-16; R. C. Haines, *Excavations in the Plain of Antioch,* II (1971), pp. 37-62; W. F. Albright, "The End of 'Calneh' in Shinar," *JNES,* III (1944), 254-55. M. C. ASTOUR

***CALVARY.** *See* HOLY SEPULCHRE, CHURCH OF THE [S].

*CANAAN, CONQUEST AND SETTLEMENT OF.

1. Introduction
2. The name "Canaan"
3. The land of Canaan
   a. As a geographic and political unit
   b. The political structure of Canaan
4. The OT traditions of conquest and settlement
   a. The textual problem
   b. The archaeological and literary problem
5. A historical synthesis
   a. The contribution of the historical documents
   b. The contribution of archaeology
   c. Conquest and settlement

Bibliography

1. Introduction. The Israelites knew that they had not always dwelt in the land of Canaan, but had occupied it at a particular point in history, when Yahweh began to fulfill the promises which he had made to the patriarchs Abraham, Isaac, and Jacob. Since the life of Israel in the land had from the beginning been under constant threat (except for the brief time of security under David and Solomon), it is understandable that the people clung to the promise and its fulfillment. It is no accident that the traditions of the occupation of the land occupy a particularly prominent place in the historical picture of the OT. *See* PROMISES TO THE PATRIARCHS[S].

2. The name "Canaan." (*See* CANAANITES §1.)

3. The land of Canaan. ***a. As a geographic and political unit.*** i. *In cuneiform texts.* One of the Mari letters reports on "Canaanite bandits" (^{lú}*ḫabbātum u* ^{lú}*Kinaḫnûm*) and so provides indirect evidence from the eighteenth century B.C. for the name Canaan. In Alalakh and Ugarit Canaanites appear in name lists as foreigners, because their place of origin is noted. Thus in the fifteenth-thirteenth centuries B.C. these cities, unlike Ammiya, the present-day Enfe ten miles SW of Tripoli in Lebanon, did not belong to Canaan (Smith).

In the fourteenth century B.C., according to the Amarna letters, Canaan was an Egyptian province ruled by Egyptian governors and local princes. In the thirteenth century the situation was essentially the same. After 1285 Ramses II made Canaan the base for a military campaign against Syria, and he arranged to meet the Hittite king, who wanted to visit Egypt, in Canaan, "in his land." *See* HITTITES §4; HITTITES[S].

ii. *In Egyptian texts.* The first mention of Canaan is from the time of Amen-hotep II (second half of the fourteenth century), who conducted a campaign in Asia in the seventh year of his reign and deported "Canaanites" (*Kn^{c}ní.w*) (*ANET* [2nd ed.], p. 246). The boundary between Egypt and Canaan passed near the fortress of Sile (Egyp. *Ṯ'rw*), not far from modern el-Qantara on the Suez Canal (*ANET,* pp. 254b, 478). The description of the "foreigners of the land *p' Kn^{c}n* (the Canaan)" begins with the mention of the "Ways of Horus" (Sile), followed by stations on the road to Palestine. In most passages, however, [*p'*] *Kn^{c}n* is a city, apparently the capital of the province of the same name. According to the contexts in which it is mentioned in connection with the campaign of Sethos I in the first regnal year, it was the city of Gaza.

iii. *In Phoenician texts.* There are no occurrences of the name Canaan in Phoenician texts prior to the Hellenistic period. In the mythological genealogies, Χνᾶ, the eponymous ancestor of Canaan, is mentioned among the cultural heros, with the information that he was the first to bear the name Φοίνικος, "Phoenician" (Philo Byblius, FHG 790 F 2:39; first or second century A.D.). The grammarian Herodianus (second century A.D.) and Stephan of Byzantium (fifth century A.D.?) also state that Phoenicia was formerly called Χνᾶ. The city of Berytus (modern Beirut) was known in the second century B.C. in Phoenician as *L'dk' 'š b-Kn'n,* "Laodicea in Canaan." *See* PHOENICIA.

iv. *In the OT.* The oldest occurrence of the term is in Judg. 5:19 (twelfth century B.C.?), where we learn that the Israelites fought at Taanach against a coalition of "the kings of Canaan." It seems that this expression reflects LB usage, and therefore designates the petty princes from the former Egyptian province of Canaan. The later author of Judg. 4:2, 23-24 derived from this the title "king of Canaan" for Jabin of Hazor, who was introduced into the story as a secondary element (cf. Josh. 11:1-15 and §4*b below*).

In the J history, Canaan as a designation for the land is found only where J adopted material from the genealogical traditions for the framework of the primordial history (Gen. 9:25-27; 10:15-19). In this context the use of Canaan and Canaanite is not uniform and is hard to explain historically. In the narrative parts of his work J speaks consistently of "the Canaanite" (הכנעני, collective singular). They are the inhabitants of the land at the time of the patriarchs (Gen. 12:6; 13:7, "the Canaanites and the Perizzites"; 24:3, 37; 34:30 [as in 13:7]; 38:2) and of the Conquest (Num. 14:43, 45; 21:1, 3; cf. Judg. 1:4 [as in Gen. 13:7]; 1:5 [secondary]). The fact that J used only the term Canaanite and did not call the land Canaan, but used the formula, "At that time the Canaanites were in the land" (Gen. 12:6; cf. 13:7), shows the extent to which J was removed in time and by national identity from the previous inhabitants, whose occupation of the land was now conceived as a mere passing episode. A similar attitude can be seen in the statements about the incomplete conquest of the land by the Israelites (Judg. 1:27-33) and in the Deuteronomic literature.

An even greater distancing from the historical reality is seen in a list of the autochthonus inhabitants of Palestine, the oldest form of which is preserved in Deut. 7:1. This list regards the Canaanites as only one group among others that were living in the land.

In contrast to the other sources, the Priestly document speaks consistently of the "land of Canaan" (ארץ כנען), except for the genealogy in Gen. 10:6, which has "Canaan." In this way it revived the LB terminology. For P, Canaan is the land that was promised to the patriarchs (Gen. 17:8; Exod. 6:4) and in which they lived for a time (Gen. 13:12; 16:3; 31:18; 37:1); it is the goal of the Israelite tribes that left Egypt (Num. 13:2, 17). The following cities are mentioned: Shechem (Gen. 33:18), Shiloh (Josh. 22:9—if this is P), Luz (Bethel, Gen. 35:6), Kiriath-arba (Hebron, Gen. 23:2), with the cave of Machpelah (Gen. 23:19). On the other hand, the cities of the plain (ככר) S of the Dead Sea (Gen. 13:12) and the land of Seir (Gen. 36:6) lie outside Canaan. The additions to P specify the Jordan as the eastern boundary of Canaan, thereby excluding Transjordan (Num. 35:14). The most detailed description of the extent of Canaan is in Num. 34:2*b*, 3*b*-12. This description does not correspond to the boundaries after 1000 B.C., but it does to those of the Egyptian territory in Asia, according to the peace treaty between Egypt and the Hittities in the thirteenth century (omitting Amurru, but including Ūpe; the S boundary is probably more recent). *See also* HURRIANS[S] §3.

The Joseph story uses, even in the parts that are not P, the concept "land of Canaan" for the homeland of Jacob and his sons (Gen. 42:5 and *passim*), and this suggests to some scholars that none of the material of the story is from J or E. The history of the transmission of Gen. 50 makes it difficult to specify the extent of the "land of Canaan" (vs. 5). The grave of Jacob, to which the text refers, was probably located at Shechem; P says it was at Mamre in the "land of Canaan" (vs. 13). Vs. 10*a* may contain another tradition, which located the grave of Jacob across the Jordan at the "threshing floor of Atad," and therefore does not mention Canaan. Only in the etiological explanation of the place name "Abel-Mizraim" in vs. 10*b*-11, in the style of J, are the "inhabitants of the land, the Canaanites," mentioned as witnesses of the great ceremony of mourning, something that does not fit the location E of the Jordan.

b. The political structure of Canaan. i. *In the Bronze Age*. The division of Canaan into many small units, each centering around a city ("city-states"), which is characteristic of the political organization of the land before the Israelite conquest, is documented in cuneiform and Egyptian texts from the beginning of the second millennium on. The earliest sources, the Egyptian execration texts of the Twelfth Dynasty, give the names of rulers, evidence of the existence of monarchical government. The basic form of this political structure survived the conquest of Palestine by pharaohs of the Eighteenth Dynasty and the setting up of Egyptian provinces. The local political realities were largely preserved, because the Egyptians interfered in the inner affairs of the city-state only when their own interests were involved. The rulers were generally regarded by their subjects as "kings," but the dynastic succession had to have the approval of the pharaoh, who probably understood this in terms of installing a royal official as "mayor," as in Egypt.

The city rulers were responsible for paying tribute regularly, maintaining military control over their territory, and, in emergencies, for supplying troops. Certain changes took place when various cities became the property of the pharaoh (Gaza and Jaffa under Thut-mose III, Simyra and Kumidi under Ramses II, and Ascalon in the period of the Ramesides) or property of the Egyptian gods, that is, temple property. On the whole, the system of indirect rule functioned well as long as Egypt was strong enough to be sure of the loyalty of the city rulers. It was, however, not a real *pax aegyptiaca*. In periods of weakness, as the Amarna letters show, the Egyptian authorities were helpless to settle the fights among the city-states. *See* TELL EL-AMARNA §2*b*; TELL EL-AMARNA [S].

The economy of the city-states was based on farming and commerce. This distinguishes them from the third political element in the land, the so-called nomads (Egyp. *Šśw;* Akkad. *Sūtû*), who are prominent in the LB texts. They were found especially in areas which the city-states did not or could not effectively control, e.g., the forested mountains. They were organized in tribes under leaders (Egyp. *wr.w*, "great men"), and their main economic activity was the raising of sheep and goats. In the texts they mainly appear in the role of robbers who make the highways unsafe, harassing the city rulers and at times even the Egyptian army; on the other hand, they served both parties as mercenaries. In reality, as anthropological and sociological studies show, the cities and the "nomads" probably had close economic relationships, and perhaps even intermarried. They were in fact interdependent, although this did not rule out occasional clashes or robberies. *See* NOMADISM[S]; HABIRU[S].

ii. *In the Early Iron Age*. Toward the end of the second millennium there appeared alongside the LB city-states and the territoral states which originated from them a new entity, peoples whose solidarity was not primarily the result of their living in the same territory, but rather the result of kinship ties. ARAM is mentioned for the first time under Amen-hotep III (fourteenth century), and again in the third year of Mer-ne-Ptah. MOAB is first mentioned prior to the fifth year of Ramses II (1285 B.C.), Israel in the fifth year of Mer-ne-Ptah (1219), EDOM in his eighth year

(1216), and the PHILISTINES in the eighth year of Ramses III (first quarter of the twelfth century).

After the end of Egyptian sovereignty in Palestine, the Philistines, who had been settled there as colonists by Ramses III, quickly established city-states on the LB model, but continued to be aware, for some time, of their origins as a single people, even sharing some common institutions. In the same period the Arameans, Ammonites, Moabites, Edomites, and Israelites transformed their tribal leagues into national states ruled by kings. This took place in part in territories on the edge of or entirely outside of the area where the LB city-states had flourished. According to papyrus Anastasi VI (*ANET,* p. 259) the Edomites belonged to the *Šˀśw,* as did the Moabites, if the Balu'ah stele (*ANEP,* no. 488) is a Moabite monument. The other peoples should probably be seen as belonging to the same milieu. In Syria and Palestine the transition from the second to the first millennium B.C. was thus marked by changes in political structures that correspond to the change from permanent nomadism to settlement and the rise of national states. This does not mean that the city-states immediately and totally disappeared, but political leadership passed from them to the national states.

4. The OT traditions of conquest and settlement. ***a. The textual problem.*** There are three blocks of material in the OT that recount the conquest and settlement of the Promised Land: (1) Num. 13–14; 21:1-3, 21-32; 22–24; 32; (2) Josh. 1–24; and (3) Judg. 1:1–2:5. To these may be added isolated passages like Deut. 2:26-37; 3:1-20; Judg. 17–21, and, in the widest sense, the traditions of the patriarchs and the judges. The events are depicted in differing ways in the texts. *See* ISRAEL, HISTORY OF §3.

i. In Numbers–Joshua the account of the Exodus leads directly into the occupation of the land. Israel, although divided into tribes, acts as a unit under unified leadership. After an unsuccessful attempt to invade Canaan from the Negeb (Num. 14:39-45), and the conquest and division of the territory E of the Jordan under the leadership of Moses, Israel crosses the Jordan under Moses' successor, Joshua. From a base camp at Gilgal near Jericho, Joshua leads a series of campaigns against cities and coalitions of Canaanite kings, and conquers large sections of the land W of the Jordan, or, according to some texts, all of it. The cities are destroyed, and their inhabitants exterminated, unless they conclude treaties with the Israelites (Gibeon, Josh. 9). The land is divided among the tribes, who, after having taken part in the great assembly at Shechem (Josh. 24), settle in the territory assigned to them.

ii. By contrast, in Judg. 1:1–2:5 it is the individual tribes who take the actions, not the nation as a whole. Nothing is said about Joshua or any other national leader, and for this reason in the editorial process the unit is placed after Joshua's death (1:1). Another striking feature is that the tribes still have to conquer their assigned territories W of the Jordan, when, according to the book of Joshua, this had already been done. This contradiction and the repetition of Josh. 24:28-31 in Judg. 2:6-9, which indicates a seam, demonstrate that Judg. 1:1–2:5 is an insertion which interrupts the continuity from the book of Joshua to the book of Judges, and which should be investigated on its own terms. *See* JUDGES, BOOK OF §C1; JUDGES, BOOK OF[S] §1.

The question of the relationships between the material in (i) and (ii) can be answered in various ways. The redactor who interpolated Judg. 1:1–2:5 believed that one followed the other; the land has been conquered and now the tribes occupy it (cf. Josh. 24:28). This view would be more logical if, with Wright, we could ascribe to Joshua a "sweeping conquest" which captured from the Canaanites a number of key strategic positions and so made it easier for the tribes to complete the final occupation of their territory. The position of Alt and Noth is, however, more probably the correct one: that the problem is not historical, but literary, involving the history of tradition. They assumed that at the beginning of Israel's history there were the tribes (cf. the stories from the days of the judges), and that national unity was achieved comparatively late. In that case, stories about what individual tribes did (as in Judg. 1:1–2:5) must belong to an earlier stage of tradition history than those that show the whole nation in action (as in Numbers and in Josh. 1–12). Also, according to Alt and Noth, we must distinguish even in Josh. 1–12 between the old traditions and the work of an editor who collected them around 900 B.C. He had already constructed the continuous narrative of the Conquest in which the main participants were Joshua and all Israel. (The Deuteronomic editor only carried this further with additions, especially description of the territories assigned to the tribes.) *See* JOSHUA, BOOK OF §§B-C; DEUTERONOMIC HISTORY[S].

The old traditions are separate accounts such as etiologies (Josh. 2–9; 10:16-27; *see* ETIOLOGY[S]) and accounts of battles (10:1-15; 11:1-15) which always have a specific locale in the territory of one of the tribes. The geographical framework and the localizing of Joshua's base camp at Gilgal reveal that the etiological sagas (except Josh. 10:16-27, which is Judean) are Benjaminite traditions that were preserved at the sanctuary in Gilgal, as was the war story in Josh. 10:1-15, while Josh. 11:1-15 is probably a Naphtalite tradition (Hazor is in Naphtali; Josh. 19:36). The original locus of the Ephramite Joshua is, according to Alt, Josh. 10:1-15, and according to Noth probably Josh. 17:14-18. It was then the "collector" of the stories who raised him to the status of leader of the armies of all Israel. Alt and Noth traced the origin of the etiological sagas back to the need of the people to explain striking contemporary geographical or social conditions in terms of determinative events of the past, especially the earliest period of the settlement in the land. An example is the huge tell at AI (Josh 8:1-29). The war stories, on the other hand, go back to clashes with Canaanites at the time of the Israelite settlement or expansion.

The explanation of most of the narratives in Josh. 2–9 as etiologies has come under heavy criticism. According to Albright, it is not possible to determine on the basis of the form of a story whether or not it can claim historicity, since "all ancient literary composition had to conform to fixed patterns of oral delivery and formal styles of writing." Bright and Childs stress the secondary nature of the etiological elements in the conquest narratives. Any solution of the problems raised by Alt and Noth would then be possible only on the basis of external evidence.

b. The archaeological and literary problem. Attempts have been made to find this external evidence in the Amarna Letters and their reports of troubles caused by the *'apiru* (HABIRU) in Canaan in the fourteenth century. The Yashuya who is mentioned in *EA* 256:18 has even been identified with Joshua. It is not possible, however, to establish a positive identification of the *'apiru* with the biblical Hebrews (עברים), and the attempt to identify Yashuya with the Hebrew יהושע runs counter to the rules of phonetics. The mention of Israel in the reign of Mer-ne-Ptah (*see* §3*b*ii *above*) has also been used to establish the date of the Exodus and the Conquest, but it is still not clear whether the biblical Israel is identical with that mentioned in the Mer-ne-Ptah stele. *See* ISRAEL, HISTORY OF §2.

For this reason the archaeological excavations in Palestine since the end of World War I take on increased significance (*see* ARCHAEOLOGY §E; ARCHAEOLOGY[S] §1). They have shown that in the thirteenth and twelfth centuries B.C. a large number of LB cities were destroyed in major conflagrations, and that the subsequent occupations of these sites in the Iron Age I differ from the earlier culture in architecture and material culture. These observations led to the general conclusion that here was external evidence for the essential correctness of the OT accounts of the Conquest (Albright; *see also* ARCHAEOLOGY §D). Almost immediately, however, difficulties arose in the application of the archaeological data to individual sites (*see* ARCHAEOLOGY[S] §2*a*iv; JOSHUA, BOOK OF[S] §5*c*). At JERICHO (Tell es-Sultan; Josh. 2; 6) the LB IIB level had been destroyed by erosion, assuming that there had been such a layer. At Ai (et-Tell near Deir Dibwan; Josh. 7–8) and ARAD (Tell 'Arad; Judg. 1:16) there were gaps in the occupation between EB and Iron I. Also at GIBEON (el-Jib; Josh. 9) and HESHBON (Hesban; Num. 21:21-31) there was no occupation layer from LB IIB. The various attempts to explain the contradictions between the conquest stories and the results of the excavations have not been convincing. The contradictions are lessened, however, when the stories are interpreted as etiologies designed to explain the presence of major ruined sites or pockets of Canaanite population in the territory settled by the Israelite tribes.

The case seems to be different with BETHEL (Beitin; Judg. 1:22-26), HAZOR (Tell el-Qedah; Josh. 11:1-15), and LACHISH (Tell ed-Duweir; Josh. 10:31-32), which were destroyed at the end of the LB age and occupied again in Iron I. It was easy to find a correlation between the results of excavations and the accounts of the Conquest, but it has still not been conclusively demonstrated that those who destroyed the LB cities are identical with the Iron Age settlers (probably Israelites). The destruction might have been caused by Israelites, or perhaps by Egyptians, Canaanites (cf. the Amarna Letters for the situation in the fourteenth century), the Sea Peoples, or even natural catastrophies. This means that the archaeological evidence is not sufficient to demonstrate the conquest of Canaan by the Israelites, and that the question still depends on the evaluation of the literary character of the texts. Judg. 1:22-26 may be based on authentic traditions. Josh 10:31-32 and 11:1-15, however, are a part of the expansion of the Benjaminite traditions in the book of Joshua, and extended Joshua's campaigns to cover the entire land. The author of Josh. 11:1-15 built on the certainly historical figure of King Jabin of Hazor (cf. Judg. 4:2, 23-24; *see also* §3*a*iv *above*), who had played a major role in the early history of Naphtali. Such quotations as Num. 21:14*b*-15 (from "the Book of the Wars of the Lord"); 21:17*b*-18*a*; and Josh. 10:12*b*-13 (from "the Book of Jashar") lead us to surmise that there were once epics of war or conquest in poetic form, which were closer to the actual events than the prose accounts. The few, poorly preserved fragments, however, give little indication of the contents of those epics.

5. Historical synthesis. §§1-4 have presented materials and analyses that deal with the problem of the Israelite settlement of Canaan from various points of view. It should be clear that a history of that process, in the sense of a chronological presentation, cannot be written. This section presents a hypothesis designed to make the settlement basically comprehensible, in terms of the contributions of the documentary and the archaeological sources.

a. The contribution of the historical documents. Both the documentary evidence (Egyptian city lists, Amarna Letters) and results of investigation into the history of the settlement of Canaan show that in the LB the cities of Palestine were concentrated in the plains, especially the coastal plain, the Valley of Jezreel, and parts of the Jordan Valley, while in the mountainous areas there were only a few cities, which depended on farming small plains or well-watered valleys, or which controlled important commercial routes. Of particular historical significance were two rows of cities running from E to W across the land. One was in the Valley of Jezreel and the other at the latitude of Jerusalem. They can be identified in the LB sources and also in the list of cities claimed by the Israelites but not conquered by them (Judg. 1:21, 27-35). They marked off the Palestinian highlands into three natural divisions: Galilee, Central Palestine (the Mountains of Ephraim), and Judah. Josh. 15–19 describes the basic territory of the Israelite tribes as lying in the mountains along these natural lines of division, and thus outside of the LB (Canaanite) areas of settlement and in the area where, according to Egyptian texts of the second millennium, the "nomads" (*see* §3*b*i *above*) were to be found.

b. The contribution of archaeology. Archaeology cannot give direct "confirmation" of the various OT conquest narratives, but it can show that the settlement of the Israelites in Canaan coincided with the transition in culture from LB to the Iron Age, when the previous city-based culture was absorbed or displaced by a new rural culture. In Palestine this process is most evident in the colonizing of the mountainous regions in Iron I, when numerous villages were begun on virgin soil or on the abandoned ruins of earlier periods. Some thoroughly excavated sites enable us to describe the process more precisely. The LB city of Hazor (stratum XIII, thirteenth century; *see* HAZOR[S] §2*a*) was totally destroyed by fire. Stratum XII (twelfth century, the first Iron Age stratum), which covers only a part of the area of the old city, is characterized by the foundations of huts or tents, with primitive fire pits and storage pits. Stratum XI (eleventh century) contains the remains of an unfortified settlement, and stratum X the first Iron Age city (tenth century, attributable to Solomon; cf. I Kings 9:15).

The situation is similar at Tell Deir'alla, E of Jordan. In LB IIB there was an unfortified sanctuary here that was destroyed in a fire caused by an earthquake. Foundations of huts and storage pits in the succeeding stratum give evidence of the efforts made by the survivors to eke out an existence among the ruins. This phase was also destroyed by fire, which was perhaps caused by seminomads, who soon thereafter settled down in the ruins, dug many storage pits, and built ovens for refining metal. Their material culture was that of Iron I.

Both examples show relatively similar processes at work: the settlement of nomads on existing city ruins and the growth of Iron Age villages out of these camps. We may surmise that elsewhere similar events took place.

c. Conquest and settlement. The assumption that the Israelites belonged to nomadic groups of the second millennium (Egyp. *Šśw*) can be supported by the OT, where there are indications that the Israelites were aware of this origin. Even a relatively late text like the "credo" in Deut. 26:5-10 speaks of the "father" (probably Israel-Jacob) who was a "nomad about to perish" (RSV "a wandering Aramean"). In Israel the Rechabite sect, centuries after the settlement in Canaan, returned to a quasi-nomadic way of life that they regarded as having been theirs originally and as being well-pleasing to God (Jer. 35:1-11). (*See, however,* RECHABITES[S].) And, finally, all layers of tradition in the Genesis accounts of the patriarchs portray Abraham, Isaac, and Jacob as wandering shepherds, with no settled abode in the territory of the Canaanite city-states. Their movements can be understood as the movement to new pastures (Gen. 12:8-9; 13:3[J]; 20:1[E]; 37:12-17). They are accompanied by their families (12:10-20; 13:1; 18:6, 9-15[J] 20:1-18[E]); they live in tents outside the cities (13:18; 18:1; 26:25[J]; 33:19[E]; cf. ch. 32 [JE]); they have extensive flocks and herds (13:2, 7-9; 26:14[J]; 27:9[E]; 47:1); and at times they quarrel with the settled population over water rights (21:25-33[E]; 26:20[J]). Episodes such as Gen. 34 indicate that the stories of the patriarchs were originally accounts of the settlement in the land, even though this attempt at peaceful coexistence failed. In the other stories almost nothing can be seen of antagonism between the two groups. Instead, there are many and varied relationships that apparently were mutually advantageous. In the present state of the texts the original character of these stories is obscured because of the combining of the patriarchal tradition with the exodus tradition, by which the sojourn of the patriarchs in Canaan became a temporary stage.

Thus the patriarchal stories can be regarded as paradigms for the migrations into Canaan of the nomads from whom the Israelite tribes developed. (The dominance of the exodus tradition, which is probably to be related to the Moses group that merged into the tribes, is a result of the strongly religious emphasis which was at work during the formation of Israel.) The seminomadic proto-Israelites could settle in the Palestinian mountains (*see* §5*a above*), for the most part peacefully and undisturbed. From time to time they conquered an isolated mountain city (Bethel, Judg. 1:22-26; Hebron and Debir, Josh. 15:13-19, cf. Judg. 1:10-15; Laish/Dan, Judg. 18; and probably Shechem, cf. Gen. 34:27); with others they merged peacefully (Gibeon, Judg. 9), or even absorbed them into the tribal kinship structures (Shechem and Tirzah, Num. 26:29-34). The plains remained out of reach as areas for settlement. The repeated reference to Canaanite "chariots of iron" (Josh. 17:16, 18; Judg. 1:19; 4:3, 13) and a tradition like that reflected in Judg. 5 are indications that, while the people of the plains did not resist seasonal migrations to find pasture, they did vigorously oppose militarily any attempts of the nomads to settle down and any Israelite attempts at expansion. In spite of occasional successes the tribes could never decisively overcome this opposition prior to the time of David and Solomon.

In spite of this fact, the military experiences became the dominant feature of the Israelite view of history and largely displaced the remembrances of the peaceful proceedings. This is understandable in psychological terms, since events that are out of the ordinary make a greater impression on the memory than the unspectacular events of everyday life. As a result it was unavoidable that when the originally limited exodus tradition was interpreted in terms of all Israel, this should lead to the portrayal of an invasion by a nation of twelve tribes that had escaped from Egypt. The existing local conquest traditions were incorporated into and subordinated to this picture, and in this way Moses and the Ephramite "hero" Joshua came to have their role as leaders of the unified tribes in the occupation of the land on both sides of the Jordan.

Bibliography. General: M. Weippert, *The Settlement of the Israelite Tribes in Palestine* (1971); S. Yeivin, *The Israelite Conquest of Canaan* (1971), §§2-3; W. F. Albright, "The Role of the Canaanites in the History of Civilization," *The Bible and the Ancient Near East* (1961), pp. 328-62; G. Buccellati, *Cities and Nations of Ancient Syria* (1967); W. Helck, "Die ägyptische Verwaltung in den syrischen Besitzungen," MDOG, XCII (1960), 1-13, and *Die Beziehungen Ägyptens zu Vorderasien im 3. und 2. Jahrtausend v. Chr.* (1962 [2nd ed., 1971]); M. Mohammad, "The Administration of Syro-Palestine during the New Kingdom," *Annales du Service des*

Antiquités de l'Égypte, LVI (1959), 105-37; R. de Vaux, "Le pays de Canaan," *JAOS,* LXXXVIII (1968), 23-30; M. Weippert, "Semitische Nomaden des zweiten Jahrtausends: Über die *Šsw* der ägyptischen Quellen," *Bibl.,* LV (1974), 265-80, 427-33. §§4-5: Commentaries on Joshua and Judges— Y. Aharoni, "New Aspects of the Israelite Occupation in the North," in *Essays in Honor of N. Glueck: Near Eastern Archaeology in the Twentieth Century,* ed. J. Sanders (1970), pp. 254-67; V. Fritz, "Das Ende der spätbronzezeitlichen Stadt Hazor Stratum XIII und die biblische Überlieferung in Joshua 11 und Richter 4," *UF,* V (1973), 123-39; F. Langlamet, *Gilgal et les récits de la traversée du Jourdain* (1969), and "Josué II et les traditions de l'Hexateuque," *RB,* LXXVIII (1971), 5-17, 161-83, 321-54; P. W. Lapp, "The Conquest of Palestine in the Light of Archaeology," *CTM,* XXXVIII (1967), 283-300, and *Biblical Archaeology and History* (1969); A. Malamat, "The Danite Migration and the Pan-Israelite Exodus-Conquest: A Biblical Narrative Pattern," *Bibl.,* LI (1970), 1-16; B. Marconcini, "Giosuè 1-12: Etiologia storica in prospettiva religiosa," *BeO,* XIV (1972), 3-12; J. A. Soggin, "Gerico: Anatomia di una conquista," *Protestantesimo,* XXIX (1974), 193-213; J. Van Seters, "The Conquest of Sihon's Kingdom: A Literary Examination," *JBL,* XCI (1972), 182-97; R. de Vaux, "On Right and Wrong Uses of Archaeology," *Essays in Honor of N. Glueck: Near Eastern Archaeology in the Twentieth Century* (1970), pp. 64-80, "The Settlement of the Israelites in Southern Palestine and the Origins of the Tribe of Judah," in *Translating and Understanding the OT,* ed. H. Frank and W. Reed (1970), pp. 108-34, and "A Comprehensive View of the Settlement of the Israelites in Canaan," *Perspective,* XII (1971), 23-33; M. Weippert, "Abraham der Hebräer?" *Bibl.,* LII (1971), 407-32, "Fragen des israelitischen Geschichtsbewusstseins," *VT,* XXIII (1973), 415-42, and "The Israelite 'Conquest' and the Evidence from Transjordan," in *Problems in the Archaeology and History of Israel at the Beginning of the Early Bronze Age,* ed. F. M. Cross (1976).

M. Weippert

CANNEH kăn' ĕ [כַּנֵּה, LXX Χαννα]. A place mentioned in Ezek. 27:23, often considered a variant of Calneh. However, assimilation of *l* to the following *n* is not very probable; to judge from the LXX Χαλαννη, the name was pronounced with a vowel between *l* and *n* (as in Assyrian *Kullani*). It is more plausible to identify Canneh with the city of Kannu', listed with other place names which suggest a location in the eastern part of N Mesopotamia, on the great trade route from Assyria to Syria via the Habur Triangle and Haran.

Bibliography. S. Parpola, "Kannu' " in *Neo-Assyrian Toponyms* (1970), for Assyrian occurrences; *DPaR* (1920), pp. 105, 115; A. T. Olmstead, *History of Assyria* (1923), p. 514.

M. C. Astour

***CANON OF THE OT.** Samaritans, Jews, and Christians are the direct heirs of Mosaic Yahwism; each group accepts as divinely sanctioned a selection of the religious writings which developed under the aegis of their common parent. Samaritans regard as canonical the Torah (Pentateuch); Jews and Protestant Christians, the Hebrew Bible; and Catholic and Orthodox Christians, slightly different forms of the OT of the late patristic church. The development of the materials included in these canons largely took place before the religions assumed their distinctive forms in late antiquity. The earliest stages of the processes of editing and appraisal that lay behind canonization are the most crucial and will be the chief concern of the present article.

1. The material of the exilic canon
   a. The oldest writings
   b. The early monarchic period
   c. The late monarchic period
2. The exilic canon
   a. The Qumran evidence
   b. The prophetic literature
3. Postexilic literature
   a. The Chronicler
   b. The Book of Truth
   c. The Megilloth and Daniel
4. The origins of the modern canons
   a. The Torah
   b. Activity in the late second temple period and after
   c. Final remarks
Bibliography

For a survey of terms relating to canon and a discussion of the contents of the canons, *see* Canon of the OT intro. and §8; for Hebrew Bible quotations in the NT, *see* §6; for theological beliefs relating to canon, *see* §9.

1. The material of the exilic canon. While little of the writing in the Bible is explicitly dated, a sizable portion of it provides historical and linguistic evidence which can be correlated with dated, extrabiblical materials. These correlations provide the basis for the advances that have been made in recent years in literary-historical study of the text.

a. The oldest writings. Recent research has shown that the oldest parts of the biblical text are poetic. A list of the principal old poems and their approximate dates follows: Exod. 15, Judg. 5, and Ps. 29 (twelfth century B.C.); Gen. 49, Deut. 33, and the poetic portions of Num. 23–24 (eleventh century B.C.); I Sam. 2, II Sam. 1, II Sam. 22 (=Ps. 18), II Sam. 23:1-7, and Ps. 2 (tenth century B.C.); and Deut. 32, and Pss. 68, 72, and 77 (ninth century B.C.).

Certain legal traditions also derive from the oldest strata of biblical writing. Among these are the Decalogue (which has, however, undergone some later systemization) and the Covenant Code (Exod. 21–23). The antiquity of the latter is best demonstrated by examination of parallel passages in Deuteronomy, in which various laws have been reshaped to render them not only comprehensible, but also serviceable to a later age (cf. Exod. 21:2 ff. and Deut. 15:12 ff.). The Ritual Code of Exod. 34 is probably also a composition of the earlier periods of Yahwism.

These two groups constitute the bulk of the materials which can be assigned in more or less their present form to the earliest period. There are other archaic materials, but these are often embedded in narratives or other types of writing designed to meet later needs and interests. Disentangling and identifying the earlier items remains a risky undertaking. The best approach is to fix the date of the finished product in the light of its responses to circumstances in the life of the people. It is this principle that makes so attractive the recent suggestion (by Mendenhall), that the Covenant Code was drawn up by Samuel to serve as a guide for Saul's monarchy. This observation takes account of the fact that literature of a semitechnical nature would only be set down and circulated in response to a concrete situation. Nontechnical literature, especially poetry, is bound to be treated in a different way, since poetry combines form and content in such an integrated fashion that it cannot easily be altered without affecting its essential character. Hence it is less susceptible than other forms of writing to periodic modernization.

b. The early monarchic period. The first part of the monarchic period coincided with an era of great prosperity all over the Near East, and just as we have many written records of the achievements of petty Oriental despots, so we should expect to find some records of the Judahite and Israelite monarchies. The traditional analysis of the Pentateuchal sources, the Yahwist (J) and the Elohist (E), is probably correct in recognizing that we do have those records, enmeshed with other, later and earlier materials, in the Torah. It has often been suggested that a common source (called G, for Ground) lies behind both J and E, but it is in the nature of the case impossible to be sure about such a hypothesis. G might have been in either verse or prose; if the former, then either a full-scale epic or a series of short narrative poems.

The YAHWIST (J) source is a prose narrative epic of Israelite history, which unifies and interweaves patriarchal stories with narratives of the Exodus, conquest, and settlement. The Mosaic covenant is deftly balanced with the Abrahamic covenant. The king is seen as both the descendant of Abraham, and thus heir and assign of the promises made to Abraham, and as the administrator of the Mosaic covenant.

The Elohist (E) source covered generally the same sweep of events as J, though with different theological interests. Some of these are: a special interest in prophecy, recognition of the name Yahweh as of Mosaic origin (for the earlier period, both E and the Priestly writer use the general term Elohim), and a decided lack of interest in Jerusalem and the Davidides. The over-all concerns of E have been partially obscured by their intermeshing with J and cannot be stated with certainty.

AMOS and HOSEA represent a new phase in the development of the Yahwist traditions. They presented a call for a complete re-evaluation of the current state of affairs in terms of the original Yahwist traditon.

ISAIAH also began to prophesy around this time. He shared the basic attitudes of Amos and Hosea, but since he lived in a less vulnerable society, with a more stable monarchic tradition, he looked for continuity alongside reform, while Amos and Hosea were forced by the circumstances they confronted to insist that a complete break with the present was the only course of action that could lead to survival.

c. The late monarchic period. The principal literary outcome of the fall of the northern kingdom was the work of the Deuteronomic school. This probably began in the reign of Hezekiah, or less likely, in that of Manasseh, as an effort to codify distinctive Yahwist traditions which had been preserved in the North. The testimony of the Chronicler about the extent and nature of Hezekiah's reforms (II Chr. 29–32) has too often been dismissed or underestimated. The compilation of Deuteronomy would fit in well not only with Hezekiah's religious activity but also with his literary interests (cf. Prov. 25:1). Furthermore, we know that he was deeply concerned about the fate of the North, and doubtless it was he who devised the policy of religious-political intervention there which Josiah carried out a century later with greater success. *See* DEUTERONOMIC HISTORY[S] §3.

Contemporary with the writing of the Deuteronomic history was the preparation of the so-called Priestly document of the PENTATEUCH (P), the most problematic of the major sources. The bulk of P is semitechnical literature, which treats paradigmatic schemata like the clean and unclean and their application in the world. The question "Was P an independent narrative source?" has been answered in the affirmative by Engnell, who regards P as the base of the Tetrateuch, the narrative which he supposes to have been added to the Deuteronomic history in order to create the Pentateuch and the Former Prophets. This solution, however, is problematic because the Tetrateuch cannot stand as an independent unit. The story of the settlement cannot end in Transjordan; indeed, the promise to the patriarchs does not include Transjordan at all. The Promised Land starts at the W bank of the Jordan, at the point reached only in the opening pages of Joshua. It seems better to return to a more or less traditional view of P, that its ending is now either buried in Joshua (from which, however, it cannot be extracted) or lost. On the face of it, the latter solution recommends itself, simply because Joshua in its present form is much more Deuteronomic than Priestly.

The position of P in the range of Pentateuchal sources is curious because it is both the oldest and youngest of them. It preserves, for example, the authentic account of the revelation of the divine name Yahweh (Exod. 6); in addition, some of P's cultic material is demonstrably ancient. That P is not older than J and the monarchy is seen in the strong bond between the patriarchs-sojourn-Exodus pattern on the one hand and that of wanderings-conquest-settlement on the other. This is the official line of all sources from the tenth century on. Further, P treats an exceptionally elaborate cultic system in a well-developed conceptual framework, the relationship of which to Mosaic Yahwism is at best tenuous. There is, however, no evidence that P is postexilic and precious little that it is exilic, as Kaufmann has shown. *See* PRIESTLY WRITERS[S].

2. The exilic canon. The bulk of the first two parts of the Bible, the Torah (Instruction) and the Nebi'im (Prophets), was in existence by 587 B.C. The material was given its finished form in the half century after that date. The Deuteronomic history was combined with something very like the so-called Tetrateuch to form the "primary history"

(PH) of Israel. At the same time, several prophetic books were edited to serve as a supplement to PH: First Isaiah, Jeremiah, Ezekiel, and a collection of minor prophets: Amos, Hosea, Micah, Nahum, Zephaniah, Habakkuk, and Obadiah. The exilic edition of First Isaiah combined materials derived from the eighth-century prophet of Judah (particularly chs. 1–12 and 28–33) and from later periods down to the Exile itself (including notably 13–14, 24–27).

The primary history and its supplement, the first edition of the prophetic corpus (PC1), were given official publication and some kind of canonization, probably in Babylonia, around 550 B.C. The two works were not accorded the same status, however, because PH was fixed at that time, never to be revised in any significant way, while the prophetic corpus was expanded and revised at least once, the work being put in final form around 500. Included in the expanded edition were Second and Third Isaiah, some more minor prophets, including Joel and Jonah (the dates of which remain uncertain), and certainly the last three prophets, Haggai, First Zechariah (i.e., 1–8), and Malachi. The suggested date for PH accords well with the plainest fact we know about it: the latest date in the narrative is around 561 (II Kings 25:27-30). Since that date does not refer to any distinctively dramatic event, it cannot be argued that it was specifically chosen by the final editor to conclude the work. The event was chosen simply because it was the most recent event worth relating in the history of Judah. The date for the prophetic corpus is rather less obvious, but certainly plausible.

a. The Qumran evidence. Is there any external evidence to support the hypothesis of the exilic canonization of the primary history and publication of the first edition of the prophetic corpus? It is unreasonable to suppose that any declaration of canonization would be preserved, since canonization is a function of a social structure which is more transient than the canon it creates. Nonetheless, there is some evidence from Qumran of the propagation of a formal text.

Since the hundreds of Qumran biblical scrolls will not be published completely for some time to come, any conclusions drawn from preliminary publications must remain tentative. Some facts are clear, however. The various hands of the Qumran documents come from a period when the Jewish script was undergoing many changes. Thanks to this fact, the relative chronology of the hands and thus of the MSS can be established. Further, due to archaeological research at Khirbet Qumran, a settlement not far from the caves, this relative chronology can be associated with the Palestinian pottery sequence and with the Palestinian coin sequence. Thus, the Qumran MSS can be dated accurately.

One of the Qumran biblical texts is particularly important because it belongs to the small group of MSS which antedate the foundation of the settlement itself, having been brought by the fugitives from Jerusalem who settled in the desert. This manuscript is called 4QSam^b (i.e., the second Samuel MS found in cave 4) and is dated conservatively to 275 B.C. It shows, unlike the other early MSS, completely uniform spelling. This is not the result of a happy accident, but of assiduous work. This labor can hardly be dissociated from some official action, and this action must pass under the rubric of canonization. The official look of the spelling is especially prominent when seen in the light of its probable model, Aramaic court spelling of the fifth century.

This MS is hardly irrefutable evidence of canonization in the mid-sixth century; but it does provide a strongly persuasive argument in the direction of our hypothesis, since it shows that by around 300 B.C., the literary history of the Former Prophets (and thus necessarily of the Pentateuch) is over and the textual history has begun.

The 4QSam^b MS and other materials from Qumran show clearly the existence of text traditions which are distinct from the Masoretic Text received today as the Hebrew Bible. Only three can be distinguished: the Palestinian text type (which survives in the Samaritan Pentateuch), the Egyptian text type (which survives in parts of the Old Greek Version), and a third which should probably be associated with Babylonia (which survives in the MT). *See* TEXT, HEBREW, HISTORY OF[S].

This circle of three traditions suggests that the common parent MS, though it must be removed some distance in time from the traditions, cannot be far removed. In fact, although there is no supertypology of MS development which could tell us how long it takes variant traditions to arise, the possibility of a fifth- or sixth-century original agrees well with the available evidence. Further, since we have several early third-century MSS which reflect at least two text types, the original cannot be later than the fourth century.

b. The prophetic literature. The surviving corpus of prophetic poems and speeches cannot be the whole or even a substantial part of the prophetic materials available in the classical period; it is a carefully considered selection made on ideological grounds. An important feature of the corpus is the exclusion of most explanations of the political background of the poems. Surely they could not long remain comprehensible without some such orientation. It seems that the poetry of the prophets supplements the primary history. Is there any evidence for this within the primary history? The constant emphasis there on Moses as prophet and on the role of the charismatic prophets is hardly susceptible of another understanding. The exact relationship between the two is more difficult to define, since the overlapping sections of PH and PC1 (cf. Jer. 52 and II Kings 24:18–25:30; and Isa. 36–39 and II Kings 18:13–20:19) suggest that the two works were in some sense distinct.

The reason for the creation of PC1 is suggested by the material itself. There was nothing in recent Judahite history to encourage the exiles. The editor of PC1 recognized that consolation would come not from writing history, but from prophecy. The material of PH prepared the ground for the belief that the prophets who were right about the Exile would be right about the return; it also provided explicit information about the return in Lev. 26:40-45 and Deut. 29:22–30:10. The editor of PC1 went further than the editor of PH could have; he went from prose to verse. He began by either preparing or taking over an edition of Isaiah, designed to show the extraordinary resemblances between the eighth- and sixth-century situations of Palestine. He then added the two great prophets of the very period he had to explain, Jeremiah and Ezekiel, and some minor prophets.

PC1 aimed at establishing the credibility of the pre-exilic prophets by showing that they had correctly analyzed the history of Israel and Judah in the context of power politics; when they saw the hand of God in all that happened, they rightly predicted the outcome. Hence their prophecies dealing with events yet to come (the editor implicitly asserts) can be relied on as well, and decisions and actions in conformity with them should be made.

The expansion of the prophetic corpus around 520-500 B.C. centered on two parts of it: the beginning and the end. The prophecies of Deutero-Isaiah were added to the Isaiah book and the later minor prophets—probably Joel and Jonah and surely Haggai, First Zechariah, and Malachi—to the end of the collection. The revision of the corpus can be dated to the period described in Haggai and First Zechariah (1–8), the period of the rebuilding of the temple and the attempted revival of the monarchy. The work of Second Zechariah (9–14) cannot be dated precisely; it probably belongs to the final edition of the corpus.

3. Postexilic literature. ***a. The Chronicler.*** The core narrative of the Chronicler's history is contemporary with the final edition of the prophetic corpus, that is, it comes from the period between 520 and 500. It is an independent Palestinian work designed to enhance the claims of the Davidic dynasty and of the second temple. It presents the claims of the Davidide Zerubbabel, the Zadokide Jeshua, and the second temple in terms of the prior claims of the corresponding ancestral figures, David, Zadok, and the first temple. The work included not only the bulk of Chronicles but also most of Ezra 1–6. (Ezra 4:6-24 and parts of chs. 5 and 6 are from the fifth century.) The genealogies which open Chronicles were probably not included in the core work, except perhaps for that of the Davidic line in ch. 3, which may originally have followed the account of David's coronation.

The final version of this history is the work of an editor around 425 B.C. He shared with the first editor an interest in Judah and Jerusalem, and in the priesthood and the temple, though he avoided the subject of the monarchy. There is thus a radical shift of emphasis, clearly reflecting the activity of EZRA AND NEHEMIAH. The most striking evidence for the distinction between two major layers of Chronicles is provided by the contrast between the model of Israelite greatness used in the core narrative (the monarchy) and that of Ezra and Nehemiah themselves (the community of the steppe wanderings). Why Chronicles was adapted to the changed situation of the fifth-century Judahite community by little more than the addition of the memoirs of Ezra and Nehemiah and of the genealogies, and not by a complete rewriting, is unknown. The editor of Chronicles certainly approved of the establishment of a Judahite commonwealth within the Persian Empire. *See* CHRONICLES, I AND II[S].

b. The Book of Truth. The first books of the Writings—Job, the Psalter, and Proverbs—are difficult to date. The book of Job reflects a non-Judahite orthographic tradition and may derive from the northern kingdom or a community with similar linguistic background. It was written in the seventh or sixth century.

Only a few psalms demand an exilic date. Some psalms, like 29, 68, and 72, undoubtedly belong to the earliest period of Israelite hymnody, the twelfth-tenth centuries. None shows the influence of the Persian, Greek, or Roman periods. The majority probably belong to the ninth-sixth centuries and were used in the cult of the first temple. If the traditional co-ordination of the Yahwist and Elohist Psalters with Northern and Southern cultic traditions is correct, then they are pre-exilic. The five-book format of the Psalter shows the influence of the Pentateuch configuration, which belongs to the fifth century. Qumran MS 11QPs[a], which contains some of the canonical psalms (numbered between 100 and 150) in a widely variant order, shows that the final arrangement of the work was either quite late or subject to considerable variation.

The book of Proverbs was composed around a core collection compiled in the time of Hezekiah; the date and even the nature of its various expansions are not clear. There is nothing in the book that demands a postexilic date, though such can hardly be excluded.

c. The Megilloth and Daniel. Of the Five Megilloth, only Lamentations can be clearly dated; it must belong to the period it describes, not only because the poet pictures himself as intimately involved in the events surrounding the siege of Jerusalem, but also because the poems reflect absolute despair, with no hope for a return. Its canonization was probably the result of its status as a Jeremianic pseudepigraph.

Pseudepigraphy is probably also responsible for the legitimization of Ecclesiastes and the Song of Songs. The Hebrew Song is a mixture of classical and archaic forms. Its final editing probably took place in the sixth century. *See* PSEUDONYMOUS WRITING[S].

The Qumran MSS of Ecclesiastes date from 150 B.C. and suggest that the book was not only known but important at that time, since its content can scarcely be accommodated to an Essene world view. Recent work which has linked the book with Phoenician sources deserves some consideration. The marked tendencies of Ecclesiastes toward speculative thought and the distinctive way this thought was expressed do suggest that the writer was a contemporary of the great Greek and Anatolian philosophers, rather than a latter-day, uncomprehending imitator of them.

RUTH probably owes its canonization to the Davidic genealogy which concludes it. The Hebrew style of the book is closely related to that of J and E, and it may therefore be dated in the ninth or eighth century. This date corresponds well to the Davidic association of the book, which can be explained only with difficulty in the post-exilic period.

ESTHER comes from the Persian period. It is a historical romance about the court of Ahasuerus (Xerxes I) of the fifth century; it was written down no later than the fourth century. It is the only book of the Hebrew Bible not represented at Qumran, though that in itself is no indication of its date. Since the Essenes did not observe Purim in their festal calendar, it is likely that they did not accept Esther as edifying, let alone canonical.

According to scholarly consensus, the book of DANIEL received its final form in 165 B.C. or thereabouts, although parts of it, especially the stories, go back to earlier times. A source comparable to the materials used in composing the biblical book has been uncovered at Qumran—the so-called Nabonidus fragment, which correctly attributes a madness story similar to the one in Dan. 4 to Nabonidus, rather than Nebuchadrezzar.

4. The origins of the modern canons. The Torah and the Former Prophets together make up the primary history, a product of the Exile. Its purpose was not to provide a blueprint for what to do after the Exile; it is largely unconcerned with the possibility of the return. It was rather to serve as a theological and historical memoir of the experience of Israel from Abraham to the fall of Jerusalem. It also sought to enable the Judahite community to remain in existence on foreign soil. As such, it was the Bible of the exiles. Contemporary with it was the first edition of the prophetic corpus, which in part shared PH's orientation toward doom and destruction, while at the same time extending its field of vision by including the Jeremianic prophecy of the new covenant and the Ezekielian renunciation of the "sour grapes" ideology of classic Deuteronomic thought.

The second edition of the prophetic corpus was designed as a vade mecum for the returnees, people spurred on by the prophecies of restoration. Contemporary with this work is the core narrative of Chronicles, the Bible of the late sixth-century settlement in Palestine. It is the work of a royalist, written for a group intent on reviving the monarchy and the other appurtenances of pre-exilic Judah. These works are the great building blocks of the modern canons, to the development of which we now turn.

a. The Torah. As has long been recognized, the Pentateuch is not a natural unit in the Hebrew Bible. To explain this configuration, we must look to a period in which the wilderness wanderings were so highly regarded as to demand a break between Moses and Joshua sufficiently sharp to take precedence over the actual shape of the narrative. This high regard is most characteristic of the period in which the Torah became a necessity for organizing a community which, like the Exodus society, lacked the ordinary features of statehood, i.e., the period of Ezra and Nehemiah. Indeed, the most obvious agent of the transformation of *torah* (correctly, "instruction," not "law"; *see* TORAH[S]) into *dāth* (a Persian loanword in Hebrew and Aramaic, meaning "law") is Ezra himself, who had the law (*dāth*) of the Most High God in his hand according to no less an authority than the Persian emperor.

The objective of Ezra and Nehemiah was to strengthen a community which lived as a minority group in an environment that was alternately hostile and seductive; strengthening the community necessarily meant clarifying its ethos. The Torah of Moses, reconceived as a legal instrument, was the chosen means. The instrument was flexible if only because of its size. The authority of Moses which, according to the Deuteronomic history, transcended that of kings, could be invoked only for the Pentateuch. At this time Genesis was probably regarded as a Mosaic composition, his prologue to his own life story. The death of Moses dictated the border between law and non-law, i.e., interpretation and commentary. Thus did Ezra carve out of the primary history a new authority for his nonmonarchic society. The rest of the primary history was subsidiary, though useful; the Former and Latter Prophets, the Psalms, and other Writings were accepted for liturgy and instruction, but could not be used as the basis for binding decisions. In all likelihood, it is the text of the Pentateuch adopted by Ezra that lies behind the three textual types mentioned earlier.

The Torah is the canonical scripture of the Samaritan sect, which was born in the travail of John Hyrcanus' reign, probably shortly before his destruction of Shechem. The reasons the Samaritans accepted only the Pentateuch are simple: at the time of the formation of the religion, it still enjoyed the special status Ezra gave it, and it was the only body of writing which was germane to the Samaritans' distinctive religious concerns.

b. Activity in the late second temple period and after. The Pentateuch would always have had a special status, given its legal character and use in the self-government of the Judahite community. It provided liturgical rules for the temple sacrifices and festivals; it set up legal bases for social operation; it offered a context for doctrinal speculation and formulations. Where it failed was in the area of prophecy; even Moses' predictions had almost all been exhausted by history. There was a need for material upon which to base hopes for the future, a need that grew in proportion to the rise in apocalyptic thought, which so largely reshaped the prophetic function. There were some Judahites who wanted no part of these forms of speculation. The others, who were in the majority, had two options. They could either create new interpretations of old prophecies to make them suitable to the present and future, or they could invent new prophecies and disguise them as old by attributing them to ancient seers and holy men, like Enoch, the sons of Jacob, and Baruch. The Essene writings from Qumran show how the first course was pursued, in the numerous *Pesharim* (*see* DEAD SEA SCROLLS §5*a*): the fixed sacred text is subjected to an entirely foreign interpretation by an exegete who was himself regarded as inspired. This tactic proved more durable and universal because most Judahites accepted the ancient texts (whose authority could be traced back to the sixth century and was thus unimpeachable), while interpretations could vary and be the object of legitimate discussion. The pseudepigraphic material was never as popular as the old writing and only by accident or dissimulation was it accepted into the canon. Daniel is in fact the only genuine pseudepigraph in the Hebrew Bible.

The Qumran findings have produced so much new information about the finalization of the Jewish and the Catholic Christian canons, that no final assessment of the picture is possible. The traditional reconstruction of these two as the descendants of Palestinian and Alexandrian canons is clearly no longer acceptable, as Sundberg has demonstrated. The validity of this reconstruction should have been suspect before Qumran, if only because there are no complete Jewish MSS of the LXX in existence and thus none which are organized according to the supposed Alexandrian canon. There are only fragments of pre-Christian date, which provide no clear information about the order of the books.

In reaction to the Qumran data, Sundberg has proposed a striking resolution of the problem of the origin of the two canons. Although it errs in that it seems to demand explicit definition from periods which are too obscure to yield up such information, it is well worth considering. Sundberg contends that there was only one canon in all of Judaism before the destruction of the second temple, i.e., the primary history and its prophetic supplement. This canon was enlarged on two occasions. The first was the result of a series of rabbinic disputations associated with the Academy at Jamnia (Jabneel), usually dated around A.D. 90. At this time, the Writings in the Hebrew Bible were defined. Sundberg believes that the early Christian community separated itself entirely from Judaism after the events of A.D. 70; indeed it was those events which stimulated the final redaction of much if not all the NT. Thus at the time of the separation, the canon of scripture consisted only of the Pentateuch, the Prophets, and an undefined group of writings. This group of writings remained undefined in the church for several centuries; during this time, the alarming gap between the Christian and Jewish Bibles was noted by Christians, who attempted to shuffle the contents of the Christian OT around to make the two match. The results are evident in most Catholic editions of the Bible; e.g., the pseudepigraphic letter of Baruch follows Jeremiah, a position which reflects the belief of the church Fathers that when the Jewish canonical list mentions Jeremiah, it also means the supposed work of his secretary. It was the result of this great shuffling operation that was more or less canonized as the Catholic and Orthodox OT in the century following the conversion of Constantine. This remains the basic canon of the Roman Catholic Church (which excluded I and II Esdras in the early Renaissance) and of the Greek Orthodox Church (which included these same books at the same time) and of its heirs.

The difficulties with Sundberg's position are manifold. Most importantly, the rabbinic debates at Jamnia do not reveal uncertainty about all the Writings, but only about Ecclesiastes and the Song of Songs. The debates about Esther and the Torah section of Ezekiel are later and largely academic. The major decisions to exclude literature more recent than Daniel were clearly made during the first centuries B.C. and A.D. The Christian canon was probably fluid in the way that Sundberg suggests, but chiefly because the varieties of thought excluded from the Jewish canon, messianic and apocalyptic, were so important to the early church.

Sundberg's hypothesis also fails to deal with the simple truth that most, if not all, of the Writings in the Hebrew Bible were in existence at the time of Ezra, except Daniel and possibly Ecclesiastes and Esther, while most of the material which is included in the Catholic and Orthodox canon but not in the Hebrew Bible is much later than Ezra. The exact formulation of a solution to this problem would have to take into account not only all the biblical data, but also additional historical information and cannot be attempted here.

c. Final remarks. The position of the prophetic writings in the Catholic Christian (LXX) canon suggests that the promise-fulfillment relationship between the two testaments was regarded as of crucial import, a regard paralleled by the Matthean use of OT quotations. The very fact that neither the LXX nor the MT correctly reflects the historical development of the canon suggests the importance of the *arrangement* of biblical materials. Both confirm the overwhelming priority of the Torah.

The different canons reflect the needs and interests of the religious communities at various stages in their histories. The first canon was created in the sixth century B.C. as a structural base for a crippled society. It was sharpened and focused by Ezra to serve a specific legal and judicial function—to integrate and sustain a community that had territory but no independent authority. The earlier canon, PH and its supplement, had been purely ideological in character, designed to hold together people who had nothing but memories and hopes. Prophecy and its stepchild apocalyptic were crucial in the formation of the later second temple period writings which were largely abandoned as a result of the disastrous experience of the First Jewish Revolt. The radical thought of the last years of the second temple period was cut back in line with strategies similar to those used by Ezra for similar purposes. Hence the elimination of the luxuriant growth of the speculation cast in apocalyptic-messianic tones which brought about the community's disaster and which later reappears in less dangerous forms in Jewish mysticism and Gnosticism.

The Christian situation was rather different. Messianism was the dominant theme, and so the focus was on prophecy and apocalyptic. For prophecy, history was the vital framework—thus I and II Maccabees and the gospels and Acts. Speculation went hand in hand with apocalyptic thought because visions and revelations must be transmuted into knowledge for survival; the two remain uneasily balanced until the rise of late patristic metaphysics.

Bibliography. F. M. Cross, Jr., *Canaanite Myth and Hebrew Epic* (1973); D. N. Freedman, "The Massoretic Text and the Qumran Scrolls: A Study in Orthography," *Textus,* II (1962), 87-102; and "The Law and the Prophets," VTSup, IX (1963), 250-65; Jack Lewis, "What Do We Mean by Jabneh?" *JBR,* XXXII (1964), 254-61; J. A. Sanders, "Cave 11 Surprises and the Question of Canon," *New Directions in Biblical Archaeology* (1971), pp. 99-112, *Torah and Canon* (1972), and "Adaptable for Life: The Nature and Function of Canon," *The G. E. Wright Memorial Volume* (1975); A. Sundberg, Jr., *The Old Testament of the Early Church* (1964); G. Mendenhall, "Ancient Oriental and Biblical Law," *BA,* XVII (1954), 26-46, and "Covenant Forms in Israelite Tradition," *ibid.,* pp. 50-76; Y. Kaufmann, *The Religion of Israel* (1960). For Engnell's views *see* G. W. Anderson, "Some Aspects of the Uppsala School of Old Testament Study," *HTR,* XLIII (1950), 239-56.

D. N. Freedman

***CANON OF THE NT.** The origin and development of the NT collection continues to be the object of intensive study and discussion.

1. The hypothesis of a core NT canon by the end of the second century
2. The demise of the hypothesis
3. A revised history of the NT canon
4. The rise of Christian writings to the status of scripture
   a. The gospels
   b. The Pauline letters
   c. The Pastoral epistles
   d. The Catholic epistles
   e. Other writings of the NT
   f. Noncanonical writings as scripture
5. Closed collections of Christian scripture
   a. The fourfold gospel
   b. The Pauline corpus
   c. The Catholic collection
6. The period of canonicity

Bibliography

1. The hypothesis of a core NT canon by the end of the second century. The application of secular historiography to biblical studies destroyed the viability of the tradition that the NT canon had been formed by the disciple John about the end of the first century, since it became evident that some NT books had not yet been written by that time. Westcott was the first to postulate the existence of a NT canon by the end of the second century. He believed this was demonstrated by the Canon Muratori in the West and the Peshitta in the East (both then dated *ca.* A.D. 170; *see* CANON OF THE NT §D6; VERSIONS, ANCIENT §4*b*), together with the usage of Irenaeus, Clement of Alexandria, and Tertullian representing the churches of Asia Minor, Alexandria, and North Africa, respectively. Soon thereafter and independently, Bleek's hypothesis of a core NT by the end of the second century was published. Bleek found witnesses to this core NT in Irenaeus, representing Gaul and (perhaps) Asia Minor; Clement of Alexandria, representing the Alexandrian church; Tertullian, representing proconsular Africa; the Peshitta, representing Syria; and the Old Latin list of Canon Muratori, representing Rome. These unanimously accepted the four gospels, Acts, thirteen epistles of Paul, I John, and I Peter. Bleek's core NT was more critical than Westcott's because he named only those books for which there was unanimous acceptance among these five witnesses. Bleek was also more forthright in acknowledging the value placed on noncanonical writings by Irenaeus, Clement of Alexandria, and Tertullian. These included Barnabas, Apocalypse of Peter, I Clement, and the Shepherd of Hermas. The criteria of canonicity, however, were the same for Westcott and Bleek. These were, first and foremost, citation with authority like that of the OT, sometimes indicated by introductory quotation formulas that included "the scripture" (ἡ γραφή or "it has been written" (γέγραπται); apostolicity; inspiration (though not clearly stated by Bleek); and inclusion in the five witnesses.

2. The demise of the hypothesis. The hypothesis that a core NT existed by the end of the second century was somewhat weakened as soon as it was shown that the Peshitta originated only in the fifth century and was therefore no witness to a second-century NT canon. At the same time, however, the old hypothesis was retained by arguing that Canon Muratori was an official publication of the Roman canon for the whole church, published by the Bishop of Rome or at his direction.

Nevertheless, evidence for a second-century core canon continues to be called into question. Clement of Alexandria has been dropped from the list of witnesses because of his wide use of noncanonical Christian writings which cannot be differentiated from his use of canonical writings; and it has been shown that Irenaeus and Tertullian also made use of writings other than those within the NT canon.

Moreover, it has become evident that the church received a much wider body of religious writings from Judaism than what it eventually canonized as "Old Testament" (*see* CANON OF THE OT; CANON OF THE OT[S]). Since the church received no OT canon from Judaism, the quotation of Christian writings with authority like the OT in the early church did not indicate that these Christian writings were canonical. Thus, what has been the basic criterion for all modern histories of the NT canon has proved erroneous. Similarly, more careful studies of quotation formulas in the NT and early Christian literature have shown that formulas containing "the scripture" or "it has been written" have no canonical connotation since they are used indiscriminately of noncanonical, heretical, and non-Christian writings as well.

Finally, the Roman provenance and late second-century date of the Muratorian Fragment have been questioned. An Eastern provenance and an early fourth-century date are more probable (*see* MURATORIAN FRAGMENT[S] §3). Thus, the evidence on which the hypothesis of a core NT by the end of the second century was postulated has eroded away.

3. A revised history of the NT canon. In spite of this erosion of evidence, the hypothesis of a second-century core canon has prevailed for over a century with only minor alterations. It is now imperative, however, to attempt to develop an alternative hypothesis, and with it, to write a revised history of the NT canon. In this revised history the development of the canon may be seen as consisting of three stages: the rise of Christian writings to the status of scripture, the conscious collection of Christian writings into closed subcollections, and the formation and standardization of NT lists—canonization proper.

4. The rise of Christian writings to the status of scripture. It is no longer satisfactory to use the terms "scripture" and "canon" synonymously. The church received "scriptures," that is, religious writings that were in some sense regarded as authoritative, from Judaism; but the church did not receive a canon, i.e., a closed collection of scripture to which nothing could be added, nothing subtracted. The DEAD SEA SCROLLS as well as the literature of earliest Christianity show what kind of materials were regarded within the Judaism of the period as somehow authoritative: a closed collection of the Law, a closed collection of the Prophets, an undefined group including the later defined collection called the Writings, books later called Apocrypha and Pseudepigrapha, and others known to us only by name. Neither in the sectarian writings from Qumran nor in early Christianity was any distinction made between those books later in the Jewish canon and those not included. It is evident that the religious writings of the church received from Judaism did not come directly from Qumran but more probably from the common usage in Judaism at that time. Melito of Sardis (*ca.* 170) is the first Christian writer to take notice of the existence of a Jewish canon, and no significant effect of that canon is felt until Origen (253), even though the Jewish canon was closed *ca.* A.D. 90. This would seem to confirm the view that the church received scriptures from Judaism but not a canon. Therefore, when Christian writings were given authority like that of the OT, these were indeed being regarded as scriptural, but not yet as canonical.

Not until *ca.* A.D. 90 is there evidence (Josephus, II Esdras) for a theory of scripture or canonization within Judaism; at this time the doctrine was promulgated that only the writings from Moses to Ezra were inspired. It is reasonable to suppose that the earlier, apparently open-ended attitude toward scripture in Judaism is what passed over into the early church, along with the Jewish scriptures themselves. The early church felt itself endued with the same inspiration that inspired Moses and the prophets (e.g., Acts 2:16-21; 15:28; I Cor. 2:4), and this sense of inspiration in word and deed carried over to their writings since they knew no limiting or restricting doctrine. Thus, Paul could commend his written instructions to Corinth by saying, "And I think that I have the Spirit of God" (I Cor. 7:40*b*). By the end of the first century the writer of I Clement thinks of Paul as having written with true inspiration (47:1-3), and also refers to his own work as "written through the Holy Spirit" (63:2).

The belief in the continuing inspiration of the Spirit endured in the church into the third century and beyond. In the first centuries no other criterion than inspiration, poured out freely upon the church, was required for a Christian writing to be regarded as scripture (Iren. Her. III.xxi.3-4). These writings were cited with authority like that of the OT, and it is only on this basis that we can understand how such works as I Clement, the Shepherd of Hermas, and Polycarp's letters, which did not fit the later criteria of canonicity, attained the status of scripture. The rise of Christian writings to this status is synonymous with the circulation and popularity of these writings in the church.

a. The gospels. All the evidence indicates that the words of Jesus were authoritative in the church from the first, and this makes it the more remarkable that such scanty attention is paid to the words or works of Jesus in the earliest Christian writings. Paul's letters, the later epistles, Hebrews, Revelation, and even Acts have little to report about them. In view of the presumed imminence of the eschaton and the immediately available guidance of the risen Lord through inspiration (cf. Gal. 1:11-12), the wonder is that gospels came to be written at all. PAPIAS (*ca.* A.D. 130), the first person actually to name a written gospel, illustrates the point. Even though he defends Mark's gospel (Euseb. Hist. III.xxxix.15-16) and had himself appended a collection of Jesus tradition to his "Interpretation of the Oracles of the Lord" (Euseb. Hist. III.xxxix.2-3), his own clear preference was for the oral tradition concerning Jesus, and the glimpses that Eusebius provides of Papias' Jesus tradition give no hint of his dependence on Mark. Neither do the more frequent citations of Jesus in the APOSTOLIC FATHERS, largely "synoptic" in character, show much dependence on our written gospels. Here, again, oral Jesus tradition is suggested. It would appear that from a very early time there was such a strong preference for the oral tradition about Jesus that this passed, together with the translation of that tradition, into Greek.

It is doubtful whether very large portions of the Jesus tradition would have been translated orally from Aramaic into Greek. It may be possible that the earliest use of written gospels in the church was as instruction books for those who would tell the Jesus tradition orally in Greek. The curious mixture of Matthean and Lukan characteristics in the gospel-like material in the Apostolic Fathers is explicable within the context of such oral transmission.

In the following decades, even though evidence for the existence of written gospels is clearer and the citations of gospel materials are more abundant, there is no attempt to identify the citations with a written gospel. The materials are cited tacitly as oral tradition, and a significant amount of material not contained in our four gospels is also used, with like authority. Not surprisingly, new gospels continued to be written, and their authors, like the gospel writers before them, used such gospel material as came into their hands. Thus, Tatian (*ca.*

175) used our four gospels in his Diatessaron just as the authors of Matthew and Luke had used Mark. The Gospel According to the Hebrews and the Gospel According to the Egyptians also apparently represented what may be called "normative Christianity" of their time. Others (e.g., the Gospels of Peter, of Thomas, of Truth, of Philip) were related in varying degrees to the form of Christianity that came to be known as Gnostic, and that flourished in North Africa during the second century.

Justin Martyr, who moved from Palestine to Rome, founded a school there, and was martyred *ca.* 165, marks an important transition in the use of gospel materials. Justin is the first Christian writer known to have appealed to written gospels, to have used them as scripture, and to have accorded them authority like that accorded to the OT. He called the gospels "memoirs" written by the "apostles and those who followed them," and remarked that in them the sayings of Christ are preserved (Apol. I, 39; *Dialogue with Trypho* 103). These memoirs were also called gospels, and on Sundays they were read together with the prophets (Apol. I, 66-67). It is probable that Justin knew our four gospels, but his citations from noncanonical materials show that he was acquainted with a wider gospel tradition.

b. The Pauline letters. Although a century passed between the writing of Mark's gospel and its first authoritative use, the letters of Paul achieved authoritative status more quickly. Before the end of the first century I Clement refers to Paul's correspondence with Corinth as written with "true inspiration" (46:3), in this respect similar to the OT (cf. 13:1; 16:2). This means that Paul's correspondence with Corinth was known in Rome before the close of the first century. Early in the second century, Ignatius, writing to Ephesus, says that Paul mentioned the Ephesians in every letter (12:2). "Every letter" does seem to imply more than I Corinthians and Ephesians, in which the Ephesians are named, but we do not know how many of Paul's letters Ignatius had in hand. (I Thessalonians, I Corinthians, Romans, Colossians and Ephesians—perhaps also II Thessalonians —appear to be reflected in the Ignatian letters.) Polycarp (*ca.* 155) shows a knowledge of Romans, Galatians, Philemon, Ephesians, and perhaps Colossians, while he actually quotes I Corinthians and alludes to Philippians and probably II Thessalonians. Like Ignatius, the writer of II Peter refers to "all of Paul's letters." Such statements tend to give credence to the early publication of the Pauline correspondence.

If the early collections of Paul's letters were complete, as some argue, it is difficult to understand the varied and incomplete listings of his letters at the end of the second and the beginning of the third centuries. Irenaeus, while quoting frequently from Paul's letters, nowhere lists them. Tertullian (*ca.* 220) lists Paul's letters as Corinthians, Galatians, Philippians, Thessalonians, Ephesians, Romans (Marcion IV.v), but then discusses them in Marcion's order: Galatians, I, II Corinthians, Romans, I, II Thessalonians, Ephesians, Colossians, Philippians, Philemon. And, while he accuses Marcion of tampering with even the number of Paul's letters (Marcion V.i, apparently referring to Marcion's noninclusion of the Pastorals), he does not correct this error in his own list. Origen, having quoted I Cor. 2:6-8, proceeds to list Paul's letters as Ephesians, Colossians, Thessalonians, Philippians and Romans; but Corinthians and Galatians go unmentioned (*Against Celsus* III.xix-xx). These circumstances do not reflect a settled list of Paul's collected letters, but suggest rather that the earlier references to "all" Paul's letters probably meant only those possessed by that writer. Marcion was probably the first to publish Paul's ten letters (*ca.* 150), but animosity toward him by the orthodox prevented his innovation from being generally utilized.

c. The Pastoral epistles. Polycarp may have known I and II Timothy, though some believe the evidence alleged for this is due instead to common tradition. Otherwise there is no sign of their use until the last quarter of the second century. Tatian is reported to have rejected some of Paul's letters but to have accepted Titus (Jerome, *On Titus,* Preface), while Athenagoras appears to allude to I Tim. 2:1-2 in his *Apology* (xxxvii). Irenaeus is the first to have used the Pastorals extensively, and thereafter they are frequently quoted as the writings of Paul. It is unlikely, however, that they were included in the third-century MS of Paul's letters now known as the Chester Beatty Papyrus (P^{46}). *See also* PASTORAL LETTERS, THE.

d. The Catholic epistles. I Peter and I John gained relatively early recognition. Eusebius says that Papias quoted I John and I Peter (Hist. III.xxxix.17), that ancient elders used I Peter in their writings (III.iii.1), and that Polycarp used testimonies from I Peter in his letter to the Philippians (IV.xiv.9). Traces of I Peter have also been noticed in Basilides (*ca.* 125) and Theodotus (*ca.* 160), a disciple of Valentinus.

Irenaeus has a single quotation from I Peter (Her. IV.ix.2), and Tertullian (*Scorpiace* xii) and Clement of Alexandria (Miscellanies III.xi; IV.xx, etc.) attribute it to the apostle. Thus soon after A.D. 200 I Peter is known and cited as a work of Peter. Similarly, I and II John come into more frequent use toward the end of the second century. Irenaeus cites from the two as though they were one letter, ascribing them to the apostle (Her. III.xvi.5, 8), and Clement of Alexandria cites I John frequently, calling it John's larger epistle (Misc. II.xv.66). There is no mention of III John in the second century.

Jude is first used in II Peter where it is utilized for most of ch. 2. Clement of Alexandria quotes it by name (*The Tutor* III.viii), as does Origen. It is mentioned by Tertullian. Origen is the first to mention II Peter and then only once, saying that it is of doubtful authenticity (*Commentaries on John* V, 3).

e. Other writings of the NT. Revelation may possibly have been known to Hermas, who parallels its imagery for church and enemy as a woman and the beast. Papias is said to have known it, but Justin is the first to name the work (Dial. 81).

Irenaeus also names and cites it as the work of John (e.g., Her. V.xxvi.1; xxx.3).

Hebrews is used already in I Clement, and it is possible that it was known by Hermas. Papias' term, "the eternal high priest," probably came from Hebrews. According to Eusebius, Irenaeus quoted from it (Hist. V.xxvi), but, according to Stephanus Gobarus (sixth century, in Photius cod. 232), he rejected Pauline authorship, as had Gaius of Rome (*ca.* 200). Origen encouraged the acceptance of Hebrews as Paul's, but concluded that only God knows who really wrote it (Euseb. Hist. VI.xxv. 13-14).

It was not possible to accept Luke and question Acts, and from Irenaeus on, the latter was attributed to the follower of an apostle who had also produced an accepted gospel.

f. Noncanonical writings as scripture. A number of other Christian writings not included in the NT canon when it was formed were used at the close of the second and at the beginning of the third centuries in ways indistinguishable from the (eventually) canonical writings already mentioned. Irenaeus used I Clement, the Shepherd of Hermas, Papias, Polycarp, and Ignatius; Tertullian, before he became a Montanist, used the Shepherd; Clement of Alexandria used the Gospel According to the Hebrews, the Gospel According to the Egyptians, Barnabas, I Clement, the Apocalypse of Peter, the Preaching of Peter, the Shepherd, the Traditions of Matthew, and the Didache. Origen, always said to be more guarded than Clement in his usage, used the Gospel of Peter, the Gospel According to the Hebrews, the Preaching of Peter, the Acts of Pilate, the Didache, the Clementine Recognitions, I Clement, Ignatius, Barnabas, the Shepherd, and the Acts of Paul (though his attitude toward the last two may have cooled in his later writings). He did reject gospels according to the Egyptians, according to the Twelve, of Thomas, Basilides, and Matthias. Five of Clement's nine and Origen's eleven extracanonical books are common to them. There is no distinguishable difference in the usage of these books and the later-named canonical ones (cf. Iren. Her. III.xxi.3-4).

5. Closed collections of Christian scripture. This stage in the process of canonization overlapped the later period of the first stage.

a. The fourfold gospel. The earliest closed collection was the fourfold gospel. Justin had held that the memoirs/gospels contained what Jesus Christ had enjoined upon the apostles, and Irenaeus further developed this doctrine. Employing fanciful quadrifid numerology, Irenaeus held that the gospels must be four in number, no more, no fewer. His argument was directed against the Gnostics and their GOSPEL OF TRUTH, and he appears also to have been defending Luke because of the Marcionite use of that gospel. It was Irenaeus' fourfold gospel doctrine that passed to Clement of Alexandria, Tertullian, and Origen, even though these latter did not completely integrate it into their usage.

b. The Pauline corpus. While Marcion published ten letters of Paul, it is probable that the Pastorals were unknown to him. Later additions to the Marcionite scriptures show that his collection was not closed. We have seen how the Pastorals came easily to be accepted as Paul's in the third quarter of the second century. It was Hebrews that became the critical issue in defining the extent of the Pauline corpus in the third century. Its rigorist teaching caused the book to come under attack in the West at the same time that the Shepherd, with its doctrine of forgiveness of one sin after baptism, was enjoying great popularity. In this connection the issue of apostolic authorship was raised. This controversy and the final closing of the Pauline corpus including Hebrews, beginning about the end of the second century, did not reach its conclusion in the West until the last part of the fourth century.

c. The Catholic collection. As distinguished from most of Paul's letters which were addressed to churches, the rest of the letters in the NT came to be regarded as encyclical and intended for the whole church. Apollonius (*ca.* 197) is the first author known to use the term, saying that the Montanist Themiso dared to compose a "catholic epistle" in imitation of the apostle (Euseb. Hist. V.xviii.5). Writers of the Alexandrian school applied the term to I John and I Peter in the first half of the third century (Euseb. Hist. VII.xxv.7-10; Origen, *Comm. on John* V, 3). In the fourth century Eusebius used the term "catholic" to designate the seven non-Pauline letters included in the NT, noting that most of them were disputed (Hist. II.xxiii; III.xxv.1-3). II, III John, II Peter, James, and Jude gained general acceptance along with I Peter and I John only in the fourth century.

6. The period of canonicity. With the fourth century the church experienced a resurgence of interest in its books. Eusebius marks the beginning of this renewed interest as he notes the Christian writings to which the church Fathers refer, and as he draws up his list of the emerging NT. Like Origen, he divides the books into "acknowledged" and "disputed," and further divides the latter into those he accepts and those he rejects. In his summary in Hist. III.xxv., Eusebius lists as acknowledged books the four gospels, Acts, the letters of Paul, I Peter, I John, and "if it seems desirable," Revelation. Disputed books, "known to most," include James, Jude, II Peter, and II, III John. "Not genuine" books are the Acts of Paul, the Shepherd, Revelation of Peter, Epistle of Barnabas, Teaching of the Twelve Apostles, and "if this view prevail," Revelation. He notes that the Gospel According to the Hebrews is sometimes included with these and identifies such gospels as those of Peter, Thomas, and Matthias, and such acts as those of Andrew and John as heretical books. The Revelation of Peter and the Epistle of Barnabas, while among the rejected books here, are called disputed in VI.xiv.1. Thus, while Eusebius was especially interested in the formation of a NT list, he himself was equivocal about some books.

Following Eusebius many other Christian writers offered canonical lists (*see* MURATORIAN FRAGMENT[S] §3). Some have suggested that the pressure of persecution forced the church to determine the exact contents of its NT, so that Christians could know what books they could give up and what books must be preserved at all costs. This, however, seems unlikely since any surrender, even of medical books, could entail the accusation of being a lapsist (Augustine, *Contra Cresconium* III, 30). It is more likely that the stimulus came from Constantine's request for fifty copies of the Christian Bible to be prepared by Eusebius for the churches of Constantinople. Eusebius, whose own NT list was compiled before Constantine's request, does not tell us what books he included in the Bibles he prepared. But their publication must have appeared as a canonizing authority that few Fathers were willing to leave to Eusebius alone. The list of Athanasius, bishop of Alexandria, set forth in his Easter letter of 367, was the first to include just the twenty-seven books finally accepted in the church.

Toward the end of the fourth century a significant portion of the Eastern church used a twenty-two book NT, omitting Revelation, II, III John, II Peter, and Jude. In Syria, Tatian's Diatessaron was read instead of the fourfold gospel. About A.D. 400 the Apostolic Constitutions listed all of our twenty-seven books except Revelation but added I and II Clement. This canon was ratified at the Quinisextine Council at Constantinople in 692. In the West a council at Hippo (393) adopted a NT list like ours except for its separation of Hebrews from Paul's letters. In 397 a synod at Carthage issued a similar NT list but provided that martyrdoms could be read on the anniversary of the martyrdom. The Carthaginian council (419) repeated the enactment but shifted Hebrews into the Pauline collection.

Bibliography. E. Reuss, *History of the Sacred Scriptures of the NT* (1842 [ET 1884]), and *History of the Canon of the Holy Scriptures in the Christian Church* (1863 [ET 1884]); B. F. Westcott, *General Survey of the History of the Canon of the NT* (1855), and "Canon, IV. The history of the Canon of the NT," in *Dr. William Smith's Dictionary of the Bible,* ed. H. B. Hackett, I (1871), 368-76, first printed in 1860; F. Bleek, *An Introduction to the NT,* II (2nd ed., 1866), 233-89, the first Ger. ed. of which was published in 1862; E. J. Goodspeed, *The Formation of the NT* (1926), *The Meaning of Ephesians* (1933), and "The Canon of the NT," IB, 1 (1952), 63-71; J. Knox, *Marcion and the New Testament* (1942), and *Philemon among the Letters of Paul* (rev. ed., 1959); E. C. Blackman, *Marcion and His Influence* (1948); R. P. C. Hanson, *Origen's Doctrine of Tradition* (1954); R. M. Grant, *The Formation of the NT* (1965); K. Aland, *The Problem of the NT* (1962); H. Von Campenhausen, *The Making of the Christian Bible* (1968); A. C. Sundberg, Jr., *The OT of the Early Church,* HTS, XX (1964), and "The Making of the NT Canon," *Interpreter's One-Volume Commentary on the Bible* (1971), pp. 1216-24.

A. C. SUNDBERG, JR.

CANONICAL CRITICISM. *See* HERMENEUTICS[S].

***CAPERNAUM** [Καφαρναούμ in P45 and POxy 847 and in Eusebius' *Onomasticon* (Klosterman, 174.25), but Καπερναούμ in W and the later traditions.] The village of Jesus (e.g., Matt. 4:13); "Cepharnōmē" (Κεφαρνώμη) or "Capernaum" (Καφαρναούμ) in Josephus (Life LXXII; War III.x.8), identified today with Tell Ḥum. Jewish sources mention "Kefar Naḥûm" [כפר נחום] (Midrash Rabbah Koheleth VII.20) or "Kefar Tanḥûm, Kefar Tanḥûmîm" [כפר תנחום, תנחומים] (Midrash Rabbah Shir. III.18; J.T. Ter. 11.7).

Recent archaeological research has greatly added to our understanding of the city and its extant remains.

1. The city. Archaeological survey indicates that in the first century A.D. the unwalled town stretched at least 500 yards E to W along the lake shore, while northward it extended only 250 yards. This translates to a population of one thousand at most.

2. The houses. In the first century B.C. extensive building occurred. Blocks of one-storied apartments or *insulae* were built in squares about 80 x 80 feet, separated from one another by streets. Within each insula the individual dwelling has rooms opening onto a central unroofed courtyard, which is provided with grinding stones, outdoor ovens, and stairways leading to the flat roofs. Fishhooks found beneath the floors in insula I suggest that this was indeed a small fishing village. *See* FISHERMEN[S].

3. The synagogue. After the first half of the fourth century A.D. the synagogue was built, entirely covering one block of houses. Thus, its platform was as high as the roofs, so that the structure itself loomed above the insulae.

The worshiping congregation faced S toward Jerusalem. New evidence suggests that two *aediculae,* or small shrines, perhaps one for the ark and one for the seven-branched candlestick or MENORAH, flanked the central entrance, as in the Sardis synagogue.

Beneath the floor of the synagogue and occasionally embedded in the mortar of the pavement were several thousand bronze coins. These date to the middle of the fifth century at the latest.

4. The octagon. It is now known that this is a church also finished by the mid-fifth century A.D. Its apse (with baptistery) is on the E side. It was probably built as a memorial church dedicated to the apostle PETER.

5. The "house church" and the "house of St. Peter." Beneath the octagon is a rectangular structure identified as a Christian "house church" or *domus ecclesia.* The excavators propose that it was built in the mid-fourth century A.D. to preserve the house of Peter, which had itself been in use as a house church since the first century. An enclosure wall forming a rectangle some 90 x 90 feet was erected above an insula first built in the first century B.C. A single dwelling of the insula (Peter's house) was isolated in the center of the rectangle and remodeled to form the house church. The interior plaster was painted, and graffiti in the plaster are in Greek, Aramaic, Syriac, and Latin, attesting to the importance of the city to Christian pilgrims in the fourth century.

Bibliography. S. Loffreda, *A Visit to Capharnaum* (2nd ed., 1973); V. Corbo, *The House of Saint Peter at Capharnaum* (1969); V. Corbo, *La Sinagoga di Cafarnao dopo gli scavi del 1969* (1970); S. Loffreda, "The Late Chronology of the Synagogue of Capernaum," *IEJ,* XXIII (1973), 37-42; M. Avi-Yonah, "Editor's Note" to the previous article, *ibid.,* 43-45; A. Neubauer, *La* *géographie du Talmud* (1868 [repr. 1967]), 221-24. *See also* SYNAGOGUE §4 and SYNAGOGUE, ARCHITECTURE[S].

J. F. STRANGE

***CARMEL, MOUNT.** In the annals of Shalmaneser III for 841 B.C., Mount Carmel appears as "the mountain of Ba'li-ra'si (KUR-*e* KUR*Ba-'-li-ra-'-si*) which is a promontory of the sea over against the land of Tyre." The Assyrian king camped there and received the tribute of JEHU of Israel. The identity of Ba'li-ra'si with Mount Carmel, made certain by a version of the annals published in 1951, is important on three accounts: it testifies to the sacral character of Mount Carmel, dedicated to the "Baal of the Promontory" (cf. I Kings 18:17-46); it confirms that Mount Carmel was the border between Tyre and Israel; and it proves that an Assyrian army crossed Israelite territory as early as 841—an event which must be put in relation with Jehu's seizure of power at that same time. *See* SHALMAN[S].

Bibliography. *ARAB,* I, §672; F. Safar, "A Further Text of Shalmaneser III," *Sumer,* VII (1951), 3-21; A. Malamat, "Campaigns to the Mediterranean . . . ," *Studies in Honor of B. Landsberger* (1965), pp. 371-72; Y. Aharoni, "Mount Carmel as Border," *Archäologie und Altes Testament* (1970), pp. 1-7; M. C. Astour, "841 B.C.: The First Assyrian Invasion of Israel," *JAOS,* XCI (1971), 383-89.

M. C. ASTOUR

CARTOGRAPHY OF PALESTINE. Cartography is the science and art of map making. Primarily because of its importance as the Holy Land, Palestine occupies a prominent place in the history of cartography and today is one of the most meticulously mapped regions in the world.

1. Ancient maps of Palestine (2500 B.C.–A.D. 400). Map making in the ancient Near East reflected both cosmological speculations and practical needs. The former were met by maps that embodied contemporary concepts of the physical world; practical concerns were reflected in maps that recorded what travelers observed. Either need could, upon occasion, find expression in linear projections such as appear in the Egyptian Book of the Dead and caravaneers' itineraries; these were not, however, maps in the proper sense, since they indicated only stopping places on a road. Probably just as early are true maps, ones that show on a plane the locations of places on or near the earth's surface.

The Egyptians may have made sketch maps of Palestine during the Old Kingdom, and it is quite likely that maps were in use during the Eighteenth Dynasty (1570-1300 B.C.), when Palestine was a part of Egypt's empire. The impetus for Egyptian cartography was practical: generals, messengers, and merchants needed to know how to get from one place to another efficiently. In addition to crude two-dimensional maps there also must have been itineraries, some of which may have indicated the distance from one place to the next. Mapping probably played much the same role in the other empires that subsequently had an interest in Palestine. Relatively few maps from these great nations have survived, and none of those extant include details of Palestinian geography.

The Hebrews seem to have had no special interest in maps of their country. A few passages in the OT allude to or suggest the possibility of the making of sketch maps. Joshua, the Yahwist relates, sent investigators "up and down the land, writing a description of it with a view to their inheritances" (Josh. 18:4); that description was, in customary fashion, structured around towns (Josh. 18:9; cf. the Priestly materials in 18:10–21:42). The account of the location of Eden (Gen. 2:10-14, Yahwist account) may imply the existence of something like a world map around the tenth century B.C. The story of David's census (II Sam. 24:1-9; cf. I Chr. 21:1-6) suggests the utilization of a map of Israel for governmental purposes.

Around the sixth century B.C. the Priestly circle in Judah may have experienced a surge of cosmological interest that created a climate of thought in which cosmological map making not only would have been possible but perhaps would have been encouraged. The prophecies of Ezekiel later in the same century indicate familiarity with surveyors' techniques (Ezek. 40–42, 47–48), and Ezek. 4:1-2 seems to allude to the prophet's making of a sketch map. From this time on, as first Greek and then Hellenistic and Roman influences were felt, the Hebrews were undoubtedly acquainted in a matter-of-fact way with both cosmological and practical cartography. No extant Hebrew maps, however, antedate the Middle Ages.

It is probable that Palestine was cursorily mapped by surveyors accompanying Alexander the Great when the conqueror passed through the country in 332 B.C. Need for maps existed during the Ptolemaic, Seleucid, and Roman occupations of Palestine, but nothing is known about the form maps may have had. The earliest surviving cartographic records of Palestine are those of the famous geographer Ptolemy of Alexandria, who compiled data (often imprecise) on the latitude and longitude of a number of towns of the region around the middle of the second century A.D. In the early fourth century EUSEBIUS OF CAESAREA prepared an onomasticon, or gazetteer, in which hundreds of Palestinian places were identified and the mileage from one place to another along the Roman roads was given. Unfortunately none of the surviving manuscripts of this important work contains a map.

2. Maps of Palestine in the Middle Ages and Renaissance (A.D. 400-1700). In the eastern Roman empire Eusebius' scholarly efforts were utilized in a number of later maps, the most famous of which is a magnificent representation in mosaic paving in a church at Madeba (ancient MEDEBA) dating from the second half of the sixth century. (*See* Fig. C2.) With the coming of Islam in the seventh century Greek culture diminished but did not disappear. The Islamic geographers themselves contributed little to the cartography of Palestine.

In the West the knowledge of the cartography of Ptolemy and Eusebius alike was largely forgotten for nearly a thousand years. Palestine itself, however, remained of interest to Europeans because of its association with the Bible and Christianity. From the fourth century onward there was an endless flow of pilgrims from Europe to the Holy Land. These travelers generally relied on itineraries

H. T. Frank

2. The Madeba mosaic map, showing Jerusalem and environs

that listed way stops rather than on true maps. The Crusades and subsequent occupation of Palestine by Europeans brought the need for improved maps. One such map, based on firsthand knowledge, has survived in a twelfth-century manuscript in Florence. The majority of maps that the Crusaders transmitted were, however, little more than late, garbled versions of the Eusebian tradition, which had remained alive in the Byzantine empire during the intervening centuries. Maps in this format continued to be used widely in Europe for several hundred years.

In the fifteenth century there was a rediscovery in the West of classical works on geography, including those of Ptolemy. Consequently there appears an influx of Ptolemaic elements on many maps, sometimes combined with details from the previous map tradition. Because no new topographical surveying had been carried out, Palestinian maps show continued deterioration in precision throughout most of the sixteenth and seventeenth centuries. As if to try to compensate for this deficiency, late Medieval and Renaissance map makers resorted to decorative embellishments that included portraits of biblical personages, scenes of salvific events, views of cities, and even heraldic motifs—all drawn from imagination. Jerusalem was the focus of interest in Palestine. Many plans and bird's-eye views of the city were produced, often highly stylized. In this age of geographical exploration world maps were particularly popular; these depicted, in keeping with the thoroughgoing Christian orientation of Western civilization at that time, Jerusalem at the center of the world. Maps of this period stand in the cosmological tradition of cartography and contain little accurate information about Palestine.

3. The modern mapping of Palestine (A.D. 1700 to the present). During the eighteenth century a transformation began that eventually led to scientifically accurate maps of Palestine. In 1714, H. Reland published a map based on a fresh study of ancient records. New mechanical devices made relatively accurate surveying possible, with the result that d'Anville's 1732 map of Palestine shows relationships that are fairly precise. By the mid-nineteenth century there were maps that approximated the actual geographical features of the country.

When the era of surface exploration of Palestine began early in the nineteenth century, the locations of hundreds of places mentioned in the Bible and in other ancient documents were still unknown. Edward Robinson identified some sites during his visits to Palestine in 1838 and 1852, and for a hundred years thereafter scholars probed the highways and byways of the region. The pages of the *Zeitschrift des Deutschen Palästina-Vereins, Palestine Exploration Fund Quarterly Statement* (later *Palestine Exploration Quarterly*), *Journal of the Palestine Oriental Society, Bulletin of the American Schools of Oriental Research,* and other pioneering journals contain many proposals for the identification of ancient sites. Among the leading scholars concerned with site-identification were H. Vincent, W. F. Albright, G. Dalman, A. Alt, F.-M. Abel, and N. Glueck.

The first thorough, professional topographical survey of Palestine was carried out by C. R. Conder and H. H. Kitchener in 1872-77 under the auspices of the Palestine Exploration Fund and published in twenty-six large sheets at the generous scale of 1:63,360, with ten accompanying volumes of text. In this work thousands of modern place names in Palestine were recorded for the first time. During the British Mandate, a survey of Palestine was published in a set of minutely detailed and scientifically precise maps at 1:10,000. In 1959 the United States Army Map Service issued a 1:50,000 set of maps of Israel and Jordan based on a new photogrammetric survey. In 1965 Israel published a 1:100,000 set of maps in Hebrew.

The governmental maps generally do not attempt to incorporate the identifications of ancient sites made by scholars. That task has been performed by several biblical geographies and atlases, including *The Historical Geography of the Holy Land* by G. A. Smith (25th ed., 1931), *The Westminster Historical Atlas to the Bible* by G. E. Wright and F. V. Filson (rev. ed., 1956), *Atlas of the Bible* by L. H. Grollenberg (Eng. ed., 1956), *Oxford Bible Atlas* by H. G. May (2nd ed., 1974), and *The Geography of the Bible* (rev. ed., 1974) and *Geographical Companion to the Bible* (1963), both by D. Baly. These works, especially the more recent ones, are not limited to topography and place-identifications but present in cartographic form other kinds of information as well, such as political divisions, demography, climatology, geology, agriculture, and commerce.

Bibliography. H. Fischer, "Geschichte der Kartographie von Palästina," *Zeitschrift des Deutschen Palästina-Vereins,* LXII (1939), 169-89; LXIII (1940), 1-111; H. M. Z. Meyer, *The Holy Land in Ancient Maps* (3rd enlarged ed., 1965); Z. Vilnay, *The Holy Land in Old Prints and Maps* (2nd ed., 1965); W. Kubitschek, "Karten," PW, X, cols. 2022-2149.

R. H. Smith

CASUISTIC LAW. *See* Law in the OT §3; Law in the OT[S] §5.

CATCHWORD. *See* Mnemonic Devices[S] §2.

***CENCHREAE.** Buildings on two promontories enclosing the harbor have been investigated. On the SW are warehouses probably dating from the early first century A.D., an apsidal building with marble pavement, and a Christian basilican church of the fourth century A.D. In the apsidal building were found panels of *opus sectile,* with pieces of colored glass mounted in plaster, which represent abstract designs, portraits, and descriptive scenes. On the NE promontory is a massive brick building, dating probably from the second century A.D. For details see the articles by R. L. Scranton and E. S. Ramage in *Hesperia,* XXXIII (1964), 134-45; XXXVI (1967), 124-86. *See also* Corinth.

C. L. Thompson

***CHAOS.** Chaos is a state of utter confusion, totally lacking in organization or predictability. It is the antithesis of cosmos.

1. The concept in ancient Near Eastern myth. Natural, political, and conceptual order depend on pattern and on change. Threats to them are imaged either as unyielding, undifferentiated mass, not amenable to change; or as dissipated, undifferentiated energy, not amenable to patterning. The Sumerian story of Ninurta and Asag is a useful paradigm of the relationship between the two images. Though told in terms of drought, wind, storm, flood, and agricultural fertility, it can as well describe disease, political tyranny, mental disorder, and related forms. Ninurta, the storm, shatters Asag, the (nether-world) mountain. The result is that the waters of the mountain are released in a destructive flood. Ninurta heaps up stones to control the flood and dedicates the now fertile earth-mound to his mother, Ninmah. A living order emerges from the combat between the two extremes.

We may call "resistant-mass chaos" that which characteristically swallows or consumes; it must be smashed open; its separated parts then sustain order. It suspends order by withholding water (Sumerian Asag) or the sun (Egyptian Apophis), by preventing fertility and growth (Hittite Hahhimas). Or it may prevent the orderly succession from father to son and from dead king to legitimate heir (Hittite Kumarbi, Greek Kronos).

We may call "dissipated-energy chaos" that which characteristically expands and must be contained. Its force, once harnessed, effects order. It disrupts by flooding, by breeding monsters (Akkadian Tiamat), by cutting off communication between vital parts of the cosmos (Hittite Ullikummi), by forever expanding (Greek Titans), by obliterating boundaries (Egyptian Seth). Creation, by contrast, is portrayed as the establishment of free yet regulated movement; time brings fulfillment as it brings death; water flows rather than floods; the sun sets and rises; sons become fathers as they engender sons.

Characteristics of chaos tend to correlate negatively with those of cosmos, so that change goes in the direction of a more comprehensive view that accommodates what had come to be experienced as irreconcilable oppositions. The effectiveness of the god is most convincingly expressed when he subsumes the powers of the monster by legitimizing its characteristic activity: Marduk, gigantic and breathing fire, assumes Tiamat's powers. As the storm, he opens her; as the sun, he contains her. As god, he releases and regulates the powers of life and growth. Vritra says to Indra "Thou art now what I was before." The dying god conquers death by making it godly (Osiris).

2. The chaos tradition in the Bible. The proper frame of reference for discussion of chaos is the drama of creation, in which cosmos is the outcome of a heroic battle between the creator and the opposing monster (*see* Myth §A1*a*, 4; Cosmogony §§A2*d*, D2*b*; for discussion of Gen. 1, *see* Creation; Deep, the). The prevailing biblical view does not locate opposition to God in natural processes, but within history and the human community. God subsumes what had earlier been conceived as the powers of chaos (*see* §*b below*). Therefore we cannot depend solely upon ancient mythic structure for the significance of direct reference or veiled allusion in the Bible to the primordial enemy of earlier tradition. On the other hand, that structure may direct the biblical poet to choices of expression in describing God's acts of creation. The chaos tradition survives in two ways: reference to known monsters may serve metaphorically to characterize historical enemies (Ezek. chs. 29, 32), or poetically to express God's sovereignty (Ps. 74:14). Images associated with the two monster-types may express the creative nature of God's activity at significant junctures in sacred history, such as the Exodus, Sinai, the "Conquest," the Exile, the Restoration, the Advent, the Apocalypse (*see* War, Ideas of §4; Water).

a. The battle myth in the Bible. Intrabiblical and comparative Ugaritic evidence suggests that independent personality was attributed to Rahab, Leviathan, the Serpent (נחש), the Dragon (תנין), Yam (Sea), the Deep (תהום), Mot (Death), Ereṣ (Earth, *see* Wakeman, *bibliog.*), and Behemoth.

Rahab is the proper name of a mythological beast associated with the sea. It is found only in Israelite tradition, and is in some passages identified with Egypt (Ps. 87:4; Isa. 30:7). He is hewn (Isa. 51:9), crushed (Ps. 89:10 [H 11]), smitten (Job 26:12), his followers subdued (Job 9:13). His fate is less ambiguous than that of the others since it is more closely tied to the historical moment of Israel's creation in the exodus from Egypt (Isa. 51:9; Ps. 89:10 [H 11]). Verbal derivatives of the name parallel to the root נגש (Isa. 14:4, reading מרהבה with LXX, Syr., Targ., 1QIs[a]; Isa. 3:5), suggest an association with the idea of oppression.

LEVIATHAN is a serpent (Isa. 27:1); Yahweh has crushed his heads and given him for food to the creatures of the wilderness (Ps. 74:14). Other passages suggest that Yahweh can draw him out with a hook and nose rope (Job 41:1-2). He is roused to battle (Job 3:8) and is Yahweh's plaything (Ps. 104:26).

DRAGON (תנין) is a generic term for the mythological monster. He is characterized as a devourer (Jer. 51:34) and associated with darkness (Ps. 44:19, NEB [H 20]).

The SERPENT in Amos 9:3 is a sea monster who bites at the command of God.

Yam (SEA) is broken (Ps. 74:13), his back is trampled upon (Job 9:8), he is muzzled (Job 26:13, reading *śām yām*), guarded (Job 7:12), cursed (Job 3:8), rebuked (Ps. 68:30 [H 31]), the object of Yahweh's indignation (Hab. 3:8). When God is the subject of the root גער ("rebuke"), the object of rebuke is paralyzed. In the NT the corresponding word is ἐπιτιμάω, which describes Jesus' command of the sea and wind (Matt. 8:26) and of unclean demons (Luke 4:35).

Yam presents difficulties because it is also the ordinary word for sea. Mythological connotation clings to it when it is the object of the verb בקע, "to break open," usually, of a body. With the possible exception of Ps. 74:15, the verb בקע used with a watery object always alludes to the account of crossing the Reed Sea. The corporeal connotation is appropriate to the sea insofar as it is regarded as a monster. The sea's being dried up translates the mythical action of killing the tyrant, to be distinguished from setting a bound on the sea as an act of cosmic ordering (cf. Prov. 8:29). The sea's covering something, usually at the behest of God, is likewise a translation of the mythical monster's swallowing (cf. Ps. 69:15 [H 16]). God's drying up the sea makes sense only if its continued existence is regarded as inimical: cf. "I saw a new heaven and a new earth; . . . and the sea was no more" (Rev. 21:1).

Though תהום (Tehom, "Deep," "ABYSS") may be related etymologically to TIAMAT, it is nowhere personified in the Bible. However, inconsistencies in the word's gender, both in its form and in its agreement with verbs and adjectives, seem to indicate that the idea was in the process of being depersonalized. Vestiges of personality cling to expressions in which the word in the singular has indications of feminine gender or definiteness. This includes all cases of תהום רבה (*see* May, *bibliog.*); תהום רבצת in Gen. 49:25; Deut. 33:13; and Ezek. 26:19, 31:15 (accusative particle). The differentiation of תהום from the sea (Exod. 15:8) gives it the autonomy of the dragon (Ezek. 32:2), the god who sits in the heart of the seas (Ezek. 28:2).

Ereṣ (Earth) swallows (Exod. 15:12), shakes (רעש, *see* Childs, *bibliog.*), trembles in fear of God (Ps. 114:7), melts in submission (Ps. 46:6 [H 7]), is trampled upon (Mic. 1:3). The difficulties are similar to those for Yam: besides being the ordinary word for earth or land, ארץ is often a synonym for the underworld, though without any implication of opposition to God.

MOT (Death) is personified in the Bible (e.g., Jer. 9:21 [H 20]), but appears only once in the OT as the Enemy: "[The Lord] will swallow up death for ever" (Isa. 25:8; cf. I Cor. 15:54; Hos. 13:14). Like Yam, he is finally defeated at the end of time when "Death and Hades were thrown into the lake of fire" (Rev. 20:14).

One may recognize behind the poetic description of "the beast" BEHEMOTH in Job a familiar figure in the ancient Near East (Asag, Vritra, etc.), the first being which emerged from the undifferentiated water, whose tyrannical reign is symbolized by drought. His relation to Leviathan is like that of Apsu (rather than Kingu) to Tiamat (*see* Enoch 60:7-8; II Esd. 6:49-50).

b. The "monstrousness" of God. God employs the monster to exercise his powers in the service of order: Aaron's rod turns into a dragon (תנין, Exod. 7:12) to swallow the Egyptian powers, to spoil their water, to split open rocks that release good water; the earth swallows Pharaoh (Exod. 15:12) or the dragon's river (Rev. 12:16); the biting serpent is sent to patrol the bottom of the sea (Amos 9:3); Leviathan and Behemoth demonstrate to Job that what is beyond his understanding is nonetheless within God's control. God subsumes the powers of the monster, exercising them for good as he brings darkness (Ezek. 32:7) and a consuming fire (Isa. 66:15; cf. Luke 12:49) upon his enemies; he makes the earth tremble (Nah. 1:5); he brings the sea up over the Babylonians (Jer. 51:42), Tehom over Tyre (Ezek. 26:19).

c. The negative correlation of images associated with cosmos and chaos in the Bible. Imagery associated with God and monster tends to polarize them as opposites. The sea monster is more evident in the Bible than the earth monster, perhaps because God's victory at the Reed Sea at the beginning of Israel's history is symbolically so central. Accordingly, God is referred to as a rock thirty-three times, the resistant body that saves from the encroaching flood of enemies within and without (e.g., Ps. 18). Of the two poles (kingship and covenant) between which biblical conceptual life swings, the imagery associated with this myth attaches to the first. It tends to revive at the junctures in Israel's history that bring it closest to the ancient hierarchical pattern, such as the establishment of the kingdom (ZION TRADITION, Davidic psalms), the hope of its restoration after the exile (the new exodus as described in Second Isaiah) and its fulfillment at the end of time (apocalyptic visions), especially when the great dragon, "that ancient serpent, who is the Devil and Satan" is vanquished (Rev. 20:2-3).

On the other hand, the giving of the Law is a creative event of equal importance to the life of Israel with the granting of the land, and is so marked by the earth-splitting theophany at Sinai (Exod. 19:16-17). The prophets who, like Moses (cf. Deut. 18:15), smite the rock (cf. Exod. 17:6; Jer. 23:29), see that it is not the nations as political reality that threaten Israel's life but the old ideology of the sacred state. Belief in the inviolability of the land undermines the true strength of Israel as a legal community under God. The Lord who speaks to Elijah (I Kings 19:11) breaks the rocks in pieces. Amos hears the Lord call for justice to "roll down like waters, and righteousness like an ever-flowing stream" (5:24). Isaiah sees God working through Assyria who will "rise over all its channels . . . sweep on into Judah . . . overflow and pass on" (8:7-8). The rock may be a foundation stone or a "rock of stumbling" (8:14). Jeremiah calls God "the fountain of living waters" (2:13; 17:13; cf. Zech. 14:4-8); and for Ezekiel "the sound of his coming was like the sound of many waters" (43:2; cf. 47:1-12). Christ is an earth-smasher. As he yielded up his spirit, "the earth shook, and the rocks were split; the tombs also were opened, and many bodies of the saints who had fallen asleep were raised" (Matt. 27:51*b*-52). Christ is the source of living water (John 4:10; Rev. 22:17); baptism into Christ (Rom. 6:3) overcomes death.

The identification of the DEVIL and SATAN with the seven-headed dragon in the Apocalypse (Rev. 12:9) reconciles archaic and biblical conceptualizations. "The Adversary" (śāṭān), who as an agent of God appears originally in legal contexts (Zech. 3; Job 1–2), comes increasingly to take on the role of the Enemy as chaos is increasingly identified with breach of covenant. The new covenant, written on the heart, entails a spiritual Enemy, who is associated with death and darkness as he prevents people from realizing their relationship with God.

Bibliography. B. W. Anderson, *Creation versus Chaos* (1967); B. S. Childs, "The Enemy from the North and the Chaos Tradition," *JBL*, LXXVIII (1959), 187-98; F. M. Cross, *Canaanite Myth and Hebrew Epic* (1973); M. Douglas, *Purity and Danger* (1966); H. Gunkel, *Schöpfung und Chaos in Urzeit und Endzeit* (1895); S. N. Kramer, *Mythologies of the Ancient World* (1961); H. G. May, "Some Cosmic Connotations of *Mayim* Rabbîm, 'Many Waters,'" *JBL*, LXXIV (1955), 9-21; P. Ricoeur, *The Symbolism of Evil* (1967); H. te Velde, *Seth, God of Confusion* (1967); M. K. Wakeman, "The Biblical Earth-Monster," *JBL*, LXXXVIII (1969), 313-20, and *God's Battle with the Monster* (1973).

M. K. WAKEMAN

CHENOBOSKION. *See* NAG HAMMADI[S].

CHIASMUS kī ăz′məs. A rhetorical term designating a reversal of the order of words in two otherwise parallel clauses, as in the literal translation of Prov. 3:10, "Then filled will be your barns with grain, and with new wine your vats will be bursting."

Biblical writers used chiasmus extensively to lend variety and charm to their parallel structures. On micro and macro levels chiasmus has been shown to be a basic element in the formal structure of biblical literature, so that critics can use it to determine the reading of a difficult text, the meaning or grammatical function of a word, or the limits of extensive pericopes, such as the flood story (Gen. 6–9) or the binding of Isaac (Gen. 22:1-19).

Simple chiasmus consisting of four members in an a.b.b′.a′ sequence is frequent, as in Jer. 6:25, literally:

Go not forth into the field,
on the road do not walk.

Less frequent is the more developed a.b.c.c′.b′.a′ pattern, as in Prov. 3:10, cited above.

Now receiving greater attention are the a.b.b.a and a.b.c.c.b.a sequences, in which the writer employs the same words or roots in both parts of the unit.

The sound of battle in the land (ארץ),	a
and of great destruction (שבר)	b
Alas, has been cut down and destroyed (ישבר)	b
the hammer of all the earth (ארץ)!	a
(Jer. 50:22-23; author's trans.)	

Make the heart of this people fat,	a
and their ears heavy,	b
and shut their eyes;	c
lest they see with their eyes,	c
and hear with their ears,	b
and understand with their hearts. (Isa. 6:10)	a

See also POETRY, HEBREW[S].

Bibliography. N. Lund, "The Presence of Chiasmus in the Old Testament," *AJSL*, XLVI (1930), 104-26, "The Presence of Chiasmus in the New Testament," *JR*, X (1930), 74-93, "Chiasmus in the Psalms," *AJSL*, XLIX (1933), 281-312, and *Chiasmus in the New Testament* (1942); M. Dahood, "Chiasmus in Job: A Text-Critical and Philological Criterion," in *A Light unto My Path*, ed. H. Bream, R. Heim, and C. Moore (1974), pp. 119-30.

M. DAHOOD

***CHILMAD.** A place mentioned in Ezek. 27:23 (to be read כלמדר, ר lost by haplography with the following רכלתך). It is to be identified with Kulmadara, one of the principal cities of the N Syrian kingdom of Unqi, annexed to Assyria in 738 B.C. (*see* HITTITES[S] §2). Perhaps it is to be located at the very large mound of Tell Jindaris, classical Gindaros, if one assumes that the Hurrian element *kulma* ("fertile place"?) was later replaced by Aram. *gin-*, "garden."

Bibliography. A. Sarsowsky, "Notizien zu einigen biblischen geographischen und ethnographischen Namen," *ZAW*, XXXII (1912), 149; *ARAB*, I, §821; R. J. Braidwood, *Mounds of the Plain of Antioch* (1937), pp. 25 (no. 58), 26 (Fig. 5).

M. C. ASTOUR

CHREIA krā′ə [χρεία, "need"]. Defined by ancient Greek rhetoricians as a concise, pointed account of something said or done by a particular person, and so named because it provided guidance for conduct, *the* most needful thing. Chreiai concerning Jesus were especially useful to early Christian preachers, although the term itself does not appear with its technical meaning in the NT.

1. Characteristics. The chreia was so designed as to be easily committed to memory. Once memorized it constituted a well-structured text that could be quoted, paraphrased, illustrated, and expounded upon at will. Chreiai were never attributed to mythological figures, and only rarely was the same chreia attributed to more than one person. When used critically along with other historical evidence, a chreia may afford valuable supplementary or confirmatory data concerning some characteristic dispositional attitude or exemplary act of its subject.

Typical are the following: "One day when

Antisthenes was censured for keeping company with evil men, the reply he made was, 'Well, Physicians are in attendance on their patients without getting the fever themselves'" (Diogenes Laertius VI.i.6). "When someone inquired [of Anaxogoras], 'Have you no concern in your native land?' 'Gently,' he replied, 'I am greatly concerned with my fatherland,' and pointed to the sky" (Diogenes Laertius II.iii.7). Some chreiai are more developed and involve dialogue, as for example those quoted by Xenophon in his *Memorabilia* III.xiii.

2. Chreiai in the Synoptic gospels. Most chreiai attributed to Jesus in the gospels have undergone literary expansion, sometimes in ways prescribed by the rhetoricians. Thus the point of Jesus' response to Peter in Matt. 18:21-22 is illustrated by the following parable. And the principle in the chreia of the widow's mite in Luke 21:1-3 is brought out in the *aitia* or "reason" in Luke 21:4. But often the expansions are glosses which must be bracketed in order to appreciate the rhetorical force of the original form. An example is one evangelist's explanation that the widow's two "mites" amounted to a (Roman) *quadrans* (Mark 12:42).

Bibliography. For further discussion and literature see W. R. Farmer, "Notes on a Literary and Form-Critical Analysis of Some of the Synoptic Material Peculiar to Luke," *NTS*, VIII (1962), 301-16. *See also* H. A. Fischel, "Studies in Cynicism and the Ancient Near East: The Transformation of a Chreia," *Religions in Antiquity*, ed J. Neusner (1968), pp. 372-411, which traces transformation of Cynic chreia forms in rabbinic literature.

W. R. Farmer

***CHRIST.** *See* Christology in the NT[S].

***CHRISTOLOGY IN THE NT.** To confess Jesus of Nazareth as the Christ is to declare that he is the basis of faith; Christology is the development and presentation of the meaning of that basis. Thus Christology is fundamentally a response to a call to faith—a response which describes that call by reference to the basis on which it was issued. The response in turn becomes a new call to faith. It is possible to distinguish between the response and the new call, but not to separate them. The major emphasis of Christology is to be found in its nature as response.

The response could be evoked by an encounter with Jesus of Nazareth, but this of course was possible only prior to Good Friday. After that the response was evoked by the encounter with the Jesus Christ who is experienced as present in the proclamation, i.e., by encounter with the kerygma.

Since the NT books were not written until after Easter, a Christology which proposes to be "New Testament" Christology in the strict sense can deal only with the response to the kerygma. It is possible, however, by means of Literary Criticism to determine pre-NT traditions with considerable certainty, and they too can be incorporated into our presentation. The opinions of scholars differ as to the age of these traditions. It is relatively certain, however, that at least the traditions of the so-called Logia source (Q) show no influence of the events of the Crucifixion and Easter. From this fact we may infer that in their substance, even though not always in their wording, they come from the pre-Easter period.

To a certain extent the differences in form of the christological expressions can be explained in the following way. The *Christ kerygma* first appeared after Good Friday. It proclaims that Christ has come (Gal. 4:4), that he has died for our sins, and that he has risen (I Cor. 15:3-4). No mention is made of the what and how of his existence. All the NT writings were affected by this Christ kerygma, and until the middle of the second century it continued to be the dominant kerygma in the church. The gospels, however, are an exception; they are oriented to the *Jesus kerygma.* Jesus is indeed proclaimed in this kerygma too, but he himself appears there as the one who proclaims and who is at work. The purpose of the Jesus kerygma is not to present a historically accurate account of Jesus' words and deeds and to hand them on with historical fidelity. It is, rather, to proclaim anew Jesus' words and deeds (precisely as *his* words and deeds) to each subsequent generation. As time passed, it was possible to preserve the content only by varying the language.

The "explicit" Christology of the Jesus kerygma is generally contrasted with the "implicit" Christology of Jesus' own preaching. This distinction is unfortunate because it obscures the fact that the Jesus traditions have come down to us as kerygma, not as historical reports. It would be better to make a distinction between a Christology that is enacted (Jesus kerygma) and a Christology that is reflected upon (Christ kerygma). Between these two there are many forms that contain elements of both. Thus the Jesus of Nazareth who speaks and acts is furnished with titles and designations of honor (Matt. 11:2; Mark 1:24; Luke 7:19, and *passim*); he is represented in his activity as a Divine Man (Mark 6:45-51); or he is portrayed mythologically (John). Here we may speak of the *Jesus Christ kerygma.*

The following discussion is arranged according to the various forms of kerygma, but it must be noted that these frequently overlap, and it is not always possible to maintain strict distinctions.

1. The Jesus kerygma
2. The Christ kerygma
   a. Before and contemporary with Paul
   b. Paul
   c. After Paul
      i. The Deutero-Pauline writings
      ii. The other writings
3. The Jesus Christ kerygma
   a. Further formations and collections
   b. The Synoptic gospels
   c. The Gospel of John
4. Conclusion
Bibliography

1. The Jesus kerygma. The Jesus kerygma is found in the NT exclusively in the context of the Jesus Christ kerygma of the Synoptic gospels, but it can be reconstructed by means of literary criticism. Since there are no absolutely sure criteria for determining the age of the individual traditions, some uncertainty remains. We may begin with the material which was revised by Q and with various small units of discourse and narrative in the Synoptics. It is important, first, to determine the distinctive form and content of the Jesus kerygma. On this basis the later developments can be made comprehensible (*see* §3 *below*).

All the traditions were formulated by believers. With the exception of Matt. 18:6, however, it is never stated that people believe *in* Jesus; rather, in the receipt and transmission of Jesus' words and deeds it is always made clear that people believe *him*, i.e., that they have submitted to his claims and that they now are speaking as those who have been influenced by him. We can ask what the historical Jesus said and did and how he understood himself and his mission. As the history of research in this area shows, however, the conclusions are far from unanimous (*see* Jesus Christ; Teaching of Jesus; Teaching of Jesus[S]). But since Christology is by nature a *response,* those conclusions are irrelevant. In the "repetition" of the preaching of Jesus and in the presentation of his activity, those who have encountered him give expression to their experiences with Jesus. In so doing they present him as the one who has appeared to them, the one who has prompted and initiated these experiences in them. Anyone who does not discern this characteristic feature of the material will always have difficulty understanding it. Thus we do not have any direct knowledge of what the historical Jesus said, but only of the way in which those who encountered him have understood what they heard from Jesus.

Jesus' words and deeds are set forth as a saving event by people who have experienced salvation in this event. Precisely here, as soteriology, Christology is enacted for us. Reflection about the one who is behind these words and deeds is found only occasionally, and then in rudimentary form. Speaking broadly, the relationship of those who are involved appears "as the reverent reserve of respectful followers before the Holy One who lives in their midst, but who in his innermost essence remains alien to them" (M. Dibelius). On the one hand, Jesus' "person" appears to be entirely human: he is hungry (Mark 11:12), eats and drinks (Matt. 11:19), is presented consistently as a teacher, and is addressed as a rabbi (Mark 11:21). But on the other hand, these human traits are repeatedly transcended: Jesus sees through the thoughts of his adversaries (Mark 2:8); he does not teach as the scribes do, but with authority (Mark 1:22; Matt. 7:29); and by his conduct he gives the impression that he is a prophet (Mark 6:15).

The key to the christological understanding of the Jesus kerygma may very well be offered by Mark 1:15: "The time is fulfilled, and the kingdom of God is at hand; repent, and believe in the gospel." In substance (though not in its formulation) this message goes back to a very early date. Scholars frequently ask whether βασιλεία means "kingdom" (thus emphasizing a state of affairs) or "rule," and whether it is to be thought of as present or as future. *See* Kingdom of God §3; Kingdom of God[S] §§2, 3.

The conception comes from late Jewish apocalyptic. The images employed there are confusing in their multiplicity and cannot be fitted into a unified system (*see* Apocalypticism[S]). The dominant idea is that of the futurity of the kingdom of God, conceived of as a state of affairs. It is the new aeon which, through earthly confusion and cosmic catastrophes, will dissolve the old aeon. The kingdom will begin with the judgment which, according to various apocalyptic systems, will be carried out by the Son of Man. Occasionally in competition with this is the idea of a (political) Messiah (from the house of David) who will set Israel free. The end time is preceded by various signs, the first of which are occasionally seen as already present or are to appear in the immediate future.

Once the background of this conception has been seen, it becomes clear that Jesus would never have been understood as an apocalyptic teacher who sought to provide information about the coming kingdom. Jesus' hearers were only too well acquainted with detailed teachings about the future. Further, we cannot tell which of the various apocalyptic systems Jesus would have opted for. It is characteristic of the Jesus kerygma that apocalyptic details are sharply reduced. It is really only the framework that remains, and questions about the coming state of affairs are rejected; it will be entirely different from the way anyone can imagine here on earth (Mark 12:25). Moreover, Jesus was not understood as an apocalyptic teacher who (like many before and after him, and like the sect of Qumran in his own time) supposed that there was still a period of time before the coming of the kingdom, even though a very brief one. Jesus' hearers understood him to mean that there was no more time. This distinctive mark of Jesus' expectation of the imminent end becomes clear when he is compared with John the Baptist. For John, repentance is a precondition for admittance into the kingdom, which is coming soon. For Jesus, the inbreaking of the βασιλεία is God's inbreaking in order to rule, with which come, simultaneously, the possibility and the necessity of Repentance. God's rule is present in the sense that now "eschatological existence" can be lived, and that it therefore must be lived.

This eschatological existence in God's presence takes away every possibility of setting one's relationship to God in order by oneself, for this possibility is no longer needed. Those who, like the Pharisee, wish to do good works are keeping God at a distance; they emphasize the distance and thus refuse to accept God's presence. Those who, like the tax collector, confess themselves to be sinners, acknowledge the nearness of God and experience salvation (Luke 18:9 ff.). We simply cannot do anything more *for* the kingdom; we can only receive it as a child (Mark 10:13-16). *In* the kingdom, of course, there is something to do. But it is not simply a doing of the Law, even when it is casuistically intensified (Mark 7:1-23). It is the doing of the will of God in all its radical demands (the antitheses of the Sermon on the Mount, Matt.

5:21-45). Where this will prevails no one can ask any longer who the neighbor is, because each one from then on always is a neighbor (Luke 10:29-37). This total submission to the will of God is rightly understood, however, only when it is understood as grace and thus as salvation. The kingdom of God belongs to the POOR (Luke 6:20); tax collectors and sinners enjoy the fellowship at the eschatological table (Mark 2:15-17); and any care about tomorrow can be left confidently until tomorrow (Matt. 6:24-34). This can be done all the more readily since the fear of judgment is removed: where anyone today has surrendered to Jesus, that one is already experiencing the (intrinsically) future acknowledgment by the Son of man (Luke 12:8; Mark 8:38).

Of course those who have encountered Jesus are aware that his call and deeds are capable of two different interpretations. Demands for a sign are rejected (Mark 8:11-12). John the Baptist's inquiry about who Jesus is shows that even the "miracles" of Jesus cannot be *proved* to be eschatological deeds. Moreover, John's question is not answered with a reference to Jesus, but with a reference to his "functions"; and then salvation is promised to the person who does not take offense at the one who is performing these functions (Matt. 11:2-6). The person who does not take offense experiences even now the presence of the kingdom of God (Matt. 12:28; Luke 11:20); however, he or she experiences this presence in the unpretentious word which is "only" a seed (Mark 4:3-9). Even the PARABLES are not intended to impart information about the coming kingdom of God (though later they were so understood). We must pay attention to their function. They are told because in them people have experienced how they have been incorporated into the kingdom of God by selling everything in order to acquire a field or a pearl (Matt. 13:44-46). And people who see themselves in this way need do nothing more *for* the coming of God's kingdom, since it now works of its own accord, automatically (Mark 4:26 ff.).

The inability of the people of Jesus' time to abandon the outline of their apocalyptic conceptions is connected with their (and Jesus') view of the world. Later on, these conceptions were further expanded (Mark 13), but even in the time of Jesus they served to prevent any misunderstanding of the presence of the kingdom of God as a particular state of affairs. Conversion was not a once-for-all event, but every day it was possible and necessary to experience it anew. Even though Jesus' presence was understood as a καιρός which does away with *our* time, there still remains for our time the constant petition, "Thy kingdom come" (Matt. 6:10).

As long as Jesus was announcing the imminence of the kingdom of God and was bringing it in by what he did, people could form ideas as to who he was, but they were not obliged to do so. It was sufficient to let him start them out on the way to the kingdom of God. Of course a problem arose when Jesus was not present, and when he was no longer present. These two conditions must be kept distinct. It is incontestable that the knowledge of Jesus and his activity was widely disseminated (Mark 1:28), even though Jesus' sending out of the TWELVE on a mission is not as such historical (Mark 6:7-13). This knowledge was reported because of a concern, but since radical rejection also expresses concern, even the effort to eliminate Jesus has to be understood as such an expression. Those who sent Jesus to the cross understood him very well; only among the Romans was there a misunderstanding in political terms. But where the knowledge of Jesus was reported because of a positive concern, the Jesus kerygma arose. This must have happened a great deal, for traditional material is abundant in the Synoptics, and it was not collected in Jerusalem but, more likely, in Galilee. Even the influence of the events that had taken place in Jerusalem was at first very limited (Q has no passion narrative and no Easter kerygma). But how can the kerygma, detached from the presence of Jesus, continue to be oriented to him? By this time at the very latest, there had to be reflection upon the person of Jesus, and thus arose the Jesus Christ kerygma (*see* §3 *below*).

The crucifixion of Jesus posed essentially the same problem, particularly for his closest followers who had come with him to Jerusalem. They faced the problem in its sharpest form: did not the Cross prove that the experiences which people had had with Jesus were simply delusions?

2. The Christ kerygma. ***a. Before and contemporary with Paul.*** Where people stood directly or indirectly under the impact of the execution of Jesus, it obviously was impossible to proclaim the Jesus kerygma any longer. Any direct connection with the past was cut off. Nevertheless, very soon after Good Friday a circle of concerned people found themselves together again. The historical events which brought this about can be reconstructed only with great difficulty (*see* RESURRECTION IN THE NT and supplementary article). It is certain, however, that—probably prompted by visions (I Cor. 15:5 ff.)—the conviction quickly prevailed: Jesus is alive! Then subsequently: He is exalted to God's presence! And finally: He is risen from the dead! This surprising experience was so unprecedented that it became the point of departure of all reflection and supplanted the earthly Jesus. The Christ kerygma arose.

A double movement, backward and forward, may be noted here. On the one hand, the Christ kerygma gives a new description of Jesus. Yet this did not involve statements *about* Jesus' history; it presupposed, rather, an orientation *to* it: to Jesus' cross, to the fact of his having lived. This is the christological aspect in the narrower sense. On the other hand, however, the Christ kerygma involved statements of function. This is expressed in particular in the many ὑπέρ statements: what happened in the past happened "for us." The "titles" of Jesus must also be understood in this way. For example, there was no intention of saying that Jesus was demonstrably and recognizably "the Messiah," but rather that he must be understood in connection with the functions of the Messiah. Conceptions known from late Judaism and apocalypticism were not uncritically transferred to Jesus. On the contrary, the functions which are encountered in Jesus determine what are to be regarded as messianic functions. It now no longer makes sense to await a Messiah, unless this would mean awaiting Jesus the Messiah who has been exalted to God's presence, is present in the Spirit, and is soon coming again. (On the wholly parallel expectation of Jesus the Son of man, *see* §3*a below*.)

Here, then, the unprecedented self-understanding of the primitive community (as over against its Jewish environment) becomes clear; its understanding of itself was christologically based. This found its decisive expression in the attitude toward the Law. While Paul was the first to formulate the thought that Christ is the end of the Law (Rom. 10:4), the essence of this idea was present quite early. The aim of the Jesus kerygma is incorporated into this understanding: the way into the kingdom (for Paul, righteousness [δικαιοσύνη]) is not found by doing something; instead, the kingdom which is present makes it possible (and demands) that now the will of God be done. Thus, Christology becomes theology; it is not the other way around.

In the Jewish Christian community at the beginning this had not yet become explicit, though it had in the Hellenistic community in Jerusalem, where there were numerous Jews from the Diaspora (*see* DISPERSION). It was against them that the attack of the Jewish authorities was first directed, leading to the martyrdom of STEPHEN (Acts 7:8 ff.), to the expulsion of the HELLENISTS from the city, and thus to the opening of the mission (Acts 8:1 ff.). The Jewish Christians remained relatively unmolested, even though they were under suspicion. Nevertheless, they held (at least in essence) the same christological view as the Hellenists. This is shown by the agreement reached later at the Apostolic Council (Gal. 2:1 ff.) and by the continuing threat to the Jerusalem church by the Jews (Gal. 2:4, 11 ff.), until the martyrdom of James the son of Zebedee (Acts 12:1-2) (*see* JAMES 1).

The relative separation of the two communities then produced a certain differentiation in Christologies, even though the boundaries between them are often fluid. (In I Cor. 11:23-25 and 15:3-5, we have Jewish Christian statements, but they are formulated in Hellenistic terms.)

The Hellenistic development can be traced particularly in Paul, whose understanding of the Cross is of Jewish Christian origin. Jesus' death was interpreted with the help of conceptions already at hand: as an expiatory (Rom. 3:25; I Cor. 15:3), covenantal (I Cor. 11:25; Mark 14:24), vicarious (II Cor. 5:14), or paschal sacrifice (I Cor. 5:7). The functional character of the christological expressions is again evident, even though the "way to the past" is opened. The OT was adduced to support the understanding of the saving significance of the Cross ("in accordance with the scriptures," I Cor. 15:3) and also the understanding of Jesus' career (the passion narrative). By means of an inversion there later arose the schema of promise and fulfillment. This, however, is misunderstood when it is taken in the modern sense as *Heilsgeschichte,* because only the fulfillment shows what can be regarded as promise. Christology, therefore, is the key to the correct understanding of the OT (II Cor. 3:14-16).

With this Judaism was confronted by a new scandal. The Law declares that anyone who is hanged on a tree is accursed (Gal. 3:13; Deut. 21:22-23). Therefore, the Jew must reject as a scandal the preaching of the Cross as a saving event (I Cor. 1:23).

From such statements a feature which runs throughout most of the NT becomes comprehensible: the members of the community live in this world as aliens (I Pet. 1:1), yet claim to be already the community of the end time by virtue of their having been granted the Spirit. This claim is christologically grounded, but because only the Cross is visible, the community's new being is still not demonstrable.

b. Paul. Paul's Christology is actually nothing other than the unfolding of his Damascus experience against the background of his activity as a persecutor. Paul did not come to grief on the Law and did not think it impossible to keep the Law, although he is often so interpreted. He himself had kept it without reproach (Phil. 3:6), even including the casuistry of the Pharisees (Gal. 1:14); and as a Christian he is still unaware of any transgressions (I Cor. 4:4). The Law declares the will of God, and therefore it is, with its commandments, holy, just, and good (Rom. 7:12). But to Paul the Jew the assertion of the Jewish Christians that one could not attain salvation by observing the Law, and hence did not need to attain it in this way, must have appeared blasphemous. Further, because God has in Christ already bestowed salvation, we may not assert our will in order to attain it; for what the Jew wants is, in the eyes of the Christians, blasphemy against God. If the Christians were right, then, paradoxically, the very person who by the most nearly perfect fulfillment of the Law sought to gain the highest praise apparently was proved to be the greatest sinner.

The Damascus experience overpowered the persecutor. It is significant to note how Paul describes that experience in Gal. 1:16. The one whom he encountered is identified as the Son, and it is in or through the Son that God meets him. This order (Son, God) is important christologically. It is reversed in the presentation only because immediately thereafter it is the function that is crucial. Through his Son, God calls the persecutor to preach the Gospel among the Gentiles. The experience is universal: the vision of Jesus (I Cor. 9:1) is a vision of the Lord who is the Son of God, and thus one is confronted by God. Further, it is not only the Jewish way of the Law that is superseded, but also the Jewish restriction of salvation to Israel.

FAITH has taken the place of the way of the Law. The concept of faith, to be sure, must be understood accurately. Faith is not a human achievement, but a trusting surrender to the call that is heard (Rom. 10:17). Thus faith is always faith *in* something, namely, in the ground and content of the summons, which in some way is always oriented to Jesus. Paul develops this orientation in a multiplicity of christological concepts, images, and metaphors, which often stand side by side, unharmonized, and therefore neither can nor may be fitted into a system. Any systematizing would take place outside of faith and would be a neutral way of looking at the matter; it would necessarily indicate tensions that go so far as to become contradictions. Therefore faith can never be an intellectual recognition of otherwise incomprehensible "objects of faith," from which one could, in a second step, draw further (more or less felicitous) consequences for conduct. (Such a *sacrificium intellectus,* incidentally, would itself be a work!) Faith is, rather, allowing oneself to be called into a movement. When Paul, caught up in this movement, looks back, he can express in various ways the things that stimulated his faith. But then he is not speaking about faith or about objects of faith from a detached position, but is confessing the basis for his faith *within* the movement of faith.

To this extent every christological utterance is complete. It can be varied, can repeat formulations that were coined before Paul or were contemporary with him, can appropriate conceptions of the people whom Paul was addressing in his epistles, or can even be developed through Paul's own mental labors. Nevertheless every individual expression *wholly* expresses the basis of faith. It is a fundamental misunderstanding to think that we are obliged to arrive at the whole by putting together the individual expressions. The so-called minimal Christology that "Jesus is Lord" (κύριος Ἰησοῦς, I Cor. 12:3) is a christologically complete utterance to the extent that it can indeed be asked how one could more precisely describe this fact of Jesus' lordship by means of other titles and conceptions; but it is not necessary to ask this. To be sure, it must be asked (and in the movement of faith it is always asked) how the lordship of Jesus becomes concrete in the existence of the believer in each new context. The believer indeed does the will of the Lord who moves him. Obedience is therefore nothing other than faith. Obedient conduct keeps the way open to the future, and therefore the one who moves the believer not only stands behind him, but at the same time stands in front of him. The futurity of the final salvation is fully maintained, but not the way it is in Judaism. We do not set out on the way to God by our own efforts; instead, the encounter with God (which is always still to be expected) has already happened and is happening now, in the movement of faith.

The gospel says that faith is possible now and can never be a "work," because in the proclaimed word the Lord is present in the Spirit. The believer actually has the Spirit already, even though in this transient world it is only as an earnest (II Cor. 1:22; 5:5) or as a first fruit (Rom. 8:23) (*see* First Fruits, NT[S]). Gift and obligation (or, more precisely, gift and the fulfillment of obligation) are not to be separated, because they are two sides of the one faith. If one side is lacking, the whole is lacking. Where the gift that is offered in the gospel is not accepted, everything that is done is a human work. This was the position of Paul the persecutor; the apostle later had to emphasize this in opposition to all Judaizing tendencies. This accent is dominant in Galatians, Phil. 3, and Rom. 1–8. Where deeds are absent, the gift is rejected or (more frequently) is not correctly recognized. Paul had to set this forth in opposition to Gnosticizing and enthusiastic tendencies (e.g., his stress on the message of salvation as the "word of the cross," I Cor. 1:18 ff.). When the situation demands, Paul can even venture one-sidedly exaggerated formulations, as when he asserts to the Galatians that the Law is not from God at all (Gal. 3:19-22); to the Romans he writes precisely the opposite (Rom. 7:12). These apparent contradictions are connected with the fact that the deficiencies of faith (ὑστερήματα τῆς πίστεως, I Thess. 3:10) lie in different places from case to case. Where there is uncertainty about conduct Paul does not argue legalistically (or even casuistically), but christologically. Where people trust in their own deeds (even to the extent of appropriating the practice of circumcision in Galatia), Paul also argues christologically.

While Paul's Christology cannot be systematized, in order to provide an overview it may be helpful to distinguish its titles from the cosmic and historical aspects of his Christology. The boundaries between these remain fluid, and the crucial matter is always the working out of the "gift."

i. The *titles* must always be understood as distinguishing functions. This cannot always be recognized in the title Christ, because for Paul this has already become a name. Most of all, formulas referring to the Cross and Resurrection are associated with this title (I Cor. 15:3-4). Paul, however, did not understand these as two saving events of equal importance; the Resurrection was not understood as a cancellation of Christ's death. That would lead to a *theologia gloriae.* It is precisely against this that Paul must wage a polemic with explicit and exclusive emphasis on the Cross (I Cor. 1:18–2:5) or on the death of Christ (II Cor. 4:10). But the apostle can also refer to the Resurrection alone. Because the Corinthians are no longer in their sins, they must also be certain of the resurrection of Christ (I Cor. 15:17). The relationship of Cross and Resurrection in Paul can be defined thus: The Resurrection makes it possible to interpret the Cross as saving event. Anyone who looks at the Cross sees it through the Resurrection, otherwise it remains a "stumbling block" (σκάνδαλον, I Cor. 1:23). Anyone who looks only at the Resurrection overlooks the fact that it is the crucified one who is risen; such a person is an "enemy of the cross of Christ" (Phil. 3:18).

The functional character is much more clearly presented in the title Lord (κύριος). As the one exalted to lordship, Jesus (Christ) is present with his community (Phil. 2:6-11; Rom. 14:9). The source of the Kyrios title is still disputed. Since the LXX translated God's name (יהוה) with κύριος, it has long been assumed that the designation of Jesus as Kyrios was meant to assign to him the OT attributes of God. But this is improbable, since this translation is first demonstrable in Christian texts of the LXX. Therefore, this title could be either an appropriation of a designation for God from Syria and Asia Minor or a translation from the Aramaic (cf. the primitive Christian acclamation formula, *maranatha* [our Lord, come], I Cor. 16:22; Rev. 22:20). In any case Paul, too, is familiar with the Kyrios title used as an acclamation: Christians call on the Kyrios Jesus Christ (I Cor. 1:2; cf. Rom. 10:13). (Prayer, however, except perhaps in II Cor. 12:8, is always addressed to God.) As Kyrios, Jesus is the permanent mediator of the relationship with God, even in the future in which the coming of the Kyrios is expected (I Thess. 4:15). Yet a comparison with II Cor. 5:10, where Paul expects that we will appear before the judgment seat of Christ, shows that a neat delimitation of the functions related to the titles is simply not possible.

The title Son, or SON OF GOD, exhibits still another aspect. It is used primarily when the subject is the mission which, understood as saving event, leads believers into the status of sonship (Gal. 4:4-7; Rom. 8:3). The idea of the sending of the Son implies pre-existence, and actually the incarnation as well. Of course the latter does not appear in Paul in the narrower sense of John 1:14, for saying that God sent his own Son "in the likeness of sinful flesh" (Rom. 8:3) is not an affirmation about the career of the earthly Jesus, who is understood as the incarnate one. In Paul's thought, it is not a continuous career of the earthly Jesus that is understood as the saving event, but the sending of the Son as such. The same thing is said of this sending that is said of the Cross. Pauline Christology is misunderstood when the two "saving points" are put in historical succession, for then an alternative would emerge: did the sending of the Son bring salvation, or did that not happen until his crucifixion? It is perilous to add together utterances which have emerged in one direction in time (backward), and then to use them in the reverse direction.

ii. The *cosmic aspect* of Pauline Christology comes into view particularly with the title "Son." The general intent is to express the other-worldly character of the saving activity, and thus the *extra nos* of faith. Jesus' person and fate do not have their significance in the perceivable character of an occurrence within this world. Here they appear as σκάνδαλον and folly. This is presented so as to say that Jesus' person and fate do not have their origin in this occurrence within the world. Faith comes from beyond, and the Beyond towers far above this world. Jesus had no worldly origin even though he was born of a woman (Gal. 4:4). A person who is blinded by the god of this aeon does not see the glory of Christ, who is the express image of God (II Cor. 4:4) and who can even be described as the mediator of creation (I Cor. 8:6).

Paul never identified the Son with the Father, not even in Rom. 9:5. The exegesis of the verse is disputed, but even so the context shows that there is no intention of expressing an equality of nature in the sense of later metaphysics. The road to the description of Christ as God leads "backward" by way of the Fathers, and if one wishes to work with the speculative christological categories of the early church, it is necessary, with reference to Paul, to speak unequivocally of a subordination of the Son to the Father (I Cor. 15:27-28). But it is anachronistic to introduce this question into Pauline Christology. Although Christ's obedience is indeed discussed, no speculation about relationships is implied, only the nature of the encounter with God (and hence of the revelation). Because the Son is God's activity in relation to the world, one meets God in him—and only in him.

The sending took place "when the time had fully come." The presentation can make use of myth, as when the Cross is described in various ways as a sacrifice (also in judicial categories; *see* §2*a above*), and also when the coming of the Son is understood as saving activity (Rom. 8:3). In the Christ hymn which Paul appropriated in Phil. 2:6-11, the career of Christ is portrayed in the course followed by the mythical bearer of salvation. The pre-existent one becomes man and is obedient even to the most extreme consequence, death itself. In the exaltation God gives to him, the bearer of the name Jesus, the name that is above every name. The apostle's interest in this myth is shown in his addition ("even death on a cross") to the earlier version as he received it. He is not interested in metaphysical or cosmic speculations, but in the fixed historical point. It is not proper here to suggest that Paul had a historical acquaintance with a path of suffering which the earthly Jesus followed from his birth to the cross; instead, the myth is used to express in concrete terms precisely what is not capable of being observed by the senses. The Son obediently takes upon himself the condescension and the cross, and because of his obedience God exalts him to be the Kyrios, and thus the one who opens the way of salvation. Elsewhere Paul expresses this with various forms of παραδιδόναι: the "handing-over" is fundamental for salvation (cf. Rom. 4:25 [RSV "put to death"], and also I Cor. 11:23 [RSV "delivered"], and *passim*).

iii. The *historical aspect,* which frequently overlaps with the cosmic (or turns into it), is likewise sketched in retrospect, in order then to make a statement with a forward thrust (starting with Christ). To put it generally, Paul places Scripture, both "persons" and circumstances within it, in the service of Christology. Thus, Abraham is used primarily as an apology for faith over against works. Christ is described as the seed of Abraham (Gal. 3:16), because Paul wants to show that in Abraham's case faith was all that mattered (Gal. 3:6-9) and that God justifies the ungodly (Rom. 4:1-8). It is a misinterpretation to find Paul here taking up affirmatively the history of God's dealing with Israel as "salvation history." The apostle explicitly rejects any continuity of such salvation history (Rom. 9:6 ff.) and, with the aid of a device well known in rabbinical exegesis (singular/plural), cancels out the entire "history" between Abraham and Christ (Gal. 3:16). The substantive point of departure for the christological argument is that faith has come with Christ (Gal. 3:23 ff.). This assertion would be convincing for anyone who accepts the Scripture as the authority, because it can be shown that even with Abraham everything hinges on faith. (Arguments which use a similar retrospective orientation to scripture occur in Gal. 4:21 ff.; I Cor. 10:1 ff.; II Cor. 3:4 ff.).

The use of the figure of Adam (whom Paul, of course, regarded as a "historical person") is not uniform. Rom. 5:12-19 exhibits a juridical pattern of thought: sin is guilt and has its origin in

Adam's disobedience. Here, however, Paul does not try to find a cause (the devil, Adam's creatureliness, etc.) which lies behind (or in) Adam and which could excuse him. The sin of people today (here lies the point of departure for reflection!) is just as inexcusable as Adam's was, and its cause is likewise disobedience. Correspondingly, the saving work of Christ is characterized as obedience, which offers the possibility of escaping the power of sin. In I Cor. 15 there is an entirely different orientation. The truth of the hope of resurrection is supposed to be christologically based on the figure of Adam. Now anthropology comes into play (though Paul does not take it up again later in Romans because in the context of his train of thought there it is unusable). It is written that the first man Adam became a living being (ψυχή, vs. 45; cf. Gen. 2:7) and received an earthly body (vs. 47). Because "flesh and blood" cannot enter into the final consummation (vs. 50) this body is mortal. But Christ, the "last Adam," became a life-giving spirit (πνεῦμα, vs. 45); he is the "second man . . . from heaven" (vs. 47). But as such, he is also the future of humankind, for in him all will be made alive (vs. 22). As they now bear the image of Adam, so in the resurrection they will bear the image of the heavenly man (vs. 49), which Christ already bears.

Thus the Christology of Paul is rightly understood only when it is understood strictly within the movement of faith. It expresses the basis of the call that has been issued, repeats it, and thus leads to theology. Hope also is founded on this faith. The ground of faith is at the same time its goal. Here, too, Christology leads to theology (I Cor. 15:28).

c. After Paul. The portrayal of Christology in the post-Pauline writings confronts a methodological difficulty which is already present in incipient form in Paul, but now becomes much more evident. A host of specific formulations and christological statements are taken over but are not always assimilated. Moreover, it is frequently unclear how these materials are to be exegeted. Are they to be interpreted in the old context, or does that context now play only a subordinate role, or perhaps no role at all? Assured conclusions are seldom possible. Since no detailed exegetical arguments can be worked out here, some of the clearer and more important points must suffice.

i. *The Deutero-Pauline writings.* The author of II Thessalonians emphasizes, in opposition to Gnostic heresies with perfectionist tendencies (2:1-2), the futurity of salvation (2:3-4). Correspondingly, Jesus' function as judge of the world (cf. II Cor. 5:10) is broadly sketched in apocalyptic fashion (1:7-12). The readers are called to obtain hereafter the "glory of our Lord Jesus Christ" (2:14), but it is nowhere noted that ethical action as Christ's gift is already possible. Faith thus becomes a knowledge of the judgment which makes action necessary. Action itself, however, is not christologically grounded, but is more or less legalistically oriented to the example of the life of the apostle (3:7-10) and to the instructions that have been handed down (2:15; 3:4). It is difficult to maintain, with the passing of time, that salvation is already a reality.

The same thing is shown in somewhat different fashion by the Pastoral epistles, whose ethic can be characterized as explicitly "bourgeois." However, it still is not an eschatological ethic; the proclamation is described as "sound doctrine" (I Tim. 1:10; II Tim. 4:3; Tit. 1:9, and *passim*) and a rationalist strain is unmistakable. Here for the first time the title Savior (σωτήρ, found in Paul only in Phil. 3:20) occurs frequently, and the concept ἐπιφάνεια (manifestation, appearance) is used. These are combined in II Tim. 1:10, which refers to Jesus' earthly appearing, and in I Tim. 6:14 in reference to the PAROUSIA. The title Savior was widely used in the emperor cult, but it probably was not taken over directly from that source, since the emperor cult itself had integrated this concept with a common way of describing deity. In a certain sense, then, we can speak of parallel developments: both the veneration of Christ and the veneration of the emperor tend toward the attribution of predicates of deity. This led to the question as to where the Savior actually is to be found; and since the assertions were mutually exclusive, Christology could set in motion the persecution of the church by the state.

In the Pastoral epistles the title Savior is used for God and for Christ (cf., among other passages, II Tim. 1:10 and Tit. 2:10). The consequence is that Christ can be forthrightly called God (Tit. 2:13). In the NT this is done very hesitantly (*see* §2*b above;* cf. John 20:28), but for IGNATIUS it was already self-evident.

The Christology of Colossians is apologetically constructed in opposition to a heresy which understands the angelic powers as guardians of the world order, to which even Christians are to be subject (2:8). By the adoption and, at the same time, the development of the ideas of the heretics, the saving work of Christ is now understood as a victory over even the cosmic forces (2:16-17; 3:15). Christ is creator and redeemer of the world (1:15-20); in him lie all the treasures of wisdom and knowledge (2:3); in him dwells the entire fullness of the Godhead (2:9), and also of the "body," the church (1:18), which now is understood as the renewed creation (2:20 ff.; 3:9-11).

This latter feature is further developed in Ephesians, where Christology is emphatically related to ecclesiology. By the use of Gnostic-mythological conceptions, Christ is portrayed as the cosmic Anthropos (2:14 ff.) who unites what is earthly and what is heavenly (1:10). Therefore he is our peace (2:14), and, as ruler of the cosmos, head of the community (1:22-23). Christ is made manifest on earth in this community (2:10) by virtue of the fact that it experiences this peace, that in its charismata it manifests a unity (4:16), and that as the Gentile Christian community it forms, with the Jewish Christians, the Una Sancta (2:11 ff.).

ii. *The other writings.* The Christ kerygma is developed from various points of view and by the stressing of various aspects. This may be illustrated by three examples.

Hebrews is usually assessed in terms of its distinctive Christology. This Christology is in fact unique in the NT. Much more interesting in this "word of exhortation" (13:22), however, is the characterization of the reader's failure to develop the christological beginnings as culpable, intellectual sloth. The readers have simply stagnated at an early form of the doctrine that has been handed down to them (5:2, 11-14). Because they have not striven to go beyond these beginnings, the author describes their sinning as willful, and says that it cannot be atoned for by a second sacrifice (10:26). The readers can really escape from sin only if they do not simply repeat what they have heard about Christ at the beginning, but advance to perfect knowledge (6:1 ff.). Thus, the effort for more comprehensive insight into the ground of faith should enable them, as the new people of God, to be on their way in concrete realization of life (ch. 12) in a manner corresponding to the old covenant (ch. 11). Thus the author, oriented to Jesus' sacrificial death, pictures the saving work of Christ as comprehensively as possible. He is the high priest (3:1; 4:14), who through his self-sacrifice has entered into the Holy Place (9:11-14) and thereby has prepared the way for his people to follow (10:19 ff.). He has become like man (2:14-18), but without falling into sin (4:15), and he is now therefore able to help those who live in the midst of temptation (2:18).

Since the high priest by virtue of his own blood has entered into the sanctuary, the Christology of Hebrews cannot include the idea of Christ's resurrection. Such a handling of the tradition in the last decade of the first century is certainly exemplary; it shows how reflectively and cautiously the author worked. (A comparable example from an earlier time is the Christ hymn in Phil. 2:6-11, which likewise does not mention the resurrection of Christ, because exaltation results from the obedience of the one who came down.) Christ has passed through the heavens, has entered into the Holy Place, and sits on the throne of God (8:1; 12:2). When the readers come to him, they will allow their conduct to be determined by him (10:22-25). One can say that in Hebrews, Christology is deliberately placed in the service of the practical life.

In principle this is also the concern of I Peter, only the author does not achieve his intention so clearly. He intends to offer comfort to churches under persecution by pointing to the baptism that has been performed. Pauline themes are adopted, though of course modified. That Christ died for our sins is indeed repeated in traditional terms (1:19; 3:18), but his death is not a salvation event which marks the present as a new time. Jesus' passion is rather an example of the way that Christians are to suffer (2:21 ff.; 4:1). Salvation is a present reality only insofar as hope now exists (3:15) as a living hope in the salvation event of the resurrection of Christ (1:3). The Parousia, which is regarded as imminent, provides strong motivation for action (4:7-11).

The Revelation to John also was written for churches undergoing severe persecution (2:3, 9-10; 7:14; 13:7). The author, wishing to encourage the readers to be steadfast and patient, appropriated various materials from late Jewish apocalyptic, even following the lines of its conceptions, as he painted in vivid colors the rewards for remaining steadfast (2:10; 7:13-17; 14:3; 22:14). The apocalyptic schema, of course, is then stoutly supported in christological terms. The certainty of hope is grounded in the death of Christ, the slain Lamb (5:6, 9; 13:8), whose blood redeems and purifies (7:14). The Lamb that has been sacrificed is alive (2:8) and holds the keys of hell and of death (1:18). Those who overcome will attain the glorious final salvation (21:7).

3. The Jesus Christ kerygma. The Jesus kerygma, separated from the personal presence of Jesus, tends now to provide a more precise characterization of the one who performed the functions, or to work out with stronger emphasis the functions themselves, in order to show that both the person of Jesus and his functions transcend what is earthly. To a large extent, contemporary scholarship agrees that this tendency was generally present. On the other hand, scholars have so far not succeeded in determining precisely in which circles these further developments emerged, in what places this happened, and how the further developments then influenced each other. Here, therefore, we can only point to certain typical forms.

a. Further formations and collections. The transition from the Jesus kerygma to the Jesus Christ kerygma is most clearly discerned in connection with the idea of the SON OF MAN. If Jesus was experienced as the one in whom the coming Son of man was already pronouncing judgment here on earth (Luke 12:8; Mark 8:38), then it was natural to understand Jesus himself as the one who was already present as the Son of man, and the returning Jesus was awaited as the coming Son of man. Significantly, the Son of man title is never used in addressing Jesus. This designation appears only on the lips of Jesus himself, and the impression is given that he is speaking of a figure who is to be distinguished from himself. Nevertheless, the group of sayings which set forth the present activity of Jesus shows clearly that he is the one to whom the title refers. For example, the Son of man has power on earth to forgive sins (Mark 2:10), he is Lord of the sabbath (Mark 2:28), he has no place to lay his head (Matt. 8:20). Parallel to this (or later), a group of sayings portray Jesus' way to suffering, death, and resurrection as the way of the Son of man (Mark 8:31; 9:9, 12, 31; 10:33, 45). In both these groups the traditionally apocalyptic conceptions are eliminated. Only the name, Son of man, is taken over and combined with the earthly activity of Jesus. In the latter group precisely the opposite occurs: the name of Jesus has been drawn into the apocalyptic expectation of the Son of man (Mark 13; Matt. 24; Luke 21). The still later development tends to make "Son of man" (like "Christ") almost a proper name, for when Jesus asks the disciples what people are saying about the identity of the Son of man (Matt. 16:13; Mark 8:27 has a different version), the answer would indeed already be included in the question, if "Son of man" had still been understood as a predicate of exaltation.

Jesus is also characterized as the SON OF GOD.

This, too, is done in various ways. The story of the Transfiguration (Mark 9:2-8) is intended to show that Jesus is recognized only when he is seen "transfigured." God made this vision possible in exceptional cases during Jesus' lifetime; faith is therefore always God's work (cf. Matt. 16:17). But faith hears the voice of God's Son in the unpretentious words of Jesus (Mark 9:7). Consequently Jesus can be recognized as Son of God even at the beginning of his activity and at the beginning of his life. In the baptismal story (Mark 1:9-11) God's "adoption formula" is pronounced over Jesus (Ps. 2:7). Elsewhere it is uttered over the king, affirming that this person, as God's Son, is acting in God's name. In Hellenistic circles the same idea is expressed in terms of the miraculous birth, which was familiar in connection with the birth of famous men in that culture. Jesus was begotten by the Spirit, or he was born of a virgin (Matt. 1:18-25; Luke 1:26-38). The two ideas are not originally identical, but they frequently overlap.

It would be incorrect to pose the question as to when Jesus became God's Son: in pre-existence (Gal. 4:4), at the time of his birth (Matthew, Luke), at the time of his baptism (Mark), or at the time of his resurrection (Rom. 1:4). All christological expressions about divine sonship are formulated in retrospect and originally stood in isolation from each other. To this extent they all say the same thing about Jesus (even though with the help of various conceptions). None of the expressions is to be understood objectively, in either a historical or a biological sense, because then they would contradict each other. The difficulty arises in placing the individual kerygmas in sequence. If this sequence is produced, as it is in the gospels, some adjustments must be made. This is clear, for example, in Matt. 1:16 where the evangelist must redirect the genealogy (which was originally handed down as a separate tradition) to Mary, though it makes sense only if Joseph was the father of Jesus.

A connection with the christological use of Davidic sonship is at least suggested in the genealogies (Matt. 1:6; Luke 3:31), but it can be more clearly recognized where the divine adoption formula for the king is appropriated for the service of Christology (Mark 1:11). Descent from David is closely connected with the idea of the Messiah, for in apocalyptic the expectation of the Messiah is to a large extent politically oriented and thus bound up with the anticipation of salvation for the nation of Israel. Although each title by and in itself is complete and comprehensible as a christological utterance, the ideas which are bound up with the titles now and again have differing accents. Therefore, difficulties emerge when the titles coalesce. This has become true not only in modern times, in the attempt to incorporate all the titles into dogmatics at once; indeed, this problem was sensed in a very early time (Mark 12:35-37).

Jesus' deeds of healing, particularly the exorcisms, which were certainly historical, were originally understood as an inbreaking of the kingdom of God (Matt. 12:28; Luke 11:20). This interpretation was not inevitable, however, and it was only possible in a direct sharing of the experience. Later on, the miraculous was more forcefully presented, not in order to give a sensational portrayal to the event, but in the service of Christology, to show that the power of Jesus is boundless. Power goes forth from him (Mark 5:30); one must and can have confidence in him as the mighty one (Mark 2:5; Matt. 8:10). Where this confidence is lacking, as in his home town, no miracles can take place (Mark 6:5-6). The stories of the feeding of the multitudes show that Jesus' gifts transcend all measure (Mark 6:44; 8:9), and the so-called nature miracles show that he is Lord over all powers (Mark 4:37-41; 6:45-51).

Even the figure of John the Baptist is employed for christological utterances. The primitive church lived at first in competition with a community of John's followers (Mark 2:18; Luke 11:1). John the Baptist did not understand himself as the forerunner of Jesus, but the church's interpretation of his appearance in these terms and its identification of him with Elijah gave Jesus an eschatological characterization (Matt. 11:10, 14; 17:10-13).

Further, the OT in general was brought into the service of Christology, as Jesus' deeds were represented in OT terms (Matt. 11:5). What was expected to occur only at the end has already come to pass in advance, through Jesus. Specific passages of scripture were found, which Matthew later employed christologically, in a fashion peculiar to him (*see* §3*b*).

The PASSION NARRATIVE is heavily saturated with OT texts and allusions (Mark 14:18, 61; 15:5, 23, 24, 34, and *passim*). Here we are probably dealing with the earliest presentation of a continuous section from the life of Jesus, compiled to a large extent from individual traditions. The Cross is not understood as salvation event as it was by Paul and earlier believers (*see* §2*a, b*). Indeed, in the whole of the synoptic material there are only two traditions which set forth Jesus' death as an atoning sacrifice or as a substitutionary sacrifice: Mark 10:45; 14:24. The passion narrative portrays, instead, Jesus' *way,* using OT language to confess the way of Jesus' suffering, such an enigma to human minds, as God's way and hence the way of salvation. Thus the community expresses understanding of DISCIPLESHIP christologically, for the Son of man takes the way of suffering. When the community now takes upon itself the way of suffering and risks its life for Jesus' sake, it is traveling on his way (cf. Mark 8:34 ff. with Mark 8:31-33). Precisely these last-named traditions (together with Mark 14–16) show that the Gospel of Mark is a passion narrative with an extended introduction.

b. The Synoptic gospels. REDACTION CRITICISM has taught us that the Synoptists were guided in the structuring of their works by different theological conceptions. In this connection the crucial christological perspectives may be accentuated. (*See* the original and supplementary articles on each gospel.)

Mark is shaped by the dialectic between hiddenness and disclosure. This is particularly evident in the motif of the messianic secret (*see* SECRET, MESSIANIC): demons are forbidden to make Jesus' messiahship known (1:34; 3:12); healings that have taken place may not be disclosed (1:44; 5:43; 7:36); even the disciples are not allowed to say who Jesus is (8:30; 9:9). Although they experience Jesus' power (6:30 ff.) and confess his messiahship (8:29), they are again and again shown to be devoid of understanding (6:52; 8:16 ff.; 9:32). The parables, which are basically quite clear, are described as dark sayings (4:11-12); and in this case it is again the disciples for whom the enigmas of the parables are solved (4:33). Hence, Mark has appropriately been called the "book of the secret epiphanies." Christian existence in the tension between faith and unbelief (9:24) is christologically grounded in the way of Jesus.

In Matthew Jesus is the authoritative teacher, whose teaching is summarized primarily in five blocks of discourses (5–7; 10; 13; 18; 23–25). But this teacher has authority because he is Israel's Messiah. His genealogy shows that he is the son of David and of Abraham (1:1). His persecution as a child corresponds to the threat to the child Moses (ch. 2). The course of his life and his deeds prove him to be the one who fulfills the announcements, understood as predictions, in Holy Scripture (cf. the stereotyped formula quotations in 1:22-23; 2:5-6, 15, 17-18, 23; 3:3; 4:14-16; 8:17; 12:17 ff.; 13:35; 21:4-5; 26:56; 27:9-10). After his resurrection all power in heaven and on earth is given to this Messiah of Israel (28:18). He himself has taken the way of righteousness (3:15), and as his historical disciples have followed him on this way, so too all who come later are to become his disciples (28:19). Matthew's Christology is a portrayal of the Lord of these disciples.

For Luke the church lives now under the leadership of the Spirit which was poured out at Pentecost (Acts 2; cf. 4:8; 6:3; and *passim*). Thereby it stands in continuity with the earthly Jesus, who during his lifetime was the sole bearer of the Spirit (Luke 4:16 ff.). Thus Luke can picture the time of Jesus as a past which (as the center of world history) was free from Satan (4:13; 22:3). Since Satan will finally be deprived of his power following Jesus' Parousia (which is not pinpointed as to time), Luke views the time of Jesus as eschatological—what is expected of the future was then already present. Thus the time of Jesus provides a foundation for hope, and the correct understanding of this time can lend certainty to faith (1:4).

c. The Gospel of John. The Fourth Gospel offers a comprehensive view of myth and history. When Jesus is described as the only way, truth, and life (14:6), typically Gnostic ideas are undoubtedly being appropriated. Although scholars still disagree about the precise religio-historical background of this gospel, the lack of consensus does not preclude our understanding its Christology. Jesus frequently says that he is imparting what he has seen and heard from the Father (3:11; 8:26, 40), yet the content of what was seen or heard is never told. Gnostic cosmology and anthropology are not component parts of a teaching which had to be accepted by faith, but rather the faith is oriented exclusively toward Jesus. The Gnostic background thus becomes a mere means of expressing the thought that Jesus' word is from the beyond and thus is an authoritative word; the Gnostic dualism is transformed in the Gospel of John into a dualism of decision. Believers are not yet taken out of the world (17:15), as in GNOSTICISM. However, they are no longer shaped and determined by this world if they remain true in the faith, which must continually be grasped anew (14:21), and if they fulfill the "new" commandment of Jesus, the sole content of which is love (13:34-35; 15:12). The new commandment is the eschatological commandment, because it is grounded in Jesus' love (13:15). This love of Jesus determines his course, from the time of his coming to the time when he surrenders his life (15:13).

There is a certain affinity with the ideas of the Christ hymn in Phil. 2:6-11. Here we are dealing with the Christ kerygma, and the modifications which the Gospel of John makes on that conception demonstrate why this gospel is to be included in the Jesus Christ kerygma. Pre-existence Christology is combined with incarnation Christology (1:14), and thereby the earthly life of Jesus, even as it unfolds in full view, takes on meaning. This is in contrast to Phil. 2:6-11. Into the essentially Gnostic schema of the descent of the redeemer and his return to the heavenly world, this evangelist incorporates many traditions (to be sure, modified and often independent) about the earthly Jesus. The one who came "in the flesh" came to his own possession, for it was through him that the world was created. But because he came as a human being, he was not recognized and not accepted by the world (1:10-11). Nevertheless, for those who are born of God (1:13; cf. 3:3), his glory (δόξα) again and again becomes visible (2:11). If Mark can be called the book of the secret epiphanies, in the Gospel of John the same dialectic is present, only in reverse form. The messianic secret (Mark) is intended to emphasize that the character of the revelation was not demonstrable and not at one's disposal; this gospel emphasizes that it was *in the flesh*, that is, in what is in itself not demonstrable, that glory became manifest. This can be expressed in various ways: Jesus is the true vine (15:1), the good shepherd (10:11, 14), the door (10:7, 9), the bread of life (6:35, 48, 51), the light of the world (8:12), the resurrection and the life (11:25). Since in Jesus salvation has come from the world beyond into this world and is present in it, believers experience final salvation as present by having faith in Jesus; judgment has already taken place, and they have passed from death to life (3:18-19, 36; 5:24; 11:25-26).

This can also be grounded in the fact that the Father has given all things into the hands of his Son (3:35). The relationship of the Son to the Father is not conceptualized to the extent it becomes a theme in this gospel, any more than it is in the other NT writings. Although it is said that Father and Son are one (10:30), the content of this utterance must be determined in accord with its intent. From the Father's point of view, it is said that he has "sent" the Son (e.g., 5:36; 7:29), that he has given all things into his hands, and that he is therefore greater than the Son (14:28). Here Jesus' origin, relationship, and authority are being expressed. When people confront Jesus, they are always dealing with the Father (8:16), and they see the Father (14:7); accordingly, Thomas can address the resurrected one quite directly as "my Lord and my God" (20:28).

The constant emphasis on Jesus' glory (δόξα) in the Gospel of John very early brought into question the idea of the Incarnation (1:14). This led to a docetic Gnosis which involved unjustifiable appeals to the gospel by Christian Gnostic groups. A Johannine school countered this tendency, on the one hand by revising the gospel in a so-called ecclesiastical redaction (Bultmann; *see* JOHN, GOSPEL OF[S] §1), and on the other hand, by writing the Johannine epistles (*see* JOHN, LETTERS OF and supplementary article). They opposed heretics who were denying the actual incarnation of the preexistent Logos (I John 4:2-3; cf. 2:22). In consequence of this kind of thinking, the Cross is bound to lose its significance (I John 1:7; 2:1-2; 4:10), and the Lord's Supper (though not baptism) presumably is rejected (I John 5:6). Anyone who disputes the Incarnation is a deceiver and antichrist (II John 7). Against this, it is emphasized that the life which has appeared (Christ) could be seen, heard, and felt (I John 1:1 ff.), and that the Cross signifies atonement for the whole world (I John 2:2).

4. Conclusion. The development of Christology within the NT is characterized by a great richness, as in each period new concepts and ideas which were familiar in the surrounding culture were appropriated. This enrichment, however, contained within it the danger that formulations which were no longer understood were simply dragged along. Thus the apparent wealth could become false riches, for now a tendency began to develop in which the functional character of Christology was more and more neglected in favor of a strong emphasis on doctrine. For instance, in place of the originally dialectical tension of belief and unbelief in the gospels of Mark and John, there appeared the juxtaposition of faith and little faith (Matthew) or of faith and false faith (the Johannine epistles). Again, the Pastoral epistles speak of "sound doctrine," and in Jas. 2:14-26 the Pauline understanding of faith (which for the apostle always includes obedience) is abandoned in favor of a doctrine to which works must be added before there is justification.

This tendency continued with intensified force in post-NT times and led, particularly in the Greek church, to passionate christological controversies, especially about the relationship of the Son to the Father and to the Spirit. These have continued, though not always with the same intensity, throughout the entire history of the church and of dogma down to the present time.

Contemporary theology needs to remain oriented to the beginnings by setting forth Christology in functional terms as kerygma. This must be done so that modern people understand the kerygma, and in fufillment of their faith they must be able to repeat it confessionally in their own words, as circumstances demand. This will be possible only if the kerygma is formulated in the language of our time. The Christology of the NT enables us to have this freedom; even the NT kerygma was never formulated other than in the language and with the aid of conceptions which were modern then and which could be understood and also repeated as familiar and well-known ideas. Remaining true to the kerygma that is oriented to Jesus does not mean repeating the old ideas, but communicating the same attitude with the help of our own language and ideas.

To put it pointedly: people may dispute the suitability, appropriateness, and comprehensibility of doctrinal formulations. Yet such disputes make sense only if thereby the christological kerygma becomes a help for others, and we are ready ourselves to suffer for it. For we can confess Jesus as Lord only when we understand what we mean and make it understandable for others. Indeed, we truly confess Jesus as Lord only if we are ready to risk our necks for this confession.

Bibliography. General: R. Bultmann, *Theology of the NT,* 2 vols. (1948-53); H. Conzelmann, *An Outline of NT Theology* (1967); O. Cullmann, *The Christology of the NT* (rev. ed., 1967); M. Dibelius, "Christologie des Urchristentums," *RGG,* I (2nd ed., 1927), cols. 1592-1607; R. H. Fuller, *The Foundations of NT Christology* (1965); F. Hahn, *The Titles of Jesus in Christology* (1966); J. Knox, *Jesus: Lord and Christ* (1958), comprising the three earlier studies, *The Man Christ Jesus* (1941), *Christ the Lord* (1945), and *On the Meaning of Christ* (1947); W. Kramer, *Christ, Lord, Son of God,* SBT, L (1963); R. Schäfer, *Jesus und der Gottesglaube: Ein christologischer Entwurf* (1970); E. Schweizer, *Jesus* (1968); G. N. Stanton, *Jesus of Nazareth in NT Preaching,* NTSMS, XXVII (1974).

On the problem of method: H. Balz, *Methodische Probleme der neutestamentlichen Christologie,* WMANT, XXV (1967); W. Marxsen, *The Beginnings of Christology: A Study in Its Problems,* FBBS, XXII (2nd ed., 1964).

W. MARXSEN

***CHRONICLES, I AND II. 1. The question of unity: I-II Chronicles, Ezra, Nehemiah.** While the view that I-II Chronicles and Ezra-Nehemiah are two separate works is still held, most modern critical scholarship has assumed that there is a single "author," "the Chronicler." This latter view is presented in various forms, ranging from a unified view of the work, in which little is attributed to later modification, to much more analytical positions, maintaining the existence of two "Chroniclers" or the presence of substantial additions (in particular, I Chr. 1–9 or large parts of these chapters; I Chr. 23–27; and the Nehemiah "memoirs" [*see* EZRA AND NEHEMIAH §3*e*]). The generally held view is that the Nehemiah memoirs constitute a separate source, already in existence and used without alteration or with only minimal adaptation by the Chronicler. Some recent linguistic, stylistic, and theological analyses of the whole work have not taken sufficient account of this. Yet, linguistic and stylistic aspects of the arguments concerning unity are hardly conclusive. Sufficient account has not been taken either of the problems of discussing such usage in a work which depends so heavily upon its sources (*see* §3), or of the textual problems (*see below*).

Arguments from the overlap of the two works (II Chr. 36:22-23 and Ezra 1:1-3*a*) are inconclusive. A single work, once divided, might be provided with a linking section to draw attention to the sequel; or, it may have been felt proper to provide a more propitious ending to I-II Chronicles than the description of the Exile. Two separate works (by the same author writing at different times or by two separate authors) might equally be provided with a link designed to point the reader to where further information could be found. More difficult questions arise in regard to the relationship of the single work or of the two works to the formation of the canon. The assumption that Ezra-Nehemiah was "canonized" first because it provided new matter, and that I-II Chronicles was later added (following Ezra-Nehemiah as the last book of the canon, as in some Hebrew MSS) is without adequate foundation. The argument for this canonical order from the reference in Luke 11:51 to murders from Abel to Zechariah depends on the (unproved) assumption that the Zechariah is the one mentioned in II Chr. 24:20-21; but even this does not demand the supposition that Chronicles stood last, for the name of Zechariah may simply represent the last named victim in the narrative books. When order of books becomes apparent in codices, Palestinian tradition places Chronicles first and Ezra-Nehemiah last among the Writings, while Babylonian tradition places Ezra-Nehemiah and Chronicles last. These two positions may reflect different views of the significance of the work. The placing of Chronicles first provides a not unfitting introduction to the Psalter (which follows immediately), in view of the former's substantial concern with David's organization of Levitical singers, and a canon closing with Ezra-Nehemiah would correspond to Josephus' definition of the canonical period as ending with the age of Artaxerxes.

The existence of part of the material in Greek (Esdras α; KJV, I Esdras), covering the section from Josiah (II Chr. 35) to Ezra's reading of the law (without Nehemiah), raises many problems. Whatever its precise textual relationship to the Hebrew and to the other Greek forms of the material, at the very least it demonstrates another way in which literary matter could be arranged. Moreover, the fact that 4QSam[a] is closer to Chronicles than is MT Samuel casts doubt on the assumption that we can say precisely what form of text the Chronicler used. The whole textual situation remains complex.

2. Date. It has been maintained that the first form of the Chronicler's work was produced in the early postexilic period. If one author is postulated, the date proposed must be later than the latest event mentioned. This will depend on the chronology of Ezra and Nehemiah and on such matters as the evaluation of lists of high priests (esp. in Neh. 12) which may show generations down to a particular moment. But such evidence is inconclusive. If the late date for Ezra is assumed (398 B.C.), then a date around 350 B.C. is possible. There do not appear to be any allusions to the fall of the Persian Empire (331) and to Greek rule, but this too is uncertain. The history of Judah during the period from 400 to 200 B.C. is too little known to be of substantial use in dating documents.

3. Sources and their use. The Chronicler used a variety of sources, though at many points the detail of his handling of them remains debatable, partly because of the textual uncertainties already noted, partly because no single explanation covers the omissions, rearrangements, and modifications. While there have been many endeavors in recent years to prove the antiquity and historical value of material not paralleled in Samuel and Kings, it remains probable that this material was of relatively late date and likely to reflect postexilic conditions rather than those of earlier times. More important is the recognition (*see* §4) that even if an older and valuable historical document has been used, the real import of the material lies not in the historical information which may be extracted, but in the manner and purpose of its use. To describe the Chronicler's work as midrash —the term used in II Chr. 13:22 (RSV "story"); 24:27 (RSV "commentary"), apparently to describe a source—is convenient, but a fully satisfactory definition of this term is yet to be established (*see* MIDRASH[S]). Recognition of the homiletic quality of the work and of the degree to which its author was endeavoring to make clear to his contemporaries the significance of the well-known traditions of the past underlines the degree to which the older material was regarded as authoritative and helps to explain some of the reorderings and modifications introduced.

4. Theological outlook and mode of presentation. The Chronicler's interest in cultic matters and his emphasis upon obedience to the stipulations of TORAH suggest an affinity with the PRIESTLY WRITERS, but a marked dependence upon the Deuteronomic history (e.g., emphasis upon God's grace and judgment) suggests an alternative alignment. Clearly, neither connection is entirely adequate in assessing what must be regarded as a presentation in its own right. The comprehensiveness and range of the Chronicler's work are greater than either P or D, and he appears to synthesize their ideas, which at some points were sharply differentiated. *See* CANON OF THE OT[S] §3*a*.

The stylizing of narratives, observable in the elaborate structures of the two other great works, is here even plainer. The tracing of ultimate origins in the prefatory genealogies reaches a climax in the themes of exile and restoration in I Chr. 9. The intent is to show to the restored community the basis for its existence. The high point of the reigns of David and Solomon is set in contrast with the disaster of Saul (I Chr. 10–II Chr. 9). The complex patterns into which the narratives of the kings are woven, so that no two are quite alike even if the underlying emphasis on faith and apostasy remains constant, provide an introduction to the moment of postexilic restoration (II Chr. 10–36). Renewal of the community and its temple is depicted as the counterpart to the age of David and Solomon (Ezra 1–6). In the larger sweep of presentation, belief in an overruling order is evident, giving coherence to what at times has seemed merely an atomistic view of history.

The theology of the Chronicler is not explicitly expressed, and so it is not surprising that it has been assessed in various ways. Like the Priestly writers, the Chronicler lays no obvious weight on the Exodus, though many allusions indicate his awareness of it. Rather, like the Deuteronomic writers, he centers upon the age of David and Solomon, reading everything else in the light of that ideal. But his reading is not narrowly political, as is seen from the fact that the theme of restoration of the monarchy finds no place in his thought. The significance of David and Solomon lies in the temple, its worship, and its organization; its sequel is the restoration after the Exile (Ezra 1–6) and the work of Ezra. The relating of the Chronicler's purpose to the problems created by the Samaritan "schism" is ill-founded, not least because of the chronological uncertainties (*see* SAMARITANS; SAMARITANS[S] §1). But, seeing that as only one expression of religious tension, we may postulate other divisive movements and see in the Chronicler a concern for unity, for orthodoxy, for the true temple and its worship. While aware of the problems of faith and obedience posed by life under the domination of the Persians, and conscious of his people's repeated failures as witnessed by tradition, he nonetheless has confidence in divine power and favor without setting out hopes for the future in precise terms. If apocalyptic may be understood as in some degree a protest against a too complacent establishment (*see* APOCALYPTICISM[S]), the Chronicler may be seen as an establishment theologian acutely aware of the need for regeneration from within. The two are not so far apart as is sometimes supposed.

To make extravagant claims for the Chronicler as theologian is unsatisfactory. But it is proper to detect in his strongly homiletic exposition of already familiar narratives, in his repetition of central themes in a variety of forms, and in his over-all patterned presentation, one who by clarifying the issues for his own day may be properly claimed as one of the great maintainers of the tradition. He is one of the more articulate of those unnamed writers who kept the community conscious of the immediacy and relevance of ancient belief and practice.

Bibliography. A comprehensive bibliog. for Chronicles, Ezra, and Nehemiah, ed. by H. Kent Richards, is to be published by the Biblical Institute Press, Rome.

Commentaries: H. Bückers, *Die Heilige Schrift,* IV/1 (1952); L. Marshal, *La Sainte Bible,* IV (1952), 5-282; K. Galling, ATD, XII (1954); W. Rudolph, *HAT,* I/21 (1955); M. Rehm, *Die Bücher der Chronik* (1954); A. M. Brunet, *DBSup,* VI (1960), 1220-61; H. Cazelles, *Les Livres des Chroniques* (2nd ed., 1961); J. M. Myers, ABi, XII, XIII (1965); F. Michaeli, CAT, XVI (1967); P. R. Ackroyd, Torch Bible Commentaries (1973); R. J. Coggins, CBC (1976).

Commentaries in one-vol. works: R. North, *JBC* (1968), 402-38; A. S. Herbert, *PCB* (1962), 357-69; C. T. Fritsch, *IOVC* (1971), 208-19; Mulcahy, *NCCHS* (1969), 352-79.

Textual studies: W. E. Lemke, "The Synoptic Problem in the Chronicler's History," *HTR,* LVIII (1965), 349-63; J. D. Shenkel, "A Comparative Study of the Synoptic Parallels in I Paralipomena and I-II Reigns," *HTR,* LXII (1969), 63-85; R. Le Déaut, J. Robert, *Targum des Chroniques,* 2 vols. (1971); L. C. Allen, *The Greek Chronicles,* VTSup, XXV (1974), with bibliog.

Special Studies: P. R. Ackroyd, "History and Theology in the Writings of the Chronicler," *CTM,* XXXVIII (1967), 501-15, *The Age of the Chronicler* (1970), "The Theology of the Chronicler," *LThQ,* VIII (1973), 101-16; D. N. Freedman, "The Chronicler's Purpose," *CBQ,* XXIII (1961), 436-42; S. Japhet, "The supposed common authorship of Chronicles and Ezra-Nehemia investigated anew," *VT,* XVIII (1968), 330-71; R. Mosis, *Untersuchungen zur Theologie des chronistischen Geschichtswerkes,* Freiburg Theologische Studien, 92 (1973); S. Mowinckel, *"Erwägungen zum chronistischen Geschichtswerk," TLZ,* LXXXV (1969), 1-8; O. Plöger, "Reden und Gebete im deuteronomischen und chronistischen Geschichtswerk" in *Aus der Spätzeit des AT; Studien* (1971), pp. 50-66, originally published 1957 in *Festschrift G. Dehn,* pp. 35-49; G. von Rad, "The Levitical Sermon in I and II Chronicles," in *The Problem of the Hexateuch and Other Essays* (1966), pp. 267-80; P. Welten, *Geschichte und Geschichtsdarstellung in den Chronikbüchern,* WMANT, XLII (1973); T. Willi, *Die Chronik als Auslegung, FRLANT,* CVI (1972).

P. R. ACKROYD

CHRONOLOGY, EGYPTIAN. *See* EGYPT, CHRONOLOGY OF[S].

CHRONOLOGY, MESOPOTAMIAN (METHOD). Writing, and thus, by definition, the historical period, began in ancient Mesopotamia about 3000 B.C., but it is not until about 2500 B.C. that there are sufficient records to permit a coherent history. Since the cuneiform cultures never developed a uniform system of dating, one of the primary prerequisites to understanding them is the construction of a coherent chronology. Generally, each regime employed its own system, so it is necessary first to recover these individual systems, then to fit them together and to date the whole in terms of years B.C.

Unfortunately, the newly developed methods of scientific dating are of little help in this process. Radiocarbon, the most useful here, has a built-in margin of error of several decades, and most major problems within this area can be dated more closely than this by historical and archaeological methods. In addition, there appears to be a fundamental flaw in the original theory. It was supposed that a constant level of cosmic-ray activity acted on a relatively fixed amount of atmospheric carbon dioxide to maintain a stable amount of radiocarbon in the environment; and so a fixed percentage of the carbon content of any living thing would, at its death, be radioactive. Since radiocarbon decays at a known rate into regular carbon, age could be determined by carefully measuring the percentage of radiocarbon yet remaining. Recent research indicates, however, that there have been fluctuations either in the levels of atmospheric carbon dioxide or, more likely, of cosmic radiation, which have produced variations in radiocarbon levels. As a result, specimens whose age can be fixed beyond doubt historically have produced radiocarbon dates centuries outside the allowable margin for error.

1. Fourteenth to second century B.C.
2. Twenty-fifth to fourteenth century B.C. and the date of Hammurabi
Bibliography

1. Fourteenth to second century B.C. The basic chronological structure for Mesopotamia from the fourteenth through the mid-seventh century is derived from Assyrian records. The Assyrians dated by means of eponyms (*limmu*) and preserved lists thereof. These lists survive for the period 911-649 B.C. The Assyrian king list has been reconstructed completely with regnal years from Enlil-nasir II (1430-1425 B.C.) through ASHURBANIPAL (668-627 B.C.) and appears generally to be quite accurate. The anchor point for this portion of the system is a solar eclipse, recorded in the eponym lists, which occurred in the month of Simanu during the eponymy of Bur-sagale in the reign of Ashur-dan III. It has been dated astronomically to June 15, 763 B.C. In addition, much chronological information can be gleaned from royal annals, building inscriptions, and business records. Assyrian documentation generally fails during the latter portion of the seventh century B.C., and both the order and relationships of the last kings are uncertain.

Babylonian chronology during this period bristles with problems. King List A originally listed the kings of Babylonia from the First Dynasty of Babylon to some time in the sixth century B.C., but it is damaged in several places. There are other fragmentary king lists, synchronistic king lists from Assyria, and chronicle texts which can be used to restore some, but not all, of the gaps.

Beginning with Burna-buriash II in the mid-fourteenth century B.C., there is a reasonably cohesive block of about four hundred years which includes the later portion of the Kassite Dynasty, the Second Isin Dynasty, and ends during the dark days of the mid-tenth century, at which point most records fail. The precise length of this period cannot be determined since Tukulti-Ninurta I's name does not appear in King List A, and it is not clear whether the seven years he ruled are omitted or are included under the name of a local prince. There might also have been an interregnum or, more likely, an overlap between the last Kassite king and the first of the Second Isin kings. The paucity of documentation following the Second Isin Dynasty may hide more problems. This floating block must be anchored primarily by synchronisms with Assyria furnished by the chronicles and the Assyrian royal annals. The Kassites prior to Tukulti-Ninurta's conquest can be moved forward or backward over a twenty-two-year period, those after him over a thirteen-year period, and the remaining kings over a ten-year period.

The mid-tenth to mid-eighth centuries were a turbulent time marked by weak kings whose sequence can be determined, but whose lengths of reign are unknown. There was an interregnum of unknown length around 800 B.C.

From Nabonassar (747-734 B.C.) onward, Mesopotamian chronology can be established with little margin for error. The Ptolemaic Canon, a classical compilation, lists the kings of Babylonia from Nabonassar through Alexander IV (316-307 B.C.) with their dates according to the Nabonassar Era (Year 1=747 B.C.). Dated astronomical observations in Ptolemy's *Almagest* provide absolute dates. King List A covers the same period through Kandalanu (647-627 B.C.), and the Babylonian chronicle series provides a historical outline with dates. Assyrian annals and correspondence offer supplementary information.

The outline for the Neo-Babylonian Dynasty, which replaced the Assyrian Empire in 609, is provided by the Ptolemaic Canon and the chronicle series. The chronicles cover fairly well the revolt against Assyria, the early years of the dynasty, and its last years prior to the Persian conquest, but there are few historical texts from its middle years.

The canon provides the basic list of Persian kings, supplemented by the classical historians and dated business texts. The canon omits the short-lived usurpers and rebel kings, but these can be allotted to the revolts against DARIUS I during 522-521 B.C. and against XERXES during 482 B.C., on the basis of Darius' Behistun inscription and changes in Xerxes' titulary.

Alexander the Great conquered the Persian Empire and assumed the kingship of Babylonia in 330 B.C. The canon breaks off after Alexander IV and follows the Hellenistic kings of Egypt, but a recently published cuneiform king list continues with the Seleucid Dynasty down through ANTIOCHUS IV (175-164 B.C.), giving their dates according to the Seleucid Era (Year 1=311 B.C.), refining the chronology already derived from classical authors. The dating under Alexander the Great is confused because the scribes sometimes counted from his accession in Macedon in 336, sometimes from his coronation in Babylon in 330 B.C.

About the mid-second century B.C. the Parthians permanently wrested control of Mesopotamia from the Seleucids and introduced a new era, the Parthian (Year 1=247 B.C.), a firm synchronism being established by a tablet from Babylon bearing the dual dates, Year 144 Parthian Era, Year 208 Seleucid Era.

While the dates of individual events within the above system may be uncertain, the over-all scheme is accurate within one or two years back to 1180 B.C. and within twenty years back to 1400 B.C.

2. Twenty-fifth to fourteenth century B.C. and the date of Hammurabi. Moving back into the fifteenth century B.C., one encounters a dark age, perhaps one to two hundred years long, in which nearly all documentation throughout Mesopotamia fails. The material preceding this time forms a cohesive block nearly eight hundred years long, which can be pushed forward or backward depending on the chronological scheme used. Efforts to fix this block usually concentrate on dating the First Dynasty of Babylon and HAMMURABI, its most powerful king.

These efforts must be accommodated to the following generally accepted historical outline. Hammurabi managed by the end of his reign to assemble an empire which comprised nearly all of Mesopotamia, including Assyria. Among his rivals were Shamshi-Adad I of Assyria, Yarim-Lim I of Aleppo, and Zimri-Lim of MARI. During the eighth year of Ammi-saduqa, Hammurabi's fourth successor, a record was made of a series of sightings of the planet Venus, and it survives in late, mistake-ridden copies. Finally, 155 years after Hammurabi's death, the Hittite Mursilis I raided Babylon and overthrew Samsuditana, last king of the First Dynasty. Meanwhile, Alalakh, a dependency of Aleppo, was destroyed about 1640 B.C., to judge from archaeological remains (*see* ALALAKH TEXTS[S]). The number and sequence of the kings of Alalakh and Aleppo are uncertain. The Hittite Suppiluliumas I can be placed about 1380 B.C. by Egyptian synchronisms, but the interval between him and Mursilis is subject to varying estimates. There is no Hittite king list. At some point during this period the Kassites entered Babylonia and the Kassite Dynasty replaced the fallen First Dynasty, but the length of their tenure and how much they may have overlapped with the First Dynasty is debated. In southern Babylonia the Sealand Dynasty ruled, a contemporary with the later First Dynasty and the early Kassite Dynasty. Also during this period the Indo-European MITANNI formed in northern Mesopotamia an empire which dominated Assyria and rivaled the HITTITES, but it is known only from its peripheral contacts, and no coherent chronology of it is possible at this time. One of its dependencies, the small Hurrian town of NUZI, flourished about 1500-1350 B.C., based on a synchronism with Mitanni and thence with Egypt. The Amarna correspondence provides synchronisms between the Pharaoh AKH-EN-ATON, the Kassite Burna-buriash II, and Asshur-uballit I (1363-1328 B.C.) of Assyria.

Both the Assyrian king list and King List A cover this obscure period, but both are damaged, and even what remains cannot always be taken at face value. King List A originally listed, in order, the First Dynasty, now almost totally missing, then the Sealand Dynasty, given a total of 368 years, then the Kassite Dynasty, the earlier portion of which is badly damaged, with a total of 576 years. The Assyrian king list preserves the canonical list of kings from Shamshi-Adad I, no. 39, onward through this period, but kings nos. 42-47 are said to have reigned *tuppishu,* a term of unclear meaning; their regnal years are not given, and the regnal years for kings nos. 65-66 are broken away in all copies. There is reason to believe that some kings who ruled directly following Ishme-Dagan I, no. 40, were omitted from the canonical list. A later king would sometimes give the length of time between his own reign and that of a predecessor, but these figures yield ambiguous and contradictory results and do not strongly favor one chronology over the others.

Most efforts to date the First Dynasty take into account the Venus sightings of Ammi-saduqa. Since the planet Venus repeats its movements in a complicated cycle every 275, 64, or 56 years, these sightings can fit a number of years between 2000 and 1500 B.C. A number of factors, e.g., the synchronism between Shamshi-Adad I and Hammurabi, render awkward alternatives outside this period. Of the three alternatives presently given most attention, the high chronology yields First Dynasty dates of 1950-1651 B.C.; the middle, 1894-1595 B.C.; and the low, 1830-1531 B.C. Following are brief sketches of the arguments and implications associated with these three different schemes.

According to the high chronology, the Kassite Dynasty lasted in Babylonia for 576 years; and thus if it fell about 1155 B.C., it began about 1730. The high chronology places this during the reign of Ammi-ditana (1739-1703, high chronology), when the power of the First Dynasty was waning; if the middle chronology is used, then this would fall during the reign of Samsu-iluna (1749-1712, middle chronology). While there was some contact with the Kassites in his eighth year, he nonetheless remained active in the Diyala and Habur areas and suppressed a widespread revolt in the S. As Kassites are nowhere mentioned in any of this, it is supposed that they were not yet established in Babylonia. The Sealand Dynasty, which ruled in southern Babylonia, cannot have been founded prior to the reign of Samsu-iluna, and it was overthrown by Ulam-buriash, probably the thirteenth Kassite king, who cannot have reigned after 1400 B.C. If its 368-year lifespan is credited, then this pushes Samsu-iluna back to high chronology dates; the middle does not allow a sufficient interval. While there is no Hittite king list, there are lists of offerings made by the kings to revered ancestors, and from these a total of nine generations have been reconstructed between Mursilis I and Suppiluliumas I. With the latter placed about 1380 B.C., and allowing thirty years per generation, this yields a date of about 1650 B.C. for Mursilis and thus for the fall of the First Dynasty. There is a similar situation at Alalakh and Aleppo, where a total of six generations are reconstructed between the fall of Alalakh about 1640 and Yarim-Lim I, who is thus dated about 1820, acceptable to the high chronology dates for Hammurabi, 1848-1806 B.C. Alalakh is assumed, consequently, to have been destroyed by the Hittites about the same time as Babylon.

Adherents of the middle chronology accept 576 years as the duration of the Kassite Dynasty, and assume the reference to Kassites in Samsu-iluna's eighth year to mark its beginning. To lower the dates of the First Dynasty any further makes it necessary either to reduce the length of the Kassite Dynasty or to assume that it was around during the reign of Hammurabi, both considered undesirable here. According to two texts, sometimes considered apocryphal, Agum II, probably the tenth Kassite king, recovered the statue of the god Marduk which had been missing from Babylon for twenty-four years following the Hittite raid. This would place the Kassites in residence at Babylon by 1570, middle chronology. The 368-year lifespan for the Sealand Dynasty is considered exaggerated, especially because of the very long reigns given its first two kings. As for Assyria, forty years are allotted for kings nos. 65-66, whose regnal years are missing, and fifty years for the confusion following Ishme-Dagan I. The 106 years provided by the high chronology is considered excessively long. There is a certain Zukrashi contemporary with the last kings of Alalakh who may be the same Zukrashi who, according to Hittite accounts, fought for Aleppo against Ḫattusilis I, grandfather of Mursilis. If so, then Ḫattusilis may have destroyed Alalakh (*ca.* 1640 B.C.) and the raid on Babylon by Mursilis would have come a generation later, about 1595.

The observations recorded in the Venus tablets fit the low chronology slightly better than either the high or middle chronologies, and its supporters stress this. The Assyrian king list also fits well if the reigns of the six *tuppishu* kings following Ishme-Dagan I in the list are reckoned as zero, and the alternate line of successors, listed in a noncanonical list fragment, is ignored. This permits dates of 1748-1716 B.C. for Shamshi-Adad I, which fits well with the low chronology dates for Hammurabi, 1728-1686, and allows a not unreasonable twenty-two years for Assyrian kings numbers 65-66. A king list compiled by the Hellenistic historian Berossos can be interpreted, with emendations, to yield low chronology dates. The 576 years attributed to the Kassite Dynasty is considered too long and is subjected to a variety of Procrustean reductions. And the sequence of kings of the allied dynasties of Alalakh and Aleppo can be reconstructed to form a block lasting from about 1740 to 1640 B.C., placing Yarim-Lim I within the vicinity of Hammurabi's low chronology dates.

It should be apparent that there is a great amount of data which must be considered in dating the First Dynasty. None of it is decisive, and much of it can be accommodated to all three solutions. Even the Venus sightings, which are commonly used to provide some structure for the problem, are so replete with errors that they could easily be ignored if there were any good evidence which would make it desirable. On the whole, the middle chronology seems the most popular, with the low receiving the next greatest amount of attention.

Babylonian affairs as far back as the accession of SARGON of Akkad can be tied relatively securely to the First Dynasty. The basic framework is derived from the Sumerian king list and the shorter king lists for Isin and Larsa, supplemented by lists of year names and subject to emendation from literary tradition and incidental references in correspondence and business texts.

About 2350 B.C. Sargon of Akkad founded the Akkadian Empire. The Sumerian king list gives for his dynasty 181 years, then 91 years during which the Guti barbarians from the mountains dominated the land, then 6 years for Utu-hegal of Uruk, 108 years for the Ur III Dynasty, and 203 years for the First Dynasty of Isin. The compilers of the Sumerian king list supposed that the entire land was subject to a single dynasty at any one time, and so dynasties which were contemporaries and rivals are listed as successors to one another. Strong historical traditions indicate that it was actually the Guti who overthrew the Akkadian Dynasty, and their assault apparently began under Shar-kali-sharri, Sargon's fourth successor. The Uruk Dynasty, otherwise unattested, is ignored for chronological purposes. Utu-hegal is credited with expelling the Guti, but his regime was shortly replaced by the Ur III Dynasty, slightly before 2100 B.C. The Ur Empire developed a sophisticated bureaucracy and is, consequently, well documented. The Empire, assaulted by nomadic Amorite invaders, began to crumble during the reign of Ibbi-Sin, the last Ur III king (*see* AMORITES; AMORITES[S]). City after city quit using the imperial dating system and declared independence under local dynasts; the most prominent were at Isin, Larsa, and Babylon. King lists, lists of year names, and references to wars and alliances establish the necessary synchronisms. It was Hammurabi who finally outmaneuvered all the other contestants and drew nearly all of Mesopotamia into the Old Babylonian Empire. The major uncertainty in the preceding schema is the length of the interval between the end of the Akkadian Dynasty and the beginning of the Ur III Dynasty; the Gutian domination is poorly documented; its duration given in the Sumerian king list cannot be confirmed elsewhere; and the extent of its overlap with the last Akkadian kings is unclear.

Little can be said for Assyria prior to Shamshi-Adad I; the kings preceding him have left few texts and the king lists do not preserve their regnal years.

It is not possible to establish a coherent chronology for the period prior to Sargon of Akkad. At Lagash a line of seven kings can be traced back to Ur-Nanshe, who must have reigned about 2550 B.C. Other isolated kings of various cities are known from brief inscriptions. The Sumerian king list is of little help; a number of the earlier kings therein are given fabulous reigns thousands of years long, and the order of the dynasties is not trustworthy.

See also ASSYRIA AND BABYLONIA[S].

Bibliography. M. B. Rowton, "Chronology: Ancient Western Asia," in *CAH* (3rd ed., 1970), I, Pt. 1, ch. vi, 193-239; and H. Tadmor "The Chronology of the Ancient Near East . . . ," in *The World History of the Jewish People,* ed. B. Mazar (1970), II, 63-101; both support the middle chronology. For the high chronology: F. Thureau-Dangin, "La chronologie de la première dynastie babylonienne," in *Memoires de l'Académie des Inscriptions et Belles-Lettres,* XLIII (1942), 229-58; A. Goetze, "On the Chronology of the Second Millennium B.C.," *JCS,* XI (1957), 53 ff. For the low chronology: W. F. Albright, "Further Observations on the Chronology of Alalakh," *BASOR,* 146 (1957), 26 ff.; F. Cornelius, "Die Chronologie . . . ," *AFO,* XVII (1956), 249-309. For radiocarbon: M. Stuiver and H. E. Seuss, "On the Relationship between Radiocarbon Dates and True Sample Ages," *Radiocarbon,* VIII (1966), 534-40.

R. D. TINDEL

***CHRONOLOGY, OT.** The scientific mind constantly searches for new understanding; hence no system is exempt from modification. Nevertheless, the article on CHRONOLOGY OF THE OT retains its essential validity. Intensive and wide-ranging discussion during the intervening period has been motivated by a response to three particular responsibilities: (1) assessing textual data from the Bible as historical evidence; (2) incorporating evaluated data into a meaningful and comprehensive structure; (3) employing new information derived from extrabiblical texts, which itself needs to be evaluated for meaning, reliability, and applicability, as a control for the interpretation of information provided by Scripture. Significant discussion has centered chiefly in the following five areas of concern.

1. The Stenring-Larrson "secret system"
2. The premonarchic period
3. The divided kingdom
4. Tishri or Nisan new year, 609–587/86
5. The date of Ezra
Bibliography

1. The Stenring-Larsson "secret system." Although quite prepared to entertain the hypothesis of sporadic alterations in the figures found in individual texts, along with the possibility of schematic numeration in specific documents or sections, OT scholars have been understandably incredulous regarding the ambitious effort of two Swedish writers, Knut Stenring and Gerhard Larsson, to correlate the entire range of biblical events from the Creation to the return from exile with an esoteric schematization theoretically devised by Hebrew scribes following the Canopus decree of 238 B.C. Influenced by his researches in Cabalistic mysticism, Stenring argued that these scribes corrected the biblical text wherever it suited their schematization, picking dates from three rival calendars, an ancient lunar calendar of 354 days, a solar calendar of 365 days, and the Canopus intercalated calendar of 366 days. Larsson, a mathematician with recognized scientific standing, has endeavored to corroborate this scheme on the basis of statistical probability.

The striking weakness of the Stenring-Larsson presentation has been its failure to apply historical and literary-critical standards to the biblical texts, or to correlate them with extrabiblical data. Larsson reveals a lack of comprehension for the theoretical basis of Stenring's scheme in arguing that certain points of correspondence with historical actuality support the schematization; if the Bible's chronology is systematically schematic, it cannot be historical except by coincidence. In matter of fact, the Stenring-Larsson dates are often widely at variance with dates attested as historical upon accepted criteria. One is justified in questioning how aimless arbitrariness can be avoided in reconstructing what was theoretically an arbitrary and "secret" picking of dates from the three calendars. Larsson's argument from statistics, awesome perhaps to the nonmathematician and intended as reassurance that Stenring has in fact hit upon the right combination, may point to elements of schematization in particular passages but leaves in serious doubt the validity of the comprehensive system.

2. The premonarchic period. Having observed this radical misconception of schematic possibilities, the biblical scholar is reminded to acknowledge ideological schematization where it in fact existed. Now more clearly than before we are in a position to assess the chronological systematization of the P writer in Genesis-Exodus (*see* CHRONOLOGY OF THE OT §1*b*). The work of Jaubert and others on the Qumran and biblical calendars (*see bibliog. for* CALENDAR), while falling short of absolute proof, suggests an element of ideology in P's dates in the patriarchal history, leaving less justification than ever for using P's figures as a basis for historical reconstruction.

The ongoing criticism of the DEUTERONOMIC HISTORY (DH) has shown that, except where it draws from annalistic or similar documentary sources, it too falls back upon a schematic chronology, though lacking perhaps the ideological bias of P. The implications of this observation have not been fully drawn out. Inasmuch as "forty" is a clearly schematic figure in the DH sections of Judges, one must seriously question whether it ought to be applied literally to the reigns of David and Solomon, or to the wilderness-wandering period (*see* CHRONOLOGY OF THE OT §2). Recent advances in the analysis of Pentateuchal traditions have made scholars wary of attempting to reconstruct the events of this remote era on the basis of schematic chronologies and itineraries. A date *ca.* 1290/1280 for the Exodus remains only an approximate possibility; a fifteenth-century date is more impossible than ever.

Noth has proposed an attractive hypothesis regarding the disparate figures in Judges-Kings, using this to support his influential theory of Deuteronomic redaction. According to Noth, the Deuteronomic figure of 480 years from the Exodus to Solomon's fourth year (I Kings 6:1), while patently schematic, is intended as the total of all the figures actually found in DH's sources or devised by himself, but does not include the twenty years of I Sam. 7:2 (because these were understood to be included in the forty years of Judg. 13:1) or three figures subsequently added to DH's text, viz., Samson's twenty years in Judg. 15:20; 16:31, and Eli's forty years of I Sam. 4:18. Though I Sam. 13:1, which provides an incomplete and confused figure for Saul, is not attested in the best LXX witnesses, Noth retains the MT's two years on the argument that DH would not have left Saul out of his chronological scheme. This produces a 481-year total. It is better to omit Saul's figure and produce a 480-year figure for the total upon the assumption that DH may have been counting Solomon's years by postdating, allowing the additional accession year to be counted in his total (*see* Table 1).

3. The divided kingdom. Thiele's chronology, tenaciously defended by himself and supported by a growing number of scholars, continues to represent the most probable reconstruction.

It is not as though there has been nothing to criticize in Thiele's work. He has been too ready to accept the historicity of specific passages and has seemed almost dogmatically committed to the MT in preference to the LXX. The two current leading rivals to Thiele's chronology are those of W. F. Albright and J. Begrich, along with modifications of each. While adherents of these two theories criticize Thiele for arguing from too many assumptions, each theory depends to a greater or lesser degree on assumptions having less objective support than those of Thiele. That is, Albright and Begrich have been willing to posit numerous errors in the biblical text as an explanation for its chronological incongruities, but seldom with any clear rationale. Wherever no pattern, tendency, or schematization can be seen, corrections on the assumption of error remain arbitrary.

Thiele has proceeded on the basis of two very

reasonable assumptions of his own: (1) the annals of the parallel Israelite kingdoms were based on historical facts, aimed at accuracy, and were guided by internally consistent principles; (2) the biblical text was carefully preserved except in rare cases of accident or tendential interference. From these assumptions he has developed a hypothesis that allows a whole array of biblical figures to be brought into a pattern of complete internal harmony, while permitting the full correlation of extrabiblical data. An intricate pattern of reigns and synchronisms, figured by different methods and based on varying ways of counting the beginning of years, sometimes involving co-regencies or rival rules (explained in CHRONOLOGY OF THE OT §3), becomes self-supporting evidence for the correctness of Thiele's assumptions.

It goes without saying that details remain open to new interpretation, especially where evidence from Near Eastern texts is forthcoming regarding synchronisms between Mesopotamian and Israelite rulers. Very recently Thiele's dates for the accession of two northern Israelite rulers, Joash and Pekahiah, have come under challenge, though in neither case with unambiguous implications. *See* JOASH[S].

A formidable threat to Thiele's chronology has come as a result of recent advances in Septuagintal criticism. Specialists have discovered that large portions of Codex Vaticanus (LXX^{B}) in Kings, including the section from I Kings 22 onward, represent not the ancient LXX but a recension (called *Kaige* from one of its peculiar readings) closely approaching the MT. In the sections mentioned, LXX^{B} is a less reliable witness to what the earliest Greek and its Hebrew *Vorlage* contained than the next-earliest recension, the Proto-Lucianic (LXX^{L}; *see* SEPTUAGINT §4*c*). Observing that Thiele was unaware that LXX^{B} from I Kings 22 onward is not a witness independent of the MT, and that he fails to reckon seriously with the pluses in the LXX at I Kings 16:28 and II Kings 1:18, Shenkel has argued that LXX^{L} represents the earliest Greek reading, with a superior *Vorlage* wherever its figures differ from those of the MT, the MT being a late normalization to an ideological schematization.

Since the issues in this debate are too complex to be analyzed in a short summation, the reader will best be served by a synoptic presentation of the variant chronological schemes developed in the MT, LXX^{B}, and LXX^{L}, respectively (Table 2). Apparent inconsistencies in the MT must be viewed in the light of the possibilities discussed in CHRONOLOGY OF THE OT §3, which, once understood, show that the MT does follow a clear and consistent scheme. LXX^{B} likewise has a rudimentary scheme: it attempts to explicate Omri's synchronism with Asa's thirty-first year by giving Zimri seven years instead of days, making Asa's forty-one years end in Omri's eleventh and adjusting all foregoing figures accordingly, then giving Ahab's accession a synchronism with Jehoshaphat's second year. The *Kaige* recension intrudes after I Kings 16, throwing complete confusion into this scheme, which subsequent scribes have vainly striven to amend. As Shenkel argues, LXX^{L} has preserved a more consistent and original scheme. Whereas LXX^{B} apparently allows two years to the rivalry between Tibni and Omri, LXX^{L} gives it nine years, after which Omri rules alone for another twelve. Since Ahab follows Jehoshaphat, Ahaziah's accession comes seven years later in Jehoshaphat's reign than in the MT or LXX^{B}. The accession of Jehoram of Israel in the second year of the other Jehoram's reign presupposes the latter's accession in Ahaziah of Israel's second year; that LXX^{L} instead reads Jehoram of Israel's fifth year in agreement with MT, coming too late in the narrative development, indicates the breakdown of the Proto-Lucianic scheme. Whether this is due to the failure of a revisionist working arbitrarily on an original chronology reflected in the MT, or to the secondary intrusion of normalizings to the MT, is the question in dispute.

Shenkel makes much of the fact that II Kings 1:17-18 dates Jehoram of Israel's accession after Jehoshaphat's death, but prior to the report of Elijah's departure in II Kings 2, as though to underscore the impossibility of the Judahite king of whom Elisha, Elijah's successor, speaks in II Kings 3:14 actually being the Jehoshaphat of the MT. LXX^{L} is consistent in omitting the duplicate Jehoram synchronism that follows the report of Elijah's departure (II Kings 3:1). Shenkel argues that LXX^{L} displays the original figures and order, explaining that a pious redactor added the name "Jehoshaphat" in ch. 3 (MT and LXX^{B}), as another scribe added "Ahaziah" in LXX^{L}. Jehoshaphat was named because neither of his next two successors would have been deemed worthy of Elisha's praise spoken in 3:14. Having made this identification, the MT/LXX^{B} redactor was obliged to carry out the elaborate adjustment that now appears in the MT figures from Asa to Ahaziah.

Although Thiele has himself offered a serious rebuttal to this thesis, the most effective counterargument has come from a Septuagintal specialist, Gooding. The essential thing to consider is that LXX^{L} is as likely to have changed figures and rearranged the text as the MT. Surely the MT's strange synchronism for Omri's accession in Asa's thirty-first year (explained by Thiele as dating from Omri's victory over Tibni, while his total reign is counted from his victory over Zimri) offers sufficient motivation for a Proto-Lucianic (and putatively LXX^{B}) reworking. The crucial evidence, as Gooding sees it, is found in I Kings 16:28 +, where both Septuagintal recensions contain summarizing and adaptive emendations, showing that the Jehoshaphat summary has been brought forward from its original place following the notice of Ahab's death.

Both Thiele and Shenkel have erred in treating II Kings 3, along with I Kings 22, as historical. Both treatments are weak with respect to literary and redaction criticism. It is too early to know whether recent investigations into the Deuteronomic regal formulas may have a bearing on the chronological problem.

4. Tishri or Nisan new year, 609-587/86. The date for the destruction of Jerusalem still depends on a choice between a Tishri and a Nisan new year for Judah's kings in its final period (*see* NEW

YEAR[S]). Though opinions continue to vary, the argument offered in CHRONOLOGY OF THE OT §3*d*, represents the greatest convergence of probabilities.

5. The date of Ezra. Some have proposed to emend Ezra 7:7 to read "thirty-seventh," according to which the date would be 428. Recent study has made it seem likely, however, that Nehemiah actually antedated Ezra by several decades, hence the Artaxerxes of this text is probably the second of that name; his seventh year is 397.

A better understanding of the Elephantine "Passover Papyrus" of 419 B.C. removes an obstacle toward dating Ezra's promulgation of the Law in the reign of Artaxerxes II. The record of the work of Nehemiah and Ezra respectively is best understood on the assumption of that order. The emendation to "thirty-seventh" in Ezra 7:7 is arbitrary. Cross's renewed plea for a 458 date, leaving unresolved the old objections, interpolates two extra high priests before Ezra without solid evidence and posits a controversial early date for Chronicles. *See* CHRONICLES, I AND II; EZRA AND NEHEMIAH[S].

Bibliography. Many titles listed in CHRONOLOGY OF THE OT (bibliog.) retain their usefulness. On the shortcomings of J. Finegan, *Handbook of Biblical Chronology* (1964), *see* S. J. De Vries' review in *JBL,* LXXXIV (1965), 76-79.

K. Stenring, *The Enclosed Garden* (1966), is intended as a provisional publication; G. Larsson's major argument is in *The Secret System* (1973). A sympathetic but devastating review by J. Meysing appears in *RQ,* VI (1967), 229-51.

On Deuteronomic chronology, *see* M. Noth, *Überlieferungsgeschichtliche Studien* (2nd ed., 1957), pp. 18-27, strongly supported by W. Vollborn, "Die Chronologie des Richterbuches," *Festschrift Friedrich Baumgärtel* (1959), pp. 192-96; W. R. Wifall, Jr., "The Chronology of the Divided Monarchy of Israel," *ZAW,* LXXX (1968), 319-37, attributes to the Deuteronomist a schematic system for the divided kingdom period.

E. R. Thiele, *The Mysterious Numbers of the Hebrew Kings* (rev. ed., 1965), is an elaborate restatement of the original ed., with minor modifications in dates. Discussions by E. R. Thiele on special problems appear in *AUSS,* I (1963), 121-38; II (1964), 120-36; *VT,* XVI (1966), 83-107. On the Joash synchronism, *see* S. Page, "A Stela of Adad-Nirari III . . . from Tell al-Rimah," *Iraq,* XXX (1968), 139-53, and "Joash and Samaria in a New Stela . . . ," *VT,* XIX (1969), 483-84; A. Jepsen, "Ein Neuer Fixpunkt für die Chronologie der Israelitischen Könige?" *VT,* XX (1970), 359-61, arguing for Begrich's chronology; A. Cody, "A New Inscription from Tell al-Rimah . . . ," *CBQ,* XXXII (1970), 325-40, arguing for a co-regency with Jehoahaz. On Menahem-Pekahiah, cf. L. D. Levine, "Menahem and Tiglath-Pileser: A New Synchronism," *BASOR,* 206 (1972), 40-42.

J. D. Shenkel, *Chronology and Recensional Development in the Greek Text of Kings* (1968), was in some ways anticipated by J. M. Miller, "Another Look at the Chronology of the Early Divided Monarchy," *JBL,* LXXXVI (1967), 276-88. D. W. Gooding's review of Shenkel appears in *JTS,* XXI (1970), 118-31; cf. also E. R. Thiele, "Coregencies and Overlapping Reigns Among the Hebrew Kings," *JBL,* XCIII (1974), 174-200; H. Weippert, "Die 'deuteronomistischen' Beurteilungen der Könige von Israel und Juda und das Problem der Redaktion der Königsbücher," *Bibl.,* LIII (1972), 301-39.

Important discussions of the late kingship are: G. Schedl, "Nochmals das Jahr des Zerstörung Jerusalems," *ZAW,* LXXIV (1962), 209-13, and "Textkritische Bemerkungen," *VT,* XII (1962), 88-119; V. Pavlovsky and E. Vogt, "Die Jahre der Könige von Juda und Israel," *Bibl.,* XLV (1964), 321-47; S. Horn, "The Babylonian Chronicle and the Ancient Calendar of . . . Judah," *AUSS,* V (1967), 12-27. Definitive is A. Malamat, "The Last Kings of Judah and the Fall of Jerusalem," *IEJ,* XVIII (1968), 137-56.

On the Passover letter, cf. K. Galling, "Bagoas und Esra," *Studien zur Geschichte Israels im persischen Zeitalter* (1964), pp. 149-84; J. A. Emerton, "Did Ezra go to Jerusalem in 428 B.C.?" *JTS,* XVI (1966), 1-19, against 428; F. M. Cross, "A Reconstruction of the Judean Restoration," *JBL,* XCIV (1975), 4-18.

S. J. DE VRIES

Table 1

The Deuteronomic Years from the Exodus to the Building of the Temple

Years of penance for former backsliding		Years of deliverance			
DH		DH		DH source material	
Wilderness wandering (Deut. 1:3)	**40**				
		Conquest of Canaan (Josh. 14:10)	5		
Cushan-rishathaim (Judg. 3:8)	8				
		Rest (Judg. 3:11)	40		
Eglon (Judg. 3:14)	18				
		Rest (Judg. 3:30)	80		
Jabin (Judg. 4:3)	20				
		Rest (Judg. 5:31)	40		
Midian (Judg. 6:1)	7				
		Rest (Judg. 8:28)	40		
Abimelech (Judg. 9:22)	3				
				Tola (Judg. 10:2)	23
				Jair (Judg. 10:3)	22
Ammon (Judg. 10:8)	18				
				Jephthah (Judg. 12:7)	6

Years of penance for former backsliding		Years of deliverance			
DH		DH		DH source material	
				Ibzan (Judg. 12:8-9)	7
				Elon (Judg. 12:11)	10
				Abdon (Judg. 12:14-15)	8
Philistia (Judg. 13:1)	40				
		David's reign (II Sam. 5:5; I Kings 2:11)	40		
		Solomon's years 1-4 (I Kings 6:1)	4+		
TOTALS	154		249+		76

Table 2

Relative Positions of Reigns from Abijam to Ahaziah According to the Major Recensional Witnesses

(All scripture references are in Kings)

Legend: Judahite kings left, Israelite kings right
ac=synchronism of accession; r=length of reign
+=additional LXX material

MT	LXX^{B}	LXX^{L}
ABIJAM ac 18 Jeroboam (I 15:1) r 3 yrs. (I 15:2)	ABIJAM (=MT)	ABIJAM (=MT)
ASA ac 20 Jeroboam (I 15:9) r 41 yrs. (I 15:10)		
	ASA ac 24 Jeroboam (I 15:9) r 41 yrs. (I 15:10)	ASA (=LXX^{B})
- - - - - -	- - - - - -	- - - - - -
ELAH ac 26 Asa (I 16:8) r 2 yrs. "	ELAH ac 20 Asa (I 16:6) r 2 yrs. (I 16:8)	ELAH (=LXX^{B})
ZIMRI ac 27 Asa (I 16:10, 15) r 7 days (I 16:15)	ZIMRI (ac omitted) r 7 yrs. (I 16:15)	ZIMRI ac 22 Asa (I 16:15) r 7 days "
OMRI ac 31 Asa (I 16:23) r 12 yrs. "	(TIBNI-OMRI)	(TIBNI-OMRI)
	OMRI* ac 31 Asa (I 16:23) r 12 yrs. "	OMRI ac 31 Asa (I 16:23) r 12 yrs. "
AHAB ac 38 Asa (I 16:29) r 22 yrs. "		
JEHOSHAPHAT ac 4 Ahab (I 22:41) r 25 yrs. (I 22:42)		
	JEHOSHAPHAT ac 11 Omri* (I 16:28+) r 25 yrs. "	JEHOSHAPHAT ac 11 Omri (I 16:28+) r 25 yrs. "

*Corrected from "Zimri" in the Greek text

MT	LXX^{B}	LXX^{L}
	AHAB ac 2 Jehosh. (I 16:29) r 22 yrs. "	AHAB ac 2 Jehosh. (I 16:29) r 22 yrs. "
	JEHOSHAPHAT ac 4 Ahab (I 22:41) r 25 yrs. (I 22:42)	
AHAZIAH ac 17 Jehosh. (I 22:51) r 2 yrs. "	AHAZIAH ac 17 Jehosh. (I 22:51) r 2 yrs. "	AHAZIAH ac 24 Jehosh. (I 22:51) r 2 yrs. " (JEHORAM)
JEHORAM ac 2 Jehoram (II 1:17) ac 18 Jehosh. (II 3:1) r 12 yrs. "	JEHORAM ac 18 Jehosh. (II 1:18+, 3:1) r 12 yrs. "	JEHORAM ac 2 Jehoram (II 1:18+) r 12 yrs. (II 1:18+, 3:1)
JEHORAM ac 5 Jehoram (II 8:16) r 8 yrs. (II 8:17)	JEHORAM ac 5 Jehoram (II 8:16) r 40 yrs. (II 8:17)	JEHORAM ac 5 Jehoram (II 8:16) r 10 yrs. (II 8:17)
AHAZIAH ac 12 Jehoram (II 8:25) ac 11 Jehoram (II 9:29) r 1 yr. (II 8:26)	AHAZIAH ac 12 Jehoram (II 8:25) ac 11 Jehoram (II 9:29) r 1 yr. (II 8:26)	AHAZIAH ac 11 Jehoram (II 8:25) ac 11 Jehoram (II 9:29) r 1 yr. (II 9:29)

CHRONOLOGY, PAULINE. The secular world took little notice of earliest Christianity. The church for its part was wrapped in its own affairs and, except for selected events susceptible of apocalyptic interpretation, paid no attention to political affairs. Thus the task of reconstructing the chronology of Paul's career is frustrating and uncertain. The standard approach is (*a*) to relate Acts to world history, and (*b*) to relate Paul's letters to Acts (*see* CHRONOLOGY OF THE NT §B). Since no significant new evidence has appeared, the continuing discussion has mainly concerned the proper balance to give to the numerous bits of evidence that have been known for several generations.

There are, however, two distinctions which are gaining increased attention. The first is that between Acts and Paul's letters (*see* PAUL THE APOSTLE[S] §1*c*). The standard approach gives each an equal voice and seeks to resolve the discrepancies between the two. More and more, however, it is being realized that these two types of sources provide information on two different levels, and that the "primary" material (the letters) must first be sifted for all the information it contains before the "secondary" evidence (Acts) is examined.

The second distinction is between absolute chronology, i.e., the dating of events by some external calendar, and relative chronology, in which events are arranged in relationship to one another. Clearly, to gain the former is to gain the latter. But the latter may be established by lines of argument different from those required by the former. Further, it is relative chronology that the interpreter of Paul's letters needs. For example, whether Paul wrote I Thessalonians before or after II Thessalonians is far more important than the actual date of either.

These two distinctions mean that the first goal of Pauline chronology is to recover the original sequence of the letters. Over the years a number of suggestions have been made about the relative order of selected letters, either apart from or in spite of the usual interpretation of Acts. It is interesting to notice that these suggestions, where they overlap, are almost completely consistent. Thus they may be added together to form a single sequence:

II Thessalonians
I Thessalonians
Previous Letter to Corinth (see I Cor. 5:9)
I Corinthians
Severe Letter to Corinth (see II Cor. 2:3; 7:8)
Philippians
II Corinthians 1–9
Galatians
Romans
Colossians, Philemon (and Ephesians, if genuine)

The only substantial disagreement concerns II Cor. 10–13. Some identify it with the Severe Letter to Corinth; others place it at some point after II Cor. 1–9. *See also* CORINTHIANS, SECOND LETTER TO THE [S].

This outline provides a framework for other events. In Galatians Paul speaks of two previous visits to Jerusalem ("after three years," 1:18; "after fourteen years," 2:1). The first visit clearly preceded all the letters. The second visit probably inaugurated the collection (2:10; *see* OFFERING FOR

THE SAINTS[S]), first announced in the Previous Letter. This visit therefore follows I Thessalonians. Rom. 15:25-32 shows that Paul was about to make a final visit to Jerusalem to deliver the collection before leaving for Rome on his way to Spain. A third visit therefore follows Romans. The later letters provide no further information beyond the fact that Paul was in prison and hoped to see at least the Colossians once more (Philem. 22). The traditions in Acts about Paul's arrest and imprisonment are to be connected most probably with this third visit to Jerusalem. The result is the following:

Conversion
First Jerusalem visit
Missionary work from Syria to Achaia
Second Jerusalem visit (collection inaugurated)
Collection journey to revisit churches
Third Jerusalem visit (collection delivered)
Imprisonment and execution

Absolute dates are, of course, desirable but uncertain. The collection was probably made in response to the famine about A.D. 46 (*see* CHRONOLOGY OF THE NT §B1*b*). II Thessalonians seems to relate to CALIGULA's attempt to erect his statue in the temple at Jerusalem in A.D. 40 (*see* THESSALONIANS, SECOND LETTER TO THE[S]).

Bibliography. G. Ogg, *The Chronology of the Life of Paul* (1968); and J. J. Gunther, *Paul: Messenger and Exile* (1972), standard approach; J. C. Hurd, "The Sequence of Paul's Letters," *CJT*, XIV (1968), 189-200; J. Knox, *Chapters in a Life of Paul* (1950), on the three-visit pattern; and most recently, A. Suhl, *Paulus und Seine Briefe. Ein Beitrag zur paulinischen Chronologie*, StNT, XI (1975).

J. C. HURD

***CITIES, GRECO-ROMAN.** Traditionally the center of human activity in the ancient world, the city in NT times had come to illustrate the distinctive results of the spread of Roman rule over the varied peoples who constituted the Empire. Each city continued to exhibit the basic signs of its origin and history in its ethnic composition and cultural tradition, and local languages often survived alongside Latin and Greek. Many of the cities, especially in the eastern lands of the Empire, were older than Rome, and had once been independent city-states. Roman rule had brought the benefits of Roman administration, with its principles of law and public order. Improved communications and widened commercial opportunities brought new prosperity to the cities, and the new conditions of Roman rule served to make the cities conscious of the link with Rome and of membership in the Empire. Yet the mark of the typical Greco-Roman city continued to be the diversity of its human element, and Roman policy permitted each city to continue to think of itself as an individual entity. The study of the Greco-Roman city thus becomes the assessment of the interaction of Roman rule and of the different local conditions which produced special social and administrative problems.

1. Archaeological evidence. Excavation at such cities as CAESAREA, ANTIOCH, SARDIS, EPHESUS, and CORINTH has furnished evidence for the physical structure and urban history of different kinds of cities and has illustrated the concern of the Roman

Scala

3. Shops in the Via dell'Abbondanza, Pompeii

authorities for improved city planning and public services.

2. Types of urban communities. Depending upon their previous history, size, importance, and location, the cities were granted different types of administrative status, viz., Roman colony, colony of Roman veterans, provincial metropolis, municipality, or "free city." There might be different degrees of local self-government, as well as direct administration by resident Roman officials. The Romans, in taking over the eastern provinces, interfered as little as possible with local usages, while in the western provinces, the cities, being of more recent origins than those in the east, tended to imitate Rome. A basic principle of Roman administration was the care taken to maintain the privileged status of the Roman citizens. The high degree of illiteracy accentuated the gulf between the ruling classes and the disadvantaged elements of the urban centers, who were unable to read and write their native languages, whether Latin, Greek, or one of the indigenous tongues.

3. Social and economic conditions. The typical Greco-Roman city exhibited a wide spectrum of status and tradition among its people. The conditions of city life emphasized the differences between Roman and non-Roman, Greek and non-Greek, free man, freedman, and slave, differences which were highly visible in terms of speech, dress, status, and social and economic opportunity, or lack of opportunity. The typical city contained a small upper class of landowners, merchants, and manufacturers and a much more numerous population of artisans, slaves, day laborers, and the chronically unemployed or unemployable. Many of those in the lower strata led a marginal existence, with little prospect of improvement. Scholars recently have studied the condition and the activities of minorities such as Jews and Christians and of the groups of the socially, economically, and politically underprivileged and disadvantaged. With this ever-present substratum of discontent, alienation, and opposition to the ruling power, there was continual need for police surveillance.

4. Religious conditions. The variety in the population was matched by the variety of cults and religious practices. While the official religion of

Scala
4. Inside of a workshop—relief, second century A.D.

Rome and the worship of the emperor claimed obligatory allegiance, their observance was in effect an expression of loyalty to the Roman state and of membership in the community of the Empire. Personal religion was found elsewhere, and the typical city offered opportunities for missionaries of various cults and for traveling holy men and philosophers. It was a responsibility of the local authorities to take note of visitors of this type and to see that public order was not disturbed.

5. The city as national and religious symbol. In a world made up of cities, Rome stood as the symbol of national history and Roman success and was the center of the official public religion. In comparable fashion, Jerusalem was a symbol for the Jews. As the Christian community developed, it conceived of itself as a special kind of "city"—that is, a community existing on earth among other kinds of communities, but at the same time possessing a heavenly "city," the New Jerusalem, envisaged as an ideal counterpart of the earthly cities of the time. The importance of true and full citizenship in the earthly cities reinforced the Christians' belief in their own citizenship in a community of a different kind. *See* JEWS, NT ATTITUDES TOWARD[S]; PHILIPPI and PHILIPPI[S]; ROME, CITY OF; ROME, CHRISTIAN MONUMENTS[S]; ROME, EARLY CHRISTIAN ATTITUDES TOWARD[S]; THESSALONICA and THESSALONICA[S]; SLAVERY IN THE NT[S].

Bibliography. M. Hammond, *The City in the Ancient World* (1972), basic comprehensive treatment, with valuable bibliography; J. B. Ward-Perkins, *Cities of Greece and Italy: Planning in Classical Antiquity* (1974), valuable for plans; A. H. M. Jones, *The Cities of the Eastern Roman Provinces* (2nd ed., 1970); A. N. Sherwin-White, *Roman Society and Roman Law in the New Testament* (1963), esp. Lecture 4, "Paul and the Cities," pp. 71-98, and *The Roman Citizenship,* (2nd ed., 1973), important for treatment of citizenship and of status of citizens and aliens in cities; R. MacMullen, *Enemies of the Roman Order: Treason, Unrest, and Alienation in the Empire* (1966), esp. ch. 5, "Urban Unrest," pp. 163-91, and *Roman Social Relations, 50 B.C. to A.D. 284* (1974), which provides insights into social conditions in the Greco-Roman city, without, however, fully utilizing the evidence of the NT; G. W. Bowersock, *Augustus and the Greek World* (1965), deals with new Roman influences on the life of the cities; H. A. Thompson and R. E. Wycherley, *The Agora of Athens: The History, Shape, and Uses of an Ancient City Center,* The Athenian Agora, XIV (1972); N. J. G. Pounds, "The Urbanization of the Classical World," *Annals of the Assoc. of Amer. Geographers,* LIX (1969), 135-57, valuable for statistics and graphic presentations.

G. DOWNEY

***CLEMENT, EPISTLES OF.** *See* APOSTOLIC FATHERS [S] §§2, 3.

***CLOUD. 1. Types.** In the OT the most common word for sky cover is *ʿānān* (ענן), which is used in prose and poetry alike. In many cases the singular clearly designates a composite type of cloud. It was found at very low altitudes, could easily dissolve, and was usually dark. In general the *ʿānān* would seem to correspond to the modern categories of *stratus* or *nimbo-stratus.*

The typical rain cloud was called *ʿābh* (עב). The word occurs almost exclusively in poetical contexts. From a modern point of view *ʿābh* is a term with a rather broad semantic scope. Usually it appears to designate thick rain clouds of the cumulus type: *strato-cumulus, cumulo-nimbus,* and *cumulus* may all have been meant.

The word *š^{e}ḥāqîm* (שחקים) is often used in poetical parallelism with "heaven," but for several reasons it cannot be a synonym of this. In spite of their great altitude, these clouds could bring rain (Job 36:28; cf. Isa. 45:8). They formed a more or less firm structure with a smooth surface (Job 37:18; Prov. 8:28). Because the root *šḥq* means "to pulverize" and the very same word *šaḥaq* denotes a layer of dust in Isa. 40:15, it would seem likely that, notwithstanding its firmness, this type of cloud made a powdery impression. All these data taken together suggest that *š^{e}ḥāqîm* may be equated with *cirro-stratus* or less stable *alto-stratus.*

n^{e}śîʾîm (נשיאים) is a poetical word for towering rain clouds which God "lifts" from under the horizon. Probably the modern equivalent would be *cumulus* or *cumulo-nimbus.*

Usually the word *ʿ^{a}rāphel* (ערפל) is interpreted as "darkness, gloom, murky cloud," but the Ugaritic cognate *ġrpl* clearly suggests something like "fog": "Remove, O Sun, the fog from the mountains" (*Ugaritica* V, RS 24.251:19). The same meaning fits all OT passages involved.

It is doubtful whether the Hebrew word *ʾēdh* (אד) in Gen. 2:6 and Job 36:27 has anything to do with vapor or mist.

2. Vesture of the divine. Everywhere in the ancient Near East the presence of the divine was thought to manifest itself by an awe-inspiring splendor which had to be screened off in order to protect mortal man from its radiance. In the OT, clouds cover Yahweh when he reveals himself (Ps. 18:11 [H 12]; 97:2), especially on Mount Sinai (Exod. 19:16 ff.; 24:15 ff., etc.), and during the Exodus. According to the sources J and E (*see* DOCUMENTS; YAHWIST[S]; ELOHIST[S] §7*b*) God guided his people through the desert in the visible form of a PILLAR OF FIRE AND OF CLOUD. Babylonians and Assyrians used to carry the emblems of their gods on a standard (*imittu*). This word is etymologically related to the Hebrew word for "pillar" (עמוד, *ʿammûdh*). Placed on a chariot, these divine emblems went before the Assyrian armies (*ālikūt* *maḫri,* "forerunners"). Since graven images were forbidden in Israelite religion, it is understandable that in this case the presence of the divine guide was indicated by a pillar of cloud.

In the final, eschatological THEOPHANY clouds again will play their protecting role. This conception may be found already in the OT (Isa. 4:5; Dan. 7:13), but it was fully developed only later in postbiblical Judaism. When Jesus manifests his divine glory, clouds overshadow him (Matt. 17:5; Mark 9:7; Luke 9:34; Acts 1:9), as will be the case when the Son of man reappears (Matt. 24:30; Mark 13:26; Luke 21:27; Rev. 1:7).

3. The Lord of the Clouds. In the Canaanite texts of Ugarit it is the weather-god Baal who commands the clouds (*CTA* 5:V.6-11; 10:II.32-33). One of his stock epithets is *rkb ʿrpt,* "Rider on the Clouds." In the OT God is likewise depicted as riding on the clouds (Deut. 33:26; Isa. 19:1; Ps. 68:33-34 [H 34-35]; 104:3). It is uncertain, however, whether *rkb bʿrbwt* in Ps. 68:4 [H 5] may be equated with Ugar. *rkb ʿrpt* (so RSV). It could be a willful distortion of the pagan epithet. The purported etymological relationship between Ugar./Heb. *ʿnn,* "cloud," and Ugar. *ʿnn,* "servant" (of Baal and other gods), does not exist (*AOAT,* XVI, 129-30).

4. Divination. The Israelites regarded the clouds and their formation in deep awe of Yahweh's creative power (Jer. 10:13; 51:16; Job 35:5; 36:26–37:24). The agriculture of Canaan was totally dependent on rainfall. Therefore rain clouds were intently observed (I Kings 18:44; Eccl. 11:4; Luke 12:54). It seems that the Canaanites, like the Babylonians, inferred even more than the Israelites from the appearance and the course of clouds. This might explain why a derivative verb *ʿnn* II became a designation of soothsaying in Hebrew.

Bibliography. K. Keyssner, "Nimbus," PW, XVII (1936), 591-624; S. Grill, *Die Gewittertheophanie im AT* (2nd ed., 1943); R. B. Y. Scott, "Meteorological Phenomena and Terminology in the OT," *ZAW,* LXIV (1952), 11-25; World Meteorological Organization, *International Cloud Atlas* (1956); R. B. Y. Scott, "Behold, He Cometh with Clouds," *NTS,* V (1958-59), 127-32; J. Jeremias, *Theophanie,* WMANT, X (1965); E. Cassin, *La splendeur divine* (1968); T. W. Mann, "The Pillar of Cloud in the Reed Sea Narrative," *JBL,* XC (1971), 15-30; J. Luzarraga, *Las Tradiciones de la Nube en la Biblia y en el Judaismo Primitivo* (1973).

J. C. DE MOOR

***CNIDUS.** The plan of late Hellenistic, Roman, and Byzantine Cnidus is rapidly being filled out by new excavations begun in 1967. A low and narrow isthmus (where prehistoric Cycladic idols have been found) joins the main body of the Cnidian peninsula to a high point of land sheltering in its lee on either side of the isthmus two fine harbors. The larger harbor on the S must have been the commercial harbor where west- or north-bound ships such as PAUL's (Acts 27:7) could wait for unfavorable weather to abate before continuing their journey beyond the windy cape. On the banks of the harbors were moorings; warehouses for the wine, vinegar, pottery, and medicines produced in the city; market places; small theaters; and a temple of DIONYSUS. On the heights to the E was the sanctuary of Demeter where a statue of the seated goddess and a damaged but beautiful head of a young woman were found. The head might represent the daughter of Demeter, but it has also been taken for an image of Aphrodite. On the highest terrace to the W overlooking both harbors was a round temple which has been identified as the landscaped shrine of Aphrodite Euploia (the Aphrodite of Good Sailing). Praxiteles' frequently copied nude statue of the goddess may have stood here (Pliny, *Natural History* 36.20).

During the Christian period when Cnidus became the seat of a bishop, several churches were constructed. The site of the temple of Dionysus by the commercial harbor became the center of a late fifth-century basilica complex. In the area of the temple of Aphrodite Euploia were found three terra-cotta flasks molded with representations of the Virgin and Child, the Foolish Virgin, and a saint holding the gospels.

Bibliography. I. C. Love, "Preliminary Report of the Excavations at Knidos," *AJA,* LXXII (1968), 137-39; LXXIII (1969), 216-19; LXXIV (1970), 149-55, 170-71; LXXV (1971), 173; LXXVI (1972), 61-76, 181, 393-405; LXXVII (1973), 183-84, 193, 413-24; LXXVIII (1974), 121; D. E. L. Haynes, "Alte Funde neu entdeckt," *Archäologische Gesellschaft zu Berlin 1971/72, Archäologischer Anzeiger* of the *Jahrbuch des deutschen archäologischen Instituts,* LXXXVII (1972), 731-37.

D. BOYD

***COLOSSIANS, LETTER TO THE.** This letter, purportedly from Paul and Timothy to the church at Colossae, is noted for its Christology (esp. 1:15-20) articulated in refutation of certain opponents (esp. 2:6-23).

1. Authorship. The authorship of Colossians (and, consequently, place and date of writing) continues to be disputed. Contributing to this debate are such factors as the peculiar vocabulary, the piling up of words and phrases in a kind of liturgical style, the curious relation to EPHESIANS, and the characteristic theology (e.g., Christ and the church, baptism, creation, reconciliation, and the powers). The pivotal issue in these and other problems is the extent and significance of difference from the acknowledged Pauline epistles.

2. Occasion and purpose. Until recently, debate on the occasion and purpose of Colossians has proceeded within approximately the same perimeters as it has for the last century (*see bibliog.*).

a. The opponents. Most scholars hold that the opponents were divergent members of the Colossian church, to some degree affected by pagan ideas prevalent at the time. A few locate the opponents outside the church. Opinions also differ on whether Gnostic perspectives are a significant part of the teachings this writer opposes. The disagreement stems from differing views of GNOSTICISM itself: Was it a distinct religious movement or simply a widely held world view? Degrees of affinity to Essenism also are generally observed. *See* ESSENES §4; ESSENES[S] §§2*c*, 3; DEAD SEA SCROLLS §§5, 6; DEAD SEA SCROLLS[S] §9.

b. Mystery initiation. Since mystery initiation was first identified as a component of the error at Colossae, most interpreters have concurred, though some few have disagreed. Recent restudy of the data (*see bibliog.*) suggests that there is no sufficient basis for holding that the Colossian Christians submitted to mystery initiation (*see* MYSTERY §§3, 4; GREEK RELIGION AND PHILOSOPHY §§4, 5). Early in this century it was erroneously postulated that in Col. 2:18 ἐμβατεύειν ("taking his stand on") was a technical term for initiation, because it appears in inscriptions found at the sanctuary of the Clarian Apollo. In fact the word was commonly used simply for entering, with a variety of nuances in different contexts.

c. Angel worship. Almost universally scholarship has assumed that the opponents worshiped angels (2:18). Recent study (*see bibliog.*) reopens the possibility seen by Luther and a few others that the opponents witnessed the angels at worship or worshiped with the angels in their visions (Heb. 12:22 ff.; Rev. 4; II Cor. 12; *see* ANGEL §C; VISION). This view has significant impact on one's understanding of the Christology of the opponents.

d. Christology. If the opponents did not worship angels or venerate the cosmic powers, then some characterizations of their false teaching frequently offered by commentators must be questioned, e.g., that Christ was subsumed in and under a cosmic hierarchy, that the powers completed the saving work of Christ, that the principalities had to be placated to make one's way to Christ, or that these spiritual forces somehow assisted one's access to Christ. In fact Colossians offers no clear evidence for any of this and nowhere directly describes the Christology of the opponents. The letter apparently does quote the opponents (2:21), but only their ascetic rules—and presumably the recipients knew as much about the asceticism of the opponents as about their Christology. Thus one is led to ask whether Christology was a prime theological issue among the opponents at Colossae after all. It is possible that some other factor in their teaching is responsible for the christological theme in Colossians, or that the writer develops this theme for his own special purpose. If so, attention must be shifted from the epistolary occasion per se to the purpose of the letter. *See also* CHRISTOLOGY IN THE NT[S] §2*c*.

e. Alternative hypotheses. A hypothesis worth exploring is that the purpose of Colossians is to assure the recipients of their spiritual well-being in the face of the ascetic, visionary practices championed by the opponents. On this hypothesis it is the writer, not the opponents, who gave these matters of piety a christological setting. Other hypotheses will probably be framed as the debate on the occasion and purpose of Colossians continues.

Bibliography. Commentaries: E. Lohse, Hermeneia (1968), the best recent commentary; H. Conzelmann, NTD (10th ed., 1965); F. Mussner, Geistliche Schriftlesung, XII, 1 (1965).

Special studies: F. Francis and W. Meeks, *Conflict at Colossae* (1973), a comprehensive review of Colossian studies including new perspectives; J. E. Crouch, *The Origin and Intention of the Colossian Haustafel, FRLANT,* CIX (1972); J. Lähnemann, *Der Kolosserbrief,* Studien zum NT, III (1971); W. Foerster, "Die Irrlehrer des Kolosserbriefes," *Studia Biblica et Semitica* (1966), 71-80; H. Hegermann, *Die Vorstellung vom Schöpfungsmittler im hellenistischen Judentum und Urchristentum, TU,* LXXXII (1961).

F. O. FRANCIS

CONFIDENCE. *See* BOLDNESS; BOLDNESS[S]; FAITH, FAITHFULNESS IN THE NT[S].

CONFLATE READINGS (OT). The combination of two or more variant readings in the Hebrew text and in the ancient versions of the OT. Conflate readings are also found in the NT, in the Qumran writings, in the biblical quotations in the Apocrypha and rabbinic literature, and possibly in other literatures of the ancient Near East. The phenomenon is also designated by the terms: alternative or double readings, and doublets.

1. Importance for the history of the Hebrew Bible text
2. Two main causes of conflate readings
3. Evidence from the Dead Sea Scrolls
4. Discernment of conflate readings
5. Impact of the transmission process
6. Classification of conflate readings in the MT
7. Original combination readings
8. Conflate readings and tradition combinations
Bibliography

1. Importance for the history of the Hebrew Bible text. Conflate readings present tangible evidence for the existence and transmission in antiquity of divergent textual traditions of Scripture. Some conflate readings must be considered to have originated in the formative period of OT literature, possibly as oral traditions, before the crystallization of definite textual formulations, and certainly before the emergence of a TEXTUS RECEPTUS of either the Hebrew original or the versions. Their preservation resulted from a variety of scribal motivations and processes. They illustrate, to a degree, the flexibility of textual formulations in the early stages of the transmission of biblical literature since they represent parallel or alternative textual traditions. They thus relate to the *Urtext* versus *Vulgärtext* controversy, i.e., to the problem of whether the relative uniformity of the major textual witnesses should be interpreted as reflecting faithfully one original text form or exemplar, or whether it resulted from a progressive selection and weeding out of variant readings, which culminated in the establishment of one officially recognized text form. *See* TEXT, HEBREW, HISTORY OF[S] §1.

2. Two main causes of conflate readings. ***a. Intentional preservation of alternative readings.*** Whenever this could not be achieved by assigning the variants to parallels of the same subject matter, such as in the Former Prophets and Chronicles, or in two versions of one and the same psalm (II Sam. 22 and Ps. 18), conflation was employed. Doublets thus illustrate the scribes' reverence for transmitted alternative readings which were invested with a measure of sacred authority.

b. Insertion of interlinear or marginal notations into the text base. Conflate readings thus give evidence to the fact that the OT text was subjected to processes of deliberate redaction, and at the same time was exposed to the textual hazards which perforce affect a given corpus of literature in the course of MS transmission.

3. Evidence from the Dead Sea Scrolls. *(See* DEAD SEA SCROLLS; DEAD SEA SCROLLS[S].) ***a. Marginal notations.*** Against the MT of Isa. 36:11, דבר־נא אל־עבדיך ארמית, which is supported by the versions, IQIs^{a} exhibits the doublet דברנא עם עבדיך עמנו ארמית. The alternative marginal reading עמנו may be reflected in ἡμᾶς of two Greek *minuscules*. The intrusion of the marginal variant into the text base most probably resulted from the lack of a system of differentiated critical symbols. Thus, the copyist was unable to decide whether the notation עמנו originally was intended to supply a word mistakenly omitted at a previous stage of copying, or as an alternative reading for עבדיך.

b. Interlinear notations. Conflate readings which ensued from the interpolation of an interlinear notation in the text base may be observed in the following instances: (i) In Isa. 41:20 the MT employs a string of four verbs: למען יראו וידעו וישימו וישכילו. The text base of 1QIs^{a} has as the third verb in the row ויבינו, which appears to represent an alternative reading from a different *Vorlage* (Hebrew original), yet mirrored in the Syr. ונתבינון, and probably also in the Gr. ἐννοηθῶσιν. וישימו was then recorded in 1QIs^{a} as a superscription, possibly by a second hand, and subsequently was disqualified by its enclosure within deletion dots. Hypothetically, this situation could have led a later copyist, who disregarded or failed to interpret correctly the deletion symbols, to consider the interlinear וישימו as a restored omission rather than as a variant of ויבינו, and therefore to include it in the text base. This would have resulted in the conflate string of verbs: למען יראו וידעו וישימו ויבינו וישכילו. (ii) Such a process presumably underlies the doublet in Isa. 44:9, ועדיהם הֵׄמָּׄה בל יראו. Here the word המה, marked redundant by the dots, appears to be the truncated notation of a variant reading preserved in the text base of 1QIs^{a}, which later was interlinearily (mis) corrected to conform with the MT:

המה
ועדיהםה בל יראו

4. Discernment of conflate readings. ***a. Comparison of multiple witnesses.*** The recognition of a doublet in the MT or in a version usually arises from a comparison of two or more witnesses to the text. A simple or short reading in one indicates that an expanded reading in the other may constitute a doublet, if the assumedly redundant component is but a reiteration of what already is expressed in the other textual component. Conflation can be most readily established when each component of the doublet has been preserved individually in the textual witnesses collated. In the Hebrew text this can be illustrated by the following examples: (i) In Jer. 52:34, דבר יום ביומו עד יום מותו כל ימי חייו, Gr. renders only the first and the second members of the triplet, while the Hebrew parallel in II Kings 25:30 records only the first and the third: דבר יום ביומו כל ימי חיו. (ii) In Judg. 19:9. הנה נא רפה היום לערוב . . . [הנה חנות היום] one Greek translation, Gr.^{B}, reflects only the bracketed, and Gr.^{A} the unbracketed, reading.

b. Juxtaposition. We may assume that both in the MT of I Kings 21:8 (not found in Gr.^{h} and OL): אל הזקנים ואל החרים [אשר בעירו] הישבים את נבות and of 21:11: אשר הישבים בעירו, the alternative readings הישבים and אשר בעירו were conflated, probably by transfer of marginal notations into the text base.

c. Different syntactical positions. In some doublets the variants were not recorded adjacent to one another but rather in different positions in the syntactical structure, as, e.g., חריה and שריה in Isa. 34:12. In yet other instances, the conflated alternative readings represent nuances in the understanding of a passage or essentially diverging interpretations which may reflect varying connotations of a word or a word cluster, or different linguistic strata *(see* §6*j*i and ii *below*).

5. Impact of the transmission process. Conflation will increase commensurate with the prolongation of the transmission chain and the proliferation of text traditions and MSS which serve as bases for new copies and for translations.

a. Version doublets which reflect conflate readings in the Vorlage. A doublet in a version may faithfully reflect a conflate reading which was already present in the Hebrew *Vorlage,* e.g., Joel 3:1 [H 4:1] בימים ההמה ובעת ההיא which Gr. renders ἐν ταῖς ἡμέραις ἐκείναις καὶ ἐν τῷ καιρῷ ἐκείνῳ. Of special interest are doublets in a version which appear to be related to or derived from an extant extra-Masoretic *Vorlage:* The eight-line Greek rendition of Deut. 32:43 results from the conflation of four sets of doublets. The individual variants of each line on the one hand reflect the MT and on the other, at least in part, alternative readings found in a Qumran fragment or mirrored in the Samar. and in the Targ. (cf. also §4*a*ii *above*).

b. Conflation by the transmitter. A doublet may be evidence of the transmitter's recalling and combining parallel expressions, or his collating different traditions: (i) In II Sam. 20:19, אנכי שלמי אמוני ישראל, Gr. conflates the rendition of שלמי by ἐγώ εἰμι εἰρηνικὰ with ἃ ἐθέντο, reflecting a reading derived from שים, which interchanges with שלם in several other instances (cf. I Sam. 2:20: ישם with Gr.: ἀποτείσαι=4QSam.: ישלם). (ii) Similarly, Deut. 32:19, וירא יהוה וינאץ, 4QPhyl. ויקנא, Gr.: καὶ ἐζήλωσεν καὶ παρωξύνθη.

c. Conflation of different interpretations. A doublet may arise from the combination of different interpretations of a common text base: (i) Jer. 4:29, בעבים and Gr.: εἰς τὰ σπήλαια καὶ εἰς τὰ ἄλση, one rendition taking the Hebrew to mean "cave" (cf. I Kings 7:46=II Chr. 4:17), and one to mean "thicket." (ii) II Sam. 12:30, ויקח את עטרת מלכם, Gr.: καὶ ἔλαβεν τὸν στέφανον Μελχὸλ (=מִלְכֹּם) τοῦ βασιλέως (מַלְכָּם) αὐτῶν.

d. Conflation of independent renditions. Two independent original renditions may be conflated by a copyist in a translation doublet, as, e.g., Judg. 20:15, איש בחור, Gr.^{B}: ἄνδρες ἐκλεκτοί, Gr.^{A}: +νεανίσκοι. Such conflations are especially numerous in revisions of the original Greek translation, such as Lucian.

6. Classification of conflate readings in the MT. In the following arrangement, a system of progressive linguistic complexity and textual comprehensiveness has been adopted. Attention is given to the position of the alternative readings in the structure of the sentence or the passage. (For a more detailed classification, consult S. Talmon, *Textus,* I, 144-84.)

a. Hybrid readings. Conflation of two possible synonymous readings, sometimes of the Qere-Kethibh type, in one word. These may be ascribed to a late stage in the standardization of the text. (i) II Kings 15:16, ההרותיה, combining determination by means of the definite article, as in Gr., with determination by means of a pronomial suffix, as in the Targ. (ii) Josh. 7:21, האהלי (cf. Gr. and Targ.). (iii) Isa. 51:9: החצבת+המחצת=המחצבת (*see* I. L. Seeligmann, VTSup, I, 109).

b. Juxtaposed grammatical alternatives. (i) Jer. 4:12, [מאלה] רוח מלא conflates מלא, which takes רוח as a masculine noun, with מלאה (transposed letters and missing in Gr.), which takes it as a feminine noun (cf. Job. 1:19). (ii) Zech. 6:12-13, ובנה את היכל [והוא יבנה את היכל יהוה] יהוה. The second reading, with the alternative imperfect יבנה for the perfect ובנה, is not extant in Gr.

c. Graphic interchanges. (i) II Chr. 28:26, [וכל דרכיו] ויתר דבריו. The MT doublet resulting from an interchange of דבר and דרכ is reflected in the versions but differs from the standard annalistic terminology (cf. I Chr. 29:29; II Chr. 9:29 and 12:15). (ii) Ps. 45:7 [H 8] אלהים אלהיך. The doublet, reflected in the versions, probably conflates alternative readings resulting from confusion of the *mēm* and the *kaph. See* Text, OT §D2*a*.

d. Spelling variants. (i) Jer. 9:16: . . . ותבואינה [ותבואנה]. The second reading is not rendered by Gr. and probably should be considered a marginal variant. (ii) Ps. 45:8 [H 9]: מני . . . מן. The recognition of the conflation makes textual emendation unnecessary.

e. Juxtaposed synonymous readings. (i) Josh. 13:17: ובית בעל מעון conflates בעל מעון (Num. 32:38; Ezek. 25:9; I Chr. 5:8) with בית מעון (Jer. 48:23). This case, however, may be an example of the break-up of stereotype phrases. (ii) Jer. 41:3: [את גדליהו] אשר היו אתו. Gr. (48:3) and the parallel in II Kings 25:25 (MT, Gr.) do not present the bracketed alternative.

f. Juxtaposed synonymous phrases. (i) The first stich of Lev. 14:31 is an alternative reading of the last stich of vs. 30, which is lacking in Gr. and Syr. (*see* KJV). (ii) I Sam. 14:25 and 26 may be conflated alternatives.

g. Variant syntactical arrangement of words and phrases. In Ps. 10:9, two variants which differed in sentence structure were conflated with the verb preceding or succeeding the noun (cf. II Sam. 17:28; I Sam. 9:13[b]; I Kings 10:28[b] [=II Chr. 1:16]). In most of these cases, one of the variants was not rendered by one or the other ancient version. In many instances of doublets, the conflated variants are distinguished by differences in word order coupled with the substitution of synonyms.

h. Complex doublets. These arise when variants of several syntactical components that exemplify diverse textual phenomena are conflated in one verse. Such conflate readings seem to underlie, e.g., the overloaded text of II Kings 5:18; 11:13 (cf. II Chr. 23:12, MT and Gr.); 22:5 (cf. II Chr. 34:10).

i. Conflation of different traditions. At times the conflated variants represent different versions of one tradition. (Such instances, however, could have resulted from the insertion of a secondary gloss into the text, rather than from a combination of pristine variant readings.) (i) I Sam. 22:6: [ברמה] ושאול יושב בגבעה תחת האשל presumably conflates two local traditions. (ii) II Sam. 15:24. Inserted into the tradition which reports Zadok the priest to have been in charge of the ark at David's flight before Absalom is a second version which appears to have mentioned another prominent priest, Abiathar (ויעל אביתר) in that context.

j. Conflation of reading with gloss. In individual cases it is difficult to decide whether a doublet arose from the conflation of two variants or from the combination of a reading with a gloss. In the following instances, the second possibility is the more probable, since we seem to be concerned with a Hebrew equivalent (bracketed) placed next to a loanword, or with the combination of an archaic word with a better known synonym: (i) Ezra 5:8 and 6:4, גלל [אבן]. Akkadian *galalu* equals Hebrew אבן="stone" (*CAD,* V, 11). (ii) Judg. 9:30: זבל [שר] העיר. Here זבל could well be the Canaanite equivalent of the Hebrew שר= "prince," "ruler," and not a personal name. זבל is known in this connotation from Ugaritic literature as a title of Baal, and also as a component of the biblical theophoric name איזבל.

7. Original combination readings. The conflate readings discussed in §6*i*, which may represent different accounts of one and the same episode, point to an aspect of this textual phenomenon which requires special attention. Scholars tend to characterize as conflate, i.e., expanded, any text which is known also in a short or pristine form in a version or MS. Even where such evidence is altogether missing, they often emend a supposedly secondary conflate reading to simplify it on the basis of meter, or even mere impressionistic stylistic considerations. This appreciation of conflate readings has its repercussions in much of biblical textual studies and exegesis. Since the discovery of the Hebrew fragments of Jeremiah from Qumran Cave IV, it has played an important role in the formulation of the theory which holds that these fragments, like Gr., which is about one eighth shorter than the MT, represent a shorter Hebrew text of the book which had been less "contaminated" by conflation than the MT. This theory is forcefully argued by Cross and his school, especially by Janzen. While the theory as such is well founded, a caveat should be sounded against the tendency to view a fuller text by definition as redundant, and routinely to judge double expressions as conflate readings. The apparent conflate text sometimes—indeed often—appears to represent an original reading, i.e., a formulation which should be ascribed to the author rather than to a reviser, redactor, or copyist, while the shorter, seemingly simple reading may have resulted from a reductionist predisposition of later generations. "Doubling," like reiteration, is not solely a textual phenomenon but also evidences a basic stylistic mood of biblical literature.

a. In a literary source. An apparent conflate reading may in fact echo a literary source in which the two components were already coupled, and which the author to whom the conflation is mistakenly attributed consciously takes up: In Jer. 29:23, ואנכי הוידע ועד, Gr.: καὶ ἐγὼ μάρτυς, does not render הוידע, probably to be read היודע, nor the immediately following copula. The resulting suggestion (*see* Janzen, *HTR,* LVII, 439) has been that the MT conflates here the variant expressions for "witness," i.e., היודע and עד. However, the suspected doublet probably echoes a similar phrase in Lev. 5:1, והוא עד או ראה או ידע, where the combination עד-ידע is reflected in the versions and we have no reason to doubt its originality. The assumed dependence of Jer. 29:23 on Lev. 5:1 suggests that the shorter reading in Gr. evidences a reductionist tendency of the translator who, like modern scholars, erroneously suspected the MT to contain a conflate reading.

b. As a stylistic device. At times, what appears on the surface to be a doublet caused by textual hazards or the conflation of synonymous variants, in fact may mirror a stylistic device by which an author consciously and intentionally combined expressions which he used alternatively in a given context. The literary unit in question can vary from a fairly short pericope to an extensive block of materials, and the combination reading can be used at the beginning, in the middle, or at the end of the unit. Such transition or summary combinations constitute tangible evidence of the interconnection of the history of the Bible text and biblical stylistics. (i) The MT reading in Deut. 12:5, לשום את שמו שם לשכנו, could readily be taken as an early conflate reading which is retained by all versions. However, further analysis makes it probable that the author introduced by prolepsis the two alternative verbs that he was to employ from this point on in reference to the sanctuary as the abode of God. In vs. 12:11, the term שכן is used, whereas in vs. 12:21 שום is employed. In later passages in Deuteronomy, the two verbs serve alternatively (cf. 14:23; 16:2, 6, 11 and 26:2 with vs. 14:24). (ii) In Jer. 44:3: ללכת לקטר לעבד לאלהים אחרים, the author may have intentionally combined the phrase לעבד לאלהים אחרים, which he uses eight times before the occurrence in the double expression, with לקטר, which is subsequently employed in the same context nine times more in ch. 44, but appears only infrequently in the first part of the book. (iii) At the end of the Gibeonites episode, Josh. 9:27: ויתנם . . . לעדה ולמזבח יהוה combines two significant terms which are employed alternatively in what are taken to be two parallel strands in the narrative (cf. vs. 21 with vss. 22-23).

8. Conflate readings and tradition combinations. In the last example, the analysis of what externally may be considered a conflate reading bears directly on basic and more comprehensive issues of biblical research. The apparent doublet here combines traditions which are ascribed to two distinguishable sources of biblical historiography. While conflate readings usually are discussed within the framework of LOWER CRITICISM, the proper context for the analysis of combined narrative traditions is the field of HIGHER CRITICISM (*see also* SOURCE CRITICISM, OT[S]). The conflux of textual and literary aspects of doubling or conflation which emerges from the foregoing discussion points up the overall importance of these phenomena for biblical research.

Bibliography. J. Herrmann, "Stichwortglossen im Buche Ezechiel," *OLZ,* XI (1908), 280-82, and "Stichwortglossen im AT," *OLZ,* XIV (1911), 200-204; A. Rahlfs, "Lucians Rezension der Königbücher," *Septuaginta Studien,* III (1911), 361-658; S. R. Driver, *Notes on the Hebrew Text and the Topography of the Books of Samuel* (1913), lv-lvii; O. H. Boström, *Alternative Readings in the Hebrew of the Books of Samuel* (1918). F. Delitzsch, *Die Lese- und Schreibfehler im AT* (1920), 132-43; J. de Groot, "Alternatieflezingen in Jesaja 24," *NTS,* XXII (1975), 153-58; B. M. Bellas, *L'importance des traductions doubles dans le texte des Septante* (1936); R. Gordis, *The Biblical Text in the Making* (1937), pp. 4-43; F. Zimmermann, "The Perpetuation of Variants in the MT," *JQR,* XXXIV (1943-44), 459-74; J. W. Wevers, "Double Readings in the Books of Kings," *JBL,* LXV (1946), 307-10; P. W. Skehan, "A Fragment of the 'Song of Moses' from Qumran," *BASOR,* 136 (1954), 12-15; S. Talmon, "A Case of Abbreviation Resulting in Double Readings," *VT,* IV (1954), 206-08, "Double Readings in the MT," *Textus,* I (1960), 144-84, "Synonymous Readings in the Textual Tradition of the OT," *Scripta Hierosolymitana,* VIII (1961), 335-83, "I Sam. XV:32—A Case of Conflated Readings?" *VT,* XI (1961), 456-57, "Aspects of the Textual Transmission of the Bible in the Light of Qumran Manuscripts," *Textus,* IV (1964), 95-132, "The OT Text," in *Cambridge History of the Bible,* I (1970), 182-91, and "The Textual Study of the Bible, A New Outlook," in F. M. Cross, Jr. and S. Talmon, *Qumran and the History of the Biblical Text* (1975); A. Jirku, "Doppelte Überlieferungen im Mythus und im Epos von Ugarit," *ZDMG,* CX (1960), 20-25; R. G. Boling, "Some Conflate Readings in Joshua-Judges," *VT,* XVI (1966), 293-98; J. G. Janzen, "Double Readings in the Text of Jeremiah," *HTR,* LVII (1967), 433-47, and *Studies in the Text of Jeremiah,* Harvard Semitic Monographs, 6 (1973); S. Jellicoe, *The Septuagint and Modern Study* (1968), *see* "Conflations, Doublets"; K. Elliger, "Dubletten im Bibeltext," in *A Light Unto My Path, OT Studies in Honor of Jacob Myers* (1974), pp. 131-39. S. TALMON

CONFLICT STORY. *See* SAYINGS OF JESUS, FORM OF[S] §6.

CONQUEST. *See* CANAAN, CONQUEST AND SETTLEMENT OF[S].

***CONSCIENCE. 1. In the Corinthian letters.** The earliest references to conscience in the NT are in connection with a controversy in the Corinthian church. A Gnostic faction held that the conscience of the weak should be strengthened in such a manner as to free them to eat meat which had been sacrificed to pagan idols (I Cor. 8). Their opponents held that one should refrain from eating such meat out of regard for the conscience of those Gentile Christians who were still bothered by the idea that eating it would mean communion with demonic forces (I Cor. 10:23 ff.). For these people "conscience" meant the uncontrollable, painful knowledge that a deed was wrong. The Gnostics, however, seem to have identified conscience with the spirit-self which must be forcibly educated for one to be saved. These radicals had embarked on a campaign of ridicule and enticement, forcing those caught by the conscience lag to violate their conscience until they were free.

Paul's discussion of these issues results in a new doctrine of autonomy. Even if the "weak" are theologically wrong in fearing the idols and restricting the goodness of meat, they should be encouraged to avoid pangs of conscience. Their "weakness" consisted not in a lack of will power, but in a lagging assimilation of the knowledge (I Cor. 8:1, 7) that the idols were powerless (I Cor. 8:4-6). To act against conscience, even though it be misguided because of prior conditioning (I Cor. 8:7), was to risk the loss of integrity and the destruction of conscience, the guardian of that integrity (I Cor. 8:7, 11, 12). To educate the conscience requires a gradual, indirect approach of exercising freedom while avoiding pangs (I Cor. 10:23-29). This may require temporary abnegation of freedom on the part of the "strong" to encourage the "weak" to avoid anything that would cause pangs of conscience. Paul's concern in I Cor. 10:29*b*-30 is that freedom not be defamed by provoking others to violate conscience and is a repudiation of the Gnostic campaign. This does not imply a permanent disavowal of freedom, because his own strategy was to free the "weak" to eat meat "to the glory of God" (I Cor. 10:31).

This doctrine provides the possibility for a community to live in mutual respect and integrity with differing conscience structures. Its premises are the recognition of the spontaneously negative function of conscience and the grounding of its authority in personal integrity rather than in divine agencies; only then can it retain autonomy even when wrong, while continuing to grow as moral perspective enlarges.

In later Corinthian correspondence "conscience" is used in an increasingly Gnostic fashion, as an agency of knowledge and judgment (II Cor. 4:2; 5:11). Paul probably wanted to facilitate debate and win the congregation back from the lures of the traveling missionaries (II Cor. 11:4-15). In II Cor. 1:12 Paul reverts to the more typical Hellenistic-Jewish usage (cf. I Cor. 4:4). Here conscience is an independent witness to Paul's integrity, although its erring, finite quality contrasts with eschatological certitude.

2. In Romans. In Rom. 13:5 submission to the state is recommended in order to avoid arousing conscience pangs. Since one knows ahead of time that disrespectful actions would arouse such pain, one can act to avoid it. Conscience here retains its basic significance as the "conscience pang" rather than the agency of conscience. In Rom. 2:15 and 9:1, however, it is the autonomous agency which marks transgressions against an internalized code. In the latter instance, Paul for the first time explicitly relates conscience to Christ and the Holy Spirit, claiming full harmony with revelation. This does not imply that conscience is controlled by the Spirit or witnesses for the Spirit. As an independent witness it simply points in this instance in the same direction as revelation; Paul is playing down its normally erring character in order to strengthen his argument.

3. In Hebrews. The Epistle to the Hebrews stresses the role of conscience as the painful knowledge of guilt which must be overcome by redemption. The legalistic cult is powerless to deal with the burden (9:9; 10:2), but the atoning work of Christ is capable of setting conscience free (9:14; 10:22). The evangelical substance of Hebrews' approach is manifest in the expression "purify your conscience from dead works to serve the living God" (9:14); the definition of these terms in 6:1 and the argument in ch. 9 indicate that "dead works" are the self-justifying acts of legalism whose burden grace overcomes. Although the concept of conscience is integrated into the salvation process, the results are not pictured in complacent terms: that the author and his colleagues "are sure" they have a "clear conscience" in 13:18 is not a claim of final certainty but a basis for requesting prayer in a problematic situation.

4. Elsewhere in the NT. I Peter 3:21 portrays the erasure of guilty conscience through BAPTISM, which places the believer under the lordship of Christ. The difficult term ἐπερώτημα is therefore best rendered as in the RSV: baptism is "an *appeal* to God *for* a clear conscience." The conscience thus cleansed by grace is to be kept intact by "gentleness and reverence" toward the authorities even during persecution, lest a conscience-pricking spirit of rebellion confuse the cause for which the church is suffering (3:14-16). The same counsel is offered in 2:19, though the word "conscience" (KJV) bears here the sense of "the shared knowledge" of God which informs the church of the meaning of its persecution.

A moralistic domestication of conscience is visible in Acts 23:1; 24:16; and II Tim. 1:3. That these references imply conformity to a code can be seen in I Tim. 1:5 and in the counterexamples of the heretics referred to in I Tim. 4:2 and Tit. 1:15, whose libertinism allegedly revealed an anesthetized conscience. By correlating conscience directly with faith, understood in a dogmatic sense (I Tim. 1:19; 3:9), these materials eliminate the possibility of respecting alternative conscience structures. The process of coercing the conscience begins here to make its way through Christian history.

Bibliography. C. A. Pierce, *Conscience in the NT*, SBT, XV (1955); J. Stelzenberger, *Syneidesis im NT*, Abhandlungen z. Moraltheologie, I (1961); C. Maurer, "συνείδησις," *TDNT*, VII (1971), 899-919; M. Coune, "Le Problem des Idolothytes et l'éducation de la *Syneidêsis*," XI (1963), 497-534; C. K. Barrett, "Things Sacrificed to Idols," *NTS*, XI (1965-66), 138-53; W. Schmithals, *Gnosticism in Corinth* (1966); R. Jewett, *Paul's Anthropological Terms*, AGJU, X (1971), includes a complete account of the scholarly debate.

R. JEWETT

COPTIC LANGUAGE. The last direct descendant of the ancient Egyptian spoken by the pharaohs; it is the final stage of a language whose history can be traced in written records for more than four thousand years.

Long before the Christian era, Coptic was spoken by the native Egyptian population, and eventually further S along the Sudanese Nile. It did not receive a standard notation, however, until about A.D. 200, when the Bible began to be translated. The surviving literature is almost exclusively Christian in content. Coptic was written in a mixed alphabet of Greek and demotic (ultimately hieroglyphic) characters. It contained a high proportion of naturalized Greek vocabulary along with inherited Egyptian stock; its grammar, however, was virtually independent of Greek.

As a literary medium Coptic survived until the fourteenth century, but as a truly living language, not much beyond the Arab conquest of Egypt (A.D. 641). A few speakers were still reported as late as the seventeenth century; thereafter Coptic totally died out, having been replaced for all secular purposes by Arabic. The Egyptian Monophysite church today sings some short passages of the liturgy in Coptic. The Gospel may also be recited in Coptic, but must be followed by the Arabic version since Coptic is no longer understood. The liturgical pronunciations are undoubtedly modern, being heavily influenced by Arabic and Modern Greek. Patriotic attempts to revive Coptic as a spoken language, begun in the late nineteenth century by Claudius (Ikladios) Labib, Eryan Muftah, and others, have borne little fruit, although encouraged by the church. Less than two hundred persons from the educated classes of Cairo and Alexandria have now learned to converse in modern (revived) Coptic, Bohairic dialect. But Coptic has not re-emerged as a medium of literature, and shows no signs of doing so.

"Coptic" is a modern word, the Europeanized form of Arabic *qubṭī*, which in turn comes from Greek αἰγύπτιος, "E-*gypt*-ian." But the ancient Copts called themselves Ⲛ̄ⲢⲘ̄Ⲛ̄ⲔⲎⲘⲈ ən-rəm-ən-kā′mĕ, "people of the Black Land," that is, Egyptians; and their language, tmənt-rəm-ən-kā′mĕ, "the characteristic of the people of the Black Land." Coptic (called simply the language of the Egyptians, οἱ κατοικοῦντες Αἴγυπτον) is mentioned in Acts 2:10 as one of the languages spoken after Pentecost. Coptic is not the language of the so-called Coptic Church of Ethiopia.

1. Proto-Coptic; adoption of the alphabet
2. Dialects
   a. Principal dialects
      i. Sahidic
      ii. Bohairic
   b. Minor dialects
      i. Fayyumic
      ii. Achmimic
      iii. Subachmimic
      iv. Oxyrhynchite
      v. Dialect P
3. Sounds and notation
4. Grammar

Bibliography

1. Proto-Coptic; adoption of the alphabet. Coptic directly descends from Late Egyptian as spoken in the sixteenth century B.C. After being adopted as the official administrative language of Egypt (since the New Kingdom, 1570 B.C.) Late Egyptian remained a conservatively written and increasingly artificial mode of expression, while the spoken idiom continued to develop and drift away from it. The demotic language, attested from 715 B.C.-A.D. 470, was an equally artificial, "literary" medium, being a later offshoot of Late Egyptian. Thus in the centuries preceding the invention of the Coptic alphabet, everyday spoken Egyptian no longer had a corresponding written form.

In 332 B.C. Alexander of Macedon conquered Egypt and established a Greek-speaking administration (*see* EGYPT §2*h*); Egyptian was thus forever doomed to remain the secondary language of the country. Many Egyptians learned Greek, especially among the middle and lower classes of the Delta; also a few Greeks learned spoken Egyptian. From the mid-third century B.C. comes the earliest surviving transcription of spoken Egyptian (or Proto-Coptic) words in the infinitely superior Greek alphabet: a Greek-Coptic glossary (Papyrus Heidelberg 414), written by a Greek. We should not imagine this was the first of such attempts, but further documentation is scarce. In the second century A.D. we find imperfectly transcribed horoscopes, magical spells, and mummy labels (in "Old Coptic").

The invention of an adequate alphabet and normative spelling system, as well as the formulation of a normative grammar and style, must be credited to the church. No doubt it formed part of a missionary program for the Egyptian countryside, organized in the episcopal reigns of Demetrius of Alexandria (A.D. 189-232) and his successors.

For propagandists of the new religion the advantages of substituting simple alphabetic transcription in place of the complicated and imperfect Egyptian scripts was obvious. Literacy would no longer be the exclusive possession of the conservative elite; the gospel could be read not only to, but by, the people; the language of the church would be the spoken idiom of daily life. Furthermore, in the struggle with heretics recourse could be made to a fixed, authoritative scripture that could be read and understood by all.

The date of the Coptic Bible, the earliest piece of Coptic literature, is uncertain. It must precede the conversion of St. Anthony (*ca.* A.D. 270), who entered the faith after hearing Matthew read in Coptic in a village church. Our earliest biblical MS perhaps dates from the same century. The monastic *Rule* of Pachomius (*ca.* 321) requires entering monks to read the scriptures in Coptic.

Because Egyptian Christianity maintained its intellectual center in Alexandria until the sixth century, almost all the original theological literature of Egypt was composed in Greek rather than Coptic. After the Arab conquest Arabic began to be used. Thus Coptic literature consists almost entirely of translations from Greek.

2. Dialects. Coptic was not a single language but a group of dialects each descended from a much older dialect of Egyptian. At least seven have substantial literary attestation (*see* Table 1).

Because the place where most Coptic MSS were copied, or even discovered, is now unknown, the centers of some dialects are not certain. However, their relative positions can be scientifically reconstructed: those that share the greatest number of

Table 1

COPTIC LITERARY DIALECTS

Name	Center
Bohairic	Western Delta and Nitria (Wadi en-Natrun)
Fayyumic	Arsinoite Nome (Fayyum Oasis)
Sahidic (Sa'idic)	Memphis (Cairo) to Heracleopolis (Helwan); possibly Thebes (Luxor)
Oxyrhynchite	around Oxyrhynchus (Behnasah)
Subachmimic	around Lycopolis (Assyut)?
Achmimic	Panopolis (Akhmim)—Thebes (Luxor)—Syene (Asswan)?
Dialect P	Thebes (Luxor)

distinguishing characteristics (isoglosses) must have existed side by side; those that share the least must have been farthest apart, etc. Other kinds of evidence then tentatively indicate where the absolute boundaries were: the historical geography of the country; nonliterary documents (graffiti, etc.) found *in situ;* modern pronunciation of Arabic place names based on older Coptic names; medieval reports; etc.

The evidence is partly self-contradictory. The relative position of Sahidic should be next to Bohairic, Fayyumic, and Oxyrhynchite, the three with which it has the most in common. But the dialect of a fourth-century papyrus codex (Papyrus Bodmer 6, "Dialect P"), when compared with nonliterary documents from Thebes, now suggests that the early dialect of Thebes was a form of Sahidic.

a. Principal dialects. i. *Sahidic* is the most important. By the fourth century A.D. Sahidic had spread to become the common "literary" language of the Nile Valley, and began to be written in a standardized spelling and style ("Standard Sahidic") such as minor dialects never attained. Sahidic's success as a national dialect depended upon the many features it shared with the local dialects and the small number unique to itself—a neutrality that facilitated comprehension and imitation. Speakers of other dialects learned Sahidic with greater or lesser correctness, depending upon their education. Many MSS contain Sahidic forms mixed unpredictably with those of a minor dialect; this probably resulted from dialectal bilingualism of the writers and from their imperfect schooling in Standard Sahidic. Among such mixed MSS are the "Sahidic" codices of the Gnostic library of Nag Hammadi (*see* NAG HAMMADI[S]), probably written by speakers of other dialects trying to imitate Standard Sahidic (with spellings that are often Sahidic; and syntax, diction, and vocabulary that are not).

The entire Bible (LXX and NT) was eventually translated into Sahidic. The earliest version dates from before A.D. 270. The MSS attest more than one Sahidic translation of certain books, now apparently conflated in the transmission. There was repeated revision against the Greek.

Most original Coptic literature (Pachomius, Shenute, etc.) was composed in Sahidic. It was the chief and official language of monasticism and nondualist Christianity. Also many nonliterary texts survive (from the early Arab period).

ii. *Bohairic* succeeded Sahidic as the ecclesiastical dialect about the eleventh century; Coptic was then a dead or dying language. Earlier, Bohairic was a dialect—probably a minor one—of the Western Delta and Nitria. The standardized, classical biblical version is almost exclusively attested in late MSS (textual critics often have to resort to thirteenth-century copies). This version is sometimes said to date from the fourth century, on the supposition that the early biblical MSS in Fayyumic were translated from it (*but see* §*bi below*).

The center of Bohairic literature and our principal source of nonliturgical texts in modern times is the library of the Monastery of St. Macarius in Nitria, patriarchal residence from the sixth to the eleventh centuries. After its destruction in A.D. 817 the library was reconstructed over a period of centuries, partly by translating Sahidic literature into Bohairic (the biblical version excepted). Apart from five non-Standard texts, the earliest surviving MS dates from A.D. 830.

b. Minor dialects. These are attested by very early MSS and, except for Fayyumic, died out as literary languages by the seventh century, presumably being replaced by Sahidic. Many of the biblical texts are translated from early Sahidic (and possibly Bohairic) versions, not directly from the Greek. This does not necessarily diminish their ultimate value as witnesses to the Greek text. Bohairic began as a minor dialect.

i. *Fayyumic* is richly attested by fragmentary literary and nonliterary texts (fourth-eleventh centuries). The entire Bible may have been translated, certain books from Sahidic, others possibly from Bohairic. But the status of the texts that coincide with the Bohairic version is uncertain; it is possible that parts of the classical Bohairic Bible were actually transposed from an early Fayyumic version at a date that is hard to determine.

ii. *Achmimic* MSS date from as early as the third century and not later than the fifth. Only a few biblical books were translated, probably all from Sahidic. Some Subachmimic texts also exhibit influence of this dialect. Although graffiti at Akhmim and nonliterary texts at Thebes show Achmimic traits, the center of diffusion remains uncertain.

iii. *Subachmimic,* the most important minor dialect, was peculiarly associated with GNOSTICISM. It spread considerably, rivaling Sahidic as a dialectally neutral, literary language. The center of diffusion is uncertain; the dialect was never standardized. Subachmimic is attested only in the fourth-fifth centuries. Its early demise as a literary language undoubtedly resulted from an intimate connection with religious movements suppressed about the time of the last known texts. The literature is almost entirely dualist or heretical: (*a*) Manichean texts (approximately four thousand

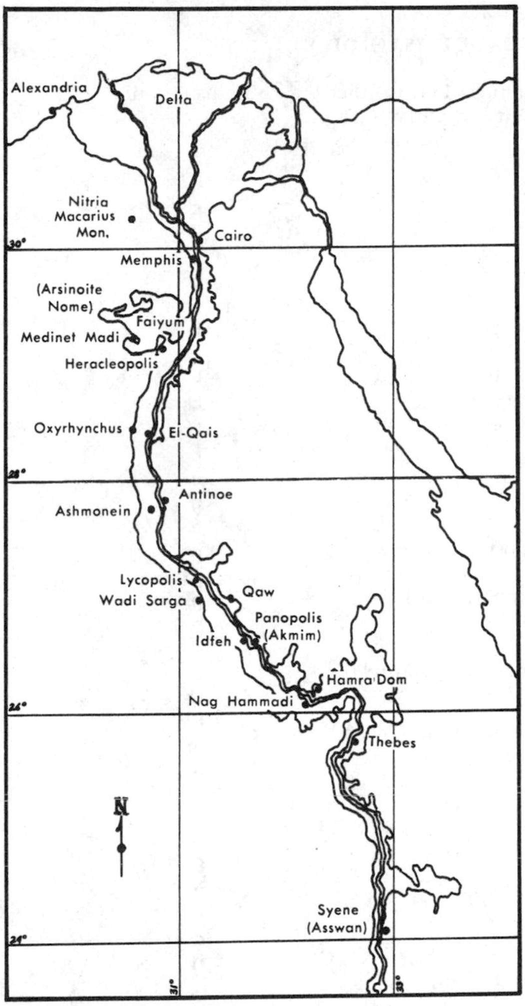

Coptic Dialect Locations

pages), now partly lost (*see* MANICHEISM); (*b*) Acts of Paul (*see* PAUL, ACTS OF); (*c*) John (translated from Sahidic), a text favored by Gnostics; (*d*) a letter on the Melitian schism; (*e*) Nag Hammadi codices CG I (GTr, OnRes, etc.), X, and part of XI; fragments of (*f*) apocryphal acts (Gnostic?); (*g*) the Gnostic OnOrgWld, also found (in impure Sahidic) at Nag Hammadi (CG II *5*, XIII *2**); (*h*) an anti-Manichean tract; (*i*) Hebrews. Other Nag Hammadi texts (ApocryJn, GTh, OnOrgWld, etc.) are translations into impure Sahidic by native speakers of Subachmimic.

The places where Subachmimic MSS have been discovered indicate its wide diffusion: Medinet Madi, El-Qais, Ashmonein, Antinoe, Hamra Dom (opposite Nag Hammadi); nonliterary evidence comes from Qaw, Ashmonein, and Idfeh. *See* map.

iv. *Oxyrhynchite* is the least known dialect (the first important text was published in 1974). The MSS, dating from the third-sixth centuries, come from not only Oxyrhynchus but also Wadi Sarga near Assyut. Thus Oxyrhynchite must have coexisted with Subachmimic and Sahidic during the fourth and fifth centuries, and its influence can be looked for in impure MSS of those dialects. A type showing Fayyumic or Bohairic influence is also known. The entire NT and at least part of the OT seem to have been translated.

v. *Dialect P* (*"Theban"*), *see* §2 *3rd paragraph.*

3. Sounds and notation. The dialects varied slightly in the number and type of phonemes they distinguished. Sahidic for example had twenty-four phonemes (seventeen consonantal, seven vocalic). These were notated by the twenty-four Greek letters, using classical rather than Koine values, and seven new letters based upon demotic signs. Of these letters eight represented no particular sound of their own: ⲝ ⲭ ⲯ ⲫ ⲑ ϯ were merely notations of ⲕⲥ, ⲕϩ, ⲡⲥ, etc. (*see* Table 2) and appeared only in certain words, mostly Greek; ⲅ, ⲇ, ⲍ, used for the traditional spelling of Greek words, had the sounds of ⲕ, ⲧ, ⲥ. The glottal stop ['] (Hebrew *'aleph* א) was notated in Sahidic by doubling the preceding vowel, ⲧⲟⲟⲧϥ, *to'tf*. The vowels *ōō* (ⲟⲩ) and *ē* probably had consonantal counterparts *w, y, ōō* (like *w*) was notated either by ⲟⲩ or ⲩ, according to complicated spelling rules; similarly *ē* (like y) = either ⲉⲓ or ⲓ.

Many Coptic syllables contained no vowel. In such syllables one of the consonants functioned "vocalically" to form the resonant peak of the syllable: cf. English *government*—gŭ'vrn-mnt, or Coptic ⲙⲛⲧⲣⲙⲛϩⲏⲧ—m*n*t-r*m*-*n*-hāt'. In Coptic MSS individual words were not separated by blank spaces, and so to faciliate the division of such strings of consonant letters into syllables, a stroke (or dot) was written above any "vocalic" consonant or its entire syllable: ⲙⲛ̄ⲧⲣⲙ̄ⲛ̄ϩⲏⲧ = mənt-rəm-ən-hāt'. Thus every written syllable contained either a vowel letter or a supralinear mark. Bohairic and Achmimic each had an additional letter (ϧ and ⳉ); dialect P, attested by a single MS, was notated in a unique mixture of demotic and Greek characters.

4. Grammar. Although the Egyptian verbal system originally resembled Semitic with its triconsonantal roots, such a system no longer operates in Coptic. The infinitive is conjugated by placing before it two elements, namely: (1) a base indicating the tense, to which is suffixed (2) the subject (pronoun or noun)—e.g., *a-f-sōtəm*, "he listened" (*a* = past tense base, *f* = "he," *sōtəm* = "listen"). Thus the base, rather than the infinitive, is inflected in conjugation.

The repertory of tenses includes a simple future ("he is going to listen") and a modal one ("he might listen" or "he shall listen!"); past progressive and past nonprogressive are formally distinct ("he was listening" versus "he listened" or "has listened"). Likewise, progressive present and aoristic present ("I am listening" versus "I listen" [as a matter of habit, ability, etc.]). Not only tenses, but also several kinds of clause subordination, are indicated by bases: "*when* he had listened" (*ntere*-f-sōtəm); "*until* he listens" (*shant*-f-sōtəm); etc.

There are four sentence patterns, distinguished by which set of pronouns is used in them, by the parts of speech that may appear as predicate, the

Table 2
THE COPTIC ALPHABET (SAHIDIC)

(a) Greek letters	Approximate pronunciation in the Sahidic dialect, third century A.D.	Transliteration
ⲁ	ŏ) “box”)	a
ⲃ	between *b* and *v*	b
ⲅ	exactly like ⲕ	g
ⲇ	exactly like ⲧ	d
ⲉ	ĕ (“set”)	e
ⲍ	exactly like ⲥ	z
ⲏ	ā (“cape”)	ē
ⲓ ⲉⲓ	ē (“*see*k”), ĭ (“h*i*t”), y (“*y*es”)	i ei
ⲕ	unaspirated k, almost g (“smo*k*y”)	k
ⲝ	exactly like ⲕⲥ (“smo*ke s*ale”)	ks
ⲭ	ⲕ followed by h (“smo*k*e *h*ard!”)	kh
ⲗ	l	l
ⲙ	m	m
ⲛ	n	n
ⲟ	ä (“c*au*ght”)	o
ⲡ	unaspirated p, almost b (“sa*pp*y”)	p
ⲯ	= ⲡⲥ	ps
ⲫ	ⲡ followed by h (“sla*p h*ard”)	ph
ⲣ	r (tip-tongue trill)	r
ⲥ	s	s
ⲧ	unaspirated t, almost d (“smu*tt*y”)	t
ⲑ	ⲧ followed by h (“hi*t h*ard!”)	th
ⲩ ⲟⲩ	o͞o (“r*u*le”), o͝o (“b*oo*k”), w (“*w*e”)	u ou
ⲱ	ō (“n*o*”)	ō
(b) Demotic letters		
ϣ	sh (“*sh*oe”)	š
ϥ	between p and f	f
ϩ	h	h
ϫ	j (“pos*t*ure”)	j
ϭ	ky (“va*cu*um”)	c *or* č
ϯ	= ⲧⲓ (“smu*tty*”)	ti

After W. Worrell, *Coptic Sounds* (1934)

form of negation, word order, etc. They may be illustrated as follows. (*a*) A-prophet + this = “he is a prophet”; a-prophet + this + Moses = “Moses is a prophet.” (*b*) *Present tense base* + he + listen (*or*: in the garden, etc.) =“he is listening” (“he is in the garden,” etc.). (*c*) *Past tense base* + he + listen = “he listened.” (*d*) [Limited to a few archaic verbs] be-big + he = “he is big” (suffixation of the subject is anomalous). In pattern (*b*), direct objects are marked by a prefix *n*-; in (*c*), alternatively they may be suffixed to the infinitive, which then undergoes vowel reduction. There is no in-progress passive form; such passives are paraphrased with a generic third person plural (they-are-building it = “it is being built”). But there is a statal passive (the “qualitative”), a verb form that differs from the infinitive in vowel pattern and sometimes by the presence of a characteristic ending; it is used in pattern (*b*)—e.g., *infinitive* kōt, “build,” *qualitative* kēt, “(be) built”: t-i-*kōt* n-ou-ēi, “I *am building* a house,” but Ø-f-*kēt* kalōs, “it is well *built*.”

Any of these four sentence types can be converted to (1) a participial clause (“[he] being a prophet”), (2) preterit time (“he was a prophet”), or (3) a relative clause (“[he] who was a prophet”) by prefixing the appropriate particle (*e-, ne-, ete-,* etc.)—e.g., a-f-kōt, “he (has) built . . . ,” but e-a-f-kōt, “(he) having built . . . .” Negation of sentence patterns (*a*), (*b*), (*d*) is effected by adding the particles *ən- . . . an* (cf. French *ne . . . pas*) or simply . . . *an;* of pattern (*c*), by substituting a corresponding negative tense base (*əmp*-f-kōt, “he did not build”), or in the case of clause subordination by inserting *-təm-* before the verb.

Special patterns and forms make it possible to distinguish unambiguously “he is a prophet” from “it is he who is a prophet”; or, “I built it upon a hill” from “it is upon a hill that I built it.” Such precisely nuanced constructions are a very common and natural feature of literary Coptic and lend it a clarity and precision resembling that of French.

There are definite, indefinite, and zero articles; grammatical gender and number (masc. and fem.

singulars, common plural) are vested in them. The genitive relationship is marked by the particle *n-* ("belonging to"). There are no adjectives like those of Indo-European languages; the adjective relationship is expressed in several other ways—e.g., by inserting the particle *n-* ("being-in-the-class-of") between two nouns: an-idol + *n-* + Ø-wood = "a wooden idol."

Bibliography. Comprehensive bibliographies: W. Kammerer, *A Coptic Bibliography* (1950); A. Mallon and M. Malinine, *Grammaire copte* (4th ed., 1956), pp. 254-401; J. Simon, "Bibliographie copte," annually in *Or,* XVIII-XXXVI (1949-67) continued by A. Biedenkopf-Ziehner in *Enchoria,* II (1972-); D. Scholer, *Nag Hammadi Bibliography, 1948-1969* (1971) and supplements in *NovT* (1971 ff.).

History: K. Sethe, "Das Verhältnis zwischen Demotisch und Koptisch," *ZDMG,* LXXIX (1925), 290-316; H. Grapow, "Vom Hieroglyphisch-demotischen zum Koptischen," *SPAW* (1938), 322-49; G. Steindorff, "Bemerkungen über die Anfänge der koptischen Sprache und Literatur," *Coptic Studies in Honor of Walter Ewing Crum* (1950), pp. 189-213.

Grammars: L. Stern, *Koptische Grammatik* (1880 [repr., 1971]), the most complete description of syntax; covers Sahidic and Bohairic. All the works of H. J. Polotsky (*Collected Papers* [1971]) are fundamental, esp. *Études de syntaxe copte* (1944), "The Coptic Conjugation System," *Or,* XXIX (1960), 392-422. "Zur koptischen Wortstellung," *Or,* XXX (1961), 294-313, and "Nominalsatz und Cleft Sentence im Koptischen," *Or,* XXXI (1962), 413-30; also, J. Vergote, *Grammaire copte* (in progress; 1973 ff.), the most up to date. Informative but grammatically unsatisfactory: W. Till, *Koptische Grammatik, Saïdischer Dialekt* (2nd ed., 1961); G. Steindorff, *Lehrbuch der koptischen Grammatik* (1951); J. M. Plumley. *Introductory Coptic Grammar* (1948).

Literature: J. Leipoldt, "Geschichte der koptischen Literatur," in C. Brockelmann, ed., *Geschichte der christlichen Literaturen des Orients* (1907), pp. 131-82; Mallon-Malinine (*cited above*), pp. 304-94; T. Orlandi, *Elementi di lingua e letteratura copta* (1970).

Dialects: W. H. Worrell, *Coptic Sounds* (1934), fundamental; P. Kahle, Jr., *Bala'izah,* 2 vols. (1954), full documentation; J. Vergote, "Les dialectes dans le domaine égyptien," *Chronique d'Égypte,* XXXVI (1961), 237-49, and *Grammaire copte* (1973), Ia, fundamental; H. J. Polotsky, *OLZ* (1969), cols. 453-54; P. Nagel, "Der frühkoptische Dialekt von Theben," *Koptologische Studien in der DDR* (1965), pp. 30-49, and "Die Bedeutung der Nag Hammadi-Texte für die koptische Dialektgeschichte," *Von Nag Hammadi bis Zypern,* Berliner Byzantinistische Arbeiten, XLIII (1972), 16-27. The complicated classification proposed by R. Kasser, "Les dialectes coptes," *BIFAO,* LXXIII (1973), 71-99, has not won general acceptance. W. Till, *Koptische Dialektgrammatik* (2nd ed., 1961) is very elementary. There are special grammars for the various dialects (*see Comprehensive Bibliographies above*); note esp. P. Nagel, "Untersuchungen zur Grammatik des Subachmimischen Dialekts" (diss., Halle, 1964); H. Quecke, "II Dialetto" [Oxyrhynchite], in T. Orlandi, *Papyri della Università degli Studi di Milano* (*P. Mil. Copti*), V (1974), 87-108, German.

Dictionaries: W. E. Crum, *A Coptic Dictionary* (1939), the standard work; W. Spiegelberg, *Koptisches Handwörterbuch* (1921), still very useful; J. Černý, *Coptic Etymological Dictionary* (1975); Wilmet-Lefort, *Concordance* (*see below*), can be profitably used as a dictionary. Dictionaries of Greek words used in Coptic (H.-F. Weiss, *Zeitschrift für ägyptische Sprache,* XCVI [1969], 79-80) and of the Gnostic texts (B. Layton and T. O. Lambdin, in the same journal, XCVIII [1972], 156) are in preparation.

Concordance: M. Wilmet and L.-Th. Lefort, *Concordance du NT Sahidique,* CSCO Subsidia, 5 vols. (1957-64).

Word frequency: B. Metzger, *Lists of Words Occurring Frequently in the Coptic NT, Sahidic Dialect* (1961).

Edition of biblical texts: [G. Horner], *The Coptic Version of the NT in . . . Sahidic,* 7 vols. (1911-24 [repr. 1969]), in part now superseded by other editions; H. Thompson, *The Coptic Version of the Acts of the Apostles and the Pauline Epistles in the Sahidic Dialect* (1932), appendix has important collation of John; H. Quecke, *Das Markusevangelium Saïdisch* (1972); F. Hintze and H.-M. Schenke, *Die Berliner Handschrift der sahidischen Apostelgeschichte, TU,* CIX (1970); [G. Horner], *The Coptic Version of the NT in . . . Bohairic,* 4 vols. (1898-1905 [repr. 1969]); A Ciasca and (for vol. III) G. Balestri, *Sacrorum Bibliorum fragmenta copto-sahidica Musei Borgiani,* 3 vols. (1885-1904). There are no complete critical editions; the scholar must collect and weigh all the scattered evidence for him/herself, using the checklists published by A. Vaschalde in *RB,* XXVIII-XXXI (1919-22), Sahidic; *Le Muséon,* XLIII (1930), and XLV (1932), Bohairic; *Le Muséon,* XLVI (1933), Fayyumic and Achmimic; supplemented by W. Till, *BJRL,* XLII (1959), 220-40. Much of the textual evidence, including important early MSS, remains unedited. The complete OT is not yet known in any dialect. P. Kahle (*cited above*), pp. 269-74, gives a list of early MSS.

Textual affinities of the biblical versions: G. Mink, "Die koptischen Versionen des NT," in K. Aland, ed., *Die alten Übersetzungen des NT . . . ,* ANT, V (1972), 160-299, surveys older works, none of which is satisfactory.

Ancient translation technique, Greek into Coptic: A. Joussen, *Die koptischen Versionen der Apostelgeschichte,* BBB, XXXIV (1969); G. Mink (*cited above*); P. Nagel, "Die Einwirkung des Griechischen auf die Entstehung der koptischen Literatur," F. Altheim and R. Stiehl, eds., *Christentum am Roten Meer,* I (1971), pp. 327-55.

The Coptic evidence has been neither fully nor accurately quoted in critical editions of the Greek Bible; its value as a witness to the pre-Constantinian text should be obvious.

Modern Coptic: Pisenti Rizkallah, *Hanouelle ənjō əmberi* (1969), poems. The report, still often repeated, that Coptic somehow "survived" into the twentieth century at the village of Zenia Bahri near Luxor is dubious. The speakers in question are now reported to have been taught crude Bohairic by an enthusiast of the language revival movement. B. LAYTON

***CORINTH.** Recent study has stressed the Roman qualities of the community that Paul visited on the narrow Greek isthmus between extensions of the Aegean and Adriatic seas. When Corinth was refounded in 44 B.C., the Roman colonists may have chosen to locate the city center, or forum, on a site different from the place of the agora in the earlier Greek city. After the re-establishment, the datable inscriptions are predominantly in Latin rather than in Greek until the third decade of the second century A.D.

N of the forum two sets of primarily Roman remains have been excavated. In a gymnasium complex are two stoas which intersect at nearly right angles and a domed building. Of particular religious interest is a structure thought to be an

American School of Classical Studies, Athens
5. The dining room at Lerna

underground bathing establishment started before the destruction of Corinth (146 B.C.) and repaired sumptuously with marble and frescoes during the early life of the Roman colony. With the partial collapse of the building in the late fourth century A.D., this apparently became a cult center, for people floated into the water basins enormous numbers of lamps, some inscribed with Jewish and Christian formulas. Further E, massive brick ruins belong to a Roman bath with marble paving and some mosaic decoration. Among the important rooms are a "cold-room" with recessed semicircular plunge baths at both ends and a "hot-room" whose floor was constructed to allow steam to circulate underneath.

S of the Roman forum, high on the sloping hill of Acrocorinth, a sanctuary of Demeter has been found, which lies on a terrace above the ancient road. Dating from the seventh and sixth centuries B.C., it has classical and Hellenistic phases that feature dining rooms lined with couches and places for washing and cooking. These are located on both sides of a staircase leading up the hill to a cultic area. Above the stairs bedrock was cut into tiers apparently to form theaters for religious spectacles in an area that was elaborately rebuilt during Roman times.

Northward on the E side of the Corinthian isthmus lies the important sanctuary of Poseidon, where the contests known as the Isthmian games were conducted for many years after their traditional founding in the early sixth century B.C. (*see* FESTIVALS, GRECO-ROMAN[S]). While Corinth remained in ruins (146-44 B.C.), the games were probably held elsewhere, but inscriptions confirm that Corinth regained control of them at the beginning of the first century A.D., when presumably their site became once again the Isthmian sanctuary. In the early Roman period men's athletic games were supplemented by contests in poetry and women's athletics. Games form the background when Paul mentions (I Cor. 9:24-27) that runners compete "in a stadium" and practice self-control to "gain a perishable wreath." A stone head carved with a victory crown of pine twigs has been found in the sanctuary. Structures at Isthmia in the later first century A.D. included a stadium, a temple of Poseidon dating from the fifth century B.C., a sanctuary of the legendary founder of the sanctuary—Melikertes-Palaimon—a theater, and cultic caves.

Considerable evidence illuminates the subject of pagan cultic meals at Corinth (*see* I Cor. 8; 10). Dining rooms with religious meanings were in use during the early Roman period in the Lerna-Asclepieum complex N of the forum of Corinth. In these dining rooms couches for reclining at meals were built along the walls. Bolsters were modeled to support the reclining diner's left elbow, while his right hand was free for eating. Tables stood near the couches, and a square block at the center of the dining room apparently supported a brazier for cooking. Facilities for dining have been discovered in originally natural caves in the Isthmian sanctuary not far from the temple of Poseidon and at the upper edge of the circle of seats in the theater. These caves were enlarged and divided into irregularly shaped chambers lined with dining couches used in the fifth and fourth centuries B.C. Cooking was done in forecourts, from which food was carried into the dining rooms. In the sanctuary of Demeter on Acrocorinth, more regularly square dining rooms like those in the Asclepieum continued in use from the sixth century to the second century B.C., although the practice of ritual meals may have been revived on the site during the Roman period. In the Greek epoch, worshipers would present animals, usually pigs, to be sacrificed, perform ritual cleansing, and then enjoy a dinner of fresh pork. Perhaps meals included as participants poorer devotees of Demeter who could afford as gifts only small clay figurines or brightly painted miniature pottery.

Corinth's later importance as the seat of the bishop of Achaia made it then as now a destination of pilgrims. At the harbor of Lechaeon N of Corinth, where the sea was said to have washed up the drowned martyr Leonidas and his seven women companions, an enormous basilican church was built. Not long afterward (A.D. 551) it was destroyed in an earthquake. Another church of the fifth century has been found, dedicated to Kodratos, a Corinthian martyr (d. A.D. 258). Remains of a sixth-century church have been found near the archaic temple of Apollo above the forum. *See also* CENCHREAE and CENCHREAE[S].

Bibliography. Surveys: "Archaeology in Greece," *AR*, IV (1957)-XIX (1972-73); "Chronique des Fouilles," *BCH*, LXXXII (1958)-XCVI (1972); "Χρονικά," *AD*, XVI (1960)-XXV (1970).

Inscriptions: *Corinth* VIII, 3, ed. J. H. Kent (1966).

Detailed reports may be found in *Hesperia*, beginning with vol. XXIX (1960).

Other: G. Roux, *Pausanias en Corinthie* (1958); F. J. de Waele, *Corinthe et Saint Paul* (1961); H. Conzelmann, *Korinth und die Mädchen der Aphrodite* (1967); O. Broneer, *Isthmia* I (1971), II (1973).

C. L. THOMPSON

***CORINTHIANS, FIRST LETTER TO THE.** This Pauline letter offers us immediate and extensive information about the problems and possibilities of the communal life of an early Christian congregation.

1. Milieu
2. Origins of the congregation
3. Unity

4. Date
5. Situation
   a. Question of parties
   b. Emergence of differences
   c. Previous exchange
   d. Trends of enthusiasm
6. Paul's response
   a. Collective identity
   b. Gifts
   c. Revelation and its mediation
   d. Ethical responsibility
   e. Role of women
   f. Worship
Bibliography

1. Milieu. In Paul's time Corinth was a relatively young city, having been refounded as a Roman colony in 44 B.C. (*see* CORINTH; CORINTH[S]). Interpreters of Paul's Corinthian correspondence have often exploited the alleged fame of Corinth as capital of vice, most of all of prostitution. Conzelmann, however, has shown that Corinth was not a center of sacred prostitution for Aphrodite even in classical times. Corinth's reputation was the result of propaganda disseminated from Athens, its major competitor in trade. The morals of Corinthians were no worse than those of any other Mediterranean city population in NT times. As in other cities the social, cultural, and religious mix was wide-ranging, and included Jews.

2. Origins of the congregation. Paul makes only general remarks about the founding of the congregation, so our knowledge is based mostly on Acts 18, according to which Paul came through Athens to Corinth in the winter of 49/50 and stayed there into the early summer of 51. He earned his own living there, collaborating with two Jewish refugees from Rome who were to become prominent members of the young church, AQUILA AND PRISCILLA (Acts 18:2, 18, 26; I Cor. 16:19). They later followed Paul to Ephesus, where they gained influence on a young Jewish Christian from Alexandria, Apollos, who according to Acts 19:1 and I Cor. 3:5-9 then came to Corinth, made converts of his own, and greatly influenced the young congregation. He stayed there only for a short time, probably returning to Ephesus (16:12). Apollos most surely had his own style and theology, but I Cor. 3 shows that Paul could see nothing in the work of Apollos which would contradict his own principles and ideas. On the contrary, Paul regarded him as a fellow worker (3:5-9; cf. 16:12). The names of other prominent Christians in Corinth are mentioned in 1:11, 14, 16; 16:15, and the Corinthians may have been partly organized into "house churches" (*see* 1:11, 16; 16:15). But certainly there was a common worship service at least every Sunday (16:2 identical with the one described in detail in ch. 14 and with the evening Eucharist in ch. 11). As in other Pauline congregations an extensive spiritual life and a communal contribution was encouraged for all members.

3. Unity. Attempts to reconstruct Paul's earlier letter to the Corinthians (mentioned in 5:9) from material in I Corinthians have not succeeded. The integrity of I Corinthians is not above question, however: 10:1-22 (23) does not fit easily with its context, especially not with ch. 8, and the relationship of 5:10-13 to 6:9-10 is also difficult. But more than any other Pauline letter, the structural arrangement of I Corinthians has been influenced by the apostle's concern to answer directly issues that the readers have raised. This is sufficient to explain the lack of system and consistency. Part of the reason why Paul's answers and tone vary in different parts of the letter is probably the different status of the questions responded to (Hurd): some react to direct information and requests from the Corinthians, others are based on hearsay. The former tend to be answered more calmly, the latter more emotionally.

4. Date. Recent research has shown that Paul's letters may be dated earlier than previously held. I Corinthians probably was written from Ephesus in 53 or 54 in response to an inquiring letter from the Corinthians to Paul and a visit of people of Chloe's (household?) to Paul. Especially from Chloe's people Paul heard about divisiveness and factions in Corinth.

5. Situation. ***a. Question of parties.*** The question about the parties in Corinth and their place in early Christianity is still the most prominent problem in the discussion of the Corinthian correspondence. The names mentioned in 1:12 have not proven helpful in defining the contending groups, and there are no traces of real parties, only particular trends. In 1:12 Paul sharpens the issue reported by Chloe's people (1:11). He intimates that, by identifying themselves with particular leaders, the Corinthians are demonstrating their failure to define their collective identity.

b. Emergence of differences. The kerygmatic basis on which Paul founded the Corinthian congregation is still commonly agreed upon in Corinth (*see esp.* 15:1-5[8]; similarly, 11:23-25). But Paul, during his missionary stay, had encouraged a lively spiritual life (cf. also the description of the beginning in Galatia, Gal. 3:3). This had expressed itself in charismatic demonstrations (11:17; esp. ch. 14), the structural implications of which the Corinthians had to experiment with after Paul's departure. Meanwhile, Paul probably made his own further explorations in the still rather uncharted realm of experience which faith in Jesus called for and provided for.

Historians of early Christianity have often overlooked the fact that I, II Corinthians are not only our most extensive, but actually—and by accident—the only extant, continuous record of the development of a community of Jesus-believers during the first three centuries. Much of what happened in Corinth must have been ordinary in the growth of any charismatic community, extraordinary in our eyes only because we are deprived of the records of the early history of other similar communities. Paul did not give his congregations a blueprint of faith and life, but with them explored the possibilities and ranges of a living message and a living faith. Problems could not always be foreseen, and there was inevitably some learning by experience. His letters make it clear that Paul taught his congregations from the beginning that both kerygma and Scripture serve as guides, but only through constant interpretation and reinterpretation. And that is what the Corinthians did.

One of the most obvious problems of collective identity was that of the degree of homogeneity within the Corinthian church itself. This was also closely related to the question of how the community was to be distinguished from the world.

c. Previous exchange. In the lost correspondence between Paul and the Corinthians (*see* 5:9 and 7:1) the problems of homogeneity and distinction were put as ethical questions, and I Corinthians in part still discusses them in that way. But the visit of Chloe's people had made Paul aware that at the base of the difficulties was an unresolved problem of communal self-understanding and its active functional expression in worship and organization. The preface and thanksgiving (1:1-9) reveal that Paul wants to discuss with the Corinthians the proper assessment of spiritual life.

d. Trends of enthusiasm. Paul refers back to his initial work in Corinth in 1:14-17 and especially in 2:1-5, and beginning in 2:6 he suggests that the proclamation of the Cross does not preclude the teaching of wisdom. It is understandable that the Corinthians, on the basis of Paul's closeness to the Jewish wisdom tradition (*see* WISDOM IN THE NT[S] §3*c*), would have drawn certain ideological and sociological conclusions from what he wrote about wisdom. The separation from the world of folly and the differentiation between teacher and students characteristic of wisdom teaching easily led in Corinth toward the adoption of an internal elitist structure and a dualistic notion of reality. The virus of Gnosticism, latent almost everywhere, was certainly more prominent in places like Corinth, where various cultural forces intersected. But the Hellenistic Jewish wisdom movement to which Paul had been exposed had already developed symptoms of the Gnostic fever, and the proclamation of the Jesus-drama could easily become a crystallizing factor for the emergence of a Gnostic consciousness, too. Its presence in the Corinthian congregation is evident. The emphatic use of the term "gnosis" (8:1-3) is the most immediate indicator, but there is also the interpretation of the spiritual experience as encouragement to communicate publicly with the angels (through speaking in TONGUES, ch. 14). This enthusiasm made these Christians claim freedom from death and from the restraints of corporeal bondage. Thus, the position criticized by Paul in ch. 15 is not the denial of the resurrection of Jesus, or even the denial of the Resurrection altogether; it is, rather, the denial of the future resurrection of the body (cf. the discussion of freedom in chs. 5–9, esp. in ch. 6). The body of Christ, a notion dear to Paul also, was interpreted by the Corinthians as the new heavenly reality (chs. 10–12). Although Paul himself thought very highly of baptism and the Eucharist, he did not regard the sacraments as magical conveyances leading immediately beyond history, where neither temptation nor responsibility exist, only the fruition of immortality (*see* IMMORTALITY[S]). Nevertheless, in a syncretistic age this was perhaps an understandable interpretation of the Easter faith. The kerygmatic formula of the institution of the Eucharist (11:23 ff.) as well as various biblical exodus stories had served as the basis for an interpretation of the spiritual reality of sacramental life in Corinth which foreshadowed the later understanding of the sacrament as a medicine of immortality. The Corinthians tried to convert their congregation from an inconsistent mystery religion into a consistent one.

In his response, Paul uses critical expressions like "pretend" (author's trans.; Gr. δοκέω, 3:18; 8:2; 10:12), "boast" (1:29, 31; 4:7; esp. 5:6) and "puffed up" (φυσιόω, 4:6; elsewhere in RSV "arrogant," 4:18, 19; 5:2; 8:1; or "boastful," 13:4). These are more than ethical metaphors. They, as well as the description of the pride of Paul's fellow believers in Corinth (4:6-21), literally (but critically) circumscribe the sense of transworldly elevation the Corinthians tended to gain from their enthusiasm. Because for them the degree of spiritual knowledge indicated the state of advancement in salvation, the Corinthians tried to differentiate between those more and those less advanced (especially with respect to the gift of speaking in tongues, ch. 14). This was not necessarily a reason for division, but this push upward could be seen by some as too fast and too far, and by others as too slow and too much hindered by the inferior believers. Thus there was discord between the strong and the weak (chs. 8–10). There is also an intimation (chs. 4, 9) that these enthusiasts had criticized Paul for not being sufficiently free and advanced, perhaps also for his holding them back.

6. Paul's response. ***a. Collective identity.*** In I Corinthians Paul tries to make the readers see that collective identity is their problem and that their fondness for religious fulfillment (even among the weak) in preference to the upbuilding of the community breaks the spiritual body asunder. The underlying theme here is the body of Christ, which Paul interprets corporately as the community of believers where, since Easter, the crucified Christ is alive. Paul can even identify the Christ and the body (12:12) as the Corinthians seem to have done. But instead of pursuing further the speculative intricacies of that mythical concept he slips suddenly to a more metaphorical treatment (12:14 ff.). Here the discussion is reminiscent of the political philosophy of the STOICS, who thought of society as an organism. Paul thus puts the body of Christ into everyday life, even giving a political aspect to the community of those who believe in Jesus.

b. Gifts. Paul radically democratizes the concepts of the body of Christ and of SPIRITUAL GIFTS. The Corinthians knew that spiritual gifts were the expression of life of the body of Christ. But Paul makes them see that all members have gifts and that all gifts are equal in rank and spiritual power. He also seems to have been the first to speak of spiritual gifts as gifts of grace (in 12:4 χαρίσματα [RSV "gifts"] instead of πνευματικά [RSV "spiritual gifts"] in vs. 1), another attempt at diffusing the elitism of the enthusiasts, with their introspective concentration on the spiritual self. The main Pauline contribution to a reassessment of the spiritual experience of the Corinthians is the emphasis on love (ch. 8, but esp. ch. 13). Not union with the deity, but the upbuilding of the community (serving one another in mutual understanding and respect) is the gift beyond all gifts.

*c. **Revelation and its mediation.*** Paul pursues his egalitarian interpretation of the Christ event as early as chs. 1–4, not only by emphasizing the self-humiliation of God in Christ, but also by depicting it as putting human pride to shame. He presents first himself and then (in ch. 3) Apollos also as ministering to the Corinthians. He dwells on the low social state of the Corinthian Christians (not as a requirement but as a symptom). He brackets his allusion to previous teaching of wisdom to the perfect (2:6-16) by critical references to the lowliness and foolishness of his work in Corinth (2:1-5) and by a sudden attack on the lack of spiritual achievement among the Corinthians (3:1-4). The point is that the very spiritual pride of the Corinthian enthusiasts betrays their continued worldliness. Paul argues that the democratization of wisdom teaching and spiritual experience is a sign of perfection, because it is the only way of reflecting the character of God's mysterious revelation in the cross of Jesus. Therefore the true apostle is not a superman but is exposed to weakness and humiliation in the ministry to the people (ch. 4).

*d. **Ethical responsibility.*** As regards the discussion of incest, the use of pagan courts for the settling of disputes among Christians, and traffic with prostitutes, Paul stresses the mutual and corporate responsibility. He even includes himself as a participant in the corporate experience (e.g., 5:4). There is no distinction between "inner" spiritual matters and other, "external," bodily matters. Everyone in the community of believers is a body and is constituted as such by the body of Christ.

Paul more than the Corinthians was influenced in his thoughts and actions by the expectation of the imminent PAROUSIA, as seen in his advice in ch. 7. However, Paul indicates that such an expectation does not require fleeing the world but, rather, facing historical conditions. Thus he suggests the unmarried state as being preferable, but he advises marriage in order to avoid fornication, and he counsels that mixed marriages be continued. He sees no harm in the practice of some who live together as couples without a sexual relationship, but he cannot ascribe to it much special spiritual value and suggests that the pair marry if the strain gets too strong (*see* MARRIAGE IN THE NT[S] §§1, 2; ETHICS IN THE NT[S] §3*d*ii). Since for Paul the Parousia implies radical change he advises against any social change now. Given the imminence of the Parousia one can possess things as though one did not have them. This very drastic eschatological prefix to the social advice in ch. 7 has on the whole been overlooked in Christian ethics (and its criticism). It should not be translated directly into a general dialectic either.

*e. **Role of women.*** Paul agrees with the Corinthian enthusiasts that corporate worship includes the right of women to participate, even as prophets. It is noteworthy that in ch. 11 Paul realizes that he has no solid argument for the veiling of women in the worship service. In his opinion, not even the idea of divinely ordained male superiority makes his argument strong enough, so he finally gives up arguing. The renewed discussion of the role of women in 14:33*b*-36, now demanding silence from women, is a second-century interpolation. The MSS show confusion, the passage does not really fit the context, and the position taken is not supported anywhere in Paul's authentic letters. *See* WOMAN IN THE NT[S] §2.

*f. **Worship.*** In discussing the LORD'S SUPPER Paul presupposes a communion meal prior to the Eucharist. But he deplores the fact that the meal had fallen into disrespect, allowing the social distinctions to show. He suggests, therefore, that the meal which was no longer truly communal be abolished, and that the Lord's Supper be celebrated after each had eaten at home. In this way the character of the Eucharist as the communal proclamation of Christ's death and the corporate anticipation of his return would again be clearly visible. In line with this notion of corporate worship and the emphasis on communal love, the open character of the Christian service is emphasized in ch. 14; here the outsider's understanding is the criterion for proper worship (vss. 16, 23-25). It is only natural that for Paul even the Resurrection is a collective phenomenon (ch. 15). Finally, he extends his plea for improved collective identity to the matter of the OFFERING FOR THE SAINTS (ch. 16). The interest in further and closer contact is pursued, and the strengthening of ties within the congregation and with the congregations in Asia is emphasized. At the close a portion of the eucharistic liturgy is quoted and this, coupled with the actual reading of the letter in the congregation, enables Paul's own active participation in its communal celebration. Thus, instead of communicating doctrinal information, this letter, in close touch with the actual dialogue in Corinth, tries to establish a correcting trend.

Bibliography. Commentaries: C. K. Barrett, HNTC (1968); F. F. Bruce, NCB (1971); H. Conzelmann, Hermeneia (1969); J. Héring (1949 [ET 1962]); J. Ruef, *Paul's First Letter to Corinth* (1971); M. E. Thrall, CBC (1965); H. D. Wendland, NTD, VII (12th ed., 1968).

Studies: G. Bornkamm, "Lord's Supper and Church in Paul" (1956), in *Early Christian Experience* (1969), pp. 123-60; H. Conzelmann, *Korinth und die Mädchen der Aphrodite* (1967); J. C. Hurd, Jr., *The Origin of I Corinthians* (1965); E. Käsemann, "The Pauline Doctrine of the Lord's Supper" (1947/48), in *Essays on NT Themes,* SBT, XLI (1964), 108-35; W. Schmithals, *Gnosticism in Corinth* (3rd ed., 1969).

D. GEORGI

*CORINTHIANS, SECOND LETTER TO THE.

1. Unity. The integrity of II Corinthians has been more successfully challenged than that of I Corinthians. The canonical second epistle appears to many to be a collection of fragments.

a. 6:14–7:1 contains non-Pauline language and seems to interrupt the context. Its views are similar to those held by the Qumran sect (*see* Fitzmeyer; DEAD SEA SCROLLS; DEAD SEA SCROLLS[S]), and its relationship to Christian faith is only superficial. The passage is probably non-Pauline, interpolated when the fragments of authentic Pauline letters were put together at a later date.

b. Other discrepancies. 2:14–7:4 (excluding 6:14–7:1) interrupts a discourse which opens in 2:1-13 and continues in 7:5 ff., and whose tone, style, and argument are rather different. The relationship between chs. 7 and 8 is also problematic; ch. 7 does nothing to prepare for the collection for the Jerusalem church, which dominates ch. 8, and ch. 8 does not pick up the reconciliation theme of ch. 7. Moreover, in ch. 7 Titus seems to have just returned from Corinth, but in ch. 8 he is on the brink of leaving for Corinth, taking ch. 8 with him (8:6, 16-24). Next, ch. 9 takes up the issue of the collection as if it had not been discussed previously, and seems to be addressed to people in the province of Achaia, not merely to the Corinthians (as had ch. 8); the delegation of ch. 8 (*see* 8:16-24) seems already to have departed (*see* 9:3-5). Finally, chs. 10–13 do not connect well with any of the previous sections. First, the sudden change in tone and style sets them completely apart. The discussion is harsh, whereas in 1:1–2:13; 7:5-16; and ch. 8 (ch. 9 does not pertain to the Corinthian problems) the opposition seems to have been already overcome. Second, the topic is different, and chs. 10–13 do not provide a suitable completion of the plea for the collection for Jerusalem (ch. 8).

c. Sequence. The following order explains best the various discrepancies noted above, as well as the particular events reflected in II Corinthians.

Letter A	2:14–7:4 (excepting 6:14–7:1 as non-Pauline)
Letter B	chs. 10–13, most probably the letter mentioned in 2:4 and 7:8 (where only the emotional circumstances of the drafting are hinted at; no summary is given)
Letter C	1:1–2:13; 7:5-16
Letter D	ch. 8
Letter E	ch. 9

d. Genres. The five fragments of II Corinthians represent as many different genres. A is close to the political speech; B is modeled after the philosophical apology (Betz), showing strong forensic elements and the use of the genre of the fool's speech of the Hellenistic mime in 11:1–12:18; C follows the genre of ordinary correspondence; D is a letter of recommendation with an elaborate preface; E is a homiletical tract.

2. A reconstruction of probable events. After dispatching what is our I Corinthians, and after Timothy's visit (announced in I Cor. 4:17 and 16:10), Paul decided to modify his earlier plans (I Cor. 16:3-9) and sent Titus to Corinth in order to speed up the collection for Jerusalem. This was done, apparently with the collaboration of the Corinthians (II Cor. 8:5, 10; 9:2; 12:18). After that visit events occurred in Corinth which made Paul change his plans completely. Christian missionaries of Jewish origin (11:22), who were also apostles (11:5, 13; 12:11), arrived in Corinth (3:1; 11:4) and took the Pauline congregation as the operational base for their activity. They exploited the admiration they seem to have found, and sowed new doubts in the hearts of the Corinthians about Paul's competence and authority.

Paul responded with Letter A, which tries to persuade the Corinthians to remain on his side. This attempt, however, was unsuccessful, so Paul decided to visit Corinth in person. The visit proved to be even more of a disaster (2:1 ff.; 7:5 ff.; 12:14; 13:1). The opposition in Corinth was at its peak, and one particular member of the congregation attacked Paul ruthlessly (2:5; 7:12). After leaving Corinth, Paul sent Letter B, in which he took the Corinthians to task (and through them the outside agitators). Titus was sent to Corinth again (2:12-13; 7:5-7), but before he returned Paul was arrested and remained in jail for several months (*see* 1:8-11). The Philippian correspondence was most probably written during this period (*see* PHILIPPIANS, LETTER TO THE §D and supplementary article §1). After his release from prison Paul hastened first to Troas, then to Macedonia, in order to meet Titus as soon as possible (2:12-13). The meeting took place in Macedonia, where Paul learned that the situation in Corinth was much improved (7:5-16). Just two things still needed clarification: the degree of punishment for the person who had offended Paul and the reason for Paul's failure to visit Corinth both on his way to, and then again on his return from, Macedonia (*see* 1:16). To respond to these two questions Paul wrote Letter C (*see* 1:17–2:4; 2:5-11).

Subsequently, Paul found Titus willing to resume the collection for Jerusalem in Corinth, and Titus was sent there, along with two other delegates and Letter D. After their departure Paul decided to send an extra letter, this one to Christians in the entire province of Achaia (Letter E). Finally, Paul himself visited Corinth again, and stayed there for several months (hinted at in Acts 20:2-3).

3. Dates. Absolute dates are not easily determined (*see* CHRONOLOGY, PAULINE[S]), but the events and correspondence outlined above could admit of the following dating.

54	Letter A written from Ephesus (summer); a visit by Paul to Corinth; Letter B written, also from Ephesus
54/5	Paul in prison in Ephesus (winter)
55	Paul in Tarsus and Macedonia (spring); Letter C written (late spring or early summer); Letters D and E written concerning the collection (summer or early fall); Paul visits Corinth again (late fall)

4. Opponents. The apostles that Paul attacked in II Corinthians had evidently been influenced by the ideology and method of Hellenistic Jewish propaganda, and now centered their message on Jesus ("another Jesus" in 11:4). Note the emphasis on the name "Jesus" in 4:10-14 and the attack on knowing Christ according to the flesh in 5:16. They were legitimate Christian missionaries, as their titles proved (11:5, 13, 23), but they retained their Hellenistic Jewish tradition (11:22; ch. 3), which was, as the Jewish apologists show, a very inclusive one. Their tradition from Moses to Jesus was seen as a storehouse of the Spirit, and the overwhelming spiritual power with which these missionaries preached allegedly proved the superiority of the religion they propagated.

In ch. 3 Paul tries to break this positive relationship between the Spirit and the tradition. His opponents seem to have regarded allegorical exegesis as the key to the treasures of the Spirit stored in the tradition; that is what they understood by turning "to the Lord" (Lord=Spirit, 3:16-17). Allegorical exegesis itself demanded skill, but it might also have afforded transcendental experiences. In any case, ecstasy and other extraordinary and miraculous achievements were seen as necessary to the competence of these missionaries (12:1-12). In this they resembled many similar "divine men" on the contemporary scene (*see* DIVINE MAN[S]), especially those missionaries who sought to prove the spiritual superiority of their particular religions. Naturally, the older the religion the better, because the greater number of "divine men" in its tradition could be claimed as evidence of its greater power. So for Paul's opponents in Corinth the preservation of close ties with the Jewish tradition and ancient figures like Solomon, Elijah, and—most of all—Moses, was essential. They were also keenly interested in the Jesus tradition, because it provided the major link between themselves and the spiritual power figures of the past. Paul charges these current itinerant missionaries with having "a different spirit" (11:4), and what they allege as a faithful imitation of the example of Jesus, Moses, etc., as miracle workers, Paul attacks as bragging and self-recommendation. For their part, the opponents find it easy to denounce Paul's own claims as mere self-recommendations, because objective testimony to the presence of the authenticating power of the Spirit in Paul seems lacking.

The opponents, presumably interested in the public acknowledgment and recording of their accomplishments, requested and used letters of recommendation (3:1). These gave them continuous proof of their spiritual status in the missionary competition and helped them gain followers. As Paul intimates, most of all in ch. 10, the competition was not only with missionaries of other religions, but also and first of all with fellow Christian missionaries. This certainly involved the need for continuous objective demonstration of one's competence, and it also cast the audience in the role of judges who would give public acknowledgment through remuneration and recommendation. Paul's refusal to accept letters of recommendation (3:1-3) or remuneration (11:7-15; 12:13-18) from the Corinthians could be taken as a sign of his incompetence, or as an insult to his audience.

5. Paul's response. ***a. Letter A (2:14–7:4, excepting 6:14–7:1).*** The Corinthian enthusiasts could be attracted to the intruding apostles because the high value that these apostles put on spiritual demonstrations and accomplishments appealed to their interest in objective spiritual experiences. But Paul notices that differences exist between the invaders and the trend-setters in the congregation, and he gets at the root of it in Letter A. He tries to drive a wedge between them by pointing out that if the Corinthians would remain true to their dualistic (Gnosticizing) premises and their interest in the transcendental character of revelation, they would stay with Paul. For this reason he stresses the antithesis between letter (tradition) and Spirit, the old and the new (3:6-18; 5:17), darkness and light (4:4-16); he also emphasizes the role of Christ as the revealer (3:18 and 4:4, 6; 5:18-21) and presents a rather dualistic anthropology (4:7-18; 5:1-10). He does not even shy away from a description of Satan which anticipates Marcion (*see* GNOSTICISM[S] §4*a*), "the god of this world" (4:4, all the more striking since the description of Satan's activity is here made parallel to that of Moses in 3:13). But Paul is careful to point out how this relates to the dialectic of the Cross and Resurrection, and how it calls for humility and responsibility in both the messengers and their audience. In this way he takes up again the points he made in I Corinthians, but with a new approach.

b. Letter B (chs. 10–13). Pushed into a corner, Paul reacts in an almost autobiographical fashion. He stresses even more than in the previous letter that life-style and theology reflect each other. His refraining from the display of power is not cowardice, but God's sovereignty working through him (ch. 10). In the fool's speech of chs. 11–12 Paul opens himself up to ridicule, but he emphasizes that to ridicule him would be to ridicule Christ, because Paul in his weakness imitates Christ. As a fool in Christ, and only as such, he conveys his power. At the end of Letter B Paul warns that another visit by him could turn judgmental, but he still hopes for reconciliation and further constructive work.

c. Letter C (1:1–2:13; 7:5-16). Because Titus has returned with good news (7:5-7, 13-16) Paul first treats the issue of continuous consolation. Next he deals with the major grudge the Corinthians hold against him: the change of travel plans. This did not imply a change of intentions, but was an affirmation of God's constancy and meant to spare the Corinthians another painful, if not destructive, experience. Paul then admonishes the Corinthians not to overcompensate for their previous opposition by crushing the one who had offended Paul, but rather to accept him again into fellowship (2:5-11; again in 7:8-12).

d. Letter D (ch. 8). This is a letter of recommendation for Titus and two other delegates who are to make renewed efforts to take a collection in Corinth. Paul reminds the Corinthians of similar efforts by the Macedonians and of the spiritual gifts they themselves had received.

e. Letter E (ch. 9). To the Christians in Achaia Paul describes the collection as a response to blessings received, as a demonstration of their wisdom and justification, and as a display of universal fellowship in the concrete celebration of thanksgiving.

Bibliography. Commentaries: In addition to those listed in the bibliog. for CORINTHIANS, FIRST LETTER TO THE[S], C. K. Barrett, HNTC (1973); J. Héring, *The Second Epistle of St. Paul to the Corinthians* (1958 [ET 1967]).

Studies: H. D. Betz, *Der Apostel Paulus und die sokratische Tradition,* BHTh, XLV (1972); J. F. Collange, *Énigmes de la deuxième épître de Paul aux*

Corinthiens, NTSMS, XVIII (1972), with full bibliog. to date; J. A. Fitzmyer, "Qumrân and the Interpolated Paragraph in 2 Cor. 6, 14–7,1," *CBQ,* XXIII (1961), 271-80; D. Georgi, *Die Gegner des Paulus im 2. Korintherbrief,* WMANT, XI (1964). D. Georgi

***CORINTHIANS, THIRD LETTER TO THE.** *See* Apocrypha, NT[S] §1.

***CORRUPTION, MOUNT OF** [הר המשחית]. A mistaken translation of the name for one spur of the Mount of Olives, where Solomon built shrines to foreign deities (II Kings 23:13; cf. I Kings 11:7), properly translated "the mountain of the Destroyer," referring to a deity worshiped there. *See* Olives, Mount of §2.

1. **Identity of the Destroyer.** "The Destroyer" is a mythological figure found widely in the extant literature (Exod. 12:23; possibly also Jer. 51:25; Isa. 54:16; Prov. 18:9 [reading בעל משחית as "Lord Destroyer"]; Wisd. Sol. 18:25; I Cor. 10:10; Deut. Rabbah 3:11). The Destroyer may have been identified with Molech, the god of the Ammonites, and Chemosh, the god of Moab, since their sanctuaries existed on his mountain throughout the monarchical period. They were regarded as West-Semitic manifestations of the Assyro-Babylonian god of death and the netherworld, Nergal. The identification, Chemosh=Molech=Nergal, all of them underworld deities, is seen from a number of considerations: (*a*) Both Chemosh (II Kings 3:27) and Molech (II Kings 23:10; Jer. 32:35; Lev. 18:21; 20:1-5) were worshiped by the burnt sacrifice of children. One of the Sumerian titles of Nergal was *(É)-gir$_4$-kù,* "pure (or sacred) oven (or stove)," and one of his Akkadian titles was *Sharrapu,* "he who burns (others)." These suggest that Nergal also received human sacrifice. (*b*) In Judg. 11:24 Jephthah, in addressing Ammonites, calls Chemosh "your god," suggesting the identity of Chemosh with Molech. (*c*) Directly W of the S end of the Mount of Olives is the valley of Hinnom, a place where Molech was worshiped (II Kings 23:10; Jer. 32:35; cf. II Chr. 28:3; 33:6; Jer. 7:31-32; 19:2, 6; Josh. 15:8; 18:16); the name of this site became the name for the underworld in Hebrew, Greek, and Arabic. (*d*) According to the Koran (Sura 43: 74-77), the ruling spirit in hell was called *Mālik,* a name etymologically identical with Molech. (*e*) The Assyrian god list VAT 10173 gives the identification "Malik is Nergal," while the list K. 4349 identifies Nergal with many other deities including ^{d}*Ka-am-muš,* i.e., Chemosh. Thus the identification Chemosh=Molech=Nergal seems established. That this deity can be called the Destroyer is seen from the large mass of material about Nergal from Mesopotamian sources.

2. **Character of the Destroyer.** The character of Nergal is both benevolent and malevolent. Hymns to Nergal represent him as one whose counsel and insight are sought by other gods; he is "gracious," "compassionate," "full of forgiveness." He can be invoked to exorcise malevolent spirits. More characteristically, however, Nergal is the god of death and the underworld; he is a mighty warrior, a furious demon, a sword, a hero among the gods, who is manifest as the raging stormtide, the great bull, the lion clothed in terror, the bringer of disease and pestilence. Nergal is the "Lord, who goes around by night, to whom locked doors open by themselves." Repeatedly Nergal is invoked in curses to bring misery, pestilence, calamity, defeat, disease, death. He is the fearful god of the netherworld, "the dreadful land," "the great city" to which all the dead must ultimately go. Such an awesome, terror-inspiring deity can quite naturally be called the Destroyer.

3. **The mount in the OT.** The cult of Chemosh-Molech-Nergal may have been imported to the Mount of Olives during the time of David. II Sam. 15:32 may be translated to say that this is where "he customarily worshiped gods." In accord with general Semitic custom, David perhaps felt it appropriate to reverence the gods of Moab and Ammon in advance of launching campaigns of conquest against them. The rationale for this practice was that, since the national gods were conceived as protectors and rulers of the nation who appointed earthly rulers to administer affairs in their names, an intended conqueror could hope for success in conquering a land only if he first befriended the deity of the land. When Solomon built shrines on the Mount of Olives to Chemosh and Molech (I Kings 11:7), he was not then importing a new cult but was only providing a permanent sanctuary for these gods much as he did for Yahweh on the temple mount.

Once the cult had been established on the mountain, the mythic matrix appropriate to the worship of Nergal saturated the popular mind so that even Josiah's violent purge of worship on the Mount of Olives (II Kings 23:13) was quite ineffectual as an effort to remove elements of the netherworld cult. For example, the strange vision of Zech. 14: 1-4, in which the Mount of Olives is split asunder and a great cleft appears between the two halves of the mountain, may reflect elements in the Nergal mythology. Zechariah's cleft in the mountain was meant to represent an exit from the netherworld for the resurrection of the dead. This interpretation is seen in a mural from the synagogue at Dura-Europos (*see* Art, Early Jewish[S] §2), which combines Ezekiel's vision of the valley of dry bones (Ezek. 37) with the cleft in the mountain motif. Fragmentary bodies appear to be proceeding from the cleft in the mountain to be assembled and revived. *See* Fig. C6.

4. **The mount in the NT.** The god Nergal was, in the Yahwistic tradition, demoted to the rank of demon and became the Destroyer, perhaps the one who went about on the night of Passover

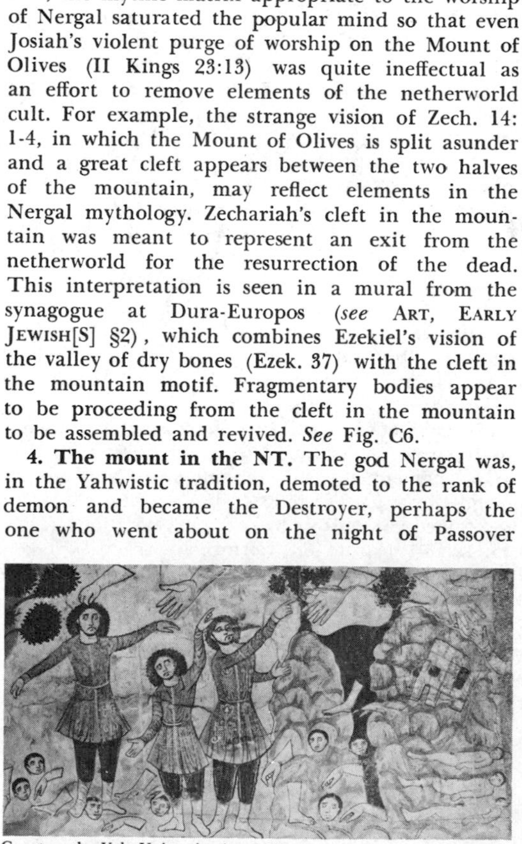

Courtesy the Yale University Art Gallery

6. Ezekiel's vision, from the Dura-Europos paintings

to slay the first-born of the Egyptians (Exod. 12:23). Thus it is appropriate that Jesus on the night of his arrest—Passover evening, according to Mark—should retire to the Mount of Olives, the mountain sacred to the god of death, to become reconciled to death (Mark 14:26-42).

The gospels (Mark 13; Matt. 24) record that on the Mount of Olives Jesus pronounced the doom of the city of Jerusalem. This act reflects an ancient tradition of denouncing the city from the mount (cf. Ezek. 11:23; Jos. War II.xiii.5; Antiq. XX.viii.6). Possibly this tradition reflects the old cult of the netherworld god: one may, while standing on the mountain, consign the city to the powers of the god of devastation.

Finally it should be noted that Jesus ascended into heaven from Bethany, a village on the E slope of the Mount of Olives (Luke 24:50-51; Acts 1:9-12), a motif possibly intended to proclaim Jesus' victory over the powers of death that were thought to inhabit the mountain.

Bibliography. For all references *see* J. B. Curtis, "An Investigation of the Mount of Olives in the Judaeo-Christian Tradition," *HUCA,* XXVIII (1957), 137-80. For a different interpretation of some of this material, *see* J. Morgenstern, "The Cultic Setting of the 'Enthronement Psalms,'" *HUCA,* XXXV (1964), 1-42.

J. B. CURTIS

***COTTON.** The only unequivocal reference to cotton in the Bible is Esth. 1:6. Its use suggests the rare exotic grandeur of King Ahasuerus' palace, since cotton fabric was not widely used in the ancient Near East. In fact, Esth. 1:6 contains one of the few literary references to the use of cotton in that region before the Christian era.

The RSV has translated the word חורי, "white [cloth]," in Isa. 19:9 as "white cotton," assuming the existence of a cotton industry in Egypt. That translation appears open to question on the basis of what is presently known about the history of cotton.

Wild cotton is indigenous to semiarid regions of the tropics and subtropics. At a very early date, the cotton plant was introduced to the Indus Valley from whence knowledge of its practical uses spread slowly throughout Asia. The prehistoric site of Mohenjo-Daro (*ca.* 3250-2750 B.C.) has yielded samples of early cotton fabric, and continued use in the historical period is well attested. It is frequently mentioned in the "Laws of Manu" (*ca.* 800 B.C.).

Harsh climatic conditions apparently inhibited northwestern migration of the cotton industry. Nevertheless, the annals of King Sennacherib of Assyria (705-681) document his attempt to introduce cotton to Nineveh. The cotton plants, for which there was apparently no Akkadian name, were described as "trees bearing wool," which "they plucked and wove as garments." Sennacherib's experiment seems to have had no lasting result. There is no further literary or archaeological evidence for the use of cotton in the Near East until the Persian period.

Herodotus (fifth century B.C.) mentions the wool of trees in describing two rare linen corselets presented as gifts by the Egyptian King Amasis (569-525). The corselets were embroidered with gold thread and cotton. Whether the garments were from India or Nubia, the description implies that cotton was a rare commodity. A cotton industry was attested by Theophrastus in Bahrein on the Persian Gulf and in Arabia by the beginning of the third century B.C. The earliest evidence for cotton cloth in Africa is provided by charred fabrics found at Karnog in Nubia, dating from the Roman period. Evidence for the use of cotton in Egypt proper is post-Christian, and hence too late to satisfy the RSV reading of Isa. 19:9.

Bibliography. G. Goossens, "Le coton en Assyrie," *Mélanges Henri Grégoire* (1953), pp. 167-76; L. W. King, "An Early Mention of Cotton," *PSBA,* XXXI (1909), 339-43; A. Lucas, *Ancient Egyptian Materials and Industries* (4th ed., 1962), pp. 147-48; J. H. Saunders, *The Wild Species of Gossypium* (1961).

O. WINTERMUTE

COUNCIL, HEAVENLY. The concept of a council or an assembly of divine beings sitting together with Yahweh, discussing and making decisions concerning affairs of heaven and earth, is clearly presented in the language and imagery of the OT. The concept is represented by *sôdh* (סוד) in Jer. 23:18; Ps. 89:7 [H 8]; Job 15:8 and 29:4 (RSV "friendship"). It appears in the word *'ēdhâ* (עדה) in Ps. 82:1. The Divine Assembly or Heavenly Council is also referred to by the term בני אלים, "the sons of the Gods," or "the divine beings," in Ps. 29:1, and by the synonymous designation בני האלהים in Job 1:6 and 2:1. The Heavenly Council is also referred to by implication in Gen. 1:26 and 11:7, as well as in Exod. 15:11. *See* SONS OF GOD; HOSTS, HOST OF HEAVEN.

Another designation is *qᵉdhōsîm* (קדשים, the Holy Ones) appearing simply or in combination as קהל קדשים, עדת קדשים, סוד קדשים, all meaning "The Assembly of the Holy Ones" (Prov. 9:10; 30:3; Ps. 89:5, 7 [H 6, 8]; Job 5:1; 15:15). As over against this concept of the Heavenly Council, there is the antithesis of "the Assembly of the Shades of the Dead," or the Council of the Netherworld, which is found in the words קהל רפאים of Prov. 21:16. *See* DEITIES, UNDERWORLD[S].

This concept of a heavenly assembly is rooted in the oldest traditions of the Near East. It appears most dramatically in the Mesopotamian and Hellenic concepts of the universe as a state, a projection of earthly political experience onto the ideal plane of eternity (Jacobsen). The state in Sumer and Babylonia consisted of the entire society governed by an assembly of the most powerful individuals. By extrapolation, the Mesopotamian conceived of the whole universe as being governed by an assembly of the immortals who were manifest in those natural forces whose power inspired the Mesopotamian with awe, and whom he therefore viewed as his "gods."

Mesopotamian literature describes the assembly as the highest authority in the universe. Here the momentous decisions regarding the course of all things and the fates of all beings were made and confirmed. Before that stage was reached, however, proposals were discussed, perhaps even heatedly, by gods who were for or against them. In the early period the leader of the assembly was the god of heaven, Anu.

The concept of the gods in council, with a king of the gods at their head, is clearly presented in the literature of ancient Greece. The gods of Olympus, gathered in council with Zeus presiding and commanding obedience, is a scene which appears frequently in the Homeric writings (e.g., *Iliad,* VIII,1-40 and XX,1-30).

Closer to the biblical milieu are the writings of UGARIT, reflecting the religious ideas of Canaan. There the council of the gods is portrayed, with "El, the Father of Years," reigning as king (*see* EL, DEITY[S]). The council of the gods in session appears most clearly in the BAAL epic.

The Ugaritic term for the assembly of the Gods is *'dt ilm* (*UT* 128:II:7, 11), identical with its Hebrew cognate *'dt El* of Ps. 82:1. A second, synonymous term used in the Ugaritic epics is *pḫr ilm* (*UT* 2:17, 34; 51:III:13-14).

The Heavenly Council appears, therefore, to have been a common concept in the ancient Near East, with almost identical structure and function in the views of the earliest Mesopotamian society, in early Canaan, in Homeric Greece, and in biblical Israel.

The prophet Jeremiah (23:18, 22) speaks of the false prophets as not having the word of Yahweh, since they have not stood in his council (סוד). It is not certain from this passage, as some claim, that the true prophets did receive their inspiration and knowledge from the council of Yahweh. *See* I Kings 22:19-23.

The idea of a Heavenly Council appears numerous times in the literature of the Dead Sea Scrolls. There the terms עדה and סוד, both in reference to the community of the faithful as well as to the Heavenly Council, figure prominently in their apocalyptic declarations.

There is a distinct difference between the biblical treatment accorded this concept and that of contemporary sources. Whereas other sources assume a polytheistic council with each member an autonomous manifestation of a force in nature, the biblical literature, consistent with its tendency to eliminate "pagan" concepts, reduces the "gods" to mere servants of Yahweh. At most, the concept of the Heavenly Council is a literary fiction to dramatize Yahweh's thought, using the analogy of a human king surrounded by his courtiers.

Bibliography. T. Jacobsen, in *Before Philosophy,* ed. H. Frankfort (1949), pp. 137-234, and "Formative Tendencies in Sumerian Religion," in *The Bible and the Ancient Near East,* ed. G. E. Wright (1961), pp. 267-78.

D. NEIMAN

***COURAGE. 1. Courage in Greek philosophy.** A prominent virtue among the Greeks, courage was distinguished from fearlessness (which is sometimes the result of nature or even ignorance); in some cases, a healthy fear of moral evil is to be valued. Plato (*Republic* IV.vii) insists that the guardians of the city, who must possess this virtue above all others, should acquire it by learning the difference between those things which ought to be feared and those which ought not to be feared. Aristotle (*Nicomachean Ethics* III.vi-viii) sees courage as the mean between rashness and cowardice and isolates five types of spurious courage. True courage is closely allied with temperance. Just as the temperate man is one who forgoes certain pleasures for the sake of achieving a greater good, so the courageous man is one who endures pain or hardship, or overcomes his fears, in order to achieve his aim. Courage was linked with wisdom (or prudence), justice, and temperance (cf. Wisd. Sol. 8:7) to form the four cardinal or basic virtues, to which the church Fathers added the three theological virtues of faith, hope, and love.

2. Courage in the NT. No NT writer uses the characteristic Greek word for courage (ἀνδρεία). Moreover, none of the synonyms are present in any of the NT catalogues of virtues, and none of them are ever used in any specifically theological sense. Perhaps this is due to the fact that the concept of courage in secular Greek was so often connected with war and the military hero, or because the popular idea of courage allowed no place for humility or dependence on God. Be that as it may, the ideal of courage is certainly exemplified by the life of Jesus and the bold witness of his apostles (*see* BOLDNESS; BOLDNESS[S]). Thus steadfastness in the face of persecution and temptation is a cardinal Christian virtue (Rom. 5:3-4; I Pet. 2:19-21; Heb. 12:2), and some are called to give their lives for the sake of the testimony of Jesus and the Word of God (Rev. 7:14; 20:4). According to Rev. 21:8, "the cowardly" (δειλοί) are among those excluded from the new Jerusalem.

Bibliography. G. Fitzer, "τολμάω, κτλ.," *TDNT,* VIII (1969), 181-86.

W. W. GASQUE

COVENANT CODE. *See* COVENANT, BOOK OF THE; LAW IN THE OT §C3; LAW IN THE OT[S] §4.

COVENANT, DAVIDIC.

1. The promise of a dynasty and the choice of Zion
2. The covenant and its terminology
3. Davidic and Abrahamic covenant—an analogous typology
4. Father-son imagery
5. The conditioning of the covenant
6. The messianic interpretation

Bibliography

1. The promise of a dynasty and the choice of Zion. The divine promise to establish a dynasty for David is found for the first time in Nathan's oracle in II Sam. 7, following the account of the transfer of the ark to Jerusalem (ch. 6). The juxtaposition of these two chapters is to indicate that it was David's devotion to the Lord and his abode that brought about the promise of eternal grace for David. Furthermore, from ch. 7 we learn that David not only provided for the transfer of the ark, but also wanted to build "a house of cedar" for it (vs. 2). The Lord appreciated this wish (cf. I Kings 8:17-18) and as a token of gratitude promised to build "a house," i.e., a dynasty, for David while declining the offer to have a temple built for himself.

A similar juxtaposition is encountered in Ps.

132. We read about the oath of David that he will not rest until he has found a dwelling place for the Lord (vss. 2-5). This is followed by an oath of the Lord to establish the throne of David forever (vss. 11-18). The promise to David is modeled after the "royal grant" which was generally bestowed upon the servant who proved his loyalty and devotion to his master. The grant to David was, then, a response to his devotion: "O, Lord, count in David's favor his great self-denial" (vs. 1, NJV; cf. II Chr. 6:42, NEB).

There is indeed a strong connection between the founding of the Davidic dynasty and the establishment of an eternal seat for God and his ark in Zion. That the Davidic dynasty cannot be separated from Zion may be deduced from Ps. 132, where we read: "The Lord swore to David . . . 'One of the sons of your body I will set on your throne. . . . Their sons also forever shall sit upon your throne.' For the Lord has chosen Zion; he has desired it for his habitation" (vss. 11-13). The establishment of the dynasty is then motivated here by the choice of Zion as the Lord's abode.

2. The covenant and its terminology. The word ברית, "covenant," is not mentioned in Nathan's oracle, although it is implied there in the word חסד (II Sam. 7:15), "grace," which is synonymous with ברית (*see* §3 *below*). A covenant sworn to David is, however, explicitly attested in various poetic sources. Thus, we find in the so-called "David's last words": "He has made with me an everlasting covenant (ברית עולם)" (II Sam. 23:5); in Ps. 89:3 [H 4]: "I have made a covenant with my chosen one, I have sworn to David my servant"; and in Jer. 33:20-21: "If you can break my covenant with the day and . . . night . . . then also my covenant with David my servant may be broken." In Ps. 132 the word "covenant" is missing; however, the oath mentioned there has undoubtedly no less power than ברית (ברית and שבועה or אלה actually constitute a hendiadys; cf. also Ps. 89:19-37 [H 20-38]; II Chr. 7:18; 21:7).

Although some of these sources are quite late, especially Jer. 33 and Chronicles, we have no right to dispute the antiquity of the concept involved, i.e., a sworn obligation by God to preserve David's dynasty. II Sam. 23:1-7 is certainly old, and Ps. 89, although later than II Sam. 7, was also crystallized during the monarchy.

As indicated above, the term for God's pledge for the Davidic dynasty in II Sam. 7 is חסד, "grace" (vs. 15), but one finds there also the terms טובה, "favor" (vs. 28 and compare I Sam. 25:30) and דבר, "word" (vss. 25, 28). All these terms denote "covenant" in the Bible as well as in Akkadian (*see below*) and Aramaic sources (עדיא וטבתא, cf. *TWAT*, I, 786-87). Ps. 89 uses for the Davidic covenant besides ברית and חסד the word אמונה, "faithfulness." The latter, which means literally "firmness," connotes covenant in Hebrew as well as in Akkadian (*TWAT*). Moreover, אמונה and חסד are the key terms for the Davidic covenant in Ps. 89. They occur SEVEN times in this psalm—a significant number—and in fact are rooted in the image of "enduring grace" (author's trans.) which prevails in II Sam. 7:15-16. The endurance of the Davidic dynasty comes also to expression in Isaiah's prophecy. Ahaz, who is afraid of his enemies who want to overthrow the Davidic government, is addressed by Isaiah with the words: אם לא תאמינו כי לא תאמנו—"If you will not believe, you surely will not endure" (7:9).

The Davidic covenant represents a gracious promise by God which is not subject to any condition (*see* §5 *below*) and therefore fits the terms "grace" and "favor," in contrast to the Sinaitic covenant, which mainly involves obligations of the people and therefore is defined as ברית and never as חסד (*see* COVENANT; COVENANT, MOSAIC[S]). The Davidic covenant is also called הברית והחסד (I Kings 8:23), which should be understood as "gracious covenant." The same expression serves as a definition of the Abrahamic covenant, which, like that made with David, represents the gracious promise of the gift of the land (cf. Deut. 7:12 [RSV "covenant and steadfast love"]).

3. Davidic and Abrahamic covenant—an analogous typology. The covenant with David constitutes a pledge given by God to establish David's dynasty forever and is typologically similar to the covenant with Abraham, which is an oath by God to give his children the land of Canaan forever. Both covenants are diametrically opposed to the Mosaic covenant, in which the people pledge loyalty to God. The Abrahamic and Davidic covenants are then a promissory type, while the Mosaic covenant is an obligatory type. The promises of God in the Abrahamic and Davidic covenants are given unconditionally, and this is especially prominent in the David covenant. The unconditionality of the gift is explicitly stated: "I will establish his royal throne forever. I will be his father and he shall be my son. When he does wrong I will punish him as any father might and not spare the rod, but my grace will never be withdrawn from him" (II Sam. 7:13-15, author's trans.). By the same token, the covenant with the patriarchs is considered as valid forever (עד עולם). Even when Israel sins and is being severely punished, God intervenes to help, because he "will not break his covenant" (Lev. 26:43-45). *See* PROMISES TO THE PATRIARCHS[S].

Like the royal grants in the ancient Near East, the covenants with Abraham and David are gifts bestowed upon individuals who distinguished themselves by serving their masters loyally. Abraham is promised the land because he obeyed God and followed his mandate (Gen. 26:5, cf. 15:6-7; 22:16-18), and similarly David was given the grace expressed in a dynasty, because he served God with truth, righteousness, and loyalty (I Kings 3:6; 9:4-5; 11:4, 6; 14:8; 15:3). The terminology employed in this context is very close to that used in the Assyrian grants. In the grant of Ashurbanipal to his servant we read: "Baltaya . . . who was devoted (lit., whose heart was whole) to his lord, served me with faithfulness, walked in perfection in my palace . . . and kept the charge (*iṣṣur maṣṣarti*) of my kingship . . . I considered his good relations with me and decreed a gift for him" (Postgate, No. 9:11 ff.). Identical formulations are to be found in connection with the promises to Abraham and David. With regard to Abraham it is said that he "kept my charge," וישמר משמרתי

(Gen. 26:5); walked before God (24:40; 48:15); and was expected to "be blameless" (17:1). David's loyalty to God is couched in phrases which are even closer to the Assyrian grant terminology: "he walked before God in truth, loyalty, and uprightness of heart" (I Kings 3:6); walked after God "with all his heart" (I Kings 14:8), etc.

"Land" and "house" (=dynasty), the subjects of the Abrahamic and Davidic covenants, are the most prominent gifts of the suzerain in the Hittite and Syro-Palestine realms; the Hittite grants, like the grant of land to Abraham and the grant of "house" to David, are unconditional. The Hittite king says to his vassal: "After you, your son and grandson will possess it, nobody will take it away from them; if one of your descendants sins, the king will prosecute him, . . . but nobody will take away either *his house or his land* in order to give it to a descendant of somebody else" (*KBo* IV, 10, obv. 8-14).

A Hittite grant typologically similar to the grant of dynasty to David is to be found in the decree of Ḫattusilis concerning Mittannamuwa, his chief scribe:

> "Mittannamuwa was a man of grace (*kaniššanza* UKÙ-*aš*) to my father . . . and my brother Muwatalli was [kindly] disposed to him, promoted him (*kanešta . . . parā ḫuitiịat*) and gave Him Hattuša. My grace (*aššul*) was also shown to him . . . I committed myself for (*šēr memiịaḫḫat*) the sons of Mittannamuwa . . . and you will keep (*paḫḫaša-dumat*) . . . and so shall the sons of my Sun and the grandsons of my Sun keep. And as my Sun, Ḫattusili, and Puduhepa, the great queen, were kindly disposed (*kanešta*) towards the sons of Mittannamuwa so shall be my sons and grandsons. . . . And they shall not abandon the grace (*aššulan anda lē daliịanzi*) of my Sun. The grace and their positions shall not be removed" (*ụeḫ*). (Goetze, *Ḫattušiliš,* pp. 40 ff.)

Like Hebrew טובה/חסד, Akkadian *ṭābtu/damiqtu,* and Aramaic טבתא, Hittite *aššul* and *kannešuụar* connote kindness and covenantal relationship. As in the case of David, so in the Hittite grant the promise is to be "kept" (שמר) with the future generations of the devoted servant, i.e., "the man of grace" (cf. חסידך in Ps. 89:19 [H 20]). The most striking parallel to the promise of David is the last sentence: "The grace and their positions shall not be removed." (*Anda*) *daliịa* equals Akkadian *ezēbu*=Hebrew עזב which is often employed in connection with חסד ואמת or חסד, while *ụeḫ*—"turn away" (remove)—equals Hebrew סור which appears in II Sam. 7 in a phrase similar to that of the Hittite grant וחסדי לא יסור ממנו, "and my grace shall not turn away from him" (vs. 15).

Similar imagery is to be found in the Assyrian grants, for example in a passage of the document quoted above:

> "I am Aššurbanipal . . . who does good (*ēpiš ṭābti*) . . . who always responds graciously to the officials who serve him and returns kindness (*gimilli dumqi*) to the officials who serve him and returns kindness (*gimilli dumqi*) to the reverent (*pāliḫi*) who keeps his royal command (*nāṣir amāt šarrūtišu*) . . . PN a man of kindness and favor (*bēl ṭābti bēl dēqti*), who from the succession to the exercise of kingship served wholeheartedly his master, I took thought of his kindness and decreed his gift. . . . Any future prince from among the kings my sons . . . do good and kindness (*ṭābtu damiqtu ēpuš*) to them and their seed. They are friends and allies (*bēl ṭābti bēl dēqti*) of the king their master." (Postgate, No. 9, pp. 27 ff.)

Like the Assyrian king who, prompted by the kindness of his servant, promises "good and kindness" (*ṭābtu damiqtu*) to his descendants, so does Yahweh to the offspring of David and Abraham; he keeps his covenant and grace (הברית והחסד) to the coming generations of his loyal servants (I Kings 8:23). Furthermore, as the official of Assurbanipal is called: *bēl ṭābti bēl damiqti,* "friend and ally" (lit., "man of kindness and favor"), so are Abraham and David "the lovers" and "friends of God."

The promise to David is given in perpetuity (עד עולם, II Sam. 7:16) and the covenant is called eternal (ברית עולם, II Sam. 23:5), concepts familiar to us from the grants and gifts in the ancient Near East. The same applies to the covenant with Abraham.

In the light of the evidence adduced it seems that both covenant traditions were crystallized at the same time, the Davidic covenant being concerned with dynasty, while the Abrahamic covenant concerns the land. The extent of the land as described in the covenant with Abraham in Gen. 15:18-21 also points to Davidic times. The delineation of borders constitutes an important part of the documents of grants in the ancient Near East.

4. Father-son imagery. The father-son imagery, as reflected in the promise to David in II Sam. 7:14 and in its counterpart in Ps. 89:26-27 [H 27-28], also belongs to the legal conventions of grants and investiture. Thus we read in the treaty between the Hittite sovereign Šuppiluliuma and his vassal Šattiwazza (for the reading of this name, *see* Zaccagnini, *OrAnt,* XIII [1974], 25 ff.): "[The great King] grasped me with his hand and said: 'When I conquer the land of Mitanni I shall not reject you, *I shall make you my son.* I will stand by [to help you in war] and will make you sit on the throne of your father . . . the word which comes out of his mouth will not turn back'" (E. Weidner, pp. 40 ff., 29-30).

The three motifs attested here—sonship, grasping the hand, and validity of the promise—are to be found in the traditions about the covenant with David. The image of David as God's son is found in II Sam. 7:14 and Ps. 89:26-27 [H 27-28] (compare Ps. 2:7). Grasping the hand of God, which ensures victory, is found in Ps. 89:21-25 [H 22-26], and is to be compared to the proclamation of the Hittite King Ḫattusilis I, that the goddess of Arinna "put him in her bosom, grasped his hand and ran in battle before him" (*KBo* X, 1, vss. 13-14). The validity of the promise, which is expressed in the words of the sovereign that his word will not be turned back, is found in Ps. 132:11: "The Lord swore to David a sure oath from which he will not turn back."

The phrase "I will be his father and he shall be my son" is an adoption formula (cf. Greengus on *verba solemnia* in connection with marriage and adoption), and actually serves as the judicial basis for the gift of the eternal dynasty. This comes to clear expression in Ps. 2:7-8 where we read, "He said to me: 'You are my son, today I have begotten you. Ask of me, and I will make the nations your heritage, and the ends of the earth your possession.'" The notion of sonship is further developed in Ps. 89, where David's rights as first-born (vs. 27 [H 28]) appear in connection with his domination "on the sea" and "on the rivers" (vs. 25 [H 26]).

As is well known, the eldest son in the ancient Near East had a privileged position in the family and was entitled to a double share in the inheritance of the paternal estate (*see* FIRST-BORN §1; FIRST-BORN[S]). The selection of David as the first-born enhances then his rights of rule and dominion.

In Mesopotamia kings called themselves "sons" of gods and goddesses, and here too the divine descent had a figurative meaning: its purpose was to give full legitimization to the dynasty and its extensive rule. Thus, we read about the "birth" of King Šulgi which actually is his coronation: "Enlil the mighty shepherd, made the young man appear, the son . . . Šulgi . . . and gave him the rule over the land . . . he tied the sceptre at his side, the shepherd of all the lands . . . he lifted up his head towards the heaven" (CT 36, 26:15-27; cf. Sjöberg). Similarly we read in an oracle by the god Adad to the King of Mari: "Am I not Adad . . . him I raised between my legs. . . . I am the master of throne, land and city. . . . I will give him throne upon throne, house upon house, city upon city, the land from east to west" (Lods).

The father-son metaphor in connection with David is even more clearly expressed in the phrase which follows the adoption formula, i.e., "When he does wrong, I will punish him with the rod of men and with the afflictions of humans" (II Sam. 7:14, author's trans.). This may be now better understood in the light of familial documents from Nuzi. In the so-called *tuppī šīmti* (testaments) documents from Nuzi we often find in connection with the provisions about obedience to the adoptive father phrases like: "If PN_1 (the adopted child) fails to show respect for PN_2 (the adoptive father), then just as a man treats his son so far shall PN_2 treat PN_1" (for references *see* Weinfeld). The idea of disciplining sons in these documents goes together with the provision about perpetual inheritance, similar to II Sam. 7:14-15. We read in a will from Nuzi (note that ברית is rendered by the LXX as *diatheke,* i.e., "will"):

> All my lands . . . to my wife Zilipkiashe have been given . . . and Zilipkiashe shall be made parent of the sons . . . whoever among my sons will not obey Zilipkiashe, Zilipkiashe shall put him in the house of detention . . . and they will be put in fetters, but their right shall not be annulled . . . and Zilipkiashe shall not give away anything to strangers. (*AASOR,* X, No. 20 [1930])

The father-son imagery has been ascribed in later Judaism to the Messiah (*see below,* the passage from the Dead Sea Scrolls) and from there passed to the NT (Heb. 1:5; Mark 1:11).

5. The conditioning of the covenant. The promise for David, which originally was unconditional, was reinterpreted in a later stage of Israelite history. The destruction of Jerusalem and the disruption of the dynasty seemed to refute the claim for the eternity of the Davidic line, and therefore a reinterpretation of the covenant was necessary. This was done by putting in a condition: The covenant will persist only if the donee keeps his loyalty for the donor. It was the redactor of the book of Kings who put the promise of David under this condition: "If your descendants take care to walk faithfully in my sight with all their heart and with all their soul, you shall never lack a successor on the throne of Israel" (NEB, I Kings 2:4; cf. 8:25; 9:4-5). Similarly this condition has been introduced in Ps. 132:12, in contrast to Ps. 89:30-31 and II Sam. 7:14-15.

Adding a condition to the promise is characteristic also of the book of Chronicles. In I Chr. 28:6-7 the author refers to the promise of eternal dynasty and the father-son image of II Sam. 7 but adds, "if only he steadfastly obeys my commandments and my laws" (NEB). In the parallel to II Sam. 7 itself, the Chronicler omits the clause about sin and punishment, since this is what makes the promise unconditional (I Chr. 17:10-14).

In spite of the limitation imposed upon the promise by the condition, the promise itself continued to be regarded as eternally valid, as may be learned from messianic belief in the second temple period.

6. The messianic interpretation. The belief in a King-Savior who will appear in the future and will bring bliss to the nation was prevalent in the ancient Near East, especially in Egypt and Mesopotamia, and even reached Rome (cf. the fourth *Eclogue* of Vergil). However, the association of this idea with David is clearly the outcome of the concept of the Davidic covenant. This comes especially to expression in the prophecies of Isaiah (9:6-7 [H 5-6]; 11:1-5; cf. also 16:5); Micah (5:2-5*a* [H 1-4*a*]); Jeremiah (23:5-6; cf. 33:15-16, 21); and Ezekiel (34:23; 37:24-25). Isaiah (11:1, 10) and Jeremiah (23:5; 33:15) use the metaphors "stump" (גזע), "root" (שרש), or "branch" (צמח) springing out of David to reflect the idea of a legitimate heir. This may be deduced from the fact that the term צמח צדיק (RSV "righteous Branch") in Jer. 23:5 (cf. 33:15 and also Isa. 4:2; Zech. 6.12) ascribed to the future king is known to us from the Phoenician royal inscriptions (*KAI* 43:11), where it denotes the legitimate crown prince. Another metaphor which symbolizes the continuity of the dynasty is "the lamp of David" (cf. I Kings 11:36; 15:4; II Kings 8:19; the term נר may have been interpreted also as yoke= dominion) since it occurs in Ps. 132:17 paired with the idea of a sprout. The prophets, especially Isaiah, endowed the concept of the Davidic dynasty with a spiritual message and universal ideology. The future scion of Jesse will rule not by an "iron rod" (Ps. 2:9; cf. 110:2) but by the rod of his mouth and with the spirit of his lips (Isa. 11:4). As a consequence of this rule, enmity will be liquidated not only among humans but also among the beasts (vss. 6 ff.). The new King will be the symbol of "justice and righteousness" in the universal sense (1:2-5) and he "shall be set up as a signal to the people; the nations shall rally to it" (11:10 NEB). The idea of David as the establisher of "justice and righteousness" was also adopted by the editor of the book of Kings (Weinfeld, *Deuteronomy*, pp. 153-54).

At the period of the second temple, the hope for renewal of the Davidic kingdom became more and more utopian and gradually became associated with a new era (*see* MESSIAH, JEWISH; MESSIAH, JEWISH[S]). Thus, for example, in a MIDRASH from the Dead Sea Scrolls on II Sam. 7 we read: "'I shall be to him as a father and he will be to me as a son' that is: the shoot of David who will arise with the Interpreter of the Law . . . in the latter days as it is written, 'And I shall rise up the tabernacle of David that is fallen'" (*DJD*, V, Qumran Cave IV, p. 53:11-12).

The hope for the re-establishment of the Davidic dynasty pervaded the Jewish liturgy and is linked to the restoration of Jerusalem. In the prayer of the Eighteen Benedicitons we find the benediction of "the shoot of David" following the one of restoration of Jerusalem. (In some circles, especially among Palestinians, both were combined in the same benediction.)

Bibliography. G. W. Ahlström, *Psalm 89* (1959), "Der Prophet Nathan und der Tempelbau," *VT*, XI (1961), 113-27; S. Amsler, *David, roi et Messie* (1963); P. J. Calderone, *Dynastic Oracle and Suzerainty Treaty, 2 Samuel 7, 8-16* (1966); A. Caquot, "Les graces de David. A propos d'Isaie 55/3b," *Semitica*, XV (1965), 45-59; R. A. Carlson, *David, the Chosen King. A Traditio-Historical Approach to the Second Book of Samuel* (1964); H. Gese, "Der Davidsbund und die Zionserwählung," *ZThK*, LXI (1964), 10-26; A. H. J. Gunneweg, "Sinaibund und Davidsbund," *VT*, X (1960), 335-41; E. Kutsch, "Die Dynastie von Gottes Gnaden," *ZThK*, LVIII (1961), 137-53; D. J. McCarthy, "II Samuel 7 and the Structure of the Deuteronomic History," *JBL*, LXXXIV (1965), 131-38; N. M. Sarna, "Ps. 89, A Study in inner Biblical Exegesis," *Biblical and Other Studies*, ed. A. Altmann, I (1963), 29-46; K. Seybold, *Das Davidische Königtum im Zeugnis der Propheten*, *FRLANT*, CVII (1972); M. Weinfeld, "The Covenant of Grant in the OT and in the Ancient Near East," *JAOS*, XC (1970), 184-203, "Addenda to *JAOS*, XC (1970), p. 184," 92 (1972), 468-69, *Deuteronomy and the Deuteronomic School* (1972), בְּרִית, *TWAT*, I (1972), 781-808, "Covenant Terminology in the Ancient Near East, *JAOS*, XCIII (1973), 190-99; A. Lods, "Une tablette inedite de Mari," in *Studies in OT Prophecy*, ed. H. H. Rowley (1950), pp. 103-10; J. N. Postgate, *Neo-Assyrian Royal Grants and Decrees* (1969); E. F. Weidner, *Politische Dokumente aus Kleinasien* (1923); A. Sjöberg, "Recension: W. Römer, *Sumerische Königshymnen Isin-Zeit*," *Or*, XXXV (1966), 286-304; S. Greengus, "The Old Babylonian Marriage Contract," *JAOS*, LXXXIX (1969), 505-32; A. Goetze, *Ḫattušiliš*, *MVAG*, XXIX (1924).

M. WEINFELD

***COVENANT, MOSAIC.** The covenant which Yahweh made with Israel through Moses at Sinai (Horeb). This is the third of the covenants made by God, which together frame the Pentateuch in its present and final form; the first is with Noah and all living creatures (Gen. 9:8-17); the second with Abraham and his descendants (Gen. 15; 17). The Mosaic covenant is the culmination in which the relationship between Yahweh and Israel is formalized. Neither the term "Mosaic covenant" nor the designation "Sinai covenant," also commonly employed, is found in the biblical literature itself, but some such term is useful for distinguishing this covenant from the others, and from the covenant with David and his heirs. *See* COVENANT, DAVIDIC[S].

1. Covenant as symbol and tradition
2. Résumé of Mosaic covenant in the Pentateuch
3. Covenant and treaty
4. International treaty
5. History of the tradition

Bibliography

1. Covenant as symbol and tradition. ***a. Forensic aspect.*** To speak of a "covenant with God" is to use figurative or metaphorical language. It is to describe a relationship with God by analogy with a particular kind of formal relationship between persons. Given the extensive use of covenants and pacts of all sorts throughout the ancient world, there is no reason to suppose that the thought of a covenant with deity was unique to Israel. That it occurred elsewhere is shown by a plaque from Arslan Tash in upper Syria, ascribed to the seventh century B.C., which seeks to ward off demons who might try to enter a dwelling: "The Eternal One has made a covenant (*krt 'lt*, cf. Deut. 29:12, 14 [H 11, 13]) with us, Asherah has made [a pact] with us" (trans. Cross and Saley).

b. Scope. Because there is more than one type of covenant between human parties, and because covenant itself represents a complex relationship, the metaphor is capable of extensive and varied application as a religious symbol. It is only because the metaphor is so widely used and so fully developed in the biblical literature that it is really possible to ask what particular models lay behind it, what religious perceptions it expressed, and under what circumstances it developed. Not only is there a series of divine covenants, but these symbolize many aspects of the relationship between God and the community, including both its establishment and its rupture, and strike the balance in several different ways between divine commitment and human obligation.

c. Epic and cultic context. In its scope the covenant metaphor is not unlike a number of others, such as marriage (and its reciprocal, divorce), to which it is closely related. Yet, in the Mosaic covenant tradition in particular, it has an aspect which these other metaphors lack, for it has a place both in the epic as an event which happened at a particular moment in the past, and in the cultus as a formulary for maintaining and renewing the fundamental relationship with God which it describes and symbolizes.

2. Résumé of Mosaic covenant in the Pentateuch. As the tradition now stands, the solemn moment in which this covenant was concluded is recounted in Exod. 19:3–24:14. God declares the terms of covenant, first directly to the people (Exod. 20:2-17, the Decalogue) and then—because they are terrified—through Moses (20:22-26; 21:1–23:19), concluding with a section which anticipates the Conquest (23:20-33). The covenant is then concluded by a complex of ritual acts, including a declaration of acceptance and obedience by the people (24:1-14).

Subsequently Yahweh makes a covenant with Israel again in Exod. 34:10-28, following the episode of the golden calf and Moses' intercession. The terms of covenant preserved here are not identical with those of Exod. 19–24, and the procedure is also somewhat different; in particular, Yahweh refers this time to the future conquest rather than the past deliverance, and there is no response by the people. Terms of covenant are given several times again without reference to previous formulations, at greatest length in Lev. 17–26 (the Holiness Code), which ends with solemn promises and warnings, the latter qualified by a concluding assurance that even in exile God will remember his covenant with the patriarchs if the people repent and return to him. The account of the sojourn at Sinai continues until Num. 10:11; this extensive block of material (Exod. 19:1–Num. 10:10), with its almost overwhelming piling up of traditions of all sorts, follows from the conviction that all of Israel's fundamental laws and religious institutions were consequent to this act of covenant.

At the conclusion of the Pentateuch, Moses, before his death (Deut. 34), recalls this covenant moment again, and exhorts Israel to obedience. Terms of covenant are set out once again (notably in Deut. 5, cf. Exod. 20; and Deut. 12–26), followed here also by solemn promises and warnings (Deut. 27; 28; 29), the latter again qualified by the assurance that a return to obedience will bring restoration to the land even from exile (Deut. 30:1-10; cf. 4:27-31).

3. Covenant and treaty. It can be seen even from this brief summary that the Pentateuchal traditions relating to the Mosaic covenant are both extensive and complex, a witness to its importance and to a long history of reflection upon its meaning. The task of tracing the history of the tradition has long occupied scholars, and a large part of the problem has been to understand the root of what was clearly a complex metaphor. The recognition that international suzerainty treaties were an analogous covenant form (*see* COVENANT §§A, C3*a*) has placed the matter on a new footing and largely shaped the course of subsequent discussion. Further investigations of the international treaties (*see* §4) and the biblical literature (*see* §5) have undertaken to test and elaborate the two sides of the analogy.

The view that covenant as a theological concept appeared only late in Israel has again found its defenders. One line of investigation has sought to establish that the theological use of ברית does not appear before the Deuteronomic tradition, building upon the argument that ברית meant originally "obligation (assumed or imposed)" and not a relationship such as the translation "covenant" suggests. The lexical argument is judged to be weakest, however, precisely at the point where it insists upon an absolute distinction between obligation and relationship. The attempt to demonstrate that all earlier references to covenant are Deuteronomic or Deuteronomistic is generally regarded as a tour de force. The line of argument is not entirely new, and carried more conviction when it could still be assumed that a covenant with deity was unique to Israel and was too subtle and developed a conception for the early period.

4. International treaty. Further research has sought to refine and supplement where possible the classic juristic analysis by Victor Korošec, on which the initial comparison with Mosaic covenant was based, and to extend it to other than Hittite treaties. These still constitute the bulk of the available evidence, however, and Korošec's work has required remarkably little modification in the light of further study and the publication of additional treaty texts and fragments.

a. Formal elements. The number of exemplars and the quite regular structure have made it possible to extract something like a prototypical form for the Hittite treaties (fourteenth-thirteenth centuries B.C.), even though each was drafted for a real political situation. Many of the texts are quite fragmentary, and not all are official documents of record (one of the treaties with the Kashkaeans, for example, is almost certainly a preliminary draft). For Korošec's analysis (six formal elements), *see* COVENANT §A. It is now generally agreed that the provision for "the deposit and public reading" of the treaty, which Korošec himself noted was lacking more often than not, should not be included. It is to be regarded, like the oath of the vassal, as a part of the procedure which only occasionally finds its way into the written text of the formal document. While it is agreed that the "historical prologue" was a typical element, there has been considerable debate over possible instances of its omission; these are few, if one grants, as one probably must, that the element could range from an extensive account which reached back several generations to a quite simple reminder that the vassal had the suzerain to thank for his investiture. Attempts to distinguish additional formal elements, such as a "statement of substance" or "general clause" concerning the future relations of the parties, or a "description of the land" detailing the accepted boundaries of the vassal's territory, have pointed more to matters of content than formal structure.

A comparable analysis of other groupings of treaties by region and period is more difficult, for the texts are fewer, are unevenly distributed, and show greater variation. A "historical prologue" seems not to have been typical, although the very fragmentary treaty of Ashurbanipal with Qedar, recently published, evidently included one. While Hittite treaties regularly stated both blessings and curses in a brief formula, the later treaties evidently contained only curses. While this is not entirely certain, because some texts are broken, emphasis certainly lay on the curses, which were extensive and detailed, sometimes dramatically enacted. The later treaties also show occasional merging of formal elements; thus the curses may be combined with the "list of divine witnesses" by linking curses appropriate to each deity with the invocation of the name, or with the "stipulations" by invoking a curse after each stipulation, in either case giving even greater prominence to curse.

Other differences appear as well, but it can be seen from these that the contrast is not merely formal. It follows rather from a difference in the way the treaty relationship itself was conceived. Treaties which included blessings and an account of the sovereign's benefactions did not rest solely upon submission to superior force and terror of divine retribution.

b. Reduction to essential elements. A different line of investigation has sought to discover which elements the ancients themselves would have regarded as the minimum essential to a treaty, and by this means to test further the extent of the difference between Hittite treaties and those of the first millennium, and to provide a minimal criterion for recognizing treaty form in the OT.

The starting point is the premise that those who drafted the documents would not have failed to include all the elements they believed essential to a valid and binding treaty. The constant elements are said to be three: the "stipulations," the "list of divine witnesses," and the "curses." These are readily inferred from the later treaties. For the Hittite treaties, however, other considerations must be invoked; thus the element "blessings and curses" is reduced to "curses" on the ground that only the curses were really operative (while this could be challenged, certainly curses alone were sufficient to make a treaty binding). The conclusion that there was a long and widespread use of the same essential treaty form rests upon this further reduction toward strictly indispensable elements. That there was some continuity is not to be denied, and would be expected, given the international use of the genre and its essential character as an expanded promissory oath. The typical forms are nevertheless quite different, and this must be the basis for any assessment of the jural concepts which lay behind them.

While these elements are common to treaties, they are not peculiar to them; they are found also in Babylonian *kudurru* texts (boundary stones) and documents of grant. The formal distinction lies in content and function, which must always be considered.

The OT contains no formal text of a covenant, political or religious (however, *see* COVENANT §C3*a*; *also* §5*d below*), although there are texts which reflect a covenant formulary. For the many references to covenant and narratives of covenant making, it has been more helpful to identify the technical terminology of treaty and the legal terms by which one referred to treaty and treaty relationship. It has been shown, for example, that the expression "peace and friendship" is used only where a treaty of friendship is involved (cf. Deut. 23:6 [H 7]; RSV "peace" or "prosperity"), and that "to make friendship" means to make a treaty (cf. II Sam. 2:6; RSV "do good"). Such terms have been taken up as theological vocabulary in the OT.

c. Reciprocity. Parity treaties detailed reciprocal obligations (*see* COVENANT §C1*b*); suzerainty treaties did not. Even so, the latter were not entirely unilateral. In exchange for his oath of loyalty, the vassal received legitimation (often explicitly mentioned) and protection, and indeed all the benefactions claimed by the suzerain in the "historical prologue" imply an obligation for the future as well. Particularly striking are those instances where the greater power bound itself by curse or oath: a vassal's right to dynastic succession sanctioned by a curse (treaty of Tudhaliyas IV with Ulmi-Tešub; some see here however a merging of the genres of treaty and royal grant); the possibility allowed that a Hittite could "transgress the oath" (treaty of Suppiluliumas with Aziras); a suzerain's reference to an exchange of oaths with a vassal (letter of Shamshi-Adad to Kuwari; cf. Deut. 26:17-19).

d. Human witnesses. The witnesses to treaties sometimes included human persons, of interest in view of Josh. 24:22 and other biblical texts. In some cases they evidently served to attest the authenticity of a copy made to replace a lost original. The publication of a series of treaties between the Hittites and the Kashkaeans which regularly name human persons as well as gods as witnesses has raised again the question whether they may sometimes have served in other capacities, perhaps as witnesses to the formal preparation of the text.

e. Process for breach of treaty. There is evidence, gathered from royal correspondence and such texts as the Tukulti-Ninurta epic, to indicate that a suzerain's proceedings against a rebellious vassal were as carefully ordered as the treaty which established the relationship. The suzerain established the justice of his case before the gods and sent formal notice to his vassal. The literary form employed was evidently a recapitulation of the relevant sections of the treaty, the broken stipulations now cast as accusations, and it was concluded either by solemn admonitions and a brief statement of proper conduct, or by an ultimatum which was virtually a declaration of war. War, if it came, was apparently viewed as the ultimate legal process by which the gods gave decision in the case.

5. History of the tradition. ***a. Premonarchic period.*** The correspondences with suzerainty treaty suggested the hypothesis that smaller kinship groups were united in a larger social and religious (perhaps better, cultic) sodality ("Israel") through a common vassalage to Yahweh (*see* COVENANT §C3*a, b*). The assumption of military obligations which this implies is now further supported by the finding that covenant making and summons to holy war employed common symbols. *See* WAR, HOLY[S].

The new sodality has been described as a sacral league, a social structure which had already been proposed on other grounds, and which provides a suitable model (on the present state of the question, *see* AMPHICTYONY[S]). Other forms of sodality may be explored, but it is hardly possible to return to the assumption that blood ties alone provided the social bond (*see* KINSHIP AND FAMILY [S] §8). It is not necessary to suppose that the new sodality was formed all at once, or that the model was taken over directly from the international political sphere.

The ground for such a development may already have existed in patriarchal society, where covenants in which the deity took the initiative were already a living social and cultic form, associated with the "god of the father" (*see* PATRIARCHS[S] §2*b*). It is likely that these were not originally free of obligation to the deity, and that the unilateral and unconditional character they have in the present epic tradition (*see* COVENANT §C2) is the result of an assimilation to the pattern of the Davidic covenant. *See* COVENANT, DAVIDIC[S] §3.

The constitution of the new sodality will have been considerably more complex than either political treaty or patriarchal covenant envisaged, and there is no simple answer to the question, Who was made vassal to Yahweh by covenant? The league model suggests tribes (or clans), and this is implied as well by the ancient poem of Judg. 5, the story of Judg. 19–21, and elsewhere. The series of three treaties which Mursilis II made at one time with peoples in one region is a somewhat analogous situation (Friedrich). If blessings and curses were once addressed to tribes, however, the custom has been forgotten. Covenant stipulations regulating the relations between tribes, if they once existed, must have been lost when the tribes ceased to function as social units. It is persons and households whose relations are regulated by the covenant traditions which have survived, and Josh. 24 suggests a covenant accepted by households (vs. 15). In Deuteronomy, however, and in the Sinai account as it now stands, it is the people (or its leaders) who accept the terms of covenant, and the blessings and curses (cf. Lev. 26; Deut. 28) also have in view the community as a whole.

b. The epic tradition (JE) gives a representation of Mosaic covenant from the period of the monarchy which is important in its own right and for the earlier tradition it incorporates (*see* YAHWIST[S]; ELOHIST[S]). The covenant is one which Yahweh initiates, following gracious acts which obligate the people; it involves stipulations binding upon the people, giving first place to the claim of exclusive loyalty (Exod. 20:3-17); it is freely accepted by a declaration of obedience (24:3, 7); and it makes continuing relationship and future benefaction conditional upon faithfulness (19:3*b*-8, attribution disputed, but probably ancient liturgical materials transmitted by E). This recalls at once the relation of suzerain to vassal, and the covenant can be recognized even in this narrative form as belonging to the same general type.

The formal structure of Exod. 19–24 has been thought to reflect the covenant formulary of an earlier cultic setting (*see* EXODUS, BOOK OF §3). Attempts to correlate this more precisely with treaty form have been only partially successful. For the historical prologue one must begin earlier, perhaps at Exod. 1; for the blessings and curses one must continue to Lev. 26, which lies outside the epic strata (in the Holiness Code) even though it has been shown to contain older material (so also the list in Deut. 28).

In the epic as a whole the Mosaic covenant has been subordinated to the patriarchal covenant. This is particularly clear in the Yahwist, which is the more fully preserved. It is the promise to Abraham (Gen. 12:1-3) and subsequent covenant with him (Gen. 15, perhaps partly E) which introduce the leading themes to which the epic repeatedly returns, and which it may originally have carried through to the Conquest. The Mosaic covenant undergoes no comparable development. The inference has been drawn, no doubt correctly, that the Yahwist made no more of it than it was obliged to, and included it only because it was already part of the existing tradition.

In this the Yahwist certainly reflects the Jerusalem royal theology (*see* YAHWIST[S]), which placed greater emphasis on the covenant with David, and which could claim the covenant with Abraham—at least in the form represented by the epic tradition—as a model and precedent. *See* COVENANT, DAVIDIC[S].

Although Sinai is connected with the Exodus in both epic strata, and therefore by inference in the older (poetic?) epic on which both have drawn, there are indications that it originally intruded; moreover, it is lacking in credal formulations which recite the saving acts of God (*see* CREDO, ANCIENT ISRAELITE[S]). The elements of an earlier covenant ritual may have been separated and recombined.

c. Prophets. Covenant form is most fully represented in the lawsuit genre, which has been shown to resemble the proceedings of a suzerain against a rebellious vassal (*see* §4*e above*). It may be inferred that the covenant and treaty forms which underlay them shared a common structure and conception. The appeal to heaven and earth (Isa. 1:2, somewhat differently Jer. 2:12; Mic. 6:1-2) recalls their role as covenant witnesses in Deuteronomy (*see* §*d below*) and provides a further link with treaty form.

It is possible to support this conclusion to some degree from the judgment speech, which is structurally simpler but more frequent than the covenant lawsuit. The prophetic announcements of judgment have been compared with the curse lists of Deut. 28, Lev. 26, and the treaties. Even allowing that descriptions of gods acting to hurt or destroy will inevitably show some similarity, there is often a remarkable correspondence in imagery, sometimes even in wording, even in the earliest prophetic material. There is also a correspondence in function, since the judgment speech, like the covenant lawsuit, makes a charge of misconduct the basis of the announced judgment.

As early as Hos. 6:7 and 8:1 there are explicit charges that Israel has scorned the covenant. If I Kings 19:10, 14 is to be credited, the same accusation had been made earlier by a northern predecessor. Hos. 8:1-3 is particularly important, for it appeals (vs. 1) to a covenant with stipulations (תורתי) which could be broken and transgressed. The people's claim to "know" God (vs. 2) is almost certainly to be understood as a claim that they acknowledge his legitimate authority as overlord. The word "to know" (ידע) is used occasionally in this legal sense to refer to mutual recognition on the part of suzerain and vassal, and has its equivalent in the treaties, although Hittite distinguishes this use by a reflexive particle.

The reciprocal usage appears, for example, in Amos 3:2, where Yahweh says of Israel, "You only have I known"; compare the phrase "I [the Su]n will know only you, Alaksandus" in a treaty of Muwattallis (Friedrich). The charge that Israel has abandoned "good" (Hos. 8:3) no doubt reflects the legal usage of טוב, טובה as "friendship, good relations," employed when a treaty relationship is involved *(see* §4*b above)*.

d. Deuteronomic tradition. Mosaic covenant is the leading theme of Deuteronomy. Its characteristic sequence of exhortation, commandments, blessing, and curse—found in individual sections and in the arrangement of the book as a whole—as well as its emphasis upon exclusive loyalty to Yahweh, the emphatic manner in which it urges gratitude as a basis for obedience, and the priority it gives to election over commandment, had all been noted before its likeness to treaty had been observed. *See* DEUTERONOMY §5.

Recent studies have shown that its language is full of the vocabulary of treaty and diplomacy, and that its curses are remarkably similar—in some cases virtually identical—to those found in treaties. While some of the same curses appear also in contexts which have nothing to do with treaty, the correspondence in form and content extends also to function: conditional curses follow stipulations, and thus provide sanctions for sworn obligations.

Deuteronomic tradition has clearly in view that Israel's obligations to Yahweh are analogous to those of a sworn vassal. Its welfare is conditional; indeed, loyalty and obedience are the conditions for realizing the gracious covenant sworn to the patriarchs (Deut. 7:12; cf. 8:18). In the later introduction to the book (1:1–4:40; *see* DEUTERONOMIC HISTORY, THE[S] §§1, 3), the balance has shifted, and the oath to the fathers is unconditional; it becomes eventually a ground for hope even in exile (4:31).

In the framework of the book the witnesses to the covenant are "heaven and earth" (4:26; 30:19; 31:28; cf. 32:1). These are frequently listed among the old gods—gods of theogony but not of cult—as witnesses to the treaties. The presence of such an element (found also in the prophets; *see* §*c above*), functional in treaty but surely vestigial here, is one of several indications of more or less conscious adaptation of treaty form, as opposed to an independent development which chanced along similar lines. It has, in fact, been argued that the central section of the book (the second discourse) was intended to be the text of a Yahweh treaty, and the same has been claimed for the book as a whole.

Some have attributed this treaty likeness to contact with the Neo-Assyrian Empire, to which both Israel and Judah were in vassalage as early as the third quarter of the eighth century. The length of the curse section (28:15-68; contrast the blessings, 28:1-14) and many of the curses do in fact resemble treaties of the eighth-seventh centuries rather than earlier ones. This may, however, only show that the analogy with treaty was still open to influence from contemporary practice. The Deuteronomic understanding of covenant gives the impression of baroque elaboration rather than innovation. The use of historical reminiscence as a basis for appeals to love, loyalty, and gratitude, and of blessings as well as curses, corresponds to the typical form of earlier treaties but seems to be quite different from the usual Assyrian practice *(see* §4*a above)*. If those scholars are correct who have on other grounds explained the characteristic structure of the book as a derivation from liturgies of covenant renewal, the basis of the analogy must lie further back in the earlier cultus.

e. The Priestly work. The question of the nature and extent of Mosaic covenant traditions in the Priestly stratum is bound up with the question whether this stratum ever existed by itself as an independent document *(see* PRIESTLY WRITERS[S] §§1-2). The place of this covenant in the final structure of the Pentateuch is nevertheless clear: it is one of three covenants which serve to divide history into four ages (Adam, Noah, Abraham, Moses). Each succeeding covenant narrows in scope as it gains in importance. The blessing of Creation (Gen. 1:22, 28) is repeated with each of the covenants, e.g., with the Mosaic in Lev. 26:9. The sabbath, instituted at Creation (Gen. 2:1-3), becomes the sign of the Mosaic covenant (Exod. 31:13-17; cf. the P expansion of the sabbath commandment, Exod. 20:11). Each covenant continues to be valid, but the Mosaic is God's ultimate self-disclosure, revealing his name and his laws, and establishing his cultus. As a mark of its special importance P employs the term עדות *(see* COVENANT §B1) for the Mosaic covenant, choosing —as it often does—an archaic word to use as a technical term, and reserves the term ברית, with few exceptions, for all others. *See* LAW IN THE OT[S] §16.

Bibliography. K. Baltzer, *The Covenant Formulary* (1971); F. M. Cross, *Canaanite Myth and Hebrew Epic* (1973), esp. pp. 265-73, 295-300; F. M. Cross and R. J. Saley, "Phoenician Incantations on a Plaque . . . from Arslan Tash," *BASOR*, 197 (1970), 42-49; F. C. Fensham, "Maledictions and Benedictions in Ancient Near Eastern Vassal-Treaties and the OT," *ZAW*, LXXIV (1962), 1-9, "Common Trends in Curses of the Near Eastern Treaties and *Kudurru*-Inscriptions compared with Maledictions of Amos and Isaiah," *ZAW*, LXXV (1963), 155-75, and "Clauses of Protection in Hittite Vassal-Treaties and the OT," *VT*, XIII (1963), 133-43; G. Fohrer, "AT—'Amphiktyonie' und 'Bund'?" *TLZ*, XCI (1966), cols. 894-901; M. Fox, "*Ṭôb* as Covenant Terminology," *BASOR*, 209 (1973), 41-42; R. Frankena, "The Vassal-Treaties of Esarhaddon and the Dating of Deuteronomy," *OTS*, XIV (1965), 122-54; A. Goetze, "Hittite *šek-/šak-* '[Legally] Recognize' in the Treaties," *JCS*, XXII (1968), 7-8; D. R. Hillers, *Treaty Curses and the OT Prophets* (1964), "A Note on Some Treaty Terminology in the OT," *BASOR*, 176 (1964), 46-47, and *Covenant* (1969); H. B. Huffmon, "The Exodus, Sinai and the Credo," *CBQ*, XXVII (1965), 101-13, and "The Treaty Background of Hebrew *Yāda'*," *BASOR*, 181 (1966), 31-37; H. B. Huffmon and S. B. Parker, "A Further Note," *BASOR*, 184 (1966), 36-38; M. G. Kline, *Treaty of the Great King* (1963); E. Kutsch, *Verheissung und Gesetz, BZAW*, CXXXI (1972); D. J. McCarthy, *Treaty and Covenant* (1963), includes trans. of selected treaties, and *OT Covenant* (1972), a survey of current opinions with bibliog.; G. E. Mendenhall, *The Tenth Generation* (1973); W. L. Moran, "A Kingdom of Priests," in *The Bible in Current*

Catholic Thought, ed. J. L. McKenzie (1962), pp. 7-20, "A Note on the Treaty Terminology of the Sefire Stelas," *JNES,* XXII (1963), 173-76, and "The Ancient Near Eastern Background of the Love of God in Deuteronomy," *CBQ,* XXV (1963), 77-87; L. Perlitt, *Bundestheologie im AT,* WMANT, XXXVI (1969); R. Polzin, "HWQY' and Covenantal Institutions in Israel," *HTR,* LXII (1969), 227-40; *ANET* (3rd ed., 1969), pp. 199-206, 318, 529-30 (Egyptian and Hittite treaties), 531-41 (Akkadian treaties from Syria and Assyria), 659-61 (Aramaic treaty), 628 (letter of Shamshi-Adad); G. M. Tucker, "Covenant Forms and Contract Forms," *VT,* XV (1965), 487-503; J. Friedrich, *Staatverträge des Hatti-Reiches in hethitischer Sprache, Mitteilungen der Vorderasiat. Ägypt. Gesellschaft,* I (1926), II (1930).

P. A. Riemann

COVENANT, NEW. *See* New Covenant[S].

COVENANT LAWSUIT. *See* Law in the OT[S].

CREDO, ANCIENT ISRAELITE. A credo is a summary statement of belief encompassing the irreducible minimum sustaining a common faith. It is necessarily confessional in nature and thus is designed to be reinforced by behavior that expresses strong conviction. The attempt to isolate such confessional statements in the OT has been made along form-literary, traditio-historical, and theological lines, often with ambiguous or conflicting results.

Some scholars have set forth such ancient credos as the basic form for the development of theological motifs and as the foundation of extensive literary complexes. Others have denied the presence of such ancient credos, arguing rather that those which have been set forth are only late summaries of developed OT faith. Yet a third group has sought to present a synthesis utilizing the insights of the two opposing groups.

1. The brief historical credo. The idea that special summaries of history and faith may provide the foundation for the literary development of parts of the OT was investigated by Jirku in 1917. He set forth the idea that a recurring pattern of "didactic expositions" *(lehrhaften Darstellungen)* may be discerned throughout the OT. These "expositions" vary in length, in sequence, and even in the number of specific points they present, but they always deal with the principal events from the call of Abraham to the entrance into Canaan, and they do so with a repeated formulaic style. Jirku believed this pattern to have been set prior to David's time, and though he never referred to the "didactic expositions" as credos, his emphasis on their use at the cultic assembly and his proposal that they became the basis of the growth of the Tetrateuch make his work foundational to the research by von Rad and Noth.

a. Gerhard von Rad. In 1938 von Rad published his theory of the brief historical credo which effectively determined both the definition of the term credo and the direction of scholarly debate concerning the concept. Von Rad was unwilling to eliminate the source documents, as Jirku had done, but like Jirku, he proposed a growth of the OT from a relatively fixed basic form.

Decrying the standstill reached in Hexateuchal studies by source and form analysis, von Rad proposed a new approach: since the essential concern of the Hexateuch is Israel's belief, why not begin with what might logically be assumed to be the irreducible minimum of that belief and then consider the whole in the light of its most fundamental form? One could call this fundamental form a "credo," von Rad held; it would be a confessional summation of the essential points of the salvation history, never subject to change in basic content from the earliest times, variable only in its external form.

Settling upon Deut. 26:5*b*-9 as the best and probably the earliest example of the brief historical credo, and adducing such parallel examples as Deut. 6:20-24 and Josh. 24:2*b*-13, von Rad proposed *(a)* a confession limited essentially to four great themes: the patriarchs, the oppression in Egypt, the Exodus, and the march to and entry of the Promised Land; *(b)* a confession formally drawn in elevated and compact language for public recitation; *(c)* a confession frequently reflected, though often in free variation, in the language of Israel's cultic worship; *(d)* a confession summarizing traditions associated with Kadesh, not Sinai, and related to the celebration of the Feast of Weeks at Gilgal, the site of Joshua's apportioning of the Promised Land.

Von Rad referred to the brief historical credo as a literary type *(Gattung)*, but his form-literary study rapidly became a traditio-historical study. A striking feature of this credo was its total lack of reference, in even its freer and fragmentary refractions, to the momentous events at Sinai. Von Rad concluded that the tradition associated with Sinai existed independently, in complete separation from the schema represented by the credo. This tradition too had a cultic locus and a cultic occasion: Shechem and the Feast of Booths. But it was not woven into the canonical pattern represented by the brief historical credo until the time of the Yahwist. This fusion of two separate bodies of tradition, probably never attempted before, was no doubt unpopular. Indeed it appears to have received wide acceptance for the first time no earlier than the Exile.

Thus was the Hexateuch, for all its complex combination of originally separate traditions, shaped primarily by preoccupation with the theme of land settlement, itself given ancient summary in the short historical credo. *See* Yahwist[S] § 3.

b. Martin Noth. Von Rad's isolation of the short historical credo became both a foundation and a point of departure for Noth's influential traditio-historical study of the Pentateuch. Noth accepted without reservation both the presence of such a literary type and also the view of formative influence upon the Pentateuch. He similarly embraced von Rad's view that the Sinai tradition, despite its own obvious antiquity, was independent of the credo until late.

The differences between the positions of Noth and von Rad are in the main differences of refinement. Noth went on to conclude that there were five separate themes which served as nuclei in the formulation of the Pentateuch. These themes (primary and basic, exodus from Egypt; subsequently, entry into Canaan, promise to the patriarchs, and guidance in the wilderness; last and latest, the revelation at Sinai) are themselves no more than refinements of the general themes isolated by von Rad, brought into sharper focus and fuller exposition. He rejected von Rad's view of the creative role of the Yahwist in uniting the traditions, holding rather that both the Sinai tradition and the patriarchal traditions were united in the common foundation *(Grundlage)* of both J and E *(see* YAHWIST[S] § 2). He similarly discounted other details of von Rad's original exposition, e.g., the primary association of the credo with the sanctuary at Gilgal.

These revisions are of small consequence for the theory of the short historical credo. The major result was a wider dissemination and acceptance of the theory. Indeed, Noth reinforced the credibility of the view that the credo formed the nucleus of the Tetrateuch (or Pentateuch, or Hexateuch) by his persuasive emphasis on the cultic context of each successive repetition of the credo.

2. A credo without Sinai? While the views of von Rad and Noth have proved stimulating, and while they have been adopted with little revision by some OT scholars, wider acceptance has been related primarily to the credo as a literary type, and to the constituent themes of such a credo. Critical reaction has been directed first of all against the separation of the credo from the Sinai tradition. Very few scholars have been able to allow this separation, not only because it does such violence to the order and emphasis of the OT text, but also because of the obvious antiquity (admitted even by von Rad and Noth) and recurrent influence of the Sinai tradition. Another objection is that the Sinai tradition, as a tradition of encounter, is different in nature from the traditions of the saving history, and therefore need not be mentioned in a credo which was part of a cultic celebration of the saving history.

That the Exodus and Sinai traditions represent events in sequence has been supported by comparative study of covenant and treaty formularies in the OT and in the state literature of the Hittite empire. A common ancient Near Eastern association of acts of protection and beneficence (history) with covenantal expectation (law) has been proposed *(see* COVENANT § A; COVENANT, MOSAIC[S]). If such a pattern can be maintained—and it has received wide acceptance and exposition—the theory that the Sinai tradition was late in becoming a part of the credo becomes still less tenable. Caution must be exercised, however, in use of the ancient Near Eastern treaty documents. Assyrian legal literature in particular has brought the more detailed outline of an ancient Near Eastern covenant or treaty formulary into question.

3. Ancient credo or late summary? Criticism of the von Rad-Noth theory has raised, in the main, two questions: *(a)* Can such a credo really be shown to be ancient? and *(b)* Did a credo, as such, ever have any place in ancient Israelite cultic life?

A crucial point in von Rad's discovery and exposition of the short historical credo is the antiquity of Deut. 26:5*b*-9. Despite an admission that this passage displays some Deuteronomic language, von Rad considered it at least earlier than the Yahwist. This assertion has been subjected to a stringent criticism by a careful comparison of Deut. 26:5-9 with the vocabulary generally regarded as Deuteronomic. These studies have prompted the view that Deut. 26:5-9 and similar passages cited by von Rad are at best a thorough Deuteronomic reworking of traditions (e.g., vss. 5 and 10*a*) or, more likely, a free composition of the Deuteronomic period. *See* DEUTERONOMY §§ 3, 7 and DEUTERONOMY[S]; DEUTERONOMIC HISTORY, THE[S] esp. §2.

More serious still is the objection that von Rad and Noth have not in fact demonstrated the presence of the credo as a literary type. The credo passages have instead been regarded as historical summaries designed for liturgical use; or catechetical sequences; or historical prologues to covenantal ceremony; or formula prayers for set occasions; or informal theological collections affirming the general perimeters of Israel's faith. Though such approaches may seem at first merely to be calling the credos by another name, they tend to deny them any role in the formation of OT literature, and thus to place serious limits on their importance. The acceptance of any such position thus undercuts completely the von Rad-Noth theory.

4. Credo and the OT. Surprisingly little attention has been given to the credo itself as a widespread OT literary type. There can be little doubt that statements of essential belief are a necessary part of the religion of an articulate people. That ancient Israel should *not* have such statements would be occasion for surprise. What is important therefore is the isolation of the vocabulary, the forms, and the recurring essential points of such statements. Only then will any consideration of the influence of the confessions upon OT literary growth become more than suggestive speculation. Underlying the form-literary considerations with which von Rad began are important questions of cultic rhetoric—the basic words and phrases of priest and prophet, of wise man and poet, of the literati of the cult, and even of the layman in whose behalf so much of the cultic literature was formed in the first place. Once these building blocks of cultic expression are better known, both the credos and the theology underlying them can be more clearly isolated.

That there was "credo" in ancient Israel now seems assured. Too detailed an assertion of its exact contents and too close an association of the credo with one cultic occasion or one particular locale must be avoided. Credo as a literary type must be allowed both considerable flexibility and broad comprehensiveness. The given form of the credo at any point in Israelite history must be regarded as determined more by the needs of the occasion and the persons involved than by a fixed outline. The credo might be as short as a single word or phrase ("Yahweh" or "Yahweh is King") or as long as the summaries of Joshua 24 or Psalms 78 or 105. By nature, the credo was always in some sense historical, but its historicality was always theological.

Bibliography. On the theory of the credo: A. Jirku, *Die älteste Geschichte Israels im Rahmen lehrhafter*

Darstellungen (1917); G. von Rad, *The Problem of the Hexateuch and Other Essays* (1966), pp. 1-78, and *OT Theology*, I (1962) and II (1965); M. Noth, *A History of Pentateuchal Traditions* (1972), and "The 'Representation' of the OT in Proclamation," in *Essays on OT Hermeneutics* (1963), pp. 76-88.

On the credo and Sinai: A. Weiser, *The Old Testament* (1961), pp. 81-99; E. Nicholson, *Exodus and Sinai in History and Tradition* (1973); W. Beyerlin, *Origins and History of the Oldest Sinaitic Traditions* (1965), esp. pp. 145-70; J. Schmidt, "Erwägungen Zum Verhältnis von Auszugs- und Sinaitradition," *ZAW*, LXXXII (1970), 1-31; H. Huffmon, "The Exodus, Sinai and the Credo," *CBQ*, XXVII (1965), 101-13.

On the credo as late summary: L Rost, *Das kleine Credo und andere Studien zum AT* (1965), pp. 11-25; T. C. Vriezen, "The Credo in the OT," in *Studies on the Psalms* (1963), pp. 5-17; N. Lohfink, "Zum 'kleinen geschichtlichen Credo' Dtn 26, 5-9," *TP*, XLVI (1971), 19-39.

On criticism of the credo as a literary type: C. Brekelmans, "Het 'historiche Credo' van Israël," *TsT*, III (1963), 1-11; J. P. Hyatt, "Were There an Ancient Historical Credo in Israel and an Independent Sinai Tradition?" in *Translating and Understanding the OT*, ed. T. Frank and W. Reed (1970), pp. 152-70.

On the credo and further inquiry: D. J. McCarthy, "What was Israel's Historical Creed?" *LthQ*, IV (1969), 46-53; J. Muilenburg, "Form Criticism and Beyond," *JBL*, LXXXVIII (1969), 1-18. J. I. DURHAM

***CRUCIFIXION, METHOD OF.** Recent archaeological evidence from Israel has thrown dramatic new light on methods of crucifixion in antiquity. The first skeletal remains of a crucifixion were unearthed from a first century A.D. TOMB found at Giv'at ha-Mivtar in Jerusalem. The tomb lies about 1½ miles N of the "Second Wall" of Roman Jerusalem.

1. The material evidence. The victim was 5 feet, 5¾ inches tall, male, between twenty-four and twenty-eight years old, and of slight build. His build perhaps implies membership in an aristocratic family that may have participated in the "Census Revolt" of A.D. 6. Both heel bones had been pierced by one iron nail, the arm bones were scratched, and the lower legs had been broken. Death was therefore caused by crucifixion.

The subject had been buried in the family tomb and later reburied in an ossuary (*see* OSSUARIES). The ossuary also contained the bones of a child three to four years old with no marks of violence or disease.

Two names appear on the ossuary. The first is "John" (יהוחנן) and the second "John son of ḥzqwl" (יהוחנן בר חזקול). The last word is unreadable as it stands, but may be read as a hypocorism or a corruption of the name Ezekiel (יחזקאל). It may also be read "the one hanged with knees apart," reading "hzqwl" (חזקול) or "h'qwl" (העקול). Thus the name of the victim was certainly "John," and his son (?) was perhaps named "John, son of the hanged."

The 4½-inch nail was still piercing the heel bones in the ossuary. Fragments of a ⅝- to ¾-inch acacia or pistacia wood plaque were found between the nail head and the heels. The point of the nail was bent ¾-inch and had bits of olivewood attached. *See* Fig. C7. Furthermore, the right radius (forearm) exhibited damage in the form of a scratch on fresh bone probably caused by the arm nails.

2. Methods of crucifixion. The evidence is subject to three interpretations, any one of which alters the traditional view of Jesus' crucifixion:

a) In the first interpretation, the feet were first nailed together parallel onto the vertical olivewood beam of the cross with a single nail. The legs were adjacent, the right knee extending past the left. Finally the arms were extended and nailed to the crossbar through the forearm between the radius and ulna.

The executioners probably added a "sedicula" or "sedecula," a small crossbar to bear the weight of the victim so as to prolong agony by preventing collapse. Because of his twisted posture probably only one buttock could rest upon it.

The lower leg bones reveal evidence of violent removal from the cross. The left leg had been severed by a single blow while the bones of the right leg had been splintered, probably by the same blow. Perhaps this was the *coup de grâce* and the method of removal from the cross.

b) In the second interpretation, the nail was

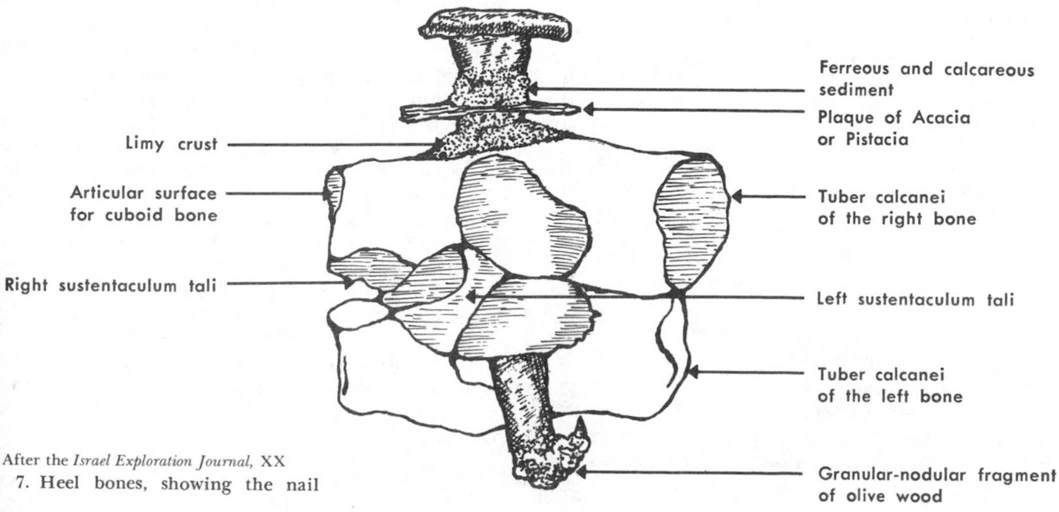

After the *Israel Exploration Journal*, XX
7. Heel bones, showing the nail

A: "Open position" crucifixion (initial restoration)

B: Crucifixion with legs adjacent (final restoration)

After the *Israel Exploration Journal,* XX

8. Two possible methods of crucifixion

driven through the plaque, the heels, and then an olivewood board, then deliberately bent over to hold the feet together. The victim was then hoisted into the air upside down and his legs looped over the top of the cross. His arms may then have been nailed to a *lower* crossbar forming a sort of "cross of Lorraine." The verb עקל (="hanged with knees apart"?) on the ossuary may suggest this.

c) Finally it is possible to interpret these data as evidence for upright crucifixion, arms nailed to the cross, and feet attached to each other but not to the cross. If the victim was not provided with the sedicula, death would be fairly swift.

Bibliography. V. Tzaferis, "Jewish Tombs at and near Giv'at ha-Mivtar, Jerusalem," *IEJ,* XX (1970), 18-32; J. Naveh, "The Ossuary Inscriptions from Giv'at ha-Mivtar," *ibid.,* pp. 33-37; N. Haas, "Anthropological Observations on the Skeletal Remains from Giv'at ha-Mivtar," *ibid.,* pp. 38-59; Y. Yadin, "Epigraphy and Crucifixion," *IEJ,* XXIII (1973), 18-22; E. M. Meyers, *Jewish Ossuaries: Reburial and Rebirth* (1971), the most useful survey on the problem of secondary burial in early Judaism.

J. F. STRANGE

***CUSH.** Cush is used as a personal name in the title of Psalm 7. Elsewhere it is a geographical term.

Modern translations render the Hebrew כוש unevenly. In a few passages it is transcribed "Cush," but in most cases it is translated "Ethiopia," misleading many contemporary readers to identify it with modern Abyssinia, which is officially named Ethiopia. The error is due to a change in the meaning of the term Ethiopia: the ancient Greeks used αἰθίοψ to designate any southern land inhabited by people with "burnt-faces."

The word כוש is most frequently used to designate the Nubian kingdom which was situated along the Nile S of Egypt. The N boundary of Cush fluctuated from period to period, but much of the time it bordered Upper Egypt just S of the Second Cataract at Semna. During the height of its political power its capital was located at Napata, near the Fourth Cataract, but after the famous Twenty-fifth Dynasty it was moved S to Meroë, about halfway between the Fifth Cataract and Khartum.

Cush is first mentioned in Egyptian texts from the Middle Kingdom (2000-1800 B.C.) as an enemy which the pharaohs fought hard to subjugate. During periods of pharaonic weakness, it broke away, but was reconquered and administered in the New Kingdom (1550-1085) by "the King's Son of Cush," an office of enormous prestige. During the weak Twenty-first Dynasty, Cush became independent and began its greatest period of power, culminating in Pi-ankhi's conquest of Egypt. Subsequently, Pi-ankhi's successors ruled all of Egypt as the Twenty-fifth Dynasty (716-656 B.C.). One of the last Nubian pharaohs, TIRHAKAH, is mentioned in II Kings 19:9 (cf. Isa. 37:9). Awareness of the political structure of the Twenty-fifth Dynasty undoubtedly contributed to the ready juxtaposition of Egypt and Cush in biblical texts (Ps. 68:31 [H 32]; Isa. 20:3-5; Ezek. 30:4, 9; Nah. 3:9).

The inhabitants of Cush were called Nḥsy by the Egyptians. In Exod. 6:25 the grandson of

Aaron is named Phinehas, which means "the Nḥsy (man)."

Once the Nubian kingdom of Cush ceased to be a familiar participant in events of the biblical world, the term Cush was used to designate a broader, remote geographical area S of Egypt, including the E coast of Africa. Cultural, linguistic, and ethnic kinship between South Arabia and the opposite coast of Africa accounts for the presence of Cush in the genealogy of Sheba and Dedan (Gen. 10:7).

The Yahwist used Cush to designate both the land (Gen. 2:13) and the eponymous ancestor (Gen. 10:8) of the Kassites. These invaders were first mentioned by Samsu-iluna, Hammurabi's immediate successor. At that time they were held back from Babylon and settled along the upper Euphrates river valley in the area of Mari. After the Hittite king, Mursilis I, made his famous raid on Babylon (*ca.* 1530 B.C. [low chronology]) and destroyed the city, the Kassites occupied and rebuilt it. They remained in power there until the Elamite king Shutruk-Naḫḫunte sacked Babylon and brought an end to the Kassite dynasty (*ca.* 1151 B.C.). At the lowest estimate, which is given above, the Kassites ruled Babylon for nearly four hundred years.

In addition to Nubian and Kassite Cush, scholars speculate about the possibility of other districts with the same name. Although they have generally rejected any extensive South Arabian Cush, many retain the name for a district in Midian. Midian is located on the NE shore of the Gulf of Aqabah and was the home of Moses' wife Zipporah (Exod. 2:16-21). In Num. 12:1, however, it is reported that Moses was married to a "Cushite" woman. Many scholars assume that both texts refer to the same woman. They support such a view on the basis of Hab. 3:7, which speaks of the "tents of Cushan" in parallelism with "the curtain of Midian."

The possibility of yet another Cushite center was proposed fifty years ago by Albright. He suggested that Pharaoh Shishak established a colony of Nubians at Gerar, and that they were responsible for the attack on Asa which is mentioned in II Chr. 14:9-15. Such a colony might also be involved in the Chronicler's notice of the "anger of the Philistines and of the Arabs who lived near the Cushites" (II Chr. 21:16 NEB).

Bibliography. W. F. Albright, "Egypt and the Early History of the Negeb," *JPOS,* IV (1924), 131-61; A. Gardiner, *Egypt of the Pharaohs* (1961); E. Lipiński, "Nimrod et Aššur," *RB,* LXXIII (1966), 77-93; E. Meyer, *Die Israeliten und ihre Nachbarstämme* (1906), pp. 315-17; A. Scharff and A. Moortgat, *Ägypten und Vorderasien im Altertum* (1950); G. Van Beek, "Prolegomenon" in the 1969 reprinting of J. Montgomery, *Arabia and the Bible,* pp. ix-xxix.

O. WINTERMUTE

CYNICS sĭn'ĭks. Members of a sect of philosophers that originated in the fourth century B.C. and flourished in the ROMAN EMPIRE. Some ancient observers held that Cynicism was a way of life rather than a philosophy (Diogenes Laertius, *Lives of Eminent Philosophers* VI.103) and that its character should be studied from the practice of its heroes rather than from their writings (Julian, *Oration* VI.189-90). Its history and teaching are closely related to Stoicism. *See also* GREEK RELIGION AND PHILOSOPHY §8*b*, *c*; STOICS.

It is not clear whether Antisthenes or his successor Diogenes was the founder of the sect. Nevertheless, Diogenes was the first to call himself κύων, "dog," thus alluding to his own independent life-style, and the name was adopted by those who emulated him. Amid discontent with the artificiality of life in Athens and despair of the customs and institutions of society, Antisthenes asserted as his basic principle the independence of the wise man. The lines of Cynic thought and the stress on individualism became more pronounced with Diogenes, who soon after his death became a legendary figure, the subject of countless anecdotes. His successor Crates gave further form to a specifically Cynic attitude toward the world. The Cynics concentrated entirely on ethics and eschewed the scientific study of logic and physics. Their goal was to live in accordance with virtue, which they held to be sufficient to happiness. The wise man, holding virtue as the only thing of value and vice as the only thing to be rejected, regarded everything else as insignificant. Governed only by reason, the sage will live naturally (κατὰ φύσιν). Stressing that this practical wisdom could be taught, and, once attained, could not be lost, they felt no need to explain what "nature" was, nor why it is good to live κατὰ φύσιν. In practice, it seems as if, for them, the man who makes his own decisions about his life is the truly wise man. He is restrained by nothing, and in his re-evaluation of everything external to himself can be said to change the coinage of convention and popular opinion (Diogenes Laertius, *Lives* VI.20, 56, 71). The Cynic therefore strives for self-sufficiency (αὐτάρκεια), which allows him to be satisfied with the simplest diet and personal furnishings consisting of a short cloak, a wallet, and a staff. It may justify his begging for a living from whomever he pleases, thus being under obligation to no one. Because of his true freedom (ἐλευθερία), no hardships (περιστάσεις) really affect him, and he can furthermore exhibit his rejection of the claims of society by repudiating the state, marriage, and the accepted sexual mores. As one who has attained such freedom, the Cynic strives to convert men by bringing them to their senses. He does so by means of bold speech (παρρησία) in which he contrasts the vices of deluded mankind with the virtues which characterize the wise man. Such an austere outlook could justify the harsh demeanor and gross conduct with which Cynics came to be identified, but with Crates, who was milder in mien than Diogenes, a more moderate strain was introduced into the sect.

Zeno, the founder of Stoicism, was a disciple of Crates. He accepted the Cynic principle that virtue is the only good, but he and his successors, especially Chrysippus, constructed a system of thought that differed markedly from Cynicism. Although retaining the profound distinction between things virtuous and vicious, they introduced a class of things which are indifferent, but among which can be distinguished some things which are natural and to be preferred, some which are unnatural, and to be rejected, and some which are truly indifferent. By nature they meant the law of the physical universe which governs all things and may also be called universal reason, destiny, providence, or Zeus, in harmony with which man should live. This scheme admitted of men, those popularly held to be philosophers, who were advancing to wisdom, but had not attained the ideal. The elaboration of this system required a knowledge of logic and physics, thus making it more theoretical and speculative than Cynicism while retaining its strict moralism.

In the third century Cynicism had notable representatives in Bion, Menippus, Menedemus, Cercidas, and Teles, who were creative on the literary level, developing the diatribe and giving special forms to parody and satire. Operating on the level of popular moral instruction, Cynicism was gradually absorbed into Stoicism. Since Cynicism had no clearly stated theoretical base that could be transmitted from generation to generation and no succession, in the strict sense of the term, it is difficult to identify specific Cynic sources or philosophers in the second and first centuries B.C. Cynicism emerges again with renewed vitality in the first century A.D., and does so because of the renewed attention it received from the Stoics.

The Stoicism of Panaetius and Posidonius, which had first come to Rome in the second century B.C., was liberal and speculative, and appealed to the nobility of the Scipionic circle. By the first century B.C., however, the Stoics turned to the masses with a practical, nontechnical philosophy aimed at reforming individuals. They did not return to the unscientific stance of the Cynics, but their insistence on the practical utility of philosophy resulted in lessening the importance of logic and physics, which nevertheless still provided the basis for their ethical theory. As their interest became more practical, Stoics tended increasingly to see the ideal in earlier Cynicism. Whereas Cynicism in Greece had been a manner of life in which one gave expression to his self-understanding and to his perception of the world, in Rome it became a norm for action. Thus in the first century A.D., the Cynic heroes, especially Heracles and Diogenes, appear in the Stoicized views of the ideal Cynic presented as models to be followed by Musonius Rufus, Epictetus, and Dio Chrysostom. Men also now appear who take up the life of Diogenes and call themselves Cynics. Seneca the Stoic provides us with information about Demetrius, whom he admired highly, the first Cynic in the Roman Empire about whom we know. Demetrius was followed in increasing numbers by others who ventured forth to correct mankind, not always with the noblest of motives, as Lucian of Samosata and other satirists make clear.

The Cynics of the first two centuries have frequently been viewed as radical Stoics whose garb and rationale differed from that of other Stoics in degree rather than in kind. There were differences in matters of class and style; the Cynics, representing the "philosophy of the proletariat," directed their attention to the masses, while the Stoics tended to confine themselves to lecture halls and the salons of the wealthy. But these distinctions were not absolute, for we know of Stoic street preachers, although they seem to have been more numerous in the first century B.C. There were, however, more fundamental differences between the two which are obscured if Cynicism is approached solely through the syncretistic descriptions of the Stoic moralists. Epictetus, and especially Dio Chrysostom, do preserve Cynic traditions of great value for understanding Cynicism, but they must be seen in the context of other Cynic traditions in such authors as Plutarch, Lucian, Maximus of Tyre, and, above all, with the writings of the Cynics themselves. There are extant a few papyrus remains of Cynic writings as well as a body of Cynic letters dating from the Augustan age under the names of Antisthenes, Diogenes, Crates, and non-Cynic philosophers such as Heraclitus and Socrates, and Anacharsis. These letters appear to have been written as propaganda pieces, and are a prime source for our understanding of Cynicism.

The Cynics held to the profound distinction between the wise and foolish, and confidently assumed that the ideal could be realized as it had been by the ancients. The Stoics, on the other hand, defined the ideal in such a way that its attainability was only an abstract possibility. The ideal sage, Seneca says, may appear like the phoenix, only once in five hundred years (*Moral Epistle* XLII.1). The Stoic philosopher is only a *proficiens* who is making progress to the ideal. Cynic individualism and confidence are also expressed in their attitude toward religion. Stoicism had made a *rapprochement* with popular piety, and its doctrine of the cosmic sympathy provided a conceptual framework for much of popular demonology, divination, dreams, magic, and astrology. Using current religious language, the Stoic expressed his concern to find his proper station in the cosmic scheme of things. For their part, the earliest Cynics scorned the popular cult, and in this they were generally followed by their successors. The high point of their opposition was reached in the systematic polemic of Oenomaus of Gadara in the second century A.D. The Cynic rejects all supra-individual points of view. He shows no interest in providence, but stresses his own free will and his own accomplishment without recourse to any physical or logical theory. His interest is solely in ethics.

Considerable diversity characterized Cynics in the Roman Empire. Serious Cynics differed from the many charlatans who also took the name, but even genuine Cynics differed among themselves. The milder form introduced by Crates and strengthened by Bion continued to find representatives who were more humane in their view of the human condition. Their perception influenced their views on how they should live, whether they should beg for their livelihood and from whom, whether they should marry or not, whether they should have disciples or not, all matters on which they disagreed among themselves. Despite Lucian's depiction of him, Peregrinus demonstrates that a Cynic could even be of a mystical bent, even though he seems to have been an exception. What remains basic to all Cynics, however, is their insistence on the individual's ability to free himself from the yearning for fame, riches, and pleasure that shackles mankind. In stressing the power of the will they demonstrate their confidence that the good can be attained by noble men.

There are many similarities between early Christianity and Cynic philosophy. Epictetus (*Discourses* III.22) describes the ideal Cynic as a messenger (ἄγγελος) sent by God as his herald (κῆρυξ) to convert men and oversee (ἐπισκοπεῖν) them. The hardships suffered by the Cynic recall those of Paul (e.g., II Cor. 6:9-10), who also makes a modified use of the Cynic description of self-sufficiency (Phil. 4:11). As do the Cynics, so Paul too uses athletic imagery to describe his labors (e.g., I Cor. 9:24 ff.). Christian preaching is also described as BOLDNESS of speech (παρρησία, cf. I Thess. 2:2), and the diatribal style, replete with lists of virtues and vices, is adopted by Paul and James (e.g., Rom. 1:16 ff.; Jas. 2:14 ff.). These similarities and points of contact do not mean that Cynics and Christians understood the terms that they used in the same way. But they do illustrate how Hellenistic philosophy contributed to a congenial climate for the transmission of early Christianity. *See also* FORM CRITICISM, NT[S]; LISTS, ETHICAL and supplementary article; PARENESIS[S].

Bibliography. D. R. Dudley, *A History of Cynicism from Diogenes to the Sixth Century A.D.* (1937); R. Helm, "Kynismus," PW, XII (1924), cols. 3-24; R. Höistad, *Cynic Hero and Cynic King* (1948); A. J. Malherbe, "'Gentle as a Nurse.' The Cynic Background to I Thess. ii," *NovT*, XII (1970), 203-17; K. H. Rengstorf, "ἀπόστολος," *TDNT*, I, (1933 [ET 1964]), 407-13.

A. J. MALHERBE

CYPROS. *See* HERODIAN FORTRESSES[S] §5.

***CYPRUS.** Human occupation is attested in the Neolithic period at several sites in the northern, central, and southern regions of the island. A pre-pottery culture dated by carbon-14 tests to *ca.* 5800 B.C. marks the earliest settlement at Khirokitia near the southern coast. At Dhali-Agridhi, on the S bank of the Yalias River near the village of Dhali, occupation dated to 5340 ± 465 has been found. The next occupation at this site is a pottery culture dated to 4465 ± 310. Neolithic pottery has also been found at Khirokitia, at Trouli in the N, and at Philia-Drakos in the W-central region.

Faunal remains lead to the hypothesis that the people practiced a mixed economy. They were herding sheep and goats and breeding pigs, and at the same time they hunted wild boar, two species of deer, and wild asses. Harvesting was also taking place, as indicated by the glossy sheen on some flint implements. These people were semisedentary herders who also hunted and harvested domesticated or wild plants. It was a community not restricted to one economic activity but was rather generalized in its adaptation to its environment.

The Neolithic communities came to an end about 3000, followed by Chalcolithic settlements. This period is represented ceramically by a red-on-white ware. Although there are some similarities between the Cypriote styles and those of Thessaly in the W and Ras Shamra–UGARIT in the E, the Chalcolithic culture is essentially a development from the Neolithic, there being no evidence of serious influence from outside the island at this time.

During the Early Cypriote period (*ca.* 2300-2000), the island was thickly settled, and numerous occupied sites have been located. Of particular interest are the sites in the vicinity of Morphou Bay. The pottery found in this area has close affinities with Anatolian pottery of the end of Early Bronze II. This lends support to the hypothesis that settlers came to Cyprus from Anatolia following the disaster that marked the end of the EB II period there. Many of the sites of the period are near sources of copper ore. There is evidence of commercial relations with Near Eastern countries and even in a limited way with Minoan Crete.

By the end of the Early Cypriote period marked changes in Cypriote culture may be noted as a result of commercial contacts with neighboring peoples. This pattern continued in the Middle Cypriote period (*ca.* 2000-1600), when Cyprus played an important role in the affairs of the Near East. At the same time, Middle Cypriote is to be seen largely as a transition period. The center of importance shifted from the N to the S with the development of important harbor towns such as Enkomi and Kition.

The Late Cypriote period (1600-1050) is marked by extensive trade with the Near East and Mycenae. By *ca.* 1200 the island was undergoing colonization by Achaean settlers, and within a century it became almost completely Hellenized. Although this colonization seems to have been peaceful, it caused radical cultural change. At Kition two Mycenaean temples have been excavated. Two altars were found, one for burnt sacrifices and one for bloodless sacrifices. Enkomi has produced a considerable number of furnaces, hearths, slags, and other industrial wastes that are clearly related to the extraction of copper from its ores. Moreover, the proximity of these industrial activities to temples, as well as the presence of votive slags at Athienou, about three miles S of the Yalias River, suggest a relationship between religion and copper production.

The history of Cyprus in the Cypro-Geometric period (1050-700) is dominated by the city of SALAMIS. The end of this period is marked by the beginning of Assyrian domination.

The Cypro-Archaic period (700-475) is largely a continuation of the previous period, with Mycenaean culture prevailing while the island was first under Assyrian and later under Egyptian and Persian domination. At Salamis, seventh-century tombs provide evidence of the sacrificial burial of chariots and horses, an Oriental and Mycenaean custom mentioned by Homer. At Idalion (modern Dhali) recent excavations have revealed domestic architecture combining apsidal and rectangular styles in the same building, hitherto unknown in Cyprus.

It is now clear that the massive stone defense wall at Idalion, formerly dated to the Roman period, was begun early in the Cypro-Classical period (475-325). Idalion was attacked by the Persians and the Kitions (under a Phoenician dynasty) *ca.* 475-450. It is therefore likely that this fifth-century defense system was erected as a response to the rising ambitions of the Kitions.

Cyprus became a part of the Hellenistic empire under the Ptolemies at the end of the fourth century. During the Hellenistic period (325-50), Cypriote culture became thoroughly Hellenistic. At the same time it is clear that a Phoenician legacy remained in such areas as Idalion and Kition. A Greek ostracon from Idalion lists four gates, two of which bear Phoenician names: Gate of the Ark of the Armies, and Gate of the Pack-bags.

The extensive Roman ruins at Salamis include a gymnasium, a theater, and an amphitheater. Salamis remained the largest center in Cyprus during the Roman period, even though PAPHOS had become the capital. Roman ruins in the form of temples, public buildings, and rock-cut tombs may be found in abundance across the island. Most spectacular are the well-preserved, high-quality mosaic floors of a third-century A.D. Roman villa at Paphos. The building had more than seventy rooms arranged around an atrium with a peristyle and including bedrooms, bathrooms, kitchens, and workshops.

Bibliography. H. W. Catling, "Cyprus in the Neolithic and Chalcolithic Periods," in *The Cambridge Ancient History,* I, Pt. 1 (3rd ed., 1970), 539-56, "Cyprus in the Early Bronze Age," *ibid.,* I, Pt. 2 (1971), 808-23, and "Cyprus in the Middle Bronze Age," *ibid.,* II, Pt. 1 (1973), 165-75; P. Dikaios, *Kirokitia* (1953); V. Karageorghis, "Recent Discoveries at Salamis (Cyprus)," *Archaeologischer Anzeiger,* LXXXI (1966), 210-55; L. E. Stager, A. Walker, and G. E. Wright, eds., *American Expedition to Idalion, Cyprus. First Preliminary Report: Seasons of 1971 and 1972* (1974); A. Westholm, *The Temples of Soli* (1936).

H. N. RICHARDSON

D

DALIYEH, WADI, MSS. *See* SAMARIA PAPYRI[S].

DAMASCUS DOCUMENT. *See* ZADOKITE FRAGMENTS.

***DAN (CITY).** The identification made by Robinson (Tell el-Qadi) in 1838 has been substantiated by excavations carried out since 1966. Located where the road from Tyre to Damascus crosses the main N-S road, Dan was already an important city in the Early Bronze period (third millennium B.C.). The massive earthen ramparts, similar to those at other sites connected with the Hyksos, belong to the Middle Bronze period (MB IIB). On the inner southern slope a number of jar burials (MB IIC) were found. On the eastern side of the mound, beneath the rampart, a tomb with four burials and some thirty vessels (MB IIA–MB IIB) was excavated. From the archaeological evidence we conclude that the large city with its massive earth ramparts represents the city (Laish) mentioned in the Egyptian execration texts and the Mari inscriptions. From the latter we learn that tin was exported to Laish from Mari. Dan-Laish is mentioned also in the Thut-mose III lists.

Occupational levels of the Late Bronze Age were also found. From the LB II period a rich tomb built of rough basalt was excavated on the inner slope of the rampart. Remains of forty-five skeletons of men, women, and children were found in complete disarray. The gifts accompanying the burials include imported Mycenaean and Cypriote ware, an oil lamp, bowls, arrowheads, and swords made of bronze. Ivory cosmetic boxes and gold and silver jewelry were also found.

There is as yet insufficient evidence for the date of the conquest of Laish by the tribe of Dan, but it may have taken place in the first half of the twelfth century B.C. The community prospered, and among items of the next two centuries was a considerable amount of pottery vessels, as well as a clay crucible with bronze sediment. On the southern slope of the mound a city gate and walls of the Israelite period were excavated, while a high place was uncovered in the N. The high place underwent a number of changes, with monumental steps added in the ninth-eighth centuries B.C. S of the steps an Israelite horned altar was found in the 1974 season. The security of the site was assured by a twelve-foot-thick city wall and a large gate. A unique feature of the city gate is an ashlar stone structure with ornamental column capitals; it probably served as a throne for the king when he "sat at the gate." A bench along the gate was possibly used by the "elders." From the eighth century B.C. a sherd with Hebrew letters "belonging to Amotz" was found near a storeroom containing some three hundred juglets. Another inscription, "belonging to Ba'al-pelet," was discovered in the last Iron Age stratum of the Phoenician period. The site continued to be occupied in the Persian, Hellenistic, Roman, and Byzantine periods.

Bibliography. E. Robinson, *Biblical Researches in Palestine, Mount Sinai and Arabia Petraea,* III (1841), p. 358; W. F. Albright, "The Jordan Valley in the Bronze Age," *AASOR,* VI (1926), 16-18; Y. Yadin, *Western Galilee and the Coast of Galilee* (1965), pp. 42-55, Hebrew; A. Biran, *All the Land of Naphtali* (1967), pp. 21-32, and "A Mycenaean Charioteer Vase from Tel Dan," *IEJ,* XX (1970), 92-94; A Malamat, "Northern Canaan and the Mari Texts," in *Near Eastern Archaeology in the Twentieth Century,* ed. J. Sanders (1970), pp. 164-77, "The Danite Migration and the Pan-Israelite Exodus-Conquest," *Bibl.,* LI (1970), 1-16, and "Syro-Palestine Destinations in a Mari Tin Inventory," *IEJ,* XXI (1971), 31-38; A. Biran, "Tel Dan," *BA,* XXXVII (1974), 26-51, 106-7. A. BIRAN

***DANIEL.** Better understanding of the Greek forms of the OT has been occasioned by the analysis of MSS found at Qumran and elsewhere. Barthélemy has shown that the Greek fragments of the minor prophets from Wadi Khabra (Naḥal Ḥever) represent a recension of the Old Greek (LXX). This recension was produced on the basis of Hebrew MSS circulating in Palestine during the first century B.C. and the early part of the first Christian century. Its translation technique is the same as the one employed in so-called "Theodotion" (generally assigned to the second century A.D.); hence, Proto-Theodotion is the common designation of this recension. It is also called the καιγε recension because καιγε is invariably used to render וגם. Barthélemy identifies Proto-Theodotion with Jonathan ben 'Uzziel, disciple of Hillel, and argues that the work was produced in Palestine between A.D. 30 and 50; others prefer a first-century B.C. dating. Research on the καιγε recension of the minor prophets, parts of Samuel-Kings, and Exodus has prompted a new look at problems of the Greek forms of Daniel. *See* GREEK VERSIONS, MINOR[S].

1. NT citations of Daniel. Two Greek forms of Daniel are extant: Old Greek (LXX), and what it now seems best to call Theodotion-Daniel. The LXX of Daniel, extant in only the Chisian MS, Papyrus 967, and the Syrohexaplar, was translated in Alexandria *ca.* 100 B.C. and was soon replaced by Theodotion-Daniel in the LXX MSS. The place and date of Theodotion-Daniel are not as certain. But as regards "Theodotion" in the other parts of the OT, some bits of information are at hand. Irenaeus (died *ca.* A.D. 202) refers to the man Theodotion as an Ephesian (*Adversus Haereses* III.xxi.1), and his own use of the "Theodotion" recension clearly contradicts Epiphanius' statement

(*De Mensuris et Ponderibus* 17) which places the translator in Commodus' reign, *ca.* A.D. 180. Montgomery dates Theod. to the early second century A.D., noting that such a late date cannot account for the citation by the NT, especially in Hebrews and Revelation, of many phrases from Theodotion-Daniel. To resolve this difficulty Montgomery and others postulated an Ur-Theodotion, perhaps a Hellenistic oral Targum (*see* THEODOTION; GREEK VERSIONS, MINOR[S]). This postulated Ur-Theodotion must not be confused with Proto-Theodotion (*see above*). J. Gwynn's hypothesis in the *Dictionary of Christian Biography* (1887) has been the most imaginative with regard to an Ur-Theodotion behind the second-century A.D. "Theodotion." He argues that side by side with the LXX of Daniel there was current among the Jews from pre-Christian times another Greek form of the book. It was the latter form that was known to the Greek translator of the apocryphal (deuterocanonical) book of Baruch, the NT authors, and the early Fathers Clement and Hermas. This form supplied the foundation for the supposedly historical Theodotion. Ziegler, however, in his splendid critical edition of Daniel notes that Theodotion-Daniel may have nothing in common with "Theodotion." Following this lead, Schmitt concludes that Theodotion-Daniel is not in the same textual tradition as Proto-Theodotion or "Theodotion." Thus, the identification of Theodotion-Daniel with Proto-Theodotion (καιγε) should no longer be maintained. A fresh approach is proposed here. Just as the LXX is not a homogeneous Alexandrian translation but differs from book to book in quality and style, it appears best to view Proto-Theodotion as only one form of Greek literary activity in the first century B.C. (Proto-Lucian being another). Theodotion-Daniel is still another type, from Palestine or Asia Minor during pre-Christian times. Perhaps it is a fresh translation with an eye on the LXX Daniel rather than a recension like the other Greek forms. Though "Theodotion-Daniel" may be a misnomer, it seems advisable to keep the title to avoid even further confusion. Moreover, there is no serious reason to question that Theodotion-Daniel, extant in nearly all the Greek MSS, is essentially what existed in the first century B.C. It is Theodotion-Daniel that appears in Greek Baruch, the NT citations, and the Apostolic Fathers mentioned above.

2. The "Additions to Daniel." It has generally been held that the Greek version which contains the apocryphal, or deuterocanonical, "Additions to Daniel" (Greek 3:25-90 and the stories of Susanna, and Bel and the Dragon) represents a canon accepted only by Jews in Egypt (where the LXX was translated). Since Theodotion-Daniel was produced in Asia Minor or Palestine, and if both the LXX and Theodotion-Daniel contained the Additions (there is no cogent reason to believe that either did not), then the ancient canonical status of the longer Greek form of Daniel needs to be re-evaluated. It would appear less than accurate to speak of the Additions as sacred only in Egyptian Jewish circles while in fact the fourteen-chapter Theodotion-Daniel was published and undoubtedly received as a holy book by many Jews in Palestine or Asia Minor.

3. Unity of the book. Most scholars have adopted one of two positions regarding the unity of Daniel: (*a*) One author of Maccabean times, reworking older materials, wrote in Hebrew and Aramaic all six midrashic stories (chs. 1–6) and the four apocalypses (chs. 7–12); so, e.g., Rowley and Frost (*see* DANIEL). (*b*) Two or more authors (third and second centuries B.C.) and possibly a redactor/compiler produced the book; so, e.g., Montgomery, Delcor, and particularly Ginsberg. A middle ground, however, may be suggested. Although there were many Daniel stories in Hebrew and Aramaic circulating in Palestine during the second century B.C. and later (e.g., the Aramaic Prayer of Nabonidus and three Aramaic pseudo-Daniel fragments from Qumran Cave IV), only the ones in the MT form of Daniel were declared canonical by the Pharisees who fixed the Jewish canon. The so-called Additions to Daniel, though written in Hebrew or Aramaic as is generally agreed, were not included in that canon; the reason for the exclusion is not known. Presumably, however, the Additions were canonical in some Jewish circles in Egypt, Palestine, and Asia Minor during the first century B.C. No critical scholar today would defend unity of authorship for the longer literary tradition found in the LXX and Theodotion-Daniel. It is proposed here that the case for the unity of the MT form is also less than overwhelming, whereas the case for multiple, like-minded authors is attractive and persuasive (position *b*). Nevertheless, the book in its short (MT) as well as its long (Greek) form has an over-all literary unity centering on the person of Daniel and a unified theological purpose, viz., to inculcate fidelity and courage in the persecuted and disheartened Jews of Maccabean times (the basic position of *a*). This hypothesis attempts a consistent explanation of enormously complex issues (the two languages of MT Daniel, the "Additions" preserved only in Greek, the different genres, the unity of outlook, the view of history, etc.), while acknowledging that a more precise verdict is not possible from the evidence currently available. *See also* SEPTUAGINT, esp. §§1, 3*b*; SEPTUAGINT[S].

Bibliography. Commentaries: J. Montgomery, ICC (1927), though old, still very valuable; N. Porteous, *Daniel* (1965); O. Plöger, *Das Buch Daniel, KAT,* XVIII (1965); M. Delcor, *Le livre de Daniel* (1971).

Special studies: J. Ziegler, *Susanna, Daniel, Bel et Draco* (1954); D. Barthélemy, *Les devanciers d'Aquila*, VTSup, X (1963); H. H. Rowley, *The Relevance of Apocalyptic* (rev. ed., 1963); D. S. Russell, *The Method and Message of Jewish Apocalyptic* (1964), excellent 25-page bibliography; C. Brekelmans, "The Saints of the Most High and Their Kingdom," *OTS,* XIV (1965), 305-29; H. H. Rowley, "The Unity of the Book of Daniel," *The Servant of the Lord* (2nd ed. rev., 1965), pp. 249-80; F. M. Cross, "The Contribution of the Qumrân Discoveries to the Study of the Biblical Text," *IEJ,* XVI (1966), 81-95; A. Schmitt, *Stammt der sogenannte "Θ"—Text bei Daniel wirklich von Theodotion? Mitteilungen des Septuaginta-Unternehmens* (1966); F. Borsch, *The Son of Man in Myth and History* (1967), a noteworthy study of a much-discussed issue; R. Hanhart,

"Die Heiligen des Höchsten," VTSup, XVI (1967), 90-101; A. Caquot, "Les quatre bêtes et le 'Fils d'homme' (Daniel 7)," *Semitica,* XVII (1967), 37-71; B. W. Jones, "The Prayer of Daniel IX," *VT,* XVIII (1968), 488-93; Z. Zevit, "The Structure and Individual Elements of Daniel 7," *ZAW,* LXXX (1968), 385-96; F. F. Bruce, "The Book of Daniel and the Qumran Community," *Neotestamentica et Semitica,* ed. E. E. Ellis and M. Wilcox (1969), pp. 221-35; J. Coppens, "La vision daniélique du Fils d'homme," *VT,* XIX (1969) 171-82; F. Dexinger, *Das Buch Daniel und seine Probleme,* SBS, XXXVI (1969), extensive bibliography; P. Grelot, "Soixante-dix semaines d'années," *Bibl.,* L (1969), 169-86; M. McNamara, "Nabonidus and the Book of Daniel," *Irish Theological Quarterly,* XXXVII (1970), 131-49; H. L. Ginsberg, "Daniel, Book of," *Encyclopaedia Judaica,* V (1971), 1277-89; C. Colpe, "ὁ υἱὸς τοῦ ἀνθρώπου," *TDNT,* VIII (1972), 400-477; A. Mertens, *Das Buch Daniel im Lichte der Texte vom Toten Meer* (1972); K. Koch, "Die Herkunft der Proto-Theodotion-Übersetzung des Danielbuches," *VT,* XXIII (1973), 362-65; J. J. Collins, "The Son of Man and the Saints of the Most High in the Book of Daniel," *JBL,* XCIII (1974), 50-66; M. Hengel, *Judaism and Hellenism* (1975).

A. A. Di Lella

***DAVID, CITY OF.** The name given to the fortified city of the Jebusites after its capture by David (*see* Jebus). The Jebusites successfully withstood the earlier stages of the Israelite infiltration (Josh. 15:63); but when David was elected king by both the northern and southern tribes, it was essential that he capture the city in order to unite his two kingdoms by the vital highway along the central hilly backbone of the country. Once captured, it was a suitable place for his personal capital, since it was not part of the patrimony of any tribal group.

The earliest stages of Jerusalem lie on the southern ends of the two ridges that run S from the present Old City. Vincent long ago suggested that the original Jebusite city was situated on the eastern of the two ridges, bounded on the E by the Kidron and on the W by the Tyropoeon Valley, since the only permanent water supply lay in the Kidron Valley. Excavation has now proved this to be correct. It was not, however, until the 1961-67 excavations that the boundaries of the original city were established. For the topography, *see* Jerusalem §2.

The early excavators believed that the ancient wall running along the eastern crest of the eastern ridge was that of the Jebusite town, repaired by David. This identification was clearly unsatisfactory. It was essential to the Jebusites to have access in time of war to the spring Gihon in the valley. Connected with the spring are a number of rock-cut channels, the most famous and latest of which is the Siloam tunnel. The earliest, explored by Warren in 1867, consists of a tunnel to the foot of a fifty-two-foot shaft, from the head of which a sloping tunnel led to steps to the surface. It is very probable that it was by this route David's forces gained access to the city (II Sam. 5:6-8). This tunnel and shaft system, however, comes to the surface some seventy-nine feet outside the line of the walls on the summit. These walls therefore did not guard access to the spring, nor could the shaft and tunnels have provided

Courtesy K. M. Kenyon

1. A view of the slopes of the eastern ridge, above the Kidron valley, on which was situated the earliest city of Jerusalem. Running down the slope is the trench cut by the 1961-67 excavations.

Courtesy K. M. Kenyon

2. The original wall, Jebusite in origin and reused by David. To the right it disappears beneath a later town wall.

a means of access to the attacking Israelites. The 1961-67 excavations in fact showed the walls to be postexilic and Maccabean.

The 1961-67 main trench down the eastern slope of the eastern ridge (Fig. D1) eventually reached the early wall some 164 feet down the slope to the E (Fig. D2). This wall, dated in origin to the eighteenth century B.C., was therefore the wall of the Jebusite town. A succession of repairs showed that it was in use until the eighth century B.C., and one of these repairs was probably the work of David referred to in I Chr. 11:8. The position of the wall is strategically sound. It could not be built to enclose the spring, since it would then be commanded by the steep slope across the valley, but it was sufficiently close to prohibit access by an enemy to the spring.

This section was the only portion of the wall exposed during the excavations. The rest of the plan shown on Fig. D3 can be inferred with considerable probability. The exposed section at its northern end turns W and disappears beneath its eighth-century successor. On the plan, A XXIV

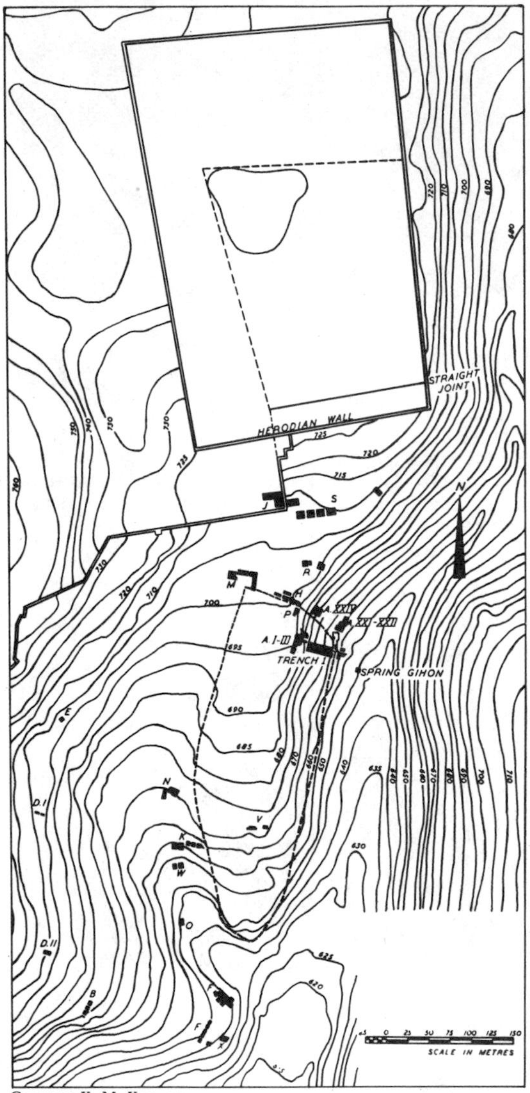

Courtesy K. M. Kenyon

3. Plan of Jebusite and Davidic Jerusalem.

is outside it, P inside and H outside, so the oblique course up the hill is certain, as is the line crossing the summit of the ridge. On the W side, sites M, N, and K are outside the early town. Site K is particularly important, since excavations were carried right up to the scarp that bounds the level area of the summit; the only traces of Iron Age occupation were sherds in cracks in the rock. The rest of the line to the S is inferred as following this scarp.

The Davidic city and that of the preceding Jebusites therefore consisted of two parts: the summit of the ridge, not much more than 328 feet wide, and the steeply sloping flank of the Kidron Valley. About the thirteenth century B.C. the latter area had been converted into terraces, supported by a complicated series of retaining walls and stone fills.

There is little textual evidence concerning Jerusalem in the period of David. He repaired the walls and MILLO (II Sam. 5:9), and built a "house" there, with the help of materials and technicians from Hiram, King of Tyre (II Sam. 5:11). He did not build the permanent home for the ark of the covenant as he had planned (I Chr. 22:8; 28:3). The other monument of David that one might expect to find is his tomb (I Kings 2:10).

It is not surprising that David did little to aggrandize Jerusalem, since most of his reign was concerned with foreign conquests. Repairs to the Jebusite E wall probably contain elements of his work, though they cannot be precisely identified. The Millo, or "filling," is probably to be identified with the massive stone fillings of the terraces on the eastern slope, to which repairs on a considerable scale were made in the tenth century B.C. Of his palace, nothing has been found, and the location of his tomb is quite uncertain; the identification of a structure on the western ridge as the tomb of David has no factual foundation.

The lack of evidence concerning the original city of David is due to two factors. The half of the town on the flank of the Kidron was dependent on the supporting Jebusite terraces. These terraces were frequently repaired during the Jebusite and Israelite periods. But the Babylonian destruction of 587 B.C. left them in complete disarray, with the result that the houses that they supported and much of the substructure were washed down the steep slope in a formless tumble of stones. Almost nothing of Jerusalem of the period of David or the monarchy therefore survives in this part of the Davidic city. The disappearance of the city on the summit of the ridge was equally complete, but for a different reason. Almost everywhere that excavations have been carried out on the summit, it has been found that the rock has been extensively quarried. A large area of quarrying was exposed in excavations carried out by R. Weill in 1913-14. The quarrying here, and probably in most other areas, belongs to the Hadrianic building of Aelia Capitolina (*ca.* A.D. 135), when the area of earliest Jerusalem was left outside the walls. Some quarrying had taken place when Herod the Great rebuilt the temple in the late first century B.C.

Among the structures destroyed by quarrying at the S end of the ridge were two tunnel-like cuttings, which Weill identified as the royal tombs. Of this there is absolutely no evidence. They are quite unlike any known tombs of the period. They were subsequently used as cisterns; and this may have been their original use, though the plan is not that of normal cisterns.

The city of David was thus on the eastern of the two ridges running S from the present Old City. Under Solomon, the temple was built on a great platform *ca.* 762 feet to the N of the original N wall, and the intervening area on the summit of the ridge was included in the city. During the period of the monarchy, there was an extension of the city to the N on the eastern slopes and some expansion to the W across the Tyropoeon Valley, the extent and plan of which is still the subject of argument. Postexilic Jerusalem shrank back onto the summit of the eastern ridge. It is reasonably certain that it was only in the Maccabean and Herodian periods that the summit of the western ridge was included within the city. The present traditional location there of Mount Zion, in II Sam. 5:7 equated with the city of David, is due to Josephus, who regarded the whole of the Jerusalem of his time as the city of David, and selected the highest point as the site of the "castle" (φρούριον) of David (War V.iv.1).

Bibliography. L.-H. Vincent, and A.-M. Stève, *Jérusalem de l'Ancien Testament* (1954); K. M. Kenyon, *Digging Up Jerusalem* (1974). K. M. Kenyon

***DAY OF THE LORD.** A poetic expression used by the prophets of Israel to describe certain momentous events. It seems to have been reserved primarily for explaining either the memory or the anticipation of war between nations. In that kind of event, the prophetic writers could clearly discern the presence of Yahweh in his ongoing activity of judgment or rescue.

1. Origin of the tradition. Mowinckel contended that the day of Yahweh should be understood primarily within the history of Israel's cultic, or worship, life, especially in the rituals of the annual New Year's celebration (*see* New Year[S]). In keeping with the patterns of ancient Near Eastern myth and ritual, the day of Yahweh was originally the event of the enthronement of Yahweh, a time of deliverance from distress and the realization of peace. Celebrated in ritual, year after year, it was the time when the reality of God's kingdom and his victory over chaos were reaffirmed for succeeding generations.

Von Rad, on the other hand, held that the origin is to be found in Israel's historical traditions of holy war. Originally, the day of Yahweh was strictly an event of war, an event involving the appearance of Yahweh to annihilate his enemies. Amos 5:18-20, where the concept first appears, is not an appropriate place to begin studying this tradition; rather, study should begin with portrayals that are broad and unequivocal, such as Isaiah 13 and 34; Ezekiel 7; and Joel 2. In these texts, von Rad found a stereotyped and consistent pattern of sacral war, characterized by (1) the call to warriors to assemble for the levy of Yahweh, (2) the sanctification of the army, (3) panic among the enemy, (4) changes in the natural order, and (5) the total destruction of the enemy (*see* War, Holy[S]).

While the approaches of Mowinckel and von Rad seem contradictory, Cross has suggested that in fact they may complement one another. While von Rad focused his study primarily on the cult in the time of the tribal league (*see* Amphictyony[S]), Mowinckel focused on the cult in the later era of the monarchy, when the themes of holy war, conquest, and kingship became united in myth and ritual patterns.

Two other suggestions concerning the origin of the tradition have been made in recent years: Fensham has suggested that covenant traditions and the event of the execution of treaty curses stand behind the tradition; Weiss suggested that theophany descriptions provide the proper context.

2. Prophetic use of the tradition. In the prophetic literature there are eighteen texts in which specific references to the day of Yahweh appear. Seven anticipate future historical or cosmic events: Amos 5:18-20; Isa. 2:12-17; 34:1-17; 61:1-3; 63:1-6; Mal. 3:13–4:6 [H 3:13-24]; and Zech. 14:1-21. In six other texts the writers use the declaration "near is the day of Yahweh!" to convey a sense of urgency and the conviction that the anticipated event may come very soon: Zeph. 1:1–2:3; Ezek. 7:1-27; 30:1-9; Obad. 1-21; Isa. 13:1-22; and Joel 1–3 [H 1–4]. But in all these texts, it is still difficult to know precisely what kind of event the prophet actually had in mind.

There are, however, five other texts in which the concept appears. In each of these, an author has described and interpreted a past event. In Lam. 1, 2 and Ezek. 13:1-9, writers used the concept as they looked back on the fall of Jerusalem in 587. The author of Lam. 1:12 depicts the woman Zion as she looks back and declares:

> Look and see
> if there is any sorrow like my sorrow
> which was brought upon me,
> which the Lord inflicted
> on the day of his fierce anger.

In a similar manner, the author of Jer. 46:2-12 reflected on the fall of an Egyptian army to the Babylonians at Carchemish in 605 and declared that this was a day of the Lord for proud Egypt. And quite certainly, the author of Isa. 22:1-14 was also reflecting on the events of the devastation of Judah and Jerusalem's narrow escape during Sennacherib's campaign in 701. Consistent with the focus on past events in the rest of that text, vs. 5 should certainly read: "For the Lord God of hosts has (had) a day of tumult and trampling and confusion."

These five texts provide a clear perspective for understanding the use of the day of Yahweh expression by the classical prophets. Because these texts describe several different past events, we can justifiably speak of various days of Yahweh throughout Israel's history. Amos announced the fall of northern Israel, convinced that the corrupt actions of the country could bring no other result (5:18-20). When Samaria and northern Israel fell in 721, those events were certainly recognized by later prophets as the fulfillment of the words of Amos; the day of Yahweh had come for northern Israel. Isaiah used the tradition to warn Judah (2:12-17) in a similar way and apparently lived to speak of the catastrophe in retrospect (22:1-14). In the years before the fall of Jerusalem, Zephaniah (1:1–2:3) and Ezekiel (7:1-27) again employed the tradition to give new and urgent warnings to Judah. The day of Yahweh concept was thus used with considerable freedom to interpret various momentous events—past, future, or imminent.

At the end of the era of the Exile, the restoration of Judah was understood to be directly dependent upon the destruction of Babylon. It is more than coincidence that the day of Yahweh concept is united with the term נקם "vindication" (not "vengeance") in three texts from this era (Isa. 34:8; 61:2; 63:4; cf. Jer. 46:10). This term can express the dual activity of a just and good king who rescues the upright while at the same time bringing punishment for those guilty of arrogance and violence. *See* VENGEANCE[S].

The day of Yahweh tradition probably had this dual character from its very origin; the prophets could emphasize aspects of judgment or rescue as they understood the realities of their own time. They were controlled in their use of the concept by their convictions about Yahweh as the ruler of all nations who has steadfast love for the upright (*see* LOVE IN THE OT §3) but who does not allow arrogance and violence among nations to continue forever.

3. The apocalyptic influence. In the late postexilic era, portrayals of the day of Yahweh tend to become more and more cataclysmic and universal in character under the influence of apocalyptic thought (*see* APOCALYPTICISM; APOCALYPTICISM [S]). But even in these late prophetic portrayals (Joel 1–4; Zech. 14:1-21; and Mal. 3:13–4:6 [H 3:13-24]), God's presence is still anticipated in the tumult of world events. When the tradition is examined in intertestamental and early Christian writings, it is important to remember that the classical prophets used this concept not to speak of the end of the world for all mankind but rather to describe a sequence of momentous events within history. That background may in fact provide important insights for understanding the various ways in which the concept is employed in later eras. *See also* DAY OF JUDGMENT; DAY OF CHRIST.

Bibliography. S. Mowinckel, *He That Cometh* (1956); G. von Rad, "The Origin of the Concept of the Day of Yahweh," *JSS*, IV (1959), 97-108; F. Cross, Jr., "The Divine Warrior in Israel's Early Cult," *Biblical Motifs*, ed. A. Altmann (1966), pp. 11-30; F. C. Fensham, "A Possible Origin of the Concept of the Day of the Lord," *Biblical Essays* (1966), pp. 90-97; M. Weiss, "The Origin of the 'Day of the Lord'—Reconsidered," *HUCA*, XXXVII (1966), 29-60; A. J. Everson, "The Days of Yahweh," *JBL*, XCIII (1974), 329-37.

A. J. EVERSON

*DEAD SEA SCROLLS.

1. Archaeological evidence
2. Editions of texts
3. Preliminary publications
4. Bible, Apoc., and Pseudep.
5. Historical theories
6. Organization of the community
7. Doctrine and religious practices
8. Eschatology and messianism
9. The Scrolls and the NT

Bibliography

1. Archaeological evidence. The archaeological evidence concerning the Qumran site and the agricultural annex at 'Ain Feshkha are discussed fully by de Vaux in his 1959 Schweich Lectures, published in French in 1961 and reissued in a revised English translation in 1973. Among the many discoveries helping to determine the chronology of the Qumran settlement, the dated coins in particular provide valuable pointers to the period during which the buildings were inhabited.

The earliest relevant phase of occupation is marked by eleven Seleucid coins, three of which can be dated precisely to three consecutive years (132-130 B.C.) of the reign of Antiochus VII. The rule of John Hyrcanus I (134-104 B.C.) and that of Aristobulus I (104-103 B.C.) are attested by a single coin each. By contrast, 143 of the coins were minted by Alexander Janneus (103-76 B.C.), one by Alexandra Salome and Hyrcanus II (76-67 B.C.), five by Hyrcanus II (63-40 B.C.), four by Antigonus Mattathias (40-37 B.C.) and ten by Herod the Great (37-4 B.C.). The ethnarchy of Archelaus (4 B.C.–A.D. 6) is attested by sixteen coins, the administration by Roman prefects (A.D. 6-41) and procurators (A.D. 44-66) by ninety-one, and the reign of Agrippa I (A.D. 41-44) by seventy-eight coins. Ninety-four bronze coins represent the First Jewish War, the majority of them dating to the second year of the revolt (A.D. 67-68), a few to the third year, and none to the fourth.

A few further coins testify to the conversion of the Qumran buildings into a Roman military post, and others attest the reoccupation of the ruins by the Jewish revolutionaries of the Second War under the leadership of Simeon ben Kosiba (A.D. 132-35). *See* BAR KOCHBA[S].

The numismatic evidence therefore yields solid backing to the thesis that the Qumran settlement was founded in the second half of the second century B.C. and remained occupied, possibly without interruption, until the war of A.D. 66-70 but more probably until A.D. 68. Such a firmly established archaeological context enables us to fix a reliable chronological framework for the dating of the scrolls possessed by the ancient inhabitants of Qumran, and for the identification of the events alluded to in those scrolls.

2. Editions of texts. At the time of the completion of the article DEAD SEA SCROLLS, the MSS of Cave I had appeared in definitive editions. Since then, three additional volumes of the series *Discoveries in the Judean Desert* (*DJD*) and a separate edition of the Targ. of Job have substantially enriched our information regarding the literature of the Dead Sea sect.

DJD III (1962) contains all the fragments discovered in Caves II, III, and V-X, the so-called "Minor Caves." In addition to a large number of small biblical and nonbiblical remains, this volume includes some minute fragments of the Hebrew Ecclesiasticus and Jubilees from Cave II. There are also several tiny scraps found in Caves V and VI (more are to follow from Cave IV) of the Zadokite Fragments or Damascus Rule (CDC), thus demonstrating the antiquity of the document preserved in two medieval MSS in the Cairo Genizah, and *mezuzoth* and *tephillin* or phylacteries from Caves V and VIII. A phylactery complete with capsule was published by Yadin in 1969.

The two most important texts appearing in this volume are the Aramaic New Jerusalem from Cave V, and the Copper Scroll from Cave III, both edited by Milik.

The New Jerusalem document (the fragments from Cave V are completed with the help of parallels from Cave IV) is inspired by Ezek. 40–48 and may be compared to Rev. 21. The author is a visionary who observes an angelic surveyor measuring the avenues, streets, houses, staircases, rooms, windows, etc. of the heavenly city. When the more extensive texts from Cave IV are published, a much fuller insight will be gained into Jewish eschatological speculation in regard to the religious capital of Israel in the world to come.

The Copper Scroll, a nonreligious composition embossed on sheets of copper in a Hebrew akin to the language of the Mishna, lists in cryptic style sixty-four hiding places where gold, silver, aromatics, and scrolls are said to have been concealed. Accepted literally, the quantity of precious metal mentioned in the scroll amounts to nearly one hundred tons. Some scholars are prepared to believe in the reality of the treasure and identify it either as the fortune accumulated by the Essene sect (Dupont-Sommer), or as the wealth of the temple of Jerusalem removed from the holy city shortly before the siege by the Romans (Rabin, Allegro). The editor (Milik), by contrast, advances the theory that it is a fictional account of hidden treasure.

It should perhaps also be noted that a few miniscule and insignificant Greek fragments from Cave VII have been blown up by the papyrologist O'Callahan into a sensational discovery of NT writings (Mark, Acts, Romans, I Timothy, James, II Peter). This argument has been repudiated as a flight of fancy by the editors of the fragments (Baillet, Benoit) and by other leading scholars in the Qumran field and Greek papyrology (Vermes, Fitzmyer, Roberts, etc.).

DJD IV (1965) contains the *editio princeps* of the Psalms Scroll from Cave XI. The MS, assigned by its editor J. A. Sanders to the second century B.C., preserves fully or in part forty-one canonical psalms (beginning with Ps. 101), the poem known as II Sam. 23:1-7, four apocryphal psalms previously available in Greek, Latin, and Syriac translations, three completely new ones, and a curious prose composition listing the number of various types of poetic works attributed to David to a sum totaling 4,050. The canonical psalms do not follow the traditional order. There are also variant readings, but few have meaningful relevance to textual criticism.

DJD V (1968) yields the first collection of fragments from Cave IV. Published by Allegro, the contents are mostly exegetical observations concerning individual books of the Bible (Genesis, Exodus, Isaiah, Hosea, Micah, Nahum, Zephaniah, Psalms), or selected extracts (florilegium, testimonia). The Nahum Commentary and a quotation from the Psalms of Joshua are of great historical significance and will be touched on below (§3).

Among the miscellaneous compositions are two fragmentary horoscopes, written from left to right in a childish cipher, and using letters chosen from various Hebrew scripts and from the Greek alphabet. The spiritual destinies of three individuals are described there as reflected by their share in light and darkness. It is interesting to remark that certain physical characteristics, such as shortness, fatness, and irregularity of features, are associated with wickedness, whereas their opposites denote virtue. An Aramaic horoscope, edited separately by Starcky, appears to be that of the royal Messiah.

The Targ. of Job from Cave XI (1971) offers an Aramaic rendering, neither fully literal nor properly paraphrastic, of substantial sections of the book of Job between Job 17:14 and 42:11. The existence of written Targs., in particular a Targ. of Job, in the days of R. Gamaliel (first half of the first century A.D.) is alluded to in J.T. Shab. 15*c* and T.B. Shab. 115*a*. The Qumran MS is attributed by its editors, van der Ploeg and van der Woude, to *ca.* 100 B.C. Their opinion that it may be identical with the Targ. rejected by Gamaliel I, and that its language is by and large the Aramaic spoken by Jesus, is, however, purely conjectural. The latest linguistic study of the document (by Muraoka) argues that this Targ. originated, not in Palestine, but in Mesopotamia between 250 and 150 B.C.

3. Preliminary publications. Among the provisionally edited texts, two deserve particular mention: the Melchizedek Document and the Temple Scroll.

The Melchizedek composition takes the form of a midrash (*see* MIDRASH[S] §3) in which Isa. 61:1 is interpreted in the light of Lev. 25:13 and Deut. 15:2. The proclamation of liberty to the captives at the end of days is understood as part of the general restoration of property in the jubilee year or universal remission of debts. The heavenly deliverer is Melchizedek, identified with the archangel Michael and leader of the sons of heaven. Designated as a "god" (אלהים), he is portrayed as presiding over the final judgment and as condemning his demonic counterpart, the Prince of Darkness, or Belial (called also Melkiresha), together with his armies. The eschatological act of liberation is expected to occur in the last Jubilee, and on the Day of Atonement. The MS sheds valuable light on the figure of Melchizedek in Heb. 7, and on the development of the concept of the heavenly Messiah in the NT and early Christianity. *See also* MELCHIZEDEK[S].

The as yet unpublished Temple Scroll is the largest of all the Qumran MSS, measuring over twenty-eight feet in length and containing sixty-six columns. It was acquired in the summer of 1967 by Yadin. A preliminary description of the contents of the MS and two small extracts have since been issued by this scholar.

The document consists of four sections. The first deals with ritual cleanness and uncleanness, the second with the festivals, the third with the building of the temple, and the fourth with the king and the army of Israel. As a source of specific laws and customs, it promises to be invaluable.

The two short passages so far released are both of considerable significance. In col. 57.17-19 we are told that even the king was subject to the rule of monogamous marriage: "He shall not take another wife in addition to her, for she shall be with him all the days of her life." Col. 64.6-13 preserves a statute according to which an Israelite guilty of treason or some similar crime against the Jewish state is to die by "hanging on the tree," i.e., in the light of the Nahum Commentary and parallel sources, most probably by crucifixion: "If a man slanders his people and delivers his people to a foreign nation and does evil to his people, you shall hang him on a tree and he shall die."

4. Bible, Apoc., and Pseudep. The eleven Qumran caves have revealed scrolls and fragments belonging to all the books of the Hebrew Scriptures except Esther, antedating by over a millennium the oldest Masoretic codices. Perhaps the most crucial feature of the biblical Dead Sea Scrolls from the point of view of Jewish history is that they represent not one but several recensional traditions. Some MSS testify to the "received text" of the later Masoretes; others echo for the first time the Hebrew underlying the Greek translations of the Bible; still others correspond to the Samaritan version. Before Qumran, it was commonly assumed that the canon of the Hebrew OT was established at Jamnia (JABNEEL) by the rabbis assembled there at the end of the first century A.D. The scrolls now show that Gamaliel II and his colleagues had to determine, not only the precise number of books to be kept on the register of sacred writings, but also which single type of recension of the text should count from then on as canonical.

Clearly, they preferred the tradition which we designate as (Proto-) Masoretic. But this simply means that, when religious authority proceeded to unify the plurality of competing textual or recensional traditions, it decided to consecrate one of the existing varieties more or less *in toto*, instead of creating, as modern biblical scholars often do, a new mosaic version with the help of what seems the best readings found in the diverse sources, readings imagined to approximate most closely the hypothetical *Urtext* of the Bible.

In brief, Qumran has disclosed that, even in the field of the transmission of the text of Scripture, plurality preceded unity. Subject to confirmation by the long-awaited release of the biblical material from Cave IV by Cross and Skehan, this new insight might lead to a veritable breakthrough, not only in textual criticism, but also in Jewish intellectual and religious history.

With the discovery of apocryphal and pseudepigraphic texts written in Hebrew and Aramaic and belonging to the period of the second temple, these writings are no longer to be seen as secondary phenomena in the literary history of Judaism, surviving only in Christian translations. They are evidence of Palestinian Jewry's own rich creativity during the co-existence of many religious parties in the pre-Destruction era. After Jamnia, the several streams of inspiration were reduced to a unity, this change being necessitated by the conditions in which Judaism was reorganized after the cataclysm of the first war against Rome, and by the way the religious leadership responded to the needs of that period of crisis in the last decade of the first and the first half of the second century A.D. The publication of the Aramaic Books of Enoch of Qumran Cave IV by Milik (and a new edition of the Ethiopic text by Knibb) is eagerly awaited. There is no sign in the pre-A.D. 70 Qumran MSS of the Book of the Similitudes of Enoch (i.e., chs. 37–72 of the Ethiopic version) with its famous references to the "Son of Man," about whom NT scholars have speculated so much. And even if Milik's dating of the relevant chapters to the third century A.D. is taken with a pinch of salt, it is doubtful, to say the least, that the "Son of Man" section existed before the destruction of the temple of Jerusalem. In that case, the historical interpretation of the corresponding gospel passages will have to be reconsidered quite independently of the Enoch evidence.

5. Historical theories. The emergence of new material and the general shift in scholarly opinion invite and even necessitate a full statement of the historical problems raised by the Dead Sea Scrolls.

In the early days of Qumran research, the dating of the history of the sect—i.e., the conflict between the Teacher of Righteousness and the Wicked Priest and the arrival of the Kittim—oscillated between the time of Antiochus Epiphanes and the age of the Crusades. During the period from 1960 to 1975, however, the extreme views have lost much ground. Protagonists of the medieval theory have been reduced to S. Zeitlin and his uninfluential circle. J. L. Teicher's Christian hypothesis has left no noticeable mark on scholarship, nor has Y. Baer's more recent restatement of the thesis endowed it with any greater verisimilitude. More significantly, no fresh attempt has been made at identifying the Kittim of the scrolls with the Seleucids. Today, experts are practically unanimous in recognizing the Kittim as Romans, and in placing the chief characters of the scrolls between the epoch of the early Maccabees (Jonathan and Simon) on the one hand, and the war of A.D. 66-70, on the other.

Within these outer boundaries, three theories with minor variations may be considered defensible.

(*a*) The Maccabean thesis situates the conflict between the Teacher of Righteousness and the Wicked Priest under the rule of Jonathan and/or Simon Maccabeus.

(*b*) The Hasmonean theory centers on the reign of Alexander Janneus or his sons Aristobulus II and Hyrcanus II.

(*c*) The Zealot reconstruction moves the majority of events alluded to in the MSS within the period of the First Jewish War.

The Zealot theory, for which the late Cecil Roth and G. R. Driver are jointly responsible, stands only a limited chance of being found correct. The Zealot chronological framework is ill-suited to the Qumran data, as it requires all the main events to be squeezed into the last few years of the existence of Qumran, whereas archaeology and literary allusions postulate prolonged occupation of the site and a lengthy internal history of the sect. Moreover, the lay character of the Zealot movement is in contradiction with the distinctly priestly features of the founding fathers of the community. It is therefore not surprising that no other scholars of repute have supported Roth and Driver by subscribing to this theory. *See* ZEALOT[S].

The Alexander Janneus thesis was once advanced by de Vaux, van der Ploeg, Delcor, Barthélemy, and others (and embraced also by Betz in IDB), but from 1960 to 1975 won no new adherents. The same may also be said of the Hyrcanus II/Aristobulus II theory championed by Dupont-Sommer, despite his renewed attempt to capitalize on the mention in the Nahum Commentary of two opponents of the sect, Ephraim and Manasseh, interpreted as the two sons of Alexander Janneus, Hyrcanus and Aristobulus.

Today the most influential and widely held theory is that which dates the history of the sect to the Maccabean era. Propounded, in chronological order, by Vermes, Milik, Cross, Winter, de Vaux, G. Jeremias, Hengel, Stegemann, and Murphy-O'Connor, its main advantage, compared with the other hypotheses, is that it accommodates without difficulty two crucial data: it can account for the establishment of the Qumran settlement some time after 140 B.C., i.e., under the reign of Simon Maccabeus, and for those literary allusions in the scrolls which associate the origin of the sect with the rise of the Hasidim at the time of Antiochus Epiphanes and the career of the Teacher of Righteousness, the founder of the community, with the initial phase of the movement's history. All the other hypotheses date his ministry to the first century A.D. or later, and thus leave a large gap at the commencement of their chronological sequence. The following figure among the more prominent hints pointing to the Maccabean theory.

The "age of wrath" (CDC 1.5) which coincided with the birth of the original nucleus of the community is best suited to the epoch of the Hellenistic crisis under Antiochus Epiphanes. The "plant root" which God "caused to spring . . . to inherit His land" (CDC 1.7-8) denotes the appearance of the Hasidim, who, as representatives of traditional Judaism, were opposed to Greek culture. The Teacher of Righteousness appeared on the scene twenty years later (CDC 1.10-11), at a time when, in our hypothesis, the war against the Seleucids had ended. The office of high priest was vacant (since the death of Alcimus in 159 B.C.), and Palestine was effectively controlled by Jonathan Maccabeus, a priest first considered good by the members of the sect, but who later betrayed God "for the sake of riches" (1QpHab. 8.9-11), no doubt when he accepted the pontifical title from the Syrian Alexander Balas in 152 B.C. With his brother Simon, the other "instrument of violence" (4QTest. 25), he fortified Jerusalem and the cities of Judea, spreading wickedness and impurity.

Jonathan was opposed by the Teacher of Righteousness, but the latter's critical stand was soon suppressed, and he was forced to retire to "the house of his exile," possibly to Qumran, where the Wicked Priest visited him when he and his followers were celebrating the Day of Atonement according to their own peculiar calendar (1QpHab. 11.4-8). Owing to the obscurity of the account, it is impossible to decide whether the purpose of this visitation was simply to humiliate the Teacher of Righteousness, or whether it intended to eliminate him and his influence altogether. Whatever the case, the Wicked Priest incurred guilt through this act in the eyes of the sectaries, and they judged that it was as a punishment for this crime that God delivered him to the enemies (1QpHab. 9.9-12), who took "vengeance on his body of flesh" (1QpHab. 9.2). The only Maccabean dynast to whom this description properly applies is Jonathan, who was captured by the Seleucid general Tryphon, the "chief of the kings of Greece" (CDC 8.11), and executed in 142 B.C.

The death of the Wicked Priest does not constitute the historical horizon of the Qumran writers. It extends, according to the Nahum Commentary, from Antiochus (no doubt Epiphanes), through Demetrius (probably Demetrius III, a contemporary of Alexander Janneus), to the coming of "the commanders of the Kittim" (4QpNah 1.2-3). Before their arrival, Israel was ruled by "the last priests of Jerusalem," whom the sectarian writer charges with having amassed "money and wealth by plundering the peoples," and who were to receive their just desserts from the Kittim (1QpHab 9.4-7). This description aptly portrays the last Hasmoneans, especially Alexander Janneus, the "furious young lion" (4QpNah 1.5), who is reproached with "hanging men alive on the tree" (4QpNah 1.7) as an act of revenge. According to Josephus, these Jewish opponents of Janneus were the Pharisees, eight hundred of whom he accused of treason in that they invited Demetrius III to invade Judea, and whom he crucified.

The Kittim, represented in the biblical commentaries of Qumran merely as God's instruments in bringing down the Hasmoneans and not as the enemies of the community, are the Romans of Pompey, who deprived the priestly rulers of Jerusalem of their wealth and of their autonomous political power.

The sect's attitude toward Rome in the years following these events is reflected in the War Rule. This MS reveals that the sons of Light were expected to remain in "exile" during the dominion of Belial (1QM 1.2), i.e., during the rule of the Romans and their Jewish allies; but, after the final forty-year-long war had been launched, Jerusalem would be reoccupied, the pure temple service restored (1QM 2.1-6), the king of the Kittim defeated (1QM 15.2-3), and the reign of light and truth inaugurated.

A variety of historical characters have been suggested for the role of the Teacher of Righteousness. Among them, in chronological sequence, are the murdered high priest Onias III; Mattathias, the father of the Maccabee brothers; Yose ben Yoezer, a priest executed in 162 B.C.; Judas Maccabeus; the Pharisee Eleazar, an opponent of John Hyrcanus I; Judas the Essene, at the time of Aristobulus I; Onias the Righteous, a charismatic person stoned to death in 65 B.C.; Jesus; and Menahem, son of Judas the Galilean, a Zealot murdered in Jerusalem in A.D. 66. *See* TEACHER OF RIGHTEOUSNESS[S].

Primarily because of the scarcity of concrete detail in the scrolls, but also because of a lack of information concerning anti-Maccabean activities in the accounts of the stories of Jonathan and Simon, which were written and transmitted exclusively by their sympathizers and partisans, none of these identifications is convincing. Indeed, the only sound conclusion at this moment of Qumran research is that the Teacher of Righteousness is still anonymous. We know that he was a priest (pPs.37 3.15), that he went into exile as a result of the persecution initiated by the Wicked Priest, Jonathan (1QpHab 11.6); but the date and the manner of his death, violent or peaceful, still remain open. We learn, however, from the Habbakuk Commentary that in the faith of his followers he occupied a unique position: *"The righteous shall live by his faith* [Hab. 2:4]. Interpreted, this concerns all who observe the Law in the House of Judah [the sect], whom God will deliver from the House of Judgment because of their suffering and because of their faith in the Teacher of Righteousness" (1QpHab. 8.1.3).

Concerning the identity of the Qumran community itself, the large majority of scholars follow Dupont-Sommer and Sukenik, with or without reservations, and recognize it as the sect of the Essenes. Minority views exercising little impact on present-day academic thinking suggest, as the people of the scrolls, the Pharisees (C. Rabin), the Sadducees (R. North), the Jewish-Christians (Teicher, Baer), and the medieval Karaites (Zeitlin, Hoenig).

6. Organization of the community. Study of the various codes, namely the Manual of Discipline or Community Rule (1QS), the Zadokite Fragments or Damascus Rule (CDC), the Scroll of the War of the Sons of Light and the Sons of Darkness or War Rule (1QM), and the Rule of the Congregation or Messianic Rule (1QSa), enables us to reconstruct the organization, governments, and life of the sect. To do this successfully, however, we have to bear in mind that the "town communities" (CDC 12.19) differed by necessity from the "camps" (CDC 12.22-23) or desert settlements, and that the various legal accounts are bound to reflect customs of successive periods.

The community of Qumran claimed, as sects generally do, to represent the genuine traditions of the religious body from which it had separated. Its members formed the true Israel and were divided like their historical model into clergy (priests and Levites) and laity (Israel). They maintained also the symbolic divisions into twelve tribes, as well as into the smaller units of thousands, hundreds, fifties, and tens.

As was generally the case in postexilic Judaism, supreme authority lay in the hands of the priests. It was they, the "sons of Zadok" or "sons of Aaron," who had the final word in matters of doctrine, justice, and property (IQS 5.2; 9.7). They nevertheless governed the sect, not entirely on their own, but through the Council of the Community, consisting of themselves, the Levites, and the lay leaders of Israel (cf. 1QSa 1.22–2.3).

The smallest unit was the group of ten. It was expected to include a priest-president to pronounce the blessing over the meals (1QS 6.2-5; CDC 13.2-3), and to perform such legal functions as were reserved to members of his class, e.g., the administration of the leprosy laws (CDC 13.4-7). The management of the community's affairs was entrusted to the guardian or overseer, who dealt with admissions, instruction, and decision making, and with determining the right conduct of every member of his unit. He was also in charge of practical matters and communal finance (1QS 6.14-23; CDC 13.7-16).

The sect as a whole was also governed by a priest-president-general and by a guardian of all the camps (CDC 14.6-12). In addition to these, the Damascus Rule mentions ten judges (CDC 10.4-10). The organization of the sect was also to have, at least in the ultimate phase of the eschatological age, a supreme lay leader, the *nasi* or prince who was, no doubt, to be identical with the royal Messiah (1QM 5.1). There was a compulsory retirement age set at fifty for the guardian of all the camps, and at sixty for other office holders (CDC 14.7, 9; 10.6-10). Association with the community began in the form of a ceremony called the "entry into the Covenant," i.e., an undertaking on oath that the person would obey all the laws of Moses according to the interpretation of the sect's priestly hierarchy (1QS 1.16–2.16; 5.1-13). Advancement in the group with a view to being admitted to the Council of the Community required two years of special training, at the end of each year of which there was a test. The final examination decided whether the candidate was to be declared a full member with the right actively to participate in all communal matters, including voting at meetings and in the common ownership of property (1QS 6.13-23).

The way to the council was barred by any deliberate transgression of the law of Moses. A member of the council found guilty of an act of disobedience, committed willfully or through negligence, was expelled and no further contact with him was tolerated (1QS 8.20-24). Minor offenses were punished with a penance entailing a reduction of the food ration, and could last from ten days to two years (1QS 6.24–7.25).

Judging from the differences in the regulations, it would appear that covenant members living in towns and villages followed the stringent rules of the sect, but were exempt from common ownership of property. They were allowed to trade with nonmembers, even with Gentiles (CDC 13.14-16; 12.9-11). A communal chest was maintained through regular contributions (two days' wages per month) and served to finance charitable activities such as support for widows, orphans, the sick, etc. (CDC 14.12-16).

The members of the council, by contrast, practiced a kind of communism: property and earnings were handed over to the financial administrator (1QS 6.19-20), who in turn provided everyone with his needs. This compulsory scheme, characteristic of the Essenes, may be compared to its optional counterpart, mentioned in the Acts of the Apostles (2:44-45; 4:32–5:2), or to the use of a common purse administered by Judas in the life of the society formed by Jesus and his apostles (John 12:6; 13:29).

The question of the marital state of the sectaries is complex. The Damascus Rule (CDC 7.6-7) and the Messianic Rule (1QSa 1.4) speak of married members and children. The War Rule does likewise, but stipulates that during the eschatological war no woman or child may enter the camp of the sons of Light (1QM 7.3-4). On the other hand, the Community Rule is silent in regard to women, and the main Qumran cemetery has yielded only male skeletons. It should be added, however, that only a small number of tombs have been opened, and that the secondary cemeteries held the remains of women and children. Assuming that the Qumran sect belonged to the Essene movement, and recalling that Josephus mentions unmarried and married Essenes, it is reasonable to conclude that the Dead Sea community also counted both varieties among its members, though the married sectaries probably outnumbered their celibate brethren.

All the members of the sect attended an annual general assembly at the Feast of the Renewal of the Covenant, when new candidates were sworn in and the ranking of the sectaries was reviewed (cf. 1QS 1–3; esp. 2.19-22). The council held a nightly study and prayer meeting (1QS 6.7). Some of the assemblies were accompanied by a solemn meal, at which bread and wine were blessed by the presiding priest (IQS 6.4-5; IQSa 2:17-21).

The Community Rule mentions also a kind of "Court of Inquiry" (1QS 6.24) designed to try offenders against the community regulations. A detailed penal code determines the punishment attached to the various transgressions, from that of speaking out of turn in public, which incurred ten-days' penance, to a deliberate breach of the Mosaic law, demanding irrevocable expulsion (1QS 6.24–7.25). The Damascus Rule refers to a tribunal of ten judges—four priests and six Israelites (CDC 10.4-10)—and specifies also the rules applying to witnesses (CDC 9.16–10.3). Among the penalties we find the death sentence. This was to be inflicted on any sectary who had willingly participated in a capital case before a Gentile court (CDC 9.1) or had preached "apostasy under the dominion of the spirits of Belial" (CDC 12.2-3).

The publication of the Temple Scroll will yield a considerable amount of additional information concerning the organization, laws, and customs of the sect.

7. Doctrine and religious practices. The members of the Qumran sect professed to belong to a "new covenant" (1QpHab. 2.3; CDC 8.21, 35) based on the message of Moses and the prophets but understood in the light of the preaching of the Teacher of Righteousness and the authoritative exegesis given by the sons of Zadok, the priestly hierarchy of the community. For their special interpretation of Scripture, both legal and prophetic, see INTERPRETATION, HISTORY OF[S] §B1.

In biblical thinking, the notion of covenant and that of chosen people are inseparable: Israelite birth is synonymous with election. By contrast, when an adult Jew joined the Qumran sect, he had—like the Gentile proselyte in mainstream Judaism—a personal and active part in the process of becoming one of God's chosen. This particular situation awakened in him an awareness of human frailty and of the all-pervading reality of divine grace, sentiments that are expressed again and again in the Qumran hymns. Another of the specific themes in these poems is the recognition in salvation of a double divine gift: the revealed knowledge of what is right and good, and the God-given power enabling the sectary to embrace truth and practice justice. Knowledge and grace were believed to lead the elect toward the way of holiness, to illuminate for them the secrets of heaven, and to allow them to contemplate even the most sacred of all visions, that of the *Merkabah,* the Chariot-Throne of God: "The Cherubim bless the image of the Throne-Chariot above the firmament, and they praise the [majesty] of the fiery firmament beneath the seat of his glory. And between the turning wheels, angels of holiness come and go, as it were a fiery vision of the most holy spirits; and about them [flow] seeming rivulets of fire, like gleaming bronze, a radiance of many gorgeous colours, of marvellous pigments magnificently mingled. The spirits of the living God move perpetually with the glory of the wonderful Chariot" (Angelic Liturgy, frag. 2).

The principal aim of the Qumran sectaries was to lead a life of continuous worship in which the sons of Light on earth joined their voices to those of the celestial choirs of the angels. Cultic acts were to be performed in the correct manner, and at the divinely prescribed moments, in conformity with the unchangeable laws of time itself governing day and night, the weeks, the months, the four seasons, and the years.

The daily prayer was to be offered at the onset of light and of darkness, i.e., at dawn and dusk. Time was measured according to a solar calendar following "the laws of the great light of heaven" (1QH 12.5); and the year was thus divided into fifty-two weeks and each season into thirteen weeks, i.e., into three months of thirty days, with an additional day linking one season to another. The result was absolute regularity: seasons and years always started on the same day of the week. Moreover, since according to the Bible the sun and the moon were created on the fourth day—a Wednesday—every New Year in the Qumran reckoning began on Wednesday. Passover, the fifteenth day of the first month, was also invariably a Wednesday. Similarly, the Day of Atonement, the tenth day of the seventh month, was always a Friday. The festivals of the Dead Sea community were in consequence celebrated on days which for other Jews were ordinary working days. This explains how the Wicked Priest could visit the Teacher of Righteousness at his place of refuge on the sect's Day of Atonement (1QpHab. 11.6-8).

As the community adhered to all the precepts of the law of Moses, the sectaries observed all the biblical feasts, but they ascribed a very special importance to the Feast of Weeks, or Pentecost. In traditional Judaism this day marks the anniversary of the revelation of the Law on Sinai; for the sect, it became the yearly occasion for the Renewal of the Covenant, the liturgy of which is described at the beginning of the Community Rule (1QS 1–3) and in an as yet unpublished section of the Damascus Rule.

The laws of cleanness and uncleanness played a significant part in the life of the community, and the ordinances concerning purification by water are clearly set out in the Damascus Rule (CDC 10.10-13), the War Rule (1QM 14.2-3), and in the Community Rule (1QS 3.4-5; 5.13). The latter passages deal with purification by means of a ritual bath in connection with entry into the covenant. In mainstream Judaism, a similar rite was administered to proselytes. In Christianity, baptism became the act of initiation par excellence.

For the sectaries, the temple of Jerusalem, singled out by Jewish law as the sole place of sacrificial worship, was a place of abomination; its precincts were considered polluted, its priests wicked, and the liturgical calendar prevailing there unlawful.

The sect therefore spiritualized its own worship until the time when the sacrificial cult, properly performed, could be restored, an event expected to take place after the reoccupation of Jerusalem by the community, in the seventh year of the eschatological war (1QM 2.5-6).

The sacred meal of the sect (1QS 6.4-5) was no doubt a substitute for the sacrificial meals of the temple. It would be celebrated again in the final age as an eschatological banquet attended by the priestly Messiah and the Messiah of Israel. The former, by virtue of his priesthood, was to have precedence over the latter (1QSa 2.17-22).

8. Eschatology and messianism. Following established Jewish patterns, the Qumran sect believed that the final triumph of justice and the establishment of the reign of God would be preceded by a period of wars and tribulations. Moreover, when the community represented the ultimate victory of the forces of good as brought about through the mediation of a Messiah, it often combined the Davidic idea with the images of a new exodus and a new Moses. The scrolls exhibit all these features, and produce an extraordinary synthesis.

According to the Damascus Rule, the messianic age was to begin approximately forty years after the death of the Teacher of Righteousness (CDC 20.13-15): the War Rule describes the fight against the armies of Darkness as also lasting forty years (1QM 2.6). If the various chronological data of these two scrolls are combined, they add up to the traditional 490 years from the first fall of Jerusalem until the triumph of the Messiah prophesied by Jeremiah (25:11; 29:10) and expounded by Daniel (9:24): 390 years from Nebuchadrezzar to the emergence of the precursors of the sect (CDC 1.5-6); 20 years of "groping in the darkness" until the manifestation of the Teacher of Righteousness (CDC 1.9-11); 40 years of his ministry and the immediate premessianic age (CDC 20.13-15); and the 40 years of the messianic war. Altogether 70 "weeks of years," or 70 times 7 years.

Before the final division of the world into armies of Light and Darkness on the eve of the new age, the sect envisaged a large-scale conversion of Jews to the community (1QSa 1.1), but after this last opportunity for repentance, no one would be able to change sides (CDC 4.11). The elect would be under the command of the Prince of Light (Michael or Melchizedek), and the rest of wicked mankind, Jews as well as Gentiles, would form the host of Darkness led by the Angel of Darkness (Belial, Melkiresha). But at the end of the forty-year struggle, "the great hand of God" would cause justice to overcome wickedness; and the Kittim and all their allies on earth, as well as Belial and his satanic forces, would be defeated forever (1QM 18.1-3).

The sect inserted into this traditional framework an idiosyncratic messianic doctrine. They expected the arrival of a Prophet, and of the two Messiahs of Aaron and Israel (1QS 9.11). The same trio is reflected in the Testimonia or Messianic Anthology, citing Deut. 18:18 ("I will raise up for them a prophet"); Num. 24:17 ("A star shall come out of Jacob, and a scepter shall rise out of Israel," i.e., the royal Messiah); and Deut. 33:8-11, the blessing of Levi (the priestly Messiah). The latter two figures appear in other Qumran texts also. The Messianic Rule refers to the Priest and the Messiah of Israel (1QSa 2.11-21); the florilegium (1.11) juxtaposes the "Branch of David" (royal Messiah) and the "Interpreter of the Law" (priestly Messiah); and a similar group of two appears in the Damascus Rule designated as the "Prince of all the Congregation" and the "Interpreter of the Law" (CDC 7.18-21).

The roles of these two Messiahs are easy to define. The lay Messiah was to defeat the Gentiles and usher in God's kingdom. He was to be inferior to the priests ("as they teach him, so shall he judge" [4QpIsa 8–10.23]), and in particular to the priestly Messiah (1QSa 2.20). The Messiah of Aaron is represented as the high priest of the final age, whose task it would be to expound the ultimate meaning of Scripture and to conduct the battle liturgy during the messianic war.

The function of the Prophet is less clear because his activity is nowhere defined. If we can rely on Deut. 18:18-19, he was to be a second Moses, a prophetic Messiah. However, if Mal. 4:5 is chosen as the Prophet's prototype, then we have a forerunner of the Messiah, a traditional element of Jewish expectation inherited also by early Christianity, where John the Baptist is described as Elijah redivivus.

To assess the true significance of Qumran messianism, it is to be remembered that in nonsectarian Judaism and Christianity the Messiah is a single individual invested with various—royal, prophetic, and priestly—features. The Dead Sea sectaries are distinguished by their refusal to amalgamate the separate streams of biblical tradition and by their consequent production of an unparalleled messianic trinity.

The recent publication of the Melchizedek Document suggests that it was also possible to conceive of a final salvation without the intervention of a human Messiah. In this writing, it is the work of an angelic Prince. It is symbolized, furthermore, not only as a war between good and evil, but essentially as a universal judgment pronounced on the eschatological Day of Atonement.

Finally, whereas there is ample evidence that the sect imagined the postmessianic age in the form of a new Jerusalem, there is no definite indication of any central belief in bodily resurrection, the cornerstone of the Pharisaic and Christian faiths. Consequently, nothing sure is known at the present time of the community's attitude to the destiny after death of the saints of past ages.

9. The scrolls and the NT. Comparison between the two bodies of literature is not only reasonable but indispensable: they date to roughly the same era and derive from the same milieu. Scholars almost without exception agree that the writings of both religious movements are in some way linked, though they differ concerning the extent and nature of the connection. At one extreme we find the theory, first propounded by Teicher and more recently restated by Baer, according to which the scrolls are Christian documents, the community is the Judeo-Christian church, and the Teacher of Righteousness is Jesus. An intermediate position holds that the community and the church are in a straight evolutionary line, i.e., that Christianity is an offshoot of Essenism, and Jesus a successor of the Teacher of Righteousness. Its chief spokesman, Dupont-Sommer, argues that Qumran confirms Renan's judgment that "Christianity is an Essenism which has largely succeeded." But the average academic view considers the Dead Sea sect and Christianity as two separate branches of the same tree and accounts for the similarities by descent from the common stock of first-century Judaism.

The identification of the scrolls as Judeo-Christian documents has so little substance that it can safely be discarded. Essene parentage of Christianity, on the other hand, still remains a distinct possibility. Yet the emphasis laid on the punctilious observance of the Mosaic law at Qumran contrasts so strongly with the peripheral importance given to it in the NT that a linear descent of the former to the latter seems unlikely. Therefore, the most sensible way to tackle the question of interrelationship is to start with the theory of two independent developments and subsequently to ask whether *all* the common features can be satisfactorily explained in this manner.

a. Major areas of contact. i. *Eschatological expectation* (*see* §8 *above*). The authors of the NT were convinced that they were witnessing the final act of the last age. Similarly, the Dead Sea literature is permeated with the idea that the *eschaton* had already begun, that the Teacher of Righteousness had ushered in the ultimate age, and that in the events taking place before their own eyes the members of the sect could detect the realization of biblical prophecies. As the consummation of time was more and more delayed, hope and perseverance became essential virtues in both communities (cf. 1QpHab. 7.9-14; II Pet. 3:3-10).

ii. *The claims to be the true Israel.* Each group believed in its own absolute and exclusive election (*see* §7 *above*). Each group was certain that it was the legitimate heir to all the divine promises made to the historical Israel and that it, and it alone, was the participant in a new covenant. The Qumran community describes itself as "that tried wall, that precious cornerstone, whose foundations shall neither rock, nor sway in their place" (1QS 8.7-8). The same metaphor, and a similar use of Isa. 28:16, are prominent in the NT (cf. esp. Rom. 9:32-33; I Cor. 3:10-13; Eph. 2:20; I Pet. 2:6). But the most notable evidence of the conviction of these minority bodies that they truly represented the "chosen people" appears in the symbolical division of their communities into twelve tribes (*see* §6 *above*). The Qumran sect was led by twelve tribal chiefs (1QSa 1.27–2.1), and the supreme council of the sect consisted of twelve laymen and three priests (IQS 8.1). Likewise, the twelve apostles of Jesus are promised that they will "sit on twelve thrones, judging the twelve tribes of Israel" (Matt. 19:28; Luke 22:30), and the church to which James wrote his letter is defined as "the twelve tribes in the Dispersion" (Jas. 1:1).

iii. *Attitude to the Bible* (*see* INTERPRETATION, HISTORY OF[S] §§B, C). The prophetic character of the Hebrew Scriptures had acquired paramount importance both for the church and for the community. The two were convinced that the words of the prophets announcing the final realities referred to the history and beliefs of their own group. Such an approach to the OT was conducive to a growing employment of biblical apologetics: the predestined character of the sect or church was proved by the conformity of its history to prophetic prediction. There was of course a certain variation in style in the presentation of these arguments. The scrolls, since they are addressed to initiates, can proceed with less emphasis and even elliptically. The NT, by contrast, directs its message to outsiders as well, and has in consequence to spell out every detail of its argumentation. Another point of obvious difference is that the early church represents Jesus as the subject of prophecies, the person in whom they are realized, while the Teacher of Righteousness at Qumran is the final interpreter, the man "to whom God made known all the mysteries of the words of his servants the Prophets" (1QpHab 7.4-5).

iv. *The significance of the Jerusalem temple.* According to biblical tradition, the sanctuary was the chosen dwelling place of the divine Presence and sacrificial worship there was the kernel of the religion of Israel. But for the Dead Sea sectaries, the temple had lost its holiness because of the wickedness of the priesthood, and they substituted for it the Council of the Community under the leadership of the sons of Zadok, their supreme institution. Atonement was to be made through the spiritual sacrifice of prayer and suffering (1QS 8.3-4; 9.4-5; 4QFlor. 1.6-7). (*See* §7 *above.*) By comparison, the behavior of Jesus and the apostles, including that of Paul when he was in Jerusalem, appears to have been conventional. They prayed in the temple and in general participated in the cult. At the same time, on the level of doctrine and belief Paul insists, like the sect, that the Christian community has replaced the old sanctuary and offerings (Eph. 2:19-22; Rom. 12:1).

One important dissimilarity nevertheless distinguishes the two theologies. At Qumran, withdrawal from the Jerusalem temple was intended as a temporary measure lasting as long as the rule of the wicked priesthood. It was expected that in the seventh year of the eschatological war sacrificial worship would be restored (1QM 2.3-6). Such is not the case in the vision of the NT book of Revelation. There is to be no material place of worship at all.

v. *Organization.* The close relationship, philological and real, of the מבקר (overseer/guardian) and the ἐπίσκοπος (bishop) has been noticed and emphasized since the publication of the Damascus Rule in 1910, but the reappearance of מבקר in the Qumran Community Rule lends the question renewed importance.

vi. *The economic system.* The use of the common purse and partial adoption of common ownership of property is also an obvious point of similarity (*see* §6 *above*). The Essenes of the classical accounts, and the full initiates of the scrolls, were required to hand over to the authorities their properties and earnings. This practice was so unusual both within and without the boundaries of Jewry that the Essene rejection of money became one of the distinctive marks of the sect. The NT nowhere imposes a similar rule: though the Fourth Gospel, at least, implies that Jesus and the apostolic community attached to him drew from a common purse held, as at Qumran, by one of their number (John 13:29; cf. 12:6). More importantly, the description of the original Jerusalem church in Acts strongly suggests that Christian property owners felt morally obliged to sell their belongings and consign the profits thus acquired to the apostles (Acts 2:44-45; 5:1).

vii. *Celibacy.* The Essenes, according to the Greek and Latin sources, rejected marriage, but literary and archaeological evidence at Qumran is contradictory (*see* §6 *above*). Be this as it may, the War Rule explicitly envisages the total separation of men and women during the last thirty-three years of the eschatological war (1QM 7.3-4; cf. 2.6). The NT does not condemn marriage, but holds celibacy or withdrawal from marital ties to be preferable (Matt. 19:10-12; Luke 14:26; 18:29; I Cor. 7:1, 7-8, 32-34). One of the reasons given is practical: family bonds must be severed by those who wish to accompany Jesus on his journeys (Luke) or to devote themselves fully to "the affairs of the Lord," i.e., the church (I Cor. 7:32-34). The second is the eschatological requirement that the chosen few, endowed with understanding, should make themselves "eunuchs for the sake of the kingdom of heaven" (Matt. 19:12). The third is a reason of convenience: the unmarried will have less trouble and worry than the married during the "impending distress" of the final upheaval (I Cor. 7:26-31; cf. Matt. 24:19). On the personal level, Paul explicitly declares himself to be wifeless (I Cor. 7:8; cf. 9:5), and the gospels give the impression that Jesus also was unmarried. Celibacy, or even a lengthy separation of the sexes, is alien to the Jewish way of life. Eliezer ben Hyrcanus, at the end of the first century A.D., went so far as to compare abstinence from procreation to murder (T.B. Yeb. 63b). This therefore could be a domain of some importance in the study of Qumran influence on Christianity.

viii. *The significance of Pentecost.* It is generally agreed that on this festival day the sect celebrated the annual renewal of the covenant, enrolled new aspirants, and admitted the initiated to full membership at the end of the two-year training period (*see* §6 *above*). Acts 2 also dates the first massive public entry into the new Christian sect to the same feast, on which occasion Peter's sermon was followed by the repentance and baptism of "about three thousand souls" (Acts 2:41).

b. Conclusions. In regard to the first of these major areas of contact between Qumran and the NT, it is undeniable that eschatological ferment was active throughout Palestine in the first century A.D. But neither the general picture of Jewish society at that time as depicted by Josephus, nor rabbinic traditions traceable with some probability to the period prior to A.D. 70, would indicate that Palestinian Jewry as such was affected by this fever to the level of intensity attested in the scrolls and the NT. On the other hand, an all-pervading eschatological expectation is more naturally found in fringe movements or sects than in the more sedate religious mainstream. It is reasonable to infer that the community and the primitive church belonged to the same socioreligious stratum of Palestinian Jewry. But we would not be justified in seeking to associate them more specifically than this.

General sectarian principles may also explain the claim made by the community and the church to be the true Israel, and their respective convictions that they were fulfilling prophecies. As these claims were of course necessarily contradictory, their separate arguments could have been influenced by controversy. There is, nonetheless, no evidence of any such confrontation in either corpus, and in the circumstances, speculation on the potential effects of polemics remains without foundation.

The temple problem is more complex. For the Qumran sect, which was dominated by priests, the sanctuary and the cult were of greater importance than for the group of unsophisticated Galileans who formed the nucleus of Christianity. This could account for the basic difference between the two doctrines, as to whether the replacement for the temple was to be temporary or permanent. Yet the resemblance of Paul's theology to that of Qumran on this point is too pronounced to be merely accidental, and it is legitimate to surmise that Paul was acquainted, directly or indirectly, with Qumran symbolism and that he adapted it in formulating his own teaching on spiritual worship. The same comment may apply to the genesis of Paul's thought on the "Israel of God" (Gal. 6:16); in shaping his own doctrine, he imitated, but simultaneously contradicted, the sectarian claims of the scrolls.

The most probable Qumran influence on the NT is associated with organization and religious practice. For the last four decades of the second temple the two communities co-existed. But Christianity during that time was no more than a nascent body, whereas the Qumran sect was a well-established institution. It would have been only sensible if, in the fields of administration and finance, the inexperienced organizers of the church had looked around for inspiration and had observed existing patterns with a view to taking them over and modifying them.

The issue of celibacy or discontinuation of marital life is less simple. The practical argument of the NT in favor of the single state, that an itinerant preacher or his follower needs freedom and mobility, is not applicable to Qumran, or (if they are different) to the Essenes of Josephus and Philo; there we are dealing largely with sedentary communities. On the other hand, the eschatological emphasis manifest in I Corinthians and the War Rule suggests once again that the scrolls may have had a direct or an indirect effect on Paul's thought. To evaluate the possibility of a Qumran influence in this respect on Jesus, we must first examine the community's justification of sexual abstinence during the eschatological era. It surely cannot lie in the misogynic tirades of Philo and Josephus, that women are selfish, jealous, skillful in seduction, licentious, and untrustworthy, and that marriage is harmful to common life and leads to discord. In fact, the only explicit reference in the scrolls to the separation of the sexes appears in a context of ritual purity (1QM 7.3-6). A ritual motivation of this sort is quite out of place in the case of Jesus, a Galilean charismatic who attached little if any importance to levitical cleanness and uncleanness. The renunciation of marriage imputed to him falls within the pattern of prophetic celibacy attested in Philo and rabbinic literature (*Life of Moses* 2.68-69; Siphre on Num. 12:1 §99).

One significant conclusion emerges from these considerations. If the scrolls exerted any influence on the NT, they will have done so not by influencing Jesus himself, to whom the bulk of Qumran doctrines would have been alien if not repugnant, but by influencing Paul, John, and other leaders of the new church. Their use, that is to say, will consist negatively in showing what Jesus was not, rather than what he was, and positively, in throwing light on the Christianity of the apostolic age.

Bibliography. Bibliographical aids: C. Burchard, *Bibliographie zu den Handschriften vom Toten Meer* I (1957), II (1965); W. S. LaSor, *Bibliography of the Dead Sea Scrolls 1948-1957* (1958); B. Jongeling, *A Classified Bibliography of the Finds in the Desert of Judah, 1958-1969* (1971); J. A. Sanders, "Palestinian Manuscripts 1947-1972," *JJS*, XXIV (1973), 74-83; J. A. Fitzmyer, *The Dead Sea Scrolls. Major Publications and Tools for Study* (1975). Works of authors not listed below can be located in these bibliographical aids.

Editions: M. Burrows, *The Dead Sea Scrolls of St. Mark's Monastery*, I (1950), II (1951); E. L. Sukenik, *The Dead Sea Scrolls of the Hebrew University* (1955); N. Avigad, Y. Yadin, *A Genesis Apocryphon* (1956); D. Barthélemy, J. T. Milik, *DJD*, I (1955); M. Baillet, J. T. Milik, R. de Vaux, *DJD*, III: *Les "Petites Grottes" de Qumrân* (1962); J. A. Sanders, *DJD*, IV: *The Psalms Scroll of Qumrân Cave 11* (1965); J. M. Allegro, *DJD*, V: *Qumrân Cave 4: I (4Q158-186)* (1968); J. P. M. van der Ploeg, A. S. van der Woude, *Le Targ. de Job de la grotte XI de Qumrân* (1971).

Preliminary editions or description of MSS: J. Strugnell, "The Angelic Liturgy at Qumran," VTSup, VII (1960), 318-45; J. Starcky, "Un texte messianique araméen de la grotte 4 de Qumrân," *Ecole des langues orientales anciennes . . . Mélanges du Cinquantenaire* (1964), pp. 51-66; A. S. van der Woude, "Melchisedek als himmilische Erlösersgestalt," *OTS*, XIV (1965), 354-73; Y. Yadin, *Tefillin from Qumran* (1969); J. T. Milik, "*Milkiṣedeq* et *Milki-resha'* dans les anciens écrits juifs et chrétiens," *JJS*, XXIII (1972), 95-144; Y. Yadin, "The Temple Scroll," *BA*, XXX (1967), 135-39; J. T. Milik, "Problèmes de la littérature hénochique à la lumière des fragments araméens de Qumrân," *HTR*, LXIV (1971), 333-78.

Zadokite Fragments: S. Schechter, "Fragments of a Zadokite Work" in *Documents of Jewish Sectaries* (1910 [repr. 1970]); C. Rabin, *The Zadokite Documents* (1954).

Vocalized edition: E. Lohse, *Die Texte aus Qumran, Hebräisch und Deutsch* (1964; [2nd ed., 1971]).

Archaeology: R. de Vaux, *Archaeology and the Dead Sea Scrolls* (1973).

Translations with introduction: G. Vermes, *Discovery in the Judaean Desert* (1956); T. H. Gaster, *The Scriptures of the Dead Sea Sect* (1957); A. Dupont-Sommer, *The Essene Writings from Qumran* (1961); G. Vermes, *The Dead Sea Scrolls in English* (1962 [2nd ed., 1975]); L. Moraldi, *I manoscritti di Qumrân* (1971).

Monograph commentaries: P. Wernberg-Møller, *The Manual of Discipline* (1957); Y. Yadin, *The Scroll of the War of the Sons of Light Against the Sons of Darkness* (1962); M. Mansoor, *The Thanksgiving Hymns* (1961); J. A. Fitzmyer, *The Genesis Apocryphon of Qumran Cave I* (1966 [2nd ed., 1971]); J. M. Allegro, *The Treasure of the Copper Scroll* (1960); M. Sokoloff, *The Targ. to Job from Qumran Cave XI* (1974); T. Muraoka, "The Aramaic of the Old Targ. of Job from Qumran Cave XI," *JJS*, XXV (1974), 425-43.

General studies: F. M. Cross, *The Ancient Library of Qumran and Modern Biblical Study* (1958 [2nd ed., 1961]); J. T. Milik, *Ten Years of Discovery in the Wilderness of Judaea* (1959); G. R. Driver, *The Judaean Scrolls* (1965); O. Eissfeldt, *The OT: An Introduction* (1965), pp. 637-68, 775-78; J. Macdonald, ed., "Dead Sea Scroll Studies 1969," in *Annual of Leeds*, University Oriental Society, VI (1969); J. Murphy-O'Connor, "The Essenes and their History," *RB*, LXXXI (1974), 215-44; G. Vermes, "The Impact of the Dead Sea Scrolls on Jewish Studies during the last Twenty-Five Years," *JJS*, XXVI (1975), 1-14.

Qumran and the NT: K. Stendahl, ed., *The Scrolls and the NT* (1957); M. Black, *The Scrolls and Christian Origins* (1961); L. Mowry, *The Dead Sea Scrolls and the Early Church* (1962); H. Braun, *Qumran und das NT*, I-II (1966); J. Murphy-O'Connor, ed., *Paul and Qumran* (1968); M. Black, ed., *The Scrolls and Christianity* (1969); J. H. Charlesworth, ed., *John and Qumran* (1972); J. O'Callaghan, *Los papiros griegos de la cueva 7 de Qumrân* (1974); G. Vermes, "A Papyrus Fragment," *The Times*, April 1, 1972; M. Baillet, "Les manuscrits de la grotte 7 de Qumrân et le NT," *Bibl.*, LIII (1972), 508-16; P. Benoit, "Note sur les fragments grecs de la grotte 7 de Qumrân," *RB*, LXXIX (1972), 321-24; J. A. Fitzmyer, "A Qumrân Fragment of Mark?" *America*, CXXVI (1972), 647-50; C. H. Roberts, "On Some Presumed Papyrus Fragments of the NT from Qumrân," *JTS*, NS XXIII (1972), 446-47; G. Vermes, *Jesus the Jew* (1974). G. VERMES

***DEATH, THEOLOGY OF.** A biblical understanding of death involves four presuppositions about life. (*a*) Psychological: the human person is a center of vitality (*nepheš*) which includes every part and element (*see* SOUL); death is the breakup of that center of vitality. (*b*) Sociological: human life is membership in a community; death is loss of full, functioning membership in the community. (*c*) Theological: life is relational; it concerns membership in a community which has a covenant with God. Life is honoring and enjoying that covenant (*see* COVENANT §§B, C, E; COVENANT, MOSAIC[S]); death is the loss of that relation. (*d*) Historical: life is understood in social, secular, political, and communal terms; death is inability to participate in such decision-demanding relations.

1. Presuppositions in a biblical understanding. In the context of those presuppositions, the term "death" is variously employed in the Bible. (*a*) Biologically, as the end of historical life. It is a natural part of life and is not particularly feared. It is enough to die in the context of one's family and community where one will be honored and remembered. One does not die in isolation but as a member of a community (Gen. 25:8; 35:29; 49:29; Deut. 32:50; Judg. 2:10; I Kings 2:10). (*b*) Mythologically, as a power, agent, or principle. Israel's environment sustained a mythology which presented

Death (Mot) as an active personal agent in combat with Yahweh. While Israel was not committed to such dualism, it used such language to speak about the struggle for the establishment of Yahweh's rule in historical affairs. (*c*) Symbolically, as the loss of rich, joyous existence as willed by God. Thus "life" refers to total well-being, and death is the loss of total well-being.

2. Death in a covenant context. Undoubtedly, in the circumstance of death Israel was tempted to assign to it fears and uncertainties like other peoples did, and to cope with it in terms of the resources and presuppositions of neighboring cultures and religions (cf. Deut. 26:14; Lev. 19:27-28; 20:6). However, Israel's normative posture can only be understood in terms of the covenant faith, which sharply contrasted with neighboring practices and beliefs. That faith affirmed that Israel's well-being was to be found in obedient relation to Yahweh. And when that relation was violated, trouble came: communal reverse or personal discomfort or misery (cf. Lev. 26; Deut. 28; I Kings 8:35-53; Job 5:17-27). Thus for Israel maintenance of covenant and not physical longevity is the optimum good, i.e., "life." "Life" sometimes means historical survival, but it also means the benefits and well-being of covenant: "See, I have set before you this day life and good, death and evil . . . that I have set before you life and death, blessing and curse; therefore choose life, that you and your descendants may live" (Deut. 30:15, 19). Conversely "death" can mean the end of historical existence, but it also means disruption of covenant. Israel's faith was able to define death in this way because of the assumptions of wholistic psychology and communal sociology indicated above.

3. Acceptance of death as the end of life. Israel fully accepted the physical termination of existence as a natural event, not to be feared. It perceived it as "sleep with one's fathers" (I Kings 2:10; 11:43; 15:8). Such a phrase reflects little interest in what happens to the dead person. While there was no doubt a popular understanding of the place of the dead (*see* Dead, Abode of the; Shades), Israel's theology has no interest in it. Death at the end of long life is simply a given. Whether the covenantal relation with Yahweh endured beyond this crisis was not a concern of Israel's unreflective acceptance of death. It is the rule of Yahweh and not life or death in a historical sense that finally matters.

4. Death and the rule of Yahweh. In Gen. 2–3, death is presented not as a natural event but as a sentence assigned by Yahweh to those who violate his covenant. The text makes clear (*a*) that death is caused by human disobedience; (*b*) death is not natural; and (*c*) at least theoretically, there might have been historical existence without death. This text is highly reflective and peculiar in the OT. It is later pursued by IV Ezra (7:62-131) and Paul (Rom. 5:12-21). In general, however, Israel is not interested in such speculative questions and the text stands alone in the OT in that regard. And even in Romans, Paul is not interested in the origin of death.

However, the concerns of Gen. 2–3 reflect a tradition concerning Retribution. This perspective, present both in Israel's historiography (Deuteronomist; Chronicler) and in its wisdom literature (*see* Wisdom in the OT[S]), interprets human experience in terms of actions and consequences. Thus death is interpreted as retribution for human choices which violate either Yahweh's covenant (in the historiography) or his created order (in wisdom) (Prov. 14:27; 15:24). The mythic expressions of Gen. 2–3 are derived from and strongly support this much broader tradition. However, in Gen. 2–3, the clearly announced sentence of death is not immediately executed. Similarly in II Sam. 12, David might expect death, but it does not come to him.

Yahweh's will toward life in covenant was more powerful than the sentence or reality of death, and his graciousness and freedom (Exod. 3:14; 33:19; 34:6) assure the power of life in a context which indicates death. *See* Grace in the OT[S].

"Why will you die, O house of Israel? For I have no pleasure in the death of any one, says the Lord God; so turn, and live" (Ezek. 18:31-32). It is this affirmation that governs prayers which seek his intervention in the face of death (Ps. 13:3 [H 4]).

It is the same affirmation which provides grist for Job's mighty protest, and which enables Paul to assert in lyrical fashion that God's will for life is stronger than every threatening alternative (Rom. 8:38-39; cf. Rom. 6:5, 23; I Cor. 15:54-56; Phil. 3:8-11).

5. God's triumph and apocalyptic imagery. Israel expressed this confident affirmation not only in its more reflective idiom but also in its boldest poetry of myth. In so doing, it employed the same language and images as its neighbors and presented death as an active agent, an alternative power which challenges Yahweh's will for life and strongly opposes him (cf. Isa. 28:15, 18). However, unlike Canaanite neighbors, Israel's normative faith did not regard this conflict as a periodic struggle to be entered into repeatedly. Rather, in Israel it is peculiarly affirmed that Yahweh is in charge of Mot. Death is still an active agent, who acts on orders from Yahweh (Hos. 13:14). Ultimately Mot is presented as not only subjected to Yahweh, but finally defeated and without power to threaten (I Cor. 15:54).

There is little doubt that Israel's understanding of death changed as time passed. The early mood of serenity gave way to vigorous and undisciplined conflict imagery. It is unlikely that the emergence of new affirmations can be explained by the intrusion of new cultural influences, either Persian or Greek. It is much more plausible that the discouraging events of the exilic and postexilic periods, when the durability and efficacy of covenant seemed much in question, drove Israel back to its earliest faith. In the earliest exodus formulations, influenced by borrowed mythic language, Israel already had the resources for speaking in radical terms about the clash between Yahweh's will for life and the forces of chaos, exile, alienation, and death (Exod. 15:4-12). The later times called for use of this language again. The times were too desperate to use the language of serenity, and so Israel's vigorous faith in the rule of Yahweh received expression in the language of conflict and victory. *See* APOCALYPTICISM[S].

Israel's late reflections continued to be organized around the fundamental conviction that Yahweh's will for an enduring covenant with his people (=life) would prevail. Several images were useful:

(*a*) Resurrection as God's overcoming of death. In early poetry, Israel had affirmed Yahweh's rule over life and death: "See now that I, even I, am he, and there is no god beside me; I kill and I make alive; I wound and I heal" (Deut. 32:39; cf. I Sam. 2:6). The theme of restoration for Israel is expressed in Hos. 6:2 and Ezek. 37. But only in the late texts of Isa. 26:19 and Dan. 12:2 is the image of rescue from the tomb utilized, though in the NT it is an accepted expression. A right understanding of resurrection requires reading it as an expression in apocalyptic imagery of God's sure rule. Resurrection has not to do with a miracle in a vacuum, but is one of a variety of images which express the undoubted affirmation that Yahweh's will for life is stronger than death. Resurrection includes nuances of (1) gathering the scattered (as in exile and return: Ezek. 11:16-17; 12:15; 20:23; 22:15; 37:21; Jer. 23:3; 29:14); (2) the restoration of a king and his re-enthronement; and (3) the fresh ratification of covenant which gives life.

(*b*) "The coming of the new age." The age-old rule of forces of oppression and chaos will be ended and God's covenantal reign will right all wrongs (Luke 7:22). The early church perceived in Jesus the coming of that age, though it waited for its full establishment in God's good time.

(*c*) The final judgment. Judgment, already expressed in Israel's oldest ceremonies (cf. Deut. 27–28), has been radicalized as ultimate judgment (cf. Matt. 25:31-46). Those who have been faithful and obedient will receive life (=covenant), and the unfaithful and disobedient will receive death (=no covenant). What has come to be called "final judgment" is in fact the covenant reckoning which Israel has faced since the beginnings at Sinai (Exod. 23:20-33).

All three images are clearly subject to perversion when removed from the context of covenant: (*a*) resurrection becomes a grave-emptying operation when not seen as restoration to covenantal life; (*b*) the coming of the new age has been perverted into spatial imagery as flight from earth to heaven when old age/new age (=out of covenant/in covenant) has been misunderstood; and (*c*) the last judgment has been turned into an ultimate senseless terror when not related to the blessings and curses of covenant.

6. Death and faithful life of submission and triumph. The NT views death in the same images used by ancient Israel with two significant additional factors. First, apocalyptic imagery is now much more widely used. Second, the death of Jesus has produced a new dimension in interpretation (*see* DEATH OF CHRIST). His death is a willing act of obedience (John 10:17-18; Phil. 2:7-8) which yields the NT's scandalous view of death: in weakness is strength, in death is life, in humiliation is exaltation. Thus a positive value is assigned to death. Now death is not only natural termination, but it is the space in which departure from the old age and entrance into the new age is experienced. Jesus, by placing himself at the disposal of the enemies of the rule of God, has triumphed and inaugurated a new age in which the power of life is supreme (Col. 2:13; Rev. 5:9-12; 12:10-11; 17:14).

This meaning of death became a characteristic way of speaking about the Christian life: (*a*) it is the language used for baptism as entrance into the new life (Rom. 6:4-7); (*b*) it is the language of discipleship which means the decision to abandon the status of the old age and the willingness to risk the new age and its demands (Luke 9:23-24).

The NT affirmation agrees with the OT conviction of God's rule over death. But now it is affirmed that death, understood sometimes symbolically and sometimes biologically, is the character and condition of faithfulness to Jesus Christ. What had been perceived as the manifestation of evil, or at least the termination of good, is now presented as a revelation of graciousness.

Death is the undoing of the old world and the entry to new life with Christ, i.e., in covenant with God. In lyrical fashion Paul can assert: "For me to live is Christ, and to die is gain. If it is to be life in the flesh, that means fruitful labor for me. Yet which I shall choose I cannot tell. I am hard pressed between the two. My desire is to depart and be with Christ, for that is far better. But to remain in the flesh is more necessary on your account" (Phil. 1:21-24; cf. Rom. 6:1-11; Gal. 2:19-21).

7. Conclusion: death and trust. With very different emphases, the OT and the NT share a central conviction: certainty about God's rule, permitting the faithful to perceive death with confidence and without anxiety. The world has been claimed for God's life-giving promises (John 16:13). Contemporary fear of death centers on fear of unbearable isolation. Biblical faith affirms that persons are never beyond the caring community of Yahweh. It is acceptance of the promises of God that permits the faithful to accept self as a historical creature, to accept death as the limit and end of life, to affirm that "you are dust and to dust you shall return."

Bibliography. L. R. Bailey, "Death as a Theological Problem in the Old Testament," *Pastoral Psychology,* XXII (1971), 20-32; H. Birkeland, "The Belief in the Resurrection of the Dead in the Old Testament," *Studia Theologica,* III (1949), 60-78; H. C. Brichto, "Kin, Cult, Land and Afterlife," *HUCA,* XLIV (1973), 1-54; J. B. Burns, "The Mythology of Death in the Old Testament," *SJT,* XXVI (1973), 327-40; J. J. Collins, "Apocalyptic Eschatology as the Transcendence of Death," *CBQ,* XXXVI (1974), 21-43; O. Cullmann, "Immortality of the Soul or Resurrection of the Dead," *Immortality and Resurrection,* ed. K. Stendahl (1965), pp. 9-53; W. Eichrodt, *Theology of the Old Testament,* II (1967), 496-529; C. F. Evans, *Resurrection and the New Testament,* SBT, 2nd series XII (1970); A. Johnson, *The Vitality of the Individual in the Thought of Ancient Israel* (1949), pp. 88-107; E. Jüngel, "Grenzen des Menschseins," *Probleme Biblischer Theologie,* ed. H. W. Wolff (1971), pp. 199-205; L. O. Mills, ed., *Perspectives on Death* (1969); J. Pedersen, *Israel I-II,* pp. 99-181, 453-96; K. Rahner, *On the Theology of Death* (1961); D. S. Russell, *The Method and Message of Jewish*

Apocalyptic (1964), ch. 14; E. Schillebeeckx and B. Willems, eds., *The Problem of Eschatology,* Concilium, XLI (1969); N. Tromp, *Primitive Conceptions of Death and the Nether World in the Old Testament* (1969); B. Vawter, "Intimations of Immortality and the Old Testament," *JBL,* XCI (1972), 158-71; G. von Rad, *Old Testament Theology* I, pp. 387-401; H. W. Wolff, *Anthropologie des Alten Testaments* (1973), ch. 12; J. Wyjngaards, "Death and Resurrection in Covenantal Context (Hos. VI 2)," *VT,* XVII (1967), 226-39; M. Martin-Achard, *From Death to Life* (1960).

W. Brueggemann

***DEBIR (CITY).** The largest and most important Canaanite city S of Hebron. It was one of the cities of the Anakim (Josh. 11:21) and was formerly known as Kiriath-sepher (Josh. 15:15; Judg. 1:11). In detailed accounts, the Bible attributes its conquest to Othniel (Josh. 15:15-19; Judg. 1:11-15), and in other passages to Joshua Son of Nun (Josh. 10:38-39; 12:13). It was one of the Levitical Cities (Josh. 21:15; I Chr. 6:58 [H 6:43]) and was mentioned with other cities in the southernmost hill country of Judah (Josh. 15:48-51).

The biblical references to Debir require an important Late Bronze and Iron Age site in the hill country of S Judea. The identification with Tell Beit Mirsim in the Shepheleh, proposed by Albright, was generally accepted, but recent archaeological research shows that Khirbet Rabud, proposed originally by Galling, suits the purpose better. It is about 7½ miles SW of Hebron at an altitude of *ca.* 2200 feet. For its water supply, it is dependent on rock-cut cisterns; the only other sources are two wells found about 1¼ miles N of the site. They provide a perfect background for Achsah's demand for the upper and the lower springs (Josh. 15:15-19; Judg. 1:11-15). Other identified sites of the same district, Jattir, Socho, Anab, Eshtemoh, and Anim (Josh. 15:48-50), are situated nearby, and the whole district is separated from adjacent districts by the watershed demarcation line.

Khirbet Rabud was occupied sporadically during the fourth and the third millennia B.C. The first walled city was built during the LB and covered fifteen acres. An Israelite Period I settlement upon LB debris well fits the conquest narrative. Remains from the tenth century represent the Levitical city. A city wall about thirteen feet wide, surrounding an area of twelve acres, was erected during the ninth century. The city was destroyed by Sennacherib in 701 but rebuilt immediately thereafter. An extramural suburb (established during the seventh century) was destroyed with the rest of the town by Nebuchadrezzar. Only scant remains from later periods have been found.

Bibliography. C. R. Conder, "The Royal Canaanite and Levitical City of Debir," *PEQ,* III (1875), 48-56; W. F. Albright, *The Archaeology of Palestine* (1932), and "Debir," in *Archaeology and Old Testament Study,* ed. D. W. Thomas (1967), pp. 207-20; M. Noth, "Die Stadt Kirjath-Seper = Debir," *JPOS,* XV (1935), 44-50; H. Orlinsky, "The Supposed Qiryat-Sannah of Joshua 15:49," *JBL,* LVIII (1939), 255-61; K. Galling, "Zur Lokalisierung von Debir," *ZDPV,* LXX (1954), 135-41; M. Kochavi, "Khirbet Rabud = Debir," *Tel-Aviv,* I (1974), 2-33.

M. Kochavi

***DEDAN** [דדן, pl. דדנים, LXX Δαδαν, Δαιδαν, old South Arab. דדן, Neo-Babylonian *Dadanu*]. Ancient name of the el-'Ula oasis in Hijaz, an important station on the "frankincense road" from Yemen to Palestine and Syria, colonized by the Mineans. Dedan first appears in the OT in prophetic passages from the sixth century. In 556 B.C. Nabonidus conquered Dadanu along with five other oases of Hijaz and settled there Babylonian subjects from both Akkad (Babylonia) and Ḫatti (Syria-Palestine). The Arabs of the sixth century B.C. referred to Syria as "Ashur" (Old South Arab. pl. אאשר; cf. Gr. *Syria*<*Assyria* and Late Egyp. *'Išwr*= Syria); hence the triple division of Dedan (Gen. 25:3) into Asshurim (new settlers from Syria-Palestine), Letushim ("metal-workers," an inferior cast), and Leummim ("nations," the full-fledged native tribesmen). It is supposed that among Nabonidus' settlers were numerous Jews, whose arrival marked the beginning of Judaism in that part of Arabia.

Bibliography. G. Ryckmans, *Les noms propres sud-sémitiques,* I (1934), 324, 328-29; W. F. Albright, "Dedan," *Geschichte und Altes Testament* (1953), pp. 1-12; C. J. Gadd, "The Harran Inscriptions of Nabonidus," *Anatolian Studies,* VIII (1958), 35-92.

M. C. Astour

DEITIES, UNDERWORLD. In the religions of the ancient Near East the underworld is the destination of the deceased, and, like the heavens, is peopled and ruled by gods. These fall into a number of different categories whose functions are not always clear and which often overlap. Indeed, the boundaries of the category "underworld deities" are themselves often blurred.

The OT preserves occasional references to the cult of underworld deities, and speaks in traditional terms of phenomena associated with death and the underworld which are attested elsewhere as part of such cults. The precise intention of these terms is often not specifiable, but they can be placed on a historical continuum which goes back to polytheistic mythologies of the underworld and which extends down to passages in the NT.

1. In the ancient Near East. Since the dead were buried beneath the surface of the earth, their post-mortem existence was necessarily in a subterranean realm (*see* Dead, Abode of the). The powers associated with death, including war, famine, and disease, were, as deities or demons, often thought to reside in the same region. But, although the earth receives the dead, it also gives birth to the vegetation that sustains life, and indeed may be conceived of as the womb of all living things. Hence the underworld is sometimes viewed as the home of the beneficent powers of fertility and healing (*see* Fertility Cults). By association, the dead may exercise inimical or beneficent powers toward the living, so that the cult of the dead and the cult of underworld deities is sometimes indistinguishable.

Ancient Near Eastern mythology also depicts certain deities as having a transient relationship with the underworld. The sun-deity passes through the underworld from W to E between setting and rising each night. Other deities visit the underworld in association with a seasonal cycle (e.g., a planet's period of invisibility), or as messengers from one realm to the other (*see* COSMOGONY). To a greater or lesser extent the underworld is opposed to, and organized on the analogy of, the celestial pantheon under a king or queen and consort, with an ambassador, gate-keeper, etc.

a. Egypt. The most distinctive and elaborate view of the underworld and its occupants is found in Egypt. The central deity is OSIRIS, who has revived after death and become ruler of the underworld. The newly dead are brought before Osiris to be judged, their hearts are weighed against justice in a balance, and the results are recorded. Osiris then pronounces final judgment and vindicates the just. The unjust are devoured by a monster who sits beside the scale (*see* Fig. D4). Osiris is also a vegetation deity, and it is the hope of the deceased to be identified with Osiris as the corn that grows anew from the dormant seed. *See* EGYPT §3*a*.

All the inhabitants of the underworld welcome the arrival of Re, the sun-god, each evening, for he brings them new life. He journeys through the twelve-gated regions of the underworld, which are described in detail, as are the various creatures he encounters. In this context it is the hope of the deceased to travel with Re in his boat, and so to reach the eastern horizon, for the sunrise is the daily demonstration of Re's power to overcome death, and by accompanying him the deceased can participate in the dawn of new life.

b. Mesopotamia. The Mesopotamian underworld is populated with several classes of gods. Its government is in the hands of a queen, Ereshkigal. Of various consorts mentioned Nergal seems to prevail. He is the bringer of death and pestilence (*see* CORRUPTION, MOUNT OF[S]). Ereshkigal's son, vizier, and messenger is Namtar, "Fate," the speedy and unwelcome messenger of death. In a vision of the underworld he is seen holding a man by the hair with one hand and grasping a sword in the other. We are also informed of a gate-keeper and a boatman of the underworld river (itself deified).

There are "killed" or "bound" gods, ancestors of the high gods An and Enlil, who have been banished to the underworld for acts of hubris. The most prominent of these is Enmesharra, who, on the occasion of the founding of a temple (an encroachment on the underworld), is invoked as lord of the underworld and is placated.

Other categories of underworld gods include vegetation deities and a select number of deified kings (e.g., Gilgamesh and Lugalbanda). Various myths deal with the movement of deities into and out of the underworld, e.g., Nergal and Ereshkigal (*ANET* [2nd ed.], pp. 103-4), and the Descent of Inanna/Ishtar (*ANET* [2nd ed.], pp. 52-57). It appears that a deity may be released from the underworld on provision of a substitute. Underworld deities are assigned a special cult in connection with deceased monarchs. *See* ASSYRIA AND BABYLONIA §G.

c. Asia Minor. More consistently than in Sumerian and Akkadian, Hittite sources make a systematic distinction between the "upper gods" or "gods of the sky" and the "lower gods" or "gods of the earth" (underworld). The ruler of the latter is Lelwani, who appears as both male and female—the latter perhaps under Babylonian influence (*see* ANDROGYNY[S] §2). A New Year festival is celebrated in her honor. The sun in its journey through the underworld is an independent "sun of the earth," who partakes totally of the nature of the underworld, being all evil and darkness, and is the very opposite of the celestial sun-deity. The Hittite underworld too knew a group of deposed

Courtesy the British Museum

4. Anubis weighs the heart of the deceased against "maat." Waiting beneath the balance is the composite devourer Thoth. A scribe records the results of the judgment as Horus presents the deceased before the shrine of Osiris. From the papyrus of Hu-nefer.

deities, the "former/primeval gods," who were once involved in the cosmogony, and remain guardians of the copper knife used to sever heaven and earth. There is a group of goddesses of fate, who seem to operate from a base in the underworld. The king regularly "became god" at death, but apparently only spent a short time in the underworld before ascending to the celestial sphere.

d. Syria-Palestine. In the preserved Ugaritic literature (*see* UGARIT §4; UGARIT[S]) the underworld deity who overshadows all others is Mot, "Death." He is designated "son of El" and "beloved of El," suggesting that he is ultimately dependent on El, and thus incorporated within the total cosmic order (*see* EL, DEITY[S]). According to the main BAAL myth Mot dwells in a city, sits on a throne, and chews up visitors like lambs. He can stretch his jaws from heaven to "earth," and even consumes Baal, the lord of life and fertility. Baal's sister, Anath, avenges Baal by annihilating Mot (cf. his annihilation in text *CTA* 23=*UT* 52). In the sequel first Baal, then Mot, reappears. They contend in a "life and death" struggle, which is finally settled by the intervention of Shapsh, the sun-goddess, who apparently assigns each to his own realm. Underworld deities are apparently the main subject of *CTA* 23. Born to El, they are insatiable, are assigned to the wilderness, but also are invoked and offered food and drink.

RESHEPH is widely attested, very popular, and evidently performed a variety of functions, including those of an underworld deity. CHEMOSH, the state god of Moab, attested also at Ugarit, is equated with Nergal, and may also therefore have an underworld role. Rapi', "Healer," may be a chthonic deity, if the *rpum* in general are the deified dead (*see* REPHAIM[S] §2). In Ugaritic narrative literature the dead are buried in "holes of the gods of the earth," and the son of the deceased has the responsibility of caring for his father's ghost and erecting a stele for his family's ancestral god. *See* PILLAR[S] §1.

2. In ancient Israel. It is the testimony of the OT that from time to time many Israelites accepted the reality of, and participated in the cult of, deities other than Yahweh. In view of the antithetic relation of Mot and Baal in Ugaritic myth, it would be surprising if Israelites who found Baal so irresistible did not also acknowledge his counterpart, Mot. Certainly Israelite literature, in its dependence on Canaanite models, made use of expressions with strong mythological associations when speaking of the underworld. In general, it is probably safe to say that such expressions were understood differently at different times and by different people—that is, sometimes as mythical realities, sometimes as purely poetic figures. In their present setting the latter understanding generally prevails. However, it is not always clear whether a given expression is the creation of an Israelite poet, a survival of specifically Canaanite mythology, or a more universal conception. In any case its significance is finally determined by the way it relates to the OT's view of Yahweh.

a. In the cult. The one underworld deity whose cult is explicitly attested in ancient Israel is Chemosh. It was introduced into Jerusalem by Solomon, according to I Kings 11:7, 33, and eradicated by Josiah, according to II Kings 23:13. For implicit testimony to the cult of underworld deities see the personal names in §*b* below.

Evidence for a hero cult in ancient Israel is lacking. The OT witnesses to necromancy (I Sam. 28), recording that the consulted dead could be called אלהים, "god (s)" (I Sam. 28:13 and probably Isa. 8:19; *see* NEB and note parallelism; *see also* FAMILIAR SPIRIT[S]). There are isolated references to food offerings for the dead (Ps. 106:28; Deut. 26:14), but the same texts express disapproval of them. While there was probably in early Israel some form of ancestor cult based on the family and its land (burial ground), it was the tendency of developing Yahwism to diminish its importance to the point where the dead are powerless SHADES. *See* REPHAIM §1.

b. In the literature. i. *Earth/Underworld* (ארץ). The concept of the "earth" as the divine mother of life and also the consumer of the dead lies behind such passages as Job 1:21 (cf. Ecclus. 40:1). In Gen. 4:10-12 the ground "opened its mouth" to receive the blood of the slain Abel. The voice of the blood then cries from the ground, which will now no longer yield its produce to the killer. In Num. 16:32-33 "the earth opened its mouth and swallowed them up, . . . So they . . . went down alive into Sheol; and the earth closed over them." If the NEB is correct at Isa. 26:19, the earth will give (a second) birth to the dead—clearly a secondary adaptation of this mythology.

ii. *Mot and Sheol.* Both appear as divine names in personal names: Sheol in Methushael ("Man of [the god] Sheol"), Gen. 4:18; Mot (in the stressed form, *Maweth*) in Azmaveth ("Mot is strong"), II Sam. 23:31; and Hazarmaveth ("Enclosure of Mot"), Gen. 10:26. The strength of Death (Mot) is already proverbial at Ugarit (*CTA* 53=*UT* 54: 11-13), and is taken up in Song of S. 8:6 (cf. Eccl. 7:26). Male and female respectively, Mot and Sheol are frequently personified in language strongly reminiscent of underworld deities (*see esp.* Isa. 5:14). Death is portrayed as a burglar (Jer. 9:21) and shepherd (Ps. 49:14 [H 15]), Sheol as the lady of a mansion rousing her staff to greet the newly deceased (Isa. 14:9). National or personal enemies can be portrayed as allies of Mot and Sheol (Isa. 28:15, 18; cf. Wisd. Sol. 1:16), or likened to them in simile (Hab. 2:5; Prov. 1:12) or metaphor (Ps. 5:9 [H 10]).

In Job 18:13 there is a reference to the first-born of Mot consuming the limbs of the wicked—perhaps recalling some now unidentifiable denizen of the underworld. The following verse either contains a title of Mot ("King of Terrors") or refers to his servants ("terrors") bringing the dead to their king (cf. NEB). *See* MOT (DEITY) [S].

iii. *Shalah.* The name in Gen. 5 corresponding to Methushael in Gen. 4 (*see* §ii *above*) is Methuselah ("Man of Shalah"). *Shalah* appears in Job 33:18 and 36:12 as the underworld river (NEB), and as such may have been a Canaanite deity. *See* SHALAH[S].

iv. *Resheph.* Resheph appears with *debher* (pestilence) as two escorts of Yahweh in Hab. 3:5. If *b^{e}nê resheph* (sons of Resheph) in Job 5:7 does not mean "sparks," it might refer to mythological progeny of Resheph flying up from the underworld as diseases (cf. NEB). The use of *debher* and *qeṭebh* (destruction) in Ps. 91:6 is in a similar tradition. *See* RESHEPH.

v. *Yahweh and underworld deities.* Certain passages have been thought to depict the underworld as outside Yahweh's sphere of influence, though without admitting a rival power. Thus the underworld does not acknowledge Yahweh (Ps. 30:9 [H 10]; Isa. 38:18); Yahweh does not exercise his power there, does not remember the dead; nor do they acknowledge him (Ps. 88:5, 10-12 [H 6, 11-13]; cf. Pss. 6:5 [H 6]; 115:17).

On the other hand, as lord of life Yahweh also controls the limits of life. It is accepted that "the Lord kills and brings to life; he brings down to Sheol and raises up" (I Sam. 2:6; cf. Ps. 104:28-29). Thus when death is desired by his faithful servants, it is to Yahweh that they appeal for it (Num. 11:15; I Kings 19:4). The mythological language of Num. 16:32-33 (*see* §i *above*) is taken literally and seen as a special creative act of Yahweh (vs. 30). Sheol is not beyond his reach (Amos 9:2) or presence (Ps. 139:8). Finally, Yahweh will treat Mot to some of his own medicine (Isa. 25:8). *See* DEATH, THEOLOGY OF[S] §4.

3. In the NT. As in contemporary Judaism so in the NT the mythology of the old underworld gods reappears in a new symbol complex. The enemy of God and man is called variously the DEVIL, SATAN, the (great) DRAGON, the ancient SERPENT (Rev. 12:9; 20:2), BELIAL (II Cor. 6:15; cf. the parallelism with Mot and Sheol in II Sam. 22:5-6 and Ps. 18:5-6, RSV "perdition"), ABADDON (Job 28:22), APOLLYON, "the angel of the bottomless pit" who is "king" over apocalyptic locusts (Rev. 9:11), and whose hosts elsewhere are the demons, serpents, and scorpions (Luke 10:17-19). In the latter passage these forces are subjected to Jesus and the seventy with whom he has shared his authority. The devil has the power of death (Heb. 2:14) and behaves like Mot (I Pet. 5:8); but in the end there is victory over death in resurrection through Christ (I Cor. 15:54-57, adapting Isa. 25:8 and Hos. 13:14). In the eschatology of Revelation Death and Hades (Mot and Sheol) are given power to kill in a quarter of the earth (6:8), but finally give up the dead, are judged, and suffer the second death (20:13-14). *See* DEATH, THEOLOGY OF[S] §6.

For the sanctuaries of underworld deities, *see* SITES, SACRED[S].

Bibliography. H. W. Haussig, ed., *Götter und Mythen im Vorderen Orient* (1965); C. J. Bleeker, G. Widengren, eds., *Historia Religionum* (1969); J. J. M. Roberts, *The Earliest Semitic Pantheon* (1972). In the three preceding works indices indicate the many relevant passages, and earlier bibliog. is indicated. E. von Weiher, *Der babylonische Gott Nergal, AOAT,* XI (1971); W. G. Lambert, "Studies in Nergal," *BO,* XXX (1973), 355-63; H. Gese *et al., Die Religionen Altsyriens,* . . . (1970), pp. 1-232; J. C. de Moor, "The Semitic Pantheon of Ugarit," *UF,* II (1970), at p. 222; W. F. Albright, *Yahweh and the Gods of Canaan* (1968); V. Maag, "Tod und Jenseits nach dem AT," *Schweizer Theologische Umschau,* XXXIV (1964), 17-37; N. J. Tromp, *Primitive Conceptions of Death and the Nether World in the OT,* BibOr, XXI (1969); J. B. Burns, "The Mythology of Death in the OT," *SJT,* XXVI (1973), 327-40; F. Vattioni, "Il dio Resheph," *AION,* NS XV (1965), 39-74; D. Conrad, "Der Gott Reschef," *ZAW,* LXXXIII (1971), 157-83; A. van den Branden, "'Reseph' nella Bibbia," *BeO,* XIII (1971), 211-25; P. L. Watson, "The Death of 'Death' in the Ugaritic Texts," *JAOS,* XCII (1972), 60-64; D. T. Tsumura, "A Ugaritic God, *MT-W-ŠR,* and His Two Weapons (UT 52:8-11)," *UF,* VI (1974), 407-13; M. Tsevat, "The Canaanite God Šälaḥ," *VT,* IV (1954), 41-49; G. Komoróczy, "Zum mythologischen und literaturgeschichtlichen Hintergrund der ugaritischen 'Dichtung §§'," *UF,* III (1971), 75-80.

S. B. PARKER

***DEMONS IN THE NT.** Hellenistic and Jewish views about demons are reflected in the NT, especially in the Synoptic gospels and Paul. In general, heaven was occupied by God and the angels, and the air by demons and the spirits of heroes, while men occupied the earth (EUSEBIUS, *Praep. Evang.* IV.5, 141*cd;* Eph. 2:2). Many kinds of demons are described, varying in their powers, their habits, and in the means by which they might be controlled (*Papyri Graecae Magicae* IV.2700 ff.). The lower demons were thicker in substance and more dangerous (Test. Sol. 20:12-17). They were often thought of as possessing bodies (*Papyri Graecae Magicae* XII.141), having physical needs (*Life of Apollonius of Tyana* VI,27), and requiring a home (Aelian, *On the Characteristics of Animals* XI, 32; Luke 11:24-26).

Demons, excluding Satan, are referred to in the Synoptic gospels nearly ninety times. The usual expression is simply "demon" (δαιμόνιον), which is used about eleven times each in Matthew and Mark and some twenty-three times in Luke (e.g., Matt. 9:33; Mark 1:34; Luke 4:35). "Unclean spirit" (πνεῦμα ἀκάθαρτον) is found twice in Matthew, eleven times in Mark and six times in Luke (e.g., Matt. 10:1; Mark 3:30; Luke 8:29). Other descriptions include "spirit," πνεῦμα (Mark 9:17), "evil spirit," πνεῦμα πονηρός (Luke 7:21), and "demon," δαίμων (Matt. 8:31). The ruler of the demons is Beelzebul (e.g., Matt. 12:24) or Satan (e.g., Mark 3:23). The demonology of Luke-Acts is more detailed and vivid than in the rest of the NT (e.g., Luke 8:2; 13:16; 22:3; Acts 16:16-18).

The Pauline emphasis is upon evil cosmic powers rather than demons causing illness through possession. They are described as "powers," ἐξουσίαι (Rom. 8:38), "rulers," ἀρχαί (I Cor. 2:8), "thrones," θρόνοι (Col. 1:16) and "lords," κυριότητες (Eph. 1:21; RSV "dominion"). Both Jewish apolcalyptic and pagan astrology seem to have contributed to these beliefs. Christ has deprived these forces of their power (Col. 2:15, 20).

See also EXORCISM IN THE NT[S].

Bibliography. T. Hopfner, *Griechisch-ägyptischer Offenbarungszauber,* I, Studien zur Paleographie und Papyruskunde, XXI (1921), sections 1-134; S. Eitrem, *Some Notes on the Demonology of the NT,* Symbolae osloensis Supp. XX (2nd ed., 1966); J. M. Hull, *Hellenistic Magic and the Synoptic Tradition,* SBT, 2nd ser., XXVIII (1974), esp. pp. 38-41, 96-104, 128-33; C. C. McCown, *The Testament of Solomon* (1922); J. Y. Lee, "Interpreting the Demonic Powers in Pauline Thought," *NovT,* XII (1970), 54-69.

J. M. HULL

DEMYTHOLOGIZING. *See* MYTH IN THE NT; MYTH IN THE NT[S].

***DESERT.** *See* WILDERNESS[S].

DEUTERONOMIC HISTORY, THE. The name given by scholars to a supposed unitary historical work contained within the Hebrew Bible and consisting of Deuteronomy and the books of the Former Prophets. The multi-faceted material of the history (henceforth DH) is held together by a theological commentary; the whole seeks to explain with ample illustrations how history works. DH was at least originally designed to shore up both the Judahite monarchy and the Mosaic tradition under the covenant rubric (*see* COVENANT, MOSAIC [S]); it sought to appeal both to those who were loyal to the Davidic line and to those who longed for a return of the Mosaic era.

The DH hypothesis has been most strikingly formulated in recent years by Martin Noth. He contends that DH was the labor of a single theologian, the Deuteronomist (Dtr), who wrote after the fall of Jerusalem and sought to explain the events of 722 and 586 B.C. According to Noth, DH aims at demonstrating that these events were the direct consequence of Israel's unrepentant following after strange gods and almost complete failure to obey divine demands and counsels.

A more cautious formulation would recognize DH as one part of the great primary history (henceforth PH) of Israel, extending from Genesis through Kings. This work was completed shortly after the fall of Jerusalem and canonized *ca.* 550 (*see* PENTATEUCH §A4*b*). The unit called DH by modern scholars was originally prepared as a programmatic justification of JOSIAH's reform; it was later slightly rewritten and extended by the exilic compiler of the primary history (henceforth PHEd). In one sense, then, DH is a meaningful unit, since we have most of its contents, largely in original form. Nonetheless, since it has been incorporated into another work, we must be cautious in trying to specify its scope and shape. Fortunately, the radical social upheaval that characterized the first half of the sixth century brought with it such great moral changes that we are able to distinguish late monarchic from exilic material with comparative ease, and thus, in large part, DH from PH. In the last analysis, however, it must be admitted that DH is not a given part of the Hebrew Bible as we have it; this caution must be kept in mind throughout. DH is closely related to the original form of DEUTERONOMY and the editors of both had similar concerns.

1. Structure
2. Problems
3. Basic approach
4. DH and the prophets
5. Summary
Bibliography

1. Structure. DH has five major sections. In the first, the editor (henceforth DHEd) provides the original book of Deuteronomy with an introduction (Deut. 1–3 belong to DH; 4:1-40, to the exilic PHEd) and various epilogues (27, 29–34; the associations of these chapters cannot be stated precisely). There may well have been more editorial work; it is, however, likely that Josiah's Deuteronomy cannot be rediscovered by critical techniques. This part of DH deals with the nature of Israel's relationship to Yahweh, consistently emphasizing a program of one God, one people, one cult. Part two of the work, the book of Joshua, narrates the conquest of Canaan, the fulfillment of the greatest of the covenantal promises of Yahweh; the coordination of exodus and conquest themes, already apparent in Judg. 5, finds its fullest expression here. The third part of DH (Judges–I Sam. 7) describes the difficulties of premonarchic Israel and traces the origins of the monarchy. This is one of the two sections of the work that most evidently reflect DHEd's distinctive theology; in fact, the entire framework of Judges was probably constructed by him. Part four details the rise of monarchic government and its greatest glories (I Sam. 7–I Kings 8). The concluding section (I Kings 9–II Kings 23:25) reviews the progressive decline of the "divided" monarchy. Like the third, it was heavily colored by DHEd, who probably composed the standardized opening and closing lines in the description of each monarch. The editor's hand is most obvious in the ideological evaluation of the consequences which each king's actions had for the nation. Again and again, the editor tells us that because Israel did not do that which was right in the eyes of Yahweh, trouble came. In sections other than three and five, the editor simply incorporated older material in pristine form, or with only minor alterations, usually insertions.

2. Problems. The substantial unity of the narrative that runs from Deuteronomy through II Kings can scarcely be questioned. Several basic problems arise in considering what to make of this fact: where does this story line start and stop, and where does the narrative come from? The problem of the unit's exact beginning is most difficult and comes down to a question that is almost as old as the documentary hypothesis itself: does the Tetrateuch (an independent work consisting of Genesis through Numbers) exist (*see* YAHWIST[S] §3)? Noth and Engnell are the most important of the many modern scholars who insist that it does. It seems, however, that to call the break between Numbers and Deuteronomy a major one is to leave the story of the first part of the Pentateuch unfinished (a few verses about the death of Moses at the end of Deuteronomy will not do). Although it might be contended that Deuteronomy would be similarly suspended if such a break were insisted upon, this is not likely; it seems rather that Deuteronomy presupposes an earlier work on which it is dependent. That is, its author assumed that everyone knew the stories up to the settlement in the land; he backtracks only to the most recent high point, the making of the covenant, the first giving of the Torah. The classic view, that Deuteronomy presupposes JE, remains defensible (*see* PENTATEUCH §§A2*c*, 4*b*). Another possibility is that the land theology of Deuteronomy is offered in order to obviate the need for the divine grant of the land to the patriarchs (*see* PROMISES TO THE PATRIARCHS [S] and CANON OF THE OT[S]).

The end of DH poses a simpler problem. Noth dates the work to the time of the last date contained in it, i.e., *ca.* 561. This approach ignores the shape of the narrative in the last part of Kings, which clearly reaches a climax in II Kings 23:25, the exaltation of Josiah. What follows that point is the embarrassed follow-up: Josiah's death at Megiddo and the subsequent chaos that continued until the release of Jehoiachin from bondage, an event that provided a soberly hopeful conclusion. This follow-up is the work of an exilic redactor (PHEd); what precedes it is the work of DHEd. The shape of the narrative in Kings was determined in advance by the story that was coming, the story of the best king of all (cf. I Kings 13:1-3). Only Josiah fulfills the promise of David's early career, a promise of piety and empire.

The incongruity of these ideals of imperialism and religiosity leads us to the third basic question: What was the origin of DH? The court of King Josiah would seem to be the most likely setting for its composition. This explanation accounts not only for the role played by political-theological thought in the world view of DHEd, but also for the influence of the wisdom tradition, most visible in I Kings 3:4-15. DH presents simple answers to two great questions: Why did Samaria fall? and Why is Josiah carrying out these alarming reforms? The answer to the first is, because of the sin of Jeroboam (I Kings 13:34); the answer to the second is, because he is the long-awaited scion of the house of David and seeks to return to its ideals. That is, Josiah is taking drastic measures to eliminate apostasies like those which led to the fall of Samaria and which, according to the prophets, threaten the survival of Judah and Jerusalem. The next question—How does Josiah know what to do?—becomes equally simple in DHEd's economy of salvation. Josiah knows that he must obey the stipulations of the covenant, to which he is completely subject. If he fails to obey the covenant, the sanctions attached to it will be imposed, and the nation will be destroyed; if he is obedient, then the nation will prosper, and all the blessings will follow. Here we see another, even more cogent reason for dating the work of DHEd to the years before 587: Deuteronomic theology became essentially untenable afterward. The most obvious testimony to this fact is offered in II Kings 23:26: "Still the Lord did not turn from the fierceness of his great wrath, by which his anger was kindled against Judah, because of all the provocation with which Manasseh had provoked him." This is a forced attempt to explain why Josiah failed. The Chronicler offers another, which is even less appealing (II Chr. 35:20-22). We cannot discuss here the more compelling testimony to the human inadequacy of Deuteronomic theology but it is not far to seek: it is to be found in the words of Ezekiel (18; 33:10-20), Jeremiah (31:27-34), and Second Isaiah (Isa. 52:13–53:12). (Job may belong with these, or it may be a similar reaction to the destruction of the northern kingdom.)

3. Basic approach. Deuteronomy is thought by most scholars to have a northern orientation. It seems likely that it was the work of a group of northern Levitic priests who fled to Judah after 722. If the work is to be dated in the early seventh century, we may suppose that they were alarmed at the speed with which Manasseh (687-642) was undoing the reforms which had been instituted by Hezekiah (715-687) in response to the utterances of Micah and Isaiah, and which had thus far averted the fall of the South. However, the abundant testimony of the Chronicler to the efficacy of those reforms (II Chr. 29–32) makes a date under Hezekiah seem more likely.

The Israelite bias of the work is most evident in the anti-monarchic polemic (Deut. 17:14-20); its immediate Judahite origin, in the concessions to Jerusalem as a worship center (12:1-14). The same tension between North and South is evident in DH, and the two works apparently belong to the same tradition. DHEd's writing, like that of the editor of Deuteronomy, is devoted to a handful of basic ideas, which are developed in an elaborate style and repeated in extended perorations. The most important of these are the graciousness of Yahweh's covenant, the evils of idolatry and a noncentralized cult, and the inevitability of punishment and reward. The primary covenant is the one made by Moses (*see* COVENANT, MOSAIC[S]). The Abrahamic, Joshuanic, and Davidic covenants (*see* COVENANT, DAVIDIC[S]) are always secondary to it. Thus, the king is always thought of as subordinate to the covenant; in this respect, DHEd's theology contrasts with the more ambiguous views of JE and early monarchic poetry (Ps. 89:35-46). If DHEd accepted the promise of the land to the fathers, he regarded it only as a simple promise, to be fulfilled once, and therefore largely devoid of content after the Conquest. His hopes are pinned exclusively to the Josianic reforms and the adherence to the Mosaic covenant they imply. PHEd, on the other hand, sees a great, irrevocable guarantee-type promise in the patriarchal narratives (e.g., in Deut. 4:31); this promise is in fact a crucial part of his approach to the dilemma of the exiles, an approach that must mediate between present existence and the promise of the future. To be sure, DHEd is aware of the possibility of covenantal sanctions so violent that only a remnant would be left after their application. The thought of such punishment is urgent even in Deuteronomy; the "us" and "today" of Moses' sermons reflect the somber mood that was the unavoidable consequence of the events of 722. Such usages do not refer so much to cultic re-enactment as to the lives of men who were becoming increasingly aware of the dangers of Judah's position, men of a pivotal generation who were being asked to believe that Josiah was able to meet the challenge of a crisis fraught with risk and opportunity.

One of the most important of Deuteronomy's "anachronisms" is the treatment of Moses as the supreme prophet. Major attention is devoted to the charismatic ninth- and eighth-century prophets in DH, most obviously in the Elijah and Elisha cycles. The importance of prophetic thought in DH is also shown by the use of prediction-and-fulfillment schemata (II Sam. 7:12-13 and I Kings 8:20;

I Kings 11:30-31 and 12:15-16; I Kings 14:7 ff. and 15:27-28; I Kings 16:1-4 and 16:9-14). DHEd's comments on the climactic moment of his history, the fall of Samaria (II Kings 17:7-18, 21-23; vss. 19-20 are exilic insertions), focus on the warnings Yahweh gave through his servants the prophets. A similar conception played a crucial part in the theology of the exilic compiler of the first edition of the prophetic corpus, who believed that the prophets who were proved right about the fall will be proved right about the return. This understanding of prophetic activity stimulated the preparation of the first full edition of the prophetic corpus, around the time of the final edition of the primary history (i.e., *ca.* 550), to which it served as a supplement. Further developments in the Deuteronomic figure of Moses, particularly his elevation from the status of God's messenger (Yahweh speaks in Exod. 20:1) to that of divinely authorized lawgiver (Moses speaks in his own name in Deut. 5:1; the only other prophet who does so is Elijah in I Kings 17:1), may reflect monarchic ideology. (The semidivine, autonomous status of MOSES is important in late postexilic thought.)

Another of Deuteronomy's anachronisms is a theology in which the name of God functions as the primary epiphanic reality. According to this scheme, Yahweh himself does not dwell on earth; rather, he causes his name to dwell (lit., pitch a tent) there. Yahweh's name is the bearer of his presence and dwells on earth in the sanctuary dedicated to him. Canaanite mythological terms formed the matrix for such ideas, but in Israel the conceptual frame was specialized to guard the aniconic understanding of Yahweh, whereby he remained, though present, invisible to his faithful. This may reflect the situation of the northern cultus after the division of the monarchy, at least in the eyes of those opposed to the shrines at Dan and Bethel.

The major differences between Deuteronomy and DH are the result of variant subject matter and theological considerations. The Deuteronomic emphasis on the election of Israel by Yahweh disappears in DH because the notion is relevant only to Israel's precovenantal beginnings. After the covenant, matters had been put on a different footing. Yahweh's gracious choice was no longer a key factor once it was formalized (*see* ELECTION §4*a*). In Deuteronomy, the land is a primary factor in the survival of Yahweh's people, and salvation is inextricably tied up with it; this theme has faded into the background in DHEd's thinking, perhaps because the notion of the inalienability of property (prominent in the story of Naboth's vineyard) had been so thoroughly diluted that it was no longer even comprehensible. Recent work contending that Deuteronomy and DH have been demythologized and secularized has tended to exaggerate minor points of disagreement with other Pentateuchal sources, while ignoring larger perspectives.

4. DH and the prophets. Writing like that of DH appears in the prose material of the book of Jeremiah (in the two complex sections, Jer. 26–29, 34–45). The material comes in all likelihood from Jeremiah's secretary BARUCH, probably in part because he was himself a Deuteronomist who sought to reconcile the more realistic theology of Jeremiah with his own; and in part simply because, like all ancient historians, he tells his tale in his own manner. The emphasis on oration and repetition links his work to Deuteronomy and DH. The difference between the theologies of Baruch and Jeremiah need not be exaggerated; both are concerned with the same phenomena, patterns of covenantal behavior. The difference between the DH historians and the pre-exilic prophets is not that of cultus and ethics. Nor do they differ in the depth or range of their historical grasp, since both deal with the whole sweep of Israel's experience and understand her present predicament in the light of her origins and obligations. The difference is rather that the historian is systematic in recounting the story from the earliest days until the present, whereas the prophet is more interested in the two end points of the spectrum, and juxtaposes them directly.

The links that connect Deuteronomy and DH to Hosea are both stylistic and ideological; in these works, the northern abhorrence of idolatry and syncretism dominates. The material of Hosea and even of Deuteronomy may have been edited in part under Hezekiah (cf. Prov. 25:1). Unlike both Deuteronomy and Hosea, however, DH lays no distinctive emphasis on the moral quality of the individual's relation to God.

5. Summary. DH as we have it is, then, the work of three editors or editorial circles. The first, the editor of Deuteronomy, wrote in the late eighth or early seventh century and was probably a refugee from the North, not directly attached to the political institutions of Jerusalem. The next two were Jerusalemite, however: the editor of the Josianic History (DHEd), and the editor of the post-Josianic addenda and of the exilic inserts in the "Tetrateuch" (PHEd). The first of these three wrote in the aftermath of the northern destruction; the second, in the days when it seemed that the South might escape the fate of the North; and the third in the days when it was clear that Yahweh had prosecuted his lawsuit (*see* LAW IN THE OT[S]) with his people and found them wanting, but not utterly beyond future redemption.

Bibliography. N. E. Andreasen, "Festival and Freedom," *Interpretation*, XXVIII (1974), 281-97; John Bright, *Jeremiah*, ABi (1965), pp. lv-lxxiii; F. M. Cross, *Canaanite Myth and Hebrew Epic* (1973), pp. 274-89; J. Milgrom, "The Alleged Demythologization and Secularization in Deuteronomy," *IEJ*, XXIII (1973), 156-59; James Muilenburg, "Baruch the Scribe," *Proclamation and Presence: OT Essays . . . G. Henton Davies*, eds. J. I. Durham and J. R. Porter (1970), pp. 215-38; E. W. Nicholson, *Deuteronomy and Tradition* (1967), pp. 107-18; Martin Noth, *Überlieferungsgeschichtliche Studien* (1943); Gerhard v. Rad, *Studies in Deuteronomy*, SBT, IX, (1953), *The Problem of the Hexateuch and Other Essays* (1966); Moshe Weinfeld, *Deuteronomy and the Deuteronomic School* (1972), esp. "Deuteronomic Phraseology," pp. 320-65, "On 'Demythologization and Secularization' in Deuteronomy," *IEJ*, XXIII (1973), 230-33. For Engnell's views *see* G. W. Anderson, "Some Aspects of the Uppsala School of Old Testament Study," *HTR*, XLIII (1950), 239-56.

D. N. FREEDMAN

*DEUTERONOMY.

1. Literary genre of the book. The Pentateuch as a unit is a story, beginning with Creation and concluding with the death of Moses. Within this framework, Deuteronomy is presented as the story of Moses' last days. The narrative elements, however, are sparse: parts of Deut. 1:3-5; 4:41-43; 5:1; 27:1, 9, 11; 29:2 [H 1]; 31:1, 7, 9-10, 14-16, 22-25, 30; 32:44-46, 48; 33:2, 7, 8, 12, 13, 18, 20, 22, 23, 24; 34:1-12. Except for 4:41-43, some verses in ch. 31, and ch. 34, all the narrative references merely note that Moses spoke the words or speeches which follow. Thus, later and rather superficially, a cloak of narration was thrown around the book. Another comprehensive form competes with the narration: the book is a kind of archive, an orderly collection of speeches organized around a system of four titles: 1:1; 4:44; 29:1 [H 28:69]; 33:1.

It is debatable whether 29:1 [H 28:69] was originally a title for chs. 29–32 or only for chs. 29–30. The passages concerning Moses' death (32:48-52; 34) and possibly also ch. 27 are not included in this system of headings. Otherwise, however, the system organizes the entire book, dividing it into four "Mosaic texts": 1–4, a speech by Moses (דברים); 5–28, the law or the teachings of Moses (תורה); 29–32, the ritual text of covenant-making in Moab (דברי הברית); 33, the blessing of Moses (ברכה). The first three texts (except ch. 32) are presented in typical Deuteronomic prose; the fourth is poetic. The "law of Moses" (5–28) consists of statutes and ordinances (5:1–11:32, historical legitimization of the law, and presentation of the main commandment to worship only Yahweh; 12:1–26:16, corpus of the laws) and a text of blessings and curses (ch. 28). From the important transitional passage between the two parts (26:17-19) it becomes clear that Deut. 5–28 is to be understood as the textual basis of a contract between Yahweh and the people of Israel (cf. §7 *below*). Thus, Deut. 29–32 contains passages and notes concerning individual incidents from the context of the ritual concluding of this contract.

2. Language of the book and milieu of the authors. Von Rad has called attention to the parenetic character of Deuteronomic language and concluded that Deuteronomy had to have come from the preachings of rural Levites (*see* DEUTERONOMY). Deuteronomic prose has since been more thoroughly examined. It is a highly rhetorical, artistic prose. Hebrew syntax, usually characterized by a co-ordinating style, has been developed into large structures which subordinate and overlap sentences. A kind of prose meter and numerous assonances give a sense of ceremony. Repetitions and systems of key words help structure the texts. Their rationality and their relation to wisdom are visible in the many phrases and clauses that express motivation. The main points of Deuteronomic theology are couched in cliché-like formulas that continually reappear. These formulas often come from a wide assortment of earlier Israelite texts, familiarity with which was probably presupposed. Stylized references to them were supposed to bring their entirety into the present for the reader or listener. That this might be the language of sermon outlines or summaries of the restorative propaganda of rural Levites is only one possibility among many, and not even the most probable one. Rather, the language of Deuteronomy shows many ties with the language of the court and with wisdom language, which were most widely known among higher officials (*see* JOSEPH STORY[S] §3; ESTHER, BOOK OF[S] §§2-3). In addition, there are legal texts, primarily in the Neo-Assyrian area, which are written in a highly rhetorical style, comparable not only in form but also in content to Deuteronomic language. Such legal texts were intended to be read in solemn public ceremonies and to make a lasting impression on the listeners. Thus we must wonder whether many texts in the book of Deuteronomy were not exactly that which they now appear to be: legal and liturgical texts which were to be read before large assemblies of Israel and which were exactly fixed in all their details. In some parts of the book, e.g., chs. 1–4, this language was probably further used for literary purposes. So, judging by the language, the origin of Deuteronomy was more likely in Jerusalem than in the country.

We are even able to indicate pre-stages of Deuteronomic formulaic language. More detailed analyses have shown that many of the so-called "Deuteronomic" additions and expansions in Genesis through Numbers do not represent (as earlier scholars often assumed) late dependence on the language and theology of the book of Deuteronomy. Rather, texts like Exod. 13:3-16 or Exod. 32:7-14 and many small "glosses" anticipate Deuteronomy. They are "pre-Deuteronomic" or—better yet—"early Deuteronomic." It is at least possible to connect these texts to the level of editing in which J and E were joined (*see* DOCUMENTS). This leads us into a relationship between literary and theological effort, and most probably to Jerusalem in the time of HEZEKIAH (*ca.* 715-687 B.C.). Hence, Deuteronomic theology and language were developed in the editing of older works of the history of Israel. Thus, at least one edition of Deuteronomic law would have to be attributed to the same theologians and writers. The priest Hilkiah and the secretary Shaphan played important roles in the discovery of the law under King JOSIAH (II Kings 22:3-10). Later the prophet Jeremiah was closely connected to the descendants of Shaphan, including Gedaliah, and there is some reason to assume that the Shaphan family had something to do with the preservation and the "Deuteronomic" edition of Jeremiah's words (*see*

JEREMIAH THE PROPHET §D7). Thus, the Deuteronomic style of writing and thinking appears to be closely related to people of the ruling class in Jerusalem.

3. Critical literary analysis. Since von Rad wrote his article (*see* DEUTERONOMY), interest in the literary analysis of the book has increased vastly. However, no one theory has won wide acceptance. This is especially true for the laws in Deut. 12–26. A critical literary theory cannot be developed without presupposing a solid evaluation of the individual criteria of differentiation or apart from clear ideas concerning the book's origin. Yet there is no agreement even on these preliminary questions. In Deuteronomy Moses sometimes speaks to Israel in the singular and sometimes in the plural. Is this a criterion for the relative age of individual passages? However, even if it were, could not the authors of later passages (e.g., Deut. 4:1-40) have thought that the inconsistency of number was typical of Deuteronomic language and imitated it consciously? The typical theological key words of Deuteronomy are not evenly distributed throughout the book. Should it therefore be assumed that texts with different backgrounds have been put together, so that one may begin to identify them by means of language statistics? In Deut. 12–26 various types of laws may be differentiated: APODICTIC, casuistic, and laws containing certain formulas (e.g., "So you shall purge the evil from the midst of you"). Beginning with formal criteria, would it be possible to identify collections of laws that were originally separate from each other but possess a unity of form? Should a relatively low number of literary editing processes be assumed, or a long and complicated process of expansion and commentary? It is important to decide to what extent one should expect logical consistency from a book like Deuteronomy. These and many other uncertainties in the method of analysis are undoubtedly responsible for the large number of critical literary theories.

Still, it must be recognized that many new observations of lasting value have been made during recent years, and there is a slowly growing consensus in some matters. It is assumed more and more often that there are large post-Josian expansions and revisions, not only in the chapters which provide a framework (1–4 and 30 ff.), but also in the central parts. Here the analysis of Deuteronomy becomes entwined with that of the Deuteronomic history (*see* DEUTERONOMIC HISTORY, THE[S]). If the first edition of that history was pre-exilic and culminated with Josiah, and then there was one or more exilic editions, each of them should have left traces in the book of Deuteronomy, with which it began. Chs. 1–3 and much of chs. 29–32 could belong to the pre-exilic edition. Some of chs. 28–29 could be claimed for a first exilic edition. However, it has also been suggested that the entire system of laws dealing with officials as it now stands in chs. 16–18 should be attributed to this latter edition, as a sort of constitutional outline that is critical of the king. It is comparable in several ways to the texts critical of the king in I Samuel (*see* SAMUEL, I AND II; contrast supplementary article §3*a*). Deut. 4, much of Deut. 7–9, and much of Deut. 30 could be late exilic. Further, it may be asked whether presenting the law as Moses' words would have made sense apart from a surrounding historical narrative. If not, the historical flashbacks in chs. 5 and 9 ff. would not have been possible before the earliest edition of the Deuteronomic history, and only a relatively small part of Deuteronomy, often very hypothetical and not yet shaped as Moses' words, would be left for Josiah's book of the law. Earlier stages of Deuteronomy would be even more hypothetical.

4. Two basic texts for Deuteronomy. The laws in Deuteronomy presuppose the "Book of the Covenant" (or a collection of laws related to it; *see* COVENANT, BOOK OF THE; EXODUS, BOOK OF §1*b*). The whole book presupposes the ancient sources of the Pentateuch, and in its later parts the stories in the books of Joshua–II Kings, as well as other legal texts no longer available to us. However, two shorter texts were probably especially important: the "cultic Decalogue" (the best known version of which is Exod. 34:10-26), and the Decalogue itself, of which one edition is quoted in Deut. 5:6-21 (*see* TEN COMMANDMENTS; TEN COMMANDMENTS[S]). For the "cultic Decalogue," the second most important text after Exod. 34 is Exod. 23:13-33. The "cultic Decalogue" is basic to the stipulations in Deut. 16, and hence probably to all centralization laws. In the parenetic ch. 7, the older level of text which was not yet influenced by the language of the Decalogue comes from the "cultic Decalogue." Its influence also appears in Deut. 12:2-3, 29-31; 14:21; 26:1-11. It appears possible that this "cultic Decalogue" constituted the earliest form of the Deuteronomic law. In any case, the Decalogue was not understood as the most basic formulation of God's will until a later phase in the development of Deuteronomy, but then it did decisively mold Deuteronomy. Some of the most frequent stereotyped phrases of Deuteronomic language come from the beginning of the Decalogue. Deut. 4:15-20; 6:10-15; 7:8-11; 8:7-20 consist of paraphrases as commentary on the first commandment. A whole series of laws (Deut. 13:1-5 [H 2-6], 6-11 [H 7-12], 12-18 [H 13-19]; 17:2-7; 19:11-13, 16-19; 21:1-9, 18-21; 22:13-21, 22, 23-27; 24:7) contains individual cases for almost all the commandments. Several characteristics separate these laws from other laws; the primary one is the formula: "So shall you purge the evil from the midst of you." Finally, in the narrative chs. 5 and 9 ff. and in the heading 29:1 [H 28:69], the explicit theory was developed that at the covenant ratification on Mount Horeb Yahweh revealed only the Decalogue to Israel. He communicated the remaining laws to Moses alone, and Moses proclaimed them to Israel only shortly before his death in the land of Moab. Also, in light of Deut. 18:16-18, that which the prophets later told Israel as the word of Yahweh was intended to be viewed only as an additional commentary on the Decalogue. Therefore, it is logical that the Decalogue should be literally quoted in Deut. 5:6-21. However, this edition of the text is probably a later one, since it stresses the sabbath commandment, which is otherwise insignificant in Deuteronomy.

5. The centralization of the cult. The greatest innovation that Deuteronomy produced was the demand to centralize the cult at the place which Yahweh chose. The historical circumstances of the centralization laws have always been controversial (Deut. 26:1-11 should be added to von Rad's list of "explicit" passages; *see* DEUTERONOMY §4). Usually they have been related to Josiah's reforms. The biblical report of a first centralization under Hezekiah was formerly believed historically inaccurate. However, the excavation of a shrine to Yahweh at Tell 'Arad appears to have shed new light on the question (*see* TEMPLES, SEMITIC[S] §2*a*). After the destruction of stratum VIII, which can be related to the time of Hezekiah, the temple was rebuilt in stratum VII, but without an altar for burnt offerings. After another destruction at the time of Josiah, the temple was not rebuilt in stratum VI. Thus, we can differentiate between an abolition of sacrifices outside Jerusalem under Hezekiah and a destruction of the sanctuaries themselves under Josiah. In that case, the essence of the Deuteronomic laws of centralization should be attributed to Hezekiah rather than Josiah. If Josiah based his more radical measures on Deuteronomy, it was most likely on those laws that demanded the complete destruction of the pre-Israelite sanctuaries.

6. The covenant of King Josiah, 621 B.C. II Kings 22–23 contains a text which was probably composed during Josiah's lifetime and may therefore be considered reliable (II Kings 22:3-20; 23:1-3, 21-23). From it we may conclude that a "Book of the Torah," the existence of which was previously known in itself, was rediscovered in the temple. In a solemn covenant ceremony, Josiah and the people bound themselves to obey the provisions of this text. This document is probably identical with an early edition of Deut. 5–28. Thus by this time at the latest, Deuteronomy became a "covenant charter." At least from 621 B.C. on, the covenant between Yahweh and Israel was periodically renewed in the cult. According to Deut. 31:10-13, the covenant was renewed every seventh year at the Feast of Tabernacles. From the record in II Kings 22–23, it is also possible that before 621 Deuteronomy was an official document and not, for example, a private literary creation. However, it is difficult to determine whether Deuteronomy served as a "covenant" document before 621. There are some signs that there was already an older covenant tradition between Israel and Yahweh. The usual designation of the Decalogue in Deuteronomy is "the Covenant" (הברית). Hosea seems to have known of a covenant related to the Decalogue. If the report in II Kings 11:17 is authentic, there was in Jerusalem a ritual related to the assumption of the throne by the king, in which a covenant was made between Yahweh, the king, and the people, and which re-established "the people of Yahweh." However, not until the time of the Assyrian domination, and only in Deuteronomy, did there develop the comprehensive theological systemization and stylization of the faith of Israel which we call "covenant theology."

7. Covenant theology in Deuteronomy. OT covenant theology cannot be understood without considering the influence of the ancient Oriental system of treaties. This was proven by Mendenhall's discovery of the similarity between Hittite vassal treaties and some texts of the OT (*see* COVENANT §C). Until recently the problem has been that the truly comparable OT texts are all very late, so that a direct influence from the Hittites would have been impossible (*see* COVENANT, MOSAIC[S]). The structure of the Decalogue is explicable without the vassal treaty (*see* TEN COMMANDMENTS[S] §3). Even the basic structure of Deut. 5–28 (history and parenesis, laws, blessings and curses) does not have to be explained by it. This becomes even clearer when one considers that the key text in Deut. 26:17-19, which interpreted Deut. 5–28 as a treaty document, imitated the legal structure of treaties between equals, not of vassal treaties, although the difference between Yahweh and Israel is clearly elaborated. The form of Hittite vassal treaties cannot be recognized with certainty in material prior to some of the late Deuteronomic texts: Deut. 4; 28–29; and Josh. 23. In the meantime, the missing link which explains the late assumption of the form of the vassal treaties has appeared. A fragment of a vassal treaty with a historical prologue between Ashurbanipal and the tribe of Qedar proves that this form of treaty was still in use in Neo-Assyrian times. However, the development of OT covenant theology did not depend on this formula but, in general, on the great significance which the taking of oaths and making of treaties had in the Neo-Assyrian Empire. They were a characteristic of the culture, and we even have evidence that the idea of covenant was transferred to the relationship between the king, the people, and a god. According to a clay tablet in the British Museum, a contract was made between the god Ashur, the king Esarhaddon, and the people of Assyria, mediated by the goddess Ishtar at a date unfortunately no longer known. That the authors of Deuteronomy were influenced in their covenant theology by Assyrian patterns of thought and institutions is adequately proven by the many terminological parallels and the direct dependence of Deut. 28:28-33 on an Assyrian treaty. (Weinfeld has prepared the best overview of this.) We have here the phenomenon of a reorganization of the old traditions of Israel with the help of a system which came from the dominant enemy culture. Probably only in this way could the old traditions be given the attractiveness needed to bring about a religious renewal and have fostered a new will toward national independence.

8. Restructuring of covenant theology in the later texts of Deuteronomy. After the fall of Judah, covenant theology with its relentless contractual logic could only serve to prove that Israel, not Yahweh, was responsible for the catastrophe. This is clear, for example, in Deut. 29:22-28 [Heb. 21-27], which is a late text (cf. I Kings 9:8-10). This logic could not produce hope for the future. However, in exile Israel found new hope. Therefore, the old covenant theology had to be restructured, even where the old concepts and patterns of presentation were kept. The texts in Deuteronomy concerning this all appear to have been developed in dialogue with other theological efforts in the closing years of the Exile. The shift in emphasis from the Sinai covenant to the one with Abraham (pure promise instead of a contract) may be found on the one hand in the Priestly writings of the Pentateuch, and on the other in Deut. 4, 7, and 9 (*see* COVENANT, DAVIDIC[S]). In addition, connections may be found from Deut. 4 to Second Isaiah, from Deut. 7 to Ezekiel, and from Deut. 30 to Jeremiah. Thus, the Pauline argument with the theology of law is actually anticipated in Deuteronomy itself.

Bibliography. N. Lohfink, *Das Hauptgebot* (1963); D. J. McCarthy, *Treaty and Covenant* (1963); J. L'Hour, "Une législation criminelle dans le Deutéronome," *Bibl.*, XLIV (1963), 1-28; N. Lohfink, "Die Bundesurkunde des Königs Josias," *Bibl.*, XLIV (1963), 261-88, 461-98; G. von Rad, *Deuteronomy* (1966); E. W. Nicholson, *Deuteronomy and Tradition* (1967); S. Loersch, *Das Deuteronomium und seine Deutungen* (1967); R. E. Clements, *God's Chosen People* (1968); P. Buis and J. Leclercq, *Le Deutéronome* (1963); M. Weinfeld, *Deuteronomy and the Deuteronomic School* (1972); G. Seitz, *Redaktionsgeschichtliche Studien zum Deuteronomium* (1971); A. Phillips, *Deuteronomy* (1973); J. McKay, *Religion in Judah under the Assyrians, 732-609* B.C. (1973); C. M. Carmichael, *The Laws of Deuteronomy* (1974); J. Halbe, *Das Privilegrecht Jahwes, Ex. 34, 10-26* (1975).

N. LOHFINK

***DIDACHE.** *See* APOSTOLIC FATHERS[S] §4.

DIDYMA. *See* MILETUS[S] §3.

***DIOGNETUS, LETTER TO.** *See* APOSTOLIC FATHERS[S] §5.

DISCIPLESHIP. 1. Jesus. ***a. Survey.*** Jesus probably gathered around himself a group of TWELVE as representatives of the eschatological Israel. Beyond this he certainly had other disciples (Mark 2:14; John 1:35-50; cf. Mark 5:18 ff.; John 10:17 ff.; Luke 9:57 ff.), distinguished from a yet wider circle of sympathizers. Discipleship as such seems to have been a special obligation rather than a general condition for acceptance of the KINGDOM OF GOD (cf. Mark 5:18-20; 10:17-22; the women who served Jesus, but were not disciples; Zacchaeus, etc.). Thus, within the larger circle of Jesus' adherents and sympathizers there was a smaller circle of disciples who shared Jesus' poverty and nomadic life (Luke 9:57-58), and for this reason renounced (until the coming of the kingdom of God?) the exercise of their occupations, the enjoyment of their family lives, etc. Since the term "disciple" rarely appears in the genuine SAYINGS OF JESUS (e.g., Luke 14:25-26, 33 is Lukan redaction), we cannot know precisely how the word was used by Jesus himself.

b. Roots of discipleship. JOHN THE BAPTIST presumably had a circle of disciples to which Jesus himself may have belonged and from which some of Jesus' disciples also perhaps came (John 1:36). This immediate background may have been more significant for Jesus than the example of the rabbi with his pupils, because Jesus was not himself an ordained rabbi and did not conduct an ordinary school. Moreover, the rabbinical *talmid* was learning (למד) the Torah exclusively. There are also other important differences between Jesus' disciples and the rabbinical pupils: rabbis and their pupils did not normally lead a nomadic life; Jesus' disciples were called by him alone and did not strive for status as pupils; ordination was not the goal of their education; discipleship does not appear to have been something temporary, and it implied the renunciation of one's occupation and of family life. Not the Law, but the person of Jesus was the crucial point of reference.

It has been suggested that discipleship derived from the messianic prophets of the Zealots, whom the people followed into the wilderness or to the Jordan, but with Jesus it was always individual men (never women) who were called to follow him (the closest parallel is the calling of Elisha in I Kings 19:19 ff.). Jesus' call to follow him cannot be understood from the environment, but must be derived from the specific form of his message.

c. The meaning of discipleship. Discipleship is best understood as special service in the proclamation of the kingdom of God (cf. Mark 1:17; Luke 9:60). The disciples share in this ministry of Jesus' and adopt his manner of life. The question then is the same for Jesus and his disciples; namely, how this manner of life is related to the proclamation of the kingdom of God. Since Jesus participated in feasts, associated with women, detached himself from John the Baptist, and was accused of gluttony (Luke 7:34), he could not have issued a call to asceticism in the usual sense. Rather, the kingdom of God is totally new and different in comparison with the world and makes a total claim upon the one who proclaims it (Matt. 10:34-37; 13:44-46; Luke 9:60, 62). Not only is its arrival as unlimited love concretized and personified in the unconditional concern which Jesus (and his disciples) showed for the poor and dispossessed, but, in addition, its alien character is made specific in the "homelessness" of Jesus and his disciples.

2. The post-Easter communities. ***a. Survey.*** In the NT the term "disciple" appears outside the gospels only in Acts, where, as a designation for Christians, "disciples" is an ecclesiological term. In the gospels (the tradition as well as in the redaction) Jesus is almost always pictured in the company of his disciples. They play a significant role in some of the special forms (*Gattungen*) of the tradition: for example, in instructions and in didactic or conflict sayings in which Jesus defends their conduct. This raises the question to what extent the community which transmitted these traditions found itself represented and portrayed in them. The development of the idea of "following" (ἀκολουθέω) in the post-Easter period exhibits a similar tendency. Although "following after Jesus" does not come into universal use as a metaphor for "being a Christian," the Fourth Evangelist is acquainted with the possibility of following the Exalted One, and the Apocalypse speaks of following the heavenly Lamb (14:4). Significant new formulations of sayings with ἀκολουθέω appear both in the community traditions and in the redaction of the Synoptic gospels, but in the epistles a theological use of the word is lacking. This leads to the thesis that in limited areas of the Christian communities "following" became a figurative concept, a code word for Christian existence, and hence increasingly lost its concreteness. For both terms, "discipleship" and "following," the connection with Jesus remained determinative.

b. The early churches. The designation of Christians as "disciples" in Acts corresponds to Lukan usage. It is difficult to disentangle the sources, so it cannot be determined whether Hellenistic Christians identified themselves as "disciples of Jesus" or were perhaps so identified by others, in distinction from the eschatological self-understanding of the Jerusalem community. The traditions of the LOGIA source (*see* Q; Q[S]) reflect a radical understanding of following and discipleship. Behind this source probably stand prophetic emissaries of the coming SON OF MAN, who, in following after him, adopt his poverty and homelessness (Luke 9:57 ff.). One can discover by reading the missionary discourse in Q (Luke 10:2-12) how this was concretely manifested. Their later successors are the wandering ascetics of the Syrian church.

c. Mark. This evangelist consciously places the role of the disciples in the service of his over-all theological concept. The disciples' lack of understanding (4:13, 40; 6:52; 7:18; 8:14-21), the idea of following into suffering, together with the disciples' protest against the suffering (8:31-34; 9:30-37; 10:32-45), and special instructions to the disciples were deliberately composed by the evangelist. There is no consensus among scholars as to the interpretation of these developments (*see* MARK, GOSPEL OF; SECRET, MESSIANIC and supplementary articles), so the question remains open whether in Mark the disciples fail to understand Jesus because there was no understanding before Easter, or because without the cross and discipleship in suffering there was no comprehension of the glory of the SON OF GOD (cf. the confession at the foot of the cross in Mark 15:39).

d. Matthew. Only Matthew has the verb μαθητεύω ("to be a disciple") along with the noun "disciple." Thus, in 28:16-20 he shows what it is to be a Christian: discipleship in obedience to the commandments of the earthly Jesus. For this evangelist, "disciple" is an ecclesiological term, and in speaking of Jesus' disciples he indicates what the state of the church actually is (of little faith) and what it ought to be (achieving understanding through Jesus' teaching, and sharing in Jesus' power and glory). The disciples' boat is the ship of the church (8:23-27); Peter, walking on the water, is the prototype of the believer (14:28-31); and Christians are the disciples of the *one* teacher, Christ (23:10). This is not simply a matter of abolishing the distance from Christ; on the contrary, only reorientation toward the teaching of the earthly Jesus can protect them from the pneumatics and wolves in sheep's clothing (7:15-23). Therefore, even more clearly than Mark, and in a manner different from that of Luke, Matthew usually understood the term "disciples" to mean the twelve disciples. This was not because the Christians of the present were not disciples of Jesus; rather it was intended to make clear that the only true discipleship was discipleship of the earthly Jesus, as was the case with the Twelve (*see* TWELVE, THE). For a different view, *see* DISCIPLE §2.

e. Luke. Luke explicitly differentiates between the Twelve (the apostles) and the rest of the disciples (6:13; Acts 6:2), a more numerous group (Luke 19:37). The differentiation between the mass of disciples (the Christians, Acts 11:26) and the Twelve corresponds to the structure of ministry in the church, which is headed first by the Twelve, and then by the elders installed by those commissioned (Acts 14:23). This differentiation is not found in Matthew. While for Luke the most important thing about the twelve apostles is their authority and their status as eyewitnesses, he uses the concept of "disciple" to make clear the radical nature of Jesus' own teaching concerning the renunciation of possessions, bearing the cross, and following Jesus (Luke 14:25-33). In Luke's day, however, the radical demands of that first period could no longer be applied without modification (Luke 22:35-38).

f. John. In John disciples "follow" the light of the world (8:12) and the Exalted One (12:26; 21:19, 22). Discipleship is identical with being a Christian—with believing (2:11), abiding in the word (8:31), practicing brotherly love (13:35; 15:8 ff.). The concept of disciple is important for John, as are all modes of thought generally which express the priority of the vertical relationship ([Father-]Son-disciples) to the horizontal relationship within the community (cf. the reduction of the whole of ethics to the brotherly love that is commanded from above). Thus the discourse in 15:1 ff. about the vine best shows what discipleship is: to abide in the vine, which is the life and the strength of any fruit. In John, too, "disciple" is an ecclesiological term, or it appears in place of ecclesiological terms. There are no allusions, as there are in Luke, to any ranks among the disciples or to a structure of office. Only two disciples are singled out: PETER, the first to enter the empty tomb (20:4 ff.) and the one to whom the leadership of the church is entrusted (21:15 ff.); and the BELOVED DISCIPLE behind whom, perhaps, the ancestor and patron of the Johannine circle is concealed.

g. Summary. After Jesus' death there was a tendency, expressed in various ways, to identify discipleship with being a Christian in a general sense. The radical character, concreteness, and eschatological reference of discipleship often tended to be lost, and, on the positive side, there was a tendency toward spiritualizing (John) and adaptation of Jesus' intention to the situation of the present (Luke). One of the earliest to react against this development, which continued throughout the history of the church, was IGNATIUS, for whom one had to be a martyr to qualify as a disciple of Jesus.

Bibliography. H. D. Betz, *Nachfolge und Nachahmung Jesu Christi im Neuen Testament,* BHTh, XXXVII (1967); K. H. Rengstorf, "μανθάνω," *TDNT,* IV, 390-461; A. Schulz, *Nachfolgen und Nachahmen,* StANT, VI (1962); E. Schweizer, *Lordship and Discipleship,* SBT, XXVIII (1955 [rev. ET 1960]).

On Jesus' teaching: G. Bornkamm, *Jesus of Nazareth* (3rd ed., 1959), ch. 6; M. Hengel, *Nachfolge und*

Charisma, BZNW, XXXIV (1968). On the early churches: P. Hoffmann, *Studien zur Theologie der Logienquelle,* NTAbh, VIII (1972); G. Theissen, "Wanderradikalismus," *ZThK,* LXX (1973), 245 ff. On Mark: E. Schweizer, *The Good News According to Mark* (1968); G. Strecker, "Zur Messiasgeheimnistheorie im Markusevangelium," *Studia Evangelica,* III, *TU,* LXXXVIII (1964), 87 ff.; T. Weeden, *Mark—Traditions in Conflict* (1971). On Matthew: U. Luz, "Die Jünger im Matthäusevangelium," *ZNW,* LXII (1971), 141-71.

U. Luz

DISCIPLINE, DIVINE. In prophetic interpretation Israel's history could be viewed as a series of disciplinary acts by which Yahweh, the God of the covenant, sought to create a faithful and obedient people. This idea is reflected also in the thought of Paul, who regarded the experience of Israel prior to Christ as a disciplinary preparation under the Law for the redemption accomplished by God in Christ (Gal. 3:23-26).

The metaphor of God as disciplinarian, which is derived from the parent-child relationship, combines the conviction that God loves his people and seeks their ultimate well-being with the belief that he demands obedience to his righteous will as the condition of human fulfillment. In this respect it is more adequate than other biblical symbols of God's relation to man, e.g., that of judge.

Divine discipline presupposes Israel's inadequacy, which consists more in sinfulness (apostasy, injustice, hardness of heart) than in ignorance. At the same time discipline presupposes the capacity of the recipient to learn, to repent, to reform. The divine discipline may take the form of prophetic instruction and reproof or experiences of deprivation and suffering. However, the latter require prophetic interpretation if they are to be morally edifying; therefore, the prophetic word always accompanies, or anticipates, the chastening event.

1. The vocabulary of divine discipline. The two Hebrew verbs that express the idea of discipline are יסר (instruct, correct, chastise), with its derivative noun מוסר, and יכח (rebuke, judge, chastise, punish), with its noun תוכחת. Both may be predicated of men as well as God and are used in a wide range of settings, from the family and school to the law court. They overlap considerably in meaning, although יסר always presupposes an educational purpose, while יכח may mean merely punishment (e.g., II Kings 19:4).

In a comprehensive study of יסר and מוסר Sanders classifies the passages where God is the subject as follows: (*a*) Israel is disciplined by suffering (e.g., Hos. 5:2; 10:10; Jer. 5:3); (*b*) Israel is disciplined by verbal instruction or warning (e.g., Jer. 7:28; 17:23); (*c*) an individual is disciplined by suffering (e.g., Jer. 10:24; Ps. 6:1 [H 2]); and (*d*) an individual is disciplined by verbal instruction or warning (e.g., Isa. 8:11; Job 33:16). These terms are never used in the OT of divine discipline of a foreign nation (*see, however,* the discussion of Isa. 53:5 in §5 *below*).

יכח is predicated of God as follows: (*a*) divine chastening, without explicit educational purpose, of Israel (all or part, Hos. 5:9; Ezek. 5:15); of foreign nations (II Kings 19:4; I Chr. 16:21); and of individuals (Prov. 30:6; Ps. 39:11 [H 12]); (*b*) divine discipline, with an express purpose of education, of individuals (Prov. 3:12; Job 5:17); (*c*) judicial judgments by God, where the specific content of the decision is not stated, with respect to Israel (Isa. 1:18; Mic. 6:2); to individuals (Job 13:10; 16:21); and to the nations (Isa. 2:4; Mic. 4:3); and (*d*) cases where it is unclear whether corrective chastening or simple punishment is intended, of Israel (Hab. 1:12), of the nations (Ps. 94:10), and of individuals (Gen. 31:42; Ps. 6:1 [H 2]).

Thus chastisement can be either for instruction (Prov. 6:23) or in wrath (Ezek. 25:17). He who rejects ordinary reproof can expect "severe discipline," which may kill (Prov. 15:10). In prophetic texts the point is made that Israel has failed to learn or to reform as a result of God's chastening, and therefore can expect harsher treatment in the future (Zeph. 3:2-8; Jer. 2:30-37). According to Jer. 31:18, Ephraim (i.e., the northern Israelite kingdom) had learned his lesson by the fall and exile of the nation (721 B.C.) and was ready finally to be brought back to God.

2. Divine discipline in prophetic and liturgical texts. Explicit use of the language of parental discipline (יסר, מוסר) to interpret the activity of God toward Israel appears first in Hosea (5:2; 7:12, 15; 10:10). It is used most frequently in the book of Jeremiah (2:19, 30; 5:3; 6:8; 7:28), which stands in direct continuity with the Hosean tradition. However, the idea had appeared already in Amos 4, couched in somewhat different terms.

Amos 4:6-13 rehearses a series of afflictions laid upon Israel by God in order to induce the nation to repent, but after each affliction Israel remained unrepentant. Therefore, God was going to bring a much worse calamity, comparable to the destruction of Sodom and Gomorrah (4:11-12; the exact meaning of vs. 12 is uncertain).

This text is regarded by some scholars as an adaptation of a liturgical tradition, perhaps from the ritual of the Jerusalem temple. Similar interpretations of Israel's history are to be found in Pss. 78; 81; 106; I Kings 8; and Lev. 26:3-13. All these texts have liturgical associations, although none may be dated with confidence before Amos 4. It seems more likely that the prophetic interpretation of historical events has been taken up by the postexilic historians and priests and made a regular feature of Jewish worship.

Other psalms rehearse the saving events of Israel's history (e.g., Pss. 44 and 105), but Pss. 78 and 106 are distinctive in viewing this history as a series of providential disciplines meant to overcome the people's perpetual faithlessness, ingratitude, and hypocrisy. Like Amos 4, these psalms regard the divine discipline as having no enduring effect. Ps. 78 concludes its somber recital with the rejection and destruction of the northern kingdom ("Joseph . . . Ephraim," vs. 67) as the people of God, and the choice of Judah as the sole bearer of the covenant tradition (vss. 68 ff.). This confidence in Judah was misplaced, according to Ps. 106, which chronicles its destruction and exile (vss. 40 ff.). Nevertheless, the psalmist confesses his confidence in the enduring love of God for his people and pleads with him for a new act of salvation following this most severe of all acts of divine discipline.

3. Divine discipline of the Davidic king. It is possible that the prophetic interpretation of Israel's history was influenced by the idea of kingship that was developed in Jerusalemite circles during and after the reigns of David and Solomon. Since the king was regarded as the representative of the nation before God, it was natural for the two sets of ideas to develop side by side.

It was believed that God had made a covenant with David, establishing his line as a permanent dynasty. The statement of this conviction in II Sam. 7 is a perfect example of the notion of divine discipline as a manifestation of parental love. "I will be his father, and he shall be my son. When he commits iniquity, I will chasten (יכח) him . . . , but I will not take my steadfast love from him, as I took it from Saul" (7:14-15). The probable need for corrective punishment is acknowledged, but the possibility of a radical break in the relationship is ruled out. (Note how the Chronicler omitted the reference to sin and chastisement when he quoted this passage, I Chr. 17:13-14. His idealized view of David required the omission. Compare the royal protestation of guiltlessness in Ps. 18:20-24 [H 21-25]).

The Davidic king as the son of God was a standard part of Judean ideology (cf. Pss. 2:7; 89:26-27 [H 27-28]), as was the notion that he could be chastened by God but not cast off (Ps. 89:32-37 [H 33-38]; and in general cf. the other royal psalms, Pss. 18, 20, 21, 45, 72, 101, 110, 144). This notion corresponds to the conviction which the people of Israel held with respect to their own covenantal relation to God, according to the picture of popular piety drawn by the prophets. The possibility that the covenant with the dynasty might be brought to an end is suggested only once in the royalist literature, namely in Ps. 132:11-12, where the endurance of the line is made conditional upon practicing the righteousness and justice demanded of a godly ruler (Ps. 72; II Sam. 23:1-7). Elsewhere the Davidic sonship to God is regarded as everlasting. The parent-child metaphor is thus made absolute and allowed to displace contractual (or adoptive) ideas of the God-king relation. In this view royal affliction, however severe, could only be interpreted as disciplinary chastening and not as radical punishment or rejection (cf. Ps. 89:38-52 [H 39-53]).

4. Parental discipline in the theology of Hosea. It is in the book of HOSEA that the idea of divine discipline receives its fullest development. Unlike AMOS, who brought the account of God's disciplinary efforts to a close with the announcement of national destruction (Amos 9:8*b*-15 is not part of the prophet's own message), Hosea plumbed more deeply the depths of divine love and proclaimed a renewal of covenant between God and his people after the destruction of the Israelite monarchy and its established cult.

Hosea's message of divine discipline is to be found not only in those passages that use the specific vocabulary of discipline but in the book as a whole. Hosea understood the relation of God to Israel as that of father and son (11:1-11) or husband and wife (1:2–3:5). The nation's experience from the time of its founding was like the education of a child by his parent, out of love (11:1-3). Unfortunately, the child rejected the lesson, together with the teacher-parent (cf. 7:15). Therefore, a sterner chastening was required (5:2, 9; 7:12; 10:10; the specific language of discipline is used in these passages). Israel would be exiled and its idolatrous institutions of state and religion would be abandoned. This event is symbolized as a second "Egyptian captivity" (11:5; 8:13; 9:3, 6).

However, this disaster was not a mere punishment ending with the death of the people. It was also a new opportunity to discover the true nature of sonship and to abandon the false gods of kingship (8:4-10), foreign alliance (7:8-11; 12:1 [H 2]; 5:13-14), ritualism (6:1-6; 7:14-16; 9:4-6), and Baalism (2:5-8 [H 7-10]; 4:15-19; 7:16; 8:5, etc.). Israel had misconstrued the gift of land and the culture that it made possible, interpreting them as objects to be exploited in terms of the Canaanite fertility cult. Only by having land, monarchy, and sacrificial system stripped away could Israel be made aware of the proper religious and ethical basis of its existence under God. Hosea represented this disciplinary chastening as a second wilderness era (2:14 [H 16]) or, under the figure of an adulterous wife, as a period of moral probation prior to the restoration of her conjugal privileges (3:1-5). The motive of God's action was love (3:1; 11:8-9), a love that transcended all human limitations or moral conditions, but which still demanded that those who were loved show moral rectitude, the necessary condition of their human fulfillment.

This disciplinary action would lead to a new exodus and covenant and a resettlement of the land (2:14-23 [H 16-25]; 3:5; 11:10-11; 14:4-7), as well as the resumption of the public worship of God, purged now of idolatry (14:2).

Hosea presents the most concise and consistent interpretation of Israel's history as a unified story of divine love and discipline. Most of the elements in his message are present, however, in the other prophetic books, although they are often couched in different terms. All the pre-exilic prophets agreed that any genuine renewal of faithfulness and justice would require the dismantling of the existing economic, political, and cultic institutions. Not all spoke in equal detail about the future prospects of the people after the fall of the nation. However, each book, in its final form, reflects the fundamental convictions that are exhibited so powerfully in the metaphors of Hosea.

5. The divine discipline of the Servant in Isaiah 53:5. Second ISAIAH goes beyond the other prophets in interpreting Israel's fall, exile, and subsequent experience among the nations not only as punishment and opportunity for renewal, but also as the means of bringing wholeness to others (53:5). The speakers here are the alien kings (52:15 ff.) who have persecuted the servant people and rejected their message about God and his relation to the created world and man. But the prophet believes that Israel's patient proclamation of this faith will eventually produce a saving result for her despisers, namely bring them to acknowledge the truth of her message and the validity of her service (cf. 42:1-7; 49:1-13; 50:4-9). Although it has appeared as though she suffered merely because of her own sin, her chastisement was intended finally as the necessary cost of her mediatorial example. By accepting this suffering she brings the nations into a right (righteous) relationship with God (53:11). This is her righteous service. By it she will help to bring all flesh to see the glory of God (40:5) and to rejoice in his gracious love (55:1-13). (Contrast the view of the editor of Jeremiah in Jer. 30:11 and 46:28.)

A further insight into the redemptive possibility of suffering is proposed by the writer of Hebrews (ch. 12). He viewed disciplinary suffering at the hand of God as a regular ingredient of Christian life and witness and as a participation in the triumph of the crucified and risen Christ. He makes use here of a number of OT quotations and allusions in this interpretation of divine discipline (cf. I Cor. 11:32; II Cor. 6:9; Tit. 2:12). *See also* Repentance in the OT[S]; Retribution[S].

Bibliography. J. A. Sanders, *Suffering as Divine Discipline in the Old Testament and Post-Biblical Judaism* (1955); G. Bertram, "παιδεύω, παιδεία . . . ," *TDNT*, V (1967), 596-625; W. Eichrodt, *Theology of the OT*, I (1961), 228-88, 457-501; II (1964), 413-95.

J. M. Ward

DISCOURSE, DIRECT AND INDIRECT. 1. "Discourse" has several technical meanings: (*a*) One is quotation, both direct and indirect (hereafter DQ, IQ). (*b*) A second, in recent linguistic and psycholinguistic studies, refers to patterned sequencing of information in and beyond the sentence—"connected discourse" (*see* Discourse Structure[S] §2). (*c*) A third, sociolinguistic "discourse analysis," involves the social rules for language use, e.g., sequencing of turns at talking in conversation. Quotation is frequent in the Scriptures, as in everyday life; much of what people say makes reference to or reports what has already been said or thought.

2. Kinds of quotation. The kinds of quotation in connected discourse differ in formal detail, but each language provides lexical and grammatical devices for quoting, and each society has rules for their use in interactions. Direct quotation and indirect quotation express most explicitly the actual words of the original speaker. More implicitly, words of saying (or thinking) refer to factors in the over-all act of speaking itself, whether reporting actual speech or representing inner thoughts. Most implicitly, some action words may include speech as a culturally expected part of some sequence of actions.

a. Direct quotation purports to give the exact words of a speaker, so his grammatical forms remain largely intact. Nevertheless, the texture of the original can be reshaped at the discretion of the quoter, drastically coloring the resultant meaning. For example, "He shrilled, 'Get on out of here!'" does not have the same pragmatic meaning as "He laughed and said, 'Get out of here!'"

b. Indirect quotation differs from DQ in grammatical and lexical form—sequence of tenses, pronominal reference, locational reference—mainly because it takes the point of view of the quoter rather than the orientation of the original speaker. Some languages have no IQ. Others, including Greek, can switch in midstream from IQ to DQ. In some languages DQ and IQ are often grammatically ambiguous.

c. Metalanguage is another quotation device. Many citations are realized implicitly in the words a language uses for referring to the act of speaking—its metalanguage. In English, "They dismissed him," refers to what was accomplished by a speech act such as, "You may go now." Frequently, however, what is implicit in one language may, in another, most naturally be explicit DQ or IQ, or be implicit in another way; for example, English "They dismissed him," could be Cashinawa (Peru) "They said, 'Go out!'" or "They caused him to go out." The content is similar; the devices for expressing the citation are different.

A quotation, whether DQ, IQ, or metalanguage, can be *reported* speech or *represented* speech. In the latter the inner thoughts, attitudes, and opinions, or mental states and processes, or stream of consciousness may be represented as DQ or IQ, or as words of thinking, feeling, etc.; again, English "He decided to go," could be Cashinawa "He said (to himself), 'I intend to go.'"

The biblical languages are rich in words referring to both reported and represented speech. Their lexical equivalents in other languages may share some features of meaning, but they will often entail culturally specific differences in expectation and understanding; English "command" is closest to Cashinawa *yunu,* "to suggest—on the part of the headman," but for a headman to command anyone is to behave inappropriately by Cashinawa values.

d. Reference to actions or a sequence of actions which, within a particular culture, entail speaking as an integral part are perhaps the most implicit kind of citation. "To gather together," for example, may first require a call to come together. Whether or not speaking is implied in the meaning of words depends on the cultural place of speech in particular situations and sequences of actions.

Combinations of any of these kinds of quotation, in most languages, can be used to refer to the same speech event.

3. Sequential structuring applies to a total discourse, whether an embedded quotation or a quotation together with its textual matrix, and shapes it into a coherent whole on these three dimensions: (*a*) reference, (*b*) attention or prominence, and (*c*) pragmatic effect or modality.

a. Reference includes devices to realize four linguistic functions: (1) Topicalization: What is being talked about? What is being said about it? Cashinawa has affixes to mark the topic in quotations and in their matrices; other devices include word order and dialogue paragraphing. (2) Delimitation: How detailed or how general is the quotation to be? (*See* §2 *above.*) Should something be left implicit or made explicit? (3) Identification of participants or events: How do you trace a participant through the vagaries of such grammatical structures as quote within quote within quote? Is this the same speaking event as that previously mentioned? (4) Information structure: Is this information assumed to be already known or new to the audience?

b. Attention has to do with whether or not a particular bit of information—a participant, an event, a description—is to have some kind of prominence in a particular segment of speech, from word and phrase to paragraph and total discourse. Information can be highlighted, backgrounded, or neutral. Quotations can be such a structural segment and can provide devices for highlighting or backgrounding information within the matrix text. Language devices can give prominence to participants, events, form, content, genre, style, etc. of a quotation.

c. Pragmatic effect affects quotation in terms of such features as the mode and intent of a quoted sentence (statement, question, command). The modal quality of a quotation may be modified pragmatically in terms of such factors as degree (insist, demand), certainty (really, doubtfully), speaker's responsibility and attitude toward what is said (hearsay, eyewitness, lying).

4. Appropriateness in quotation has to do with the social, interactional rules for language use; it is often implied in metalanguage meanings. Cultural judgments of effectiveness and rightness are tied to social meaning, to the speech expectations associated with specific cultural situations (testimony at a trial); with participants, their roles and status (terms of address—honorifics are universal); with their purposes (prophecy, exhortation) and tone (fearful, sincere); with the style level (formal, informal) and genre (riddles, letters, parables, sermons), etc.

5. Translating quotations—as well as nonquoted material—has as its goals accuracy of exegesis in the source language and naturalness in the target language, naturalness of form (grammatical and generic structures), of content (referential and social meaning), and of style (sentence length, levels of usage, frequencies, etc). Thus translation is a function of the language-specific kinds of quotation and sequencing systems, and culture-specific expectations on which appropriateness is judged.

Bibliography. J. Beekman, *Translating the Word of God* (1974); K. Callow, *Discourse Considerations in Translating the Word of God* (1974); R. Cromack, *Language Systems and Discourse Structures in Cashinawa*, Hartford Studies in Linguistics, No. 23 (1968); E. Nida and C. Taber, *Theory and Practice of Translation* (1969).

R. Cromack

DISCOURSE STRUCTURE. Communication through language, whether spoken or written, is a structured event; discourse structure is the way in which words, phrases, clauses, sentences, and whole compositions are joined to achieve a given purpose.

1. Universal features of discourse
   a. Markers for beginning and end
   b. Markers for internal transition
   c. Temporal relations
   d. Spatial relations
   e. Logical relations
   f. Successive references to the same objects, events, or qualities
   g. Foregrounding and backgrounding
   h. Author involvement
2. Factors involved in a discourse event
   a. Source (sender)
   b. Receiver
   c. Channel
   d. Form of the message
   e. Code
   f. Topic
   g. Context

Bibliography

1. Universal features of discourse. In a language that a person knows well, it is easy to distinguish between a well-constructed discourse and a badly constructed one, though he may not be able to give precise reasons for his intuitive judgments. A well-constructed discourse in any language must respect certain constraints, which give structure to the discourse. These constraints may be called universals of discourse. There are at least eight of them, and they fall into four categories. Some have to do with the discourse as a whole (§§*a, b*); a second category has to do primarily with events (§§*c–e*); a third grouping relates primarily to the objects within the discourse (§§*f, g*); and a final category relates to the attitude and viewpoint of the author (§*h*). Although these features of discourse are called universals, this does not mean that all languages make use of the same devices to express these universals. Moreover, a given device within a single language generally serves more than one function. Language is highly complex and flexible, and the essential differences between languages do not consist of what can be said, but of the manner in which things are permitted to be said.

a. Markers for beginning and end. The markers themselves often indicate the nature of the contents. In English a story that begins "Once upon a time" indicates that it is not true; and the reader will not at all be surprised if it ends, "And they lived happily ever after."

Similarly, the biblical languages have a multiplicity of patterns for the opening and closing of discourse, some of which are problematic to present-day readers because their structure seems unnatural. One such formula is "and it came to pass," which often leaves the reader with the question, "What came in order to pass by?" Luke is particularly fond of this phrase; he sometimes uses it to introduce or to conclude a narrative, or even to mark the climax or transition in a narrative. When translated into other languages it may be rendered in a number of different ways, depending on its function in the context and on the way that the receptor language marks that particular function. For example, "and it came to pass on another sabbath" (Luke 6:1) is used to introduce a narrative, and is translated simply "on a sabbath" by the RSV; while "and it came to pass, that as soon as the days of his ministration were accomplished" (Luke 1:23 KJV), which indicates the conclusion of a section in a narrative, appears as "and when his time of service was ended."

Occasionally, certain discourse units are characterized by a particular formulaic pattern at the beginning and the conclusion. Jesus' parables of the kingdom sometimes begin, "The kingdom of God (or heaven) is like . . ." But even this apparently clear and lucid statement may lead to a misunderstanding of the comparison intended in the parable. The meaning intended is, "It is the same with the kingdom of God (or heaven) as it is with . . ." So then, in Matt. 22:2 the kingdom of heaven is not like a king, but like the situation depicted in the wedding feast, and the parable may be introduced, "When God establishes his rule, the situation will be like that of a king who prepared a wedding feast for his son." *See also* Matt. 13:24, 45; 18:23; 20:1; 25:1.

b. Markers for internal transition. Some transitional expressions frequently used in English are, "On the other hand, however"; "The next day"; "Then suddenly"; and, "Not only that, but." Job 1:13-22 is an example of a text artistically woven together through the use of transitionals. Four times "and I alone have escaped to tell you" serves as the climax for one scene and the marker for the beginning of the new scene. In vss. 16-18 the transition to the next scene is indicated by "while he was yet speaking," which is replaced in vs. 20 with "then Job arose." The narrative has a double climax (the words of Job in vs. 21, followed by the comment of the narrator in vs. 22); in vs. 21 the transition to the climax is marked by "and he said," while in the next verse "in all this" serves the same function. Although I Kings is a separate book from II Samuel, it actually begins with a transitional marker, "Now King David was old," assuming King David of I, II Samuel as old information. Judges also begins with a transitional, which links the narrative with that begun in Joshua: "After the death of Joshua." On the other hand, Job opens as new information: "There was a man in the land of Uz, whose name was Job."

One of the most frequent errors made by translators is that of translating the Hebrew *wāw* and the Greek *kai* as "and" in their every occurrence. *Wāw,* when used as a transitional marker, may have many different meanings (e.g., "when," "so," "then," "thus," "although," etc.), and the translator should respect the meaning in the context rather than attempt verbal consistency throughout. In Mark 1 the RSV begins twenty-six sentences with either "and" or "and immediately," which gives the impression that the narrative may have been written for children. Another pitfall is the Semitic idiom "and behold," which is often used merely as an intensifier. The verb "he arose" (Heb. *qûm*) often simply is an auxiliary to the main verb. In the Gospel of John *oun* ("therefore," "then," "thus," "so") occurs more than two hundred times, often serving as a transition marker, but rarely needing to be rendered by any specific word in the receptor language.

c. Temporal relations. Temporal relations may be indicated (1) by temporal conjunctions (e.g., "after," "while," "when"), (2) temporal phrases (e.g., "the next day," "the following year"), (3) relative verb tenses (e.g., the future perfect and the past perfect), (4) sequence of tenses (e.g., "He said he did it" as opposed to "He said he was going to do it"), and (5) order of events, based on the assumption that unless otherwise indicated the linguistic order represents the historical order as well.

Note the problem of the sequence of tenses in John 4:45 (italics added): "So when he *came* to Galilee, the Galileans *welcomed* him, *having seen* all that he *had done* in Jerusalem at the feast, for they too *had gone* to the feast." The time of "came" precedes "welcomed," while "having seen" and "had done" precede in time both "came" and "welcomed," but "had gone" is chronologically prior to all events recorded, though appearing in final position in the sentence. For some receptor languages it may be necessary to restructure this verse somewhat as follows: "The people in Galilee had gone to the Passover feast in Jerusalem, and they saw everything that Jesus had done during the feast. So, when Jesus arrived in Galilee, the people there welcomed him." *See also* Mark 6:14-29 and John 1:32-33.

d. Spatial relations. The primary markers of spatial relations are three: (1) prepositions (e.g., "in," "at," "on," "under"), (2) expressions of distance (e.g., "a foot high," "three miles wide," "three days' journey"), and (3) verbs which imply direction or motion. Spatial relations may not appear to be problematic, but difficulties often arise. Sometimes the order of description may not be natural to the reader (e.g., the description of the size and shape of the altar in Ezek. 43:13-17; *see also* Jer. 52:21-23). On other occasions the writer of the biblical text shared with his readers information not known by present-day readers. The story of the rape of Tamar (II Sam. 13:1-22) presupposes certain basic information about the shape and construction of the room where the event took place. It would be helpful to know this, but it is not given, because the original readers knew these details. Occasionally a spatial relation is defined in an idiomatic way that is unusual to the reader. Such an expression is "a sabbath day's journey away" (Acts 1:12), which appears as "about half a mile away" in the TEV, and as "about a kilometer away" in a number of translations that use the metric system.

In a number of languages difficulties arise when verbs of motion are used, because the concepts of "going" and "coming" frequently require subtle shifts in verb usage, depending either on the real or assumed position of the narrator, or on some shift in focus. The gospel writers may say "Jesus went *up* to Jerusalem," because in the NT, as in the OT, going or coming *"up"* is the normal way of speaking of a journey to the holy city. However, in some languages one must first ask, "Is the writer assumed to be in or away from Jerusalem at the time of narration?" Only then may the decision between "went" and "came" be made in the receptor language.

e. Logical relations. Logical relations may be marked (1) by special kinds of "logical conjunctions" such as "moreover," "therefore," or "nevertheless"; (2) by conjunctions which introduce dependent clauses (e.g., "if," "because," "although"); (3) by the use of verbal forms such as participles, which indicate dependency; and (4) by lexical units (e.g., "that is why he behaved that way"; "he concluded").

A logical relation that is clear in the source language may not always be clear in the receptor language, unless the form is completely restructured. For example, a literal translation of the last part of John 5:13 ("for Jesus had withdrawn, as there was a crowd in the place") makes a misunderstanding possible. This could intimate that Jesus left because of the crowd. NEB avoids this ambiguity by translating "the place was crowded and Jesus had slipped away," making clear that the presence of the crowd made it possible for Jesus to slip away. A literal translation of a verse as John 5:16 ("And this was why the Jews persecuted Jesus, because he did this on the sabbath") is awkward in many languages, including English. "And this was why" is actually redundant information and may be omitted. For some languages it may even be necessary to place the cause or reason before the result, so one must translate, "Because Jesus did this on the sabbath, the Jews began to persecute him." Cf. John 5:18.

f. Successive references to the same objects, events, or qualities. This may be done in at least the following ways: (1) by the use of pronominal references (e.g., "he," "she," "it"); (2) by the use of references that point back (e.g., "this," "that"); or (3) by the use of synonyms (e.g., "Mary . . . his wife . . . that woman").

Pronominal ambiguities are abundant in many translations. Occasionally the receptor language requires a pronoun where the biblical text has a noun, but more often the problem is that the biblical text uses a pronoun where it is more natural to use a noun in the receptor language. In the Markan account of the healing of the epileptic boy (9:14-29) Jesus is referred to by a pronoun at least nine times before being mentioned by name in vs. 23; whereas in many languages it would be more natural to mention him by name first and then follow with pronominal references. Note also the problems in a passage like John 12:39*b*-41:

For Isaiah again said,
"*He* has blinded their eyes and
hardened their heart,
lest they should see with their eyes
and perceive with their heart,
and turn for *me* to heal them."
Isaiah said this because *he* saw *his* glory and spoke of *him*.

In vs. 38 the Lord (God) was mentioned in a scripture quotation, but there is no marker to indicate that he is now being referred to by the pronouns *he* and *me* of vs. 40 (except for the quotation marks); and, although Jesus is mentioned in the larger context, there is no grammatical marker to suggest that *his* and *him* of vs. 41 refer back to Jesus, while *he* of the same verse is a reference to Isaiah.

g. Foregrounding and backgrounding. In any account not all the participants and events are of equal importance. In a number of languages the matter of who or what is in focus is as basic as the question, "Who did what, where, and when?" So then, the translation of an apparently simple sentence like Acts 12:13 ("And when he [Peter] knocked at the door of the gateway, a maid named Rhoda came to answer") may become quite complex, if it is necessary to know the event or person in focus—whether Peter, the maid, the act of knocking, the act of coming to answer, or the name of the maid.

The matter of focus is handled in a number of different ways: by the position of a lexical item in the discourse; by the shift from active to passive (or vice versa); by the use of intensifiers (e.g., "I myself" as opposed to "I"); by the use of particles; by the use of a separate lexical item for the subject in languages such as Greek and Hebrew which include the subject in the verb form; by unusual word, clause, or sentence order; by repetition; by ellipsis; by "flashbacks," etc. However, a construction indicating emphasis or focus in one language may operate precisely the opposite way in another language. According to the Hebrew mind the use of parallelism in poetry not only added to the poetic beauty, but it added stress as well. But in some languages the use of this type of parallelism is regarded as unnecessarily repetitious, and so has the opposite effect.

h. Author involvement. The author's involvement may be indicated in one of two ways: (1) autobiographical (whether real or unreal), through the use of first person pronominal forms; or (2) judgmental, as in Job 1:22 ("In all this Job did not sin or charge God with wrong").

A noted example of the author's involvement through the use of first person pronominal forms is found in the so-called "we-sections" in Acts, where the writer suddenly shifts from the third to the first person in his narrative (16:10-17; 20:5-15; 21:1-18; 27:1–28:16). Some scholars question whether Luke was actually present during these events, or whether he simply used the "we" forms to add vividness to his account. But in any case, the author evidently intends for his readers to assume that he was present, and so the first person form should be maintained in translation.

Even though the prophetic books represent a long history of editorial work, the use of the first person form for the prophet is an essential feature of some books (e.g., Ezekiel; Dan. 7–12). In lengthy, disconnected passages where there are a large number of unmarked participants there occasionally appears a prophetic oracle or prayer in the first person; in such passages it is good to set this off by a section heading and maintain the first person form for vividness. However, especially in narrative sections, some languages may more naturally shift to the third person, where the Hebrew has the first, or from the third person to the first, depending on the context. Changes in either direction should always be made on translational grounds, either for the sake of making sense or of marking participants, and never for dogmatic reasons, as, for example, with translations which shift into the first person "I" for the beloved disciple of John 21.

The Gospel of John is notorious for the way in which the author shifts from the speaker's words to his own comments without indicating this shift for the reader (e.g., 3:14-21). In such cases the translator must follow the exegesis which he believes is best and open and close the quotations accordingly.

2. Factors involved in a discourse event. The structure of a given discourse is determined not only by the constraints imposed on it by the nature of language itself (that is, by the universals of discourse), but by certain other factors operative in all communication events. Every discourse is tied to a specific historical and cultural context, and so there are certain nonlinguistic factors which must be taken into consideration when attempting to understand the structure and meaning of any discourse. These may be termed "nontextual" or extralinguistic factors, as opposed to the "textual" or linguistic features termed universals of discourse, and there are at least seven.

a. Source (sender). In every communication event it is helpful to know such details as the age, sex, nationality, educational background, motives, and attitude of the person who is the source of the discourse. And, where books have a long history of editorial reworking, it is useful to know all the information possible about the person or persons involved at the various stages of revision, especially about the final editor or editors, for this information also gives clues to understanding the structure of the discourse. *See* REDACTION CRITICISM, OT[S]; REDACTION CRITICISM, NT[S].

To understand a writer's purpose it is necessary to understand the manner in which he used the sources available to him, that is, the way in which he structured his writing. The structure of the Gospel of Matthew is not the same as that of Mark, for example, but the structure of each book gives important clues to the intention of the author, and consequently, to a "picture" of the author himself. Through a careful study of the book's structure valuable insights may be gleaned about the author that will help in the interpretation of his writing.

b. Receiver. It is just as valuable to have information about the recipients of a message as it is to have information about the source. We possess certain general information about the intended recipients of the biblical writings—the OT books were directed to the Jewish community of faith, while the NT books were written for the Christian community. But it is important to have more specific knowledge about the recipients of each individual writing. For example, the psalms date from different situations and periods in Israel's history; and the prophetic books in their present form represent a long history of editorial work, in the course of which time oracles dating from later periods have been included. Jesus' parables were spoken to one audience during his ministry, but they appear in different settings in the various gospels, because the audience has changed. The persons to whom James addressed his words about "faith and works" are not the same people to whom Paul wrote about the relation between "faith and works"; and, indeed, the "works" which James demands of his readers are not the same as those "works" which Paul so ardently opposes.

c. Channel. The channel or medium of communication may be of various types (e.g., radio, television, books, newspapers, etc.), but here we are concerned solely with a written medium, that is, with the scriptures. Several problems emerge. In certain cultures the concept of sacred literature is foreign, and people learn primarily through the practice of ritual, not by being instructed through the use of a written medium. Other problems arise because the scriptures are now appearing in different formats, such as cartoon-style adaptations; while still other problems relate to the production of selections and portions in which a passage is removed from its setting and linked with a group of other passages, either on thematic or other grounds. Care must be taken not to skew the focus and intent of the original author, or else the altered channels may result in a distortion of the message.

d. Form of the message. The form of the message is a vital factor in any communication event; but a given form in one language setting may not carry the same emotive impact that it does in another linguistic and cultural context. Traditionally translators have attempted to reproduce the Hebrew poetic form wherever it occurs in the Hebrew text, without asking whether or not that particular form is appropriate for the subject matter in the receptor language. In the OT, poetry was used to express prophetic messages of warning or doom, as well as instruction and philosophical reflection; but for the contemporary English-speaking community these same forms would be inappropriate for this subject matter, and in most situations would receive a negative reaction. On the other hand, the poetic form is still considered appropriate for themes of love and of mourning for a comrade lost in some tragedy, as well as for hymns and songs of private and public worship.

Another form that needs some attention is the LETTER form of the NT. The Pauline correspondence, e.g., follows the letter form of the first century; but the letter openings and closings in particular do not awaken for the contemporary reader the same emotions that these same forms would have aroused for first-century readers. Attention must be given to the fact that the letter is a total discourse unit, and that meaning (especially the emotive impact conveyed in the letter opening) has priority over form.

The Bible also contains forms not found in some other cultural settings. One of these is apocalyptic literature, as represented by Daniel 7–12 and by the book of Revelation (*see* APOCALYPSE, GENRE[S]; APOCALYPTICISM and APOCALYPTICISM[S]). Consideration must be given to ways in which the contemporary reader can realize the purpose and intent of the apocalyptic form and avoid the extremes of faulty interpretation.

The gospels (*see* GOSPEL, GENRE[S]) have frequently been misunderstood because they have some of the formal features of a biography, and so have been interpreted in this light. The Hebrew tradition of expressing religious truths through the medium of the narrative form, especially when combined with their freedom in weaving together various strands of tradition, has been a source of concern for the careful and devout reader, who assumes that he is reading an account such as he might find in a history textbook.

e. Code. The code used in the Bible is in the form of Hebrew and Greek, and, in a few places, Aramaic. These languages, like all other languages, have unique features which may be disturbing to the person who is not familiar with their structure and idiomatic expressions. Long and complex sentences are frequent, both in the OT and in the NT. Examples could be multiplied, but note Ezek. 34:7-10*a,* which takes sixteen lines in the RSV, 18:5-9, eighteen lines, and Rom. 1:1-7, which extends through twenty lines. Since Hebrew prefers direct discourse to indirect discourse (*see* DISCOURSE, DIRECT AND INDIRECT[S]), the result is often a series of quotations within quotations, as in Jer. 7:1-4. This is particularly disturbing in languages which mark direct and indirect discourse in ways different from Hebrew. Rhetorical questions are misleading in languages which do not use them, but sometimes also even in languages as English, where they are used. For this reason, they sometimes are better translated as statements. (Compare "For to what angel did God ever say . . . ?" (RSV) with "Nor did God say to any angel . . ." (TEV) in Heb. 1:5). Biblical languages sometimes use constructions in which words linked by "and" are not really in a co-ordinate and balanced relation as the construction implies, but rather are essentially one thought. For example, "wicked and sinners" (KJV) of Gen. 13:13 means "wicked sinners," while "spirit and life" (RSV) of John 6:63 would be better rendered as "(God's) life-giving Spirit." NT Greek frequently uses nouns where verbs, or noun-verb constructions, are more appropriate in the receptor language (e.g., Mark 1:4, "a baptism of repentance for the forgiveness of sins"). Biblical idiomatic expressions may sometimes be confusing or completely misinterpreted when a literal translation is given (e.g., "horn of my salvation," Ps. 18:2; "Do not lift up your horn," Ps. 75:4; "make a horn to sprout," Ps. 132:17). Occasionally mixed figures are used, and need to be restructured entirely, as TEV has done in Jer. 48:11. Although all language codes are different from one another, whatever can be said in one language can also be said in another language, if the unique features of each language code are respected.

f. Topic. The topic of a discourse is important, since at the discourse level form and content are closely related. Certain subject matter may be well suited for one form, while quite unsuited for another. The apocalyptic form is a much more dynamic way to depict the demonic forces that threaten God's people than is the form of a philosophical essay. And the problem of the suffering of the righteous comes through more dramatically in the dialogue form selected for the book of Job than it would in an alternative form.

One of the aspects of topic in biblical literature that is confusing to the modern reader is the matter of sudden shifts without any overt markers to indicate the new subject matter. A hymn in the praise of wisdom suddenly interrupts the dialogues in the book of Job (ch. 28), and there is no grammatical marker to indicate the shift; and Psalm 19 deals with two distinct topics (vss. 1-6 and 7-14). Though the change of subjects is not so shaking as in Job, this is, nevertheless, helpful information for the modern reader to have, since the reading matter that he is accustomed to in daily life does not follow this pattern. Some passages in the gospels sound extremely strange, because Jesus suddenly changes from one subject to another for no apparent reason. If the Bible is to make much sense to today's reader, then thought must be given to the preparation of appropriate formats and of reader helps, as is being attempted in some of the modern translations.

g. Context. Every event is conditioned by the particular historical and cultural context in which it occurs; but the presuppositions of the reader are also conditioned by his contextual setting, and problems arise when the cultural presuppositions of the original context and of the reader are not the same. A reader who is not familiar with the OT account of Moses may well assume, on the basis of John 3:14, that Moses actually picked up a live snake with his bare hands! In the traditional translations of Gen. 1:2 the reader misses completely the picture in the mind of the writer, because "the waters" are mentioned as old information, without any indication of the relation between the water and the earth—whether the water is on it, under it, or surrounding it. This was information known and shared by the writer and his intended readers, but the world view of the modern reader makes it impossible for him to picture in his mind what was clear to the writer and the reader in the original context. In Jer. 23:23 the Lord sounds as if he is declaring himself to be a God who is far removed from the affairs of men ("Am I a God at hand, says the Lord, and not a God afar off?"), though the reader is helped some by reading the following verse. The meaning is that God is no insignificant deity, tied to a local sanctuary, but a God high in the heavens, who can look down and see all that takes place. The integrity of the original cultural context must never be compromised, but attention should be given to making the original setting clear for the modern reader, for whom the biblical setting may be quite foreign.

Bibliography. K. R. Crim, "Translating the Poetry of the Bible," *TBTr,* XXIII (1972), 102-9, "Hebrew Direct Discourse as a Translation Problem," *TBTr,* XXIV (1973), 311-16; H. G. Grether, "Translating the Questions in Isaiah 50," *TBTr,* XXIV (1973), 240-43; D. Hymes, *Language in Culture and Society* (1964), pp. 215-20; J. P. Louw, "Discourse Analysis and the Greek New Testament," *TBTr,* XXIV (1973), 101-18; B. M. Newman, "Some Suggested Restructurings for the New Testament Letter Openings and Closings," *TBTr,* XXV (1974), 240-45; E. A. Nida, *Toward a Science of Translating* (1964), pp. 206-13; E. A. Nida and C. H. Taber, *The Theory and Practice of Translating* (1969), pp. 121-62; H. M. Orlinsky, *Notes on the New Translation of The Torah* (1969), pp. 10-40; P. C. Stine, "On the Restructuring of Discourse," *TBTr,* XXV (1974), 101-6.

B. M. NEWMAN

***DIVINATION.** The art of determining the purposes, will, or attitudes of the gods. Whereas revelation means divine self-disclosure to men, the diviner always takes the initiative in discovering the import of divine communication (*see* REVELATION). The practice presupposes that the gods, or the god in a monotheistic religion, provide signs which, if interpreted properly, divulge something of divine intentions.

In general, divinatory methods in the ancient Near East may be divided into two categories. In the one, a diviner manipulates objects such as oil, water, or lots so as to derive the omens. In the other, he observes phenomena such as animal entrails or dreams that take place without any action on his part and interprets them as divine communication. Both methods involve the belief that man has certain power to influence his life. Omens consequently are warnings of impending disaster or indicate a choice between fortune and misfortune. It is not a question of inflexible destiny, but rather of an opportunity to engage in proper action so as to avoid calamity or remove conditions offensive to the gods.

Though diviners practiced their art in all areas of the ancient Near East, most of the extant literary remains derive from Mesopotamia of the second and first millennia. There are extensive texts, but owing to complex historical developments, technical vocabulary, regional preferences, and diverse techniques, we still do not know precisely how the diviner determined his verdict. Judging from the sheer numbers of omen collections, however, it must have involved sophisticated training and lengthy search for appropriate matching of phenomena with traditional interpretation. Later literary references have drastically simplified the procedures when they simply report that a king inquired of the gods through divination and received an answer. Aside from these references, we possess collections of omina typically consisting of a series of statements positing various associations between events: "If there is seen in a house the dead owner of the house, his son will die" (Saggs, p. 321). For oneiromancy (*see* DREAM): "If a man in a dream eats a raven (*arbu*), income (*irbu*) will come in. . . . If a man in his dream ascends to heaven, his days will be short. If he descends to the netherworld: his days will be long" (Oppenheim, *Dreams,* pp. 241, 267). In addition to these compendia, actual records of hepatoscopy, the most important means of divination for Babylonian and Assyrian kings, have survived. These texts typically enumerate the omens observed, record the verdict (favorable or unfavorable) and the subject of inquiry, sometimes cast in the form of questions put to the gods by the monarch. "Given: a liver part, a two-fold path, the left path lying upon the right path. The enemy will furiously vent his weapons over the weapons of the princes. . . . Five unfavorable signs here. Favorable do not appear. It is unfavorable. . . . Will he go, will he with warriors, troops of Ashurbanipal, wage armed conflict . . . fight with them? Not good" (Klauber, pp. 103-5).

Certain segments of Israelite society prohibited divination, or at least severely criticized its deficiencies (Deut. 18:14; Ezek. 13:4-7; 22:28). Yet the practices seem to have been diverse and rather more widespread than many earlier scholars would have admitted. The allusions in the OT are well known (*see* DIVINATION). In addition to leconomancy (divination by means of liquid in a cup; Gen. 44:5), belomancy (divination by means of arrows; Hos. 4:12), and oneiromancy (I Sam. 28:6; Gen. 37:5-11; 41:1-36), one hears of divining by observing the action of animals (I Sam. 6:7-12) or budding plants (Num. 17:1-11). The recent discovery of clay liver models at Hazor now makes it impossible to rule out hepatoscopy in Israel as well (cf. Ezek. 21:21-22). We know also of the chance oracle, corresponding to the Babylonian *egirrû* and Greek κληδών, from I Sam. 14:8-10, where Jonathan takes a remark by the Philistine guard as an omen (אות) that Yahweh has guaranteed victory for the Israelites (cf. Gen. 24:14; I Kings 20:33). The practice of necromancy is reflected in I Sam. 28. There, King Saul, wishing for some omen of the outcome of an impending battle, consults a medium (בעלת אוב, lit. mistress of the pit), who calls up from earth the departed spirit of Samuel. The word אוב means the divining pit from which spirits are summoned, but sometimes the necromancer (I Sam. 28:3, 9; Lev. 19:31), or the spirit itself (Isa. 29:4). It apparently has its background in Hurro-Hittite culture, and is cognate with Hittite *a-a-bi,* the pit from which the spirits rise. Similarly, Hebrew תרפים, some sort of object used in the mantic arts (Zech. 10:2; Hos. 3:4), now appears to be cognate with Hittite *tarpiš,* a spirit which on some occasions was thought to be benevolent, and on others malevolent. *See* TERAPHIM.

The best attested, and apparently officially sanctioned, technique of divination was ארים ותמים, the sacred lots cast by priests in Israel. (*See* URIM AND THUMMIN.) The *locus classicus* for this institution is Num. 27:21, where the priest Eleazar is authorized to inquire of God by the practice of Urim in a sanctuary. Ordeals by which a priest would determine guilt or innocence are surely related divinatory practices (Num. 5:14-30). *See* JEALOUSY, ORDEAL OF.

Prophets, too, practiced divination. Mic. 3:6-7 castigates the prophets of the eighth century for abusing their office. Because they speak comfort when their bellies are full and malevolence when hungry, they shall become confused: "It shall be night to you, without vision (חזון), and darkness to you, without divination (קסם)." Earlier texts portray a seer, or a "man of God," as the one to whom a man could go to "inquire of God" (דרש את-אלהים) or to seek an oracle of Yahweh. Similar expressions apply to Egyptian divination (Isa. 19:3) and necromancy in Israel (I Sam. 28:7). One would inquire about sickness (I Kings 14) or military crisis (II Kings 3), or a lost animal (I Sam. 9), and the like. The intent was for the seer to reveal the future or to deliver the decision of the deity in a specified situation. The practice may still be reflected in Ezek. 14 and 20. However, in Jer. 21:2; 37:3, 6, the phrase "inquire of Yahweh" already has come to mean intercessory prayer in times of distress. Similarly, Ezek. 14 and 20 have something to do with petition for relief in the despair of the exile; cf. Ezek. 36:37. After Ezekiel's time, we hear nothing more of prophetic divination in this form.

The only hint of the procedure followed appears in II Kings 3:15, where music and a suggestion of ecstatic experience accompany the prophet's answer. Seeing a vision was apparently involved as well. Vision (חזון) and divination (קסם) belong together in Mic. 3:6. Just as the necromancer "sees" the spirit of Samuel (I Sam. 28:13), so Elisha in response to an inquiry says "The Lord has shown me (הראני) that he [the king] shall certainly die" (II Kings 8:10). In a similar situation of prophetic inquiry, Micaiah ben Imlah responds with a full report of vision (I Kings 22:17-23).

It is no accident that something of this world of prophetic divination adheres to later reports of visions. Though many clearly function simply as prophetic announcement, their inner logic recalls the presuppositions of the diviners. Amos "sees" a supramundane scene of destruction and immediately responds as though it were an omen, a portent of a future event in the mundane realm (Amos 7:1-6; cf. Ezek. 9:1-9). The vision of Amos 8:1-2, though mainly carrying a direct word from God, develops from a rather fortuitous linkage with a visionary object and predicts a future state of affairs (קיץ, a summer fruit, suggested קץ, the "end" of Israel). In visions, what is seen by the prophet often is a sign for the future, just as in Mesopotamian omen series what is observed about animal behavior or dreams is interpreted by the diviner as a warning of something yet to materialize in the lives of men. Of course, visions were understood in Israel as the word of a free and transcendent Yahweh. This meant that the appropriate human response was worship and petition, not prophylactic ritual as in Babylon.

Bibliography. A. Caquot, ed., *La Divination* (1968); H. A. Hoffner, "Hittite Tarpis and Hebrew Teraphim," *JNES,* XXVII (1968), 61-68, "Second Millennium Antecedents to the Hebrew *'ôb,*" *JBL,* LXXXVI (1967), 385-401, and *TWAT* (1970), 141-45; E. G. Klauber, *Politisch-religiöse Texte aus der Sargonidenzeit* (1913); Recontre assyriologique internationale, XIV, *La divination en Mésopotamie ancienne et dans les régions voisines* (1968); W. Z. Lauer, *La divinazione nel VT* (1970); E. Lipiński, "Urim and Tummim," *VT,* XX (1970), 495-96; B. O. Long, "The Effect of Divination upon Israelite Literature," *JBL,* XCII (1973), 489-97; A. L. Oppenheim, *Ancient Mesopotamia* (1964), pp. 206-27, *The Interpretation of Dreams in the Ancient Near East* (1956), and "A Babylonian Diviner's Manual," *JNES,* XXXIII (1974), 197-220; H. W. F. Saggs, *The Greatness That Was Babylon* (1962); F. Schmidtke, "Träume, Orakel, und Totengeister als Kunder der Zukunft in Israel und Babylonien," *BZ,* XI (1967), 240-46; H. Tadmor and B. Landsberger, "Fragments of Clay Liver Models at Hazor," *IEJ,* XIV (1964), 201-17.

B. O. Long

DIVINE MAN. The term θεῖος ἀνήρ originated in the Hellenistic world as a designation for a truly wise man, whose wisdom manifested a perception of and a harmony with ultimate reality. Both historical (e.g., Socrates) and mythological (e.g., Apollo) figures were accorded this status, and in the third and fourth centuries A.D. Iamblichus, Diogenes Laertius, and Porphyry portray Pythagoras as the model divine man. How accurately these late traditions represent an earlier divine man conception cannot be determined.

At the beginning of our era, and largely in Egypt, attempts were made to demonstrate the divinity of kings (e.g., Augustus, Alexander) and wise men by attributing to them prescience or miracles. At the same time, among the educated classes, the divine man was regarded as a paragon of virtue and wisdom. Lucian of Samosata (second century A.D.) satirizes attempts to blend these two traditions (e.g., *Lover of Lies; Alexander the False Prophet*) and draws on popular MIRACLE STORIES for evidence of what he regards as the ridiculous claims made on behalf of such charlatans.

In Hellenistic Judaism, and above all in the works of PHILO, OT worthies such as Moses, Enoch, Melchizedek, and Elijah came to be viewed as belonging to a special category of humankind. Thus, for instance, Moses (called ἄνθρωπος θεοῦ, a "man of God," in the LXX [e.g., Deut. 33:1]), is honored by Philo (*Life of Moses*) as a paradigm of obedience and having special access to the divine will. His being taken up to God at his death is regarded as a resolution of soul and body into pure mind; but the biblical accounts of Moses' miracles are explained either rationally or allegorically by Philo and are not integrated into Moses' divine man role.

Some scholars (Hadas, Smith) have held that the gospels present Jesus according to the divine man model. Others have argued that a divine man Christology was championed by certain opponents of Mark (Weeden) or Paul (Georgi). Yet firm documentation of the concept in Christian or pagan literature of the first century A.D. is lacking, and in the Gospel of Mark (*see* MARK, GOSPEL OF §9*b*) Jesus' miracles are valued, in accord with Jewish apocalyptic views, as signs of the inbreaking kingdom.

See also MIRACLE WORKERS[S]; ARETALOGY[S]; SIGN IN THE NT[S].

Bibliography. H. D. Betz, "Jesus as Divine Man," in *Jesus and the Historian,* ed. F. T. Trotter (1968); L. Bieler, ΘΕΙΟΣ ΑΝΗΡ (1935 [repr., 1967]); D. Georgi, *Die Gegner des Paulus im 2.Korintherbrief,* WMANT, XI (1964); M. Hadas and M. Smith, *Heroes and Gods: Spiritual Biographies in Antiquity,* Religious Perspectives, XIII (1965); H. C. Kee, "Aretalogy and Gospel," *JBL,* XCII (1973), 402-22; T. Weeden, *Mark—Traditions in Conflict* (1971).

H. C. KEE

***DIVINERS' OAK** [אלון מעוננים, *'ēlôn me'ôn^{e}nîm*]. There is some uncertainty with regard to the species of tree involved. Some scholars favor the translation OAK, but others prefer TEREBINTH. The newer Hebrew dictionaries cautiously assign the meaning "mighty tree" to Heb. *'ēlâ, 'ēlôn,* and *'allôn.* However, texts like Isa. 2:13; 6:13; 44:14; Ezek. 27:6; Hos. 4:13; Amos 2:9; Zech. 11:2 prove beyond doubt that at least *'ēlâ* and *'allôn* must be specific tree names. It is fairly certain that *'allôn,* like its Akkad. cognate *allānu,* is the oak. The hardness of its wood is alluded to in Amos 2:9. According to reliable ancient traditions *'ēlâ* (pl. *'ēlîm,* Isa. 1:29; 57:5; 61:3) is the terebinth. It is much more difficult to establish the meaning of *'ēlôn.*

The *'ēlôn m^e'ôn^{e}nîm* of Judg. 9:37 was situated in the vicinity of Shechem. This tree should be distinguished from the oak that stood *in* Shechem. The latter is meant in Judg. 9:6, where we have to read *'allôn* with LXX, and in Josh. 24:26 (cf. 24:25) where it is called *'allâ.* The conspicuous tree outside Shechem, however, was an *'ēlâ* according to Gen. 35:4. This would seem to indicate that *'ēlôn* and *'ēlâ* were very much alike. Josephus' statement that the *'ēlôn* near Hebron (Gen. 13:18, etc.) was a very old terebinth (War IV.ix.7) points in the same direction. Apparently both *'ēlâ* and *'ēlôn* were members of the pistachio family. The very old and isolated tree called *'ēlôn* could be the *Pistacia atlantica,* var. *latifolia,* which sometimes attains a height of fifty to sixty-five feet. The lower tree or shrub called *'ēlâ* may be the *Pistacia terebinthus* L., var. *palaestina,* which does not rise above twenty-three feet. The latter is an important associate of oaks in the maquis on hills (cf. Hos. 4:13; the same combination occurs in an Assyrian text: 4R 56, III.37=KAR 239, II. 13).

Gen. 12:6 mentions an *'ēlôn môrê* near Shechem (cf. Deut. 11:30). Because it is hardly believable that this would be a third well-known tree in the same area, *'ēlôn môrê* or "the Teacher's Terebinth" might be a later, less offensive Israelite name for the *'ēlôn m^{e}'ôn^{e}nîm,* "the Diviners' Terebinth." Hab. 2:18-19 suggests that an idol could be called a "teacher" by its worshipers. (On speaking idols, see the parallels collected by J. Cerny, *BIFAO,* XXX (1931), 491 ff.; O. Kaiser, *ZRGG,* X (1958), 193 ff.)

Holy stones and trees (*see* ASHERAH §3) were often found together in ancient Canaanite and pre-Israelite places of worship (e.g., Exod. 34:13; Deut. 7:5; 12:2-3; Josh. 24:26). According to the Canaanites of Ugarit, stones and trees were able to murmur messages (*CTA* 3:C.19-20; *PRU,* II, 1:Rev.7, 12-13). Similarly, the Greeks, consulting the oracle of Dodona, heard their fortune told in the rustling of leaves and branches. Thus it may well be that the diviners of Canaan obtained oracles through their holy stones and trees. In Mic. 5:12-14 [H 11-13] the diviners, the holy stones, and the Asherim are mentioned in the same breath.

It is possible that, at an early stage of Israelite religion, DIVINATION by means of rustling trees was not regarded as pagan. David got the signal to attack the Philistines from the sound of footfalls in the tops of *bākhâ*-shrubs (II Sam. 5:24). It may be significant that this shrub is another member of the pistachio family (*Pistacia lentiscus* L.).

Bibliography. W. W. Baudissin, *Studien zur semitischen Religionsgeschichte,* II (1878), 184-230; M.-J. Lagrange, *Études sur les religions sémitiques* (2nd ed., 1905), pp. 169-80; J. G. Frazer, *Folk-Lore in the OT,* III (1919), 46-54; I. Löw, *Die Flora der Juden,* I (1928), 192, 622; IV (1934), 28, 416; F. Stummer, "Convallis Mambre und Verwandtes," *JPOS,* XII (1932), 6-21; G. Greiff, "Was war ein elōn?" *ZDPV,* LXXVI (1960), 161-70; J. A. Soggin, "Bemerkungen zur alttestamentlichen Topographie Sichems," *ZDPV,* LXXXIII (1967), 189-91, 194-95; M. Zohary, *Flora Palaestina,* II (1972), 296-99.

J. C. DE MOOR

***DIVORCE.** The officially recognized dissolution of a marriage. It is this element of official recognition by the society which, in some societies, distinguishes divorce from casual separation.

1. Initiative. In OT law, the initiative in instituting divorce proceedings lay entirely with the husband (Deut. 24:1-4). There is no hint of a divorce being initiated by a wife. This is in keeping with the double standard which characterized Israel as well as most of its contemporaries in the Mediterranean region.

The ELEPHANTINE PAPYRI, reflecting various foreign influences in a later period (sixth century B.C.), do seem to permit a wife to initiate a divorce. But in the reports of the teachings of Jesus in the Synoptic gospels (Matt. 19:9; Mark 10:11-12; Luke 16:18), only Mark mentions the possible initiative of a wife; this provision probably reflects a foreign influence. As for Paul, he seems to consider, in the Gentile context, that divorce would be legally available to a wife (I Cor. 7:10-11), but that a Christian wife should not divorce a non-Christian husband (or vice versa); though RSV translates χωρίζω in vs. 10 as "separate" and ἀφίημι in vs. 11 as "divorce," the distinction cannot be pressed, since both terms are used in the papyri to refer to divorce.

2. Grounds. The only legal passage in the OT which refers to grounds for divorce (Deut. 24:1-4) is extremely vague: "if then she finds no favor in his eyes because he has found some indecency in her, . . ." This, as is well known, gave rise to a prolonged debate between rabbinic schools of thought in later generations. One school interpreted this condition so broadly as to include incompetent cooking; the opposite school understood "indecency" to refer only to infidelity. The term ערוה means literally "nudity," and is often used to refer to a shameful uncovering of the genitals, especially the female genitals; it is therefore used by extension to refer to sexual intercourse, especially in contexts where illegitimate intercourse is meant (Lev. 18:7-19; also Gen. 9:22-23), as in incest or homosexuality. However, the legal texts uniformly prescribe the death penalty for voluntary infidelity, whether of wife or fiancée (Lev. 20:10; Deut. 22:22-24); divorce is not mentioned in these contexts. A fiancée raped under circumstances where she could not obtain help was judged to be innocent (Deut. 22:25-27), but it is not said what her fiancé could or should do about it. Similarly, if a man at the time of the consummation of his marriage accused his bride of not being a virgin, her parents were bound to provide the proof of her virginity in the form of a blood-stained cloth. If they were able to do this, the husband was fined one hundred shekels, whipped, and forbidden to divorce his wife forever. However, if the parents were unable to furnish proof of their daughter's virginity, she was to be stoned (Deut. 22:13-21). In the case of a husband's suspicion of adultery without proof or witnesses, the wife underwent a trial by ordeal (Num. 5:11-31; *see* ORDEAL, JUDICIAL[S] §3). The consequences for a wife found guilty were pain, swelling of the body, an unspecified ailment of the thigh, and execration by the people; whether or not this brought about death or entailed the death penalty is not specified. In other words, it is not at all clear under what circumstances a wife or fiancée could be unfaithful and yet incur only divorce.

However, the accounts of actual cases seem to indicate a much greater degree of flexibility in practice than the law suggests. In the case of David's adultery, the consequences were that the first child he had from Bathsheba died (II Sam. 12:11-18); it is also said that the subsequent sordid history of the offenses of David's sons was linked to David's sin; in other words, there were penalties short of death, and these were inflicted directly by divine intervention, not by society. Likewise, Hosea took the option of initially divorcing his unfaithful wife (if we understand Hos. 2:2*b* as a statement, as in RSV, rather than as a question, as in NEB), though he later forgave her and took her back. It may be thought, however, that his conduct was atypical, as the conduct of the prophets often was, precisely to the extent that it was intended as a jolting object lesson to Israel; so that we may not rest too strongly on Hosea as an example of normal conduct.

Undoubtedly, in earlier times, adultery on the part of the husband was not cause for divorce by the wife, because it was considered that the person offended by a man's adultery was not his wife, but the husband of his partner in adultery. It must not be thought, however, that a man could commit adultery with impunity or with general approval. Later writers especially urged husbands to be faithful to their wives as such, not just to avoid the revenge of a cuckolded husband.

There were two situations in which a man could never divorce his wife: the case when she was exonerated of his charge of nonvirginity (Deut. 22:13-19) and the case when he was forced to marry her after raping her (Deut. 22:28-29).

In the later years of the OT period it became increasingly frowned upon to divorce one's first wife (Mal. 2:14-16); this attitude continued into NT times, so that in spite of the rabbinic debate, by the first century A.D. divorce was generally instituted only for infidelity (Matt. 1:19). This is reflected in the Matthean version of Jesus' words on the subject (Matt. 5:31-32; 19:1-9), but not in the versions in the other Synoptics (Mark 10:1-12; Luke 16:18), possibly because they were written for Gentiles whose standards of reference were different. Paul (Rom. 7:1-3) says that in Jewish law a woman had no option to divorce, but says nothing about the husband's option. In the other extended passage about marriage and divorce (I Cor. 7), he says that neither partner, if a Christian, should initiate divorce; but that the Christian partner in a mixed marriage could not prevent the non-Christian from doing so.

3. Procedures. The only relevant passage again is the legal one (Deut. 24:1, quoted in Matt. 5:31; 19:7; Mark 10:4). The rule was that the husband must give his wife a document which spelled out the fact that she was divorced and hence free of any claims he might have upon her. Another passage (Hos. 2:2*b*) gives a formula which may have been used in such a document. This paper was, of course, an advantage to the wife, since she now had proof of her freedom.

4. Remarriage. The law said (Deut. 24:2-4; cf. Jer. 3:1) that a woman properly divorced was free to marry another man. However, if her second husband died or divorced her, she was not free to remarry her first husband. Two cases might be cited as counterexamples, but in fact they are not. Though Saul had given his daughter Michal, David's wife, to another man (I Sam. 25:44), David never divorced her, and so was legally justified in taking her back (II Sam. 3:13-16). Hosea, though he had divorced his wife, could take her back because she had not formally married another man in the meantime.

4. Conclusion. It is generally agreed that divorce was never frequent among the Hebrews. Since the family unit was so important, its stability was most carefully defended, and the fidelity of both husband and wife was highly valued (Prov. 6:20-35). In other words, the realities of interpersonal relationships and of concrete social pressures went a long way to mitigate the apparent permissiveness of the law. *See also* SEX, SEXUAL BEHAVIOR[S].

Bibliography: *See bibliog.* for MARRIAGE[S].

C. R. TABER

DOCUMENTARY HYPOTHESIS. *See* SOURCE CRITICISM, OT[S]; SYNOPTIC PROBLEM; SYNOPTIC PROBLEM[S].

***DOCUMENTS.** *See* YAHWIST[S]; ELOHIST[S]; PRIESTLY WRITERS[S].

***DOLMENS.** The name is derived from two Old Breton (French) words: *dol*=table, *men*=stone. Originally applied to man-built structures of which the simplest form resembles a massive stone table consisting of two heavy, unworked blocks with a third placed horizontally across them (a simple trilithon), the term was subsequently applied to more complicated structures.

In the nineteenth century, travelers and explorers in the Holy Land were struck by the many "rude stone monuments" they encountered, and it was natural that they should describe them by the word with which they were familiar. This does not necessarily imply that there is a direct connection between the dolmens of Europe and those of the Near East or elsewhere, although such a hypothesis cannot be ruled out.

1. Diffusion. Dolmens are found throughout widespread regions of the Near East, especially on the high plateau lands which lie E of the Jordan Rift and between it and the desert. These and other forms of megalithic tombs are likewise known from other parts of the world, including North Africa, South Russia (Caucasus), and Europe. Relatively few are known from W Palestine, mostly in the N. The majority of those recorded are located in northern Moab, Gilead, Bashan, and the Golan, where hundreds and thousands of dolmens of various shapes and sizes are concentrated in what are known as dolmen fields. Throughout the ages these imposing piles of stone have attracted attention and aroused curiosity. Many were disturbed in antiquity by would-be treasure hunters; in many instances they were re-used as tombs in later periods. Dolmens are a prominent feature of the landscape, so that succeeding generations living in their vicinity cannot but have been aware of their existence. Thus it may well be that the biblical references (Deut. 2:10-11, 20-21) to various tribes of half-legendary tall people, collectively referred to as ANAKIM or REPHAIM (Heb. "giants"), reflect a folklore which grew out of the desire to explain the huge megalithic structures. It is interesting to note a similar tendency in modern times: many dolmen fields and other megalithic remains are known today as *qubur bani Isra'il* (Arab. "the tombs of the Children of Israel").

2. Structure and size. Eleven different types of dolmens have been distinguished, with many intermediate or hybrid forms. Regardless of size, the chamber is usually rectangular in plan—sometimes square or trapezoidal. The dolmen is built in dry-stone technique of large blocks of unworked stone, each of which has been carefully selected in accordance with its function in wall or roof. The orthostatic wall stones are placed side by side, varying in size according to the dimensions of the chamber. This is usually closed at one end by a single transverse block, the entrance being at the opposite narrow end, sometimes preceded by a short approach corridor. Some dolmens are closed at both ends, entry being by means of a narrow passage which runs below the tumulus (cairn) and opens into one of the long walls. In some closed dolmens in Transjordan, entry was effected through "porthole" apertures cut in one of the short sides. In most dolmens the floors are paved and the roofs constructed of one or more heavy slabs placed horizontally, either directly upon the wall blocks or on the uppermost wall course laid above them. The roof stones are placed either side by side or rest partially one upon the other. Sometimes they rise in step-like tiers so that the roof, forming a corbeled ceiling within, towers about the whole structure (Fig. D5). Dolmens were built of the natural rock which lies strewn over the surface. Their position was determined by the facility with which the heavy stones could be moved, taking into account the natural contours of the terrain, rather than, as has been suggested, by considerations such as their proximity to water or orientation toward the sun's rays at specific times of the day or seasons of the year.

The chamber of a medium-sized dolmen is some 11½ feet long, 5 feet wide, and 5 feet high; but many are considerably larger, having a total length of 24½ feet and more, other measurements being in proportion. There are also many small trilithons (open at both ends) built of two basic wall stones and a single heavy roof block. This type of structure is usually set up on the surface with no more than a hint of a surrounding tumulus or encircling outer wall.

Courtesy C. Epstein

5. Large dolmen with towering roof. Note tumulus wall courses behind the measuring stick.

The dolmen is frequently surrounded and partially hidden by a tumulus built of piled-up stones, having an outer ringwall of larger stones laid in distinct courses. The size of the tumulus is usually determined by the size of the dolmen and in most cases it is considerably larger. A tumulus may be 65 feet in diameter and built to a height of some 6½ feet above the surrounding terrain. Most have a flattish surface above, which reaches to the top of the dolmen roof and is often partly visible. Sometimes an additional, nonfunctional capstone is added to the dolmen, doubtless to mark the position of the structure below. The tumulus was intended not only to cover and screen the dolmen, but also to stabilize the heavy pile which was frequently set on a slope.

3. Function and date. For many decades opinions of scholars were divided regarding the function of the dolmen, but today it is generally accepted that it served as a tomb. Since there are no remains of associated houses in the vicinity of the dolmen fields, the indications are that the dolmens were built by pastoral nomads who roamed the steppe lands between the desert and the sown areas, each tribe erecting a specific type of dolmen in accordance with age-old custom. There was far greater controversy regarding the date of the dolmens: Albright, followed by Glueck, considered that they were preceramic in date, while Stekelis and others were of the opinion that they should be dated to the latter half of the fourth millennium B.C. Until recently relatively few structures had been excavated, yielding for the most part inconclusive evidence. During the last few years excavations in some thirty dolmens situated in six different sites in the Golan have brought to light datable funeral gifts which had originally been placed on the paved floor within. The assemblages, which were found together with disarticulated bones indicating secondary burial, include pottery vessels, weapons, and personal ornaments (many of the latter being of copper) dating to Middle Bronze I (also known as the Intermediate EB-MB period). Since this is the earliest material found in these dolmens, it can be deduced that they were built in this period, during the last quarter of the third and the very beginning of the second millennia B.C. It is, however, possible that some may have been built by related tribal groups a little earlier. But it is significant that no older material has been found in the excavated structures. A re-examination of the reports of artifacts found during the past hundred years or so in dolmens which were cleared in a less scientific manner has revealed material which can be similarly dated.

It was during the MB I period that the major walled towns in W Palestine were destroyed by seminomadic tribes who only gradually became sedentary. These tribes are known chiefly from the shaft tombs which they laboriously cut into the rock below ground, these being of different shapes and sizes, indicating differences in tribal customs. The extensive effort required suggests that great importance was attached to the final burial place. In many of them no complete skeletons were found, there being, rather, scattered bones from a secondary burial, round which a few pots had been placed together with weapons and personal ornaments, many of them made of copper. The similarity of the burial practices in the dolmens and the shaft tombs is striking, and both date to the same period. It would thus appear that there is a connection between them. In both, secondary burial is found, this being common among nomadic groups; both are characterized by comparatively few grave goods, and these often include metal objects with a high percentage of copper, indicating that they were the work of people well-versed in metallurgy. The essential difference between them was determined by the nature of the terrain where they were situated. In the areas which extend E and especially NE of the Jordan, which are characterized by the ubiquitous basalt whose volcanic hardness makes it difficult to work, the traditional form was the dolmen. Further W, where softer rock is found, the shaft tomb below ground took the place of the megalithic structure. At the same time it should be noted that the existence of dolmens built of limestone both E and W of the Jordan (e.g., in Galilee) indicates that age-old traditions died hard and were only gradually superseded.

For another type of dolmen *see* DOLMEN, Fig. 35; *see also* TOMB[S].

Bibliography. G. Schumacher, *Across the Jordan* (1886), pp. 65-69, 149-50, *The Jaulan* (1888), pp. 123-28; C. R. Conder, *The Survey of Eastern Palestine* (1889), pp. 126-33, 159-71, 188-89, 202-3, 229-36, 254-74; G. Schumacher, *Northern 'Ajlun* (1890), pp. 131-34, 169-77; P. Karge, *Raphaim* (1925), pp. 315-20, 412-63; F. Turville-Petre, "Dolmen Necropolis near Kerazeh, Galilee," *PEFQS* (1931), 155-66; M. Stekelis, *Les Monuments Mégalithiques de la Palestine* (1935), "Megalithic Culture," in *Encyclopaedia of Archaeological Excavations in the Holy Land* (in preparation); N. Glueck, *Explorations in Eastern Palestine, IV, AASOR*, XXV-XXVIII (1951), *passim;* W. F. Albright, *The Archaeology of Palestine* (1960), p. 64; C. Epstein, "Golan," *IEJ*, XXIII (1973), 109-10, "The Dolmen Problem in the light of recent excavations in the Golan," *Eretz Israel*, XII (1975), Hebrew with English summary.

C. EPSTEIN

***DOMINION OVER CREATION.** In the OT, the idea of human dominion over the creation appears in Gen. 1:26-28; 9:1-7; and Ps. 8:6-8 [H 7-9]. This idea, especially as expressed in Gen. 1:28, has recently become controversial in the debate over ecology. Some suggest that the biblical text encourages a sense of human detachment from, and superiority to, nature; this sense has entered the consciousness of the West and become the cause of uncontrolled technological advance whose baleful consequences we now see (White). Others reply that this is a false understanding of a biblical text which plainly sets dominion in the context of universal harmony and goodness, in which the human vocation is care and responsibility for nature. This controversy provides an appropriate framework for interpretation of the texts. What is meant by dominion, and is it lost in the FALL?

Gen. 1:26-28 uses two words for human dominion: רדה for the relationship to animate beings (reading in vs. 26, with the Syriac, "wild beasts" for "earth," to restore the animal list of which vs. 28 gives a truncated version) and כבש for the relationship to the earth. רדה in the OT most often refers to the rule of a monarch. כבש means "subdue, bring into bondage," with strong connotations of force, and often refers to the conquest of lands in war. Vocabulary, therefore, suggests humanity's rule to be in general that of a monarch, and specifically coercive. This agrees with the understanding of the IMAGE OF GOD accepted by many, that its conceptual background is the ancient Near Eastern belief that the monarch is the representative of the ruling deity. Futhermore, the link between dominion and "filling the earth" suggests that humanity's rule grows and develops in history. In summary, Gen. 1:26-28 enjoins humanity to impose its kingly rule more and more widely.

Thus understood, this text is at odds with its context. The large picture of harmony, completeness, and goodness agrees poorly with subjugation. In particular, the implied injunction to vegetarianism in vs. 29 sets an unexpected and stringent limit to human dominion. If we move into the separate creation account of ch. 2 we find stress on human oneness with the earth (vs. 7) and responsibility for its keeping (vs. 15). Gen. 1:26-28 has on other grounds, including stylistic, been regarded as an addition to the six-day creation, presumably replacing a briefer account of the creation of people. It is plausible to see the dominion formulations as serving to link the story of the creation of humans with its context, by ascribing rule over the animals created on the fifth and sixth days. As we now have it, Gen. 1 presents a dialectical tension between dominion over nature and harmony with it.

Gen. 9:1-7, stemming like 1:26-30 from the P source (*see* DOCUMENTS; PRIESTLY WRITERS[S]), is closely related to it; but the divine injunctions after the Flood are different. Dominion is not mentioned in Gen. 9:1-7; instead people inspire "fear" and "dread" in animals (vs. 2). Does this suggest that the primal "dominion" has been replaced by a less harmonious relationship between humanity and nature? Probably not. רדה and כבש, as noted above, are not appropriate words to express harmony, and in any case their omission from Gen. 9:1-7 is probably due to textual error, since the emendation ורדו for ורבו in vs. 7 is widely accepted (e.g., JB and NEB). Genesis therefore does not imply that human dominion, any more than the divine image, was lost in the Fall.

Ps. 8:6-8 [H 7-9] agrees closely with Gen. 1 in its view of dominion. Royal ideology is very clear ("crown," vs. 5 [H 6]; "put under one's feet"). The extent of human dominion is even wider in the psalm, covering "all things." But the suggestion of triumphant subjugation of nature is absent. The psalm does not use רדה or כבש, but the more general word for ruling, משל. It speaks of a single event of enthronement, rather than the giving of an ongoing injunction to rule. And it maintains a dialectic between divine and human rule, between human greatness and smallness, similar to the tension between Gen. 1:26-28 and its context.

The NT alludes only rarely to the OT theme of dominion over creation and almost always implies that it is lost or lacking in the present. Two minor exceptions are Rom. 1:23—idolatry is doubly foolish when practiced by those to whom everything has been subjected—and Jas. 3:7-8—those who can control everything else cannot control themselves. Most allusions are christological. Ps. 8:6*b* [H 7*b*], "Thou hast put all things under his feet," is referred to in I Cor. 15:27; Eph. 1:22; Phil. 3:21; and I Pet. 3:22. Early Christians linked these words with Ps. 110:1 to express Christ's victory over the cosmic powers of evil (*see* ANGEL; DOMINION; POWER §5*b*; PRINCIPALITY). Some have linked the power (ἐξουσία) of the Son of man in the Synoptic gospels with the "son of man" in Ps. 8:4 [H 5]. But this link is tenuous, since "son of man" in Ps. 8 is a figure of weakness, and nowhere do the gospels explicitly relate Jesus' power over nature to the dominion theme of the OT.

Two NT passages are important. Rom. 8:20 speaks of the "subjection" of creation to futility, and it is most tempting to see this as a combination of Gen. 1:28 and 3:17: subjection to humanity became, through the Fall, subjection to futility. Paul goes on to declare that this subjection will be reversed through human salvation in Christ. Heb. 2:5-9 quotes a large section of Ps. 8 (curiously omitting vs. 6*a* [H 7*a*]) and argues that, since present human experience does not bear out what the psalm says about dominion, it must seek its fulfillment elsewhere, and is, in fact, fulfilled in the victory of Christ.

Early interpretation of the OT texts did not see in them a charter for technological advance, but held that dominion was one of the gifts lost to humanity through the Fall. Many Christian interpreters drew on Greek philosophy and much preferred the theism of the Stoics, with its harmony between gods, people, and nature, to the view of the Epicureans that these entities are at enmity and that human "progress" is a successful overcoming of restrictions placed upon humanity by malevolent gods. Only much later, in medieval and modern times, has the link been regularly made between Gen. 1:28 and human progress.

The dominion formulations in Gen. 1:26-28 might in isolation be interpreted as allowing unrestricted human use, even abuse, of the earth and its creatures. But in the immediate context this rule is part of a universal divine hierarchy and harmony, people being charged with peaceful coexistence with, and responsibility for, nature. Gen. 1 and Ps. 8 in their present form present a dialectical tension between humanity's supreme dignity over and radical oneness with the rest of creation. The fate of the created world depends on humanity's situation before God, a theme further pursued especially in Gen. 3:17-19 and Rom. 8:19-23.

Bibliography. D. T. Asselin, "The Notion of Dominion in Genesis 1-3," *CBQ*, XVI (1954), 277-94; P. Trible, "Ancient Priests and Modern Polluters," *Andover Newton Quarterly*, XII (1971), 74-79; L. White, "The Historical Roots of Our Ecological Crisis," *Science*, CLV (1967), 1203-7; H. Wildberger, "Das Abbild Gottes: Gen 1, 26-30," *Theologische Zeitschrift*, XXI (1965), 245-59, 481-501.

D. JOBLING

***DOR.** For new information on Dor, *see* J. Leibovitch, "Dor," *IEJ*, I (1950-51), 249, and "The Reliquary Column of Dor," *Christian News from Israel*, V, nos. 1-2 (1954), 22-23; G. Foerster, "Dor," *Encyclopedia of Archaeological Excavations in the Holy Land* (1970), pp. 130-32, Hebrew.

***DUMAH (CITY).** The Judean site is at Deir ed-Dômeh, to the E of the town of Dûmā.

Bibliography. M. Kochavi, "The Land of Judah," *Judaea, Samaria and the Golan, Archaeological Survey, 1967-1968* (1972), pp. 21, 74, Hebrew.

A. F. RAINEY

DURA-EUROPOS. *See* ART, EARLY JEWISH[S].

E

EBIONITES. *See* Poor[S]. §4.

***ECCLESIASTES. 1. Critical positions.** The present consensus is that the book is the product of an urbane Jewish sage living in Jerusalem between 350 and 250 B.C., writing in Hebrew. He was well acquainted with the cosmopolitan currents of the Hellenistic world, but was essentially located in his own Jewish culture. That his work has received modest editorial alteration is also generally assumed, though the extent of that activity remains debated.

2. Literary structure. Analysis of the formal structure of the book remains a vexing problem. Careful attempts to detect some inner unity have been made from both literary and form-critical approaches (*see* Form Criticism, OT and Form Criticism, OT[S]). Though the issue remains un settled and the form-critical approach shows signs of bearing fruit, all efforts to show a logical sequence have attained only partial success. Within smaller units logical sequences do obtain, but taken as a whole, the book does not seem susceptible of such formal analysis. There does seem to be, however, an inner unity to the book which can be discerned from the thought or mood of the author.

3. Problems of interpretation. One of the major problems is the book's deviation from the mainstreams of OT faith and religion. Though there is no single theology of the OT, two features permeate the diverse strands of the biblical outlook: (*a*) God was active in history, indeed history was the primary medium of the disclosure of his will and purpose, and (*b*) there was a divinely given law, conformity to which resulted in the blessings of God for the community and also for the individual. In a later period this second affirmation was understood by some to apply not only to a revealed law but also to an understanding of the orders of the world which could be learned by human experience. This approach shifted the locus of the requisite norms, but did not alter the fundamental truth that certain forms of behavior did cause certain results. Koheleth, as the writer of Ecclesiastes is known, forthrightly denies the validity of such explanations.

The writer stands squarely within the wisdom tradition, employing the methodology of empirical observation, rational analysis, and reflection upon available phenomena. Things must be so to be true. But his observations, analyses, and reflections led him to conclusions diametrically opposed to the official religion. For instance, he categorically denies that the regularity observed in nature should lead one to trust the God/Providence behind that regularity (1:5-9; 11:3-8). Nor does any meaning appear in the historical process (1:4, 10-11; 4:13-16; 6:10-12; 9:13-15); the events of history are ephemeral and soon forgotten. It simply is not true that the good are rewarded and sinners punished (7:15; 8:10-11, 14; 9:1-3). If nature, history, and law are of no avail, what then of wisdom?

Koheleth was a sage. Would not, then, wisdom avail when other legitimations of society proved lacking? Not so! To be sure, wisdom was better than folly (2:13), but in the final analysis, even wisdom is only proximate (2:14-16; 7:23-25; 8:16-17; 9:1-6) and can provide no ultimate meaning to life. Other sources of meaning are suggested: pleasure (2:1-8), companionship (4:9-12), one's own work (5:18-20); yet finally each of these is nothing but vanity and a striving after wind. Some things *are* better than others; the wise and prudent man chooses the better, but in the long run, it really doesn't make any difference. Everything is transitory, everything adds up to zero. In sum, Koheleth hated life (2:17; 4:2-3; 6:3-6), but he did not counsel suicide. Why?

The one thing to which Koheleth could hold on was life itself. Many passages which are sometimes considered "pious" interpolations seem to indicate that he recognized that though life might not in the long run be much, it was our only possession, so it should be lived fully (2:24-26; 5:18-20; 8:15; 9:4-10; 11:7; 12:1-8). Some of these passages may be editorial additions, and many of them temper the admonition to enjoy life with the reminder that such enjoyment is temporary, but taken together they indicate that Koheleth, lacking a philosophy of life, could still teach a philosophy for living. This philosophy was not resigned hedonism; its basis was theological and existential. God existed, and man existed, and the purpose of religion is to bring these two existences into some meaningful relationship.

The religious teachings of his day were too superficial for so consistent a thinker as Koheleth. Wisdom and righteousness did not necessarily lead to a good end. Caprice and chance (*see* esp. 2:14; 3:19; 9:2, 3, 11) affected human lives just as much as obedience to the law or attention to the counsels of the wise. God was not present in history; he simply did not care. He had become the omnipotent determinative power, the great amoral Personality. The ideological world of Koheleth had become too small for the larger questions he was forced to ask. He could only conclude that all was enigma and mystery (3:11). Consequently, Koheleth must be seen as a skeptic and even a pessimist. The fact of death overrides all proximate values (2:15-16; 3:19-22; 6:12; 9:2-6, 11-12; 12:7). Wealth, wisdom, pleasure, and progeny are all swept away by the immutable fact of death, which renders all human strivings, acquisitions, and even dreams empty and vacuous.

4. Estimate of the book. How then do we interpret the over-all message of Koheleth within the context of the biblical tradition? One solution has been to suggest that he represents a completely aberrant, individualistic point of view. If this is so, we may read him with interest, but need not weary ourselves overmuch with attempting to relate his thinking to the biblical tradition as a whole. Others, both ancient and modern, have proposed that the real value of the book is that it teaches the emptiness of life without a firm faith in God. In this sense, it is almost a "messianic prophecy," calling men to the Redeemer who will lift them beyond the seeming antinomies of existence. Another modern interpretation is that Koheleth represents the bankruptcy of humanistic, secular wisdom, and calls the wisdom movement back to genuine Yahwism, which is its source. Either or both these points of view may possess truth; but, it seems possible to approach the enduring value of the book from a different perspective. All too often "religious" people tend to overlook the painful discrepancies between their faith and the facts of life. Koheleth reminds us all that religious affirmations which cannot be looked at squarely, with honesty and integrity, will not finally sustain us in the vicissitudes of life. He raises with vigor and precision the very questions which must be asked. One need not share his answers, stemming from his lack of an answer, but beliefs which avoid his questions are revealed again and again as shallow, if not false.

Even for those who do not share either Koheleth's views or those he contradicts, the book remains a source of wonder and delight. The hauntingly beautiful phrases, the cynical and ironical deflating of beliefs too easily held, and the heartfelt sorrow for a world gone sour continue to stimulate and irritate all who look beneath the surface. *See also* WISDOM IN THE ANCIENT NEAR EAST[S]; WISDOM IN THE OT[S].

Bibliography. Excellent references to the latest periodical material may be found in the notes in von Rad and Crenshaw (*see below*).

E. Bickermann, *Four Strange Books of the Bible* (1967), esp. pp. 139-67; *The Five Megilloth and Jonah,* ed. H. L. Ginsberg (1969), esp. pp. 52-78; E. Good, *Irony in the Old Testament* (1965), esp. pp. 168-95; R. Kroeber, *Der Prediger* (1963); D. B. Macdonald, *The Hebrew Philosophical Genius* (1936), esp. pp. 68-93; J. Paterson, *The Book That Is Alive* (1954), esp. pp. 129-50; G. von Rad, *Wisdom in Israel* (1972), esp. pp. 226-39; R. B. Y. Scott, *Proverbs-Ecclesiastes,* ABi (1965); J. L. Crenshaw, "The Eternal Gospel (Eccl. 3:11)," in *Essays in Old Testament Ethics,* ed. J. L. Crenshaw and J. T. Willis (1974), pp. 25-55; J. Priest, "Humanism, Skepticism and Pessimism in Israel," *JAAR,* XXXVI (1968), 311-26; A. Wright, "The Riddle of the Sphinx: The Structure of the Book of Qoheleth," *CBQ,* XXX (1968), 313-34.

J. F. PRIEST

***ECCLESIASTICUS.** Study of the text of Ecclesiasticus has entered a new phase in recent years with added discoveries of Hebrew fragments, with critical editions of the Greek and Latin texts, and with the first publication of a Hebrew concordance.

1. Hebrew fragments. Of these, the most important are those recovered at MASADA in 1964, containing portions of 39:27–44:17 from a scroll written in the early first century B.C., thus about a hundred years after the composition of the book. These fragments give impressive testimony to the general faithfulness and integrity of the grandson's (Greek I) translation and to the basic authenticity of the medieval Hebrew copies recovered earlier in MSS A to E from Cairo. At the same time they help to illustrate the many accidents of transmission and instances of deliberate paraphrase into a later and more colloquial form of Hebrew that have infected all later copies, including the archetypes for all existing translations. (*See* MANUSCRIPTS FROM THE JUDEAN DESERT §§2*c,* 4.) This is true to an even higher degree of the text of 51:13-20, 30 found in the early first century A.D. Psalter MS from Khirbet Qumran (11QPs[a]). This is from the alphabet-acrostic poem with which Ecclesiasticus ends; its first half is preserved in the Qumran MS in a sound and dependable text. By contrast, the Hebrew text of this poem in Cairo MS B is in especially poor condition and is rather generally viewed as having been partially retranslated from the Syriac some time after A.D. 800. Also from Khirbet Qumran is a fragment that furnishes the ends of lines from 6:20-31 in a copy from the late first century B.C. (*see* Baillet). This MS was written, like that from Masada and the Cairo MSS B and E, in a stichometric arrangement with two cola, or half-lines, of Hebrew verse making up each line in the copy. In 1958 and 1960 a few additional leaves of the medieval MSS B and C were identified at Cambridge by J. Schirmann (*see* Di Lella). While these several sources do little to fill the lacunae in the Hebrew text as previously known, they do permit critical scrutiny of that text and its versions to proceed with greater assurance and clearer perspectives.

2. Greek and other versions. Control of the Greek evidence has been amplified and enhanced by Ziegler's critical edition, which supplies both Greek I and its later reworking (Greek II) in a carefully established text with extensive collations. Convergent evidence of early recensional activity on the Greek rendering of the OT books of the Hebrew canon has come to light with the progress of publication of DSS fragments in both languages (*see* DEAD SEA SCROLLS[S] §2; GREEK VERSIONS, MINOR[S]). This confirms the dating of the secondary materials of Greek II of Ecclesiasticus, with Kearns, to about 70-60 B.C. The Old Latin text as it appears in the Vulgate has also been critically edited of late; but in this direction there is no doubt much to be gleaned from the broader collations of the *Vetus latina* project at Beuron, still awaiting publication. There is perhaps less to be hoped for from further critical work on the Syriac of this book. An edition combining full running texts of the Hebrew (basically from I. Lévi), the Greek (Ziegler's), the Latin (from the Benedictine Vulgate), and the Syriac (from P. Lagarde) has been published by Vattioni. While this is a useful working instrument, its Hebrew and Greek readings need careful verification before they can be accepted as definitive.

3. Exegetical and translation problems. The improved textual evidence for the acrostic poem in 51:13-30 has led Sanders, in publishing 11QPs[a], to a reappraisal of this composition. He finds it highly erotic in tone; and not for that reason, but because of its appearance in a "Davidic" compilation, he denies that Ben Sirach is its author. In the first of these evaluations a number of writers concur. It is possible, however, to see the poem as much less perfervid in its imagery than this view would have it; and the links with the authentic work of Ben Sirach are quite substantial (*see* Skehan). The many problems surrounding the text of Ecclesiasticus have led translators to opt for divergent approaches to the book. Thus while RSV, NEB, and the JB reflect the Greek of the grandson's translation, with the added material from Greek II in the footnotes, the NAB and the Italian translation by Duesberg and Fransen work out from the Hebrew wherever possible and use the versional evidence primarily as an aid to reconstructing or supplemeeting that basic text.

Bibliography. M. Baillet *et al.*, *Les 'petites grottes' de Qumrân, DJD,* III (1962), *Textes,* pp. 75-77, and *Planches,* Pl. xv; D. Barthélemy, O. Rickenbacher, *Konkordanz zum hebräischen Sirach* (1973); *Biblia sacra juxta latinam vulgatam versionem ad codicum fidem,* XII: *Sapientia Salomonis; Liber Hiesu filii Sirach* (1964); A. A. Di Lella, *The Hebrew Text of Sirach* (1966), and "The Recently Identified Leaves of Sirach in Hebrew," *Bibl.,* XLV (1964), 153-67; H. Duesberg, I. Fransen, *Ecclesiastico,* La sacra Bibbia, ed. S. Garofalo (1966); C. Kearns, "Ecclesiasticus," *A New Catholic Commentary on Holy Scripture* (1969), 541-62; H. P. Rüger, *Text und Textform im hebräischen Sirach, BZAW,* CXII (1970); J. A. Sanders, ed., *The Dead Sea Psalms Scroll* (1967), pp. 74-77, 112-17, "The Sirach 51 Acrostic," *Hommages à André Dupont-Sommer* (1971), pp. 429-38, and "The Qumran Psalms Scroll (11QPs^a) Reviewed," *On Language, Culture and Religion: In Honor of Eugene A. Nida* (1974), pp. 88-95; P. W. Skehan, "The Acrostic Poem in Sirach 51:13-30," *HTR,* LXIV (1971), 387-400; J. Strugnell, "Notes and Queries on the Ben Sira Scroll," *Eretz Israel,* IX (1969), 101-19; F. Vattioni, *Ecclesiastico* (1968); Y. Yadin, *The Ben Sira Scroll from Masada* (1965); J. Ziegler, *Sapientia Jesu filii Sirach,* Septuaginta, XII, no. 2 (1965).

P. W. SKEHAN

EDEN ē'dən [עדן]. Three separate Aramean entities appear under this name in the OT.

1. In Ezek. 27:23, Eden, one of the trading partners of Tyre, is generally recognized to represent Bit-adini of Neo-Assyrian records. Formed *ca.* 1000 B.C. by an Aramean tribe, but retaining the use of Hittite hieroglyphs, the state of Bit-adini was located on both sides of the great bend of the Euphrates and controlled its crossings. Its capital was Til-Barsib (Tell Aḥmar); for its extent and the major towns, *see* HITTITES[S] and the map. It was conquered and annexed to Assyria by Shalmaneser III between 857 and 855. A plausible conjecture emends ארץ בני-עמו, "land of the sons of his people," the location of PETHOR (Num. 22:5; RSV "the land of Amaw") to ארץ בני-עדן, "land of the Adini tribe." *See* BETH-EDEN.

Bibliography. *DPaR* (1920), pp. 25-26; R. Dussaud, *Topographique histoire de la Syrie* (1927), pp. 462-64; F. Thureau-Dangin and M. Dunand, *Til-Barsib,* 2 vols. (1936); W. F. Albright, "The Home of Balaam," *JAOS,* XXXV (1915), 386-90.

2. In Amos 1:5, "the scepter-bearer of Beth-eden" (בית-עדן) in the oracle against Damascus clearly designates the king of that state. Beth-eden cannot refer here to the remote Euphratean Bit-adini (*above*), which does not fit into an utterance about Damascus and, moreover, ceased to be a state more than a hundred years before Amos' prophecy. Note that Ezek. 28:13-16; 31:3-18 placed "Eden, the garden of God" in the Lebanon, i.e., on the western border of Damascus (cf. the Wadi Brisa inscription of Nebuchadnezzar II: "the Lebanon, the [Cedar] Mountain, the luxurious forest of Marduk"); local medieval traditions regarded the Anti-Lebanon, N of Damascus, as the site of the Garden of Eden.

Bibliography. A. Malamat, "Amos 1:5 in the Light of the Til Barsip Inscriptions," *BASOR,* 129 (Feb. 1953), 25-26, a different interpretation from the one proposed above; *ANET* (2nd ed.), p. 307 (Wadi Brisa inscription); G. Le Strange, *Palestine Under the Moslems* (1890), pp. 252-53, 259.

3. In Isa. 37:12 (=II Kings 19:12), "the people of Eden who are in Tel-assar" (*see* TEL-ASSAR[S]) correspond to Bit-adini, a branch of the Aramean tribe of Bīt-Dakkuri in Babylonia. According to the Aramaic ostracon from Assur, אללי, Ululai (the Babylonian name of Shalmaneser V) drove away prisoners from בית עדן (Bit-adini). A letter from the time of Sargon II speaks of Bit-adini in Babylonia. Sennacherib lists Bit-adini among the participants of the Babylonian-Elamite coalition which opposed him at Ḫalule in 691 B.C.

Bibliography. *KAI,* no. 233; J. A. Brinkman, *A Political History of Post-Kassite Babylonia* (1968), p. 244; M. Dietrich, *Die Aramäer Südbabyloniens* . . . (1970), p. 11.

M. C. ASTOUR

***EDOM.** The original entry on Edom, while remaining substantially correct, needs modification in the light of recent biblical scholarship and field archaeology. It is not at all sure that the southern boundary of Edom was the scarp of the Neqb esh-Shtar; nor can the W or E boundaries be given with any accuracy in the absence of positive geographical features (such as the Wadi el-Ḥesa to the N). By Neo-Assyrian times, Edom's southern territorial limits must have extended as far as the N shore of the Gulf of Aqabah to include Ezion-geber (Tell el-Kheleifeh).

Literal interpretation of Gen. 36:31-39 would suggest that there were kings in Edom, thereby implying a settled, powerful kingdom between the thirteenth and eleventh centuries B.C. It might be more accurate, however, to regard them as tribal chieftains, particularly since the various kings mentioned in this passage are not referred to in later historical or prophetic writings. Also, apart from a reference to Edom and Seir (which many scholars consider to be synonymous) by Pharoahs Mer-ne-Ptah and Ramses III, there is nothing in New Kingdom period (*ca.* 1570-1075) records to suggest that Edom had any subtantial status as a kingdom, or indeed that it was a kingdom.

Although biblical passages referring to the Exodus (Num. 20:14-21; Deut. 2:29) suggest that by *ca.* 1250 Edom was a state with which to reckon, it is significant that there is mention neither of a specific king nor of a city in Edom. Furthermore, recent archaeological research has shown not only that there is no evidence prior to the end of the ninth century B.C. or the beginning of the eighth for capital cities, but also that there is none for any sedentary occupation in the thirteenth-eleventh centuries. Ezion-geber may have been a later Solomonic creation.

It has been suggested that much of Edom's importance at this time was a result of her mining activities in the Wadi el-Arabah and the Negeb, perhaps in association with the Kenites and Kennizites, the traditional smiths with whom the Edomites (Gen. 36:11, 42) had close ties.

Recent excavations have demonstrated that it was the Egyptian pharoahs from Seti I (1302-1290) to Ramses III (1195-1164) who controlled the copper mines in the Negeb, perhaps with Kennizite, Kenite, and Edomite labor. The mines in this area were not exploited in Solomonic times, and this has brought into question the dating and interpretation of period I of EZION-GEBER. The idea of its being a Solomonic smelting center for the mines at Timna' has been rejected by the excavator (*see* TELL EL-KHELEIFEH[S]). It was, however, a center for finished objects to be transported by sea or overland (I Kings 9:26; 10:11, 22). The prosperity of Edom lay not in her control of the mines but of the caravan routes from India and South Arabia to Egypt. For this reason, Israel and Judah at various times campaigned against Edom and hence the see-saw of Edom's political fortunes.

Recent archaeological researches have necessitated some revision of previously accepted statements. According to II Kings 14:7, King Amaziah of Judah achieved a partial conquest of Edom as far S as Sela. The site of Sela has been identified as Umm el-Biyara, the rock massif overlooking Petra from the W. Excavations there, however, have proved an occupation in the mid-seventh century, at least one hundred years too late for Amaziah. A more suitable candidate for Sela is a village still bearing that name. *See* SELA (OF EDOM) [S].

Another identification frequently made is that of TEMAN with Tawilan, a modern village near Elji on the eastern outskirts of Petra. Excavations have uncovered a large, unfortified, prosperous, agricultural settlement of the Iron Age II period, but nothing to indicate its being the southern capital of Edom. De Vaux concludes that nowhere in the Bible is the word Teman used to designate a town. Rather, according to the etymology of the word, it applied to southern Edom, a sense which was perhaps kept in Ezek. 25:13. In other texts Teman had become a poetic designation for all of Edom. It is useless therefore to seek a specific site with which it may be identified.

Amos 1:12, when compared with 2:2, suggests that Bozrah is a town in Teman (part of the state of Edom), thus balancing Kerioth as a town in Moab.

Excavations NW of present-day Buseira have uncovered a large fortified town, which, in all probability, is to be identified with biblical BOZRAH. The absence of tangible evidence here for a settled kingdom in the mid-thirteenth century B.C. is worthy of note. The ancient site was a highly fortified city, with a casemate type city wall, encompassing an area of *ca.* nineteen acres (*see* BOZRAH IN EDOM[S]). Typical Iron Age II houses of the eighth and seventh centuries B.C. surrounded the acropolis or citadel. Buildings on the acropolis had been destroyed by fire and completely sacked, likely during the campaigns of Nebuchadrezzar. There is evidence of later Persian occupation and use of the site in Roman times. The archaeology of Edom accords much more happily with the later books of the Bible, reinforced by the Assyrian Annals, than it does with the earlier biblical books.

Bibliography. J. R. Bartlett, "The Rise and Fall of the Kingdom of Edom," *PEQ* (1972), pp. 26-37; C.-M. Bennett, "Fouilles d'Umm el-Biyara, rapport preliminaire," *RB*, LXXIII (1966), 372-403, "Ṭawilân (Jordaine)," *RB*, LXXVI (1969), 386-90 and LXXVII (1970), 371-74, and "Excavations at Buseirah, Southern Jordan," *Levant*, V (1973), 1-11; VI (1974), 1-24; VII (1974); R. de Vaux, "Téman, ville ou région d'Édom?" *RB*, LXXVI (1969), 379-85; M. Weippert, *Edom* (1972); B. Rothenberg, *Timna: Valley of the Biblical Copper Mines* (1972).

C.-M. BENNETT

***EGLON (CITY). 1. Tell 'Aiṭûn?** With the location of DEBIR at Khirbet Rabud in the hill country, Noth's suggestion to place Eglon at Tell 'Aiṭûn (Tel 'Eton), WSW of Lachish, becomes a serious possibility. This would give a more logical geographic sequence for Josh. 10:34-36, since Tell 'Aiṭûn is on the natural route from Lachish to Hebron. Tell 'Aiṭûn had Late Bronze as well as Iron Age occupation. Elliger was unaware of this when he proposed to identify Eglon with the slightly smaller Tell Beit Mirsim (Tel Mirsham).

Bibliography. K. Elliger, "Josua in Judäa," *PJ*, XXX (1934), 66-68; M. Noth, *Das Buch Josua* (2nd ed., 1953), p. 95; "Tell 'Aitun," *IEJ*, XVIII (1968), 194-95; V. Tsaferis and G. Edelstein, "Tell 'Aitun," *RB*, LXXVI (1969), 578-79; D. Ussishkin, "Tombs from the Israelite Period in Tell 'Eitun," in *Excavations and Studies*, ed. Y. Aharoni (1973), pp. 31-47.

A. F. RAINEY

2. Tell el-Hesi? The site was first excavated in 1890 by Petrie, who, on the basis of Arabic town names, identified the site as Lachish (*see* SITES, ANCIENT[S]). By relating the changing forms of pottery to the stratigraphy of the site, he laid the foundations of modern archaeology. In 1891-92 Bliss removed a third of the acropolis area, exposing eight cities with three subcities. When Tell ed-Duweir became equated with LACHISH, Hesī went nameless until W. F. Albright suggested that it was Eglon.

Since 1970 an interdisciplinary team has been investigating the thirty-seven-acre tell with its seven-acre acropolis. The four seasons (1970, '71, '73, '75) have concentrated on the acropolis, on a wall system at the base of the acropolis, and on a survey and probing of the larger tell.

On the acropolis five distinct phases have been identified. The first three are: recent military trenching activities from Turkish, Egyptian, and Israeli times; a phase of Moslem burials of which over four hundred complete or nearly complete burials have been removed for study; and an earlier Arab phase of poor remains, almost totally decimated by the burials. Phase 4 is Hellenistic, with three subphases. The two earlier subphases each had a substantial building, one of stone and one of mud-brick, and the earliest also had a fine associated drain and cistern. Phase 5, the Persian period, had four subphases, which promise to make an important contribution to this little-known period. The later three subphases are built around similar mud-brick wall lines and represent an early agricultural use period, a rebuilding period, and a late period of pit digging. The earliest Persian period is a major building phase when those at Hesī dug down through and removed earlier materials to found their own buildings on a strange pier system which Petrie called a "long range of chambers." This activity may be related to the Persian fortunes in Egypt.

The wall system at the southern base of the acropolis involves a double rebuilding of an earlier wall, most likely from the Persian period. The earliest wall had bonded to its interior face a series of piers on top of which was a mud-brick capping, forming a platform for additional living area or erosion control. The final rebuilt wall was forty feet wide, creating a formidable defensive system. Earlier walls have been identified but not excavated.

The survey and probes have indicated a gap in occupation in the Middle Bronze period (*see* ARCHAEOLOGY §F). The Early Bronze period is well represented by at least three phases in the lower city. After abandonment toward the end of the EB period, Hesī was refounded in the Late Bronze period on the acropolis, where it continued until Hellenistic times. This pattern is similar to that of other sites in southern Palestine where large EB populations also disappeared. Whether this was due to historical or environmental factors is a question which can only be answered by further investigation.

Little epigraphic material has been found and the identification of the site is still uncertain. Wright suggested that Hesī formed part of a defensive ring around Lachish, and Hesī does have many things in common with Tell ed-Duweir. However, especially in the Persian period, it shows affinities with Tell Jemmeh and Tell el-Far'ah (South), both of which were large grain storage areas. The lack of Philistine sherds raises questions about the control of the city during the period of the united kingdom of Israel.

Bibliography. W. F. Petrie, *Tell el Hesy (Lachish)* (1891); F. J. Bliss, *A Mound of Many Cities* (1894); G. E. Wright, "A Problem of Ancient Topography: Lachish and Eglon," *BA,* XXXIV (1971), 76-85; L. E. Toombs, "Tell el-Hesi, 1970-71," *PEQ,* CVI (1974), 19-31 and pls. I-VI; D. G. Rose and L. E. Toombs, "Tell el-Hesi, 1973 and 1975," *PEQ,* CVIII (1976), and "Tell el-Hesi, 1970-75," *AASOR,* XLIII (1976).

D. G. ROSE

***EGYPT, CHRONOLOGY OF.** The chronological scheme of Egyptian dynasties is an ancient device which was worked out by Manetho, an Egyptian priest, in the third century B.C. His thirty-one dynasties, spanning the time from the unification of Egypt (*ca.* 3000 B.C.) under Menes to its conquest by Alexander the Great (332 B.C.), are used by modern historians as a convenience and are utilized to form named periods which correspond with eras of flowering and decadence.

1. Determining dates. Like other peoples of antiquity, the Egyptians did not have a way of expressing dates in absolute terms but ordinarily dated official documents by the regnal year and the day of the season. The Egyptian year had three seasons, each with four months of thirty days. The 360 days were supplemented by five epagomenal days, which were regarded as birthdays of various deities.

A period of some 1,460 years, known as the Sothic cycle, was sometimes used to date historical references. This period was related to the heliacal rising of the Dog Star, Sirius, the Greek Sothis (Egyp. "Sopdet"). The divergence of one fourth of a day between the civil calendar of 365 days and the astronomical calendar meant that New Year's Day worked its way through the calendar, with an advance of one day every four years, so that in 1,460 years the calendar New Year again coincided with the rising of Sothis at dawn. The occurrences of Sothic dates enable astronomers to calculate absolute dates in terms of our modern calendar, so that we have a few astronomically fixed dates in Egyptian history.

In practical matters, such as agriculture, the Egyptians relied on the regularity of the Nile inundation, which afforded a seasonal calendar and provided the basis for naming the three seasons in agricultural terms.

2. The sources. Primary documents are numerous and diverse, but the most explicit and informative among them are lists of kings or of events which distinguished a regnal year in a sort of annal. They contain many errors, discrepancies, and variants, and give the names of a number of kings whose existence is not corroborated by monuments contemporary with them. The earliest of these lists is the Palermo Stone, which dates from the Fifth Dynasty. This monument, in the Palermo Museum, is incomplete, but another fragment of it is preserved in the Cairo Museum. An important hieratic list, the Turin Papyrus, comes from the reign of Ramses II (thirteenth century B.C.). Unfortunately, the papyrus was seriously damaged between the time of its acquisition and its study by Egyptologists. Restored as much as possible by competent papyrologists, the Turin Papyrus remains one of the basic works of Egyptian chronology in the Egyptian language.

Other valuable king lists have been found carved in stone on the walls of temples or tombs. Gardiner regarded as the most important of these the record found in the temple of Seti I at Abydos. Here Seti and his son, Ramses II, are shown venerating seventy-six of their royal predecessors, who are represented by cartouches bearing their names. The Sakkarah king list comes from a Memphite tomb dating to the reign of Ramses II. In the temple of Karnak there is a list from the time of Thut-mose III; it names kings not found in other lists, but as the order is incorrect, the usefulness of this record is limited.

The king lists exhibit certain peculiarities as to what was given or what was omitted. None of these lists gives the names of the Hyksos rulers (Fifteenth-Sixteenth Dynasties); they also omit the "heretic" Akh-en-Aton and his three immediate successors.

The chronicle of Manetho, from a much later time, exists only in excerpted form in still later works, such as Josephus (first century A.D.), Africanus (third century A.D.), Eusebius (fourth century A.D.), and Syncellus (*ca.* A.D. 800).

Chronicles, or annals, of individual kings, such as those of Thut-mose III in the temple of Karnak, not only provide information of historical interest but also help establish chronology. Any dated document or incidental record of date such as those written on dockets of storehouse jars may prove useful. They can, for instance, substantiate a date late in the reign of a king for whom the highest regnal year is in doubt. An imperfectly written or poorly preserved specimen of a date may be the basis for extended debate among chronologers.

Egyptian chronology receives some assistance from synchronisms, correspondences, or cross references from historical materials from other countries of the ancient world. The Amarna Letters, international treaties or agreements, and other records of diplomatic relations, business transactions, or military engagements supply chronological data which are useful in correlating events in various regions.

Although archaeology has often been the means of recovering dated monuments, archaeological finds aside from written records have not been as useful for the historic period in Egypt as they have been for other areas of the Near East. Due to the abundance of written remains from Egypt, pottery chronology, stratigraphy, and the newer techniques of the physical sciences give way to the more precise dates provided by the ancient documents.

Sothic dates are calculated from the writings of Censorinus, who recorded that a Sothic cycle began in A.D. 139. This would mean that previous cycles began in 1317 B.C. and in 2773 B.C. Hieroglyphic records refer to Sothic dates during the reign of Thut-mose III, and in year 9 of Amen-hotep I. A papyrus document from the Faiyum mentions a Sothic date in year 7 of Senusret III.

3. Chronological problems. Discrepancies, omissions, and other shortcomings in the king lists and other remains result in many difficulties for the chronologist. As one would expect, the data for the most stable periods are the most numerous, complete, and reliable, but for even the Eighteenth Dynasty there remain some widely argued issues (e.g., a possible co-regency between Amen-hotep III and Akh-en-Aton).

Times of instability or disintegration, commonly called "intermediate" periods, are obscure, records are confused, and documentation is inadequate. In spite of these problems, they have been the subject of intensive investigation. The Second Intermediate Period, comprising the Thirteenth-Sixteenth Dynasties, has been thoroughly studied by von Beckerath. More recently attention has been devoted to what is now called the Third Intermediate Period, the Twenty-first through Twenty-fifth Dynasties. Among those who have concerned themselves with this research have been Kitchen and Wente (particularly the Twenty-first Dynasty). Also significant is H. E. Winlock's *The Rise and Fall of the Middle Kingdom at Thebes,* which covers part of the First Intermediate Period and the entire Second Intermediate Period.

Generally, the more distant the time, the more imprecise and inaccurate are the dates. Dates after 690 B.C. and certain Middle Kingdom dates based on Sothic references (*see* §1 *above*) may be accurate to within one year. Before about 2200 B.C. the margin of error is roughly ± fifty years and the date for the beginning of the dynastic period (First Dynasty) still shows wide variation among historians.

4. Egyptian chronology and Bible history. Egyptian kings characteristically bore five titles and five names, of which the last two were most commonly used in official records. It is unfortunate for historians that biblical authors seldom referred to the Egyptian ruler by name, but simply spoke of him as "the king of Egypt" or as "Pharaoh." (The term pharaoh, meaning "Great House," was originally applied to the palace and later was transferred to the ruler, much as Sublime Porte in Turkey.) The few exceptions to this general rule occur in the later years of Israel's existence, during the divided kingdom.

The first Egyptian king mentioned by name in the Bible is SHISHAK (Sheshonk I) of the Twenty-second or Libyan Dynasty, who invaded Judah in the fifth year of Rehoboam (I Kings 14:25). This event can be dated to 926 B.C.

Another reference is to "Tirhakah king of Ethiopia" (II Kings 19:9; Isa. 37:9), who must be Taharka of the Twenty-fifth (Kushite or Ethiopian) Dynasty, although there seems to be problems of synchronism here.

A third Egyptian king named in the Bible is NECO of the Twenty-sixth (Saite) Dynasty, who came to help the Assyrians fight the Babylonians. King Josiah of Judah went out to oppose the Egyptian but was killed at Megiddo (cf. II Kings 23:29 ff.; II Chr. 35:20-24). Supported by documents from Mesopotamia, the date of this event can be fixed at 609 B.C.

The Egyptian king who was father-in-law to Solomon and who captured Gezer and presented it as dowry to his daughter (I Kings 9:16) cannot be identified with certainty, but must have been a king of the Twenty-first Dynasty.

The problem of the kings of the Oppression and the Exodus is far too vexing and complicated a matter for discussion here. There is great latitude in the dating of the Israelite exodus from Egypt, but the event must have fallen in the Eighteenth or Nineteenth Dynasty. *See* EXODUS, BOOK OF §2; EXODUS, THE[S].

The ruler of Egypt at the time of Abram's descent into that land (Gen. 12:10-20) cannot be identified either, but this is usually assigned to the time of the Middle Kingdom, although not to any specific king.

A reference to Egyptian chronology appears in Num. 13:22, "Hebron was built seven years before Zoan in Egypt," but this does not lead to a definite date, as the time of the founding of Zoan is not known.

Israel's close relationship with Egypt covered a number of centuries and led eventually to a sense of dependence upon Egypt during the later years of the Jewish monarchy. However, the chronological notices are few, so there is comparatively little Egyptian support for a definitive biblical chronology.

Bibliography. C. Aldred, *Akhenaten, Pharaoh of Egypt* (1968), "Two Monuments from the Reign of Ḥoremḥeb," *JEA,* LIV (1968), 100-106; J. von Beckerath, *Untersuchungen zur politischen Geschichte der Zweiten Zwischenzeit in Ägypten,* Ägyptologische Forschungen, XXIII (1964); F. Campbell, *The Chronology of the Amarna Letters* (1964): J. Černý, "Note on the supposed beginning of a Sothic period under Sethos I," *JEA,* XLVII (1961), 150-52, and "Three Regnal Dates of the Eighteenth Dynasty," *JEA,* L (1964), 37-39; H. W. Fairman, "A Block of Amenophis IV from Athribis," *JEA,* XLVI (1960), 80-82; A. H. Gardiner, *Egypt of the Pharaohs* (1961); J. R. Harris, "How Long was the Reign of Ḥoremḥeb?" *JEA,* LIV (1968), 95-99; H. W. Helck, *Die Beziehungen Ägyptens zu Vorderasien in 3. und 2. Jahrtausend v. Chr.,* Ägyptologische Abhandlungen, V (1962); E. Hornung, *Unter suchungen zur Chronologie und Geschichte des Neuen Reiches,* Ägyptologische Abhandlungen, XI (1964); M. F. Ingham, "The Length of the Sothic Cycle," *JEA,* LV (1969), 35-36; K. A. Kitchen, *Suppiluliuma and the Amarna Pharaohs* (1962), and *The Third Intermediate Period in Egypt (1100-650 B.C.)* (1973); J. Leclant, *Récherches sur les monuments thébains de la XXVe dynastie, dite éthiopienne* (1965); R. A. Parker, "The Calendars and Chronology," in *The Legacy of Egypt,* ed. J. R. Harris (2nd ed., 1971), pp. 13-26; D. B. Redford, "The Coregency of Tuthmosis III and Amenophis II," *JEA,* LI (1965), 107-22; *History and Chronology of the Eighteenth Dynasty of Egypt* (1967); M. B. Rowton, "Comparative Chronology at the Time of Dynasty XIX," *JNES,* XIX (1960), 15-22; T. Säve-Söderbergh and I. U. Olsson, "Dating and Egyptian Chronology," in *Radiocarbon Variations and Absolute Chronology,* ed. I. U. Olsson, *The Nobel Symposium,* XII (1970), 35-55; T. C. Skeat, "Notes on Ptolemaic Chronology," *JEA,* XLVI (1960), 91-94, XLVII (1961), 107-12; XLVIII (1962), 100-105; John Van Seters, *The Hyksos: A New Investigation* (1966); J. Vergote, *Toutankhamon dans les archives hittites* (1961); E. F. Wente, "On the Chronology of the Twenty-first Dynasty," *JNES,* XXVI (1967), 155-76; J. Yoyotte, "Les principalites du Delta en temps de l'anarchie libyenne," in *Mélanges Maspero* I, 4 (1961), 121-81.

C. DeVries

***EGYPTIANS, GOSPEL ACCORDING TO THE.** *See* Apocrypha, NT[S]; Nag Hammadi[S] §3.

***EKRON.** Identification with Khirbet el-Muqanna' (Tel Miqne) is confirmed by the presence of an extensive Byzantine site in the open field NW of the Iron Age tell; this is the "large village of Jews," Euseb. Onom. 22:9-10. The Gallaia of Euseb. Onom. 72:6-7 is obviously Jîlyā, just W of el-Muqanna'. The buildings of Jonathan's estate (I Macc. 10:89; Jos. Antiq. XIII.iv.4) are apparently located just N of the Iron Age site on the banks of the wadi.

Bibliography. J. Naveh, "Ekron," *Encyclopaedia Biblica,* VI (1971), cols. 339-43, Hebrew.

A. F. Rainey

***EL.** One of several words for "God" found in biblical Hebrew (*see* God, Names of §C1). The word is common to all the Semitic languages except Ethiopic, yet, despite numerous attempts, no satisfactory etymology has been suggested. It is probably a primitive noun like *'im,* "mother" or *šim,* "name." In addition to its general appellative meaning "God," El is also used as the proper name for a specific deity.

1. Outside the Bible. This dual usage is not a late development. It is already attested in our earliest Semitic sources, the Old Akkadian personal names from Pre-Sargonic cuneiform texts (before 2350 B.C.). The appellative usage is common in these names, but they also contain numerous examples of the undeclined stem *il-* in constructions where the form can be explained syntactically only as a divine name. A similar usage probably continues in the later Sargonic (2350-2150 B.C.) and Amorite names (the majority from the eighteenth century B.C.), but the evidence for Il as a proper name is more ambiguous here than in the earlier period. El also occurs as a divine name in Old South Arabic, but it is the Ugaritic texts (*see* Ugarit §4; Ugarit[S] §4) which provide the most reliable evidence for this usage. While the appellative use is attested, it is comparatively rare. The normal use at Ugarit is as the proper name.

a. Old Akkadian Il. The evidence does not permit one to say much about the character of the Old Akkadian Il. He was a high but gracious god, interested in man's welfare and particularly active in the giving of children. Whether he was the head of the pantheon in the Pre-Sargonic period is uncertain; he was not in the Sargonic period.

b. Ugaritic El. Any attempted characterization of El based on the Amorite or South Arabic evidence would be just as inadequate as the preceding characterization of the Old Akkadian Il. Only the Ugaritic sources permit a relatively full portrait of the deity. Nevertheless, the continuity of the name and of the epithets attributed to him suggest a close resemblance between the Ugaritic El and the Il or El of these other language groups. There can be even less doubt that the picture of El given in the Ugaritic texts corresponds in most essentials to the conception of that deity throughout the Canaanite cultural sphere, even if the linguistic classification of Ugaritic remains unsettled.

i. *As benign.* The Ugaritic evidence agrees with the Old Akkadian material in presenting El as basically favorable toward humanity. Two of his most common epithets stress this benevolent aspect of his character: *lṭpn il dpid,* "the Kind One, El the Compassionate One." And like the Old Akkadian Il, Ugaritic El is active in human childbirth. He is called *ab adm,* "father of mankind," and *bny bnwt,* "creator of all creatures," and both Keret and Daniel (*see* Ugarit §4) finally acquire heirs only through El's intervention.

ii. *As supreme.* The Ugaritic pantheon lists, as well as the literary compositions, make El the head of the pantheon. A certain *ilib* precedes him in the pantheon lists, but this obscure deity, perhaps the divine (dead) ancestor, is not a major god of the cult. Some of the mythic texts give more prominence to BAAL than to El, but even in them Baal clearly reigns by the consent of El as Sanchuniathon, the ancient Phoenician religious historian, also states. When the divine assembly (*see* COUNCIL, HEAVENLY[S]), presided over by El, surrenders Baal to Prince Sea, Baal is unable to contest the decision, and Baal's later desire for a palace cannot be fulfilled without first receiving the permission of El. Moreover, even Baal's enemies, though they may at times challenge it, recognize El's authority. The mere threat of El's intervention is enough to force Mot (*see* MOT[S]) into seeking a reconciliation with Baal.

iii. *As warrior*. Mot's reaction is understandable. El had literally hacked his way to the head of the pantheon in the bloody cosmogonic battles recorded in Sanchuniathon and in Hittite texts contemporary with Ugarit. If no longer dominant, El's martial virtues were still to be respected.

iv. *As patriarch*. El's continuing role is as patriarch, however, not as warrior. The gods may be referred to en masse as the family or assembly of El's sons (*dr bn il* or *mpḫrt bn il*). El is called *ab bn il,* "father of the gods," and his chief consort, ASHERAH is designated *qnyt ilm,* "creatress of the gods." As the progenitor of such a large clan, El is portrayed as quite ancient, yet still animated by the prodigious sexual appetite that created the divine assembly. He is *mlk ʿlm,* "eternal king," *ab šnm,* "father of years," and possessed of a gray beard, but he also plays the lead in the sacred marriage text (Shahar and Shalim) where he makes love to two thoroughly aroused goddesses. Moreover, when Asherah comes to lobby for Baal's palace, El offers her food or sex, and his excitement over her arrival indicates clearly El's preference. Another text speaks of Asherah's interest in Baal, but such dalliance on her part, far from proving El's alleged impotence, points rather to Asherah's own strong sexuality and may suggest El had neglected her for younger goddesses.

Nevertheless, despite his lustiness and an occasional drunken spree, El's wisdom befits his age. He is the patriarch whose wise decree brings a life of good fortune. Though a number of texts refer to him as king, El's kingship is most often sketched with features resembling an OT patriarch or judge. He normally lives in a tent, not a palace, and his rule takes the form of judicial decrees to be executed by other members of the divine council. It is a rather primitive kingship, comparable at best to that of Saul.

v. *El's abode*. The location of El's tent sanctuary remains a subject of dispute. The Ugaritic texts customarily place it at the "springs of the two rivers, midst the sources of the two deeps" (*mbk nhrm qrb apq thmtm*). Presumably this site had a mountain setting, since El is elsewhere located "in the midst of the mountain" (*tk ḫršn*), "in the midst of Mount Ks" (*ǵr ks*), and he presides over the divine assembly on Mount Ll (*ǵr ll,* some scholars emend the text to read *ǵr il,* "mountain of El," but justification for this emendation is lacking). Nevertheless, the constant mention of the aquatic nature of El's abode compared to the relative scarcity of references to his mountain suggests the place was more impressive as a water source than as a mountain. A location of the site at Khirbet Afqa in the Lebanon fits the Ugaritic evidence quite well. There, nestled in a majestic mountain setting, the Nahr Ibrahim emerges from a cavern to plunge into a deep and verdant gorge, while a scant 7½ miles away, on the other side of the mountain, a similar spring feeds the lake, Birket el Yammûneh, "The Little Sea."

An alternative location on the N Syrian coast in the Amanus Range is also possible, though it has less to commend it. The absence of unambiguous Ugaritic references to Mount Amanus (*ḫmn*) as El's mountain is a major problem. The contrast with the frequent references to Baal and his Mount Zaphon (*see* ZAPHON, MOUNT[S]) cannot be ignored. Moreover, one cannot compensate for this lack by a premature appeal to Hurrian evidence. Hurrian (*see* HURRIANS §1) is still too little understood to add much clarity to the question. *in ḫmnd* may mean "to (the divine mountain) Haman," but it does not connect El to the mountain. *il pbnḫwn ḫmn* is syntactically obscure, and even if one accepts the highly uncertain translation "El the One of the Mountain Ḫaman," the question remains whether this refers to the Canaanite El or simply gives evidence of syncretism between El and a native Hurrian deity of the Amanus. Finally, the much later biblical texts, shaped as they are by a different tradition and subject to consequent distortion, can only be cited as secondary evidence. Though Ezekiel uses the expression *yrkty ṣpwn* in a vague way to refer to the region N of the Amanus (38:6, 15; 39:2, "the uttermost parts of the north"), this is hardly its primary meaning, and his usage should not be invoked to locate the "mount of assembly" of Isa. 14:13-15 in the Amanus. The Isaiah passage still retains the primary mythological context of the expression, and the polarity with *yrkty bwr,* "the depths of the Pit" (vs. 15), requires that *yrkty ṣpwn* be translated, "the heights of Zaphon" (RSV "the far north"), analogously to *yrkty lbnwn,* "the heights of Lebanon" (II Kings 19:23; Isa. 37:24).

2. Biblical usage. The word *'ēl* occurs 238 times in the OT, appearing in both early and late texts. Many of its occurrences are clustered in the Psalms (77) and Job (55), though Genesis (18), Second Isaiah (15), and Deuteronomy (13) also use it frequently. The plural *'ēlîm* is rare (Exod. 15:11; Pss. 29:1; 89:6 [H 7]), and the feminine *'ēlat,* though well known in the cognate languages, does not appear in the Bible.

a. As an appellative. The normal biblical usage of *'ēl* is as a simple appellative. It is a synonym of the more common noun Elohim, "God," and it may take the article (Deut. 7:9; 10:17) or the first singular pronominal suffix (Exod. 15:2; Isa. 44:17), just as Elohim does. The latter construction is used to stress the personal attachment between an individual or group and their god, but when used as a vocative, even the form without suffix often carries the same connotation (Pss. 16:1; 17:6, etc.).

As an appellative *'ēl* may either refer to God or to one of the pagan gods. The idolater says "my god" to the idol he has made (Isa. 44:17). Note also the expressions "other god" (אל אחר, Exod. 34:14); "strange god" (אל זר, Ps. 44:20 [H 21]); "foreign god" (אל נכר, Deut. 32:12; Ps. 81:9 [H 10]), and "a no god" (לא־אל, Deut. 32:21). The plural is used of the pagan gods in a question originally at home in polytheism, "Who is like thee . . . among the gods?" (Exod. 15:11), and similar statements of Yahweh's incomparability using the singular *'ēl* are numerous (Deut. 3:24; II Sam. 22:32; Mic. 7:18). The term also appears in passages which stress the radical difference between God and man (Num. 23:19; Isa. 31:3).

Whether *'ēl* appears in the idiom לאל יד, "in the power of" (Gen. 31:29; Deut. 28:32) remains uncertain. Despite its clear meaning, the precise semantic analysis of this idiom is obscure, and אל in this expression may derive from a completely different word.

b. As a proper name. In addition to the appellative usage, El occasionally appears in the Bible as the equivalent of a proper name. Apart from the divine names constructed with El in the patriarchal narratives (*see* God, Names of §C2), the clearest example is the altar name El-Elohe-Israel, "El is the God of Israel" (Gen. 33:20), but there may be other occurrences which reflect a conscious identification of El and Yahweh. Josh. 22:22's solemn heaping up of divine elements should perhaps be read as a creedal affirmation: "Yahweh is El of the Gods! Yahweh is El of the Gods! He knows, and let Israel itself know." A similar interpretation has been suggested for Ps. 95:3: "For Yahweh is the Great El, the Great King over all the gods." The use of אל in the Balaam oracles, the Psalms, and Job in parallel with other designations such as Elyon also suggests a proper name rather than an appellative.

c. Yahweh and El. Though this use of El undoubtedly stems from a Canaanite background, Yahweh and El have been thoroughly merged. When used as a proper name, El never designates a deity clearly distinct from Yahweh. Even in the relatively few passages which show a strong influence of Canaanite mythology the El=Yahweh equation seems to be assumed.

In Ezek. 28:2 the ruler of Tyre exalts himself as though he were El, and both his vaunted wisdom and the characterization of his abode as "the seat of the gods, in the heart of the seas," recall features of the El mythology. Ezekiel may have been aware of this background, but if so, he obscures it by interchanging El and Elohim, thereby reducing El to a simple appellative, "yet you are but a man, and no god."

Isa. 14:13 mentions the "stars of El." From the context these are clearly the highest stars. Like the parallel Akkadian expression "the heavens of Anu" (*see* Assyria and Babylonia §G), this idiom is dependent on El's status as head of the pantheon. The etymology of El has no bearing on the meaning, and the same must be said for the related expressions "cedars of El" (=tallest cedars, Ps. 80:10 [H 11]) and "mountains of El" (=highest mountains, Ps. 36:6 [H 7]). These last two expressions are simply inherited phrases, coined in the world of Canaanite mythology, but carried over into biblical usage with little thought to their origin. The "stars of El" still occurs in a strongly mythological passage, but the mythology is mixed, and there is little doubt Isaiah identified El and Elyon with Yahweh.

The "assembly of El" (עדת אל, Ps. 82:1) also comes from a Canaanite background, as does the expression "sons of El" (בני אלים, Pss. 29:1; 89:6 [H 7]). The plural form is to be explained either as a misunderstood form with enclitic *-m* or as a plural of majesty (*see* Sons of God). But again, if these expressions betray their Canaanite origin, they are still defused by El's complete identification with Yahweh. Moreover, the biblical tradition so thoroughly strips independent personality from the "sons of El" that one may speak of their demotion to mere servant status; Ps. 82:6-7 even proclaims their impending death.

Yahweh's debt to El's Canaanite past is more extensive than these few overtly mythological expressions indicate, however. Though Yahweh did not maintain El's reputation for sexual prowess, most of the other features of the Canaanite god are passed on to Yahweh, quite often in epithets that still contain the word El. Yahweh's benevolence toward man is expressed in the epithet אל־רחום וחנון, "a God merciful and gracious" (Exod. 34:6; Ps. 86:15); אל אלהי הרוחת לכל־בשר, "O God, the God of the spirits of all flesh" (Num. 16:22), underlines his role as creator; אל גדול ונורא, "great and terrible God" (Deut. 7:21), stresses Yahweh's majestic standing; and אל גבור, "mighty God" (Isa. 10:21), designates Yahweh as a mighty warrior. His great age is suggested by the epithets אל עולם, "Everlasting God" (Gen. 21:33), and מלך עולם ועד, "king for ever and ever" (Ps. 10:16). One should also note Ps. 90:1-4 and Daniel's vision of the "ancient of days" (Dan. 7:9-14). The latter reads like a description of gray-haired El. Finally, Yahweh's wisdom is registered in the epithet אל דעות, "a God of knowledge" (I Sam. 2:3).

Some of the other epithets formed with El have a less obvious connection to the Canaanite god. אל אמונה, "God of faithfulness" (Deut. 32:4; cf. 7:9) and אל אמת, "faithful God" (Ps. 31:5 [H 6]) could derive from El's suggested connections to covenant; אל גמלות, "God of recompense" (Jer. 51:56), אל נקמות, "God of vengeance" (Ps. 94:1), and אל־צדיק, "victorious (RSV "righteous") God" (Isa. 45:21), could go back to El the warrior; and האל הקדוש, "Holy God" (Isa. 5:16) might also stem from El. The epithet אל חי, "living God" (Josh. 3:10), however, is more likely derived from a dying and rising god like Baal, and אל כבוד, "God of glory" (Ps. 29:3), is adapted along with the whole psalm from Baal theology. אל קנא, "jealous God" (Exod. 20:5), may not go back to a Canaanite origin at all. Yahweh's fierce jealousy which tolerates no rival is unparalleled in the religious literature of the ancient Near East. "Forgiving God" (אל נשא, Ps. 99:8) also seems to be a distinctive Israelite creation.

Moreover, a number of the El names in the patriarchal narratives may not stem from the Canaanite El. El Shaddai may be a distinct Amorite deity, and El Elyon may simply be an Israelite creation. Two distinct gods, El and Elyon, mentioned separately in Sanchuniathon and as a pair in an eighth-century B.C. Aramaic inscription, have been compounded in an effort to exalt Yahweh by identifying him not only with El, but also with an older god whose very name means "Most High."

The Israelite identification of Yahweh with El took place without the bitter conflict which characterized the confrontation of Yahweh and Baal. Yahweh also absorbed many of Baal's features, but did so through a terrible religious struggle extending over several centuries. The difference in the two cases probably lies in the Israelite perception of the essential identity of El and Yahweh. Though Yahweh does not inherit all the features of the Canaanite El, and while Yahweh's nature has become more complex due to his usurpation of all the divine functions, he may still be perceived as a development of El. Indeed, the very name Yahweh may have originated as a cultic epithet for El (Cross).

Bibliography. F. M. Cross, *Canaanite Myth and Hebrew Epic* (1973), pp. 1-75, "אֵל 'ēl," *TDOT*, I (1974), 242-61; D. N. Freedman, "Early Israelite History in the Light of Early Israelite Poetry," *Unity and Diversity*, ed. H. Goedicke and J. J. M. Roberts (1975); P. W. Miller, "El the Warrior," *HTR*, LX (1967), 411-31; M. H. Pope, *El in the Ugaritic Texts* (1955); J. J. M. Roberts, *The Earliest Semitic Pantheon* (1972), pp. 31-34, 121-44, "The Davidic Origin of the Zion Tradition," *JBL*, XCII (1973), 329-44, and "The Religio-Political Setting of Psalm 47," *BASOR* (1975, forthcoming); W. H. Schmidt, "אֵל 'ēl Gott," *Theologisches Handwörterbuch zum Alten Testament*, ed. E. Jenni, I (1971), 142-49.

J. J. M. Roberts

***ELATH;** ELOTH. A village near the modern city of Aqabah, on the N shore of the Gulf of Aqabah (Aelanitic Gulf). The early Hebrew tribes encamped there (Deut. 2:8). Uzziah (Azariah) captured Elath and rebuilt it (II Kings 14:22; II Chr. 26:1-2), and later the king of Edom captured it from Judah (II Kings 16:6). In Nabatean and Roman times Elath was known as Ailah; architectural remains of a Christian church have been discovered there. *See* Tell el-Kheleifeh[S]; Ezion-geber; Ezion-geber[S].

E. K. Vogel

***ELECTION, NT.** "Election" is the equivalent of Gr. ἐκλογή, cf. the adj. ἐκλεκτός, "chosen," from the verb ἐκλέγομαι "choose," "select."

1. Jesus. The designation "my elect one," which in the OT Yahweh gives to David (Ps. 89:3) and to his servant (Isa. 42:1), is similarly given to Jesus on the Mount of Transfiguration in Luke 9:35 [ἐκλελεγμένος] and ironically echoed by the "rulers" at his crucifixion: "Let him save himself, if he is the Christ of God, his Chosen One [ἐκλεκτός]!" (Luke 23:35). In John 1:34 some authorities read "Elect [ἐκλεκτός] of God" for "Son of God." In I Pet. 2:4, 6 Jesus is identified with the "chosen" [ἐκλεκτός] cornerstone of Isa. 28:16 (LXX). Whether the designation of the Son of Man as "Mine Elect One" in the Similitudes of Enoch (I Enoch 45:3, etc.) influenced the NT usage is very doubtful. As applied to Jesus, the designation is synonymous with the more common "my beloved," spoken of him by the heavenly voice at his baptism and transfiguration (Mark 1:11; 9:7).

2. The eschatological remnant. In the eschatological sense, the elect are those chosen to survive the troubles of the end time (cf. Isa. 4:3, "recorded for life"). In Jesus' eschatological discourse the days of trouble are shortened by God "for the sake of the elect, whom he chose" (Mark 13:20, 22, 27; Matt. 24:22, 24, 31). The troublous time gives encouragement to false prophets whose persuasive words, with supporting signs, are calculated (if such a thing were possible) to seduce even the elect; nevertheless, they maintain their loyalty and are gathered by the angels to "stand before the Son of man" (Luke 21:36).

A similar reference is appended to the parable of the importunate widow in Luke 18:7, 8. If even an unjust judge can be badgered into seeing justice done to a widow, much more will God see that speedy justice is done to his elect, "who cry to him day and night."

The proverb in Matt. 22:14, "Many are called, but few are chosen [ἐκλεκτοί]," implies a close connection between election and perseverance. One might compare the mystery adage quoted by Plato, "The wand-bearers are many but the initiates are few" (*Phaedo* 69c), or two Gnosticizing sayings from GTh: "There are many around the opening but no one in the well" (No. 74, ascribed to the Ophite *Heavenly Dialogue* by Celsus, according to Origen, *Against Celsus*, viii.16) and "Many stand outside at the door, but it is only the single ones who enter the bridal chamber" (No. 75). But the saying in Matt. 22:14 is tantamount to that in Mark 13:13; Matt. 10:22; 24:13: "He who endures to the end will be saved" (cf. Luke 21:19).

In Rev. 17:14 the associates of the Lamb in his victorious progress are "called and chosen [ἐκλεκτοί] and faithful"; the three terms are practically synonymous. But if their calling and election are divine acts, their faithfulness is their own responsibility (cf. Rev. 2:10*b*, "Be faithful unto death, and I will give you the crown of life"). So, in II Pet. 1:10, those who have been called and chosen presumably by God are exhorted to "confirm" their "call and election [ἐκλογή]" in order to ensure full and free admission to the eternal kingdom.

3. The church. The Christian community is referred to comprehensively in the NT as "God's elect [ἐκλεκτοί]" (Tit. 1:1); they are destined to "obtain salvation in Christ Jesus with its eternal glory" (II Tim. 2:10). To them is applied the language of election used of Israel in the OT (e.g. Isa. 45:4; cf. Acts 13:17). The church is "a chosen race [γένος ἐκλεκτόν], a royal priesthood, a holy nation, God's own people [λαὸς εἰς περιποίησιν]" (I Pet. 2:9; cf. Isa. 43:20, 21; Exod. 19:4-6). To the same effect Tit. 2:14 (echoing Exod. 19:5) says that Jesus "gave himself for us to . . . purify for himself a people of his own [λαὸς περιούσιος] who are zealous for good deeds" (cf. Eph. 2:10).

The sovereignty of God's election appears in his choosing people of little account by worldly standards to be the recipients of his grace and agents of his service (I Cor. 1:26-30; cf. Jas. 2:5).

There is a distinctive depth in Paul's treatment of the subject. The election of the people of God is bound up with their union with Christ and has in view their conformity to his character. Paul's teaching is summarized in Eph. 1:4, where the new people of God (comprising Jewish and Gentile believers) have been chosen [ἐκλέγομαι] in Christ before the world's foundation to be "holy and blameless before him." In Rom. 8:29 Paul affirms that God has predestined [προώρισεν] his people "whom he foreknew [προέγνω] . . . to be conformed to the image of his Son."

We may compare the description of Christian readers in I Pet. 1:2 as "chosen and destined [ἐκλεκτοῖς . . . κατὰ πρόγνωσιν] by God the Father and sanctified by the Spirit for obedience to Jesus Christ"—the purpose of this divine act being that the chosen people should be holy, like the God who chose them (I Pet. 1:15, 16, quoting the refrain of the OT law of holiness, Lev. 11:44, 45, etc.).

That this purpose is to be fulfilled now, not only at the end time, appears from Paul's ability to discern in the present conduct of his Thessalonian converts the evidence of their election: "We know, brethren beloved by God, that he has chosen [ἐκλογή] you; . . . And you became imitators of us and of the Lord" (I Thess. 1:4-6; cf. II Thess. 2:13). In Col. 3:12 it is because they are "God's chosen ones [ἐκλεκτοί], holy and beloved," that Christians are to cultivate qualities worthy of him: "compassion, kindness, lowliness, meekness, and patience." If the initiative in the fostering of such qualities rests with divine grace, personal responsibility plays a necessary part: those from whose lives they are absent are not elect but reprobate (I Cor. 6:9, 10; II Cor. 13:5).

The minority of Israelites who, in Paul's day, shared his faith in Jesus constituted "a remnant, chosen by grace"—"the elect" [ἐκλογή] who by faith attained the righteousness before God which the others vainly sought (Rom. 11:5-7). The existence of this "remnant" guaranteed the eventual restoration of the whole community. The election of some means the salvation of others, not their perdition. For Paul, the status of the church of the new age as God's elect people does not abrogate the election of Israel. Even in their refusal to acknowledge Jesus as the Christ, they remain "as regards election [ἐκλογή] . . . beloved for the sake of their forefathers. For the gifts and the call of God are irrevocable" (Rom. 11:28-29). That this is not the logical conclusion of Paul's argument in Rom. 9–11 is conceded by him when he calls it a "mystery," a new revelation of God's hidden purpose (Rom. 11:25).

4. The apostles. The Twelve are said to have been chosen by Jesus from the wider number of his disciples (Luke 6:13). In John 6:70 Jesus himself claims to have chosen them, but later Judas' treachery disqualifies him from the "chosen" band (John 13:18). The deeper significance of Jesus' choice of them is unfolded in his upper room discourse: "You did not choose me, but I chose you. . . . I chose you out of the world" (John 15:16, 19).

After the Resurrection, those whom Jesus had already "chosen" (Acts 1:2) selected two suitable men to replace Judas and prayed the risen Lord to show by means of the lot which of the two he had "chosen" to fill the vacancy. "The lot fell on Matthias; and he was enrolled with the eleven apostles" (Acts 1:23-26).

Later in Acts, Paul is described by the risen Lord as "a chosen instrument [σκεῦος ἐκλογῆς] of mine to carry my name before the Gentiles and kings and the sons of Israel" (9:15); compare Paul's own claim that God had set him apart (ἀφορίσας) before his birth to proclaim his Son "among the Gentiles" (Gal. 1:15-16; cf. Rom. 1:1).

At the Council of Jerusalem, Peter reminds the apostles and elders how God "made choice [ἐξελέξατο]" among them that by his mouth "the Gentiles should hear the word of the gospel and believe" (Acts 15:7).

5. Special instances. Rufus is called "eminent [ἐκλεκτός, KJV "chosen"] in the Lord" (Rom. 16:13). If the word had the sense which applies to all Christians, there would be no point in using it here of one individual; perhaps the adjective "choice" would be appropriate.

The "elect lady" [ἐκλεκτῇ κυρίᾳ] of II John 1 is a local congregation, her "children" being its members. The "children" of her "elect sister" (vs. 13) are the members of the church in the place where the writer was staying.

See also ELECTION and bibliography there.

Bibliography. G. Quell and G. Schrenk, "ἐκλέγομαι," *TDNT*, IV (1942 [ET 1967]), 144-92; L. Coenen, "Erwählung," *Theologisches Begriffslexikon zum NT* (1967), 282-91.

F. F. BRUCE

***ELOHIST.** The anonymous author or compiler of one of the four principal narrative sources of the PENTATEUCH. The term is derived from a Hebrew word for God, Elohim (אלהים), the use of which is characteristic of the source, especially prior to the revelation of the name Yahweh in Exod. 3:14-15. Both source and compiler are designated by the siglum E. *See* SOURCE CRITICISM, OT[S]; DOCUMENTS.

1. Independent character
2. Tradition history
3. Date
4. Provenance and scope
5. Subsequent redaction
6. Structure and scope
7. Theology
Bibliography

1. Independent character. In the early years of Pentateuchal criticism E was not separated from the Priestly source (P) because both used Elohim to refer to God prior to the time of Moses (*see* PRIESTLY WRITERS[S]). When the P material had been isolated on other grounds, E stood alone as an independent source in the classical documentary hypothesis. *See* BIBLICAL CRITICISM; BIBLICAL CRITICISM, HISTORY OF.

Some scholars have questioned the independence of E within the old Pentateuchal tradition (J and E). (*See* YAHWIST[S].) It has been suggested that E represents a new edition of J, or consists of parallel, independent traditions which have been interpolated into J, or is a redaction of J based on variants of J materials which emerged over the years (Volz; Rudolph; Mowinckel). Others suggest that in the epic tradition we have to do, not with the interweaving of literary strands, but with the preliterary growth of diverse traditions (Engnell). Still others do not deny E's independence, but consider it to be so fragmentary that little can be learned concerning its character (Noth).

Most scholars, however, view E as an independent source which is sufficiently intact to merit full characterization. The primary evidence is as follows:

a. Doublets. The same narrative materials in different versions occur throughout the non-Priestly portions of the Pentateuch: e.g., the expulsion of Hagar (Gen. 16; 21); Sarah's being placed in jeopardy (Gen. 12; 20); the introduction of the name Yahweh (Gen. 4:26; Exod. 3:13-15).

To postulate a new edition of J is not satisfactory, for that leaves unexplained why the older versions, often with highly divergent elements, were retained along with the new ones. Nor is the supplementary hypothesis likely, for this assumes the addition of new materials rather than the same materials in a new version. Moreover, to understand E as an independent development of J traditions fails to consider seriously enough either the extent of the differences between J and E or the likely priority of much of the E material.

b. Compositeness. Many texts are composite. It needs to be considered in each instance whether this is due to a preliterary or a literary convergence. Firm decisions for the latter can be made only if there is evidence of unity (at the level of language and point of view) in the larger context of the tradition to which parts of a composite text may be related. The evidence suggests that literary convergence is common (*see* §§1*c*, 7 *below*).

Sufficient explanation for two literary strata is provided by the division between North and South. A form of the tradition would have continued in northern circles both before and after the division of the kingdom. Given the dynamics of the relationship between the kingdoms, J, with its special southern interests, would hardly have been acceptable to northerners (*see* §§2, 4 *below*).

c. Unity. It should not be assumed that the E materials, when isolated from their present contexts, form a fully unified narrative. This has led to a hypercritical dissection of the materials. The JE redactor appears to have used his sources in such a way that neither J nor E is complete (*see* §5 *below*).

With this precaution in mind, it is possible to say that evidences exist of unity among the E materials. Beginning with the doublets, other traditions can then be isolated that bear the same or similar characteristics. Peculiarities of language and perspective begin to emerge.

Distinctive vocabulary items include, besides Elohim, the use of Horeb (instead of Sinai), Amorites (instead of Canaanites), and Jethro (instead of Hobab). Stylistically, careful attention is given to linking the various accounts to earlier or later narratives, as with Joseph's bones (Gen. 50:25; Exod. 13:19; Josh. 24:32), or in the Jacob story (Gen. 28:20-22; 31:13; 35:1-3). E has a fondness for dialogue and detail (Gen. 20; 40–42), and anticipates D with a merging of narrative and parenesis (Exod. 20:18-20; Gen. 45:5-15).

Unity is especially evident in recurring themes (e.g., the fear of God; prophecy) and a distinct theological perspective (*see* §7 *below*).

2. Tradition history. Much of the material within the major sources did not originate with the compilers who gave them their decisive form. The compilers were working with traditions which had been passed down for generations. It was primarily at cultic centers during the period of the judges that these traditions began to be shaped in such a way as to bring into being the basic form and content of the later Pentateuch. Early Israelite confessions of faith (e.g., Deut. 26:5-9) provided the pattern: patriarchs; Egyptian sojourn; Exodus and wilderness wanderings; occupation of the land. *See* CREDO, ANCIENT ISRAELITE[S].

The narrative which emerged is called G (*Grundlage*). Originating *ca.* 1100 B.C. in oral form, it was decisively shaped by leaders within the boundaries of the later northern kingdom, and thus was fundamentally a northern product. *See* PENTATEUCH §A2.

Because J and E have essentially the same structure, it has been suggested that both used G as the basis for their work. It is probable, however, that E, being northern (*see* §4 *below*), would have had the greatest continuity with G. With J, more changes would have been introduced in order to conform the traditions more closely to southern perspectives. This would help explain why E commonly represents an earlier stage in the history of tradition than J.

Other sources utilized by E are occasionally identifiable: old poetic pieces (Exod. 15:21; Num. 21:14-15, 17-18, 27-30; 23:7-10, 18-24), the Decalogue and Book of the Covenant (Exod. 20–23), and perhaps the Song and Blessing of Moses (Deut. 32–33).

3. Date. It has been suggested that E completed his work in the wake of the secession of the North under Jeroboam. The northern kingdom would have needed its own edition of the epic tradition to rival J in the South, just as it needed a new cultic center. However, G would have constituted just such an edition. The North, given its conservative tendencies, would have held tenaciously to the *traditional* shape in the face of "modernizing" trends in the South. A later date for E must be envisioned.

The classical hypothesis proposed an eighth-century dating, while recent scholarship has suggested the ninth century. The latter seems more probable.

The understanding of prophecy in E (the Mosaic model) is more mature than the earlier charismatic movement, but is not as developed as that of classical prophetism. The problem of idolatry assumes a shape that implies the cult established by Jeroboam (Exod. 32; I Kings 12), but it has not reached a stage where the end of Israel is clearly in view. The strong affirmation of charismatic and democratic leadership suggests that the principle of such leadership was endangered (Exod. 18; Num. 11–12); this may imply a struggle against dynastic forms of kingship and institutionalized prophetism (I Kings 22). Politically and militarily, there is no indication of internal or external threats to security (Num. 23:21).

4. Provenance and scope. The delineation of E's provenance must proceed chiefly from a determination of those traditions with which E has the greatest affinity. Matters which reflect regional interests in more specific ways may supplement such a comparative study of traditions. The evidence suggests an origin in the North, perhaps among prophetic circles.

a. Joshua. It has long been common to trace the Pentateuchal sources into Joshua. Recent scholarship has moved away from such a course, setting the Former Prophets (Joshua, Judges, I and II Samuel, I and II Kings) within the DEUTERONOMIC HISTORY (Noth). Yet the sources of the Deuteronomist remain unclear, and new attempts to identify the Pentateuchal sources among them have emerged (Mowinckel).

It is probable that G contained traditions regarding the occupation of the land. Given the relationship between G and E (*see* §2 *above*), the latter may also have included such a narrative (embedded in Josh. 1–12; 24). This would account for the connections between Num. 25:1-5 and Josh. 2:1, and provide for greater continuity with the land promise (Gen. 15:13-16) and the settlement of some of the tribes in Transjordan (Num. 32). Yet, except for ch. 24, literary contacts between E and Joshua are relatively infrequent.

Thus, while we can speak of the probability of Pentateuchal sources among those used by the Deuteronomist in Joshua, successive redactions have made a literary solution highly problematic. *See* JOSHUA, BOOK OF[S].

From a broader traditio-historical perspective, however, there are significant affinities between E and these portions of Joshua. The traditions are in large part of Benjaminite origin and almost always related to the northern sanctuaries of Gilgal (Amos 5:5; Hos. 12:11) or Shechem. The Ephraimite Joshua has functions parallel to those of E's Mosaic model (Josh. 8:30-35; 10; 24). (*See* §7 *below.*) Moreover, the "all Israel" orientation, the concern for total conquest conceived within a concern to avoid the dangers of apostasy, the emphasis upon obedience, all presented in a hortatory fashion, connect these chapters with the E tradition.

b. Judges-Kings. The Pentateuchal sources are almost certainly not to be traced into Judges, Samuel, and Kings. There are, however, traditio-historical affinities between E and parts of Judges (6:7-10; 8:22-23; 9:7-15), the antimonarchic source in I Samuel (chs. 7; 8; 10:17-27; 12; 15; cf. 1:1–4:1*a**; 13:7-15; 16:1-13; 28), and the Elijah-Elisha narratives (I Kings 17 ff.). (The symbol * indicates that the assignment to a source is problematic in whole or part.) Emphases in these chapters suggest that they originally emanated from northern circles: charismatic/prophetic leadership with antimonarchic tendencies (cf. Samuel); obedience to God in the face of dangers from Canaanite religion; idealization of persons and events; and the general congruence with tribal league emphases. *See* JUDGES, BOOK OF[S]; SAMUEL, I AND II[S]; KINGS, I AND II[S].

c. Hosea and Deuteronomy. While it has been common to assert Hosea's literary dependence upon E, nothing more can be claimed than commitment to the same traditions. This is most evident in the prophetic conception of the Mosaic office (12:13 [H 14]), emphasis upon covenantal obedience, and an antimonarchic stance.

While much work remains to be done on the antecedents of the Deuteronomic tradition, numerous ties with E suggest a common northern provenance: the Sinaitic covenant; the Mosaic office; key theological emphases; the antimonarchic perspective; and a religious interpretation of history that merges narrative and parenesis.

d. Regional interests. Aspects of E which reflect northern ties are most evident in narratives where J and E are parallel. Thus, Reuben is the leader of Joseph's brothers, not Judah (Gen. 37). In the Abraham cycle attention is focused on Beer-sheba (cf. Amos 5:5; 8:14), not on Hebron. Northern cultic centers and burial places such as Bethel and Shechem predominate, as do the roles given Joseph and Joshua.

5. Subsequent redaction. The fall of the North in 721 B.C. inevitably had its effect upon northern traditions. Northerners fleeing S would have brought traditions such as E with them. Under HEZEKIAH attempts at a religious and political reunification of Israel and Judah surfaced (II Chr. 30), perhaps accompanied by a merger of literary traditions. The JE redaction was the result. *See* REDACTION CRITICISM, OT[S].

It has usually been assumed, chiefly from the placement and volume of J material, that the JE redactor used J as the basic source, adding E largely for enrichment. Yet caution is in order here, for the original scope of the E tradition is unknown. Moreover, because the redactor has often interwoven J and E so closely, it is sometimes impossible to determine the source upon which he is primarily dependent.

It is possible that there were redactions of E prior to JE. This is suggested by passages which have a Deuteronomic cast (e.g., Exod. 13:3-16; 23:20-33; 34:11-16). Though these may belong to the Deuteronomist or even to the JE redactor, the possibility of an earlier redaction needs serious consideration.

6. Structure and scope. Structurally, the narrative centers on the covenant at Sinai (Exod. 19–24*). The preceding narratives are idealized and preparatory, focusing especially on Joseph and Moses. The calf episode is virtually a "fall" story (Exod. 32–34*), with subsequent narratives sketching Israel's struggles with sin and obedience, issuing finally in paradigmatic covenant renewal (Josh. 24). *See* COVENANT §3; COVENANT, MOSAIC[S] §5*b*.

The following delineation of E is tentative in its detail; much work remains to be done.

a. Preparation. i. *Abraham:* Gen. 15:1-4*, 5-6, 13-16; 20:1-17; 21:1*, 6, 8-34; 22:1-19. ii. *Jacob:* 25:25-27*, 29-34; 27:1-45*; 28:11-12, 17-18, 20-22; 29:1, 15-23, 25-28*a*, 30; 30:1-8*, 13*, 17-20*a*, 22-40*; 31:2, 4-16, 19-42, 43-55*; 32:1-2, 13*b*-21*; 33:5-11*, 18*, 19-20; 35:1-5, 6*b*-8, 14, 16-20. iii. *Joseph:* 37:3-4*, 5-11, 13*b*-20*, 22-24, 28-36*; 39:1-6*; 40:1-23; 41:1-33, 34-56*; 42:1-12*, 13-26, 29-37; 45:2-3, 5*b*-27; 46:1*b*-5*a;* 48:1-2, 7-9*a,* 10*b*-12, 15-16, 20-22; 50:15-26.

iv. *Egyptian sojourn:* Exod. 1:11-12*, 15-22; 2:1-10; 3:1, 4*b*, 6, 9-15, 19-22; 4:10-16*, 17-18, 20*b*-23, 27-28, 29-31*; 5:1-2, 3-5*, 9-14*, 22-23*; 6:1*; 7:15*b*-17*, 20*b*, 23; 9:22-35*; 10:12-15*, 20-23, 27; 11:1-3; 12: 35-36. v. *Exodus and wilderness wanderings:* 13:17-19; 14:5-7*, 10-12*, 15-16*, 19-20*, 31*; 15:20-21, 25*b*-26; 17:3-6, 8-16; 18:1-27.

b. Covenant. 19:2*b*-8, 9-19*; 20:1-26; 21:1–23:19; 23:20-33*; 24:1-15*a*, 18*b*; 31:18*b*.

c. Sin and its consequences. i. *Golden calf:* 32:1-35; 33:2-3*, 4-11, 12-23*; 34:1-5*, 6-9, 11-31*. ii. *Wilderness wanderings:* Num. 11:1-3, 11-12, 14-17, 24-30; 12:1-15; 13: 17*b*-20*, 22-24*, 26*b*-31*; 14:3-4*, 8-9*, 11-25*, 39-45*; 20:1*b*, 14-18, 21; 21:4-9, 11*b*-20*, 21-32; 22:2-3*a*, 8-21*, 36-41*; 23:1-26, 27-30*; 25:1-5*. iii. *Occupation of the land:* 32:1-42*; Deut. 31:14-15, 23, 16-22*; 32:1-44; 33:1-29; 34:5-6, 10-12*; Josh. 1-12*; iv. *Covenant renewal:* 24:1-33*.

7. Theology. The theology of E is decidedly northern in its emphases, and has been shaped in decisive ways by the idolatrous situation to which it was addressed.

The most pervasive theological issues, which give striking importance to the human factor, are: (*a*) God's word and deed are mediated chiefly through charismatic leaders; (*b*) God's gift of salvation is conditioned by Israel's continued obedience.

a. God and human agency. God's activity, while occasionally mediated by heavenly messengers (Gen. 22:11; 32:1; Exod. 23:20), is primarily accomplished through human agency. Human actions are necessary vehicles for divine activity, even if not well-intentioned or so recognized (Gen. 50:20; Exod. 2:10).

Though any Israelite could function as the vehicle of the divine word and deed (Exod. 1:20-21; 19:6), it is primarily the prophetic or charismatic leader who is so considered. Figures such as Abraham and Joseph stand out (Gen. 20:17; 41:38), but MOSES is the leader par excellence (Exod. 11:3; Num. 12:3-8; Deut. 34:10-12). Yet E manifests considerable interest in the decentralization of his office (Exod. 18:21-23; 32:29; Num. 11:24-30; cf. Deut. 17–18). This may be a reaction against centralizing tendencies and realities in both North and South.

It is not man, however, who is to be worshiped for such accomplishments (Gen. 50:19); it is God's continuing, though unobtrusive, activity which is to be confessed (45:5-8).

b. God and human response. E centers his narrative around FAITH (FEAR) and OBEDIENCE. He begins with Abraham. God's promise stands at the beginning of the account (Gen. 15:5), accompanied by Abraham's response of faith (15:6). This constitutes a paradigm for all that follows. Israel is elected in Abraham, receives the same promise, and is called upon to make the same response.

The climax of E's narrative is the establishment of the covenant at Sinai (Exod. 19–24*), where a spiritual bond between God and Israel is established (3:12; 19:4-6). Within this relationship the gracious gift of the commandments points the way for a truly human life. While indicating how covenant faithfulness may be expressed, they also guard against that which would injure Israel's life with God and in the world.

An obedient people receive the benefits of the covenant (Gen. 22:16-18; Exod. 23:23-33*), but judgment for a disobedient people is inevitable (Exod. 32:9-10, 30-34; 33:5; cf. Gen. 15:14, 16). Thus the promises of God are not unconditional; they must be seen within the framework of the Sinai covenant (Exod. 19:5; 23:21-22; 32:33). The promise cannot be permanently embodied in any particular national or institutional expression. Therefore, while the promise motif is carried throughout the narrative, it is tied to a worshiping community, and only concessively to a land or a nation. *See* PROMISES TO THE PATRIARCHS[S].

Given E's perception of a breakdown in this relationship in his day, he has an overriding concern with sin and judgment, with repentance and forgiveness. It is raised in the first major E narrative (Gen. 20) and is pursued in the stories of Jacob and Joseph (35:1-4; 42:21-22; 50:15-17). It reappears in warnings connected with the making of the covenant (Exod. 20:5, 20) and is given special attention in connection with the golden calf apostasy and its aftermath (32:7-10, 14, 30-34; 33:4-6; 34:7-9; Num. 14:11-20; 21:4-9; Josh. 24:19-20).

The fundamental effect of this concern is to show the utter seriousness of disobedience. Accompanying this, however, is a picture of the incredible patience of God (Num. 14:19-22). Through the intercessory prayer of the prophet (Gen. 20:17; Exod. 32; 34; Num. 12; 14), God again and again responds with forgiveness and healing (*see* GRACE IN THE OT[S]). Even punishment is used as a means to the restoration of relationship (see the response in Exod. 33:4-6). Yet E seems to suggest (e.g., Num. 14:20-23) that there may be a limit to God's patience. *See* DISCIPLINE, DIVINE[S].

This gives a sense of urgency to E's call for faith and obedience. To this end the patriarchs serve as models of the obedient response, as their faith, like Israel's, is put to the test (Gen. 22:1; 42:15-16; Exod. 15:25; 20:20). Abraham's "fear of God" expresses itself largely in personal relationships (e.g., Gen. 22:12); Jacob's in matters relating to worship (e.g., 35:1-4); and Joseph's in matters relating to administration, including tribal relationships (42:18). This emphasis is continued in Exodus (1:17, 21; 4:31; 14:31; 18:21).

The definition of acceptable worship is of special interest to E. He makes frequent allusion to cultic practice, both to condemn and commend. The calf incident provides a special focus for condemnation, given the similar situation in the North (Exod. 20:4-5, 23; 32; cf. I Kings 12). Other practices are similarly castigated (Exod. 20:24-26; 23:24-33*; 34:11-16*). Still other aspects of worship are commended: acts of purification, vows, tithes, sacrifices, covenant ceremonies (Gen. 28:20-22; 35:2-4; Exod. 18:12; 19:10-23*). This concern accounts for the emphasis upon awe in the presence of God (Gen. 28:17; Exod. 3:6; 20:18), restraint in the use of anthropomorphic language when speaking of God, and emphasis upon dreams, visions, cloud pillars, and heavenly messengers (Gen. 20:3; 46:2; Num. 12:5). The point is not so much that God is distant; rather, it is that Israel must use greater care in her approach to God—a necessary emphasis in the face of Canaanite influence.

It is this factor which also explains E's unusual interest in the form of God (Num. 12:8; Exod. 24:9-11; 33:17-23*). This may have been occasioned by the calves erected by Jeroboam and emerging understandings of the possibility of divine representation.

The message to the people of Israel is clear: they are to put away all idolatrous practices and renew their covenant vows. Joshua 24, which perhaps constitutes a conclusion to E's narrative, is not simply a reminder of past ceremony, but a call to renewed commitment, so that Israel might truly experience the gift of God's salvation.

Bibliography. General introductions: S. R. Driver, *An Introduction to the Literature of the OT* (9th ed., 1913); A. Bentzen, *Introduction to the OT* (5th ed., 1959); A. Weiser, *The OT: Its Formation and Development* (1961); O. Eissfeldt, *The OT: An Introduction* (1965); G. Fohrer, *Introduction to the OT* (1968).

Pentateuchal criticism: J. Wellhausen, *Prolegomena to the History of Ancient Israel* (1885), and *Die Composition des Hexateuchs* (3rd ed., 1899); J. E. Carpenter and G. Harford-Battersby, *The Hexateuch According to the Revised Version*, 2 vols. (1900); O. Eissfeldt, *Hexateuch-Synopse* (1922); C. R. North, "Pentateuchal Criticism," in *The OT and Modern Study* (1961), pp. 48-83; S. Mowinckel, *Erwägungen zur Pentateuch Quellenfrage* (1964), and *Tetrateuch-Pentateuch-Hexateuch* (1964); G. von Rad, *The Problem of the Hexateuch and Other Essays* (1966), pp. 1-78; I. Engnell, *A Rigid Scrutiny* (1969), pp. 50-67; M. Noth, *A History of Pentateuchal Traditions* (1972).

Studies of the Elohist: O. Proksch, *Das nordhebräische Sagenbuch: Die Elohimquelle* (1906); P. Volz and W. Rudolph, *Der Elohist als Erzähler: Ein Irrweg der Pentateuchkritik? BZAW*, LXIII (1933); W. Rudolph, *Der "Elohist" von Exodus bis Josua, BZAW*, LXVIII (1938); A. W. Jenks, *The Elohist and North Israelite Traditions* (diss., Harvard University, 1964); L. Ruppert, "Der Elohist: Sprecher für Gottes Volk," *Wort und Botschaft des Alten Testaments* (1967), pp. 108-17; R. Kilian, "Der heilsgeschichtliche Aspect in der elohistischen Geschichtstradition," *ThGl*, LVI (1966), 369-84; H. W. Wolff, "The Elohistic Fragments in the Pentateuch," *Int.*, XXVI (1972), 158-73.

T. E. FRETHEIM

***EMENDATIONS OF THE SCRIBES** [תקוני סופרים, *Tiqqune Sopherim*].

1. The usual explanation. A list of eighteen passages in the MT which have undergone emendation for theological motives. The more recent and fuller lists may be found in the MASORA to certain MSS, while traces of earlier and less complete lists may be found in rabbinic writings. Apart from certain differences in some of the Masoretic lists, the eighteen emendations are: Gen. 18:22; Num. 11:15; 12:12; I Sam. 3:13; II Sam. 16:12; 20:1; I Kings 12:16; II Chr. 10:16; Jer. 2:11; Ezek. 8:17; Hos. 4:7; Hab. 1:12; Zech. 2:8 [H 12]; Mal. 1:12; Ps. 106:20; Job 7:20; 32:3; Lam. 3:20. The emendation in each case is minimal. It may have been the omission or alteration of one or more consonants (עליך emended to עלי in Job 7:20; אלהים emended to להם in I Sam. 3:13 אפי emended to אפם in Ezek. 8:17). It may have consisted of the inversion of consonants (אלהיך emended to אהליך in I Kings 12:16; II Chr. 10:16; cf. II Sam. 20:1) or the inversion of the word order (Gen. 18:22). Thus emended, the MT avoids what would have been anthropomorphic, irreverent, or idolatrous expressions in relation to God. One of these cases is directly related, not to God, but to Moses (Num. 12:12).

2. Ambiguity of the Masoretic lists. At first sight these lists appear invaluable for the textual critic. However, closer examination reveals a number of problems. The lists do not always agree in the number of emendations, nor in the order in which they are presented, nor in the actual passages listed, nor in the proposed "original reading" when this is given. Slight differences occur in the titles of the lists. Some MSS carry the title תיקון סופרים or תקוני סופרים or תיקון עזרא. Others carry the heading כנויי סופרים (*Kinnuye Sopherim*, "Euphemisms of the Scribes"), and indicate that the text was never emended (לא שתיקנו אותם); rather, the scribes were supplying what they considered would have been written had Scripture not expressed itself euphemistically. Such discrepancies and differences in interpretation should warn textual critics that the lists of eighteen "scribal emendations" may not be a simple statement of fact.

3. Earlier sources for these lists. Ambiguity and apparent contradiction in the Masoretic lists reflect a difference of opinion already present in the earlier sources. The *Kinnûyîm* interpretation is present in the Mek. of R. Ishmael (*ca.* A.D. 90-130) on Exod. 15:7, which lists eleven passages, and in the Sifre on Num. 10:35, which lists eight passages. The *tiqqûnîm* interpretation is present in Shemoth Rabbah XIII.1 and XXX.15; in Tanḥ. Yelammedenu §16, and in other rabbinic works dependent on the earlier Midrashim. In these too, there is great variety in the number of passages given.

4. Genuine scribal emendations? If it can be established that some of the eighteen passages usually listed are indeed the emended forms of originally blasphemous or disrespectful expressions, then it follows that there really was emendatory initiative on the part of the scribes. But it would be naïve to equate this initiative with the official lists of medieval times and with these lists only.

In the case of two of the passages mentioned in both rabbinic and Masoretic lists, I Sam. 3:13 and Job 7:20, a number of factors help to establish that the MT form must have been emended at an early stage in its textual history for theological motives. First, the reading of the LXX coincides with the "original reading" proposed in the lists of scribal emendations. Moreover, a study of the immediate context of each passage reveals: (*a*) that while the MT does not involve any irreverent or theologically incorrect statement, neither does it conform to normal Hebrew idiom or modes of expression, (*b*) that the reading of the LXX best suits the context and does give rise to what might be considered as irreverent statements relating to God, and (*c*) that the emendation of the original text to the MT form required very little surgery.

The case of Zech. 2:8 [H 12] is not as clear-cut as the preceding two. Yet, the fact that the reading of a minor section of the Greek textual witnesses (Quinta, Codex W, and certain citations of Justin) coincides with the "original reading" of Masoretic lists could throw more light on both the nature and the antiquity of scribal emendation.

Since the bulk of the Greek tradition contains the "emended" reading for Zech. 2:8 [H 12], this would carry the phenomenon back into the third and second centuries B.C. It could then be linked with the mentality of the author of Chronicles, and with the tendencies of the Old LXX and Targumim, where there was a conscious effort to eliminate the anthropomorphisms and gross expressions of an earlier mentality. That the phenomenon of scribal emendation was by no means completed at the time of the LXX is shown by the fact that the *Vorlage* for I Sam. 3:13 and Job 7:20, and for a minor section of textual witnesses for Zech. 2:8 [H 12], was still "unemended." These variations in the Greek textual tradition are important, for they help to pinpoint within a definite historical context, and in an objective fashion, the activity of the scribes. They are also independent, to a large extent, of rabbinic traditions.

5. Transmission of *tiqqûnîm* traditions. To emend the biblical text was a delicate matter. It required great prudence, especially when one takes into consideration the minute rules and regulations to which scribes and copyists were expected to conform (*see* TEXT, OT §A3*a*). This would have been particularly true in the first century A.D., in view of the official promulgation of the freshly standardized text (*see* TEXT, HEBREW, HISTORY OF[S]). It was probably within such a climate that the formula *Kinnuye Sopherim* (*see* §2 *above*) was used to interpret the *tiqqûnîm* phenomenon. Since scribal emendation could not be spoken of openly in certain circles, it was inevitable that, in the course of time, the procedure would be open to different kinds of contamination. Closer examination of the official lists reveals that many, if not most of them, are not genuine emendations. In most cases (apart from I Sam. 3:13; Zech. 2:8 [H 12]; and Job 7:20) the MT and its context present no serious difficulty. Futhermore, the proposed alternative "original reading" does not have significant textual support from the versions, and it is usually possible to unravel from the Midrashim and rabbinic commentaries ways in which imaginative interpretation created so-called *tiqqûnîm*. Given the variety of "emendations" in the official lists, and the complexity of rabbinic sources, it is not possible to know at what stage each false *tiqqûn* came to be. But this infiltration nevertheless began at an early age, since even the earliest lists contain a number of false "emendations."

6. Value of these lists for textual criticism. The apparently comprehensive Masoretic lists of eighteen scribal emendations must not be accepted as a simple statement of fact. But neither must they be rejected as wholly untrustworthy. They preserve reminiscences of an emendatory initiative of scribes of an earlier age—an initiative more widespread than the impression given by these lists, and concerning which later traditions were to remain prudently vague. The real value of these *tiqqûnîm* traditions lies more in the phenomenon to which they draw attention than in the accuracy of their lists. A parallel phenomenon in the history of LXX substantiates this conclusion. Shemoth Rabbah V.5 contains mention of "eighteen passages which the sages changed for King Ptolemy." Of these passages, which can be easily and objectively checked, only six are in fact genuine emendations of the MT in the LXX. Consequently, recognition of the existence of some genuine emendations within the official lists provides a springboard for investigation into "unofficial emendations" not listed under the heading *Tiqqune Sopherim*, but which surely qualify for this title. For example, the MT of II Sam. 12:9, 14 and of I Kings 9:8 may be considered as emended in order to preserve respect for God. The MT of II Sam. 5:8 may be considered as emended out of respect for David. The MT of I Sam. 2:22 and 14:14 could also be considered as emended in a pejorative sense, in order to lessen the "good" name of less desirable people. Meanwhile, the "unauthentic emendations" remain interesting illustrations of Midrashic interpretation.

Bibliography. C. D. Ginsburg, *The Massorah* (1880-1905), letter ת, vol. II, p. 710, secs. 204-6; *Introduction to the Massoretico-Critical Edition of the Hebrew Bible* (1897), pp. 347-62; W. E. Barnes, "Ancient Corrections in the Text of the OT (*Tiḳḳun Sopherim*)," *JTS,* I (1900), 387-414; A. Geiger, *Urschrift und Übersetzungen der Bibel* (1857), pp. 308-50; S. Lieberman, *Hellenism in Jewish Palestine* (1950), pp. 27-32; D. Barthélemy, "Les Tiqquné Sopherim et la Critique Textuelle de l'Ancien Testament," VTSup, IX (1963), 285-304; B. Keller, "Fragment d'un traité d'exégèse massorétique," *Textus,* V (1966), 60-83. C. MCCARTHY

ENCROACHMENT. In the OT, encroachment is attested in both the secular and the sacred realm. The former is expressed by the term הסיג גבול, literally, "moves a boundary" (RSV "landmark"). Its prohibition is found once in a law code (Deut. 19:14). However, since it contains no penalty, it must be understood as a moral injunction. That it could not be enforced in the courts is confirmed by its inclusion among the curses (Deut. 27:17), i.e., surreptitious crimes generally undetectable by man and hence punishable only by God.

Encroachment is also forbidden in wisdom literature (Prov. 22:28; 23:10; Job 24:2). That Deuteronomy was informed by wisdom teaching and not the reverse is suggested by its ubiquitousness in the legal and sapiential instructions of the ancient Near East, much of which antedate the Deuteronomic literature.

From the Middle Assyrian Laws it is clear that the apprehended encroacher upon property is subject to severe penalties, including fines, mutilations, beatings, and forced labor (tablet B, §§8-9, 20; cf. *ANET* [2nd ed.], pp. 185-86). However, the boundary stones (*kudurru*) found in Babylonia (beginning with the Kassite period) make it likely that encroachers were rarely apprehended. These stones, engraved with the symbols of the protector gods and inscribed with curses (*see* LANDMARK Fig. 12), indicate that the property owner was dependent upon the fear of the divine and not of the courts to prevent any tampering with his land. That the gods were thought to punish encroachers is evident from the belief that this crime was a cause of severe illness (e.g., *Shurpu* II, 45-46; cf. III, 53-54). Indeed, in the Hittite Code, the apprehended encroacher not only must idemnify his victimized neighbor with part of his own land, but must pacify either the storm-god or sun-god with a fixed sacrifice (§§168-69, *ANET,* p. 195). In Egypt, the "Instruction of Amen-em-opet" implies that the encroacher upon property is subject to divine jurisdiction (ch. 6, *ANET,* p. 422). The Greeks likewise invoke "Zeus the Protector of Boundaries" in cases of encroachment (Plato, *Laws* 842E).

The second realm of encroachment—upon sacred property—finds its most detailed description in the Hittite "Instructions For Temple Officials" (*ANET,* pp. 207-10). This text lists types of encroachment by those most capable of it, the temple staff (I, 46-66; II, 12-58) or the farmers and herdsmen employed on the temple fields (IV, 1 ff.). Encroachment is committed by keeping, eating, using, selling, gifting, delaying, or exchanging the temple's animals, fields, or grain; by expropriating, altering, or wearing the temple's implements or garments; or by changing the time fixed for rites. Women, children, and servants, even of the priests, as well as all foreigners, are considered encroachers if they enter the sacred precincts, whereas important Hittite men are granted access provided they are accompanied by a priestly appointed guard (II, 9-12).

In Israel, encroachment upon sanctums must be distinguished by the criteria of literary genre and historical development. The narratives record the lethal power of the ark. Uzzah's touching the ark (II Sam. 6:6-7) and the Beth-shemeshites' viewing it (I Sam. 6:19), both unpremeditated acts, are punished by God with death. P's earliest traditions on the wilderness period also reflect this belief: the Kohathites will be struck down for accidentally touching covered sanctums (Num. 4:15) or viewing uncovered ones (Num. 4:20). However, P's laws indicate a change by positing inadvertance (*šᵉgāgâ*) as a mitigating factor in all forms of trespass (*ma'al*) upon sanctums (Lev. 5:14-16). Moreover, P further reduces the contagious power of the sanctums. Though it still prohibits nonpriests (and disqualified priests) from entering the shrine, it does not penalize them for making contact with the sacrificial altar which stands in the open court. This concession can be ascertained from the use of the verbs קרב/נגע, which are to be rendered not as "approach" but "encroach" (e.g., Exod. 28:43; 30:20; Lev. 21:23; Num. 1:51; 3:10). Thus only one who usurps the priestly monopoly to officiate at the altar is subject to divine sanctions, but not if he only touches the altar, even deliberately. This leads to the corollary deduction that the formula כל-הנגע ב . . . יקדש must be rendered "whatever (not whoever) touches . . . is sanctified" (cf. Exod. 29:37; 30:29); i.e., only objects that contact the sanctums absorb their holiness, but not persons. The specific reasons for P's reduction of sanctum contagion may lie in P's refusal to grant altar asylum to fugitives from justice (cf. I Kings 1:50-53; 2:28-34), and P therefore devised in its place the institution of city asylum (Num. 35:9-28).

P's notion of encroachment finds its most significant articulation in its formula הזר הקרב יומת (Num. 1:51; 3:10, 38; 18:7), which should be rendered "the unauthorized encroacher shall be slain." The context of the formula invariably is the elaboration of the guarding duties of the priestly and Levitic cordons in and around the tabernacle. Num. 18 in particular specifies the hierarchy of responsibility in the shared custody of the tabernacle. The priests are responsible for the encroachment of disqualified priests at the altar and within the shrine (Num. 18:1, 7*a*; cf. 3:10). Both priests and Levites guard the sanctums against possible encroachment by the Levites (Num. 18:3, 5*a*). When, however, the sanctums are in transit, the Kohathite Levites who carry them by shoulder (Num. 4:15-20; 7:9) must protect them from Israelite encroachment (Num. 4:18-19). Finally, the Levite cordon stationed outside the tabernacle guards against possible incursions by Israelites (Num. 18:3, 22-23). The gradations of responsibility are in accordance with the physical realities—the actual distribution of the sacral guards.

The most significant aspect of this formula is its penalty. Whereas God alone punishes for cultic sins (*yāmûth* [*qal*]), in the case of encroachment upon sanctums, death is imposed by man (*yûmath* [*hophal*]). The graded scale of tabernacle responsibility (*above*) clarifies this alleged exception: the wrath of God kindled by the Israelite encroacher does not vent itself on the people but vents itself on the negligent Levite guards. The latter, therefore, are empowered to kill the encroacher; he is their potential murderer, and they slay him in self-defense. Indeed, according to P, it is the Levites' mortal risk in guarding the tabernacle that entitles them to the largesse of the tithes as their reward (Num. 18:21, 31). Such ransoming of Israelites by Levites is not an instance of vicarious atonement, i.e., the innocent suffer for the sake of the wicked. The formula implies the reverse: encroaching Israelites are ransomed only by the guilty Levites, i.e., the negligent Levite guards. Whereas the doctrine of collective responsibility is the cornerstone of P's theology, a concession is made within the sanctuary to limit its destructiveness to the clergy alone. Thus Num. 18 is a fitting appendix to the Korahite rebellion (chs. 16–17). In the wake of the rebellion, God inflicts a plague upon the entire camp (Num. 16:46-50 [H 17:11-15]). The people panic; henceforth, they will have nothing to do with the tabernacle (17:13 [H 28]). Num. 18 is both the remedy and consolation. Thereafter, the sacral guards will bear the responsibility for lay encroachment. The doctrine of collective responsibility is compromised for Israel's sake so that it may again worship at the sanctuary without fear.

Bibliography. *RLA,* III (1957-71), under "Grenze"; J. Milgrom, *Studies in Levitical Terminology,* I (1970), 1-59.

J. MILGROM

***ENOCH, BOOK OF.** Alternately: I ENOCH; ETHIOPIC ENOCH. A collection of pseudepigraphic writings composed in the third to first centuries B.C. under the names of ENOCH, son of Jared, and Noah (*see* PSEUDONYMOUS WRITING[S]). The collection is extant in its entirety only in an Ethiopic translation of a Greek translation of Aramaic originals. The discovery of fragmentary

Aramaic MSS of Enoch among the DEAD SEA SCROLLS, as well as the renewed discussion of apocalyptic, make the re-evaluation and reinterpretation of these materials both necessary and possible.

1. Qumran MSS. The following MSS have been identified and dated.

4Q	chs. 1-5	6-36	72-82	83-90	91-105	106-7
Hen^{a} (200-150)	]x	x[				
Hen^{b} (± 150)	]x	x[				
Hen^{c} (30-1)	]x	x[		]x[	]x	x[
Hen^{d} (30-1)		]x[		]x[		
Hen^{e} (100-50)		]x[		]x[		
Hen^{f} (150-125)				]x[		
Hen^{g} (± 50)					]x[	
Henastr^{a-d} (200-±1)			]x[			

[ ] indicate MS is mutilated at beginning or end of section

2. Contents: ***a. Introduction (chs. 1–5).*** The presence of these chapters in early Qumran MSS indicates that originally they introduced a shorter writing: either chs. 1–19 or 1–36.

b. The Book of the Watchers (chs. 6–36). Chs. 6–11 conflate two traditions about the origin and judgment of sin. The first, a narrative expansion of Gen. 6:1-4, depicts the rebellion of the angel *Šemiḥazah* and his hosts. Their intercourse with women produces a race of half-breed giants, whose devastation of the earth and the human race triggers divine judgment. The pathos evident in the lengthy, angelic plea in behalf of mankind and the world (9:4-11), as well as the lengthy description of the judgment and the *eschaton* which follows it (10:11–11:2), strongly suggest that we have here not an etiology of sin in general, but an apocalyptic allegory which describes the demonic origin of the mighty of the author's own time and announces their impending destruction. A date at least well back into the third century B.C. is required by the evidence of the second-century MSS (4QHen^{ab}) in which this tradition has been combined with others and prefaced by the introduction.

The *Šemiḥazah* story has been expanded by a tradition in which the angelic rebellion consists in the revelation of heavenly secrets to mankind. Detailed similarities to Greek traditions about Prometheus are evident. The angelic chief here is Azazel or *'Asa'el* (cf. 6:7). He is identified with the AZAZEL of Lev. 16, and motifs from this chapter have informed Enoch 10 (especially vss. 4-8).

Chs. 12–16, Enoch's ascent to heaven and commission, stress that the irregular intercourse between spirit and flesh was bound to result in disaster, viz., the demonic presence on earth, and underscore the certainty of the judgment.

Enoch's journey to the ends of the earth (chs. 17–19) culminates in a vision of the angels' place of punishment. An evident subscription in 19:3 indicates the end of an earlier work. In chs. 20–32, a second journey tradition repeats material in chs. 17–19 and expands it with information of eschatological interest (22; 24:4–27:5). Chs. 33–36 are a compression of the astronomical material in chs. 72–82.

c. The Book of Parables (chs. 37–71). This modern title is somewhat deceptive, since Enoch's transmission of revelation in the form of a "parable" is mentioned also in 1:2; 93:1, 3 (all attested in Aram. MSS). The theme of the whole of chs. 37–71 is the coming judgment, which is anticipated and described in a series of heavenly scenes. Interspersed among these are brief references to the revelation of heavenly (astronomical) secrets, descriptions of journeys to the places of punishment for men and angels, and narrative material about Noah and the Flood. Thus, the types of material in chs. 37–71 closely parallel those in chs. 1–36.

Peculiar to the eschatology of this book is the SON OF MAN or "Elect One," a mysterious, angel-like figure (46:1) who champions the cause of the righteous and executes the final judgment. He is introduced in a scene closely related to Dan. 7:9-10, 13 (46:1-3; 47:3) and is "named" in a scene that is dependent on the call of Second Isaiah's Servant (ch. 48; cf. Isa. 49:1-8). His titles are drawn from Dan. 7:13, Isa. 42:1 (cf. Enoch 49:4), and perhaps Isa. 53:11 (cf. Enoch 38:2). The principal judgment scene (Enoch 62–63) has a close parallel in Wisd. Sol. 5, and both are variations of a traditional expansion of Isa. 52–53, in which the exalted one executes judgment on his former persecutors. Enoch identifies this figure with Daniel's "one like a son of man," there the exalted, angelic patron of righteous Israel, and attributes to him the execution of judgment against "the kings and the mighty"—the persecutors of the righteous.

d. The Book of the Heavenly Luminaries (chs. 72–82). Enoch's special connection with astronomical instruction is widespread and very old (cf. Jub. 4:17; 1QapGen 19.25; Euseb. *Preparatio Evangelica* IX.xvii.8-9). In chs. 72–82, the angel Uriel reveals to Enoch the movement of the heavenly bodies according to a 364-day calendar. This latter fact would have made the book of great interest to the Qumran community. The book is preserved alone in four MSS ranging from 200 B.C. to the turn of the era, in a much fuller form than in the Ethiopic book.

e. The Dream Visions (chs. 83–90). The second dream vision is a typical historical apocalypse which describes events down to the present crisis, which will be resolved by an imminent judgment that will inaugurate the *eschaton*. Like several of its sister apocalypses (Dan. 10–12; Assumption of Moses; Jub. 23:17 ff.), it dates from the time of Antiochus Epiphanes (*see* ANTIOCHUS §4).

f. A book of exhortations and woes (chs. 92–105). 4QHen^{g} indicates the following order for this section: 91:1-10, 18-19; 92:1-5; 93:1-10; 91:11-17; 93:11-14 (in a much fuller form); 94:1 ff. 4QHen^{c} contains ch. 105, previously thought to be a Christian interpolation. The reprise of themes from 92:1 in ch. 105 suggests that these chapters delimit a separate book of Enoch that circulated independently (as indicated by the Chester Beatty papyrus of this section). The book reflects a time of bitter antagonism in which the rich and the mighty ("the sinners") are oppressing the poor ("the righteous"). The theme of a coming judgment which will resolve this problem is carried in three forms which are the warp and weft of the book: *woes* that enumerate the sinners' deeds as the basis for their judgment; *exhortations* for the righteous to stand fast in view of the coming judgment; *descriptions* of the judgment and the events connected with it. The verbs used in the exhortations ("Have faith!" "Hope!" "Fear not!") indicate that the author is responding to a crisis in faith triggered by the disparity between faith and experience. The climax of the book (102:4–104:8) is a disputation on the problem of evil (*see* FUTURE LIFE IN INTERTESTAMENTAL LITERATURE[S] §2).

g. *The birth of Noah (chs. 106–107).* In this conclusion to the Enochic corpus, the miraculous birth of Noah is interpreted as a portent of salvation, in reality the salvation promised throughout the book. The Genesis Apocryphon of Qumran (*see* DEAD SEA SCROLLS §5*e*) recounts the same story, there told by Noah's father, LAMECH. His suspicion of his wife, detailed in that version, is paralleled by the same motif in the story of Melchizedek's birth at the end of II Enoch.

h. *The Book of the Giants.* This cycle of tales about the fallen angels and their progeny, hitherto known only from Manichean writings, has survived in at least six Aramaic copies among the DSS. While analysis must await more complete publication, it is evident that the Ethiopic corpus represents only part of a wider Enochic-Noachic tradition.

3. Apocalyptic. (*See* APOCALYPSE[S]; APOCALYPTICISM[S].) The Enochic corpus is a series of revelations of eschatological and cosmological secrets. Common to the eschatological material is a situation of persecution or oppression, the promised remedy of which is an imminent divine judgment which is the subject of the revelation. Presumed throughout, but emphasized in varying degrees, are two levels of reality: the mythical and the historical. The earliest strata in chs. 6 ff. deal primarily with the mythical. They attribute the presence of evil to angelic rebellion and focus on the judgment of these angels. In chs. 85–90, this rebellion is one episode in primordial history, but it has its counterparts in the wicked deeds of the postexilic angelic shepherds. Over against and related to this angelic level, the deeds of human history are recited. Judgment will be dispensed to all the principals: human and angelic. The parables pay primary attention to "the kings and the mighty," the historical foes of the author and his people, but they do so primarily in the mythical context of the final judgment. They also devote considerable space to the angelic rebels. Chs. 92–105 focus almost exclusively on the level of history and human deeds, although reference is made to the angelic mediation that will trigger the judgment. In all these writings, final judgment is executed by God or his heavenly agent (s), and this involves an end to history and the beginning of a new and final era or situation described in heavenly or mythical superlatives.

Within their present literary setting, cosmological revelations must be interpreted with reference to this eschatology. Descriptions of the places of judgment, the resting places of the righteous, and the new Jerusalem provide a locative reference and reassurance to the temporalized announcements of the judgment. The temporal and spacial dimensions flow together in the parables, where the seer is witness to the judgment and the events leading up to it. The geographical details in 17:1–18:5 and 28:1–32:2 may have the literary function of documenting Enoch's trip to places of eschatological interest. Nonetheless, behind these literary purposes, there was a much broader interest in cosmological and "scientific" matters, the revelatory contexts and aspects of which must still be investigated in the light of catalogues of revealed (and nonrevealed) things in other apocalyptic and in wisdom literature.

4. Provenance. Essential to most of Enoch is a distinction between the righteous and the sinners, which at times suggests a genuine sectarianism (*see* APOCALYPTICISM[S] §3*d*). Least typical in this respect are the older materials in chs. 6–16, where the primary antithesis is between beleaguered humanity as a whole and the semidivine giants and their fathers. The distinction does appear in 10:14, 17, however, and the introduction to the section (chs. 1–5) is a salvation-judgment oracle, announcing vindication for "the elect" and "the righteous" and punishment for "the sinners." The animal apocalypse contrasts the awakened *hasidim* with the deaf and blind Hellenizers (90:6-7) (*see* HASIDEANS). The Apocalypse of Weeks (93:1-10; 91:11-17), a traditional piece utilized in chs. 92–105, depicts the foundation of the hasidic community as an eschatological event (93:9-10), and we are not far removed from the viewpoint of Qumran sectarianism (cf. CD 1.3-12). The rest of chs. 92–105 are probably contemporaneous with the early years of the Qumran community (± 100 B.C.) and speak against a common foe, the Hasmonean rulers and their friends. Moreover, the religious and theological concerns expressed in 98:9–99:10 and the inclusion of this section in Qumran MSS suggest a point of origin within the orbit of the ESSENE community. But typical features of Qumran sectarian documents are missing: clear references to a community and the use of the term "the elect"; a pronounced dualism; references to the priestly or temple connections and abuses of the opponents.

The parables were unknown at Qumran, if we may judge from the MSS. However, the hypothesis of a Christian origin seems highly unlikely in view of a total lack of christological references in the son of man passages. Occasional historical references (56:5-7; 67:8-13) suggest a date around the turn of the era. The frequent use of "the elect" as a designation for the righteous, and the occurrence of expressions like "the congregation of the righteous" (38:1; cf. 53:6; 62:8) may reflect a genuine sectarianism.

The Enochic corpus arose and was reworked and transmitted in circles that can be identified only partly with known Jewish groups. As such it witnesses to the complexity of sectarian and quasi-sectarian Judaism in this era. *See also* PSEUDEPIGRAPHA; PSEUDEPIGRAPHA[S].

Bibliography. M. Black, ed., *Apocalypsis Henochi Graece, Pseudepigrapha Veteris Testamenti Graece,* III (1970), extant Greek texts; J. T. Milik, "Problèmes de la littérature hénochique à la lumière des fragments araméens de Qumrân," *HTR,* LXIV (1971), 333-78,

"Turfan et Qumran: Livre des Géants juif et manichéen," *Tradition und Glaube*, ed. G. Jeremias *et al.* (1971), pp. 117-27, and "Fragments grecs du livre d'Hénoch (P. Oxy. XVII 2069)," *Chronique d'Égypte*, XLVI (1971), 321-43. On the traditions about the Elect One, see G. W. E. Nickelsburg, Jr., *Resurrection, Immortality, and Eternal Life in Intertestamental Judaism*, HTS, XXVI (1972), 70-75.

G. W. E. NICKELSBURG, JR.

ENOCH, SECRETS OF. Also known as the Slavonic Book of Enoch, or the Slavonic Apocalypse of Enoch, or II Enoch. *See* PSEUDEPIGRAPHA §2 (II,E); PSEUDEPIGRAPHA[S] §2*d*.

***EPHESIANS, LETTER TO THE. 1. Authorship.** This question hangs with that of the letter to the COLOSSIANS, for which Pauline authorship is less generally accepted today than in the beginning and middle of this century. If Colossians, but not Ephesians, was written by Paul, the imitation would in some respects be more "Pauline" than the authentic letter. Thus, an increasing number of scholars tend to think that Paul was the author of neither of these letters—or of both of them.

The style of Ephesians is peculiar, with long chains of loosely appended prepositional phrases, subordinate clauses, etc. But in some respects Colossians departs even more from the style of the undisputed letters; cf., e.g., the paucity of causal and adversative conjunctions. Themes like the Holy Spirit, grace and works, and Israel and the Gentiles are more prominent in Ephesians than in Colossians, and in Ephesians a "cosmic Christology" has been more thoroughly integrated with Paul's idea of the church as one body with many interdependent members (Eph. 4:7-16, 25; 5:30; contrast Col. 1:15-17; 2:10, 19).

Ephesians resembles a mosaic, but the pieces are not all taken from the letters of Paul. OT allusions, quotations, and interpretations presuppose earlier usage (Eph. 2:13-22; 4:8-10; 5:28-33; 6:14-17, etc.). Statements like Eph. 1:20-23, that Christ is enthroned above all cosmic powers, and Eph. 2:5-7, that Christians have been made alive and enthroned with him, are likely to be derived from early hymns. In I Cor. 15:25-28 and Rom. 6 Paul qualifies this type of realized eschatology. Traditional warnings against fellowship with evildoers are reproduced in Eph. 5:5-13, but without the clarifying interpretation added in I Cor. 5:9-12. A common topic, that ignorance of God causes moral decay, is used in a much more conventional way in Eph. 4:17-20 than in Rom. 1:18-31. Similarities with I Peter and other writings confirm that Ephesians draws upon the phraseology, patterns, and themes of early Christian worship and teaching.

The author's familiarity with Colossians does not fully explain the combination of verbal similarities and differences. The two letters are likely to have originated in the same linguistic environment. Two main options deserve consideration: (*a*) Different assistants of the imprisoned apostle wrote three letters: to PHILEMON, to the Colossians, and our Ephesians, possibly destined for HIERAPOLIS and LAODICEA. (*b*) Colossians and, somewhat later, Ephesians were both written by members of a "Pauline school" which continued to exist after the death of the apostle, perhaps in Ephesus. The first theory operates with the fewest unknown factors. The second accounts better for the absence of any specific epistolary situation and what seems to be a post-Pauline perspective in Ephesians (cf. esp. Eph. 2:20; 3:2-11; 4:11-14).

Remarkable analogies to Ephesians can be found both in the devotional language of Palestinian Judaism and in the more philosophical terminology of PHILO. The author himself was probably a Jew, younger than Paul, though converted to a Pauline form of Christianity. Some, but not many, persons of this type are known to us (cf. Col. 4:10-11).

2. Composition and scope. In spite of its lack of specific statements, Ephesians is not a theological tractate or a meditation upon the theme Christ and the church. It belongs to a type of Greek letters—genuine and spurious—which substitute for a public speech rather than for private conversation. The epistolary purpose is to overcome separation and establish contact between sender and recipients, or even to mediate the apostle's presence to Gentile Christians who are separated from him in time rather than in space.

The opening praise of God strikes a congratulatory note (Eph. 1:3-14; cf. I Pet. 1:3-12; II Chr. 2:11-12). The benediction, assertions of thanksgiving and intercession, and a doxology form the framework for a panegyric that recounts the implications of God's call, the working of his power, the privileges bestowed upon former Gentiles, and the special grace given to Paul (Eph. 1:3–3:21). In the second part of the letter the recipients are urged to live up to their calling and are reminded of what they have been taught (4:1–6:20). Little or no new information is communicated. There is no argumentation in the style of forensic speeches or popular diatribe. The content of the letter is recollection and EXHORTATION, anamnesis and PARENESIS, rather than theology and ethic.

The theory that Ephesians presupposes a coherent, Gnostic redeemer myth has not proved tenable. But the author does use the lofty language of esoteric knowledge and cosmic religion to celebrate redemption in Christ. He represents Paul as the mediator of revealed wisdom and the church as the body of Christ, in whom Israel and the Gentiles have been made one, and in whom the "re-capitulation" of the universe has begun. The "great mystery" of Christ's sacred marriage with the church serves as the basis for injunctions to mutual subordination in conjugal love (Eph. 5:21-33). The author does not combat deceiving "winds of doctrine" (cf. Eph. 4:14). He rises above them by demonstrating the superiority of what is given in Christ, as proclaimed by Paul, in order that all members of the church may grow in common faith, love, and knowledge.

3. Problem of interpretation. Ephesians has been seen as the mature fruit of Paul's thought, as the beginning of its distortion, or as an inspired reinterpretation. The Pauline paradox of wisdom and foolishness, power and weakness, is no longer explicit, but it is implicit, insofar as wisdom, glory, riches, and unity are ascribed to Christians who lacked any unified organization and who had little influence in a world where it was in no way manifest that all powers had been made subject to Christ. But terms like "the church," "the saints," or "Israel," which Paul uses to refer to identifiable social realities, have become more vague and abstract. One might say that Ephesians is utopian, whereas Paul is paradoxical.

One line of development leads from Paul via Ephesians to second-century Gnostics, to whom "the church" (ἐκκλησία) was a spiritual and heavenly entity. Another development leads to Irenaeus and other antiheretical fathers, to whom the unity of the catholic church is guaranteed by apostolic tradition and episcopal succession. Later church history amply demonstrates how much the interpretation of Ephesians depends upon the context in which the letter is read and upon the presuppositions of its readers.

Bibliography. Commentaries: H. Schlier, *Der Brief an die Epheser* (1957), major Ger. work; J. A. Allan, *The Epistle to the Ephesians,* Torch Bible Commentaries (1959); J. Gnilka, HTKNT (1971), representative of contemporary Ger. interpretation; M. Barth, ABi, 2 vols. (1974), independent, excellent bibliographies.

Special studies: E. Käsemann, "Ephesians and Acts," *Studies in Luke-Acts,* ed. L. E. Keck and J. L. Martyn (1966), pp. 288-97; J. C. Kirby, *Ephesians, Baptism and Pentecost* (1968), liturgical background; J. P. Sampley, *"And the two shall become one flesh": A Study of Traditions in Eph. 5:21-33,* NTSMS, XVI (1971); H. Merklein, *Das kirchliche Amt nach dem Epheserbrief,* StANT, XXXIII (1973); K. M. Fischer, *Tendenz und Absicht des Epheserbriefes, FRLANT,* CXI (1973); D. Smith, "The Two Made One: Some Observations on Eph. 2:14-18," *Ohio Journal of Religious Studies,* I (1973), 34-54; A. van Roon, *Is Ephesians authentic?* NovTSup, XXXIX (1974), detailed investigation; N. A. Dahl, "Cosmic Dimensions and Religious Knowledge (Eph. 3:18)," *Jesus und Paulus,* ed. E. E. Ellis and E. Grässer (1975), pp. 57-75; A. Lindeman, *Die Aufhebung der Zeit,* StNT, XII (1975).

Unpublished dissertations: D. C. Smith, "Jewish and Greek Traditions in Eph. 2:11-22" (Yale, 1970); W. H. Rader, "The Church and Racial Hostility" (Basel, 1970), Eph. 2:11-22 in the history of interpretation; H. J. Lester, "Relative Clauses in the Pauline Homologoumena and Antilegomena" (Yale, 1973), syntax and style.

N. A. DAHL

***EPHESUS.** Recent excavation, conservation, and restoration at Ephesus have added tremendously to the appearance of the ancient city. The atmosphere of the city and the various aspects of ancient life which can be observed here now make Ephesus the rival of ATHENS, Pompeii, ROME, and Ostia.

1. The altar and temple of Artemis. One of the most important results of the recent excavations has been the discovery of the great altar of the Artemision. The rectangular altar precinct stood before the W façade of the Archaic temple, on axis and parallel to it. In the excavator's reconstruction the altar comprised a large sacrificial stone table approached by a rampway. During the late Archaic period a low wall was thrown around three sides of the table, including the side facing the temple, leaving open only the fourth side toward the sea on the W. The courtyard so formed was approximately fifty feet deep and one hundred feet broad, broader then than the similar but later Altar of Zeus at PERGAMUM. In late Classical times the enclosure on the same foundations consisted of a base sculptured with reliefs above which stood a series of Ionic columns.

In hopes of solving the long-standing controversy over the ground plans and reconstructions of the early and later temples, the Artemision itself has received more attention. Suggestions have been made for restoring the original Archaic Artemision with double rows of columns on the four sides of a structure divided into forehall, large central area, and reserved rear chamber. The later Classical temple remained essentially the same except for some enlargement and modification, including the addition of a third row of eight columns on the W which served to advance the façade of the temple; by this means an epiphany of the goddess through doors in the pediment of the temple's roof could be seen more easily over the walls of the altar's court. The central unroofed area was entered down a flight of stairs from the front porch of the temple. In this central area stood a small shrine for the cult image of ARTEMIS Ephesia, a stiff, pillar-like figure wearing a corselet of eggs and a long, fitted skirt worked with various animal figures. The suggested reconstruction makes the Artemision very similar to the temple of Apollo at Didyma near MILETUS, which did in fact have the same architect, Paionios of Ephesus (Vitruvius, *On Architecture* VII, Preface [16]).

After being destroyed by the Goths in A.D. 263 the temple of Artemis may have been partially repaired, but with the advance of Christianity the temple gradually became no more than a quarry for materials reused in Late Antique, Medieval, and Turkish constructions in Selçuk (Church of St. John) and Istanbul (Hagia Sophia).

2. Civic agora. The ceremonial center of the city established by ALEXANDER's general Lysimachus was the shrine of Hera Boulaia on the saddle between Mounts Pion and Koressos. In this shrine a sacred hearth representing the well-being of the city was kept constantly burning. Here also was the assembly hall for the city councilors (*bouleuterion*), offices for the duty officials (*prytaneion*), and a large three-aisled hall (*basilica*) for transaction of business and legal proceedings as well as for the display of the laws and public announcements. Numerous portrait heads from commemorative statues set up here have been found; several, including one of AUGUSTUS, had been mutilated by zealous Christians who hacked crosses into the foreheads of the portraits (Fig. E1). Within the great square below the basilica stood a small temple built in the late first century B.C. and demolished in the time of Theodosius. A black stone head of AMMON and the rattle from a sistrum indicate that the temple may have been dedicated to the Egyptian gods, while a large portrait head of Antony discovered in the area suggests that Antony and Cleopatra commissioned its construction.

3. Baths of Scholastikia. During the rule of Theodosius at the end of the fourth century, ma-

Austrian Archaeological Institute, Vienna

1. Bust of Augustus, with the cross subsequently carved on his forehead

Austrian Archaeological Institute, Vienna

2. Fresco portrait of Socrates from Ephesus

terial was robbed from the sanctuary of Hera Boulaia and surrounding buildings by a Christian woman named Scholastikia, in order to renovate a large bath at the intersection of the "Street of the Kouretes" and the "Marble Road" in central Ephesus. Two statues of Ephesian Artemis (one carved from translucent Parian marble and bearing traces of gilding) were found carefully buried beside the robbed buildings. It would seem that certain persons objected to burning the images into lime for mortar, because they at least did not believe Paul's dictum that "gods made with hands are not gods" (Acts 19:26). The Baths of Scholastikia included almost every facility for bodily comfort: eating places, dressing rooms, hot and cold baths, massage and anointing chambers, a lavatory, and even a large *paidiskeion* (brothel) decorated with mosaics and frescoes.

4. Residences. On the S side of the so-called Street of the Kouretes running between the civic agora and the lower, commercial agora, a number of well-preserved houses crowded together on a series of ascending terraces have been excavated. These upper-middle-class residences had a multistoried appearance not unlike certain apartment buildings in Rome and Ostia. The apartment block is fronted by a colonnade sheltering stores and taverns. Passageways between the shops lead from the street up to the entrances of individual living quarters. Each section usually centers around a small open colonnaded courtyard from which subsidiary rooms are entered. The standard of living varied from section to section, but generally the apartments seem to have been fairly comfortable. At least two had heated bathrooms; several boasted colored marble wall revetments and floor mosaics, as well as glass, ivory, bronze, and marble adornments; such amenities as running water and wall frescoes were common. The construction and refurbishing of these apartments continued from the first into the seventh century A.D.

5. Churches and mosques. The major Christian shrines at Ephesus symbolically link the ancient world with late medieval and modern times. The Church of St. John, the study of which is now being continued with excavation and restoration, stands close by the Sultan İsa Bey Camii (Mosque of Sultan Jesus I of the Aydınoğlu dynasty) erected in A.D. 1375. In 1955 a cave-like chapel on Mount Koressos above the city to the S was discovered, and graffiti here attest for the first time in Ephesus the invocation of PAUL as a saint. The controversial last home of the Virgin (Meryem Ana or Panaya Kapulu, S of Ephesus) was visited by Pope Paul in 1967. The Church of Mary in Ephesus proper was built inside a Roman structure which has been recognized as the stock exchange for the bankers of ancient Ephesus. The Third Ecumenical Council held in this church in A.D. 431 established a secure cult position for the Virgin as the divine Mother of God; she thereby completely usurped the status of Artemis, "Mother of the Gods."

Bibliography. New final reports in *Forschungen in Ephesus* VI-VII, *Österreichisches Archäologisches Institut in Wien* (1971 ff.); annual preliminary reports in *Anzeiger der phil.-hist. Klasse der Österreichischen Akademie der Wissenschaften Wien,* and articles on various aspects of the city in *Jahreshefte des Österreichischen Archäologischen Instituts in Wien, Hauptblatt* and *Beiblatt;* D. Knibbe, W. Alzinger, and S. Karwiese, "Ephesos," *PW, Supplementband* XII (1970), cols. 248-364; J. Keil, *Ephesos, Ein Führer durch die Ruinenstätte und ihre Geschichte* (5th ed., 1964); A. Bammer, "Der Altar des jüngeren Artemisions von Ephesos," *Archäologischer Anzeiger* of the *Jahrbuch des deutschen archäologischen Instituts,* LXXXIII (1968), 400-423; LXXXVII (1972), 714-28, *Die Architektur des jüngeren Artemision von Ephesos* (1972), "Die Entwicklung des Opferkultes am Altar des Artemis von Ephesos," *Istanbuler Mitteilungen* 23/24 (1973/

1974), 53-63; R. Fleischer, *Artemis von Ephesos und verwandte Kultstatuen aus Anatolien und Syrien* (1973); O. F. A. Meinardus, *St. Paul in Ephesus and the Cities of Galatia and Cyprus* (1973).

D. Boyd

EPICTETUS ĕp ĭk tē'tŭs. Greek philosopher born *ca.* A.D. 50 in Hierapolis in Phrygia. As a young slave he was taken to Rome, where he came under the influence of the Stoic philosopher Musonius Rufus. Later he was set free. At an indeterminate time he was banished by Domitian and took up residence in Nicopolis in southern Epirus, where he lived to the end of his life, attracting students to a school in which he gave instruction in philosophy. His reputation spread far and wide during his lifetime, and he was highly regarded by pagans and Christians in late antiquity. He died *ca.* 125.

Epictetus himself wrote nothing. His teaching was preserved in two works by his disciple Arrian, the historian of Alexander the Great. The *Discourses* or *Diatribes,* originally in eight books of which four and some fragments are extant, are Arrian's account of Epictetus' instruction. They are important examples of the diatribe. Epictetus' adaptation of the diatribe style has more in common with the style of an earlier period than with that of his contemporaries. The *Manual* or *Encheiridion* consists of a collection of Epictetus' philosophical sayings which Arrian regarded as most useful to urge the soul to virtue.

Epictetus' philosophy is Stoic (*see* Stoics) with a strong Cynic coloring (*see* Cynics[S]). This is most clear in his idealization of the Cynic (*Discourses* III.xxii), in his attitude toward scientific learning, and in his stress on ethics. In his philosophical system logic and physics are subservient to ethics. One must study Stoic logic in order to examine the decisions of one's will, but only those logical principles are necessary which enable one to get rid of fear, grief, passion, and so to attain freedom. The philosopher's lecture room is a hospital for sick souls in which the listeners become aware of their own weakness (*Discourses* III.xxiii.30; II.xi.1), a consciousness of which enables them to see what the work that leads to virtue is. A person experiences a conversion (ἐπιστροφή) when he comes to his senses and realizes the state he is in. He then questions, in each instance, whether his external impressions are in accordance with nature. Moral progress can only be made when one has turned to one's own moral choice (προαίρεσις) and strives to perfect it and make it harmonize with nature. Our moral choice consists in limiting our desires to things in our power, and is the basis of ethics. Only things within our power have to do with virtue. Such things as possessions, health, and family and social relationships appear to be goods, but are really indifferent.

One is free only when living in accordance with one's moral choice. This shows the desire to be of one mind with God and in fellowship with him. The philosopher is God's witness, scout (κατάσκοπος), and messenger, sent by God to show people that they have gone astray and to instruct them in the true meaning of the good (*Discourses* I.xxix.46-49; III.xxii.23-24; IV.viii.30-32). This is a task undertaken only with the conviction that it is God's will. Then one can with confidence assume one's assigned place in the ordered universe. By acceding to the divine will freedom is not forfeited; rather, it is found when one aligns oneself with God.

Epictetus' religious language has led to the suspicion of interdependence between him and the NT. Furthermore, the NT attests the existence of Christians in Hierapolis, Rome, and Nicopolis, the three cities where he was active, and Epictetus does speak of Christians, calling them Jews and Galileans (*Discourses* II.ix.19-21; IV.vii.6). Nevertheless, Epictetus' piety is basically that of Stoic pantheism; there is no evidence that he actually came in contact with Christians; and his comments on them are not favorable. There are, however, parallels between him and the NT: various elements of the diatribe style are found in both: both use lists of virtues and vices and *Haustafeln* (*see* Lists, Ethical §2*b*; Lists, Ethical[S] §2*b*), and they both describe the messenger sent by God to convert mankind in similar terms. Rather than showing direct dependence on each other, these similarities reflect the Christian appropriation of the language and literary devices of the ethical philosophers of the period, of whom Epictetus is a major representative.

Bibliography. *Epicteti dissertationes ab Arriano digestae,* ed. H. Schenkl (1916), critical text with index of Greek words; *Arrian's Discourses of Epictetus,* 2 vols., LCL, ed. W. A. Oldfather (1928), text and trans.; T. Zahn, *Der Stoiker Epiktet und sein Verhältnis zum Christentum* (2nd ed., 1895); A. Bonhöffer, *Epiktet und das NT* (1911); D. S. Sharp, *Epictetus and the NT* (1914); R. Bultmann, "Das religiöse Moment in der ethischen Unterweisung des Epiktets und das NT," *ZNW,* VIII (1912), 97-110, 177-91; M. Spanneut, "Epiktet," *RAC,* V (1962), cols. 599-681.

A. J. Malherbe

***ESCHATOLOGY OF THE NT.** "Eschatology" literally means the doctrine of the end or of the "last things." The term was first used by scholars of the nineteenth century as an alternative title for that section of theology which spoke about the doctrines of the physical death of individuals, the intermediate state of the soul, and the promised resurrection of the dead at the end of the world. Thus it is basically a term in systematic theology.

The NT texts do not focus primarily on the question of individualized eschatology, the death of a person, and the state after death. Instead they speak about the end of the world and of history. An investigation of the adjective "eschatological" (ἔσχατος) underlines this aspect: Christians wait for the coming of the last day, which will be announced by the last trumpet (I Cor. 15:52). Eschatological plagues will precede this final day (Rev. 15:1; 21:9); then the last enemy, death, will be overcome (I Cor. 15:26), and the resurrection of the dead, the last judgment, and final salvation will take place (John 6:39-40, 44, 54; 11:24; 12:48; I Pet. 1:5). In the NT perspective this final end time had already been inaugurated by the coming of Jesus Christ (Heb. 1:2; I Pet. 1:20). Therefore, the time of the Christians is the last time. They have received the eschatological gift of the Spirit (Acts 2:17; *see* HOLY SPIRIT §3*e*) and experience the eschatological tribulations (II Tim. 3:1; Jas. 5:3; I John 2:18; Jude 18; II Pet. 3:3). Scholars agree, therefore, that according to the NT the eschatological events are in some sense present and in some sense future. But after acknowledging the tension between the "already" and the "not yet" the scholarly consensus rapidly dissolves. Since the tension between the present and future is interpreted in very different ways, the term "eschatology" has been qualified with adjectives such as consistent, imminent, apocalyptic, thoroughgoing, futuristic, proleptic, realized, in the process of realization, inaugurated, or fulfilled, that indicate how the concept is understood (*see* §3 *below*).

Since the end of the nineteenth century, exegetes have more and more recognized that eschatological language is not a peripheral element of the NT, but is central for understanding Jesus as well as the theological perspective of the early Christian community. The history-of-religions school has pointed out the pervasive influence which Jewish APOCALYPTICISM had upon early Christian theology. NT eschatology is expressed in apocalyptic-cosmological concepts and images: the last tribulations, the great last day of the Lord, the PAROUSIA, the coming of the MESSIAH, the Last Judgment, the RESURRECTION of the dead, the future bliss and happiness. As in apocalypticism, eschatological salvation for the individual has as its condition a new heaven and earth, a new creation and paradise. Like apocalyptic language, eschatological imagery in the NT impresses us as strange and fantastic: stars fall from heaven, fire destroys the earth, the SON OF MAN comes on the clouds of heaven, or the works of the righteous are found recorded in heavenly books. Schweitzer therefore distinguished between *apocalypticism,* which binds Jesus to the concepts of his own time, and *eschatology,* which expresses the true meaning of these apocalyptic concepts and makes the message of Jesus valid for all times. This distinction between apocalypticism and eschatology has become normative for most serious theological inquiry, so that "apocalyptic" is often used in a pejorative sense. "Eschatology" is then used with reference to things eternal, and the real content of eschatology is strictly differentiated from the varying ideas and images of apocalypticism. The concept of eschatology, thus detemporalized, may be cast in existential terms. For example, in Bultmann's opinion the meaning of Jesus' eschatological message is that persons *now* stand under the necessity of decision. The real understanding of human existence and eschatology means that every hour is the "last hour."

Recent scholarly discussion, however, has pointed out that it is impossible to divorce apocalyptic language from its eschatological content. Against the pervasive reductionistic treatment of eschatological language, Doty stresses that this figurative and evaluative language expresses a visionary wholeness. It unites past experiences and anticipated futures and elicits comprehensions and expectations about the purpose of history and the world as well as of individual existence. NT eschatology is not only concerned with the future of the individual, but with that of the whole creation, as well as the whole of human history. In the NT eschatological language is apocalyptic language; as such it is cosmological, universal, political, and mythological.

The history-of-religions (*religionsgeschichtlich*) categories upon which scholars once based their reconstruction of primitive Christian history are widely questioned today, and it is therefore inadvisable to base an analysis of NT eschatology upon them. If methodological considerations preclude an investigation of NT eschatology starting with the "historical Jesus" or the different, culturally determined stages of the primitive Christian church, then we must reconstruct the eschatology of the NT literature itself. Such an approach reveals two kinds of eschatological understanding and hope. On the one hand are those writings which stress, often in apocalyptic language and imagery, the *future* aspect of eschatological salvation. This type includes also those writings that reflect on the interim time between the life of Jesus and his parousia. On the other hand are those NT writings which underline the experience and conviction that in Jesus Christ eschatological salvation is already a *present* reality. Yet it has to be emphasized that none of the NT writings stress one eschatological aspect to the total exclusion of the other. The two types of early Christian eschatology appear to have developed independently, but in dialectical tension with one another.

1. Eschatological salvation as future event
   - *a.* Paul
   - *b.* The synoptic tradition
     - i. The Logia source
     - ii. Mark
     - iii. Luke
     - iv. Matthew
   - *c.* The book of Revelation
2. Eschatological salvation as present
   - *a.* Enthusiastic eschatology
   - *b.* Colossians and Ephesians
   - *c.* The Fourth Gospel
3. Eschatological expectations of the "historical Jesus"
   - *a.* "Thoroughgoing eschatology"
   - *b.* "Apocalyptic eschatology"
   - *c.* "Realized eschatology"
   - *d.* "Inaugurated eschatology"

Bibliography

1. Eschatological salvation as future event. ***a. Paul.*** According to Paul's teaching, the cross and resurrection of Jesus Christ constitute the turning point of the ages. The time is fulfilled (Gal. 4:4), and anyone who is in Christ is "a new creation"; the old has passed away and the new has come (II Cor. 5:17; I Cor. 10:11). On the other hand, Paul also stresses the "not yet" of salvation. We are saved "in this hope" (Rom. 8:24); Christians baptized into the death of Christ will participate in the resurrection only in the future (Rom. 6:1 ff.). As heirs and fellow heirs the Christians will be delivered from the wrath to come (Rom. 5:9-11) and will be glorified with Christ (Rom. 8:17). Paul reminds the Corinthians that the world is passing away (I Cor. 7:31) and promises the Romans that creation itself will be set free from its bondage to decay (Rom. 8:21). The parousia of Christ will bring about the completion of the cosmic redemption which he inaugurated.

Paul uses apocalyptic imagery in order to maintain the difference between faith and sight. He is convinced that the "day of Christ" (Phil. 1:6, 10; 2:16; cf. I Cor. 4:5; II Cor. 5:10; Rom. 14:4) and the coming salvation are very near (Rom. 13:11 ff.; 2:3 ff.; 14:12) and will take place in his own lifetime. In I Thess. 4:13-18 Paul comforts the Thessalonians who are concerned about those who died before the "day of Christ." He promises that at the Lord's descent from heaven at the last day the dead will arise first, and together with those who are alive they will be "caught up . . . in the clouds to meet the Lord in the air" (vs. 17). In I Cor. 15 the imagery is somewhat different. Paul is still convinced that not all will have died at the day of the Lord (15:51). Both those who have fallen asleep and those still alive will attain the life of the resurrection only through a change into a celestial and spiritual body. Paul does not conceive of resurrection and new life in individualistic but in universal-cosmic terms. At the Parousia, when the end comes, after Christ has destroyed every authority and power, including even the last enemy, death, he will deliver the kingdom to God the Father (15:24-26). In Phil. 1:23-24 (and perhaps also in II Cor. 5:1 ff.) Paul associates his being "with Christ" with his own death. This text cannot be used as evidence that Paul changed his apocalyptic eschatological expectations, since in II Cor. 4:14 as well as in Phil. 3:11 Paul also expresses the hope for the future resurrection. (For a different view *see* PAUL THE APOSTLE[S] §2*a*, *b*.) Paul is confident that God's power will overcome the present evil forces exercising their dominion over people (cf. Rom. 5–7). For the righteous, the last day will be a day of salvation (Rom. 13:11-12) and glorification (Phil. 3:21; Rom. 8:18, 21; II Cor. 4:17); for the principalities and powers now ruling this world it will be a day of destruction.

God's power which transcends the present age and stands over and against the powers of this age is nevertheless already operative in the life of the Christians. They have already received his Spirit, and, as representatives of the new age, it is the ground of their hope (Rom. 8:11). Paul insists, however, that even while Christians are oriented toward the coming age and called thereby to freedom, they remain in this world and in danger of falling prey to its powers. Here Christian existence is understood in an apocalyptic context; eschatological and apocalyptic thought are intertwined. *See* PAUL THE APOSTLE §B10.

b. The synoptic tradition. i. *The Logia source.* In Q Jesus is the eschatological messenger and bringer of salvation. As eschatological prophet he casts out evil spirits (Luke 11:14-22; 17:20; Matt. 12:22-29; Mark 3:22-27), announces the coming of the KINGDOM OF GOD and inaugurates its establishment on earth (Luke 7:19-23; Matt. 11:2-6). Since Jesus is the eschatological messenger, each person's destiny is determined by the response that each makes to him. Thus the parenetic tone of the source is rooted in its eschatological outlook. The demands of eschatological DISCIPLESHIP are given in absolute terms: to follow Jesus means to give up one's home and to hate one's family (Luke 9:57; 14:25 ff.), to undergo tribulations and persecutions (Luke 12:2-12). Those who remain faithful will be vindicated on the last day. The time during which one may enter the New Age is brief (Luke 13:25-28) and God's judgment is imminent. Jesus teaches the disciples not only to pray for the coming of God's kingdom but also to pray that they will not have to live through the eschatological tribulations (Luke 11:1-4). The eschatological parables insist that since the coming of the Son of man cannot be predicted, one ought always to be prepared for the Parousia; the eschatological day comes suddenly but certainly (Luke 13:20-21). For Q, eschatological salvation means the reversal of the present conditions: the poor will inherit the kingdom (Luke 6:20-21); the persecuted disciples of Jesus will later rejoice (Luke 6:22-23) and take their rightful place in the kingdom, participating in judgment (Luke 22:29-30).

In summary, while Q reflects the expectation that the end is imminent, it also evidences the conviction that Jesus' ministry has already inaugurated eschatological salvation. This conviction forms the basis for the eschatological PARENESIS. Eschatological warning and promise are expressed in apocalyptic language and imagery.

ii. *Mark.* According to this gospel, the eschatological kingdom of God has drawn near in the work and life of Jesus (1:14-15). The kingdom is present, but hidden (4:26-29, 30-32) and will soon come in power (9:1). Since the kingdom does not at present manifest itself in power and glory, it is comprehensible only to those to whom its mystery is entrusted. There is a growing consensus among scholars that Markan redaction is discernible in 13:1-4, 28-37. Here the evangelist interprets the apocalyptic tradition, and thus reveals most clearly his own eschatological outlook. The tradition itself describes the tribulations of the interim before the eschaton (vss. 5*b*-23) and announces the parousia of the Son of man (vss. 24-27). Wars, earthquakes, famines, and persecutions are only the beginnings of the "birth-pangs" of the coming age. Only after the final tribulation will the end come, and that will mean the destruction of the cosmos and the vindication of the elect.

In the last section of the discourse, Mark spells out his own eschatological understanding. Vss. 28-31 answer the question of the disciples expressed in vs. 4: When will the end come? Mark stresses that the destruction of the Jerusalem temple is a sign that the kingdom is very near, to be expected within the lifespan of this generation (vss. 29-30). Nevertheless no one, not even Jesus, knows the exact day or hour. Vss. 33-37 draw the consequences for the behavior of the disciples: like the doorkeeper in the parable, the disciples must constantly watch, because the master will come suddenly (vss. 33, 35, 37).

Mark understands the time and fate of Christians during the interim to be analogous to that of

Jesus. The time for the proclamation of the gospel (13:10; 4:14) inevitably provokes persecutions and sufferings for the community. Those who have heard and accepted the message must now take up their cross and follow Jesus on his way to death (8:34-38). In this faithless and corrupt age the temptation is to be ashamed of Jesus and his words (8:38).

In order to strengthen the faith and endurance of this community Mark stresses both that the time of the end is very near and that everyone must remain watchful, because the Lord will come suddenly. The emphasis on the nearness and suddenness of the eschatological end thus serves parenetical purposes. *See* MARK, GOSPEL OF §9*d*; MARK, GOSPEL OF[S] §4*a*iii, *b*v, *c*.

iii. *Luke.* Conzelmann's interpretation of Lukan eschatology has been widely influential. In his view, Luke's eschatology represents not only a historicizing of the traditional eschatology but also a division of salvation history into periods. By distinguishing three periods in this history Luke replaces the traditional apocalyptic pattern of an imminent end of the age and points out the function of the church in God's plan. The evangelist interprets the apparent delay of the Parousia positively insofar as he characterizes the present time as the age of the world-wide mission of the church. Conzelmann maintains that the Little Apocalypse of Luke 21 reflects a tendency to distinguish between historical events and cosmic, supernatural events of the end time. Thus, while marking off distinct periods of salvation history to emphasize the historical events, Luke can at the same time emphasize the apocalyptic events by intensifying their apocalyptic features.

Conzelmann's view of salvation history and eschatology in Luke have been challenged, however. Critics maintain that Luke shows the same eschatological urgency as his sources and that he does not relegate eschatological matters to some distant future. Luke does not detemporalize early Christian eschatology but retains an urgent eschatological tension insofar as he connects the past ministry of Jesus, the missionary efforts of the community, and the future coming of the kingdom. This evangelist, like Mark, understands himself as living in the "last days" (Acts 2:17 ff.). He is convinced of the imminence of the end, but denies that it would come immediately (cf. Luke 19:11; 10:9, 11; 21:31-32). Luke expressly denies that one can assume a delay of the Parousia: God will not long delay but will vindicate his elect "speedily" (18:1-8). The disciples, therefore, have always to "be ready; for the Son of man is coming at an unexpected hour" (12:40; cf. vss. 41-46). *See* LUKE GOSPEL OF[S].

iv. *Matthew* adopts and intensifies the urgent expectancy and apocalyptic language of his sources. He places Jesus in the history of the church and expressly links eschatology with ecclesiology. Like Paul, he distinguishes between the kingdom of the Son and the kingdom of the Father. Matthew stresses the lowliness of Jesus and the hopes for his future appearance in glory. Even when he speaks of the kingdom as having come (with a saying derived from Q, 12:28), he retains the future nature of the judgment (12:27, 36-37), characterizes the present as a time of decision (12:30), and clearly distinguishes between this time and the future aeon (12:32).

Matthew links the eschatological expectation and the ethical parenesis. He alone gives a detailed description of the final judgment (25:31 ff.; 13:36 ff.; 7:21 ff.), which is inevitable and makes all persons accountable for their deeds (16:27). The interpretation of the parable of the "weeds among the wheat" (13:24-30, 36 ff.) points out that the church is not the assembly of the elect but a mixed group which is also subject to judgment. The Son of man will judge all according to one single standard—namely whether or not God's will was done (22:11-14; 16:27). Since the Parousia and the last judgment will come suddenly (24:43), Christians must watch and be ready (24:42, 44; 25:13). Matthew therefore concludes his apocalyptic discourse with the parables of the faithful and wicked servants (24:45-51), the wise and foolish maidens (25:1-13), and the talents (25:14-30), all of which demonstrate what faithfulness, zeal, and readiness mean. On the one hand, Matthew warns his readers not to rely on the delay of the eschatological coming of the Lord; he characterizes the words of the wicked servant, "my master is delayed" [χρονίζει μου ὁ κύριος] as an illusion (24:48). On the other hand, he criticizes the foolish young women for counting on the immediate arrival of the bridegroom and praises the wise ones for taking into account that their master would be away a long time. Matthew concludes the whole section with a portrait of the judgment of the world. All are judged by whether or not they have shown love to those who were in need. Eschatology and parenesis are clearly intertwined. *See* MATTHEW, GOSPEL OF §7; MATTHEW, GOSPEL OF[S] §3.

c. The book of Revelation. Here the conviction that Christ in heaven has assumed dominion over the world is combined with the expectation that he will soon manifest his dominion on earth. All the visions of Revelation stand under the sign of this imminent expectation. The eschatological end means the destruction of the antidivine powers, the judgment of the dead, and the vindication of the suffering of Christians.

By the use of apocalyptic materials and the application of traditional eschatological schemata, Revelation describes the present as the "short time" before the end. Although the parousia of Christ and the end are imminent, a certain time must elapse before they occur. Whereas in Mark the task for this interim is the proclamation of the gospel, in Revelation the duration of the "short time" depends upon the Christians' martyrdom (6:9-11). The task of Christians in the interim is to go into captivity or to death (13:10). Just as the victory of the Lamb in death was the prerequisite for his heavenly reign, so also the victory of the Christians in death is the prerequisite of the establishment of God's kingship on earth. Final salvation presupposes a new heaven and a new earth; after death, Hades and all antidivine forces are destroyed. *See* REVELATION, BOOK OF §E; REVELATION, BOOK OF[S] §2.

2. Eschatological salvation as present. Alongside

a temporal-futuristic eschatological expectation, the NT exhibits a strain of *realized* eschatology. This springs from the conviction that certain aspects of the future salvation are already experienced by Christians within present historical and worldly conditions. The expression "realized eschatology" does not imply a complete realization of eschatological salvation, since all Christian eschatologies, even those of the Gnostics, have both present and future aspects. But while futuristic eschatology understands the "already" of salvation in christological rather than anthropological terms, realized eschatology stresses the "already" of salvation as experienced by true Christians in the present.

a. Enthusiastic eschatology. It is no longer possible to ascribe futuristic eschatology to apocalypticism and realized eschatology to GNOSTICISM, since both strains of eschatology are found in the literature of Qumran (*see* DEAD SEA SCROLLS[S]). Kuhn has pointed out that the THANKSGIVING PSALMS use elements of the paradise tradition in order to conceptualize eschatological salvation as present reality. Here salvation manifests itself in the possession of the Spirit of God, in the experience of eschatological knowledge and joy, in the forgiveness of sins and in the cessation of sorrow. Five specific eschatological events were experienced by the Qumran community as present reality: resurrection, communion with angels, deliverance from the final power of death, a new community, and proleptic eschatological transference to heaven. This realized eschatology is rooted in the self-understanding of the community as being the eschatological temple and the dwelling place of God and the angels.

Traces of an early Christian self-understanding as rooted in the present experience of eschatological salvation are found in most of the NT writings. Research pertaining to Paul's "opponents" and to those of Mark, Luke, Matthew, the Pastoral epistles, and Revelation has uncovered remnants of such an early Christian enthusiasm. II Tim. 2:17*b*-18 contains the remark that there are Christians who hold that the resurrection has already occurred. In Paul's lifetime the same eschatological conviction probably existed in the Corinthian community, where enthusiasts believed that they were already rich and already kings (I Cor. 4:8). Since they believed that they possessed all that was hoped for, they denied the necessity of a future resurrection of the dead (15:12). If Jesus was exalted, so were his followers who have received the eschatological gift of the Spirit and who were thus able to speak in the tongues of angels (cf. 13:1). A similar eschatological enthusiasm has been suggested for the opponents alluded to in I and II Thessalonians and Philippians. Thus, it becomes increasingly apparent that Paul as well as other NT authors (e.g., those of Luke, Matthew, Mark, Pastorals, I John, and Revelation) developed their futuristic eschatology in dialogue and controversy with a realized eschatological perspective. Basic theological consequences of enthusiastic forms of realized eschatology are the detemporalizing, the spiritualizing, and the individualizing of eschatological hope in order to maintain its present reality. Such a realized eschatology is clearly expressed in the Deutero-Pauline tradition and in the Fourth Gospel.

b. Colossians and Ephesians. The most significant change in the Deutero-Pauline literature is the alteration of the Pauline future tenses into past tenses: Christians have been buried in baptism with Christ but have also been raised with him through faith (Col. 2:12). Eph. 2:5-6 maintains: "[God] made us alive together with Christ . . . and raised us up with him, and made us sit with him in the heavenly places." Even though elements of a temporal perspective are still found (e.g., Col. 1:21, 22-23; 3:3; Eph. 2:7), spatial concepts predominate.

In COLOSSIANS Christ is Lord of the cosmos, since he has overcome the cosmic powers and reconciled the world to himself (1:15-20; 2:9-15). By appropriating this event through BAPTISM (2:12; cf. 2:20 and 3:3), believers are emancipated from the cosmic powers and transferred to the kingdom of Christ (1:13). This redemption means forgiveness of sins (1:14; 2:13). Salvation has become available through the gospel, which has revealed the hidden mystery of God (1:26; 4:3). The content of the mystery is nothing other than God's plan of salvation (1:25 ff.). The gospel has not only revealed this mystery, but has also proclaimed "the hope laid up for you in heaven" (1:5). Salvation is present in the church, the body of Christ, yet the church has still to show that it is the real body of Christ by holding fast to him in suffering (1:24), in mutual instruction (3:16), in thanksgivings and songs (1:12; 2:7; 4:2), and in the ministry of love (3:14). Thus in Colossians the paradox of "already present" and "still future" salvation is maintained for the sake of parenesis. The statement of the new condition, "if then you have been raised with Christ," is followed by the imperative, "set your mind on the things that are above" (3:1-4).

EPHESIANS further develops this eschatological conception. In addition to the alteration of tenses (2:4-7), there is the notion that salvation is present in the church. Ephesians combines the mythical conception of the body of Christ with that of the "redeemed redeemer." Christ is head of the cosmos and head of the church in which Jews and Gentiles have become one. However, for the sake of ethical admonitions, Ephesians also maintains the tension between the "already" and "not yet." Although believers have been raised with Christ and enthroned in heavenly places, they must still put off their "old nature which belongs to [their] former manner of life" (4:22). They are freed from the cosmological powers, but they still have to fight against them (6:10 ff.). As in Colossians there is a warning that present salvation can be lost. The parenesis maintains that Christians are "heavenly beings" and as such must live in accordance with what they already are in Christ Jesus.

c. The Fourth Gospel. This evangelist views eschatological salvation as realized in the present. Believers already possess eternal life and no longer come under judgment (5:24). It is debated whether the so-called future, apocalyptic statements (5:28; 6:27; 12:25; 14:2-3; 17:24) are a genuine element of the evangelist's theology or whether they are added by an ecclesiastical redactor (Bultmann).

Even if these statements did originally belong to the gospel text, they are outnumbered, and the basic mood of the gospel reflects realized eschatology. This evangelist believes that the work of salvation is complete in Jesus Christ who is the "savior of the world" (4:42) and is its judge (3:1-21; 5:22-24). The judgment does not happen as a dramatic cosmic event but takes place in Jesus' word and the response of faith to it.

Those who believe in Jesus are no longer "of the world," even though they are still in the world (17:11, 14, 16). They have already gone through judgment, have left death behind them (8:51; 11:25), and have eternal life (3:36). According to the Fourth Gospel, the "already" of eschatological salvation is a present reality not only in Jesus Christ but also in the life of Christians.

Like Paul, John uses "this world" [ὁ κόσμος οὗτος] in order to characterize the radical opposition of the cosmos to God and Jesus. Yet the evangelist never contrasts "this world" with the "future age," the world to come. Here the time element has been eliminated. The essence of "this world" is darkness, falsehood, death, and bondage. The "ruler of this world" is the devil (12:31; 14:30; 16:11), and bondage to him is synonymous with bondage to sin and death. In distinction and opposition to "this world" Jesus is the light, the truth, the freedom, the life, and the resurrection.

The cosmological dualism in John is not absolute, since this world is the creation of God (1:3) and the object of his love (3:16). The cosmological dualism of apocalypticism has become a "dualism of decision" (Bultmann). Before the light came into the world the whole world was in darkness and death. But by sending his Son into the world, God asked people to decide for the light and against the darkness. Whether one belongs to the light or to the darkness is determined not by fate or by nature, but by one's decision for Jesus and against "this world." Such a decision is the transition into eschatological existence. Salvation, which took place once in the life of Jesus, continually takes place anew from above. Believers have nothing more to expect from the future than what they already have: life, glory, peace, love, and community.

The "not yet" of Christian salvation is maintained in the Farewell Discourses (chs. 13–17). The disciples are still in the world and still exposed to it. They are separated from their Lord and experience sorrow, trouble, persecution, and rejection. The farewell of Jesus means that he has gone in advance to prepare places in heaven for his own. In the time between Jesus' departure and his parousia the PARACLETE will represent him among the disciples.

The Fourth Gospel uses apocalyptic-eschatological language (e.g., judgment, the coming of the Lord, eternal life) in order to announce eschatological salvation as a present reality. This salvation is thus radically individualized and detemporalized. *See* JOHN, GOSPEL OF §D; JOHN, GOSPEL OF[S] §4.

3. Eschatological expectations of the "historical Jesus." The oldest synoptic traditions ascribe two different eschatological perspectives to Jesus. Some texts indicate that Jesus shared the hopes of Jewish apocalypticism and expected the end of the world, the coming of the Son of man on the clouds of heaven, and the establishment of the kingdom of God in the very near future (e.g., Mark 9:1; 13:30; Matt. 10:23). Other texts indicate that in the person and ministry of Jesus the time of salvation has already come and the kingdom of God is already a reality (e.g., Luke 11:20; 17:20-21; Matt. 11:12). Exegetes have dealt with these two opposite eschatological Jesus traditions in four different ways.

a. "Thoroughgoing eschatology." The expressions of imminent expectation and apocalyptic eschatology have been accepted as authentic words of the historical Jesus, whereas statements of realized eschatology have been explained away as expressions of the post-Easter church. This position contains two theological problems: First, if Jesus expected the end of the world and the coming of the kingdom in the lifetime of his hearers, then history has proven him wrong. Thus, the main theological problem of the early church must have been the "delay of the parousia." The author of I Clement addresses the problem (23:3-5), and so does the author of II Peter, who argues that "with the Lord one day is as a thousand years, and a thousand years as one day" (3:3-9). Exegetes have therefore proposed that the various dogmatic rationalizations and expressions of eschatological expectation were attempts to come to terms with the "delay of the end" (Werner, Grässer).

Second, if Jesus expected the imminent end of the world, then he was not only mistaken, but he ceases to be relevant for us. Weiss raised the crucial question of the relationship between the apocalyptic Jesus and our contemporary situation, maintaining that we have to rely on our own theological understanding and not on that of the historical Jesus, since the resurrected Lord is now guiding his community. Bultmann agrees with Weiss that Jesus' preaching is controlled by his imminent expectation. There can be no doubt that Jesus, like his contemporaries, expected a tremendous eschatological upheaval in the immediate future. Jesus' expectation implies for us that the eschatological time has come in the here and now. Through Jesus we are confronted by the immediacy of God and challenged to decision; the nearness of the kingdom confronts us with the ultimate "either-or." What is important is not the accuracy of Jesus' eschatological expectations but the validity of his understanding of life and human existence.

b. "Apocalyptic eschatology." Another exegetical position recognizes the apocalyptic-eschatological elements in the oldest synoptic traditions. Christian apocalyptic theology did not originate with Jesus, but in the post-Easter enthusiasm of the primitive church. Jesus began with the same burning eschatological expectation as JOHN THE BAPTIST, but Jesus was speaking of the coming of the kingdom in a different sense from that of John and contemporary Judaism. Jesus' preaching does not distinguish between the God who is near and the God who is far away; he preaches the forgiving, helping, and comforting God. Thus, REPENTANCE is not oriented toward God's wrath and judgment but toward his grace. Jesus' eschatology understands all life as lived before God. It is not the message of the historical Jesus, but rather the Christian kerygma that has an apocalyptic context. Apocalypticism is the "mother of all Christian theology" (Käsemann). The primitive church applies the title "Son of man" to Jesus and preaches him as the exalted one, the coming judge who will inaugurate the last day and final salvation.

*c. **"Realized eschatology."*** A third position is that Jesus taught that the kingdom and eschatological salvation were realized in his own ministry, that he did not understand the kingdom of God as an event or an era, but as an order "beyond space and time." Dodd, the chief proponent of this position, de-eschatologizes Jesus' message in that he considers Jesus' eschatological imagery as only symbolizing the "moral universe" or the "eternal realities." Similarly, Wilder speaks of Jesus' references to the eschatological kingdom as "stylistic" or "symbolic" of ineffable realities intended to dramatize his message. Perrin maintains that the kingdom is not a stenosymbol, but a tensive symbol, whose meaning cannot be reduced to any literal interpretation. "Kingdom of God" is not a sign which refers to only one identifiable event in a certain time, but a symbol which cannot be exhausted in any one event which all persons experience in their own time.

*d. **"Inaugurated eschatology."*** The fourth position is that the presence of the kingdom is evoked and anticipated in Jesus' ministry, but that its consummation remains in the future. Only then will the eschatological salvation present in and through the life of Jesus be manifested universally or cosmically. In the ministry of Jesus the decisive battle has been won, but the war will continue until the final victory is achieved and Jesus returns as judge of the world.

Some students of Bultmann also speak of a dialectical tension between present and future elements in Jesus' eschatological teaching (present/future, hungry/satisfied, lost/found), but they understand the tension existentially rather than temporally. All scholars who maintain the "both-and" position are, however, hard pressed to formulate the theological focal point of the "already" and "not yet" (Moltmann).

All four of the positions identified attempt to come to terms with both future and present aspects of the eschatological statements in the oldest synoptic traditions. All four tend to de-emphasize apocalyptic elements and to explain the eschatological message of Jesus in existentialist or spiritual terms. As a result, the cosmic-universal and social-political dimensions of the apocalyptic world view are eliminated from Jesus' message and from early Christian theology. Moreover, the whole discussion demonstrates that exegetical results depend largely on the systematic presuppositions and interests with which scholars approach the texts. The search for the eschatological outlook of Jesus confronts the same methodological difficulties which have doomed as a futile exercise both the "old" and the "new quest" for the historical Jesus. It no longer appears to be possible to "distill" the eschatology of the historical Jesus from its NT interpretation.

See also KINGDOM OF GOD; KINGDOM OF GOD[S].

Bibliography. General: D. E. Aune, *The Cultic Setting of Realized Eschatology in Early Christianity,* NovTSup, XXVIII (1972); R. Bultmann, *The Presence of Eternity: History and Eschatology* (1957), and *Theology of the NT,* 2 vols. (1948-53); W. D. Davies and D. Daube, eds., *The Background of the NT and Its Eschatology* (1956); W. G. Doty, "Identifying Eschatological Language," *Continuum,* VII (1970), 546-61; J. Gager, *Kingdom and Community* (1975); E. Grässer, *Die Naherwartung Jesu,* SBS, LXI (1973); R. H. Hiers, "Eschatology and Methodology," *JBL,* LXXXV (1966), 170-84; G. Klein, "The Biblical Understanding of 'The Kingdom of God,'" *Int.,* XXVI (1972), 387-418; J. Körner, *Eschatologie und Geschichte: Eine Untersuchung des Begriffes des Eschatologischen in der Theologie R. Bultmanns,* Theologische Forschung, XIII (1957); H. W. Kuhn, *Enderwartung und gegenwärtiges Heil,* SUNT, IV (1966); W. G. Kümmel, "Futuristic and Realized Eschatology in the Earliest Stages of Christianity," *JR,* XLIII (1963), 303-14; J. Moltmann, "Probleme der neueren evangelischen Eschatologie," *Verkündigung und Forschung,* XI (1966), 100-124; A. L. Moore, *The Parousia in the NT,* NovTSup, XIII (1966); N. Perrin, "Eschatology and Hermeneutics," *JBL,* XCIII (1974), 3-14; A. Strobel, *Kerygma und Apokalyptik* (1967); A. Vögtle, *Das NT und die Zukunft des Kosmos* (1970); M. Werner, *The Formation of Christian Dogma* (2nd ed., 1953).

The synoptic traditions: G. Bornkamm, "End-Expectation and Church in Matthew," *Tradition and Interpretation in Matthew* (1960); H. Conzelmann, "Present and Future in the Synoptic Tradition," *JTC,* V (1968), 26-44; C. H. Dodd, *The Parables of the Kingdom* (1936 [rev. ed., 1961]); F. O. Francis, "Eschatology and History in Luke-Acts," *JAAR,* XXXVII (1969), 49-63; E. Grässer, *Das Problem der Parusieverzögerung in den synoptischen Evangelien und in der Apostelgeschichte,* BZNW, XXII (2nd ed., 1960); L. Hartman, *Prophecy Interpreted,* Coniectanea Biblica, NT Series, I (1966), esp. on Mark 13; R. H. Hiers, *Jesus and Ethics* (1968), and *The Historical Jesus and the Kingdom of God* (1973); N. Perrin, *The Kingdom of God in the Teaching of Jesus* (1963); J. T. Sanders, "The Question of the Relevance of Jesus for Ethics Today," *JAAR,* XXXV (1970), 131-46; A. Schweitzer, *The Quest of the Historical Jesus* (1906); C. H. Talbert, "The Redaction-critical Quest for Luke the Theologian," *Jesus and Man's Hope,* ed. D. G. Buttrick (1970), pp. 171-222; J. Weiss, *Jesus' Proclamation of the Kingdom of God* (1892 [ET 1971]); A. Wilder, "Social Factors in Early Christian Eschatology," *Early Christian Origins,* ed. A. Wikgren (1961), pp. 67-76.

Special Studies: On Pauline eschatology, H. R. Balz, *Heilsvertrauen und Welterfahrung,* BEvT, LIX (1971); G. Klein, "Apokalyptische Naherwartung bei Paulus," *NT und Christliche Existenz,* ed. H. D. Betz and L. Schottroff (1973), pp. 241-62; H. M. Shires, *The Eschatology of Paul in the Light of Modern Scholarship* (1966). On the Fourth Gospel, J. Blank, *Krisis: Untersuchungen zur johanneischen Christologie und Eschatologie* (1964); R. Bultmann, *The Gospel of John: A Commentary* (rev. ed., 1957, supplement, 1966 [ET 1971]); L. von Hartingsveld, *Die Eschatologie des Johannesevangeliums* (1962). On apocalyptic eschatology, E. Käsemann, "The Beginning of Christian Theology," and "On the Topic of Christian Apocalyptic," *JTC,* VI (1969), 17-46 and 99-133; K. Koch, *The Rediscovery of Apocalyptic,* SBT, 2nd ser., XXII (1970).

E. SCHÜSSLER FIORENZA

***ESSENES. 1. Sources.** PHILO JUDEUS describes the Essenes as an outstanding example of a free and virtuous life. The best and most explicit report on the Essenes, however, is given by Flavius Josephus (*see* JOSEPHUS, FLAVIUS) who claims that in his youth he had been a member of the three Jewish religious groups. Important for its geographical references is a brief description of the Essenes by Pliny the Elder (*see also* Dion of Prusa, *ca.* A.D. 80-120, preserved by Synesius of Cyrene). The report by Hippolytus is an expansion of Josephus, *The Jewish War* (II.viii). All later references to the Essenes are dependent on either Josephus or Pliny.

2. History. ***a. Date.*** Josephus first mentions the Essenes in the time of the Maccabean high priest Jonathan (152-143 B.C.) and says that they enjoyed the favor of Herod the Great, but suffered martyrdom at the hands of the Romans. This means that the Essenes must have existed from the middle of the second century B.C. until A.D. 68.

b. Location. According to Josephus there were Essenes in all the cities, while Philo says they lived as farmers and craftsmen in the villages of Palestine. According to Pliny, however, they used to dwell by the shore of the Dead Sea, near the city of En-gedi. This location, together with the evidence from the DEAD SEA SCROLLS and also the excavations at the ancient site of Qumran, leads to the conclusion that the Essenes must be identified with the members of the Qumran sect. They had a kind of monastic center in the desert settlement of Qumran and groups and camps in other parts of Palestine.

c. Organization. Josephus classifies the Essenes—like the Pharisees and Sadducees—in a Hellenizing fashion as a αἵρεσις, "religious party," thereby comparing them with Greek philosophical schools (φιλοσοφίαι.) In addition, he uses the term τάγμα, "unit, order." Both terms are reminiscent of the Hebrew word *serekh,* "order" (cf. MANUAL OF DISCIPLINE[S], *Serekh Hayyaḥadh*). But the Qumran people understood themselves as a "community" *(edhah)* and as a "union" *(yaḥadh);* they claimed to be the holy remnant of Israel and the nucleus of God's people at the end of the times. This idea is expressed in the hierarchical order in which priests and elders had a higher rank than the laity and the novitiates. There is much emphasis on obedience to supervisors and elders and on discipline at the sessions of the council. The sectarian aspect, not mentioned by either Philo or Josephus, is important also: the withdrawal from the mainstream of culture under the guidance of priests (in the middle of the second century B.C.); the life in the desert; and the critical position toward the religiously dominant Sadducees and Pharisees and the Jerusalem temple, which led to a spiritualized understanding of the sacrificial worship and of the temple.

3. Eschatological existence. Philo and Josephus described the community in Hellenistic terms, placing the exterior phenomena in the foreground; the true apocalyptic motivation of the Essene way of life becomes apparent only through the Qumran texts. According to Philo, to love God, virtue, and one's fellow man were the guiding principles of Essene life; similarly, Josephus speaks of reverence for God and justice toward man, whereby one should harm nobody, should hate the unjust, and should support the struggle of the righteous. This is reminiscent of the main rules, mentioned in the beginning of the Manual of Discipline: to seek God and to do what is good and right before him, to love all the children of Light, and to hate all the children of Darkness. This attitude toward their fellow man is founded on a strong belief in divine election, which Josephus explains with the term εἱμαρμένη. However, he omits the dualistic structure of the Essene world view: the teaching about the two spirits of Truth and Error and about the realms of Light and Darkness with their rulers Michael and Belial (1QS 3:13–4:26), probably because one cannot compare it with the dualism of Plato. A Stoic rendering is given by Philo.

a. Piety. Concrete expressions of Essene piety are the prayer toward the rising sun, the prayer of the priest at the beginning and end of the meal, the strict observance of the sabbath, and especially the remarkable practices of ritual purity: the daily ritual bath, the linen garments, the sacredness of the refectory, the holy meal prepared by priests, the prescriptions for cleanliness, the ritual separation of the four classes, and the long period of probation for the novitiates. Economic relations with the outside world were avoided, and even in desperate situations, an Essene tried to keep himself undefiled, by rejecting food or help from other people. According to Josephus, the Essenes believed in the immortality of the soul, which after the death of the body will be rewarded by being brought to a beautiful place or punished by being thrown into Hades.

b. Ethics. Essene ethics are highly praised by both Philo and Josephus, but are incorrectly explained. The remarkable common life is rightly emphasized and considered by Philo a guarantee of genuine freedom. This common life was realized by the sacrifice of private property and a central administration of all goods, by common work, prayer, consultation, and communal meals. There was also a strong emphasis on chastity or celibacy. Josephus explains it in Stoic terms by relating it to the avoidance of lust and to the ideal of ascetic self-control. Philo relates it to a critical attitude toward women, who by their selfishness and immodest demands of their husbands prevent men from true fellowship with each other. The common ownership of property was then the result of Essene love of the simple life and served as a defense against avarice. This philosophical and psychological analysis of the Essene way of life is incorrect. Their practice of holiness must be attributed to eschatological hopes and to strict obedience of the OT law. The Essenes believed that God's coming was at hand. Therefore, it was necessary to establish a well-prepared, sacred people with clean bodies and pure hearts. The rules for preparing Israel's encounter with the holy God at Mount Sinai (Exod. 19:1 ff.), for the priests when serving in the temple (Ezek. 44:9-31), and for Israel's camp during a holy war (Deut. 23:10-15) shaped the eschatological existence of the Essenes in a decisive way. Together with the expectancy of the final judgment, these rules could lead to celibacy, to the rejection of private property, and to the observance of sacred meals. Philo and Josephus mention the study of the scriptures by the Essenes. But the fundamental importance of exegesis and fulfillment of the Law, which was re-enforced by the strong eschatological hope (1QS 8:14-15), is not evident in their reports. Moreover, Philo has obscured the preparation for holy war by his emphasis on the Essene love of peace. *See also* DEAD SEA SCROLLS §6; DEAD SEA SCROLLS[S] §§5, 6, 7.

Bibliography. Texts: A. Adam, *Antike Berichte über die Essener* (2nd ed., 1972); E. Schürer, *Geschichte des jüdischen Volkes im Zeitalter Jesu Christi* (4th ed., 1907), II, 651-80 (contains the Gr. and Lat. texts on the Essenes).

General Works: O. Betz, *Offenbarung und Schriftforschung in der Qumransekte,* WUNT, VI (1960); A. Dupont-Sommer, *The Essene Writings from Qumran* (1962); M. Hengel, *Judentum und Hellenismus* (1969); S. Wagner, *Die Essener in der wissenschaftlichen Diskussion vom Ausgang des 18. bis zum Beginn des 20. Jahrhunderts, BZAW,* LXXIX (1960).

Special Studies: O. Betz, "The Eschatological Interpretation of the Sinai-Tradition in Qumran and in the New Testament," *RQ,* VI (1967), 89-107; G. Vermes, "The Etymology of Essenes," *RQ,* II (1960), 427-43, and "Essenes and Therapeutai," *RQ,* III (1962), 495-504.

O. BETZ

***ESTHER, BOOK OF.** The OT book which describes the Jews' deliverance from persecution in the Persian Empire by Esther and Mordecai, an occasion which became the basis for the institution of the feast of Purim. Both the names Esther (אסתר; Akkad. *Ishtar;* cf. Pers. *stara,* star) and Mordecai (מרדכי; Akkad. *Marduk*) have as prototypes the names of Babylonian deities. Esther is also called Hadassah (Heb. "Myrtle") in Esth. 2:7, which seems to be regarded as her Jewish name.

1. Contents
2. Literary analysis
3. Theology and purpose
4. Historicity
5. Place in the canon

Bibliography

1. Contents. Angered by Queen Vashti's refusal to display her beauty, the Persian King Ahasuerus (Xerxes) had her banished. Esther, a young Jewish girl who was under the guardianship of her relative Mordecai, was selected to become queen. Mordecai, who had instructed Esther not to reveal her Jewish identity, uncovered a plot to assassinate the king and, through Esther, had him informed. The plot was foiled and Mordecai's part recorded, but he was not then rewarded. He later incurred the hatred of the new vizier, Haman, by refusing to prostrate himself before him as everyone was commanded to do. Haman sought permission from the king to destroy not only Mordecai, but all of a people scattered throughout the empire who had different laws and did not keep the king's law, implying that this would fill the royal coffers as well. Permission was granted, and after Haman had determined the date for the pogrom by casting the lots (*pur*), royal edicts were sent throughout the empire. Mordecai had Esther appear before the king unsummoned; she did so and was warmly received. Being told that any request she made would be granted, she invited the king and Haman to a banquet she was preparing for that evening. When the king again extended his offer, she invited them to a second banquet the next day. Haman boasted to his wife and companions of his grandeur, but concluded by saying that it all turned to gall when he encountered an unrepentant Mordecai in the palace gate. Advised to strike at once, he built a huge gallows and returned that night to the palace for permission to hang Mordecai on it. Meanwhile, the king, unable to sleep, had the royal journal read to him, and was reminded that Mordecai had earlier saved his life but had never been rewarded. The king sought the advice of Haman, who suggested that the one whom the king wished to reward be given highest royal honors. "Do so to Mordecai the Jew who sits at the king's gate" (6:10), ordered Ahasuerus. And Haman did. Crestfallen he returned home, only to be summoned to the second banquet. There Esther revealed her Jewish identity and Haman's plot. Haman made an inept appeal to Esther for his life, but was hanged by the enraged king on the gallows which he had built for Mordecai. Mordecai was then given Haman's estate and office, and new edicts were sent out permitting the Jews to defend themselves. On the thirteenth day of Adar—and on the fourteenth also for the Jews of Susa—they successfully did so. It was then determined that the deliverance was to be celebrated each year with a feast called Purim. And so "Mordecai the Jew was next in rank to King Ahasuerus, and he was great among the Jews and popular with the multitude of his brethren, for he sought the welfare of his people and spoke peace to all his people" (10:3).

2. Literary analysis. The book of Esther now appears as the festal legend for the Jewish feast of Purim, the origins of which are obscure (*see* PURIM §2). However, the links with this feast within the narrative are tenuous. With the exception of the notice in Esth. 3:7, they are found only in the ninth chapter, which is much more discursive and prosaic than the body of the book. It appears that an existing tale of Esther and Mordecai was taken over to provide a basis for the celebration of a festival already popular among the Jewish communities of the eastern Diaspora (*see* DISPERSION §3; EXILE §3). The festival was quite possibly of pagan origin. A natural conclusion for the tale is found in ch. 8, in which Haman's position and property are given to Mordecai and the pogrom is thwarted. This tale is in essence one of conflict between courtiers, in which officials battle for position and power. The emphasis is on action and story development. The tale is well constructed, with a whole series of seemingly chance happenings and ironies that hold the reader's attention and that entertain. The characters are rather stereotyped and two-dimensional; action, rather than personal motivation or feeling, is stressed. The rapid narrative pace is broken only when the author lovingly dwells for a time on the personages and trappings of the royal court (1:3-9, 13-14; 2:12-14, etc.), in what seems to be an attempt to provide his story with an appearance of historicity.

Critical analysis of this tale has found three separate parts that may originally have been unrelated. There is first the short and independent tale of Queen Vashti (Esth. 1), which serves as an introduction to the Persian court and provides the occasion for the entrance of Esther into the royal harem. The second tells of the adventures of a lovely young Jewish girl who rises to become the favorite of the king and delivers her people from persecution. The third, interwoven with the second, is a tale of conflict between two courtiers. The second and third are so intertwined that, in spite of the presence of some seams and seeming doublets (*see* esp. ch. 2), they cannot be separated with any certainty. However, it is to be noted that some early lines of tradition placed more emphasis on the role of Mordecai (*see* "Mordecai's day" in II Macc. 15:36; the exclamation "let Mordecai be blessed" in T.B. Meg. 7b; as well as the mention of Mordecai, but not Esther, in Esth. 10), while others seemed to underscore the part taken by Esther (*see* esp. Add. Esth. 15:1-16). Yet, in the tale as now constructed the two figures are too closely bound in purpose and situation to be separated (Esth. 2:7, 10-11, 19-22; 4:1-17).

This tale of court conflict and intrigue is most likely a product of the late Persian Diaspora. Later, probably in the early Hellenistic period, the tale was taken up by some of these Jewish communities and utilized as a foundation for the popular festival of Purim—a festival not mentioned in the Torah, thus historicizing it and providing a legitimate basis for its observance. This was done through the insertion of the notice in Esth. 3:7 about Haman's casting lots (*pur*) to determine the most propitious day for his intended pogrom, reference to which is not found again until Esth. 9:23-28. The emphasis moves in ch. 9 from the conflict between courtiers to the broader themes of the Jews' overcoming the destruction that threatened them and the fixing of the dates and forms for the celebration of Purim. It is possible that several hands are to be seen in Esth. 9, as attempts were made to reconcile different dates and practices in the celebration of Purim among the scattered Jewish communities.

Several further additions made in the later Hellenistic period are found inserted in the LXX, but not in the MT (*see* ESTHER, APOCRYPHAL).

3. Theology and purpose. At every level in its development the tale of Esther and Mordecai clearly has entertainment as an essential purpose. This is true of the short tale of Vashti in the first chapter and of the book as a whole, as attested by the book's reception at its annual reading at Purim down through the years. The fast-paced action, the exotic setting, the intrigue, scheming, and suspense, the sudden reversals and delightful ironies, the happy ending: all are the ingredients of popular storytelling. Both the tale of Vashti and the tale of Esther and Mordecai reflect a type of literature about courtiers that was quite popular in the ancient Near East and early Judaism, as witnessed by the popularity of the JOSEPH STORY, the tales in Dan. 1–6, and the extrabiblical tale of Ahikar (cf. Tob. 1:21-22; 14:10; *see* AHIKAR and AHIKAR, BOOK OF). The inner workings of the royal court, where the lines of authority were ill-defined, and where great power and wealth were to be won if one had the wits to master the situation, have always fascinated readers. And Gaster has suggested that the tale of Vashti is a harem story satirically showing how the willfulness of one pretty woman compelled the king and highest officials of the realm to marshal all the instruments of government to assure male supremacy in the home.

While providing entertainment, the court tale of Esther and Mordecai also presents a distinctive theological understanding and presupposes a particular style of life for Diaspora Judaism. It has often been noted that there are no references to God or to specific Jewish religious practices as these are developed in the Torah. An awareness of a divine purpose is evidenced in Esth. 4:14 ("For if you keep silence at such a time as this, relief and deliverance will rise for the Jews from another quarter. . . . And who knows whether you have not come to the kingdom for such a time as this?"), and some understanding of providence is presupposed in the work (cf. Jos. Antiq. XI.vi.11). But events seem to work themselves out on the human plane, and there is no sudden and miraculous divine intervention into the course of human history. Moreover, the Jewishness of Esther and Mordecai did not prevent them from living full and effective lives in interaction with their pagan environment. Esther is the Persian queen and Mordecai a royal courtier. There is no concern for the difficult legal problems that arose as later Jewish circles pondered the situation of these two Jews so highly placed in the royal court and harem (contrast Dan. 1:8-16; the book of Judith; and later developments of Esther in the LXX, Josephus, and the Midrash). Their success and the deliverance of their people are dependent, not on their keeping customs and practices distinctive to Judaism, but on their effective aciton in the slippery and dangerous confines of the royal court. The central conflict itself is as much a result of the courtier's characteristic concern over rank and authority (3:1-5) as it is a result of the Jewishness of Mordecai (3:4*b*; cf. Dan. 1; 3; 6) and the fact that Haman is an Agagite (3:10).

This absence of particular Jewish customs and legal practices and of clear reference to the deity and to divine intervention in human affairs has led to the suggestion that this tale was formed under wisdom influence which flourished in the royal courts (*see* WISDOM §1*a, b, c*; WISDOM IN THE ANE[S] and WISDOM IN THE OT[S]). This has been strengthened by the observation that there are affinities between the tale of Esther and Mordecai and the Joseph narrative of Genesis, both in over-all narrative form and development and in linguistic usage and idiom. In essence, this tale affirms to the Jew of the Diaspora that it is possible to live a rich and creative life in the pagan environment and to participate fully in that world. As Esth. 10:3 suggests (cf. also Jer. 29:1-7; the Joseph narrative in Genesis; the figure of Nehemiah), the Diaspora Jew could serve both king and people at the same time and even reach the heights of authority as well.

This latter characteristic of the tale was radically overturned when it was brought into conjunction with the feast of Purim, which placed emphasis on the conflict between Jew and pagan and on the joy at the defeat of the latter. Survival of the Jews under persecution became the central concern at this level in the development of the book (ch. 9), and the line between Jew and pagan was more sharply drawn. A tension appears in the book, perhaps revealed most strikingly in the almost absurd figure of the malleable and foolish king who first permits the destruction of many of his subjects and then must destroy great numbers of others to spare the first. Esther now becomes less an example of effective and creative interaction between the Jew and the foreign world and more a symbol of hope in the face of persecution, although the vindictive quality that in part accompanies this change has disturbed many.

Even in its incorporation into the festivities associated with Purim the book remained free from any direct reference to God. This may reflect a concern to avoid any unintentional abuse of the divine name in the unrestrained celebration and feasting that is essential to the festival. Additions in the LXX and developments in later Jewish tradition supply what many seemed to find lacking in the book: clear reference to the deity, to divine purpose and operation in human history, and to Jewish practice and piety.

4. Historicity. *See* Esther §3; Moore, *Esther,* pp. xxxiv-xlvi.

5. Place in the canon. See Esther §5; Canon of the OT[S] §§3*c*, 4*b*; Moore, *Esther,* pp. xxi-xxxi.

Bibliography. Commentaries: L. B. Paton, ICC (1908); H. Ringgren and A. Weiser, ATD (1958); H. Bardtke, KAT (1963); C. A. Moore, ABi (1971).

Other studies: T. H. Gaster, *Purim and Hanukkah in Custom and Tradition* (1950); H. Cazelles, "Note sur la composition du rouleau d'Esther," in *Lex tua veritas: Festschrift für Hubert Junker* (1961), pp. 17-29; S. Talmon, "'Wisdom' in the Book of Esther," *VT,* XIII (1963), 419-55; H. Bardtke, "Neuere Arbeiten um Estherbuch. Eine kritische Würdigung," *JEOL,* XIX (1965-66), 519-49; W. L. Humphreys, "A Life-Style for Diaspora: A Study of the Tales of Esther and Daniel," *JBL,* XCII (1973), 211-23; C. A. Moore, "On the Origins of the LXX Additions to the Book of Esther," *JBL,* XCII (1973), 382-93.

W. L. Humphreys

***ETHICS IN THE NT.** It is not proper to speak of *the* NT ethic because, in spite of all the lines of convergence and the constant elements, it is necessary to treat the various writings and authors separately and to inquire into their ethical motifs and criteria and the way these are applied. Our concern here is not so much with an ethos that is lived or with descriptive ethics (*see* Ethos of Early Christianity[S]), but rather with normative ethics, that is, with the presentation of the underlying reasons, motivations, orientations, and contents of earliest Christian ethics.

1. Jesus and the Synoptic gospels. ***a. Eschatology and ethics*** belong indissolubly together in the Teaching of Jesus. The preaching of the Kingdom of God forms the fundamental presupposition and basis of Jesus' ethics, regardless of how his eschatology is defined. Even if eschatology and ethics are regarded as two distinct entities relatively isolated from each other, or if no direct connection is seen between the two complexes, some suggestions must be made as to how the two are related. Both the future and the present components of the kingdom of God are to be taken into account here. Crisis parables like that in Luke 12:58-59 demonstrate the necessity of proper conduct in the last hour. The so-called admission sayings, which make entrance into the kingdom of God dependent on particular conditions (Matt. 18:3 and similar passages), or the threats of judgment, according to which people must give an account of themselves at the end (Matt. 5:22; 7:1; Mark 12:40), show the eschatological orientation of Jesus' ethic. Above all, the promises of reward (Mark 10:21; Matt. 5:46; 6:19-20) belong to the series of eschatological motifs, and thus special emphasis is given to the idea of the individual's obligation to serve (Luke 17:7-10). The kingdom of God, however, is not simply an event yet to come which serves to motivate people to right conduct. Rather, according to Matt. 13:44-46, it is also a discovery, already joyously affirmed, which brings them to a decision. Because God's mercy has already been bestowed on men and women, they are called upon to show mercy (Matt. 18:23-35; cf. also Matt. 5:44-45; Luke 7:41-50; 15:1-32). Therefore, the ethic of Jesus is not intended simply as a preparation for the eschaton; it arises out of the mercy of God which is already experienced in Jesus. This means that the interpretation of the ethic of Jesus as a so-called "interim ethic" is inappropriate. Jesus is not a prophet of the decline and end of the world, and the decisive motive and profoundest reason for Jesus' demands are not to be found in the imminent end of the world or in fear of the end. They are to be found in the God who brings salvation near in Jesus, and in the will of God which Jesus proclaims with authority.

This does not mean that we may isolate the content of the demands of Jesus and regard it as unaffected by eschatology. Indeed, the tradition contains a natural ethic, the contents of which are in tension with the eschatology, e.g., the almost rationalistic appeal to reason and experience which stems from the wisdom literature (cf. Matt. 6:19 ff.). But this is only one argument among many. Sound human reason may question the abiding value of earthly treasures, or it may provide insight into the senselessness of anxiety, but it can hardly draw the inference that we should lay up "treasures in heaven" or achieve freedom from anxiety. The wisdom tradition, therefore, with its prudence and good sense about life, is repeatedly shattered by eschatology (cf. Matt. 10:26). *See* WISDOM IN THE NT[S].

b. Repentance and discipleship. The appropriate response to the coming kingdom of God is first of all REPENTANCE (μετάνοια; cf. Mark 1:15, which is to be regarded as a secondary but apposite résumé). It requires a wholehearted turning toward God, not a legalistic zeal for penance or an obedience to the Torah. God comes to us without reservations or preconditions, and we must respond to him in the same way; he wants nothing halfhearted or partial, but wants total and undivided obedience (cf. Matt. 6:24 and *passim*). In this one respect Jesus' ethic can be interpreted as an "ethic of attitude," emphasizing that he is not concerned with peripheral details, but with the center of our being. The pure heart (Matt. 5:8) is the undivided heart. However, it would be incorrect to set this in antithesis to works and deeds, because Jesus is also concerned with obedience shown in our actions (Luke 6:43 ff.; Matt. 21:28 ff.).

Because the coming of the kingdom is inseparable from the person of Jesus, repentance is manifested in DISCIPLESHIP. There is no analogy here to the schools in Judaism for, in contrast to the rabbis, Jesus associated with sinners, prostitutes, and tax collectors, and in his teaching discipleship was not merely a transitional stage that led to becoming a teacher. Moreover, the learned atmosphere of the house of instruction is lacking, as is a fixed place for teaching. Following Jesus, as a relationship with his person and his cause, does not mean imitating him; nor does it always imply an outward companionship with Jesus (thus Mark 1:16-20; 2:14), but rather a readiness to accept the consequences (cf. Matt. 8:19-22) and a commissioning for, initiation into, and inclusion in the mission of Jesus (Mark 6:7-13; Matt. 9:37-38; Luke 9:60*b*).

c. The Law. While in postbiblical Judaism the Law had come more and more to be the crucial element in life and for salvation, and had acquired ever-increasing independence and absoluteness, Jesus' attitude toward it was consistently free. Because the idea of the Law was stressed in a variety of ways in the early church, it is difficult to distinguish Jesus' own view. Yet it can be said with some certainty that he neither rejected the Law nor fully accepted it, but combined acceptance with criticism. It is evident first of all that for Jesus God's commandments in the Decalogue were the point of departure and of orientation for his own demands (cf. Mark 10:17-22), even though in Matt. 5:18-19 this is sharpened by strict, law-observing Jewish Christianity. Clearly discernible also is a radicalizing of the Law's demand for obedience: not only murder but even anger, not only adultery but even a lustful look, not only perjury but even an oath is evil (Matt. 5:21-26, 27-30, 33-37). Along with the quotation of the Law and its intensification, it is contrasted to tradition (cf. Mark 7:9-13), and in this at least the criticism of tradition goes back to Jesus himself, as the conflicts over the sabbath confirm (Mark 2:23-28; 3:1-6).

Jesus' sovereign freedom, however, goes further and touches not only the interpretation and practice of the Law, but the Law itself. This is evident first in the fact that one passage of scripture is played off against another (Mark 10:2-9). But Jesus, without any support from the Scripture, also violated and annulled both the law of retaliation attested in the Law (Matt. 5:38) and the cultic and ceremonial commandments (Mark 7:15). It was not as though the will of God cannot be discovered in the Law, or that Jesus understood his mission as clarification of a misunderstanding concerning the Law. Rather, he rejected the identification of the Law and God's will and the return to the letter of the Law. For him, the criterion by which even the Law must be measured is the commandment to love both God and neighbor.

d. The Great Commandment. It is disputed whether the summary of the Law in the dual commandment of love (Mark 12:28-34; Luke 10:25-28) goes back to Jesus himself. It is certain that the interpretation in Matthew (22:40), according to which "all the law and the prophets" depend on the two commandments, is the result of redaction (cf. also the insertion of the GOLDEN RULE in Matt. 7:12 and of Hos. 6:6 in Matt. 9:13 and 12:7), as is the apologetic and rational version of the tradition in Mark 12:28-34. Further, in Hellenistic Judaism there were already attempts to advance beyond the splintering of moral demands and to interpret love as the summation of obedience to the Torah (cf. Test. Iss. 5:2; 7:6; Philo, *On the Special Laws* II, 63; cf. also T.B. Jebam 49a). In the end these attempts were destined not to succeed, and they never were phrased as a combination of Deut. 6:4-5 and Lev. 19:18. In substance, however, the placing of the commandment of love in a pre-eminent position is entirely in harmony with Jesus' own intention (cf. also Mark 3:4; Matt. 23:23).

For Jesus, love is first of all love for one's neighbor. In the OT the meaning of "neighbor" was restricted to the people of Israel and the foreigners who dwelt in the land, and in Judaism in the time of Jesus the discussion on this point was not settled (Jewish documentation for the universal application of the term can be demonstrated only from the second century A.D. onward). But Jesus' parable of the good Samaritan (Luke 10:29-37) reveals the unlimited scope of the obligation to love (cf. Luke 10:25-28). Against the background of the irreconcilable hatred between Jews and Samaritans, the choice of a Samaritan here is an indication that love dares to transcend prejudices, conventions, and national and religious limitations, and is able to discern in everyone the person who is commanded to show sympathy for others, and to provide concrete assistance (cf. also Matt. 25:31 ff.).

Removal of the limitations on who is one's neighbor is climaxed by the inclusion of one's enemy (Matt. 5:44). This universalizing of love not only makes it clear that love is not a "preference" (Kierkegaard) or a love based on reciprocity (Matt. 5:46-47); it also transcends the identification (possible in the context of love of neighbor) of the object of love with family, circle of friends, or homeland.

The co-ordination of love of God and love of neighbor should not be understood, however, as meaning that they are identical. This cannot be claimed even on the basis of Matt. 25:31-46. Obedience to God certainly cannot be practiced without regard to one's neighbor; it is to be substantiated and made concrete in the encounter with the neighbor. The original intention of the parable probably was that the king represents God, and so God is identified precisely with "the least of these my brethren." But God is not wholly represented by concern for others, and he does not appear only in hidden form in the figure of the neighbor in distress; he also will appear in the future, no longer hidden, as Judge of the world. Conversely, however, love of neighbor is so little directed toward God in its practice, that those who do good works are not at all aware that they have done them to God. Thus, the two are to be distinguished but not separated. Even Matthew, who, in contrast to Mark, says explicitly that the "second" commandment is "like" the first (Matt. 22:39), does not say that the two are the same.

e. Specific teachings. For Jesus all structures and institutions of the world are provisional (cf. Mark 12:25), but he did not conclude that we should therefore sabotage them or withdraw from them, or that we should try to stabilize and sanction them. In case of conflict one must be willing to abandon all (cf. Matt. 10:37-38; Luke 14:26), but this did not lead Jesus to show contempt for the world. It was not wholly without reason that he was criticized as a glutton and a winebibber (Matt. 11:19). Jesus certainly opposed divorce, referring back to his belief about creation, but this is not the same as a defense of the *status quo.* This is evident in the conflicts over the sabbath and in his sharing meals with tax collectors and sinners, a practice offensive to many around him (Mark 2:15). He neither saw his distinctive task as that of reforming society (cf. Luke 12:13-14) nor did he simply preach an inwardness and a piety of the heart (cf. also the healings). It is hardly possible then to apply to Jesus' words the Lutheran distinction between a spiritual and a wordly kingdom, or between person and office. From the outset this distinction between private and public spheres blunts the point of many radical sayings of Jesus. It is also impossible to distill from Jesus' words a two-level ethic or to interpret them as enunciating impossible demands meant only to prompt repentance. Rather, they seek to clarify, by examples, the meaning of radical obedience.

i. *Relations between men and women.* In his teachings and his practice Jesus clearly dissociated himself from the general religious and social discrimination against women. His summons was addressed to men and women alike (cf. the parables drawn from the world of women's work). Altogether untypically, moreover, women are found in his entourage (Luke 8:1-3; vs. 3 is a case of Lukan stylizing and generalizing; cf. also Mark 15:40-41; Matt. 20:20); they are healed by Jesus (Matt. 8:14-15; 9:18-26), or are held up as examples of true faith (e.g., Matt. 15:28).

Marital union is something provisional and temporary (Mark 12:25); indeed, some refrain from marriage for the sake of the kingdom of God (Matt. 19:12 is to be understood in this way and not as meaning self-castration or incapacity for marriage), but such celibacy does not arise out of ascetic and dualistic motives or for the sake of gaining merit, and it is not a binding rule. For example, Peter was married and remained so (I Cor. 9:5). Even less did the eschatological relativizing of marriage lead Jesus to denounce sexuality and marriage. Rather, he recognized them as in harmony with the creative will of God and sought to guard against divorce (Mark 10:2-9). Here Jesus distinguished his own position from the easy practice of divorce, particularly of the followers of Hillel, but also from the harsher view of the school of Shammai, which allowed divorce in the case of unchastity (cf. the secondary softening of the rule pertaining to this in Matt. 5:32 and 19:9). Jesus offered protection to women, who at that time were under a serious disadvantage with respect to the Law. He also sharply condemned adultery (Matt. 5:27 ff.). *See also* WOMAN IN THE NT[S] §3; MARRIAGE IN THE NT[S] §2.

ii. *Possessions.* In harmony with the apocalyptic woes (cf. I Enoch 94:7-8; 96:4-8), the gospels also contain woes for the rich and promises for the POOR (Luke 6:20, 24), but above all clear warnings against the danger of riches. It is true that Jesus hardly demanded in general terms a renunciation of possessions (cf. Mark 1:29; 2:14 ff.), but in individual cases he called upon people to sell (Mark 10:17-22) or to abandon everything (cf. Mark 10:28). It is impossible to serve God and mammon simultaneously (Matt. 6:24). Warnings are frequently given against collecting earthly treasures (Matt. 6:19-21; Luke 12:13-21; 16:19-31). Possessions are to be used for the benefit of the poor and of those who have fallen among robbers (cf. Mark 10:21; Luke 10:35; cf. 16:9; 19:8).

iii. *The state.* In spite of the fact that those who followed Jesus were already governed by a power other than that of the state (cf. Mark 10:42-45), Jesus did not oppose the Roman state in the spirit of the ZEALOT revolutionaries. While the Zealots consistently refused to pay the imperial tax, because they regarded it as an infringement upon God's sovereignty, Jesus regarded it as the emperor's rightful due (Mark 12:13-17). Indeed, without being asked he added to the saying, "Render to Caesar the things that are Caesar's," the further admonition, "and to God the things that are God's." Thereby the admonition about obeying God is given priority above any other. Jesus' saying occupies a middle position between the two extremes of rebellion on the one hand and glorification or unconditional and uncritical affirmation of the emperor (cf. also Luke 13:32; 22:25, and similar passages) on the other; but vs. 17 is directed essentially against the Zealots. Even though Jesus did not belong to the Zealots' liberation movement, his message must have held a certain attraction for its members (cf. Luke 6:15, among others). But in spite of some points of contact, there can be no doubt about the distance between his movement and that of the Zealots. His exhortation to love one's enemies and to renounce violence, his table fellowship with the tax collectors, and many of his individual sayings (cf. Matt. 26:52) are irreconcilable with the Zealots' use of violence.

See also Teaching of Jesus[S] §3*d*; Rome, Early Christian Attitudes Toward[S] §1.

2. The earliest church. It is not easy to achieve any certainty about the pre-Pauline communities, yet the Cross and the Easter event, as well as the experience of the Spirit and the expectation of the imminent end, must be regarded as the common presupposition of any post-Easter ethic. Along with the voice of prophecy (*see* Prophecy in the Early Church[S]), the words of Jesus were regarded as the supreme norm and guideline for Christian conduct. Even though the Logia source as a whole hardly goes back to the earliest church and though the sayings of the Lord were not collected exclusively for parenetic purposes, it is still true that Parenesis was a central component of Q (*see* Q; Q[S]; Sayings of Jesus, Form of[S]). Particularly evident is the parenetic reshaping of texts that were originally otherwise oriented, but it is difficult precisely to localize and date the reshaping. Further, even before the time of Paul more than one attitude can be observed, particularly on the question of the validity of the Law. Thus the Hellenists who are criticized in Matt. 5:19 appear to have adopted a freer attitude toward the Law. The so-called communism of the early church also probably goes back to the circle of the Hellenists, though this practice as portrayed in the summary statements in Acts 2:42-47 and 4:32-37 is hardly historical; it is, rather, a generalization of individual cases of renunciation of possessions, like that of Barnabas as presented by Luke (Acts 4:36-37). But since Barnabas was probably one of the Hellenists expelled from Jerusalem (cf. Acts 11:29-30), this shows that in Stephen's circle there was not only freedom of the spirit but also freedom to renounce possessions. Very early the problem was posed as to the limits of what was tolerable in a Christian community (cf. Acts 5:1-6). It appears that even before Paul certain schemata and the contents of ancient ethical teachings, such as the catalogues of virtues and vices (*see* Lists, Ethical; Lists, Ethical[S]), had been appropriated and integrated into missionary preaching (cf. Gal. 5:19-24; I Thess. 4:2-8). Parts of the parenetic chs. of Paul's epistles in particular are to be regarded as belonging to the ethical tradition, even though we can hardly posit a primitive Christian moral catechism.

3. Paul. ***a. Basis and motivation.*** Paul frequently divided his letters into two parts, thus stressing that God's saving action in Jesus Christ is the basis and ground of action for the Christian. The relation of the indicative, in the word of salvation, and the imperative, in the moral demand, is not that of ideal and actuality, or of theory and practice, but a substantively necessary paradox which is rooted ultimately in the eschatological dialectic. The immediate juxtaposition in I Cor. 5:7 and Gal. 5:25 shows how far from inconsistent Paul is here. Christ is the one by whom the Christian lives (cf. Gal. 2:20) and he ultimately gives charismatic dimension to all that the Christian does (cf. I Cor. 12:11 and *passim*). Therefore, the conduct corresponding to the imperative cannot be understood as completing or realizing something only potentially given, nor can the gift of the indicative be separated from the Giver.

The content of the indicative cannot be found by isolating individual elements and classifying the entire Pauline ethic as "pneuma ethic," "sacramental ethic," "*telos* ethic," or such. Rather, the various motivations belong together. The most we can say is that God's eschatological saving action in Jesus Christ is the all-inclusive basis of the Pauline ethic. The Christian is both set free by Christ and taken into Christ's service, and so the Christian life is determined by Christ (II Cor. 5:14-15; I Cor. 3:21-23). This means that the ethical dimension is not something secondary, but already is implied in the relationship with Christ. This is confirmed by, e.g., the use of Pauline *Kyrios* title (cf. Rom. 14:8-9; 16:18, and *passim*), the parenetic introductory formulas (II Cor. 10:1; Rom. 15:30 and *passim*), and the pattern of conciliation and conformity (Rom. 15:2-3, 7).

If baptism makes the Christ event real for believers (cf. Rom. 6) by releasing them from the power of sin and making them partakers in Christ's destiny, it is also a part of the basis of Christology. And since Paul's doctrine of the Spirit is also related to Christology (cf. II Cor. 3:17; Rom. 8:9), the charismatic activity of the Spirit is another ground for ethics for the Christian. By the miraculous power of the Spirit Christians are enabled to live a new life, and the entire Christian life is to be regarded as the "fruit of the Spirit" (Rom. 8; Gal. 5). The idea of a "gift" (charisma) which belongs with the gift of the Spirit stresses yet more pointedly the bestowal of individual gifts and responsibilities (I Cor. 7:7; 12:7, 11). If Christology ultimately sets the context even for eschatology (cf. the idea of "being with the Lord" as the central element of the Pauline expectation), the motif of future salvation, which is central for ethics, can also be cited here (Rom. 13:11-14; I Thess. 5:1-11); in any case, even in Paul, ethics is not a compensation for a receding eschatology, but is a consequence of a lively and vital eschatology.

b. The new obedience. The transformation of human nature (Rom. 12:2) as renewal of the whole person and the overcoming of the divided condition of the self described in Rom. 7 are in harmony with the wholeness and unity of God's demand and of human obedience (cf. the striking change in number in Gal. 5:19, 22 ["works," "fruit"]). But that transformation and renewal are both manifested in specific demands and deeds. Various facts related to the particular situation play a role, especially in I Corinthians. Yet even the usual character of Pauline parenesis, with its individual admonitions, which for the most part are strung together loosely and without order, indicates that a pure situation ethic does not suffice. Not all of the admonitions are tailored to fit specific, individual cases (cf. the catalogues of virtues and vices, or I Thess. 4:1 ff.), and Paul is often looking beyond the moment and the individual congregation (cf. I Cor. 4:17; 7:17; and other similar passages). This does not detract from the concrete character of the apostolic admonitions. These do not contradict the bestowal of the Spirit and the personal character of obedience. Nor are they merely solutions designed for an emergency or a transitional situation, because they are also addressed to those who both know and practice what is required (I Thess. 4:1, 10). This only underscores the fact that Christians continue to be people under threat of attack (Gal. 4:9; 5:17; I Cor. 10:1-13). Freedom from the Law as a way of salvation (Rom. 6:14; 7:1-6; Gal. 2:19) and freedom "from all men" (I Cor. 9:19; cf. 3:21-23) do not mean a dispensation from "keeping the commandments of God" (I Cor. 7:19), which Paul does not distinguish from the apostolic instructions (I Thess. 4:1-2). In spite of the significance of self-examination (I Cor. 11:28; Gal. 6:4), reason (Rom. 12:1; Phil. 1:10), and the judgment of conscience (I Cor. 8-10), the Christian cannot unequivocally and definitively judge him/herself (I Cor. 4:1 ff.); nor can we absolutize our own style and pattern of life or make it a matter of purely private concern. To be sure, there is a diversity in ethical decisions (cf. I Cor. 6:1 ff. and chs. 8–10), but Paul strongly insists on seeking together for the will of God and striving to do it (cf. Rom. 15:5-6; Phil. 2:2 and *passim*).

c. Material criteria. In spite of the knowledge of an ethical norm, even on the part of non-Christians (cf. Rom. 2:14-15; 13:3; I Cor. 5:1); in spite of a congruence between the Pauline ethos and that of antiquity (this is presupposed, e.g., in I Thess. 4:12; I Cor. 10:32); and in spite of the unequivocal acceptance of ethical norms and content from the environment (cf. Phil. 4:8), we still cannot speak of a simple identity between the Pauline ethic and that of the surrounding environment.

It is possible to cite several different factors which are responsible for the content of the Pauline ethic. Among these is the OT belief about creation (cf. I Cor. 10:26; Rom. 14:20 and the references to "nature" in Rom. 1:26; I Cor. 11:14), to which eschatology forms a certain corrective (e.g., in the estimate of marriage; *see* §dii *below*). Other OT demands are found primarily in parenetic proverbial material (cf. Rom. 12:16, 17, 19, 20), and these are in part quoted explicitly (cf. Rom. 12:19, and further I Cor. 6:16; II Cor. 8:15; 9:9). In this process, to be sure, various implicit modifications are made. I Cor. 9 shows that a word of the Lord (vs. 14) is an authority that stands above the OT (vss. 8-9).

A clearly delineated saying of the Lord is acknowledged in I Cor. 7:10-11 as a superior authority. In addition to the relatively few sayings of the Lord (cf. I Cor. 7:25) which Paul quotes, one can also count some points of agreement which are not noted as such (Rom. 12:14, 17; 13:8-10, etc.). However, it is not the concrete example of the earthly Jesus, but the imitation of Christ (μίμησις τοῦ Χριστοῦ) that is of crucial significance for Paul (cf. I Cor. 11:1; I Thess. 1:6; Rom. 15:2-3, 7): conformity to and harmony with the Christ event.

From this it follows that Paul, like Jesus, places great emphasis on the commandment to love, which not by accident can also be called "the law of Christ" (Gal. 6:2; cf. Rom. 14:15 also with 15:5). Love means being free from oneself and being available to others, and this is the quintessence and center of all the individual demands (Rom. 13:8-10; Gal. 5:14). This central position of love is also repeatedly exhibited in the individual admonitions, e.g., in the discussion of the right relationship of the strong to the weak in Rome and Corinth (Rom. 14–15; I Cor. 8–10). Love as the motivating and guiding force is demonstrated not only within the confines of the community, but also in interpersonal relationships: in the relationship of master and slave (cf. Philem. 16, "in the flesh and in the Lord"), in marriage (I Cor. 7:4), in love for one's enemies, and in refraining from taking revenge (Rom. 12:17-21). Although Paul knows all about the hidden character of love (I Cor. 13:3), it does not continue to be hidden, and he is thoroughly familiar with its signs (I Cor. 13:4 ff.).

d. Concrete admonitions. i. *The individual.* The idea of community and solidarity in the OT and Jewish tradition, although it takes seriously the individual's responsibility, still does not admit an ethic that is oriented primarily to the individual. For this reason also the Greek concept of virtue is absent from Paul's ethic (in Phil. 4:8-9, ἀρετή is used in an utterly non-Greek way). The term "body," which is central for Pauline anthropology and ethics (*see* Body[S] §2), does not have reference to a relationship to oneself, but signifies primarily a person in his or her capacity for interpersonal relationship and communication (I Cor. 6:12-20). Of course Paul is familiar with the struggle against the real self to achieve self-discipline and self-mastery (I Cor. 9:25), or inner freedom and independence from needs (Phil. 4:11-13). The socioethical dimension of Paul's ethic is dominant, however, though one must not set up false alternatives here (cf. Gal. 5:22-23). Paul's position respecting labor and property is typical. On the one hand he practices manual labor (cf. I Cor. 4:12), which he does not idealize, in order not to be a burden to anyone (I Thess. 2:9) and to avoid being confused with the materialistic behavior of popular Christian or syncretistic propagandists (cf. II Cor. 12:14; I Thess. 2:5); on the other hand he sets labor within the context of brotherly love (I Thess. 4:9-12; cf. later, Eph. 4:28). He uses the intrinsic transience of everything earthly as a basis for inner freedom, even with respect to possessions (I Cor. 7:30; cf. Phil. 4:11-12), but he also urges commonality with respect to earthly goods (Gal. 6:6; cf. also the matter of the collection, particularly in II Cor. 8–9).

ii. *Relations between men and women.* Since all values that belong to this world are overcome in Christ (Gal. 3:28), man and woman have the same rank before God (*see* WOMAN IN THE NT[S] §2). This overcoming of the inferiority of woman also has practical consequences, evident from women's sharing in the work of the community (cf. Rom. 16:1, 3, and *passim*) and their prophetic preaching (I Cor. 11:5). I Cor. 11:2-16 is a difficult passage. There Paul uses a number of rather inconclusive arguments, apparently to counter an emancipation of Corinthian women that shows signs of enthusiasm. In so doing, particularly in vss. 7-8 (as distinguished from vss. 11-12), he is clearly on a level beneath that of Gal. 3:28, even though we may note that here, as always, Paul talks about freedom as freedom for service.

Paul's undeniable reservations about marriage are not based on a depreciation of sexuality or of the human body. He places a high value on celibacy, which according to I Cor. 7:25-31 makes possible an undivided commitment to the Lord in the age that is coming to an end, and which as a *charisma* (I Cor. 7:7) affords a special possibility for service to others, but he clearly warns against the dangers of sexual asceticism (I Cor. 7:2). Marriage is bodily communion also, in which the body of either marriage partner is at the disposal of the other (I Cor. 7:3-4), an arrangement that is to be suspended only upon agreement and only for a limited time (I Cor. 7:5). Another feature of marriage is its indissolubility; hence Paul rejects divorce, borrowing a saying of the Lord (I Cor. 7:10-12).

iii. *Slavery*. While the slave in antiquity was usually regarded as a piece of property (*res*), and therefore is counted in enumerations of possessions, along with money, real estate, and the like (*see* SLAVERY IN THE NT[S] §§1-3), Paul relativized slavery and made it outdated by the idea of brotherhood. He did not preach the emancipation of slaves, but neither did he interpret slavery as a divinely ordained institution. For him the main thing was, during the short time yet remaining, to demonstrate obedience in the "state" in which the call of the Lord had been received (I Cor. 7:17-24). Even the master is a slave of Christ, and the slave a freedman of Christ (I Cor. 7:22), and this not only has consequences within the community (observance of the Lord's Supper together, the fraternal kiss, etc.), but it also affects the institution of slavery itself. Thus, Paul desires forgiveness of the runaway slave ONESIMUS, who according to Roman law had to expect severe physical punishment, branding, and even worse (Philem. 12 and 17). His request that the slave be relinquished indicates that for him it is not a matter of unassailable rights and property.

iv. *The state.* Rom. 13:1-7, which is often overemphasized and for which the content was supplied in large measure from traditional material, was probably prompted neither by Zealot nor revolutionary tendencies in Rome nor by apologetic intentions. Instead, it is a part of two parenetic chs. in which Paul is urging the fundamental principle that his readers should take seriously their earthly obligations in everyday life, regardless of their provisional character (Rom. 13:11-14). The earthly authorities, who are put in their positions by God, are not to be undermined but respected. Obedience is not to be confused with an uncritical spirit of submissiveness, particularly since Paul himself had come into conflict with political authorities (cf. II Cor. 11:23-25, 32-33). Paul mentions only indirectly that the state's rationale and function is to protect and promote the good. This involves the maintenance of law and justice, thus making possible a well-ordered community life, and the warding off of evil, i.e., by the exercise of judicial and punitive power (Rom. 13:3-4). Because Christian obedience does not result from compulsion or fear, but from freedom and insight (cf. vs. 5), Christians fulfill even such prosaic obligations as the payment of taxes (vs. 7). Even the renunciation of judicial decisions by the state (I Cor. 6:1-6) is no disqualification of the state's aim to maintain law and order; it is a manifestation of love, which does not renounce justice, but voluntarily renounces its own rights.

4. The Deutero-Pauline letters. ***a. Colossians and Ephesians.*** In Colossians and Ephesians also the indicative provides the foundation for the imperative, and this pattern is reflected in the structure of the epistles, cf. Col. 3:3, 5; Eph. 4:32; 5:2. The theme has, however, a different accent, insofar as a modification of eschatology and Christology is to be observed: in the foreground now stands the dominion which Christ has already achieved over the powers. In specific opposition to a heresy that regarded the world as demonic and placed a taboo on Christians' dealing with the world (cf. Col. 2:16-19) it is emphasized that the strength of the powers has been broken by Christ and that he is the head of all powers (Col. 2:10, 15; cf. Eph. 1:21). From this Christology arises the demand for obedience to this Lord in all areas of human life (Col. 3:17). In details there are various points of contact with Paul: the establishment of the new life through baptism (Col. 3:1-3), the old and the new nature (Col. 3:9-10), the idea of charisma (Eph. 4:7), the significance of reason (Col. 1:9-10; Eph. 5:17), references to the OT (Eph. 4:25-26; 5:31-32; 6:2-3), love as the decisive criterion (Col. 3:14), and rejection of asceticism (Col. 2:16-17). But there are also obvious differences: the plural "works" (Eph. 2:10), the strong connection of ethics with the church (Eph. 4:1 ff.; cf. also 2:14-22), and the emergence of new forms such as that of the HAUSTAFEL.

The injunctions of the *Haustafel* (probably taken over from Hellenistic Judaism; *see* LISTS, ETHICAL[S] §2) correspond in part to what was conventional at that time, e.g., that wives should be subject to their husbands. Of course a critical sifting and reshaping also took place, and there are also specifically Christian injunctions which make it evident that the structures and relationships of the world are understood as the place and opportunity for love; precisely in this the lordship of the *Kyrios* is made manifest. The idea of analogy, which was already potentially present in the motifs of the *Haustafel*, is given new expression in this process, particularly in Ephesians; thus, marriage between man and woman is analogous to the relationship of Christ and the church (Eph. 5:25; cf. 5:2; 6:5, 7). For Christians the *Kyrios* Christ is a prototype and a point of reference in social structures also.

b. The Pastoral epistles. The atmosphere is much more prosaic, moralistic, formal, and bourgeois in the Pastoral epistles, which are striving for a consolidation of the church on the foundation of the apostolic tradition. In the dispute with a Judaizing Gnosis, which, e.g., forbade marriage (I Tim. 4:3), they have the merit of having held soberly to mundane obligations in the face of the speculative and the ascetic. Moreover, it is not forgotten that ethics is grounded in soteriology (Tit. 2:11-14). Yet the correction of enthusiasm is provided not by eschatology, but by the idea of holding office; the Spirit is not primarily a gift and the sign of the dawning eschaton, but is closely bound up with church offices (II Tim. 1:6-7). Nothing more is said of the multiplicity of gifts. The content and criteria of the ethical teaching accord, in general, with the ideals of Hellenistic morality (cf. especially the admonition to a respectable and pious manner of life [εὐσέβεια]). But the doctrine of creation (cf. I Tim. 4:3-4) and respect for the natural orders is also present, and the ethic of the family (I Tim. 3:4-5; 2:15) and the interweaving of ethic and church order are predominant motifs (cf. I Tim. 3:2, 8-13).

In the specific injunctions as well we find clear differences from Paul: characteristic for the relationship of husband and wife is I Tim. 2:8-15 (corresponding to the secondary passage in I Cor. 14:34-35; *see* WOMAN IN THE NT[S] §2*a*), in which the sole guilt for the fall is ascribed to the woman, and rules from civil life apply now also in the service of worship. It speaks only of the love of the wife for her husband and children (Tit. 2:4), no more of the love of the husband for his wife. New and detailed rules are given for the care of widows (I Tim. 5:3-16), who at that time were under grave disadvantages. In the admonitions regarding slaves (I Tim. 6:1-2; Tit. 2:9-10) the absence of any admonitions to the masters is striking. The appeal to pray for kings and all those in authority (I Tim. 2:2), which also appears here for the first time, harks back to Jewish customs.

5. The Catholic epistles. ***a. I Peter.*** The coordination of kerygma and parenesis in I Peter corresponds to the dialectic of indicative and imperative in Paul; even though the motivation usually follows rather than precedes, the basis for the ethic is that salvation is both present and future. In some cases christological statements in the form of a confession or a hymn (cf. 1:17-21; 3:17-20) and references to baptism predominate (1:22-23; cf. 1:2, 3; other motivations in 1:15-16; 5:5). In other cases, eschatology is the chief motivating force (4:7-8; 1:13). According to the superscription of the *Haustafel* here, Christians are aliens and exiles, who in the provisional situation of this world fulfill their earthly obligations in civil life and in the home (2:11 ff.). A considerable role is played, insofar as content is concerned, by the OT (cf. 1:15-16; 3:5-6 and *passim*), of which the author regards the church to be the heir (cf. 2:9-10). Of course, in some cases the Christian reinterpretation of OT texts is involved (e.g., the reshaping of Prov. 24:21 in 2:17, and the eschatological interpretation in 3:10-12 of vss. from the Psalms which were originally understood as a practical rule of prudence). Still more important is the analogy to the suffering Christ (cf. esp. 2:21-25 but also 3:9; 4:1). In I Peter, Christ is ascribed an exemplary significance, although the idea here of following in the "steps" of Jesus (2:21) must be distinguished from the idea of copying or imitating him. In the persecution that is beginning the author also insists upon the missionary and apologetic motive of regard for the opinion of non-Christians (cf. 2:12; 3:16; 4:14-15). In 3:1-2 the Christian manner of life is even credited with what the word was unable to do: the "winning" of non-Christians, which of course is not to be confused with mere conformity, but rather includes a break with earlier practices (cf. 4:2-4).

The author's primary concern is with brotherly love (1:22; 2:17; 4:8) and good works (1:17; 2:12). The *Haustafel* here (2:13 ff.) has some peculiarities when compared with those in Colossians and Ephesians. For instance, in 2:13-17, where the underlying tradition is similar to that of Rom. 13, some peculiar emphases are inescapable: obedience is to be offered to "creatures" (RSV "every human institution"); there is no parallel to Rom. 13:1*b*-2; freedom is the basis and mode of obedience (vs. 16). The admonition to the women (3:1-6) lacks any special Christian coloration, except for the comment about missionary responsibility in mixed marriages (vss. 1*b*-2) and the exhortation not to be terrified (vs. 6). The warning against outward adornment (3:5) has many parallels (cf. I Tim. 2:9; Isa. 3:18-24, and others). The exhortation to the men (3:7), on the other hand, is less traditional, and is aimed at consideration and understanding; a lack of consideration and love for others also burdens and disrupts the relationship with God (vs. 7*b*). In 2:18-25 the slaves are admonished, and, particularly in the case of harsh and unjust treatment by unreasonable masters, are referred to the example of the innocent sufferings of Jesus.

b. James. The epistle of James is a hortatory and didactic writing with a primarily ethical orientation. In terms of form criticism, it belongs to the category of parenesis, and it lists admonitions and warnings without any discernible continuity.

It draws from a broad parenetic stream of tradition which is fed by various elements of ethics from antiquity. The author wages a polemic against justification by faith alone and makes works once again a factor in salvation (2:14-26). Certainly, Christians are recipients (1:17), but faith is not understood as the root and basis of works or, as in Gal. 5:6, of love. Instead, it is seen as a purely theoretical and intellectual persuasion that something is true (2:19; a different position is reflected in the passages 1:3, 6; 2:1, that stem from the tradition). This perhaps points back to a degenerate Paulinism. The author, however, is not so much concerned with a new doctrine of justification or a different concept of faith as with the realization of a practical and concrete obedience. His warning against the separation of hearing and doing (1:22-25; cf. also Matt. 7:24-27) shows no recognition of the problematical aspect of doing, whether in terms of the priority of hearing the message of salvation (cf. Luke 10:42) or in terms of the blind alley of the way of the law (Paul). Like Jesus, the author touches upon eschatological motivation (5:1 ff.), but this stands alongside the awareness of the transitoriness of human nature without any reconciliation of the two (4:13-17).

The author regards the OT Law in its ethical parts as obligatory and views these as comprising the whole and perfect Law (2:8-13). By ethicizing the cultic ideas (1:26-27) and by not observing the ceremonial law he levels an indirect criticism of the Law, in which he is evidently thinking primarily of social obligation (in addition to 1:27, cf. also 2:15-16 and the sharp criticism of wealth in 5:1-6; 2:1-7). Other central points in his parenesis concern the exclusiveness and unequivocal character of obedience (1:7-8; 3:10-12), the polemic against sins of the tongue (3:1-9), and self-assurance (4:13-17).

6. The Johannine literature. The unmistakable reduction of ethical issues in the Johannine writings (especially in the Fourth Gospel) also signifies a concentration and integration of ethics into the whole of theology. Nowhere else is ethics so exclusively grounded in God's eschatological saving act in Christ; this is in harmony with the exclusivity and absoluteness of the revelation given in Christ and the salvation that is bestowed in him. The Christian life bears fruit only by abiding in him (John 15:1-11, where also the dialectic of indicative and imperative is reflected). Christology is the dominant theme not only of the indicative, but also of the imperative, to the extent that the basic stance of the Christian is his relationship with Christ. This can be expressed by hearing, abiding, knowing, etc., but also by keeping the word and the commandments (8:51; 14:15; 15:10). This also implies an orientation to the example of Jesus' conduct: "For I have given you an example, that you also should do as I have done to you" (13:15); the reference here is to the lowly, humbling, loving act of foot-washing, not to a cultic act. In I John, Jesus' exemplary function is elucidated in other concepts also (3:3, 7, 16), and in 2:6 the idea of such correspondence with his conduct is stated in a fundamental way: we are to "walk in the same way in which he walked."

The keeping of the commandments and the obligation that arises therefrom (cf. John 13:34; 15:12) is usually described in terms of love for one's brethren. Thereby Jesus' radical removal of limitations is reversed, though the basis and meaning of this reversal are not altogether clear. Nevertheless, for John, too, love is the loftiest quality. Indeed, it is unique, and even here it is not an emotion or affection. It is, in a comprehensive sense, living for others, even to the point of laying down one's life (I John 3:16). Since there is no middle position between love and hatred, hatred can be equated with murder (I John 3:15), and love can be the basis for recognition of the sphere of salvation and life (John 13:35; I John 3:14). Dualistic expressions declare all "flesh" and everything worldly to be vain, irrelevant, and of no avail (John 6:63, etc.) and warn against any love of the world (I John 2:15-17), but in spite of this according to I John love also is to prove itself precisely in the needs of everyday life (I John 3:17-18).

7. The book of Revelation. The entire book of Revelation is permeated with apocalyptic eschatology and an intense expectation of the imminent end (cf. 1:1, 3; 22:20). Of crucial importance is the connection of this expectation with the present Christ, whom the community already has encountered as Savior and Lord, whose love is constant (1:5*b*), and whose victory is already hailed proleptically in hymns (11:15-18; 12:10-11, and *passim*). This also determines the ethic of the book, particularly in the seven letters (chs. 2–3). Promises and threats of judgment are by far the most prominent elements (though on the other hand there are reminders of what the community has already received, 3:3). The seer is concerned primarily with repentance (2:5, 16, 21-22, and *passim*), which is manifested in works (2:5, 19, and *passim*) and in total and undivided commitment (3:15-16). Hardly ever is a position taken on concrete ethical questions, though in ch. 18 an undertone of social criticism may be detected.

At the center of the ethical considerations stands the impending conflict with Rome and its cult of the emperor (cf. 2:13; 6:9-11; 17:6; 20:4). In ch. 13 the seer sketches the fantastic picture of a demonic monster which symbolizes the Roman state. With its seven heads and ten horns it is the earthly image of the dragon (=the devil; cf. 13:1 with 12:3), and thus the embodiment of satanic power on earth. But it is also a devilish caricature of Christ (cf. 13:3, 12 with 2:8; 5:6; 13:2 with 3:21). This means that the Roman state demands what belongs to God (cf. 13:4), and as such is of the devil. It is satanic, because it is a totalitarian state. By means of propaganda and "signs" a second beast (13:11-17) promotes the veneration of the first beast as divine, and thus provides for an ideology, for metaphysics, and for symbolism appropriate to the state. It provides also for state policy, in that it subjects to economic boycott (13:17) or puts to death (13:13) those who reject the state cult. The attitude of Christians toward such a perverted and deified state can only be disobedience, endurance, and passive resistance (13:10). *See also* ROME, EARLY CHRISTIAN ATTITUDES TOWARD[S] §6.

Bibliography. General studies: L. H. Marshall, *The Challenge of NT Ethics* (1946); H. Preisker, *Das Ethos des Urchristentums* (2nd ed., 1949 [repr. 1968]); R. Völkl, *Christ und Welt nach dem NT* (1961); W. G. Kümmel, "Sittlichkeit im Urchristentum," *RGG,* VI (3rd ed., 1962), cols. 70-80, with bibliog.; R. Schnackenburg, *The Moral Teaching of the NT* (2nd ed., 1965); H. D. Wendland, *Ethik des NT,* NTD Ergänzungsreihe, IV (1970); V. P. Furnish, *The Love Command in the NT* (1972).

On Jesus and the Synoptics: H. Windisch, *The Meaning of the Sermon on the Mount* (rev. ed., 1937 [ET 1951]); A. N. Wilder, *Eschatology and Ethics in the Teaching of Jesus* (2nd ed., 1950); E. Neuhäusler, *Anspruch und Antwort Gottes* (1962); W. D. Davies, *The Setting of the Sermon on the Mount* (1964).

On Paul: M. S. Enslin, *The Ethics of Paul* (1930 [repr. 1962]); W. Schrage, *Die konkreten Einzelgebote in der paulinischen Paränese* (1961); V. P. Furnish, *Theology and Ethics in Paul* (1968); O. Merk, *Handeln aus Glauben. Die Motivierung der paulinischen Ethik,* Marburger Theologische Studien, V (1968).

On the Deutero-Paulines: E. Lohse, "Christologie und Ethik im Kol," *Apophoreta,* ed. W. Eltester, BZNW, XXX (1964), 157-68; J. E. Crouch, *The Origin and Intention of the Colossian Haustafel, FRLANT,* CIX (1972); W. Schrage, "Zur Ethik der neutestamentlichen Haustafeln," *NTS,* XXI (1974), 1-22.

On the Catholic epistles: E. Lohse, "Kerygma und Paränese im 1 Petr," *ZNW,* XLV (1954), 68-89; K. Philipps, *Kirche in der Gesellschaft nach dem 1. Petrusbrief* (1971); G. Eichholz, *Glaube und Werke bei Paulus und Jakobus,* Theologische Existenz Heute, NF LXXXVIII; E. Lohse, "Glaube und Werke. Zur Theologie des Jak," *ZNW,* XLVIII (1957), 1-22.

On the Johannine literature: O. Prunet, *La morale chrétienne d'apres les écrits Johanniques* (1957).

On the book of Revelation: R. Schütz, *Die Offenbarung des Johannes und Kaiser Domitian, FRLANT,* L (1933); E. Käsemann, *Jesus Means Freedom* (3rd ed., 1968), pp. 132-43; W. Schrage, *Die Christen und der Staat nach dem NT* (1971), pp. 69-76.

W. SCHRAGE

ETHOS OF EARLY CHRISTIANITY. In the world of classical and Hellenistic Greek, ἦθος (only I Cor. 15:33 [proverbial] in NT, but cf. I Clem. 1:2; 21:7 and ἔθος) refers to "character" or "habitual way of life." To the Stoic, for example, it denotes that which is the source of behavior.

1. Definition
2. Problems of formation
3. Ethos and form criticism
4. The symbolic world of early Christianity
   a. The ethos of Pauline Christianity
   b. John's Gospel and John's world
   c. Conclusions

Bibliography

1. Definition. In its modern use the term has a somewhat fluid status in cultural anthropology. Early descriptions of ethos as national or cultural "character" were impressionistic, an unwarranted extension of individual habits and dispositions to entire groups or races. More recent and fruitful is the use of ethos to describe the perceived emotional quality or force of cultural acts and the motivation behind them, or to describe the relationship among a range of values within a given culture or social unit.

All theories of culture which refer to ethos seek to distinguish it from an ethic, which is a body of principles on the basis of which moral actions can be taken and recommended. Ethos differs from an ethic by involving not only moral but also cultural and communal values. Unlike an ethic, an ethos cannot be reduced to a set of principles for behavior, since the reasons for actions may be implicit rather than explicit. An ethic tells the member of a group what he or she is to do. The ethos of the group reinforces that by also saying who and where one is.

This leads to a more specific working definition of ethos as the tone and style of a group's (or culture's) entire range of values, the quality of its life. It exists in close connection with a more external element, the way the universe is perceived or what is sometimes called "world view." A people's world view is a perception of actuality in its many dimensions: personal, social, and natural. The relationship of ethos to world view is the relationship of the moral, aesthetic, and evaluative aspects of a culture to the cognitive and experiential aspects.

Religious groups, like other social and cultural units, live in the interconnection between ethos and world view. Some interpreters will regard the metaphysics of a religious system as basic, and others will emphasize its ethics, but a religion is never either of these in isolation. It is a response to a perceived reality of the sort which stresses that the nature of reality as a given carries implicit obligation. The religious community is persuaded that the fulfillment of obligations is itself a way of sustaining and enhancing that which is real. The "ought" is firmly grounded in the "is."

Such a view is not peculiar to religious groups but is characteristic of the mutuality of the concepts "ethos" and "world view," regardless of the setting to which they are applied. As a bundle of values comprehending an entire tone or mood of life, ethos does not merely respond to the world view with which it is associated. It also at the same time underwrites and thus guarantees that world view, enhancing the "reality" of that which is considered real. In similar fashion, a world view can so thoroughly penetrate the ethos of those who subscribe to it that the ethos itself embodies the world view and renders the heightened sense of reality operative in the ordinary here and now. Each, in effect, borrows authority from the other while lending authority to the other.

Between ethos and world view, co-ordinating them and encouraging their mutual influence, stand *symbols.* These may be simple objects or more complex rituals and myths. Such symbols comprehend both the meaning of reality and the quality of life considered appropriate to it. Sacred symbols thus provide the mechanism by which a religious community will relate ontology and cosmology to aesthetics and morality. When these symbols become arranged in a more or less comprehensive whole we may speak of a "religious system."

2. Problems of formation. The idea of an ethos of early Christianity entails certain difficulties beyond the obvious ones stemming from the number and particular interests of historical sources and questions of their reliability. Christianity arose out of the relatively coherent and comprehensive ethos of Judaism, but immediately called much of that heritage into question. As a result, three characteristics mark the emerging Christian sensibility.

First, the question of social identity became a central issue requiring clarification; the new experience demanded a new social expression. Second, materials for constructing a new world view and ethos came, in part, from the more variegated world of HELLENISM. As a result, the development of a more or less unified Christian world view and ethos required several generations, during which pluralism was a notable fact. Third, although Christianity early began to separate itself from Judaism, it never completely severed the symbolic ties to that cultural and religious world, as is evident from early Christianity's insistence that it was the "new" Israel. While such symbolism is not wholly antithetical to a Hellenistic environment, as the earlier prosperity of Judaism in such a context makes clear (*see* JUDAISM, HELLENISTIC[S]), the maintenance of elements of an older ethos alongside those of a new setting creates tensions. Only when these are resolved or significantly reduced may we begin to speak of something approaching a single, characteristically Christian ethos. In the earliest stages the picture is fragmented and diverse.

3. Ethos and form criticism. It seems apparent from this description that the study of the ethos of a group which is in rapid transition, and of multiple groups which are only loosely related to one another organizationally, will need to identify as far as possible both the internal and external elements that shape the group and help it achieve self understanding. Much of what happened along these lines in the first centuries of Christianity has been lost from view, but hints remain in both the form and the substance of its literature. That such is the case has long been recognized by FORM CRITICISM and its newer offspring, REDACTION CRITICISM.

Nevertheless, form criticism shows signs of atrophy at the point where a crucial question, that of the social function of forms, literary types, and finished literary works, arises (*see* BIBLICAL CRITICISM, NT[S] §4*c*). At the beginning of the form critical method, Gunkel, for example, regarded the setting (*Sitz im Leben*) of a discrete "form" as its wider cultural and social setting, one which enabled the group to use the form for its own purposes. The setting thereby provided a new meaning or interpretation for an older tradition. On this understanding the form is very nearly equivalent to "symbol" as that term is used above. Setting and form represent multiple realities, external and internal, social as well as literary. This understanding has been obscured in more recent form-critical work. The problem is already evident in the earliest stages of NT form criticism represented by Dibelius, who narrowed the idea of setting to the cultic. Within that area he paid particular attention to the sermon. After Dibelius there was little further exploration of the sociological dimensions of the Christian use of oral and literary traditions. As a result, social functions came to be regarded somewhat parochially as cultic function, while *Sitz im Leben* was gradually construed as "historical context." The question of the setting of a tradition came to be regarded as an invitation to choose among indistinct historical alternatives such as the ministry of Jesus, Jewish Christianity, Hellenistic Christianity, Hellenistic-Jewish Christianity, etc.

It has also been noted that form criticism is reductionistic in another sense as well. It too easily assumes a single correlation between the setting and one particular literary type (*Gattung*). Even a socially restricted and specific setting such as cult will provide a home for numerous literary types (e.g., sermon, hymn, prayer, etc.), so that the true nature of the setting cannot be understood without attention to the mutual relationship of these components. Much the same may be said for a larger literary effort which orchestrates various specific forms and thereby becomes itself a "setting." If a gospel, for example, is to be seen as a cultural and social item as well as a literary category, the traditional forms that are its components will appear to function as symbols inside a more or less comprehensive system. Such comprehensiveness may be difficult to suggest for some NT texts. It is more likely to be evident in groups of texts or groups of symbols used across the boundaries of several texts. The closer we come to being able to speak of such symbolic unity or affiliation, the closer we come to being able to speak of an ethos.

4. The symbolic world of early Christianity. To uncover the ethos of various groups within earliest Christianity requires identifying and analyzing a wide variety of literary forms, terms, myths, rituals, and objects which can serve as symbols. What is required is that the device chosen be able to compress in a single nexus that which is experienced and that which is regarded as a style of life appropriate to the experience. Two examples, one from Paul and one from John, will provide an illustration using quite different kinds of symbols. The latter case also exemplifies the often implicit nature of ethos where a world view is dominant.

a. The ethos of Pauline Christianity. The statement that the "ought" of an ethos is firmly grounded in an "is" sounds similar to the common exegetical observation that Pauline ethics is constructed on an "indicative-imperative" scheme. In Gal. 5:25 Paul urges, "If we live by the Spirit, let us also walk by the Spirit." To Paul it seems evident that the life of the Christian is constituted by the gift of a new reality which he refers to as Spirit (e.g., Rom. 5:5; 8:16; Gal. 3:2). That the term has a symbolic status is suggested by the variety of particular expressions Paul can use in referring to the same phenomenon. In addition to the "Spirit of God" (Rom. 8:9), we find the "spirit of faith" (II Cor. 4:13), the "Spirit of his Son" (Gal. 4:6), and the "Spirit of Christ" (Rom. 8:9), all of which are related to the "Spirit of holiness" (Rom. 1:4) conceived as the source of life in a new age.

Paul's use of this term to contrast the realms of FLESH and SPIRIT (Gal. 5:16 ff.; Rom. 8:5) suggests the true force of the indicative-imperative scheme. The Spirit negotiates the relationship between the actual world which exists for the Christian and the obligations grounded in that world. This world is ruled by Christ as Lord, the sovereign of a realm to which the Christian belongs.

What values does such a realm of existence certify? Which values will underwrite and make visible its reality, which will suggest its nature as a world inhabited by real people? Among many suggestions in the letters two are particularly arresting for the combined light they shed on one aspect of the ethos of Pauline Christianity.

The first of these is freedom, frequently described as freedom from the law. The law cannot be subscribed to innocently, for it belongs to an old order of existence and is antithetical to the new realm (Gal. 3:23-29). But freedom means more than the relegation of law to a day now past, to a kingdom ruled by sin. It also means the emancipation of the Christian *from* that whole realm. For this reason, on an issue such as whether or not Christians may eat meat sacrificed to idols (I Cor. 8:4-6) Paul stresses that they are free not just from law but from an entire world that is now rendered meaningless.

At the same time Paul's treatment of this issue shows the weight he assigns to a quite different value which seems no less securely tied to that world view from which the idea of freedom is derived. Although the Corinthians may eat such meat, they ought also to consider one another and "take care lest this liberty . . . somehow become a stumbling block to the weak" (I Cor. 8:9). If a brother wounds another's conscience on this matter he sins (8:12) and so forsakes the very world which his freedom was supposed to reflect and underwrite.

The role of the Spirit in Paul's letters suggests how this apparent conflict of values is to be seen as deriving from a single view of reality. In fact, the relationship between the values further specifies that reality: The "world" which is real for the new person in Christ is a communal world, not merely an individualistic one. This is made clear when Paul invokes the symbol of Spirit within the context of the image of the body of Christ (I Cor. 12). Just as the Spirit behind the many individual gifts is one, so the body of many members is a single body of Christ. In I Cor. 6:7 we find a similar sentiment cast in a different image. Christians could well afford to forego the strife of litigation among themselves, suffering wrong instead. The power for individuals of the new reality stored in the image of the Spirit is modified by the social nature of that reality, indicated by the close association of Spirit and "body" (as in I Cor. 6:12-20).

Thus it is not surprising to find that Paul can interpret his own indicative-imperative scheme by urging the Galatians to "bear one another's burdens," suggesting that to do so fulfills the law of Christ (Gal. 6:2). On this matter, at least, the ethos of Pauline Christianity includes something more than just the notion that a Christian's individual ethical behavior based on his freedom from the law is what constitutes the new life. The Pauline ethos also values the community and expresses a conviction that this new life has a coercively social and communal orientation. Paul's indicative and imperative are not one-dimensional statements of gift and obligation. They reflect the complexity which is characteristic of world views and natural for an ethos as the expression of an entire style of life. For that reason the symbol of Spirit must itself be of sufficient scope to connect the multiple strands between indicative and imperative, between world view and ethos.

It is common to say of Paul's imperatives that they do not recommend a course of action toward the indicative, as if this indicative were a goal to be achieved. This is particularly true if we think of the imperatives as individual moral obligations. It appears, however, that the imperative contains a fuller range of obligations, *some of which have goals within the ethos itself*. Such is the nature of admonitions about the common life of Christians. Whether Paul himself conceived of this as a long-range goal may be questioned, since part of his world view seems to involve an imminent eschatology. But adjustments in that picture of reality as experienced by subsequent generations served to underscore the vitality of communal concerns within the developing ethos of the church. This is signaled by symbolic shifts in the period after Paul. The role of some symbols, such as the Spirit, diminishes. Others are transformed, as is the case with the body of Christ. Still others, like the *Haustafeln* (*see* LISTS, ETHICAL §§1-4; LISTS, ETHICAL[S] §2), make their initial appearance.

This can happen because Paul strikes not a single note but a chord. Some of the individual notes within it recur in subsequent generations while others disappear. The resulting difference in harmonies is nevertheless not wholly discontinuous with the Pauline period, when some of those whom he addresses in his letters (especially in I Corinthians) understood the Spirit in a way which did not sound right to him.

b. John's Gospel and John's world. John's Gospel offers a quite different study in early Christian perception of social identity. Unlike the Pauline letters, this document does not take us inside the community's discussion of the values appropriate to the Christian life, but focuses instead on the origin of a community as a distinction between the world and the circle of those who believe in Jesus. That distinction is drawn so clearly and stressed so persistently that it becomes constitutive of the new identity of believers.

Jesus as the descending and ascending Savior is the symbolic means by which this new world is articulated. Of heavenly origin, he comes to "his own," but they do not receive him (1:11). The matter of his origin outside of this world is repeatedly stressed, not in order to indulge speculation about his nature but in order to display the curious fate of this other-worldly savior. He is not comprehended, but finally rejected. Even

Nicodemus, who regards Jesus as having "come from God" (3:2) and is willing to approach him as a teacher, cannot receive his "testimony" (3:11) and will never know of the "heavenly things." What these might be is not as important for the author as the barrier which proves insurmountable for Nicodemus. This is underscored by the adamant hostility of the "Jews" who do not accept what even Nicodemus saw, that Jesus is from God (9:16), and yet do not know where he comes from (vs. 29).

Obviously, some do "comprehend," so that it can be said of those "who received him, who believed in his name" (1:12) that they "beheld his glory" (vs. 14). The fate of one of these, the blind man whom Jesus heals (ch. 9), is instructive. Because he persists in saying that the one who healed him comes from God, he is cut off from the Jewish community (9:34) in accordance with the decision of the Pharisees that "if any one should confess him to be Christ, he was to be put out of the synagogue" (vs. 22).

It is apparently this experience of the expulsion of Christians from the synagogue (cf. also 12:42; 16:2) which necessitates a new sense of identity and occasions the gospel which supplies it (*see* JOHN, GOSPEL OF[S] §2). That the ethos of such a group should be essentially negative, in the sense that its identity is achieved through contrast with the disbelieving world, is not surprising. But just as there is a motif of the descent of the Savior, so is there one of his ascent, with which the second half of the gospel is primarily concerned. While the community cannot immediately follow Jesus in his departure, it is assured internal unity and fellowship with him, and is promised the "Counselor . . . the Spirit of truth" (14:16-17). Furthermore, what is said about this figure and about the believers themselves links, through the symbol of the other-worldly Savior, an ethos with an appropriately stark yet consoling sense of reality. Like Jesus, the Spirit of truth is one "the world cannot receive, because it neither sees him nor knows him" (14:17), a characteristic which, finally, can be applied to the community itself: "If you were of the world, the world would love its own; but because you are not of the world . . . the world hates you" (15:19).

Believing in Jesus translates the believer from one social world into another. This happened historically, apparently, when believers were excluded from the synagogue. The historical event continues to exist as symbolic fact through the role played by the gospel, which uses this trauma as a platform to provide a new social identity for the believers. That identity is not revealed in nuance and detail. John presents less the taxonomy of the Christian community than its general anatomy. But the gospel itself, as literary form, plays a decisive role in the projection of the new identity. As an aggregate literary form it becomes the "setting" in which various older traditions take on new life and meaning. More than that, the gospel recapitulates in the life of the community the actual experience of Jesus and functions for its members as its hero functions in the story it tells. Even the literary structure of the gospel, with its enigmatic discourses, repetition, and *double-entendre* is a reflection of the nature of the new reality which has emerged from the older story. Thus the ambiguity of and about Jesus which progressively leads to his rejection, his death, and his ascent is paralleled by the ambiguity of belief on the part of those whose first limited understanding, frequently misunderstanding, leads to gradual initiation into the truth of Jesus and finally produces their alienation from this world which has been hostile to him and to them. He has made them his own by calling them out of this world.

c. Conclusions. The contrast between these two examples is instructive. The Pauline ethos appears confident, linked as it is with a world viewed as having been freed from the inevitability of an evil age. Such "heroic" posture accords with missionary zeal, rapid growth, and, perhaps, a certain looseness of organization, all of which seem on other evidence to be part of a Pauline pattern within early Christianity. The Johannine picture reveals a community somewhat more static or at least more stable, certainly less robust and probably less well adapted to a missionary milieu. John's images tend toward sustenance and intensification rather than toward growth by extension. Comprehensive analyses of ethos and world view in these and other early texts may confirm or modify the suggestions sketched here, but certainly such analyses should broaden understanding of the social setting and social significance of early Christianity.

Bibliography. The definition of ethos used is based on C. Geertz, *Interpretation of Cultures* (1973), pp. 89-90; 125-41, and *Islam Observed* (1968), pp. 90-114. On the general social setting of early Christianity: U. Kahrstedt, *Kulturgeschichte der römischen Kaiserzeit* (2nd ed., 1958); M. Rostovtzeff, *Social and Economic History of the Hellenistic World,* 3 vols. (1941), and *The Social and Economic History of the Roman Empire,* 2 vols. (2nd ed. rev. by P. M. Fraser, 1957).

Specific studies: S. J. Case, *The Social Origins of Christianity* (1923), and *The Social Triumph of the Ancient Church* (1933); E. von Dobschütz, *Christian Life in the Primitive Church* (1902); J. Gager, *Kingdom and Community* (1975); E. A. Judge, *The Social Pattern of Christian Groups in the First Century* (1960); L. Keck, "On the Ethos of Early Christians," *JAAR,* XLII (1974), 435-52, basic; H. Preisker, *Das Ethos des Urchristentums* (2nd ed., 1949); C. Schneider, *Geistesgeschichte des antiken Christentums,* I (1954), 486-530.

On Pauline Christianity: V. P. Furnish, *Theology and Ethics in Paul* (1968), esp. pp. 44-50; 81-91; 224-27; D. Georgi, *Die Gegner des Paulus im 2. Korintherbrief,* WMANT, XI (1964); W. Meeks, "The Image of the Androgyne: Some Uses of a Symbol in Earliest Christianity," *History of Religions,* XIII (1974), 165-208; G. Theissen, "Legitimation und Lebensunterhalt: Ein Beitrag zur Soziologie Urchristlicher Missionäre," *NTS,* XXI (1975), 192-221, "Soziale Schichtung in der korinthischen Gemeinde," *ZNW,* LXV (1974), 232-72, and "Wanderradikalismus. Literatursoziologische Aspekte der Überlieferung von Worten Jesu im Urchristentum," *ZThK,* LXX (1973), 245-71.

On Johannine Christianity: W. Meeks, "The Man from Heaven in Johannine Sectarianism," *JBL,* XCI (1972), 44-72, on which the interpretation above is based; H. Leroy, *Rätsel und Missverständnis,* BBB, XXX (1968); J. L. Martyn, *History and Theology in the*

Fourth Gospel (1968); D. M. Smith, "Johannine Christianity: Some Reflections on its Character and Delineation," *NTS*, XXI (1975), 222-48. J. H. Schütz

ETIOLOGY ē tē ŏl' ə jē. Properly, the study of causes (Gr. αἰτία, cause); the term commonly used to designate stories which are designed to explain how some existing phenomenon in nature, custom, or institution came into being by recounting a past event which is taken to be the effective cause of that phenomenon.

1. Classification and OT examples. Many different schemes of classifying the various types of etiological stories have been proposed, but since, in biblical studies, the analysis of Gunkel has been and remains, with some modifications, the most influential, a brief outline of his classification is in order.

Gunkel took as his starting point the position that etiological stories are answers to questions; men look at things and ask why. He proceeds to classify etiological types in terms of the kinds of questions which he assumes to lie behind the answers embodied in the narratives. He concludes that there are four basic types: (1) ethnological etiologies, which give reasons for relations among tribal groups; (2) etymological etiologies, which explain the names of persons or places; (3) ceremonial or cultic etiologies, which account for the origin of religious rites and customs; and (4) geological etiologies, which explain the origin of a particular locality or geological formation. Stories explaining other natural phenomena, e.g., the origin and meaning of the rainbow (Gen. 9:12-17), should also be included in this category. Finally, Gunkel observed that in some stories various types are combined, resulting in a mixed form. Gunkel's typology remains dominant in biblical studies (*see* Legend §§2, 3).

Examples illustrating these types abound. The subservient lot of the Canaanites and the incorporation of the Philistines into the Israelite empire is explained in the story of Ham, Shem, and Japheth in Gen. 9:20-27; the conflict between Israel and Edom is explained by Gen. 25:23; the child's question about the meaning of certain details of the Passover ceremony (Exod. 12:26; 13:14) lies behind the immediately preceding narratives (Exod. 12:21-25; 13:11-13); a peculiar rock formation is accounted for by the act of Lot's wife (Gen. 19:26); and so on. Etymological notes, often philologically erroneous (e.g., the derivation of Moses from Heb. *māšâ*, Exod. 2:10) are especially numerous, particularly in the earlier literary strata. The following list is illustrative but by no means exhaustive. Personal names: woman, Gen. 2:23; Eve, Gen. 3:20; Cain, Gen. 4:1; Ishmael, Gen. 16:11; Abraham, Gen. 17:5; Isaac, Gen. 17:19; Esau, Gen. 25:25, 30; Jacob, Gen. 25:26. Place names: Babel, Gen. 11:9; Beer-lahai-roi, Gen. 16:14; Zoar, Gen. 19:22; Beer-sheba, Gen. 21:31; Marah, Exod. 15:23.

2. Etiologies and general OT interpretation. Recognition of the nature and function of etiological stories was an important step in tracing the preliterary stage of early Israelite tradition. Serious questions have been raised, however, as to the propriety of utilizing the etiological motif as the primary key for interpreting all materials which contain an etiological element. Put simply, should all narratives which contain an etiological theme, or from which an etiological theme may be deduced, be interpreted primarily as accounts designed to supply an answer to the question stated or implied? Are there other factors which are more important than the etiology that must be utilized by the interpreter? The issue may be put this way: In a narrative which contains an etiology, to what extent is the etiology itself central; to what extent has it simply been tacked on as a secondary element; or, to what extent has an earlier etiology been radically modified for a totally new and different purpose? The answers may result in widely divergent interpretations of biblical material.

A classic case study is the story of Jacob's wrestling with the angel (Gen. 32:22-32). Four different etiological themes have been isolated in this account: (1) explanation of a peculiar cultic dance at a particular shrine (vss. 25, 31); (2) explanation of a place name (vs. 30); (3) explanation of a dietary regulation (vs. 32); and (4) explanation of Jacob's new name, Israel (vs. 28). It is probable that all four existed in the preliterary stage of the material, but the interpreter must attempt to assess their respective weights in evaluating the present form of the narrative. In this instance there seems little doubt that the giving of the new name is primary.

In this example, etiologies are clearly present, and the problem is to determine which etiology is dominant. Another narrative, the judgments pronounced against the serpent, the woman, and the man (Gen. 3:14-19), raises another kind of problem. No doubt ancient etiologies are employed, answering questions about why snakes crawl on their bellies, why women have pain in childbirth, and why there is so much difficulty in bringing forth produce from the earth. The intention of the present form of the narrative, however, would be seriously misconstrued if attention were centered on these original etiological themes. The author has utilized them for an altogether different theological purpose. Etiology is secondary.

3. Etiologies and historical narrative. A somewhat different issue arises in interpreting historical narratives which contain etiological references. For example, does the story of Joshua's execution of the five kings and their burial in a cave at Makkedah evolve from an attempt to explain the great stones at the mouth of a well-known geographical locale, or is there a genuine historical tradition behind the account (Josh. 10:16-27)? This issue has been debated with respect to the historical reliability of the narratives of the era of the settlement (conquest) of Canaan. Some scholars have concluded that if a story possesses an etiological element, it is, in most instances, a methodological error to attempt to recover historical data from the narrative. The etiological theme has been formative of the tradition, and one errs in attempting to go beyond the obvious etiological interest in evaluating the material. Thus, such stories in Josh. 1–12 as the heap of stones at the Jordan (4:1-24); the place names Gilgal (5:8-9) and Achor (7:1-26);

the destruction of Ai (8:1-29); the social status of the Gibeonites (9:3-27) are etiological tales and cannot be utilized in reconstructing the history of Israel. Other scholars have sharply dissented from this view (*see* JOSHUA §D1). Their contention is that presence of an etiological motif does not necessarily mean that the etiological purpose has given rise to the narrative. Rather, it is maintained that in many instances the etiological reference is a secondary element and that the historicity of the account must be determined on other grounds. This view admits that some stories are indeed primarily etiological, but insists that etiology has not been the primary factor in shaping an entire historical tradition, i.e., the settlement (conquest) of Canaan.

While it remains true that each individual narrative must be evaluated separately with respect to the primacy of the etiological intent, recent detailed studies of etiological narrative indicate that, on the whole, the latter view outlined above rests on more solid foundations. The prevailing opinion is that in most instances etiological themes are not decisive as criteria for historical evaluation. The historicity of a narrative, thus, is not to be decided simply upon the presence or absence of etiological elements. Other criteria are more significant.

Some writers have extended the definition of etiology considerably beyond the limits defined by Gunkel and commonly employed. For instance, the whole of Exod. 1–15 has been described as a cultic etiology of the Passover (*see* PASSOVER §3). I and II Samuel have been characterized as an etiology of the Davidic dynasty (*see* SAMUEL, I AND II §C1*a*, 5); I and II Chronicles as an etiology of the structure of the postexilic Jewish community (*see* CHRONICLES, I AND II §3); and the whole of the Deuteronomic history as an etiology of Josiah's reform or the destruction of the Judean state (*see* KINGS, I AND II §C6, 7). As interpretive devices such perspectives are illuminating, but they probably stretch the term etiology so far as to render it methodologically unmanageable. It would seem more appropriate to define such purposes as legitimations rather than etiologies. Legitimation denotes the sanctioning of a broader socioreligious complex than is present in a proper etiological story.

4. Etiology and the NT. Thus far etiology has been discussed within the OT context and primarily in connection with the earlier strata of the OT. This was done because etiologies occur much more frequently in the beginning periods of a people's tradition since it is precisely at that time that the broad foundations are laid. Nevertheless, etiological references, both within the more formal definition and in the broader usage referred to in the preceding paragraph, are to be found in the NT.

The first set of examples is found in the birth narratives. Luke tells of the naming of John (1:13) and of Jesus (1:31). The giving of the name is often found in etiological stories, but in neither instance does Luke explain the meaning of the name, nor does the name seem to shape the accompanying narrative. Matt. 1:21 explains the name Jesus, "for he will save his people from their sins" (the Heb. or Aram. root means "to save"), but the narrative betrays no etiological influence.

The Markan account of the appointing of the disciples (3:13-19) contains two name changes; Simon is surnamed Peter (vs. 16), and James and John are surnamed Boanerges, that is, "sons of thunder" (vs. 17; *see* BOANERGES). Here there is no apparent interest in etymology as such and certainly this etiological reference has had no effect on the form of its narrative. Matt. 10:2 and Luke 6:14 also mention that Simon is called Peter, but like Mark, give no reason for the change. Both omit the surnaming of the sons of Zebedee.

Finally, John 1:42 says that Simon will be called Cephas, and it is noted that Cephas means Peter. Again no reason is given for the change of name and it is not possible to discern any effect of the etymological note on the narrative. Indeed in all of the narratives it is probable that we do not have examples of etiology proper at all. It has been suggested that a theological purpose, showing that in giving the new names Jesus was displaying his sovereign ability to create something new underlies the surnaming narratives, but this seems to go beyond the intention of the texts.

Matt. 16:13-20, Peter's confession at Caesarea Phillipi, requires a separate examination. Here Jesus confers upon Simon the new name, and it is probable that a twofold etiology is implicit. The supposed etymology of Peter is explicitly given. He is Peter (*petros*) for he is to be the rock (*petra*) upon which the church will be built. The wordplay is clearer in Palestinian Aramaic, which uses the same word, *Kepha,* for both the proper name and the common noun. It is probably the intention of the story to denote a shift in Peter's character and to provide dominical authority for his supremacy in the early Christian community. Indeed, this latter interest may well account for the insertion of vss. 17-19, which are lacking in the parallel accounts in Mark 8:27-30 and Luke 9:18-22. However, the historicity of the account is hardly to be decided simply by its obvious etiological nature.

Another change of name is noted in Acts 4:36-37, where the generosity of a certain Joseph led the apostles to give him the new name Barnabas, "Son of encouragement." It is to be doubted if this etiological reference played any considerable role in the narrative in which it is found (Acts 4:32-37). Both Matt. 27:3-10 and Acts 1:16-20 utilize etiology in narratives of Judas' death. They vary in details but agree that his burial place came to be called the "Field of Blood." The existence of such a place may well have supplied some details in the shaping of the narratives, but it is difficult to conclude that it exercised a primary influence. All the NT examples cited contain formal elements of etiological material, whether etymological or geographical. With the possible exception of Matt. 16:17-19, however, it does not appear that the etiological reference played any significant role in shaping the narrative in which it is embedded.

5. The gospels as extended etiologies. Quite a different claim has been made for the influences of cultic etiology on NT narratives, particularly in the gospels. It is assumed that the Christ portrayed is not the historical Jesus but the Christ of the faith and cult of the Christian community. For example, the narrative in John 13:2-11 is an etiology explaining cultic foot washing; the stories of Jesus' baptism (Matt. 3:13-17; Mark 1:9-11; Luke 3:21-22; John 1:31-34) are etiologies for Christian baptism; the accounts of the Last Supper are etiologies for the Lord's Supper, etc. In its most extreme form this position suggests that as a whole the gospels may be viewed as expanded cult legends in which etiology is the dominant though not the exclusive factor (*see* MYTH IN THE NT §§3, 4).

Such a position seems subject to the same reservation mentioned with respect to the role of etiology in shaping the settlement (conquest) narratives discussed above. It is probable that some details in the present form of the narratives do reflect cultic practices and that these practices have resulted in a reshaping of the tradition itself. The tradition gave rise to the cult, which in turn reacted back upon the detailed formulation of the tradition. To be sure, the historicity of the tradition itself must be the object of careful scrutiny, but its historicity is not to be decided solely upon the criterion of cultic etiology.

6. Summary. Etiological stories provide considerable information about the early Israelite world view and some insight into the formation of the present form of certain biblical accounts. Recognition of etiological motifs may assist in interpreting particular narratives, but caution should be exercised in assuming that the presence of an etiology explains the function of the entire narrative of which it is a part. Both the possibility of genuine historical tradition to which an etiology has been secondarily added and awareness of the present function of the narrative in the larger literary complex must be given as much attention by the interpreter as analysis of the etiology itself.

Bibliography. J. Bright, *Early Israel in Recent History Writing* (1956); R. Bultmann, *History of the Synoptic Tradition* (1963), esp. pp. 244-302; B. S. Childs, "A Study of the Formula 'Until This Day,'" *JBL*, LXXXII (1963), 279-92, and "The Etiological Tale Re-examined," *VT*, XXIV (1974), 387-97; M. Dibelius, *From Tradition to Gospel* (1935), pp. 104-32; H. Gunkel, *The Legends of Genesis* (1964), pp. 24-36; B. Long, *The Problem of Etiological Narrative in the OT* (1968); M. Nilsson, *A History of Greek Religion* (1925), pp. 48-75; M. Noth, *Das Buch Josua*, 3rd ed., *HAT* (1971). For a brief summary of his position see *The History of Israel* (1958), esp. pp. 68-84; J. A. Soggin, "Kultätiologische Sagen und Katachese im Hexateuch," *VT*, X (1960), 341-47.

J. F. PRIEST

EUSEBIUS OF CAESAREA ū sē'bĭ əs [Εὐσέβιος]; **EUSEBIUS PAMPHILI** păm'fĭl ī [ὁ τοῦ Παμφίλου]. Early fourth-century bishop of CAESAREA on the coast of Palestine; historian, biblical scholar, and theologian; the "Father of Church History." He wrote a history of early Christianity covering the first three centuries; compiled a unified chronology of general ancient Near Eastern, Greek, and Roman history; and wrote other works on biblical geography, gospel parallels, interpretation of scripture, apologetics, and contemporary theological issues.

1. Life. Born *ca.* A.D. 260, possibly in Caesarea itself, where it is known he spent his later life. He developed his massive scholarship in the libraries of Bishop Alexander at Jerusalem and the presbyter Pamphilus in Caesarea. Eusebius is often identified simply as Eusebius Pamphili, "Pamphilus' Eusebius." The two engaged in text-critical work on biblical manuscripts, both being admirers of Origen's methods. When the great persecution began under Diocletian in 303, Pamphilus was eventually martyred, but Eusebius escaped. After the emperor Constantine declared a pro-Christian policy and triumphed at the battle of the Milvian bridge in 312, Eusebius became one of the chief spokesmen for the new vision of a Christian world empire. He had personal access to Constantine and at times acted as his agent.

Eusebius was made bishop of Caesarea *ca.* 313. At the Council of Nicaea in 325, which officially affirmed the full divinity of Christ, he subscribed to the conciliar decision, though with hesitation. His behavior in the years immediately afterward was typical of the majority of moderate theologians in the East at that time. He did not adopt the views of Arius, whom the council had condemned, but he feared that the conciliar decree undercut the real distinctions between the three persons of the Trinity, and he therefore participated in attempts to undo the work of the council.

He survived Constantine and died around A.D. 339 or 340, regarded by all as the greatest Christian scholar of his time.

2. Eusebius as historian. Eusebius had a well-developed philosophy of history. He believed in an Origenistic doctrine of pre-existence of souls. He argued for human free will against classical Greek fatalism and contemporary astrology and Gnosticism. He affirmed a divine providence that controlled the affairs of emperors and kings. He rejected the idea of a future millennial kingdom of Christ on earth (cf. Iren. Her. V.xxxiii.3; *see also* MILLENNIUM §2) in favor of a more Platonic concept of immortal life in some supercosmic realm. The end of this world he placed several centuries, or at least several generations, in the future. In what we might call an "expanded eschatology" he spread out the biblical events of the last days over hundreds of years. He believed for example that the Pax Romana begun under the emperor Augustus was the predicted eschatological kingdom of peace (Isa. 2:1-4; Mic. 4:1-4), and that the emperor Constantine and his descendants were "the saints of the Most High" (Dan. 7:18), who were to rule Rome, the fourth kingdom (Dan. 2:31-45), until the end. Then the world would be destroyed and the last judgment held.

Eusebius' *Church History* was the first full-length, continuous narrative history written by a Christian; it is therefore one of the four or five seminal works in the history of Western historiography. It recounts the history of Christianity from the time of Jesus to Eusebius' own day, and is a mine of information on the period of the NT and early church. He "picked from the flowered meadows" of early church history, as he says (Euseb. Hist. I.i.4), a host of long and short quotations from ancient writers, which he included verbatim in his *Church History*. Eusebius cites such sources as

Hegesippus, PAPIAS, Quadratus, the Legend of ABGAR, and Clement of Alexandria's lost work, the *Hypotyposes.* There are almost 250 passages in all, of which nearly half are preserved in Eusebius' work alone, and would otherwise have been completely lost. Eusebius also preserves traditions about such things as the early history of the church at Jerusalem, earliest Syriac Christianity, the Ebionites, and individuals such as Pontius Pilate, the evangelists Matthew and Mark, James the brother of the Lord, Simon Magus, Valentinus, and Marcion. Some information comes from still-extant sources like Justin and Irenaeus, but a good deal is preserved today only in Eusebius' text. Certain of the earlier traditions contain some legendary or improbable material, but they still may be used, with the aid of modern critical methods, to help in reconstructing early Christian history. Eusebius further records information about the development of the NT canon: which books were used by the earliest orthodox writers, which were read publicly in orthodox churches, and which were disputed (see, for example, Euseb. Hist. II.xxiii.24-25, III.iii, III.xvi, III.xxiv.2, III.xxiv.17-18, III.xxv). *See* CANON OF THE NT §D4.

Another work by Eusebius, the *Chronicle,* endeavored to lay out a scientific, comparative chronology for ancient Near Eastern, Greek, Roman, and biblical history (the latter, with good critical sense, attempted only from the time of Abraham). It contains material which was of value in our own modern period for reconstructing the history of the ancient Near East, and also some valuable dates and other information for Greek and Roman history. Other historical works were the *Martyrs of Palestine* and a eulogistic imperial biography, the *Life of Constantine.*

3. Other works. Eusebius' *Onomasticon* was a work on biblical place names, giving geographical locations of some six hundred towns, historical sites, districts, mountains, and rivers, and connecting them with contemporary Roman place names. (*see* CARTOGRAPHY OF PALESTINE[S] §1). The *Eusebian Canons,* still printed in standard critical texts of the NT, were invented by Eusebius as a means of indicating parallel passages in the gospels (*see* HARMONY OF THE GOSPELS). In *Against Hierocles* Eusebius argued (on the Christian side) as to whether Jesus or Apollonius of Tyana was the true DIVINE MAN. Other works survive, in which we can see Eusebius' exegesis of scripture, his arguments in defense of Christianity against both pagans and Jews, and his position in the fourth-century trinitarian controversy.

Bibliography. Texts and translations: *Die Kirchengeschichte,* GCS, IX, 3 vols., Gr. and Lat., ed. E. Schwartz and T. Mommsen (1903-1909); *The Ecclesiastical History,* LCL, 2 vols., Gr. and Eng., trans. K. Lake and J. E. L. Oulton (1926-32); *The Ecclesiastical History and the Martyrs of Palestine,* 2 vols, trans. H. J. Lawlor and J. E. L. Oulton (1927-28)—the second vol. contains historical notes, including a discussion by Eusebius on NT canon, pp. 100-104; *Die Chronik: aus dem armenischen übersetzt,* ed. and trans. J. Karst (1911); *Die Chronik des Hieronymus,* ed. R. Helm (1956); *Das Onomastikon der biblischen Ortsnamen,* ed. E. Klostermann (1904); *Against Hierocles,* Gr. and Eng., in Vol. II of Philostratus, *Life of Apollonius of Tyana,* LCL, trans. F. C. Conybeare (1912).

Studies: Johannes Quasten, *Patrology,* III (1960), 309-45, offers a description of all Eusebius' writings, with full bibliog.; D. S. Wallace-Hadrill, *Eusebius of Caesarea* (1960) discusses Eusebius' life and work (bibliog.); E. Schwartz, art. on Eusebius in PW, VI (1907), cols. 1370-1439; Richard Laqueur, *Eusebius als Historiker seiner Zeit,* Arbeiten zur Kirchengeschichte, XI (1929); Hendrik Berkhof, *Die Theologie des Eusebius von Caesarea* (1939); Robert M. Grant, "Early Alexandrian Christianity," *Church History,* XL (1971), 133-44; Glenn F. Chesnut, "Fate, Fortune, Free Will and Nature in Eusebius of Caesarea," *Church History,* XLII (1973), 165-82, and "The Pattern of the Past: Augustine's Debate with Eusebius and Sallust," in *Our Common History as Christians: Essays in Honor of Albert C. Outler,* ed. J. Deschner, L. T. Howe, and K. Penzel (1975), pp. 69-95; C. U. Wolf, "Eusebius of Caesarea and the Onomasticon," *BA,* XXVII (1964), 66-96, an excellent summary of modern critical work. G. F. CHESNUT

EXEGESIS ĕk sə jē′ səs. The process by which one comes to understand a text. The same methods of exegesis are applicable to the Bible as to any other document. Each of the many special methods and tools of research (e.g., TEXTUAL CRITICISM, SOURCE CRITICISM, lexicography) has been developed to facilitate the process of understanding the text. In addition, exegesis is fundamental to other tasks, such as historical reconstruction of the history of Israel and the early church, theological appropriation of biblical faith and religion, or preaching. Exegesis is both a science and an art. As a science, it proceeds according to acknowledged principles and controls; as an art, its "rules" are transcended by the creative insight and interpretation of the exegete.

1. Terminology
2. The necessity of critical exegesis
   a. Why the Bible requires exegesis
   b. The critical and historical orientation of exegesis
3. The limits of critical exegesis
4. The exegetical process
   a. Text and method
   b. The process itself
5. The impact of exegesis
   a. Historical understanding
   b. Theological appropriation
   c. Exegesis and preaching
Bibliography

1. Terminology. The definition of exegesis stated above is narrower than that found throughout the history of exegesis. Exegesis transliterates a Greek term, ἐξήγησις, meaning the process of bringing out—hence, bringing out the meaning. The noun is not used in the NT; but in Luke 24:35; John 1:18; Acts 10:8; 15:12, 14; 21:19 the verb ἐξηγέομαι occurs, meaning "recount, tell, or make known." The other NT term for interpretation, ἡρμηνεύω, generally introduces an explanation of a Semitic name (e.g., Matt. 1:23). In the OT, both the noun *pesher* and the verb *pāthar* are used, especially for interpreting dreams and visions (e.g., Gen. 41:8, 12; *p*ᵉ*shār* in Dan. 2:4), that is, making clear what is obscure or symbolic. *Pesher* became a technical term for that type of exegesis emphasized at QUMRAN, in which the meaning of the text was identified as some aspect of the community's own experience or expectation. *Pesher* was used also by the rabbis, but without the sectarian focus. In rabbinic Judaism, the key term was MIDRASH (from *dārash,* to search out). In II Chr. 13:22 midrash means story, but in II Chr. 24:27 it means commentary. Though originally oral, rabbinic exegesis was later written down; the resultant commentaries are known as the midrashim. Many rabbinic methods of exegesis appear also in the NT. *See* INTERPRETATION, HISTORY OF[S] §C1*b*.

When exegesis is distinguished from exposition, the former refers to the process of ascertaining the original meaning, and the latter, to meaning for today. The distinction, though useful, should not be pressed. Traditionally, the principles of exegesis and interpretation are called HERMENEUTICS.

Although exegesis is a discipline in its own right, there is also a tacit exegesis. For example, when Christian lectionaries offer a set of passages for a given Sunday, the selection itself expresses an unstated exegesis of the texts. Furthermore, translation also involves exegesis. Important exegeses of the Hebrew Bible are embodied in the LXX (*see* SEPTUAGINT) and in the TARGUMS. Both translations are of special importance for understanding how the Hebrew Bible was being interpreted by various Jewish communities in NT times.

2. The necessity of critical exegesis. Exegesis is unnecessary where there is understanding, except to test it. Although one can say that an intuitive exegesis is present wherever a text is understood, even a letter from a friend begins to require exegesis as soon as the meaning is not understood ("What did she mean by that?"), or as soon as the assumed meaning becomes problematical ("But before, you said . . ."). In other words, exegesis is necessary whenever the meaning of a text is not self-evident.

a. Why the Bible requires exegesis. Biblical writings become problematical, and so require exegesis, for a variety of reasons. First, the text itself may lack clarity, perhaps because of the vicissitudes of its transmission (e.g., words may have been left out, or the text may incorporate several writings), or because the writer did not express himself clearly to begin with. Second, there is a gap between the text and today's reader—linguistic, cultural, ethnic, or socioeconomic. The ideas and idioms of ancient Semites in semiagricultural Palestine are foreign to modern urbanites in a technological culture. None of us has ever seen an EPHOD, or participated in animal sacrifice. Third, in the course of centuries, we have forgotten what the text was supposed to be and do, tending to read it as the private theology of creative individuals. E.g., recently we have come to see that some of the Psalms were really part of a script for rituals. Fourth, the reader may discover that an assumed, inherited understanding is not the only possibility, perhaps because contrary understandings have been discovered, or because someone is using the text to support a claim which another cannot accept. Each of these factors can induce the reader to ask, "But what does the text really mean?" At that point, the necessity of exegesis becomes evident.

b. The critical and historical orientation of exegesis. Exegesis is a process by which one enables the text's own meaning to come forth in its own terms. Exegesis (leading out) is often contrasted with eisegesis (reading meaning into the text); the aim of exegesis is to give the text its own voice. Given the cultural distance between the biblical text and the reader, the exegete learns to expect the unexpected, to encounter ways of thinking which appear strange and difficult. Recognition of this strangeness is fundamental to fruitful exegesis if we are to be kept from assuming that the meaning of the text is already self-evident, and from attempting to support a preconceived notion about it. The more sound and sensitive the exegetical process, the more accurately the reader can "hear" the text.

Exegesis must be critical so that the appropriateness of one's understanding can be assessed. Criticism means comparison and judgment based on publicly accessible evidence and principles. Critical exegesis makes no appeal to private knowledge, belief, or inspiration which must be accepted before the text can be understood rightly. Exegetes working with the same texts, relying on the same methods, and adducing the same data reach differing conclusions only because they weigh the evidence differently and have varying sensibilities and insights.

Given the fact that the biblical texts are rooted in the history of Israel and the early church, it is also necessary for critical exegesis to be historically oriented. Exegesis seeks to locate meaning in the text's original setting. The distinction between what the text meant and what it means is fundamental, even though it should not be pressed. Nor can the original meaning be permitted to prohibit subsequently discerned meanings, since all significant texts come to mean more than the original writers intended. Nonetheless, by understanding the text historically, we have criteria for evaluating the appropriateness of what is subsequently believed to be its meaning. For example, the seventh commandment (Exod. 20:14) is commonly interpreted as prohibiting a wide range of illicit sexual activities. But the historical meaning of the Hebrew text quite clearly understands adultery as violations of sexual taboos by married persons only, not as "fornication" generally. So the historical meaning becomes a standard for evaluating subsequent interpretations of the text. Once we embark on the quest of historical meaning, we often find that there is more than one such meaning, for the simple reason that the present text itself has a history behind it. Thus in the case of the seventh commandment, it is likely that it meant one thing as an independent prohibition, another as part of the Ten Commandments, and still another when the Ten Commandments were placed in their present literary context. *See* REDACTION CRITICISM, OT[S].

One cannot even read a Bible, whether in translation or a printed edition of the Hebrew or Greek text, which does not depend upon the results of historical-critical work. Even readers who know only the KJV depend on the historical-critical work of its translators and textual critics. Modern translations of all sorts rest even more clearly on the broad range of historical-critical exegesis and the disciplines which it has spawned, such as historical grammar and philology, lexicography, studies of Hebrew meter, and the like. Historical-critical work is both necessary and unavoidable.

3. The limits of critical exegesis. Despite two centuries of increasingly intense and sophisticated work, biblical exegesis has reached no permanent conclusions, nor are such to be expected. It is evident that significant limitations are built into the process.

i. The text is more than an "object." The common understanding of "objectivity" applies primarily to the process of explaining the text as an object by means of various critical methods. The exegete takes nothing for granted, but persists in asking why the text says this and not that, why it says it at all, and how this particular way of saying it is related to other ways of saying similar things at the time. In principle, there are historical answers (explanations) for all such questions, though in many cases lack of evidence frustrates a solution. Discovering which questions can and which cannot be answered is an important aspect of exegesis.

But a text is also more than an analyzable object; biblical texts are also expressions of beliefs, values, rituals, and world views of particular persons in communities of faith. Explanation is not yet understanding. One can describe the ideas and account for their use, but this is not the same as grasping their content.

Understanding involves rethinking the subject matter of the text on the basis of what one has come to learn about it as an object of inquiry, and on the basis of one's preunderstanding of the subject matter. "Preunderstanding" is that level of perception of the subject matter—whether ethical principles, theological beliefs, or other content—which one brings to the text. In the process of rethinking the subject matter in conjunction with what one has come to know about the text, one enters into "conversation" with the text in order to understand its content. In this process one's own preunderstanding may be enriched, corrected, or confirmed. It is not necessary to agree with the text in order to understand it, any more than it is necessary to agree with a person in order to understand him or her. In fact, increased understanding may lead either to greater agreement or disagreement. On this level of the exegetical process, "objectivity" does not mean detachment or disinterest, but does mean openness to the text and to the possibility of being corrected by it. One reason why exegesis is never completed is that our preunderstanding is not static. It is not only the historicity of the text that puts limits to understanding, but the historicity of the exegete as well; both are conditioned by history. Some exegeses are better than others, not simply because some exegetes are more knowledgeable, but also because some are more attuned to the subject matter. There are no "final" answers in exegesis, but there are varying degrees of perceptive understanding.

ii. Given the nature of biblical literature (*see* §4*a below*), it becomes evident that recovery of the original meaning is a far more complex enterprise and its results far more tenuous than commonly expected. Many texts (e.g., Genesis, Isaiah, Matthew, John) contain several "original" meanings because each of their component parts, whether literary sources or stages of composition and editing, has its own meaning (*see* REDACTION CRITICISM[S]; TRADITION CRITICISM, OT[S]). In principle, historical exergesis can recover the meaning at each stage in the development of the text in relation to its historical context. In most cases, however, that context must itself be inferred from the emphases of the stratum in view. The test of such work is finally the degree to which the results illumine the text.

iii. Within the foregoing limitations, exegesis can ascertain the theological beliefs of the texts and their antecedents, oral or written; but exegesis itself cannot answer the question of the truth of those beliefs. Exegesis can answer the question, What did the text mean by saying that God brought Israel out of Egypt, or that he raised Jesus from the dead? But it cannot establish the truth of those beliefs, nor can the truth of one passage be established by exegeting another. Before the rise of historical-critical exegesis (and where it is still resisted), the exegete did (does) indeed establish the truth of religious beliefs by quoting and exegeting the Bible. But such a procedure is possible only when there is prior commitment to the view that whatever the Bible says is true because it is the Bible that says it. Historical criticism neither requires this view nor precludes it, nor can exegesis itself establish it. One's decision with regard to the truth of the Bible, whether an *a priori* view or a decision evoked by what exegesis exposes, is grounded in one's over-all theological stance. *See* §5*a below*.

iv. Some hold that it is possible to exegete a text—in the sense of ascertaining and understanding the original meanings—without posing the question of current meaning, and thus relegate that issue to a separate step or to theologians or preachers. Others regard it as part of their exegetical task to bring out the meaning for today (*see* HERMENEUTICS[S] §3). In the latter case, the sensibilities and commitments of the exegete as a person are explicitly involved. Even in the former case, however, it is seldom possible to exegete a theological text without tacitly involving one's sense of what is of abiding importance. Moreover, since the text exists at all because it was preserved and canonized in order to address the community, something of the ongoing import of the text must be disclosed if one is to be faithful to its intent.

It would be unfortunate if one were to conclude that the limitations enumerated above outweigh the possibilities, and so revert to a direct reliance on "what the text means to me" apart from exegesis. The quest for personal meaning is continually enriched by attending to the questions posed by the exegetical process, even if they cannot always be answered satisfactorily. More important, if those responsible for public interpretation of Scripture, especially in church and synagogue, short-cut exegesis in order to focus on personal meanings, they cheat their people out of the Bible. Actually, because exegesis is an ongoing process, it remains a major mode of personal and corporate growth in perception and understanding. To declare exegesis bankrupt because it does not produce personal wholeness is like declaring psychology bankrupt because people are still frustrated.

4. The exegetical process. Critical exegesis involves a stance toward the text in which the reader is aware of those principles and preconceptions which inform his or her reading; all who read the Bible become critical exegetes when they raise their assumptions about the text to the level of consciousness. Furthermore, the process and the results of exegesis are guided by the interpreter's own experience, history, and social context. Oppressed minorities, for example, have always gained understanding and strength through the interpretation of apocalyptic texts such as Daniel and Revelation. Individuality and experience are not to be left aside in the exegetical process, but rather the reverse: what one is capable of understanding will be limited but also deepened by personal and social experience. It is difficult to comprehend many of the Psalms which cry against impending death, or Eccl. 12:1-8 which describes it, unless one has viewed death at close quarters. Those who have experienced "the absence of God" will understand the book of Job in ways not available to those who have not.

a. Text and method. The methods and procedures of exegesis must be adjusted to the nature of the text. One does not approach legal contracts in the same way as poetry, nor all kinds of poetry in precisely the same way. Similarly, it is important to appreciate the character and the diversity of biblical texts in order to ask the appropriate questions and use the proper methods to answer them.

i. *It is the text which must be understood, not a person.* All biblical literature is the result of compiling and editing; relatively few biblical books now stand as the literary expressions of a single author's creativity. Moreover, the identity of all the compilers and editors as well as that of most of the authors remains unknown. Some books are compilations of diverse materials, and some books are purposely pseudonymous (*see* Pseudonymous Writing[S]). Consequently, the exegete focuses attention on the text, not an elusive author or compiler or editor behind the text.

ii. *The function of the text in the community needs to be determined.* It is extremely unlikely that any of the biblical literature was produced for a general public, as are novels or histories today; it was produced in and for communities of faith. Since biblical literature was written across a span of some ten centuries, it reflects an exceedingly rich range of functions in worship, exhortation, or instruction. Since in a compiled text, each of the parts may have functioned differently before its inclusion, the exegete must be sensitive to the ways in which the compiling and editing have themselves affected the function of the materials used. For example, Phil 2:6-11 is probably an early Christian hymn, originally sung or chanted in worship. Paul, however, quotes it in order to undergird moral exhortation. The exegete is obliged to understand both settings and both functions.

iii. *Texts may be multilayered.* Many biblical texts are themselves exegetical because they interpret older traditions in a variety of ways, ranging from simple appropriation to self-conscious reinterpretation. For example, if Matthew used Mark, then Matthew is at least tacitly exegeting Mark. Moreover, Mark itself took up older cycles of traditions and interpreted them. Furthermore, each item in the cycle received a new nuance by being joined with others in the cycle. Thus, a given passage in Matthew is the result of an interpretive process which reaches back several decades. More explicit interpretation of earlier texts can be seen in the Chronicler's use of the book of Kings and in the exegesis of the OT in the NT. The more fully one is able to trace the layers of material in the text, the more complex becomes the exegetical process, and the richer the results. *See* Interpretation, History of[S] §§A, C.

Exegetical work moves backward as well as forward. It moves backward by beginning with the text as it has come to be, and ascertains the stages of its history and the elements that came into it at each step. Then one can begin with the earliest stratum and move forward toward the text as it now stands. The decisive thing, however, is that one no longer reads the text in a "flat" way, but perceives its depth and textures resulting from the process of its emergence.

The exegetical process is complex and cannot be reduced to a single question or a single method. Rather, the process must be guided by a number of factors, including the particularities of the text, the goals of the interpreter, and the exegete's own individuality, as well as the context within which one reads and unfolds the text. Nevertheless, the process has a certain logic in which all the individual steps are related to one another. The results of each step may correct and not simply supplement the results of others.

b. The process itself. The process of exegesis requires establishing a working text and preparing a translation (*see* Textual Criticism, OT[S]; Textual Criticism, NT[S]). Recent advances in linguistics, semantics, and communication theory have increased our understanding of both the science and art of translating, and have underlined the necessity of disciplined work if translating is to be on the same level as other areas of biblical study (*see* Discourse Structure[S]; Discourse, Direct and Indirect[S]; Semantics[S]; Versions, English[S]). Exegetes who do not read the original biblical languages can recognize some of the more serious text critical problems through the footnotes in modern translations, the more extensive notes in such tools as a harmony of the gospels, and from commentaries. Textual criticism attempts, not to spell out the meaning of the text, but simply to determine which words actually stood in it.

Given a translation, the exegesis of any passage must then grasp the structure of the book or larger unit, e.g., the Deuteronomistic history (Deuteronomy through II Kings) or Luke-Acts. One looks for clues which indicate major transitions so that the larger blocks or units begin to emerge. Once these are in view, one can take the next step of learning how each of the larger units is built up; e.g., one may recognize the different narrative patterns in the gospels or the process of an argument in an epistle. In this way, the exegete can discover how a particular passage is related to the whole—whether it is the climax of a unit, its turning point, conclusion, or introductory element. Learning the structure of a book is the fundamental way of ascertaining how the final editor or author intended the reader to understand the material.

It is not always clear what the over-all structure is, however, or what conclusions should be drawn from recognizing it. Nonetheless, critics are beginning to see the compositional techniques more clearly (*see* MNEMONIC DEVICES[S]). Some books are composed by chiastic principles (a. b. b′. a′.) (*see* CHIASMUS[S]); others by themes; some by the line of a plot. Sometimes analysis of the structure uncovers evidence of compilation, though structure and sources do not always coincide. In any case, one must apply source and redaction criticism: when, where, and by whom was the book written, and what message was conveyed by the selection and arrangement of the material? Detailed analysis of the structure will begin to reveal the shorter elements inherited by the final writer or editor. Here the form-critical questions become crucial: what is the genre of the whole and the parts, what are their sociological backgrounds, and what purposes did they serve in their contexts? (*see* FORM CRITICISM; FORM CRITICISM[S]). For example, Matt. 5:17-20 is composed of discrete sentences, each of which is a distinct form, suggesting diverse original settings and functions.

Thus, one wants to discover, not only the place of the unit within its literary framework, but also its location in the history of traditions and in its environment. It must be determined whether individual units were created by the final editor to bring coherence to the inherited material, or whether individual traditions had been structured previously.

One should be careful about making value judgments concerning the content of the text on the basis of authorship, age of oral tradition, or editorial activity. Critics of the late nineteenth and early twentieth centuries often assumed that additions, e.g., to the prophetic books, were less valuable than the original words of the prophets; likewise some form critics seem to assume that older oral traditions are more important than the work of compilers and editors. Neither of these assumptions is valid. The purpose of determining authorship and recognizing different traditions is simply to discern the different voices in the text and its tradition. The relative importance of the stages in the text's development depends on the question in view. But one should not lose sight of the shape and content of the final form of the text—including all additions—in the search for its component parts.

Once the structure and its history have begun to emerge, the exegete raises questions concerning historical, sociological, and religious background. Historical questions concern not only the date of the material but also political and other forces which shaped human experience. What, for example, was the impact of the Babylonian exile on the writers of that time and their audiences? The temple was lost; the holy city destroyed; the chosen people uprooted from the Promised Land. The literary works and traditions emerging from the Exile both reflect and respond to these crises of faith and religion. Moreover, some texts reflect worship in the temple, and begin to take on flesh and blood when that environment with its ritual and sense of sacred time and place are reconstructed. The gospels and the letters of Paul come alive when set against first-century Judaism and the culture of the Roman world, and when viewed in the context of early church struggles; the Pastoral epistles reflect the emerging institutional structures of the young Christian church.

When the unit under consideration has been placed in its matrix, then the exegete turns attention to the individual elements (sentences) and words within it. Technical vocabulary may appear, e.g., "covenant," "kingdom of God," "righteousness," "eternal life." The etymology of a word and the usage of its cognates in related languages can tell us much about its history, but only the contexts in which it is used can define its meaning. The context is fundamental, and can be investigated by the use of a proper concordance. A significant word should be compared with other biblical and nonbiblical occurrences, especially within works of the same author or within a given historical period or tradition, e.g., the use of "the law" in the letters of Paul, or Hosea's particular use of "knowledge of God." Note should be taken of formulas (e.g., the greetings in epistles or the various stereotyped expressions in prophetic speeches), of the lines and strophes in poetry, of the syntax and content of each sentence. Every important word in every line of the text under consideration will be examined. But important as word studies are, the exegete's attention must be focused upon units of thought, sentences and paragraphs. Individual words seldom convey meaning apart from sentences, so syntax must be analyzed in order to avoid being atomistic and paragraphs in order to avoid lifting expressions out of context. In the case of Hebrew poetry, the exegete must be aware of the principles of parallelism, in which the unit of thought is almost always at least two lines.

Involvement with the text must have in view not only the ancient world but the modern as well, including particular audiences and purposes within both worlds. Thereby exegesis inevitably entails a measure of theological reflection. This may include what has been called "content criticism" (*Sachkritik*). The question, "How adequately has the message (or the story, or the argument) been presented?" should be pursued with reference to both the original matrix and today's. This may involve weighing Paul's words against what he says elsewhere, or evaluating various elements or stages of the gospel tradition against one another. Here the exegete will need to be particularly conscious of the assumptions and criteria on which such evaluations are based. When one goes beyond the ancient meaning of the text and begins to evaluate it for theological understanding today, exegesis releases the Bible to become an anvil upon which contemporary theology is hammered out.

Exegesis is enriched by examination of the history of interpretation, which begins in the literature itself, as form and redaction criticism have shown (*see* INTERPRETATION, HISTORY OF[S] §§A, C). It is self-deception to assume that the contemporary exegete can vault over twenty centuries of interpretation and confront the text directly. The history of interpretation can present possibilities for meaning which had not occurred to the interpreter, and it can make the exegete aware of his or her own preunderstanding.

5. The impact of exegesis cannot be controlled in advance, and often not predicted, since the meaning of the text is a matter of repeated discovery. It is useful to consider this with regard to three closely interrelated areas.

a. Historical understanding. Two aspects of historical understanding of the Bible must be distinguished. One concentrates on recovering and reconstructing past events, such as the conquest of Canaan (Josh. 1–12; Judg. 1–2) or the council at Jerusalem (Acts 15; Gal. 2), as accurately as possible. In pursuit of this aim, one uses the texts as sources of information about the past. To be sure, most biblical narratives were designed, not to be historical accounts in the modern sense, but to articulate a particular understanding of events. Yet the original intent of the text does not preclude using the text for other ends. In fact, some of the most valuable historical sources are precisely those which had no intent whatever of providing accurate information. Poetry, songs, legends, and theological statements may well provide primary evidence for the historian who is trained to use them sensitively. Conversely, those reports which were intended to provide the original readers with a definitive account inevitably reflect the perspectives and concerns of the times, and were sometimes written from a clearly discernible partisan standpoint (e.g., the Deuteronomistic historical work or Acts). Every text is a primary source for some aspect of historical reconstruction, whether it reports an event or is itself an event in the history of understanding. The second aspect of historical understanding of the Bible, then, is the history of beliefs, assumptions, values, rites, or social conditions. Because these two aspects are intertwined in the texts themselves, they must be distinguished even if they cannot be neatly separated.

In the task of reconstructing past events like the conquest of Canaan, exegesis is fundamental, for without it the historian does not understand the sources or know how to use them properly. The impact of exegesis, however, differs from case to case. Sometimes the accumulated evidence, including nonbiblical data from archaeology or contemporary accounts, indicates that the biblical narrative, while written from a particular theological viewpoint, also reports events accurately, if not fully. Sometimes, however, it becomes apparent that the biblical account is historically inaccurate, even if one may grant the religious truth conveyed by writing it that way. This phenomenon can emerge from the exegesis of two conflicting biblical accounts (e.g., the understanding of the conquest of Canaan in Judg. 1 and 2 conflicts with that in Josh. 1–12, or the account of the Jerusalem council in Acts 15 conflicts with that of Gal. 2—assuming that both refer to the same meeting). Whether the discrepancies are real or only apparent is precisely what must be determined case by case. The historical inaccuracy of a particular account can also emerge from internal considerations of a single account; commonly, historians have regarded accounts of the miraculous as historically inaccurate. In any case, the texts must be exegeted before the historian can use them to reconstruct what happened.

The more precise and sensitive the exegesis of biblical narratives has become, the more difficult it has become to use them as straightforward historical evidence. This is especially clear in the case of the gospels and Acts. The tension between John and the Synoptics, evident all along, is not to be explained by saying that John is "the theologian." All the gospels are theologically shaped, and differences lie in the kind of theology, not in the amount. Moreover, form and redaction criticism have shown that the order of the material in the Synoptics results from editing and compiling traditions and texts; the particular contexts of Jesus' words and deeds are not known. Likewise, we do not know the historical sequence of Israel's tribal heroes, because the present order of the stories in the book of Judges is the work of an editor. In either case, it is important not to confuse knowing that we do not know the correct sequence and context, and knowing that the present sequence is wrong.

The distinction between reconstructing what probably happened and exegeting the reports of what happened is fundamental to all historical work. Before the development of historical criticism in general and of BIBLICAL CRITICISM in particular, it could be assumed that the two tasks coincided—that exegesis of the narrative discloses what happened. This may no longer be assumed; in some cases what actually happened may be quite different from any biblical account of it. For example, although we have four accounts of the trial of Jesus, what actually took place may have been quite different; after all, none of the disciples was there. In the case of the Exodus, many historians are persuaded that only a few of the tribes were in Egypt, and that the present account reflects the fact that later all twelve tribes understood themselves to have been there, so that the experience of some provided the founding event for all (*see* CANAAN, CONQUEST AND SETTLEMENT OF[S]). When the portrayal of an event and the reconstruction of it differ, the result is not merely negative, as if historical reconstruction controverted or corrected the biblical account. The result is also positive, for now one understands the account in a new way, and the particular theological understanding of the event comes into sharper relief.

It is now clear why the second aspect of historical understanding—that having to do with biblical theology—is profoundly affected by historical exegesis. The historian of the religious faith of Israel or early Christianity does not, of course, limit himself or herself to biblical texts, but relies also on nonbiblical texts and on nonliterary evidence as well—temples, cult practices and objects, etc. The same is true of the social historian of Israel and early Christianity. In either case, the faith and praxis of the biblical communities are understood in relation to their antecedents and contemporaries. When the theological ideas and motifs, whether assumed or expressed, are exegeted and understood historically, three other things are understood. (1) There are many theological standpoints in the Bible, some of which are logically in tension with others (*see* HERMENEUTICS[S] §5). (2) Some of these tensions result from the fact that theological ideas were grounded in particular historical situations and hence changed in the course of the ten centuries during which the Bible was being written. Historical-critical exegesis has destroyed the impact of old arguments against the Bible because there were "contradictions" in it. Diversity and tension are to be expected. (3) Many theological ideas in the Bible are found also in its several environments; at almost no point can one identify a theological idea which is wholly peculiar to the Bible.

Frequently, what is distinctive about the theologies in the Bible is the way they give nuance to, restate, or challenge prevailing ideas of the time, inside and outside the communities for which the literature was written. Sensitive exegesis exposes the concrete ways in which such forms of interaction occurred. Well-known examples are the biblical accounts of Creation, the polemic against idolatry (which uses the vocabulary of Canaanite cults), or Paul's dialectical appropriation of and rejection of the theological tendencies among the Corinthians. The impact of exegesis on the effort to trace the historical development of the theologies in the Bible is a deepened and sharpened understanding of both their similarity with and divergence from their environments.

b. Theological appropriation. The impact of exegesis on theological appropriation depends on the role of Scripture in a particular religious tradition and on the importance of theology in it. Judaism, being concerned primarily with TORAH (instruction), has never had a creed in the Christian sense nor emphasized theological doctrines. For Protestants and Catholics, however, the growth of biblical criticism since the Enlightenment has required a fundamental reconsideration of the relation between the Bible and doctrine. *See* BIBLICAL CRITICISM, HISTORY OF; INTERPRETATION, HISTORY OF[S] §§H, I.

First, it has caused a reassessment of what Christians call the "Old Testament." The OT is not a Christian book, nor does understanding and appropriating it require reading it through the lens of the NT. Christian and Jewish scholars use the same methods, adduce the same evidence, and may reach the same general conclusions. The differences in their results are determined, not necessarily by their being Jewish or Christian, but by the diversity of the individuals and of the schools of thought to which they belong. Nonetheless, with some notable exceptions, Christians have steadfastly insisted that the Bible of the synagogue must be retained as part of Christian scripture—a place granted to the scriptures of no other religion.

Precisely how the synagogue Bible and the distinctly Christian canon cohere into one Bible has been a theological problem almost from the start, and several ways of holding them together have been developed, including naming the larger part "Old Testament." Among them are prophecy (or, promise) and fulfillment; law and gospel; Christ as latent in the Old, manifest in the New; and the more recent liberal Protestant view of "progressive revelation." While each has something to commend it, none comports easily with the results of critical exegesis. The OT is more than prophecy; it includes "gospel" (proclamation of grace) as well as law—indeed, the law itself is understood as a sign of grace (*see* TORAH[S]). Critical exegesis cannot show that Christ is latent throughout the OT, apart from allegory; nor does the NT itself teach progressive revelation. Developing a theological understanding of the place of the OT which does not violate the integrity of the synagogue Bible or Christian theology remains high on the agenda of Christian theology.

Second, whereas the older Christian orthodoxy held that the Bible was the basis of a coherent system of doctrine, critical exegesis has shown that the Bible includes not only a long development but a rich pluralism, and that both Testaments contain internal critiques. For example, one may regard the wisdom theology of the OT as a critique of the theocratic covenant theology of the prophets and the Deuteronomistic history; and, even within the wisdom tradition, Job protests against the wisdom theology of suffering. In the NT, the Johannine emphasis on the presence of salvation, as well as the interpretation of the return of Christ as the Spirit-Paraclete, provides an alternative to the theology of Matthew, Hebrews, Revelation, and to some extent Paul as well. Critical exegesis has made it impossible to speak of *the* theology of the OT or of the NT. Attempts to ascertain a single overarching theme, such as "salvation history," or a particular understanding of human existence, do not do justice to the whole range of biblical material; they only express particular viewpoints in modern theology. Critical exegesis, then, makes some form of content criticism necessary (*above* §4*b*). The Christian theologian must, on nonexegetical grounds, determine what theological understanding is most adequate. Then the degree to which the truth of Christian faith is expressed in a particular text or by a given writer must be ascertained by critical evaluation. All biblical texts are equally canonical, but not all are equally profound.

Critical exegesis not only poses the problem of theological pluralism but suggests a way of dealing with it. It discloses how the various biblical theologies were occasioned by particular circumstances. This means that the logical tension between writers and books is itself relativized, for no given text was ever designed to say everything that the writer/editor deemed true or important. Moreover, by canonizing diverse theologies the church affirmed a range of possibilities within which diversity could flourish. To affirm that the Bible is the norm of faith and life is to affirm that the Christian community is subject to a diversified norm, and thereby to preclude the tyranny of a homogeneous sacred book. By staying in dialogue with such a canon, Christian systematic theology is constantly renewed. *See* BIBLICAL THEOLOGY[S].

Third, critical exegesis affects the understanding of the authority of the Bible (*see* SCRIPTURE, AUTHORITY OF[S]) . Since the Enlightenment, it has become increasingly prevalent to distinguish the Word of God from the words of the Bible, and to regard the Word of God as the religious meaning (and the occurrence of meaning) which emerges through the text. On this basis, the exegete, who analyzes the text and factors it into its component strata in order to relate them to their respective contexts, is not dissecting the Word of God but is trying to understand as precisely as possible the text through which religious meaning (Word of God) occurs. "Word of God" is now seen as a religious confession that through this text one has been grasped by a decisive meaning. The authority of the Bible has not been destroyed by critical exegesis but it has been recast. Many regard critical exegesis as the means by which the authority of the Bible has been released from misplaced expectations in order to exercise a more proper role.

c. Exegesis and preaching. Wherever the Bible is regarded as canon and not merely a source book for early theological ideas, critical exegesis is fundamental to preaching. The overview of the exegetical process sketched above should indicate the variety of ways by which the preacher can ascertain the biblical message. All the critical methods and tools are justified only to the extent to which they provide access to the meaning of the text. Competence in critical exegesis is as fundamental to the vocation of the preacher as any other skill. *See* HERMENEUTICS[S].

The more one perceives the historical character of the text through each of its stages of development into its present form, the more possibilities emerge for preaching. Nowhere is this clearer than in the Synoptics. For example, once we see that a given parable has taken on different meanings in each of its contexts—Jesus, the stage of oral transmission, Mark, Matthew, Luke—the possibilities for preaching are multiplied, because a sermon can emerge from each of them. In principle, one could preach five sermons, each developed from a different setting of the same parable. Likewise one could preach from a given OT text and also from its use in the New. Or one could preach a series of sermons on the Exodus, each from a different text where this event is reinterpreted. Indeed, preaching from the Bible extends the interpretive process which the biblical texts themselves represent.

The degree of exegetical thoroughness which a given sermon requires depends on whether the sermon is developed from a particular metaphor, a narrative, a theological motif, or a parenetic passage. Moreover, the impact of exegesis on such preaching depends to a great extent on the imagination with which the preacher does the exegesis and on the extent to which one discerns situations today which are analogous to those in which the text (and its strata) emerged in the first place.

Perhaps most important, exegesis becomes fruitful for preaching when one engages in it steadily and with whole books in view. Simply "looking up" a passage in commentaries is not exegesis. Sustained study of the text builds a cumulative understanding which will manifest itself in the depth of perception and range of appropriation. Above all, the preacher must be grasped by the import of the text; otherwise one simply gossips about what others have heard through it.

Bibliography. O. Kaiser and W. G. Kümmel, *Exegetical Method: A Student's Handbook* (1963); G. Fohrer *et al., Exegese des AT: Einführung in die Methodik* (1973); V. P. Furnish, "Some Practical Guidelines for NT Exegesis," *PSTJ,* XXVI, 3 (1973), 1-16; G. M. Landes, "Biblical Exegesis in Crisis," *USQR,* XXVI (1971), 273-98; J. White, R. Casto, and D. Hester, "Conversing with the Text," *Duke Divinity School Review,* XXXIX (1974), 153-80, and XL (1975), 18-50; R. E. Murphy, ed., "Theology Exegesis, and Proclamation," *Concilium,* VII (1971); L. E. Keck, "Listening To and Listening For: From Text to Sermon (Acts 1:8)," *Int.,* XXVII (1973), 184-202; L. R. Bailey, " 'From Text to Sermon': Reflections on Recent Discussion," *Concilium,* XI (1975); B. S. Childs, "Interpretation in Faith: The Theological Responsibility of an OT Commentary," *Int.,* XVIII (1964), 432-49; M. Mezger, "Preparation for Preaching—The Route from Exegesis to Proclamation," *JTC,* II (1965), 159-79. For good models of exegetical work, see the following commentaries: Hermeneia (series); B. S. Childs, *The Book of Exodus: A Critical, Theological Commentary* (1974); J. L. Mays, *Amos: A Commentary* (1969), and *Hosea: A Commentary* (1969); C. K. Barrett, *The First Epistle to the Corinthians* (1968); R. Bultmann, *The Gospel of John: A Commentary* (rev. ed., 1957, suppl. 1966 [ET 1971]); E. Haenchen, *The Acts of the Apostles* (rev. ed., 1965); E. Schweizer, *The Good News According to Mark* (1968).

L. E. KECK
G. M. TUCKER

***EXHORTATION IN THE NT.** The Greek verb παρακαλέω can mean (*a*) to summon to one's side for help (e.g., Acts 28:20; Luke 8:41; II Cor. 12:8) ; (*b*) to exhort (e.g., Acts 16:40; Heb. 3:13) , implore or request (e.g., II Cor. 12:18; Mark 1:40) ; (*c*) to comfort (e.g., II Cor. 1:4) ; and (*d*) to conciliate (e.g., Acts 16:39) . In the NT *a* is the most frequent meaning, while in the LXX *c* predominates.

The verb often introduces parts of Paul's letters (e.g., Rom. 12:1-2) , perhaps following a Hellenistic epistolary convention (*see also* LETTER[S] §4) . Bjerkelund argues that the Pauline passages do not stress the apostle's authority and are not hortatory in nature.

The meaning of the verb in the NT, however, requires a consideration of the history of the tradition as well as of the origin of the epistolary formula. (*a*) The churches are exhorted in reference to a tradition (I Thess. 4:1-2) which from the beginning contained both doctrinal and ethical teachings (Rom. 6:17; 16:17). (*b*) Exhortation is regularly associated with the prophetic witness (I Cor. 14:31; Acts 15:31) and the presentation of the gospel (Acts 2:40). (*c*) Because the frequent admonitions to exhort and establish one another in the faith (Acts 16:40; Heb. 3:13; II Cor. 10:1) have definite ethical implications (I Thess. 2:11-12), the verb seems to be expressing a strong, personal appeal, i.e., an exhortation. The authority of the appeal does not rest in the authority of the apostles, however, and in this respect Bjerkelund's study is helpful. The authority and basis of the appeal is Jesus himself; exhortation is a strong personal plea to accept Jesus' call to faith and to a Christian life, i.e., to discipleship (II Cor. 5:20; I Thess. 2:3-4).

Bibliography. *See* bibliog. for PARENESIS[S] and also C. J. Bjerkelund, *Parakalō,* Bibliotheca theologica norvegica, I (1967); V. Furnish, *Theology and Ethics in Paul* (1968), esp. pp. 68-111 and bibliog.; A. Grabner-Haider, *Paraklese und Eschatologie bei Paulus,* NTAbh, NF IV (1968); H. Schlier, *Die Zeit der Kirche* (1962), pp. 74-99; O. Schmitz and G. Stählin, "παρακαλέω, κτλ.," *TDNT,* V (1954 [ET 1968]), 773-99.

D. SCHROEDER

***EXODUS, THE.** All the information on the exodus of Israel from Egypt, as well as on their settlement and oppression in that land, comes from the Bible alone. Certain data on the history and geography of Egypt and the peninsula of Sinai can testify to the special circumstances which existed at the time of the event and served as a background for it, but they contain no testimony, either direct or indirect, concerning the event itself. The information in the Bible is found mostly in the narratives of the Pentateuch, where its character is distinctly legendary. Nevertheless, there is no reason to doubt the historical reality of the event itself.

1. The religious significance of the Exodus
2. The historical framework
   a. The store-cities
   b. Mention of Israel in the Egyptian sources
   c. The Transjordanian kingdoms
   d. Chronological data
3. The route of the journey
   a. The southern route
   b. The northern route
   c. Routes in Sinai
   d. Varying sources
Bibliography

1. The religious significance of the Exodus. According to the Bible (Exod. 1:1-7; Deut. 10:22) the family of Jacob became a people even before the Oppression began. There is a kernel of truth in the assumption that Israel took form as a national group even before the Exodus, but the exodus from Egypt marks the first appearance of the people Israel in the historical arena. The Bible, however, does not perceive the event merely as a national-historical matter, but first and foremost as an event having religious significance. It was not an ordinary occurrence which could be explained as the result of previous events. God himself is the one who caused it to happen and had a specific intention in doing so. While the Bible puts a teleological interpretation on all historical events connected with Israel, in the case of the Exodus there is something more—Yahweh has demonstrated clearly how he caused the event, thus showing to the whole world that he is the one standing behind it.

The historical-realistic aspects of the event (political conditions, form of the Oppression, and the route of the journey) are thus restricted to a minimum. In their place an atmosphere of legend prevails in nearly the whole of the narrative: popular imagination (also accompanied by a measure of wit and irony), miraculous deeds, and the feeling of the unlimited power of God, for whom the war against the Egyptians becomes somewhat like a game. The plagues which Yahweh sends against Pharaoh and his kingdom are depicted as punishments and also as signs and miracles. They are punishments because God executes vengeance on the heathen nation, its king, and its magicians; they are signs and miracles because he makes known in advance the coming of each plague and also its cessation, and thus reveals that all the plagues are the work of his sovereign will. Some of the miraculous deeds are only signs, e.g., Aaron's rod turning into a serpent (Exod. 7:9-12). However, it is not impossible that in all this there is some kernel of historical reality, even if covered with a thick layer of vibrant imagination and miracle stories, by means of which religious meditation seeks for itself poetic, intuitive expression.

Since the Exodus is perceived in the Bible as a divine event, it serves as one of the most significant symbols of the biblical faith. One of the axioms of this faith is that Yahweh, and not any other deity, brought Israel out from Egypt: "I . . . who brought you out of the land of Egypt, out of the house of bondage" (Exod. 20:2; Deut. 5:6). The significance of these words is that the deity who brought Israel out of Egypt was the one who now spoke to them and laid on them obligations and commandments (*see* COVENANT, MOSAIC[S]). The memory of the Exodus is embedded in the injunction to celebrate the festivals and in many day-by-day commandments, not only in the particular phraseology of D (Deut. 10:19; 15:15; 16:3, 12; 24:22, etc.), but also in the language of the other sources (Exod. 13:8, 14; 22:21 [H 20]; 23:15; Lev. 23:43, etc.).

2. The historical framework. One approach to determining at which time and in which reign the Exodus occurred is to try to account for the fact that, according to the biblical tradition, there was no trace of an Egyptian presence in the land of Canaan when the tribes of Israel conquered it. If we accept this testimony we might search for a period of decline in Egyptian power in Canaan. However, it must be remembered that even in periods of great Egyptian power on the Asian front, control in conquered areas was not direct and administrative in character, but was exercised through local rulers who became vassals of the pharaoh. (*See* CANAAN, CONQUEST AND SETTLEMENT OF[S] §3*b*.) Furthermore, the mountain regions of Canaan, which until the beginning of the monarchy were the effective limit of conquest and settlement by the tribes of Israel, were in fact situated on the edges of the area under the supervision of the Egyptians, whose influence was recognized more especially along the principal highways in the coastal area and in the valleys. It is characteristic that almost all the Canaanite cities which are mentioned in the Egyptian sources, even cities located in the interior of the country, such as Jerusalem and Shechem, are according to the testimony of the Bible itself among those which were not conquered by Israel in the period of the settlement. Consequently, we cannot exclude the possibility that the beginning of the settlement and the exodus which preceded it took place during the reign of a strong pharaoh.

The determination of the date of the Exodus is contingent on a prior decision concerning several questions. What is the time of the conquest of Canaan? Was it accomplished, at least in essence, in one onslaught, or was it the result of an extended process, so that it could be accompanied by quiet settlement? (*See* CANAAN, CONQUEST AND SETTLEMENT OF[S].) Did the tribes enter the land as a unit, or in two main waves? Where and at which point or points did the entrance occur? What is the significance of the archaeological findings in this matter and how do they agree with the biblical testimony? The main evidence for determining the date is as follows.

a. The store-cities. According to Exod. 1:11 the Israelites built for the pharaoh the "store-cities," Pithom and Raamses (RAMESES). The name Pithom is undoubtedly derived from *pr-Itm,* meaning "house (temple) of Atum" (the sun god). As is made clear from the inscriptions, this was the name of Tell el-Maskhutah in the eastern part of the Delta at the end of the fertile belt of Wadi Tumilat (*see, however,* PITHOM). Tell el-Maskhuta is identified with Theku, the capital city of the eighth district of Lower Egypt, and is the biblical Succoth. It is probable that the temple of Atum was located in the center of the city, and in accordance with the custom of the Ramesside period of calling places by the name of the principal temple found in them and not by their older names, the name Pithom was applied as an epithet of this city. In Tell el-Maskhuta was found a large granite statue of Ramses II; and from the excavations which were carried on at the site it became clear that the city had a quadrilateral form, with heavy walls. Inside it were found right-angled compartments which served as places of storage. This was, therefore, a "store-city" (or "city of storage places") intended to serve as a supply base for the armies of Ramses II when leaving for the E and also as a protection for the eastern frontier.

The site of Rameses is in dispute. From the testimony of the papyri the city of Tanis (the biblical ZOAN), which is in the vicinity of the NE corner of the Delta, and whose remains are found today near the village of San el-Hagar at the S shore of Lake Menzaleh, was called *Pr-R'mssw,* "House of Ramses." If Zoan existed before the time of Ramses II, it was he at least who rebuilt and adorned it to the extent that he was considered as its second founder. If Ramses II is the one who erected it originally, then "House of Ramses" is its older name which in the time of the Twenty-first Dynasty was changed to Zoan (Gardiner made a similar suggestion). If Zoan was not built until the time of the Twenty-first Dynasty (as perhaps may be concluded from the excavations carried out at the site by J. Yoyotte from 1965 to 1969), then apparently it was built upon the site of the "House of Ramses" which had stood there formerly. Some say, therefore, that the biblical Rameses is surely Tanis-Zoan, but this identification is fraught with difficulties. Zoan is situated N of Tell el-Maskhutah, but from the statement that in their exit from Egypt the Israelites journeyed from Rameses to Succoth (Exod. 12:37), it is clear that the site of Rameses was to the W of Succoth. Also, Zoan was not a store-city. Alt advanced the hypothesis that the city of Rameses extended from Zoan to Qantir, about twelve miles S of San el-Hagar, and thus encompassed a large area (like the capital city of Amen-hotep IV at Tell el-Amarna, which extended over twelve miles from W to E and about nine miles from N to S), but even this is not sufficient to remove the difficulties. Moreover, it is probable that many of the places in the Delta which were built by Ramses II bore his name. It would appear, therefore, that those who say that the biblical Rameses is to be looked for in one of the tells W of Tell el-Maskhutah are correct. Perhaps Petrie was right when he identified Rameses with Tell er-Retaba, about nine miles W of Tell el-Maskhutah. Although the identification of this latter place with Succoth and Pithom is nearly certain, some have made a distinction between Pithom and Succoth and argue that Tell er-Retaba is Pithom (Gardiner and Albright); but they had to assume that Rameses is Zoan (*see* PITHOM; RAMESES, CITY).

In any case, these witnesses may lead to the conclusion that the pharaoh in whose time Israel was oppressed in Egypt was Ramses II. And if so, then the Exodus also took place in his reign or in that of his successor (*see, however, below*).

b. Mention of Israel in the Egyptian sources. It may be that in lists from the time of Thut-mose III and Ramses II mention is made of a place in Canaan by the name of Jacob-El and perhaps also Joseph-El. And some scholars say that the name Asher also appears in Egyptian lists. But these data are either doubtful or are not sufficient to produce substantial conclusions. The only real evidence of this kind is the mention of Israel on the victory stele of Mer-ne-Ptah, the only mention of the name Israel in any of the Egyptian sources (*see* MER-NE-PTAH Fig. 40). It portrays in ornate style the defeat of the king's enemies in the fifth year of his reign: "The Hittite land is pacified, Canaan is taken captive . . . Ashkelon is plundered, Gezer is seized upon, Yanoam is reduced to nothing, The people Israel is destroyed, it has no offspring; The Horite land has become like a widow for Egypt."

The date on the inscription is from the year 1230 or 1229 B.C., and this is a solid point of control, proving that Israel was already in Canaan. That Israel is marked with the determinative of "foreign people" and not "foreign land" does not weaken at all the validity of the evidence, since it is possible that the borders of Israel's settlement were still shifting, and since the tribal confederation of Israel was located in the mountain regions and did not have control over the central walled cities which dominated the inhabited area of these "lands" and cities mentioned alongside Israel in this inscription. It is far-fetched to assume, as various scholars have done, that the inscription refers to an Israel still wandering in the wilderness, or to Israelite tribes that did not go down to Egypt, or even to an Israel which was seized just as it was coming out of Egypt.

The view (based on Exod. 2:23) that the pharaoh of the Exodus arose only after the death of the pharaoh of the Oppression is by no means proven, since the biblical witness at this point is built on ancient traditions overlaid with fantasy and legendary distortion. It is thus not impossible that the Exodus occurred in the time of Ramses II himself. This is the hypothesis of Albright, who fixes the Exodus (in his opinion—of the Leah tribes only, under the leadership of Moses) at approximately 1290 B.C., at the beginning of the reign of Ramses II, when this king was absorbed in his building enterprises (while the conquest of Canaan would have taken place in the second half of the same century).

Since, however, the biblical evidence is in legendary story form and not annalistic, it is equally possible that the Oppression began earlier. Ramses II was the most outstanding and well-known king of the Nineteenth Dynasty (his reign was also the longest—sixty-seven years); therefore it is possible that he cast his shadow over the biblical perspective. The Oppression may therefore have begun earlier, *ca.* 1350 B.C., with the rise to power of the Nineteenth Dynasty whose most outstanding king was Ramses II; it is even likely that the beginning of the Oppression was connected with the change of dynasties. But the king in whose time the conquest of Canaan occurred was of necessity Ramses II, because he preceded Mer-ne-Ptah, in whose fifth year Israel is mentioned as a living entity. It cannot have been an earlier pharaoh, since Lachish and Bethel were still Canaanite during at least part of Ramses' reign. In the burned Canaanite stratum at Lachish a scarab of Ramses II was found, and there are a number of indications that Bethel, too, was destroyed close to the end of his reign. So if the Conquest occurred in the time of Ramses II, then the Exodus should have taken place some decades earlier.

At the same time, not to be excluded from consideration is the possibility that the Exodus took place in the time of the weakness and decline of the Eighteenth Dynasty, or during the transition to the Nineteenth Dynasty, about 1350 B.C. In this case, "the pharaoh of the Oppression" would be the kings of the Eighteenth Dynasty, who were known as great builders. The entrance of the Hebrew tribes into Egypt may have occurred with the coming of the HYKSOS, while the rise of the Eighteenth Dynasty (*ca.* 1580 B.C.) marked the change in status and the beginning of the Oppression. As to the statement about Pithom and Raamses in Exod. 1:11, there is the possibility that it is a mere anachronism from the time of the literary crystalization of the biblical narrative in this part of the Pentateuch. The narrative uses geographical terms, not as they were current at the time of the event, but as they were widely recognized at the time of the narrator, or were still remembered from the immediately preceding period. If the place name Rameses lasted until the end of the Twentieth Dynasty (i.e., until the beginning of the eleventh century), then it is not far removed from the end of the period of the Judges, when some ancient biblical traditions were already taking shape. Such anachronisms are fairly frequent in the Pentateuchal narratives.

c. The Transjordanian kingdoms. According to the biblical tradition, Moab and Ammon were settled in their territories before Israel reached Canaan. According to J (*see* DOCUMENTS), Israel was forced to go around these territories because they had been refused permission to cross them (Num. 20:14-21; 21:11-13; cf. Judg. 11:17-18). According to D they passed through them in peace after having been authorized to do so (Deut. 2:2-13, 29). From the viewpoint of historical reality the two descriptions are of equal cogency. A group of nomads could make its way either by going around settled territories or by crossing them if permitted to do so and if it actually restricted itself to "the King's Highway" without deviating "to the right or to the left" (Deut. 2:27). Therefore, we cannot know which of these two traditions corresponds to historical reality. It appears that the viewpoint of D lies also at the base of the tradition of P, which in its list of encampments (Num. 33:41-49) puts together the route of passage through the territories of Edom and Moab. In this priestly list there is no evidence, in spite of the claims of some scholars, of a first wave of Israelite penetration, which is supposed to have preceded the settlement of Edom and Moab. The Bible also records that the Ammonites settled in their territory prior to the entrance of Israel into the land of Canaan (Num. 21:24; Deut. 2:19-21).

The survey which N. Glueck carried out in areas of Transjordan showed that within the limits of these kingdoms there is no sign of permanent settlements before the thirteenth century B.C. This indicates that the settlement of Israel also did not occur earlier than that, and hence that the Exodus could not have taken place before the Nineteenth Dynasty (*see, however,* AMMON, AMMONITES [S]; EDOM[S]; MOAB[S]; RABBAH[S]). Perhaps it is even possible to conclude that the settlement of Israel took place only a short time after Moab settled in its land. This conclusion holds if "the first (RSV "former") king of Moab" (Num. 21:26) is interpreted in the sense of "the first king to rule over the Moabites" and not "the earliest king who ruled in Moab before this time." If Sihon fought against the first king of the Moabites, and afterward Israel came and fought against this same Sihon, then the settlement of both Moab and

Israel in their respective territories took place within the course of one generation. In any case it is probable that there was no long interval between these two events.

d. Chronological data. In the Bible there are certain chronological data relating to the Exodus, but there are also grave questions as to their validity. In a Priestly chapter heading it is said that the construction of Solomon's temple, which began in the fourth year of his reign (about 970 B.C.), took place 480 years after the Israelites came out of Egypt (I Kings 6:1). If this number were realistic, the Exodus would have taken place about 1450 B.C., that is, in the time of Thut-mose III, but this is unlikely. It is probable that the number 480 is merely forty years multiplied by twelve, forty years from the biblical perspective being reckoned as one generation. This, therefore, is a typological combination which has no historical significance (*see* NUMBER §5). Moreover, we are not entitled to suppose that from the Exodus to the beginning of the construction of the temple twelve "real" generations elapsed, for the number twelve is itself typological. In addition it is hard to believe that in the time of Solomon records of generations of priests could be found and that such records could reach back to the dimly remembered times of the Exodus.

Likewise typological is the mention of four generations, which according to biblical tradition elapsed from the time when Jacob and his household went down to Egypt until Israel went out from there (Exod. 1:2; 6:14-20). Thus from the historical point of view nothing whatever is to be learned from this tradition. This number is already found in the story of the covenant in which God assures Abraham, "And they shall come back here in the fourth generation" (Gen. 15:16). It is probable that in the patriarchal stories one generation was considered not as forty years, but as a hundred years, since the life spans of the patriarchs were considered to be longer than those of ordinary men; this would explain why it says in the same passage that the oppression in Egypt will last four hundred years (Gen. 15:13). In a manner characteristic of P, the round number of four hundred years receives a more exact form of 430 years (Exod. 12:40). (Similarly, the round number of 600,000, which the earlier sources recognize as the number of those leaving Egypt [Num. 11:21; Exod. 12:37, "about 600,000"] receives in P a more precise form of 603,550 [Exod. 38:26; Num. 1:46; 2:32].) Nevertheless, the more precise number does not establish historical credibility. To be sure, Albright claimed that if we subtract 430 years from the era of Tanis-Zoan, which began about 1750 B.C., we reach approximately the time when the exodus from Egypt occurred. But this is an inappropriate mixing of categories, in which numbers based on an epic-narrative tradition are combined with a chronological system which belongs to another culture.

Likewise the number put into the mouth of Jephthah, that until his time Israel had been able to dwell three hundred years in the areas N of the Arnon (Judg. 11:26), is certainly typological and rounded off, and cannot be the basis for computing the beginning of the settlement of Israel in Transjordan or the date of their exit from Egypt.

3. The route of the journey. The information on the route followed by the fugitives from Egypt, like that on the Exodus itself, comes only from the Bible. However, it is possible, to some extent, to supplement this information with data connected with the terrain of the area and the natural pathways that cut across the peninsula of Sinai. The biblical information is not uniform, but varies according to the sources which make up the Pentateuch. Furthermore, the description put together in each of the sources does not necessarily constitute a complete picture. J and E have been preserved in fragmentary form; the description in D is deficient in some details; the descriptions in P are vague and it is impossible to pinpoint many of the locations. Accordingly, it is not surprising that scholars have proposed conflicting routes.

a. The southern route (Wright, Grollenberg, May *et al.*). In leaving Egypt, Israel turned directly S-SE toward Jebel Musa, on the road which led to the copper and turquoise mines among the mountains in the S part of the peninsula of Sinai (*see* EXODUS, ROUTE OF §2). The chief support of this route is the identification of Mount Sinai with Jebel Musa, which has been accepted in Christian tradition since the Byzantine period. But this tradition has no connection with the biblical period and even less with the time of the Exodus (*see* SINAI, MOUNT). Moreover, according to the biblical tradition itself, Israel intended at first to reach Canaan, and only after they were already at Mount Sinai (or Horeb) and after they had sent out the spies was it decreed that they should wander in the wilderness (Num. 13–14; Deut. 1:19-28, 34-40). A group intending to reach Canaan would have no reason for turning toward the S of the peninsula.

b. The northern route (Eissfeldt, and in essence accepted by Noth and others). The route of the fugitives turned N, crossed the coastal road, and entered the belt of dry land separating Lake Sirbonis from the Mediterranean Sea. Among the arguments for this are the identification of BAAL-ZEPHON (Exod. 14:2, 9; Num. 33:7) with the place called Mohammediyeh, a small hill at the western corner of Lake Sirbonis, or with Ras Kasrun, a place about twenty-five miles to the E; likewise the identification of MIGDOL (mentioned in the same passages) with Tell el-Her, along the road extending from Kantara, about twelve miles to the NE. Another argument is based on the supposition that "the sea" which was divided before Israel was only a lake, and if the lake was called *Yam Suph* (literally "Sea of Reeds," sometimes translated as "Red Sea"), then it was only later that this name came to be transferred to the great sea at the S of the peninsula of Sinai (as a matter of fact, in the narrative of P as it is woven into Exod. 14:1-15, the sea which was divided before Israel is not called "Sea of Reeds" but simply "the sea").

But this theory also will not stand close examination. No lake could account for the name *Yam Suph* (Sea of Reeds) being transferred to the Red Sea unless that lake was originally connected to that sea. And even though the sea which was divided is called in P simply "the sea," nevertheless in addition to this P mentions *Yam Suph* as one of the stopping places which were encountered on the route of Israel after the miracle of the crossing (Num. 33:8-11). Apparently "the sea" at which according to P the miracle was experienced by Israel was in the vicinity of the modern Lake Timsah, near the E end of the Wadi Tumilat. Counting against the northern theory is also the fact that there is no natural route connecting Lake Sirbonis with, for example, Kadesh, which is one of the important stopping places along the line of Israel's journey. Furthermore, nearly impassible sand dunes to the S of the coastal road cut it off from the interior of Sinai. The identifications of Baal-zephon and Migdol mentioned above are little more than conjectures.

c. Routes in Sinai. The two theories just discussed also do not take into account the decisive fact that biblical testimony is not at all uniform, but varies according to the sources, each one of which has its own particular conception of the route. In different circles and in different times this great historic event was portrayed in different geographical terms. Each narrative was based on an actual geographical possibility, but each contains a measure of anachronistic projection. Thus we are not able to describe the exact route over which the fugitives actually passed; we can only trace how Israel conceived of this route after they had settled in the land of Canaan and their ancient traditions had been put into literary form. At that time the geographical understanding of the journey was no longer connected with one particular route, and the differing conceptions were already influenced by the conditions which existed at various periods of the monarchy.

Also, the above theories, especially the northern theory, do not take sufficient account of the natural trails that have cut across the peninsula of Sinai from ancient times to the present. Only these trails were suitable for the passage either of nomads or of an army with iron chariots, and upon a combination of them the route of Israel must be based. The names of the trails were determined, as a rule, according to the destination, and therefore it was possible for one route to be called by two names; for anyone who travels in the reverse direction, the beginning has become the end, and therefore the name of that road is changed.

Three trails cut across the breadth of the peninsula of Sinai (*see* Map 1); (1) The coastal road beginning at the fortress of Sila (Zilu? Sile?) near the E arm of the Nile and extending beyond Gaza and Megiddo. Perhaps for one traveling on this road from Palestine in a SW direction it would be called "the way to Egypt" (*see* Isa. 10:24 [RSV "as the Egyptians did"], 26; Jer. 2:18 in Heb. and KJV). (2) The central road going off from Lake Timsah, passing by Kadesh ('Ain el-Qudeirat), extending to Beer-sheba, then going up to Hebron and Shechem. It is probable that this road is the one called in Exod. 13:17 "the way of the land of Philistines" and that the reference is to "the land of the Philistines" of the Negeb, mentioned in the patriarchal narratives, on the border of which Beer-sheba was thought to be situated (Gen. 21:32-34; 26:23-33). In the opposite direction this same road was called "the way to Shur" (Gen. 16:7), that is, the road that goes down to the chain of fortresses on the border of Egypt (cf. Gen. 25:18; Exod. 15:22; I Sam. 15:7 27:8). (3) The southern road extends from Suez to Elath and is identical with Darb el-Hajj, the route of the pilgrims to Mecca. It is probable that for one traveling E this route was called in the Bible "the way of the wilderness" (Exod. 13:18).

In addition, there are three lengthy trails running diagonally across Sinai. They are subsidiary to "the way of the wilderness," and two of them join at Kadesh. These are: (4) a road going up from the way of the wilderness and ending at Kadesh. It is called "the way to the hill country of the Amorites" (Deut. 1:19) because at Kadesh began the dominion of the Amorite hill country (Deut. 1:6-7, 20). (5) A road going down from Kadesh to the end of the gulf of Elath (Gulf of Aqaba), and called "the way to the Red Sea" (or Sea of Reeds) (Num. 14:25; 21:4; Deut. 1:40; 2:1). (6) The road that extends N to the end of the Dead Sea, called "the way to the Arabah" (Deut. 2:3, 8 [RSV "Arabah road"]), since it ends in "the Arabah" (with the definite article), the biblical designation for the Jordan Valley (Deut. 1:7; Josh. 18:18; II Sam. 4:7; II Kings 25:4 and *passim*). *See* Map 1.

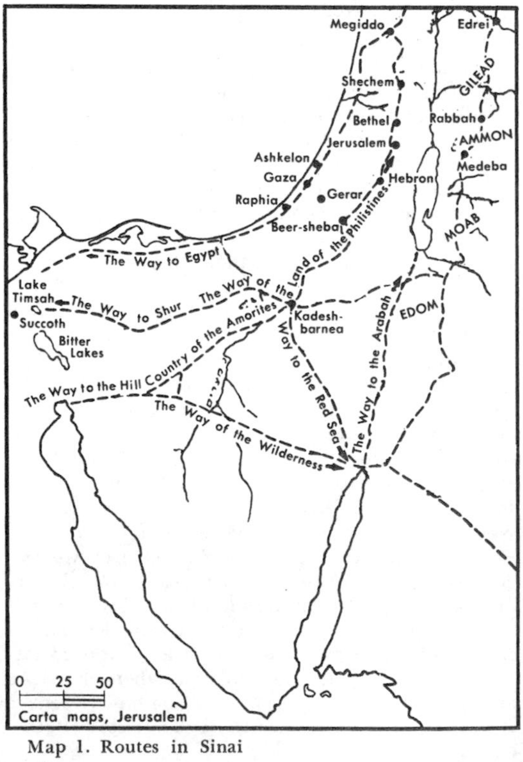

Map 1. Routes in Sinai

d. Varying sources. In order to understand the distinct conceptions of the route in the various sources, it is fitting to point out that E and D agree, since the latter depends on the former, that is, the narrative portions of D (Deut. 1:9–3:29;

9:8–10:11) are based upon the narrative of E alone. And the E narrative, preserved in fragmented form, is brought to partial completion by what is related in D.

i. According to E, after Israel crossed the Sea of Reeds and went up "the way of the wilderness" (Exod. 13:18; and fragments of E in ch. 14) they reached Mount Horeb, in the vicinity of which were found also the stopping places of Massah-Meribah and Rephidim (Exod. 17:2-13). The route beyond Horeb is summed up by D, which says that from there Israel traveled along "the way to the hill country of the Amorites" and reached Kadesh-barnea (Deut. 1:19). From Kadesh-barnea the spies were sent out, and there it was decreed that Israel should wander in the wilderness until the whole generation of those who came out of Egypt had died (Num. 13–14, with interruptions; Deut. 1:20-39).

From Kadesh-barnea they journeyed on "the way to the Sea of Reeds" (Num. 14:25; Deut. 1:40; 2:1); and from there they kept marching around "the hill country of Seir many days" (Deut. 2:1). After the completion of their period of wandering, they turned N (Deut. 2:3) on "the road to the Arabah," which runs N from Elath and Ezion-geber, and crossed the territory of the people of Esau living in Seir (Deut. 2:4, 6, 8, 29). After that they went around Moab on the E side (Deut. 2:8), but at Ar they entered the territory of Moab so that they could reach the land of Sihon the Amorite (Deut. 2:18, 24). Finally the lands of Sihon, king of the Amorites (Deut. 2:26-37), and Og, king of Bashan (Num. 21:33-35; Deut. 3:1-3), fell before them. *See* Map 2.

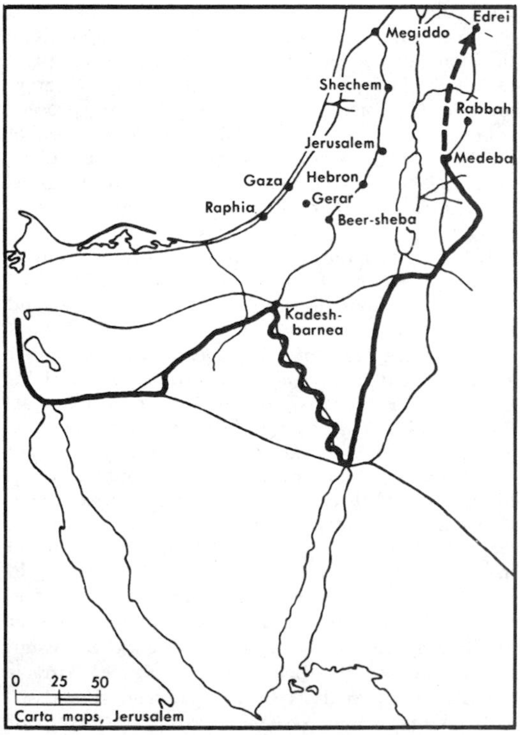

Map 2. The exodus route according to ED

ii. According to J, after crossing the Sea of Reeds, Israel went on to the wilderness of Shur, and the first stopping places they found were Marah and Elim (Exod. 15:22-25*a*, 27). After that they reached Mount Sinai, and perhaps also according to J this was on "the way of the wilderness." Their journey from Mount Sinai is described in Num. 10:29-36. The narrative of J concerning the spies is preserved in fragments only (Num. 14:3β-4, 8-9, 11-24), and they do not indicate the place from which the spies were sent out.

From Kadesh Israel attempted to cross the territory of Edom, but permission was denied them (Num. 20:14-21); therefore, they went down "the way to the Sea of Reeds" in order "to go around the land of Edom" (Num. 21:4; the words "and they set out from Mount Hor" are from the Priestly editing). They next went around Moab on the E and did not enter its territory (Num. 21:11β; cf. Judg. 11:18). After more stops they reached the top of Pisgah, which looks down on the valley of the Jordan (Num. 21:20). Then they conquered the country of Sihon, king of Heshbon (Num. 21:21-32; cf. Judg. 11:19-22), and finally the clans of Manasseh (Machir, Jair, and Nobah), went on to conquer the land N of the Jabbok (Num. 32:39-42). *See* Map 3.

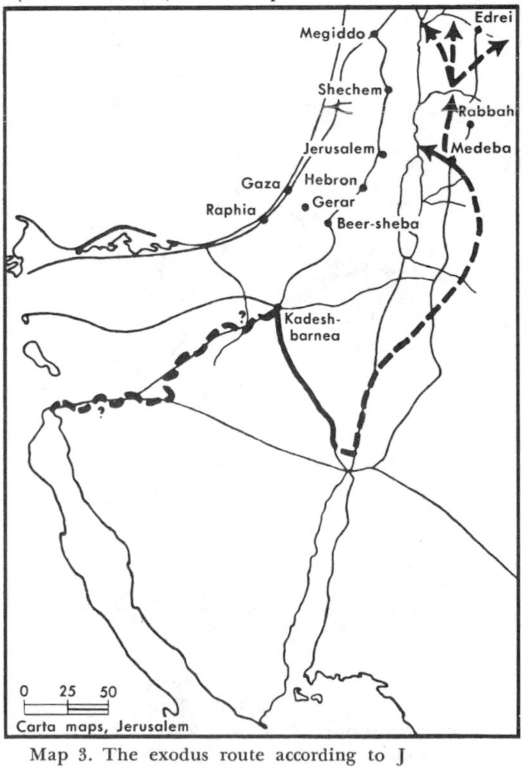

Map 3. The exodus route according to J

iii. The testimony of P is twofold: narratives and editorial verses in Exodus and Numbers, and the list in Num. 33:1-49, which enumerates no less than forty stopping places. None of the places which the list mentions between the Sea of Reeds and Ezion-geber (Num. 33:11-35) can be located with certainty, but the itinerary possibly agrees in essence with Darb el-Hajj (*see* §*c* (3) *above*). The distance between Ezion-geber and Kadesh is conceived as though it was covered in one short march without any stop in between (Num. 33:36). The natural trail connecting these two places is the road which in the opposite direction was called "the way to the Sea of Reeds" (*see* §*c* (5) *above*).

After Kadesh Israel crossed the territories of Edom and Moab (Num. 33:37-47). Certain signs indicate that P's route in this section is the principal ancient road which extended from Kadesh eastward, crossed the valley of El-Arabah S of the Dead Sea, entered the territory of Edom, and continued from there to Moab. After that P refers clearly to the principal road that extended along the heights of Transjordan ("the King's Highway") and passed through the territory of Moab and "the tableland" (Deut. 3:10; 4:43), which is N of the Arnon. The last stopping place was by the Jordan opposite Jericho, where the Israelite camp stretched "from Beth-jeshimoth as far as Abel-shittim" (Num. 33:48-49). *See* Map 4.

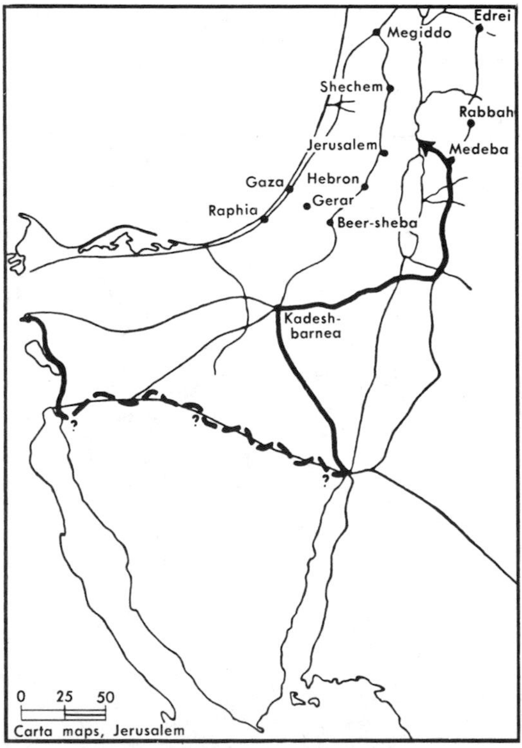

Map 4. The exodus route according to P

iv. Certain aspects of the route are similar in each account, and in all of them Kadesh is a turning point—although the character of its role changes from source to source. On the question of the course of the journey, at least to the border of Edom, the conception of J is not very far from that of ED. But these two conceptions are at variance with respect to timing. Both conceptions postulate that from Kadesh (-barnea) Israel attempted to enter Canaan; but according to ED this occurred at the beginning of the period of the wanderings, and Israel had its penalty imposed there; according to J this occurred at the end of the period of the wanderings, and from there Israel was forced to go around Edom.

P's view differs to a considerable degree from the other two, but with respect to the question of timing it is close to J. Kadesh, which marks the beginning of Israel's penetration of the land of Canaan, also marks the end of the wanderings.

Bibliography. E. Naville, "The Geography of the Exodus," *JEA,* X (1924), 18-39; A. H. Gardiner, "The Geography of the Exodus: An Answer," *JEA,* X (1924), 87-96, and "Tanis and Pi-Ramesse: a Retraction," *JEA,* XIX (1933), 122-28; O. Eissfeldt, *Baal Zaphon, Zeus Kasios und der Durchzug der Israeliten durchs Meer* (1932), and "Palestine in the Time of the Nineteenth Dynasty: (a) The Exodus and the Wanderings," *CAH,* II, ch. 26a (1965); W. F. Albright, *From the Stone Age to Christianity* (1940), pp. 194-95, 212, and *The Biblical Period from Abraham to Ezra* (1963), pp. 10-15; H. H. Rowley, *From Joseph to Joshua* (1950), *passim;* A. Alt, "Die Delta-residenz der Ramessiden," in *Kleine Schriften,* III (1959), pp. 176-85; H. Cazelles, "Les localisations de l'Exode et la critique littéraire," *RB,* LXII (1955), 321-64; D. B. Redford, "Exodus 1:11," *VT,* XIII (1963), 401-18; W. Helck, "Tkw und die Ramses-Stadt," *VT,* XV (1965), 35-48; S. Herrmann, *Israel in Egypt* (1973), pp. 25-28, 38-50; M. Haran, "The Exodus Routes in the Pentateuchal Sources," *Tarbiz,* XL (1971), 113-43, Hebrew, and *Ages and Institutions in the Bible* (1972), pp. 37-76, Hebrew.

M. HARAN

***EXODUS, BOOK OF.** The book of Exodus has attracted a considerable degree of attention in the past two decades because of the centrality of its message for the faith of Israel and the special complexity of its historical problems. While some important new material has come to light from archaeology, the most intensively examined area has been the history of the traditions contained in the book in the period of oral transmission prior to their incorporation into the main literary sources. It is most helpful therefore to proceed from a survey of research into the composition of the book to an examination of the structure of its main component themes, and to use this to assess its historical background and theological significance.

1. Literary composition. The basic literary sources of the book of Exodus are widely recognized as the three main documentary strands, J, E, and P (*see* PENTATEUCH §§3, 5). Both Eissfeldt and Fohrer have re-affirmed their conviction that a further extended source, called L by Eissfeldt and N by Fohrer, is also to be found here, although this view has not been followed by most other scholars. The material ascribed to this source is otherwise largely regarded as belonging to J. Besides these three, or four, main source documents most scholars also recognize the presence of material which has been introduced by editors of the Deuteronomic school, although the extent of this material is variously estimated (*see* DEUTERONOMIC HISTORY[S]). A marked feature of recent literary criticism has been a tendency to assign much more of the book to this source. This is notable in the analysis by Zenger, who traces two main Deuteronomic revisions of the earlier J and E material, one pre-exilic and one postexilic. A more radical attempt to overthrow the accepted results of literary analysis has been proposed by Fuss, who regards chs. 3–17 as composed from two main sources: an original (JE) narrative and an extensive editing and supplementation of this by a Deuteronomic redactor. Of the two analyses, that by Zenger remains more convincing.

Of considerable importance for an understanding of the revelation and covenant-making at Sinai, which forms the second half of the book, has been the question of the source to which the Decalogue (20:2-17) and the Book of the Covenant (20:22-23:19) should be ascribed. Eissfeldt, Beyerlin, and Newman regard both law collections as having been incorporated into the early E document, but Noth and Zenger have argued that, while both law collections are of an early date, their incorporation into the book of Exodus is the work of Deuteronomic editors, almost certainly after the Exile.

2. Component traditions. The method of traditio-historical analysis has increasingly dominated over the purely literary-critical study of the history of the book. Its aim is to study the formation of the narrative traditions in the stage of oral transmission, before their incorporation into the major written sources. In Exodus the first main block of such traditions is to be found in chs. 1–15 and centers on four main events: the call of Moses, a series of plagues on the Egyptians, a celebration of the feast of Passover, and the deliverance from Egyptian pursuit at the Sea of Reeds. The finished narrative is made up from J, E, and P sources. Fohrer has attempted a fresh literary analysis to include recognition of his source N, and has strongly opposed the view, advocated earlier by Pedersen and Noth, that the controlling theme is the celebration of Passover, so that the whole may have originated as a development of the Passover liturgy. Fohrer contends that there is no clear evidence that the Passover had a central position in the earliest sources; nor can it be claimed that the plague narrative has been developed out of features associated with the celebration of Passover. Herrmann has examined chs. 1–15 to determine the historical setting in which the events took place.

The second main narrative section, chs. 16–18, concerns a period spent in the wilderness (resumed in the book of Numbers after the interval created by the story of God's revelation at Mount Sinai). The picture of life in the wilderness centers upon two main themes: Israel's rebellion against God, and God's providential provision of food and water. The wilderness stories have been examined by Fritz, who looks at each in its probable original setting. He argues that originally they did not belong to a narrative describing a journey from Egypt to Canaan, but drew upon memories of seminomadic life in the desert region S of Judah, where Israel's ancestors had lived before their settlement in the land. The chronological scheme and itinerary were therefore secondary developments in the editing of stories which originated over a more extended period of time. Coats is concerned with the theological implications of the tradition of Israel's rebellion, showing how it developed from a theme with a primarily political motive to one more directly religious and spiritual, concerning the nature of human sin and ingratitude.

The story of the theophany on Mount Sinai, which occupies the remainder of the book (chs. 19–40), is integrally connected with the making of a covenant and the disclosure of the laws which govern it. It readily divides into separate sections dealing with different aspects of God's revelation, and it is evident that an original brief narrative account has been expanded later by the inclusion of many instructions and regulations. Those which deal with the making of a tabernacle (chs. 25–28) and the installation of its priesthood (chs. 29–31) are drawn from the P source, and the account of how these were carried out (chs. 35–40) derives largely from a supplement to this (P^s). However, underlying such instructions there were undoubtedly older traditions, and the study of the tabernacle by Görg endeavors to trace an old nucleus in the instructions for building it. Similarly the study by Walkenhorst looks at the traditions concerning the cultic ceremonies for the installation of the Aaronide priests, and seeks to trace an early core in them.

Much discussion has centered upon the structure, scope, and significance of the earliest (JE) account of God's revelation at Sinai. Three issues stand out as of most importance. The first is whether the earliest account of the Sinai event described the making of a covenant between Yahweh and Israel, or simply an appearance of Yahweh in a theophany. The latter view is strongly contended for by Perlitt. The second issue is whether the earliest Sinai narrative included the Decalogue of 20:2-17. Several scholars (Noth, Zenger, Gerstenberger) have come to deny this (*see* CREDO, ANCIENT ISRAELITE[S] §§1, 2). A third issue is whether, accepting that the earliest Sinai narrative included the Decalogue and described what took place as the making of a covenant, this was adapted from the form of ancient Near Eastern vassal treaties, as Mendenhall has argued (*see* COVENANT §C3*a;* COVENANT, MOSAIC[S]). The whole discussion evidences wide disagreements and has given rise to an extensive literature.

3. Historical background. Discussion has revolved around the part played by MOSES in the events described and varying estimates of the significance of evidence from Egyptian documentary sources relating to the period. The problem concerning the work of Moses arises out of the reconstructions put forward by von Rad and Noth of the way in which the separate stories were connected into a sequential history, and from the evident fact that the later the tradition, the more the work of Moses is emphasized. Hence, by reduction to the original nucleus, it appears that we can know very little about the part originally played by Moses in the events described. On the other hand, Beegle maintains a positive and conservative stance in claiming that we can recognize behind each of the main events the impact of the figure of Moses. A middle position has been proposed by Herrmann.

Concerning Egyptological material, two points are significant. The first is whether we should expect to find references to people and events which are directly identifiable with those described by the OT. This not only concerns whether Egyptian sources are likely to have recorded Israel's departure, but also whether we should expect to be able to identify the pharaoh under whom Joseph rose to greatness (one of the Hyksos kings or Akh-en-Aton?). Against Vergote, Herrmann argues that the JOSEPH STORY shows many elements of folklore which leave little confidence that it offers the real reason why Israelites went down to Egypt and became slaves. Rather the reason must be found in the general search by Israel's Aramaean ancestors for lands in which to settle. Furthermore, we must recognize that the employment of these ancestors for state building projects and their subsequent escape were on a small scale. It is only in later religious and theological developments that they became of major importance. Hence it is unlikely that contemporary Egyptian annals made any record of what took place. What we can find in the Egyptian material, and in many circumstantial details in the book of Exodus, is a basic framework of historical knowledge into which the OT tradition fits very convincingly, without direct corroboration being possible.

A particular problem relates to the often accepted identification of the Hebrews of the OT with the *'apiru* in Egyptian sources, who are referred to as *ḫabiru* in several Mesopotamian sources. Herrmann argues that such an identification cannot be sustained. The Egyptian *'apiru* were evidently people of a particular social class or status, who were drawn upon to provide groups of slave workers (*see* HABIRU; HABIRU[S]). In the OT, however, the term "Hebrew" has a genealogical and racial significance, and indicates a person who was descended from an eponymous ancestor Eber (Gen. 10:21). There would not therefore appear to be any sure ground for making an identification of two groups of people who are in one sphere a social class and in the other a clan and kin group.

In spite of such limitations imposed by the nature of the evidence offered by Egyptian material, Herrmann argues that Israel's ancestors were involved in the building projects of Ramses II, and escaped from this slavery to migrate northward into Canaan, where they were able to link up with other Aramean tribes, and eventually to establish themselves as Israel. The God to whom they ascribed this deliverance was Yahweh, who became the God of all Israel.

4. Theological significance. The exodus from Egypt provides a focus for the OT, and has influenced its entire understanding of God. He had brought Israel, his people, "out of Egypt." Thus the recollection of this event established a basic understanding of the nature and purpose of Israel's God, which could be used to interpret other events and situations. The use of this "exodus pattern" is very marked in the prophecies of Isaiah 40–55 relating to the forthcoming release of exiles from Babylon in the sixth century B.C.

Aside from the significance of the exodus pattern, the book of Exodus moves into the forefront of theological discussion because of the centrality of the idea of covenant. In the structure, growth, and interpretation of God's revelation at Sinai are to be found a long history of reflection on, and theological elaboration of, the relationship between Yahweh and Israel. Questions have emerged concerning the meaning of the term "covenant" itself (examined by Kutsch) and concerning the relationship of covenant to law and to particular collections of laws, especially the Decalogue. This raises major issues concerning the connections between law and grace (*see* GRACE IN THE OT[S] §§1, 2). Certainly the connection between the laws of Sinai and the deliverance of the Exodus show that neither the book of Exodus in particular nor the Pentateuch as a whole can be interpreted as law in a thoroughgoing legalistic sense.

It is a reflection of this central theological interest of Exodus that Childs has sought to introduce a new theological dimension to the task of exposition. By examining the history of both Jewish and Christian interpretations of the book, and by seeking to view it in the light of its position in the entire canon, Childs seeks to uncover the theological significance which the book as a whole possesses today.

Bibliography. Commentaries: B. Childs, OTL (1974); R. Clements, Cambridge Commentaries (1972); J. P. Hyatt, New Century Bible (1971); M. Noth, OTL (1962).

Special studies: B. Anderson, "Exodus Typology in Second Isaiah," in *Israel's Prophetic Heritage,* ed. B. Anderson and W. Harrelson (1962), pp. 177-95; D. Beegle, *Moses the Servant of Yahweh* (1972); W. Beyerlin, *Origins and History of the Oldest Sinaitic Traditions* (1965); G. Coats, *Rebellion in the Wilderness* (1968); G. Fohrer, *Überlieferung und Geschichte des Exodus* (1964); V. Fritz, *Israel in der Wüste* (1970); W. Fuss, *Die deuteronomistische Pentateuchredaktion in Exodus 3–17* (1972); E. Gerstenberger, *Wesen und Herkunft des apodiktischen Rechts,* WMANT, XX (1965); H. Gese, "Bemerkungen zur Sinaitradition," *ZAW,* LXXIX (1967), 137-54; M. Görg, *Das Zelt der Begegnung* (1967); S. Herrmann, *Israel in Egypt* (1973); E. Kutsch, *Verheissung und Gesetz* (1973); G. Mendenhall, *The Tenth Generation* (1973); M. Newman, *The People of the Covenant* (1965); E. Nicholson, *Exodus and Sinai in History and Tradition* (1973); M. Noth, *A History of Pentateuchal Traditions* (1972); J. Pedersen, "Passahfest und Passahlegende," *ZAW,* LII (1934), 161-75; L. Perlitt, *Die Bundestheologie im AT,* WMANT, XXXVI (1970); G. von Rad, *The Problem of the Hexateuch* (1966), pp. 1-78; J. Vergote, *Israel en Égypte* (1959); K. Walkenhorst, *Der Sinai im liturgischen Verständnis der deuteronomistischen und priesterlichen Tradition,* BBB, XXXIII (1969); G. Widengren, "What Do We Know about Moses?" in *Proclamation and Presence,* ed. J. Durham and J. Porter (1970), pp. 21-47; E. Zenger, *Die Sinaitheophanie. Untersuchung zum jahwistischen und elohistischen Geschichtswerk* (1971).

General works: O. Eissfeldt, *The OT* (1965); M. Noth, *The History of Israel* (1960); E. Sellin and G. Fohrer, *Introduction to the OT* (1968).

R. E. CLEMENTS

***EXORCISM IN THE NT.** Exorcism is the expulsion of demons from persons or places. It is prominent in the ministry of Jesus when he heals the Capernaum demoniac (Mark 1:21-28; Luke 4:31-37), the Gerasene madman (Mark 5:1-20; Luke 8:26-39; Matt. 8:28-34), the Syrophoenician's daughter (Mark 7:24-30; Matt. 15:21-28), and the epileptic boy (Mark 9:14-29; Luke 9:37-43; Matt. 17:14-21). It is difficult to distinguish sharply between exorcisms and other healings, since some of the latter may exhibit features of exorcism, e.g., Luke 4:38-39; 13:10-17; Mark 7:32-37. Exorcism is referred to in the summaries of Jesus' healing (e.g., Mark 1:34; 3:10-11; Luke 7:21; Acts 10:38), was entrusted to his disciples (e.g., Mark 6:7; Luke 9:1), and became part of the Christian mission (Matt. 7:22; Mark 16:17; Luke 10:17; Acts 5:16; 8:7; 16:16-18; 19:11-17). There is however no specific reference to exorcism in the NT outside the Synoptic gospels and Acts.

1. Exorcism in the pagan and Jewish world. Exorcism originated, as did astrology (*see* ASTROLOGY[S]), in ancient Mesopotamia and became widespread in Egypt during the Ptolemaic period (*ca.* third century B.C.). Although rare in ancient and classical Greece, exorcism became a central feature of Hellenistic magic, which was common to the Greco-Roman world and well developed before the birth of Jesus.

Accounts of individual exorcisms are rare in the pre-Christian period. One of the earliest is found on an inscription from the time of RAMSES II 1290-1224 B.C.). In TOBIT the hero is protected by magical means against the attack of the demon Asmodaeus, and JOSEPHUS describes the exorcism of Saul (Antiq. VI.viii.2) and one performed by Eleazar, a Jewish exorcist, with the aid of Solomon's ring (Antiq. VIII.ii.5). Such stories are more common during the early Christian centuries, the most familiar being those recounted by Lucian of Samosata (born *ca.* A.D. 120) and Philostratus (born *ca.* A.D. 170). Lucian describes the exorcisms of "the Syrian from Palestine" (*Lover of Lies* 16), and in the *Life of Apollonius of Tyana,* Philostratus describes five exorcisms performed by the sage (II, 4; III, 38; IV, 10, 20, 25) which have similarities to those by Jesus. Exorcism was often carried out by the Jewish rabbis and is common in Christian apocrypha and hagiography. Although the most important Greek magical papyri come from the third and fourth centuries A.D., they contain material which is much older and may be used with caution to understand, both by contrast and similarity, the gospel accounts.

2. Interpretation of the exorcisms of Jesus. The main problem is whether the deeds of Jesus should be seen in the light of eschatology or of magic.

a. The eschatological interpretation. In Jewish eschatological belief, particularly during the intertestamental period, the final triumph of God is considered to be dispossessing and excluding the evil powers. The advent of Messiah is accompanied by the overthrow of demons. This background is highly relevant to the interpretation of the exorcisms offered by the Synoptics. Mark 1:21-28 illustrates the authority of Jesus before whom the unclean spirits flee. Satan's kingdom "is coming to an end" (Mark 3:26), the strong man's house is plundered (Mark 3:27), and John the Baptist's question about "he who is to come" is answered by reference to the exorcisms as part of a general messianic activity (Luke 7:20-23). The granting of the powers of exorcism to the disciples is placed in the same context as the coming kingdom (Luke 9:1-2), and in their success Jesus sees the overthrow of Satan (Luke 10:17-18). Jesus answers his critics by saying, "If it is by the finger of God that I cast out demons, then the kingdom of God has come upon you" (Luke 11:20; cf. Matt. 12:28), and the comment about the feats of the Jewish exorcists (Luke 11:19-20; cf. Matt. 12:27-28) indicates that the deeds of Jesus are not outwardly different from those of others, their meaning being available only to faith.

b. The magical interpretation. Almost every reference to exorcism in pre-Christian and first-century literature is associated with magic. (The Jewish apocalypses offer no exception, since they deal almost entirely with the general overthrow of demons and not with the expulsion of those causing sickness in individuals.) Parallels between the exorcisms of Jesus and those of the pagan magicians are found in the magical papyri. These include (1) use of the formula "I know who you are" (Mark 1:24; cf. *Papyri Graecae Magicae* VIII.13, "I know you, Hermes, who you are and whence you come"); (2) the expression "I adjure you by God" (Mark 5:7; cf. *Papyri Graecae Magicae* XXXVI.189-190, "I adjure you by the great name Ablanatha"); (3) the importance of making the demon speak to disclose his name (Mark 5:9); and (4) the need to prevent the discovery and use of the exorcist's name by the demon (hence, perhaps, the commands in the gospels to the demons to be silent). Magical contexts include words such as φιμόω ("Be still!" Mark 4:39), στενάζω ("he sighed," Mark 7:34), ἐμβριμάομαι ("sternly charged," Mark 1:43), λύω ("released," Mark 7:35), and several others, but are lacking for other significant words such as ἐπιτιμάω ("rebuked," Mark 9:25, etc.). Weight is given to the magical context by the fact that the name of Jesus was added at a very early stage to the repertoire of the professional exorcist (Mark 9:38; Acts 19:13). The name of Jesus occurs in exorcisms in *Papyri Graecae Magicae* IV.3019 and 1228-29 and probably is to be read on a leaden cursing tablet giving fever to an enemy, which comes from the first or second century. It would be a serious mistake to think that the magical tradition is mere hocus-pocus. Magic, including power over evil spirits, was thought of as a gracious revelation of the gods, given through figures such as Zoroaster and Solomon for the salvation of men. Although its commercial use brought it into disrepute with the educated classes, its significance for the ordinary people of the time should not be underestimated.

3. Conclusions. Neither the magical nor the eschatological interpretation can be excluded. It seems most likely that Jesus made restrained use of methods typical of magical exorcism but thought of them in relation to his own role in the bringing of the kingdom. He thus extended the general, eschatological expulsion of demons to cases of immediate, individual suffering. As the stories circulated, the magical aspects were emphasized, particularly in Mark and Luke-Acts. The danger that this might swamp the broader theological perspective may have led later writers (Matthew and John) to reduce or even omit the exorcisms. *See also* MIRACLE WORKERS[S]; DIVINE MAN[S];

Aretalogy[S]; Demon, Demonology §C; Demons in the NT[S].

Bibliography. General: O. Bauernfeind, *Die Wörte der Dämonen im Markusevangelium* (1927); S. V. McCasland, *By the Finger of God* (1951); J. M. Hull, *Hellenistic Magic and the Synoptic Tradition,* SBT, XXVIII (1974).

For §1: J. Bidez and F. Cumont, *Les mages hellénisés* (1938); F. Cumont, *L'Égypte des Astrologues* (1937); F. Lexa, *La Magie dans l'Égypte antique* (1925); T. Hopfner, *Griechisch-ägyptischen Offenbarungszauber,* 2 vols., Studien zur Paleographie und Papyruskunde, XXI, XXIII (1921, 1924); K. Preisendanz, *Papyri Graecae Magicae,* ed. A. Henrichs, 2 vols. (new ed., 1973-74); H.-D. Betz, *Lukian von Samosata und das NT, TU,* LXXVI (1961); D. Daube, *The NT and Rabbinic Judaism* (1956); W. L. Knox, "Jewish Liturgical Exorcism," *HTR,* XXXI (1938), 191-203.

For §2*a*: C. K. Barrett, *The Holy Spirit and the Gospel Tradition* (1947), pp. 57-58; R. H. Hiers, "Satan, Demons and the Kingdom of God," *SJT,* XXVII (1974), 35-47; A. Dupont-Sommer, "Exorcismes et guérisons dans les récits de Qumrân," VTSup, VII (1960), 251-53; H. C. Kee, "The Terminology of Mark's Exorcism Stories," *NTS,* XIV (1968), 232-46.

For §2*b*: C. Bonner, "Traces of Thaumaturgical Technique," *HTR,* XX (1927), 171-81, and "The Technique of Exorcism," *HTR,* XXXVI (1943), 39-49, as well as Bauernfeind, Hull, and Kee (listed above). Also, R. Wünsch, *Antike Fluchtafeln* (2nd ed., 1912), no. 1.

For §3: C. H. Cave, "The Obedience of Unclean Spirits," *NTS,* X (1964), 93-97, an interpretation of the Gerasene demoniac entirely in terms of the OT.

J. M. Hull

***EXPIATION.** *See* Atonement in the OT[S].

***EZEKIEL.**

1. Composition
2. Form and tradition history
3. Ezekiel's personality
4. Message

Bibliography

1. Composition. The prophet Ezekiel was among those taken into Babylonian exile with King Jehoiachin. Wiseman's *Chronicle of Chaldaean Kings* shows that the first conquest of Jerusalem occurred on the second of Adar in the seventh year of Nebuchadrezzar (March 16, 597 B.C., according to Parker-Dubberstein). An administrative document from Babylon (*ANET* [2nd ed.], p. 308) verifies the fact that Jehoiachin was recognized as king even during his captivity (II Kings 25:27-30), which in turn explains Ezekiel's use of the year of Jehoiachin's reign for the numerous dates which he gives.

When examined closely, the book of Ezekiel appears to have a dual nature. First, it has a clear over-all composition: the prophecies of calamity (1–24), the commentary on the foreign nations (25–32), and the prophecies of salvation (34–38, introduced in 33). Similar to the construction of Isa. 1–35, Jer. 1–51 (according to the LXX), and Zephaniah, the structure of Ezekiel reveals the final editor's intent: the preaching of judgment upon Israel is followed by the pronouncement of judgment upon the foreign nations, and then by the proclamation of salvation for Israel. Even the fifty units that comprise the book are so clearly defined that they create no problem. These units are introduced either by a specific date calculated to the day (this occurs twelve times, thirteen including 3:16) or by the formula: "And the word of the Lord came to me." There are only two instances where this proclamation is not found: one in ch. 19, which probably comprised the conclusion of ch. 17 before ch. 18 was inserted, and the other in the vision, 37:1-14, whose content marks it as an extraneous passage.

On the other hand, this clear structure is in contrast to the fact that these individual passages reveal a long history of revision. An example is 1:15-21, which transforms into a carriage with wheels the image of four supernatural beings carrying God's throne. Other examples are the repetition in ch. 10 of a slightly modified form of the vision of God in ch. 1 and the confusing similarity of the prophecy in 12:1 ff. to the reported fate of Zedekiah in II Kings 25:4-7. In various instances the words of the prophet have undergone radical revision by those who transmitted the text. We may label them the "School of Ezekiel."

Furthermore, there are clear indications that independent groupings at one time existed. The six sections that deal with Egypt and are introduced by dates once formed a collection of Egyptian oracles (chs. 29–32). The undated section, 30:1-19, the content of which separates it from the other elements, has been inserted to obtain the number Seven. The same is true of the three oracles about Tyre in 26:1–28:19, which are tied together by the refrain in 26:21; 27:36*b*; and 28:19*b*.

The tendency toward rounding out to the number seven is evident again in the incorporation of all the statements on the foreign nations. In the structure of chs. 25–32, seven political powers are addressed (Ammon, Moab, Edom, Philistia, Tyre, Sidon, and Egypt). The unexpectedly general oracle about Sidon (28:20-23) has been added to obtain the number seven. However, it is noteworthy that the verses that conclude these oracles about the nations are found in 28:24-26 after only six nations have been addressed, and not at the end of ch. 32 as would be expected. The passage dealing with Egypt clearly is a closely knit construction, which was incorporated as a whole without revision. A probable reason for this arrangement is the concern with the sequence of dates, which extend in the Egyptian oracles (tenth-twelfth year of Jehoiachin) beyond the date of the Tyre collection (eleventh year).

Ch. 29:17-20 (21), dated in the twenty-seventh year, does not fit into the sequence of dates in the Egyptian oracles. These verses are also unique in that they connect the political conditions in Egypt with those in Tyre. This joining the fates of two foreign nations is not found anywhere else in Ezek. 25–32. In addition, these verses are unique because they contain a revised statement of the earlier pronouncement about Tyre. The promised booty from Tyre (26:1–28:19) is to be replaced by booty from Egypt, because Nebuchadrezzar's battle against Tyre did not bring the expected success. This updated oracle, formulated fifteen years after the original one, did not lead to a change in the tone of the older text. This shows how firmly the wording of the prophets was entrenched and, subsequently, how little others dared to tamper with it. Thus we have a strong indication of the authenticity of the prophetic texts and simultaneously of the accuracy of the dates given. These dates therefore become reliable sources of information. At the same time, these verses establish how keenly Ezekiel, whose prophecy often appears to be rigidly constructed, is aware of the freedom of his God to change history, as the earlier prophets had proclaimed. *See* HERMENEUTICS [S] §5.

There is little that we can say with certainty about the genesis of chs. 1–24. A desire to arrange the dates in 1:1-2 (3:16); 8:1; 20:1; 24:1; 26:1; 33:21; and 48:1 chronologically is readily apparent. On chs. 29–32, *see above*.

A second report of the call of the prophet to be a "watchman" (33:1-9) begins the section 33–48. A similar reference to the prophet in this capacity is to be found in 3:17-21, subsequent to the initial report on his call in 1:1–3:15. There is an obvious break at the end of ch. 39. General statements summing up God's treatment of Israel (39:23-29) have been added to the Gog pericope. These verses are somewhat reminiscent of the summary in 28:24-26. The concluding vision of the new temple, the temple services, and new temple regulations (chs. 40–48) forms traditional elements into a unified whole. This section contains much post-Ezekiel material. It is impossible to delve any further into the chronology of the postexilic material, as has been recently attempted anew with the proposal of a Deutero-Ezekiel (Garscha).

2. Form and tradition history. The beginning of the call vision (1:1–3:15) brings to mind Isaiah's call (ch. 6), where he meets Yahweh enthroned in majesty in the temple. The continuation, in which the prophet is given the scroll to eat and is summoned not to fear, reminds the reader of Jeremiah's call (Jer. 1). With regard to the tradition behind Ezek. 2:8–3:3, we find that the metaphors and images in the confessions of Jeremiah (15:16) and in the Psalms (19:10 [H 11]; 119:103) become a dramatically experienced reality for Ezekiel, who physically eats God's word. The fact that the prophet receives the word of God in the form of a scroll indicates that he was already familiar with prophetic material in written form. However, the original context of the vision of Yahweh's glory in the plain (3:22-27) remains unclear. The prophet's second vision (chs. 8–11) has been enhanced by the addition of chs. 10–11. It is constructed according to a dual scheme. Ch. 8 reports on the abominations the prophet sees in the temple, and in turn lays the foundation for the judgment brought down on Jerusalem by the "executioners" in chs. 9–10. The enormity of the sin is depicted through the symbolic use of the number four, which also occurs many other times in Ezekiel. *See* NUMBER §5.

Comparatively more closely knit is the vision of the valley of dry bones (ch. 37). An image which the prophet has heard in the cry of the people—"Our bones are dried up" (37:11)—becomes a fully developed scene. In the raising up of the dry bones to become living men, we can see an act of creation similar to that of Gen. 2:7.

Finally, we see a special form of old Zion tradition (chs. 40–48), where the prophet views the perfect proportions of the newly built temple that is free from all contact with the profane and unclean—the palace district and memorial stelae of deceased members of the royal family (43:7-9). However, it is striking that the name Zion does not appear at all in Ezekiel.

The means through which Ezekiel is to proclaim Yahweh's words are worthy of note. In most instances the prophet limits himself to quoting God's directions. The actual carrying out of the directions is seldom reported (12:1 ff.; 24:15 ff.). Ch. 4:1-3 relates that the prophet is to inaugurate the siege of Jerusalem, utilizing a brick which portrays the plan of the city. By eating a sparse ration of unclean food, Ezekiel is to symbolize the starvation of the besieged city (4:9-17). In the act of cutting and destroying his hair, he is to symbolize the destruction of the city's besieged population (5:1-4); a verse used symbolically in Isaiah (7:20) thus becomes a dramatic reality in Ezekiel's act. By leaving his house with the usual provisions for exile, Ezekiel portrays the deportation of the surviving population of Jerusalem (21:23 ff.). And, finally, Ezekiel's uncontrolled mourning over the sudden death of his wife becomes symbolic of the imminent mourning of the people at the fall of Jerusalem (24:15-24). Other prophecies announce the realities of exile—lying powerless (4:4-8), the trembling fear of the inhabitants of the land (12:17-20), and the wailing in the face of impending news of calamity (21:8-13).

The prophet uses images that occasionally assume a strongly allegorical character. The statement about useless vines in ch. 15 mirrors the situation of Jerusalem between 597 and 587; the images of the unfaithful wife (ch. 16) and the two unfaithful wives (ch. 23) become the means for unfolding a broad historical theology. The tendencies of Hosea (9:10; 13:5-8), Isaiah (1:21-26), and Jeremiah (2:23; 3:6-14) are continued here in powerful fashion. The proximity of chs. 16 and 23 illustrates clearly how traditions that were formerly separated begin to be fused in Ezekiel. Ch. 16 speaks of Jerusalem, which Yahweh raises as a foundling abandoned by its parents and then takes in marriage; the previous Canaanite history of the city is vividly depicted (16:3) and is used as an explanation of Jerusalem's depravity (cf. Isa. 1:21-26 for a similar focus upon the Zion tradition). However, in ch. 23 the origins of both women are traced back to Egypt, where Israel's past remains clouded. (The Israel-Egypt tradition in Hosea establishes this quite clearly.) The image-free, historical-theological text of ch. 20 proceeds along the lines of the Egypt-Exodus tradition, for in it (vss. 1-31) we see the obstinacy of Israel from her beginnings portrayed in unexcelled sharpness. Thus the streams of tradition still separated in Isaiah and Hosea flow together in Ezekiel.

Zedekiah's breach of trust with Nebuchadrezzar is described in an allegory (ch. 17). Ch. 19 joins the allegorical form with that of a lamentation for the dead, a form which is frequently used in Proverbs. This is true, for example, in the description of Tyre as an elaborate ship (ch. 28), in the representation of Pharaoh as a crocodile (29:3-5; 32:2-8) or as a cedar in Lebanon (ch. 31). In all of these cases we can clearly see the uniqueness of Ezekiel's language. While Hosea and Jeremiah constantly vary a wealth of metaphors in kaleidoscopic fashion, Ezekiel remains with one thematic image and often carries it out in all its variations to its logical extreme. Such thematic descriptions can be found apart from the allegories. Examples of this are in ch. 6, which treats the theme of the "mountains of Israel" (judgment over the idolatry in the high places); ch. 7, "the end has come" (related historically and traditionally to Amos 8:2); ch. 13, "prophets"; ch. 21, the "sword" in three different ways; 24:3-14, the metaphor of Jerusalem's fate as a kettle on the fire; and ch. 34, the "shepherds of Israel."

We should also consider the form of the so-called "word of proof" which characterizes so much of Ezekiel. Prophetic statements about future acts of Yahweh often conclude with the formula, "You will know that I am the Lord." The purpose behind this is a definite one: to lead to the concrete realization that Yahweh acts in judgment and salvation, and that Israel might recognize in these actions the God who is revealing himself to her. Fully expressed in this is the aim of prophecy: a true acknowledgment of God, which according to Hebraic usage of "know" is simultaneously a clear perception of God. *See* KNOWLEDGE §1*b*.

3. Ezekiel's personality. Firsthand reports about the character and life of the priestly prophet Ezekiel are scarce (*see* EZEKIEL §A). What we know of him is for the most part intertwined in his message. Many characteristics seem to be signs of sickness, so that it has been felt necessary to analyze him by psychological methods (Broome). Such characteristics include his loss of the power of speech (3:15, 26-27; 24:27; 33:21-22), his lying bound (3:25; 4:4-8), his trembling at Yahweh's commands (12:18), and his somberness at the death of his wife (24:15-18). Even the renowned psychiatrist-philosopher Karl Jaspers believed that Ezekiel suffered from schizophrenia. No doubt exists that we are dealing here with an unusually sensitive person. The cases referred to above, where metaphoric language was transformed into a dramatically experienced reality, bear this out. The capability of visionary experience as well as the symbolic and strongly articulated expressiveness of his prophecy point in the same direction. But other elements can unmistakably be ascribed to a language that is richly stylized and pervaded by divine influence. In these and other characteristics the personal life of the prophet is hidden behind his message, which is his only concern.

4. Message. The coming fall of Jerusalem dominates the first phrase of Ezekiel's proclamation. The fact that the only section of the book which is not depicted as the word of God contains the report of the fall of the city by a survivor (33:21) underscores the importance of this event.

The message of God's judgment, and above all the execution of that judgment, achieves its most concrete formulation in Ezekiel's oracles. For this reason he can be labeled the definitive theologian among the prophets of judgment. Whereas Hosea, Jeremiah, and Isaiah (1:21-26) contrasted the wickedness of contemporary Jerusalem with a better past, Ezekiel portrays the entire history of Jerusalem and of Israel as one of continuous rebellion and sin against Yahweh. Ezekiel approaches the symbol of the vine, which Israel customarily used to refer to her nobility (Ps. 80), only from the perspective of wood for the fire. The pronouncement of judgment in 20:23-26 is made even more harsh by the fact that Yahweh had already decided to scatter his people among the nations at the time they were in the wilderness. In an otherwise unheard-of pronouncement, Ezekiel says that Yahweh had afflicted his people with "statutes that were not good and ordinances by which they could not have life" (vs. 25), e.g., the command to sacrifice the first-born. In similar predestined severity, Ezekiel speaks of the inevitable fall into sin of Israel and Jerusalem, the "bloody city" (ch. 22), both of which no longer should expect salvation. "And I will set my face against them; though they escape from the fire [597 B.C.], the fire [587 B.C.] shall yet consume them; and you will know that I am the Lord, when I set my face against them. And I will make the land desolate, because they have acted faithlessly, says the Lord God" (15:7-8).

However, the event of 587 signifies the turning point in Ezekiel's prophecy. The pronouncements of judgment against the neighboring nations, which likely are to be dated between 588-586, mark this turning point in the view of those who edited the book (*see* §1 *above*). The change is most clearly expressed in the vision of the dry bones (ch. 37). Yahweh's action is not to be understood as healing and raising up a people who in itself still possesses something of a possibility for and right to life. It is the resurrection from a justly imposed death, and the creator of life alone can make it possible. In all this the meaning is not individual resurrection but, as an exegesis of the vision (37:11-14) clearly shows, a restoration of the community to their homeland. This act of being led back is also portrayed in 20:32-44, which was added to 20:1-31 after 587. In the "wilderness of the peoples," which is typologically contrasted with the "wilderness of the land of Egypt" and should therefore not be given a geographical location, Yahweh separates the nations (the model for Matt. 25:31-41) and leads his purified people to his holy mountain where he will be worshiped properly. The concept of a new exodus has been created, which will, in very different language, dominate the thought of Deutero-Isaiah. The prospect of a new, pure temple service will be developed in the complex vision of chs. 40–48. Other prophecies treat the inner renewal of the nation (36:25-32), the end of the misery of being a divided kingdom, and the new, just leadership of a new David (34; 37:24-28). Whether the Gog pericope (chs. 38–39), which depicts a final threat from the enemy from "the north" after the return to the land of Israel, stems from Ezekiel remains controversial; unfulfilled prophecies of Jer. 4–6 and Isa. 10 may be referred to in 38:17 and 39:8. This prophecy of final liberation points the way to the postprophetic apocalypses. *See* APOCALYPTICISM; APOCALYPTICISM[S].

In ch. 18 (cf. 33:1-20; 3:17-21) we have a general teaching on just recompense to the individual (*see* EZEKIEL §E2*d*). This text has to be understood in terms of the situation after 587. A series of quotations from Ezekiel's neighbors (18:2, 25, 29; 33:10, 17, 20) shows how the danger of resignation, whether out of godlessness or piety, can begin to spread. Ezekiel confronts the resignation by listing a series of concrete commands which are perhaps modeled on the temple entrance liturgy prescribed for those who desired entrance to its "life" and "blessing" (cf. Pss. 15; 24:3-6). The present generation is not to let itself be deterred from the way of obedience and the promised life by fatalistically looking back to the wickedness of the nation's early history or to an individually sinful past. The purpose of the warnings is, not the coming to terms with a new teaching of individual recompense, but the hearing of a call to repentance. This fact is emphasized by the statement that God desires not the death of the guilty one but rather repentance and life (18:23, 31, 32; 33:11).

Bibliography. W. Eichrodt, *Ezekiel,* OTL (1970); J. Garscha, *Studien zum Ezechielbuch* (1974); W. von Rabenau, *Die Entstehung des Buches Ezechiel in formgeschichtlicher Sicht,* Wissenschaftliche Zeitschrift der Martin Luther-Universität Halle-Wittenberg, V (1955-56); J. B. Taylor, *Ezekiel* (1969); J. Wevers, *Ezekiel* (1969); W. Zimmerli, *Ezechiel,* BKAT, XIII (1969), *Ezechiel, Bibl. Stud.,* LXII (1972), *Gottes Offenbarung* (2nd ed., 1969), *Studien zur alttestamentlichen Theologie und Prophetie* (1974), and "The Message of the Prophet Ezekiel," *Int.,* XXIII (1969), 131-57; E. Broome, "Ezekiel's Abnormal Personality," *JBL,* LXV (1946), 277-92; R. Parker and W. Dubberstein, *Babylonian Chronology 626* B.C.–A.D. *45* (2nd ed., 1956).

W. ZIMMERLI

***EZION-GEBER.** According to the Bible, Ezion-geber was located near Eloth (ELATH), on the N shore of the Gulf of Aqabah. It was a station on the route of the Exodus (Num. 33:35-36; Deut. 2:8). Solomon had a fleet constructed there (I Kings 9:26-28; II Chr. 8:17), and Jehoshaphat's ships were wrecked there (I Kings 22:48). *See* TELL EL-KHELEIFEH[S]. E. K. VOGEL

***EZRA AND NEHEMIAH (BOOKS AND MEN).** The books of Ezra and Nehemiah are our main source of information for the crucial period of the return from the Babylonian exile. This was the formative time of transition between the biblical age of the first temple, which came to an end in 586 B.C., and the emerging second Jewish commonwealth. The fragmentary picture which emerges from these books can be supplemented for the first part of the period by bits of information and impressions gathered from the books of the three postexilic prophets HAGGAI, ZECHARIAH (chs. 1–8), and MALACHI, as well as from several psalms (e.g., Pss. 85; 126; 137; etc.). Some genealogical lists found in Chronicles (*see* GENEALOGY §§5*c*-7) extend beyond the events recorded in Ezra and Nehemiah, and the book of ESTHER conveys an impression of life in the Persian Diaspora.

The men of that period highly esteemed the traditions of Israel's past, trying to utilize them as the material base for forging the life of the reborn Jewish society. Their endeavors to shape the Jewish consciousness of their contemporaries linked up, in some measure, with the efforts of king JOSIAH (cf. I Esd. 1:1-55), whose short-lived cultic and social reforms had been aimed at safeguarding the religious and political identity of his people. However, although predominantly characterized by the attempt to preserve tradition, the age is not devoid of genuine creativity in the fields of literature, religious thought, and cultic organization. Ezra's and Nehemiah's actions and decrees may be seen as the beginning of an ongoing reinterpretation of tradition in its application to changing circumstances, e.g., in the introduction of the public reading of the Law (Neh. 8), public confession (Ezra 9–10; Neh. 9), the enforcement of the observance of the sabbath (Neh. 13:15-21), or the form in which the Succoth festival is observed (Neh. 8:13-18) and the statutes against intermarriage are applied (Neh. 13:23-28). Here are the beginnings of the exegetical and hermeneutical techniques of the midrash halachah later fully developed and applied by the sages to the interpretation of biblical, legal literature. *See* INTERPRETATION, HISTORY OF[S] §§D, F.

1. Authorship and place in the canon
   a. Authorship
   b. Place in the canon
   c. Extracanonical Ezra literature
2. The historical framework
   a. Persian history
   b. Jewish history
   c. Historical problems
3. Literary problems
   a. Constituent literary units
   b. Literary devices indicating structural components
4. Historical reconstruction
   a. The era of Sheshbazzar and Zerubbabel
   b. Ezra's leadership
   c. Nehemiah's terms of office

Bibliography

1. Authorship and place in the canon. ***a. Authorship.*** Early Jewish tradition considered Ezra and Nehemiah as one work written, together with (most of) Chronicles, by Ezra but completed by Nehemiah (T.B. B.B. 15a; cf. Sanh. 93b). However, this ascription may have resulted from the prominence accorded to Ezra by the early Jewish sages, who considered him a second Moses. Ezra and Nehemiah are reckoned as one work in the traditional count of twenty-four books which make up the canon in the Jewish-Masoretic tradition (*see Diqduqe ha-Teamim* XXVIII, and the Masoretic summary notation at the end of Nehemiah). The unity seems to be implied by the author of Ecclesiasticus, who refers to Nehemiah in his praise of famous men (49:13) but makes no mention of Ezra. No clues have come forth so far from the published Qumran material. From the one fragment of Ezra no conclusions can be drawn with regard to the book of Nehemiah. Nor can any judgment be made on the grounds of the summary at the end of the book of Nehemiah (13:30-31; contra Myers). Also the LXX tradition as exhibited in the ancient uncials presents Ezra-Nehemiah as one work. The same pertains to the earliest Christian roster of the OT books given by Melito of Sardis (second century).

However, Origen (third century) already knew the two books as First and Second Ezra. So did Jerome (fourth century), who introduced the division into the Vulg., from which it was adopted into a Hebrew MS dated 1448 and thereafter in most printed editions. This division may well be original, as indicated by the fact that while the book of Ezra bears no superscription, Nehemiah's book is introduced by the caption: "The narrative of Nehemiah son of Hacaliah" (NEB). In some Masoretic MSS the marginal notation ספר נחמיה is found (*Biblia Hebraica*), but it cannot be considered original. Luther, too, refers to the book of Nehemiah as a separate entity. If indeed Ezra and Nehemiah at one time were two separate works written by different authors, this could help in explaining the duplication of some events and literary units in both, such as the list of returning exiles (Ezra 2=Neh. 7), and the intermingling of constituent components when the two entities were combined, e.g., the placing of Ezra material in Neh. 8–9.

There is reason to assume that the book of Nehemiah actually was composed before the book of Ezra took form. This must be taken into account in the comparison of these books with Chronicles, and in the repeated ascription of their authorship to the Chronicler.

b. Place in the canon. Historically and chronologically, Ezra and Nehemiah are a sequel to Chronicles, since they open with the report of Cyrus' decree (Ezra 1:1-3*a*) with which Chronicles ends (II Chr. 36:22-23). However, according to the Talmudic passage mentioned above, Ezra-Nehemiah directly precedes Chronicles in the canonical order. This order is maintained in most Ashkenazi MSS and printed editions. But in the Masoretic treatise *Adath Deborim* (thirteenth century), in some predominantly Spanish MSS, and most importantly in the famous Aleppo Codex (tenth century), which Maimonides considered most accurate, Chronicles opens the collection of the Hagiographa while Ezra-Nehemiah are put at its close (*see* Ginsburg, pp. 6-8). This is most probably the original arrangement. It may be surmised that the transfer of Chronicles to the end of the Hebrew Bible resulted from its being considered, as Jerome termed it, "the chronicle of the whole sacred history."

The repetition of Cyrus' decree at the close of II Chronicles (36:22-23) may well represent an attempt to provide an optimistic ending for the OT canon (Talmudic order), or it can be viewed as a signpost to call to the reader's attention the onetime proper chronological order: Chronicles, Ezra-Nehemiah. It can hardly be adduced as proof for the often voiced assumption that "Ezra was intended from the start as an integral part of Chronicles" (Myers), or that these books were penned by the same author (Torrey, A. Kapelrud) whom A. von Hoonacker identified as Ezra. The latter view was accepted by Albright and many of his students (Cross, Freedman). Nehemiah's memoirs are held to be characteristically different from the writings of the Chronicler and secondarily appended to the Chronicles-Ezra block (Cross), though composed earlier. This theory now seems to have won the upper hand over the previously widespread assumption that the Chronicler was also the author of the books of Ezra-Nehemiah (*see* CHRONICLES §5; Japhet), together designated "the chronistic historiography." The latter proposal had encountered weighty objections based on differences of style, literary techniques, and general outlook between Chronicles on the one hand and Ezra-Nehemiah on the other. The challenge came from W. de Wette, E. König, M. H. Segal, and others, and recently has been systematically presented by Japhet, who concludes that linguistic and stylistic differences and oppositions prove that the books could not have been written or compiled by the same author and that they were probably separated by a certain period of time. Acknowledging the persuasive evidence marshalled by Japhet, Cross attempted to account for the stylistic, linguistic, and conceptual differences as well as the similarities between Chronicles, Ezra, and Nehemiah by positing three successive editions of the expanding chronistic history: "Chronicles 1 composed in support of Zerubbabel shortly after 520 B.C., Chronicles 2 written after Ezra's mission in 458 B.C., and Chronicles 3 edited about 400 B.C. or shortly after." Both Japhet's and Cross's position require further detailed investigation.

c. Extracanonical Ezra literature. *See* ESDRAS, BOOK OF.

2. The historical framework. In their present arrangement, the books of Ezra-Nehemiah span approximately a century, from 538 B.C., shortly after the accession of the Persian emperor CYRUS the Great (550-530) to the throne in Babylon, to about 420, the beginning of the reign of Darius II Nothus (423-404).

a. Persian history. From a Jewish vantage point, this period in Persian history can be subdivided into two major blocks: (1) From the proclamation of King Cyrus in 538, which made possible the return to Zion, to the completion of the rebuilt temple in Jerusalem in 515, early in the reign of DARIUS I Hystaspes. Included in this time span are the reign of Cambyses II, who conquered Egypt in 525, and the short-lived attempt of the rebellious Gaumata to capture the Persian throne in 522 (*see* PERSIA §D3*a*). The names of these kings are not mentioned in our sources, which, however, may well contain references to events which occurred in their time. (2) The second block of events is set in the days of ARTAXERXES I Longimanus (464-424), with possibly one short reference to Darius II in Neh. 12:22 which, however, has also been taken to refer to Darius I.

Events pertaining to the period between 516 and 458, i.e., the better part of the reign of Darius I and the whole of the reign of XERXES (485-465), are not reported, except for the mention in Ezra 4:6 of Ahasuerus, who is taken to be Xerxes.

b. Jewish history. From the viewpoint of internal Jewish history, the books of Ezra and Nehemiah cover three major periods which are identified by the personalities who stood at the head of the people in those times: (1) The age of SHESHBAZZAR, a prince of Judah and governor of the province, and ZERUBBABEL, the Davidide who headed the first (or the second) wave of returnees and also became governor at a time when Jeshua (Joshua) officiated as high priest (Ezra 2:2= Neh. 7:7; Neh. 12:1; etc.; *see* JESHUA 5) and the prophets Haggai and Zechariah were active. (2) The time of Ezra the scribe, an Aaronide (Ezra 7:1-4) who led a group of returning exiles in the seventh year of King Artaxerxes (Ezra 7:7), whose identification is open to discussion (*see* §cii *below*), when Jehochanan the son of ELIASHIB and grandson of Jeshua was priest (*see* JEHOCHANAN 4). (3) The days of Nehemiah, from the twentieth year of King Artaxerxes (Neh. 1:1; 2:1). Nehemiah served two terms as governor, with an intervening visit to the court to report to the king (Neh. 13:6). At that time, one Eliashib (Neh. 3:1; 13:4), and probably also his son JOIADA and grandson Johanan (Neh. 12:22-23; Ezra 10:6; cf. I Esd. 9:1), also called Jonathan (Neh. 12:10-11; *see* JOHANAN 9; JONATHAN 12), served as high priests.

c. Historical problems. The reports on the activities of the main dramatis personae in the case of Sheshbazzar and Zerubbabel, as well as in that of Ezra and Nehemiah, do not give a clear picture of the chronological relationships, nor do they provide a sure definition of the spheres of competence of the contemporaneous leaders. The resulting uncertainties have provoked an ongoing debate.

i. *The relation of Sheshbazzar and Zerubbabel.* The problems concerning the relationship between Sheshbazzar and Zerubbabel arise from the absence of a clear chronology in Ezra 2–4, the paucity of information on the former, and the fact that what is reported about Sheshbazzar is also reported about Zerubbabel. Both are of royal descent, both are presented as governors of the province of Judah: Sheshbazzar in Ezra 5:14 and Zerubbabel throughout the book of Haggai. Sheshbazzar, whose ancestry is not given, is designated "the prince of Judah" in Ezra 1:8. His name has been explained by Albright as a corruption of Sin-ab-uṣur, of which the Hebrew SHENAZZAR mentioned in David's genealogy (I Chr. 3:18) would be an alternate form. Sheshbazzar (=Shenazzar) thus is identified as a Davidide, a son (or grandson) of the exiled King Jehoiachin and an uncle of Zerubbabel (I Chr. 3:19). Zerubbabel was considered a descendant of the royal house (Zech. 3:8), was invested with messianic glory (Hag. 2:23), and was regarded as the divinely appointed head of his people (Haggai; Zechariah; Ezra 2–5 *passim;* Neh. 12:1, 47). In the genealogical list (I Chr. 3:19) his father's name is given as Pedaiah, whereas in the books of Ezra (3:2, 8; 5:2), Nehemiah (12:1), and Haggai (1:1, 12, 14; 2:2; 23) he is invariably presented as a descendant of SHEALTIEL, who is Sheshbazzar's elder brother (or uncle) according to I Chr. 3:17. This causes some difficulties in the identification of Zerubbabel which cannot be solved by the assumption that Pedaiah begot a son by the widow of his deceased, childless elder brother Shealtiel (on levirate marriage, *see* MARRIAGE §1g), or by the conjecture that our sources refer to two men (possibly related) called Zerubbabel, a fairly common name in Babylon as shown by inscriptions from the time of Darius. According to Ezra 2:2 (=Neh. 7:7) and Neh. 12:1, Zerubbabel headed the major wave of returning exiles. However, our sources are ambiguous with respect to whether this event occurred in the reign of Cyrus or in that of one of his successors, probably Darius I, as the books of Haggai and Zechariah and Ezra 4–5 seem to imply. Sheshbazzar likewise is connected, in an official capacity, with the first contingent of returnees who were inspired by Cyrus' edict. He received, on behalf of the Jewish community, the restored holy vessels of the temple from the Persians' treasurer (Ezra 1:7-8). However, the verb העלה (vs. 11) does not permit a clear-cut decision as to whether he himself "took them all up to Jerusalem" (NEB; cf. LXX: τὰ πάντα ἀναβαίνοντα μετὰ Σασαβασαρ) as explicitly stated in Ezra 5:15-16, or whether he only "caused" them to be taken there "when the exiles were brought back (העלות) from Babylon" (1:11, NEB; the second verb was not translated in the LXX). Scholars get around these uncertainties by presuming two initial waves of return, one in 538 led by Sheshbazzar, the other several years later, led by Zerubbabel after Sheshbazzar's assumed death, probably after 530 B.C., i.e., after the reign of Cyrus.

A more vexing problem is that our sources variously accredit either Sheshbazzar or Zerubbabel with laying the foundation of the temple, which would presuppose that Sheshbazzar, too, made the trek back to Jerusalem. Against this, we find no reference whatsoever to the participation of Sheshbazzar in the ensuing building operations, which are unanimously ascribed to Zerubbabel and Joshua the priest (Ezra 3–5, Haggai and Zechariah, *passim;* cf. I Esd. 6:2; Ecclus. 49:11-12), though without connecting them with the completion of the temple (Ezra 6:14-15). The discrepancy with regard to the laying of the foundations can hardly be resolved by the explanation (Galling) that Zerubbabel renewed, under Darius, operations which were begun by Sheshbazzar but had been discontinued because of the hostile intervention of the local population (Ezra 3:3) in the reign of Cyrus or later under Cambyses. But the reference there concerns only the resumption of sacrifices on the altar and makes no mention of the temple. H. Graetz proposed that Sheshbazzar and Zerubbabel are two names of the same person. Both names are mentioned in the genealogical list in I Chr. 3:18-19, if Shenazzar can be identified with Sheshbazzar. It should be noted that the name Zerubbabel turns up throughout the Hebrew passages of Ezra (1–5) and in the books of Haggai and Zechariah, which do not once refer to Sheshbazzar. Sheshbazzar is mentioned in the Hebrew passage Ezra 1:7-11 with reference to the temple vessels which he brought, or sent, to Jerusalem, but information about his participation in the laying of the temple foundations comes solely from the Aramaic source Ezra 5:1–6:18, in a quotation from a letter written by the foreign governor Tattenai to Darius (Ezra 5:16; cf. I Esd. 6:20) whose historical accuracy is not above doubt. If this bit of evidence is discounted, one can conclude that if Sheshbazzar preceded Zerubbabel as "prince of Judah," and governor of the province (Ezra 5:14), he lived there only a short time, and that he had no hand in the attempt to rebuild the temple, which was wholly Zerubbabel's endeavor. This would go far toward explaining the absence of any reference in Ezra 1–6 and other contemporaneous biblical sources to any connection of Sheshbazzar with Joshua the high priest, who is always mentioned in association with, or possibly in opposition to, Zerubbabel (Zech. 3–4).

ii. *The relation of Ezra and Nehemiah.* Even more perplexing is the relationship between Ezra and Nehemiah. According to the biblical sources, both were active in the time of Artaxerxes. In following the biblical presentation of events, this king must be identified as Artaxerxes I Longimanus. The date of Ezra's coming to Jerusalem in the seventh year of the king's rule then would be 458 B.C. Nehemiah's arrival in the king's twentieth year would fall in the year 445/44 (E. Bertheau); and his return to Persia, after a term of twelve years as governor, in the thirty-second year of Artaxerxes I (Neh. 13:6) would have occurred in 433, followed by a second term of office of undetermined duration beginning in 432. However, doubt has been cast on the identification of Artaxerxes as Artaxerxes I in reference to Ezra, or else on the date given for Ezra's arrival in Jerusalem, since they seem to clash with the information given about Nehemiah, which can be substantiated from external sources. A letter written in 407 B.C. by the Jewish garrison in Elephantine is addressed "to Delaiah and Shelemaiah the sons of Sanballat the Governor of Samaria," Nehemiah's archenemy, who by that time appears to have been replaced by his sons due to his advanced age. The same source refers to Jochanan the grandson of Eliashib, who was high priest in Jerusalem in Nehemiah's days. Thus one can reasonably be assured that Nehemiah's patron was Artaxerxes I (Bright). Therefore the biblical dates concerning Nehemiah are constants to which the items concerning Ezra must be adjusted. The absence of any reference to Nehemiah in the Ezra material is surprising. In the Nehemiah memoirs only one definite mention of "Ezra the scribe" is found (Neh. 12:36), and this may well be a later insertion (Myers). Since their functions are not coordinated, they presumably were not active in the same period. Therefore, it has been proposed to identify the Artaxerxes of the Ezra narrative (Ezra 7:1 ff.) with Artaxerxes II (403-359) or even Artaxerxes III (358-338). The latter position has not found many adherents, but many hold that Ezra's arrival in Jerusalem should be dated in 396 B.C. However, the above considerations do not constitute valid objections to the contemporaneity of Ezra with Nehemiah, as presupposed by the biblical sources. By the same token one would have to conclude that Haggai and Zechariah, who both began their prophetic careers in Jerusalem in 520, should be chronologically separated, since one does not mention the other. Equally unconvincing is the argument that the turbulent early years of Artaxerxes I were not a propitious time for a mission like the one Ezra undertook. We have nothing to substantiate this objection. Also, the fact that Ezra deferred the reading of the Law for thirteen years, until the arrival of Nehemiah (Neh. 8:1-8; *see* §4*b below*), or that his reform measures seemingly had only a temporary effect, afford no tangible evidence for dating Ezra after Nehemiah (*see* Vernes, pp. 572-91; A. von Hoonacker). It is likewise precarious to date Ezra in the reign of Artaxerxes II or Artaxerxes III by presenting him as the author of the book of Chronicles, which was not composed before 400 or even 350 B.C. This argument runs in a vicious circle, since it depends on a series of disputed assumptions (*see* §1*b above*). Not much is gained by Albright's modified view, based on an emendation of Ezra 7:7, that Ezra arrived on the scene in the *thirty*-seventh year of Artaxerxes I, assuming that the number thirty dropped out of the text. (Wellhausen previously had suggested that the text might have read originally "the twenty-seventh year.") This assumption, which ties in with Pavlovsky's suggestion that Ezra accompanied Nehemiah on his second mission in 428/27, has no textual warrant (Freedman). A variation on W. Rudolph's proposal, previously put forward by Kosters and Bertholet, is that Ezra's mission came between the two ministries of Nehemiah, i.e., that it should be dated in 433 B.C.

Such tenuous argumentation does not warrant a reordering of the biblical presentation of events and certainly cannot justify the profound skepticism voiced by Torrey, partly following Bellangé, Vernes, and Kosters, over the historicity of the Return, or even the existence of Ezra, or the dates given in the books of Ezra and Nehemiah.

With only a very few exceptions (*see* EZRA AND NEHEMIAH §§3, 4), scholars have abandoned this radical view, and returned to the more "conservative" dating of Ezra to 397 (Stinespring). Today, a more optimistic appreciation of the basic validity of the biblical presentation seems to be gaining ground. In defending the biblical sequence of Ezra and Nehemiah, Kaufmann and M. H. Segal base themselves almost exclusively on literary considerations, although the Elephantine material is not ignored. Recently, this school has derived support from newly discovered archaeological material. The Wadi Daliyeh Samaritan Papyri help better to date SANBALLAT the Horonite and his descendants (*see* SAMARIA PAPYRI[S]). A silver bowl dated not later than 400 B.C., inscribed "Qaynu son of Gašm king of Qedar" (*see* Rabinowicz), helps in fixing the time of Gashum, the adversary of Nehemiah and an ally of Sanballat (Neh. 2:19; 6:1-6) in the second half of the fifth century, if indeed his identification with the father of Qaynu is certain (*see* Cross). Most recently, Avigad has brought to light a collection of bullae, confidently dated by him in the sixth century B.C., some of which refer to members of Zerubbabel's immediate family who were connected with other Jewish governors who followed him. These latest finds reaffirm the historicity and the accuracy of the numerous יה(ו)ד (*see* Albright, *JPOS;* Avigad, *IEJ*) and especially the פחוא stamps found at Ramat Raḥel and other early postexilic sites, the reading of which had been mistakenly questioned.

It appears that the new archaeological evidence, fragmentary and partial as it is, when taken in its totality provides new perspectives to the old problem of the accuracy and historicity of the information contained in the books of Ezra and Nehemiah. The hypercritical attitude which has reigned supreme since the middle of the nineteenth century is losing ground, and the traditional view that Ezra preceded Nehemiah in the days of Artaxerxes I is steadily gaining credibility. However, this new school, in contrast to the fundamentalist conception, reaffirms the necessity of viewing critically the literary materials of which these books are composed, arriving at its historical and chronological conclusions by a process of re-evaluating and reordering the individual components.

3. Literary problems. There is practically unanimous agreement that the books of Ezra and Nehemiah are a compilation of diverse sources and documents. This circumstance, probably more than any other, may account for the discontinuous presentation of historical events over more than a century. There is the major gap of about sixty years between ch. 6 and ch. 7 in Ezra, i.e., between the end of Zerubbabel's days and the return of Ezra. Moreover, some chronological difficulties are eased if one assumes discontinuities within the principal sections as, e.g., between chs. 2 and 3, and between the components of ch. 3 (*see* §4*a below*). The composite character of the Ezra-Nehemiah complex as a whole manifests itself in Ezra 1–6 in the interweaving of a Hebrew with an Aramaic historiographical account. All the material from Ezra 7 to the end of Nehemiah is in Hebrew. However, neither the Hebrew nor the Aramaic material displays stylistic or linguistic features sufficiently distinct to allow for a more precise dating within the over-all chronological limits established on grounds of historical considerations.

a. Constituent literary units. In addition to the Sheshbazzar-Zerubbabel section (Ezra 1:1–6:18 or 22, hereafter designated S-Z), there are two large blocks of material. One may be designated the Ezra memoirs (EM) and the other the memoirs of Nehemiah (NM). Both are written in part in an autobiographical, and in part in a narrative-descriptive, style. All three blocks display a similarity in structure and in the type of literary units of which they are composed.

i. *Documents.* S-Z contains the Aramaic edict of Cyrus (Ezra 6:3-5), and its Hebrew variant (1:2-4). The authenticity of both versions was defended by Bickerman, who explained the differences in tone and subject matter as arising from the different audiences to which they were addressed. The matter-of-fact Aramaic document presumably was to be delivered in writing to the royal officials in Persia and Palestine. The Hebrew version was intended to make the king's proclamation known to the Jews in the Diaspora and probably was made public orally by announcers or town criers (1:1*b*). Of the same type is the letter given to Ezra by Artaxerxes (EM), also preserved in Aramaic (7:12-26), and authentic. No such material is found in NM.

ii. *Letters.* In S-Z and in EM the epistolary literature is represented by exchanges of letters in Aramaic between officials in Palestine and the Persian court. These include the letter that Rehum and Shimshai sent to Artaxerxes and the latter's reply, which were wrongly placed in Ezra 4:8-22 (*see* §4*a below*), and an exchange of messages between Tattenai and Darius (5:7-17; 6:6-12), in which the Cyrus Aramaic memorandum is quoted (6:3-5). All these are characterized by a common epistolary style. At least some of these documents must have come from the Persian state archives by ways which can no longer be ascertained. There are also Hebrew messages and notes in NM sent by Sanballat to Nehemiah and vice versa (Neh. 6:2-9).

iii. *Lists.* These are found in all three blocks. They are written invariably in Hebrew and, like the items mentioned in (ii) above, may stem from temple archives and/or from the Jewish governors' files.

1) Inventories of the temple vessels (a) handed to Sheshbazzar by the King's treasurer (Ezra 1:9-11) and (b) brought back by Ezra (8:26-27).

2) Rosters of returnees: (a) those who came back under Zerubbabel (2:1-70 and Neh. 7:7-72*a*) and (b) family heads who returned with Ezra (Ezra 8:1-14).

3) Lists pertaining to the repatriated community: (a) men who had married foreign wives (10:18-44); (b) the builders of the city wall (Neh. 3:1-32); (c) residents of Jerusalem (11:3-24); (d) resettled inhabitants of the cities of Judah and Benjamin (11:25-36); and (e) a comprehensive list of priests and Levites from the time of Zerubbabel to Nehemiah (12:1-26).

4) Roll of signatories to Nehemiah's covenant (9:38–10:27 [H 10:1-28]).

5) Text of the covenant in which are enumerated the obligations undertaken by the returnees (10:28-39 [H 29-40]).

iv. *Prayers.* These are (1) ascribed to Ezra (Ezra 9:6-15); (2) offered by the whole congregation, the Levites, or possibly by Ezra (Neh. 9:6-37); and (3) Nehemiah's prayer (1:5-11); cf. Dan. 9:4-19.

v. *Others.* To the above may be added the descriptions of the reading of the Law (Neh. 7:73*b* [H 72*b*]–8:18), of the ceremony of the dedication of the city walls (12:27-43), and possibly of the observation of the Passover (Ezra 6:19-22*a*).

b. Literary devices indicating structural components. The complexity of the sources indicates that the present arrangement of Ezra-Nehemiah is the result of an intricate and probably multiphase process of literary structuring. Like the redactors of other biblical books, the arranger of Ezra-Nehemiah did not inform his readers of the considerations which guided him in his work or the techniques which he used. However, some stylistic and textual phenomena help in delimiting some components and disclose traces of the process of literary compilation.

i. *Closing invocations.* Nehemiah's memoirs conspicuously display the formula "remember to my good" (NEB) or "to my credit" (Myers), by which God's benevolence is invoked at the completion of a specific action or matter of concern. In all these instances, the formula marks the end of a textual unit (5:19; 6:14; 13:14, 22, 29) or of the book as a whole (13:31, *see* §4*c below*).

ii. *Summary notations.* Also of importance are the condensed summaries at the end of a given unit. These notations recapitulate the contents, and thus also delineate the extent of a preceding textual unit. The catchphrases catalogue major issues touched upon in the unit and thus help in identifying it.

1) The simplest form of such a notation is the summary found in Neh. 12:26, which digests the roster of priests and Levites presented in 12:10-25 (cf. also 12:47 in reference to 12:44-46).

2) A more distinct example of a concluding formula is Ezra 4:4-5*b*α, which defines 3:1–4:3 as a unit by directly referring to obstructions placed by local groups before the returnees in their efforts to rebuild the temple in the days of Cyrus (cf. 4:4 with 3:3). The last part of 4:5—"until the reign of Darius king of Persia"—serves as a prolepsis of events to be related in 5:1 ff.

3) Of a similar character is the notation in 6:13-14, which gives the gist of events related in detail in the pericope 5:1–6:12, which also is set apart from the Hebrew narrative in 1:1–4:5 by being written in Aramaic.

4) Of even greater interest is the tersely phrased catalogue of Nehemiah's reforms at the end of the book (13:29*b*-31), which reflects exclusively issues previously mentioned in chs. 10–13. There is a conspicuous absence of any reference to events in Nehemiah's career related in earlier chapters (1–7) or to the cultic institution of reading the Law described in the Ezra insertion (chs. 8–9). Thus chs. 10–13 are shown by the summary to be a separate entity (*see* §4*c below*). The summary notation records only cultic reforms and therefore does not reflect, as could be expected, the contents of the diverse lists. It can further be ascertained that the pericope which describes Nehemiah's actions during his second term of office, i.e., 13:4-28, which displays interim subscripts for each of its subunits (13:13, 22, 29), is not reflected at all in the final summary notation.

iii. *Repetitive resumptions.* These seem to mark the insertion of a self-contained unit into a given context. This technique is characterized by the partial repetition after the insert of the verse which closed the preceding part of the comprehensive unit, generally with some textual variation.

1) Ezra 4:6-24 is thus recognized as an interpolation by the resumption of the last words of the summary notation 4:4-5, in Aramaic in 4:24*b*.

2) Ezra 6:22*b* resumes in Hebrew the Aramaic reference to the rejoicing over the completion of the temple in vs. 16*b* and thus shows the Passover pericope (vss. 19-22*a*) to be a distinct unit (vss. 17-18 must be discussed separately).

3) Again, the similarity of Ezra 2:1*b* with 2:70 suggests that the list of returnees (2:2-67 or 69) was originally a separate entity (cf. Neh. 7:7-70 or 72 [H 69 or 71]), and that in the narrative sequence Ezra 2:1 is continued directly in 3:1.

4) Similarly, the reference in Neh. 11:1 to the ballot under the supervision of the leaders of the people to designate recruits for settlement in Jerusalem clearly harks back to 7:4-5, where those leaders are referred to and the motivation for the ballot is spelled out. The complex 7:5*b*–10:39 [H 40], which for other reasons must be considered a separate entity, thus is also set apart structurally.

Some of these textual remarks most probably concern features in the basic components that were combined in the present books of Ezra and Nehemiah. Others obviously pertain to the process of compilation and structuring. In any case, they can serve as important guideposts in the attempt to re-arrange the constituent units so as to achieve a better picture of the sequence of events in the period reviewed in Ezra and Nehemiah.

4. Historical reconstruction. For lack of unequivocal objective criteria, any attempt to reconstruct the historical sequence of events must remain subjective and hypothetical. Some measure of control and corroboration can be attained, however, not only by considering one type of analytical tool, such as the literary techniques identified above, but also by combining the variety of approaches taken by different scholars. Thus, one should take into account internally specified dates, foremost in the Ezra narratives, as suggested by Gelin, internal issues and developments throughout the century described in the books (Pavlovsky), and the results of historical and archaeological investigations (for a survey of diverse systems, *see* Myers).

a. The era of Sheshbazzar and Zerubbabel.

Ezra 1:1-4	The decree of Cyrus (cf. 6:3-5; II Chr. 36:22-23).	538
1:5-11	Sheshbazzar returns (with?) the holy vessels.	
2:1-67	List of returning exiles under Zerubbabel and Jeshua at an undefined date in the reign of Cyrus.	before 530 (?)
[2:68-69]	To follow 3:6.	
2:70	Settling the cities.	
3:1-3	Soon after, on the first of the seventh month of an unspecified year, the altar is reconstructed and sacrifices reinstituted, but no attempt is made to build the temple for fear of the local population.	
3:4-6	The Sukkoth festival is	

	observed. From this point on, the biblical text tacitly assumes the regular offering of sacrifices and the observance of the festivals, although the temple foundations were not yet laid (3:6*b*). Building activities are interrupted for several years, probably throughout the reign of Cambyses.	
[2:68-69]	Some family heads contribute to the building of the temple. Delete "when they came [to build (sic!)] the house of the Lord which is in Jerusalem" (vs. 68), which is missing in the parallel Neh. 7:71 [H 70]. The remark was inspired by the similar phrase in 3:8 and the general tenor of 1:1-4 and Hag. 1:2-6 and facilitates the anchoring of the passage in its present context after 2:67.	
	Renewal of activities, but no reference to the reign of Darius or to the initiatives of the prophets Haggai and Zechariah (Hag. 1:1 ff.; cf. Ezra 5:1).	521 (?)
3:7	Phoenician craftsmen are employed to prepare building materials. The idealized presentation reflects the influence of passages describing the building of Solomon's temple (I Kings 5:1 ff. [H 15 ff.]; cf. II Chr. 2:1 ff. [H 1:18 ff.]; II Kings 22:3 ff. = II Chr. 34:8 ff.). A more realistic report is given in Hag. 1:8.	
3:8-9	In the second month (or possibly sixth, if we emend שני to ששי; cf. Hag. 1:15: "twenty-fourth day of the . . . sixth month") of the second year of preparations for building the temple, which is identical with the second year of Darius, Zerubbabel and Jeshua appoint Levites as supervisors of actual building operations (cf. 5:2; Hag. 1:14-15), invoking Cyrus' decree.	520
3:10-13	Foundations are laid, according to Hag. 2:1, on the twenty-first of the seventh month. During the ceremony some of older generation express disappointment over the small size of the building (cf. Hag. 2:1-3; Zech. 4:8-10). The prophets encourage the people (Hag. 2:4-9; Zech. 1:1-6, in the eighth month).	
4:1-3	Building operations progress and "the adversaries of Judah and Benjamin," presumably Palestinian remnants of the northern kingdom, ask to participate, but are rejected. This occurred on the twenty-fourth of the ninth month, according to Hag. 2:10-19, as interpreted by Rothstein. The intervention has no effect. The prophets continue to encourage the people (Hag. 2:20-24; Zech. 8:1-17). A relevant oracle of Zechariah is dated on the twenty-fourth of the eleventh month (Zech. 1:7 ff., esp. vss. 16-18).	
4:4-5	Summary notation concerning interventions from the days of Cyrus (3:3) to the reign of Darius. The passage is a prolepsis of events reported in the Aramaic source 5:3–6:12, and possibly also in the insert 4:6-24.	
[4:6-24]	Insert with resumptive repetition and based on topical association—accusations against returning exiles (cf. the accusations of Haman against the Jews of Persia in Esth. 3 ff.). 4:6, and equally 4:7-23, should possibly follow 6:18. 4:7-23, however, may perhaps refer to events in the days of Nehemiah.	
5:1-2	Aramaic parallel of 3:8-9	
5:3–6:13	Intervention in the days of Darius I by Tattenai, the governor of "the province Beyond the River," which included the province of Judah. The extended Aramaic account expands on, and possibly links up with, the short Hebrew summary in 4:4-5*a*. In contrast to the	519 or later

Hebrew historiographical and the Hebrew prophetic sources, which throughout credit Zerubbabel and Jeshua the high priest with initiating and supervising the building of the temple, the Aramaic report ascribes these actions to Sheshbazzar (5:15-16), without mentioning Zerubbabel and Jeshua. The crucial statement in 5:16 most probably is a quotation from the Persian governor's report to the king and may reflect a standard official version, which also underlies 1:7-11, rather than historical realities. The king reaffirms the permission granted by Cyrus and operations proceed. 6:13 harks back to 5:3.

6:14-15 After an unspecified length of time, the temple is completed on the third of Adar in the sixth year of Darius I under the leadership of the Judean elders. Again Zerubbabel and Jeshua are not mentioned. 6:14*a* echoes 5:1, and 6:15***b*** links up with 4:24*b*. Thus 4:24*b*–5:3 and 6:13-15 demarcate the extent of the "Tattenai document." 6:14*b* is a summary notation which echoes 4:5*b*-7. Together these verses envelop the Aramaic section. 516

6:16-18 This short description of the inauguration ceremony probably should be viewed as an appendix.

[6:19-22*a*] The Hebrew report on the observance of the Passover is an independent unit, as indicated by the repetitive resumption of

6:22*b* vss. 14-15 in 6:22*b* which refers to the rejoicing over the completion of the temple. The piece was appended here possibly because of the reference to the rejoicing over the Mazzoth festival (vs. 22*a*), the suggestive sequence of dates: third Adar (vs. 15) and fourteenth Nissan (vs. 19), and the impact of a tradition in which the rededication of the temple is followed by a Passover (II Chr. 30:13 ff.; 35:1 ff.). The concern about separation from the impurities of the people of the land (Ezra 6:21) seems to suggest that the episode belongs in the Ezra memoirs. By a transfer of this pericope to follow Ezra 10:44 a topical continuity is re-established (cf. 10:18 ff.) as well as a similar sequence of dates: twentieth of the ninth month (10:9), first of the tenth month (10:16), and first of the first month (10:17).

4:6 As suggested, the report about an unspecified accusation against the Judeans and Jerusalemites in the days of Xerxes I (for which cf. the book of Esther), probably should be placed after 6:18. The same may apply 486–465

4:7-23 to the intervention by Bishlam and his confrères (early?) in the reign of Artaxerxes I (i.e., before 458), against an otherwise unknown attempt to fortify Jerusalem, before the arrival of Nehemiah. However, the suggestion to transfer this piece to some place in the Nehemiah memoirs has equal merit. 458

The consecutive narrative of events in the book of Ezra breaks off with the dedication of the temple in 516 (6:18), or in 515 if the Passover pericope (6:19-22) is retained in its present place, and is resumed in 7:1 with a report on Ezra's return in 458, the seventh year of Artaxerxes I (7:7). There results a gap of some seventy years in the biblical history of the period of the Return which, however, can be bridged to some extent if, as suggested, the Aramaic piece 4:6 (8)-23 is placed after 6:18 (or 6:22). This gap usually is explained as giving evidence of a deterioration of the returnees' community as a result of steps taken by the Persian government to curb the attempts of the Judeans to achieve political independence that had become apparent in the messianic or quasimessianic glorification of Zerubbabel. Scholars have held that the independence of the province of Judah under a Jewish governor, within the framework of the Persian Empire, effectively came to an end after Zerubbabel, who followed Sheshbazzar, and was renewed only several generations later when Nehemiah was appointed governor in 435 by Artaxerxes I. In the interim Judah was incorporated into the province of Samaria (Rudolph, Myers; *see* Provincial Systems

IN THE ANE[S] Map 2) or had been a part of it from the outset (Alt). Nehemiah's effort to establish, or re-establish, the autonomy of Judah is seen as the root of the measures taken by Sanballat, the Samaritan governor, to forestall such a development. Scholars who raise objections against this theory point out the expression "province of Judah" (Ezra 5:8; cf. 2:1) and Nehemiah's reference to "governors who preceded him" (who cannot be identified with Sheshbazzar or Zerubbabel since he views them rather critically, Neh. 5:15) as proof that Judah indeed was an autonomous province ruled by Jewish governors between the times of Zerubbabel and Nehemiah (Kaufmann; Liver; M. Smith).

The debate remained unresolved for lack of material that would present decisive proof one way or the other. Such proof now is forthcoming in the form of a collection of sixty-five inscribed bullae and two seals, together with several uninscribed pieces. Although the find is of unknown provenance, Avigad could date it confidently in the late sixth and the early fifth centuries B.C. by epigraphical evidence, terminology characteristic of the period, and identifiable personal names. Of special importance for our present discussion are ten bullae which exhibit the Aramaic designation for the Persian province Judah—יה(ו)ד. Four of these (one fragmentary) further display the personal name חננה, a shortened, possibly hypocoristic, form of חנני(ה), the name borne by Nehemiah's brother or compatriot (Neh. 1:2; 7:2), the commander of the Jerusalem citadel and the emissary who communicated the Passover edict of Darius II to the Jewish garrison in Elephantine (*see* Cowley, no. 12, pp. 62-63), and who possibly should be identified with the חנני mentioned in Neh. 1:2. Together with the approximately 350 jar handles and coins bearing the impression יה(ו)ד which were discovered at Ramat Raḥel, Tell en-Nasbeh, Jericho, En-gedi, Gezer, Bethany, Moza^c and in Jerusalem (*see* Cross, *Eretz Israel,* IX; Avigad, pp. 35 ff.), the new discovery gives irrefutable evidence for the existence of an autonomous province of Judah within the Persian Empire.

Even more important are the two seals in the collection. One inscribed לאלנתן פחוא gives the name of yet another governor of the province of Judah, who can be dated, most opportunely, by means of the inscription on the other seal—יהד לשלמית אמת אלנתן. One can hardly go wrong in identifying the owner of the seal, as Avigad was quick to recognize, with Shelomith the daughter of Zerubbabel (I Chr. 3:19), who most probably was the wife (taking אמה as an expression of court etiquette) of her father's successor to the governorship of Judea. This identification suggests that the aforementioned impression יהוד חננה, found also on fragments of storage jars at Ramat Raḥel (*see* Aharoni, *IEJ,* VI), refers to Zerubbabel's son, the brother of Shelomith whose name is recorded next to hers (I Chr. 3:19) in the Davidic genealogy and who probably was a tax collector. It further may be presumed that one Baruch, named on eleven additional bullae—לברוך בן שמעי—is the son of Zerubbabel's brother, although this cannot be proved. From all this it follows that Elnathan governed the province of Judah from about 515 B.C. to the beginning of the fifth century. Into the emerging picture we can now fit several more stamped jar fragments. One group, found at Ramat Raḥel, bears the impression יהוד/יהועזר/פחוא. The other, found on the same site (with one item stemming from Tell en-Nasbeh), bears the legend לאחזי פחוא, a hypocoristic form of Ahaziah. Both are dated by Avigad later than the Elnathan seals and therefore belong to two of this governor's successors: Jeho^cezer in the first, and Ahazy in the second, quarter of the fifth century B.C. It is probably in his days that Ezra came to Israel.

Here we can again pick up the thread left off at Ezra 6:18 with the dedication of the temple in 515 B.C.

b. Ezra's leadership.

Ezra 7:1–8:36	The preparations for the return of the group led by Ezra to Jerusalem begin on the first of the first month in the seventh year of the reign of Artaxerxes I (7:9). They set out on the twelfth of the same month (8:31) and arrive in Jerusalem on the first of the fifth month (7:8). Ezra's function is that of a "scribe skilled in the law of Moses" officially recognized by the Persian king (7:6). Although of high-priestly stock (7:1-5) he does not officiate in the cult; nor is he the holder of a specific political office. Neither does he carry the title of פחוא which probably was held at the time by Ahazy, who is not mentioned in the biblical records. The assumed lacuna after ch. 8 can be filled by the transfer of Neh. 8–9 into the present context.	458
Neh. 7:72*b*-9:37 and 13:1-3	About two months after the arrival, in the beginning of the seventh month of that same year, the returnees congregate in Jerusalem to hear Ezra read out to them the Law, with Levites serving as interpreters. (The reference to Nehemiah the "governor" in 8:9*a* must be deleted, having probably been added after the insertion of the Ezra document into the Nehemiah memoirs.) The next day, after the reading of the relevant passages, it is	

decided to observe the Sukkoth festival, which is concluded on the twenty-fourth with Ezra's solemn prayer (9:1-37). Into this context fits a short piece in Neh. 13:1-3 which also treats of marriages with foreign women and refers to the reading of the Law "on that day" (13:1*a*). We propose to insert Neh. 13:1-3 after 9:1. The linkage is indicated by the doubling of "they separated from Israel all who were of foreign descent" (13:3) in 9:2*a*: "And the Israelites separated themselves from all foreigners."

Ezra 9:1–10:44 The opening words of 9:1 refer to the events related in Neh. 8–9, and the apparent abruptness in the transition from Ezra 8:36 to 9:1 is overcome. Strengthened in their interpretation of Jewish identity by the reading of the Law, the leaders of the returnees approach Ezra in the matter of the the marriages of men who are reckoned among the "holy seed" with daughters of the unclean "peoples of the land" (9:1-2). Ezra's prayer leads the people to repent. After Ezra's public fast in the chambers of the high priest, a public meeting is set for the twentieth day of the ninth month to deliberate on the matter, but pouring rain prevents the taking of effective steps. It is therefore decided to appoint a committee to look into the matter. They sit for two months, from the first of the tenth to the first of the first month of the next year. The account is rounded out with 457
a detailed roster of the exiles who agreed to dissolve their marriages (10:18-44).

6:19-22*a* It would appear that at this juncture the undated report on the observance of the Passover should be inserted (*see* §4*a above*). Thus, the Ezra memoirs would end early in the year 457, after about one year of activity under Ezra's leadership, when Ahzai (?) was governor.

c. Nehemiah's terms of office.

Neh. 1:1–7:73*a* [H 72*a*] Twelve years later, in the month of Kislev, i.e., in the ninth month of the twentieth year in the 445
reign of Artaxerxes I, begin "the memoirs (RSV 'words') of Nehemiah the son of Hacaliah" (Neh. 1:1). After having been alerted by a messenger to the plight of Jerusalem, Nehemiah sets out for Jerusalem in the month of Nissan. The narrative proceeds smoothly up to 7:5, i.e., to the mention of Jerusalem being too thinly populated (vs. 4), without any dates being given. It is possible that the misplaced piece Ezra 4:7-23 could find its proper setting somewhere in this part of the memoirs, e.g., after Neh. 5:7 or 5:9.

7:6-73*a* [H 72*a*] Here follows the roster of returnees with Zerubbabel (cf. Ezra 2:1-70), which serves as the basis of the census taken by Nehemiah to repopulate Jerusalem.

[7:73*b* (H 72*b*) – 9:37] *See* §4*b above.*

[9:38–10:39 (H 10:1-40)] Also, Nehemiah's covenant appears to be out of place. *See below* after 12:43.

11:1–12:26 11:1-2, which reports the measures taken by Nehemiah to resettle Jerusalem, connects most suitably with 7:73*a* [H 72*a*]. All the materials relate directly or indirectly to the building of the city wall, most probably to the time after one half of the wall had already been reconstructed (3:38). It may be assumed that several years were needed for this work, probably the better part of Nehemiah's first term of office.

12:27-43 Thus the dedication or inauguration ceremonies of the completion of the wall took place *ca.* 435. 435

9:38–10:39 [H 10:1-40] "Because of all this," i.e., after the necessary security preparations, Nehemiah turns his attention to internal reforms (cf. 5:1-13), especially with regard to the temple cult and the revenues of the temple personnel. A document which records the stipulations (10:28-39 [H 29-40]) is drawn up and signed by the dignitaries (9:38–10:27 [H 10:1-28]).

12:44-47 The document ends with a concluding notation which connects the contemporary reforms in the period from Zerubbabel to Nehemiah with cultic laws and rules established by King David.

13:30-31 These two verses appear to be the onetime summary notation of the over-all covenant unit, which consisted of 9:38–10:39 [H 10:1-40] and 12:44-47. The notation consists of catchphrases which recapture some of the salient points of Nehemiah's reform.

[13:1-3] The short reference to another reading of the Law which results in the separation from all who were "of foreign descent" (vs. 3*b*) is to be inserted after Neh. 9:1 (*see above*).

13:4-29 The rest of the chapter and the book is set several years later, after Nehemiah's return to Jerusalem for a second term of office. The earliest this could have happened is the thirty-third year of Artaxerxes (13:6-7), i.e., 432. In some matters, such as the reordering of tithes and offerings (vss. 10-14) and the reference to mixed marriages (vss. 23-28), the account of Nehemiah's actions in his second term parallels the covenant document (9:38–10:39 [H 10:1-40]; 12:44-47). The pericope closes in vs. 29*b* with a notation which refers back to the subject matter dealt with in the immediately preceding text unit (vss. 23-27), namely the marriage with non-Judahite women. It is prefaced by a liturgical formula of the type that seems to have been favored by the author of the Nehemiah memoirs (cf. 5:19; 6:14; 13:14, 22, 31) but is not found in the Ezra material. 432

[13:30-31] The transfer of these verses from their suggested original place after 12:47 (*see above*) to the present context may have been caused by their summary character, which makes them a suitable ending for Nehemiah's memoirs.

The results of this inquiry can be presented in a chart showing the succession of Davidids, synchronized with the roster of high priests and governors of the province of Judea and a genealogy of Sanballatids (the rulers of the neighboring province of Samaria). The chart is based on the biblical sources (Ezra-Nehemiah, Haggai, Zechariah, and I Chronicles), the information gleaned from the Judean stamps and jar handles from the early Persian period (especially the seals and bullae most recently published by Avigad), the Samaritan Wadi Daliyeh documents analyzed by Cross, and the Elephantine papyri.

Dates	*High priests*	*Davidids*	*Governors*	*Sanballatids*
538		Sheshbazzar		
-515	Yeshua^{c}	Zerubbabel		
515-	Yoyaqim	Ḥananiah	Elnathan	
	(brother of)			
ca. 490-	[Eliashib I]		Yeho^{c}ezer	
ca. 470-	[Yohanan]	Shechaniah	Aḥzai	
	Eliashib II	Ḥattush	(Ezra)	
445-420 (?)	Yoyada^{c} I	'Elyoenay	Nehemiah	Sanballat I
	Yoḥanan II	^{c}Anani		Delaiah
408	Yaddua^{c}		Bagohi	Sanballat II

This synoptic table can be further extended for several generations after Nehemiah to the end of the Persian period by the addition of four generations of high priests, three generations of Sanballatids, and one more Judean governor known from coins.

Dates	*High priests*	*Governors*	*Sanballatids*
			Yeshua[c] (?) (brother of)
390	Yoḥanan III		Ḥananiah (?)
360	Yaddua[c] II		Sanballat III
330	Onias I	Yeḥezqia	
300	Simon I		

Nothwithstanding the gaps in our information, the available evidence strongly suggests that the province of Judea existed as an autonomous entity within the Persian Empire down to the days of Alexander of Macedonia. *See also* SANBALLAT[S].

Bibliography. Commentaries: E. Bertheau, *Die Bücher Esra, Nehemia und Ester* (1862); C. C. Torrey, *The Composition and Historical Value of Ezra-Nehemiah* (1896); W. F. Stinespring, Prolegomenon to the reissue of C. C. Torrey, *Ezra Studies* (1970), pp. xi-xxvi; H. Schneider, *Die Bücher Esra und Nehemia, übersetzt und erklärt* (1959); A. Gelin, *Le livre de Esdras et Néhémie,* La Sainte Bible (1960); S. Mowinckel, *Studien zu dem Buche Ezra-Nehemia I-III* (1964-65); J. M. Myers, *Ezra-Nehemiah,* ABi, XIV (1965).

Authorship: D. N. Freedman, "The Chronicler's Purpose," *CBQ,* XXIII (1961), 436-42; P. Ackroyd, "History and Theology in the Writings of the Chronicler", *CTM,* XXXVIII (1967), 501-15; S. Japhet, "The Supposed Common Authorship of Chronicles and Ezra-Nehemiah Investigated Anew," *VT,* XVIII (1968), 330-71; J. D. Newsome, Jr., "Toward a New Understanding of the Chronicler and his Purposes," *JBL,* XCIV (1975), 201-17.

Place in canon: C. D. Ginsburg, *Introduction to the Massoretic-Critical Edition of the Hebrew Bible* (1897); N. Ararat, "Ezra and his Activity in the Biblical and Post-biblical Sources," *Beit Mikra,* XVII (1972), 451-92, Hebrew; P. Höffken, "Warum schwieg Jesus Sirach über Esra," *ZAW,* LXXXVII (1975), 184-201.

The historical framework: C. Bellangé, *Le Judaïsme et l'histoire du peuple juif* (1889), pp. 180-88; M. Vernes, *Précis d'histoire juive depuis les origines jusqu'à l'époque persane* (1889), pp. 572-91; W. M. Kosters, *Die Wiederherstellung Israels in der persischen Periode* (1895); J. Wellhausen, "Die Rückkehr der Juden aus dem babylonischen Exil," *Nachrichten von der Königlichen Gesellschaft der Wissenschaften zu Göttingen* (1895), pp. 166-86; W. F. Albright, *From the Stone Age to Christianity* (1940), pp. 254 ff., and *Archaeology and the Religion of Israel* (1968), pp. 162-68; A. T. Olmstead, *History of the Persian Empire* (1948); M. Noth, *The History of Israel* (1958); J. Liver, "The Return from Babylon, Its Time and Scope," *Eretz Israel,* V (1958), 114-19, Hebrew; J. Bright, *A History of Israel* (2nd. ed., 1972); G. E. Mendenhall, "Biblical History in Transition," in *The Bible and the Ancient Near East: Essays in Honor of W. F. Albright,* ed. G. E. Wright (1961), pp. 32-53; P. R. Ackroyd, *Exile and Restoration* (1968); Y. Kaufmann, *History of the Religion of Israel,* IV (1969), Hebrew; M. Smith, *Palestinian Parties and Politics that Shaped the OT* (1971); S. Herrmann, *Geschichte Israels in alttestamentlicher Zeit* (1973); F. M. Cross, Jr., "A Reconstruction of the Judean Restoration," *JBL,* XCIV (1975), 4-18.

The era of Zerubbabel: S. A. Cook, "The Age of Zerubbabel," in *Studies in OT Prophecy,* ed. H. H. Rowley (1950), pp. 19-36; E. Sellin, *Serubbabel—ein Beitrag zur Geschichte der messianischen Erwartung und der Enstehung der Judentums* (1898); G. Sauer, "Serubbabel in der Sicht Haggais und Sacharjas," *Das Ferne und Nahe Wort. Festschrift für L. Rost* (1967), pp. 199-209; J. Gabriel, *Zorobabel* (1927); S. Mowinckel, *He That Cometh* (1955), pp. 119-22, 155-62; S. Talmon, "Typen der Messiaerwartung um die Zeitwende," in *Probleme Biblischer Theologie, Gerhard von Rad zum 70. Geburtstag,* ed. H. W. Wolff (1971), pp. 571-88; J. Theis, *Geschichtliche und literarkritische Fragen in Esra 1–6,* Alttestamentliche Abhandlungen, II. Band, 5. Heft (1910); J. S. Wright, *The Building of the Second Temple* (1958); K. Galling, "Serubbabel und der Hohepriester beim Wiederaufbau des Tempels in Jerusalem," *Studien zur Geschichte Israels im persischen Zeitalter* (1964), pp. 127-48; A. Gelston, "The Foundations of the Second Temple," *VT,* XVI (1966), 232-35; D. L. Petersen, "Zerubbabel and Jerusalem Temple Reconstruction," *CBQ,* XXXVI (1974), 366-72.

The period of Ezra and Nehemiah: F. de Saulcy, *Études chronologiques des livres d'Esdras et de Néhémie* (1862); V. Pavlovsky, "Die Chronologie der Tätigkeit Esdras. Versuch einer neuen Lösung," *Bibl.,* XXXVIII (1957), 275-305, 428-46; J. Bright, "The Date of Ezra's Mission to Jerusalem," *Y. Kaufmann Jub. Vol.* (1960), pp. 70-87; J. Morgenstern, "The Dates of Ezra and Nehemiah," *JSS,* VII (1962), 1-11; U. Kellermann, "Erwägungen zum Problem der Esradatierung," *ZAW,* LXXX (1968), 55-87.

The Ezra memoirs: F. Arlemann, "Zur Esra Quelle," *ZAW,* LIX (1943), 77-98; S. Mowinckel, " 'Ich' und 'Er' in der Esrageschichte," *W. Rudolph Festschrift* (1961), pp. 211-33; U. Kellermann, "Erwägungen zum Esragesetz," *ZAW,* LXXX (1968), 373-85; W. T. In der Smitten, *Esra: Quellen, Überlieferung u. Geschichte,* Studia Semitica Neerlandica, XV (1973).

The Nehemiah memoirs: W. Bayer, *Die Memoiren des Statthalters Nehemia* (1937); G. von Rad, "Die Nehemia-Denkschrift," *ZAW,* LXXVI (1964), 176-87; U. Kellermann, *Nehemia: Quellen, Überlieferung und Geschichte, BZAW,* CII (1967); W. T. In der Smitten, "Die Gründe für die Aufnahme der Nehemiaschrift in das chronistische Geschichtswerk," *BZ,* NF XVI/2 (1972), 207-21.

Lists and documents: E. Bickerman, "The Edict of Cyrus in Ezra 1," *JBL,* LXV (1946), 249-75; L. Rost, "Erwägungen zum Kyroserlass—Esr 1," *W. Rudolph Festschrift* (1961), pp. 301-07; R. Smend, *Die Listen der Bücher Esra und Nehemia* (1881); H. L. Allrik, "The Lists of Zerubbabel (Neh. 7 and Ezra 2) and the Hebrew Numeral Notation," *BASOR,* 136 (1954), 21-27; U. Kellermann, "Die Listen in Nehemia 11, eine Dokumentation aus den letzten Jahren des Reiches Juda?" *ZDPV,* LXXXII (1966), 209-27.

Archaeological sources: E. Meyer, *Der Papyrusfund von Elephantine* (1912); A. Cowley, *Aramaic Papyri of the Fifth Century* B.C. (1923); J. B. Pritchard, *Ancient Near Eastern Texts Relating to the OT* (1950, 1956); I. Rabinowicz, "Aramaic Inscriptions of the Fifth Century B.C.E. from a North-Arab Shrine in Egypt," *JNES,* XV (1956), 1-9; B. Porten, *Archives from Elephantine* (1968); W. F. Albright, "Notes on Early Hebrew and Aramaic Epigraphy," *JPOS,* VI (1926), 93-102; N. Avigad, "A New Class of *Yehud* Stamps," *IEJ,* VII (1957), 146-53, and *A New Discovery of an Archive of Bullae from the Period of Ezra and Nehemiah,* Qedem IV, Monographs of the Institute of Archaeology, The Hebrew University of Jerusalem (1975); F. M. Cross, "Papyri of the Fourth Century B.C. from Dâliyeh: A Preliminary Report on Their Discovery and Significance," in *New Direction in Biblical Archaeology,* ed. D. N. Freedman and J. C. Greenfield (1969), pp. 41-62, "Judean Stamps," *Eretz Israel,* IX (1969), 20-27; E. Stern, *The Material Culture of the Land of the Bible in the Persian Period 538-332* B.C.E. (1973), Hebrew; Y. Aharoni, *Excavations at Ramat-Rahel, 1959-1960* (1962), *1961-1962* (1964).

S. TALMON

F

***FAITH, FAITHFULNESS IN THE OT.** In addition to what the OT says explicitly about persons believing/trusting and disbelieving/distrusting, there are innumerable passages that bear upon the question implicitly. The present article concentrates on those in which the reference is explicit.

1. The Hebrew verb האמין
2. Nonreligious contexts of "believing/trusting"
3. Religious contexts
4. Faith and the exodus tradition
5. Abraham's faith
6. "Faith" in the oracles of Isaiah
7. Faithfulness

Bibliography

1. The Hebrew verb האמין. Biblical Hebrew lacks a noun equivalent to the English word "faith." A possible exception occurs in Isa. 26:2 (i.e., in the latest stratum of the book): "Open the gates, that the righteous nation which keeps faith may enter in." In the context of vs. 3 ("whose mind is stayed on thee, . . . trusts in thee"), the phrase "keep faith" here refers more likely to believing/trusting in God than to keeping his commandments or the like (i.e., being faithful in a moral sense). (On Hab. 2:4, *see* §5 *below.*) Elsewhere, however, it is the *hiph'il* of the verb אמן that expresses "faith."

Studies of a few decades ago that sought to interpret האמין in terms of the etymology of the root אמן, or of the meaning of the *qal* or *niph'al* forms, or of an alleged fundamental meaning lying beneath all the forms, or of general theological considerations, have now been rejected as untenable. For the most part, these studies tended to eliminate the element of believing in favor of that of being steadfast (i.e., identifying the *hiph'il* with the *niph'al,* as in the case of Isa. 7:9, where the prophet's assertion is thereby made into a tautology: "If you do not stand firm you will not be firm"), or to dissolve statements about the inward human act of believing/trusting into mere declarations of the reliability of God (i.e., the interpretation of the verbal form as a declaratory *hiph'il*). Barr's reassertion of the view of the older grammarians, that האמין is an internal transitive verb denoting the mental act of being sure about something or someone, is supported by the actual usage of the verb in the OT. It is this usage, determined in literary context, that is decisive for exegesis, and not the hypothetical etymology of the root, or deductive theological reasoning, or a choice among the several possible meanings of *hiph'il* forms generally.

Neither the word האמין nor either of the other Hebrew words for trusting (בטח, "trust," חסה, "seek refuge") implies anything in itself about the moral qualities or worth of the one of whom it is predicated or of the object of belief/trust. A fool may believe (Prov. 14:15), and one may believe a liar (I Sam. 27:12). Believing/trusting does not necessarily involve the ethical commitment of the believer to the object, or the evocation of a deep or lasting emotional response. *True* faith *in God* entails these things, as the OT affirms, but this is a religious conviction and not a meaning inherent in the word "believe" itself. There is no more hidden theological or ethical significance in the Hebrew word than in the English equivalent. האמין means simply to be certain in the mind (Barr).

2. Nonreligious contexts of "believing/trusting." The nonreligious contexts in which האמין is employed may be classified under six headings. (*a*) Where the words of another person are believed to be true or false. Jacob disbelieved his sons' report about Joseph's being alive in Egypt (Gen. 45:26). The Queen of Sheba disbelieved the reports about Solomon's wisdom and glory, until she saw him for herself (I Kings 10:7). Cf. Jer. 12:6; 40:14. (*b*) Where belief in another's words and trust in him as a person are implied. Achish of Gath believed David's lies and therefore trusted him as an enemy of Israel (I Sam. 27:12). Cf. Prov. 14:15; 26:25. (*c*) Where trust is placed in another person or thing as being reliable (faithful, righteous). Cf. Mic. 7:5 (anyone); Job 15:31 (vanity); 39:12 (the wild ox); 4:18 and 15:15 (angels). In these particular cases the subject does not, or is warned not to, trust in a particular object, but the negative character of the statement is not inherent in the verb itself (contra Jepsen). The verb means being certain in the mind, but in these instances such certainty is judged by the writer to be lacking or unwarranted. The subject is God in Job 4:18 and 15:15, where it is asserted that God does not trust even his angels, let alone mortal men. (*d*) Where someone believes that something is (or is not) taking place (Lam. 4:12; Job 15:22; 29:24). These passages (cf. Ps. 27:13; Job 9:16; Exod. 4:5, 31) show that in the OT "believing" is not necessarily directed toward persons—let alone toward God, the transcendent person. (*e*) In the phrase "have confidence in [one's] life." The meaning of the phrase is to expect to continue to live (Job 24:22; Deut. 28:66). (*f*) In Job 39:24 the verb is used of the battle horse that cannot "stand still" (RSV), or, better, "be held in" (NEB). Here the meaning of the *hiph'il* does approach that of the *niph'al* (be firm).

3. Religious contexts. (*a*) Believing a prophetic oracle or a report of a revelatory event (Exod. 4:1, 5, 8, 9, 31; 14:31; Isa. 7:9; 28:16; 53:1; Hab. 1:5; Jonah 3:5). (*b*) Believing in a prophet as a generally reliable messenger of God (Exod. 19:9; II Kings 17:14; II Chr. 20:20). (*c*) Believing/trusting in God's promises and his ability to fulfill them (Gen. 15:6; Num. 14:11; 20:12; Deut. 1:32; 9:23; Ps. 78:22, 32). (*d*) Believing that something involving God is or will be the case (Isa. 43:10; Ps. 27:13; Job 9:16; cf. Exod. 4:5, 31). (*e*) Believing God's commandments (Ps. 119:66).

4. Faith and the exodus tradition. Texts dealing with the exodus tradition are perhaps the most significant for understanding the OT view of faith. The issue is not whether to believe in the existence of God, something that ancient Israelites took for granted, but whether to acknowledge his presence as Savior and Lord, to believe God's chosen mediator and the promises he conveys, and to trust God as continuously willing and able to fulfill these promises and to rule the life of his people. This faith is the foundation of commitment to God and to his demands; indeed, faith in God is not complete if it does not produce such commitment. However, faith and commitment are not synonymous. Believing in God, or trusting him, is not the same thing as obeying him. Faith and faithfulness are intimately related, and they constantly affect each other, but they are distinguishable in OT usage.

When Moses was commissioned by God to return to Egypt to lead the Israelites to freedom and the worship of Yahweh (Exod. 3), he protested that the people would not believe that Yahweh had actually appeared to him and therefore would not follow him out of Egypt (4:1 ff.). He had previously been assured that the God who addressed him was none other than the God of Abraham, Isaac, and Jacob (3:6, 15), thereby placing the present experience in continuity with the previous experiences of Israel. As confirming evidence that God had indeed appeared and given the stated commission, Moses was given the power to work miraculous signs and was assured that Israel would "believe the signs," even if they disbelieved Moses' report (4:2-9). This proved to be the case. "And the people believed; and when they heard (better, "realized") that the Lord had visited the people of Israel and that he had seen their affliction, they bowed their heads and worshiped" (4:31). The greater sign of God's saving presence is that when Moses has led Israel out of Egypt, they are to worship God at the mountain in the wilderness (3:12). There the experience of encounter with God will be repeated. But it will be deepened by the intervening experience of flight from oppression in an idolatrous culture. This flight will be successful only because of the determinate purpose of God, working against enormous opposition from the powers of the world, but it will require a venture of faith on the part of the people.

Here, then, are all the ingredients of the revelatory and redemptive event—the "faith event": memory of the God of the fathers (with all that this implies about religious knowledge, cultic practice, and moral commitment), intense human need, strong leadership by a man of God, worship of God at the beginning and the end, acceptance of a hazardous venture toward freedom (and the concomitant responsibility) and toward a largely unknown future. The act of commitment, which includes obedient action, is based upon previous conviction (belief in the God of the fathers), but it serves to deepen and enrich faith—and the understanding of God—at the same time. Thus faith builds upon faith. (Cf. Isa. 43:10: by serving God as witnesses—prophets, teachers, lawgivers—Israel herself comes to know and believe more fully.)

Subsequently, Israel lost confidence in Moses and Yahweh, in the face of massive, visible danger (the Egyptian pursuers), and regretted the decision to flee (Exod. 14:10-12). It is really only after the great deliverance by God at the Sea of Reeds that the people's skepticism gives way to genuine conviction, and they fear the Lord and believe in him and his servant Moses (14:31). Believing in them means both believing the truth of what they have said about the purpose and promise of God and trusting God to fulfill his word.

Exodus 14:14 has often been used to justify a passive or quietistic view of faith ("The Lord will fight for you, and you have only to be still"). But the destruction of the Egyptian soldiers in the sea is only one episode in the story. The faith event taken as a whole demands action by the people; indeed, it involves a radical transformation of their entire way of life.

The people's faith in Yahweh and in Moses proves to be wavering, and in the wilderness wandering that follows the Exodus there are repeated occasions when it must be renewed. The priestly writer even represents Moses as losing faith in God's power, in the episode of the water-producing rock (Num. 20:12). In the Sinai narrative God is cited as saying to Moses, "Lo, I am coming to you in a thick cloud, that the people may hear when I speak with you, and may also believe you for ever" (Exod. 19:9).

But the struggle between faith and unbelief continues throughout the life of the people, as both the writers of the Pentateuch and the psalmists represent the tradition (Num. 14:11; Deut. 1:32; 9:23; Pss. 78:22, 32; 106:12, 24). Pss. 78 and 106 are especially revealing of the OT understanding of faith. In both psalms it is clear that faith in God involves the *memory* of God's previous acts of deliverance, *confidence* in his continuing ability to preserve his people, *obedience* to his commandments (and his appointed leaders), and *avoidance of idolatry*. And it issues in *praise*.

By all accounts of this tradition, faith is not a static condition of life or consciousness but a dynamic activity of the mind, heart, and will; not a virtue perfectly or permanently attained but a commitment to be continually renewed. It is not so much a human achievement as a response to God's grace. And above all it is acknowledgment of his lordship over all other powers, visible and invisible, and reliance upon his will and power to direct, support, and fulfill the life of his people.

5. Abraham's faith. At a time when Abraham and his wife Sarah were childless, God appeared to him by night and promised that he would give him a son from whom would spring eventually a great people (Gen. 15:1-5). "And he believed the Lord; and he reckoned it to him as righteousness" (vs. 6). Believing God here means believing that his promise is true. But it can only be true if God is able to bring it to pass. Therefore, it is equally legitimate to translate the verb here as "trust in" the Lord (Amer. Trans.), or "put faith in" the Lord (NEB, NAB, JB). This faith is not merely faithfulness understood as a moral achievement of Abraham. The statement that Abraham's faith is accounted as righteousness means simply that believing in God's promise is the right thing for Abraham to do. It is what God expected of him in the circumstances. But the virtue all belongs to God. Abraham merely receives the promise, both when it is first made and when it is (initially) fulfilled (Gen. 21:1-3).

The related text, Hab. 2:4, is ambiguous. The MT reads, "He whose soul (self) is not upright is puffed up (RSV and JB n.), but the righteous lives by his אמונה (faith or faithfulness)." The noun אמונה usually means firmness, faithfulness, steadfastness, and elsewhere never means belief/trust. Yet the contrast here between being puffed up and being faithful suggests that the latter means humble trust.

Gen. 15:6 should be read together with Gen. 22, the story of the offering of Isaac. Although the explicit terms of believing/trusting are not used here, the account is all about faith. God asks Abraham to sacrifice the child of promise, although Isaac had been given him as an extraordinary gift, when he and Sarah were too old to expect a child by ordinary conception. He makes the offering—although he is stopped at the last moment from actually killing the boy—and thus surrenders the gift, returning him to God. When Abraham has shown that he can make this offering, yielding any claim upon the child as his own possession, the child is allowed to live, to carry on the line of Abraham, and to inherit the promise.

Isaac is Abraham's whole life at this point, his name, his fortune, his future, the most precious thing he has—the one thing he really would not want to and could not afford to give up. His own life could easily be sacrificed instead of the boy's. But this is not enough. It is precisely the center of Abraham's world that must be surrendered to God. God must become the center, and Abraham must live in absolute reliance upon God and absolute commitment to his will. Grateful acceptance of the gift freely given and willing surrender of the whole to God's disposition—this is the meaning of Abraham's faith, and, thus, of the faith of his descendants (cf. Rom. 4).

6. "Faith" in the oracles of Isaiah. Twice Isaiah gave oracles of promise to the Judeans of the eighth century B.C. and called for a radical act of faith in response (Isa. 7:9; 28:16). At the time of the Israelite-Aramean invasion of Judah (Isa. 7:1 ff.; II Kings 16:1 ff.) Isaiah gave king Ahaz of Judah an oracle from Yahweh assuring Ahaz that he had nothing to fear from the invaders (7:3-8). Isaiah concluded the oracle with the famous line, which plays on the *hiph'il* and *niph'al* forms of the verb אמן, "If you will not believe, surely you shall not be established" (7:9). The parallel to Moses' experience with the Israelites in Egypt is close (Exod. 4:1; 14:31). It is the word brought by the messenger of God that is to be believed, that is, Isaiah's oracle (7:3-8). This involves also believing that Yahweh has truly spoken to the prophet and is able to bring to pass what he promises. Believing the prophet implies trusting in God as the effective Lord of history, who keeps his word, but it means first of all believing the word of the prophet (*see* §3 *a, b above*).

Isaiah does not try to tell Ahaz what are the specific implications of this faith for political action—whether he should defend the city of Jerusalem, try to drive out the invaders, or merely wait quietly and let the danger pass. Thus we may not legitimately deduce a general theory of social ethics or political action from Isaiah's oracle.

In Isa. 36–37 (taken from II Kings 18:13–19:37) Isaiah is said to have prophesied divine intervention, by means of a rumor, to save Jerusalem from the Assyrian siege of 701 B.C. and thus vindicate Hezekiah's trush in Yahweh (36:15; 37:10). Another source attributes the actual deliverance to an angelic devastation of the Assyrian army (37:36-38). Cf. II Chr. 20:1-25, where Jehoshaphat merely stands by (20:17; cf. Exod. 14:13-14) and watches, while God causes his enemies to destroy each other (20:22-23). These are late, partly legendary accounts. Jeremiah rejected the reliance on divine miracles to protect Jerusalem as a vain superstition (Jer. 7:16).

Isa. 28:16 seems to make a similar point to that of 7:9. Whoever believes/trusts the prophet's assurance that God is establishing Zion (which represents the religious community of those faithful to Yahweh) and will not let it be wholly destroyed by the powers of the world will be secure (NEB "shall not waver"). Isaiah says nothing about the possible cost of such faith nor the specific political decisions that it might entail. The faithful must always be prepared to suffer for their convictions and to take responsibility for their actions, in the face of constantly changing circumstances.

7. Faithfulness. This is a quality exhibited fully and consistently only by God, to whose faithfulness the OT writers constantly refer (e.g., Pss. 33:4; 100:5; Isa. 61:8). Men, on the other hand, are not to be trusted (Mic. 7:5; Prov. 29:25). God is trusted especially to rescue the oppressed and afflicted from the power of their enemies, whether it is Israelite slaves from Egyptian tyranny (Exod. 3 ff.) or sick and persecuted persons from disease and evildoers. The language of trusting (בטח) and seeking refuge (חסה) in a faithful God is used frequently in the Psalms in this latter connection (בטח about thirty times, including Pss. 9:10 [H 11]; 25:2; and חסה about twenty-five times, including 7:1 [H 2]; 11:1). The main burden of these psalms is appeal for divine help and praise for receiving it. But another recurrent theme is the assertion that God discriminates between the righteous faithful and the wicked by blessing the one and not the other—in the short or long run (cf., e.g., Pss. 1; 32:10). However, Ps. 73 shows that this faith was not always simplistic or materialistic but could discern the consequences of trust in ultimate religious terms. Cf. Jeremiah's conviction that God would preserve him to do his prophetic work but would not give him a comfortable life or otherwise alter his outward circumstances (Jer. 15:10-21; 16:1 ff.; and *passim*).

Bibliography. J. Barr, *The Semantics of Biblical Language* (1961), pp. 161-205; W. Eichrodt, *Theology of the OT,* II (1967), 268-315; A. Jepsen, *Theological Dictionary of the OT,* I (1974), 292-323; R. Smend, *Hebräische Wortforschung,* VTSup, XVI (1967), 284-90; H. Wildberger, *ibid.,* 372-86; T. C. Vriezen, *An Outline of OT Theology* (2nd ed., 1970), pp. 153-75; J. Ward, *Amos and Isaiah* (1969), pp. 181-91, on Isa. 7:9 and related texts; A. Weiser, *TDNT,* VI (1968), 182-96.

J. M. Ward

***FAITH, FAITHFULNESS IN THE NT.** A relationship to a person (or thing) involving understanding, belief, trust, and obedience, grounded in that person's faithfulness, and often expressed in fidelity and steadfastness. Especially, in the NT, a "response term," presuming the initiative of grace by God, but also, as "faithfulness," a term characterizing God and his servant-son, Jesus; and an ethical expression in the believer's life. The terms occur with frequency and remarkable evenness throughout the NT (*see* Faith, Faithfulness §A3, to which should be added derivatives from πείθω, πεποίθησις, "trust in, [have] confidence"; *see* Boldness[S]).

1. Overview
2. Jesus and the synoptic tradition
3. Paul
4. The later epistles
5. The Fourth Gospel
6. The book of Revelation

Bibliography

1. Overview. The NT concepts reflect extensive prior development (*see* Faith, Faithfulness §§B, C; Faith, Faithfulness in the OT[S]). (1) NT concepts are sometimes pre- or non-Christian (cf. Heb. 11:6; 10:23-25; Jas. 2:18-26). (2) Specifically Christian "Easter faith" stands out as response to the kerygma of the early church about Jesus' death and resurrection (cf. Faith, Faithfulness §D3). Early Christian preaching was a call to faith in Christ (πιστεύειν εἰς Χριστόν, πίστις Χριστοῦ) who "died for us" and is "raised from the dead," often employing a "*pistis* formula" (Rom. 10:9*b*; 5:8; I Cor. 15:3*b*-5; II Cor. 5:15). From this kerygmatic background come gospel verses like John 20:31 and Mark 1:15. (3) In light of these two influences, a variety of ways can be identified in the NT in which "faith/faithfulness" is understood, some unreflective and others more developed (Paul, John).

Continuing debate concerns (1) the best rendering of πίστις in specific vss.; (2) whether, esp. in Paul, πίστις Ἰησοῦ Χριστοῦ means "faith in Jesus Christ" (objective genitive) or "the faith(fulness) of Jesus" (subjective genitive); and (3) the place of the historical Jesus' own πίστις (reflecting the "new quest"; *see* Biblical Criticism, NT[S] §4*c*).

2. Jesus and the synoptic tradition. ***a. The historical Jesus*** assumed the faith and trust in God's kingship, power, providence, and justice so characteristic of ancient Israel. This is clear even if isolated vss. like Mark 11:22; Matt. 21:21 may be redactoral: "Have faith in God" (ἔχετε πίστιν θεοῦ). What Jesus speaks of is above all "prayer faith" (Mark 11:24) and "miracle faith" (Mark 4:40; 5:34, 36; 10:52), which may even be vicarious (2:5), taking seriously the power of God in specific situations here and now.

No new definition of faith is announced. Those who worry over food and clothing are persons of little faith, as in rabbinic usage. People are to believe John the Baptist and his preaching; publicans and harlots did, while priests and scribes did not (Mark 11:31; Matt. 21:32). Jesus' word of forgiveness is occasionally an object of faith (Luke 7:50; Mark 2:5). But when Jesus himself becomes the object of faith, we are more clearly dealing with the assertions of the early church (Matt. 18:6; cf. Mark 9:42; 15:32), post-Easter assertions (Luke 24:25; Mark 16:13, 14, 16, 17). There can also be false belief (Mark 13:21) and unbelief (Mark 6:6; 9:19, 24).

There are boundless possibilities which Jesus' trust and confidence in God open up, for himself and for his circle of followers. He elicits, by his word and presence, faith that can change creation itself (Mark 11:23; Luke 17:6). Jesus' sayings emphasize the power of faith and connect it with healings, often via the formula, ἡ πίστις σου σέσωκέν σε, "Your faith has made you whole/saved you" (author's trans.; Matt. 9:22; Mark 5:34; Luke 8:48). Jesus awakens faith; he summons people to saving faith in God through their concrete encounters with himself. This faith gives certainty to existence, over against doubt or fear; a Christology in embryonic form is present here.

Fuchs, representative of the "new hermeneutic," has contended that Jesus, in his own faith, "was sure of God" (cf. Mark 9:23) and "prayed *for* his own." At Easter, God "confirmed that the faith of Jesus was a faith which would benefit them," so that now "to believe in Jesus means to believe *like* Jesus that God grants prayer." According to this view, faith "*is* the future," as promise; it believes, "as Jesus did, in the victory of love," and confesses "that Jesus occurred 'for us' by following his way" (Achtemeier). Others would prefer to speak of Jesus' "trust" (a more universal and social term than "faith"): Jesus trusted God, and "to trust Jesus is to appropriate him as the index of God" (Keck).

These tendencies, safeguarded as they are in various ways from the dangers inherent in the "old quest," plainly stress Jesus as exemplar of trust and faith—i.e., *fides qua,* rather than *fides quae* ("how Jesus believed," rather than "Jesus as object of faith"). However, at least two questions arise, one of them historical, the other theological: Can we recover sufficient "Jesus material" to tell us "what Jesus was like"? And, did the gospel tradition intend to convey such data?

b. The synoptic evangelists. Here firmer conclusions can be drawn.

i. *Mark* reflects at points the kerygmatic use of πιστεύειν as belief in the gospel (1:15), and there are also passages on faith which go back to Jesus, usually with an OT-Jewish ring (*see* §2*a*). Mostly, however, Mark regards πίστις as "saving power," the theme of the Miracle Stories.

ii. *Luke* uses πιστεύειν at times in the sense of

"believe the Christian message" (8:12-13; cf. Mark 4:15, 17); ἡ πίστις is used for "the [Christian] faith" (18:8), ἄπιστοι for "unbelievers" (12:46; cf. 24:11; 22:67, contrasting 24:25; 22:32; 17:5). In Q emphasis had been placed on DISCIPLESHIP as faithfulness to Jesus and his message, to be rewarded in the eschaton, and on the faith of Gentiles as a warning to the Jews.

iii. *Matthew* generally preserves the views of faith found in his sources, but his particular achievement was to take a concept already present in the miracle stories, "Your faith has saved you" (Mark 5:34; 10:52), and to use it as a formula of his own (cf. 8:13; 9:29; 15:28) to shape these stories as paradigms showing what πίστις is. The principle, "to you according to your faith," informs 9:27-31 and determines abbreviations in 9:18-26; Mark 5:21-43. As a theme in the story about the centurion's servant (*see* 8:8-10), it controls both the conclusion (8:13) and introduction (8:5-7): the centurion's initial request shows faith; Jesus tests him, "Am I to come [into a pagan's house] and cure him?" (8:7, NEB n.); faith persists and is rewarded. The same pattern is seen in 15:21-28. Faith is the power which "opens the way for Gentiles to Jesus" (Held).

While Matthew thus takes the concept of πίστις that supplicates and develops it as trust in Jesus' miraculous power, he also combines this concept and "understanding" as a presupposition for faith. "Understanding" and "trust" are a complementary sequence in Matthew, and those of "little faith" (always disciples, in trying situations) "understand" but "doubt" or do not trust (14:31-33; 16:5-12; 28:17—the eleven worshiped *and* doubted).

iv. *Summary*. For the Synoptics generally, faith includes human faithfulness (Luke 16:10-12), "prayer faith" in God, credence in a prophet (Mark 11:27-33), and obedience (Luke 16:31). Above all it means trust in Jesus and God's power working through him, and belief that he is the Messiah (Mark 8:29; Matt. 16:16; Luke 9:20). πίστις is primarily faith/trust in God's power, active in Jesus, grasping after help from God, with an element of will (Mark 10:51; Matt. 15:28), prayerfully expressed.

3. Paul uses πίστις/πιστεύειν to mean, above all, belief in the Christ kerygma, knowledge, obedience, trust in the Lord Jesus. It comes by hearing with faith the gospel message (Gal. 3:5, ἐξ ἀκοῆς πίστεως; cf. RSV and NEB), by responding with a confession about Christ (ὁμολογεῖν, Rom. 10:9-10), and by the "obedience of faith" (Rom. 1:5, ὑπακοὴ πίστεως, "the obedience which faith is"). The importance Paul attaches to the human response of "faith" leads him to insert this notion into pre-Pauline formulas (e.g., Rom. 3:25) and to stress it as "justification-faith," i.e., "belief" with reference to God's justifying power in Christ's cross. Christians are "those who believe" (οἱ πιστεύοντες, Rom. 3:22; I Cor. 1:21). The kerygma is an object of faith (I Cor. 15:2, 11, 14, 17), but there is often a combination of *fides quae creditur* and *fides qua creditur* (cf. Rom. 1:8 and I Cor. 2:5). At times πίστις denotes God's faithfulness (Rom. 3:3), God's being true; human "believing" or "trust" is to acknowledge the truth of God. It can also denote human fidelity or faithfulness, as when Paul quotes a list of "virtues" (Gal. 5:22).

a. The place and "structure" of faith in Paul's thought is still debated. Some, following Bultmann, regard it as central, with "obedience" its primary side. Others stress the priority of grace (e.g., Rom. 4:16) and challenge the emphasis on "obedience" at the expense of trust and intellectual acceptance. It has been observed that Paul never makes faith the subject of an imperative ("Believe!") and never speaks of "faith *alone*" (but cf. Rom. 11:20, RSV; Rom. 3:28, where commentators since Origen have felt the sense demanded it).

Alternatives to balance Bultmann's individualistic and anthropocentric view of πίστις as "the attitude of man in which he receives the gift of 'God's righteousness'" have been proposed. H. Binder insists on faith as an action of God centered in the Cross and Resurrection, so that it becomes a transsubjective faith event originating with God, in the new covenant. Similar are efforts to interpret πίστις ['Ιησοῦ] Χριστοῦ not as "faith [by persons] in [Jesus] Christ" (objective genitive) but as "the faithfulness of Christ" (subjective genitive) who was the incarnate truthfulness of God; Jesus becomes "believer—for us, vicariously," and Rom. 1:17 (ἐκ πίστεως εἰς πίστιν) is rendered, "from God's faithfulness to man's faith embraced in it" (Torrance). Others who translate the genitive as subjective stress far more "Christ's trusteeship" (*fidei commissum*) or the "loyalty" of Christ to the promise to Abraham (Rom. 3:22). Still others can make of Christ a model believer whom we are to imitate. The majority of interpreters, however, continue to read the genitive as objective (for believers' trusting, obedient response to Christ; cf. Philem. 5), even though Bultmann's view is often acknowledged to be one-sided.

b. Faith and ethics. Faith determines the existence of believers; it is part of the indicative in the new relation to God, which is the basis for the imperatives. Faith works itself out in the form of love for others (Gal. 5:6; cf. I Thess. 1:3) and, directed to the future, is manifest as hope. When I Cor. 13 (from an earlier source?) presents faith as part of a triad with "hope" and "love," the sense is that of wonder-working faith (13:2; cf. Matt. 17:20). Neither there nor in I Cor. 12:9 (where faith is a charismatic gift some Christians have to work miracles) is the usual Pauline meaning of "justification-faith" present.

4. The later epistles. In these, πίστις comes to mean more commonly "the faith which is believed," as in Colossians (1:23; 2:7), a basis for the steadfast life of believers (1:4; 2:5). In Ephesians Paul's "justification-faith" is formally present (2:8; cf. 3:17), but πίστις seems on its way to becoming one virtue among many (6:16, 23); at 4:5, "one Lord, one faith, one baptism" can be taken to refer to Christ's death on the cross as baptism/circumcision for all peoples (cf. Mark 10:38-39; Col. 2:11-15), but more likely it means a church ritual, water baptism. The trend is toward "unity of faith and knowledge" (Eph. 4:13).

The Pastoral epistles, while reflecting usages found in Paul's unquestioned letters, tend to accentuate πίστις objectively as "the common faith" of the emerging church (Tit. 1:4; I Tim. 4:1, 6; 6:21). This was manifested in God's word, the kerygma, with which Paul, now guarantor of the tradition, was entrusted (ἐπιστεύθην, Tit. 1:3; cf. II Tim. 1:12). The kerygma is to be shared with trustworthy persons (πιστοί, II Tim. 2:2), who must receive "the trustworthy message as taught" (Tit. 1:9, author's trans.). The apostle's mission was to transmit the faith and thus "further the faith" (Tit. 1:1). In these letters "faith" also appears as one virtue among others (II Tim. 3:10; Tit. 2:10, fidelity; I Tim. 1:5, "sincere faith"; Tit. 2:2, "sound in faith," cf. 1:13). At times, "in Christ [ἐν Χριστῷ]" seems to be a synonym for "in [by] faith [ἐν πίστει]" (II Tim. 2:1, 10; 3:12). The five sayings introduced by a "citation-emphasis formula" (πιστὸς ὁ λόγος [the saying is sure]; I Tim. 1:15; 3:1; 4:9; II Tim. 2:11; Tit. 3:8) reflect the community's conscious faith about salvation, godly living, and church order (Knight).

James can be termed a "Pauline epistle" if it is assumed it was written to counter misuse of Paul's "justification-faith" by pupils who maintained his formula "by faith," but not his gospel (*see* JAMES, LETTER OF §1*e*). Instead of Paul's view of πίστις as a total response of belief, trust, and obedience, faith has been understood as mere intellectual assent to doctrines (2:19). That view is a caricature of Paul and also differs from Matthew's πίστις-concept (G. Barth). The author of James (2:14-26) seeks to correct this misunderstanding by carrying it to absurd conclusions; now Pauline πίστις can be understood only as faith *and works.* The danger is that this daring corrective by James will be taken as the norm.

Hebrews, when not read in the shadow of Paul, exhibits its own view of πίστις, one not specifically Christian (*see* FAITH, FAITHFULNESS §D6), but rooted in the OT, late Judaism, and Qumran (*see* DEAD SEA SCROLLS, DEAD SEA SCROLLS[S]) (though lacking the OT's personal relationship—6:1 and 11:6 specify only that "God exists" and "rewards seekers"); Philo often clarifies passages in Hebrews (*see* FAITH, FAITHFULNESS §A2). In Hebrews faith means chiefly "holding firm" (3:14; 11:1), "keeping faith" (10:37-38=Hab. 2:3-4; 10:39), hence "patient endurance" (10:36-39; 12:1). The pilgrim people press on, just as in the OT (4:1-11; 10:19 ff.; hence the examples in ch. 11), but now with the exalted Christ as leader (12:2). As they do so they need "[bold] confidence" and hope (3:6; 10:35), a "full assurance of faith" and "of hope" (10:22; 6:11). Faith is the integrating component for this people living by God's promises "between the times," en route to a "heavenly calling." The message heard in the community is to produce faith once again (4:2) in God's promises; πίστις has become the virtue suitable to such promises—faithfulness or steadfastness on the part of those who believe; it is "belonging to the community" (Grässer).

5. The Fourth Gospel. In the Fourth Gospel the explicit, developed christological faith of the early church is projected back into the life of Jesus in the light of later experiences. In the "signs source" or "gospel" upon which many recent scholars believe this evangelist to have drawn (*see* JOHN, GOSPEL OF[S] §2; SIGN IN THE NT[S] §3), faith would have been viewed as the *result* of Jesus' miracles ("signs"; σημεῖα; 2:11; 4:54; 20:30-31; cf. 6:14); miracles legitimize his messianic status. The emphasis is on the effect of the signs on witnesses: people see (or read, 20:31) that as wonder worker he is Messiah; and so they become believers (4:53; 11:45).

The evangelist himself further develops the idea of faith through signs (6:26; 11:41-42; 14:11), but at the same time criticizes it, notably in 4:48 ("Unless you see signs and wonders you will not believe," inserted into the miracle about the nobleman's son). John also reckons with the hard fact of nonbelief (12:37, 42). Above all, alongside the possibilities of "seeing and believing" (characteristic of the source), "seeing, yet not believing," and "not seeing and therefore not believing" (20:25), he introduces a fourth: "not seeing and yet believing" (20:29). This is the superior form of faith. Moreover, believing can lead to seeing in a deeper way (cf. 11:40; 1:50; and the communal confession of 1:14*b*, 18). To this extent there are, in John, degrees of faith. But all are based on perceiving Jesus' death as his glorification; his death discloses who he really is in relation to the Father, and that he is the source of salvation and life.

6. The book of Revelation issues a call to fidelity and endurance (13:10), to "the faith of Jesus" (14:12, meaning either confession of him as Lord or to his faithfulness as a martyr [1:5], or both). Faithful followers must keep the faith (2:10, 13); the faithless will later be punished (21:8). Faithfulness by Christians is becoming, amid persecution, one of a series of "works" (2:19).

Bibliography. General: H. Braun, "Glaube III. Im NT," *RGG,* II (3rd ed., 1958), cols. 1590-97; R. Bultmann, "πιστεύω, κτλ," *TDNT,* VI (1959), 174-228, and *Theology of the NT,* 2 vols. (1948-53); W. Kramer, *Christ, Lord, Son of God,* SBT, L (1963), pp. 19-64; W. Marxsen *et al., The Significance of the Message of the Resurrection for Faith in Jesus Christ,* ed. C. F. D. Moule, SBT, 2nd ser., VIII (1968); O. Michel, "Glaube," *Theologisches Begriffslexikon zum NT,* I (1967), 560-75; T. Torrance, "One Aspect of the Biblical Conception of Faith," *ET,* LXVIII (1957), 111-14.

On Jesus and the synoptic tradition: P. Achtemeier, *An Introduction to the New Hermeneutic* (1969), pp. 101-15; G. Bornkamm, G. Barth, H. J. Held, *Tradition and Interpretation in Matthew,* NTL (1960); R. Bultmann, *History of the Synoptic Tradition* (3rd ed., 1958 [ET 1968]); G. Ebeling, *Word and Faith* (1960), pp. 201-46; E. Fuchs, "Jesus and Faith," *Studies of the Historical Jesus,* SBT, XLII (1960), 48-64; L. E. Keck, *A Future for the Historical Jesus* (1971), esp. pp. 47-99, 177-92; E. D. O'Connor, *Faith in the Synoptic Gospels* (1961).

On Paul: H.-W. Bartsch, "The Concept of Faith in Paul's Letter to the Romans," *BR,* XIII (1968), 41-53; H. Binder, *Der Glaube bei Paulus* (1968); G. Bornkamm, "Faith and Reason in Paul," *Early Christian Experience* (1969), pp. 29-46; H. Conzelmann, *An Outline of the Theology of the NT* (1967), pp. 171-73; V. P. Furnish, *Theology and Ethics in Paul* (1968), pp. 181-206; H. Ljungman, *Pistis: A Study of Its Presuppositions and Its Meaning in Pauline Use* (1964); F. Neugebauer, *In Christus: Eine Untersuchung zum Paulinischen Glaubensverständnis* (1961); P. Stuhlmacher, "Glauben und Verstehen bei Paulus," *EvT,* XXVI (1966), 337-48; G. M. Taylor, "The Function of

ΠΙΣΤΙΣ ΧΡΙΣΤΟΥ in Galatians," *JBL*, LXXXV (1966), 58-76; D. E. H. Whiteley, *The Theology of St. Paul* (1964).

On the later epistles: E. Grässer, *Der Glaube im Hebräerbrief* (1965); G. W. Knight III, *The Faithful Sayings in the Pastoral Letters* (1968).

On the Fourth Gospel: R. E. Brown, *The Gospel According to John*, ABi, XXIX (1966), 512-15 and XXIX A (1970), 1048-51. J. Reumann

***FAMILIAR SPIRIT** [אוב; for etymology *see* final paragraph *below*]; RSV Medium (but Spirit in I Sam. 28:8; Ghost in Isa. 29:4). Has to do with necromancy, a form of Divination. Recent comparative studies have cast fresh light on both the institution and the terminology.

1. The institution. The clearest picture afforded by the Bible is in I Sam. 28. Saul, having vainly sought guidance from Yahweh by more conventional means, resolves to get in touch with the dead Samuel. He goes to a necromancer, requesting that she divine for him by an אוב, and bring up Samuel. The woman proceeds to describe what she sees: a divine being (אלהים; similarly Isa. 8:19) coming up from the ground in the form of an old man in a cloak—which is enough for Saul to recognize Samuel. Samuel asks why Saul has disturbed him, and Saul tells him his plight, only to hear words of rejection. The emphasis in this literary account is on Saul's fate outside Yahweh's favor and on the true word of the prophet. But the account reflects enough of necromantic practice to be aligned with similar practices attested elsewhere.

An Akkadian text gives instructions for going to a soothsayer's house with food for the spirits of the dead in order to elicit an oracle, and others speak of food offerings being placed in a pit (*apu*). In the twelfth tablet of the Gilgamesh Epic (and its Sumerian original) Gilgamesh opens a hole in the ground, and the spirit of the dead Enkidu emerges to answer questions about existence in the underworld. Hittite ritual texts speak of a sacrificial pit (*a-a-bi*) being opened and gifts lowered into it, including food offerings (designed to lure up chthonic deities) and certain silver objects: a model ladder, suggesting a means for the deity to ascend to the upper world; and a model ear, suggesting the readiness of the waiting mortals to hear a message from below. *See* Deities, Underworld[S] §2*a*.

It is uncertain to what extent the sparse biblical picture may be legitimately filled out with details from these other sources. But necromancy was clearly practiced in pre-exilic Israel (I Sam. 28; II Kings 21:6; cf. II Chr. 33:6), and equally clearly condemned, at least from Deuteronomic times onward (Deut. 18:11; II Kings 21:6; 23:24; Lev. 19:31; 20:6, 27; I Chr. 10:13-14). Cf. also the presumably derogatory references to the "chirping" and "murmuring" of the voice from beyond in Isa. 8:19; 29:4.

2. The terminology. אוב occurs with ידעני as a hendiadys eleven times, and without ידעני four times. Both words may refer to the spirits of the dead in every case (so NEB), though in some it is possible that the necromancer is referred to (so exceptionally NEB in II Kings 23:24). Traditionally ידעני (from ידע, "know") was supposed to allude to the esoteric knowledge of the practitioner (cf. KJV and RSV "wizard"), but it could equally well connote the privileged knowledge possessed by the dead. After all, necromancy is "enquiry of the dead" (Deut. 18:11; Isa. 8:19), who were consulted especially for their knowledge of the future (I Sam. 28).

The etymology of אוב is less transparent. The pit referred to in the Hittite texts is called *a-a-bi*, which may be related to Sumer. *ab*, Akkad. *ap(t)u* (both meaning "hole"), as well as Heb. אוב. (If this is so, the root would be non-Semitic, and may have been borrowed by all these languages.) אוב may still bear this sense in I Sam. 28:7-8. The reference to the spirit that emerges from the pit would then be a transferred sense, and the application to the necromancer a further development. Because of the common institutional setting this etymology seems preferable to older suggestions, despite the philological irregularities.

Bibliography. O. Eissfeldt, "Wahrsagung im AT," *La Divination en Mésopotamie ancienne* (1966), pp. 141-46, esp. 144-45; F. Schmidtke, "Träume, Orakel und Totengeister als Künder der Zukunft in Israel und Babylonien," *BZ*, XI (1967), 240-46; H. A. Hoffner, Jr., "Second Millennium Antecedents to the Hebrew *'ôḇ*," *JBL*, LXXXVI (1967), 385-401, and art. "אוב" in *TDOT*, I (1973), 130-34. Hoffner's work is the main source for the institutional and philological comparisons drawn above. For comparable phenomena from Greece and elsewhere see T. H. Gaster, *Myth, Legend and Custom in the OT* (1969), pp. 462-75. S. B. Parker

***FAMILY.** *See* Kinship and Family[S].

***FEAR OF ISAAC.** An archaic phrase used to designate the God of Isaac by whose name Jacob swore an oath (Gen. 31:53, cf. 31:42). Since the dialect of the patriarchs was not biblical Hebrew, the meaning of the phrase remains somewhat obscure. Scholars who interpreted it on the basis of later biblical phrases such as פחד יהוה, "the fear of Yahweh" (II Chr. 19:7), and פחד אלהים, "the fear of God" (Ps. 36:1 [H 2]), assumed that Isaac was the name for a deity from whence fear proceeded.

Alt has questioned whether the explanation can be based "so straightforwardly on a later meaning of פחד," and has explained the epithet as "an archaic title of the numen whose appearance terrified Isaac and thereby bound him to himself forever" (p. 26). Some scholars have seen "the Fear of Isaac," in that sense, as an allusion to the earlier sacrifice of Isaac in Gen. 22.

Albright has proposed to translate the phrase as "Kinsman of Isaac," which seems appropriate as a designation for the God of a patriarchal clan. More recently, however, Hillers has seriously challenged this etymology and opted for retaining "Fear of Isaac."

Hillers' translation still leaves open the precise nuance intended by the Hebrew word *paḥad*, "fear." Speiser translated it "the Awesome One of Isaac." Kopf proposed "the Refuge of Isaac," which he supported by a semantic parallel with the Arabic root *faziʿa*, meaning both "to fear" and "to take refuge." Hillers himself suggests that a better semantic parallel is to be found in Syriac *deḥla,* which means both "fear" and "object of worship." Hillers' view is close to that of Becker, who understands that by metonomy the word *paḥad* represents the object of fear (i.e., veneration).

Bibliography. W. F. Albright, *From the Stone Age to Christianity* (1957), p. 248; A. Alt, "The God of the Fathers," in *Essays on Old Testament History and Religion* (1966), pp. 3-77; J. Becker, *Gottesfurcht im Alten Testament* (1965), pp. 7-8, 177-79; D. Hillers, *"Paḥad Yiṣḥaq," JBL,* XCI (1972), 90-92; L. Kopf, "Arabische Etymologien und Parallelen Zum Bibelwörterbuch," *VT,* IX (1959), 257; E. A. Speiser, *Genesis,* ABi (1964), pp. 243, 247. O. WINTERMUTE

FESTIVALS, GRECO-ROMAN. Holy days and festivals dedicated to the gods were prominent features of the organized religious life of the Greek city-states, and by the seventh century B.C. various contests (athletic, musical, oratorical, dramatic) had become part of the religious celebrations. These competitions, originally secular in nature, were thereby placed under the protection and patronage of the gods and given a distinctly religious aspect. Augustus provided new support for the traditional festivals and competitions, and especially in the cities of the eastern provinces these celebrations retained their civic and religious importance.

Two significant changes in the character of the festivals took place under the Empire. First, they were more often dedicated to the emperor than to the gods, and second, the old Greek ideal of pure competition (ἀγῶνες) gave way increasingly to the Roman taste for entertainment *(ludi)*. Professional competitors itinerated from one city to another, and the games and associated contests tended to be designed more for the spectators than for the participants. The Romans introduced chariot and horse races, boxing, bullfights, and gladiatorial shows. These latter were brought even to the strongly Hellenic cities of Asia Minor when Lucullus sponsored a gladiatorial spectacle at Ephesus (71-70 B.C.) to celebrate a military victory. The public games instituted by Herod in Jerusalem *(see* Jos. Antiq. XV.viii.1) are typical of the Roman provincial festivals. *See* GAMES, NT.

Bibliography. E. Norman Gardiner's *Greek Athletic Sports and Festivals* (1910) and his more popular *Athletics of the Ancient World* (1930) are still valuable discussions of the public games. L. Robert, *Les gladiateurs dans l'orient grec* (1940) is unsurpassed on this special topic. Irene V. Ringwood (Arnold) has dealt with Greek festivals in her *Agonistic Features of Local Greek Festivals Chiefly from Inscriptional Evidence* (1927), and in a series of articles in *AJA* (1929-60); *see also* her "Festivals of Ephesus," *AJA,* LXXVI (1972), 17-22. A. C. Bouquet, *Everyday Life in NT Times* (1954), pp. 180-90, is a popular account of amusements and recreations. Oscar Broneer envisions what Paul might have seen of the Isthmian Games during his residence in Corinth, "The Apostle Paul and the Isthmian Games," *BA,* XXV (1962), 2-31; but Victor C. Pfitzner, *Paul and the Agon Motif: Traditional Athletic Imagery in the Pauline Literature* (1967) shows that the apostle's agonistic metaphors do not derive primarily from direct observation, but are related instead to the traditional use of such imagery by the Hellenistic popular philosophers and in Hellenistic Judaism. Similarly, Abraham J. Malherbe, "The Beasts at Ephesus," *JBL,* LXXXVII (1968), 71-80. V. P. FURNISH

***FIRST FRUITS, OT.** The first issue of all life, whether from the womb *(see* FIRST-BORN[S]) or the soil, called בכורים (πρωτογένημα) or ראשית (ἀπαρχή), was considered intrinsically holy. It had to be transferred to the deity, the rightful owner, before human beings were permitted to use the crop. Moreover, its transfer to the deity was considered a prerequisite for the assurance of divine blessing on the remainder of the crop. Both factors, the intrinsic holiness of the first fruit and its pragmatic purpose, are exemplified by the law of the first edible yield of fruit trees: "And in the fourth year all their fruit shall be holy, an offering of praise to the Lord. But in the fifth year you may eat of their fruit, that they may yield more richly for you" (Lev. 19:24-25). Similar is the law of the first fruits of the barley harvest: "You shall bring the first (ראשית) sheaf of your harvest to the priest . . . to gain acceptance for yourselves" (Lev. 23:10-11 NEB). Note also the advice of Wisdom: "Honor the Lord with your substance and with the first fruits (ראשית) of all your produce; then your barns will be filled with plenty, and your vats will be bursting with wine" (Prov. 3:9-10).

The gift of the first fruits is due not only from the first-ripe crops of the soil but also from certain foods processed from these crops, i.e., grain, new wine, new (olive) oil, fruit syrup, leavened food, and bread dough. The Priestly source preserves the terminological distinction between these two kinds: בכורים, "the first-ripe," and ראשית, "the first-processed." Thus, "All the best of the oil, and all the best of the wine and of the grain, the first processed [RSV "fruits"; ראשית] that they give to the Lord, I give to you. The first ripe (בכורים) of all that is in their land, which they give to the Lord, shall be yours" (Num. 18:12-13; cf. Ezek. 44:30). Grain, wine, and oil as well as fruit syrup, leaven, and dough, are clearly processed from plants and are termed ראשית in P (Num. 18:12; Lev. 2:12—cf. II Chr. 31:5; Num. 15:20-21—cf. Ezek. 44:30; also wool in D, Deut. 18:4). עמר ראשית קצירכם, (RSV "the sheaf of the first fruits of your harvest," Lev. 23:10) is not an exception. ראשית here is not a technical term for first fruits, but simply the adjective "first." Its use emphasizes that the omer is not to be selected from among the many sheaves of the first-ripe harvest but must be the very first sheaf (Deut. 16:9; cf. Exod. 23:19; 34:26). The use of ראשית as first-processed fruits seemed to have continued at Qumran. Outside of P, ראשית has two other meanings: either it is equivalent to בכורים, "first-ripe" (e.g., Deut. 26:2, 10; Jer. 2:3) or it means "the best" (e.g., I Sam. 2:29*b*; 15:21; possibly, Exod. 23:19; 34:26, but *see above*).

On the other hand, בכורים consistently refers to the first-ripe fruit in all the biblical sources (Exod. 23:16, 19; 34:22; Num. 13:20; Neh. 10:36 [H 37]). The term לחם בכורים (Lev. 23:17, 20; II Kings 4:42) means bread made from first-ripe grain, and מנחת בכורים (Lev. 2:14) refers to the *minḥâ* offering made from first-ripe barley. The use of בכורים in tannaitic literature is also restricted to first-ripe (unprocessed) fruits (e.g., M. Bik. 3.1).

The most significant festival involving the first of a crop to ripen was that of the first-ripe wheat, which was made to coincide with the Pentecost or Feast of Weeks (Exod. 23:16*a*; 34:22*a*; Lev. 23:15-22; Num. 28:26; Deut. 16:9-12). However, it is known from the Temple Scroll (*see* DEAD SEA SCROLLS[S] §3) that the Qumran sectarians also observed two similar festivals for the new wine and the new oil, set apart by fifty-day intervals. Thus in accordance with the Qumran calendar of twelve months of thirty days each, with one added day at the end of every three months, the omer (the first-ripe barley) was counted on Sunday (month 1, day 26, the first Sunday after the Passover); Pentecost (the first-ripe wheat) was celebrated on Sunday (month 3, day 15); the new wine on Sunday (month 5, day 3); and the new oil on Sunday (month 6, day 22). There is a possibility that the practice of multiple *bikkûrîm* festivals goes back to Nehemiah (13:31), for he mentions appointed "times" in connection with the wood offering and the first-ripe fruits.

Bibliography. J. Felix, *Agriculture in the Land of Israel in the Period of the Mishna and Talmud* (1963), p. 172, Hebrew; J. Milgrom, in *Zer Li'gevurot,* ed. B. Z. Luria (1973), p. 46, n. 28, Hebrew. For Qumran: S. Poznanski, "Philon dans l'ancienne littérature Judeo-Arabe," *REJ,* L (1905), at 26-27; J. Milik, "Le travail d'édition des mss. du désert de Juda," VTSup, IV (1957), at 25; E. Vogt, "Kalenderfragmente aus Qumran," *Bibl.,* XXXIX (1958), at p. 76; Y. Yadin, "The Temple Scroll," *BA,* XXX (1967), 135-39, and *The Temple Scroll* (1976).

J. MILGROM

FIRST FRUITS, NT [ἀπαρχή]. The expression occurs eight times in the NT (Rom. 8:23; 11:16; 16:5 ["first converts"]; I Cor. 15:20, 23; 16:15 ["first converts"]; Jas. 1:18; Rev. 14:4).

Paul uses the term in a missionary as well as in an eschatological context. In Rom. 16:5 and I Cor. 16:15 he characterizes the converts of certain provinces as first fruits. They appear to have authority within the community, not only because they were the first to believe in Jesus Christ, but also because they were actively engaged in the service of other Christians. In I Cor. 15:20, 23 the term clearly characterizes the risen Christ as the first in a series of those to be resurrected. Christ is not only the first in a numerical sense but also in a qualitative way. His RESURRECTION is constitutive for the resurrection of the other dead. Moreover, contrary to the enthusiast's belief, Christ is the first and the only one who already participates in the resurrection of the dead. Rom. 8:23 calls the eschatological gift of the Spirit first fruits. The expression is here equivalent to the notion of ἀρραβών in II Cor. 1:22. Rom. 11:16 contains a double metaphor which stresses that the beginning or the origin is determinative for the whole process and for its outcome. The first metaphor relates the dough as first fruits to the whole lump. Paul develops only the second metaphor, which speaks of roots and branches. Both metaphors stress that if the origin of Israel was holy, then Israel as a whole is holy, despite appearances to the contrary.

Outside of the Pauline literature the term is also used in the sense of first in time and quality. The Christians addressed by the letter of James are described as the first fruits whom God brought forth by the word of truth (1:18). The Christians are the first among God's creatures, as Israel, according to Philo, is the first among the nations. In Rev. 14:4 the expression has retained its cultic overtones familiar from the OT (*see* FIRST FRUITS, OT[S]). The 144,000 on Mount Zion are not only called first fruits but also qualified as spotless [ἄμωμος], a term also found in the sacrificial cult of Israel. The 144,000 are ransomed as first fruits for God and the Lamb. As God has accepted the Levites in the place of the first-born sons in Israel (Num. 8:14-18) to be a symbol for the holiness of the whole nation, so the 144,000 are a sign that all humankind belongs to God and Jesus Christ. Those who have the name of God and Christ written on their foreheads signify the promise of universal salvation for the whole world.

E. S. FIORENZA

***FIRST-BORN. 1. Terminology.** The first-born male of human beings and animals is usually called בכור, less frequently פטר רחם, and, in the case of human beings, occasionally רב (Gen. 25:23) and ראשית אוני (Gen. 49:3). The denominative בכר (*pi'ēl*) is also found (Deut. 21:16; cf. Keret B.iii.16, *ANET* [2nd ed.], p. 146). The animal "first-born" is always that of the mother. For human beings בכור can be either of the mother or the father, or even a metaphor (e.g., Exod. 4:22); פטר רחם, "the first issue of the womb," refers exclusively to the first-born of the mother; the remaining terms refer only to the first-born of the father. In most instances, the first-born is of the father. The first-born of the mother occurs in three limited instances: (1) to stress the child's sanctity (e.g., Exod. 34:19); (2) to emphasize that he is not his father's first-born (e.g., I Chr. 2:50); and (3) to underscore the mother's status at the time of his birth (Deut. 25:6; cf. Jos. Life 76; Luke 2:7).

2. The family status of the first-born. The genealogical lists point up the importance of the first-born male. He is first in the list, even if the genealogical line is given for all the sons (e.g., I Chr. 6:16-29 [H 1-14]). The family line is continued through the first-born, even if other sons are named (e.g., I Chr. 7:1-4); at times, the first-born is the only one named (e.g., Gen. 11:12-13). Daughters, even the first-born (בכורה), are listed at the end (e.g., I Sam. 14:49). More significantly, the status of the first-born is indicated by the formula "father/mother/brother/sister of" (e.g., Gen. 36:22), indicating that he is the base of reference for the rest of the family.

The hegemony of the first-born is reflected in the early narratives (e.g., Gen. 27:1-45; 37:22; cf. 29:32), as in the literature of the ancient Near East (e.g., *Shurpu,* II, 35, 89; IV, 58; VIII, 59; Hymn to Enlil, l. 32—*ANET* [3rd ed.], p. 574; Legend of Naran-Sin, l. 40). More important, it is concretized in his rights of inheritance. In Israel, the law of Deut. 21:15-17 ordains that the first-born should receive double the portion allotted to each of his brothers (that פי שנים means "two portions" of the estate, *see* LXX, Targ. Onkelos, Targ. Jonathan [*ad loc.*]; Philo, *On the Special Laws* II, 130; Jos. Antiq. IV.viii:23; T.B. B.B. 122b-23a). This division also obtained in the ancient Near East (e.g., Middle Assyrian Laws B §1), but other systems are also attested, e.g., one tenth more, the entire inheritance, the same amount. *See* NUZI[S] §2.

The polemic wording of Deut. 21:15-17 indicates that in practice fathers discriminated in favor of other sons. Indeed, the right of the father to transfer the birthright is evidenced among Israel's neighbors (e.g., Nuzi: Harvard Semitic Series XIX, 37; Egypt: *see* Mattha, p. 114; Ugarit: RS 8.145). However, Israel differed in this respect: though a younger brother might gain the birthright (בכורה), he never acquired the title בכור (cf. I Chr. 26:10-11, where he is called "chief," ראש; II Chr. 11:22, "chief prince," נגיד). The reason for this may be that elsewhere the first-born's status was defined in purely economic terms, but in Israel he held a sacred status (*see below*). Thus the transfer of the birthright—even without the title—is generally recorded as taking place, not by the whim of the father or intrigue of the brothers, but solely by the intervention of God (e.g., Jacob, Gen. 25:23; Ephraim, Gen. 48:19; David, I Chr. 28:4; Solomon, I Kings 2:15). In the ancient Near East as well, Ashurbanipal, the youngest son, supports his right to the throne because of divine election (Parpola, letter 132).

3. The sanctity of the first-born. The laws declaring the sanctity of the first-born consist of a general statement (Exod. 13:1-2; 13:12*a*; 34:19*a*; Num. 18:15) and a threefold application: to pure animals, impure animals, and human beings (Exod. 13:12*b*-13; 34:19*b*-20; Num. 18:16-18; cf. Exod. 22:29-30 [H 28-29]; Lev. 27:26-27; Deut. 15:19-23). In the case of the pure animal the law codes (*see* DOCUMENTS) differ: in JE (Exod. 13:12-13; 22:29-30 [H 28-29]; 34:19), the first-born is transferred (העביר, נתן) to the Lord, i.e., sanctified either as an עלה or as the שלמים of the priest; P holds that it is the priest's שלמים (Num. 18:17), whereas D maintains it is the owner's (Deut. 15:20). The law codes again differ in the case of the impure animal: JE requires that only the ass be ransomed, but P extends the ransom requirement to all impure animals (on this case D is silent). Here, however, the difference may reflect socioeconomic changes: in JE's time, the ass may have been the only domestically impure animal (cf. Ibn Ezra on Exod. 13:13). The ransom also varies: in JE it is a sheep; however, P's law of Lev. 27:26-27 stipulates that it is ransomed (פדה) by its worth as evaluated (בערכך) by the priest, but if the owner redeems it (גאל), he adds one fifth to its value. Since the value of an ass is greater than a sheep, the change from JE to P is in favor of the sanctuary.

The verbs used in the laws of the human first-born, "העביר, קדש, נתן to the Lord," as well as the use of פדה, "ransom," clearly indicate that the first-born male is the property of the Deity. This may be a literary reflex of an ancient rule whereby the first-born was expected to care for the burial and worship of his deceased parents. Traces of ancestor worship are found in Mesopotamia; e.g., the first-born inherits the family gods at Nuzi and cultic objects at Nippur; the *kudurru* curses (*see* ENCROACHMENT[S]) include lack of a son who will pour a libation after death. Ancestor worship is also attested in Egypt, among pre-Islamic Arabs, and in Israel (e.g., Isa. 8:19; cf. Deut. 26:14). Thus the Bible may be preserving the memory of the first-born bearing a sacred status, and his replacement by the Levites (Num. 3:11-13, 40 ff.; 8:14-18) may reflect the establishment of a professional priestly class. The ransom of the first-born is unspecified in JE, but P sets it at five shekels (Num. 18:16; cf. Lev. 27:6). The theory that the first-born was originally offered as a sacrifice is without support. *See* FIRST-BORN.

Bibliography. General: G. Brin, *The First-Born in Israel in the Biblical Period* (diss., Tel-Aviv, 1971), Hebrew. Mesopotamia and Syria: P. Koschaker, "Drei Rechtsurkunden aus Arrapḫa," *ZA,* NF 14, XLVIII (1944), 161-221; E. Reiner, *Surpu* (1958); R. O'Callaghan, "A New Inheritance Contract from Nippur," *JCS,* VIII (1954), 137-41; O. Gurney, "The Sultantepe Tablets," *AnSt,* V (1955), 93-113; J. Klíma, *Untersuchungen zum altbabylonischen Erbrecht* (1940); F. Kraus, various articles in *Essays on Oriental Laws of Succession* (1969), pp. 1-57; E. Weidner, "Eine Erbteilung in mittelassyrischer Zeit," *AFO,* XX (1963), 121-24; D. Wiseman, "Syria: Alalakh," in *Archaeology and OT Study* (1967), ed. D. Winton Thomas, pp. 119-35; F. Rundgren, "Parallelen zu Akk. *šinēpūm* '2/3'," *JCS,* IX (1955), 29-30; S. Parpola, *Letters from Assyrian Scholars to the Kings Esarhaddon and Assurbanipal* (1970); F. Thureau-Dangin, "Trois Contats de Ras Shamra," *Syria,* XVIII (1937), 245-55.

Egypt: G. Mattha, "Rites and Duties of the Eldest Son," *Bulletin of the Faculty of Arts, Cairo University,* XII (1958), 113-18; P. Pestman, "The Law of Succession in Ancient Egypt," *Essays on Oriental Laws of Succession* (1969), pp. 58-77.

On sacrifice of the first-born: M. Weinfeld, "The Worship of Moloch and of the Queen of Heaven," *UF,* IV (1972), 133-54; R. de Vaux, *Studies in OT Sacrifice* (1964), pp. 63-90; J. Henninger, "Zum Erstgeborenenrecht bei den Semiten," *Festschrift Werner Caskel* (1968), pp. 162-83; M. Smith, "A Note on Burning Babies," *JAOS,* XCV (1975), 477-79. J. MILGROM

FIRST-PROCESSED. *See* FIRST FRUITS, OT[S].

***FIRST-RIPE.** *See* FIRST FRUITS, OT[S].

FISHERMEN (NT). 1. Fisher and fishing. Depending on the kinds of fish and tools used (*see* FISHING) there are in Greek different designations for fishermen and fishing. The NT uses only the collective term "fishermen" (ἁλιεῖς), either literally (Mark 1:16; Matt. 4:18; Luke 5:2) or metaphorically (Mark 1:17; Matt. 4:19). The use of ships for fishing led to the equating of fishermen with sailors (*see* SHIPS AND SAILING IN THE NT §§1, 3). As was the case with other craftsmen, the social reputation of fishermen was traditionally very low. Because the occupations used similar tools, the Bible employs fishing and hunting or fowling metaphors interchangeably for the ministries of kings, judges, prophets, priests, wise men, and apostles.

Individual fishermen used spear, angle rod,

wicker basket, or casting net. In groups, large drag nets and boats were used. The catch was sorted (small or large; ordinary or delicatessen; clean or unclean), processed (cured, dried, salted), and finally traded and sold (*see* TRADE AND COMMERCE §4). Places for these activities in Palestine were SIDON, BETH-SAIDA, and MAGDALA. In Jerusalem (*see* JERUSALEM §§6*d*, 7*b*) the fish traded were from Tyre (Neh. 13:16) and other coastal fishing areas, from the Sea of Galilee (*see* GALILEE §2; GALILEE, SEA OF §3), Lake Huleh, the Jordan River, and perhaps fish ponds. Trade guilds ("partners" in Luke 5:7) of all kinds were subject to strict Roman Imperial legislation. Fishing ventures were underwritten by investment brokers ("tax collectors") who then assessed a tax on the catch. Some rabbis, and perhaps also an occasional Levite or even priest, were fishermen. The economic power and social status of fishermen changed with population growth, urbanization (*see* CITY §B2*h*), and greater demand for supplies in NT times. The Galilean fishermen disciples of Jesus were anything but poor at the time of their call (they employed hired hands in Mark 1:20; *see* JAMES §1; JESUS CHRIST §§B1, E5*j*, *k*).

2. Fish. The literature of antiquity lists the known kinds of fish and forms of fishing. While the Bible speaks mostly in the generic sense of fish (ἰχθύς), Gen. 1:21 and Matt. 13:47 do refer to a variety of fish and their species. Mythical fish serve various symbolic functions (e.g., LEVIATHAN at the messianic banquet).

Fish was eaten as staple food (Mark 6:38; Matt. 14:17; Luke 9:13; John 6:9 on bread and fish; *see also* John 21:9; Luke 24:42, and the logion in Matt. 7:10; Luke 11:11; and FOOD §1*a*). In Jewish communities fish without fins and scales were regarded as unclean (Lev. 11:9-12; *see* CLEAN AND UNCLEAN §3*b*). On the sabbath special fish were eaten and fish oil was used. Delicatessen fish were served on special social occasions and exported for similar use elsewhere. Fish broth was used at popular drinking parties, and fish and parts of fish were used in magic and medicine.

3. Symbolism. Christian symbols derive their meaning from the symbolism of ancient Near Eastern and Greek cultures, channeled to Christianity in part through Judaism. The NT includes the parable of the fish net (Matt. 13:47-50) and stories of the miraculous fish catch, with (Luke 5:1-11) and without (John 21:1-14) the commission to the disciples to catch human beings. A connection of fish with the Eucharist is especially apparent in the Markan accounts of the feeding of the multitudes (6:30-44; 8:1-10). In the latter half of the second century, fish figures, the angler, and the ΙΧΘΥΣ ACROSTIC (*see* SYMBOL §3*e*; FISH §B3*c*) appear as Christian symbols. Believers are represented as fish "caught" (brought to life, cf. Luke 5: 1-11) through baptism, and the apostles—subsequently also bishops and popes—are portrayed as fishers of persons. There is also reference to the gospel as fishing for fish in a sea of sin (or the world) and to the catch as divine judgment in history (as often in the OT) or at the end of history.

Bibliography. J. Engemann, "Fisch," *RAC,* VII (1968), cols. 959-1097; E. R. Goodenough, *Jewish Symbols in the Greco-Roman Period,* 13 vols. (1953-68); W. H. Wuellner, *The Meaning of "Fishers of Men"* (1967).

W. H. WUELLNER

***FLESH IN THE NT.** The Pauline understanding of "flesh" (σάρξ) as evil self-dependency reflects the apostle's conflicts with Judaizers and libertinists.

1. "Flesh" as the object of trust. It has often been claimed that Paul identified "flesh" with the lower, material nature of persons, and that "fleshly" temptations counter one's higher impulses. Although they may strive to dissociate this concept from Hellenistic dualism, those who begin by saying "man is composed of flesh and . . ." stand in the Greek tradition, and this hinders comprehension of the Hebraic usage in the NT. Bultmann was responsible for moving the discussion past this deadlock, suggesting that Paul used σάρξ to depict the natural, earthly realm, which becomes evil only when one places ultimate trust in it. Thus sin originates in the flesh, not because of sensual temptations, but because one seeks salvation in one's own accomplishments. This approach to σάρξ as an object of trust suggests two distinct norms: the spirit and self-love. Since references to σάρξ as an independent, demonic force (e.g., Gal. 5:16-17) are viewed as rhetorical, critics of this approach have noted the connection between flesh and the old aeon. The question of whether Paul adapted his concept from the Gnostic idea of hostile spheres, from the cosmic dualism of Hellenistic Judaism, or from the demonic impurity which Qumran writings ascribe to the flesh may never be satisfactorily resolved, because only imprecise parallels have been found.

2. Variations in Pauline usage. The varied situations in the early congregations account in part for the peculiar variations in Pauline usage. The struggle with Judaizers in Galatia evoked Paul's first use of σάρξ as the circumcised flesh, which becomes a demonic source of boastful opposition to the new age (Gal. 6:12-15; 4:21-31). Thus the personal, legalistic, and cosmic connotations arise from Paul's creative response to a theological crisis. This response was conditioned partly by the apocalyptic tradition in which he stood and partly by the necessity of communicating with a Hellenistic audience predisposed to view σάρξ as a polemical term. The enmity of flesh as a power in the old age required a polemic also against libertinism (Gal. 5:13-25), but since Paul's premises were apocalyptic rather than Gnostic, the essential goodness of the creation was not questioned. In later situations a neutral understanding of σάρξ as simply the creaturely sphere (Phil. 1:22, 24), even as a synonym for "body" (I Cor. 6:16; 15:39; II Cor. 7:1 [NEB]), remains possible. The semantic fluctuations can be explained by the rapidly developing controversy with Gnostic radicals (I Cor. 1:26, 29; 3:1, 3; 5:5; 9:11) and with the invading missionaries (II Cor. 5:16; 10:2-3; 11:18; 12:7). The polemical sense of flesh as a demonic power or of the "fleshly" realm as impervious to the spirit is used to advance Paul's argument; but it is avoided when it might mislead a congregation toward a dangerous kind of Hellenistic dualism.

3. **Romans.** In Romans, the negative connotations of σάρξ as the basis for legalistic self-righteousness are crucial for an understanding of 2:28; 3:20; 4:1; and chs. 9–11. In 1:3-4 and 8:3-4 Paul corrects creedal formulations of the Hellenistic church which employed flesh and spirit as mutually exclusive realms; in 7:14–8:7 he appears to adapt Gnostic materials which conveyed the idea of a deliverance of the inner man from bondage to the material flesh. By defining life "in the flesh" in legalistic terms, Paul shifts the explanation of the human dilemma from materiality to self-righteousness. As Rom. 7:13-25 and 10:1-18 indicate, the dilemma is that in seeking righteousness through legalistic obedience one comes into opposition to God's righteousness. As long as one depends on fleshly accomplishments, salvation through grace is impossible and the will to accomplish the good is thwarted. Σάρξ in this context is neither sensuality nor lack of will power but the actual physical flesh whose circumcision provides a means of self-justification. Similarly, the "mind that is set on the flesh" (8:5-7) becomes a power of the old aeon, whereby the legalist is destroyed through self-righteousness.

4. **Elsewhere in the NT.** The distinctive Pauline usage is rarely reflected in the rest of the NT. While a connection between flesh and circumcision is visible in Col. 2:11 and Eph. 2:11, the distinctive anti-Judaizer thrust is absent; σάρξ denotes not self-righteousness but sensual temptation (Col. 2:13, 18, 23; Eph. 2:3) overcome by Christ (Col. 1:22; 2:11; Eph. 2:15). The trend toward Hellenistic dualism is checked in these two letters by the continued neutral use of flesh (Col. 2:1, 5; 3:22; Eph. 2:11; 6:5; in most of these instances the RSV uses some other word than "flesh" to translate σάρξ). The Hellenistic premise of separate spheres of flesh and spirit surfaces, however, in I Tim. 3:16 and in the Johannine literature. "Flesh" in John 1:13; 3:6; 6:63; 8:15; I John 2:16 designates the human realm inherently incapable of insight into spiritual reality. On apparently similar premises, "flesh" in Heb. 5:7 and 10:20 is the earthly life the great High Priest took up in order to lead his people to salvation. The ascetic interpretation of flesh as the source of sinful lusts, increasingly typical for postbiblical usage, is visible in II Pet. 2:10, 18; Jude 23.

See also SPIRIT §6; SPIRIT[S]; BODY; BODY[S]; MAN, NATURE OF, IN THE NT and supplementary article.

Bibliography. W. D. Stacey, *The Pauline View of Man* (1956); R. Bultmann, *Theology of the NT,* 2 vols. (1948-53); E. Schweizer *et al.,* "σάρξ," *TDNT,* VII (1964), 98-151; S. Sand, *Der Begriff "Fleisch" in den paulinischen Hauptbriefen,* Biblische Untersuchungen, II (1967); E. Brandenburger, *Fleisch und Geist,* WMANT, XXIX (1968); R. Jewett, *Paul's Anthropological Terms,* AGJU, X (1971), complete history of the scholarly debate; E. Käsemann, *Perspectives on Paul* (1969); E. J. Cooper, "Sarx and Sin in Pauline Theology," *Laval Théologique et Philosophique,* XXIX (1973), 243-55.

R. JEWETT

***FLOOD (GENESIS).** Significant studies of the Genesis flood include W. F. Albright, "The Babylonian Matter in the Pre-Deuteronomic Primeval History (JE) in Gen. 1–11," *JBL,* LVIII (1939), 91-103; W. W. Hallo, "Antediluvian Cities," *JCS,* XXIII (1970), 57-67; A. Heidel, *The Gilgamesh Epic and OT Parallels* (2nd ed., 1949); T. Jacobsen, *The Sumerian King List* (1939); W. G. Lambert and A. R. Millard, *ATRA-ḪASĪS: The Babylonian Story of the Flood* (with *The Sumerian Flood Story,* M. Civil) (1969); M. E. L. Mallowan, "Noah's Flood Reconsidered," *Iraq,* XXIV (Autumn 1964), 62-82; E. Schmidt, "Excavations at Fara, 1931," *Museum Journal,* Museum of the University of Pennsylvania, XXII, nos. 3-4 (1931), 193-217, esp. p. 200 and illustrated section on p. 201; E. Sollberger, *The Babylonian Legend of the Flood* (1962); L.-Ch. Watelin, "Rapport sur les Fouilles de Kish," *Journal Asiatique,* CCXV (1929), 103-16, and *Excavations at Kish, IV* (1934), p. 53; C. L. Woolley, "Excavations at Ur, 1928-29," *Antiquities Journal,* IX (1929), 304-43, at pp. 327, 329, and illustrated section opposite p. 330, *Ur Excavations,* V (1939), and *Ur Excavations, IV, The Early Periods* (1955) p. 15 and pl. 83, also p. 165.

M. E. L. MALLOWAN

***FOLLY** [Gr. μωρία, adjective μωρός, verb μωραίνω; and ἀφροσύνη, adjective ἄφρων]. The background of the NT concept is to be found in the Israelite and Jewish wisdom movement. *See* WISDOM and supplementary articles.

Matt. 7:26; 25:2, 3, 8; Rom. 2:20 (perhaps 1:22); Eph. 5:17; and I Pet. 2:15 express the idea of folly common to circles that stress experiential wisdom. Folly is understood as a particular form of godlessness: the aggressive denial of God's power, and of the value of the fear of God and of righteousness. Thoughtlessness, lack of restraint, and the immediate submission to the impulses of greed, lust, pride, and comfort are its characteristics. Such folly is usually seen as incorrigible, a dangerous disease (similarly in many Greek and Hellenistic texts). Therefore it is understandable why in Matt. 5:22, "fool" is taken to be the worst curse (cf. Matt. 23:17).

In theological wisdom, the fateful nature and aggressive character of folly caused it to be hypostatized (e.g., Prov. 7 and 9). Subsequently, in Wisd. Sol. 1–5, fools appeared as a class of people metaphysically distinct from the wise (and righteous). Folly in this dualistic view became identical with the world of death. In Hellenistic paganism, there was also the idea of folly as fate.

The dualism of wisdom and foolishness as developed in the Jewish wisdom movement is also clearly behind Paul's dialectic approach to folly, e.g., as that is formulated in the question: "Has not God made foolish the wisdom of the world?" (I Cor. 1:20*b*). There is still the antithesis of experiential wisdom in I Cor. 1:18, where the divine message is foolishness to those who perish. But in vs. 20*b* Paul uses the antithesis of wisdom and foolishness in a cosmic sense: God versus this world. Earlier, sapiential thought had played with the difference between the obvious and the real, and in the Wisdom of Solomon, this was used as the description of revelation (an illusory reality is replaced with a true one). Now in I Corinthians, the clear reversal of the obvious by the real is the vehicle of revelation: through God's revelatory action in Jesus Christ, what appeared to be wise turned out to be foolish, and vice versa.

In I Cor. 1–3 the Christ event is described, paradoxically, as God's "foolishness" which is wiser than worldly wisdom, and this is related to the way that event is proclaimed (e.g., 1:18–2:5); then in I Cor. 4:10 the paradox is extended to include the apostles. In his "fool's speech" in II Cor. 11–12, Paul uses the structure of the ancient mime with its critical irony to elaborate on the role of the apostle as a fool—but as a fool in Christ and like Christ. Paul's practical aim in this passage was to overcome what, in view of the Christ event, he understood to be the major symptom of godless folly—pride or boastfulness.

Bibliography. G. Bertram, "μωρός, κτλ.," *TDNT,* IV (1943 [ET 1967]), 832-47, and "φρήν, κτλ.," *TDNT,* IX (1973), 220-35, esp. 230-32. D. Georgi

***FOREST. 1. General description.** *Ya'ar* (normally "forest") means wild, untilled land carrying permanent vegetation, i.e., not open steppe where the grass dies in summer. It included the towering forests of Lebanon, open woodlands, thickets and scattered shrubs, and merged finally into the arid *midhbār* (usually "desert," but better "wasteland"). Together *ya'ar* and *midhbār* formed a continuum of uncultivated land, encountered everywhere beyond the village or town. Both words connote disorder, and consequently terror, for the absence of clearly defined roads and the constant menace of savage beasts frightened the settled farmer.

No absolute distinction was drawn between them. The *ya'ar* of Gilead (II Sam. 18:8) is described as *midhbār* (17:29). Ezekiel classed the two together, promising that wild beasts would be banished, so that men might "dwell securely in the *midhbār* and sleep in the *ya'ar*" (Ezek. 34:25). In Isaiah, in otherwise parallel passages, the forest of Lebanon in 29:17 is replaced by *midhbār* in 32:15. In times of strong government, villagers might take their flocks into the uncultivated countryside, but this was always temporary. *Ya'ar* and *midhbār* provided regions of refuge for "every one who was in distress, and every one who was in debt, and every one who was discontented" (I Sam. 22:2). War caused the *ya'ar* to swallow up the cultivated fields, which reverted to brambles and thorns (Isa. 7:23-25; Hos. 2:12).

2. Distribution. *Ya'ar* existed wherever the annual rainfall exceeded eight inches, and true forests were much more widespread than today. Only the driest regions had the naked appearance modern visitors associate with the country. From the Judean highlands the transition eastward to *midhbār* was fairly rapid, but elsewhere the intervening zone of thicket and scrub was wide and indeterminate. Roughly speaking, the greater the rainfall, the denser the forest, but less rainfall does not always mean fewer trees. It means less undergrowth and fewer kinds of trees. Yet the oaks, pines, and terebinths covering much of ancient Palestine protected the soil from erosion as effectively as the stately cedars of Lebanon.

The character of the underlying rock also affected the forest cover. The rich alluvium of the lowlands carried thick forest, as did the Cenomanian limestone of W Galilee, Carmel, Ephraim, and (less densely) Judah. The less fertile chalky limestone of the Shephelah, the Carmel ridge behind Megiddo, and SW Galilee had oak and fig sycamore (I Kings 10:27). After the trees had been cut down, these latter regions remained covered with almost impenetrable shrubs, for the soil has often a hard crust, called *nari,* which makes it unattractive to the farmer.

By the late Bronze Age much of the lowland had been cleared for farming, although the easily flooded plain of Sharon remained uninhabited forest and marsh up to Roman times. The soft chalky valleys and some of the slopes of the Shechem region had been cleared, for the soil was easier to till than that on the Cenomanian highlands further S. Some clearing had begun on the saddle of Benjamin, between Bethel and Jerusalem. Cypress and pine were still available there for building at Gibeah in the late eleventh century B.C., but three centuries later almond wood was used instead. The highlands N of Beer-sheba were then almost entirely wooded, except for the eastern slopes. Upper Galilee had, throughout the biblical period, the richest forests S of the Lebanon mountains. The basalt plateaus N and SW of the lake were also forested. The soil here is rich, but excessively difficult to plow, and not until the NT period were serious efforts made to clear these areas for agriculture.

The Huleh basin was always marsh, surrounded by rich, though not impassable, forest. S of the Lake of Galilee, the Jordan flowed through an impenetrable jungle of tamarisk, famous for its lions (Jer. 12:5; 50:44; Zech. 11:3), and even recently the haunt of wild boar.

The forests of fertile Bashan were cleared early, though stands perhaps remained in the hills of Geshur and Maacah. The oaks mentioned in the prophetic writings (Isa. 2:13; Ezek. 27:6; Zech. 11:2) belonged to the Jebel Druze, or "mountain of Bashan" (Ps. 68:15 [H 16]); they cannot have been tall, since basalt gives little room for roots to develop.

The Cenomanian limestone of Gilead carried a dense forest similar to that of Ephraim (II Sam. 18:6). The Ammonite hills to the SE probably had terebinth, though immediately beyond lay steppeland. To the SW the scarplands of the Abarim had a thick cover of oak and pine. The tableland of Moab was sheep country (II Kings 3:4), i.e., open *ya'ar* and steppe, though with woodland on the plateau edge and perhaps the slopes of Jebel Shihan. Further S the heights of Edom carried much oak, juniper, hawthorn, and carob. This forest was confined to the ridge, being limited on the W by open sandstone gorges, and on the E by sudden transition to desert.

3. Disappearance of the forest. Forest clearance began about 2500 B.C. and has proceeded ever since. It is false to blame this process on either the Bedouin or supposed biblical attitudes toward nature. The chief enemies of trees have always been increased accessibility and the political security which makes this possible. Settled populations, once granted access to the forests, always do more harm than nomads. Certainly forest clearance increased with the more general use of iron tools during the Israelite monarchy, but this same period was marked by careful terracing of the agricultural land, which the felling of trees made available.

Major forest clearance, causing serious erosion and silting of river mouths, began with the Greeks and continued under the Romans. But two thousand years later there were still extensive woodlands. The most savage destruction has occurred during the last hundred years, though much reforestation is being done today.

See also FLORA §§A9, B.

Bibliography. *Atlas of Israel* (1970); A. Alon, *The Natural History of the Land of the Bible* (1969); D. Baly, *The Geography of the Bible* (rev. ed., 1974); D. Baly and A. D. Tushingham, *Atlas of the Biblical World* (1971); M. B. Rowton, "The Woodlands of Ancient Western Asia," *JNES,* XXVI (1967), 261-77.

D. BALY

***FORGIVENESS.** *See* REPENTANCE IN THE OT[S]; REPENTANCE IN THE NT[S].

***FORM CRITICISM, OT.** Form criticism is a means of analyzing the typical features of texts, especially their conventional forms or structures, in order to relate them to their sociological contexts. Thus, form criticism is best understood as a literary-sociological method.

1. Scope and aims
2. *Sitz im Leben*
3. Methods
4. Gains and implications
Bibliography

1. Scope and aims. Form criticism is one of the tools of EXEGESIS, one of the means of interpreting OT literature within its own frame of reference. It is a procedure, not a theology or an ideology, although it, like any other method, will entail a certain hermeneutic of language and particular assumptions concerning man, the world, knowledge, and perhaps even God. To characterize form criticism as a literary-sociological discipline is to call attention to its special focus on texts in terms of their social context or contexts. But at its best it does not use texts to reconstruct social situations, but rather the reverse: it seeks to understand texts by relating them to whatever recurring human situations or patterns of behavior and thought may have contributed to their shape. The form critic's interest in the history of literature, literary types, and oral traditions is finally for the sake of explaining and unfolding the texts in which they are embedded.

Form criticism is one method of interpretation among others. That is, it is not to be equated with exegesis, nor are all literary disciplines—source criticism, redaction criticism, tradition criticism, etc.—to be viewed as aspects of or operating in the service of form criticism. While form critical study may be carried on independently to resolve particular questions, the exegete will pose the form critical questions to the text before him in concert with the questions raised by other disciplines.

Above all, form criticism is interested in questions concerning the typical nature of linguistic entities and whatever gave rise to that nature. It is occupied with what is typical in the form or shape of expression as well as its content, with what is usual as well as what is unusual in a particular text. Thus, form criticism is founded on the observation that human language is formed according to typical structures or types of expression, corresponding to typical or recurring human situations or thought processes. The elucidation and analysis of such structures or genres is therefore an indispensable step in understanding individual expressions. For example, the OT hymns share many common elements because they were stamped by the recurring occasion of Israelite worship. And the recognition of the different types of OT narrative will not only give the interpreter insight into the occasions which lie behind the telling of the stories, but also the distinct purposes or intentions articulated through the various types.

What sorts of linguistic entities does the form critic investigate? What is form, and what constitutes it? Ambiguity concerning such fundamental concepts has been implicit in the discipline from the beginning. But clarification and some redefinition have begun to emerge in recent years concerning two points. First, it has been recognized that the term "form" has been applied far too loosely in two senses which must be distinguished from one another. On the one hand, it refers to the structure or pattern or framework of an individual text or a genre. On the other hand, it has been used in reference to genre or type or *Gattung* itself. For the single word "form" most OT form critics now have substituted the terms "structure" and "genre." The former refers to the (often typical) outline or framework of a text. The latter refers to the types of literature or oral expression, such as the hymn, the speech, the wisdom saying, and the like. The two are by no means identical, since genre is constituted not only by structure but also by setting, content, mood, intention, and other factors.

Second, until quite recently it was assumed that the distinctive concern of form criticism was with the expressions which had been formed by the oral stage in the development of biblical literature (*see* TRADITION, ORAL; TRADITION, ORAL[S]). This often led to the restriction of form criticism to the analysis of very short units. While the recognition and analysis of the preliterary materials must remain an important aspect of the form-critical endeavor, it is only a part of the task. There is a growing awareness that the form-critical questions, i.e., the search for what is typical in the linguistic expressions, can and should be applied to all stages of the literature, including material which did not have an oral prehistory. Thus, the form critic does not look first for the oral material embedded in literature, but at the literature itself. Not only oral tradition, but also literary expression, which is formed according to typical structures, can and must be classified according to genre if it is to be fully understood. For example, the novel, the news story, the editorial, and the letter are distinct literary genres, as are the apocalypse, various types of "books," and perhaps many other types of OT literature. The form critic no longer assumes either that all OT literature had an oral prehistory or that the method is limited to preliterary materials, but instead investigates all the material form-critically. In fact, it is part of the task, not one of the assumptions, to distinguish between literature and oral tradition.

2. *Sitz im Leben.* Since form criticism intends to relate texts or genres to their sociological contexts, the concept of *Sitz im Leben* ("setting in life" or simply "setting") has been fundamental to the methodology from the outset. Often there is a direct relationship between the form of OT texts and the institutions in which they were employed. Thus the setting was seen to have determined the genre. Often, genres of speech and literature, as well as the short formulas within them, arise and become stereotyped within institutional contexts. For example, hymns and psalms of complaint bear the marks of the services of worship in which they were employed; and laws were formed—at least in part—by the legal process itself.

Throughout the history of the discipline the relationship between genres and settings has been understood in various ways. Gunkel emphasized the analysis of literature itself, to be sure, in relationship to its setting, but many of his successors have tended to assume that every genre must have a setting in a narrow sense, that is, in terms of a particular institutional location. For instance, Mowinckel pushed the form-critical analysis of the Psalms in the direction of what he called a "cult-functional" approach, in which virtually every psalm was viewed in terms of a particular function which it served in Israelite worship. Thus, on the basis of the valid observation that many texts and genres were shaped by institutional life, some scholars have led form criticism in the direction of a sociological determinism, assuming that all formed language was shaped by its setting, viewed in a narrow sense.

In recent years, however, in part because of the application of the form-critical method to literature and not simply to oral tradition, it has been recognized that genres are determined not only by setting understood in terms of particular institutions, but also by setting understood as tradition, the prelinguistic activity of the human mind, by the spirit of an age, by particular literary concerns, and by actual performances or by specific creative occasions. It appears that biblical form criticism must either restrict itself to dealing with only one aspect or one kind of formed language, that which was shaped by institutions, or broaden its understanding of setting. The latter, while more complicated, is preferable. This approach is consistent with the basic assumption of form criticism that texts can be better understood by appeal to external sociocultural and intellectual data, and with the directions of contemporary linguistics and sociology, which emphasize that meanings are determined culturally in a broad sense and transmitted through the structure of expression. Consequently the exegete as form critic will not assume that every genre or structure was formed by a particular institutional setting, but will ask whether or not such is the case, and if not, what kind of sociocultural or intellectual matrix accounts for genre or text. Texts and genres are indeed intrinsically related to their setting, but we are only beginning to recognize the various kinds of settings which determined those materials.

3. Methods. It is implicit in the above remarks that form criticism operates inductively, on the basis of the analysis of specific OT texts. That is, it is not assumed that the OT is composed of various hypothetical, ideal genres of literature and speech, but rather the texts are analyzed to determine their place in the history of the transmission of material and their relationship to the sociocultural factors which shaped them. As generally practiced today, OT form-critical analysis can be divided into four steps: the analysis of the structure, the determination of the genre, the elucidation of the setting, and the description of the intention or purpose of the genre and the specific text. The steps are interrelated and interdependent; none is sufficient without the others. However, there is a logic in the sequence as described; the movement from structure to genre to setting to intention corresponds roughly to a movement from description and analysis to classification and reconstruction.

a) The first step in the analysis of the *structure* of a text is the determination of the unit. A book of the OT usually will consist of a great variety of types of expression, which in many cases are simply juxtaposed. One must ask, What is the appropriate unit for analysis and interpretation? It has long been recognized that the divisions into chapters and verses—and often also into books—seldom correspond to divisions according to sense or genre, so they must be ignored. In the past, the determination of the unit often carried with it the assumption that one had thereby uncovered an original unit of the oral tradition. But that can no longer be taken for granted. Units may represent original elements of oral or written tradition, various stages in compilation or composition, or even chapters or paragraphs of written works. *See* REDACTION CRITICISM, OT[S]; TRADITION CRITICISM, OT[S].

Units can and should be recognized at various levels, from the smallest to the largest. For example, the entire book of Genesis is a unit in a much larger composition, but the book of Exodus is not a unit. It has been argued that the larger unit to which the book of Genesis belongs must be defined variously as PENTATEUCH, tetrateuch, or HEXATEUCH, depending on the different stages of composition. Or at one level, Isa. 1:2-26 appears to be a unit, but as such it is the systematic composition by a redactor of five originally independent speeches attributed to the prophet.

Seldom are the units designated as such in the OT, but there often are indirect yet clear indications of beginnings and endings. Some such indications are the introductory and concluding formulas for speeches or stories and changes in speaker, addressee, tense, mood, or even subject matter. Furthermore, once the more or less typical patterns of different genres have been recognized, such outlines can be employed as aids to recognizing units. For example, stories will be structured according to plot. Once the unit has been established, it should then be outlined according to the structure, that is, the formal elements—including formulas—which compose it.

b) The identification of texts according to *genre* (*Gattung* or type) aims at finding the most appropriate and specific category by which the unit is to be understood. It involves analysis, comparison, and classification. The procedure may move from very broad to more precise observations. For example, to identify a segment of material as a prophetic speech is only to begin understanding it generically. Is it a prophecy of punishment or salvation, a woe speech, or an admonition?

Comparison of the unit with other examples of the genre will reveal which elements are constant (the formal elements) and which are variable. For instance, all the OT reports of a call, whether of prophets or of leaders, have many elements in common, but it has been argued that they should be subdivided into two categories depending upon the kind of experience described. And of course every example has its distinctive features. In fact, the comparison with other examples of the genre begins to place in sharp focus the particular elements and concerns of each text.

It will be recognized that some genres are more formalized than others. Seldom do the OT poetic genres follow rigid patterns of meter, but the dirge or *qina* always has a distinctive three-plus-two meter. *See* POETRY, HEBREW §D.

c) The designation of texts according to genre leads directly to conclusions concerning their *setting*. This step in form-critical analysis has developed from Gunkel's observation that every genre belonged to a distinct side of the life of the people of Israel. Setting in this sense does not refer to the date of the composition of the text; that is the concern of SOURCE CRITICISM as such. Nor does it refer necessarily, as we have seen above, to a particular institutional location in the narrow sense, for example to a specific service of worship or to the functions of a specific office, but rather to whatever sociocultural factors contributed to or determined the shape of the genre and the specific instance of it.

Since we know far less about the society of ancient Israel than we do about our own, such decisive factors in the text's background must be reconstructed or re-enacted. Often the texts contain allusions to the activities of which they were a part, but more often they give only subtle allusions to the side of the communal life to which they belonged. Furthermore, the mood or tone of the genre helps to reveal the setting, as does its intention or purpose.

Seldom can a genre be related simply and directly to a single setting in life. More often than not various factors have shaped it through a long history. Moreover, in many cases texts which originated in one context have been adapted or modified in another. For example, the prophets employed genres from virtually every side of Israel's life, and laws which may once have been used in the legal process have been embedded in cultic materials.

d) The final step in a form-critical analysis is to determine the *intention* of a genre and of the particular example of it. Just as the conventions of language, literature, and speech arise in particular social contexts, likewise each genre serves a particular intention, function, or purpose. The focus of attention here is not on the intention in the mind of a particular writer or speaker but, as in the case of setting, on the social context. In the consideration of a genre's intention, the audience or hearers are equally as important as the writers and thinkers. Some types of narrative were meant to edify, others to entertain, and others to explain the meaning of present realities by accounting for their origins. Some genres establish the law, either as divine or human regulations, while others were designed to make the law effective by forming in the hearer an attitude of obedience.

It is possible to agree on the structure and even setting of a particular genre, but still disagree about its intention. For example, there is general consensus concerning the main contours of the prophecy of punishment (also called the prophetic judgment speech), but was its intention to activate divine judgment, given the Israelite understanding of the power of the prophetic word to change history, or was it to bring about repentance, and thus avert the doom announced by the prophet? In the determination of such issues many factors in addition to those mentioned above must be considered, including the mood, tone, and literary subtleties of the material. For instance, in Amos 4:4-5 the prophet issues a call to worship, but the irony of the expression reveals that the text does not intend to initiate worship, but rather to criticize it. Thus it is necessary to distinguish between the intention of genres in general and of the particular examples or uses of them.

So the form-critical question concerning intention speaks directly, if not always definitively and decisively, to the central issue of exegesis, namely, what does the text mean to say? This raises the question of the relationship between form and content. Form criticism often has been accused of neglecting the latter for the former. While the allegation may be justified in some instances, in principle it is unfounded. Form criticism has only insisted that the form (seen as both structure and genre) of texts is as fundamental to their interpretation as content. The two are always interrelated, and it must be insisted that mere formed language alone does not constitute a genre. On the one hand, structure and genre will limit—if not determine—content which can be communicated. On the other hand, the content will shape the selection of structure and genre. For example, the dirge is hardly an adequate vehicle for communicating the content and sentiments usually associated with a love song.

4. Gains and implications. Form criticism has made and continues to make significant contributions to the interpretation of the OT. These contributions are perhaps most obvious in the case of the Psalms, where a previous concern with date and authorship has been supplemented by the interest in classifying the various psalms into hymns, songs of thanksgiving, laments, complaints of the individual and the community, and others. On the basis of this classification the reader begins to hear voices as they were raised in the worship of the temple and on other occasions, and therefore is better able to identify with the literature. And the understanding of the prophetic books has been deepened, primarily by the recognition of the distinct units of speech and narrative which they contain and by the recognition of the major genres of prophetic address. Many OT narratives have been recognized for what they are, not history in the modern sense at all, but folk and family stories, legends with distinct religious purposes, and other types. Perspectives have also been opened up on the wisdom literature, though in this case the question of setting remains quite problematic. All these results have definite implications for the historian of ancient Israel, the historian of Israelite religion, and the biblical theologian.

Above all, form criticism contributes to the task of relating the OT texts to the life of the people who produced them. Primarily as a result of form-critical work, interpreters are no longer satisfied simply to link texts to particular creative individuals—though there were many—but must take account of the decisive contributions of the community of Israel, understood both historically and sociologically. Form criticism thus militates against an individualistic in favor of a communal interpretation of the OT. The life which flows through the OT is not simply that of a genius or two, but of a large company of men and women of faith and without faith; not just prophets, but their disciples and their detractors; not simply historians and novelists, but families and clans and groups which told and heard and retold the stories we find before us.

Bibliography. K. Koch, *The Growth of the Biblical Tradition* (1969), the most extensive intro. to the method available, including the application of the procedure to both OT and NT texts; see the 3rd Ger. ed., *Was Ist Formgeschichte?* (1974) for an extensive discussion of the relationship between form criticism and linguistics (pp. 289-342); G. M. Tucker, *Form Criticism of the OT* (1971), a student's intro. to the method, updated in part by the present article; J. H. Hayes, *OT Form Criticism,* Trinity University Monograph Series in Religion, II (1974), an important collection of essays which list the major bibliog. in the discipline and discuss major trends and results according to different types of literature; R. Knierim, "OT Form Criticism Reconsidered," *Int.*, XXVII (1973), 435-68, an excellent treatment of the present status of methodological reflection; *see also* the other articles in *Int.*, XXVII (1973) for applications of the method to various types of OT literature; W. Richter, *Exegese als Literaturwissenschaft; Entwurf einer alttestamentlichen Literaturtheorie und Methodologie* (1971), and W. Richter, "Formgeschichte und Sprachwissenschaft," *ZAW*, LXXXII (1970), 216-25, a distinctive approach to form criticism which links the method to certain developments in linguistics; E. Güttgemanns, *Offene Fragen zur Formgeschichte des Evangeliums* (1970), an important work for OT as well as NT form criticism; A. Ohler, *Gattungen im AT: Ein Biblisches Arbeitsbuch,* 2 vols. (1972-73), a summary of the major genres of the OT; D. A. Knight, "The Understanding of 'Sitz im Leben' in Form Criticism," *SBL Seminar Papers,* I (1974), 105-25, proposes to replace the concept of *Sitz im Leben* with that of matrix; J. Muilenburg, "Form Criticism and Beyond," *JBL*, LXXXVIII (1969), 1-18, argues that form criticism must be supplemented with a concern for the rhetorical, stylistic features of texts; D. Greenwood, "Rhetorical Criticism and Formgeschichte: Some Methodological Considerations," *JBL*, LXXXIX (1970), 418-26; R. Lapointe, "La Valeur Linguistique du Sitz im Leben," *Bibl.*, LII (1971), 469-87; H. W. Hoffman, "Form-Funktion-Intention," *ZAW*, LXXXII (1970), 341-46; W. G. Doty, "The Concept of Genre in Literary Analysis," *SBL Proceedings,* II (1972) 413-48; D. A. Knight, *Rediscovering the Traditions of Israel, SBLDS,* IX (1973), considers the relationship between form criticism and traditio-historical research; H. Gunkel, "Die Israelitische Literatur," in *Die Kultur der Gegenwart,* I/VII (1925 [repr. 1963]); H. Gunkel, *The Legends of Genesis* (1901 [repr. 1964]); W. Klatt, *Hermann Gunkel: Zu Seiner Theologie der Religionsgeschichte und zur Entstehung der formgeschichtlichen Methode, FRLANT,* C (1969), includes a treatment of Gunkel's contributions to the form-critical method; K. H. Bernhardt, *Die Gattungsgeschichtliche Forschung am AT als exegetische Methode* (1959).

G. M. TUCKER

***FORM CRITICISM, NT.** The form-critical study of the NT has recently developed in many ways, including the refinement and proliferation of categories, both within and outside the gospels.

1. Form criticism of the gospels. While it is still recognized, with Dibelius, that the gospels are neither histories nor biographies, there is a growing tendency to accept as at least roughly parallel a variety of Hellenistic forms, especially "lives" of the philosophers (*see* GOSPEL, GENRE[S]). Major stress is laid, however, on the smaller units comprising the gospels (form criticism) and on the literary and theological tendencies of the individual writers (*see* REDACTION CRITICISM, NT[S]) rather than on the formal analysis of the gospels as literary wholes.

One important example of greater refinement within the categories used in the synoptic tradition is the "sentence of holy law" (Käsemann). Such sentences, first attested by Paul but clearly antecedent to him (I Cor. 3:17; 14:38) and reflected in various strata of the NT (often in attenuated form, Rom. 2:12; II Cor. 9:6; Rev. 22:18-19; Mark 8:38; Matt. 10:32-33; Mark 4:24; Matt. 5:19) show that eschatological judgment (God's action) may be solemnly pronounced (sometimes by repetition of the same verb) in terms reminiscent of the offense committed (the person's action). Though later forms of these sentences may be gnomic or parenetic, the original intention shows through: Christian prophets, speaking in the name of the risen Lord, combine charismatic activity and law—in the earliest days of the church. The existence of any such fixed forms and the possibility of deducing a prophetic-enthusiastic setting for them have been vigorously disputed (Berger). *See* SAYINGS OF JESUS, FORM OF[S].

While other similar refinements could be cited, Bultmann's form-critical categories within the synoptic tradition still predominate. Doty's useful suggestions for the Fourth Gospel (hymnic materials; editorial remarks; descriptive narrative; sayings of Jesus; dialogues; signific narratives; OT allusions and quotations; and theological discourses) have not been widely accepted, though no good alternatives have been offered.

2. Form criticism outside the gospels. Greater advances have been made in the analysis of non-gospel NT materials. To be included here are acclamations, doxological statements, confessions, hymns, sermons, and different kinds of parenetic materials.

The "acclamation" is known primarily from the Pauline corpus (I Cor. 12:3; Rom. 10:9; Phil. 2:11; cf. also Acts 19:28, 34 with Rev. 7:10), but it lies behind materials scattered throughout the NT, both as brief liturgical expressions common to Jewish worship (Amen: I Cor. 14:16; Rev. 1:6; 5:14; 22:20; Eph. 3:21; Phil. 4:20; Hallelujah: Rev. 19:1, 3, 4, 6) and specifically Christian terms and phrases (MARANATHA: I Cor. 16:22; Did. 10:6; LORD [Kyrios]: Rom. 10:9; I Cor. 12:3; Phil. 2:11; "Worthy . . ." [ἄξιος εἶ; ἄξιός ἐστιν]: Rev. 4:11; 5:9, 12).

Epistolary greetings and doxological materials seem to rest on (partially Hellenized) Jewish practice (Deichgräber; Pss. Sol. 17:3; Enoch 22:14; 36:4; 39:9-13; 81:3; 84:1-3; Tob. 13:18; Prayer Man. 15*b*; 1QH 2.30, 31; 4.5; 5.20; 7.6-7; 10.14-15; 14.23; 16.8; 17.20), modified by the christological and ecclesiastical beliefs of the primitive church ("Thanks be to God": Rom. 7:25; I Cor. 15:57; II Cor. 2:14; 8:16; *see also* Luke 2:14; Gal. 1:5; Eph. 3:20-21; Did. 9:2-3; I Clem. 38:4). Praises may be offered to God (Rom. 11:33-36; Eph. 3:20-21; I Pet. 5:11; Rev. 7:12; 11:17), to Christ (II Pet. 3:18; Rev. 1:5-6; Mart. Polyc. 21), or to both (Rev. 5:13; 7:10; I Clem. 65:2). Quite advanced stages of liturgical development are sometimes reflected (II Pet. 3:18; I Clem. 61:3; 64; Mart. Polyc. 14:3 and, in a different way, I Tim. 6:15-16; Rev. 7:12). In these instances the influence of the worshiping community on its liturgical forms and literary deposits is clear.

The confessional materials are far more complex. Here too a Jewish base is evident, but the church's growth has influenced both the terms and the concepts used. The differentiation of the one true God from idols (I Thess. 1:9-10) is, as in Judaism, important, its polemic against the "many 'gods' and many 'lords'" of Hellenism (I Cor. 8:5-6) self-evident. And the basic Christian teachings, some of which perhaps formed patterns of catechesis rather than confessional materials as such, show some formal similarity with the usages of Hellenistic Judaism (cf. Rom. 1:3-4; II Tim. 2:8; Heb. 6:1; I Pet. 3:18-22; Ign. Eph. 18:2; Trall. 9:1-2; Smyr. 1:1-2). Essentially, however, Christian confessions are concerned with Jesus and with the saving events of his ministry; that Jesus is the MESSIAH, the CHRIST (cf. Mark 8:27 ff. with John 1:20; *see also* I John 2:22; 5:1; Acts 9:22; 18:5, 28), or SON OF GOD (Matt. 16:16; John 1:34; I John 4:15; cf. Acts 8:37 [RSV n.] as well as Acts 9:20; Heb. 4:14), or, in Hellenistic terms, that Jesus is Lord (Rom. 10:9; I Cor. 12:3; Phil. 2:11; cf. Acts 11:20 and contrast the pagan creed, "Caesar is Lord" [κύριος καῖσαρ] in Mart. Polyc. 8:2) is the fundamental affirmation required of converts. It is possible, though unproven, that confessions in the technical sense began at the junction of Jewish and Hellenistic Christianity with the affirmation that the Messiah is the Lord (Χριστὸς Κύριος; Luke 2:11; cf. Acts 2:36). Other early creedal affirmations connect various christological titles with the Crucifixion and the Resurrection (Acts 2:36; Luke 24:25 ff., 46 [Χριστός]; the "passion predictions" in Mark 8:31; 9:31; 10:33-34 [the SON OF MAN]; in Rom. 10:9-10 the Resurrection has become a second item of belief; cf. also I Cor. 15:3-8). That the most primitive Christology connected Jesus with the PAROUSIA and conceived of him as merely "Messiah designate" until that time (J. A. T. Robinson) is highly unlikely. Primitive Christian controversy (I John 2:22; 4:3—note the variant λύει, a conative present?; II John 7; John 17:3; Acts 4:9-12), preaching (II Cor. 4:5; Acts 5:42; 17:3; 18:5; II Tim. 2:8; Heb. 4:14; 10:23), and catechesis (Luke 24:45 ff.; Acts 17:2-3; 18:5, 28; 26:22-23) contributed significantly to the way various early creedal statements were elaborated.

The hymnic element in the NT is particularly important. It is now generally recognized that (*a*) the use of hymns in Christian worship (Acts 16:25; I Cor. 14:15, 26; Col. 3:16; Eph. 5:19; cf. the formal liturgical setting in Rev. 4, 5 and the examples in Rev. 15:3-4; 19:5, 6-8) antedates all NT documents; and (*b*) while the origin of specifically christological hymns may well lie on the fringes of early Christianity in Hellenized Jewish-Christian or Gnosticizing circles, deposits of hymnic materials—either fragments or brief hymns as a whole—are reflected in many strata of the canonical as well as the postcanonical literature. The hymns in the birth stories (Luke 1:14-17, 46-55, 68-79; 2:29-32 [35]) may have been composed by the evangelist himself, though they could also reflect pre-Lukan (Baptist? Jewish? Jewish-Christian?) sources (Laurentin). But several passages in the rest of the NT are widely regarded as having originated (in some form) *before* the composition of the documents in which they are now found. Such passages are characterized by some or all of the following: (*a*) an introductory demonstrative or relative pronoun, often followed by participial clauses (Eph. 2:14 ff.; Col. 1:15-20; I Tim. 3:16; Heb. 1:3; I Pet. 1:3 ff.); (*b*) rhythm, brevity, sonorous language, and a spirit of exultation or ardor (Matt. 11:25 ff.; Luke 10:21-22 [Q]; Rev. 11:17-18; Eph. 2:4-7); (*c*) balanced strophes or clauses (Col. 1:15-20; I Pet. 3:18-19; I Tim. 3:16; Rev. 11:17-18); and (*d*) a pattern related in some way to the coming, ministry, exaltation, and heavenly enthronement of Jesus (I Pet. 3:18-19; Heb. 1:3; Phil. 2:6-11 [whether in two stanzas—descent/ascent—or three—pre-existence/earthly life/exaltation]) and arranged chronologically; this is probably not true in I Tim. 3:16). Note, however, that: (*a*) the line between hymns and confessions is impossible to draw; (*b*) John 1:1-12[13](18?) is clearly poetic, though many of the above criteria are missing; hence a different, possibly non-Christian, origin must be postulated for the hymn proper; (*c*) conversely, Col. 1:15-20 meets practically all of the above criteria but also has so little specifically Christian content that we must similarly postulate a non-Christian origin for the basic hymn. In sum, we must recognize that both the literary forms and the specific content of some NT hymns rest on various kinds of non-Christian antecedents, although they have been thoroughly Christianized.

Examples of early Christian preaching are rare and of uncertain significance. The sermons of Acts, which may be roughly divided into two types, depending on whether the hearers are Jewish or Gentile (Wilckens), are almost certainly compositions based on models from the worship of the author's own time, though the similarities between Acts 7, 13 and Heb. 11 suggest at least a tradition of sermons about "faithful witnesses and unfaithful people." The structure of some Pauline letters (I Thessalonians, Romans, Galatians; cf. Colossians, Ephesians) may also reflect early sermonic practice.

Parenetic materials of many kinds are found scattered in almost all levels of the NT (*see* PARENESIS[S]). Some (I Pet. 1:3-5; 2:22-25; 3:18-22; 5:5-9; less probably, Heb. 13:1-17 and the book of James) may well rest on prebaptismal catechetical practice. Others, like the list of vices and virtues (Rom. 1:28-31; Gal. 5:19-23) condemned or commended, reflect no fixed form, but rest on a wide variety of (largely Hellenized, yet predominantly Jewish) antecedents. A probable exception is the master/slave, husband/wife, parent/child triad in the *Haustafeln* (*see* HAUSTAFEL [S]) in I Pet. 2:13–3:7; Eph. 5:21–6:9; Col. 3:18–4:1. The admonitions to church officers (*see* esp. the Pastoral epistles) reflect the institutional needs of the developing church, not fixed cultural forms.

Finally, form-critical methods have made possible some separation of tradition and redaction in Acts. *See* ACTS OF THE APOSTLES[S].

3. Critique of form criticism. Reservations about the theory and practice of form criticism have been expressed from its beginnings. The earlier critique tended to agree that the method is "in the strict sense applicable only to the Synoptic gospels" (Fascher) and to object to the form-critical analysis of the gospels on the following grounds, among others: (*a*) the proposed "forms" were neither so widespread nor so pure as proponents of the study insisted; (*b*) the relationship between literary form and theological use was oversimplified; (*c*) an "antisupernaturalistic bias" was more significant than formal analysis in predetermining form-critical judgments about the authenticity of materials; and (*d*) the whole notion of a "community product" is *a priori* implausible and incompatible with the unity and power of the concepts lying behind the materials of all categories, which point toward a single creative mind.

Objections (*b*) and (*c*) are less common today, as it is generally recognized that liturgical, catechetical, and missionary use do affect the forms by which the tradition is passed on, while (*d*) is seen to rest on a misunderstanding: "community product" means composed (or modified) so as to serve the interests of a specific community and reflecting the theological interests of the author's tradition, not "written by a committee."

But more serious objections are added in terms of anthropological and sociological categories, themselves not yet fully worked out. The Parry-Lord study of Yugoslav songs, it is held, shows that (*a*) oral materials are always modified to suit the interests of both the teller and the audience (a confirmation of a basic form-critical insight), which makes the prehistory and authenticity of particular materials very difficult to judge; (*b*) there is a fundamental difference between oral and written materials, so that small collections of written materials before the gospels (as posited by many form critics) would have served little purpose (Güttgemanns); and (*c*) nonliterary (i.e., oral) forms may owe much to the internal habits ("deep structure") of the human psyche, so that we must broaden the cultural and anthropological base of the materials studied (Güttgemanns and a variety of "structuralists"). *See* TRADITION, ORAL [S]; LITERATURE, BIBLE AS[S] §4*a*.

While the need for a broader history-of-religions base may be freely granted, it is apparent that "deep structure" is an extraordinarily elusive and questionable concept, and that the materials from the Near East at the beginning of our era must provide most of the form-critical base (Koester). Further, nothing in the Parry-Lord hypothesis renders impossible or even improbable a gradual transition from oral to written forms, while patient literary analysis (redaction criticism) makes it evident that not only Mark (Kuhn, Carlston) and Q (Hoffmann, Lührmann, Schulz) but perhaps even some of their (written) sources had a prehistory.

See also LITURGICAL MATERIALS, NT[S].

Bibliography. General: W. G. Doty, "The Discipline and Literature of NT Form Criticism," *ATR*, LI (1969), 257-321, very extensive bibliog. with critical comments; G. Bornkamm, "Formen und Gattungen. II. Im NT," *RGG*, II (3rd ed., 1958), cols. 999-1005; H. Conzelmann, "Formen und Gattungen: II. Im NT," *EKL*, I (1956), cols. 1310-15; E. Käsemann, "Liturgische Formeln im NT," *RGG*, II (3rd ed., 1958), cols. 993-96.

On form criticism of the gospels: K. Berger, "Zu den sogenannten Sätzen Heiligen Rechts," *NTS*, XVII (1970/71), 10-40; G. Bornkamm, "Evangelien, formgeschichtlich," *RGG*, II (3rd ed., 1958), cols. 749-53; M. Dibelius, "Zur Formgeschichte des Evangeliums," *Theol. Rundschau*, NF I (1929), 185-216; E. Käsemann, "Sentences of Holy Law in the NT," *NT Questions of Today* (1969), pp. 66-81.

On form criticism outside the gospels: M. E. Boismard, *Quatre hymnes baptismales dans le première épître de Pierre*, Lectio divina, XXX (1961); H. Conzelmann, *Die Apostelgeschichte*, HNT, VII (1963); R. Deichgräber, *Gotteshymnus und Christushymnus in der frühen Christenheit*, SUNT, X (1967); M. Dibelius, "Zur Formgeschichte des NT (ausserhalb der Evangelien)," *Theol. Rundschau*, NF III (1931), 207-42, and *Studies in the Acts of the Apostles* (1951); E. Haenchen, *The Acts of the Apostles* (14th ed., 1965); R. Laurentin, *Structure et théologie de Luc I-II, EB* (1957); V. H. Neufeld, *The Earliest Christian Confessions*, NTTS, V (1963); J. A. T. Robinson, "The Most Primitive Christology of All?" *Twelve NT Studies*, SBT, XXXIV (1956), 139-53; J. T. Sanders, *The NT Christological Hymns: Their Historical Religious Background*, NTSMS, XV (1971);

U. Wilckens, *Die Missionsreden der Apostelgeschichte,* WMANT, V (2nd ed., 1963).

Earlier critiques of form criticism: P. Benoit, "Reflections on 'Formgeschichtliche Methode,'" *Jesus and the Gospel,* I (1961), 11-45; B. S. Easton, *The Gospel before the Gospels* (1928); E. Fascher, *Die formgeschichtliche Methode,* BZNW, II (1924); X. Léon-Dufour, "Formgeschichte et Redaktionsgeschichte des Évangiles synoptiques," *RSR,* XLVI, (1958), 237-69; L. J. McGinley, *Form-Criticism of the Synoptic Healing Narratives* (1944); E. B. Redlich, *Form Criticism, Its Value and Limitations* (2nd ed., 1948).

More recent critiques of form criticism: C. E. Carlston, *The Parables of the Triple Tradition* (1975); E. Güttgemanns, *Offene Fragen zur Formgeschichte des Evangeliums,* BEvT, LIV (1970); P. Hoffmann, *Studien zur Theologie der Logienquelle,* NTAbh, VIII (1972); A. Jolles, *Einfache Formen . . . ,* (3rd ed., 1965); H. Koester, "One Jesus and Four Primitive Gospels," in J. M. Robinson and H. Koester, *Trajectories through Early Christianity* (1971), pp. 158-204; H. W. Kuhn, *Ältere Sammlungen im Markusevangelium,* SUNT, VIII (1971); A. B. Lord, *The Singer of Tales* (1960); D. Lührmann, *Die Redaktion der Logienquelle,* WMANT, XXXIII (1969); G. Schille, "Der Mangel eines kritischen Geschichtsbildes in der neutestamentlichen Formgeschichte," *TLZ,* LXXXVIII, (1963), cols. 491-502; S. Schulz, *Q: Die Spruchquelle der Evangelisten* (1972); Jan Vansina, *Oral Tradition: A Study in Historical Methodology* (1961). C. E. CARLSTON

FORTRESSES, HERODIAN. *See* HERODIAN FORTRESSES[S].

***FRIEND, FRIENDSHIP IN THE NT.** "Friend," "friendship" appear about thirty times in the NT. Half these occurrences are in Luke.

1. Jewish and Greek models. Josephus indicates that the Essenes were noted for the way in which they had all things in common and, of all Jewish groups, they had most consistently practiced mutual friendship (War II.viii.2 ff.). The willingness to give up everything for the sake of the other indicates that no other group had so fully, outside of marriage, carried out the Pythagorean mandate of community of goods. Epicurus rejected it because it implied mutual distrust and "without confidence there is no friendship" (Diogenes Laertius X, 11). In spite of this, it was the Epicureans who more than anyone else praised friendship, for "he who is noble makes wisdom and friendship his first concern; of these wisdom is a mortal good, but friendship immortal" (*Vatican Sayings* 78). To Epicurus is attributed the statement: "Friendship dances across the world calling on us to awake and praise our happy life" (*Vatican Sayings* 52), and these words of praise were backed up by his own success in founding a new family in a world where the traditional frameworks of city and family were disappearing.

2. Jesus as friend. Jesus is described as a "friend" of sinners and tax collectors (Matt. 11:19; Luke 7:34) because he associates with them. It is indicative of Jesus' association with people who were outsiders (*see* TEACHING OF JESUS[S] §3*b*). The disciples, however, can also be called "friends" of Jesus (Luke 12:4). In John 15:13 ff. the three ideas of loving one another as Jesus loved his disciples, laying down one's life for friends, and following that which Jesus has bid his disciples do are closely related. The disciples will be called "friends" rather than "slaves" (RSV "servants") because they have been informed of all things from God the Father (John 15:15). Jesus not only tells his disciples about union with him, he actually imparts it. The friends here are those who are bound together by *agape;* they are his friends by choice, and the friendship is sealed by his act of laying down his life for them (John 15:16). Through Christ's supreme act of *agape,* they are being incorporated with him into the *agape* of God.

3. The new Christian model. The disciples are called "friends" of Jesus but never "friends" of God, even though this traditional Jewish description of Abraham does appear in Jas. 2:23. In Acts pagan dignitaries are once referred to as Paul's friends (19:31), and the term appears again as a general category to describe Christians (Acts 27:3). In III John 15 the writer sends greetings to "friends," apparently using that term instead of "brothers" or "saints." But by and large, the term "brothers" crowds out the term "friend" in early Christian usage, perhaps because of its greater inwardness and warmth. It is only among the Gnostics that the term "friends" seems to be preferred.

The new Christian model is clearest in the letters of Paul where each associate is regarded as a co-laborer sharing a common task; all are equal under the lordship of Christ. A sense of mission and the conviction that each is bound to his brother as a fellow member of the body of Christ pervades the early Christian self-understanding. Indirectly, then, the Stoic model of human relationships is rejected in favor of a model similar to that found in the Greek mystery religions and at Qumran. Friendship is not rejected, but rather deepened: each member of the church shares with the others a common life. The fellow Christian is the brother for whom Christ died (Rom. 14:15).

Bibliography. G. A. Panichas, *Epicurus* (1967); H. C. Baldry, *The Unity of Mankind in Greek Thought* (1965); A. J. Festugière, *Epicurus and His Gods* (1946); A. Harnack, *Mission and Expansion of Christianity,* I (2nd ed., 1906), 419-21; H. Clay Trumbull, *Friendship, The Master-Passion* (1892); G. Stählin, "φιλέω," *TDNT,* IX (1973), 113-69. W. KLASSEN

FUTURE LIFE IN INTERTESTAMENTAL LITERATURE. According to different anthropologies and eschatologies, the future life begins during this life, immediately upon death, or after a resurrection.

1. Presuppositions. The presuppositions for this complex of beliefs are twofold. (1) Yahweh is a God of justice who rewards the righteous and punishes the wicked. (2) His power to execute this justice transcends even death. As Lord of life and death (Deut. 32:39; I Sam. 2:6), he brings back from the gates of Sheol those who are seriously ill or in grave danger (Ps. 30:1-3 [H 30:2-4]; Hos. 6:1-2; Jonah 2:2-9 [H 2:3-10]), and on rare occasions he has raised the dead (I Kings 17:17-22; II Kings 4:18-37). ENOCH and ELIJAH escaped death when he "took" them to himself (Gen. 5:24; II Kings 2:6-12).

2. Function: the enactment of God's justice. The first personal confessions of the belief that Yahweh's justice transcends physical death appear, though not without ambiguity, in the Isaianic apocalypse (Isa. 24–27) and in Ps. 73. When Yahweh comes forth from his place to judge (Isa. 26:20-21), the oppressed righteous will arise from the dust of death (26:19), while their dead overlords will remain in Sheol (26:13-14; *see* DEAD, ABODE OF THE). The psalmist reflects on the prosperity of the wicked and his own suffering (Ps. 73:2-14), but in spite of these inequities, he affirms divine justice, contrasting the coming destruction of the wicked with the reward that awaits him when his God "receives" him to glory (לקח, 73:24; cf. Gen. 5:24; II Kings 2:3).

The problem of affirming God's justice and omnipotence becomes particularly acute during Antiochus Epiphanes' persecution (167 B.C.) (*see* ANTIOCHUS §4). Not only are the righteous not receiving the just reward for their faithfulness to TORAH, and the wicked the deserved punishment for their apostasy; but, just the contrary, the righteous are being put to death because of their piety, and the apostates are escaping because of their faithlessness—a sheer confounding of all biblical canons of divine justice. The hasidic authors of this time (*see* HASIDEANS §2) solve the resultant crisis in faith by asserting that God's justice transcends death.

An early tradition, at least from the time of Antiochus, is preserved in Wisd. Sol. 2–5. It conflates the last Servant Song (Isa. 52:13–53:12) with Isaiah's taunt against the king of Babylon (ch. 14), identifying the persecuted leaders of the community with the servant and their persecutor with the king whose demon tries to seize God's throne and is cast down to Sheol. The conflate tradition is read as a postmortem judgment scene in which the Servant, now gloriously exalted to power in the heavenly courtroom, confronts his former persecutor and condemns him.

Dan. 10–12 describes the events culminating in the persecution and announces an imminent judgment (11:45–12:3). Antiochus, who has attempted to storm heaven (11:36; cf. 8:10-11), will be struck down (11:45; cf. 8:25). The righteous Jews who are still alive will be delivered (12:1), and the dead principals of the Hellenistic-hasidic controversy will be raised from Sheol, "the land of dust" (12:2, Goodspeed). The righteous will be vindicated for their faithfulness ("everlasting life") and the apostates punished for their faithlessness ("everlasting contempt"). The hasidic leaders, cast in the role of the Servant (12:3; cf. Isa. 52:13; 53:11), will be elevated to heaven, not to judge (this is Michael's function, Dan. 12:1), but to receive the special honor due their position. They will shine in glory forever. The author of Jub. 23:11-32, a contemporary of "Daniel," also posits an imminent judgment as the solution for the troubles of his time. The spirits of the righteous will have "much joy," and their enemies will be cursed (vss. 30-31).

The theme of the righteous person(s) condemned to death for faithfulness to Torah, but rescued, exalted, and vindicated, is embodied in narrative form in the old tales preserved in Dan. 3 and 6. The same theme (minus the exaltation) occurs in the story of the seven brothers and their mother, which is set in Antiochian times (II Macc. 7). The brothers, condemned in a human court and put to death because of their faithfulness to Torah, will be raised from the dead and thus vindicated by the divine judge. Significantly different from the Daniel stories where the heroes are rescued at the brink of death, here the brothers are rescued and vindicated in spite of and after death. Their mother, cast in the image of Second Isaiah's Mother Zion, awaits the restoration of her sons in the resurrection, when the Creator will re-create and thus redeem his servants.

Quite probably reflecting conditions in Palestine *ca.* 100 B.C., Enoch 92–105 depicts the oppression of the poor ("the righteous") by the rich ("the sinners"). Chs. 102:4–104:8 constitute a disputation in which the author contests the Deuteronomic view of divine justice. One's lot in this life is no index of piety. After death the tables will be turned. The righteous will receive the reward denied them in this life, and the sinners, who have prospered in this life, will be punished.

In the texts cited, immortality and its equivalents function as an essential part of the divine adjudication of the inequities of this life. Elsewhere, eternal life and eternal destruction function as the appropriate REWARD and punishment of the righteous and the sinners regardless of whether or not they were rewarded or punished during their lifetimes (Pss. Sol. 3:11-12; 13:11; 14:9-10; 15:12-13; Sib.Or. IV, 176-91; II Esd. 7:32-37; Test. Benj. 10:6-9; *LAB* 3:10; Test. Abr. 11-13, Recension A [8-11, Rec. B]). As the focus moves away from the narrower contexts of persecution and oppression, the tendency is toward a universal judgment (and resurrection).

This reward and punishment function occurs in the theology of the two ways, which is rooted in the biblical covenant theology, where the blessings and curses are spelled out as "life" and "death" (Deut. 30:15-19; cf. Jer. 21:8). This theology is often carried in a variation of the covenant form: (1) Prologue=Creation; (2) the deeds comprising the two ways and the blessings and curses; (3) an eschatological section=God's visitation of the earth or the annihilation of evil. Examples of this form include: 1QS 3:13–4:26; the Testament of Asher (a reworking of Ps. 73, a "Two Way" psalm, and Ps. 74); Wisd. Sol. 1–5; the Mandates of HERMAS; Barn. 18–20. Life and death are here construed, at least in part, as eternal life and eternal destruction (cf. also Pss. Sol. 3, 13, 14, 15). The Testament of Abraham describes the two ways and the gates leading to them (11, Recension A [8-9, Rec. B]).

3. Time and mode. The texts differ in their understanding of the time and mode of recompense after death, according to their specific conceptions of what constitutes the person (body, soul, spirit, body and soul, etc.).

In Jub. 23:31, the "spirits" of the righteous will experience much joy (in heaven), while their bones will rest in the earth. According to Enoch 102:4–103:8, the "spirits" or "souls" (the texts disagree) of the righteous (see 102:5 for the anthropological dichotomy) "will come to life" (103:4) and, evidently, ascend to heaven (cf. 104:1-5), while the souls or spirits of the sinners will burn in Sheol. According to Test. Asher 6:4-6 and Test. Abr. 11-13, Recension A (8-11, Rec. B), the *soul* goes to its eternal destiny at the time of death. For the Wisdom of Solomon, "death" is that power which the wicked summon to themselves while still in this life (1:12, 16), while "immortality" (1:15; 2:23; 3:4) belongs to the righteous. Their souls are in the hand of God, and physical death is in reality the passing of their souls to the fruition of their immortality (3:1-4). A similar view occurs in IV Maccabees (*passim*), which rewrites II Macc. 7, consistently eliminating the references to bodily resurrection and stressing the immortality and incorruptibility of the soul. The heavy influence of Greek thought is evident in the Wisdom of Solomon and IV Maccabees, although for both writings immortality is not an inherent quality of the soul, but a divine reward for righteousness. Greek influence is perhaps also present in the Testament of Asher and the Testament of Abraham (cf. Plato, Republic X.xiii ff.; Phaedo 107D–108C), but this influence is not at all obvious in Palestinian documents such as Jub. 23 and Enoch 102–103. *See* IMMORTALITY[S].

Resurrection of the body is indicated in Isa. 26:19 and probably in Dan. 12:2 and Enoch 51:1; 61:5. The most explicit references to such a resurrection occur in II Macc. 7:9, 11, 14, 23 (cf. 14:37-46), where the resurrected body is identified with the body tortured and put to death. This identification gives expression to the idea of vindication. The earthly king punishes the brothers' obedience to Torah by destroying their bodies. The cosmic King will vindicate this obedience by restoring their bodies. II Esdras combines two eschatologies. At death the soul departs from the body (7:78, 88) and experiences in a preliminary manner its appropriate reward or punishment (7:79-101). At the end of time, the bodies will be raised and presumably reunited with the souls (7:26-38), and universal judgment will follow.

The early texts witness to a variety of anthropologies, but there seems to be some trend toward bodily resurrection by the early part of the Common Era. However, with the exception of II Macc. 7 and 14 and their own peculiar formulation, the body of the resurrection is conceived of as qualitatively different from the earthly body. This difference functions at times as a constitutive part of apocalyptic conceptions of the qualitative differences between the present sinful or corrupt age and the age to come.

An interest in the intermediate state is rarely evident in the texts, but the references in Dan. 12:2 to "those who sleep" and in Enoch 102–103 to the righteous who "grieve" in Sheol do imply such a concept. While Enoch 22:3 indicates rewards and punishments for the "spirits of the souls" of all mankind immediately upon death, it also posits a resurrection of some of the wicked and presumably of the righteous. Ideas of death and resurrection as the separation and reuniting of body and soul are rare and appear only in late texts (*LAB* 44:10; II Esd. 7:78).

4. The Dead Sea Scrolls: realized eschatology. (*See* DEAD SEA SCROLLS[S] §8; ESSENES[S] §3.) The eschatological views in the Qumran Scrolls have their own peculiar character and problems of interpretation. Two of the hymns express a highly realized eschatology. Events normally ascribed to the eschatological future are here depicted as present realities: exaltation to the eternal height and access to the angelic assembly (1QH 3.19-22); resurrection from the level of dust and worms to the divine realm and the company of the angels (1QH 11.11-14). When the sectarian enters the community, he passes from death and alienation from God to life, knowledge of God, and communion with the angels. Although a certain tension remains and he still lives in an evil world, he is nevertheless already participating in the eternal life. Whether the Qumranites nourished a belief in a future resurrection is highly doubtful. The sectarian texts normally cited as evidence for such a belief do not bear the weight of this interpretation (1QH 6.29-30, 34; cf. also 4Q ps-Dan. 4Q181 1.3-6 may be an exception). Physical death, the presupposition for such a resurrection, is scarcely mentioned in the scrolls and is evidently of little concern. The reinterpretation of eschatological conceptions and their application to one's entrance into, and existence in, the community indicates that at least the author(s) of these hymns believe that the significant eschatological event has already occurred.

The use of the concept of the two ways in 1QS 3.13–4.26 may point in the same direction. The theology of this period (MANUAL OF DISCIPLINE; HERMAS, Mandates; WISDOM OF SOLOMON) stresses the *fact* of reward and punishment, life and death, and, for the most part, is singularly elusive on the question of how and when. Somewhat parallel to the realized eschatology of the hymns, "life," "immortality," and "death" are not only ultimate destinies beyond physical death, but also permeate and characterize one's present life-style and existence (Wisd. Sol. 1:12, 15-16; 2:23; 3:4). The imagery of the "way" is suggestive of this kind of continuity: life/immortality and death in the present continue unbroken through the relatively insignificant event of physical death to their fruition. If we accept the identification of Qumranites with the ESSENES, the attribution of this viewpoint to the scrolls finds support in JOSEPHUS, who describes Essene eschatology in terms of immortality of the soul (War II.viii.11; Antiq. XVIII.i 5).

A view of realized eschatology closely approximating that in the Qumran hymns is expressed in Joseph and Asenath 8:10-11; 15:3-4, and Philo attributes such a view to the Therapeutae (*On the Contemplative Life* xiii).

5. Other views. Early tannaitic traditions generally envision a resurrection of the body within the broader context of a universal judgment. Different from most of the texts cited above, and typical of the rabbinic materials, is an explicit dependence on biblical texts, often texts that originally did not refer to a literal resurrection (e.g., Deut. 32:39; I Sam. 2:6). Similar reinterpretations occur in the Targums (and in the Greek Bible.)

Josephus' description of Pharisaic belief in resurrection of the body (War II.viii.14; Antiq. XVIII.i.3) accords well with the rabbinic texts and with the post–A.D. 70 apocalypses (the Apocalypse of Baruch [*see* BARUCH, APOCALYPSE OF] and II ESDRAS). The PSALMS OF SOLOMON, often described as Pharisaic, are vague as to the form of resurrection.

The Sadducees' denial of the resurrection (Jos. War II.viii.14; Antiq. XVIII.i.4; Mark 12:18-23; Acts 23:6-8, etc.) may reflect not only their theological conservatism, but also their high social status, which removed them from the kind of problems that spawned and nourished a hope for recompense after death (cf. Enoch 102:4–104:8 as discussed in §2 above). The silence of many texts with regard to resurrection, immortality, and eternal life must be judged contextually. Do the authors face the situations and deal with the problems that elsewhere are answered with these hopes for a life to come?

See also DEATH; DEATH, THEOLOGY OF[S]; ESCHATOLOGY OF APOC. AND PSEUDEP.; LIFE; RESURRECTION; RESURRECTION IN THE NT[S]; IMMORTALITY[S].

Bibliography. R. Martin-Achard, *From Death to Life* (1956), exegesis of the OT texts; H.-W. Kuhn, *Enderwartung und gegenwärtiges Heil,* SUNT, IV (1966), eschatology of the Qumran hymns; G. W. E. Nickelsburg, Jr., discusses the traditions, their forms and functions in *Resurrection, Immortality, and Eternal Life in Intertestamental Judaism,* HTS, XXVI (1972), and "Eschatology in the Testament of Abraham," *1972 Proceedings, Septuagint and Cognate Studies,* II, ed. R. A. Kraft (1972), 180-227; G. Stemberger, *Der Leib der Auferstehung,* AnBib, LVI (1972); H. C. C. Cavallin, *Life after Death,* Coniectanea Biblica: NT Series, VII, 1 (1974), the Jewish literary and epigraphic evidence related to I Cor. 15; B. Vawter, "Intimations of Immortality," *JBL,* XCI (1972), 158-71, possible early biblical allusions

G. W. E. NICKELSBURG, JR.

G

***GALATIANS, LETTER TO THE.** The letter written by the apostle Paul (1:1; 6:11-18) and co-senders "to the churches of Galatia" (1:2) is a carefully composed apology in epistolary form. It was prompted by the Galatians' decision to shift their allegiance away from Paul to his opponents (1:6-7). In his defense Paul argues that as Gentile believers in Christ (2:3-5; 3:2-5; 4:8; 5:2-3; 6:12-13) the Galatians have heard the "gospel" (3:2, 5) and received the Holy Spirit (3:2-3, 14; 4:6, 29; 5:5, 16-18, 22, 25; 6:1, 8) and that this is sufficient for their salvation (1:1-5; 3:26-29; 4:6-7, 31; 5:1*a*, 13*a*, 25*a;* 6:8, 15-16). The argument is directed against the theology of Jewish-Christian missionaries opposed to Paul who have nearly won over the Galatians by persuading them that they remain "sinners" (2:15-17, 21) outside of salvation, unless they accept Circumcision (2:3; 5:2-3, 6; 6:12-13, 15) and Torah (3:2, 5; 4:9-10, 21; 5:2-4, 18). Galatians constitutes one of the most important theological documents of early Christianity. Basing Christian existence radically upon the gift of the Spirit and "justification by faith" (*see* Justification §3*c*; Faith, Faithfulness, §D4; Faith, Faithfulness, NT[S]), the letter separates in principle and as far as we know, for the first time, Christianity from Judaism. Many of the points made here reappear, expanded and sometimes modified, in Romans. Historically, Gal. 1–2 is the only extant primary source of information in regard to the earliest period of Christianity.

1. The anti-Pauline opponents. The studies by Crownfield and Munck showed that the problem of precisely who Paul's Galatian opponents were had remained unsolved. Was there one type of opponent or two (Lütgert); were they Christian Jews or non-Christian Jews or Gentiles; were they resident Galatians or intruders, and if the latter, where did they come from and why? Crownfield described them as Jewish-Christian syncretists favoring circumcision for a symbolic reason. Munck held them to be not Jews but Gentiles who had recently become circumcised members of a Judaizing Christian movement in Galatia, which without connections to Jerusalem had developed as a "heresy" within Paulinism. Schmithals launched the most vigorous attack against the lingering consensus that the opponents were "Judaizers," that is, Christians who demanded the acceptance of the Jewish Torah, including circumcision, as a condition for salvation. Showing that this consensus does not match with the sources, Schmithals proposed that the opponents be regarded as (Christian or non-Christian) Jewish Gnostics (*see* Gnosticism §2; Gnosticism [S]), promoters of the ritual of circumcision, but "libertines" in regard to the moral demands of the Torah. Subsequent discussions of Schmithals' thesis led to its modification by Bornkamm, Wegenast, Koester, and Georgi, who assume that the opponents were Jewish-Christian missionaries rooted in a syncretistic brand of Asia Minor Judaism. Bronson tried to connect the Galatian agitators with political pressures in Jerusalem and a nationalistic tendency of the men around James, while Jewett speculated that Zealot pressures might have caused Jewish Christians in Judea to organize a campaign to "Judaize" Gentile fellow-Christians and thus to offset the Zealot reprisals. H. D. Betz proposed that II Cor. 6:14–7:1, long recognized as a *non*-Pauline interpolation, in effect represents an *anti*-Pauline theology diametrically opposed to Galatians; this theology is Jewish-Christian and close to Qumran Judaism (*see* Dead Sea Scrolls §6; Dead Sea Scrolls[S]), and could be identical with the theology of Paul's Galatian opponents. For the literature and state of research, *see bibliography.*

2. Composition. Galatians is an "apology" in epistolary form (*see* Letter; Letter[S]). The epistolary "frame" consists of the prescript (1:1-5) and the postscript (6:11-18). The prescript follows the basic pattern of other Pauline letters, with *superscriptio* (1:1-2*a*: name of the principal sender, his official title, a definition of the title, stating of co-senders); *adscriptio* (1:2*b*); *salutatio,* expanded by christological and soteriological formulas (1:3-4); doxology, with the concluding "amen" (1:5). The postscript, written by Paul's own hand (6:11), presupposes that the preceding letter was written by an amanuensis. The postscript is intended to authenticate the letter and to sum up finally the points Paul wants to make, thus serving as the *recapitulatio* (*peroratio*) of the "apology."

The body of the letter (1:6–6:10) is composed as a defense speech, with its traditional sections. The introductory *exordium* (1:6-9) at once introduces the "cause" (1:6-7) and Paul's reaction, the reissuing of a previous curse against apostates from the Pauline gospel (1:8-9). Between this conditional curse and a corresponding conditional blessing upon those who remain loyal to Paul (6:16), the defense itself is presented. It has three parts: the *narratio* (1:12–2:14) covers the events preceding and leading up to the present situation; these events are presented with a partisan point of view, so as to support the main line of the defense (1:11-12). The *narratio* ends with the same dilemma now facing the Galatians (2:14*b*). Next comes the *propositio* (2:15-21), stating the material points to be proved in the main part, the "presentation of proof" or *probatio* (3:1–4:31). The most important proof, undeniable evidence, is presented first in the form of an *interrogatio* (3:1-5). Next come proofs from scripture (3:6–4:11), then admonitions and pleas belonging to the theme of "friendship" (*see* FRIEND, FRIENDSHIP IN THE NT[S]) which was very popular in letters (4:12-20), and concluded by an argument from "allegory" (4:21-31). The third part is an exhortation (*parenesis,* 5:1–6:10; *see* PARENESIS[S]). Each of the three subsections (5:1*a,* 13*a,* 25*a*) begins with a restatement of the indicative of salvation (3:26-28), the first two being warnings against taking up the yoke of the Torah (5:1-12) and against corruption by the FLESH (5:13-24), the third providing positive advice in the form of gnomic sentences (5:25–6:10).

3. **Function.** The letter represents Paul, who cannot be present in person with the Galatians to deliver his defense (4:18-20); in effect, the letter carries his defense to the Galatians who have to make their final judgment. In addition, in carrying a conditional curse and blessing (1:8-9; 6:16), Galatians functions as a "magical" letter, confronting the addressees once again with the choice between salvation and condemnation; depending on what they will choose, curse or blessing will automatically be activated.

Bibliography. Commentaries: H. Lietzmann, HNT (4th ed., 1971); A. Oepke, Theologischer Handkommentar (3rd ed., 1973); H. Schlier, Meyer (5th ed., 1971); P. Bonnard, CNT (2nd ed., 1972); H. N. Ridderbos, NICNT (1953); R. Bring, *Commentary on Galatians* (1958); J. Bligh, *Galatians* (1969); F. Mussner, HTKNT (1974).

Introductions: W. G. Kümmel, *Introduction to the NT* (rev. ed., 1973 [ET 1975]), §18; A. F. J. Klijn, *An Introduction to the NT* (1965), ch. 8; W. Marxsen, *Introduction to the NT* (1964), §5; A. Wikenhauser and J. Schmid, *Einleitung in das NT* (1973), §18.

Studies: W. Lütgert, *Gesetz und Geist* (1919); F. R. Crownfield, "The Singular Problem of the Dual Galatians," *JBL,* XLIV (1945), 491-500; J. Munck, *Paul and the Salvation of Mankind* (1954); K. Wegenast, *Das Verständnis der Tradition bei Paulus und in den Deuteropaulinen,* WMANT, VIII (1962); D. Georgi, *Die Geschichte der Kollekte des Paulus für Jerusalem,* Theologische Forschung, XXXVIII (1965); W. Schmithals, *Paul and the Gnostics* (1965), ch. 1, and *Paul and James* (1963); D. B. Bronson, "Paul, Galatians, and Jerusalem," *JAAR,* XXXV (1967); G. Bornkamm, *Paul* (1969); J. M. Robinson and H. Koester, *Trajectories through Early Christianity* (1971), pp. 144 ff.; R. Jewett, "The Agitators and the Galatian Congregation," *NTS,* XVII (1971), 198-212; J. Eckert, *Die urchristliche Verkündigung im Streit zwischen Paulus und seinen Gegnern nach dem Galaterbrief,* Biblische Untersuchungen, VI (1971); H. D. Betz, "2 Cor. 6:14-7:1: An Anti-Pauline Fragment?" *JBL,* XCII (1973), 88-108, "Spirit, Freedom, and Law: Paul's Message to the Galatian Churches," *SEA,* XXXIX (1974), 145-60, and "The Literary Composition and Function of Paul's Letter to the Galatians," *NTS,* XXI (1975), 353-79.

H. D. BETZ

***GAMES, NT.** *See* GAMES, NT; FESTIVALS, GRECO-ROMAN[S].

***GATH.** Excavations at Tell Sheikh Aḥmed el-ʿAreinī (sometimes called Tell el-Menshîyeh; now Tel Erani) near ʿArâq el-Menshîyeh proved that the Iron Age settlement was much too small for an important city such as Gath; Philistine ware was scarcely in evidence. Tell en-Nejîleh (Tel Nagila), a more southerly candidate, was also disproved by excavation; there was no real Iron Age town there at all. Wright's new equation with Tell esh-Sherîʿah (Tel Seraʿ) is too far S; ZIKLAG is a more likely identification for that site. Re-examination of the written sources—biblical, Assyrian, and Byzantine—indicates that Gath was located in the N of Philistia. Tell eṣ-Ṣâfī (Tel Ẕafit) is the only reasonable candidate for identification with Gath.

Bibliography. S. Yeivin, *First Preliminary Report of the Excavations at Tel "Gat"* (1961); G. E. Wright, "Fresh Evidence for the Philistine Story," *BA,* XXIX (1966), 70-86, and "A Problem in Ancient Topography: Lachish and Eglon," *HTR,* LXIV (1971), 437-48 (= *BA,* XXXIV [1971], 76-86); A. F. Rainey, "Gath of the Philistines," *Christian News from Israel,* XVII, nos. 2-3 (Sept., 1966), 30-38, no. 4 (Dec., 1966), 23-34, and "A Problem in Source Analysis for Historical Geography," *Eretz Israel,* XII (1975). A. F. RAINEY

***GAZA.** New information on the site can be found in A. Ovadiah, "Excavations in the Area of the Ancient Synagogue at Gaza," *IEJ,* XIX (1969), 193-98; U. Rappaport, "Gaza and Ascalon in the Persian and Hellenistic Periods in Relation to their Coins," *IEJ,* XX (1970), 75-80; M. Benvenisti, *The Crusaders in the Holy Land* (1970), pp. 189-94.

***GEHENNA.** The underworld (*Sheʾôl*), the peaceful abode of all the dead according to the literature of the OT (*see* DEAD, ABODE OF THE), was replaced, in some of the intertestamental literature, by a place of fiery punishment for the wicked (*see* GEHENNA). Why it then assumed the name of the valley of Hinnom S and W of Jerusalem (gê-hinnōm; LXX^{B} Josh. 18:16, γαιεννα; NT γεεννα; *see* HINNOM, VALLEY OF THE SON OF) is not entirely clear. The often repeated description of the Valley of Hinnom as a public garbage heap and incinerator, into which "unclean" corpses were thrown, is apparently without archaeological foundation and seems to have originated with David Qimḥi's commentary on Ps. 27 (*ca.* A.D. 1200). Thus it is doubtful that Jesus applied the term "Gehenna" to the underworld merely by analogy.

While the tendency to place eschatological events at well-known places is often attested in Israel's literature, there may be another dimension to the identification of the final place of punishment with the infamous valley against which Jeremiah prophesies. Since an altar often memorializes the appearance of a deity at a given place (*see* THEOPHANY IN THE OT[S] §1*ai*), and since it was often viewed as an entrance to the realm of the particular deity to whom it was dedicated (Wainwright), those of chthonian deities were often placed in deep valleys (Lehman; *see* Isa. 57:5-6; SITES, SACRED[S]). Hence human sacrifices were offered to MOLECH in the deep Valley of Hinnom (*see also* CORRUPTION, MOUNT OF[S]). The belief that there was an entrance to the underworld in this valley is attested even in Talmudic times (T.B. ʿEr. 19a). Just as, in Assyrian thought, Nergal's cult city Kutu gave its name to the realm of Nergal beneath it (*see ANET* [2nd ed.], p. 107, l. 40), the altars to chthonian deities in Hinnom ultimately resulted in the transfer of the name to the realm beneath.

Bibliography. M. Lehman, "A New Interpretation of the Term שרמות," *VT,* III (1953), 361-71; J. Montgomery, "The Holy City and Gehenna," *JBL,* XXVII (1908), 24-47, discusses the idea of Jerusalem as a microcosm, in which the deep ravines nearby would suggest Sheol situated at the roots of the mountains which uphold the earth; G. Wainwright, "Jacob's Bethel," *PEFQS* (1934), 32-44.

L. BAILEY

***GENEALOGY.** *See* GENERATION, SEVENTH[S].

***GENEALOGY (CHRIST).** For details of the two NT genealogies (Matt. 1:1-17; Luke 3:23-38) see the original article; here the concentration will be upon their theological import for the evangelists.

1. Matthew. This evangelist does not transmit a factual family tree; for, while Jesus may well have been of Davidic descent, he was not the dauphin of a princely family. Either Matthew has created the genealogy himself, or, more probably, he has added the names of Joseph and Jesus to an existing genealogy of the expected Davidic Messiah, a genealogy which Matthew joined to a pre-Davidic era list resembling those in Ruth 4:18-22 and I Chr. 2:1-15. Since the omissions in the monarchical sections may have arisen through confusions about the Greek names of the kings, a hypothetical pre-Matthean genealogy would more likely have existed in Greek and have been of a popular rather than archival nature. The appearance of priestly names in the postexilic period (e.g., Zadok) may reflect a vague remembrance of the transfer of political power in the fifth century B.C. from the Davidic heirs to the high priests. Matthew calls attention to the pattern of fourteen generations in the genealogy (1:17); he may have found this pattern already in the pre-Davidic and monarchical sections and have realized that the addition of Joseph and Jesus extended the pattern to the postexilic period. For him the numerical pattern reflected the carefulness of God's planning for the Messiah. If Matthew knew that the ancient Hebrew orthography of David's name gave a numerical value of fourteen, his awe at God's planning would have been increased. Thus, the genealogy reflects the same appreciation of God's providence attested in the Matthean "fulfillment citations," so prominent in the infancy narrative.

In the heading of the genealogy the twofold designation of Jesus as "son of David" and "son of Abraham" may be directed to Matthew's composite community. "Son of David" is an assurance to Jewish Christians that God's promise to Israel of a Davidic Messiah has been fulfilled. "Son of Abraham" tells Matthew's Gentile Christians (cf. 8:11; 21:41) that in Jesus as the seed of Abraham all the nations of the world have been blessed, and not only Israel (3:9). If the section 1:18-25 will show how Jesus through Joseph's acknowledgment is the son of David, the section 2:1-12 will show how his birth attracts magi from the East, the ancient land of Abraham. Four women (Tamar, Rahab, Ruth, and the wife of Uriah) have been introduced by Matthew into the genealogy as a sign of God's planning for the role of Mary in the birth of Jesus. These women have in common: (a) an extraordinary or irregular marital union which was scandalous in the eyes of outsiders but which continued the blessed lineage promised by God; (b) taking the initiative in bringing about God's plan; (c) being popularly regarded as instruments of God's Spirit. For instance, in first-century Jewish piety it was thought that God's Holy Spirit led Tamar to seduce Judah, and that the same Spirit selected the prostitute Rahab even before Israel entered the Promised Land. Besides seeing these women as foreshadowing Mary, Matthew may have been interested in them as non-Israelites (or married to a non-Israelite, as the wife of Uriah). In the genealogy of Israel's Messiah there were already signs of a wider salvation.

2. Luke. Matthew gives his genealogy before beginning the story of Jesus, just as Gen. 5 lists Noah's ancestors before the story of Noah (chs. 6–9). Luke relates first Jesus' birth and youth and the inauguration of his ministry before giving a genealogy (3:23-38), even as Exodus tells of Moses' birth and youth and his inaugural call before it lists his Levitical ancestors (Exod. 6:14-25). In Luke and in Exodus the genealogy authenticates the mission; and in Jesus' case, where the genealogy goes back to God, it explains how he is the Son of God, as the heavenly voice has just proclaimed (Luke 3:22). The position of the genealogy suggests that it may have been part of the gospel before Luke prefixed chs. 1–2. Indeed, the phrase "as was supposed" in 3:23 may represent a modification to make the genealogy agree with the motif of virginal conception in 1:26-38.

While Luke has a more plausible number of generations covering the span of time between David and Jesus (forty-two to Matthew's twenty-eight), the names he gives for the monarchical period are of a type common in postexilic Judaism. And the names Luke gives for the postexilic period reflect Levitic descent (e.g., Levi, Mattathias), a curious feature in a Davidic lineage. Moreover, there are suspicious duplicates in the Lukan list (cf. Jesus, Joseph, Heli, Matthat, Levi in 3:23-24; Joseph, Matthathias in 3:24-25; and Jesus [Joshua], Eliezer . . . Matthat, Levi in 3:29). There is little need to harmonize the Matthean and Lukan lists (*see* GENEALOGY, CHRIST §3) if we realize that the Lukan list has little more claim than Matthew's to be factual. Luke's tracing of Jesus' Davidic descendancy through Nathan (3:31) rather than through Solomon (Matt. 1:6-7) is consonant with Luke's interest in Jesus as a prophet—Nathan the Davidic prince (II Sam. 5:14) was popularly confused with Nathan the Davidic prophet (II Sam. 7:2). The extension of Jesus' ancestors to Adam and thus beyond Hebrew history may reflect the Gentile orientation of Luke's gospel.

Bibliography. J. Jeremias, *Jerusalem in the Time of Jesus* (3rd ed., 1962), pp. 275-97; M. D. Johnson, *The Purpose of Biblical Genealogies,* NTSMS, VIII (1969).

R. E. BROWN

GENERATION, SEVENTH. The OT has preserved, on occasion, differing versions of the same lineage.

It can be shown, in some cases, that the genealogies were restructured in order to transpose into the seventh slot an individual deemed especially worthy of attention. In light of the enormous attention accorded by the Semites in general, and the Hebrews in particular, to the number SEVEN, it is not surprising that the seventh position in a genealogical tree became particularly favored. To a degree, the fifth position was accorded secondary importance.

Clear examples of the manner in which this convention operated are obtained by comparing the order of Israelite tribes as listed in various books of the OT.

1) Gen. 46 presents Israel, at the time of the journey to Egypt, as a community of seventy males. The number seven and its multiples are frequently invoked. Gad (גד), whose descendants numbered precisely seven, is placed in seventh position, very likely because his *gematria* (*see* WORDPLAY IN THE OT[S] §1) added up to 7 (ג=3, ד=4).

2) The census list preserved in Num. 26:5-51 records Joseph in the favored (seventh) slot. His is the only line which is carried into the seventh generation, that of Zelophehad's daughters, who, according to Num. 27:1-11, elicited from Moses an innovative juridical decision.

3) Num. 13:4-15 lists the *neśî'îm* sent on a mission into Canaan. It has long been recognized that vss. 10-11 belong before vs. 8 in order to secure the sequence Manasseh-Ephraim (de Vaux). Consequently, seventh place would go to the hero Hosea (Joshua), son of Nun.

The following instances are also noteworthy.

1) There are two listings in Genesis which preserve the names of mankind's antediluvian ancestors: one, of seven "cultural heroes," reflects the development of human institutions (4:17-24); the other, consisting of ten "eponymous ancestors," details the human links between Creation and the Flood (5:3-31). These are paralleled by Mesopotamian concepts (Hallo). Despite minor alterations in spelling, the lists from Genesis were developed from a single source. In each case, the genealogist placed in the seventh position an ancestor who received special notice in the tradition.

S (ethite) tradition (5:3-31)		K (enite) tradition (4:17-24)	
I	Adam		
II	Seth		
III	Enosh	(1)	Adam
IV	Kenan	(2)	Cain
V	Mahalalel	(3)	Enoch
VI	Jared	(4)	Irad
VII	Enoch	(5)	Mehujael
VIII	Methuselah	(6)	Methusael
IX	Lamech	(7)	Lamech
X	Noah		

In K, Lamech is placed in seventh position, likely because he was remembered in the famous "sword-dance" of Gen. 4:23-24 as "avenged seventy-sevenfold" (cf. also 5:31 where he is said to have lived 777 years). In S, however, the seventh slot is given to Enoch because of the description of his singular fate: "God took him" (5:23-24). The changes in genealogical order thus were minimal; while most of the ancestors were kept to their proper slots, the positions of Enoch and Mehalalel/Mehujael were switched. This not only permitted Enoch to occupy, in S, the favored position, but preserved Mahalalel in the fifth spot, the same as that enjoyed by Mehujael in K.

2) Gen. 11:10-20 lists eponymous ancestors from the postdiluvian period. Eber, after whom the Hebrews (*'ibhrî*) were named, is accorded the fourteenth (2x7) position since Creation. In the MT, Abraham is reckoned as seventh from Eber; while in the LXX, he is placed in the twenty-first slot (3x7) since Creation.

3) Gen. 36 lists thirteen Edomite descendants of Esau (vss. 11-14), then fourteen clans issued from him bearing the same names, plus one (vss. 15-18). By inserting the name "Korah" at the secondarily important fifth position of the clan list, the genealogist not only reminded his audience of a notable "villain" (Num. 16) but also pushed AMALEK, Israel's foremost foe, one slot down into the seventh position. Note also that Korah, as the fifth son of Esau (vs. 5), now also occupies slot fourteen (7x2) of the clan list.

4) David's line as preserved in Ruth 4 has Boaz in seventh spot. Since he is the hero of the tale, this is hardly surprising. A proper appreciation of the "seventh-generation" convention indicates that the lineage was specifically tailored for inclusion in Ruth and, therefore, should not be considered as a secondary addition to that narrative. In order to preserve Boaz in the seventh slot, the genealogist must begin his line with Perez and not, as he logically might have, with the more illustrious Judah or Jacob. The mention of Perez in 4:12 thus anticipates the genealogy.

5) I Sam. 9:1-2 preserves the genealogy of Saul: Saul ← Kish ← Abi'el ← Zeror ← Becorath ← Aphiah ← a Benjaminite landowner. To place Saul in the seventh position, the genealogist must begin his line with an individual whose name had been forgotten (RSV "a Benjaminite, a man of wealth"). Most modern translations mistakenly delete either בן or איש.

6) In Matthew's delineation of Jesus' ancestry (1:2-16), it is possible that the convention was still operative. In order to obtain fourteen (2x7) ancestors in each of three "ages" (1:17), Matthew (1) begins with Abraham rather than with Adam, Noah, or Shem; (2) omits a few names transmitted by the Chronicler (I Chr. 3:5, 10-16); (3) repeats (counts again) the name of Jechoniah, last of the second "age," in first position of the third "age." Note also that Mary (1:16) is the fifth woman to be mentioned in the lineage.

7) Luke (3:23-38) reckons Jesus as the seventy-seventh (7x11) human descendant of Adam. The following are given prominence: Enoch (seventh), Shelah (fourteenth), Abraham (twenty-first), Admin (twenty-eighth), David (thirty-fifth), Joseph son of Jonam (forty-second), Jesus/Joshua son of Eliezer (forty-ninth=7x7), Shealtiel (fifty-sixth), Mattathias son of Semein (sixty-third), Joseph son of Mattathias (seventieth), Jesus son of Joseph

(seventy-seventh). To be noted: all the occurrences of the names Joseph, Jesus, and Mattathias fall in the seventh spot or its multiples; Enoch, David, and Abraham are similarly honored. By "Mattathias" (sixty-third), Luke may have been reminded of the Hasmonean patriarch whose grandfather was named Simeon (I Macc. 2:1).

Bibliography. W. W. Hallo, "Antediluvian Cities," *JCS,* XXIII (1971), 57-67; R. de Vaux, *Histoire ancienne d'Israël, II: la période des juges* (1973), p. 43; J. M. Sasson, "A Genealogical Convention in Biblical Chronography," *ZAW* (*forthcoming*); A. Malamat, "King Lists of the Old Babylonian Period and Biblical Genealogies," *JAOS,* LXXXIII (1968), 163-73. J. M. SASSON

***GENESIS.** The book of Genesis contains the primeval history (chs. 1–11) and the history of the patriarchs (chs. 12–50). Although the critical search for the sources of Genesis did not emphasize this division (*see* SOURCE CRITICISM, OT[S]; DOCUMENTS), more recent research has recognized that they are two completely separate complexes of tradition.

A. Primeval history (Gen. 1–11)
  1. Main types of interpretation
  2. Biblical primeval history in the context of similar stories
  3. The uniqueness of the biblical primeval history

B. History of the patriarchs (Gen. 12–50)
  1. Main types of interpretation
  2. Preliterary traditions
  3. The three parts of the patriarchal history
  4. The environment and times of the patriarchs

Bibliography

A. PRIMEVAL HISTORY (GEN. 1–11). **1. Main types of interpretation.** ***a. Traditional interpretation*** (until about 1850). This approach viewed the stories as historical reports of the beginnings of the world. The biblical primeval history, on the one hand, was thought to be universally known. Parallels from other religions (Hesiod, Berossos) were explained by the assumption of an original revelation from which they had evolved. On the other hand, Christian dogmatics produced a strong emphasis on the first three chapters (Creation and Fall) and isolated them from the rest of the primeval history. These chapters in particular were interpreted in light of salvation through Jesus Christ. This interpretation was shaken by modern natural science, especially by biology and Darwinism. *See* SCIENCE AND THE BIBLE[S].

b. Critical literary interpretation (dominant, 1860-1920). The historical-critical method approached the biblical primeval history purely as a literary problem. For it, the history consisted of two (or three) great literary works which run through the entire Pentateuch. The content of the history was explained entirely in terms of the time of composition of these works; i.e., it does not provide genuine information about the patriarchal age. It was thought that the attacks of natural science could be avoided by distinguishing between a historical nucleus and the "religious content." Material from other religions, especially from Mesopotamia, was usually examined only from the perspective of mutual literary dependence (*see* BIBLICAL CRITICISM, HISTORY OF §2*b*). Recently, a kind of "salvation-history" approach has been linked to the critical literary interpretation. It is especially interested in the theology of the source writings and views the primeval history entirely from the perspective of the later "salvation history" of Yahweh's dealings with Israel (cf. Delitzsch, von Rad, etc.).

c. Form- and traditio-critical interpretation (starting with Gunkel, 1910). In this approach, it was recognized that the primeval stories had a long, usually oral, history before their fixation in writing (*see* TRADITION, ORAL[S]). Many of the motifs were widespread among early peoples (e.g., creation of a human being out of clay, the story of the Flood; *see* Frazer, Baumann). Thus, it was helpful to interpret the stories in a universal context. The question of historicity was dismissed as irrelevant to be replaced by the form-critical question of the function of the stories in the community (*see* Eliade, Maag). *See* BIBLICAL CRITICISM, HISTORY OF §3; TRADITION CRITICISM, OT[S].

2. Biblical primeval history in the context of similar stories. ***a. Individuality and unity.*** The primeval stories of all cultures are not intended to be historical reports but rather to present those fundamental realities concerning the world and humanity which precede the ethnic, national, political, and social differentiations under which people living in historical time find themselves. Hence, primeval history, which has to do with all people, is fundamentally separate from the history of God in dealings with the one people Israel (Gen. 12 ff.; Exod. 3 ff.). The unity of the former does not consist of a cohesive pattern of development; there is no real progression of plot (contrast von Rad's "sin increasing like a landslide"). On the contrary, that which seems to be narrated in a sequence is only the development of those fundamental realities and should not be understood chronologically. A prominent characteristic of many primeval stories is that they present such realities in a complementary manner; i.e., something positive and negative simultaneously (cf. Pandora's box). According to this model, biblical primeval history and also the Babylonian Atrahasis epic (Gilgamesh Epic) are dominated by the contrast between creation and destruction of the created world by the Flood (*see* Table 1).

b. The structure of biblical primeval history. The account of the YAHWIST (J) and the Priestly writings (P) consist of two components: (i) stories, (ii) genealogies.

i. *Stories.* In both J and P there are two kinds of stories: stories of creation, and stories of guilt and punishment, thus expressing the complementary character of primeval history.

P is the most stylized and therefore has the clearest structure. The two types of story stand opposite each other, connected only by genealogies: the story of the creation of the world and human beings (1:1–2:4*a*), and the story of the destruction of Creation by the Flood (chs. 6–9). This contrast is also the center of J, which elaborates on the

Table 1

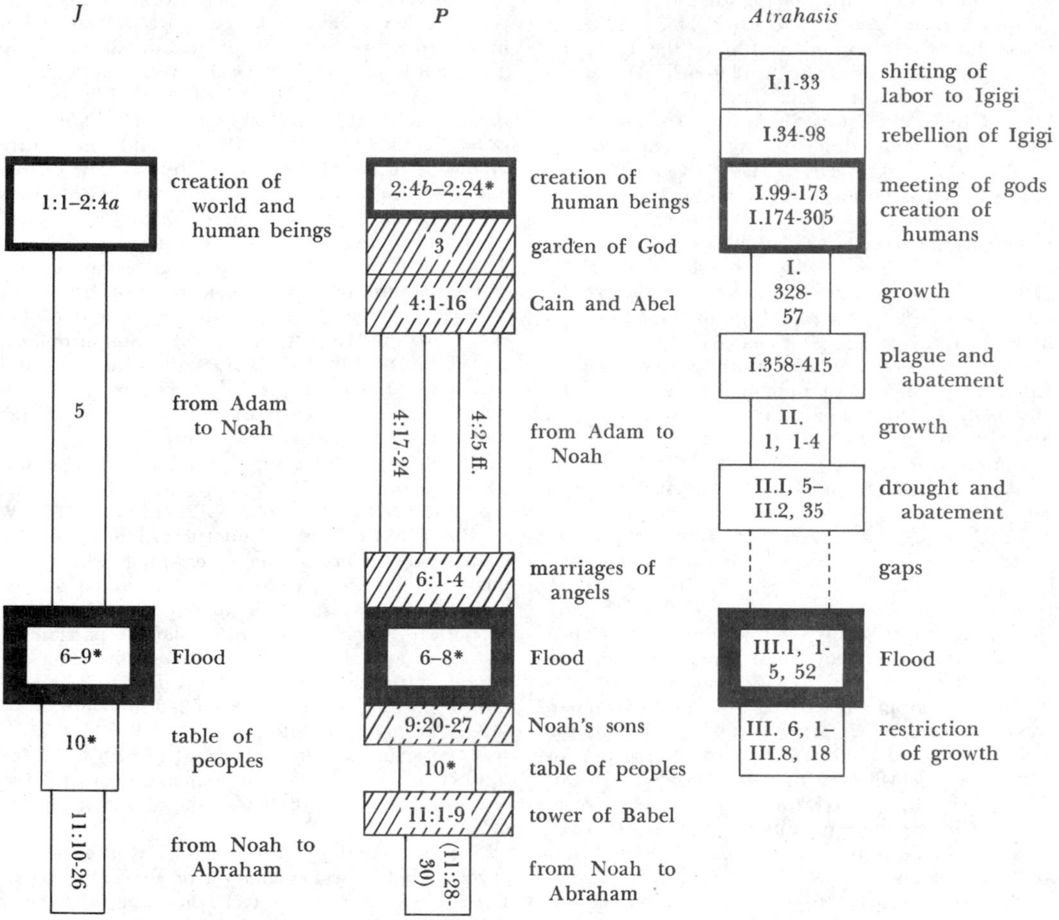

various aspects of being human (ch. 3; 4:2-16; 6:1-4; 9:20-27; 11:1-9). While P only generally states the evil in humanity (6:11-12), J expounds the many ways of going astray. People were hardly created before they tried to increase the possibilities of their lives and overcome their limits, thus offending their Creator. Ch. 3 tells of human misdeeds in the relationship between man and woman; ch. 4 tells of those in the relationship between brothers (a competitive struggle to the death); 9:20-27 tells of an offense within the family; and 11:1-9 of an attempt of people to overcome their limitations. In 6:1-4 a transgression of the border between the human and the divine sphere is intimated. In all cases, the Creator sends the people back within their bounds. He drives them out of his presence (3:24); he limits the length of their lives (6:3); he scatters them throughout the earth (11:8). Meaningless labor (3:18-19) and painful birth (3:16) are traced back to primeval time. No matter how much effort human beings make, as God's creatures they remain within the limits God imposed.

In addition to the creative and limiting action of God, there is a third element: God continues to surround his creatures with his care (2:8-9, 15). The story of the Flood tells not only of the destruction of humanity but also of the saving of Noah. The stories of guilt and punishment are conspicuously inconsistent (cf. God's gift of clothing in 3:21; the sign of protection for the murderer Cain in 4:15).

ii. *Genealogies.* The genealogies are related to primeval history in two ways. (a) They show the continuing effect of the blessing (i.e., fertility) which the Creator has granted to human persons (1:28; 5:1-3). The blessing ensures that people will spread to the farthest reaches of time (ch. 5; 11:10-26) and space (ch. 10).

(b) Humanity proceeds in the chain of generations; J used the genealogies to present the progress of human culture (4:1, 17-26; 5:29; 10:8-12). However, progress not only eases and improves human life; it also increases its dangers: the working of iron (4:22-24), the processing of wine (5:29; 9:20-27), and the building of cities (11:1-9). Thus the genealogies are also characterized by the ambivalence of the entire primitive history.

c. Structure of the Atrahasis epic (Gilgamesh Epic). The old Babylonian Atrahasis (Utnapishtim) epic (*ca.* 1700 B.C.) is also characterized by the contrast between the creation of human beings and a flood, and by the ambivalence of the creation and limitation of humanity. However, the arena of action shifts to the mythological level (action between gods). The Anunnaki, the greater gods, shift the labor of culture to the Igigi, the lesser gods (I. 1-33). The work soon becomes too difficult even for them, and they revolt against the king of the gods, En-lil (I. 34-98). To resolve the conflict, the gods decide to create human beings who will labor for them (I. 174-305). People have hardly taken over the work when they become so numerous and noisy (I. 328-57) that En-lil tries to destroy them with a flood (III. 1, 1-5, 52). The creator, Ea, prevents this from happening. He gives Atrahasis advice as to how he can avert the catastrophes (e.g., I. 364-415) and finally saves him from the flood. The plan of destruction is averted. However, human reproduction and the dangerous dynamics of human civilization are reduced by different kinds of childlessness and by high infant mortality.

d. Stories of creation. Except for the Flood, the biblical creation account has the largest number of religio-historical parallels. An overview of all the material shows that the stories of the creation of human beings were once independent from those of the creation of the world. While the former type may be traced back to primitive religions, the latter appear only in the highly developed cultures (e.g., the Babylonian Enuma elish). The reports of Creation by J and P fit into this pattern of development. Gen. 2 is a story of human creation; Gen. 1 is a story of the creation of the world, which was added to that of the creation of human beings. Yet even in P the earlier independence of the human creation story may be recognized. The creation of human beings (1:26-30) does not fit into the schema of P, because they are not created by a word. *See* CREATION §2*a*.

The distance between the two traditions is also shown in the manner in which God creates. While in ch. 2 God creates like a craftsman, in ch. 1 he calls the world into being by a command (1:3), although P also kept the older conception in many parts of his report (e.g., 1:7). Similarly, in the cosmogony of Memphis (Egypt), creation by a word appears only at the end of a long theological development (*see* Koch; *ANET* [2nd ed.], pp. 4-6). When P related Gen. 1 to his genealogy (תולדות; RSV "generations"; 2:4) schema, he made covert reference to the "more primitive" conception of creation by birth. Since the authors and those who passed on the biblical traditions purposely left such contrasting conceptions side by side, we may conclude that they wished to imply that none of the conceptions adequately depicted the creation of the world and human beings. The creation remains a mystery.

3. The uniqueness of the biblical primeval history. Those who are not aware of the religio-historical background often overestimate the originality of the biblical history. Gen. 1–11 relates that which is true for all people and which was told by many religions. Nevertheless, the formative influence of Yahwism may be recognized in the details. Thus, the notion of creation as the birth of gods was repressed, and with it, the difference between Creator and created became clearer than it was in Egyptian religion. Mythological material was absorbed only in a muffled form (Gen. 6:1-4; *see* CREATION §1*a*), and kingship was not anchored in the primeval time as it was in Sumer. The monotheistic faith in Yahweh precluded any history of the gods, and, because of this, human beings acquired a greater significance. They became genuine partners of God, and the entire drama of primeval history took place between the one God and his creatures. However, the decisive characteristic is that primeval history was added to the beginning of Yahweh's history with Israel. Thus, this particular history was given a universal background. Yahweh, who saved Israel out of Egypt, is the creator of all people and of the entire world. His activity for the one people is the result of his activity for all humanity, and will again at the end involve all people (apocalypticism). For this reason, the biblical primeval history lends itself better than most passages in the Bible to the role of bridge between Christians and non-Christians.

B. HISTORY OF THE PATRIARCHS (GEN. 12–50). **1. Main types of interpretation.** *a*) In the traditional understanding, everything which was related about the patriarchs was regarded as historical. In contrast, Wellhausen, a representative of critical literary research, explained patriarchal history as a projection backward in time from the period of the monarchy and assumed that it contained nothing historical. *See* §A1 *above*.

b) The mythical interpretation (Winckler, Meyer), trying to explain patriarchal history from the context of Babylonian or Canaanite mythology, saw original figures of gods behind the names of the patriarchs.

c) Some scholars (Ewald, Stade, Guthe, Steuernagel) sought the explanation of the entire patriarchal history in the fact that the names of individuals were also names of tribes, e.g., the names of the sons of Jacob (Gen. 35:23-26). It was the history of the tribes which was actually being told in the stories about their ancestors. In this case birth would mean the origin of a tribe, and marriage would mean the union of two tribes. (Eissfeldt and Kaiser also represented a limited tribal-historical theory in the story of Joseph.)

d) A new direction was begun in the explanation of patriarchal history as individual legends (Gunkel, Gressmann). This gave the oral phase of the tradition a new significance. Alt proceeded further in this direction when he concluded from the special type of patriarchal religion that there was a historically demonstrable religion of the patriarchs before the settlement in the Promised Land. *See* PATRIARCHS[S] §2*b*.

e) Interpretation from the perspective of archaeology was especially represented by Albright and his students (Wright, Bright, and Cross). The time, the life style, and the historical background of the patriarchs began to be explored in the context of the second millennium B.C. Archaeological access to patriarchal history is also very important for Cazelles and other French scholars, including de Vaux.

f) Noth (1948, 1966) established the dominance

of the traditio-historical viewpoint (*see* TRADITION CRITICISM, OT[S]). Its concern is the origin, growth, continued formation, and combination of the traditions about the patriarchs. These developed in various places (*Haftpunkte*) and in certain circles (tribes or groups of tribes) until their final written form in Genesis. (Noth presupposes, however, the division of the text into sources.) Many scholars have continued this traditio-historical research (Jepsen, Seebass). Works on parts of the patriarchal history have tried to achieve a connection between the critical literary and the traditio-historical methods (Kilian, Gen. 12–25; Eising, Gen. 25–36; Ruppert, Gen. 37–50).

2. Preliterary traditions. Gunkel and Gressmann recognized that the individual stories in the patriarchal history once had an independent life and were passed down independently in oral fashion before becoming a part of a comprehensive written work (*see* TRADITION, ORAL[S]). Usually, they were labeled "legends," but some people thought that they were closely related to fairy tales or myths. However, the patriarchal stories can be clearly distinguished from tales and myths, and further discussion has shown that the label "legend" was too broad and indefinite.

According to recent studies Gen. 12–50 contains three groups of individual traditions: stories, lists (including genealogies and itineraries), and texts of promise (e.g., 12:1-3) which connect the patriarchs with the history of Israel. The material may be divided into stories of families (Westermann) or of holy places, and larger contexts of stories. The genealogies and the itineraries may be divided into primary and secondary forms. The primary ones preserve memories of wanderings or of descent; the secondary ones are literary forms that provide transition. In addition, there are several other forms of oral tradition.

3. The three parts of the patriarchal history. In the form in which it has come down to us, patriarchal history consists of three parts which were previously independent: the Joseph story (Gen. 37–50, which differs greatly from Gen. 12–36), the Abraham cycle (Gen. 12–25), and the Jacob-Esau cycle (Gen. 25–36). The organization of the three parts is reflected in their different themes. The Abraham cycle is concerned with the progression from parents to children, the Jacob-Esau cycle with the relationship of two brothers, and the Joseph story with differentiated relationships: the father, the brothers, the brother in the family. The three parts also differ in form. Gen. 12–25 consists primarily of individual stories, 25–36 is dominated by larger groups of stories, and 37–50 is one long story. From a theological point of view, promise is emphasized in 12–25, blessing in 25–36, and peace in 37–50 (שלום as the state of well-being of a community).

a. Abraham (Gen. 12–25). Today it is generally assumed that Abraham was an individual who lived at a time which cannot be precisely determined (*see* PATRIARCHS; PATRIARCHS[S]). At first, the Abraham tradition consisted of separate stories, and from them the existing history of Abraham grew in a long, slow process. A certain loose thematic resolution may be found in that the cycle begins in Gen. 11:30 with Sarah's infertility and almost ends in 21:1-7 with the birth of Sarah's son. These stories tell directly or indirectly of the continuing concern for the next generation. Almost all of them deal with the basic parent-child relationship. The Lot-Sodom complex and the late MIDRASH (as most scholars call it) of the battle of the kings and Melchizedek (Gen. 14) were added later. A special problem is created by the promises and the stories of the promises, of which some belong to the time of Abraham and some could have been added much later (*see* PROMISES TO THE PATRIARCHS[S]). The promise (12:1-3) which introduces the Abraham cycle in J connects the primeval history (1–11) with the patriarchal history (12–50), and at the same time points toward the history of the people of Israel (von Rad, Wolff).

b. Jacob and Esau (Gen. 25–36). There are four different groups of texts (according to Gunkel, Gressmann, de Vaux): the stories of Jacob and Esau, of Jacob and Laban, of holy places and theophanies, and of the sons of Jacob. The Jacob and Laban complex has been inserted into the Jacob and Esau complex by use of the themes of flight and return. The stories of holy places and theophanies (28:10-22; 32:1-2; 32:22-32; 35:1-7; 35:9-15[P]) are different from the first two groups in that Jacob alone appears in them. The fourth group presents the sons of Jacob as the fathers of the tribes of Israel (34; 35:23-29; 36). The most important theological concept in chs. 25–36 is that of blessing. In the Jacob-Esau stories, the conflict which dominates the whole cycle grows out of the blessing given by the father (ch. 27). In the Jacob-Laban stories, the conflict grows out of the blessing of wealth in the form of herds. The heart of the Jacob traditions may have come from the time of the patriarchs. The life-style of small, half-nomadic groups is presupposed, as is shown by the fact that only in this part of Genesis is God's presence promised to the wanderer. But *see* NOMADISM[S].

The stories of holy places and theophanies belong in another traditio-historical context (*see* THEOPHANY IN THE OT[S]). The accounts of God's revelations to the patriarchs often indicate the gradual takeover of the Canaanite holy places (*see* SITES, SACRED[S]), while the stories of the sons of Jacob connect patriarchal history with the history of the tribes.

c. Story of Joseph (Gen. 37–50). The story is a single, closed framework, and is called a *novella* by many interpreters (e.g., Gunkel, von Rad). This clearly separates it from Gen. 12–25 and 25–36, and scholars are agreed that it developed independently of those passages. However, it is related to the rest of patriarchal history in terms of its sources (J, E, and P) and content. It is a family story which begins with conflict and ends with reconciliation. Thus, it is actually not a "story of guidance" (cf. von Rad, Ruppert, etc.) which tells of God's wonderful guidance toward a good end (*see* JOSEPH STORY[S]). Rather, it is a story of a family whose "well-being" (שלום) is destroyed by the brothers' attempt to commit murder and the subsequent deception of their father, but is restored in the end by God's providence.

The special character of Gen. 37–50, as opposed

to chs. 12–36, is in the encounter of the new people of Israel with the world power, Egypt, and its new, overwhelming possibilities. A connecting motif is the avoidance of famine, which is handled in a manner entirely different from that in which the same motif is treated in 12:12-20.

All the types of interpretation mentioned above (§B1) have been applied to the Joseph story: a backward projection from the time of the monarchy (Wellhausen), the mythical interpretation (reflected in Thomas Mann's *Joseph* novels), the tribal history interpretation (Steuernagel, Kaiser), the historical interpretation (Albright and Wright place it in the Hyksos era [1800-1550 B.C.]; while Procksch and Rowley place it in the Amarna era [fourteenth century B.C.]). Egyptology offers its own interpretation (formerly represented by Yahuda, now by Vergote and especially Redford). Von Rad's attempt to explain the Joseph story as reflecting older Israelite wisdom has been accorded much respect. But recent writers (Crenshaw, Redford, Coats) have viewed the influence of wisdom in Gen. 37–50 more critically.

The question of the literary character of Gen. 37–50 was first posed by form-critical research (Gunkel, 1922; Gressmann, 1923). According to Gressmann, it is a legend of the king; according to Gunkel it is a family story expanded from motifs of legends. Gunkel called it a *novella* and this label was adopted by von Rad. Coats also understood the Joseph story as a *novella,* but he saw chs. 39–41 as an originally independent political legend with a didactic purpose and assumed the influence of wisdom only in this passage.

The majority of scholars have continued to hold the theory that the Joseph story was composed from different literary sources (Simpson, Gunkel, von Rad, Eissfeldt, Cazelles, and especially Ruppert). Rudolph (1933) tried to prove the literary unity of the Joseph story, and some scholars have followed him in this (e.g., Mowinckel, Brueggemann, Coats). Some have recently tried to distinguish several layers of tradition rather than several literary sources (Jepsen, Mowinckel, Redford). The question remains open.

4. The environment and times of the patriarchs. Efforts to determine the precise time of the patriarchs have not yet been successful. The suggestions range between 2200 and 1200 B.C. An attempt has been made to relate the nomadic wanderings of the second millennium to the wanderings of the patriarchs. However, the patriarchal stories do not contain any direct traces of such a relationship. *See* PATRIARCHS[S] §1.

Knowledge of the countries and peoples of the ancient Near East of the second millennium has increased enormously in recent decades, and this has served to illuminate the background of the patriarchal history (for limitations, however, *see* MARI[S] §8; NUZI[S] §2). Such biblical names as Abraham and Jacob have been found in ancient Near Eastern documents covering a long period of time in the second millennium. This surely shows that the names of the patriarchs refer to individuals, and that they lived before the settlement in the Promised Land. For the religion of the patriarchs, *see* PATRIARCHS; PATRIARCHS[S] §2*b*; for the promises, *see* PROMISES TO THE PATRIARCHS[S].

Bibliography. §A: C. Westermann, *Genesis, Biblischer Kommentar,* I, 1 (1974); G. von Rad, *Das erste Buch Mose. Genesis,* ATD, II-IV (9th ed., 1972); H. Gunkel, *Genesis,* HKAT I, 1 (7th ed., 1966).

§1: C. Westermann, "Genesis 1–11," *Erträge der Forschung,* VII (1972); H. W. Wolff, "Das Kerygma des Jahwisten," *EvT,* XXIV (1964), 73-98, also in *Gesammelte Studien zum AT,* Theologische Bücherei, XXII (1964), 345-73; J. G. Frazer, *Folklore in the OT,* 3 vols. (1919); H. Baumann, *Schöpfung und Urzeit des Menschen im Mythos der afrikanischen Völker* (1936 [2nd ed., 1964]); M. Eliade, "Structure et fonction du mythe cosmogonique," *Sources orientales,* I, *La naissance du monde* (1959), 469-95; V. Maag, "Sumerische und babylonische Mythen von der Erschaffung der Menschen," *Asiatische Studien,* VIII (1954), 85-106.

§2: C. Westermann, "Die theologische Bedeutung der Urgeschichte," *Forschung am AT II,* Theologische Bücherei, LV, (1974), 96-114; W. G. Lambert and A. R. Millard, *Aṭra-Ḫasīs: The Babylonian Story of the Flood* (1969); W. H. Schmidt, *Die Schöpfungsgeschichte der Priesterschrift,* WMANT, XVII (2nd ed., 1967); K. Koch, "Wort und Einheit des Schöpfergottes in Memphis und Jerusalem," *ZThK,* LXII (1965), 251-93; R. Albertz, *Weltschöpfung und Menschenschöpfung. Untersucht bei Deuterojesaja, Hiob und in den Psalmen,* Calwer theologische Monographien, III (1974); W. G. Lambert, "A Middle Assyrian Medical Text," *Iraq,* XXXI (1969), 28-39.

§3: C. Westermann, *Creation* (1974).

§B: For older literature, *see* H. Weidmann, *Die Patriarchen und ihre Religion, FRLANT,* XCIV (1968); A. Alt, "Der Gott der Väter," *Kleine Schriften zur Geschichte des Volkes Israel,* I (1953), 1-78; H. G. May, "The Evolution of the Joseph Story," *AJSL,* XLIV (1930), 83-93; E. A. Speiser, "Ethnic Movements in the Near East in the Second Millenium," *AASOR,* XIII (1933), 13-54; P. Volz and W. Rudolph, *Der Elohist als Erzähler: ein Irrweg der Pentateuchkritik?, BZAW,* LXIII (1933); P. Humbert, "Die neue Genesisforschung," *ThRev,* VI (1934), 147-66; C. H. Gordon, "The Story of Jacob and Laban in the Light of the Nuzi Tablets," *BASOR,* 66 (1937); W. F. Albright, *From the Stone Age to Christianity* (1940 [2nd ed., 1957]), and *Archaeology and the Religion of Israel* (1942 [3rd ed., 1952; 4th ed., 1956]); H. Eising, *Formgeschichtliche Untersuchungen zur Jakoberzählung der Genesis* (1940); M. Noth, *Überlieferungsgeschichte des Pentateuch* (1948 [3rd ed., 1966; ET, B. W. Anderson, *A History of Pentateuchal Traditions,* 1972]); H. H. Rowley, *From Joseph to Joshua* (1950); N. Glueck, "The Age of Abraham in the Negeb," *BA,* XVIII (1955), 1-9; G. E. Wright, *Biblical Archaeology* (1957 [2nd ed., 1962]); C. H. Gordon, "Abraham and the Merchants of Ura," *JNES,* XVII (1958), 28-31; G. von Rad, "Josephgeschichte and die ältere Chokma," *Gesammelte Studien zum AT* (1958 [3rd ed., 1965]), pp. 272-80; J. Bright, *A History of Israel* (1959); O. Kaiser, "Stammesgeschichtliche Hintergründe der Josephgeschichte," *VT,* X (1960), 1-15; H. Cazelles, "Patriarches," *DBSup,* VII (1961), 81-156; O. Eissfeldt, "Stammessage und Novelle in den Geschichten von Jakob and von seinen Söhnen," *Kleine Schriften,* I (1962), 143-49; A. Parrot, *Abraham et son temps* (1962 [ET, *Abraham and His Times,* 1968]); J. M. Holt, *The Patriarchs of Israel* (1964); C. Westermann, "Arten der Erzählung in der Genesis," *Forschung am AT. Gesammelte Studien,* Theologische Bücherei, XXIV (1964), 9-91; L. Ruppert, *Die Josepherzählung der Genesis,* StANT, XI (1965); R. Kilian, *Die vorpriesterliche Abrahamsüberlieferung in der Genesis,* BBB, XXIV (1966); H. Seebass, *Der Erzväter Israel, BZAW,* XCVIII (1966); C.

Westermann, "Die Josepherzählung der Genesis," *Calwer Predigthilfen,* V (1966), 11-118 [ET, *The Genesis Accounts of Creation,* 1966]); W. Gross, "Jakob, der Mann des Segens," *Bibl.,* XLIX (1968), 321-44; R. Martin-Achard, *Actualité d'Abraham* (1969); G. Wallis, "Die Tradition von den drei Ahnvätern," *ZAW,* LXXXI (1969), 18-40; D. B. Redford, *A Study of the Biblical Story of Joseph,* VTSup, XX (1970); R. de Vaux, *Histoire ancienne d'Israël* (1971), pp. 157-73; F. M. Cross, *Canaanite Myth and Hebrew Epic* (1973); G. W. Coats, "The Joseph Story and Ancient Wisdom," *CBQ,* XXXV (1973), 285-97, and "Redactional Unity in Genesis 37–50," *JBL,* XCIII (1974), 15-21; T. L. Thompson, *The Historicity of the Patriarchal Narratives, BZAW,* CXXXIII (1974); C. Westermann, *Genesis 12–50,* Erträge der Forschung (1975), *see* bibliog.

C. WESTERMANN
R. ALBERTZ

GENRE. *See* ACTS, GENRE[S]; APOCALYPSE, GENRE [S]; GOSPEL, GENRE[S]; LETTER; LETTER[S]; LITERATURE, EARLY CHRISTIAN[S].

***GERIZIM, MOUNT.** At the E end of the valley which separates Mount Gerizim from Mount Ebal to the N (*see* EBAL, MOUNT) lie the remains of ancient SHECHEM (Tell Balata), Jacob's Well (Bir Ya'qub), and the village of Balatah, while at its W end is the city of Nablus (ancient Neapolis). Though Mount Ebal is higher, Mount Gerizim has played a more important role in the history of the region, due partly to the fact that at least ten springs flow from the N base of Mount Gerizim, while the S side of Mount Ebal has no source of water except Ain 'Askar on its SE slope. The forested N face of Gerizim and the barren slopes of Ebal are both recent phenomena. Both mountains had trees on them in the Roman period but by the nineteenth century they were denuded.

The most ancient structures on the mountain are the excavated remains of a fifty-five-foot square temple of the sixteenth century B.C. and adjacent remains, also probably a tribal league shrine, of the seventeenth century B.C. Both are located on the low, NE slopes of the mountain above the remains of Shechem.

Josephus (Antiq. XI.viii.2, 7; XII.v.5; XIII.ix.1) affirms the existence of the Samaritan temple on Mount Gerizim (*see* SAMARITANS §C1*d*), declaring that it was built by permission of Darius III and Alexander the Great, modeled after the temple in Jerusalem, but called by different names until its destruction by John Hyrcanus in 128 B.C. The present-day Samaritans revere a flat rock on the highest peak of the mountain as the place where their temple stood, although no ancient remains have been found there. On top of the northernmost peak of Mount Gerizim, at Tell er-Râs, however, a large building complex centered around a half cube, sixty-six feet wide, sixty-six feet long, and thirty feet high, constructed of large unhewn stones, laid without cement and without internal structuring, has been excavated. This structure rests on the bedrock of the mountain in the midst of a 135-foot-wide, rectilinear courtyard built with walls of unhewn stone. The latest pottery taken from the foundation trenches of the walls is from the third century B.C.

The discovery of this monumental structure dating from the Hellenistic period on Mount Gerizim above Shechem, the chief city of the Samaritans, has led the excavator to call the complex the Samaritan temple and the unhewn stone half cube, the Samaritan altar of sacrifice. The remains of this altar would have been visible to Jesus and the Samaritan woman from Jacob's well (John 4:20), as it is today.

On the S slopes of the mountains a walled town, probably Samaritan Luza, with foundations from the Hellenistic period has been surveyed.

In the second century A.D. HADRIAN built on Mount Gerizim a temple to Zeus Hypsistos with a stairway of over 1500 marble steps leading to it. This temple, depicted on second-century coins minted at Neapolis, has been found at Tell er-Râs, built on top of the remains of the Samaritan temple. Apart from the church built by Zeno in A.D. 485 and the fortification built round it in the sixth century by Justinian, there are no other known ancient structures on the mountain.

Bibliography. R. G. Boling, "Bronze Age Buildings at the Shechem High Place: ASOR Excavations at Tananir," *BA,* XXXII (1969), 82-103; E. F. Campbell, Jr., and G. E. Wright, "Tribal League Shrines in Amman and Shechem," *BA,* XXXII (1969), 104-16; R. J. Bull, "A Preliminary Excavation of an Hadrianic Temple at Tell er-Ras on Mt. Gerizim," *AJA,* LXXI (1967), 387-93, "The Excavation of Tell er-Ras on Mt. Gerizim," *BASOR* 190 (1968), 4-19 and (same title) *BA,* XXXI (1968), 58-72.

R. J. BULL

***GEZER.** The earlier article on Gezer contains an adequate description of the site, as well as a summary of the literary sources and of the previous excavations. The present article corrects and supplements it.

1. The Late Chalcolithic period. The earliest occupation (stratum XXVI) is on the bedrock and in some of the natural caves. It is extensive but characterized mainly by campsites, hearths, rock-cuttings, and the most elementary domestic installations. It is clear that the village was unfortified. The material culture is closest to that of the Ghassul-BEER-SHEBA sites of the last half of the fourth millennium B.C., particularly in the ceramic (the "cream ware") and lithic industries.

2. The Early Bronze period. The first occupation followed that of the Late Chalcolithic after a brief hiatus, re-using some of the structures and showing continuity in certain elements of material culture. The fullest evidence is from Cave I.3A in Field I (stratum XXV), which was first used for a dwelling and then later for storage. In addition to an assemblage of pottery and stone vessels, it contained charred grain which yielded a radiocarbon-14 date of 3045 B.C. ± 180. This would correlate well with the other sites of this horizon, Wright's "EB IB" and Kenyon's "Proto Urban" periods.

The main phase of EB occupation was represented by strata XXIV–XXIII, which extended from the twenty-ninth into the twenty-sixth century B.C. The town was now rather densely built up, and the pottery and other artifacts show a considerable degree of prosperity. Although this period at comparable sites is characterized by massive city walls, it is clear that Gezer remained undefended. Two phases of occupation were discerned, coming to an end contemporary with most other sites in Palestine about 2500 B.C., in a manner as yet unexplained. The site lay deserted throughout the EB III-IV and MB I periods, *ca.* 2500-1900 B.C., with only sherds marking the gap ("stratum XXII").

3. The Middle Bronze II period. This period (strata XXI-XVIII) represents Gezer's zenith, as one of Palestine's greatest Canaanite city-states. In MB IIA the build-up was gradual and the town was not yet fortified. By MB IIC, however (*ca.* 1600 B.C.), a massive defense wall (Macalister's "Inner Wall") circled the site, reinforced by a series of stone towers and a plastered glacis (or ramp). The gate on the S side was of the typical three-entry-way type, flanked by two towers of cyclopean masonry more than fifty feet thick. Macalister's "High Place" has been conclusively dated to this period. This unique installation consists of ten enormous standing stones (or masseboth of the OT), some more than ten feet high (*see* PILLAR[S] Fig. 5). It can no longer be interpreted with Albright and others as a mortuary shrine, but must have been rather an open-air sanctuary.

4. The Late Bronze period. The long MB period having been brought to a violent end by a destruction possibly attributable to Pharaoh Thut-mose III *ca.* 1479 B.C., Gezer was virtually deserted for most of the LB I period in the fifteenth century B.C. (stratum XVII). A revival accompanied the LB IIA period (stratum XVI, fourteenth century B.C.). This is witnessed independently by ten letters from three different kings of Gezer in the Amarna archives (*see* TELL EL-AMARNA §2; TELL EL-AMARNA [S] § 2). The town evidently overflowed its walls, for a new defense system (Macalister's "Outer Wall") was built farther down the slopes, equipped with its own glacis. Domestic levels revealed hints of considerable wealth but were mostly robbed out later. A cave in Field I (I.10A) yielded several dozen well-preserved burials, accompanied by both local and imported pottery and small objects, some of Egyptian derivation. It is possible that the great water shaft and tunnel were constructed during this period, but a date in the Iron Age cannot be ruled out.

A destruction ended the Amarna period, followed by a rather poor domestic occupation during most of the thirteenth century B.C. (stratum XV). A further disturbance toward the end of the century was followed by a period of squatter occupation and deep pitting and trenching operations (stratum XIV). This may be due to a partial gap following the destruction which Pharaoh MER-NE-PTAH claims on the well-known "Israel Stele" *ca.* 1220 B.C.

5. The Philistine era. Strata XIII–XI of the twelfth-eleventh centuries B.C. represent the Philistine era. The period is characterized by the typical painted bichrome pottery, as well as by several fine courtyard houses (*see* Fig. G2), a public granary, and a series of unique stone wine vats. The period began without major disturbances but was divided internally by several destructions, after which (from the mid-eleventh century B.C. onward) there was a marked decline until the mid-tenth century B.C. (strata X–IX).

6. The Israelite period. After a final destruction ending the Philistine period, the earliest Israelite

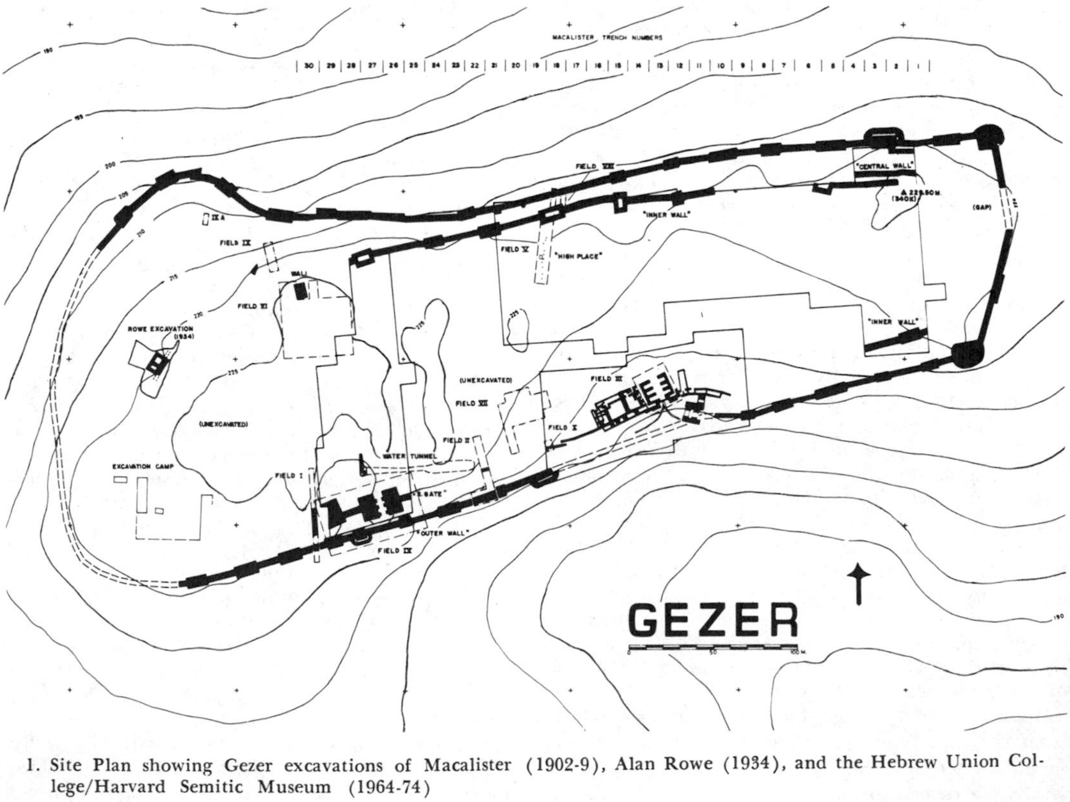

1. Site Plan showing Gezer excavations of Macalister (1902-9), Alan Rowe (1934), and the Hebrew Union College/Harvard Semitic Museum (1964-74)

Robert B. Wright

2. Twelfth-century B.C. courtyard house in Philistine stratum VC, Field VI, on the acropolis at Gezer

structures appeared, accompanied by the characteristic hand-burnished pottery. Stratum VIII saw the repair of the "Outer Wall" with a series of ashlar towers being inserted; the addition of a casemate wall near the destroyed city gate; and the construction of a four-entryway gate nearly identical to those known at HAZOR and MEGIDDO (*see* Fig. G3). This is a striking confirmation of I Kings 9:15-17, which records an Israelite takeover of the site and its refortification following an Egyptian destruction. Stratum VIII appears to have been destroyed by Shishak *ca.* 918 B.C.

Strata VII–VI mark the Iron II period until the Assyrian destruction in the late eighth century B.C., which is vividly witnessed. Stratum V in turn ended with the Babylonian destruction *ca.* 587/586 B.C., again well attested. The evidence indicates that after the Solomonic period Gezer was a relatively unimportant city.

Robert B. Wright

3. Solomonic four-entryway city gate, Field III at Gezer

7. The Persian, Hellenistic, and Roman periods. Strata IV–I represent these periods, in which Gezer enjoyed a revival only briefly during the mid-second century B.C., when it played a rather prominent role in the Maccabean wars. At this period the gate was rebuilt a final time and semicircular bastions were added to the "Outer Wall." The well-known boundary inscriptions belong to the Herodian era, when occupation on the site seems to have ceased and the area belonged to a large Roman estate. Many Byzantine and a few later tombs brought its history to a close.

Bibliography. R. A. S. Macalister, *The Excavation of Gezer,* 3 vols. (1912); W. G. Dever, H. D. Lance, G. E. Wright, *Gezer I. Preliminary Report of the 1964-66 Seasons* (1970); W. G. Dever *et al., Gezer II. Report of the 1967-70 Seasons in Fields I and II* (1974). See also the introductory articles and preliminary reports by W. G. Dever, H. D. Lance, and J. F. Ross in *BA,* XXX (1967), 34-70; and by W. G. Dever *et al.* in *BA,* XXXIV (1971), 94-132.

W. G. DEVER

***GIBEAH (OF BENJAMIN).** In 1964 the ancient remains on the summit of Tell el-Ful, the likely site of ancient Gibeah of Benjamin, were excavated by Lapp under the aegis of the American School of Oriental Research and Pittsburgh Theological Seminary.

1. Saul's fortress. This excavation aimed at uncovering evidence to settle a number of controversies arising from prior excavations. Discussion had centered on a massive rectangular tower which Albright attributed to King Saul and from which he projected the plan for a huge fortress (*see* GIBEAH 2 and Fig. 27). Others suggested that this was a lone tower or was constructed by a Philistine garrison (I Sam. 13:3, reading "Gibeah" for "Geba"). Some objected that the contours of the mound would not support a fortress with so broad a W-E axis such as Albright projected.

Unfortunately, most of the evidence which might have decided these and other questions with finality no longer existed. Most of the structures contemporary with the tower were subsequently dug out by builders of the Israelite and Hellenistic periods in order to found their structures firmly on bedrock. Lapp, however, did discover a ten-foot portion of a five-foot-wide wall N of the tower. Datable pottery and similarity of construction show that this fragment belongs to the same building complex as the tower. It may well be a portion of the W wall of the projected fortress, for it is of similar width and almost in line with the "fortress" wall running N from the tower. Thus, it is clear that there was more than a single tower here. Nor is it unreasonable to view the complex as a "fortress" of some sort, since the wall fragment is fully five feet wide. The wall, however, is too far N to support Albright's projected plan. The N-S axis was more likely longer than the W-E axis. In addition, the absence of any evidence for an inner wall makes it necessary to abandon the supposition that this was a casemate or double-walled construction during Saul's time.

2. Occupation. On the basis of the pottery, the occupation layers are now to be dated as follows:

Pre-fortress period	*ca.* 1200-1150 B.C.
Fortress period	*ca.* 1025-950
City with casemate wall	late seventh, early sixth century
Rebuilt city	middle sixth century
Populous Hellenistic town	last two thirds of second century

On this dating it is unlikely that the Philistines constructed the first phase of the fortress, for Gibeah was apparently unoccupied during the height of Philistine power (*see* PHILISTINES[S]). We may assign its construction to King Saul with as much assurance as is ever possible where documentary evidence is lacking. If a Philistine garrison was at Gibeah, it was either on temporary bivouac or housed in an installation on some point of the mound not yet excavated.

In the late seventh century the city was rebuilt and fortified by a casemate wall (containing chambers, formed by two parallel walls joined by transverse walls). Sections of this were discovered both on the W and the NE. After destruction, presumably by the Babylonians, Gibeah flourished in the sixth century. Its houses spilled outside the fortifying city walls. This was a period when Judah to the S lay in ruins, and the population center moved N (cf. Jer. 40:11-12). Gibeah's final period of occupation, during Maccabean times, was also one of its most populous ages. The relatively small area excavated at Gibeah produced no less than twenty-four storage silos, probably dug at the time of Saul and then reused down into the Hellenistic age.

Bibliography. P. Lapp, "Tel el-Fûl," *BA,* XXVIII (1965), 2-10; L. Sinclair, "An Archaeological Study of Gibeah: Tell el-Ful," *AASOR,* XXXIV-XXXV (1954-56), 1-52.

C. GRAESSER, JR.

GLOSS. *See* ABBREVIATIONS, HEBREW TEXT[S] §3*d*; INTERPRETATION, HISTORY OF[S] §A1*c*.

GLOSSOLALIA. *See* TONGUES, GIFT OF; TONGUES, GIFT OF[S].

GNOSIS. *See* GNOSTICISM; GNOSTICISM[S].

***GNOSTICISM.** Usually designates a religious or philosophic movement widespread in the first three centuries A.D. The diverse teachers, groups, and systems described as Gnostic share the conviction that, although mankind exists in ignorance and illusion, one can, through *gnosis,* attain spiritual liberation, that is, recognition of one's own identity with the divine.

1. The problem of definition
2. The scope of the discussion
3. Sources
   a. Patristic works against Gnosticism
   b. Original Gnostic texts
4. Gnostic doctrines
   a. Marcion of Pontus
   b. Valentinus
   c. Basilides
5. History of interpretation
Bibliography

1. The problem of definition. Irenaeus, bishop of Lyons (*ca.* 180), described Gnostic groups and teachers that he saw proliferating among his contemporaries: he said of the members of a single sect (Valentinian) that "you can hardly find two or three that agree on anything: they all contradict each other, both in the terminology and substance of their teaching" (Her. I.xi.1). Epiphanius (*ca.* 375) listed more than sixty Gnostic leaders, most of them unknown except by name; extant sources offer specific characteristics of at least twenty distinct teachers or sects. The second-century evidence reveals a diversity in ethical practice that ranges from ascetic to antinomian and libertarian, in ritual from the mystery religions to Jewish and Christian practice, and in theology from metaphysical philosophy to myth and magical incantations.

What justifies classifying such disparate groups together as Gnostic? For one thing, members of some groups called themselves Gnostics (literally, "those who know"). The Naassenes, for example, claimed that they alone knew "the secrets of the holy way" since, as they said, "they alone knew the deep things" (Hippolytus, *Refutation* V.vi.4). Followers of the teacher Marcellina similarly "call themselves gnostics" on the basis of secret doctrines, as do the Valentinians who claim "to know the deep things of God" and to have "perfect knowledge of God" (Iren. Her. I.xxv.5; I.vi.1; xix.1–xxi.4). Members of the groups that Irenaeus and Hippolytus described considered themselves to be Christians, but claimed to have surpassed the faith they held in common with other believers, which they contrasted with the "higher gift" of gnosis, "knowledge" or "insight."

One received gnosis through a process of initiation. The initiate passed thereby from identification with "the many" who remained ignorant into the circle of "the few" to whom was given "to know the mysteries of God." Some groups (notably certain Valentinians) offered doctrinal instruction to prepare the candidate for the secret ritual of "redemption" which conveyed gnosis. Such secret rituals took diverse forms; even within a single sect practice varied from second baptism to the "bride-chamber" ritual. Others dispensed entirely with ritual, considering the attainment of gnosis itself to be the "redemption."

Gnostic teachers insisted that it was impossible to describe the specific content of gnosis: "Because it is not static, it cannot be explained simply or in one word. So there are as many systems of redemption as there are teachers of these mystical doctrines" (Iren. Her. I.xxi.1). Nevertheless, receiving gnosis characteristically occurred as an act of self-discovery. One Valentinian writer explained that "it is not the bath [baptism] which liberates, but it is *gnosis* of who we were, what we have become; whence we were; into what we have been cast; whither we hasten; whence we are redeemed; what birth is, and what rebirth" (*Excerpts from Theodotus* 78.2).

Receiving gnosis, one learned the secret of one's true identity: that the inner self is unalterably divine. The initiate thereby rejected the view common to Jewish and Christian tradition, that mankind, having been made by God the creator, always remains distinct from the divine nature. Instead the Gnostic learned to recognize himself as a child generated from the true Father and the true Mother; hence his inner nature belonged to that divine harmony. Those "redeemed," then, were released from the creator's dominion; they might declare independence from his authority as they asserted their newly found identity: "I am a son from the pre-existent Father. . . . I know myself, and I know whence I am" (Iren. Her. I.xxi.5). In certain Valentinian circles, the ritual described as "the mystery (or: sacrament) of marriage" initiated the recipient into union with the divine; one was thus transformed and enabled to anticipate the full realization of the divine nature.

Many Gnostic groups traced the authority for such esoteric traditions to the Savior himself, and specifically to the secret teaching he gave to certain disciples. The Naassenes, for example, said that their tradition came from Jesus through James, his brother, then through Mariamne; the followers of Basilides traced theirs to Matthew; the Valentinians to Paul through his disciple Theudas. Included in these secret traditions were techniques for reading and interpreting "the scriptures," that is, the Hebrew Scriptures and many of the Christian writings, which, in these circles, often included esoteric writings. Such groups considered themselves to be "the spiritual," "the elect," or "those who have transcended," in contrast to the ignorant masses outside their circle.

Certain affinities in structure and religious conception exist, therefore, between different Gnostic sects: the discrimination of an inner circle of "those who know"; secret writings and oral traditions of doctrine, exegesis, and rituals; the concern with knowledge as the primary means of redemption; the characteristic identification of self-knowledge with knowledge of God.

2. The scope of the discussion. "Gnosticism" is a modern term. As long as the polemic writings against the Gnostics remained the primary sources for research, Gnosticism generally was considered a Christian heresy. In the eighteenth and nineteenth centuries, with the discovery of some original Gnostic texts, certain scholars suggested that Gnosticism may not have been primarily Christian, but possibly was an independent, even pre-Christian movement. Some, noting affinity between Gnostic sources and a wide range of other religious phenomena, proceeded to redefine Gnosticism in terms of specific doctrines or "attitudes" which, in their view, characterize it. On this basis the HERMETIC LITERATURE has often been classified as a type of Gnostic literature. Similarly, MANICHEISM, the dualistic theology that arose in the third century combining Christian and Iranian religious conceptions, may be regarded as a form of Gnosticism. MANDAEISM, a baptist sect that continues even today, may represent a Gnostic system. Certain movements within Judaism seem to demonstrate striking, if diverse, affinities with Gnostic sources: Scholem cites as examples the Qumran community of the DEAD SEA SCROLLS, PHILO, the Merkabah mysticism (*see* PSEUDEPIGRAPHA[S] §2*c*) of the school of Johanan ben Zakkai, and even the medieval doctrines of the Kabbalah. Certain currents within Islam, such as Sufism, may contain phenomena parallel to Gnosticism. Some scholars see Gnostic influence in certain occult or theosophic traditions, even those continuing to the present; others see parallels between Gnosticism and some esoteric Buddhist schools.

3. Sources. Two types of sources offer information on Gnostic sects and doctrines: the accounts of the church Fathers, written to refute Gnosticism, and original Gnostic works, including many discovered since 1946.

a. Patristic works against Gnosticism. Irenaeus' *Against Heresies,* or *Unmasking and Refutation of the False Gnosis,* is the most important of those that are extant. Irenaeus and his predecessor Hegesippus (whose lost work, the *Memoirs,* is often quoted in the *Ecclesiastical History* of EUSEBIUS) relate information gained by discussion with Gnostics, by hearsay, and by reading Gnostic works. Tertullian (d. 220) wrote five books *Against Marcion,* one *Against Valentinus,* the *Prescription of Heresies,* and the *Scorpiace* ("remedy for the scorpion's sting" of Gnosticism). Clement of Alexandria (d. before 215) includes quotations from Valentinus, Basilides, and others in his *Miscellanies* and quotes extensively from Theodotus (*Excerpts from Theodotus*). Hippolytus of Rome (d. 235) used Irenaeus' writings and other sources in his own *Refutation of all Heresies.* The works of Origen (d. 253/254), notably his *Commentary on John,* contain citations especially from Heracleon. Eusebius' *Ecclesiastical History* and the *Panarion* of Epiphanius (d. 403) also offer much useful information.

b. Original Gnostic texts. The patristic materials have clear disadvantages as sources for the study of Gnosticism, because their authors are writing specifically to "attack and destroy" what they intend to unmask as "false gnosis." With the discovery of the Askew Codex, acquired by the British Museum in 1785, original Gnostic texts became available for the first time. Since then an extraordinary range of Gnostic texts have been discovered.

The Askew Codex contains four books, including the PISTIS SOPHIA, a third-century text which purports to narrate secret conversations between the risen Jesus and his disciples. The Bruce Codex, which includes the Two Books of Jeu, was discovered in 1769 and published in 1891. The Berlin Codex, discovered in 1896, disclosed several remarkable texts, including a Gospel of Mary, the Sophia of Jesus Christ, and the Secret Book of John (*see* JOHN, APOCRYPHON OF[S]).

Far more significant than any earlier find was the discovery in 1945-46 of thirteen Coptic codices near Nag Hammadi in Egypt. For a discussion *see* NAG HAMMADI[S] and other articles cross-referenced there.

4. Gnostic doctrines. Irenaeus describes how Gnostic groups proliferate and rival each other's claims: "Since those who are considered more contemporary among them endeavor to describe something new every day, and to invent what no one ever thought of before, it is difficult to describe their opinions" (Iren. Her. I.xxi.5). While members of more conventional Jewish and Christian groups stress their fidelity to archaic tradition, Gnostics (rather like members of artistic circles today) regard innovation as the mark of spiritual creativity. Yet gnosis always involves a definite understanding of God and the world which is of decisive importance and which may be characterized as follows:

(1) There is an irreconcilable contradiction between the cosmic system of this world and the absolutely transcendent God. That God is often described negatively: the indescribable, unknowable, or nonexistent One; alternatively, the Abyss, Source, or Primal Beginning of all things.

(2) The "I" of the Gnostic, the "spirit," or "inner man" is unalterably divine, and belongs to that divine being which transcends all creation.

(3) The "spiritual" element, however, has become mingled with two distinct lower elements, and bound into the lower order of creation with them: first, with the body, dominated by sensual passions: second, with the soul, the center of psychic functions. The spirit, hidden within soul and body like marrow within two layers of bone and flesh (*Excerpts from Theodotus* 51-61), has been entrapped within these lower elements. The person in whom it is hidden remains unaware of its presence.

(4) Only an emissary from the divine world above—a savior, a redeemer, or a "call"—can release these bonds of confinement. Through gnosis the spiritual spark that lies dormant within the Gnostic is ignited, and the inner spirit is liberated so that one becomes aware of one's own true nature.

A consideration of the views of Marcion, Basilides, and Valentinus will illustrate several ways in which such a schema could be adapted to different religious systems and practices.

a. Marcion of Pontus, one of the most distinctive heretics, often classified as a Gnostic, came to Rome *ca.* 130-44, apparently accepted as a member of the Christian community. His opponent Tertullian says that he became preoccupied with the problem of evil: he came to reject the belief that God the creator is both good and just, that mankind, created good, introduced corruption into the world by an act of willful disobedience. Marcion concluded that the Creator, if just, is neither omnipotent nor good; that Christ's message of his good, loving Father therefore must refer to a God hitherto entirely unknown. Marcion read Paul's contrast of law and gospel as a confirmation of his conclusions: his work *Antitheses* contrasts the just, wrathful creator of the OT with the Good Father of Jesus. Marcion presented his own edited version of "the gospels and the apostle," which he claimed to have shorn of the secondary accretions added by "Judaizing" Christians. Expelled from the Roman church, he founded an institutional church whose members strove to attain perfect adherence to the Father by rejecting the creator and his works, including sexual intercourse, meat eating, and drinking of wine. *See* MARCION, GOSPEL OF.

Marcion's teaching bears certain clear affinities with Gnostic teaching; for example, his distinction between the Unknown Father and the creator, and his claim of a relationship between the Father and those who attain a "new recognition" of him through Christ. Nevertheless, according to the sketch of Gnostic doctrine given above, Marcion could not be described as a Gnostic teacher, for he does not consider the inner self to be divine prior to redemption. Furthermore, his teaching lacks the mythological and allegorical elaboration that characterizes many Gnostic teachings; and, unlike many, it leads to specific ascetic practices within an institutional structure.

b. Valentinus, the most influential Gnostic teacher of his time, came from Egypt to Rome *ca.* 140-60. His many writings have been lost, except for a few fragments, although some scholars suggest that GTr (*see* TRUTH, GOSPEL OF[S] §§1, 5) and OnRes (*see* RESURRECTION, THE TREATISE ON[S] §3) discovered at Nag Hammadi are his original writings. Tertullian says that Valentinus had expectations of becoming the leader of the Christian community in Rome, but that he subsequently separated from the church and taught independently. His followers include Ptolemaeus, author of the *Letter to Flora,* who also wrote an exegetical commentary on the Johannine prologue; Heracleon, author of the first known commentary on the Johannine gospel (and possibly of the Tripartite Tractate from Nag Hammadi); Florinus, a presbyter and teacher in Rome; Theodotus, excerpts of whose writings are found in the works of Clement of Alexandria; and Marcus, whose ritual practice and doctrine Irenaeus describes.

His followers claimed that Valentinus' teacher was Theudas, a disciple of Paul who, they said, received the apostle's secret teaching. They represented themselves, therefore, as transmitters of "wisdom" (cf. I Cor. 2:6), or as the "elect few" among the larger circle of Christian believers, whom they termed "the many," or the "ecclesiastics." They offered to teach gnosis to those they considered ready for it, and to initiate them into the Gnostic circle by means of secret rituals. While they themselves insisted that their esoteric teaching disclosed the "true meaning" of the Scriptures, Irenaeus attempted to repudiate their claims, declaring instead that their teaching undermined Christian faith and contradicted its basic premises.

Valentinus' own teaching, according to Irenaeus, begins with the doctrine of the primal Dyad, one element of which is called Indescribable, and the other, Silence. From their relationship proceeds the Father and Truth, Logos and Life, Mankind and Ecclesia, and from these proceed the whole fullness of the divine being. Describing the divine being as a harmonious relation of masculine and feminine hypostases, Valentinus relates that the twelfth and youngest of these, Sophia, having separated from her counterpart, Theletos, sets in motion the devolution of the divine being. Thereby a portion of the spiritual being becomes intermingled with the ignorance, fear, confusion, and grief she experiences in her separation from the divine being. The creation of the cosmos then becomes a means of repairing the effect of Sophia's transgression. The savior, sent from the "PLEROMA," transforms her four "passions" into the elements of air, earth, fire, and water. Through the demiurge, himself created by the Savior, and Sophia as the unwitting instrument of cosmic creation, the "seed" of the divine spirit receives a structure, the "cosmic system," within which it is planted and may grow to maturity (i.e., receive gnosis concerning its divine origin).

Those persons who became aware of the presence of the spirit (*pneuma*) within them were, the Valentinians explained, pneumatic, the elect seed. The rest were classified according to their identification either with matter (as *hylics*) or with the soul (as psychics) by contrast with the spiritual ones (pneumatics). Valentinian teachers differed, apparently, on questions of ecclesiology and eschatology. Most frequently they described how the pneumatic seed, scattered into the cosmos since Sophia's fall, was to be regathered and purified. All material elements of creation were to be annihilated and the psychic elements discarded as the pneumatic seed, reconstituted in Sophia, were restored to the harmony of the divine being. Although Valentinian theology persisted in various Christian communities through the fourth century (as Origen's works and the texts from Nag Hammadi indicate), it is difficult to trace beyond that period.

c. Basilides, active in Rome from the time of Hadrian to Antoninus Pius (*ca.* 115-45), wrote a gospel, twenty-four books of exegesis on the gospel (only fragments of which remain), and hymns and prayers (which have been lost). His followers include Isidore, who declared that gnosis is to be understood not as philosophy but as prophetic insight. Irenaeus and Hippolytus offer sharply contrasting accounts of Basilides' teaching. According to Irenaeus, Basilides described the origin of all things from the God who originated five forces (Nous, Logos, Phronesis, Sophia, and Dynamis). From these were formed angels who created 365 heavens, all ruled by Abraxas, and ranked in desending order. The lowest of these heavens was ruled by the Jewish God who introduced strife into his creation. To rectify this situation, the highest God sent his Nous, that is, Christ, who appeared in spiritual form to liberate those who recognize him from the oppression they suffer from the rule of angelic powers and their chief, the Jewish God.

Hippolytus' account, on the other hand, relates that Basilides taught a monistic doctrine. Like the Valentinian teaching, Basilides' doctrine attempted to account for the dispersal of the divine seed within cosmic creation, and to anticipate its final restoration into its divine source. According to this account, the ineffable God put forth the seed of the world, which contained within it potentially all elements of the future creation. Within this world seed were included three Sonships; the Sonship of light, which ascends immediately to God; the Sonship mingled with darkness, which needs to be purified through the Holy Spirit; and the third Sonship, which needs revelatory teaching to achieve its final purification. The Son of the High God descended with the gospel message to the lower regions ruled by the demiurge, the Great Archon, to reveal the true nature of the sonships and to purify and finally to liberate those who belonged to each, so that all might finally reascend to the place of divine origin.

5. History of interpretation. Von Harnack's classic definition of Gnosticism as "the radical Hellenizing of Christianity" was based primarily upon heresiological sources. From these he inferred that Gnostic teachers, attempting to interpret Christian doctrine by means of the terms and concepts of Greek philosophy, became in one sense "the first Christian theologians," yet in another, propagators of false, spurious, hybrid forms of Christianity. Although this definition continues to exert its influence (Leisegang, Wilson), it has been challenged by some scholars who have asked, first, whether Gnosticism is essentially Christian at all, and, second, whether its primary sources are indeed Hellenistic. Some (e.g., Bousset) have concluded that Gnosticism was a pre-Christian movement, an independent religion derived from ancient Iranian tradition, and that such Christian elements as are found are late, superficial additions. Others (e.g., Wilson, Scholem), while agreeing that the antecedents of Gnosticism are pre-Christian, stress the influence of Jewish sources. Certain of the Nag Hammadi texts in particular (such as The Nature of the Archons, The Testimony of Truth) continuously cite Jewish scriptures with little or no reference to Christian sources. Still other scholars view Gnosticism as a syncretistic movement arising simultaneously—but independently—with Christianity in the first and second centuries A.D.

This whole quest for origins has itself come under attack as a method of research that leads to a potentially infinite regress of ever remoter "origins." Instead, it has been argued, the impetus for the development of Gnosticism must be sought in specific events or experiences: in the shattering of eschatological hope after the fall of Jerusalem in A.D. 70 (Grant); in "the experience of the self," then mythically projected (Quispel); or in a certain "attitude toward existence" (Jonas). Present research is less concerned to construct comprehensive theories than to investigate the remarkably diverse body of Gnostic literature that is becoming available from Nag Hammadi—some of it distinctively Christian, some showing little or no Christian influence, some few writings with a pagan origin, and some (perhaps more than expected) with a Jewish origin. Publication of these materials remains the first priority of scholars of Gnosticism, who generally agree that earlier theories will have to be revised in the light of these newer resources.

Bibliography. W. Völker, ed., *Quellen zur Geschichte der Christlichen Gnosis* (1932); for eds. of the Askew, Bruce, Berlin, and Nag Hammadi Codices, *see:* D. Scholer, *Nag Hammadi Bibliography, 1948-1969,* Nag Hammadi Studies, I (1971), with supplements in *NovT* (1971 ff.); U. Bianchi, *Le Origini dello Gnosticismo,* Supplements to Numen, XII (1967); W. Eltester, *Christentum und Gnosis,* BZNW, XXXVII (1969); R. M. Grant, *Gnosticism and Early Christianity* (1959); H. Jonas, *The Gnostic Religion* (2nd ed., 1963); H. Langerbeck, *Aufsätze zur Gnosis* (1967); G. MacRae, "Gnosis, Christian," and "Gnosticism," *New Catholic Encyclopedia,* VI (1967), 522-28; J. M. Robinson and H. Koester, *Trajectories through Early Christianity* (1971); K. W. Tröger, *Gnosis und NT* (1973); G. Quispel, *Gnosis als Weltreligion* (1951); F. L. Sagnard, *La Gnose valentinienne et le témoignage de saint Irénée,* Études de philosophie médiévale, XXXVI (1947); E. Pagels, *The Gnostic Paul* (1975); R. M. Wilson, *The Gnostic Problem* (1958), and *Gnosis and* *the NT* (1968); G. G. Scholem, *Jewish Gnosticism, Merkabah Mysticism, and Talmudic Tradition* (2nd ed., 1965).

E. H. PAGELS

***GOD, NATURE OF, IN THE OT.** As a symbolic mode of disclosure, theological language presents God in relationship to Israel, to humankind, and to the individual. This language belongs to different genres which span centuries of traditions and carry diverse perspectives. It is culturally conditioned speech which draws from a variety of experiences. Thus the OT does not describe God as God. Instead, it appropriates both andromorphic and gynomorphic images to portray a God who relates to human concerns. Though often neglected in OT theology, the female images are especially important for an expanding knowledge of ways in which the divine and the human meet.

1. Womb imagery. ***a. The root rḥm.*** Designating a place of protection and care, the womb (*reḥem*) is a basic metaphor of divine compassion. The metaphor begins with a physical organ unique to the female and extends to psychic levels in the plural noun רחמים (mercies), in the adjectival form רחום (merciful), and in uses of the verb רחם (to show mercy). It moves from the literal to the figurative, from the concrete to the abstract.

b. The creedal formula. Distinctive in Mosaic faith is the assertion that Yahweh is merciful (רחום) and gracious (Exod. 34:6; cf. 33:19). Used only of the deity, רחום is not language for a father who creates by begetting but for a mother who creates by nourishing in the womb. Often as part of a set phrase, the term occurs in descriptions of God's saving acts in history (Ps. 111:4; Neh. 9:17), and in petitions for deliverance (Ps. 86:15), calls for repentance (Joel 2:13; Jonah 4:2), and proclamations of unmerited forgiveness (Pss. 78:38; 103:8).

c. Some prophetic contributions. Hosea employs uteral speech in both negative and positive ways (e.g., 1:6, 7; 2:1, 4, 19, 23 [H 3, 6, 21, 25]). Jeremiah intensifies this language in a poem replete with female imagery (31:15-22). Over against Rachel's lament is the word of Yahweh: "Is Ephraim my dear son? Is he my darling child? For as often as I speak of him, I do remember him still. Therefore my inner parts yearn for him; I will surely have motherly compassion on him (*raḥēm ʾᵃraḥᵃmennû*), says the Lord" (31:20, author's trans.). As Rachel mourns the loss of the fruit of her womb, so God yearns from her own inner parts. While the human mother refuses comfort, the divine mother changes grief into grace (cf. Jer. 12:15; 30:18). This vocabulary of the feminine continues in the final strophe. There Jeremiah calls the nation "virgin" and "daughter." Not only do these epithets replace a masculine one (vs. 20), but also they lead to the revolutionary reversal of sex roles. In the new creation a merciful (*rḥm*) God overturns male dominance: "For the Lord has created a new thing on the earth: a woman protects a man" (31:22*b*).

Both physical and psychic meanings of womb appear in Isa. 49:15. Juxtaposing Yahweh and a mother, the word hints at the unfathomable depths of transcendent love.

d. Conclusion. Uteral imagery is used extensively in the OT. This language functions as a major symbol throughout the history of Israel. In this symbol, divine mercy is analogous to the womb of a mother. As Yahweh's creative activity, maternal compassion signifies the thought, feeling, attitude, and action which results in life and well-being for nations, individuals, and the world (cf. Ps. 145:8, 9). It suggests a natural and spontaneous relationship between the divine and the human, in contrast to one based on adoption, duty, or law. It embodies God's intimate embrace.

Yet this analogy does not restrict the love of God to a female attribute; rather it establishes that semantic value from which a wide range of meanings extend. And among these meanings is paternal love: "As a father pities (*kᵉraḥēm*) his children, so the Lord pities (*riḥam*) those who fear him" (Ps. 103:13). Hence, from its literal base in the uterus, this metaphor expresses the love of female, male (cf. I Kings 3:26 with Gen. 43:30), and deity. Neither definition nor limitation, it contributes a major component to the meaning of mercy.

2. Related female images. ***a. Womb and breasts.*** In addition to the womb itself, other gynomorphic language enhances an understanding of God in relationship. Gen. 49:25 parallels the God of the fathers with the God Shaddai. These epithets balance masculine and feminine symbols. Cross holds that Shaddai had the original meaning of female breasts, a meaning that is preserved here through paronomasia (*see* WORDPLAY IN THE OT [S]). The God of the breasts gives the blessings of the breasts (*shādayim*; cf. Hos. 9:14). Elsewhere, the deity is both midwife and mother. She takes the infant from the womb and places it safely upon maternal breasts; in turn, she becomes the very one upon whom the child is cast from birth (Ps. 22:9-10 [H 10-11]). Although this poetry stops short of equation, its female imagery corresponds to divine activity (cf. Ps. 131:2).

b. Travail. What Ps. 22 suggests, Deut. 32:18 makes explicit: "You were unmindful of the Rock that begot you, and you forgot the God who gave you birth." While the first verb (*yld*) is used for both the bearing of the mother and the begetting of the father (e.g., Prov. 23:22, 25), the second verb (*ḥyl*) describes only a woman in labor pains (e.g., Isa. 51:2). God is such a woman, bearing Israel in travail. Similarly, Second Isaiah interprets destruction as "the birth pangs of God." Out of divine labor comes a new creation: "Now I will cry out like a woman in travail, I will gasp and pant" (42:14*b*). In Job 38:29 the gynomorphic metaphor is ironic: "From whose womb did the ice come forth, and who has given birth to the hoarfrost of heaven?" A woman's giving birth is not comparable to the cosmic work of God; yet this human analogy alludes to divine creativity. From the divine womb came the ice and the hoarfrost (cf. Job 38:8).

c. Comfort. Proclaiming the unprecedented birth of a new people to Zion, Yahweh identifies with that event: "Shall I bring to the birth and not cause to bring forth? says the Lord; shall I, who cause to bring forth, shut the womb? says your God" (Isa. 66:9). This poem continues with a joyful description of Jerusalem the consoling mother (vss. 10-11). Then the deity speaks: "As one whom his mother comforts, so I will comfort you; you shall be comforted in Jerusalem" (vs. 13). Whereas this metaphor focuses primarily on the nation as a child being comforted, its second level pertains to the agent of that comfort, God as mother.

d. Conception. In Num. 11, when Israel complains of hunger and thirst, an angry Moses reproaches God (cf. II Esd. 1:28-30): "Did I conceive all this people? Did I bring them forth that thou shouldst say to me, 'Carry them in your bosom, as a nurse carries the sucking child, to the land which thou didst swear to give their fathers'?" (11:12). The first two verbs depict a woman becoming pregnant and giving birth. Indirectly, Moses ascribes that activity to God. Moreover, he sees Yahweh providing food for the infant. Although the word for nurse is masculine (*hā'ōmēn*), the imagery surrounding it favors a feminine meaning. Indeed, an alternate pointing reads *hā'immōn,* a hypocorism for *'ēm,* mother (*see bibliog*).

3. Conclusion. All these passages disclose an invaluable vocabulary of female imagery for God. Recovery of this meaning tempers any assertion that Yahweh is a male deity. It expands our understanding of the divine-human relationship, for which both female and male images are appropriated. Yet Israel knows the inadequacy of all analogies to the freedom and transcendence of Yahweh (cf. Num. 23:19; Isa. 40:25; Hos. 11:9*b*), and OT faith has no final resting place in God the mother, or in God the father. The One to whom these epithets witness goes before Israel in otherness to make all things new: "For my father and my mother have forsaken me, but the Lord will take me up" (Ps. 27:10).

See also EL[S] §2*c*; SEMANTICS[S] §§1, 2.

Bibliography. D. N. Freedman, "God Compassionate and Gracious," *Western Watch,* VI (1955), 6-24, and "The Name of the God of Moses," *JBL,* LXXIX (1960), 151-56; J. Muilenburg, "Isaiah (chs. 40–66)," IB, V (1956); A. Jepsen, "Gnade und Barmherzigkeit im Alten Testament," *Kerygma und Dogma,* VII (1961), 261-71; W. Holladay, "Jer. xxxi 22B Reconsidered: 'The Woman Encompasses the Man,'" *VT,* XVI (1966), 236-39; M. Noth, *Numbers* (1968), pp. 86-87; F. Cross, *Canaanite Myth and Hebrew Epic* (1973), pp. 54-55; P. A. H. de Boer, *Fatherhood and Motherhood in Israelite and Judean Piety* (1974), esp. p. 35 for the pointing *hā'immōn.*

P. TRIBLE

***GOD, OT VIEW OF.** *See* PRESENCE OF GOD, CULTIC [S].

***GOLDEN RULE, THE. 1. Background.** The maxim enjoining one to treat others as one would like to be treated, in both the positive and negative form, is, in the Hellenistic world, a product of the Sophistic movement (late fifth century B.C.). It resulted from the Sophists' penchant for encapsulating popular morality in pungent aphorisms. It is, accordingly, an expression of popular morality rather than of philosophic ethics, based on the ancient idea of retribution or reciprocity, a notion which, in turn, arises out of an understanding of the world of moral action as a balance of obligations. The Golden Rule is related to primitive ideas like blood revenge, which Greek and Hellenistic philosophic ethics quickly transcended in their quest for the good as such. It is clearly inadequate as a guide to conduct unless there is also present a notion of the good to enlighten and control the reciprocity; to give a vivid example, a masochist following the rule naïvely would wreak moral havoc.

The Rule occurs for the first time in Greek literature in Herodotus (III.142; VII.136), who was influenced by the Sophists. From the fourth century B.C. onward it was an essential part of the gnomic popular ethics encountered in the Greek and Latin literature influenced by rhetorical schools, but is absent for the most part in philosophic writings (cf. Aristotle's *Rhetoric* II.vi.19). It does not occur in Jewish literature before the Hellenistic period (Aristeas 207; Tobit 4:15), although it could be seen to be implied in texts like Deut. 15:13. Despite this latter possibility, one must conclude that the Golden Rule is the product of Greek popular morality as formulated by the Sophists, and was taken over from there by Jewish thought in the Hellenistic period. In early Christian literature the Golden Rule was popular, mostly in the negative form.

2. In the NT. *a. Luke.* The Golden Rule occurs in a puzzling context in the Third Gospel as part of an exhortation to love one's enemies (Luke 6:27-36; cf. Matt. 5:38-48). The very attitude of reciprocity which the rule seems to advocate in vs. 31 is condemned in the vss. immediately following (32-34). The Golden Rule would appear to be a rather loose summary of vss. 27-30. It is interpreted, in turn, by vss. 32-34, in such a way as to minimize the element of reciprocity which it entails. Luke, therefore, like Hellenistic philosophic ethics in general, is transcending the relatively naïve popular ethic of the Golden Rule by means of the radical religious ethic of love for enemies. The background of Luke's thought in this regard is the tradition about Jesus and the humanitarian climate of Greco-Roman philosophic culture.

b. Matthew. In Matthew the Golden Rule summarizes the teaching of the SERMON ON THE MOUNT that precedes it. Davies suggests that the section of the Sermon from 5:17 to 7:12 was composed as a counterpart to the three pillars of Judaism (AB. 1.2)—Torah, worship, and deeds of loving-kindness. In 5:17-48 we find the Torah of Jesus, in 6:1-16 the true worship, and in 6:19–7:11 deeds of loving-kindness. All this is summarized by the Golden Rule in 7:12, which is called, in turn, the epitome of "the law and the prophets." This statement [οὗτος γάρ ἐστιν ὁ νόμος καὶ οἱ προφῆται] recalls the opening of the section in 5:17-18, and the great twofold commandment in 22:40.

By qualifying the Golden Rule as "the law and the prophets" and linking it with the preceding sermon, Matthew achieves the same correction of the ethic of naïve reciprocity as Luke does. They link the Golden Rule with a clear statement of the content of the good, thus providing an idea of the good by which reciprocity might be guided and controlled.

Bibliography. W. D. Davies, *The Setting of the Sermon on the Mount* (1964); A. Dihle, *Die Goldene Regel: Eine Einführung in die Geschichte der antiken und frühchristlichen Vulgärethik,* Studienheft zur Altertumswissenschaft, VII (1972); V. P. Furnish, *The Love Command in the NT* (1972); E. Lerle, "Realisierbare Förderungen der Bergpredigt?" *Kerygma und Dogma,* XVI (1970), 32-40.

R. G. Hamerton-Kelly

***GOLGOTHA.** *See* Holy Sepulchre, Church of the[S].

***GOLIATH.** The MT of I Sam. 17:4 gives the height of Goliath as "six cubits and a span," and this is followed by most modern translations. (Cf. NEB "over nine feet in height.") Two LXX MSS, however, read "four cubits and a span," and one reads "five." The reading "four" is supported by the still unpublished Heb. MS 4QSam[a], and was accepted by NAB, which translates "six and a half feet tall." Many other readings from this scroll are followed by NAB in I Sam., especially where they agree with LXX.

GOSPEL, GENRE. "Gospel" was first introduced as a literary term by late first-century Christians, who adopted it as a short title for the Gospel of Mark (*see* Gospel [Message] §1). The title was transferred to other literary works which had many similar features and so came to designate a group of writings. The modern consensus has been that the canonical gospels are unique in antiquity, not only by reason of their title, but also as a type of literature. Recent developments have put the consensus in doubt and have led to a renewed investigation of the genre issue.

1. The individuality of the gospels and the problem of genre. ***a. Canonical gospels.*** Genre is determined by the interrelation of form, style, and content. Writings grouped together by content may belong to the same genre, but similarity of content alone is not a sufficient criterion. Since dogmatic content was a more important criterion than literary form in the canonizing process (*see,* e.g., Iren. Her. III), scholars have challenged the opinion that Matthew, Mark, Luke, and John represent the same genre. For example, Matthew has been viewed as a "church manual" because of its concern for ecclesiastical rules. However, the formal divergence of Matthew from known manuals (such as the Didache) is extreme, and Matthew's retrojection of ecclesiastical concerns into speeches by Jesus is probably only a special case of the gospels' general tendency to interpret the ministry of Jesus in terms of postresurrection experience.

b. Noncanonical "gospels." In comparison with the remnants of other ancient gospel literature, the canonical four appear to constitute a distinct class. Apart from fragmentary examples (e.g., Gospel of the Ebionites [*see* Ebionites, Gospel of] and the Secret Gospel of Mark), other writings to which the title has been applied are clearly not of the same type. The Infancy Gospels belong to the realm of romantic fantasy. The so-called Gnostic gospels (e.g., Pistis Sophia) are a species of revelation discourse (*see* Apocrypha, NT; Apocrypha, NT[S] §3). Even the synoptic-like teaching tradition in the Gospel of Thomas (*see* Thomas, Gospel of[S]) is embedded in an identifiable genre ("The Sayings of the Sages") with roots in the Jewish wisdom movement. Such considerations, although they do not settle all issues raised by the differences among the canonical gospels, caution against concluding that they do not belong to the same genre.

c. The individuality of the evangelists. Emphasis on the distinctiveness of each gospel is, perhaps, the primary scholarly development requiring reevaluation of the question of genre. The judgment that the gospels represent a unique genre initially relied on their identification as "folk literature" and the consequent minimizing of the self-awareness of the evangelists as authors. The form-critical observation that the Synoptics largely consist of small, independent units which are frequently brought together by devices characteristic of the process of tradition (such as catchword association) encouraged the view that the gospels were not so much compositions as deposits. Thus, the genre, gospel, was seen to have evolved under the influence of some special feature of the tradition (usually, the kerygma of Cross and Resurrection). From this standpoint, the gospel becomes an expanded cult legend. Still, evidence which points in another direction was recognized: the specific concerns of individual evangelists (e.g., Mark's messianic secret [*see* Secret, Messianic], Luke's fondness for dividing history into periods, the literary claims of Luke's prologue, and John's freedom to impose a significant unity on his material). Redaction critics have reassessed the role of the evangelists and no longer regard them as mere collectors, but as writers with imaginative and purposeful control of their sources (*see* Redaction Criticism, NT[S] §§3, 4). This judgment requires re-examination of the sense in which the gospel can be seen as a new type of "evolved" literature.

2. Genre identification, gospels, and gospel sources. The hypothesis of a genre without roots in antecedent literary types presents theoretical problems. Since genre is a sociolinguistic convention through which meaning is conveyed, a genuinely *sui generis* writing is not congruent with its milieu. Both ancient and modern endeavors to define the genre of the gospels recognize that fact. Justin Martyr's references (e.g., Apol. I, 66) to "memoirs (ἀπομνημονεύματα) called Gospels" provided a clue to the character of these writings, whose designation was unintelligible to most people in the mid-second century. Justin probably meant to evoke comparison with the Socratic *Memorabilia* (Ἀπομνημονεύματα) of Xenophon. The analogy does not provide an accurate identification of genre, since in Xenophon's composite work sections of dialogue, anecdotes, and aphorisms comprise an appendage to an introductory rhetorical defense. In light of Xenophon's claims to direct knowledge (e.g., I.iii.1; II.v.1.), Justin may have meant that the gospels were dependable eye-witness memoirs. Even so, this apologetic is appropriate only to such literary types as history and biography.

a. "Sayings of the Sages." The modern search

for genre relationships has also extended to the sources of the gospels. The sayings source (*see* Q; Q[S]) may be an example of the genre "Sayings of the Sages," found in the Gospel of Thomas at a later stage (*see* §1*b above*). Since the "Sayings" genre is deficient in narrative elements, it is not directly antecedent to gospels of the canonical type; at the same time, the Christology of Q (for which Jesus functions primarily as the bearer of revealed truth) effectively illustrates the intimate relation of form and content.

b. Aretalogy. Because of miracle stories in the gospels, considerable attention has been given to reports of the mighty deeds of gods and wonder workers in antiquity. As may be seen from such material as Oxyrhynchus Papyrus 1381 (apparently an introduction to a record of Asclepius' healing miracles), Lucian of Samosata's exposé, *Alexander, the False Prophet,* and a tradition behind Philostratus' *Life of Apollonius of Tyana,* the purpose of the reports was to accredit divine power to their heroes. In modern practice, accounts of these mighty deeds have been designated aretalogies; a human subject honored in an aretalogy is said to be a DIVINE MAN. Sources of both Mark and John have been plausibly linked with such accounts. The signs source of John and a chain of miracles taken up by Mark appear to have advanced Jesus as a thaumaturgic divine man. While both evangelists sought to subordinate this view of Jesus to a more comprehensive Christology, the aretalogy (in the sense of a record of mighty deeds) has significantly affected the structure of the canonical gospels (but *see* ARETALOGY[S]).

c. Aretalogical elements in narrative literature. The "divine man" ideology was a widespread feature of Greco-Roman culture. Indeed, it was probably sages, rather than wonder workers, who were first described as divine. The moral giant whose status was attested by his teaching and by his adherence to it presents an alternative to the divine man conceived as thaumaturge and authenticated by miraculous deeds. The difference may be seen by comparing Lucian's Peregrinus (the false Cynic) or Demonax with his Alexander. Yet, though these positions were in conflict, they also had much in common. There was a confluence of aretalogical traits associated with divine men from shamans to statesmen: heroic motifs (drawn especially from the Heracles myth), miraculous birth, prodigies at death, divine wisdom, supernatural manifestations. Such traits had a pervasive influence on Greco-Roman narrative types from biography to romance.

3. The gospel as aretalogical biography. ***a. Aretalogical biography.*** To the average modern reader the gospels present the appearance of biography, and they probably left the same impression on readers in antiquity. The term "memoirs," which commended itself to Justin as a description of the gospels, suggests a type of biographical literature; the Third Evangelist's evaluation of his predecessors pointed in a similar direction (Luke 1:1-4). Scholarly resistance to such classification is in part a reaction against efforts to treat the gospels as modern historical biography even though, as in most ancient biography, the sequences of events in the gospels do not depict the natural unfolding of their subject's personality. The issue also has been clouded by rigid views of Greco-Roman biographical literature. The skillful chronological narrative of Plutarch's best performance was not standard, but contrasts sharply with the many credulous anecdotal biographies of antiquity, which had an artificial sequence or none at all. The rhetorical origins of ancient biography, especially its indebtedness to the encomium, left it formally flexible and amenable to the introduction of aretalogical features. Philo's *Life of Moses,* Porphyry's *Life of Pythagoras,* and Philostratus' *Life of Apollonius of Tyana* exhibit such features, though none is an aretalogy (*see* §2*b*). Among Philostratus' sources was an aretalogy of Apollonius as wonder-working divine man, although Philostratus (I.ii) sought to subordinate thaumaturgy to moral excellence as a criterion of divine power. Eunapius (fourth century) perceptively observed that Philostratus' *Life of Apollonius* might be called "The Visit of God to Mankind" (*Lives of the Philosophers* 454).

b. The gospel as adapted genre. If a place can be found for the gospels in the context of ancient biographical literature, that place would appear to be the biography with aretalogical traits. The alleged lack of literary expertise on the part of the evangelists is not a valid objection to this classification; books of any genre may be poorly written. More significant is the question of the relation of the gospel genre to the kerygma of the Cross and Resurrection. The view that the gospel "grew" out of a tradition impelled by the kerygma does not really explain how complex traditions and sources were combined in a form which resembles a life of Jesus. A more natural explanation of that combination is that in the first-century Mediterranean world, accounts of founding prophets, sages, and wonder workers were a cultural requirement, that the aretalogical life was becoming an established convention, and that the gospel is a response to that setting. The thematic dominance of the gospel by the kerygma of the Cross and Resurrection (at least in Mark and John) suggests that the response was not a blind adoption of the available convention but an adaptation of it. The description of Mark as a passion narrative with a long introduction, though inaccurate in terms of form, points to the kerygma's fundamental thematic modification of the genre. The gospel is distinctive as an adaptation of an existing genre, not as a *sui generis* phenomenon. Most of the earliest readers would have taken the gospels as accounts of Jesus' life, even though they might not have acknowledged their reliability, and the elite would have noted a weakness of discrimination and style. Speaking broadly, the gospels would have been taken as biographical; and, in spite of the kerygmatic element, they were probably so intended.

See also LITERATURE, EARLY CHRISTIAN[S] §§7, 8.

Bibliography. P. J. Achtemeier, "Toward the Isolation of Pre-Markan Miracle Catenae," *JBL,* LXXXIX (1970), 265-91, and "The Origin and Function of the Pre-Marcan Miracle Catenae," *JBL,* XCI (1972), 198-221, uses "catena" to describe a collection of miracles resembling an aretalogy; H. D. Betz, "Jesus as Divine

Man," in *Jesus and the Historian,* ed. F. Trotter (1968), pp. 114-33, outlines alternative ancient conceptions of divine man; F. F. Bruce, "When is a Gospel not a Gospel?" *BJRL,* XLV (1962-63), 319-39; R. Bultmann, "The Gospels (Form)," in *Twentieth Century Theology in the Making,* ed. J. Pelikan, I (1969), 86-92, trans. from *RGG,* II (2nd ed., 1928); H. Conzelmann, "Present and Future in the Synoptic Tradition," *JTC,* V (1968), 26-44; M. Hadas and M. Smith, *Heroes and Gods* (1965), offers an overly schematized presentation of aretalogy as "spiritual biography"; W. R. Farmer, "Jesus and the Gospels," *Perkins School of Theology Journal,* XXVIII (1975), 35-61, sees the gospel as product of the interaction of Scripture interpretation and rhetorical models; R. T. Fortna, *The Gospel of Signs,* NTSMS, XI (1970), finds an aretalogy-like source behind John.

H. C. Kee, "Aretalogy and Gospel," *JBL,* XCII (1973), 402-22, rejects attempts to establish the form of the aretalogy because of the diversity of types of aretalogies; W. Marxsen, *Mark the Evangelist* (1956 [ET 1969]), pp. 117-50, stresses the distinctiveness of the gospels, but does not see clearly the distinction between lexical analysis of "gospel" as a term and literary analysis of the gospel as a genre; J. M. Robinson and H. Koester, *Trajectories through Early Christianity* (1971), includes several important essays on genres of sources as well as of canonical and noncanonical gospels, oriented toward the gospel as "evolved" literature; K. L. Schmidt, "Die Stellung der Evangelien in der allgemeinen Literaturgeschichte," in ΕΥΧΑΡΙΣΤΗΡΙΟΝ, II, ed. H. Schmidt, *FRLANT,* XXXVI (1923), 50-134, the definitive statement of the consensus position; W. Schneemelcher, "Gospels . . . Introduction," in E. Hennecke and W. Schneemelcher, *NT Apocrypha,* I (1959), 71-84; M. Smith, "Prolegomena to a Discussion of Aretalogies, Divine Men, the Gospels, and Jesus," *JBL,* XC (1971), 174-99; G. N. Stanton, "The Gospel Traditions and Early Christological Reflection," in *Christ, Faith, and History,* ed. S. W. Sykes and J. P. Clayton (1972), pp. 191-204, gives a sober assessment of the gospels in relation to contemporary biography; C. H. Talbert, *Literary Patterns, Theological Themes, and the Genre of Luke-Acts,* SBLMS, XX (1974), regards Luke-Acts as an example of Greco-Roman lives of philosophers; D. L. Tiede, *The Charismatic Figure as Miracle Worker,* SBLDS, I (1972); C. W. Votaw, "The Gospels and Contemporary Biographies," *AJT,* XIX (1915), 45-73, 217-49 (reprinted in FBBS, XXVII [1970]), sees the gospels as "popular" biographies.

M. J. Suggs

***GOVERNMENT, ISRAELITE.** Government in general can be defined as the exercise of continuous sovereign authority over a political unit. Since at least the Bronze Age, governments have operated through the means of war for external security, law for internal security and control over the production and distribution of goods. In the ancient world, continuity of sovereignty usually was expressed in the concept of dynastic succession from father to son. The legitimacy of a regime was based historically on a superiority, if not a monopoly, of force and fear, and ideologically upon the myth of a "divine charter" (i.e., the king had been chosen by a god or a committee of gods to exercise rule). Kingship in all our written sources is presented as the clearest and most important expression of the "will of the gods," except in ancient Israel before the monarchy (cf. Judg. 9:8-15). *See* King §2.

Government can also be defined more broadly as that complex of social institutions, laws, and customs through which the maintenance of a social order is carried out in a specific social unity. Whatever the social control system, it is inevitably linked to the ideology as well as the technology of the culture. As a result, if one of these three aspects of culture changes, there will inevitably be changes in one or both of the other aspects. Ancient Israel went through at least four major phases characterized by radically differing kinds of social organization and government.

1. Bronze Age governments
2. Early Israel
3. The monarchies
4. The exilic reformation
5. Postexilic priestly rule
6. The NT reformation
Bibliography

1. Bronze Age governments (*see* Canaan, Conquest and Settlement of[S] §3*b*). ***a. City-states.*** The typical political unit in Mesopotamia and Syria in prehistoric times was an urban center surrounded by a cluster of villages (*see* Prehistory in the ANE and supplementary article). Ideally, the surplus productivity of the villages supported and made possible the specializations of the city: arts and crafts, political administration, scribal activity, and elaborate ritual.

Prior to the emergence of centralized monarchical control, specific Mesopotamian urban complexes were regarded as the "estate" (common Semitic *bēth,* "house") of a deity, administered by a "steward." It is probable that many of the place names in the OT that consist of the word *Beth-* followed by a divine name reflect a similar type of religious and socioeconomic organization. Thus the concept of the divine ownership of available land, so characteristic of early Israel, may not have been a radically new idea; instead, it may have been a re-adaptation of archaic concepts that reach back into prehistoric times.

b. Empires. It is probable that the transition from the "temple state" to monarchy was a result of increasing competition between urban complexes in a rapidly rising population during the course of the Early Bronze Age. Since military success had undeniable economic advantages for the urban base of the successful conqueror, in the form of "spoils" (looting) and "tribute" (taxation in kind), it is not surprising that in the Early Bronze Age, city-states had already succeeded in becoming centers of short-lived empires. But since they were based largely on superior military force and judicious allocation of the economic surplus available to the king, large-scale identification of local populations with the central government was not common. In other words, modern "nationalism" likely did not exist.

c. Suzerainty treaties. A "divine charter" mythology was the easiest religious ideology for legitimizing the royal monoply and use of force, short of deifying the king himself. The contrary concept of rule based upon the voluntary consent of the governed may have originated with the biblical tradition (*see, however,* Jacobsen).

Attempts were made to base political authority

upon voluntary consent in the Late Bronze Age, for which the Hittite suzerainty treaties give us the best evidence. But those treaties were between a "Great King" and his vassals, some of whom seem to have owed their small royal domain to the Great King, i.e., they were puppets. These puppets received no more allegiance from their subjects than they had for the Great King. Such covenants were only attempts to regularize, to make predictable in public life, a temporary coincidence of collective local interests. *See* COVENANT §C1*a*; COVENANT, MOSAIC[S].

Since the empires existed only by collecting the surplus productivity of villages in foods and raw materials and did not support the symbiotic relationship between local villages and urban centers, they became parasitic. Under attack by the Sea Peoples (*see* PHILISTINES §4*a*; PHILISTINES[S]) at the end of the Late Bronze Age, virtually all of the great empires collapsed into social chaos. Such destruction prepared the way for a new religious ideology, a new concept of society, and an equitable social economy.

2. Early Israel. ***a. Sinai and the traditions of wandering.*** The nineteenth-century scholarly idea of a nomadic origin of the people of ancient Israel cannot be maintained (*see* WILDERNESS[S]; RECHABITES[S]; NOMADISM[S]). The "murmurings" traditions may suggest that the little band under Moses was not a people adapted to desert existence. Further, some sort of symbiosis was achieved with the Midianites, into which group Moses had married.

This period marks the beginnings of the specifically biblical religious tradition, and of a systematic rejection of the old Bronze Age religious ideologies and the political institutions that perpetuated them: the royal court and royal temple bureaucracy. The Sinai covenant traditions are the only available source for the unique religious tradition of ancient Israel, although they have been obscured by later attempts (under the monarchy) to harmonize them with the revived and re-adapted tradition of the divine charter (*see* COVENANT, DAVIDIC[S]). The results of the Exodus-Sinai events included at least the following traits that were never entirely obscured.

i. The rejection of "other gods." This is the only important similarity to the alleged monotheism of AKH-EN-ATON's reform, and the contrasts are enormous. Most gods in the Late Bronze Age were symbols for various social power structures, and Akh-en-Aton merely substituted one symbol for another. Moses and early Israel refused to identify Yahweh with any social power structure.

ii. The necessary cause and effect relationship between grace and gratitude (*see* GRACE IN THE OT[S]). The LB suzerainty treaties already emphasized this. In situations where the benefactor was in a position of great power and authority, he had a recognized claim to define what he wished to receive. This would not ordinarily be true among equals, except by mutal negotiation: the few ancient parity treaties come under this rubric.

iii. It follows that obligations are stipulated by Yahweh and are accepted by the new community because of what had already happened—the deliverance from slavery in Egypt. Contrary to some traditional interpretations, all the early obligations under the Sinai covenant are ethical. Ritual traditions have to do only with those customary and mutually understood symbolic acts whereby persons commit themselves to permanent relationships and obligations.

iv. Enforcement of obligations by the social organization was not even contemplated in the earliest sources and narratives; instead, we have a succession of narratives about miracles by which Moses was upheld and his various enemies or challengers punished or annihilated. Although these narratives cannot have been put into their present form before the monarchy, it is likely that they have a historical nucleus: a Moses who had no social coercive power over a tiny band of refugees from Egypt, refugees who merged into the nascent community of the Israel of God.

v. Voluntary servitude to a political authority, Yahweh the King. This introduces the theme of the KINGDOM OF GOD, which is so essential to the entire biblical tradition. Only upon this religious foundation can the existence of ancient Israel be understood either theologically or historically. *See* KING, GOD AS[S].

vi. Perhaps most important because of its enormous potential for development and adaptation over the centuries was a "sense of history": the affirmation that certain acts have necessary consequences over a long range of time (e.g., to the fourth generation, Deut. 5:9). Such a perspective contains the grounds for social and individual self-criticism, illustrated beautifully in the eleventh-century poem of Deut. 32. This is adumbrated in the blessings and curses formulas of the LB suzerainty treaties, but in a much narrower ideological context.

b. The twelve-tribe federation. As a society of village peasants and shepherds (as was also most of the rest of the Eastern Mediterranean world at the time), the Israelite federation had little need for government in the sense of continuous, centralized bureaucracy. Yahweh was King, and his concerns were ethical, not material. Village courts are the largest unit contemplated in the old Covenant Code; conflicts between tribal groups may have called for action by the federation leaders (e.g., Judg. 19), or may have been referred to some local prestigious personality for arbitration (the "judges"), though we have no direct evidence.

The federation made itself manifest only when a specific occasion called it into action, and this is again characteristic of peasant society solidarities. A common cultic symbol (the ark) and priesthood served as a meeting place. When an emergency arose, the call went out to all who were near enough, or sufficiently involved, to render assistance.

The analogy to the amphictyonies of early Greek society seems now clearly to have outlived its usefulness. The contrasts are greater than the similarities, though it seems quite possible that the amphictyonies may actually be a relatively late adaptation of earlier forms of political alliance that could well have been more nearly analogous to the Israelite federation. *See* AMPHICTYONY[S].

As leader in war, as the supreme court of appeal where injustice had been done, as the ultimate source of economic weal or woe, Yahweh had all the important roles of the old Bronze Age kings, except for presiding over a bureaucracy, and even this was at some time attributed to him in the concept of the "Divine Council."

c. Polytheism vs. monotheism. The nature of the early Israelite community was inseparable from the new monotheism that stemmed from the Sinai covenant (*see, however,* MONOTHEISM[S]). The only important contrast between Israelites and non-Israelites was a contrast between the adherents to a monotheist ethical faith, and those who wanted to perpetuate the Bronze Age political institutions (e.g., the war lords of the Canaanite states, or the relatively new military aristocracies of the coastal regions, of which the Philistines are the best known example).

The oldest sources in the OT either state or imply that Israel was the "creation" of Yahweh, or was "found" by Yahweh in the wilderness. The concept of an "elect people" did not exist until half a millennium later (*see* ELECTION §4), and could not have existed until a long experience of community had taken place.

3. The monarchies. In the period from 1050 to 950 B.C., the old ideology of the Yahwist federation was discredited by the capture of the ark and the destruction of SHILOH. The demand for a political organization able to cope with the Philistines was irresistible and the chiefdom of Saul was created in imitation of similar chiefdoms of the eastern Mediterranean region. Saul fell as a truly tragic figure who simply could not combine the old Yahwist ideology and society with a centralized monopoly of power. *See* SAMUEL, I AND II[S] §4.

a. Political and ideological change. During the regimes of David and Solomon the political government (centered in the old city-state of Jerusalem) became assimilated to Near Eastern traditions in almost every respect. The ideological base was changed from the Sinai covenant to the "divine charter" tradition of the Middle Bronze Age, and old traditions concerning Abraham were invoked as authority (*see* COVENANT, DAVIDIC[S]). It seems probable that an indigenous Jerusalemite prophet (Nathan) was the engineer of this ideological adaptation. The conclusion is strongly reinforced by the fact that he was behind the events that led to the coronation of Solomon (I Kings 2). Solomon's regime reflects many continuities with Bronze Age city-states: the temple (*see, however,* ZION TRADITION[S]); almost certainly the priesthood (*see, however,* ZADOK[S]); the temple sacrifical ritual; and sacral prostitutes in the temple.

b. The prophetic reaction. Under these circumstances, at the instigation of Yahwist prophets, the northern tribes broke away from Jerusalemite rule, only to experience comparable political regimes of their own. Not long afterward little or nothing was left of the old tribal organization that had posed a threat to the centralized political regimes of both North and South. The old tribes no longer had sociopolitical functions, although some survived for a time as genealogical traditions. *See* TRIBES[S].

The Yahwist prophets never stopped trying to bring the political regimes under the control of the old Mosaic/Yahwist ethic, but had only slight and temporary success. In the South the result seems to have been a systematic attempt to merge the Mosaic covenant tradition with the "divine charter" tradition, in which the legitimizing function of the latter was made conditional upon faithful adherence to the former. *See* COVENANT, DAVIDIC[S] §5.

Isaiah, in his famous "messianic" prophecies (chs. 9 and 11) had a vision of such a combination, describing an era of peace and well-being that subsequently has been a constant inspiration. Unfortunately, what came instead was Manasseh, probably the worst king Judah ever had. The preexilic canonical prophets without exception predicted the destruction, first of dynasties in the North, then the destruction of the state, both North and South. Almost always, however, they tempered their message with a plea for "return," i.e., REPENTANCE, but evidently with increasing pessimism.

4. The exilic reformation. After the destruction of state and temple there was little left as a basis for the identity and continuity of the community other than the Mosaic-prophetic tradition. (To be sure, some persons hoped for restoration under a Davidic descendant.) Chastened by experience and deprived of realistic hopes for power, Israel was now able to maintain community with virtually no "governance" other than the complex of common understandings and traditions derived from the remote past. The result was a time of creativity in religious thought unparalleled since Moses: Jeremiah, Ezekiel, Lamentations, Job, the Priestly Code, and Deutero-Isaiah, in approximately that order (although the Priestly Code perhaps should be placed in the early postexilic period).

Thus the community, diverse as it must have been, again demonstrated the possibility of survival without a king (i.e., state), and at the same time experienced and transmitted insights that have been of permanent value to those who came after.

5. Postexilic priestly rule. After the return there was evidently a serious division of opinion concerning the wisdom of or necessity for the re-establishment of the Davidic dynasty. A struggle for power now replaced the mature and creative thought of the exilic poets and prophets. There is little in the postexilic prophets that could not have derived from the prophets of Bronze Age Mari, except for the theme of one God's ruling over history and a particular emphasis on ethical demands.

Kingship was discontinued and for half a millennium the expectation of an ideal ruler (Messiah) played a minor role in Judean thought (*see* MESSIAH, JEWISH[S]). For the priestly ruler that succeeded the monarchy, *see* AARON, AARONIDES [S].

6. The NT reformation. A small, but rapidly growing new community recognized Jesus of Nazareth as the long-expected Davidic Messiah. Through submission to the high priest and later the Roman procurator, as well as through his teachings, Jesus made it clear that the kingdom of God had nothing to do with political power structures. (For the antecedents of this idea, *see* PHARISEES[S].) As at the time of Moses, such power structures were now secularized; or better, they all received divine legitimacy (a status which they had long sought through myth): "The powers that be are ordained of God." But none could be deified as the ultimate source of security and well-being and peace, nor as the power to which members of the "New Israel" must subject their every concept of right and ethic.

What happened in the early Christian movement was a complete merging of the old Mosaic ethical covenant and the "divine charter" (e.g., the title "son of God"). But it could be done only by a complete separation of the latter from its pagan associations (which survived for so many centuries in the old doctrine of the "divine right of kings").

The early Christian community was thus based entirely upon a voluntary commitment to a religious and ethical value system that was completely separated from any possession of, or desire for power, and was best illustrated in the crucifixion of Jesus.

Bibliography. J. Bright, *A History of Israel* (2nd ed., 1972), esp. pp. 140-75; A. Glock, "Early Israel as the Kingdom of Yahweh: The Influence of Archaeological Evidence on the Reconstruction of Religion in Early Israel," *CTM,* XLI (1970), 558-608; G. Mendenhall, *The Tenth Generation* (1973), "The Conflict Between Value Systems and Social Control," in *Unity & Diversity* (1975), pp. 169-80; T. Jacobsen, "Primitive Democracy in Ancient Mesopotamia," *JNES,* II (1943), 159-72.

G. E. MENDENHALL

***GRACE IN THE OT.** Grace is a characteristic of God in biblical faith. It is closely associated with such categories as "love" and "mercy" (*see* LOVE IN THE OT §3 and MERCY, MERCIFUL §2*a*), but "grace" implies God's love to his people when it is undeserved. In contrast to the NT, in which there is a specific Greek word, χάρις (*see* GRACE §1), the OT offers not specific words so much as a perception expressed in various ways. The OT offers diversity of opinion about whether it is God's grace which prevails or his justice (wherein he deals with his people as they deserve); and it offers diversity, too, as to whether God expresses his grace or his justice to a total community or to persons individually. And all this we must discern not so much from abstract affirmations as from narrative of God's personal interaction with people. Even with all these difficulties of definition, however, the impression one gains of God's grace in the OT is very strong.

1. The idea of grace in the OT. The attitude and action of deity toward people are variously understood on a spectrum between two extremes. At one extreme the deity is perceived to give to people automatically what they think they need, regardless of their own conduct. In this view the deity gives to his or her devotees willy-nilly, responding to the people's economic or political or military cravings. This was the assumption of the FERTILITY CULTS (cf. Hos. 2:5 [H 7]; Jer. 2:27). At the other extreme God is perceived to reward and punish persons mathematically according to their conduct. This view is a characteristic, for example, of some of the historical material in Chronicles (*see* CHRONICLES, I AND II §2*a*), so that the evil king Manasseh's long life and the good king Josiah's short life are satisfactorily explained (II Chr. 33:10-13; 35:22). But this view of rewards and punishments neither conforms to experience (there is too much unrewarded good and too much unpunished wickedness in the world), nor allows for the personal initiative of God with human beings which the Israelites felt they experienced (it is too impersonally mathematical). The Israelites, then, normally saw God's attitude to be at neither extreme. Certainly their conduct was crucial to God's attitude; nevertheless, his attitude was more loving, more gracious, than their conduct strictly would elicit. This perception of the relation of grace to justice was expressed in classic form in Exod. 34:6-7: "The Lord, the Lord, a God merciful and gracious, slow to anger, and abounding in steadfast love and faithfulness, keeping steadfast love for thousands, forgiving iniquity and transgression and sin, but who will by no means clear the guilty, visiting the iniquity of the fathers upon the children and the children's children, to the third and the fourth generation." Thus we deal first with this expression.

2. Exod. 34:6-7. This passage offers a surprising "propositional" theology, without direct reference to historical events such as the Exodus found in other "credos" (cf. Exod. 20:2; Deut. 26:5-9; *see* HISTORY and SALVATION §2, esp. *b*); but this proposition was a distillation of Israel's experience in history.

The first phrase states that the Lord is a God who is "merciful" (רחום and "gracious" חנון). These words are applied in the OT only to God and are chosen at least partly for their assonance. The word "gracious" (חנון) exhibits a Semitic root meaning "show favor"; the Hebrew noun (חן) from this root is almost always translated by χάρις in the LXX (*see* GRACE §1). A person in authority grants favor: a king "shows mercy" to the oppressed (Dan. 4:27 [H 24]); fathers may "grant" daughters as a favor (RSV "graciously," Judg. 21:22). So Yahweh, as protector of the helpless, shows favor to them (Exod. 22:27 [H 26]): חנון here is translated "compassionate." The other word in the pair, "merciful" (רחום), is very close in meaning (*see* MERCY §§1, 2). Since, however, the related word רחם means "womb," it is at least possible that "merciful" was understood to be a motherly attribute, and "gracious" a fatherly attribute, of God. And not only God: a good man also is gracious (RSV "kind") to the poor (Prov. 14:21).

"Slow to anger" is found in Proverbs as well (16:32); though Yahweh does become angry, it takes him a long time to reach the point of wrath.

"Abounding in steadfast love and faithfulness" repeats in parallelism the ideas of earlier phrases. "Steadfast love" (חסד) (*see* LOVE IN THE OT §3) moves beyond the context of the simple showing of favor and implies the rights and obligations of the covenant: Yahweh pre-eminently keeps up his end of the bargain with his people. The further "gracious" phrases in vs. 7 reinforce what has been said, and the "punitive" phrases express in succinct form the tension between God's grace and his justice (*see* God, OT View of §D3-5).

The phrases of Exod. 34:6-7 are repeated approximately eighteen times in the OT, testifying to the popularity of the expression, particularly in the exilic and postexilic periods. The usage in Jonah 4:2 is particularly noteworthy: here, ironically, the prophet expresses distaste for a God who is more gracious (to the hated Ninevites!) than human views of justice suggest he ought to be.

3. Testimony to the grace of God in OT material. The narratives of Genesis offer strong testimony to God's grace. Creation itself implies grace: God is sovereign and brings the world into being by his word, without constraint; no creature earns the right or deserves to be created (*see* Creation §2). By the same token the P narrative of the making of a covenant after the flood (Gen. 9:8-17) is evidence of grace: never again will God exert his wrath in a universal flood. And though the story of the Tower of Babel (in which men tried to make a name for themselves, Gen. 11:4) leaves the impression that God's grace is exhausted (vss. 8-9), still the story serves as a backdrop for the narrative of the call to Abraham (whose name God will make great): Abraham will become a blessing to all mankind (Gen. 12:2-3). Rather than abandon humankind to the consequences of its sins, God takes the initiative for a solution.

The struggle between the claims of grace and justice is dramatized in the bargaining between Abraham and God over Sodom: God finally agrees that it would take only ten righteous men in Sodom to stay his punitive hand (Gen. 18:16-33).

Further patriarchal stories emphasize God's grace in spite of man: Isaac is a child of the old age of Abraham and Sarah, so that the covenantal family line is in no sense attributable to human effort (Gen. 18:9-15; 21:1-7). Jacob, though again and again a trickster with his kinsmen (25:26-34; 27:1-46; 30:25-43) and a wrestler with the stranger who stands for God, becomes by God's calling the father of the covenant people (32:22-30 [H 23-31]). Joseph's brothers, though they mean to harm him, are saved by their very deed of selling him into slavery, because God intends it (50:20).

God's rescue of Israel from Egypt and his consequent covenant with her were seen in retrospect to be the act of God's grace par excellence. This conviction is strikingly portrayed in the old poem of Deut. 32 (now dated to the eleventh century):

> He [God] found him [Israel] in a desert land,
> and in the howling waste of the wilderness;
> he encircled him, he cared for him,
> he kept him as the apple of his eye (vs. 10).

Other portions of the poem (e.g. vss. 15, 36) reinforce this conviction. The prophets also pick up this theme of the helplessness of Israel when God took up the people in the wilderness: Hos. 9:10 expresses it, and in a striking allegory in Ezek. 16 the prophet depicts Israel as an exposed infant girl whom Yahweh adopted and to whom he was later married when she came of age.

Then the wilderness traditions speak of the manna and quails by which God fed the Israelites even when they were complaining that they had left the full larders of Egypt behind (Exod. 16), and of the water that gushed from the rock, again in spite of complaints (Exod. 17:1-7).

The book of Deuteronomy is particularly insistent that both Yahweh's election of Israel and his giving of the land to her were acts of grace: Israel had no intrinsic value and attractiveness that Yahweh should choose such a people; it is simply that God loves her and keeps his promise to the patriarchs (Deut. 7:6-8). Again, Israel should not assume that it was by her own efforts that she would gain riches in the land; it is Yahweh who gives her wealth (Deut. 8:7-18). And this perception of grace in the giving of land is implied also in the prophets (*see* Jer. 2:7).

There are other modes by which the Israelites testified to God's grace in the giving of the land. One is by the commandment to "devote" the spoils of the conquest to destruction (e.g. Josh. 6:17, 21; cf. vs. 24; *see* Devoted) so that they may not be taken for personal profit (cf. Deut. 13:17). Another is the legal tradition that the land does not "belong" to Israel at all but to Yahweh; Israel is simply a tenant (Lev. 25:23).

Meditation on other aspects of Israel's life likewise brought evidence of grace. Thus while the election of Israel was an act of grace, the consequent covenant at Sinai brought stipulations which were to be obeyed, so that the stress in this covenant was on God's justice rather than his grace: he rewards the obedient and punishes the disobedient (Deut. 28). (*See* Covenant; Covenant, Mosaic [S].) But in contrast to the Sinai covenant, the covenant with David was seen to be an act of grace entirely (II Sam. 7:13-15); God is bound to the Davidic line forever, whatever the conduct of a given king may be (*see* Covenant, Davidic[S]). Various sacrificial observances likewise were understood to be effective regardless of the spontaneous feeling of the priest or worshiper. The danger in this conviction was of course the temptation to manipulate God's forgiveness, but the positive feature is the chance to recognize God's grace.

While the Deuteronomic historian (*see* Deuteronomic History, The[S]; Judges, Book of §D; and Kings, I and II §C2) saw the events of Israel's history in the time of the judges and kings purely as the working out of God's justice, others, especially prophets, saw scope for God's grace. Thus Amos, though insisting on God's justice, still prayed that God would stay his punishment (Amos 7:1-6; *see* Amos §7). Hosea clearly saw God struggle with his basic love for Israel in spite of her sin (Hos. 11:1-9: "How can I give you up, O Ephraim!" vs. 8). (*See* Hosea[S].) Jeremiah heard God speak sadly of great hopes he had had for Israel, spoiled now by her faithlessness (Jer. 3:19-20). And after God's punishment, Jeremiah picked up the note of grace from the event of the first exodus and applied it to a new one for the exiles (31:2-6); indeed God would draw up a fresh covenant in which sin would be nothing but a nightmare from the past (31:31-34; *see* New Covenant, The[S] §2).

For these prophets, then, justice and grace were not opposites but were correlative.

Deutero-Isaiah was pre-eminently a prophet of grace (*see* Isaiah §B2). It is proclaimed with great clarity in Isa. 55:1-2 ("Come, buy wine and milk without money and without price"), but the total message of this prophet is of the marvelous mercy of God to go to any length to rescue his people (43:3-4), to effect a new exodus (51:9-11) to bring them home again (49:14-18); and because he is who he is, he restrains his anger (48:9).

The psalms offer language that is often even more allusive than some other portions of the OT, but the total impression given is of a God of marvelous grace (e.g., Ps. 103).

If Jonah had complained that God is more merciful than he should be, Job complains that God is more cruel than he should be. In Job the problem of faith is explored in a fresh way, in the experience of a single individual. Job begins by demanding justice from God (Job 7:20; 9:13-20), but he reaches beyond this to a God of grace. He looks for an umpire to vouch for him before God (9:32-33). He imagines himself dead and God groping after him (10:1-12), yearning for what he had created (14:13-17). He dreams of a heavenly witness who will keep his case open before God and finally show him God as he is (19:25-27).

And while the end of the OT period and the intertestamental period saw a resurgence of the doctrine of just rewards and punishments, the conviction of the grace of God had not disappeared. We note Asmp. Moses 12:7: "For not for any virtue or strength of mine, but of His (God's) good pleasure have His compassion and longsuffering fallen to my (Moses') lot."

The strong perception of grace throughout the whole witness of Israel then forms the backdrop to the NT perception.

Bibliography. Theology, beginning with Exod. 34:6-7: D. N. Freedman, "God Compassionate and Gracious," *Western Watch,* VI (1955), 6-24; Th. C. Vriezen, *An Outline of OT Theology* (1970), pp. 321-23.

Detailed analysis of Exod. 34:6-7: J. Scharbert, "Formgeschichte und Analyse von Ex 34,6f und seiner Parallelen," *Bibl.,* XXXVIII (1957), 130-50; R. C. Dentan, "The Literary Affinities of Exodus xxxiv 6f," *VT,* XIII (1963), 34-51.

The root חנן: D. N. Freedman and J. Lundbom, "חנן," *TWAT* (in press).

Grace in the OT in general: G. von Rad, *OT Theology* (1962, 1965); W. Eichrodt, *Theology of the OT* (1961, 1967), esp. Vol. I—see citations under "Grace" in Index of Subjects; E. M. Good, *Irony in the OT* (1965); N. Glueck, *Ḥesed in the Bible* (1967). Suggestive word study: A. Jepsen, "Gnade und Barmherzigkeit im AT," *Kerygma und Dogma,* VII (1961), 261-71. Grace in specific prophets: G. Farr, "The Concept of Grace in the Book of Hosea," *ZAW,* LXX (1958), 98-107; H. L. Creger, "The Grace of God in Second Isaiah," in *Biblical Studies in Memory of H. C. Alleman,* ed. J. M. Myers *et al.* (1960), pp. 123-36.

W. L. Holladay

***GREECE.** *See* Hellenism[S].

***GREEK RELIGION AND PHILOSOPHY.** *See* Hellenism[S]; Cynics[S]; Judaism, Hellenistic[S].

***GREEK VERSIONS (MINOR).** The third quarter of the twentieth century has seen great development in scholarly understanding of the history of the OT text, both Hebrew and Greek. New MS discoveries have exploded old theories, resolved serious problems, and given rise to new and more complex questions about the biblical texts. The present state of knowledge is impressive, but still fragile and incomplete.

1. A quarter-century of discovery
   a. Qumran and Naḥal Ḥever
   b. Other MSS
   c. Local texts and successive revisions
2. New scholarly perspectives
   a. Characteristics of *Kaige*/Theodotion
   b. Members of the *Kaige*/Theodotionic group
   c. *Kaige*/Theodotion's relation to other versions
3. Detailed analyses
4. The versions today and tomorrow
Bibliography

1. A quarter-century of discovery. ***a. Qumran and Naḥal Ḥever.*** In 1947 the first biblical MSS were discovered in Cave I at Qumran (*see* Dead Sea Scrolls; Dead Sea Scrolls[S]). Five years later, Hebrew MSS of Samuel were discovered in Cave IV at Qumran and a Greek MS of the minor prophets was found at Naḥal Ḥever. Although 4QSam[a,b,c] have not yet been fully published, they have changed the shape of Hebrew textual history. Now scholars know that the divergent LXX version of Samuel is not simply a free paraphrase of a difficult Hebrew text, but a reliable reflection of a variant Hebrew tradition once at home in Palestine and subsequently lost or suppressed (*see* Samuel, I and II[S] §2*c*). Similar evidence now also exists for Jeremiah and other books of the OT (*see* Text, Hebrew, History of[S]). The Greek minor prophets scroll proved to be equally significant. Its text was not the standard LXX, but a systematic revision to reflect the Hebrew text. And this Hebrew text, in turn, was not identical with the MT. This revision is called "R" or *Kaige,* because it used the Greek word καίγε to translate Hebrew גם or וגם. Further translational features of *Kaige* have been isolated, and related materials have been identified in the majority Greek recension of II Sam. 11:1–I Kings 2:11 and I Kings 22–II Kings (Thackeray's sections βγ and γδ of LXX Reigns) and in the version of Theod. (i.e., cited from the sixth column of Origen's Hexapla) for many LXX books. In addition, *Kaige* was proposed as the text on which the revision of Aquila was based (*see* §2*c below*).

b. Other MSS. Some Egyptian texts provide similar evidence. Among those receiving attention recently are the fifth/sixth-century Giessen parchment fragments discussed by Tov (1971; published by Glaue and Rahlfs in 1911) and Papyrus Fouad 266 from pre-Christian times (published most fully by Dunand in 1966). Although limited in scope, these texts are further evidence that the development of Greek versions through deliberate revision was a widespread and complex process.

c. Local texts and successive revisions. Prior to the Qumran discoveries, biblical scholars were divided on the nature of LXX MSS. The majority followed Lagarde in supposing that a single translation was represented more or less faithfully in all MS copies. A significant minority held, on the contrary, that various translations or partial translations were made independently over the years and that the major divergences within the LXX MS tradition have come from these different translations (so, e.g., Kahle). (*See* SEPTUAGINT §5.) The versions of Aq. and Symm. were often described as new translations, while Theod.'s version was regarded as a revision of an earlier, presumably independent version. *See* VERSIONS, ANCIENT §2*b*; SEPTUAGINT §3.

Just as the various Hebrew traditions known from Qumran can now be explained as relatively independent developments—during the fourth to first centuries B.C. and, according to Cross, in the geographic isolation of Alexandria, Palestine, and Babylon—so the nonaccidental variants within the LXX witnesses can be understood as due almost entirely to deliberate and often successive revisions of a single translation from the Hebrew.

By the end of the second century B.C. at the latest, the Babylonian and Alexandrian Hebrew versions were brought into Palestine, because witnesses to all three text types are found for at least some OT books at Qumran. About the same time, too, some users of the LXX (based upon the Alexandrian Hebrew text) became aware that their Greek text did not correspond exactly to the Hebrew text(s) available to them. Various efforts at revision were begun, some sporadic and some systematic. The process continued in Jewish circles for some two centuries, until the definitive fixing of the MT (*see* TEXT, HEBREW, HISTORY OF[S] §1). In Christian circles, revisional activity apparently continued for another century or more.

In the Lucianic MSS for Samuel and Kings (boc_2e_2), Cross has found evidence for an early stratum that represents a revision of the LXX to the Palestinian Hebrew text attested in $4QSam^{a,b,c}$. While the existence of this early stratum is generally admitted today, some scholars argue that it is nothing more than the LXX for Samuel-Kings (*see* §§2*c*, 3 *below*). The early stratum of boc_2e_2 has itself been revised toward the MT tradition, though not in its final form. For Cross, this Proto-MT is a product of the Babylonian Hebrew tradition. The revision to the Proto-MT ("R" or *Kaige*) was systematic and detailed, and its characteristic features can be found in the Theodotionic material generally, as well as in the minor prophets scroll from Naḥal Ḥever. In Samuel-Kings, however, this *Kaige* revision has replaced the LXX in most MSS, though only in Thackeray's βγ and γδ sections (Shenkel has since shown that βγ should begin at II Sam. 10:1 rather than 11:2 as proposed by Thackeray).

The *Kaige*/Theod. revision was itself further revised by Aq. at the end of the first century A.D. to reflect the present MT. Aq.'s revision took over many *Kaige*/Theod. elements, extended them, and introduced further literalistic features. Symm.'s version shares some readings with *Kaige*/Theod. or with Aq., but the precise nature of his version has not yet been explored. There is limited evidence for further revisional activity on *Kaige* by second-century Theod. The precise contributions of third-century Lucian to the first-century Proto-Lucianic material which he took over are not clear, but genuine revision seems to have been involved. Text-critical interest will be directed less to these figures from the second and third centuries, whose textual changes are to the normative MT, and more to their Proto-Lucianic and *Kaige*/Theodotionic antecedents, since these are the sources of evidence for Palestinian and Proto-MT Hebrew variants.

2. New scholarly perspectives. ***a. Characteristics of Kaige/Theodotion.*** When Barthélemy published the Greek minor prophets scroll, he drew together a number of distinctive features to identify the new *Kaige* recension there and elsewhere. Several had already been noted much earlier for βδ (=βγ+γδ) by Thackeray. In addition to the regular introduction of καίγε to represent Hebrew גם/וגם, the most important *Kaige*/Theod. characteristics proposed by Barthélemy are: (1) the use of ἀνήρ rather than Old Greek (=OG) ἕκαστος to represent Hebrew איש, even when the latter is used idiomatically to mean "each"; (2) the tendency to replace ἀπό or ἐπάνω with ἐπάνωθεν or ἀπάνωθεν for Hebrew מעל; (3) the restriction of OG σάλπιγξ to Hebrew חצצרה and the introduction of κερατίνη to represent Hebrew שופר; (4) the elimination of the OG historical present in favor of the aorist for the Hebrew converted imperfect in narration; (5) an emphasis on the atemporal character of Hebrew אין by using οὐκ ἔστιν to translate it, even in the midst of a series of aorist verbs; (6) the introduction of the phrase ἐγώ εἰμι as a unit, often as the subject of a finite verb, to represent Hebrew אנכי in contrast to אני; and (7) an avoidance of OG εἰς ἀπάντησιν as the equivalent of Hebrew לקראת.

The list has since been extended, e.g., (1) φωτίζειν for הורה, the *Hiph'il* of ירה (Smith); (2) ἐν ὀφθαλμοῖς to translate בעיני when the object is Yahweh (Shenkel; the OG often uses ἐν ὀφθαλμοῖς for human objects, but avoids it with Yahweh); (3) θυσιάζειν in place of OG θύειν for זבח (Shenkel); (4) ῥομφαία for חרב, where OG has μάχαιρα or ῥομφαία, or other equivalents, and Aq. and Symm. have μάχαιρα (O'Connell); (5) νῖκος for נצח (Grindel); (6) words from the root δουλ- for forms of Hebrew עבד (O'Connell); (7) transliterations to translate unknown words (Tov); (8) the tendency to systematize the Greek equivalents of specific Hebrew words or roots, frequently by taking one of several OG renditions and using it regularly.

One example of *Kaige*/Theod. revisional activity may be given. In Exodus the Hebrew verb פרע occurs three times. The MT forms and corresponding OG equivalents are פרע הוא/διεσκέδασται and כי פרעה/διεσκέδασεν γὰρ αὐτούς in 32:25, and תפריעו/διαστρέφετε in 5:4. The *Kaige*/Theod. revisions are διεσκεδασμένος ἔστιν, ὅτι διεσκέδασεν αὐτόν, and διασκεδάζετε, respectively. The OG correspondence in 32:25, διασκεδάζειν=פרע, has been extended back to 5:4 (twenty-seven chapters earlier), and other changes have been made to express the Hebrew forms more closely. Aquila, for his part, uses a different, non-OG verb throughout and chooses αὐτός rather than ἔστιν to reflect MT הוא still more literally: ἀποπετάσμενος αὐτός, ὅτι ἀπεπέτασεν αὐτόν, and ἀποπετάζετε, respectively.

b. Members of the Kaige/Theodotionic group. Barthélemy identified the following members of the *Kaige*/Theod. group along with the minor prophets scroll: (1) the Greek translations of Lamentations and probably also of the Song of Songs and Ruth, (2) the majority recension for sections βγ and γδ in LXX Reigns, (3) the version of Judges found in MSS $irua_2$ and Befsz, (4) the Theodotionic edition of Daniel, (5) the Theodotionic additions to the LXX of Job and the frequently anonymous additions to the LXX of Jeremiah, (6) the Theodotionic (=sixth) column of Origen's Hexapla generally, though not in the minor prophets or Samuel-Kings, at least, and (7) the Quinta (=seventh) column of the Hexapla for Psalms as well as for the minor prophets. Traces of the revision could also be found in other LXX witnesses. The *Kaige* character of βγ and γδ in Reigns and of the Theodotionic material in Exodus has already received thorough confirmation.

c. Kaige/Theodotion's relation to other versions. While Barthélemy saw the basis for the *Kaige* revision in βδ of Samuel-Kings as simply the OG now preserved primarily in MSS boc_2e_2, Cross argued vigorously for the presence of a prior (Proto-Lucianic) revision of the OG toward the Palestinian Hebrew text there, and Tov suggested that the boc_2e_2 text had departed somewhat from the OG without having undergone a systematic revision prior to its use by *Kaige*/Theod. Further investigations have brought these positions somewhat closer together, but differences of interpretation remain (*see* §3 *below*).

Barthélemy argued cogently that Aq. used the *Kaige*/Theod. revision as the basis for his further revision, adopting such *Kaige* features as καίγε for גם and ἀνήρ for איש="each," further systematizing Greek-Hebrew correspondences, making *Kaige* translations even more exactly literal, and introducing further features such as the Greek particle σύν to represent the Hebrew accusative particle את. O'Connell's analysis of the Theodotionic material in Exodus has provided even stronger support for Aq.'s use of the *Kaige*/Theod. revision as the basis for his own version. The following example illustrates the relationships (Exod. 5:16):

id.=same as previous column; *om.*=omission, no form

OG	Theod.	Aquila	MT
καὶ	*id.*	*id.*	-ו (*wᵉ-*)
ἰδοὺ	*id.*	*id.*	-הנה (*-hinnê*)
οἱ	*id.*	*om.*	*om.*
παῖδές	δοῦλοι	*id.*	-עבדי (*ʿᵃbhādhê-*)
σου	*id.*	*id.*	-ך (*-khā*)
μεμαστίγωνται	*id.*	πεπληγμένοι	מכים (*mukkîm*)
om.	καὶ	*id.*	-ו (*wᵉ-*)
om.	ἡ	*om.*	*om.*
ἀδικήσεις	δοῦλοι	*id.*	-חטאת (*-ḥāṭā'th*)
οὖν	*om.*	*om.*	*om.*
om.	εἰς	*om.*	*om.*
τὸν	*id.*	*om.*	*om.*
λαόν	*id.*	λαῷ	-עמ (*ʿamme-*)
σου	*id.*	*id.*	-ך (*-khā*)

Theod. differs from the OG only in the replacement of παῖδες with δοῦλοι for MT (ך)עבדי and in the recasting of the second phrase (Theod. καὶ ἡ ἁμαρτία εἰς τὸν λαόν σου vs. OG ἀδικήσεις οὖν τὸν λαόν σου) enough to represent MT וחטאת עמך more closely. Aq.'s version agrees with Theod. on δούλοι and the general recasting of the second phrase, but omits elements not explicitly supported in the MT (οἱ, ἡ, εἰς τόν—with change of λαόν to dative case) and replaces the finite verb μεμαστίγωνται with the participle πεπληγμένοι to represent the Hebrew participle מכים.

Barthélemy provided some evidence for a similar dependence of Symm. on the *Kaige*/Theod. revision, rather than on the OG directly, but the question of Symm.'s exact place within recensional history remains unresolved.

Although the so-called Theodotionic edition of Daniel was included within the *Kaige*/Theod. group by Barthélemy, Schmitt's analysis has provided evidence for a distinction between that material and the sixth column of the Hexapla for Daniel. This may point to the existence of two layers within *Kaige*/Theod. *See* DANIEL[S].

An index to Aq. has appeared (Reider), but its usefulness is somewhat limited. The new insights into Aquila's use of the *Kaige*/Theod. revision as the basis for his own work and the evidence for some dependence of Symm. on the same revision complicate the interpretation of readings cited from two or three of these versions together (both those cited jointly as a single note —α'θ', α'σ'θ', etc.—and those attributed separately to more than one version). Where Aq. or Symm. agrees with Theod., the evidence cannot be used to argue for characteristics of Aq. or Symm., but only for their unwillingness or failure to change what was in the base text. Moreover, variants from the OG in Aq. or Symm. where no corresponding reading from Theod. is preserved do not necessarily reveal characteristics of Aq. or Symm., either. They may simply be survivals from the now lost Theodotionic text. Any discussion of Aq. or Symm. that does not deal constantly with the possibility of influence from Theod. is in danger of inaccuracy. All previous discussions of Aq. must be revised with that in mind. Thus when a reading from Aq. is at variance with his pattern elsewhere, the possibility of a survival from *Kaige*/Theod. must be investigated carefully.

3. Detailed analyses. Various further studies have been done on specific questions of LXX textual development (*see* SEPTUAGINT[S] §A1*d-e*). Some of these analyses relate to the understanding of the minor Greek versions and may be summarized briefly. Lemke has shown that differences between the narratives of Chronicles and Samuel-Kings are sometimes due to differences in Hebrew text traditions, rather than to deliberate adaptations. Klein discovered that I Esdras frequently reflects a Hebrew text older than that represented by Hebrew and Greek Ezra. He also found that Greek Chronicles reflects Lucianic boc_2e_2 rather than majority LXX *Kaige*/Theod. for II Kings. Harrington uncovered similarities between the Hebrew text used in Pseudo-Philo's *Liber Antiquitatum Biblicarum* and the Palestinian text reflected in Lucianic witnesses and in Josephus. Bodine has studied the B family in Judges as a representative of the *Kaige*/Theod. group. Ulrich has argued that the Lucianic witnesses in Samuel preserve evidence of an early revision to the Palestinian Hebrew text of $4QSam^a$ and that this revision is distinct from both MT and OG. There are instances in Thackeray's sections α, ββ (I Sam. 1–II Sam. 9) where the majority recension preserves the OG, an OG not in need of revision, and yet the Lucianic witnesses boc_2e_2 preserve revisions toward $4QSam^a$ that are not identical with the MT. This supports Cross's view that boc_2e_2 agreements with $4QSam^a$ where the OG no longer survives are also to be seen as revisional. The evidence for this Proto-Lucianic revisional activity is still fragile, and the existence of a genuine revision can still be disputed. But the presence within Lucian of some revisional activity toward the Palestinian text of Samuel-Kings can no longer be doubted. The recensional nature of the developed Lucianic text has been demonstrated independently by Brock, who has shown that the final form of the text reflects the time and place of the martyr from Antioch.

In the Pentateuch, where a Palestinian Hebrew text distinct from the Proto-MT can also be identified, the possibility of finding a Proto-Lucianic Greek revision has been seriously reduced by Wevers' recent conclusion that no Lucianic recension at all can be identified securely within the textual evidence for Greek Genesis. The only true recension surviving for Genesis, according to Wevers, is that of Origen.

4. The versions today and tomorrow. In summary, the following Greek versions of the LXX are now known and their recensional nature at least partially understood: (1) first-century B.C./first-century A.D. Proto-Lucianic revision of the OG, at least in Samuel-Kings, to conform to the Palestinian Hebrew text; (2) early first-century A.D. *Kaige*/Theod. revision of the LXX—of the Proto-Lucianic revision in Samuel-Kings, of an already slightly revised LXX in Exodus, perhaps of a slightly revised LXX elsewhere—to the Proto-MT; (3) late first-century A.D. revision by Aq. of the *Kaige*/Theod. revision to the MT; (4) Symm.'s late second-century A.D. revision of *Kaige*/Theod. —or influenced by *Kaige*/Theod. and perhaps also by Aq.—to the MT; (5) second-century A.D. Theod.'s adoption and apparently limited further revision of *Kaige*/Theod. to the MT; (6) early third-century A.D. Origen's collection of the versions known to him (MT, LXX, Aq., Symm., Theod., and occasionally one to three further versions) into the Hexapla (*see* VERSIONS, ANCIENT, §2*b*; SEPTUAGINT §4*a*); (7) late third-century A.D. Lucian's revision of the Proto-Lucianic material and perhaps other materials to the MT; (8) third-century A.D. Hesychius' recension of Origen's LXX text (identified by Jellicoe with MS B or Vaticanus); (9) third-century A.D. Eusebius' recension of Origen's LXX text.

Traces of other recensional activity can be found in various witnesses. Further research will focus on these traces, as well as on more detailed investigation of the versions listed above. It is not to be assumed that the material attributed to any version in one biblical book will necessarily share the characteristics of material attributed to that same version elsewhere. The distinctive nature of θ′ material in Samuel-Kings or the minor prophets in comparison with the *Kaige* text attributed to θ′ elsewhere is a case in point. The picture of Greek versions will almost certainly grow more complex as scholarly investigations continue, for the period from which they came is now known to have included intense and repeated efforts at control of the Hebrew and Greek OT texts.

Bibliography. *See* S. P. Brock, C. T. Fritsch, and S. Jellicoe, *A Classified Bibliography of the Septuagint* (1973).

D. Barthélemy, *Les devanciers d'Aquila* (=*DA*), VTSup, X (1963)—*see* reviews by S. Jellicoe in *JAOS*, LXXXIV (1964), 178-82, by R. Kraft in *Gnomon*, XXXVII (1965), 474-83—also "A Reexamination of the Textual Problems in 2 Sam 11:2–1 Kings 2:11 in the Light of Certain Criticism of *DA*," *1972 Proceedings: IOSCS and Pseudepigrapha*, ed. R. Kraft, LXX and Cognate Studies 2 (1972), pp. 16-89; W. R. Bodine, "ΚΑΙΓΕ and Other Recensional Developments in the Greek Text of Judges" (diss., Harvard, 1973); S. P. Brock, "Lucian *redivivus:* Some Reflections on Barthélemy's *DA*," *SE*, V [=*TU*, 103] (1968), 176-81, "The Recensions of the LXX Version of I Samuel" (diss., Oxford, 1966); C. M. Cooper, "Theodotion's Influence on the Alexandrian Text of Judges," *JBL*, LXVII (1948), 63-68; F. M. Cross, Jr., *The Ancient Library of Qumran and Modern Biblical Studies* (2nd ed., 1961), "The Contribution of the Qumrân Discoveries to the Study of the Biblical Text," *IEJ*, XVI (1966), 81-95, "The Evolution of a Theory of Local Texts," *1972 Proceedings: IOSCS and Pseudepigrapha*, ed. R. Kraft, LXX and Cognate Studies 2 (1972), pp. 108-26, and "A New Qumran Biblical Fragment Related to the Original Hebrew Underlying the Septuagint," *BASOR*, 132 (1953), 15-26; F. Dunand, *Papyrus grecs bibliques (Papyrus F. Inv. 266), Volumina de la Genèse et du Deutéronome*, Recherches d'archéologie, de philologie et d'histoire, XXVII (1966)—the text and a critical apparatus are found in *Études de Pap.*, IX (1971), 81-150, *see also* the comments by G. D. Kilpatrick, 221-26, and by Z. Aly, 227-28; P. Grelot, "Les versions grecques de Daniel," *Bibl.*, XLVII (1966), 381-402; J. A. Grindel, "Another Characteristic of the *KAIGE* Recension: נצח/νικος," *CBQ*, XXXI (1969), 499-513; D. J. Harrington, "The Biblical Text of Pseudo-Philo's *Liber Antiquitatum Biblicarum*," *CBQ*, XXXIII (1971), 1-17; G. Howard, "Frank Cross and Recensional Criticism," *VT*, XXI (1971), 440-50, "*Kaige* Readings in Josephus," *Textus*, VIII (1973), 45-54, "Lucianic Readings in a Greek Twelve Prophets Scroll from the Judaean Desert," *JQR*, LXII (1971-72), 51-60, and "The Quinta of the Minor Prophets: A First Century Septuagint Text?" *Bibl.*, LV (1974), 15-22; S. Jellicoe, "The Hesychian Recension Reconsidered," *JBL*, LXXXII (1963), 409-18, and *The LXX and Modern Study* (1968) —*see* reviews by K. O'Connell in *JBL*, LXXXVIII (1969), 230-32, by R. Kraft in *JQR*, LXI (1970), 167-71, and by E. Tov in *RB*, LXXVII (1970), 84-91—also, "Some Reflections on the ΚΑΙΓΕ Recension," *VT*, XXIII (1973), 15-24; P. E. Kahle, *The Cairo Geniza*

(2nd ed., 1959), and "The Greek Bible MSS Used by Origen," *JBL*, LXXIX (1960), 111-18; R. W. Klein, "New Evidence for an Old Recension of Reigns," *HTR*, LX (1967), 93-105, "Studies in the Greek Text of the Chronicler" (diss., Harvard, 1966), and *Textual Criticism of the OT* (1974); W. E. Lemke, "Studies in the Chronicler's History" (diss., Harvard, 1963), and "The Synoptic Problem in the Chronicler's History," *HTR*, LVIII (1965), 349-63; B. M. Metzger, "Lucian and the Lucianic Recension of the Greek Bible," *NTS*, VIII (1961/62), 189-203, and "The Lucianic Recension of the Greek Bible," *Chapters in the History of NT Textual Criticism* (1963), pp. 1-41; T. Muraoka, "The Greek Texts of Samuel-Kings: Incomplete Translations or Recensional Activity?" *1972 Proceedings: IOSCS and Pseudepigrapha*, ed. R. Kraft, LXX and Cognate Studies 2 (1972), pp. 90-107; K. G. O'Connell, *The Theodotionic Revision of the Book of Exodus*, Harvard Semitic Monographs, 3 (1972); A. Rahlfs, *Lucians Rezension der Königsbücher*, Septuaginta Studien 3 (1911), and "Über Theodotion-Lesarten im Neuen Testament und Aquila-Lesarten bei Justin," *ZNW*, XX (1921), 182-99; J. Reider, *An Index to Aquila*, completed and rev. by N. Turner, VTSup, XII (1966)—*see* E. Tov, "Some Corrections to Reider-Turner's *Index to Aquila*," *Textus*, VIII (1973), 164-74; A. Schmitt, *Stammt der sogenannte "θ'"-Text bei Daniel wirklich von Theodotion?*, *Mitteilungen des Septuaginta—Unternehmens*, IX (1966); J. D. Shenkel, *Chronology and Recensional Development in the Greek Text of Kings*, Harvard Semitic Monographs, 1 (1968), and "A Comparative Study of the Synoptic Parallels in I Paraleipomena and I-II Reigns," *HTR*, LXII (1969), 63-85; M. Smith, "Another Criterion for the καίγε Recension," *Bibl.*, XLVIII (1967), 443-45; H. St. J. Thackeray, *The LXX and Jewish Worship*, Schweich Lectures 1920 (1923)—*see also* his series of articles in *JTS*, IV (1902/3), 245-66, 398-411, 578-85; VIII (1906/7), 262-78; IX (1907/8), 88-98; R. Thornhill, "Six or Seven Nations: A Pointer to the Lucianic Text in the Heptateuch, with Special Reference to the Old Latin Version," *JTS*, NS X (1959), 233-46; E. Tov, "Lucian and Proto-Lucian: Toward a New Solution of the Problem," *RB*, LXXIX (1972), 101-13, "Pap. Giessen 13, 19, 22, 26: A Revision of the LXX?" *RB*, LXXVIII (1971), 355-83, "The State of the Question: Problems and Proposed Solutions," *1972 Proceedings: IOSCS and Pseudepigrapha*, ed. R. Kraft, LXX and Cognate Studies 2 (1972), 3-15, and "Transliterations of Hebrew Words in the Greek Versions of the OT: A Further Characteristic of the *kaige*-Th. Revision?" *Textus*, VIII (1973), 78-92; E. C. Ulrich, "The Qumran Text of Samuel and Josephus" (diss., Harvard, 1975), and "4QSam[a] and Septuagintal Research," *Bulletin No. 8* of the IOSCS (Fall 1975), pp. 24-39; A. Vaccari, "The Hesychian Recension of the Septuagint," *Bibl.*, XLVI (1965), 60-66; J. W. Wevers, "A Lucianic Recension in Genesis?" *Bulletin No. 6* of the IOSCS (Fall 1973), pp. 22-35.

K. G. O'CONNELL

GRIESBACH HYPOTHESIS grēs'bäk. The theory that the Gospel of Mark was written later than Matthew and Luke and in direct dependence upon them. First proposed by J. J. Griesbach in 1783, the hypothesis was subsequently elaborated and defended by him and since the 1960s has been the subject of renewed discussion.

Griesbach, who presumed but did not explicitly argue that Luke had used Matthew, believed that Mark's use of the two earlier gospels had been deliberate and careful enough that his method of following first one, then the other, may be readily observed. Mark has reformulated their material "in his own way," sometimes omitting and abbreviating, but at other times adding and expanding. Griesbach explicitly rejected Augustine's view that Mark's purpose was to epitomize Matthew, and that Mark in turn had been used by Luke (*see* SYNOPTIC PROBLEM §B1). Rather, Mark's purpose was to compose a gospel appropriate to the needs of his own readers, using materials selected from both Matthew and Luke.

Griesbach regarded his hypothesis as a plausible explanation for three particular characteristics of Mark: its order, its contents, and its alternating conformity to Matthew and Luke. As to order (which is especially emphasized), Mark seems to have followed Luke's narrative at every point where he departed from Matthew's, and then to have returned to Matthew's when leaving Luke's. In a long series of notes to a table of synoptic passages, Griesbach sought to account for each of Mark's moves back and forth and for other particular features of his gospel, including his omissions. To Griesbach, Mark's dependence upon Matthew and Luke seemed to be assured also by its contents, virtually all of which are parallel to materials in Matthew or Luke. Since Mark would have known so many things about Jesus' life and teachings (Griesbach did not question the attribution of the Synoptics to Matthew, Mark, and Luke respectively), his selection of almost the same materials for inclusion in his gospel as are present in the other two could have been due only to Mark's deliberate use of them. And finally, Mark's alternating conformity, now to Matthew, now to Luke, requires the conclusion that Mark "had both seen and compared the works of each simultaneously."

Griesbach's detailed defense of his hypothesis won it many adherents, and it was the prevailing view of German critical scholarship until the mid-nineteenth century, when the two-document hypothesis replaced it (*see* SYNOPTIC PROBLEM §§B 2-3). The modern consensus has recently been challenged, however, by Farmer and others, who have revived certain parts of Griesbach's hypothesis and have directed new attention to his arguments. *See* SYNOPTIC PROBLEM[S].

Bibliography. J. J. Griesbach, "Inquisitio in fontes, unde euangelistae suas de resurrectione domini narrationes hauserint" (1783), and "Commentatio qua Marci Euangelium totum e Matthaei et Lucae commentariis decerptum esse monstratur" (1789/90 [rev. ed., 1794]), both reprinted in *Opuscula academica*, ed. J. P. Gabler, II (1825), 241-56 and 358-425 respectively; W. R. Farmer, *The Synoptic Problem* (1964), bibliog.; C. H. Talbert and E. V. McKnight, "Can the Griesbach Hypothesis Be Falsified?" *JBL*, XCI (1972), 338-68; G. W. Buchanan, "Has the Griesbach Hypothesis Been Falsified?" *JBL*, XCIII (1974), 550-72.

V. P. FURNISH

***GUEST ROOM.** In Philem. 22 the phrase translates ξενία which, though more commonly a reference to the hospitality shown a guest, could also be used for the place where the guest was housed (cf. Acts 28:23). Hospitality for itinerant apostles and teachers was an important responsibility of early Christian congregations. V. P. FURNISH

H

***HABAKKUK COMMENTARY** (1QpHab). A scroll from Cave I at Wadi Qumran, containing a commentary (*pesher*) on the first two chapters of Habakkuk. On its discovery *see* DEAD SEA SCROLLS §1. For its meaning and significance *see* DEAD SEA SCROLLS §5*a*; DEAD SEA SCROLLS[S] §5 and bibliog.; and especially INTERPRETATION, HISTORY OF[S] §B1*ai*, *b*iii.

***HABIRU** or, more correctly, **HAPIRU.** A term applied to certain groups of people in second-millennium records from Cappadocia, Babylonia, Mari, Alalakh, Ḫattusas, Nuzi, Ugarit, several other cities of Syria-Palestine, and Egypt. Despite considerable evidence and discussion of the problem since 1890, no firm solution has been reached on the cardinal questions: (*a*) etymology and semantics of the term; (*b*) whether the Hapiru were an ethnic, social, occupational, or legal entity; (*c*) the relation between the Hapiru and the Hebrews.

1. Name. ***a. In cuneiform script.*** i. *Ideographic writing:* SA.GAZ (variants: SA.GAZ.ZA, SA.GA.AZ, SAG.GAZ, GAZ), which is a Sumerian borrowing of Akkadian *šaggāšu,* "killer, aggressor, violent person." It was also read *ḫabbātu;* "robber" or "migrant," sometimes used as an Akkadian synonym of the West Semitic loanword *ḫapiru.* ii. *Phonetic writing: ḫa*-BI-*ru;* fem. (Nuzi) *ḫa*-BI-*ra-tu;* aberrant spellings: *ḫa*-'-BI-*ru* (Alalakh VII, not certain); *ḫa*-AB-BI-*ri* (Hittite). The initial *ḫ* could transcribe the West Semitic phonemes *h, ḫ,* or ʿ; the second syllable could be read, in the orthography of the second millennium, *bi* or *pi.* The ethnic *Ḫa-bir-a-a* in two Babylonian letters seemed to point to the pronunciation *ḫabiru;* but we are probably dealing with natives of a Babylonian town whose name is only accidentally similar to the term *ḫa*-BI-*ru.*

b. In Egyptian. The Egyptian transcription is ʿ*pr,* pl. ʿ*pr.w.* It shows that the initial pharyngeal in *ḫa*-BI-*ru* corresponded to ʿ (ע), although there have been attempts to explain the *p* as an Egyptian rendering of Semitic *b.* But numerous Egyptian transcriptions of foreign names and words always preserve the original *b,* with one exception (*ḥrp*= חרב, "sword"), in which, however, the final position of *b* may have caused its loss of sonance, which does not apply to the intervocalic position of the labial in *ḫa*-BI-*ru.*

c. In Ugaritic. In parallel lists of towns of the kingdom of UGARIT, written in Akkadian syllabic and in Ugaritic alphabetic scripts, the syllabic ^{URU}*Ḫal-bi* $^{LÚ.MEŠ}$SAG.GAZ corresponded to alphabetic *Ḫlb* ʿ*prm.* This proved that *ḫa*-BI-*ru* was read *ḫapiru* and that its West Semitic original was ʿ*apiru.* Efforts were made to preserve the connection with the root ʿBR (*see* §*d below*) by invoking the interchange *b*/*p* in Semitic, but this phenomenon normally occurs *between* languages, not within the same language, except in certain specific cases. In Ugaritic, *b* can shift to *p* only by regressive assimilation in contact with an unvoiced consonant. Nor can the form ʿ*prm* be blamed on the phonetic influence of Hurrian; were this the case, it would have lost the ʿayin. Ugaritic possessed the root ʿBR, and there was no reason for Ugaritian scribes to spell one of its derivatives with a *p.*

d. Etymology. Two early etymologies, which presupposed the reading *ḫabiru,* derived it from the roots ḤBR, "to bind, join," or ʿBR, "to cross, pass," which made *ḫabiru* the equivalent of, in the former case, חברים, "confederates," and in the latter, עברים, "Hebrews," originally "migrants, transients." The Egyptian and especially the Ugaritic spellings rule out these derivations (*see also* §5). The root of *ḫapiru*/ʿ*apiru* is now generally recognized as ʿPR, but there is no agreement as to its semantics. One theory sees in ʿPR the West Semitic cognate of Akkadian *epēru,* "to provide with food," which would explain *ḫapiru* as persons who receive food rations; but the relevant West Semitic root, as shown by Ugaritic, is ḤPR. Another theory proceeds from the use of *epēru,* the Akkadian cognate of West Semitic ʿ*pr,* "dust," in the sense of "territory," and sees the ʿ*apiru* as people of undeveloped, wooded areas; but *epēru* does not have this connotation and simply refers to the land of a town or village. A more plausible etymology derives ʿ*apiru* from ʿ*pr* in its basic meaning "dust": it would signify "dusty," people covered with dust from long journeys. In Arabic the corresponding root (ʿ*afara*) has also the meaning "to be wicked, ferocious, terrible," which is close to the semantics of Akkadian *šaggāšu,* the prototype of SA.GAZ, the ideogram for *ḫapiru;* but there is no instance of such meaning of ʿPR in an ancient West Semitic text.

2. Survey of evidence. ***a. Eighteenth century.*** The Hapiru are first mentioned in documents from the eighteenth century (low CHRONOLOGY OF THE OT). The Mari texts attest to their activities in N Mesopotamia. They were engaged in military operations in the service of local kings, or in pillaging on their own, or in alliance with a city. Once they co-operated with a group of revolted *muškênu* (semifree peasants) who fled into the steppe. They sometimes appeared in large units; we hear of "two thousand Hapiru of the country" as a garrison on the upper Euphrates. A detachment of Hapiru was composed of members of the Amorite tribe of Yamutbal. Some Mari texts use the Akkadian equivalent *ḫabbātu:* a "son of a *ḫabbātu*" was appointed governor of a steppe district; a troop of *ḫabbātu* and Canaanites occupied a town. An Old

Assyrian tablet from Alişar speaks of wealthy Hapiru connected with Assyrian commercial colonies in Cappadocia. Hapiru are attested at Larsa (southern Babylonia) as soldiers who are issued rations.

b. Seventeenth century. Tablets from Alalakh, level VII, speak of a *ḫabbātu* chieftain who waged war against a king of Yamḫad. One of his subordinates called himself on his seal "general of *ḫabbātu*," which shows that this term could be used without a pejorative meaning. A date formula of another king of Yamḫad commemorates the conclusion of peace between him and Hapiru troops (ERIN.MEŠ *Ḫa-'-pí-ru,* probable reading and interpretation).

c. Sixteenth century. A Hittite king concluded a formal treaty with Hapiru, taking them into his army and promising them equal treatment with native royal troops. Three thousand Hapiru soldiers in Hittite service were placed as a garrison against the Hurrians. *Ca.* 1510-1500, a fugitive prince of Aleppo, Idrimi, spent seven years among Hapiru in northern Phoenicia before recovering his ancestral kingdom with their help.

d. Fifteenth century. Census lists from Alalakh, level IV, frequently mention "Hapiru who own arms." A "house of Hapiru" consisted of 1,436 men, including eighty charioteers. A Syrian city on the edge of the steppe was transferred by a Mitannian king to a prince who was a Hapiru. Hapiru men and women entered into contracts of voluntary servitude with rich citizens of Nuzi. Other Hapiru at Nuzi were in the service of the government; one commanded a squad of ten soldiers. The occurrence at Nuzi of a "Hapiru scribe" seems to indicate that the Hapiru spoke a language which was distinct from Hurrian and Akkadian. About the same time, Pharaoh Amen-hotep II listed 'Apiru among prisoners taken in Palestine and southern Syria.

e. Ḫatti and Ugarit. In the fourteenth century the Hittites reappeared in Syria and renewed their contact with Hapiru. Large groups (presumably prisoners of war) were assigned to Hittite temples, but other Hapiru (presumably allies) possessed their own territory under Hittite sovereignty. The "gods of the Hapiru" were included in Hittite enumerations of gods. A "Hapiru town" existed in Cilicia. Few Hapiru, apparently, were present in the kingdom of Ugarit. We learn from a legal document of *ca.* 1300 that a Hapiru as well as an *ubru* (foreign resident) could be billeted in private houses. A Hapiru was thus under royal protection and was distinguished from a foreign resident. One of the five towns of the kingdom named Ḫalbi was known as "Ḫalbi of the Ḫapiru (*'prm*)" (*see* §1*c*), and was in no way different as to its status and obligations. *'prm* seem to have served in the Ugaritian navy during the invasion of the Peoples of the Sea (*ca.* 1200; *see* PHILISTINES[S]).

f. Amarna letters. The largest body of evidence comes from the Amarna correspondence (*ca.* 1375-1345; *see* TELL EL-AMARNA esp. §2*b*; TELL EL-AMARNA[S]). It shows the Hapiru as a major force in central and southern Syria, Phoenicia, and Palestine. They formed the bulk of the armed forces of the usurper Abdi-Ashirta, the founder of the kingdom of Amurru; but his grandson speaks instead of Sutu (Bedouin), as though these terms were equivalent. The Egyptian commissioner of southern Syria, Biriawaza, had both Hapiru and Sutu in his army. A city ruler begged the pharaoh to deliver him from the hand of the Hapiru, the *ḫabbātu,* and the Sutu, the mighty enemies. Several local kings or pretenders were allied with Hapiru, who seized towns and territories, and often killed loyal city rulers. A recurring complaint is that the land of the Egyptian king has been taken over by the Hapiru.

g. Egyptian sources. Two identical letters (in Akkadian) from a pharaoh of the Amarna period were discovered in Kumidi (Kāmid el-Lōz in southern Lebanon). They instruct the vassal kings of Damascus and a city in the Biqa' to send *ḫapiru aburra* to Egypt so they can be settled in Nubia. *Aburra* seems to be a diptotic genitive of *aburru,* "pasture." The people in question must have been prisoners; cf. the 'Apiru captives of Amen-hotep II (*see* §1*d*). Egyptian texts of the New Kingdom mention 'Apiru in Egypt itself, employed as vineyard workers or at hauling stones for construction. The Beth-shan stele of Seti I (1318-1304) speaks about that pharaoh's action against 'Apiru in southern Galilee. The latest mention of 'Apiru in Egypt comes from the middle of the twelfth century, and with it the 'Apiru/Hapiru forever disappear from the historical scene.

3. Hapiru as foreigners, refugees, or outlaws. The Hapiru were at first mostly regarded as a people and were often identified with the Hebrews (*see* §5 *below*). But in 1924, B. Landsberger and J. Lewy independently proposed to see in *ḫabiru* (as they continued to read it) a nonethnic, generic appellation. For Landsberger, the Habiru (from Canaanite *ḥābēr,* "member of a band") were uprooted individuals of varied origins, without tribal or family ties, who joined in bands which could be hired as soldiers by organized states, or acted on their own. For Lewy, the Habiru were foreign immigrants who were subject to special laws, were segregated from the native population, and found employment as soldiers of a "foreign legion"; hence their name, which derives from West Semitic *'ābir,* "one who had crossed the border"="immigrant foreigner." Both etymologies, as noted in §1*d,* turned out to be wrong. Most recent definitions of the term *ḫapiru* are variants of the Landsberger-Lewy view: "foreigners who are also enemies," "stateless persons," "soldiers of fortune," "uprooted persons who work for food," "displaced persons," "refugees," "outlaws," "rebels against the lawful ruling power." A separate theory (by W. F. Albright) saw the Hapiru/'Apiru as professional donkey caravaneers, whom lack of business compelled to become bandits or soldiers; but none of the approximately 250 pieces of evidence ever connects them with donkeys or commerce.

There are serious objections to understanding the Hapiru as an underprivileged social or legal category: (*a*) None of the definitions cited above fits all, or even most, of the contexts. (*b*) No legal discrimination of foreigners is attested in any state of Mesopotamia or Syria in the second millennium. Documents from Ugarit, in particular, show that the city contained numerous immigrants from other states who were well integrated into the economic life of the kingdom. To be sure, numerous ancient Near Eastern texts mention fugitives: runaway slaves, embezzlers, insolvent debtors, political refugees; but such persons were either extradited (as stipulated in all state treaties), or else granted asylum and naturalized. (*c*) At no time were gangs of outlaws of mixed origin a major factor in the Near East. Pillaging raids, destructions of towns, seizure of territories—all these were until recently perennial features in the struggle between the desert and the sown land; but the perpetrators of these acts of violence were organized tribal units (*see* NOMADISM[S]). (*d*) If, as is claimed, Near Eastern societies contained large agglomerations of people who had dropped out from normal social life (Mendenhall), it is impossible to explain why the Hapiru are attested for only six hundred years (*ca.* 1750-1150) and why there is no later mention of them, or of massive bands of outlaws and stateless persons under any other name.

4. Hapiru as nomadic tribesmen. In view of the contradictions of the sociolegal view of the Hapiru, de Vaux posed the question whether one should not, after all, consider the Hapiru as one of the West Semitic ethnic elements which roamed the fringes of the desert. Here a reservation must be made: *ḫapiru* was not an ethnic term; if it were, it would have been written in Ugaritic **ʿprym,* not *ʿprm;* nor is it ever spelled **ḫapirû* or **ḫapirāya* in Akkadian (the Middle Babylonian ethnic *Ḫa-bir-a-a,* as noted in §1*a*, probably does not belong here). Nevertheless, if one is looking for a social group which would combine all these features: love of war and violence; mobility; predilection for military career; economic status ranging from considerable wealth to extreme poverty; tendency to keep together, often in large units; hospitality; efforts to seize areas and settle in them; possible connection with pastures; possession, at times, of territories under their own jurisdiction; chieftains who are proud to be called *ḫabbātu;* preservation of group identity even inside cultivated land—one cannot but think of nomadic tribes in the fringe areas and inside Syria and Mesopotamia. Granted that the Hapiru were not full-fledged citizens of the country of their sojourn; however, it was not their being strangers that made them Hapiru, but their being Hapiru that made them strangers. Immigrants from civilized countries entered the civic society by joining one of its cells (a town or a corporation); the Hapiru remained members of tribal communities who were resisted if they came as plunderers or conquerors, but tolerated and rewarded if they chose to enter the royal service against other states or tribes. The distinction between sedentary subjects and Hapiru tribesmen was indeed, to an extent, a legal one; yet it was not imposed by the state within a single system of law but was a self-imposed adherence of the Hapiru to their independent system of tribal law. *Ḫapiru* was indeed a designation of a peculiar way of life—like "Bedouin," and like the earliest meaning of "Arab"—but, like these, it had a *de facto* ethnic connotation. Nomads, in our time as in the second millennium B.C., appear only within the framework of tribes, and these tribes, in a given period, belong to one of the branches of the Semitic family which succeeded each other in this role: Amorites, Arameans, Arabs. The activities of the Hapiru in the Amarna Age are closely comparable to the penetration of Syria by Arabs during the collapse of the Seleucids. It is significant that the six hundred years of Hapiru presence in the Near East start with the end of Amorite invasions and conquests and end with the start of the Aramean expansion. The Hapiru are no longer mentioned after 1200-1150 because by that time their turbulence was spent: like their predecessors and successors, they ended by settling down. If the Hapiru are both associated with and distinguished from the Sutu, the difference probably consisted in the Sutu being Bedouin of the desert, while the name *ḫapiru* was given to those nomads who had already infiltrated cultivated lands; however, this distinction was not very rigid.

5. Hapiru and Hebrews. As shown in §1, the view that *Ḫabiru* was the same word as Heb. *ʿibri,* "Hebrew," had to be abandoned because of indubitable evidence that the original form of this term was *ʿapiru,* which cannot be plausibly explained as a phonetic variant of **ʿabiru.* Nor is it probable (as hypothesized by Albright) that around the turn of the first millennium the pronunciation shifted from *ʿapir-* to *ʿabir-,* in part under the influence of the root ʿBR, "to cross, to pass," and then from *ʿabir-* to *ʿibr-* by the same mechanism by which an earlier *malik-* became the Canaanite *milk-,* "king." The latter example is unconvincing because *milk-* is attested (in Amorite names) as early as the Ur III period; *milk-* and *malik-* (the latter used only as a divine name) are parallel formations. A dual transformation, both consonantal and vocalic, of *ʿapir-* into *ʿibr-* is difficult to admit. *ʿApiru* and *ʿibrî* are in all likelihood etymologically and semantically unrelated. *ʿIbrî* is a regular ethnic derived from the geographical term *ʿibr-* (>Masoretic *ʿēber*), "land beyond the river." It is seldom encountered in the OT, was not a normal self-designation of the Israelites, and may have been of a relatively late origin. If it is unwarranted to interpret the Hapiru, wherever one finds them, as Hebrews, it is equally wrong to explain the term "Hebrew" in the OT by the alleged sociolegal meaning of *ḫapiru.* Could there have been, however, a historical connection between the Hapiru and Israel? If the Hapiru, as this is often assumed (§3), were disparate bands composed of outlaws of various ethnic origins, then there was no relation whatever between them and the Israelites who, during their early history in Palestine, displayed all the characteristic features of a normal tribal society of nomadic background in the process of becoming sedentary. If, on the other hand, one accepts the view outlined in §4, then the penetration of the Hapiru into Syria-Palestine of the Amarna Age presents a close analogy to the settlement of Israelite and cognate tribes, as it was still remembered in certain pre-Deuteronomic passages, and it becomes permissible to assume that this settlement was an episode of the final stage of the Hapiru movement.

Bibliography. An excellent survey is provided by J. Bottéro, *Le problème des Ḫabiru* (1954). Similar is M. Greenberg, *The Hab/piru* (1955 [2nd, augmented ed., 1961]). More recent literature is quoted in R. de Vaux, "Le problème des Ḫapiru après quinze années," *JNES*, XXVII (1968), 221-28. The article "Habiru" by J. Bottéro in *RLA*, IV, fasc. 1 (1972), 14-27, contains a full list of documents, a brief supplementary list of studies, and a new discussion of the evidence.

M. C. ASTOUR

***HADRACH** [חדרך, Old Aram. חזרך, Assyr. *Ḫat(a)-rikka, Ḫat(a)rakka*]. A city mentioned with Damascus (Zech. 9:1). Identified with the very large mound of Tell Āfis, *ca.* twenty-eight miles SW of Aleppo (*see* HITTITES[S] map); here was discovered an Old Aramaic inscribed stele of Zakir, king of Hamath and *L'š* (*ca.* 800 B.C.) which reports the unsuccessful siege of *Ḥzrk* by a coalition of Syrian kings headed by Bar-hadad (BEN-HADAD), king of Aram. Hadrach was the capital of Luḫuti or *L'š*, allied with Hamath from 854 to 773. After seceding from the then pro-Assyrian Hamath, Hadrach opposed Assyria till it was conquered by Tiglath-pileser III in 738 and turned into an Assyrian province. In 720 it rose against Sargon II, along with Hamath, Arpad, Simirra, Damascus, and Samaria, but the revolt was suppressed the same year (these events are probably hinted at in Zech. 9:1-6).

Bibliography. KAI, no. 202; *ANET*³, pp. 655-56; A. Malamat, "The Historical Setting of Two Biblical Prophecies on the Nations," *IEJ*, I (1950/51), 149-59; R. de Vaux, "La chronologie de Hazaël et de Benhadad III. . . ," *Bible et Orient* (1967), pp. 75-82; S. Parpola, "Ḫatarikka," in *Neo-Assyrian Toponyms* (1970), for Assyrian occurrences. M. C. ASTOUR

HADRIAN hā'drĭ ən. Publius Aelius Hadrianus, Roman emperor (A.D. 117-138). Hadrian was born, probably in Rome, on January 24, 76. His family came from Italica in Spain (near Seville), the birthplace of his predecessor TRAJAN (98-117). Left fatherless in 85, he became the ward of Trajan, his father's cousin, and of Acilius Attianus, also from Italica, who played a significant role early in Hadrian's reign. A favorite of Trajan's wife, Plotina, Hadrian was also linked to the emperor through his marriage to Sabina (A.D. 100), Trajan's grandniece. His career followed a traditional course of civil and military appointments which included service in Trajan's Dacian campaigns (101-102, 105-106), the consulate in 108 and, in 117, at a critical stage in the Parthian wars, command of the important Syrian army while Trajan returned to Rome. When Trajan died en route (August, 117), Hadrian was proclaimed emperor by the troops in Syria and then recognized, somewhat reluctantly, by the Roman senate.

As emperor, Hadrian abandoned Trajan's Parthian conquests and thereafter maintained a policy of peace based on fortified border defenses (e.g., Hadrian's Wall in Britain), a highly disciplined army, and no further imperial expansion. In Rome, his reign opened inauspiciously with the execution of four senators—upon suspicion of treason—by Attianus, now prefect of the PRAETORIAN GUARD.

Courtesy the Museum of Roman Ships, Ostia
1. Hadrian

When Hadrian himself reached Rome, in the summer of 118, he removed Attianus from office, blaming him for the executions, and took several measures designed to counteract his own unpopularity. The most spectacular was the remission of 900,000,000 sesterces worth of debts to the state, an act recorded on his coins of 118. Restless, inquisitive (Tertullian later called him *omnium curiositatum explorator*), and perhaps never fully comfortable in the capital, Hadrian spent extended periods away from Rome: 121 to 125; 128 to 132 or 133; briefly in 134 in connection with the Jewish revolt in Judea (*see* GERASA Fig. 19). His travels enabled him to inspect the army, to attend to provincial affairs in person, and to indulge a penchant for Greek culture which, in childhood, had earned him the nickname "Greekling" (*Graeculus*).

In matters religious, Hadrian's reign was of varying significance. He was himself a devotee of astrology and an initiate of the Eleusinian mysteries (*see* GREEK RELIGION AND PHILOSOPHY §5). His homosexual affair with Antinoüs, a Bithynian youth, ended unhappily when the boy was drowned in the Nile in 130. Cults of Antinoüs sprang up throughout the Empire in response to Hadrian's grief—and soon became a stock example in Christian polemic against Roman paganism. Toward the Christians, as a surviving rescript shows (Just. I Apol. 68), Hadrian continued Trajan's lenient policy. His legislation against CIRCUMCISION, however, helped to provoke the Jewish revolt under

Bar Kochba (132-135). The founding of the Roman colony of Aelia Capitolina at Jerusalem in 130 may also have contributed to Jewish resentment of Rome (contra Euseb. Hist. IV.vi, it was not a punitive reaction to the revolt). In neither case, however, is it clear that Hadrian acted with deliberate intent against the Jews.

Himself a poet of some skill, a musician, and an amateur architect, Hadrian exercised great influence on the culture of the Empire. His preference for the archaic (he is reported to have preferred Ennius to Virgil) set the rhetorical and literary style for his period. He cultivated a repristination of Hellenistic art which verged on the romantic (especially evident in statues of Antinoüs). An avid builder, his architectural achievements include, in Rome, the reconstruction of the Pantheon, the Temple of Venus and Rome, and his own mausoleum (the Castel Sant' Angelo). His architectural masterwork, however, was the personal villa which he created at Tibur (Tivoli), outside of Rome, during the final years of his rule. Among Hadrian's provincial buildings were the Temple of Jupiter Capitolinus erected on the site of the Jewish temple and the Temple of Aphrodite (Venus) built over Jesus' tomb, both in Jerusalem. Under Constantine, the Temple of Aphrodite was removed to make way for the Church of the Holy Sepulchre (Eusebius, *Life of Constantine* III.xxv-xxix).

Complex, enigmatic, always changeable (*semper in omnibus varius* reports the *Historia Augusta*), Hadrian is a difficult figure to assess. His profound philhellenism marks a high point in the melding of Greek culture with Roman power. But he himself was always regarded and remembered with ambivalence. His reign ended (July, 138) under a cloud: two candidates were put to death before he settled the succession on Antoninus Pius. Only with great difficulty was Antoninus able to persuade the senate to vote Hadrian the honor of posthumous deification.

Bibliography. Sources: Dio Cassius, *Roman History* LXIX (ed. Boissevain), preserved only in Byzantine epitomes; "Life of Hadrian" in the *Historia Augusta* (ed. Hohl). On Dio: F. Millar, *A Study of Cassius Dio* (1964). On the *Historia Augusta:* A. Chastagnol, *Recherches sur l'Historie Auguste* (1970). Selected inscriptions: E. M. Smallwood, *Documents Illustrating the Principates of Nerva, Trajan and Hadrian* (1966).

Studies: B. W. Henderson, *The Life and Principate of the Emperor Hadrian* (1923) and S. Perowne, *Hadrian* (1960), neither fully reliable; R. Syme, *Tacitus,* 2 vols. (1958); E. M. Smallwood, "The Legislation of Hadrian and Antoninus Pius against Circumcision," *Latomus,* XVIII (1959), 334-47. Art: R. Bianchi Bandinelli, *Rome: The Center of Power* (1970).

W. S. Babcock

***HAIR.** In the ancient world hair represented one's essence, probably because it endures beyond death; therefore, numerous restrictions and customs clustered about it.

1. Hair worn long. *a*) Heroic figures like Esau, Samson, Absalom, Gilgamesh, and anonymous heroes of ancient art are pictured with long hair, sometimes with seven locks (Samson). *See* Fig. H2.

The Louvre

2. Bust of head with seven locks. Phoenician, 6th-4th century B.C. from Carthage

b) Kings allowed hair to grow as a sign of potency. Even Queen Hatshepsut in statuary art possessed a stylized beard. Assyrian kings grew long, curly hair with great, square beards.

c) Gods were imagined as possessing long side locks and hair. The bull symbol of Ur's moon-god had a beard, indicating potency.

d) The expression "there shall not one hair of his head fall to the ground" (I Sam. 14:45; cf. II Sam. 14:11; I Kings 1:52) shows the significance of hair to one's well-being.

e) Disheveled hair represented mourning (Lev. 10:6) as well as reckless abandon. Priests' hair was not to be disheveled (Lev. 21:10), while the leper was to let his hair hang loose (Lev. 13:45). A woman accused of infidelity was to have her hair unbound by the priest when she appeared before God to test her innocence (Num. 5:18).

f) Israelites, as a sign of their distinctiveness, were to leave the hair of the temples and beard untrimmed (Lev. 19:27).

g) A Nazirite (Num. 6:1-21) was obligated to leave his hair uncut as an act of dedication. Samson's strength derived from his vow; the shaving of his seven locks removed his vow's last vestige; therefore, the Lord "left him" (Judg. 16:20).

h) The statement that "the leaders took the lead in Israel" (Judg. 5:2) may suggest dedication to God by growing hair. The term used, פרע, is cognate to the usual Akkadian word for hair (*pertu*) and appears elsewhere in the OT with this connotation (Lev. 10:6; Num. 6:5).

i) Married women and those otherwise set apart were to cover their hair with a veil.

2. Hair to be cut. *a*) Shaving the Levites' bodies was an essential part of purification (Num. 8:5-7). The name Korah means "bald," perhaps indicating tonsure (Num. 16). Priests and physicians of the ancient world often were shaven.

b) Hair was offered as a sacrifice by a Nazirite on completion of his vow or when he inadvertently violated it (Num. 6:9-18), and by the person completing a journey or pilgrimage. Lepers shaved as part of the ritual for restoration (Lev. 14:8, 9).

c) Israelite prophets advised their listeners to cut their hair in mourning for the coming destruction (Isa. 3:24; Jer. 7:29).

d) Priests in Ezekiel's "Temple Ordinances" must not shave their heads or let their hair grow long (44:20). They may only trim their hair and beards, which suggests avoidance of the tonsure, a characteristic of foreign priests (*see* Lev. 21:5). The prophetic mantle (I Kings 19:19; II Kings 2:8, 13) was hairy (Zech. 13:4), reminiscent of the hairy kilt worn by bald-headed priests of Sumerian times.

e) Ezekiel (5:1-4) cut his hair to symbolize the coming destruction and exile. Prophets may earlier have been marked by tonsure as indicated by Elisha's being called "baldy" (II Kings 2:23), or by the prophet who bandaged his head as a disguise (I Kings 20:35-43). *See also* VEIL; BEARD.

Bibliography. W. R. Smith, *The Religion of the Semites* (2nd ed., 1894), pp. 324-31, 481; H. W. F. Saggs, *The Greatness That Was Babylon* (1962), pp. 183-85; J. G. Frazer, *Adonis, Attis, Osiris*, I (3rd ed., 1914), 38, 225; J. Lindblom, *Prophecy in Ancient Israel* (1962), pp. 68-69; A. T. Olmstead, *History of Assyria* (1923), pp. 71, 120-21, 567.

W. C. GWALTNEY, JR.

***HARAN (PLACE). 1. Historical references.** The eighteenth-century B.C. texts found at MARI refer to Asditakim, king of Haran, and the alliance made between local kings of Zalmaqum and elders of the tribe of Benjamin (*see* BENJAMIN, BENJAMINITES[S]) in the temple of Sin at Haran. In this same century Haran is referred to as a staging post on an important caravan route between Mesopotamia and the northwest.

The moon-god Sin of Haran was invoked as a guarantor of treaties between the HITTITES and MITANNI, and the town was involved in a three-way struggle between Hatti, Mitanni, and Assyria in the fourteenth century. It was annexed by Assyria under Shalmaneser I (1274-1245 B.C.). Until the sacking of Haran in 610 B.C., the city was the capital of one of the most important provinces in the empire and gradually acquired privileges including the right of exclusion from military levies. Throughout this time the cult and temple of Sin remained important, and restorations of the temple are twice recorded.

The Babylonian ruler NABONIDUS had a deep veneration for Sin and his temple at Haran, and his monumental inscribed slabs record the rebuilding of the temple in the sixth century. Well into the Christian period a pagan cult of the moon-god continued to flourish in the region. The city had strategic importance in these later times also.

2. Excavations. The investigations in the 1950s were primarily concerned with the Islamic remains, and the limited excavations on the large tell in 1959, being restricted to one deep trench, revealed only sketchy traces of its early history. The artifacts show that the town was established by at least the middle of the third millennium, but its origins are probably much earlier. The evidence reflects a well-to-do town with mud-brick houses existing for the following five hundred or so years. But for the entire second and first millennia, a period otherwise so well documented, the evidence is thus far restricted to a few sherds and fragmentary inscriptions. One fragmentary text of Assyrian date refers to the temple. Excavations in the neighborhood at Aşagi Yarimcâ and Sultantepe have revealed fairly extensive Assyrian towns or cult establishments dedicated to Sin, and this has led to suggestions that the site of ancient Haran might have been located away from the Roman, medieval, and present site. This view seems unnecessary however, for it is clear that most sizable towns of the region would have had subsidiary temples dedicated to this paramount deity. It has been suggested that the ancient temple of Haran lies beneath the Great Mosque where Nabonidus' stelae were found, but the contours of the top of the hill may indicate that the tell became a podium for the temple, which Assurbanipal records he restored on a wide platform with stone foundations, raised high in the center of the city and approached by a stairway. The contemporary town would thus lie below at the sides of the tell, and now be hidden beneath as much as twenty-three feet of Roman and Islamic debris. The stratifaction in the excavation indicates that this transformation of the early tell could have taken place at any time after the end of the third millennium.

Bibliography. S. Lloyd and W. C. Brice, "Harran," *Anatolian Studies*, I (1951), 77-111; D. S. Rice, "Medieval Ḥarrän," *Anatolian Studies*, II (1952), 36-84; C. J. Gadd, "The Harran Inscriptions of Nabonidus," *Anatolian Studies*, VIII (1958), 35-92; K. Prag, "The 1959 Deep Sounding at Harran in Turkey," *Levant*, II (1970), 63-94.

K. PRAG

***HARMONY OF THE GOSPELS.** A four-gospel harmony of the Greek text in current use is K. Aland, ed., *Synopsis Quattuor Evangeliorum* (7th ed., 1971) which includes parallels from apocryphal gospels and patristic sources. These latter are not incorporated in the Greek-English ed., *Synopsis of the Four Gospels* (1972), which adds the RSV text and notes KJV and ERV variants.

HAUSTAFEL hous′ tä fĕl. A technical term for NT passages in which persons are admonished concerning their stations in life. *See* LISTS, ETHICAL §§1–4; LISTS, ETHICAL[S] §2. D. SCHROEDER

***HAZARMAVETH.** For etymology *see* DEITIES, UNDERWORLD[S] §2*b*ii.

***HAZOR.** Between 1955 and 1958 extensive excavations were conducted at Hazor on behalf of the Hebrew University under the directorship of Y. Yadin. During the four seasons various areas were excavated both on the tell (the upper city) and the rectangular plateau (the lower city) at the foot of the tell (*see* HAZOR Fig. 8). The strata of the upper and lower cities were allocated independent numbers. In the summer of 1968 a fifth season was conducted.

Courtesy Y. Yadin

3. Topographical map of Hazor showing excavated areas

1. The lower city. C, D, E, "210," F, H, K, and P were excavated, revealing the following five occupation levels (numbered bottom to top):

Stratum 4: MB IIB period (eighteenth century B.C.)

Stratum 3: MB IIC period (seventeenth-sixteenth centuries B.C.)

Stratum 2: LB I period (sixteenth-fifteenth centuries B.C.)

Stratum 1B: LB IIA (TELL EL-AMARNA period; fourteenth century B.C.)

Stratum 1A: LB IIB period (thirteenth century B.C.; city destroyed by fire at end of thirteenth century).

a. Area C. (i) Stratum 4. During this period the lower city's first fortifications and the rampart were constructed. (ii) Stratum 3. The city was destroyed by a great fire. Infant burials in store jars were discovered beneath some of the houses, as in the previous stratum (*see* MEGIDDO Fig. 28). (iii) Stratum 2. A number of dwellings were unearthed. (iv) Stratum 1B. During this phase the city flourished. On the inner slope of the rampart a small temple was found with a rectangular room containing small stelae and a statue (*see* TEMPLES §2*a*; TEMPLES, SEMITIC[S] §1*a*). Around the temple a number of buildings were uncovered, probably workshops to serve the temple's needs. (v) Stratum 1A. This town rose upon the ruins of the town preceding it, and its structures are similar to, but somewhat poorer than, those of stratum 1B. The temple from the previous city was reconstructed, and all its components replaced in their original positions.

b. Area D. The main finds here included rich tombs from the MB IIB period and attractive dwellings. An important discovery was a shard with two letters in the Proto-Canaanite script of the LB II period.

c. Area E. This small area is of special importance for its rich find of pottery of the LB I period. Some of the ceramics, showing Anatolian influence, are of a type never before discovered in Israel.

d. Area 210. A 17x17 foot trial dig was conducted to prove that the chronology of the strata was in fact identical in every area, and that the entire enclosure had been inhabited.

e. Area F. (i) Stratum 4. Rock-hewn tombs were discovered (all MB IIB), connected by a wide network of tunnels. All have basically the same plan: a deep rectangular shaft, at the bottom of which are a number of entrances (*see* TOMB[S] §3). (ii) Stratum 3. A large "double temple" with thick walls and rectangular in shape was constructed here (*see* TEMPLES, SEMITIC[S] §1*a*). A wide network of channels connected the temple to the earlier tombs, and formed a drainage complex. (iii) Stratum 2. The main building discovered was a square temple, similar to that discovered at Amman in Jordan. (iv) Stratum 1B. An altar made of a large ashlar block was discovered here, around which stood other structures related to this cultic object, as well as many cult vessels (*see* ALTAR Fig. 21). (v) Stratum 1A. The majority of structures surrounding the altar were reconstructed during this period; many cult objects and vessels were discovered.

f. Area H. A series of four temples was discovered, one above the other. All, like the temple in area C, are close to the inner slope of the rampart. (i) Stratum 3. The temple in this stratum has a wide room with a niche in the N side. Two columns in the center of the room supported the roof. The whole area in front of the temple entrance was paved with a fine pebble floor. (ii) Stratum 2. This temple is identical to that of the previous stratum, even though the building is a new structure. A number of small platforms were found, including a rectangular *bamah* or altar in the courtyard. To the E of the latter a large heap of broken cult objects and vessels was unearthed, including a most unusual find—inscribed fragments of clay liver models used by priests (*see* DIVINATION Fig. 32). (iii) Stratum 1B. The temple now comprises three main parts running from N to S, their doorways on a single axis leading to each chamber in succession. Generally, it is reminiscent of Solomon's temple in Jerusalem (*see* TEMPLE OF SOLOMON[S] §2*c*). The lower parts of the walls of the holy of holies and the porch were lined with large, well-dressed basalt slabs (orthostats). A huge lion orthostat was found, which, together with its missing counterpart, stood once at the entrance of the porch. (iv) Stratum 1A. This is virtually the same temple as in 1B with a few additions and changes. In the "holy of holies" a rich find of cult vessels was uncovered, including a basalt incense altar upon which was engraved the emblem of the storm-god (circle with cross) and a small basalt statue of a man sitting on a chair. *See* Fig. H4.

© Y. Yadin

4. Implements from the "holy of holies" of a Canaanite temple, 13th century, as found at Hazor. Probably destroyed by Joshua.

g. *Area K.* Here five city gates were unearthed, one above the other. (i) Stratum 4. Little remains of this, which was flanked by a tower on either side. The gate and the wall were built of bricks on a stone foundation. (ii) Stratum 3. In the gate passage were three pairs of pilasters, while two large towers flanked the sides of the gate. Close to the gate the remains of the earliest type of casemate wall known in Israel were unearthed. In front of the gate was a large platform enabling chariots to enter. This in turn was supported by a revetment wall built of huge basalt stones. (iii) Stratum 2. The gate of this phase is identical in plan to that of stratum 3, but is built of large, well-dressed stones. (iv) Stratum 1B. This gate is like that of stratum 2, but includes a number of alterations. The floor of the passage is now built of cobblestones, and in the S some workshops and cult objects including stelae were discovered. The casemate wall gave place to a brick wall, *ca.* ten feet thick. (v) Stratum 1A. This is the same gate as in the previous phase, with minor repairs and additions. The floor was found covered by a thick layer of ashes.

h. *Area P.* A similar set of gates was found here.

2. The upper city. The areas excavated in this part of the city included area A in the center of the tell (this is where Garstang conducted his trial dig in 1928); area AB situated close to area A; area B which lies in the W; area G in the E; and area L, which is situated SW of area A. Twenty-one occupational levels were discovered.

a. *Area A.* (i) Strata XXI-XIX may be attributed to the various stages of the EB period. Pottery was the main find in the levels, such as was the case in stratum XVIII (MB I). (ii) Strata XVII-XVI correspond to strata 4 and 3 in the lower city respectively. Remains of a large structure, possibly a palace, and remains of a great wall were uncovered here. The wall is twenty-five feet thick and is built of plastered bricks on a foundation of stone. (iii) Stratum XV corresponds with stratum 2 in the lower city. Here were unearthed sections of a large palace. Adjacent to it, a rectangular temple was found. Its entrance was built of orthostats. (iv) Stratum XIV corresponds to stratum 1B in the lower city. The main discovery in this phase were the remains of the palace with courtyards and squares paved in pebblestones. Close to the palace was a large reservior, to which rain water was carried through special channels. (v) Stratum XIII corresponds to stratum 1A in the lower city. Its destruction in the thirteenth century B.C. brought an end to the Canaanite occupation of Hazor. Very few buildings were constructed during this phase, but buildings from the previous stage were added to and reconstructed. (vi) Stratum XII. After a gap, the beginnings of Israelite occupation appear above the ruins of the thirteenth-century B.C. city: stone foundations of huts or tents and storage pits. Stratum XI is as poor as its predecessor. (vii) Stratum X. Hazor was rebuilt as a large city. Signs of its importance can be found in the casemate wall and the big gate which had six chambers (three on each side) and was flanked by a tower on each side. These fortifications may be attributed to King Solomon (*see* I Kings 9:15), since they are similar to those built by Solomon at GEZER and Megiddo (*see* MEGIDDO Figs. 36-37). (viii) Stratum IX. There is a decline in the standard of construction during this stage, which may be ascribed to the period between Solomon and Omri. This city was destroyed by an extensive conflagration. (ix) Stratum VIII. This phase excels in its wealth of public buildings and installations. Dominating the central part of the city was a large building, at the center of which stood two rows of columns. This stratum is assigned to the dynasty of Omri, and was most probably built by Ahab. (x) Stratum VII. The large pillared building was still in use during this stage, but other structures around it were altered. This level was razed to the ground, and its buildings were never reconstructed. (xi) Stratum VI. An area of public structures from an earlier stratum now became an area of living quarters and workshops. This city was probably destroyed in the earthquake which struck Israel during the period of Jeroboam II (Amos 1:1). (xii) Stratum V. During this period most of the houses of the previous level were reconstructed. The city was destroyed by a great fire, which may be attributed to the conquest of Tiglath-pileser III in 732 B.C. (*see* II Kings 15:29). Thus ended the fortified Israelite occupation of Hazor.

Few remains of importance were unearthed in strata IV-I (Assyrian-Hellenistic periods).

b. *Area B.* During the Israelite period a series of citadels occupied most of this area. The remains of the citadels were not removed, and therefore all knowledge of the area before the Israelite period was obtained from trial digs on the E side. (i) Stratum XII. This was the first Israelite occupation, and as in area A it was a poor and unwalled settlement. Although this type of life style continued in stratum XI, the latter is a far more permanent settlement. Finds of cult vessels around a "high place" seem to point to a cult center. (ii) Stratum X. Solomonic remains include the casemate wall surrounding the tell. A citadel was built on the W end, but little can be learned about it, since the citadel of stratum VIII was constructed directly above it. (iii) Stratum IX. Very little remains of this level. (iv) Stratum VIII. A massive fortress was unearthed (*ca.* 69 x 82 feet) with walls almost one foot thick. Two long halls with rows of rooms represent the basement of the citadel. The upper floors, built of bricks, have not been preserved. Buildings close by likely served the administrative staff. Proto-Aeolic capitals were found here. The outer walls of the structures served as a defense wall for the citadel. The fort constructed in the middle of the ninth century B.C. was used in strata VII-VI without significant changes. (v) Stratum V. Anticipating an Assyrian attack, the citadel was strengthened by an "offsets/insets" wall in the S, W, and N. In order to construct this wall a number of existing buildings had to be demolished. Stratum V was destroyed completely by Tiglath-pileser III (732 B.C.). (vi) Stratum IV. After the destruction of the fort, an open, unwalled settlement was established during the eighth-seventh centuries B.C., most probably occupied by Israelite squatters. (*See* Fig. H5.) (vii) Stratum III. A new citadel was constructed, probably by the Assyrians. Its plan consists of an open inner courtyard surrounded on all sides by halls and rooms. (viii) Stratum II. This layer belongs to the Persian period, during which the fort of stratum III continued to exist, but with many alterations. It may be dated to the fourth century B.C. (ix) Stratum I shows signs of yet another citadel which may be assigned to the Hellenistic period (second century B.C.).

c. Area G. The excavations in this section throw more light on the extent of development of the upper city.

i. *The Canaanite period.* The most important discovery of the MB II period was a line of fortifications on the NE corner of the tell. Of special note is the round corner bastion whose external walls sloped to form a stone glacis defended by a deep and narrow moat.

ii. *The Israelite period.* The earlier Solomonic town stretched over only a small part of the tell in comparison to the period of the dynasty of Omri (stratum VIII), when it spread out to encompass most of the area. This fact received further proof during the 1968 season of excavations in area M (NE of area A).

© Y. Yadin

5. Israelite house, Hazor, 8th century B.C.

d. Area L. During the fifth season of excavations (1968), an underground water system was unearthed, situated in areas A and B. It consists of three main sections.

i. *The shaft.* The upper section of the shaft cut through the early layers, reaching bedrock. It was revetted by a huge supporting wall built of large, rough stones. The lower section was entirely quarried into the soft natural rock. Along the sides was a rock-cut staircase measuring up to one foot in width. The shaft at Hazor is twice as big as that of Megiddo (*see* MEGIDDO[S] §2).

ii. *The sloping tunnel.* A tunnel, about thirteen feet wide and high, is the continuation of the flights of stairs. At the end a "pool" with clear water was found. The entire depth of the water system from the peak of the tell is about 131 feet.

iii. *The entrance structure.* To the E of the shaft, a building was discovered through which one could descend from the city to the shaft down two ramps specifically constructed for this purpose. Access from the entrance structures to the shaft was through a monumental gate. *See* Figs. H6, H7.

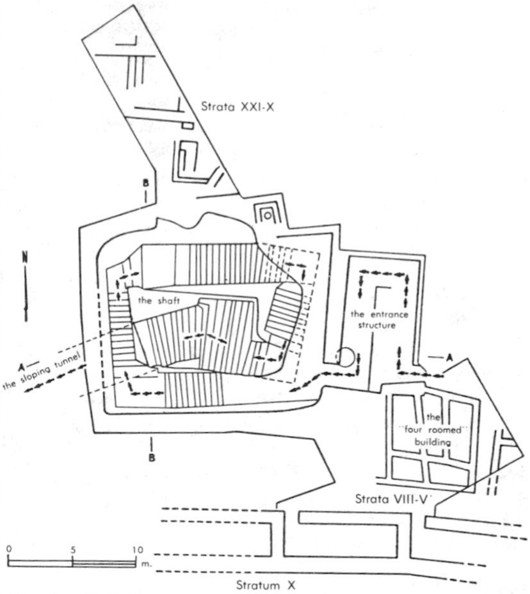

Courtesy Y. Yadin

6. The water system and the adjacent buildings and sections, Hazor

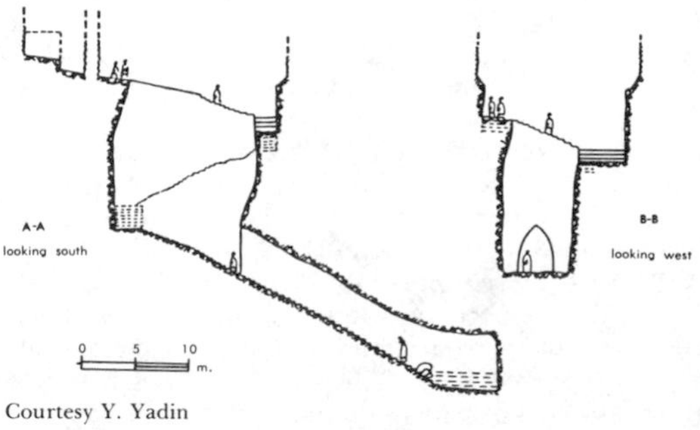

Courtesy Y. Yadin

7. Sections of the water system

It was possible to date this gigantic water system to the ninth century B.C. (i.e., dynasty of Omri) based on the similar water system found in Megiddo, the ceramic evidence, and stratigraphic examinations of the area. The system was in use until the final destruction of Hazor by Tiglath-pileser III in 732 B.C. *See also* ARCHAEOLOGY[S].

Bibliography. W. F. Albright, "The High Place in Ancient Palestine," VTSup, IV (1957), 242-58; K. Galling, "Erwägungen zum Stelenheiligtum von Hazor," *ZDPV,* LXXV (1959), 1-13; J. Gray, "Hazor," *VT,* XVI (1966), 26-52; Y. Yadin, *Hazor* (The Schweich Lectures; 1972). Y. YADIN

HEAD COVERING. During the biblical period priests and royalty are described as wearing a "turban" (צניף or מצנפת). No biblical or talmudic source, however, commands the covering of the head when entering a sanctuary, or participating in or performing a religious ceremony.

In Palestine during the biblical and rabbinic periods it was the custom to go bareheaded. When Antiochus Epiphanes forced Jewish young men to "wear the Greek hat" (II Macc. 4:12), Palestinian rabbis resented it as a sign of Hellenization.

It seems likely that it was in Babylonia that Jews developed the custom of covering the head. Rabbis and scholars there, affected by foreign customs, came to regard the practice as a sign of humility before God and of respect for prominent men.

Modern scholars disagree on how the custom spread. There is clear evidence that a head covering was not required in medieval France, but by the twelfth or thirteenth century it seems to have become deeply rooted throughout the rest of the Jewish world.

In modern times, especially in the United States, the issue of covering the head during worship has aroused controversy between traditional Jews and Reform Jews. The majority of Reform Jews in the U.S. pray bareheaded, whereas it is the practice for Orthodox Jews at all times and Conservative Jews during worship to wear either a hat or a skull cap, usually called a *yarmulke.* This word is of Polish origin *(jarmulka)* and has been adapted into Yiddish יארמעלקע; the Hebrew equivalent is כיפה. L. M. BARTH

***HEAVE OFFERING** [תרומה, *t^e^rûmâ*]. The sacred gifts called *t^e^rûmâ* are: the right hind thighs of the priestly consecration offering, מלאים, and "well-being" offering, שלמים (Exod. 29:27-28, RSV "priest's portion"; Lev. 7:32, 34; 10:14-15; Num. 6:20); the breast of the well-being offering (Exod. 29:27); the materials for the building of the tabernacle (Exod. 25:2-3; 35:5, 21, 24; 36:3, 6 [RSV "offering"]); the census silver (Exod. 30:13-15); the cakes of the thank offering, תודה (Lev. 7:12-14); the first yield of baked bread, ראשית הערסה (Num. 15:19-20; *see* FIRST FRUITS, OT[S]); the tithe and its tithe (Num. 18:24-29); the portion of the war spoils assigned to the sanctuary (Num. 31:29, 41, 52); sacred gifts in general (Num. 5:9; 18:8) and gifts of lesser sanctity in particular (Lev. 22:12, 15; Num. 18:11-19). Ezekiel adds to this list the land allotted to the priests and Levites (45:1; 48:8-21 [RSV "portion"]) and the sacrificial ingredients levied on the people (45:13, 16).

The tannaitic interpretation that *t^e^rûmâ* is a ritual whereby the offering is subjected to a vertical motion (cf. M. Men. 5.6) is responsible for the accepted rendering "heave offering." This rendering, however, is questionable, since in the cultic texts of the Priestly source, the verb *hērîm,* used exclusively with the preposition *min* and with the synonyms *hēsîr* (e.g., Lev. 4:8-10, 31, 35) and *nibhdal* (Num. 16:21, 45 [H 17:10]), never means "raise, lift," but only "set apart, dedicate." Consequently, the noun *t^e^rûmâ* can refer only to that which is set apart or dedicated, and hence must be rendered "dedication, contribution." This rendering is confirmed by the Targ. (אפרשותא), by the LXX (ἀφαίρεμα), and by the Akkadian *tarīmtu* (an exact cognate) and *rīmūtu* from the root *râmu* III (Assyrian *riāmu*).

The function of the *t^e^rûmâ* is to transfer the object from its owner to the deity. In this respect it is similar to the *t^e^nûphâ* (*see* WAVE OFFERING [S]), but with this crucial distinction: the *t^e^nûphâ* is performed "before the Lord" *(liphnê Yhwh),* whereas the *t^e^rûmâ* is never "before" but always "to the Lord" *(l^e^ Yhwh).* Thus the *t^e^nûphâ* and *t^e^rûmâ* comprise two means of dedication to the Lord: the former by a ritual in the sanctuary, and the latter by a dedication without ritual outside the sanctuary, effected either by an oral declaration (e.g., Judg. 17:3) or by a physical act (e.g., Lev. 27:32). This distinction serves to resolve the alleged ambiguities resulting from the same object undergoing both *t^e^nûphâ* and *t^e^rûmâ* (e.g., Exod. 29:22-24, 27; 35:24; cf. 38:24), a distinction which can be formulated into this rule: every *t^e^nûphâ* (ritual) is preceded by *t^e^rûmâ* (being set apart, designated as an offering).

The thigh of the well-being offering constitutes a special problem: the text which defines it (Lev. 7:32-33) assigns it directly to the officiating priest without the mediation of the *t^e^nûphâ,* whereas three other passages dealing with this thigh require the *t^e^nûphâ* (Lev. 8:26-27; 9:21; 10:15). The first of these passages (Lev. 8:26-27) concerns the thigh of the priestly consecration, which is incinerated on the altar and not given to the officiating priest. This unique disposal of the thigh requires the dedicatory rite of the *t^e^nûphâ.* Textual analysis of the remaining two passages (Lev. 9:21; 10:15) points to the possibility that "and the right thigh" is a later interpolation, whose historical motivation may be reconstructed by comparing Lev. 7:30-33 with I Sam. 2:13-17. Both pericopes share two postulates: (1) the officiating priest is recompensed by a portion of the well-being offering which does not undergo a ritual, and (2) the Deity receives his portion (via the altar) first, ahead of the priest. Such was the practice at Shiloh and, probably, at bamah sanctuaries. At the Jerusalem temple, however, the thigh was subjected to the *t^e^nûphâ* ritual in order to enhance the standardization and pomp befitting the national-royal shrine. Then it was ordained that the thigh should be distributed equitably to the entire priestly staff rather than becoming the due of the officiating priest, in order to prevent contention over its ownership. Early in second-temple times, the two traditions, the t^e*rûmâ* and the t^e*nûphâ,* were harmonized by blending them into a single ritual (perhaps through a Midrash Halachah on Exod. 29:27; cf. Sifra, Tsav 11.11) whereby the thigh was swung vertically and horizontally, as the rabbis attest was the practice during the last years of the second temple.

Bibliography. A. Vincent, "Les rites, du balancement (*tenoûphâh*)," *Melanges syriens offerts à Monsieur René Dussaud,* I (1939), 267-72; Y. Muffs, *Studies in the Aramaic Legal Papyri From Elephantine* (1969), p. 132, n. 2; W. von Soden, "Mirjam-Maria 'Gottes-(Geschenk),'" *UF,* II (1970), 269-72; J. Milgrom, "The שוק התרומה," Hebrew, plus English summary, and "An Akkadian Confirmation of תרומה Meaning 'Gift,'" *Tarbiz,* XLII (1973/74), 1-11, XLIV (1975-76), 189.

J. MILGROM

***HEBREW LANGUAGE. 1. Types of Hebrew.** Biblical Hebrew is divisible into dialects, depending on time, place, and category of literature.

a. Time differences. For example, Persian loan words, such as *dāth* (דת), "law, custom, religion," and *pithgam* (פתגם), "word, saying," do not appear until the Achaemenian conquest of the Near East in the second half of the sixth century B.C.

b. Local differences. Tribal dialects were recognized by the Israelites themselves, who noted that the Ephraimites did not distinguish *š* (ש) from *s* (ס) and accordingly said סבלת instead of שבלת (Judg. 12:6). The northern dialect at Samaria reduced the diphthong *ay* to *ê,* even in closed accented syllables where the Judeans retained the *y;* in the Samaria ostraca, the word for "wine" is written ין instead of MT יין.

c. Genre differences. Categories of literature call for their own conventional language. Poetry often preserves archaisms peculiar to itself. Thus the use of *yqṭl* verbs to express past time (often in Psalms, e.g., Ps. 78:26, 29, 38, 40, 45, 47, 49, 58, 64, 72) instead of *qṭl* or **wan+yqṭl* (ויקטל), continues an early poetic usage typifying the Late Bronze Age poetry from Ugarit. The definite article *ha(n)-* (ה) is an innovation that spread and became normal in Hebrew prose during the Iron Age (after 1200 B.C.), but old or archaizing poetry tends to avoid it (e.g., Ps. 68, where it is used very sparingly). Words like חרוץ, "gold," instead of the normal Hebrew זהב, and זו, instead of אשר, "which" (relative pronoun), are limited to poetry. Listings may be given in accordance with bookkeeping usage, without sentence structure. The thirty-one kings conquered by Joshua are identified by their city-states, each followed by the numeral "one" (Josh. 12:9-24). The total is added at the end. Descriptions of art and architecture (see Exod. 25–40 for the construction and furnishings of the tabernacle, and I Kings 5–7 for the temple) evoke special modes of expression different from narrative prose like the Joseph story or a love poem like Song of Songs. Diplomatic agreements have formulas found nowhere else; thus King Jehoshaphat of Judah agrees to be a military ally of the King of Israel by saying: "I am as you are, my people as your people, my horses as your horses" (I Kings 22:4).

2. Historical outline of Hebrew. *a. Biblical Hebrew.* The Ugaritic tablets, unearthed since 1929, make it abundantly clear that the Hebrew language, including even its poetic structures, was taken over by the Hebrews from the earlier Canaanite population. Indeed in the OT, the language is called not "Hebrew" but "the language of Canaan" (Isa. 19:18). The mainstream of the Hebrew people, according to biblical tradition, was Aramean (Gen. 31:47; Deut. 26:5); they learned Canaanite after migrating to Canaan.

Ancient Hebrew did not come to an end with the latest books of the OT canon in Hellenistic times, but continued to be spoken and written as the native language of many Jews, especially in Palestine. Apocryphal books such as Ecclesiasticus were composed in a natural, classical Hebrew (*see* ECCLESIASTICUS[S]). The caves at Qumran have yielded parts of the Hebrew originals of a number of apocryphal and pseudepigraphical books. The Qumran compositions were written in language essentially the same as biblical Hebrew, showing that this stage of the language survived in Roman Palestine until at least the dawn of the Christian Era. *See* DEAD SEA SCROLLS[S] §§2, 3.

b. Mishnaic Hebrew. The main representative of postbiblical Hebrew is the MISHNA, compiled in Palestine about A.D. 220. Its style is terse, but the language is that of the common people rather than the elite for whom Ecclesiasticus wrote. Mishnaic Hebrew is not a continuation of the literary OT language, but is rather the development of the colloquial language of OT Palestine. That it was not an artificial creation is shown by its containing words that appear in Ugaritic but not in the OT, e.g., *daq* (little), to designate small cattle (i.e., sheep and goats). Since the rabbis had no access to the long-dead Ugaritic language, the term must have survived in colloquial speech. Similarly, a certain marriage endowment is called מלוג in the Mishna. Though the word is ultimately of Akkadian origin, it had already been borrowed into Canaanite by the Late Bronze Age when it appears as *mlg* in Ugaritic literature.

Uncommon OT usage is often the norm in the Mishna. Thus the usual feminine singular demonstrative pronoun in the OT is זאת (this); occasionally זה or זו appears, and it is זו that serves regularly in the Mishna. In many other ways, the Mishnaic dialect diverges from classical OT Hebrew. The verbal system illustrates this well. In classical OT Hebrew verbs were inflected for aspect (perfective or imperfective), but not for tense. The Mishna uses the perfect (קטל) to express the past, the participle (קוטל) to express the present, and the imperfect (יקטל) or a periphrastic future composed of עתיד+ל+infinitive to express the future. Moreover the Mishna has progressive tenses made by adding participles to finite forms of the verb "to be"; thus הוא היה אומר, "he was saying," usually in the sense of "he used to say."

We also know from recently discovered letters of Bar Kochba (who rebelled against Rome during A.D. 132-35) that Hebrew was still a living language. *See* BAR KOCHBA[S] §4*b;* MANUSCRIPTS FROM THE JUDEAN DESERT[S] §2*a, b.*

c. Medieval Hebrew. Down through the centuries,

there were always Jews who could read, write, and speak Hebrew. Some writers (e.g., the author of the medieval Book of Jashar) could successfully imitate biblical style. Others wrote clumsy, artificial Hebrew compositions that in no way reflected living speech, but were intelligible because they employed the morphology and for the most part the vocabulary of the earlier stages of the language. Skillful writers—especially in creative periods such as the Golden Age of Spain and the centuries that immediately followed—could compose elegant prose and poetry that made medieval Hebrew the vehicle of belles-lettres second only to the OT. In this development, Arabic models were particularly important in inspiring metric forms of poetry, rhymed prose, and philosophical and scientific terminology. *See* INTERPRETATION, HISTORY OF[S] §F.

d. Modern Hebrew. Modern Hebrew, the official language of the state of Israel, is a creation of the nineteenth and twentieth centuries, under the influence of Western literary, intellectual, and scientific trends. It is a medium of expression ranging from common speech to the writing of all aspects of prose and poetry on a par with the languages of the world that have never undergone serious interruption. The tendency during the formative period was to draw on any or all of the earlier stages of the language. Contemporary Hebrew is still developing, and has attained qualities that differentiate it even from the Hebrew spoken and written during the era of the British Mandate between the World Wars. As the population comes to consist more and more of those for whom Hebrew is their first language, ancient and medieval usages often become less acceptable and even unintelligible.

3. Comparative Hebrew linguistics. Hebrew belongs to the family of Semitic languages, which embraces Akkadian, Arabic, Ethiopic, Syriac-Aramean, etc., as well as the Canaanite dialects. Every Semitic language thus has a bearing on Hebrew linguistics. Obscure or rare Hebrew words and formations have in many cases been clarified through comparative Semitic evidence. For example, אחדים, the plural of אחד, "one," means "pair, set," in Ezek. 37:17. This rarely attested usage, not to be confused with אחדים, "a few, several," which is common in postbiblical Hebrew, is familiar in Akkadian, where *iltēnūtu,* "pair, set," is the adjectival plural of *iltēn,* "one," and was reflected in Canaanite as early as Ugaritic *aḥdm,* "pair, set."

The linguistically conservative nature of Arabic makes it valuable for comparative studies. Prov. 17:22 states that a happy heart improves the גהה: a word that appears only once in the OT (RSV "medicine"). In Arabic *wjh* is the root of the word for "face"; the common nominal formation of roots beginning with *w-* yields for *wjh* the feminine *jihat,* to which Hebrew גהה corresponds exactly. This gives an appropriate meaning for the Hebrew phrase, "a happy heart improves the countenance."

At every level, the study of Ugaritic is revolutionizing our understanding of the Hebrew language. Illustrations are legion. Hebrew יפח or יפיח, once thought to be verbal forms, are now known to be nouns meaning "witness," like Ugaritic *ypḥ,* as is borne out by the OT contexts in which they occur (e.g., Prov. 6:19; Ps. 27:12). כושרות (a *hapax legomenon* in Ps. 68:6 [H 7]; RSV "prosperity") is at last clarified by Ugaritic *kṯrt,* "the songstresses [who gladden joyous occasions such as weddings and births]."

Ugaritic does not normally employ מן to express "from"; ב, "in," and ל, "to, for," serve also to express "from." ב and ל in the sense of "from" have been recognized in Hebrew only since Ugaritic was deciphered in the 1930s. Some examples: באדם העיר (Josh 3:16), "from the city Adam" (Qere: מאדם); ויאסרהו . . . במלך (II Kings 23:33), "and he stopped him from ruling" (Qere: ממלך); ובא לציון גואל (Isa. 59:20), "and a redeemer will come from Zion," as interpreted in Rom. 11:26 (ἐκ Σιών). *See* UGARIT; UGARIT[S]; POETRY, HEBREW [S].

4. Historical orthography. As late as the Early Iron Age II (900-600 B.C.) the general tendency was to write only consonants (as remained the rule in Phoenician). Not until Early Iron Age III (600-300 B.C.) were long vowels often indicated by *matres lectionis* (=vowel letters). Final vowels were the first to be indicated graphically; they appear in the Moabite Stone of the ninth century B.C. (e.g., בנתי, I built, versus Phoenician בנת) and in early Hebrew inscriptions such as the Gezer Calendar of the tenth century B.C. (ירחו, two months—in the construct state) and the Siloam Inscription of the late eighth century B.C. (e.g., היה, כי). In the Lachish Letters of the early sixth century B.C., medial long vowels, as well as final vowels, are sometimes indicated orthographically; thus, העירה, "to the city." *See* INSCRIPTIONS, SEMITIC [S] §2*a*.

Variants within the MT are often no more than alternative spellings; thus לא (not) is sometimes written לוא with no change in pronunciation or meaning; in the Qumran Scrolls, לוא is the normal spelling. The MT normally represents long *u* and *o* by ו, and long *i* and *e* by י; thus, קום (arise!), קול (voice), שיר (song), ריק (empty). However, if two long vowels occur in the same word, sometimes only one of them is represented by a vowel letter; e.g., שָׂמוּ (they set) but שָׂמֻנִי (they set me) in Song of S. 1:6. Long *a* is represented by a vowel letter only at the end of a word: קָם, "he arose," but קָמָה, "she arose."

With the passage of time, starting in the OT itself, there was a tendency to indicate even short *u, o,* and *i* with *matres lectionis;* thus postbiblical מילה for OT מִלָּה (word).

5. History of pronunciation. *a. In antiquity.* The keys to the pronunciation of Hebrew in antiquity are many; e.g., transliterations into foreign vocalized systems of writing. Sennacherib's *Annals* spell the name of the city of Ekron (עֶקְרוֹן) thus *am-qar-ru-na,* with *qq* dissimilated to *mq̈*. This shows that at the time (701 B.C.) words formed like חֶסְרוֹן were still pronounced חַסָּרוֹן*; cf. LXX Ἀκκαρών. Thus, in nouns of the *qaṭṭalān* type, the shift from *ā* to *ô* had already taken place by 701 B.C. (actually, we know from Canaanite glosses in the Amarna tablets that it happened before 1400 B.C.), but not the shift from *a* to *i* in closed unaccented syllables. The latter is normal in Masoretic Hebrew; thus Arabic *yaqṭul* appears as יִקְטֹל in Hebrew, and Arabic *majdal* as מִגְדָּל (tower, fortress). Yet the change had not taken place in all dialects, as we see from NT Magdal (Mary Magdalene is so called because she came from Magdal). Even Jerome (d. A.D. 420) retains the original *a*. *See* MAGDALA[S].

The most extensive external source of pre-Christian Hebrew pronunciation is the LXX (second century B.C.). The transliteration of proper names throws light not only on the vowels but also on the consonants. עזה is rendered Γάζα (Gaza), showing that the initial ע was still pronounced *gh* (retained to this day in the Arabic pronunciation of the town name).

b. In the MT. Jews in the Greco-Roman world gradually lost the ability to pronounce Hebrew in accordance with the system of earlier times. For example, Jews could no longer pronounce final ח as in *rûḥ*, "spirit, wind" unless it followed an *a*-vowel. Therefore the Masoretes inserted an anaptyctic *a* (furtive pataḥ) because phonetic habits made it possible for the Jews to pronounce רוּחַ (*rûaḥ*). That this device was artificial can be seen in two feminine singular forms of the perfect of roots with final ח or ע. Corresponding to קָטַלְתְּ is שָׁמַעַתְּ (thou [fem.] hast heard) with the second pataḥ introduced to avoid the final cluster -*ᶜt* which the Jews could no longer pronounce. Note that the dagesh in the final תְּ- is retained in spite of the preceding vowel, which would ordinarily spirantize the תּ *(t)* to ת *(th)*. The aim of the Masoretes was to save what they could, even if they had to avoid following through on the normal consequences of their stopgap measures.

The MT follows the Tiberian system of vocalization. Its main rival was the Babylonian or supralinear system, which places more vowel signs above the line than does the Tiberian (*see* HEBREW LANGUAGE §4). There are phonetic differences between the two systems. In the Babylonian, *e* (segol) falls together with *a* (pataḥ). Thus the suffix *-tem* (as in קְטַלְתֶּם) appears as *-tam* in the Babylonian system. Another difference is that, in the Tiberian system, initial *w*- followed by two consonants shifts to *û*-, e.g., וּקְטַלְתֶּם; but in the Babylonian system, *w*- under those conditions is followed by *i*, so that the form appears as *wiqṭaltam*. Similarly, note Babylonian *wilʿôlām* for Tiberian וּלְעוֹלָם.

c. Modern pronunciations. The most familiar pronunciations are the Ashkenazic (perpetuated by the Jews of Germany and East Europe) and the Sephardic (perpetuated by the descendants of the Jews from Spain and Portugal). The official pronunciation in Israel is often called Sephardic, though the Ashkenazic has left many marks on it. Occasionally Ashkenazic pronunciation preserves ancient features. The rendering of every *qameṣ* as *o* is corroborated by *matres lectionis* in texts from Talmudic Babylonia in which בָּרוּךְ is spelled בורוך; עוֹלָם is spelled עולום, etc. Official Israeli pronunciation follows the Sephardim in this regard, pronouncing every *qameṣ* derived from *a*, as *a*.

Bibliography. General: *Encyclopaedia Judaica* (1971), VIII, 77-175; XVI, 1352-1408, 1560-1662 (various articles on all aspects of Heb. language, with bibliog.).

Grammar: R. Meyer, *Die hebräische Grammatik* (3rd ed., 1966); A Sperber, *A Historical Grammar of Biblical Hebrew* (1966).

Dictionary: L. Köhler and W. Baumgartner, *Lexicon in Veteris Testamenti libros* and *Supplementum* (3rd ed., 1967).

Babylonian Masora: P. Kahle, *Masoreten des Ostens* (1913).

Ugaritic: C. H. Gordon, *Ugaritic Textbook* (1967).

C. H. GORDON

***HEBREWS, LETTER TO THE. 1. General.** The structure and theology of the letter have been illuminatingly treated by A. Vanhoye.

H. W. Montefiore has revived and supported with fresh arguments an earlier suggestion that the letter was sent to Corinth. He finds a clue to its context in I Cor. 16:12, where Paul mentions Apollos' inability to visit Corinth just then. Instead of visiting Corinth, Montefiore thinks, Apollos sent from Ephesus this letter which arrived shortly before I Corinthians, when the situation with which Paul deals there had not fully developed. "Those who come from Italy" who send their greetings in Heb. 13:24 are Priscilla and Aquila (cf. Acts 18:2), who were in Ephesus at the time (cf. I Cor. 16:19).

2. OT and Philonic influence. The LXX text used by the writer has been studied by K. J. Thomas, who finds about two-thirds of his citations agreeing with the A-recension and about one-third with the B-recension, which indicates that he used a text type earlier than these recensions. J. C. McCullough, pressing his research farther back, finds that the citations from the Pentateuch, Psalms, and Jeremiah show textual affinities respectively with the Origenic, Egyptian, and Q-recensions.

The writer's OT exegesis has been the subject of several monographs (*see bibliog.*). That the writer was acquainted with Alexandrian Jewish literature, like Wisdom, IV Maccabees, and Philo's works, becomes increasingly probable. His dependence on Philo has been exaggerated, especially when verbal similarities (relatively numerous) received more attention than coincidences in thought (relatively few). A sober reassessment has been made by R. Williamson, who concludes with good reason that the writer's thought is independent of Philonic influence.

3. Qumran influence. The literature of the QUMRAN sect has been thought to provide help with the problems of Hebrews. Some have suggested that the letter deals with particular tendencies apparent in the sect, and Yadin has argued that it was actually addressed to former members of the sect, who even after conversion to Christianity retained some of their old beliefs. H. Kosmala proposed that the addressees were Jews holding views very similar to those of the Qumran sectaries and other Essene groups, who had made some progress toward Christianity but stopped short of full commitment. (The main objection to this is that the writer, while certainly urging his readers to press forward, exhorts them to maintain their faith in Christ.)

C. Spicq, who earlier supported the view that the recipients were former Jewish priests, like those of Acts 6:7, later argued further that these converted priests were "Esseno-Christians," including former members of the Qumran sect, whose ideas, interests, and methods of biblical interpretation were well known to the writer. J. W. Bowman suggested that the addressees were Hellenistic Jewish Christians living near Sychar, where John the Baptist, Jesus, and later Philip had preached. Since Philip's mission (Acts 8:5-25), the center of Christian evangelization had moved north to Antioch, bypassing Samaria; there were thus defects in those Hellenists' understanding of Christianity which the writer undertook to correct.

The new sanctuary in Hebrews, while it is presented in Platonic terminology as situated in the supracelestial sphere, is probably identified with the fellowship of believers, "who share in a heavenly call" (Heb. 3:1-6). This identification appears elsewhere in the NT (cf. I Cor. 3:16; Eph. 2:19-22; I Pet. 2:4-8) and is paralleled in the Qumran literature, where the community is a living sanctuary and its priestly nucleus a holy of holies (1QS 8:5, 6). But in Hebrews there is no distinction between priests and laity within the believing fellowship; all have equal access to God through Christ, their high priest (Heb. 10:19-22). The priesthood of Christ is not related to the Qumran expectation of a Messiah of Aaron; in Hebrews the nonlevitical descent of Christ is emphasized and his priesthood is contrasted with Aaron's, being interpreted in terms of the priesthood of Ps. 110:4, "after the order of Melchizedek" (Heb. 7:11-14). While it is conceivable that the recipients of Hebrews entertained an angelology in which Melchizedek was a herald of the eschaton, as in 11QMelch (*see* MELCHIZEDEK[S] §2 and bibliog. there), in fact there is no essential affinity between the argument of Hebrews and the portrayal in the Qumran fragment. In Hebrews, Melchizedek, "resembling the Son of God," is a very great man (Heb. 7:3, 4), but it is Jesus, not Melchizedek, who is exalted to the heavenly throne to administer salvation and, eventually, judgment (Heb. 9:11-28).

J. Coppens has cautioned against the tendency to be carried away by real or imagined affinities between Hebrews and the Qumran literature.

4. A new appraisal. G. W. Buchanan treats the letter (except ch. 13) as a homiletical midrash on Ps. 110, addressed to a celibate community of diaspora Jews who had come to live near Mount Zion, called "the heavenly Jerusalem" in Heb. 12:22 because its origin is divine, even if its location is earthly. There they waited for the inheritance which God had promised to Abraham; the "rest" that remained for them (Heb. 4:9-11) was the land of Canaan.

Buchanan sees no reason to identify this community with the Qumran sect; there were several Jewish groups around this time who believed that the current situation demanded an ascetic life, that the temple was polluted by an impious priesthood, and that the time was at hand for the godly remnant to receive the fulfillment of the promises made to their ancestors (cf. Luke 1:54-55, 68-75). The writer exhorts his readers to take courage from the fact that Jesus, by his self-offering, has procured the definitive atonement; not to go back to the place from which they came but to maintain their hope, which would soon be vindicated by the arrival of the Coming One. By such obedience they would gain the "rest" which the Exodus generation forfeited by disobedience.

5. Conclusion. There are in Hebrews features characteristic of nonconformist Judaism in contrast to what was to become mainstream Judaism, such as the "instruction about ablutions" in Heb. 6:2. The study of the Qumran texts has made us more sensitive to these. But Jewish nonconformity was not confined to Qumran, or indeed to Palestine. The presence of these features in Hebrews can readily be explained if the letter was intended for a Jewish-Christian household church in Rome. As late as the *Apostolic Tradition* of Hippolytus (*ca.* A.D. 215), Roman Christianity retained a number of Jewish practices (e.g., the purificatory bath on Maundy Thursday for those who were to be baptized on Easter day) which had a rather close affinity to the nonconformist tradition in Judaism. Probably such nonconformist elements were present in early Roman Judaism and in the Jewish foundation of the Roman Church. *See also* ALTAR, NT[S] §§2, 3; CHRISTOLOGY IN THE NT[S] §2*c*ii.

Bibliography. Commentaries: J. W. Bowman, Layman's Bible Commentary (1962); H. W. Montefiore, HNTC (1964); F. F. Bruce, NICNT (1964); G. W. Buchanan, ABi (1972).

Studies: Y. Yadin, "The Dead Sea Scrolls and the Epistle to the Hebrews," *Scripta Hierosolymitana,* IV (1958), 36-55; C. Spicq, "L'Epître aux Hébreux: Apollos, Jean-Baptiste, les Hellénistes et Qumrân," RQ, I (1958-59), 365-90; H. Kosmala, *Hebräer, Essener, Christen: Studien zur Vorgeschichte der frühchristlichen Verkündigung,* SPB, I (1959); J. Coppens, *Les affinités qumrâniennes de 1 Épître aux Hébreux,* ALBO (1962); A. Vanhoye, *La structure littéraire de l'Épître aux Hébreux,* StudNeot, I (1963), and *Situation du Christ: Hébr 1-2,* LD, LVIII (1969); K. J. Thomas, "The OT Citations in Hebrews," *NTS,* XI (1964-65), 303-25; J. C. McCullough, "Hebrews and the OT" (unpublished Ph.D. thesis, Queen's University of Belfast, 1971); S. Kistemaker, *The Psalm Citations in the Epistle to the Hebrews* (1961); S. G. Sowers, *The Hermeneutics of Philo and Hebrews* (1965); F. Schröger, *Der Verfasser des Hebräerbriefes als Schriftausleger* (1969); R. Williamson, *Philo and the Epistle to the Hebrews* (1970).

F. F. BRUCE

***HEBRON (CITY IN JUDAH).** For recent literature, *see* M. Avi-Yonah, "Greek Inscriptions from Ascalon, Jerusalem, Beisan and Hebron," *QDAP,* X (1944), 160-69; P. C. Hammond, "Hebron," *RB,* LXXIII (1966), 566-69, LXXV (1968), 253-58.

HELEB. *See* HELDI 1.

***HELLENISM.** The complex of ideals and institutions that came to maturity in fifth-century Athens and has had, in one form or another, a profound effect on the intellectual, artistic, and religious history of the Near East and the Mediterranean world from that day to this. Indeed, when one says "Western," nothing less is being described than the orbit of Hellenism.

The Greek ideal of what constituted the nature and end of human life and the social, political, and moral means to that end already appears in the earliest preserved literary statement of the Hellenes —the Homeric poems—but its most cogent and fully realized expression is in the life and art of Periclean Athens. The portrait of that time and place has been idealized by its heirs, but even for their non-Hellenic contemporaries the Greek manner of viewing the universe and of living in it was enormously attractive, and what later came to be called Hellenism began to spread, without benefit of either arms or preaching, among the Greeks' neighbors in ITALY, MACEDONIA, and ASIA (Anatolia). The Greeks were not much impressed by the flattering imitation; in their view the gulf between Hellene and BARBARIAN could not be bridged by aping Greek manners or importing Greek intellectuals and soldiers to grace courts and stiffen armies. Whether clad in chiton or even speaking Greek, the Oriental autocrat with his horde of subservient subjects was simply a parody of Hellenism.

1. The transmission of Hellenism
   a. The polis
   b. Hellenism as a literary good
2. Hellenism in Palestine
   a. Jewish resistance
   b. The Nabateans
   c. Herod
3. Hellenism and early Christianity
4. The transformation of Hellenism in the East
   a. Gnosticism
   b. Greco-Oriental art
   c. Hellenism and the Eastern mysteries
5. The impact of Hellenism on Christian theology
6. The revival of local cultures
Bibliography

1. The transmission of Hellenism. It was precisely just one such Hellenized non-Greek, ALEXANDER of Macedon (d. 323 B.C.), who bridged that gulf by his political conquest of the older "barbarian" civilizations of the Near East in Anatolia, Syria, PALESTINE, EGYPT (*see* §2*h*), Iraq, Iran, and beyond. For the first time Greeks and Hellenized Macedonians had to rule non-Greeks. At hand were two political institutions that might serve that end, the Macedonian kingship and the Greek *polis.* The first blended with and was modified by its contact with the traditions of PHARAOH and Shah, the latter of which Alexander himself found particularly attractive, but it was the polis, a purely Greek conception, that in the end served as the chief instrument of a new Near Eastern prosperity and of the diffusion and consolidation of Hellenism.

V. P. Furnish
8. Priene, the council chamber altar, 4th century B.C.

a. The polis. The polis or city-state was an urban social unit composed of free citizens enjoying at least some degree of political and economic autonomy (*see* CITY §C2*a*; CITIES, GRECO-ROMAN[S] §2). It was at the same time the locus of those moral and intellectual ideals that lay at the heart of Hellenism: that free people can govern themselves and can both understand and achieve the perfection of the human faculties which constitutes the ultimate end of humanity. To gain those ends the polis had spawned various institutions of governance and social association: a senate composed of the local aristocracy; an assembly where all the citizens could gather and express their political will; elected municipal magistrates to execute the laws of the city and assure its economic and social well-being; theaters, gymnasia, baths, hippodromes, and, in the new post-Alexandrian polis, schools where the ideals of Hellenism could be transmitted to new generations which now included non-Greeks eager to gain entrance to the privilege and prosperity of the Near Eastern *poleis.*

b. Hellenism as a literary good. That the ideals of Hellenism could be sublimated into literary goods that could be publicly taught was one of the most remarkable of the Greek achievements. Hellenism was no longer a matter of birth; if it could be taught, it could be taught to anyone, and thus the way lay open for the formerly despised barbarians of the East to be initiated, through the study of the canonized masters of literary Hellenism and by adopting the externals of the Greek life-style, to membership in the new *poleis* and, indeed, in the new Hellenic *oikoumene* that would eventually stretch from Britain to the Indus.

Alexander's reputation as a polis-builder has been exaggerated, but at least one of his foundations, ALEXANDRIA in Egypt, became the center of the newly intellectualized and academicized version of Hellenism that transformed the Near East. From Alexandria, which in sheer size far transcended anything a Periclean Greek would recognize as a polis, came the new texts, commentaries, curricula, handbooks, grammars, and lexica from which generations of Egyptians, Syrians, Jews, Iranians, Romans, and others would learn everything from the rudiments of Greek literacy to the subtle mysteries that lay at the end of the curricular highroad to human wisdom and human perfection: logic, physics, mathematics, and theology.

From the beginning, the Greek vision of the good—and here we are at the heart of Hellenism—was a highly intellectual one (*see* EDUCATION, NT §2). It was tempered, to be sure, by the concomitant ideal of the human being as a balance of physical and spiritual perfections, but in the end it was the latter that triumphed; in late antiquity the gymnasia, where they were still being built, were the resort of professional athletes. Schools and not gymnasia were the final bearers of the Greek legacy, and it was in the former that the barbarians learned, from the texts of the masters, that people could achieve happiness in this world through the exercise of their purely human faculties and particularly through the exercise of that faculty which set them apart in the order of creation, the human intellect. From the foundation of the intellect arose the impressive structure of the Greek sciences, the various but strictly subordinated routes to the truth which at their end led to the highest science, theology or the knowledge of God.

For all its rationalism, Hellenism was by no means irreligious; the Greeks worshiped with as much fervor as the non-Greeks, and each polis had its divine patrons and splendid temples in which they were housed in the highly anthropomorphized manner typical of the humanity-centered Hellenes. These gods went back to deep antiquity and were enshrined in the great body of myth that was close to the center of Greek religious sensibilities. They had little resistance, however, to the increasingly profound Hellenic pursuit of rationalism, and in the end the Hellenized intellectual recognized that the traditional gods were little more than symbols of more spiritual beings or even different manifestations of a single divine principle that was spiritual and transcendental but nonetheless comprehensible through the exercise of human reason and without benefit of special revelation or divine illumination. *See* GREEK RELIGION AND PHILOSOPHY.

The issue with this and other postulates of Hellenism was joined by representatives of the indigenous cultures of the Near East as the successors of Alexander in Egypt and Syria covered their domains with a network of newly established *poleis*. The Ptolemies of Egypt (*see* PTOLEMY), descendants of Alexander's Macedonian general who in Egypt reserved their Hellenism for Alexandria and played the pharaoh elsewhere along the Nile, were particularly active city founders in their Palestinian province. Many of the Greek cities along the Mediterranean coast and the cluster of *poleis* in the TRANSJORDAN, the nucleus of the later DECAPOLIS, were raised under their auspices, possibly as a Hellenic anchor against the neighboring Jewish temple state in JUDEA or the Arab kingdom of the NABATEANS, while from ANTIOCH eastward across northern Syria and MESOPOTAMIA the rival Seleucids (*see* SELEUCIA) lay down the foundations of their own *poleis*.

Some of these *poleis* were close to being entirely new foundations, Alexandria and Antioch, for example, while others were simply transformations of older settlements with an appropriate change of name to celebrate a reigning dynast (PHILADELPHIA, Berenice, Ptolemais [*see* ACCO], Seleucia) or some nostalgically remembered town in Macedonia (Pella, Edessa). Many of the *poleis* began life simply as a Greek or Macedonian garrison town (κατοικία), but for the full juridical status of polis what was required was a registered body of citizens (δῆμος) characterized by a certain economic and social status and their assimilation to Hellenism, a city council (βουλή) drawn from the upper class of the δῆμος, the appropriate city magistrates (ἄρχοντες) and the public facilities already described. To this day the remains of those latter buildings, temples, theaters, and baths, long colonnaded boulevards leading to or from a central marketplace (ἀγορά), and the magnificent paved roads that connected one polis with another testify to the taste, skill, and prosperity of these urban creations of the Greeks and their Roman successors in the Near East.

The *poleis* remained the linchpin of the economic and social policies of the Greeks and Romans from their foundation down to the Moslem invasion. They were semiautonomous urban islands floating in a sea of state and crown land which was administered directly by the central governments of the Ptolemies, Seleucids, and Romans. There was little outside interference in the life of the Near Eastern *poleis* until the end of the third century A.D., and even after Diocletian they continued to be governed, provisioned, and adorned largely from the resources of their own citizens. A polis might indeed profit from imperial notice—the fortunes of Shohba, a somewhat obscure town in the Hawran, improved considerably as Philippopolis after the accession of one of its native sons to the Roman purple—but it profited even more from the spirit of its citizens and the wealth of its own enterprises, agricultural and commercial.

Part of the price of this prosperity was paid by those of the inhabitants who by reason of inferior social and economic status could never aspire to be enrolled as members of the δῆμος. In a sense, Hellenism institutionalized class differences, where the poor and disenfranchised peasantry were precisely the native population of the area. The fellahin of Egypt, Palestine, and Syria were aliens in their own land.

2. Hellenism in Palestine. The transformation of one older settlement into a polis and its revolutionary effects can be traced in some detail. At the request of some of its more prosperous and already partially Hellenized rulers, in 175 B.C. ANTIOCHUS IV Epiphanes raised the former temple state of JERUSALEM (*see* §8) to the status of polis as Antioch in Judea. The local council, the prototype of the later SANHEDRIN, became its βουλή and a list of enfranchised citizens was drawn up. Antioch's magistrates were its rulers of old, the temple priesthood—Judea remained in fact, if not in judicial theory, very much a temple state whose economics were closely tied to the temple corporation—but, somewhat extraordinarily, its constitution or πολιτεία remained what it had been, the Mosaic law.

a. Jewish resistance. There was resistance to this. The temple priesthood with its Hellenic, pagan ways and its Hellenized adherents was not a popular institution, and the creation of the polis, for all its promise of a new Hellenic prosperity, served also to underline growing social and economic differences between the urban wealthy and the poor agricultural peasantry in Judea. (*See* ECCLESIASTICUS §3*c*.) But events moved too quickly for adjustment. Antiochus scented treason in his new polis—there remained a considerable pro-Ptolemaic faction in Jerusalem—and in 169 or 168 B.C. he cashiered it back to the status of κατοικία. To insure its security he stationed in Jerusalem a garrison of Syrian troops and suspended the Mosaic law, in effect, the practice of Judaism.

If the earlier resistance to polis status was social and economic, the issue was now clearly ideological.

R. Schoder, S. J.; courtesy the Archaeological Museum, Pella

9. Krateros saves Alexander the Great during a lion hunt near Susa; pebble mosaic from Pella, Greece, late 4th century B.C.

So at least it was preached by the MACCABEES, who saw the very existence of Judean Judaism threatened by the policies of Antiochus. They spearheaded an insurrection that in the end won for Judea its independence as a kingdom, one of many which arose out of declining Seleucid fortunes in the Near East.

The existence of all of these petty kingdoms was ephemeral. The far more potent Romans were already in the Near East and so the glories of Hasmonean Palestine barely spanned a century. It is an interesting century, nonetheless, in the history of Hellenism, since the petty kingdoms that came into existence between the decline of the Seleucids and their expropriation by the Romans were local phenomena governed by native dynasts, Jews, Syrians, and Arabs, and each in its own way continued to display with pride its progress down the ways of the Greeks. The kingdoms of Edessa and Commagene, the Ituraeans of BAALBEK and Chalcis (*see* ITURAEA §2), the Nabateans of PETRA, and the HASMONEANS, lately the Maccabees, of Judea were all officially and openly philhellene.

b. The Nabateans. Apart from the Hasmoneans, the Nabateans provide the clearest example of the extent, though not always of the means, of the early penetration of Hellenism into the culture of the Semites. The Nabateans, originally Bedouin of the North Arabian steppe, found success as traders and middlemen in the growing international trade that was another product of the Hellenic *oikoumene*. Their commercial interests carried the Nabateans all over the Mediterranean, and though they never adopted Greek as their language—Aramaic remained, perhaps, more useful at that point—their coinage, their art, their temple architecture, and even their gods succumbed to the lure of Hellenic assimilation when the Nabatean kings took their place in that fellowship of Hellenized monarchs that the Romans tolerated for a season on the fringes of their expanding Eastern empire. Petra, the Nabatean capital in the former EDOM, with its rich juxtaposition of temples, theaters, and tombs, continues to bear silent testimony to the attractiveness and malleability of what the Greeks had to offer to their Semitic neighbors and subjects in the Near East.

c. Herod. HEROD ruled in Judea (37-4 B.C.) under similar Roman auspices and exploited an even more classical form of the Greek style. CAESAREA Maritima, HEBRON, and HERODIUM all bear traces of his immense and skilled building activities; his temple at Jerusalem could probably have stood with insouciant ease upon the Palatine in Rome or at the foot of the Athenian acropolis (*see* TEMPLE, JERUSALEM §C; TEMPLE OF HEROD[S]). Herod the builder and benefactor of Greco-Roman ostentation is well known, but these were not his only interests in the ways of the Greeks and the Romans. An important member of his entourage was Nicolaus of Damascus, the historian and Peripatetic philosopher who was a Hellenized Aramaean from Damascus and who displays in his writings as surely as Herod did in his buildings the continued progress of Hellenic transformation. Whatever his ethnic origins, Nicolaus, like many of his predecessors and innumerable of his successors in the Near East, thought and wrote in Greek for an audience who shared the experience of Hellenic schooling in Rome, Athens, Pergamum, Ephesus, Antioch, and Alexandria.

3. Hellenism and early Christianity. And yet for every Herod and Nicolaus there were countless numbers in the new *Imperium Romanum* who remained disenfranchised and unlettered in Greek ways beyond the orbit of Hellenism. Herod's progeny built TIBERIAS, CAESAREA PHILIPPI, and Beth-saida-Julias (*see* BETH-SAIDA) as Greek-style settlements in the northern parts of the Jewish kingdom, but around the Galilean countryside, the appeal and penetration of cultural and political Hellenism was

J. M. Ward
10. The baths at Ostia, the port by which Paul entered Italy

probably feeble indeed. Jesus appears to have been little affected by it, for example, and it was only after his death, when the nascent Christian community began to include Hellenized Jews (*see* HELLENISTS) among its members, that Christianity had to face the clash of ideals between a profoundly Jewish Christianity represented by the pious and traditionalist JAMES, the brother of the Lord, and the startlingly different perceptions of a PAUL, equally a Pharisee but reared in the Diaspora.

The newly emerging histories of the "church from the circumcision" and the "church from the Gentiles" are not in the first instance an example of the clash between Hellenism and Judaism, but as the latter drew apart from the "Hebrew" succession in Jerusalem, Hellenic notions of theology, morality, liturgy, art, and architecture all began to assert themselves among Christian intellectuals (*see* ART, EARLY CHRISTIAN[S]). Origen in Egypt and Caesarea, the Cappadocian Fathers in Anatolia, the beginnings of Christian art in the catacombs, and Constantine's buildings in Rome and Palestine were simply the most visible signs of the foundations of a new Christian culture or παιδεία that drew heavily upon the spiritual and physical legacy of Hellenism.

The third and fourth centuries A.D. ring with the consequences, when Christian ideals, themselves in the process of transformation, confront and are confronted by those of the older, more traditional Hellenism. In the West, pagan intellectuals were more inclined to regard Christianity as a threat to the political foundations of the ROMAN EMPIRE, but the Eastern Hellene was far more concerned with Christianity's apparent challenge to the Hellenic culture; for someone like Libanius (*ca.* A.D. 314-393), the death of Apollo was necessarily the death of Homer, and the sight of Christian mobs razing the temples of the old gods must have appeared an act of cultural parricide. That Apollo was already dead, or at least displaced by other, far less Hellenic perceptions, was revealed in the failure of the Emperor Julian's (d. A.D. 363) necromantic attempt at breathing new life into what was by then a very old corpse.

4. The transformation of Hellenism in the East. Julian was a religious antiquarian who failed to observe that even before the appearance of Christianity the traditional Hellenism was suffering the pains of erosion. Its contact with Near Eastern religions of great antiquity that promised a higher truth and a more sacral religion than that achieved by human reason alone, when joined with Hellenism's waning confidence in its own powers, sapped the foundations of Greek rationalism and made Hellenism more attentive to other voices from other worlds on high or here below. The MIRACLE WORKERS and Eastern sages took their place with the philosophers, and the GREEK LANGUAGE too had to yield its claim to absolute preeminence. Even in Hellenism's most sacred bastion, the Academy at Athens, Plato's successors gave ear to the alien call of theurgy and the Oriental mysteries.

a. Gnosticism. Another product of the clash of Hellenism with some other powerful force alien to its own spirit was GNOSTICISM. Whatever its origin, Gnosticism represented a view of the world which, in its profound pessimism regarding the cosmos and humanity's place in it, was directly and deeply antithetical to the optimism of Hellenism. For the Greeks the cosmos was an intelligently designed and functioning organism which served as the paradigm for mankind's own moral aspirations. The Gnostic, on the other hand, regarded the sensible universe as a place of moral terror whose existence could only be explained by the creative activity of a malign god. The presence of mankind in such a setting was thus the result of a "fall," a lapse in the fullness of spiritual perfection (πλήρωμα).

For the genuine Hellenic notion of perfectability through the perfection of one's intellect, the Gnostic substituted the concept of salvation, of rescue from an alien environment by the bestowal of a special knowledge (γνῶσις). Greek wisdom was a public wisdom approached through a public and rigorous dialectic; γνῶσις was a hermetic and elitist understanding of sacred texts. What that understanding was, however, when it emerged from beneath the Gnostic μῦθος, was little more than an elaborate and somewhat imaginative version of Greek metaphysics. Deprived of its Greek epistemological foundation in a purely human intellection, this baroque metaphysics of the πλήρωμα flourished under Christian, Jewish, and Islamic auspices and remains today, under the rubric of "the philosophy of illumination," as the most vital metaphysical force in the world of Islam.

b. Greco-Oriental art. Hellenism was transformed in other ways as well. The Greek city-states of the Mediterranean coastal areas flourished, albeit under Christian auspices, until the Moslem invasion and in a form recognizable to their founders a millennium earlier. But out in the hinterland the mix was richer and the transformations far more complex. Parthian and Sassanian art translated the Hellenic prototype into new hybrids which stare from the crypts of Semitic Palmyra and the walls of Parthian Dura-Europos and Indian Gandhara. The Jews of Beth Alpha decorated the floor of their sixth-century Palestinian synagogue with an elaborate zodiac pattern in which traditional Greek mythological figures sit easily next to Abraham and Isaac, all executed in a careful and highly sophisticated folk idiom. (*See* SYNAGOGUE §3*a*, Fig. 100; ART, EARLY JEWISH[S]; SYNAGOGUE, ARCHITECTURE [S].) In the early eighth century the Moslem Umayyads used Byzantine craftsmen to execute the mosaics of their mosque in Damascus and the results echo some of the finest landscape frescoes of Greco-Roman antiquity. The same is presumably true of their winter palace and bath at Khirbet al-Mafjar near JERICHO, and while the mosaics there are likewise in the finest Hellenic tradition, the preserved sculpture reveals odd, un-Hellenic figures in vaguely Greco-Roman costume; the caliph himself is portrayed in the raiment of the Shah of Iran.

c. Hellenism and the Eastern mysteries. The mystery religions of the East had made their first impression on the Greco-Roman world in a crude and unassimilated form that often shocked the religious sensibilities of those accustomed to the more familiar and comfortable niceties of the traditional religion. But soon those same mysteries fell under the power of the Hellenic intellectuals, as Eastern religious goods had for centuries, and a Plutarch (*ca.* A.D. 46-120) could soon produce a perfectly rationalized version of the ISIS-OSIRIS myth, for example. Having once been rationalized, these same Eastern mysteries were then further spiritualized by their competitive contact with Christianity, itself the product of the infiltration of Hellenism into a Semitic religion. *See* GREEK RELIGION AND PHILOSOPHY §§4, 5.

5. The impact of Hellenism on Christian theology. Christianity's own testimony to the influence of Hellenism is frequently contradictory. Christian intellectuals educated in Hellenic schools fell eagerly to the task of constructing a Christian theology, that is, to converting the scriptural witness of the gospels into the currency of Hellenic scientific discourse about God. The task may have appeared deceptively easy and inviting at first, and there were many at Alexandria, for example, who were fluent in both idioms, the scriptural and the philosophical. But the incompatibility of the two modes began to appear quickly enough, and Arius' perfectly reasonable—in the Hellenic sense—discussion of the relationship of the Father and the Son in terms of principles was felt by many to violate the sense of the gospels. And it was merely the beginning. Once set in train, the growth of a Christian theology left the believer with little choice but to adhere to a kind of scriptural fundamentalism, with its attendant rejection of the entire scientific and intellectual tradition of the day, or to proceed painfully onward toward converting the God of Abraham, Isaac, and Jacob into the God of the philosophers. The task of passing judgment on the results fell to the ecumenical councils from the fourth to the sixth centuries, and there the debates were increasingly couched in terms which were unknown to the evangelists but were the common currency of the philosophical schools at Athens and Alexandria.

There was little place for Christianity to conceal itself from Hellenism, even when it chose to do so. In Egypt and Syria early Christian pietists fled from the worldly morality of the Hellenic metropolis to the remote fastness of the countryside where they practiced the virtues of scriptural Christianity. Early Christian asceticism, with its emphasis on the training of the will and its ideal of the imitation of Christ, had little to do with Hellenic philosophical ethics. But within a century, particularly in the work of Evagrius of Pontus (d. A.D. 399), the training of the will and the view of virtue as something to be acquired by a continuous practice (πρᾶξις) was joined to another notion, that of the illumination of the intellect whereby asceticism became the prelude to the higher stages of "grace." At first these latter were simply a series of insights into one's relationship with God and the world, but it came to term in a true THEOPHANY where God manifests his own essence in the purified and unified intellect of the mystic.

Christian mysticism, particularly after its contact with the disguised Neoplatonism of DIONYSIUS "the Areopagite," drew deeply from later Greek theories of illumination, and the "lights" besought with such fervor by hermits in the Sinai were in fact reflections from distant Alexandria and Athens, where pagan theologians had long since given over the old Aristotelian idea of virtue as an acquired habit in favor of a divine descent from on high. The Hellenes had arrived on the summit of Mount Tabor long before the first Christian mystic struggled onto those heights.

6. The revival of local cultures. But Christianity was likewise responsible for the revival of the native cultures of the East that had been submerged by the pervasive Hellenism of an earlier age. The gospels were soon translated from Greek into Coptic and Syriac (*see* COPTIC LANGUAGE[S]; SYRIAC VERSIONS[S]), and in Egypt the most determined resistance to the Hellenism of Alexandria was to be found among the non-Greek-speaking monks of the desert who pondered the Coptic gospels and lives of the saints while the Christian theologians of Alexandria, Gnostic and orthodox alike, were feeding on the most sophisticated Neoplatonic thought of their day. Origen and Plotinus, the Christian and the pagan theologian, may have sat at the feet of the same teacher in Alexandria, but both were equally foreign to the monks who were even then beginning to populate the wildernesses of Egypt.

In Syria the choice was less simple. Here too Christianity brought about a revival of the native Aramaic culture, but the new Syriac-speaking-and-writing Christianity of Edessa, though it had its share of Hellene-baiters and semiliterate ascetics, produced new and sensitive literary voices like that of Ephraem the Syrian (d. *ca.* A.D. 373) and even theologians who looked to Christian but Hellenic Antioch to supply them with the foundations for a new Christian theology in Syriac. Through translation—and it was the first major effort to translate the intellectual goods of Hellenism into the Semitic idiom—Syrian theologians followed every turning in the great christological disputes at Antioch, Alexandria, and Constantinople. Edessa had its own theological school where the students read both the pagan Aristotle and the Christian Theodore of Mopsuestia (d. *ca.* A.D. 428) in Syriac translation. When its orthodoxy fell under question in the fifth century, the faculty at Edessa migrated to the safer confines of the Sassanian Empire and recommenced its work at Nisibis. Thus was opened to the Sassanians a major passage to the Hellenism of their Romano-Byzantine rivals and neighbors. Not only theology but also Greek science and medicine came to Iraq and Iran through those talented Syrian Christians who centuries later passed their own Hellenic heritage on to the new Moslem masters of the Near East. Aristotle was being read in Baghdad in A.D. 900 only because there were present there Syrian Christians skilled in Greek, Syriac, and Arabic who could instruct these new converts in the gospel of Hellenism.

See also JUDAISM, HELLENISTIC[S].

Bibliography. W. W. Tarn, *Hellenistic Civilization* (3rd rev. ed., 1952); M. Nilsson, *Geschichte der griechischen Religion, II: Die hellenistische und römische Zeit,* Handbuch der Altertumswissenschaft, V (2nd ed., 1961); H. I. Marrou, *A History of Education in Antiquity* (3rd ed., 1964); F. E. Peters, *The Harvest of Hellenism* (1970); S. Tcherikover, *Hellenistic Civilization and the Jews* (1959); M. Hengel, *Judaism and Hellenism,* 2 vols. (2nd ed., 1973); S. K. Eddy, *The King is Dead* (1961); A. D. Nock, *Essays on Religion and the Ancient World,* ed. Z. Stewart, 2 vols. (1972); A. H. M. Jones, *The Cities of the Eastern Roman Provinces* (2nd ed., 1971); D. Schlumberger, "Descendents non-méditeranéens de l'art grec," *Syria,* XXXVII (1960), 131-66, 253-318; W. Jaeger, *Early Christianity and Greek Paideia* (1961); P. Brown, *The World of Late Antiquity* (1971); F. E. Peters, *Allah's Commonwealth* (1974).

F. E. PETERS

HELLENISTIC JUDAISM. *See* JUDAISM, HELLENISTIC[S].

***HEM.** In the ancient Near East, the hem of the garment was closely identified with the person of the wearer. It was regarded as an extension of the owner's personality and authority. One could put a signature to a clay tablet by impressing it with the hem (*see* Fig. H11). By means of the hem, a person could cast magic spells or perform oracular divination. The hem was cut during rites of

Courtesy the University Museum

11. Fragment of bulla (clay on which the seal impression is stamped), showing hem impression in lieu of a cylinder sealing

exorcism and procedures for divorce, signifying the breaking of close personal bonds. Many idioms reflect the significance of the hem. The "right of the hem" denotes surety which a creditor might demand. A gift of money or the so-called "bride-price" (*terḫatu*) was "bound in the hem" (VAB V, 209:20). In order to take a person to court, one "seized the hem" of his garment. A vassal would grasp the hem of his overlord's garment as a sign of submission (ARM VI, no. 26). Nebuchadrezzar II states, "Because I grasp the hem of Marduk ('s garment), Marduk, my lord, loves me." Nabonidus described himself as one who "in order not to commit any sin (cultic error), grasps the hem of the gods."

When David encountered Saul near En-gedi, he sliced off the hem of Saul's garment (I Sam. 24:4 [H 5]). By this symbolic action, David declared that Saul had lost the kingship. David regarded the act as more than a mere warning or a dangerous prank (vs. 5 [H 6]), and Saul recognized the significance of the severed hem when he said, "And now, behold, I know that you shall surely be king, and that the kingdom of Israel shall be established in your hand" (vs. 20 [H 21]).

In I Sam. 15, Samuel announced that Yahweh had rejected Saul's kingship (vs. 26). The text is ambiguous regarding the initiator of the action, but the hem of a garment was seized and torn. The RSV understands it to be Samuel's garment; according to the KJV, Samuel seized Saul's hem. Whichever is the case, the symbolism is clear. Samuel might have torn Saul's hem signifying that Saul had been deprived of his authority. Conversely, Saul might have seized Samuel's hem as would a vassal before his overlord.

Other OT passages which may be consulted with regard to the significance of the hem include I Kings 11:29-33; Ezek. 5:1-4; Zech. 8:20-23; Hag. 2:10-19.

According to the gospels (Matt. 9:20=Luke 8:44), a woman touched the hem of Jesus' garment and was healed. Her action may be based on the belief that the power of a person is transferred to clothing (Matt. 14:36=Mark 6:56; Acts 19:12). In analogous fashion, impurity could be transferred through garments (Lev. 15:27; 17:15; Hag. 2:13).

T.B. Ta'an. 23b provides an example in post-biblical Judaism. A certain Ḥānān was so well-known for his piety that, during periods of drought, the rabbis would send children to seize the hem of his garment and implore him to ask God for rain.

Bibliography. For references to the Akkadian literature see S. Langdon, *Die neubabylonischen Königsinschriften, VAB,* IV (1912), 110-11, 142-43, 262-63; W. von Soden, *Akkadisches Handwörterbuch* I (1965), 114*a*; II (1972), 897*a*, 1042*b*, 1050-51; *CAD,* VIII (K), 258*a;* XVI (Ṣ), 17*b*, 223*b*. For Mesopotamian background and comments on I Sam. 24 see J. Lewy, "Les textes paléo-assyriens et l'Ancien Testament," *RHR,* CX (1934), 31-33, and M. Noth, "Remarks on the Sixth Volume of Mari Texts," *JSS,* I (1956), 327-31. For hem used in signing documents as well as in magic and divination see J. R. Kupper, *ARM,* VI (1954), 123; H. Huffmon, "Prophecy in the Mari Letters," *BA,* XXXI (1968), 101-24; W. G. Lambert in *La divination en mésopotamie ancienne et dans les régions voisines* (1966), pp. 120-21. For the NT see H. van der Loos, *The Miracles of Jesus* (1965), pp. 317-21.

R. A. Veenker

***HENA.** *See* Sepharvaim[S].

HEREM. *See* Devoted.

***HERMAS, THE SHEPHERD OF.** *See* Apostolic Fathers[S] §6.

HERMENEUTICS. From Greek ἑρμηνεία meaning interpretation, translation, or explanation; the Gr. verb in the biblical period also meant to proclaim or discourse upon a topic. As used today it signifies (1) the principles, rules, and techniques whereby the interpreter of a text attempts to understand it in its original context; (2) the science of discerning how a thought or event in one cultural context may be understood in a different cultural context; and (3) the art of making the transfer.

1. The communities' book. The believing communities engage in dialogue with the Bible as canon, out of their own ever-changing contexts, asking two questions: Who are we and what are we to do? The fact that the biblical canon functions in this way issues in three basic observations. (*a*) In a lengthy process of canonization the Bible emerged out of the experiences of ancient Israel, early Judaism, and the early church, when they asked those two questions of their own authoritative traditions (*see* CANON OF THE OT, NT[S]). (*b*) It was shaped in and by those communities in their common life, cultic and cultural. (*c*) Its proper function continues to be that of being in dialogue with the heirs of those same communities as they continue to seek answers to those two questions (identity and life-style, faith and obedience). Essential to that dialogue is hermeneutics, and the hermeneutics most valid is that which can be discerned in the Bible's own history (i.e., canonical hermeneutics; *see* §§3, 4), through the tools of biblical research.

Canonical hermeneutics has two basic tasks: determining valid modes of seeking the meaning of a biblical text in its own setting, and then determining a valid mode of expression of that meaning in contemporary settings. It addresses the problem of how to bridge the gap between biblical meanings and contemporary cultural categories of thought. For Western Christians this has meant translating biblical meanings into modern, Western philosophical thought patterns.

2. Recent discussions. In the nineteenth century Schleiermacher and others based their work in hermeneutics on the common humanity of author and interpreter: the latter could have confidence in an intuitive grasp of what the author intended. Modern categories of understanding were considered fully capable of seizing biblical meanings.

Rudolf Bultmann followed directly in Schleiermacher's wake; but he sought to define more precisely the pre-understanding or presupposition asserted by Schleiermacher. Reacting against what he viewed as simplistic historicism in the early twentieth century, Bultmann stressed an existentialist position informed by the early work of the philosopher Martin Heidegger. Bultmann attempted to discount theological presuppositions by resting his case for pre-understanding solely on technical biblical criticism and the then regnant existentialist philosophy. Criticisms of his work have been lodged principally on two grounds: that he indeed had theological suppositions and that his method was not adequate for the whole Bible, especially not for the OT.

Over against Bultmann was Karl Barth, who worked out a church dogmatic wherein his pre-understandings were an imposing neo-Reformationist dogmatic of the Word of God derivable from the words of the Bible. Whereas Bultmann's work has seemed to many as anthropological, even nontheological, Barth's has seemed to others as mythic and traditionalist. One of Barth's late essays, "The Humanity of God," seemed to stress the human more than the divine and has given rise to attempts to build bridges between Barth and Bultmann. While Barth's theology was Christocentric, much of his dogmatic theology focused on the OT. This was also the case with Dietrich Bonhoeffer, whose hermeneutic issued in a nonreligious interpretation of biblical faith. A criticism of both Bultmann and Bonhoeffer is that their hermeneutics have led to a kind of humanism. One result of the confluence of the work of Bultmann and Bonhoeffer and the essay cited by Barth was the so-called death-of-God movement.

Students of Bultmann continued to read Heidegger as the latter moved from existentialism to ontology. In that move Heidegger revalued the import of language for humanity's understanding of itself, elevating language from a secondary position to primal authority. Language became the home of human being. The importance of this move for proclamation of the Word, that is, for biblical and theological hermeneutics, was recognized by Ernst Fuchs and Gerhard Ebeling. In their view the Christ event was, indeed is, a language event. James Robinson focused their work into *A New Quest of the Historical Jesus*. This involves not just translation of words from one linguistic idiom (the biblical languages, Greek and Hebrew) to another (modern tongues), but a transculturation of the Word, as perceived in the text, to new words.

Criticism of the "new quest" centered in questioning language as a valid vehicle of biblical revelation. Barth, with others, had been acclaiming history, or time, as the vehicle of revelation (*see* REVELATION IN HISTORY[S]). Wolfhart Pannenberg then attempted to meet this criticism by focusing on hermeneutics which can read both the Bible and human experience in the world. Sensitive to the criticisms of OT scholars and of Jews toward the Bultmannians and the post-Bultmannians, Pannenberg shifted attention to a theology of world history, in which the historical process was sought in a continuum connecting past and present. Reality could thus be viewed as a unity grounded in the biblical affirmation of the oneness or unity of God. The gap between biblical past and human present is spanned by a view of a continuing history or story of God's unfolding plan not only for the ongoing communities of believers but for the world. Jürgen Moltmann pressed Pannenberg's case into a "theology of hope" wherein the future aspect of universal history was stressed and stated as God's future continually invading the human present. Thus Moltmann recognized the eschatological aspect of biblical thought.

3. The task today. The task of biblical hermeneutics today is to seek a mid-point between the hermeneutical task of the historical-critical method, which seeks original biblical meanings, and the hermeneutical task of spanning the gap between those recovered meanings and modern cultural systems of meaning. And that task is called canonical hermeneutics: the means whereby Israel, Judaism, and the church spanned the gaps between inherited faith and new cultural settings.

The canon includes the process whereby early authoritative traditions encountered ancient cultural challenges, were rendered adaptable to those challenges, and thus themselves were formed and re-formed according to the needs of the believing communities. (It was in this process, e.g., that ancient Near Eastern wisdom was adapted into biblical literature.) That process itself is as canonical as the traditions which emerged out of it.

Therefore, the Bible may be read as a paradigm not only of God's truth but of how those who find their identity in it should pursue the integrity of reality in their own later contexts. *Canonical* hermeneutics is the means whereby early believing communities pursued, and later believing communities may yet pursue, the integrity (oneness) of God, both ontological and ethical. It is in this sense that the Bible is, canonically viewed, a monotheizing literature.

Hermeneutics, therefore, is as much concerned with the contexts in which biblical texts were and are read or recited as with the texts themselves. It is in this sense that one must insist that the Bible is not the Word of God. The Word is the point that is made in the conjunction of text and context, whether in antiquity or at any subsequent time. Discernment of context, whether then or now, is thus crucial to biblical interpretation (*see* §8*a below*). The greater the knowledge we have of the ancient contexts, the clearer becomes the impact the (words of the) text had; and the greater the discernment of current contexts, the clearer one's choice of hermeneutics for transmitting the point originally made.

4. The Bible as canon. It is the nature of canon to be both stable and adaptable. It is stable in the sense that once its structure was set and its contents determined, nothing was to be added to it or subtracted from it (Deut. 4:2; 12:32 [H 13:1]; Rev. 22:18-19). (The OT canon was closed for Judaism sometime near the end of the first century A.D., and the NT canon sometime in the fourth century A.D. *See* CANON OF THE OT[S] §4*b*; CANON OF THE NT[S] esp. §6.) But it is also the nature of canon to be adaptable, i.e., it is believed to speak to the communities generation after generation.

Hermeneutics is the mid-point between the Bible's stability and adaptability as canon. In this sense hermeneutics is the art of interpreting the Bible for the ongoing believing communities. It is the means whereby the professional interpreters within those communities demonstrate the Bible's relevance and help the faithful (and the doubting) to hear its message for their time and situation.

But hermeneutics is also the science whereby the trained interpreter attempts to understand a text in terms of its ancient, original contexts; this is the prior task of biblical hermeneutics. The believing communities have always been interested in what Moses or Jesus "really meant" in their time, as well as in the implications for later believers of what they said. The uncritical reader assumes the earlier and later meanings to be the same, with the conviction that the plain meaning discernible in the text "now" was what it meant then. One result of the Enlightenment has been the development of tools and techniques for probing carefully back to the original meanings. This has resulted in what has been called LOWER and HIGHER CRITICISM. *See* BIBLICAL CRITICISM and supplementary articles; TEXTUAL CRITICISM, OT, NT[S]; TRADITION CRITICISM, OT[S]; REDACTION CRITICISM, OT, NT[S]; FORM CRITICISM, OT, NT[S]; SOURCE CRITICISM, OT[S].

5. Canonical hermeneutics. The history of "biblical interpretation" begins early in the history of the formation of the Bible itself (*see* INTERPRETATION, HISTORY OF[S] §§A, C). The biblical thinkers often cited earlier authoritative traditions in order to validate what they themselves had to say. Most commonly the traditions cited were those which told Israel's epic history; and the most common reason they were recited was (*a*) to remind Israel who she was and what was expected of her because of that identity, or (*b*) to remind Israel who God was and what might be expected of him in the covenantal relationship (*see* TORAH[S]). Where the ancient contexts in which these traditions were recited are available, we are able to discern what the hermeneutics of the biblical author were. The most common hermeneutic rule employed was that of historical analogy or TYPOLOGY, sometimes accompanied by another, the *qal waḥomer* argument, or *argumentum a fortiori*.

One obvious example of this is found in Ezek. 33. The shocked and despondent exilic community is quoted as consoling itself over the recently received news that Jerusalem had fallen. Ps. 137 records, in another form, their shock and despair at the same news: they hung their harps upon the trees of the camps where they were interned and refused to sing the old authoritative Torah traditions which reminded them of God's gracious acts in history in creating an Israel for himself. They undoubtedly felt that God had abandoned them and let them down. But others, trying to take heart, cited an old tradition about the call of Abraham: "Abraham was only one man, yet he got possession of the land; but we are many; the land is surely given us to possess" (Ezek. 33:24). Their ancestors had apparently engaged in the same sort of consolation when Samaria fell to the Assyrians in 722 B.C. (Isa. 9:10). Ezekiel here records an excellent example of the hermeneutic rules of typology and *qal waḥomer,* but Ezekiel himself disagreed with the argument.

A little later, after it had become clear that Persia was to be the new international power in the Middle East, the Second Isaiah consoled the descendants of those same exiled Jews with exactly the same argument which Ezekiel had rejected: "Look to Abraham your father and to Sarah who bore you; for when he was but one I called him, and I blessed him and made him many. For the Lord will comfort Zion" (Isa. 51:2-3). The argument Ezekiel disputed and the argument the Second Isaiah supported were exactly the same, indeed employing the same hermeneutic rules. The difference was context.

The Second Isaiah lived in the same sort of exiled, dispossessed community as Ezekiel had, but he lived some forty years later, and that made an immense difference. In Ezekiel's time it was still possible to deceive the people into thinking that the fall of Jerusalem had been an insignificant event. In Ezekiel's thinking, it was still necessary for the shock to be absorbed and accepted as part of God's agenda and purpose. Not until that point had been made and accepted, without any false hopes remaining, could Isaiah's subsequent message of restoration be heard properly.

The argument advanced by Ezekiel's contemporaries, which he disputed, had been advanced a few years earlier by a prophetic colleague of Jeremiah's, Hananiah of Gibeon. He argued, in a fully prophetic manner and apparently on the basis of Israel's legitimate authoritative traditions, that God would bring the deportees back home "within two years" (Jer. 28:2-4). As a member of the same covenant community as Hananiah, Jeremiah much preferred Hananiah's message to his own (28:6-9); but he sharply disputed Hananiah's message in the same terms with which Ezekiel disputed the same sort of message only ten years later.

Eva Osswald, following Martin Buber, has put it succinctly: "The true prophet must be able to distinguish whether a historical hour stands under the wrath or the love of God." The self-same message, based on the same authoritative traditions about what Israel can expect of God (because of what he has done in the past), in the one context was false while in the later was true. In other words, to derive consolation from the Torah story of God's gracious acts, without also deriving the obligations of the covenant relationship, is falsehood. Conversely, the "true" prophets, with the possible exception of Amos, when declaiming their messages of God's challenges and judgments (always based on the Torah story), went on to state how the impending adversity would also have the purpose of purging, refining, disciplining, or healing them (cf. Jer. 30:12-17; Ezek. 36:26-31). *See* DISCIPLINE, DIVINE[S]; GRACE IN THE OT[S].

6. Hermeneutic modes. Behind whatever hermeneutic rules the biblical thinkers employed there were two basic modes: the constitutive and the prophetic, and both were valid. Recent scholarship has shown that in the ambiguity existing at the time a prophecy is made, one cannot so easily distinguish a true from a false prophet as one can by hindsight, after reality has taken shape (Jer. 28:9; *see* PROPHECY, FALSE[S]). Both used the prophetic-messenger formulas, both cited the authoritative Torah-story traditions, both had great faith, both came out of the people and identified with them; but they had quite opposing messages because their basic hermeneutic modes were different. The one tended to read the tradition in a constitutive or supportive way, while the other permitted the tradition to be read in a challenging way.

At those historical moments when Israel was weak and needed reconstituting, the Bible in its canonical shape seems to indicate that the constitutive mode was proper: our father Jacob was a wandering Aramaean (Deut. 26:5); we are lost and wandering like him (in Exile); maybe like him we mark another beginning and not the end of Israel. But if that same mode of rereading the tradition about Jacob, or Abraham, was read at a time when Israel had power, and had somehow confused it with God's power, then Jeremiah and Ezekiel, as well as the other prophets, called it false prophecy. To continue to draw strength from the tradition would only harden the heart into further irresponsibility. At that historical moment the prophetic mode is indicated: it may be we must wander, once more, like Jacob, long enough to rediscover our true identity.

7. Theology of canonical hermeneutics. The debates between the so-called true and so-called false prophets always seem to have reached a crucial theological juncture. The so-called false prophet apparently believed that the God who had freed Israel from Egypt, guided her in the wilderness, and brought her into Canaan was strong enough and faithful enough to keep her there. His theology was one familiar in the Bible: that of emphasizing the grace of God in the midst of human sin. Even if we are not faithful, God is. He will keep us here. The so-called true prophet went a long way with that theology. But he apparently believed that the God who had freed Israel from Egypt, guided her in the wilderness and brought her into Canaan was powerful enough to take her out again and into exile! He recited the same Torah story, but in the prophetic mode.

Not by any means abandoning the doctrine of God's redemptive grace, he instead put it in the larger framework of the doctrine of God the creator. "It is I who by my great power and my outstretched arm have made the earth, with the men and animals that are on the earth, and I give it to whomever it seems right to me. Now I have given all these lands into the hand of Nebuchadnezzar, the king of Babylon, my servant" (Jer. 27:5-6). God still loved his people, and later would restore them handsomely, but some clear demonstration of God's integrity (unity) and freedom to reject as well as to elect was sometimes indicated by the historical moment. The prophetic indictments of the people were not only that they did not act like Israel, or live up to their true identity, but also that they presumed on God. *See* PRESENCE OF GOD, CULTIC[S].

These same hermeneutic modes (as well as the same hermeneutic rules) persist into the NT, where the evidence is mounting that Jesus, as a Jew among Jews in the first third of the first century, interpreted scriptural (OT) traditions in the prophetic mode, stressing the integrity and freedom of God in the coming eschaton (*see* §9 *below*).

8. Principles and rules. ***a. Context.*** As already stressed (§5) the interpreter must be able to discern the contemporary context so as to know which message is needed, that of constitutive support or that of prophetic challenge. The challenge may vary in intensity from challenge of life-style to threat to identity (canceling of election), just as the support may vary from the blessed assurance of divine presence to exhortation to believe in God's plans and power in a very evil situation.

b. Covenant identity. In either case, the ancient interpreter had the same essential covenantal identity as the people he addressed. Even Amos, who prophesied in the northern kingdom rather than in his homeland of Judah, nonetheless addressed people of the same basic covenantal identity as his own. Whether the biblical interpreter used the constitutive mode or the prophetic mode, he or she did so as a member of the group.

c. Memory. A distinctive characteristic of canonical hermeneutics was that of reading or reciting Israel's Torah story *in memory*. To recite the Torah story, in whatever form or in whatever circumstance, was to remember Yahweh's mighty acts in creating the world and Israel. To put God in remembrance of those same mighty acts was to petition or induce him to do the same sort of act again. But the retelling of that epic story of Israel's origins entailed such intensive identification with those in the past who benefitted from God's mighty acts in the story that, in cultic terms, time and space were in that moment of recital transcended. Those recalling or remembering the story understood themselves *actually* to be the slaves freed from Egypt, guided in the desert, and brought into the promised land; that is, the holy story became present reality in them.

When the evangelist recounted the command of Jesus to his disciples to engage in the Eucharist "in remembrance of me," the evangelist fully meant that in the moment of that cultic act, accompanied by some form of recital of the Torah-gospel story, the whole scene of the passion account would be actualized, made present, in the believers so "remembering." The Word or message received, however, will depend directly upon whether one identifies with Jesus, the Romans, the Jews, or with the disciples in actualizing the story (*see* following sections).

d. Dynamic analogy. To attempt to make the same points again today one must employ the basic rule of dynamic analogy. If a prophet challenged ancient Israel, or if Jesus challenged his own Jewish, responsible contemporaries, then a prophetic reading of the Bible today should challenge those dynamically equivalent to those challenged in the text: if the priests and prophets of Hosea's day or the Pharisees in Jesus' day, then the church establishment today, since prophets, priests, and Pharisees represented the responsible church leaders and groups of their time. Dynamic analogy also means that one reads the text for oneself and not only for others. It should not be read to identify false prophets and Pharisees with another group or someone else, but with one's own group and with oneself, in order to perceive the right text in the right context. In fact, there would have to be real humility (*see* §*g below*) on the part of modern Christians to identify with the Pharisees, since we hardly ever measure up to Pharisaic devotion and piety, much less their intense desire to please God. But to read the text as though Jesus were condemning either those Jews in their time or condemning some other group than one's own today is to read the text by static analogy. Put another way, to identify with Joseph, Jeremiah, and Jesus in the biblical accounts, without careful discernment of one's present-day context, is to miss what Joseph, Jeremiah, and Jesus have to say to believers today. Conceivably a new movement (one that feels it needs the strength to aid and to forgive those who had earlier sold them into slavery?) might identify with Joseph; but when that movement has become established, such a reading would only induce self-righteousness. The challenge then needed could come only from identifying with the brothers. The climactic point of Amos' address recorded in Amos 1:3–3:2 is that whereas autochthonous Israel should have treated the poor and weak and dispossessed in their own land the way Yahweh had treated Israel when they had been dispossessed slaves in Egypt, they were actually treating them the way Pharaoh had dealt with the Hebrew slaves in the Torah (Exodus) story.

e. Ambiguity of reality. Dynamic analogy means also that one must breathe the ambiguity of reality into the ancient situation or context. To read Amos as though what he said was "right" because, after all, he ended up being included in the canon, and as if those he addressed were "wrong" in some absolute sense, would be to miss the realism of the Bible as canon. Good, responsible folk in ancient times held another viewpoint on God's promises and expectations and in all sincerity and good faith considered Amos, Jeremiah, and Jesus to have been wrong. "The tradition works . . . not only to illuminate and to identify the Christ, but also to reject and resist the Christ" (J. Barr). We must read biblical texts in terms of the ambiguity of reality which any situation has; this means that we must be able to discern present contexts dynamically, and then read the biblical text in the same dynamic way.

f. Mirrors for identity. Most biblical texts must be read, not by looking in them for models for morality, but by looking in them for mirrors for identity. To look for models for morality in the Bible is very nearly a futile task, since a basic emphasis of the canon is on the grace and faithfulness of God and on the sin and faithlessness of Israel as well as of the disciples in the NT. There are hardly any moral models in the Bible as it is canonically shaped, except for a few characters viewed principally through ancient Wisdom thought, e.g., Joseph after he gets to Egypt. Abraham and Sarah lied out of fear for their lives and both snickered at the annunciation of Isaac's birth (Gen. 17–18); Jacob was a deceiver and supplanter and yet became Israel (Gen. 27); Moses was a murderer and fugitive from justice and yet became our savior from slavery and our lawgiver (Exod. 2); the disciples forsook Jesus (Matt. 26:56) and denied him (Mark 14:66-71); etc. The point is not that we should be liars, cheats, and murderers in order to be elect; on the contrary, to read the Bible in that way is to moralize statically on the basis of the text.

g. Theologizing and moralizing. One must read the Bible theologically before reading it morally. The primary meaning of redemption is that God has caught up human sinfulness into his plans and made it a part of those plans. This theologem pervades the Bible, OT and NT, and so all texts must be understood theologically (in the light of that theologem) before any indication for obedience be drawn from it.

The tendency to moralize first has resulted in dishonest readings of the Bible. Not to accept the clear biblical signal that Abraham feared for his own existence and lied about Sarah is to engage in white-washing the story. Not to accept what the Bible so clearly says about Jacob's devious character is to concentrate on how bad Esau was to sell his birthright (Heb. 12:16), which is to miss the point of Genesis altogether. But to seek to find the proper place of a passage in full canonical context by theologizing first (God's grace in the midst of human sin; God's free acts in electing "sinners") permits the reader then to ask in a fully canonical sense what the passage might indicate for current programs of obedience or life-style, without doing violence to the Bible, and without being misled by a false reading of it.

One should read the Bible not only with honesty but also with humility and humor. Humility means one identifies in the stories and episodes not with Joseph, Jeremiah, and Jesus, but with those who heard their challenging messages and learned from them. Whenever our reading of a biblical passage makes us feel self-righteous, we can be confident we have misread it. Humor means that in reading the biblical texts we take God a little more seriously than usual and ourselves a little less so.

9. The Bible as paradigm. If the story of Jesus' sermon at Nazareth (Luke 4:16-30) is read constitutively, that is, if one identifies with Jesus, then almost certainly one will read the passage anti-Semitically, get angry with the mob for trying to stone Jesus and then wonder, missing the point entirely, how Jesus was able to walk through the midst of them unharmed. But if one identifies with the good, responsible folk of Nazareth who attended the service, listens to Jesus' sermon from their standpoint, hears the terrible offense of it, and gets the feelings which the congregation got because of it, then one may want to lynch Jesus also. The question, What did Jesus say that made them so angry? becomes, What does Jesus say that makes us so angry? He said that when the great herald, or Elijah, would come finally, he would do the same sort of thing he and Elisha did in ancient Israel (I Kings 17; II Kings 5); he would take his blessings, not to our community, but to foreigners, even to our enemies. That is not the sort of message any congregation wants to hear, especially today, whether conservative or liberal. What is the use of being a member of the in-group if, when God intervenes to sort everything out, he takes his blessings to sinners, or outsiders? There is a deep injustice in paying those who work only one hour the same wages as those who have borne the burden and heat of a full day's work. But the Bible is full of the insistence on God's freedom and generosity (Matt. 20:1-15). Such a reading of Luke 4 (or of almost any passage in the Bible) would bring the church today to ask who it really is and what its self-understanding, or essential identity, ought truly to be. To read the Bible in this way is to engage in biblical "memory."

Even a passage like John 14:6, "No one comes to the Father, but by me," can be read either constitutively or prophetically. Reading in the constitutive mode one assumes one to be "by" or "in" Christ. For young, struggling churches who are not at all sure of survival, such a reading can be a correct one and a genuine encouragement not to assimilate or defect. But for established churches which have confused their identity with the dominant culture (so that, e.g., they think, because of the Puritan heritage, that to be a good Christian is to be a good American, and maybe even vice versa!), to read the verse in that way is to sponsor self-righteousness and pride and to encourage confusion of identity. To read it prophetically would be to hear in it the challenge that indeed the churches are not coming to the Father, and this is precisely because they are not, despite all their confessions and lessons learned by rote, coming "by me." Read in that way, the passage somehow no longer seems to sponsor notions of exclusivity at all, but rather sponsors a further step into understanding what the freedom of God means. Minimally it means that God is not a Christian in the sense that the churches habitually co-opt him to be. "A judge who is the God of all" (Heb. 12:23) read constitutively seems to say, "Our god is the judge of all them" (and the book of Revelation seems to say something like that to persecuted Christians under the Roman heel). But read prophetically the passage challenges all tribal, sectarian, and denominational ideas of God.

Conclusion. The Bible itself gives indications of how to make again today the points originally made and then to move on in our contexts to further theological horizons (views of truth). The two basic modes are the constitutive and the prophetic, according to context. The crucial distinction between them is theological: the freedom of God on the one hand, and his generosity and grace on the other; and his apparent bias for the powerless, those who have not yet confused his power with theirs. The Bible, read as a paradigm of the verbs of God's activity, permits us to conjugate in our own contexts the verbs of his continuing activity and how we may pursue, in our time, the integrity of truth, i.e., God's oneness both ontological and ethical.

Bibliography. P. Achtemeier, *An Introduction to the New Hermeneutic* (1969); J. Barr, *Old and New in Interpretation* (1966), pp. 149-200, and *The Bible in the Modern World* (1973), pp. 75-181; C. Braaten, *History and Hermeneutics* (1966), pp. 130-59; R. E. Brown, "Hermeneutics," *JBC,* II (1968), 605-23; B. Childs, *Memory and Tradition in Israel* (1962), and *Biblical Theology in Crisis* (1970); J. Crenshaw, *Prophetic Conflict* (1971); J. W. Doeve, *Jewish Hermeneutics in the Synoptic Gospels and Acts* (1954); R. Funk, *Language, Hermeneutic and Word of God* (1966), pp. 1-122; J. Moltmann *et al., The Future of Hope* (1970); E. Osswald, *Falsche Prophetie im AT* (1962); W. Pannenberg *et al., History and Hermeneutic* (1967); J. M. Robinson, *A New Quest of the Historical Jesus* (1959); J. M. Robinson and J. B. Cobb, Jr., *The New Hermeneutic* (1964), and *Theology as History* (1967), pp. 1-133; J. A. Sanders, *Torah and Canon* (2nd ed., 1974), "The Ethic of Election in Luke's Great Banquet Parable," *Essays in OT Ethics,* ed. J. Crenshaw and J. Willis (1974), pp. 245-71, and "Reopening Old Questions about Scripture," *Int.,* XXVIII (1974), 321-30; C. Westermann, ed., *Essays on OT Hermeneutics* (1963), pp. 160-99, 314-55. Examples of application of above hermeneutic principles: J. A. Sanders, "The Banquet of the Dispossessed," *USQR,* XX (1965), 355-63, "Promise and Providence," *USQR,* XXI (1966), 295-303, "In the Same Night," *USQR,* XXV (1970), 333-41, and *The New History: Joseph, Our Brother* (1968).

J. A. Sanders

HERMETIC LITERATURE hûr mĕt'ĭk. A variety of theosophical writings ascribed to Hermes Trismegistos ("thrice-great"), the Greek title of Thoth, the Egyptian god of wisdom. Composed originally in Greek in Egypt, the Hermetica were translated into Latin, Arabic, and Armenian, and were esteemed in medieval times by Albertus Magnus and Paracelsus.

1. Types and MSS. The "vulgar" Hermetica are astrological, magical, and alchemical works preserved in MSS of the thirteenth through the fifteenth centuries. The "learned" Hermetica are religious and philosophical in character. These are preserved in the Greek Corpus Hermeticum (CH), the Latin Asclepius, the Coptic NAG HAMMADI Codex VI, and in extracts in Stobaeus and other writers. The CH is an extensive collection of seventeen tractates composed in the second and third centuries A.D., numbered I–XIV, XVI–XVIII. An early editor had placed extracts from Stobaeus as CH XV. Hermetic works in Nag Hammadi Codex VI are: Authoritative Teaching (not explicitly Hermetic but probably a popular form of it); the Discourse on the Eighth and Ninth (an important new initiation liturgy comparable to CH XIII); the Prayer of Thanksgiving (also found in Asclepius 41 and the Greek Papyrus Mimaut); and the Apocalypse from Asclepius (cf. Asclepius 21-29).

2. Teachings. The Hermetica show borrowing from both dualistic Platonism and pantheistic Stoicism. The monistic tractates (CH V, VIII, XI, XIV) maintain that the invisible god may be discerned in the Cosmos, especially in the celestial order. The dualistic tractates (CH I, IV, VI, VII, XIII) teach that the world is not the direct creation of the First God. CH IX, X may be called "mixed."

The important tractate CH I, called Poimandres, reveals that God gave birth to a Second Mind who made the planets, and also to the Anthropos who united with Nature to produce seven androgynous persons from whom came humanity (*see* ANDROGYNY[S]). Therefore, one's body imprisons one's soul and subjects it to astrological fate.

The Hermetic who is reborn by receiving *nous,* "intelligence," and by suppressing the bodily senses may ascend at death through the seven circles and join the company of the celestial gods. In the Nag Hammadi tractates there is reference to a brotherhood of Hermetic saints who have broken the bonds of fate (On8th9th), as well as references to kissing, and to eating holy and "unbloody" food (PrThank). ApocAscl refers to a mystery of *synousia,* "living together."

In spite of Reitzenstein's attempt to suggest that the Poimandres is the source of Johannine thought, the Anthropos of CH I is not a savior like Christ. Though some of the CH tractates are almost Gnostic, the Hermetica lack the radical dualism of GNOSTICISM. Creation is not regarded as in itself evil, and the demiurge is not a rebel but the son of the supreme God.

Bibliography. R. Reitzenstein, *Poimandres* (1904); W. Scott and A. S. Ferguson, eds., *Hermetica,* I-IV (1924-36); C. H. Dodd, *The Bible and the Greeks* (1935); A. J. Festugière, *La révélation d' Hermes Trismégiste,* 4 vols. (1949-54); A. D. Nock and A. J. Festugière, eds., *Corpus Hermeticum,* 4 vols. (1945-54); A. J. Festugière, *L'Hermetisme* (1948); G. van Moorsel, *The Mysteries of Hermes Trismegistus* (1955); K.-W. Tröger, *Mysterienglaube und Gnosis in Corpus Hermeticum XIII, TU,* CX (1971); L. S. Keizer, *The Eighth Reveals the Ninth* (1974).

E. M. YAMAUCHI

HERODIAN FORTRESSES. Herod the Great fortified Judea against invasion from without and insurrection from within. Apart from strengthening cities such as JERUSALEM and Sebaste, he constructed eleven remarkable fortresses, mostly on relatively inaccessible but strategic wilderness mountaintops. Only the Herodium SE of Bethlehem was wholly new (not to be confused with another Herodium at El Hubbeisa in Peraea). Alexandrium, Hyrcania, Machaerus, Cypros, and MASADA were built upon Hasmonean foundations. These major citadels in the Jordan Valley could signal to one other at least. Herodium, Cypros, and Machaerus could signal directly to Jerusalem.

The S of Herod's domains, the object of envy of his archrival, Cleopatra VII of Egypt, saw a concentration of smaller fortresses also on ancient foundations. In the wilderness above En-gedi were Carmel (Khirbet Kermel) and Zif (Khirbet Ziph). Oresa (Khirbet Istabul? Khirbet Harissah?) and Adora (Dura) were S of Hebron.

1. The Alexandrium (Khirbet Sarbata, fifteen miles SE of Shechem) is a vital point on the central Jordan Valley road. Built by Alexander Jannaeus, for whom it is named, it became a refuge for his son, Aristobulus, who in 63 B.C. resisted Pompey there (Jos. War I.vi.5). Six years later his grandson, Alexander, surrendered Alexandrium to Gabinius and Marc Antony, who demolished it (War I.viii.4, 5; Antiq. XIV.v.3, 4). Herod rebuilt it in 38 B.C. (War I.xvi.3; Antiq. XIV.xv.4) and gave it a sinister reputation as a place for the incarceration of political enemies. In 30 B.C. Herod visited Octavian at Rhodes, putting his mother-in-law, Alexandra, and his wife, Mariamne, as well as their children, in the Alexandrium and giving orders to kill Mariamne should he not return (War I.xxii.4; Antiq. XV.vi.5). The discovery of this secret set in motion events which led to the woman's death. Twenty-three years later when Herod ordered the death of his two sons by Mariamne (Alexander and Aristobulus) they were buried on this brooding height among many of their Hasmonean ancestors (Antiq. XVI.xi.7). While several of the fortresses served as treasuries, it was at the Alexandrium that Herod kept much of his vast fortune.

Mishna and Talmud mention Sarbata, where beacons were lit to announce the new moon. The summit contains ruined walls, cisterns, an olive press, and rock-cut tombs. At its base are remains of the Herodian town of Alexandrium and its ancient aqueduct.

2. The Herodium. At Jebel el-Fureidis, which commanded the desert road from Jerusalem to En-gedi, Herod erected a curious fortress which he named for himself (Jos. War I.xiii.8; Antiq. XIV.xiii.9). The easternmost of twin hills was used to heighten the western summit. Upon this cone-shaped mount a round castle was constructed (War I.xxi.10), contained within double circular walls 180 feet in diameter. Upon all "wealth was lavished in profusion." Here Herod was buried (War I.xxxiii.9). The Herodium was, says Josephus, "a memorial to himself." *See* HERODIUM; HERODIUM[S]; for a photo, *see* TEKOA Fig. 7.

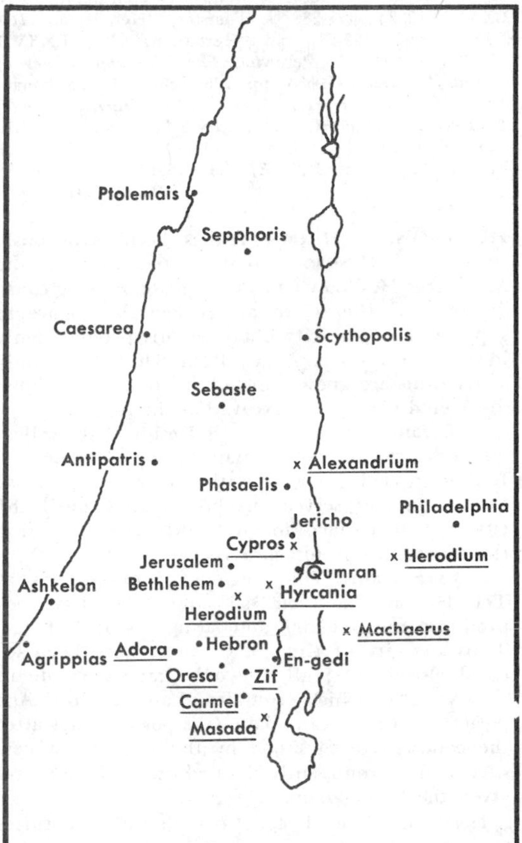

HERODIAN FORTRESSES

3. **Hyrcania** (Khirbet Mird, in the desolate wilderness eleven miles N of Jericho) was built by John Hyrcanus (or perhaps Alexander Jannaeus). Destroyed by Gabinius in 57 B.C. (Jos. War I.viii.5; Antiq. XIV.v.4), it was rebuilt by Herod before 32 B.C. The grimmest of the desert fortresses and that with the most evil reputation, it continued as a state prison where secret executions and burials took place (Antiq. XV.x.4). Here Herod, in his last week of life, had his son Antipater murdered and unceremoniously buried (Antiq. XVII.vii.1).

After the Jewish revolts Hyrcania fell into ruin. In A.D. 492 St. Sabas founded a monastery (*Castellion*) on the site. In 1953 Belgian archaeologists recovered a number of MSS there, mostly from the fifth to eighth century A.D.: codices including Mark, John, and Acts; portions of the Bible in Aramaic; and fragments of Euripides' *Andromache.*

Mird contains extensive Roman and Byzantine ruins including mosaics and parts of an aqueduct and a bridge.

4. **Machaerus** ("The Sword," Targ. Michvar; Arab. Mukawer and Qasr el-Mishneneq) is E of the Dead Sea thirteen miles SE of Judean Herodium. Built to take advantage of the natural cleft of the Arnon Valley, it effectively guarded Herod's vulnerable frontier with the Nabateans. Its soaring towers (approximately 100 feet high), joined by massive ramparts, enclosed spacious royal apartments magnificently appointed, with hugh cisterns furnishing an abundance of water. *See* Jos. War VII.vi.2.

Machaerus' most famous prisoner was John the Baptist, beheaded there by order of Herod Antipas (Matt. 14:1-12; Mark 6:14-29; Luke 9:7-9; Jos. Antiq. XVIII.v.2).

After Jerusalem fell in A.D. 70 the Romans beseiged Machaerus; it was taken by a ruse and subsequently destroyed (Jos. War VII.vi.4). Remains of the Roman siege wall and camps as well as portions of the Herodian aqueduct, fortress and town below are still visible. *See* MACHAERUS.

5. **Cypros** (Tell el-Akabe), named for Herod's mother (Jos. War I.xxi.9), stood 800 feet above the Jericho Plain on the S side of the Wadi Qelt, guarding the road from Jerusalem to Jericho. Building on earlier, probably Ptolemaic foundations, Alexander Jannaeus constructed three forts in the vicinity. One was Docus, on the summit of "the Mount of Temptation," while the other two, Threx and Taurus, flanked the Wadi Qelt. All three were dismantled by Pompey in 64 B.C. Cypros was a reconstruction of Threx. It was, according to Josephus (Antiq. XVI.v.2), "a place notable for its security and most pleasant to stay in." It did not have the sinister history often associated with Herod's wilderness fortresses.

Bibliography. F.-M. Abel, *Géographie de la Palestine,* II (1938), pp. 241, 350, 371; S. Applebaum, "The Initial Date of the Limes Palestinae," *Zion,* XXVII (1962), 1-10, Hebrew; W. J. Moulton, "A Visit to Qarn Sarṭabeh," *BASOR,* 62 (Apr. 1936), 14-18; N. Glueck, "Explorations in Eastern Palestine. III," *BASOR,* 65 (Feb. 1937), 23-29; M. Grant, *Herod the Great* (1971), pp. 110-14; A. H. M. Jones, *The Herods of Judaea* (1938), pp. 75-79; S. Perowne, *The Life and Times of Herod the Great* (1956), pp. 105-8, 121-23; A. Schalit, *König Herodes* (1969), pp. 341-43; E. Schürer, *The History of the Jewish People* (rev. ed., 1973), I, 3-4.

H. T. FRANK

*__HERODIUM.__ The name of two fortresses established by Herod the Great, the only ones which he built *de novo.*

1. **Herodium in Peraea.** The date of construction is uncertain, but Josephus indicates that Herod built the first Herodium on a "mountain toward Arabia" prior to building the one by the same name near Bethlehem (Jos. War I.xxi.10). Ruins of a small fortress known as El Hubbeisa, "the little prison," are the likely location. It was constructed close to the foot of Mount Nebo, near an agricultural settlement which Herod called

Livias, in honor of Caesar Augustus' wife. Along with Machaerus, its purpose was to defend Herod's frontier against the Nabateans.

2. Herodium near Bethlehem. The Arabic name of this site is *Jebel el-Fureidis,* which means "mountain of small paradise." In the materials from Murabba'at the spelling is "Herodis" for which some scholars maintain Fureidis is an Arabic corruption. Sometimes the location is referred to as "Frank Mountain" from a tradition that a body of Franks held out there for forty years after the Crusader kingdom of Jerusalem fell in A.D. 1187. There is, however, no archaeological evidence to substantiate this.

Construction on the Herodium began in 24/23 B.C., when Herod was fifty years old, and was completed prior to Marcus Agrippa's state visit to Herod's realm in 15 B.C. (Jos. Antiq. XV.ix.4). Located on a hill 3½ miles S of Bethlehem, this palace-fortress was constructed on a conical plan. A very steep glacis provided the base for the outer of two circular walls. From the outer wall protruded three semicircular towers to the S, N, and W. The eastern wall was dominated by a round tower, the ruins of which still stand over 50 feet high. From the valley below, a stairway of 200 marble steps led up to the outer wall.

The building complex, which had a maximum diameter of 262 feet, had three floors above the semiunderground level. All walls except the outer one were covered with stucco, the ground floor level being in polychrome, the upper levels in white. Paintings in both distemper and fresco have been discovered. Well-sculptured columns and capitals in both the Corinthian and Ionic orders were employed. Both marble and mosaic floors have been uncovered.

As is typical of Herodian fortresses, huge subterranean cisterns were constructed to store rain water. To augment the water supply for the Herodium and the small town at its base, a conduit was built from Solomon's pools just S of Jerusalem.

Although Herod is known to have been buried here, his tomb has not been identified.

During the First and Second Jewish Wars Herodium was occupied by Jewish rebels. During the First Revolt the rebels found it in excellent condition, but those who settled there during the Second Revolt dwelt among ruins of the destroyed buildings. It is difficult to discriminate between the evidence left during the two rebel occupations. However, the occupants during the Second Revolt can be credited with construction of new rooms in three of the towers and the conversion of a dining hall into a synagogue.

Some scholars have concluded from letters found at Murabba'at that Simeon bar Kochba, the rebel leader, personally commanded the garrison at Herodium before his retreat to Bether. *See* BAR KOCHBA[S] §3.

Rooms which best withstood the ravages of two Roman sieges were the baths. They were occupied not only by Jewish rebels but subsequently by a community of Christian monks, whose occupancy lasted until the seventh century A.D. The walls of the baths contain an intriguing mixture of graffiti written by the first inhabitants, the Jewish rebel soldiers, and the monastic occupants. The monks built a small church in the palace courtyard.

See HERODIUM; HERODIAN FORTRESSES[S] §2.

Bibliography. P. Benoit, J. T. Milik, R. de Vaux, DJD, II, *Les Grottes de Murabba'ât* (1961), pp. 124-32; C. Corbo, "Gebel Fureidis (Hérodium)," *RB,* LXXV (1968), 424-28; G. Foerster, "Herodium," *IEJ* XIX (1969), 123-24, and "Herodium," *RB,* LXXVII (1970), 400-401; S. Perowne, *The Life and Times of Herod the Great* (1956), pp. 106, 121-23; E. Vardaman, "The History of Herodium," *The Teacher's Yoke: Studies in Memory of Henry Trantham,* ed. E. Vardaman and J. Garrett (1964), pp. 58-81; Y. Yadin, "Expedition D," *IEJ,* XI (1961), 51-52

T. O. HALL, JR.

***HESHBON. 1. History.** It has been erroneously stated (*see* HESHBON) that at the time of the Maccabees Heshbon had the right of striking coins. There is no literary or archaeological evidence to support this. The city obtained this privilege only in the third century A.D., from which time only a few coins are known, including one fine specimen discovered during the excavations in 1973.

In Byzantine times Esbus, as Heshbon was called, was the seat of a Christian bishop. During the Islamic period it became the district capital of the Belqa and served in this capacity until the city was abandoned for unknown reasons during the fourteenth or fifteenth century A.D.

2. Excavations. Four seasons of excavations at Tell Ḥesbân (between 1968 and 1974) have not produced any remains antedating the Iron I age. Thus the city of King Sihon must have been located elsewhere. Jalul, the only important site in the vicinity which contains Late Bronze Age pottery, is a good candidate. It is possible that after the conquest of Heshbon by the Israelites a new site, more prominently located, was chosen and given the former name, Heshbon.

Heshbon's Iron I age (twelfth-tenth centuries B.C.) is represented by what seems to have been a fortification wall built of rough, tightly fitting boulders, as well as by a large plastered cistern which contained only Iron I sherds in its water-laid silt.

Pottery of the early Iron II period (ninth-eighth centuries) has come to light in two sites on the mound. One is an open-air water reservoir (so far only partially excavated) at least fifty feet long, forty feet wide, and fifteen feet deep. It probably was one of the pools mentioned in Song of S. 7:4 [H 5].

The late Iron II age (seventh-sixth centuries) is well represented. Part of the ancient defense wall has been discovered, founded on the original bedrock. In the reservoir, filled in during Hellenistic times, Ammonite pottery, known previously only from tombs excavated in and around Amman, was recovered. This fill also contained ostraca from the seventh and sixth centuries B.C. which have enriched our knowledge of the Ammonite dialect and script (*see* AMMON, AMMONITES[S]; INSCRIPTIONS, SEMITIC[S] §3*c*).

From the sixth to the third century B.C. Tell Ḥesbân seems to have been abandoned, but it was resettled in the second century, probably by the Maccabees. The most extensive remains came from the Roman period. They included an impressive perimeter wall around the acropolis; a tower; a paved flagstone floor; and a wide monumental stairway which gave access to a public building on the acropolis, probably a temple. The temple most likely is depicted on the reverse of coins minted at Esbus in the third century A.D., which show the façade of a four-columned building with a female deity standing between the central columns (*see* Fig. H12). To the Roman period belong also the earliest rolling-stone tombs of the first century A.D. thus far discovered E of the Jordan River.

Eugenia L. Nitowski; courtesy the Andrews University Archaeological Museum

12. The Esbus coin, found during the 1973 Hesbon expedition.

The most noteworthy remains from Byzantine times are the foundations of a basilica-type church, erected in part on the foundations of earlier Roman structures. It was probably destroyed during the Persian invasion in A.D. 614.

Structures dated to the Umayyad and Ayyubid/Mamluk times include vaulted rooms surrounding a central plaza on the summit and a well-preserved bathing complex.

Bibliography. W. Vyhmeister, "The History of Heshbon from Literary Sources," *AUSS*, VI (1968), 158-77; R. S. Boraas, S. H. Horn *et al.*, *"Heshbon* 1968," *AUSS*, VII (1969), 97-239; S. H. Horn, "The 1968 Heshbon Expedition," *BA*, XXXII (1969), 26-41; A. Terian, "Coins from the 1968 Excavations at Heshbon," *AUSS*, IX (1971), 147-60; E. N. Lugenbeal and J. A. Sauer, "Seventh-Sixth Century B.C. Pottery from Area B at Heshbon," *AUSS*, X (1972), 21-69; R. G. Bullard, "Geological Study of the Heshbon Area," *AUSS*, X (1972), 129-41; R. S. Boraas, S. H. Horn *et al.*, "Heshbon 1971," *AUSS*, XI (1973), 1-144; J. A. Sauer, "Heshbon Pottery 1971," *Andrews University Monographs*, vol. VII (1973); A. Terian, "Coins from the 1971 Excavations at Heshbon," *AUSS*, XII (1974), 35-96; F. M. Cross, "Ammonite Ostraca from Heshbon," *AUSS*, XIII (1975), 1-20; R. S. Boraas, S. H. Horn *et al.*, "Heshbon 1973," *AUSS*, XIII (1975), 101-247. S. H. Horn

***HIERAPOLIS.** Although Hierapolis had previously been explored and surveyed, regular campaigns of excavation and restoration were begun only in 1957. One of the most important discoveries of the recent excavations has been the recognition of the deadly Plutonium with its entrance to the underworld (*see* Hierapolis). The Plutonium area is located beside and below the temple of the oracular Apollo Archegetes in the center of the city and focuses on a doorway or large niche from which the sound of rushing water and the unpleasant smell of chemicals still come forth.

A second outstanding discovery is a martyrium, possibly that of Philip the apostle, but more likely belonging to Philip the evangelist, who is reported to have spent his last days in Hierapolis and been buried there along with his prophetic virgin daughters (Acts 21:8-9; Eusebius, Hist. III.xxxi). The martyrium of Philip stood in a dominating position above the city, just outside the walls to the NE, and was approached by a broad flight of steps. Over 180 feet square in plan and bounded on all sides by a series of small chambers (intended perhaps for the accommodation of pilgrims), the martyrium had at its center an octagonal chamber more than sixty feet in diameter, roofed by a lead-plated dome. From this chamber radiated eight chapels and corridors each with twin marble columns in its doorway. The complex was built in the early fifth century.

Bibliography. P. Verzone, "Le chiese di Hierapolis in Asia Minore," *Cahiers Archéologiques*, VIII (1956), 37-61, "Il martyrium ottagono a Hierapolis di Frigia," *Palladio*, NS X (1960), 1-20, "Grandi martyria dell'oriente e problemi relativi alla loro struttura originaria," *Atti del VI Congresso Internazionale di Archeologia Cristiana, Ravenna 1962* (1965), pp. 611-40, "Le campagne a Hierapolis di Frigia," *Annuario della Scuola Archeologia di Atene*, NS XXIII-XXIV (1961-62), 633-747, and XXV-XXVI (1963-64), 351-433, and "Hierapolis christiana," *Corsi di Cultura sull'Arte Ravennate e Bizantina*, XII (1965), 613-727; E. S. Equinni, *La necropoli di Hierapolis di Frigia* (1972).

D. Boyd

HIGHER CRITICISM. Distinguished from Lower Criticism, whose work it carries forward, by its concern to understand documents in relation to their original historical setting; sometimes understood as virtually equivalent to historical criticism (*see* Biblical Criticism §5*d*). Higher criticism relies more on internal than on external evidence. E.g., in determining whether Peter wrote the epistles, it assesses the intrinsic probability in light of their contents rather than relying on the epistles' own claim to authorship or on external attestation in other texts. The higher critic who concludes that Peter is not the author then proceeds to infer the probable time, place, and occasion of the epistles. The nineteenth- and twentieth-century controversies over biblical criticism have concentrated on the legitimacy of higher criticism because it appeared to threaten the authority of the Bible. *See* Biblical Criticism, History of; Biblical Theology, History of; Scripture, Authority of[S].

L. E. Keck

HILLEL. 2. Father of Abdon, one of the Israelite judges (Judg. 12:13, 15). He was from the town of Pirathon in the tribal territory of Ephraim.

***HITTITES.** An Indo-European people of the second millennium, creators of a strong kingdom in E central Anatolia, which grew into a powerful empire and fell *ca.* 1200 B.C.; also, their descendants in SE peripheral areas from *ca.* 1200 to 700 (Neo-Hittites).

1. The Bronze Age Hittites. The name *Ḫatti* originally designated the native, non–Indo-European population of central Anatolia. Speakers of western

Indo-European *(centum)* languages are attested in Anatolia since early in the second millennium. Those who settled in its central part adopted the name *Ḫatti* as the political appellation of their kingdom, but they called their own language Nesite (also known as "cuneiform Hittite" in modern literature). Two other Indo-European languages spoken in Anatolia were Luwian (in the S and SW) and Palaic (in an undetermined northern area). After 1600 the Hittites took over the cuneiform script from northern Syria, as well as the use of Akkadian and Hurrian. About the same time the royal residence was moved from Kussara (as yet unidentified) to Ḫattusas (Boghazköy). The first historical ruler of the Old Kingdom, Ḫattusilis I (*ca.* 1570-1540, low CHRONOLOGY OF THE OT), began the Hittite drive for the conquest of northern Syria. His successor, Mursilis I, captured Ḫalab (Aleppo) and sacked Babylon (1531). But soon the Hurrian offensive (*see* MITANNI[S]; HURRIANS; HURRIANS[S]) and a long series of palace revolutions weakened the Hittite state. *Ca.* 1420 a new, stable dynasty laid the foundations of the New Kingdom. Suppiluliumas I (*ca.* 1386-1356) restored Hittite supremacy in Anatolia, conquered northern and central Syria, and established a protectorate over Mitanni, thus creating the Hittite Empire. His successors were involved in wars with Egypt, which tried to recover its lost possessions in Syria. The culminating battle took place in 1300 at Kadesh on the Orontes and resulted in an indecisive victory of King Muwatallis over Pharaoh Ramses II. A peace treaty was concluded in 1279 between Ramses II and Ḫattusilis III. The Hittites retained their Syrian dominions, but they could not prevent the conquest of Mitanni by Assyria.

Scala
13. The Lion Gate at Boghazköy

Ca. 1200 the Hittite Empire was overthrown by the invasion of the People of the Sea (*see* PHILISTINES §1). Ḫattusas was destroyed, never to rise again, and the very memory of the great Anatolian Empire was forgotten till the start of excavations at Boghazköy early in this century. These excavations, which are still going on, have revealed great monuments of architecture, works of art, and an enormous archive of cuneiform tablets of all genres. *See* Fig H13.

2. The Neo-Hittites. Some traditions of the Hittite Empire were preserved for another five hundred years in the Taurus region and in northern Syria. The number of Hittites there was probably increased by an influx of refugees from Anatolia. The cuneiform script and the "cuneiform Hittite" language disappeared, but the Hittite hieroglyphic writing, occasionally used under the Empire, survived and spread to new areas. The language of the Hittite hieroglyphs is very close to Luwian. However, Luwian-speaking elements had been an integral part of the Hittite state, and their descendants were known as Hittites to their Assyrian, Urartian, and Hebrew contemporaries. We shall therefore retain for them the conventional designation "Neo-Hittites" (preferable to "Syro-Hittites," because they were not limited to Syria). S of the Taurus, they were a minority in a predominantly Semitic environment. The power in most of their states in Syria gradually passed to the Arameans, who initially continued the Neo-Hittite traditions. The Assyrian conquest of Syria put an end to the Neo-Hittite court culture.

In the ninth and eighth centuries, the Neo-Hittite area was divided into several small states, some of which are mentioned in the OT (*see* map). Bit-adini (*see* EDEN[S] §1) was annexed by Assyria in 857-855, and the other states between 740 and 708, except the southwestern part of Tabal, which remained autonomous.

The Assyrians called northern Syria *Ḫatti* (Hittite land), and along with their military advance this geographical term extended to the rest of Syria and to Palestine, interchangeably with the older name of the region, *Amurru,* or combined with it in the hendiadys "Ḫatti and Amurru" or "Ḫatti of Amurru."

3. The Hittites in the OT. The Hittite conquests never reached Palestine, and no ethnic Hittite elements ever settled there. In the historical books of the OT, "Hittites" always designate the Neo-Hittites of northern Syria.

When Ezekiel (16:3, 45) said to Jerusalem that "your father was an Amorite, and your mother a Hittite," he simply followed the geographical terminology of his time which assigned Jerusalem to the land of Ḫatti or "Ḫatti and Amurru." The same Neo-Babylonian usage underlies the appellation "Hittites" for the population of Canaan in the patriarchal stories of P (Gen. 23:3; 26:34; 27:46). There is no reason to see a genuine survival of imperial Hittite law in the courteous procedure of concluding a deal as described in Gen. 23. As a Syrian people, the Hittites were assigned to the descendants of Canaan in the table of nations, Gen. 10:15, and included in the

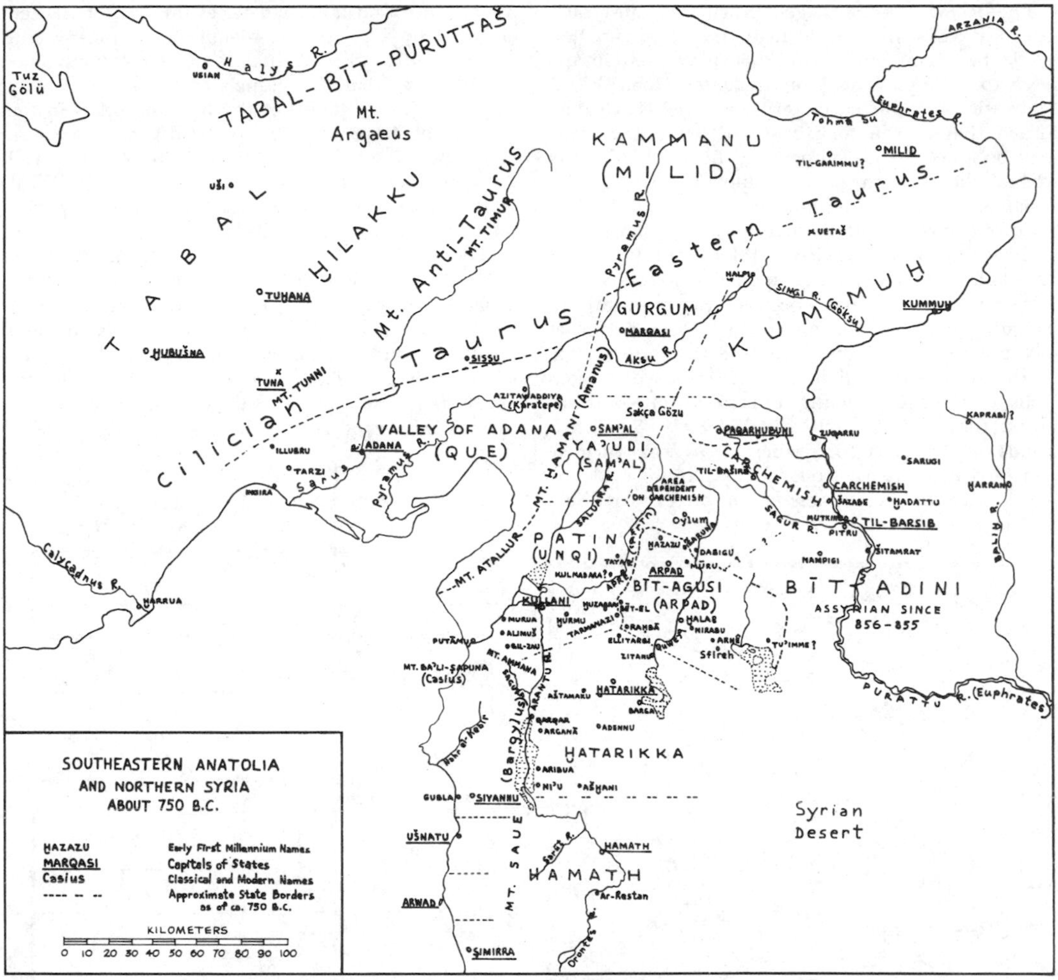

standard enumerations of the peoples whose land was promised to Israel (Gen. 15:18-21 and elsewhere).

Bibliography. The Bronze Age Hittites: A. Goetze, *Hethiter, Churriter und Assyrer* (1936); J. Garstang and O. R. Gurney, *The Geography of the Hittite Empire* (1959); O. R. Gurney, *The Hittites* (2nd ed., 1961); H. Otten, "Das Hethiterreich," in *Kulturgeschichte des alten Orient,* ed. H. Schmöckel (1961), pp. 311-446; F. Cornelius, *Geschichte der Hethiter* (1973); *CAH*³, II, Pt. I, chs. 6, 15 (by O. R. Gurney); Pt. II, chs. 17, 21(a), and 24 (by A. Goetze). A representative selection of Hittite texts is given in *ANET* (3rd ed.).

The Neo-Hittites: I. J. Gelb, *Hittite Hieroglyphic Monuments* (1939); D. G. Hogarth, C. L. Woolley, R. D. Barnett, *Carchemish. . . ,* I (1914), II (1921), III (1952); W. Orthmann, *Untersuchungen zur späthethischen Kunst* (1971); J. D. Hawkins, "Assyrians and Hittites," *Iraq,* XXXVI (1974), 67-83.

The Hittites in the OT: J. C. L. Gibson, "Observations on Some Important Ethnic Terms in the Pentateuch," *JNES,* XX (1961), 224-27; M. R. Lehman, "Abraham's Purchase of Machpelah and Hittite Law," *BASOR,* 129 (Feb. 1953), 15-18; contrast G. Boyer, "Étude juridique," in J. Nougayrol, *PRU,* III (1955), 297, and G. M. Tucker, "The Legal Background of Genesis 23," *JBL,* LXXXV (1966), 77-84.

M. C. Astour

***HIVITES.** *See* Hurrians[S] §3.

***HOBAB, THE KENITE.** *See* Arad[S] §2.

HODAYOTH. *See* Thanksgiving Psalms[S].

HOLINESS CODE. *See* Leviticus §3*e*; Leviticus[S] §4.

***HOLY SEPULCHRE, CHURCH OF THE.** An ecclesiastical complex in the walled Old City of Jerusalem that comprises the traditional locations of Golgotha (Calvary) and the tomb of Jesus, which according to John 19:41 were located close to one another. The church was constructed by the emperor Constantine in the fourth century (*see* Art, Early Christian[S] §4*a*) and subsequently has undergone numerous alterations, some of them extensive. Although many historical records pertain to the church, the history of this complex could not be written satisfactorily until extensive archaeological explorations were undertaken as a part of restorations begun in 1960 by the Greek Orthodox, the Armenian, and the Roman Catholic churches, the three principal Christian communities that share the edifice.

The Romans often staged crucifixions just outside city walls and beside main roads, where they would be prominently visible. Such a situation appears to be implied in John 19:20 (cf. Heb. 13:12). Excavations conducted in Jerusalem in 1961-68 confirmed that at the time of Jesus' death the areas now occupied by Golgotha and the tomb of Jesus within the Church of the Holy Sepulchre were situated 100-150 yards outside the city wall. This discovery obviates the most serious objection to the authenticity of the traditional location. It is also now known that the place upon which the church was built had formerly been a quarry, into the irregular terrain of which tombs had been cut prior to the expansion of Jerusalem and the construction of the third city wall in A.D. 41, some years after Jesus' passion. Although there is no incontrovertible proof that the Church of the Holy Sepulchre stands on the exact spots where Jesus was crucified and buried, there is strong circumstantial evidence for the essential correctness of the places memorialized in the church. *See* Fig. H14.

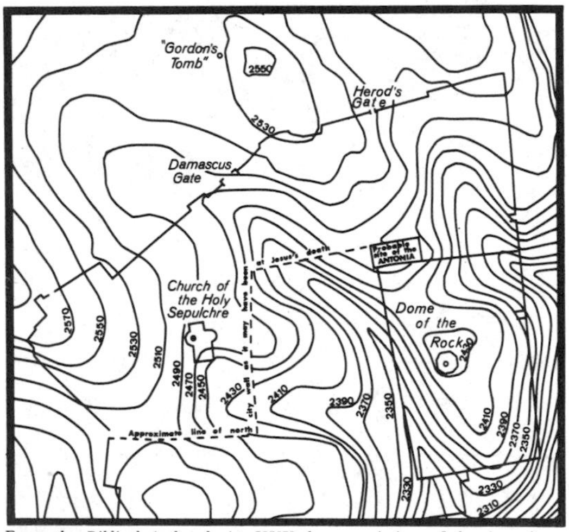

From the *Biblical Archaeologist,* XXX, by permission of the American Schools of Oriental Research

14. Contour map of Jerusalem. Drawing by R. H. Smith based on the topographical map by C. Warren.

The small second-story Golgotha chapel in the church preserves at best relatively little of the original ground on which Jesus was crucified. Glimpses of rock may be seen in the floor and on the ground level below the chapel. Not much is yet known archaeologically about this spot, but test borings near it have shown that the quarry drops off to the E around Golgotha. Golgotha may therefore have been a highly visible pinnacle. Fourth-century masons probably left standing only an irregular part of this knoll. Any original contours that might have given the place its designation of "skull" in Jesus' day no longer exist.

Even less, presumably, remains of the tomb of Jesus, located on the ground level of the church. To form a courtyard, Constantinian masons cut away most of the hillside around the tomb, and subsequently pilgrims and enemies alike hacked away much of the surviving rock that formed the tomb. Since Constantinian times the tomb has been enclosed by a small mausoleum-like shrine, several times rebuilt. The original form of the tomb may be inferred from the gospels and from the many surviving Jewish tombs of the Roman period in the vicinity of Jerusalem. It can hardly have been so elaborate as the large Hellenistic tombs that still stand in the Kidron Valley. (*See* TOMB Fig. TOM 70.) It had a typically small inner doorway that may have been closed with a millstone-like disk that rolled in a slot (*see* Fig. TOM 71; cf. Mark 15:46; 16:3-4 and parallels; John 20:1). Inside was perhaps a single chamber with rock-hewn mortuary slabs against the three walls that faced the door and possibly typical burial slots at right angles to the walls of the chamber, although these latter do not figure in the accounts in the gospels. *See* Fig. H15; GOLGOTHA; JERUSALEM §11; JERUSALEM[S].

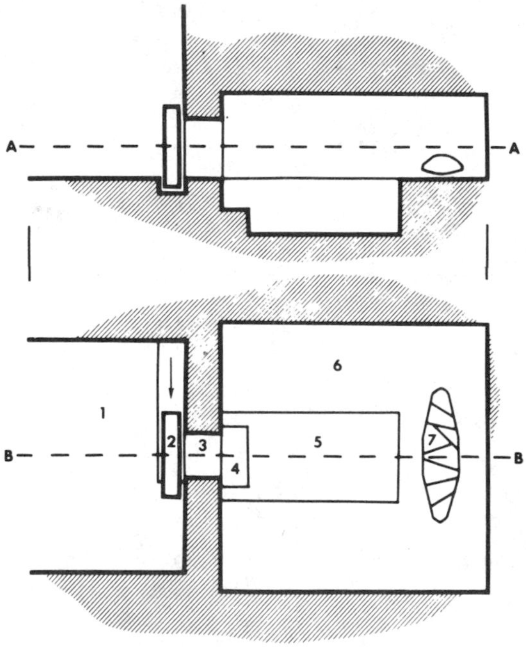

Drawing by R. H. Smith

15. Hypothetical reconstruction of the tomb of Jesus from archaeological evidence of Jewish tombs at Jerusalem during the time of Jesus. At the top is a cross section (through plane B-B) and at the bottom is the plan (through plane A-A). 1: Forecourt. 2: Disk-shaped closing stone in a slot; the arrow indicates the direction of downward slope of the slot, whereby the stone rolls into place by gravity but cannot be rolled back except with the expenditure of much energy. 3: Entrance to the burial chamber. 4: Stone step. 5: Central pit to permit one's standing erect in the chamber. 6: Stone benches in the bedrock on three sides of the chamber. 7: Possible elevation of Jesus' shrouded body. The chamber is taken to be a little more than eleven feet wide and slightly less than six feet in height.

Bibliography. C. Couasnon, *The Church of the Holy Sepulchre Jerusalem* (1974); V. Corbo, "La Basilica del S. Sepolcro a Gerusalemme," *Liber Annuus,* XIX (1969), 65-144; R. H. Smith, "The Church of the Holy Sepulcher: Toward an Ecumenical Symbol," *The Yale Re-*

view, LV (1965), 34-56, and "The Tomb of Jesus," BA, XXX (1967), 74-90; K. M. Kenyon, *Jerusalem: Excavating 3000 Years of History,* (1968), pp. 146-54 and Fig. 15, and *Digging Up Jerusalem* (1974), pp. 226-34, 261-67; L. E. C. Evans, "The Holy Sepulchre," PEQ, C (1968), 112-36. R. H. SMITH

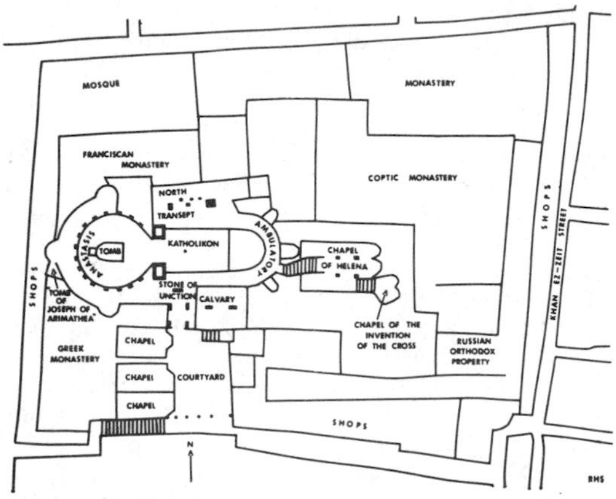

From the *Biblical Archaeologist,* XXX; by permission of the American Schools of Oriental Research

16. Plan of the Church of the Holy Sepulchre and adjoining buildings. Redrawn by R. H. Smith from a plan by Conrad Schick and C. Mommert.

HOMILY. *See* FORM CRITICISM, NT[S].

***HOMOSEXUALITY.** The previous article cited the study of D. S. Bailey but took no notice of its arguments and conclusions. Bailey argued that the homosexual interpretation of the sin of Sodom is not found in the OT, the Apocrypha, or the Talmud, but was a reinterpretation developed by Pseudepigraphists, Josephus, and Philo which was then accepted by the church and made the basis of its teaching that those who indulge in homosexual acts bring on themselves and all who tolerate such depravity the vengeance of God. Bailey regarded it as significant that none of the biblical condemnations of homosexual practices (Lev. 18:22; 20:13; Rom. 1:26-27; I Cor. 6:9-10; I Tim. 1:10) mention the Sodom story. The references to the wickedness of Sodom in Jer. 23:14 and Ezek. 16:49-50; Wisd. Sol. 10:8; and Ecclus. 16:8 do not suggest homosexuality. Only in the late NT books, II Peter and Jude, are homosexual practices connected with the sin of Sodom. It is the Palestinian Pseudepigrapha which reflect the development of the sexual and homosexual interpretation of that sin. The references discussed by Bailey include passages from Jubilees (7:20-21; 13:17; 16:5-6; 20:5-6) and the Testaments of the Twelve Patriarchs (Naph. 3:4-5; 4:1; Asher 7:1; Benj. 9:1; Levi 14:6), II Enoch 10:4; 24:2; III Macc. 2:5. Philo of Alexandria expressly associated the sin of Sodom with pederasty, attributing to the verb "know" in Gen. 19:5 homosexual coital connotation (*Quaestiones et Solutiones in Genesin* iv. 37, and in the treatise *De Abrahamo* (xxvi. 134-136) Philo tells us that the Sodomites in their mad lust violated not only the marriages of their neighbors, "but also men mounted males without respect for the sex nature which the active partner shares with the passive." The result of this activity was sterility for the aggressors while the passive partners were saddled with the curse of a female disease. Philo's Sodom, according to Bailey (p. 22), reflects not so much the biblical city of the plain as later life on the Mediterranean shores (depicted in lurid detail by Petronius and Juvenal), and similarly with Josephus' references to Sodomite abuses (Antiq. I.xi.1 [194-195], 3 [200]).

It is striking that rabbinic literature knows little of the homosexual interpretation of the sin of Sodom. The offense of the Sodomites was mainly that they were mean, inhospitable, uncharitable, and unjust (T.B. Sanh. 109a; Er. 49a; Keth. 103a; B.B. 12b, 59a, 168a; AB. 5). The single midrashic reference to homosexual activity (Genesis Rabbah 50.7) by the Sodomites explains that they subjected strangers to sexual assault and robbed them. The Fathers of the church, however, had no doubt that the Sodomites were addicted to pederasty and that this was the ground for the wrath visited on them. The homosexual interpretation has profoundly influenced Western attitudes and legislation, but Bailey argued that the Sodom story has no bearing on the modern problem, that it cannot be held that the divine wrath on Sodom is still determinative for the attitude of church or state toward sexual inversion.

Whatever the influence of Jewish reaction to the homosexual practices encountered in the Diaspora, there can be no question that the understanding of the Pseudepigraphists and the church Fathers was well founded, that the Sodomites' offense, like that of the men of Gibeah (Judg. 19:22), was the demand for carnal knowledge of a neighbor's guests (cf. ABi, I on Gen. 19:5).

The previous article mentioned sacral homosexual prostitution in connection with foreign cults and suggested that this may have been a factor in the strong biblical repudiation of homosexuality. The adjective "foreign" is questionable, since these cults were doubtless long established in Syria-Palestine, and all over the ancient Near East, in pre-Israelite times. The term *qādhēsh,* "holy one" (cf. Deut. 23:17 [H 18]; I Kings 14:24; 15:12; 22:46; II Kings 23:7) rendered "sodomite" by KJV and "male cult prostitute" by RSV, may designate the catamite homosexual, as Jerome assumed in the rendering of Job 36:14 (*inter effeminatos*). The excesses of these hierodules apparently reduced their life expectancy (cf. ABi, XV on Job 36:14). Religious sanction for phenomena associated with homosexuality is better documented in ancient Mesopotamia than in other parts of the Near East. The *assinnu, kulu'u,* and *kurgarrû,* cult functionaries of the love and war goddess Inanna/Ishtar, are mentioned in terms suggestive of homosexuality. Of the *assinnu* and *kurgarrû* we are told (Erra IV. 55) that the goddess "changed them from men to women in order to show the people piety." The technique by which the change was effected may well have been castration. Eunuchs figured prominently in the goddess cults of the Near East, in the worship of Cybele, the Dea Syria, Hecate, Aphrodite of Aphaca, and the Scythian mother goddess. The ancients apparently believed that certain sacred functions could only be properly performed by one qualified for them by perfect continence, hence many cults required as ministers virgins living in chastity or children who had not attained puberty. The eunuch castrated himself in enthusiasm at the sacred festival of the goddess in order to be perfectly fitted to serve the object of his devotion throughout life. The paradox of the infertile serving a fertility deity need not detain us here. Eunuchs after the transformation dressed distinctively and to some degree acted as women, thus the classical characterizations *in mulieres transformantur* or *emolliuntur in feminas* correspond to the earlier Akkadian "change from a man into a woman" (cf. entry "zikrūtu" 2, in *CAD*, XXI, 117a).

Transvestitism, prohibited by biblical laws (Deut. 22:5), is commonly associated with sexual inversion. In a sacred marriage hymn of Iddin Dagan (cf. D. Reisman, *JCS*, XXV [Oct. 1973], No. 4, 187) the hierodules are described as parading before the goddess, primping and decorated with colored bands, skipping rope, and adorned on the right side of the body with women's dress and the left side with men's. The bilateral combination of male and female clothing suggests either androgyny or sexual ambiversion, or both. Of overt homosexual activity on the part of the hierodules we have no witness, although there is reference to a man having intercourse with an *assinnu* (cf. *CAD*, I, part 2 [A] 431b). The *kulu'u*, a sort of actor-dancer-musician, is called "bedfellow" and "lover" of the goddess, yet it is said of a certain member of the profession, one Ninurta-tukulti-Ashur, "he is a *kulu'u*, not a (he-) man" (*CAD*, VIII, 529a). It is not clear what a *kulu'u* might do for the goddess as lover and bedfellow. For the *assinnu* and *kurgarrû*, *CAD* (A II, 341-42 and VIII, 557) denies that there is any specific evidence that they were homosexual and suggests that the Erra passage may mean simply that Ishtar changed their interest from the male to the female role. *See* ANDROGYNY[S].

Secular homosexual activity, casual or otherwise, is not well documented for ancient Mesopotamia, but there are occasional hints. We are told that the hero Gilgamesh continually imposed himself with unbridled arrogance on males as well as females, "Gilgamesh leaves not the son to [his] father" (cf. Tablet I [ii] lines 16-17, 22-23, *ANET* [2nd ed.], pp. 73-74), but we are not explicitly informed that the imposition was sexual. The friendship of Gilgamesh and Enkidu has been suspect since Enkidu, created as a match for Gilgamesh, was lured from his animal associates by a sacred prostitute and became Gilgamesh's companion after being rejected by his former associates, the animals. The Mesopotamian legal codes virtually ignore homosexual acts. The Middle Assyrian laws prescribe that a man who spreads a rumor against his neighbor that people have lain with him repeatedly, and is unable to prove it, may be flogged, sentenced to a month's royal corvée, marked (castrated?), and fined a talent of lead (Tablet A #19). If a man is convicted of lying with a neighbor, they shall lie with him and turn him into a eunuch (Tablet A #20; *ANET*, p. 181).

Among the Hittites there was apparently no prohibition of homosexual activity as such, but if a man violated his son, it was an abomination, or a capital crime. The concern in this instance was not the homosexual act, but incest which, like bestiality, was an abomination (cf. *ANET*, pp. 196-97).

From Ugarit we get no information on homosexuality or social attitudes toward it. There is reference in one of the mythological texts to conduct of the divine servant girls which was so disgusting that Baal rose and spat in the midst of the assembly of the gods, but there is no hint as to the nature of the offense, only that it was a banquet or sacrifice (*dbḥ*) characterized by shame (*bṯt*) and lewdness (*tdmm*) on the part of the serving wenches (*amht*; 4 [51]. III. 11-22). Since Baal was not noted for delicacy in such matters, we may wonder what manner of misconduct could have so offended him.

Among the ancient Egyptians, pederasty was not approved. The negative confession or protestation of guiltlessness in the 125th chapter of the Book of the Dead, which is one of the few sources of information on Egyptian social law, twice presents the protestation "I have not had sexual relations with a boy" (A 20, B 27, cf. *ANET*, pp. 34-35). The myth of Horus and Seth, however, presents an episode which suggests that homosexual abuse of a defeated foe was practiced occasionally. In the course of their protracted contest, Seth tricked Horus by pretending to seek reconciliation, invited him to his house, sodomized him as he slept, and then claimed dominion on the ground that he had performed doughty deeds of war against his opponent (cf. J. Gwynn Griffiths, *The Conflict of Horus and Seth* [1960], pp. 41-46). It thus appears that humiliation of a defeated foe or a helpless stranger was practiced in places other than Sodom and Gibeah. In the book of Job there are a couple of passages, 19:22*b* and 31:31-32 which are suggestive of sexual abuse of the stranger (cf. ABi [3rd ed.], XV, 143 and 236-37).

Among other biblical passages open to homosexual interpretation is the story of Joseph and Potiphar. There was rabbinic suspicion that Potiphar's interest in Joseph was sexual (T.B. Sot. 13b). Whether the term *sārîs* applied to Potiphar meant that he was a eunuch (so NEB, Gen. 39:1), impotent, or effeminate, is moot. The behavior of Potiphar's wife is understandable apart from this possible factor.

The friendship of David and Jonathan has provoked suspicion because of the line in David's lament, "Your love to me was wonderful, passing the love of women" (II Sam. 1:26). Whether there was any sexual involvement in the intimacy with Jonathan, David's heterosexual character is well attested and his ample experience with women enhances the tribute to Jonathan's love.

Evidence for female homosexuality in the biblical world is sparse, apart from Sappho of Lesbos and her school. Biblical law forbade a woman to lie with an animal (Lev. 18:23; 20:16), but says nothing about lying with another woman. The attachment of Ruth and Naomi (Ruth 1:16) has been cited by contemporary champions of Lesbianism, but on very slender grounds. Paul's strictures against women who exchanged natural use for that contrary to nature (Rom. 1:26) may include tribadism or other forms of sexual contact between women, since the corresponding charge against men who do "likewise" manifestly refers to homosexual practices. It has been suggested, however, that the female perversion envisaged may have been merely reversal of the succumbent coital position, regarded as natural to the female, for the incumbent ("missionary") position deemed natural by and for the male. It seems likely, despite the ambiguity, that Rom. 1:26 alludes to female homosexual activity parallel to that of males, this being the sole biblical allusion of the sort. Lack of concern about female homosexuality, in contrast to the serious view taken of such activity among males, was doubtless due in large measure to belief in the sanctity of semen. Without understanding of ovulation and the female role in conception, the ancients supposed that the semen supplied the essential material which coagulated with menstrual fluid to produce the embryo or fetus. The woman's part was to serve as a receptacle and incubator in which the semen was planted, like seed in a field. Human semen was regarded as almost a person (*met' oligon anthrōpon,* as Clement of Alexandria put it), and should not be profaned, misused, wasted, or lost whether by *coitus interruptus,* masturbation, homosexual coitus, *fellatio,* or any other "unnatural" or improper means. Rabbinic concern about defilement through accidental and involuntary emission was doubtless related to the notion of the sanctity of semen. This notion has been a major factor in the serious view of male homosexual activity and comparative unconcern for parallel phenomena among females up to the present.

There are other biblical references and terms which have sexual implication and may include homosexual as well as heterosexual offenses. The "dog" of Deut. 23:18 [H 19], whose wages were unacceptable in the house of the Lord, appears to be synonymous with the male cult prostitute proscribed in the previous verse. The term "dogs" (*klbm*) is applied to cult functionaries of an Ashtarte temple in Cyprus (*KAI* 37B, line 10). The suggestion (cf. *BASOR,* 216, 56a) that these "dogs" were cult personnel dressed like dogs does not explain why they should be associated with whores and their revenue excluded from the temple (Deut. 23:18 [H 19]). Whether the "dogs" (κύνες) of Rev. 22:15 refer to male prostitutes, holy or profane, is uncertain. In Rev. 21:8 ἐβδελυγμένοις has been taken to refer to sexual perverts, but there is no proof of this. More provocative is the expression γενέσεως ἐναλλαγή "change of kind/sex," in Wisd. Sol. 14:26 which RSV renders "sex perversion," JB "sins against nature," and NAB "unnatural lust." It has been argued that this "change" refers merely to the general effects of syncretism, intermarriage, and the like, which obliterated distinctions between Jews and non-Jews, without particular reference to sexual inversion or perversion. The context, however, favors RSV's explicitly sexual and implicitly homosexual interpretation. The ἐναλλαγή recalls the Akkadian terminology applied to the change of Ishtar's hierodules from male to female.

Paucity of precise terminology for distinction of different modes of homosexual practice makes it all the more important to preserve differentiations where found. In I Cor. 6:9 the terms μαλακοί and ἀρσενοκοῖται are rendered by KJV as "effeminate" and "abusers of themselves with mankind." Moffatt more precisely rendered "catamites and sodomites," but RSV lumped the two terms together in the first edition as "homosexuals" and in the second edition as "sexual perverts," both translations imprecise and unlikely to find favor in the present climate of concern in this matter.

Claims have been made in recent years that Jesus was a sexual invert. Arguments in support of this view have been—and will in the nature of the case continue to be—too subjective for review in a brief article. Reference is given below to some of the discussions in news media and other literature.

Bibliography. J. Z. Eglinton, *Greek Love* (1971), pp. 50-55, on antisexual and antihomosexual orientation of the Bible; W. B. Parker, *Homosexuality: A Selective Bibliography of over 3,000 Items* (1971), the following items follow his enumeration: (41) J. H. Foster, *Sex Variant Women in Literature* (1958); (457) C. Larere, "The Passage of the Angels through Sodom," in *New Problems in Medical Ethics,* ed. Peter Flood (1955); (962) "Playboy Forum," *Playboy,* XV (Sept. 1968), 82, 220-221; (1042) "The Sins of Sodom," *Time,* LXXXII (Sept. 6, 1963), 54; (1094) "Was Jesus an Outsider?" *Newsweek,* LXX (Aug. 7, 1967), 83; (1134) "The Bible and the Homosexual," *Christianity Today,* XII (Jan. 19, 1968) 24-25; XII (March 1, 1968), 33; (1238) B. L. Smith, "Homosexuality in the Bible and the Law," *Christianity Today,* XIII (July 18, 1969), 7-10; (1252) H. Williamson, "Sodom and Homosexuality," *Clergy Review,* XLVIII (Aug. 1963), 507-14, and reply, XLVIII (Oct. 1963), 650-51; (2963) R. W. Wood, "Homosexual Behavior in the Bible," *One Institute Quarterly,* V (1962), 10-19.
M. H. Pope

***HOPE IN THE OT. 1. Terminology.** In contrast to the NT, where hope as a theological concept is expressed by the noun ἐλπίς and the verb ἐλπίζειν (e.g., Rom. 5:3-5), the OT does not have such clearly defined terminology. The nouns תקוה and תוחלת and the corresponding verbs קוה and יחל are widely used. קוה denotes tense expectation, a looking forward to some event. An element of tension is suggested by the nouns from the same root, קו and תקוה, which mean "cord" or "rope." This element is not found in the verb יחל, which merely signifies waiting to see what is to come. Noah waits seven days each time he sends out the doves from the ark in order to assess the changing situation (Gen. 8:10, 12). Other verbs denoting "waiting" can incorporate the idea of hope in certain circumstances, e.g., שבר in Ps. 104:27: "These all look [wait in hope] to thee, to give them their food in due season." מורש, which may be translated "hope" in Job 17:11, contains an element of desire. The component of futurity in hope is expressed very clearly when תקוה is either directly connected with, or given in parallel with, the word אחרית, meaning "result, future" (Jer. 29:11; Prov. 23:18; 24:14). The concept of hope includes a good outcome. Similarly, the word "hope" today not only signifies the subjective process of inner tension with regard to what is hoped for, but also can objectively mean the object of hope toward which this inner tension is directed. Etymologically מבט denotes the idea of being on the lookout for something. The three times it appears in the OT (Isa. 20:5-6 and Zech. 9:5), it is used graphically to mean the military power upon which the various nations believed they could rely. This leads to another aspect of hope in the OT to which the LXX especially points. Of the one hundred places where the Hebrew equivalent of the Greek ἐλπίζειν can be determined, not less than forty-seven come under בטח, which is usually translated "trust." This indicates that hope can refer not only to an object, but also to another person.

2. The concept of hope suggested by OT terminology. ***a. Wisdom literature.*** By psychological observation, it can be affirmed that hope (תוחלת) is something which promotes life (Prov. 13:12). Good upbringing represents a "hope" (תקוה) for the formation of a young person (19:18). More important are verses which base hope upon righteous behavior: "The desire [תאוה] of the righteous ends only in good; the expectation [תקוה] of the wicked in wrath" (11:23). The truly wise man knows that "the fear of the Lord is the beginning of knowledge" (1:7). Thus it can also be said of this wisdom that, if you find it, you have a future (אחרית) and your hope (תקוה) will not be cut off (23:18). Fear of the Lord also includes a trust in God which dares to forego retaliation for evil: "Do not say, 'I will repay evil'; wait for [קוה] the Lord, and he will help you" (20:22).

The book of Job is critical of assertions that human beings may have hope because of just actions. Eliphaz insists that fear of God and integrity always make hope possible. "Is not your fear of God your confidence, and the integrity of your ways your hope [תקוה]? Think now, who that was innocent ever perished? Or where were the upright cut off?" (4:6-7; cf. 8:13; 11:14-18). Job, who scarcely has enough strength to wait in hope, rejects this view. His only "hope" is to be called from life by God (6:8-9). Bitterly he remarks: "He breaks me down on every side, and I am gone, and my hope [תקוה] has he pulled up like a tree" (19:10; cf. 14:19). "But when I looked [קוה] for good, evil came; and when I waited [יחל] for light, darkness came" (30:26). The bond between fear of God and hope as a human possibility is entirely destroyed. Only if God himself did the impossible could Job's hope persist: "Oh that you wouldest hide me in Sheol, that thou wouldest conceal me until thy wrath be past. . . . All the days of my service I would wait [wait in hope, יחל], till my release should come. Thou wouldest call, and I would answer thee; thou wouldest long for the work of thy hands" (14:13-15). The possibility of hope lies only in a new, freely willed gift of the Creator.

A skeptical judgment of human possibility as regards hope can be found in Eccl. 9:4-6. Here death is the power which makes any human hope appear questionable.

b. The Psalms. Ps. 119 views Yahweh's word as the basis for hope. "Remember thy word to thy servant in which thou hast made me hope [יחל]" (vs. 49; cf. vss. 74, 81, 114, 147). However, most of the time God himself is the object of hope in the Psalms: "I am weary with my crying; my throat is parched. My eyes grow dim with waiting [יחל] for my God" (69:3 [H 4]). References to hope can be found in the descriptions of individual waiting (62:5 [H 6]; 130:5-6), in the general formula of trust "let none that wait [קוה] for thee be put to shame" (25:3; cf. vss. 5, 21), and in appeal to others (130:7) or to oneself (42:5 [H 6]; 43:5). They are also present in the song of thanksgiving, sung by the one who has endured suffering and has received help (40:1-2 [H 2-3]).

In Psalm 39 the inescapable reality of death is soberly captured and clarified; there can be no existential hope for man (vss. 5-6 [H 6-7]). The Psalmist asks himself the question: "And now, Lord, for what do I wait [קוה]?" and then answers, "My hope [תוחלת] is in thee" (vs. 7 [H 8]). A similar inner tension can be found in Lam. 3, where the one making the prayer states after the fall of Jerusalem: "Gone is my glory, and my expectation from the Lord" (vs. 18), only to confess afterward: "This I call to mind, and therefore I have hope [יחל]: The steadfast love of the Lord never ceases. . . . 'Therefore I will hope [יחל] in him.' The Lord is good to those who wait for him [קוה], to the soul that seeks him" (vss. 21-25; cf. 27, 29).

The question inevitably arises as to why the speakers in the Psalms and Lam. 3 are confident that those who are condemned to death can have hope in Yahweh. To find the answer we must investigate the phenomenon of hope in the OT aside from specific terminology.

3. Hope in the narrative, prophetic, and apocalyptic writings. ***a. The narrative writings.*** In Job and in the Psalms the validity of hope cannot be established by human means or achievement, but only by Yahweh. The PENTATEUCH exhibits a similar view, especially in two of its sections. First, there is the story of the patriarchs in Gen. 12–50. The YAHWIST (J) has joined a series of accounts showing man's guilt and God's reactions (Gen. 3–11) with the story of the promise to Abraham (Gen. 12:2-3). A nation descending from Abraham and possession of the land of Canaan are the content of God's promise, for which the patriarchs must wait. The PRIESTLY WRITERS (P) tell the story with a different flavor, creating the theological concept of "sojourn in a foreign land," during which time the patriarchs are called by God to wait for the fulfillment of the promise. The episode in which Abraham acquires a grave for Sarah (Gen. 23) presents an impressive act of hope. Patient waiting for possession of the whole country is combined with the certainty that this is the Promised Land; therefore, the dead can be laid to rest here in the period of waiting. Both accounts are governed by the knowledge that it is God's word of promise that provides the actual power for all hope. *See* PROMISES TO THE PATRIARCHS[S].

The same can be said for the second Pentateuchal section: the exodus from Egypt and the wandering in the desert. Here the nation is under way, but has not yet reached the Promised Land. It wanders toward its desired goal, facing the constant danger of the temptation to betray its call. Maag correctly perceives that Israel's migrations prior to taking possession of the land have helped to shape all subsequent belief. "God leads to a future which is not just a repetition and confirmation of the present. . . . The goal gives meaning to the wandering and its difficulties; the present decision to trust in God is symbolic of what is to come." Preuss also views the hopeful waiting for the future, which typifies Israel's belief, as based upon the exodus proclamation.

Taking possession of the land of Canaan appears to bring the hope of the patriarchs and of the exodus generation to its fulfillment. The DEUTERONOMIC HISTORY shows, however, how the land is lost again as the result of Israel's disobedience. But the writer lets a hope shine forth in the concluding episode that recounts the raising up of the deported Davidic king (II Kings 25:27-30), a hope based upon the promise to the house of David through the prophet Nathan (II Sam. 7).

b. The prophets. Although it might seem as if Amos had for Israel only a stern "no," or at most an "it may be that the Lord, the God of hosts, will be gracious to the remnant of Joseph" (5:15), there is nevertheless in Hosea a hope that the nation will be restored after a new period of judgment in the desert (2:16-23; cf. 11:8-9; *see* HOSEA[S] §5). In Isaiah hope for a new work which Yahweh will do on Zion (14:32; 28:16-17*a*) and through the house of David (9:6-7; 11:1-3) can be seen among the sharp pronouncements of judgment (*see* ISAIAH[S] §2*b, e-f*). Popular expressions of hope (קוה) are rejected by Jeremiah (14:19–15:1). Yet, at the time of the imminent catastrophe, he buys land in Anathoth and proclaims: "Houses and fields and vineyards shall again be bought in this land" (32:15). In the supplement to the letter which Jeremiah sent to the exiles (probably post-Jeremiah), there is much said about hope: "For I know the plans that I have for you, says the Lord, plans for welfare and not for evil, to give you a future and a hope [אחרית ותקוה]" (29:11). To speak of hope and salvation becomes the great commission of Ezekiel after 587, and of the somewhat younger Deutero-Isaiah. Ezekiel turns sharply against the people remaining in the country in 587, because they appeal to Abraham as a figure of hope without changing their lives: "Abraham was only one man, yet he got possession of the land, but we are many; the land is surely given us to possess" (33:24). But to those who sigh, shattered by punishment, "Our bones are dried up, and our hope [תקוה] is lost; we are clean cut off" (37:11), he proclaims his unprecedented vision of the raising of the dried bones. A more detailed description of the return to the Promised Land becomes the task of Deutero-Isaiah, who can speak of hopeful expectation being fulfilled. "But they who wait [קוה] for the Lord shall renew their strength, they shall mount up with wings like eagles" (40:31; cf. 49:23; 51:5). *See* DISCIPLINE, DIVINE[S].

3. Apocalyptic. Hope becomes the focal point of apocalypticism, nourished by the expectation of a great crisis soon to befall the whole world, when God will call everyone to judgment. The apocalyptic visions which Daniel sees are pervaded by eschatological impatience for the establishment of a "kingdom which shall never be destroyed" (Dan. 2:44), and which is given to "the holy people of God."

It is easy to understand how such suspenseful expectation has its roots in prophetic proclamation of judgment and new beginning (*see* APOCALYPTICISM; APOCALYPTICISM[S]; TORAH[S]). Ezek. 38–39 portrays destruction of an enemy from the N "in the latter years," reflecting the belief that Jeremiah's prophecy about the enemy from the N and Isaiah's expectation of the destruction of the Assyrians on Yahweh's mountain were not limited to past fulfillment, and thus could be applied anew. The so-called Isaiah apocalypse (Isa. 24–27) speaks of judgment over all the powers of heaven and earth (24:21-23) and of the invitation to the great feast of nations on the mountain of the Lord (25:6-8). Thus hope was sustained that Yahweh was not allowing his old promises to go unfulfilled.

In all of this we see that the hope of Israel according to the OT does not exist through human works, but exists solely through Yahweh's faithfulness to his promise.

Bibliography. C. Westermann, "(Das Hoffen im Alten Testament) Eine Begriffsuntersuchung," *Theologia viatorum*, IV (1953), 19-70 (=*Forschung am Alten Testament*, Theol. Bücherei, XXIV [1964], 219-65); T. Vriezen, "Die Hoffnung im Alten Testament," *TLZ*, LXXVIII (1953), cols. 577-86; J. van der Ploeg, "L'espérance dans l'Ancien Testament," *RB*, LXI (1964), 481-507; V. Maag, "Malkût Jhwh," VTSup, VII (1960), 129-53; H. Preuss, *Jahweglaube und Zukunftserwartung*, V/7 (1968); W. Zimmerli, *Man and His Hope in the OT* (1971).

W. ZIMMERLI

***HORITES.** *See* HURRIANS[S] §3.

HORNS OF MOSES. Jerome's translation of Exod. 34:29 (in the Vulg.) reads: "When Moses came down from Mount Sinai . . . he did not know that his face was horned (*ignorabat quod cornuta esset facies sua*) because of his conversation with the Lord." Modern scholars have debated the correctness of his translation, often unaware of the explanation which he makes in his commentary on Ezekiel: Moses' face "had been 'glorified' (*glorificata erat*), or as it says in the Hebrew, 'horned' " (*Corpus Christianorum, SL*, LXXV, 557, lines 262-64). Thus he is using the term metaphorically (Mellinkoff), as is often done in the OT (e.g., I Sam. 2:1; Ps. 89:17, 24 [H 18, 25]; I Chr. 25:5) and in accordance with the LXX (δεδόξασται, "glorified"; so also at Exod. 15:2).

Most modern scholars had suggested that Jerome's translation was in error and that the Hebrew original (*qāran 'ôr pānāw*) means, "the skin of his face shone" (thus RSV and most modern versions). This seems to have been the understanding of the Byzantine artists who, as early as the sixth century, depicted Moses with a halo (Mellinkoff, Figs. 6-7), and most rabbinic texts reflect the same interpretation. Rashi, adhering more closely to the etymological meaning of *qāran*, speaks of light radiating from Moses' face in horn-shoped beams (cf. Mellinkoff, Fig. 68). This understanding is found in the Great Bible (1539): "the skinne of his face shone in manner of an horne."

Support for the "shining face" interpretation includes the ancient versions (e.g., the LXX read in accordance with II Cor. 3:7-18); the Arabic cognates *qarn* (the first visible part of the rising sun) and *qarîna* (eclampsia: medical condition which sometimes includes the perception of blinding light); the *melammu* (Heb. *kābhôdh*?), a radiant aureole which was said to surround Assyro-Babylonian deities and (occasionally) kings; and parallels in other cultures (Suhr). However, this interpretation is uncertain since the verb *qāran* (in the *qal*) occurs only in this one ambiguous context (Exod. 34:29, 30, 35). Its one other occurrence (in the *hiph'il*) clearly means "to display horns": Ps. 69:31 [H 32]. The noun from which it is derived (*qeren,* "horn"), used *ca.* eighty times in the OT, does not mean "light" (with one possible exception, the problematic Hab. 3:4 [RSV "rays"]), but rather denotes a horn-shaped object or is a metaphor for strength or pride.

A few modern scholars had suggested that Jerome rendered the text properly (preceded by the literalistic Aquila's κερατώδης ἦν), since horns or a horned turban are traditional ancient Near Eastern iconographic symbols for divinity (*see* Fig. H17) or for a deified king (*see* KING §7*c-d*; ASSYRIA AND BABYLONIA Fig. 96; MARI Fig. 14). Alexander (who claimed descent from Zeus) is shown on Greek coins with conspicuous horns, whereas only gods had been so depicted previously. This iconographic tradition continued until the time of Jerome and beyond, as shown by the horned gods of the Romans and the Parthians, NT descriptions of a horned devil (Rev. 12:3-9), and the description of Alexander in the Koran as "the two-horned one" (18:82, 85, 93; cf. the commentaries of Baidhawi, Zamakhšari, Jalalludin *et al.*), an epithet which was extended to Arab rulers (Freytag). It has also been suggested that Moses wore a ritual mask with horns, a practice attested in the ancient Near East (Jirku). However, such literal interpretations are problematic since deities or kings are depicted with horns growing from the forehead (*mēṣaḥ*), not from the face (*pānîm*); moreover, the subject of the verb is *'ôr* (skin) rather than *pānîm.* And thus the meaning of the Hebrew original remains uncertain.

Following Aelfric's Old English translation of *cornuta* as "gehyrned," artists in eleventh-century England began to depict Moses with a horned helmet such as nobility wore (Mellinkoff, Fig. 13), then later with horns projecting directly from his forehead (*see* Fig. H 18). Jerome's translation is the basis for medieval exegesis of the passage and is reflected in English translations prior to the Geneva Bible (1560) and thereafter in the Douay Version.

Bibliography. F. Dumermuth, "Moses strahlendes Gesicht," *TZ,* XVII (1961), 241-48; G. Freytag, *Lexicon Arabico-Latinum,* III (1837), 435, under *"qarn"*; A. Jirku, "Die Gesichtsmaske des Mose," *ZDPV,* LXVII (1944-45), 43-45; J. de Fraine, "Moses 'Cornuta facies' (Exod. 34, 29-35)," *Bijdragen Tijdschrift voor filosophie en theologie,* XX (1959), 28-38; J. MacCulloch, "Horns," *Encyclopedia of Religion and Ethics,* VI (1913), 791-96; R. Mellinkoff, *The Horned Moses in Medieval Art and Thought* (1970); J. Morgenstern, "Moses with the Shining Face," *HUCA,* II (1925), 1-27; L. Oppenheim, "Akkadian *pul(u)ḫ(t)u* and *melammu,*" *JAOS,* LXIII (1943), 31-34; G. Redslob, "Über den 'Zweihörnigen' des Koran," *ZDMG,* IX (1855), 214-23; I. Scheftelowitz, "Das Hörnermotiv in der Religionen," *Archiv für Religionswissenschaft,* XV (1912), 451-87; E. Suhr, "The Horned Moses," *Folklore,* LXXIV (1963), 387-95; E. Van Buren, "Concerning the Horned Cap of the Mesopotamian Gods," *Or,* XII (1943), 318-27.

L. R. BAILEY

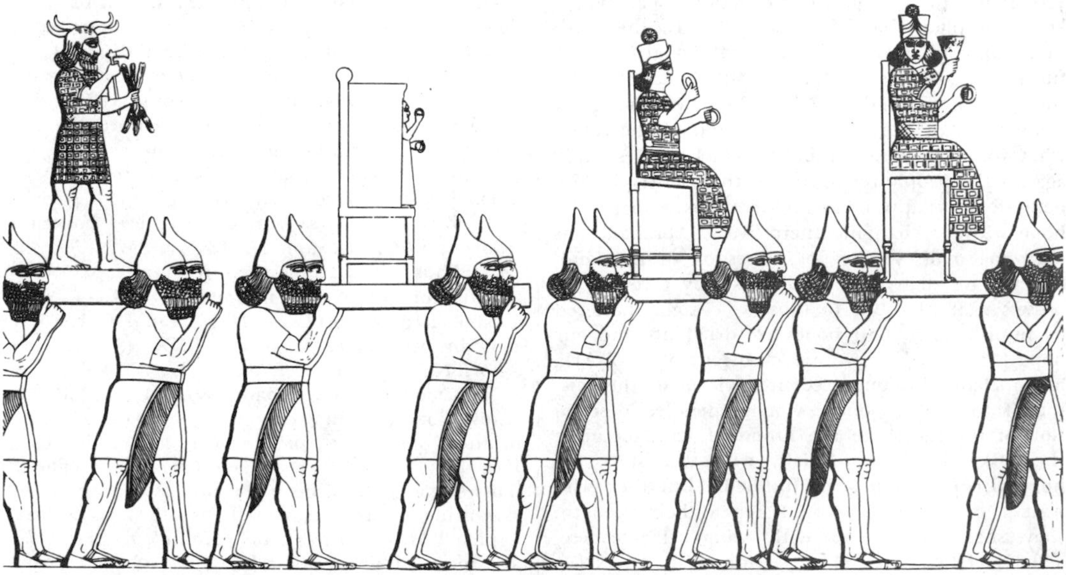

17. Assyrian soldiers of Tiglath-pileser III carry away the gods of a captured town. Horned god at left; deities with horned turbans at right. Wall relief from Nimrud.

Archives Photographiques

18. Bust of Moses, the old Carthusian Monastery of Champol, Dijon; sculpture by Claus Sluter

***HOSEA. 1. The historical setting of Hosea's oracles.** In addition to the editorial superscription (1:1), the principal clues to the historical background of Hosea's ministry are contained in 5:8-15 and 7:3-7. Alt's interpretation of the former passage has been almost universally accepted by commentators. It is that these lines condemn the kingdoms of Judah and Israel for their military acts against each other in the Syro-Ephraimite crisis of 735 B.C. and its aftermath, and for their international policies vis-à-vis Assyria during this period (cf. II Kings 15:37; 16:5-9; and Isa. 7:1-9). The Judean reprisal against Israel (Hos. 5:8-10) for her part in the invasion of the southern kingdom is in one sense a just punishment of the earlier act, but in another sense is fully culpable. Therefore, Judah will also be punished. Both kingdoms have resorted at various times to dependency upon Assyria as a means of national security, but in so doing have lost sight of the religious and moral dimensions of their corporate life, which have been undermined to the point of social collapse. The outward conquest of the two kingdoms will complete the divine judgment upon them.

Hosea 7:3-7 seems to reflect the dynastic chaos which prevailed in the northern kingdom from the time of Zechariah's murder in 746 B.C. (II Kings 15:8-10) to the reign of Hoshea, which began in 732, after his assassination of Pekah (II Kings 15:30). If this inference is correct, it means that Hosea's ministry extended into the last decade of the kingdom (732-722 B.C.). Whether he lived until Assyria conquered it in 722 is not indicated explicitly in the book, but it is not impossible. Indeed, in the judgment of some scholars it is likely that he did.

In addition to the light which this dating throws upon aspects of Hosea's oracles of judgment, it raises an important possibility for the critical estimate of the promises of renewal in the book (1:10-11; 2:1, 14-23; 11:10-11; and 14:1-8). These are regarded by some critics as postexilic additions to the book, on the ground that such a message of reassurance would have been inappropriate in the time when Hosea was condemning the nation for her moral, cultic, and political crimes, but would have been highly appropriate in a later time, when the remnant of the nation—or of the Judean kingdom which followed it into ruin—was broken and in despair. However, since Hosea may have witnessed the fall of Israel himself, and in any case did observe the last years of its life, it is not unreasonable to take the oracles of salvation as his own last word. It is important to see, however, that these oracles do not contradict the prophet's threat of destruction. They presuppose that the fall of the nation will have occurred.

2. Hosea's use of historical tradition. Hosea's proclamation of judgment and subsequent renewal is modeled on the ancient story of the exodus from Egypt, the wandering in the wilderness—where the covenant with Yahweh was made—and the settlement in the land of Palestine. This series of experiences would be repeated, in a sense, in the future. He proclaimed the impending exile of Israel as a return to "Egyptian" captivity (11:5; 7:16; 8:13; 9:3, 6, 17), and the eventual renewal of covenant and restoration of the nation as a second Exodus and settlement (2:14-23; 11:10-11; 14:4-7; cf. 1:11; 3:5). Thus he drew more fully than any other eighth-century prophet upon the historic traditions preserved in the Pentateuch. Furthermore, unlike AMOS, for example, who cited these traditions in order to dispute the popular view of their significance (Amos 3:1-2; 9:7-8*a*), or to support his condemnation of Israel (Amos 2:9-11), Hosea saw in them the fundamental clue to the way of God with Israel, not only in the past but also in the future. The future would not be merely a repetition of the past, but it would resemble it in certain essential respects. Hosea was thus the first prophet of a new Exodus and the first of the canonical prophets to interpret the whole of Israel's life—past, present, and future—in terms of a single, coherent, historical scheme.

3. Hosea 1–3. The romantic interpretation of Hosea's marriage has all but disappeared from current treatments of the book. The impossibility of recovering the history of his marital associations, particularly their interior dimensions, is acknowledged on all sides, and the oracles in chs. 1–3 are treated primarily as prophetic proclamations. Ch. 2 is entirely an allegory of Israel's covenantal history, and not a set of allusions to the prophet's marriage. The woman in ch. 3 may or may not be Gomer, Hosea's wife, but the meaning of the action, which is directly stated in the report, is what really matters. The symbolical names of Hosea's children (ch. 1) convey the substance of his judgment of Israel, but chs. 2 and 3 are each a representation of his full message of the "return to Egypt" and the new Exodus of salvation.

4. Liturgy and sacrifice. Criticism of the Israelite

cult is a persistent theme among the pre-exilic prophets, and it is nowhere more evident than in the book of Hosea (2:5-13; 3:1; 4:4-19; 5:1-2, 5-7; 5:15–6:6; 8:11-14; 9:1-5; 10:1-2; 13:1-3). The interpretation of this criticism which dominated OT scholarship prior to about 1950 was that the prophets rejected the ritual of the altar categorically as a corrupting factor in Israel's religion. The dominant view today is that the prophets did not reject the cult per se but only a Baalized cult—and one which was unaccompanied by moral uprightness and the pursuit of justice. This change in interpretation has been accompanied by a growing conviction on the part of many that the pre-exilic cult was much richer in verbal content—including moral exhortation and even prophetic proclamation—than the prescriptions for ritual in the Pentateuch suggest, devoted as they are to the forms of sacrifice, ritual purification, etc.

It is doubtless true, as is often said, that a cultless religion would have been inconceivable to the prophets, since some form of cult is universal in communal religious practice. However, there is a radical quality to the prophetic condemnation of the rituals built around the sacrifice of animals—and the manipulation of their blood—and products of the soil that cannot be denied. According to Hosea this system, along with the kingship which supported it, was an obstacle to faithful obedience and the knowledge of God. And since true reformation was beyond the will or capacity of priesthood, court, or people, only a destruction of the cultic and political institutions by conquest would suffice to make a genuine renewal possible. This destruction would be an act both of divine justice and of divine grace, that is to say a punishment brought about by the moral, political, and social dissolution of the covenant community, and, at the same time, an opportunity for covenant renewal. Hosea—like all the pre-exilic prophets—makes no prescription for the forms of public worship in the future community, but he does suggest, both by the implications of his oracles of doom and by the actual words of the last oracle in the book, that God should be approached in the time of return with an offering of words alone, without material sacrifices (14:2). The MT reads, "We will render the *bulls* of our lips." This is commonly emended to "fruit of our lips," but the Hebrew may be correct. The meaning is that the proper "bulls" to be offered to God in future are merely verbal offerings—prayer and praise. *See* GRACE IN THE OT[S].

5. The message of Hosea. Hosea's prophecy of doom for the kingdom of Israel and its cult was unconditional. He did not offer the possibility of a reprieve in return for repentance. Rather he viewed the destruction of state and cult as the necessary precondition of repentance. Thus, the people's only real hope lay on the far side of calamity. Yet it was a real hope—grounded in the undying love of God for his children (11:8-11; 2:14-23; 1:10-11). By speaking of God's relation to Israel in terms of the most intimate human relations—parent-child and husband-wife—Hosea deepened and enriched the biblical witness of faith and influenced subsequent prophetic tradition profoundly. Perhaps his other most notable theological contribution is his insight into the personal and social dynamics of behavior—the relationship of action to will and disposition, the pervasive self-destruction worked by the apostate heart, the moral interdependence of all the members of a community, for good or ill, and the need for divine initiative to break the web of corporate self-enslavement. In this, as in his understanding of the judging-saving grace of God, Hosea is unsurpassed among the writers of the OT.

See also DISCIPLINE, DIVINE[S].

Bibliography. Commentaries and general works: W. Brueggemann, *Tradition for Crisis, a Study in Hosea* (1968); E. Jacob, *Osée,* CAT, XI*a* (1965); J. Mauchline, IB, VI (1956), pp. 553-725; J. L. Mays, *Hosea: A Commentary* (1969); G. C. Morgan, *Hosea: The Heart and Holiness of God* (1960); W. Rudolph, *Hosea, KAT,* XIII/1 (1966); N. H. Snaith, *Mercy and Sacrifice* (1953); J. M. Ward, *Hosea: A Theological Commentary* (1966); H. W. Wolff, BKAT, XIV/1 (1961 [2nd ed., 1965]).

Special studies: P. R. Ackroyd, "Hosea and Jacob," *VT,* XIII (1963), 245-59; A. Alt, "Hosea 5,8-6,6. Ein Krieg und seine Folgen in prophetischer Beleuchtung," *NKZ,* XXX (1919), 537-68=*Kleine Schriften* II (1953), 163-87; M. J. Buss, *The Prophetic Word of Hosea, a Morphological Study, BZAW,* CXI (1969); R. B. Coote, "Hosea XII," *VT,* XXI (1971), 389-402; J. F. Craghan, "The Book of Hosea, A Survey of Recent Literature," BThB, I (1971), 81-101, 145-70; W. Eichrodt, "The Holy One in Your Midst: The Theol. of Hosea," *Int.,* XV (1961), 259-73; H. L. Ginsberg, "Studies in Hosea 1-3," *Yehezkel Kaufmann Jubilee Volume,* ed. M. Haran (1960), pp. 50-69; E. M. Good, "The Composition of Hosea," *SEA,* XXXI (1966), 21-63, and "Hosea 5,8-6,6: An Alternative to Alt," *JBL,* LXXXV (1966), 273-86; J. L. McKenzie, "Divine Passion in Osee," *CBQ,* XVII (1955), 287-99, and "Knowledge of God in Hosea," *JBL,* LXXIV (1955), 22-27; E. H. Maly, "Messianism in Osee," *CBQ,* XIX (1957), 213-25; D. Ritschl, "God's Conversion, an Exposition of Hosea 11," *Int.,* XV (1961), 286-303; W. F. Stinespring, "A Problem of Theological Ethics in Hosea," *Essays in Old Testament Ethics,* ed. J. L. Crenshaw and J. T. Willis (1974), pp. 131-43; *Studies on the Books of Hosea and Amos,* by Members of Die OT Werkgemeenskap in Suid-Afrika, 1964-65; J. M. Ward, "The Message of the Prophet Hosea," *Int.,* XXIII (1969), 387-407; J. Wijngaards, "Death and Resurrection in Covenantal Context (Hos. VI 2)," *VT,* XVII (1967), 226-39; H. W. Wolff, "Guilt and Salvation, a Study of the Prophecy of Hosea," *Int.,* XV (1961), 274-85.

J. M. WARD

***HUMILITY IN THE NT.** The terms ταπεινός, πραΰς, and their cognates designate in the NT a kind of humility and gentleness which are part of the gift of the Holy Spirit (Gal. 5:22-23).

1. Greek concepts of humiliation. The form of God's servanthood through Jesus, which is seen as worthy of imitation, finds a distinct antecedent in various Greek humiliation traditions about their hero-kings: Heracles, Odysseus, Cyrus, and Alexander. All these kings became exemplary, some as early as the time of Antisthenes (Diogenes Laertius VI.i.4), because of the humiliation they endured. Since this motif was isolated by the CYNICS and STOICS, it is possible that Paul had it in mind when in the Corinthian correspondence he alluded to the suffering role of the apostles. The Corinthians had already entered into their kingly role, but the apostles were "weak" and in "disrepute" (I Cor. 4:8 ff.). For Paul, establishing his authority over the Corinthians meant abasing himself by denying himself financial support (II Cor. 11:7). Just as in the earlier Greek poetry (e.g., Pindar, Nemean Odes I, 31 ff.) Heracles is portrayed as the figure who embodies *philanthropia* through suffering, as the victim of fate (Sophocles, *Trachiniae*), as slave though king, so Dio Chrysostom (Discourses VIII, 35) depicts his cleaning of the Augean stables as a deliberate humiliation with a moral purpose. Any humiliation according to Cynic values of the first century could have a positive good, particularly if voluntarily accepted (Epictetus III.xxii.54-59, xxvi.31-32). Poor, naked, and alone Heracles may be, but he is still held up as the righteous king. The Cynic portrait of Cyrus also stands alone in stressing the servant motif of his kingship. The Cynic Antisthenes regarded Cyrus as the ideal king who moved through afflictions and humiliations to kingship and turned disadvantages into advantages. The attributes of the ideal Cynic were defenselessness, voluntary suffering, self-abasement, and adaptability. Accordingly, Cynics believed that only the abased king was qualified to rule, e.g., Odysseus, mistreated by his slaves, himself attired in slave's garb, personally humiliated by the taunting Ajax. This contrast between inner tranquillity and external affliction, inner riches and external poverty, was central to Cynic conceptions of power, and was apparently in Paul's mind when he wrote to the Corinthians. For the Cynics the highest model for this behavior was Socrates, for Paul it was Jesus (Phil. 2:3-11). Because the humiliated one can triumph, the attitude of humility becomes a positive virtue.

2. Humility as a virtue. The vocabulary of humility was used by such major ethical writers as Aristotle, and as early as the Homeric poems one finds evidence of the value placed on humility by Greek writers. They advocated the golden mean in which persons viewed themselves not as gods but as men, avoiding both the errors of *hubris* as well as the errors of deliberate and paralyzing self-abasement.

The oppression, poverty, and political captivity under which the Jews suffered for the several centuries immediately preceding the rise of Christianity also contributed to the NT understanding of humility. The lowly dove became symbolic of God's people (e.g., II Esdras 5:23 ff.), and, most important, the hope arose that temporary humiliation would lead to eventual vindication after the model of Joseph (Test. Benj. 5:1-5). It was also affirmed that God chooses lowly people and seeks to achieve his highest goals with those who, in meekness and lowliness, retain an upright faith in the fulfillment of his purposes and promises despite all contrary evidence (*see* Moses, Assumption of). The NT writers, like the Essenes (1QS 5.3–6.25; 8.2), counsel the faithful to live in humility with each other and toward God (e.g., I Pet. 5:5-6); but now humility is thought of especially as an aspect of the lowliness of Jesus (e.g., Phil. 2:3 ff.; II Cor. 10:1).

Bibliography. A. Nissen, *Gott und der Nächste im antiken Judentum* (1974); A. Gelin, *The Poor of Yahweh* (3rd ed., 1959); S. Rehrl, *Das Problem der Demut in der profan-griechischen Literatur,* Aevum Christianum, IV (1961); R. Höistad, *Cynic Hero and Cynic King* (1948); A. Büchler, *Studies in Sin and Atonement* (1967), ch. 2; G. F. Moore, *Judaism,* II (1927), 272-75; W. Grundmann, "ταπεινός," *TDNT,* VIII (1969), 1-27; A. Dihle, "Demut," *RAC,* III (1957), cols. 735-78.

W. Klassen

***HURRIANS.** A people who first entered Mesopotamia from the NE during the late third millennium and then descended in large numbers in the centuries before 1500 B.C. to produce the powerful state of Mitanni. They are perhaps related to the Horites of the OT. They were an important factor in the spread of Sumero-Akkadian culture, particularly literature and religion, to the W, notably to the Hittites. Their characteristic sociojuridical customs, especially family law, have been seen as the background for a number of features of the patriarchal narratives. *See* Nuzi; Nuzi[S]; Mari[S] §8; Patriarchs[S] §1; Music[S].

1. Origin and language. *See* Hurrians.

2. History and geographical distribution. Hurrians first appear in Late Akkadian times, *ca.* 2300 B.C., at Urkish, a kingdom located in the hilly region of Upper Mesopotamia which remained the center of Hurrian civilization throughout their history. In this early period they had already borrowed the cuneiform syllabary and adapted it for writing their own language. All other evidence prior to 2000 B.C. shows the Hurrians confined to the region E of the Tigris and N of the Upper Zab, although a few individuals appear sporadically in Babylonia during the Ur III period.

During the centuries succeeding the fall of Ur III (*see* Sumer §2*c*), the Hurrians slowly penetrated into Upper Mesopotamia and northern Syria. Amorites form the vast majority of the population of Mari, the Hurrian influence being minimal. But in the N the Hurrian presence is much stronger: at Chagar Bazar they constitute about one third of the population. As the centuries pass, the Hurrian presence constantly increases and moves southward. The texts from Alalakh level VII (*see* Alalakh Texts[S]), *ca.* 1700, show that the Hurrians constitute more than a third of the population. By the time of Alalakh level IV in the fifteenth century, the Hurrians form the vast majority of the population and the society is Hurrianized in every respect. Further S at Ugarit in the fifteenth century the West Semites are in the majority but Hurrian influence is significant. In the eighteenth and seventeenth centuries, however, southern Syria and Palestine show no trace of Hurrian penetration.

In the light of the limited extent of Hurrian penetration into Syria prior to the sixteenth century, there seems little likelihood that they (and especially the Indo-Aryans associated with them in the later Mitanni kingdom) could have played any role in the Hyksos interlude in Egypt.

Almost no written evidence exists from NW Mesopotamia for the seventeenth and sixteenth centuries B.C. When our sources take up again *ca.* 1500, the Hurrian penetration into Syria has become a flood, and the Hurrian kingdom of Mitanni has united all of Upper Mesopotamia into one state, controlling territory from the Mediterranean to E of the Tigris. *See* MITANNI[S].

The Mitanni-Hurrians and their Indo-Aryan aristocracy seem to have introduced the composite bow and the defense for it, a type of scaled armor used on men, horses, and chariots (the Hurrian name of which appears in Egyptian, Akkadian, Hittite, Ugaritic, and Hebrew). These new weapons revolutionized warfare and became decisive in battle from the fifteenth century on.

Although the hegemony of the state of Mitanni was short lived, falling to the Hittite New Kingdom (*see* HITTITES[S]), the Hurrian immigration continued throughout the Near East. The TELL EL-AMARNA tablets from the fourteenth century reveal their presence in Palestine, but here they represent nothing more than a ruling class, imposed in feudal style on the city-state system. Texts from Palestine show no trace of the Hurrian substratum which now appeared everywhere N of the Biqa^{c} in central Syria. In fact, the majority of the non-Semitic names in these texts are Indo-Aryan, revealing the presence of the Mitannian military aristocracy, a fact which explains why the Egyptians could call Syria-Palestine, increasingly under the Nineteenth Dynasty, "Ḫuru-land." Cities which we can document as having been ruled by these Mitannian overlords, or having had such elements in their population, were all in Cisjordan and primarily in the N and the coastal region: Jerusalem, Shechem, Taanach, Megiddo, Acco, Achshaph, and in the S Ashkelon and possibly Hebron. The tenuous nature of the Hurrian presence in southern Syria and Palestine renders impossible the hypothesis that the spirantization of the labial, dental, and velar stops in Hebrew and Aramaic could be due to Hurrian influence, apart from the formidable linguistic problems involved. *See* HURRIANS §2.

3. The Hurrians and the Horites of the Bible. The Bible speaks of the "Horites," the Hebrew term *ḥôrî* being the exact equivalent of cuneiform *Ḫurri* (*see* HORITE). However, its usage presents us with a special problem when we attempt to relate it to the extrabiblical Hurrians. In the OT the Horites are described as the original population of Seir who were displaced by the Edomites (Deut. 2:12, 22; Gen. 36:20-30). Yet, the names of the Horites given in Gen. 36 are all Semitic. This, combined with the fact that we have no evidence in extrabiblical texts for Hurrians in this area, makes it extremely difficult to relate the two groups.

In the areas in Cisjordan where our extrabiblical evidence would suggest that Hurrians be found, the OT locates Hivites: at Shechem (Gen. 34:2), Gibeon (Josh. 9:7; 11:19), the mountains of Lebanon (Judg. 3:3), and below Hermon (Josh. 11:3). (*See* HIVITE.) In Gen. 36:2 the Hebrew text identifies Zibeon, son of Seir the Horite (Gen. 36:20, 29), as a Hivite and some LXX texts read Horites (MT Hivites) in Gen. 34:2 and Josh. 9:7.

The solution to these apparently conflicting facts is not apparent. Some scholars have simply reversed the roles of Hivites and Horites, hypothesizing that the two very similar names have become confused. This seems at best a desperate solution. Another attempt accepts the LXX reading of Horites for Hivites in Gen. 34:2 and Josh. 9:7 as correct, thus regarding Hurrians and Hivites as synonymous. The Horites of Gen. 36 would then be an unrelated Semitic tribe with a homophonous name. This hypothesis is preferable to the other, but it is based upon textual variants that may be mistaken readings. Thus, the Greek text of Aquila and Symmachus agrees with the MT in Gen. 34:2 while several MSS of the LXX, the Old Latin, the Syriac, and the Ethiopic agree with the MT at Josh. 9:7. Further, besides the Semitic names of the Shechemites in Gen. 34, they are identified as Canaanites in Gen. 34:30; while the Gibeonites are identified as Amorites in II Sam. 21:2.

The most recent hypothesis attempts a solution by recognizing the problem of the Israelite use of older nomenclature. Having rightfully reserved "Canaan" for Cisjordan, the Israelites applied Ḫuru, i.e., Horites, to southern Transjordan, for which area the received nomenclature had no term. The solution most probably must be sought along the lines of this last suggestion.

Bibliography. On the people and their culture: E. A. Speiser, "The Hurrian Participation in the Civilizations of Mesopotamia, Syria and Palestine" in *Oriental and Biblical Studies,* ed. J. Finkelstein and M. Greenberg (1967), pp. 244-69; H. G. Güterbock, "The Hurrian Element in the Hittite Empire," *Journal of World History,* II (1954), 383-94.

On the Hurrian expansion: I. J. Gelb, "The Early History of the West Semitic Peoples," *JCS,* XV (1961), 27-47; R. T. O'Callaghan, *Aram Naharaim* (1948); R. de Vaux, *Histoire ancienne d'Israël* (1971), pp. 69-71, 86-91; J.-R. Kupper, "Northern Mesopotamia and Syria," *CAH* (3rd ed.), II, ch. I; O. R. Gurney, "Anatolia c. 1750-1600 B.C.," *CAH* (3rd ed.), II, ch. VI; M. S. Drower, "Syria c. 1500-1400 B.C.," *CAH* (3rd ed.), II, ch. X; W. F. Albright, "The Amarna Letters from Palestine," *CAH* (3rd ed.), II, ch. XX.

On the Hurrians and the Horites: R. de Vaux, "Les Hurrites de l'histoire et les Horites de la Bible," *RB,* LXXIV (1967), 481-503; W. F. Albright, "The Horites in Palestine," *From the Pyramids to Paul,* ed. L. Leary (1935), pp. 9-26; E. A. Speiser, *Genesis* (1964), pp. 282-83; J. C. L. Gibson, "Observations on Some Important Ethnic Terms in the Pentateuch," *JNES,* XX (1961), 217-38.

F. W. BUSH

***HYKSOS.** A term used in Manetho's Hellenistic history *Aegyptiaca* to refer to a dynasty of foreign rulers of Egypt during the second intermediate period. By the Hellenistic period "Hyksos" was understood to mean "shepherd kings" but it actually corresponds to Egyp. *ḥq3w ḫ3swt,* "rulers of foreign lands," and refers primarily to rulers beyond the borders of Egypt. The term has no ethnic or geographic significance. The Turin canon of kings from the thirteenth century B.C. also designates a group of six rulers of Egypt as Hyksos, to be identified with Manetho's fifteenth dynasty (*ca.* 1670-1562 B.C.).

Josephus' version of the Manethoan tradition presents the rise of the Hyksos to power as the result of a great invasion and their eventual overthrow as an expulsion, and he associates these events with the biblical stories of Joseph and the Exodus. But such traditions of an invasion and expulsion, drawn primarily from folklore, have little historical value.

There are two basic factors in the Hyksos rise to power in Egypt. On the one hand, in the Middle Bronze Age (MB II, *ca.* 1900/1800-1550) a rather advanced urban and largely West Semitic culture, often called Amorite (*see* AMORITES[S]) developed numerous strong kingdoms throughout the Fertile Crescent. At the same time Egypt declined into a state of weakness and disunity at the end of the Middle Kingdom (*ca.* 1800 B.C.), permitting a considerable penetration of Asiatics into the eastern Delta. Toward the end of the Thirteenth Dynasty (after *ca.* 1725), disintegration of centralized authority resulted in a proliferation of local rulers in Lower Egypt, many of whom were Asiatic. The ruler of Avaris, a city in the Delta, gained sufficient power to put all Egypt under his control.

There is no evidence either for a mass invasion by Indo-Aryans and HURRIANS or for a military elite using horses and chariots to conquer Egypt. The foreign names in Egypt in this period are West Semitic, and the Hurrian migration into Palestine did not take place in significant numbers before the sixteenth century B.C. Military use of the chariot is not attested before the Late Bronze Age.

For a long time it was thought that the Hyksos capital (Avaris) was located at the later site of Tanis (biblical ZOAN), but recent study has made this view untenable. A more likely location is Tell ed-Dab'a near the village of Qantir. In four seasons of excavation (1966-69) a large city was uncovered (Thirteenth Dynasty) with continuous occupation to the Ramesside period. It is significant that this city represents an extension of MB II culture from Syria-Palestine into Egypt, with only gradual assimilation into Egyptian culture. This seems to confirm the political development outlined above. Small objects bearing the names of Hyksos kings were found, as well as an inscribed building block with the name of the god Seth, a deity specially honored by the Hyksos, who apparently identified him with the Semitic god BAAL.

There is no justification for the notion that the foreign population was expelled with the rise of the Eighteenth Dynasty. The rulers were defeated in a civil war begun by Ka-mose of Thebes and completed by Ah-mose. Places like Tell ed-Dab'a suffered damage and decline, but, to judge from the artifacts, the same Asiatic population continued to reside in the eastern Delta and to be the focal point for diffusion of Semitic cultural influence in Egypt from that time onward.

Bibliography. *CAH*³, II/1, chs. 2 and 8; J. Van Seters, *The Hyksos, A New Investigation* (1966); D. B. Redford, "The Hyksos Invasion in History and Tradition," *Or,* XXXIX (1970), 1-51; M. Bietak, *Mitteilungen des Deutschen Archäologischen Instituts, Kairo,* XXIII (1968), 81-114, XXVI (1970), 15-42, for the preliminary reports on the excavations at Tell ed-Dab'a.

J. VAN SETERS

HYRCANIA. *See* HERODIAN FORTRESSES[S] §3.

I

***IGNATIUS, EPISTLES OF.** *See* Apostolic Fathers [S] §7.

***IMMORTALITY.** Immunity to dissolution or death. In Greek Religion immortality was in the first instance the quality which distinguished divine beings from men. Ascription of immortality to the rational life-principle (soul) in men by Plato and other Greek thinkers thus signified not merely that the self survives death in some form, but that, unlike body, soul is naturally akin to the divine, shares its eternity and incorruptibility (ἀφθαρσία), and is capable of sharing its blessedness. Hence in the NT immortality is used naturally, if very rarely, (*a*) to characterize God, and (*b*) to characterize the quality of resurrected human existence as a sharing in the life of God's spirit. Later Christian thinkers grounded the possibility of such existence in an original human immortality, or capacity for immortality, lost through sin but restored in Christ.

1. Greek philosophy. While Greek religion always described the gods as immortal and saw this quality as definitive of the divine way of being, the abstract term "immortality" came into current use with Plato. He employed it in the first instance to describe soul (ψυχή) for cosmological purposes as the eternal, self-moving source of orderly motion in the universe. Soul according to Plato is a divine principle mediating between the unchanging, intelligible realm of Ideas (Being) and the changing, sensible realm of visible reality (Becoming), but essentially akin to the former in virtue of its capacity for contemplative knowledge of the Ideas (*Phaedrus* 245C-E; *Timaeus* 30C-D, 34B-35A). In its several forms, soul is thus an eternal life-principle animating the cosmos—without beginning or end, "ingenerate (ἀγένητος) and immortal" (*Phaedrus* 246A).

This cosmological vision brings with it a view of humanity which is also formed in part by Orphic influences. The human being is a rational soul, linked to an inferior, mortal, and passionate soul, and animating or using an earthly body. This association with earthly body, however, represents for the soul a kind of exile, and carries with it the threat of alienation from the celestial life of contemplation which is proper to an immortal being and which soul must seek to realize. Thus Plato's doctrine of immortality says at least three things. First, it presupposes that body, being intrinsically mortal, is alien to soul, and hence no essential factor in the constitution of human selfhood. Second, it means that soul is unaffected as far as its existence is concerned by the dissolution of the body. Third, it means that soul fulfills its given nature only in the achievement of the divine life of changeless contemplation appropriate to an eternal and intelligent being. The doctrine of immortality thus not only speaks of the survival of soul, but specifies its nature and its ideal state as well.

Prior to its revival in the first century B.C., this Platonist doctrine of immortality underwent severe qualification in philosophical circles. Aristotle, for whom the word "soul" denoted the formative principle of a particular organism, denied that soul is separable from the body which it animates, and so held that it does not pre-exist or survive the organism whose life it is. Immortality he ascribes to "active intellect," the highest phase of soul, which is "separable, impassible, unmixed . . . immortal, and eternal" (*On the Soul* III.v). It seems, however, that this intellect transcends all individual souls and is common to all. Hence there is no individual survival of death. People live the immortal (i.e., divine) life insofar as they identify themselves in and with active intellect, which is "something divine . . . present in" them (*Nicomachean Ethics* X.vii.8).

Among the Hellenistic schools, the Epicureans are reported to have held that soul is dissolved in death along with body. The Stoics, for whom the individual soul is a spark of the "fiery spirit" which is the active, formative principle of things, taught that either at death, or at any rate at the end of each cosmic cycle, the soul is resolved into its element. The wise man, however, in the practice of virtue, realizes his oneness with the divine Reason (Fate) which penetrates and governs all things. The basic idea that soul is akin to the divine thus persists.

2. Hellenistic religion. The social and cultural conditions of the later Hellenistic era encouraged a new interest in the idea of immortality, occasioned by the increasing isolation of the individual and the pessimistic belief that the earthly life is controlled by alien and even hostile forces—chance, fate, and the stars. In this setting, the promise of immortality signified liberation from fate and from the mechanism of nature so that we may have a divine and celestial life. The mystery cults ministered to this hope, with their promise of immortality to be gained not after death but upon initiation into the cult of the god or goddess. A revived Platonism, critical of determinism and affirming the goodness of the cosmic order, offered an intellectual and moral training as the way to fulfillment of the soul's immortal nature. In Gnosticism, however, the stream of pessimistic religion continued and reached a culmination. The soul's immortality was seen to mark it as a displaced member of a transcendent spiritual cosmos alien to this world of error and evil.

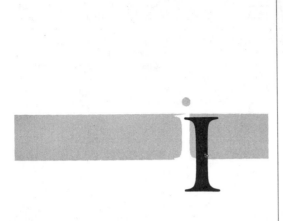

3. The NT. "Immortality" occurs only three times in the NT. In one of its occurrences, it is used to describe God as the one "who alone has immortality" (I Tim. 6:16). This use follows Greek custom, which makes immortality the attribute par excellence of deity. In I Timothy, however, it is God *alone* to whom immortality properly belongs. What for Plato and others in the Greek tradition was an attribute of a class of beings (including soul) becomes for this Christian writer an attribute which sets the unique God apart from other sorts of beings.

In another passage, however, immortality is used to describe a condition of human existence. In I Cor. 15:53-54 Paul employs the words "immortal" and "incorruptible" to describe the quality of the existence of those who share the resurrection of Christ in the new age. These terms express for Paul the goal of the transition from "psychic" to "spiritual" life, from an earthly to a heavenly humanity. Immortality thus marks the result of a change in the human condition which occurs in, and is dependent on, Christ, the second Adam; and it denotes the quality of a human life whose informing principle is not the power of death and sin, but the power of the HOLY SPIRIT. Immortality, then, signifies human life transformed by participation in the power of divine life; and the Christian hope of RESURRECTION is implicitly presented as the fulfillment of the human desire for final victory over the powers which destroy and deform life.

The contrasts between this idea of immortality and that of the Platonist tradition are clear. What they have in common is the understanding of death, the dissolution of the human self, as the frustration of the human capacity for fellowship with the divine. On the other hand, immortality for Paul is not, as for Plato, a matter of "nature." It belongs to humanity in virtue of a certain relation to God in Christ, not in virtue of what human beings are in and of themselves. Further, the self whose death is feared is not, for Paul, SOUL as distinct from BODY. It is the total human person as animated body. Finally, Paul does not work with a dualism of changelessness and mutability, immaterial and material. His is a dualism of present and future, this age and the age to come. Consequently, immortality for him is a "new thing"—God's transformation through the Spirit of the mode of human existence as a totality.

4. Early Church Fathers. In the writings of the so-called APOSTOLIC FATHERS, immortality is used in its Pauline sense to denote the new life which God gives in Christ, considered both as future consummation and as present reality. "Life in immortality" is one of the gifts of God for which Christians wait (I Clem. 35:1-4). Immortality is "[made] known" in Jesus (Did. 10:2). The eucharistic bread for Ignatius is "the medicine of immortality" because it enables men to "live in Jesus Christ" (Ign. Eph. 20:2). Only in the Letter to DIOGNETUS is there allusion to the natural immortality of the soul (6:8); and the context makes it clear that this immortality is not simply to be identified with the salvation for which Christians wait.

In fact, the doctrine that the soul is immortal in the sense of being ingenerate and incorruptible is rejected by all Christian writers of the second century except the Gnostics. Justin Martyr speaks disapprovingly of those who think that because the soul is immortal in its own right, it needs nothing from God (Dial. i.5). The soul, he says, is not immortal because it is not, like God, ingenerate—uncreated (Dial. iv.2; v). Immortality is the gift of Christ at his second coming, when believers will become "impassible and immortal as God is" (Dial. cxxiv.4).

This denial that soul is uncreated and the understanding of immortality as an eschatological sharing in the divine life did not, however, entail rejection of the commonplaces of late Hellenistic anthropology. The early Fathers seem to presuppose that man is a compound of soul and body, that death is the separation of soul and body, and that soul survives this separation (e.g., Tertullian, *Treatise on the Soul* xiv.1-2). Such survival, however, is a merely natural fact, and not the eschatological immortality which is promised in Christ for soul and body alike.

Thus Tatian, Justin's disciple, denies in his *Address to the Greeks* that soul enjoys immortality in its own right (xiii.1). Immortality consists in knowledge of the truth and communion with the Logos (vii.3), which Adam enjoyed until he sinned and thus became subject to death (cf. Rom. 5:12). This position, however, does not lead Tatian to question the soul's survival of death. Similarly Irenaeus—who generally follows Theophilus of Antioch in teaching that Adam was created immature and thus only *capable* of immortality (see Theophilus, *To Autolycus* II.xxiv, xxvii)—nevertheless asserts that the soul survives the death of the body for "a long series of ages" (Iren. Her. II.xxxiv.2). This prolonged existence, however, is not true immortality; for "being in subjection to God is continuance in immortality, and immortality is the glory of the uncreated One" (Her. IV.xxxviii.3). Moreover, eschatological immortality includes, for Irenaeus as for other Christian writers of this time, body as well as soul.

Underlying these positions is the principle that true immortality—because it is God's and consists, for human beings, in fellowship with God—is essentially a gift of God. The position of the Fathers approaches the Platonist idea that the soul is immortal by nature only to the extent that later writers assert that humanity received the gift of immortality at creation and then lost it through sin. In general, moreover, except perhaps in Origen, the soul's survival of death is carefully distinguished from immortality in the proper sense, which remains an eschatological reality and encompasses body as well as soul. The primary barrier in Christian thought to adoption of a pure Platonism was not, as Cullmann thought, a Pauline or biblical anthropology, but the doctrine that God alone is ingenerate and immortal, and that creaturely beings possess immortality only in relation to, and dependence on, him.

See DEATH; DEATH, THEOLOGY OF[S]; FUTURE LIFE IN INTERTESTAMENTAL LITERATURE[S]; RESURRECTION IN THE NT; RESURRECTION IN THE NT[S].

Bibliography. O. Cullmann, *Immortality of the Soul or Resurrection of the Dead?* (1956), setting out the inconsistencies between the idea of immortality and the idea of resurrection; E. Rohde, *Psyche* (7th/8th ed., 1921), a basic survey of Greek ideas of immortality; A. H. Armstrong and R. A. Markus, *Christian Faith and Greek Philosophy* (1960), pp. 43-58, for a useful treatment of patristic anthropology; F. M. Cornford, *Plato's Cosmology* (1937), for the developed Platonic idea of soul; A.-J. Festugière, *La Révélation d'Hermès Trismègiste,* III: *Les Doctrines de l'âme* (1953), for later Greek speculation on the soul; H. Diels, *Doxographi Graeci* (1929 [repr. 1958]), and J. von Arnim, *Stoicorum Veterum Fragmenta,* 3 vols. (1903-5 [repr. 1964]), for the traditions of Hellenistic philosophy.

R. A. NORRIS, JR.

***INHERITANCE IN THE NT.** The OT language dealing with inheritance reveals a richly varied content in Israel's history. It moves from legal concerns for property to such theological affirmations as the land of Canaan as Israel's inheritance, Israel as Yahweh's inheritance, and Yahweh as Israel's inheritance (*see* INHERITANCE §§2-5). Further, later Jewish writings can refer to the Law as Israel's inheritance (e.g., Ecclus. 24:23; Enoch 99:14), speak of inheriting life or eternal life (e.g., Pss. Sol. 14:7; Enoch 40:9; cf. Secrets of Enoch 50:2; Apocal. Bar. 44:13), or view the inheritance as mystical unity with God (Philo in *Who Is the Heir of Divine Things?*). The DEAD SEA SCROLLS relate inheritance to the new covenant community of elect persons (cf. IQS 4.23-26; 1QpHab 2.3), and Enoch relates it to the coming SON OF MAN (71:14-17). Such variety indicates how changing historical contexts may produce multiple understandings. These then are part of the background for NT writers as they deal distinctively with inheritance language in their own varied settings.

In the NT, inheritance terms (κληρονομία, inheritance; κληρονομεῖν, to inherit; κληρονόμος, heir; συγκληρονόμος, joint heir) can move the distance from an earthly concern for property (Luke 12:13) to a heavenly, imperishable inheritance beyond history (I Pet. 1:4; cf. Rev. 21:7; note other uses in I Pet. 3:7, 9), but the coming of Jesus Christ provides the decisive point of reference for NT writers.

1. The Synoptic gospels and Acts. All three Synoptics relate the inheritance of eternal life to the story of the rich man (Matt. 19:29; Mark 10:17; Luke 18:18), but Matthew gives "inherit" a distinctly eschatological emphasis by using it only after the story itself in relation to the "new world" and the coming of the Son of man (Matt. 19:28; cf. Dan. 7:13; Enoch 71:14-17). In contexts oriented to the future, Matthew supports this emphasis further with "shall inherit the earth" (Matt. 5:5; cf. Ps. 37:11; Enoch 5:7*b*) and "inherit the kingdom" (Matt. 25:34; cf. Jas. 2:5; Secrets of Enoch 9:1).

In the allegorized parable of the wicked tenants, all three Synoptics use "heir" and "inheritance" (Matt. 21:38; Mark 12:7; Luke 20:14) with particular christological significance. Early Christians saw Jesus as the Son and heir, and with his death they viewed the inheritance (i.e., the vineyard; cf. Isa. 5) as passing to them. Matthew explicitly sees the vineyard as God's kingdom (Matt. 21:43), and with the death of God's Son and heir, this inheritance is entrusted to those "producing the fruits of it."

In Acts, Luke denies any relationship of "inheritance" to Abraham (7:5), affirms its historic connection to Canaan (13:19), and finally interprets it as given to "all those who are sanctified" (20:32; i.e., to the church). For Luke, Christ culminates Israel's history and brings an inheritance of life in the church.

2. Paul. In his letters Paul never refers to the inheritance of Canaan, but he does relate inheritance language to the promise of Abraham (Gal. 3:18; 4:30; Rom. 4:13-14) and sees that promise fulfilled in Christ. For him, it is those with faith in Christ who are Abraham's true heirs (Gal. 3:29). Through God's justifying deed in his Son, they are (by adoption; cf. Gal. 4:5; Rom. 8:15) God's sons and heirs (Gal. 4:7), "fellow heirs with Christ" (Rom. 8:17). Christ as the offspring of Abraham (Gal. 3:16) is the heir; but as the fulfillment of the promised blessing of Abraham (Gal. 3:14) he also is the inheritance. As heir and inheritance he is both the means to and the essence of the unifying life which believers have in him (cf. Gal. 3:26-29).

However, Paul also can use "inherit" of future events in referring to those who shall not inherit the kingdom (I Cor. 6:9-10; Gal. 5:21; cf. Eph. 5:5) and in affirming (concerning the Resurrection) that "flesh and blood cannot inherit the kingdom of God" (I Cor. 15:50).

3. Ephesians speaks of inheritance in the future (1:14, 18; 5:5; cf. Col. 3:24—the RSV's "inheritance" in Col. 1:12 should read "lot"; Tit. 3:7) with the Spirit as present "guarantee" (ἀρραβῶν). Ephesians sees Christ as the means to an inheritance which ultimately is the unity of all things (cf. 1:9-10). However, in a concern for the church's unity, Ephesians speaks of the Gentiles as "fellow heirs" (3:6) and sees the unity of Jew and Gentile in the church as revealing (cf. 3:4-6) and witnessing to (cf. 3:10) the final inheritance of cosmic unity in Christ.

4. Hebrews portrays Christ as the Son and heir of all things (1:2; cf. 6:17; 11:7, 9; in 1:4 the Son "inherited"—RSV "obtained"—a more excellent name). As the high priest and mediator of a new covenant, he is the means to "the promised eternal inheritance" (9:15; cf. Secrets of Enoch 10:6; 55:2; note also "inherit [RSV "obtain"] salvation" in Heb. 1:14 and "inherit the promises" in 6:12). This inheritance is the heavenly city (11:8-10). Hebrews can relate inheritance terms to Abraham (6:15—RSV has "obtained"; 11:8), but his inheritance is not the land of Canaan (Hebrews also reinterprets the conquest; cf. 4:8); it is the city "whose builder and maker is God" (11:10).

A decisive concern in Hebrews is the legal argument that only through the death of the eschatological (cf. 1:2) Son and heir does the inheritance-enacting will or covenant (διαθήκη) take effect (9:16-17). That death is the means to the inheritance of the city.

5. Conclusion. What was originally legal language is richly theologized in both OT and NT, but in the NT Jesus Christ as the Son provides the major focus for inheritance language. (The concept, significantly, is absent from the Gospel and Letters of John.) Whether understood as present or future or both, for NT writers the content of the inheritance relates crucially to Christ.

Bibliography. P. L. Hammer, "The Understanding of Inheritance [ΚΛΗΡΟΝΟΜΙΑ] in the NT," (diss., Heidelberg, 1958), and "A Comparison of *KLĒRONOMIA* in Paul and Ephesians," *JBL,* LXXIX (1960), 267-72; J. D. Hester, *Paul's Concept of Inheritance, SJT,* Occasional Paper, XIV (1968); W. Foerster, "κληρονόμος, κτλ.," *TDNT,* III (1938), 767-85.

P. L. HAMMER

*INSCRIPTIONS, SEMITIC.

1. Introduction
2. The value of the inscriptions for biblical study
   a. Philology
   b. History, religion, and civilization
3. Survey of new inscriptions (including new interpretations of some previously known inscriptions)
   a. Hebrew
   b. Moabite
   c. Ammonite
   d. Aramaic
   e. Phoenician
4. Conclusion

Bibliography

1. Introduction. Semitic epigraphy has been well served in the past decade and a half through the issue of a number of up-to-date manuals, including two textbooks of inscriptions with commentary and illustrations. As a result, today's students have readier access than their predecessors to a wide range of texts from Palestine and adjacent lands.

2. The value of the inscriptions for biblical study. *a. Philology.* The most obvious dividends in OT studies have been and will probably continue to be earned at the technical levels of writing, phonology, grammar, and vocabulary. This evidence is enabling the Hebraist and biblical scholar to pierce with growing precision behind not only the vocalized Hebrew text of Masoretic times but the consonantal text of a millennium or so earlier (*see* TEXT, OT; MASORETIC ACCENTS; QERE-KETHIBH[S]). It is now widely accepted that the latter text is our best guide to the language of the original writers, but it should not be assumed that it directly reflects it any more than the vocalized text does. Its formation indeed was closely bound up with a process of standardization in spelling and grammar which began soon after the return from the Exile and which accommodated many older orthographic practices and dialectal forms to the current Hebrew of the postexilic community in Jerusalem. (*See* TEXT, HEBREW, HISTORY OF[S].) The recovery of these older practices and forms involves internal backward reconstruction using the strict methods of diachronic or historical linguistics, but it also requires an external criterion that gives scope for the comparative method to be brought into play as well; it is this criterion that the inscriptions, the non-Hebrew no less than the Hebrew, are increasingly supplying.

In the sphere of writing considerable advance can be recorded, and we now have an exceptionally clear picture of the development of the Hebrew script and orthography from their beginnings in the time of the Gezer "calendar" (tenth century B.C.) down to the NT period and beyond. (*See* ALPHABET; ALPHABET[S]. For a table of the Old Hebrew scripts, *see* ALPHABET Table 1; WRITING AND WRITING MATERIALS Fig. 34.) The relation of the Hebrew writing system to those of its near neighbors, the Aramaic especially, is also becoming much better understood. Ancillary questions for which inscriptions supply evidence are:

1) How widespread was the ability to write in ancient Israel and Judah? Considerably more widespread than was once thought; it was not simply the prerogative of an elite scribal profession.

2) How long did the Old Hebrew script survive before being superseded by the "square" Aramaic script? Again, much longer than used to be assumed; both scripts seem to have been employed side by side for several centuries for their respective languages, and it was only in the Greek period that the Aramaic script began to be used for writing Hebrew. *See* SAMARITAN PENTATEUCH[S] §1*d*; §3*a*ii *below*.

3) Are the Hebrew and related scripts really alphabets? The present writer is one who believes that they are more accurately described as syllabic than alphabetic; each sign stands not for a consonant alone, but for a syllable or, more exactly, a syllable part, consisting frequently of a single consonant but just as frequently of a consonant plus a vowel.

In the spheres of phonology, grammar, and vocabulary, the results of studies in the 1960s and early 1970s are more difficult to evaluate, and there is much controversy over methodology. As examples I cite the rather different work of Beyer and Dahood.

1) In his *Althebräische Grammatik* (1969) Beyer attempts to reconstruct the phonology and grammar of the Hebrew of the biblical period, basing himself on the consonantal text and the Old Hebrew inscriptions. From what I have said above it will be clear that I sympathize with Beyer's aim; the unvocalized Hebrew in which the OT was first written was not at all the same as the vocalized Hebrew of our Masoretic MSS. But Beyer's dismissal of the Tiberian and other vocalization systems as artificial and contrived goes too far, and in supplying the missing vowels in my *Textbook* I have kept rather closer to the model of these systems. They may postdate the biblical pronunciation by many centuries but were, I believe, ordered and natural developments out of it, or at any rate out of the stage it had reached when the consonantal text was formed (*see* HEBREW LANGUAGE §4).

2) Dahood's primary interest lies in the close linguistic and stylistic affinities he finds between the Ugaritic tablets and the OT (*see* POETRY, HEBREW[S]). But he also makes considerable use of the Semitic inscriptions alongside his Ugaritic

sources, particularly of early Phoenician texts like those from Karatepe and Zenjirli. Like Beyer he tends to be too critical of the Masoretes and not critical enough of the consonantal text; he moves from a Ugaritic or epigraphic allusion to a biblical passage without discussing the often very different contexts of each; he lists biblical parallels without distinguishing between those he himself considers most likely and those he thinks just possible, and so on. But in spite of these weaknesses, his basic case is sound, namely that in these early Northwest Semitic sources there is evidence which will illumine many facets of the OT text and the Hebrew language. Moreover, they will show how wrongheaded were many of the postexilic datings and conjectural emendations beloved by a previous generation of biblical critics.

b. History, religion, and civilization. Less directly helpful to the student of the Bible, but nonetheless welcome, is the information that can be gleaned from the inscriptions on matters of history, religion, and civilization. By their very nature, epigraphic texts are usually short and sometimes also summary and cryptic. The largest proportion of them in fact is composed of no more than labels or dockets identifying the purpose or place of origin or capacity of an object, or giving the personal name of an owner or manufacturer or user. The private letters are often jejune and of interest to few beyond the first recipients. Legal documents record single cases and do not necessarily tell us much of the systems behind them. Texts on gravestones do not explain in detail beliefs in a life after death that were the common currency of the time. Royal inscriptions are potentially more exciting, but their allusions are rarely sufficient to satisfy our curiosity, and their occasional boastful tone arouses our suspicions about their trustworthiness. Inscriptions mention the names of deities, but do not enlarge on their characteristics or on their positions in specific pantheons. Taken as a whole, the Semitic inscriptions provide only a small portion of the data required for sustained research into the ancient history and society of the region.

3. Survey of new inscriptions. This section describes the most important or interesting Semitic inscriptions discovered or published since the late 1950s; it also includes a brief discussion of several inscriptions known before that time of which fresh or fuller interpretations have recently been put forward.

a. Hebrew. Dialectally, three divisions can be seen: no. i below representing an archaic southern dialect; nos. ii-iv, the dialect of the northern kingdom; and nos. v-x, the dialect of Judah (*see* HEBREW LANGUAGE[S] §1*b*). The finds mentioned under xi and xii give valuable evidence of the continuing vitality of Hebrew as a spoken tongue for many centuries after the Exile.

i. *Gezer.* Although it was discovered in 1908, the interpretation of this tiny tenth-century inscription, the earliest in the Old Hebrew script, is still uncertain. It gives a list of months designated according to the agricultural activities that took place in them; they are arranged in a rough chronological order—vintage, sowing, spring pasture, flax pulling, barley harvest, wheat harvest, pruning, summer fruit—but begin rather peculiarly from the farming standpoint in the middle of the soft fruit harvest. The fact that the ancient Hebrew New Year (*but see* NEW YEAR[S]) began in the autumn (Exod. 23:16) probably had something to do with this, but it is doubtful whether the tablet can properly be regarded as a calendar. It can only be made so by taking an ending *w* attached to four of the eight occurrences of the word "month" (*yrh*) as a dual or a suffix to the dual, whereas it is more likely to be an archaic nominative plural construct ending, "months of." This would give more than twelve months, but by allowing overlapping, would accord better with the facts of farming life. In any case, farmers do not need a calendar to remind them when to do their various tasks, and it would only be helpful to nonfarmers to have their months named after such tasks if twelve tasks were chosen. It is surely therefore the sequence of the activities rather than their dates that is significant. Perhaps the inscription was a "blessing" tablet placed in the local sanctuary during some religious ceremony at New Year and left there as a visible prayer to Yahweh (the proper name, Abijah, in the marginal line shows that the scribe was Israelite) to grant favorable seasons in the coming year; cf. Gen. 8:21-22; Deut. 28:8-9; Jer. 5:24; etc.

ii. *The Samaria ostraca.* These ostraca, sixty-three in number, have also been known a long time (since 1910), but there is as yet no agreement about their purpose. They belong to the early eighth century B.C. and record the delivery of wine and oil from certain places near Samaria to the royal palace. Bewildering fluctuations in the formulas make it unlikely that all of the ostraca were, as was formerly thought, official taxation documents. The mention of clan territories on some ostraca would be well explained on this supposition; cf. I Chr. 5:17, which gives information about a census by clans carried out by Jeroboam II, to whose reign many of the texts can in fact be dated. Recently, however, it has been suggested that the recipients were not administrators but courtiers or other high-ranking persons to whom the income from certain estates was allotted as a reward for services to the crown (cf. I Sam. 8:14-15; II Sam. 9:7). Both these interpretations depend on the preposition *l* (prefixed to many of the personal names) having the meaning "[for delivery] to"; but it could just as well mean "[belonging] to," in which case the names are simply those of the local landowners who farmed and prepared the produce. Perhaps the dockets record several different kinds of transaction and were found together only because the merchandise was the same and was therefore stored in the same room.

iii. *Hazor.* Eight very short inscriptions on potsherds were discovered in 1956, four belonging to the ninth century, and four to the eighth. They consist chiefly of proper names with the preposition *l,* which clearly here identifies the owners of the jars. The word *smdr* (a variety of wine) on one inscription occurs in Song of S. 2:13, 15, where it is thought to mean "vine blossom." These texts are the first Hebrew inscriptions to come from Galilee. *See* HAZOR[S].

iv. *Nimrud.* Traces of a Hebrew inscription were discovered in 1961. It probably was a plaque dedicating a votive offering, and it contains the first letter of the divine name Yahweh: "May Y[ahweh] shatter (?) . . ./. . . after me, from great king [to private citizen, who . . ./. . . to] come and deface [this inscription]!" The material used and the careful chiseling of the words witness to a high standard of craftsmanship in Samaria, from which the plaque was doubtless carried away as booty after the crushing of the revolt in 721 B.C. The date of the writing is a little earlier than this.

v. *Siloam Tomb.* The inscription was discovered in 1870 at the entrance to the village of Selwan (Siloam), but was largely undeciphered until a successful restoration in the 1950s. The writing belongs to the same period as the famous Siloam Tunnel inscription (*ca.* 700 B.C.). It reads: "This is [the tomb of Sheban]iah, who is over the house. There is no silver or gold here,/only [his bones] and the bones of his maidservant with him. Cursed be the man who/opens this!" Elaborate inscribed tombs from the pre-exilic period are rare in Israel and Judah, no doubt because they could be ill afforded by the bulk of the population, but perhaps also because they offended against the ethos of the Hebrew faith. The fierce oracle in Isa. 22:15-16 against Shebna (whose tomb inscription this may in fact be; cf. the title in vs. 15) lends some credence to the latter opinion.

vi. *Yavneh-yam.* An ostracon of fourteen lines was discovered in 1960 in the remains of an ancient fortress about a mile S of Yavneh-yam near Jamnia (JABNEEL). The cursive writing is earlier than that of the Lachish letters (beginning of the sixth century) and suggests a date in the second half of the seventh century, probably in the reign of Josiah. The document preserves an appeal from a farm worker to the governor of the district against a sentence imposed by a minor official. The phrase *lpny šbt* used to specify the time of the offense should possibly be translated "before Sabbath" (cf. Amos 8:5), but may simply mean "before stopping." The minor official is said to have "taken away your servant's garment," a phrase that is repeated so that the governor may be in no doubt about how badly the man felt he had been treated; cf. Exod. 22:25-27, Deut. 24:10-13, according to which confiscation of a garment is the regular distraint in Mosaic law for nonpayment of a debt or obligation by a poor person.

vii. *Wadi Murabba'at.* In 1952 a papyrus palimpsest with the faint remains of two inscriptions, one a private letter, the other a list of names, was discovered in a cave in the Wadi Murabba'at S of Qumran; it was published in 1961. It is the only papyrus text surviving from pre-exilic times (for later finds at the site *see* §xii *below*). The excavations reveal an occupation of caves in the vicinity during the latter part of the eighth and the whole of the seventh century B.C., and the papyrus must belong within that period. We can only guess what disaffected group was responsible for it—perhaps a sect of religious loyalists or nationalists who fled there during Manasseh's long reign.

viii. *Tell 'Arad.* Excavations begun in 1962 have uncovered a rich treasure of ostraca, from several Iron Age strata (*see* ARAD[S] §4). One letter begins: "To my lord Eliashib./May Yahweh ask/ for your peace!" The greeting is odd; unlike those on the Lachish ostraca, it is paralleled in the Bible (Gen. 43:27; I Sam. 10:4), though not with God as subject. Biblical phrases occurring on other ostraca include: "a homer of wine" (cf. Exod. 16:33) and "two mules' burden" (Judg. 19:10; II Kings 5:17). A jar discovered in the first season is interesting for its short inscription, which may contain a new name of a Hebrew month ("month of *ṣaḥ*"); this word occurs in Isa. 18:4, where it seems to mean "clear or shimmering heat." This interpretation has, however, recently been challenged.

ix. *Other pre-exilic finds.* Some sixty jar handles, inscribed with names and dating to the late seventh century, were unearthed in the late 1950s at el-Jib, the ancient Gibeon. More recently we have three small tomb inscriptions of the eighth and seventh centuries from Khirbet el-Qom near Hebron and some names on jugs and sherds from Beer-sheba.

The number of Hebrew seals, stamps, and weights has also been considerably increased in the last two decades. One of the most interesting of the new seals contains the inscription, "[Belonging] to Manasseh, son of the king." It probably belonged to a prince or noble of the late Judean period. Another seal is inscribed, "[Belonging] to Azariah [of] the Locust [clan]"; there is a splendid picture of a locust beneath the name. This seal has enabled some names ("partridge," "gadfly," etc.) on the enigmatic Ophel ostracon, discovered in Jerusalem in 1924, to be interpreted as clan or family crests or emblems rather than as a father's or ancestor's personal name.

Two weights published in the 1960s are much larger than any known hitherto, having the numbers twenty and thirty inscribed on them alongside the characteristic shekel loop sign. They represent, however, respectively sixteen and twenty-four shekels, and seem to confirm a recently advanced theory that Hebrew weights, which traditionally mounted by multiples of four, began at some point in the late monarchy (probably the reign of Josiah) to be marked by their equivalents in the Egyptian system, which was based on the multiple five. An international agreement to standardize trade practices may have lain behind this change.

x. *Khirbet Beit Lei.* Several graffiti were discovered in 1961, scratched on the wall inside a burial cave near Lachish. They include rough drawings of human figures, ships, various geometric designs, and a number of rather strange inscriptions in the Old Hebrew writing. The inscriptions are difficult both to date and to decipher. The first editor (Naveh) placed them in the seventh century, but F. M. Cross and the present writer prefer the sixth century. The longest text, which is the first Hebrew inscription to mention Jerusalem by name, is translated as follows by Naveh: "Yahweh is the God of the whole earth;

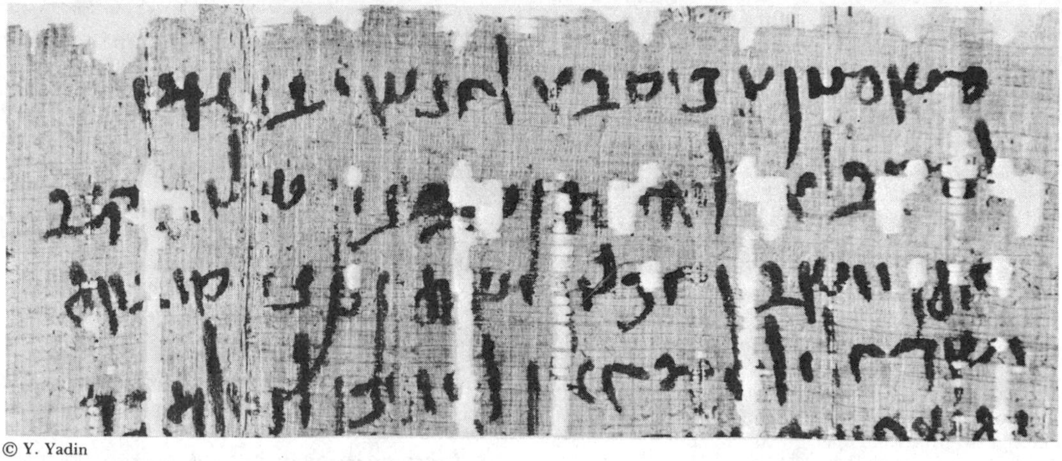

© Y. Yadin

1. Bar Kochba's letter to the men of En-gedi

the moun/tains of Judah belong to him, to the God of Jerusalem." Cross's revised rendering is considerably different: "I am Yahweh thy God; I will accept/the cities of Judah, and will redeem Jerusalem." A second inscription, in which Naveh found an allusion to Mount Moriah, is treated by Cross as a prayer for mercy. It is doubtful whether the two texts are funerary inscriptions. As in the case of the Murabba'at papyrus (§vii *above*), we should probably think of refugees or chance travelers taking shelter in the cave. If the inscriptions belong to the early sixth century, it is tempting to suppose that their writers were fleeing from the advancing Babylonian army; but the sentiments they express would sound just as fitting at the end of that century at the time when the temple was being rebuilt (cf. Isa. 43:3; 52:9; 62:12).

xi. *The Persian period.* If the Khirbet Beit Lei inscriptions are indeed postexilic, they indicate that the older Hebrew writing was not so quickly abandoned in favor of the Aramaic script as used to be thought (*see* §2*a above*). Since (if we discount Khirbet Beit Lei) the meager inscribed finds from this period are nearly all Aramaic (*see* §3*d* viii *below*), this opinion is based on the merest scraps of evidence, e.g., that two bullae sealing Aramaic papyri from fourth-century Samaria bear Hebrew legends written in Hebrew characters. Nevertheless, it is likely to be correct. It not only closes meaningfully the gap between the preexilic period and the appearance of the Old Hebrew script on Jewish coins of the Hasmonean era, but goes far toward explaining the emergence in the early Christian centuries of a style of writing in the Samaritan community showing many points of contact with the older script. Neither the coin script nor the Samaritan script need now be considered new archaizing creations.

xii. *The Bar Kochba finds.* Hebrew began to be written extensively in the "square" Jewish script of Aramaic origin in the Greek period, as is shown by the biblical and other scrolls from Qumran, and more recently by finds from the Wadi Murabba'at (1950s) and the "Cave of Letters" in Naḥal Ḥever (1960-61), which date to the times of the Jewish revolts against Rome in A.D. 66-73 and 132-35. These finds also include scrolls, but the bulk comprises smaller items like letters or legal deeds on papyrus, which the freedom fighters composed or took with them during their retreat into the desert. Most of the documents and letters are in Aramaic, but a few, including some of Bar Kochba's, are in Hebrew (*see* Fig. I1). On the significance of these finds for the history of the period *see* BAR KOCHBA[S]. Here it is enough to state that the Hebrew letters are written in a late form of the language approximating to that used in the MISHNA; the so-called Copper Scroll from Qumran is in the same dialect. Mishnaic Hebrew was once thought by most scholars to be an artificial academic language created by and used only in learned circles, though a few were of the opinion that it reflected a continuing development of a Hebrew vernacular in Palestine from the Exile into NT times (*see* HEBREW LANGUAGE[S] §2*b*). The discovery of these Hebrew letters, documents that can in no way be described as academic, strongly suggests that the latter were right. *See further* MANUSCRIPTS FROM THE JUDEAN DESERT[S] §§2, 5, 6.

b. Moabite. A fragment of a ninth-century stele in the Moabite language, known from the famous Mesha stone to be closely related to Hebrew, though it has some affinities with Aramaic and also some independent features, was discovered at el-Kerak in 1958 and published in 1963. It contains only a few words, one of which is the name "Chemosh-yat," now probably to be restored in Mesha, line 1, as that of the king's father. Chemosh was the national deity of the Moabites (Num. 21:29).

c. Ammonite. The most important items are a fragment of a ninth-century stele, discovered in 1961 during excavations at the citadel mound of Amman (*see* Fig. I2), and a bronze bottle with an inscription of eight lines dating to about 600 B.C., found in 1972 at Tell Sīrān. None of the lines on the citadel fragment is complete, and interpretation is very difficult, but the stele seems to have been set up to commemorate the building of a temple to the chief Ammonite deity, Milcom (I Kings 11:5; Jer. 49:3), whose name can be

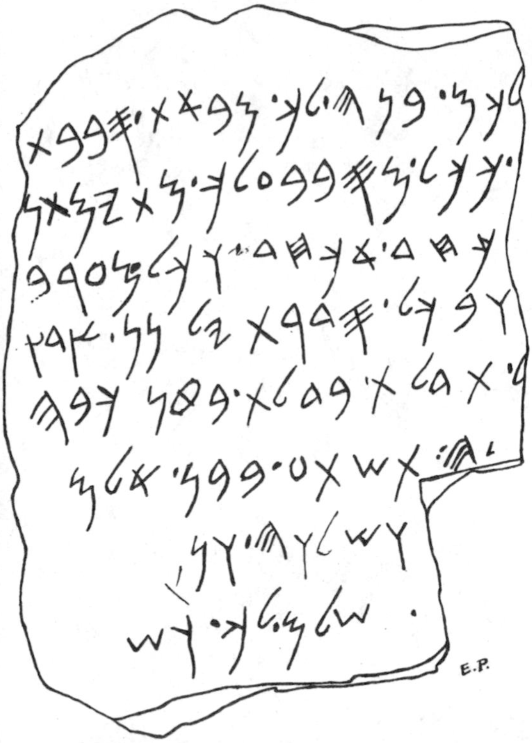

Courtesy Emile Puech

2. Inscription from the citadel mound of Amman

restored in the first line. The inscription on the bronze bottle, which was probably cultic or dedicatory in purpose, speaks of the building works of a king called ʿAmmi-nadab: "May he exult and rejoice/for many days to come/and in years far off!" With the parallelism between "many days" and "far-off years" we may compare Ezek. 12:27. The Ammonite language was, as far as we can tell from these two short pieces, a near-relative of Hebrew, though one scholar (Garbini) has argued for an affinity with North Arabic. *See* HESHBON[S].

d. Aramaic. Aramaic epigraphy falls into three easily separable stages. The first is represented by inscriptions of the early first millennium B.C. (*see* i-iv *below*); these are closely related except for the dialect of Zenjirli (ancient Sam'al), which shows several archaic features and in some other features is more akin to the Canaanite dialects than the Aramaic (*see* YA'UDI[S]). The second is represented by many scores of inscriptions, ostraca, clay tablets, and papyri, written in the standardized dialect adopted by the Assyrians and after them by the Babylonians and Persians as a lingua franca (v-viii). The biblical books of Ezra and Daniel contain portions written in this official or imperial Aramaic. After the fall of the Persian Empire regional differences began to reassert themselves (stage three); one of the new dialects was the Palestinian, employed in the TARGUMS and TALMUD. The Aramaic letters and documents of Bar Kochba (*see* §*a* xii *above*) and some of the Judean scrolls are in an earlier form of this dialect. *See further* ARAMAIC; ARAMAIC[S].

i. *Barhadad.* This inscription, dedicated to Melcarth, the chief deity of Tyre, and belonging to the ninth century B.C., was discovered in 1939 near Aleppo. However, it was drawn up by a king of Damascus and therefore reflects the dialect of that kingdom. The veneration, in an Aramean kingdom, of a Tyrian deity can be compared with events in contemporary Israel, where Jezebel introduced the cult of the Tyrian Baal (I Kings 16:31-32). The second line, which is badly faded, was brilliantly restored by Albright to read: "Barhadad, son of Tobrimmon, son of Hezion, king of Aram" (cf. I Kings 15:18). This interpretation has recently been challenged by a number of scholars, but the alternative solutions they propose yield rather peculiar formulas; thus, e.g., "Barhadad, son of Ezer, the Damascene, son of the king of Aram" (Cross); "Barhadad, son of Iḏri-Šamš, who [was] the father of the king of Aram" (Lipiński). According to the first of these interpretations Barhadad is a son of [Hadad]ezer, and according to the second, a brother of Hazael. The existence of either Barhadad is not elsewhere attested. In my opinion Albright's restoration should still stand.

ii. *Northern Israel.* Two short inscriptions were discovered at Ein Gev and Tell DAN in Galilee in the 1960s. That from Ein Gev reads "For (the use of) the wine butlers" (cf. Gen. 40:1; Neh. 1:11); that from Dan "For [the use of] the butchers or cooks" (cf. I Sam. 9:23). The scripts belong to the ninth century and probably witness to the Aramean occupation of towns in this area by Barhadad during the reign of Baasha (I Kings 15:20).

iii. *Sefire.* One of the three long inscriptions from Sefire near Aleppo was edited as long ago as 1931, but full study of these very important texts has had to wait for the excellent editions of Dupont-Sommer (1956-68) and Fitzmyer (1967). They date to the mid-eighth century B.C. Stelae i and ii record two treaties between Barga'yah, king of an unknown city or territory called *Ktk,* and the local king, Matiʿel of ARPAD. Only part of stele iii survives; it was clearly a similar treaty, perhaps drawn up between Matiʿel and some other king, though the partners' names are not preserved. The contents of the three texts include, in addition to the detailed stipulations, lists of the gods of the contracting parties, who are called upon to witness the treaty, and series of curses to be enacted against the king of Arpad should he violate it; there are also descriptions of magical rites with wax models to be made effective under the same circumstances. Of special interest to OT students are the parallels in format and phraseology between the Sefire stelae and Hittite and Assyrian treaties of the late second and the first millennia B.C., and between all of these and a number of biblical passages in which the themes of covenant or of blessing and curse are prominent (*see* COVENANT, MOSAIC[S]). Among the gods mentioned are El and Elyon (cf. Gen. 14:9; Ps. 78:35), and also vague entities like "Heaven and Earth" (cf. Deut. 4:26; 30:19; Job 16:19) or "Abyss and Springs" (cf. Isa. 44:27). The curses may be compared with Deut. 27 and 28 and Lev. 26. The stipulations of the treaties evidence the concern for a peaceful succession which so occupied

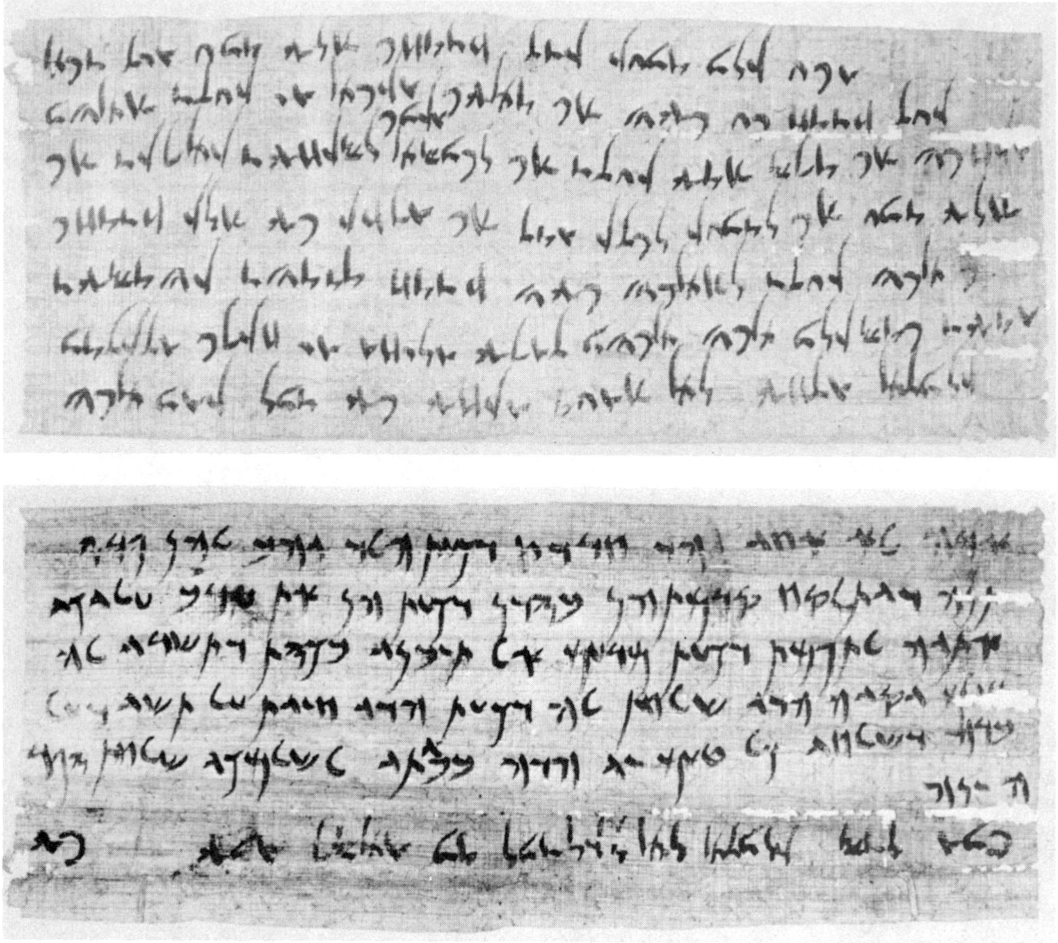

Courtesy Edda Bresciani

3. Aramaic papyrus from Hermopolis

monarchs in that bloody era; cf. Solomon's execution of Adonijah, Joab, and Shimei (I Kings 2); I Kings 16:11; II Kings 10:6-7; 11:1, etc.

iv. *Luristan.* Two tiny inscriptions on a bronze juglet and cup from Luristan, north of Elam, were published in 1964. The articles belong to the eighth century B.C., and may have been taken to Luristan by a group of ethnic Arameans emigrating from Babylonia, where the Kaldu (Chaldeans) and other tribes had established themselves early in the millennium. They are our earliest evidence of an eastern Aramaic dialect.

v. *Tell el-Maskhuta.* A number of fifth-century inscribed silver bowls, acquired in the 1950s, were reported to have been found at this site near Ismailia in Lower Egypt. They witness to the presence in the Delta region of a community of N Arabs belonging to the tribal confederacy of Kedar (Gen. 25:13; Isa. 60:7). One bowl (*see* KEDAR Fig. 2) was presented to the community shrine by the chief of the confederacy on a visit; his name shows him to have been the son of Nehemiah's archenemy (Neh. 2:19; 6:1-2). The inscription reads: "That which Qainu, son of Geshem, king of Kedar, offered to han-Ilat." The goddess han-Ilat is known from later Nabatean inscriptions and is mentioned in the Koran.

vi. *Asia Minor.* Two new inscriptions of the fifth-fourth centuries B.C. were published in the 1960s, one from a boundary stone discovered in 1957 at Bahadirli in Cilicia, and one from a funerary stele found in 1965 at ancient Daskyleion near the Bosporus. The stele is decorated with secular scenes in relief and adjures passers-by in the name of the Mesopotamian deities Bel and Nebo not to disturb the grave. If, as a recent study suggests, the dead man was a Jew, one Elnaf son of Ishyahu, we have an indication both of the wide westward outreach of the Diaspora not two centuries after the fall of Jerusalem and of a laxity of religious practice not dissimilar to that evidenced by the Elephantine papyri from contemporary Egypt.

vii. *Papyri from Egypt.* Eight well-preserved papyri were discovered at Hermopolis in 1945, though not published till twenty years later (*see* Fig. 13). They were written in Memphis, and comprise private letters addressed to relatives resident in either Syene or Thebes. The writers were probably soldiers in the employ of the Persian administration in Egypt, who belonged to Aramean communities in these two places. Those from the former place would belong to the "Arameans of Syene," mentioned several times in the documents from Elephantine. The chief importance of these papyri lies in the sphere of language, where in several particulars they present a different picture from the ELEPHANTINE PAPYRI; this is probably because the writers were, unlike the Jews of Elephantine, not simply using an official language but, being native Arameans, were still speaking their ancestral tongue.

Another interesting papyrus, found in Egypt at the beginning of the nineteenth century and published in 1960, was written by a Jewish resident in Migdol to his son on military service in Elephantine. A reference to the temple of Yahu (Yahweh) dates the papyrus prior to its destruction in 410 B.C. The writer encourages his son "to be a man," and informs him that some difficulty over his salary had been cleared up.

viii. *Palestine.* Two tiny fourth-century ostraca from Tell 'Arad and Nebi Yunis were unearthed in Israeli excavations in the early 1960s, providing a welcome supplement to the scant written remains from postexilic Judah. The one from Arad reads: "The cave of Anani/and his straw shed/and his ox stable"; if, as seems likely, the man himself lived in the cave, this little text vividly illustrates the poverty of the times. On the discovery of a number of fragmentary papyri from Samaria, also belonging to the fourth century, *see* SAMARIA PAPYRI[S]; SAMARITANS[S] §1.

e. Phoenician. The last couple of decades have seen a revival of Phoenician and Punic epigraphic studies, partly because of the impetus of the Ugaritic discoveries. There have been a number of articles re-examining older finds like the Nora stone, the Arslan Tash incantation text, and the Karatepe and Kilamuwa inscriptions, many of them drawing parallels with biblical constructions and motifs.

i. *Pyrgi.* The most important new Phoenician find (1964) is a fifth-century votive text from Pyrgi, N of Rome, which witnesses to the close relations between the Etruscans, who ruled that area, and the Phoenicians and Carthaginians. It announces the building by an Etruscan king of a "holy place" or cell in a temple of Astarte; this cell contained an image of the goddess, the dedication being made on the "day of the burial of the deity," probably some cultic occasion. The last lines read: "And [may] the years for the votive gift of the deity in her temple [be] years like these stars (*km hkkbm 'l*)!" Noting the difficulty that commentators have had in finding a referent for the final phrase, Dahood has proposed "like the stars of El" (cf. Isa. 14:13), which certainly improves the sense. The definite article is idiomatically prefaced to the whole phrase, and the *m* is enclitic.

ii. *Seville.* A statue of Astarte with an inscription on the pedestal was discovered near Seville in 1963. It belongs to the eighth century B.C. and adds to the growing evidence of early Phoenician colonization in Spain. Recently, also, C. H. Gordon has reawakened an old controversy over a Phoenician text from Paraíba in Brazil, which had long previously been pronounced a forgery. Gordon argues that it is genuine, proving that the Phoenicians did not only reach the far W of the Mediterranean, but sailed across the Atlantic as well. Most scholars have, however, been unconvinced by his arguments.

iii. *Other finds.* Several more Phoenician and Punic inscriptions were discovered during the 1960s in the course of excavations at Sidon (the temple of Eshmun) in Phoenicia proper, and on the islands of Sardinia (Monte Sirai), Sicily (Motya), and Malta (Tas Silg), but unfortunately few of them are complete or clear.

4. Conclusion. These inscriptions are so varied in content and originate from so many widely scattered places that their impact on the study of the Bible is less immediately felt than that of major finds at a single site like Qumran or Ras Shamra. They are nevertheless vital if the ongoing interpretation of biblical truth is to be anchored solidly in the ancient Semitic world from which the Bible came.

Bibliography. Students' and other important collections of texts: H. Donner and W. Röllig, *Kanaanäische und aramäische Inschriften,* I: *Texte,* II: *Kommentar,* III: *Glossare, Indizes, Tafeln* (1962-64 [2nd ed., 1966-69]); J. C. L. Gibson, *Textbook of Syrian Semitic Inscriptions,* I: *Hebrew and Moabite Inscriptions* (1971), II: *Aramaic Inscriptions, Including Inscriptions in the Dialect of Zenjirli* (1975), III: *Phoenician and Punic Inscriptions* (in preparation); J. Fitzmyer, *The Aramaic Inscriptions of Sefire* (1967); P. Grelot, *Documents araméens d'Egypte* (1972); M. G. Guzzo Amadasi, *Le iscrizioni fenici e puniche delle colonie in occidente* (1967).

Individual inscriptions: The text with bibliography of all but the most recent discoveries can be found in the collections of Donner-Röllig and Gibson. For the Bar Kochba material and the Samaria papyri, *see* BAR KOCHBA[S] and SAMARIA PAPYRI[S]. On the Ammonite inscriptions, S. H. Horn, "The Amman Citadel Inscription," *BASOR,* 193 (1969), 2-13; F. Cross, *ibid.,* pp. 13-19; G. Garbini, *Le lingue semitche* (1972), ch. vi; H. O. Thompson and F. Zayadine, "The Ammonite Inscription From Tell Siran," *Berytus,* XXII (1973), 115-40. On the Seville inscription, F. M. Cross, "The Old Phoenician Inscription From Spain," *HTR,* LXIV (1971), 189 ff.; a useful study of other important recent Phoenician texts is W. Röllig, "Beitrage zur nordsemitischen Epigraphik (1-4)," in *Die Welt des Orients,* V (1969), 108-25. On the Phoenician inscription from Brazil, C. H. Gordon, "The Authenticity of the Phoenician Text from Parahyba," *Orientalia,* XXXVII (1968), 75-80; the latest study is by G. I. Joffily, "L'inscription Phoenicienne de Parahyba," *ZDMG,* CXXII (1972), 22-36.

Translations: Selections are given in J. B. Pritchard, ed., *ANET* (2nd ed., 1955, and suppl. vol., 1969); D. Winton Thomas, ed., *Documents from OT Times* (1958).

Illustrations: Plates or figures of many inscriptions are included in most of the collections mentioned in the first paragraph above, and in the books by Diringer, Birnbaum, and Michaud mentioned in the seventh and eighth paragraphs below. A useful selection is available in J. B. Pritchard, ed., *The Ancient Near East in Pictures* (1954 and suppl. vol., 1969).

Grammars and studies on language: K. Beyer, *Althebräische Grammatik* (1969); B. S. J. Isserlin, "Epigraphically Attested Judaean Hebrew," *AJBA,* II (1972), 197-203; J. A. Emerton, "The Problem of Vernacular Hebrew in the First Century A.D. and the Language of

Jesus," *JTS,* NS XXIV (1973), 1-23; R. Degen, *Altaramäische Grammatik der Inschriften des 10-8 Jh. v. Chr.* (1969); E. Lipiński, *Studies on Aramaic Inscriptions and Onomastics* (1975); A. van den Branden, *Grammaire phénicienne* (1969); J. Friedrich and W. Röllig, *Phönizisch-Punische Grammatik* (2nd ed., 1970); G. Garbini, *Il semitico di nord-ovest* (1960).

Dictionary: C. F. Jean and J. Hoftijzer, *Dictionnaire des inscriptions sémitiques de l'ouest* (1965).

Script and orthography: D. Diringer, *The Story of the Aleph Beth* (1958); F. M. Cross, "The Development of the Jewish Scripts," in *The Bible and the Ancient Near East,* ed. G. E. Wright (1961), pp. 133-202; S. A. Birnbaum, *The Hebrew Scripts,* 2 vols. (1954-57, 1971); J. C. L. Gibson, "On the Linguistic Analysis of Hebrew Writing," *Archivum Linguisticum,* XVII (1969), 131-60; J. Naveh, "Hebrew Texts in Aramaic Script in the Persian Period?" *BASOR,* 203 (1971), 27-32, and "The Development of the Aramaic Script", *Proceedings of the Israel Academy of Sciences and Humanities,* V, 1 (1970); T. Wahl, "How did the Hebrew Scribe form his Letters?" *JANES,* III (1970-71), 9 ff.; A. R. Millard, "The Practice of Writing in Ancient Israel," *BA,* XXXV (1972), 98-111; J. B. Peckham, *The Development of the Late Phoenician Scripts* (1968); G. R. Driver, *Semitic Writing: From Pictograph to Alphabet* (1948); I. J. Gelb, *A Study of Writing* (rev. ed., 1963); L. A. Bange, *A Study of the Use of Vowel-Letters in Alphabetic Consonantal Writing* (1971).

The inscriptions and the Bible: The work of M. Dahood may be studied in "Qoheleth and Northwest Semitic philology," *Bibl.,* XLIII (1962), 349-65; *Proverbs and Northwest Semitic Philology* (1963); *Psalms I-III,* ABi, XVI, XVII, XVIIA (1965, 1968, 1970). Studies by pupils of Dahood are A. C. M. Blommerde, *Northwest Semitic Grammar and Job* (1969); K. J. Cathcart, *Nahum in the Light of Northwest Semitic* (1973). For criticism of his position, *see* J. Barr, *Comparative Philology and the Text of the OT* (1968), index, under "Dahood."

The following studies are less controversial: H. Michaud, *Sur la pierre et l'argile: Inscriptions hébraiques et Ancien Testament* (1958); S. Gevirtz, "West Semitic Curses and the Problem of the origins of Hebrew Law," *VT,* XI (1961), 137-58; D. R. Hillers, *Treaty-Curses and the OT Prophets* (1964); J. F. Ross, "Prophecy in Hamath, Israel, and Mari," *HTR,* LXIII (1970), 1-28; J. C. Greenfield, "Scripture and Inscription: The Literary and Rhetorical Element in Some Early Phoenician Inscriptions," in *Near Eastern Studies in Honor of W. F. Albright,* ed. H. Goedicke (1971), pp. 253-68; E. Lipiński, "From Karatepe to Pyrgi: Middle Phoenician Miscellanea," *Rivista di studi fenici,* II (1974), 45-61.

General background: D. Winton Thomas, ed., *Archaeology and OT Study* (1967); D. J. Wiseman, ed., *Peoples of OT Times* (1973); Y. Aharoni, *The Land of the Bible: A Historical Geography* (1967); A. H. van Zyl, *The Moabites* (1960); M. F. Unger, *Israel and the Aramaeans of Damascus* (1957); B. Mazar, "The Aramean Empire in its Relations with Israel," *BA,* XXV (1962), 98-120; B. Porten, *Archives from Elephantine: The Life of an Ancient Jewish Military Colony* (1968); D. B. Harden, *The Phoenicians* (1962); S. Moscati, *The World of the Phoenicians* (1968); W. A. Ward, ed., *The Role of the Phoenicians in the Interaction of Mediterranean Civilization* (1968).

New periodical: *Neue Ephemeris für semitische Epigraphik* (1972-).

Bulletin: For up-to-date bibliographical information, the annual "Bulletin d'épigraphic sémitique," by J. Teixidor, published in the periodical *Syria* from 1967 onward, should be consulted. J. C. L. GIBSON

*INTERPRETATION, HISTORY OF.

A. Within the OT
  1. History and folklore
  2. Law
  Bibliography
B. At Qumran and in the Targums
  1. Qumran
  2. The Targums
  Bibliography
C. NT interpretation of the OT
  1. External data
  2. Hermeneutics
  3. Exegetical results
  4. How OT interpretation developed
  Bibliography
D. Early rabbinic
  1. Oral Torah
  2. Hermeneutic rules
  3. Akiba and Ishmael
  4. Haggadah
  Bibliography
E. Early Christian
  Bibliography
F. Medieval Jewish
  1. In the Eastern Mediterranean
  2. In Spain
  3. In France
  Bibliography
G. Medieval Christian
  1. Jerome
  2. The fifth-eleventh centuries
  3. The twelfth-fifteenth centuries
  Bibliography
H. Reformation and Enlightenment
  Bibliography
I. Nineteenth- and twentieth-century Christian
  1. The nineteenth century
  2. The twentieth century
  Bibliography

A. WITHIN THE OT. Certain passages in the OT contain literary elements which were originally not part of the text. These addenda may be identified as modes of interpretation. A similar judgment is reached from a comparison of duplicated or related texts, where a later version puts a different construction on, or redresses a deficiency in the earlier one.

To appreciate the procedures underlying interpretation within the OT, reference to the broad principles of the rabbinic system will be helpful. There are two main categories of exposition, designated by the terms *peshat* (*pšṭ,* "to make plain") and *derash* (*drš,* "to inquire, search"). In the former the intent may be to explain a seeming obscurity or anomaly in a biblical text or to extend its range in a manner akin to exegesis. In the latter category, however, nonrational as well as logical methods of interpretation may be applied in order to derive scriptural authority for a rabbinic prohibition or ordinance, or to embellish themes in biblical folklore and point to moral teachings. These two categories are to be found, in rudimentary forms, in the OT itself.

1. History and folklore. Under this broad heading, types of *peshat* interpretation are found as follows.

a. Parallel or related passages. In Num. 20:12 and Deut. 32:50-52 we learn that Moses was denied entry into the Promised Land because he disobeyed God's explicit command to speak to the rock at Meribah. In Deut. 1:37, however, the blame for this ban is laid on the people. This passage (Deut. 1:22-39) recalls the discouraging report brought back by the spies (Num. 13:25-33), the resulting mass agitation against Moses and Aaron (Num. 14:1-10), and the consequent divine punishment by which the adult population died in the wilderness (Num. 14:22-24). It looks as if the Deuteronomist included Moses in the category of condemned adults and thus exonerated him from any fault to which the ban on his entry into Canaan could be attributed.

Ps. 106:32-33 acknowledges that the divine ban on Moses' entry into Canaan resulted from the incident at Meribah, but again it is the people, and not Moses, who are censured. "They (the people) angered him (God) at the waters of Meribah, and it went ill with Moses on their account; for they made his spirit bitter." In the consonantal Hebrew text (before vowel points were devised) the word *hmr* could be read as either *himrû,* as in the Masoretic text, from the root *mrh* and meaning "they rebelled," or *hēmārû,* as scholars generally adopt, from the root *mrr* and meaning "they embittered." Perhaps the poet intended that both notions should be understood. In rabbinic homiletic interpretation a dual meaning of a word is often induced by accepting both the *kethibh* (the word in a text) and the *qere* (the oral substitute; *see* QERE-KETHIBH[S]), thereby implying a dual meaning.

In II Sam. 7:2 (and I Chr. 17:1) David intimated to the prophet Nathan his desire to build a temple, but a divine revelation to the prophet denied him this honor, which was to be reserved for his son (II Sam. 7:12, 13). No explanation is offered for this disqualification, but this omission is remedied in I Chr. 22:8 and 28:3. In the first passage David explained to Solomon, and in the latter passage to the assembled leaders of Israel, that his disqualification was due to his having "shed so much blood." The Hebrew expression implies willful killing. Recalling how David arranged for the elimination of Uriah (II Sam. 11:14-17) and the murder of Saul's surviving sons, with the exception of Mephibosheth (II Sam. 21:7-9), the phrase aptly describes David's ruthless acts. The Chronicler, however, associates David's bloody exploits with the necessities of war and thus slurs over the sordid side of his character.

b. Editorial notes. Exod. 20:12 and Deut. 5:16, versions of the Decalogue commandment to honor one's parents, offer the promise "that your days may be long" (in itself an addition to the statement of the commandment). The Deuteronomy text adds the assurance "and that it may go well with you," as does the LXX in both passages. The additional note was evidently meant to assure the reader (or the listener) that the promised long life would be a happy one. The tendency to make explicit what is obviously implicit is characteristic of rabbinic exposition, and here we find its prototype in the OT. The fact that this additional note appears in the LXX of both passages indicates that this kind of interpretation was well established before the second century B.C. Furthermore, the addition to the Masoretic text of Deuteronomy indicates that this method was applied to sacred texts long before the final editing of that book.

Ps. 1:3 provides an example of interpretation, in practical terms, of what the poet meant to convey in poetical imagery. The psalmist describes the happy lot of the man who shuns the company of sinners, and whose delight is in God's Torah. "He is like a tree planted by streams of water, that yields its fruit in its season, and its leaf does not wither." At the end of the verse is a line out of harmony with this poetical picture—"in all that he does, he prospers." This is an editorial expository note.

c. Glosses. A gloss may be recognized primarily by its interrupting the flow of thought, so that its elimination restores a smooth sequence. Yet glosses are of interest, in that they represent types of interpretation or comments on words or phrases in the text. A simple example is found in Josh. 1:15. In this chapter Joshua reminds the tribes of Reuben and Gad and the half-tribe of Manasseh of the pact they had made with Moses (Num. 32). They were allotted territory E of the Jordan, but had agreed to join the rest of the tribes in the conquest of the territory W of Jordan. Once they fulfilled their commitment, they would be free to return to their allotted lands. The text under consideration may be translated: "Then shall you return to your inherited land, *and you shall possess it* which Moses, the servant of the Lord, gave you beyond the Jordan." The italicized words destroy the smooth reading of the line; their removal restores an even flow of thought. The judgment that we have here a gloss is confirmed by the absence of these words in the LXX. The interposed note makes explicit what is clearly implicit in the verse, namely, that returning implied taking possession.

An explanatory gloss designed to avoid anthropomorphism is found in Ps. 18:6 [H 7]. It may be translated: "My cry before him (God) enters his ears." The rules of parallelism in Hebrew poetry make it clear that this line read, "My cry enters his ears." The extra word לפניו, meaning "before him," breaks the flow of thought and is therefore a gloss. The annotator explained that what is meant by the seeming anthropomorphic phrase "enters his (God's) ears" is "enters his presence." The avoidance of such phrasing by the interpolation of a word is characteristic of the Aramaic TARGUMS. A typical example is Gen. 6:9 where the Hebrew expression "Noah walked with God" is rendered by both Targs. as "Noah walked in the fear of God."

The differences between an editorial note and a gloss are that: (1) An editorial note deals with the subject matter of the text, while a gloss comments on a word or phrase. (2) An editorial note was apparently consciously added to the verse, since it becomes a continuum with it, while a gloss, because it breaks the smooth flow of thought, was apparently meant to be external to the text but was subsequently incorporated into it by faulty copying.

2. **Law.** The rabbinic device of securing scriptural authority for a prevailing prohibition by artificially deriving it from a biblical text was anticipated by the narrative in Gen. 32:32 [H 33]. To take an example of the rabbinic method first, the prohibition of eating meat and milk together is associated with the negative command in Exod. 23:19 (and elsewhere), "You shall not boil a kid in its mother's milk." The forbidding of mixing meat and milk in this special case was sufficient, in the rabbinic system of *derash,* to warrant the deduction of the general prohibition current in their time. The biblical narrator states that the angel "touched the hollow of his (Jacob's) thigh, and Jacob's thigh was put out of joint" (Gen. 32:25). "Therefore to this day the Israelites do not eat the sinew of the hip which is upon the hollow of the thigh" (vs. 32). One is led to the conclusion that (1) in ancient Israel the prohibition against the eating of this membrane of an animal was operative before the final editing of the Pentateuch, and (2) the folk tale was sufficient warrant to derive the prohibition from this incident. Thus this passage provides an early example of what became a widespread rabbinic mode of interpretation.

Often a dilemma caused by conflicting legal texts was resolved by the rabbis by merging the two discrepant texts into one composite directive. An illustration of this method is provided by Exod. 21:2-6 as modified in Deut. 15:12-18.

The Exodus law states, "When you buy an עברי slave, he shall serve six years, and in the seventh he shall go out free, for nothing." The term עברי is usually translated "Hebrew," but it seems more likely that the law refers, not to an Israelite slave, but to a HABIRU. The Habiru were a rootless society whose members engaged themselves as mercenaries in time of war, but entered menial service in peace time. The Exodus law regulated the terms of service of Habiru with an Israelite master. The Habiru apparently disappeared after the eleventh century B.C. and even their name was not known to later generations. Because of such designations as "Abram the עברי" in Gen. 14:13 and the "God of the עברים" in Exod. 3:18, the term came to be identified with "Israelite."

The dilemma which presented itself to the Deuteronomic legislator was this. With the Hebrew term עברי identified with "Israelite," the Exodus law seemed to be expressly contradicted by Lev. 25:39-46. This latter law laid down that an impoverished Israelite could voluntarily enter the service of a fellow Israelite, but he was to be treated as a hired servant and not as a slave. The problem was solved by interpreting the Exodus law in the light of the Leviticus law, so that the Exodus law was made to refer to an impoverished Israelite selling himself into the temporary service of an Israelite master.

The following translation of Deut. 15:12-18 (with interpolations) adheres to the Hebrew text more closely than the standard translations. "If your brother, a Hebrew (i.e., an Israelite) man—or a Hebrew (i.e., an Israelite) woman—sells himself to you (i.e., according to the law in Lev. 25:39), and he serves you six years, and in the seventh year you let him go free from you (i.e., as laid down in the law of Exod. 21:2), then, when you let him go free from you, you must not let him go free empty-handed. You must furnish him liberally out of your flocks, your threshing floor, and your wine press; . . . for at half the cost of a hired servant (as in the Leviticus law), he has served you six years (as in the Exodus law)."

This is only one example of the several biblical laws and historical incidents recorded in Exodus, Leviticus, and Numbers which have been modified or extended in Deuteronomy. This phenomenon can best be explained by postulating the existence and operation of an oral TORAH (like the later MISHNA), a corpus of law and history outside and co-existing with the written Torah, of which authorized interpretation of the sacred text was a part. Because Deuteronomy was the accepted official interpretation of the Torah, it came to be endowed with divine inspiration and was attached to the earlier books.

Neh. 8:1-8 describes the scene in which, under the direction of Ezra, the Levites instructed the assembled people in the Torah. "[They] helped the people to understand the law" (vs. 7). "And they read from the book, from the law of God clearly (or, with interpretation—RSV n.); and they gave the sense, so that the people understood (or, they, the Levites, gave understanding to) the reading." It is likely that Ezra extended to the public the practice, which may have earlier been confined to selected groups, of teaching the Torah by means of a uniform exposition.

The significant conclusion reached by the study of interpretation within the OT is that, during the period of the formation of the OT, a system of expounding the Hebrew Scriptures was already established and that it continued in a direct line of tradition into the early rabbinic era.

Bibliography. N. Sarna, "Psalm 89: A Study in Inner Biblical Exegesis," *Biblical and Other Studies,* ed. A. Altmann (1963), pp. 29-46; J. Weingreen, "Rabbinic-type Glosses in the OT," *JSS,* II (1957), 149-62, "Exposition in the OT and in Rabbinic Literature," in *Promise and Fulfilment,* ed. F. F. Bruce (1963), pp. 187-201, and "The Deuteronomic Legislator—a Proto-Rabbinic Type," in *Proclamation and Presence,* ed. J. Durham and R. Porter (1970), pp. 76-89; F. F. Bruce, "The Earliest OT Interpretation," *OTS,* XVII (1972), 37-52.

J. WEINGREEN

B. AT QUMRAN AND IN THE TARGUMS.

1. **Qumran.** A great variety of writings belonging to the literary genre of Bible interpretation have survived among the documents concealed in the Qumran caves. Our purpose is to distinguish the diverse forms of exegesis used by the Dead Sea sectaries and to reconstruct and evaluate their methods.

a. The forms of Qumran exegesis. i. *The pesher.* This Hebrew term (pl. *pesharim*), the etymological meaning of which is "interpretation," has acquired a twofold technical significance. It may designate a literary work in which a biblical book is quoted continuously verse by verse (or unit by unit), each citation being accompanied by exegesis. Or it may denote a certain type of nonliteral interpretation (*see* §aiii *below*).

It cannot be proved theoretically that the literary form of *pesher* was restricted at Qumran to the interpretation of prophecy alone, but the fact is that the only surviving and published examples belong to this class. The most important *pesharim* relate to Habakkuk, Nahum, Isaiah, Hosea, and Ps. 37.

From the point of view of structure, the *pesharim* belong to one or the other of two categories: the interpreter either deals with each biblical unit separately or seeks to establish a connection between the successive verses.

In the first instance, the MS opens with a biblical text followed by a formula introducing the exegesis, such as, "Its interpretation: . . ."; "Its interpretation concerns. . ."; "The interpretation of the saying concerns," etc. When the exposition is completed, the next section of Scripture is quoted, and the same process recommences. The treatment of Hab. 2:3*a* in 1QpHab 7.5-8 may serve as an illustration.

> *For there shall be yet another vision concerning the appointed time.*
> *It shall tell of the end and shall not lie.*
> Interpreted, this means that the final age shall be prolonged and shall exceed all that the Prophets have said; for the mysteries of God are astounding.

Occasionally, the biblical excerpt consists of more than one verse and is too long for an uninterrupted exegesis. In such cases the interpreter first expounds the initial part of the unit, then, employing a special introductory formula (usually, "As for that which He said"), repeats the next section of Scripture and appends to it his further comments. For example, 1QpHab 6.14–7.5 interprets Hab. 2:2 in the following manner:

> *And the Lord answered* [*and said to me,*
> *Write down the vision and make it plain*] *upon the tablets that* [*he who reads*] *may read it speedily.*
> God told Habakkuk to write down that which would happen to the final generation, but He did not make known to him when time would come to an end. And as for that which he said, *That he who reads may read it speedily,* interpreted, this concerns the Teacher of Righteousness, to whom God made known all the mysteries of the words of His servants, the Prophets.

In the less frequent second category of *pesharim,* the interpreter links his exegesis of the previous verse to the subsequent quotation. In 4QpIs[b] 2.13 on Isa. 5:10 we read:

> [*For ten acres of vineyard shall produce only one* bath, *and an* omer *of seed shall yield only one* ephah.]
> Interpreted, this saying concerns the last days, the devastation of the land by the sword and famine. At the time of the Visitation of the land there shall be
> *Woe to those who rise early in the morning to run after strong wine* (Isa. 5:11).

ii. *Midrashic paraphrase of large units.* The most important example of a full-scale midrashic paraphrase at Qumran is the Genesis Apocryphon (1QapGen). Instead of quoting and explaining the biblical narrative, the author recasts the story so that Scripture and its interpretation form an undivided whole.

Gen. 12:17	*1QapGen 20.16-17*
But the Lord afflicted Pharaoh and his house with great plagues because of Sarai, Abram's wife.	And on that night the Most High God sent a spirit of affliction, an evil spirit, to afflict both him and his house. He was afflicted and all his household, and he could not approach her and he knew her not.

The author of 1QapGen not only provides a more vivid description, but also makes it plain that the virtue of Sarah was unquestionably safeguarded through God's direct intervention.

iii. *Midrashic interpretation of smaller units.* The Damascus Rule (CDC) frequently adduces sundry short citations from the Bible to demonstrate the particular issue under discussion. For instance, in CDC 6.11-13, Mal. 1:10 serves to justify the withdrawal of the sect's priests from active service in the temple of Jerusalem.

> None of those brought into the Covenant shall enter the Temple to light His altar in vain. They shall bar the door, forasmuch as God said, *Who among you will bar its door?* And, *You shall not light my altar in vain.*

iv. *Collection of proof texts.* The only relevant document so far edited is the Messianic Anthology or 4QTest. Its aim is to provide scriptural backing for the community's expectation of a "Prophet and the [two] Messiahs of Aaron and Israel" (1QS 9.11). According to our text the prophet is announced in Deut. 5:28-29; 18:18, 19; the king in Num. 24:15-17; and the priest in Deut. 33:8-11. For further remarks, *see* DEAD SEA SCROLLS[S] §8.

v. *Collection of legal texts arranged according to subjects.* The well-established Jewish custom of explaining one text of Scripture by another is attested at Qumran. In the legal domain, one of the most striking illustrations is furnished by the Damascus Rule when it demonstrates (CDC 4.20–5.2) the absolutely binding nature of monogamy. The opponents of the sect are accused of committing fornication in "taking a second wife while the first is alive, whereas the principle of the creation is, *Male and female created He them* (Gen. 1:27). Also, those who entered the ark went in two by two (Gen. 7:9). And concerning the prince, it is written, *He shall not multiply wives to himself* (Deut. 17:17)."

vi. *Collection of doctrinal texts arranged according to themes.* Apart from the incidental combination of such passages in the Damascus Rule (e.g., Num. 21:18 and Isa. 54:16 in CDC 6.3-8; or Amos 5:25-26; 9:11 and Num. 24:17 in CDC 7.14-21), two principal compositions must be mentioned in this context. First, the Midrash on the Last Days, or 4QFlor, expounds II Sam. 7:10-14 with the help of Exod. 15:17-18 and Amos 9:11, and Ps. 1:1 by means of Isa. 8:11 and Ezek. 44:10.

Secondly, the Melchizedek Document, or 11QMelch, establishes a link between Isa. 61:1; Lev. 25:13; and Deut. 15:2, to conflate their respective messages into a single eschatological doctrine. *See* MELCHIZEDEK[S] §1.

The sectarian interpreters were convinced that these six classes of exegesis constituted a highly technical and sophisticated system that enabled them to clarify the obscurities of the Bible and to prove "scientifically" that their laws and beliefs had been divinely ordained. For them, Bible interpretation was an indispensable tool in the construction of a theological or apologetic edifice.

b. Methods of Qumran exegesis. To evaluate the exegetical methods of the Dead Sea community, it will be of help to recall that ancient Jewish Bible interpretation had a dual purpose: on the one hand, it aimed at rendering the message of the text intelligible, coherent, and acceptable (pure exegesis); on the other, it sought to discover in Scripture answers to nonbiblical questions by searching for hidden general principles which could be applied to new situations and fresh problems (applied exegesis).

i. *Midrashic supplement to a story.* a) Pure exegesis. In the Genesis account of Abram's journey to Egypt, the biblical author fails to indicate how the patriarch learned of the danger that he would incur should he and his beautiful wife cross the southern frontier of Canaan. The Genesis Apocryphon introduces a premonitory dream as a result of which Abram keeps his wife out of the sight of the Egyptians for five years. Her attractions are discovered only when three princes of Pharaoh are dispatched explicitly to make inquiries concerning the foreign couple (1QapGen 19.14-24).

b) Applied exegesis. In their endeavor to prove that their community had replaced the Jewish people as God's elect and that their council had been substituted for the Jerusalem temple, the sectaries discovered in Hab. 2:17, "for the violence done to Lebanon shall overwhelm you," the evidence they needed. To understand how they managed to render this text as, "For Lebanon is the Council of the Community" (1QpHab 12.3-4), it should be borne in mind that there was already in existence a popular Jewish tradition identifying Lebanon with the temple. The application, therefore, of the same Lebanon metaphor to the council simply proclaims the community's belief that the replacement of Jerusalem by the spiritual sanctuary of the sect was predestined by God and foretold by Habakkuk.

ii. *Halachic reinterpretation.* a) Pure exegesis. In ch. 30 of Numbers, the biblical legislator proclaims that a vow made on oath by a man is always binding, but one made by a woman may be annulled by a male guardian, viz., her husband or father. The law recorded in the Damascus Rule introduces a moral distinction, and limits the right of the husband or father to cancel the vows in question by stipulating that they may revoke only those which should never have been made.

> Concerning the oath of a woman. Inasmuch as He said, *It is for her husband to cancel her oath* (Num. 30:9), no husband shall cancel an oath without knowing whether it should be kept or not. Should it be such as to lead to transgression of the Covenant, he shall cancel it and shall not let it be kept. The rule for her father is likewise (CDC 16.10-12).

b) Applied exegesis. Conflict between a man's duty toward his dependents and piety toward God, expressed in the form of gifts to the temple, must have been a familiar dilemma in the intertestamental period (cf. Mark 7:9-13; Matt. 15:3-6). The author of the Damascus Rule demonstrates by means of a punning exegesis of Mic. 7:2 that the sectary's obligation to his parents takes precedence over his obligation to send gifts to the sanctuary. In poetic language, the prophet accuses the Israelites of hunting one another with a "net" (*ḥerem*). The same Hebrew word can, however, also mean a "votive offering." The Damascus Rule therefore has only to substitute the one meaning for the other: "No man shall consecrate the good of his house to God, for it is as He said, *Each hunts his brother with a votive offering*" (CDC 16.14-15).

iii. *Fulfillment of prophecy.* The Qumran sectaries, like all protagonists of an eschatological outlook at the turn of the eras, were convinced that the final age had already begun, and that they themselves were witnessing the last act of the human drama about which the prophets had spoken. As a consequence, they were able to detect in the events of their own time the realization of ancient predictions. The words of Habakkuk or Nahum, for instance, were seen to adumbrate the end of world history in general, and the sect's destiny in particular, but to make such hints fully intelligible the interpreter had to correlate the prophetic announcements with fulfillments. Peculiar though this kind of interpretation may be, it is still to be regarded as "pure exegesis." Nevertheless, when the logical sequence is reversed, and the starting point is a disconcerting contemporary event, we are faced with a specimen of "applied exegesis."

By interpreting Hab. 1:6*a*, "For behold I rouse the Chaldeans, the bitter and hasty nation," as announcing the coming of "the Kittim [who are] quick and valiant in war, causing many to perish" (1QpHab 2.10-13), the Qumran exegete believed that he was merely spelling out the full eschatological meaning (or *pesher,* cf. §*ai above*) of the words of Habakkuk. The prophet thought that the final conquerors of the world would be the Chaldeans, but the sectaries recognized the enemy's true identity and knew that they were the "Kittim," i.e., the Romans.

By contrast, when a fairly general utterance of Hab. 2:8*b*, "Because of the blood of men and the violence done to the land, to the city and to all its inhabitants," is explained in 1QpHab 9.8-12 as referring to "the Wicked Priest whom God delivered into the hands of his enemies because of the iniquity committed against the Teacher of Righteousness and the men of his Council," the exegete does not proceed to explain the text by means of a contemporary illustration, but adopts a dogmatic stand. The event, he asserts, is the fulfillment of

Hab. 2:8*b*, and as such it was foreordained by God from all eternity.

It should be noted that the interpreter occasionally takes liberties with the text of Scripture in order to ensure that it conveys the meaning he intends it to have, as for instance in his reshaping, in CDC 7.14-20, of Amos 5:26-27—originally a divine threat—to read as a promise of salvation. This is, however, exceptional. The usual attitude is so respectful that at times it presents the exegete with difficulties. For example, in Hab. 2:16, the commentator reproduces the Hebrew text with a LXX-type variant, "Stagger!" (*hērāᶜēl*), instead of the Masoretic reading, "Show your foreskin!" (*heᶜārēl*). He writes:

> You have filled yourself with ignominy more than with glory. Drink also and stagger!

Yet his exegesis discloses knowledge of both textual traditions:

> Interpreted, this concerns the Priest whose ignominy was greater than his glory. For he did not circumcise the foreskin of his heart, and he walked in the ways of drunkenness that he might quench his thirst (1QpHab 11.12-14).

This rendering not only implies an acquaintance with the variants; it also shows an inability or unwillingness to choose between them. Both readings are cleverly mingled, revealing that, far from being free with the biblical text, the interpreter held in profound esteem every witness of what in his view was the sacred record of the word of God.

2. The Targums. The translation of the Hebrew Bible into vernacular Aramaic was intended to render its message easily intelligible to the ordinary Jew. It was not merely offered as reading material—in fact, if the Mishna is to be believed, the Targ. was to be recited without a script—but as an uncontroversial guide for practice and belief. The Targumists adopted different styles of presentation which vary according to the nature of the scriptural books and also according to the interpreter's notion of his own particular role. The Targ. therefore oscillates between a fairly straightforward translation and a rich, homiletic paraphrase. Our analysis, based on the earlier and more important Targs. to the Pentateuch and the Prophets, will first outline matters relating to Targumic form and structure, and will follow this with a succinct account of Targumic exegetical principles. *See also* TARGUM; TARGUM[S].

a. Targumic form and structure. Although no Aramaic version of Scripture can be described as strictly a literal translation, the Targ. ascribed to Onkelos comes nearest to such a genre. The Palestinian Targs. (Pseudo-Jonathan, Fragmentary Targ., Neofiti, and Cairo Genizah fragments) often contain large midrashic additions, whereas the Jonathan Targ. to the Prophets occupies an intermediate position.

The Targ. of Onkelos, which was finally compiled in Babylonia, offers, in a literary language, a verse-by-verse translation of the Torah with only a small amount of paraphrase, apart from obscure poetic passages where it scarcely differs from the more expansive Palestinian Targs. The intention of the final redactor was to keep the Aramaic as close as possible to the Hebrew. He sought, for instance, to translate one Hebrew by one Aramaic word, preferably always the same. (In this respect, Onkelos is comparable to the Greek version of Aquila, and foreshadows the modern German version of the OT by Buber and Rosenzweig; *see* VERSIONS, ANCIENT §2*b*; VERSIONS, MEDIEVAL AND MODERN, NON-ENGLISH §3.) Again, wishing to remain closely linked to the biblical original, Onkelos attempted to explain its legal and doctrinal difficulties as laconically as possible, as the following example illustrates. The age-old taboo against boiling a kid in its mother's milk, recorded in Exod. 23:19, developed in time into a legal principle, which first prohibited the use of milk in the cooking of meat, and later became one of the foundations of rabbinic dietary law in which meat and milk must be kept absolutely apart. Onkelos, in rewriting the Exodus passage, took all this evolution into account and rendered it quite simply as, "You shall not eat flesh with milk."

In the doctrinal field, Onkelos used key words and short allusions to suggest complex haggadic developments. Gen. 4:24, "If Cain is avenged sevenfold, truly Lamech seventy-sevenfold," was transformed by Onkelos into, "If seven generations were suspended for Cain, shall there not be seventy-seven for Lamech, his son?" The Targumist tried to convey in a limited number of words the doctrine expounded in the Palestinian Targs. and midrashic literature that God never punishes without offering an opportunity for repentance, and that during this period the sinner lives as it were under a suspended sentence.

The unlearned, to be sure, required still further clarification after listening to the "literal" type of Targ., but through his skillful choice of words, Onkelos provided teachers and preachers with material to which they could easily attach any additional commentary that they needed.

The midrashic, or fully paraphrastic, Targ. represented by the Palestinian variety may take two different forms. Either the Targumist appended a developed exegesis to every part of the scriptural account, or he selected a few key verses and enlarged on them without significantly altering the rest of the narrative. In the interpretation of the sacrifice of Isaac (Gen. 22:1-18), Pseudo-Jonathan testified to the former method. Neofiti, by contrast, chose vss. 8, 10, and 14, which no doubt originally inspired the midrash, and built on them an elaborate HAGGADAH.

b. Targumic exegetical principles. As has been stated, the primary purpose of Bible interpretation is to clarify obscurities, harmonize contradictions, and identify predictions. To achieve these aims, the exegete employs accepted principles of interpretation, a number of them devised to cope with philological or stylistic problems, and others to deal with more complex exegetical topics.

In the field of language, one obvious difficulty is posed by the use of a foreign word in the Hebrew text. "Babel" is one such term. The Bible itself contains a pointer to its meaning by ignoring its original Akkadian significance, "gate of the deity," and expressing it by means of a vaguely similar-sounding Hebrew verb, *balal,* to confuse: "Because there the Lord confused the language of all the earth" (Gen. 11:9). Onkelos followed, and even improved on, the biblical pattern by choosing the corresponding slightly cleverer Aramaic pun, *balbēl*. The Palestinian Targs., on the other hand, introduced a more ordinary Aramaic term conveying the idea of mingling or mixing (*ʿarbēb*), but concealing the fact that the original exegesis was construed on a play on words. Likewise, the Egyptian word uttered by heralds to announce the arrival of Joseph is explained in the Palestinian Targs. (Gen. 41:43) from the Hebrew, by a process called *notrikon,* the artificial division of a word into several parts which are then separately interpreted (*see* WORDPLAY IN THE OT §1). Thus, the Egyptian *abrek* (probably, "pay homage") is split into *ab* and *rek,* "father," and "tender," and the verse becomes: "Long live the father of the king, who is great in wisdom, although tender in years."

Other linguistic problems may spring from genuine textual corruptions; or they may be invented by the interpreter himself when, for religious reasons, he is unwilling to accept that the Bible may be formulating an archaic view; or they may derive from an elliptic phrase requiring supplementation.

Furthermore, it is common in the Targ. to replace symbols by the object symbolized. This type of conversion is often simple: seed=children, lion=king, etc. Sometimes it is more complex, as may be seen in the Targ. to Hos. 1:2.

Hosea	*Targ.*
Go, take to yourself a wife of harlotry and have children of harlotry, for the land commits great harlotry by forsaking YHWH.	Go and prophesy a prophecy about the inhabitants of the erring city who continue to sin. For the residents of the land err indeed away from the worship of YHWH.

The elimination of anthropomorphisms belongs to the same type of exegesis: "sons of God" become "sons of the judges" (Gen. 6:2); "YHWH came down"="the glory of the Shekhinah (Presence) of YHWH revealed itself" (Gen. 11:5). Apropos of the Targumic substitutes for the Tetragrammaton, especially *Shᵉkhina* (Presence) and *memra* (word), it has been recently argued that originally they were not used haphazardly, but fulfilled particular purposes, the former appearing in contexts of manifestation and divine residence, the latter in circumstances of speech and communication. They tended, however, to lose their special connotations and to be used in an indeterminate manner.

Geographical terms are either modernized or interpreted symbolically. Thus "Erech, Accad and Calneh in the land of Shinar" of Gen. 10:10 (Goodspeed) are replaced in the Palestinian Targs. by, "Edessa, Nisibis and Ctesiphon in the land of Babel (or Pontus)." In the second alternative, a simple geographical description may be transformed into a detailed story, as in the Targumic exegesis of Deut. 1:1.

Deut.	*Targ.*
These are the words that Moses spoke . . . in the wilderness, in the Arabah, over against Suph, between Paran and Tophel, Laban, Hazeroth, and Di-zahab.	These are the words that Moses spoke. . . . He reproved them because they sinned in the wilderness, and had angered [God] in the plain (*Arabah*), over against the sea of Reeds (*Yam Suph*); because they had scorned (*ittappalu*=*Tophel*) the manna (Laban=white) and had angered [God] in Hazeroth on account of meat, and had made the golden calf (*Di-zahab*=that which is of gold).

One of the basic principles of all forms of Jewish exegesis is to assemble parallel passages and explain one with the help of the other. Pseudo-Jonathan follows this custom in respect to Exod. 21:7 by reinterpreting the old legislation of the Code of the Covenant, according to which Hebrew slave women were not granted emancipation in the sabbatical year, in the light of later scriptural rulings.

> If a man, a son of Israel, sells his daughter, a minor, to be a bondmaid, she shall not go out as do the Canaanite slaves who gain liberty through [the loss of] a tooth and an eye (Exod. 21:26-27), but in the years of release (Deut. 15:12), through the tokens [of puberty], at the Jubilee (Lev. 25:40), the death of her master (Lev. 25:45-46) and through payment of money (Exod. 21:8).

A final Targumic characteristic concerns the interpreter's attitude to prophecy. When Pseudo-Jonathan explains that Balaam's description of the king of Israel as "higher than Agag" (Num. 24:7) refers to Saul's victory over the Amalekite king in question, he propounds an exclusively historical exegesis. Against this, Neofiti and the Fragmentary Targ. stress the messianic significance of the same words: "He shall be stronger than Saul, who showed mercy to Agag king of Amalek, and the kingdom of the king Messiah shall be exalted."

Here, as in many other instances, the interpreter advances a comprehensive view of history in which past and future are perceived at a single glance. The best example of this kind is afforded by Pseudo-Jonathan on Deut. 34:1-3, where Moses's contemplation of the Promised Land is transformed, through a combination of space and time, into a complete history and eschatology of Israel.

> Moses went up from the plain of Moab to Mount Nebo, the high peak opposite Jericho, and the Word of YHWH showed him the mighty ones of the land: the acts of valor that Jephtha of Gilead would do and the victories of Samson son of Manoah of the tribe of Dan; the thousand officers of the house of Naphtali who would associate themselves with Barak, and the kings whom Joshua son of Nun of the tribe of Ephraim would kill, and the acts of valor of Gideon son of Joash of the tribe of Manasseh; and all the kings of Israel and the kingdom of the house of Judah who would rule over the land until the last Temple would be destroyed; and the king of the south who would associate himself with the king of the north to ruin the inhabitants of the land, and the Ammonites and the

Moabites, the inhabitants of the plain who would oppress Israel; and the exiles of the disciples of Elijah who would be exiled from the vale of Jericho and the exiles of the disciples of Elisha who would be exiled from the city of the palm trees by their brethren, the house of Israel, two-hundred-thousand men; and the affliction of each generation and the punishment of the wicked Armalgos (Armillos) and the battle of Gog: and in the time of this great tribulation, Michael would arise to save with his arm.

Bearing in mind the exegetical contents of the Targs. and their common teaching function in the weekly liturgy, we can safely reassert the widely held thesis that the main body of Targumic exegesis reflects the ordinary, nontechnical understanding of the message of the Bible current among Aramaic-speaking Jews in the first two or three centuries of the Christian era.

Bibliography. Qumran: F. F. Bruce, *Biblical Exegesis in the Qumran Texts* (1959); O. Betz, *Offenbarung und Schriftforschung in der Qumransekte* (1960); G. Vermes, *Scripture and Tradition in Judaism* (1961 [2nd ed., 1973]), and *Post-Biblical Jewish Studies* (1975), pp. 35-56.

Targums: G. Vermes, *Scripture and Tradition in Judaism;* M. McNamara, *The NT and the Palestinian Targ. to the Pentateuch* (1966); J. Bowker, *The Targs. and Rabbinic Literature* (1969); A. M. Goldberg, *Untersuchungen über die Vorstellung von der Schekhinah in der frühen rabbinischen Literatur* (1969); R. Le Déaut, "Un phénomène spontané de l'herméneutique juive ancienne: le targoumisme," *Bibl.*, LII (1971), 505-25; P. Vermes, "Buber's Understanding of the Divine Name Related to Bible, Targ. and Midrash," *JJS,* XXIV (1973), 147-66; R. Hayward, "The *Memra* of YHWH and the Development of Its Use in Targ. Neofiti I," *JSS,* XXV (1974), 412-18; G. Vermes, *Post-Biblical Jewish Studies* (1975), pp. 59-146.

G. VERMES

C. NT INTERPRETATION OF THE OT. Interpretation of the OT in the church of NT times involved complex methods and processes only partly discernible to modern research, but there can be no doubt of the enormous and enduring effect of the OT on primitive Christianity.

1. External data. The NT contains over 1,600 citations of the OT and many more allusions to it. Among the direct quotations, 239 are introduced by formulas which usually underline their authority. It must be assumed that the appearance in early Christian documents of OT concepts, images, turns of phrase, and deliberate quotations is only the visible tip of an iceberg that profoundly influenced the sea of early church life and thought. Yet church use of the OT awakened controversy and occasionally outright repudiation (MARCION and certain Christian Gnostics), and some early Christian writings refer to it only rarely (e.g., I and II Thessalonians, Colossians, the Pastorals, the Johannine and Ignatian letters).

Unlike some sources behind the NT whose existence and character can only be matters of conjecture, the OT writings exist today in probably about the form or forms known to the first Christians. Generally the NT quotes the OT according to the LXX; but there are numerous departures from the LXX text, which may in particular cases stem from faulty recollection, intentional rewriting, or reliance on the MT, on other versions, or on intermediate sources ("testimony books," etc.). *See* QUOTATIONS §1.

2. Hermeneutics. The historical question is not "What is there about primitive Christian interpretation of the OT that moderns can approve or appropriate?" but simply "What were the working principles and procedures of that ancient exegesis?" (*see* HERMENEUTICS[S] §§7, 9). The general principles and procedures cannot be understood in isolation from the specific religious interests directing the exegesis (*see* §3 *below*), but a number of interpretive approaches used in the early church can be identified and often related to contemporary (mainly Jewish) hermeneutics.

a. General assumptions. In Rom. 15:4, Paul declares, "Whatever was written in former days was written for our instruction, that by steadfastness and by the encouragement of the scriptures we might have hope." He thus expresses perhaps the most basic hermeneutical principle of the early church, viz., that the OT was written for the sake of the church. Further, its "instruction" is designed not merely to inform but to inspire confidence in the future. Finally, the passage suggests that scriptural study must be coupled with steadfastness, a divine gift bound up with faith in Christ (15:5, 13; cf. 5:1-5). Early Christian interpretation of the OT is typically a venture of faith seeking deeper understanding and conviction. The general attitude seems to have been that Jesus as the Christ opens up the true meaning of the OT, and it, in turn, offers a major path toward comprehension of Christ and the church (e.g., Luke 24:44-47; Ign. Phila. 8:2–9:2).

The exegetical methods of early Christianity must often have appeared dubious or arbitrary to non-Christians. Exegetes like Paul, however, claimed that authentic interpretation required the spiritual perspective of believers in Christ (II Cor. 3:14-17). Theirs was an aggressive, authority-claiming, pneumatic exegesis. The Jews were recognized as historical recipients of God's oracles, but the standard Christian view came to be that adherents of the synagogue misread their scriptures by failing to perceive that they bore witness to Jesus (John 5:39-47; cf. Mark 12:24).

An eschatological attitude prevailed in most early Christian exegesis, as Paul suggests in a comment on a Pentateuchal narrative: "Now these things happened to them (Israelites led by Moses) as a warning, but they were written down for our instruction, upon whom the end of the ages has come" (I Cor. 10:11; cf. II Cor. 1:20; 6:2).

b. Particular methods. In the light of the NT church's sense of existing "in the last times," its general tendency to regard the OT as a book of promises and prophecies "now" in the process of being fulfilled (e.g., I Pet. 1:10-12) is not altogether strange.

This "prophecy-fulfillment" schema finds vivid expression in direct NT statements that various events in the life of Jesus and the church were anticipated in the OT (e.g., Mark 1:2-3; Acts 2:16-21). A special group of eleven fulfillment quotations appears in Matthew (e.g., 1:22-23; 27:9-10), and a similar set of thirteen in John. These sets of citations are introduced by distinctive formulas and characterized by an interpretive approach having important affinities with the midrash *pesher* attested in certain QUMRAN texts (e.g., 1QpHab), where the text forms of OT passages are selected or altered to bring out the commentator's interpretation and those passages are conceived to be apocalyptically "fulfilled" in the days of the TEACHER OF RIGHTEOUSNESS and his community (*see above* §B1*b*; DEAD SEA SCROLLS §5*a*; DEAD SEA SCROLLS[S] §8). The apostle Paul also seems to shape his OT citations in *pesher* fashion in some instances (e.g., I Cor. 15:54-55). *See* MIDRASH[S] §5*c, d*.

Less direct use of the prophecy-fulfillment pattern is found in NT narratives that allude to the OT without quoting it. The first two chapters of Luke are outstanding in this regard (the hymnic materials are especially noteworthy; the Magnificat, e.g., powerfully recalls Hannah's song without ever directly quoting I Sam. 2:1-10).

A related exegetical approach that also presupposes a two-aeon view of history is TYPOLOGY, which correlates OT persons, events, or things with counterparts in the age of fulfillment. Some key instances connect Adam and Christ (Rom. 5:12-21; I Cor. 15:21-22, 45-49; probably Phil. 2:6-11), Melchizedek and Jesus (Heb. 7:1-17), Noah's deliverance and Christian baptism (I Pet. 3:21; *see* BAPTISM[S] §2*f*), Israel under Moses and Joshua, and the church under Jesus (I Cor. 10:1-13; Heb. 3:7–4:10). *See* MOSES IN THE NT[S].

It is difficult and quite likely illegitimate to make a sharp differentiation between typology and ALLEGORY as the latter is practiced in the NT church. Paul explicitly says that the story of Sarah and Hagar is allegorical (Gal. 4:24), signifying the conflict between law-bound Judaism and spirit-freed Christianity. Similarly, the singular "seed" promised to Abraham is identified with Christ (Gal. 3:16), and primeval words about marriage are judged a "mystery" concerning Christ and the church (Eph. 5:32). Allegory is not always related to crucial events of salvation history: Paul can say that Mosaic words apparently dealing with oxen really are meant to express God's concern for human ministers (I Cor. 9:8-10; cf. I Tim. 5:18). All such interpretations imply that a secret "spiritual" lesson underlies the OT text, but the hidden meaning is usually eschatological in character rather than oriented to a domain of timeless realities (as in the typical allegories of PHILO). The Epistle of Barnabas employs typology and allegory lavishly to extract an eschatological *gnosis* concealed in the Jewish Scriptures (e.g., 9:8-9).

A number of hermeneutic methods common in rabbinic literature are utilized in the NT. The technique of building an interpretation on a single detail in a text is seen in Mark 12:26, 35-37; John 10:34; Gal. 3:16. The practice of constructing a chain of OT quotations dealing with a single theme or term is well illustrated in Rom. 3:10-19; 10:18-21; I Pet. 2:6-8. The general rabbinic principle that scripture should be interpreted from scripture is practiced in Christian passages joining OT texts in intricate webs of elucidation. A fine example is Rom. 10:5-13, where Paul pits Deuteronomy against Leviticus and then introduces citations from Isaiah and Joel to draw out a firm conclusion about justification by faith. In this passage and in several gospel pericopes (e.g., Matt. 5:21-48; Mark 7:15), the truth of certain OT texts seems disputed or denied. More commonly, however, an early Christian writer sets OT texts side by side without questioning the validity of any, a procedure more in line with Pharisaic practice. Finally, whether early Christians heeded the rabbinic precept that scripture be interpreted with regard to original context is still a subject of controversy among scholars.

3. Exegetical results. Christians of the NT era used the OT for many purposes: to praise the God of Israel (using the Scriptures directly as a liturgical resource of the church), to think through religious and theological problems, to give depth to teaching within the church, to support positively the main points of missionary preaching, and to defend the *kerygma* against objections from both Jews and Gentiles. The exegesis was functional, generally aimed at affirming, clarifying, or defending beliefs about Christ and the church.

a. Christology (*see also* CHRISTOLOGY IN THE NT [S]). Early Christian images of Jesus as the bringer of SALVATION were very largely formed with OT materials. Many of the central christological titles were taken more or less directly from the scriptures: MESSIAH, SON OF MAN, SON OF GOD, son of David, the SERVANT OF THE LORD, the high priest, "the prophet."

Most of the christological references to the OT in the NT affirm or argue that Jesus is the Messiah; they do not seek to prove that God needed to send a deliverer or Messiah (perhaps that was widely regarded as self-evident). Presumably the matters most in need of scriptural explanation from the start were Jesus' death and resurrection (cf. Acts 17:3). This view is supported by I Cor. 15:3-5, which many scholars regard as substantially a pre-Pauline creed: here the parallel declarations that Jesus died "for our sins" and was raised on the third day are each accompanied by the phrase "in accordance with the scriptures." The passage neglects to specify any particular scriptural texts, but it at least implies that at a very early date the OT was used to express and perhaps explain Jesus' death and resurrection as in accord with God's salvation plan.

The NT regularly connects Jesus' resurrection with his exaltation as LORD and SAVIOR, and most of the OT passages cited in regard to the Resurrection bring out this soteriological orientation (e.g., Pss. 8:6; 68:18; 110:1).

Jesus' suffering and death must have early been a prime subject for Christian reflection and apologetic. Isa. 53, of vast importance in later Christian centuries, is oddly unused in much of the NT. The most clear-cut linking of that passage with an atoning view of the death is in a relatively late passage, I Pet. 2:21-25, although passages like Mark 10:45; 14:24; and Rom. 4:25 may reflect much earlier thinking along those lines. The passion narratives in the gospels offer a large number of OT quotations and allusions (especially to passages in the Psalms and in Zechariah); the result is, if not a full theory of atonement, at least a powerful assertion that Jesus died by the predetermined will of God (cf. Mark 14:21*a*; Matt. 26:24*a*; Luke 22:22). The formation of the passion narratives (*see* PASSION NARRATIVE[S]) was probably marked by some historicizing of these OT "predictions" (i.e., events connected with Jesus' death were invented or modified to bring them into line with expectations based on the OT). In only a few other places in the NT is Jewish Scripture directly referred to in order to show the necessity or meaning of his death (*see* particularly John 3:14; Gal. 3:13; Heb. 9).

Major events connected with Jesus' birth, pre-Passion career, and ministry are also set forth as fulfilling OT prophecy, particularly in summary or programmatic statements (e.g., Luke 4:16-21; Matt. 8:17; 12:17-21). The OT is also used to articulate convictions about Christ's pre-existent roles in creation (Heb. 1:10-12) and salvation history (I Cor. 10:4; Heb. 11:26), as well as his future parousia (Mark 13:26; 14:62; Matt. 24:30; Luke 21:27; Matt. 26:64; Luke 22:69; Rev. 1:7; etc.).

Not the least christological contribution of OT interpretation may have lain in the area of enabling the church to affirm the uniqueness of Jesus as Savior while also maintaining a staunch monotheistic faith in a sovereign Creator (cf. I Cor. 15:25-28; Heb. 1:1-14; 2:5-13).

b. Ecclesiology. OT exegesis also had a decisive impact on the development of reflection on the church. In the act of claiming the OT as God's word for them, the earliest Christians identified themselves as members of God's chosen people, the true Israel (*see* ISRAEL, CONCEPTIONS OF[S] §4). They rapidly appropriated other OT descriptions for the church—e.g., children of Abraham, God's flock, the vine, the bride of the Lord (*see* CHURCH, IDEA OF). The critical implication was that the Christian movement was no merely human religious society (or loosely knit group of societies); the church was rather a unified community miraculously founded and sustained by grace (Rom. 9:6-33; Eph. 2:11-22; I Pet. 2:9-10). At the same time the OT could help the church recognize its imperfections, its liability to temptations and suffering (I Cor. 10:12-13), and its burgeoning history of success (Rom. 10:18), failure (Acts 13:41), and surprise (Acts 15:15-18).

OT study also gave the church primary impetus and guidance in formulating an interpretation of past salvation history (e.g., Acts 7:2-53; Gal. 3:6–4:3; Rom. 5:12-14). At the same time it helped the church define its sense of universal mission (e.g., Rom. 4:11-17) and its final eschatological hopes (e.g., Rom. 8:19-22; 11:7-36; the book of Revelation, which is saturated with OT allusions; etc.).

c. Ethical responsibility. The deontological emphasis of primitive Christian ethics is grounded in the OT attitude that man discovers his true being through submission to God's kingdom and will (Matt. 4:10; Luke 4:8). Jesus' summons to repentance and the calls of early Christian preachers for Christians to live out a radical trust in God as manifested in Christ echo the demands of OT prophets for inner transformation and trust (*see,* e.g., I Cor. 1:31). The early church generally took over the OT moral law, above all the command to love one's neighbor as oneself. Apart from marriage regulations, however, the OT social, economic, and political teachings were usually ignored by Christians in the NT period. The cultic laws of the OT were by and large viewed as having been abrogated. OT personages were readily cited as moral examples, sometimes in extended haggadic homilies (Heb. 11; I Clem. 9–12). *See also* ETHICS IN THE NT and supplementary article.

4. How OT interpretation developed. In a vital sense, NT exegesis of the OT begins with the statements about scripture that the gospels attribute to Jesus. Severe critical problems arise when one attempts to determine whether these particular attributions are historically true. Since the communities that produced the gospels obviously studied the OT intensively in their efforts to understand Jesus, there is great difficulty in deciding where his scriptural interpretations end and those of the church begin.

Still, there is no reason to doubt that Jesus studied the OT closely, and in all probability it played a vital role in his teaching and deeply conditioned his sense of personal mission. Scholarship is sharply divided on the issue of whether early Christian exegesis of the OT was directly influenced by Jesus' interpretations. It is at least probable, however, that what early Christians thought Jesus had said on particular issues related to the OT (e.g., I Cor. 7:10) had a significant impact on their thinking.

a. The question of intermediate sources. Study of OT exegesis in the early church has uncovered some important indications of unity in interpretation. For example, early Christians cite certain scriptural texts with a frequency that can hardly be due to simple coincidence, and there is considerable unanimity regarding their interpretation (some of the most prominent texts are Pss. 2:7; 8:6; 110:1; 118:22; Isa. 8:14; Jer. 31:31-34).

No single collection of OT quotations ("testimony book") can have guided all or most of the exegesis found in early Christian writings. Yet, particularly in the light of discoveries of biblical florilegia at Qumran (especially 4QTest.; *see* §B1aiv *above*), there is little reason to doubt that early Christians may have often worked and traveled with brief or lengthy collections of OT quotations. Copies of the entire OT cannot have been accessible everywhere. Probably, too, Christian exegesis was shaped to some degree by other kinds of documents or fixed traditional materials underlying the surviving documents of the NT age, particularly liturgical confessions or hymns (*see* LITURGICAL MATERIALS, NT[S]) incorporating OT references (e.g., I Pet. 3:18-22; Polyc. Phil. 2:1). Perhaps, too, the early church produced some extensive commentaries on OT passages resembling Jewish midrashes; such materials might lie behind John 6:31-58 or Rom. 4:1-22.

b. Diversity despite unity. While there are unifying features in primitive Christian OT interpretation, there are also remarkable differences in detail and in the general attitude toward the OT. Even where separate Christian authors cite the same OT text, each usually gives it a unique nuance of meaning. Shifts in application occur, although the development of these cannot be charted with much probability. Christian exegetes follow no single party line in method or results; at most they are unanimous only in believing that the OT speaks of Jesus and the church.

Plainly the "workshop of early Christian theology" was one in which many different patterns of thinking were stimulated and guided by the Jewish Scriptures. Missionaries like Paul and the congregations with whom they communicated must have been occupied with ongoing exegetical explorations, sometimes with conflicting conclusions. There is evidence that several different "schools" or traditions of OT exegesis emerged in the church of the NT period.

Recent study of the gospels has emphasized their use of the OT as a major clue to the distinctive theological views of the evangelists and the traditions on which they rely (*see* REDACTION CRITICISM, NT[S]). MATTHEW, for example, lays consummate stress on Jesus as fulfilling the Mosaic law and the expectations of OT prophets. JOHN, if possible, gives even greater emphasis to Jesus' relation to the OT, but at the same time draws the hardest line in the NT between Jewish and Christian interpretations of the OT. Paul, perhaps the most ingenious and flexible among NT exegetes, cites the OT for a multitude of purposes; but he does so most characteristically and forcefully in declaring it a witness to a revelation of God's righteousness apart from the Law (Rom. 3:21-22; *see* TORAH [S]). The Letter to the Hebrews (*see* HEBREWS, LETTER TO THE) weaves a rich argumentative tapestry portraying Christianity largely with OT threads; yet the author regards the OT as containing revelation that is meaningless or obsolete apart from its witness to the New Covenant in Jesus' blood (e.g., 7:18-19; 8:6, 13; 11:39-40).

Modern scholarship has increasingly demonstrated that early Christian exegetes, despite their varied reservations about Judaism, owed much to the results and the methods of contemporary Jewish scriptural interpretation. The new religion's acceptance of the OT necessarily kept alive the issue of Jewish-Christian relations. Some church exegesis was polemically addressed to Jews; the "Pharisees" in the gospels may often symbolize the "synagogue on the other side of the street" offering alternative interpretations. Yet a considerable portion of early Christian scriptural study was also motivated by a desire to convert Jews, and tolerant biblical discussions may have sometimes materialized when proselytizing failed (cf. Just. Dial. 142).

Bibliography. R. Harris and V. Burch, *Testimonies,* 2 vols. (1916, 1920); C. H. Dodd, *According to the Scriptures* (1952); K. Stendahl, *The School of St. Matthew,* ASNU, XX (1954); E. E. Ellis, *Paul's Use of the OT* (1957); M. D. Hooker, *Jesus and the Servant* (1959); J. A. Fitzmyer, "The Use of Explicit OT Quotations in Qumran Literature and in the NT," *NTS,* VII (1960-61), 297-333; B. Lindars, *NT Apologetic* (1961); P. Prigent, *Les testimonia dans le Christianisme primitif: l'Épitre de Barnabé I-XVI et ses sources,* Études Bibliques (1961); B. W. Anderson, ed., *The OT and Christian Faith* (1963); P. Borgen, *Bread from Heaven,* NovTSup, X (1965); J. Barr, *Old and New in Interpretation* (1966); W. A. Meeks, *The Prophet-King,* NovTSup, XIV (1967); D. M. Smith, "The Use of the OT in the New," in *The Use of the OT in the New and Other Essays,* ed. J. M. Efird (1972), pp. 3-65, the best recent survey of research; D. M. Hay, *Glory at the Right Hand: Ps. 110 in Early Christianity,* SBLMS, XVIII (1973); R. Longenecker, *Biblical Exegesis in the Apostolic Period* (1975), a lucid intro.; M. Rese, *Alttestamentliche Motive in der Christologie des Lukas,* StNT, I (1969); K. Berger, *Die Gesetzesauslegung Jesu, Teil I; Markus und Parallelen,* WMANT, XL (1972); M. McNamara, *Targum and Testament* (1972), a suggestive intro. to the ancient Aramaic paraphrases of the OT and their influence on the NT. D. HAY

D. EARLY RABBINIC. Biblical scholarship among the rabbis of Roman Palestine or Sassanian Babylonia was not cultivated in isolation from other activities in guiding the social, political, economic, cultural, and religious life of the people. In the synagogues where they preached, the law courts where they passed judgment, or the academies where they studied, the rabbis sought to uncover the timeless significance of Scripture by making it respond to contemporary issues and problems. They accomplished this by reading Scripture as if the meaning of its idiom were not limited to the ancient Near Eastern culture that produced it and by assuming that the pertinence of the biblical laws and message was not restricted to the historical situation they once actually governed and addressed. It was their exegetical task to permit Scripture to meet the needs and satisfy the diverse ideological, moral, and aesthetic sensibilities that had emerged in Jewish life and thought during the fateful turmoil of the period prior to and following upon the destruction of the temple in A.D. 70.

To animate Scripture with the same immediacy and self-evident freshness that it had possessed for their ancestors, the rabbis first needed to explain biblical *realia* and translate difficult or rare words into a simpler Hebrew or Aramaic. Since for linguistic purposes they considered the entire Bible a single unit, they often explained one passage in the light of another, e.g., the use of Isa. 31:5 (RSV "He will spare . . . it") to interpret Exod. 12:13 ופסחתי to mean "I will protect you" (RSV "I will pass over you"). They also had resort to Phoenician, Coptic, Syriac, and other languages to elucidate difficult terms in Scripture (*see* Lieberman, pp. 48-53).

1. Oral Torah. More complicated is their treatment of the customs and traditions already well established in Jewish life, but not explicitly mentioned in Scripture. In Antiq. XIII.x.6 Josephus reports that the "Pharisees had passed on to the people certain regulations received from their forefathers but are not recorded in the law of Moses" (*see* PHARISEES[S]). Rabbinic willingness to allow the "oral laws" to stand independently without seeking to supply them with a scriptural proof text is a characteristic of early exegetical activity, i.e., before A.D. 70.

Perhaps it was the rabbis' view of Scripture as a revealed, universally applicable prescription of God's unchanging, yet eternally normative will, together with the constant demand for new legislation and the need to refute the Saduccean (and later the sectarian and Christian) refusal to submit to their interpretations of Scripture, that led them to search for biblical bases, both for the old laws rooted in tradition and for the new laws they generated while governing the people. Although biblical literature itself could not explicitly account for Jewish life and thought as they had developed in Roman Palestine or Sassanian Babylonia, it became axiomatic in rabbinic exegesis that everything in Jewish life and thought could be shown to have scriptural warrant if only the scholar had mastered the "correct" methods of interpretation. "Search it (i.e., Torah), and search it, for everything is in it" (M. AB. 1.5). Especially after the destruction of the temple in A.D. 70, the task was to derive and deduce oral Torah from the written. It was the function of MIDRASH to produce these derivations and deductions.

2. Hermeneutic rules. The best known of the midrashic methods used by the rabbis to derive new laws from the (written) Torah and to find support for old ones stemming from the "oral tradition" are the seven rules associated with Hillel the Elder and their expansion into the thirteen rules of Rabbi Ishmael. Lieberman and others have explored the possible Hellenistic provenance of several of these methods. The seven rules are: (1) inference *a minori ad majus;* (2) inference by similarity of language in two different passages; (3) constructing a general principle on the basis of a single passage; (4) constructing a general principle on the basis of two passages; (5) the general and the particular, the particular and the general; (6) exposition by means of another similar passage; (7) deduction from the context. Rule 3, e.g., uses Deut. 17:2, 6 to establish that two or three witnesses are also required in the cases mentioned in Deut. 18:10; 22:22; and 24:7 (on the basis of the recurring idiom כי ימצא, "if there be found"). Scholars are generally agreed that the rabbis used these and other methods only to create biblical support for already existing norms and practices. Hillel himself did not convince the Bene Bathyra by employing his exegetical ingenuity until he informed them that he was merely transmitting the traditional law as he had learned it from his teachers. Indeed the range of rule 2 is severely limited by the rabbis, who permit its use only in the case of a well-established law.

3. Akiba and Ishmael. The classical period of midrashic activity is that of Rabbi Ishmael and Rabbi Akiba. In the second century these two scholars, together with their colleagues and disciples, perpetuated and perfected the means by which Johanan ben Zakkai had reconstructed and consolidated Jewish life after the destruction of the temple. It is largely to Akiba that we are indebted for what Heinemann has termed "creative philology" and "creative historiography," or what Moore has described as "atomistic exegesis, which interprets sentences, clauses, phrases, and even single words, independently of the context or the historical occasion" (vol. I, p. 248). As Goldin states: "Not a curlicue, not a peculiarity of the biblical text was devoid of higher meaning to the man. Conjunctions, particles, repetitions were to him sources of most significant implication. Protest as his notable colleague Rabbi Ishmael might, that Torah must be interpreted only by means of established hermeneutic rules, that Hillel's formulas plus a few more were all that was needed, that many peculiarities of Scripture were no more momentous than similar peculiarities in human speech, Akiba persisted in his own course" (p. 157).

A single passage (T.B. Sanh. 646) will illustrate both Rabbi Akiba's method and Rabbi Ishmael's opposition. Interpreting Num. 15:31 ("that person shall be utterly cut off," הכרת תכרת), the Talmud takes the absolute infinitive to mean that the idolator "shall be cut off in this world" and the finite verb to mean that he shall be cut off "in the world to come." This is Rabbi Akiba's view. But Rabbi Ishmael said: "But the previous verse (Num. 15:30) has already stated that 'the person shall be cut off.' Are there then three worlds?" Rabbi Ishmael proceeded to use the phrase from vs. 30 to refer to being cut off from this world, and the infinitive from vs. 31 to refer to being cut off from the world to come. As for the repetition of the finite verb, Rabbi Ishmael invokes the principle that the "Torah speaks in the language of man," by which he means that Rabbi Akiba should desist from deriving matters of law from mere stylistic embellishments in scriptural syntax. Epstein identifies no less than thirteen major differences between the exegetical methods employed by Rabbi Akiba and his school and those exploited by Rabbi Ishmael and his school (pp. 521-36).

In accounting for their divergencies, some scholars, e.g., Finkelstein, point to the social and economic interests represented by each school. In his view, Rabbi Ishmael was "pro-agrarian, pro-patrician, and pro-property" (p. 167). Rabbi Akiba, by contrast, represented the plebeian class. Other scholars, most notably Heschel, correlate their exegetical tendencies with theological presuppositions and religious typologies, identifying Rabbi Ishmael as the sober, rationalistic thinker, and Rabbi Akiba as the theocentric, almost mystical visionary.

4. Haggadah. Compared to the exegetical methods by which the rabbis adjusted legal material to contemporary life, their treatment of the nonlegal portions of Scripture is marked by a dramatically larger measure of freedom and imagination. The same rabbi may offer any number of interpretations of a single verse, thereby illustrating the rabbinic view that Scripture possesses a multiplicity of meanings, as long as the verse in question is not a legal one, i.e., a matter of halachah (law). In Rabbi Ishmael's school, Jer. 23:29 was understood to mean that just as a rock "is split into many splinters, so also may one biblical verse convey many teachings" (T.B. Sanh. 34a). Even the so-called thirty-two hermeneutic rules of the Haggadah (nonlegal material) reflect less a set of methodological controls than a summary of the most widely applied rhetorical devices for interpreting biblical narratives or poetry. Among these methods are reading Scripture symbolically or allegorically; paronomasia; *gematria* (computing the numerical value of words); cryptography (substitution of letters according to a set pattern); *notrikon* (individual letters of a single word are taken as the initial letters of other words, i.e., acrostics); and anagrams (cf. Lieberman, pp. 68-82; WORDPLAY IN THE OT[S] §1). Moreover, Ginzberg's *Legends of the Jews* clearly shows that the rabbis borrowed vast amounts of foreign folklore, which they utilized in describing various biblical figures and situations. Anachronisms and outright fabrications also abound in midrashic literature.

In every case something in Scripture itself, or the occasion on which it is read, and the other biblical texts that are read with it trigger and justify the commentary supplied by the rabbis (*see* LECTIONARY CYCLE, RABBINIC[S]). A seemingly superfluous word in Scripture, the juxtaposition of sections, an apparent contradiction, the order of words in a sentence, even the spelling of a word, all underlie many a rabbinic homily. For the rabbis, what the Bible means is inseparable from how it means. Gen. 6:9, e.g., teaches that Noah was a righteous man, blameless or perfect in his generation. Reading Scripture through rabbinic eyes uncovers an ambiguity in the words "his generation." Either it suggests that he would not be blameless had he lived in any other age or it means that his righteousness is all the more noteworthy for he was blameless despite the moral standards of his time (T.B. Sanh. 108a).

When a midrash weaves Deut. 6:20-25; Exod. 12:26-27; 13:14; and 13:7 into a sermon about a father's obligation to recount the Exodus to his children by assigning the verses respectively to a wise son, a wicked one, a simple-minded one, and one who lacks the ability to inquire at all; or when it discovers in the abrupt style of Exod. 6:1-4 a dialogue between God and Moses in which the prophet convinces God to shorten his name so that the people will not be burdened by anxieties over their future fate (T.B. Ber. 9b); or when it justifies the apparent superfluity of Gen. 22:2 in identifying Isaac by reference to God's concern for Abraham's psychological reaction to the command; or transforms Gen. 4:13 into an audacious challenge of God's mercy by reading it as a rhetorical question rather than as a declarative statement of Cain's confession; rabbinic literature signals an acute literary and aesthetic sensibility born of an unsurpassed intimacy with Scripture and a heightened moral awareness of man's nature. Midrash haggadah reflects the rabbinic recognition of and response in kind to the characteristics of biblical literature: "certain parts brought into relief, others left obscure, abruptness, suggestive influence of the unexpressed, 'background' quality, multiplicity of meanings and the need for interpretation, universal-historical claims, development of the concept of the historically becoming, and pre-occupation with the problematic" (Auerbach). As a creation of Hellenistic culture, midrash haggadah also emerges as the Bible rewritten to conform in many respects with Auerbach's Homeric basic type, i.e., that style which favors "fully externalized description, uniform illumination, . . . all events in the foreground, displaying unmistakable meanings."

Even this does not exhaust the richness and complexity of the Haggadah. There is the esoteric midrashic activity based on the opening chapters of Genesis, the chariot visions of Ezekiel, and the theosophical rendering of the Song of Songs; discussions of doctrinal and creedal matters, including those concerning the pre-existence of Torah, the name of the Messiah, etc.; and various attempts to find in Scripture predictions of "future events" which the interpreter knew had already taken place either in biblical or postbiblical times, as well as considerable attention to eschatological speculations based on Scripture. And there is still more: cosmological and scientific asides on a wide variety of subjects; theological discussions concerning the phenomena of prophecy and revelation; and debates on the nature of interpretation.

Early rabbinic interpretation was collected in anthologies, recorded in the Talmuds, and embedded in the liturgy of the synagogue. It was cited as authoritative in medieval Jewish exegesis, was influential in Christian and Islamic literature, and is relied upon in contemporary scholarship. There is no gainsaying its genius and its continued influence.

Bibliography. J. N. Epstein, *Introduction to Tannaitic Literature* (1957), Hebrew; L. Finkelstein, *Akiba* (1962); J. Goldin, "The Period of the Talmud," *The Jews,* ed. L. Finkelstein (1949); I. Heinemann, *Methods of the Haggadah* (1954), Hebrew; A. J. Heschel, *The Theology of Ancient Judaism,* vol. I (1963), Hebrew; M. Kadushin, *The Rabbinic Mind* (1936); S. Liberman, *Hellenism in Jewish Palestine* (2nd ed., 1962); G. F. Moore, *Judaism* (1927-30); J. Neusner, *From Politics to Piety* (1973); G. Scholem, *The Messianic Idea in Judaism* (1971); H. Strack, *Introduction to the Talmud and Midrash* (1931); H. Wolfson, *The Philosophy of the Church Fathers* (1967); E. Auerbach, *Mimesis* (1968), p. 23.

K. P. BLAND

E. EARLY CHRISTIAN. In addition to the original article (§§*2a-c*, 3), *see* BIBLICAL CRITICISM §1.

Bibliography. General: J. N. S. Alexander, "The Interpretation of Scripture in the Ante-Nicene Period," *Int.*, XII (1958), 272-80; H. Chadwick, "The Bible and the Greek Fathers," and J. N. D. Kelly, "The Bible and the Latin Fathers," in *The Church's Use of the Bible, Past and Present,* ed. D. E. Nineham (1963), pp. 25-39 and 41-56 respectively; W. J. Burghardt, "On Early Christian Exegesis," *TS,* XI (1950), 78-116; R. M. Grant, *A Short History of the Interpretation of the Bible* (rev. ed., 1963), pp. 57-115, and IB, I (1952), 106-14; R. P. C. Hanson, "Biblical Exegesis in the Early Church," *CHB,* I (1970), 412-53, and bibliog., 595; M. Elze, "Schriftauslegung," *RGG,* V (3rd ed., 1961), cols. 1520-24; G. W. H. Lampe, "The Exposition and Exegesis of Scripture to Gregory the Great," *CHB,* II (1969), 155-83.

Special studies: Two monograph series, Beiträge zur Geschichte der biblischen Exegese (1955 ff.) and Beiträge zur Geschichte der biblischen Hermeneutik (1959 ff.), include studies of individual early Christian interpreters and of specialized topics, with detailed bibliogs.; M. F. Wiles, H. F. D. Sparks, G. Bonner, and J. A. Lamb, *CHB,* I (1970), 454-558, deal with the interpretation of the Bible by Origen, Theodore of Mopsuestia, Jerome, and Augustine, and in the liturgy, bibliogs., 595-98. *See also* E. Aleith, *Paulusverständnis in der alten Kirche* (1937); F.-M. Braun, *Jean le théologien et son évangile dans l'église ancienne,* 2 vols. (1959); M. Comeau, *St. Augustin exégète du quatrième évangile* (1930); W. H. C. Frend, "The OT in the Age of the Greek Apologists, A.D. 130-180," *SJT*, XXVI (1973), 129-50; D. A. Hagner, *The Use of the Old and New Testaments in Clement of Rome*, NovTSup, XXXIV (1973); A. Kerrigan, *St. Cyril of Alexandria: Interpreter of the OT* (1952); O. Linton, "Interpretation of the Psalms in the Early Church," *TU*, LXXIX (1961), 143-56; E. Pagels, *The Gnostic Paul: Gnostic Exegesis of the Pauline Letters* (1975), and *The Johannine Gospel in Gnostic Exegesis* (1973); M. Pontet, *L'exégèse de S. Augustin predicateur* (n.d. [1946]); J. S. Preus, *From Shadow to Promise: OT Interpretation from Augustine to the Young Luther* (1969), pp. 9-23, on Augustine; R. Simpson, *The Interpretation of Prayer in the Early Church* (1965), focuses on interpretations of the Lord's Prayer.

V. P. FURNISH

F. MEDIEVAL JEWISH. The prime interest of Jewish scholars in the period after the canonization of the Bible was not so much in the written book as in the oral law, the HALACHAH, i.e., the legal conduct of the way of life as derived from biblical sources. Their purpose was to find authority for the rules and teachings of Judaism. There was little concern with free interpretation or the original meaning of the text. Simultaneously, however, the HAGGADAH, homiletic exposition, flourished.

The interpretation of the Bible in the Middle Ages encompassed linguistic studies, philosophical explanations, and homiletic expositions. The linguistic evaluation of the text and context was objective; the other modes were more subjective and even dependent upon current notions.

1. In the Eastern Mediterranean. Islamic culture and the Arab conquests soon opened new vistas. In imitation of Moslem study of the Koran and the prevailing interest in philosophy and poetry, biblical research expanded to include the reconciliation of philosophical thought with traditional teachings and the portrayal of the poetic and aesthetic contents of the Bible.

a. Karaites. The Karaite sect, by rejecting the Talmud and pursuing the dictum "search the Scriptures diligently," helped extend freedom of interpretation still further. Among the outstanding Karaite authors were Anan (*ca.* 770), Benjamin Nahawendi (*ca.* 830), Judah the Persian, Hivi al-Balkhi (*ca.* 880), Salmon ben Yeruham, Sahal ben Masliah, Daniel al-Qumisi (*ca.* 900), al-Kirkisani, Japheth ben Ali, and Eliyahu ha-Melammed.

b. Saadiah. The Rabbanites made every effort to offset the vast Karaite research by promoting their own investigations. The outstanding Rabbanite protagonist, who set the course for the Judeo-Arabic scholars and may be regarded as the founder of the philosophical and philologic schools, was Saadiah Gaon (882-942). His translation of the Bible into Arabic, which removed all anthropomorphisms, and was free from literalism, stimulated the study of later scholars. He wrote short and long commentaries for the laymen and for the learned, and in special introductions explained the purpose of each book and the incidents it contained, seeking particularly to reconcile apparent contradictions. He commented profusely on biblical passages in his philosophical tome *Emunot ve-De'ot*, finding in the Bible support for his concepts of theology and demonstrating thereby that Torah can be explained in rational terms. To him there were essentially three authorities for the basis of exegesis: reason, tradition, and Scripture itself. His translation, *Tafsir*, is still read in its original by Oriental Jews.

Saadiah's methodology was carried on by Samuel ben Hophni, the last Gaon of Sura (*ca.* 1000). He was more literal than his predecessor in his translation, though he endeavored to interpret such incidents as Jacob's wrestling with the angel or the speech of Balaam's ass as being only dreams. Only fragments of his works survive.

c. North Africa. Soon the scene of biblical research shifted to Africa, to Kairawan (Tunis). The philosopher Isaac Israeli (*ca.* 950) wrote an Arabic commentary on Genesis. Judah ben Koreish, the grammarian, drew on Targumic insights and revived the Talmudic adage, "The Torah uses human forms of speech." The Talmudists Hananel ben Hushiel and his contemporary Rabbi Nissim (*ca.* 1000) coupled midrash with their scope of exegesis. Fragments reveal their concern with explaining the Jewish calendar on the basis of Exod. 12. *See* MIDRASH[S].

2. In Spain. Activity in biblical research abounded. This community at first was dependent for its traditions on the Babylonian Gaonate, and Palestinian Jewry had little impact on Spanish culture. After the Gaonic period Spanish Jewry attained critical independence. Great interest developed in poetic writing, utilizing biblical prose and poetry as the criterion. The poet thus had to be both philologist and exegete.

a. Philological studies. The basic biblical study in Spain was in philology, grammar, lexicography, syntax, analysis of uni-, bi-, and tri-literal roots, accentuation, classification of nouns, conjugation of verbs, determination of antonyms, synonyms, and homonyms, and evaluation of the consonants. Such probing resulted at times even in ignoring the Masoretic text or in suggesting textual emendations. Menahem ibn Saruk (910-970), who discovered the parallelisms in biblical verse, expanded his scientific investigation in his dictionary *Mahberet*, written in Hebrew. He was severely criticized by his contemporary Dunash ben Labrat (920-990). Their debates heightened interest in Hebrew grammar and provided the tools for future exegetes eager for the correction of misinterpretations resulting from lexicographical errors. Their work was also continued by Judah ben David Hayyuj (*ca.* 1000), who set up the standards for the fixing of the consonantal nature of the verb and its root. These endeavors were also promoted by Jonah ibn Janah (*ca.* 1000), who demonstrated in his *Sefer ha-Rikmah* over two hundred textual omissions and interchanges of letters in the Scriptures. He formulated the syntactical laws of biblical Hebrew in his lexicon of roots, *Sefer ha-Shorashim*, thereby removing guesswork in rhetoric and lexicography. He likewise did not hesitate to set tradition aside in favor of the natural and literal sense of the text. Moses ben Samuel Gikatilla (d. 1080) was the first to suggest the lateness of some Psalms and also to indicate a Deutero-Isaiah from ch. 40 on. He is also remembered for his translation of earlier scientific works from Arabic into Hebrew. He endeavored to show that the prophets spoke of their own times and not of the messianic era, and that the biblical miracles are to be explained rationalistically. Judah ibn Balaam (d. 1090) similarly contributed to the understanding of Hebrew accents and philology. Most of the early Arabic writings were lost but are mentioned by Abraham ibn Ezra (1092-1167) and David Qimḥi (*see* §3*b below*). Only in the last generation have scholars published fragments of these compositions.

Their scientific biblical investigation was primarily directed toward finding the sense of a passage without sacrificing the inviolability of the received text. Textual "corruptions," ellipses, word or sentence sequences, vocalization, haplography, omissions, or substitutes were rationalized on the basis of the Talmudic rules for hermeneutics and exegesis as set by the tanna, Rabbi Eliezer ben Yose ha-Gelili (second century).

Comparative studies of languages also were undertaken. Saadiah had already used this methodology to explain *hapax legomena.* The Karaite lexicographer David ben Abraham al-Fasi had employed Persian, and Judah ben Koreish had probed the similarity in vocabulary and the grammatical formations and rules of Hebrew and Arabic. Textual criticism in the modern sense was unknown.

b. Ibn Ezra. One of the most versatile of biblical commentators was Abraham ibn Ezra (1092-1167), who also engaged in poetry and philosophy. His method, combining scientific investigation and traditional interpretation, led him to probe every text according to verse context, grammar, philology, and simple literal meaning. He demonstrated boldness and critical independence in a biting and curt style, and he opposed allegorical interpretations, any full reliance on midrash, or even the introduction of unnecessary secular learning. He also disdained the Karaite mode of explaining Scripture by ignoring tradition. His commentary is in substance a condensation of the achievements of the past, making this knowledge available to scholars in France and Germany (*see* §3 *below*). In addition, he wrote several books, including an outline of grammar, and dealt specifically with explanations of the vowel system.

A relative, Moses ibn Ezra (d. 1139), studied the poetry of the Bible from an aesthetic point of view, stressing its artistic expression of the human spirit. Similarly, Solomon ibn Gabirol (1021-69), the poet and philosopher, is said to have written a commentary on the Pentateuch in an allegoric mystic fashion, portraying Adam, Eve, and the serpent as symbols of the rational, animal, and vegetative souls, respectively. These writings have now been lost, but are referred to by later medieval authors.

c. The Bible and philosophy. Another aspect of biblical interpretation may be found in the works written to reconcile revelation and reason. Bahya ibn Pakuda (*ca.* 1000), Abraham ben Hiyya (1065-1136), and Joseph ben Zaddik (d. 1149) are among those who included explanations of verses in their philosophical expositions. Judah Halevi (1086-1141), on the other hand, in his *Kuzari* emphasized the fundamentalist approach against the rationalistic. He held that nothing in the Bible contradicted that which is manifest, and that Scripture is to be interpreted only according to tradition and historical experience. Philosophical truths are to be uncovered in the text; allegory is to be spurned.

Another philosophical commentary was by Levi ben Gershom (1288-1344), who sought rationalism but indulged in astrology. He even introduced a mystic vein to most of the Bible text, stressing the moral lesson derived from it.

d. Maimonides. The outstanding philosopher of the age was Moses ben Maimon, or Maimonides (1135-1204), whose *Guide to the Perplexed* is full of biblical quotations, utilizing antonyms and homonyms as part of his philological-philosophical exegesis. His major concern was to promote reason, and so he read Aristotelian metaphysics into Scripture. He maintained that the Bible utilized all of the resources of human language, including metaphors and figures of speech to convey meaning. Prophecy is explained in terms of psychic experiences, and in Scripture there is both exoteric and esoteric meaning. In his code book, the *Yad,* he derived the halachah from the direct interpretation of Scripture.

e. Nahmanides. One who blended the secular scholarship of Spanish Jewry with the religious learning of the French rabbis (*see* §3 *below*) was Moses ben Nahman, or Nahmanides (1194-1270). He sought to reconcile the traditional rabbinic interpretation and the plain sense of Scripture in order to demonstrate the rationale of rabbinic precepts. Yet he severely rebuked the rationalism of ibn Ezra (*see* §*b above*). He also combined a mystical approach and Cabalistic insight with his rabbinic and philological analysis.

Following Nahmanides was Bahya ben Asher (d. 1340), who explained verses in four ways: midrashic, philosophical, mystic, and by use of the literal meaning (*peshat*). Much of his commentary was borrowed from his predecessors. Jacob ben Asher (d. 1340), on the other hand, based his interpretations on the numerical value of the consonants (*gematria; see* Wordplay in the OT §1). Also of importance from this era are the commentaries of Simeon ben Zemah Duran in the spirit of *peshat* and the homiletic interpretations by Isaac Arama (*ca.* 1490). The Tibbon family, by translating many medieval Arabic texts into Hebrew, contributed to better comprehension of the Bible. The Talmudic studies of Menahem ben Solomon Meiri (1249-1306) and the works of Joseph ibn Kaspi (1280-1340), who quoted ibn Ezra in his glosses, demonstrated particularly how, even in rabbinic research, biblical exegesis was not ignored.

f. Abarbanel. The last of the Spanish-Jewish exegetes was Don Isaac Abarbanel (1437-1509), who opposed the rationalism of Maimonides and the notions of Levi ben Gershom. He shunned Cabalah (*see* §3*c below*) and the methodology of the philosophical, allegoric school. He also avoided philologic and grammatical probings, devoting more attention to the biblical contexts by writing prefaces and excursuses on the dates and historic nature of events. He utilized contemporary social and political patterns to explain the Bible. In addition, perhaps because of the turbulence of the era, he wrote messianic tracts and strenuously refuted those who found Christian messianic teachings in the Bible.

3. In France. Unlike Spain, where topical, philological, and philosophical issues were stressed, there was little interest in secular studies in France. Above all, the basic rabbinic traditions were cultivated there, and the major activity was in Talmudic pursuits. The earlier rabbinic and midrashic homiletic explanations were used profusely. In their attempts to give the student a clear understanding of the literal meaning in the text, the scholars drew on the writings of Menahem and Dunash for knowledge of grammatical forms (*see* §2*a above*). N France was influenced by the German Talmudists, and S France by the Spanish teachers. Thus geographic influence is evident in the resultant modes of *derash* (homiletics) and *peshat.*

Menahem ben Helbo was one of the first French commentators to stress *peshat,* but he had little feeling for grammatical nuances. Another was Moses ha-Darshan (the Preacher) of Narbonne (eleventh century) whose forte was homiletical exposition. Gershom ben Judah, known as the "Light of the Exile" (*ca.* 1000), and Joseph Bonfils were primarily concerned with copying Masoretic lists and transmitting the correct readings.

a. Rashi. From these precedents the most prominent of biblical commentators, Solomon ben Isaac, called Rashi (1040-1105), emerged. He utilized both *peshat* and *derash* to produce a full running commentary by word and verse, while recognizing the differences between biblical and rabbinic linguistic style. Conciseness was his special quality. Depending much on his predecessors, he also followed closely the Aramaic translation of Onkelos in the Pentateuch and that of Targ. Jonathan in the Prophets. He did not hesitate to employ current French expressions to clarify a text. Basically, his approach was rabbinic, and he viewed the text with a literal simplicity. His dictum was that the biblical text does not depart from its plain meaning (based on T.B. Shab. 63a). Because of the popularity of his commentary, it was the first Hebrew book printed in Italy in 1475, and through the work of Nicolas of Lyra and the school of St. Victor, Rashi's work later influenced Martin Luther's German translation of the Bible, as well as the King James version. *See* INTERPRETATION §2*d*; §G3*c below.*

The French school of biblical commentators followed Rashi's synthetic methodology closely. His disciples, Joseph Kara (1113-40) and Shemaiah, added to their master's work. The grandson of Rashi, Samuel ben Meir (called Rashbam), especially encouraged simplicity by his interpretations. At times he disagreed even with rabbinic tradition. He also noted that his grandfather had sought to rewrite his commentary with more clarity, because new insights arise daily. Moreover, the growing christological interpretations of that period necessitated more careful literal explanation of questionable texts.

In the subsequent era anthologies of commentaries were compiled by scholars of the Rashi school known as Tosafists (from *tosefet,* addition); these eclectic comments are generally included in a work known as *Hadar zekenim.* Outstanding among the Tosafists was Rabbi Joseph ben Isaac of Orleans, known as Joseph Bekhor Shor (twelfth century). His perspective was rationalistic; he used the vernacular; and he reduced biblical miracles to natural phenomena (for example, he explained the pillar of salt of Lot's wife as an encasement of lava that overtook her). He also opposed the use of allegory, explained away anthropomorphisms, refuted christological notions, and interpreted the Bible in terms of social conditions. As the last important representative of *peshat,* he also commented on the duplicate accounts found in the Pentateuch.

b. Qimḥi. The Spanish commentators wrote in Arabic. The new literary activity in France used Hebrew and also made translations into the vernacular. The Qimḥis (thirteenth century), were the most prominent writers. David Qimḥi's extensive commentary presented the literal meaning, yet was permeated with rabbinic lore. Like his father, Joseph, he dealt with the *qere-kethibh* (*see* QERE-KETHIBH[S] §8*b*). His commentary on Psalms, because of its polemics against Christian exegesis, was one of the first Hebrew books to be published, though with many deletions.

c. Other schools. The di-Trani family (*ca.* 1200), although immersed in Talmudic investigations, was also concerned with philology and emendations, in addition to the traditional approach, as evident in a commentary on the book of Judges. Another synthetic work wherein the chronological aspects were evaluated was prepared by Tanhum of Jerusalem, one of the last authors of this era.

Exegesis may also be noticed in the holiday liturgy, where the *payyetanim* (poets) paired biblical verses, demonstrating thereby their own research. As a result, later exegetes referred back to them to substantiate their own interpretations of the Bible.

Despite the tendency to literalism in interpretation, interest in midrashic collections never waned, as is evident in the emergence of an anthology known as *Yalkut Shimoni* (thirteenth century). Similarly, the appearance of the Zohar as a running midrashic commentary stimulated mystic lore, and Menahem Recanati (fourteenth century) drew from it to write his Cabalistic work.

The accepted tendency throughout was to encourage interpretation on the basis of *pardes,* a mnemonic which included a fourfold approach: (1) *peshat,* literal, plain sense; (2) *remez,* allusion or allegory; (3) *derash,* homiletics; and (4) *sod,* secret, mystical sense.

Modern scholars have now recognized their indebtedness to these medieval traditional Jewish commentators. Their early contributions have paved the way for present-day scientific biblical investigations and research.

Bibliography. I. Abrahams, *Chapters on Jewish Literature* (1899); W. Bacher, "Die Jüdische Bibelexegese vom Anfange des Zehnten bis zum Ende des Fünfzehnten Jahrhunderts," in Winter and Wuensche, *"Die Jüdische Litteratur seit Abschluss des kanons,* II, (1894-96), and "Bible Exegesis," *Jewish Encyclopedia,*

III, 162-74; S. W. Baron, "Restudy of the Bible," in *A Social and Religious History of the Jews,* VI (2nd ed., 1952-69), 235-313; S. Posnanski, "Kommentar zu Ezechiel: eine Abhandlung über die nordfranzösischen Bibel Exegeten eingeleutet," *Schriften des Vereins Mekize Nirdamim,* 3rd series, no. 15 (1913); N. Sarna, "Hebrew and Bible Studies in Medieval Spain," *The Sephardi Heritage,* ed. R. D. Barnett (1971-); M. H. Segal, *The Exegesis of the Bible* (1943), Hebrew; B. Smalley, *The Study of the Bible in the Middle Ages* (2nd ed., 1952). S. B. HOENIG

G. MEDIEVAL CHRISTIAN (from Jerome to the end of the fifteenth century). The period is marked by the development of literal interpretation, with its emphasis on the importance of the direct and original meaning of the biblical text, and by the study of Hebrew and the consulting of Jews in the search for a more complete understanding of scripture. Literal interpretation, however, forms only a part of the vast spectrum of medieval interpretation.

1. Jerome. Jerome (*ca.* 347-420) drew the material for his exegetical works from many different sources (*see also* LATIN VERSIONS[S] §2*b*). As a young man he studied the classics at Rome; he attended lectures in Antioch, and thus he was acquainted with the principles of that exegetical school; he was also influenced by the Alexandrians and frequently quoted Origen; and finally, when he was about thirty years old, he began to learn Hebrew from a converted Jew. His literary ability caused Pope Damasus to ask him to undertake a revision of the Latin text of the NT of which there existed "almost as many versions as codices." For this revision, which much later (in the sixteenth century) was to become known as the Vulgate, Jerome used what he himself calls "ancient" Greek MSS. After settling with his small community in Bethlehem (385), he continued his work of collating and revising the text of Scripture. With the help of Origen's Hexapla, he revised the existing Latin version of the books of the Hebrew canon, which was originally based on the LXX. In all his OT studies Jerome shows an implicit faith in the Hebrew text, the *Hebraica veritas,* as he calls it.

Jerome was not a systematic thinker, and he did not compose a formal treatise on the interpretation of Scripture. Occasionally he refers to a threefold interpretation, but, in general, exegesis for him is divided into literal or historical interpretation and spiritual exposition, also called tropology or anagoge. According to him each of these senses requires the other, the spiritual developing naturally from the literal. But while the literal sense gives the interpreter no liberty, "tropology is free and is limited only by these laws. It must yield a pious meaning, keeping close to the language of the context and must not violently conjoin really disparate matters" (PL XXV, 1281D-1282A). During the course of his life Jerome moved further and further away from the fanciful allegorical exposition as put forward by Origen; in his last unfinished commentary, that on Jeremiah, spiritual interpretations are comparatively rare. Apart from his biblical commentaries, Jerome's works most used by later exegetes are: *Liber de Nominibus Hebraicis,* a collection of interpretations of all the proper names of both OT and NT; *Liber de Situ et Nominibus Locorum Hebraicorum,* a geographical dictionary of towns, mountains, rivers, and other relevant names occurring in the Bible; *Liber Hebraicorum Quaestionum in Genesim,* a book of explanations of selected passages, and of corrections of faulty opinions about the Hebrew text in the Greek and Latin codices.

Jerome, with his interest in the literal interpretation of Scripture, especially the OT, and his discussions with Jews concerning their explanations, was very much an exception. The great majority of interpreters concerned themselves primarily with the typological meaning of Scripture, where the events and personalities of the OT foreshadowed those of the NT, where the church stood for virtue, the synagogue for vice. (*See also CHB, II,* 80-101.)

2. The fifth-eleventh centuries. *a. Gregory.* From the fifth to the eighth century it was in the monasteries of western Europe that Bible study and interpretation took place. The main aim of the monk, apart from leading a holy life, was the contemplation and understanding of Scripture, and while he grew in purity of heart, he increased his perception of the spiritual senses. It is hardly surprising therefore that in this atmosphere the main stress in exegesis fell on allegory, i.e., on the discovery of the hidden, spiritual meaning of the text.

The master of spiritual interpretation was undoubtedly Gregory the Great (d. 604). Many of his biblical works (commentaries on Job, Ezekiel, Kings, and the gospels) are based on sermons and lectures to clergy and laity. His famous comparison of interpreting Scripture to erecting a building was frequently quoted in the Middle Ages. First, according to Gregory, we lay the historical foundation; next we steady our faith by pursuing the typical sense; and, lastly, by the grace of moral teaching, we color the whole structure. For him the whole of Scripture, OT as well as NT, is really concerned with one subject only: the revelation of God in Christ. Everything in the Bible is inspired; therefore its deeper spiritual meaning should always be sought beneath the letter. But this search does not for Gregory take the form of theoretical speculation; above all he was a practical man and a moralist, who finished his sermons on Ezekiel while a barbarian army stood before the gates of Rome. "We hear the words of God," he said in his *Moralia in Job,* "when we act upon them." And also: "Throughout Scripture God speaks to us for this purpose alone, to lead us to the love of himself and of our neighbour."

In the latter half of this period many reference books were produced, for example the *Etymologiae* of Isidore of Seville (d. 636), a kind of encyclopedia based on Scripture which became very popular with later commentators. We also find many so-called florilegia, collections of extracts from the Bible with their interpretations.

b. The Carolingian revival (ninth-eleventh centuries). In the second half of the eighth century, at the beginning of the Carolingian era, we see a renewed, though not particularly original, exegetical activity in the monastic and cathedral schools. Some of the best-known commentaries of the period are those of Rabanus Maurus, but they are mainly a compilation of the writings of the Fathers and Gregory. Also of importance is the revision of the text of the Vulg. which Alcuin undertook on request of Charlemagne, and for which he made use of ancient MSS. (For an extensive discussion of this text, *see CHB,* II, 133-40.) Two features of the Carolingian revival, however, did influence the development of later medieval exegesis. First, an interest in linguistics, based on a concern for the correct text of the Bible, with a few attempts here and there to learn Hebrew; second, a "questioning" of obscurities and contradictions in the patristic authorities, which gave rise to the production of many collections of so-called *Quaestiones.*

3. The twelfth-fifteenth centuries. ***a. Victor.*** Toward the end of the eleventh century we find a revival of Bible study in cathedral schools such as Chartres and Laon. In the latter the brothers Anselm and Ralph taught. The most famous product of this school is the Gloss (*Glossa Ordinaria*), which can be best described as a text of the Bible in which extracts of patristic and earlier medieval commentators are written in the margin or between the lines. The Gloss soon gained popularity, and it became the standard work of reference for interpretation.

Until the second half of the twelfth century the Bible, with its various aids of study, was the only set book in the schools. The growing interest, however, in science and pagan philosophy made a wider frame of reference necessary. Books of sentences came into being in which opinions or weighty statements on theological questions of the schoolmasters were collected. The most authoritative collection, the *Liber Sententiarum,* was compiled by Peter Lombard, *ca.* 1150; it covered the whole field of theology as it was then taught.

The most important Paris school in the twelfth century was undoubtedly St. Victor, a house of canons regular under master Hugh (d. 1141). Hugh was a deeply religious person, a mystic, but a scholar too. Before embarking on the study of the Bible he advised his pupils to acquire a wide knowledge of contemporary science: "Learn everything; you will find nothing superfluous; a narrow education displeases." Then, when progressing to Scripture, the student should start with the literal, historical sense. For Hugh this was so vital, because he saw biblical history as reflecting God's handling of events. History thus becomes history of salvation (*historia salutis*). Therefore, according to him, in order to understand this deeper meaning of the events mentioned in Scripture, the student ought to come to grips first with the basic, literal sense. And on this knowledge he can then base his allegorical interpretations. In stressing the fundamental importance of the letter of the biblical text, Hugh reacted strongly against an uncritical use of allegory which was all too common in his days:

> The mystical sense, is in the first place gathered from what the letter suggests. . . . [But some say:] "We do not care for the letter, we teach allegory." But how can you read Scripture and not the letter? . . . "The letter," they say, "means one thing according to the literal sense, another according to the allegorical. Lion, for example, is according to the historical sense a beast, but allegorically it means Christ. . . ." But I ask you, who approves of this, why lion means Christ? Perhaps you answer, as one should in such a case when the meaning has been derived from a likeness: "because a lion sleeps with open eyes," or something like that. Thus a lion signifies Christ because he sleeps with open eyes! (PL CLXXV, 13A-C).

Allegory, according to Hugh, should be based on facts as narrated in Scripture, not on single words taken out of their context. Having mastered the historical and allegorical sense, Hugh then lets his pupil progress to tropology, which will lead him away from knowledge to meditation and contemplation of the works of God.

Hugh put his ideas concerning the literal sense into good practice. He compiled two chronicles and a map of the world in order to facilitate the understanding of historical and geographical references in the text. And, more important, he made an attempt to learn Hebrew, the results of which can be found in his *Notulae,* a collection of literal interpretations on parts of the OT, in which there are a number of references to the Hebrew text and Jewish explanations. *See also* INTERPRETATION §2*d.*

His pupil Andrew (d. 1175) followed his master's footsteps in that he too studied Hebrew and concentrated exclusively on the literal interpretation of the OT. In doing so he claimed to have used as his sources, first, Jerome, then what his own studies had shown him, and lastly whatever information he could gather from contemporary Jews. However much he may at times seem to have been influenced by Jewish exposition, he used their interpretations only as aids for understanding the literal sense of Scripture and never had any intention of denying its deeper spiritual meaning. This has not always been sufficiently appreciated.

By stressing the importance of a knowledge of Hebrew for a scholarly understanding of the text of the OT, and by his consistent references to Jewish interpretation, Andrew opened up a whole new field of biblical studies which was soon to be integrated in the curriculum of the Paris schools.

b. The masters of the biblical-moral school. In Paris three masters continued to work out the Victorine program: Peter Comestor (d. 1179), Peter the Chanter (d. 1197), and Stephen Langton (d. 1228). They had in common a lively interest in biblical studies and in practical moral questions. Peter Comestor, so called because he had "eaten and digested" the whole of Scripture, made a compendium of sacred history, the *Historia Scholastica,* which became a standard textbook. All three masters left glosses on both the OT and NT. In their expositions they were much concerned about what should and should not be included in the literal sense; on the whole they decided that whatever was in the writer's mind belonged to the literal sense. For example, Num. 24:17, "A star shall come forth out of Jacob, and a scepter shall rise out of Israel," can, according to Langton, be taken literally as referring to Christ. It is interesting to note that later he gives the spiritual interpretation: allegorically the star is the Blessed Virgin, the scepter her son; tropologically the star is the light of good works, the scepter the chastisement of conscience. In spite of their interest in literal exposition, the spiritual interpretations of the three were the more popular ones, and the confusion remained of what did and did not belong to the literal sense. In fact it was not until the work of the friars in the thirteenth century that literal interpretation became more generally accepted.

c. The friars. In the thirteenth century we also see a multiplication of aids to study in the form of concordances to the Bible and the Fathers, biblical dictionaries, and geographies of Palestine. The Dominican Hugh of St. Cher, who taught in Paris from 1230-35, supplemented the Gloss on the whole Bible with more excerpts from patristic and medieval commentators in his *Postilla.* Robert Grosseteste lectured in Oxford and did much to promote biblical studies there. He realized the value of studying Greek for biblical scholarship. Indexes became more efficient, references more accurate, and one is aware of a greater concern for the correct biblical text. Thomas Aquinas (d. 1274) finally succeeded in making the literal sense acceptable by defining it as the writer's full original meaning, even if he expressed himself by means of prophecy, parable, or metaphor. One should no longer think of the letter as superficial only, but as having a rich, deep meaning in its own right, which could contain both prophecy and moral instruction. The spiritual meaning Thomas defined as what God, the divine author of Scripture, made known through the events related by the human author, these events being sometimes understood better by later interpreters in the light of subsequent revelation than by the original author.

In the next century, roughly between 1310 and the outbreak of the black death in 1348/49, the friars were again active in Bible study in all the great centers of Europe: Paris, Oxford, Cambridge, Toulouse, Avignon, Cologne, Florence, Bologna, and Padua. The most influential product of their efforts is the *Postilla litteralis* on the whole Bible by the Franciscan Nicholas of Lyre (d. 1349), in which he made frequent use of Jewish interpretations, in particular those of Rashi. *See* Interpretation §2*e*.

In the end of the fourteenth century, masters not belonging to a religious order entered the field of theology, for example John Wyclif (d. 1384), who studied at Oxford. In his exegetical work he shows a critical attitude toward much of the traditional interpretation and toward the monopoly in this respect claimed by the religious orders. Like John Gerson, who revived biblical studies in Paris, Wyclif thought that Scripture had been understood better in the early days when it was still free from later explanations.

In the late fourteenth and fifteenth centuries a desire arose among devotional groups of lay people in England, and even more so in Germany and the Low Countries, to be able to read Scripture in the vernacular. In England the work of translation was begun by Wyclif. The church, however, regarded these vernacular versions with the utmost suspicion, unwilling to lose the monopoly of interpretation, and afraid that the availability of Scripture to theologically untrained people would lead to heresy, as was indeed considered to have happened in Wyclif's circle.

Bibliography. "The West from the Fathers to the Reformation," in *CHB,* II, ed. G. W. H. Lampe (1969); B. Smalley, *The Study of the Bible in the Middle Ages* (2nd ed., 1952). G. A. C. Hadfield

H. REFORMATION AND ENLIGHTENMENT. In addition to the original article (§§2*f*, 3), *see* Biblical Criticism §§1-4; Biblical Criticism, History of §1; Biblical Theology, History of §1.

Bibliography. General: In *CHB,* III (1963), R. Bainton, B. Hall, N. Sykes, and F. J. Crehan discuss, respectively, "The Bible in the Reformation," 1-37, with bibliog., 536-37; "Biblical Scholarship: Editions and Commentaries," 38-93, with bibliog., 538-39; "The Religion of Protestants," 175-98, with bibliog., 543-44; and "The Bible in the Roman Catholic Church from Trent to the Present Day," 199-227, with bibliog., 544-45. In *The Church's Use of the Bible, Past and Present,* ed. D. E. Nineham (1963), E. G. Rupp and E. Carpenter discuss, respectively, "The Bible in the Age of the Reformation," pp. 73-87, and "The Bible in the Eighteenth Century," 89-124. *See also* R. M. Grant, *A Short History of the Interpretation of the Bible* (rev. ed., 1963), pp. 128-52; H.-J. Kraus, *Die Biblische Theologie: Ihre Geschichte und Problematik* (1970), esp. pp. 15-59, through the discussion of J. P. Gabler; H. Liebing, "Schriftauslegung," *RGG,* V (3rd ed., 1961), cols. 1528-33; IB, I (1952), 123-32, sections of arts. by J. T. McNeill and S. Terrien.

Enlightenment, general: A. Brown, "John Locke and the Religious 'Aufklärung,'" *Review of Religion,* XIII (1948/49), 126-54; E. Cassirer, *The Philosophy of the Enlightenment* (1932 [ET 1951]), esp. pp. 134-96; G. R. Cragg, *Reason and Authority in the Eighteenth Century* (1964), with full bibliog.; H. W. Frei, *The Eclipse of Biblical Narrative: A Study in Eighteenth and Nineteenth Century Hermeneutics* (1974); P. Hazard, *The European Mind: The Critical Years, 1680-1715* (1935 [ET 1953]), esp. pp. 180-97, on R. Simon and the birth of biblical criticism, and *European Thought in the Eighteenth Century: From Montesquieu to Lessing* (1946 [ET 1954]), esp. pp. 59-73, on the rationalist attack on revealed religion, and pp. 393-434 on various strains of Deism; E. Hirsch, *Geschichte der neuern evangelischen Theologie,* I (1949), esp. 204-306; II (1951), esp. 169-86, 417-32, which deal with biblical interpretation in England and France as well as Germany, from the mid-seventeenth through the eighteenth centuries; K. Scholder, *Ursprünge und Probleme der Bibelkritik im 17. Jahrhundert,* FGLP, XXXIII (1966), esp. helpful for this period.

Reformation, special studies: The series, Forschungen zur Geschichte und Lehre des Protestantismus (1927 ff.), includes several monographs on Reformation interpreters and related topics. *See also* H.-J. Kraus, "Calvins exegetische Prinzipien," *Zeitschrift für Kirchengeschichte,* LXXIX (1968), 329-41; G. Krause, *Studien zu Luthers Auslegung der Kleinen Propheten,* BHTh, XXXIII (1962); J. S. Preus, *From Shadow to Promise: OT Interpretation from Augustine to the Young Luther* (1969), pp. 153-271, on Luther; D. Schellong, *Calvins Auslegung der synoptischen Evangelien,* FGLP, XXXVIII (1969), provides a very full bibliog.

Other special studies: L. Bouyer, "Erasmus in Re-

Princeton University Press

(a) **Torah shrine; fresco, west wall, the synagogue at Dura-Europos.**

Courtesy Mrs. George Ellis

(b) **Frescoes on the north wall, the house church at Dura-Europos. Shown here are women approaching the tomb of Christ, Christ healing the paralytic, and Christ walking on the water.**

PLATE XXXIII

The Brooklyn Museum

(a) Head of a gazelle; mosaic of the first to second century A.D., possibly from the pavement of the synagogue at Hamman Lif, Tunisia.

J. M. Ward

(b) Christ; mosaic from SS Cosma e Damiano, Rome.

PLATE XXXIV

The Brooklyn Museum

(a) Stylized lion; mosaic from the pavement of the synagogue at Hamman Lif, Tunisia (second half of the fifth century A.D.).

J. M. Ward

(b) Mosaic ceiling, Sta. Constanza, Rome.

© *Y. Yadin*

(c) Frescoes on the lower terrace, Masada. Plaster has been painted to resemble marble.

PLATE XXXV

Princeton University Press

(a) **Samuel anoints David; fresco, west wall, the synagogue at Dura-Europos.**

J. M. Ward

(b) **Mosaic from the apse, Sta. Maria Maggiore, Rome.**

PLATE XXXVI

J. M. Ward

(a) **The Good Shepherd; mosaic from the Mausoleum of Galla Placida, Ravenna.**

Courtesy Mrs. George Ellis

(b) **The Good Shepherd; fresco above the baptismal font, the house church at Dura-Europos.**

PLATE XXXVII

Princeton University Press

(a) Elijah's sacrifice; fresco, south wall, the synagogue at Dura-Europos.

Scala

(b) Gold cup, in the Archaeological Museum, Teheran.

PLATE XXXVIII

Scala

(a) **Painted decoration for the Malgatta Palace. Tutankhamen and His Time Exhibit, Paris.**

Scala

(b) **Throne of the daughter and royal spouse Satamon. Tutankhamen and His Time Exhibit, Paris.**

PLATE XXXIX

Scala

(a) **Mosaic, part of the story of Jonah; Aquileia Museum.**

B. Brenk

(b) **The Lateran Baptistry.**

PLATE XL

lation to the Medieval Biblical Tradition," *CHB,* II (1969), 492-505; V. P. Furnish, "The Historical Criticism of the NT: A Survey of Origins," *BJRUL,* LVI (1974), 336-70; G. Hornig, *Die Anfänge der historisch-kritischen Theologie: Johann Salomo Semlers Schriftverständnis und seine Stellung zu Luther,* Forschungen zur systematischer Theologie und Religions-philosophie, VIII (1961); H.-J. Kraus, *Geschichte der historisch-kritischen Erforschung des AT von der Reformation bis zur Gegenwart* (2nd ed., 1969); W. G. Kümmel, *The NT: The History of the Investigation of Its Problems* (2nd ed., 1970), esp. pp. 20-119; O. Merk, *Biblische Theologie des NT in ihrer Anfangszeit: Ihre methodischen Probleme bei Johann Philipp Gabler und Georg Lorenz Bauer und deren Nachwirkungen,* Marburger Theologische Studien, IX (1972); T. H. L. Parker, *Calvin's NT Commentaries* (1971).

V. P. FURNISH

I. NINETEENTH- AND TWENTIETH-CENTURY CHRISTIAN. The question is how scholars understood the biblical witness to God to be related to historical event. In the preceding centuries, dogmatic orthodoxy had equated the two.

1. The nineteenth century (*see also* BIBLICAL CRITICISM, HISTORY OF §2; BIBLICAL THEOLOGY, HISTORY OF §§2, 3). Fundamental attacks were made on the historical credibility of the biblical witness. H. E. G. Paulus, in *Leben Jesu* (1828), questioned all supernaturalism, while D. F. Strauss, in *The Life of Jesus* (1835 [ET 1946]), saw the gospel's Christ as the mythical creation of early Christian messianic expectation derived from the OT. F. C. Baur, leader of the Tübingen school (1826-60), maintained in a series of writings that the simple Jewish Christianity of Jesus and the apostles had been overlaid with Paul's universalistic theology and a later second-century Catholic synthesis. In England, *Essays and Reviews* (1860) called for a purely scientific approach to the Bible, while in Germany, A. Harnack's *What Is Christianity?* (1901 [ET 1902]) posited a humanistic understanding of Jesus, and W. Wrede's *The Messianic Secret* (1901 [ET 1971]) maintained that messianism was a post-Resurrection creation of the Christian community. The Roman Catholic Church defended the Scriptures as inerrant and inspired, principally in M. J. Lagrange's *La Méthode historique* (1904) against A. Loisy's modernistic attack on the church's interpretive authority, in *L'Évangile et l'église* (1902).

In every field the century was characterized by developmentalism, history, and scientific criticism. The definitive result of these emphases in OT interpretation was Wellhausen's philosophy of Israelite history, *Prolegomena to the History of Ancient Israel* (2nd ed., 1883 [ET 1957]), and *Israelitische u. jüdische Geschichte* (1894). Rejecting all supernatural causes, Wellhausen understood Israel's history to be a natural development of human institutions and thought from primitive to higher forms. OT studies subsequently took the form of histories of Israel's religion, understood in developmental and naturalistic terms. The first of these was R. Smend's *Lehrbuch der alttestamentlichen Religionsgeschichte* (1893), while Oesterley and Robinson, *Hebrew Religion, Its Origin and Development* (1930), was characteristic of English works. Some scholars tried to point to the theological witness of the OT, but the fifth edition of H. Schultz's *OT Theology* (1896 [4th ed., ET 1895]) and A. B. Davidson's *The Theology of the OT* (1904) were the last attempts to write OT theologies, in German and English respectively, for almost thirty-five years.

In the NT field, the teachings of Jesus were considered most important, and Christianity was understood largely as a natural, historical phenomenon, within the context of the ancient Jewish and Hellenistic world. H. J. Holtzmann's *Die synoptischen Evangelien* (1863) was the first important liberal life of Jesus, although O. Pfleiderer's *Primitive Christianity* (1887 [ET 1906-11]) was considered the father of German religio-historical theology. K. Lake, in *The Earlier Epistles of St. Paul* (1911), introduced this German scholarship to the English-speaking world, with W. Bousset's *Kyrios Christos* (1913 [ET 1970]) forming perhaps the definitive summary of such NT interpretation.

The Roman Catholic Church would have none of this modernism. Its defense of the inerrancy of the Scriptures and the authority of tradition and church to interpret them is seen in the papal encyclicals *Providentissimus Deus* (1893), *Pascendi Dominici Gregis* (1907), and the decree of the Holy Office, *Lamentabili* (1907).

2. The twentieth century (*see also* BIBLICAL CRITICISM, HISTORY OF §3; BIBLICAL THEOLOGY, HISTORY OF §4). A new approach was signaled by attacks on a purely historical understanding of the NT. M. Kaehler's *The So-called Historical Jesus and the Historic, Biblical Christ* (1892 [ET 1964]) and J. Weiss's *Jesus' Proclamation of the Kingdom of God* (1892 [ET 1971]) pointed to the theological character of the NT. Schweitzer's *The Quest of the Historical Jesus* (1906 [ET 1910]) made it clear that it was impossible to write a historical account of the life of Jesus, while E. C. Hoskyns and N. Davey, *The Riddle of the NT* (1931), and R. H. Lightfoot, *History and Interpretation in the Gospels* (1935), emphasized the theological nature of the gospels. But the decisive call to hear the Word of God through the Scriptures came from Karl Barth in *The Epistle to the Romans* (1918, rewritten 1921 [ET 1932]), *The Word of God and the Word of Man* (1924 [ET 1928]), and *The Doctrine of the Word of God* (1932 [ET 1936]).

The problem was, however, how to relate the witness of the Bible to a scientific understanding of its history. After much debate in German periodicals, Eichrodt's comprehensive *Theology of the OT,* 3 vols. (1933-39; rev. ed., 1957 [I, ET 1961; II, ET 1967]), pioneered in the demonstration of method. This unleashed a flood of OT theologies in Europe: W. Vischer, *The Witness of the OT to Christ,* 2 vols. (1934 [I, ET 1949]); L. Koehler, *OT Theology* (1935 [ET 1957]); O. Procksch, *Theologie des AT* (1950); E. Jacob, *Theology of the OT* (1955 [ET 1958]); T. C. Vriezen, *An Outline of OT Theology* (1954 [rev. ed., ET 1958]); and G. A. F. Knight, *A Christian Theology of the OT* (1959). Eichrodt portrayed the covenant relationship as the structural center of OT faith in every period and formed his theology around it. In contrast, on the basis of tradition criticism, von Rad pointed to the dynamic character of the Word of God to Israel in *OT Theology,* I (1957 [ET 1962]) , II (1960 [ET 1965]) , and *Wisdom in Israel* (1972, posthumous) . Roman Catholic contributions came from P. Heinisch, *Theology of the OT* (1940 [ET 1950]) , and P. van Imschoot, *Theology of the OT,* I (1954 [ET 1965]) , II (1956) , the first major Roman Catholic theology after the papal encyclical of 1943, *Divino Afflante Spiritu.*

Important NT theologies were P. Feine, *Theologie des NT* (1913) , and E. Stauffer, *NT Theology* (1941 [ET 1955]) ; but NT theology found its most comprehensive expression in G. Kittel, *Theological Dictionary of the Bible* (1932-73 [ET 1964-74]) .

In Britain and the United States, the result of the recovery of the Bible's witness to God was the biblical theology movement, which emphasized the unity of the Bible, the revelation of God in history, the Hebrew mentality of the Bible, and the uniqueness of biblical faith over against its environment. For bibliog. and full discussion *see* BIBLICAL THEOLOGY[S].

At the same time, the Roman Catholic Church accepted the methods of modern criticism in the encyclicals *Divino Afflante Spiritu* (1943) and *Humani Generis* (1950) . The Dogmatic Constitution, *Dei Verbum,* from Vatican II (1962) gave full freedom to Roman biblical scholars so that their methodology now differs little from that of Protestants and Jews.

The principal weakness of the biblical theology movement was its failure to define the nature of the history with which it purported to deal. One of its sharpest critics has been J. Barr in *The Semantics of Biblical Language* (1961) , *Old and New in Interpretation* (1966) , and *The Bible in the Modern World* (1973) .

The writings of Bultmann have attempted to solve the problem of the relation of faith to history by demythologizing the biblical text and interpreting the Christian faith in existentialist, eschatological terms: *Jesus and the Word* (1929 [ET 1934]) ; *NT and Mythology* (1941, in *Kerygma u. Mythos,* I, 1948 [ET 1957]) ; *Theology of the NT,* I (1948) , II (1951) , III (1953) , 2 vols. in ET, 1951-55; and *The Presence of Eternity: History and Eschatology* (1957) . B. W. Anderson, ed., *The OT and Christian Faith* (1963) , is a discussion of Bultmann's treatment of the OT.

The new hermeneutic attempts to unite history and faith in the gospels by using the later Heidegger's understanding of the function of language include E. Fuchs, *Hermeneutik* (1954) , *Zum hermeneutischen Problem in der Theologie* (1959) , *Studies of the Historical Jesus* (1960 [ET 1964]) , *Marburger Hermeneutik* (1968) , and *Jesus, Wort und Tat* (1971) ; G. Ebeling, "Hermeneutik," *RGG,* III (3rd ed., 1959) , 242-62, *The Nature of Faith* (1959 [ET 1962]) , *Word and Faith* (1960 [ET 1963]) , *Einführung in theologische Sprachlehre* (1971) ; J. M. Robinson and J. B. Cobb, eds., *New Frontiers in Theology,* I (1963) , II (1964) , III (1967) ; R. W. Funk, *Language, Hermeneutic, and Word of God* (1966) ; P. J. Achtemeier, *An Introduction to the New Hermeneutic* (1969) .

Most NT scholars recognize that the NT's history is the product of faith, and recently there has been much work on the methods and theology manifested by the NT evangelists (*see* REDACTION CRITICISM, NT[S]; BIBLICAL CRITICISM, NT[S] §2*c*) . Yet, many believe that there is a possibility of getting behind such faith to something of the historical Jesus. On the new quest for the historical Jesus, *see* BIBLICAL CRITICISM, NT[S] §4*c*.

But the problem of the relation of the Bible's faith to its history remains. In the latest, still largely unjudged interpretive works, historical criticism is largely ignored. Structuralism, using the methods of Lévi-Strauss, interprets the Scriptures in terms of structures of human thought, usually binary and often defined in a seemingly arbitrarily manner (*see* LITERATURE, BIBLE AS §4*a* and bibliog.) . Canonical exegesis, as represented by B. S. Childs' *Biblical Theology in Crisis* (1970) and *The Book of Exodus* (1974) , abandons the findings of historical criticism for an acceptance of the interpretation imposed upon any text by the total canon and church. J. A. Sanders' *Torah and Canon* (1972) is more moderate.

Bibliography. E. C. Blackman, *Biblical Interpretation* (1957); R. Davidson and A. R. C. Leaney, *Biblical Criticism* (1970); R. C. Dentan, *Preface to OT Theology* (1950); R. M. Grant, *A Short History of the Interpretation of the Bible* (1963); H. F. Hahn, *The OT in Modern Research* (2nd ed., 1966); S. C. Neill, *The Interpretation of The NT, 1861-1961* (1964); J. D. Wood, *The Interpretation of the Bible* (1958).

E. ACHTEMEIR

*ISAIAH.

1. The book as a whole
   a. The diversity of the book and the canonical process
   b. Computer studies and the unity of the book
2. First Isaiah
   a. The man Isaiah
   b. The David and Zion traditions in Isaiah
   c. Isaiah and wisdom
   d. Other literary genres
   e. Isaiah 6 and the purpose of prophecy
   f. Isaiah 7—faith and Immanuel
   g. Isaiah 24–27
3. Second Isaiah
   a. Nationalism and universalism in Isaiah 40–55
   b. Cyrus
   c. The Servant of the Lord
   d. Literary forms in Isaiah 40–55
   e. Isaiah 56–66

Bibliography

1. The book as a whole. ***a. The diversity of the book and the canonical process.*** The rich diversity of the book of Isaiah is unequaled elsewhere in the prophetic canon. It is the result of re-presentation and expansion of the tradition that arose with the great prophet of the eighth century and extended through several centuries of the life of the Judean and postexilic Jewish community. It is customary to speak of a First and Second

Isaiah (chs. 1–39 and 40–66, respectively), but it has become increasingly evident that a long series of writers are responsible for the book. Interest in discerning the witness of Isaiah in the context of eighth-century Judah remains high, but there is today an equal or greater interest in tracing the book's dynamic development amid the crises and challenges of subsequent centuries.

There is almost no explicit information available about the origin and growth of the components of the book; therefore, there is no sure way to account for its richness and diversity—in form, contents, and historical background—as compared to the other prophetic books. One can only suppose that it is due to the intrinsic power of Isaiah's witness and to the formation of a group of disciples who maintained that witness in the next generation (Isa. 8:16-17), and who gave rise to a "school of Isaiah" that persisted into the postexilic era.

It is likely that older strata in the tradition were preserved, not for antiquarian reasons, but because they continued to be reapplied and reinterpreted in each new phase of the community's life. Thus the eighth-century oracles of judgment against Judah (1:2-26; 2:6–4:1; 5–8; 9:8–10:34; 22:1-14; 28:1–29:16; 30:1-8; 31:1-5) would have seemed painfully relevant to sensitive persons during the decades before and after the fall of the Judean kingdom (598-586 B.C.). We can also imagine that the oracles concerning foreign nations were adapted and expanded during this era, as the nations of the Near East were thrown into turmoil in the power struggles marking the transition from the Assyrian to the Neo-Babylonian empire (cf. Isa. 13–23). And then, as the Isaianic tradition was enlarged by the addition of the great cycle of exilic poems (chs. 40–55), the older collection provided the historical-theological presuppositions for the new proclamation of salvation. From this point on the process is relatively easy to imagine. The corpus was large and varied and susceptible to adaptation by means of additions. The early postexilic oracles (most of chs. 56–66) were an effort by several writers to make sense prophetically of the ambiguous realities of the age anticipated by the exilic poet. The addition dealing with Isaiah, which was taken from the exilic historical work (II Kings 18:13–20:19; cf. Isa. 36–39), was a natural move in an age of extensive scribal activity. Chs. 24–27 are difficult to date, but the incorporation of these universalist-eschatological oracles is perfectly understandable in either the Persian or Hellenistic period, when cosmic speculation and eschatology were rife.

At each stage in this process of expansion, the older portions of the tradition would have been allowed to speak anew to the religious community, alongside, and partly by means of, the new words which were formed in response to the demands of faith in changing circumstances.

b. Computer studies and the unity of the book. Electronic computers have been used recently to analyze statistically the linguistic phenomena of the book, especially with the aim of establishing the unity or diversity of authorship. However, contradictory results have been produced so far by this method. Therefore we must continue to rely upon the established methods of historical and literary criticism to deal with the question of authorship, until such time as objective criteria for computer programming have been agreed upon.

2. First Isaiah. ***a. The man Isaiah.*** As awareness of the complexity and vitality of the canonical process has increased, confidence in older deductions about Isaiah the man has decreased. The common inference that Isaiah was an aristocrat (witness his exalted literary style), who had access to if not membership in the royal court (witness his dialogue with Ahaz in ch. 7), must be questioned. (The late, legendary account of Isaiah's activity in Hezekiah's court [Isa. 36–39] is an unreliable witness to the actual circumstances of his ministry.) The only explicit indication of Isaiah's relationship with the court is that he had to accost Ahaz while the king was (apparently) inspecting the water supply of Jerusalem (7:3). If anything, this implies the *in*accessibility of the court to Isaiah.

It is also dubious to conclude from the images in Isaiah's vision (ch. 6) that he was in the temple when the visionary experience occurred, let alone that he was a cultic prophet there (an inference sometimes drawn). The vision presupposes familiarity with Yahwistic cultic practice, but nothing more. In short, all we know about Isaiah is that his father's name was Amoz (1:1) and that he gave symbolic names to two of his children (7:3; 8:1 ff.), one of whom was born to a woman referred to as "the prophetess" (8:3). But we have his oracles, and their meaning does not depend upon knowledge of the man.

b. The David and Zion traditions in Isaiah. These traditions are prominent in First Isaiah (Zion in 1:12-31; 2:1-4; 4:2-6; 10:12, 27-34; 14:28-32; 17:12-14; 29:1-8; 30:27-33; and 31:1-9; the Davidic king in 9:1-7; 11:1-9; and 32:1-5). However, they are variously interpreted. One view is that the oracles proclaiming the inviolability of Zion and the glories of the future king are later additions. The Zion oracles are taken correspondingly as reflecting in part the legend of the miraculous deliverance of the city from Sennacherib in 701 B.C. (II Kings 19:20-37; Isa. 37:21-38), and in part the ardent hope for the restoration of the city and temple that marked the piety of exilic Jews. The royal oracles, then, are regarded as examples of postexilic messianism (*see* MESSIAH, JEWISH §3*b*).

At the other end of the critical spectrum is the view that much of this material originated with Isaiah and rested upon a deeply rooted tradition concerning the twofold divine election of the Davidic line and of the city of Jerusalem (cf. II Sam. 7; I Kings 8:12-21). The truth may lie somewhere between these extremes. Zion surely appears to be a prominent symbol of the faithful religious community in Isaiah's message, a community he believed God would preserve, even though only as a remnant, against all threats of destruction. However, the superstition that the city and temple were proof against military conquest is incompatible with the oldest Isaianic corpus (e.g., 1:2-8; 2:6-22; 3; and 5:24-30), as well as the unanimous witness of the other pre-exilic writing prophets (*see* ZION TRADITION[S]).

Assessment of the messianic oracles is more difficult. Isa. 11:1-9 incorporates the prophetic insistence upon maintenance of justice as the chief obligation of the agent of God. In its present form, however, it appears to presuppose the eclipse of the Davidic dynasty in 586 B.C. (11:1). Isa. 9:1-7 [H 8:23–9:6] is less easily datable. It shares motifs common in the royal psalms (e.g., Pss. 2, 72, 89) and, like them, could well be a pre-exilic composition. But whether it is Isaiah's cannot be determined on purely objective grounds. Alt's theory that 9:1-7 is an oracle addressed to the northern Israelite territories conquered by Assyria in 732 B.C. (the Plain of Sharon, Transjordan, and Galilee, cf. 9:1), on the occasion of the birth (or coronation) of a new Judean king (perhaps Hezekiah), is a brilliant possibility.

c. Isaiah and wisdom. Isaiah, like Amos (*see* AMOS[S] §3), was influenced by the wisdom traditions of ancient Israel. This can be seen in his use of literary forms prominent in these traditions: parables (1:3; 5:1-7; 28:23-29), proverbial sayings (or, disputation fables, 10:15 and 29:16), and summary appraisals (14:26 and 28:29); and in his appropriation of the wisdom terms "counsel/plan" (verb יעץ, noun עצה), especially in the sense of a (fixed) divine plan or counsel (e.g., 5:19; 14:24; 28:29; 30:1-5). The woe oracle, employed more often by Isaiah than any other prophet (nineteen times; e.g., 3:9, 11; 5:8, 11, 18, 20, 21, 22), is regarded by some as a further sign of wisdom influence, but the origin of this form is still being debated (the main options are the curse, the funeral lament, and wisdom—either of court or clan). In order to recognize Isaiah's use of wisdom motifs it is not necessary to determine whether and to what extent these motifs derived from professional wise men in the kingdoms of Judah and Israel (a question currently under discussion; *see* WISDOM IN THE OT[S]).

By challenging the older view that the direction of influence was entirely from the prophets to the wisdom writers, contemporary scholars have effected the same kind of corrective as that of a generation ago with regard to the relationship between the prophets and the Pentateuch. In both instances it has become clear that there was mutual interaction among the various literary traditions and institutions of Israel.

d. Other literary genres. The study of the literary genres used by the prophets has advanced rapidly in recent years (*see* FORM CRITICISM, OT[S]; PROPHECY IN ANCIENT ISRAEL[S]). The genre occurring most often in First Isaiah is the oracle of judgment, which is generally regarded as the basic type of address originating in prophetic circles. However, Isaiah did not always use it merely in its conventional two-part form (accusation plus announcement of punishment), but sometimes adapted it creatively. Thus Melugin has shown how he mixed words of promise or disputation with the standard judgment form, to heighten the effect of the latter (28:7-13; 28:14-22; and 30:15-17), or interwove the traditional elements of the oracle of judgment in new ways, in order to show a cause-and-effect relationship between Israel's evil desires and their (unexpectedly) destructive fulfillment.

e. Isaiah 6 and the purpose of prophecy. The once conventional view that the purpose of the prophets' preaching was to call Israel to repentance in order to avert the national disaster which they threatened is only partly accurate at best. They did indeed call for repentance and reform. However, the eighth-century prophets all announced the unconditional destruction of the political and cultic establishments of the northern and southern kingdoms. Whatever reformation or revitalization of the religious community they envisioned was to take place in spite of or as a consequence of the fall of the monarchy, that is, through the response of a REMNANT (express or implied). This idea is explicit in Isaiah's message (7:3; 10:20-23). Therefore, the terrible recognition by Isaiah, at his commission, that his proclamation would be an instrument of national disaster, by hardening the people's hearts (6:9-13), should not be explained away as the retrospective rationalization of a disappointed reformer, as has commonly been done.

Isaiah believed that the new obedience of God's people would come only after the experience of radical purgation—a sapling growing from a burned-out stump (6:13) (*see* DISCIPLINE, DIVINE [S]). (There are no objective grounds for deleting vs. 13 as a late addition. Contrary to an often repeated opinion, the final clause *is* present in the majority of Greek manuscripts of the LXX; and, in the case of the two in which it is missing, it can be shown that the omission is due to a simple scribal error.)

f. Isaiah 7—faith and Immanuel. In recent study of the Immanuel oracle (7:13-17), the view that the child to be born was Isaiah's has gained considerable support. "Immanuel" would thus be viewed as a third child of the prophet to bear a prophetic name (along with Shear-jashub, 7:3, and Maher-shalal-hash-baz, 8:1-4).

On the meaning of the famous oracle in 7:9 ("If you will not believe, surely you shall not be established"), *see* FAITH, FAITHFULNESS IN THE OT[S] esp. §6.

g. Isaiah 24–27. The judgment that this section was very late (second-first century B.C.), disjointed, and apocalyptic—a view that dominated criticism for decades and is still influential—has been displaced in significant respects in more recent study. Considerable literary unity has been perceived, at least in over-all design, whether it be the alternation of eschatological poems (24:1-6; 24:16*b*-20; 25:6-10*a*; 26:20-21; 27:12-13) with responsive songs of thanksgiving (24:7-16*a*; 25:1-5; 26:1-14; 27:2-11) (Lindblom), or the linking together of three prophetic liturgies (24:1-20; 24:21–25:10*a*; 27:1-6, 12-13) with a song (26:1-6) and a prayer (26:7-21) (Fohrer), or the building of an oracular crescendo through the series oracle, song, oracle, song, prayer, climactic oracle (24:21–27:1) (March). Since many distinctive features of late Jewish apocalyptic are absent, and many features of earlier prophecy are evident, the prevailing judgment today is that Isa. 24–27 should be characterized as eschatological prophecy, or at most, proto-apocalyptic, rather than apocalyptic. Current dating varies from fifth to third century B.C. Isa. 24:1-20 is closely related to the oracles on the nations in chs. 13–23; and 24:21 ff. may be viewed as a fitting conclusion to this whole collection of oracles. *See* APOCALYPTICISM; APOCALYPTICISM[S] §3.

3. Second Isaiah. ***a. Nationalism and universalism in Isaiah 40–55.*** Modern interpreters have generally regarded Second Isaiah as proclaiming the universal establishment of God's justice and the conversion of all peoples to faith in him. However, on the basis of such passages as 42:10-17; 43:3-4; 45:14-17; and 49:22-26, several scholars have argued that Second Isaiah was a fervid nationalist, interested only in dispersed Jews, their ingathering to a restored Jerusalem, and the humbling of their oppressors. In this view, though the prophet's monotheism was intrinsically universalistic, he did not carry out its ethical implications.

To the extent that previous expositions have smoothed over the harsh words in the passages listed above, this challenge is a timely corrective. Nevertheless, these passages are not the touchstone by which to judge all others. The universal scope of salvation is set already in the opening poem: *"all flesh"* shall see the glory of God (40:5). And it is recapitulated in the concluding poem: *"every one* who thirsts" is invited to the eschatological banquet (55:1 ff.). Between these passages there are many others that require a universalist interpretation: 42:1-4—the servant's mission is to establish justice for the nations and the earth and bring *torah* (RSV "law"; *see* TORAH[S]) as far as the coastlands (*torah* here meaning true religion—the story of God's grace and his demands); 42:6—the servant is a light to the nations; vs. 5 confirms the universal scope of vs. 6; 49:6—the salvation of God is to reach the ends of the earth; 45:22-23—every knee shall bow, every tongue confess Yahweh's sole godhead and righteousness; *see also* 45:6; 52:10; 52:15 ff.

The universal acknowledgment of Yahweh cannot be dismissed as a mere admission by the nations that Israel's god is greater than theirs; for Yahweh is God alone—all alternatives are illusions (*see* MONOTHEISM[S]). Therefore, to acknowledge him—to see his glory (40:5)—is to share the prophet's faith, and this is the final measure of salvation (though it includes also release from bondage, etc.). The reversal of fortunes between conqueror and conquered is indeed depicted—the proud despoilers of peoples will be led in captives' chains (45:14), and Babylon will surely be humiliated (ch. 47). But these acts are not the final ones in the age of salvation announced by the prophet.

b. Cyrus. Isa. 44:28 and 45:1 represent the Persian king as a second agent, alongside Israel, of God's rule in history. The world conqueror defeats the tyrant Babylon, releases the prisoners, and enables Israel to fulfill her mission. Most commentators regard Cyrus also as the one referred to in 41:2, 25 and 46:11. However, Smart has recently revived Torrey's theory that the original figure was an Israelite messiah, descendant of Abraham (the prototype of the one called from the E, 41:2, etc.), and that Cyrus' name was added to 44:28 and 45:1 retrospectively by a scribe who mistook Cyrus' achievements as the fulfillment of Second Isaiah's prophecy. In this view military-political and legislative-religious leadership were both to be vested in Israel.

Although few adherents have been won to this interpretation, it provides a corrective to an overemphasis upon the role of Cyrus. There is a universal scope and finality in the prophet's expectation that exceeds anything accomplished by Cyrus, who did not call upon the name of Yahweh (41:25). Some would say that Second Isaiah was disappointed by Cyrus and therefore recast his prophecy after 539 B.C. (when Cyrus conquered Babylon and acknowledged the Babylonian god Marduk). Isa. 49–55 does not mention Cyrus, and there is a more somber note here in the representation of Israel's mission than in 40–48, perhaps reflecting a measure of disillusionment on the prophet's part. In this view, then, Second Isaiah turned, in his later years, more fully toward the future as the time when the promised salvation would be completed —"to the ends of the earth." In the views of Torrey and Smart, his message had this eschatological quality from the outset; but the resultant proclamations are similar in the two views.

c. The Servant of the Lord. The interpretation of the Servant as Israel, both in the Servant Songs (42:1-4; 49:1-6; 50:4-9; 52:13–53:12) and elsewhere (e.g., 41:8; 42:19), holds the field today, though a few regard the figure as the prophet himself (and many Christians believe the Servant's mission was completed only by Jesus). The fluctuation between passages in which he is clearly a symbol of Israel and others in which he is a minister to Israel (49:6) are explained less in terms of the social psychology of ancient Israel (the theory of "corporate personality," according to which Israelites allegedly made less distinction between a group and its individual members than we do) and more in terms of the poetic-dramatic character of Isa. 40–55. Thus, the Servant is viewed as a representative figure, the holder of a prophetic office, the paradigm of the faithful covenanter, the symbol of the true man/people of God. His office is that of mediator to Israel of the prophetic word of salvation and to the nations of the *torah* and justice of God. This second dimension of the office is one that Israel herself is responsible for as well; so the Servant merely represents the people in this ministry.

Several scholars recently have challenged the idea that 52:13–53:12 describes the Servant as a vicarious sufferer for the redemption of others, or as dying and being revived. The second idea is perhaps debatable, since the text does not say unambiguously that he died or was killed. Nevertheless, it is clear that he has suffered to the very point of death, at least, in faithful discharge of his task. The first idea, however, can hardly be denied, in the face of 53:4-5, 10-11. The Servant's affliction has made others whole and healed (vs. 5) and brought them into a right and righteous relationship with God (vs. 11), overcoming their sinfulness.

The text does not tell us precisely what has led the speakers of 53:1-10 to change their minds about the Servant's affliction—that is, instead of regarding it as God's punishment of a guilty one, perceiving it as the means of their own redemption by one who is innocent of wrongdoing—unless it is the extremity of his suffering or his willingness to bear it. Nor does this passage spell out the full meaning of their healing, wholeness, and justification. However, in the light of the other Servant Songs, and of the total proclamation of Isa. 40–55, this can only be their acknowledgment of the truth about the Lord as the sole creator, judge, and redeemer of all things, and their obedience to him as a consequence of this faith. The speakers of 53:1-10 are to be identified with the "kings/many nations" referred to in the introduction to this confession (52:13-15).

It should be noted that the famous references to Nebuchadrezzar as the servant of Yahweh in Jer. 25:9; 27:6; and 43:10 are textually very insecure. The LXX does not call him this in any of these passages, and it is probable, in the light of the latest textual study, that the Hebrew text is corrupt at this point.

d. Literary forms in Isaiah 40–55. There has been a definite trend in the last decade away from the atomizing of literary components in Second Isaiah toward an appreciation of the unity of the whole complex of poems, including the Servant Songs. Yet study of the prophet's use of various genres in the literary tradition continues to be fruitful. The main ones are these: (1) oracle of salvation (41:8-13; 41:14-16; 43:1-4; 43:5-7; 44:1-5; 54:4-6) often following a popular lament form and containing an address to the audience, assurance of salvation, substantiation of the assurance (the power of God, his former saving acts, etc.), description of the immediate outcome, and indication of the final goal (e.g., rejoicing in Yahweh); (2) proclamation of salvation (41:17-20; 42:14-17; 43:16-21; 46:12-13; 49:7-12; 49:14-26; 51:1-8; 51:9-16; 51:17-23; 54:7-10; 54:11-17; 55:1-5) including introduction, allusion to a collective lament, proclamation of God's turning toward Israel or his intervention on her behalf, and indication of the final goal; (3) trial speech (e.g., 41:1-5; 41:21-29; 42:18-25; 43:8-13; 43:22-28; 44:6-8; 45:18-25; and 50:1-3), containing a variety of the usual elements of court procedure; and (4) disputation (40:12-31; 44:24-28; 45:9-13; 46:5-11 [13]; 48:1-11; 48:12-15 [16]; and 55:8-13), a monologue in loose form used to justify the message of salvation to a discouraged audience. Hymns are also used in the book (e.g., 43:10-13; 44:23; 52:9-10; 54:1-3). *See* FORM CRITICISM, OT[S].

e. Isaiah 56–66. It is generally agreed that these chs. come from the generation after Second Isaiah (i.e., the writer of 40–55) and reflect the conflict of viewpoints in the Palestinian Jewish community during and after the rebuilding of the temple of Jerusalem (520-515 B.C.). According to Westermann's analysis the following strands may be distinguished: (1) the nucleus (60–62), composed by a disciple of Second Isaiah and reflecting his theology, set within two communal laments (59 and 63–64), and associated with other utterances from the same writer (57:14-20; 65:16*b*-25; 66:7-14; and possibly 58:1-12); (2) a series of independent sayings reflecting a split in the community between those who regarded themselves as devout Yahwists and those whom they regarded as transgressors (56:9–57:13; 57:21; 59:2-8; 65:1-16*a*; 66:3-4; 66:5, 17); (3) a group of judgments against foreign nations (60:12; 63:1-6; 66:6, 15-16, 20, 22-23), meant to counteract the positive view of foreigners shown in the first strand, together with some apocalyptic additions to 60:19-20; 65:17, 25; 66:20, 22 ff.; and (4) additions in 56:1-2, 3-8 and 66:18-19, 21, exhibiting openness toward Gentiles and concern for sabbath observance.

Bibliography. On the unity of the book: Y. T. Radday, "Vocabulary Eccentricity and the Unity of the Isaiah," *Tarbiz,* XXXIX (1970), 323-41, Hebrew, and *The Computer Bible,* II, *Isaiah* (1971); L. L. Adams, "A Statistical Analysis of the Book of Isaiah . . . ," *Dissertation Abstracts,* XXXII A (1972), 4701-A.

Commentaries and general studies on First Isaiah (chs. 1–39): S. H. Blank, *Prophetic Faith in Isaiah* (1958); B. S. Childs, *Isaiah and the Assyrian Crisis,* SBT, II/3 (1967); O. Kaiser, *Isaiah 1–12* (1972), and *Isaiah 13–39* (1974); E. A. Leslie, *Isaiah* (1963); G. von Rad, *OT Theology,* II (1965), 147-75; T. C. Vriezen, "Essentials of the Theology of Isaiah," *Israel's Prophetic Heritage* (1962), pp. 128-46; J. M. Ward, *Amos and Isaiah* (1969); H. Wildberger, *Jesaja 1–12,* BKAT, X/1 (1972).

Special studies on First Isaiah: A. Alt, "Jesaja 8, 23-9,6," *Kleine Schriften,* II (1953), 206-25; I. Engnell, *The Call of Isaiah, UUA,* IV (1949); G. Fohrer, "The Origin, Composition and Tradition of Isaiah I–XXXIX," *ALUOS,* III (1961-62), 3-38, and "Die Aufbau der Apokalypse des Jesajabuchs (Is. 24–27)," *CBQ,* XXV (1963), 34-45; N. K. Gottwald, *All the Kingdoms of the Earth* (1964), 147-207; J. Jensen, *The Use of tôrâ by Isaiah,* CBQMS, III (1973); J. Lindblom, *Die Jesaja-Apokalypse, Jes. 24–27* (1938); W. E. March, "A Study of Two Prophetic Compositions in Isaiah 24, 1-27, 1," *Dissertation Abstracts,* XXVII (1966/67), 1916-17; R. Melugin, "The Coventional and the Creative in Isaiah's Judgment Oracles," *CBQ,* XXXVI (1974), 301-11; B. Otzen, "Traditions and Structures of Isaiah XXIV-XXVII," *VT,* XXIV (1974), 196-211; J. W. Whedbee, *Isaiah and Wisdom* (1971); H. Wildberger, "Jesajas Verständnis der Geschichte," VTSup, IX (1963), 83-117.

Commentaries and general studies on Second Isaiah (chs. 40–66): D. Baltzer, *BZAW,* CXXI (1971); P. de Boer, *OTS,* XI (1956); K. Elliger, BKAT, XI/1 (1970); Y. Kaufmann, *The Babylonian Captivity and Deutero-Isaiah* (1970); J. L. McKenzie, ABi (1968); C. R. North, *The Second Isaiah* (1964); H. L. Orlinsky and N. H. Snaith, *Studies on the Second Part of the Book of Isaiah,* VTSup, XIV (1967); A. Schoors, *I Am God Your Saviour: A Form-Critical Study of the Main Genres in Is. XL–LV,* VTSup, XXIV (1973); U. E. Simon, *A Theology of Salvation* (1953); J. D. Smart, *History and Theology in Second Isaiah* (1965); C. Stuhlmueller, *Creative Redemption in Deutero-Isaiah,* AnBib, XLIII (1970); E. von Waldow, "The Message of Deutero-Isaiah," *Int.,* XXII (1968), 259-87; C. Westermann, *Isaiah 40–66* (1969).

Special studies on Second Isaiah: B. W. Anderson, "Exodus Typology in Second Isaiah," *Israel's Prophetic Heritage* (1962), pp. 177-95; W. Brueggemann, "Isaiah 55 and Deuteronomic Theology," *ZAW,* LXXX (1968), 191-203; R. Davidson, "Universalism in Second Isaiah," *SJT,* LVI (1963), 166-85; G. R. Driver, "Isaiah 53:13–53:12 . . . ," *BZAW,* CIII (1968), 90-105; O. Eissfeldt, "The Promises of Grace to David in Is. 55:1-5," *Israel's Prophetic Heritage* (1962), pp. 196-207; A. Gelston, "The Missionary Message of Second Isaiah," *SJT,* LVIII (1965), 308-18; M. Haran, "The Literary Structure and Chronological Framework of the Prophecies in Is. 40–48," VTSup, IX (1963), 127-55; M. D. Hooker, *Jesus and the Servant* (1959); H.-J. Kraus, "Die ausgebliebene Endtheophanie. Eine Studie zu Jes. 56–66," *ZAW,* LXXVIII (1966), 317-32; T. Ludwig, "The Traditions of the Establishing of the Earth in Deutero-Isaiah," *JBL,* XCII (1973), 345-57; R. Melugin, "Deutero-Isaiah and Form Criticism," *VT,* XXI (1971), 326-37; D. W. Thomas, "A Consideration of Isaiah LIII in the Light of Recent Textual and Philological Study," *ETL,* XLIV (1968), 79-86; R. N. Whybray, *The Heavenly Counsellor in Isaiah XL 13–14* (1971). J. M. Ward

***ISHBAAL.** *See* Ishbosheth[S].

***ISHBOSHETH** [איש בשת, man of Bashtu]. *See* Ishbaal for personal history.

The element *bosheth* derives from *bashtu,* later *baltu,* a theophoric element meaning "genitals, sexual potency, abundance, dignity, pride." *Bashtu,* in Assyrian lexical lists, is identified with *shēdu,* a winged male figure who holds a pine cone and bucket for the purpose of bestowing fertility. *Bosheth,* in the names Ishbosheth and Mephibosheth, is a divine epithet designating Baal as giver of life. It need not be considered a late scribal substitute showing contempt for Baal.

Mesopotamian names making use of *bashtu* fall into five categories: (*a*) *bashtu* plus suffix (Baltānu [O, our potent one!]; Bashtia [O, my potent one!]); (*b*) god name plus *bashtu* ([d]Abba-bashti, Ishtar-bashti, Sin-balti [god X is my potent one]; compare Mutibashti [my husband is my potent one]); (*c*) *bashtu* plus god name ([f]Balti-Adad, Baltu-Shamash [My potent one is god X]); (*d*) *bashtu* plus verb ([f]Balti-libur [may my potent one be strong]); (*e*) *bashtu* in a three-element name (Ashur-baltu-nishe [Ashur is the potent one of the people], Nabu-baltu-ilani [Nabu is the most potent of the gods]). Also the verbal root *BŠ* appears in Akkadian names with similar meaning.

The Ugaritic cognate *bṯt* means "richness" (RS 22.225:6, 12, 13 in CRAI (1960), 180-86).

The word *bashtu* (pronounced *bosheth* in biblical Hebrew) came to mean "shame," often retaining sexual connotation (Mic. 1:11). Thus a name like Ishbosheth would no longer be understood in a positive, theophoric sense, but might evoke amusement or repugnance.

Bibliography. M. Astour, "Second Millennium B.C. Cypriot and Cretan Onomastica Reconsidered," *JAOS,* LXXXIV (1964), 240-54, *"Bashtu," CAD,* II (B), 142-44, "Bashtu," *AHW,* I, 112; J. Lewy, "Amunnitica," *HUCA,* XXXII (1961), 36-37; M. Tsevat, "Studies in the Book of Samuel V: Ishbosheth and Congeners," *HUCA,* XLVI (1975). W. C. Gwaltney, Jr.

ISRAEL, CONCEPTIONS OF. "Israel," the new name given to Jacob (Gen. 32:28; 35:10), designates both this biblical forebear and those descended from him. The people Israel are the corporate body of central concern and attention of the OT, regarded as occupying a special role in God's economy.

1. Origin of the concept. The clue to the rise of a conception of Israel lies in the development of monotheistic-universalistic views about the Israelite deity. Perhaps the scholarly view is right that there are clear indications in biblical literature of a development whereby Yahweh was initially a tribal god of some associated clans, then became a "national god," thereafter traversing a period of henotheism (i.e., the notion of one god in one land, with Yahweh the god of the land of Canaan), and emerging into a view that he was the god of all peoples, of all the world, and indeed the only god. In a situation of many peoples and only one God, the biblical conception of Israel is the response to the question: What is the special role of this one people to the God of all the peoples and all the world? If universalistic monotheism had not arisen, no "conception of Israel" would have arisen.

2. OT views. Two different (though inseparable) themes mark this conception of Israel. One is historical, i.e., a matter of origins and of the flow of events. The Pentateuch sets forth such a view: From the three sons of Noah the world was repopulated after the flood. From the eldest son, Shem, whose descendants settled in the eastern area ultimately called Chaldea, there was born Abraham, the first of three patriarchs. He left his native land, and after a sojourn in Haran, migrated to Canaan, the land divinely destined for his descendants. Abraham had several offspring, Isaac by his wife Sarah, Ishmael by Hagar, and Zimran, Jokshan, Medan, Midian, Ishbak, and Shuah by Keturah (Gen. 25:1-2). From Abraham's nephew Lot the kindred Ammonites and Moabites were descended. However, the preferred line went from Abraham through Isaac.

Isaac had two sons, Esau and Jacob-Israel, the preferred line going through the latter.

Jacob-Israel had twelve sons, the ancestors of the twelve tribes. On Jacob's move to Egypt, the collective family numbered seventy; these are called the "children" (KJV) of Israel (Gen. 46:8-27). Between the time of Jacob and the time of Moses the children of Israel—at times called the Hebrews—increased to 600,000 men, apart from women and children. Enslaved in Egypt, they were freed through Moses and led to Sinai-Horeb, where a covenant (*see* Covenant, Mosaic[S]) was concluded by which Yahweh became Israel's special deity and Israel his special, chosen people. Under Joshua (Son of Nun), this people conquered Canaan and in the period of the Judges settled in the land.

Many modern scholars assert that the foregoing is not reliable history. Rather, what took place was the gradual infiltration of Canaan by related Hebrew tribes, bound to each other in a confederation (Amphictyony), and only as a sequel to this confederation did a collective, corporate Israel arise.

Further to complicate the somewhat obscure matter of origins, the pre-exilic prophetic literature seems completely unacquainted with an eastern origin (i.e., Abraham coming from Ur), but instead attributes the origin to the wilderness (which, in the Pentateuchal narrative, is not the place of origin but only a transitory phase through which the people passed; *see* Jer. 2:1-2; Deut. 32:10).

A second, related view is essentially theological. Canaan had had its deity, the Baal. Through conquest Canaan had come to belong to Yahweh, who demanded an exclusive fidelity from his people. In the thought of the pre-exilic prophets, the Baal was no god, and the worship of him by Israel violated its covenantal requirement of fidelity to Yahweh. Through the speeches and writings of the pre-exilic prophets, the view became common that

Israel was God's people, and not the Baal's. As God's people, chosen by him for his purposes, Israel had unique responsibilities to him which other peoples did not have. Moreover, as God's special people, Israel was assured of his beneficent guidance and protection, at least so long as it abided by the responsibilities implied by fidelity. Infidelity to Yahweh relieved him, as it were, of his obligation to beneficent guidance and protection, thereby allowing Israel to become a prey to invaders. Cumulative corporate guilt could bring the two-way relationship to a crisis, and even end it.

In time the view arose that a righteous remnant could and would escape the corporate doom. Moreover, the view that infidelity could be cumulative implied that prior to the climax, the deity exercised tentative forbearance; hence, he was characterized by prolonged mercy as well as strict, immediate justice. Indeed, insofar as he was characterized by mercy and grace, his abstention from immediate punishment raised the issue of theodicy, an issue destined to flower in various ways (e.g., the punishment of the innocent along with the wicked; the forgiveness, by grace, of the culpable; and, on an individual basis, the observed prosperity of the wicked and the misery of the righteous).

The unfolding of such matters, which are traceable in the prophets, is best explained by the often tacit premise of the special relation existing between the deity and his people. Israelite thinking, no matter how universalist it became, began with Israel and centered in it. Thus, though AMOS declares that Israel is like the Ethiopians, and the Philistines, and the Syrians (9:7) to the deity, he also declares, "You only have I known of all the families of the earth" (3:2*a*). He adds, significantly (3:2*b*), "therefore I will punish you for all your iniquities." In prophetic thought, the ELECTION of Israel always carried with it a sense of special obligation from which other nations were exempted; the supposition that election meant capricious privilege is denied in this passage in Amos and in many other passages. *See* PROPHET, PROPHETISM §D2.

In the view of Amos, Israel's infidelity had cost it the deity's protection, so that an invader (Assyria) would be allowed to devastate the land and send the northern kingdom into exile (Amos 3:11; 9:9). But in ISAIAH, the deity, rather than passively permitting the invader to attack, actively controls him, bringing him in to invade as a tool by which God punishes his people (Isa. 10:5-14). Isaiah also appears to envisage a saved or even saving remnant, thereby modifying the earlier view of total corporate punishment (10:20-23).

An often repeated theme tells that the land promised to Abraham had a special place in God's economy, as the place where his special people was to dwell. At one stage in Hebrew thought, God, people, and land were deemed inseparable. The Babylonian conquest (598) and the EXILE (587) wrought a significant change. Now the connection was primarily between deity and people, though concern for land never completely disappeared. The change is explicit in Jeremiah (29:7). It is heightened in Second Isaiah (42:1 ff.; 43:14-24) where the Exile is viewed as part of Yahweh's plan, openly announced from earliest times. In that plan Israel is God's servant in the working out of God's universal salvation. Whereas Jeremiah had viewed the Exile as a means of purifying a defective Israel, Second Isaiah proceeded to declare Israel forgiven for its past trespasses as an act of divine grace (43:25).

3. A special people. It is in Second Isaiah that the concept of Israel as the special people of the one and only God, whose sway is universal, gets its clearest initial expression: Israel is God's elect people, chosen by him for his divine purposes.

Subsequent times preserved this sense of a special people in a variety of ways. On the one hand, it was envisaged that Gentiles could, as proselytes, enter into the elect people (Zech. 8:20-23; Isa. 2:2-3; Mic. 4:1-2). On the other hand, passages in Ezra and Nehemiah (e.g., Ezra 4:3 ff.) reflect the deliberate exclusion from the people of God of the SAMARITANS, and also extreme steps of purging the restored postexilic community of the intrusion into its midst of "Gentiles" (Neh 13:23-30). Against such exclusivism were raised the tolerant views of the book of Ruth and the universalistic book of Jonah. If the Pentateuch, as modern scholars assert, reached its full form in the age of Ezra and Nehemiah (utilizing older materials), perhaps the recurrent hostility expressed against the ancient Canaanites is in part a retrojection into the patriarchal and Mosaic ages of the postexilic exclusivism and hostility; the Canaanites are depicted in the Pentateuch as destined for and worthy of complete annihilation; this was, lamentably, imperfectly carried out by Joshua, who was deceived into sparing the Canaanite Gibeonites (Josh. 9).

The concept of Israel as God's chosen, elected for obligation, but first in divine concern and affection, became a cornerstone of Israelite thought. In the variety of abundant passages reflecting the concept (e.g., in Psalms), one voice might stress God's universalism, virtually ignoring the particular people, while another voice might stress the particular people, virtually ignoring the heritage of universalism.

A by-product of the view of God as the universal deity is the prophetic denunciation not only of Israel, but of other nations, especially Edom, as part of the divine concern (*see* Jer. 46–51).

The Samaritans, excluded by the Judeans (see the basis provided in II Kings 17:24-41), made their implicit response by appropriating the Pentateuch as their own, and by exalting their temple on Mount Gerizim as the true sanctuary of God. The Samaritan schism reflects the emergence of a new kind of question, namely, which people is truly God's chosen? The Samaritans and Judeans shared in common the view that God indeed had his own people, but each contended that it was the chosen, the Israel of God.

4. Early Christian views. Within the NT, which concedes that Christianity arose out of Judaism, the view is expressed in a variety of ways that now "Christians" rather than Jews have become the elect of God, for the Jews have been supplanted in God's economy as his special people. Paul, for example, expresses this in his allegorizing (Gal. 4:21-31; cf. Rom. 9:6-13) of Sarah and Hagar as the matriarchs from whom respectively the "free" (the Christians) and the "slaves" (the Jews) are descended. In the gospels, the genealogies provided in Matt. 1:1-17 and Luke 3:23-38 imply the continuity of Christendom with the OT forebears, especially Abraham (*see also* GENEALOGY, CHRIST and supplementary article). The explicit identification by Paul of Christians as now the true Israel (Gal. 6:16) is expressed in the gospel narrative in which John the Baptist asserts that God can raise true descendants of Abraham from stones (Matt. 3:7-9). Christians are deemed the spiritual descendants of Abraham, superior to the supplanted Jews whose descent from him was only of the body. Rarely is the Christian claim of being God's Israel expressed in the gospels without a denial of a Jewish right to that status.

This contention of supplanting is expressed in a variety of tones (*see* JEWS, NT ATTITUDES TOWARD [S]). In Paul, the expression is ordinarily one of painful regret (Rom. 9:1-2) accompanied by the caution that Gentiles are branches engrafted in the tree (Rom. 11:17), while Jews are the true branches that were broken off but who, in some future time, would be returned into God's favor and affection (Rom. 11:25-27). In Luke-Acts, Christianity is the unbroken continuity of the ancient Judaism, and never marred by infidelity to any Jewish requirement or sensibility. Rather, the Jews are the ones who have gone astray, as a result of their failure to see how law grew into gospel. In Mark, the Jewish opponents of Jesus are blindly hostile, and his Jewish disciples are blind and disloyal. In Matthew, "the kingdom of God" is in some passages the "church" from which exclusion or expulsion is possible, e.g., Matt. 7:15-23. More explicitly than Mark, Matthew treats the Jews with unrelieved denunciation, especially the Pharisees (*see* Matt. 23). In John, the opponents of Jesus, though occasionally Pharisees, are usually "the Jews." Though "salvation is from the Jews" (4:22), especially in view of invalid Samaritan claims (4:21), the Jesus of John seems conceived of as not a Jew at all ("your" synagogue, etc.).

Perhaps the clearest expression of Christianity as the Israel of God is I Pet. 2:9-10. "But you are a chosen race, a royal priesthood, a holy nation, God's own people. . . . Once you were no people but now you are God's people."

The Epistle to the Hebrews (1:1-2) expresses the view that Christianity is the climax in the history of revelation that had begun with the Jews; in Hebrews, Judaism is the imperfect foreshadowing now outmoded by the perfection characteristic of Christianity.

Unflattering to Judaism and to Jews as are many NT, especially gospel, passages, they do not approach in virulence the Epistle of BARNABAS or the strictures of such church Fathers as John Chrysostom of Antioch (of the fourth century).

5. Later Christian views. While outside the NT, some voices (e.g., the second-century MARCION) seem to have regarded Christianity as historically unconnected with Judaism, this view was uncongenial to others in the church. The normal view was that Christians had supplanted Jews as God's elect and the OT promises were really addressed to Christians. For this reason the Jewish Bible was retained by Christians, but viewed now as their own Scripture, their OT. OT and NT constituted a single, continuous scripture. Later Christians ordinarily regarded themselves either as the "third race," differentiated from Jews and Gentiles, or more usually as *Verus Israel,* "the true Israel" of God.

6. The nonelect. In both OT and NT, and in the ancient rabbinic literature roughly contemporaneous with NT writings, the often felicitous view of election as a demand for a higher morality carried with it an unexpressed doctrine, that there were the nonelect who merited God's curse and wrath. The claim of divine election is thus sporadically blemished by the omission of the usual demand for a higher morality, and by the substitution of a dismal arrogance instead.

Bibliography. The best historical study is M. Simon's *Verus Israel: étude sur les relations entre Chrétiens et Juifs dans l'Empire romain* (2nd rev. ed., 1964), pp. 135-425. P. Richardson, *Israel in the Apostolic Age,* NTSMS, X (1969), presents much material, frequently in an idiosyncratic way. S. Sandmel, *The Several Israels* (1971), deals with aspects of claims of both Jews and Christians of being God's Israel. *See also* H. H. Rowley, *The Biblical Doctrine of Election* (1952).

S. SANDMEL

***ISRAEL, HISTORY OF.** The original article by Rowley exemplifies his well-known concern for precision, thoroughness, and balance, and does not call for extensive correction or revision. Archaeological activity over the last few years, however, has provided a welcome supplement to our previous knowledge (*see* ARCHAEOLOGY[S] §§1-2). For example, a destruction layer found at HAZOR can most probably be associated with the Israelite conquest; on the contrary, the stratigraphy at SHECHEM reveals no such layer, confirming the assumption, based on biblical evidence, that the city passed into Israelite hands without a major battle. Recent work at JERUSALEM has clarified the history of its fortifications and water system, and excavations at BEER-SHEBA have revealed a well-planned late Israelite city. A casemate wall and gate from the Solomonic period at GEZER are also of interest in confirming that city's connection with Hazor and Megiddo (I Kings 9:15), where similar remains have been found. In addition to these sites, mention must be made in particular of AI, ARAD, ASHDOD, DAN, EGLON (Tell el-Hesi), En-Gedi, LACHISH, TAANACH, SHILOH, and ZARETHAN. Occasionally fresh investigations have cast doubt on the earlier identification and attribution of certain archaeological features; for example, it is now probable that the famous "Solomonic stables" at MEGIDDO should be associated rather with the building activity of Ahab, and that the evidence for flues of copper smelters at TELL EL-KHELEIFEH (*see also* ELATH; EZION-GEBER) is to be reinterpreted rather as gaps left by burned-out beams.

New inscriptions have also cast light on the history of Israel, as well as on the life and customs of biblical times (*see* INSCRIPTIONS, SEMITIC[S]). In this connection the SAMARIA PAPYRI are particularly important. They contain information, especially in the form of proper names, which will be of considerable help in interpreting the postexilic history of Palestine in general and the history of the SAMARITANS in particular. Inscriptions discovered in neighboring lands continue to provide data of interest to the biblical scholar. For example, a stele found in 1967 at Tell er-Rimaḥ in Iraq tells of a campaign by Adad-nirari III (811-784 B.C.) to the W after which the Assyrian king received tribute from "Mari' (Ben-Hadad?) of the land of Damascus . . ., Ia-'a-su (or Iu-'a-su) of the land of Samaria, the [ruler] of Tyre, and the [ruler] of Sidon." This is the first occurrence of the name of King Joash/Jehoash (801-786 B.C.) in an Assyrian text, and also the first designation of the northern kingdom as "Samaria"; the usual Assyrian term is "Bit Humri," i.e., "house of Omri" (*see* JOASH §8; JOASH[S]). Finally, recently published Dead Sea Scrolls continue to cast at least indirect light on the later history of Israel and especially its religious sects and parties. *See* DEAD SEA SCROLLS[S]; MANUSCRIPTS FROM THE JUDEAN DESERT[S].

In addition to assessing the significance of discoveries such as these, the historian of Israel must continually re-evaluate the biblical sources. Recent study of the PENTATEUCH has brought into sharper relief the distinctive contributions of its various oral and literary traditions, and has emphasized the theological significance of Israel's attempts to understand history as God's "mighty acts" (*see* YAHWIST[S]; ELOHIST[S]; PRIESTLY WRITERS[S]). Furthermore, the great importance of the DEUTERONOMIC HISTORY is now becoming quite clear. Rather than being merely a continuation of the earlier Pentateuchal sources, it is a new attempt, not only to bring Israel's history up to date, but also to make it relevant for the needs of the current generation (*see also* JUDGES, BOOK OF[S]). Finally, the work of the Chronicler (*see* CHRONICLES; EZRA AND NEHEMIAH) is now receiving new attention. It has long been known that in spite of its relatively late date it contains a great deal of authentic data for the historian. But recent studies have concentrated on the sources and various editions of the work, and have helped to explain some of its inconsistencies and confusions which have long plagued the study of postexilic history.

These two concurrent enterprises—the appropriation of new data and reassessment of old—have brought about certain changes of perspective in the study of most of the major periods of Israelite history.

For many decades scholars have held widely differing opinions on the date and background of the PATRIARCHS, with a few denying any historicity to the narratives of Genesis. Extrabiblical inscriptional evidence (*see esp.* MARI[S] §8; NUZI[S] §2, but note the cautions contained therein) and the discoveries of Palestinian archaeology seem now to locate them in the Middle Bronze Age; here we find a period to which we can attribute with some confidence patriarchal names, customs, and style of life and religion. Some are inclined to place them early in the period and regard them as donkey caravaneers (Albright); others suggest MB II and stress the patriarchs' connection with the great folk movements associated with the AMORITES.

Israel's entry into Canaan may now be seen with greater clarity as a penultimate phase of this larger movement, and thus as a stage in a continuous process that lasted for many centuries. The biblical historians concentrate on the last act of this continuum, depicted as a military conquest of the Canaanite city-states in three lightning campaigns under the leadership of the traditional figure of Joshua. But this conquest was most probably preceded by decades of infiltration, intermarriage, and peaceful co-existence; various archaeological surveys (*see* Aharoni) have provided evidence of this, and placed in new perspective other data usually associated with the Israelite destruction of certain cities. Such a view also helps to interpret other traditions in the OT, such as Judg. 1:1–2:5 and certain variant texts even in the book of JOSHUA, which imply that the Israelite settlement was not as rapid and unified as it first appears. All of this makes it unlikely that one can assign a precise date to the exodus from Egypt; indeed it is probable that Israel's departure took place in two or more stages, and that the wanderings in the wilderness and Transjordan followed several different routes and were associated with different tribal groups. *See* CANAAN, CONQUEST AND SETTLEMENT OF[S].

There has been increasing criticism of the once popular thesis that Israel under the judges was organized as a "tribal league" or AMPHICTYONY; in this connection the role and function of the judge has been widely discussed (*see* JUDGES, BOOK OF[S] §3). Studies of the Israelite monarchy have centered on such topics as the nature of kingship and the character of David (*see* COVENANT, DAVIDIC [S]), the "enlightenment" under Solomon, and the correlation of Israel's history with that of her immediate neighbors and the great empires of the ancient Near East. The Exile is now seen to be one of Israel's most productive and creative eras, and the postexilic period has been illuminated from new finds and fresh perspectives, leading some to conclude that the traditional order of Ezra and Nehemiah may after all prove to be correct.

Bibliography. New eds. and/or trans. of older works: J. Bright, *A History of Israel* (2nd ed., 1972); *CAH* (3rd ed., 1970-75), esp. vol. II, Pt. 2; M. Noth, *The History of Israel* (2nd ed., 1960); *The OT World* (1966); J. B. Pritchard, ed., *ANET,* 3rd ed., with supplement (1969). New works: Y. Aharoni, *The Land of the Bible* (1967); W. F. Albright, *Yahweh and the Gods of Canaan* (1968); S. Herrmann, *A History of Israel in OT Times* (1975); B. Mazar, ed., *The World History of the Jewish People,* II, *Patriarchs* (1970), III, *Judges* (1971); J. M. Myers, E. F. Campbell, Jr. *et al.,* "The History of Israel and Biblical Faith: In Honor of John Bright," *Int.,* XXIX (1975); R. de Vaux, *Histoire ancienne d'Israël,* 2 vols. (1971-73). Bible atlases: Y. Aharoni and M. Avi-Yonah, *The Macmillan Bible Atlas* (1968); H. G. May, ed., *The Oxford Bible Atlas* (2nd ed., 1974).

Special topics: W. Hallo, "From Qarqar to Carchemish: Assyria and Israel in the Light of New Discoveries," *BA,* XXIII (1960), 34-61, repr. in *BAR,* II (1964), 152-88; S. Herrmann, *Israel in Egypt* (1973); A. D. H. Mayes, *Israel in the Period of the Judges* (1974); D. S.

Russell, *The Jews from Alexander to Herod* (1967); M. Weippert, *The Settlement of the Israelite Tribes in Palestine* (1971). J. F. Ross

*ISRAEL, SOCIAL AND ECONOMIC DEVELOPMENT OF.

1. Sources and methods of study; socioeconomic structure
2. Major turning points in socioeconomic history

Bibliography

1. Sources and methods of study; socioeconomic structure. The still unrealized project of reconstructing the social and economic history of Israel has at its disposal considerable biblical data, largely unsystematized, to which can be added a growing fund of information on Syro-Palestinian society and economy derived from material remains and from extrabiblical texts. What has been lacking is the sustained and systematic application of social scientific method (from anthropology, sociology, economics, and political science) in conjunction with adjunct disciplines for recovering the material base of society (cultural or ethnological ARCHAEOLOGY, cultural geography, demography, climatology, metallurgy, agronomy, etc.). In particular, sociological theory concerning such historical phenomena as peasant revolts, tribal organization, the pre-industrial city, class composition and class struggle, and premodern bureaucratic empires can provide analytic and synthetic grids for cross-sectional and temporal reconstructions of Israel's socioeconomic life. These reconstructions must also be viewed in relation to adjacent Near Eastern peoples and to peoples observed first-hand at similar stages of socioeconomic development.

In brief, the basic societal component of ancient Israel was a populace engaged primarily in intensive rain and spring-irrigated AGRICULTURE, practicing supplemental forms of stock-breeding and handcrafts, and eventually selectively engaged in state-promulgated light industry and commerce (*see* TRADE AND COMMERCE §§2-3). The populace was village-based and organized tribally on pseudo-KINSHIP lines, an infrastructure progressively overlaid and fractured by political hierarchy and social stratification. Increasing urbanization, confined to a few centers, dominated and exploited the countryside but failed to draw a majority of the populace into the cities. The Israelite socioeconomic system was solidified and legitimated, and its internal conflicts heavily surcharged, by a highly developed religious ideology that was in part continuous with ancient Near Eastern religious ideologies and in part highly idiosyncratic.

2. Major turning points in socioeconomic history. In its initial tribal form, Israel's socioeconomic relations were egalitarian in the sense that the entire populace was assured of approximately equal access to basic resources by means of its organization into extended families (*bêth-'abhôth*), protective associations (*mishpāḥôth,* not to be construed as exogamous "clans"), and tribes (*shebhāṭîm* or *maṭṭôth*), federated as an intertribal community ("Israel," "Israelites," or "tribes of Israel"). Political hierarchy, introduced by the monarchy, gave impetus and protection to "creeping" social stratification. Increasingly, the former, communally owned means of production, vested in extended families, fell into the hands of a minority of state officials, merchants, and large landholders, who never constituted more than five to ten per cent of the total populace. Between the tenth and the early sixth centuries, the conjunction of domestic social conflict and imperial aggression destroyed this mixed tribal-statist social system, in both the northern and the southern kingdoms. Israelite/Judean survivors of the downfall of the two states, including those who returned to Palestine under Persian sponsorship, retained features of tribal existence vis-à-vis the great empires to which they were subordinated (Persia, Macedonia, Seleucids, Ptolemids, Rome), while simultaneously incorporating internal social stratification in which disproportionate wealth and power were vested in native elites.

There were four primary turning points in the social and economic development of Israel.

a. Revolutionary tribal origins. Prevailing models of Israel as an invading or immigrating seminomadic people of a distinct ethnic type have singularly failed to provide a plausible account of Israelite beginnings. More convincing is the hypothesis that Israel burst into Near Eastern history as an ethnically and socioeconomically heterogeneous coalition of insurgent mercenaries and freebooters (*'apiru; see* HABIRU[S]), tribally organized farmers and pastoral nomads (*Shosu*), depressed, "feudalized" peasants (*ḫupshu*), assorted craftsmen (including Kenite-Rechabite metallurgists; *see* RECHABITES[S]), and renegade priests, all of whom joined in rebellion against the imperial and quasi-feudal sociopolitical structures of Egyptian-dominated Canaan. *But see also* CANAAN, CONQUEST AND SETTLEMENT OF[S].

The first Israelites were peasants. Evidence from prehistory and ethnology, combined with close scrutiny of the biblical text, indicates that pastoral nomadism was no more than a minor component in the Israelite economy. Israelite pastoral nomads were integrated with the vast peasant majority in a symbiosis dictated by the dependence of sheep, goat, and ass breeding on contractual pasture and water rights in the settled regions. The pastoral nomadic component in Israel, serving in part as a mode of political escape and asylum, fluctuated according to changing economic and political conditions but probably never exceeded ten per cent of the total population. *See* NOMADISM[S].

Indigenous Israelite tribalism must be accounted for, not by the chimerical extension of seminomadism into Canaan, but by the organized resurgence of suppressed rural and village independence against the drafting and taxing powers of the hierarchic state as exercised by the Egyptian Empire, Canaanite city-states, Midianites who attempted a commercial empire in eleventh-century Transjordan, the nascent national states of Ammon, Moab, and Edom, and the Philistine military oligarchy. In Israel, diverse segments of the Canaanite underclasses, previously divided and at odds, gathered in the hill country and united in free agriculture based on regional mixes of grains, wine, oil, and assorted fruits and vegetables, supplemented by small bovine herds and larger sheep and goat herds, only a fraction of which were tended by seasonal nomadic movements into the steppes. The basic unit of material production and reproduction was the extended family, which consumed or bartered what it produced. The larger groupings into protective associations, tribes, and intertribal confederacy served the needs for mutual aid, external defense, and a comprehensive religious ideology of covenanted or treaty-linked equals. Tribal leadership was largely patriarchal, although women as a whole—relative to Canaanite class society—benefitted from their participation as members of the tribal production and defense systems.

b. Monarchic superstructures. The centralized military leadership that arose in Israel to cope with the Philistine threat did not disband after the defeat of Philistia (*see* KING, KINGSHIP; SAMUEL, I AND II[S] §4). Instead, it rapidly imported a state apparatus for fiscal and military administration and embarked on fateful wars of expansion and domination in a totally new departure from Israel's immediate tribal past (*see* WAR, HOLY[S] §§1*c*, 2*c*). Unable to reverse this hierarchic-imperial growth, the tribes at least slowed the process by breaking up the united monarchy. The surviving parts, however, continued as monarchic states.

The continuing tribal infrastructure stood in accommodation, tension, and contradiction to the superimposed political structures in N and S, often fiercely contesting and openly resisting arbitrary state powers. To varying degrees and at differing tempos, state power in the divided kingdoms of Israel and Judah strengthened and validated the social stratification, which penetrated more and more into the egalitarian tribal structure in a bitter seesaw struggle. Tribally guaranteed access to basic resources for all Israelites slowly gave way before the concentration of wealth in the state treasury and in the hands of merchants and landlords who were largely urban-based and backed by explicit or implicit state power, including a judicial system largely compliant to the newly enriched speculators.

As elsewhere in the ancient Near East, it is probable that the Israelite state apparatus, while protecting and furthering the vital interests of the new propertied classes it had brought to power, also strove to stand above sectoral conflict by occasional redress of the most vocal grievances of the disadvantaged segments of society. The "benign neutrality" and periodic "reforms" of the state (including Josiah's effort) failed to alter or to stem the accelerating social stratification, and may never have been fully intended to bring about fundamental changes in the socioeconomic structures.

c. Intrusion of the great empires. Tribal Israel and early statist Israel capitalized on a period when no great empires imposed their wills on the ancient Near East. From the mid-ninth century, however, Assyria, and later Neo-Babylonia, intruded on the autonomy of Syro-Palestinian states in programs of economic and political domination intended to maximize the production, circulation, and concentration of international wealth to the advantage of the imperial metropolis.

This intervention in Israel and Judah coincided with protracted internal social strife. To strengthen their positions vis-à-vis the threatening foreign powers, the Israelite states centralized and deployed their limited wealth—necessarily extracted from the peasants' precarious "surpluses"—for armaments and a favorable balance of trade. Monarchic war against foreign states was simultaneously and ineluctably war against the mass of Israelite peasants. Land, the primary mode of production for the vast majority of Israelites, became subject to excessive taxation and to predatory merchant capital offered at exorbitant interest rates and issuing in debt SLAVERY for growing numbers of impoverished Israelites. *See also* JUBILEE, YEAR OF[S]; SABBATICAL YEAR[S].

So skewed was the socioeconomic structure of Israel and Judah in favor of a rapacious minority —a minority no doubt fully convinced of the wisdom and virtue of their policies in the name of "national security"—that by the time of the culminating Assyrian and Neo-Babylonian interventions in 722 and 587 B.C. the rural population was so demoralized and impoverished as to offer only feeble resistance and, with the connivance of some urban elements, to welcome the conquerors as a possible or probable respite from the unrelenting depredations of their own domestic ruling class (rather similar to the way that Jews later embraced Pompey and the Romans as a relief from corrupt and oppressive Hasmonean rulers).

The prophets of the eighth through the early sixth centuries, widely construed as religious mystics or utopian dreamers, were in fact articulate spokesmen for the grievances of the suffering Israelite masses. They effectively invoked the weighty and rich resources of the society's religious ideology in order to steer the Israelite states toward a socioeconomic and political course that would heal the fractured tribal infrastructure and restore the social unity of the people. The prophets astutely perceived that the insatiable longings of the Israelite ruling classes to emulate world empires were totally unrealistic. The sole lasting result would be the destruction of tribal egalitarianism, which was the material and spiritual foundation of Israelite autonomy and vitality.

d. Renewed socioeconomic autonomy and conflict. The old infrastructure of tribal egalitarian life, fueled by its resourceful religious ideology, continued to inform the consciousness of Israelites and Judeans, both those left in their homeland and those deported to Mesopotamia. The Neo-Babylonian deportation policies were not so destructive of conquered and transplanted communities as Assyrian policies had been. The Jews in Babylonian detention lived contiguously and retained a measure of self-rule (*see* EXILE §2). These deportees had been the elite in the former state of Judah; when some of them returned to set up a semiautonomous Jewish community under Persian tutelage, class struggle was renewed in a triangular form among the peasant masses and two rival elite classes. A Samaritan Jewish elite (surviving from the downfall of the northern kingdom) had penetrated into Judah during the exile, filling the leadership vacuum left by the deported Judean upper classes and taking control of deserted properties. A fierce contest was joined between the Samaritan and the Judean elite for socioeconomic and political hegemony over the peasant masses. *See* SAMARITANS §§A3, B1.

In spite of bold efforts by some of the new leaders, such as Nehemiah and Ezra, to prevent the recurrence of socioeconomic inequities (cf. Neh. 5:1-13), the Israelite lower classes once again faced economic repression at the hands of the native elite, this time backed by Persian authority. This lengthening class struggle can be traced through the Maccabean-Hasmonean, Herodian, and Roman periods in Palestine. Increasingly, however, the internal socioeconomic contest was eclipsed by Jewish ethnic and religious self-consciousness as a marginal people of status, by turns privileged or disadvantaged, but in all events distinctively rooted in a historical consciousness and identity interpreted and validated by a religious ideology of extraordinary tenacity and vitality with its touchstone in a sacred literature of unusual historical scope and socioreligious richness. One of the unfinished tasks of a social and economic history of Israel is to discern in greater detail the postexilic contradictions between the group and class struggles within the community and the external ethnic-status struggle between the community as a whole and its various political overlords.

Bibliography. On socioeconomic methods and models: S. N. Eisenstadt, *The Political Systems of Empires* (1969); M. H. Fried, *The Evolution of Political Society* (1967); C. Geertz, "Ideology as a Cultural System," *Ideology and Discontent,* ed. D. Apter (1964), pp. 49-76; M. Harris, *The Rise of Anthropological Theory* (1969); M. J. Herskovits, *Economic Anthropology* (1960); G. Lenski and J. Lenski, *Human Societies* (2nd ed., 1974); M. Nash, *Primitive and Peasant Economic Systems* (1966); M. D. Sahlins, *Tribesmen* (1968); G. Sjoberg, *The Preindustrial City: Past and Present* (1960); E. Terray, *Marxism and "Primitive" Societies* (1969); S. Thrupp, ed., *Millennial Dreams in Action: Studies in Revolutionary Religious Movements* (1970); E. Wolf, *Peasant Wars of the Twentieth Century* (1966).

On ancient Near Eastern social and economic history: R. M. Adams, *The Evolution of Urban Society* (1966); R. Braidwood and G. Willey, eds., *Courses Toward Urban Life* (1962); B. C. Brundage and W. F. Edgerton in *Feudalism in History,* ed. R. Coulborn (1956), pp. 93-132; G. Buccellati, *Cities and Nations of Ancient Syria,* Studi Semitici, XXVI (1967); I. M. Diakonoff, ed., *Ancient Mesopotamia: Socio-Economic History* (1969); I. J. Gelb, "Approaches to the Study of Ancient Society," *JAOS,* LXXXVII (1967), 1-8; F. Heichelheim, *Ancient Economic History,* I (1959); M. Heltzer, "Problems of the Social History of Syria in the Late Bronze Age," *La Siria nel Tardo Bronzo,* ed. M. Liverani (1969), pp. 31-46; W. Helck, *Die Beziehungen Aegyptens zu Vorderasien im 3. und 2. Jahrtausend v. Chr.* (2nd ed., 1971); H. Klengel, ed., *Beitraege zur sozialen Struktur des alten Vorderasien* (1971); A. L. Oppenheim, "A New Look at the Structure of Mesopotamian Society," *JESHO,* X (1967), 1-16; K. Polanyi, "On the Comparative Treatment of Economic Institutions in Antiquity . . . ," in *The City Invincible,* ed. C. H. Kraeling and R. M. Adams (1960), pp. 329-50; K. Polanyi *et al.,* eds., *Trade and Market in the Early Empires* (1957); M. B. Rowton, "The Topological Factor in the *Ḫapiru* Problem," *Studies in Honor of Benno Landsberger* (1965), pp. 375-87; W. J. van Liere, "Capitals and Citadels of Bronze-Iron Age Syria in their Relationship to Land and Water," *Les annales archéologiques de Syrie. Revue d'archéologie et d'histoire,* XIII (1963), 109-22; W. M. Watt, *Islam and the Integration of Society* (1961).

On Israelite social and economic history: A. Alt, *Kleine Schriften,* II (1953), 316-37; III (1959), 348-81; D. Baly, "The Wheat and the Barley, the Oil and the Wine," in *Geographical Companion to the Bible* (1963), pp. 60-77; P. Berger, "Charisma and Religious Innovation: the Social Location of Israelite Prophecy," *American Sociological Review,* XXVIII (1963), 940-50; S. H. Bess, "Systems of Land Tenure in Ancient Israel," (diss., Univ. of Mich., 1963); P. Bird, "Images of Women in the OT," in *Religion and Sexism,* ed. R. Ruether (1974), pp. 41-88; W. Claburn, "The Fiscal Basis of Josiah's Reforms," *JBL,* XCII (1973), 11-22; M. Cogan, *Imperialism and Religion,* SBLMS, XIX (1974); C. J. de Geus, "The Importance of Archaeological Research into the Palestinian Agricultural Terraces . . . ," *PEQ,* CVII (1975), 65-74; R. de Vaux, *Ancient Israel: Its Life and Institutions* (1961); H. Donner, "Die soziale Botschaft der Propheten im Lichte der Gesellschaftsordnung in Israel," *OrAnt,* II (1963), 229-45; J. Dus, "Moses or Joshua? On the Problem of the Founder of Israelite Religion," *Radical Religion,* II (February 3, 1975); G. Fohrer, "Zur Einwirkung der gesellschaftlichen Struktur Israels auf seine Religion," *Near Eastern Studies in Honor of W. F. Albright,* ed. H. Goedicke (1971), pp. 169-85; F. S. Frick, "The City in the OT" (diss., Princeton, 1970); F. S. Frick and N. K. Gottwald, "Orientation Paper for the SBL Consultation on the Social World of Ancient Israel," *SBL Seminar Papers,* I (1975); A. E. Glock, "Early Israel as the Kingdom of Yahweh," *CTM,* XLI (1970), 558-605; R. Gordis, "The Social Background of Wisdom Literature," *Poets, Prophets and Sages* (1971), 160-97; N. K. Gottwald, *All the Kingdoms of the Earth: Israelite Prophecy and International Relations in the Ancient Near East* (1964), "Domain Assumptions and Societal Models in the Study of Pre-Monarchic Israel," VTSup, Edinburgh Congress Vol. (1975), pp. 1-12, *A Sociology of the Religion of Liberated Israel, 1250-1000* B.C., 2 vols. (1976), and "Were the Early Israelites Pastoral Nomads?" in *Rhetorical Criticism,* ed. J. Jackson and M. Kessler (1974), pp. 223-55; H. Hahn, *The OT in Modern Research* (rev. ed., 1966), pp. 44-82, 157-84; K. Henry, "Land Tenure in the OT," *PEQ,* LXXXVI (1954), 5-15; B. Kovacs, "Is There a Class-Ethic in Proverbs?" *Essays in OT Ethics,* ed. J. Crenshaw (1974), pp. 171-89; H.-J. Kraus, "Die Anfänge der religionssoziologischen Forschung in der altt. Wissenschaft," *Biblisch-theologische Aufsaetze* (1972), pp. 296-310; A. Kuschke, "Arm and Reich im Alten Testament, mit besonderer Berücksichtigung der nachexilischen Zeit," *ZAW,* LVII (1939), 31-57; M. Lurje, *Studien zur Geschichte der wirtschaftlichen und sozialen Verhältnisse in israelitisch-jüdischen Reiche* (1927); G. E. Mendenhall, *The Tenth Generation* (1973), and "The Hebrew Conquest of Palestine," *BAR,* III (1970), 100-120; H. Mottu, "Jeremiah vs. Hananiah: Ideology and Truth in OT Prophecy," *Radical Religion,* II (February 3, 1975), pp. 58-67; P. A. Munch, "Verwandtschaft und Lokalitaet in der Gruppenbildung der altistraelitischer Hebräer," *Kölner Zeitschrift für Soziologie und Sozialpsychologie,* XII (1960), 438-58; E. Neufeld, "The Emergence of a Royal-Urban Society in Ancient Israel," *HUCA,* XXXI (1960), 31-53; N. Peters, *Die soziale Fürsorge im AT* (1936); T. H. Robinson, "Some Economic and Social Factors in the History of Israel," *ET,* XLV (1933-34), 264-9, 294-300; J. R. Rosenbloom, "Social Science Concepts of Modernization and Biblical History: the Development of the Israelite Monarchy," *JAAR,* XL (1972), 437-44; H. E. von Waldow, "Social Responsibility and Social Structure in Early Israel," *CBQ,* XXXII (1970), 182-204; F. Walter, *Die Propheten in ihrem sozialen Beruf und das Wirtschaftsleben ihrer Zeit* (1900); M. Weber, *Ancient Judaism* (1921 [ET 1952]); R. R. Wilson, "The OT Genealogies in Recent Research," *JBL,* XCIV (1975), 169-89.

N. Gottwald

'ITTURE SOPHERIM. *See* Qere-kethibh[S] §3.

IVVAH. *See* Sepharvaim[S].

J

***JACHIN AND BOAZ.** The two pillars Jachin and Boaz are believed by most scholars to have served a purely decorative or symbolic purpose. The archaeological evidence usually adduced in support of this theory consists of the following: two stone bases flanking the entrance to the main room of the sanctuary excavated at Arad, conical pillar bases found inside the porch of the Late Bronze Age II temple at Hazor, and a relief from Quyunjiq (Nineveh), on which one can distinguish two big and apparently freestanding pillars topped with fleur-de-lis capitals.

Preoccupation with the symbolism of the pillars seems to have detracted the attention of scholars from significant details in the textual tradition available to us. The two words לבית חלוני (*labbāyith ḥallônî*, JB "windows for the Temple") in I Kings 6:4 may describe the *'ûlām* (RSV "vestibule") as a *bît ḫilâni* type, i.e., a N Assyrian type of portico with one, two, or even three columns often placed at the top of a low flight of steps. No scholar has claimed that such columns had to be freestanding. This argument is further supported by a reading preserved in LXX III Kings 7:9 which states that an architrave (μέλαθρον) rested on top of the two pillars. It might then be proper to describe the Solomonic structure as a temple with columns *in antis* (in front) without having to visualize Jachin and Boaz as freestanding pillars.

Bibliography. W. Kornfeld, "Der Symbolismus der Tempelsaüle," *ZAW*, LXXIV (1962), 50-57; J. Ouellette, "Le vestibule du Temple de Salomon," *RB*, LXXVI (1969), 365-78; R. D. Barnett, "Ezekiel and Tyre," *Eretz-Israel,* IX (1969), 6-13 and pl. I; Th. A. Busink, *Der Tempel von Jerusalem* (1970), pp. 299-321; J. Ouellette, " *'Aṭumîm* in I Kings 6:4," *BIJS* (1974), 99-102.

J. Ouellette

***JAMES, LETTER OF. 1. Form, language, and style.** James consists largely of parenetic material, and many believe that the epistolary form does not extend beyond the salutation in 1:1. Recent study of the form and function of Hellenistic letters, however, has reopened the possibility of assessing James as a letter. For example, the parenetic letter, established by the first century A.D. as a form of exhortation, may have provided the cultural form for the author's interests. Nevertheless, in distinction from such letters as those of Paul, the letter of James lacks situational immediacy. *See* Letter §§2, 3*a*; Letter[S].

There is no doubt that James was written in Greek, especially in view of the fact that the author employs frequent wordplays (2:22; 4:13), catchword connections (1:4, 5, 12, 13), alliteration (1:2), and other linguistic devices which can only be explained if Greek were the original language. But James is also characterized by many instances of Semitisms, including direct, spontaneous Semitisms unrelated to the LXX. For example, 1:19 where ἔστω δὲ πᾶς ἄνθρωπος τάχυς εἰς τὸ ἄκουσαι (Let every man be quick to hear) appears as a rather literal rendering of וכול איש ימהר לשמע; the LXX always renders מהר and the infinitive by ταχύνειν τοῦ and the infinitive. With reference to sentence syntax James displays more Semitisms—in distinction from septuagintisms—per page of the text than any other NT letter except I-III John. The author knew ordinary Koine Greek as it was written by people of some education, but he also had recourse to a Semitic style.

2. Traditional material and message. Parenesis is avowedly traditional, and James' exhortations reflect a variety of traditions found in Christian, Jewish, and other Hellenistic-Roman literature (*see* Parenesis[S]). Many of the parenetic precepts in James would be congenial to a wide audience and are not distinctively Christian. Thus the exhortation to regard trials joyfully as a testing of faith (1:2-4) is paralleled in I Pet. 1:6-7, is in keeping with Ecclus. 2:1-6, and is similar to Seneca's maxim "Disaster is virtue's opportunity." But it must also be observed that the author has selected critically from traditional material, and he has shaped these traditions according to his interests. Thus, for example, James does not draw on parenetic traditions concerning sexual behavior, but he does draw on traditions related to hospitality (2:15, 25). James draws on Jewish judicial tradition in 2:2-4, but he has used this tradition, not to give court instructions, but to warn against divisive partiality in the community.

The recognition of the use of traditional material brings into question the relationship of James to other Christian literature. Parallels with such writings as I Peter, I Clement, and Hermas are best explained as due to the use of common traditions, rather than literary borrowing. James shares traditions with Matthew and Luke, but in some instances James preserves a more primitive form. Thus the prohibition of oaths in 5:12 represents an earlier form than that which appears in Matt. 5:34-35. And the sharp distinction between rich and poor in 2:6-7 is closer to the sources of Luke-Acts than to the view of the redactor of Luke-Acts.

James' knowledge of the Pauline letters or a misunderstood Paulinism continues to be affirmed by many interpreters, but it is questioned by others. The crucial passage, 2:14-26, can be understood as developed from a wisdom tradition or parenetic traditions concerning hospitality without presupposing a controversy with Paul.

The parenesis of James is sometimes informed by eschatological expectation (e.g., 2:5; 5:7), and in the sections which betray the most *creative* work of the author (e.g., ch. 2) there is a concern for proper, well-ordered fraternal relations within the elect community. James relies heavily on the Jewish wisdom tradition in its understanding of man and the world, and his Christology may be a wisdom Christology. *See* WISDOM IN THE NT[S].

3. Text. Papyrus Bodmer 17 (P^{74}), a seventh-century MS, offers a significant variant reading to 1:27. Instead of ἄσπιλον ἑαυτὸν τηρεῖν (to keep oneself unstained), P^{74} reads ὑπερασπίζειν αὐτούς —"to protect them" (the needy) from the world. This reading makes better sense in context, for it regards the world as dangerous (cf. 4:4) but not polluting, and it underscores the social interest elsewhere evidenced in the letter.

Bibliography. Commentaries: M. Dibelius, rev. by H. Greeven, Hermeneia (1964 [ET 1976]); F. Mussner, HTKNT (1964); B. Reicke, ABi (1964).

On form, language, and style: A. Wifstrand, "Stylistic Problems in the Epistles of James and Peter," *ST,* I (1948), 170-82; K. Beyer, *Semitische Syntax im Neuen Testament,* SUNT, I (1962); F. O. Francis, "The Form and Function of the Opening and Closing Paragraphs of James and I John," *ZNW,* LXI (1970), 110-26.

On traditional material and message: E. Lohse, "Glaube und Werke," *ZNW,* XLVIII (1957), 1-22; J. B. Soucek, "Zu den Problemen des Jakobusbriefes," *EvT,* XVIII (1958), 460-68; R. Walker, "Allein aus Werken. Zur Auslegung von Jakobus 2, 14-26," *ZThK,* LXI (1964), 155-92; B. Noack, "Jakobus wider die Reichen," *ST,* XVIII (1964), 10-25; U. Luck, "Weisheit und Leiden. Zum Problem Paulus und Jakobus," *TLZ,* XCII (1967), 253-58; R. B. Ward, "The Works of Abraham. James 2:14-26," *HTR,* LXI (1968), 283-90, and "Partiality in the Assembly: James 2:2-4," *HTR,* LXII (1969), 87-97; J. A. Kirk, "The Meaning of Wisdom in James: Examination of a Hypothesis," *NTS,* XVI (1969), 24-38; D. O. Via, Jr., "The Right Strawy Epistle Reconsidered: A Study in Biblical Ethics and Hermeneutic," *JR,* XLIX (1969), 253-67.

R. B. WARD

***JAMES, PROTEVANGELIUM OF.** *See* APOCRYPHA, NT[S].

***JAPHETH. 1. Japheth in J.** In the J story (*see* YAHWIST[S]) of Noah's drunkenness, Gen. 9:20-27, the sons of Noah are Shem, Japheth, and Canaan ("Ham, the father of" in vs. 22 is a harmonizing gloss). This etiological narrative (*see* ETIOLOGY[S]) sees in the three sons the ancestors not of mankind but merely of the three population groups of Palestine. With Canaan standing for the subjugated natives, and Shem for the Israelites (cf. "Shem, the father of all children of Eber," i.e., Hebrews, Gen. 10:21), Japheth can only represent the Philistines. The benevolent attitude shown toward the Philistines has puzzled some commentators, but it must be remembered that after David's victories over the Philistines the relations between them and Judah were generally peaceful. The idea of friendly coexistence underlies the narratives of alliance and delimitation between Abraham and Isaac and the Philistine king Abimelech (Gen. 21:22-34; 26:26-33).

2. Japheth in P. In the genealogy of P, the three sons of Noah are Shem, Ham, and Japheth (now Noah's youngest son). In the table of nations (Gen. 10), Japheth is the ancestor of northern peoples and countries: Gomer (Cimmerians), Magog (taken from Ezek. 38:2; 39:6, probably <Akkad. **māt-Gugi,*" "the land of Gyges," or Lydia), Madai (Media), Javan (Ionians, and by extension all Greeks), Tubal (Tabal), Meshech (Phrygia), and Tiras (Tyrsenians=Etruscans), as well as of the "sons" of Gomer: Ashkenaz (<*Ashkuz, Scythians), Riphath (unidentified), and Togarmah (a city in eastern Anatolia), and the "sons" of Javan: Elishah (Alashya=Cyprus), Tarshish (Tartessus in southern Spain), Kittim (Cition in Cyprus), and Dodanim (preferably Rodanim [Rhodians] with I Chr. 1:7). The Philistines, conversely, were relegated by P to the descendants of Ham through Egypt.

3. Japheth and Iapetos. What is the relationship between Japheth and his virtual namesake Iapetos (Hesiod, *Theogony* 133-34), one of the six Titans who ruled the world before the ascent of Zeus? Iapetos was the father of Prometheus; Prometheus was the father of Deukalion, the survivor of the Flood, whose son was Hellen, the eponymous ancestor of the Greeks. The flood motif suggests that the connection of Japheth with Iapetos transcended mere onomastic resemblance. On the other hand, it is not Iapetos but his grandson who is the hero of the flood myth; of Iapetos, only the name remained in the genealogy, with no narratives or concrete characteristics attached to it. It has been surmised that Iapetos may have played a larger role among the pre-Greek inhabitants of the Aegean, and that the Philistines may have brought him to Palestine as their mythical ancestor. But epigraphic discoveries have failed so far to reveal his name in Greece and Crete of the Bronze Age, and the hypothesis remains unconfirmed.

Bibliography. E. Meyer, *Die Israeliten und ihre Nachbarstämme* (1906), pp. 219-21; E. Dhorme, "Les peuples issus de Japhet. . . ," *Recueil Eduard Dhorme* (1951), pp. 167-89; "Iapetos," *PW,* IX (1916), cols. 721-24.

M. C. ASTOUR

***JEREMIAH THE PROPHET.** The summary by Muilenburg of the issues surrounding the prophet Jeremiah and the book bearing his name is an admirable reflection of the consensus at the end of the 1950s (*see* JEREMIAH THE PROPHET). Since then we have seen an updating of the German commentaries of Rudolph and Weiser and the appearance of a new one by Bright. Research has gone on in many areas; four will be dealt with here—the chronology of Jeremiah, form criticism of Jeremianic material, the content of Jeremiah's message, and the text and composition of the book. No synthesis of the results of such work has appeared, so that representative literature is scattered (*see bibliog.*).

1. Chronology. From several quarters doubts have been raised regarding the traditional dating for Jeremiah's ministry, namely that he began to prophesy in 627/6 B.C. and therefore that many of the oracles in the first few chapters of the book (e.g., in chs. 2–4) are from the period 626-621. Instead a "lower" chronology has been proposed, by which the prophet would have begun to prophesy in 609, when Josiah was killed, or even in 605, at the time of the battle of Carchemish. One suggestion is that the "thirteenth year" of Josiah (627/6; *see* Jer. 1:2) is the date of the prophet's birth. Theologically Jeremiah perceived the basic encounter with God to have been before his birth (1:5), and this event may then be what is marked by the "thirteenth year" of Josiah. In this way difficulties raised by the traditional chronology are removed: the seeming silence of Jeremiah about Josiah's reform (ch. 11 can hardly be a reference to it); the prophet's presumed silence during the period 621-609; the puzzle of the identity of the foe from the north (the hypothesis that they were SCYTHIANS must be abandoned). Such a dating would also bring into focus Jeremiah's understanding of himself as the prophet like Moses (cf. Deut. 18:18 with Jer. 1:7, 9): it was the reform by Josiah in 621 which turned people's attention to Moses, but Josiah's death in 609 put Moses' instruction in limbo (cf. 7:9), so that 609 would be a plausible date for the beginning of Jeremiah's ministry. But the matter is not settled among scholars.

2. Form criticism. Aware of uncertainties in the chronology of Jeremiah, and aware, too, that to ask the date of a given oracle is not always to ask the most important question about it, scholars have moved their attention to using form-critical methods on the material (*see* FORM CRITICISM, OT[S]). They raise the question of what literary category Jeremiah was employing in a given instance, and whether he was reshaping an older category for a fresh purpose. Form criticism alerts us to how much we might have been using modern psychological assumptions in separating Jeremiah from his own culture.

This reminder came in an extreme form in a study in which Reventlow tried to show that Jeremiah was the holder of a cultic office and that the "I" of Jeremiah's words, especially in the so-called "confessions," was simply a way to say "we" on behalf of the people. By this reading, then, Jeremiah's own personality could not be known by us at all. This view, however, has been refuted by Bright and Berridge; Jeremiah is still an individual prophet with a unique voice. But Reventlow's work was a needed corrective, indicating the peril of an overromanticized reconstruction of the prophet.

Form-critical work in other directions has brought permanent gains. Thus scholars examining the "foe from the north" material in 4:5-12 point out that the passage assumes the themes of "holy war" (*see* WAR, IDEAS OF §§1, 3): the sounding of the horn, the battle cry, the flight of the enemy and his terror and demoralization. Jeremiah here has taken the old category of an appeal to holy war and applied it against Judah: Yahweh now declares war against his own people.

Again the "confessions," though the utterances of Jeremiah personally, are not simply an ancient equivalent of a private diary. Jeremiah voiced them as an individual, but also as one bearing the judgment of God in the context of his people. Thus the reply of God (15:19-21) to one of Jeremiah's confessions (15:15-18) involves the vocabulary of holy war ("fortified wall of bronze"). The wording of 1:17-19, which is very similar, suggests the same understanding ("gird up your loins," 1:17; cf. I Kings 20:11). In his life and ministry Jeremiah symbolically represents that holy war which Yahweh will wage against Judah.

3. The content of Jeremiah's message. Fresh exegesis of specific passages has in many cases brought into sharper focus Jeremiah's message and his understanding of God. Thus it is now clear that a phrase in 12:1 must be translated "yet I would pass judgment upon thee" instead of "yet I would plead my case before thee" (RSV); for the Hebrew idiom, cf. H 39:5. If God can pass judgment on the people because they did not keep their promise to him, then Jeremiah for his part feels free to pass judgment on God because he did not keep his promise to deliver Jeremiah (cf. 1:8). Again, it seems likely that 9:2 (H 9:1) is spoken not by Jeremiah but by God; Jeremiah has wished that his eyes might be a fountain of tears, that he might weep for his people (9:1 [H 8:23]), but then God, mimicking Jeremiah's diction, wishes to have a shelter in the desert, far away from his people.

Jeremiah seems to have loved ambiguity in words. This trait is exhibited in his use of double meanings, puns, and assonance. It may be, then, that in a given case any argumentation over two interpretations of a phrase is beside the mark—Jeremiah may have had *both* in mind. For example, in 14:8 and 17:13 does *miqwê* mean "hope of" (RSV) or "pool of" Israel (Dahood)? Linguistically, it could be either, and "pool of" would fit the imagery of 2:13; 2:31 (by implication), and 15:18. The answer doubtless is that in Jeremiah's mind the word carried both meanings.

In addition to fresh exegesis, scholars have been reassessing the judgments of earlier commentators that certain passages in Jeremiah were not genuine. The majority have now accepted the genuineness of 4:23-26, and of most if not all the poetic material in chs. 30–31. A few scholars have even argued that 10:1-16 is authentic to Jeremiah.

The image of God which emerges from Jeremiah's oracles is that of a deity who is radically innovative, never bound by the decisions of the past. He is willing to destroy Jerusalem in Jeremiah's day, even though he was understood to have guaranteed the safety of Jerusalem in the time of Isaiah (Jer. 7:1-15; cf. Isa. 37:33-35). Correlatively, Jeremiah emerges all the more clearly as a highly innovative person himself, turning old patterns of thinking and speaking into new directions. It is arguable that the catastrophe of the fall of Jerusalem in 587 was so shattering (cf. Lam. 4) that only such an innovative person could offer a theology with enough flexibility to carry people into the novel circumstances of the exilic and postexilic periods.

4. Text and composition of the book. Spurred by the discoveries of biblical texts among the Dead Sea Scrolls (*see* DEAD SEA SCROLLS §4; DEAD SEA SCROLLS[S] §4), scholars have made a fresh attack on the problem of the divergent Hebrew text traditions before the first century A.D. (*see* TEXT, OT; TEXT, HEBREW, HISTORY OF[S]). In this regard the text of Jeremiah offers noteworthy problems, since the LXX of this book differs quite markedly from the MT (*see* JEREMIAH THE PROPHET §D11). Janzen has concluded that the MT of Jeremiah, originating in Palestine, is full of secondary expansions (sometimes single words like the specification of the missing subject of a verb, sometimes longer phrases or even verses), while the LXX, originating in Egypt, gives in most cases a "purer," less expanded text tradition; and that the traditions began to diverge in the period 450-350 B.C. Argumentation in these matters continues lively.

When we turn from the issue of text transmission to that of the composition of the book, we note progress in scholarly investigations, but as yet no overall theory that brings consensus; the process by which the book took shape was complex in the extreme. We take note of three recent efforts, out of many, to deal with aspects of the process.

Rietzschel has offered a closely reasoned study, concentrating on the process by which large "blocks" of material were added to the book and on the motives which led the collectors of each of these successive blocks to supplement the growing collection. Rietzschel located the original scroll (cf. Jer. 36) in chs. 1–6, and found the "Deuteronomistic" material, Mowinckel's source *c* (*see* JEREMIAH THE PROPHET §D7) to be not a source at all but a literary category present in several of his blocks of material. His analysis is impressive, but perhaps overconfident in its preciseness.

Fresh doubts have been raised about earlier assumptions regarding that "Deuteronomistic" material. H. Weippert has demonstrated, by a careful examination of the typical phrases of that material in their contexts, that it is not at all related to the prose of the Deuteronomic school but fits the message of Jeremiah after all, and is simply another literary category ("formal prose"; German: *Kunstprosa*) through which Jeremiah's message was preserved.

The present writer has suggested that rhetorical criticism (cf. LITERATURE, BIBLE AS[S]) may be useful in analyzing the way by which the oracles and other units were originally collected, and that such an analysis might lead to greater certainty as to the contents of the original scroll described in Jer. 36. It remains for the future to show whether these attempts and others can lead us with certainty to a clearer understanding of the composition of the book.

Bibliography. Commentaries: Most recently: W. Rudolph, *HAT*, XII (1968); A. Weiser, ATD, XX/XXI (1969); J. Bright, ABi, XXI (1965). General survey: W. L. Holladay, *Jeremiah: Spokesman Out of Time* (1974); cf. P. R. Ackroyd, *Exile and Restoration* (1968).

Chronology: For a lower dating: J. P. Hyatt, IB, V (1956), and most recently, "The Beginning of Jeremiah's Prophecy," *ZAW*, LXXVIII (1966), 204-14; C. F. Whitley, "The Date of Jeremiah's Call," *VT*, XIV (1964), 467-83; W. L. Holladay, "The Background of Jeremiah's Self-Understanding," *JBL*, LXXXIII (1964), 153-64, and "Jeremiah and Moses," *JBL*, LXXXV (1966), 17-27; further (but partial) literature in J. B. Berridge, *Prophet, People and the Word of Yahweh* (1970), p. 75, n. 5. For the traditional dating, see the literature in Berridge, same note, and a brief summary of argumentation in T. W. Overholt, *The Threat of Falsehood* (1970), p. 96, n. 26 with literature; see also the commentaries of Rudolph, Weiser, and Bright.

Disproof of the Scythian hypothesis: R. P. Vaggione, "All Over Asia?" *JBL*, XCII (1973), 523-30 with literature.

Form criticism: In the prophets generally: C. Westermann, *Basic Forms of Prophetic Speech* (1967); K. Koch, *The Growth of the Biblical Tradition* (1969), esp. pp. 183-220. For the view that Jeremiah cannot be known as an individual: H. Graf Reventlow, *Liturgie und prophetisches Ich bei Jeremia* (1963); refutation: J. Bright, "Jeremiah's Complaints," J. I. Durham and J. R. Porter, eds., *Proclamation and Presence* (1970), pp. 189-214; Berridge. On holy war themes in the prophets generally: R. Bach, *Die Aufforderungen zur Flucht und zum Kampf im alttestamentlichen Prophetenspruch* (1962). On aspects of form criticism in Jeremiah: Berridge, with much literature; and specifically, on Jeremiah's use of holy war motifs against Judah, see there pp. 73-113, and on the confessions, pp. 114-83.

On 12:1: W. L. Holladay, "Jeremiah's Lawsuit with God," *Int.*, XVII (1963), 280-87; Berridge, pp. 161-62; cf. J. Bright, "A Prophet's Lament and Its Answer," *Int.*, XXVIII (1974), 62, n. 10. On 9:2 [H 9:1]: W. L. Holladay, *The Architecture of Jer. 1-20* (1976), pp. 110-13. For an elaborate use of ambiguity in Jeremiah: W. L. Holladay, "The Covenant with the Patriarchs Overturned," *JBL*, XCI (1972), 305-20. On *miqwê*="pool of" in 14:8 and 17:13: M. Dahood, "The Metaphor in Jeremiah 17,13," *Bibl.*, XLVIII (1967), 109. On the genuineness of 4:23-26 and the material in chs. 30-31 cf. the treatment in Hyatt's and Bright's commentaries; on 10:1-16: T. W. Overholt, "The Falsehood of Idolatry," *JTS*, NS XVI (1965), 1-12. On God as innovative: W. L. Holladay, *Jeremiah: Spokesman;* on Jeremiah as innovative: W. L. Holladay, "Jeremiah in Judah's Eyes and Ours," *Andover Newton Quarterly*, XIII (1972-73), 115-32.

On text: Cross's theory of text types: F. M. Cross, "The History of the Biblical Text in the Light of Discoveries in the Judean Desert," *HTR*, LVII (1964), 281-99, and "The Contribution of the Qumran Discoveries to the Study of the Biblical Text," *IEJ*, XVI (1966), 81-95. Critique of the theory: G. Howard, "Frank Cross and Recensional Criticism," *VT*, XXI (1971), 440-50. On the text in Jeremiah: J. G. Janzen, *Studies in the Text of Jeremiah* (1973).

On composition: General survey: T. R. Hobbs, "Some Remarks on the Composition and Structure of the Book of Jeremiah," *CBQ*, XXXIV (1974), 257-75. On the historical context for the emergence of the prose: E. W. Nicholson, *Preaching to the Exiles* (1970). On "tradition blocks": C. Rietzschel, *Das Problem der Urrolle* (1966). On aspects of the problem of the "Deuteronomistic" prose: M. Weinfeld, *Deuteronomy and the Deuteronomic School* (1972); H. Weippert, *Die Prosareden des Jeremiabuches* (1973). On rhetorical analysis of Jer. 1-20: W. L. Holladay, *Architecture.*

W. L. HOLLADAY

***JERICHO. 1. The name.** The toponym Jericho is composed of the personal name of the West Semitic moon-god, Yara/iḫ, plus the terminative *-ō* (< *-ā*), whose precise signification is disputed. This explanation seems better than relating the word to Assyro-Babylonian *yarḫu*, "water hole, pond," despite Jericho's situation next to the strong spring of ʿAin es-Sultan. Moreover, *yarḫu* never seems to refer specifically to a spring, and its consistent orthographic representation without an "i"-vowel suggests caution in identifying it as the etymon of Jericho. Curiously, Jericho is never mentioned in extant epigraphic sources of the third and second millennia B.C.; and though it may be present under a different name, this has never been demonstrated. Its absence may be due to the fact that at the time our epigraphic material was written Jericho was either unoccupied or only sparsely settled. The place name bears some relationship to the clan name Yariḫû, one of the subtribes of the Banū-yamīna mentioned in the Mari correspondence (*see* BENJAMIN, BENJAMINITES and supplementary article §2). However, despite the identity in name between the biblical and Mari Benjaminites, it is not clear, without further evidence, that the Jordan Valley Benjaminite town of Jericho took its name from some far-spread offshoot of the N Mesopotamian Yariḫû (note that the final -û in this name would expectedly remain -û in Canaanite and Hebrew, certainly not become -*ô*).

2. Prebiblical Jericho. Carbon-14 tests of burned material uncovered in Kenyon's 1952-58 excavation indicate that Jericho's earliest occupation must be pushed back into the Mesolithic (Palestinian Natufian) era, *ca.* 8000 B.C. Permanent sedentary life on the site, however, did not begin until the prepottery Neolithic period (*ca.* 7000 B.C.), when the earliest fortified town so far known was established at Jericho. Its well-built defense system, featuring a massive circumvallation wall with lookout towers and moat, bespeaks a well-organized and prosperous community (*see* PREHISTORY IN THE ANE[S] §2*a*). After the end of the Neolithic period (*ca.* 4000 B.C.), Jericho was abandoned until the Early Bronze Age, when once again significant town life flourished on the site for some six centuries (2900-2300). The last major sedentary occupation was during the so-called HYKSOS period of the late Middle Bronze Age (*ca.* 1750-1560), when a comparatively simple culture existed there, defended in typical Hyksos fashion by a strong mud-brick wall crowning a massive sloping plastered stone revetment. After the complete destruction of MB Jericho, *ca.* 1560 B.C., the town was not reoccupied until the beginning of the fourteenth century, but archaeological evidence for this is extremely slender. Three nearby tombs yielding Late Bronze pottery clearly datable to the fourteenth century also support some kind of LB occupation, but there is nothing to suggest that Jericho had once again become a fortified town. Though the disappearance of much more extensive LB remains has been attributed to wind and rain erosion, it is nonetheless strange that in the erosion tip lines at the base of the tell there is almost no LB pottery. Since there is no evidence at all of a thirteenth-century occupation (the few samples of local imitations of Mycenean pottery types found principally in tombs away from the mound are best assigned to a fourteenth- rather than thirteenth-century context), it would seem that Jericho had again become an abandoned site by the last quarter of the fourteenth century.

3. OT Jericho. Biblical traditions referring to the conquest and destruction of Jericho presuppose its existence as a walled town (Josh. 2, esp. vss. 15, 18 [LXX]; 24:11; 6). Because of a lack of any archaeological evidence for a thirteenth-century occupation of Jericho (seemingly the most probable date for the Hebrew exodus and conquest, *but see* EXODUS, BOOK OF §2), if there is any historical validity to the Joshua traditions they refer either to the fourteenth-century destruction or to a later overturn of such a small settlement that its remains have totally disappeared or have not yet been discovered by archaeologists. It is possible that the tradition about Jericho's fall is only an ETIOLOGY, i.e., an explanation of the site's impressive ruins, created long before Joshua's day, but subsequently attributed to the invasion under his leadership (as may have been the case with respect to AI).

It is striking that most of the remaining OT references imputing some kind of sedentary life at Jericho (cf. Judg. 3:13; II Sam. 10:5; I Kings 16:34; II Kings 2:5, 15, 18; Ezra 2:34; Neh. 3:2; 7:36) are likewise without any archaeological support. After the fourteenth century, occupation at Jericho is not substantially attested again until the eighth, but principally the seventh century B.C. At the base of the W side near the N end of the mound, the Austro-German expedition (1908-11) uncovered what seems to have been an unfortified settlement which developed through three building phases, the middle of which represented a rather significant structure. Archaeologically, this is the last time we have any indication of settled life at Tell es-Sultan, correlating possibly with reference to Jericho in II Chr. 28:15 from the time of Hezekiah. It may well be that this occupation continued until the coming of Nebuchadrezzar's army in the early sixth century B.C. (cf. II Kings 25:5; Jer. 39:5; 52:8).

4. Hellenistic Jericho. Among the Testimonia from Cave IV at Qumran, there is a pseudepigraphic work called the Psalms of Joshua, which, in quoting and interpreting Josh. 6:26, bears witness to the Hellenistic rebuilding of Jericho (at Tulul Abu el-ʿAlayiq) by "a cursed man, a man of Beliel" and his two sons, presumably a reference to Simon the Maccabee and his sons, whose death in Jericho at the hand of Ptolemy in 134 B.C. is interpreted by the Qumran community as a reapplication of Joshua's curse in their own time.

Bibliography. E. Anati, *Palestine Before the Hebrews* (1962), esp. pp. 240-50; H. J. Franken, "Tell es-Sultan and OT Jericho," *OTS,* XIV (1965), 189-200; G. L. Harding, *The Antiquities of Jordan* (rev. ed., 1967), esp. pp. 166-76; K. M. Kenyon, *Digging Up Jericho* (1957), *Excavations at Jericho,* I (1960), II (1965), *Amorites and Canaanites* (1966), and "Jericho" in *Archaeology and OT Study,* ed. D. W. Thomas (1967), pp. 264-75.

G. M. LANDES

***JEROBOAM** [Heb. ירבעם "may the people multiply" or "he who fights the people's battle" (viz., against the tyranny of Rehoboam King of Judah)]. The first king of the northern kingdom following partition of the united kingdom after Solomon's death (928-907 B.C.); son of Nebat. His mother, Zeruah ("leprous"), is described as a widow in I Kings 11:26, while in LXX III Kings 12:24*b* she is called Sarira and depicted as a harlot. Whether deliberate vilification was intended by either the MT or the LXX is an open question. It is also doubtful whether Jeroboam was of humble origin or—as may be indicated in I Kings 11:28 (גבור חיל)—an affluent landowner. His ability was recognized by Solomon, who put him in charge of the *corvée* of the tribes of Ephraim and Manasseh.

Jeroboam's rise to power is reported in two contradictory versions. The MT records that the prophet AHIJAH of Shiloh, predicting the imminent collapse of Solomon's kingdom, assured Jeroboam that he would become king over the ten northern tribes. Encouraged by this prophetic support, Jeroboam rebelled, but was forced to flee to Egypt, where Shishak (Shoshenk) I, founder of the Twenty-second Dynasty, provided asylum to Solomon's enemies (cf. I Kings 11:14-22, 40).

After Solomon's death, Jeroboam headed a delegation of tribal leaders who petitioned Rehoboam to reduce the onerous burdens imposed by his father. When this petition was contemptuously rejected, the northern tribes seceded (I Kings 12:1-16; II Chr. 10:1-16). According to another account, however, it was only after the secession that Jeroboam was summoned by the northern tribes to be crowned king of Israel (I Kings 12:20).

The LXX offers an entirely different narrative (III Kings 12:24). Jeroboam fortified the town of Sarira and assembled three hundred chariots in an abortive uprising against Solomon. Having taken refuge in Egypt, he was given Pharaoh's sister-in-law in marriage, presumably to tie him more closely to Pharaoh's political ambitions. However, in view of the extraordinary similarity of this part of the narrative to MT I Kings 11:14-22 (where Hadad the Edomite, another enemy of Solomon's, is depicted as Pharaoh's favorite and brother-in-law), it is likely that some confusion has crept into the LXX text.

When Jeroboam returned to his homeland, he assembled his fellow tribesmen and again fortified Sarira. At this point the LXX changes the entire chronological order of the MT. The sickness of Jeroboam's son and the visit by Jeroboam's wife to consult the prophet Ahijah—which in the MT occur at a much later time (I Kings 14)—precede Jeroboam's assumption of kingship. Ahijah's role is reversed, and instead of announcing Jeroboam's rise to power, he predicts the ruin of his dynasty. Since Jeroboam had not yet made the golden calves (which in the MT are the primary reason for the prophetic denunciation of him), one may assume that the (Alexandrian) LXX author, reflecting the views of his own time, wished to convey the idea that Jeroboam's Egyptian marriage was the central cause of the curse pronounced by the prophet upon his dynasty. Nevertheless, the LXX does record prophetic support for Jeroboam's ascent to power: Shemaiah (cf. RSV I Kings 12:22-24; II Chr. 11:2-4) announces that Jeroboam is to reign over the ten tribes. The historical reliability of the LXX account has been a matter of dispute, though it is probable that it contains at least some historical basis. It is no more tendentious than the MT.

Jeroboam, conscious of security considerations, rebuilt or fortified the cities of Shechem, Penuel, and possibly Tirzah (I Kings 12:25; 14:17). The latter seems to have been his capital (although some believe that it was during Baasha's reign that Tirzah became the capital; cf. 15:21), conceivably because Shechem lacks strong natural defense lines.

Jeroboam felt insecure while Jerusalem continued its religious hegemony over the entire country. The threat of a reawakened loyalty to the Davidic dynasty if pilgrimages to Jerusalem continued induced Jeroboam to establish an independent Yahweh cult at Bethel and Dan. To counter the prestige of the Jerusalem temple, Jeroboam—probably harking back to an old northern tradition which regarded Aaron as the originator of an Israelite cult—built two golden calves (or bulls) to serve as pedestals for the enthronement of Yahweh just as the ark and cherubim served at Jerusalem. *See* CALF, GOLDEN[S].

Jeroboam also asserted his religious and political authority by appointing a new, non-Levitical priesthood dependent on himself, thereby imitating Solomon, who had deposed Abiathar and appointed ZADOK as a subservient court priest (I Kings 2:35). Furthermore, Jeroboam postponed the Festival of Ingathering (Succoth) by one month, probably because of the later harvests in the north. As the climactic symbol of his supremacy, Jeroboam himself performed the priestly office (I Kings 12:32; 13:1).

Although Jeroboam maintained an authentic form of Yahweh worship, his challenge to the supremacy of the Jerusalem temple was uniformly condemned by the later court annalists of the Davidic dynasty. It is exclusively the view of the Judahite Deuteronomic-prophetic school which is reflected in the negative evaluation of Jeroboam and his successors in the books of Kings. The partition of the monarchy and the establishment of the bull cult were the cardinal "sins of Jeroboam which he sinned and which he made Israel to sin" (I Kings 15:30 and *passim*).

Jeroboam's position was seriously weakened by Shishak's invasion of Palestine (*ca.* 924 B.C.). According to an inscription at Karnak, Shishak captured a considerable number of Israelite cities, and archaeological evidence indicates that Gezer, Beth-shan, Taanach, Megiddo, and many other cities were destroyed (*ANET* [3rd ed.], pp. 242-43). The invasion was disastrous for the country, weakening its economy and undermining its military strength. Henceforth Jeroboam and his son and successor, Nadab, were involved in frequent border warfare with the resurgent Philistines and with a militarily strong Judah under Rehoboam and Abijah (II Chr. 12:15; 13:2-20; cf. I Kings 14:30; 15:6-7).

While the author of the books of Kings is remarkably reticent concerning the wars between Jeroboam and the kings of Judah, the Chronicler adds many details—derived in the main from the chronicles of the kings of Judah. Thus, he describes a major victory over Jeroboam (II Chr. 13:2-20). While the Chronicler's account includes many embellishments and exaggerations (e.g., 500,000 Israelite battle casualties [vs. 17]), the list of cities captured seems genuine enough. It was probably as a result of this crushing defeat that the northern kingdom lost the disputed territory of Benjamin and, temporarily at least, parts of southern Ephraim. Although King Baasha of Israel seems to have regained southern Ephraim, he was unable to reconquer the land of Benjamin (I Kings 15:17-21).

Jeroboam was further weakened by the erosion of prophetic support. Even Ahijah turned against him. When Jeroboam sent his wife to ask whether her sick son would recover, Ahijah prophesied the extermination of Jeroboam's dynasty (I Kings 14:1-16). The reason given for this radical change of attitude is that Jeroboam had made himself "other gods, and molten images" (vs. 9). Although the golden calves are not expressly mentioned here, it is evident that Jeroboam's cultic innovations brought about the loss of prophetic support. This, combined with the military setbacks, which must have had serious economic consequences, undermined Jeroboam's regime. While he died a natural death, apparently as a result of a plague (II Chr. 13:20), his son Nadab was overthrown and killed, along with Jeroboam's entire family (I Kings 15:27-29).

Bibliography. J. A. Montgomery and H. S. Gehman, *ICC, Kings* (1951); J. Gray, *I and II Kings* (1963); B. Mazar, "The Campaign of Pharaoh Shishak to Palestine," VTSup, IV, (1957) 57-66; M. Aberbach and L. Smolar, "Aaron, Jeroboam, and the Golden Calves," *JBL,* LXXXVI (1967), 129-40, "Jeroboam's Rise to Power," *JBL,* LXXXVIII (1969), 69-72; D. W. Gooding, "The Septuagint's Rival Versions of Jeroboam's Rise to Power," *VT,* XVII (1967), 173-89 and a rejoinder by M. Aberbach and L. Smolar, "Jeroboam and Solomon: Rabbinic Interpretations," *JQR,* LIX (1968), 118-32; J. W. Wevers, "Exegetical Principles Underlying the Septuagint Text of I Kings ii 12-xxi 43," *OTS,* VIII (1950), 310-11, 321; B. Oded, "Jeroboam," *Encyclopaedia Judaica,* IX (1971), cols. 1371-73.

M. Aberbach
L. Smolar

***JERUSALEM. 1. The Israelite period.** It is concerning this period that the largest amount of new information has come as a result of the recent excavations. The most important discovery is a 130-foot stretch of city wall, 23 feet thick, excavated in the Jewish Quarter. Such a wall, situated on the upper part of the E slope of the W hill, is indeed a great surprise, but seems to be in accord with the previous scholarly opinion (the "middle view") that only the areas in the Tyropoeon Valley were encompassed within the walled city during the time of the Judean kingdom. The excavator of the new city wall, Avigad, dates it by stratigraphic position to the end of the eighth century B.C. (*see* Fig. J1). Pertinent are the rock-cut tombs found at the foot of the E slope of the W hill. Mazar dates them to the second half of the eighth century and the first half of the seventh century B.C. Since tombs would have been placed outside the walled city, we must assume that the part of the W hill which is within the Avigad wall was incorporated after the initial use of these tombs.

The fact that floors, walls, and sherds of the Israelite period were found in every excavation throughout the Old City, from the Citadel to the Armenian Garden and Mount Zion, seems to indicate that the whole W hill was inhabited during that period, though most probably not walled until (as the new line of wall proves) the middle of the eighth century B.C.

New explorations to the N and the W of the Old City revealed various tombs of the Israelite period, such as those in the grounds of École

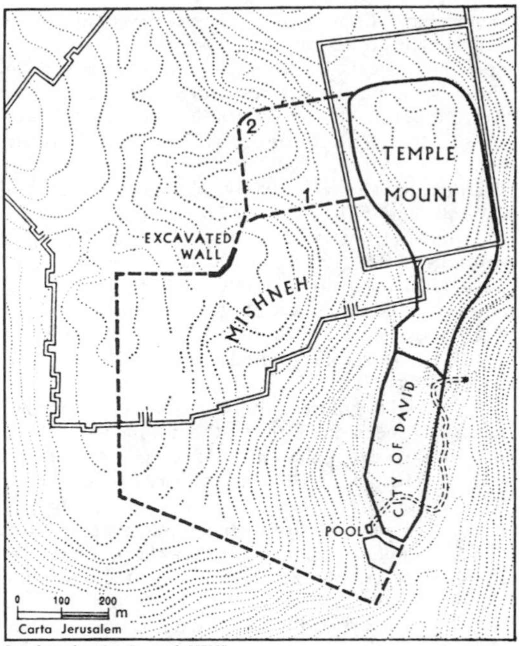

Israel Exploration Journal, XXII

1. Excavations in the Jewish Quarter, Jerusalem

Biblique, or in the area of Mamilla, or those recently discovered at the foot of the W slope of the W hill.

2. The Persian period. New information has come mainly from Kenyon's excavations on Ophel (*see* David, City of[S]). These excavations revealed the existence of late Iron Age houses beneath the "Jebusite Wall" (R. A. S. Macalister) —a fact which proves that this wall is at the earliest of the Persian period. Kenyon ascribes it to Nehemiah. Thus, this seems to be the E city wall of Jerusalem in the period of the return to Zion. All the recent excavations, however, have not brought about a definite answer to the problem of the extension of the city toward the W. The problem is whether the city was confined to the SE hill (known as Ophel), or whether it included part of the W hill, that part which is enclosed within the newly discovered city wall (the Avigad wall).

3. The Hellenistic period. Most of the Hellenistic remains which have been recently uncovered in the Jewish Quarter, in the Citadel, and on Mount Zion belong to the Hasmonean period. Pre-Hasmonean remains are known mainly on the Ophel, discovered long ago by Macalister and Duncan (*PEF Annual,* 1923-25; *see also* David, City of). In the other parts of the city, the remains are as follows: (*a*) In the Jewish Quarter a tower assignable to the Hasmonean period was discovered, built on top of the remains of the city wall of the first-temple period. (*b*) In the citadel extensive remains of the Hasmonean period came to light. The first city wall, which had been excavated on its outside by C. N. Johns, was now excavated on its inside face. It contained an inwardly projecting tower, the length of which is over 33 feet. Adjacent to the tower and the wall, rooms have been found, one preserved almost to full height, containing a doorway with its lintel and jambs. (*c*) In the excavations S and W of the temple mount cisterns and water installations were found. They were built into cave tombs which date back to the eighth-seventh centuries B.C.

Finds of special interest include two colossal capitals and a base of the Ionic order found in the Jewish Quarter (not *in situ*). They belong to columns at least 39 feet high, and may have been part either of the Temple of Apollo built by Antiochus IV or of one of the Hasmonean palaces. Both were located somewhere on the W hill.

4. The Herodian period. ***a. The temple.*** *See* TEMPLE OF HEROD[S].

b. Herod's palace. The location of the palace has never been in dispute: the whole area of the present-day citadel, to the SW corner of the city wall, an area about 985 feet long and 330 feet broad. The recent excavations by Kenyon-Tushingham, Amiran-Eitan, and Broshi-Bahat have proved that this location is right, and they have discovered some features of the engineering method. The clearest evidence, from within the Hasmonean city wall in the courtyard of the Citadel (Amiran-Eitan), shows that the whole palace stood upon a platform (podium) raised considerably above the floor levels of the Hasmonean houses. The foundations are walls 33 feet thick and 10-13 feet high, filled in with huge quantities of soil mixed with stones and sherds. In the Armenian Garden (Kenyon-Tushingham and Broshi-Bahat) similar foundation walls came to light, proving that the podium extended throughout the area of the palace. A few rooms escaped the fate of the rest of the palace, thanks to the fact that they were located at the very edge of the podium in the NW corner of the city wall. Vessels, coins, and other objects found on their floors date them to the first half of the first century A.D.

c. Private dwellings. Recent excavations on the W hill have uncovered a number of private dwellings from the Herodian period. These large-scale, magnificent houses of the well-to-do families are in accord with the evidence of Josephus. The houses had two or more stories built around a central court, beneath which was a basement containing cisterns and ritual baths. The rooms have mosaic floors or *opus sectili,* and the plastered walls often have frescoes which imitate marble panels or typical Herodian masonry. The walls contain niches for use as cupboards. Small objects include pottery, metal objects, inscribed weights, and a large quantity of vessels made locally of soft chalk. Special mention should be made of magnificent stone tables resting on one foot.

On the E slope of the hill the houses were built in steps, or terraces. Along their N boundary a street extended from about the middle of Herod's palace to the flight of stairs which lead to the temple mount (Robinson's Arch; *see* TEMPLE OF HEROD[S]). These houses existed until the eighth of Elul, A.D. 70, when they were destroyed along with the temple. Evidence of a great conflagration may be seen in the ruins of these houses.

5. The walls (*see* IDB, Vol. I, map XXIV). ***a. The first wall.*** The alignment and parts of the W and S first wall are known since the work of Maudslay (1871-75) and Bliss and Dickie (1894-97). Johns discovered the NW corner of the first wall in his excavations in the courtyard of the Citadel. He established the method by which the Herodian Phasael tower was inserted into the then-existing first wall (Hasmonean). In the fragments of the wall that Johns discovered he distinguished two types of construction, assigning both to the Hellenistic period. In the recent excavations (Amiran and Eitan, 1968-69), a tower belonging to the same city wall has been discovered (*see* §3*b* *above*). The two types of building seem to belong to the Hasmonean period (150-30 B.C.). The Herodian engineers made use of the Hasmonean wall in various ways. Sometimes they left it unchanged; sometimes they thickened it; and sometimes they built new segments to replace the previous ones. Excavations along the outside face of the present (Turkish) city wall (by Broshi) produced analogous results: the present wall makes use of the Hasmonean-Herodian wall at many points along the W side.

b. The second wall. The alignment of the second wall is one of the most controversial problems of the historical topography of Jerusalem, mainly because of its close connection with the problem of the location of the HOLY SEPULCHRE (*see also* JERUSALEM §11). Not much factual data has been added recently, but some negative information should be mentioned. Kenyon has found that the area she has excavated in the vicinity (site C) was outside the city area until the middle of the first century A.D., which pushes the N-S stretch of the second wall eastward.

Hennessey's clearance of Hamilton's excavations (1937-38) outside the present Nablus Gate reopened the magnificent Aelia Capitolina Gate, the remains under which may go back to a gateway of the second wall.

c. The third wall. Excavations carried on in 1965 (Kenyon-Hamrick) and in 1972-73 (Ben Arieh and Netzer) have added new information. Work was done in two areas, one of which had been excavated in 1927 and 1940 (Sukenik and Mayer); the other area was a little to the W of the first. Foundations of a 197-foot stretch of the wall and the bedding of two oblong towers (one is 29 x 36 feet) were uncovered. Avi-Yonah has summarized the evidence for the identification of this wall with the third wall mentioned by Josephus.

Excavations in 1971-72 (Bahat and Ben Ari) outside the NW corner of the present city wall (outside the Tancred Tower, sometimes called Goliath Tower) produced no trace of a city wall earlier than the Crusader period. Thus, the problem of the alignment of the third wall still remains.

6. Cemeteries. The line of cemeteries stretching from Haqal Dama in the S, to the Kidron Valley, the Mount of Olives, and Mount Scopus continues without interruption toward Sanhedria, since a large number of tombs have recently come to light on Giv'at ha-Mivtar and on Mount Scopus. Most are of the usual type; a central room and niches (*kôkhîm*) with a courtyard in front. Interment is in ossuaries (*see* TOMB[S] §3). Among the most important finds are: (1) A tomb on Giv'at ha-Mivtar with an ossuary inscribed with "Simon builder of the Temple." (2) Another tomb on ha-Mivtar with a skeleton of a crucified man (*see* CRUCIFIXION, METHOD OF[S]). (3) A tomb on Mount Scopus, with a beautifully carved sarcophagus of hard stone, and some ossuaries, one incised with the inscription, "Hanania son of Jonathan the Nazir." (4) An unusual cave tomb on Giv'at ha-Mivtar with a long inscription in Aramaic (but in Paleo-Hebrew script) by one "Abba son of the priest Eleazar, son of Aaron the great . . ., who was born in Jerusalem and went into exile into Babylonia and brought Mattathia son of Jud[ah] . . . [and buried him in the cave]."

Bibliography. §1: B. Mazar, *The Excavations in the Old City of Jerusalem* (1971), pp. 24-34; N. Avigad, "Excavations in the Jewish Quarter . . . 1971," *IEJ*, XXII (1972), 193-200. §2: K. M. Kenyon, "Excavations in Jerusalem," *PEQ*, XCVIII (1966), 73-88; XCIX (1967), 65-73; C (1968), 97-109. §3: Y. Yadin, ed., *Jerusalem Revealed* (1975), arts. by N. Avigad, R. Amiran and A. Eitan, and B. Mazar. §4*b*: A. D. Tushingham, "The Armenian Garden," *PEQ*, XCIX (1967), 71-73; C (1968), 109-11; Y. Yadin, ed., *Jerusalem Revealed*, arts. by R. Amiran and A. Eitan, D. Bahat and M. Broshi. §4*c*: Y. Yadin, ed., *Jerusalem Revealed*, arts. by N. Avigad and M. Broshi. §5*a*: C. N. Johns, "The Citadel, Jerusalem," *QDAP*, XIV (1950), 121-90; Y. Yadin, ed., *Jerusalem Revealed*, art. by R. Amiran and A. Eitan. §5*b*: K. M. Kenyon, "Excavations in Jerusalem, 1962," *PEQ*, XCV (1963), 14-15; M. Avi-Yonah, "The Third and Second Walls of Jerusalem," *IEJ*, XVIII (1968), 98-125; J. B. Hennessey, "Preliminary Report of Excavations at the Damascus Gate Jerusalem, 1964-66," *Levant*, II (1970), 22-27. §5*c*: E. L. Sukenik and L. A. Mayer, *The Third Wall of Jerusalem* (1930); E. W. Hamrick, "New Excavation at Sukenik's 'Third Wall,'" *BASOR*, 183 (1966), 19-26; Y. Yadin, ed. *Jerusalem Revealed*, arts. by S. Ben Arieh, M. Avi-Yonah, and D. Bahat and M. Ben Ari. §6: J. Haas, "Anthropological Observations. . . ," *IEJ*, XX (1970), 38-59; V. Tzaferis, "Jewish Tombs. . . ," *IEJ*, XX (1970), 18-32; Y. Yadin, ed., *Jerusalem Revealed*, pp. 66-67, 73-74.

R. AMIRAN
Y. ISRAELI

***JESUS CHRIST.** *See* CHRISTOLOGY IN THE NT[S]; TEACHING OF JESUS[S]; SAYINGS OF JESUS, FORM OF [S].

JEWS, NT ATTITUDES TOWARD. Earliest Christianity was a movement in Judea, of and by Jews, for a Jewish purpose. In a relatively short time it spread outside Judea and became a movement primarily of Gentiles. The NT attitude toward Jews is a complex of many factors, primarily disputes over the messiahship of Jesus and Paul's view of the Law, but with attendant conflicts and mutual Jewish-Christian hostilities. Ultimately the church came to believe that it was a discrete entity, and that God had cast off the Jews as his people and replaced them with Christians (*see* ISRAEL, CONCEPTIONS OF[S] §§4, 5). Jews and Judaism figure in Christian scripture, but Christians and Christianity do not, of course, figure in Jewish scripture.

1. The gospels. The gospels present Jesus in a Jewish setting and in varying kinds of relations with his fellow Jews, including the severely critical (*see* TEACHING OF JESUS[S] §§2, 3*b*). Assuming full historical reliability here, Jesus can thus be viewed as being in the loyal line of the pre-exilic prophets (e.g., Amos, Isaiah, Jeremiah) who criticized their people from within their common traditions and common assumptions. Only a few scholars have insisted that Jesus really stood over against the Jews and Judaism, and that the polemic attributed to him was, and is, justified.

Because the canonical gospels were written *ca.* A.D. 70-100, many scholars believe the attitude toward Judaism reflected in them indicates as much about the church's situation in this period as about the nature of Jesus' own ministry. In this period there was acute antagonism between Jews and Christians: the Jews resented the nonparticipation of Jewish Christians in the rebellion against Rome in A.D. 66; Christians contended that the Roman destruction of the temple in A.D. 70 was both a punishment of the Jews for having "rejected" Jesus and a vindication of their own Christian claims. These same scholars also stress the shift of attention from temple to synagogue in postbellum Judaism, resulting in the reorganization of Judaism by rabbinic leaders at Jamnia and increased emphasis upon the scrupulous observance of the Mosaic laws and secondary regulations derived from them. It is claimed that laxity in observing these regulations by Jewish Christians led to the punishment by flogging of Christians, to their exclusion from synagogues, or even to their persecution. There are some NT echoes of this latter, e.g., John 16:2.

Yet early rabbinic sources (the "tannaitic literature") lack the term "Christian" and the hostility found in these sources is directed to the enigmatic *minim.* These could have been pagan, Jewish, or even Christian Gnostics. Local harassment of Christians by Jews is recurrently described in Acts, where Christian preaching in a particular synagogue elicits opposition, punishment, and even violence. But there is no evidence for any determined, directed Jewish persecution of Christians. No Jewish decrees or hortatory statements that might have spurred deliberate maltreatment are extant. Indeed, in Acts the stoning of Stephen (6:1–7:60) and the events in Iconium and Lystra (14:1-19) are treated as lamentable but unplanned uprisings. The same author also shows how Gamaliel persuaded the Sanhedrin against killing the apostles (Acts 5:17-42). Though beaten and forbidden "to speak in the name of Jesus" (vs. 40), the apostles were released and continued "teaching and preaching Jesus as the Christ" (vs. 42). Although "a great persecution . . . against the church in Jerusalem" is mentioned (8:1), the peace and progress of the church "throughout the region of Judea and Samaria" is also noted. Incidents of hostility and mean treatment of Christians there were; but the Jews pursued no consistent, over-all policy of persecution toward the Christians. That Jewish stringencies after A.D. 90 resulted in the exclusion of Christians from synagogues is not confirmed in Jewish sources, but reasonably inferred from Christian writings. If the gospels reflect the bitter church-synagogue feelings, then the question of the historical reliability of the gospel accounts of conflicts between Jesus and the Jews of his time must remain uncertain and moot.

a. Mark. Scholarly inquiry into anti-Jewish sentiments in the gospels has usually fixed on certain limited materials: e.g., the TRIAL OF JESUS or the parable of the wicked tenants (Mark 12:1-12; Matt. 21:33-46; Luke 20:9-19). But attention to limited pericopes or sections, though valid, surely needs supplementing by attention to the totality of a gospel, of its tone and accentuations.

Mark, usually regarded as the earliest of the gospels, is no less than a thorough disparagement both of Jews (who are blindly hostile) and of Jesus' Jewish disciples (who are opaque, lacking in full understanding, and disloyal). Mark's Jesus is kindly and noble, opposed by Jews of each and every sort, ranging from ordinary people in synagogues to Herodeans, scribes, Pharisees, Sadducees, and priests. These opponents are portrayed as vicious, pitiless hypocrites and villains. The disciples—Jews—are portrayed as ineffectual, unreliable and finally disloyal. Only a Roman centurion, a Gentile, recognizes Jesus for what he is (Mark 15:39). The anti-Jewish tone of Mark is more than sporadic pericopes; it is the warp and woof of the gospel.

b. Matthew. Here the hostility to Jesus is more overt. Ch. 23 is a collection of woes against the scribes and Pharisees. The title rabbi is not to be used (vs. 8); the scribes and the Pharisees are hypocrites who "shut the kingdom of heaven against men" and neither enter themselves "nor allow those who would enter to go in" (vs. 13). In traversing sea and land to make a single proselyte, they make him "twice as much a child of hell" as themselves (vs. 15). They swear not by the temple, but by its gold (vss. 16 ff.). They "tithe mint and dill and cummin," but "have neglected the weightier matters of the law" (vs. 23). And Jerusalem kills the prophets (vss. 29 ff.). In the PASSION NARRATIVE, Pilate, to show his innocence, "washed his hands before the crowd," and the Jews responded, "His blood be on us and on our children!" (27:24-25). (Most modern Christian scholars deny the validity of the medieval interpretation of this passage which held that all Jews, of whatever time or geography, are culpable for the death of Jesus.)

c. Luke-Acts. The hostility to Jews is more subtle here. Jesus and his followers are represented as never having trespassed against Judaism; but the Jews are portrayed as having trespassed against Christians. The narrative of the rejection at Nazareth is expanded and placed earlier (4:16-30; cf. Matt. 13:54-58; Mark 6:1-6) as if to imply that this Jesus, faithful in his synagogue attendance, was rejected by the Jews at the very start of his career. In the parable, the Samaritan (10:29-37) was a good neighbor when a priest and a Levite (both Jews) were not. When the prodigal son returns home, his elder brother (Judaism) is angry and refuses to attend the feast (15:11-32). The view in Luke-Acts is that the Law grew naturally into the gospel and that the Way (e.g., Acts 9:2) became true Judaism, for Jews had lost their position of favor with God (cf. the parables of the marriage feast, Luke 14:16-24, and of the rich man and Lazarus, Luke 16:19-31).

d. John. Jesus' opponents are usually called "the Jews." (Some scholars interpret "the Jews" in John to mean only "the people," thus attempting to mitigate the apparent "anti-Semitism," an anachronistic word.) Jesus is depicted in controversy with Jews who had (once) believed in him, and whom he charges with being descended from the devil rather than from Father Abraham (8:31 ff.). Jesus is greater than Abraham was and Abraham rejoiced to see his day (vss. 53-57). In this gospel, to be sure, certain affirmative notes are struck (4:22, "salvation is from the Jews"; 1:47, "an Israelite . . . in whom is no guile"). And, more than in the Synoptic gospels, the quarrels and animosities between Christians and Jews seem historically rooted in the evangelist's own day (e.g., 6:41-51; ch. 9; 16:2; *see* JOHN, GOSPEL OF[S]).

In the gospels, the animosities are clearly two-sided. The most significant anti-Jewish motif of all was (and is) the contention that while the Romans did the crucifying, the Jews were the true culprits. In Christian writings a progressive shift in blame from Romans to Jews culminates in an unreserved blame of the Jews and the unreserved exoneration of the Romans for the death of Jesus (Riddle).

2. The letters of Paul. As distinct from the portrayal of Paul in Acts, only an occasional passage in his own letters reflects focused hostility toward Jews. The charge in I Thess. 2:14-16 that the Jews killed both Jesus and the prophets and have suffered the wrath of God is sometimes regarded as an interpolation, largely because it seems so out of keeping with the apostle's ordinary views, and seems to reflect a later time (especially if "wrath" alludes to the destruction of the temple in A.D. 70). The attacks in Phil. 3:2 and Gal. 5:12 may be against Gentile Judaizers, not Jews. Significantly, Paul is critical of Judaism, as distinct from Jews, holding Judaism to be unable to provide salvation. Not by the observance of laws (self-reliance) but only through faith can true salvation come. But since Paul himself is a Jew, even in his denigrating Judaism he reserves some praise for it, and he expresses the hope that all Israel, though hardened in heart, will be saved (Rom. 11:25-26). By implication, a Jew is an adherent of an ineffective and superseded religion.

3. Elsewhere in the NT. Hebrews deals with Judaism, not Jews, and argues that Christianity is perfection, superior to the imperfect Judaism which prepared its way. While scorn is expressed about "Jewish myths" in Tit. 1:14 no evidence has yet been discovered for the actual existence of such. In Rev. 2:9, allusion is made to slanderers "who say that they are Jews and are not, but are a synagogue of Satan" (cf. 3:9). Such passages served in medieval times for identifying Jews and Satan.

4. Conclusions. It is probable that hostility toward Christians surfaced in some Jewish literature just as hostility toward the Jews is apparent in the NT and following. Although no such Jewish sources have survived, overtones may be recovered from Celsus, *True Word.* Jewish denunciations of paganism (e.g., LETTER OF JEREMIAH) and second-century Christian attacks on Greek culture (e.g., Pseudo-Justin, Discourse to the Greeks), and Christian attacks on fellow Christians (e.g., Irenaeus, *Against Heresies*) show that religious controversies in the early centuries of the church's life were never genteel. The anti-Jewish tones of the NT are products of a particular age and set of historical circumstances. Many modern Christians are disquieted by these anti-Jewish sentiments and regard them as passing, angry outbursts, historic curiosities, possessing no ongoing validity, and surely not normative for a modern Christian's attitude toward Jews.

Bibliography. Augustin Cardinal Bea, *The Church and the Jewish People* (1966); D. R. A. Hare, *The Theme of Jewish Persecution of Christians in the Gospel According to St. Matthew,* NTSMS, VI (1967); J. Isaac, *Jesus and Israel* (1948 [ET 1971]); R. Ruether, *Faith and Fratricide: The Theological Roots of Antisemitism* (1974), contains an intro. by G. Baum which disavows the negative thesis in his *Is the NT Anti-semitic?* (rev. ed., 1965), strongly affirming now the presence of anti-Semitism in the NT; D. W. Riddle, *Jesus and the Pharisees* (1928); S. Sandmel, *We Jews and Jesus* (1973), *We Jews and You Christians* (1967), and "Myths, Genealogies, and Jewish Myths and the Writing of Gospels," *Two Living Traditions* (1972), pp. 158-65.

S. SANDMEL

***JOASH, KING OF ISRAEL.** The discovery of a stele honoring the Assyrian king Adad-nirari III (810-783 B.C.) at Tell er-Rimaḥ (N Mesopotamia) made Joash the sixth king of Israel to be named in an Assyrian record. Its line 8 mentions tribute from ^{m}*Ia-'a-su* ^{KUR}*Sa-me-ri-na-a,* i.e., Joash of the land of Samaria. *Ia-'a-su* is a defective writing of **Ia-ú-'a-su* (cf. in Tiglath-pileser III's annals *Ia-ú-ḫa-zu* instead of **Ia-ú-'a-ḫa-zu* for Jehoahaz=Ahaz); *s* stands here, according to the Assyrian usage, for *š*. The new piece of evidence raised questions relating to both Assyrian and Israelite chronology. The likeliest date of Joash's payment of tribute to Adad-nirari III is 796, when the Assyrian king invaded Manṣuate (the Biqa' Valley N of Israel). *See* CHRONOLOGY, OT[S].

Bibliography. S. Page, "A Stela of Adad-nirari III and Nergal-ereš from Tell al Rimah," *Iraq,* XXX (1968), 139-53; A. R. Millard and H. Tadmor, "Adad-nirari III in Syria," *Iraq,* XXXV (1973), 57-64; H. Tadmor, "The Historical Inscriptions of Adad-nirari III," *ibid.,* 141-50.

M. C. ASTOUR

***JOB, BOOK OF.** While recent studies of Job can hardly claim to have solved any of the major technical or interpretive problems, new evidence has been brought to bear, new approaches have been suggested, and older ones have been revised.

1. Evidence from Ugarit. The most significant evidence has come from texts discovered at UGARIT (modern Ras Shamra). Many of these celebrate the exploits of gods and goddesses in poems of epic length. Although they considerably predate the writing of Job, it is clear that these or similar sagas were known by the author, and that they influenced both his mode of expression and his literary iconography. They have also led scholars to a clearer grasp of the many mythological allusions which fill the book.

It is now certain that Leviathan (לויתן), mentioned in 3:8 and described extensively in ch. 41, is not a whale or a fantastic crocodile but rather a mythological sea serpent with seven heads (cf. Ps. 74:13-14). Indeed one of his epithets, "the fleeing serpent" (Job 26:13; cf. also Isa. 27:1), reproduces exactly an ancient title now known from the Ras Shamra tablets. The gruesome description of the wicked man's end at the hands of "Death's first-born"/"the King of Terrors" in 18:13-14 (ABi) is given clearer comprehension through reference to the ravenously hungry god MOT (Death).

2. New parallels proposed. Other parallels or influences have long been proposed, particularly Mesopotamian literary works (*see* JOB §7). Recently further parallels have been suggested. Holland has called attention to the Attic comedy as exemplified by the plays of Aristophanes. He argues, rather unconvincingly, that the structure of Job and that of the Greek comedies are similar and likely stem from the same or similar origins in "Phoenician-Canaanite traditions."

The recent suggestion of Hoffner that a parallel may be found in the Hurrian-Hittite myth of Appu is somewhat more likely. Appu's complaint is childlessness, and this causes him to suffer severely. Like Job, Appu must endure the chiding of an unsympathetic wife. Finally he declares: "You are a woman and of a woman's temperament—you know nothing at all" (cf. Job 2:10). However, the Appu story appears to have more affinities with the Cain and Abel narrative than with Job. Hoffner therefore does not press the parallel too far. Rather, he suggests that if Appu and Job are one and the same, the Appu tale may be a traditional story which portrays a further incident in the life of the righteous Job of folk legend (cf. Ezek. 14:4; *see* JOB §5). The slight resemblance of the names Appu and Job (i.e., Ayyabu; *see* JOB §1) lends some shaky support to this proposal.

3. Qumran. The ancient biblical scrolls from Wadi Qumran include manuscripts of Job. While some of these still await publication, a Targum, or Aramaic translation from the eleventh cave, was published in 1971. The scroll (11QtgJob) preserves parts of thirty-eight columns of text and contains a translation of about one third of Job over-all, running intermittently from 17:14 to 42:11. This Targ., which probably should be dated to the first century B.C. or perhaps the latter half of the second century, is the oldest Job MS of any extensive length so far known. Along with two small unpublished fragments from Qumran Cave IV (one from yet another Aramaic translation of Job), it is also the earliest known exemplar of a Targ. of any sort. *See* JOB §2; DEAD SEA SCROLLS[S] §2.

The discovery of this scroll not only gives insight into the textual history of Job but also greatly aids our understanding of the Aramaic language, and is invaluable evidence for targumic research. For the most part the basic text type and order is the same as found in the traditional Hebrew (MT). The notable exception is the prose Epilogue (ch. 42, col. 38, in 11QtgJob). Here the indications are that the Job Targ. preserves a text ending at 42:11, six verses short of the MT version. (We can further contrast this with the LXX, which has an even fuller Epilogue than that found in the Hebrew.)

Most of the numerous variants from the MT appear to be secondary, and hence can be employed only occasionally to improve the text (*see* TEXTUAL CRITICISM, OT[S]). Modifications appear consistently to be employed to soften the picture of a rebellious Job and to place blame instead on the three friends and Elihu. For example, where Elihu remarks about Job, "God may vanquish him," the Targum renders, "but God will condemn us" (Job 32:13=11QtgJob 21:5).

Some scholars (Tuinstra, Caquot) have argued that 11QtgJob was composed in the context of the Essene sect at Qumran, with their spirtual leader, the "Teacher of Righteousness," as the model for the portrayal of Job. It is further suggested that this Targum may well be the same as the text ordered buried by Rabbi Gamaliel (Tosef. Shab. XIII.2). While both of these proposals are possible, the evidence is not decisive.

4. Structure, unity, and date. A new defense of single authorship has been recently mounted by Gordis. He argues that the Elihu speeches—most suspected of being an interpolation from a second author (*see* JOB §10)—were in fact added by the original author in a later period of his life. Freedman accepts the predominant view that the Elihu speeches are a later interpolation, but he does not think that they were all intended by their author to be placed at the end of Job's final speech. Instead, he believes that each was meant to be inserted at a turning point in the Dialogue section: the first three Elihu speeches respectively at the end of the first three "cycles" of the debate, and the last speech where all of Elihu's remarks now stand. To support this argument, Freedman cites close correlations between each of Elihu's speeches and the sections of Job with which each was meant to be grouped.

A "structuralist" approach has been presented by Polzin. He side-steps the historical issue of the unity or disunity of Job and endeavors to approach the book as a *de facto* unit for the purpose of analysis. This done, he is able to view the book as a "confrontation of inconsistencies," i.e., a framework in which an original equilibrium is upset by a conflict which, in being resolved, engenders yet another conflict, and so on in succession until the original equilibrium is re-established when Job receives double his wealth in the Epilogue. The main drawback to Polzin's theory is that it requires a number of *ad hoc* technical and interpretive assumptions, none of which can be objectively verified. If one rejects even one of them, the analysis falls apart.

An inquiry into the date of the Prologue and Epilogue by Hurvitz has advantages that Polzin's study lacks, namely external and hence largely objective criteria. Employing, as a standard for dating, linguistic elements found in biblical books unmistakably datable in the exilic/postexilic period (Esther, Ezra, Chronicles), he compares these with similar linguistic elements in the Prologue-Epilogue. Hurvitz is thus able to point to a date no earlier than the Exile (sixth century B.C.) for the composition of these sections as we now have them. One must therefore conclude that whatever patriarchal or epic substrata are found in this prose work are either survivals from an earlier form of the story or are archaisms. Beyond this, certain implications may be drawn, depending on whose views are followed. If one agrees with Pope's tentative dating of the Dialogue to the seventh century B.C., for example, it follows that the Prologue-Epilogue was added by a redactor at a later period. If on the other hand one accepts Cross's view that Job contains archaic material probably reworked by the poet in the sixth century B.C., one may well see a single author for Dialogue and prose sections.

5. Interpretations. For most readers the more technical difficulties are incidental to the central question: What is the point of the book? Recent studies have focused upon the THEOPHANY section as a key. One view declares that, though on a strictly rational level God's reply to Job is not very satisfactory, on a level beyond the bounds of man's intellect it is able to reach and indeed to bring peace to Job. This argument was probably given its best treatment some time ago by Otto, who speaks of "the sheer absolute wondrousness that transcends thought, . . . the *mysterium* presented in its pure non-rational form," which Job finds in his encounter with God. When Scott speaks of "wisdom of the soul, . . . not the same thing as intellectual knowledge," or Gordis of "a sense of reverence for the mystery and miracle of life," or Polzin of Job's "assent to the sphere of belief" after being "overwhelmed by the theophany," they are largely voicing similar ideas.

Yet one must ponder whether this is a sufficient answer. One cannot help recalling that it is precisely an overwhelming burst of divine power (such as is found in the Theophany) which Job begged God not to unleash (13:21-22; cf. 9:34). Job well knew that without such forbearance (or lacking this, some guarantor or umpire who could offer protection, cf. 9:33; 16:19; 19:25) his position was hopeless (9:15).

In view of this difficulty, one must consider the interpretation by Tsevat, who denies a resolution in a nonrational sphere. He believes that the confrontation between mortal and divine compels the reader to the logical conclusion that the world is an amoral environment in which man's standards of right and wrong cannot be imposed upon God. Job loses his belief in justice, but gains in its place a closer relation to the Deity, an appreciation of his accessibility to man.

Tsevat's argument is attractive, yet problematical. Amorality implies indifference, a world where, as Koheleth says, "God is in heaven, and you upon earth" (Eccl. 5:2). Yet God is depicted as far from indifferent; can the author therefore have implied that he is amoral?

What these remarks demonstrate is that any interpretive analysis of Job is open to question. Every point one can make tends to have an equally defensible counterpoint. As Zophar states, "There are two sides of wisdom" (Job 11:6, Pope's trans.) and in Job the cross current of ideas is particularly strong. A solution to the book perhaps is not really desirable. We should rather understand Job as a penetrating insight into the deepest thoughts of mankind, and recognize that the dark ponderings engendered by this insight are as inevitable as life itself.

Bibliography. Commentaries: G. Fohrer, *KAT,* XVI (1963); R. Gordis, *The Book of God and Man* (1965); F. Horst, BKAT, XVI (1968); A. Guillaume, *Studies in the Book of Job* (1968); M. Pope, ABi (3rd ed., 1973).

Ugaritic and Job: M. Dahood, "Northwest Semitic Philology and Job," in *The Bible in Current Catholic Thought,* ed. J. L. McKenzie (1962), pp. 55-74, and "Hebrew Ugaritic Lexicography, I-XII," continuing article in *Bibl.,* XLIV-LV (1963-74); *Psalms,* ABi, 3 vols. (1965-70); A. C. M. Blommerde, *Northwest Semitic Grammar and Job* (1969); N. J. Tromp, *Primitive Conceptions of Death and the Nether World in the OT* (1969); the most balanced study of Job employing Ugaritic is Pope's.

Parallels: J. A. Holland, "On the Form of the Book of Job," *AJBA,* II (1972), 160-77; H. A. Hoffner, "Some Contributions of Hittitology to the OT Study," *Tyndale Bulletin,* XX (1969), 27-55, esp. 52 ff.

11QtgJob: *editio princeps:* J. Van der Ploeg *et al., Le Targum de Job de la Grotte XI de Qumran* (1971); major studies: E. M. Tuinstra, *Hermeneutische Aspecten van de Targum van Job uit Grot XI van Qumran* (1971); M. Sokoloff, *The Targum to Job from Qumran Cave XI* (1974), the best commentary to date; J. Fitzmyer, "Some Observations on the Targum of Job from Qumran Cave 11," *CBQ,* XXXVI (1974), 503-24, best introductory article with extensive bibliog.; S. A. Kaufman, "The Job Targum from Qumran," *JAOS,* XCIII (1973), 317-27; A. Caquot, "Une écrit sectaire de Qoumran: le 'Targoum de Job,'" *RHR,* CLXXXV (1971), 9-27; J. Gray, "The Masoretic Text of the Book of Job, the Targum and the Septuagint Version in the Light of the Qumran Targum (11QtgJob)," *ZAW,* LXXXVI (1974), 331-50.

Structure and unity: H. H. Rowley, *From Moses to Qumran* (1963), pp. 139-83, a good summary; D. N. Freedman, "The Elihu Speeches in the Book of Job," *HTR,* LXI (1968), 51-59; P. Skehan, "Job's Final Plea (Job 29–31) and the Lord's Reply (Job 38–41)," *Bibl.,* XLV (1964), 51-62; R. Polzin, "The Framework of the Book of Job," *Int.,* XXVIII (1974), 182-200; A. Hurvitz, "The Date of the Prose-Tale of Job Linguistically Reconsidered," *HTR,* LXVII (1974), 17-34; F. Cross, *Canaanite Myth and Hebrew Epic* (1973), p. 169.

Interpretations: N. Glatzer, "The Book of Job and Its Interpreters," *Biblical Motifs,* ed. A. Altmann (1966), pp. 197-221, an excellent survey of rabbinic interpretations through the medieval period; N. Glatzer, ed., *The Dimensions of Job* (1969); P. Sanders, ed., *Twentieth Century Interpretations of the Book of Job* (1968); C. G. Jung, *Answer to Job* (1954); R. Otto, *The Idea of the Holy* (1923), esp. pp. 77-81; R. B. Y. Scott, *The Way of Wisdom in the OT* (1971), esp. pp. 136-64; G. von Rad, *Wisdom in Israel* (1971), esp. pp. 206-26; H. L. Ginsberg, "Job the Patient and Job the Impatient," *Conservative Judaism,* XXI (1967), 12-28; M. Tsevat, "The Meaning of the Book of Job," *HUCA,* XXXVII (1966), 73-106.

B. ZUCKERMAN

***JOHN, APOCRYPHON OF.** Considered the most important work of mythological GNOSTICISM. Within the framework of a revelation by the resurrected Christ to John, the son of Zebedee, a remarkably clear description is given of the transcendent God, the light realm, the origin of the evil Creator, the creation of the spiritual world rulers and of man, and the struggle to rescue man from his imprisonment in the body and the material world. Though much of the content was already known from reports of the church Fathers, it appears here in a form and context which shed new light on the unresolved problem of the relationship between Gnosticism and Christianity. The heterogeneous body of Gnostic tractates which share themes or details with ApocryJn raises the question of the origin and function of these writings.

1. Text and date. Four copies of ApocryJn are extant, representing three independent translations from Greek into Sahidic COPTIC. Codex Berolinensis 8502 (BG) and NAG HAMMADI Codex III (NH III,*1*) contain the shorter and probably older version, while NH II,*1* and IV,*1* represent two copies of the same Coptic translation of the longer version. BG has been the basis of the discussion up to now, since it is the best preserved and the only one available in a dependable edition. It probably dates from the fifth, the NH copies from the fourth century A.D. The teachings of the Gnostics described in Iren. Her. I.xxix are largely identical with the cosmological section of ApocryJn. At the end of this section the tractate shows a possible literary seam (BG 44,19), since it changes from a revelation discourse to a dialogue. Though Irenaeus apparently did not know ApocryJn in its present form with its Christian title and framework, but only the first part with some significant differences in detail, it is certain that the main teaching of the tractate existed before A.D. 185, the date of Irenaeus' Heresies. ApocryJn was still used in the eighth century A.D. by the Audians in Mesopotamia.

2. Purpose and content. ApocryJn supplies answers to two basic questions posed not just by Gnostics: What is the origin of evil? How can we escape from this evil world to our heavenly home? The cosmogony, in spite of its exotic details, also serves this purpose. The supreme deity is defined in terms of an abstract Greek concept of perfection which excludes all anthropomorphisms and involvement in the world. From him emanated a series of light beings which include Christ and Sophia.

The Fall occurred when Sophia desired to bring forth a being without the approval of the great Spirit and her consort. She produced the monstrous Creator-God Ialdabaoth, who possessed some of the light power of his mother. He created angels to rule over the world and to aid in the creation of man. Man is fashioned after the image of the perfect Father which was mirrored on the water. He comes to life when Ialdabaoth is tricked to breathe his light power into him. This initiates a continuous struggle between the powers of light and of darkness for the possession of the divine particles in man. The evil powers put man in a material body to keep him imprisoned. They also create woman and sexual desire to spread the light particles, and so to make escape more difficult. Christ is sent down to save men by reminding them of their heavenly origin. Only those who possess this knowledge and have lived ascetically can return to the light realm; others are reincarnated until they also come to saving Gnosis.

The longer version includes a lengthy enumeration of the angels who created the different parts of the human body, and the powers who rule in these parts, said to come from some "book of Zoroaster" (NH II 15, 29–19, 12). We probably have here a typical example of how Gnostic writings were changed and expanded. The syncretistic interest of the anonymous author and redactors in esoteric books knew few bounds. The other major addition is a remarkable section spoken in the first person by the perfect Protonoia relating his three descents into the world (II 30, 14–31, 25).

3. Relationship to Christianity and Judaism. The Christian framework is not integral to the revelation. It appears that also the revelation itself has been Christianized. Christ and the Holy Spirit have been given a prominent though not essential role. There is little more than a crude identification of the savior-revealer with a Christ who lacks his characteristic NT features. The mythology is developed largely in terms of the early chapters of Genesis with the dramatic value reversals typical of this kind of Gnosticism. The vilification of the OT God is not a sign of anti-Semitism, but a necessary consequence of the belief that the world is evil by nature. The OT itself is not rejected, for it reveals, when correctly interpreted, not only the evil nature of the Creator, but also the beginnings of the Gnostic race. The knowledge of Jewish traditions is too extensive to deny that mythological Gnosis in its pagan and Christian forms derived, in some way, from Judaism.

4. Place within Gnosticism. The NH library contains many tractates which share some themes or details with ApocryJn. These are the Nature of the Archons, On the Origin of the World, the Gospel of the Egyptians, Eugnostos the Blessed, the Sophia of Jesus Christ, the Apocalypse of Adam, the Concept of our Great Power, the Second Treatise of the Great Seth, the Three Steles of Seth, Zostrianos, the Letter of Peter to Philip, Melchizedek, the Thought of Norea, the Testimony of Truth, Allogenes, and Trimorphic Protennoia. Yet the agreements are mostly incidental and are few, compared with the differences. It is impossible to claim that they represent the teachings of a specific sect or even closely related sects. It is questionable whether any of these writings meant to present normative teaching. More likely they were written by visionaries whose main aim was to aid believers in reaching mystical Gnosis. By assuming that these books presented the doctrinal statements of heretical groups the church Fathers mistakenly concluded that the Gnostic movement was fragmented into many separate sects. The heresiological tradition has attached the name Barbelo-Gnostics to the group whose teaching Irenaeus reports in Her. I.xxix. It is doubtful that such a sect ever existed or that there was ever a group which possessed ApocryJn as its distinctive teaching. It is characteristic of the Gnostic movement and its literature that ApocryJn could appeal to a wide variety of Gnostics. *See also* ADAM, APOCALYPSE OF[S].

Bibliography. Text ed.: W. C. Till, *Die gnostischen Schriften des koptischen Papyrus Berolinensis 8502* (2nd ed., 1972), with intro. and dependable trans.; S. Giversen, *Apocryphon Johannis,* Acta theologica danica, V (1963), inferior ed. of NH II,*1* with Eng. trans. and commentary; M. Krause, and P. Labib, *Die Drei Versionen des Apokryphon des Johannes* (1962), ed. of NH copies, needs to be redone; several synopses are in preparation.

Eng. trans. of BG in R. M. Grant, *Gnosticism, An Anthology* (1961), pp. 69-85, and M. Krause in W. Foerster, *Gnosis,* I (1969), pp. 100-120.

On Iren. Her. I.xxix: C. Schmidt, "Irenäus und seine Quelle in adv. haer. I,29," *Philotesia,* ed. A. von Harnack *et al.* (1907), pp. 317-36; H.-M. Schenke, "Das literarische Problem des Apokryphon Johannis," *ZRGG,* XIV (1962), 57-63; F. Wisse, "The NH Library and the Heresiologists," *VC,* XXV (1971), 205-23. A good but outdated intro. by H.-Ch. Puech in Hennecke/Schneemelcher, *NT Apocrypha* I (1959 [2nd ed., 1968]), pp. 314-31. Further bibliog. in D. M. Scholer, *Nag Hammadi Bibliography 1948-1969* (1971), with supplements in *NovT* (1971 ff.).

F. WISSE

***JOHN, GOSPEL OF.** The Fourth Gospel gained canonical status only when it was generally recognized as the work of John the apostle.

Among the problems posed by the traditional view of authorship none is greater than the Fourth Gospel's differences from the Synoptics. Such differences extend not only to the order of events and content, but also and particularly to the style and form of Jesus' speech (*see* JOHN, GOSPEL OF §§C1, D2*a*). The disparity between the Johannine Jesus, who constantly speaks of his own role and dignity, and the synoptic tradition of Jesus' sayings is difficult to reconcile, and it is generally agreed that the Synoptics represent more accurately the mode and themes, as well as the style, of Jesus' speech. Nevertheless, the Fourth Gospel is not without historical value, and some Johannine data (e.g., the dating of Jesus' crucifixion) may be superior to what is found in the Synoptics.

John was probably written near the end of the first century and after the Synoptics (surely after Mark). Quite possibly the author was not acquainted with any of the Synoptics. Moreover, it is generally acknowledged that he did not use any canonical gospel as his source in the way Matthew seems to have used Mark, but relied mainly on sources or traditions not otherwise known. The evangelist clearly represents a distinct theological perspective, but one nevertheless influenced by traditional Christian, Jewish, and perhaps other concepts and ways of thinking. The uniqueness of his work may account for a hesitancy in some quarters of the early church to accept it as authoritative and canonical. Possibly this historic bulwark of orthodoxy was itself at one time suspected of heterodoxy.

1. Sources and composition of the Gospel of John
2. Traditional and theological developments underlying the gospel
3. Principal religious and cultural influences upon the gospel
4. Purpose and historical setting of the gospel

Bibliography

1. Sources and composition of the Gospel of John. Taking up numerous suggestions of earlier scholarship, Rudolf Bultmann proposed in his epoch-making commentary (1941) that the Fourth Gospel was composed on the basis of several major sources (revelation-discourse source, *semeia* or miracle source, passion and Easter sources) and that its present form is the result of an apparently accidental disarrangement of the original text and its subsequent infelicitous restoration and editing by means of a process called "ecclesiastical redaction." His elaborate analysis, in which every sentence of the gospel is ascribed to the evangelist, one of his sources, or the redaction, has not gained general acceptance, but it embraces critical elements which are widely regarded as well-established results of Johannine research, e.g., the existence of a collection of miracle stories upon which the evangelist drew, as well as a passion tradition or source, the substantial independence of the gospel from the Synoptics, the secondary character of ch. 21, and the reversal of the order of chs. 5 and 6.

The use of sources in the Fourth Gospel can be most convincingly demonstrated in the miracle and passion narratives, where Johannine redaction may sometimes be clearly distinguished from a traditional narrative. Moreover, the enumeration of the signs in 2:11 and 4:54 has the appearance of a vestigial remnant of an earlier source. Although written sources for the discourses seem less likely than for the narratives, it is possible that they embrace traditional patterns and forms of speech. Thus, discourses of much the same type appear again in the Johannine epistles, although these may not be the work of the same author. Moreover, chs. 15–16 (17) follow awkwardly after 14:31 ("rise, let us go hence") and may represent traditional materials added rather late in the process of composition.

2. Traditional and theological developments underlying the gospel. The distinctiveness of the Fourth Gospel in relation to the Synoptics, the existence of the related Johannine letters, and the likely incorporation of earlier sources or traditions into the gospel suggest the possibility of analyzing and describing a history of the Johannine tradition. That I John differs somewhat theologically and in other respects from the gospel (*see* JOHN, LETTERS OF[S] §1) in no way militates against such an analysis, since the discrepancies are what might be expected in documents representing the life and thought of a living community. In recovering the tradition-history of the gospel, it is necessary to consider the evangelist's use of narrative sources, particularly a miracle source; the possible divergence of his own theological perspective from that of his sources; the significance of "the Jews" in the Fourth Gospel; and the possibility of placing the gospel, its constituent parts, and related documents in the context of the development of early Christianity.

Although the evangelist is critical of shallow faith in miracles, he does not reject the positive view of miracles as signs pointing to the divinely given authority of the miracle worker (*see* SIGN IN THE NT[S] §3). The greater sophistication of the gospel in matters of miracle and faith is related to the way the miracle stories serve as points of departure for the theologically pregnant discourses and debates in which Jesus plays the central role. The existence of a Johannine miracle source and tradition presupposes a community, in which the individual stories likely served more than one function. Thus the hypothesis of a development in reflection upon and use of miracle stories within the Johannine community seems to be warranted. In addition, raising the question of the purpose of *collections* of miracle stories leads to a fruitful hypothesis regarding their relation to the Jewish environment of the gospel. *See also* MIRACLE STORIES, NT[S]; MIRACLE WORKERS[S].

If the pervasive Jews of the Fourth Gospel are not of symbolic significance only, they must afford some clue to the milieu from which the gospel arose. Their presence probably reflects a historical setting in which efforts to convert Jews led to charges and countercharges between Johannine Christians and other synagogue members (cf. 5:17-18; 6:41 ff.; 7:40-43; 8:33 ff.), culminating in the exclusion of those who confessed Jesus to be Christ from synagogue fellowship (9:22; 12:42; 16:2). (*See* JEWS, NT ATTITUDES TOWARD[S].) The suggestion that the Johannine miracle or sign stories were originally compiled to convince a Jewish audience that Jesus was the Messiah corresponds to their present context in the gospel, where they lead to debate with the Jews about Jesus' identity and issue in such statements as 12:37 and 20:30-31. The difficulty that miracle-working played no major role in contemporary Jewish messianism is offset somewhat by a recognition that such activity was expected of an anticipated eschatological prophet like Moses (Deut. 18:15-22), and that this figure may have colored some Jewish messianic expectations. Moreover, Jesus was known as a miracle worker, and in all probability in this as in other respects what he said and did contributed to the understanding of his messianic role, i.e., the articulation of Christology, among his followers.

The passion tradition and related material in the gospel include scriptural testimonies (e.g., 12:13, 14-15, 38, 40; 13:18; 15:25; 19:24, 28, 36-37) that are primitive and presuppose a Jewish mentality, for which scripture was authoritative. Even if the apparent apologetic intention of such testimonies only answers to the Christians' own need to put the passion in a positive light as the fulfillment of God's will, it bespeaks the Jewish milieu and presuppositions of the tradition. The implicitly anti-Jewish episodes of the PASSION NARRATIVE (e.g., 18:38-40; 19:4-7, 12-16) and the polemical exchanges between Jesus or his followers and Jews (or Pharisees) elsewhere in the gospel (e.g., 8:31-59; 9:24-34) support rather than disprove a Jewish provenance, for such deeply felt polemics are best explained on the basis of genuine, experienced confrontation and conflict.

The gospel is not, however, concerned solely with Jewish-Christian identity and relations. Although after the conclusion of the public ministry (ch. 12) the theme of Jewish hostility recurs (e.g., in 15:18–16:4 as well as in 18:38–40; 19:4-7, 13-16), from ch. 13 onward the focus shifts to subjects of distinctly Christian character: the relationship of Jesus' followers to one another (13:34-35; 15:12 ff.) and their continuing communion with Jesus after his departure from them. In this regard the promise of the PARACLETE, the Spirit of Truth, becomes especially important (14:15 ff., 25 ff.; 15: 26-27; 16:7 ff.). The gospel's abandonment of the fervid apocalyptic expectation typical of much primitive Christianity is accompanied by an awareness of the continued presence of Jesus in the community (14:18-24), mediated by the Spirit. Thus in chs. 13–17 the postresurrection community of Jesus' disciples occupies the center of attention. In the Johannine letters certain pastoral and even organizational questions become explicit, as with the passage of time problems of church doctrine and discipline inevitably emerge. Such matters are adumbrated in the gospel itself, although there they are subordinated to the evangelist's dominant christological interest.

The author of Revelation (*see* REVELATION, BOOK OF §B and supplementary article) can scarcely have been the evangelist or the author of the letters of John, for the literary styles are quite different and the colorful apocalypticism of Revelation is foreign to the other books. Nevertheless, Revelation contains striking parallels with concepts or terms found in the gospel, and the possibility of some significant traditional relationship between it and the other Johannine books is worthy of serious consideration.

3. Principal religious and cultural influences upon the gospel. The content and character of the Gospel of John were shaped by a form of Christian preaching which developed where Christians were in close touch with the synagogue, whether in Palestine or elsewhere. The Jewishness of the Fourth Gospel is reflected not only in its citation of the OT and the frequent polemical and other references to Jews, but also in the way Jesus is constantly compared with the leading figures of Jewish history, particularly Moses (e.g., in 1:17), and in the familiarity with Jewish scriptures, custom, and tradition which it manifests (e.g., 7:40-41; 7:51-52). *See* MOSES IN THE NT[S] §5.

Recent archaeological and manuscript discoveries have underscored the Jewishness of this gospel. The distinctive documents of the sectarian community of Qumran (*see* DEAD SEA SCROLLS §5 and supplementary article) contain remarkable terminological and conceptual parallels to the gospel (cf. esp. the dualism of the MANUAL OF DISCIPLINE). Such similarities show that certain Johannine features once thought characteristic only of pagan Hellenism were not foreign to Judaism, even Palestinian Judaism. The Qumran parallels do not, however, exclude the possibility of Hellenistic influences in the Fourth Gospel, nor do they guarantee a Palestinian provenance of the gospel, although the Johannine tradition probably originated there. The Qumran community's rather narrow sectarian bias perhaps also finds a parallel in the Johannine Jesus' injunction to love one another (13:34-35), meaning one's Christian brother, rather than the neighbor generally, and there is in both a similar emphasis on the oneness or unity of the community. Yet the Qumran community, unlike Johannine Christianity, is based on obedience to the law, and the vivid apocalypticism of some of its documents (e.g., the War Scroll) differentiates it from John's gospel. The eschatology of this gospel, with its claim to realization and accompanying emphasis on union with God (and Christ), finds closer parallels in PHILO, the WISDOM OF SOLOMON, and the HERMETIC LITERATURE than in the Qumran scrolls. John's characteristic emphases on individual faith and the attainment of salvation in the form of eternal life, as well as the language of (mystical) union with the Savior, can indeed be paralleled in Judaism, particularly Hellenistic Judaism, but they also serve to show the gospel's participation in the broader religious currents of the Greco-Roman world.

The Mandaean documents (*see* MANDAEISM[S]) contain striking parallels with the Gospel of John (terms such as "knowledge," "life," "truth"; dualism; and perhaps also the redeemer figure). In view of the character of its esoteric teaching and because the name "Mandaean" seems to be derived from a Semitic word meaning knowledge, this literature has been widely acclaimed as representative of (pre-Christian) GNOSTICISM and has therefore stimulated considerable interest in the Gnostic affinities and possible Gnostic milieu of Johannine Christianity. It is impossible, however, to date these documents in the period of Christian origins or earlier, although they themselves have not been influenced by the NT in obvious ways. In their present form they are later than the Fourth Gospel by many centuries. Moreover, their treatment of John the Baptist appears to be derivative from Christianity. Yet very old tradition may be preserved in the Mandaean books, especially the liturgical material, and the claim of a Palestinian Jewish origin of the sect (and subsequent migration eastward) has won the support of modern Mandaean research. At best, however, the historical relationship of ancient Mandaeism to the Fourth Gospel remains unclear, and its literature may be used only with great caution to illuminate the milieu of Johannine Christianity.

Since mid-century, interest in possible Gnostic influence upon the Fourth Gospel has again been stimulated by the discovery of a library of Coptic Gnostic documents at NAG HAMMADI in Upper Egypt. Most of these documents were known previously, if at all, only through references in patristic authors. One of them, the GOSPEL OF TRUTH, is a narration of the revelatory and saving work of Jesus, told without much reference to the familiar gospel story. Yet its Christology is closer to the Fourth Gospel than to any of the Synoptics. Some of the documents contain "I am" sayings similar to those ascribed to Jesus in the Fourth Gospel. Neither the library nor its constituent parts may be dated earlier than the Fourth Gospel, and most are at least a century or more later. Yet they may afford evidence of a basically non-Christian Gnosticism to which Christian language and interpretation have been added secondarily, while at the same time they contain some isolated features strikingly similar to the Fourth Gospel. Some of the documents manifest decidedly Jewish characteristics apparently not mediated through the NT. This suggests the possibility of a Jewish Gnosticism, or a Gnosticism in which Jewish elements were more primitive than Christian.

The Nag Hammadi documents and the Mandaean sources have in common Jewish as well as Gnostic features, and both bear certain conceptual and linguistic similarities to the Fourth Gospel. This gospel, which arose out of Jewish-Christian dialogue, has some relation, possibly in origin and certainly in earliest use, with Gnosticism. Affinities or connections with Judaism and Gnosticism, as well as with Johannine Christianity, have also been found in the letters of IGNATIUS and in the early Christian ODES OF SOLOMON. Yet to trace all the historical relationships that are thereby suggested is a task for which the evidence is probably not sufficient.

Significant parallels to Johannine thought have also been found in certain Jewish mystical speculations (e.g., III Enoch), in Jewish wisdom books and traditions (*see* WISDOM IN THE NT[S]), and in Samaritanism, where interest in Moses and, accordingly, in the eschatological Mosaic prophet call to mind corresponding aspects of the Fourth Gospel (*see* MOSES IN THE NT[S]). That the fourth evangelist or his tradition has a special interest in Samaria and Samaritans is clearly evident (cf. John 4). Moreover, John the Baptist plays a role in John (cf. 1:6-8, 15, 19 ff.; 3:22 ff.), which suggests that he or his followers are of some importance for understanding the gospel's origins. Difficult as it may be to put all the possibly relevant historical materials into a single picture of the religious and cultural matrix of the Fourth Gospel, it is nevertheless clear that Johannine Christianity has links with several forms of Judaism and sources influenced by Judaism. Thus the continuing search for its roots within Judaism or at its boundaries remains a fascinating, fruitful, and necessary, if complex, task. But to locate the germinal ground of Johannine Christianity there is not to deny its Hellenistic character or development. Just such a complex and syncretistic setting, nominally Jewish as it may have been, typified the Hellenistic world of antiquity.

4. Purpose and historical setting of the gospel. If a basic outline of the origin, pattern, and development of Johannine Christianity now suggests itself, it remains to be asked why and under what circumstances the gospel in its present form was composed. Its original conclusion (20:30-31) is an important statement of purpose, but it leaves open the question of whether the gospel was intended to arouse faith, as the aorist tense of πιστεύειν (believe) suggests, or to sustain faith, as is also possible. Although the statement is a valid index of John's emphasis upon faith in Jesus as the way to salvation, i.e., eternal life, it is so general as to be applicable also to other gospels. Moreover, 20: 30-31 does not suggest any peculiar circumstances or problem that may have evoked the writing of the gospel.

Interpreters have often demurred from attempting a more precise definition because of the gospel's apparent intention of presenting a universally applicable version of the Christian message. Nevertheless, it has been suggested that the Gospel of John was written as a missionary tract for Jews generally, for Hellenistic Jews, for disciples of John the Baptist, or for one-time adherents of the Qumran community. Alternatively, it has been regarded as a book designed to interest and attract adherents from a philosophically oriented piety of late Hellenism. It has been seen either as Gnostic or as anti-Gnostic (or anti-Docetic) in intent; or again, either as the product of a sectarian, Spirit-inspired, and somewhat heterodox Christianity defending itself against incipient institutionalism or as a bulwark of Christian orthodoxy. There may be some truth in each of these proposals, but they cannot all be correct. Some relative assessment is necessary.

The various efforts to relate John's gospel to a Jewish milieu or to a first-century dialogue and controversy between Judaism and Christianity point in the right direction insofar as the origin and milieu of Johannine Christianity are concerned. But the sharp polemic against the Jews, particularly Pharisees and other authorities, and the finality of the Jewish rejection of Jesus (18:28–19:16) do not comport well with the view that the extant gospel is a missionary tract for Jews. Furthermore, the farewell discourses and prayers (chs. 13–17) focus attention upon the community of Jesus' followers and on his promise that they will not be separated from him. The continuing relationship of the community to Jesus comes into focus again in the original conclusion of the gospel, where Thomas' desire to touch Jesus (20:24-29) and confirm the reality of his resurrection becomes the occasion for Jesus' commendation of those who have not *seen* him, and yet believe (20: 29). The Gospel of John was intended to reassure Christians that through faith the reality of Jesus is accessible and the eternal life, which only he brings (14:6), attainable.

Moreover, there are hints within the gospel that it was addressed to a community facing a crisis of faith. Precisely such situations elicit the most genuine and significant theological affirmations. If a period of friendlier relations with the synagogue had come to an end, perhaps because of the missionary efforts of Johannine Christians, the role played by the Jews in the Fourth Gospel is still significant. While they are indeed surrogates for the hostile world in its rejection of Jesus, their prominence nevertheless suggests that Judaism remains within the evangelist's environment and purview, if only as a part of that hostile world that opposes Jesus, persecutes his followers, and thus makes the question whether to have faith in him an urgent one. The gospel conveys the unmistakable impression of a closely knit community, at least as a desideratum. The solidarity of that community, and the necessity of its solidarity, was in some measure a result of pressure from without.

If, however, a community is held together only by external pressure, it soon disintegrates. The Johannine community had a center of allegiance and solidarity in Jesus, while it also faced questions about his accessibility and even his reality. The gospel was written for a community under duress at a time near the end of the first century when the original apocalyptic expectation of the triumphant return of Jesus was no longer a source of reassurance but, because of its delay, a problem. The appendix (esp. 21:20-23) indicates that John was published among Christians facing such a problem, as does the deliberate juxtaposing of traditional apocalyptic hopes with the present eschatological reality of Jesus (11:23-27). A major purpose of the farewell discourses (chs. 14–16) is to show Jesus addressing himself to the problem of his departure from the disciples by redefining the traditional apocalyptic eschatological terms so that they refer to possibilities in the present rather than to an indefinite future.

Nevertheless, the evangelist does not reduce significant time to the present. The future of Jesus' followers is assured even beyond death (14:1-4; 17:24-26). The past is also significant as the time of Jesus' earthly ministry, unfulfilled as that was until his glorification (2:22; 7:39; 12:16; 16:7). For apart from his death, departure, and the coming of the Paraclete or Spirit, the revelation of God in Jesus was incomplete. After his departure the Spirit continues the revelation and mediates the reality of Jesus among his followers. Thus in the community of faith the giver, Jesus, and the gift, eternal life, continue to be real and accessible amidst a hostile world (cf. 17:3, 14 ff.; also 14:6; 11:25).

The date and place of composition cannot be established with certainty. Nevertheless, the last decade of the first century is late enough to take account of the gospel's developed perspective on the events it narrates and of the familiarity with post-Jamnian controversies between Jews and Christians reflected in it. Such a dating agrees both with critical insights and with ancient tradition. The traditional place of publication, Ephesus, remains a possibility, particularly if the gospel was not ascribed originally to John the son of Zebedee. Otherwise, Ignatius' failure to mention John as he mentions Paul in his letter to the Ephesians (*ca.* A.D. 110) becomes a serious difficulty. Wherever the place of composition may have been, a Syrian or Palestinian origin of the Johannine tradition seems likely. *See also* CHRISTOLOGY IN THE NT[S] §3*c*.

Bibliography. Commentaries: R. Bultmann, *The Gospel of John: A Commentary* (rev. ed., 1957; suppl., 1966 [ET 1971]); R. E. Brown, ABi, 2 vols. (1966, 1970); R. Schnackenburg, HTCNT (1965), covers chs. 1–4 only; B. Lindars, NCB (1972).

Other works: C. H. Dodd, *Historical Tradition in the Fourth Gospel* (1963); D. M. Smith, *The Composition and Order of the Fourth Gospel* (1965); F. Mussner, *The Historical Jesus in the Gospel of St. John* (1965); W. A. Meeks, *The Prophet-King,* NovTSup, XIV (1967); J. L. Martyn, *History and Theology in the Fourth Gospel* (1968); E. Käsemann, *The Testament of Jesus* (1966); R. H. Fortna, *The Gospel of Signs,* NTSMS, XI (1970); B. Lindars, *Behind the Fourth Gospel,* Studies in Creative Criticism, III (1971); J. H. Charlesworth, ed., *John and Qumran* (1972); W. A. Meeks, "The Man from Heaven in Johannine Sectarianism," *JBL,* XCI (1972), 44-72; G. Reim, *Studien zum alttestamentlichen Hintergrund des Johannesevangelium,* NTSMS, XXII (1974); D. M. Smith, "Johannine Christianity," *NTS,* XXI (1974/75), 222-48; *see also bibliographies* for BELOVED DISCIPLE[S]; JOHN, LETTERS OF[S]; PARACLETE[S]; SIGN IN THE NT[S].

D. M. SMITH

***JOHN, LETTERS OF.** As early as the third century Bishop Dionysius of Alexandria argued that all three letters and the GOSPEL OF JOHN, but not the Revelation of John (*see* REVELATION, BOOK OF and supplementary article) were from the same hand. While this view has long been the predominant one in critical scholarship, the common authorship of the gospel and epistles should not be taken for granted. The three letters did not gain canonical recognition as a group, or with the gospel, the longer I John taking precedence over the other two.

1. The relation of the letters to the Gospel of John and to each other. While the question of authorship remains undecided and there is a distinct possibility that the gospel and letters are the work of more than one writer, it can safely be said that most of the difficulties in ascribing the Fourth Gospel to John the son of Zebedee apply also to the letters (*see* JOHN, GOSPEL OF §§E, F). Moreover, the author of II and III John describes himself as an elder rather than an apostle. If he is also the author of I John, none of the letters is likely the work of an apostle, despite the statements of I John 1:1-3.

The question of authorship aside, the letters appear to be later than the gospel. Although they contain no specific data or references which allow us to date them absolutely, their relation to the gospel may be inferred from several lines of evidence. The Jews, who play so prominent a role in the gospel, have disappeared from the letters altogether, and no OT testimonies are adduced. The author of I John cites the love commandment (cf. John 13:34) as the old, rather than the new, commandment (I John 2:7-8; 3:11; II John 5); it is the commandment his readers have had from the beginning. Moreover, he plays upon the meaning of "new" in relation to "old" (I John 2:7-8). Jesus' word in the gospel about laying down one's life for his friends (15:13) is seemingly taken up in I John's injunction to lay down one's life for the brethren (3:16). Although the gospel is nowhere explicitly quoted, its teaching or the tradition behind it appears to be assumed as the basis for the author's exhortation.

The prologue of I John (1:1-4) is apparently modeled on the gospel prologue (John 1:1-18), but the "word of life" is not the pre-existent Word of the gospel. Rather it seems to be the Christian message, and "from the beginning" (instead of the gospel's "in the beginning") refers to the origin of the gospel preaching in Jesus' life and ministry. The author also repeatedly refers to doctrine which he regards as well established (2:13-14; 4:1-3; cf. II John 9).

Against such evidence favoring the priority of the gospel must be weighed I John's futuristic eschatology (2:18, 28; 3:2) and apparently primitive doctrine of the vicarious atonement by Jesus' blood (1:7; 2:2), neither of which is emphasized in the gospel. Although both teachings might be regarded as signs of the letter's earlier date, they also comport well with the view that I John is more indebted to a developing conventional church doctrine than is the gospel. The Johannine letters are probably correctly characterized as Johannine pastorals.

2. Questions of orthodoxy and church order as reflected in the letters. The doctrinal and disciplinary emphases of the Johannine letters, including the exhortations to love, are to be seen against the background of heterodox teaching and practice. The opponents hovering in the background are perceived as miscreants who have departed from good and approved conduct (I John 2:3-6, 10-11; 3:4-10), as well as from the true teaching (I John 2:18-19; II John 9). Invective is not spared. They are "antichrists" (I John 2:18, 22; 4:3) who teach that Christ has not come in the flesh (I John 4:2-3); they practice hate rather than love (I John 1:6-7; 2:3-11, esp. 9-11; 4:20-21). The doctrinal heresy is apparently understood as fundamental, while disobedience and hate are seen as the natural consequences of it. In any event, I John reflects a situation in which doctrine is developing along incompatible lines; thus there emerges the struggle between orthodoxy and heresy, with each side believing in its own rectitude.

III John does not deal with the same set of problems as I and II John, but rather with questions of church polity or governance. Controversy centers around DIOTREPHES (9-10), whose willingness to exercise authority against other Christians has affected the author. He is generally thought to be a claimant to the powers of the monarchial episcopate in his church, but it is not clear whether the elder objects to him because his own customary supervisory role over a number of churches (perhaps in a geographic area) is challenged, or because he himself represents a basically antihierarchical approach to church polity, whereas Diotrephes wishes to be a bishop. The hypothesis that Diotrephes has excommunicated the elder because of the latter's flirtation with Gnosticism as a potential vehicle of Christian thought is suggestive, but the slim evidence at our disposal is scarcely sufficient to confirm it.

3. The relationship of the letters to contemporary religious movements. The battle joined by the author of I John with Gnostic or Docetic opponents probably did not leave him unaffected, if indeed he did not originally share some ideas with them (*see* JOHN, LETTERS OF §1*b, c*). Similarities to the DEAD SEA SCROLLS also appear, particularly in the dualism and dualistic terminology (e.g., Spirit of Truth/Spirit of Falsehood). Certain of these affinities may be stronger than in the case of the Fourth Gospel, even though the severe rejection of the world (I John 2:15-17) is more Gnostic than Essene. Nevertheless, the Johannine letters, especially I John, stand closer in language, style, and conceptuality to the Fourth Gospel than to any other extant document or body of literature.

Bibliography. Commentaries: R. Schnackenburg, HTKNT (3rd ed., 1965); R. Bultmann, Hermeneia (1967); J. L. Houlden, HNTC (1973). See also: C. H. Dodd, "The First Epistle of John and the Fourth Gospel," *BJRL,* XXI (1937), 129-56; H. Conzelmann, "Was von Anfang war," *Neutestamentliche Studien für Rudolf Bultmann,* BZNW, XXI (2nd ed., 1957), 194-201.

D. M. SMITH

***JOHN THE BAPTIST.** Recent research has focused more on the origin of traditions about John the Baptist and their use by the evangelists than on his own life and work.

1. The origin of the traditions about John the Baptist. John did not intend to found a sect, but by BAPTISM across sectarian lines, to prepare a people for the baptism of the Coming One (Matt. 3:11-12; Mark 1:7-8; Luke 3:16-18). The inner circle of adherents who assisted in his work had their own style of life, to be sure, including fasting, sobriety, fixed forms of prayer, and ethical norms appropriate to a repentant life (Mark 1:6; 2:18; Matt. 11:16-18; Luke 11:1; 3:7-14). But the vast majority of those baptized by John returned to their regular occupations to await the expected one (cf. Luke 3:8, 10-14). To one or the other of these circles Jesus and most (or all?—Acts 1:22) of his first disciples belonged.

In the early period of the church, John's disciples continued to be regarded fraternally, since both groups fully endorsed the ministry of John. For the most part the Baptist movement was absorbed into the Christian church. The remaining holdouts first protested that the MESSIAH had not come; then in defensive reaction some proclaimed John Messiah, apparently meaning thereby the eschatological prophet. Using Christian sayings against Christians, they asserted John's superiority over Jesus by means of Jesus' own words (*see* esp. Matt. 11:11*a*; Luke 7:28*a*).

In response, the church hedged about its traditions concerning John with various defense mechanisms, the purpose of which was not only to safeguard belief in Jesus as the Christ, but to preserve John for the church. On the whole, though, John's position in Christian theology was already secure by virtue of continuing veneration by those in the church who had come to Jesus by way of John, and because the tradition itself was so uncompromising and unanimous in its declaration that the actual events proclaimed as "gospel" by the church had begun with John.

In short, the church stood at the center of John's movement from the very beginning and became its one truly great survivor and heir. The church thus already possessed a full store of authentic traditions about John from its inception and continued to be the primary locus for their legendary and theological elaboration. As John's followers continued to convert to the church, they no doubt brought with them oral traditions with which to supplement the church's treasury of lore about John. Some of these traditions may have eventually made their way into the NT. There is no evidence, however, that written documents or "gospels" about John existed or were employed by the evangelists.

2. The use of Baptist traditions by the church. Explicit polemic against the remnant of John's disciples is present only in the Fourth Gospel and Q. Traces of apologetic are clearly present in Luke's sources, but Luke himself appears not to be engaged in struggle against John's followers. And in Matthew and Mark there are no signs of antagonism against a Baptist sect.

It is rather John's role as "the beginning of the gospel" which accounts for his positive religious significance for the writers of the NT. Under this formula each successive evangelist has developed his own peculiar understanding of John's role.

Mark portrays John as ELIJAH incognito, whose sufferings prepare the way of the Lord and serve as an example to the persecuted Christians of Rome. In his introductory narrative Mark creates every conceivable presumption that John is Elijah. Yet even in 9:11 John is not explicitly called Elijah; his identity in God's purpose must remain, like that of Jesus, hidden until the resurrection (9:9*b*).

But John also suffers, and it is only in order to underline this fact that the bizarre account of John's beheading is included in such detail. By uniting the fate of John with that of Jesus, Mark succeeds in saying that John's suffering is not meaningless, any more than is that of the Christians in Rome. He too, like Jesus and the church, struggled in obscurity and humiliation. His true identity was concealed from the world. He too suffered ignominious death. But he suffered as Elijah, and in that suffering shares the fate of Jesus and his elect. What "they" (HEROD and Herodias, 9:13) did to John, so also "they" (contemporary opponents of the church, 13:9) will do to Christians now. This is as it must be, but this epoch of suffering and humiliation will soon give way to the day of vindication, when humiliation will be swallowed up in victory.

Matthew's treatment of the Baptist, supplemented as it is by materials from Q, is quite different from that in Mark. Matthew is polemically involved against contemporary Jewish authorities in proving that God's promises have been fulfilled in the church. Therefore he removes all doubt about John's identity; John *is* Elijah (Matt. 17:12-13). By this open identification Matthew is able to validate the messiahship of Jesus by reference to John according to the proof-from-prophecy schematism. But there is another reason; for if John is Elijah, then his rejection by the Jewish authorities becomes all the more inexcusable. Matthew uses John's fate to illustrate the hostility of "pseudo-Israel" to every overture from God. John and Jesus are brought into the closest possible relationship; words of Jesus are even placed on John's lips, and vice versa. John's fate prefigures the fate of Jesus. Together they stand against the wall of opposition thrown up by the authorities. John thus is made to witness against both "that" generation (John's) and "this" (Matthew's) that they have rejected the will of God and have lost the keys of the kingdom (21:32). Claim is therefore laid on John for the "true" people of God, the church. It is this deep gulf dividing the "false" from the "true" Israel which accounts for the way Matthew "Christianizes" John and quarters him in the Christian camp.

Luke also used the Baptist traditions of Q and Mark, along with sources of his own (especially for the infancy narratives), but his treatment of John is altogether different from Matthew's. Luke, in fact, makes very little change in the conception of John already present in Q. Luke also pictures John as the forerunner of the Messiah, the preacher of judgment and REPENTANCE; and as in Q, Luke does not explicitly identify John with Elijah. In other respects Luke simply follows Mark. Luke's greatest innovation lies in the manner in which he incorporates John into his grand scheme of redemptive history. John occupies a niche all to himself as the one who inaugurates the time of fulfillment, but his ministry is completely separate from that of Jesus. His work as preparer of the way marks the first stage in the central epoch of salvation history. Luke's contribution therefore lies in placing the figure of John within a panoramic theology of history.

Finally, the Fourth Evangelist divests the Baptist of every known role in the Jewish expectation. He becomes simply "the voice." As such he witnesses to Jesus as the Christ. He points continually away from himself to Jesus. John is not the bridegroom but only the friend of the bridegroom, who hears him and rejoices greatly at the bridegroom's voice (3:22 ff.). John is not the light, but only came to bear witness to the light, that all might believe through him (1:6-8). Indeed, the Baptist's last words stand as a motto over the entire representation of him in the Fourth Gospel: "He must increase, but I must decrease" (3:30). John's only wish, in short, is to be transparent, invisible—a voice which no one sees, but which directs everyone to Christ. The evangelist thus makes John the Baptist the first confessing Christian and the ideal image of the true missionary of Christ.

Behind this striking diversity in the evangelists' treatments of John lies a surprising unity: each continues to make him the "beginning of the gospel." Jesus himself appears to have been the source of this estimate of John's role in God's saving activity. The conviction that John is "the beginning of the gospel," and all of the Christian elaborations thereof, are but the theological expression of a historical fact, that through John's mediation Jesus perceived the nearness of the KINGDOM OF GOD and his own relation to its coming. Each evangelist has developed this tradition in the light of urgent contemporary needs, but also in faithfulness to Jesus' basic conception of John as the one through whom the eschatological event is proclaimed to be "at hand" even though it may seem to be indefinitely remote.

The early church used the figure of John typologically, as a means of setting forth its conception of its own role in "preparing the way of the Lord." John is the archetype of that moment before the light dawns (Luke 1:76 ff.), the catalyst for a sort of chaos out of which God creates something new. The image of John thus personifies the frontier character of the Christian proclamation as it encounters persons at the border of the times and calls them to receive the kingdom.

Bibliography. Recent monographs on the life of John: C. H. H. Scobie, *John the Baptist* (1964); R. Schütz, *Johannes der Täufer,* ATANT, L (1967); C. H. Kraeling, *John the Baptist* (1951), remains definitive.

Redaction critical studies: H. Conzelmann, *The Theology of St. Luke* (1957); W. Trilling, "Die Täufertradition bei Matthäus," *BZ,* III (1959), 271-89; W. Wink, *John the Baptist in the Gospel Tradition,* NTSMS, VII (1968), with complete bibliog.

W. WINK

***JONAH, BOOK OF. 1. The figure of Jonah ben Amittai.** That the author of the book of Jonah took as his hero (or perhaps better, anti-hero) Jeroboam II's court prophet, Jonah ben Amittai, seems beyond serious doubt, though why he selected this particular, obscure prophet remains elusive. Outside his name, no other detail has apparently been appropriated from the Deuteronomic historian's preserved tradition about Jonah (II Kings 14:25), and this has led some scholars to propose that it was precisely the emblematic significance of the name (meaning "dove," and as such, a suggestive symbol for Israel) which moved him to choose Jonah as the chief protagonist for his story. Hosea appears to be the first to introduce the figure of the dove as a metaphor for Israel in both a pejorative and positive sense (cf. Hos. 7:11; 11:11), but while the author of Jonah doubtless did intend a significant group within Israel to see their own views reflected in the recalcitrant prophet, the story does not seem originally designed as an allegorical representation of all Israel. Perhaps of greater interest to the author was the fact that the historical Jonah ben Amittai was a successful "prophet of salvation," a feature which he uses in an ironical way by portraying him as the reluctant instrument of a far more amazing divine deliverance than is associated with him in II Kings 14:25. The author has broadened both the extent and nature of the prophetic task, and through a remarkably bad example (perhaps chiefly the product of his own literary imagination, though possibly some unwritten tradition associated with the historical Jonah ben Amittai should not be ruled out), has depicted by implication what a true "prophet of salvation" should be.

2. The literary analysis of the book. ***a. Its form.*** Form-critically, the book of Jonah is a short story or *novella,* distinguished by mythical and folkloristic motifs as well as a definite didactic aim that essentially set it apart from historical biography. Though reminiscent of so-called prophetic legends among the stories of Samuel (cf. I Sam. 7:2–8:22; 10:17-27; 12), Elijah and Elisha (I Kings 17–19; II Kings 4–6), Ahijah (I Kings 11:29-39; 14:1-18), and certain anonymous "men of God" (I Kings 12:33–13:32), the book should probably not be classified as the compilation of one or more legends, primarily because its chief figure is not, in the final analysis, presented as an exalted example for emulation. Moreover, the prophetic legends in Samuel and Kings would appear to have a more substantial historical nucleus than does the book of Jonah. *See* Form Criticism, OT[S].

Because the author has placed on the lips of Jonah (in 4:2*b*) a traditional description of the gracious and merciful character of Yahweh (cf. Exod. 34:6; Num. 14:18; Pss. 86:15; 103:8; 145:8; Nah. 1:3; Joel 2:13; Neh. 9:17), some scholars have wanted to see the whole book as an attempt to probe the meaning and implications of this scriptural tradition, so that the work has the function, if not precisely the form, of what was later to be called a midrash (*see* Midrash[S]). As early as the fifth century B.C. there existed a type of literary work known as the midrash of a prophet (cf. II Chr. 13:22 [RSV "story"]; also note II Chr. 24:27 [RSV "commentary"]). However, the form and character of these *midrashim* can only tentatively be inferred from the rather meager evidence the OT offers, and lacking any certain surviving examples, it is impossible to say whether in the fifth century or earlier a work like the book of Jonah might have been called a midrash. In any case, the central theological thrust of the book is related to the way in which the author understood the implications of 4:2*b*.

In light of its obvious didactic purpose, the book might perhaps best be described literarily as a short story in the form of a parable, or in OT terms, as an example of one type of *mashal.* Though somewhat longer than the typical biblical parable, the book nonetheless illustrates all the distinctive features of the parable form: a comparatively short, simple, dramatic story, not necessarily historically factual, designed to teach a lesson embodied in basically one central point, emphasized and broadened by several subsidiary points, climaxing directly or indirectly in a call for decision on the part of the hearers or readers, motivated by a mutually understood analogy between the characters and events portrayed and real-life persons and events.

b. Its structural composition and the problem of the psalm. The author has constructed his story in two major parts (chs. 1–2 and 3–4) which are virtually parallel detail for detail until 4:8*b* is reached. There is also a thematic parallelism between the major motifs, with the focus initially upon the non-Israelites (the sailors in ch. 1, the Ninevites in ch. 3), then upon Jonah (chs. 2 and 4). Thus in chs. 1–2, both the sailors and Jonah are threatened with destruction; they respond with prayer to Yahweh; Yahweh reacts to their prayers by rescuing them; and they conclude by worshiping Yahweh. In chs. 3–4, the Ninevites and Jonah are confronted by a crisis involving destruction (for Jonah the crisis is not his own destruction, but the fact that Nineveh apparently will not be destroyed!); they respond to Yahweh: the Ninevites with faith and repentance, Jonah with anger, complaint, and a request for death; this is followed by Yahweh's response: to the Ninevites by changing his mind about destroying the city, to Jonah by encouraging the prophet to change his mind about wanting the city to be destroyed. Thus, structural analysis presupposes the integral relationship of the psalm (2:2-9 [H 3-10]) to the book as a whole, contrary to the general scholarly consensus which has rather seen it as the inept interpolation of a later editor. Though the vocabulary and linguistic characteristics of the psalm indicate that the author did not compose it especially for his story, its formal, structural, and meaningful compatibility with other elements in the prose parts suggests that it could well have been the writer himself who inserted it precisely in its present position. Moreover, as a psalm of declarative praise, it is typologically appropriate to the context. As one who has just experienced deliverance from death in the sea, it is fitting that Jonah express his gratitude to the Deity rather than petition the latter for release from the fish, which, as the psalm itself makes clear, never posed a threat to him. Finally, the usage of the "three days and three nights" motif in 1:17 [H 2:1] to describe the temporal limits of a journey between the nether and upper worlds (cf. the Sumerian myth of the Descent of Inanna to the Nether World, *ANET* [2nd ed.], p. 55) further strengthens the thesis that it was the author of Jonah who inserted the psalm with its explicit reference to the underworld (cf. 2:6 [H 2:7]) as the place from which Jonah was rescued. The contextual interpretation of the psalm adds certain dimensions to the character and personality of Jonah which prevent him from being interpreted too consistently and simplistically, thereby denying the complexities and contradictions in his actions and beliefs which the author seems deliberately to have intended.

c. Implications of the structural analysis for the message of the book. At the end of the first half of the story, when the sailors and Jonah have been faced with similar perils, they both supplicate Yahweh, are rescued by him, and cultically respond to him in similar fashion. But in the last two chapters, the conduct of the Ninevites and Jonah is radically distinct, so that the conformity in chs. 1–2 serves to heighten and emphasize the lack of it in chs. 3–4. The most striking contrast is that Jonah, unlike the Ninevites, does not repent. Though the writer clearly wants to emphasize the limitless character of the merciful divine will to save, offered equally to non-Israelite and Israelite, he wants also to stress the link between the two parts of the human response—prayer and repentance. With respect to prayer, Jonah was on the same plane as the sailors, but with respect to repentance, his response does not match the Ninevites', and at the end he is contemplating death instead of life. Hence the original thrust of the author's message may well have been this: given the divine compassion to save all who repent, repentance is easier for the most wicked non-Israelite metropolis imaginable than for one Israelite who has been treated mercifully. The author seeks to underline the difficulty some Israelites have in bringing any change in attitude toward what Yahweh wants of them. Thus the purpose is not to remind the Israelites of their mission to foreigners but to get them to see how incongruous their conduct is, and, it is hoped, to elicit a more favorable response. But the story's ending suggests that the writer is not hopeful about what his intended audience will do. All he can say is that Yahweh is unswerving in offering his pity and compassion to repentant sinners, whether they are Ninevite or Israelite. Without repentance they may be left to their doom, though Yahweh will persist to the end to bring about a change of mind and heart.

3. Date and setting. Nothing in either the language or content of the book points decisively to a particular period in Israel's history. Reference is often made to a group of so-called Aramaisms in the book, deemed an indication of a postexilic milieu. However, closer scrutiny of these terms in light of comparative Semitic philological data has tended to show that most of them stem from northern Israelite-Phoenician usage rather than Aramaic. But since both northern Israelite-Phoenician and Aramaic linguistic phenomena were in use in Hebrew both before and after the Exile, and almost none of those occurring in Jonah can be clearly demonstrated to have only postexilic currency, they are not very helpful for dating. The use of the perfect tense ("was") form in 3:3 with Nineveh as subject does not necessarily mean that the city had long since been destroyed by the time of the writer, since the same form is often used simply as a regular narrative tense form (cf., e.g., Gen. 29:17; Exod. 9:11; Num. 14:24). Also we should probably abandon the assumption that the author's alleged unhistorical use of the expression "the king of Nineveh" in 3:6 means that he was remote from Assyrian customs of royal titulature. Not only is the identification of kings with their chief royal residence attested in Israel (cf. I Kings 21:1; II Kings 1:3), but also in the Neo-Assyrian inscriptions. Finally, the various literary affinities between the book of Jonah and other biblical writings are not very useful for dating, since they occur in both pre- and postexilic works, and it is hard to demonstrate that the author of Jonah was actually dependent upon any of these for particular expressions or ideas.

There has long been agreement among OT scholars that the book was written to combat certain narrowly nationalistic and exclusivistic tendencies as a result of the work of Ezra and Nehemiah (*see* JONAH, BOOK OF §3*e*). Though it is obvious how the book may have been used to address that situation, there is actually nothing in the content of the book that unequivocally indicates that the author wrote it primarily to persuade his fellow Jews to be more open and merciful to Gentiles in the postexilic period. Increasingly, evidence seems to suggest that substantially the entire prophetic corpus of the OT had been written and collected by *ca.* 500 B.C., which would mean that the book of Jonah was most likely a creation of the sixth century, either before or after Deutero-Isaiah (*see* CANON OF THE OT[S] §2*b*). Since the book's universalism is expressed somewhat differently from that of the latter prophet, and in no way shares in Deutero-Isaiah's exclusive monotheism and polemic against idolatry, there is no evidence that the author of Jonah was directly under the influence of the great exilic prophet. If it is correct that the writer had an overriding concern about the lack of repentance within the Israelite community, a motif which finds its most prominent stress precisely in the writings of several of the sixth-century prophets, then it would seem he was breathing the same theological air, so to speak, as Jeremiah, Joel, and Ezekiel, some of whose ideas he definitely shared (note esp. Jer. 18:7 ff.; Joel 2:13; Ezek. 33:11). It may even be that he wrote especially against the background of Israel's early sixth-century crisis, whose life-or-death implications convinced him that his people's survival in the land was contingent upon their bearing the fruits of repentance.

Bibliography. E. J. Bickerman, *Four Strange Books of the Bible, Jonah-Daniel-Koheleth-Esther* (1967); M. Burrows, "The Literary Category of the Book of Jonah," in *Translating and Understanding the OT*, ed. H. T. Frank and W. L. Reed (1970), pp. 80-107; G. H. Cohn, *Das Buch Jona* (1969); A. Jepsen, "Anmerkungen zum Buche Jona," *ATANT*, LIX (1970), 297-305; Y. Kaufmann, *The Religion of Israel* (1960), esp. pp. 282-86; E. G. Kraeling, "The Evolution of the Story of Jonah," in *Hommages à André Dupont-Sommer,* ed. A. Caquot and M. Philonenko (1971), pp. 305-18; G. M. Landes, "The Kerygma of the Book of Jonah," *Int.,* XXI (1967), 3-31; O. Loretz, "Herkunft und Sinn der Jona-Erzählung," *BZ,* NS V (1961), 18-29; W. Rudolf, *Joel-Amos-Obadja-Jona, KAT,* XIII (2nd ed., 1971); H. W. Wolff, *Studien zum Jonabuch* (1965).

G. M. LANDES

JOSEPH STORY, THE. The material in the last part of the book of Genesis which relates the adventures of Joseph, son of Jacob, in the land of Egypt and his relations with his brothers and father. Most broadly, it includes chs. 37–50, but ch. 38 (the story of Judah and Tamar) and ch. 49 (the so-called "blessing of Jacob") deal with quite different matters.

1. Contents. The Joseph story opens with the presentation of a family torn by destructive tensions: a doting father who lavished favors on a spoiled youngest son, arousing the envy and hatred of the other sons, who were even more incensed when their younger brother related his dreams which indicated that they all would do obeisance before him. Sent on one occasion to report on his brothers, Joseph was seized by them, and eventually was sold in Egypt to an official named Potiphar. The grieving father, deceived by his sons, presumed Joseph to be dead. In Egypt, Joseph's abilities soon became apparent, and he was placed in a position of total authority over his master's estate. But his fortunes suddenly turned as he attracted the enamored attention of his master's wife. Rejecting her advances, he found himself accused of attacking her and was cast into prison. There he came to the attention of the royal butler and baker by interpreting their dreams. Events happened as he predicted, and, although forgotten for a while, he was later summoned when the pharaoh had two dreams that none of his courtiers could interpret. Joseph interpreted the dreams—warnings of a seven-year famine coming after seven years of plenty—and offered advice on how to meet the danger. His display of ability made him the obvious candidate to put such advice in operation: thus he became the vizier of Egypt, subject only to the pharaoh himself. His actions were effective, and when the famine came, only in Egypt was there a store of grain.

In time Joseph's brothers came to Egypt seeking supplies. He recognized them, but they did not recognize the harsh official who accused them of being spies, threw Simeon into prison, and told them not to come back without their youngest brother, Benjamin. Only when all supplies were gone was their reluctant father persuaded to permit a second trip. They took Benjamin along, were politely received, and Simeon was restored to them. Yet, fortune turned again: Benjamin was accused of theft, and the brothers found themselves once more able to resolve a difficult situation by giving up a younger brother. However, they had changed; Judah offered himself in place of Benjamin, and the tension was finally broken as Joseph revealed his identity. The good news was reported to Jacob, and he and the rest of the family moved to Egypt. Jacob died in time and was buried in Palestine, and the tale came full circle as the brothers were reassured of Joseph's good will and prostrated themselves before him. The narrative ends with a notice of Joseph's death in Egypt.

2. Literary analysis. Critical study of Genesis has long noted that chs. 37–50 stand apart from what precedes them, both in terms of subject matter and literary style. They form, not loosely gathered, short, independent units such as comprise the cycles dealing with Abraham and Jacob, but an organically constructed and artfully tailored romance or *novella,* where plot development and complex characterization extend over many chs., and the parts are interdependent and cannot stand alone. Yet it must also be noted that the story falls into two parts. Gen. 37, 42–48, and 50 deal with the internal affairs of the family of Jacob, while Gen. 40–41 relates the adventures of Joseph in the Egyptian court and contains no clear reference to the brothers or to the tensions and developments of the former material. In Gen. 40–41 a new set of characters and problems appears, and only when these are finally dealt with does the narrative return to those presented and left hanging in Gen. 37. These two parts are, however, carefully blended: while Gen. 40–41 could stand independent of Gen. 37, 42–48, 50, the latter builds upon this unit and forms the framework for it. It must be noted further that, as the Joseph story now stands, it is divided by literary criticism among the sources designated J and E, and to a lesser extent P (*see* DOCUMENTS). This suggests three stages in the literary development of the Joseph story.

a. Joseph the Egyptian courtier. Gen. 40–41 comprises a courtier tale of small beginnings and a happy ending. A foreign youth rises from life's lowest rung to become the highest official in the land. Gen. 47:13-26 and 50:26 might have been part of this tale. The former, which breaks into its present context, graphically illustrates this courtier's effective service for the pharaoh. The latter tells of the courtier's death at 110 years and his proper burial, an important element in the story of any Egyptian courtier. The bulk of the Egyptian elements in the Joseph story are found in this tale (*see* §5 *below*), and it is here that Joseph acts most fully as a model for the wise (*see* §3 *below*). While the story is set in the Egyptian court, the fact that the hero is a foreigner, along with the picture of the pharaoh as awesome, but not a divine king, and the understanding of royal dreams presented in Gen. 41 suggest that this tale was formed and circulated in a non-Egyptian setting. A Late Bronze Age city-state in Palestine, which throughout the Eighteenth and Nineteenth Dynasties was under Egyptian political and cultural influence, might be proposed as a home for this tale.

b. Joseph and his brothers. The tale of Joseph the Egyptian courtier was later utilized as a kernel around which the story of Joseph and his brothers was constructed, possibly using older traditions about the sons of Jacob. The hatred of the brothers became the occasion for Joseph's being sold into Egyptian slavery, and his position in the court of the pharaoh became the critical factor in the later resolution of the story. This forms a tightly constructed story with complex characterization and high tension and drama. The interest in the psychic dimension, some affinities with wisdom, and the understanding of divine providence revealed in this story (*see* §4 *below*) suggest that its place of origin was possibly the court of Davidic or Solomonic Jerusalem.

c. J, E, and P. In time this story of Joseph and his brothers was taken up within the sacred story of ancient Israel, where it served as an elaborate transition piece between the patriarchal material and that dealing with Moses and the Exodus. Thus, it found a place in both J and E (and possibly, with some differences, in P, cf. 37:2) and now appears in a form that is the result of the redactional combination of these sources (*see* GENESIS §B4; PENTATEUCH §B1*b*; contrast Whybray, "The Joseph Story," pp. 522-28). The tightly knit structure of the story was broken, especially at the conclusion, as additional materials were added dealing with Joseph (Gen. 39, a traditio-historically secondary addition of possible Egyptian provenance and set apart by style and vocabulary; Gen. 48 and 41:51-52), the other sons of Jacob (Gen. 38; 46:8-27), and Jacob's last days and death (Gen. 46:1-7; 49; 47:29-31 and 50:1-14).

3. The Joseph story and wisdom. Drawing upon Egyptian instruction literature and upon the book of Proverbs, G. von Rad has sought to demonstrate that the Joseph story is steeped in wisdom themes and motifs, and that the picture of Joseph presents, as a didactic model, the educational ideal of the court wisdom schools. Joseph is a skilled interpreter of dreams (41:15; cf. Dan. 2; 4) and a sage adviser to the pharaoh, self-disciplined (cf. Prov. 14:29; 15:18), restrained (cf. Prov. 10:19; 14:30; 15:33), courteous (cf. Prov. 10:12; 24:29), yet forceful in speech (cf. Prov. 15:23; 16:21-24), and Pharaoh describes him as "discreet and wise" (41:39; cf. 41:33; Prov. 1:2-6). Von Rad's thesis has received some criticism and modification, but it has much to recommend it. It is especially in Gen. 40–41; 47:13-26 that Joseph appears as the model wise courtier and that most of von Rad's examples are to be found. And, while he is hardly such a model in much of Gen. 37, 42–48, 50, the material dealing with Joseph and his brothers is not without examples as well; e.g., the speech of Judah (44:18-34) is a model of courtly petition. Wisdom schools flourished in the setting of the royal courts (*see* WISDOM IN THE ANE[S] and WISDOM IN THE OT[S]), and especially in the court of Solomon, whose patronage of the wise made his own wisdom legendary (cf. I Kings 4:29-34; 10:1-10; Prov. 10:1; 25:1).

4. Theology and purpose. The prevalence of wisdom motifs in the tale of Joseph the Egyptian courtier suggests that it was intended to function as a didactic piece, designed to appeal to the youths in the wisdom schools and to recommend the model of the wise courtier. It serves to entertain and at the same time to inculcate a particular style of life.

Von Rad has called attention to the notices in Gen. 45:5-8; 50:20 concerning divine control of human events, and he suggests that they represent an understanding of providence characteristic of wisdom thought in particular (cf. Prov. 16:1, 2, 9; 19:21; 20:24; 21:30-31). Here is expressed a belief in a divine purpose that is at times beyond comprehension and is apparent only below the surface of human history. Yet, this understanding turns the brief references to God in Gen. 40:8 and 41:16, 25, 32 into confessions about a pervasive divine providence and gives added dimension to the dreams of Joseph in Gen. 37 (cf. 42:9; 50:18).

As this story is incorporated into the sacred story of ancient Israel, attention is moved from Joseph to the traditio-historically more critical figure of the patriarch Jacob. As a transition piece within the sacred story, certain of its themes receive new accentuation. The divine promise of progeny is again affirmed (cf. Gen. 12:2; 15:4-6; 26:3-5; 28:14); the patriarchal line, threatened by famine, is preserved by the God of the patriarchs (48:4-5); Israel is seen functioning as a source of blessing for the nations (cf. 12:1-3). This narrative is remarkably open to the possibility of creative interaction with the Egyptians; it is in Egypt that the sons of Israel find sustenance, it is for the pharaoh (47:13-26) that Joseph works, and the patriarch Jacob himself blesses the Egyptian ruler (47:7, 10). This is a far cry from the later situation when "there arose a new king over Egypt, who did not know Joseph" (Exod. 1:8).

5. Historicity. In light of the development and function of the Joseph story outlined above, it is clear that its central concerns are literary, didactic, and theological, rather than historical. Thus, the degree to which the historian can utilize this material in the reconstruction of the life of a historical Joseph, let alone early Israelite intertribal relations, is quite limited. The "rags to riches" motif that governs the tale of Joseph the Egyptian courtier is a popular one in folk literature. Even if the author of the story of Joseph and his brothers drew upon earlier traditions about the twelve tribes, these have been fully reworked and submerged in the story. And there is no mention of a Joseph in Egyptian court records; yet the tale does show affinities, not only with such Egyptian materials as the story of Si-nuhe and the shipwrecked sailor, but with the so-called tomb biographies of Egyptian courtiers as well.

Traces of Egyptian coloring are found in Gen. 40–41; 47:13-26; 50:26 (Egyptian loan words, elements in the dreams, court customs, officials, and titles, onomastica, economic situation, age at death, burial practices, etc.). They function as integral parts of the tale, while the two prominent notices of supposed Egyptian practice in the remainder of the story, Gen. 43:32 and 46:34, find no support from Egyptian materials and are intrusive and artificial in the narrative, creating an impossible situation if pressed to their logical conclusion. Thus, the author of the tale of Joseph the Egyptian courtier seems acquainted with Egypt, while the author of the story of Joseph and his brothers reveals both a limited knowledge of Egypt and a desire to provide some sense of verisimilitude for his story by bringing in these two notices that reflect an outsider's awe and fear of that dangerous and mysterious land.

Bibliography. H. Gunkel, "Die Komposition der Josephgeschichte," *ZDMG,* NF I (1922), 55-71; H. Gressmann, "Ursprung und Entwicklung der Josephsage," *Eucharisterion: Studien zur Religion und Literatur des Alten und Neuen Testaments,* I (1923), 1-55; G. von Rad, *Die Josephsgeschichte* (1954), "The Joseph Narrative and Ancient Wisdom," in *The Problem of the Hexateuch and Other Essays* (1966), pp. 292-300, and *Genesis: A Commentary* (rev. ed., 1973); J. Vergote, *Joseph en Égypte: Genèse chap. 37–50 à la lumière des études égyptologiques récentes* (1959); L. Ruppert, *Die Josephserzählung der Genesis: Ein Beitrag zur Theologie der Pentateuchquellen* (1965); R. N. Whybray, "The Joseph Story and Pentateuchal Criticism," *VT,* XVIII (1968), 522-28; J. L. Crenshaw, "Method in Determining Wisdom Influence Upon 'Historical' Literature," *JBL,* LXXXVIII (1969), 129-42; D. B. Redford, *A Study of the Biblical Story of Joseph,* VTSup, XX (1970); G. W. Coats, "The Joseph Story and Ancient Wisdom: A Reappraisal," *CBQ,* XXXV (1973), 285-97, "Redactional Unity in Genesis 37–50," *JBL,* XCIII (1974), 15-21. W. L. HUMPHREYS

***JOSHUA, BOOK OF.** (*See* JOSHUA, BOOK OF for an outline of its contents.)

1. Joshua and the Deuteronomic history
2. Composition
3. The conquest narratives
4. The city and boundary lists
5. Historical issues
Bibliography

1. Joshua and the Deuteronomic history. Joshua has a very close affinity to Deuteronomy. It might be summarized, in fact, as an account of the completion of the program anticipated by Deuteronomy: the conquest of the land (chs. 2–12), the allotment of territory to the tribes (chs. 13–21), and the establishment of the Yahwistic cult (8:30-35; 24:1-28). The theological motifs which characterize Deuteronomy—e.g., covenant and law, the holy-war ideal—find further expression in Joshua. A common literary style is apparent even in translation. Both books emphasize the role of Joshua as Moses' successor.

Deuteronomy-Joshua can be read as a conclusion to the account of Israel's origins presented by Genesis–Numbers. Thus earlier scholars favored the term HEXATEUCH and sought to trace J, E, and P through Joshua. This approach has not been abandoned entirely, but most contemporary critics doubt that these sources can be traced in Joshua, even if they are present there, since the materials have been so thoroughly reworked by Deuteronomic editors. *See* YAHWIST[S] §3; ELOHIST[S] §4*a*.

The five books which follow in the Hebrew canon (Judges, I-II Samuel, I-II Kings) also have been edited from a Deuteronomic perspective, and when read in sequence with Deuteronomy-Joshua, they provide a continuous survey of Israel's history from Moses to the Exile. The essential unity of this survey was emphasized by M. Noth in 1943. While recognizing that the survey incorporates numerous traditions from various periods, he insisted that the over-all unity of plan and theological perspective is such that its compilation must have been essentially the work of a single Deuteronomic compiler-historian during the Exile—i.e., roughly contemporary with the last events recorded in the survey (cf. II Kings 24–25). In short, as far as their literary history is concerned, Deuteronomy and Joshua are not to be understood as the conclusion to the Hexateuch but as the beginning of the DEUTERONOMIC HISTORY.

2. Composition. The statement in Josh. 13:1*a*, "Now Joshua was old and advanced in years," prepares the reader for his farewell address in 23:1*b*-16, which is introduced with virtually the same statement. Thus Noth was probably correct in identifying the long excursus on the tribal allotments which interrupts this sequence as a secondary appendix. That this excursus also derived from Deuteronomic circles is indicated by the characteristically Deuteronomic summary and transition in 21:43–22:6. The report of Caleb's allotment (14:6-15) probably does not belong to the appendix, but was transferred from 11:21-22 to its present position when the appendix was added. The transferral would have been invited by the fact that Caleb's allotment (Hebron and vicinity) fell within the territory which the appendix assigned to Judah (cf. esp. 15:54).

The two passages which focus on the sanctuary at Shechem (8:30-35; 24:1-28) are to be associated with each other. Yet both are problematic in relation to the remainder of the book. The account of the establishment of the altar (8:30-35) has no recognizable connection with its present context. The account of the second Shechem assembly (24:1-28) is redundant and anticlimactic to Joshua's farewell address (ch. 23). Shechem plays no cultic role elsewhere in the book; Gilgal (4:19 ff.) and Shiloh (18:1 ff.) are the usual places of tribal assembly. Probably both passages should be read together (8:30-35 immediately following 24:1-28) and understood as another Deuteronomic appendix which was introduced with reference to the instructions given in Deut. 27:2 ff.

Any analysis of the composition of the book of Joshua must take Judg. 1:1–2:5 into account. (1) This bloc of material contradicts the contention of the Deuteronomic editor(s) that the whole land was conquered by a unified Israel under the leadership of Joshua. (2) It appears to be connected with the Deuteronomic survey only loosely, having been attached by means of a second summary statement regarding Joshua's death and burial (cf. Josh. 24:29-33 with Judg. 2:6-10). (3) Most of the traditions which are combined in Judg. 1:1–2:5 appear also in Joshua. They are introduced separately in Joshua, however, sometimes in significantly different versions and generally at the expense of considerable redactional effort. For example, the report of the defeat of Adoni-zedek in Josh. 10:1 ff. is clearly related traditio-historically to the report of the defeat of Adoni-bezek in Judg. 1:4 ff. The report of Caleb's and Othniel's conquests in Hebron and vicinity is almost word for word the same in Josh. 15:13-19 and in Judg. 1:11-15. Note that this report conflicts with Josh. 11:21-23; 14:6-15, which attributes the conquest of the whole land including Hebron to Joshua. The conflict has been eased somewhat, but not removed entirely, by the editorial gloss in 14:12*b*, "for you heard on that day how the Anakim were there, with great fortified cities: it may be that the Lord will be with me, and I shall drive them out as the Lord said." Finally, the cities which appear in the so-called "negative conquest list" of Judg. 1:21, 27-35 have been incorporated for the most part into the description of the tribal allotments (*see* §4 *below*).

3. The conquest narratives. The conquest narratives in Joshua 2–11 have been so thoroughly reworked and edited from the Deuteronomic perspective that it is difficult to reach any secure conclusions regarding the history of their pre-Deuteronomic transmission. However, there is widespread agreement among critical scholars on the following points.

a. The narratives. Most of these narratives pertain to the territory of Benjamin (10:16 ff. are the exceptions) and probably circulated independently among the Benjaminites during the earliest stages of transmission. Occasionally more than one version of a tradition existed—e.g., there appear to have been two versions of the story about the execution of the five kings at Makkedah: one in which the kings were buried alive in the cave, and one in which they were hanged on five trees (10:16-17). There are indications as well that motifs and details were sometimes transferred from one tradition to another. Note the striking similarity between the description of the military tactics employed at Ai and at nearby Gibeah (cf. Josh. 8 and Judg. 20).

b. Pre-Deuteronomic collection. Most of these narratives probably were already collected into essentially their present arrangement before being re-edited and incorporated into the Deuteronomic history. Whether this pre-Deuteronomic collection included the non-Benjaminite traditions (10:16 ff.) or presumed an initial conquest of the whole land by all Israel under the leadership of Joshua is uncertain. Joshua as leader of a unified Israel has in any case been superimposed upon most of the narratives. This is especially evident in the account of the covenant with Gibeon (ch. 9), where Joshua tends to fade into the background, even in the present form of the narrative.

c. Etiology. These narratives reflect a strong interest in ETIOLOGY, e.g., the explanations for the names "Gibeath-haaraloth" and "Gilgal" provided in Josh. 5:2-9. Some narratives may be entirely etiological in origin. But caution is in order. Recent studies have demonstrated that an etiological explanation can be secondary to the structure and central theme of a narrative.

d. Cultic factors. The possibility must be taken into account that some of these narratives are basically cultic in origin; chs. 3–4 come into special consideration in this regard. The holy-war ideal must be counted among the cultic influences. Not only does it play a major role in the Deuteronomic theology, but it appears to have been a significant element in some of these narratives in their pre-Deuteronomic stage of transmission. Thus the narrator of the account of the fall of Jericho was very much concerned to depict the incident as a divine victory rather than the result of human might. Israel's only responsibilities in the affair were to perform the proper rituals and to maintain the holy-war regulations.

4. The city and boundary lists. Josh. 10:29-39 is generally recognized as an authentic list which harks back to some early campaign. Vs. 10:42 probably belongs to this itinerary rather than to the concluding Deuteronomic summary (vss. 40-43). The original historical context of the itinerary cannot be established. It is tempting to associate it with Saul's conquests; except that Lachish, according to the archaeological evidence, was virtually unoccupied between *ca.* 1200-1000 B.C. But the summary of W Jordanian conquests in Josh. 12:7-24 is generally suspected of being an artificial list, the names of which would have been derived primarily from the traditions preserved in chs. 2–11 (including the itinerary of 10:29-39, 42). A problem with this explanation is that some of the names in the list do not appear in the preceding chapters, and in fact are not associated with the Conquest anywhere else in the OT. If the list is authentic, and a fairly strong case can be made in its favor, it is probably to be associated with King Solomon's reign.

Discussion of the Judean district list (15:20-62; 18:21-28) focuses on the first subgrouping of Benjaminite cities (18:21-24). Since the territory to which this subgrouping pertains normally belonged to the northern kingdom, some scholars contend that the subgrouping originally represented the Benjaminite district of the northern kingdom and has been attached to the Judean district list secondarily. This is of course possible, but by no means a necessary conclusion. The list is internally consistent as it stands now (i.e., including 18:21-24) and the boundary between the two kingdoms is known to have fluctuated from time to time.

We noted above that data from the "negative conquest list" (Judg. 1:21, 27-35) have been incorporated into the description of the tribal allotments (cf., e.g., Josh. 15:63; 16:10; 17:11-13). This created editorial problems in that the tribal holdings presupposed by the list did not always correspond to those presupposed by the allotment system. Note, e.g., that the list associates Gezer with Ephraim (Judg. 1:29; Josh. 16:10), although Gezer was situated in the very heart of the territory allotted to Dan (Josh. 19:40-48). One detects in the description of Joseph's (Ephraim's) southern boundary (16:1-3) a not entirely successful effort to deal with this contradiction. On the basis of the allotment system, one would expect this boundary to (1) correspond to Benjamin's northern and western boundary to the point where it meets Judah's northern boundary (Josh. 18:12-14); (2) follow Judah's northern boundary from that juncture to the vicinity of Beth-shemesh (Josh. 15:9*b*-10); and then (3) turn to the NW via Aijalon (Arab. Yalo) and Jehud (el-Yahudiyeh) to the Mediterranean Sea—i.e., in order to allow for Dan's allotment (Ir-shemesh in Josh. 19:41=Beth-shemesh in 15:10). The description begins as expected, following Benjamin's northern boundary as far as Lower Beth-horon. But then we are told simply that it extended "then to Gezer, and it ends at the sea" (16:3). Apparently the original boundary description has been curtailed and replaced with this vague editorial gloss in an effort to bring Gezer within the bounds of Ephraim. A similar editorial problem occurred in connection with Manasseh's allotment and explains the curious statement in Josh. 17:11-13: "Also in Issachar and in Asher Manasseh had Beth-shean and its villages, and Ibleam and its villages" (cf. Judg. 1:27-28). *See* TRIBES, TERRITORIES OF; TRIBES, TERRITORIES OF[S].

Scholarly opinion remains widely divided regarding the list of Levitical cities recorded in Josh. 21 (cf. the slightly different version in I Chr. 6). Some view it as an entirely artificial and utopian list without any historical basis. Those who attribute historicity to it express various opinions regarding its date and the circumstances of its origin. In any case the list is highly schematized. Four cities are listed for each tribe. The only exceptions, Judah and Naphtali, offset each other and probably are to be attributed to corruptions in the text.

5. Historical issues. The question of historicity must be raised at two levels. First, do the individual narratives and lists reflect actual historical events or circumstances? Second, does the Deuteronomic presentation of the conquest and settlement, under which these narratives and lists have been subsumed, have any claim to historicity?

a. The pre-Deuteronomic narratives and lists. We have already noted that several of the lists are probably authentic historical sources, although the dates and circumstances of their origin cannot be established with certainty. In any case they generally derive from later periods of Israel's history than their present context in the book of Joshua would imply. Thus, while the district list in Josh. 15:20-62; 18: (21-24), 25-28 is an extremely valuable source of historical information regarding the administrative system of the southern kingdom, it is only indirectly relevant for the study of the premonarchial period. Some of the narratives in chs. 2–11 probably also hark back to actual historical events. For example, the account of the covenant with Gibeon (ch. 9) apparently preserves the memory of an early agreement which was broken later by Saul (II Sam. 21:1-14). But other traditions preserved in these chapters may be entirely etiological or cultic in origin; and even those which are based on actual historical events have undergone such significant changes during the process of transmission that their historical basis is no longer clearly discernible.

The account of the conquest of AI is a case in point. The opening scene (7:2 ff.) continues the holy-war theme which dominates the preceding account of the conquest of Jericho: victory was to be given by Yahweh and was in no way dependent upon human might. The initial defeat at Ai illustrates Israel's helplessness when the holy-war regulations were not maintained. We have already observed that the description of the tactics employed during the second attack (8:3 ff.) is related traditio-historically to the account of the conquest of nearby Gibeah (Judg. 20). Both stories circulated orally among the same folk population, and it is not surprising that elements of one would have been transferred to the other. Finally, the account of the conquest of Ai provides an etiological explanation for the prominent ruin situated SE of Bethel. The Hebrew name "Ai" means "the ruin." According to Josh. 8:24-28, the ruin resulted from Joshua's destruction of a massive Canaanite city at the time of Israel's conquest of the land. Excavations have demonstrated that the massive ruins had already been standing for hundreds of years before Israel appeared on the scene. Possibly Israel did fight a significant battle in the vicinity, but if so, the memory is preserved so indirectly that the possibility must remain in the realm of speculation.

b. The Deuteronomic presentation of the Conquest. The Deuteronomic editor (s) of the book of Joshua wished to emphasize that the whole land of Canaan was conquered by a unified Israel under the leadership of Joshua. This view is not supported by the narratives in chs. 2–11. Even if taken as historically accurate sources, they account for the conquest of only a portion of the land. Certain non-Deuteronomic traditions strongly suggest, moreover, that Israel took possession of the land by means of a less unified and more gradual process. The traditions preserved in Judg. 1:1–2:5 imply that the various tribes acted on their own, and that their initial attempts were only partially successful (cf. esp. Judg. 1:21, 27-35). The distinction maintained between the "Leah" and "Rachel" tribes suggests that the settlement occurred in at least two major phases (cf. esp. Gen. 29:31–30:13 + 35:16-20). Even within the book of Joshua there are hints that the Deuteronomic presentation of the Conquest is more ideal than historically accurate (cf. esp. 11:13; 13:1-13; 17:14-18).

In view of the apparently contradictory nature of the biblical evidence, it is not surprising that scholars have reached widely divergent conclusions regarding the conquest. *See* CANAAN, CONQUEST AND SETTLEMENT OF[S].

c. The archaeological evidence. Evidences of Late Bronze (*ca.* 1500-1200) destructions have been uncovered at Tell Deir'alla (biblical Succoth?), Megiddo, Beth-shan, Bethel, Gezer, Beth-shemesh, Lachish, Tell Beit Mirsim, Tell Abu Hawam, and Ashdod. Some would associate these destructions with Joshua's campaign, but this involves both an overextension and an oversimplification of the archaeological evidence: (1) It cannot be assumed that these LB destructions occurred in a single wave or were due to a single cause. None of the destructions can be dated precisely; and the end of the LB age was a politically turbulent period for Palestinian city-states apart from whatever pressures Israel exerted. (2) The destroyed cities are for the most part not the ones which the biblical texts associate with Joshua's conquests. The two unquestionable exceptions are Lachish (Josh. 10:3 ff.) and Hazor (11:1 ff.). Gezer and Bethel are listed in the summary list of Josh. 12:7-24. But Josh. 10:33 carefully avoids the notion that Joshua actually took the city of Gezer itself (cf. also 16:10; Judg. 1:29; I Kings 9:16-17); and the account of the taking of Bethel does not appear prior to the summary, as one would expect if its conquest were to be credited to Joshua, but in Judg. 1:22-26, where the deed is credited to "the house of Joseph." Actually, one need not assume that the taking of Bethel as described in Judg. 1:22-26 involved the city's destruction. (3) Excavations at sites which do figure prominently among the conquests attributed to Joshua have, with the exception of Hazor, produced only negative evidence. Jericho and Ai appear to have been unoccupied during the LB age. Gibeon may have been occupied at that time; but if so, all the evidence escaped the excavators except four tombs.

d. Shechem and the amphictyony. It was observed above that 8:30-35 and 24:1-28 stand apart from the remainder of the book of Joshua in that they presume SHECHEM to have been the place of tribal assembly (i.e., rather than Gilgal and Shiloh). It is often held that 24:1-28 preserves the remembrance of an ancient ceremony by which the tribes bound themselves together into amphictyonic union, a ritual which may have been repeated at regular intervals during the premonarchial period. According to the hypothesis, Shechem would have served as the first amphictyonic center. Gilgal, Bethel, and Shiloh may have served as amphictyonic centers at later periods.

The amphictyonic hypothesis is falling under increasing attack and not without good reason (*see* AMPHICTYONY[S]). One of the least convincing aspects of the hypothesis is the role it ascribes to Shechem. There is no direct evidence that it was an early Irsaelite cultic center aside from the two problematic passages in Joshua. These two passages are clearly Deuteronomic in their present form, and appear to be secondarily Deuteronomic at that (*see* §2 *above*). The claim that 24:1-28 is based on a very old, pre-Deuteronomic tradition is possible, but cannot be satisfactorily demonstrated.

Bibliography. Commentaries: J. Alberto Soggin, OTL (1972); J. M. Miller and G. M. Tucker, CBC (1974). Special studies: Y. Aharoni, "The Province-list of Judah," *VT,* IX (1959), 225-46; M. Haran, "Studies in the Account of the Levitical Cities," *JBL,* LXXX (1961), 45-54, 156-65; E. Jenni, "Zwei Jahrzehnte Forschung an den Büchern Joshua bis Könige," *Theol. Rundschau,* XXVII (1961), 1-32, 97-146; W. Herzberg, "Adonibesek," *Beiträge zur Traditionsgeschichte und Theology des Alten Testaments* (1962), pp. 28-35; N. Lohfink, "Die deuteronomistische Darstellung des Übergangs der Führung Israels von Moses auf Josue," *Scholastik,* XXXVII (1962), 32-44; B. S. Childs, "A Study of the Formula, 'Until This Day,' " *JBL,* LXXXII (1963), 279-92; W. M. Roth, "Hinterhalt und Scheinflucht (Der stammespolemische Hintergrund von Jos 8)," *ZAW,* LXXV (1963), 296-304; S. Mowinckel, *Tetrateuch-Pentateuch-Hexateuch, BZAW,* XC (1964), identifies J and P in Joshua; J. Blenkinsopp, "Are There Traces of the Gibeonite Covenant in Deuteronomy?" *CBQ,* XXVIII (1966), 207-19; J. A. Soggin, "Gilgal, Passah, und Landnahme. Eine neue Untersuchung des kultischen Zusammenhangs der Kap. III-VI des Josuabuches," VTSup, XV (1966), 263-77; P. W. Lapp, "The Conquest of Palestine in the Light of Archaeology," *CTM,* XXXVIII (1967), 283-300; B. O. Long, *The Problem of Etiological Narrative in the Old Testament, BZAW,* CVIII (1968); V. Fritz, "Die sogenannte Liste der besiegten Könige in Josua 12," *ZDPV,* LXXXV (1969), 136-61, associates the list with King Solomon's reign; D. J. McCarthy, "The Theology of Leadership in Joshua 1–9," *Bibl.,* LII (1971), 165-75; M. Weippert, *The Settlement of the Israelite Tribes in Palestine,* SBT, XXI (1971), a compelling response to J. Bright's criticism of Alt and Noth; G. M. Tucker, "The Rahab Saga (Joshua 2)," *The Use of the Old Testament in the New and Other Essays,* ed. J. Efird (1972), pp. 66-86; V. Fritz, "Das ende der spät bronzezeitlichen Stadt Hazor Stratum XIII und die biblische Überlieferung in Joshua 11 und Richter 4," *UF,* V (1973), 123-39; A. N. Radjawane, "Das deuteronomistische Geschichtswerk," *Theol. Rundschau,* XXXVIII (1973), 177-216.

J. M. MILLER

***JOTHAM (KING OF JUDAH).** The seal bearing the inscription *lytm* (*see* JOTHAM §3, with Fig. 31; the reading *ltym* is in error) was discovered at TELL EL-KHELEIFEH. This site cannot be positively identified with Ezion-geber.

***JUBILEE, YEAR OF** [יובל, etymology uncertain; traditional: a word for "ram"; some scholars compare, rather unconvincingly, the root *ybl,* "to bring (a gift)"; the word has no relation to Lat. *jubilare,* "to raise a shout," and its English derivations]. שנת היובל, the year concluding a cycle of seven sabbatical years.

1. The word. In Exod. 19:13 a musical instrument, היבל, is mentioned; the same instrument is called קרן היובל in Josh. 6:5, whereas vss. 4, 6, 8, 13 of this chapter speak of שופרות היובלים, "trumpets of rams" (?). According to the Mishna (R.H. 3:3) the trumpet of the New Year was made of a straight horn of a mountain goat; Rabbi Judah maintained (3:5) that this instrument was used at the beginning of the year of jubilee only, whereas at all other New Year festivals the ram's horn was blown.

2. Legislation. The legislation concerning the year of jubilee—sometimes called simply "the jubilee"—in Lev. 25:8-17, 23-25 stands in close connection with regulations for every seventh year, Lev. 25:1-7, 18-22 (*see* SABBATICAL YEAR and supplementary article). Though the jubilee has some characteristics of its own, all that is prescribed for the sabbatical year applies to the jubilee as well. This is already an argument in favor of assuming the identity of the jubilee and the seventh sabbatical year, as in the Book of Jubilees. This identity was maintained by Rabbi Judah (T.B. Ned. 61a) against the majority of the rabbinical authorities who concluded from Lev. 25:10, 11, where the jubilee is called "the fiftieth year," that the jubilee was the year following the seventh sabbatical year. It is more probable, however, that we have to understand "fiftieth" in the same way as Christ is said to have risen "on the third day," though the resurrection took place on the second day after his death. The jubilee begins on the tenth day of the seventh month, on the Day of Atonement, and is inaugurated by "sending abroad the loud trumpet (שופר, not יובל) throughout the land" (Lev. 25:9). In such a way "liberty" is proclaimed to all the inhabitants (vs. 10). This word, דרור, indicates the manumission of slaves, i.e., of those Israelites who, because of poverty, had sold themselves either to fellow Israelites (vss. 39-43) or to non-Israelites dwelling in Israel (vss. 47-54). In Ezek. 46:17 "the year of liberty" is another name for the jubilee.

It has often been said that the manumission in the year of jubilee contradicts Exod. 21:2-6, which prescribes the manumission of a Hebrew slave after his sixth year of bondage (cf. Deut. 15:12-17). One should, however, note the differences. Exod. 21:2-6 has to do with a private contract between a hopelessly poor man and his wealthy neighbor, but Lev. 25 belongs to public law, general measures for which the whole community is responsible. The laws of Exodus and Deuteronomy leave open the possibility that a Hebrew slave, if he wished, might remain a slave after the expiration of the period of six years; in the jubilee, however, such slaves are also set free. Moreover, while the laws of Exodus and Deuteronomy apply only to an Israelite slaveowner, the public law of Leviticus applies to the non-Israelite slaveowner as well. Even if the ordinances of Exod. 21:2-6 were always obeyed—which may be doubted—there was ample scope for a general public law restoring liberty to every Israelite.

In the jubilee all land sold during the preceding years returns to the original owners or to their descendants. If the land were not returned to the newly freed slave, he could find himself compelled to enter bondage again. This law, however, has a wider application: it also benefits those who have sold their land, or part of it, without selling themselves into slavery. The motivation, therefore, is different from that of the gifts to be presented to the freed slave according to Deut. 15:14. The aim of jubilee is the restoration of the position as it was of old: free persons living on free land.

This does not mean that Israelite society during the forty-nine years following a jubilee could follow a policy of *laissez-faire*. The next of kin of the seller had the duty, if he had means enough, to redeem the land; the seller, if he became prosperous again after the sale, had the same duty (Lev. 25:25-27). Though it is not said explicitly, it is evident that in such cases the buyer had to comply. In the same way, an Israelite who had sold himself as a slave to a non-Israelite resident in the country had to be redeemed or could redeem himself (vss. 47-49). The price of redemption, both of slaves and of land, was to be calculated in accordance with the years during which the buyer had the use of the property (vss. 15-17, 27) or of the labor of the slave (vss. 50-52). The general principle is that what is sold is not the land or the person, but their use, as it says in vs. 16: "for it is the number of the crops that he is selling to you." In the case of a person selling himself into slavery, the buyer should regard his bondsman "as a hired servant and as a sojourner" (vs. 40). It would be better still if the wealthy man sustained his poor neighbor by an interest-free loan (vss. 35-38).

Vss. 29-31 define a difference between a house in a walled city, which may be redeemed only in the first year after the sale, and a house in a village, which may be redeemed at any time, and which in any case will return to the original owner in the jubilee. It is not said why such a distinction is made. Probably the house in the village was considered part of the field, while such a relation did not exist between a field and a house situated in a walled city. The houses of Levites, even in a walled city, could be redeemed at any time (vs. 32). If a Levite other than the original owner exercised the right of redemption (so the Hebrew text of vs. 33), he could retain it until the jubilee, when it was returned to the original owner. The fields of the Levites, as designated in the regulations concerning the Levitical cities, could not be sold (vs. 34). These special regulations are to be explained by the position the Levites had in Israelite society.

The jubilee is mentioned incidentally in two other legislative sections. Lev. 27:16-25 deals with an owner's voluntary dedication of a field to the sanctuary; in principle also this is not a transfer of property, but of a fixed number of harvests. If the owner wants to redeem it, one fifth is to be added to its value, computed in accordance with the number of years between the moment of redemption and the next jubilee. If not redeemed, or if sold to somebody else, the field will become the absolute property of the sanctuary in the jubilee. Num. 36:1-12 prescribes that "every daughter who possesses an inheritance in any tribe" (vs. 8; cf. Num. 27:1-8) is not allowed to marry outside her tribe, because her inheritance would be added to the tribe into which she has married, "when the jubilee of the people of Israel comes" (vs. 4). Not only is the ownership of an individual and his inheritors safeguarded, but also the tribal boundaries are fixed once and for all.

3. Theory and practice. The occurrence of the word jubilee in Lev. 27:16-25 and Num. 36:4, sections which do not deal expressly with this institution, is an indication that Lev. 25 is not a utopian speculation by a single late theorist, as has often been maintained by Western commentators during the last two centuries. These scholars, apparently influenced by the Western capitalistic structure of society, had no idea of the practicability of other economic and social structures. Their main argument was that the jubilee is mentioned only in what were considered to be late parts of the Pentateuch. Its occurrence in Lev. 27:18, 21 and Num. 36:4, in contexts which deal with other matters, speaks for the real existence of the institution. The antiquity of the institution is attested by the fact that no convincing etymology of the word יובל was known in postexilic times. Had a late utopian coined the word, its meaning would have been known to his contemporaries. Another argument may be derived from the Nuzi texts in which Gordon has found traces of similar customs. In Nuzi contracts it is often stipulated that a transfer of property, e.g., took place "after *šûdûtu*" or "after *andurâru*." The latter word is etymologically related to *d*ᵉ*rôr*, "liberty" (Lev. 25:10). Since *šûdûtu* occurs far more frequently than *andurâru*, Gordon equates the former with the sabbatical year, the latter with the jubilee. One could also compare the proclamation of *andurâru* by Akkadian kings, often in the year of their ascension to the throne (*see* Kraus). It is feasible that after the introduction of kingship in Israel the proclamation of "liberty" and the carrying out of its implications became the duty of the king.

There are a few indications that the institution was known and sometimes carried out. Whether Isa. 37:30 (cf. II Kings 19:29) alludes to either a sabbatical year or a jubilee is not certain. The manumission of Hebrew slaves in the year 588 (Jer. 34:8-22) could be a belated jubilee, the same jubilee as alluded to in Jer. 31:26, though the reference is to Deut. 15, not to Lev. 25. According to Sarna the year 588 was a sabbatical year, but, as we have seen, the jubilee was a sabbatical year with additional implications.

This does not mean that the jubilee was always observed; there were too many kings who neglected their duties in this respect. According to II Chr. 36:21 (cf. Lev. 26:34, 35) the sabbatical year had often been neglected; the same applies *a fortiori* to the jubilee.

4. Theological relevance. The jubilee restored equality among the citizens and gave new opportunities to those families which had become so impoverished that they had lost their possessions or even their liberty. On the other hand, the rich were reminded that there would come a time when their Israelite slaves would once more be their equals who could bring them to court for maltreatment during the years of bondage. When a king reigned in justice, he was to proclaim the jubilee in due time, delivering the needy (cf. Ps. 72:4, 12-14). Justice, in Israelite law, is primarily the protection of the weak.

The institution was based on definite theological insights. Ownership of land was not absolute; the land was given to the Israelites as a fief. God is the liege lord, and the individual head of a family is his vassal. God wants the country to remain equally divided among all his bondsmen, as was done in the days of Joshua. A vassal should not acquire permanent possession of the fiefs of his fellow vassals. "The land shall not be sold in perpetuity, for the land is mine; for you are strangers and sojourners with me" (Lev. 25:23). God does not allow permanent strife between classes; all the members of his chosen nation are equally dear to him. The dominance of the rich over the poor is a breach of God's covenant with the whole nation.

In the same way, God does not want some of his bondsmen to be the slaves of others. He has delivered all Israelites from the bondage in Egypt and wants them to be free from permanent servitude to men. They are his servants and this service is their freedom. If some of them become the servants of others, God's own rights over them are infringed upon by the slaveowners (Lev. 25:55). Nobody can serve God and at the same time oppress God's servants.

God's gifts to Israel (liberty and a country) have been given conditionally. Israelites cannot do with the land what they wish, naming lands their own (Ps. 49:11); neither should one person's liberty infringe upon that of another. If God's laws concerning land and liberty are not recognized, the nation will forfeit both, as happened in the Exile.

For Christianity, these laws, extended over the whole of mankind, retain their basic value. Within any region and society the need for social reform, taking away the injustice inherent in all human developments, should always be recognized. Such reforms should take place in accordance with God's will and without creating new injustices, in contrast to reform which is brought about through violence. Applied to nations, the principles underlying the jubilee condemn permanent colonialism and unbridled exploitation of the soil to the detriment of its inhabitants. One nation should not be subjugated to another, stronger, nation. The proclamation of a "solemn rest for the land" in the sabbatical year (Lev. 25:5) and therefore in the jubilee as well (Lev. 25:11) also has meaning in the present-day struggle against the destruction of natural resources, for "the earth is the Lord's and the fulness thereof" (Ps. 24:1).

Bibliography. A. Jirku, "Das israelitische Jobeljahr," in *Von Jerusalem nach Ugarit* (1966), pp. 319-29; C. H. Gordon, "Parallèles nouziens aux lois et coutumes de l'Ancien Testament," *RB,* XLIV (1935), 34-41; J. Lewy, "The Biblical Institution of *Derôr* in the Light of Akkadian Documents," *Eretz-Israel,* V (1958), 21-31; R. North, *Sociology of the Biblical Jubilee* (1954); F. R. Kraus, *Ein Edikt des Königs Ammi-ṣaduqa von Babylon* (1958); N. Sarna, "Zedekiah's Emancipation of Slaves and the Sabbatical Year," in *Orient and Occident,* H. Hoffner, ed. (1973), pp. 143-49.

A. VAN SELMS

***JUDAH, FORMATION OF.** The name Judah, linked by popular etymology to the root ידה, "to thank" or to "praise" (Gen. 29:35), perhaps derives from *yhd* (Arab. *whd*), meaning "lowland," referring to coastal plains and wadis in the region. From the terrain the name may have been transferred first to the people and then their eponymous hero in the traditional accounts of the Israelite tribes. Judah's position as Leah's youngest son suggests the late development of the group associated with his name, while Leah's secondary status as a wife (Gen. 29:21-30) may reflect the originally inferior status of the groups descended from her.

The picture of the tribes as self-aware entities moving from the desert to the conquest of Canaan represents an idealized retrojection based upon the political realities of a period no earlier than the united monarchy. The purpose of such retrojection was to provide the various sociopolitical units ("tribes") that had developed in the land with the ideological benefits accruing from a claim to corporate continuity going back to the wilderness and even to patriarchal times. *See* CANAAN, CONQUEST AND SETTLEMENT OF[S]; TRIBE; TRIBE[S]; GENEALOGY §3.

The case of Judah provides an excellent example of the development of an Israelite "tribe." The growth of Judah was characterized demographically by a continuing blend of the original invading nucleus with the indigenous populations of Canaan; geographically, by the gradual expansion of these blended populations over most of the region S of a boundary running roughly from the N end of the Dead Sea W toward the coast at Jamnia; politically, by the gradual creation of numerous independent polities of varying size, cohesiveness, stability, and strength; and ideologically, by the gradual extension to all groups of Yahwistic allegiance and Judahite identity.

The mingling of the invading groups with the local population is exemplified eponymously in the account of Judah's marriage to the daughter of Shua (who lived in the region of Timnah, Adullam, and Achzib), and in his relations with his daughter-in-law, Tamar ("palm tree," perhaps a totem; Gen. 38; *see* TOTEMISM[S]). The Shelanites, who were descendants of the first union, and the Perizzites and Zerahites, descended from the second, represent groups amalgamated with the Judeans, who were already possibly composed of various Hebrew ethnic blends (*see* HABIRU; HABIRU[S]). The process of absorption also included Kenite elements (*see* KENITES), the Kenizzite clans of Othniel and Caleb (possibly of Edomite origin), and the Jerahmeelites living in the Negeb, ethnically akin to the Calebites, since Jerahmeel is said to have been Caleb's brother (I Chr. 2:42). Among the Calebite areas absorbed was Ephrathah, personalized as Caleb's second wife (I Chr. 2:24, 50; 4:4). Ephrathah is identified with Bethlehem, which appears to have been a later and geographically more comprehensive name for the city. In their expansion, the Judahites eventually pushed the Reubenites across the Jordan and confined the Simeonites and the Levites to small areas. They appear also to have participated in the containment of Dan, and at least in a minor way in the events leading to the decimation of Benjamin. In this regard, the abuse of the Judahite concubine (Judg. 19) suggests a successful Benjaminite military violation of the population of Judah rather than an organized and active participation of the latter in the decimation of Benjamin.

The story of the theft by Achan (Josh. 7; Achar in I Chr. 2:7), reflecting the treason of an entire clan, or, at least, one of its major components, suggests intense competition at an early period in the conquest, although the narrative cannot be further elucidated or located historically or geographically.

It was not until the time of David in the tenth century that the various Hebrew elements in Judah were united into a single polity. David's father, it should be recalled, is described as an Ephrathite of Bethlehem (I Sam. 17:12), not a Judahite. The actual creation of the state can probably be connected with David's flight from Saul's court after his failure to effect a palace coup. The new state, called Judah, with its capital at Hebron, provided David with a base to mount opposition to Saul's kingdom and, eventually, to subdue it after Saul's death. The figures for the population of Judah, 74,600 for the first census (Num. 1:27; 2:4) and 76,500 for the second (Num. 26:19-22), belong most appropriately to the period of the united monarchy.

The absence of Judah from the roll of the tribes in the Song of Deborah (Judg. 5) may indicate that the tribe did not exist at the time, while its mention in a pre-Davidic context elsewhere in the Bible suggests in each case a retrojection from post-Davidic times. The town and boundary lists of Judah in Josh. 15, purporting to record an allotment by Moses, are probably post-Davidic, and yield no information about conditions of earlier centuries. Jacob's blessing of the tribes (Gen. 49) is a *benedictio post eventum* which, in Judah's case, reflects attainment of "the scepter" and "the ruler's staff" among the tribes and the realistic hope that this hegemony "shall not depart." Such a position was not attained by Judah until sometime after David's establishment of the united monarchy. The blessing of Moses (Deut. 33) represents a similar retrojection. Though some scholars have dated this composition as early as the eleventh century B.C. on the fragile evidence of style, others, on the same evidence, place it three centuries later. Still others suggest the use of older forms by a later writer to create the impression of antiquity. It has also been suggested that the present composition represents the embellishment of an original eulogy of a limited number of tribes, in which the present section on Judah was not included. In any event, it is impossible to determine whether or not the section on Judah represents a plea for help from a nascent state struggling with Israel, or a powerful state with marauding armies away at war, or a weakened state struggling with its foes.

Bibliography. "The Role of the Shilonite Priesthood in the United Monarchy of Ancient Israel," *HUCA,* XXXVI (1965), 59-98. M. A. COHEN

***JUDAISM, EARLY RABBINIC.** Rabbinic Judaism is that mode of Jewish belief and observance molded by the Palestinian and Babylonian rabbis of the early centuries of the Common Era, and ultimately embodied in compendia of Jewish law and lore, most notably the TALMUD. Many scholars trace the origins of rabbinic Judaism back into the Hellenistic if not Persian periods, or even to the time of the Babylonian exile. Often termed "scribism" (*see* SCRIBE) or "Pharisaism" (*see* PHARISEES [S]) in its formative phases in Palestine, it remained generally inchoate in nature until the late first century A.D., when the destruction of the Jerusalem temple by Rome occasioned a radical reorientation of life in Judea. The priestly hierarchy and SADDUCEES now faded along with the sacrificial cult, but Pharisaism survived and flourished. Its leaders, by now having assumed the title RABBI (in the sense of "teacher"), emerged as the recognized authoritative interpreters of Scriptures.

1. Essential elements
  a. Twofold law
  b. Nature of God
  c. Nature of man
  d. Israel and the nations
  e. The hereafter
  f. Essentials of personal, domestic, communal living
2. Historical origins and development
3. Relation to Christianity
Bibliography

1. Essential elements. While no systematic description of rabbinic Judaism is presented by its literature, the following fundamental elements emerge:

a. Twofold law. The hallmark of early rabbinic Judaism was its view that God at Mount Sinai had imparted to Moses a twofold revelation: The written Law (תורה שבכתב, i.e., the Pentateuch; *see* TORAH[S]), declaring God's will for the world, also detailed the duties and obligations devolving specifically upon the Israelite people as a "holy nation"; by virtue of its written form, this revelation was readily accessible to all. Also imparted, but never promulgated, was an unwritten Law (תורה שבעל פה), preserved through oral tradition by Moses and Joshua, and transmitted by the prophets to especially eminent and authoritative personages of later times. The unwritten Law could be recovered through the application to the written text of specific hermeneutic or exegetical principles (*see* HERMENEUTICS[S]; INTERPRETATION, HISTORY OF, [S] §D), the development and unique mastery of which enabled the rabbis to establish themselves as the authoritative interpreters of God's revelation.

Through these principles, the rabbis derived scriptural support not only for laws, regulations, and institutions already operative in society, but for new enactments required by changing conditions of their own day. Biblical laws no longer susceptible of observance or possessing significance were often reinterpreted exegetically so as to assume new relevance; others were suspended altogether in the belief that they would someday reacquire importance. The rabbis thus attempted to uphold the written Law as eternally valid and divinely sanctioned, and yet, through the skillful application of the oral tradition, to harmonize the Scriptures with the ever-changing realities of life (*see* LAW IN FIRST-CENTURY JUDAISM).

b. Nature of God. The existence of but one God, eternal, indivisible, incorporeal, omnipresent, omnipotent, and omniscient, who created the universe, whose creative powers continue to function in the processes of nature, and whose presence pervades human affairs, was accepted axiomatically. The promulgation and preservation of this belief, together with a relentless campaign against polytheism and idolatry, were conceived of as the purpose of the Jewish people. Twice daily the Jew affirmed his belief in monotheism (Deut. 6:4 ff.; cf. Mark 12:28 ff.) and his willing submission to divine injunctions (*see* SHEMA, THE). He conceived of God as a loving father, supramundane yet not extramundane, ever-near to mortal man in his need; no intermediary was needed or tolerated between man and God.

c. Nature of man. The human race, in both its physical and spiritual dimensions, was considered God's pre-eminent creation, the singular blend of the earthly and the divine. There was no inherent impurity in the flesh as opposed to the spirit (*see* JUDAISM, HELLENISTIC[S] §§3, 6); the body, in its marvelous construction, was perceived as itself a masterpiece. While it might induce one toward sensual desires, the body by no means compelled one to sinfulness. Rather the human soul, the spiritual force within, was endowed with free will, enabling each one to choose the good and reject the evil. Sin was thus an erring from the path of virtue, and not the depraved state of mankind.

Active in every human being were two urges—one to goodness (יצר הטוב), the other to evil (יצר הרע); a person's free will determined which was to have dominance. Nor was the evil impulse without positive purpose, for it allowed people to have a moral sense, thus elevating them above the animals; without the possibility of consciously doing what was evil, righteous deeds ceased to be righteous in any meaningful sense.

Those who attempted to live a righteous life received assistance of two kinds. First, the commandments (מצות; singular מצוה), 613 in all, encompassed within the twofold law, guided them along the paths of virtue. God also provided the option of sincere repentance, a procedure by which persons could neutralize their wrongdoings. God not only anxiously awaited their repentance but also facilitated it; for God's attribute of compassion and pardon (מדת הרחמים) supplanted his disposition toward stern justice and punishment (מדת הדין). The decision to repent nevertheless resided with human beings: they could sin; they could atone; then God could forgive.

At the same time, the attribute of justice demanded that the righteous be rewarded and the unrepentant wicked punished, if not in this life then in the life to come. While cognizant that motives of reward and punishment were not the loftiest incentives toward ethical conduct, the rabbis hoped that righteous behavior so induced would ultimately condition people to righteousness for its own sake.

d. Israel and the nations. The biblical theme of intimate and unique interrelationship between God and the Israelite people (*see* COVENANT §C2, 3; ELECTION §4) was richly amplified by the rabbis. Small in numbers, weak in possessions, and repeatedly the victims of exile and persecution, the Jewish people had but one treasure: they had been made the guardians of the twofold law bequeathed in the wilderness. No favoritism need be imputed to God, for all other nations had long before refused acceptance of God's guidance (*see,* e.g., *Mek. Baḥodesh,* Yitro, §5; *Sifre Deut.,* Berakah, §343, 142b; and, later, *Exod.R.,* Yitro, xxvii, 9; *Pes. K.* 199b fin–200a; *Tanh.B.,* Yitro, 38b).

Israel, however, by accepting the Law, assumed favored status before God, henceforth being considered the chosen depository and guardian of his universal truths. To keep these truths forever intact, Israel was obliged to accept laws and rites specifically national in character—ritual and cultic laws, hygienic and dietary practices, and calendrical observances which had for their major object the shielding of the Jewish people from all heathen inducements to idolatry and impurity; only so detached could Israel maintain itself as "a kingdom of priests and a holy nation" (Exod. 19:6).

Though receipt of the Torah sealed the covenant between God and Israel, yet the Torah was not Israel's exclusive possession. For through Israel the Torah was to be promulgated to all nations. The door was thus open to any Gentile seeking entry to the Hebrew people out of pure motives. Gentiles not disposed to enter the fold could yet merit divine approval by abiding by the sevenfold Noachian code (Tosef. 'A.Z. VIII.4; Sanh. 56a: practicing social justice; refraining from blasphemy, idolatry, incest, bloodshed, robbery, eating flesh torn from a living animal; cf. Gen. 9:3-6). Ultimately, all nations would accept the Torah's teachings, and God's kingdom would be recognized as established on earth, the righteous of all peoples inheriting the bliss of the hereafter.

e. The hereafter. It is not possible to systematize rabbinic notions of the hereafter; both in conception and terminology, there is a lack of clarity and consistency. Generally speaking, an imperfect conflation or overlapping of two schemes emerges—one supernatural and cosmic in dimension, the other political and national. Presupposed in the one was a separation, at death, of the souls of the righteous from those of the wicked, the former going to a blessed abode, the latter to Gehinnom (*see* GEHENNA). At the appointed time, the bodies of the dead would be restored and, upon rising from their tombs, become rejoined to their respective souls, the whole person now being summoned to a last judgment before God, the verdict determined in accordance with the individual's conduct in the former life.

The completion of this pattern of events was contingent upon an earlier, interim age of national and international crisis and resolution thereof. During this period, accordingly, the final destiny of Israel and the nations would be determined. While externally Israel was to recover independence and power from the rule of foreign oppressors, internally the people were to undergo religious and moral regeneration. A golden age was to ensue, patterned not upon the detested Hasmonean or Herodian dynasties but rather on the glorious Davidic monarchy of old, represented by the person of the Messiah of the Davidic line, who would preside over the whole world in an era of universal peace and prosperity, rectitude and pious fidelity to God and his Law. Jews in other countries would be miraculously gathered to the Holy Land to partake of the bliss of the messianic age.

While resisting precise delineation, the term "KINGDOM OF GOD" (מלכות שמים; literally, "Kingdom of Heaven") in rabbinic literature often seems to connote universal recognition of God's kingship. While God was already—indeed had always been—king over all the earth, Israel alone of all the nations had acknowledged his sovereignty; but ultimately all nations would acknowledge it, and the universal reign of God would find realization in the relations of all men to God and their fellows. The messianism of rabbinic Judaism, with the exception of the Bar Kochba period (*see* BAR KOCHBA [S]), thus anticipated fulfillment only in the remote future, in contrast to certain expressions of imminent messianism encountered in, e.g., the Pseudep. and NT. Nor do the rabbinic notions so extensively partake of apocalyptic imagery (*see* APOCALYPTICISM[S]; ESCHATOLOGY articles). In particular, the Messiah generally emerges not as antemundane or supernatural but rather as an earthly personage.

f. The essentials of personal, domestic, and communal living. The wholesome life, according to rabbinic Judaism, could be achieved not only through faithful adherence to the Torah's injunctions but also through pious imitation of God himself. While God had revealed the Torah, the Torah also revealed God as the exemplar of holiness, righteousness, compassion, and loving-kindness. Imitation of God was possible since every person was created in his image. When people fashioned their lives after the divine model, they experienced a feeling of complete kinship with the Creator. Thus the adage, "You shall be holy; for I the Lord your God am holy" (Lev. 19:2), emerges as the heart of the Law. Underpinning this concern with holiness were the many precepts of rabbinic law—its moral directives, its hygienic, dietary, and marriage laws, its calendrical observances and the like.

The rabbis were mindful that the stability of a society and the piety of life within it depended ultimately on the integrity and holiness of the domestic family unit. They thus preferred wedded life as the natural state; celibacy was disapproved of. A name of the marriage relation was קדושין ("holiness" or "consecration"), reflecting the chastity and purity which the rabbis viewed as inhering in the union of man and woman—the precise figure which God himself had chosen to illustrate his bond to Israel (*see* MARRIAGE §§3, 4). This union was to be essentially spiritual; at the same time, since the flesh was also God's creation, sexual union was itself deemed proper and sacred.

The legal status of WOMAN under rabbinic law represents a noticeable advance over that in contemporary civilizations and in the biblical legislation. No longer was the woman sold from father to husband, transferred from one subjection to another (*see* MARRIAGE; WOMAN IN THE ANE[S]; WOMAN IN THE OT[S]); marriage was a voluntary union dependent on the woman's consent. The rabbis developed new legal institutions to aid and protect wives and daughters, in particular the כתובה, a document given to the bride by the groom at the marriage ceremony, affording wife and children financial protection in various contingencies. With respect also to DIVORCE, the husband's right to dismiss his wife at pleasure was progressively limited and restricted by the rabbis.

A major purpose of marriage was the rearing of children, who would in turn transmit the religious heritage unimpaired to later generations. A system of universal education was adopted toward this end. Adults meanwhile were to assemble on the sabbath day in special houses (*see* SYNAGOGUE §§2, 6) where sections of the Torah were read and interpreted by exegetes, followed by the *haftarah,* a reading from the Prophets.

The rabbis emphasized that people were intended to live not in isolation but as members of society, and that, consequently, many duties devolved upon them with respect to one another. The social order depended in particular on the maintenance of justice, truth, and peace.

The administrators of justice bore a heavy responsibility; only their integrity guaranteed honest enforcement of the duties and rights safeguarding society's classes and individuals. Public justice was administered impartially, and the accused was presumed innocent until proven guilty, elaborate precautions being taken to prevent wrongful conviction.

Any deviation from the truth was vigorously censured in rabbinic literature. Every man was to be inwardly exactly what he appeared outwardly. Integrity in business dealings was particularly emphasized. The rabbis denounced every mode of deception and fraudulent dealing, every gain secured by gambling or economic speculation, every breach of promise, every act of calumny.

Only on a foundation of peace could a community enjoy stability and well-being. The Hebrew שלום meant not simply "peace" but fulfillment of every kind: contentment and health, security and prosperity. Only these were productive of that harmony essential to the welfare of all components of society. The principle "You shall love your neighbor as yourself" (Lev. 19:18; cf. Mark 12:28-31) was the only true standard of human relationship. Hence, pre-eminence was given to גמילות חסדים ("deeds of loving-kindness"): the alleviation of the burdens of the afflicted and the extension to all one's fellows of gestures of friendship and heartfelt concern.

2. Historical origins and development. Rabbinic literature manifests little concern with historical data and offers no systematic presentation of rabbinic Judaism's origins and growth. Even when historical episodes are narrated, testimony may be incomplete, inaccurate, or overlaid by legend. Josephus' treatment of the Persian, Hellenistic, and Roman periods generally confines itself to *political* developments through the fall of the temple; he is thus of somewhat limited assistance in reconstructing the history and institutions of rabbinic Judaism, and problems attend even to his descriptions of the Pharisees. While the NT—especially the gospels—mentions scribes and Pharisees frequently, such testimony may be utilized only with the greatest caution (*see* §3 *below*). Because the evidence is so incomplete, classical reconstructions of the history of early rabbinic Judaism must be viewed with great reserve; these usually present the following general picture:

Jews in Babylonia, during and after the Exile, being without a temple, developed a new institution, the synagogue, where they gathered to hear scripture read and expounded. Their interest in the study of these writings thus awakened, a demand arose for men equipped with the learning to qualify them to act as teachers. These instructors became known as סופרים (scribes), and foremost among them, in the middle of the fifth century B.C., was EZRA, "a scribe skilled in the law of Moses" (Ezra 7:6).

Ezra traveled to Jerusalem during the reign of Artaxerxes I (465-424 B.C.) with a royal warrant to reform religious conditions. He instituted public reading of the Torah on the sabbath, festivals, and all public occasions, accompanied by learned interpretation, the latter required so as to bring the Torah into harmony with changing societal conditions. Ezra's system of interpretation (later termed Midrash) would thus render him the founder of scriptural exegesis.

Ezra commissioned a special synod of teachers, so tradition relates, called the Great Assembly (כנסת הגדולה; *see* SYNAGOGUE, THE GREAT[S]) to receive the corpus of doctrine preserved till their day and to adapt and develop it so as to suit the new conditions of their age. This Great Assembly ceased to exist sometime in the third or second century B.C. (AB. 1:1-2) and was followed by another organization, called the SANHEDRIN (*see also* SANHEDRIN[S]), which took charge of the affairs of the community in Judea. The sanhedrin was headed by a series of five זוגות ("pairs [of sages]"), ending, with Hillel and Shammai, about A.D. 10; one of each pair was נשיא ("Prince," i.e., president), and the other was אב בית דין ("Father of the Court of Law," i.e., vice-president).

HILLEL, a Babylonian by birth, reputedly descended from the Davidic dynasty, personified the Jewish ideal of peace and loving-kindness; he epitomized the ethics of Judaism in one famous maxim: "Do not unto others that which is hateful to thee" (Shab. 30b-31a; *see also* GOLDEN RULE, THE; GOLDEN RULE, THE[S]). It was Hillel who gave a heightened impetus to exegetical activity by introducing implementation of seven hermeneutic rules by which HALACHAH was to be derived. Shammai, according to rabbinic depiction, was a sterner man and more conservative in nature, as reflected in his interpretations of the Law.

Down to the destruction of Jerusalem in A.D. 70, the halachah proliferated and the successors of Hillel and Shammai, called respectively בית הלל (House of Hillel) and בית שמאי (House of Shammai), struggled to impose their particular legal interpretations. Ultimately, the Hillelites prevailed because, we are told, their teachings were more adaptable to life and grounded in sounder logic.

The youngest of Hillel's disciples was said to be Johanan ben Zakkai. Convinced of the futility of the Jews' rebellion against Rome, which began in A.D. 66, he counseled surrender but went unheeded; thereupon he adroitly secured from the Roman general VESPASIAN permission to establish a school at Jamnia (or Jabneh; *see* JABNEEL) which he later fashioned into an academic sanhedrin, thus guaranteeing Judaism's survival (*see esp.* Git. 56ab and ARN 4). This court was modeled after and considered a continuation of the Jerusalem sanhedrin which had earlier met within the temple precincts.

Following the period of Johanan's leadership, the office of *nāśî'* was held by a succession of patriarchs of the family of Hillel; the *nāśî'* became considered the nation's accredited representative to Rome, and his jurisdiction was recognized by Jews throughout the DISPERSION (*see also* JUDAISM, HELLENISTIC[S] §1*b*). He traveled extensively outside the Holy Land, often with certain other eminent scholars; visits to Rome most likely involved a presentation of Jewish interests to imperial authorities.

Under strong leadership, the sanhedrin at Jamnia exercised a powerful centralizing influence, especially in its regulation of the calendar for the whole Dispersion as well as Palestine. Liturgy became defined and canonized by the leaders, and the contents of the final section of Hebrew Scriptures were determined. Above all, efforts began to be made to control and systematize the ever-proliferating volume of halachic material. *See also* TALMUD.

At the same time, patterns of worship and assembly became structured around the decentralized synagogue, which replaced the temple and its sacrificial cultus. Liturgical features rooted to the temple were detached where possible and adapted to synagogue observance—such as the blowing of the shophar (*see* MUSICAL INSTRUMENTS §B2*e*) on New Year's day (*see* NEW YEAR[S] §3) and marching with palm branches and willows at Tabernacles (*see* BOOTHS, FEAST OF). Divine forgiveness was now to be secured through prayerful repentance and good deeds rather than through animal sacrifices.

Hadrian's decision to erect on the remains of the temple a new structure to Capitoline Jupiter provoked a revolt by the Jews in A.D. 132 under Simeon BAR KOCHBA, acclaimed by the eminent Rabbi Akiba as Messiah. Hadrian reacted by suppressing the sanhedrin and forbidding on pain of death the study and practice of Torah. Akiba, publicly defying the prohibition, was executed.

Antoninus Pius, succeeding Hadrian in 138, revoked a number of prohibitions, thus allowing rabbinic activity again to spring to life. A new academic sanhedrin was established in Galilee, which had been spared much of the ravages of the Hadrianic wars. Simeon ben Gamaliel II was recognized as supreme head of the Jews; his son, succeeding him, was Judah Hanasi ("the Prince"; died 217), often called simply "Rabbi" (i.e., the teacher, par excellence).

The proliferation of halachic material during the period from Hillel onward prompted eminent scholars to compile private collections. Compendia produced by the schools of Akiba and Ishmael ben Elisha evolved into nuclei of later works of halachic midrash (*see* MIDRASH; MIDRASH[S]). Akiba himself was the first to systematize on a wide scale the contents of the earlier traditional Law according to subject matter with divisions and subdivisions. To this MISHNA collection, Akiba's disciples attached comments by their master himself and by his contemporaries—and thus prepared halachic collections for their individual use. As the number of these private collections multiplied, variants and divergences of transmission began to occasion considerable confusion. This prompted Judah Hanasi and his colleagues to collate the traditions of the different academies and to produce the authoritative edition of the Mishna. This work served both as a code and a digest of the oral Law, indicating the accepted decisions while preserving worthy divergences of opinion. *See* TALMUD §§3, 4.

The classical understanding of early rabbinic history as outlined in the preceding paragraphs takes its cue mainly from the reconstruction of same attempted by Sherira, Gaon of Pumbedita in the tenth century A.D. In response to a query concerning the origins of the Mishna, Sherira fashioned a historical outline by recourse to narrative episodes and sayings in the Mishna itself, supplemented by like material in other rabbinic works, all of which he arranged in a simple chronological order. Sherira stressed that the laws ultimately incorporated into the Mishna by Judah Hanasi had their origins in antiquity, but through memorization had been accurately transmitted in oral form throughout an uninterrupted chain of tradition, from Sinai, through the men of the Great Assembly, to later times, each master teaching his disciples the exact words of his own instructor before him. Initially, these laws had been fully understood so that disputes over them never arose; later, however, sages began to vary their language when teaching the laws; poor discipleship and the turbulence produced by war contributed further to an unsettled state. Accordingly, disputes began to arise over the provisions of the laws and the reasons behind them. Akiba and his disciples, Meir in particular, played an instrumental role in preserving the accurate halachah, setting the stage for Judah Hanasi to produce his authoritative corpus.

Sherira's reconstruction maintains influence disproportionate to its credibility. Since the early nineteenth century, scholars have learned to take a skeptical view of historical and biographical narrative imbedded in biblical literature. Such reserve should be applied to the study of rabbinic traditions as well.

It should be realized, e.g., that to the ancient mind religious credentials, to be authentic, required a grounding in antiquity. The rabbis' ascription of halachoth to Ezra and the Great Assembly—let alone to Moses himself—thus emerges as suspect, as do the early origins assigned the synagogue or the sanhedrin or the office of *nāśî'*. Some have thus questioned whether the Great Assembly ever existed, or, if so, whether it, not to mention Ezra himself, actually bore any connection with incipient rabbinic Judaism. Sherira himself, it must be noted, was an ardent opponent of Karaism—a movement denying the authenticity of rabbinic Judaism—and he was thus naturally disposed to demonstrate how the oral Law went back, uninterrupted, through the men of the Great Assembly to Sinai. He thus gravitated toward those rabbinic traditions which rooted rabbinic institutions in the remote past and accepted these traditions at face value. A more convincing speculation would hold, by contrast, that the pioneers of rabbinic Judaism emerged not in the Babylonian or Persian periods but much later—most likely in the second century B.C.—surfacing in some fashion or another on the successful tide of the Hasmonean revolt.

There is, moreover, the problem of bias. While the alleged Pharisaic dominance over the Sadducees before A.D. 70 may be factual, the many traditions to this effect were recorded, preserved, and ultimately included in rabbinic literature by sages Pharisaic in sympathy, and at a time when the Sadducees had faded from the scene. The pro-Hillelite slant of rabbinic literature may have similarly colored traditions about Shammai and his followers, while embellishing those about Hillel and Beth Hillel. All these considerations should serve to focus scholars' attention on developments after A.D. 70, the formative period of Jamnia and following, when the process of collecting and reworking traditions concerning earlier Pharisaism and developing halachah was undertaken on a wide scale. Only through the application of form and redaction critical perspectives to this material can a more viable picture of the history of early rabbinic Judaism emerge. But the process is fraught with problems, especially in that the material itself resists such analysis. It is particularly taxing to determine how much the image of pre-70 Judaism, its teachings and institutions—particularly the sanhedrin and its make-up and procedures—may be only a retrojection of the post-70 period, or, in some respects, purely an idealization of beliefs and practices never actively implemented (*see* SANHEDRIN).

3. Relation to Christianity. For many years, the image Christian scholars accepted of rabbinic Judaism was determined largely by NT testimony. They noted Jesus' frequent denunciation of the scribes and Pharisees for zealousness over the letter of the Law and asserted that Jesus came to restore the heart to such barren religion. Paul's denigration of Pharisaic life under the Law was presumed an echo of Jesus' own sentiments. Excerpts from rabbinic literature in translation served to confirm for many the alleged absurdities of the rabbinic preoccupation with the Law, invidious comparisons being drawn between rabbinic literature and Christianity's authoritative writings, with an eye toward establishing the latter's superiority (*see,* e.g., PHARISEES, an article severely criticized, in print, by Jewish scholarship).

Several twentieth-century Christian scholars, however, pre-eminently Moore and Herford (*see bibliog.*), themselves proficient in rabbinic texts in the original, drew attention to whole strata of rabbinic literature treating purely of moral and spiritual teachings in terms as lofty as those advanced by Jesus himself and suggested that even legalisms of the Talmud reflected high spirituality. Special focus was assigned to ethical maxims which documented beyond refutation that many of Jesus' teachings were similar if not identical to those of the rabbis. In particular, many parables of Jesus, especially when pared down from their extended allegorical form, were seen virtually to duplicate rabbinic parables.

These observations all served to establish Jesus' proximity to rabbinic Judaism and thus also to temper at least somewhat the one-sided portrayal of rabbinic authorities in the gospels. At the same time, certain form critics have suggested that many of the gospel controversies between Jesus and the rabbinic leaders—scribes and Pharisees—may actually reflect confrontations of the later church with Jewish authorities, rather than Jesus' own relations with them; some scholars have ventured that the Pauline denigration of the Law was attributed, in the gospels, to Jesus instead, and that Jesus himself had actually valued the Torah's teachings and significance. Alongside these skeptical views, the more conservative outlook has persisted.

Careful study reveals that Matthean and Lukan portrayals of scribes and Pharisees are explicable as merely extensions of the Markan usage and that a number of Markan passages that mention scribes and Pharisees are themselves secondary to the pericopes in which they are imbedded, at least some of these (particularly the appearance of "scribes" in 2:16 and 7:1, 5) inserted in the interest of a literary accommodation of Mark's sources to one another. The artificial distinction of scribes from Pharisees in Mark (and hence the Synoptic gospels as a whole) also essentially derives from Mark's dependence on sources for this material, two of these (one the pre-Markan passion narrative) using only "scribes" as the term for rabbinic leaders, and the third only "Pharisees"; Mark, unfamiliar with who scribes were, failed to detect the synonymity of the usage and presents us with two groups rather than one. The appearances of the scribes and Pharisees in the Synoptic gospels, not even to mention John, are thus often the result of improvisation, artificial construction, and literary artistry by writers themselves largely unfamiliar with Jewish leaders in Jesus' own day. Hence, we cannot determine whether traditions of controversy between Jesus and rabbinic authorities are historically reliable, or whether, instead, pericopes regarding the controversies reflect in good measure tensions between Christians and Pharisees in the apostolic period, retrojected by the tradition to the time of Jesus' ministry. The latter view has much to commend it; Jesus' foremost enemies would most likely have been within the priestly establishment, and the grounds of such confrontation political. Controversy over the validity of the law of Moses as interpreted by rabbinic spokesmen reflects a later context.

Attention to rabbinic literature has also prompted reconsideration of the gospel accounts of Jesus' trial (*see* TRIAL OF JESUS[S]). Rabbinic literature is sharply at variance with gospel testimony in describing the nature of the sanhedrin and the procedures it followed in capital cases. Some scholars, fully accepting the rabbinic portrayal, have questioned whether the gospels' trial narratives can be adjudged reliable. While doubts must be entertained on this score, the discrepancies between the sources can be better resolved by viewing the sanhedrin mentioned in the gospels as a (perhaps *ad hoc*) political institution serving the interests of the procurator and headed by his appointee, the high priest (*see* Jos. Antiq. XVIII. ii.2; iv.3), and not at all related to the religious בית דין portrayed in rabbinic literature, whose procedures may themselves be something of an idealization. *See* SANHEDRIN; SANHEDRIN[S].

See also ART, EARLY JEWISH[S]; HAGGADAH.

Bibliography. On the nature of rabbinic Judaism: S. Schechter, *Some Aspects of Rabbinic Theology* (1909); G. F. Moore, *Judaism in the First Centuries of the Christian Era,* 3 vols. (1927-30); A. Marmorstein, *The Old Rabbinic Doctrine of God,* 2 vols. (1927, 1937), and *Studies in Jewish Theology* (1950); C. G. Montefiore and H. Loewe, *A Rabbinic Anthology* (1938); A. Cohen, *Everyman's Talmud* (1949); G. Horowitz, *The Spirit of Jewish Law* (1963).

Historical studies: G. F. Moore, "The Rise of Normative Judaism," *HTR,* XVII (1924), 307-73; R. T. Herford, *The Pharisees* (1924); J. Z. Lauterbach, *Rabbinic Essays* (1951); R. A. Marcus, "The Pharisees in the Light of Modern Scholarship," *JR,* XXXII (1952), 153-64; H. Mantel, *Studies in the History of the Sanhedrin* (1961); L. Finkelstein, *The Pharisees,* 2 vols. (3rd ed., 1962); E. Rivkin, "Defining the Pharisees: the Tannaitic Sources," *HUCA,* XL-XLI (1969-70); A. Guttmann, *Rabbinic Judaism in the Making* (1970); J. Neusner, *The Rabbinic Traditions about the Pharisees before 70* (1971).

In relation to Christianity and Christian scholarship: G. F. Moore, "Christian Writers on Judaism," *HTR,* XIV (1921), 197-254; I. Abrahams, *Studies in Pharisaism and the Gospels,* Ser. I-II (1917-24; 1967 ed. includes intro. by M. S. Enslin); D. W. Riddle, *Jesus and the Pharisees* (1928); C. G. Montefiore, *Rabbinic Literature and Gospel Teachings* (1930; 1970 ed. includes intro. by E. Mihaly); W. O. E. Oesterley, H. Loewe, and E. I. J. Rosenthal, eds., *Judaism and Christianity,* 3 vols. (1937-38; 1969 ed. includes intro. by E. Rivkin); S. Sandmel,

We Jews and Jesus (1965), ch. 4, and "Understanding and Misunderstanding: Prepossession versus Malice," and "Parallelomania," *Two Living Traditions: Essays on Religion and the Bible* (1972), pp. 108-19, 291-304.

M. J. COOK

***JUDAISM, HELLENISTIC.** In its general sense, the experience of the Jewish people dispersed in communities throughout the Greco-Roman world during the period beginning with Alexander the Great (reigned 336-323 B.C.) and extending several centuries into the Common Era; in a more restricted sense, the process by which Jews in these communities accepted and assimilated Hellenistic language, manners, and culture, thus fusing Hellenism with characteristic modes of Jewish thought and observance. While Hellenism made substantial inroads also into Palestine itself, under the Seleucids in particular, its penetration and influence were in some measure checked by the success of the Hasmonean revolt in the mid-second century B.C. (*see* MACCABEES, BOOKS OF) and the subsequent development of rabbinic Judaism. *See* JUDAISM, EARLY RABBINIC[S].

1. The Diaspora
   a. Development in Greco-Roman period
   b. Ties to Palestine
2. Nature of Jewish communities
   a. Organization
   b. Status
3. Essentials of religious outlook
4. Relations with Gentiles
5. Jewish-Hellenistic literature
6. In relation to Judaism in Palestine

Bibliography

1. The Diaspora. ***a. Development in Greco Roman period.*** The term διασπορά denotes the process by which Jews gradually came to be distributed in lands outside Palestine, primarily as a consequence of war and foreign domination (*see* DISPERSION). In the Hellenistic period, Greek rulers intermixed populations as a means of consolidating (cf. Jos. Antiq. XII.iii.4) and populating their territories. Over succeeding centuries, myriads of prisoners of war were transported from Palestine to the West—paticularly after Jewish insurrections under VESPASIAN, TRAJAN, and HADRIAN. Frequently, they were sold as slaves on the world market (cf. Jos. War VI.viii.2; ix.3); but where settled together in sufficient numbers, they survived to form nuclei of later Jewish communities, especially in Italy, Spain, and Gaul (*see* Philo, *On the Embassy to Gaius* XXIII).

Meanwhile, developing commercial opportunities encouraged formation of Jewish colonies outside Palestine. Conquests by ALEXANDER widened channels of commerce, by sea routes in particular, thus rendering attractive the prospect of dwelling along Mediterranean coasts. The achievements of Greco-Roman art and civilization, promoting cultural interests, also contributed to emigration from Palestine to Diaspora lands, while enticing those visiting there to remain.

Once established, the Jewish presence in the Diaspora ultimately assumed enormous dimensions both in terms of geographic expanse and population; a high rate of natural reproduction, plus effective proselytism, probably rendered Jewish population in the first-century Diaspora considerably in excess of that in the mother country.

b. Ties to Palestine. Strong ties nevertheless persisted between these outside communities and Jerusalem. Male Jews twenty years and older annually contributed a half-shekel (Exod. 30:11-16; cf. Matt. 17:24-27; Mishna Sheḳalim, entire) or two Greek drachmas for maintenance of the Jerusalem temple's sacrificial cult (Philo, *On the Embassy to Gaius* XXIII; *On Monarchy* 2.3; Jos. Antiq. XIV.vii.2; XVIII.ix.1); even Egyptian Jews preferred the Jerusalem cult to the temple of ONIAS at Leontopolis (Jos. Antiq. XII.ix.7; XIII.iii.1-3, x.4; XX.x.1; Jos. War I.i.1; VII.x.2-4; cf. Sib. Or. V, 501). Moreover, on the three pilgrimage festivals, huge crowds flocked to Jerusalem (*see* Jos. War VI.ix.3; *On Monarchy* 2.1). Even after the temple's destruction, the patriarchate in Palestine, hereditary among Hillel's descendants (*see* JUDAISM, EARLY RABBINIC[S] §2), served as a center of religious solidarity for Jews the world over. The temple tax, however, was now channeled by imperial authority for support of the temple of Jupiter Capitolinus (Jos. War VII.vi.6; Dio Cassius 66.7).

2. Nature of Jewish communities. ***a. Organization.*** Wherever Diaspora Jews lived together in sufficient numbers, they organized themselves into societies protective of their interests and ancestral religious customs. The precise mode of organization in the Greco-Roman world was not, however, everywhere identical. At Alexandria, they formed a single great semiautonomous political corporation, termed a πολίτευμα, seemingly a small state within the state, with administrative, financial, and judicial functions (Ep. Aris. §310). In Rome, by contrast, Jews were more modestly organized into private societies safeguarding their religious interests, small associations of worshipers, including proselytes. These were each designated by the term συναγωγή, and served political as well as religious functions. The term πολίτευμα is found in the case of Alexandria, and Berenice in Cyrenaica; the synagogue mode of organization seems characteristic of most other Jewish communities. Almost everywhere we find the managing committee of the community bearing the title ἄρχοντες. The appearance of the terms γερουσιάρχης or γερουσιάρχων on Italian tomb inscriptions implies the existence also of a γερουσία ("assembly of elders") in many communities in Italy and most probably elsewhere as well. The presence of these terms indicates that organization of Jews in these Diaspora communities largely modeled itself on the communal constitution of the Greek cities.

b. Status. Almost everywhere in the Dispersion, the Jews were extended toleration by Greek and Roman authorities. Under the Ptolemies and the Seleucids, they enjoyed religious freedom and certain political privileges; the repressive policies of ANTIOCHUS IV Epiphanes accordingly emerge as exceptional. Roman legislation, also, permitted the Jews free exercise of their religion and other privileges, and forfended against attempts at their suppression (Jos. Antiq. XIV.viii.5, x, xii.3-6; XVI.vi.2-7); Judaism enjoyed legal status as a *religio licita* throughout the Roman Empire (Tert. Apol. 21; cf. *On the Embassy to Gaius* XXIII).

The Jews were specially excused from participation in the cult of the emperor, an exemption seriously menaced only under Caligula (Jos. Antiq. XIX.v.2-3). Other exceptional privileges included permission to administer their own funds (including the collection and export of dues to the Jerusalem temple; cf. *On the Embassy to Gaius* XXIII, XL; Jos. Antiq. XVI.vi.2-7), and to settle their own legal affairs in civil suits involving one Jew against another; even Jews possessing Roman citizenship preferred submission of such disputes to their own tribunal (cf. Jos. Antiq. XIV.x.17). Certain correctional authority may also have been conceded Jewish communal leaders (e.g., II Cor. 11:24; cf. Acts 18:12-16).

Deference to Jewish sabbath observance occasioned a wide range of other privileges including exemption from military service (Jos. Antiq. XIII.viii.4; XIV.x.11-14, 16, 18-19) and from court appearances on the sabbath (Jos. Antiq. XVI.vi.2, 4); distributions of money or grain falling on the sabbath day were deferred, in the case of Jewish recipients, till the morrow (*On the Embassy to Gaius* XXIII). Allotments of pagan oil, use of which was forbidden Jews by their law, were rendered to Jews in monetary equivalent (Jos. Antiq. XII.iii.1).

It remains unclear, however, whether the Jews possessed the civic right in the Greek cities—i.e., municipal rights of citizens to participate in the city's public life, election of magistrates, determination of municipal affairs, and the like. The affirmative view relies primarily on the testimony of Josephus, who repeatedly asserts that Jews and Greeks possessed equal rights (ἰσοτιμία, ἰσονομία, ἰσοπολιτεία): Alexander rewarded Jews for assistance in conquering Egypt, placing them on equal footing with the Macedonians when he founded Alexandria (Jos. Apion ii.4; cf. Jos. Antiq. XIX.v.2) and allowing them to refer to themselves as Macedonians (Jos. War II.xviii.7; *see* ALEXANDER)—while the Egyptian masses were consigned to an inferior status. These equal political rights were confirmed to them by Caesar (here, most likely Augustus) who set up a brass pillar in Alexandria declaring the Jews Alexandrian citizens (Jos. Antiq. XIV.x.1; Jos. Apion ii.4). A similar situation prevailed with regard to Antioch and certain other cities (Jos. War VII.iii.3, v.2; Jos. Antiq. XII.iii.1; cf. XVI.vi.1; Jos. Apion ii.4).

An opposing viewpoint holds that, since the acquisition of citizenship carried with it special status and advantages, including exemption from certain taxes, traditions naturally arose in Jewish circles alleging that Jews had received equivalent rights. Such allegations become especially misleading in the hands of so apologetic a writer as Josephus, who seeks to persuade Gentiles that their own forebears had held the Jews in highest affection and esteem. Since Josephus generally copied or interpreted his sources uncritically, we cannot assess the extent to which his testimony here is reliable. Moreover, Josephus was expert in neither Greek law nor correct usage of Greek legal terms; Philo himself employed such terms loosely, often straying from their precise juridical significance. While Jews did enjoy significant privileges in deference to their ancestral religious customs, Josephus has perhaps misconstrued these rights as the actual rights of citizenship. It is difficult to conceive of Greek cities bestowing citizen rights on people who refused to acknowledge the city's official cult; most likely, Jews were eligible to become full citizens only if, renouncing their ancestral religion, they worshiped the gods of the πόλις.

3. Essentials of religious outlook. The Hellenistic world was hospitable to a diversity of religious expression; from the Greek standpoint, Judaism was just another cult which had been transplanted, accepted, and absorbed into the Hellenistic milieu. The essentials of Judaism as perceived among Hellenistic Jewish writers were obedience to the law of Moses (*see*, e.g., IV Macc. 5:19-26; 9:2; Jos. Apion ii.39; Philo, *Life of Moses* 2.3, 5; III Macc. 2:31-33; Sib. Or. III, 573-85, 762-71) and faithful adherence to their ancestral customs. Specially stressed were the injunctions toward monotheism and imageless worship, moral ideals and precepts for ethical conduct, sabbath observance, circumcision, and avoidance of swine meat. Their belief in a sole, universal, just, omnipotent Creator of the universe was inevitably contrasted by Diaspora Jews with what they perceived to be the crass pagan polytheism surrounding them. Their resultant pride in Jewish adherence often reflected itself in ridicule of pagan polytheism and worship of images (Wisd. Sol. 13:10-19; 15:7-17; Jos. Apion ii.34-35) and attempts to account for the origins of such paganistic outlook (Wisd. Sol. 13:1-9; 14:12-21; Jos. Apion ii.36).

At the same time, the Jews could hardly escape the influence of the Hellenistic milieu, in particular the Greek language. Around 250 B.C., Greek-speaking Jews were numerous enough, and sufficiently estranged from knowledge of Hebrew, that they found it necessary to render the five books of Moses into Greek (*see* SEPTUAGINT; SEPTUAGINT[S]); in due course the remainder of Hebrew Scripture was translated. Greek was the language of the synagogue service, and it was the Greek Bible which was used in the synagogue (*see* Just. Apol. i.31; Just. Dial. 72; Tert. Apol. 18).

While the Torah, or Pentateuch, embodies narrative history plus teachings, customs and observances, as well as fundamentally legal material, Greco-Jewish writings most commonly render תורה simply as νόμος (*see* TORAH[S]). Just as pagan Greeks had compiled law codes of their own, and attempted to justify their philosophical validity, so also Hellenistic Jews presented Moses as a lawgiver and came to focus on Judaism as though it were both in essence and as a totality law and nothing but law. The preservation of Jewish-Hellenistic literature by the church has perpetuated this misidentification of Judaism with Law, so that even rabbinic Judaism, which never availed itself of this identification, is still commonly so misconstrued. *See* JUDAISM, EARLY RABBINIC[S].

Similarly, through the prism of allegorical interpretation, certain Jewish-Hellenistic writers dissolved the literal meaning of the Pentateuch by investing, indeed saturating, Scripture with meanings suggested by Greek language, habits, and philosophy, by Greek views on the nature of man, of sin, of righteousness, faith, and the like (*see* GREEK RELIGION AND PHILOSOPHY). Often they accounted for the resultant similarities between Greek philosophy, on the one hand, and the Law of Moses, on the other, by the suggestion that Greek philosophers had themselves learned and then usurped these eternal universal truths of reality from their Jewish predecessors, the patriarchs and Moses. By thus appropriating and assimilating Greek notions as their own, and then claiming prior possession of these ideas by their own forebears, Hellenistic Jews managed to maintain loyalty to their Scripture and ancestral practices, and yet also to feel at ease with Greek modes of thought.

The Greeks conceived of man's spiritual soul as the captive of the material, and hence evil, body. A leitmotiv of Greek religion was the soul's escape from bondage to bodily passions and sensual desires. In the writings of Philo (*see* PHILO JUDEUS), Judaism, replete with its ritual and regimen—especially sabbath observance, circumcision, and dietary restrictions—becomes the symbolic vehicle through which the individual's soul or mind can prevail over the lusts and passions of the body and attain to spiritual freedom and immortality. The specific laws, thus rendered allegorically, emerge reshaped as reflective of universal spiritual truths; the external requirements of Jewish practice remain, but their spiritual utility is thus reappraised.

It cannot be determined to what extent Jews in the Dispersion actually continued to abide by the Law. Abroad, subject as they were to an alien culture and religious environment, the Jews found their fidelity to ancestral faith and practices severely tested. The eagerness with which they rendered the Hebrew Scriptures into Greek clearly evinces determination by many to preserve the Judaism of old even while dressing it in Hellenistic garb. Problematic, however, is the extent to which the Law could have been followed. Many of the observances enjoined in the Pentateuch focused on the temple in Jerusalem. But most Jews dwelling in the Dispersion, especially those in the more remote regions, could not undertake expensive and difficult pilgrimages, and, while they may have considered it important to contribute the temple tax, yet the many individual prescriptions dealing with the sacrificial cult probably could elicit only sentimental attachment. While Philo applauds those who, through recourse to allegorical interpretation, have penetrated to the higher philosophical or ethical sense of the commandments, he yet laments the consequent neglect by some—we cannot gauge how numerous they were—of the literal observance of scriptural injunctions, for all these, even the ceremonial and dietary, are based upon reason and nature (Philo, *De Migratione Abraham* 89 ff.). Even cases of more substantive defection, however, probably seldom resulted in an actual break from the organized community—especially where there was no guarantee that the defector could attain Greek citizenship; the Jewish community had been accorded so many special privileges that this alone may have impelled Jews to maintain their communal affiliation if not also their religious conformity.

At the same time, the religious life of the majority was probably regulated by adherence to the Law of Moses insofar as was practicable. Jews had the privilege of erecting, within those quarters where they lived, association halls for purposes of reading the Law, common worship and education (Philo, *On the Special Laws* ii.62), festive celebration, or simple assembly. Native synagogues seem to have functioned actively as centers of Jewish education and expression in the Dispersion. Larger cities had more than one, and Alexandria a great many (*On the Embassy to Gaius* XX); Acts portrays Paul encountering synagogues throughout his journeys.

4. Relations with Gentiles. Also sustaining Judaism in the Dispersion was extensive proselytism. Even aside from missionary activity, Jews—by their very presence and contacts, and their synagogues open to all—commanded favorable notice among many Gentiles. Particularly appealing was Judaism's emphasis on monotheism, the original oneness of the human race, ethical conduct, judgment by God, the promise of eternal salvation, plus Judaism's opposition to polytheism, idolatry, and wickedness. To some, Judaism appeared a philosophy, and synagogue worship as an assembly of teachers and disciples of a foreign philosophical school; to others, Judaism resembled the Oriental mystery cults offering eternal life. Especially alluring were fidelity to sabbath observance and lights, fasts, and dietary prohibitions.

Circumcision, however, proved a deterrent, and accounts for the fact that most proselytes were women. Besides those formally received into Judaism, many Gentiles attached themselves in a loose form as "God-fearing (σεβόμενοι, φοβούμενοι τὸν θεόν), and constituted a kind of appendage to the Jewish community. Undoubtedly, the extremely rapid Hellenization of Christianity is in large measure traceable to inroads made by Jewish proselytism; and, very likely, many who were deterred from Judaism mainly because of required circumcision were all the more receptive to the preaching of Gentile Christianity.

At the same time, much hostile sentiment accrued against Jews. Though Hellenism was hospitable toward innumerable cults and their gods, the Jews were unable to reciprocate and denied recognition and tolerance to the Greek and Roman pantheon. Their religious particularism was frequently represented as atheism; their social particularism was often misconstrued, sometimes deliberately, as a hatred of mankind. The special privileges and exemptions allowed Jews by Roman authorities aroused envy and ill will; so also did the continuous flow of Jewish funds toward Jerusalem. Proselytes to Judaism cut themselves adrift from family and friends, intensifying resentment among those remaining Gentiles.

5. Jewish-Hellenistic literature. Such tension reflected itself on the literary plane. Manetho, Cheremon, Lysimachus, and Apion, among others, produced severely negative and distorted assessments of Judaism and its origins; these are cited and refuted by Josephus (Apion i.26 ff.; ii.1 ff.). The Jews were also the butt of Roman satirists, such as Horace, Persius, Martial, and Juvenal, and were maligned by the historian Tacitus as well. Much Jewish-Hellenistic literature thus serves apologetic ends—the defense of Judaism through assertion of its antiquity and glorification of its credentials and accomplishments.

Aside from the LXX, this literature falls mainly into three major classifications: history, poetry, and philosophy. The historical writings include the works of JOSEPHUS, and Philo's *Against Flaccus* and *On the Embassy to Gaius* (*see* PHILO JUDEUS). Earlier, JASON of Cyrene produced a history of the Maccabean wars, of which II Maccabees is basically a condensation (*see* MACCABEES, BOOKS OF). Alexander Polyhistor, Josephus, Clement of Alexandria, and Eusebius preserve for us fragments from a number of others, including Demetrius, Eupolemus, Artapanus, and Cleodemus. III Maccabees and the Letter of ARISTEAS, although fictional, are historical in form.

Christian writers, especially Eusebius, preserve reference to works of poetry and drama: an epic on Jerusalem by a poet named Philo, a long poem on Shechem by Theodotus, a work on the Exodus by the dramatist Ezekiel. In the SIBYLLINE ORACLES, Jewish poets attributed to ancient, oracle-giving sibyls verses teaching the truths of Judaism and directed at reformation of paganism.

The WISDOM OF SOLOMON, an exhortation to seek wisdom, is reminiscent of Palestinian wisdom literature (*see* WISDOM; WISDOM IN THE OT[S]), but reflects as well the influence of Greek philosophy, especially Stoicism. IV Maccabees is also a Stoicizing work, extolling the supremacy of devout reason over the passions (*see* MACCABEES, BOOKS OF). A work by ARISTOBULUS represents an early attempt (mid-second century B.C.) to expound the law of Moses through ALLEGORY. Alexandrian Jewish philosophy, along with allegorical interpretation, reached its culmination with Philo of Alexandria, whose works have been preserved to us in great numbers.

6. In relation to Judaism in Palestine. Broad contrasts emerge between Hellenistic Judaism and the two fundamental modes of Judaism contemporaneous with it in Palestine—Pentateuchal Judaism, functioning under the postexilic theocracy, succeeded by emerging Pharisaic or early rabbinic Judaism.

For Hellenistic Jews, the Pentateuch was a Greek work of law, revealing a God of refined philosophic reason, and suffused with philosophic concerns: Logos (*see* WORD, THE), universals and particulars, causality, chance and fate, the individual's plight, resurrection, immortality, and the like. Its specific laws enabled individual man to triumph over his passions, ensuring his soul's escape from bondage and attainment of life eternal in the realm of the incorporeal. Such motifs, however, are foreign to Pentateuchal Judaism functioning in Palestine. At face value, the Pentateuch actually addresses itself not to sophisticated Greek Jews in the vibrant Greek cities, nor, to be sure, to any urban environment at all, but rather to a seminomadic wilderness community ultimately to adopt agricultural pursuits in Canaan. Here an anthropomorphic and anthropopathic immanent God (*see* GOD, OT VIEW OF §C4) intervenes in nature, is personally in touch with his people, and even addresses Moses face to face. Focus rests on God's COVENANT with Israel as a people, not with the plight of the individual and his soul's quest for resurrection and immortality. Only when refracted through the lens of Hellenistic allegory does the God of the Pentateuch become transcendent and purest reason, totally spiritual and free of passions; only then does Moses emerge as philosopher, statesman, and lawgiver par excellence, rather than as one plagued by insecurity and imperfection, and the patriarchs emerge as paradigms of the laws of nature.

So also is Hellenistic Judaism noticeably incongruent with Pharisaism. The concept of unwritten law to Philo signified the law of nature, and in no sense was this equivalent to the rabbinic תורה שבעל פה, the category of traditional HALACHAH functioning parallel to the written Law. While the Pharisees for years conveyed their teachings only orally, and conceived themselves as a scholar class in an unbroken chain of authorities extending back to Moses himself, Jewish-Hellenistic spokesmen communicated in writing, as individuals, many citing as their motivation only personal inclination and disposition. Rabbinic Judaism is clearly at variance with many Hellenistic conceptions, as, e.g., regarding evil and fate and the nature of God and man; the rabbinic conception of Torah is, moreover, considerably broader than the Greek designation νόμος suggests (*see above* §3; *see also* TORAH [S]; JUDAISM, EARLY RABBINIC[S]).

The question naturally arises whether Hellenistic Judaism and the modes of Judaism in Palestine experienced contact with each other. Clearly, it was the deep penetration of Hellenistic influence into the heart of Palestine itself under the Seleucids which set Jerusalem society astir, ultimately provoking the HASMONEAN revolt. Archaeological finds and other substantive evidence indicate that despite the rebellion's political success, Greek influence, albeit diminished, persisted in Palestine in subsequent centuries, becoming especially noticeable again during the reigns of Herod the Great and Archelaus. Hundreds of Greek loan words found in tannaitic sources also attest to assimilation of some overtones of Greek culture in Palestine during the early rabbinic period. Yet this Hellenistic presence, while seemingly extensive, must be judged as essentially superficial.

Far-reaching in import is the opposite problem: Pharisaism's incursion into the Diaspora. We remain ill informed concerning this penetration—as to precisely when and where it commenced and what form it took. Paul of Tarsus, a native of the Diaspora (Acts 21:39; 22:3; cf. 9:11, 30; 11:25), informs us he was Pharisaic in upbringing (Phil. 3:5; cf. Gal. 1:14). The author of Acts links Paul's Pharisaic upbringing with Gamaliel I in Jerusalem (22:3; cf. 26:4-5). Paul's genuine epistles, however, in no way confirm this portrayal and, if read independently of Acts, could be construed as indicating that Paul was never in Jerusalem during his upbringing (Gal. 1:13-14, 22; cf. PAUL §A2*a-c*). If we rely on the epistles, we may infer that whatever Paul himself means by his Pharisaic background, he received it in the Diaspora. The content or nature of Pharisaism as known to the apostle Paul cannot be gauged from what we know of Pharisaism in Palestine, because, on the one hand, it is difficult to reconstruct the nature of Pharisaism in Palestine before A.D. 70, and, on the other hand, we have no assurance that Pharisaism in the Diaspora in the time of Paul was identical with its counterpart in Palestine. Even if we presumed that Pharisaism had spread into Asia Minor as early as the period of Paul's youth, we could not assess precisely how it interacted with and was affected by the Hellenistic milieu which determined so much of Paul's own thinking. We are informed that, in later times, rabbinic emissaries traveled from Palestine into the Diaspora, but we are uncertain how early this practice began and how it affected the spread of Pharisaism. Clearly our understanding of the nature of Diaspora synagogues, of the dynamics of Jewish proselytism, and of many other dimensions of the Jewish experience in the Dispersion, hinges very basically on how this general problem is to be resolved.

Bibliography. General treatments: E. Schürer, *A History of the Jewish People in the Time of Jesus Christ* (1891), Div. II, Vol. II, §31, Vol. III, §33; P. Wendland, *Die hellenistisch-römische Kultur in ihren Beziehungen zu Judentum und Christentum* (2nd and 3rd eds., 1912); J. Juster, *Les Juifs dans l'empire romain,* 2 vols. (1914); M. Radin, *The Jews among the Greeks and Romans* (1915); C. Guignebert, *The Jewish World in the Time of Jesus Christ* (1939), pp. 211-37; R. Marcus, "Selected Bibliography (1920-1945) of the Jews in the Hellenistic-Roman Period," *Proceedings of the American Academy of Jewish Research,* XVI (1946-47), 97-181; R. H. Pfeiffer, *History of NT Times with an Introduction to the Apocrypha* (1949); V. Tcherikover, *Hellenistic Civilization and the Jews* (1959); E. R. Goodenough, *Jewish Symbols in the Greco-Roman Period,* 12 vols. (1953-65); S. Sandmel, *The First Christian Century in Judaism and Christianity* (1969), pp. 107-42 and *The Genius of Paul* (2nd ed., 1970), chs. 1–2.

Hellenistic influence in Palestine: S. Lieberman, *Greek in Jewish Palestine* (1942); *Hellenism in Jewish Palestine* (2nd ed., 1962).

Specialized studies: I. Levy, "Le proselytisme juif," *REJ,* LI (1906), 1-29; A. Bludau, *Juden und Judenverfolgungen im alten Alexandria* (1906); H. I. Bell, *Jews and Christians in Egypt* (1924); H. A. Wolfson, "Philo on Jewish Citizenship in Alexandria," *JBL,* LXIII (1944), 165-68; G. La Piana, "Foreign Groups in Rome during the First Centuries of the Empire," *HTR,* XX (1927), 183-403, esp. 341-93; S. L. Guterman, *Religious Toleration and Persecution in Ancient Rome* (1951).

Jewish-Hellenistic literature: J. Freudenthal, *Alexander Polyhistor und die von ihm erhaltenen Reste judäischer und samaritanischer Geschichtswerke* (1875); W. N. Stearns, *Fragments from Graeco-Jewish Writers* (1908); H. B. Swete, *An Introduction to the OT in Greek* (2nd ed., 1914); H. St. John Thackeray, *Josephus: The Man and the Historian* (1929 [repr. 1967]); E. R. Goodenough, *An Introduction to Philo Judaeus* (1940); H. A. Wolfson, *Philo,* 2 vols. (1947); M. Hadas, *Aristeas to Philocrates* (1951); L. Feldman, *Recent Research on Josephus and Philo* (1964); S. Sandmel, *Philo's Place in Judaism* (1971); B. Z. Wacholder, *Eupolemus: A Study of Judaeo-Greek Literature* (1974). M. J. COOK

***JUDGES, BOOK OF.** A remarkable collection of folklore, tribal traditions, and hero tales combined with historical fragments, theological insight, and editorial opinion. Though efforts to unravel the threads of this composition have been fruitful, many questions yet remain to be answered.

1. Introduction
2. Narratives of the major judges
3. The minor judges
4. Appendixes
5. Composition
Bibliography

1. Introduction. The book can be divided into four sections: (1) a prelude (1:1–2:5) which describes the extent of Israelite occupation of the land; (2) an introduction (2:6–3:6) to the main body of the book; (3) a collection of narratives dealing with individual judges (3:7–16:31); and (4) two appendixes recounting the origin of the tribal sanctuary of Dan (17–18) and the deplorable behavior of the Benjaminites of Gibeah (19–21).

a. Prelude. Though 1:1–2:5 contains passages which have parallels in the book of Joshua (1:12-15 with Josh. 15:13-19; 1:21 with Josh. 15:63; 1:29 with Josh. 16:10; 1:27-28 with Josh. 17:11-13; and 1:34-35 with Josh. 19:47), in its present position this section appears to stand in sharp contrast with the description in Joshua of a sweeping conquest of the land. According to 1:1–2:5 there were many areas that were not conquered (*see* JOSHUA, BOOK OF[S] §2). Some scholars now hold that this section once functioned as the conclusion of the book of Joshua when that book served as the final portion of the HEXATEUCH.

The Hexateuch was of short duration; once Joshua was removed, the resultant PENTATEUCH concluded with the account of the death of Moses. In order that the book of Joshua might also end with the death of its hero, its conclusion was placed at the beginning of the book of Judges, thus creating the impression of a contrasting view of the Conquest. Support for this view is the possibility that the source strata of the Pentateuch (*see* DOCUMENTS) may continue through Joshua and Judg. 2:5. (*See* §4*b below.* For another perspective, *see* JOSHUA, BOOK OF[S] §1; DEUTERONOMIC HISTORY, THE[S] §§1-2; YAHWIST[S] §3; ELOHIST[S] §4*b*.) Following this shift in position, the parallel passages noted above were then interpolated from Judg. 1 into the book of Joshua, most likely in the postexilic period (Fohrer). Earlier, 2:6-9 served as an introduction of the book of Judges, providing a link to Josh. 23:16.

b. Theological interpretations. The remainder of the introductory section (2:11–3:6) contains two theological interpretations of history. The first (2:11-19) describes the apostasy of the people, their subsequent punishment, and their deliverance. Upon the death of the deliverer, however, the pattern of apostasy, punishment, and deliverance is repeated. This pattern differs from the theological framework of the hero narratives (e.g., 3:12-15*a*, 30; 4:1*a*, 2, 3*a*, 23) in that the latter pattern contains an additional element of repentance. The interpretation in 2:11-19 is more recent and depicts the deliverance as an undeserved act of Yahweh's mercy.

The second of the two theological interpretations (2:20–3:6) understood the series of crises which Israel experienced as a period of probation which tested Israel's proficiency in warfare and her will to obey Yahweh's commandments.

2. Narratives of the major judges. The traditions dealing with the major judges (3:7–16:31) originated as single stories, each circulating individually before being combined into larger narratives. The major judges were associated with particular tribes in the early cycles. Later their heroic deeds were made to refer to Israel as a whole (probably during the time of the united monarchy).

It has recently been proposed (Richter) that the pre-Deuteronomic collection of hero tales consisted of 3:12–9:55 and first existed in the form of a northern Israelite deliverer book *(Retterbuch).* The geographical area encompassed by this collection extended from Benjamin in the S (3:15) through Manasseh and Ephraim in the central portion (6:11; 7:23-24; 8:2) to Naphtali, Asher, and Zebulon in the N (4:10; 7:23). Issachar and the Israelite tribes of Transjordan play no role in this book, or at least there is no example of a deliverer from these groups. According to this view the deliverer book was compiled at a time when Gilead no longer formed a part of Israel—probably during the second half of the ninth century B.C.

The compiler of the deliverer book edited his traditions where it seemed advisable. He combined the prose and poetic versions of the Deborah-Barak tradition and reworked the Gideon material, identifying the latter with Jerubbaal, the father of Abimelech. He arranged the material in such a way that the refusal of the kingdom by Gideon in 8:22-23 contrasts sharply with the Abimelech tradition. Thus Abimelech exemplified the worst that one might fear in the monarchy, and this is further emphasized by Jotham's fable (9:5*b*, 7-21). The intent of the deliverer book was to portray the strength of the war of Yahweh and the deliverers whom Yahweh called forth; its thrust was directed against the monarchy in which the war of Yahweh could no longer be implemented spontaneously (*see* WAR, IDEAS OF §1; WAR, HOLY[S]). Placing the prophet Deborah on a par with the deliverer Barak is thought to indicate that the editor of the deliverer book was someone within the prophetic circles of the North.

Whether or not the pre-Deuteronomic collection of hero tales can be limited to 3:12–9:55 remains problematic. Another proposal based upon I Sam. 12:11 suggests that the earliest form of the pre-Deuteronomic deliverer book consisted of the traditions of Jerubbaal (Gideon), Bedan (RSV "Barak"), Jephthah, and Samuel. In a secondary expansion, Jerubbaal and Jephthah were combined with the narratives of other deliverers. The tradition of Bedan was set aside and lost completely; that of Samuel, which was closely linked to the Saul tradition, was removed from the collection (Fohrer).

a. Othniel. The tradition of Othniel (3:7-11) remains something of an enigma. Though this narrative is possibly derived from an early tradition, no earlier form has thus far been identified. Given its strong Deuteronomic influence and schematic nature, the narrative in its present form is thought to have originated no earlier than the Exile.

b. Ehud. The tradition in its earliest form consisted of 3:15*b*-26. Its expansion through vss. 27-29 was intended to associate all Israel with the hero's feat. The so-called "double" entrance of Ehud in 3:19-20 has caused some to suggest the possibility that two sources are combined in this narrative.

c. Shamgar ben Anath is unique in that no information is provided about his call, tenure in office, place of burial, or tribal connection. The name Shamgar is possibly Hurrian (occurring in certain NUZI texts) while ben Anath, "son of Anath," is Semitic. On the basis of the MARI texts, where there is evidence that worshipers of the warrior-goddess Anath often served in military capacities, it has been suggested that Shamgar ben Anath was a mercenary (Craigie). Perhaps Anath came to be associated with mercenaries in general as the expression "ben Anath" might indicate. The reference to Shamgar in Judg. 3:31 seems to be secondary, and the name may have been suggested by the brief reference in 5:6.

d. Deborah and Barak. The earliest tradition concerning Deborah and Barak consists of Judg. 4:4*a*, 6-9*a*, 9*c*-10, 12-16. Vss. 4*b*-5 which mention Deborah's role as arbiter appear to be an editorial expansion likely based upon the memory of a sacred oak associated with another Deborah, Rebekah's nurse in Gen. 35:8 (Gray). The tradition of Jael's murder of Sisera was originally an independent narrative. It has been proposed that two traditions have been fused in the prose account of ch. 4, as might be reflected in the two locations of the muster—one at Mount Tabor (4:6, 12, 14) and the other at Kadesh (4:9-10). The tradition of Jabin, whose defeat has already been attributed to Joshua (Josh. 11:1-11), has been secondarily joined to that of Sisera.

The Song of Deborah (ch. 5) is the most authentic source we have dealing with the time of the Judges. A victory song composed soon after the battle it commemorates, it has been variously described as a thanksgiving psalm (Bentzen), a cultic drama and liturgy for covenant renewal within the AMPHICTYONY (Weiser), or (omitting vss. 1-5 and 31) a propaganda song (Richter). Ch. 5 is primarily devoted to extolling the victory of Yahweh, while ch. 4 provides a broader historical account. The catalog of tribes in 5:14-18 has been thought to include the potential participants in this engagement (Smend). Those tribes that did not respond were censured or derided for their disloyalty. In view of the celebratory nature of the Song of Deborah, 5:14-18 has also been taken simply as a tribal roll call intended to maintain solidarity among members of the amphictyony, and thus, with the possible exception of vs. 18, is not directly related to the military effort of Barak and Deborah (Weiser). According to this view, only vss. 19-30 in ch. 5 are relevant to the military encounter. Based upon 4:6, 10, and possibly 5:18, only the tribes of Zebulun and Naphtali actually participated in the campaign; and even their participation is secondary to the main purpose of the Song—the praise of Yahweh's victory.

e. Gideon. The most complicated use of source materials is found in the account of Gideon (chs. 6–8) and the Abimelech episode (ch. 9). Various traditions and fragments were deftly combined around the theme of apostasy. The tradition of Gideon's call (6:11*b*-17) has been combined with that of the sanctuary of Ophrah (6:11*a*, 19-24) and further enhanced by a legend of an unknown sanctuary that was later identified with Ophrah (6:25-32) (Haag). It is in this latter passage that Jerubbaal first appears. Vs. 32 provides an ETIOLOGY for Jerubbaal and the name change. Haag has seriously questioned any connection between Gideon and Ophrah. It is more likely, however, that Jerubbaal, who is named only four times in chs. 6–8 (6:32; 7:1; 8:29, 35), originally belonged to the Shechem tradition of ch. 9. Gideon was not connected with Shechem. The conclusion of the vocation narrative (6:11*b*-17) is found in 6:36-40.

Gideon's heroic effort against the Midianites as preserved by his clan Abiezer is described in 7:11*b*, 13-21 (expanded by vss. 9-11*a*, 12, 22). The war cries of 7:18 and 7:20 are thought to represent two variant traditions. In 7:24–8:3 we may have two versions of an awkward episode that occurred between Gideon and Ephraim. The Abiezer version (7:24-25) of the slaying of two Midianite chiefs contains etiologies of "Raven Rock" (rock of Oreb) and "Wolf Winepress" (winepress of Zeeb). The Ephraimite version (8:1-3) was preserved because of the compliment which Gideon paid Ephraim in 8:2.

The memory of Gideon's raid into Transjordan is preserved in 8:5-9, 13-21*ab*, 28*a* (expanded by vss. 4 and 10-12). The campaign against the chiefs Zebah and Zalmunna represents an original element in the tradition as over against the etiologies in 7:25.

Though Gideon's connection with Ophrah has been questioned, Deuteronomic judgment on his activity (8:27*b*) would seem to attest to the genuineness of this tradition. The account of Gideon's refusal of the kingship, however, is problematic. Earlier critics saw his refusal as indicative of northern resentment of the monarchy as voiced within prophetic circles during the eighth century B.C. Such resentment was shared by the Deuteronomic theologians. Gideon's refusal of the kingship has also suggested two other possibilities: (1) he may have accepted the power without the title; or (2) his emphatic refusal may as a matter of principle have preceded his acceptance of the kingship (cf. Gen. 23:11 ff. and II Sam. 24:21 ff.) (Davies). Our text (8:22-23) may not contain the entire tradition of this incident, but only its beginning which suited the purpose of the pre-Deuteronomic compiler.

Despite Gideon's fashioning an ephod, he died "in a good old age" and was buried with honor. No doubt, this was due to his stature and success as a deliverer. It has been suggested that the account of his making an ephod was an etiological legend explaining the tradition of an ephod at Ophrah. Others have noted, however, that given Gideon's position of influence, it is more likely that the historicity of this account lay with his claim of access to the oracle of God which the ephod in part represented (I Sam. 14:3; 23:6, 9; 30:7) (Gray). 8:31 is a Deuteronomic insertion which provides a literary link to ch. 9.

f. The Abimelech episode, which is made up of several originally independent stories (9:1-5*a*, 6, 23-24; 9:26-40; 9:41-45; 9:46-49; 9:50-54), was preserved because of the identity of Jerubbaal with Gideon. A pre-Deuteronomic summary is offered in 9:55-57*a*. The fable of Jotham has been interwoven through the first portion of the cycle (9:5*b*, 7-21). It has been suggested that the earliest version may have consisted of 9:5*b*, 7, 16*a*, 19*b*-21. It could have been cited in a shorter form originally, or suggested by a passage like vs. 20.

Abimelech's quest for power provided the compiler an opportunity to assail the concept of the hereditary monarchy. In addition, it also offered the Deuteronomist an opportunity to portray the retribution incurred by Gideon through his making of an ephod at Ophrah (8:27).

g. Jephthah. The position of the Jephthah cycle (10:6–12:7) in the midst of the notices of five minor judges (10:1-5; 12:8-15) may be related to the nature of his selection by the elders of Gilead. It has been suggested that Jephthah's appointment is that of a minor judge, since only later (11:29) is the charismatic nature of his position mentioned (Gray); *see also* §3 *below*. The lengthy and detailed introduction (10:6-16) distinguishes this cycle from the earlier narratives.

Jephthah's campaign against the Ammonites (10:17–11:29, 32*b*-33*a*) appears to combine two separate traditions: (1) Jephthah's appointment as a minor judge or ruler at the sanctuary of Mizpah, the military threat by the Ammonites, and Yahweh's victory over the Ammonites (11:1-11, 29, 32*b*, 33*a*β); and (2) a more recent report involving a dispute over Moabite land (10:17; 11:12-28, 32*a*, 33*a*α) which, even though edited to agree with the above, is strongly reminiscent of Num. 20:14-21; 21:13, 21-24*a*.

Combined also within this narrative complex is the story of Jephthah's vow (11:30-31, 34-40). Some have seen the vow as an act of desperation following an unsuccessful recruiting effort (11:29*a*). The prototype of the story may be rooted in mythology rather than history. What may originally have been a rite connected with the annual mourning for the death of a deity is explained etiologically by this tradition (Burney).

An episode involving the Ephraimites (12:1-6) recalls an earlier incident connected with Gideon (8:1-3). In the case of Jephthah, however, the threat to "burn your house over you with fire" was far more serious. The Ephraimites apparently were opposed to the independent military action of Jephthah's people, whom they called "fugitives of Ephraim." Given the overwhelming victory of the Gileadites, this would appear to be a Transjordan tradition that was likely associated with the sanctuary at Mizpah. The report of Jephthah's death is in a form (12:7) similar to those of the five minor judges (10:2*b*, 5; 12:10, 12, 15).

h. Samson. Though the Samson cycle (13–16) was not a part of the pre-Deuteronomic deliverer book, many of the stories contained therein are of great antiquity. Two separate collections (13–15 and 16) are suggested by the presence of two separate summary statements in 15:20 and 16:31*b*.

Chs. 14 and 15 combine folkloristic episodes, riddles (*see* RIDDLE[S]), and anecdotes into a single narrative with an over-all theme which reveals the secret role of Yahweh (14:4) in the deliverance of his people (15:8) (Wharton). Indicative of this scheme are feats of strength originally credited to Samson's prowess which are now attributed to the spirit of Yahweh (14:6, 19; 15:14), and the prayer in 15:18 in which Samson acknowledges his dependence upon Yahweh. Another indication of the editorial art can be seen in the interpolation of Samson's parents into this narrative (14:5, 6, 9, 16) in order to relate chs. 14 and 15 more closely to ch. 13 and the role of Yahweh in all that transpires.

Ch. 13 may contain the original introduction to chs. 14 and 15, plus later insertions that have been made to further the theological interests of the editor (13:4-5, 7*b*, 14*a*, 16*b*-18, 19*b*, 21, 24*b*-25) (Eissfeldt). The disruptive effect of vss. 4-5 and 7*b* upon the relatively uncomplicated narrative of ch. 13 was necessitated by the introduction of the Nazirite theme of uncut hair, which is crucial to the dramatic unfolding of 16:4 ff. (Wharton). Vss. 4, 5, and 7*b* were likely added by the same hand that combined chs. 13–15 with 16.

The narrative in these chapters is fully resolved with the two etiologies of Ramath-lehi (jawbone hill) and En-hakkore (the spring of him who called) in which Samson confesses complete dependence upon Yahweh for his strength in performing his feats. The summary formula in 15:20 clearly concludes this literary unit.

It has been proposed that the rustic episode in 16:1-3 was used by the editor as a culmination of Samson's prowess when he was victorious over the entire city of Gaza. This episode served to offset the impact of betrayal and humiliation (16:4 ff.) which Samson subsequently experienced at Gaza prior to his final act of vengeance (Wharton).

The narrative of 16:4 ff. may have originally attributed Samson's strength simply to his uncut hair without any mention of his role as a Nazirite (16:13, 19). If this were the case, his strength would have returned as his hair grew (16:22). Once the theological scheme was superimposed, however, Samson fell prey to the Philistines because "Yahweh had left him." In his final act of vengeance, Samson regained his strength only after praying to Yahweh; no mention is made of his hair. The summary formula in 16:31*b* agrees with its counterpart in 15:20 concerning a period of twenty years.

The abbreviated introduction in 13:1 is closely modeled after 6:1, and was probably added along with 15:20 when chs. 13–15 were incorporated into the first Deuteronomic revision of the deliverer book (*see* §5 *below*). Ch. 16 was included through a subsequent revision. Even within the theological scheme which has been superimposed upon these literary pieces, it is clear that Samson did not function as a judge or deliverer. He neither organized nor led any military campaign against a foreign enemy or oppressor. Yet, the end result is the reaffirmation of the presence of Yahweh (Wharton).

3. The minor judges. A second group, consisting of five leaders, is mentioned in 10:1-5 and 12:8-15. The lack of information about their activities stands in sharp contrast with the often lengthy accounts given concerning the deliverers. This points up two basic scholarly understandings of the function of the שפט: (1) a judicial and administrative official (judge), and (2) the deliverer or military hero. שפט as "judge" is thought to include such functions of civil administration as governing or ruling and dispensing justice, excluding military activities (Richter, Smend). The term שפט seems originally to have applied primarily to the five minor judges, each of whom is specifically said to have "judged Israel." The minor judges likely gave their title to the deliverers (Smend) through a Deuteronomic redactor who no longer distinguished between the two.

The only heroic figure who likely "judged" in addition to his role as deliverer was Jephthah. The concluding note on his tenure as judge and his death (12:7) corresponds closely with the notices of the other five. It is probably no coincidence that the minor judges are placed adjacent to Jephthah. This note on his role as a minor judge may have prompted a later redactor to include at that point the notices of the other minor judges, since Jephthah's playing of both roles possibly obscured any significant distinction between the two types, and since some effort may have been made to achieve a total of twelve leaders (even though the present text does not reflect this).

The record of Jephthah's exploits as deliverer is recounted at length. When the account shifts to his role as judge (12:7), there is little to be reported (Smend). Even the number of years assigned (six) corresponds with the random numbers attributed to the five minor judges, whereas the deliverers are assigned multiples of forty years. All this would seem to suggest that the role of minor judge represented a regular office that was well documented. Beyond this, opinion is currently divided. One approach is to see this list as an old document of genuine historical value. Accordingly, these figures in sequence occupied a permanent office in the Israelite tribal league (Noth).

A second approach considers the design of this list to be influenced in part by records of the early monarchical period (I Sam. 13:1 and I Kings 11:41-42). The time sequence is seen as secondary; these minor judges may have ruled simultaneously. Their primary association with towns or cities is thought to indicate the transition from the tribal state to district and city rule. Within this view, Israel is understood as a concept of political geography and not as an amphictyony of twelve tribes (Richter).

4. Appendixes. ***a. Chs. 17 and 18.*** Variations within the text seem to indicate a lengthy period of transmission. An earlier hypothesis of parallel sources for this section (Eissfeldt) has been questioned by those who contend for its essential literary unity (Noth). The adherents of both positions, however, acknowledge the presence of changes made by later hands.

This narrative is comprised primarily of three themes: (1) the origin of a cultic object in the tribal sanctuary at Dan (17:1 ff.); (2) the role of a Levite from Bethlehem (17:7 ff.); and (3) exploration and conquest by the tribe of Dan (18:1*b*-29). Though this remarkable composition ostensibly describes the founding of the Danite tribal sanctuary, it does so in a way that subtly disparages each of the three themes it embodies. The cultic object made from silver stolen by Micah is in turn stolen from Micah's private shrine. A Levite who was hired by Micah to attend the shrine is made a priest among the Danites, much to his delight, and his ungrateful behavior is duly noted. Even in the conquest of a new tribal territory, emphasis is so placed upon the defenseless and unsuspecting nature of the indigenous people that their subsequent slaughter can hardly be seen as courageous or praiseworthy.

Previously, chs. 17–18 were understood as an effort to discredit the royal cult of Jeroboam I with its sanctuaries at Bethel and Dan (I Kings 12:28-29). However, as Noth has shown, these chapters are likely the work of the royal priesthood of Dan in an effort to represent every phase of the earlier tribal cult in an unfavorable light. This view would appear to be supported by 17:6, "In those days there was no king in Israel; every man did what was right in his own eyes" (cf. 18:1*a*). Both passages seem to look favorably upon the role of the king (such as Jeroboam I) in the installation of priests.

Of the two concluding verses (18:30-31), 30 and 31*b* are later glosses which attempt to identify the otherwise nameless Levite with the priesthood of Moses. The gloss in vs. 30 would seem to indicate that the tribal priesthood of Dan was later a rival of the royal cult. Repeated mention of EPHOD and TERAPHIM (17:5; 18:14, 17-18, 20) may be intended to indicate that, in the time of the royal cult, the tribal priesthood had been reduced to the practice of delivering oracles. In its earliest form, the narrative likely ended with 18:31*a* (Noth).

Given this favorable view of the king and especially of his role in cultic affairs, the description of the untrustworthy Levite and the slaughter of a defenseless city by the Danites, it is readily apparent why this narrative was not included in early editions of the book of Judges (*see* §5). Yet, with its account of the migration of Dan, the ridicule of Micah's cultic object and the apparent premonarchical setting, it was added by a later redactor who may have been unaware of its polemical nature.

b. Chs. 19–21 raise anew the question of source strata (*see* §1*a above*). Positions vary from the view that this appendix is comprised of parallel Hexateuchal narratives—L and J (Eissfeldt)—to the more recent proposal that we have here an authentic historical memory only partially preserved at the time of its postexilic composition (McKenzie). Between these extremes is the view which assumes the combining of two major traditions from the shrine of Mizpah and the sanctuary of Bethel plus additions by a postexilic redactor (Burney). Repetitions and parallels within such episodes as the fall of GIBEAH and the provision of wives for Benjamin are thought to support the last position. In the latter episode, for example, wives for Benjamin are provided by a reprisal raid on JABESH-GILEAD (21:1-12, 14*a*, 24*a*) and by the rape of the daughters of SHILOH (21:16-23). The Jabesh-gilead incident has been seen as an etiological explanation of the appeal which that group made to Saul (I Sam. 11:1-4; 31:11-13; II Sam. 2:4-5) when besieged by Nahash the Ammonite. The rape of the daughters of Shiloh may be an effort to provide a historical basis for a local vintage festival noted for its rites of sexual license or ritualistic rape.

The major literary themes of this narrative are (1) outrage in Gibeah (19:1-30); (2) war between Israel and Benjamin at Gibeah (20:1-48); and (3) the survival of Benjamin (21:1-25). In the first of these themes, action is directed toward an episode in Gibeah. Reference to Benjamin occurs only twice (19:14, 16*c*), and 19:16*b* ("sojourning") is likely a redaction based upon Gen. 19:9*b*. In its earliest form this tradition may have dealt solely with Gibeah; the actual crime involved may have been unknown to later writers, who thus turned to Gen. 19:4 ff.

In the second theme, the fall of Gibeah is reminiscent of the destruction of Ai (Josh. 8). This has prompted two proposals: (1) the initial defeats suffered by Israel (20:19 ff.) may have involved circumstances, now lost, similar to those of Joshua's initial defeat at Ai (Josh. 7) (McKenzie); and (2) more recently, the view that the fall of Ai is not historical at all but is based upon the account of the fall of Gibeah (de Vaux). (*See* AI; AI[S] §5.) In evaluating the significance of this report on the fate of Gibeah and Benjamin, it is often recalled that SAUL, Israel's first king, was from the city of Gibeah and the tribe of Benjamin. It has been widely accepted that we have here a strong bias against the kingship of Saul, reflecting a Judean recension (Fohrer) which can also be seen in 20:18. Such a bias has been understood by many as a later reflection upon an unfortunate experience with the monarchy. Others insist that this opposition was likely expressed at the outset of Saul's rise to power and may be traced in part to Samuel himself (Bright). However, it must be remembered that in the wake of David's success as king, Saul was a figure of little significance in Judah. If this antimonarchical bias was early rather than late, its origin was likely not in Judah, but rather among the centers of Yahwistic influence in the N.

The traditions preserved in ch. 21 make no mention of Gibeah and likely had no connection with that city in their earliest forms. The attack upon Jabesh-gilead seems to attest to a unique relationship between this city and Benjamin. In all likelihood the traditions in ch. 21 do represent authentic memories of intertribal conflicts involving Benjamin. It is much less likely, however, that all the other tribes of Israel were originally involved. The same would hold for the size of the military forces mentioned and the complete mobilization of all Israel as recorded in 20:1-2.

The narrative in 19–21 in its present form is a product of the postexilic period in which it was fashioned from several early traditions and motifs (cf. Judg. 19:29 with I Sam. 11:7). Various redactors contributed a number of passages (21:12*b*, 19*b*), certain of which are reminiscent of P (20:1; 21:10, 13, 16) (Fohrer). It has been proposed that this narrative is midrashic in nature (*see* MIDRASH [S] §§1-3), aimed at eliminating corruption in Israel, even though an entire tribe is faced with possible annihilation (McKenzie). Thus its *raison d'être* may be primarily theological rather than historical. This is further reflected in 20:19 ff. where, despite overwhelming odds, Israel is twice defeated by Benjamin; and only after Yahweh promises to "give them into your hand" (vs. 28) is there victory.

In 19:1*a* and 21:25 are two formulas we have encountered earlier in 18:1 and 17:6 respectively. In the first appendix these formulas appear to relate directly to the preceding passages and thus play a significant role in that context. In 19:1*a* and 21:25, however, they appear to be redactional, even superfluous (Noth). Here they serve as the opening and concluding verses in an effort to relate this narrative to chs. 17–18 which had been added in an earlier recension.

5. Composition. The present book of Judges can best be traced from the pre-Deuteronomic collection of hero narratives which circulated individually prior to the monarchy. There is broad consensus that the old deliverer book underwent at least two Deuteronomic revisions. The first revision, in the spirit of Deuteronomy, produced the theological framework for each of the narratives in 3:12–9:57, probably during the Exile. Also added at this time were the Othniel narrative (3:7-11), the Jephthah narrative (10:6-10*a*, 16; 10:17–12:7), and a portion of the Samson narrative (13–15).

The second Deuteronomic revision incorporated the expanded deliverer book into the larger scheme of the Deuteronomic history. Numerical data were added to provide a chronological order corresponding to the 480 years which elapsed, according to I Kings 6:1, between the Exodus and the beginning of Solomon's temple. This revision included a new introduction (2:11-19) which omitted any mention of the people's repentance and understood Yahweh's deliverance as an act of mercy. A second complex of Samson materials (13:4-5, 7*b*; 16:1-31) was also added. Possibly as a later part of this second revision were added an introductory link with the book of Joshua (2:6-9) and an additional theological interpretation (2:20–3:6) which viewed the crises of the deliverers as a period for testing Israel. It has been suggested that at this point the over-all Deuteronomic scheme was likely projected beyond the deliverers to include Eli, Samuel, and the latter's sons. The editor(s) of the second revision may well have felt that the degeneration of the office of deliverer had led directly to the selection of the deliverer Saul to be king (Richter).

Following the Deuteronomic revisions, the book of Judges consisted of 2:6–16:31, excluding the notices of the minor judges (10:1-5 and 12:8-15), which were included in the postexilic era under the influence of the notice pertaining to Jephthah (12:7). Other postexilic additions are the appendixes of chs. 17–18 and 19–21 and the former conclusion of the Hexateuch (1:1–2:5).

Bibliography. Commentaries: R. G. Boling, ABi (1975); C. F. Burney, *The Book of Judges* (1903); J. Gray, *The Century Bible* (1967).

Special studies: A. Alt, *Essays on OT History and Religion* (1966), pp. 79-132; G. Bacon, "The Book of Judges," *Encyclopaedia Judaica,* X (1972), 442-50; A. Bentzen, *Introduction to the OT* (5th ed., 1959); J. Bright, *A History of Israel* (2nd ed., 1972); P. C. Craigie, "A Reconsideration of Shamgar ben Anath (Judg. 3:31 and 5:6)," *JBL,* XCI (1972), 239-40; G. H. Davies, "Judges VIII 22-23," *VT,* XIII (1963), 151-57; R. de Vaux, *Histoire ancienne d'Israël* (1971); O. Eissfeldt, *The OT* (1965); G. Fohrer, *Das Alte Testament,* I (1969); E. Sellin-G. Fohrer, *Introduction to the OT* (1968); H. Haag, "Gideon—Jerubbaal—Abimeleck," *ZAW,* LXXIX (1967), 305-14; O. Kaiser, *Introduction to the OT* (1975); J. McKenzie, *The World of the Judges* (1967); M. Noth, "The Background of Judges 17–18," *Israel's Prophetic Heritage,* ed. B. W. Anderson and W. Harrelson (1962), pp. 68-85, and *Überlieferungsgeschichtliche Studien* (2nd ed., 1957); W. Richter, *Die Bearbeitungen des "Retterbuches" in der Deuteronomischen Epoche* (1964), and "Zu den 'Richtern Israel,'" *ZAW,* LXXVII (1965), 40-72; R. Smend, *Yahweh War and Tribal Confederation* (1970); A. Weiser, "Das Deboralied, eine gattungs- und traditionsgeschichtliche Studie," *ZAW,* LXXI (1959), 67-97; J. Wharton, "The Secret of Yahweh: Story and Affirmation in Judges 13-16," *Int.,* XXVII (1973), 48-66.

M. G. ROGERS

JUNG CODEX. *See* NAG HAMMADI[S] §2*a*.

JURIDICAL PROCEDURE. *See* LAW IN THE OT [S].

K

KAIGE RECENSION. *See* Greek Versions, Minor[S]; Daniel[S]; Samuel I and II[S] §2*c*.

KHAMSIN. *See* Palestine, Climate of §6.

KHIRBET. *See* Tell[S].

***KING, GOD AS.** The idea of God as king in the OT has two meanings and apparently two origins. The meanings can be distinguished by the different answers to the question: King of whom? One answer is: of the gods; the other: of the people. The first, the mythical meaning, is found primarily in the Psalms; elsewhere its occurrence is sporadic or uncertain. In most of the Hagiographa neither usage is found.

The mythical concept originated outside of Israel. The religion of Israel was henotheistic from the beginning and as such has had little occasion for, and no interest in, the development of a pantheon which provides for the position of a king over the other members (*see* Council, Heavenly[S]; Sons of God; Hosts, Host of Heaven). In its later, monotheistic phase no conditions for the creation of this position were present.

In the Bible the mythical meaning is most clearly stated in Ps. 95:3, "The Lord is a great (i.e., the supreme) God, and a great King above all gods." But such statements of relatively pure mythical kingship are few (Ps. 89:5-10 [H 6-11]; 103:19-22?). (Occasional motifs from supernatural battles, familiar fixtures in the regions of the eastern Mediterranean, are further indications of the origin of the mythical meaning.) More frequent is the tendency to describe or praise Yahweh as the king of the cosmos. The transition follows easily from the notion that Yahweh's mythical officials (cf. I Kings 22:19, 21-22), i.e., gods of lower or lowered rank (cf. Ps. 82), appear as powers of nature (Ps. 104:4). It follows in turn that those who praise him—other than men—are not only the mythical beings, attendants of the heavenly court (Isa. 6:3), but the whole cosmos in all its parts, and its praise is its recognition of God as king (Pss. 96–99). A further extension presents God as the king of the universe, which comprises nature and humanity alike. Expressions of this extended perception are usually eschatological in various degrees, although Israel is not always accorded much attention (Jer. 10:7, 10; Zech. 14:9, 16-17; Ps. 22:28 [H 29]; 47).

The line that has been plotted so far will converge with the line spun from the other meaning of the kingship of God. A paraphrase of Isa. 24:21-23 may show this: The one who commands mythical, cosmic, and historical forces will rule as king in Zion amidst his people Israel.

The other, the societal meaning, expresses the concept that God is king of a society, Israel. In telling contradistinction to the first meaning, this meaning entails the people's recognition of God as king with all the resulting commitments, duties, and prohibitions. (Even an individual member of the people may personally commit himself and call God "my king" [Ps. 5:2 [H 3], etc., and personal names; *see* Name §C2*c*].) It is often said that this meaning arose during the later time of the monarchy or in the Babylonian exile. This position is to be rejected. Although there are pertinent passages of significance (Exod. 15:18; Num. 23:21; Judg. 8:23; I Sam. 8:7; 10:19; 12:12) that refer to early Israel, their time of origin is controversial (*see* Samuel, I and II[S] §3), and the argument will therefore rest only (*a*) on personal names and (*b*) on the general idea of gods as kings in the ancient Near East.

a) In the premonarchial names Abimelech (Judg. 8:31, etc.), Ahimelech (I Sam. 21:1 [H 2], etc.), Malchishua (14:49), and, probably, Malchiel (Num. 26:45, etc.) the components *-melech* and *malchi-* (king) cannot refer to a human monarch but only to a deity. Even if the names were borrowed from other peoples—and there is no indication that they were—they had an unequivocal meaning for their givers and bearers: the kingship of God, that is, the kingship of Yahweh. *See* Names, Religious Significance of[S].

b) Even if there were no scriptural attestation to the idea that God is the king of Israel, one would be tempted to suppose its existence. Excepting the Egyptians, virtually every people of the ancient Near East, Semites and non-Semites alike, held that a god was the king of their polity. This fundamental idea, religious, social, and political, is expressed numerous times from Urukagina (Uruinimgina) of twenty-fourth-century Sumer to the Phoenicians and Carthagenians of Roman times. Urukagina and the Sargonic rulers Rimush and Naram-Sin a century later say that their respective chief gods, Ningirsu and Enlil, had entrusted to them land to hold and administer. The Old Assyrian king Ṣulili (*ca.* 2000?) says: "[The god] Ashur is the king, and Ṣulili is the governor of Ashur." The idea is also documented in several small Mesopotamian states of the eighteenth century, viz., Warum, Mari, and Der. A Hittite text (fourteenth century?) is explicit: Kingship is the storm god's, who has given the government to his human deputy. The application of this principle to early Israel is not refuted by maintaining that in the premonarchical period Israel did not have the specific experience that would enable it to give that shape to its religious ideal. *Malk* and other forms or words conventionally translated "king" in fact denote the highest ruler, chief, or leader of the political organization of a given kind of society. The question is not primarily one of this or that ancient lexeme. The *abbū* of the Ḫaneans in the area of eighteenth-century Mari are also called *šarrānu*. The first word is usually translated "sheiks" (literary "fathers"), the second "kings." The Midianites, no less nomadic than contemporary Israel, were ruled by *m*e*lāchîm* ("kings"; Judg. 8:12) as well as by *sārîm* ("princes"; Judg. 7:25). The basic question is in whom the chief authority of the polity is vested. If it is God, concentration of power in one man for more than a fleeting moment is excluded, and the formation of firm and permanent institutions of leadership, lawgiving, and decision-making is hardly tolerated. *See* SAMUEL, I AND II[S] §4.

A combination of arguments (*a*) and (*b*) makes it quite probable that the societal meaning of the kingship of God is early and genuine Israelite. In practice it differed from similar phenomena of other Near Eastern civilizations, as far as they are known to us, in the consistency and dedication with which the ideal was held and with which its implementation was tried again and again.

Later the societal meaning was fused with the mythic meaning (as in Isa. 41:21-24; 44:6-7; Ps. 47), in a characteristic expression of monotheism.

Bibliography. J. A. Soggin in *Theologisches Handwörterbuch zum AT,* I (1971), cols. 914-15.

M. TSEVAT

***KINGDOM OF GOD.** This remains a central topic in biblical, especially NT research. In addition to the bibliography with the original article, the following representative studies are important.

1. The kingdom of God in OT and Jewish Sources. J. Bright, *The Kingdom of God* (1953); A. Schweitzer, *The Kingdom of God and Primitive Christianity* (1951 [ET 1968]), Pt. I; J. Bonsirven, *Palestinian Judaism in the Time of Jesus Christ* (1950 [ET 1964]), chs. 8-10.

2. Jesus and the Synoptic gospels. ***a. Future and apocalyptic interpretations.*** H. S. Reimarus, *The Goal of Jesus and His Disciples* (ET 1970), also trans. as *Fragments* (ET 1970), was first published by G. E. Lessing in 1778. Reimarus held that Jesus was thinking mainly of a political kingdom. J. Weiss, *Jesus' Proclamation of the Kingdom of God* (ET 1971), was a major event when it first appeared in 1892. A. Schweitzer (cited in §1 *above*), Pt. II, presents his fullest account of Jesus' eschatological message. *See also* R. H. Hiers, *The Kingdom of God in the Synoptic Tradition* (1970), and *The Historical Jesus and the Kingdom of God* (1973).

b. The kingdom of God as present. J. A. T. Robinson, *Jesus and His Coming* (1957), argues that Jesus did not expect significant future eschatological occurrences. C. H. Dodd, *The Parables of the Kingdom* (rev. ed., 1961), maintains the viewpoint set forth in his earlier works. N. Perrin, *Rediscovering the Teaching of Jesus* (1967), and *Jesus and the Language of the Kingdom* (1975), emphasizes a present, experiential kingdom of God.

c. Both future and present. Several excellent studies find Jesus' understanding of the kingdom of God both future and present, but like W. G. Kümmel, *Promise and Fulfilment,* SBT, XXIII (3rd ed., 1956), finally claim the latter essential, while tending to subordinate the former; H. Ridderbos, *The Coming of the Kingdom* (1950 [ET 1962]); G. Lundström, *The Kingdom of God in the Teaching of Jesus* (1947 [ET 1963]); N. Perrin, *The Kingdom of God and the Teaching of Jesus* (1963); R. Schnackenburg, *God's Rule and Kingdom* (1959); G. E. Ladd, *The Presence of the Future* (rev. ed., 1974); J. Reumann, *Jesus in the Church's Gospels* (1968), chs. 6-8.

3. Early Christianity. *See* R. Bultmann, *Theology of the NT,* 2 vols. (1948-53); A Schweitzer (cited in §1 *above*), Pts. III, IV, as well as his classic, *The Mysticism of Paul the Apostle* (1911 [ET 1931]); E. Käsemann, *NT Questions of Today* (1964), ch. 5. D. E. Aune, *The Cultic Setting of Realized Eschatology in Early Christianity,* NovT Sup, XXVIII (1972), proposes that early Christians experienced eschatological salvation through worship as evidenced, e.g., in the Gospel of John and the ODES OF SOLOMON. Problems and consequences deriving from the fact that the kingdom of God did not come are examined by M. Werner, *The Formation of Christian Dogma* (1941 [ET 1957]); E. Grässer, *Das Problem der Parusieverzögerung in den synoptischen Evangelien und in der Apostelgeschichte,* BZNW, XXII (2nd ed., 1960); and J. G. Gager, *Kingdom and Community* (1975), ch. 2. H. Conzelmann, *The Theology of St. Luke* (1957), and W. C. Robinson, Jr., *Der Weg des Herrn,* Theologische Forschung, XXXVI (1964), see the delay of the PAROUSIA as a basic Lukan concern.

4. The kingdom of God and ethics. C. Walther, *Typen des Reich-Gottes-Verständnisses,* FGLP, XXII (1961), treats nineteenth-century interpretations (Kant, Fichte, Hegel, Schleiermacher, Rothe, and Ritschl). A. N. Wilder, *Eschatology and Ethics in the Teaching of Jesus* (rev. ed., 1950), urges that Jesus' announcement of the coming kingdom was only a formal, symbolic and secondary sanction for his ethics. R. H. Hiers, *Jesus and Ethics* (1968), reviews the positions of Harnack, Schweitzer, Bultmann, and Dodd. C. E. Braaten, *Eschatology and Ethics* (1974), relates biblical eschatology to current issues.

5. The kingdom of God and contemporary theology. J. Moltmann, *The Theology of Hope* (1964), W. Pannenberg, *Theology and the Kingdom of God* (1969), and C. E. Braaten, *Christ and Counter-Christ* (1972), exemplify the "new" theology or "theology of hope," blending biblical research, Reformation doctrines, and contemporary theological concerns.

See also articles and bibliographies on APOCALYPTICISM; APOCALYPTICISM[S]; ESCHATOLOGY OF THE OT; ESCHATOLOGY OF THE NT; ESCHATOLOGY OF THE NT[S]; MESSIAH; SON OF MAN; SON OF MAN[S].

R. H. HIERS

***KINGS, I AND II. 1. Kings as part of the "Former Prophets."** That the two books of Kings form a single unit is evident from the continuity in the Elijah cycle of narratives (I Kings 17–II Kings 2), itself part of a major section running from I Kings 17 to II Kings 13, in which primary place is given to prophetic material (*see* §3 *below*). It is also clear that the opening of I Kings forms a continuous narrative with that of II Sam. 9–20, interrupted only by appendixes to the books of Samuel (*see* SAMUEL, I AND II §§5-6 and supplementary article). In their turn these books are closely linked with Joshua and Judges. Thus as it stands, the section of the Hebrew Bible known as the "Former Prophets" has a literary unity; consideration of any one of its component parts cannot ignore the implications of such an over-all unity of final redaction. As regards structure, the question is whether the very evident differences between the four books (Joshua to Kings) are sufficiently explained as due to the differences of the materials utilized by their compiler(s) or require the supposition of quite independent redactional activity; as regards purpose, whether differences of emphasis are again sufficiently accounted for if they are viewed as belonging to the prior stages through which the material has passed, and whether they may be seen as subsumed within a single recognizable and definable ultimate intention on the part of a final redactor whose activity cannot be placed earlier than the mid-sixth century B.C. (later than the latest event recorded in II Kings 25:27-30). *See* DEUTERONOMIC HISTORY, THE[S].

2. Redactional activity in Kings. The widely accepted "two edition" view of the books of Kings (*see* KINGS I AND II §§5-6) endeavors to resolve the contradiction between passages which clearly envisage the exilic situation and those (e.g., II Kings 22:20 on the death of Josiah) which appear to be unaware of it. It is clear that account must be taken of the degree to which earlier material retains its original form even when incorporated in a framework or a larger work which offers a different, even a contradictory, interpretation. Such a survival of contradiction may be seen in the positive statements concerning Jeroboam II in II Kings 14:25-29 (*see also* §3 *below*); the principle is in any case familiar in other parts of the OT, notably in the PENTATEUCH. Detailed examination of particular sections of the work—for example the Hezekiah narratives—suggests that a greater degree of redactional unity was given to the work in the exilic age than has sometimes been supposed. As with other kinds of material, notably psalmody and prophecy, the provision of a new context, or a minimum of verbal change, may invite the reader to see a quite different meaning in words which originally applied to a situation other than his own. *See* REDACTION CRITICISM, OT[S].

Detailed study of the framework material—the formulas which introduce and close the reigns of individual rulers—suggests that it is not all of one piece, though it may be doubted whether the verbal differences are sufficient to establish precise stages in the redaction. It is clear that Deuteronomic and Deuteronomistic are terms which should not be regarded as suggesting a single moment or a single process, but more precise definition may not be possible on the basis of the limited evidence available. The textual problems (*see below*) alone forbid too simple a delineation of the process. Moreover, it may with justice be affirmed that, in a period before strict and meticulous copying was enjoined, each copy of a work may in some degree be equivalent to a new edition. And such clues as we have point to a multiplicity of text forms in the earlier stages. Thus the two forms of the Hezekiah-Isaiah narrative (II Kings 18:13–20:21; Isa. 36–39) reveal different "editorial" stages: the absence of II Kings 18:14-16 from the latter, and the addition of a "prayer of Hezekiah" in Isa. 38 (plus deviations in other respects in that narrative) make this clear.

The supposition that the last part of II Kings represents a shortened version of Jer. 37–44 hardly does justice to the complex relationship between these two sharply divergent forms of the same or similar material; it may be better to think in terms of two alternative endings to one work. The same applies to the slighter differences to be seen in Jer. 52.

The textual situation also remains unresolved. The MT, LXX, and Qumran texts illustrate the variety and complexity of the textual evidence, and the Qumran texts provide support for a more positive evaluation of the LXX *Vorlage* (*see* SEPTUAGINT[S] §A1; TEXT, HEBREW, HISTORY OF[S] §1). The relationship between the texts of Kings and Chronicles is a matter of great complexity. At some points it is probable that the text of Kings has been influenced by the Chronicles text; a two-way process of influence may have continued until a relatively late date. We are not able either to trace a completely coherent history of the textual development or to adjudicate firmly between one form of the text and another. *See* CHRONICLES, I AND II[S].

These considerations make it evident that while we may observe certain main points in the development of the present form of Kings, we must also acknowledge that a precise definition in terms of two or more "editions" does less than justice to the facts. We may need to recognize that the text, in any of the forms known to us, represents a certain element of accident, of fixation at a point which is not neat and well-rounded, but leaves unevenness and inconsistency.

3. Prophetic material in Kings. It is evident that a crucial part is played in the narratives by prophets, named and unnamed. A pattern of judgment and promise, already begun in Judg. 6 and in the Samuel narratives, develops into a much closer correlation between prophetic intervention and the sequence of events. The reign of Solomon is set in the prophecies of Nathan (I Kings 1) and Ahijah (I Kings 11); his successor Rehoboam in Judah and the line of rulers in the N come under prophetic comment in I Kings 12–16. The whole section from I Kings 17 to II Kings 13 is dominated by the complex twofold cycle of Elijah and Elisha, with the indications of overlap in the portrayals of these two nevertheless distinctive figures; the former's traditions are interwoven with the separate prophetic elements of I Kings 20 and 22, the latter's with material concerning prophetic bands, depicted as associated with Elisha, who nevertheless, like Elijah, appears also as a lone figure.

From this point on, a different question emerges. While there is much prophetic material, and frequent allusion to prophetic activity, the absence of reference to the major prophets with the exception of Isaiah (II Kings 18–20) and the less significant mention of Jonah (II Kings 14:25) presents a curious problem. Various solutions have been proposed, ranging from the supposition that a prophetic canon was already sufficiently established for such reference to be unnecessary (but if so, why the inclusion of the Isaiah material?), to the idea that in some degree the books of Kings offer a critique of prophetic judgment, with II Kings 14:25-27 as a denial of the doom oracles of Amos. In reality the situation is considerably more complex. The presence of the Isaiah material in II Kings 18–20 is all the more remarkable because of the absence of allusions to Isaiah in the Ahaz narrative of II Kings 16 (cf. Isa. 7). The existence of an alternative narrative form in Jer. 37–44 shows evidence of a presentation in which Jeremiah is a full participant (*see* §2 *above*). The form of the text again in this respect suggests a moment of fixation which has in it both an element of chance (the Isaiah material present) and an element of choice (the Jeremiah material not included); the final form would thus be in some degree related to the existence of a prophetic collection, but not consistently ordered with that in view. *See* Canon of the OT[S] §2*b*.

What is more, we may observe in the prophetic material that is included a variability of editorial method. In the case of Isaiah there is a substantial, though not a full, measure of editorial integration. In the Elijah and Elisha material, there is in general much less evidence of such reworking, though it is not entirely absent. For the most part the reinterpretation of those narratives depends on their context, their being fitted into the framework so that they become comments on the reigns of particular rulers, while retaining much of their earlier form.

4. Problems of chronology. No one solution appears to meet all the chronological problems presented by the figures given for individual reigns and for synchronisms between the two kingdoms. Suppositions regarding calendar change at the time of the Neo-Babylonian conquest open up some possibilities of clarification; the probable practice of co-regency, or at least its use in some specific cases such as that of Uzziah and Jotham, offers another approach; the recognition that numerical symbols or number-words, especially if abbreviated, are readily susceptible of error, adds a third possible element (*see* Abbreviations, Hebrew Texts[S]). Intractable inconsistencies remain, and no one of these or other suggestions can resolve all the difficulties. We have a sufficiently close chronology for general purposes; the endeavor to work out a detailed scheme, even for the last years of Judah where we have a great deal of information, must inevitably remain hypothetical at many points. *See* Chronology of the OT and supplementary article.

5. The nature and purpose of Kings. The continuity of material from the preceding books inevitably means that any comment on the books of Kings alone is inadequate. Yet within this particular section of the narrative presentation of what led up to the final collapse of the kingdoms of Israel and Judah, we may observe the degree to which the compiler or compilers have engaged in a process of selection, clearly taking up only a part of the material which must have been available to them; they have offered a patterned presentation, not as highly stylized as that of the later Chronicler (*see* Chronicles, I and II[S] §4), but nevertheless in some respects artificial. The reign of Solomon is clearly a high point because of the building of the temple, which is a central theme of the work; for the compiler, loyalty to Yahweh is substantially equated with loyalty to the Jerusalem sanctuary. This section incorporated the markedly homiletic prayer of Solomon (I Kings 8), which provides a significant punctuating moment. The whole account of Solomon is set within the initiating prophecy of Nathan and the judgment of Ajihah, and might in this respect almost be said to epitomize the whole. The pattern of the kings of the North, universally condemned, is broken by the interventions of Elijah and Elisha, which obliquely say so much about the nature of Yahwistic faith in that area. With the decline and collapse of the North, there is both the occasion for the introduction of one of the major commenting discourses (II Kings 17, comparable with such an earlier passage as I Sam. 12) and the moment for introducing a more stylized pattern into the reigns—bad and good alternating (Ahaz, Hezekiah, Manasseh-Amon, Josiah, Jehoahas-Jehoiakim-Jehoiachin-Zedekiah) to the first moment of doom in 597. That these judgments are in some measure artificial is clear from a close examination of the material. The description of Hezekiah begins to move to that greater degree of idealization typical of later accounts. This may explain the inclusion of the Isaiah material, which centers around him, whereas the books of both Isaiah and Micah (cf. Jer. 26) suggest a much more negative appraisal. It is too simple a judgment to see Ahaz as evil because his temple reforms (II Kings 16) are negatively assessed; or Manasseh (II Kings 21) because his reign is associated only with apostasy. The complexities of politics and religion are not in reality so readily unraveled, and Manasseh in particular has been utilized as a counterpart for Judah of the Jeroboam ben Nebat who "caused Israel to sin." We may note that in the later presentation by the Chronicler the emphasis has shifted: Ahaz has become the supreme example of evil, whereas Manasseh has been transformed into a penitent and a reformer (II Chr. 28 and 33).

Such stylizing marks a homiletic exposition and cautions against too simple a reconstruction of history based upon it. Whatever may have been the motivation of the compilers of earlier structures, its ultimate form is directed toward providing instruction and encouragement for those who looked back on Judah's total collapse. The books of Kings give, not simply in the somewhat equivocal ending with Jehoiachin's release, but in the whole presentation with its repeated hints of warning and promise, a look at the past which holds within itself a rethinking of the community's life for the future.

Bibliography. For a survey to 1961, *see* E. Jenni, "Zwei Jahrzehnte Forschung an den Büchern Josua bis Könige," *Theol. Rundschau,* XXVII (1961), 1-32, 97-146.

Commentaries: J. Gray, *I and II Kings* (1963 [2nd ed., 1970]); J. Fichtner, *Das erste Buch von den Königen* (1964); K. D. Fricke, *Das Zweite Buch von den Königen* (1972); H. A. Brongers, *Eerste Koningen* (1967), *Tweede Koningen* (1970); M. Noth, *Könige,* BK IX/1 (1968); J. Robinson, CBC, I (1972); II (1976).

Commentaries in one-volume works: J. Mauchline, *Peake's Commentary on the Bible* (rev. ed., 1962), pp. 338-56; *JBC* (1968), pp. 179-209; *IOVC* (1971), pp. 181-207.

Textual studies: J. D. Shenkel, *Chronology and Recensional Development in the Greek Text of Kings* (1968); T. Muraoka, "The Greek Texts of Samuel-Kings: Incomplete Translations or Recensional Activity?" *Septuagint and Cognate Studies,* ed. R. Kraft, II (1972), 90-107; D. W. Gooding, *Relics of Ancient Exegesis: a Study of the Miscellanies in 3 Reigns 2,* Soc. for OT Study Monographs, 4, 1975.

Chronology: *see* CHRONOLOGY OF THE OT and supplementary article.

Special Studies: P. R. Ackroyd, "Historians and Prophets" *SEA,* XXXIII (1968), 18-54, and "An Interpretation of the Babylonian Exile: A Study of 2 Kings 20, Isaiah 38–39," *SJT,* XXVII (1974), 329-52; S. R. Bin-Nun, "Formulas from Royal Records of Israel and of Judah," *VT,* XVIII (1968), 414-32; G. Braulik, "Spuren einer Neubearbeitung des deuteronomistischen Geschichtswerkes in I Kön. 8, 52-53, 59-60," *Bibl.,* LII (1971), 20-33; G. Buccellati, *Cities and Nations of Ancient Syria,* Studi Semitici, 26 (1971); F. Crüsemann, "Kritik an Amos im deuteronomistischen Geschichtswerk: Erwägungen zu 2 Könige 14,27," in *Probleme biblischer Theologie* (1971), pp. 57-63; J. Debus, *Die Sünde Jerobeams, FRLANT,* XCIII (1967); O. Eissfeldt, "Die Komposition von I Reg 16.29–II Reg. 13.25," in *Das Ferne und Nahe Wort, BZAW,* CV (1967), 49-58=*Kleine Schriften,* V (1973), 21-30; J. Lindblom, *Erwägungen zur Herkunft der Josianischen Tempelurkunde* (1971); B. Porten, "The Structure and Theme of the Solomon Narrative (I Kings 3–11)," *HUCA,* XXXVIII (1967), 93-128; H. Weippert, "Die 'deuteronomistischen' Beurteilungen der Könige von Israel und Juda und das Problem der Redaktion der Königsbücher," *Bibl.,* LIII (1972), 301-39; M. Weippert, "Fragen des israelitischen Geschichtsbewusstseins," *VT,* XXIII (1973), 415-42; D. J. Wiseman, *Chronicles of Chaldaean Kings* (1956); E. Zenger, "Die deuteronomistische Interpretation der Rehabilitierung Jojachins," *BZ,* XII (1968), 16-30.

P. R. ACKROYD

KINSHIP AND FAMILY. A system in each society which structures and labels those interpersonal relationships, with their attendant rights and duties, which are based on real or putative ties of genealogy or marriage. A kinship system may also, depending on the defining principles involved, specify certain bounded groups (family, lineage, clan, etc.) which may function collectively. In most human societies, kinship ties are the most important ties between persons, and the obligations they entail override all others. There are even societies in which kinship ties are the only ones which bind the society together.

In general, societies which have the simplest subsistence patterns (hunting and gathering) have the fewest nonkinship associations, but kinship organization itself in such societies ranges from the minimal (Eskimos) to the extremely elaborate (Australian Aborigines). Societies which practice pastoralism tend to have highly developed kinship systems but little other social structure. Agricultural societies typically have complex kinship systems, and may also have highly developed nonkin associations based on age, sex, or other considerations (much of traditional Asia and Africa). Modern industrial societies tend to elaborate a high number of associations but to simplify their kinship systems.

1. Learning one's kinship system
2. Descent systems and kinship groups
   a. Bilineal systems and kindreds
   b. Unilineal systems and resulting groups
   c. Double descent and ambilineal systems
3. Kinship terminology
   a. Principles involved
   b. Types of systems
4. The regulation of marriage
   a. Exogamy
   b. Endogamy
   c. Preferred and prescribed marriages
   d. Resulting relations between groups
5. The family
   a. The nuclear family
   b. The composite family
   c. The extended family
6. Residential units
   a. The household
   b. Nomadic units
   c. Sedentary units
7. Functions of kinship
   a. Social identity
   b. Socialization
   c. Social security
   d. Economic co-operation
   e. Social order
   f. Descent and inheritance
   g. Regulation of marriage
   h. Religious and ceremonial functions
8. Kinship in ancient Israel
   a. Patriarchal times
   b. After the Exodus
   c. The kingdom
   d. After the return from exile

1. Learning one's kinship system. As a child (Ego) becomes gradually aware of the social world in which he lives, he or she first recognizes the existence and some of the significance of the people he sees around him: parents, siblings, perhaps grandparents, aunts and uncles, and so forth. He learns that these people have distinctive labels that make them "relatives" or "kin" to separate them from all others. He learns that each labeled relationship between him and other persons entails a set of expected attitudes and behaviors, a set of rights and duties. He learns that his relatives are often—depending on the system—related to each other. Some of his kin are related to him by descent ("blood"), some by marriage. As male Ego grows up, he learns that some women are sexually taboo because of kinship. Female Ego learns that some men are sexually taboo. Both learn that some partners are taboo for marriage, while others are preferred or even prescribed. In short, Ego learns his or her kinship system: the rules for deciding who is related to him and in what way, and the attitudes and behaviors that these relationships involve.

2. Descent systems and kinship groups. Though each person normally feels that his own kinship system is the "right" or "natural" one, in fact human societies operate with every possible kind of system, based on every possible view of the nature of descent. These systems illustrate the fact that kinship is fundamentally a social, not a biological, reality. That is, each society agrees upon what factors shall be taken into consideration in deciding who are kin. The American system, in which biological relationship is crucial, is only one possibility among others; and it is a *social* agreement that makes biology predominate, just as by social agreement some societies partially ignore biology.

a. Bilineal systems and kindreds. Bilineal systems (sometimes called bilateral) such as the American system give equal weight to relationships through Ego's father and mother. Though recent findings in genetics give biological support to this view, the system long antedates knowledge of genetics. The terminology reflects the sameness of relations on both sides by using the same terms, for example, for father's father and for mother's father.

Two facts characterize bilineal systems and the kinship "groups" they generate: (1) The system can be extended in all directions and to all generations to the limits of one's interest and available information without coming to any boundary across which people are not related; in other words, the *kindred* generated by a bilineal system is not a bounded group. (2) The set of persons who are related to any given Ego and his full siblings is unique: I am related to everyone who is related to my father, but my father is not related to everyone who is related to me. Since a kindred is not bounded there is no possibility of its ever functioning corporately. It is also possible in such a system for Ego to be caught in the middle of a conflict between people to whom he is related but who are not related to each other. Since a kindred is so weak, societies with bilineal systems assign great responsibility to the nuclear family, which is the only unit with any degree of boundedness and coherence.

Bilineal systems exist typically (though by no means exclusively) at the two extremes of the subsistence ladder: among hunters and gatherers, and in modern industrial societies. Both of these otherwise totally different kinds of societies require a high degree of flexibility and mobility for the minimal unit, the nuclear family; in the first, there often seems no need for some of the functions fulfilled by elaborate kinship systems, in the latter many of the necessary functions are fulfilled by nonkinship associations.

b. Unilineal systems and resulting groups. An alternate approach is to select as crucial relationships established through only one parent. In other words, biological relationships which exist through the other parent are ignored or even denied, whether or not the people involved have the relevant genetic knowledge.

i. *Matrilineal systems.* A matrilineal system says that Ego is related to his mother and her kin, but not to his father and his kin. Such a system, of course, emphasizes the already obvious cruciality of the mother for the birth and early survival of her child and de-emphasizes the role of the father. Society may, for instance, deny biological paternity; or it may recognize it but deny that it has important social consequences. In a number of such societies, the father is an indulgent adult, or he may be largely absent and have no significant relationship with Ego. In many such situations, it is mother's brother who is the male authority figure.

ii. *Patrilineal systems.* Though the patrilineal system appears to be a mirror image of the matrilineal one, in that the child is related to father and his kin, but not to mother, it is in fact not just a mirror image because of the irreducibly different biological roles of father and mother. Whereas in a matrilineal system father can be reduced to a virtual zero, there is no way of similarly reducing mother's role. Thus, at least in Ego's subjective experience, the relative importance of the two parents tends to be more balanced in a patrilineal system. But in jural terms, the child belongs unequivocally to his father. Because of the greater indispensability of the mother, the nuclear family is often more important and more stable in patrilineal than in matrilineal societies.

iii. *Lineage, clan, moiety, phratry.* In one respect, unilineal systems are alike and together contrast with bilineal ones: they both produce defined, bounded groups, such that each individual belongs to one group only. It is (in principle if not always in reality) possible to list the members of such a group and to tell unambiguously whether a given person is a member or not. There are several types of such groups.

A *lineage* consists of all descendants of a real, known, historical ancestor. The depth in generations varies with the ability of society to keep records, but it rarely exceeds four or five generations.

A *clan* consists of the real or putative descendants of a legendary, mythical, or very remote ancestor, so that there may be reason to doubt the strict accuracy of genealogies. When the ancestor is a mythical creature or an animal, it may continue to have a special relation to the clan and its members in the form of a totem. *See* TOTEMISM[S].

A *moiety* is one of two complementary and exogamous groups into which an entire society is divided for the reciprocal exchange of women. A *phratry* is like a moiety except that there are more than two phratries in the society.

Within a given unilineal society, it is possible for lineages, clans, and moieties (or phratries) to coexist, each fulfilling certain roles in the total scheme. In such a case, a moiety (or phratry) is divided into clans, and a clan into lineages. Each lineage may, in some societies, be further divided into sublineages.

Roughly two thirds of the societies of the world are unilineal, the large majority being patrilineal. Pastoral societies without known exception are patrilineal; agricultural societies may be either patrilineal or matrilineal.

c. Double descent and ambilineal systems. These are much rarer than the others.

In double descent, Ego is related to both parents, but in quite different ways and for different social purposes. Each individual belongs to one patrilineage (or clan) and one matrilineage (or clan), but only full siblings belong to the same pair.

In ambilineal (sometimes called nonunilineal) systems, male Ego chooses, subject to the approval of present members, whether he will belong to the kinship group of his father or to that of his mother. The group thus constituted, called a ramage, is bounded like a clan, but not unilineal. Ego may also, for convenience or social prestige, and with the consent of present members, choose to belong to the ramage of his wife (via her father or mother). Though a person may belong to two or more ramages, only one is fully functional at any period of his life. This system is found in the Pacific, notably in Samoa.

3. Kinship terminology. This is the set of terms used to designate or to address all persons categorized as kin. Terminology obviously reflects kinship structures—that is, the patterned statuses and prescribed interpersonal relations, though not always with total accuracy. In any system, some terms are particularizing, in that they designate a single person (e.g., "father" in English), others are classificatory, in that they lump together a number of persons who occupy quite distinct places in the genealogical chart (e.g., "cousin" in English). Clearly, the emotional flavor of relations between two individuals will be in some ways unique to the pair; but in the structural sense, it is generally true that the kin who are lumped under a single term, however different they may be in all other respects, owe the same duties to Ego and expect the same privileges from him or her.

a. Principles involved. We have already seen that biology can be ignored in favor of a social reality structured along different lines. A broader statement is that although all societies make use of a set of universal categories or dimensions in grouping or splitting kin types and in defining kin terms, each system uses a particular subset of these categories and applies them in a unique way. The categories most commonly used are as follows:

1. *Difference of generation.* Contrast "father" and "son."
2. *Difference between lineal and collateral kin.* Contrast "father" and "uncle."
3. *Difference in sex.* Contrast "brother" and "sister."
4. *Difference between consanguineal and affinal kin.* In English, "husband" and "wife" are exclusively affinal; all others are consanguineal unless followed by "-in-law."
5. *Difference in sex of linking relative.* This category, not used in English, characterizes unilineal systems because it distinguishes kin through father from kin through mother.
6. *Difference in age within same generation.* This is found in societies conscious of seniority, where it may be important to distinguish older brother from younger brother.
7. *Difference in sex of Ego.* In such systems, which are rare, men and women use different terminologies.
8. *Same sex vs. opposite sex.* This distinction, which is fairly rare, obtains only for siblings. A man calls his brother and a woman calls her sister by a term meaning "sibling of same sex"; a man will call his sister and a woman her brother by a term meaning "sibling of opposite sex."

No system uses all of these, nor will they be used by the same rules. English uses only 1-4.

b. Types of systems. The interplay of these categories with the different descent rules generates a potentially enormous number of distinct terminologies (disregarding the trivial matter of the actual phonetic forms used). But in fact all terminologies can be classified into six broad groups, depending upon which kin are lumped together and which are differentiated in parents' generation; which are lumped and which are differentiated in Ego's generation; and the operation of certain skewing rules which reflect descent and marriage rules. In what follows, I will use the most elementary kin terms in a strictly genealogical sense and compound them for more remote kin.

i. *The Hawaiian system* (also called the generational system) lumps people of the same generation and distinguishes people of adjacent generations. Thus, a single term covers father, father's brother, and mother's brother, and a parallel term covers mother, mother's sister, and father's sister. Similarly a single term (or a pair of sex-distinguished terms) covers all siblings and first cousins. Such a system, of course, is used in a bilineal society, since kin of both sides are treated in the same way.

ii. *The Eskimo system* (also called the lineal system) lumps father's brother and mother's brother, but has a distinct term for father; it lumps mother's sister and father's sister, but has a distinct term for mother; and it has a single term for first cousins, but distinguishes them from siblings. This is obviously the American system. It reflects a bilineal society in which the nuclear family is the fundamental unit, by distinguishing lineal from collateral kin.

iii. *The Iroquois,* iv. *Crow, and* v. *Omaha systems* all have in common that they reflect unilineal societies. They lump father's brother with father but distinguish mother's brother; they lump mother's sister with mother but distinguish father's sister; and they lump parallel cousins (father's brother's children, mother's sister's children) with siblings but distinguish cross cousins (father's sister's children, mother's brother's children). Such a treatment shows that these societies consider parallel cousins to be the same as siblings, but do not so consider cross cousins; the latter may even be preferred marriage partners. The skewing rules which distinguish these systems from each other are complex, but their effect is to make the Iroquois system weakly correlated with matriliny, the Crow strongly correlated with matriliny, and the Omaha strongly correlated with patriliny.

vi. *The Sudanese system* has the most particularizing terms, in that there are separate terms for father, father's brother, and mother's brother; for mother, mother's sister, and father's sister; and for siblings, parallel cousins, and cross cousins. This is the rarest of all the terminologies.

4. The regulation of marriage. Some consider the regulation of marriage to be the most important function of kinship systems. This begins with the incest taboo, but goes much further, in that it specifies rules of exogamy, rules of endogamy, and even, in some cases, rules which pinpoint a particular kin position whose occupant (s) is/are the preferred or prescribed spouse.

a. Exogamy. This is the rule that one may not marry a fellow-member of a particular group, usually a kinship group. In all societies this includes the nuclear family, and usually the extended family. It is rare in bilineal societies that the rule goes further; but in unilineal societies it is not uncommon for lineages or even clans to be exogamous, even when they number in the millions. In societies with moieties and phratries, these are by definition exogamous. The origin and rationale of exogamy are in dispute, but one effect is to force each exogamous group to find wives outside itself.

b. Endogamy. This is the rule that one should marry a fellow-member of one's own group. This may be a kinship group, as when certain pastoral peoples, including ancient Hebrews in patriarchal times, practiced lineage endogamy to keep women, their future children, and their property in the lineage. Many societies practice community endogamy, or social class/caste endogamy, or religious endogamy, or society-wide endogamy, so that marriage with foreigners or outsiders is forbidden or frowned upon.

c. Preferred and prescribed marriages. Many societies have more specific rules than exogamy and endogamy. In some cases, kinship groups have between themselves long-standing arrangements for the direct exchange of women: e.g., you marry my sister, I'll marry yours. Some societies practice deferred but still direct exchange in alternate generations. In still other instances, three or more groups, such as phratries, have a circular system whereby group A gives wives to B, B gives wives to C, and C gives wives to A. Finally, the rules may be so precise that the preferred or prescribed marriage narrows down to a particular position in the kinship network; in some patrilineal societies, the preferred bride is mother's brother's daughter (she is not of one's group, since she is not of father's group). Obviously, the more specific the rule, the more often it happens that no one occupies the preferred position. But in such cases all societies make provision for alternative marriages; in societies with the most restrictive rules, the "preferred" marriages are in fact statistically rare. In other words, societies can either define a broad class of available women within which it is easy to find a suitable mate; or they can make narrow rules and provide for many exceptions.

d. Resulting relations between groups. Relations between groups which exchange women, either directly or indirectly, are often ambivalent. On the one hand, there must be a minimum of civility to permit the often complicated negotiations that precede marriage. On the other hand, unilineal groups are often competitive and even hostile outside marriage arrangements. Thus, one finds two motifs in explanations of intergroup marriage relationships: "We marry our enemies" and "We marry to cement alliances." Groups which have exchanged women are often regarded as having enduring rights and obligations in their relationships; these can be an important factor in maintaining a sometimes precarious superkin unity within society as a whole. It is hardly ever the case that marriage is regarded as a purely private arrangement between the spouses themselves.

Another dimension of this question is that a group which has given a woman to another is at that moment in a creditor, that is, a superior position, with respect to the receiving group. If the exchange is direct and immediate, there is no problem. If the exchange is deferred, the receiving group is in an inferior-debtor position until the balance is restored. But in the case of complex exchange, each group remains in a permanently inferior position in relation to the group that always gives it wives and in a permanently superior position with respect to the group to which it gives wives. This aspect of the question is only partially altered in the case of societies which practice bride wealth payment. *See also* DIVORCE[S]; MARRIAGE[S].

5. The family. The family is that kinship unit which lives together on a fairly continuous basis. It should not be confused with the household, however, since the latter often includes nonkin.

a. The nuclear family. In most societies, a nuclear family is established when a man and a woman marry; in some, it does not begin until the birth of the first child; and in a very few, it is hard to identify such a unit at all. In some societies, the nuclear family endures until the last child gets married or otherwise leaves home; in others, it lasts until the death of one spouse; in many, it can end with divorce. Whatever the precise social definition of the beginning and end of a nuclear family, it is clearly a relatively temporary and unstable unit. Furthermore, each individual during his lifetime normally belongs to two such units, the one into which he or she is born and the one founded when he or she marries; and it is not unusual for the interests of these to be in conflict and for the individual to be torn between incompatible obligations. Societies provide different resolutions to these conflicts, whether in favor of one's natal family or of one's conjugal family.

b. The composite family. This type of family exists whenever one marriage partner has more than one spouse (polygamy). The commonest pattern is polygyny, in which a man has more than one wife. In such a situation, each wife with her children constitutes an important unit, while the husband is the single tie that binds the whole together. The composite family may itself be merely a unit in a still larger family.

c. The extended family. This may be defined as a sublineage which lives together. In a typical patrilineal extended family, a patriarch will be at the head; with him live his wife or wives, his married sons and their wives, their married sons and their wives, and all unmarried children, grandchildren, and so on. The mirror image obtains in a matrilineal society, though authority is often in the hands of the brothers and sons of the core women rather than in the hands of the women themselves. In such a system, there is normally a sharp distinction between insiders (men and their children in a patrilineal system, women and their children in a matrilineal one) and the outsiders who have married in. In some societies, spouses are given full rights and are received with much affection; at the opposite extreme are cases where bitter hostility continues between spouses and affinal kin even after the marriage, and the in-marrying persons are harshly treated.

6. Residential units. Though residential units are not in themselves necessarily kinship groups, in almost all societies kinship and marriage are the most important factors on which co-residence is based.

a. The household. This is the smallest residential unit. The core is typically a family (in any of the above senses); but the household often includes unrelated persons such as servants or slaves and long-term guests.

Not all members actually need dwell in the same building, though they may (a typical example would be the pueblos of the matrilineal extended families of the Hopi, Zuni, and other Southwestern peoples). Composite or extended families often live in a cluster of huts, perhaps surrounded by a fence or hedge.

In addition to co-residence, the household is characterized by centralization of authority and of family activities, including economic activities and the management of family assets.

b. Nomadic units. When nomadic—that is, hunting and gathering or pastoral—peoples have residential units larger than the household, they are called, in order of increasing size, the camp and the band. The camp includes one or more households that stay together most of the time; they may be tied together by kinship, but need not be. The band comprises several camps that recognize their special relationship by getting together periodically—often annually—for social, economic, and religious purposes.

Nomadic units are often fairly unstable, since a marked increase in population or a decrease in resources often requires fission. This was the case when Abraham and Lot had to separate when pasture and water were insufficient for their animals (Gen. 13:1-13). *See also* NOMADISM[S].

c. Sedentary units. Sedentary peoples often live together in units larger than households. In order of increasing size, they are the neighborhood or ward, the village or town, and the district. The extent to which kinship is involved in these groupings varies all the way from total determination to virtual lack of correlation.

In some cases, sedentary peoples reflect their kinship relationships not only in residential patterns, but also in patterns of land distribution and use, so that the closer the kinship between farmers, the closer together their fields. Something of this kind appears to have resulted from the initial distribution of the land of Canaan among the Israelites after the Exodus. *See* TRIBES, TERRITORIES OF[S].

7. Functions of kinship. Scholars debate hotly which is the predominant function of kinship; some emphasize descent and inheritance; others the regulation of marriage; others, especially cultural materialists, emphasize economic considerations; still others emphasize ideological, mythical, and religious factors. What is clear is that kinship in most societies plays multiple roles, and their relative importance varies widely. The following list includes those functions which are most commonly fulfilled, in whole or in part, by kinship systems.

a. Social identity. By defining the conditions of legitimacy and affiliation, the rules of marriage and kinship provide each person with his social identity. A child who for any reason is not recognized by the rules is a social outcast in many societies; in others, the rules function in such a way as to assign legitimate parentage to every child, regardless of biology.

b. Socialization. Whether or not a society has formal schools (a small minority do), the bulk of the socialization process is carried out by the kin group, especially the family.

c. Social security. In most non-Western societies, kinship provides for each member's social security in the broadest sense. This includes co-operation and mutual aid, both routine and emergency, co-operation and mutual defense in litigation and conflicts with other groups, the acceptance of collective responsibility for the actions of members, provision for orphans and widows, and so forth. In societies which have no social structure apart from kinship, protection of members extends even to military action (Gen. 14:13-24).

d. Economic co-operation. The rational pooling of major resources, especially land and water, and co-operative labor make possible large undertakings with a minimum of nonkin structure, as can be seen from the extensive mountainside irrigation terraces of the Ifugao (Philippines). Ownership of land by a kinship group is almost the norm, on a world-wide basis. And all sorts of enterprises, whether pastoral, agricultural, commercial, or industrial, can be and often are owned and operated by kin groups

e. Social order. Kin groups are often involved in ensuring internal order by enforcing rules and penalizing deviants.

f. Descent and inheritance. We have already discussed descent; it remains to say something about inheritance. The orderly passage to other persons of the rights and possessions of the dead is almost always regulated in terms of kinship, though the specifics vary widely.

g. Regulation of marriage. *See* §4 *above.*

h. Religious and ceremonial functions. Certain types of religious functions, including totem cults and ancestor cults, are by definition tied to kinship groups. But many other types of religious and ceremonial activities center on the kin group or take it seriously into consideration. One also finds fairly often that religious specialization is assigned on the basis of kinship (cf. the role of the Levites and the Aaronic family in Israel).

8. Kinship in ancient Israel. Kinship played an especially crucial role among the Hebrews as the very foundation of the entire society: they considered themselves descendants of Abraham, Isaac, and Jacob, and circumcision of males was the sign of their being one people, the "children of Israel." This explains their pre-occupation with genealogy throughout their history: if one could not trace physical descent from Jacob, his status was in jeopardy (cf. §2 *above*). Examples of a whole society considering itself to be one enormous kinship group are rare, at least when the society numbers more than a few thousand people. What is likely is that at some stage a mechanism was invoked to incorporate related smaller peoples into the "children of Israel."

a. Patriarchal times. In the lifetimes of the three patriarchs, the whole people was simultaneously a sublineage, an extended family, and a vast household/camp. Though ties for marriage purposes were maintained with the patrilineage in Haran, the camp was in every other way self-contained, self-sufficient, and autonomous. The patriarchs moved about as they pleased and ruled their households with absolute authority. The kinship group provided fully for every one of the functions listed in §7 above. In a time of emergency, Abraham was able to mobilize 318 adult male household members, no doubt mostly servants and slaves (Gen. 14:14). By the time Jacob moved to Egypt, the extended family (only kin) is said to have contained seventy persons (Gen. 46:26-27).

b. After the Exodus. By the time of the Exodus, the twelve sons of Jacob had become, by the multiplication of their descendants, the ancestors of twelve "tribes," which in our terms should be called clans. One clan, that of Levi, was set apart for religious functions; that of Joseph was split into two to maintain the number of twelve. Apart from the personal charismatic leadership of Moses, then Joshua, and the religious unity in the worship of Yahweh centralized in the Aaronic priesthood, the people continued to think of themselves primarily in terms of their clans, lineages, and sublineages; national unity was thus fairly tenuous and continued to be through the time of the Judges. Clans often failed to co-operate, and sometimes actually fought. The land of Canaan was apportioned on the basis of kinship groups, right down to the family (e.g., Josh. 17:1-6). The "Judges" themselves seem to have been mostly *ad hoc* clan heroes rather than national leaders.

c. The kingdom. With the advent of the monarchy, political dominance began to slip away from the clans in favor of the centralized power, somewhat in the way that religious power had been centralized earlier. But the clans remained strong enough to serve as the basis for the split between the northern and southern kingdoms under Rehoboam. Apparently the lower order units (lineages, extended families, etc.) continued to fulfill most of their functions in providing social identity, socialization, social security, and so forth.

d. After the return from exile. The Jews who returned from Babylon attempted to re-establish their former system, and in particular Ezra enforced again national endogamy and restored the temple worship and the priesthood. This required the reconstruction to his satisfaction of the genealogies on which the priesthood depended (Ezra 2:36-63).

In the Diaspora, the synagogue gradually evolved and assumed a significant role in the education of children, thus supplementing but not replacing the socialization function of the home. But throughout the biblical period the Hebrews/Israelites/Jews continued to be a strongly patrilineal society which assigned first place of honor and responsibility in all of society to the family and the home. As society became more complex, religious and political institutions evolved to take over certain spheres; but these served to supplement, not to supplant, the kinship groups.

See also SEX, SEXUAL BEHAVIOR[S]; AGING, ATTITUDES TOWARD[S].

Bibliography. *See* MARRIAGE[S]. C. R. TABER

***KIR** (in Mesopotamia). A place whither Tiglath-pileser III transplanted the people of Damascus (II Kings 16:9; an editorial gloss in Amos 1:5). In the Deuteronomic interpolation Amos 9:7, Kir is mistakenly called the place of origin of the Arameans. In Isa. 22:6 (written in 539 B.C.) Kir figures along with Elam (i.e., Persia) as enemies of Babylon (cf. Isa. 21:2, where the enemies of Babylon are Elam and Media). No place called *Qîr* is mentioned in ancient records; however, *Qîr,* West Semitic for "wall," should be understood as a translation of the city name *Dēr* with the same meaning (var. of Akkad. *dūru*). The name was ideographically written BÀD.DINGIR^{KI}, "wall of the gods," or simply BÀD^{KI}, "wall." Tiglath-pileser III, who called it *Dūru,* transferred its inhabitants to northern Syria (after 738); it would thus be natural if they were replaced, a few years later (in 732), by exiles from Damascus. Dēr, an important ancient city E of the lower Tigris (now Badrah), on the main road from Elam to Babylon, was in the Neo-Babylonian period the capital of the province of Gutium. Its governor, Gubaru, joined Cyrus in 539 and was the first, with his troops, to enter the city of Babylon.

Bibliography. *ARAB,* I, §772; *DPaR* (1920), pp. 89, 96-97; A. T. Olmstead, *History of the Persian Empire* (1948), p. 49; J. van Dijk, "Le site de Guti'um. . . . ," *AFO,* XXIII (1970), 71-72; S. Smith, *Babylonian Historical Texts* (1924), pp. 98-123. M. C. ASTOUR

***KNOWLEDGE IN THE NT.** The idea of knowledge is expressed by the noun γνῶσις and the more frequently used verbs γινώσκω and οἶδα. Virtually synonymous (Mark 4:13; cf. Mark 15:10 and Matt. 27:18), these verbs can refer to such rudimentary concepts as the acquiring of information and the ascertaining of facts (Mark 10:42; Matt. 20:25; Acts 19:35). The OT idea of personal involvement in knowledge forms the background of the NT concept, illustrated by the use of "to know" for sexual intercourse in Matt. 1:25; Luke 1:34 (Gr.). The NT also echoes the OT understanding of the intimate relationship between God and his people (II Tim. 2:19; John 10:14), grounded in the priority of God's knowledge (cf. Jer. 1:5 and Gal. 1:15). God knows the needs of his people before they ask (Matt. 6:8, 32; Luke 12:30).

The NT is also influenced by concepts of knowledge current in the Hellenistic environment; by means of mediators and "divine men" (*see* DIVINE

Man[S]), secrets and mysteries are conveyed from the distant deity to chosen recipients. Thus Jesus, displaying supernatural knowledge (Matt. 9:4; Luke 5:22), is sometimes described as a dispenser of cryptic teachings (Matt. 10:26-27; 13:11; Luke 8:10). In later christological reflection, Christ himself is viewed as the embodiment of the divine mystery (Col. 2:3). Texts like these have led many interpreters to conclude that NT writers have used Gnostic expressions (*see* Gnosticism[S] §1) to communicate Christian concepts and to do battle with "what is falsely called knowledge" (I Tim. 6:20). In contrast to Gnosticism, the NT stresses God's acts of revelation in history culminating in Jesus Christ (Heb. 1:1-2). In response to him, Christians can confess, "I know whom I have believed" (II Tim. 1:12; cf. Acts 2:36).

Paul frequently uses verbs of knowing and employs the noun γνῶσις twice as often as the rest of the NT. Like the OT writers, Paul stresses the priority of God's self-disclosing action. God foreknows his people (Rom. 11:2; 8:29) and makes known to them "the riches of his glory" (Rom. 9:23). Thus, the knowledge of God is granted on the basis of a relationship which God creates (Gal. 4:9; I Cor. 8:3). God's will is made known in the law (Rom. 2:18) and possibly in nature (Rom. 2:14). According to Rom. 1:19-21, the knowledge of God has been shown to the Gentiles in the things which he has made. Elsewhere Paul insists that the heathen "do not know God" (I Thess. 4:5; cf. Gal. 4:8). What is revealed in the creative acts of God is "his invisible nature, . . . his eternal power and deity" (Rom. 1:20). Proof of the Gentile failure to appropriate this revelation is seen in their devotion to visible and powerless idols. Though they are able to know of God's transcendence, they do not acknowledge him as God (Rom. 1:21).

The frequency of the term γνῶσις within the Corinthian correspondence (fourteen times) is explained by Paul's opposing the false understanding of knowledge advocated by sponsors of a type of incipient Gnosticism (I Corinthians). The knowledge which they claim "puffs up" (I Cor. 8:1), and they express pride in a charismatic gift of knowledge (12:8; 1:5). In I Cor. 2:6-16, Paul borrows their language to refute them, claiming that he imparts wisdom to the mature, and that the gift of the Spirit makes known the "depths of God" (vs. 10). For Paul, the "secret and hidden wisdom of God" (vs. 7) is embodied in God's redemptive plan and revealed in history in the crucifixion (vs. 8); and consequently the wisdom of his opponents does not impart the knowledge of God. *See* Wisdom in the NT[S]; Folly[S].

Although he never uses the noun γνῶσις, the author of the Fourth Gospel employs verbs meaning "to know" more often than any other NT writer. He stresses that Jesus is the one who reveals God (cf. 1:18). Like the Hellenistic "divine man," Jesus performs signs and wonders (3:2) and displays his omniscience (1:48; 2:25; 16:30). He can serve as revealer since he has come from above (3:31; 6:38, 41, 50). Because he has been sent by God (3:17, 34; 5:36), Jesus knows God (8:55; 17:25) and enjoys a special relationship with him (10:15). "If you knew me," he says, "you would know my Father also" (8:19; 14:31). John uses the metaphor of seeing to express the idea of knowing (cf. 6:46 and 17:24). In ch. 9, Jesus is presented as the light of the world who gives sight to the blind, so that "those who do not see may see, and that those who see may become blind" (vs. 39). Authentic sight, like true knowledge, is seeing with the eyes of faith (20:29). Although he uses Gnostic motifs, John affirms historical revelation. The glory of the Logos is disclosed in the flesh (1:14), and the hour of his glory is the hour of his death (12:27, 33). Faith in Jesus leads to knowledge and knowledge leads to life (10:38). "And this is eternal life, that they know thee the only true God, and Jesus Christ whom thou hast sent" (17:3). This knowledge provides not a way of escape but a responsible life of obedience (13:17) to the command of love (13:34-35). *See also* John, Gospel of and John, Gospel of[S] §3.

Bibliography. R. Bultmann, "γινώσκω, κτλ.," I (1933 [ET 1963]), 689-719; R. C. Dentan, *The Knowledge of God in Ancient Israel* (1968); W. D. Davies, "'Knowledge' in the Dead Sea Scrolls and Matt. 11:25-30," *HTR,* XLVI (1953), 113-39; B. Reicke, "Da'at and Gnosis in Intertestamental Lit.," *Neotestamentica et Semitica,* ed. E. E. Ellis and M. Wilcox (1969), pp. 245-55; B. Gärtner, *Areopagus Speech and Natural Revelation,* ASNU, XXI (1955); D. M. Coffey, "Natural Knowledge of God," *TS,* XXXI (1970), 674-91; U. Wilckens, *Weisheit und Torheit,* BHTh, XXVI (1959); R. Baumann, *Mitte und Norm des Christlichen,* NTAbh, V (1968); W. Schmithals, *Gnosticism in Corinth* (2nd ed., 1965 [ET 1971]); H. Schlier, "Glauben, Erkennen, Lieben nach dem Johannesevangelium," *Besinnung auf das NT* (1964), pp. 279-93; J. Gaffney, "Believing and Knowing in the Fourth Gospel," *TS,* XXVI (1965), 215-41; E. Fascher, "Christologie u. Gnosis im vierten Evangelium," *TLZ,* XCIII (1968), cols. 722-30.

W. Baird

***KUE.** Eastern Cilicia was known to the Neo-Assyrians as *Qaue* or *Que,* to the Hebrews and Arameans as קוה, and to the Neo-Babylonians as *Ḫume* (pronounced *Ḫuwe*). But its native population called it for its central city, Adana (which still bears that name): *Adanawa* in hieroglyphic Hittite; עמק עדן, "the Plain of Adana" in Phoenician; the ethnic designation of its inhabitants was, in Phoenician, דננים, "Danunians." This, and much other information about the country, was learned from the long bilingual (in Phoenician and hieroglyphic Hittite) which was discovered in 1945-47 at Karatepe and which belongs to the ninth or eighth century B.C. The inscription sheds much light on the social and political life of a typical half-Semitic Neo-Hittite state on the confines of Syria (*see* Hittites[S] §2 and map), and particularly on the Canaanite religion of its inhabitants.

Bibliography. The Karatepe inscription, Phoenician version: *KAI,* no. 26; *ANET*³, pp. 653-54; S. Parpola, *Quwe,* in *Neo-Assyrian Toponyms* (1970), for Assyrian occurrences; D. J. Wiseman, *Chronicles of the Chaldaean Kings* (1956), pp. 39-42, 74-77, 86-88; W. F. Albright, "Cilicia and Babylonia under the Chaldaean Kings," *BASOR,* 120 (Dec. 1950), 22-25; A. Goetze, "Cilicians," *JCS,* XVI, (1962), 48-58; M. C. Astour, *Hellenosemitica* (2nd ed., 1967), pp. 1-69.

M. C. Astour

L

***LACHISH. 1. Recent excavations.** Explorations at Lachish (Tell ed-Duweir) in 1966 and 1968 have added considerably to our understanding of the Hebrew cultus during and after the period of the monarchy.

a. The Jewish temple. Archaeologists returned to Lachish primarily to study the stratification of a structure which Starkey had interpreted to be a "Solar Shrine." Recent excavation at Tell 'Arad had uncovered an Israelite temple of the monarchial period, and its similarity in architecture to the "Solar Shrine" prompted further investigation (*see* TEMPLES, SEMITIC[S] §2). Expeditions sponsored jointly by Tel Aviv University and the University of North Carolina, and directed by Y. Aharoni, restricted operations to the shrine and its immediate environs.

The structure consists of two main rooms and a court, corresponding to those in the Arad temple, as well as to biblical descriptions of Solomon's temple and the tabernacle in the wilderness. It now seems certain that the structure is to be interpreted as a Jewish temple dating *ca.* 200 B.C. Further excavation beneath the court and in the area adjacent to the temple walls revealed a Late Bronze level (stratum VI) as well as four Iron Age levels (strata V-II) and postexilic levels.

b. The Israelite sanctuary. Beneath the temple a steeply inclined street extended in an E-W direction, on either side of which were rooms and industrial installations.

The street came to an end at a terrace which was constructed *ca.* 900 (stratum IV) and on which were erected the buildings of the acropolis. The terrace partially overlaid a sanctuary (stratum V) —a rectangular room of about ten by sixteen feet with a rich assemblage of cultic vessels of the tenth century including a horned stone altar, four incense burners, chalices, lamps, offering bowls, etc., but no figurine or other artifact that would negate the conclusion that it was a place of Yahwistic worship.

c. The high place (bamah). Just SE of the sanctuary and partially covered by the Holy of Holies of the Jewish temple a raised platform was discovered which, in view of the sacred nature of the place, is interpreted to be a *bamah* (*see* HIGH PLACE). Just S of the Holy of Holies, there is a large stone standing upright and held in place by three smaller stones fixed against its base. It was set into the debris of stratum VI only four inches below the floor level of stratum V. Thus this massive stone remained standing throughout strata IV and III. Clearly it is a massebah (*see* PILLAR §3 and PILLAR[S]). Directly in front of it there was a rounded heap of black ashes, the charred remains of a tree trunk. Possibly archaeology has at long last discovered the remains of an ASHERAH. Perhaps it was this *bamah* which occasioned Micah's bitter indictment of Lachish as "the beginning of sin to the daughter of Zion" (1:13).

d. The temple of the Persian period. Excavations resumed at Lachish in 1973. There is strong evidence of another temple situated *ca.* 44 yards SE of the Jewish temple. Pottery finds, including an incense stand, indicate that the structure belongs to the Persian period, and was abandoned at about the same time the Jewish temple was built. Exploration continues in this area as well as in the general area between the "Governor's Palace" and the gate.

2. Conclusions. The discovery of four places of worship within so severely restricted an area, spanning at least nine hundred years, is unprecedented. Clearly there was an ancient tradition of a sacred area at Lachish. It must now be assumed that during the period of the united monarchy the Solomonic temple was by no means the only Israelite temple in the land.

Bibliography. Y. Aharoni, "Trial Excavation in the 'Solar Shrine' at Lachish, preliminary report," *IEJ*, XVIII (1968), 157-69; Y. Aharoni *et al.*, *Lachish V* (in press); O. Tufnell *et al.*, *Lachish III* (1953), pp. 141-45.

B. BOYD

LA'IR lä ĭr' [לעיר]. It has been suspected that the awkward לעיר in Isa. 37:13 (=II Kings 19:13) does not mean "of the city" but represents a toponym. It was proposed, as early as 1912, to identify לעיר with Laḫiru, a city on the upper Diyāla River. This assumption is confirmed by Aramaic letters of the fifth century, in which (no. VI, line 1) Laḫiru is spelled לער. Laḫiru was annexed to Assyria by Sargon II in 712 B.C. Understanding לעיר as a place name requires the restoration of <ומלך> between it and ספרוים. *See* SEPHARVAIM[S].

Bibliography. A. Sarsowsky, "Notizien zu einigen biblischen geographischen und ethnographischen Namen," *ZAW*, XXXII (1912), 146; G. R. Driver, *Aramaic Documents of the Fifth Century* B.C. (1957), pp. 27-28, 56-57; *DPaR* (1920), pp. 46-47, 95-96, 98; S. Parpola, "Laḫiru," in *Neo-Assyrian Toponyms* (1970), for Assyrian occurrences.

M. C. ASTOUR

***LAODICEA.** Despite the historical importance of Laodicea, its attractive ruins remained completely unexcavated until 1961-63. During the excavations an elaborately ornamented nymphaeum (public fountain) was uncovered on one corner of a paved intersection of the city's streets near the center of the flat-topped mound. At first, discovery of a fairly complete, colossal statue representing the goddess Isis or one of her priestesses led to the supposition that the building was a sanctuary of Isis, but the structure's true character through its various phases of use and alteration between the third and fifth centuries A.D. soon became apparent. See Fig. L1.

Laodicea Excavations, Université Laval, Quebec
1. Statue of Isis, from the nymphaeum at Laodicea

In the mid-fourth century when Laodicea was the foremost bishopric of PHRYGIA, the nymphaeum was laid out with façades facing N and W, each with marble-lined semicircular niches serving as fountains to one side, and sharing a large rectangular basin between. The basin was faced with a marble parapet ornamented with scenes of Theseus and the Minotaur, ZEUS and Ganymede. Behind the basin rose a high colonnade framing statues of Roman officials. Probably as the result of an earthquake in the late fifth century the entire city of Laodicea including the nymphaeum was heavily damaged.

Subsequently the basin was filled in with debris (including the statue of Isis), and walls were erected over the basin's parapets to create an elevated and enclosed room entered by a stairway and door on the N. Crosses carved on various blocks suggest that the new construction was used by the Christians of the city whose earliest converts had met in the house of NYMPHA (Col. 4:15). The niches to either side of the former basin, although altered, continued to serve as public fountains, now decorated with at least two stone plaques carved with simple, modified motifs of Christian symbolism: a vase and the monogram of Christ.

In relation to the newly discovered nymphaeum the much older study of the high-pressure stone pipeline and aqueduct at Laodicea takes on new importance. This Roman Imperial feat of engineering transported water over five miles from springs near the well-watered Turkish city of Denizli on the S to a distribution tower prominent among Laodicea's ruins. From here the water would have been apportioned to the luxurious thermae (baths) and nymphaea of the city. NNE of Laodicea the white mineral cascades of the hot springs and modern bathing resort at Pamukkale, ancient HIERAPOLIS, are visible.

Bibliography. J. des Gagniers *et al., Laodicée du Lycos, Le nymphée, Campagnes 1961-1963,* Université Laval Recherches Archéologiques Série I (1969); G. Weber, "Die Hochdruck-Wasserleiting von Laodicea ad Lycum," *Jahrbuch des kaiserlich deutschen archäologischen Instituts,* XIII (1898), 1-13; XIX (1904), 95-96.

D. BOYD

LATIN VERSIONS.

1. The Old Latin Bible
   a. Origins: the African text
   b. European recensions
   c. Critical editions
   d. The character of OL MSS
   e. Significance of the OL tradition
2. Jerome and the Vulg.
   a. Terminology
   b. Jerome's career
   c. Other translators
   d. Jerome and the canon
   e. Critical and literary value
3. History of the Vulg. in the church
   a. Earliest times
   b. The centuries of the great MSS
   c. The rise of humanism

d. Critical editions
e. Modern revisions of the Vulg.
Bibliography

The OL versions date back to the period of Christian origins; for the NT, the earliest examples can be safely dated to the century that followed the creation of the Greek text.

1. The Old Latin Bible. ***a. Origins: the African text.*** For some centuries, Greek was the written language of western Christianity—from Mark's Gospel and the Letter to the Romans through Clement of Rome, Hermas, Irenaeus, and Hippolytus. Whatever may have been the Oriental element in the membership of Christian communities (e.g., slaves), it is clear that the Latin language maintained a certain position, though, for some time simply as a spoken language. If written documents did exist, they were not considered worth preserving. Latin Christian literature really began in Africa with Tertullian, who wrote between A.D. 197 and 222. Numerous scriptural quotations are found in his writings, but they are based on the Greek text, and cannot stem from any well-defined Latin version, whether such a version already existed or not. The situation changed, however, with Cyprian, bishop of Carthage. His quotations, more than 1500 in number (representing 950 different texts), are taken from a well-established Latin text, substantially identical with that found in later MSS, e.g., **k** (Bobbiensis) for the gospels, and Vulg. for Wisdom of Solomon and Ecclesiasticus. This version, which first appears at Carthage, is commonly called African. The name is not intended to define the area where it originated or circulated or the provincial character of its language. It certainly did not originate with Cyprian; his use of it is already marked by certain retouching. Different translators were responsible for the various biblical books, but there are certain common characteristics. First, the Greek text they translated represents the Western textual tradition—which, with its many glosses and harmonizations, is a good example of a text that circulated in cultural milieus free from rigid controls. It could still, however, preserve valuable readings, by virtue of the fact that it had not passed through the sieve of the Alexandrine philologists. This same textual tradition also finds support in the Syriac versions, and in certain ancient or very popular citations by Greek writers (*see* TEXT, NT §E5*d* and TEXT, NT[S]). For the OT, Lucian's LXX recension has preserved something of this ancient tradition (*see* SEPTUAGINT[S] §B). Second, the translation is marked more by respect for the letter than by intelligent freedom, and uses popular and distinctive vocabulary. Some scholars have sought to identify in this version traces of a Latin text of Marcion or of Tatian's Diatessaron—as if a heretical initiative underlay the church's version. All in all, their arguments cannot stand up under searching criticism. Finally, any attempt to discover vestiges of Jewish pre-Christian Latin versions, made on an analogy with the LXX, must fail for total lack of evidence.

b. European recensions. As early as the time of Cyprian, Novatian preserves citations where the vocabulary is less markedly African. The evidence, first by way of citations and later of MSS, increases, till, by the latter part of the fourth century, we are faced with a great variety of versions. Such a situation is understandable in view of the rapid evolution of Christian communities, on both the social and the literary levels; and, since knowledge of Greek was widespread, everyone was tempted to make his own improvements in the Latin text. These versions are commonly called European. Augustine, it is true, once used the expression *Itala,* but this term can scarcely be understood as referring to a well-defined type, or be applied as a geographical description to recensions found in Rome, Milan, or Spain. In fact, so numerous are the variants that many think we are dealing with two or three independent versions, especially since common traits can be explained by reference to the same basic Greek text. However, from one book to the next, residual "Africanisms" are too numerous to be satisfactorily explained merely by accidental contacts. A more balanced explanation would take into account the prior existence of a Christian vocabulary with local variations, and of traditions engendered by viva-voce liturgical translation. Hence, when an "African" text came into being in a given locality, it was soon adopted everywhere, with necessary adaptation to local usages. During the period prior to the appearance of the first witnesses which have been preserved, constant use entailed further development. The resultant pluralism thus seems normal. However, ill-regulated attempts at emendation only produced futher textual corruption and the net result was confusion. By the end of the fourth century the situation had become intolerable.

c. Critical editions. P. Sabatier edited in three large folio volumes the principal textual material known in his time: *Bibliorum sacrorum latinae versiones antiquae seu Vetus Itala* (Reims, 1745-49)—a work still indispensable. It is impossible to list here the editions of individual MSS that gradually came to light, or the monographs devoted to individual patristic sources. A. Jülicher (and, after his death, W. Matzkow and K. Aland) edited a collection of the OL MSS of the gospels in *Itala* (Berlin, 1938-72). However, citations are not included, and the classification adopted is problematic and needs further critical study. B. Fischer, assisted by W. Thiele, H. J. Frede, and the editorial staff at Beuron, undertook the monumental task of preparing a rigorously critical edition of the whole corpus of material, in *Vetus Latina* (Freiburg, 1949—). Vol. I contains a list of sigla, which can be kept up-to-date through loose-leaf insertions. Vols. 2, 24, and 26/1 (Genesis, Ephesians, Philippians, Colossians, Catholic Epistles, 1949-71) have been published. Vols. 7/2, 11, and 25/1 (Judith, Wisdom of Solomon, Ecclesiasticus, and Thessalonians through Hebrews) are in preparation. The work so far accomplished has set the problems of the Latin Bible in much sharper focus than heretofore and has completely revised the techniques employed in earlier scholarly editions. Considerable effort by way of initiation is demanded of the reader, but he or she will be repaid a hundredfold. Besides these general editions, a few specialized collections deserve mention: *Old-Latin Biblical Texts* (7 vols.; Oxford, 1885-1923); *Collectanea Biblica Latina* (14 vols.; Rome, 1912-72); *Aus der Geschichte der lateinischen Bibel* (8 vols.; Freiburg, 1957-74). The *Bulletin de la Bible latine,* an appendix to the *Revue Bénédictine,* contains a survey of current bibliography by M. Bogaert.

d. The character of OT MSS. The OL MSS that have come down to us are frequently mutilated, and not very numerous, since the success of the Vulg. tended to eliminate them. At best they represent only certain books. There exists one copy of the Heptateuch. Apart from that, and setting aside palimpsests and papyri, the OT is represented principally by Psalters, with collections of canticles appended—for local recensions continued in use in the liturgy. Frequently the OL version of OT books or parts is to be found tucked away in MSS predominantly Vulg. in character. Often enough OL texts were preserved after the fashion of relics, since people believed they had been written by, or had belonged to, some saint. This is particularly true of the OL gospels, which are somewhat more familiar to the biblical scholar, for they are frequently cited in critical editions of the Greek NT, or in specialized studies involving textual criticism. We shall now enumerate the chief witnesses to the European text, grouping them by "families" rather than listing them by sigla in alphabetical order.

Palatinus (**e,** fifth century) has a text recognizably African in character, but behind it lies a long history, marked by corrections not always well understood. Colbertinus (**c**), though very late (twelfth century), also preserves an African basis, especially in Luke; but this is overlaid by borrowings both from the European text and from the Vulg. A group of MSS, principally **a** (Vercellensis, fourth century), **n** (Sangallensis, fifth century), and **s** (Ambrosianus, 0.210 sup., fifth century), include a number of "Africanisms" in their text, which is related to that of Novatian, and, for John, to that of Lucifer of Cagliari. Another group, however, **b** (Veronensis, fifth century), $\mathbf{ff_2}$ (Corbeiensis, fifth century), and **i** (Vindobonensis, fifth century), is the best representative of the text current in Italy in 350-80. This is the text of Ambrose and Ambrosiaster, and, for Luke, of Lucifer of Cagliari. It also lay behind Jerome's Vulg. The Hiberno-Gallican text, used, e.g., by Hilary of Poitiers, has come down to us in **h** (Claromontanus, fifth century), **r** (Usserianus, *ca.* 600, from Ireland), and **g** (Sangermanensis, ninth century—example of a fine Vulg. text blended with an OL tradition, especially in Matthew). Finally, moving farther E, there is **q** (Monacensis, seventh century) from Illyria or Pannonia, containing the text used *ca.* 400 by the Latin Arians.

Mention must also be made of the well-known bilingual Codex Bezae (fifth century). The Greek part is virtually the only surviving representative of the Western text. The Latin (**d**) has been carefully edited to conform closely to the Greek, but without entirely eliminating earlier OL readings. Codex Bezae covers not only the gospels, but also Acts. The latter is also found in another bilingual MS, **e** (Laudianus, sixth century), known to St. Bede. The Latin text here is closer to the Vulg., but it, too, is artificial and made to conform to the Greek. For Acts, Revelation, and Catholic Epistles, we have the palimpsest fragments of Fleury (**h**, fifth century) — an African text, slightly revised. The remarkable Gigas (**g**, thirteenth century), a massive Bohemian Vulg. Bible, contains Acts and Revelation in a version reminiscent of that used by Lucifer of Cagliari *ca.* 350.

For the Pauline corpus, there are especially the great bilingual uncials, of which Claromontanus (**d**, fifth century) is the best example. The Greek part is a noteworthy witness to the Western text. The Latin derives from a very ancient version that has been adapted to the facing Greek. Its primitive form, however, can be reconstituted by reference to Lucifer of Cagliari's citations, and to a MS from Budapest, recently discovered and published.

The OL Psalters are designated by minuscule Greek characters. We shall not attempt an enumeration, but simply single out for mention the bilingual MS of Verona, with Greek text written in Latin characters (fifth or sixth century). These Psalters were conveniently published by R. Weber, together with the old Roman Psalter, in *Psautier Romain* (Rome, 1953).

e. Significance of the OL tradition. All these MSS clearly tell us something about the period when they were written and used, but, in general, the text they reproduce is older. The Greek text to which they bear witness can be dated to the second century, if, that is, they have preserved the primitive version, or if the changes they have undergone are due to liturgical usage, not to comparison with another Greek prototype. Hence, use of their readings for textual criticism presupposes the following: knowledge of the history of the Latin Bible; utilization of the entire evidence, including patristic citations; and a grasp of the significance of "clusters" formed by agreement among the authorities. A hundred testimonies drawn from one and the same widely circulated version do not have the same weight as a single witness taken, for example, from a palimpsest which represents an archaic version. Patristic citations, moreover, are often made with a freedom that seems capricious. However, in some cases, e.g., the *Speculum de Divinis Scripturis* of Pseudo-Augustine, quotations are taken with great accuracy from a written Bible. Finally, the specialist who knows the characteristics of each author and is trained to make the best use of citations will frequently uncover genuine elements of tradition underlying free quotations from memory. One conclusion clarifies another, and so the history of the text bears a certain consistency, however freely it may have been used.

Linguistic and literary factors played a large part in this evolution of the Latin text. Another factor was the authority of the Greek text that was adopted, not without good reason, by the philologists and the churches of the East. The great Greek uncials, which have survived precisely because they were rightly acknowledged as valid witnesses, give us a good idea of the textual standard attained by fourth-century culture. Church leaders in the West could hardly escape the influence of this standard. In fact their literary education led them to correct the popular versions, which found more favor in other social strata. Hence, there arose, almost spontaneously, a process of fermentation, marked by a quest for readings at once more literary, more intelligible, more uniform, and more faithful to the Greek—qualities difficult to bring together. The *Vetus Latina* of Beuron—not without some occasional over-simplification—has marshalled all these revisions under two or three major heads, and so isolated the various trends at work. Finally, the Vulg. appeared. It gained acceptance on its own merits, for it corresponded well to the bulk of these tendencies.

2. Jerome and the Vulg. ***a. Terminology.*** Originally the term "vulgata" designated simply the most widely-circulated text. Jerome never used it to describe his own work. He used it, first, to refer to the common Greek text as opposed to Origen's critical edition (the Hexaplaric text, i.e., his recension of the LXX collated with the Hebrew, part of a monumental synopsis in six columns of all known witnesses to the text). Secondly, he used the term to denote the Latin version current in his time. This version he was always inclined to disparage, contrasting its material dissemination with its poor intrinsic value. It was an irony of fate that led to the "vulgarizing," or broad dissemination (with consequent corruption), of his own version, which in turn became the butt of criticism from those who clamored for yet another revision. One good aspect of this subsequent "vulgarizing" was that biblical books never translated by Jerome himself were inserted into the corpus of his translations.

b. Jerome's career. Jerome (Hieronymus) is the prince of translators (*see also* INTERPRETATION, HISTORY OF[S] §G1). Born *ca.* 347 and blessed with an exceptional literary education, he became proficient in Greek and learned Hebrew during his stay at Antioch (374-80). Both then and later he had the opportunity of listening to teachers from the best exegetical schools of the East: Apollinaris of Laodicea, Gregory of Nazianzus, Didymus the Blind, and various rabbis. On his return to Rome he soon became the oracle of a pious circle of aristocratic ladies, who both sponsored him financially and encouraged him in his work. He spent the last part of his life (385-420) in Palestine, in direct contact with the Holy Land, and within reach of the excellent library established at Caesarea by Origen and Eusebius. His creative work, it is true, is not very original—yet, in the course of history, few Western scholars have had his opportunity of imbibing at the sources of the Greek and Semitic East with the same curiosity, the same ample documentation, and the same enthusiasm. However, one must admit that this enthusiasm produced more solid results when curbed by the demands of public good, as in his biblical translations, than when given free rein in literary and polemical pursuits.

The authority of the Vulg. has sometimes been explained in terms of a direct commission from Pope Damasus. This would have established it from the first as the official version of the Roman Church. This opinion takes too seriously the dedicatory letter, *Novum opus,* that accompanied the revised version of the gospels (383). In it Jerome certainly credits the Pope with the initiative for the work. Yet even if Damasus effectively sheltered the enterprise against criticism, it is nowhere stated that he did so in his official capacity. In any event, his commission would only have applied to the gospels. One other book, the Psalter, was revised (according to the Greek) before the death of Damasus. This version has been lost, there being no grounds for identifying it with the Roman Psalter, long used in Italy and England, but now only in St. Peter's Basilica in Rome. Its disappearance would be inexplicable if it had been officially adopted by the Pope. Subsequently Jerome's relations with Pope Siricius and the Roman clergy so deteriorated that he resolved to quit Rome and settle down at Bethlehem. There could no longer be any question of completing a commissioned work. It was according to his own ideas that Jerome set about revising the OT on the basis of the Hexaplaric Greek text, which he found at Caesarea. Such an undertaking was calculated to meet with complete approval from men like Rufinus of Aquileia or Augustine. They wished, in effect, to eliminate the corruptions that disfigured the Latin MSS and be guided by the best available Greek text, yet without any radical departure from a usage traditional in the churches since the apostles' time. Of this revision according to the Hexapla, we possess the Psalter, later named Gallican, after Charlemagne adopted it for the liturgy of the Frankish Empire. Previously it had circulated widely in Ireland. Its subsequent acceptance by the Franciscans ensured its use in the whole Western church until the time of Pope Pius XII. Job, Song of Songs, and many quotations of Proverbs have also survived, for the wisdom books were accepted as almost definitive for church usage. Jerome claims (*Epistulae,* CXXXIV) that he corrected the whole Latin Bible by the Hexapla, and complained that the work was "stolen"; however that may be, he does not seem to have regretted the loss.

In the years 389-90, after touring Palestine, he compiled, in imitation of Philo, Origen, and Eusebius, two learned compositions, lists of proper names of persons and places. This led him to a new and more concrete type of interpretation. He undertook a careful investigation of the different Greek versions in the Hexapla, and went on to compose his *Quaestiones Hebraicae.* No sooner had he completed revising the book of Genesis than he decided to abandon the Greek Hexaplaric text in favor of the Hebrew, as clarified by Aquila, Symmachus, and Theodotion. Toward 391 he published his version of the Prophets, a very literal translation of a difficult original. There followed, before 395, Samuel and Kings, in a more flexible rendition, and the *Psalterium juxta Hebraeos.* Job, with Ezra-Nehemiah, appeared in 394, and, two years later, Chronicles. However, Jerome's recourse to the original Hebrew (the *Hebraica veritas*) was far from meeting with an enthusiastic welcome. The Origenist controversy, which was to distract Jerome's attention for some time, was not without some bearing on the new Bible. An incomplete Greek version of it by Sophronius met with no success. In 398 Jerome translated the three books of Solomon—in eight days, so he claimed. The Octateuch, begun the same year, was completed only in 405, at the same time as Esther. Meanwhile, at the request of his friends, Jerome had translated, in somewhat offhand fashion, two of the Apocryphal (deuterocanonical) books, Tobit and Judith.

c. Other translators. It is now generally admitted that the revision of the Epistles, Acts, and Revelation is not the work of Jerome. However, the guiding principles of this revision are the same as those laid down by Jerome in his preface to the revised gospels. The difference is that these principles are now applied much more methodically, without erratic stylistic changes. The author appears to be Rufinus the Syrian, a disciple of Jerome at Bethlehem, who returned to Rome a little before 400. The work was completed in Rome *ca.* 405. It was possibly begun around 386 under the direction of Jerome, for, beginning at this time, he has quotations from the Catholic Epistles that herald the Vulg. text. It may be that Jerome began the work himself, then relinquished it in favor of his translation from the Hebrew, and finally entrusted its completion, more or less explicitly, to one of his disciples.

d. Jerome and the canon. By his choice of the *hebraica veritas,* Jerome excluded from his biblical canon the Apoc. (deuterocanonical books) of the OT. However, they were soon introduced and appear in all the MSS. The only exception is Baruch, which, in four different forms, passed imperceptibly into a few MSS in isolated sectors of the church; the definitive text arose only *ca.* 800, in the Bibles of Theodulf of Orléans. Wisdom of Solomon and Ecclesiasticus obviously follow the OL African text as a basis, with a few additions modeled on the Greek, and many more accidental changes. Maccabees, on the other hand, is clearly an anonymous revision.

e. Critical and literary value. The critical value of the Vulg. and also its literary quality thus vary considerably from one book to another, and even within the same book. It has been remarked that in the course of the same book, e.g., Genesis, Jerome showed greater respect for the OL in the case of oracles, prayers, and formulas already consecrated by the liturgy or by popular Christian piety. This left him more elbowroom, so to speak, in rendering the narratives. Thus the Vulg. cannot serve as a source book for a course on linguistic evolution or on the development of religious belief before or after the Babylonian exile. It is not a rigorously scientific tool for the study of the original text. Its true historical importance lies elsewhere. It made use of the best available Greek text and of a Hebrew text almost identical with the MT, but five centuries older. Jerome's rabbinic education did not deprive him of a Christian perspective on the unity of the two testaments. Since, moreover, the Vulg. Bible had been completed by the translation of some books from the LXX, and since it became familiar to medieval readers in the context of the liturgical year, with many elements (e.g., anthems, responsories, and commentaries) inspired by the OL, it underwent a certain adaptation and synthesis. Its literary quality—restrained by respect for the language of the OL, marked by numerous Semitisms, and refined by constant use, sacred and secular—unquestionably served to open up the Bible to the Western world and to make it the most influential of books.

3. History of the Vulg. in the church. ***a. Earliest times.*** Jerome used his new version as the basis for his learned commentaries, side-by-side with a version made from the Greek. He himself, however, habitually quoted from the OL, and so did his friend Chromatius of Aquileia, to whom he dedicated several of his translations, and so too, as is evident, did Rufinus. Augustine followed the same practice, at least for books translated from the Hebrew; while for the gospels and the Hexaplaric revision of the Psalms he readily used Jerome's work. At Rome, Pelagian circles were possibly the first to exploit the Vulg., not without some deliberate "improvements," i.e., retaining OL Italian readings which seemed as good as those of the Vulg. This kind of textual cross-influence took place in the years immediately following publication of the Vulg. It is, indeed, to be expected that mixed texts will arise once a new revision is presented to a public already familiar with an existing translation.

We still possess important fragments of a book of the gospels (Saint Gall MS 1395), which could have been written in Jerome's lifetime. There is some hope of supplying the missing portions, thanks to an early ninth-century copy made direct from the MS. Some 485 scribal errors have been counted—this represents a high degree of textual purity. Deserving of special attention are the marginal variants (apparently by the same hand as the text), frequently drawn from Jerome's commentaries. Here we see how, at a time when criticism was held in honor, texts could not be handed on without retouching.

b. The centuries of the great MSS. In the centuries that followed, sustained efforts to revise from the Greek seemed to have been exhausted, perhaps for want of capable translators. It is interesting to compare this with the situation in the Syrian Church, where such revision was in progress in the fifth century (NT Peshitta, to be attributed to Rabbula, despite some denials), and continued till the seventh (Philoxenian and Harclean revisions, and Syro-Hexaplar version). In the West, the fifth and sixth centuries seem to be characterized by an abundance of prologues and *capitula,* the remains of partial editions, which found their way into later Bibles. One example is well known. In 547, Victor, bishop of Capua, had a NT MS copied and corrected—a work today preserved at Fulda. In it he went to the trouble of collating a gospel harmony (*Diatessaron*) with the Vulg. text, rather than simply taking over Jerome's work. Cassiodorus (d. 570) mentions three complete Bibles: an OL copy in nine volumes, a large volume containing Jerome's Hexaplaric version, and a Vulg. in smaller format. The Vulg., however, made rapid progress. The oldest complete Vulg. Bible is the celebrated Amiatinus, copied at Jarrow in Northumbria by Abbot Ceolfrid (d. 716). Intended as a present for the Pope, it was taken to St. Peter's at Rome perhaps in exchange for certain valuable Italian MSS, on which it had been modeled. Its text is of exceptional value, though of unequal merit, and less pure than the MSS of southern Gaul, where John Cassian and Eucherius were very early witnesses to the Vulg. After that, MSS multiplied; for details the reader should consult specialized works. With the eighth century, the art of illumination produced de luxe editions. Churches and monasteries spared no expense to honor God's Word and to dignify both worship and culture. At the beginning of the ninth century, strenuous effort was expended on textual criticism at Charlemagne's court, at Tours (Alcuin), Orléans (Theodulf), Corbie, and Saint Gall, with its bilingual MSS and pride in Greek learning. The most damaging variants, of course, were not those blunders that a careful reader could easily dispose of, but intelligent and untimely corrections, facile readings that are contagious. In Spain, and in the entourage of Theodulf or Rabanus Maurus, recourse was had to the rabbis. The best texts came from Italy, while, on the confines of the W, in Spain and Ireland, isolated traditions were maintained, usually more bizarre than pure, which occasionally returned to influence the center of Christendom. As early as the eighth century, the Latin text was glossed by versions in Anglo-Saxon, Irish, and German, a foreshadowing of the multiplication of glossed medieval versions of the Vulg., from Italian and Spanish to Scandinavian languages. Finally, brief mention must be made of the continued work of Cistercians, Franciscans, and Dominicans, and of the universities, in setting up a standard text and providing it with necessary aids, such as divisions, dictionaries, and concordances. The first book printed by Gutenberg (1456?) was the forty-line Mainz Bible.

For further information on the Peshitta and the Philoxenian and Harclean revisions, *see* SYRIAC VERSIONS[S] §2*c, d, e*.

c. The rise of humanism. The rise of humanism, and the literary studies that accompanied it, together with renewed access to the original texts, followed by the crisis of the Reformation—all this meant that the authority of the Vulg. soon came under attack. As early as 1440, Lorenzo Valla composed his *Annotationes in latinam Novi Testamenti interpretationem,* subsequently printed by Erasmus in 1505. New translations were made from the Greek, e.g., by Erasmus in 1516, and from the Hebrew, e.g., by Santes Pagnini (completed in 1518, printed in 1527), and by Cajetan (published 1530-32). On the Protestant side, versions from the Hebrew were made by Sebastian Münster (Zurich, 1539), Leo Jud (Zurich, 1543), and Sebastianus Castellio (Basel, 1551). Editions of the Vulg., corrected by the Hebrew, were published by Osiander (Nuremberg, 1522, 1527, 1529) and Pellicanus (Zurich, 1582); and, on the Catholic side, by J. Rudel (Cologne, 1527), A. Steuco (Venice, 1529), I. Clario (Venice, 1542), and others. Controversy followed. It was very likely the teaching of J. Driedo, in *De ecclesiasticis Scripturis* (Louvain, 1535), that formed the basis of the decree *Insuper* of the Council of Trent (April 8, 1546), in which—among all the Latin translations in circulation—the Vulg. was acknowledged as the authentic version of the Catholic Church. This decree occasioned some surprise in Rome, where men were more accustomed to humanism and its criticism of the errors of the Vulg. The Council theologians, however, were trying to express their theological perspective of the authority of the church. The traditional Bible of the church, they argued, could not be in error as regards revealed truth—though obviously, as a version, it necessarily referred back to the original texts. A somewhat rigid interpretation of the Council's decree occasioned much pointless polemic. At the Council's request, the Popes set about preparing an official edition of the Vulg., an undertaking that entailed fifty years of meticulous work. The Sistine edition (1590), the work of Sixtus V, took little account of the MSS or of the learned commission that had consulted them. The Pope died soon after, and the edition was withdrawn, to be replaced by the Clementine Vulg. (1592, reprinted 1593 and 1598).

d. Critical editions. A critical edition of the NT was begun by J. Wordsworth, and continued by H. J. White and H. F. D. Sparks: *Novum Testamentum Domini nostri Jesu Christi latine secundum editionem S. Hieronymi* (Oxford, 1889-1954). A commission appointed by Pius X, and, later, the abbey of San Girolamo, established by Pius XI, undertook the *Biblia Sacra . . . ad codicum fidem* (Rome 1926—; fourteen volumes so far, up to Baruch). An *editio minor,* with critically revised text, has been published under the direction of R. Weber: *Biblia Sacra juxta vulgatam versionem* (Stuttgart, 2nd ed., 1975). A series of *concordantiae* has been invaluable for the study of the Vulg. A new concordance, based on the critical text and variants, will be published in connection with the Stuttgart Bible.

e. Modern revisions of the Vulg. In 1945 Pope Pius XII authorized for use a new version of the Psalter, prepared by the professors of the Biblical Institute under the direction of A. Bea. At the request of the Second Vatican Council, Paul VI commissioned a new version of the Vulg., corrected by the original texts, entitled *Neovulgata.* The first volume appeared in 1969. This version will be used henceforth in the Vatican's official Latin documents.

Bibliography. The most recent scholarly studies, with ample bibliog., are those of B. Fischer, H. Frede, and M. Thiele, in *Die alten Übersetzungen des Neuen Testaments,* (1972); cf. also the introductions to the major eds. of the texts, esp. *Vetus Latina.* In Eng.: *The Cambridge History of the Bible,* vols. I-II (1969-70); H. W. Robinson, ed., *The Bible in its Ancient and English Versions* (1940); F. Kenyon, *Our Bible and the Ancient Manuscripts* (2nd ed., 1958); B. Smalley, *The Study of the Bible in the Middle Ages* (2nd ed., 1952). Some older works are still indispensable, e.g., for the Renaissance versions, F. Kaulen, *Geschichte der Vulgata* (1868), details need checking.

J. GRIBOMONT

*LAW IN THE OT.

1. The range of the law
2. Ancient law codes and biblical parallels
3. The origins of biblical law
4. The age of the Covenant Code
5. The function of case law
6. The use of writing in law

1. The range of the law. The laws written down in the OT do not encompass the full range of procedures, statutes, and regulations that governed ancient Israelite society. Narrative and other nonlegal portions of the Bible reveal areas of legal life that are not in the laws, e.g., sale of children for debts of parents (II Kings 4:1; Isa. 50:1), ADOPTION (I Chr. 2:34-36; Ps. 2:7 ["begotten"]; *see* Kraeling 8), division of spoil in warfare (I Sam. 30:23-26).

Comparison of OT law collections with similar materials, i.e., ancient Near Eastern laws, reveals additional gaps. The Bible, e.g., has no laws dealing with craftsmen, professions, or merchants. Some of these omissions can be explained by the observation that ancient Israelite society was not as developed as that of its neighbors.

But there are gaps and omission that cannot be explained in this way. To cite one example: a law governing the hire of a wet nurse is recorded in Eshnunna Laws 32, but it is omitted in the Hammurabi Laws. (For law codes cited in this article, *see ANET* [2nd ed.] and supplement.) There can be no question as to the use of wet nurses in Hammurabi's society, since §194 of his laws regulates the case of a wet nurse who concealed the death of the infant from his parents—a case which, in turn, is not covered by the Eshnunna Laws. Wet-nurse laws are totally absent in the OT (and in the Hittite Laws), but there can be no doubt as to the use of wet nurses in ancient Israel (cf. e.g., Gen. 24:59; Exod. 2:7; II Kings 11:2). There doubtlessly existed customs and regulations regarding her fees and responsibilities; but these laws, along with so many others, have simply not been preserved among the extant OT laws.

The study of Israelite law lacks the resources of private records which could reveal the everyday practice of law in ancient Israelite society. These documents exist in Mesopotamia, and they have shown that there are many areas of legal life that the extant laws do not discuss.

A hint of what data could be forthcoming is seen, e.g., from comparing the references to "the sealed deed of purchase, . . . and the open copy" in Jer. 32:11 with the bills of sale found among the Dead Sea Scrolls; cf. Hos. 2:2 [H 4] with the marriage formula, "She is my wife and I am her husband from this day and forever," found in the Jewish Aramaic papyri from Elephantine; and the possibility of DIVORCE proceedings initiated by women (Cowley 15; Kraeling 2, 7, 14). In sum, the field of Israelite law is much broader domain than the areas discussed by the biblical laws; the laws of ancient Israel included many more concepts and categories than the OT actually records. The Pentateuchal compositions are collections of laws and not codes; comprehensive codes in the modern sense simply did not exist in the ancient Near Eastern world.

2. Ancient law codes and biblical parallels. Many scholars have regarded the written Pentateuchal laws as expressions of sterility, rigidity, and decline in religious idealism in Israelite society. They believe that ancient Israel took a false turn when it began to concretize its sense of religious affinity with God into specific, prescribed written forms. The discovery of the laws of Hammurabi and similar collections with parallels to Israelite traditions brought scholars to the recognition that fixed written laws played a more vital part in ancient Semitic societies than was formerly imagined. *See* LAW IN THE OT §B; HAMMURABI.

In many instances, the laws are so close that the offenses and penalties are described in identical fashion. This is so in laws about false witness (Exod. 23:1-3; Deut. 19:16-20; Hammurabi Laws 1, 3, 4), kidnaping (Exod. 21:16; Hammurabi Laws 14), loss of deposited animals (Exod. 22:10-13 [H 9-12]; Hammurabi Laws 266-67), the responsibility for borrowed animals (Exod. 22:14-15 [H 13-14]; Hittite Laws 75), an ox goring another ox (Exod. 21:35-36; Eshnunna Laws 53).

Identical or near-identical formulations are also found in cases of sexual relations with a stepmother in the lifetime of the father (Lev. 18:8; 20:11; Deut. 27:20; Hittite Laws 190), sexual relations with a stepmother after the father's death (I Kings 2:13-22; Hittite Laws 190; Hammurabi Laws 158), sexual relations with a daughter-in-law (Lev. 18:15; 20:12; Hammurabi Laws 155), sexual relations with one's mother (Lev. 18:7; Hammurabi Laws 157; Hittite Laws 189), sexual relations with a daughter or granddaughter (Lev. 18:10; Hammurabi Laws 154; Hittite Laws 189), sexual relations with two sisters (Lev. 18:18—the OT has no stated penalty—Hittite Laws 191-92), rape of a betrothed woman (Deut. 22:25-27; Eshnunna Laws 26; Hammurabi Laws 130; Hittite Laws 197), BESTIALITY (Lev. 18:23; 20:15; Deut. 27:21; Hittite Laws 187-88, 199), personal injuries (Exod. 21:23-25; Hammurabi Laws 196-97, 200), brawling men causing a miscarriage to a bystander (Exod. 21:22-23; Sumerian Laws; Hammurabi Laws 209, 210; Hittite Laws 17; Assyrian Laws A 21, 50-52), an ox goring a person (Exod. 21:28-32; Eshnunna Laws 54-55), sorcery (Exod. 22:18 [H 17]; Deut. 18:10-12; Hammurabi Laws 2; Assyrian Laws A 47), and the protection of the rights of a first wife whose husband marries another (Exod. 21:10; Lipit-Ishtar Laws 28).

There are other instances where the biblical laws and the ancient Near Eastern laws are close but not identical; the offensive act is universally condemned but the penalties or some other detail of handling may differ. This is so in cases involving debt SLAVERY (Exod. 21:2-11; Deut. 15:12-18; Hammurabi Laws 117), ADULTERY (Deut. 22:22-24; Ur-Nammu Laws 4; Hammurabi Laws 129; Hittite Laws 197-98; Assyrian Laws A 13-16, 22-23), setting a careless fire or letting one's animal graze in a neighbor's field (Exod. 22:5-6 [H 4-5]; Hittite Laws 98-107), rape or seduction of an unmarried girl (Exod. 22:16-17 [H 15-16]; Deut. 22:28-29; Assyrian Laws A 55-56), murder (Exod. 21:12-14; Lev. 24:14, 21; Assyrian Laws A 10), striking one's parent (Exod. 21:15; Hammurabi Laws 195), sexual relations with a mother and daughter (Lev. 18:17; 20:14; Hittite Laws 191, 194, 200), a woman seizing a man's genitals in a fight (Deut. 25:11-12; Assyrian Laws A 8), sexual relations between males (Lev. 18:22; 20:13; Assyrian Laws A 19-20; *see* HOMOSEXUALITY[S]), and regulation of punishment of a debt slave (Exod. 21:20-21; Lev. 25:43, 53; Hammurabi Laws 115-16; Assyrian Laws A 44).

And finally, there are a number of cases where the biblical laws and the pagan laws both address the same problem. The common focus demonstrates a shared, underlying cultural background, but the respective legal treatments are different. This group includes illegal entry and theft (Exod. 22:1-4 [H 21:37–22:3]; Eshnunna Laws 12-13; Hammurabi Laws 21-22; Hittite Laws 57-70, 93-97), community responsibility for a slain murder victim (Deut. 21:1-9; Hittite Laws 6), the eating and use of fruit from a young tree (Lev. 19:23-25; Hammurabi Laws 60), a wife suspected of adultery (Num. 5:11-31; Ur-Nammu Laws 11; Hammurabi Laws 131-32; Assyrian Laws A 17), violation of a slave girl (Lev. 19:20-22; Ur-Nammu Laws 5; Eshnunna Laws 31), sale and redemption of a house (Lev. 25:29-34; Eshnunna Laws 39), return of lost articles or animals (Deut. 22:1-3; Hittite Laws 45), a female debt slave (Exod. 21:7-11; Hammurabi Laws 117; Assyrian Laws A 48), mixed seeding in the same field (Lev. 19:19; Deut. 22:9; Hittite Laws 166-67), and sexual relations with a sister-in-law plus LEVIRATE marriage (Lev. 18:16; 20:21; Ruth 4:4-11; Gen. 38:8; Deut. 25:5-10; Assyrian Laws A 30; Hittite Laws 193, 195).

3. The origins of biblical law. The similarity between the Israelite and pagan laws is remarkable and unexpected. The language in which the respective laws were formulated is at times so close that questions have arisen as to the originality and independence of the Israelite legal traditions. Many scholars argued that Israelite law was an outright borrowing from Mesopotamia. Others maintained that Abraham or the ethnic unit he represents brought this knowledge with him from Ur. But still other scholars, worried about how to explain the long interval between the patriarchs and the composition of the PENTATEUCH (*see* DOCUMENTS), posit a more gradual intermediate influence—the existence of a common Near Eastern legal tradition developing in Mesopotamia and spreading northward to Anatolia and westward to Syria and Palestine. They would see the Israelites learning this Near Eastern law from their more sophisticated Canaanite neighbors, after entering the Promised Land. This view has won widespread favor and remains the working hypothesis of many scholars today. But it must be remembered (1) that there is no evidence for Canaanite law of any kind; (2) the legal traditions of the ancient Near East, of which the OT is a part, were alive and functioning over a long period of time. Mesopotamian laws of the Neo-Babylonian period have also been discovered (*see ANET,* pp. 197-98); these are not extensively preserved, but the existence of these later laws, as well as the continued scribal study of more ancient collections like the Hammurabi Laws in Chaldean times, makes it impossible to assign the Israelite-Mesopotamian connection to a particular point in time.

4. The age of the Covenant Code. It is widely assumed that the Covenant Code (*see* LAW IN THE OT §C3) belongs to the oldest part of Israelite history because it contains the greatest number of parallels to the pagan laws. This is only partly true. Out of twenty-seven cases cited above where similarities are present, twelve relate to the Covenant Code alone, another five have parallels with the Covenant Code and with another part of the Bible, but the remainder have no connection with the Covenant Code and find their correspondence in either Leviticus or Deuteronomy. Scholars have at times assigned parts of Deuteronomy to the Covenant Code, which have their parallels to the ancient Near Eastern laws: such similarities, they claim, are a characteristic of the Covenant Code. But this is circular reasoning. Scholars have also taken those parts of the Holiness Code (*see* LAW IN THE OT §D3) which have parallels with the ancient Near Eastern laws to represent the oldest materials in that collection—again using the argument that the parallels are proof of antiquity.

5. The function of case law. Most of the OT laws which have parallels in the ancient Near Eastern law collections are formulated in case or casuistic form (*see* LAW IN THE OT §C3): cf. e.g., "If a man strikes his father they shall cut off his hand" (Hammurabi Laws 195), and, "If a man steals an ox or a sheep and kills it or sells it, he shall pay five oxen for an ox, and four sheep for a sheep" (Exod. 22:1 [H 21:37]). It is said that casuistic laws are essentially secular and represent instruction for the day-to-day work of lawyers and judges. Recent research, however, has raised questions about the use and application of ancient Near Eastern law collections in their settings. In reading through thousands of ancient legal documents which are contemporary to these codes, it has been noted that the documents never refer to the codes and often differ from the regulations contained in them. Even the kings who published them take no special notice of them in their historical records. The repetition of similar laws in collections by succeeding rulers suggests that the codes were written not for judges or government officials but for literary purposes, in documents addressed to the gods or to some distant human posterity who will read the text and recognize how just and righteous the rulers have been.

The changing image of non-Israelite case law gives reason to re-examine the role of case law in ancient Israel. If it cannot be shown that casuistic law served judges or courts in the teeming centers of Babylonia, Assyria, and Asia Minor, then there is little reason to claim this function in ancient Israel. One must search anew to understand the purpose of writing down these laws in the Bible; one cannot simply assume that they belong to the administration of justice in the monarchy or, indeed, any other period.

6. The use of writing in law. The Bible preserves historical memory of periods in Israelite history when writing was not yet an integral feature of legal life and procedure. Abraham purchased the cave of Machpelah without writing a document (Gen. 23:7-16). Symbolic gestures rather than writing were employed for the transfer of the levirate and the redeeming of property in Ruth 4:7-11. The use of written deeds is first encountered in the redemption and transfer of real estate in Jer. 32:9-14. Written documents were used for divorce in Deut. 24:3; Isa. 50:1; and Jer. 3:8; but this is not the ancient custom for, as late as the fifth century B.C., the Elephantine Papyri still preserve a ceremony of divorce accomplished by the recitation of oral formulas (*see* §1 *above*). It appears that the custom of writing legal documents came into widespread use during the monarchy, and probably only toward the end of that period (cf. further Isa. 8:16; Job 31:35). There is no reason to assume the need for law books prior to the emergence and use of writing in the general conduct and practice of legal affairs. The ancient Israelite judges apparently never came to rely upon written laws; when a judge was puzzled about the law, he was to seek the help of a higher official in the capital (Deut. 17:8-11).

7. The Ten Commandments. There are traditions in the Bible about laws first being inscribed upon stones; one finds this in connection with the Ten Commandments (Exod. 31:18; 32:15-19; 34:1-4, 28-29; Deut. 5:22; 10:1-5) and in connection with unspecified larger corpora (Deut. 27:4-8; Josh. 8:32). These traditions are reminiscent of the writing down of the Twelve Tables at Rome and the Laws of Gortyna in Crete. The purpose of these monumental records was not for the dissemination of the laws via written media but rather to preserve a fixed text, at least in one place, should dispute ever arise as to their wording and intent. At ancient Rome, the setting up of the Twelve Tables preceded the general use of writing by several centuries; as in ancient Israel, the conduct of legal affairs remained an oral matter. *See also* TEN COMMANDMENTS[S].

8. The forms of the law. Most ancient Near Eastern laws are presented in case or casuistic form (*see* §5), but most of the OT laws are not set in this form. They occur in the form of prohibitions, prescriptions, instructions, and commands—sometimes spoken in second person—enjoining or forbidding a certain activity most usually without stating a penalty, which is almost always present in casuistic laws. (For examples, *see* Exod. 21:13-17; 22:18-24 [H 17-23]; 23:6-19; Lev. 18:7-23; Deut. 27:15-26.) These "categorical" or "apodictic" legal statements (*see* LAW IN THE OT §C3) are not unknown in the ancient Near Eastern law codes. They occur in the Eshnunna Laws (10-11, 15-16, 51-52), the Hammurabi Laws (36, 38-40), the Assyrian Laws (A 40, 57-59), and in the Hittite Laws (48, 50-52, 54-56). Second-person statements are not found among these law collections, but they do commonly occur in ritual and magical manuals, where priests, diviners, or magical experts are told how to proceed with their tasks. Negative prohibitions are rarer in the non-Israelite literature, but excellent parallels to the biblical prohibitions have been found in the Hittite vassal treaties of the latter part of the second millennium B.C.

One cannot claim, as some scholars do, that these apodictic or declarative laws are uniquely Israelite in contrast to casuistic formulations. At the same time, however, it remains true that the Bible does use the former style to a much greater extent than found elsewhere. This use is probably best explained by a setting of oral address in situations where listeners are being informed and instructed. The Bible repeatedly utilizes the scenario of the priests reading the Law to Israel on special occasions (Deut. 31:9-13; Neh. 8:1-8; 13:1-3); the book of Deuteronomy is stylistically presented as the public address of Moses to the people; and the Decalogue, the Covenant Code, and indeed all of the laws are presented as materials for public address.

9. Law and authority. The Bible has preserved record of a number of authority groups: family, elders, tribes, kings, prophets, and priests, who had a claim to regulate the life of Israelites in some way. At the earliest level, there was family and tribe (§14 *below; see also* KINSHIP AND FAMILY[S] §8); subsequently, monarchy developed and, with the loss of political independence, disappeared (§§11-12). The family units persisted throughout Israelite history (cf. Ezra 2, 8), but tribal leadership dissolved soon after the monarchy was established. The elders also survived the transition from kinship to contiguity, and they continued to function throughout the centuries (Deut. 22:18; I Kings 21:8-14; Ruth 4:2-12) regardless of shifts in authority at the top of the social ladder (§14). Priestly authority seems to have been of little importance during the tribal phase (cf. Judg. 17, 18) but gained strength toward the end of the monarchy (§10), as the political fortunes of Judah sank, and especially after the Exile, when secular and religious power was given to them by the Persian kings (*see* AARON, AARONIDES[S] §2). The prophets seem to have flourished during the monarchy (§13); and while there is occasional mention of prophets earlier—Moses and Abraham are called prophets (Gen. 20:7; Deut. 18:18; 34:10)—the galaxy of prophetic heroes is most visible during the period between Saul and Zerubbabel. Prophecy seems to come to an abrupt end in the days of the second temple; its disappearance may be linked to the firm establishment of priestly authority and the Law in Israel. The power of the prophet to communicate with heaven was no longer needed and indeed was felt to be disruptive, once the Law was established and fixed (cf. Deut. 13:1-5; 18:15-22).

10. The law and the priesthood. The oral character of the apodictic or declarative laws and the pronounced emphasis of the OT laws in general upon ritual and cultic matters are a result of the important role of the priesthood in developing the written Pentateuchal laws. It is for this reason that the term "Torah" (RSV "law," "instruction"), which is intimately associated with priestly lore (e.g., Deut. 17:8-13; Jer. 18:18), comes to describe the Pentateuch as a whole (*see* TORAH[S]). The Bible's emphasis on religious rather than secular matters is a natural outgrowth of the priestly point of view and priestly desire to establish the public maintenance of the centralized cult. The Bible thus extensively addresses itself to the observance of festivals, expiations, sacrifices, tithes, benefices, questions of rank, hierarchy, and the like. One must not underestimate the historical role of the priests in shaping the Scriptures, for only after their participation is fully evaluated is it possible to look for the contributions of other authority groups. *See* PRIESTLY WRITERS[S].

11. Law and kingship. After the priesthood, the monarchy is the next most important source of authority and law. Monarchs are certainly the most active agents for the promulgation of law in the pagan cultures of Sumer, Babylonia, Asia Minor, and Rome, as well as in early medieval Europe. The reforms of JOSIAH, and the probable connection of these reforms with the origin of the book of DEUTERONOMY, are one clear link between monarchy and law. Yet, here too, the priests also play a significant role (cf. Deut. 17:14-20). Some scholars would connect the Covenant Code to the activities of the monarchy; that code, after all, bears the closest resemblance to the ancient Near Eastern laws. This remains a plausible even if not yet a provable hypothesis. *See* KING §6*a;* GOVERNMENT, ISRAELITE[S].

12. The law and the state. It may be possible to detect evidence of the advancing power of the state in the biblical laws of *talion* (Exod. 21:23-25; Lev. 24:19-20; Deut. 19:21), which customarily have been considered a relic from Israel's nomadic past (*see* LEX TALIONIS[S]). Recent discoveries, however, have supplied new perspectives. In the Eshnunna Laws (42-48) and the Ur-Nammu Laws (15-19), which precede the Hammurabi Laws in time, the penalties for assault and personal injury are all monetary. The later Hammurabi Laws (196-205) punish assaults against free men by *talion* or public beating, while injuries to persons of lower class and slaves are punished by monetary penalties. *Talionic* sanctions continue to be found in the later Assyrian Laws as well. From comparison with old Saxon law, Diamond argues that the sociocultural progression is not from *talion* to monetary penalties but the reverse. As the state becomes more powerful and central authority grows, it intrudes into the private domain, declaring an increasing number of wrongdoings (murder, rape, adultery, wounding, grand larceny) to be crimes against the state (and God). In archaic societies, the trauma of these wrongs is assuaged by compensation; in the advancing state, the state punishes the wrongdoer (often severely, by death) but the victims are now without remedy (cf. Assyrian Laws A 21).

13. Law and the prophets. The prophets do not seem to function as sources for law except in the Pentateuch, where Moses brings the laws to the people in the manner of a prophet (Deut. 18:15; 34:10; Hos. 12:13 [H 14]). The prophets, however, are definitely aware of the Law; their condemnations contain numerous references to specific actions which are also the subject of laws in the Pentateuch. To cite only a partial list of categories: false weights (Amos 8:5; Mic. 6:10-11; Deut. 25:13-15; Lev. 19:35-36), taking interest in the form of food (Amos 5:11; Deut. 23:19 [H 20]), taking garments in pledge (Amos 2:8; Exod. 22:26-27 [H 25-26]), withholding wages (Jer. 22:13; Lev. 19:13; Deut. 24:14-15), eating swine and other forbidden foods (Isa. 65:4; 66:17; Lev. 11:7; Deut. 14:8), catching a sneak thief (Jer. 2:34; Exod. 22:2 [H 1]), remarrying a divorced wife after she has been married (Jer. 3:1; Deut. 24:1-4), writing a bill of divorce (Isa. 50:1; Jer. 3:8; Deut. 24:1-4), circumcision (Jer. 4:4; 9:25-26; Gen. 17:10-14), observance of new moons, sabbaths, and festivals (Amos 8:5; Isa. 1:13; 56:4; Jer. 17:22-27; Ezek. 20:12-21; Exod. 20:8-11; etc.), the Nazirite (Amos 2:12; Num. 6:1-21), child sacrifice (Jer. 19:4-5; 32:35; Lev. 18:21; 20:2).

It is not possible to assume (1) that the literary prophets came before the development of the Law, or (2) that the prophetic position was antithetical to the Law. The prophets, however, were responsible for a new emphasis on morality which forever set Israel apart from her neighbors who, while by no means insensitive to morality and justice, nevertheless believed in a fundamentally amoral universe. The ancient Israelites no doubt came to believe that a God who asked for righteousness and justice would also supply the means of instructing his people in his ways. One may see the emergence of the written laws as a partial response to this search for divine guidance. The fall of the northern kingdom in the eighth century probably accelerated this process; the people of Judah came to hearken more soberly to the message of those prophets who preached that destruction was a consequence of the lack of morality, and they accepted the commandments emanating from the "prophet" Moses, by which they hoped to gain God's favor and blessing.

14. Before the monarchy. There is no evidence for any promulgation of laws during the tribal phase of Israelite history. That is not to say that there were no laws during this period; there were certainly norms, traditions, and customs. Many of the later written laws, cultic, secular, and ritual, may be older than the time of their becoming incorporated into the written collections; and some of them were surely in existence during the tribal period. But there is no clear way to attach any of the OT laws to the leadership or authority of the tribes. There are those who reconstruct the existence of a tribal AMPHICTYONY or religious federation which functioned during the tribal epoch. Similar institutions have been suggested for Greece and for Sumer; these other amphictyonies, however, did not produce any laws.

During the tribal period, chieftains were active in leading the people and in making decisions (cf. Judg. 20, 21), but they were not lawgivers. The same can be said of the judges who led Israel into battle, and who administered justice in cases of disputes. There is no way of knowing whether any of the laws of the Pentateuch derive from their judicial activities. *See* JUDGES, BOOK OF[S].

The elders appear to have played a passive role and never appear as originators of policy or law (cf. Deut. 22:18; I Kings 21:8-14; Ruth 4:2-12); rather, they carried out the existing laws of the land under the leadership of higher authorities (cf. Ezra 10:7-8).

The family would seem to be a group far removed from the activities of lawgiving. Nevertheless, Gerstenberger has looked for links between the family or clan and the law. He draws attention to affinities between the negative prohibitions of the laws and exhortations found in the wisdom books and parallels to be found in Egypt and Babylonia. From contexts like Prov. 3:5-12, 27-31; 22:17–24:22; and Jer. 35:6-7, where advice is given by a father to his children, Gerstenberger suggests that the negative apodictic prohibitions are remnants of clan or family wisdom, which was taught to the young as a catechism to be learned prior to their being accepted into adulthood (*see* PROVERBS, BOOK OF[S] §2*c*). This is possible, but it must be remembered that a good deal of what is called wisdom in the ancient Near Eastern sources is in reality court literature: the education of young noblemen in the arts of flattery, caution, and humility before their all-powerful lords (cf. also Prov. 23:1-5; Eccl 8:2-4; 10:20; *see* JOSEPH STORY[S] §3). Then, too, the speaker of wisdom appeals to the good sense of the listener, frequently adding motive clauses to explain his admonitions; the lawgiver possesses an implied authority to speak and to direct the lives and actions of his listeners. For other possible remnants of familial jurisdictions, compare Gen. 31:32, 37; 38:24; 48:5-6. *See also* WISDOM IN THE ANE[S] §§1*a*, 2*a*; WISDOM IN THE OT[S] §3.

15. Corporate and individual identity. The emergence of the written law caused a change in the Israelite viewpoint on responsibility. Earlier, the group or community could legitimately suffer for the wrongdoings or sins of one of its members. This is true in the narratives (e.g., Josh. 7:24-25; II Sam. 12:14; 21:1-6; 24:10-15) and in the Pentateuch (e.g., Exod. 20:5; 34:7; Num. 14:18; Deut. 5:9), and the concept is implied in the prophetic predictions of disaster overtaking the entire nation of Israel because of the sins of the wicked among them. The promulgation of written laws laid open the requirements and preconditions for securing God's favor; each person could learn the commandments, and it became his responsibility to do so. People came increasingly to believe that each person should suffer for his own sins (cf. Gen. 18:23-32; Deut. 24:16; Jer. 31:29-30—contrast 32:18; Ezek. 14:12-20; 18:1-20; 33:1-20), thus laying the groundwork for the idea of individual reward and punishment. *See* EZEKIEL[S] §4.

16. Law and covenant. The new emphasis on individualism and the growing power of the central government eroded any remnants of kinship and tribalism that may have survived the formation of the state. The units of tribe and clan had fit in well with the older concept of communal or corporate identity. There was a need for a new framework which could integrate the individual into the nation and, at the same time, maintain the primacy of God, who was the supreme ruler of a moral universe. The concept of the national covenant came into prominence at this time, modeled after the great international treaties between Israelite kings and their Assyrian overlords (*see* Frankena). This covenant supported individuality by incorporating the written Pentateuchal laws into stipulations of agreement between God and the people of Israel; at the same time it offered the notion of the community of the covenant to replace the old communality which was based on kinship. The covenant was not the catalyst for the laws. The concept of covenant existed independently of the laws, as can be seen by the strong biblical tradition of covenants without stated stipulations (cf. Gen. 9:8-17; 15:17-21; Num. 25:13; II Sam. 23:5). The concept of Israel's special relationship with Yahweh was of course not a new idea. What was new is the expression of this relationship in the form of a formal agreement between God and each individual Israelite.

The national covenant became a dynamic principle of faith only during the late monarchical period, and hence the prophets do not make extensive use of this concept. There are those who would reconstruct this later national covenant as a part of the premonarchic and preprophetic phases of Israelite history (*see* COVENANT; COVENANT, MOSAIC[S]; COVENANT, DAVIDIC[S]). These theories are complete speculation; if the national covenant can be Mosaic, then one can likewise attribute the Pentateuchal laws to Moses, for there is certainly more biblical evidence for this position than for ascribing the covenant to the period of Moses or of the tribal federation.

Bibliography. B. Porten, *Archives from Elephantine* (1968), pp. 212, 234 on adoption, 260-62 for a discussion of women's right to divorce in the Aramaic papyri; P. Benoit, J. T. Milik, R. de Vaux, *DJD*, II [Texte] (1961), 104, 244-46 has a discussion on double documents in the Dead Sea Scrolls; M. Civil, "New Sumerian Law Fragments," AS, XVI, (1965), at 2, 4-6 on Lipit-Ishtar Laws 28 and Sumerian laws relating to miscarriage; J. J. Finkelstein, "The Laws of Ur-Nammu," *JCS*, XXII (1969), 66-82, "Ammisaduqa's Edict and the Babylonian 'Law Codes,'" *JCS*, XV (1961), 91-104, and "Ancient Near Eastern Law," *Encyclopedia Biblica*, V (1968), 588-614, 1138-40, Hebrew; Z. Falk, *Hebrew Law in Biblical Times* (1964); S. E. Loewenstamm, "Biblical Law," *Encyclopedia Biblica*, V (1968), 614-37, Hebrew; J. J. Stamm, with M. E. Andrews, *The Ten Commandments in Recent Research* (1967); E. Gerstenberger, "Covenant and Commandment," *JBL*, LXXXIV (1967), 38-51; A. S. Diamond, "An Eye for an Eye," *Iraq*, XIX (1957), 151-55; D. McCarthy, *Treaty and Covenant*, AnBib, XXI (1963); R. Frankena, "The Vassal Treaties of Esarhaddon and the Dating of Deuteronomy," *OTS*, XIV (1965), 122-54; R. Bergren, *The Prophets and the Law* (1974), pp. 97-116, 181-85; W. Zimmerli, *The Law and the Prophets* (1965); A. Cowley, *Aramaic Papyri of the Fifth Century* B.C. (1923); E. Kraeling, ed., *The Brooklyn Museum Aramaic Papyri* (1953).

S. GREENGUS

LECTIONARY CYCLE, RABBINIC. Deut. 31:10-13 and Neh. 8:1-8 are the earliest references to the Jewish practice of a liturgical or didactic public reading of appropriate passages from the TORAH (i.e., Pentateuch) as the central element of communal worship during festival celebrations (cf. T.B. Meg. 32a). By A.D. 200 the practice had developed into an established tradition of Pentateuchal readings for every Monday, Thursday, and sabbath; special readings for all the festivals, including Hanukkah and Purim; and special readings for fast days. M. Meg. 3.4-6, which identifies these readings, also includes the special readings assigned to each of the four sabbaths immediately preceding the Passover festival. According to Elbogen, the practice of weekly sabbath readings grew by extending the pre-Passover custom to every sabbath. (cf. Acts 15:21; Jos. Apion II.175; Philo, II *Somniis* 27). It was only as a result of these weekly sabbath readings that the Torah came to be read serially in its entirety.

Two different lectionary systems emerged: the one associated with Palestine, the so-called "triennial cycle," and the other associated with the Babylonian Jewish community, in which the Pentateuch was divided into fifty-four *parashoth* (e.g., Gen. 1:1–6:8; 6:9–11:32; 12:1–17:27, etc.; note the siglum פרש in the margin of *Biblia Hebraica*) and completed in a single year. The Palestinian system divided the Pentateuch into either 141, 153, 155, or 167 weekly *sedarim* depending upon the particular synagogal list (e.g., Gen. 1:1–2:3; 2:4–3:21; 3:24–4:26; 5:1–6:8, etc.; note the siglum ס in the margin of *Biblia Hebraica*) and therefore required from three to three and one half years to complete the Pentateuch. The pioneering arguments of Buechler (*see* Petuchowski) and Mann for a uniform Palestinian cycle have been refuted, with most scholars today agreeing on the co-existence of many different cycles.

Historically, it was the Babylonian system of annual completion that became the standard Jewish practice, even within Palestine itself.

The second main stage in the incorporation of the Bible into Jewish liturgy was the "completion" (*Haphtarah*) of the Pentateuchal reading by a selection from such books as Isaiah, Jeremiah, I and II Kings, Ezekiel, etc. Though the origins of this practice are shrouded in mystery, we may assume that it emerged only after the Pentateuchal reading was already established. As suggested in Luke 4:16-21, prophetic readings for an ordinary sabbath were originally not fixed. According to Tosefta and T.B. Meg. 31a-b, *Haphtarah* readings were determined only for the festivals and the four pre-Passover sabbaths. As in the case of the Torah itself, the practice was extended to every sabbath of the year as well as to other special days, e.g., the Ninth of Ab. Hence there emerged a fixed prophetic reading for each sabbath or festival or fast day on which the Torah was read. The criterion for selection was merely that the prophetic reading somehow resemble the Pentateuchal portion in content or language (T.B. Meg. 29b). E.g., Isa. 42:5 was assigned to Gen. 1:1 ff. and Mic. 5:6 ff. to Num. 22 ff. It is also clear that the Palestinian "triennial" cycle demanded three times the number of *Haphtarah* readings required in the Babylonian annual system. As the later cycle became the dominant pattern, it usually selected the first of the three *Haphtarah* readings assigned to its particular *parashah* (weekly portion).

The impact on midrashic literature and on the development of Jewish homiletics cannot be overestimated. It has been shown that many rabbinic homilies are largely the result of weaving together the Pentateuchal and prophetic readings of a given day into complex sermonic fabrics.

The final stage in the full development of the Jewish lectionary system was the assignment in Talmudic times of Esther to Purim, and later the assignment of Ruth to Shavuoth (Pentecost), Song of Songs to Passover, Lamentations to the Ninth of Ab, and Ecclesiastes to Sukkoth (Booths). Some have argued for a "triennial" reading of Psalms, basing this claim on its 150 chapters, five books, and significant internal midrashic evidence, but this is difficult to prove.

Bibliography. I. Elbogen, *Der Jüdische Gottesdienst in Seiner Geschichtlichen Entwicklung* (1913); J. Mann, *The Bible as Read and Preached in the Old Synagogue* (1971), preface by Wacholder and Sonne; J. Petuchowski, ed., *Contributions to the Scientific Study of Jewish Liturgy* (1970).
K. P. BLAND

*__LETTER.__ The letter is one of the oldest and most common types of written texts. Letters have long been recognized as important documentary sources for most areas and branches of historical research. Less attention has been paid to the ancient history and phenomenology of letter writing, in spite of some pioneering works; but interest in epistolography is increasing among biblical and other scholars.

1. Source materials. All letters in the Bible and most letters from ancient Greece and Rome have been preserved by way of literary tradition. Unfortunately, it is often hard to know the extent to which letters contained in collections or in historical works (e.g., I and II Maccabees, Josephus) are authentic.

Modern archaeology has vastly increased the source materials, but the number of recovered letters does not reflect the frequency of letter writing. Akkadian letters on clay tablets and brief notes on potsherds (*see* OSTRACA) have resisted decay, in contrast to Greek and Latin letters on waxed wooden tablets (diptychs; *see* WRITING AND WRITING MATERIALS §B1). PAPYRUS letters have been found primarily in Egypt and—in much smaller quantities—in the desert of Judah and other places with a dry climate. On letters of importance for various periods of the history of Israel and Judaism, *see* esp. MARI, TAANACH, TELL EL AMARNA, LACHISH, BAR KOCHBA, and supplementary articles; *also* ELEPHANTINE PAPYRI. *See further, bibliog.*

2. Written message and oral text. As indicated by the terms used, the concept "letter" includes both a message conveyed and a written document (*see* LETTER §1). As the written text of spoken words the letter could—in Israel and elsewhere—open with the messenger formula, "Thus says. . ." (e.g., Ezra 1:1-2; cf. Rev. 2:1). Only the context makes it clear whether or not a letter is implied by the clause "A sends to B, saying" (cf. II Kings 19:9, 14). Throughout antiquity, the sender's name was placed at the beginning, as in oral messages.

The written document authenticated the message,

especially when signed with the sender's seal (cf. I Kings 21:8; Esth. 8:8), which also made it possible to send an order without revealing it to the courier, as in II Sam. 11:14-15. With increased use of letters the distinction between oral and written messages became sharper—a development which had at an early date taken place in Assyria. Many papyri are petitions (probably handed in by the applicant), contracts and other legal documents in letter form.

Even in later periods letters and oral reports often supplemented one another. Individuals who were not able to employ special couriers had to entrust their letters to occasional travelers. Phoebe might be one example (Rom. 16:1-2). The letter carrier could add informal information about the sender, whether the letter itself was a conventional token of affection or an elaborate document (cf. Col. 4:7-9). The separation of PAUL from his churches was overcome by exchange of delegates as well as of letters (e.g., I Cor. 16; II Cor. 7 and 8; Phil. 2:19-30, cf. Acts 15:22-33; III John 9-10).

3. Addressors and addressees. The form and function of letters depend upon the relationship between senders (addressors) and recipients (addressees). Letters to and from kings, especially orders and decrees, are prominent in the OT (e.g., I Kings 5 and II Chr. 2; II Kings 10:1-6; Ezra 4–7). Exchange of letters between superiors and subordinates became increasingly common at all levels of administration and also during military operations (cf. JOSEPHUS' *Life* and the letters of BAR KOCHBA).

Corporate bodies, e.g., city-states and councils, could receive and issue edicts and encyclicals, or engage in diplomatic correspondence with monarchs and with one another (e.g., I Macc. 8:22-30; 12:1-23; 14:16-23). They could also be addressed by absent individuals in letters which substituted for a speech (e.g., letters of Demosthenes).

Many letters were neither purely private nor strictly official, e.g., business letters, legal briefs, letters from counselors or "friends," oracular responses, and prophetic letters (II Chr. 21:12-15; Jer. 29), letters from scholars and philosophers (Plato, Epicurus, and others), and even the letters of Paul.

The idea of the "familiar letter" as the most genuine type of letter originated among the Greeks. According to rhetorical theory, the style of a letter should be dignified but only moderately ornate, since the letter was a gift among friends, a substitute for personal conversation, and a medium for spiritual presence (παρουσία, cf. I Cor. 5:3; Col. 2:5).

4. Composition. The purpose of letters is in general (*a*) to maintain contact, (*b*) to provide information, and (*c*) to make requests. The form is both highly conventional and extremely flexible.

The maintenance of contact and fostering of good relations can be taken care of by opening and closing greetings. Optional items include other good wishes, assertions of intercession and thanksgiving, expressions of joy or shared grief, of confidence in the addressees and of hope for reunion, polite compliments and reminders of previous good relations, greetings from or to other persons. "Philophronetic" statements (φιλοφρόνησις, friendly disposition) occur mainly in opening and closing segments of a letter and are most elaborate in familiar letters and diplomatic correspondence. Paul combines epistolary conventions with the language of thanksgiving, blessing, and prayer (e.g., I Thess. 1–3; Philem. 1-7, 21-25; cf. II John 1-3, 12-13; III John 4-6*a*, 13-15). In certain circumstances "philophronetic" statements give way to expressions of disappointment and embarrassment (often introduced by θαυμάζω, "I am surprised"), reproach, irony, and warnings (e.g., Gal. 1:6-9; 3:1-5; 4:8-11; 5:2; 6:17).

The nature and specific content of information and requests depend upon the occasion for and purpose of a letter and range from personal matters and business to policy and philosophy. Conventional phraseology is often used for purposes of introduction and transition, as in "disclosure formulas"—"I want you to know" (e.g., Rom. 1:13)—or simply "concerning" (περὶ δὲ, I Cor. 7:1, etc.; I Thess. 4:9). Requests can be formulated as commands or petitions, but are frequently introduced by polite clichés, such as "I appeal to you" (παρακαλῶ, e.g., Rom. 12:1; cf. Philem. 8-10) or "You will do well to" (καλῶς ποιήσεις, III John 6). Paul uses these epistolary conventions with considerable freedom, as do highly literate letter writers like Cicero.

In more elaborate letters, including some private papyrus letters, the issues at hand are illuminated by references to general human experience, by proverbs and maxims, by quotations and historical paradigms, and by rules for proper conduct. In a similar way, NT letters include scriptural passages and examples; kerygmatic, hymnic, and catechetical traditions, etc. *See* LISTS, ETHICAL §3; LISTS, ETHICAL[S]; PARENESIS[S]; LITURGICAL MATERIALS IN THE NT[S].

In antiquity the composition of letters was treated as part of rhetoric. The influence of forensic, deliberative, and laudatory ("epideictic") rhetoric is most prominent when a letter is intended to persuade. Classical models were provided by the letters of Plato, Isocrates, and Demosthenes—authentic or not. Examples from the first century A.D. include Agrippa's written plea to Caligula on behalf of the Jews (Philo, *On the Embassy to Gaius* XXXVI-XLI) and Paul's letters, especially those to the Corinthians, Galatians, and Romans.

5. Types of letters. Letters can be classified according to several criteria which often overlap: writing materials; mode of preservation; private, official, or public character; levels of style; and what was most important to ancient letter theory—occasion, scope, and mood. A main distinction was made between "familiar" letters and "negotial" letters, those which discussed issues. There were also more or less fixed patterns for some special genres, like petitions, reports (cf. Acts 23:26-30), communication of official decisions (cf. Acts 15:23-29), letters of consolation, etc. Handbooks on epistolography list quite a number of types, but several of them are likely to represent the style to be used for various purposes rather than distinct subgenres.

Paul's letters were written in his capacity as an

apostle of God and addressed to "the saints" or "the church" at various places. But he appeals to the experience and judgment of the recipients (Philem. 8-9; Rom. 15:14 ff.). The structure and style are more akin to familiar and diplomatic letters than to official orders and decrees. The individual letters, or more often parts of them, conform more or less exactly to recognized types: the letter of recommendation (Philemon; Rom. 16:1-2; cf. II Cor. 3:1-3); the letter of thanksgiving (Phil. 1:3 ff.; 4:10 ff.) or a response (I Cor. 7–14); the didactic (esp. Rom. 1–11) or the apologetic letter (esp. Gal. 1–2, II Cor. 10–13, even I Cor. 1–4 and Romans); the parenetic letter of exhortation (esp. I Thessalonians); and the symbouleutic letter of advice (Galatians; cf. I Cor. 7; II Cor. 8). Philophronetic features predominate in II Cor. 1–7, in spite of strained relations.

Later Christian letter writers, e.g., IGNATIUS and POLYCARP, were influenced by Paul. But other models were also important. Letters from Jewish authorities about fasts, festivals, and other matters must have been common practice (cf. I Kings 21:9; II Chr. 30; Esth. 9:20-22; II Macc. 1–2; TB Sanh. 11a; Acts 9:2; 28:21). Several NT letters are in the form of encyclicals (Acts 15:23; Rev. 1:4-7; I and II Peter; James). I Clement is a letter of advice from the church of Rome to the church in Corinth.

III John is a familiar letter and II John is written in the style of one. But the letter form can also be used for writings which otherwise belong to different genres: sermons (Hebrews; cf. I John), WISDOM and parenesis (James), mandates for ministers of the church (I Timothy, Titus), literary testaments (most clearly II Timothy and II Peter), prophecy and apocalyptic (Rev. 2–3 and also 1:4-6; 2:21; cf. e.g., II Bar. 78–87). *See also* LITERATURE, EARLY CHRISTIAN[S] §4.

6. Publication and literary fiction. Royal and other official letters of general interest were published by oral proclamation, posted, and even cut in stone as inscriptions. Other letters could be copied and forwarded, kept in archives, occasionally even used as models of style. The correspondence of Aristotle (now lost), of Cicero, and of many after them was eventually published. The letters of Paul are likely to have been copied and circulated before they were edited as a collection. Ignatius' letters were almost immediately collected (cf. Polyc. Phil. 13).

The distinction between "true letters" and literary "epistles" (*see* LETTER §4) has a limited validity. As a technical term "epistle" should be reserved for writings which are in the style of a letter but intended for a general public, so that the specific address, if any, is a literary fiction or a propagandistic device. It is contrary to ancient theory and practice to make spontaneity and confidentiality part of the definition of a true letter. Even familiar letters could be of more than personal and ephemeral interest; some were written by masters of style, many by professional scribes.

Sometimes letters were forged in order to deceive the recipients (cf. II Thess. 2:2). More frequently, fictitious letters were composed as part of rhetorical school exercises or for literary purposes, entertainment, historical fiction, or propagation of ideas. Historians felt free to compose letters as well as speeches, and there was no great step from a literary "dialogue" to an imitated letter (*see* PSEUDONYMOUS WRITING[S] §3). For the most famous example of Jewish literature in letter form, *see* ARISTEAS.

Among the NT apocrypha the correspondence between Paul and Seneca is fiction in letter form, the "Letter to the Laodiceans" an attempt to substitute for a letter that was assumed to have been lost. Among the letters or "epistles" included in the NT canon, II Peter is certainly spurious. In other cases, it is possible that the author drew upon genuine traditions from the alleged addressor ("Deutero-Pauline" epistles, I Peter, James[?]).

The frequency of fictitious as well as of genuine letters in early Christianity is remarkable. Within the fellowship of scattered believers, letters and writings similar to letters were the most appropriate form for written communication and exposition of the common faith. Up to the time of the second-century apologists (and Gnostics) only the narrative form of the gospels had an equal importance.

Bibliography. Editions and translations (examples): A. L. Oppenheimer, *Letters from Mesopotamia* (1967); J. B. Pritchard, ed., *Ancient Near Eastern Texts* (3rd ed., 1969), pp. 475-92; P. Benoit *et al.*, eds., *Discoveries in the Judean Desert,* II (1961), pp. 115-69, letters from Murabba'at; J. A. Fitzmyer, *JBL,* XCIII (1974), p. 206, n. 37, other letters from the Bar Kochba period; R. Hercher, *Epistolographi Graeci* (1873 [repr., 1965]), comprehensive collection of Gr. "literary" letters (cf. critical eds. and translations of individual authors); V. Weichert, ed., *Demetrii et Libanii qui feruntur* τυποι επιστολκοι et επιστολομαιοι χαρακτηρες (1910), "handbooks"; C. B. Welles, *Royal Correspondence in the Hellenistic Period* (1934); A. S. Hunt and C. C. Edgars, *Select Papyri, LCL,* 2 vols. (1932-34); B. Olsson, *Papyrusbriefe aus der frühesten Römerzeit* (1925); A. V. Tcherikover and A. Fuks, eds., *Corpus Papyrorum Judaicarum,* 3 vols. (1957-64); G. Ghedini, *Lettere christiane dai papiri greci del III e IV secolo* (1923); E. Hennecke and W. Schneemelcher, *NT Apocrypha,* II (1964), 111-12, 128-66.

General: W. G. Doty, *Letters in Primitive Christianity,* Guides to Biblical Scholarship, VII (1973); F. X. J. Exler, "The Form of the Ancient Greek Letter" (diss., Catholic Univ. of America, 1923); J. Fitzmyer, "Some Notes on Aramaic Epistolography," *JBL,* XCIII (1974), 201-25, with index of sources; R. W. Funk, *Language, Hermeneutic and Word of God* (1966), pp. 250-74; H. Koskenniemi, *Studien zur Idee und Phraseologie des griechischen Briefes bis 400 n. Chr.* (1956); H. Leclercq, "Lettres chrétiennes," *DACL,* VIII (1929), cols. 2683-85; B. Rigaux, *The Letters of Paul* (1962); J. Schneider, "Brief," *RAC,* II (1954), cols. 563-85; J. Sykutris, "Epistolographie," PWSup, V (1931), 185-220; K. Thraede, *Grundzüge griechisch-römischer Brieftopik,* Zetemata, XLVIII (1970).

Special studies: C. Andresen, "Zum Formular frühchristlicher Gemeindebriefe," *ZNW,* LVI (1965), 233-59; G. H. Bahr, "Paul and Letter Writing in the Fifth Century," *CBQ,* XXVIII (1966), 465-77, and "The Subscriptions in the Pauline Letters," *JBL,* LXXXVI (1968), 27-41; K. Berger, "Apostelbrief und apostolische Rede," *ZNW,* LXV (1974), 190-231; C. J. Bjerkelund, *Parakalô,* Bibliotheca Theologica Norvegica, I (1967); N. A. Dahl, "The Particularity of the Pauline Epistles as a Problem in the Ancient Church," *Neotestamentica et Patristica,* NovTSup, VI (1962), 261-71; F. O. Francis, "The Form and Function of the Opening and Closing Paragraphs of James and I John," *ZNW,* LXI

(1970), 110-26; R. W. Funk, "The Apostolic Parousia," *Christian History and Interpretation,* ed. W. R. Farmer *et al.* (1967), 249-68, and "The Form and Structure of II and III John," *JBL,* LXXXVI (1967), 424-30; C. H. Kim, *The Familiar Letter of Recommendation,* SBLDS, IV (1972); T. Y. Mullins, "Formulas in NT Epistles," *JBL,* XCI (1972), 380-90, "Petition as a Literary Form," *NovT,* V (1962), 46-54, "Disclosure: A Literary Form in the NT," *NovT,* VII (1964), 44-50, and "Greeting as a NT Form," *JBL,* LXXXVII (1968), 418-26; M. L. Stirewalt, "Paul's Evaluation of Letter-Writing," *Search the Scriptures,* ed. J. M. Myers *et al.,* Gettysburg Theological Studies, III (1969), 179-96; R. D. Webber, "The Concept of Rejoicing in Paul" (diss., Yale, 1970), pp. 96-200; J. L. White, *The Form and Structure of the Official Petition,* SBLDS, V (1972), and *The Body of the Greek Letter,* SBLDS, II (1972).

N. A. DAHL

***LEVITICUS** [Heb. ויקרא; LXX λευιτικόν]. The book is more aptly described by its tannaitic name תורת כהנים, "The Priests' Manual." It is thematically an independent entity. In Exodus, the P code (*see* PRIESTLY WRITERS[S]) describes the construction of the cultic implements (the tabernacle and the priestly vestments), whereas Leviticus converts this static picture into scenes from the living cult. Numbers then concentrates on the cultic laws of the camp in motion, e.g., the military arrangement of the tribes, the censuses of the warriors, the transport of the sanctums and their protection against encroachment (*see* ENCROACHMENT[S]). Since the latter is the main function of the Levites, it is striking that all the laws pertaining to the Levites are in Numbers, and none are in Leviticus.

Although "The Priests' Manual" focuses on the priests, few laws are reserved for them alone (Lev. 8–10; 16:1-28; 21:1–22:16). Their role is defined in pedagogic terms: to teach the distinctions "between the holy and profane, between the pure and impure" (10:10; cf. 14:57; 15:31). They must do this, because Israel's moral sins and physical impurities lead to the defilement of the sanctuary and its eventual abandonment by God (*see* ATONEMENT IN THE OT[S]; ATONEMENT, DAY OF[S]). The priests, then, are charged with a double task: to instruct Israel not to cause defilement, and to purge the sanctuary whenever it is defiled. However, Leviticus is not just a collection of rituals. On the contrary, the ethical element fuses with and even informs the ritual so that one may seek a moral basis behind each ritual act.

From the point of view of literary criticism, Leviticus is relatively uncomplicated: it is a single source (*see* SOURCE CRITICISM, OT[S]). Even if another stratum is recognized (*see* §4 *below*), it has been thoroughly assimilated by P. Furthermore, the text has been excellently preserved; the few divergencies in the versions are nearly all secondary to the MT. The difficulty lies in the terminology used to describe the cult. It is a conservative vocabularly whose meaning was sometimes already lost on those who lived in the age of the second temple and even more so on subsequent generations.

1. Chs. 1–7: the sacrificial system
2. Chs. 8–10: the inaugural service at the sanctuary
3. Chs. 11–16: the laws of impurities
4. Chs. 17–26: the Holiness Source (H)
5. Ch. 27: commutation of gifts to the sanctuary
Bibliography

1. Chs. 1–7: the sacrificial system. In chs. 1–5 the sacrifices are listed from the point of the donor: chs. 1–3, the spontaneously motivated sacrifices (*'ōlâ minḥâ, šelāmîm*); chs. 4–5, the sacrifices required for expiation (*ḥaṭṭā'th* and *'āšām*). Chs. 6–7 regroup these sacrifices in order of their sanctity in the daily ritual, i.e., most-sacred: *'ōlâ, minḥâ, ḥaṭṭā'th, 'āšām;* sacred: *šelāmîm.* The common denominator of the sacrifices discussed in these chapters is that they arise in answer to an unpredictable religious or emotional need, and are thereby set off from the sacrifices of the public feasts and fasts that are fixed by the calendar (chs. 9, 16, 23; cf. Num. 28–29). *See* SACRIFICES AND OFFERINGS, OT[S] §§1*b,* 2-3, *for* §§*a-g below.*

a. 1:1-2: general introduction. The Hebrew particles for introducing general and particular statements in legal formulation indicate that chs. 1 and 3 were originally a single unit which was later split by the insertion of ch. 2. The conditional construction of 1:2*a* underscores the voluntary basis of the sacrifices. Though these verses are addressed to Israel alone, the sacrifices were made available to the resident alien (Lev. 17:8; 24:15-22; Num. 15:14-16, 29).

b. 1:3-17: the whole offering ('ōlâ; RSV "burnt offering"). It is the only sacrifice which is entirely consumed on the altar, hence the translation "whole" (cf. Deut. 33:10; I Sam. 7:9). Vss. 3-5 encapsule the major concepts of the sacrificial system: laying on of hands, acceptance, EXPIATION, slaughter, blood manipulation, entrance to the tent of meeting. The donor is an active participant in the ritual. The whole offering must be chosen from male, unblemished and eligible species of the herd, flock, or birds. The *'ōlâ* is probably the oldest and most popular sacrifice (Tosef. Zeb. XIII.1). Its function here is expiatory (vs. 4; cf. 9:7; 14:20; Job 1:5; 42:8; *UT* 9:1, 7), but in P, whenever it is offered by an individual, the motivation is joyful (e.g., Lev. 22:17 ff.; Num. 15:1-11).

c. Ch. 2: the tribute (cereal) offering (minḥâ). In the non-Priestly texts, *minḥâ* connotes both "a present made to secure or retain goodwill" (Driver; e.g., Gen. 32:13-21 [H 14-22]), and a tribute brought by subjects to their overlords, both human (Judg. 3:15-18) and divine. It could be either animal or vegetable (Gen. 4:3; I Sam. 2:17). In P, however, it is exclusively cereal, either choice flour (Lev. 2:1-3), or cakes of choice flour (vss. 4-10), or roasted grain (vss. 14-16). Because leaven and honey (fruit syrup) ferment, whereas salt preserves, the first two were forbidden, and salt was required on the altar (vss. 11-13). Leaven, however, was permitted as a FIRST-FRUIT offering to the priest (23:17; II Chr. 31:5). The restriction to cereal emphasizes that man's tribute to God should be from the fruit of his labors on the soil. In daily life, however, the aspect of appeasement may also have been present (I Sam. 26:19; cf. *ANET* [2nd ed.], p. 439, 1. 51). Because cereal was abundant and cheap, it became the poor man's *'ōlâ* (Philo, *On the Special Laws,* I.271; Lev. Rabbah 8:4), and probably replaced it in popularity and function.

d. Ch. 3: the well-being offering (šᵉlāmîm; RSV "peace offering"). This offering never serves as expiation. Its basic function is simply to permit the consumption of flesh. It was usually spontaneous and motivated by elation. The rules are similar to those of the whole offering, except that the victims may be female but not birds. Also, being of lesser sanctity, its portions were assigned to the donor as well as to God. The choicest internal fats (suet) were turned to smoke.

e. Ch. 4: the purgation offering (ḥaṭṭā'th; RSV "sin offering"). Its purpose is to remove the impurity inflicted upon the sanctuary by the inadvertent violation of prohibitive laws (but not ethical violations). The brazen violation of these laws is punishable by death through divine agency (כרת, RSV "cut off," Num. 15:27-31). Other instances specify the nature of the violations: holy days (e.g., Passover, Day of Atonement), contamination of sanctums (e.g., Lev. 7:20-21), prohibited cultic acts (e.g., 17:3-4, 8-9) and illicit sex (18:29). The last mentioned is among the ritual sins, since it leads to the pollution of the land (18:27).

f. 5:1-13: borderline cases of the purgation offering. Rabbinic tradition distinguishes between the purgation offering of ch. 4 and that of 5:1-13, calling the latter "the scaled offering" (RSV "guilt offering") geared to the financial means of the offender (not his status, as in ch. 4). This separate *ḥaṭṭā'th* probably arises from the failure or inability to cleanse impurity immediately upon its incurrence.

g. 5:14–6:7 [H 5:14-26]: the reparation offering ('āšām; RSV "guilt offering"). It is prescribed for trespass (מעל) upon the property of God or man, the latter through the use of a false oath. The sin to which it relates is desecration: the sanctums or the name of God have become desanctified (as opposed to cases of the purgation offering, ch. 4, where the sin is contamination of sanctums).

h. Ch. 6–7: supplementary instructions. Since the well-being offering is eaten chiefly by the donor, the rules pertain mainly to him (7:11-34, esp. vss. 23, 29). Otherwise they are the concerns of the officiating priest. The subjects are: the altar fire (6:8-13 [H 1-6]); the manner and place for eating the tribute offering (6:14-18 [H 7-11]); the daily tribute offering of the high priest and the voluntary one of the ordinary priest (6:19-23 [H 12-16]); safeguards in sacrificing the purgation offering (6:24-30 [H 17-23]); the ritual for the reparation offering (7:17, missing in ch. 5); the priestly share in the whole and tribute offering (7:8-10); the types of well-being offering and their taboos (7:11-21); the prohibition against eating fat and blood (7:22-27); the priestly share of the well-being offering, set aside by the donor (7:28-36); the summation (7:37-38). The inclusion of the consecration offering before the well-being offering in this summation suggests that a section based on Exod. 29 originally preceded 7:11.

2. Chs. 8–10: the inaugural service at the sanctuary. This section follows logically and chronologically on Exod. 35–40; the priests are inducted into service after the priestly vestments and the tabernacle are completed. It is not Aaron, however, but Moses who dominates the scene. He is the one who conducts the inaugural service, consecrates the priests, and apportions all tasks. Aaron is clearly answerable to him, as seen from their confrontation in 10:16-20. Strikingly, the superiority of prophet over priest is insisted upon by the Priestly document! *See, however,* AARON, AARONIDES [S].

a. Ch. 8: the consecration of the priests. "To ordain you" (vs. 33) is literally "to fill your hands." In Scripture this phrase is used exclusively for the consecration of priests (Exod. 32:29; Judg. 17:5, 12; I Kings 13:33), but in the archives of MARI it refers to the distribution of booty. Thus, the Hebrew idiom indicates that installation rites officially entitle the priests to their share of the revenues and sacrifices brought to the sanctuary. "As the Lord commanded Moses" concludes each phase of the consecration ceremony, a reminder that this chapter is a repetition of the instructions in Exod. 29.

b. Ch. 9: the priests assume office. On the eighth day following the week of consecration, the priests begin their official duties. They offer up special sacrifices for the people "that the presence (RSV "glory") of the Lord may appear" (vs. 6; also vss. 4, 23). Indeed, the whole purpose of the sacrificial system is revelation, the assurance that God is with his people. However, God's presence is never assumed to be a co-efficient of the cult (in contrast to other religions); it is always viewed as an act of his grace. *See* PRESENCE OF GOD, CULTIC[S] esp. §§1-4.

c. 10:1-11: the sin of Nadab and Abihu. That the fire was "alien" could be charged either to the offering or the offerer. Most likely, the fire was taken from elsewhere, not from the altar (16:12; Num. 16:46 [H 17:11]).

d. 10:12-20: the consumption of the initiatory offerings. This section continues ch. 9. The tribute and well-being offerings are eaten by the priests in accordance with 6:16 [H 9] and 7:28-34. But the procedure for the purgation offering is switched from the individual to the communal form: the disposal of blood (9:9, 15; 10:18) has been according to 4:30 but not the disposal of its flesh (vs. 11), which follows 4:12 rather than 6:26 [H 19] and despite 6:30 [H 23]. The death of Nadab and Abihu has intervened. Aaron follows the more stringent procedure of destroying rather than eating the sacrificial meat because it has been doubly polluted by the sin and death of his sons. Its ingestion would not be "acceptable in the sight of the Lord," and it must be burned outside the camp.

3. Chs. 11–16: the laws of impurities. Knowledge of contagion is clear from the following procedures: (1) Lustration is limited to impurities arising from animal cadavers and certain human skin diseases and fluxes, all prime sources of putrefaction and infection. (2) One who contracts the impurity from a human being washes at once (antisepsis through washing is effective only the first few hours), even though ritual impurity lasts till nightfall; the one who is afflicted is removed from the camp (Num. 5:2-4) and washes only after he is healed. (Lustration serves no medical purpose once infection sets in.) (3) Living animals never transfer impurity (in contrast to the Egyptian attitude toward swine: Herodotus II.47). The carcass, however, must be disposed of; hence its handling is never prohibited, but anyone contaminated by it must purify himself with water. For details, *see* CLEAN AND UNCLEAN.

a. Ch. 11: animal impurities. The food prohibitions are certainly older than the rationale given for them. Regardless of their origin, the fact remains that no punishment befalls anyone who violates them. In P, there is not even a prohibition against eating carrion: demons, formerly thought to have caused such death, have been banished.

The laws themselves offer but one rationale: holiness (Lev. 11:44-47; 20:22-26; cf. Exod. 22:31 [H 30]; Deut. 14:21), a word which bears the dual connotation of "sanctification" (by emulating God's nature, 11:44*a*) and "separation" (from the impurities of the pagans, 20:23-26; cf. comment on chs. 18–20, §4*a below;* SACRIFICES AND OFFERINGS, OT[S] §3*b*). The food and blood prohibitions form a united dietary code allowing humans to consume meat and not be brutalized in the process. (i) *11:1-8: land animals.* Compare vss. 3-4 with Deut. 14:4-6, where the permitted quadrupeds are named. The classification is the result not of empirical medical knowledge (Albright) but of the universal need to classify the world into beneficent and destructive categories (Douglas). (ii) *11:9-12: fish.* That neither the prohibited nor permitted fish are enumerated (nor in Deut. 14:9) may be explained by the relative absence of sea life in the Mediterranean prior to the Suez Canal. Fish—alone among the creatures—were not named by Adam (Gen. 2:19-20). (iii) *11:13-23: birds and winged insects.* No classification is given for birds, probably because none was known. A number of the identifications (translations) are conjectural. (iv) *11:24-40: impurity by contact with carcasses.* This section is an insertion from another source, since it interrupts the fourfold classification (vs. 46) of creatures that may not be eaten. Nonporous articles are polluted by cadavers of the eight species listed in vss. 29-30 and must be washed, but contaminated earthenware (porous and absorbent, 6:28 [H 21]) may never be reused. Food and seed grain are immune to impurity except when moist, since water is an impurity carrier. (v) *11:41-47: swarming things and summation.* Continues 11:23.

b. Ch. 12: the impurity of childbirth. For seven days following the birth of a male and fourteen days for a female no conjugal relations are allowed. For an additional period of thirty-three and sixty-six days respectively, contact with sanctums is proscribed. That sacrifices are brought only subsequently indicates that earlier ideas of demonic control of this period have been rejected. The rite certifies that passage of the prescribed time has removed impurity, and it is scaled to economic circumstances (cf. 5:7-13; 14:21-32).

c. Chs. 13–14: the impurity of skin diseases. The priest is instructed to identify and isolate those who are afflicted with contagious skin diseases. The word translated "leprosy" actually refers to a variety of afflictions. The noncontagious kind is probably vitiligo or, less likely, psoriasis (*see* LEPROSY). Lev. 13:47-59 describes the deterioration of garments probably because of mildew or fungus, and 14:33-53 describes the infection of houses because of the spread of saltpeter or moss, in which case quarantine procedures are also enforced. Unusual considerations for property are reflected in vs. 36: the priest clears the house prior to his inspection so that the contents will not be condemned with the house.

d. Ch. 15: the impurity of genital discharges. This chapter is composed of two sections: natural discharge of men and women (vss. 16-18, 19-24, respectively), whose impurity is simply removed by bathing, and pathological discharges (vss. 2-15, 25-30, respectively), which require sacrificial expiation.

e. Ch. 16: the impurities of the sanctuary and the nation. According to vs. 1, ch. 16 follows upon ch. 10. Thus, chs. 11–15 are an insert listing the specific impurities that will contaminate the sanctuary (15:31) for which the purgation ritual of ch. 16 is mandated. *See* ATONEMENT, DAY OF[S].

4. Chs. 17–26: the Holiness Source (H). The remainder of the book of Leviticus, it is often held, consists largely of an independent code in which moral and ritual laws alternate, and whose motivation is holiness. This, however, is to be doubted. Ch. 17, the alleged beginning of the code, is connected thematically and verbally with the preceding chapters. Chs. 25–26, the alleged conclusion, form an independent scroll, to judge by the unique vocabulary (e.g., 25:18-19; 26:5), theme (25:8-13; 26:34-35, 43), and redaction (25:1; 26:46). Nonetheless, much of the language and some ideas in chs. 17–26 differ with the first part of Leviticus. Most likely P incorporated into these chapters an earlier document which might be called the Holiness Source (H).

a. Ch. 17: killing for food. Whosoever kills a sacrificial animal outside the sanctuary is guilty of murder (vss. 3-4). Two ends are thus achieved: Sacrifice to "satyrs" is abolished (vss. 5-9), and expiation for killing the animal is assured through a ritual by which its lifeblood is returned to its creator, either upon the altar (vss. 10-12), or by being drained and covered by earth, in the case of hunt animals (vss. 13-14; cf. Deut. 12:16). The inescapable conclusion to be drawn from the context is that vs. 11 has nothing to do with the expiation of sin in general. *See* SACRIFICES AND OFFERINGS, OT[S] §3*b*.

b. Chs. 18–20: on being holy. Though these three chapters were originally independent, they are thematically united: ch. 20 prescribes the penalties for the illicit relations and homicidal cult practices of ch. 18 (cf. 20:1-5) and for violating the ban on magic of 19:31 (cf. 20:6). Moreover, the entire unit is framed by a single goal: separation from the Canaanites, whose idolatry and immoral practices pollute the divinely chosen land (18:3, 24-30; 20:22-24). That the arraignment of Ezek. 22 contains a mixture of ethical and ritual sins based solely on those chapters shows that their written formulation is pre-exilic.

The key word in this section is קדש, "holy." A קדש cluster is found in the food prohibitions (Lev. 11:44-47; 20:23-26) and only one other context—the rules concerning the priesthood, 21:6-8. This fact is significant. The priesthood, Israel, and man, respectively, form three rings of decreasing holiness about the center, God. The biblical ideal is that all Israel shall be "a kingdom of priests and a holy nation" (Exod. 19:6). If Israel is to move up to a higher sphere of holiness, it is enjoined to a more rigid code of behavior than practiced by the nations, just as the priest lives by more stringent standards than his fellow Israelites. Holiness, then, implies separation, and is so defined in 20:26. The positive aspect of holiness is discussed in ch. 19.

i. *Ch. 18: illicit sexual relations.* The list of prohibitions is encased by a framework (vss. 1-5; 24-30) which castigates the sexual mores of the Egyptians and the Canaanites. They worshiped and deified sex, applying the term "holy ones" to cult prostitutes (*see* PRIESTS[S] §1). In contrast, Israel is charged with an exacting code of family purity whose violation means death (cf. 20:10-16). Only the Holiness Source proclaims the sanctity of the land of Canaan; hence the responsibility of both Israelites and resident strangers to maintain its sanctity (18:26-27; 20:2; 24:22). The moral justification for its conquest (18:27-28; 20:22) is also a warning: if guilty of the same infractions, Israel, too, will be "vomited out."

ii. *Ch. 19: Imitatio dei—positive holiness.* For Israel, "holy" means more than that which is unapproachable. It becomes a positive concept, an inspiration and a goal associated with God's nature and his desire for humans: "You shall be holy; for I . . . am holy" (vs. 2). That which man is not, nor can ever fully be, but which he is commanded to emulate and approximate, is what the Bible calls "holy." Holiness means *imitatio dei*—the life of godliness.

How can human beings imitate him? The answer of Lev. 19 is given in a series of ethical and ritual commands, soaring above which is the commandment to love all persons (vs. 18), including aliens (vs. 34). Such love must be concretely expressed in deeds: equality in civil justice (20:2; 24:16, 22; Num. 35:15), free loans (25:35-55; cf. Deut. 10:18), and free gleanings (19:9-10).

iii. *Ch. 20: penalties for certain infractions in chs. 18–19.* The penalties for illicit sex relations are graded according to the severity of the punishment: vss. 9-16, death by man; vss. 17-19, death by God; vss. 20-21, childlessness. Since there had been such apparent and notable violators as Abraham (vs. 17; cf. Gen. 20:12) and Amram (vs. 19; cf. Exod. 6:20), the offender may only be reprimanded; God alone would settle with him. Of the idolatrous varieties, only MOLECH worship and oracles through mediums are singled out, the former because of its monstrousness, and the latter because of its prevalence (Deut. 18:9-12; I Sam. 28:9; Isa. 8:19). That the lofty pronouncements of ch. 19 are not in this list is mute evidence that ethics are really unenforceable.

c. Chs. 21–22: the disqualifications of priests and sacrifices. Restrictions are placed upon the priests in order to guard against moral and ritual defilement which might inflict dire consequences on them and the people (22:9, 15-16; cf. 4:3; 15:31).

d. Ch. 23: the festivals. P's listing of the festivals is distinguished from JE (Exod. 23:14-17; 34:21-23) and D (Deut. 16) by emphasis on natural and agricultural data. Because Lev. 23 is addressed to the lay farmer rather than the priest, the New Moon festival is omitted (on this day the Israelite had no special duties or prohibitions). Indeed, with the exception of vss. 13 and 18-20, all requirements of the priestly, public cult are ignored, and only the offerings of the individual farmer are enumerated. *See* PASSOVER AND FEAST OF UNLEAVENED BREAD; WEEKS, FEAST OF; NEW YEAR; NEW YEAR[S] §2; ATONEMENT, DAY OF[S].

e. Chapter 24: Miscellany. i. *24:1-4: the lamp oil.* Since the lampstand stood inside the sanctuary building, its greater sanctity required the use of pure oil, and that it be lighted by the high priest (Exod. 30:7; Num. 8:1-4; "sons" in Exod. 27:21 is a probable error). *See* MENORAH[S] §1.

ii. *24:5-9: see* BREAD OF THE PRESENCE.

iii. *24:10-14; 23: the law of blasphemy.* Blasphemy means more than speaking contemptuously of God, for which there is no stated penalty (Exod. 22:28 [H 27]). It must involve the additional offense of uttering the TETRAGRAMMATON, and it is the combination of the two (vss. 15-16) that warrants the death penalty. The Tetragrammaton's power affects not only the speaker but the hearers; their contamination is literally transferred back to the blasphemer by the ritual of laying on the hands.

iv. *24:15-22: an appendage of civil-damage laws.* That LEX TALIONIS (Exod. 21:23-25; Deut. 19:21) was extended to the stranger is one of the great moral achievements of P's legislation. Every distinction is eradicated not only between the powerful and the helpless but even between the Israelite and the non-Israelite. The interpolation of these civil statutes, with their emphasis upon the resident alien, is due to the legal status of the half-Israelite offender.

f. Ch. 25: the sabbatical and jubilee years. Each seventh year is a sabbath of liberating rest for Israelite slaves (Exod. 21:2-6; Deut. 15:12-18), debtors (Deut. 15:1-11), and the land (Exod. 23:10-11). In P, this "full" sabbatical is reserved for the jubilee, whereas the seventh-year sabbatical applies only to the land. *See* JUBILEE, YEAR OF[S]; SABBATICAL YEAR[S].

g. Ch. 26: the concluding exhortation. The threat of total destruction and exile appears in three other books of the Bible: Deuteronomy, Jeremiah (while he was still a Deuteronomic evangelist), and Ezekiel (whose eschatology is largely based on Lev. 26). These also share with this chapter the pre-prophetic view that cultic sins alone determine the nation's collapse—idolatry (vs. 1) and the neglect of the sabbatical system (vss. 2, 34-35) are specified here. Since chs. 25–26 are attributed to Israel's sojourn at Mount Sinai (25:1; 26:46), they may constitute the text of the Sinaitic covenant according to the Holiness Source.

5. Ch. 27: commutation of gifts to the sanctuary. This chapter is a P appendix to the Holiness Source. The following gifts are discussed: persons (vss. 1-8), animals (9-13), houses (14-15), land (16-25), firstlings (26-27), devotions (28-29), and tithes (30-33). The organizing principle of this chapter is that gifts offerable on the altar may never be desanctified, but nonofferable gifts (with the exception of devotions) may be desanctified by their sale or redemption. *See* SANCTIFICATION IN THE OT[S].

Bibliography. Commentaries: S. R. Driver (ET 1898); D. Hoffmann (1905-06), German, (1953), Hebrew; M. Noth (ET 1965); K. Elliger (1966), German; N. Snaith (1967). Studies: For a comprehensive bibliog., until 1968, *see* J. G. Vink, "The Date and Origin of the Priestly Code in the OT," *OTS,* XV (1969), 1-144. Post-1969: J. Milgrom, "The Function of the Hatta't Sacrifice," *Tarbiz,* XL (1970), 1-8, Hebrew, "A Prolegomenon to Lev. 17:11," *JBL,* XC (1971), 149-56, "Sin Offering or Purification Offering?" *VT,* XXI (1971), 237-39, *Cult and Conscience* (1976), "Two Kinds of ḥaṭṭāt," *VT* (forthcoming), "Israel's Sanctuary: The Biblical 'Picture of Dorian Gray'," *RB* (forthcoming); A. Cody, *A History of the OT Priesthood* (1969); S. E. McEvenue, *The Narrative Style of the Priestly Writer* (1971); R. J. Thompson, *Moses and the Law in a Century of Criticism Since Graf* (1970); F. M. Cross, *Canaanite Myth and Hebrew Epic* (1973), pp. 195-215, 293-325; B. A. Levine, *In the Presence of the Lord* (1974); cf. also J. Milgrom, "The Biblical Diet Laws as an Ethical System," *Int.,* XVII (1963), 288-301; M. Douglas, *Purity and Danger* (1966), pp. 40-57; W. F. Albright, *Yahweh and the Gods of Canaan* (1968), pp. 172-82.

J. MILGROM

LEX TALIONIS lĕks tăl ĭ ō′nəs. The term derives from a provision in the Twelve Tables, the first compilation of Roman law (450 B.C.): "If a man has broken a limb (i.e., of another man), unless he makes his peace with him (i.e., by making a pecuniary compensation) there shall be like for like (*talio esto*)." The principle of punishing a wrongdoer with exactly those injuries or damages he has inflicted upon someone else is known in a number of ancient and primitive laws. It is most often—but not exclusively—applied to cases of bodily injury. Whereas *talion* emphasizes the kind of punishment warranted in such cases, the principle of blood feud—which is occasionally mistaken by modern writers as *talion*—denotes the persons within the group of the victim of murder or manslaughter who are required to execute punishment against the person who committed the act or against other members of his group.

The only ancient Near Eastern laws besides those in the OT in which *talion* is clearly represented are the laws of Hammurabi (secs. 195-204; probably also secs. 116 and 153). *Talion* is found neither in the older laws of Ur-Nammu and Lipit Ištar nor in the laws of Eshnunna. The Middle Assyrian laws stipulate sympathetic sanctions for a number of offenses (e.g., sec. 9, cutting off a man's lower lip for kissing a married woman), but these do not qualify as *talionic* in the strict sense. Secs. 1-18 of the Hittite laws, often cited in discussions of *talion,* represent a stage where monetary compensation for manslaughter or murder has superseded the ancient custom of blood feud. *Talion* is part of the pre-Islamic Arabic tribal laws (Caskel), and is adapted with certain restrictions into the Koran (Sura 2).

Some writers have viewed the *talion* as a primitive principle of law which was gradually replaced by a more humane system of monetary compensation (Driver and Miles). However, other scholars regard the opposite as true: *talion* has replaced an earlier system of monetary compensation whereby wrongs formerly regarded as merely private civil offenses now become criminal, as the state assumes greater responsibility for the welfare of its members (Diamond, Finkelstein).

Talionic sanctions are found in three places within the OT: Exod. 21:23-25; Lev. 24:17-21; Deut. 19:21. They are phrased in an abstract and apodictic style (an eye for an eye, etc.; *see* LAW IN THE OT[S] §5) in contrast to the casuistic formulation of the laws of Hammurabi. Each context is different, and careful textual analysis shows that the *talion* serves as a generalization for sanctions resulting from the possibilities of the individual case. Exod. 21:23-25 refers to injuries suffered by a pregnant woman who was accidentally caught in a fight between two or more men. The resulting miscarriage is treated in casuistic style in vs. 22, but in case of additional bodily injuries summary reference is made to the *talionic* formula, which is an obvious interpolation in this context (Alt, Diamond). The contrast with the casuistically styled laws of the bulk of the Book of the Covenant (Exod. 20:23–23:33) is evidence that the *talionic* sanctions of the OT originated in tribal law. In Lev. 24:19, the *talionic* regulation concerning bodily injury is in a secondary position after a regulation concerning restitution in kind for herd animals killed. It likely was added because of the words "life for life" in vs. 18. In Deut. 19:21 the *talionic* formula is again only a generalization of the sanctions stipulated for false or malicious accusations, which means that a person who cannot prove his accusations suffers the penalty the accused would have suffered if found guilty. For this principle of *calumnia,* widely attested in ancient Near Eastern laws, *see* Petschow.

No specific mention is made in the OT of the actual implementation of the *talionic* punishments.

The rabbinic abrogation of the *talion* results from the conflict between the commitment to follow the Mosaic laws and the obvious impossibility of executing the *talionic* sanction. The argument for abrogation is based on the assumption that no two persons have identical bodily members, and *talion* therefore could not be applied fairly. *Talion* was replaced by a system of monetary compensation (T.B. B.K. 83b-84a; Mekilta).

Jesus expands and reverses the *talion* (originally restricted to bodily injury) by exhorting his disciples, when they fall victim to wrongdoing and malicious treatment, not to retaliate but to endure it (Matt. 5:38-42; Luke 6:29-30).

Bibliography. A. Alt, *Kleine Schriften zur Geschichte des Volkes Israel,* I (1953), 341-44; W. Caskel, "Der arabische Stamm vor dem Islam und seine gesellschaftliche und juristische Organisation," *Dalla Tribù allo*

Stato (1962), pp. 139-51; A. S. Diamond, "An Eye for an Eye," *Iraq,* XIX (1957), 151-55; P. Doron, "A New Look at an Old Lex," *JANES,* I (1969), 21-27; G. R. Driver and J. C. Miles, *The Babylonian Laws,* I (1952), 406-16; J. Finkelstein, "Ammiṣaduqa's Edict and the Babylonian 'Law Code,'" *JCS,* XV (1961), 91-104, esp. 98; S. Paul, *Studies in the Book of the Covenant,* VTSup, XVIII (1970), 75 ff. H. Petschow, "Altorientalische Parallelen zur spätrömischen calumnia," *Zeitschrift der Savigny-Stiftung für Rechtsgeschichte,* Romanistische Abteilung, XC (1973), 14-35; R. Yaron, *The Laws of Eshnunna* (1969), pp. 173-77.

J. M. Renger

***LIBNAH (CITY).** With Ekron firmly established at Tell el-Muqanna', the identification of Libnah with Tell eṣ-Ṣâfī (Tel Zafit) becomes impossible. Sennacherib took Ekron first (*ANET,* 287*b*) and then went on to besiege other Judean towns; only after taking Lachish did he turn on Libnah (II Kings 19:8). No intelligent strategist would have left a hostile outpost at Tell eṣ-Ṣâfī to threaten his supply lines while mounting a siege of the proportions required to reduce Lachish. He surely would have taken Tell eṣ-Ṣâfī and probably also Azekah, thus securing the Vale of Elah before moving against Lachish. Besides the fact that eṣ-Ṣâfī means "the shining one," not "white," the original name evidently goes back to Aramaic *Ṣâphîthâ* (Gr. *Saphitha* on the Madeba Map), "watch tower."

Bibliography. W. F. Albright, "The Nebuchadnezzar and Neriglissar Chronicles," *BASOR,* 143 (1956), 33; A. F. Rainey, "A Problem in Source Analysis for Historical Geography," *Eretz Israel,* XII (1975).

A. F. Rainey

***LISTS, ETHICAL. 1. Catalogues of virtues and vices.** Some have sought the origin of the NT catalogues in an early Jewish proselyte cathechism (Klein, Carrington), but the existence of such is problematic (Vögtle). Others have emphasized Stoic origins, but Christian borrowing from Stoicism is limited: the Stoic ethic is informed by what is natural, the NT ethic by love (*agape*) and faith; there is no Stoic parallel to Paul's identification of virtues with "fruit of the Spirit"; the four cardinal virtues and corresponding vices of Stoicism are not present in NT catalogues; and many of the virtues in the NT lists were regarded as vices in Stoicism.

Kamlah has refined Wibbing's notion of an Iranian origin of the NT catalogues by distinguishing two forms, the "descriptive" catalogues which close with a promise of salvation and a threat of destruction (e.g., Gal. 5:19-23) and the "parenetic" ones which depict a "putting off" of the old and a "putting on" of the new (e.g., Col. 2:20–3:17). He posits a background in Hellenistic syncretism for the latter and a background in the dualistic cosmology of Iranian religion for the former. But in Judaism and the NT God remains sovereign Lord and there is no place for a dualistic cosmology of the Iranian type. The NT catalogues manifest, rather, the sort of ethical dualism implicit in Israel's expectation of the Day of the Lord which will bring salvation for some and judgment for others, and in such OT passages as Deut. 27 ff. where a catalogue of curses and blessings has been incorporated into a hortatory setting closing with the appeal: "See, I have set before you this day life and good, death and evil . . . blessing and curse; therefore choose life" (30:15, 19; cf. Jer. 21:8; Ezek. 18:5-9, 15-17).

2. NT station codes. ***a. Types.*** Three types of literature have been grouped together under the term Haustafel, but they are so different in form, content, and function that they must be distinguished.

i. *Station codes proper.* These are in Col. 3:18–4:1; Eph. 5:22–6:9; I Pet. 2:13–3:7 and Rom. 13:1-7. Christians are addressed in their stations in life as wives, children, or slaves, with the subordinate member of each reciprocal relationship mentioned first. The emphasis is on being subordinate (ὑποτάσσομαι) and the form is that of direct address, followed by an exhortation in the imperative mood and supported by a motivating statement.

ii. *Church-order regulations.* These address church officers (bishops, deacons) or members of the church (old, young, widows) with respect to their stations in the church and deal with life in the church, not in society. To this form belong I Tim. 2:8-15; 6:1-2; Tit. 2:1-10; I Clem. 1:3; 21:6-9; Ign. Pol. 4:1–6:1; Polyc. Phil. 4:2–6:3.

iii. *The Didache and Barnabas.* Although the exhortations in Did. 4:9-11 (parallels in Barn. 19:5-7) are addressed to stations in society (fathers, children, slaves, masters), they stand materially and formally closer to the wisdom tradition and to the Two-Ways doctrine than do the NT station codes. Only Did. 4:11 contains a remnant of these latter.

b. Origin. (*See also* Parenesis[S].) i. *Stoicism.* The evidence does not support the view that the form and content of the NT station codes were taken over from Stoicism, either directly or via Hellenistic Judaism. There are, first, important formal differences. In Stoic texts the stations are not addressed directly, nor is the imperative mood employed; the naming of the station was sufficient to indicate the appropriate conduct. Similarly, motivating phrases are lacking. There are also differences in content. The stations emphasized in the NT (wives, children, slaves) are seldom if ever mentioned in the Stoic lists; the NT codes use ὑπακούω not πείθομαι for obedience; and the ἀνῆκεν ("it is fitting") is not left to stand alone (Col. 3:18, "as is fitting *in the Lord*").

ii. *Hellenistic Judaism.* Some scholars argue that the relationship of the NT station codes to Jewish proselyte literature indicates a Hellenistic Jewish origin. But in addition to questions about the existence of a Jewish proselyte catechism, the sharp distinction between Hellenistic and Palestinian Judaism this view presupposes does not hold up. Further, the differences between station codes in the NT and in Hellenistic Judaism have not been fully appreciated; and what similarities remain are better explained by positing a common dependence upon OT and Jewish traditions.

iii. *Multiple roots.* The NT station codes reflect the influence of diverse traditions. Formally (direct address, imperative mood, motivating statements) they are indebted to the OT apodictic law (Deut. 5:16). The stating of the ethic in terms of stations in life is typically Hellenistic, especially Stoic. The content is drawn basically from the OT,

Judaic tradition, although with the addition of certain Greek (what is fitting) and Christian (*agape*) concepts. The basic ethical conception of the NT codes—that without belonging to the world as such, one has responsibilities within the structures of society—takes us back to the teaching and example of Jesus himself.

See also ETHICS IN THE NT §6; ETHICS IN THE NT[S] §§3*d*, 4, 5*a*; CYNICS[S].

Bibliography. In addition to the original bibliog., *see* on ethical catalogues: E. Kamlah, *Die Form der katalogischen Paränese im NT,* WUNT, VII (1964); G. Klein, *Der älteste Christliche Katechismus und die Jüdische Propaganda-Literatur* (1909); A. Vögtle, *Die Tugend- und Lasterkataloge im NT,* NTAbh, XVI, 4/5 (1936); S. Wibbing, *Die Tugend- und Lasterkataloge im NT, BZNW,* XXV (1959).

On "Haustafeln": J. E. Crouch, *The Origin and Intention of the Colossian Haustafel, FRLANT,* CIX (1973), with further bibliog.; L. Goppelt, "Prinzipien ntl. und systematischer Sozialethik heute," *Die Verantwortung der Kirche in der Gesellschaft,* ed. J. Baur *et al.* (1973), pp. 7-30, and "Jesus und die 'Haustafeln'-Tradition," *Orientierung an Jesus,* ed. P. Hoffmann (1973), pp. 93-106; J. P. Sampley, *'And the Two shall become one Flesh,' A Study of Tradition in Eph. 5:21-33,* NTSMS, XVI (1971); W. Schrage, "Zur Ethik der ntl. Haustafeln," *NTS,* XXI (1974-75), 1-22; D. Schroeder, "Die Haustafeln des NT: Ihre Herkunft und ihr theologischer Sinn" (diss., Hamburg, 1959).

D. SCHROEDER

LITERARY CRITICISM. Analyzes texts in order to determine their structure and composition, possible use of sources (oral or written), integrity (whether the text is composite), and style. The more questions of genre are pursued, the more literary criticism merges with FORM CRITICISM, since the latter can no longer be limited to oral or pre-literary traditions. In biblical scholarship, literary criticism early became intertwined with historical or HIGHER CRITICISM, since the prevailing desire was to write the biblical history the way it "really happened." To do so, it was necessary to relate the biblical books and their sources to their own times and places.

Recently, a "new criticism" has been applied to biblical literature. This understands texts as aesthetic objects in their own right, and finds the key to meaning in the logic intrinsic in the form and structure of the writing rather than in its historical situation, use of sources, or the intention of the writer. *See* LITERATURE, BIBLE AS[S].

The earlier literary criticism, however, being concerned with genetic relationships between texts and parts of texts, attempted to recover sources (assumed to be texts) as precisely as possible. Hence older discussions tend to equate literary criticism with SOURCE CRITICISM. Literary criticism has shown that the books of the Bible are the end products of sometimes long and always complex processes of writing, compiling, and editing. *See* BIBLICAL CRITICISM §5*c*; BIBLICAL CRITICISM, NT[S] §2; BIBLICAL CRITICISM, OT[S] §2.

L. E. KECK

***LITERATURE, THE BIBLE AS.** This phrase designates a point of view taken by a relatively small but increasing number of biblical scholars toward the writings contained in the Old and New Testaments. These scholars, who come from diverse philosophical and theological traditions, are united in considering the Bible primarily and fundamentally as a literary document (as opposed, e.g., to considering it as a historical or theological document). Despite this unity, however, they employ often very different and even incompatible methodologies for the study of literary texts and usually disagree markedly about the implications of their work for the understanding of the Bible.

Generally speaking, they do not feel that their work invalidates other approaches to the Bible. Yet it is clear that their enterprise, viewed in the context of Western culture as a whole, is part of a turning away from a preoccupation with history and a turning toward a concern with language. For this reason, they believe that their studies provide a helpful corrective to a prepossession with history among biblical students. Because of their concern with language, they find themselves looking to such fields as linguistics and semiology (the study of the use and meaning of signs) for basic presuppositions and methodological tools.

The movement to consider the Bible as literature may be part of the general secularization of Western culture. It is noteworthy that many of its practitioners are teachers in secular institutions who have no specifically religious or theological interest in the Bible. Their study of it as literature is rooted in an appreciation of the biblical portrayal of the human situation. There are other advocates of a literary approach to the Bible, however, whose final concern is religious. They believe that the literary appreciation of the Bible is one more way of appropriating God's word spoken through documents centuries old.

1. Literature as paradigm
2. Consequences of paradigm change
3. Objections to literary study of the Bible
4. Current research
   a. Structuralism
   b. Nonstructuralist criticism
Bibliography

1. Literature as paradigm. The exceptional literary merit of the Bible has been recognized from the earliest times. Both Jewish and Christian commentators from the founding fathers on have noted the simple grandeur of its prose narrative, the evocative power of its imagery, and the penetrating insight of its characterizations. Furthermore, LITERARY CRITICISM has long been recognized and practiced as an important part of biblical interpretation (e.g., its delineation of genres of literary speech). Yet the new literary critics distinguish their work from that of the older criticism, while at the same time acknowledging their own indebtedness to that which form and source analysts have been doing.

Contemporary sociologists of knowledge have used the word "paradigm" to describe any idea or set of ideas that provides the framework within which a given set of phenomena are understood. One can say, then, that the *paradigm* which has governed practically all modern research on the Bible is history. Scholars operating under this paradigm have either remarked on the literary quality of a text as an aside or have engaged in literary tasks for the purpose of answering historical questions (e.g., the attempt to establish the authentic sayings of Jesus by form criticism). The paradigm, or controlling idea, guiding the research of literary critics is, on the other hand, literature. Consideration of the Bible as literature is itself the beginning and end of scholarly endeavor. The Bible is taken first and finally as a literary object. It is because of this shift from history to literature as paradigm that contemporary literary critics wish to distinguish themselves from their predecessors. They claim that it is possibly the most significant change of paradigm in biblical studies since the adoption of the historical model sometime after the Middle Ages, and that it will revolutionize the way the Bible is assimilated into modern culture. An analogy with Homer is often made. The questions an ancient Greek would have asked, believing the *Iliad* both a sacred text narrating the activities of the gods and a historical document reporting the Trojan War, are far different from those asked by a modern Homeric critic.

2. Consequences of paradigm change. With a change in paradigm goes a shift in criteria governing the type of problems that are studied, the selection of methods used to solve these problems, and the legitimacy and adequacy of proposed solutions. Thus, for help in framing questions to be asked of biblical materials, for tools of analysis, and for basic notions of what an acceptable answer looks like, practitioners of the new literary criticism tend to call upon a broader field of general literary and linguistic studies. Exod. 1–15 can be used as an example to illustrate how this new literary analysis works, although it should be kept in mind that what follows is only one among numerous ways the passage might be studied by these critics.

An initial reading indicates that Exod. 1–15 has many features of literary comedy, especially dramatic comedy. By a comparison of this material with other examples of this genre, and a study of various critical analyses of comedy in literature, some basic tools with which to test the initial hypothesis may be gained (e.g., theories of characterization and plot structure typical of comedy). Thus, one is able to see, for instance, that the *dramatis personae* in Exodus conform very neatly to the characterization found in the comedy genre. Pharaoh is a typical *alazon* (an imposter, one who tries to be more than he is), and Moses a typical *eiron* (one who subverts the *alazon*). Yahweh is a good example of the behind-the-scenes initiator and sustainer of the comic action, Aaron a characteristic hero's helper, and the Egyptian army an exemplary *pharmakos,* or scapegoat. Moreover, the verbal contest, or *agon,* between Moses and Pharaoh is a recurring feature of comic plots, as is the final outcome of the action: a move from one society to a more authentic alternative.

Further testing of the hypothesis that Exod. 1–15 is a literary comedy would have to lead to an assessment of the internal consistency of the narrative so viewed, and to a comparison with other acknowledged examples of the genre. This comparative study is crucial. If one encounters no significant negative evidence, the hypothesis gains the status of a theory and is used to examine certain larger questions of meaning, including the meaning of comedy and its function within human societies.

This illustration, brief as it is, points to several common characteristics of the new literary criticism of the Bible. First, no extraliterary hypotheses (e.g., that Exod. 1–15 is Scripture, that it is historical reportage, or that it originally had a place in the cultic celebrations of ancient Israel) are introduced to account for any features of the text or as evidence in support of any conclusions drawn. That Exodus is considered by some to be a sacred text is irrelevant to the discussion. That the events it describes are considered by many to be historical is also irrelevant. For the literary critic nothing depends on the truth or falsity of these historical claims. The situation is exactly comparable to reading, e.g., Gibbon as literature. Gibbon intended to write history, and his initial readers certainly read him that way. The literary critic simply brackets this intention and reads him in a wholly different context, one in which the accuracy of his account of ancient Rome never comes into question. Finally, that the *Sitz-im-Leben* out of which Exod. 1–15 came was a cultic one would not surprise the literary critic, since much literature may have such an origin. But, if it were proved that this hypothesis were false, it would not influence his findings one way or the other. The situation in this case is comparable to the study of Greek drama in relation to its reputed origin in Greek religion. Such information might give the critic some clues about the social significance of drama, but would otherwise be unhelpful.

Second, literary critics in general do not believe it is necessary to use the traditional disciplines of biblical research (e.g., source, form, or tradition criticism) or to employ the findings of those disciplines. Upon occasion a critic may indeed make use of these—if, e.g., there is a special interest in analyzing the JE version of the Exodus. Source criticism would then be employed in order to establish the text. But much more often the text is simply taken in its received form, so that information about its construction from smaller units (whether these units are oral or written) is not likely to be crucial. In any case, wherever literary critics do make use of these disciplines, it is for their own purposes.

Third, the new literary criticism may be described as inherently ahistorical. For instance, should a text be available in several recensions, the choice of which recension to study is essentially idiosyncratic, depending on the interests of the critic, and is unrelated to assumptions about greater value lying in greater antiquity or in closer proximity to original author(s). Also, since such critics consider that all individual works comprise one vast body of literature, they normally feel quite free in studying a particular work in relationship to any other, of whatever date or from whatever place. It follows, moreover, from this same assumption that these critics freely employ modern ideas as explanatory concepts in the attempt to comprehend ancient texts. They do not assume that the viewpoint of the author(s) or of the original audience is privileged over the point of view of any other reader.

Fourth, to adopt the paradigm of literature in one's interpretation of the Bible usually also involves an assumption about the nature of symbols, namely, that their final direction is inward not outward. Symbols are understood to have been used, not instrumentally, but imaginatively, to construct a fictive world where actions are not real actions but imitations of real actions, and where ideas do not apply directly to the real world but to the fictive world. Ideas in literature are hypothetical constructs, and the route one would take in transferring them from fictive to real world is most circuitous. This of course has implications for the thorny question of "truth" in literature. Generally speaking, a question about the truth of an action or idea expressed in a work of literature resolves itself into a question of its rightness or appropriateness in context. The truth of Jesus' resurrection, e.g., becomes a question of how fitting it is as the climax of the narrative action told in the gospels and is parallel to the rightness of Hermione's return to life in *The Winter's Tale*. Likewise, the truth of a biblical theme like the fall of man is parallel to the problem of the truth of Keats' proclamation in "Ode on a Grecian Urn" that "beauty is truth, truth beauty." In both these cases the question is whether a truth claim is valid, not in the real world, but within the fictive world that the work creates. The Bible's significance as literature is closely tied to the power of the literary symbolism present in its various books. The centripetal force of literary symbols draws the reader into the work, and, through an effort to unite its symbols in a total realization of its structure, one is led finally to surrender oneself to the force of the work.

3. Objections to literary study of the Bible. Two closely related objections are often made to studying the Bible as literature. It is said that such study entails an essential distortion of the meaning of biblical texts because it makes them into something they were not meant to be. The second objection is that literary methods of analysis are successful only on works self-consciously written as literature. Literary critics do not deny that they place the biblical materials in a context alien to those in which they were originally written. They argue, however, that the designation of these texts as Scripture (another clear instance of a paradigm shift) also places them in an alien context, and that such changes in contextual frameworks are inevitable as history changes the concerns of mankind. In response to the second objection, one may simply observe that critics have for generations successfully studied numerous materials not self-consciously written as literature (e.g., Donne's sermons, C. Wesley's hymns, Milton's political tracts, the King James translation of the Bible).

4. Current research. Although certain presuppositions held in common by sponsors of the new literary criticism of the Bible have been identified, it is not surprising to find also some important differences. The liveliest debate among interpreters interested in moving from the history to the literature paradigm centers on the validity and usefulness of structuralism as a critical methodology.

a. Structuralism. Two presuppositions are crucial to structuralism both as a philosophy and as a critical methodology. The first is that appearances are not reality. Phenomena (like literary texts) as they meet the eye are to be explained by phenomena below the surface, called deep structures. The second assumption is that deep structures express themselves as codes. All human activities, from kinship patterns to literary texts to fashions, are coded expressions of the deep structures of the human brain. The fundamental model for understanding all codes is language, which explains the peculiarly important place that linguistics plays in structuralist theory. By decoding human activities one can not only discover the reality behind the appearances of everyday life, but can also, potentially, map the structure of the mind.

One particular implication of these presuppositions is of special importance for structuralist literary criticism: in order to break codes one must pay attention to wholes. One should not, as has been the case so often in the past, dissect wholes into parts and then consider that these parts have meaning apart from the whole. The proper procedure, rather, is to study works as wholes by showing the interrelation of their parts.

For the structuralist, then, at one pole is the literary text as it meets the eye, a text capable of being reduced to very small units, like words, images, metaphors. At the other pole are the deep structures which have been coded in the text. In between are a series of intermediate structures of ever increasing abstraction, like narrative sequences, plot structures, genres. The entire model should be compared to the analysis of language into phonemes, morphemes, words, phrases, sentences, groups of sentences, etc. Structuralist criticism may begin at any one of these levels, but it finally always proceeds from whole to ever larger whole.

Structuralists have done significant work at many different levels, e.g., on genre, style, metaphor, narrative, and characterization. Since it is not feasible to discuss their methodology in each of these areas, a hypothetical example will be used to illustrate certain of their basic procedures. Typically they assign the major functional elements in a story (i.e., characters, objects, conditions, feelings, etc.) to one of six different roles: subject, object, recipient, ordainer, helper, opponent. When these roles are placed in relation to actions, one arrives at the following schematized plot (of which there are innumerable refinements): a subject, aided by a helper and hindered by an opponent, wants to possess an object or render it to a recipient, the object and possibly even the entire action proceeding from an ordainer. Usually the outcomes of potential actions represented by this plot are arranged into binary sets (reflecting a general propensity within structuralism to understand things in terms of binary opposition): subject does/does not possess object, recipient takes/refuses to take object, etc.

Using the above schemata and others like them the structuralist critics, from their own intuition and from the example of their predecessors, attempt to identify the meaningful units of a given text, e.g., a parable of Jesus. These units may be specific actions, episodes, themes, relationships between characters, or the like. For simplicity the meaningful units of a particular parable may be represented by the symbols *a, b, c*. Next, choosing similar texts (e.g., the remaining parables of Jesus), the critic performs the same analysis and may arrange the findings in a chart:

Parable 1	a	b	c		
Parable 2	a		c	d	e
Parable 3	a	b		d	
Parable 4		b	c	d	e
Parable 5		b		d	e

This chart, taken as a whole, represents the set, parable of Jesus, and read across line by line it shows the relation of one parable to the set. It is easy to see that reading any one parable will give only part of the total message. One would need to read the entire set to understand the fuller meaning. In fact, it is possible that the meaning units of any one parable may be so arranged as to mislead the reader. In this case, the parable would have a surface meaning and a deeper meaning. One could discover this latter meaning only by comparing the parable with the entire set. It is even possible, maybe even the rule, according to structuralists, that the meaning units of a given series of texts will be so arranged that the real meaning of the whole series is obscured. In this case, the surface meaning of every text in the series is different from its deep meaning. Even a serial reading of the entire group will not yield the deep meaning. Only when a serial reading (horizontal axis in the above chart) is combined with a formal reading (vertical axis) will the true meaning become clear.

This analysis of Jesus' parables could be carried a step further by producing a similar set for the parable genre. This set would be what is called the generative matrix out of which all parables come by means of certain laws of transformation. The process is similar to the one by which specific English sentences are generated from the matrix, English language, by means of the laws of grammar. One of the major objects of structuralist activity is to discover the laws of transformation governing all aspects of human behavior. Knowing these laws for parables, the critic, by comparing Jesus' actual parables (his performance as a maker of parables) with the generative matrix, can draw conclusions about Jesus' competence (or his ability to generate parables). In less abstract terms, such a procedure would allow the critic to discover the distinctiveness of Jesus' style and message.

Clearly this is a very different type of analysis from that undertaken in the context of historical study. Given a particular text the historian will ask what conditions in the context caused it to be the way it is. For the structuralist, on the other hand, both the generative matrix and the human mind that is ultimately the locus of that matrix are transtemporal and transspatial. When structuralist critics, therefore, draw conclusions about Jesus' parables, they are not making historical statements, but drawing comparisons between one set of structures and other sets, and also with the pool that includes all possible sets.

b. Nonstructuralist criticism. Much of the literary criticism of this century, especially that known as new criticism, has been principally concerned with the text as it presents itself to the reader. The hallmark of this type of criticism is "close reading," the meticulous, detailed analysis of the verbal texture of the work, paying particular attention to patterns of imagery, use of metaphors, and the type of interplay between words that generates wit, paradox, and irony. These critics emphasize the way the verbal interrelations within the text work together to produce an organic whole that is more than the addition of the parts. It follows that each work is indivisible and unique, so that paraphrase is heresy and even translation grossly inadequate. Furthermore, since the poem is unique, each experience of the poem, accomplished by an intense "close reading," is also utterly unique, and is characterized by a heightened integration of body and mind and self and world. New criticism agrees with structuralism in its concentration upon the text as object and in its willingness to divorce the text from its historical moorings, but it abhors the tendency of structuralism to dissolve the particularity of the object in ever larger abstractions.

"Close reading" works best on texts that are written out of an intense self-consciousness and so possess a very dense aesthetic surface (e.g., the poems of Donne). Since there are few texts within the Bible that are so written, application of new criticism to biblical materials has been sporadic and uneven. Some interesting analyses have been done on books like Job, Jonah, Mark, and Revelation. In the long run it may be that work done by new critics on narrative style may be more useful in biblical criticism. Unlike the structuralists, who tend to abstract narrative elements from the text in a process called normalization, new critics concern themselves with the actual language of the text, with such matters as choice of syntactic constructions and vocabulary, point of view, and tone of voice.

As interest in new criticism has waned, scholars have turned their attention increasingly to classificatory schemes for literature, especially to the notion of genre. Some but not all of this activity has been structuralist oriented (*see above*). Biblical scholars have been concerned both with the smaller genres found within larger works (e.g., songs, stories, proverbs) and with the larger works themselves. Studies of the smaller units, in many ways related to form criticism, have tried, by comparing these units with certain traditional genres, to come to a fuller understanding and appreciation of the distinctive qualities of biblical speech. Investigation of the larger units has, for the most part, amounted to the study of biblical books as wholes (e.g., gospels, letters, histories) and is related to redaction criticism. An attempt has been made to show that these books belong to genres and to discover the basic conventions of these genres. The notion that the writing of history is itself a literary genre governed by literary conventions is particularly exciting, and illustrates, once again, the tendency of literature to swallow up history.

One attempt to isolate the units of which larger wholes consist depends not upon traditional classification of genre but upon the rhetorical strategies used by their authors. With works very obviously oratorical (e.g., Second Isaiah) this method has produced significant results. Efforts to apply it more broadly have not, as of yet, been very successful.

See also ACTS, GENRE[S]; APOCALYPSE, GENRE[S]; DISCOURSE STRUCTURE[S]; FORM CRITICISM, OT, NT [S]; GOSPEL, GENRE[S]; LETTER[S]; PARABLE[S]; POETRY, HEBREW[S]; REDACTION CRITICISM, OT, NT[S]; SOURCE CRITICISM, OT[S].

Bibliography. The most useful bibliography of works on literary criticism is that published in annual volumes by the Modern Language Association. J. D. Crossan, "A Basic Bibliography for Parables Research," *Semeia,* I (1974), 236-73, is useful for the biblical student interested in structuralism.

Literary criticism: There are numerous anthologies of literary criticism from Plato to the present; a good one is H. Adams, *Critical Theory Since Plato* (1971). Biblical students should begin with N. Frye, *Anatomy of Criticism* (1957), to which the present discussion is heavily indebted. Other important studies are: I. A. Richards, *Principles of Literary Criticism* (1924) and *Practical Criticism* (1929); K. Burke, *The Philosophy of Literary Form* (1941); G. Bachelard, *The Poetics of Space* (1957), a very good example of phenomenological criticism; M. Krieger, *The New Apologists for Poetry* (1956), a useful summary of literary critical debate through the first half of this century, and *A Window to Criticism* (1964), which has a fascinating discussion of the relation of poem to reality; F. Kermode, *The Sense of an Ending* (1967), for a discussion of the meaning and significance of fictions; and R. Wellek and A. Warren, *Theory of Literature* (3rd ed., 1963), for basic orientation. Additional critics who are likely to be helpful to biblical students are J. C. Ransom, R. P. Blackmur, and C. Brooks (all new critics); G. Santayana and A. W. Levi (for philosophical orientation); R. S. Crane (a neo-Aristotelian formalist); G. Poulet and J. H. Miller (both phenomenologists); G. Steiner (for the implications of modern linguistic theory for literary criticism); as well as the prose writings of T. S. Eliot, Ezra Pound, and Wallace Stevens.

Structuralism: There are four helpful anthologies of structuralist writings: R. Macksey and E. Donato, eds., *The Languages of Criticism and the Sciences of Man* (1970); J. Ehrmann, ed., *Structuralism* (1970); M. Lane, ed., *Introduction to Structuralism* (1970); and R. and F. DeGeorge, eds., *The Structuralists from Marx to Lévi-Strauss* (1972). The latter two contain excellent introductions. One should begin with the three founding fathers: K. Marx, *Capital* (3rd ed., 1887); S. Freud, *The Psychopathology of Everyday Life* (1904), only one of numerous possible selections; and F. de Saussure, *Course in General Linguistics* (1916 [ET 1959]). After them one should turn to the giants of structuralism as a self-conscious movement: R. Jakobson and M. Halle, *Fundamentals of Language* (1956); R. Jakobson, *Selected Writings,* vol. I (1962); R. Barthes, *Writing Degree Zero* (1953 [ET 1968]), *Elements of Semiology* (1953 [ET 1968]), and *On Racine* (1960); C. Lévi-Strauss, *Structural Anthropology* (1958) and *The Savage Mind* (1962); E. Leach, *Claude Lévi-Strauss* (1970), helpful in understanding the man and his work; N. Chomsky, *Language and Mind* (1968). Among structuralist examinations of individual genres V. Propp's *Morphology of the Folktale* (1928 [ET 1968]) should probably be singled out as most important for biblical students. In order to pursue individual interests beyond the above basic list, Crossan's bibliography should be consulted.

Literary criticism of the Bible: James Barr, "Reading the Bible as Literature," *BJRUL,* LVI (1973), 10-33, offers a general survey with references to a number of pertinent studies. Much of the work is to be found in journals. One should pay special attention to *Linguistica Biblica* and *Semeia,* two journals devoted exclusively to literary criticism of the Bible and related matters. Also, *Interpretation,* XXVIII (1974), a special issue on structuralism, should be consulted. Several general books in the field are: R. G. Moulton, *The Literary Study of the Bible* (rev. ed., 1899), a pioneering and still useful study; D. B. McDonald, *The Hebrew Literary Genius* (1933); T. Henn, *The Bible as Literature* (1970); S. Sandmel, *The Enjoyment of Scripture* (1972); A. Wilder, *Early Christian Rhetoric: The Language of the Gospel* (1971), a basic work on the literary art of the NT; L. Alonso-Schökel, *The Inspired Word* (1965). For structuralist and/or linguistic oriented studies see: R. Funk, *Language, Hermeneutic, and Word of God* (1966); E. Güttgemanns, *Offene Fragen zur Formgeschichte des Evangeliums* (1970); E. Leach, *Genesis as Myth and Other Essays* (1969), a fascinating and potentially revolutionary study of several biblical stories from the point of view of a structuralist anthropologist; D. Via, *The Parables* (1967) and *Kerygma and Comedy in the NT: A Structuralist Approach to Hermeneutic* (1975). Other useful studies are: W. Beardslee, *Literary Criticism of the New Testament* (1970), a fine study of the larger genres like gospel and apocalypse; E. Good, *Irony in the Old Testament* (1965); E. Auerbach, *Mimesis* (1946), which includes a classic study of Hebrew narrative style. J. Muilenburg's exegesis of Isa. 40–66, IB, V (1956), 381-418, 422-773, introduces the concept of "rhetorical criticism." See also S. E. McEvenue, *The Narrative Style of the Priestly Writer,* AnBib, L (1971); D. Redford, *A Study of the Biblical Story of Joseph,* VTSup, XX (1970).

Sociology of knowledge: Those interested in this subject and in the idea of paradigm should begin with T. Kuhn, *The Structure of Scientific Revolutions* (1962) and P. Berger and T. Luckmann, *The Social Construction of Reality* (1966). D. ROBERTSON

***LITERATURE, EARLY CHRISTIAN.** Most of the writings from the first 150 years of Christian history (*ca.* A.D. 30-180) belong to collections which are referred to by certain traditional designations: the twenty-seven writings of the NT canon (*see* CANON, NT; CANON, NT[S]) ; the APOSTOLIC FATHERS, writings which were believed to have been written by disciples of the apostles; and the NT Apoc., writings which usually bear the name of an apostle, but were not admitted to the canon of the NT (constantly increasing in number through new discoveries; *see* APOCRYPHA, NT[S] §1; NAG HAMMADI[S]) . Some of the works of the Apologists, as well as some of the Acts of Christian martyrs must also be included.

These writings are of very different types. They include brief letters as well as long treatises comprising several "books." They belong to several distinct literary genres, and not all of them were written in order to be published. Yet all of these Christian writings share the features which generally characterize other literature of the period—features which in many instances were mediated through the Hellenistic-Jewish literature of that time. Moreover, all these Christian writings served particular purposes in the development and history of Christian communities (propaganda, edification, organization, polemics). Their function usually determines their literary genre.

1. Preservation
2. Cultural context
3. Written literature and oral tradition
4. Letters
5. Wisdom books
6. Apocalyptic literature
7. Aretalogy, biography, romance
8. Passion narrative and "gospel"
9. Church orders
10. Apologies and theological treatises
Bibliography

1. Preservation. Even though Jesus apparently did not write anything himself, among the earliest Christian writings some must have been composed in ARAMAIC. This is generally assumed for the synoptic sayings source used by Matthew and Luke (*see* Q; Q[S]), for the collection of parables used in Mark 4, and perhaps for the Gospel of Thomas (*see* THOMAS, GOSPEL OF[S]). Some scholars also believe that certain sources of the Gospel of John were originally written in Aramaic; however, no such sources of the known gospels have survived. Without exception, all writings which are preserved were originally written in Greek, and it seems that the production of Christian writings in languages other than Greek (Latin, Syriac) did not begin until late in the second century.

Of the several hundred Christian writings from this period known to have existed, all the autographs are lost; only copies are extant. In the case of the canonical writings of the NT, one very small papyrus fragment of such a copy can be dated as early as the first half of the second century A.D. (P^{52}), a few more papyri of parts of the NT come from the late second and third centuries, and the oldest MSS of the whole NT date from the fourth century, with an ever increasing number of NT MSS in Greek and in translations from subsequent centuries (*see* TEXT, NT §B; TEXT, NT[S] §1). In contrast, most of the works of the Apostolic Fathers and Apologists are preserved only in one or two MSS which are sometimes of a rather late date. Of some we possess only fragments, e.g., the Preaching of Peter (*see* PETER §12), the Apology of Quadratus (*see* APOSTOLIC FATHERS[S] §10), and the Interpretations of the Lord's Oracles by PAPIAS, all as early as some of the later books of the NT. The preservation of the NT Apoc. is even worse, though some are known from fragments of papyrus which were written as early as the second century (an "Unknown Gospel" fragment in the Papyrus Egerton 2, the Gospel of Thomas in several papyrus fragments from Oxyrhynchus). Of many others the original Greek text is lost and only translations into other languages (Latin, Syriac, Coptic, Ethiopic) survive. It is therefore often difficult to be certain about their original text, and in many instances even the original scope and content of such works is not sufficiently known.

2. Cultural context. Early Christianity developed within a literary culture. The Hellenization of the whole eastern half of the ancient Mediterranean world since the time of Alexander the Great had brought with it a marked increase of literacy, especially in the hundreds of Greek cities which had been founded in the areas ruled by the successors of Alexander (*see* HELLENISM[S] §§5, 6). The Roman conquest of these countries did not bring any major changes; indeed, it renewed the strength of the Hellenization process. Most of the cities had public schools and libraries. Writing, no longer the privilege of priestly, prophetical, or philosophical schools and traditions, had become democratized. Literature was produced and widely distributed, often for the sole purpose of entertainment. Written communication was a matter of course for most people, and many genres of formal and informal writing developed and became firmly established—from the private or business LETTER to the various genres of political and religious propaganda, philosophical treatises, scientific and medical handbooks, didactic poetry and entertaining novels, to name only a few.

Jews of the Hellenistic period had fully participated in these developments, not only the Jews of Alexandria living in the center of culture and scholarship, but also, to various degrees, those living in other areas—Asia Minor, Rome, Antioch, Babylon, and markedly in Palestine itself (*see* JUDAISM, HELLENISTIC[S] §5). Christianity's missionary efforts were most successful in the major cities, so the majority of early Christian writings come from those urban centers which reached the highest level of civilization and literacy during the Roman Imperial period: Antioch, the cities of western Asia Minor and Greece, and Rome, later also cities in eastern Syria, Egypt, and Africa. It was in these centers and among their largely literate populations that the use of the written medium of communication was most likely to be effective.

The literary genres employed by early Christian writers were quite distinct from those of classical Greece (tragedy, comedy, epic, etc.), but parallels to the classical literature of Israel are equally rare. In the late Hellenistic and Roman Imperial periods, however, the differences between Christian, Jewish, and pagan literary genres are less striking. This is particularly true of the functional literature that serves the needs of apologetics, propaganda, community organization, education, and edification (as distinct from that which is primarily artistic, philosophical, or scientific). Most of the genres of such functional literature had been adopted by Jewish circles during the Hellenistic period. Often Christianity could simply adopt them from Judaism and rely on their continuing effectiveness within a culture that remained largely "Hellenistic."

3. Written literature and oral tradition. Because of the functional role of early Christian literature, it is closely related to the various forms of oral communication and oral tradition (*see* TRADITION, ORAL[S]; FORM CRITICISM, NT[S]). Oral tradition preceded literature and continued to co-exist with it, because worship and prayer, preaching and teaching, polemics and community organization provided a natural situation for oral forms in the life of the church. It is probably wrong to see the expectation of Christ's imminent PAROUSIA as the cause of a preference for oral tradition. Indeed, it is Paul, who certainly expected Christ's coming in the immediate future, who produced the earliest Christian writings which have been preserved (*see* §4 *below*). Literature comes into existence wherever special circumstances require it; e.g., the need to communicate with a newly organized church from which the apostle is physically separated, the desire to introduce oneself or a fellow missionary to another community in advance of one's arrival, the attempt to produce manuals for church order that would be binding for churches in different cities. Early examples of such literature soon served as models and stimuli for subsequent literary productions; Paul's letters were imitated by the authors of the Deutero-Pauline epistles; later, gospels and church orders used and expanded earlier exemplars of such literature.

Because the situations for oral tradition and written literature were often analogous in the life of the churches, large amounts of oral materials appear in early Christian literature. Some writings are primarily collections of oral traditions, both sayings and narratives (e.g., the DIDACHE; to a certain degree the Synoptic gospels, the ACTS OF THE APOSTLES, and the Epistle of James). Hymns and other LITURGICAL MATERIALS are quoted and used frequently. Parenetic sections in many epistles utilize and interpret catalogues of vices or virtues and tables of duties for the members of the household (*see* LISTS, ETHICAL; LISTS, ETHICAL[S]; PARENESIS[S]). Such writings also reflect the style of oral communication. Paul's letters consistently reveal the language of his preaching (the style of the Cynic and Stoic diatribe); prophetic writings not only contain traditional sayings of Christian prophets (*see* PROPHECY IN THE EARLY CHURCH[S]), but also imitate their style in the production of apocalyptic literature (*see* APOCALYPTICISM; APOCALYPTICISM[S] §3*e*).

4. Letters. The earliest preserved Christian writings are the letters of Paul. In their external form, these letters correspond to the private letter of the Hellenistic and Roman period (*see* LETTER §2; LETTER[S] §§3-5). There are, however, several peculiar features in the Pauline letters which distinguish them from the common private letter form. (*a*) The sender introduces himself with his title ("Apostle")—a feature otherwise found only in official letters, not in private correspondence. (*b*) In addition to personal information which usually appears in the expanded proem (it often includes the "travelogue," cf. II Cor. 1:3–2:11; I Thess. 1:2–3:13), the body of the letter presents mostly "official" information. (*c*) Paul utilizes literary genres and oral materials which are not normally parts of private correspondence: church-order materials (I Cor. 5:1–14:40; I Thess. 4:1-12), eschatological treatises (I Cor. 15; I Thess. 4:13–5:11), apologies (II Cor. 10–13; Galatians). This demonstrates that the Pauline letters are not private correspondence, but political instruments in the organization of mission congregations.

A special kind of church-political letter is the letter of recommendation, frequently found in private and official letters in antiquity. The opponents of Paul in II Corinthians apparently used letters of recommendation from other churches where they had worked successfully (II Cor. 3:1). Rom. 16, perhaps an originally independent writing (*see* ROMANS, LETTER TO THE[S] §1*b*), is a letter of recommendation for Phoebe, a Christian minister from CENCHREAE; a long list of greetings is attached in order to reaffirm the leadership and good standing of those named. The letter to PHILEMON recommends a runaway slave and instructs the addressee to accept him back "no longer as a slave, but . . . as a beloved brother" (Philem. 16); the official form of the letter—addressed to the whole church—indicates that what is recommended is meant to have general validity.

The letter genre as developed by Paul became normative for almost all later epistolary literature in ancient Christianity. Colossians, Ephesians, and I Peter contain primarily interpretations of liturgical traditions, together with church order and other parenetic traditions (catalogues of vices, tables of duties for the household). These letters, as well as other Deutero-Pauline epistles which contain similar materials (the Pastoral Epistles, I Clement, Polycarp to the Philippians) imitate and vary the Pauline prescript and proem. Paul's use of letters as instruments of church politics also influenced Ignatius of Antioch; through his letters he tried to propagate the institution of the monarchic episcopate as the only guarantee for the true "gospel" and the effective use of the eucharist. As collections of Pauline letters became more widely known and accepted, the "official" letter was established as an important medium, not only of communication, but also of propaganda, polemics, and organization; cf. the letters of Bishop Dionysius of Corinth (fragments preserved in Euseb. Hist. IV.xxiii), the letters of Bishop Cyprian of Carthage, and many others.

The letter form has also been used as an external dress for writings which actually belong to a different literary genre: II Timothy is better understood as a TESTAMENT. Hebrews, Barnabas, and I John are theological treatises (*see* §10 *below*). The letter to Rheginos is a tractate on the immortality of the soul (*see* RESURRECTION, THE TREATISE ON[S]).

5. Wisdom books. Israel had long since known a literature in which the sayings of the wise men were collected, edited, and transmitted (*see* WISDOM §2). Later, such writings not only served as a repository of wisdom traditions, but also became books in which the religious convictions of particular groups ("wisdom movement") found expression (Ecclesiasticus, Wisdom of Solomon). Usually, such writings present sayings in only externally connected form, but thematic ordering also occurs (*see* WISDOM IN THE OT[S]).

Jewish wisdom literature apparently served as a model for the compilation of sayings of Jesus into Christian wisdom books in which Jesus appears as a teacher of wisdom (*see* SAYINGS OF JESUS, FORM OF[S] §1). Later on catechetical material and prophetic sayings were included in such collections. This is evident in the source ("Q") from which Matthew and Luke drew the sayings materials for their gospels. In a related wisdom book, the (Coptic) Gospel of Thomas, a considerable number of wisdom sayings have been added to the older stock, and the whole writing is dominated by the concept that is typical of this genre: secret sayings of wisdom which give life. That the transmission and composition of such sayings collections continued into the second century A.D. is also demonstrated by the work of Papias (*ca.* 130 A.D.), who composed five books of Interpretations of the Lord's Oracles. II Clement, Justin Martyr (Apol. I, 15-17), and the author of the Pseudo-Clementine Homilies had access to such books which were, in part, compiled on the basis of the canonical gospels. *See also* WISDOM IN THE NT[S].

6. Apocalyptic literature. Beginning with the Exile, apocalyptic began to replace prophecy, and an apocalyptic literature evolved which, though it is by no means uniform, has a number of characteristic features (*see* APOCALYPTICISM[S] §§2-3; APOCALYPSE, GENRE[S]). Of these features the following recur in Christian apocalyptic writings: the setting for the revelation is usually a remote place (e.g., Rev. 1:9), often a mountain (e.g., Mark 13:3); the revelations are given in the form of visions (also "parables" or "similitudes") which are then explained by an angelic interpreter (in Christian apocalypses and in Gnostic revelations it is often Christ himself who assumes that role); the interpretations give the opportunity to raise theological problems which will be solved by the interpreter or revealer; the conclusion occasionally contains an oath formula which protects the inviolability of the writing (Rev. 22:18-19) or its secrecy.

This literary genre influenced at an early date the collection of sayings of Christian prophets whose pronouncements were given and transmitted under the authority of the "Lord" (e.g., I Thess. 4:15-16). The setting in which such prophetic sayings appear in Mark 13—Jesus with selected disciples, seated on the Mount of Olives and answering questions about the events of the future—indicates that this collection was understood as an "apocalypse" (cf. also Matt. 24–25 where an apocalyptic setting has attracted additional materials of a similar kind). Similar apocalypses, usually containing traditional materials, have been added to writings of a different character: the Didache (*see* §9 *below*) concludes with an apocalypse (ch. 16; cf. also the apocalyptic sections at the end of several letters: I Thess. 4:13–5:11; I Cor. 15; II Pet. 3:1-13).

Major apocalyptic writings in Christianity follow the patterns established by the Jewish apocalypses. The earliest of these Christian books is the Revelation of John (*see* REVELATION, BOOK OF §§A-C; REVELATION, BOOK OF[S]; APOCALYPSE, GENRE[S] §1; APOCALYPTICISM[S] §1), written at about the same time as two of the later Jewish apocalypses, Baruch and IV Esdras (in the last decades of the first century A.D.). Two Christian apocalyptic books which appear in the Latin translation of IV Esdras as chs. 1–2 and 15–16 (V, VI Esdras) are direct continuations of this Jewish apocalyptic tradition (*see* ESDRAS, BOOK OF §3*b*). This genre also had room for the incorporation of typically Hellenistic speculations about the various punishments of the wicked in the afterlife or Hades, which occur for the first time in the Apocalypse of Peter (*see* PETER, APOCALYPSE OF) and became a very significant element in later Christian piety. The ties between Jewish and Christian and pagan eschatology are equally obvious in the related genre of the SIBYLLINE ORACLES. Apologetic and apocalyptic materials are here presented in the form of (often crude) hexameters, written by Jews and later by Christians in imitation of the pagan oracle books of the several Sibyllae.

Another kind of apocalyptic literature is found in the Gnostic books of revelations. These were imperfectly known until recently, when many such writings were discovered in the library of Nag Hammadi. The setting is often the same as in the apocalypses: the mountain, appearance of Jesus from heaven, an esoteric group, revelations in questions and answers (the revealer functions as angelic interpreter), and an oath formula (the Apocryphon of John, the PISTIS SOPHIA, etc.). The contents of such revelations are actually theological treatises, containing interpretations of Genesis, wisdom material, and church orders (Eugnostos the Blessed presents the same materials in the form of a treatise which the Sophia of Jesus Christ presents in the form of a revelation dialogue).

7. Aretalogy, biography, romance. The origin of the ARETALOGY, an account of the powerful deeds of a hero or of a god, is the typical Hellenistic belief that divine power is present in the miraculous or marvelous deeds (the ἀρεταί) of a DIVINE MAN. This is expressed in the character of such writings—enumerations of marvelous accomplishments—and in their typical endings (cf. John 20:30-31, the original ending of an aretalogical source used by John; I Macc. 9:22; cf. Ecclus. 43:27). Aretalogical features are also predominant in ancient biographies, such as Suetonius' *Lives of the Emperors,* Philo's *Life of Moses* and *Life of Abraham,* and Philostratus' *Life of Apollonius of Tyana* (cf. also the *Parallel Lives* of Plutarch). The similarities in the narrative materials of the gospels of Mark and John are best explained if one assumes that both evangelists used closely related source materials which were aretalogies of Jesus. In the Gospel of John, this is the well-known "signs source" which contained the stories of the wedding feast at Cana (John 2:1-11), the official's son (John 4:46-54), the paralytic (John 5:1-9), the feeding of the multitude (John 6:1-13), the walking on the sea (John 6:16-21), the blind man (John 9:1-7), and Lazarus (John 11) (*see* SIGN IN THE NT[S] §3). The author of the Gospel of Mark, in addition to a similar aretalogy (cf. Mark 6:34-52; also 8:22-26), used still another source of the same type from which he drew stories that present Jesus as an exorcist (e.g., Mark 1:23-28; 5:1-20; *see* EXORCISM IN THE NT[S]). The genre of aretalogy is further developed in the Infancy Gospel of Thomas, in the stories of martyrs and saints, and in the Acts of the Apostles.

A new component, however, has contributed to the latter genre. A popular type of literature in the Hellenistic and Roman period was the romance, which reflected the new experience of life that Hellenism had made possible. The heros of the romance travel by land and by sea (even encountering shipwrecks! cf. Acts 27) to strange countries, see untold marvels, encounter numerous obstacles which they overcome miraculously, and speak of the ideals of love and morality to foreign kings and barbarian audiences. Thus, the readers' horizons are extended far beyond the traditional city-state. A number of motifs from older Greek literature recur, but the chief concentration is upon the individual's fate, experiences, troubles, and ultimate success. That Judaism also was influenced by the Hellenistic romance is evident from TOBIT and Joseph and Asenath (though in the latter, only the love motif is utilized).

Not only the apocryphal Acts of the apostles (*see* ACTS, APOCRYPHAL), but also the canonical Acts of the Apostles are modeled after this literature (*see* ACTS, GENRE[S]). Aretalogical motifs are clearly present, e.g., in the miracles which the apostles do (cf. Acts 3:1-10; 5:1-11). But from the romance derives the travel motif (Paul's journey to Rome takes up several chs. of Luke's Acts, and in the Acts of Thomas the apostle travels all the way to India), and the ascetic life of the apostle corresponds to the love motif of the Hellenistic romance. The most elaborate romance is preserved in the Pseudo-Clementine literature which uses the typical motif of "recognitions"; members of the same family, divided by fate, finally are brought together and recognize each other—which provides the climax of the story.

8. Passion narrative and "gospel." There is no obvious non-Christian analogy to the Christian literary genre known as the "gospel" (εὐαγγέλιον), a complex literary phenomenon. The gospels used sources which belong to quite different literary genres: aretalogy, wisdom book, apocalypse (*see above*). Mark, the earliest, is actually a PASSION NARRATIVE (from the entry into Jerusalem, ch. 11, to the Crucifixion, ch. 15) with a comparatively brief biographical introduction which consists mostly of aretalogical materials, interspersed with sayings (4:1-34; 7:1-23) and an apocalyptic discourse (ch. 13). The model for the passion narrative, however, is the Christian kerygma of Jesus' suffering, death, and resurrection which earlier had been called "gospel" by Paul (I Cor. 15:1-5). The term certainly originated here, and not until the middle of the second century A.D. is there evidence that it was used for the writings which we now know under that name. Literary models are absent, unless one assumes that Jewish stories of martyrdom had already developed into a distinct literary genre; but that is uncertain (despite IV Maccabees). Yet, Christian experience of martyrdom has certainly influenced the later development of Jesus' passion narrative, especially in the gospels of John and Luke. Further expansion of the narrative and sayings materials in the gospels, and in particular the adding of birth narratives (Matt. 1–2; Luke 1–2), have given these writings the appearance of biographies. As such, these gospels have made it possible that the central Christian presentation of the event of revelation remained the story of a human being and of his experiences. *See* GOSPEL, GENRE[S].

A large number of noncanonical writings from the second and third centuries are also known as "gospels." Only a few of these could have belonged to the same genre as the canonical gospels, and only fragments have been preserved (Gospel of Peter, the "Unknown Gospel" of Papyrus Egerton 2, Secret Gospel of Mark). All others are works of a different character: theological treatises (Gospel of Philip, Gospel of Truth), revelations (Gospel of Mary, and many other so-called Gnostic gospels), aretalogies (Infancy Gospel of Thomas, Proto-Gospel of James). But the proliferation of literature under this title gives evidence for the authority and influence which the literary genre of gospel had gained. *See* APOCRYPHA, NT; APOCRYPHA, NT[S] §3.

9. Church orders. Church order materials were incorporated into the gospels and epistles quite extensively. In the case of genuine Pauline letters such sections (e.g., Rom. 12–14; I Thess. 4:1-11) rest on materials which were used and transmitted orally. The Gospel of Matthew makes an attempt to mold such traditions into a written church order: instructions for individual behavior, concluding with a reference to the "Two Ways" (Matt. 5–7), instructions for missionaries (Matt. 9:35–10:42), regulations for the community life (Matt. 18), and teaching about the eschatological events (Matt. 24–25). Matthew may be following an already established genre which also appears in the Didache, a writing that begins with the "Two Ways," i.e., a traditional description of the way of life and the way of death, adds instructions for baptism, prayer, and eucharist, and regulations for church officers, and concludes with an eschatological chapter. That the same topics (especially also the "Two Ways") constituted even earlier the Manual of Discipline from Qumran demonstrates the direct introduction of a Jewish model into this Christian literature. Occasionally Christian church orders are presented in the form of an epistle (I Timothy and Titus) or of a prophetic writing (the Shepherd of Hermas). But the Didache became also the prototype of a special literary genre of which several examples are preserved (Didascalia, APOSTOLIC CONSTITUTIONS, Apostolic Order, Apostolic Tradition of Hippolytus).

10. Apologies and theological treatises. Christian apologetic literature is a direct continuation of Jewish apologies (Letter of ARISTEAS, WISDOM OF SOLOMON, cf. the apologetic writings of Philo [*see* PHILO JUDEUS §2]) which in turn depend upon the Greek philosophical apology and the *protrepticus* (an invitation to a philosophical life, known since the time of the Sophists). Patterns of apologetic writings appear in Paul's letter to the Romans (Rom. 1:18–3:20), and apologetic motifs are found in the use of the argument from Scripture in the speeches of the book of Acts (e.g., Acts 2:14-36; 7:2-52) and in the Epistle to the Hebrews. A Christian literature to which this term "apology" can be applied begins around the turn of the first century, when the written defense of and propaganda for the Christian kerygma or creed (the "gospel") makes its appearance. The oldest apology, the Preaching of Peter, seems to rely primarily on a pattern of argument in which scriptural proof is provided for the events which are proclaimed in the kerygma. The Apology of Aristides adds the defense of monotheism, which was to become the first article of the creed. The basic pattern is fully developed in Justin Martyr, who gives full quotes both of scriptural passages (OT) and of the events of fulfillment (written gospels). He uses as the ordering principle the creedal formula of his church, which was similar to what later became known as the Apostles' Creed. In the further development of this literature, renewed dependence upon the Greek *protrepticus* (Clement of Alexandria, Augustine) and of legal arguments (Tertullian) are important factors.

Each single *topos* of the creed, however, could also be developed into an apologetic or parenetic writing in its own right. This is the origin of the theological treatise. Topics of the creed treated most frequently are the creation (Origen's *On First Principles;* cf. Philo's *On the Creation of the World;* Gnostic literature has focused particularly on this topic, with obvious attention to the interpretation of the book of Genesis, e.g., The Nature of the Archons and the Apocryphon of John), the origin of the soul (Tertullian's *On the Soul*), the Resurrection (Athenagoras, also the Gnostic Treatise on Resurrection). A comprehensive theological treatise from the second century A.D., anti-Gnostic in its orientation, is the Epistle of the Apostles (*see* APOSTLES, EPISTLE OF THE). This begins with an explanation of the first article of the creed, continues with an account of Jesus' birth, ministry, death and resurrection, and finally, of the church (including church order material and eschatological sections). Here various genres are welded together in the defense of the creed. This became the primary concern of much Christian literature, and has provided the basic outline of systematic theological writings ever since.

Bibliography. The best comprehensive history of early Christian literature in English is still M. Dibelius, *A Fresh Approach to the NT and Early Christian Literature* (1926 [ET 1936]), but see now P. Vielhauer, *Geschichte der urchristlichen Literatur* (1975). Important older works are F. Overbeck, *Über die Anfänge der patristischen Literatur* (1882 [repr. 1955]), and P. Wendland, *Die urchristlichen Literaturformen,* HNT (1912).

For bibliog. on the individual genres of early Christian literature *see* ACTS, GENRE[S]; APOCALYPSE, GENRE [S]; GOSPEL, GENRE[S]; LETTER; LETTER[S], as well as the introductions in E. Hennecke and W. Schneemelcher, *NT Apocrypha,* I (2nd ed., 1968), II (1964).

The most convenient survey of non-Christian literature of this period can be found in A. Lesky, *A History of Greek Literature* (2nd ed., 1963), pp. 642-897.

H. KOESTER

LITURGICAL MATERIALS, NT. Form criticism and literary analysis have given access to the meaning of the worshiping life of the earliest Christian communities. The results are seen in the following classifications of fragmentary data which we may assume formed part of the worship current in the period.

1. Acclamations. From the Jewish traditions in the temple and synagogue, Christians brought over such ejaculations in praise of God as *Amen* (I Cor. 14:16) and *Hallelujah* ("Praise Jah," Israel's covenant God). The latter is found at Rev. 19:1, 6 in the song of triumph to celebrate the victory of the heavenly host, but reflects the joy of the church on earth in its worship.

More specifically Christian forms are Abba—a caritative form of *'Ābh* ("father")—used as a child's title for his earthly parent and meaning "dear father" and MARANATHA ("Our Lord, come," a prayer as in Rev. 22:20; Did. 10:6). Both Abba and Maranatha played significant roles in NT prayer (*see* ABBA; ABBA[S]). The presence of Abba in Gal. 4:6; Rom. 8:15 seems to indicate that the invoking of God as Father passed early into the religious vocabulary of Gentile churches.

Acclamations of Jesus as LORD (Kyrios) are found in I Cor. 12:3 (in a polemical setting), Rom. 10:9 (in a baptismal context), and at Phil. 2:11 (a eucharistic or baptismal milieu has been postulated). The affirmation "Jesus is Lord" contains the elemental Christian confession of faith. The "Son of God" formula has been traced to a baptismal origin in Jesus' own baptism (Mark 1:11; Matt: 3:17; Luke 3:22) and the parallelism with the Christian experience of sonship worked out in early hymns (Col. 1:12-14 seen as an introit to the citation of the hymn in 1:15-20; cf. Acts 8:37 [RSV n.]). The so-called ἄξιος acclamations in Rev. 4:11; 5:9, 12 ascribe worthiness to God or the exalted Christ.

2. Hymnic confessions are more extensive tributes of praise to God and the enthroned Christ. The distinction between hymns and confessions of faith is not absolute. Confessions are short, simple sentences such as "Jesus is Lord," whereas the hymns represent a longer statement of the person and achievement of Christ. One-member confessions developed into two-member statements (I Tim. 2:5) and then into a triadic structure under pressure of polemical situations (Eph. 4:5) or through the rise of baptismal formula (Matt. 28:18-20). Other confessional formulas are directed against incipient Gnosticism in its Docetic form (esp. I John 4:2*b*). Paul had earlier warded off a Gnosticizing denial of the Cross at Corinth by asserting in a creedal formulary the main elements of the tradition (I Cor. 15:3-5). Scattered through the Pauline corpus are creedal snatches that highlight chiefly the atoning (Rom. 4:24-25; II Cor. 5:21) and soteriological (Rom. 8:34; cf. Gal. 1:4; 2:20; Eph. 5:2, 25; I Tim. 2:5-6; Tit. 2:14; I Thess. 1:10; I Cor. 1:30) significance of the Christ-event.

Some hymnic forms show the influence of the Greek-speaking synagogues of the Diaspora (Rev. 4:8, 11; 11:17, 18; 14:7; 15:3, 4). Distinctively Christian hymnic creations are chiefly christological, incorporating a twofold summary of Christ's existence, denoted by the terms "flesh-spirit" (Rom. 1:3-4; I Pet. 3:18; cf. II Tim. 2:8). The clearest example is in I Tim. 3:16, a confessional statement in solemn, hieratic style composed as a hymnic tribute. Eph. 5:14 is identified as hymnic with its introductory formula ("Therefore it is said") and its swinging, trochaic rhythm. Its *Sitz im Leben* is most likely baptism for which it provides the accompanying choral chant.

Longer hymnic specimens are in Phil. 2:6-11 (a hymn embracing the three states of the Lord's existence as premundane, incarnate, and victorious); Col. 1:15-20 (a tripartite hymn to Christ as the agent in the creation and preservation of the world and in redemption); and John 1:1-18 (where the much debated issue is how far we are able to detect a hymn already in use which the biblical author has edited and so adapted to his own purpose). Fragmentary hymns have been detected in I Peter (1:18-21; 2:21-25; 3:18-22) and Hebrews (1:1-4; 7:26-28).

3. Sacramental and ecclesiastical procedures and ceremonies. Prayer-speech, partly based on the Jewish "blessing" of God in the synagogue liturgy (II Cor. 1:3; Eph. 1:3; I Pet. 1:3) and partly indebted to Greek models (e.g., Phil. 1:3), has been isolated. Paul's custom of using liturgical language in the opening paragraphs of his letters may reflect his desire to link himself with the congregation at worship (I Cor. 1:2), and it is the same with the doxologies scattered through the NT (Rom. 1:25; 9:5; II Cor. 11:31; Phil. 4:20, praising God; II Pet. 3:18; Rev. 1:6, praising Christ). *See also* LETTER[S].

Baptismal and eucharistic hymns and confessions may be read in the light of a developing insistence on the need to hold fast to the apostolic kerygma and homology (Heb. 3:1; 4:14; 10:19-25) in time of testing and in the face of false teaching. Attempts to find a fixed, detailed liturgy, whether baptismal (I Peter) or eucharistic (I Cor. 16:21-24) in the NT have not been too successful. Just as problematical have been the endeavors to locate a "church order" in the NT. I John supposedly contains allusions to the catechumenate, confirmation, first communion, and a confessional system. More likely is the hypothesis that a free, charismatic ordering of worship in the pre-Pauline churches (I Cor. 14:26-27) developed into a more fixed and orderly sequence, both in structure and personnel (Eph. 4:11-16). Part of the evidence for church life and worship in the "early catholic" period is seen in the emphasis on ordination (the Pastorals), church officials (Eph. 4; Heb. 13:17; I–III John) —both men (I Pet. 5; I Tim. 3:1-10) and women (I Tim. 3:11-12)—a concern to deal with lapsed church members and their restoration (Hebrews), the use of the creeds as a bastion against heresy (Eph. 4:3; Hebrews; I–III John), and an incipient sacramental system.

See also FORM CRITICISM, NT[S]; WORSHIP IN NT TIMES, CHRISTIAN.

Bibliography. C. F. D. Moule, *Worship in the New Testament,* Ecumenical Studies in Worship, IX (1961); G. Delling, *Worship in the New Testament* (1952 [rev. ET 1962]); F. Hahn, *The Worship of the Early Church* (1970); O. Cullmann, *The Earliest Christian Confessions* (2nd ed., 1949); J. T. Sanders, *The New Testament Christological Hymns,* NTSMS, XV (1971); R. P. Martin, *Worship in the Early Church* (2nd ed., 1975).

R. P. MARTIN

***LORD.** *See* CHRISTOLOGY IN THE NT[S].

***LORD'S DAY.** W. Rordorf, *Sunday* (1968), provides a full discussion of the topic and an extensive bibliography (to 1967). See also C. S. Mosna, *Storia della domenica dalle origini fino agli inizi del V secolo,* Analecta Gregoriana, CLXX (1969); Paul K. Jewett, *The Lord's Day: A Theological Guide to the Christian Day of Worship* (1971). The pertinent texts, with an introduction, translation, and commentary, are assembled in W. Rordorf, *Sabbat und Sonntag in der Alten Kirche,* Traditio Christiana, II (1972).

***LOVE IN THE NT.** The distinctiveness of the NT view of love resides in the centrality given to the commandment: "Love your enemies" (Luke 6:27; Matt. 5:44).

1. Jesus' command: "Love your enemies." Scholars agree that the command to "love your enemies" goes back to Jesus, and that it is most often quoted in the second century. Its popularity among early Christians probably stems from the openness which first-century Jewish and Greek society had toward the idea, rather than the conviction of the church that it was the most important element in the TEACHING OF JESUS. Those Jewish writers who had been influenced by Stoic and Pythagorean thought (TESTAMENTS OF THE TWELVE PATRIARCHS, Joseph and Asenath, Josephus, the Assumption of Moses [*see* MOSES, ASSUMPTION OF]) and who rejected violence are close to the NT teaching.

The NT concept of love shares with its Hellenistic environment an inclusivenes of object. Just as Jesus actually associated with sinners and ate and drank with the despised, so the practice of love among the Epicureans and STOICS was more important than discussions about it. Within Judaism as well, the theology of narrow particularism was yielding to an understanding that, as God's love encompassed all persons, so those who sought to follow God must be prepared to love even their enemies. The idea of loving enemies is not found in Greek thought before Socrates. Lysias (458 B.C.) had expressed the common folk morality: "I considered it ordained that one should harm one's enemies and serve one's friends" (*For the Soldier* 20; cf. 14). But this idea was gradually overthrown by Greek ethical teachers, especially by Socrates, but also, according to Thucydides, by Pericles, who urged victory over foes through generosity (IV.xix.1-4); and later Musonius Rufus (X [79, 3 ff., C. E. Lutz ed.]) refers to forgiving the offender instead of taking vengeance. Indeed, vengeance begins to assume the form of showing love toward the enemy and thus "overcoming evil with good" (e.g., Test. Benj. 4:3; Test. Iss. 7:7; Test. Joseph 18:2-3).

The new element in the teaching of Jesus is that he *commands* love, even toward the enemy. Like Pythagoras, he called into being a community, instructing them to practice benevolence toward enemies yet refusing to predict the outcome of such action. Pythagoras saw this as a way of transforming enemies into friends (Diogenes Laertius VIII.i.23), and in the DIDACHE the command to love is given along with a promise that then "you will have no enemy" (1:3). But in the NT itself this expectation is lacking, and the command stands without any prudential grounds attached to it, even though various injunctions of ancient wisdom literature are used to make it concrete: give the hungry enemy food and drink; if he is in need, provide him with money; if he curses, respond with a blessing.

The admonition to return a blessing for a curse shows most strikingly the new element in the teaching of Jesus. While the curse-blessing formula found in Deuteronomy was applied by the Qumran community both to outsiders and to defectors (1QS 2.2-17), Jesus urges that his followers *return* blessings for curses (Luke 6:28; cf. Rom. 12:14; I Cor. 4:12). Thus, passive acceptance of reviling and insults is also rejected, for the disciple of Jesus is to respond actively to hostile action with love.

Even though one is commanded to love the neighbor (singular), the command to love *enemies* always uses the plural. The intent of this is apparently to include all enemies, "national" as well as "personal."

2. The NT idea of love. The Johannine literature prefers to speak of "loving the brother," without relinquishing love for the enemy. Even the Apocalypse does not give up the idea of loving the enemies, for the dominant symbol of the book, the Lamb, overcomes by absorbing suffering and conquers his enemies by the Word of his mouth (Rev. 19:13-15). The followers of the Lamb are to overcome in the same way (12:11). Vengeance here, as throughout the NT, is left entirely in the hands of God, although during the continuing persecution there is restlessness about when God will avenge the innocent (6:10).

With the NT writers a significant shift has taken place in the model of love. The synoptic writers depict Jesus as one who eats and drinks with sinners, just as he does with the righteous. Likewise, God is impartial in his love; he loves both the sinner and the just, and allows rain to fall and sun to shine on everyone (Matt. 5:45). Similarly, the followers of Jesus are to love their enemies. Luke uses an enemy, a Samaritan, to show what it means to love the neighbor (Luke 10:25 ff.). Just as the profoundest view of love in the OT is found in Hosea in connection with the prophet's marriage, so in the NT, the profoundest view of love comes in the command to love one's enemies. God, too, loved his enemies and thus reconciled them (Rom. 5:10).

Bibliography. P. Minear, *Commands of Christ* (1974), ch. 4; A. Nissen, *Gott und der Nächste im antiken Judentum, Untersuchungen zum Doppelgebot der Liebe,* WUNT, XV (1974); V. Furnish, *The Love Command in the New Testament* (1972); G. Outka, *Agape,* Yale Publications in Religion, XVII (1972); V. Warnach, *Agape: die Liebe als Grundmotif der neutestamentlichen Theologie* (1951); D. Lührmann, "Liebet eure Feinde," *ZThK,* LXIX (1972), 412-38; O. J. F. Seitz, "Love Your Enemies," *NTS,* XVI (1969-70), 39-54; W. C. van Unnik, "Die Motivierung der Feindesliebe in Luke VI, 32-35" *NovT,* VIII (1966), 284-300; W. Klassen, "Vengeance in the Apocalypse of John," *CBQ,* XXIX (1966), 300-316; H. Hunger, "Philanthrōpia," *Anzeiger der phil.-hist. Klasse der österreichischen Akademie der Wissenschaften* (1963), pp. 1 ff.; W. Klassen, "Love Your Enemy," *Biblical Realism Confronts the Nation,* ed. Paul Peachey (1963), pp. 1 ff.; W. Klassen, "Love Your Enemy," Love Thy Neighbour as Thyself," *NovT,* V (1962), 157-70; W. Thimme, "Eros im NT," *Verbum Dei Manet in Aeternum,* ed. W. Foerster (1953), pp. 103-16.

W. Klassen

LOWER CRITICISM. Undertakes to establish the identity, extent, and best text of a given document, relying heavily on external evidence; commonly equated with Textual Criticism. Matters of grammar and lexicography also belong to lower criticism. In contrast with Higher Criticism, lower criticism evaluates the credentials of the text, not the credibility of its content. The distinction between "higher" and "lower" criticism, seldom used today, entered biblical scholarship through the work of J. G. Eichhorn (1752-1827; *see* Biblical Criticism §3*a*).

L. E. Keck

***LUKE, GOSPEL OF.** Recent Lukan study has been concerned especially with the theology of the author of Luke-Acts; this has been due primarily, in the case of the gospel, to H. Conzelmann's influential work (*see* §§1, 2 *below*).

1. Conzelmann's interpretation of Luke. While using and acknowledging previous studies, Conzelmann shifted the focus from literary criticism's search for sources and from form criticism's efforts to construct a social history of the traditions, and focused on an analysis of Luke's literary achievement seen as a whole—which Marxsen later labeled Redaction Criticism. Conzelmann incorporated earlier recognition of Luke's dominant emphasis on the will and plan of God (e.g., Cadbury; this was also the main point of Schubert's "proof from prophecy" interpretation). This is expressed in a "sense of direction" in divinely led history (Dibelius) which Luke conceived as a salvation history in three parts: the epochs of Israel, of Jesus ("the middle of time"; cf. the German title of Conzelmann's book, *Die Mitte der Zeit*), and of the church (von Baer). Luke portrayed Jesus' ministry as a peaceful period during which Satan withdrew (between Luke 4:13 and 22:3, von Baer). In this period danger was distant (contrast the "now" of Luke 22:36 [buy a sword] and the "then" of Jesus' time, 22:35, when lambs were safe among wolves [Luke 10:3] without any need to be "wise as serpents" [contrast Matt. 10:16]), and the very essence of the Kingdom of God was exhibited (Luke 4:18-22; 7:21-23; Acts 10:35, Noack).

Conzelmann directed these insights, together with the analysis of numerous passages and concepts in Luke, toward accomplishing the principle of historical interpretation set out fifty years earlier by W. Wrede: "The first task must always be the thorough illumination of the accounts in the spirit of those accounts themselves, to ask what the narrator in his own time wanted to say to his readers, and this task must be carried to its conclusion and made the foundation of critical historiography." Luke was concerned with the theological legitimacy of the Christian church near the end of the first century, when the passage of time had made it difficult to continue defining Christian existence on the basis of the expectation of Jesus and the earliest Christians that the kingdom was soon to come.

Luke was not the first to experience this difficulty; that the delay of the Parousia had already become a problem is evident in the sources he used. Nor is Luke's distinctiveness to be found in the way he, like his sources, sought to avoid implying the imminence of the Parousia. Rather, Luke's own achievement, as Conzelmann showed, was in facing the problem and in offering a solution in which "eschatology was no longer the decisive, all-inclusive force" (Wilckens). In the gospel the immediate expectation of the end no longer defined the kingdom, the church, or the Christian life. Instead, Luke's emphasis was on the nature of the kingdom (*see above* and also Luke's treatment of Mark 1:15; 9:1; 14:62: Luke 4:14 ff.; 9:27; 22:69). For him the church was legitimated because it was within the will and plan of God, and so was led and empowered by the Spirit. While eschatology still functioned in exhortations to watchfulness and prayer (Luke 18: 1; 21:36), it did not perform that function because the end was known to be near, but because the time of its coming could not be known (Luke 17:20; 12:40, 46). Conzelmann's interpretation quickly gained widespread acceptance.

2. Critiques of Conzelmann's views. Conzelmann's interpretation has been criticized, chiefly on the basis of certain statements in Luke's gospel which seem to anticipate an imminent Parousia, e.g., 10:9, 11; 18:8; 21:32 (*see* §2*a below*). Some of these have been explained as tradition which Luke took over unchanged from his sources (e.g., Cadbury), but this explanation has been unacceptable to others who think Luke would have omitted them if his aim actually had been to de-eschatologize the tradition (e.g., Kümmel). To disallow such an explanation is fundamental to Conzelmann's most radical critics (*see* §2*b below*), although they permit themselves similar explanations in attempting to deal with those passages not congenial to their interpretation, where a delay of the Parousia is implied (Luke 12:38, 45; 13:8).

a. Lukan reinterpretation. It should be noticed that some of these statements of imminence, though retained verbatim by Luke, have been reinterpreted in his recasting of the material. Thus, in his usage they do not imply that he expected the kingdom to come soon. The most troublesome to Conzelmann's interpretation, Luke 21:32 ("this generation will not pass away till all has taken place"), is the same in position and almost the same in wording as in Luke's source (Mark 13:30), but the sense is different. Luke has reworked Mark's apocalypse so that most of it (Luke 21:5-24) refers solely to Jerusalem's destruction and only the predictions from Luke 21:25 on refer to the end. Thus, the common practice of interpreting all of Luke 21:7 ff. on the basis of Luke 17:20 ff. is wrong; Luke 17:20 ff. should be taken only with Luke 21:25 ff. Luke separated the final events from Jerusalem's downfall (*pace* Francis) by omitting Mark's linking statements (Mark 13:24; contrast Luke 21:25) and by distinguishing the signs in the cosmos (Luke 21:25-26) from those on earth (Luke 21:7 ff.; Robinson). Thereby he profoundly altered the meaning of the Markan material used in Luke 21:25 ff.; he has projected it into that final time when the universe totters and the SON OF MAN appears (Luke 21:25-27). *Then* the final redemption of believers will be literally near (Luke 21:28). "This generation" (Luke 21:32) no longer meant (as in Mark) those of Jesus' lifetime, but those at that incalculable future time (Luke 17:20) of the coming of the Son of man. That generation would, literally, "not pass away until all has taken place" (Luke 21:32).

The statements that when Jesus came near (Luke 10:1), the kingdom was near (Luke 10:9, 11) fit Luke's conception of Jesus' ministry as a proleptic manifestation of the kingdom of God (Noack, Conzelmann), in which Jesus' presence was a divine visitation (Robinson; cf. Francis) which required a response and imposed consequences on negative response (Luke 19:37-44). In short, when Jesus came near, the kingdom was near (Noack, Robinson), and Luke 10:9, 11 assert nothing about imminence from Luke's place in time. Ott has argued that Luke 18:1-8 is yet another illustration of Conzelmann's point that one consequence of giving up the near expectation is increased emphasis on the suddenness of its coming. This passage agrees with other Lukan exhortations to pray and therefore fits easily into Luke's eschatology as Conzelmann has presented it.

b. Conzelmann's radical critics. The most radical criticism of Conzelmann has come from Bartsch and his followers. They claim that Luke, far from seeking to solve problems resulting from an acknowledged delay of the Parousia, "consistently maintained the near expectation." He was thereby correcting a view which put the Parousia in the past by believing it occurred with Jesus' resurrection, a belief useful to early Christian GNOSTICISM (Bartsch, Talbert). This view, however, is not convincing. First, as noted above, such critics use a double standard in holding Luke less strictly accountable for retaining implications of delay than for retaining those of imminence. Second, they refuse to allow that the theme of the suddenness of the Parousia, based on inability to calculate the end in advance (Luke 17:20; cf. 12:40, 46), does not require an expectation of its nearness though it is compatible with it. Finally they exclude the nuances by reducing to a single sense all language that sounds eschatological. In this way they rule out in advance the possibility that exhortations to "watch at all times, praying . . ." (Luke 21:36, which Bartsch used as the title of his book) or "always to pray and not lose heart" (Luke 18:1) are Lukan means for dealing with the offense arising from the delay of the Parousia (Ott, Wilckens).

c. Assessment. Conzelmann's interpretation of Luke seems to be correct in the main, even though it claims too much Lukan concern to remove all implications of imminence and is unconvincing in its treatment of John the Baptist (Robinson). Conzelmann is also right in identifying Luke's theology as salvation history (*Heilsgeschichte*), yet his claim that the evangelist articulated this in three epochs is problematical (*see* §3 *below*).

3. Luke's "salvation history." As noted above (§1), Conzelmann's interpretation made use of von Baer's argument that in Luke salvation history is presented as consisting of three epochs. Von Baer had found evidence for the first of these (the epoch of Israel) in chs. 1–2, but Conzelmann could not use this evidence, since he questioned the authenticity of those chapters. Conzelmann's own attempt to use Luke 16:16 as the basis is not convincing. The aspects of Luke's work which, on comparison with his sources, appear most obviously to be his innovations are (1) Acts and (2) the travel narrative in Luke 9:51 ff. In both instances a journey is involved, not just movement incidental to storytelling. Travel is a major structural element in Luke's presentation of the providential leading of history (where the church has its rightful place) and in the qualification of the witnesses (Acts 13:31), from which the church could offer its message with assurance. Therefore, the metaphor which best describes Luke's theology is not "the middle of time" (Conzelmann) but, rather, "the way of the Lord." This metaphor is more appropriate to Luke's own presentation, and the phrase itself appears in Luke 3:4 in a quotation from Isa. 40 which Luke took over from Mark. But Luke has gone beyond Mark's quotation (Luke 3:5-6) to include the all-encompassing assertion, "And all flesh shall see the salvation of God." Luke concluded his two-volume work with similar words (Acts 28:28) and by showing how the word of God had actually reached Rome.

Luke viewed salvation history, therefore, as a course of events following a schedule of times set by God and directed by God toward all people. In Jesus' ministry the way led from Galilee to Jerusalem (Luke 23:5; Acts 10:37), during which the Christian witnesses became qualified (Acts 1:21-22; 13:31), and in Acts it led from Jerusalem to Rome (Luke 24:47; Acts 1:8), when "the word of God increased" (Acts 6:7; cf. 12:24; 19:20), empowered by the Holy Spirit (Luke 24:49; Acts 1:8; 2:1 ff.). In Jesus' ministry Luke presented the paradigm of God's gracious reign (*see* §1 *above*), so that the Christian's present life might be marked by joy (Luke 2:10; Acts 2:46; 8:8; 13:52; 15:3) rather than by anxiety about the things of the world (Luke 8:14; 10:41-42; 12:11, 22-24, 25-26; 21:34). Hence, Christians need not fear the future: when the end does come, believers—knowing the gracious nature of God's kingdom from Luke's portrayal of it in Jesus' ministry—are to "look up and raise [their] heads, because [their] redemption is drawing near" (Luke 21:28; cf. the terms used in Acts 3:19-21: "times of refreshing," "time for establishing").

Since Luke connected the "restoration" (RSV "establishing") with the Parousia (Acts 3:21) rather than with the outpouring of the Spirit (Acts 2:1 ff.), the disciples' question about the time of the restoration of the kingdom (Acts 1:6) is in effect rejected. A separation in time is made between the outpouring of the Spirit and the final restoration (von Baer). While the outpouring of the Spirit "in the last days" (Acts 2:17) was for Luke an eschatological aspect of his own time, it was a "prolepsis of the end" (Cullmann), not "the eschatological gift, but the substitute in the meantime for the possession of ultimate salvation" (Conzelmann; vs. Francis). Calculation of the time of the end being impossible, the only way to be ready is to stay ready (Luke 21:34-36; 17:26 ff.; 12:35 ff.), and this meant regular practice of the Christian life (Luke 12:40 ff.; "daily": 9:23; 11:3; Acts 2:46-47*a*; 5:42; 16:5), especially in prayer (Luke 11:1-13; 18:1-8; 21:34-36; 22:31-34, 39-46) and in reliance on the gift of the Spirit (*see* the key scenes early in each of Luke's writings, Luke 4:16 ff. and Acts 2:1 ff.).

See also Synoptic Problem[S].

Bibliography. Recent commentaries in English: F. W. Danker, *Jesus and the New Age According to St. Luke, a Commentary on the Third Gospel* (1972); E. E. Ellis, NCB (1966). Studies: H. von Baer, *Der Heilige Geist in den Lukasschriften* (1926); H. W. Bartsch, *Wachet aber zu jeder Zeit! Entwurf einer Auslegung des Lukasevangeliums* (1963); H. J. Cadbury, *The Making of Luke-Acts* (1927 [2nd ed., 1958]; H. Conzelmann, *The Theology of St. Luke* (1957); O. Cullmann, "Geschichtsschreibung im NT," *RGG,* II (3rd ed., 1958), cols. 1501-03; M. Dibelius, *Studies in the Acts of the Apostles* (1951); F. O. Francis, "Eschatology and History in Luke-Acts," *JAAR,* XXXVII (1969), 49-63; W. G. Kümmel, "Current Theological Accusations against Luke," *ANQ,* XVI (1975-76), 131-45; K. Löning, "Lukas—Theologe der von Gott geführten Heilsgechichte," in *Gestalt und Anspruch des NTs,* ed. J. Schreiner (1969), pp. 200-28; B. Noack, "Das Gottesreich bei Lukas. Eine Studie zu Luk. 17, 20-24," *SBU,* X (1948), 47 ff.; W. Ott, *Gebet und Heil. Die Bedeutung der Gebetsparänese in der lukanischen Theologie,* StANT, XII (1965); W. C. Robinson, Jr., *Der Weg des Herrn. Studien zur Geschichte und Eschatologie im Lukas-Evangelium,* Theologische Forschung, XXXVI (1964); P. Schubert, "The Structure and Significance of Luke 24," *Neutestamentliche Studien für Rudolf Bultmann,* BZNW, XXI (1954), 165-86; C. H. Talbert, "The Redaction Critical Quest for Luke the Theologian," *Jesus and Man's Hope,* I (1970), 171-222; U. Wilckens, "Interpreting Luke-Acts in a Period of Existentialist Theology," *Studies in Luke-Acts,* ed. L. E. Keck and J. L. Martyn (1966), pp. 60-83; W. Wrede, *The Messianic Secret* (1901 [ET 1971]).

W. C. Robinson, Jr.

M

*__MACEDONIA.__ Recent discoveries illustrate the transitions between the classical and Hellenistic periods and between pagan and Christian culture.

Excavation on the central Macedonian plain at Leucadia has uncovered a large Macedonian tomb built in the late fourth century B.C. Like other Macedonian tombs, it has a vaulted structure and a temple-like façade, but its painting is unusually brilliant. Chance finds at Pella, *ca.* twenty-four miles W of Thessalonica, have resulted in systematic study of the Hellenistic capital of Macedonian royalty. The spacious ancient houses, built in orderly blocks, are notable for their pebble mosaics depicting such lively scenes as a lion hunt and the god Dionysus riding a panther. At Derveni, *ca.* six miles N of Thessalonica, rich graves dated by coins to the fourth century B.C. have been uncovered. Their contents included a papyrus sheet on which was copied an Orphic cosmogony, a large gilded bronze vase decorated with scenes of revelry, and much precious jewelry and armor.

More has been discovered about sites visited by Paul in a westward journey (Acts 16–17). In NEAPOLIS remains of the late archaic and classical sanctuary of a virgin goddess identified with Athena have been studied. Macedonian tombs have been found in Philippi and Amphipolis, and important buildings and graves of Hellenistic and Roman times have been uncovered below the modern cities in Thessalonica and Beroea. Many elaborate churches from the early Byzantine period discovered at various sites witness to Macedonian Christianity.

See also PHILIPPI; PHILIPPI[S]; THESSALONICA; THESSALONICA[S].

Bibliography. Surveys: "Archaeology in Greece," *AR,* IV (1957)–XIX (1972-73); "Chronique des Fouilles," *BCH,* LXXXII (1958)–XCVI (1972); "χρονικά," *AD,* XVI (1960)–XXV (1970); Μακεδονικά, VII (1966-67), 277 ff., IX (1969), 101 ff.; M. Paraskevaidis, "Archaeological Research in Greek Macedonia and Thrace 1912-1962," *Balkan Studies,* III (1962), 443-58. Other: *Ancient Macedonia,* ed. B. Laourdas and C. Makaronas (1970); P. E. Davies, "The Macedonian Scene of Paul's journeys," *BA,* XXVI (1963), 91-106; N. G. L. Hammond, *History of Macedonia* (1972-).

C. L. THOMPSON

*__MADMANNAH.__ Though the ancient name is echoed in the Arabic name Khirbet Umm ed-Deimneh, there are no suitable Israelite remains at that place. Furthermore, it is situated in the hills rather than in the Negeb. Not far away is a large antiquity site, actually in Negeb territory, with ample Iron Age ceramics (as well as Hellenistic and later), viz., Khirbet Tatrît, about 4½ miles S of eẓ-Ẓāherîyah on the Beer-sheba road. Placing Madmannah here confirms the accuracy of the regional distinctions in Josh. 15 between the Negeb and the hill country.

Bibliography. M. Kochavi, "The Land of Judah," in M. Kochavi, ed., *Judaea, Samaria and the Golan, Archaeological Survey 1967-1968* (1972), pp. 80-81, Hebrew.

A. F. RAINEY

*__MAGDALA.__ Probable town of Mary Magdalene (Μαγδαληνή = "of Magdala"). Generally identified with Migdal Nûnyâ (מגדל נוניא="Tower of [salted] Fish") of the Babylonian Talmud (T.B. Pes. 46b) and the Tarichea (Ταριχήα="[Place of] Salted Fish") of Josephus (War II.xxi.8; III.ix.7–x.5) and perhaps Migdal Ṣebʻiyâ (מגדל צבעיא = "Tower of Dyers") of the Jerusalem Talmud (J.T. Taʻan. IV.8), today usually identified with Mejdel on the W shores of the Sea of Galilee.

Recent excavations at Mejdel have uncovered possible early Roman, i.e., first-century A.D. structures. These include a small synagogue at the intersection of two well-paved Roman streets or roads just S of a large, unidentified building. W of the synagogue is a Roman period masonry tower.

The putative synagogue is only 26.8 x 23.8 feet and equipped with five stone benches (risers) on the N wall. The interior is in the form of a small basilica with nave and two aisles the length of the building and an aisle across the back or S side. The size of the building implies a small congregation, as there is room for perhaps thirty on the risers, and the nave will accommodate about twenty-five comfortably.

A harbor has been located and plotted. Thus this was surely a fishing village that perhaps supplied dried fish to the region, hence the name Migdal Nûnyâ. *See also* SYNAGOGUE, ARCHITECTURE[S].

Bibliography. M. Avi-Yonah, *The Holy Land from the Persian to the Arab Conquest* (1966), pp. 97, 106, 111; A. Neubauer, *La Géographie du Talmud* (1967 [1868]), pp. 216-18; B. Bagatti, *Antichi villaggi cristiani di Galilea* (1971), pp. 80-83; V. Corbo, "Scavi Archeologici a Magdala (1971-1973)," *Liber Annuus,* XXIV (1974), 5-37; M. Nun, "Ancient Anchorages and Harbors in the Sea of Galilee," *Nature and Land,* V (1974), 212-19, Hebrew.

J. F. STRANGE

MAHALATH. 1. A daughter of Ishmael. She became one of Esau's wives (Gen. 28:9).

2. A daughter of Jerimoth, one of King David's sons. She became the wife of Rehoboam, her father's half brother (II Chr. 11:18).

*__MAN, NATURE OF, IN THE NT.__ The person, male or female, is the creature whose body is made alive by God's breath, whose divine image can be defaced by sin and redeemed by the apportioned Holy Spirit, and whose historical destiny is defined by relationships from birth to death.

1. Introduction. The OT legacy is generally

carried over into the NT, in that man is viewed as a totality, with terms such as heart, soul, flesh, or spirit denoting not a portion but the entire person from a particular point of view. It is assumed that humans are sexual creatures and that flesh is intrinsically good, so long as one does not boast in its prowess. Since all NT writers assume the human dilemma lies in disobedience rather than materiality, the crucial differences between them arise in conceptualizing sin and its cure. (*a*) A tendency to divide the world between saints and sinners along predestinarian, moralistic lines is common to Revelation and the Pastorals. (*b*) A tendency toward moral gradualism through obedience to ethical norms is a mark of Luke, Matthew, and James. (*c*) A doctrine of relationship, in which the line between saint and sinner is marked by faith in God or lack of faith is typical for the historical Jesus and the Pauline and Johannine traditions.

Each approach to sin implies a different concept of man's destiny and salvation. Since option (*c*) has the strongest claims to originality and consistency with the Christ event, it will be developed more fully below.

2. Discipleship and servanthood. That "no one can serve two masters" (Matt. 6:24) presupposes that some form of servanthood is intrinsic to man. He is determined by whom he serves, whether God or mammon. Freedom is not absolute autonomy but release from idolatrous forces which distort life. Jesus' struggle against legalism (Mark 2:27), Paul's attack on justification by works (Rom. 3), and the struggle in Hebrews and Colossians against the veneration of cosmic forces (Heb. 1–2; Col. 2) all aim at restoring man to proper servanthood. The images of stewardship (Matt. 25:14-30; Luke 17:10), DISCIPLESHIP (Mark 6:8-11), sonship (Gal. 4), and being begotten by God (John 3; I John 3) imply high levels of independent initiative for those who know their Father's will. To stand fast in freedom (Gal. 5:1) is to fulfill one's destiny through service in love (I John 3), to reject continuously all conformity, while being impelled by grace to render service to the world (Rom. 12:1-2). For those set free by Christ, socially imposed subservience is no longer determinative, and equality is the result (Gal. 3:28). One is free to discover an appropriate form of servanthood that brings fulfillment (I Cor. 9:19; 7:22; Eph. 6:6).

3. Finitude and ethics. Freedom does not include release from the essential conditions of bodily, historical existence. Man remains "body" (Rom. 8:10); his life is "in the flesh" (Philem. 16; Rom. 7:5); even the "inner/outer nature" categories (II Cor. 4:16; Rom. 7:22) indicate Paul did not think of a real self in contrast with fallen flesh, for these categories were borrowed from opponents and were redefined within the context of Pauline theology. So constitutive is bodily existence that each person must find an appropriate way to express sexual inclinations (I Cor. 7). Each must work for daily bread (I Thess. 4:11-12; II Thess. 3:6-13). The alienation which these relationships produce is overcome by Christ, but we remain finite. Thus, although there are remarkable efforts to overcome inequalities (I Cor. 7:4; Luke 10:41-42), Paul once found it necessary to reimpose traditional sex roles temporarily in face of Gnostic demands to eradicate such finite factors from Christian self-identity (I Cor. 11:2-16). Each person's sexual "gift" (I Cor. 7:7; cf. Matt. 19:12) must be exercised in holiness (I Cor. 6:12-20; I Thess. 4:4), i.e., display the love of Christ (Eph. 5:21-33; I Cor. 7:4).

The love ethic (John 13:34-35) is not legalistic; it requires the full use of rational judgment (I Cor. 7:6, 33-38). The gift of the Spirit (I Cor. 14:14-15) unleashes rather than subordinates the practical intellect. Man is called to exercise prudence, particularly in relation to the future, whose trials and judgment are unpredictable (Matt. 25:1-13; Mark 13:32-33; I Thess. 5:1-11). Man is the creature who moves toward God's future (Phil. 3:12-14; Heb. 13:13), whose deeds and values face judgment (I Cor. 4:3-5), and whose virtues can therefore never be an occasion for boasting (Eph. 2:9). Even the most exalted spiritual insights are finite and need eschatological fulfillment (I Cor. 13:12). To be human requires faith rather than perfect certainty, hope rather than present fulfillment. As a pilgrim, man is to "[go] out, not knowing where he [is] to go" (Heb. 11:8). With adversity his expected lot (Matt. 8:20; Heb. 11:32-40), he remains vulnerable until the eschaton (II Cor. 12:5-10; Rom. 8:18-30; Heb. 13:3).

4. Reconciliation and resurrection. It follows that SALVATION involves RECONCILIATION *in* rather than release *from* finitude. Each person repeats the choice of Adam to sin by disregarding his limits (Rom. 5:12-21). Those under the Law fall into self-righteousness while those outside the Law violate conscience and fall prey to idolatry (Rom. 1:18-32; 3:23). The essence of SIN is not rule-breaking but alienation—the refusal of the creature to acknowledge the creator. "Flesh" in this context denotes the tendency to mistake one's accomplishments for the good, and thus to enter into conflict with divine righteousness (Rom. 7:13-25; 10:1-10). The human dilemma is therefore not weakness but mistaken strength, which relates closely with Paul's critique of misguided zeal (Rom. 10:1-4) and Jesus' opposition to unbridled anger (Matt. 5:21-26). The Cross reveals the depths of this alienation, and the RESURRECTION gives the power that persons need to break free (Eph. 2:12-16; Rom. 3:21-26).

When anyone receives this gospel and is reconciled with God, the righteousness of God is restored (Rom. 1:17-18), and that person regains his rightful role in the creation (Rom. 8:12-25; 12:1-2; I Cor. 6:3). He takes up responsibility in the world (Heb. 13:1-16) and extends reconciling love into his economic, family, and political obligations (Eph. 5:21–6:9; I Pet. 2:13-25; I Cor. 7; Rom. 13:1-7). He is set free to enjoy creaturely existence (Matt. 11:19; Phil. 4:8) and to find "rest" in his encounter with God's word day by day (Heb. 3:7–4:13). Man thus restored exhibits an alert, resourceful vitality as he moves in hope toward the fulfillment only God can provide (Matt. 24:42; Phil. 3:8-16; Heb. 11–12). He is reconciled to the exigencies of historical life (Heb. 13:1-6; Phil. 1:14-26) and thus can face death with courage, expecting the resurrection of the body (I Cor. 15), but knowing that nothing in his power can pass unscathed through the judgment (I Cor. 3:12-15). Man's situation is therefore decisively shaped by the tension between present reconciliation and future fulfillment (I Cor. 7:29-31; Rom. 8).

Bibliography. R. Bultmann, *Theology of the NT,* 2 vols. (1948-54); W. D. Stacey, *The Pauline View of Man* (1956); W. G. Kümmel, *Man in the NT* (rev. ed., 1963), and *The Theology of the NT According to Its Major Witnesses: Jesus—Paul—John* (1969); R. Scroggs, *The Last Adam: A Study in Pauline Anthropology* (1966); J. Jeremias, "ἄνθρωπος," *TDNT,* I (1933 [ET 1964]), 364-67; K. H. Schelkle, *Theology of the NT,* 4 vols. (1968 ff.); H. Conzelmann, *An Outline of the Theology of the NT* (1967); E. Schweizer, *Beiträge zur Theologie des NT* (1970); R. Jewett, *Paul's Anthropological Terms,* AGJU, X (1971); M. Hengel, "Was ist der Mensch?" *Probleme Biblischer Theologie* (1971), pp. 116-35; E. Käsemann, *Perspectives on Paul* (1969); G. E. Ladd, *A Theology of the NT* (1974); P. K. Jewett, *Man as Male and Female* (1975).

R. Jewett

MANDAEISM măn dē′ĭzm. A syncretistic, Gnostic religion whose adherents constitute the sole surviving sect of ancient Gnosticism.

1. The Mandaeans. There are about 15,000 Mandaeans in Iraq and a much smaller number in SW Iran. Their texts are written in Mandaic, an eastern Aramaic dialect, in a script which resembles the Elymean and Characenian scripts of the second century A.D. The earliest of their texts are amulets in lead strips from the third century A.D. and inscribed magic bowls from *ca.* 600. The religious MSS are mainly from the eighteenth and nineteenth centuries, with the oldest MS dating to the sixteenth century. The most important work is the *Ginza,* which relates the creation of the cosmos and the fate of the soul after death. The book of John describes John the Baptist as a Mandaean, but the traditions about John are quite late. The Mandaeans regard Christ as a false Messiah.

2. Teachings. The Mandaeans believe not only in the First Life but also in a second (*Yoshamin*), a third (*Abathur*), and a fourth (*Ptahil*). In their dualistic cosmogony Ptahil creates the world (*Tibil*) with the aid of the evil Spirit (*Ruha*), the Seven (planets), and the Twelve (signs of the zodiac).

Ptahil also creates man, who is a dual being, comprised of physical Adam (*Adam pagria*) and secret Adam (*Adam kasia*). Manda ḏ-Haiye, "Gnosis of Life," reveals himself to man as an incarnation of three Uthras, "heavenly spirits." At death the soul of the Mandaean leaves behind his "stinking" body and ascends through the seven hostile planetary spheres back to the world of light.

3. Cult. In contrast with other Gnostic sects the Mandaeans observe elaborate rituals which are administered by the head priest (*ganzibra*) or priests (*tarmide*). There is a clear distinction between the *mandaye,* the semi-ignorant laity, and the *naṣoraye,* the initiated clergy.

The Mandaeans observe a magically purifying rite of baptism (*maṣbuta*), celebrated in the precinct of a cult hut with a "Jordan" (*yardna*) of running water flowing through it (*see also* Baptism [S] §1*b*iii.) At death a sacramental meal (*masiqta*) is celebrated to assist the soul in its journey to the world of light.

4. Ethics. The Mandaeans have a highly developed code of ethical and ritual behavior. Their emphasis on marriage for the purpose of procreating as many children as possible is unique among Gnostic groups.

5. Origins and significance for the NT. Many scholars have argued for a pre-Christian, Palestinian origin of the Mandaeans, and some have made use of Mandaean texts to reconstruct a pre-Christian Gnosticism, which they have then assumed in their interpretation of the NT.

Though Rudolph and Macuch are convinced that the Mandaeans originated in pre-Christian Palestine (*see bibliog.*), their position is based largely on alleged parallels with Johannine texts (*see* John, Gospel of[S] §3). There is no objective evidence of the establishment of Mandaeism earlier than the second century A.D.

Bibliography. M. Lidzbarski, *Das Johannesbuch der Mandäer,* 2 vols. (1905-15), and *Ginzā* (1925); E. S. Drower, *The Mandaeans of Iraq and Iran* (1937), *The Haran Gawaita and the Baptism of Hibil-Ziwa* (1953), and *The Canonical Prayerbook of the Mandaeans* (1959); K. Rudolph, *Die Mandäer,* 2 vols., *FRLANT,* LVI (1960-61), *Theogonie, Kosmogonie und Anthropogonie in den mandäischen Schriften, FRLANT,* LXXXIII (1965), "Problems of a History of the Development of the Mandaean Religion," *History of Religions,* VIII (1969), 210-35, and "Mandaean Sources," *Gnosis,* II, ed. W. Foerster (1971), 121-319; E. S. Drower and R. Macuch, *A Mandaic Dictionary* (1963); R. Macuch, *Handbook of Classical and Modern Mandaic* (1965); E. Yamauchi, *Mandaic Incantation Texts,* AOS, XLIX (1967), and *Gnostic Ethics and Mandaean Origins,* HTS, XXIV (1970).

E. M. Yamauchi

MANUAL OF DISCIPLINE. (1QS). A scroll from Cave 1 at Wadi Qumran, containing the rules and doctrines of the Qumran community. It is also known as Rule of the Community, and sometimes identified as 1QSer. *See* Dead Sea Scrolls §5*b*; Dead Sea Scrolls[S] §6 and bibliog.; Interpretation, History of[S] §B1*a*iv.

MANUSCRIPTS FROM THE JUDEAN DESERT. Before the Qumran discoveries it was an axiom among archaeologists that no document written on perishable material (leather, parchment, papyrus) could survive in Palestine. But once the theory was contradicted by the Qumran facts, determined individuals—amateur Bedouin scroll hunters and professional explorers—set out to look for further ancient documents and managed to uncover various caches in scattered corners of the wilderness of Judea. The finds made in caves situated in Wadi Murabba'at (1951-52 and 1955), in Naḥal Ḥever, Naḥal Ẓe'elim, and Naḥal Mishmar (1960-61), and at Masada (1963-65) are securely dated by coins and explicit literary evidence to the first and early second century A.D.

1. Qumran
2. Other discoveries
   - *a.* The Murabba'at documents
   - *b.* Documents from Naḥal Ḥever, Naḥal Ẓe'elim, and Naḥal Mishmar
   - *c.* Documents from Masada

3. The biblical MSS
4. Apoc. and Pseudep.
5. Legal documents prior to the Second Revolt
6. Documents relating to the Second Revolt
Bibliography

1. Qumran. *See* DEAD SEA SCROLLS; DEAD SEA SCROLLS[S].

2. Other discoveries. ***a. The Murabba'at documents.*** First discovered by Ta'amireh Bedouin, and subsequently excavated by de Vaux and Harding, the caves of Murabba'at have yielded leather and papyrus fragments and ostraca with Hebrew, Aramaic, Greek, and Latin texts. Biblical remains (Genesis, Exodus, Numbers, Deuteronomy, Isaiah, minor prophets) form only a small part of the total find. The majority of the texts are nonliterary, namely, lists of goods, contracts, and letters. The most significant of these are legal and historical documents belonging to the era of the second Jewish war against Rome under Hadrian (A.D. 132-35) and providing for the first time direct and contemporary Jewish evidence concerning Bar Kochba, the leader of the revolt, and his men. After being occupied by rebels in the second century, the caves were occasionally visited in later times, as is indicated by Arabic documents dating between the ninth and the fourteenth centuries, among them a receipt from A.D. 938/939, and Christian Greek fragments, written on paper and belonging to the tenth and eleventh centuries. *See also* BAR KOCHBA[S] §4*b*.

b. Documents from Naḥal Ḥever, Naḥal Ze'elim, and Naḥal Mishmar. In 1960 and 1961 Israeli archaeologists organized a systematic exploration of the caves between En-gedi and Masada and found a few biblical fragments representing a phylactery and Pss. 15 and 16, an important collection of Hebrew, Aramaic, and Greek letters from the time of Bar Kochba, and an archive of thirty-five Nabatean, Aramaic, and Greek documents dating from A.D. 93/94 to 132 dealing with the affairs of a certain Jewish lady by the name of Babata, daughter of Simeon, and her family. Naḥal Ze'elim produced eight papyrus fragments in Greek giving lists of Jewish names in Hellenized forms; and another fragment of the same type, and no doubt issued by the same office, has been found in Naḥal Mishmar. Finally, thirteen shreds of parchment were discovered in Naḥal Ḥever itself belonging to a Greek version of the twelve minor prophets. The bulk of this MS, twenty-four fragmentary columns extending from Jonah 1:14 to Zech. 9:4, was removed from the cave in question in 1952 by Bedouin who sold it to the Palestine Archaeological Museum in Jerusalem. A preliminary edition of the text was published by Barthélemy in 1963. *See also* BAR KOCHBA[S] §4*c-f*.

c. Documents from Masada. The famous rock fortress, which was constructed by Alexander Janneus, embellished and enlarged by Herod the Great, and held during the first war by the Zealots in their courageous stand against the Romans even after the fall of Jerusalem, was thoroughly excavated between 1963 and 1965 by an international team of volunteers under the direction of Yadin. Their work brought to light important written documents, none of which can have originated later than A.D. 74, the recently suggested date of the conquest of Masada, previously thought to have taken place in A.D. 73.

The Bible is represented by a fragment each from Genesis and Leviticus, and by a somewhat larger relic of a Psalms scroll (Pss. 81:3–85:10). The Apoc. are attested by twenty-six fragments of Ecclesiasticus, or the Wisdom of Ben Sirach, forming thirteen columns, and corresponding to Ecclus. 39:37 to 44:20. A small scrap of the Qumran Angelic Liturgy has also been unearthed, as well as a Hebrew papyrus written in archaic script, but it is too damaged for identification. We have also a Greek letter written on papyrus from an Abascantos to a Jew called Judah. The several Latin papyri found here derive from the Roman garrison of Masada. Finally there are over two hundred ostraca in Hebrew and Aramaic, indicating mostly the contents of a vessel and the name of its owner. *See also* MASADA[S] §2.

Before discussing the particular significance of the various finds, we should consider two general points which affect our understanding of the Dead Sea Scrolls. (1) At Masada and in the caves occupied by the revolutionaries of Bar Kochba, the biblical and other religious texts are outnumbered by the secular documents, whereas at Qumran the literary deposit is almost exclusively religious. This is an external confirmation of the special nature of the Dead Sea Community. (2) The presence at Masada of a sectarian Qumran writing—the Angelic Liturgy—can be explained in three ways: it can be interpreted to mean either that the Qumran sectaries were Zealots; or that the Qumran Essenes joined the Zealots in the struggle against Rome, as appears to be implied by Josephus' mention of John the Essene among the Jewish generals, and of the heroism of the members of the sect when subjected to Roman torture; or that the Zealots occupied the Qumran site after its evacuation by the Essenes and transferred to Masada some of the MSS found there. The first hypothesis, as has been shown earlier, is unlikely (*see* DEAD SEA SCROLLS §5), but the second and the third seem equally plausible.

3. The biblical MSS. The biblical fragments from Masada have not yet been published, but according to a preliminary account Gen. 46:7-11 may contain some variants; Lev. 4:3-9 agrees with the MT; and so, with one exception, does the Psalms scroll. A Psalms fragment from Naḥal Ḥever is also in line with the received version apart from the omission, possibly accidental, of four words from Ps. 16:3. According to Yadin it may predate the Bar Kochba war by several decades and belong to the same period as the Masada specimen.

The biblical documents from Murabba'at are to all intents and purposes the same as the Masoretic version of the OT. They attest, not only a Masoretic consonantal text, but also the same internal divisions of the text into sections, the same type of script, and the same format and arrangement of the writing on a leather scroll. Likewise, the Murabba'at phylactery—and that from Naḥal Ẓe'elim—follow the traditional rules, whereas those found at Qumran depart from them considerably.

This would suggest that the decisions concerning the Bible taken at the academy of Jamnia (Jabneel) at the end of the first century A.D. were implemented without delay; in MS deposits of the Bar Kochba age, only one generation after Jamnia, the scriptural text is Masoretic, and not a single fragment represents either the Apoc. or other noncanonical literature.

4. Apoc. and Pseudep. Masada, by contrast, which fell before the work of Jamnia was undertaken, testifies to noncanonical Jewish writings. Its most important contribution in this respect comes from a fragmentary scroll of the Hebrew Ecclesiasticus which is considerably more substantial than the small Qumran fragments. This discovery has removed once and for all any doubts that may still have lingered concerning the authenticity and antiquity of the Hebrew text revealed by the medieval copies of the Cairo Genizah. If the date proposed by the editor, Yadin—namely, the end of the second century B.C.—is accepted, the Masada MS falls to within a hundred years of Ben Sirach's original composition (habitually dated to around 190 B.C.) and is roughly contemporaneous with the Greek translation prepared by the author's grandson. The Masada fragments were published in 1965 and have since been used, together with the Genizah and Qumran MSS, in a new edition of Ben Sirach issued in 1973 by the Academy of the Hebrew Language and the Shrine of the Book in Jerusalem.

Apart from Ecclesiasticus, Masada has yielded other pseudepigraphic writings, as yet unidentified and unpublished, in addition to the fragment from the Qumran Angelic Liturgy already mentioned. This would imply that the otherwise strictly observant Zealots had no scruples about keeping, and presumably reading, books which received official disapproval a decade or two later at Jamnia.

5. Legal documents prior to the Second Revolt. Murabba'at and the southern caves have provided us with dated contracts and other documents in Hebrew, Aramaic, and Greek that shed unprecedented light on Jewish legal customs and terminology prior to the legislation codified in the Mishna. They include an Aramaic acknowledgment of debt, dated to the second year of the emperor Nero (A.D. 55/56), that expressly stipulates that the sum borrowed must be repaid in full, even in a sabbatical year. We have a bill of divorce from the sixth year of the province of Arabia (A.D. 111), an Aramaic marriage contract from the eleventh year of the same era (A.D. 117), and another the date of which is missing. And we have thirty-five papyri constituting the family archive of Babata (A.D. 93/94-132), records which represent various types of legal texts, from Babata's marriage contract to property deeds and other occasions of litigation. Among the papyri is Babata's tax or census declaration made in Greek, on December 2, 127, before the Roman district governor at Rabbath Moab, and sworn "by the Tyche of the Lord Caesar," although from what is known of her financial affairs it was probably incorrect. It is noteworthy that besides Hebrew and Aramaic, Greek and even Nabatean were used by legal scribes in a Jewish territory, and that the dating of the documents followed the secular era in force at the time in question.

Belonging to the Babata collection are also several tied deeds. In these, the text has been copied twice on the same papyrus, and the upper half then rolled up and tied with knots, against each of which a witness put his signature at the verso of the papyrus. The lower half was left untied for consultation. A similar custom existed already in the time of Jeremiah (Jer. 32:11-14).

6. Documents relating to the Second Revolt. Until the Bar Kochba discoveries, the history of the Jewish rebellion against Rome under Hadrian was known only from a brief notice of the Roman historian Dio Cassius, and from occasional rabbinic and patristic references. The new texts, though too scanty to allow a proper account of the war to be written, afford a valuable fresh insight into the system of administration adopted by the rebels, and into the discipline imposed by the leader of the revolt on his men and the ideals which inspired the anti-Roman fight.

Before the recent find, it was already known, thanks to the coins minted by him, that the name of the chief of the insurgent was Simeon, nicknamed later by his supporters, according to Jewish and Christian sources, Ben or Bar Kochba (Son of the Star=Messiah), and by his rabbinic critics, Bar Koziba (Son of the Lie=False Messiah). It is only now that we are able to determine that his real name was Simeon ben Kosiba. (The pronunciation can be ascertained from a Greek text.) Furthermore, his title of *nasi* (head of government), which appears on coins, is also confirmed by our papyri.

The outbreak of the war (A.D. 132) was chosen as the start of another era, that of the "Liberation of Israel," and various documents are dated to the first, second, third, and fourth year of the new age. The territory under rebel control was divided into districts, and their command entrusted to the care of military governors. Four of these are named: Jonathan bar Ba'ayan and Masabala bar Simeon were in charge of the En-gedi region; and Judah bar Manasseh, of Kiriath Arabayya. The command of Joshua ben Galgula is not named, but doubtless it too was situated in the Judean Desert.

Each community was administered by *parnasin,* or leaders, whose duties entailed, in addition to those of normal local government, the leasing of land belonging to the state and yearly rent collections: the *nasi* seems to have appropriated all property formally owned by the Roman emperor. The *parnasin* were also in control of liaison with the military commander of the district.

Simeon ben Kosiba was authoritarian, as excerpts from several of the letters issued in his name make abundantly clear. He threatened, for example, the people of Tekoa with punishment for wasting their time on repairing their houses. When the inhabitants of the same town and those of Tel Arazin were reported to be unwilling to fight, they received a stern warning: "Let it be known to you that I will inflict punishment on you!" Ben Kosiba's menaces, as other evidence demonstrates, were no empty words: we know of named individuals, among them Joshua bar Tadmorayya, who were arrested on his order.

High-ranking officers were handled equally firmly. The two district commanders of En-gedi were told: "You sit, eat and drink from the property of the House of Israel, and care nothing for your brothers." A brief message addressed to another commander, Joshua ben Galgula, ends with the following ominous words: "I call Heaven as my witness that if anyone among the Galileans who are with you is ill-treated, I will put your feet in irons, as I did to ben Aphlul."

The letters so far published nowhere refer to the actual conduct of hostilities. The Romans are only rarely mentioned, once by name, and on a few other occasions as "the *goyim*" (the Gentiles). For instance, two local dignitaries explain to the same Joshua ben Galgula that they would have reported to him in person if "the *goyim*" had not been so close.

In regard to geographical data, some of the localities appearing in the letters are otherwise unknown, but those which are identifiable, e.g., En-gedi, Herodium, Tekoa, are all situated in the Judean Desert. According to rabbinic tradition, the last stand of the revolutionaries took place there, and Simeon was himself killed in the battle of Bether, S of Jerusalem.

One of the most fascinating features to emerge from these papyri is the considerable importance which the leader of the revolt attached to the strict observance of Jewish religious practices. In a letter, Simeon ben Kosiba directs that a certain Eleazar bar Hitta should be sent to him "before the Sabbath." According to another, his messengers are to be provided with accommodation so that they can rest on the sabbath, and not travel until the following day. A legal document specifies that taxes are to be paid in nature with tithed corn; in several deeds, reference is also made to the sabbatical year.

One final message from the *nasi* deserves to be quoted for its sheer irrelevance to the perils of the moment. "Simeon to Judah bar Manasseh at Kiriath Arabayya. I am sending you two donkeys and you shall dispatch with them two men to Jonathan bar Ba'ayan and Masabala in order that they pack and send you palm branches and citrons for the camp. You shall send other men from your place to bring you myrtles and willows. Tithe them and send them to the camp." These are instructions to collect and deliver to headquarters all that was required for the proper celebration of the Feast of Tabernacles, no doubt in the autumn of A.D. 134, a few months before the final collapse of the rebellion.

Though costly, the subsequent Roman victory was total. The few surviving revolutionaries fled to inaccessible caves which with the passing of time became the burial places, not only of their MSS, but also of their families and themselves. The cave appropriately designated by the archaeologists as the Cave of Horrors has revealed the tombs, and also a large number of skulls and skeletons, of refugees who died of starvation. To one of them, a potsherd stands as a pathetic memorial. On it is written simply: "Saul the son of Saul. *Shalom* [Peace]!" *See also* BAR KOCHBA[S] §4*f*.

Bibliography. Editions of texts: P. Benoit, J. T. Milik, and R. de Vaux, *DJD II: Les grottes de Murabb'at* (1961); Y. Yadin, *The Ben Sira Scroll from Masada* (1965).

Preliminary editions and descriptions of discoveries: N. Avigad, Y. Yadin *et al.*, "The Expedition to the Judean Desert, 1960," *IEJ*, XI (1961), 1-72, and "The Expedition . . . 1961," *IEJ*, XII (1962), 167-262; Y. Yadin, "The Excavation of Masada—1963/64," *IEJ*, XV (1965), 1-120.

Archaeology: Y. Yadin, *The Finds from the Bar Kokhba Period from the Cave of Letters* (1963).

General studies: Y. Yadin, *Masada: Herod's Fortress and the Zealots' Last Stand* (1966), and *Bar-Kokhba* (1971); J. A. Fitzmyer, "The Bar Cochba Period," *Essays on the Semitic Background of the NT* (1971), pp. 305-54; E. Schürer, G. Vermes, F. Millar, *The History of the Jewish People in the Age of Jesus Christ (175 B.C.–A.D. 135)*, I (1973), 512, 515, 534-57.

Monographs: D. Barthélemy, *Les devanciers d'Aquila. Première publication intégrale du texte des fragments du Dodécaprophéton* (1963); E. Koffmahn, *Die Doppelurkunden aus der Wüste Juda* (1968).

G. VERMES

MAPS AND MAPPING. *See* CARTOGRAPHY OF PALESTINE[S].

MARCION. *See* MARCION, GOSPEL OF; GNOSTICISM §2*b*; GNOSTICISM[S] §4*a*.

***MARESHAH (CITY).** The present name, Tell Sandahannah, is probably an Arabic corruption of the crusader Church of St. Anna which was constructed in the vicinity. *See* MARESHAH for a survey of the city's history.

Excavations have revealed a typical Hellenistic city which flourished from the third to the first century B.C. Streets intersected at right angles, and buildings were constructed around an open court in each block. The city was divided into industrial, administrative, and religious sections. In the eastern quarter a building thought to be a temple has been discovered. Almost square, 450 by 480 feet, it was surrounded by two walls, the inner near the mound's edge and the outer a few feet below on the tell's slope. A revetment between the walls strengthened the inner one. Four corner towers constructed of brick-like soft limestone added to the city's defenses. Circumstantial evidence based on the account of the Nabatean destruction of the city in 40 B.C., after which Mareshah ceased to be occupied, has led some to conjecture that Herod the Great was born there and held family property in the vicinity.

Painted tombs found between Tell Sandahannah and Beit Jibrin provide valuable data for reconstructing the history and culture of Mareshah. Objects and graffiti, in Greek, Nabatean, and Aramaic, date the use of the tombs from the third to the first century B.C. Access is through a stone door, from which steps lead down into an entrance hall and then to burial rooms. Single rows of perpendicular, triangular-topped burial niches, each high enough to hold two bodies, are cut into the walls of the burial halls. The triangular or gabled roofs of the burial niches probably represent a temple. Some tombs contain larger vaults probably intended as sarcophagi for the chief figures buried there. A ledge extends around the burial halls, with small square niches below to contain the bones of decomposed corpses. The painted friezes of the tombs exhibit a wide variety of African animals, human forms, and Cerberus of Greek and Roman mythology. Among the inscriptions there is a reference to the Idumean god Qos, and to a Sidonian, Apollophones, who ruled Marissa (Mareshah) for thirty-three years. One of the most celebrated finds is a small terra-cotta figurine of Aphrodite, which some scholars date several centuries after the destruction of Mareshah.

In the area around Mareshah, 132 carefully cut *columbaria* (lit. dovecotes) caves have been explored. Some scholars maintain they were for human burial, others that they were for raising doves sacred to the Aphrodite-Atargatis cult. Approximately one third of the caves are cross shaped; in them row upon row of cubical niches have been cut, with one cave containing over two thousand. Archaeological evidence dates these *columbaria* from the third to the first century B.C. The other caves are circular or square, and have, in addition to the carved niches, tall conical pillars, generally in the center. These caves continued in use until the fourth century A.D. Niches in both types of caves are eight inches in height, width, and depth. Discoveries at other sites prove that pillars and doves were sacred to Aphrodite and Atargatis. This, plus the fact that the niches were too small to contain burial remains, gives support to the cultic view. Other scholars, however, claim the niches are sufficiently large to hold ashes of the deceased.

Bibliography. M. Avi-Yonah, "A Reappraisal of the Tell Sandaḥannah Statuette," *PEQ* (1967), pp. 42-44; Y. Ben-Arieh, "Caves and Ruins in the Beth Govrin Area," *IEJ*, XII (1962), 47-61; B. Couroyer, "Inscription Coufigue de Beit Gibrin," *RB*, LXXI (1964), 73-79; E. Goodenough, *Jewish Symbols in the Greco-Roman Period*, I (1953), 65-75, 80, 83, 127, 143-44; E. Oren, "The 'Herodian Doves' in the Light of Recent Archaeological Discoveries," *PEQ* (1968), pp. 56-61.

T. O. HALL, JR.

*MARI.

1. Location
2. Excavations
3. The royal archives
4. History
5. Economy
6. Society and administration
7. The cult
8. Mari and biblical research
Bibliography

For 1 and 2 *see* MARI.

3. The royal archives. Some twenty thousand cuneiform tablets were found in the palace levels of *ca.* 1800-1760 B.C. The bulk of these date from the time of Iasmaḫ-Adad and Zimri-Lim. A smaller corpus of texts dates to the time of Sumū-Iamam, and a few scattered documents stem from the reign of Iaḫdun-Lim. Most of the documents were administrative in content, concerned with the care of the palace and the feeding of its occupants. These, together with juridical, economic, and epistolary texts were found scattered throughout the vast palace. Except for a very few examples written in Hurrian, the tablets were composed in Akkadian. Divergence from the "classical" Akkadian of Hammurabi of Babylon, lexical peculiarities, and nouns that were obviously West Semitic indicate a population that spoke Amorite.

4. History. Although the first unequivocal reference to Mari was not inscribed earlier than the reign of Eannatum I of Lagash (*ca.* 2450), archaeological remains indicate the area of Mari to have been settled in the Jemdet Nasr period.

A recent discovery (1965) enhances the possibility that the beginning of Mari's history may have to be sought around 2600 B.C. A large jar was found which contains fifty-two objects, some of which are stylistically similar to artifacts from the famous royal graves of Ur. (*See* UR [CITY].) An inscribed lapis lazuli "pearl" states that it was dedicated by Mesannepada, king of Ur (*ca.* 2600). Two levels indicate periods of destruction attributed to Lugalzaggesi of Uruk and Sargon of Agade. These destructions inaugurate a period, half a millennium long, in which Mari was dependent on various Mesopotamian powers (2400-1900 B.C.). We do possess the name of a number of *šakkanakkû* (governors). Kupper offers some evidence to reconstruct plausible chronological sequences for reigns, beginning in the Ur III period and ending with the arrival of the Lim dynasty.

Iaggid-Lim was probably not the Amorite leader who established a dynasty in Mari of the Old Babylonian period, but he is the first about whom we have historical information. A remarkable letter sent to a god tells us that Iaggid-Lim was occupied in battling the king of neighboring Terqa. His son, Iaḫdun-Lim, made an expedition to the Mediterranean. Although the latter boasted of exacting tribute from enemies he had subdued on his journey homeward, it is likely that no permanent benefits were obtained by Mari.

Shamshi-Adad, a native of Terqa who had managed to occupy the throne of Asshur, probably instigated a palace revolt which ultimately ended with his son, Iasmaḫ-Adad, becoming the new ruler of Mari. The legitimate heir to the throne, Zimri-Lim, escaped to find shelter, probably in Aleppo-Iamḫad. It is likely that Iasmaḫ-Adad's control of Mari lasted not more than a decade. With Shamshi-Adad's death, Zimri-Lim recovered his throne, aided by his father-in-law, the powerful king of Iamḫad, Iarim-Lim. Recently published documents indicate that the struggle, requiring a number of campaigns, ended in the escape of Iasmaḫ-Adad.

After the death of Iarim-Lim, king of Iamḫad, relations between Mari and Aleppo deteriorated. The new ruler, Hammurabi, directed a reordering of alliances, favoring his namesake in Babylon over Zimri-Lim. Difficulties between the allies developed mostly as a result of Mari's economic policies. Additionally, evidence indicates that after the death of Iarim-Lim, Mari was no longer acting as dutiful vassal. Babylonian troops destroyed Mari in two stages. Hammurabi of Babylon, in the thirty-second through thirty-fourth years of his reign, with the tacit approval of Iamḫad, dismembered Mari (*ca.* 1757, "middle" CHRONOLOGY) and divided the spoils with Aleppo. Although a small settlement remained there, at least five hundred years later, the glorious days of Mari had ended.

5. Economy. The period following the demise of the Ur III Empire saw a redistribution of economic power from the hands of S Mesopotamian (i.e., Sumerian) rulers to those of dynasts who settled all along the Euphrates. (*See* SUMER §2*c*.) Because of its geographical situation Mari was in a position to benefit from the transfer of goods and raw materials from one area to another. Heavy taxes were levied on raw products such as wood, stone, and cereals, as these were shipped between the nations. Tin trade, in particular, seems to have prospered the kings of Mari, as Mari distributed Elamite tin to Levantine markets. The manufacturing of clothing, leather objects, metal vessels, and weaponry were other profitable ventures. Not the least source of Mari's income were the tribute payments from minor allies and numerous vassals rendered in exchange for security.

6. Society and administration. The Mari texts speak of *awīlum, muškēnum,* and *wardum,* the three "classes" of the Hammurabi law code. This terminology should not be forced into specific definitions. F. R. Kraus tries to show that the term *awīlum* in Old Babylonian refers to a "privileged, elite person." This view holds well, in a number of instances, for Mari. The term is also used in a more social and legal context to mean: "a messenger from [X], a ruler of [X]." *Muškēnum,* sometimes contrasted to *awīlum,* at Mari refers to the "common citizenry," and not to "serfs" as it is sometimes claimed. Whereas the king, his family, and his top administrators certainly belonged to the elite class, it is not possible to ascertain the proper position for the officers, merchants, messengers and traveling artisans who are mentioned in the texts. As to *wardum,* "slaves," most of the Mari references indicate that this group consisted of those who failed to repay loans or who were captured in military clashes.

a. The king. One of the famous Mari wall paintings depicts the ceremony which took place whenever a prince, at the death of his father, was invested with the symbols of kingship. The temple area, in which the king is depicted as meeting the goddess Ishtar, is remarkably reminiscent of Solomon's house of worship. One document (ARM X:10) hints that in another ceremony the king received the acclamation of his soldiers.

The king was constantly on the move. Records of rations for the king's table generally indicate that only during the months of December through May was the king likely to remain in his capital. The rest of the year was devoted to his activities in the provinces and in foreign lands. The warmer months were set aside for warfare. While away on expedition, the king kept in touch with developments at home by means of fast couriers. Particularly during those days, the king sought advice from the gods, sent to him through "prophets." Other travels of the king saw him visiting shrines of provincial gods, dispensing justice, meeting with foreign potentates, and visiting foreign courts and temples. To ease the burden of such travel, palaces were built in four localities outside of Mari. These palaces were equipped with miniature courts complete with wives, bureaucrats, attendants, and workers.

A letter informs Zimri-Lim of the king of Ugarit's desire to have his emissary visit the Mari palace. According to archaeological evidence, the palace was a remarkable building of over 250 rooms and open courtyards, covering an area of some eight acres. Within it, one finds not only the royal and guest chambers but also workshops, a scribal school, storehouses, and kitchens. Many of the walls were decorated with frescoes. One document tells us that at least four hundred persons were employed in the palace. Meals were prepared by a large kitchen staff. Meats were not plentiful, probably eaten only after the offering of sacrifices. Seasonal bounties, however, included pickled grasshoppers, wild truffles, and choice fish. Good wine, honey, and olive oil were shipped from the N. Even in the summer's heat, an ingenious structure stored ice that had been transported by night from cooler climates. For entertainment, the king hunted lions and deer, enjoyed watching performances of trained (?) bears, and personally selected attractive maidens for his large corps of dancers and singers.

b. The queen. The future queen was probably selected for the prince by a reigning monarch eager to cement political relations with a ruler of equal status. A first wife could not easily be repudiated, or indeed even slighted. This is confirmed by a letter in which Shamshi-Adad scolds his son for neglecting his wife, hence ultimately humiliating her father, the king of Qatna.

Our documents most often speak of Šiptu, daughter of Iarim-Lim of Iamḫad and Zimri-Lim's queen. Šiptu's correspondence reveals her to have performed as an "acting king" while her husband was away from the capital. Her letters to Zimri-Lim, published mostly in ARM X; are full of encouragement, advice, and solicitous exhortations: "May my Lord protect his body from sun-blisters" (X:11); "May my Lord act according to the god's order" (X:11). In general, however, most of Šiptu's letters concern her activities as a palace administrator. Responding to her husband's requests, she directed the dispatch of foodstuffs, wine, and other objects to her husband and to other potentates (X:131); made sure that garlic was properly dried before storage (X:136); supervised the division of an estate (X:134); kept watch over political hostages (X:124); took action to prevent the spread of a contagious disease (X:129, 130); controlled access to sealed storerooms (XIII:22; XIII:14; X:12); prevented officials from remaining idle (X:157, 154); and acted in moments when quick decisions were needed (X:160).

But it is in her cultic involvement that Šiptu appears to be most unusual. One text (X:120) records Zimri-Lim's order for the queen to offer sacrifices to a goddess. Additionally, Šiptu receives precise instruction from her husband on the process of extracting information from the gods. It was her responsibility, too, to collect prophetic utterances and to communicate them, together with necessary proofs of authority, to the king. In X:4, one even notes the queen's readiness to promote her own interpretation of a divine revelation.

c. The royal family. Zimri-Lim's children, it appears, were all female, although at least one male child died young. Some of his daughters were married to vassals who might best promote the king's cause, and some were married to court officials. We are fortunate to possess a number of letters written by these ladies, for they add a dimension to our knowledge of Near Eastern society rarely attested to elsewhere. Some of the girls, happily married, wrote to bolster their husbands' positions before the king. Others bitterly complained about their fate, threatened to come back home, or even talked of suicide. Two sisters, like the daughters of Laban, even married the same person; one was desperately unhappy, while the other basked in her husband's favor.

A number of girls were dedicated as priestesses to gods, local and foreign. One princess was sent to Sippar as a "daughter-in-law" of the god Shamash. Two others remained, unmarried, in the palace. Zimri-Lim's sister became the high priestess of Adad. *See* WOMAN IN THE ANCIENT NEAR EAST[S].

d. Administrative personnel. For convenience' sake, the government of Mari could be divided into two branches: that of Mari proper and that which ruled the provinces. The bureaucrats, however, easily moved from one position to another. For this reason, it is not surprising to note the presence of the same functionary at a number of localities. Bureaucrats survived, largely undisturbed, the upheavals brought about by changes in dynasties. Obviously administrative talent was rated higher than allegiance to individual leaders.

Kupper and Marzal have provided us with the greatest insight into the administration of the provinces. Two terms seem to be used for the governor: *merḫum* and *šāpiṭum*. The first title seems to include an additional power, that of a military commander. While the etymology of the first term is unclear, the second term is undoubtedly derived from a root similar to biblical *šāphaṭ* (to judge). One cannot, however, equate the activities of the Mari *šāpiṭum* with the biblical *šōpēṭ* (Judge). The former was only incidentally concerned with administration of justice. Rather, he performed the king's will in areas where the king was not likely to be present. The *šāpiṭum's* authority ranged widely over a number of personnel who were probably appointed by the king. The *abu bītim* may have been an aide to the governor, yet probably reported to the king any unusual activity. A third-level rank was that of the *ša sikkatim,* whose specific functions are yet to be determined. These bureaucrats, established as leaders of provincial districts, acted through the agency of local authorities, whether village chieftains (*suqāqu*), elders, or leaders of townships. As executors of the king's decision, the *šāpiṭum* and the *merḫum* were provided with police, soldiers, and scribes. Their decisions dealt as much with keeping the district safe from nomadic invasion as with collecting taxes due to the palace, repairing canals and dikes on royal land, and when needed, ministering to the needs of local gods.

Mari and the palace were administered by the king; but when he was absent, by the queen or by a high official. The king apparently had a private secretary whose powers were wide. There were also persons given the titles of "king's bodyguard," "friends," "beloveds," and "acquaintances." It is this group, probably, that shared the king's table and it is from this group, very likely, that the king chose emissaries to foreign potentates. Such was the *ḫazannu* sent to vassals as a "resident delegate." The *šandabakkû* and the *šatammu* also lived in Mari, and, together with other officials, these illiterate officials could be considered all-purpose bureaucrats, able to shoulder a variety of responsibilities, not the least being the dispensation of materials stored within the palace under their supervision. Additionally, they controlled workshops in which were produced textiles, jewelry, furniture, and armament. There were, however, a few "specialists"—officials who directed scribal, musical, and dance instruction.

e. The military. The military was drawn from the citizenry, the number of soldiers being considerably enlarged by levies on "nomadic" groups. The act of registering and tallying the citizens for military purposes involved scribes and officials in a ceremony called the *tēbibtum.* This subject was studied by, among others, Speiser and Kupper. While Speiser highlighted the military connotation of the term, Kupper emphasized the religious involvement in a purification ceremony. Some scholars have found parallelism with biblical institutions detailed in Exod. 30 and Deut. 20.

The conscript's time of duty probably lasted throughout the hostilities, which diminished as cold weather approached. The forces on either side of the battle could reach enormous proportions. One of Shamshi-Adad's wars saw him raise some sixty thousand men. Military organizations, theoretically headed by the king, included the following commissioned personnel: the *rabi amurrim* (general; literally, "leader of the Amurru people"); the *rabi pirsim* (squad leader); the *laputtûm* (lieutenant); the UGULA 10.LÚ (corporal); the *rēdûm* ("privileged" soldier); the *bā'irum* and the *be'rum,* (draftee and "tenant" draftee). One West Semitic term, *baddum,* probably refers to "leader of a scouting team."

The weaponry employed included throw sticks, bows and arrows, slings, spears/lances, axes, maces, swords, and daggers. Heavy weaponry included a variety of chariots, siege towers, breach-mines, rams. Flaming arrows and torches were also used to attack any city defended by ramparts. The soldier wore a helmet, hauberk, and a codpiece; he carried a large shield and a ram's horn.

Elaborate rituals, both religious and political, preceded military undertakings. The king wrote a letter to the gods and to his protective spirits (cf. I:3; IV:68), sacrificed at local shrines, consulted the omens, and collected oaths of support from his officers. Data about the enemy were gathered from itinerant artisans, friendly merchants, and affected vassals. Ambassadors at foreign courts kept their ears open, seeking information from "secret sources." Evidence was gathered from intercepted documents and from spies. Occasionally fifth columnists and rumor-mongers were injected into disputed areas to demoralize the citizenry. Assassination was attempted as a quick solution to a thorny issue.

Defeat meant a dismantled rampart, burnt fields, and destroyed homes. Prisoners were led away to slavery. There was a possibility, however, for ransoming the males. Females entered the workshops of the victors. Those of nobler blood were either killed or taken as hostages. At religious ceremonies some prisoners were released.

f. Nomads. One of Mari's important contributions is undoubtedly the light its archives shed on Near Eastern nomadism. (*See* NOMADISM[S].) Kupper was the first to evaluate the nature and extent of nomadic culture among the Amorites of the Old Babylonian period. Additionally, our understanding has appreciably deepened due to a large extent to the works of M. B. Rowton and A. Malamat. Malamat studied the tribal terminology, *ummatum, ḫibrum,* and *gâ'um,* and showed that all three terms have Hebrew cognates and refer to nomadic conglomerations. Terms such as *nawum* and *ḫaṣārum* seem to retain their full meaning, "settlement," even beyond patriarchal time. Rowton distinguishes between "enclosed" and "bedouin" nomadism. While the latter type is to be found in Central Asia and in the Arabian deserts, the former was prevalent in the areas that concerned Mari and the biblical writers. In these last regions, no sharp distinction is to be made between the world of nomads and that of sedentary folk. Urban settlements were encircled, if not pockmarked, with pastoral land. Mari's nomads depended not on the camel, but on the sheep, an animal whose nature did not allow for long and deep forays into desert regions. Constant return to well-watered regions, particularly in the warmer period, was necessary. Additionally, the conveniences of the settled regions were needed even in winter, for sheep do not weather well the cold season in the mountains to the N. The ensuing interaction between the state and the *nawum,* the migratory group within the tribe, fostered mutual dependence and, at the same time, mutual hostilities. Our records from Mari disclose the existence of tribes that had, in this atmosphere, struck a balance of varying proportions between these two antithetical positions. Depending on the strength, determination, and independence of the tribal leadership, the rulers of Mari would, with varying degrees of success, extend their authority and usurp the right to determine the pattern of seasonal migration.

7. The cult. Although we possess data on the pantheon at Mari before the Old Babylonian dynasty, this survey will concentrate on the era of the Lim dynasty (*ca.* 1800-1760 B.C.). The most striking document dating to this period enumerates the distribution of sacrificial sheep to the various temples and gods of Mari. The largest consignment, seven sheep, was offered to the goddess Diritum. This is a bit surprising, since her main shrine was located in Dēr, a village about a day's journey from the capital. Six sheep were offered to each of the following deities [(f) indicates females]: (f) Bēlet-ekallim ("The Lady of the Palace"), Dagan, (f) Ninhursagga, Shamash, Itur-Mer, (f) Annunitum, and Nergal. Two sheep each were given to: Shamash of the Heavens, Sin, IGI•-KUR, (f) Nanni, (f) Ḫanat ("Anat"), (f) Ishtar, (f) Bēlet-Agade, Numušda, (f) Kišitum ("Lady of Kish"), (f) Ḫišamitum ("Lady of Hišamta," a local village), (f) Marat-Altim. A sheep each was granted to (f) Ishtar of the Palace, (f) Ninkarrak, (f) Išḫara, and (f) Bēlet-ḫiṣari ("Lady of the Enclosure").

It is interesting to note the heterogeneous nature of this pantheon. Some deities are Sumerian in origin; others Amorite in background. A few are known to have been worshiped in S Mesopotamia; some are named after cities in which they reigned; others are unique, as yet, to Mari. The archives and the personal names contained therein reveal Mari's knowledge of over 140 deities. Among the West Semitic deities known are: Abba, Addu, Amurru, Ašar, Ašmun, Askur, Dagan, Epuḫ (Yapuḫ), Eraḫ (Yareḫ), Ešuḫ (Yašuḫ), Ḫal ('Al), Ḫammu ('Ammu), (f) Ḫanat ('Anat), Ḫatta, Ḫawran (Ḫoron), (Y) akrub-El, El, (Y) atur-Mer (?), (f) Lab (w) a, Laban, Malik, Nas (s) i, Naru, Neḫim, Rasap (Rešep), and Salim. Hurrian deities such as Tešub, Ḫepat, and Allai were worshiped in the area of Saggaratum, one of the king's residential cities.

Many festivals in honor of individual deities are known to have been celebrated. Preserved in a somewhat fragmentary condition is the following description of a ritual for Ishtar. An early meal is followed by presentation of offerings before the gods and their emblems. The king dressed in a special garment and sat on a sailor's seat, flanked by his "favorite" and by his bodyguard. As chanting, accompanied by musical instruments, was performed by the priests, acrobatic feats and dramatic performances were presented. Libations and display of provisions ended the ceremony.

Of temple personnel we know the following: priestesses, *kalû* (singers), *bārû* (diviners), *āpilum* (prophets), *muḫḫum* (ecstatics), *assinu* (transvestites), *kumru* (priests), and lower-level temple functionaries. It is unlikely that the average Mari citizen played a role in cultic presentations, except possibly to observe the statues of the deities as they were carried outside their temples. The *kispu* ceremony required the king, at least once a month, to offer sacrifices to the spirits of his ancestors.

8. Mari and biblical research. The fact that preliminary reports on Mari's archives indicated the nature of the documentation to be concerned with the activities of Middle Bronze Age Amorites from the Middle and Upper Euphrates Valley attracted early the attention of those who were predisposed to place the patriarchal age within a similar context. (*See* PATRIARCHS[S].) It would be fair to state that attempts to use Mari documentation to confer historicity on the patriarchal narrative have largely failed. Success has been achieved, however, when some Mari institutions were compared with those drawn from the OT.

a. Geography, ethnology, onomastics. The Mari archives have given us valuable information on Upper Mesopotamia, the region which included ARAM-NAHARAIM, home of the biblical patriarchs.

Two cities, Naḫur and Haran, play a large role in the politics of Mari. Haran was an important trading center. The Mari archives have also furnished us with substantial information concerning movements of tribal and ethnic groups around 1800 B.C. Still at issue is the connection between one tribe, the DUMU-Iamina, and the BENJAMINITES of the OT.

Mari's onomastica provide the biblical scholar with the most potent arguments in favor of dating the patriarchs into the second millennium. The names of Abi-ram (Abraham), Laban (cf. also Aḫi-Laban, Il-Laban), Iaḫqub-el (Jacob), etc. occur in lists from the Sumū-Iaman period.

b. Covenant making. *See* Ass[S] §2.

c. Census. Speiser, who studied the Mari institution of *tēbibtum,* believes that a connection could be made with the Hebrews' *kippurîm,* a personal (*nepheš*) tax of half a shekel aimed at warding off a plague in the wake of a census (Exod. 30:12). Speiser further points to the narrative of II Sam. 24 which records the outbreak of a pestilence among the Israelites following a census ordered by David. Speiser suggests that this occurred precisely because no *kopher* was offered by David's people after the tallying was completed.

d. Prophetic texts. *See* PROPHECY IN THE ANCIENT NEAR EAST[S] §5*c*.

e. Law, patrimony. In the OT the term *naḥălâ* (patrimony) implies a property whose transfer is affected only within a family or a tribe. The twelve tribes, in sharing the Promised Land, received territory which was expected to remain whole and unbroken. In Mari, six texts make allusion to the verb *naḫālum* with a meaning which parallels biblical usage.

f. Adoption. ARM VIII:1, a text dating to the Assyrian period (trans., *ANESTP,* p. 545), records that an adopted son would receive a double share of the inheritance should his adopters choose to acquire more sons. Mendelsohn believes this practice, attested also in the OT, originated among seminomadic, agricultural societies. On this problem, however, *see* De Vaux, *Histoire ancienne d'Israël,* I, pp. 238-39.

Bibliography. Extensive bibliographies are in H. Huffmon, *Amorite Personal Names in the Mari Texts* (1965), pp. 274-77; 281-99; A. Malamat, *BA,* XXXIV (1971), 22. The "Keilschriftbibliographie" of *Orientalia* is a yearly index with items on Mari often found under sections 33 and 45. *See also* A. Malamat, *IEJ,* XXI (1971), 37-66, *Orientalia,* XL (1971), 75-89, and in *Near Eastern Archaeology in the Twentieth Century,* ed. J. Sanders (1970), pp. 164-77; G. Dossin, *RA,* LXIV (1970), 17-44, 97-106, 163-68, *Syria,* XLVIII (1971), 1-19, and L (1973), 1-12; J. R. Kupper, *RA,* LXV (1971), 113-18; M. Birot, *RA,* LXVI (1972), 131-34, *Syria,* L (1973), 1-12; F. R. Kraus, *Vom Mesopotamischen Menschen der Altbabylonischen Zeit und seiner Welt* (1973); W. H. Ph. Römer, *Frauenbriefe über Religion, Politik, und Privatleben in Māri* (1971); J. M. Sasson, *Iraq,* XXXV (1972), 55-67, *JCS,* XXV (1973), 59-78; M. B. Rowton, *Orientalia,* XLII (1973), 247-58, *JNES,* XXXII (1973), 201-15, and *JESHO,* XVII (1974), 1-30; M. Held, *BASOR,* 200 (1970), 32-40; A. Marzal, *Orientalia,* XLI (1972), 359-77, and *JNES,* XXX (1971), 186-217; E. A. Speiser, *Oriental and Biblical Studies* (1967), pp. 160-186; I. Mendelsohn, *BASOR,* 156 (1959), 38-40.

J. M. SASSON

***MARK, GOSPEL OF.** Before the general acceptance of FORM CRITICISM it was possible to argue from the PAPIAS tradition of the early church that the evangelist Mark had been a companion of Peter and that he had composed his gospel largely from eyewitness reminiscence of the ministry of Jesus, particularly that of Peter himself. The gospel would then be interpreted as essentially a chronicle of the ministry of Jesus. For such an interpretation *see* MARK, GOSPEL OF esp. §§2, 8. But such a view is held today only by a small minority of scholars, who either reject form criticism or seek to minimize its findings. Beginning with the work of Lightfoot and Marxsen (*see* §2 *below*), the interpretation of this gospel has proceeded with a full acceptance of form criticism.

1. Form criticism and the Gospel of Mark. So far as the Gospel of Mark is concerned form criticism made two points, one concerning the nature of the gospel *material* and one concerning the work of the evangelist, and hence the nature of the *gospel.* Form critics saw the material in the gospel, the SAYINGS OF JESUS and the stories about him, as having been formed, and in no small part actually created, in the tradition of the early Christian communities where it served a variety of purposes: missionary preaching and propaganda, catechetical instruction, exhortation, liturgical practice, and so on. This material had a long history of transmission, use, and interpretation in the early Christian communities, and when it reached the hand of Mark any element of historical reminiscence had long since been lost. The evangelist himself was primarily a collector and organizer of this traditional material, and his purpose in writing was to unite the characteristic Hellenistic Christian kerygma of Jesus as the crucified and risen Savior of men with the traditional Jesus material. The Gospel of Mark, therefore, is narrative proclamation.

This view of the gospel carried full conviction with regard to the nature of the gospel material; subsequent research has strengthened and refined the form-critical understanding of the sayings of Jesus and the stories about him. But the view of the work of the evangelist carried less conviction. The pioneer form critics were more interested in the traditional material and the history of its use in the early Christian communities than they were in the Gospel of Mark itself, and their statements about the evangelist and his work tended to be rather perfunctory. So far as the interpretation of the gospel was concerned, the way forward was shown by two scholars: R. H. Lightfoot in England and W. Marxsen in Germany.

2. Lightfoot and Marxsen on the Gospel of Mark. In a series of works (*see bibliog.*) Lightfoot introduced English readers to form criticism and set out to interpret the Gospel of Mark in light of its findings. He pioneered in the treatment of the evangelist as an author, paying particular attention to his compositional techniques, e.g., intercalation, and to his symbolic use of geographical references (especially Galilee). Lightfoot insisted that Mark be treated as a literary unit and any one part interpreted in light of its function in the whole. His work may be said to have reached a climax in the commentary on the gospel written by his pupil Nineham.

In Germany, Markan compositional techniques were also a special concern of Lohmeyer, and this concern for Markan composition led to the work of Marxsen. In a series of studies (on John the Baptist, the geographical outline in Mark, the word *evangelion,* Mark 13) Marxsen concerned himself with the evangelist's editing and compositional use of traditional material. In each instance he went on to consider the further editing of the Markan material by Matthew and Luke. Marxsen coined the term *Redaktionsgeschichte* (*see* REDACTION CRITICISM, NT[S]) to describe this method of approach to the gospels and so ushered in a new era in their interpretation.

3. From redaction criticism to literary criticism. Since redaction criticism is concerned to investigate the evangelist's editing and use of traditional material, it has been naturally accompanied by the attempt to isolate pre-Markan material in the text of the gospel and then to observe how it has been redacted. Such a procedure, however, is not only difficult to carry out, but also has obvious limitations. Consequently, although the attempt has not been abandoned, there is a growing tendency to turn to Markan composition of the gospel as a whole. This involves a study of the structure and the function of the various parts within it and observation of the themes the evangelist pursues, i.e., a general literary criticism of the gospel. More and more the evangelist is being considered as an author who has made extensive use of traditional material, but nonetheless *an author,* and a conscious attempt is being made to develop a literary-critical method that would be appropriate to the interpretation of the text he has created. An early move in this direction was made by Best, and it is a particular feature of the American interpretation of the gospel represented by such scholars as Weeden and Perrin.

4. Some issues in the most recent discussion. ***a. The question of a model.*** If, as many believe, this evangelist is the first to write a gospel, and hence the creator of a new literary genre, one must consider first of all what sort of a model he might have been following (*see* GOSPEL, GENRE[S]). Among the possibilities are the following.

i. The ARETALOGY, understood as a cycle of stories exhibiting the power of a hero figure, possibly concluding with an account of his death as an apotheosis. Koester and Robinson suggest that this was Mark's model.

ii. The PASSION NARRATIVE. A popular dictum concerning the gospel is that it is a "passion narrative with an extended introduction." Some scholars claim that the passion narrative in Mark is essentially pre-Markan, and that the evangelist composed the remainder of the gospel as an introduction to it (Marxsen, Burkill).

iii. Apocalyptic. Ch. 13 clearly plays an important role in the gospel, and the evangelist has an overall concern for the apocalyptic PAROUSIA of Jesus as SON OF MAN. This has led some scholars to suggest that Mark is modeling his work on Jewish Christian apocalyptic (so, in different ways, Kee and Perrin). *See* APOCALYPTICISM; APOCALYPTICISM [S].

b. Thematic concerns. A major feature of current interpretation of the gospel is recognition of the fact that the evangelist is an author who systematically pursues thematic concerns. Among the Markan themes being studied are:

i. The messianic secret. *See* SECRET, MESSIANIC[S].

ii. Christology, which many interpreters (e.g., Weeden, Perrin) see as a, if not the, major concern of the evangelist.

iii. Discipleship. It is clear that disciples and discipleship play a large role in the gospel (*see* DISCIPLESHIP[S]). Two extended and very different treatments of the theme are offered by Weeden and Meye.

iv. Galilee and the Gentile mission. Lightfoot and his pupils (Boobyer and Evans) have shown that two of the major concerns in the Gospel of Mark are for Galilee and the Gentile mission, and that the former is used symbolically for the latter.

v. Eschatology. Mark's understanding of the KINGDOM OF GOD and this understanding as a theme in the gospel has been investigated by Kelber.

c. Mark's purpose in writing. The older form-critical judgment that Mark's intention was to unite the Hellenistic kerygma and the Jesus tradition is too general. Increasing knowledge of the evangelist as an author has made more precise statements possible, even though recent discussion has not reached a consensus, except perhaps for recognition of the fact that any understanding of the purpose of the evangelist must take into account and integrate all facets of the gospel uncovered by the redaction- and literary-critical investigation. If Mark is an author exercising control over his material, then all that material must be embraced in a statement of his purpose in writing.

Although there is no scholarly consensus, there is some agreement that the evangelist is writing for a community or communities of Christians caught up in a period of apocalyptic fervor occasioned by the circumstances of the Jewish War, and that he is writing either shortly before or shortly after the fall of Jerusalem in A.D. 70. His purpose is to help his readers prepare themselves for the coming of Jesus as Son of man, an event both he and they regard as imminent. To this end he composes what is essentially a *didactic history;* he tells the story of Jesus in such a way as to instruct his readers. He and his readers face the prospect of suffering as a prelude to the coming of Jesus as Son of man and the consequent glory which will be the reward of those who endure to the end. But Mark sees Jesus himself as having, of divine necessity, suffered his passion as a prelude to being redeemed out of his death, and quite literally out of his tomb, to be with God in the heavens until the moment of his coming on the clouds of heaven as Son of man. So his purpose is to prepare his readers to face the necessity of following their Master through the reality of suffering to the equal and indeed surpassing reality of the glory they will share with him at his (second) coming. In all probability Mark is writing specifically against a Christology which understood Jesus only in terms of glory, one which played down the reality of his suffering and of the prospective suffering of the believer, as only the necessary accompaniment to an apotheosis. For Mark, both the suffering and the glory are equally real. They were so for Jesus and they are to be so for the believer.

Bibliography. Commentaries: E. Lohmeyer, Meyer (1937); D. E. Nineham, *The Gospel of Saint Mark,* The Pelican Gospel Commentaries (1963); E. Schweizer, *The Good News According to Mark* (1968), specifically from a redaction-critical viewpoint.

Studies: E. Best, *The Temptation and the Passion: The Markan Soteriology,* NTSMS, II (1965); G. H. Boobyer, "Galilee and Galileans in St. Mark's Gospel," *BJRL,* XXXV (1952-53), 334-48; T. A. Burkill, *Mysterious Revelation* (1963), and *New Light on the Earliest Gospel* (1972); J. R. Donahue, *Are You the Christ? The Trial Narrative in the Gospel of Mark,* SBLDS, X (1974), argues for extensive Markan authorial activity in the passion narrative; C. F. Evans, "I will go before you into Galilee," *JTS,* NS V (1954), 3-18; H. C. Kee, *Jesus in History* (1970), pp. 104-47; W. Kelber, *The Kingdom in Mark* (1974); H. Koester and J. M. Robinson, *Trajectories through Early Christianity* (1971); R. H. Lightfoot, *History and Interpretation in the Gospels* (1935), *Locality and Doctrine in the Gospels* (1938), and *The Gospel Message of St. Mark* (1950); R. P. Martin, *Mark: Evangelist and Theologian* (1972), reviews the recent discussion and offers a conservative response to it; W. Marxsen, *Mark the Evangelist* (1956 [ET 1969]); R. P. Meye, *Jesus and the Twelve* (1968); F. Neirynck, *Duality in Mark: Contributions to the Study of the Markan Redaction,* BETL, XXXI (1972); N. Perrin, "The Christology of Mark: A Study of Methodology," *JR,* LI (1971), 175-87, "Towards an Interpretation of the Gospel of Mark," in *Christology and a Modern Pilgrimage,* ed. H. D. Betz (rev. ed., 1974), pp. 1-52, *The NT: An Introduction* (1974), esp. pp. 143-67, and *A Modern Pilgrimage in NT Christology* (1974); T. J. Weeden, *Mark: Traditions in Conflict* (1971).

N. PERRIN

MARK, SECRET GOSPEL OF. A title derived from an eighteenth-century Greek MS, discovered in 1958, which purports to transmit a section "from the letters" of Clement of Alexandria (*ca.* A.D. 150-215) to a certain (otherwise unknown) "Theodore" (Pl. I, line 1). In the process of warning about "the unspeakable teachings of the Carpocratians" (a second-century Gnostic sect), the author urges that their false version of Mark's Gospel must be distinguished from the evangelist's "secret Gospel" (II, 6-10). The latter is described as an expanded version of Mark's original gospel, prepared by him as "a more spiritual Gospel for the use of those who were being perfected" (I, 21-22). One narrative, said to have been included between Mark 10:34, 35, is quoted in full (II, 21–III, 11), as well as one sentence said to have been added after Mark 10:46*a* (III, 14-16).

The MS of Clement's letter, discovered in the library of the desert Monastery of Mar Saba near Jerusalem by Smith, occupies two and a half pages in the back of a printed book of the seventeenth century. The text breaks off in midsentence (III, 18). On the basis of orthography, an eighteenth-century date seems assured, and there has been general agreement that the MS preserves part of a previously unknown, but authentic, letter of the Alexandrian theologian.

Scholarly discussion has focused primarily on the significance of the narrative which Clement quotes here from the Secret Gospel. It tells of Jesus' raising a young man from the dead at Bethany, and mentions that the youth, six days later, came to Jesus at night and was "taught . . . the mystery of the kingdom of God" (III, 10). Smith has argued that this story derives from an early Aramaic source common to Mark and John (cf. the story of the raising of Lazarus in John 11), and that it discloses that the historical Jesus practiced an esoteric baptism of certain disciples, singly and at night, perhaps with erotic aspects. There has been a virtually unanimous rejection of Smith's interpretation, however, as incautious and unfounded. Other scholars have pointed out fundamental errors in Smith's methodology and his misuse of ancient texts. The consensus is that this newly discovered fragment is indeed from Clement, but that it does not provide evidence of an ancient gospel source. What it brings to light, instead, is a hitherto unknown version of the Gospel of Mark, an esoteric gospel approved by Clement. It is to be classed with the other second-century apocryphal gospels. *See* APOCRYPHA, NT; APOCRYPHA, NT[S].

Bibliography. M. Smith, *Clement of Alexandria and a Secret Gospel of Mark* (1973), plates, transcription, translation, and commentary, with an interpretation of the significance of the discovery, and *The Secret Gospel* (1973), a popularized account and discussion; R. M. Grant, "Morton Smith's Two Books," *ATR,* LVI (1974), 58-64, outlines an alternative interpretation; H. Merkel, "Auf den Spuren des Urmarkus?" *ZThK,* LXXI (1974), 123-44, to date the most detailed examination of the evidence since Smith's, and the most extensive critique of Smith's interpretation, answered by Smith in *ZThK,* LXXII (1975), 133-50; R. E. Brown, "The Relation of 'The Secret Gospel of Mark' to the Fourth Gospel," *CBQ,* XXXVI (1974), 466-85.

V. P. FURNISH

***MARRIAGE.** Marriage is in almost all societies that institution by which the nuclear family is established; this is so even in the frequent case in which the nuclear family is only a unit in a larger kin group such as the lineage or the clan. It is to be distinguished from mating in that it is formalized, and in that it has important functions in addition to the sexual gratification of its members. The functions of marriage in the OT are similar to those found for the majority of human societies: (*a*) the regulation of sexual behavior, especially of women; (*b*) companionship between husband and wife (Gen. 2), though this was often modified by the working of the double standard; (*c*) economic functions through family enterprises; (*d*) religious functions, in that the majority of festivals centered on participation by households; (*e*) most importantly, the procreation, legitimation, and socialization of children. In the absence of any clear doctrine of personal immortality, the Hebrews believed that a man lived on through his posterity. Thus, children were the supreme example of divine favor (Gen. 12:2; Deut. 28:9-11; Ps. 127:3-5), and childlessness was a curse (Gen. 15:2; Deut. 28:18, 30). The desire for large families is characteristic of both pastoral and horticultural societies. So crucial was the need for sons to perpetuate the lineage that in one case a man without sons gave his daughter to a slave so she could bear children (I Chr. 2:34-35).

Marriage was regarded as man's normal estate, and there was no recognized status for celibates (Isa. 4:1), who could be considered socially irresponsible. In this context, Jeremiah's divinely commanded celibacy (Jer. 16:1-4) becomes a sinister sign of impending judgment in which family lines will be cut off. In the NT, marriage is again seen as normal and honorable (Heb. 13:4), and Paul goes so far as to call compulsory celibacy a heresy (I Tim. 4:1-3). When he advises against marriage (I Cor. 7:26), it is clearly specified as being because of impending hard times.

1. **Who could or should marry?** Throughout the OT, it is taken for granted that Ego, the person taking the initiative, is the man (or his family), and all rules are so stated.

a. Incest taboo. The INCEST taboo prohibited marriage to certain women (Lev. 18:6-18): one's mother and stepmother, sister and half sister, granddaughter, father's and mother's sisters, and the wives of brother, father's brother, and son; also wife's mother, sister, daughter, and granddaughter. It is clear that all these prohibitions have as their aim the avoidance of conflicts within the nuclear family and the lineage.

A number of these seem not to have been operative in patriarchal times. Instances of marriage to half sister (Gen. 20:12), wife's sister (Gen. 29:21-30), and father's widow (I Chr. 2:24) are cited without reproach.

b. Endogamy. Hebrews were supposed to marry only within the twelve tribes, though this was often disregarded. The reason given was to avoid cultural-religious syncretism (Exod. 34:15-16; Deut. 7:3-6; Josh. 23:11-13); there was no "racial" basis for this taboo, as can be seen from the marriage of Moses with a Cushite (=black) woman, for which God defended him from the accusations of Miriam and Aaron (Num. 12:1-16). Throughout Israel's independent history, intermarriage was practiced, especially by kings, though it was condemned in the "official" view. Tribal exogamy may be inferred from the story (Judg. 21) of the tribe of Benjamin, to which the other tribes had vowed not to give wives. It proved necessary to find a city which had not made the vow, kill the men and nonvirgins, and give the virgins to Benjamin as wives. Ezra and Nehemiah (Ezra 9–10; Neh. 10:28-30) restored ethnic endogamy after the Exile. But by NT times (Acts 16:1-3; 24:24), Jews of the Diaspora married non-Jews.

c. Parallel cousin marriage. In the patriarchal period, there was a special form of preferential marriage within the patrilineage: the ideal mate was one's paternal parallel cousin (father's brother's daughter). Failing this specific person, another woman of one's patrilineage would do: one's half sister (Gen. 20:12), father's brother's granddaughter (Gen. 24), or even mother's brother's daughter (Gen. 29:21-30), since she was, in this case, also a member of the patrilineage by descent from Abraham's brother. There is another case (Exod. 6:20) in which a man is said to have married his father's sister. Though in most other societies, and in later times in Israel, many of these marriages would be considered incest, in a few societies they are normal. Specifically, they are found where there is a strong patrilineal lineage structure, a slight or nonexistent political structure apart from the lineage structure, and the custom of permitting women to inherit in their own right (Num. 27:1-11; 36; *see also* Lev. 22:12-13, where a woman loses certain rights when she marries outside her patrilineage). The effect of this custom is to keep within the lineage the wealth and the fertility of the woman, both important in interlineage conflicts. In Israel, as among Bedouin tribes, this custom persisted until the development of urbanism and the state (Josh. 15:16-19; Judg. 1:12-15), but it then largely disappeared, as among urbanized Arabs. At this later time, a number of the women became taboo, though not first cousins; and there are cases, especially among royalty, of paternal parallel cousin marriage (II Chr. 11:20-22).

d. The levirate. One could obtain wives also through the levirate, which specified (Gen. 38:6-26; Deut. 25:5-10) that when a married man died childless, his brother should marry the widow; the purpose was to beget children in the name of the dead man and to preserve lineage property (Ruth 4:1-6). Implicit, but certainly important, was the obligation to provide for the economic, social, and sexual needs of a widow still young enough to marry and to bear children. Though the obligation fell first on the brother of the dead man, it was in fact a corporate responsibility of his lineage, so that Judah accepted the blame for not providing for Tamar (Gen. 38:26). There was a recognized order of priority among the kin, in case there was no brother or in case someone chose not to do his duty (Ruth 2:20; 3:2, 12, 13; 4:1-10). Naomi had suggested to Ruth, since Naomi could have no more sons, that she was free to return to her father's home; but the fact that Ruth stayed with Naomi was highly regarded (Ruth 2:11-12). The levirate, then, functioned for some of the same purposes as parallel cousin marriage, though it lasted much longer (Matt. 22:23-28; Luke 20:27-33). In the first century, marriage to brother's wife during the brother's lifetime continued to be regarded as incest (Mark 6:16-19). Widows past child-bearing age were less fortunate (Ruth 1:12); they were classed with orphans and strangers who had no natural defenders, so that God took the responsibility (Ps. 146:9). It is not clear whether or not Caleb's marriage to his father's widow (I Chr. 2:24) is an extension of the levirate; though of course the rationale of providing children for a childless man would not be operative.

e. Marriages for alliance. Kings not infrequently, after the example of their neighbors, married foreign princesses to cement alliances (I Kings 3:1). Solomon merely carried this policy to extremes.

f. Captives and slaves. An important source of secondary wives, in times of external warfare (from the time of the Conquest through the time of the kingdoms), consisted of women taken captive. Since slavery was an accepted institution, it followed that victorious soldiers and wealthy men would have a ready supply of women who as their property could be used at their will (Num. 31:18-19; Deut. 21:10-14; *see* SLAVERY IN THE OT[S]). The patriarchs also took slaves as concubines, but these were the property of their wives (Gen. 16; 29:24, 29; 30:3-13), and they were used explicitly as surrogate ovaries and wombs to produce children who would belong to their mistresses. The story of Sarah and Hagar (Gen. 16:4-6) shows that human emotions can get in the way of accepted social practice.

2. Selection. Initiative in making a specific selection could be taken by the man's family, especially if he was young and was taking his first wife (Gen. 24). Or the man could take the initiative (Gen. 29; Judg. 14:1-2). In a few cases, a prominent man promised his daughter to whoever would perform some valorous feat (Josh. 15:16-19; I Sam. 17:25; 18:17-27). There is no case of marriage being initiated by a woman, at least on her own behalf.

3. Solemnization. The solemnization of marriage included the payment of bride wealth or suitor service, the engagement, and the wedding; not all parts were equally elaborate in all periods.

a. Bride wealth or suitor service. Like many other societies, the Hebrews felt that a man owed his prospective father-in-law compensation for the loss of his daughter, and especially of her progeny, which would strengthen another lineage. This compensation usually took the form of bride wealth (Gen. 34:12; Exod. 22:16), the amount of which is unspecified except in the case of a forced marriage after rape (Deut. 22:29). This bride price, or better, progeny price, should not be confused with the gifts made to the bride and to members of her family at the time of betrothal (Gen. 24:22, 30, 47, 53). It was rather the sign of a valid marriage and of the legitimacy and lineage affiliation of the subsequent children. Nor should it be confused with a dowry, which was rarely if ever practiced by the Hebrews, except in the form of slaves given to a bride by her father at the time of her marriage (Gen. 24:59; 29:24, 29; Josh. 15:18-19). It is said that Pharaoh gave his daughter the city of Gezer when she married Solomon (I Kings 9:16).

When a young man was deserving but poor, he could work for his father-in-law instead of paying bride wealth (Gen. 29:15-30).

b. Engagement. Once the matter of bride wealth was settled, the father of the bride made a solemn commitment to the groom (I Sam. 18:21*b*), which initiated the engagement. This was a serious matter. The groom enjoyed all rights of marriage short of cohabitation, and it required a divorce to break the engagement. Engaged men were exempt from military duty (Deut. 20:7). Rape of an engaged woman was treated as adultery (Deut. 22:23-27), and an engaged woman guilty of infidelity was punished for adultery. It was grounds for divorce (Matt. 1:18-19).

c. Wedding. A marriage could be solemnized with a minimum of fuss (Gen. 24:66-67). But as social life became more elaborate, so did weddings. At the appointed time, the groom and his friends would go to the bride's house (Song of S. 3:6-11), where they would find her veiled, richly dressed, and adorned with jewels (Ps. 45; Isa. 61:10). They would escort her, with singing and dancing, to the groom's home (Gen. 24:67; Ps. 45; I Macc. 9:39; Matt. 25:1-13). There would be a great feast (Gen. 29:22; Judg. 14:10) lasting seven to fourteen days, and including the singing of love songs (Song of Solomon). At some stage of the proceedings, there was, according to the Elephantine documents, the use of a solemn formula by the groom: "She is my wife, I am her husband, from this day forever." The marriage was consummated on the first night (Gen. 29:23), at which time it was the responsibility of the bride's family to preserve the tokens of her virginity (*see* VIRGINITY, TOKENS OF[S]).

Since marriage was an arrangement between families for their mutual benefit, it could happen that one party might for his own advantage try to alter the terms at the last minute; this was usually the bride's father, as Jacob (Gen. 29:23-26), Samson (Judg. 14:15–15:2), and David (I Sam. 25:44) discovered to their chagrin.

4. Residence. In patriarchal times, as might be expected, the prevalent residence pattern was patrilocal; that is, the new couple lived with the groom's family (Gen. 24:67; Judg. 12:9). Exceptions were due to special circumstances (Gen. 31:26, 43). Later, as the Hebrews in Canaan became town dwellers, the single nuclear family became relatively more independent, and sons built their own houses.

5. Polygyny. From the earliest times for which we have reliable records, polygyny was known and accepted. However, it was never statistically prevalent, if only because of the normal demographic balance between men and women. Economic considerations would also make it hard for most men to have more than one wife. Abraham apparently had only one wife at a time (Gen. 16:1-4; 25:1-6), though he also had concubines. Isaac seems to have married only Rebekah (Gen. 24:67). Esau had two Hittite wives (Gen. 26:34) and one wife who was a granddaughter of Abraham (Gen. 28:9). Jacob had two wives and two concubines (Gen. 29:21–30:13). It is not until Gideon that we hear of a man with "many" wives (Judg. 8:30), but their number is unspecified. However, it was with the institution of the monarchy that polygyny came to be practiced on a large scale. David had six wives whose names are recorded (I Sam. 25:39-43; 27:3; II Sam. 3:2-5), and Solomon had a genuine Oriental royal harem of seven hundred wives and three hundred concubines, most of them to cement alliances. However, the "proper" attitude was that a king should not have many wives, because of their bad moral influence (Deut. 17:17).

Concubinage was a recognized status decidedly lower than that of a wife, and a concubine's children did not have the rights of a wife's children, unless their mother was a stand-in for her mistress, in which case they were the mistress' children (Gen. 21:14; 25:5-6).

As do most polygynous people, the Hebrews recognized that relations between co-wives could be strained and hostile. Jealousy over the husband's favors and over privileges for their children often pitted wife against wife. The contempt of a fertile wife for a barren one was a source of hatred. One approach to a solution was to require a kind of "equal time" between the wives, and the law required that the first-born son of an unloved wife be given his rights rather than the younger children of a beloved wife (Deut. 21:15-17).

Wives and concubines of a deposed or conquered king were booty for his conqueror (II Sam. 12:8; I Kings 20:3). For this reason Absalom's act of going in to his father's concubines during the latter's flight (II Sam. 16:20-22) was considered such a great insult, and Adonijah's request to be given Abishag was tantamount to a demand that he be given the throne (I Kings 2:13-25).

In NT times, monogamy seems to have been the normal practice, though there is no explicit prohibition of polygyny except for church leaders (according to a possible exegesis of I Tim. 3:2, 12; Tit. 1:6).

6. Rights and obligations. The respective rights and obligations of spouses seem, at first sight, to be totally lopsided. The husband has authority and freedom, especially in sex, and the wife is subject to him and liable to divorce or other penalty for displeasing him. An adulterous wife was punished for violating her husband's rights; an adulterous man was punished only if he had infringed upon some other man's rights.

But it must not be thought that the wife had no rights. Especially in the case of polygyny, minimal fairness was enforced on the husband. Furthermore, wives had property rights of their own, e.g., in slaves given them by their fathers. Finally, a wife always had ways of asserting herself, including the withholding of sexual favors, if her rights were neglected.

In a more positive sense, the picture of the ideal wife (Prov. 31:10-31) is hardly that of a weak, secluded, compliant child. She clearly has a great deal of authority and knows how to use it, and her economic role is extremely important. And even in the case of sharply defined specialization in the roles of the sexes, this very fact has been found to give each sex certain exclusive prerogatives which can be translated into leverage.

The NT, while it does not eradicate the double standard, does give teachings which undermine it just as surely as they undermine slavery: the spiritual equality of the sexes "in Christ" (Gal. 3:28) and the teaching that husbands ought to love their wives "as Christ loved the church" (Eph. 5:25) both clearly imply that though rights and duties may not be identical, they are essentially equal. *See also* FAMILY; WIDOW; SEX, SEXUAL BEHAVIOR[S]; DIVORCE[S].

Bibliography: S. Baron, *A Social and Religious History of the Jews,* I (2nd ed., 1952); C. S. Ford and F. A. Beach, *Patterns of Sexual Behavior* (1951); R. Fox, *Kinship and Marriage* (1967); C. Lévi-Strauss, *The Elementary Structures of Kinship* (1969); G. P. Murdock, *Social Structure* (1949); R. Patai, *Sex and Family in the Bible and in the Middle East* (1959); E. L. Peters, "Aspects of the Family among the Bedouin of Cyrenaica," in M. N. Nimkoff, *Comparative Family Systems* (1965), pp. 121-46.

C. R. TABER

MARRIAGE IN THE NT. From the few references to marriage in the NT it is not possible to assemble a specific Christian teaching about marriage and the marital relationship. In general, marriage is accepted and the partners urged to love and care for each other; doubtless most early Christians continued to live within and create new families, regardless of the sometimes intense expectation of the end of history. Nevertheless the church was not all of the same view, and differences both of substance and nuance can be seen.

1. The esteem accorded to marriage in the early NT period. The basic tone is set by the dispute about DIVORCE in Mark 10:2-9, the nucleus of which may go back to Jesus himself. There marriage is said to be an indissoluble bond between two persons, whose selves are altered by virtue of the sexual union. The bond has its sanction in God's will as expressed in the created order; that is, it is rooted in the very nature of humankind (Gen. 1:27; 2:24). In the gospels, the joyous marriage feast gives rise to metaphors which describe the joy and bliss of life in the kingdom of God (*see* MARRIAGE §3).

Paul, while encouraging unmarried people to remain single (*see* §2 *below*), nevertheless accepted marriage as a positive and caring relationship between two people (I Cor. 7:32, 35) and exhorted both husband and wife to express this care in their sexual relations (I Cor. 7:3-5). It appears that most church leaders of his day were married (I Cor. 9:5). *See* ETHICS IN THE NT[S] §3*d*ii.

2. Tendencies toward the single life. At the same time there is evidence of an early dethronement of marriage from the all-important place it held in Jewish society. Jesus and Paul, as John the Baptist before them, do not appear to have been married. Some Corinthian Christians apparently believed that because sex was evil marriage should not be consummated, if, as is likely, I Cor. 7:1 cites their view rather than Paul's own. In the following verse Paul objects to this view. Nevertheless he does promote the single state for any of the unmarried or widows who would not find such celibacy disturbing (I Cor. 7:8-9, 36-40). The interpretation of I Cor. 7:36-38 is uncertain. It refers either to fathers who have refused to offer their daughters in marriage or, more likely, to engaged couples who have hesitated to take the final step of formal marriage. In either case it evidences an inclination by some Corinthians toward the single state. Contrary to the Corinthian ascetics, Paul's reasons for remaining unmarried are (1) the avoidance of the inevitable split in loyalty between spouse and church which a married person confronts (I Cor. 7:32-35), and (2) the imminent end of this world (I Cor. 7:27-31).

In Mark 12:25 Jesus echoes a common apocalyptic notion that there is no sexuality and therefore no marriage in heaven. Such a view, coupled with belief that the kingdom of God is already manifested within the Christian communities, could have formed another basis for the movement away from marriage, especially among the Gnostics. In its present place in Matthew, the unusual saying about people becoming eunuchs for the kingdom of God may be a comment on the kind of life necessary after a person has separated from his or her spouse (i.e., no remarriage is permitted; cf. Matt. 19:9-12). In the oral tradition, however, it must have been an exhortation to, or defense of, believers (or of Jesus?) who practiced celibacy, either because they thought they were living already *in* the kingdom of God, or in order to give complete devotion to work *for* the kingdom. *See* EUNUCH; ETHICS IN THE NT[S] §1ei.

This early tendency toward the single state was continued in some segments of the later church. The silence about marriage in the Gospel of John and Johannine epistles may indicate uncertainty in that circle about marriage. In the book of Revelation the redeemed in heaven are said to have been celibate, assuming the language is intended literally rather than metaphorically (14:4). Nowhere else in the book, however, is the idea repeated; thus it plays no important role in the thought of the final author. Only Gnostic Christianity seems to have stressed celibacy, though the evidence for this is largely of post-NT date. The author of I Timothy, however, is already fighting a view of Christianity in which marriage is prohibited along with certain kinds of foods (I Tim. 4:1-3); here he stands against an ascetic movement which may have connections with emerging GNOSTICISM. A fully formed, extreme position against marriage can be found in such late second-century writings as the Acts of Thomas (e.g., 12–14; *see* THOMAS, ACTS OF).

3. Emphasis upon marriage in the later NT church. The tendency toward the single state did not deflect the mainstream church, however, from preserving the validity and sanctity of marriage. In fact, the dispute with Gnostic groups may have intensified the insistence upon marriage in this period. A popular form of ethical admonition in the later first century, the "rules for the household," simply assume the validity of marriage and procreation (*see* LISTS, ETHICAL §§1–4; LISTS, ETHICAL [S] §2; ETHICS IN THE NT[S] §§4*a*, 5*a*). Heb. 13:4 exhorts its readers to honor marriage. It is in the Pastoral epistles, however, that the greatest stress is laid upon marriage, an emphasis which may actually imply that remaining single was fairly widespread in actual practice (*see also* ETHICS IN THE NT[S] §4*b*). Marriage is asserted to be an order of creation and therefore good (I Tim. 4:4); bishops, deacons, and elders are assumed (and perhaps encouraged) to be married and to have children (I Tim. 3:2, 12; Tit. 1:6); the function of woman seems to be narrowed to the bearing and raising of children (I Tim. 2:15); and younger widows are encouraged to remarry and have children (I Tim. 5:14; cf. Paul's more reluctant concession about the remarriage of widows, I Cor. 7:39-40).

4. The quality of the marital relationship. Wherever marriage is accepted, it is accepted in all its dimensions. Sexual relationships are highlighted by Paul (I Cor. 7:3-5) and assumed in the later traditions. For Paul, peace is necessary to marriage, and he is sensitive to the care each partner bestows on the other. Likewise he stresses the equality and mutuality within the marriage bond (I Cor. 7). The later rules of the household highlight, on the one hand, the need for tenderness and love on the part of the husband and, on the other, the willing subordination of the wife to him. For the author of Ephesians the model for the husband's love is the total self-giving of Christ for the church (5:25). *See* WOMAN IN THE NT[S] §2*b*.

Paul, however, sounds a warning against the possible usurpation through marriage of one's primary allegiance to Christ (I Cor. 7:29-31). When one allows marriage and spouse to become the ultimate concern, he or she is still living in that old order now being transcended in the new creation. *See also* Luke 14:26.

Bibliography. For the most detailed treatment, *see* H. Baltensweiler, *Die Ehe im Neuen Testament,* ATANT, LII (1967). Further, J. P. Sampley, *'And the Two Shall Become One Flesh': A Study of Traditions in Ephesians 5:21-33,* NTSMS, XVI (1971); J. O'Rourke, "Hypotheses Regarding I Cor. 7:36-38," *CBQ,* XX (1958), 292-98; P. Trummer, "Einehe nach den Pastoralbriefen," *Bibl.,* LI (1970), 471-84. For the understanding of Matt. 19:12, Q. Quesnell, "'Made Themselves Eunuchs for the Kingdom of Heaven' (Mt. 19, 12)," *CBQ,* XXX (1968), 335-58. R. SCROGGS

***MASADA.** After the surveys conducted at Masada in 1953 and 1955-56 it was decided to hold full-scale excavations at the site. In these excavations (1963-65) nearly all the structures on Masada were uncovered and partially reconstructed; the water system was examined; and one of the Roman camps encircling Masada was surveyed and partially excavated. The finds belong to three main periods: the Herodian period (37-4 B.C.), the period of the Revolt (A.D. 66-73), and the Byzantine period (fifth-sixth century A.D.). No remains of pre-Herodian structures were uncovered.

1. The Herodian period. Most of the structures on Masada belong to this period and can be divided into two groups: the N group which comprises the northern palace, the storerooms, the bathhouse, and three structures, the administrative building, the residential building, and the apartment building, and the SW group, which includes the western palace, smaller palaces (XIII, XII, and XI), the *columbarium,* and the swimming pool. *See* Fig. M1.

a. The water system. There is no permanent source of water near Masada, and therefore water was the first problem Herod had to deal with on building the fortress. The water system has three basic components: storm-water drains from the wadis in the W, reservoirs for this water on the NW side, and a system of cisterns on top of the mountain. The cisterns at the NW side were quarried in two rows—eight in the upper row and four in the lower. All these together held 1,400,000 cubic feet of water. The water was carried by people or pack animals over a winding path which led from the cisterns to the vicinity of the N palace. *See* Fig. M2.

b. The wall and gates. Although Masada enjoys a naturally defensible position, a casemate wall fifteen hundred yards long was built to encircle the entire top of the mountain. Thirty towers and four gates were set in it. The gates are all

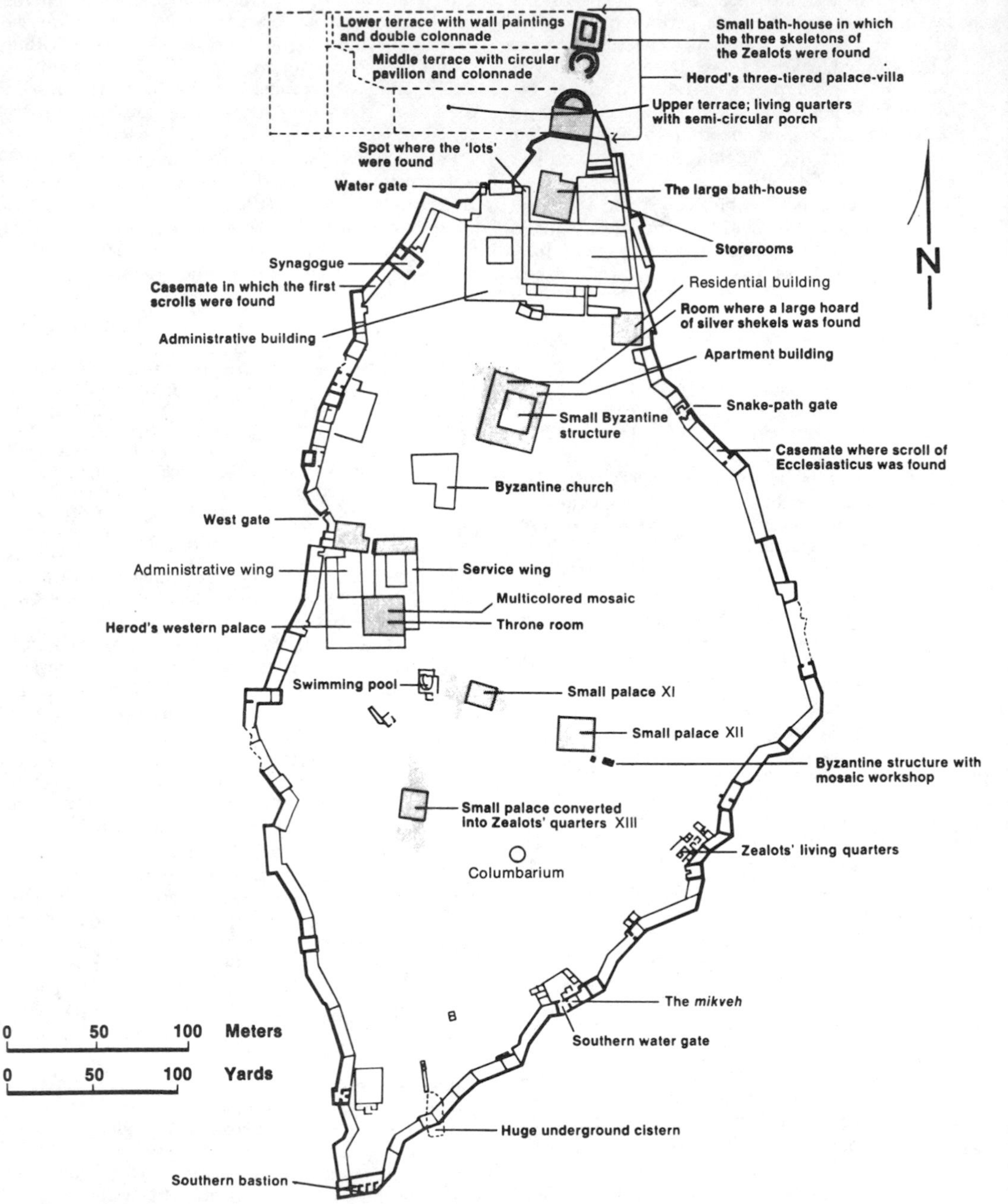

Courtesy Y. Yadin

1. Site plan of Masada

similar, with a square room and an opening in the internal and external walls. The Snake-Path Gate is situated in the NE section of the wall; its internal walls are plastered in white and decorated with false "panels" imitating Herodian masonry, and its floor is built on slabs of stone. The W gate is situated in the middle of the W wall. The S gate (Cistern Gate) is situated NE of the southern end of the cliff; it served for the conveying of water from the SE cisterns. The NW gate (Water Gate), situated at the end of the NW wall, served as an entrance for the water carriers from the upper row of cisterns.

*c. **Public storerooms.*** Situated in the N block, they are divided into a northern part composed of long rooms (66 x 12 feet), most of which have only one entrance (from the S), and a southern part, which is larger and comprises eleven long storerooms (88 x 13 feet) with entrances in the N side. Here was stored wine, oil, flour, etc. Three storerooms were constructed encircling the administrative building on the W and S, and others were

© Y. Yadin

2. One of the large cisterns, excavated from solid rock, which supplied water to Masada. Sunbeam is coming through a hole through which water filled the cistern; staircase is on the right.

later added to the SE side. These were all constructed at a later stage to increase the capacity of the main storerooms.

d. The palaces. The northern palace resembles a private villa intended only for the king and his entourage. Herod's western palace was used for administrative and ceremonial purposes, and a group of smaller palaces housed the king's family and the court ministers.

i. The northern palace was built on three terraces of the N cliff. The upper terrace held only a few rooms, while on the two others were luxurious buildings. The upper terrace was composed of two main parts: a semicircular platform bounded by two concentric semicircular walls upon which was probably built a portico of two rows of columns. To the S of the platform are the dwelling structures consisting of only four rooms. Their walls were decorated with plant and geometrical designs, and the floors were paved with a black-and-white mosaic. The entrance to the entire palace was on the E side of this terrace.

The middle terrace is located 66 feet below the upper one and contains two main elements, a circular building and a complex to the S of it. The only remains of the former are the foundations of the two concentric walls which supported the upper structure. It seems that the circular building had the form of a cupola, with two rows of columns supporting its roof. The southern complex comprises three parts, a staircase at the W, a big hall at the E, and an open area between. Here too the walls were decorated with paintings. The staircase was hidden from view from the outside and connected the middle to the upper terrace. This complex served as an entertainment area.

The lower terrace is about 50 feet below the middle terrace. Its buildings were constructed on a raised, square platform (57 x 57 feet), built on the edge of the cliff with the aid of supporting walls. The main structure was a square central space surrounded by porticoes, the inner walls of which had columns interspaced by windows. The S wall was formed by a plastered rock face with half columns attached to it. They have Corinthian capitals painted in gold. The portico walls are decorated with wall paintings imitating panels. It seems that the central courtyard was open, while the space between the two concentric porticoes was roofed. To the E of the square building was a small but complete bathhouse with hot, tepid, and cold rooms, while to the W a staircase led from the middle to the lower terrace. The structures on this terrace were also designed for pleasure and not as living quarters. *See* Pl. XXXV (c).

The northern palace has the air of a private, intimate villa. Its special architectural character seems to carry the personal stamp of Herod the Great.

ii. The western palace is the biggest complex of living quarters on Masada (its over-all area encompasses about 36,000 square feet), and it was the main administrative and ceremonial palace. It was composed of four blocks: the SE block (the living quarters and throne room), the NE block (the service and work rooms), the SW block (the storerooms), and the NW block (the administrative wing). The main entrance was at the N.

The living quarters were constructed around a big central court, S of which was a large covered hall separated from the court by two columns. From here one passed into the throne room through a triple entrance in the SE corner. Most of the palace walls were covered with white plaster imitating panel designs, and the floors of the waiting room and bathroom were decorated by multicolor mosaics with plant or geometrical patterns. In this section there was also a small bathhouse which served those living in the palace.

The service and work rooms were also built around a large court. The storeroom block comprises one very long storeroom (230 feet) in the W and three smaller storerooms between this block and the palace. The administrative block is located in the NW and comprises three buildings.

iii. The small palaces were probably inhabited by the royal family and high officials. The apartment building, situated S of the storerooms, differs from the others. It chiefly consisted of a row of groups of rooms placed around a central court, and served, most probably, as the family quarters of the royal guard.

iv. Other buildings. Besides the two small bathhouses attached to the main palaces, Herod also built a large and luxurious bathhouse W of the northern group of storerooms. It consisted of four rooms and one big, open courtyard. A swimming pool is situated alongside one of the small palaces and is cut out of the bedrock and covered in plaster. The *columbarium* is a round structure on the S of Masada. Its diameter is 25 feet, and its internal area is divided in two by a wall with an entrance. Hewn into the internal face of the walls are small niches (about 6 inches wide, high, and deep) in straight rows. These apparently served as a depository for the ashes of non-Jewish members of the Herodian garrison.

Between the Herodian period and the revolts of A.D. 66-73, a garrison stayed on Masada, leaving only a few coins behind them. It is possible however that some of the changes in the Herodian structures were made during this period.

2. The Revolt (A.D. 66-73). During this period most of the Herodian structures underwent great changes at the hands of the Zealots, who tried to adapt them to their needs. Similarly, primitive structures were erected in other parts of Masada, particularly in the casemates of the wall encircling the fortress. Most of the architectural elements such as columns and their capitals were used by the Zealots as building material. They also used much of the wooden parts of the structures. The northern palace was probably used by the Zealots as their military headquarters, for a large amount of arrows and other weapons were found there (*see* ZEALOT; ZEALOT[S]). Beneath the layers of debris in the bathhouse three skeletons were uncovered, as well as ostraca written in Aramaic and fragments of a prayer shawl.

The western palace was used mainly for administrative purposes. Hundreds of burnt arrows, coins from the days of the Revolt, and ostraca with personal names were found here. When found, most of the palace was covered with the ashes—a result of a great conflagration.

The smaller palaces were inhabited by the families of the Zealots, and remains of ovens were discovered in most rooms. During this period interior walls had been built to divide rooms into smaller units. The baths and bathhouses continued to be used, but the Zealots made a few changes in them. All the rooms in the walls and towers were inhabited by their families. Among the rich finds in these rooms were much pottery, clothes, leather articles, basketware, glass, stone, bronze ware, remains of food, as well as fragments of scrolls and ostraca. The scrolls include fragments of the Holy Scriptures, Ecclesiasticus, and Qumranic literature. Because of the dry climate on Masada, most of these articles were very well preserved. *See* MANUSCRIPTS FROM THE JUDEAN DESERT[S] §§2*c*, 4.

In addition, the Zealots also constructed religious buildings including two *mikveh* (ritual baths) and a long room in palace XIII which may have been used as a "religious study house." Along three of the room's walls were benches and between them a table. The synagogue built by the Zealots is also of great importance. Situated in the NW section of the wall, it is a rectangular structure 41 x 34 feet facing W, that is, toward Jerusalem. Along three walls of the room, four rows of benches were built one above the other out of architectural elements removed from the northern palace. In the W, there was only one bench. Two rows of columns supported the roof. Parts of scrolls of the Scriptures were found here—deliberately buried under the floor—as well as ostraca containing writings cultic in nature. This is the earliest synagogue ever found.

The finds from the period of the Revolt include some seven hundred ostraca, most written in Hebrew and Aramaic and a few in Greek and Latin. Some of them may have been used as food coupons distributed during the siege. Some had single names on them, including the name of Ben Yair, who was known to have been the Zealot leader at Masada; these ostraca may have served as "lots." Some of the remains discovered on the ash layer indicate that a Roman garrison remained behind after the final conquest. From the beginning of the second century A.D. Masada was deserted until the Byzantine period.

3. The Byzantine period. In the fifth and sixth centuries A.D. monks settled on Masada. They built a church mainly consisting of an elongated hall with an apse in the E wall. The floor of the hall was made of colored mosaics, as were the floors of the other rooms which adjoined the hall. During this period other buildings were repaired, and signs of occupation have been found in a few caves hewn in the S cliff, alongside of which the monks built a few rooms and cells.

Bibliography. I. A. Richmond, *JRS,* LII (1962), 142-55; Y. Yadin, "The Excavations of Masada 1963/64, Preliminary Report," *IEJ,* XV (1965), 1-120; Y. Yadin, *Masada* (1966). Y. YADIN

MASORA. *See* TEXT, OT §A4; MASORETIC ACCENTS; QERE-KETHIBH[S]; EMENDATIONS OF THE SCRIBES[S].

MASORETIC TEXT. *See* TEXT, OT.

***MATTHEW, GOSPEL OF.** Advances in our understanding of the gospel have been achieved primarily by means of redaction criticism (*see* REDACTION CRITICISM, NT[S] §3). By paying special attention to the way the final work is composed scholars have gained new insight into its background, its structure, and its teaching. There has also been renewed discussion of the possible primacy of Matthew among the synoptic sources.

1. Background
2. Structure
3. Teaching
4. Sources

Bibliography

1. Background. The creative milieu (*Sitz im Leben*) of Matthew contained the opposing forces of conservatism and radicalism. This evangelist seeks to steer between the two extremes. His most obvious criticism is directed against "the scribes and Pharisees" who represent the conservative element (23:13-36); but the disagreement with "enthusiasts" is also clearly discernible (7:15-23). The author presents himself as one who is able to profit from both the Law and the gospel, both the tradition and the Spirit, as a "scribe who has been trained for the kingdom of Heaven," who "like a householder brings out of his treasure what is new and what is old" (13:52).

The designation of himself as a "scribe" suggests

that the author worked in a "school," and that his gospel issued from this kind of scholarly milieu. Such a background would seem to be confirmed by the way this evangelist used quotations from the OT and the perceived similarity between his usage and that of the exegetes of QUMRAN (Stendahl). (*See also* INTERPRETATION, HISTORY OF[S] §§B1, C2*b*; ESSENES §4*g*.) Davies has claimed to see in Matthew's handling of the tradition in the SERMON ON THE MOUNT a procedure similar to the Gemara of the post-Jamnian rabbis, i.e., an extension or modification of the scope of a commandment to make it applicable to present circumstances (e.g., the "antitheses" of Matt. 5:18 ff.). Gerhardsson has argued that the temptation narrative and the famous parable chapter (13) are constructed on the basis, firstly, of the SHEMA, secondly, of texts from the OT, and thirdly, in the case of the temptation narrative, on rabbinic moral theology. The method used was that of the rabbinic MIDRASH. The assumption that this gospel comes from a scholarly milieu, roughly analogous to a rabbinic house of Midrash, has, therefore, proved fruitful in understanding many of its features.

Such a background might explain Matthew's polemic against the "scribes and Pharisees." As a rival to a rabbinic "school" of interpretation, the Matthean church claimed that its acceptance of Jesus as the MESSIAH and its understanding of the tradition in the light of his words and deeds made it the true Israel (cf. the temptation narrative in which Jesus, as God's son, withstands all the temptations to which Israel, as God's son, succumbed in the wilderness, and thus shows himself to be the true Son of God, heir to the promises, and, accordingly, shows his followers to be the true Israel of God). (*See* ISRAEL, CONCEPTIONS OF[S] §4.) Likewise, the church's moral teaching is a righteousness higher than that of the Pharisees (5:20). The Matthean church claims, vis-à-vis the "synagogue across the street," to be the true Israel living the truly righteous life. This is the "conservative" element.

The radical element in Matthew's milieu is discernible by contrast in the strictures against lawlessness (ἀνομία: 7:23; 24:11-12). The purveyors of this lawlessness are called "false prophets" (ψευδοπροφῆται: 7:15, 24:11), and their "evil fruit" (7:18-19) is the cooling off of all love (24:12), or, in the context of the Sermon on the Mount, the contravention of the GOLDEN RULE, which, in turn, is said to be the epitome of all religious obligation laid down in the Law and the Prophets (7:12). Jesus' magisterial interpretation of the Law and Prophets is summed up in the binding obligation to love, even one's enemies (5:44), and certain false prophets in Matthew's community have made such love difficult. Hence they are in contravention of the Law of the Messiah and so guilty of lawlessness. Schweizer has shown that Christian prophets (*see* PROPHET IN THE NT; PROPHECY IN THE EARLY CHURCH[S]) and their "charismatic" activity were an important part of this gospel's milieu. The references to false prophets imply the existence of the true; their coming in disguise, as wolves in sheep's clothing, shows that they were part of the Christian community and not outsiders. They call Jesus "Lord" (7:15, 21).

The presence of true "prophetic" or "charismatic" Christianity in the Matthean church can also be seen from the following: in 4:23 and 9:35 a frame is set around the picture of Jesus as the Messiah of word and deed, which summarizes his activity as teaching, preaching, and healing. In 10:1 the disciples are given the same authority "to heal every disease and every infirmity," the same expression that was used in 4:23 and 9:35. In chs. 8 and 9 Matthew collects MIRACLE STORIES from Mark and Q and at the end adds two more, the healing of two blind men (9:27-31) and one dumb man (9:32-34), all of which he tells again later (20:29-34 and 12:22-24). He makes this collection in order that the answer to the disciples of John in 11:4-5, "Go and tell John what you hear and see: the blind receive their sight and the lame walk, lepers are cleansed and the deaf hear, and the dead are raised up, and the poor have good news preached to them," might be precisely illustrated from the deeds of Jesus. The answer to John's question, which chs. 8 and 9 illustrate, is placed, however, not immediately after ch. 9, but only after ch. 10. Why? Because ch. 10 tells how the healing power of Jesus, which will convince the followers of John, continues to be exercised by Jesus' disciples. Charismatic healing, therefore, was a mark of the disciple of Jesus, a sign that the Spirit of the Lord continued to operate through his disciples. A further illustration of this point occurs in 10:40-42 where we find the identification of Lord and disciple explicitly stated—"He who receives you receives me"—along with the self-designations chosen by the Matthean Christians: "prophet," "righteous man," and "little ones" (cf. 25:40, 45, author's trans.). Matthew's was the church of the "little ones" who were also prophets and righteous folk.

The background of the gospel is to be found, therefore, among people who considered themselves bound to the Law as interpreted by Jesus, obliged in its terms to be righteous, yet free to reinterpret it for new occasions by means of the spirit of Jesus guiding them, folk who were both scribes and prophets, little ones who followed Jesus and by his power were great enough to teach, preach, and heal.

Schweizer suggests that the most likely provenance for such a gospel was Syria, which also gave us the DIDACHE—so explicit in its interest both in Christian prophets and in church order (another characteristic of Matthew). Recently, Schweizer claims, this conjecture about provenance has been confirmed by the discovery of the Apocalypse of Peter at NAG HAMMADI, which represents a group of "these little ones who are seen (by God)" and opposes those "who let themselves be called bishops, and also deacons" (ApocPet 79, 19 ff.; cf. Matt. 23:6-10; 18:10). The Matthean church, therefore, was "the body of these little ones who are ready to follow Jesus, a group with an ascetic and charismatic character, that found its continuation in the Church of Syria, finally merging into the monastic movement of the Catholic Church" (Schweizer).

2. Structure. Bacon's analysis of Matthew into five great discourses, punctuated by the phrase "And when Jesus [had] finished" (7:28; 11:1; 13:53; 19:1; 26:1), with a preamble (chs. 1–2) and an epilogue (chs. 26–28), and patterned on the Mosaic Pentateuch (*see original bibliog.*), has not stood the test of time. Two arguments have proven fatal to the hypothesis. First, to place the infancy narratives and the passion and resurrection accounts outside the main structure of the gospel is to overlook the fact that Matthew presents his gospel as history, not as a law code or a church manual, and that he views the Cross and Resurrection as marking a climax in the historical process. Second, since ch. 11 is a collection of logia, and between ch. 23 and chs. 24–25 there is a complete change of setting, there are actually six or seven, rather than five, great discourses. Bacon and his many followers have mistakenly taken the gospel as a code of religious instruction topically arranged, and nothing more. Consequently, they have overlooked the fact that Matthew works within the usual biblical concept of salvation as history (*Heilsgeschichte*).

The structure of Matthew's gospel is being restudied at present, and lasting new results have not yet emerged. One of the proposals offered as an alternative to Bacon's long-accepted hypothesis may be worth considering, nevertheless, as an example. Kingsbury suggests that 4:17 and 16:21, "From that time Jesus began," mark the points of new departure in Matthew. This insight produces the following division of the gospel: (1) The Person of Jesus the Messiah (1:1–4:16); (2) The Proclamation of Jesus the Messiah (4:17–16:20); (3) The Passion, Death, and Resurrection of Jesus the Messiah (16:21–28:20). This scheme has the advantages of including the birth narrative and the passion narrative within the main structure, which Bacon's proposal could not do, and of enabling one to take the element of "saving history" into account—salvation is given in and through the history of Jesus the Messiah. It also enables one to give a persuasive account of Matthew's teaching.

3. Teaching. The theology of the gospel is focused on Christ, as Kingsbury's proposed outline shows. It is in the first place Christology; but the Christology unfolds in the events of Jesus' history and then merges into the doctrine of the church, as the power of Jesus is believed to be passed on to his disciples.

Many have argued that Matthew divides the history of salvation into three epochs: of Judaism, of Jesus, and of the church, respectively (Trilling, Walker, Strecker). However, it seems preferable, with Kingsbury, to see only two epochs in the gospel: of Judaism, and of Jesus. The epoch of the church is an extension or subcategory of the epoch of Jesus. Especially by means of the formula quotations from the OT, the evangelist shows that the period of prophecy is over and the time of fulfillment has come. The phrase "[in] those days" (3:1; 24:19, 22*a, c,* 29) shows that the time of fulfillment extends from the period of John and Jesus to the end of the age, thus leaving no room for another epoch (of the church). Positive evidence for the exclusion of a church epoch is provided by the emphasis on Jesus' abiding presence with the disciples (1:23; 14:27; 18:20; 28:20) and the presentation of the ministry of the disciples as a recapitulation and continuation of the ministry of Jesus.

If this twofold pattern of Matthew's salvation history is accepted, then the center of his thought cannot be the church, as Bacon and many others aver. It must be, rather, the Christ, thus making the church a corollary of the Resurrection presence of Jesus (Kingsbury). Whether or not we accept Kingsbury's further analysis, namely, that upon the twofold *Heilsgeschichte* Matthew has superimposed a threefold topical organization of (1) the Person, (2) the Proclamation, and (3) the Passion, there is good reason to believe that Kingsbury is correct in identifying the central interest of Matthew to be Christology.

The keynote of the gospel is in 1:23: Emmanuel, "God with us." Jesus Christ is "God with us" for the Matthean church because he is God's Son (1:1, 18, 20, 23). Gerhardsson has shown brilliantly that the temptation narrative (4:1-11) with its repeated phrase, "If you are the Son of God" (4:3, 6), and its constant reference to Deut. 6–8 (4:4=Deut. 8:3; 4:7=Deut. 6:16; 4:10=Deut. 6:13) contrasts Jesus, the faithful Son of God, with God's unfaithful son, Israel, whose temptation in the wilderness is described in Deut. 6–8. The temptation narrative is a skillful midrash on the Deuteronomy passage, dominated by the theme of Sonship.

In the Sermon on the Mount, as Davies has shown, Jesus is portrayed in comparison with Moses. He is not Moses redivivus, a prophet like Moses à la Deut. 18:15, however, but greater than Moses. As Emmanuel, "God with us," Jesus gives the Torah of the Messiah, which supersedes the Torah of Moses by bringing it to radical fulfillment in the command to love—the so-called Golden Rule (7:12—"for this is the law and the prophets").

But the climax of Matthew's exposition of "Emmanuel" is the identification of Jesus with the Wisdom of God (Suggs). In passages like Matt. 11:18-19, 28-30; 23:34-36, 37-39, Jesus is identified as the pre-existent Sophia (Wisdom) which, in Jewish circles, had been identified with the Torah. The great invitation in 11:28-30—"Come to me, all who labor and are heavy laden, and I will give you rest. Take my yoke upon you, and learn from me"—is like something Wisdom would say in the tradition (Ecclus. 51:23-30; 24:19-22; Prov. 1:20-23; 8:1-21). Davies calls this text "the quintessence of the Matthean interpretation of Christianity as Gospel and Law." Jesus is "God with us" because he is the very Wisdom/Torah/Son of God, incarnate. The chapter on church discipline (18) is controlled by the same ideas. In 18:20 Jesus is the SHEKINAH (cf. AB. 3.2).

As 11:28-30 shows, there is also a strong emphasis on the humility of the incarnate one (8:17; 12:17-21; 21:4-5). But the humble one is he to whom all authority in heaven and earth has been given, through his death and resurrection. He will be with his disciples until the end of the age (28:18-20), and in the end this humble one will use his authority to judge all the nations (7:21-23; 13:36-43, 25:31-46).

4. Sources. The problem of the synoptic sources has been reopened, and although there are no conclusive results to date, sufficient doubt has been cast on the traditional two-document hypothesis to warrant caution (*see* SYNOPTIC PROBLEM[S]). The renewed discussion focuses on the agreements between Matthew and Luke against Mark. In the case of a triple tradition (one attested by all three gospels) it has usually been assumed that Mark provides the middle term. But there are instances in which it seems that Matthew performs this function (e.g., Matt. 8:4; 13:22; 17:17), and a few where Luke does (Luke 12:1; 23:52). This, along with other considerations, raises at least the possibility of the chronological priority of Matthew (Farmer), and, in any case, the need to recognize that the relationships among the Synoptic gospels are more complex than the received two-document hypothesis allows.

Bibliography. E. P. Blair, *Jesus in the Gospel of Matthew* (1960); G. Bornkamm, G. Barth, H. J. Held, *Tradition and Interpretation in Matthew* (1960); W. D. Davies, *The Setting of the Sermon on the Mount* (1964); W. R. Farmer, *The Synoptic Problem* (1964), and "Jesus and the Gospels: A Form-critical and Theological Essay," *PSTJ,* XXVIII, 2 (1975), 1-62; B. Gerhardsson, *The Testing of God's Son (Matt 4:1-11 & Par),* Coniectanea Biblica, NT Ser., II (1966); J. D. Kingsbury, "Form and Message of Matthew," *Int.,* XXIX (1975), 13-23, and "The Structure of Matthew's Gospel and His Concept of Salvation-History," *CBQ,* XXXV (1973), 451-74; E. P. Sanders, "The Overlaps of Mark and Q and the Synoptic Problem," *NTS,* XIX (1973), 453-65; E. Schweizer, "Observance of the Law and Charismatic Activity in Matthew," *NTS,* XVI (1970), 213-30, "The Matthean Church," *NTS,* XX (1974), 216, and *The Good News According to Matthew* (1973); K. Stendahl, *The School of St. Matthew and Its Use of the OT* (1968); G. Strecker, *Der Weg der Gerechtigkeit—Untersuchung zur Theologie des Matthäus, FRLANT,* LXXXII (1962); M. J. Suggs, *Wisdom, Christology, and Law in Matthew's Gospel* (1970); W. G. Thompson, *Matthew's Advice to a Divided Community: (Mt. 17, 22-18, 35),* AnBib, XLIV (1970); W. Trilling, *Das Wahre Israel; Studien zur Theologie des Matthäus-Evangeliums,* SUNT, X (1964); R. Walker, *Die Heilsgeschichte im ersten Evangelium, FRLANT,* XCI (1967).

R. G. HAMERTON-KELLY

***MEGIDDO.** After the publication of the results of the 1925-39 excavations at Megiddo, a few problems concerning the stratigraphy of the site still remained unsolved. In the light of excavations conducted at Hazor and a study of Gezer, Y. Yadin decided to take another look at the wall which had been attributed to Solomon and at the stratigraphical problems of the tell during the Israelite period. Excavations were conducted during 1960, 1966, 1967, and 1971.

In 1960 the area selected for the trial dig was in the N side of the E half of the tell, to the E of the "Schumacher Trench" and the DD area. In this section an "offsets/insets" wall had been well preserved, and Yadin's assumption that this wall (stratum IVA) was not Solomonic (based on the fact that at both Hazor and Gezer the wall from the time of Solomon was a casemate wall) could now be checked.

1. Structures of the Solomonic period. It soon became clear that the offsets/insets wall was constructed in this area upon the foundations of a large structure, probably a palace (no. 6000 in Yadin's report), whose courses were mainly built of ashlar stones. This building also stretches beneath the foundations of the northern stable complex (407) which is situated alongside the area under discussion. (*See* Fig. M3.) Furthermore,

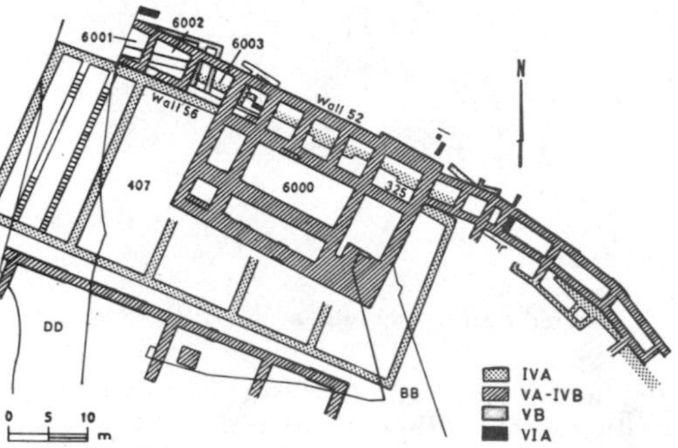

Courtesy Y. Yadin

3. Megiddo excavations of 1960, 1966-67; the new Solomonic palace and the casemate walls. Note position of strata VB, VIA.

on both sides of this palace a casemate wall was discovered. The offsets/insets wall was constructed upon this casemate wall and upon its rooms which had been filled in. It became clear that the northern stable complex (also called "Solomon's stables"), the wall, and the building are later than the Solomonic period and can definitely be attributed to stratum IVA, that is, to the period of the dynasty of King OMRI. From this it could be seen that the palace and the casemate wall belong to IVB-VA (Solomonic period) as does the palace. The S palace is similar to palaces found in Zinjirli and at sites along the Phoenician coast, all from the early centuries of the first millennium B.C. This kind of structure, known from Assyrian sources as the "Bit Hilani," functioned mainly as a ceremonial palace. The presence of such a building at Solomonic Megiddo is yet more evidence to the biblical assertion of the Phoenician influence upon Solomon's building projects.

It was now possible to attribute gate 2156, which has six chambers and two towers, definitely to Solomon and to associate it with the casemate wall. In this manner the other Israelite gates previously discovered at Megiddo fell into their correct stratigraphical periods. We may now attribute gate 500B to the offsets/insets wall, that is to sub-stratum IVA (the dynasty of Omri), and gate 500 to stratum III. *See* Fig. M4.

2. The water system. Various questions relating to the water systems at Megiddo were also cleared up. In the SW section of the tell the previous excavators had unearthed a structure which they labeled "gallery 629": a narrow passage just over three feet in width, leading outside the city to the SW slope of the tell where a spring is situated. The passage walls were built of well-dressed ashlar stones, laid header-and-stretcher fashion. Strati-

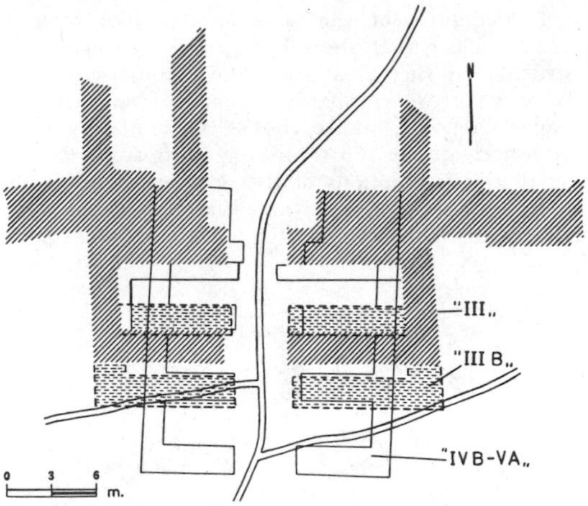

Courtesy Y. Yadin

4. Megiddo city gates, strata VA-III

graphically speaking, the passage is situated underneath the offsets/insets wall which the excavators considered Solomonic, and they therefore concluded that the gallery was pre-Solomonic. Finding it impossible to assign this magnificent structure to earlier meager strata, they attributed the gallery to stratum VIIA (the days of Ramses III, twelfth century B.C.). *See* Fig. M5.

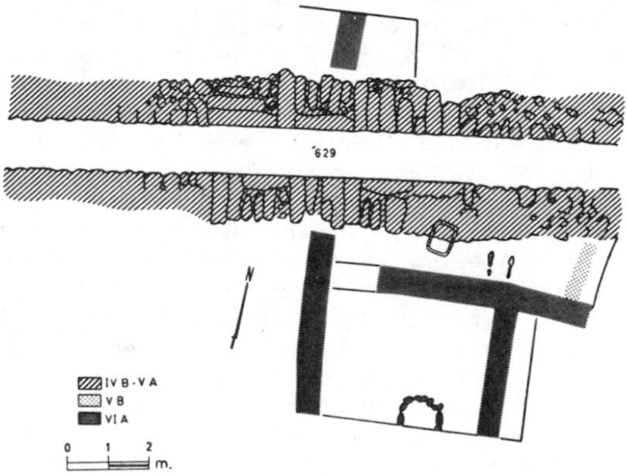

Courtesy Y. Yadin

5. The 1967 excavations near gallery 629

This erroneous assumption resulted, in turn, in an incorrect dating of the great water system, which consists of two parts: a vertical shaft and a long horizontal tunnel (*see* MEGIDDO Fig. 30; WATER WORKS Fig. 7). The purpose of the tunnel was to convey the spring waters from the natural cave at the foot of the tell to the bottom of the vertical shaft, where the city's inhabitants could draw water in times of siege.

On the basis of pottery found in the cave, the latest of which was typical of stratum VIIA (thirteenth-twelfth centuries B.C.), and other data, the excavators decided the water system could not have been constructed before the thirteenth century B.C. Because they attributed the quarrying of the shaft and tunnel to the twelfth century, they automatically assigned the gallery to the period prior to the completion of the water system, for after this there was no need for a gallery leading to the spring outside the wall.

When it was ascertained that wall 325 was later than Solomon's period, the gallery beneath it could then be attributed to his rule for the following reason. During the trial dig (1960, and especially 1966) it became clear that the foundation of the gallery was cut into the fallen burnt bricks of stratum VIA and VB (eleventh century B.C.). It is possible to conclude therefore that the gallery was constructed before the wall, but after the destruction of strata VIA and VB, that is, during Solomon's reign. Thus we may ascribe the later great water system to the dynasty of Omri (ninth century B.C.), when both the stables and the offsets/insets wall were built. *See* Fig. M6.

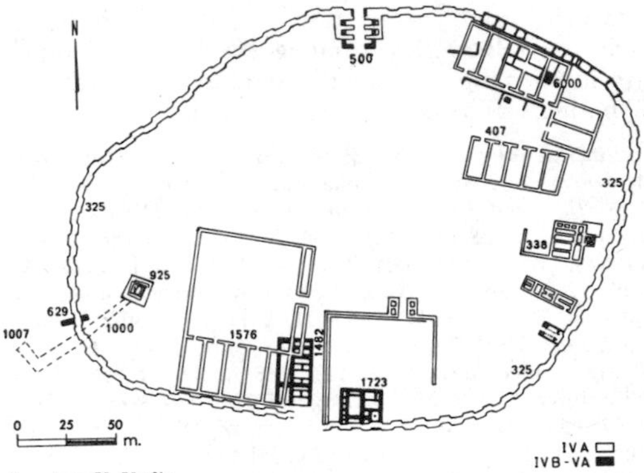

Courtesy Y. Yadin

6. Site plan: key plan of Megiddo in strata IVA; IVB-VA

Stratum IVA was therefore constructed under the dynasty of Omri, during the second quarter of the ninth century, and because it is quite clear that repairs and additions were made to the stables, we may presume that the city continued to exist until it was destroyed in 733 B.C. by the Assyrians.

An additional water system was discovered during the 1960 trial digs. Below the city gates a well-built staircase was unearthed which seemed to incline with the path leading to the gates. The previous excavators of Megiddo had not completed their investigation of this system (which incidentally seemed to have been roofed), and claimed that the stairs served as a pedestrian entrance into the city. On further examination, however, it became clear that these stairs led to yet another source of water in the N, which had possibly been connected to Megiddo's second water source close to the tell. The continuation of the staircase was discovered running E toward a well-plastered pool. This water system can be attributed to the dynasty of Omri (ninth century B.C.) and probably served as a supply of water only during days of peace, since it is situated beyond the city's fortifications, while the large, subterranean water system served the city during days of siege. *See also* ARCHAEOLOGY[S].

Bibliography. K. M. Kenyon, "Megiddo, Hazor, Samaria and Chronology," *Bulletin of the Institute of Archaeology of the University of London,* IV (1964),

143 ff.; Y. Yadin, *IEJ*, XVI (1966), 278-80, XVII (1967), 119-21, "Megiddo of the Kings of Israel," *BA*, XXXIII (1970), 66-96, and *Hazor* (The Schweich Lectures; 1972), pp. 150 ff. Y. YADIN

***MELCHIZEDEK. 1. In the Dead Sea Scrolls.** Fragments of a MS found in 1956 in Qumran Cave 11 give us details of a Melchizedek tradition which was alive in certain circles of late Palestinian Judaism. Of thirteen fragments, nine or ten can be arranged to form the greater part of one column of the original MS and a few words of the next column. For paleographic reasons, the fragments are to be dated toward the beginning of the Common Era. This text is an example of an eschatological MIDRASH in which, by means of associative interpretation of texts, various scriptural passages are grouped together thematically and interpreted as relating to the coming eschaton. Because in the extant part of the original MS Melchizedek plays a central role, the document was designated 11QMelch by its editor.

Isa. 61:1-2 supplies the most important themes for the scriptural exegesis of 11QMelch (the acceptable year; the vengeance exacted by Melchizedek; the bringer of good tidings). First, the author finds in Lev. 25:13 and Deut. 15:2 prophecies not only of the return from the DIASPORA, but also of the time of the proclamation of release from captivity and sin. In the view of the interpreter, the jubilee year ("*yôbhēl*-year") mentioned in Lev. 25:13 refers to the last or tenth jubilee year, with which (as in Dan. 9) a period of seventy weeks of years, i.e., 490 years, comes to a close and the awaited time of salvation dawns. Then the atonement of all the faithful children of God will occur, for "that is the time of the acceptable year of Melchizedek" (line 9). Because of the fragmentary nature of the extant text, it is difficult to determine whether this atonement occurs by Melchizedek's agency and whether he acts as priest. But in the sequel the author relates Ps. 82:1 to him: "The Heavenly One (*'aelōhîm*) standeth in the congregation of God (*'ēl*)" (line 10). In this quotation *'aelōhîm* is interpreted as referring to Melchizedek, who stands in the assembly of God and judges among the heavenly ones (angels). Thus the author has designated Melchizedek as a heavenly, angelic figure, something he could doubtless do only because this tradition was known to him. Correspondingly, in the whole MS God is referred to as *'ēl*, never as *'aelōhîm*. In 11QMelch, then, Melchizedek is neither a purely earthly figure of the past (cf. Gen. 14:18) nor an earthly man whose appearance is expected in the future.

It is incorrect to explain the figure allegorically as a "copy" of the figure in Gen. 14, or even as a person who merely has the same name as the former priest-king of Salem. Because Melchizedek suddenly appears in Gen. 14, and because Abraham —as Levi's ancestor—gives Melchizedek a tenth of all his booty and thus acknowledges Melchizedek's superiority over Levi, the thought had sooner or later to arise that Melchizedek was exalted above even the most blessed of men. Melchizedek's designation as "priest of the Most High" allowed him to appear as God's heavenly high priest officiating in the heavenly sanctuary. But because he is also a king, the author of 11QMelch can also declare, with reference to Pss. 7:8-9 [H 9-10] and 82:2, that at the eschaton Melchizedek "will exact the vengeance of the judgments of God and will rescue all the Children of Light from the power of Belial and from the power of all spirits of his lot," and that "all the heavenly gods are for his help" (lines 13-14).

This rescuing of the Children of Light is, elsewhere in the Qumran writings, ascribed to an angelic prince who is designated as "Prince of Light (s)" (1QM 13; CDC 5.18) or as "His (= God's) Angel of Truth" (*mal'akh 'amittô:* 1QS 3.24; 4QCatena[a] 12-13, col. I, 7), and who appears as the adversary of the Angel of Darkness (1QS 3.20). From 1QM 17.5-9 it is clear that by this "Prince of Light (s)" only the archangel MICHAEL can be meant. According to late Jewish tradition, Michael not only is the guardian angel of Israel and is commissioned by God to pass judgment upon the spirits of Belial, but he is also the heavenly high priest who offers sacrifice in the heavenly temple and intercedes for the pious before God (T.B. Ḥagiga 12b; Zebhāḥîm 62a; Menāḥôth 110a). Consequently Melchizedek is also later expressly identified with Michael in some parts of the Jewish tradition. The appearance of Melchizedek in the final battle, and his annihilation of Belial's angelic hosts, mean the beginning of the time of salvation prophesied—according to the author of 11QMelch (lines 15-16)—by Isa. 52:7. Here our author interprets the "bringer of good tidings" as the one "anointed with the Spirit" of Isa. 61:1 (cf. Luke 4:18-19), who proclaims the appearance of *'aelōhîm*, the Heavenly One. Unfortunately the text breaks off just at the point where it explains who is meant by this *'aelōhîm;* but the word "Belial" in the sequel makes it probable that Melchizedek is meant. The column ends with a quotation of Lev. 25:9 (cf. I Thess. 4:16).

2. In the Letter to the Hebrews. From 11QMelch new light falls on the designation of Christ as "high priest after the order of Melchizedek" (Heb. 5:5-10; 6:20; cf. Ps. 110:4) and especially on Heb. 7.

In 7:2 "Melchizedek" is interpreted as "king of righteousness," and "king of Salem" as "king of peace." ("Righteousness" and "peace" are eschatological gifts.) Unique in this context is especially Heb. 7:3, where it is said of Melchizedek that "he is without father or mother or genealogy, and has neither beginning of days nor end of life, but resembling the Son of God he continues a priest for ever." Apart from "resembling the Son of God," all these epithets can now be explained by looking at 11QMelch. As a heavenly angelic figure he has no genealogy or parents, as humans do, and he does not die, as they do. The author of Hebrews here doubtless quotes a text which was also known to his readers and which he thus could use to describe Christ's high-priestly office. Consequently, in 7:4-10 the author tries to prove Melchizedek's superiority to Abraham, Levi, and Aaron. He remarks, first, that Melchizedek received tithes from Abraham, and therefore also from Levi (whose priestly descendants ask tithes from the people). Consequently, Melchizedek is superior to (Abraham and) Levi. Secondly, the author emphasizes that Melchizedek blessed Abraham, who received God's promises. Melchizedek therefore must be greater than Abraham and Levi. A third argument is taken from 7:3. The Levitical priests are mortals, but of Melchizedek we may say that "it is testified that he lives" (7:8). The new priesthood after the order of Melchizedek has been predicted. If the Levitical priesthood had been destined to bring perfection, God would not have spoken of another priest "after the order of Melchizedek."

Now a change of priesthood means a change of law (7:15 ff.). On the basis of Ps. 110:4 it is pointed out that the "covenant" of which Jesus is "the surety" is far superior to the previous one (7:22): the priests of the old order "took their office without an oath" (7:21) and had after their death to be succeeded by others (7:23), but Christ "was addressed with an oath" (7:21) and "holds his priesthood permanently" (7:24). He is the perfect high priest who always lives to "make intercession" for "those who draw near to God" (7:25). Thus Christ's greater dignity and the superiority of his high-priesthood to that of the Levitical priests is emphasized in Heb. 7 by reference to the Melchizedek tradition. On the other hand, however, the words about Melchizedek's "resembling the Son of God" (7:3) emphasize the subordination of the archangel Melchizedek to the pre-existent Son of God: the former is only a "copy" of the Son of God whose absolute superiority to all angels has been established in Heb. 1–2. The similarity of both is found in their "continuing for ever" (cf. 7:3, 24).

Thus, on the basis of 11QMelch it is no longer necessary to suppose that the strong anti-Aaronite conception of a heavenly high priest in Hebrews was influenced by Jewish-Gnostic or Philonic traditions.

Bibliography. A. S. van der Woude, "Melchizedek als himmlische Erlösergestalt in den neugefundenen eschatologischen Midraschim aus Qumran-Höhle XI," *OTS,* XIV (1965), 354-73; M. de Jonge and A. S. van der Woude, "11Q Melchizedek and the NT," *NTS,* XII (1966), 301-32; J. A. Fitzmyer, "Further Light on Melchizedek from Qumran Cave 11," *JBL,* LXXXVI (1967), 25-41; M. P. Miller, "The Function of Isa. 61:1-2 in 11Q Melchizedek," *JBL,* LXXXVIII (1969), 467-69; M. Delcor, "Melchizedek from Genesis to the Qumran Texts and the Epistle to the Hebrews," *JSJ,* II (1971), 115-35; J. Carmignac, "Le Document de Qumrân sur Melkisédeq," *RQ,* VII (1970), 343-78; D. F. Miner, "A Suggested Reading for 11Q Melchizedek 17," *JSJ,* II (1971), 144-48; F. Laubscher, "God's Angel of Truth and Melchizedek: A Note on 11QMelch 13b," *JSJ,* III (1972), 46-51; J. T. Milik, "Milkî-sedeq et Milkî-reša' dans les anciens écrits juifs et chrétiens," *JJS,* XXIII (1972), 95-144; K. Berger, "Der Streit des guten und des bösen Engels um die Seele: Beobachtungen zu 4QAmr^b und Judas 9," *JSJ,* IV (1973), 1-18; J. A. Sanders, "The OT in 11Q Melchizedek," *JANES,* V (1973), 373-82.

A. S. VAN DER WOUDE

***MENORAH.** Hebrew מנרה is a generic term for the repository or support of a lamp or source of light. KJV "candlestick" is anachronistic. Although there is one instance (II Kings 4:10) of the secular use of such a lampstand, the term normally indicates a cultic object found in the central Israelite sanctuaries. *See* LAMPSTAND.

1. The tabernacle menorah. It has long been supposed that because the Priestly texts (Exod. 25:31-40 and 37:17-24) which describe the menorah date in their final form from exilic or postexilic times, the menorah (if not the tabernacle itself) is to some degree a projection into the wilderness period of what existed in the second temple (*see* PRIESTLY WRITERS[S] §4). However, the wealth of detail given in its description allow it to be placed, in light of archaeological and artistic motifs, at the end of the Late Bronze Age. Furthermore, its exceptional status indicates that it is an object of symbolic value above and beyond its ritual function.

a. Construction. The functional value of the lampstand resides in the central portion, the ירכה וקנה (Exod. 25:31; 37:17). These words together represent a cylindrical stand with a flaring lower portion which typified ceramic and metallic stands (*see* LAMPSTAND Fig. 9) from the third millennium until the sixth century B.C., when tripodal stands become ubiquitous. "Menorah" is used in the priestly texts to refer to this portion alone (Exod. 25:31-35; 37:17-21) as well as to the total object (Exod. 26:35; 40:4, 24; Num. 8:2-3). To the central portion are added six branches, which seem to have no functional value; the lamps, not an integral part of the description of the lampstand, are nowhere said to be placed at the end of each branch. Thus, where the lamps are said to be placed on the menorah (as Lev. 24:4), the central portion may be the intention.

The vocabulary describing the branches, as well as the decorative elements, is firmly rooted in architectonic language. In addition, many of the terms (such as קנה, פרח, כפתר, משקדים) have a vegetal origin, indicating the translation of plant forms into architectural features.

The triple rendition of the floral capital (Exod. 25:33) can be related to a similar development in cylindrical cultic stands at the end of the Late Bronge Age. The bowl element (גבעים; RSV "cups") can be related to the double-bowl lamp (a bowl containing a smaller cylindrical form of one piece with it, also called "cup-and-saucer" lamp), most common in Palestinian contexts in the LB II period. This receptacle, with antecedents in Egypt and the Aegean, may have served originally as a source of light for the tabernacle or tent of meeting (*see* Exod. 27:20; Lev. 24:2), with the use of discrete lamps dating to a later period. The instructions in P concerning the direction in which light is to fall (Exod. 25:37; Num. 8:2-3), seem to indicate the use of nozzled lamps, a fifth-/fourth-century development in Palestine (*see* LAMP).

The workmanship indicated by the use of the terms "pure gold" (Exod. 25:31, 36; 37:17, 22) and "one piece of hammered work" (Exod. 25:36; 37:22) is rooted in ancient metallurgic technology. The former term, when set against other references to gold in the Bible, reflects an independent gold-working tradition allied with Egyptian practices. It is distinctly different from the northern technical influences involved in the construction of the Solomonic temple and its furnishings. The second term is also technical and indicates the use of sheet gold or gold foil rather than gold leaf and thus implies the use of a wooden model.

b. Symbolism. Since there is no functional necessity for the six side branches or the elaborate floral capitals, a symbolic purpose must be supposed. Three pairs of branches are a convention in Near Eastern iconography as far back as the Old Akkadian period. By far the most common theme expressed by branched forms of any kind is that of fertility and the sustenance of life. The association of life trees with celestial symbols is a recurrent pattern. The form that most closely parallels the menorah is found in the Late Bronze Age culture of the MITANNI Empire, from whence it was disseminated to the E Mediterranean areas, including Palestine. The tabernacle artisan, in drawing this form from the symbolic lingua franca of his age, was introducing into the Israelite cult a powerful symbol—whatever specific meaning attached to it. *See* Fig. M7.

The menorah in the tabernacle is singled out (Exod. 25:40; cf. Num. 8:4) as having its pattern revealed "on the mountain." This invocation of the mountain paradigm, along with the epithet

7. Mitanni-type theme of seven-ball branch on a seal, cut and laid out like a scaraboid; from Lachish, LB II

8. Metopic design on Ajjul ware showing tree and antithetical animals; from Lachish, LB II

9. Six-branched tree with ledged stem plus human figures and assorted symbols on a Cypriote common-style seal; from Salamis, LB II

"pure" (Exod. 31:8; 39:37) as an indication of cosmic brightness, serves to place the menorah within the realm of indicators of sacred space, the dwelling of the Lord in his heavenly abode or its earthly counterpart. As a visual expression of an arboreal form, within a culture in which the fertility and immortality themes associated with life trees are negated, it is transformed into a symbolic assurance of God's presence.

2. Solomonic temple menorahs. One would expect the ten menorahs of the Solomonic temple (I Kings 7:49) to have been cylindrical stands of the same sort as the central portion of the tabernacle menorah, since that sort of cultic stand still predominated at the beginning of the Iron II period. They also seem to have possessed some sort of floral capital; however, the text does not mention the branches, which are a predominate part of the composite tabernacle menorah. The lamps which surmounted the first temple lampstands were perhaps of the seven-lipped variety such as are typical in Palestine, especially in cultic contexts, from the Middle Bronze Age through the Iron Age; the lampstand in Zechariah's vision (Zech. 4), though of a more elaborate nature, seems to reflect such a possibility.

3. Second temple menorah. Zechariah's vision exhibits the second temple emphasis on continuity with the past. The still uncompleted temple is depicted, in its reversion to a single menorah, as following the prescriptions of the tabernacle texts. Yet the divergency of Zechariah from later sources such as Josephus perhaps indicates that Zechariah is preserving a historical memory of Solomonic lampstands. However, changes in technology (e.g., in refining of gold, use of closed lamps) and artistic tradition (use of tripodal stands) since the time of the wilderness cult meant that the second temple menorah could not duplicate in a technical way the tabernacle archetype. Furthermore, the language of the Exodus texts, as the somewhat confused LXX renderings may indicate, was not fully understood. Possibly more than one menorah was constructed because of lootings of the temple before its final destruction by the Romans in A.D. 70. With the cessation of the Jerusalem cult, the menorah emerged into the everyday symbolism of the people, in synagogues and tombs, amulets and lamps, thus demonstrating the continuing power of this ancient symbol of the divine presence.

Bibliography. P. R. Ackroyd, "The Temple Vessels—a Continuity Theme," VTSup, XXIII, 166-81; E. R. Goodenough, *Jewish Symbols in the Greco-Roman Period* (1954-68), IV, 71-98; M. Haran, "The Complex of Ritual Acts Inside the Tabernacle," *Scripta Hierosolymitana,* VII, 272-302, and "The Priestly Image of the Tabernacle," *HUCA,* XXXVI (1935), 191-226; E. O. James, *The Tree of Life* (1966); C. L. Meyers, "The Tabernacle Menorah: A Synthetic Study of a Symbol from the Biblical Cult" (diss., Brandeis, 1974); R. Noth, "Zechariah's Seven-Spout Lampstand," *Bibl.,* LI (1970), 183-206; N. Perrot, "Les representations de l'arbre sacré sur les monuments de Mésopotamie et de l'Élam," *Babyloniaca,* XVII (1937), 5-144; D. Sperber, "The History of the Menorah," *JJS,* XVI (1965), 135-59; L. Yarden, *The Tree of Light* (1971).

C. L. MEYERS

*MESSIAH, JEWISH. Although the belief in a Messiah was to become the foundation of Christianity and, ultimately, an essential belief within Judaism, its roots in the OT are tenuous. It is nowhere to be found in the Pentateuch, and is only intimated in the historical, prophetic, and hagiographic books. This idea lay dormant in Jewish writings until the Hasmonean age and flowered only during the turbulent years of Roman rule which followed the death of Herod (4 B.C.).

1. The emergence of the messianic idea
2. The eclipse of the eschatological idea
3. The emergence of alternative viewpoints
4. The contribution of the Pharisees
5. A new set of alternatives for the Jews
6. Jesus and the Pharisees
7. Subsequent developments in Judaism

Bibliography

1. The emergence of the messianic idea. To understand the emergence and the development of the Messiah idea in Israel we must distinguish the various stages in the evolution of the religion of Israel. None of the patriarchs, or Moses, or Joshua, or any of the Yahwistic leaders were "anointed." The prevailing assumption throughout Israel's early history was that Yahweh would bring his people to a land flowing with milk and honey, where he would make his will known through divinely chosen spokesmen like Abraham, Moses, and Joshua. Neither an "anointed" king with a special divine destiny nor an idyllic end-of-days was anticipated. Only when the Philistines threatened to overwhelm Israel did the need for a military leader impel Samuel to "anoint" first Saul (I Sam. 9:16; 10:1; 15:1-17), and then David, as king (I Sam. 16:3, 12-13; *see* SAMUEL, I AND II[S] §4). It was here that the idea of a Messiah was born.

Yahweh promised his beloved David that his descendants would sit on the throne forever (II Sam. 7:8-29). Even though some of them might prove disloyal, Yahweh would never annul his covenant (II Sam. 7:14-15). It was this divine commitment to David which planted the seed that was subsequently to flower as the messianic idea. *See* COVENANT, DAVIDIC[S].

The commitment was given a radically new meaning by passages in Amos, Hosea, Micah, and Isaiah, which envisioned a perfect and righteous king who would reign over Israel in an idyllic future. This new meaning was articulated in response to a set of grave internal and external problems. Internally there was rampant disloyalty to Yahweh, economic and social distress, and political and moral corruption. Externally there were imperial powers which threatened the land with devastation and the people with death and exile. The optimal solution was a perfect king, a perfect society, perfect peace among the nations, and perfect harmony throughout God's creation. Swords would be beaten into plowshares, the lion would lie down with the lamb, war would be unthinkable, and justice, righteousness, mercy, and the knowledge of the Lord would be the norm. Over such a perfect society, a shoot from the stock of Jesse would reign as the wonderful counselor, Mighty God, Everlasting Father, Prince of Peace. The throne of David would be synonymous with justice and righteousness (Isa. 2:1-4; 9:2-7; 11:1-9; Amos 9:11; Jer. 33:14-22; Ezek. 37:24-28).

Although virtually all the prophets shared similar visions of the future, some prophetic books made a greater impression on subsequent generations. Of these, none was more influential than Isaiah, the First Isaiah for his unsurpassed vision of the ideal David and the idyllic future and the Second Isaiah for his proclamation of good tidings and for his picture of the Suffering Servant. Also, the Davidic motifs employed by the Psalmist (Pss. 89; 132) and the bold expression "Son of man" used by Ezekiel were to find strong echoes in the interpretation of Jesus in the gospels.

2. The eclipse of the eschatological idea. These prophetic dreams were rudely shattered by the economic, political, and social reality following upon the Babylonian exile and Judean restoration. Although CYRUS was hailed by the Second Isaiah as Yahweh's anointed (45:1), the restoration which his decree made possible bore little resemblance to the serene end-of-days so alluringly pictured by the prophets. Instead, there were bitter struggles for power between priests and Davidites, struggles which the contemporary prophets deplored while seeking to adjudicate and ameliorate them (cf. Zech. 3:1–4:10). Where righteousness was to have flourished, corruption abounded; where justice was to have reigned, there was exploitation; and where an ideal king was to have mounted the throne, the monarchy itself was being effectively undermined. The prophets of the restoration had no other recourse than to dream away the present. Malachi reassures the people that though corruption among the Levitical priests may now be the rule, there will come a day when their offerings "will be pleasing to the Lord as in the days of old and as in former years" (Mal. 3:4), and that though evil-doing is now rife, Yahweh "will send you Elijah the prophet before the great and terrible day of the Lord comes" (Mal. 4:5).

Paradoxically, the final outcome of these decades of turmoil, indecision, and disillusionment was a restored community which no prophet, with the partial exception of Ezekiel (chs. 40–48), had even remotely envisaged—a restructured society under priestly hegemony. There was to be no king at all. Even more startling, there were to be no prophets. In their stead was the canonized PENTATEUCH with its proclamation that God had revealed immutable laws. The Pentateuch gave a mandate to the priests, the "sons of Aaron," to exercise hegemony over the cultus, over the Law, and over the congregation of Israel, hence negating the need for kings. The priest, and not the king, was the "anointed" one. With the promise of agricultural abundance, long life, and many children, there was no longer a need for a radically transformed future. *See* AARON, AARONIDES[S].

The dissolution of the eschatological vision is confirmed by Ecclesiasticus. The author's overriding interest is the Pentateuch, and in the Pentateuch it is the role of Aaron as the father of the priesthood that stirs him most deeply (45:6-22). He is not unmindful of David or of God's promise to him (45:25; 47:11), but a verse or two is all that he can spare. The prophets are held in awe, but neither their teaching nor their vision of an idyllic future captivates him. Their prophecies had, so it seemed, been meant for an earlier day, for a sinful Israel. Neither they nor their admonitions had much relevancy for a community that lived by the Torah and was devoted to Yahweh, his cultus, and his priesthood.

3. The emergence of alternative viewpoints. This long period of eschatological dormancy came to an end with the take-over of Palestine by the Seleucids (*ca.* 197 B.C.) and the promulgation by ANTIOCHUS Epiphanes of his infamous decrees (168 B.C.) aimed at shattering the religion of Israel by demanding worship of Greek deities. These upheavals dealt a mortal blow to the authority of the high priesthood. First Jason and then Meneleus bought the sacred office from Antiochus, and they confronted the Jews loyal to God with a problem for which there was no easy answer. Antiochus and the radical Hellenists demanded, on pain of death, that all Jews transfer their loyalties from God to gods. Trapped between apostasy and an utterly unforeseeable outcome, loyal Jews desperately searched for a constructive resolution of their dilemma. *See* ISRAEL, HISTORY OF §14.

Four basic solutions emerged: (1) faith in God's power to save and a readiness to die rather than violate his law (the Hasidim); (2) revival of prophetic vision, but assigning this vision to a prophet-like figure who had lived during the years when prophecy was both alive and credible (DANIEL; *see* APOCALYPTICISM; APOCALYPTICISM[S]); (3) armed uprising (the HASMONEANS; *see* MACCABEES, MACCABEAN REVOLT); (4) a mutational form of Judaism which shifted the focus from earthly rewards and punishments to heavenly ones (Pharisaism; *see* PHARISEES[S]).

Of these four, armed uprising under the Hasmoneans, combined with an enthusiastic response to the novel teachings of the Pharisees, formed the solution which most Jews favored. Nevertheless, the pseudepigraphic device for reviving prophecy was used with such success by the author of the book of Daniel that it was resorted to again and again when visionaries (Enoch, Testaments of the Twelve Patriarchs, Psalms of Solomon, IV Ezra, Baruch, the Syballine Oracles) glimpsed solutions to ongoing problems which were at odds with those advocated by the dominant Pharisaic leadership who rejected these books as spurious. *See* PSEUDONYMOUS WRITING[S].

Daniel is important for the development of the messianic idea since its author used such enigmatic expressions as "Son of man," gave sanction to the reality of specific angels such as Gabriel and Michael, spoke of an "anointed" prince (*māshîaḥ nāgid*), conjured up the puzzling image of the "ancient of days," and held out a hope for RESURRECTION.

Although only the book of Daniel gained scriptural status, this approach was appealing whenever conditions were turbulent. In some pseudepigraphic writings there are visions of deliverance through a Son of man, a Messiah, and of a sweeping away of the alien tyrants and the establishment of the kingdom of God on earth.

4. The contribution of the Pharisees. The Pharisaic solution to the problem posed by Roman persecution and by the agonizing grip of the Roman procurators was a steadfast faith in *'Ôlām habbā'* (the world to come) and *tᵉḥîyath hammēthîm* (the resurrection of the dead). The focus was on individuals and their eternal life, and not on the shifting configurations of an unsteady and unreliable external world. Those who adhered to the twofold law comprised the true community of Israel, which was not dependent for its viability on either the land or the temple but on its selection by Yahweh. Pharisaism was transnational, universal, and oriented toward the individual's yearning for salvation. For the Pharisees, a Messiah who would liberate the Jews from the Roman yoke and restore the throne of David would be far more a problem than a solution. For them the key issues were not liberation from pain and suffering, but the life beyond the grave; not national independence, but true and steadfast belief; not Israel of the flesh, which would necessarily include nonbelieving Sadducees, but Israel of the spirit—those who were steadfastly loyal to the twofold law and the salvation which it promised.

This focus can be clearly discerned in the decision of the Pharisaic leadership to acknowledge the right of the Roman governor to take a census and levy tribute. They believed that as long as the Pharisaic sages were permitted to teach freely the twofold law (*see* MISHNA; TORAH[S]) and to preach the good news of life eternal, Rome had a right to collect the tribute for Caesar. For the Pharisees, the Roman imperium was an exercise of authority over this transient world and did not cut off access to the enduring world to come. Those scholars who refused to accept this decision, but insisted that allegiance to Rome was disloyalty to God, were forced to promulgate a fourth philosophy of their own which differed, according to Josephus, from that of the Pharisees on this issue alone (cf. Jos. Antiq. XVIII.i.1-2, 6).

It is thus evident that Pharisees did not look upon themselves as resurrected prophets. They did not rely on fresh dreams of an idyllic end-of-days or of a righteous shoot from the stock of Jesse to provide solutions to the ongoing problems of the people of Israel.

5. A new set of alternatives for the Jews. Although the majority of the Jews held fast to the salvation system of the Pharisees, large numbers of them were drawn to alternative solutions, since living under the procurators proved to be an increasingly stressful experience. These alternatives were: (1) the revolutionary doctrines of the Fourth Philosophy or Sicarii, which called for continuous terrorist activity against Rome and for an egalitarian society (*but see* ZEALOT[S]); (2) a revolt against Rome and the establishment of a Jewish polity which would be nonoppressive and quasi-democratic; (3) a charismatic leader, a Messiah, who would sweep away the tyranny of Rome and usher in the kingdom of God—as foretold by the prophets of old and as reiterated in the pseudepigraphic visions (cf. Jos. War VI.v.2-viii.3; Antiq. XVIII.v.2).

The messianic alternative, however, was risky since neither the prophetic visions nor the pseudepigraphic foretellings were specific. They did not spell out names and they did not give dates. They were even unclear as to whether the Son of man was to be a descendant of David or whether there was to be a specific person at all. Many were disillusioned as now this and now that would-be Messiah was caught by the Romans and put to death, and as the anticipated kingdom did not come.

6. Jesus and the Pharisees. It was in this climate of messianic uncertainty that Jesus began his ministry. As a Jew, Jesus had been nurtured on the teachings of the Pharisees and had absorbed their faith in the world to come and their firm belief in the resurrection of the dead. He had also absorbed the Pharisaic mode of using scripture—a mode which drew freely on any verse which it deemed appropriate to a specific situation, wherever it might be in Scripture, and without any regard for its contextual setting. This mode may best be designated as situational exegesis. Such a mode was not a commentary on Scripture, but on events. A verse from Isaiah joined to a verse from Deuteronomy joined to a verse from Daniel was deemed to be far more helpful in elucidating the divine meaning of an event than the next verse in Isaiah or Deuteronomy or Daniel. To the extent that Jesus himself drew on Scripture as illustrative of his teaching or his messianic role, he invariably used the situational exegesis of the Pharisees. And so, too, did his disciples and Paul. *See* INTERPRETATION, HISTORY OF[S] §§B, C-D.

But Jesus deviated radically from the Pharisees insofar as he based his "new" teaching of the approaching kingdom on his own personal authority, as though he were the Son of man or a prophet like Elijah, or a son of God, or the Messiah. Such claims the Pharisees could not tolerate, and in seeking to refute them the Pharisees had to develop some concept of the Messiah, since they were confronted with scriptural proof texts indicating that a Messiah had indeed been foreseen by the prophets. This concept, however, was thoroughly defensive; i.e., it was a concept that, while affirming that a Messiah, son of David, will come, indeed, must come, set conditions that no would-be Messiah, least of all Jesus, was ever likely to meet. Among these were (1) an impeccable, unchallengeable genealogy of Davidic descent, (2) a public display of signs and wonders, (3) the return of Elijah prior to the advent of the Messiah, (4) fulfillment of his messianic mission during his lifetime, demonstrated as having been implicitly or explicitly spelled out by the prophets. To all intents and purposes, therefore, the messianic idea of the Pharisees, whom the majority of the people followed, was a negative one. It supported the belief even as it undercut its contemporary relevance. By Pharisaic criteria, Jesus could not be, or have been, the Messiah since, (1) he appears to disclaim Davidic descent ("How can the scribes [Pharisees] say that the Christ [Messiah] is the son of David? David himself, inspired by the Holy Spirit, declared, 'The Lord [God] said to my Lord [the messiah-King], Sit at my right hand, till I put thy enemies under thy feet.' David himself calls him [the messiah] Lord; so how is he his [David's] son? And the great throng heard him gladly" [Mark 12:35-37]); (2) he did not perform persuasive signs and wonders ("The Pharisees came and began to argue with him, seeking from him a sign from heaven, to test him. And he sighed deeply in his spirit and said, 'Why does this generation seek a sign? Truly, I say to you, no sign shall be given to this generation' " [Mark 8:11-12]); (3) it was not agreed that Elijah had appeared prior to Jesus' ministry ("And they asked him, 'Why do the scribes say that first Elijah must come?' And he said to them, 'Elijah does come first to restore all things; . . . But I tell you that Elijah has come, and they did to him whatever they pleased, as is written of him' " [Mark 9:11-13]); (4) he was crucified, and this form of execution utterly nullified his claims. Although the gospels insisted that Jesus was a descendant of David, did indeed perform persuasive signs for those who had faith in him, that Elijah had in fact already come, and fully confirmed that he was the Messiah by his resurrection, neither the people at large or the Pharisees in particular were impressed or convinced by the gospel writers, or by Paul.

Paradoxically, it was the core teaching of the Pharisees that made the gospel claims for Jesus as the Christ credible. The Pharisees had made possible the fundamental belief of the Christian faith (that Jesus was the Messiah because he had been resurrected) since belief in the Resurrection is not based on the OT, but on Pharisaic doctrine. Unlike the many prophetic utterances referring to the restoration of David's throne and visions of an idyllic end time, there was no prophetic anticipation of the agonizing death of the son of David and his resurrection as the necessary prelude to those events. The only scriptural support for the belief in the Resurrection is that which follows from the situational exegesis of the Pharisees, an exegesis which Jesus drew upon to confute the Sadducees and win the approbation of the listening scribe (Pharisee) (Mark 12:18-27). What, for the Pharisees, had been a defense against the claims of would-be Messiahs, namely, that the pretensions of a Messiah dissolve with his death, was regarded by the Christians as their most telling proof, a proof made credible by the Pharisees themselves.

If, then, we seek to account for the breakthrough of Christianity to novel messianic ground, and seek to discover the Jewish roots which made such a breakthrough possible, we would posit that there was fusion of (1) the belief that God had made a promise to David, his anointed, to establish his throne forever (cf. Mark 11:8-10); (2) the prophetic linkage of an ideal Davidic king with an idyllic future; (3) the Pharisaic belief in the world to come and the Resurrection; (4) the Pharisaic mode of applying disconnected scriptural verses to ongoing events.

And if we seek to explain why ideas so long dormant were revived in so fresh and compelling a manner, we need only note the agonizing experience of the Jews under the procurators, an experience that was ultimately to drive even the most loyal followers of the Pharisees into a suicidal war against Rome. In these circumstances, so reminiscent of the agony which had stirred Amos, Hosea, Isaiah, and others to frame a perfect solution to such relentless distress, it is little wonder that the hope for a kingdom of God and the wish for a perfect king should have been revived and believed.

What must be stressed is that insofar as the gospel record is concerned, the roots of the Christian messianic idea are deeply embedded in the Pharisaic system of Judaism and not in the pseudepigraphic writings. Like the Pharisees, Jesus and his followers considered these writings to be spurious and therefore at no time did they cite them.

7. Subsequent developments in Judaism. However for most Jews, the messianic alternative, even in its highly novel and audacious Christian message of a risen Christ and a second coming, was rejected. The majority continued to adhere to the Pharisaic faith in the world to come and the resurrection of the dead, and in the verifications which the Pharisees demanded of the Messiah and which they alone would evaluate.

Whereas the belief in the world to come and the resurrection are affirmed in the Mishna as binding on every Jew (cf. M. Sanh. 10.1), the belief in the Messiah has no doctrinal status whatsoever. The term Messiah occurs only twice in the Mishna (Ber. 1·5; Soṭ. 9.15).

The messianic idea in Judaism did subsequently gain the status of a dogma, but not during the Pharisaic and tannaitic periods. To be sure, the highly esteemed teacher of the twofold law, Rabbi Akiba, hailed Simon Bar Koziba as the Messiah, calling him BAR KOCHBA ("Son of the Star," alluding to Num. 24:17-19), and supported his ill-fated revolt (132-135 A.D.) against the Roman emperor HADRIAN. But even R. Akiba did not look upon Bar Kochba as other than a mortal leader.

It was not until the time of Maimonides (1135-1204) that the belief in the Messiah was declared to be a fundamental principle of faith.

In grappling with the messianic idea during the years following the Hasmonean revolt, it is necessary to evaluate the relevance and the significance of the DEAD SEA SCROLLS. These scrolls do indeed reveal a keen interest in the Messiah, whom they refer to as the *moreh tsedek* (teacher of righteousness), and they are fraught with eschatological concerns. Yet one hesitates to use these materials in the same way as one would use the pseudepigraphic literature. Scholarly discretion demands that we regard the scrolls as sources which are still being processed and that we refrain from integrating them into our reconstructions of Jewish history. *See* DEAD SEA SCROLLS[S] §9.

Bibliography. A. H. Silver, *History of Messianic Speculation in Israel* (1927); L. Ginzberg, *The Legends of the Jews,* vol. 7 (1938), pp. 306-9 (index); G. Scholem, *The Messianic Idea in Judaism* (1971); E. Rivkin, "The Meaning of Messiah in Jewish Thought," *USQR,* XXVI (1971), 383-406.

E. RIVKIN

MESSIANIC BANQUET. A great feast for the faithful in the age to come was a feature in Jewish and Christian speculation about the end time. Where the Messiah is not mentioned, it may more properly be called the eschatological banquet.

1. Jewish sources contemporary with the NT period. It is often stated that such a banquet was a common feature of Jewish apocalyptic thought. This is probably correct, though direct and explicit references are comparatively few. Apocal. Bar. 29:4-8 and Enoch 62:14 are regularly cited. Strictly speaking, the former refers not so much to the eschatological banquet as to an abundance of food in the eschatological era. The flesh of the mythical creatures Leviathan and Behemoth, the manna, and fruit, the food of Adam in paradise, will be fare for the redeemed. The latter passage says of the righteous "with that Son of Man shall they eat/And lie down and rise up for ever and ever." Two later (perhaps A.D. 250-300) apocalypses, III Enoch and the Apocalypse of Elijah, also speak of eating with the Messiah. A text from Qumran supplies important evidence. 1QSa 2.17-22 describes a community meal presided over by the Priest and the Messiah of Israel. Allusion to the messianic banquet is apparent. (Presence of the Priest *and* the Messiah of Israel refers to the Qumran expectation of two messianic figures.) At the end of the passage, however, the provision is given, "And they shall act according to this decree at every me-[al when] at least ten men are gathered." Thus, at Qumran the regular common meal of the community, described also in 1QS 6.4-6, seems to have been considered an anticipation of the future messianic meal. Other passages in apocalyptic writings contain partial allusions and reminiscences of the theme, implying that it was more widely a part of the "common knowledge" of apocalyptic speculation than the few explicit references might indicate.

2. NT evidence. Witness to the banquet in the NT may be summarized under the following classifications.

a) Some passages indicate that the motif, apparently well-known to Jesus and his hearers, could be used as a general illustration without detailed explanation or specific connection with Jesus the Messiah (Matt. 8:11-12=Luke 13:28-30; and probably the parables in Matt. 22:1-10=Luke 14:16-24; and Matt. 25:1-13). Such general usage was early given a messianic interpretation in the tradition (*see* Luke 14:15 and the setting of Matt. 8:11-12).

b) Two passages clearly refer to Jesus as host at the messianic banquet (Luke 22:28-30; Rev. 19:9).

c) The Last Supper was considered to have a peculiar relationship with the coming banquet, as Jesus refers to eating and drinking with his disciples afterward in the kingdom (Matt. 26:29; Mark 14:25; Luke 22:15-18. *See* LAST SUPPER §3; PASSOVER §2).

d) Less direct, but significant, are the miraculous feeding narratives (Matt. 14:13-21; 15:32-39; Mark

6:35-44; 8:1-10; Luke 9:12-17; John 6:1-14) and the post-Resurrection accounts in Luke 24:28-43 and John 21:9-14. All these seem to have been understood as anticipations of the banquet of the end time.

e) Further, it appears that in some early Christian circles celebration of the Lord's Supper was considered both a commemoration of the death of Jesus and an anticipation of the coming messianic feast (I Cor. 11:23-26).

f) Finally, Rev. 19:17-18 treats the theme in an entirely different way. Depicted is the great eschatological supper of God, but the emphasis is on the judgment and destruction of God's enemies rather than the joy of his redeemed.

3. **OT backgrounds.** Detailed examination of OT motifs which contributed to the picture of the eschatological banquet goes beyond the scope of this note. Attention may be directed, however, to Isa. 25:6-8 which, in an eschatological context, speaks of a feast to be enjoyed by all peoples on the day when the Lord has vanquished death, and to the summons to eat and drink in Isa. 55:1-5, a passage which is usually interpreted eschatologically. Two other themes in the OT also had considerable influence. A number of passages (e.g., Zeph. 1:7-9; Jer. 25:15-34; 46:10; Isa. 34:5-7; Ezek. 39:17-20) mention the sacrificial slaughter of God's enemies on the day of his triumph. In some of these, eating is associated with the sacrifice, though the participants at the meal are not the members of the redeemed community. The emphasis is on judgment, not joy (cf. Rev. 19:17-18). A variation of this theme portrays the mythical beast Leviathan as the object of the sacrifice (Ps. 74:12-17; cf. Ezek. 29:3-5; 32:2-8), though no mention is made of the redeemed as sharers in the feast. (The Leviathan myth is well attested in many cultures and its Ugaritic [Canaanite?] version no doubt influenced biblical usage. *See* LEVIATHAN.) Jewish and Christian apocalyptic writers drew from all these themes (and others, e.g., marriage imagery) and interwove them into the varied descriptions of the eschatological banquet discussed above.

Eating and drinking was a common OT manner of expressing joyous fellowship, both on the human level and in a covenantal context between the worshiping community and God (*see* MEALS §4*a*). Thus the messianic (eschatological) banquet served as a striking pictorial representation of God's final triumph, which would be characterized by communion between him and the faithful in the New Age. The meal stood as a symbol of triumph and of joy.

Bibliography. Convenient summaries of Pseudep. material in R. H. Charles, *Apocrypha and Pseudepigrapha of the Old Testament* (1913), vol II, and G. F. Moore, *Judaism* (1927), vol. II, pp. 363-65. Good discussions of NT evidence in J. Jeremias, *Eucharistic Words of Jesus* (1966), and *The Parables of Jesus* (1963). T. H. Gaster, *Thespis* (2nd rev. ed., 1961), pp. 137-53 and 232-35 discusses OT material in broad mythological background. The Qumran evidence is summarized in J. Priest, "The Messiah and the Meal in 1QSa" *JBL,* LXXXII (1963), 95-100.

J. F. PRIEST

MESSIANIC SECRET. *See* SECRET, MESSIANIC[S].

***METALLURGY.** *See* TELL EL-KHELEIFEH[S].

METEORITES. Sanchuniathon, the Phoenician priest whose account of Canaanite religion was preserved by Philo of Byblos, said that, as Astarte was traveling through the world, she encountered "a star falling through the air," took it up and consecrated it on the holy island of Tyre. Tyrian coins from the third century A.D. portray two stones with the inscription ΑΜΒΡΟΣΙΕ ΠΕΤΡΕ, "divine stones." Acts 19:35 refers to the city of EPHESUS as the "temple keeper of the great Artemis and of the sacred stone that fell from the sky." The black stone revered in the Ka'ba sanctuary at Mecca is, like these others, a meteorite, and was in pre-Islamic times revered as divine, a portion of himself sent by a sky god to serve as the sacred center of a city consecrated to him. These are but a few of the many examples found in ancient Greece and the Middle East of the worship of sacred meteorites.

In Canaanite religion, the meteorite-god seems to have been called Bethel (god-house), and was worshiped in Israel also (*see* BETHEL, DEITY). One of the gods of Tyre is named Baitilani (a plural form of Bethel). Sanchuniathon lists Baitulos as a son of Heaven and Earth and states that Ouranos (Heaven) used *baitulia,* which are λίθοι 'εμψῦχοι (stones with souls), as weapons in his unsuccessful struggle against his son EL.

Gen. 28:10-22 relates the story of Jacob's dream of a "ladder" reaching to heaven. The stone upon which he slept, possibly a meteorite, he declared to be "God's house" and thus he named the place "Bethel." Material from Egypt contains a number to motifs which appear similar to those in this biblical story. The stone would thus have "opened" the heavens to Jacob, as did the meteorite of Thebes for its high priest. The "ladder" would be like the iron or meteorite ladders of Egypt, on which the divinized pharaohs walked. On awakening, Jacob exclaimed, "This is the gate of heaven," words identical to those used in connection with Pharaoh's ladder and reminiscent of the title of the high priest at Thebes, "the Opener of the Gates of Heaven."

Bibliography. P. Clemen, *Die Phoenikische Religion nach Philo von Byblos* (1939); A. B. Cook, *Zeus,* III (1940), 881-942; H. Lewy, "Origin and Significance of the Mâgên Dâwîd," *ArOr,* XVIII, Pt. 3 (1950), 346-49; Comte du Mesnil du Buisson, "Origine et évolution du panthéon de Tyr," *RHR,* CLXIV (1963), 133-63; G. A. Wainwright, "Jacob's Bethel," *PEFQS* (1934), 32-44.

R. A. ROSENBERG

***METHUSELAH.** *See* SHALAH[S].

***METHUSHAEL.** For etymology *see* DEITIES, UNDERWORLD[S] §2*b*iii.

***MICAH THE PROPHET.** Recent study of the book of Micah, as of other prophetic writings, centers on the identification of the varieties of tradition utilized in the book—and their literary affinities and social settings—and the setting and purpose of the book in its final, edited form.

1. The final edition of the book. In contrast to the atomizing criticism of a previous generation, contemporary scholars have sought the unifying features in the arrangement of the book. The most comprehensive investigation of this has been made by Willis. He holds that the editor, who may have been among the disciples of Isaiah left in Judah after the fall of Jerusalem in 586 B.C., arranged the book in a series of three groups of alternating (and composite) oracles of doom and salvation. In the first and third groups the doom oracles are extensive (1:2–2:11 and 6:1–7:6), and the oracles of hope are brief (2:12-13 and 7:7-20), while the reverse is true in the middle group (doom, 3:1-12; hope, 4:1–5:15). His purpose was to persuade the exilic Jewish community that God had not abandoned them. Since the portions of the collection deriving from Micah had been uttered in the Assyrian crisis of 734-700, their republication in and after the Babylonian crisis of 605-586 was a fitting appropriation of prophetic tradition. These portions were supplemented with anonymous oracles of salvation reflecting the Davidic and Zionistic traditions of Jerusalem (*see* ZION TRADITION[S]). To this analysis may be added the observation that the oracles of doom would have functioned in the exilic situation to justify the destruction of Judah, which had already occurred, as a divine punishment for iniquity, and to elicit a spirit of contrition among the survivors.

2. Older traditions. Following the lead of Gunkel, several scholars have recognized ch. 7 as a liturgical composition, deriving originally from the northern kingdom of Israel. Thus Reicke argues that 7:1-6 is a communal lament (not an oracle of judgment), in which the speaker identifies himself with the sin and suffering of the people in the manner of the royal psalms of lamentation, and 7:7-20 is the prophetic response. The whole is modeled after a liturgy of penance from the autumnal New Year's festival, or perhaps the Day of Atonement. The description of distress (7:1-6) utilizes in part the conventional language of ancient Near Eastern eschatological texts (e.g., the dissolution of family solidarity).

Others have interpreted the mixture of oracles of doom with oracles of salvation in the book as a whole as the result of its origin in the public worship of the pre-exilic period, i.e., Micah's own time. However, the argument for an exilic date for the final collection, and some of the oracles of promise, is more convincing.

Bibliography. H. Gunkel, "The Close of Micah: A Prophetical Liturgy," *What Remains of the Old Testament and Other Essays* (1928), pp. 115-49; J. Jeremias, "Die Deutung der Gerichtsworte Michas in der Exilzeit," *ZAW*, LXXXIII (1971), 330-54; A. S. Kapelrud, "Eschatology in the Book of Micah," *VT*, XI (1961), 392-405; B. Reicke, "Liturgical Traditions in Micah 7," *HTR*, LX (1967), 349-68; A. S. van der Woude, "Micah in Dispute with the Pseudo-prophets," *VT*, XIX (1969), 244-60; J. T. Willis, "The Structure of the Book of Micah," *SEA*, XXXIV (1969), 5-42. J. M. WARD

*__MIDRASH__ mĭd'räsh [מדרש, from דרש, *dāraš, see* §1 *below,* perhaps related to Arab. *darasa,* "to tread," "to study" and Akkad. *darāsu-darāšu,* "to trample upon," "to press hard"]. The most important and characteristic term in the ancient rabbinic milieu for interpretation of scripture, including its aims, methods, and results. An understanding of midrash can be approached by tracing the semantic development of the term, the historical factors which contribute to its development, its presuppositions, aims, and characteristics, and the forms in which it comes to expression in rabbinic literature. In addition, recent study has focused on the history of midrash with the result that the term is currently associated with the whole phenomenon of biblical interpretation in early Judaism, and its importance in the milieu in which Christianity arose.

1. Semantic development
2. Historical factors
3. Presuppositions, aims, and characteristics
   a. Hermeneutical rules
   b. Rational and mantic characteristics
4. Rabbinic Midrashim
   a. Composition and date
   b. Types and characteristics
5. Recent study of midrash
   a. Origins
   b. Evolution
   c. Varieties
   d. Comparative midrash
   e. Problem of definition
Bibliography

1. Semantic development. The verbal root *dārash* has several meanings in the OT among which "to seek, inquire," "to investigate" are prominent, and most important for the semantic development of the term. The seeking of God's will (Ps. 119:10; II Chr. 17:4; 22:9), the inquiry of God through prophetic oracle (I Sam. 9:9; I Kings 22:8; II Kings 3:11; Jer. 21:2), and the thorough investigation of a matter (Judg. 6:29; Deut. 13:15; 17:4; 19:18) develop in the course of time into the particular type of seeking, inquiry, and investigation associated with the interpretation of scripture.

The transition to a later usage can be seen when one compares the different objects which the verb takes in similar phrases found in II Chr. 30:19 and Ezra 7:10. In the former, King Hezekiah had prayed for "everyone who sets his heart to seek God" (לדרוש האלהים). In the latter, Ezra the scribe "had set his heart to seek the law of the Lord" (לדרוש את תורת יהוה). While we should probably not attribute an explicitly exegetical sense to *dārash* in Ezra 7:10, nor assume that the techniques associated with later rabbinic interpretation of scripture are already implied in the verb (though procedures akin to later midrash are already found in the Bible, *see* §5*a below*), we do have the first instance of *dārash* applied to an authoritative text and signifying, at the least, the thorough study of the Torah in conjunction with its teaching and practice (cf. Ps. 119:45, 94, 155; I Chr. 28:8; Ecclus. 32:15).

By the first century B.C., there are instances in Qumran and associated writings where *dārash* clearly has an exegetical meaning. Legal conclusions were drawn from the interpretation of scripture and made binding on the sect (CDC VI.7; VII.18; 4QFlor 1.11; 1QS 6.6; 8.12). The extent to which interpretation was recognized as a basis for deriving legal ordinances in scribal and Pharisaic circles prior to the destruction of the temple is debated. In any case, this practice receives new impetus with the influential figure of Rabbi Akiba (active *ca.* A.D. 110-135) who derived *halachoth* (rabbinic prohibitions and ordinances) from the interpretation of particles in the biblical text. *See* INTERPRETATION, HISTORY OF[S] §D.

Though one finds instances of an earlier and more general usage in rabbinic writings, the exegetical meaning of *dārash* becomes dominant and is associated with the full range of methods employed in the interpretation of scripture. In addition to this, there is one other distinctive meaning of the verb in rabbinic writings: "to convey" or "declare to others," thus, to preach a sermon, give a public oration, to pronounce a *halachah,* recite a midrashic text.

The noun *midrāsh* appears twice in the OT and in both cases in the *status constructus.* The Chronicler refers to מדרש הנביא עדו ("story of the prophet Iddo," II Chr. 13:22) and to מדרש ספר המלכים ("Commentary on the Book of the Kings," II Chr. 24:27). The meaning of *midrash* in the Chronicler's work is uncertain. Although RSV translates "Commentary" at II Chr. 24:27, it is unlikely that this is already the meaning of the term. The LXX translates "book" and "writing" respectively, and many modern commentators follow this view. It is possible that the Chronicler has coined the word *midrash* to cover both a historical narrative and an account of prophecy (cf. Gertner). If this is correct, *midrash* has the notion of conveyance before it comes to mean interpretation.

The later development is again evidenced in Qumran writings where in several instances *midrash* refers to study and interpretation of Torah (1QS 8.15; CDC XX.6; cf. 4QFlor 1.14 where *midrash* stands as a heading for a contemporizing interpretation of Ps. 1:1. In contrast to this usage, cf. 1QS 6.24; 8.26). (*See also* INTERPRETATION, HISTORY OF[S] §B1.) The NT may also have the term *midrash* in view in passages which concern questions or matters (ζήτησις, ζήτημα) of scripture (Acts 25:19-20; 23:29; 18:14-15; 26:3; cf. I Tim. 1:4; 6:4; II Tim. 2:23; Tit. 3:9).

In the rabbinic writings, *midrash* becomes the characteristic term for interpretation of scripture, denoting both the activities involved and the results produced. In the latter sense, it can refer to a single biblical text with its interpretation, and to a collection or book of *midrashim.* It also refers to the school or college (בית מדרש) where Torah was studied and interpreted. In addition, early rabbinic usage often equates *midrash* with biblical חק (statute). This equation stems in part from the semantic relationship between the Hebrew verbal roots חקק (to cut in, engrave, or to decree statutes) and דרש, both of which are found in the Bible as synonyms of חקר ("to investigate, search out, examine," Judg. 5:15, 16; Deut. 13:15). Similarly, Qumran circles equate the Lawgiver (מחקק) with the Interpreter of the Law דורש התורה; see CDC VI.7; VII.18; cf. T.B. Sanh. 5a).

2. Historical factors. The semantic development of *dārash/midrash* is symptomatic of the pervasive and deep-rooted historical and conceptual changes which mark the long development from the biblical period to the beginnings of rabbinic Judaism. In pre-exilic Israel, the will of God was largely ascertained by means of inquiry through priestly and prophetic oracle. By the beginning of the rabbinic period (*ca.* end of the first century A.D.), the mantle of inspiration and authority had passed to those responsible for discerning the will of God through interpretation of sacred texts.

Among the factors contributing to this change in the Persian and Hellenistic periods are the decline of prophecy, the final editing of Israel's epic, legal, and prophetic traditions, their collection in a twofold canon of Torah and Prophets, and the emergence of lay scholar groups to compete with the traditional teaching authority of the priests. The development of biblical interpretation by the rabbis parallels the work of the Alexandrian grammarians on the sacred texts of Homer, and coincides with the standardization of the Hebrew Bible text (*see* TEXT, OT §A3*b*). The weakening or destruction of other institutions of Israel's religious and national life also affected the development of midrash. Following the destruction of the temple in A.D. 70, the Bible was the only part of Israel's national heritage that remained intact. To the creative interpretation of this source, the rabbis devoted their energy, skill, and ingenuity to find a basis for customs and legal precedents which, at least in part, had arisen independent of the Bible, and to provide comfort and instruction that would both forge a link with the biblical past and make scripture relevant to the present.

3. Presuppositions, aims, and characteristics. This general aim of midrash is rooted in a certain understanding of scripture, and operates in the historical distance that separates the world of the Bible from the world of the rabbis. The Bible was not merely a revered record of the nation's past, but the single and complete revelation of God's will for the nation in all generations, the unshakeable ground of action and identity, the mystery of man and the world, and the vision of Israel's destiny. From this perspective, scripture was productive of an inexhaustible wealth of meaning which could be uncovered and made relevant through intensive meditation and proper probing of the biblical text. The spirit which had spoken through Moses and the prophets spoke now in the creative reflection on scripture, in midrash, which, from another angle, was but the appropriate transmission of what was received from scripture in the context of the present needs and circumstances of the community.

Yet the world in which the Bible was thus understood was no longer the world out of which the Bible had emerged. As a record of a bygone age composed of diverse traditions transmitted, reworked, and combined over generations, the Bible presented for a later age a strange and often obscure world, and at the same time the contemporary voice of God in which their own world was reflected. Contradictions in the biblical text, both real and apparent, had to be resolved and the unity of scripture unfolded. The legal corpora of the Bible had to yield directives for new cases under new conditions. The biblical narratives had to be updated, ethical and cultural perspectives modernized, and new tales composed out of the "silence" of scripture. By means of midrash, the Bible was wrapped in the garment of contemporary perceptions, issues, and concerns, and thus transformed; in turn, the contemporary world was perceived in the light of scripture, and thereby illuminated.

a. Hermeneutical rules. In postbiblical Judaism, the formulation of a list of rules for interpretation of scripture is found only in the rabbinic tradition. Seven *middōth* (hermeneutical rules) are ascribed to Hillel (Tosef. Sanh. VII.11). The terminology of several of these rules appears to be influenced by formulations of the Alexandrian grammarians for interpretation of the Greek classics. An expanded edition in the form of thirteen *middōth* is attributed to R. Ishmael (*Mek. deRabbi Simeon bar Yoḥai* on Exod. 21:1). These rules involve various types of inference and analogy and are largely confined to the derivation of rabbinic *halachoth* from the written Law of the Pentateuch (*midrash halachah*). A late tradition ascribes thirty-two *middōth* to R. Eliezer ben Jose Ha-gelili. These are largely confined to the interpretation of the nonlegal portions of scripture (*midrash haggadah*). *See* INTERPRETATION, HISTORY OF[S] §D.

b. Rational and mantic characteristics. Though these rules do not encompass all the procedures employed in midrash, as a whole they do reflect two general features of midrash which can be distinguished, yet which often figure in the same tradition. The rabbis, like modern readers, often found the text of the Bible obscure, and in general recognized that scripture spoke with an economy of language. Obscurities in the text were elucidated, gaps filled in, and situations clarified, partly by comparison with words and verses from other biblical loci, partly by what appeared appropriate from the perspective of the rabbis. Thus, on the one hand, midrash invokes the principle of learning the unknown from the known, and in this connection sometimes proceeds via logical inference and sound philological observations, yet usually without making the clarification of a biblical text a goal distinct from the actualization of that text in the present.

On the other hand, there is a distinctly mantic characteristic which is pronounced in midrash. The Bible is regarded as a vision and portent of the future. Its language is not only laconic, but intentionally elliptical and ambiguous, the language of dreams and oracles, those direct modes of divine communication known from antiquity. (Cf. the earlier biblical meaning of *dārash,* "to inquire of God.") As an oracular text, scripture is not bound by the grammatical proprieties, semantic possibilities, literary contexts, and temporal sequences of ordinary texts. Hence, especially in the atomistic interpretation of words and letters and the variety of wordplay, midrash proceeds in a manner similar to magical and symbolic procedures employed in interpretation of dreams and oracles in the contemporary Greco-Roman world and known from high antiquity.

This view of scripture as divine oracle is certainly not limited to the rabbinic tradition. It is important for the general phenomenon of biblical interpretation, its methods and goals, in early Judaism, and it is especially evident in eschatological and mystical interpretation—e.g., in Qumran *pesharim,* NT christological interpretation, and Philonic allegory. In the rabbinic tradition, such methods are clearly popular and not confined to passages thought to have eschatological or mystical import. Indeed, in rabbinic midrash, there is a tendency to organize in scientific-like classification the results of interpretation gained by such methods.

4. Rabbinic Midrashim. The major midrash books (Midrashim) of the rabbinic corpus can be broadly classified along the lines of content and literary genre. Thus, one speaks of halachic and haggadic Midrashim according to whether the contents are largely of a legal or nonlegal character, and of exegetical, homiletical, and narrative Midrashim. Exegetical Midrashim are verse-by-verse commentaries on large portions of biblical books, and present a variety of individual traditions which are not organized in any larger structural patterns. As the name implies, homiletical Midrashim develop sermonic themes which are presented on only the first verse (or first few verses) from the weekly sabbath portion of the Pentateuch read in the synagogue, or from the Pentateuchal and Prophetic lections for festivals. Narrative Midrashim are not commentaries, but gather legendary material associated with biblical stories and with the history of biblical and postbiblical times.

a. Composition and date. The rabbinic Midrashim in their extant form are largely a composite literature. A single midrash book may evidence structural features of more than one genre, and the time and place of composition may vary in different sections of the work. The date of final editing itself is often difficult to determine with any precision. Even more difficult to determine is the date of the individual traditions which compose a Midrash. One cannot rely on the date of final editing. Nor is it possible to rely on the ascription of traditions to known rabbinic authorities without testing this evidence by other internal criteria.

b. Types and characteristics. The halachic Midrashim belong to the category of exegetical midrash. They are the earliest rabbinic Midrashim, generally thought to have received their final editing in the third century A.D. Since large portions of Exodus-Deuteronomy are treated in these works, not all the biblical material commented on is legal, and therefore one finds sections of haggadic midrash as well. On the basis of the different authorities cited and differences in technical terminology and hermeneutical rules, it has been shown that the halachic portions of these Midrash books derive from the Palestinian schools (disciples) of R. Akiba and R. Ishmael.

The haggadic Midrashim are dated from the fifth through the twelfth centuries. The characteristic feature of the homiletical Midrash is the proem or introduction to each homily. Since most homilies begin with a series of proems, it is very unlikely that each chapter in a homiletical Midrash was drawn from a single sermon as it was actually delivered in the synagogue. Rather, the literary homilies of the Midrashim have probably been compiled from parts of many sermons delivered in the synagogues. The proem has a distinct rhetorical structure. It begins with a biblical text (the proem verse), often drawn from the Hagiographa and seemingly remote in content from the opening verse of the Pentateuchal lection. From this proem verse, a chain of expositions is evolved, often on the basis of a verbal tally or play on words with the lection verse, until the connection is finally made with the lection verse with which the proem closes. By means of this chain of expositions, proem and lection verses are linked, and both are thereby seen in new perspective.

Although the narrative Midrashim are late, several are closer to the pre-Christian genre of rewritten Bible (i.e., to Jubilees, the Genesis Apocryphon, Pseudo-Philo) than to the exegetical or homiletical Midrashim. They embellish biblical stories, sometimes with legendary material otherwise unknown. (For a listing of the major Midrashim, *see* MIDRASH; for fuller listings with pertinent information on editions, translations, etc., *see bibliog.*)

5. Recent study of midrash. Since the end of World War II, the term *midrash* has increasingly come to be associated with study of the origin, evolution, and varieties of biblical interpretation in early Judaism, including the NT. From this perspective, the study of midrash is not limited to the rabbinic literature, nor to the direct antecedents of the rabbinic movement.

a. Origins. The origins of midrash are found in the Bible (*see* INTERPRETATION, HISTORY OF[S] §A). The indications are especially clear in the exilic and postexilic periods with the emerging consciousness of a canon. The adaptation of the words of Deutero-Isaiah by the writer of Trito-Isaiah, the apocalyptic appropriation of Jeremiah's prophecy of the seventy years in Dan. 9:2 ff., the harmonizing of earlier texts by the Chronicler and by the final redactors of the Pentateuch, the creation of new contexts in the historicizing headings of certain psalms all evidence responses to the consciousness of a canon, and are akin to procedures used in later midrashic literature. The authority of earlier biblical texts becomes independent of their original contexts and function. The unity of Torah is presupposed, and data from other scripture provide specific historical settings for originally cultic texts. Thus, the process of attributing unique and permanent authority to earlier tradition, i.e., the process of canon, and the emergence of midrashic procedures belong in their initial phases to study of the formation and shape of the Hebrew Scriptures.

b. Evolution. Study of the evolution of biblical interpretation in early Judaism has been affected by three major factors since World War II: (1) The discovery of the DEAD SEA SCROLLS with their importance for the history of the biblical text and their eschatological contemporizing of biblical prophecy, and the discovery of a complete Palestinian Targum to the Pentateuch (Codex Neofiti I) resulting in a re-evaluation of the targumic literature for the evolution of Jewish exegesis (*see* TARGUMS[S]). (2) The recognition that the multifaceted character of Jewish exegesis is not merely the product of individual creativity, but develops within traditions whose evolution can be traced. (3) The application of historical-critical methods for tracing the history of exegetical traditions in the literature of early Judaism and in the rabbinic Midrashim. It is not a closer definition of midrash which is of primary concern in such study, but the manifold types of evidence that are relevant for tracing the history of exegetical traditions. (Among the earliest of such evidence are glosses on the biblical text, editorial expansions and harmonizations, and the Bible versions.) The recognition of exegetical traditions which often cross the boundaries of particular communities and which are present in different literary forms provides a larger historical context from which to assess the common ground and distinctive features, as well as the issues at stake, in particular applications of biblical texts.

c. Varieties. The varieties of biblical interpretation in early Judaism must also be stressed (*see* INTERPRETATION, HISTORY OF[S] §B). This applies to content (e.g., legal, historical, prophetic, apocalyptic, allegorical, mystic christological) and form (e.g., narrative, anthological, *pesher,* homiletic, targumic), and also to exegetical techniques, hermeneutics, and *Sitz im Leben.* The authority of scripture was not only common ground in early Judaism, but, in the very impulse to meditate on and live out of what was uncovered in scripture, a source of sectarian division. The sectarian tendencies of Judaism prior to the destruction of the temple reflect the social as well as the intellectual impact of biblical interpretation. Creative exegesis and the formation and maintenance of community are closely linked in this milieu.

d. Comparative midrash. This comparative study of midrash has developed out of the recognition of the formative role of biblical interpretation for the historical shape and creative thought of early Judaism. Nowhere is this role more apparent than in the formation of christological traditions in the NT which recent study has shown are marked at every stage by the creative use of scripture (*see* INTERPRETATION, HISTORY OF[S] §C). Comparison of exegetical traditions, midrashic structures and techniques, and the social settings of biblical interpretation provides important avenues of access to the literature, history, and thought of early Judaism. Such study must also take full account of the larger Greco-Roman milieu. The influence on midrash of Alexandrian textual scholarship and of Greco-Roman rhetorical forms has been recognized in recent scholarship.

e. Problem of definition. When the study of midrash was largely confined to the rabbinic tradition and literature, the varied nuances, emotive force, and broad cultural resonance of the term nonetheless had a point of reference in a particular tradition with its associated concepts, and in a certain type of literature where the word itself was for the most part to be found. The more recent tendency to associate midrash with the whole phenomenon of the use of scripture in early Judaism, and thus with groups, traditions, and literature which differ markedly from the rabbinic, has raised the problem of what is properly denoted by the term. The suggestion has recently been made to apply the term exclusively to the special characteristics of a literary genre. However, such a modern limitation, whatever the gains in clarity—and this itself is doubtful—involves a serious attenuation of traditional usage. In its ancient loci, midrash refers to the activity as well as the results of biblical interpretation, and even in rabbinic tradition comes to expression in different literary forms.

At present, there appears to be no wholly satisfactory way to resolve this problem. On the one hand, midrash as the characteristic term for biblical interpretation in the rabbinic milieu has clear analogues with respect to presuppositions, procedures, and functions in literature outside and prior to the rabbinic movement. On the other hand, the term tends to lose its descriptive power when applied to a variety of uses of scripture in early Judaism, especially where the task is to discern the distinctive traditions of biblical interpretation. In this circumstance, it would perhaps be best to retain a broad, synthetic use of the term for describing the general characteristics and evolution of biblical interpretation in early Judaism, and to develop more specific classifications for distinguishing the special types and traditions. *See also* JUDAISM, EARLY RABBINIC[S] §1; CANON OF THE OT.

Bibliography. M. Gertner, "Terms of Scriptural Interpretation: A Study in Hebrew Semantics," *Bulletin of the Schools of Oriental and African Studies,* XXV (1962), 1-27, a full discussion of semantic development of *dārash/midrash* as well as of other technical terms of interpretation; S. Lieberman, *Hellenism in Jewish Palestine* (2nd ed., 1962), 47-82, discusses the Hellenistic influences on rabbinic hermeneutical terminology and the similarities between methods of dream interpretation and methods of scriptural interpretation; I. Heinemann, *Darkhê Ha-Aggadah* (2nd ed., 1954), Hebrew, the major treatment of methods of midrash haggadah; E. E. Halevi, *Sha'arê Ha-Aggadah* (1963), 32-41, Hebrew, an excellent general treatment of midrashic method; J. N. Epstein, *Introduction to Tannaitic Literature* (1957), 521-44, Hebrew, detailed discussion of differences of technical terminology and hermeneutical rules originating in schools of Rabbi Akiba and Rabbi Ishmael; J. Heinemann "The Proem in the Aggadic Midrashim—A Form-Critical Study," *Studies in Aggadah and Folk-Literature,* ed. J. Heinemann and D. Noy, *Scripta Hierosolymitana,* XXII (1971), 100-122; J. T. Townsend, "Rabbinic Sources," *The Study of Judaism,* ed. J. Neusner (1972), 35-80; G. Vermes, "Rabbinic Literature," in Schürer's *The History of the Jewish People in the Age of Jesus Christ,* ed. G. Vermes and F. Millar, I (rev. ed., 1973), 68-118; J. Bowker, *The Targums and Rabbinic Literature* (1969), 40-92; I. L. Seeligmann, "Voraussetzungen der Midraschexegese," VTSup, I (1953), 150-81; B. Childs, "Midrash and the OT," *Understanding the Sacred Text, M. Enslin Festschrift,* ed. J. Reumann (1972), 47-59; G. Vermes, "Bible and Midrash: Early OT Exegesis," *Cambridge History of the Bible,* I (1970), 199-231; R. Bloch, "Midrash," *Supplément au Dictionnaire de la Bible,* V (1957), cols. 1263-81, "Ecriture et Tradition dans le judaïsme—Aperçus sur l'origine du Midrash," *Cahiers Sioniens,* VIII (1954), 9-34, and "Note méthodologique pour l'étude de la littérature rabbinique," *RSR,* XLIII (1955), 194-227; G. Vermes, *Scripture and Tradition in Judaism* (1961); M. P. Miller, "Targum, Midrash, and the Use of the OT in the NT," *JSJ,* II (1971), 29-82; H. A. Fischel, *Rabbinic Literature and Greco-Roman Philosophy* (1973); W. S. Towner, *The Rabbinic "Enumeration of Scriptural Examples"* (1973); J. Neusner, *The Rabbinic Traditions About the Pharisees Before 70,* 3 vols. (1971), esp. Pt. III, pp. 39-42; 62-64; 76-78; 97-99 on Pharisaic and early rabbinic exegetical forms; A. Wright, *The Literary Genre Midrash* (1967); R. Le Déaut, "Apropos a Definition of Midrash," *Int.,* XXV (1971), 259-82.

M. P. MILLER

***MILETUS.** In the reactivated excavations, new evidence both for "older" Miletus (the earliest Iron Age settlement) and for "oldest" Miletus (principally the Minoan and Mycenaean Bronze Age occupations) has been produced.

1. Oldest Miletus. Sherds and miniature vessels (votives?) from a house near the temple of Athena have been dated to the transition from the middle to the late Minoan periods (roughly the sixteenth century B.C.) and are said to be Cretan imports. This house, in view of its superior construction, decoration, and votives, may have been a shrine representing the founding of the cult later to be recognized as belonging to Athena. The Mycenaean colonists who immediately succeeded the Minoan traders seem to have felt completely secure on the unfortified site until the thirteenth century B.C. when they stretched a wall around the city. Although the full extent of the fortification has not been absolutely determined, the area enclosed seems rather extensive and may contain a palace and archives.

2. Older Miletus. The Mycenaean wall was destroyed *ca.* 1100 B.C., and this destruction marked a partial change in the city's population. A Mycenaean megaron beneath the Athena temple seems to have been refurbished and re-used as a temporary shrine until new cult installations were established in the Protogeometric and Geometric periods. Because Homer (*Iliad* II.868-69) mentions that Miletus was occupied by Carians at the time of the Trojan War, the new population has been tentatively identified as Carian. The seventh-century Archaic temple of Athena, due to its light construction and poor preservation, was regarded until recently as an unimportant, makeshift building. The recent excavations, however, have shown that it was a noteworthy megaron-shaped building with a single line of columns along the central axis, but no surrounding colonnade (more like a Mycenaean house than a classical Greek temple). This temple was destroyed at the end of the Ionian Revolt in 494 B.C. after the Persian sea victory by the island of Lade (just offshore from Miletus). Only after the corresponding Persian defeat in the Battle of Mycale (N of Miletus) in 479 B.C. was a new temple of Athena erected in a "modern" Greek form.

3. Sanctuaries of Apollo in Miletus and at Didyma. The principal divinity of Miletus was actually not Athena but Apollo. On the waterfront of the northernmost and best of Miletus' four harbors was an open sanctuary dedicated to Apollo Delphinios, protector and guide of all who cross the sea. PAUL probably walked by here when he landed in Miletus (Acts 20:15). A processional road led from this sanctuary through the city and sacred gate to Miletus' most important shrine of Apollo miles to the S at Didyma, where recent excavations have also increased our knowledge of Miletus' early history. Directly below the later temple, the earliest structure was a late Geometric enclosure which probably contained the sacred spring and laurel tree of Apollo. In the Archaic period a small shrine or *naiskos* replaced the enclosure, and around the *naiskos* was constructed the first colossal temple of Apollo, which was also destroyed by the Persians in 494 B.C.

After being freed by ALEXANDER, the Milesians planned a new temple at Didyma on such a magnificent scale that it proved impossible to finish the building despite the distinguished patronage which the project received. Alexander aided the rebuilding; SELEUCUS NICATOR (312-281 B.C.) continued the work and restored to Didyma the cult statue of Apollo Philesios, which the Persians had carried off to Ekbatana; and later the Roman emperor CALIGULA (A.D. 37-41) also attempted to complete the temple. Both TRAJAN (98-117) and HADRIAN (117-138) held the honorary position of chief priest while contributing to the construction. Diocletian (284-305) must have made some contribution after the oracle here advised him to continue the persecution of the Christians (Caecilius, *De mortibus persecutorum* XI.vi.7). Julian the Apostate (361-363) tried to revive the oracle by ordering the governor of Caria to burn the superstructure and dig up the foundations of the Christian chapels which had arisen inside Apollo's sanctuary (Sozomenus, *Ecclesiastical History* V.xx). Nevertheless, the Didymaean oracle seems to have foreseen the victory of Christianity, because when Licinius petitioned the oracle concerning his struggle with Constantine (*ca.* A.D. 308), he received two lines from Homer (*Iliad* VIII.102-3) as a reply: "Old man, you are beset by young warriors, your strength is gone, and grievous old age is upon you" (Sozomenus I.vii). After the promulgation of the Edict of Theodosius (A.D. 385), a basilica was erected inside the temple of Apollo. *See* Fig. M10.

Bibliography. Preliminary reports of the most recent excavations can be found in C. Weickert, G. Kleiner *et al., Istanbuler Mitteilungen* 9/10 (1959/1960 and following); Kleiner, *Alt-Milet* (1966), *Die Ruinen von Milet* (1968), and *Das römische Milet* (1970); K. Tuchelt, *Die archaischen Skulpturen von Didyma,* Istanbuler Forschungen, XXVII (1970), and *Vorarbeiten zu einer Topographie von Didyma,* Istanbuler Mitteilungen, Beiheft IX (1973); W. Günther, *Das Orakel von Didyma in hellenistischer Zeit, ibid.,* Beiheft IV (1971); W. Voigtländer, *Der jüngste Apollontempel von Didyma, ibid.,* Beiheft XIV (1975).

D. BOYD

Courtesy the State Museum, Berlin

10. The Byzantine church in the temple of Apollo, Didyma (the church was demolished in 1918)

MIRACLE STORIES, NT. In the gospel tradition the miracle stories are generally presented as aspects of the inbreaking kingdom of God. The closest formal and material parallels to these stories are found in the rabbinic and Hellenistic popular stories of the first century A.D. which include, typically, a description of the incurable nature of the disease, its duration, mode of cure and the visible consequences. Form critics have classified the more compact narratives as either paradigms (Dibelius) or apothegms (Bultmann) and the more extensive accounts as tales (Novellen [Dibelius]) or simply miracle stories (Bultmann).

See also DEMONS IN THE NT[S]; EXORCISM IN THE NT[S]; FORM CRITICISM §§3, 4; MIRACLE WORKERS[S]; ARETALOGY[S]; SIGN IN THE NT[S] §1.

Bibliography. In addition to bibliographies with related articles: L. J. McGinley, *Form-Criticism of the Synoptic Healing Narratives* (1944); R. H. Fuller, *Interpreting the Miracles* (1963); H. van der Loos, *The Miracles of Jesus,* NovTSup, VIII (1965).

H. C. KEE

MIRACLE WORKERS. 1. OT and Jewish miracle workers. In the OT and the intertestamental writings the deeds performed by miracle workers or in their behalf (by direct divine intervention) serve to confirm them as chosen instruments of God. The prototype is Moses, through whom "signs and wonders" accomplish the deliverance of Israel from bondage. The divine sanction of the prophetic roles of Elijah and Elisha is likewise provided through miracles performed by them or at their word. In the apocalyptic tradition, God acts in a miraculous way to vindicate his people and is expected to act through signs and wonders (Dan. 6:27) to defeat the enemies of his people and establish his eternal rule (Dan. 7; 9:15 ff.). Eschatological deliverers working redemptive miracles are expected in a range of texts from 200 B.C. on (e.g., Ecclus. 48:5-10; Test. Levi 5:2 ff.; Apoc. Baruch 71:1–75:8).

2. Hellenistic miracle workers. The closest analogy to the itinerant ministry of Jesus and his disciples as portrayed in the gospels—and probably to the actual course of Jesus' peripatetic ministry of preaching and healing—is that of the Cynic-Stoic wandering teacher-preachers of Asia Minor and Syria (first and second centuries A.D.). There are also reports of miracles worked by certain rabbis, of whom Haninah ben Dosa is the best-known. Although there are formal analogies between stories of miracles attributed to these Jewish and pagan charismatics and those told of Jesus, the functions they serve are significantly different. The pagan miracles are presented either as the acts of tricksters and charlatans exploiting a gullible public (so Lucian) or as demonstrations of the independence of these itinerant wise men from all earthly claims and limitations (as in Philostratus' *Life of Apollonius of Tyana*). The miracles preserved from the tannaitic traditions of Judaism concern chiefly the personal authority of the rabbi as interpreter of the Law or his insight concerning the future or the identity of his demonic opponents.

3. Miracle workers in the NT. The gospels interpret Jesus' miracles as an essential part of a larger undertaking: the defeat of the evil powers in preparation for the coming of God's kingdom (e.g., Mark 3:22-26; Luke 11:19-20). His disciples are commissioned to extend his ministry (e.g., Mark 3:14-15), yet the authority of Jesus' name is reported to have been exploited by his followers (Acts 3:6) and also others (Mark 9:38). Paul views miracle-working as a gift of the Spirit (I Cor. 12:9-10).

See also MIRACLE STORIES, NT[S]; ARETALOGY[S]; DIVINE MAN[S]; DEMONS IN THE NT[S]; EXORCISM IN THE NT[S]; SIGN IN THE NT[S].

Bibliography. In addition to bibliographies with the related articles: C. F. D. Moule, ed., *Miracles: Cambridge Studies in their Philosophy and History* (1965).

H. C. KEE

***MITANNI.** A powerful empire in N Mesopotamia and surrounding regions, one of the four great powers in the Near East during most of the Late Bronze Age. Also known as Ḫanigalbat (mainly in Akkadian texts), Ḫurri, and Naharina (in Egyptian texts). The circumstances of Mitanni's rise are obscure. It seems to have been formed *ca.* 1600 B.C. (low CHRONOLOGY OF THE OT) through unification of numerous Hurrian (*see* HURRIANS; HURRIANS[S]) and Amorite states, under a dynasty of Indo-Aryan origin (a splinter of the Aryan migration to India). The number of Indo-Aryans in N Mesopotamia was relatively small, and their impact on the native population was limited: twenty to forty personal names of Sanscrit derivation; four Indian gods in the Mitannian pantheon; and about a dozen words, mainly relating to horses and chariotry, which entered the Hurrian language (often with Hurrian suffixes). One of the latter, *maryannu*, "charioteer," was also adopted by the West Semites of Syria and by the Egyptians. Otherwise, Mitanni was predominantly Hurrian in language, religion, and culture. But the role of the Indo-Aryans as political unifiers and military innovators must not be underestimated.

During the Hittite Old Kingdom (*see* HITTITES[S] §1), Ḫurri/Ḫanigalbat was strong enough to invade Anatolia at the time of Ḫattusilis I, to attack Mursilis I on his way back from Babylon, and to wrest northern Syria from his successors. *Ca.* 1520, under Thut-mose I, the first Egyptian ruler to have reached the Euphrates, the name *Mitanni* makes its appearance in Egyptian records and opens a century of intermittent warfare between the two powers for the control of Syria. *Ca.* 1500, the overlordship of the Mittannian king Barattarna was recognized by Alalakh (*see* ALALAKH TEXTS[S]) in northern Syria, Kizzuwadna in southeastern Anatolia, and Arrapḫa in the Trans-Tigris. In the next fifteen years, Mitannian influence spread into southern Syria and Palestine. Many Canaanite cities received Mitannian garrisons and rulers, whose successors continued to bear Hurrian and Indo-Aryan names over a century later. Thut-mose III reconquered Palestine in 1482, southern and central Syria in 1476-1474, but his domination of northern Syria was short-lived (altogether six years). King Shaushshatar of Mitanni (mid-fifteenth century) still reigned over a vast empire

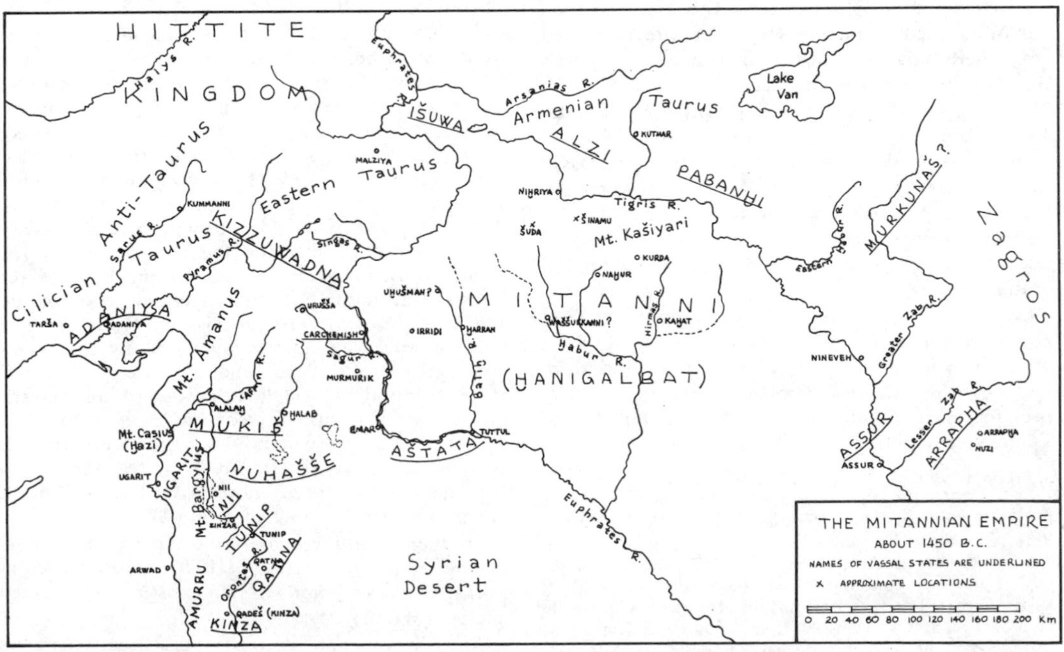

The Mitanni Empire *ca.* 1450 B.C.

from the Zagros to the Anti-Taurus and the Mediterranean and from southern Armenia to the middle Orontes. His successor Artatama concluded peace with Thut-mose IV (*ca.* 1420), and relations between the two empires became cordial. Tushratta, the great-grandson of Artatama, repelled the first attack on northern Syria by the Hittite king Suppiluliumas (*ca.* 1386), but twenty years later Suppiluliumas invaded Mitanni from the N, sacked its capital, and deprived it of its Syrian dependencies (*see* HITTITES[S] §1). This humiliation was followed by the murder of Tushratta and a civil war between his successors. Suppiluliumas, by backing one of the pretenders, was able to impose a Hittite protectorate over Mitanni. However, the decline of Mitanni played into the hand of its former vassal, Asshur. The Assyrian king Adadnirari I, early in the thirteenth century, invaded Mitanni and made it his tributary; and his son Shalmaneser I destroyed the last remainders of Mitannian statehood and annexed it to Assyria. The massive resettlement of N Mesopotamia by Arameans in the following two centuries obliterated the last traces of the Hurrian ethnic element.

The capital city of Mitanni was Washukkanni, plausibly identified with the huge mound of Tell Fekheriyeh near Rās el-'Ain, at the principal source of the Habur. Limited excavations conducted at that site failed to disclose the royal palace or any Mitannian documents.

Mitanni had a profound influence on the Hittites, especially at the time of the New Kingdom. Hurrian deities and cults were adopted, and Hurrian myths and tales were translated into the Hittite language. Many Hurrian words also entered the Assyrian dialect of Akkadian. Some scholars found parallels between the family law of Nuzi and the marriage practices of the patriarchs as described in Genesis, and believed that the Hebrews had borrowed them from the Hurrians. Others denied that there was any particular similarity between the two sets of customs (*see* NUZI §2; NUZI[S]; MARI[S] §8). Besides implanting a number of Indo-Aryan and Hurrian names in Palestine, one of which may have survived to the time of David (*see* ARAUNAH), they transmitted to the Canaanites the tactics of chariotry warfare (associated with the Canaanites in Judg. 1 and 5) and the ensuing rise of charioteers as an upper class. Even though ethnic Hurrians formed a small minority in the S Canaanite society, the Egyptians applied the term *Ḫuru* to the whole population of Palestine long after the end of Mitanni. This term was, in turn, taken over by certain sources of the OT to designate pre-Hebrew populations in southern Palestine and Edom (*see* HORITE).

Bibliography. A. Goetze, *Hethiter, Churriter und Assyrer* (1936); R. O'Callaghan, *Aram-Naharaim* (1948); H. G. Güterbock, "The Hurrian Element in the Hittite Empire," *Cahiers de l'Histoire Mondiale,* II (1954/55), 383-84; F. Imparati, *I Ḫurriti* (1964); M. Mayrhofer, *Die Arier im Vorderen Orient—ein Mythos?* (1974); R. de Vaux, "Les Ḫurrites de l'histoire et les Horites de la Bible," *RB,* LXXIV (1967), 481-503; I. M. Diakonoff, "Die Arier im Vorderen Orient: Ende eines Mythos," *Or,* XLI (1972), 91-120. M. C. ASTOUR

MNEMONIC DEVICES. 1. The alphabetic acrostic. The use of the successive letters of the alphabet to introduce consecutive verses is an external principle of arrangement which, at times, subordinates sequence of thought to a formal literary structure. Though some have attributed this device to the magical power of letters (Löhr), it is more likely an expression of the skill of the writer, who, in his attempt at conveying the idea of totality or comprehensiveness of an emotion or a belief, utilizes a pedagogic memory scheme, which may have its roots in wisdom circles (Munch, Gottwald).

In the Hebrew Bible there are fourteen literary units which completely or partially employ the letters of the alphabet; all but one (Nahum) are to be found in the Hagiographa. The complete abecedaries, consisting of all twenty-two letters of the Hebrew alphabet, are Ps. 111 (note the use of *sîn* for *šîn* in vs. 10*b*) and Ps. 112, where successive letters initiate each half verse; Ps. 119, an acrostic tour de force, which consists of stanzas of eight lines apiece headed by the same letter; Prov. 31:10-31, where the initial letter heads each full verse; and the first four chapters of Lamentations. Lam. 3 consists of twenty-two stanzas of three lines apiece, each headed by the same letter. The last chapter of Lamentations also consists of twenty-two verses, but is not arranged alphabetically. An interesting transposition of the letters *'ayin* and *pēh* occurs in Lam. 2:16-17; 3:46-51; and 4:16-17. This variant order of letters also lies behind the LXX's translation of Prov. 31:25-26, where the Hebrew *'ayin* and *pēh* verses are reversed. It has also been reasonably suggested that the order *pēh, 'ayin* was original to Ps. 34:15-16 [H 16-17], since the subject of the *zadi* verse (17 [H 18]) refers back to the subject of the *'ayin* verse (15 [H 16]), and not to that of the *pēh* verse (16 [H 17]).

An incomplete alphabetic arrangement is found in Ps. 25, where both the *wāw* and *qôph* verses are missing, and the letter *rêš* heads two separate lines. Possible reconstructions of both missing verses, however, have been offered by modern critics. Ps. 34 also lacks a line for the letter *wāw,* and both Pss. 25 and 34 conclude with an additional verse beginning with the letter *pēh*. Ps. 37, where the letters begin alternate verses, lacks a verse beginning with the letter *'ayin,* which has been reconstructed in vs. 28*b* on the basis of the LXX's translation. In the Hebrew text of Ps. 145 only the *nûn* verse is missing. However, here too the verse can be supplemented by the Greek and Syriac translations, and a similar *nûn* verse is now found in 11QPs[a]. Traces of an acrostic arrangement are also present in Pss. 9–10, possibly a single psalm as evidenced by the Greek translation, and in Nah. 1:2-9. To be noted also is the sequence of the three consecutive letters *lāmedh, mēm,* and *nûn* in Song of S. 4:9-11.

Another incomplete acrostic composition is found in the Apoc., in Ecclus. 51:13 ff. Acrostic literary works are also found in Hellenistic and Roman poetry (Marcus).

The phenomenon of word and sentence acrostics is also present in cuneiform literature. The "Babylonian Theodicy" (*ANET* [2nd ed.], pp. 438-40) (dated between 1000-800 B.C.) is an acrostic poem originally consisting of twenty-seven stanzas of eleven lines each. Each line in each stanza starts with the same sign, and when completely restored (only nineteen stanzas have been preserved) spells out the authorship of the work. Five other acrostics are known from Akkadian literature, with the two dated examples coming from the reigns of Ashurbanipal and Nebuchadrezzar II, seventh and sixth centuries B.C. For attempts to discover acrostic devices purporting to convey the name of the author in biblical psalms, see Driver (pp. 206-8).

2. Concatenation of catchwords, phrases, or ideas. Associative reasoning was well known to students of Talmudic literature and is now being more and more recognized as a key to unraveling the arrangement of otherwise disparate prose, legal, prophetic, psalm, and wisdom sections. A few selected examples from different literary genres will be noted.

The legal portion of the Book of the Covenant (Exod. 21:12–22:16) has an arrangement of its individual sections and laws based upon the principle of associative reasoning: (*a*) 21:12-27, laws pertaining to crimes committed by one man against another; (*b*) 21:28-32, laws pertaining to crimes committed by a man's property (an ox) against another man; (*c*) 21:33-36, laws pertaining to damages caused by one man's property (a pit) against another's property (an ox); (*d*) 22:1-17 [H 21:37–22:16], laws pertaining to crimes committed by one man (directly or indirectly) against another's property and cases of natural forces. In sum: (*a*) man against man; (*b*) property against man; (*c*) property against property; (*d*) man and natural forces against property. The individual laws in each section are also linked together by similar principles (Paul). It has also been suggested that an associative external and internal ordering is present, too, in the various cuneiform legal corpora.

In the book of Numbers the regulation of the priestly dues (5:5-10) is followed by the ordeal of jealousy (5:11-31), which in turn precedes the laws pertaining to the Nazirite (6:1-21). These three originally unconnected sections are linked to one another by key phrases central to each unit: the first two by למעל מעל, "breaking faith" (5:6; cf. vs. 12, "acts unfaithfully"), and the second two by ופרע . . . ראש (5:18, "unbind the hair"; 6:5, "hair . . . grow long"). (Cassuto has called attention to many such literary attractions in his commentaries to Genesis and Exodus.) Num. 15:22-23 serves as a prologue to the laws pertaining to those who unwittingly fail to observe the commandments. A sin offering is then prescribed, which must be brought by the community (vss. 24-26) or by the individual (vss. 27-29) for inadvertent sins. This section is followed in turn by the law for anyone who "with a high hand," that is, willfully and defiantly, violates the commandments. He is to be "cut off from among his people" (vss. 30-31). The immediately following literary unit, pertaining to a man who is caught gathering wood on the sabbath day, serves as an illustration of such a defiant act, and, as to be expected, the sinner is put to death (vss. 32-36). Finally, the chapter concludes with a seemingly totally disconnected section, the instructions for making fringes upon the corners of the garments (vss. 37-41). The key to the understanding of the position of this unit is actually provided by the reason for this specific law. Its religious motive states that the man is to wear fringes so that when he sees them he will "remember all the commandments of the Lord, to do them." In other words, the fringes serve as a reminder for the observance of the Law, and thus constitute the antithesis of the preceding prescriptions, which pertain to those who inadvertently or willfully disregard it. Compare vs. 22, "if you fail to observe any one of the commandments," and vs. 40, "thus you shall be reminded to observe all my commandments" (Paul).

Such mnemonic devices are prevalent in prophetic literature as well. For example, the six oracles against the nations, which are placed at the beginning of the book of Amos (1:3–2:3), are arranged in accordance with an internal literary order which weaves the separate oracles into a cohesive and sequential pattern. Each link in this chain of prophecies is connected to the next by the concatenation of key words, phrases, and ideas common only to the two oracles contiguous to one another (Paul). The prophetic book which most clearly demonstrates such linguistic and thematic associations is Second Isaiah. Key words present within the individual prophecies pass from one prophecy to another, forming a remarkable literary bond (Mowinckel, Kaufmann).

For another illustration, note how the unit which concludes with Isa. 1:9 mentions Sodom and Gomorrah. The topically unrelated unit 1:10 ff. begins with these same names. The sequencing of the units may reflect the aid to memorization which such "catchwords" provided. On the transmission of the prophetic materials, *see* LITERATURE §6; *see also* TRADITION, ORAL and supplementary article.

Such aids to the memory are also noticeable in the arrangement of many of the psalms and proverbs, and even, at times, in the arrangement of the individual sections in the Song of Songs. Note, for example, that almost all the literary units which contain the word לבנון (Lebanon) are to be found in ch. 4 (vss. 8, 11, 15), and that the first of these sections is preceded by a lyrical section which contains, toward its conclusion, the somewhat similar-sounding word לבונה (frankincense).

Bibliography. For Talmudic and post-Talmudic usages of acrostics and other mnemonic devices, *see Encyclopaedia Judaica* (1971), II, cols. 230-31; XII, 187-90; and XVI, 1424-25. These authorities, as well as medieval biblical interpreters, frequently used inferences from the juxtaposition of sections as an exegetical principle.

M. Löhr, "Alphabetische und alphabetisierende Lieder im AT," *ZAW*, XXV (1905), 173-98; S. R. Driver, *An Introduction to the Literature of the OT* (9th ed., 1913), pp. 337, 367-68, 456-57, 459; F. Dornseiff, *Das Alphabet in Mystik und Magie* (2nd ed., 1925); P. A. Munch, "Die alphabetische Akrostichie in der jüdischen Psalmendichtung," *ZDMG*, XC (1936), 703-10; S.

Mowinckel, "Die Komposition des deuterojesajanischen Buches," *ZAW,* XLIX (1931), 87-112, 242-60; R. Marcus, "Alphabetic Acrostics in the Hellenistic and Roman Periods," *JNES,* VI (1947), 109-15; G. R. Driver, *Semitic Writing* (1954), pp. 181, 200-208; N. K. Gottwald, *Studies in the Book of Lamentations* (1954), pp. 23-32; W. G. Lambert, *Babylonian Wisdom Literature* (1960), pp. 63, 66-67; Y. Kaufmann, *The Babylonian Captivity and Deutero-Isaiah* (1970), pp. 75-88, 193-98; S. M. Paul, *Studies in the Book of the Covenant in the Light of Cuneiform and Biblical Law,* VTSup, XVIII (1970), 106-11, and "Amos 1:3–2:3: A Concatenous Literary Pattern," *JBL,* XC (1971), 397-403; U. Cassuto, "The Sequence and Arrangement of the Sections in the Bible," *Biblical and Canaanite Literatures* (1972), pp. 200-204, Hebrew; D. N. Freedman, "Acrostics and Metrics in Hebrew Poetry," *HTR,* LXV (1972), 367-92.

S. M. Paul

***MOAB.** Knowledge of Moab in the earlier periods, the Proto-Urban (or the transition between the Chalcolithic and the Early Bronze) and, again, between the end of the latter period and the beginning of Middle Bronze, has expanded in recent years, partly because of excavation and partly because of increased scholarly interest in the problem of the Amorites and the historical setting of the patriarchs.

1. The Bronze Age. At Bab edh-Dhra', on the Lisan peninsula, a vast cemetery covering the range of these prehistoric periods has been found, complementing a walled city of the EB period which had been discovered in the 1920s. This cemetery was probably used as a communal burial ground for different groups dwelling in the area—perhaps in the Cities of the Valley. *See* Tomb[S].

An alternative name for the fortified city on the Lisan is Tell el Alawiyin, "the tell of the giants," thus continuing the biblical tradition (Deut. 2:10-11) that the predecessors of the Moabites were a race of giants known as the Emim.

The findings at Bab edh-Dhra' will have an important bearing on the history of Palestine during the twenty-fourth to nineteenth centuries B.C. and may help to solve the problem of the Amorites and the part they played in the eclipse of the EB urban civilization and the subsequent urban revival. The excavations at Aroer have underlined the theory that much of Moab was unoccupied during the greater part of the second millennium. *See* Moab §3*b*.

2. Iron Age. In the Iron Age, Aroer played an important function as a fortress, either in conjunction with Dibon and/or as a vital link in the security chain of communications along the King's Highway. The earliest occupation at Dibon coincides almost exactly with King Mesha (*ca.* 840-830 B.C.). Excavations at Tell Hesban have provided no archaeological substantiation for the traditional identification with biblical Heshbon, the capital of Sihon, king of the Amorites (Num. 21:26). In the Neo-Assyrian period, there were flourishing communities at both Dibon and Heshbon, and both testify to a general decline in sedentary life from the end of the sixth down to the end of the fourth century B.C.

3. Religion. From Moab comes attestation of a cultic practice which, though attested W of the River Jordan at places such as Gezer and Hazor, has not been discovered in the other states making up Transjordan: a series of stones, or monoliths, usually unadorned, either in a straight or in a slightly curved N/S line. So far, they have been found at Bab edh-Dhra', Ader, Khirbet Iskander, El Mugheirat, and Lejjun, all of which sites have EB/MB occupation. These monoliths are a well-recognized and common feature in Semitic religions, and references to them in the OT are manifold. *See* Pillar; Pillar[S]; Moab §3*a,* with Figs. 57-58.

Bibliography. P. W. Lapp, *The Dhahr Mirzbâneh Tombs* (1966), pp. 94-96, and "Bâb edh-Dhrâ', Perizzites and Emim," in *Jerusalem Through the Ages,* The Twenty-Fifth Archaeological Convention, 1961 (1968), pp. 1*-25*; E. Stockton, "Stones at Worship," *AJBA,* I, no. 3 (1970), 58 ff.; A. D. Tushingham, *The Excavations at Dibon (Dhībân) in Moab, AASOR,* XL (1972).

C.-M. Bennett

MONOTHEISM. The belief in and the exclusive worship of one god. Strict monotheism, which implies the denial of the existence of other gods, is a fairly rare phenomenon represented primarily by Judaism, Christianity, and Islam, and to a certain extent Zoroastrianism.

The long-prevailing evolutionistic school of comparative religion held monotheism to be the last and highest stage in the evolution of religions. An opposite view has been advocated by such scholars as Lang and Schmidt, who argue in favor of primitive monotheism as the origin of religion. A useful distinction was introduced by Pettazzoni, who maintained that strict monotheism comes into existence only as a protest against polytheism. Primitive monotheism, which is found among many illiterate peoples and tribes, is much more vague and never worked out theoretically. It involves the belief in a high god, who is often located in or identified with the sky and who is believed to be the master of man's destiny (Widengren). This, however, does not exclude the belief in other gods of a lower rank, but the high god is usually accepted as superior.

The historical origin of Israelite monotheism is a matter of debate. Even the traditionally accepted role of Moses in the formation of Israelite religion is called into question by many, and there is in any case no consensus as to what elements in Israel's faith really go back to Moses. *See* Moses[S]; Credo, Ancient Israelite[S].

If the Decalogue (*see* Ten Commandments) and the laws of Exod. 34 are accepted as documents of early Mosaic religion, it must be admitted that they do not teach strict monotheism. The first commandment (Exod. 20:3; Deut. 5:7) forbids Israel to worship gods other than Yahweh, but the existence of these gods is not questioned. The same is true of Exod. 34:14. In other words, this amounts to monolatry (rather than to monotheism): Yahweh is the God of Israel, and they shall worship him exclusively, but other peoples may have other gods and be allowed to worship them. Accordingly, Judg. 11:24 presupposes Chemosh to be the god of the Moabites, just as Yahweh is the god of

Israel, and I Sam. 26:19 states that David had to serve other gods dwelling outside Israel. II Kings 5:17 shows that, in the opinion of Naaman the Syrian, Yahweh could be worshiped properly only on Israelite soil. Not even Deut. 6:4, "Hear, O Israel, Yahweh our God, Yahweh is one (or: is one Yahweh)," expresses strict monotheism. Either it refers to the oneness of Yahweh in contradistinction to the many gods of other nations, or it can be taken to emphasize that there is only one Yahweh and not several local deities as there were local forms of BAAL. The emphasis is on the oneness of Israel's God, not on his being the only and exclusive God of all the world.

There are, however, several traits in the early Israelite conception of God that could easily develop into strict monotheism. First of all, Yahweh appears as an ambivalent high god, from whom both good and evil derive. In the song of Hannah (I Sam. 2), we learn that Yahweh "kills and brings to life; . . . makes poor and makes rich; he brings low, he also exalts" (vss. 6-7). The same is later stated by Deutero-Isaiah: "I form light and create darkness, I make weal and create woe" (45:7). Thus a monistic view pervades the religion of Israel. Yahweh is not only the giver of good gifts, wealth, victory, and happiness, but also the evil in human life comes from him (Amos 3:6). Deut. 32:39 had developed the statement "I kill and I make alive; I wound and I heal" in a monotheistic direction: "There is no god beside me." It is only in later Judaism that a dualistic view develops, deriving evil from a separate being, SATAN.

Secondly, the Song of the Sea (Exod. 15) contains the question of incomparability: "Who is like thee, O Lord?" (vs. 11). A similar question is found in Ps. 113:5-6*a*: "Who is like the Lord our God, who is seated on high, who looks far down?" Such questions are common in Akkadian hymns in a polytheistic environment, proclaiming the absolute superiority of the deity in question. In Israel this question extols Yahweh above the gods of other nations and brings out his superiority.

Thirdly, the Psalms praise the greatness of Yahweh as the king of the world, which implies that he is the creator and ruler of the whole world and "a great King above all gods" (Ps. 95:3). Sometimes such psalms contain a reference to the futility of other gods, e.g.: "All the gods of the peoples are idols; but the Lord made the heavens" (Ps. 96:5). The word for "idols," *'aelîlîm,* sounds very much like *'aelōhîm,* "god," but has a pejorative sense: futile gods who are not really gods. There are also statements which call the other gods *lō' 'aelōhîm,* i.e., "not-gods." One example is in Deut. 32:16-17: "They stirred him to jealousy with strange gods; . . . they sacrificed to demons which were no gods, to gods they had never known." Similar statements are found in Jer. 2:11; 5:7. The context in these passages indicates that the "non-gods" are powerless and of no avail.

The prophets sometimes allude to the fact that the other gods are nothing but "the work of men's hands" (Hos. 8:6; 13:2; Isa. 2:8, 20; Mic. 5:13 [H 12]). Hosea even adds: "it is not God" (8:6). Even if these polemic statements lack the positive assertion that Yahweh alone is God, they come very close to a monotheistic attitude. It should also be kept in mind that in the prophetic literature there are allusions to Yahweh as the sovereign master of world history. Amos 9:7 asserts that just as Yahweh brought Israel out of Egypt, he also brought the Philistines from Caphtor and the Syrians from Kir. The majestic poem in Isa. 10 makes mighty Assyria the instrument of Yahweh's wrath without any initiative of its own; it is Yahweh who is active in and behind the military exploits of Assyria. This of course excludes the activity of other gods. Explicitly monotheistic statements, however, are not found earlier than Deutero-Isaiah. He repeats the argument that the gods of the nations, especially of Babylon, are nothing but stone, wood, gold, and silver, and have no power at all (40:18-20; 44:9-20; 46:6-7). The question of incomparability recurs: "To whom then will you liken God, or what likeness compare with him?" (40:18; cf. 40:25). "To whom will you liken me and make me equal, and compare me, that we may be alike?" (46:5). The answer is self-evident: there is none. Accordingly, there are also positive statements: "I am God, and there is no other; I am God, and there is none like me" (46:9); "I am the Lord, and there is no other, besides me there is no God" (45:5). In a way, this monotheism is the result of opposition to the polytheism of the surrounding nations and corresponds to Pettazzoni's definition cited above.

Two similar statements in Deuteronomy are probably approximately contemporaneous with Deutero-Isaiah. One is 32:39, "There is no God beside me," immediately following a monistic statement. The other is ch. 4, the latest chapter of the prologue, which contains clear allusions to the Exile: "The Lord is God; there is no other besides him" (vs. 35; cf. vs. 39). It is probable that both these statements are dependent on the same cultic tradition as Deutero-Isaiah.

Express references to monotheism are comparatively rare in the postexilic books of the OT. In the book of Malachi there is a reference to Yahweh receiving true worship and pure sacrifices all over the world (1:11), but the meaning of this verse is somewhat obscure. The book of Daniel contains several allusions to Yahweh's superiority to the gods of Babylon (2:21, 47; 3:29; 4:35 [Aram. 32]; 6:26 [Aram. 27], but none of these passages deny the existence of these gods; they do state, however, that Yahweh is the almighty ruler of the world, while the other gods are completely useless.

In the intertestamental literature, monotheism is taken for granted. It is typical that the God of Israel is often referred to not by his proper name, Yahweh—even the pronunciation of the divine name was avoided—but by means of several circumlocutions: the Almighty One, the Lord, the Holy One, the Name, etc. Strangely enough, this monotheistic attitude is coupled with a tendency toward a dualistic view, insofar as evil is ascribed to a being different from God, called Satan, Mastema, the Angel of Darkness, etc. At the same time, certain divine activities acquire semi-independence as hypostases, e.g., Wisdom and the Word (*memra*); and the importance of the angels is increased.

None of these phenomena, however, is regarded as an infringement on monotheism.

Bibliography. A. Lang, *The Making of Religion* (1898); W. Schmidt, *Der Ursprung der Gottesidee* (1912); R. Pettazzoni, *Dio* (1922), and *The All-Knowing God* (1956); G. Widengren, *Hochgottglaube im alten Iran* (1938); W. F. Albright, *From the Stone Age to Christianity* (1957), pp. 168-71, 257-72; T. J. Meek, *Hebrew Origins* (1960), ch. 6. H. RINGGREN

***MOSES** [משה, from Egyp. *mśy,* "to be born"]. The quest for the historical Moses continues, with no evidence that scholars are approaching a consensus. The article MOSES can still be accepted as a fair and balanced study of critical problems, while taking a moderate position on important issues. But much significant work has been done in the intervening years.

1. Methodological matters. For those who accept the biblical traditions as a literal and accurate historical account there are few problems. Scholars who employ the critical tools of biblical research, however, are not so blessed. SOURCE CRITICISM has led to the position that reliable information concerning Moses in the PENTATEUCH is preserved by and large in the J and E documents rather than D or P. Relying on source analysis, archaeological data, and geographical considerations, Beegle constructs a biography of Moses which generally accepts the JE epics as providing fairly detailed and accurate information. Employment of FORM CRITICISM and TRADITION CRITICISM, however, complicates the quest. Von Rad and Noth delineate four major themes in the Pentateuch connected with Moses: exodus from Egypt, revelation at Sinai, wandering in the wilderness, and entrance into the Promised Land. If, in its preliterary existence, the Sinai tradition was formed as the cult legend of a covenant festival, and the other themes also developed in separate settings among the various tribes, then the question emerges as to whether Moses could have been involved in more than one of these (*see* CREDO, ANCIENT ISRAELITE[S]). If these traditions preserve the memory of separate historical experiences of different tribes, the answer would apparently be in the negative. Noth concluded that the only authentic Mosaic tradition concerned his tomb in Transjordan, and subsequently, Koch announced the death of the view that Moses was in any sense the founder of Israel's religion. Thus a great gulf would exist between the historical Moses and the Moses portrayed by J and E, to say nothing of D and P. Such minimal conclusions need not lead to theological nihilism, as is evinced by the creative commentary by Childs, which deals with literary and theological matters but virtually no historical questions. Many other scholars who have followed this general critical path have been less skeptical concerning the historical value of the traditions, but have tended to locate Moses in either the Sinai or the Exodus themes. For example, von Rad and Seebass (at least in his first book) opted for Sinai, while Smend and Schnutenhaus located him in the Exodus event.

2. Sinai and the suzerainty treaty. An important contribution was made by Mendenhall, who contended that Moses used an international suzerainty treaty form to express the covenant relation between Yahweh and his people under Moses at Sinai (*see* COVENANT §§1*a*, 3*a;* COVENANT, MOSAIC[S]). The preamble, in which the king identifies himself, may parallel Exod. 20:2*a*: "I am the Lord your God"; and the historical prologue, in which the suzerain recounts the benevolent deeds he has performed for his vassal, recalls Exod. 20:2*b*: "who brought you out of the land of Egypt." Acceptance of this position would lead to the conclusion that Moses was involved in both the Sinai and the Exodus events. If so, there would seem little reason to deny his original connection with the others as well.

Subsequent research, particularly by McCarthy, has rendered this position less compelling than originally believed. He pointed out that the blessings and curses, essential elements of the suzerainty treaty, do not appear in the Decalogue. Equally important, two essential elements of the covenant at Sinai—the theophany and the ritual for sealing the compact—are not found in the suzerainty form. One might add that the J covenant tradition in Exod. 33–34, a parallel of the E account in Exod. 19–24, reveals almost no evidence of treaty influence. While there may be traces of such influence in the E tradition about Sinai, in Josh. 24 and unquestionably in the book of Deuteronomy, whether Moses himself used such a form is quite uncertain. *See* EXODUS, BOOK OF[S] §§2, 3.

3. A portrait of the historical Moses. Even apart from heavy reliance on the suzerainty treaty hypothesis, it is possible for scholars to sketch a portrait of Moses which may not be too far removed from the historical man. This has been done by Schmid, Hermann, de Vaux, and Newman (who no longer holds that Moses made use of a suzerainty treaty at Sinai).

The recognition that the major traditions developed independently during their early oral existence does not preclude the possibility that Moses was involved in all of them. The crucial experiences of Moses and of the Hebrews under his leadership could have been remembered on different cultic occasions, just as in the Christian church the birth of Jesus is remembered in one season with certain liturgical traditions and the death and resurrection of the same Jesus at other times with different traditions. The traditions of the plagues and escape from Egypt could have been formed in connection with the Passover; the Sinai legend involving the same group and the same Moses could have developed separately in connection with covenant worship, and so on. These traditions would have been brought together over an extended period in premonarchical times and eventually resulted in the J and E epics.

Viewing the stories in such a way does not permit the writing of a detailed biography, but it opens up the possibility of sketching the general contours of his life and work. And those contours in broad outline conform to the present text of the OT account.

See also HORNS OF MOSES[S].

Bibliography. G. Auzou, *De la Servitude au Service* (1961); D. M. Beegle, *Moses: The Servant of Yahweh* (1972); W. Beyerlin, *Origins and History of the Oldest Sinaitic Traditions* (1965); J. Bright, *A History of Israel* (2nd ed., 1969), pp. 105-66; H. Cazelles, "Moïse devant l'histoire," *Moïse: L'homme de l'alliance* (1955), pp. 11-27; B. Childs, *The Book of Exodus* (1974); G. Fohrer, *Überlieferung und Geschichte des Exodus, BZAW,* XCI (1964); S. Hermann, *Israel in Egypt, SBT,* 2nd Series, XXVII (1973); J. P. Hyatt, *Commentary on Exodus* (1971); K. Koch, "Der Tod des Religionsstifters," *Kerygma und Dogma,* VIII (1962), 100-123; D. McCarthy, *Treaty and Covenant,* AnBib, XXI (1963); G. Mendenhall, "Law and Covenant in Israel and the Ancient Near East," *BA,* II-III (1954) 26-46, 49-76; M. Newman, *The People of the Covenant* (1962); E. Nicholson, *Exodus and Sinai in History and Tradition* (1973); M. Noth, *Exodus* (1962), *A History of Pentateuchal Traditions,* (1972), and *The History of Israel* (1960), pp. 127-38; E. Osswald, *Das Bild des Mose in der kritischen alttestamentlichen Wissenschaft seit Julius Wellhausen, Theologische Arbeiten,* XVIII (1962); G. von Rad, *The Problem of the Hexateuch and other essays* (1966), pp. 1-78, *Moses* (1960), and *Old Testament Theology,* I (1962), pp. 3-14, 289-96; H. Schmid, *Mose: Überlieferung und Geschichte, BZAW,* CX (1968); F. Schnutenhaus, "Die Entstehung der Mosetraditionen" (diss., Heidelberg, 1958); H. Seebass, *Der Erzvater Israel und die Einführung der Jahweverehrung in Kanaan, BZAW,* XCVIII (1966), and *Mose und Aaron, Sinai und Gottesberg* (1962); R. Smend, *Yahweh War and Tribal Confederation* (1970); R. de Vaux, *Histoire ancienne d'Israël* (1971), pp. 277-440.

M. NEWMAN

***MOSES IN THE NT.** Moses is named seventy-eight times in the NT (not counting John 8:5), most frequently in citing or alluding to the scriptures attributed to him. As in contemporary Greek Jewish writers, he appears most frequently as lawgiver and prophet. TORAH in its narrow sense can be called "the law of Moses" (Luke 2:22; 24:44; John 7:23; Acts 13:39; 15:5; 28:23; I Cor. 9:9; Heb. 10:28) or "the book of Moses" (Mark 12:26) or simply "Moses" (Luke 16:29, 31; 24:27; Acts 15:21; II Cor. 3:15). A citation may be introduced by "Moses commanded," "Moses said," or the like (Mark 1:44; Matt. 8:4; Luke 5:14; Mark 7:10; 10:3-4; Matt. 19:7-8; Mark 12:19; Matt. 22:24; Luke 20:28, 37; John 1:45; cf. 5:45; Acts 3:22; 26:22; Rom. 10:5, 19; Heb. 8:5). More carefully expressed, the law was not given *by* Moses, but *through* him (John 1:17); he was its "mediator" (μεσίτης, Gal. 3:19). "Moses said" (Mark 7:10) is the equivalent of "God said" (Matt. 15:4, from Gr.); Moses is the one to whom "God has spoken" in a unique way (John 9:29; Acts 7:44; Rom. 9:15; cf. Num. 12:7-8; Deut. 34:10). In short, he was the prototypal prophet. The early Christians seized on this aspect of the tradition in order to legitimate their reinterpretation of Pentateuchal texts as prophecies of the events which had constituted their own faith.

Since not only individual commandments and the five books of the Torah but all the "customs" (τὰ ἔθη) of Judaism were thought to have been transmitted by Moses (Acts 6:14; 15:1), the whole institutional and ritual structure of Judaism could be identified with his name (Acts 6:11; 21:21). When Matt. 23:2 speaks of "the chair (καθέδρα) of Moses" (JB) and John 9:28 of "disciples of Moses," they are probably reflecting the tendency of the rabbinic academy to present itself as a "school" whose founder was "Moses our master."

The early Christian writers used elements of the story of Moses in a variety of ways: as examples for admonitions to the community, as tacit or explicit features in their portraits of Jesus, and for both positive and invidious comparisons to clarify the relationship of Christianity to Judaism.

1. Moses in the Pauline letters. In I Cor. 10:1-10 a parenetic homily (*see* PARENESIS[S]) presents a series of incidents from the Exodus story (Passover Haggadah?) as cautionary "models" (τύποι, vs. 6, author's trans.; cf. vs. 11, τυπικῶς συνέβαινεν). Paul's summary (vs. 11) closely resembles the eschatological exegesis in the *pesharim* from Qumran (*see* DEAD SEA SCROLLS[S] §8; MIDRASH[S] §3; INTERPRETATION, HISTORY OF[S] §C). Paul appears to move in the direction of an explicit Moses/Christ typology in vs. 2, yet nowhere else in the undisputed letters of Paul are Moses and Christ paralleled in such a way that the one could be called a "type" of the other. In Eph. 4:7-11 there is perhaps an implicit typology, for Ps. 68:18 (LXX 67:19), applied here to the "gifts" of Christ following his exaltation, refers in rabbinic midrash to Moses' gift of the Torah, which he received in heaven after ascending from Sinai.

In II Cor. 3:7-8 Paul contrasts Moses with Christ, but compares him with himself as apostle of the "new covenant." His peculiar exegesis of Exod. 34:29-35 is a parody of Jewish interpretations, which took the shining of Moses' face to represent the glory of God's image, lost by Adam but restored in the giving of the Torah. There is probably an allusion in 3:18; 4:6, and in I Cor. 13:12 to Num. 12:8. In at least one other place Paul compares himself with Moses: his rhetorical offer to sacrifice his own salvation for that of Israel (Rom. 9:3) echoes Moses' intercession after the sin of the golden calf (Exod. 32:32).

2. Presynoptic tradition. Moses and ELIJAH appear together in the Transfiguration narrative (Mark 9:2-10; Matt. 17:1-9; Luke 9:28-36), presupposing the tradition that Moses like Elijah was assumed into heaven at the end of his life. Matthew and Luke strengthen the allusion to Exod. 34:29 (Matt. 17:2; Luke 9:29). Other elements in the story are also reminiscent of the Sinai THEOPHANY: the mountain, the cloud that overshadows the group, the voice of God (quoting Deut. 18:15*b*?), Peter's desire to erect tents (*sukkoth*?); note also Mark 9:2, "after six days" (cf. Exod. 24:16); Luke 9:31, *exodos* (*see below*).

The stories of the miraculous feeding (Mark 6:32-44; Matt. 14:13-21; Luke 9:10-17; Mark 8:1-10; Matt. 15:32-39) may have contained from the outset some allusions to the manna miracle, which become explicit in the Johannine version (*see below*). THE TWELVE disciples inevitably recall Israel's TWELVE tribes and could suggest Moses' installation of twelve tribal leaders (cf. Num. 1:4; 7:84), but NT texts make nothing of this except perhaps in Matt. 19:28; Luke 22:30. The Q version of Jesus' temptation contains a secondary allusion to Moses' forty-day fast (underlined by Matthew's addition, "and forty nights").

3. Luke-Acts. The fullest recital of the Moses

saga in the NT is in the speech of Stephen (Acts 7:17-44), which contains traces of the elaboration of the story known from extant Jewish writings in Greek. The author emphasizes Moses' rejection by the people whom he was sent to save (vss. 27, 35, 39-41). The summation (vss. 51-53) asserts that the same treatment was accorded all the prophets, culminating in Jesus, whose coming, betrayal, and murder not only repeat the pattern, but also fulfill the prophets' predictions. The parallel between Moses and Jesus is emphasized by the formal structure of statements about them (compare 7:35 with 2:36; 3:14; 4:10; 5:30-31), while the fulfillment of prophecy is specified by the quotation of Deut. 18:15 both here (vs. 37) and in 3:22. The numerous references to Jesus' prophetic mission, beginning with the solemn appropriation of Isa. 61:1-2 in the Nazareth sermon (Luke 4:16-30), must be read in the same light. Like Moses, Jesus was the "prophet mighty in deed and word" (Luke 24:19; Acts 7:22) and more: the anointed ruler and leader who was destined "to redeem Israel." Luke could call that redemption Jesus' *exodos* (Luke 9:31). Luke's account of Jesus' ascension in Acts 1:9-10 may have been modeled after legends of Moses' translation. The seventy missionaries of Luke 10:1-12 may be related to the seventy elders of Num. 11:24-30. The Pentecost account in Acts 2 contains imagery found in haggadic versions of the Sinai theophany.

4. Matthew. In the Matthean infancy narrative, not only the direct verbal allusion to Exod. 4:19 in Matt. 2:20 but also the hostility of the king, the slaughter of children, the warning dreams, and perhaps the initial impulse of the father to divorce the mother all echo motifs found in haggadic accounts of Moses' birth. In late versions of the latter the portentous star and the astrologers who interpret it also appear, but this element originated, so far as Jewish folklore is concerned, in the Abraham legends. Matthew's setting of the SERMON ON THE MOUNT suggests a deliberate allusion to the Sinai theophany (compare 5:1 with Exod. 19:3), but attempts to find an elaborate typology portraying Jesus as "the new Moses" and the five discourses in Matthew as "the new Torah" are not convincing.

5. John. The Fourth Gospel shows a remarkable ambivalence toward the Moses traditions, to which it makes numerous allusions. The law which was given through Moses is both parallel to and supplanted by the "grace and truth" which came "through Jesus Christ" (1:17). Jesus is the one of whom "Moses in the law . . . wrote" (1:45; 5:46) so that a faithful comprehension of the scriptures would discover testimony to Jesus (5:39, 46-47). Like Moses, Jesus conveyed to his disciples both God's words and "new commandment" and God's *name* (17:6, 8, 11-12, 26). Also the manna (6:31-58) and Moses' lifting up of the serpent (3:14) are supplanted by Jesus. In each case John insists that Jesus' gift—finally identical with himself, given in the crucifixion—grants eternal life, qualitatively superior to the sustenance or temporal healing brought by the corresponding gift of Moses. Like Moses in Samaritan and Jewish tradition, Jesus is the agent of God. He is the expected prophet like Moses (6:14; cf. 4:19, 25*b*, 29; 7:40-52; 9:17), yet greater than Moses as he is greater than Jacob (4:12 ff.) and Abraham (8:53 ff.), so believers are forced to choose between being disciples of Moses and being disciples of Jesus (9:28). Those who put their trust in Moses (as advocate on the last day) will find him instead their accuser (5:45); those who rely on Moses' heavenly revelations are misled, for "no one has ascended into heaven but he who descended from heaven, the Son of man" (3:13).

6. Hebrews. A certain ambivalence toward the Moses tradition is evident also in Hebrews; the author wants to show not only that Jesus, *like* Moses, is superior to the angels (chs. 1–2), but also that Jesus as Son of God and anointed high priest of the heavenly sanctuary is far superior to Moses the servant of God, who founded the earthly copy of that sanctuary. He accomplishes this by an ingenious midrash (3:1-6) combining Num. 12:7 with the Nathan oracle (I Chr. 17:12-14) and the Eli oracle (I Sam. 2:35). Other references to Moses as leader of the Exodus and mediator at Sinai (3:16; 8:5; 9:19; 10:28; 12:18-21) all serve the principal warning theme that runs through Hebrews: if the old law and cultus mediated through Moses, though a mere shadow of the heavenly reality, brought such severe penalties to those who were unfaithful to it, how much more must constant faith and endurance be required in the new covenant mediated through Jesus? In 11:23-28, on the other hand, Moses becomes a direct paradigm of the requisite faith and endurance.

7. Other passages. As Moses led a hymn of triumph beside the Sea of Reeds, according to an early rabbinic midrash, so he will lead Israel in song when the dead are raised. Thus in Rev. 15:3 the Christian witnesses who have conquered "the beast" (ch. 13) sing in heaven "the song of Moses, the servant of God, and the song of the Lamb." Features of Moses and Elijah are used to portray the "two witnesses" of ch. 11; certainly the plagues of vs. 6, like the other plagues mentioned in Revelation, recall those of Moses. Exodus motifs are prominent in 12:13-16, but Moses is absent. Legendary expansions of the Moses saga are taken up in both II Tim. 3:8 and Jude 9. In the former, the Egyptian magicians who opposed Moses (unnamed in scripture, but provided by folklore with names and histories) become types of Christian heretics. In Jude the restraint shown by Michael as he struggled with Satan for Moses' corpse (recounted in the ASSUMPTION OF MOSES, according to Origen *et al.*) becomes a model for proper piety toward angels, violated by those whom the author opposes. *See also* INTERPRETATION, HISTORY OF[S] §C.

Bibliography. General: A. F. Gfrörer, *Das Jahrhundert des Heils* I/2 (1838), pp. 318-44, is still basic, though sometimes idiosyncratic; critical surveys are: J. Jeremias, "Μωϋσῆς," *TDNT,* IV (1942 [ET 1967]), 848-73; J. M. Kastner, "Moses im NT" (diss., Munich, 1967); somewhat more specialized, H. M. Teeple, *The Mosaic Eschatological Prophet,* SBLMS, X (1957).

Special studies: R. Le Déaut, *La nuit pascale,* AnBib, XXII (1963), 298-338; M. M. Bourke, "The Literary Genus of Matthew 1-2," *CBQ,* XXII (1960), 160-75; J. Dupont, "L'arrièrefond biblique du récit des tentations de Jésus," *NTS,* III (1956-57), 287-304; S. Schulz, "Die Decke des Moses. Untersuchungen zu einer vorpaulinischen Überlieferung in II Cor. 3:7-18," *ZNW,* XLIX (1958), 1-30; D. Georgi, *Die Gegner des Paulus im 2. Kor.,* WMANT, XI (1964), esp. pp. 258-82; T. F. Glasson, *Moses in the Fourth Gospel,* SBT, XL (1963); W. A. Meeks, *The Prophet-King: Moses Traditions and the Johannine Christology,* NovTSup, XIV (1967); M. R. D'Angelo, *Moses in Hebrews* (diss., Yale, 1975).

W. A. Meeks

MOT. The word for death, *māweth, môth* (*mawth*), is several times personified in the OT (e.g., Jer. 9:21 [H 20]; Job 18:13, NEB). In some instances, the term is a personified place name, standing in synonymous parallellism with Sheol, or with another term for the abode of Death (Isa. 38:18; Hos. 3:14; Job 28:22; 30:23). "Death" as a designation of the infernal realm derives from the name of its ruler, Mot, alluded to under a variety of epithets, such as "king of terrors" (Job 18:14), "Ravenous One" (Job 18:12, ABi) and "first-born" (Job 18:13). Cf. ABi, XV (3rd ed.), 134-35.

Philo of Byblos mentioned a deity Muth, Death, compared to Pluto. Texts from ancient Ugarit have brought us fuller information on Mot/Death as the chief foe of Baal.

Mot's realm in the Ugaritic texts is commonly designated simply as "earth," *arṣ*. The entrance to his infernal abode is marked by twin mountains with names still unexplained, corresponding apparently to the "dark mountains" of postbiblical Jewish lore. The fullest characterization of Mot and his abode is given in Baal's instructions to his messengers:

Then set face
Toward Mount TRǴZZ,
Toward Mount ṮRMG,
Toward the mounds that plug Earth.
Lift the mount on your hands,
The hill on top of your palms;
And descend to the pest house (*bt ḫpṯt*) of Earth.
Be counted with those who descend to Earth.
Then set face
Toward his city Oozy (*hmry*);
Low, the throne of his see,
Slime, the land of his heritage.
But beware, O servitors of the gods;
Do not get close to divine Mot,
Lest he make you like a lamb in his mouth,
Like a kid in his gullet's breech you be crushed (Baal Cycle 4 [51].VIII.1-37)

The "pest house" (*bt ḫpṯt*) is virtually identical with the בית החפשית in II Kings 15:5=II Chr. 26:21 (KJV "several house"; RSV "separate house") used of an isolation ward for lepers who are unclean and as good as dead. The term rendered "Oozy" (*hmry*) is cognate with the *hapax legomenon* מהמרות of Ps. 140:10 [H 11], (slimy) "pits" from which one cannot rise. The watery, slimy, filthy character of Mot's abode explains the remark by Philo of Byblos that the term Muth itself denotes slime or a putrescent watery mixture. Mot applies the same term to his esophagus when he invites Baal to dinner both as guest and as main course:

You shall go down the throat of divine Mot,
The gullet (*mhmrt*) of El's beloved hero. (5 [67].I.6-8).

The opposition between Baal and Mot, the conflict between fertility and sterility, life and death, is apparently seasonal. Baal meekly acquiesces to Mot's summons to be swallowed. Baal's sister-consort, the violent virgin Anath, however, pines for her lost lover and accosts Mot:

She seized Mot by the hem of his garment,
Grabbed him by the end of his robe.
"Thou, Mot, give [up] my brother."
Divine Mot replied:
. . . .
"I met Mighty Baal.
I put him like a lamb in my mouth,
Like a kid in my gullet's breech was he crushed.
The god's lamp, Sun, glows,
The skies gleam in the power of divine Mot.
. . . .
She seized divine Mot.
With a sword she split him,
With a sieve she sifted him,
With fire she burned him,
With millstones she ground him,
In the field she sowed him.
His flesh the birds ate,
His parts sparrows consumed.
Flesh to flesh did cry (6 [49].II.9-37)

In text 23 [52].8-9 there is reference to "pruning" of the god:

Death-and-Evil sits,
In his hand the rod of bereavement,
In his hand the rod of widowhood.
Let the pruners prune him [like] a vine,
Let the binders bind him [like] a vine,
Let them lop his tendrils like a vine.

The word *šdmt,* rendered "tendrils," occurs several times in the OT and has evoked considerable and continuing discussion. It has been taken as a compound meaning "field (s) of Mot," but the occurrences in Deut. 32:32; Hab. 3:17-18; and Isa. 16:8 in parallelism or association with the vine, as in the Ugaritic passage cited, suggest "tendrils," or the like.

Aspects of Anath's treatment of Mot suggest a grain ritual and recall the Israelite offering of the first fruits in the form of crushed grain parched with fire (Lev. 2:14-15), further described by Philo of Alexandria (*On the Special Laws* II, 20), Josephus (Antiq. III.x.5), and in the Mishna (Men. 10). The women of Haran, according to Ibn an-Nadīm, wept for Tammuz because he was ground and strewn to the wind. Thus it has been supposed that Mot had a dual character, like other chthonic deities such as Tammuz-Adonis, Osiris, Pluto, Demeter, and Kore (*see* Deities, Underworld[S]). The figure of death, resurrection, and fertility in the planting, germination, and increase of grain is applied to the death of Jesus in John 12:24. There is, however, no corroborative evidence in the Ugaritic texts for beneficent fertility function on the part of Mot. Destruction and sterility are his concern and fear is the natural response to Mot, both for gods and people. Mot's standard epithet *ydd* (Yadid), "Beloved," must be euphemistic for the opposite sense. Mot's power is sufficient even to overcome mighty Baal, to halt his life-giving rain, and to turn the blazing sun into an instrument of death. The expression "strong as Hell" has an ancient background. A private letter from Ugarit contains the pregnant lines "and the hand/love of the gods here [is] like Mot/Death exceeding strong." Whether the grapheme *yd* here (54:11) represents "hand" or "love" (more likely the former in the sense of plague or other calamity), the comparison is with the strength of Mot/Death. In Song of S. 8:6 it is love that is affirmed strong as Mot/Death and Sheol/Hell, and this assertion may be more than a mere superlative statement since love, fecundity, and faith are the only defenses against the dread power until the final victory, the death of Death and Hell's destruction (cf. I Cor. 15:54-55; Rev. 20:14).

We have no sure representation of Mot in early art. A strange stele from Ugarit (*Ugaritica* II, pl. 22 right; *ANEP,* p. 489) has been thought to depict Mot, among other deities, but this is highly conjectural. Among verbal characterizations, we have reference to Mot's rod (*ḫṭ*=Akkad. *ḫaṭṭu*), but it is clear only that it is an implement for bereavement, *ṯkl* and widowhood, *ulmn* (23 [52].8-9). The Angel of Death, *ml'k mwt',* is depicted on an Aramaic magic bowl with sword and spear in his hands and these have been related to the rod(s) of bereavement and/or widowhood of Death-and-Evil, *Mt-w-Šr* of the Ugaritic text.

Bibliography. N. Tromp, ***Primitive Conceptions of Death and the Nether World in the OT*** (1969); T. H. Gaster, "The Combat of 'Aleyan Ba'al and Mot," *JRAS* (1934), pp. 677-714; (1935), pp. 1-44; (1936), 225-35; V. Jacobs and I. Jacobs, "The Myth of Mot and 'Al'eyan Ba'al," *HTR,* XXVIII (1945), 77-109; T. Worden, "The Literary Influence of the Ugaritic Fertility Myth on the OT," *VT,* III (1953), 273-97; J. Finkel, "An Interpretation of an Ugaritic Viticultural Poem," in *The Joshua Starr Memorial Volume* (1953), pp. 29-58; M. R. Lehmann, "A New Interpretation of the Term *šdmwt,*" *VT,* III (1953), 361-71; M. Dahood, "Ancient Semitic Deities in Syria and Palestine," in *Le Antiche Divintà Semitiche,* ed. S. Moscati (1958), pp. 65-94, at p. 92; J. S. Croatto and J. A. Soggin, "Die Bedeutung von *šdmwt* in AT," *ZAW,* LXXIV (1962), 44-50; H. Schmid, "Tod II. Tod und Totenreich im AT," *RGG,* VI (3rd ed., 1962), cols. 912-13; U. Cassuto, "Baal and Mot in the Ugaritic Texts," *IEJ,* XII (1962), 77-86; A. Kapelrud, "Baal and Mot in the Ugaritic Texts," *IEJ,* XIII (1963), 127-29; V. Maag, "Tod und Jenseits nach dem AT," *Schweizerische Theologische Umschau,* XXXIV (1964), 17-37; H. Kosmala, "Mot and the Vine," *Annual of the Swedish Theological Institute,* III (1964), 147-51; M. H. Pope, "The Word *šaḥat* in Job 9, 31," *JBL,* LXXXIII (1964), 269-78; M. H. Pope and W. Röllig, "Mot," *Wörterbuch der Mythologie,* ed. H. W. Haussig, I (1965), 300-303; A. Jirku, "Die Vorstellungen von Tod und Jenseits in den alphabetischen Texten von Ugarit," *Ugaritica* VI (1968), 303-8; P. Watson, "The Death of 'Death' in the Ugaritic Texts," *JAOS,* XCII (1972), 60-64; W. Michel, "Death in Job," *Dialog,* XI (1972), 183-89; D. Tsumura, "A Ugaritic God MT-w-ŠR, and His Two Weapons," *UF,* VI (1974), 407-14. M. H. Pope

***MOUNT, MOUNTAIN.** To be added to the IDB list of Hebrew terms for "mountain" is צור. In many cases the translation "rock" or "crag" is appropriate (e.g., Isa. 8:14, צור in parallelism with אבן). However, in other occurrences of the word, both context and poetic parallelism require the translation "mountain." In Job 14:18, for example, צור and הר are clearly synonymous. In Num. 23:9, where the context indicates that Balaam is standing on an elevation of some significance, the nouns גבעות and צרים are parallel to each other. Significantly, גבעה is the regular synonym of הר, the most common Hebrew word for mountain (Hab. 3:6; Ps. 114:4, 6). Hebrew צור and Aramaic טור are cognate to Ugaritic *ǵr,* "mountain."

The fact that צור may be translated "mountain" is of more than philological interest. It is well known that the Hebrews referred to their God as צור ישראל (II Sam. 23:3; cf. 22:33; Deut. 32:30; Ps. 78:35). Though the traditional "Rock of Israel" is not impossible (cf. Gen. 49:24), "Mountain of Israel" is preferable. The Mesopotamians referred to various gods by the epithet "great mountain" (Akkad. *šadû rabû;* Sumer. *kur. gal*). Among these gods were Addu, Amurru, Asshur, Enlil, and Girra. Clearly, the epithet emphasizes the protective power and formidability of the deity. Thus an Akkadian name such as *Aššur-šad-nišēšu,* "Asshur-is-the-mountain of his people," is very similar to the Hebrew name types צוריאל, "El [God]-is-my-mountain" (Num. 3:35), and פדהצור, "The-mountain-has-redeemed" (Num. 1:10).

More problematical is the question of whether to include the divine name Shaddai (שדי) among mountain epithets. As early as the nineteenth century, proposals were made to relate the Hebrew name to Akkadian *šadû,* "mountain," and thus to elucidate the origin of the deity. Speakers of Akkadian distinguished between *ilī māti,* "lowland [valley] gods," and *ilī šadî,* "mountain gods" (*TCL* 3:315). In Asia Minor and Syria, literary and nonliterary sources demonstrate that mountains were deified, worshiped, invoked as witnesses to treaties, and given offerings along with other deities. A particularly well-studied example is the Syrian divine mountain Zaphon (*see* Zaphon, Mount[s]), which received divine homage and was employed as a theophoric element in such names as Ugaritic *ʿbdṣpn,* "Slave-of-Zaphon," *bdṣpn,* "In-the-hand [care]-of-Zaphon," as well as Phoenician גרצפן, "Client-of-Zaphon." However, the simple equation of *šadû* and Shaddai fails to account for the doubling of the second Hebrew consonant as well as for the final diphthong (Albright). The same objection may be made against the equation of אל שדי with Amorite *bēl šadê,* "Lord of the Mountain[s]," an epithet of Amurru (Bailey). Furthermore, unlike *bēl šadê,* each element of אל שדי may stand alone. It thus appears to be a composite name along the lines of אל עליון and אל בית אל. The Amorite epithet, on the other hand, is a construct genitive, similar in form to בעל שמם, "Lord of of Heaven" (e.g., *KAI* 4:3), and בעל בת, "Lord of the dynasty" (*KAI* 24:16). A related hypothesis is to equate the Hebrew with Akkadian *šaddā'u,* "mountain dweller." Linguistically sound, this proposal is in harmony as well with Yahweh's association with mountains (e.g., Deut. 33:2; I Kings 20:23). It must be cautioned however that Akkadian *šaddā'u* is poorly attested and never as a divine epithet (cf. God, Names of §C2*a*; Almighty).

Hebrew religion was, by its nature, antithetical to some elements of Near Eastern mountain mythology. Clearly, mountains could not be deified without infringing on Yahweh's right to Israel's exclusive worship. Yet, other elements of Near Eastern mountain myth made their way into Hebrew religious literature, some merely as poetry, others as vestiges. A good example is the הר מועד, "mount of assembly" (Isa. 14:13). Though it was at one time thought that Isaiah's description reflected Babylonian notions, it has been shown that Canaanite mythology underlies the chapter. Accordingly, the "mount of assembly" can be traced back to the mountain (*Ll*) upon which sat the divine assembly of Ugarit (*pḫr mᶜd*, "assembled gathering," e.g., *CTA* 1:II:20). In fact, it has been suggested that בהר מועד be emended to בפחר מועד.

Scholars have suggested that the Hebrews shared with the ancient Mesopotamians the concept of a *Weltberg*. That notion, known from comparative folklore, describes the world as a huge mountain at whose peak is heaven and at whose base is the underworld. It is difficult to find support for this view in the OT. Moreover, there is no clear evidence that the Mesopotamians actually held such a belief (Clifford). Sargon II, for example, describes a mountain, *ša ēliš rīšāša šamāmi endāma šaplānu šuršūša šukšudū qereb aralli*, "whose peaks above lean against the heavens, while below, its roots reach the heart of the nether world" (*TCL* 3:19). As the context demonstrates, Sargon is merely conveying the viewer's awe of majestic mountains which dominate the landscape, and which can be scaled only with great difficulty. In Akkadian and Sumerian literature the idea of greatness may be expressed by saying that a particular object has its base in the underworld and its top in the heavens. These objects may be as diverse as a god, a temple, a god's weapon, a mythical tree, or the speaker of an incantation. Even those mountains which are explicitly identified as the gateways to the nether world (e.g., Ugar. *trǵzz* and *ṯrmg*, *CTA* 4:VIII:3:1-9) are not necessarily indications of Near Eastern belief in a *Weltberg*. Rather, they may be taken as expressions of the widespread view that mountains (usually in the N) mark the edge of the world. Naturally, then, beyond that edge the underworld is located.

Yet Hebrew religion knew of sacred mountains. Among these were BASHAN (Ps. 68:15-16 [H 16-17]), GERIZIM, HOREB (Exod. 3:1), and of course SINAI and ZION. The mythology of Mount Zion provides a clear example of how the Israelites appropriated earlier religious traditions and made them their own. Prior to the discovery of Ugaritic it was difficult to understand why an author would locate Mount Zion in the "far north" (ירכתי צפון, Ps. 48:2 [H 3]). However, it is now known that Zaphon was the proper name of Baal's holy mountain, the site of his temple, and itself divine. Accordingly, צפון in our passage should be treated as a proper name as in Ugaritic (cf. NEB n.). Yahweh's mountain is here identified explicitly with Zaphon. Accordingly, the Psalmist has no difficulty in applying to Zion the grandiose terminology of myth.

Bibliography. W. F. Albright, "The Names *Shaddai* and *Abram*," *JBL*, LIV (1935), 173-204, "Baal-Zephon," *Festschrift Alfred Bertholet* (1950), pp. 1-14, *From the Stone Age to Christianity* (1940), pp. 188-89, and *Yahweh and the Gods of Canaan* (1968), pp. 24-25, 188-89; L. Bailey, "Israelite *'Ēl Šadday* and Amorite *Bêl Šadê*," *JBL*, LXXXVII (1968), 434-38; R. Clifford, *The Cosmic Mountain in Canaan and the OT* (1972); F. M. Cross, *Canaanite Myth and Hebrew Epic* (1973); pp. 44-60; T. Gaster, *Thespis* (1950), pp. 197-99; H. L. Ginsberg, "Reflexes of Sargon in Isaiah after 715 B.C.E.," *JAOS*, LXXXVIII (1968), 47-53; J. Hayes, "The Tradition of Zion's Inviolability," *JBL*, LXXXII (1963), 419-26; M. Held, "Philological Notes on the Mari Covenant Rituals," *BASOR*, 200 (Dec. 1970), 34, n. 16, and "Hebrew *maᶜgāl*: A Study in Lexical Parallelism," *JANES*, VI (1974), 111, n. 50; T. Jacobsen, *Toward the Image of Tammuz* (1970), pp. 117-18; P. Jensen, *Die Kosmologie der Babylonier* (1890), pp. 201-12; H.-J. Kraus, *Psalmen*, I (1960), 342-45; W. G. Lambert, *Babylonian Wisdom Literature* (1960), p. 327; M. Noth, *Die israelitischen Personennamen im Rahmen der gemeinsemitischen Namengebung* (1928), pp. 127-31, 156-57; J. Ouellette, "More on 'Ēl Šadday and Bêl Šadê," *JBL*, LXXXVIII (1969), 470-71; M. Pope and J. Tigay, "A Description of Baal," *UF*, III (1971), 123; J. Stamm, *Die akkadische Namengebung* (1939), p. 82; K. Tallqvist, *Akkadische Götterepitheta* (1938), pp. 64, 221, 251; N. H. Tur-Sinai, *The Book of Job* (rev. ed., 1967), pp. 71-74; E. D. van Buren, "Mountain-Gods," *Or*, NS XII (1943), 76-84; M. Weippert, "Erwägungen zur Etymologie des Gottesnamens *'El Šaddaj*," *ZDMG*, CXI (1961), 42-62; H. W. Haussig, ed., *Wörterbuch der Mythologie*, I (1965), 160-61, 256.

D. SPERLING

***MURATORIAN FRAGMENT.** This partial list of NT books, previously held to have originated in Rome about the end of the second century, must now probably be regarded as Eastern, dating from the early fourth century.

1. Rise to importance. The fragment, discovered in an eighth-century codex at Milan, is a mutilated list of NT books now beginning with the third gospel and ending abruptly. Portions are found also in four Latin MSS (eleventh or twelfth century) at Monte Cassino which were not copied from the Milan MS. Campos has shown that the Latin of the MF was influenced by the Vulg., assuring its Greek origin.

Nineteenth-century scholars associated the MF with the Peshitta and the Old Latin versions as representative lists dating from about A.D. 170. Harnack endowed the fragment with new importance when he claimed that it was an official list published in Rome as the NT canon for the whole church. Despite subsequent discrediting of these claims, the fragment has retained the prominence it first attained through Harnack's claims.

2. Re-evaluation. Recent scholarship has determined that an early fourth-century date and an Eastern provenance are more probable than the view which has become traditional.

a. The case against Rome. The argument for a Roman origin of the fragment was built chiefly on its use of specific phrases and words. It has been shown, however, that the expression *catholica (ecclesia)* should not be limited to Rome, because Cyprian applied it to the Christian community in each city, and that Roman writers referred to their city with *hic in urbe Roma*, not with *cathedra urbi Romae ecclesiae*, as in the MF. Moreover, the use of the word *urbs* for Rome (lines 38-39) is dependent upon Rom. 15:24, 29; Acts 28:14*b*-31, and in any case such a usage is not limited to writings of Roman origin. Other linguistic arguments have likewise been seriously questioned or refuted.

b. The case against the late second-century dating. The early dating of the fragment has been based almost exclusively upon the phrase *nuperrime temporibus nostris,* usually translated "very recently, in our time," and taken to mean, within a generation of Pius I. But this interpretation is tendentious. It could also mean "most recently," with respect to the previously named books; and "in our time" could therefore just as well refer to postapostolic times in general (cf. Euseb. Hist. IV.xxii.4; III.xxxi.6–xxii.1; Iren. Her. V.xxx.3). Thus, the date of the MF must be determined in some other way.

3. The Eastern provenance and fourth-century date of MF. It is significant that the fragment does not approve the Shepherd of Hermas for public reading in the church, because, except for Tertullian (a special case due to his Montanism), the work was highly regarded in both East and West until Eusebius and is first called into question in the East (Euseb. Hist. III.iii.6-7; xxv.4). MF also conforms to the Eastern tendency in excluding the Wisdom of Solomon from the OT and including Jewish apocrypha in NT lists. For example, Eusebius, illustrating Irenaeus' use of NT books, mentions his quotations from the Wisdom of Solomon among them (Hist. V.viii.1-8); Epiphanius (d. 403) included Wisdom of Solomon and Sirach in his NT list (Her. III.i.5); and the index of Codex Alexandrinus (probably Palestinian) concludes the NT list with Psalms of Solomon. An Eastern provenance and later date for MF are also indicated by its placing of the book of Revelation, along with the Apocalypse of Peter, on the fringe of the canon, following the Wisdom of Solomon. The book of Revelation was only questioned in the East following Dionysius (265). Moreover, scant evidence of acquaintance with the Apocalypse of Peter is found in the West, and its inclusion in the canon was considered only in the East (e.g., Euseb. Hist. VI.xiv.1-2; II.xxv.4, 6-7).

Apart from MF, the earliest NT list we possess is that of Eusebius. Thus, if the fragment does date from the end of the second century, it must have been composed in a corner and preserved by chance; it surely had no influence on the developing NT canon in the West. The evidence suggests, rather, that MF is to be dated in the fourth century and regarded as an Eastern list.

Bibliography. A. C. Sundberg, Jr., "Canon Muratori: A Fourth-Century List," *HTR,* LXVI (1973), 1-41, provides the full argumentation and evidence for the view that MF is an Eastern list from the fourth century. *See also* A. von Harnack, "Das Muratorische Fragment und die Entstehung einer Sammlung Apostolisch-Katholischer Schriften," *Zeitschrift für Kirchengeschichte,* III (1879), 358-408, 595-98; J. Campos, "Epoca del fragmenta Muratoriano," *Helmantica, Revista de Humanidades Clasicas,* XI (1960), 485-96.

A. C. SUNDBERG, JR.

***MUSIC.** Assyriological research since 1959 has led to the discovery of four Akkadian cuneiform texts that describe ancient Near Eastern music theory and practice from *ca.* 1800 B.C. to *ca.* 500 B.C. Dating to the Old Babylonian, Middle Assyrian, and Neo-Babylonian periods, they demonstrate that the ancient Mesopotamian musical scales were heptatonic and diatonic. Thus, our evidence for the antiquity of Western music has been pushed back some 1400 years earlier than the earliest Greek evidence.

Fourteen Akkadian terms are known as names of musical intervals—seven names for intervals of fifths and fourths, seven for thirds and sixths.

String Designations	fifths and fourths	
1-5	*nīš gabarî*	"rise of the duplicate"
2-6	*išartu*	"normal"
3-7	*embūbu*	"reed-pipe"
4-1	*nīd qabli*	"fall of the middle"
5-2	*qablītu*	"middle"
6-3	*kitmu*	"closed"
7-4	*pītu*	"open"
String Designations	**thirds and sixths**	
7-5	*šēru*	"song"
1-6	*šalšatu*	"third"
2-7	*rebūtu*	"fourth"
1-3	*isqu*	"throwstick/lot"
2-4	*titur qablītu*	"bridge of the middle"
3-5	*titur išartu*	"bridge of the normal"
4-6	*serdû*	(a type of music)

These terms do not indicate differences between major or minor thirds, perfect or augmented fourths, etc.; in other words, these terms do not reflect the position of semitones in the scale. This position depends on the tuning. There are seven tunings:

									Corresponding Greek Octave-Species
išartu	"normal"	E	F	G	A	B	C	D	Dorian
kitmu	"closed"	E	F♯	G	A	B	C	D	Hypodorian
embūbu	"reed-pipe"	E	F♯	G	A	B	C♯	D	Phrygian
pītu	"open"	E	F♯	G♯	A	B	C♯	D	Hypophrygian
nīd qabli	"fall of the middle"	E	F♯	G♯	A	B	C♯	D♯	Lydian (=our major scale)
nīš gabarî	"rise of the duplicate"	E	F♯	G♯	A♯	B	C♯	D♯	Hypolydian
qablītu	"middle"	E♯	F♯	G♯	A♯	B	C♯	D♯	Mixolydian

Tuning was accomplished by a series of fifths and fourths, which produced a diatonic scale in Pythagorean tuning. Each tuning was named for the fifth or fourth that began the series; in each tuning the tritone, hence the semitones, was located in a different place.

One complete piece of music, a syllabic cuneiform Hurrian cult hymn to the goddess Nikkal, dating to *ca.* 1400 B.C., has been found at ancient UGARIT. This piece, written (as its colophon tells us) in the *nīd qabli* (=major) scale uses a notational system based on the Akkadian terminology discussed above. No directions for rhythm or tempo are given. The notation consists of interval names followed by numerals. It is thought that the numerals indicate the number of times the dichord (i.e., the two notes of the interval sounding simultaneously) is to be played or sung. Analyzing the notation thus, the hymn from Ugarit appears to be provided with heterophonic music as shown in Fig. M11. It is assumed that the top melodic line was to be sung, and that the bottom notes represent the harmonic accompaniment. Until additional texts with explicit notation are brought to light, this interpretation of the notational system in Ugarit must remain hypothetical.

In the Neo-Babylonian period (middle to late first millennium B.C.), a different but related system of notation appears to have been in use. There, notations are placed directly next to the lines of the hymnic literature and apparently amount to abbreviated directions. But this late system is not yet understood by scholars.

Bibliography. R. D. Barnett, "New Facts about Musical Instruments from Ur," *Iraq,* XXXI (1969), 96-103; R. D. Biggs, "The Sumerian Harp," *American Harp Journal,* I (1968), 6-12; M. Duchesne-Guillemin, "Découverte d'une gamme babylonienne," *Revue de Musicologie,* XLIX (1963), 3-17, "A l'aube de la théorie musicale. Concordance de trois tablettes babyloniennes," *Revue de Musicologie,* LII (1966), 147-62, "La harpe à plectre iranienne: son origine et sa diffusion," *JNES,* XXVIII (1969), 109-15, and "Note complémentaire sur l' instrument algar," *JNES,* XXIX (1970), 200-201; O. R. Gurney, "An Old Babylonian Treatise on the Tuning of the Harp," *Iraq,* XXX (1968), 229-33; H. G. Güterbock, "Musical Notation in Ugarit," *RA,* LXIV (1970), 45-52; H. Hartmann, *Die Musik der sumerischen Kultur* (1960); A. D. Kilmer, "The Strings of Musical Instruments," *Studies in Honor of Benno Landsberger,* Oriental Institute of the University of Chicago, Assyriological Studies No. XVI (1965), 261-68, "The Discovery of an Ancient Mesopotamian Theory of Music," *PAPS,* CXV (1971), 131-49, and "The Cult Song with Music from Ancient Ugarit: Another Interpretation," *RA,* LXVIII (1974), 69-82; H. M. Kümmel, "Zur Stimmung der babylonischen Harfe," *Or,* XXXIX (1970), 252-63; W. G. Lambert, "The Converse Tablet: A Litany with Musical Instructions," *Near Eastern Studies in Honor of William Foxwell Albright,* ed. H. Goedicke (1971), pp. 335-53; E. Laroche, "Documents en langue hourrite provenant de Ras Shamra," *Ugaritica,* V (1968), 462-96, and "Études hourrites: notation musicale," *RA,* LXVII (1974); J. Rimmer, *Ancient Musical Instruments of Western Asia in . . . the British Museum* (1969); A. Spycket, "La musique instrumentale mésopotamienne," *Journal des Savants* (July-Sept. 1972), pp. 153-209; W. Stauder, *Die Harfen und Leiern der Sumerer* (1957), *Die Harfen und Leiern Vorderasiens in babylonischer und assyrischer Zeit* (1961), "Ein Musiktraktat aus dem zweiten vorchristlichen Jahrtausend," *Festschrift für Walter Wiora* (1967), pp. 157-63, and "Die Musik der Sumerer, Babylonier und Assyrer," *Orientalische Musik, Handbuch der Orientalistik* (1970), pp. 171-243; D. Wulstan, "The Tuning of the Babylonian Harp," *Iraq,* XXX (1968), 215-28, and

Lyrics (in Hurrian)

1. [x (x)] ḫan[u]ta niyaša ziwe š[i]nute zuturiya ubugara [ḫub]urni tašal killa [z]ili šipri ḪUMARUḪAT UWARI
2. ḪUMARUḪAT UWARI wanda[n]ita ukuri kurkurta išalla ulali kabgi a[l]l[i]bgi širit m[u]rnušu WEŠAL TATIB TIŠIYA
3. WEŠAL TATIB TIŠIYA unu[g]a kabšili unugat akli šamšam me[l]il uklal tununitak[a ḫanu]ka KALITANIL NIKALA
4. KALITANIL NIKALA niḫ[ur]ašal ḫana ḫanuteti attayaštal attari ḫ(u)weti ḫanuka [(x)xxxxxxxx]-šati *WEWA ḪANUKU*

Notation (using Hurrianized Akkadian terms)

5a. qablite 3 irbute 1 qablite 3 ša/ini?

5b. titimišarte 10 uštamari

6. titimišarte 2 zirte 1 šaḫri 2
zi[rt]e 2 irbute 2

7. umbube 1 šaššate 2 irbute [1] ša[šš]ate
2? titarqabli 1 titimišarte 4

8. zirte 1 šaḫri 2 šaššate 4 irbute 1
nadqabli 1 šaḫri [2]

9. šaššate 4 šaḫri 1 šašš[at]e 2
šaḫri 1 šaššate 2 irb[ute] 2

10. kitme 2 qablite 3 kit[me] 1
qablite 4 kitme 1 qablite 3?

= notation for REPEATED REFRAINS (7 syllables each) [5a]

= notation for *CLOSING PHRASE* (5 syllables repeated) [5b]

= notation for long lines 1 & 4 of lyrics (based on approximate matching of word syllables to the numbers of dichords) [6–8]

= notation for short lines 2 & 3 of lyrics (based on approximate matching of word syllables to the numbers of dichords) [9–10]

Colophon (in Akkadian)

11. [ann]û zammaru ša nid-qibli s/za[luzi ša DINGIR.MEŠ TA ᵐUrḫia] ŠU ᵐAmmurapi — "This is a song of the Fall-of-the-Middle (scale), a hymn (?) of the gods, from Urḫiya; copied by Ammurapi."

11. Transcription of clay tablet from Ugarit (Ras Shamra), with notation—the earliest specimen of notated music

"The Earliest Musical Notation," *Music and Letters,* LII (1971), 365-82. A. D. KILMER

MYSTERY RELIGIONS. *See* GREEK RELIGION AND PHILOSOPHY.

***MYTH IN THE NT.** The term "myth" designated originally an "account" or "story," but it came to mean "rumor" or "fable," and in the NT is always used in this negative sense. However, in some NT writings (e.g., Revelation), mythological imagery is used to convey the Christian message. The question therefore arises: To what extent is myth present in the NT and how is mythological material to be interpreted?

The question was sharply focused by Bultmann's program of demythologizing, formally advanced in 1941. He argued that the earliest Christians used mythological expressions in formulating their Christology and eschatology. The task of interpretation, he concluded, is to disclose the Christian message (*kerygma*) expressed there and to expose its meaning for human existence. Bultmann's view of myth as the prescientific depiction of transcendent reality in this-worldly, objective terms has been widely debated, and a variety of alternative definitions of myth have been offered. Most influential has been the work of Eliade, for whom myth is the recital of a sacred history. By describing events of a primordial time, myth tells the beginning of existence; retelling the myth then makes it possible to participate in the basic sources of being. On this basis, Tillich, Gilkey, and Aulén have insisted that myth or symbol is essential to religious expression, and Knox has even described the biblical drama of redemption as "the Christian myth."

Although it is widely agreed that the NT world view includes mythological elements, some interpreters believe that much of what Bultmann calls myth, e.g., the miracles and the Resurrection, should be identified as history. The resulting charge that Bultmann has abandoned the historical basis of the *kerygma* seems oblivious to his stress on the historical event of Jesus. Some of Bultmann's followers are engaged in a "new quest of the historical Jesus," in which the words and deeds of Jesus are recognized as an essential part of the Christian proclamation (*see* BIBLICAL CRITICISM, NT[S] §4*c*). At the same time, Bultmann's contention that the NT uses a pre-Christian, Gnostic redeemer myth in formulating its christological confessions has been called into question by recent research into GNOSTICISM.

Much of the demythologizing debate has failed to recognize that Bultmann intends to interpret rather than eliminate myth. Nevertheless, his use of existentialism as a method of interpreting the meaning of myth has led to the claim that Bultmann has exchanged the old myth for a new philosophical or scientific one. While Bultmann actually believes the *kerygma* to be independent of any objective (mythological) formulation, his concern with the method of interpretation has provoked a lively interest in HERMENEUTICS. Some of his followers, influenced by the later writings of M. Heidegger, are engaged in the "new hermeneutic." According to their view, the revelation of God occurs in the "language-event" of Jesus, and the texts which witness to his words are not objects to be interpreted, but the Word which interprets the hearer, offering authentic existence. Other interpreters take a literary approach (*see* LITERATURE, BIBLE AS[S]), insisting that the meaning of myth is intrinsic to the mythological form (Wilder), or that religious language needs to be enriched by mythological expression so that the poverty of the modern imagination may be overcome (Ricoeur). Structuralists have sought to apply the theories of Lévi-Strauss and to show that myths reflect patterns of narrative structure which correspond to basic structures of human life and thought.

Bibliography. G. Stählin, "μύθος," *TDNT,* IV (1942 [ET 1969]), 762-95; G. Bornkamm, "Theologie R. Bultmanns in d. neueren Diskussion," *Theol. Rundschau,* XXIX (1963), 35-141; H. Bartsch, ed., *Kerygma u. Mythos,* I–VI (1951-74 [ET vols. I, II 1972]); C. Braaten and R. Harrisville, eds., *Kerygma and History* (1962), *The Historical Jesus and the Kerygmatic Christ* (1964); C. Kegley, ed., *Theology of Rudolf Bultmann* (1966); W. Schmithals, *Introduction to the Theology of R. Bultmann* (1966); A. Malet, *The Thought of Rudolf Bultmann,* Nouvelle série theologique, XIV (1962); M. Eliade, *Myth and Reality,* World Perspectives, XXXI (1963); P. Tillich, "Myth and Mythology," *Twentieth Century Theology in the Making,* ed. J. Pelikan, II (1970), 342-54; L. Gilkey, *Religion and the Scientific Future* (1970); G. Aulén, *The Drama and the Symbols* (1965); J. Knox, *Myth and Truth* (1964); J. Robinson, *New Quest of the Historical Jesus,* SBT, XXV (1959); J. Robinson and J. Cobb, eds., *New Frontiers in Theology,* 2 vols. (1963, 1964); P. Achtemeier, *Introduction to the New Hermeneutic* (1969); A. Wilder, *Early Christian Rhetoric: The Language of the Gospel* (1971); P. Ricoeur, "The Language of Faith," *USQR,* XXVIII (1973), 213-24; C. Lévi-Strauss, "Structural Study of Myth," *Myth: A Symposium,* ed. T. Sebeok (1958). W. BAIRD

N

NAG HAMMADI näg həm mä'dē. A site in the vicinity of the modern city of Nag Hammadi in Upper Egypt, where an extensive collection of fourth-century Christian and non-Christian Gnostic writings in Coptic was discovered in 1946. The modern history of the discovery is quite complex and in some details still unclear. On the ancient history of the library of papyrus codices, little can be known except by inference; archaeological excavations at the site of the find may help clarify the origin of the books. The contents of the library are extremely rich and varied, representing many literary types of Gnostic literature as well as diverse forms of Gnosticism itself. The importance of the collection for the history of religions, the history of early Christianity, the study of the Coptic language, and many other fields is incalculable. For the first time, students of Gnosticism have at hand a large collection of original Gnostic writings with which to understand the movements so bitterly and successfully combated by church authorities in the early centuries of our era. Such major problems as that of the origin of the Gnostic religion are enlightened by these documents, and the Christian, Jewish, and pagan contributions to the syncretistic amalgam of Gnostic myth can be distinguished with greater clarity.

1. Description of the codices
2. History of the discovery
   a. The Jung Codex
   b. The other codices
   c. Major publications
3. Contents of the library
4. Preliminary classification of the writings
   a. Literary genres
   b. Types of Gnosticism
      i. Sethian
      ii. Valentinian
      iii. Other Gnostic types
      iv. Hermetic
      v. Non-Gnostic writings
5. Issues in interpretation
   a. Christian and non-Christian origins
   b. Jewish materials
   c. Gnosticism and the NT
Bibliography

1. Description of the codices. The Nag Hammadi codices represent some of the oldest extant examples of what corresponds to the modern bound book. They consist of folded PAPYRUS leaves assembled into one or more quires and sewn into a leather cover. The earlier literature on the collection has spoken of thirteen codices, but Robinson has shown that Codex XIII, which consists of one tractate plus a few lines of another on its last page, was placed in antiquity as a set of eight folios within the cover of Codex VI. Thus one should properly speak of twelve codices (of which much of Codex XII is missing, perhaps lost in modern times) and parts of a thirteenth. The covers of Codices II-XI are preserved, along with the pages of all the codices, in the Coptic Museum of Old Cairo; the cover of Codex I is in the collection of the Institute for Antiquity and Christianity, Claremont, California. Because of the extremely fragmentary nature of many of the leaves, calculations of the total number of extant inscribed pages vary considerably. Thus far at least 1,139 complete or partial pages have been identified.

The codices contain several different copyists' hands, some of them very elegant and all of them remarkably clear and legible. Because Coptic literary hands varied only slightly over long periods of time, it is difficult to date MSS on paleographic grounds. In such cases one has recourse to the papyrus scraps, often letters or other documentary papyri, used to stiffen the leather covers of books. Preliminary analysis of the contents of the cover of Codex VII by J. Barns uncovered the dates 339 and 342, and while a complete study of all the covers is under way, one may safely date the collection to the middle of the fourth century. Of itself this date does not determine the date of origin of the literary works contained in the codices; in some cases it is known with virtual certainty that individual writings are much older.

The language of the codices is not entirely uniform. All are in Coptic, the late form of Egyptian written mostly in Greek uncial letters and used in Christian times, but the dialects are neither uniform nor, in the sense of modern grammarians, pure. The bulk of the codices are in a form of Sahidic, but Codices I and X and part of Codex XI are in the Subachmimic dialect (*see* COPTIC LANGUAGE[S] §2*ai*, *b*iii). The apparently "mixed" quality of the dialects may be a sign of an early stage in their development or evidence of influence from neighboring dialects. The effect of this large amount of early Coptic documentation on the study of the language has yet to be assessed. The working hypothesis of almost all scholars is that we are dealing with Coptic translations of works originally written in Greek. In a few cases such as the Gospel of Thomas, fragments of the Greek are extant elsewhere. Sporadic attempts to demonstrate a Semitic original or a Coptic original for certain of the works have not won general acceptance.

Most of the codices contain more than one tractate, varying from two in Codices IV, VIII, and apparently XIII to eight in Codex VI. Codex X, which is only poorly preserved, apparently contained only one work. In some cases writings are grouped by literary genre, e.g., four "apocalypses" in Codex V, or by origin, e.g., three consecutive Hermetic works in Codex VI, but for the most part no principle of arrangement is immediately evident. Not all the tractates have titles, but because of lacunae we cannot be sure that all the original titles survived. Those that are extant appear either at the beginning or at the end, or, in some cases, in both positions, without apparent systematic arrangement.

2. History of the discovery. Precise details of the manner and site of the discovery are not available, but scholars have been able to piece together much of the story. The codices were found in 1946 by a local peasant in one of a number of caves or tombs in the lower face of the Gebel et-Tarif cliff about 6.2 miles NE of the city of Nag Hammadi, near the village of Hamra Dom. A number of references in the papyrus cartonnage of the covers indicate that they come from the region around Chenoboskion, an early center of monastic life. The codices were presumably sold to middlemen and eventually came into the hands of antiquities dealers.

a. The Jung Codex. Codex I, commonly called the Jung Codex, has its own distinct history. A large portion of it along with the cover came into the possession of an antiquities dealer named Albert Eid and disappeared from Egypt. In the winter of 1948-49 it was offered for sale to the Bollingen Foundation in New York, but the transaction had not taken place when the owner died. After long delays and considerable detective work, the codex was discovered in Brussels, examined, and in 1952 purchased there by Gilles Quispel of Utrecht on behalf of the C. G. Jung Institute in Zurich. It was known that some of the folios of Codex I were in the Coptic Museum at Old Cairo, and in exchange for the right to publish them along with the bulk of the codex, the Zurich authorities agreed to return the Jung Codex folios to the museum to rejoin the rest of the collection once they had been published. The codex has now been completely published and the whole returned to Cairo.

b. The other codices. In 1946 a middleman brought Codex III to the attention of the curator of the Coptic Museum, Togo Mina, who purchased it for the museum. The contents were identified by the French scholar Jean Doresse in 1947, and the discovery was made public in Cairo and in Paris in early 1948. Meanwhile an antiquities dealer in Cairo assembled the remaining codices and fragments from several middlemen, and the collection was offered for sale to the museum in 1948. Doresse again examined and identified the material, and the museum agreed to its purchase. Doresse announced this discovery in Paris in mid-1949. The codices were kept sealed for security while funds were being raised. There they remained through the Egyptian revolution and the reorganization of the Department of Antiquities, and it was not until 1956 that they were declared national property and study of them could be resumed.

c. Major publications. In the first twenty-five years after existence of the collection was reported, publication was complicated and incomplete. Only a sketch of major projects can be given here (for details *see bibliog.*). The contents of Codex I were completely published in five volumes and one supplement from 1956 to 1975. These contain facsimiles, transcription, translations into French, German, and English, introductions, notes, and indexes.

Plans made in 1948 to publish Codex III never materialized, but some knowledge of its contents was made available in 1955 by Till, who published the first edition of Berlin Codex 8502 and in footnotes printed the variant readings of three of the tractates of Codex III which were related to parts of the Berlin Codex. In 1956 the Coptic Museum, under its director (Labib), undertook the preparation of a photographic facsimile edition of the entire corpus, but only the first volume appeared. It contained photographs of those pages of Codex I that were not in Zurich and also of the first 110 pages of the voluminous and unnumbered Codex II. At that time and at various periods during the next fifteen years the aid of UNESCO was enlisted in the appointment of an international committee of scholars to publish critical editions of the material. As none of these efforts was successful, the director of the Coptic Museum turned to scholars present in Cairo to edit and publish some of the texts. Thus all or parts of Codices II, III, IV, V, VI, and VII were published at intervals between 1956 and 1973 by Labib and other scholars, including Doresse, Till, Krause, Böhlig, and Giversen. In the meantime a certain amount of scientific photographic work was undertaken under the auspices of the UNESCO committee.

By 1970, in response to the initiatives of J. M. Robinson, the UNESCO committee had been reactivated and reorganized with the result that a proper facsimile edition began to appear in 1972, and the work of placing unidentified fragments, properly photographing the papyri, and ensuring their proper preservation went rapidly forward. Under Robinson's general editorship preparation of an international English edition of the complete library was undertaken by an international board.

3. Contents of the library. An accurate table of contents of the entire collection has emerged only slowly, as the placement of fragments and decipherment and translation work has gone forward. In the process, several systems of numbering the codices have been used; the one used below has now been generally accepted, and a collation with previous systems may conveniently be found in the Nag Hammadi bibliography by Scholer and in the introduction to the facsimile edition by Robinson. The table indicates the codex number, tractate number, page and line references, the ancient titles of the tractates or in some cases titles assigned by modern scholars, and the system of abbreviated titles used by the English-language edition. Square brackets indicate missing pages and lines and asterisks designate conjectural pagination in the case of fragmentary codices.

The codices are now referred to by the siglum CG, for (Codex) Cairensis Gnosticus, in imitation of the designation BG, (Codex) Berolinensis

Gnosticus, used for Berlin Codex 8502. The latter was first brought to light by Carl Schmidt in 1896, but because of a long history of unfortunate accidents was never published until Till's edition of 1955. It is a Coptic codex, dated by Schmidt and others to the fifth century, which is close to the Nag Hammadi collection in contents, two of its four tractates being also found in CG III (cf. also II, IV, and V). It is therefore appropriate to include BG 8502 in the following table, as it is included in the English-language edition of the Nag Hammadi library.

The Nag Hammadi Library

(Completing and correcting the list of Chenoboskion writings printed in IDB, Vol. A-D, p. 169)

Codex, tractate, pages, lines	*Title*	*Short title*
I,*1*:1,1–16,30	The Apocryphon of James	ApocryJas
I,*2*:16,31–43,24	The Gospel of Truth	GTr
I,*3*:43,25–50,18	The Treatise on Resurrection	OnRes
I,*4*:51,1–140,25	The Tripartite Tractate	TriTrac
I,*5*[141,1–142,end]143,1–144,9	The Prayer of the Apostle Paul	PrPaul
I,*5a*:144,10-11	Colophon	
II,*1*:1,1–32,9	The Apocryphon of John	ApocryJn
II,*2*:32,10–51,28	The Gospel of Thomas	GTh
II,*3*:51,29–86,19	The Gospel of Philip	GPh
II,*4*:86,20–97,23	The Nature of the Archons	NatArch
II,*5*:97,24–127,17	On the Origin of the World	OnOrgWld
II,*6*:127,18–137,27	The Exegesis on the Soul	ExSoul
II,*7*:138,1–145,19	The Book of Thomas the Contender	ThCont
II,*7a*:145,20-23	Colophon	
III,*1*:[1,1-13]1,14–40,11	The Apocryphon of John	ApocryJn
III,*2*:40,12–69,20	The Gospel of the Egyptians	GEgypt
III,*3*:70,1–90,13	Eugnostos the Blessed	Eug
III,*4*:90,14–119,18	The Sophia of Jesus Christ	SJC
III,*5*:120,1–149,23	The Dialogue of the Saviour	DialSav
IV:*1*:1,1–49,28	The Apocryphon of John	ApocryJn
IV, *2*:50-1–81,2[81,3-end]	The Gospel of the Egyptians	GEgypt
V,*1*:1,1–17,18	Eugnostos the Blessed	Eug
V,*2*:17,19–24,9	The Apocalypse of Paul	ApocPaul
V,*3*:24,10–44,10	The First Apocalypse of James	1 ApocJas
V,*4*:44,11–63,33	The Second Apocalypse of James	2 ApocJas
V,*5*:64,1–85,32	The Apocalypse of Adam	ApocAd
VI,*1*:1,1–12,22	The Acts of Peter and the Twelve Apostles	AcPetTwAp
VI,*2*:13,1–21,32	The Thunder: Perfect Mind	Thund
VI,*3*:22,1–35,24	Authoritative Teaching	AuthTeach
VI,*4*:36,1–48,15	The Concept of our Great Power	GrPow
VI,*5*:48,16–51,23	Plato, Republic 588B-589B	PlatoRep
VI,*6*:52,1–63,32	The Discourse on the Eighth and Ninth	On8th9th
VI,*7*:63,33-65,7	The Prayer of Thanksgiving	PrThank
VI,*7a*:65,8-13	Scribal Note	
VI,*8*:65,14–78,43	The Apocalypse from Asclepius	ApocAscl
VII,*1*:1,1–49,9	The Paraphrase of Shem	ParaShem
VII,*2*:49,10–70,12	The Second Treatise of the Great Seth	GrSeth
VII,*3*:70,13–84,14	The Apocalypse of Peter	ApocPet
VII,*4*:84,15–118,7	The Teachings of Silvanus	Silv
VII,*4a*:118,8-9	Scribal Note	
VII,*5*:118,10–127,27	The Three Steles of Seth	3StSeth
VII,*5*a:127,28-32	Colophon	
VIII,*1*:1,1–132,9	Zostrianos	Zost
VIII,*2*:132,10–140,27	The Letter of Peter to Philip	PetPhil
IX,*1*:1,1–27,10	Melchizedek	Melch
IX,*2*:27,11–29,5	The Thought of Norea	Nor
IX,*3*:29,6–74,31[. . . 75,xx or 76,xx]	The Testimony of Truth	TestimTr
X,*1*:1,1–72,18	Marsanes	Mar

Codex, tractate, pages, lines	Title	Short title
XI,*1*:1,1–21,35	The Interpretation of Knowledge	InterpKn
XI,*2*:22,1–39,39	A Valentinian Exposition	ValExp
XI,*2a*:[40,1-7]40,8-29	On Baptism A	OnBapA
XI,*2b*:40,30–41,38	On Baptism B	OnBapB
XI,*2c*:[42,1-9]42,10–43,20	On Baptism C	OnBapC
XI,*2d*:43,21-38	On the Eucharist A	OnEuchA
XI,*2e*:[44,1-14]44,15-37	On the Eucharist B	OnEuchB
XI,*3*:[45,1-4]45,5–69,20	Allogenes	Allog
XI,*4*:69,21–72,33[. . . 72,37]	Hypsiphrone	Hyps
XII,*1**:[1*,1-14*,end]15*,1-34*,28[35*,1–39*,xx]	The Sentences of Sextus	SSext
XII,*2**:[39*,xx–53*,18]53*,19–60*,30[61*,1–67*,end]	The Gospel of Truth	GTr
XII,*3**:[68*,1 . . .] . . .	Fragments	Frm
XIII,*1**:35*,1–50*,24	Trimorphic Protennoia	TriProt
XIII,*2**:50*,25-34[51*,1-79*,xx]	On the Origin of the World	OnOrgWld
BG 8502,*1*:[1,1 . . .]7,1–19,5	The Gospel of Mary	GMary
BG 8502,*2*:19,6–77,7	The Apocryphon of John	ApocryJn
BG 8502,*3*:77,8–127,12	The Sophia of Jesus Christ	SJC
BG 8502,*4*:128,1–141,7	The Acts of Peter	AcPet

4. Preliminary classification of the writings. No definitive classification of the Nag Hammadi tractates can be undertaken, either in terms of literary genre or in relation to types of Gnosticism, until they have been submitted to thorough and painstaking analysis. The following paragraphs are therefore provisional approaches to categorization, intended only to describe further the materials contained in the codices.

a. Literary genres. The collection contains a striking variety of literary genres, many of them typical of Gnostic literature, others imitative of existing genres in Christian and other literatures. The following list of types is based in part on the titles in the codices and in part on comparison with other works. The genres are often mixed and rarely found in a pure form, so that individual tractates might appropriately be considered under several headings. In addition, some of them are so fragmentary as to render classification premature if not impossible.

i. *Gospels.* Of the works entitled "gospel" in the library, namely GTr, GTh, GPh, GEgypt, and GMary, none corresponds to the gospel genre of the NT (*see* APOCRYPHA, NT[S] §3; GOSPEL, GENRE [S]; PHILIP, GOSPEL OF[S]; THOMAS, GOSPEL OF[S]; TRUTH, GOSPEL OF[S]). GTr, for example, is a meditation on the person of Christ and his saving work. GMary is a combination of dialogue between the risen Jesus and his followers and of revelation discourse. The most important in terms of genre is GTh, a collection of sayings of Jesus, most of which are introduced with the formula "Jesus said" without any narrative framework. Such a "gospel" may be the lineal descendant of the type of sayings collection that one supposes the hypothetical Q document may have been. *See* *Q*[S] §3.

ii. *Apocalypses.* Several of the tractates are titled "apocalypses," and a number of others should best be described this way: e.g., ApocPaul, 1 ApocJas, 2 ApocJas, ApocAd, ApocPet, and ApocAscl, NatArch (in part at least), ParaShem, and others (*see* APOCALYPSE, GENRE[S] §§1, 2). The best example of the genre, though itself a mixed one, is the ApocAd (*see* ADAM, APOCALYPSE OF[S]), a revelation of the future course of Gnostic history which Adam receives from celestial visitors and transmits to his son Seth. Some of the works, such as ApocPaul, which is not identical with the NT apocryphal work of the same title (*see* PAUL, APOCALYPSE OF), describe the visionary experiences of NT personages with typically Gnostic features or background.

iii. *Acts.* Two of the tractates use the name "acts" in their titles, the AcPetTwAp and the AcPet (*see* ACTS, GENRE[S]). The latter is not a Gnostic work at all, but a fragment of the larger body of apocryphal acts of Peter which had wide currency and a complicated history in the early church. Though it is entitled "The Letter of Peter to Philip," VIII,*2* is really modeled on the NT book of Acts; the title applies only to the begining of the work.

iv. *Letters.* Several of the tractates are often referred to as epistles because they are addressed directly to readers, among them OnRes (the "Letter to Rheginos") and Eug. These are more properly treatises, however, and it is notable that the collection does not include any imitations of the Pauline letter form. PetPhil contains a letter in imitation of the letters embedded in narratives.

v. *Dialogues.* One of the most characteristic genres of Gnostic literature is the dialogue between the risen Jesus and his disciples in which Gnostic teaching is revealed. In the Nag Hammadi library the SJC and the DialSav exemplify the genre, but it is also represented in many other works with ostensibly different genres. Codex VI also contains a Hermetic dialogue in the classical form.

vi. *Secret books.* The term "apocryphon" is used in the titles of two works, the ApocryJas and the ApocryJn, of which four copies, in two recensions, survive (*see* JOHN, APOCRYPHON OF[S]). Strictly speaking it does not identify a genre but can be applied, as in the latter case, to a combination of apocalypse and revelation dialogue.

vii. *Speculative treatises.* Many of the tractates fall into this category, some of them, such as OnOrgWld and Eug, beginning formally with a brief discussion of divergent or erroneous opinions which are to be contrasted with the true explanation that follows.

viii. *Wisdom literature.* The presence of a Coptic version of the SSext in Codex XII provides an example of a work of aphoristic wisdom literature that is not of Gnostic provenance but presumably was subject to an interpretation congenial to the compilers of the library. Silv is an important witness to the survival of the wisdom literature genre in Christian, possibly monastic, circles; it is modeled on the OT wisdom literature and is perhaps not of Gnostic origin.

ix. *Exegesis.* The tractate of Codex II entitled ExSoul is unique in the collection in that it sets forth a mythical explanation of the fate of the soul trapped in the world, with numerous citations from the OT, the NT, and the *Odyssey* of Homer as proof texts.

x. *Revelation discourses.* Under this heading are grouped documents in which a revealer figure such as Sophia speaks in the first person. There are fragmentary examples in such passages as the ending of the long version of ApocryJn and elaborate ones like the TriProt. The most striking of all, however, is Thund, in which the voice of the thunder represents the revealing voice from the world of the divine expressing itself in a long series of I-am sayings with antithetical and paradoxical predicates.

xi. *Prayers.* Finally, the collection contains a number of prayers of different types. There are brief scribal prayers in colophons and there are whole tractates, some Christian and some non-Christian, in prayer form. Codex I ends with a prayer of the apostle Paul, Codex VI contains a Hermetic prayer of which both Greek and Latin versions were previously known, and Codex VII has an important and elaborate prayer under the title 3StSeth.

b. Types of Gnosticism. It is probably more important but certainly more speculative to undertake to classify the materials of the collection according to the types of Gnosticism they represent. The enterprise is difficult in part because the types of Gnosticism described by the church Fathers themselves are insufficiently distinct to allow us to construct a satisfactory typology (*see* GNOSTICISM [S]) . Moreover, for some scholars the very existence of the Nag Hammadi library has called into question the attempts of Irenaeus and others to distinguish a variety of Gnostic "systems" in the second century. The following divisions are therefore tentative and merely suggestive.

i. *Sethian.* The fact that a number of the tractates such as GEgypt, ApocAd, ParaShem, GrSeth, 3StSeth, and others give a prominent place to the figure of Seth as channel of the gnosis, or resemble some features of the patristic descriptions of Sethianism, led Doresse and others to regard the library as basically a Sethian collection with a generous admixture of other writings. This may yet be the case, but it is important to note that virtually none of the tractates corroborates in detail the patristic accounts of Sethianism. The ParaShem, a difficult but important Gnostic apocalypse, has much in common with Hippolytus' description of the Sethian doctrine and the "Paraphrase of Seth," but it does not allow the interpreter to conclude that it is the source of Hippolytus' account.

ii. *Valentinian.* There seems to be little reason to question the patristic descriptions of Valentinianism as referring to a distinct group in the second century, though it is a complex group with important internal variations. The Nag Hammadi library contains a number of works that can be classified as Valentinian with varying degrees of certainty, some of them quite clearly in close affinity to the *Excerpta ex Theodoto* and other works. Among the Valentinian works one should enumerate perhaps all of Codex I, certainly the GPh from Codex II, 1 ApocJas from Codex V, and at least some of the tractates of Codex XI. *See also* GNOSTICISM[S] §4*b*.

iii. *Other Gnostic types.* It is not the intention here to suggest specific Gnostic sects represented in other tractates of the collection, but it is plain that many of the works, including some of the most important such as the GTh, Eug, Thund,

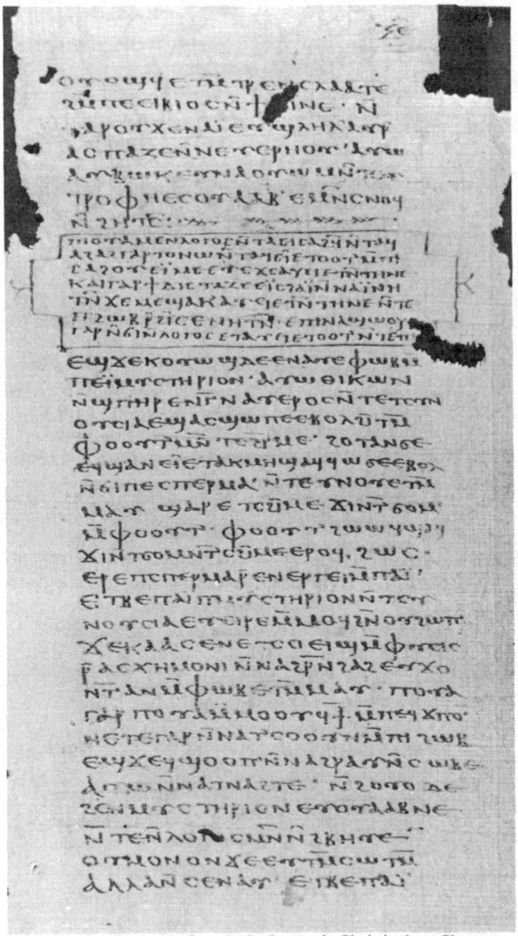

Courtesy the Institute for Antiquity and Christianity, Claremont Graduate School

1. Nag Hammadi Codex VI, p. 65, with scribal note concerning the copying of Hermetic tractates. This 7-line scribal note appears between the Prayer of Thanksgiving and the Apocalypse of Asclepius.

Melch, etc., do not clearly fit the world either of Sethian or of Valentianian systems. The Gnostics were syncretistic, as is well known, but there is reason to think that the Nag Hammadi library deliberately collected a variety of writings. The suggestion that the collection was made to provide material for a comprehensive refutation of the patristic type recurs in the literature on Nag Hammadi. It tends to be supported by the colophon of Codex VI but not by the prayerful colophons of other codices. The collectors may indeed have been fourth-century Gnostics interested simply in any literature they found congenial.

iv. *Hermetic.* The last suggestion derives some support from the fact that Codex VI contains three pieces in succession which unmistakably belong to the type of purely pagan gnosis known as Hermetism (*see* HERMETIC LITERATURE[S]). These include a typical Hermetic dialogue, part of the Asclepius preserved otherwise only in a Latin translation, and a well-known Hermetic prayer. Contacts between Hermetism and Christian Gnosticism have not been well attested, and this dimension of the Nag Hammadi corpus may prove to be an important one for the study of religions in Egypt in the early Christian period.

v. *Non-Gnostic writings.* The greatest surprises in the Nag Hammadi library came from the recognition of works that are not Gnostic at all. Among these is the rather inferior Coptic translation of a passage from the *Republic* of Plato in Codex VI, which one must suppose to have had a Gnostic interpretation. The same must be said of the moralizing SSext, and perhaps one should include Silv, possibly a relatively orthodox monastic work, part of which corresponds to a Coptic fragment preserved in the name of St. Anthony, and the AuthTeach, another treatise on the dangerous existence of the soul in the world. That there existed a tradition of Gnostic exegesis of biblical texts is well attested and universally accepted. The possibility that other literature received a peculiarly Gnostic interpretation should not be surprising (e.g., PlatoRep).

5. Issues in interpretation. In addition to the suggestions already made, it is possible here to mention only a few of the more general questions to which the Nag Hammadi library gives rise. These are important issues in that they contribute to the long-standing debate about the role of Gnosticism in the formation of the Christian tradition and to the "Gnostic problem" itself. *See* GNOSTICISM[S] §§1, 2, 5.

a. Christian and non-Christian origins. Whether Gnosticism is properly understood as a Christian heresy or a non-Christian religion that made a serious impact when it confronted nascent Christianity has been debated for over a century. The Nag Hammadi collection significantly contributes to the debate in that it contains several works that apparently are not of Christian origin, or at least do not contain obvious Christian elements. In this connection such tractates as Eug, ApocAd, ParaShem, and Allog, among others, are of prime importance. To conclude that these are pre-Christian Gnostic works would be unjustified, especially in view of the relatively late date of the collection. But that they are non-Christian seems undeniable (as of course are the Hermetic works in the collection). Yet they represent a fully developed Gnostic myth with a Gnostic redeemer figure who is not inspired by the Christ of the NT. *See* ADAM, APOCALYPSE OF[S] §§2, 3.

Considerable importance must be attributed to the one example in the collection in which the transition from non-Christian to Christian Gnosticism can be documented. This is the case of the work called Eug in which there is no apparent Christian influence. In the SJC this treatise is transformed into a revelation of the risen Jesus to his disciples. Krause has demonstrated convincingly that the literary relationship between the two documents proceeds in the direction of Christianization. Perhaps an analogous relationship must be seen between the apparently non-Christian ApocAd and the Christian GEgypt in which Christ is seen as a manifestation of the Gnostic Seth. The extrinsic character of the Christian elements of the ApocryJn, the NatArch, and other writings points in the same direction. The Nag Hammadi library cannot yet be said to prove conclusively the non-Christian origin of Gnosticism, but it adds a great deal of probability to this classic position.

b. Jewish materials. Interpreters of Gnostic literature are not surprised to find in it considerable use of the Genesis story as a basis for the Gnostic myth of origins, but many have discovered in the Nag Hammadi writings elements of Jewish haggadic tradition that point to a prominent role of Judaism itself in the formation of Gnosticism, especially in the documents of the Sethian type. In addition, there is evidence of considerable Jewish influence on the structure of the Sophia myth, the techniques of biblical interpretation, the apocalyptic schematization of history, and many other features of the contents of a large number of tractates. Such Jewish influence has reopened the discussion whether some type of Judaism that was oriented to wisdom and apocalyptic may have served as a matrix for the evolution of Gnostic myth. Specific attempts to identify the Judaism in question have not been successful, however; nor are there solid grounds for thinking that the basic anticosmic dualism of any Gnostic system is itself to be derived from Jewish tradition. In the syncretistic process of Gnostic origins, nevertheless, the Nag Hammadi library points to a much more prominent Jewish role than previously acknowledged.

c. Gnosticism and the NT. The most important contribution of the Nag Hammadi library to the history of religions lies in the light that it sheds on the nature and variety of the Gnostic phenomenon itself. In addition, one can anticipate the possibility of answers to some other questions in the field, e.g., the suggestion that in Allog, Zost, 3StSeth, and perhaps other tractates one has access to the Gnostic sources used by Plotinus in his anti-Gnostic polemic. From the first announcement of the discovery of the codices, NT scholars have also shown great interest in them. The debate about the possible interaction between Gnosticism and early Christianity within the formative period of the NT itself is an old one, and it was not unreasonable to expect a collection of original Gnostic writings to shed some light on it. Indirectly it does so by strongly reinforcing the view that Gnosticism is non-Christian in origin. Whether it is pre-Christian in a chronological sense has not been demonstrated on the basis of the Nag Hammadi library, but it seems at least contemporaneous with nascent Christianity.

In several more specific ways individual Nag Hammadi tractates impinge upon the study of the NT. This is obvious in the case of the GTh, where comparison of the Jesus sayings with the synoptic tradition has even resulted in the inclusion of the GTh in some recent synopses of the gospels (*see* THOMAS, GOSPEL OF[S]). In other cases it is less obvious but possibly more significant, and these can be expected to remain under study for some time. The ApocPet of Codex VII, e.g., which contains some polemic against the church, seems to admit the reader to the debates about authority and legitimacy in the early second century which also underlie II Peter in the NT. Again, the variety of attitudes toward baptism in some of the texts, often quite negative ones, makes it possible to reconstruct a theory of the interaction of Jewish, Christian, and Gnostic motifs in baptist and anti-baptist circles of the first century. Several of the Nag Hammadi revelation discourses, such as Thund and TriProt, provide clearly Gnostic models for the type of revelation discourse found throughout the Fourth Gospel. But the evidence does not permit us to suggest that we have in such documents access to the source of the Johannine discourses. To give one final example, if the non-Christian character of ApocAd, ParaShem, and other tractates proves to be correct, then the NT scholar has evidence of a redeemer myth outside of the Christian message which must be examined for its possible influence on some forms of NT Christology.

The first quarter of a century since the Nag Hammadi discovery has been dominated by efforts to edit, translate, and publish the materials, with only modest efforts at interpreting them and weighing their significance. It remains the task of scholarship for years to come to carry on the work of interpretation.

Bibliography. An exhaustive bibliog. of materials pertaining to the codices may be found in D. M. Scholer, *Nag Hammadi Bibliography 1948-1968,* Nag Hammadi Studies, I (1971) and in the same author's annual supplements in *NovT* (1971 ff.). The more specialized bibliographies of the articles on individual tractates (ApocAd, ApocryJn, GPh, OnRes, GTh, GTr) are not repeated here.

The principal publication of the texts is *The Facsimile Edition of the Nag Hammadi Codices* (1972 ff.). P. Labib, *Coptic Gnostic Papyri in the Coptic Museum at Old Cairo,* I (1956), is also valuable for its early photographs of parts of Codices I and II.

Other editions and translations: *The Coptic Gnostic Library,* general ed., J. M. Robinson, Nag Hammadi Studies (1975 ff.); M. Malinine *et al., Evangelium Veritatis* (1956) and successive vols. on each tractate of Codex I; A. Böhlig and P. Labib, *Koptisch-gnostische Apokalypsen aus Codex V von Nag Hammadi* (1963); R. A. Bullard, *The Hypostasis of the Archons,* Patristische Texte und Studien, X (1970); A. Böhlig and P. Labib, *Die koptisch-gnostische Schrift ohne Titel aus Codex II von Nag Hammadi* (1962); M. Krause and P. Labib, *Gnostische und hermetische Schriften aus Codex II und Codex VI* (1971); M. Krause, edition of VII, *1, 2, 3, 5,* in *Christentum am Roten Meer,* ed. F. Altheim and R. Stiehl, II (1973); W. Foerster, *Gnosis,* II (1971); W. Till and H.-M. Schenke, *Die gnostischen Schriften des koptischen Papyrus Berolinensis 8502* (2nd ed., 1972).

Studies: In addition to the series Nag Hammadi Studies (1971 ff.), F. L. Cross, ed., *The Jung Codex* (1955); J. Doresse, *The Secret Books of the Egyptian Gnostics* (1958-59); J. M. Robinson, "The Coptic Gnostic Library Today," *NTS,* XIV (1967-68), 356-401; A. K. Helmbold, *The Nag Hammadi Gnostic Texts and the Bible,* Baker Studies in Biblical Archaeology, V (1967); W. C. van Unnik, *Newly Discovered Gnostic Writings,* SBT, XXX (1958); G. MacRae *et al., Essays on the Coptic Gnostic Library* (1970); H.-C. Puech, "Gnostic Gospels and Related Documents," in *NT Apocrypha,* ed. E. Hennecke and W. Schneemelcher, I (2nd ed., 1968), 231-362; R. M. Wilson, *Gnosis and the NT* (1968); U. Bianchi, ed., *Le origini dello gnosticismo,* Supplements to *Numen,* XII (1967); K. Rudolph, "Gnosis und Gnostizismus, ein Forschungsbericht," *Theol. Rundschau,* XXXIV (1969), 121-75, 181-231, 358-61, XXXVI (1971), 1-61, 89-124, XXXVII (1972), 289-360, and XXXVIII (1973), 1-25; A. Böhlig, *Mysterion und Wahrheit,* AGJU, VI (1968); A. Böhlig and F. Wisse, *Zum Hellenismus in den Schriften von Nag Hammadi* (1975); M. Krause, "Das literarische Verhältnis des Eugnostosbriefes zur Sophia Jesu Christi," in *Mullus: Festschrift Theodor Klauser,* Jahrbuch für Antike und Christentum, Ergänzungsband, I (1964), 215-23.

G. MACRAE

***NAMES, RELIGIOUS SIGNIFICANCE OF.** The giving of personal names in ancient Israel was not merely for the purpose of providing a distinctive label for an individual but was also commonly an occasion for expressing religious convictions associated with the birth of a child or its future. As such, personal names provide an invaluable source for the religious ideas of the ordinary Israelites. Even those names that do not directly express religious feelings often have importance for an understanding of Israelite religion. In the late periods, however, names came to have less immediate religious significance.

The meaning of many names remains unclear, in part because of their archaic character, in part because of our limited knowledge of classical Hebrew vocabulary, and in part because of a lack of comprehension of Israelite naming practices. *See* NAME §C for general discussion.

1. The structure of personal names. Typical of Semitic names is the utilization of a variety of structures. Many names are themselves sentences, and others represent phrases. The shorter, one-element names may be either abbreviations of longer names or full names in themselves.

a. Sentence names. Names may embody any type of simple sentence used in Hebrew. For example, verbal sentence names with a perfect verb, such as Shemaiah="The Lord has heard [the parents' prayer]," and Benaiah="The Lord has built [a family line]," make a statement. Names with an imperfect verb are less clear. Ishmael may mean, "May God hear [the child]"; "God will hear [the child]"; or "God has heard [the parents]." The case of Ibnijah="May the Lord build [a line]," or "The Lord will build/has built [a line]," and parallel names is similar. It is clear that some names do express a wish; for others, the underlying grammatical structure may be unclear, or may be inappropriate for a wish.

Tobiah="The Lord is good," and Elijah="The Lord is my God," are names based on nominal sentences. An example of an interrogative sentence is Michael="Who is like God?" Names with an imperative are quite rare, but Shubael (Shebuel) ="Turn [to me], oh God" is one example. Another rare type, with three elements, is Eliehoenai/Elihoenai="My eyes are on the Lord."

b. Construct-phrase names. By their nature as expressions of possession, these names express a quality of the name bearer or his relationship with God. Typical examples are Obadiah="Servant of the Lord," and Solomon's other name, Jedidiah ="Beloved of the Lord."

c. Hypocoristic names. For the compound names illustrated above, hypocoristica or abbreviated forms may also exist. The hypocoristic names may either be given as regular names or be used alongside the compound name. Occasionally both name forms are attested, as with King Ahaz (=He has taken [for protection]), for whom the longer form, equivalent to Jehoahaz (=The Lord has taken), occurs in Assyrian sources. It is often impossible to determine whether a one-word name is a hypocoristicon. Hypocoristic names frequently make use of a special ending, often expressing endearment, such as with Abdon="[Little] servant."

d. One-word names. Simple names that are not hypocoristica of compound names include gentilics such as Judith="The [female] Judean"; animal or plant names such as Deborah="Bee," and Hadassah="Myrtle"; names which mark the bearer as a substitute for a person who has died, Menahem="Comforter."

2. The semantics of personal names. Although the interpretation of many individual names is unclear, general classes of names can be distinguished. The special symbolic names that the prophets Hosea and Isaiah give their children are not discussed here; *see* MAHER-SHALAL-HASHBAZ; SHEAR-JASHUB; IMMANUEL §1; LO-AMMI; LO-RUHAMAH; JEZREEL §2.

a. Names with divine elements. More than one tenth of the Israelite names make direct reference to Yahweh. The divine name appears in four different shortened forms: initially as *yô-* or *yᵉhô-* , as in Jonathan/Jehonathan="The Lord has given [a child]," and—much more commonly—finally as *-yāhû* or *-yâ,* as in Zedekiah="The Lord is righteous for me," for which the English rendering does not distinguish the two Hebrew spellings.

Another common divine element is *'ēl,* which means simply "god." However, it was also the name of the head of the Canaanite pantheon, El, though Baal had replaced El in immediate significance and everyday power. Also, El was a well-known deity among the Amorites of Mesopotamia and other Semitic language groups. Accordingly, the use of *'ēl* in Israelite names, where it is exceeded in frequency only by forms based on Yahweh, is of considerable interest. Names such as Eliezer="My God is help," and Nathaniel="God has given [a child]," indicate that awareness of El as a Canaanite deity was not strong enough to inhibit the use of the common word "god" in Israelite names. El worship apparently was not a threat to Yahwism in the same way that Baal worship was. Some interpreters conclude in addition that the naming practices fit into a picture of accommodation between Yahweh and El, and even of derivation of Yahwism from circles where El was worshiped. *See* GOD, NAMES OF §C1-2; EL[S].

A third divine element, which occurs in only three names, is Shaddai, as in Zurishaddai="Shaddai is my protection." This divine name, in the form El Shaddai, is connected with the patriarchal time (*see* Exod. 6:3) and was not seen as in opposition to Yahwism.

The element *ba'al* represents both a common noun, "lord, husband," and the name of the Canaanite deity BAAL. It occurs in only seven Israelite names in the OT, and its meaning was disputed. The older sources show that the element was regarded by the tradition as improper for an Israelite name, so in the DEUTERONOMIC HISTORY all such names are given a tendentious etymology or have an altered form, which substitutes a word meaning "shame"; e.g., Saul's son, Ishbaal="The lord/Baal exists," became Ishbosheth="Man of shame" (*see, however,* ISHBOSHETH[S]). Jerubbaal, doubtless meaning, "May the lord/Baal exalt [the child]" (*see* §1*a above*), is explained by the tradition as, "Let Baal contend against him" (Judg. 6:32). Baal obviously became identified so closely with opposition to Yahwism that the element could not be used in its common meaning, assuming that it was used among Israelites in the time of Saul and David in the sense, "lord, master." (In the Chronicler the names with *ba'al* were left unchanged.) In the Samaria ostraca, dating from the eighth century B.C., after the battles with Baal of Elijah's time, names containing a form of Yahweh only slightly outnumber those containing *ba'al.* This suggests something of Baal's popularity in the northern kingdom two hundred years or more after the time of Saul and David.

Many names contain a divine epithet such as *'ādhôn,* "lord, master," *melekh,* "king," *ṣûr,* "rock," or one of the kinship terms discussed below, in place of the divine element. The names are otherwise parallel.

b. Names with elements expressing kinship. Elements such as *'ābh,* "father," *'āḥ,* "brother," and, less frequently, *'amm-,* "kindred, paternal uncle," are generally theophoric, the deity being identified as a protective relative. For example, the name Abishua="My [divine] father is help," is paralleled by Joshua="The Lord is help," and Malchishua="My [divine] king is help." Other names with kinship elements, but without such parallels, may represent substitution names.

c. Expressions of trust. Many names express the trust that the individual's parents have in the deity. Note such names as Adonijah="The Lord is my master"; Uzziah="The Lord is my strength"; Bezalel="In God's protection"; and perhaps also Ibneiah="The Lord will build [a line]" (*see* §1*a above*).

d. Expressions of thanks. The birth of a child elicited parental thanks, and many names so indicate. Note Shemaiah="The Lord has heard [the parents' prayer]," Azariah="The Lord has helped," and Abinadab="My [divine] father inclined himself [to me]."

e. Expressions of acknowledgment. Names such as Saul="Asked [of God]," Baruch="Blessed [by God]," Abdeel="Servant of God," and Benaiah="Son of the Lord," acknowledge the person as closely tied to the deity. Similarly, names such as Micaiah="Who is like the Lord?" and Malchiel="God is my [divine] king," confess qualities of the deity.

f. Expressions of wishes. The interpretation of the names discussed here is disputed (*see* §1*a above*). Names expressing wishes clearly exist in related onomastic corpora, and the tradition is surely correct in understanding the name Joseph as, "May the Lord add to me another son" (Gen. 30:24). Names such as Jeberechiah="May the Lord bless [the child]," Jacob="May he [the deity] protect [the child]" (cf. the tendentious etymology as, "He will supplant," given in Gen. 27:36; cf. also Gen. 25:26), Iphdeiah="May the Lord redeem [the child]," and Ishmaiah="May the Lord hear [the child]," illustrate this type.

g. Substitution names. A child was often welcomed as replacing a deceased relative, as able to keep alive something of the deceased person's character. The personal names reflect this basic concern for the continuity of life. For examples note Ahikam="My brother has arisen [again]"; Jashobeam="May my paternal uncle return [in me]"; Eliashib="May God bring back [the deceased]" (cf. §1*a above*); and Meshullam="Given as a replacement." The name Solomon may be of this type, meaning, "His [the deceased elder brother's] wholeness," though other interpretations are possible.

Also, some names that express sorrow, such as Job="Where is the father?" and Ichabod="Where is the glory?" (note the explanation given in I Sam. 4:21), point to the family's sense of loss and the desire that the child provide continuity for the future.

h. Animal and plant names. Animal names as personal names, such as Rachel="Ewe," Jael="Mountain goat," and Jonah="Dove," have formerly spurred some interpreters to see evidence of totemism (*see* TOTEMISM[S]). However, the widespread use in the ancient Near East of animal names, and of plant names such as Habakkuk (though the precise identification of the plant is uncertain), suggests a playful sense of continuity between the human and the natural worlds rather than totemism, fear of plant spirits, or the like.

i. Personal qualities as names. Many names point to personal characteristics: Haggai="Born on a festival day," Hashum="Flat nose," and Amon="Reliable," are a few examples.

3. Naming practices. Habits in name giving changed in terms both of the individual names which were in favor and the types of names. For example, names with imperfect verbal elements fluctuated in popularity, as did names with perfect elements. Likewise, simple and compound names varied in esteem. Some name types even go almost completely out of use.

One custom that endured throughout the OT was that of feminine names having theophoric elements much less frequently than masculine names, a practice that may well reflect the very minor involvement of women in Israel's cult.

A number of Israelites bear foreign names. Moses, clearly an Egyptian name, is the best known, and the priestly names Phinehas, Hophni, and Pashhur are also Egyptian. Later, during the exilic and postexilic periods, Aramaic and Akkadian names are found, even among Davidic descendants, e.g., Zerubbabel, an Akkadian name meaning "Offspring of Babylon." In the late period Persian names are also found. The use of foreign names points to a somewhat less than rigid tie between religious and linguistic identity.

A major change in the practice of name giving was a shift during the postexilic period away from emphasis on the meaning of names and toward the giving of names because of the persons who had borne them previously. This seems to have happened fairly early in the priestly families, where names recur several times, and, to a more modest extent, among royalty. A specific practice of this type, which may have originated in Aramaic customs, was papponymy, i.e., naming a child after its grandfather. It was widely practiced during the Persian and Hellenistic ages.

Bibliography. J. J. Stamm, "Hebräische Ersatznamen," in *Studies in Honor of Benno Landsberger,* AS, XVI (1965), 413-24, and "Hebräische Frauennamen," VTSup, XVI (1967), 301-39.

H. B. HUFFMON

NAVEL OF THE EARTH. The JB uses this expression to translate טבור הארץ (Ezek. 38:12; cf. Judg. 9:37, "Navel of the Land"). טבור is apparently identical with Mishnaic Hebrew and Late Aramaic *ṭibbûr* (navel) and thus a synonym of שרר (e.g., Song of S. 7:2 [H 3]; Ezek. 16:4). Though the translation suggests a connection with Near Eastern and Hebrew cosmogonies (*see* COSMOGONY), it is not clear that the biblical Hebrew phrase has any cosmic significance. Complicating matters is the fact that ארץ need not refer to the entire earth (γῆ) in contrast to heaven, but may refer only to a particular geographical or political entity—"land," "country," "region" (χώρα; so RSV at Judg. 9:37).

The belief was widespread in antiquity that shrines, principal cities, and even private homes were located at the center of the world. Each of these domains could constitute the bond which linked the various components of what modern people call the universe. Thus, ancient Mesopotamians referred to the city of Nippur as "the bond of heaven and earth." Such a bond is often described as a "navel," indicating the centrality and prominence of the locale as well as its function as a link between the realms of heaven, earth, and underworld. The conical stone omphalos (navel) at Delphi was said to mark the earth's center. (Greek myth claimed that Zeus had released two eagles of equal speed from opposite ends of the earth, and these had met at Delphi.)

L. R. Bailey
2. Omphalos, Delphi Museum

(*See* Fig. N2.) Similar omphali have been found elsewhere in the Greco-Roman world.

The idea of Jerusalem as a "navel" is reflected in Jewish Midrashim: "God created the world like an embryo. Just as the embryo begins at the navel and continues to grow from that point, so too the world. The Holy One, blessed be He, began the world from its navel. From there it was stretched hither and yon. Where is its navel? Jerusalem. And its [Jerusalem's] navel itself? The altar" (Jellinek, *Beth ha-Midrash,* V, 63). Clearly the above midrash employs the symbolism of the navel to indicate the centrality of Jerusalem and its altar within the cosmos. Still earlier, Jub. 8:19 (cf. Enoch 26:1) refers to Mount Zion as "the center of the navel of the earth."

These Jewish images have parallels in Greek and Latin sources as well as among Buddhists, Celts, and Hindus. In fact, the translations of the two biblical attestations by the LXX and Vulg. (ὄμφαλος τῆς γῆς; *umbilicus terrae*) suggest that the biblical and nonbiblical conceptions be equated.

Cults at earth-navel sites often involved serpent imagery, chthonian rites, and, at least covertly, sexual symbolism. Accordingly, some scholars allege that snake worship, chthonian rites, male prostitution, and androgyny were all to be found at Delphi and other Greek earth-navel shrines as well as at Jerusalem. Inasmuch as earth-navel mythology fuses the earthly, chthonian, and heavenly realms, we would not be surprised to find elements of each in its cult and ritual. Furthermore, sexual symbolism connected with fertility rites would be appropriate at a shrine which claimed to be at the center of the world and its point of origin.

The above hypothesis must, however, be treated with caution. It must first be demonstrated that each of the features suggested is indeed related to earth-navel symbolism; secondly, that each is actually found both at Jerusalem and at undisputed earth-navel shrines; and, thirdly, that whatever elements are in fact common play similar roles in the myths and rituals which are being compared. Thus, the serpent was important at Delphi and in Israelite religious sources. Yet within the Bible itself serpent symbolism is polyvalent (*see* SERPENT; SERPENT[S]). In the cult it is found only as a healing figure (*see* NEHUSHTAN; SERPENT, BRONZE). Morever, it is uncertain that the serpent was part of the temple worship in Jerusalem.

Regarding the remaining items suggested for comparison, (*a*) there is no evidence of chthonian rites associated with the Jerusalem temple (*see* DEITIES, UNDERWORLD[S]). (*b*) The attribution of male prostitution and ANDROGYNY to Israelite cult depends on the proper identification of the קדשים, whose function is by no means certain. The Ugaritic *qdšm,* presumably related to the biblical *qdšm,* are known only to have been cultic personnel (*see* PRIESTS[S] §1). (*c*) Solar worship, though attested at Jerusalem (*see* SUN), was seen by Greeks as a hallmark of barbarian worship. The solar cult at Rhodes was unique, and was universally viewed as a foreign importation.

Accordingly we must examine the two biblical attestations of טבור הארץ to see if the earth-navel comparisons can be substantiated.

In Judg. 9:36 a group of invaders is described as "coming down from the mountain tops." In the following verse, what appear to be these same forces are described as "coming down from the center of the land [טבור הארץ]." The context indicates that the phrases are synonymous. The verb employed, "coming down," suggests that the distinctive feature is height rather than centrality. Scholars have therefore suggested that the reference must be to Mount Gerizim, in line with Samaritan tradition that Gerizim was indeed the navel of the earth, the blessed mountain which was not submerged by the Deluge. Here again caution is warranted. The relevant Samaritan traditions date only from the early centuries of the present era and cannot be considered infallible evidence of authentic reminiscences of premonarchic Shechem. Secondly, the very identification of Gerizim with the "navel" would be open to question on the grounds that Mount Ebal, opposite Gerizim, is actually some two hundred feet higher.

In Ezek. 38:11, an invader has assembled his host in order to "go up against the land of unwalled villages" and "fall upon the quiet people who dwell securely." In vs. 12 these same intended victims are described as living on the navel of the land (RSV "who dwell at the center of the earth"). The alternation of phrases indicates that emphasis is not upon privileged position in the cosmos but rather upon vulnerability. The intended victims are as unprotected as the human navel in the center of the body. Old Babylonian omen texts describe an invasion as a penetration to the "navel of the enemy's land" (*abunnat māt nakrim:* YOS, X.33,iii. 41; cf. 34:15). All that is described is an incursion which has passed through the outer defenses into the center. Needless to say, we learn nothing of the victim's cosmology.

Apparently, then, we should see no more than poetic personification in the Ezekiel passage. To ancient speakers of Hebrew, and related Semitic languages, the earth had an eye (Exod. 10:15), a face (Gen. 11:9), a mouth (Num. 16:32), hands (Gen. 34:21) and even a nakedness (Gen. 42:9; RSV "weakness"). Note that Judah has a neck (Isa. 8:8). In none of these cases should we infer that a mythology underlies the personification. In this vein it should be mentioned that Josephus relates that his contemporaries referred to Jerusalem as the "navel of the country" (Χώρα; War III.iii.5). A similar intention must have motivated the pun of Rabbi Jeremiah (T.B. Meg. 6a), who explains that in his day (fourth century), biblical Rakkath was properly called Tiberias inasmuch as it was located on the navel of the land of Israel. He meant simply that Tiberias was the center of Jewish Palestine in his time.

Bibliography. W. Caspari, "Tabur (Nabel)," *ZDMG*, XI (1933), 49-65; G. A. Cooke, ICC (1937), pp. 412-13; E. Dhorme, *L'emploi métaphorique des noms de parties du corps en Hebreu et en Akkadien* (1923), p. 107, the standard work on the metaphorical use of body terms; M. Eliade, *The Sacred and the Profane* (1959), pp. 42-47; T. H. Gaster, *Myth, Legend, and Custom in the OT* (1969), p. 533; W. Guthrie, *The Greeks and Their Gods* (1950); H. Herrmann, *Omphalos* (1959), numerous illustrations of omphali; G. F. Moore, ICC (1895), p. 262; W. von Soden, "Zur Stellung des 'Geweihten' (*qdš*) in Ugarit," *UF*, II (1970), 329-30; S. Terrien, "The Omphalos Myth and Hebrew Religion," *VT*, XX (1970), 315-38, extensive bibliog., and *Bibl.*, LV (1974), 445-46 (review art.); N. H. Tur-Sinai, *The Language and the Book*, III (1955), 233-41; A. Wensinck, *The Ideas of the Western Semites Concerning the Navel of the Earth* (1916), the basic work, although most of the sources are medieval; G. Wright, "The Mythology of Pre-Israelite Shechem," *VT*, XX (1970), 75-82, good bibliog.

D. Sperling

***NEHEMIAH.** *See* Ezra and Nehemiah[S].

NEW COVENANT, THE. A phrase ברית חדשה first appearing in Jer. 31:31-34 which became basic for the Christian faith.

1. The background
   a. "Covenant" in the OT
   b. Jeremiah's message of judgment and restoration
2. Jer. 31:31-34
3. The "new covenant" in subsequent material
   a. Absence of reference in subsequent OT material
   b. The intertestamental literature
   c. The NT

Bibliography

1. The background. ***a. "Covenant" in the OT.*** The idea of a "new covenant" must be seen against the general Israelite background of "covenant" (*see* Covenant §C). Israel was convinced that God had taken the initiative in covenanting (contracting) with her for a special purpose. This covenanting was pre-eminently at Sinai by the mediation of Moses and implied God's protection and blessing in war and peace (*see* War, Ideas of §1; Peace in the OT §§2, 3; King, Kingship §7). It also stipulated that Israel was to conform to ethical norms set forth in the Ten Commandments and other legal collections (*see* Law in the OT §§C, D, E). Israel was further convinced that this covenant which God had initiated with her set her apart from all other nations (*see* Election §4). This concept, then, is basic in OT theology.

The consciousness of covenant obligations and privileges was powerfully reinforced for the inhabitants of Judah by the reform of Josiah in 621 b.c. This reform, based on the discovery of a scroll (I Kings 22–23) which evidently became the core of Deuteronomy (*see* Deuteronomy §8), meant a rediscovery of Moses and of the Sinai covenant at a time when many aspects of religion and society in Judah had become conformed to pagan patterns. Many evidently assumed that once reforms had been carried through according to the stipulations of the scroll, God would protect and bless the nation as he had in the past. This conclusion was reinforced by the centrality of Jerusalem and the temple in the reform: altars outside Jerusalem were destroyed and sacrifice officially could take place only at the temple in Jerusalem. Since on an earlier occasion, when Jerusalem had been under siege by Sennacherib in 701 b.c., the city and its temple had survived unscathed, it was widely assumed in Josiah's day and thereafter that Jerusalem would be a haven from any impending destruction. *See* Presence of God, Cultic[S] §3.

b. Jeremiah's message of judgment and restoration. Jeremiah saw the matter differently, as Jer. 7:1-15 and 26:1-24 make clear (*see* Jeremiah the Prophet §B). The people had turned their backs on God (Jer. 2:27), so that God had no other recourse than to declare holy war against his own people, war in which land and cities would be devastated, including Jerusalem (4:5-8; 7:14); there seemed only a slim chance, if the people repented totally, that the execution could be stayed (4:14). In Jeremiah's view, the covenant had been so broken by the people as to leave no basis for a "business-as-usual" relation with God (6:27-30).

Jeremiah was convinced that the victories of the Babylonian king Nebuchadrezzar over Judah in 597 and 587 b.c. were the carrying out of God's punishment (Jer. 28–29; 37–40, e.g., 38:1-3). Events therefore gave the lie to more complacent folk within the nation, like Hananiah (Jer. 28). Both Jeremiah's theology and his perception of history suggested to him that the Sinai covenant was dead.

But Jeremiah also saw the possibility that God would restore the covenant. Just before the final fall of Jerusalem, the prophet returned to his village to buy a tract of land which was in danger of being lost to his family (Jer. 32:1-15), because "thus says Yahweh: . . . Houses and fields and vineyards shall again be bought in this land" (vs. 15). Most of his hopeful oracles are found in chs. 30–31, and most of these are authentic to the prophet (cf. Jeremiah the Prophet §D8). Two passages here employ the word "new." The first is 31:21-22, in which Jeremiah looks forward to a restoration of the community socially and politically: "For Yahweh has created a new thing on the earth: a woman protects a man"—that is, sex roles will be reversed, so that the prostration of the army (cf. 30:5-6) will no longer be a curse or cause for shame but a blessing for the restored community. The second is the "new covenant" passage, 31:31-34.

2. Jer. 31:31-34. Though commentators disagree

as to how authentic these exact words are to Jeremiah, there is no doubt that the substance of this novel idea goes back to the prophet himself. The first section of the passage is rounded off in the middle of vs. 33 (with "says the Lord") and simply states in legal diction that God will make a new covenant with the people unlike the old one which had been broken. The second section, beginning "I will put my law within them" (vs. 33) and continuing to the end of vs. 34, breaks into poetic form. Because of the theological importance of the passage, it is necessary to understand clearly what each phrase means.

The expressions "I will put my law within them" and "I will write it upon their hearts" (vs. 33) are parallel. The law (or instruction) stipulated in the Sinai covenant had of course been written on tablets of stone (Exod. 24:12; 34:1). Now, by contrast, God will write it on the "heart" or "inward parts" (KJV) of the people. The conception of HEART in the OT centers more on volition than on emotion. The heart is the center of planning and the carrying out of plans; see e.g., Isa. 10:7, where the Hebrew text reads, "But it is not thus that he plans, and it is not thus that his heart devises." The words "inward parts" (RSV "within them") are no different. The passage suggests that a law outwardly written on tablets of stone may elicit disobedience, or else grudging or insincere obedience; next time, therefore, God will write the law inwardly, making it a part of the total will of the people, so that they obey God, not because they are supposed to, but because they want to. Thus God's will permeates the people's will, so that each conforms perfectly to the other. Is this coercion? Jeremiah does not say.

What is the result of God's action? First, says God, "I will be their God and they shall be my people." This simple formulation was a traditional mode of expressing the covenantal relationship (e.g., Exod. 6:7; Lev. 26:12), a relationship now broken by the people (cf. Hos. 1:9). God has forsaken his people (Jer. 12:7) because they have forsaken him (2:19); but soon the relationship will be restored.

Then there will be no necessity for the people either to teach one another of the obligation to know God or to be reminded of it (31:34): it will come naturally to everyone. "Know" has intimate overtones in the OT (cf. Gen. 4:1); to "know God" implies, not knowledge about him, but a relationship with him (*see* KNOWLEDGE §1*b*). Hosea had complained that "there is . . . no knowledge of God in the land" (Hos. 4:1). Teaching the lore of God was always an obligation in Israel, particularly teaching that lore to one's children (Deut. 11:18-21); but this will become unnecessary. Because God's will has been grafted into the will of his people, everyone in the community, from top to bottom, will know God.

Finally, God will forgive the iniquity of the people and remember their sin no more (31:34). The iniquity of the people was what had led them to break with God (cf. Jer. 5:7 where the word translated "pardon" is the same word as "forgive" in 31:34). Now God will restore the relationship, and all the nightmarish past with its rupture between God and his people will be gone. In Jer. 2:2 we hear that he "remembers" the honeymoon loyalty of Israel to him, a loyalty which died away (2:5); now we hear that God will not "remember" this sin any more, so that a fresh relationship like that of the honeymoon time will be established.

This idea of a new covenant is an extraordinary one; such a radical solution to the problem between God and his people suggests how radical the problem is. For one thing, it hints that God did not take adequate steps the first time to ensure people's loyalty; there were loopholes in the first contract which God will now close. This image of a God who, it is implied, learns by his mistakes must have been shocking to Jeremiah's hearers. (The question in 2:5, "What wrong did your fathers find in me that they went far from me?" hints at the same image of God.) For another thing, it suggests that the rock-bottom certainty which some traditions affirmed about covenant-making in the past needs modification. (For example, the covenant with Abraham and that concerning circumcision are described as an "everlasting covenant," Gen. 17:7, 13, 19; "[God] is mindful of his covenant for ever," Ps. 105:8. There are many such expressions in the OT.)

3. The "new covenant" in subsequent material. ***a. Absence of reference in subsequent OT material.*** The notion of the new covenant was so extraordinary that there is no further reference to the idea in subsequent OT material. It often happens with important ideas in scripture that there are echoes of them as later generations re-express them; thus the "swords into plowshares" passage in Isa. 2:2-4; Mic. 4:1-3 turns up as "plowshares into swords" in Joel 3:10 [H 4:10]. But the new covenant is not mentioned in later OT material. The idea was perhaps too unsettling, not meeting the religious cravings of the people. Rather, it was the unending stability of God's promises which was emphasized; e.g., Deutero-Isaiah writes a half century after Jeremiah, "The word of our God will stand for ever" (Isa. 40:8; *see* ISAIAH §B2*g*). The idea of the new covenant is not picked up again until the time of the intertestamental literature and of the NT.

b. The intertestamental literature. The term "new covenant," after Jeremiah, is found first in Hebrew writings of the DEAD SEA SCROLLS. In the so-called "Damascus Scroll" (CDC; *see* ZADOKITE FRAGMENTS; DAMASCUS, COVENANT OF), the phrase "new covenant" occurs three times (6.19; 8.21 =19.33-34; 20.12; the citations as they appear in *APOT* are viii.15; ix.28, 37 of the Zadokite Fragments). In addition, there is a passage in the Habakkuk Commentary containing the word "new" with a lacuna in the MS where scholars suspect the word "covenant" stood (IQpHab 2.3; *see* DEAD SEA SCROLLS §5*a*).

These passages make it clear that those in the Dead Sea community understood themselves to be members of a "new covenant" ("all the men who entered into the new covenant in the land of Damascus," CDC 8.21—it is uncertain whether "Damascus" here refers to the actual location of a branch of the sect or is a code name for members located elsewhere). Those entering the sect separated themselves from the main body of Jews and by prayer, fasting, study, and ritual cleansings understood themselves to be outside the range of Israel's sin and therefore to be fulfilling the words of Jeremiah.

The Jeremiah passage is also reflected in I Bar. 2:35 and Jub. 1:17-18, 23-25, as well as in other passages in the Dead Sea Scrolls, but without the specific words "new covenant."

c. The NT. The phrase "new covenant" (in Greek, ἡ καινὴ διαθήκη) appears in the tradition about Jesus, particularly in connection with the Last Supper. The earliest citation is I Cor. 11:25; this letter of Paul's is dated A.D. 55 (*see* CORINTHIANS, FIRST LETTER TO THE §9). Paul gives the words of Jesus at the Last Supper on the basis of careful oral tradition (11:23); his version of the words over the cup are: "This cup is the new covenant in my blood. Do this, as often as you drink it, in remembrance of me" (11:25). The wording in Mark, dated not long after A.D. 65 (*see* MARK, GOSPEL OF §3), is slightly different: "This is my blood of the covenant, which is poured out for many. Truly, I say to you, I shall not drink again of the fruit of the vine until that day when I drink it new in the kingdom of God" (Mark 14:24-25). Matthew (26:27-29) enlarges on this phrasing slightly, but neither Mark nor Matthew, in the earliest and best MSS, use "new" with "covenant" (though later MSS do offer "new" at that point). Luke (22:17-20) offers two text traditions, a shorter one which does not mention "covenant" at all, and a longer one which mentions "the new covenant" (cf. RSV footnote to vs. 19). It is altogether likely that the traditions in Paul and in Mark rest on reliable historical information. If Jesus said "new covenant," he had Jer. 31:31-34 in mind; if he said "covenant" without "new," he had Exod. 24:8 in mind, a covenant secured by shedding blood; but he might also have had Jer. 31:31-34 in mind, as the earliest Christian church certainly did in handing down the tradition (*see* LAST SUPPER, THE §3).

Paul mentions the "new covenant" once more, in II Cor. 3:5-6: "Our sufficiency is from God, who has qualified us to be ministers of a new covenant, not in a written code but in the Spirit." This passage reflects the basic dichotomy in Paul's thinking between "law" and "faith" (cf. PAUL THE APOSTLE §6*a*) and affirms that all those in the church serve to mediate the new covenant.

The work in the NT which reflects Jer. 31:31-34 in the greatest detail, however, is the Letter to the Hebrews. Heb. 8:8-12 quotes the whole passage (as it appears in the LXX) and applies it to the sacrifice of Jesus Christ.

The first-century Christian community was thus profoundly moved by the conviction that God has acted in a new way through Jesus Christ, a way which left them so completely in God's debt (Rom. 8:12; I Cor. 7:23) that their love for each other, for God, and for the world results from God's love for the world (I John 4:19). In this understanding, doing God's will flows out of God's loving relationship with mankind (Rom. 14; I Cor. 8), a relationship signaled and sealed by the Cross (Heb. 4–10). Such ethical freedom is derived from Jesus' own stance and life (cf. Mark 2:27-28). This total Christian perception was congruent on a very deep level with Jeremiah's idea of God's law planted within the people's heart; after all, Jesus is remembered as saying in the Garden of Gethsemane, "Yet not what I will, but what thou wilt" (Mark 14:36). The idea was generalized in the naming of the two parts of the Scripture, the Old "Testament" and the New "Testament," because *testamentum* is Latin for "covenant." *See* TESTAMENT; TORAH[S].

Bibliography. In general: B. W. Anderson, "The New Covenant and the Old," in B. W. Anderson, ed., *The OT and Christian Faith* (1963), pp. 225-42, and further literature there; J. Coppens, "La Nouvelle Alliance en Jer 31,31-34," *CBQ*, XXV (1963), 12-21, and further literature in n. 1; G. von Rad, *OT Theology*, vol. II (1965), pp. 215-17; J. Bright, "An Exercise in Hermeneutics, Jeremiah 31:31-34," *Int.*, XX (1966), 188-210; D. R. Hillers, *Covenant, the History of a Biblical Idea* (1969), esp. pp. 167-68; W. L. Holladay, *Jeremiah: Spokesman Out of Time* (1974), esp. ch. 8.

On the Dead Sea Scrolls: H. Ringgren, *The Faith of Qumran* (1963), pp. 128, 201.

On the NT: J. Jeremias, *The Eucharistic Words of Jesus* (1966), pp. 171, 185, 194-95; W. G. Kümmel, *The Theology of the NT* (1973), pp. 91-92, 94, 129, 133, 252.

W. L. HOLLADAY

***NEW YEAR.** New Year is taken to mean here both New Year's day and the season of New Year. The date of New Year in Israel naturally depended on the CALENDAR employed from time to time. It is clear that in postbiblical times a festival of New Year was in existence; the character of that festival is well-attested in the rabbinic sources. But the nature and even the existence of such a festival in pre-exilic times remains hypothetical.

1. In the ancient Near East
   a. Babylonia
   b. Assyria
   c. Egypt
   d. Canaan
2. In Israel and Judah
   a. The date of New Year
   b. A New Year's day?
   c. A New Year festival?
3. In postbiblical Judaism
Bibliography

1. In the ancient Near East. Most Near Eastern civilizations observed New Year celebrations.

a. Babylonia. In Babylon a New Year festival (the Akîtu festival) was celebrated in the spring, on Nisan 1-11. A ritual text for days 2-4 survives (*ANET*, pp. 331-34), but it is not comprehensive since it concerns only the role of the leading priest. Moreover it is not always reliable evidence for Babylonian practice of Israelite times, since it comes from the Seleucid period (third and second centuries B.C.). However, from it and other references to the festival, we know that the celebration included the following: recitation of the Babylonian Creation Epic to the statue of Marduk; purification of the temple; ceremony of renewal of the king's authority—including a ritual humiliation of the king; procession to the Akîtu house outside the city; probably a ritual drama there depicting Marduk's primordial victory over Tiamat, the chaos monster (*see* CHAOS[S] §1); upon return to the city, a ritual marriage (*hieros gamos*) of Marduk in the temple Esagila. It is doubtful that the king played the role of the god in these ceremonies, as is sometimes claimed, and it is almost certainly incorrect that the festival included a celebration of Marduk's death and resurrection. Elsewhere in Babylonia there is evidence also of autumn Akîtu festivals.

b. Assyria. The celebrations were similar to those at Babylon, with some exceptions: the festival lasted about twenty days; there is no evidence of a ritual humiliation of the king; and a sacred banquet of the gods (*tākultu*) may have been a feature of the rites. References also exist to Akîtu festivals in other months of the year, so it is unwise to regard all the details of Akîtu rituals as proper to New Year celebrations.

c. Egypt. New Year rituals are best known from the late (second-century B.C.) inscriptions of the temple of Edfu. Prominent among the rituals was the bringing forth of the statue of Horus from his temple to be exposed to the rays of the sun, a reuniting of the soul of the god with his body.

d. Canaan. The autumn harvest festival played an important, and probably the most important, role in the religious life of the CANAANITES (*see also* UGARIT; UGARIT[S] §4). But it has not yet been convincingly shown that the Canaanites celebrated that festival as a festival of New Year. It is far from certain that the BAAL myth, telling of the building of a temple for Baal as a symbol of his kingship and of his resurrection and victory over MOT, the god of death, had a special connection with the autumn festival or with a celebration of New Year.

2. In Israel and Judah. ***a. The date of New Year.*** The prevailing view distinguishes—often tacitly—the regnal New Year and the liturgical or agricultural New Year. The regnal New Year, by which the reigns of kings were reckoned, is usually believed to have begun in the month of Nisan (spring) in Israel, and in Tishri (autumn) in Judah throughout the greater part of the monarchical period (*see* CHRONOLOGY OF THE OT §3*a*). Many think, however, that the Assyrian spring calendar was adopted by Judah in the eighth or seventh century B.C. The liturgical year corresponded more closely to the cycle of the agricultural year, which is thought to have begun in the autumn. None of the above statements has gone unchallenged, however.

i. *The regnal New Year. a*) Solomon's temple was begun in the second month of his fourth year and completed in the eighth month of his eleventh year (I Kings 6:1, 37-38), but I Kings 6:38 also says that he spent seven years in building it. If the usual inclusive manner of counting is employed—whereby the fractions of years at beginning and end counted as full years—"seven years" makes sense only if his regnal years were reckoned from Tishri, the seventh month, while the years during which the work was carried out were reckoned from Nisan. However, it seems that the "seven years" are not inclusive, since they form part of a total of Solomon's reign (*see* I Kings 9:10; 11:42), and inclusive reckoning is not employed when adding figures. Moreover, the "seven years" may be a schematic and symbolic figure. *See* SEVEN, SEVENTH, SEVENTY.

b) In the account of Josiah's reforms (II Kings 22–23), the discovery of the book of the law occurred "in the eighteenth year" of Josiah (22:3), while the Passover that concluded his reforms also occurred "in the eighteenth year" (23:23). On Nisan reckoning, all the events of these chapters must have occurred in the improbably short time of two weeks; a Tishri reckoning allows six months. Yet it is clear from II Chr. 34 that not all the events of II Kings 22–23 occurred in the eighteenth year, and again the figures seem to be too schematic for sure chronological inferences to be drawn.

c) Jeremiah wrote prophecies in a scroll in the fourth year of Jehoiakim, and had them read in the temple in the fifth year, in the ninth month (Jer. 36:1, 9). Clearly the months are numbered from the spring, for the ninth month is wintry (cf. 36:22). But if the regnal year was reckoned from the spring, Jeremiah must have waited at least nine months for the public reading of his scroll. It might seem more likely that a Tishri reckoning was in force, involving an interval of only three months. But even so, why did Baruch not read the scroll on the fast day in the seventh month? If a three-month interval is inexplicable, a nine-month interval is perhaps no less likely.

ii. *The agricultural and religious New Year. a*) The autumn Festival of Ingathering (*see* BOOTHS, FEAST OF) occurred, according to the ancient festival calendars, at the "going out" (צאת) or the "turn" (תקופה) of the year (Exod. 23:16; 34:22). Whether these terms signify not only that the agricultural year ended with the last harvest festival but also that the next year began immediately thereafter, as is usually assumed, is open to question. For the correlative of the "going out" of the year is the "return" (תשובה) of the year in the spring (II Sam. 11:1; I Kings 20:22, 26; I Chr. 20:1), and the "turn" of the year probably means simply the transition from summer to winter, for it is used also for the vernal transition from winter to summer (II Chr. 36:10).

b) The Gezer calendar (*see* CALENDAR §3*b*), which lists the chief agricultural activities of the year, begins in the autumn. But it is noteworthy that it begins with two months of "ingathering," which is the final element in the Israelite festival calendars (Exod. 23:14-17; 34:18-23). So if the Gezer calendar represents the beginning of the agricultural year, it is out of step with the Israelite religious year. It is more probable, however, that the Gezer calendar, written rather crudely as it is, has no normative status for establishing the time of the year Israelite peasants regarded as the beginning of the year.

c) The festival calendars (Exod. 23:14-17; 34:18-23) stress that the Festival of Unleavened Bread is to be kept in the month Abib (later Nisan). Is is hard to see why the month of observance should be mentioned in the case of this festival alone unless the month had some special significance, e.g., as the first month. Exod. 12:2, indeed, specifically requires Israel to count Abib as the first month of the year, but many scholars regard this passage as postexilic and therefore of no evidential value for the pre-exilic period. Others believe that premonarchic Israel observed a spring New Year. What is clear, however, is that the festival calendars enumerate three chief festivals beginning in the spring, which would be strange if pre-exilic Israel usually began its religious New Year at the time of the autumn festival. But because the current view is that Israel reckoned at least its religious New Year from the autumn, it is now necessary to examine the evidence for that view.

b. A New Year's day? Tishri 1, the first day of the "seventh" month—months always being numbered from the spring—is often thought to have been regarded as New Year's day in pre-exilic Israel, as it was in postbiblical times. Though the first day of every month, the NEW MOON day, was a religious festival (cf. Hos. 2:11 [H 13]; Amos 8:5), the first day of the seventh month was observed with more impressive ritual (Lev. 23:23-25; Num. 29:1-6). Work was forbidden, a cultic assembly was held, and sacrifices additional to those prescribed for the other new moon days were offered. These Priestly texts probably embody pre-exilic practice, though many scholars still believe they were first reduced to writing in the exilic or postexilic period (*see* PRIESTLY WRITERS[S] §§1-2). But there is no suggestion that the significance of this day lay in its being the New Year's day; it was rather that it introduced the month of two most solemn observances, the Day of Atonement (*see* ATONEMENT, DAY OF and supplementary article) on the tenth, and the Festival of Tabernacles (*see* BOOTHS, FEAST OF) on the fifteenth to the twenty-first or twenty-second.

Tishri 1 was also the date of Ezra's reading of the Law (Neh. 8:2), but since that was a unique occasion, it is somewhat speculative to infer that the day was chosen because it was New Year's day.

The term "beginning of the year" (ראש השנה) occurs only in Ezek. 40:1, where it probably designates not New Year's day, but the season of the year. Comparison of the chronology with the Babylonian Chronicle shows that a spring date is here intended.

c. A New Year Festival? If no New Year's day is attested, may there have been celebrations for the season of New Year? Those who have identified a New Year festival in pre-exilic Israel have by no means claimed that they had discovered a hitherto unknown festival additional to the well-attested festivals of the liturgical year—Passover, Weeks, and Booths. They have rather insisted that the New Year celebrations are only one aspect (albeit, for most scholars of this opinion, the most important aspect) of the regular autumn Festival of Ingathering, or, in one or two opinions, of the spring Festival of Passover. They are therefore freed of the necessity of demonstrating the existence of the festival; they have only to show that the rituals and ideology of the festival signify that it bore the character of New Year celebrations. Here the New Year rituals of the ancient Near East are given greater or less weight by different scholars, and the degree to which an Israelite festival may have modified non-Israelite practices is variously assessed. An Israelite New Year festival has been understood in various ways.

i. *A festival of Yahweh's enthronement.* This view, propounded principally by Mowinckel and accepted in many circles of biblical scholarship, holds that the New Year festival was primarily a celebration of an enthronement of Yahweh (*see* KING, GOD AS[S]). Many of the Psalms, especially those concerned specifically with Yahweh's kingship (e.g., Pss. 47, 93, 96, 97, 99), are assigned to the liturgy of this festival. The frequent phrase יהוה מלך in these psalms would mean: "Yahweh has become king" (in the cultic ritual just performed). This need not mean that Yahweh ever ceased to be king; indeed Ps. 93:2 affirms that the kingship that Yahweh has just now entered upon has been his "from of old." Crucial to this understanding is the conception of cult as creative drama, which not only brings reality into being, but also is a representation of primordial reality. Thus the enthronement of Yahweh that is celebrated and made a present reality at the New Year festival is his entering upon kingship at the time of creation, when he stilled the unruly waters of chaos (cf., e.g., Ps. 93:3-4). The New Year is therefore the time when Yahweh re-creates and makes all things new. The most prominent ritual of the festival was a procession of the ark, re-enacting the ark's removal to Jerusalem by David and dramatizing Yahweh's entry into his palace. Other features of the ritual included the reconsecration of the temple (cf. Ps. 93:5) and the communal acclamation of Yahweh as king (Ps. 47:1-2 [H 2-3]).

Some have emphasized rather more strongly the dramatic character of the ritual and have found it possible to reconstruct from a number of psalms a liturgical cycle such as would have been employed at the festival. Thus Johnson finds evidence for a ritual battle between the forces of light, led by the Davidic king, and the forces of darkness, chaos, and death. Ps. 89:38-45 [H 39-46] presents then the ritual humiliation and defeat of the king, Ps. 101 his protestation of loyalty and righteousness, Ps. 18 his thanksgiving after deliverance from the forces of death, and Pss. 2 and 110 his re-enthronement as the climax of the ritual drama. The outcome of the drama portrays at the same time Yahweh's primordial defeat of chaos and darkness and his own enthronement as king.

Nevertheless, while Yahweh's kingship was undoubtedly celebrated in the cult—quite possibly by means of ritual and dramatic actions—there is no clear link between celebration of Yahweh's kingship and the autumn Festival of Ingathering. One late postexilic text (Zech. 14:16) indeed mentions both together, but even if their conjunction is more than accidental, it does not prove that in the pre-exilic period the festival was largely concerned with that theme. Some have argued that the psalms of Yahweh's kingship were more probably used as sabbath psalms than as psalms for the autumn festival (Snaith), but perhaps it would be wiser to acknowledge that we do not know the occasion on which such psalms were sung, or indeed whether they were intended for one particular occasion. It can also be persuasively argued that the phrase יהוה מלך does not mean "Yahweh has become king," but rather "It is Yahweh who is king," focusing attention on the fact that it is Yahweh, and not Baal nor even the human king, who fully deserves that title.

ii. *A typical Near Eastern New Year festival.* This view, not so influential as that previously mentioned, is associated chiefly with adherents of the myth and ritual school (e.g., Engnell and Hooke; *see* MYTH, MYTHOLOGY §B). They believed it possible to identify traces in the OT of a New Year festival identical in many respects to those of the rest of the ancient Near East. In addition to the elements of the re-enthronement of Yahweh and the ritual battle, the liturgy of the festival will have included: a period of chaos in which law and order are abolished and roles are reversed, with the king being humiliated and deposed and the god depicted as descending into the underworld; the cultic portrayal of the god in his death and resurrection by the king; a celebration of the *hieros gamos,* "sacred marriage," by the king and his consort, symbolizing and creating fertility and prosperity; the fixing of the destinies for the ensuing year; and the recitation of creation myths as a means of ensuring the renewal of creation. A variant upon this view portrays the king in the role of the resurrected sun-god on New Year's day, the autumn equinox (*see* NEW YEAR).

Two principal objections can be raised against this hypothesis:

a) The ritual pattern it invokes is much more fragmentary than has been claimed. Recent studies in Near Eastern religions emphasize the differences in ritual and belief between cultures, and the scarcity of information about the rituals and especially about their significance. Hence there is no fixed Near Eastern pattern from which gaps in our knowledge about Israelite religion can be filled. The question remains whether New Year observances in the Near East exhibit sufficient unity to enable us to reconstruct such observances in Israel —when little specific OT evidence exists.

b) The relation between mythological texts and rituals is complex. Myth is not simply the spoken accompaniment of ritual. Near Eastern myths are often essentially literary productions, with only distant connections to particular ritual acts. Even when they were recited during a ritual—as was the case with the Babylonian Creation Epic—the ritual activities cannot be safely reconstructed from the myths. Equally hazardous are inferences about Israelite festivals based on OT Psalm texts.

iii. *An agricultural New Year festival.* The autumn festival, whatever else it was, was primarily a harvest festival. In the earliest OT references, it is called the "feast of ingathering" (Exod. 34:22; 23:16). It has been argued—notably by Snaith—that a festival that marks the end of one agricultural year will also mark the beginning of the next. While it commemorates the blessings of the past, it must also invoke blessings for the coming year. In that sense the autumn festival in Israel will have had the character of a festival of the New Year. Principal among its concerns will have been anxiety for the coming of the rains, especially the EARLY RAIN (*see also* PALESTINE, CLIMATE OF §5) which is expected in October, i.e., within a few weeks of the autumn festival. It is not surprising that prayers for rain figure in the later Jewish liturgy for New Year (*see* §3 *below*).

Though there is no direct biblical evidence for such an element in the celebration of the autumn festival, it is quite probable that the major festival of the year did not pass without prayers for the future, and, to be more specific, for the ensuing new agricultural year. Whether that probability constitutes sufficient grounds for calling the Festival of Ingathering or Booths a New Year festival is, however, open to doubt—especially because the biblical sources never refer to the festival in such terms.

It may be concluded that even if pre-exilic Israel and Judah did reckon their liturgical year from the autumn—and that is by no means self-evident, as we have seen above—the evidence that they celebrated the autumn festival as a New Year festival is far from compelling, however attractive and imaginative some of the resultant interpretations of OT texts may be.

3. In postbiblical Judaism. For reasons as yet unclear, the beginning of the year, reckoned from the spring by the early postexilic community, came to be celebrated in the autumn in Judaism. The sounding of the ram's horn (שופר; *see* MUSICAL INSTRUMENTS §B2*e*) figured prominently in the ritual of the festival, held on Tishri 1-2, while the liturgy emphasized the themes of judgment, God's kingship, and creation.

Nisan 1 continued to be recognized as New Year's day for the reckoning of the reigns of Jewish kings and for festivals. Thus, although the calendar year began with Tishri 1, Passover was regarded as the first festival of the year. Of minor significance were the New Year's days on Elul 1 and Shebat 1, for the tithing of cattle and for trees respectively.

Bibliography. General: S. H. Hooke, ed., *Myth and Ritual* (1933), and *The Origins of Early Semitic Ritual* (1938); T. H. Gaster, *Thespis* (rev. ed., 1961); H. Frankfort, *The Problem of Similarity in Ancient Near Eastern Religions* (1951).

In Israel: P. Volz, *Das Neujahrsfest Jahwes* (1912); S. Mowinckel, *Psalmenstudien,* II (1922); H. Schmidt, *Die Thronfahrt Jahves am Fest der Jahreswende im alten Israel* (1927); N. H. Snaith, *The Jewish New Year Festival* (1947); G. Widengren, *Sakrales Königtum im AT und im Judentum* (1955), esp. pp. 62-79; H. Ringgren, *Israelite Religion* (1966), pp. 185-200; S. Mowinckel, *The Psalms in Israel's Worship,* I, ch. 5 (1962); A. R. Johnson, *Sacral Kingship in Ancient Israel* (2nd ed., 1967); I. Engnell, *A Rigid Scrutiny* (1969), pp. 180-84; H. Cazelles, "Nouvel an (fête du). IV. Le nouvel an en Israël," *DBSup,* VI (1960), cols. 620-45. Less sympathetic to the autumn New Year: R. de Vaux, *Ancient Israel* (1961), pp. 502-6; H.-J. Kraus, *Worship in Israel* (1966), pp. 61-68; G. Fohrer, *History of Israelite Religion* (1972), pp. 142-45; J. B. Segal, *The Hebrew Passover* (1963).

Date: E. R. Thiele, *The Mysterious Numbers of the Hebrew Kings* (rev. ed., 1965); J. Finegan, *Handbook of Biblical Chronology* (1964), pp. 33-37; D. J. A. Clines, "The Evidence for an Autumnal New Year in Pre-exilic Israel Reconsidered," *JBL,* XCIII (1974),

22-40, and "Regnal Year Reckoning in the Last Years of the Kingdom of Judah," *AJBA*, II (1972), 9-34.

In Judaism: Mishna, Tractate Rosh Hashanah; A. Michel, "Nouvel an (fête du). III. Dans le Judaïsme," *DBSup*, VI (1960), cols. 597-620; L. Jacobs, "Rosh Ha-Shanah," *Encyclopaedia Judaica*, XIV (1971), cols. 305-10.

In the ancient Near East: H. Ringgren, *Religions of the Ancient Near East* (1973), esp. pp. 83-89; E. Drioton and R. Largement, "Nouvel an (fête du). I. Dans l'Égypte ancienne. II. Dans la religion suméro-akkadienne," *DBSup*, VI (1960), cols. 556-97; F. Thureau-Dangin, *Les rituels accadiens* (1921); S. A. Pallis, *The Babylonian Akitu Festival* (1926); A. Falkenstein, "akiti-Fest und akiti-Festhaus," *Festschrift Johannes Friedrich*, ed. R. von Kienle *et al.* (1959), pp. 147-82; W. G. Lambert, "The Great Battle of the Mesopotamian Religious Year: the Conflict in the Akītu House," *Iraq*, XXV (1963), 189-90; G. van Driel, *The Cult of Aššur* (1969), pp. 139-69; J. C. de Moor, *New Year with Canaanites and Israelites*, 2 vols. (1972).

D. J. A. Clines

***NOMADISM.** Pastoral nomadism, a socioeconomic mode of life that is based on intensive domestication of livestock and requires movement in a seasonal cycle dictated by the need for pasturage and water, is well attested in the ancient Near East and in the Bible. Unfortunately, historians and exegetes have acquired and clung to erroneous and inexact conceptions of the place of pastoral nomadism in social evolution, the numbers of pastoral nomads, their self-sufficiency and isolation from settled peoples, their role as presumed bearers of major historical, social, and cultural changes, and the supposed socioeconomic and cultural equivalence of village tribalism and pastoral nomadism.

1. Ancient Near Eastern pastoral nomadism. ***a. Origins of pastoral nomadism.*** Data from prehistory and ethnology have clarified the secondary and limited adaptive development of pastoral nomadism out of a prior mixture of agriculture and animal husbandry in the settled zones. Humans first entered the river valleys of Mesopotamia, not from the Arabian Desert, but from the Anatolian and Iranian hills and grasslands. Animals were domesticated within the Neolithic farming village. Under specific economic and political conditions, some groups specialized in herds of goats, sheep, and asses that were grazed on the marginal desert steppes, both to take advantage of the otherwise unexploited winter growth and to escape oppressive political authorities in the settled regions. *See* Agriculture; Prehistory in the ANE, and supplementary articles.

b. Numbers of pastoral nomads. In modern times no more than ten per cent of the total populace in the Middle East has been composed of pastoral nomads. Extrapolating backward, there appear to be no ecological or technological factors that would have increased that percentage at any time throughout recorded history. Before the advent of camel and horse nomadism, which permitted deeper penetration into the Arabian Desert (from the twelfth century B.C. on), the number of ass nomads was probably far fewer.

c. Self-sufficiency of pastoral nomads. The degree of self-sufficiency and isolation of pastoral nomads varies markedly. It depends upon the animals that are bred, distances traveled, terrain traversed, frequency and types of exchange of goods and services with settled peoples, the total mixture of economic modes among the nomads, language and other cultural similarities or differences between nomads and the settled people they contact, and the presence or absence of state boundaries or police powers and other political factors. In some cases the same community has pastoral nomadic and farming segments; in other cases a whole people alternates pastoral nomadism with crop cultivation in half-yearly cycles. A gamut of nuanced relations between pastoral nomads and settled peoples may range from virtually complete merger, except for the peculiarity of the periodic trek (which in transhumance pastoralism may be led by a small number of herders in a basically agricultural community), to frequent or stated periodic contacts between demographically and culturally similar or dissimilar people for the purpose of exchange of goods and mutual services (e.g., grazing rights over field stubble in return for the fertilization of the fields by animal manure). These contacts are as often friendly and symbiotic as they are hostile and hegemonic. On occasion pastoral nomads try to build commercial empires by controlling trade routes and imposing tribute (e.g., Midianites in the eleventh century B.C. and Nabateans in Greco-Roman times).

d. Pastoral nomads as major change agents. Historical and sociological reconstructions of the ancient Near East, and of Israel in particular, have been obscured and distorted by the "pan-nomadic" hypothesis which posits the Arabian Desert as an inexhaustible source of population influxes, military conquests, dynastic changes, cultural departures, and religious mutations. Recent study of the Amorites, for example, shows that they have been carelessly subsumed under the broad heading of "pastoral nomadism" which has in turn, with no concrete evidence, been attributed to an origin in the desert. Amorites at Mari, who were indeed pastoral nomads of a sort, were integrated into village communities and their restiveness and conflict with the state was not due to their invading or infiltrating from the desert but rather to their rural-based resistance to the drafting and taxing powers of the state. Again and again migration due to uprooting because of natural and historical circumstances has been naïvely equated with nomadism as regular movement in the exercise of a socioeconomic mode of life.

e. Village tribalism and pastoral nomadism. In socioeconomic and cultural terms, features of tribal organization and typical elements of rural life have been mistakenly identified as specifically pastoral nomadic traits. Often this disastrous confusion derives from unfamiliarity with anthropology (*see* Tribe[S]) which has made abundantly clear that village tribalism is exhibited in societies with a wide range of economic modes.

The great majority of supposed pastoral nomadic indicators have no singular diagnostic value. Asses were used as favorite riding animals and reliable beasts of burden throughout the ancient Near East. Sheep and goats were kept by settled peoples.

Tents were used by merchants, armies, and royal hunting parties, and by farmers for guarding and harvesting distant fields or where building materials were scarce. For that matter, nomads often lived, not in tents, but in grass or wood huts, mud houses, windscreens, or caves. Moreover, evidence in Israel, and among other ancient Near Eastern peoples, of blood revenge and hospitality, brotherly covenants, and solicitude for strangers, orphans, and widows, "democratic" or egalitarian social institutions and behavior, and warfare by ambush, feigned flight, single combat, and destruction of captives and booty (*see* War, Holy[S]) has been customarily attributed to distinctively pastoral nomadic origins. But every one of these traits, and often all of them together, can be found throughout a range of tribal social organization in which not a single pastoral nomad is present.

2. Israelite pastoral nomadism. ***a. Limited incidence.*** A careful reading of the biblical text shows that a component of pastoral nomadism as a socioeconomic phenomenon existed in Israel, probably in two forms: (1) winter treks into the steppes lying S and E of Canaan, and (2) spring/summer treks into the well-watered uplands of Canaan. Owing to the close proximity of steppe and cultivable zone in Canaan, as well as the fluctuating line between them governed by erratic rainfall, agricultural and pastoral nomadic modes of life were closely juxtaposed and interwoven. Many pastoral nomads were part-time or seasonal, and there were farmers who took to pastoral nomadism and returned to farming as economic and political circumstances dictated. There is no reason to believe that the Israelite people—at any time of their existence—included more than ten per cent pastoral nomads.

On the other hand, numerous traits of rural village life and of tribal social organization long assumed to be "pastoral nomadic" have been profusely cited without justification. Mention of asses and tents (*see* §1*e above*), flocks and herds, wells and stockades, as well as a host of customs and laws reflecting tribal practice, can no longer be equated with pastoral nomadism unless there are specific indications of seasonal movement by herders. When there are such indications, it must be further determined, if possible, what specific forms of pastoral nomadism are referred to, since references may be to a trek conducted by a handful of herders from a farming community or to the pastoral movements of one segment of a community in which half or more of the populace is fully resident and engaged in farming.

b. Patriarchs as pastoral nomads? Migration is not *ipso facto* pastoral nomadism (contrast Nomadism §§3, 4*a*). People move for many other reasons than to tend herds; they move because of famines, debts, political turmoil, war, and marriage, and for purposes of religious pilgrimage. The reasons given for the movements of the patriarchs are more often than not precisely such factors. Moreover, the form-critical and traditio-historical cautions against reading the text of Genesis on a single spatiotemporal plane, coupled with the dominant retrojected motif of wandering on an as-yet-unpossessed promised land, should warn us against making snap judgments about the socioeconomic and cultural context of the patriarchs.

c. Wilderness wandering as a nomadic trek? The movement of Israelites out of Egypt and across the wilderness, long taken for granted as a pastoral nomadic trek, fails to satisfy the appropriate criteria. The departure from Egypt was flight, expulsion, or armed escape—not a herding trek. The mass of people are pictured as unfamiliar with desert terrain and modes of survival. Animals and people perish. Only the intervention of a Midianite familiar with the environment saves the disoriented fugitives. They settle for long years around the oases at Kadesh where agriculture was certainly practiced. The diet of fish and vegetables which they recall was hardly pastoral nomadic fare. In every way the desert is presented as an alien place.

d. Nomadic conquest of Canaan? Did land-hungry nomads conquer Canaan? What is the evidence for this "obvious" assumption? Positively, it consists essentially of no more than the superficial assumption that a people whose patriarchs had been nomads (but *see* §2*b above*), and who had managed to flee Egypt and cross the wilderness to Canaan, must have been pastoral nomads. This conclusion begs all the questions and flies in the face of all the counterindications and caveats referred to above. Insofar as they may have adopted some pastoral nomadic survival measures, it was more by compulsion than by advance preparation or preference.

The logical alternative is to look for the origins of Israel in the land of Canaan itself, for it is not to be forgotten that even those who came out of Egypt had once lived in the land of Canaan. In particular it will be necessary to examine the Canaanite matrix of those features of village and rural life and those traits of tribal organization which the pastoral nomadic mirage has so long monopolized. In a model of early Israel as a rift within strife-torn Canaanite society there will be room for a moderate dash of Israelite pastoral nomadism as a subspecialization and outrunner of a basically agricultural people organized in tribal egalitarianism (*see* Israel, Social and Economic Development of[S] §§1, 2*a*; Canaan, Conquest and Settlement of[S]).

e. "The nomadic ideal." The widely-hailed "nomadic ideal" of Israel evaporates once it is recognized that what is praised is not a pastoral nomadic mode of life but an egalitarian tribal society in which religious ideology and praxis and social ideology and praxis were complementary and harmonious aspects of a cultural totality. *See* Wilderness[S] §§1*e*, 2; Rechabites[S]; Habiru[S] §§ 3-4.

Bibliography. On ethnology of pastoral nomadism: D. H. K. Amiran and Y. Ben-Arieh, "Sedentarization of Beduin in Israel," *IEJ*, XIII (1963), 161-81; E. E. Bacon, "Types of Nomadism in Central and Southwest Asia," *Southwestern Journal of Anthropology*, X (1954), 44-68; H. Charles, *Tribus moutonnières du Moyen-Euphrate*, Documents de L'Institut Francais de Damas, VIII (1939); J. I. Clarke, "Studies of Semi-nomadism in North Africa," *Economic Geography*, XXXV (1959), 95-108; L. Febvre, *A Geographical Introduction to His-*

tory (1925), pp. 261-94; L. Krader, "Ecology of Central Asian Pastoralism," *Southwestern Journal of Anthropology,* XI (1955), 301-26; L. Krader, "Pastoralism," *International Encyclopaedia of the Social Sciences,* XI (1968), 453-61; D. L. Johnson, *The Nature of Nomadism* (1969).

On prehistory and ancient Near Eastern pastoral nomadism: R. Braidwood, "The Early Village in Southwestern Asia," *JNES,* XXXII (1973), 34-39, and *Prehistoric Men* (7th ed., 1967); R. Braidwood, B. Howe *et al.,* eds., *Prehistoric Investigations in Iraqi Kurdistan* (1960), pp. 1-8, 129-38; C. Coon *et al.,* "Badw," in *The Encyclopaedia of Islam,* I (new ed., 1960), 872-92; O. Eissfeldt, "Protektorat der Midianiter ueber ihre Nachbarn im letzten Viertel des 2. Jahrtausends v. Chr.," *JBL,* LXXXVII (1968), 383-93; M. de Goeje, "Arabia," in *The Encyclopaedia of Islam,* I (1913), 372-77; W. Dostal, "The Evolution of Bedouin Life," *L'antica società beduina,* ed. F. Gabrieli (1959), pp. 11-33; R. Giveon, *Les Bédouins Shosou des Documents Égyptiens,* Documenta et Monumenta Orientis Antiqui, XVIII (1971); A. Haldar, *Who Were the Amorites?* (1971); J. T. Luke, "Pastoralism and Politics in the Mari Period" (diss., Univ. of Mich., 1965); M. B. Rowton, "Autonomy and Nomadism in Western Asia," *Or,* XLII (1973), 247-58, "The Physical Environment and the Problem of the Nomads," *La civilisation de Mari,* ed. J.-R. Kupper (1967), 109-21, and "Urban Autonomy in a Nomadic Environment," *JNES,* XXXII (1973), 201-15.

On Israelite pastoral nomadism: F. S. Frick, "The Rechabites Reconsidered," *JBL,* XC (1971), 279-87; N. K. Gottwald, "Were the Early Israelites Pastoral Nomads?" *Rhetorical Criticism: Essays in Honor of James Muilenburg* (1974), pp. 223-55; P. A. Riemann, "Desert and Return to Desert in the Pre-exilic Prophets" (diss., Harvard, 1963); M. S. Seale, *The Desert Bible* (1974); S. Talmon, "The 'Desert Motif' in the Bible and in Qumran Literature," *Biblical Motifs,* ed. A. Altmann (1966), pp. 31-63; J. van Seters, *Abraham in History and Tradition* (1975), pp. 13-38.

See also bibliog. under NOMADISM.

N. GOTTWALD

***NUMBERS, BOOK OF.** The Greek and Latin names *arithmoi* and *Numeri* agree with the Talmudic designation of the book as *ḥômeš happiḳḳûdîm* (T.B. Soṭ. 36b) "the 'fifth' of the census," i.e., that one of five Torah books containing the wilderness census.

The variegated materials incorporated in Numbers and its tenuous literary structure make a two-stage analysis desirable. The non-Priestly materials will be studied independently in order to assess their historical and religious significance, followed by a detailed examination of the Priestly (P) materials. *See* PRIESTLY WRITERS[S].

1. Non-P materials
2. Historical significance of the non-P materials
3. Religious significance of the non-P materials
4. P materials

Bibliography

1. Non-P materials. *a*) Numbers contains continuous sections from the YAHWIST and ELOHIST, including excerpts from early collections of Hebrew poetry. *See* CANON OF THE OT[S] §1*a*.

i. 10:29–12:16: a series of narratives epitomizing Moses' leadership as divinely ordained, reminiscent of Exod. 16–18.

ii. 20:14–25:5 (except 20:22-29; 22:1): attempts to penetrate Canaan from the KADESH area, the subsequent circumvention of Edom, and events in the steppes of Moab.

b) Edited non-P sections where early materials have been worked into a later account.

i. Chs. 13–14: the dispatching of advance scouts to spy out S Canaan as far as Hebron (13:22). The P writer(s) provided an introduction (vss. 1-16, or 17*a*), and by inserting 13:21 extended the area to be surveyed all the way to Hamath, an interpretation of the mission predicated on the theoretical description of the Promised Land (cf. Num. 34:1-2). Original is the attempt to approach S Canaan by proceeding W from Kadesh along the way to the wilderness of Shur, which was repulsed by the AMALEKITES (14:40-45). It is probably the P writer, however, who introduced Yahweh's wrathful edict against the wilderness generation (14:26-39).

ii. Ch. 16: the attempted rebellion against Moses' leadership, a theme prominent in 10:29–12:16. The P writer made of this an internecine struggle among the Levitical clans. Early material is found in 16:1, 12-15, 25-34. (Ch. 17 is probably all the work of P writers.)

iii. Ch. 32: the request of Reuben, Gad, and half of Manasseh to settle in Transjordan. Source criticism of this chapter has been unsuccessful. Noth has stressed the historicity of vss. 39-42. The tradition of Num. 32 was utilized in Deut. 3:8-9.

2. Historical significance of the non-P materials. Numbers preserves early historiography otherwise unavailable for the period prior to the entry of the Israelites into Canaan. The Midianite connection in the pre-Canaanite period, first encountered in Exodus, is presented in Numbers. Despite differences in detail, both traditions place the Israelites and Midianites together in NE Sinai. This correlates with the dispatching of the scouts from Kadesh (13:26-27), and with the attempt to reach Canaan by moving W along the road to the wilderness of Shur, again from Kadesh (14:40-45). Finally, the request for passage through Edom also came from Kadesh (20:14-21). Thus the early historiography of Numbers is the principal source on the function of Kadesh-barnea as the Israelite base in Sinai.

All attempts to penetrate Canaan apparently failed until after the circumvention of Edom. De Vaux's conclusion that the Israelite victory over the Amalekites (recorded in Exod. 17:8-13) is historical must be questioned. More reliable is the account in Num. 14:44-45, which records an Israelite defeat (cf. Deut. 25:17-19). The Exodus account incorrectly places the event at Rephidim in S Sinai, whereas Numbers has it at Hormah in the Negeb. The battle against the king of ARAD is problematical (21:1-3). It is unlikely that the Israelites were victorious, and vss. 2-3, which echo holy-war themes (*see* WAR, HOLY[S]), represent a later tradition. It is improbable that, afforded an opportunity to penetrate the Negeb directly, the Israelites would have resorted to a route around Edom that took them all the way to Elath (21:4 ff.).

Of obvious historical importance is the Israelite advance from Kadesh to the steppes of Moab. They ended up controlling Transjordan up to the Ammonite border, including Jazer, N of HESHBON

(21:4-32). The battle of Edrei, in the Bashan (21:33-35), would have taken them far afield, and is probably the record of a later event.

The poetic excerpts fit into the historical reconstruction. De Vaux interprets 21:27*b*-30 as a ballad celebrating the Israelite defeat of Sihon, against the refrain of Sihon's earlier defeat of the Moabites. In effect this meant that Moabite claims to parts of Transjordan need not be honored in principle because they had lost hegemony over them even before the advent of the Israelites.

It was Albright who first pointed out that references to the Kenites and the characterization of the Seir area in the Balaam oracles would be more understandable if these poems reflected a twelfth-century situation, or even the late thirteenth century. The oracles thus antedate the narrative framework by a considerable period of time.

Archaeological excavations and historical research have shed new light on the situation in NE Sinai and Transjordan during the thirteenth and twelfth centuries B.C. Giveon's recent study of the Shosu nomads has clarified relations between the pharaohs Seti I, Ramses II, and Mer-ne-Ptah and nomads in the Dead Sea area and Transjordan. Rothenberg's excavations at Timna', near Elath, show extensive Egyptian mining activity during the fourteenth through twelfth centuries. Surveys of Transjordan initiated by Glueck and continuing excavations indicate that there was little permanent construction in Edom, Moab, or further N in Gilead during a period of six hundred years prior to the Iron Age. Biblical traditions which speak of cities and permanent settlements in these areas are, therefore, products of a later time, probably the period of the Judges. There were active overland trade routes in NE Sinai and Transjordan before the Iron Age, and the availability of ample water in the Kadesh area made it suitable as an Israelite base.

The early accounts in Numbers do not resolve the problem of the S route of migration indicated by Rephidim (Exod. 17:1, 8; 19:2), Hazeroth (Num. 11:35; 12:16), and Dizahab (Deut. 1:1). The interpretation of significant passages in Numbers depends on whether we posit a unified penetration of the Israelite tribes into Canaan. *See* EXODUS, THE[S].

3. Religious significance of the non-P materials. The early sections of Numbers highlight the charismatic leadership of Moses as judge, administrator, and intercessor on behalf of a recalcitrant people. Moses' personal virtues are brought out more fully in Numbers than in Exodus, despite the dramatic saga of the Egyptian encounter. The Deuteronomist drew on Numbers in dealing with this theme.

The BALAAM oracles (chs. 22–24) are an epitome of Yahweh's providence, a theme introduced in the story of the manna (ch. 11). They also afford us an exceptional glimpse into early notions of prophecy. Balaam employed DIVINATION as well as sacrifices, and actively sought divine communications rather than simply waiting for a response.

4. P materials. *a*) The P materials in Numbers represent a variety of genres, and Gray was correct in positing more than one stratum. In addition to Priestly editing in chs. 13–14, 16 (and 17), and 32, already noted above, the following mostly narrative sections take their cue from the earlier traditions in Numbers.

i. 20:1-13: events in the Kadesh area.

ii. 20:22-29: the death of Aaron and the transfer of priestly authority to his son, Eleazar.

iii. 25:6-18: the zeal of the priest Phinehas in stemming a plague resulting from Yahweh's wrath over the Baal-Peor episode.

iv. 27:12-23: the designation of Joshua as Moses' successor.

v. Ch. 31: another version of the Midianite war (cf. 25:16-18).

vi. Ch. 33: a P version of the route of the Israelites from Egypt to the steppes of Moab, drawing on traditions of Exodus and Deuteronomy as well as Numbers.

vii. Chs. 34–36: matters related to the anticipated division of Canaan. This material is loosely related to ch. 32, which introduced the theme of tribal territories.

All of the above sections bear a clear Priestly stamp. The Midianite war of ch. 31 (cf. 25:16-18) may be a later echo of the situation during the period of the Judges (cf. Judg. 6:1–8:9), inserted here because the Balaam and Baal-Peor episodes were associated with the Midianite-Moabite alliance against Israel.

The theme of the division of the land allows for the introduction of a census list in ch. 26, additional to the one provided in ch. 1 (*see below*). The delineation of Canaan (34:1-12) corresponds to the Egyptian province of Canaan as defined in the treaty of Kedesh, *ca.* 1270 B.C. (*see* HITTITES; HITTITES[S]). As demonstrated by Kaufmann, this territorial description never matched any actual program of occupation or conquest, but was merely an idealized conception of the Promised Land. Alt and Albright, followed by Mazar, have considered the lists of LEVITICAL CITIES in Num. 35:1-8 (cf. Josh. 21; I Chr. 6:54-81) as reflecting an ancient institution. Note the reference to such properties in Leviticus (25:33-34) as part of an early system of land tenure. Similarly, the cities of refuge (*see* CITY OF REFUGE), which, according to Num. 35:6, account for six of the forty-eight Levitical cities, are related to the ancient right of asylum stipulated in the Book of the Covenant (Exod. 21:13-14), mentioned in I Kings 1:50, and provided for in Deut. 4:41-43. Num. 36, referring to the settlement of the clan of Machir (cf. 32:39-42), introduces a series of estate laws thematically associated with the case of Zelophehad's daughters (27:1-11). These laws attest the principle that, as a general rule, sons inherit ancestral property, and that such real estate cannot pass out of the control of the clan. This again points to Lev. 25, with its provision for the JUBILEE YEAR.

Num. 16–17 in their final P version deserve special comment. The P writers present a rebellion against Moses and Aaron by a rival Levitical clan (Kohath). They charge Aaron and his clan with arrogating all the priestly offices to themselves. Here we have early notions on divine selection (the sprouting of a rod, or the acceptance of an incense offering). Haran has interpreted the role of the censers in this story within the framework of graduated taboos affecting specific areas of the sanctuary and courtyards. Num. 16:25-34 belongs, together with vss. 1*b*-2*a* and 12-15, to the non-P material, and presents an alternate mode of destruction for the usurpers. The name of Korah was inserted by the P writer. *See* AARON, AARONIDES[S].

b) Numbers presents a plethora of P materials, which fall into two categories.

i. *The Israelite camp.* Num. 1–4 constitutes a loose literary unit. Ch. 1 contains a census list; ch. 2 a prescribed encampment according to a unit called *deghel,* and a marching order; and chs. 3–4 prescribe the Levitical assignments according to tribal subdivisions. Related thematically to chs. 1–4 are 9:15–10:28, and of course the census list in ch. 26. (Num. 26:52-56 concerns the division of the land, and belongs with chs. 27 and 32 ff.).

Speiser's brief study on the technical term *'ᵃbhôdhath mattānâ,* "a service of dedication" (Num. 18:7), and Liver's observations on the specialized sense of *'ᵃbhôdhâ* in certain P sources, have now been followed by Milgrom's more extensive investigation of Levitical terminology. The terminology of these P sections is not fabricated, and has its analogues in cognate Near Eastern usage. A good example is the array of the Israelite camp according to the *deghel* unit. Hebrew *deghel* is usually rendered "banner, standard," but the evidence on the organization of the military colony at Elephantine (*see* ELEPHANTINE PAPYRI) shows that, in Egypt under the Persian administration, the *deghel* represented an actual military unit, which Porten estimates as consisting of one thousand men. Aharoni has discovered an Aramaic ostracon at ARAD, also dated to the Persian period, which lists one person as belonging *ldgl 'bdḥy,* "to the unit of *'Abdîḥai.*" In this light, one is tempted to regard Ps. 20:5 [H 6] against a military background: "May we shout for joy in your victory, arrayed by 'units' in the name of our God" (author's trans.). The translation "unit" is preferable in Numbers as well.

The traditions employ the term *ṣābā'* and its derivatives to connote a team of workers, in this case Levites. Elsewhere this term almost always refers either to a military force or to the heavenly "hosts" (*see* HOSTS, HOST OF HEAVEN). The distinctive Priestly usage closely follows Akkadian where *ṣābu,* the cognate of Hebrew *ṣābā',* often designates groups of personnel.

Of central importance are the census lists of chs. 1 and 26. Mendenhall suggests that Priestly writers were aware of the procedure of assigning tribal quotas for the Israelite militia in the premonarchic period. Thus, the term *'eleph* originally designated a tribal subdivision or clan, a sense attested in early biblical sources. The exaggerated numerical totals preserved in Numbers may reflect a later interpretation of *'eleph* as "one thousand," the normal strength of a royal military unit. What we have in Numbers is a P reconstruction of a premonarchic system, under which the militia was mustered according to tribe, and the units commanded by the tribal chieftain, the *nāśî'.*

Speiser's study of the office of the biblical *nāśî',* in which he also discusses the subtribe called *bêth-'ābh,* "patriarchal clan," strengthens the conclusion that we have in the Priestly reconstruction a background reality, recast by later writers, but certainly not a fabrication. The office of *nāśî'* is mentioned in the Book of the Covenant (Exod. 22:28 [H 27]), and the patriarchal narratives also attest to its earliness (Gen. 23:6; 34:2). We even read of the *nāśî'* in the early monarchy (I Kings 11:34). As Speiser noted, it was Ezekiel who envisioned a restored Israel governed by a *nāśî',* not a *melekh,* "king" (Ezek. 34:24; 46:18). Ezekiel thus expresses the Priestly outlook on ideal government, the system which had once obtained in ancient Israel and would arise again.

The social connotation of the term *bêth-'ābh,* which can merely designate a place of residence, is unambiguous in Judg. 6:15, where it is synonymous with *'eleph,* "clan," and in I Sam. 22:1, where it is synonymous with *'aḥ,* "kinsman." The P writers revived premonarchic notions of tribal organization, and built upon them an elaborate portrayal of the wilderness period. We encounter lists of tribal chiefs in Num. 7 (*see below*); in 10:11-21; 13:1-16. Not all of the lists derive from the same source. Excluded from all lists in the book of Numbers are the Levites, who are always listed separately. They are deprived of the usual *naḥalâ,* "homestead," in Canaan, and have special duties.

ii. *Cultic rites and laws.* Of the P materials in Numbers, there remain only certain rites and codes of cultic praxis, all associated at least tangentially with maintaining the purity of the Israelite camp and its cult place.

Num. 7 records the dedication of the tabernacle altar, and is to be linked with the tabernacle texts in Exodus (chs. 25–30, 35–40). Levine has classified Num. 7 as an archival record presented narratively and listing the uniform donations of each chieftain. Of all the P accounts, Num. 7 is the closest in format to an original temple record, in which the numerals were originally ideographic, which accounts for the inverted order of listing items and quantities: "oxen, 2; rams, 5; he-goats, 5; yearling lambs, 5," etc. Levine also reconstructed Num. 7 as a two-dimensional record, reading down and across in several columns, a convention employed at various periods by cuneiform scribes. Once the introduction is read (vss. 1-11), there are few verbs, and only formulaic features characteristic of a record.

Num. 8:5-26 prescribes the consecration of the Levites, and as such is a companion to Lev. 8–9, the installation of the Aaronide priests (*see* PRIESTS[S]; AARON, AARONIDES[S]).

Num. 18 is a roster of gifts which the priests are to receive from the offerings of the people, in return for their responsibility in maintaining the purity of the sanctuary and its altars. Ch. 18 draws on diverse traditions, Levitical and Deuteronomic. It includes a section on Levitical gifts (vss. 21-24) and represents the tithe both as compensation for the service of the Levites and as a grant in lieu of a land inheritance.

Directly related to the purity of the sanctuary and its priesthood are the provisions of ch. 19, which prescribe procedures for ridding the camp of impurity resulting from contact with a dead body, considered sufficiently severe as to endanger the sanctuary itself (vs. 20). Levine has treated the religio-magical conceptions involved in such purificatory rites, where sacrificial blood was employed in order to ward off contamination. In this case, some of the sacrificial blood was sprinkled at the entrance of the tent of meeting (vs. 4) as a means for protecting the sanctuary and its resident deity from impurity. The expiatory sacrifice prescribed here (*ḥaṭṭā'th*) is of the type usually reserved for expiating offenses by the chief priest or the community as a whole (*see* ATONEMENT IN THE OT[S]). Its utilization here is due to the unusual seriousness of contact with dead bodies in the Priestly conception of purity. This same type of *ḥaṭṭā'th* was prescribed for the periodic purification of the sanctuary (cf. Lev. 16). The concern for purity is also reflected in Num. 5:1-4 (cf. Lev. 15), which requires the removal from the camp of those having bodily eruptions or discharges.

Numbers preserves three sacrificial codes: 9:1-14; ch. 15; and chs. 28–30. All of them are composites based on earlier P sources and are probably to be assigned to the final stratum of the P redaction. *See* SACRIFICES AND OFFERINGS, OT[S].

Num. 9:1-14 is a code for the PASSOVER festival, based on Exod. 12–13. Absent from the code of Exodus is the provision for a deferred Passover in the second month (for those distant from the temple or impure at the appointed time in the first month). This provision appears to have Deuteronomic overtones (cf. Deut. 12:21; 14:24), and is the source for the tradition of the second Passover ordered by Hezekiah (II Chr. 30:3, 17-18).

Num. 15 can be linked quite clearly to earlier P sections. Vss. 22-31 are a précis of Lev. 4–21, the only addition being a concern for the resident alien (*ger*, vss. 16, 29-31). Num. 15:1-16 represents a sacrificial code dealing with the *zebhaḥ* (slain offering) and can serve as a complement to Num. 28–30 where this type of sacrifice is conspicuously excluded. The basis is a statement in the Holiness Code (Lev. 19:5-8), and the more complete prescriptions of Lev. 1–3; 7:11-38.

Num. 15:17-21 deals with the FIRST FRUITS and employs late terminology, most notably the term *'arîsâ* ("baking"?), otherwise attested only in Ezek. 44:30 and Neh. 10:38. Num. 15:32-36 represents a didactic account on the observance of the sabbath. Of interest is the reference to a detention facility (*mišmār*), one of the two exceptional cases (cf. Lev. 24:11-12) of such use of prisons for offenders against the TORAH. There is an implicit reference in Num. 11:28.

Finally, Num. 15:37-41 instructs the Israelites to wear fringes on their garments as a reminder of Yahweh's commandments. This section was incorporated into early Jewish liturgy in the period of the second temple as part of the SHEMA prayer, a recitation composed entirely of Torah passages (Deut. 6:4-9; 11:13-21; and Num. 15:37-41; cf. M. AB. 2.3).

Num. 28–30 presents a calendar of appointed times for sacrificial offerings, which is clearly subsequent to Lev. 23, and dependent on it. Num. 28–30 incorporates interpolations already inserted in Lev. 23 (vss. 12-13, 18-20). In its original version, Lev. 23 refers only to an *'iššê* for each sacred occasion. Hebrew *'iššê* is a general term applied to burnt, altar offerings. Num. 28–30 adds the *tāmîdh* (daily offering), and prescribes an entire regimen of sacrifices including the holocaust, grain offering, libation, and a preparatory expiatory sacrifice (*ḥaṭṭā'th*) whose purpose was to rectify any offenses on the part of the priests that would have prevented their officiating on festivals and other sacred days. Rainey has pointed out that, in using such cultic texts for establishing the order of sacrifices in the public cult of ancient Israel, one must distinguish between the administrative order of listing materials allocated for sacrifices and the operative order in which they were presented as sacrifices. The operative order was: *ḥaṭṭā'th*, where required; holocaust, and its accompanying grain offerings and libations; and slain offering (*zebhaḥ*), where appropriate.

There are three remaining sections in Numbers which require comment. Num. 5:11-29 is a cultic ordeal for determining the innocence or guilt of a wife suspected of adultery (*see* ORDEAL, JUDICIAL [S]).

Num. 6:1-21 and 30:2-17 are codes reflecting the votive system of ancient Israel (cf. Lev. 27) and the institution of the NAZIRITE. The P tradition is concerned primarily with what the Nazirite devotes to the cult and with his purity. Num. 30:2-17 deals with the duties of a father vis-à-vis his daughter and a husband vis-à-vis his wife in fulfilling votive obligations undertaken by women.

Numbers is the least coherent of all the Torah books. Yet from a meager repository of early historiography and epic poetry, the P writers developed a full-blown portrayal of the wilderness period. In so doing they revived early notions of cult, social organization, and government, and focused attention on the central importance of the priests and Levites in Israelite life. For further discussion of the dates and *Sitz im Leben* of the P traditions, *see* PRIESTLY WRITERS[S].

Bibliography. Commentaries: M. Noth, *Numbers* (1968); N. H. Snaith, Leviticus and Numbers, *The Century Bible* (new ed., 1967).

Geographical data: Y. Aharoni *et al.*, *The Macmillan Bible Atlas* (1968).

Major studies on the contents of Numbers: B. A. Levine, *In the Presence of the Lord: A Study of Cult and Some Cultic Terms in Ancient Israel* (1974); J. Milgrom, *Studies in Levitical Terminology*, I (1970); R. de Vaux, *Histoire ancienne d'Israël*, I (1971); Y. Aharoni, "Arad: Its Inscriptions and Temples," *BA*, XXXI (1968), 2-32; W. F. Albright, *Yahweh and the Gods of Canaan* (1968), pp. 1-46, "The List of Levitic Cities," *Louis Ginzberg Jubilee Volume* (1945), pp. 49-73, and "The Oracles of Balaam," *JBL*, LXIII (1944), 207-33; A. Alt, *Kleine Schriften*, I (1953), 176-202; I. Caine, "Numbers, Book of," *Encyclopaedia Judaica*, XII (1971), 1249-54; F. M. Cross, *Canaanite Myth and Hebrew Epic* (1973), pp. 195-215; L. Geraty, "The Excavations at Tell Hesban, 1974," *American Schools of Oriental Research Newsletter*, no. 5 (November 1974), pp. 1-8; R. Giveon, *Les Bedouins Shosou des documents Égyptiens* (1971); N. Glueck, *The Other Side of the Jordan* (1940), pp. 114-57; M. Greenberg, "Levitical Cities," *Encyclopaedia Judaica*, XI (1971), 136-37 (see map); M. Haran, "The Uses of Incense in the Ancient Israelite Ritual," *VT*, X (1960), 113-29, and "The Priestly Image of the Tabernacle," *HUCA*,

XXXVI (1965), 191-226; Y. Kaufmann, *The Biblical Account of the Conquest of Palestine* (1953); B. Levine, "The Descriptive Tabernacle Texts of the Pentateuch," *JAOS,* LXXXV (1965), 307-18; J. Liver, "The Ransom of the Half Shekel," *Yehezkel Kaufmann Jubilee Volume,* (1960-61), pp. 54-67, Hebrew, English trans. in *HTR,* LVI (1963), 182-198, and "Korah, Dothan, and Abiram," *Scripta Hierosolymitana,* VIII (1961), 189-217; B. Mazar, "The Cities of the Priests and Levites," VTSup, VII (1960), 193-205; M. Noth, *Aufsätze zur biblischen Landes- und Altertumskunde,* ed. H. W. Wolff (1971), vol. I: 53-110, 183-209, 345-543; vol. II: 1-132, sections containing discussions relevant to Numbers; B. Porten, *Archives from Elephantine* (1968), pp. 29-35; A. F. Rainey, "The Order of Sacrifices in OT Ritual Texts," *Bibl.,* LI (1970), 485-98; B. Rothenberg, *Timna'* (1970); E. A. Speiser, "Unrecognized Dedication," *IEJ,* XIII (1963), 69-73, and "Background and Function of the Biblical *Nāśī',*" *CBQ,* XXV (1963), 111-17; J. P. Weinberg, "Das *Bēit 'Ābōt* im 6.-4. JH. v.u.Z.," *VT,* XXIII (1973), 400-414.

B. A. LEVINE

***NUZI. 1. New texts.** More than four fifths of the approximately five thousand Nuzi tablets recovered from excavations at Yoghlan Tepe (ancient Nuzi) and from the city of Kirkuk (ancient Arrapkha) have been published. New sites have also yielded tablets which from their provenance, form, script, and contents may be classified as Nuzi-type texts. Over 840 such tablets have been unearthed in the first two excavation campaigns (1967-69) at Tell al-Faḫḫār, which is located about nineteen miles SW of Nuzi. A study of the texts argues for an identification of this site with Kurrukhanni, mentioned in the Nuzi texts, rather than with the city of Arwe as first assumed. Two Nuzi-type texts were also found W of the Tigris at Tell er-Rimaḥ (ancient Karanā), located approximately 115 miles NW of Nuzi. The major portion of the over 250 texts which have been published during the last thirteen years relate to family law.

2. Bearing on the Bible. A re-evaluation of the importance and usefulness of the Nuzi material for biblical studies has begun (*see also* MARI[S] §8). It must be borne in mind that proponents of Nuzi parallels have admitted from the outset that often a certain disparity does exist between the Nuzi and biblical accounts. It is assumed that this disparity is due to distortion which resulted because the biblical redactor misunderstood ancient traditions. Arguments for re-evaluation of suggested parallels must thus be based either on the testing of previously advanced interpretations of the Nuzi data or on ascertaining the uniqueness of the Nuzi data within Mesopotamian sociolegal traditions. If an interpretation becomes untenable, the parallel can no longer be drawn. If, however, the interpretation is still valid, but the Nuzi data can be shown to be no longer uniquely Hurrian but rather reflect common Mesopotamian practice, the parallel is of less value in resolving historical and chronological issues of biblical inquiry.

Based upon re-examination of old evidence and upon data from recently published documents, a few previously advanced interpretations can no longer be maintained with any degree of certainty. One is the role of the Nuzi house gods as symbols of inheritance rights. It may be inferred from the texts that upon the death of the head of the household and the subsequent division among the heirs, each new household would normally make new house-god images. The ancestral images were usually bequeathed to the chief heir, although one text records their bequeathal to a secondary heir. Although it is clear that the house gods were symbols of the unity of the household and the integrity of its membership, there is no evidence that they also functioned as tokens of inheritance rights. Their only attested function specified in the texts is of a cultic nature.

Similarly, new evidence has weakened the assumption that in Nuzi a husband could have the concurrent status of brother by adopting his wife from her natural brother. It is clear from the texts that, presumably in the absence of the father, a brother assumed certain rights and obligations over an unmarried sister, including the right to assign her in marriage or in adoption with her consent. Through adoption into sistership, a brother could transfer his rights over an unmarried sister to another, who was then empowered to assign his newly acquired sister to a third party in marriage and receive her price. The evidence indicates that the rights and obligations of either the natural or adoptive brother terminated with the subsequent marriage of the sister to another party. Since the brother of a married woman no longer possessed legal rights over his sister, his sister's husband could not acquire such rights from him. One could argue that the concurrent status of husband and brother could be achieved by first adopting a sister and then marrying her. However there is no evidence that sistership adoptions entailed the granting of conjugal rights to the adoptive brother, and hence he did not *ipso facto* possess the right to marry his adopted sister himself. From all indications, the marrying of one's adopted sister would first necessitate the ceding of one's adoptive rights.

Lastly, it should also be noted that there is no new data to corroborate the thesis that at Nuzi the transfer of a pair of shoes was a symbolic act validating an irregular legal practice.

The attempt to delineate the uniqueness of Nuzi sociolegal traditions within the orbit of Mesopotamian civilization is hampered by the nature and extent of presently available source material. A major difficulty in defining any Mesopotamian sociolegal institution is due to the terse, static, and tenacious nature of the legal formulary of cuneiform contracts. In addition, the Nuzi texts constitute one of the rare private archives from Mesopotamia, especially distinguished in its quantitative representation of family law. Thus the discernment of distinctive characteristics of Nuzi sociolegal practice is impeded by the nature of the source material in general, and in particular by the lack of equal documentation from chronological periods and geographic sites other than Nuzi.

The customs of inheritance and concubinage may serve to illustrate this problem. In Nuzi, the "eldest" son was entitled to a double portion of the paternal estate. This practice is also attested in Middle Assyrian legal tradition. Although the laws of Hammurabi seem to reflect a tradition in which sons normally divided property in equal shares, some Old Babylonian private documents also refer to the additional share of the "eldest" son. A close examination of the Nuzi documentation reveals, however, that the term "eldest" does not refer to chronological priority, but rather it refers to legal primacy created by paternal decree. Such a definition is not as clearly evident from the scant documentation of the Old Babylonian and Middle Assyrian periods. *See* FIRSTBORN[S] §2.

Similarly, a custom of concubinage was practiced in Nuzi, whereby the childless wife provided her husband with a handmaiden to bear children in her stead. Such a custom is also cited in the laws of Hammurabi with reference to a priestess-wife. The contention that such concubinage was not applicable to other marriages is based on an argument from silence, and certain Old Babylonian documents may indeed reflect such general practice. Old Assyrian marriage contracts also record similar provisions of concubinage, although the nature of the relationship between the chief wife and the handmaiden's children cannot be presently ascertained for comparison with the Nuzi data.

Bibliography. For a comprehensive bibliog. of the Nuzi texts and related studies, consult M. Dietrich, O. Loretz, and W. Mayer, *Nuzi-Bibliographie* (1972).

Biblical studies utilizing Nuzi material include: M. Burrows, "The Complaint of Laban's Daughters," *JAOS*, LVII (1937), 259-76, and "The Ancient Oriental Background of Hebrew Levirate Marriage," *BASOR*, 77 (1940), 2-15; D. Daube and R. Yaron, "Jacob's Reception by Laban," *JSS*, I (1956), 60-62; A. E. Draffkorn, "Ilāni/Elohim," *JBL*, LXXVI (1957), 216-24, but cf. M. Greenberg, "Another Look at Rachel's Theft of the Teraphim," *JBL*, LXXXI (1962), 239-48; O. Eissfeldt, "Der Beutel der Lebendigen," *Berichte über die Verhandlungen der Sächsischen Akademie der Wissenschaften*, CV (1960); C. H. Gordon, "A New Akkadian Parallel to Deuteronomy 25:1-12," *JPOS*, XV (1935), 29-34, "Fratriarchy in the OT," *JBL*, LIV (1935), 223-31, and "The Patriarchal Narratives," *JNES*, XIII (1954), 56-59, but cf. J. van Seters, "The Problem of Childlessness in Near Eastern Law and the Patriarchs of Israel," *JBL*, LXXXVII (1968), 401-8, and "Jacob's Marriages and Ancient Near East" (sic), *HTR*, LXII (1969), 377-95; O. Loretz, "Ex 21,6; 22,8 und angebliche Nuzi-Parallelen," *Bibl.*, XLI (1960), 167-75; I. Mendelsohn, "The Conditional Sale into Slavery of Free-born Daughters in Nuzi and the Law of Ex. 21:7-11," *JAOS*, LV (1935), 190-95, and "On the Preferential Status of the Eldest Son," *BASOR*, 156 (1959), 38-40; S. Paul, "The Patriarchate in the Light of the Nuzi Documents," *Diné Israel*, II (1970), 23-28, Hebrew; E. A. Speiser, "The Wife-Sister Motif in the Patriarchal Narratives," *Biblical and Other Studies* (1963), pp. 15-28, but cf. A. Skaist, "The Authority of the Brother at Arrapha and Nuzi," *JAOS*, LXXXIX (1969), 10-17; R. de Vaux, "Les patriarches Hébreux et l'historie," *RB*, LXXII (1965), 5-28.

B. L. EICHLER

O

ODES OF SOLOMON. An early hymnbook, neither pre-Christian and Jewish nor late and Gnostic, which reflects the joyful thanksgivings of the early Jewish Christians and contains metaphorical language characteristic of the Dead Sea Scrolls and the Johannine literature.

The Odes, which were listed by Nicephorus and Pseudo-Athanasius and quoted by Lactantius and the author of the Pistis Sophia, were discovered by J. Rendell Harris in one of his Syriac MSS, now John Rylands Library Cod. Syr. 9. Subsequently Syriac MS B.M. Add. 14538 and Papyrus Bodmer XI were found to contain versions of the Odes.

1. Original language. Early arguments for a Greek original were undermined by recognition of the Semitic quality of the Odes, whereupon a Hebrew original was proposed. But there are impressive data to indicate that Syriac may itself be the original language. On the one hand, most of the reasons for a Greek original have lost their persuasiveness: occasional dependence upon the LXX, parallels with Gnostic literature, and the style of the extant Greek. On the other, the reasons against a Syriac original were suggested early in the century when Syriac was often denigrated and when some scholars anachronistically judged the Syriac poetry of the Odes according to the late classical norms of Ephraem. The most impressive argument for a Syriac original is the intrinsic quality of the Syriac: the play on words, some of which is possible only in Syriac (viz., 19:9), assonance, parallelisms, metrical scheme, and rhythm. Numerous variants between the Coptic, Greek, and Syriac are evidently explained by a Syriac *Urtext: maryâ* for *m^{e}raimâ* in 5:2 and 23:4, *brk* for *krk* in 22:6; and *raḥmâ* for *rûḥâ* in 25:8.

2. Date. Dating is difficult because the Odes neither quote nor are quoted in literature composed during the first two centuries; they do not refer to historical events; and they are defined by religious experience not dogma. The attempts to place them within the sect that composed the DSS have failed to convince specialists, since Christian elements permeate the hymns and are not merely redactional. They cannot be earlier than A.D. 30, and since significant parallels are not with patristic literature but with the Pseudepigrapha and especially the DSS, they are probably not later than A.D. 150. The impressive parallels with the sectarian scrolls and the apparently close but not dependent relationship with the Johannine literature suggest that the most probable date is A.D. 100. This date is supported by the Odes' joyfulness, strong Jewish nature (the term "Gentiles" is used negatively, 10:5; 23:15 [N]; 29:8), and primitive Christology.

3. Provenance. Affinities between the Odes and the Fourth Gospel (*see* John, Gospel of[S] §3) make either Ephesus or Antioch a likely place of origin. Either Antioch or Edessa is probable if the original language is Syriac. The Odes' relationship with the Johannine literature, parallels to the DSS, early date, and affinities with Ignatius support the hypothesis that the Odes were composed in or near Antioch.

4. OT. Although the odist never quoted the OT, he often borrowed a phrase or metaphor (cf. Ode 6 and Ezek. 47). Ode 41:9 seems dependent upon Prov. 8:22, and Odes 8:19; 16:12; and 22:9 are influenced respectively by Isa. 58:8; Gen. 2:2; and Ezek. 37:4-6. The odist's major dependence is upon the Psalms, which he probably knew in Hebrew and Greek. Odes 7:10 and 9:8-9 are based apparently upon the LXX of Psalms 50:3 [H 51:1] and 20:4 [H 21:3]. In at least two places he seems to have diverged from the LXX; Odes 5:8 and 29:10 follow the Hebrew, or Syriac, not the Greek of Psalms 21:11 and 1:4. As expected in a Christian hymnbook that rejoices in Christ's passion, the most influential psalm is the twenty-second (28:14=Ps. 22:16; 28:18=Ps. 22:18; 31:8-13=Ps. 22:16-18).

5. Dead Sea Scrolls. The Odes are strikingly parallel to many ideas and images in the DSS, especially the Hodayoth. The Odes contain a dualism similar to that developed in 1QS 3.13 ff., notably the paradigm opposing light and truth to darkness and perversity, with hypostatic creatures in polemical confrontation but subordinate to a creator. The Odes and the major sectarian scrolls contain a consciousness of being "the Way," the dwelling place of the holy ones which God has founded upon the rock, and God's planting for his glory. Likewise both employ "knowledge," "the war," "crown," "living water," and "the sun" as symbols. It is difficult to attribute all these similarities to a shared milieu within sectarian Judaism; perhaps the Odes were influenced by the ideas developed in the DSS.

6. NT. The NT is not quoted in the Odes, but it, or the traditions recorded therein, is evidently behind many of the poetic phrases. The traditions that praise Jesus' birth from a virgin, baptism, and walking on the water motivate the odist in Odes 19, 24, and 39 respectively. The Passion and Crucifixion are celebrated in Odes 8:5, 27; 28:9-20; 31:8-13; 42. The tradition behind Matt. 16:18 is reflected in Ode 22:12:

> And the foundation of everything is Thy rock.
> And upon it Thou hast built Thy kingdom,
> And it became the dwelling-place of the holy ones.

The most significant, striking, and numerous parallels are between the Odes and John. It is possible that both come from a community in western Syria that was characterized by a Word Christology, an emphasis upon love, and which expressed eternal life through the drinking of "living water."

7. Gnosticism. Few scholars would attribute the

Odes to the fully developed Gnostic systems of the second century, but many would place them within proto-GNOSTICISM. They seem to be a tributary to Gnosticism since their concept of knowledge is akin to the Qumran idea that God has made known his mysteries to an elect few who will enjoy a new covenant relationship (cf. 1QpHab 7 and 1QS 1.1-20 with Odes 8:8 ff. and 9:6 ff.).

8. Theology. The Odes' Christology is related to the concept of the Trinity (cf. 19:2; 23:22), but is not necessarily Docetic, as some scholars argue. Passages once considered Docetic are better seen as praises of Christ's pre-existence, virginal birth, and victorious death (e.g., 28:17-18), because the Odes do not deny that Christ has come in the flesh. The Docetism of the Acts of John (*see* JOHN, ACTS OF) is quite different.

The most prominent feature of the Odes is an expression of joy in the presence of eternal life and love. This salvation is achieved by Christ, through the Incarnation (7:1-6), Crucifixion (e.g., 42:1-2), descent into hell (e.g., 42:15-20), and Resurrection (e.g., 42:6-13). Note, e.g., the words attributed to Christ in 31:6-9, 12-13.

> Come forth, you who have been afflicted,
> And receive joy.
> And possess yourselves through grace,
> And take unto you immortal life.
> And they condemned me when I stood up,
> Me who had not been condemned.
> Then they divided my spoil,
> Though nothing was owed them. . . .
> And I bore their bitterness because of humility;
> That I might redeem my nation and instruct it.
> And that I might not nullify the promises to the patriarchs,
> To whom I was promised for the salvation of their offspring.

Bibliography. For the text, with trans., notes, and bibliog., J. H. Charlesworth, *The Odes of Solomon* (1973), whose versification has been followed here. Also, R. Harris and A. Mingana, *The Odes and Psalms of Solomon*, 2 vols. (1916, 1920).

J. H. CHARLESWORTH

***OFFERING FOR THE SAINTS.** A collection of money undertaken by the apostle Paul for the benefit of Christians in Jerusalem. Direct references to it appear in I Cor. 16:1; II Cor. 8:4; 9:1; and most fully in Rom. 15:26. Very probably Paul and the Jerusalem apostles agreed on the project during the meeting described in Gal. 2:1-10: "they would have us remember the poor" (vs. 10). Paul then communicated with his churches. His letter to the Corinthians is mentioned in I Cor. 5:9. Paul planned to revisit all his churches to promote the collection, supervise its reception, and arrange for its transfer to Jerusalem. At Ephesus he received a letter from the Corinthians indicating their willingness to participate. In response he directed them to set aside money weekly until his arrival (I Cor. 16:1-2). Paul was intending to travel N and W to Macedonia when Pentecost (late May?) was past, and thence S to Corinth in the fall (16:5-9). For reasons of safety and for symbolism the churches were to supply representatives to form a party which would carry the money to Jerusalem before winter (16:3-4).

Paul's plans, however, went awry. While he was still in Ephesus a crisis occurred in which he "despaired of life itself" (II Cor. 1:8). How long this "deadly peril" lasted Paul does not say, but eventually he made his way to Macedonia. There he intercepted Titus, who was returning with news of the Corinthians—good news except about the collection. Paul then wrote a letter (II Cor. 1–9) pleading with the Corinthians "to complete what a year ago you began not only to do but to desire" (8:10). They seem to have suspected that Paul was intending to divert some of the funds for his own expenses. Paul responded, "We intend that no one should blame us about this liberal gift which we are administering, for we aim at what is honorable" (8:20-21).

The next mention of the collection is in Romans. There Paul speaks of the imminent completion of the project, of his obligation to accompany the money to Jerusalem, and of his plans to leave his former area of mission to begin anew in Spain (15:24-28). He expressed apprehension about his safety in Jerusalem and even whether his "service for Jerusalem" would be "acceptable to the saints" (15:31). If, as some scholars think, II Cor. 10–13 was written in this period, Paul's final words to the Corinthians include a further protest about his honorable intentions (II Cor. 12:14-18).

At this point the evidence in the letters breaks off. Acts makes no direct reference to the project (24:17 is a mere hint). Acts does, however, preserve a list of names of men from various churches, traveling companions for Paul on his last and ultimately fatal visit to Jerusalem (20:4). These may have been the representatives carrying the collection according to Paul's original plan.

The collection had several purposes. (*a*) There was genuine need, perhaps a result of property sharing (Acts 4:34–5:11), famine (*see* CHRONOLOGY OF THE NT §B1*b*), or apocalyptic excitement (II Thess. 3:6-13). (*b*) The project gave Paul a concrete opportunity to respond to the Jerusalem apostles in gratitude for their entrusting him with the Gentile mission (Gal. 2:7-9). (*c*) It served as a thank offering from the Gentile churches for their share in the salvation originally given to Jewish Christianity (II Cor. 9:12; Rom. 15:27). The undertaking had no real antecedent, although alms and gifts for religious purposes were common. The Jewish temple tax (*see* TAX, TAXES) is the closest parallel.

Bibliography. K. F. Nickle, *The Collection,* SBT, XLVIII (1966); D. Georgi, *Die Geschichte der Kollekte des Paulus für Jerusalem,* Theologische Forschung, XXXVIII (1965).

J. C. HURD

***OMEN.** *See* DIVINATION; DIVINATION[S].

OMISSIONS OF THE SCRIBES. *See* QERE-KETHIBH [S] §3*b*.

***OMRI, KING.** *See* MEGIDDO[S]; HAZOR[S] §2*a, c, d.*

ORDEAL, JUDICIAL. Trial by ordeal is an appeal to divine judgment to decide otherwise insoluble cases that cannot be allowed to remain unresolved.

1. The nature of ordeals. An individual at law

is subjected to a physical test and is adjudged loser or winner on the basis of a bodily response. Such trials were used by all the great historical civilizations with the exception of ancient Egypt and China. They are purely Old World phenomena and are found in the Americas only in a few isolated and obviously borrowed instances.

There are many forms of trial by ordeal. The most common involve immersion in water, drinking or otherwise coming into contact with various potions, or ordeals by heat, in which the individual must retrieve a given object from a boiling liquid, or touch, lick, walk upon, or carry a red-hot object a given distance. There have been many explanations offered for the efficacy of such trials, and parallels have been drawn between them and modern physiological measuring devices such as the polygraph. Whatever scientific validity that these tests may (or may not) have, the common denominator among them and the rationale consistently offered by the practitioners is the belief in the supernatural character of the trial. The supernatural agent may be the element itself, or a god embodied in the element, or a more transcendent god, but in all cases there is some divine agent whose superior knowledge is being invoked to help solve the case.

2. Ordeal, divination, and oath. The supernatural character of trial by ordeal indicates its close affinity to two other well-known procedures for appealing to the supernatural: DIVINATION and oath. The three procedures may utilize the same natural elements and may as a consequence appear markedly similar, but they are distinguished from each other by the roles they play in the legal system, and the role played by the divine.

Divination and ordeal are both methods of invoking the special knowledge of the supernatural agent in order to decide upon a course of action. Divination, however, is used as a preliminary procedure to identify a suspect and provide a prima-facie case against him, whereas the ordeal is used to decide the guilt or innocence of the accused. The classic case of legal divination in the Bible, the story of Achan (Josh. 7:10-26), is a clear illustration of their different functions. Joshua has announced that the defeat at Ai was due to a crime committed by a member of Israel, and Achan is thereafter chosen by lots, one of the major forms of biblical divination. He does not stand guilty of the charge, however, and is not convicted or punished until after he has confessed. This is in clear distinction to the ordeal, which is used when there is no confession, and when the case cannot be decided in any other way.

An oath may also be used to resolve unsolvable cases. The defendant may take a "purgatory oath" in which he swears his innocence and is thereupon cleared by the court, on the assumption that he would be punished by the divine agent if he swears falsely. The chief difference between these oaths and the ordeal is the mode in which the divine enters the case. The ordeal sets up a specific test in which the divine manifests his verdict, revealing the individual undergoing trial to be innocent or guilty. The jurisdiction over the accused rests with the court, which almost invariably retains the right to pass sentence. The oath is fundamentally different: jurisdiction is transferred to the power in whose name the oath is sworn, and the court has no further power over the defendant. It can only adjourn the case to the higher court, which will ultimately pass judgment and sentence the wrongdoer. The oath cannot therefore be used when matters cannot be left in abeyance indefinitely, either because public feeling runs high or because the crime is considered intolerable by society at large. In such cases the ordeal will be imposed.

3. The biblical ordeal. ***a. Description.*** The one ordeal prescribed in the Bible is the trial of a woman whose husband accuses her of adultery. This ordeal, sometimes called the "ordeal of jealousy" or "ordeal of bitter waters," is prescribed in Numbers 5:11-31 (*see* WATER OF BITTERNESS). The procedure has two parts: the "jealousy offering" that the husband brings for his wife, and the drinking of the "bitter, curse-bearing waters" (vs. 18). The offering (one tenth of an ephah of flour) may be seen as a form of payment for the trial itself, in which the woman, upon solemn declaration of innocence, drinks a special potion composed of "holy water" and "dust that is on the floor of the tabernacle" (vs. 17) and into which a scroll bearing the legal curse has been immersed until the writing has dissolved (vs. 23). The innocence or guilt of the woman will then be determined by her physical reaction to the waters. If she is guilty "her belly will swell and her thigh will fall off," whereas if she is innocent no harm will befall her and "she will bear seed" (vss. 27, 28). The allusion may be to the sexual organs, which the waters will destroy if the woman is guilty, while leaving the innocent woman fertile.

b. The critical problem. Numbers 5:11-31 is not a homogeneous section, but is rather composed of two distinct literary strands. The portion is repetitive and disjunctive, with no way to tell which of the two strands was original. The major difference seems to be the order of events: one strand records the offering of the sacrifice before the drinking of the potion (vs. 16) and the other, afterward (vss. 24-26). The writing of the curse is only mentioned once, and for this reason some scholars have sought to distinguish between a phase of the ordeal in which there was simply an oral adjuration and a potion of water and dust, and another, perhaps later, phase in which the curse was dissolved in the water. These conjectures do not seem to have any substantive weight, and it is best to consider the ordeal as one procedure described in two originally separate literary strands.

c. The form of the ordeal. The form of the biblical ordeal presents a problem in comparative analysis. Biblical law is usually seen as arising out of, and in juxtaposition to, the great cuneiform legal tradition (*see* LAW IN THE OT §B and LAW IN THE OT[S]). We should therefore expect the biblical ordeal to be the same as the ordeal by river. In this ordeal, which is found in pre-Sargonic and classical Sumer, in Old Babylonian Elam, Esnunna and Mari, in Nuzi, Assyria, Babylonia, and among the Hittites, the accused plunges into the river and is acquitted if he or she successfully floats or navigates the river. The Bible may possibly be alluding to this practice in Isa. 43:2, although it seems more likely that this passage is an allusion to the crossing of the Red Sea. In either case, the only ordeal prescribed in Israel is one of drinking a potion, and we are therefore dealing with a different family of trials, that of the "poison" ordeal and, most specifically, a special subcategory of this ordeal, that of drinking specially prepared water.

In the "poison" ordeal, which should perhaps better be called a "potion ordeal," the individual drinks a medicinal concoction which may be (but is frequently not) actually poisonous. The medicine is considered a mystic reagent which will demonstrate the innocence or guilt of the individual by causing various physical reactions. The ordeal by special water is distinguished from the other potion ordeals in that there is no pharmacological agent. The water is rendered potent by ritual action which imparts to the water the power and attributes of the divine agent invoked. The closest parallel to the biblical ordeal is one prescribed in the Code of Vishnu. The accused must drink water in which the statues of the gods have been washed. The results are manifested in a few weeks.

The distribution of these potion ordeals is extremely limited. The "poison" ordeal was prominent in African tribal legal systems, where it was the most common form of ordeal. It is found in the Indian law books, and was practiced in Arab tribes, but does not seem to have been used elsewhere. The ordeal of drinking "sanctified" water is even rarer, although oaths are frequently accompanied by the drinking of sacred substances.

Judicial drinking may not have been totally unknown in the ancient Near East. We have one incomplete text from Mari (ARM X:9) in which several minor deities appear to be taking an oath before Ea, promising fealty to the city and ruler of Mari and drinking a potion of water mixed with dust and cornerstone (sic!) of the gate of Mari. The concept behind the potion is markedly similar to that in Num. 5, with the dust imparting the essence of the place to both potions. The legal nature of the act, however, is different, for the Mari text does not involve an ordeal. The gods swear by the water in much the same manner as the gods of Greece swear by the river Styx: Should the oath be false the power of the oath will ultimately catch up with those who take it and punish them. The one true potion ordeal in the Near East seems to be among the Hittites: "drinking the rhyton of the life of the god" (contra *ANET* [2nd ed.], p. 210 #18). There is no way of knowing what the potion consisted of, or any of the details of its use, but it does seem to be partially parallel to the biblical trial.

d. Practice. The only information that we have about the ordeal in early Israel is the passage from the book of Numbers. There are two major sources for the later use of the ordeal, the Mishna and Tosefta Soṭah, "the Errant woman," which contain specific and concrete information about the procedures and materials used. Although these sources are tannaitic, and thus compiled after the destruction of the temple and the abolition of the ordeal by Johanan ben Zakkai (M. Soṭ. 9.9), they record architectural details about cultic installations and specific locations within the temple bearing on the ordeal. The potion was drunk at the Nicanor (eastern) gates of the temple (M. Soṭ. 1.5). The officiating priest, who was chosen by lot (Tosef. Soṭ. 1.7), prepared the potion. Holy water was poured from the laver, and the dust was taken from underneath a slab, one cubit square, that was located within the sanctuary to the right of the entrance. The slab had a ring attached so that it could be lifted to get the dust (M. Soṭ. 2.2). Rather than have the priest go each time to open the scroll of the Law in order to copy the proper verses, the portion was inscribed on a golden tablet which hung on the far wall of the sanctuary visible from the ouside (Tosef. Soṭ. II.1). A golden tablet for this purpose is recorded elsewhere (M. Yoma III.10) as one of the gifts presented to the temple by Queen Helena, Queen Mother of Adiabene. Such architectural details appear to be authentic and indicate that the ordeal of the errant wife was considered a living legal procedure. The Mishna, however, records so many restrictions and prerequisites that, if the Mishna can be taken as an indication of second temple practice on this issue, ordeals must have been very rare. The situation would be analogous to that of capital punishment, which, although not only permitted but required by the Law, was imposed extremely rarely (M. Mak. 1.10). There are rabbinic accounts of an occurrence of the ordeal (M. Eduyot 5.6; T.B. Ber. 19a; J.T. Soṭ. 18a), but we cannot be certain about the precise circumstances.

e. Legend. The relationship of God to Israel is often seen as a marital union, with Israel frequently portrayed as a faithless wife. The Jewish tradition interprets the incident of the golden calf in this light, and Exod. 32:20, where Moses grinds the calf into powder, places it on water and makes the Israelites drink, is explained by the Talmud as an ordeal of Israel as an errant wife (T.B. 'A.Z. 44a). The biblical passage does seem to record a potion ordeal for the nation, and thus the analogy to the ordeal of the wife may be very early, and may be embedded in the prophetic images of the "cup" that Israel drinks. It is fully and explicitly developed in later Midrashic writings.

We would expect the pregnancy of the betrothed Mary to have given rise to speculations about an ordeal, and both the gospel of Pseudo-Matthew (XII) and the Protoevangelium of James (XVI) record variant legends of such a trial of Mary as a suspected adulteress.

Bibliography. In general: T. Frymer, "Studies on Trial by River Ordeal" (diss., Yale Univ., 1976).

"Poison" ordeal: T. Gaster, *Myth, Legend and Custom in the OT* (1969), pp. 280-300.

The biblical ordeal: H. Cohn, "Ordeal," *Encyclopaedia Judaica* (1971), XII, 1448-49; M. Weinfeld, "Ordeal of Jealousy," *Encyclopaedia Judaica,* XII, 1449-50; B. Stade, "Beitrage zur Pentateuchkritik," *ZAW,* XV (1895), 157-78; J. Hempel, "Die Israelitischen Anschauungen von Segen und Fluch im Lichte altorientalischen Parallelen," *ZDMG,* LXXIX (1925), 42-44; R. Press, "Das Ordal im alten Israel," *ZAW,* LI (1935), 122-26; J. Morgenstern, "Trial by Ordeal Among the Semites and in Ancient Israel," *Hebrew Union College Jubilee Volume* (1925), pp. 113-43.

T. S. FRYMER

P

***PALACE.** *See* Hazor[S]; Megiddo[S]; Beth-haccherem[S].

***PAPIAS.** *See* Apostolic Fathers[S] §8.

***PARABLE.** Redaction Criticism has greatly enhanced our understanding of how the individual evangelists used parables in their gospels, and linguistic and literary criticism have opened up new possibilities for appreciating the nature of the parable.

1. Redaction criticism and the NT parables. Three generalizations may be made. (i) The extensive modifications of the parables, in both context and wording, introduced by all three synoptic evangelists make it abundantly clear that the first question to be asked is not, "What did Jesus mean?" but, "What did the individual evangelist mean?" or even, "What does the present text mean?" (ii) Similarly, since all of the parables have passed through the alembic of the early church and particularly the individual evangelist, we become less sure of the interpretation of individual parables the farther back we attempt to go. (iii) While no one denies that Jesus spoke in parables or that the substance of much of the parabolic material in the gospels rests on the authentic Teaching of Jesus, we are far less certain today than we formerly were how much of it can be ascribed to Jesus or interpreted in the light of his teaching. Every successive retelling has introduced another layer over the original parable, so that, even in the case of authentic parables (and not all need to have originated with Jesus), it is difficult to separate the various layers of tradition and recover the original form. Redaction criticism makes us aware of the various layers and may, if practiced with sufficient patience, illuminate some of them, but it by no means leads infallibly to the teaching of the historical Jesus.

The role of redaction criticism in the study of the parables may be illustrated with reference to the so-called "hardening theory" of Mark (*see* Parable §4*b*). It can easily be shown that Matthew and Luke, who take over and modify Mark 4:10-12, do so for quite different purposes, none of which have much to do with the view that Jesus taught in parables in order not to be understood. Matthew's concern is clearly that the true disciple should understand (cf. Matt. 13:16-17, 19, 23, 51), a view that is probably implicit in Mark's source for ch. 4 (cf. Mark 4:33) but rejected by Mark himself (4:34). Luke, on the other hand, restricts the question about the "parables" (Mark) to the single parable of the sower (Luke 8:9); he notes that for the "others" (which?) something (unspecified—cf. Mark's "all things") is "in parables" (i.e., not understood, 8:10); and he puts the entire discussion in the context of the true hearing of the word of God (cf. Luke 8:15, 19-21). In addition, Mark does not really say that only the parables (which he sees as somehow obscure, as in apocalyptic) are given in order to harden human hearts; Jesus' words, acts, and indeed his entire ministry serve that purpose. Note "everything," not "everything I say" in Mark 4:11 and the insistence in vs. 34 that everything Jesus said—whether parabolic in form or not—was a "parable" needing explanation.

Finally, the statement in Mark 4:11-12 does not really say that parabolic speech in our sense was intended to prevent belief, but rather that the withholding of the "secret" (μυστήριον) of the kingdom of God was so intended. Even the pre-Markan tradition (from which the saying surely comes) cannot be understood as saying that Jesus used parables in order to be misunderstood; it says that Jesus' entire ministry is intended, in the purpose of God, to condemn those whose hearts have been hardened. Since this is not compatible with what we know of the teaching and intention of Jesus, and since for various technical reasons the statement cannot be retranslated into an Aramaic saying which can be plausibly ascribed to Jesus (Carlston), we must probably see Mark 4:11-12 as originating in connection with the theological problem created by Jewish rejection of the Christian message and elaborated in different ways in Mark's source and in our three Synoptic gospels.

Such multiple layers—in this case at least four—are behind most of the gospel parables, and any particular parable can be understood "historically" only in terms of its setting in each of these layers. So far as one is committed to "historical" questions, therefore, redaction criticism is indispensable for understanding the early history (and thus provenance) of any particular parable.

2. Linguistic and literary criticism. It is only possible here to make some generalizations about the various ways in which linguistic and literary criticism have shifted the emphasis of contemporary parabolic interpretation.

a) Neither a parable nor any other metaphor "says one thing and means another." A parable is a particular way of speaking, not a code, and what it means is what it says (Black).

b) Parables, like all metaphorical speech, rest to some extent on common cultural assumptions and experiences. The varying degrees to which those assumptions and experiences are shared thus results in varied apprehensions of a parable's nuances. Further, while some degree of nonmetaphorical interpretation may be desirable in individual cases, such interpretation shifts the kind of response evoked and thus the "meaning" of the parable.

c) "Historical" questions, as commonly asked in modern biblical studies, stand in constant danger of misunderstanding the text in any or all of the following ways: (i) by "atomizing" the text; (ii) by seeing the text only as a formal unit, subject to laws of transmission and historical forces (FORM CRITICISM); (iii) by interpreting the text as simply a modification of its sources (redaction criticism). What is lost in all three cases is the integrity of the text itself as well as its character as a text, i.e., as a particular statement with its own validity.

Structuralism, which specifically elaborates this last point in various ways, attempts to understand a text primarily in terms of its structure. Structuralism is concerned, not simply about the organization or movement of a text, but about its organic wholeness. It has devised a particular method of analysis in order to disassemble and then reassemble the text so that its inner unity may be understood. Many structuralists go even further, arguing that, while the possibilities of language are enormous, they are still finite, and seeking to determine the "deep structure" of the human psyche that seems to have imposed some kind of limited order on those possibilities. *See* LITERATURE, BIBLE AS[S] §4*a*.

It is by no means clear how the various new approaches to linguistic and literary criticism will develop, or how their varied forms will affect future interpretation of the parables. But many of their basic insights—if not always their specific methods and esoteric vocabularies—will surely become part of the tools of parabolic interpretation in the next generation.

Two other points must be noted. (i) Most practitioners of such newer methods understand their techniques as corrective supplements to other methods rather than substitutes for them. (ii) So far as Christian theological reflection rests on the method, speech, or action of Jesus, it must accept the fact that parables are a part of Jesus' ministry, but only a part. No sound critical method will allow us to attribute much more (or less) of the parabolic than of the nonparabolic materials of the gospels to Jesus. Insofar as the NT parables are parables of Jesus, they come from a context which included nonparabolic statements as well, and each kind of statement must be interpreted in the light of the other.

Bibliography. On OT parables: J. L. Crenshaw, "Wisdom," *OT Form Criticism,* Trinity University Monograph Series in Religion, II (1974), 225-64 (229-39 are on the Heb. *māšāl*). *See also* the brief arts. under "Gleichnis und Parabel," in *RGG,* II (3rd ed., 1958): C. M. Edsman, "Religionsgeschichtlich," cols. 1614-15, G. Fohrer, "Im AT," cols. 1615-16, and E. L. Dietrich, "Im Judentum," cols. 1616-17, each with an extensive bibliog.

On redaction criticism and the NT parables: C. E. Carlston, *The Parables of the Triple Tradition* (1975), with bibliog.; J. Gnilka, *Die Verstockung Israels: Isaias 6, 9-10 in der Theologie der Synoptiker,* StANT, III (1961).

On linguistic and literary criticism: E. Auerbach, *Mimesis: The Representation of Reality in Western Literature* (1946); M. Black, *Models and Metaphors: Studies in Language and Philosophy* (1962); J. D. Crossan, *In Parables: The Challenge of the Historical Jesus* (1973); R. W. Funk, *Language, Hermeneutic, and Word of God: The Problem of Language in the NT and Contemporary Theology* (1966); M. Lane, ed., *Introduction to Structuralism* (1970); E. Linnemann, *Parables of Jesus* (3rd ed., 1964); S. TeSelle, *Speaking in Parables: A Study in Metaphor and Theology* (1975); D. O. Via, Jr., *Kerygma and Comedy in the NT: A Structuralist Approach to Hermeneutic* (1975), and *The Parables: Their Literary and Existential Dimension* (1967); A. Wilder, *Early Christian Rhetoric: The Language of the Gospel* (1971). The journal *Semeia* (1973 ff.) is devoted to "the exploration of new and emergent areas and methods of biblical criticism" and contains much of the ongoing discussion in literary criticism and the NT.

C. E. CARLSTON

***PARACLETE.** This distinctively Johannine term does not occur in the LXX but is found in other Jewish writings contemporary with the NT. Outside the NT it most commonly means "advocate," "mediator," or "intercessor," one who appears in another's behalf. Such a meaning finds support in rabbinic sources and is appropriate in I John 2:1, where Christ's role as advocate before God the Father is clearly meant.

Because of the way in which the Paraclete's functions are described in the Fourth Gospel a number of translations have been proffered, e.g., "Comforter" (KJV), "Counselor" (RSV), as well as "Advocate" (NEB). None of the titles is entirely satisfactory, however, and it is doubtful that purely linguistic research will prove conclusive. Recently efforts have been made to understand the term on the basis of its conjectured historical background. The Mandaean figure of the "helper" and also the figure of the archangel Michael as described in Qumran texts have each been adduced as models (*see* MANDAEISM[S]; DEAD SEA SCROLLS[S]).

The safest course is to attempt to understand the Paraclete on the basis of the gospel itself. Clearly the Paraclete, the Spirit of truth (John 14:17; 15:26) or HOLY SPIRIT (14:26), is sent from the Father (14:16; 15:26) after the departure of Jesus (16:7) to be with his followers forever (14:16). He remains unknown to the world (14:17), but he teaches the disciples and reminds them of what Jesus has said, thus glorifying him (14:26; 16:14). He imparts truths from Jesus that the disciples could not have borne during his earthly ministry and declares things that are to come (16:12-15). He bears witness concerning Jesus (15:26) as the disciples who have been with him from the beginning bear witness (15:27). He confutes and exposes the world concerning sin, righteousness, and judgment (16:8-11). In fact, the Paraclete functions in the absence of Jesus' physical presence to make his guidance and power real among his followers. Thus with some reason he is called *another* Paraclete (14:16), having succeeded Jesus (I John 2:1).

The specificity of the gospel's description of the Paraclete's role conveys a sense of vivid, concrete reality. The figure of the Paraclete seems to be neither a mere object of hope nor a creation of the imagination, but rather the literary distillation of a living experience and discrete function within the community. Quite possibly the evangelist had in view a prophetic office exercised in the Christian church whereby the Paraclete became accessible to the community. In this connection it is significant that the seven letters of Rev. 2–3, in which the risen Jesus instructs the prophet (1:3, 10; 22:6-7, 9-10, 18-19) what to write to the churches (1:11), contain certain parallels to the Johannine Paraclete. Each letter is a word from the living Christ (1:17-19; described in various ways at the beginning of each letter: 2:1, 8, 12, 18; 3:7, 14), but also a word of the Spirit (2:7, etc.), so that Christ and Spirit merge, much as they do in the Johannine figure of the Paraclete. Although there are many differences between Revelation and the Fourth Gospel, their portrayals of the Spirit (Paraclete) are in some respects mutually supportive.

Bibliography. C. K. Barrett, "The Holy Spirit in the Fourth Gospel," *JTS,* I (1950), 1-15, esp. 7 ff.; O. Betz, *Der Paraklet,* AGJU, II (1963); J. Behm, "Παράκλητος," TDNT, V (1954 [ET 1967]), 800-814; H. Windisch, *The Spirit-Paraclete in the Fourth Gospel* (1927, 1933 [ET 1968]); G. Johnston, *The Spirit-Paraclete in the Gospel of John,* NTSMS, XII (1970).

D. M. Smith

PARENESIS pâr ĕ nē′ sĭs [Gr. παραίνεσις, advice; παραινέω, advise, exhort]. Commonly used as a technical term to refer to all general exhortations of an ethical or practical nature. Only the verb appears in the NT (Acts 27:9, 22). Elsewhere (e.g., Luke 3:18; Acts 2:40; 11:23) παρακαλέω (to exhort) is used in much the same way (*see* Exhortation in the NT[S]).

Parenesis is common in the literature of Stoicism and Hellenistic Judaism (Tobit, Pseudo-Phocylides, Testaments of the Twelve Patriarchs, Pirke Aboth) and also in the church fathers (Didache, I Clement, Barnabas, Hermas). In the NT, major portions of Paul's letters consist of parenesis (I Thess. 4–5; Gal. 5–6; I Cor. 6–7; Rom. 6, 12–15), whereas other epistles have it distributed throughout (Hebrews, I Peter) or are almost entirely parenetic (James).

NT parenesis ranges over various topics (e.g., love, Gal. 5:13-14; marriage, fidelity, and celibacy, I Cor. 7; interpersonal relationships, Rom. 12:19-21; 14:1–15:7; II Thess. 3:6-10; Heb. 12–13; I Pet. 5:1-5) and includes various ethical catalogues and station codes indicating how one ought to live in society (*see* Lists, Ethical; Lists, Ethical[S]). Parenetic materials are typically eclectic and loosely arranged, formulated with an eye not to specific situations but to what is universally applicable. Parenesis, therefore, provides information about the church and its traditions in general rather than about particular congregations being addressed.

Once the traditional nature of NT parenesis was recognized it became necessary to inquire about its origin. Those who have traced this to an early baptismal liturgy (Perdelwitz) or catechism (e.g., Seeberg, Selwyn) cannot fully explain why the same parenesis appears in such varied contexts within the NT. Moreover, these parenetic materials were undergoing constant development and change: e.g., the station code, not yet fully born in I Cor. 7:17-24, comes to full fruition in Col. 3:18–4:1, but is absorbed into a church-order regulation in I Timothy (*see* Lists, Ethical[S] §2*a,* esp. ii). Equally unsatisfactory is the view that the church developed its ethical teaching only when faced with a delay of the Parousia, and that it had then to draw on readily available Jewish and Hellenistic sources (Wendland, Dibelius). On the contrary, ethical as well as doctrinal material was part of the apostolic tradition from the beginning (*see* Exhortation in the NT[S]).

It is more realistic to regard the various elements of NT parenesis as due to various life settings: (*a*) the teaching and ministry (practice) of Jesus himself (I Cor. 7:10; 11:2-3; Jas. 2:7); (*b*) oral traditions formulated within the earliest church, setting forth the implications of Jesus' life and teaching for Christian faith and practice (I Thess. 4:1-2; Rom. 6:17; 16:17); (*c*) apostolic instructions called forth by the problems of specific congregations and conveyed with a sense of divine authority (I Cor. 7:40); (*d*) opinions or judgments offered in response to given circumstances (I Cor. 7:25-35).

See also Ethics in the NT; Ethics in the NT[S]; Cynics[S].

Bibliography. In addition to the bibliog. for Lists, Ethical[S] and Exhortation[S] *see:* A. Seeberg, *Der Katechismus der Urchristenheit* (1903); P. Wendland, *Anaximenes von Lampsakos,* Studien zur ältesten Geschichte der Rhetorik (1905); R. Perdelwitz, *Die Mysterienreligion und das Problem des I Pet.* (1911); M. Dibelius, *A Fresh Approach to the NT and Early Christian Literature* (1926 [ET 1936]), pp. 215-37, *From Tradition to Gospel* (1919 [ET 1934]), pp. 233-65, and *James,* rev. H. Greeven (1964 [ET, Hermeneia, 1976]), pp. 1-11; E. Selwyn, *The First Epistle of St. Peter* (1946); D. Bradley, "The Topos as a Form in the Pauline Paraenesis," *JBL,* LXXII (1953), 238-46; H. Thyen, *Der Stil der Jüdisch-Hellenistischen Homilie, FRLANT,* LXVII (1955); L. Nieder, *Die Motive der Religiös-sittlichen Paränese in den paulinischen Gemeindebriefen,* Münchener Theologische Studien, XII (1956); W. Schrage, *Die konkreten Einzelgeboten in der paulinischen Paränese* (1961), for bibliog.

D. Schroeder

PARONOMASIA. *See* Wordplay in the OT[S].

PASSION NARRATIVE. The title given those chapters of the gospels which depict the last days and hours of Jesus' life (Mark 14–15; Matt. 26–27; Luke 22–23; John 18–19). While there is ample testimony that the suffering and death of Jesus was the subject of early Christian preaching and confession (Acts 2:23, 36; 4:10; 5:30; 10:39; Rom. 8:32; I Cor. 1:23; 15:3) and was liturgically celebrated (Rom. 6:3-5; I Cor. 11:23-26; Phil. 2:6-11), the gospels contain the only extended narrative of these events.

1. Formation of the narratives. Different facts point to the formation of a narrative tradition older than the gospel accounts. While John and the Synoptics differ radically in their pictures of the public ministry of Jesus, there is remarkable convergence of the four evangelists in those sections of the passion narrative which follow the arrest of Jesus (Mark 14:43; Matt. 26:47; Luke 22:47; John 18:2). The second and third predictions of the Passion in the Synoptics begin with the "handing over" of Jesus (Mark 9:31; 10:33; Matt. 17:22; 20:18; Luke 9:44; 18:32), as does the tradition of Paul in I Cor. 11:23. A suggested development of the passion traditions would be: (*a*) a short kerygmatic account, much like I Cor. 11:23-26; (*b*) a longer account which began with the arrest of Jesus, recounted his appearance before religious and civil officials, and included the crucifixion and burial; (*c*) longer accounts to which incidents such as the Last Supper and Gethsemane were added; and (*d*) the gospel accounts.

Though previous critics tended to identify the longer account, (*c*), with the Markan account, recent work on the literary sources such as that of Taylor and the work of the form critics (Bultmann, Dibelius, Linnemann, *see bibliog.*) indicates clearly that Mark created his account out of existing traditions.

2. Characteristics of the accounts. *a. Mark.* The passion narrative occupies roughly twenty per cent of Mark. Mark's hand is especially evident in the temporal and topological notations which link the pericopes and give a structure to the account (14:1, 3, 12, 17, 26, 32, 42, 53, 72; 15:1, 16, 25, 33, 34). Mark writes from the viewpoint of the Easter faith; his passion theology is rooted in the paradox of faith. The Cross is salvation; the humiliation of Jesus is his exaltation; the way of discipleship is the way of suffering; a Gentile centurion confesses Jesus as the Son of God (15:39); he who dies, forsaken by God, is fulfilling the will of God (15:34; 14:36). The christological thrust is of prime importance. Throughout Mark's gospel Jesus conceals his identity by ordering silence (1:25, 34, 44; 3:12; 5:43; 7:36; 8:26) and by private teaching (4:10-12; 13:3-37), and his own disciples misunderstand the nature of his mission (8:32-33; 9:32; 10:35-45). This messianic secret (*see* SECRET, MESSIANIC) is unveiled in the Passion. In the Sanhedrin trial (14:53-65), in response to the question, "Are you the Christ, the Son of the Blessed [God]?" Jesus answers with the revelational formula "I am," and qualifies the SON OF GOD title by affirming that he is the SON OF MAN. In Mark, the Son of man is he who exercised authority on earth (2:10, 28), followed the way of suffering (8:31; 9:12, 31; 10:33, 45; 14:21, 41), and will be revealed in glory to his elect (8:38; 13:26; 14:62). By unveiling the secret in the TRIAL OF JESUS, Mark conveys to his readers that only those who follow Jesus on the way of the Cross will understand who he is. In place of the disciples who flee and deny Jesus during the Passion (14:50, 66-72), faithful women follow Jesus to the cross (15:40-41), and to them is given the news of the Resurrection (16:1-7). Therefore, in Mark, passion traditions become a passion theology. The reader is called on to affirm in faith that the lowly one is the Messiah, that the way of discipleship is the way of the Cross, and that the small band who wait in Galilee will be the temple "not made with hands" (14:58).

b. Matthew. Matthew's passion is to be viewed in the context of the whole gospel. Matthew writes a Jewish-Christian work which articulates a theology for a community in the process of separation from Judaism (*see* MATTHEW, GOSPEL OF §8). Jesus is the new Moses (*see* MOSES IN THE NT[S] §4) who teaches a new Torah (chs. 5–7) and is the founder of the new ecclesia or community of Israel (16:18). In the infancy narratives Matthew tells his readers that Jesus is the Christ, the scion of David (1:1), the fulfillment of prophetic hope (1:22), and the one to whom Gentile lords give homage (2:1-12).

The heightened christological status and the church as the new Israel influence Matthew's passion. In Matthew "Jesus" is not simply a name, but a title—he who will save the people from their sins (1:21). In contrast to Mark, Matthew introduces the major parts of the passion narrative with the title "Jesus." Matthew stresses Jesus' foreknowledge of events (26:2, 25). In the arrest Jesus exercises control over events. He addresses Judas as "friend" and only "then" (26:50) can the arrest occur. He has the power to summon angels to his aid, but does not because he is aware that scripture must be fulfilled (26:53, 54, 56). In the temple saying Jesus is the one who is able to destroy the temple (26:61), and the high priest ironically affirms Jesus' dignity by using the Christian form of confession, "the Christ, the Son of God" (26:63).

The trial before PILATE (27:11-26) achieves special significance since here the separation of the new and old Israel takes place. Prior to the trial Matthew inserts the story of the death of JUDAS (27:3-10). By throwing the "blood money" into the temple, Judas symbolically transfers the responsibility for Jesus' death back to the Jewish leaders. The intervention of Pilate's wife, while emphasizing the righteousness of Jesus (27:19), also anticipates the mission of the new Israel to the Gentiles (28:19). Matthew adds the explicit gesture by which Pilate disclaims responsibility and with the cry, "His blood be on us and on our children!" (27:25), shifts the blame for the death to the old Israel. Caution should be observed in interpreting this cry of the people apart from its historical context. This saying represents a secondary polemical motif of Matthew's theology in its struggle with Judaism after the destruction of the temple and should not be used as a historical indication of the attitude of the Jewish people at the time of the death of Jesus, nor as a prophecy for subsequent generations of Jewish people.

Matthew addresses his church with a picture of Jesus who goes to death as lordly master of his own fate, and whose death signals to the Christian of his time that he or she is a member of the new Israel.

c. Luke. While it is usually agreed that Matthew used Mark as a source for his passion account, the relation of Luke to Mark is problematic. Though the passion narratives in Mark and Luke are about the same length, only twenty-seven per cent of Mark's vocabulary appears in Luke, and Luke has thirty-four verses from his own tradition. Also, while in the body of the gospel Luke carefully follows the Markan order, in the passion narrative there is constant transposition and alteration of this order. These divergences raise the question as to whether Luke had a particular source (Proto-Luke), and, if so, whether he revised Mark in light of the source or reworked Mark into the content and order of his source (*see* SYNOPTIC PROBLEM §B3*c* and SYNOPTIC PROBLEM[S]). While there is no consensus on this subject, a definite Lukan theology does emerge in the passion narrative.

Luke is distinctive in not ascribing a directly salvific significance to the death of Jesus. He omits Mark 10:45 from the body of his gospel and the originality of 22:19*b*-20 (the redemptive aspect of the meal) is uncertain. Instead, Luke stresses Jesus as the paradigm of the innocent martyr. Pilate proclaims him innocent three times (23:4, 14, 22), as do Herod (23:15), one of the criminals at the cross (23:41), and the centurion (23:47). Another theme is that, in the Passion, Jesus achieves final victory over Satan. After the third temptation (4:13) Satan leaves "until an opportune time" but returns during the Passion, entering into Judas (22:3). He is ready to capture Peter (22:31), and the Passion is the assault of the power of darkness (22:53). However, Satan's attacks are futile, both against the disciples and against Jesus. Unlike the Markan portrayal, the disciples do not fail during the Passion, but are described as "those who have continued with me in my trials" (22:28). Luke does not have the prophecy of scandal (Mark 14:27); Jesus prays for Simon that his faith will not fail, even after the denial (22:32). The sleep of the disciples is excused (22:45-46), and Jesus is followed to his cross not only by faithful women but by "acquaintances" (23:49) from Galilee. The attacks against Jesus are also futile. At his arrest Jesus remains a healer (22:51); he teaches the disciples (22:35-38); he prophesies to the women of Jerusalem (23:28-31); and he offers salvation to the good thief (23:43). At the death agony Luke omits the cry of dereliction, and Jesus dies with words of filial trust, "Father, into thy hands I commit my spirit" (23:46). Jesus is the model for those who suffer innocently; just as suffering did not destroy Jesus, neither will it destroy those who follow him (cf. 21:13-14).

d. John. John's passion narrative is the shortest of the accounts (eighty-two vss.) and, while it has points of contact with the Synoptics, is not directly dependent on them (*see* JOHN, GOSPEL OF §C1; JOHN, GOSPEL OF[S] §1). The narrative is characterized by a doctrinal concern—the Christology; an apologetic concern—an intensified picture of the Jews as the agents of Jesus' death; and a dramatic concern—carefully constructed narratives such as the trial before Pilate (18:28–19:16). The theology of the passion narrative emerges not only from the narrative itself, but also from the farewell discourses (chs. 14–17), which function as an extended commentary on the Passion.

In John the harsher aspects of the sufferings of Jesus are softened (the scourging and mocking are reduced to two verses, 19:2-3). The Passion is therefore less a story of degradation than the triumphal return of the Word to the Father and the hour of glorification (17:1), as well as a prelude to the sending of the PARACLETE (15:18-26). Authority and majesty characterize Jesus in the Passion. At his arrest Jesus knows what is to befall him (18:4), and his captors fall before his majesty (18:6). He has the power to protect the disciples (18:8-9; cf. 17:12). His death is the willing acceptance of the cup his Father has given him (18:11). In the hearing before Jewish officials, in contrast to the silence or cryptic answers in the Synoptics, Jesus interrogates his captors (18:20-24). In the Pilate sequence Jesus confounds the powers of the world (19:10-11) and Pilate is reduced to the role of powerless questioner (18:38; 19:9). John sees the saving significance of the Passion in the victory Jesus achieves over the powers of the world (cf. 15:18-26), in the picture of Jesus as a model of love, the good shepherd who lays down his life (cf. 10:1-18), and in the fact that, when Jesus is lifted up, he will draw all men to himself (cf. 12:32; 8:28).

3. Conclusion. The passion narratives are not primarily history but theology of the history of the events surrounding the suffering and death of Jesus. Mark invites the reader to an act of faith in the paradox of the cross. Matthew calls for adoration and worship of the Lord who is master of his fate. Luke invites participation in and imitation of the suffering of the martyred Jesus. And John proclaims that we must celebrate the victory of one who, as a model of love, followed the Father's will to the end.

Bibliography. R. E. Brown, ABi, XXIXA (1970), contains massive bibliographies not only on John, but on Synoptics; R. Bultmann, *The History of the Synoptic Tradition* (3rd ed., 1958 [ET 1968]), esp. pp. 262-84; H. Conzelmann, "History and Theology in the Passion Narratives of the Synoptic Gospels," *Int.*, XXIV (1970), 178-97; M. Dibelius, *From Tradition to Gospel* (2nd ed., 1933); J. A. Fitzmyer, "Anti-Semitism and the Cry of 'All the People' (Mt 27:25)," *TS*, XXVI (1965), 667-71; E. Haenchen, "History and Interpretation in the Johannine Passion Narrative," *Int.*, XXIV (1970), 198-219; J. Jeremias, *The Eucharistic Words of Jesus* (3rd ed., 1960 [ET 1966]); X. Leon-Dufour, "Passion [Récits de la]," *DBSup*, VI (1960), cols. 1419-92, excellent on growth of passion traditions and relations between accounts; E. Linnemann, *Studien zur Passionsgeschichte*, *FRLANT*, CII (1970); M. Ramsey, *The Narratives of the Passion* (1962); G. Schneider, *Die Passion Jesu nach der drei älteren Evangelien* (1973); V. Taylor, *The Gospel According to St. Mark* (1965), pp. 644-67 for special studies on passion narrative, and *The Passion Narrative of St. Luke* (1972); A. Vanhoye, *Structure and Theology of the Accounts of the Passion in the Synoptic Gospels* (1967).

J. R. DONAHUE

***PATRIARCHS** [אבות, πατριαρχαι; Lat. *patriarchae*]. The Hebrew term אבות, "fathers," is somewhat ambiguous. It can mean the previous generations of the people, often used in a derogatory way by the prophets (Jer. 7:14, 22-26; 11:7-10; 16:10-13). It can also refer to the founders of the people, either to the first generation who came out of Egypt (Jer. 2:4-8; 11:3-5; Ezek. 20:1-8), or to the triad of ancestors, Abraham, Isaac, and Jacob. It is this last meaning of patriarchs corresponding to the modern usage which will be dealt with here. (On the wider usage in OT and NT *see* PATRIARCHS.)

1. The historicity of the patriarchs
   a. The patriarchs as nomads
   b. Personal names, peoples, and places
   c. The customs of the patriarchs
   d. Archaeology and the patriarchs
   e. The patriarchs in world events
   f. Conclusion

2. The tradition-history of the patriarchal stories
   a. The stories as oral tradition
   b. The religion of the patriarchs
   c. The patriarchs and the settlement
   d. Critique
3. The patriarchs in written sources

Bibliography

1. The historicity of the patriarchs. The notion that the patriarchal stories in Genesis reflect the second millennium B.C. has long been accepted as a tenet of OT scholarship, even though opinion varies greatly on the precise limits of their period within the Middle Bronze or Late Bronze Age. Over the past few decades many scholars have taken up the task of comparing new epigraphic and archaeological knowledge of the second millennium with the patriarchal stories. It is helpful to examine the nature and limits of some of these parallels. *See* PATRIARCHS §3*a*.

a. The patriarchs as nomads. To the casual reader of Genesis, the patriarchs, especially Abraham, appear to lead a nomadic way of life, grazing their flocks, living in tents, and moving from place to place. This picture has invited comparison with the sheep-breeding nomads (often called semi-nomads) mentioned in the second-millennium sources. The stories are thus believed to reflect an early presettlement phase of nomadic life carried on by the forefathers of the later Israelites.

Such a view, however, encounters many problems in the present stories. They tell of the patriarchs' possession of camels and tents, features more appropriate to the desert nomads of the first millennium. On the other hand, the patriarchs also possess cattle, animals belonging to a sedentary way of life. Isaac is pictured in Gen. 26:12 ff. as a successful farmer, the envy of the Philistines. Laban (Gen. 29–31) and Jacob (Gen. 37) are owners of large flocks; their families remain in one location while their sons take the sheep to distant pasturage. All the patriarchs have households of slaves and hired hands, but, except for Lot's brief stay with Abraham, there are no accompanying clansmen. It is for this reason that both Isaac and Jacob must obtain wives from the old homeland in Aram-naharaim. Even Abraham's movements do not reflect the nomadic seasonal change of pasture, but only an artificially constructed itinerary to tie the story units together. Thus, while the stories may reflect a rural and pastoral setting, they do not suggest a presettlement form of nomadic life. *See* NOMADISM[S].

b. Personal names, peoples, and places. It is often argued that the names of the patriarchs fit very well with those of West Semitic names in the second millennium. The names Abram (in the form *Abi-ram*) and Jacob (as a component in such names as *Ya'qub-ilu*) occur in both the early and late second millennium. Some of the names of the twelve tribes, such as Simeon, Ashur, and Benjamin, may also be attested. But the antiquity of a tribal name by itself counts for very little, since the tribes may antedate by many years the stories about their eponymous ancestors. And the nontribal, personal name Abi-ram also belongs to a name type common in the first millennium as well, as is evident in the very similar Phoenician name *Aḫi-ram.* The form ABRAHAM is not found in the second millennium and is best explained as an Aramaic dialectical variant of Abram.

The names TERAH, NAHOR, and SERUG in Abraham's genealogy are also cities in Upper Mesopotamia in the region of Haran, from which Abraham is said to have set out for Canaan. Of these cities, Nahor, Haran, and also Ur in southern Mesopotamia, are known from early second-millennium sources. But Terah and Serug, as well as the others, are found in inscriptions of the first millennium, and Ur *of the Chaldeans* and Haran in *Aram-naharaim* point, by these designations, directly to the great prominence these cities attained in the late Assyrian and Neo-Babylonian times (the eighth to sixth centuries B.C.). Likewise, the close relationship of the patriarchs to the sedentary northern ARAMEANS and the nomadic Arabs (*see* ARABIANS), with their accompanying genealogies (Gen. 22:20-24; 25:1-18), reflect the circumstances and importance of these two peoples in the mid-first millennium.

The terms for the indigenous inhabitants of Palestine (Amorite, Hittite, Canaanite, and Horite) all have their origins in the second millennium. But the way these terms are used does not fit the historical realities. Instead, they represent a tendency toward the use of archaisms common to many first-millennium sources. Thus in the late cuneiform texts the terms *Ḫatti* (Hittite) and *Amurru* (Amorite) were artificially applied to the population of Syria-Palestine as a whole. Similarly, the terms Canaanite and Horite seem to correspond to the Egyptian archaic terms for this region. The reference to PHILISTINES in Genesis has been widely recognized as anachronistic for any period prior to their coming to Palestine (*ca.* 1200 B.C.). *See* AMORITES[S]; HITTITES[S]; HURRIANS[S].

c. The customs of the patriarchs. Another argument for the antiquity of the patriarchal traditions has been the citing of parallels to the social customs of the second millennium. Recent studies have cast considerable doubt upon such parallels. First, a number of distinctive customs reconstructed from cuneiform sources never actually existed. Examples of these are the so-called *errebu* marriage, a special "wife-sister" marriage, and a use of the household gods (*teraphim*) as a claim to property rights. (*See* NUZI; NUZI[S]; MARI[S] §8.) Second, there has been a tendency to supply the stories of Genesis with missing elements to make the comparison complete. Thus parallels have been drawn to the Jacob story on the assumption that he was adopted by Laban, but nothing in the story itself warrants such an assumption. Third, parallels were often drawn to second-millennium sources while ignoring the extant first-millennium evidence for a given custom. In fact, there are no customs of the second millennium parallel to the Genesis stories which are not also attested from the first millennium. (For works on the current state of this debate *see bibliog.*)

d. Archaeology and the patriarchs. Some attempts have been made to associate the patriarchs with various archaeological periods in the second millennium but it is difficult to make any one period fit all the relevant stories. Some scholars have suggested MB I (2200-1900 B.C.) as a background for the "age of Abraham." They point to the evidence of an extensive settlement in Transjordan and in the Negeb, followed by a gap in occupation until the Iron Age. This would make only MB I suitable for such stories as the Sodom tradition (Gen. 14; 18–19). But a lack of urban settlement in this period would cause many difficulties for other stories. Others have associated the cultic installations at SHECHEM in MB II with the building of altars there by Abraham and Jacob. But the cultic interpretation of some of the architectural features is disputed and nothing points specifically to the patriarchal stories (*see* JOSHUA, BOOK OF[S] §5*d*). On the other hand, recent excavations at BEER-SHEBA have revealed that there was no settlement there before the Iron Age, even though the place name is closely associated with all three patriarchs. This fact alone would raise grave doubts about the use of archaeology in elucidating the background of the patriarchs.

e. The patriarchs in world events. Few patriarchal stories make any mention of the broader world events of the day. The story of Abraham's victory over the kings of the E in Gen. 14 is an exception, but opinions vary greatly on its historical value. The names of some of the persons and places seem quite enigmatic. The story seems to suggest that a great coalition of four world powers (Elam, Babylonia, Assyria, and the Hittites) conducted a campaign throughout Transjordan and the Negeb, explicitly for the purpose of punishing a group of rebellious kings in the region of the Dead Sea. These foreign invaders were in turn routed by Abraham and his 318 servants. Such a course of events, however, cannot be reconciled with our extensive knowledge of the political history of the second millennium. Neither Elam nor any other eastern or northern power had a foreign empire in Palestine or Transjordan in the second millennium. A coalition between these powers cannot be imagined, since they were enemies whenever there was any mutual contact. Finally, a campaign into this western region would have been totally pointless, for there was scarcely anything there at the time to warrant it. In fact it is more likely that the story reflects the knowledge of the domination of this region by the successive empires of Assyria, Babylonia, and Persia in the first millennium B.C.

Even the setting of the JOSEPH STORY in Egypt gives us no name of any pharaoh nor any other clue as to the time of the events. The Egyptian coloration in the story is more characteristic of the first millennium than any earlier period. Attempts to establish specific connections with such periods as the Hyksos rule of Egypt, first proposed by Josephus, fail for lack of any specific evidence. *See* HYKSOS[S].

f. Conclusion. The presence in the patriarchal stories of such features as camels and Philistines has been regarded in the past as an anachronism which "updated" the original stories. But these features would appear to be far more numerous than could be covered by such an explanation. They call into question the whole scholarly search for parallels with the second millennium and suggest instead that the traditions were largely molded by and for the social and religious community of a later date, including the period of the Exile.

2. The tradition-history of the patriarchal stories. Another approach to the patriarchal traditions, tradition-history, has recently attained widespread acceptance. *See* TRADITION CRITICISM, OT[S].

a. The stories as oral tradition. The method as applied to the patriarchal traditions arises out of Gunkel's commentary on Genesis in which he traced the origins of the various stories back to legends (*Sagen*) handed down and transformed by oral tradition (*see* TRADITION, ORAL[S]). Such legends were originally separate from one another and belonged to various life-settings and localities. Some were non-Israelite in origin but, in time, were adapted by Israelites to their own perspective. In identifying and describing the earliest legend form, the most important criterion for Gunkel was the presence of etiology in the stories (*see* ETIOLOGY[S] esp. §3; FORM CRITICISM, OT[S]). Most of the traditions were viewed as various kinds of etiology, reflecting a seminomadic or early settlement period of Israel's history (either native to the Israelites or taken over from the indigenous population).

b. The religion of the patriarchs. One of the earliest attempts to use Gunkel's analysis for religious history was by Alt. According to Alt, the OT consistently represents Yahweh as the God who was in covenant with the tribes of Israel as a whole when they were settled in the land. But such a religion would not reflect the earliest nomadic period of the patriarchal traditions which even the OT seems to recognize as religiously distinct from the later period (Exod. 3:13 ff.; 6:2-3). Alt identified two religious forms of worship in the tradition prior to Yahwism. One was the worship of EL in various local forms at the different sanctuaries throughout the land. This was the religion of the indigenous population. Each particular form of El, along with its cultic traditions, especially those having to do with sacred trees, pillars (*maṣṣeboth*), and altars, was tied to a specific cult center. The other form of religion was the "God of the fathers," which Alt reconstructed by analogy with the personal deities of Nabatean religion and which he regarded as reflecting the original cult of a nomadic community. Thus the patriarchs were regarded as individuals who founded their personal cults, i.e., the God of Abraham, the God of Isaac, and the God of Jacob, among nomadic peoples on the edge of the arable land of Palestine before the Israelite settlement. When these originally distinct cults entered the land with different clan groups, they became associated with a local sanctuary and merged their traditions with those of the El deity of the place. Eventually, by interaction among the various clans, the three cults of the patriarchs were combined by the fiction of genealogical connection, and thus resulted in the one God of the fathers: the God of Abraham, Isaac, and Jacob. *See* GOD, NAMES OF §C.

One consequence of this view was to assert the personal and individual identity of the patriarchs against the view that they were merely the personification of tribes. This would mean, in the case of Jacob, that the tribal and national use of the name is secondary to its original designation of an actual person. Another result of Alt's view has to do with the theme of the divine promises to the patriarchs, which are presented throughout Genesis as coming from the God of the fathers. Alt suggested that these promises originated in the promise of land made by the deity of the personal cult to the land-hungry nomads. *See* PROMISES TO THE PATRIARCHS[S].

c. The patriarchs and the settlement. Noth expanded upon Alt's thesis by making the themes of both the land promise and the promise of numerous progeny the primary focus of the early traditions of all three patriarchs. In distinction from Alt's view, however, the patriarchal tradition did not develop its unity separate from the other Pentateuchal traditions. Instead, the Jacob tradition, with its divine promises, first combined with the exodus-conquest traditions of the house of Joseph in such a way that the promise of land to Jacob was viewed as fulfilled in the Conquest (*see* YAHWIST[S] §3). Similarly, the combined Abraham-Isaac traditions with their promise themes were taken up by the tribes settling in the S. The total union of the patriarchal traditions expressed in the genealogical chain of Abraham, Isaac, and Jacob represents the latest stage in the development of the Pentateuchal tradition which came about only with an all-Israel confederation of tribes. Thus for Noth, the patriarchal traditions also reflect the complex history of Israel's settlement in the land. *See* CANAAN, CONQUEST AND SETTLEMENT OF[S].

d. Critique. In spite of the current popularity of this approach, a number of questions have arisen. First, the degree to which oral tradition lies behind the stories of Genesis has not yet been settled. Gunkel's primary criterion of etiology to identify the legend form has become very doubtful, but nothing else has adequately taken its place. This also means that Alt's use of cult etiologies as the means of explaining the attachment of traditions to certain places (*Ortsgebundenheit*) is greatly weakened. The fact that Beer-sheba, a prominent cult center in the patriarchal traditions (Gen. 21:22 ff.; 26:23-33; 46:1-4), did not come into existence until the Iron Age points up this same weakness. Also against Alt, the designation of a deity as the "god of [name]" does not exclude its being used of a high god like El or Yahweh, and it is not necessarily nomadic nor primitive; such usage is also common in later Israel. Furthermore, even Alt recognized that the form "God of the fathers" and the theme of promises scarcely have any trace in the oldest extant traditions but instead constitute the framework for the literary composition of the patriarchal tradition. Finally, against Noth's reconstruction, it remains unexplained how the house of Joseph, with its conquest tradition, is to be related to the Jacob group with different traditions of identity and land-claim. Between such groups one would naturally expect protracted conflict rather than an artificial rationalization of traditions and claims.

3. The patriarchs in written sources. The two concerns of historicity and tradition-history have largely overshadowed any interest in the stories of the patriarchs as literature. They have largely assumed the literary analysis of the PENTATEUCH established by J. Wellhausen, with the modification that the written sources originated in a basic body of fixed oral tradition. On this view the authors were reduced to editors and compilers of ancient lore. But a decline in these dominant methods could result in a revival of interest in the literary aspects of the stories. *See* LITERATURE, BIBLE AS[S].

Closely related to any literary reappraisal is the role of the written tradition in the life of the people. Recent studies have viewed the so-called Yahwistic source (J) of the Pentateuch, dated to the early monarchy, as using the themes of promises and covenant to Abraham to support the dynastic ideology of the monarchy (*see* YAHWIST[S]). But no text dealing with royal ideology makes any reference to Abraham. The role of the Abrahamic tradition and of the patriarchal promises as a means of expressing the community's identity and destiny are found, outside the Pentateuch, only in sources from the exilic period, and it is in fact to this period that the J source belongs. With the demise of the monarchy, its author skillfully transferred the royal covenant and ideology to Abraham, the father of the people, and so to the people as a whole. Thus comparisons must be made with J's contemporary, Deutero-Isaiah, in which the patriarchs symbolize the hope of a new day (Isa. 41:8-10; 51:1-2).

Bibliography. On arguments for a patriarchal age in the second millennium B.C.: J. Bright, *A History of Israel* (2nd ed., 1972); E. A. Speiser, *Genesis* (1964); R. de Vaux, *Histoire ancienne d'Israël* (1971), contains the best comprehensive treatment of all the arguments. Critical of arguments for historicity is the work of T. L. Thompson, *The Historicity of the Patriarchal Narratives* (1974).

On tradition-history: H. Gunkel, *The Legends of Genesis* (1901); A. Alt, "The God of the Fathers," *Essays on OT History and Religion* (1966), pp. 1-77; M. Noth, *A History of Pentateuchal Traditions* (1972).

On the dating of J: compare R. E. Clements, *Abraham and David* (1967); N. E. Wagner, "Abraham and David?" *Studies on the Ancient Palestinian World,* ed. J. W. Wevers and D. B. Redford (1972), pp. 117-40.

For my own fuller review of these questions see *Abraham in History and Tradition* (1975).

J. VAN SETERS

***PAUL, ACTS OF.** *See* APOCRYPHA, NT[S] §3.

***PAUL, APOCALYPSE OF.** *See* APOCRYPHA, NT[S] §§3, 4; NAG HAMMADI §4*a*ii.

***PAUL THE APOSTLE.** The influence of this extraordinary man, author of the earliest surviving Christian writings, continues unabated, and, in spite of all that has been written about him, new insights continue to appear.

1. The sources
   a. Paul and the computer
   b. Letter structure
   c. Paul's life from the letters
   d. Theological development?

2. Biography and theology
a. Apocalypticism
b. The death of the body
c. Christians and the law
Bibliography

1. The sources. ***a. Paul and the computer.*** Statistical treatment of vocabulary and syntax is an important technique for ascertaining authorship and is now made practical by the availability of the computer. The approach is still in its infancy; there are as yet relatively few workers, and not unexpectedly the results are uneven. Unfortunately, when applied to Paul this approach has two limitations. (1) Paul's letters, particularly the disputed ones (EPHESIANS, II THESSALONIANS, COLOSSIANS), are uncomfortably brief for statistical treatment. (2) To decide whether Paul or some unknown person probably wrote a given letter is considerably more difficult than to decide, for example, whether a particular Federalist paper is closer to the style of Madison or of Hamilton, each author known by a large body of undisputed text. This new technique supplements the standard tools of historical research, and, as it becomes more widely understood, its usefulness will rapidly increase.

b. Letter structure. Paul's letters are related to common Greek letters of the day in their salutation, greeting, and polite opening (*see* PAUL THE APOSTLE §A1*a*). But recent study indicates that the relationship is much richer and the common letter far more structured than had previously been supposed (*see* LETTER[S] §§4, 5). The study of other genres, e.g., homilies and benedictions, has revealed further structural parallels. Attention is also being given to internal patterns. One of the most interesting of these is Paul's use of CHIASMUS, i.e., a.b./b.a. (or even a.b.c.d. . . ./. . .d.c.b.a.) structures. In I Thess. 2:19-20, for example, appear "joy . . . crown . . . you . . . before our Lord Jesus/at his coming . . . you . . . glory . . . joy" (Greek word order), and there are many other examples. Paul had a habit of winding his way into a passage and then unwinding it so as to end where he began. One should not, however, try to press all Paul into this single mold. (For a.b.a. patterns *see* THESSALONIANS, FIRST LETTER TO THE[S]).

c. Paul's life from the letters. For Paul's life the letters are our "primary" historical sources and Acts is a later, "secondary" historical source (*see* PAUL THE APOSTLE §A1*b*). Increasingly it is recognized that the two different kinds of information gained from these two different types of sources should not be mingled. Courts of law in general admit only firsthand evidence; hearsay is rejected. The historian cannot afford to be as fussy and must use all the evidence. However, before the secondary evidence is admitted, as much information as possible must be squeezed from the primary sources. Otherwise the secondary material will dominate, precisely because it was written to be more helpful (cf. the supremacy of Acts in most "lives" of Paul).

The first problem posed by the letters, once one has dealt with their genuineness and integrity, is their original sequence. Their order in the NT canon is not chronological. Over the years a variety of sequences have occurred. At present the letters are arranged in order of descending length, first those to churches, then to individuals. When the letters are arranged according to data they themselves provide, and this sequence is integrated with the pattern of Paul's Jerusalem visits similarly derived (*see* CHRONOLOGY, PAULINE[S]; OFFERING FOR THE SAINTS[S]), the following outline of Paul's biography is possible.

Conversion (Gal. 1:15-16; I Cor. 15:8)
Sojourn in Arabia (Gal. 1:17)
Escape from Damascus (II Cor. 11:32-33)
First Jerusalem visit (Gal. 1:18-19)
Mission in Syria and Cilicia (Gal. 1:21)
Illness in Galatia? (Gal. 4:13-14)
Persecution in Philippi (Phil. 4:15; 1:5, 30)
Opposition in Thessalonica (Phil. 4:16; I Thess. 2:2)
Mission in Corinth (II Cor. 1:19; 10:14; 11:9)
II Thessalonians
Work in Illyricum? (Rom. 15:19) Elsewhere?
Stay in Athens (I Thess. 3:1-5)
I Thessalonians
Second Jerusalem visit—Apostolic Council and start of the collection journey (Gal. 2:1-10)
Previous Letter to Corinth (I Cor. 5:9)
Trouble in Antioch (Gal. 2:11-14)
Visit to Galatia (I Cor. 16:1)
Stay in Ephesus (I Cor. 16:8, 19)
Response letter from Corinth (I Cor. 7:1)
I Corinthians from Ephesus
News of trouble in Corinth (II Cor. 2:5-10)
"Painful" visit to Corinth (II Cor. 2:1)
Severe Letter to Corinth (II Cor. 2:3-4; 7:8-12)
"Affliction" (prison) in Ephesus (II Cor. 1:8-9)
Money from Philippi (Phil. 4:14-18)
Epaphroditus' illness (Phil. 2:25-30)
Philippians from an Ephesian prison
Release; trip to Troas (II Cor. 1:10; 2:12)
Meeting with Titus in Macedonia (II Cor. 2:13; 7:5-6)
Collection officials from Jerusalem (II Cor. 8:18-24)
II Corinthians 1–9 sent via Titus and officials
News of Judaizers in Galatia
Galatians
Romans; plans for Spain (Rom. 15:24, 28)
"False apostles" in Corinth (II Cor. 11:13)
II Corinthians 10–13
Last visit to Corinth (II Cor. 12:14; 13:1)
Third Jerusalem visit to deliver collection
Arrest and imprisonment
Colossians, Philemon (and *"Ephesians"*?)
(Transfer to Rome; execution)

Variations are, of course, possible. What is important is that the evidence come first from the letters.

d. Theological development? To give primacy to Paul's letters leads directly to a chronological view of his writing and raises the question whether one should look for theological change or development. Those who start with Acts date the letters late in Paul's career and in general do not allow development in that period of Paul's thought. But as more attention is given to the uniqueness of each individual letter—its historical occasion, content, and structure—the differences among the letters become clearer. How should we think of these differences? Some nineteenth-century writers cast Paul's thought in an evolutionary mold. Others think of Paul's letters as occasional expressions of a single theology. A better way lies between. Most would agree that at the level of personality, religious experience, and theological orientation it is the same Paul throughout the letters. But in the course of his ministry Paul interacted with events and sought theological explanations for them. These reactions came more from Paul's basic religious attitude than from the logic of his previous utterances (not that he was unaware of the latter). And as Paul confronted a particular issue, he added lines of argument and associations for key words to his intellectual equipment. One may reasonably expect to see the effect of such struggle in his subsequent writing. "Development" is perhaps not the best word if it invokes logical or biological images. The process was not the unfolding of a logically coherent system. Rather, we may attempt to trace how Paul learned from experience.

2. Biography and theology. Several exemplary ways in which Paul's biography and theology are related may be noted. ***a. Apocalypticism.*** Behind Paul's earliest letters lies his original, apocalyptic message. He taught that the "Lord Jesus Christ" would soon appear. His arrival (the PAROUSIA) will be preceded by a series of disasters: social anarchy, appearance of Satan's "man of lawlessness," opposition to all religion, delusion of the damned, and desecration of the Jerusalem temple. Then the Lord with his mighty angels will slay the man of lawlessness and all non-Christians (II Thess. 2:3-4, 8-10; 1:7-10). Christians, on the other hand, will enjoy "the presence of the Lord" in his kingdom (II Thess. 1:9; I Thess. 4:17). Battle with the forces of evil will continue until even death is destroyed (I Cor. 15:24-26). In the great judgment which will follow, Christians will serve as judges over the world and even over angels (I Cor. 6:2-3).

The message is similar to the SON OF MAN apocalypticism found, e.g., in Mark 8:38–9:1; 13:24-27, but with two key differences. The resurrection of Jesus meant to the early church (1) that Jesus was this expected Son of man, and (2) that the apocalyptic sequence which would end this age had actually begun. God himself had given the church the sign which Jesus had refused his hearers (Mark 8:12; Matt. 12:39).

The messianic age was clearly future and not present, for wickedness flourished unchecked outside the church. But the community looked toward the kingdom and tried to put some of its ways into practice. MARRIAGE would have no place in the kingdom (Mark 12:25). Therefore Paul had advocated asceticism both for the unmarried (I Cor. 7:8, 25-26, 38) and the married (I Cor. 7:5-6). Women enjoyed considerable freedom (e.g., to preach; I Cor. 11:5), since in the kingdom sexual differences would disappear (cf. Gal. 3:28; *see* WOMAN IN THE NT[S] §2). Within a few years, however, Christianity began the necessary process of adapting to changing times, and the apocalyptic fervor faded.

b. The death of the body. Paul had not anticipated that Christians would die before the Parousia. In I Thess. 4:13-18 he deals with the problem for the first time, making a simple pastoral statement. Just as Jesus had been raised prior to the general resurrection, so too Christians who die will be raised in time to enter the kingdom with their fellows. A similar statement must have been included in the "Previous Letter" to Corinth (cf. I Cor. 5:9). The Corinthians objected to the materialism of bodily resurrection. Paul responded with I Cor. 15, where he explained that at the Parousia fleshly bodies would be instantly transformed into spiritual bodies.

Then occurred Paul's "crisis in Asia." In a time of intense personal conflict Paul came to believe that the bond binding Christians to God through Christ was far more of a present reality than his apocalyptic mode of preaching expressed. He came to reflect on his present suffering and possible death, and on the humility, obedience, and death of Jesus (Phil. 2:5-11). He came to base his hope of resurrection on likeness to Christ (Phil. 3:7-11).

In Phil. 3:20-21 he still speaks of spiritual bodies as given at the Parousia, but II Cor. 1–9 shows a new approach. Instead of the instantaneous change he substituted a gradual transformation. As suffering erodes the flesh, spirit is granted in its place (II Cor. 3:18; 4:7–5:5). In a sense Paul "demythologized" his eschatology. Instead of using the apocalyptic model to describe the relation of the believer to God, he substituted analogies drawn from personal relationships: e.g., adoption as sons (Gal. 4:1-7; Rom. 8:14-17), manumission (Gal. 5:1; Rom. 6:16-23), and marriage (Rom. 7:1-6; II Cor. 11:2; Eph. 5:21-33). The end of the age receded into the indefinite future.

c. Christians and the Law. At the apostolic council the Jerusalem apostles decided that circumcision would not be required of Gentile converts (Gal. 2:1-10). Paul's trouble with Judaizers in Antioch (Gal. 2:11-14; cf. 2:3-5) indicates, however, that not all Jewish Christians were content with this decision. Nothing more is heard about the problem until Paul's imprisonment in Ephesus. There Paul, writing an otherwise loving and generous letter, warns against those who "preach Christ from envy and rivalry" (Phil. 1:15, 17) and who seek to "mutilate the flesh" (3:2). Shortly later we discover that the Jerusalem church has sent representatives ("apostles"; II Cor. 8:23 [RSV "messengers"]) to help administer the collection. It is hard to resist the conclusion that Paul's imprisonment had something to do with this outbreak of Jewish-Christian activity. News about Paul had probably reached Jerusalem. Leaders there may well have considered that their agreement to stay out of Paul's territory was therefore suspended.

With his release the Judaizing problem seemed to fade in Paul's mind, although he continued to think about the claim of the Mosaic law (II Cor. 3). Then, however, he heard the news from Galatia. Paul's response (Galatians) is so angry that it is easy to exaggerate the difficulties there. Because Paul considered these Judaizers his enemies does not mean that they presented themselves as his enemies. On the contrary, Paul seems to be fighting the suggestion that he also was a Jerusalem missionary (Gal. 1:11–2:14) who preached circumcision (5:11). They seem to have advocated circumcision for its symbolic and practical (avoidance of persecution; 5:11; 6:12) value. Paul had to insist that this partial observance of law necessitated the whole Law (5:3).

Paul felt so keenly the interference from Jerusalem that he decided to move to Spain. Yet out of his conflict over the Law he produced his greatest achievement, his doctrine of justification by faith. Here we see Paul's greatness.

Bibliography. G. Bornkamm, *Paul* (1969); C. H. Buck and G. Taylor, *St. Paul: A Study in the Development of His Thought* (1969); and C. H. Dodd, "The Mind of Paul: II," *NT Studies* (1953), pp. 83-128, on development; M. S. Enslin, *Reapproaching Paul* (1972); D. E. H. Whiteley, *The Theology of St. Paul* (1964); V. P. Furnish, *Theology and Ethics in Paul* (1968), and "Development in Paul's Thought," *JAAR*, XXXVIII (1970), 289-303, questions development; E. Käsemann, *Perspectives on Paul* (1969); W. Schmithals, *Paul and the Gnostics* (1965); R. Jewett, *Paul's Anthropological Terms*, AGJU, X (1971); A. Q. Morton and J. MacLeman, *Paul, the Man and the Myth* (1966), on computers; J. Bligh, *Galatians* (1969), on chiasmus.

J. C. Hurd

***PELLA OF THE DECAPOLIS.** The most notable feature of this ancient caravan city is an oval mound of ruins more than 400 yards long and about 100 feet high. At the S foot of the mound is a copious spring that was undoubtedly the most important reason for habitation at this spot for thousands of years. In addition, the site enjoys one of the most satisfactory climates to be found in the Jordan Valley; although the valley is hot during the summer, Pella's mean maximum temperature is lower than that of most other locations in the valley, and its particular situation on the lower slopes of the eroded Transjordanian plateau keeps it free of frost during the winter, an advantage over most locations on the valley floor proper.

Much information about Pella has been obtained in recent years as a result of excavations, soundings, the clearing of tombs, and occasional discoveries of seals and previously unknown coin-types from the site. Pella was probably occupied very early, though just how far back in prehistory has not yet been determined. Excavations have yielded Chalcolithic sherds that attest occupation by about 3400 B.C. In Canaanite times (MB and LB) Pella was a flourishing city. Many of the surrounding slopes were utilized for rich tombs, eleven of which were discovered in 1964 and two more in 1967. Some of Pella's pottery in those times was apparently imported from Cyprus and other E Mediterranean localities.

The 1958 and 1967 excavations showed that Pella was inhabited during the Iron I and Iron II periods (*ca.* 1200–600 B.C.). This evidence is particularly welcome, since the absence of historical references to Pella during these periods had previously prompted some scholars to suppose that Pella was not occupied throughout this time. The city took on fresh vigor in Hellenistic times, although the much later assumption by Stephen the Byzantine that Alexander the Great himself founded Pella cannot be substantiated. Pella was wrested from Ptolemaic control by the Seleucids in 218 B.C. and prospered as a commercial link between Arabia and the Mediterranean region. Jars from Rhodes are known to have been a part of the commerce that flowed through the city. Pella's capture by the Hasmonean king Alexander Janneus in 83-82 B.C. resulted in adversity for the inhabitants, but Josephus' statement that Pella was destroyed by Alexander must be regarded as an exaggeration. It was at this time, if not before, that Pella gained the reputation of being hostile to Jews.

Courtesy the Wooster Expedition to Pella © 1973

1. Female figurine found in a Christian tomb at Pella. Having pierced ears, a beak-like nose, outstretched arms, a prominent coiffure, and a long dress, it shows continuity with pre-Christian religious images from Transjordan and Syria.

Marching through the Jordan Valley in 63 B.C., the Roman general Pompey liberated Pella from Jewish control and may have organized the ten commercial cities bordering on Arab territory into the DECAPOLIS, a loose federation that was to last for several centuries. The Roman period seems, from archaeological remains, to have been one of increasing population and prosperity for Pella, made possible by the Roman government's improvement of roads and protection of trade routes. On Tell el Husn, a towering conical hill lying immediately S of Pella, a massive temple was constructed in Roman style, perhaps dedicated to an old local deity who by then had become identified with Jupiter. Pella began minting its own coins in A.D. 82-83, a practice that lasted intermittently until 219-220. Several tombs uncovered in the East Cemetery have contents that reflect the prosperity of the city. A small plain that extends W from the city became a popular place for wealthy Pellaeans to construct mausoleums. A forum may have been laid out in the little valley that lies between the city and Tell el Husn, an area that was embellished with colonnaded streets, an elegant two-story nymphaeum (fountain), and other structures in provincial Roman style. None of the present evidence, whether literary or archaeological, contravenes the tradition that Christians of the Jerusalem church fled to Pella on the eve of the first Jewish revolt (A.D. 66-70); indeed, some circumstantial evidence tends to support that tradition, although by no means demonstrating it conclusively.

During the Byzantine period the city expanded, most notably to the northwestern slopes of Tell el Husn. On the plain W of the city a large church was constructed above part of the existing cemetery. This West Church is thought by some to have been the cathedral of the city. Pella probably reached its greatest size in the fifth and sixth centuries. From the early seventh century onward the city declined. In 635 Islamic invaders fought a great battle with the Byzantine army in the Jordan Valley between Pella and Beth-shan and subsequently occupied Pella. The conquerors did not insist that all the inhabitants convert to Islam, and for several centuries thereafter the population was mixed Arab and non-Arab. Pella continued to be inhabited throughout the Middle Ages and was not totally abandoned until a few centuries ago. By that time its exact location had been forgotten in the West, and it was not until the mid-nineteenth century that the site, then in complete ruins, was rediscovered. *See* PELLA; DECAPOLIS.

Bibliography. R. H. Smith, ***Pella of the Decapolis, Vol. I: The 1967 Season of The College of Wooster Expedition to Pella*** (1973); R. W. Funk and H. N. Richardson, "The 1958 Sounding at Pella," *BA,* XXI (1958), 82-96; P. H. Williams, Jr., *American Schools of Oriental Research Newsletter* 4 (1964-65).

R. H. SMITH

***PENTATEUCH.** Source strata: *see* YAHWIST[S]; ELOHIST[S]; DEUTERONOMY[S]; PRIESTLY WRITERS[S]; J. Tigay, "An Empirical Basis for the Documentary Hypothesis," *JBL,* XCIV (1975), 329-42. Canonization: *see* CANON OF THE OT[S] §§1-2; contrast J. Sanders, *Torah and Canon* (1972), ch. I. Recent research: H. Cazelles, "Theological Bulletin on the Pentateuch," *BThB,* II, no. 1 (1972), 3-24.

***PENTECOST.** *See* HOLY SPIRIT §3*e*; TONGUES, GIFT OF §1; TONGUES, GIFT OF[S].

***PERGA.** Research at Perga has been continued in regular campaigns since 1967. The excavations at the city gate, by the nymphaeum, in the market place, and along the main streets have yielded rich architecture, well-preserved sculpture, and historically informative inscriptions. The search for the elusive temple of ARTEMIS Pergaia and the study of her cult image have also been continued.

1. The city gate. The main entrance to the city was on the S toward the sea and comprised two consecutive gateways at either end of a long plaza. The outer element, a passageway built into the fourth-century A.D. extension of the city walls, incorporated arched and columned façades erected during the reigns of HADRIAN (A.D. 117-138) and Septimius Severus (193-211). The inner Hellenistic gate consisted of two round towers flanking the entrance to a horseshoe-shaped courtyard which opened toward the center of the city. (*See* Fig. P2.) During the early second century A.D. a benefactress of the city, Plancia Magna, daughter of the governor of BITHYNIA, embellished this courtyard with statues of the principal divinities of the city (Apollo, Aphrodite, Hermes, Herakles, etc.), the legendary founders of Perga (Mopsos, Kalchas, and Machaon, among others), and the honorary founders (including Plancia Magna, her father, and her brother). Plancia Magna was also responsible for the tripartite arch at the open end of the courtyard. An inscription in bronze letters informs us that Plancia Magna dedicated the gateway to her "fatherland," apparently meaning Perga. Cuirassed male and draped female figures from the monument are identified by inscriptions as the divine TRAJAN, Hadrian, and other members of the Roman Imperial family. The tomb of Plancia Magna, who was both high priestess of the city goddess, Artemis, and of the cult of the emperor, is located just outside the gateway complex.

2. Nymphaeum. From the S gateway a broad avenue led northward to the city's acropolis. At the foot of the acropolis stood a monumental, U-shaped nymphaeum (fountain) which complemented the open horseshoe-shaped gateway at the opposite end of the avenue. Colonnaded wings held statues both of gods and emperors and

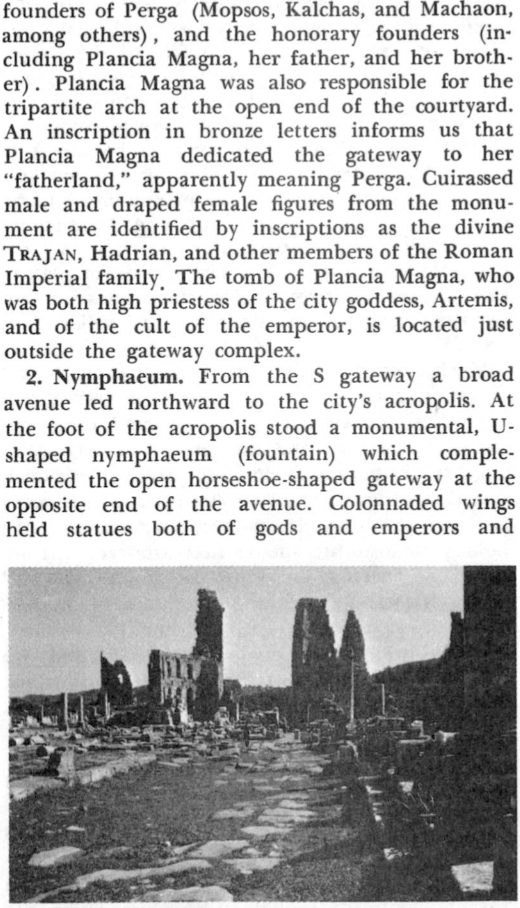

V. P. Furnish

2. The inner Hellenistic gate at Perga: view from the center of the city

Dionysiac reliefs. The fountain proper comprised three vaulted niches flanked by doorways. A pedestal in front supported a reclining statue representing the river god Cestrus. Since the Cestrus River provided easy communication and transport between the city and the sea, PAUL probably sailed the seven miles up this river to a landing E of Perga (Acts 13:13-14; 14:25). *See* Fig. P3.

V. P. Furnish

3. The nymphaeum at Perga, with the reclining statue of Cestrus

3. Market. The food market of Roman Perga was an open area well over two hundred feet square NE of the city gate. The square was enclosed by Corinthian porticoes behind which were lines of shops. Entrances to the square were located in the center of each side. In the middle of the open area stood a circular building bounded by sixteen Corinthian columns; it seems to have been the focus of the market's activities and may also have had some religious function. Sculptures representing Artemis, Attis, and a priest of the emperor cult have been recovered from the market area. During the Byzantine period the N entrance to the market was converted into a chapel.

4. Artemis Pergaia. The most renowned monument of ancient Perga, the temple of the city goddess, has still not been found. Ancient descriptions indicate that the temple of Artemis Pergaia was situated in a high place near the city and that it was outstanding in size, quality of workmanship, and beauty. At one point, the discovery of a Hellenistic Doric temple less than one mile S of Perga gave rise to hopes that Artemis' temple had finally been found, but none of the expected votives and inscriptions were discovered. Moreover, the famous temple should be either Ionic or Corinthian rather than Doric according to the representations of it on coins. We also know that at the end of the third century A.D. the statuary in the sanctuary of Artemis was destroyed by a band of Christians (martyred); therefore, the temple, too, may eventually have been leveled.

Representations of Artemis Pergaia have been found in various places within the city. Artemis Pergaia in her most primitive form was represented either as a squarish block of stone, perhaps a meteorite, or a rather formless wooden statue. The gold stripped from the goddess in 79 B.C. by the Roman governor Gaius Verres (Cicero, *Against Verres* II, I.xx.54, III.xxi.54, IV.xxxii.71) may have covered this primitive idol. The goddess was also represented in the manner of Artemis of EPHESUS, or even like a Greek Artemis with bow, quiver, the crescent moon, and stars. The celestial nature of Artemis Pergaia is indicated by a relief disc sculptured with a bust of the goddess surrounded by the twelve signs of the zodiac, and by an inscription referring to solar discs in the goddess' temple treasury. Perhaps the astronomical aspect of the cult is connected with the success of the third-century B.C. mathematician and astronomer Apollonius of Perga who, through his study of ellipses, came very close to a true understanding of the form and movement of the solar system.

5. The transformation of Artemis. The central avenue of Perga was lined with shops fronted with Ionic columns. One remaining column bears a relief representing Apollo in his chariot, and a second is carved with his virgin sister Artemis. During the Byzantine period a church was built into the shops behind these columns, but the images of Artemis and Apollo were not effaced. In the case of this Artemis, her representation with a halo-like crown and crescent must have made possible her identification with the Virgin, and Apollo in his chariot might easily have been taken for one of the prophets. In such a manner the transition of religious allegiance was facilitated in Perga.

Bibliography. A. M. Mansel, preliminary reports yearly in the journals *Belleten* (Türk Tarih Kurumu), *Türk Arkeoloji Dergisi, Anatolian Studies,* and through M. J. Mellink's "Archaeology in Asia Minor" in *AJA;* S. Onurkan, "Artemis Pergaia," *Istanbuler Mitteilungen* 19/20 (1969/1970), 289-98, pls. 55-58; H. Lauter, "Das hellenistische Südtor von Perge," *Bonner Jahrbücher,* CLXXII (1972), 1-11; A. Pekman, *History of Perge* (1973); J. İnan, "Neue Porträtstatuen aus Perge," *Mélanges Mansel* (1974), pp. 643-61, pls. 195-218.

D. BOYD

***PERGAMUM.** Recent work at Pergamum concerns the *heroon,* the sanctuary of Demeter, the "Red Hall," and the sanctuary of Asclepius (Asclepieum). One important result of this work has been the development of a fairly comprehensive picture of the wide range and varying degrees of religious experience in Pergamum.

1. Heroon. A building just outside the upper citadel has been recognized as a sanctuary dedicated to the cult of the heroized kings of Pergamum.

The sanctuary was centered on a colonnaded courtyard roughly sixty feet square. On the NE was a broad chamber where services related to the cult probably took place. Behind this chamber lay a smaller room characterized as a mausoleum by a podium set against the rear wall in the interior and by a high, columned attic on the exterior. ATTALUS I (241-197 B.C.), who defeated the marauding Galatians and was the first to take the title of King of Pergamum, and EUMENES II (197-159), who brought Pergamum to its height of power and cultural pre-eminence, received special honors here as semidivine heroes. Such reverence was a prelude to the divine status accorded the Roman emperors. TRAJAN, HADRIAN, and Caracalla were so honored in Roman Pergamum, and the presence of Rome represented by these cults made Pergamum in a sense "Satan's throne" for the early Christians (Rev. 2:12-13).

2. Demeter sanctuary. A cult in which the women of Pergamum, like those of CNIDUS, took a special interest was that of Demeter, whose Pergamene sanctuary lay on the S slopes of the acropolis. To the W, inside a long courtyard enclosed by colonnades, stood Demeter's temple and altar. These structures were originally dedicated by Philetairos (281-263 B.C.) and his brother Eumenes I (263-241) in honor of their mother, Boa. A bank of steps to one side between the temple and the gateway of the sanctuary probably served as a grandstand for participants in the mystery rites of Demeter, Kore, and Hades. Just outside the gateway and flanking the approach were a semicircular nymphaeum (fountain) and a stone-lined pit; here the worshipers, before entering the sanctuary, made their ablutions and deposited their offerings.

4. The "Red Hall." The large building to the S of Pergamum's acropolis derives its modern name, the "Red Hall," from the color of the bricks in its exposed core. At the time of its erection during the second century A.D., however, the building was veneered with colored marble. At one end of an approximately six-hundred-foot-long courtyard, underneath which the Selinus River was channeled, stood the monumental rectangular structure flanked by two tower-like buildings. On either side of the central structure and in front of the "towers," courts containing long pools were bounded by rows of columns sculpted with human figures in an Egyptian style. The Egyptianizing figures, the presence of numerous pools and basins throughout the complex, and the tripartite division of the architecture suggest that the building was a temple dedicated to the Egyptian trinity Serapis, ISIS, and Harpocrates, divinities popular in the Roman world.

The central rectangular building was entered through an enormous doorway on the W. The interior was lighted by means of five great windows on either side high above the marble floor. The E end, however, was left in semidarkness. In the center of the hall was a shallow basin beyond which a broad podium supported the base for the cult statue. A hole in the base gave entry to a subterranean tunnel through which the priests may have entered the cult statue in order to speak in the god's person. The Red Hall was used as a church during the Byzantine period.

5. Asclepieum. The cult of Asclepius was carried to Pergamum from Epidaurus in Greece during the fourth century B.C., and in time the sanctuary of Asclepius in Pergamum became the second most renowned health center in the ancient world. The Asclepieum, located on the outskirts of the city to the SW, was approached by a splendid avenue almost a mile long. Beyond the gateway to the sanctuary was a broad courtyard flanked by colonnades. Immediately to the right was a building used as library and cult center for the deified Roman emperors; farther on was a small open-air theater. To the left rose first the dome of the round temple of Zeus-Asclepius, built on the model of the Pantheon in Rome, and then the roof of the rosette-shaped "treatment center." A subterranean tunnel connected the "treatment center" with sacred wells and pools in the center of the courtyard. Cures were effected here through the physical means of baths and mud packs, diet and exercise, as well as through the use of psychological treatment in the form of dream analysis, isolation, and faith healing.

Also outside the city, burial tumuli and simple shrines have been investigated. The Hellenistic and Roman tumuli with internal chambers remind one in general concept of the much earlier tumuli in PHRYGIA. One of the sanctuaries outside the city was dedicated to the Phrygian goddess Cybele, who in various forms was much worshiped in Pergamum. The heart of this sanctuary was a small cave-like compartment with rock-cut niches and shelves for votives. Nearby stood a structure probably devoted to the worship of Mithras.

Bibliography. E. Boehringer, ed., *Altertümer von Pergamon,* vols. IX-XI (1937-68), and *Pergamenische Forschungen,* vols. I-II (1968, 1972). Current excavation reports may be found in *Neue deutsche Ausgrabungen im Mittelmeergebiet und im vorderen Orient* (1959), pp. 121-71, with extensive bibliography, and *Archäologischer Anzeiger* of the *Jahrbuch des deutschen archäologischen Instituts* (1966, 1970, 1973). Also, R. B. McShane, *The Foreign Policy of the Attalids of Pergamum* (1964); E. Ohlemutz, *Die Kulte und Heiligtümer der Götter in Pergamon* (2nd ed., 1968); R. Salditt-Trappmann, *Tempel der ägyptischen Götter in Griechenland und an der Westküste Kleinasiens* (1970); E. V. Hansen, *The Attalids of Pergamon* (2nd ed., 1971); W. Radt, *Guide to Pergamon* (1973).

D. BOYD

***PESHITTA.** *See* SYRIAC VERSIONS[S] §2*c*.

***PETER. 1. Peter in the Pauline Letters.** Significantly, the symbolic designation "Petros" or "Cephas," i.e., "Rock," which is not a known personal name, dominates in the NT over "Simon" (*see* PETER §1). While only Matt. 16:18 offers an explanation of the symbolic name (Simon is the rock on which Jesus founds the church), the tradition of the changed name is widely known. Paul, the most ancient Christian writer, never uses "Simon" but always refers to Cephas or Peter. Early usage is attested in Paul's description of his visit to "Cephas" at Jerusalem some three years after his conversion, when he *acquired information* (the verb ἱστορῆσαι in Gal. 1:18). The formula in I Cor. 15:5, which lists first an appearance to "Cephas," may be one of the oldest items of traditional information received (15:3) by the newly converted Saul-Paul. The similarity between the wording of that passage ("He was raised . . . he appeared to Cephas") and Luke 24:34 ("The Lord has risen indeed, and has appeared to Simon") suggests the possibility that the changing of the name is to be associated with the appearance of the risen Jesus to Simon. Matthew would then be plausible in relating the "rock" symbolism, not to Peter's character, but to his confession of faith and his role in the church; for both confessions of faith and assignment of "church-founding" missions are typical of postresurrection appearances.

Also significant is the frequent reference to Cephas in Galatians. Although Paul characterizes Peter's ministry as being to the circumcised (2:7), he assumes that Peter is an authority well known to this Gentile congregation. Thus, even when a community was evangelized by a noneyewitness of Jesus' ministry (e.g., Paul), information about Cephas was part of the Christian heritage. True, Paul is sarcastic about "those who were reputed to be something," the so-called "pillars" (2:6, 9); but that reference grudgingly implies how well established the repute was. And Paul cites as a paradigm for his own apostolate to the uncircumcised the apostolate of Peter (2:7-8), which seemingly was accepted as a fact by all, even by Galatian Gentiles who had not been evangelized by Peter and by those who questioned Paul's apostolate. Paul felt free to oppose Cephas (2:11); but his letter boasting of this, when read between the lines, tells us much about the fame of Peter in the 50s.

In the Corinthian community there is a Cephas faction (I Cor. 1:12). Had Cephas visited Corinth in the 50s (a plausible implication of 9:5)? If so, his ministry was more widespread than we might have judged from the mission to the circumcised allowed by Paul in Gal. 2:7. If not, the existence of a Cephas faction is all the more indicative of his importance and authority. That there were Apollos and Paul factions at Corinth is intelligible, since these men had preached there; that there was a Christ faction is also intelligible. But why a Cephas faction if he had not been there? Had he sent missionaries? Or was the name of the first among the Twelve so widespread that even those who had no personal contact with him would adhere to him in opposition to factions loyal to local missionaries? That Cephas or his emissaries might be the "superlative apostles" attacked by Paul in II Cor. 11:4-5 for preaching another gospel is unlikely in the light of I Cor. 15:11, where Paul joins himself to Cephas as a fellow preacher of the same kerygma.

2. Peter in Mark. MARK is the earliest gospel (the 60s?) and the only one that may have been written during or just after Peter's lifetime; yet it gives the least exalted gospel picture of Peter. While he is depicted as the most prominent among the Twelve, his confession of Jesus as the Messiah receives no real acceptance; rather Jesus accuses him of being on the side of men rather than of God (8:27-33). Though at the Transfiguration Peter is the spokesman for the special three disciples (*see* PETER §4), Mark points out his lack of understanding (9:2-13). Peter's denials are dramatically reported, even to the point that he may have cursed Jesus, if that is the meaning of 14:71. In Gethsemane (14:37) Jesus singles Peter out, rebuking him for failing to stay awake and watch. Only one passage unique to Mark can be interpreted as giving Peter a special honor, namely, the instruction at the empty tomb (16:7): "Go, tell his disciples *and Peter* that he is going before you to Galilee; there you will see him"—perhaps an echo of the tradition that the first appearance of the risen Jesus was to Peter. It is exaggerated to claim that Mark regarded Peter as an adversary. Rather, in Mark the incipient stages of Peter's faith and his failures during the ministry of Jesus have not yet been heavily overlaid by the memory of his subsequent apostolic career. In the later gospels Peter fares much better, so that it is clear that his image among Christians continued to grow after his death, and in some communities more than in others.

3. Peter in Matthew. Here Peter is made a spokesman in scenes that Mark or Q attributed to the disciples (cf. Matt. 15:15 and Mark 7:17; Matt. 18:21-22 and Luke 17:4), so that Peter initiates the occasion for having Jesus explain things to his disciples. Similarly, in 17:24-27 Peter is deeply involved in drawing forth Jesus' solution to a tax problem faced by his disciples. For MATTHEW, then, Peter emerges as an intermediary through whom Jesus teaches the church. At Caesarea Philippi (16:13-20) Peter confesses Jesus not only as the Messiah but also as the Son of the living God, and this insight does not originate with flesh and blood but is a special revelation from God. Jesus now reacts positively, designating Peter as the rock on which he will found the church. The Matthean language here is similar to that of Paul when he describes his experience of the risen Jesus in terms of a revelation from God which was not through flesh and blood (Gal. 1:12-16). Granted the common opinion that the Matthean Caesarea scene is composite (*see* PETER §5), this parallelism in terminology favors the hypothesis that Matthew has enlarged Mark's more negative scene by interpolating elements from a postresurrection scene where Jesus appeared to Simon, who made a confession of faith, was given a special apostolic role, and had his name changed to rock (*see* §1 *above*). Thus the rock on which the church is built is the Peter who had postresurrection faith. Matthew was written in the subapostolic period of the last third of the century when the metaphor of the apostles as a foundation was popular (Eph. 2:20; Rev. 21:14), and so Peter as the most prominent of the Twelve is pictured as the foundation par excellence. The power of binding and loosing (excommunicating? making doctrinal decisions?) is another image assigned both to Peter and to the other disciples (Matt. 18:18; John 20:23), but the image of the keeper of the keys is related to Peter alone (Matt. 16:19). Some would derive this image from Isa. 22:15-22 and the description of the prime minister in the Davidic kingdom of Judah. In any case, it seems that Peter has a type of ecclesiastical priority in the outlook of Matthew.

4. Peter in Luke-Acts. Although drawing upon Mark, LUKE omits many Markan details unfavorable to Peter; e.g., there is no rebuke of Peter's messianic misunderstanding (9:20-22), no special rebuke of Peter's sleepiness in Gethsemane, and a milder presentation of Peter's denials. In this last context, Jesus prays that Simon's faith will not fail despite Satan's testing and that, when he has turned, he will strengthen his brethren (22:31-32). Some would detect here an earlier tradition in which Peter did not deny Jesus (a theory that treats "when you have turned again" as a gloss), but more likely Luke is preparing for the role to be attributed to Peter in ACTS as a spokesman of and sufferer for the gospel. Luke 5:1-11 introduces into the Markan scene of the call of the disciples a miraculous catch of fish and specifies that Jesus said to Simon (not to the group, as in Mark 1:17-18): "Henceforth you will be catching men." This too seems to prepare for the career of Peter in Acts, where he is the most active missionary among the Twelve and takes the lead in the acceptance of a Gentile into the Christian community (*see* PETER §7).

Christians have long and acrimoniously debated the relative importance of Peter, JAMES, and PAUL as reconstructed from Acts 1–15 and the Pauline letters (*see* PETER §9), debates influenced by the claim of the Bishop of Rome to be the successor of Peter in jurisdiction over the whole church. It is important not to read later problems into the biblical accounts and to recognize the possibility of contemporaneous and different roles for these men. The Twelve are never described by Luke as local church administrators despite later traditions making them bishops. Acts 6:2 is a rejection by the Twelve of administrative tasks necessitated by the development of a community large and enduring enough to warrant established structure. Drawing upon the information that the DEAD SEA SCROLL sectarians celebrated "Weeks" or Pentecost as a feast of covenant renewal, we may suspect that the post-Pentecostal Christian community first saw itself as a renewed Israel living in the brief time of repentance allotted until God should send Jesus, the appointed Messiah (Acts 3:19-20). In this period when little structure was required, the Twelve served as leaders; their role, however, was not permanent but eschatological. They were not to be replaced after death, for their destiny was to eat and drink with Jesus in his kingdom and to sit on thrones judging the tribes of Israel (Luke 22:30). When duration, numbers, and diversity eventually necessitated structured administration for the Jerusalem community, that role fell to men other than the Twelve. Acts 6 describes how the Seven were appointed as administrators among the Hellenist Christians; simultaneously James and the elders may have become administrators for the Hebrew Christians (11:30; 12:17; 15:6, 13, 22; 21:18). Thus, James would not have been the successor of Peter as "bishop" of Jerusalem or as "pope" of the church (both ideas anachronistic for this early period). Rather, Peter was first among the Twelve (as in all the lists and specifically in Matt. 10:2), while James, the brother of the Lord, was the first administrative leader of the mother church at Jerusalem—a function later designated as a bishopric.

Variant analyses have been offered for Acts 15. It is possibly a composite scene, with only 15:1-12 representing the same meeting described in Gal. 2:1-10. Peter, Paul, and James (and John) would then all have agreed on the decision to admit Gentiles without their becoming Jews—a decision touching the very nature of Christianity and affecting all, including the Twelve, missionary apostles, and local church leaders. But, as obvious in Gal. 2:11 ff., this decision did not determine the way that Jews and Gentiles would interrelate once Gentiles had been admitted. Paul resisted any demand that Gentiles conform to Jewish sensibilities, seeing it as an infringement on gospel freedom; Peter wavered, perhaps because he may have seen it only as a question of how to keep peace, rather than a gospel issue. If Acts 15:13 ff. is interpreted as a second Jerusalem meeting (with Paul absent) provoked by the kind of problem raised at Antioch and described in Gal. 2:11-13, James was intervening as administrator and pastor of Jerusalem and of neighboring communities with a large Jewish-Christian population, evangelized from Jerusalem. His intervention forced Gentiles *in this area* to observe the better-known Jewish practices in order to avoid scandal (15:19-21). Paul, on the other hand, did not impose similar observances in the churches he had founded (I Cor. 8). Such a reconstruction is hypothetical, but it illustrates the possibility of seeing Peter, Paul, and James as having different kinds of authority and areas of influence, as distinct from a solution involving their succession to or displacement of one another in leadership.

5. Peter in John. Simon Peter remains the most prominent of the identified disciples; and he features in scenes not recorded in the synoptic tradition, e.g., with Andrew in the Jordan valley (1:40-42); at the washing of the feet (13:6-11). But the evangelist's greater concern is to show the prominence of the unidentified BELOVED DISCIPLE who is the source of the community's tradition. In the section of JOHN directed to Jesus' "own" (chs. 13 ff.), at the major scenes, namely, the LAST SUPPER, the Jewish interrogation of Jesus, the CRUCIFIXION, the empty tomb, and the postresurrection appearance, this disciple, precisely as the disciple whom Jesus loves, appears in a more sympathetic and perceptive role than does Simon Peter. He is closer to Jesus, does not desert him, perceives the significance of the tomb for faith, and is the first to recognize the risen Jesus. The Johannine community may not have derived its somewhat different traditions about Jesus from a "name" apostolic source, but it insists that its source was an authentic eyewitness (19:35), even closer to Jesus than the best known of the Twelve. In 21:15-23 the comparison comes to a head. As foreseen by Jesus, Peter has glorified God by dying a martyr's death and is thus par excellence a witness (μάρτυς=martyr, witness) in the following of Jesus (21:18-19). A similar death was not willed by Jesus for the beloved disciple (in fact, some mistakenly did not expect him to die at all); yet he remains a μάρτυς (21:24) since his career was also foreseen by Jesus (21:22). In consistently setting these two figures side by side, John is not really disparaging or demeaning Peter. Indeed, in ch. 21 (written by a redactor?) Peter remains the great fisherman, bringing to shore an amazing catch of fish made with Jesus' help, as well as a shepherd who loves Jesus and is entrusted with caring for Jesus' sheep—a church-directed role with some resemblance to that given Peter in Matt. 16:18 and Luke 22:32.

6. Images of Peter. We know little of Peter's historical career after A.D. 50 and the meeting at Jerusalem. The tradition that he ultimately went to Rome, was martyred and buried there in the 60s, is solid, as attested by the trophy that 150 years later stood in his honor on Vatican Hill (*see* PETER §11). Whether that trophy marks his actual grave is uncertain, despite Pope Paul VI's acceptance (1968) of the archaeological opinion that Peter's bones had been found. A key to Peter's subsequent importance for Christians may lie in the shift of imagery from fisherman to shepherd in John 21. When they died, the great apostles (not only the Twelve) were idealized as models for meeting the needs of church life (*see* §1 *above* for the tendency to describe them as the foundations of the church). Just as in the PASTORAL LETTERS (80s or 90s?) Paul the missionary becomes a pastor worrying about structure in the churches that grew from his mission, so also in the Petrine letters Peter, once a fisherman-missionary, is portrayed as a shepherd-pastor with the care of established flocks as a primary concern. In I Pet. 5:1 he is depicted as a presbyter establishing ideals for the presbyter-bishops of the last third of the century. In II Pet. 1:16-21 his participation at the Transfiguration and the direct revelation he received from God enable him to correct new myths and pseudo-prophecies that are emerging in the early second century. This image of authentic apostolic teacher and source of tradition, which would become dominant by the time of Irenaeus (A.D. 200), had a predecessor in the portrait of Peter as true confessor of the Christian faith in Matt. 16:16-17 and Acts 1–5. Already in II Pet. 3:15-17, this image is so strong that Peter's name can be invoked to correct those who are misinterpreting the Pauline letters. Thus, in the community from which II Peter was written (Rome may be involved, if we can judge from I Pet. 5:13; *see* II Pet. 3:1), the trajectory of Peter's image has begun to outstrip the trajectory of Paul's image. This trajectory would be continued beyond the NT literature and era; and eventually, when the see of Rome had emerged as the most prominent bishopric in the empire, it would be invoked by the bishops of that city, where Peter had died, to justify the leadership they exercised. The debate on the validity of this claim to "succession," even when thus understood in terms of the trajectory of an image, goes beyond the biblical evidence and belongs to church history and theology.

See also BELOVED DISCIPLE; BELOVED DISCIPLE[S]; ROME, CHRISTIAN MONUMENTS[S] §2.

Bibliography. D. W. O'Connor, *Peter in Rome* (1969); R. E. Brown *et al., Peter in the NT* (1973).

R. E. BROWN

*PHARISEES.

1. Definition
   a. In Josephus
   b. In the NT
   c. In tannaitic literature
2. Scribes and Pharisees
3. Teachings
   a. The twofold law
   b. Content
4. Innovations
   a. The Great Senate
   b. The synagogue
   c. The calendar
   d. Priestly procedure
5. Origin and history
6. The Pharisees and early Christianity
Bibliography

1. Definition. A scholarly class dedicated to the teaching of the twofold law (the written and the oral) and to the dissemination of their belief in the world to come and the resurrection of the dead. They are not mentioned in the Hebrew Scriptures, they taught laws and doctrines not set down in those scriptures, and they promised salvation to the individual in a life beyond the grave, a concept not formulated in the Pentateuch. Yet these Pharisees were so successful in winning over the people to their innovational teachings that in the time of Jesus they are sitting in the chair of Moses, and legitimately so (cf. Matt. 23:1-3).

Unfortunately, this simple definition of the Pharisees has eluded scholars, who have pictured them as a sect of ritual purists, separating themselves from the negligent masses, the *'Am Ha'arez.* On the basis of M. Ḥag. 2.7, which reads that the garments of an *'Am Ha'arez* are a source of midrash uncleanness for *pᵉrûšîm,* even as the garments of *pᵉrûšîm* are the source of midrash uncleanness to those who eat the heave offering, the majority of scholars have concluded that *pᵉrûšîm* in this text means Pharisees. And since the *pᵉrûšîm* are juxtaposed to the *'Am Ha'arez,* the scholars have further concluded that these *pᵉrûšîm* are to be identified with the *ḥᵃbhērîm,* who likewise separate themselves from the masses (M. Dem. 2.3). If, then, *pᵉrûšîm=Pharisees=ḥᵃbhērîm,* the Pharisees are a sect of ritual purists who separate themselves from the masses.

The Hebrew word *pᵉrûšîm,* however, is sometimes used as a common noun; i.e., separatists, and sometimes as a proper noun, i.e., Separatists, or Pharisees. In the crucial text, Ḥag. 2.7, the word does not refer to the Pharisees at all, but to individuals who have taken upon themselves restrictions not required by the oral law (HALACHAH). Like the *ḥᵃbhērîm* of Dem. 2.3, they are mistrustful of the ritual practices of the masses and voluntarily choose to avoid contact with them. That these are not Pharisees is made clear by a comparison of Ḥag. 2:7, where the *pᵉrûšîm* are juxtaposed to the *'Am Ha'arez,* with other tannaitic texts (cf. M. Yad. 4:6-7; Tosef. Yad. 2:20; T.B. Yoma 19b; Tosef. Ḥag. 3:35), with Josephus

(War II.viii.2, 14; Antiq. XIII.ix.9, viii.5, cf. xv.5; XVIII.i.3-4; Life 4-12) and with the NT (Matt. 22:23-40; cf. Mark 12:18-27; Luke 20:27-40; Acts 23:6-10) where they are contrasted with the Sadducees, and never with the masses. Indeed, Josephus stresses (Antiq. XIII.ix.6, xiv.5; XVIII.i.3-4) that the masses were so solidly behind the Pharisees that they were willing to rise up against their Hasmonean rulers when the teachings of the Pharisees were abrogated.

Methodologically, therefore, the definition of the Pharisees must be constructed from Josephus, the NT, and those tannaitic texts where the meaning "Pharisees" is attested to by the juxtaposition of the *perûšîm* with the *ṣedhûkhîm,* i.e., the Sadducees. For unlike *perûšîm, ṣedhûkhîm* is always a proper noun.

a. In Josephus. Josephus refers to the Pharisees in the *The Jewish War, The Antiquities of the Jews,* and in the *Life,* where they are described as the exponents of the dominant "philosophy" among the Jews and are contrasted to the Sadducees, to the Essenes, and to the Fourth Philosophy. The Pharisees (Antiq. XIII.x.6; cf. XIII.xvi.2) "had passed on to the people certain regulations *handed down* (παρέδοσαν) by former generations and not recorded in the law of Moses, for which reason they are rejected by the Sadducees, who hold that only those regulations should be considered which were written down, and those which had been *handed down* (παραδόσεως) by former generations should not be observed." They were, he affirms, the most accurate expositors of the Law (War I.v.2; II.viii.14), held the position of the leading school of thought (War II.viii.14), offered to believers a total system of governance (Life 2), preached the immortality of the soul and the resurrection of the body (War II.viii.14; III.viii.5; Antiq. XVIII.i.3; cf. Apion II:31), and affirmed the interplay of fate and free will (War II.viii.14; Antiq. XVIII.i.3). One of their distinguished leaders, Simon the son of Gamaliel, is referred to as an unrivaled expert in the laws (Life 38).

b. In the NT. The NT, though hostile toward the Pharisees, presents the same picture. This is most striking in Phil. 3:5-6, where Paul affirms that "as to the law" he had been a Pharisee, and as to righteousness under the law he had been blameless. He echoes this affirmation in Gal. 1:13-14 as one extremely zealous for the traditions (παραδόσεων) of the fathers, the technical expression used by Josephus (Antiq. XIII.x.6, xvi.1) and by the gospel writers (Mark 7:3, 8-9, 13; Matt. 15:2-3, 6) to denote the oral law. The Pharisees thus must have been the teachers of the twofold law, a scholar class, whose interpretation of the Law was viewed by Paul as the authentic one.

The Synoptic gospels and Acts likewise picture the Pharisees as the scholar class of the twofold law. In Mark 7:5, the Pharisees are the exponents of the "traditions of the elders" (παράδοσιν τῶν πρεσβυτέρων), traditions which are not written down in Scripture. They appear as authorities over the Law, e.g., when they rebuke Jesus for allowing his disciples to pluck ears of corn on the sabbath (Mark 2:23-27); admonish him for allowing his disciples to transgress the traditions of the elders (Matt. 15:1-9); challenge him on the legality of divorce (Matt. 19:1-9) and the payment of tribute to Caesar (Matt. 22:15-22); applaud him for his masterful refutation of the Sadducees, who deny resurrection (Matt. 22:23-34); and differ with him on the question as to whether the Messiah must be the son of David (Matt. 22:41-45). Most striking is Jesus' statement that "the Pharisees sit on Moses' seat; so practice and observe whatever they tell you, but not what they do; for they preach, but do not practice" (Matt. 23:2-3). Here the Pharisees are explicitly confirmed as the authoritative spokesmen for the Law—and legitimately so. This, despite whatever hostile feelings they engender in the followers of Jesus and however hypocritical they may seem to be. (They may indeed wish all their deeds to be seen by men; they may indeed wear their phylacteries broad and their fringes long; they may relish the place of honor at feasts, the best seats in the synagogue, and being called rabbi, but withal they sit in Moses' seat and exercise authority over the Law legitimately [Matt. 23 *passim*].)

The Pharisees in Matthew are thus identical with the Pharisees in Mark, just as they are with the Pharisees in Paul: the prestigious and authoritative teachers of the twofold law who rejected the claim that Jesus was the Messiah, the Son of man, and that, following his crucifixion, he was raised from the dead. Neither Paul, nor Mark, nor Matthew defines the Pharisees as preeminently concerned with laws of ritual purity, or as ranged against the common masses. Indeed, the one instance in which the Pharisees engage Jesus in controversy over ritual purity is in the matter of the washing of the hands (Mark 7:1-8), a tradition of the elders which had been devised so as to lighten the strict laws of purity set down in the Pentateuch. While the written law required a ritually unclean individual to take a ritual bath at sunset, the oral law prescribed the washing of the hands as sufficient, except for a priest who was to eat the heave offering. This portrayal is further confirmed in Luke and John, and in Acts 5:33-34; 22:3.

c. In tannaitic literature. The third major source, the tannaitic literature, when critically analyzed yields the same definition as do Josephus and the NT. However, since it was the failure to discriminate between the two meanings of *perûšîm,* separatists or Pharisees, which largely accounts for the prevailing misconceptions, it is essential that the methodology for differentiation be made explicit.

Only one fact has not been challenged: that the Sadducees were in conflict with the Pharisees. Since this alone is secure, only those tannaitic texts in which the *perûšîm* are juxtaposed to Sadducees can be used for constructing the tannaitic definition of the Pharisees. These texts are few in number, but they are sufficient to allow us to draw a clear picture of who the Pharisees were.

The tannaitic texts fall into two categories: those which have the formula "The Sadducees say, 'we complain against you Pharisees'" followed by "The Pharisees say, we complain against you Sadducees!" (M. Yad. 4.6-7; Tosef. Yad. II.20, equating Boethusions with Sadducees), and those which simply have the Sadducees and Pharisees involved in controversy or disagreement. (T.B. Yom. 19b; Tosef. Hag. III.35; T.B. Nid. 33b; Tosef. Yom. I.8). In spite of this difference in form, there is complete congruity in the image of the Pharisees that emerges. In all these texts the Pharisees are, without exception, the source of the Law, never its object. The laws which they expound are oral laws—laws which are not written down in the Pentateuch (e.g., Holy Scripture renders the hands unclean: M. Yad. 4.6). These laws they hold to be binding on all Jews, not simply on themselves. The laws deal with the whole range of legislation: cultic, criminal, and civil. Not one of them pertains to rules for ritual purity binding on the Pharisees but not on the common people; nor is there any provision made for a legal barrier between the Pharisees and the masses. And all these laws are rejected by the Sadducees.

The picture which emerges from these texts is that of a class of scholars who teach, with authority, the twofold law. In a word, they sit in the chair of Moses. And those who challenge them are the Sadducees, who reject in principle the claim of the Pharisees that God had revealed to Moses oral laws as well as written laws. This definition from the tannaitic literature thus squares with that which can be drawn from Josephus and from the NT.

The Mishna, Tosefta, and the *b^eraithôth* (tannaitic texts which were not included in the Mishna and Tosefta but which are cited in the Palestinian and Babylonian Talmuds) use the term *p^erûšîm* for the scholar class only when they are juxtaposed to the Sadducees. In all other instances these authorities refer to the scholars of the twofold Law in the period before A.D. 70 as *Sôph^erîm* (scribes), *ḥ^akhāmîm* (sages), or *z^ekhēnîm* (elders).

This discriminating usage can be clearly demonstrated when we analyze two Mishna texts which deal with the question as to whether Holy Scripture renders the hands unclean. In M. Yad. 4.6, the Sadducees complain against the Pharisees for saying that Holy Scripture renders the hands unclean. Here the Sadducees are juxtaposed to the *p^erûšîm*. When, however, in the same tractate (3.2), the Sadducees are not arrayed against the *p^erûšîm,* the dictum "Holy Scripture renders the hands unclean" is affirmed to be the words of the scribes and, as such, enjoys an equality of status with the Scripture itself. A close analysis of relevant tannaitic texts likewise yields equivalent synonymity between *p^erûšîm*-Pharisees and sages, *p^erûšîm*-Pharisees and elders, and *p^erûšîm*-Pharisees and the anonymous oral law. (*See* E. Rivkin in bibliog. for an analysis of all the texts.) The care with which the tannaitic teachers refrained from using the term *p^erûšîm* to mean Pharisees except in juxtaposition to Sadducees allows us to conclude that for these teachers the term *p^erûšîm* must have been a slur coined by the Sadducees to brush aside the teachers of the twofold law as "separatists," "deviants," "heretics."

2. Scribes and Pharisees. The equation of *p^erûšîm*-Pharisees with scribes within the tannaitic texts is of great importance for shaping a definition of the Pharisees which is thoroughly objective. Furthermore, it makes clear that the scribes and the Pharisees in the NT are one and the same. The gospels use the terms interchangeably and an analysis of the gospels and Paul reveals that the scribes and the Pharisees invariably hold identical views with respect to the Law and are pictured as the opponents of the Sadducees (cf. Matt. 22:34 [Pharisees] with Mark 12:28 [scribe]; Matt. 12:24 with Mark 3:22, etc.). This identity is underlined in Matt. 23. Indeed, one may even go so far as to suggest that the passages in Mark where the scribes are mentioned without the Pharisees reflect Palestinian Jewish usage which avoided the term Pharisees when the Sadducees were not involved. It is thus likely that in the early form of the gospel story, the Hebrew honorific title *sôph^erîm* (scribes) was used exclusively, but as the story unfolded and spread outside Palestine and amongst the Gentiles, the term Pharisees came to be used more frequently. Whereas γράμματοι (scribes) for Greek listeners and readers conveyed no notion of legislators or scholars, Pharisees did, at least, evoke an image of leaders. But since the term Pharisees itself meant nothing to the average Greek or Roman, Luke went further and equated Pharisees with the teachers of the Law, νομοδιδάσκαλοι (5:17).

Drawing on the equation scribes=Pharisees=teachers of the Law, we can now add those verses where the term scribes, but not Pharisees, is used, in order more fully to elaborate the definition of the Pharisees as derived from the NT. These passages confirm those already analyzed: the scribes are the teachers of the twofold law and of the resurrection which it promises (Mark 12:18-28). They reject Jesus' claim to a personal authority (Mark 1:21-22), attribute his power to drive out demons to Beelzebul (Mark 3:22), insist that the Messiah must be the son of David (Mark 12:35-37), assert that Elijah must come first (9:11), adhere to the traditions of the elders, a term which is synonymous in the Mishna with scribes-Pharisees (Mark 7:1-8), and are horrified that Jesus would blaspheme God by arrogating to himself the right to forgive sins (Mark 2:6-7).

Nowhere in these texts do the scribes oppose the masses, or display any special concern for the laws of ritual purity. They express astonishment that Jesus would sit with publicans and sinners, but they nowhere espouse separation from the masses or a level of ritual purity beyond that which the Law prescribed for *all* Jews.

3. Teaching. ***a. The twofold law.*** We can now spell out the substantive teachings of the Pharisees as derived from the previous sources:

i. God had given to Moses a twofold law, the written and the oral. This twofold law had been transmitted from Moses to Joshua to the elders to the prophets to the men of the Great Synagogue and then to the scholar class (M. AB. 1.1). It had not been transmitted to the priests; nor had the priests been assigned authority over it. They were meant to be sacred functionaries, not authoritative teachers.

ii. Although the written law was not to be altered by so much as an iota, the oral law was not so fixed. The authoritative teachers in each generation were invested with full authority to determine what the oral law was to be in that generation. The oral law was not so much an immutable body of law as a concept of ongoing authority over the Law as instituted by Moses himself. In this sense, the teachers of the twofold law in every generation sat in the chair of Moses. Whereas the written laws are called מצות (commandments), תורות (teachings), חקים (statutes), משפטים (judgments), עדות (testimonies), פקודים (precepts), the oral laws are called *halachoth* (pathways [to salvation]), *gezeroth* (decrees), *takkanoth* (ordinances). The scribes-Pharisees never used biblical terms for their oral laws.

iii. This array of laws was transmitted orally and not put down in writing till Judah ha-Nasi promulgated the Mishna at the beginning of the third century A.D. Since the oral law, unlike the written law, was continuously in flux, and since most of the unwritten laws were set down anonymously in the Mishna and the Tosefta, it is difficult to determine whether a particular oral law was operative at an earlier time, unless specific teachers are named, or specific historical situations are presupposed. The fact, however, that the oral laws cannot in each individual case be dated does not nullify the assumption that a system of such laws was operative from the time of the Hasmonean Revolt (*see below*).

iv. The form of transmitting the oral law was unique, because the Pharisees did not take biblical forms as their model. Biblical law is set within a narrative framework and is associated with a specific historical setting, but the oral law was framed as individual items. Each item could circulate separately or could be combined with other items at the discretion of the teacher. Although there may have been a tendency long before the promulgation of the Mishna to combine these items logically and categorically, they never were set within a narrative framework. Furthermore, the oral laws never used any biblical formula for law, such as "If . . . , then," or "Thou shalt" or "Thou shalt not." Rather, they are phrased as simple declarative sentences, e.g., "There are four principal kinds of damage" (M. Baba Kama 1.1), or as questions raising a legal issue, e.g., "From what time do we read the Shema in the evening?" (M. Ber. 1.1). Similarly, whereas the Pentateuchal law leaves no doubt that it is coming directly from God through Moses, the oral laws are either anonymous or attributed to the scribes, to the sages, to the schools of Shammai and Hillel, or, after A.D. 70, to individual teachers such as Simeon ben Gamaliel, Akiba, etc.

v. Since the oral law is co-equal with the written law, it needs no scriptural proof texts for legitimazation (cf. M. Yad. 3.2; M. Sanh. 11.3), but proof texts are still used frequently. This is a radical departure from scriptural models, since as late as Eccelesiasticus no author supported his views with citations from Scripture. Biblical laws and concepts may have been assumed, but they were not directly quoted. By contrast, the Pharisees frequently cite Scripture to undergird or to clarify an oral law, or to elicit the larger meaning of some situation or event (cf. M. Ber. 1.3, 5; 7.3; 9.5; Pe'ah 5.6; 7.3; 7.7; 8.9, and *passim* throughout all tractates).

In addition to oral law (HALACHAH), there was also oral lore (HAGGADAH). The Haggadah, like the Halachah, was transmitted as free-floating items without benefit of a narrative framework. As such, the haggadic form was nonbiblical and, like the Halachah, frequently underscores its point with situational exegesis.

Because all biblical writings were believed to be divinely inspired, every verse was regarded as saturated with divine insight. Each could be detached from its context and freely joined to other verses from other books to support or elucidate either a halachic or haggadic dictum. Indeed, the fact that verses so far removed from one another as Deuteronomy, Isaiah, and Psalms, seemingly displayed the identical thought was taken as stunning proof of the coherence and consistency of God's revelation. The Pharisees shattered the contextual framework of the biblical books and thereby liberated the verses for situational exegesis. Jesus and his disciples, as well as Paul and the other writers of the NT books, all bear eloquent testimony to this Pharisaic procedure. *See* INTERPRETATION, HISTORY OF[S] §D; MESSIAH, JEWISH[S].

Whether teaching law (halachah) or lore (haggadah), the Pharisees did not commit their teachings to writing. This gave rise to confusion among non-Jews, who would never imagine that γράμματοι, literally "secretaries," "writers," could possibly be legislators who were committed *not* to write down any of their teachings.

b. Content. The fundamental teaching of the Pharisees was a triad: (1) God, the Father, so loved the individual that (2) he revealed his twofold law to Israel, so that (3) each individual who *internalized* this twofold law and obeyed the teachings of the scholar class could anticipate that after death his soul would enjoy life in the world to come, alongside God the Father, and that in the distant future his soul would be restored to his resurrected body. On this foundation other doctrines were erected:

i. The true community of Israel consisted of all those who affirmed the triad and who adhered to the twofold law (cf. M. Sanh. 10.1; Pe'ah 1.1; Jos. War II.viii.14; II.xvi.4; Apion II.30). Those Israelites who, like the Sadducees, had been born Israelites in the flesh but who rejected the triad were deemed sinners and were to have no share in the world to come. (M. Sanh. 10.1-4; Jos. Antiq. XVIII.i.3; War II.viii.14; XVI.4) By contrast, those Gentiles who had been born pagans in the flesh but had been stirred to convert to the twofold law of Judaism were deemed to be co-citizens in the community of Israel (cf. Jos. Apion II.28, M. Yad. 4.4; Matt. 23:15) and entitled to a share in the world to come and to the resurrection of their bodies. The Pharisees thus had already, long before Paul, distinguished between Israel of the flesh and Israel of the spirit (cf. Jos. Apion II.28).

ii. No longer was the ultimate fate of the individual bound up with the fate of the community at large. Although every other Israelite might sin, and the people might lose its land and its temple, the individuals who adhered loyally to the teachings of the twofold law which they had internalized would not be deprived of eternal life.

iii. Without faith that God had indeed revealed the twofold law and without faith in eternal life and resurrection, the law itself was meaningless. Obedience to the law was the only way in which this faith could be shown to be real and not spurious. *See* TORAH[S].

iv. This world was transient, uncertain, unreal. The world to come, by contrast, was permanent, secure, and suffused with untarnished serenity and joy. For this reason the Pharisaic leaders acknowledged the legitimacy of all terrestrial rulers, as long as they allowed the teachers of the twofold law to teach the way to eternal life. The Pharisees were teachers of salvation for the individual through a community of true believers in the twofold law, and not nationalists focusing on the land, or on the temple, or on a sovereign state. Their kingdom of God was an internalized kingdom of those who affirmed God's unity (cf. M. Ber. 2.5) and adhered to his laws wherever they were living—Jerusalem, Corinth, Ephesus, or Rome —and under whatever conditions prevailed.

4. Innovations. ***a. The Great Senate.*** To generate and disseminate the twofold law, the Pharisees created a novel institution which they called the *Bêth Dîn HagGādôl,* the Great Boulé, or Senate. It consisted of seventy-one distinguished teachers presided over by a *nāśî'* who, it seems, represented the majority opinion, and by an *ābh bêth dîn,* who presumably represented the minority position (cf. M. Hag. 2.2). The *Bêth Dîn HagGādôl* was the body which determined the status, at any given moment, of the system of twofold law. *See, however,* SANHEDRIN[S] §3.

b. The synagogue. The most durable of institutions which the Pharisees created was the synagogue, but its origins are obscure, and there is no evidence of its existence in Palestine prior to the Hasmonean period. It is mentioned for the first time in sources deriving from the time of Augustus and later.

The synagogue seems to have sprung up originally as the meeting place (*bêth ha-kenesseth*) of the Pharisees and their followers during the Hasmonean Revolt (*see, however,* SANHERDRIN[S] §3*b*). Subsequently these meeting houses became gathering places for the so-called *ma'amadot.* These *ma'amadot* had been established by the Pharisees to give the Jews at large a sense of participation in the temple worship. The people were divided into twenty-four *ma'amadot* to parallel the twenty-four watches of the priesthood. While representatives of the *ma'amadot* went off to Jerusalem to be present while the daily offering was being sacrificed by the particular priestly watch with which the *ma'amadot* was associated, the other members of that *ma'amadot* would gather in the synagogues and read from the first chapter of Genesis. Since the daily sacrifice offered in the morning and the evening was for the entire people, it was felt that their representatives ought to be present (M. Ta'an. 4.1-4). This insistence on public participation was opposed by the Sadducees.

In contrast to the temple, the synagogue was a highly decentralized institution which was superbly tailored to the Pharisaic focus on individuals and their salvation. The synagogue encouraged fellow believers to come together for the reading of Scripture, the mandatory prayer, and mutual support. It allowed the individual to have, through prayer, a direct and ongoing relationship with God the Father. Little wonder, then, that it looms so large in the gospels, and that the followers of Jesus were angry and bitter when they were expelled (Matt. 23:34). Nor is it surprising that Paul, in preaching the risen Christ, sought out the synagogues to reach those Jews who were most likely to hear this gospel. The synagogue was, after all, the gathering place of the followers of the Pharisees. It was an exclusively Pharisaic instituiton, and no Sadducees were ever found there.

c. The calendar. Among the most audacious innovations of the Pharisees was a lunar-solar calendar which was dependent on the testimony of eyewitnesses and which involved the intercalation of both months and years. No such calendar is attested in the Pentateuch. By loosening the festivals and holy days from the grip of the Pentateuchal calendar the Pharisees determined even on which day the Day of Atonement was to fall. It is also interesting to note that the Pharisees, not the Pentateuch, designate the first day of the seventh month as New Year, along with three other New Years (M. R.H. 1.1).

d. Priestly procedure. The ultimate revolutionary act of the Pharisees was to insist that the high priest follow Pharisaic procedures on the Day of Atonement. Whereas the Sadducees required the high priest to light the incense before he entered the holy of holies, the Pharisees insisted that he light the incense only after he entered. And the Pharisaic procedure was the one operative in Jesus' day (cf. Jos. Antiq. XVIII.i.2; Tosef. Yom. I.8).

5. Origin and history. Although we know something about the Pharisees in the time of Jesus, we know nothing precise about their origins or any details of their subsequent history. Even Josephus tells us nothing of when and how they came into existence. They simply appear without any introduction in his account of Jonathan the Hasmonean's wars against the Seleucids (Antiq. XIII.v.9). And even after he mentions them for the first time, he fails to follow through with any connected history of their activities. Except for those occasions when the Pharisees became directly involved in political affairs, or when Josephus feels the need to explain who they were, he does not consider them to be relevant to the kind of political history that he was writing. As for the Pharisees themselves, they left no historical records. This is not surprising, for, as we have seen, they were a non-writing scholar class which deliberately refrained from following biblical models or forms for their teachings. Just as their prayers were prose, not poetry, and just as their law and lore were items and bits, not connected narrative discourse, so their factual data of the past were episodes, anecdotes, and illustrative paradigms, not chronicles. Indeed, since the Pharisees focused on the world to come, they considered history to be irrelevant, except insofar as individuals and events might serve as illustrations of how salvation might be gained or lost. But for such purposes, imagined facts were no less efficacious than real facts. History as continuity, sequence, and process was, for them, pointless, and so they had no interest in preserving the history of their movement.

The NT likewise throws no direct light on the origins and the history of Pharisaism. The gospels are interested in the Pharisees only to the degree that they were involved with Jesus. The Pharisees show no interest in the question as to when or how they got into the chair of Moses. For us, however, this is a core question, and we may be able to hazard some suggestions.

There is no mention of Pharisees in any book of the OT. No pre-Hasmonean source makes any mention of them. Indeed, prior to the Hasmonean Revolt the Aarondies sat securely in the chair of Moses and exercised full authority over the Law (*see* AARON, AARONIDES[S]). This absolute hegemony is enthusiastically affirmed and endorsed by Ben Sirach (Ecclus. 45:6-22), who does not accord to the scribes of his day any authority over the Law. Furthermore, Ben Sirach knows nothing of an oral law, indulges in no exegesis whatsoever, has no compunction about setting down his wisdom in writing, and has no hesitation in following appropriate biblical models.

The Pharisees, however, are in the chair of Moses during the early years of John Hyrcanus' reign, when he regarded himself as a disciple of theirs (Jos. Antiq. XIII.x.5). That their oral law was fully operative is evident from the fact that when John Hycanus broke with the Pharisees and went over to the Sadducees, he "abrogated the laws which they (the Pharisees) had established for the people" (*ibid.*, x.6). These laws, Josephus immediately makes clear, were those unwritten laws which the Pharisees had transmitted to the people "from the Fathers," and which were, on that account, "rejected by the Sadducees" (Antiq. XIII.x.6). It is also evident from the fact that, following the abrogation of these laws, the people rose in revolt (Antiq. XIII.x.7; War I.ii.8), first against John Hyrcanus and subsequently against Alexander Janneus (Antiq. XIII.xiii.5; XIII.xv.5). So tenacious was the loyalty of the people to the Pharisees and the twofold law that the civil war could be brought to an end only when Salome Alexandra made peace with the Pharisees and restored "whatever laws introduced by the Pharisees in accordance with the traditions of the Fathers had been abolished by her father-in-law Hyrcanus" (Antiq. XIII.xvi.2).

We may therefore conclude that the Pharisees came to power sometime during the Hasmonean Revolt, but no later than the high priesthood of Jonathan (Antiq. XIII.v.9). They were a revolutionary class since they had no Pentateuchal sanction for their authority. They were no less revolutionary in their unseating the Aaronide priests from the chair of Moses and reducing them to temple functionaries. Indeed, by recognizing Simon, the Hasmonean, as a legitimate high priest even though he was not a direct descendant of the high priestly line and by recognizing the legitimacy of all high priests, even when they were appointed by Herod and the procurators, the Pharisees displayed their utter independence of the written law. It was for this reason that the spokesman for the exclusive authority of the written law and for the exclusive right of the sons of Zadok to minister as high priests denounced the teachers of the twofold law as *p^erûšîm,* separatists, heretics.

Following the grand compromise which was worked out between Salome Alexandra and the Pharisees, a compromise which distinguished between the realm of state sovereignty on the one hand and religious sovereignty on the other, the Pharisees ceased to play an active role in affairs of state. For this reason, Josephus has little occasion to include them either in his *Wars* or *Antiquities.* Indeed, he draws them in only when he indicates that they did not challenge Cyrinius' right to take a census and exact tribute (Antiq. XVIII.i.1, 6) and when he pictures the Pharisaic leaders as urging the people not to revolt against Rome (War II.xvii.3-4).

The Pharisaic system underwent three structural phases: (1) That of the *zugôth,* or pairs, who served as *nāśî'* and as *ābh bêth dîn* of the *Bêth Dîn HagGādôl.* During this phase, only the names of those who filled these offices have been preserved; they were not called rabbi; and the oral laws were promulgated by a majority decision of the *Bêth Dîn HagGādôl,* with dissenting views having no legal status. (2) That of the schools of Shammai and Hillel and the establishment of a hereditary *nāśî'* of the *Bêth Dîn HagGādôl,* a descendant of Hillel. During this phase, the *nāśî'* was called rabban (our teacher), but the scholars were not yet called rabbi. Each of the schools could publicly teach oral laws in the name of the school, even when the schools had very different notions as to what the laws should be. (3) That of the free-teaching individual scholar who was ordained and authorized to teach oral laws in his own name. It was during this phase that the title "rabbi" was first used to designate an ordained teacher of the twofold law.

6. The Pharisees and early Christianity. Jesus' ministry fell during the second phase, and it is for this reason that the scribes-Pharisees are referred to as a class. The only individual who is mentioned by name is Gamaliel, which is quite understandable since he was the *nāśî'* and therefore legitimately singled out.

As the authoritative teachers of the twofold law, the scribes-Pharisees were both puzzled by and ultimately angered at Jesus. Although they recognized him as a teacher and although they were pleased with his refutation of the Sadducees and his affirmation that God was one and that one should love one's neighbor as oneself, they were hostile to his teaching of doctrines they had not authorized; to his taking the law in his own hand; to his forgiving sins; to his exorcising demons; and, above all, to his affirming, or allowing his disciples to affirm of him, that he was the Son of man, the Messiah. The Pharisees were especially angry over his unwillingness to heed them when they confronted him with his deviations. This rejection, first of Jesus, and then of his disciples who claimed that Jesus had been resurrected, was bound to stir up animosity toward the Pharisees in both Jesus and his followers. This animosity was exacerbated when the Pharisees proclaimed the early Christians to be heretics and threw them out of the synagogue. Such deepening hostility turned the early Christians against the Pharisees, and unleashed such virulent epithets as "hypocrites" and "whitewashed tombs." For these early Christians, the Pharisaic hallmark of righteousness had been marred by their rejection of Jesus, and by their hounding the Christians out of the synagogue.

As to the role of the Pharisees in the trial and crucifixion of Jesus, only a few aspects are relatively clear. Although the Pharisees had no love for Jesus, they did not bring Jesus to trial before one of their courts, a *bêth dîn* (Βουλή). Rather, he was brought to trial before a sanhedrin, a council, of the high priest. This sanhedrin must have been a political, not a religious body; for it was presided over by the high priest Caiaphas, a Sadducee who had been appointed by the procurator. This council was concerned with Jesus' religious teachings only insofar as they had political ramifications and only insofar as they might be interpreted as a challenge to Roman authority. The issue was whether Jesus claimed to be the king of the Jews. Having ascertained that this was indeed the case, the Sanhedrin of the high priest turned him over to Pontius Pilate for final judgment. *See* TRIAL OF JESUS[S]; SANHEDRIN[S].

Although the Pharisees rejected the claims made for Jesus, it was their tenacious belief in eternal life and resurrection which had opened the hearts and minds of Jesus' disciples to the credibility of their witness that Jesus had risen from the dead. Resurrection was not an impossibility; it was the chief cornerstone of the Pharisaic faith. The Pharisees could deny that Jesus had been resurrected, but they could not mock the belief in resurrection. Why did Paul cast off the law when he was stunned into the belief that Jesus had risen from the dead? For him, the system of the internalized twofold law did not guarantee salvation; only Jesus, the Christ, could now give this assurance. It was Christ alone who could dissolve sin and lead the way to God the Father. For Paul, the twofold law was now a fraud. It was a barrier—not the road—to eternal life, because it deluded man into thinking obedience to the law is triumph over sin, when the law is the shield of sin and its most provocative instrument (cf. Rom. 7).

The power of Pharisaism has throughout the centuries been made manifest not only in the continued vitality of Judaism (all subsequent forms of Judaism are derivative of Pharisaism), which alone of the religions of antiquity proved immune to the Christian gospel, but also in the vitality of Christianity itself. For Pharisaism transmitted to Christianity its threefold belief structure: (1) God, the Father, so loved the individual that (2) he revealed his will so that (3) the individual might hope for eternal life and resurrection. For the Pharisees the revealed will was the twofold law; for the Christians it was Christ. This belief was the enduring achievement of Pharisaism—a belief which was a true mutation from earlier Judaism.

Bibliography. For scholarly efforts at defining the Pharisees, *see* the comprehensive art. and bibliog. by A. Michel and J. LeMoyne, "Pharisiens," *DBSup,* Fascicles 39-40 (1964), cols. 1022-1115, as well as R. Marcus, "The Pharisees in the Light of Modern Scholarship," *JR,* XXIII (1952), 153-64. Of special impact have been E. Schürer, *A History of the Jewish People in the Time of Jesus Christ* (1902), second division, vol. II, 10-28; R. T. Herford, *The Pharisees* (1924); G. F. Moore, *Judaism,* I (1927), 56-71; L. Finkelstein, *The Pharisees,* 2 vols. (3rd ed., 1962); and most recently, J. Neusner, *The Rabbinic Traditions about the Pharisees before 70,* 3 vols. (1971).

The definition developed in this article is based on that first set down by S. Zeitlin, *The History of the Second Jewish Commonwealth: Prologomena* (1933), pp. 41-56, "Hasduquim we-ha prušim," *Horeb,* II (1936), 56-89, and elaborated in my own writings: E. Rivkin, "The Internal City," *JSSR,* V (1966), 225-40, "The Pharisaic Revolution," *Perspectives in Jewish Learning,* II (1966), 26-51, Prologomenon to Oesterley and Loewe, *Judaism and Christianity* (1969), pp. vii-lxx, "Pharisaism and the Crisis of the Individual in the Graeco-Roman World," *JQR,* LXI (1970-71), 27-52, "Defining the Pharisees: The Tannaitic Sources," *HUCA,* XL-XLI (1969-70), 205-49, *The Shaping of Jewish History* (1971). Although close to Zeitlin on definition, there is no agreement on historical reconstruction; cf. Zeitlin, *The Rise and Fall of the Judean State,* I (1962), 178-87 with E. Rivkin, "Solomon Zeitlin's Contribution to the Historiography of the Interestamental Period," *Judaism,* XIV (1965), 354-67.

E. RIVKIN

***PHILEMON, LETTER TO.** Recent research notes that the letter addresses three persons rather than one (Philemon, APPHIA, and ARCHIPPUS), indicating it is not a private communication but an apostolic letter. For a parallel, cf. Ep. 142 of Isidore of Pelusium (PG 78, 277).

Debate continues on the question of the letter's place of writing, with increasing preference for Ephesus over Caesarea and Rome, and on the letter's purpose: was Paul simply requesting Onesimus' reinstatement or was he asking Philemon to free Onesimus for missionary service?

The letter effectively shaped early Christian attitudes toward slavery for four centuries. On the one hand it supported laws on slavery respecting the return of runaway slaves; on the other it challenged conventional mores by calling for a new sense of brotherhood (Philem. 16) between master and slave. *See also* SLAVERY IN THE NT[S].

Bibliography. Commentaries: E. Lohse, *Colossians and Philemon,* Hermeneia (1968); G. Friedrich *et al., Die Kleineren Briefe des Apostels Paulus,* NTD, VIII (1962); W. Hendriksen, *New Testament Commentary: Exposition of Colossians and Philemon* (1964); A. Stoeger, in J. Reuss and A. Stoeger, *The Epistle to Titus and the Epistle to Philemon* (1971).

Special studies: H. Bellen, *Studien zur Sklavenflucht im Römischen Kaiserreich* (1971), pp. 78-82; F. F. Bruce, "St. Paul in Rome: The Epistle to Philemon," *BJRL,* XLVIII (1965), 81-97; T. Preiss, "Life in Christ and Social Ethics in the Epistle to Philemon," *Life in Christ,* SBT, XIII (1954), 32-42; W. J. Richardson, "Principle and Context in the Ethics of the Epistle to Philemon," *Int.,* XXII (1968), 301-16; U. Wickert,

"Der Philemonbrief—Privatbrief oder apostolisches Schreiben?" *ZNW*, LII (1961), 230-38.

W. G. Rollins

***PHILIP, GOSPEL OF.** A Valentinian document discovered in the Gnostic library of Nag Hammadi. The passage which Epiphanius quotes from a "Gospel of Philip" is not contained at all in the Nag Hammadi text, and must therefore be from a completely different work.

1. Text. The text is contained in Codex II of the Nag Hammadi library, immediately after the Gospel of Thomas. The Coptic MS is dated *ca.* A.D. 400, but the gospel itself probably goes back to a Greek original dating from the second half of the second century. There are indications to suggest a Syrian origin, probably in Antioch or its neighborhood. The text is on the whole well preserved, but there are lacunae at the bottom of every page.

2. Structure and composition. Opinions differ regarding the structure of the work. An editorial division into 127 "paragraphs" is generally employed for convenience of reference. These "paragraphs," however, are not "sayings of Jesus" like those in Thomas, nor can they be considered a Gnostic counterpart. It is probably better to regard the gospel as a didactic and hortatory treatise, presenting the Gnostic message through a series of loosely linked aphorisms and meditations. While the document is certainly not just a string of disconnected sayings, there are abrupt transitions and breaks in continuity. A notable feature is a kind of spiral movement, in which certain favorite themes constantly recur: Adam and Paradise, creation and begetting, the meaning of the names of Jesus, the mystery of the bridal chamber, etc. That the construction is not entirely random is suggested by the fact that the "gospel" reaches something of a climax in §125, and is then quietly rounded off in §§126 and 127.

3. Character and contents. This work is not a gospel in any accepted sense, since it does not contain any account of the life and work of Jesus, nor does it present (like many Gnostic "gospels") revelations allegedly given to his disciples by the risen Jesus before his ascension. The ascription to Philip appears only in the title appended at the end, which may be secondary. This may be because Philip is the only disciple mentioned (§91), but it should be noted that in the Pistis Sophia (ch. 42) he is one of the three disciples charged with the writing down of all that Jesus said and did.

The nature and structure of the document make it impossible to summarize its contents in brief compass. There is no connecting thread of argument or unifying theme. The document is, however, clearly Valentinian in character, and a knowledge of the Valentinian system as known from the accounts of Irenaeus is sometimes essential for understanding certain allusions. Although it is not yet possible to identify the gospel with any particular branch of that school, the closest affinities appear to be with the Marcosians and the *Excerpta ex Theodoto*. The Manichean parallels noted by Ménard do not necessarily place the work as late as the third century.

The author counts himself a Christian, and contrasts his present state, and that of his readers, with the period before they became Christians (§§6, 102). His knowledge of the NT is difficult to assess, since the evidence ranges from clear and unmistakable quotations to possible echoes and allusions which appear significant to some readers yet quite unconvincing to others. He certainly quotes from Matthew, John, I Corinthians, and I Peter. A reference to the Good Samaritan suggests knowledge of Luke, while his use of such themes as priesthood, the sanctuary, and the veil may reflect knowledge of Hebrews. But these allusions do not necessarily imply direct knowledge of the book in question, and other echoes are even less certain. At most, the evidence suggests a period when several of the NT books were known but not yet "canonical." This points to the second century rather than the third.

Whatever his knowledge of the NT, the author's theology is distinctly different. Language and imagery familiar to us in a NT context have been transposed into a Gnostic key, as a few examples may serve to show:

a. The world and man: This world came into being through a transgression (§99) and is dominated by archons who wish to deceive man (§13). These archons think they do everything of their own will, but in fact the Holy Spirit is working through them (§§16, 34; cf. Sophia in the Valentinian system). The names employed in this world are deceptive (§11); its good is not good, and its evil not evil (§§10, 63). The only true realities are those of the other world, described as "the kingdom of heaven" (§24) or "the aeon" (§11).

In this world the soul is captive to the "robbers" (§9). Like a pearl dropped in the mud, however, it does not lose its value (§48), even though it is imprisoned in "a despised body" (§22). The same disparagement of the world and the flesh appears in the admonitions "Love not the world, but love the Lord" (§112), "Be not fearful of the flesh, nor love it" (§62). A distinction is drawn between the sons of Adam and those of "the perfect man" (§28). The condition of natural man is bestial (§84): "There are many beasts in the world which bear the form of man" (§119). The state of man unredeemed is frequently described in terms of slavery. In contrast, he who has the knowledge of the truth is a free man, exalted above the world (§110). With the coming of the light, the slaves are set free and the captives delivered (§125), and this must happen even in this world: if a man does not receive the light while he is in this world, he will not receive it in the other (§127). But for the man who has received it, the world has already become "the aeon." He cannot be detained by the hostile powers and is immune from their attacks.

b. Salvation: Christ is the perfect man (§15) whom the Gnostic must put on (§101). He came "to redeem some, to save others, to deliver others" (§9). At several points he is contrasted with Adam (§83). But Philip's Christ comes not to save the world by giving his life but to restore things to their proper places (§70) and become the father of a redeemed progeny (§§74, 120). The fundamental evil in the human situation is not sin but ignorance. Deliverance comes through knowledge (cf. §110), not through the Cross (although there are references: the Cry of Dereliction is quoted in §72, and §91 contains the curious story that Joseph made the cross). Similarly, death is not the wages of sin but the result of the separation of the sexes (§§71, 78); hence Christ came to remove the separation and effect a reunion. Separately, man and woman are exposed to the attacks of unclean spirits, but united they are immune (§61).

c. The sacraments: The gospel provides little or no evidence for any "church" structure or organization, but the numerous references to sacraments give it significance for an aspect of Gnosticism not otherwise well documented. In §68 five sacraments are mentioned, apparently in ascending order: baptism, chrism, eucharist, redemption, and bridal chamber. Eucharist and redemption *(apolutrosis,* cf. the Marcosians) do not figure very prominently. Chrism is expressly said to be superior to baptism (§95: it is from the chrism we are called Christians, not because of the baptism), and apparently olive oil was used (§92). The redemption may have been a sacrament for the dying (Iren. Her. I.xxi.5). The highest sacrament, the bridal chamber, must be interpreted in the light of the Valentinian theory (Iren. I.vii.1): at the consummation Achamoth will enter the Pleroma (i.e., the bridal chamber) to become the bride of the Savior, while the "spiritual" who derive from her become brides of the Savior's angels. This is in some way symbolized or prefigured in the sacrament, but whether the reference is to marriage as such or to a separate rite is not clear. It has been suggested that this too was a sacrament for the dying.

4. Significance. The chief importance of the book is that it adds to our original sources for the study of Valentinian Gnosticism, and so helps to shed light on a still obscure period of early church history. It is also of interest for the way in which NT themes and ideas are taken up, interpreted, and transmuted in a Gnostic context. Finally, it is important as helping to show what Gnosticism meant to a Gnostic.

Bibliography. The Gospel of Philip was first published in P. Labib's photographic ed., *Coptic Gnostic Papyri in the Coptic Museum at Old Cairo,* I (1956). From this a German trans. was made by H. M. Schenke, *TLZ,* LXXXIV (1959), 1-26 and English trans. by C. J. de Catanzaro, *JTS,* XIII (1962), 35-71, and R. McL. Wilson, *The Gospel of Philip* (1962; with a commentary). See also *The Facsimile Edition of the Nag Hammadi Codices: Codex II* (1974; with plates); J. E. Ménard, *L'Évangile selon Philippe* (1967); H. G. Gaffron, *Studien zum koptischen Philippusevangelium* (1969); W. Foerster, *Gnosis,* II (1971), 76-101, new Eng. trans., 1974. For other literature see D. M. Scholer, *Nag Hammadi Bibliography 1948-1969* (1971) and supplements in *NovT* (1971 ff.).

R. McL. Wilson

***PHILIPPI.** Excavation under and around the monumental Roman forum has yielded small finds which confirm Hellenistic occupation of the site and has uncovered a series of eleven Roman shops to the S. Clearing of the theater to prepare for modern performances led to discovery of the ancient entryways on both sides and staircases beyond them, all of Roman date.

In addition to the two basilican churches explored earlier, three more early Christian churches have been found. The earliest is a fourth-century basilica outside the city walls on a little river to the E, a site which may have been traditionally associated with Paul's preaching (Acts 16:13). This small church, constructed with many materials from earlier, pagan buildings, had a semicircular apse lined with three marble steps in the E, from which a nave extended westward, separated by a single row of columns from aisles on both sides. Within the walls of Philippi N of the Via Egnatia a fifth-century Christian basilica, similar in dimensions to one previously studied to the E of it, has now been investigated. A newly discovered complex S of the Via Egnatia to the E of the Roman forum centered on an octagonal church. Built over the remains of an earlier basilican church, the octagon was entered from the W, where a triple colonnade led N to a monumental gateway onto the Via Egnatia. A baptistery, with a font in the form of a Maltese cross, could be reached both from the octagon to the S and from the N, where lay an extensive bathing establishment with typical features such as steam rooms and pools for hot or cold water. A vaulted Macedonian tomb of the third century B.C. was found beneath a room near the baptistery. To the E and S of the octagonal church a large group of rooms has been identified as an episcopal palace.

Bibliography. Surveys: "Archaeology in Greece," *AR,* IV (1957)–XIX (1972-73); "Chronique des Fouilles," *BCH,* LXXXII (1958)–XCVI (1972); "Χρονικά," *AD,* XVI (1960)–XXV (1970); Πρακτικὰ τῆς . . . Ἀρχαιολογικῆς Ἑταιρείας (1958-64, 1966-71); Ἔργον (1958-64, 1966-72); S. Pelekanides, "Excavations in Philippi," *Balkan Studies,* VIII (1967), 123-26, and "Ἡ ἔξω τῶν τειχῶν παλαιοχριστιανικὴ βασιλικὴ τῶν Φιλίππων," Ἀρχαιολογικὴ Ἐφεμερίς (1955), 114-79; R. F. Hoddinott, *Early Byzantine Churches in Macedonia and Southern Serbia* (1963), pp. 99-106.

C. L. Thompson

***PHILIPPIANS, LETTER TO THE.** A composition of three letters of the apostle Paul directed to the church founded by him in the Macedonian city of Philippi, now transmitted as one of the Pauline letters in the NT canon. Recent research has been concerned with the place of this correspondence within the missionary work of Paul in the Aegean, the composite nature of the document, and the interpretation of the Christ hymn in Phil. 2:6-11.

1. The place of Philippians in the mission of Paul. The probability that this correspondence dates from the period of Paul's stay in Ephesus, and not from his later Roman imprisonment, has become more widely accepted. The receiving of support from Philippi (4:10-15), seen as analogous with the support which Paul received from the same church during his stay in Thessalonica (4:16), and the sending of Timothy and Epaphroditus (2:19-30; 4:18) cannot be explained satisfactorily if Paul was indeed in Rome at that time.

If the Philippian correspondence does in fact reveal that Paul sent three letters to that church within a brief period, and that he also received additional information from Philippi before sending the third letter, the Ephesian imprisonment is the most likely time during which these letters were written. In a letter written when he had left Ephesus, and while he was on his way to Corinth via Macedonia, during the last year of his Aegean activity, Paul refers to the mortal danger he had faced in Asia (II Cor. 1:8-11). Phil. 1:12-26 seems to speak about this same threat to his life.

2. The composite nature of the document. Philippians contains several seams, the most obvious one between 3:1 and 3:2 (while 4:4 repeats 3:1 in part); the situation with respect to Epaphroditus has changed after the writing of 4:18, which knew nothing of the sickness reported in 2:25-30; nothing in 1:1–3:1 (and certainly not 1:15-18) prepares the reader for the merciless attack on opponents which one finds in 3:2-21. Several scholars have therefore suggested that the canonical Philippians contains three fragments of Pauline epistles. (The assignment of the several pieces now preserved in 4:1-9 and 4:21-23 must remain uncertain).

i. Phil. 4:10-20 was written early during the Ephesian imprisonment in order to acknowledge the receipt of a gift which the Philippians sent through Epaphroditus. This letter emphasizes the apostle's independence in terms closely reflecting concepts of Cynic philosophy (4:11-12; *see* CYNICS [S]). Paul wants to point to God as the source of all gifts (4:19-20) and refuses to focus attention upon his own personal fate.

ii. In the second letter, 1:1–3:1 and 4:4-7 (perhaps 4:21-23), the situation has changed. There are more hopeful prospects for a successful defense in court (1:12-14) and Paul expresses his determination to continue the work for his churches (1:22-26). He begins to make plans for his own travel, and sends Timothy ahead to prepare for his own visit (2:19-24). This, no doubt, resumes the plans which Paul had already discussed in I Cor. 16:10-11; it gives evidence that he now is reorganizing the collection for Jerusalem. But meanwhile Epaphroditus has fallen sick, and Paul has to apologize for his delay in returning (2:25-30).

iii. The third letter, 3:2–4:3 and 4:8-9, presupposes that Paul has received another communication from Philippi about the arrival of a new group of Christian missionaries and about a quarrel between two influential church leaders in Philippi —Euodia and Syntyche (4:2). This letter is directed primarily against the missionaries, probably Jewish Christians who preached law and circumcision as a means for reaching perfection. Because of the Gnosticizing views of these opponents, it is unlikely that they were identical with the opponents in Galatia against whom Paul wrote at about the same time (*see* GALATIANS, LETTER TO THE and supplementary article), though it is noteworthy that Paul refers to his conversion in Phil. 3:4-10 as well as in Gal. 1:13-16. The question of law and justification, which Paul was to move into the center of the debate in his Epistle to the Romans, written about a year later, is treated for the first time in these two polemic writings.

3. The interpretation of the Christ hymn, 2:6-11, has led to the thesis that neither Isa. 52:13–53:12 nor non-Jewish Hellenistic myth provided the background for the Christology expressed in this hymn, but rather it was provided by a version of the Suffering Servant theme which developed in the speculative wisdom of Judaism (*see* WISDOM OF SOLOMON §3). While the hymn in that setting spoke about the humiliation and ultimate vindication of divine "Wisdom," who is the true representative of the fate of each wise person, Paul reinterprets the hymn so that it now points to humiliation and obedience as the fundamental expression of the Christian ethos. Christ, who demonstrated this new ethos, is not, like Wisdom, the mythological representative of human fate, but is the crucified Lord, who is worshiped (2:10-11). Paul's reshaping of the older hymn is visible in several prose phrases (2:7*a*, 8); and because of this reshaping, it is no longer possible to reconstruct the original poetic form.

Bibliography. Commentaries: F. W. Beare, HNTC (1959); P. Benoit, *La Sainte Bible de Jerusalem* (1959).

On the place of Philippians in the mission of Paul: D. Georgi, *Die Geschichte der Kollekte des Paulus für Jerusalem,* Theologische Forschung, XXXVIII (1965), 46-51.

On Philippians as a collection of letters: J. Müller-Bardorff, "Zur Frage der literarischen Einheit des Phil.," *Wissenschaftliche Zeitschrift der Fr. v. Schiller Universität Jena,* VII (1957-58), 591-604; W. Michaelis, "Teilungshypothesen bei Paulusbriefen," *TZ,* XIV (1958), 321-26; B. D. Rahtjen, "The Three Letters of Paul to the Philippians," *NTS,* VI (1959-60), 167-73; G. Bornkamm, "Der Philipperbrief als paulinische Briefsammlung," in *Neotestamentica et Patristica,* NovTSup, VI (1962), 192-202.

On Paul's opponents in Phil. 3: H. Koester, "The Purpose of the Polemic of a Pauline Fragment," *NTS,* VIII (1961-62), 317-32, where other literature is given.

The most important recent contributions to the understanding of the Christ hymn: D. Georgi, "Der vorpaulinische Hymnus Phil 2,6-11," in *Zeit und Geschichte,* ed. E. Dinkler (1964), pp. 263-93; G. Bornkamm, "On Understanding the Christ-Hymn," *Early Christian Experience* (1959 [ET 1969]).

H. KOESTER

***PHILISTINES.** Caphtor, the home of the Philistines according to biblical tradition, is now firmly identified as Crete on the basis of a recently published topographical list of Amen-ophis III (*ca.* 1400 B.C.); but no archaeological data connecting the Philistines and Crete has been found. Tablets discovered at UGARIT and archaeological finds on CYPRUS give evidence of the troubled period when the Sea Peoples in the late thirteenth century ravaged the area. From Late Bronze Age Cyprus we now have depictions of warriors in kilts and plumed headdresses typical of the Philistines and other Sea Peoples. Mycenean III C1 wares similar to those found at Enkomi and Sinda on Cyprus have been found at Ashdod, Gezer, Azor, Tell 'Aiṭûn, and other sites are closely related in appearance and function to objects from the Aegean. These consist of *kernoi,* kraters with cups, rhyta, figurines (of which heads are usually the only remnant), etc. A clay statuette of a female deity with Philistine decorative elements was found in a twelfth-century stratum at Ashdod. The goddess is schematically portrayed as a seated woman, her body forming part of the chair (*see* ASHDOD[S] §2 and Fig. A24). This is in the Mycenean tradition. Of prime importance for the study of Philistine cultic remains are the ritual incense stands discovered at Ashdod and Tell Qasileh (*see* ASHDOD[S] Fig. 25). These stands, as well as other ritual objects from Tell Qasileh (stratum X), were found in a temple excavated in 1971-72. This is the only building of its kind which can be attributed to the Philistines. The excavator has characterized it as a long house with a "bent-axis" plan and has noted that the principal architectural elements resemble those of other temples in Canaan and of a small temple recently discovered at Mycenae; but he has also pointed out that the layout of rooms, entrances, raised platforms, and pillars has no parallel. Two round stone bases supported the wooden pillars on which the roof rested; this has led to a comparison with the temple in Gaza (Judg. 16:29).

Philistine pottery has been subjected to intensive study, and the various types and styles have been classified. Analysis has shown that from the beginning Philistine pottery was a local product using local techniques but with strong influence from Mycenean III C1 ware. The anthropoid coffins which had earlier been identified as Philistine are now shown by finds from Deir el-Balaḥ to have been first introduced for burial of Egyptian officials in the Late Bronze Age, and that later in the Early Iron Age they were adopted by the Philistines. The same conclusion has been drawn from renewed study of the anthropoid coffins from Beth-shan (*see* BETH-SHAN Fig. 38). An Aegean prototype has been proposed for some of the Philistine tombs at Tel Sharuhen. A form of embalmment was found in the tombs (twelfth century) at Tell es-Sa'idiyeh which have been ascribed to the Sea Peoples. *See* ZARETHAN[S].

Clay tablets inscribed with a form of the Cypro-Minoan script have been found at Deir'alla in the Jordan valley. These have not been deciphered, but they have been taken by some to be possibly Philistine in origin, since Philistine pottery was discovered in the overlying level. Seals inscribed with Cypro-Minoan characters were found in twelfth- and eleventh-century levels at Ashdod, but these also remained undeciphered. No further light has been cast on other aspects of Philistine language or culture, but it has been proposed that there was a relationship between Hebrew סרן (which designates the Philistine rulers and is assumed by most scholars to be Philistine in origin) and Neo-Hittite (or late Luwian) *tarwanas*, a title borne by rulers from the eleventh to the seventh century. Two epigraphic items from later periods are important; both were excavated at Ashdod. The first consists of fragments of an inscribed basalt victory stele erected by Sargon which has its parallels in inscriptions from Assyria proper; the second is a late-fifth-century ostracon inscribed in Aramaic script reading *krm zbdyh*, "the vineyard of Zebedia." This has raised speculation that a document in "Ashdodite" has been discovered.

Bibliography. Note the items listed in the IDB, and the select bibliographies in R. Hestrin, *The Philistines and Other Sea Peoples* (1970), pp. 18-20, Hebrew; K. A. Kitchen, "The Philistines," in *Peoples of the OT Times*, ed. D. J. Wiseman (1973), pp. 53-78; to which should be added: T. Dothan, *The Philistines and their Material Culture* (1967), Hebrew; J. B. Pritchard, "New Evidence on the Role of the Sea Peoples in Canaan at the Beginning of the Iron Age," in *The Role of the Phoenicians in the Interaction of Mediterranean Civilizations*, ed. W. Ward (1968), pp. 99-112; M. Dothan, "Ashdod of the Philistines," in *New Directions in Biblical Archaeology*, ed. D. N. Freedman and J. C. Greenfield (1969), pp. 15-24; T. Dothan, "Anthropoid Clay Coffins from a Late Bronze Age Cemetery near Deir el-Balah," *IEJ*, XXII (1972), 65-72; XXIII (1973), 129-46; A. Mazar, "Excavations at Tell Qasile 1971-72," *IEJ*, XXII (1973), 65-71.

J. C. GREENFIELD

***PHRYGIA.** Aspects of the distinct and well-developed early Iron Age Phrygian civilization are becoming clearer year by year as excavations continue at such sites as Gordion, Ankara, Pessinus, and Boğazköy (Hattusha). Advances in the study of the Phrygian language have been coupled with research into the incompletely resolved problems

German Archaeological Institute, Istanbul Division

4. Statue of Cybele-Kubaba with musicians

of Phrygian origins and religion. In aspects of material culture, the stout citadel and megaron houses at the Phrygian capital, Gordion, as well as the colossal burial tumuli both at Gordion and Ankara have been recognized as monuments typical of Phrygian architecture. Phrygian sculpture is now known in the form of cult reliefs of Cybele-Kubaba and by the limestone statue of Kubaba standing between two youthful flute and lyre players from Boğazköy. *See* Fig. P4.

One millennium after their creation the enormous rock-cut tombs of the Phrygians were taken over and reused by the Christians, albeit with the addition of a cross or inscription and the substitution of the Virgin for Cybele. The Christians also cut into the rock multiroomed houses, individual cells, and even entire churches, just as they did farther W in the Göreme area of CAPPADOCIA.

Bibliography. A. Gabriel, ed., *Phrygie, Exploration archéologique,* vols. I-IV (1941-65); R. S. Young, reports on Gordion in *AJA,* LVI (1952 ff.); M. J. Mellink, "Archaeology in Asia Minor," *AJA,* LIX (1955 ff.), for annual reports on the progress of other excavations in Phrygia; E. Akurgal, *Phrygische Kunst* (1955), and *Die Kunst Anatoliens* (1961), pp. 70-121; R. D. Barnett, "Phrygia and the Peoples of Anatolia in the Iron Age," *CAH,* II, ch. 30 (1967); C. H. Emilie Haspels, *The Highlands of Phrygia,* 2 vols. (1971).

D. BOYD

***PILATE, PONTIUS.** As elsewhere in the PASSION NARRATIVE, Jesus' trial before Pilate reflects each evangelist's theology.

1. The Synoptic gospels. In Mark, Pilate three times calls Jesus "king of the Jews" (15:2, 9, 12), which is the titulus on the cross (15:26). For Mark, Jesus *is* the proclaimer of God's kingdom (1:14-15), but this kingdom is not recognized by the powerful (10:14) or the rich (10:24-25), and is a mystery to outsiders (4:11). In condemning Jesus as king, Pilate is the ironical agent who paves the way for the true meaning of Jesus as king, the one who establishes his kingdom by suffering. Matthew substitutes "Jesus who is called Christ" (Matt. 27:17, 22) for two of the Markan references to Jesus and king. This substitution, as well as the intervention of Pilate's wife (Matt. 27:19), illustrates the Matthean theme that it is the "nations" who will ultimately confess Jesus (cf. Matt. 2:1-12; 28:19). A significant alteration in Luke's trial before Pilate is that Jesus is charged with two clear political crimes: (*a*) urging nonpayment of the tribute to Caesar (23:2) and (*b*) stirring up the people (23:5). Luke is anxious to portray the death of Jesus as a juridical murder and to stress that Jesus was innocent of both the civil and religious charges.

2. The Fourth Gospel. Here the trial before Pilate is especially important (John 18:28–19:16). It is structured into seven scenes with a clear alternation between outside (18:28-32, 38*b*-40; 19:4-8, 12-16*a*) and inside (18:33-38*a*; 19:1-3, 9-11) scenes. Three main theological themes emerge: (*a*) the true nature of Jesus' kingship, (*b*) the crisis that Jesus poses to the powers of the world, and (*c*) Pilate as a symbol of one who, having failed to believe in the truth, ends up serving only the world.

See also PROCURATOR; TRIAL OF JESUS §2; TRIAL OF JESUS[S] §2.

Bibliography. S. G. F. Brandon, "Pontius Pilate in History and Legend," *History Today,* XVIII (1968), 523-30; R. E. Brown, *The Gospel According to John,* ABi (1970); J. F. Quinn, "The Pilate Sequence in the Gospel of Matthew," *Dunwoodie Review,* X (1970), 154-77; G. S. Sloyan, *Jesus on Trial* (1973), excellent study of historical problems and development of traditions.

J. R. DONAHUE

***PILLAR.** Inscribed stones, or stelae as they are technically called, are the rule in Mesopotamia and Egypt, while uninscribed stones, termed pillars or masseboth, are extremely rare. In Palestine, however, plain masseboth are the rule. Virtually all of the few inscribed stelae discovered in Palestine are demonstrably of foreign origin. They are victory or offering stelae bearing Egyptian or Akkadian texts, erected by invading or occupying forces. The Palestinian tradition apparently preserves the form which standing stones had before writing was common. The lack of strong empires in Palestine apparently contributed to the tradition, since stelae were propaganda tools which glorified kings and officers.

Because they do not bear self-explanatory inscriptions, Palestinian pillars are often difficult to interpret. We must deduce the function and meaning of a particular pillar from hints in the archaeological context, from possible parallels among inscribed stelae elsewhere, and from biblical comments.

1. Typology. The pillar was basically a marker; it caught the attention of the onlooker. It performed one or more of four functions: memorial, legal, commemorative, and cultic. Memorial stones perpetuated the memory of the deceased (Absalom, II Sam. 18:18) or marked the place of burial (Gen. 35:20). Legal stones marked the relationship between individuals or groups; they might be treaty stones (Jacob and Laban, Gen. 31:44-50; God and Israel, Josh. 24:27) or boundary markers. Commemorative stones were most common, marking some past event, such as a victory (Saul, I Sam. 15:12) or a sacrifice or vow (Jacob, Gen. 28:20-22), and honoring the participants. The cultic stone marked the immanence of the deity in a sacred area, the point where the deity could be invoked and reached through cultic or sacrificial activity.

An alternate typology sees the pillar as a surrogate, either of the deity or one of the worshipers. The stone either effects the presence of the deity in the sacred place or perpetuates the presence of a worshiper there.

2. Recently excavated pillars. Re-excavation has discovered that the ten pillars at GEZER, misnamed "the Great High Place," were erected simultaneously in a large open area within the city wall not long after the major refounding of the city and remained in use for several centuries. This suggests that they served a public, city-wide function as legal stones, marking a treaty by which ten clans (or cities?) joined to form this huge city. (Compare the twelve stones of the twelve tribes at Gilgal, Josh. 4.) The large stone socket before the alignment either held an emblem of the deity or formed an altar (*see* Fig. P5). (Compare the stones and altar at Sinai, Exod. 24:4.)

Robert B. Wright

5. The masseboth at Gezer

A most striking pillar is the single massebah found in the "holy of holies" of the ARAD sanctuary, clearly a cultic stone indicating the presence of the deity and marking the focus of worship. Its presence in a sanctuary originally constructed under Solomon indicates the general use of such pillars even in the worship of Yahweh, before they were proscribed during the reformation instituted by Josiah (II Kings 23).

A number of miniature masseboth have been found at the sacred precincts of HAZOR and Tell Taanach, measuring only six to fourteen inches high. Their size rendered them cheaper, portable, and easily re-usable. Probably they were not used in public worship, where size was important for viewing, but in private, meant only for the eyes of the worshiper and his deity. Presumably they served to create a "holy place" for worship and as a focus for worship and prayer or were left in the sanctuary to remind the deity of a vow, prayer or the piety of the worshiper.

Bibliography. C. Graesser, Jr., "Standing Stones in Ancient Palestine," *BA,* XXXV (1972), 34-63; E. Stockton, "Stones at Worship," *AJBA,* I (1970), 58-81.

C. GRAESSER, JR.

***POETRY, HEBREW.** Perhaps the most significant advances registered in recent study of Hebrew poetry concern parallel pairs and the techniques used by biblical poets. The discovery and analysis of Ugaritic poetry (*see* UGARIT; UGARIT[S]), with its varied assortment of formal devices, have sharpened the consciousness of biblical scholars, obliging them to inspect OT poetry more intently. Some of the more important formal techniques will be treated here. (All translations are by the author.)

1. Parallel word pairs
2. Conditioned meaning
3. Abstract-concrete pairing
4. Breakup of composite phrases
5. Double-duty modifier
6. Inclusion
7. Ellipsis
8. Enjambment
9. Conclusion

Bibliography

1. Parallel word pairs. Since parallelism of thought and corresponding word mass characterize Hebrew poetic expression, the poet needed numerous pairs of words to sustain his composition. The identification in Ugaritic of nearly a thousand word pairs that also occur in OT poetry, and usually in the same order, discloses that OT poets had fallen heir to a parallelistic tradition which they adapted for the composition of Yahwistic poetry. The Ugaritic word pairs, moreover, enable the critic to recover in the OT braces of words misinterpreted by tradition. Thus Ugar. *'d,* "seat," *//ksu,* "throne," favors this rendition of Ps. 89:29 [H 30]:

> And I will put his offspring upon his seat (לעד),
> and his throne (כסאו) will be like the days of heaven.

2. Conditioned meaning. By reason of their antithetic parallelism (*see* POETRY, HEBREW §C1*b*), some words assume a conditioned meaning. E.g., when contrasted with ימין, "right hand," יד, "hand," sometimes specifically designates the left hand, as in Judg. 5:26:

> Her left hand (ידה) she stretched out for the tent peg,
> and her right hand (ימינה) for the workmen's mallet.

3. Abstract-concrete pairing. Closely related to the preceding phenomenon is the poetic practice of pairing an abstract with a concrete noun, both of which translate concretely. Thus the balance with concrete תירוש, "new wine," points to a concrete signification for abstract שבע, "satiety," in Prov. 3:10, where the following literal rendition attempts to reproduce the complete a.b.c.//c'.b'.a' CHIASMUS of the Hebrew:

> Then filled will be your barns with grain (שבע),
> and with new wine (תירוש) your vats will be bursting.

Commentators have long noticed that barns are not properly said to be filled with "satiety," and have accordingly appealed to LXX σίτον, "wheat," to uphold the emendation of MT שבע, "satiety," to שבר, "grain." The appearance, however, in the eighth-century B.C. Phoenician inscription from Karatepe of the phrase *b'l śb' wtrsh,* "possessors of grain and new wine," vindicates MT and reveals that the biblical writer broke up (*see* §4) a composite phrase composed of an abstract and a concrete noun and distributed its components over the parallel stichs of the verse.

4. Breakup of composite phrases. Biblical poets sometimes split up the elements of composite or stereotyped expressions for the sake of parallelism. In Isa. 11:2 the prophet employs the phrase עצה רוח, "the spirit of counsel," but in 19:3 he distributes its components over the parallel stichs.

> Egypt's spirit (רוח) will gush out of his belly,
> and his counsel (עצתו) will I confuse.

The frequency of this formal device in Isaiah suggests that tradition has missed the meaning when failing to recognize the breakup of the construct chain "the spirit of counsel," in Isa. 40:13:

Who has meted out Yahweh's spirit (רוח),
what man has taught him his counsel (עצתו)?

The phrases קול רם, "a roaring voice," in Deut. 27:14 and קולו רום, "his roaring voice," in Hab. 3:10, suggest that the suspiciously long *hapax legomenon* רוממתך in Isa. 33:3 be broken up into two words, רם מתך, "the roar of your soldiers," and the verse read as a distich with an a.b.c.d./ /a'.b'.'c'.d' sequence:

At the voice (*qôl*) of your army, may
peoples flee,
At the roar (*rôm*) of your soldiers, may
nations be scattered!

This verse illustrates several features: the breakup of קול רום to form an assonant parallel pair רום//קול; the use of the double-duty suffix whereby suffixless המון, "army," shares the suffix of its counterpart מתך, "your soldiers"; the alliteration (*see* POETRY, HEBREW §§E1, 2) of נפצו//נדדו; and the rhyme of גוים//עמים.

The construct chain כסא קדשו, "his holy throne," in Ps. 47:8 [H 9] appears with its components separated to produce an uncanny instance of delayed identification (*see* §9 *below*) in Ps. 11:4:

Yahweh—in the temple is his holy,
Yahweh—in the heavens is his throne.

A prose writer would merely state that Yahweh's holy throne is in the heavenly temple, but the psalmist, by means of the split construct chain, obliges the listener to wait till the end of the verse to learn what "his holy" modifies. In both halves of the verse the writer also uses the suspended subject construction—here, Yahweh—to heighten the suspense.

To sustain the parallel structure of his prayers, the poet drew from the rich thesaurus of composite divine names and separated the components over the balancing halves of the verse. The original full name of Israel's God, יהוה אל, "Yahweh El," lent itself to this practice in Jer. 15:15:

O Yahweh, remember me and visit me,
take vengeance for me on my persecutors, O El!

In this verse, by repointing MT negative *'al,* "not," to *'ēl,* one recovers the composite divine name יהוה אל with which the prophet forms an inclusion (*see* §6 *below*), beginning and ending the line with a divine name. The psalmist employs the same components in Ps. 143:7:

Hasten to answer me, O Yahweh,
my spirit fails, O El (*'ēl;* MT *'al*)!

5. Double-duty modifier. This is one of the most engaging formal devices uncovered by recent research and illustrates the skill and subtlety of the Israelite poets. Also termed the "two-way middle," this device creates an interpenetrating and, as it were, fluid entity, in which phrases will go both with the sentence before and after with no break in the movement of thought. The Elizabethans were trained to use lines that went both ways (Shakespeare's *Sonnets* and John Donne's *Corona* furnish good examples), and now it appears that biblical poets were also familiar with this technique.

I will thank you, my Lord, my God,
with all my heart
I will indeed glorify your name, O Eternal! (Ps. 86:12)

As traditionally understood, the wholeheartedness of the psalmist formally modifies only the first stich, but in this scansion, "with all my heart" modifies both what precedes and what follows.

The appreciation of this prosodic and semantic technique precludes the emendation adopted by some modern versions in II Sam. 1:21. The verse can be translated naturally as follows:

O mountains of Gilboa,
no dew and no rain upon you,
O upland fields!

This two-way curse is addressed both to the mountains of Gilboa and to the upland fields in a 6-9-6 syllabic sequence. In this analysis, vocative "O mountains of Gilboa" balances "O upland fields," whose initial *wāw* parses as the vocative *wāw,* attested in Arabic and Ugaritic. Such careful syntactic and syllabic parallelism tells against the emendation proposed by H. L. Ginsberg in 1938 and accepted by RSV, "Ye mountains of Gilboa / let there be no dew or rain upon you / nor upsurging of the deep!"

The Israelite poets often combined CHIASMUS with the double-duty modifier, as in Ps. 109:14:

Recorded be the iniquity of his father
by El Yahweh
the sin of his mother never erased!

Between the two chiastically arranged stichs the psalmist sets אל יהוה as the two-way middle with the syntactic function of the accusative of agency with two passive verbs. The syllable count numbers 8-3-8. Plural אבתיו might be taken as numerical plural, but pairing with singular אמו, "his mother," favors its parsing as a plural of majesty, and thus singular in meaning, as in Isa. 14:21 and the Phoenician inscription from Karatepe.

6. Inclusion. Repetition characterizes Hebrew poetry and one special use of repetition has been termed "inclusion." This figure also receives the labels "envelope figure" or "cyclic composition," in which the author returns to the point where he began. In its basic form inclusion consists of the exact repetition of key words or phrases. Ps. 12 concludes with the phrase בני אדם, "the sons of men," the same phrase that ends its opening verse. The repetition may also appear at the beginning and at the end of a distich, as in Song of S. 1:2*b*-3*a*:

How much sweeter your love than wine,
than the scent of your oils how much sweeter?

This distich also illustrates the use of the double-duty כי, "How!" whose force extends from the first to the second stich (*see* §7).

A less obvious type of inclusion consists not of

repetition of terms but of the resumption or completion of a thought in other words. Synonymous imperatives at the beginning and end of a unit recur often in prayers, such as Ps. 70, whose first line ends with the plea, "Yahweh, hasten to help me!" and whose last words are "Yahweh, do not tarry!"

An inclusion can also be formed by setting the same root at the ends of a line but in different formations, as in Job 37:16:

> Do you know how the clouds are balanced,
> the wondrous works of the Perfect in Knowledge?

Using the same root ידע, "to know," at the extremities of the verse, the poet contrasts the finite knowledge of Job with the infinite knowledge of God.

An even subtler and more sophisticated inclusion results from placing the members of a fixed word pair, not in the parallel stichs of a verse, but in the first and last lines of a larger poetic segment. The roots *l'y*, "to prevail, vanquish," and *ḥtt*, "to defeat, break," which form a fixed pair in Ugaritic and in I Sam. 2:3-4, appear at the beginning and end of the unit in Isa. 9:3-4 [H 2-3]:

> You have multiplied the nation, O Vanquisher,
> you have increased the joy. . . .
> The oppressor's rod
> you have broken as on Midian's day.

Unexplained MT *lō'*, "not," takes on meaning when repointed to *lē'*, "the Vanquisher," here a fitting appellative because it was God who broke (*haḥittōthā*) the rod of the oppressor.

Hebrew poets also fashioned inclusions by playing on roots containing the same three consonants but arranged in a different sequence. The consonants מצא occur in the verb meaning "to find," but in the sequence אמץ these consonants express the idea of strength. Note the inclusion in the first and fourth stichs of Ps. 89:20-21 [H 21-22]:

> I have found David, my servant. . . .
> my arm also shall strengthen him.

7. Ellipsis. The omission of a word or words which would complete or clarify the construction has long served as one criterion for distinguishing Hebrew poetry from prose. The highly elliptical quality of Ugaritic poetry, with its double-duty suffixes, prepositions, negatives, etc., has alerted scholars to look for similar phenomena in biblical poetry.

The sense of the fourth parallel stich in Ps. 135:16-17 changes when "they have," repeated three times in the first three stichs, is seen to belong semantically to the fourth stich as well, even though it is omitted.

> They have mouths, but do not speak,
> they have eyes, but do not see.
> They have ears, but do not hear,
> nostrils, but there is no breath from their mouths.

Since the final stich already contained as many words as the others, the psalmist may have resorted to ellipsis to avoid overburdening it.

The recognition of the double-duty negative, that is, a negation extending its force from the first to the second stich, uncovers two pointed and coherent questions in Job 22:11:

> Or will you not see the darkness,
> and will (not) the cascading waters cover you?

Eliphaz is warning Job that his callousness toward widows and orphans will bring him to the gloom of Sheol, where rushing waters will overwhelm him. One might add that Job's elliptical style helps explain why this book bristles with problems of translation and interpretation. A double ellipsis creates an exegetical problem in Prov. 19:22:

> What is desired in a man is loyalty,
> and a poor man is better than a liar. (RSV)

To make complete sense of the second stich, one must mentally supply two adjectives omitted by the author who is really saying, "a poor *truthful* man is better than a *rich* liar."

8. Enjambment. A widely held view finds expression in the article POETRY, HEBREW (§C2, p. 834): "We can be sure that no enjambment or 'run-on' lines, typical of Western poetry, will occur in Hebrew poetry." Some modification of this judgment now seems needed. While biblical poets did not employ enjambment nearly as much as do Western poets, they were not strangers to this device.

Zeph. 3:19 illustrates an enjambment which is brought out in a literal translation: "And I will convert for them into praise and renown / in all the earth their humiliation," i.e., "For their sake I will convert their humiliation throughout the world into praise and renown." The direct object of the verb, "and I will convert for them," with a dative suffix of advantage, is forthcoming only with the last word of the line, "their humiliation."

The double-duty modifier or two-way middle discussed above (*see* §5) may be considered a type of enjambment, as illustrated by Isa. 11:9*b*:

> For the earth shall be filled with
> the knowledge of Yahweh
> shall be like the waters covering the sea.

When the line is scanned as a tristich with a 7-5-8 syllable count, the two-way middle, "the knowledge of Yahweh," serves a double syntactic role. With the first stich it functions as the accusative of material, but of the stich that follows it becomes the subject. The use of a phrase with a double grammatical role in a run-on line indicates the skill of Israelite poets and the refinement of their aesthetic sense.

The frequency of the a.b.b.a chiastic pattern, which usually extends over two successive verses, further shows that Hebrew poets were adept at running the thought from one line to the next.

9. Delayed identification. To create suspense the poet reserves explicit mention of the subject or object until the latter part of the verse. Elihu asks Job in Job 34: 17:

> Can it be he will bind up a hater of justice,
> or will you condemn the Just Mighty One?

The identity of "he" in the first stich becomes evident only with the mention of the Just Mighty One in the second stich. Whereupon it also appears that "the hater of justice" is Job himself. The semantic chiasmus is noteworthy: in the first stich God is the subject and Job the object, whereas in the second Job is the subject and God the object.

The prophet shows to what heights of complexity Hebrew poetry could be brought by employing a double-duty negative, a two-way middle, and delayed identification in Isa. 57:12-13:

> And they will not avail you
> when you cry out
> your pantheons will not rescue you.

The subject of "avail" does not become explicit until "your pantheons" are mentioned at the end of the line. 1QIs[a] grasped the sense but not the technique, inserting an explicit subject in the first stich: "And your pantheons will not avail you/ when you cry out your pantheons will not rescue you."

9. Conclusion. Because of a growing awareness that the Israelite poets inherited from their predecessors in Canaan a refined poetic tradition with a varied assortment of techniques, modern scholars treat biblical poetry with increased respect. The literary and rhetorical conventions at their disposal enabled the poets and prophets of Israel to give to their religious and theological message a subtlety and sophistication whose extent continues to unfold.

Bibliography. General: L. A. Schökel, "Poésie hébraïque," in *Dictionnaire de la Bible Supplément,* VIII (1972), cols. 47-90; M. Dahood, *Psalms III* (1970), pp. 361-456; D. N. Freedman, "Prolegomenon," to G. B. Gray, *The Forms of Hebrew Poetry* (reprinted 1972), pp. vii-lvi.

On parallel pairs: R. G. Boling, "'Synonymous' Parallelism in the Psalms," *JSS,* V (1960), 221-55; M. Dahood, *Psalms III,* pp. 445-56, "Ugaritic-Hebrew Parallel Pairs," in *Ras Shamra Parallels,* I (1972), 71-382, and "Ugaritic-Hebrew Parallel Pairs," in *Ras Shamra Parallels,* II (1975), 3-39.

On abstract-concrete pairing: E. König, *Stilistik, Rhetorik, Poetik* (1900), pp. 65-69; W. van der Weiden, "'Abstractum pro concreto': phaenomenon stilisticum," *Verbum Domini,* XLIV (1966), 43-52.

On breakup of composite phrases: E. Z. Melamed, "Breakup of Stereotype Phrases as an Artistic Device in Biblical Poetry," in Ch. Rabin, ed., *Studies in the Bible (Scripta Hierosolymitana),* VIII (1961), 115-53; Y. Avishur, "Pairs of Synonymous Words in the Construct State (and in Appositional Hendiadys) in Biblical Hebrew," *Semitics,* II (1971-72), 17-81; M. Dahood, "The Breakup of Stereotyped Phrases: Some New Examples," in *Theodor Gaster Festschrift* (= *The Journal of the Ancient Near Eastern Society of Columbia University*), V (1973), pp. 83-89.

On double-duty modifier: M. Dahood, "A New Metrical Pattern in Hebrew Poetry," *CBQ,* XXIX (1967), 574-79; W. Kuhnigk, *Nordwestsemitische Studien zum Hoseabuch* (1974), pp. 75-80.

On inclusion: L. J. Liebreich, "Psalms 34 and 145 in the Light of their Key Words," *HUCA,* XXVII (1956), 181-92, esp. *Addendum,* 190-92, and "The Compilation of the Book of Isaiah," *JQR,* XLVIII (1956-57), 114-38, esp. 127 ff.

On delayed identification: M. Dahood, "Ugaritic-Hebrew Syntax and Style," *Ugarit-Forschungen,* I (1969), 15-36, esp. 27. N. Airoldi, "Esodo 22, 28*a*: Esplicitazione ritardata," *Bibl.,* LIV (1973), 63-64. M. DAHOOD

POLYCARP, EPISTLE OF. *See* APOSTOLIC FATHERS [S] §9.

***POLYCARP, MARTYRDOM OF.** *See* APOSTOLIC FATHERS[S] §9.

***POOR.** The term refers first of all to the actual socioeconomic state of persons and groups; later it came to have distinct religious meanings, and eventually became a self-designation of a Jewish-Christian sect.

1. Poverty and wealth in the OT. The OT has a richer vocabulary for poor persons than does the NT. Certain words (דל, lean, thin, poor; רוש, and אביון) refer to economic deprivation; the virtually synonymous terms, עני (bowed down, lowly, downtrodden) and ענו (afflicted, humble), imply also the dehumanizing impact. In the development of the religious meaning of poverty, *'ebhyôn* is associated with *'ānî* and *'anāw;* given the phenomenon of *parallelismus membrorum* (*see* POETRY, HEBREW §C), it is not surprising that these terms are combined in various ways. In Ps. 82:3-4 all four terms occur virtually interchangeably.

The disparity between the rich and the poor developed in distinctive ways during the Israelite monarchy. Though beggary was known, it was never regarded as a holy state; rather, the social and economic well-being of every Israelite was assumed to be the norm (Deut. 15:4). Still, the norm was mocked by reality, "for the poor will never cease out of the land" (Deut. 15:11). This disparity between norm and reality elicited laws for the protection of the poor and produced diverse theological understandings of poverty and wealth.

Among the legal provisions to protect the poor were the law of release, according to which debts were to be cancelled every seven years (Deut. 15), the right of the poor to harvest what was left in the fields (Lev. 19:9-10; etc.; the sojourner, fatherless, and widow are assumed to be poor), prohibition of interest on loans to fellow Israelites, and regulations governing collateral (Exod. 22:25-27; Deut. 23:19-20). In addition, charity to the poor was emphasized (Prov. 14:31; Amos 5:12; Ecclus. 4:1-6).

Given the diverse socioeconomic conditions from the Conquest to Maccabean times, the attitudes and theological understandings of poverty and wealth in the OT vary. First, because prosperity was interpreted as God's blessing, as his reward for fidelity (e.g., Ps. 112), poverty and disaster were viewed as signs of God's negative response to infidelity (especially clear in Deut. 28). Thereby prosperity was given a moral and religious meaning, though sometimes the sages could formulate a straightforward "work ethic" as well (Prov. 20:13; 28:19). At other times, they are quite aware of the ambiguity of wealth and poverty (Prov. 28; Ecclus. 18:25-26; 25:2; 29:22), and the dangers of both are seen (Prov. 30:8-9; Ecclus. 14:3-10), as is the tendency of the rich to exploit the poor (Ecclus. 13:3-13). However, this common-sense correlation between rectitude and prosperity was too simple

(Ecclus. 27:1), as the book of Job makes clear. *See* JOB, BOOK OF §11.

Second, the sense of justice, grounded in Yahweh's own rectitude, induced the prophets to denounce all wealth gained at the expense of the poor (e.g., Amos 2:6-7; 5:10-12; 8:4-6; Isa. 3:13-24; Jer. 6:26-29; Mic. 2:1-2). The prophets' protest is grounded in the same conviction as the simple reward-punishment scheme—that Yahweh rewards rectitude and punishes injustice. New with the prophets is the moral discernment that there is no necessary connection between righteousness and prosperity, since the experience during the monarchies showed that wealth generated power through which the poor were robbed of their rights. (Job 24 is a poignant portrait of the exploited poor.) Therefore the justice of God would lead him to destroy such wealth.

Third, since Yahweh will destroy the nation because of injustice to the poor (as well as for the corruption of Yahwism by the cult of BAAL), it is natural that the expectation of the future would include a portrayal of equity and prosperity for all, and that the ideal ruler would be expected to safeguard the rights of the poor (Isa. 11:3-5). Isaiah's hope of a remnant which would survive disaster comes to be understood by Zephaniah as a remnant of the lowly and poor (עני ודל, Zeph. 3:11-13). During the Exile, Deutero-Isaiah can call God's people the poor (עניים, Isa. 49:13; RSV "afflicted"), though he does not emphasize this; the same understanding of the people of God is found in Trito-Isaiah (Isa. 61:1-2) and Ps. 140:4.

Fourth, given the Hebrew understanding that a just judge not only determines who is in the right but undertakes to rectify the inequity of the case before him, and given the conviction that Yahweh is committed to justice and righteousness, Israelite piety came to believe that God is especially concerned to rectify the plight of the oppressed poor. They are understood to be the special "clients" (*gērîm*) of God. This view is expressed frequently in the Psalter (e.g., Pss. 10; 25; 34; 37). Whether these psalms come from a distinct group (the poor), as has been asserted repeatedly, is doubtful. In any case, these psalms articulate two things simultaneously: a refusal to accept one's lot as fate or as God's will, and a confidence that God will "judge" (vindicate, set right) the plight of the oppressed poor (e.g., Ps. 70; so also Ecclus. 21:5; 35:13-17). Thus the poor person comes to be understood as counting on God, as specially devout because he or she does so in the midst of poverty, and as, therefore, humble and expectant before God.

Finally, given the religious understanding of lowliness before God, humility (ענוה; Gr. πραΰτης) is praised as a virtue, especially by Ben Sirach (e.g., Ecclus. 3:17-20). Humility can be attained by the rich as well as the poor, just as it is seen that poverty can generate greed as well as humility (Ecclus. 31).

2. Qumran. The covenanters at Qumran regarded themselves as the true Israel of the end time. Besides developing a dualistic self-understanding (e.g., the Sons of Light against the Sons of Darkness or of Belial), they applied to themselves a wide range of scriptural terms and motifs, such as saints, covenant, elect, and (God's) people. Not surprisingly, they also claimed to be the poor for whom God was especially concerned. This has led many scholars to conclude that the Qumran covenanters used "the Poor" (either אביונים or ענוים) as a technical title for themselves. In view of their communal life, it has been claimed that Qumran provides a virtually complete precedent for the earliest church in Jerusalem (*see* §4 *below*). However, such a view goes beyond the evidence. (1) Most occurrences of the terms for poverty merely describe a concrete social status (e.g., IQH 2.32; 6.15-16; 1QM 11.13). (2) When the Habakkuk Commentary accuses the Wicked Priest of destroying the poor (1QpHab 12.2), the phrase can mean the community itself (the Poor), but need not be restricted to it. (3) When other terms are used as self-designations (e.g., the community, היחד), the definite article appears. The only text which actually speaks this way is 4QpPs 37: "The Congregation of the Poor." Its importance should not be overemphasized, however, because the Qumranian view of Scripture and the language of Ps. 37 made coining this phrase virtually inevitable. (4) Texts which discuss regulations for sharing property and wealth do not refer to "the poor," while those which speak of "the poor" do not deal with economic arrangements.

In sum, the community at Qumran understood itself as God's poor people, not because members divested themselves of private possessions in order to become the community of "the Poor," but because they may in fact have been poor and harassed, and because they read the Psalms as referring to themselves. *See* DEAD SEA SCROLLS §5; DEAD SEA SCROLLS[S] §§8, 9.

3. Jesus and the gospels. There is no reason to think that Jesus deliberately impoverished himself in order to lead a mendicant life, or that he was unusually poor by contemporary standards. II Cor. 8:9 speaks metaphorically of the Incarnation, not of Jesus' lack of wealth after leaving his trade. Since for John the Incarnation is not a state of lowliness, as for Paul (see also the hymn quoted in Phil. 2:6-11), John's gospel ignores the matter; the Synoptics do not emphasize Jesus' poverty, and only Luke explains how his needs were met (Luke 8:1-3).

Jesus' concern for the poor is emphasized by Luke, largely in the Q material which he used. For Q, Jesus as the Son of man on earth is homeless (Matt. 8:20; Luke 9:58) and directs his mission to the poor (using language of Isa. 61:1; *see* Matt. 11:4-5; Luke 7:22). If, as is likely, the woes originally followed the Beatitudes in Q (Luke 6:22-26), then, for Q, Jesus was convinced that the kingdom would bring about a reversal of present circumstances. Q probably preserved Jesus' own understanding that the kingdom would rectify everything now perverted. Thus Jesus' concern for the poor is not simply the reflex of his own socioeconomic background, nor an expression of a "proletarian" view of the kingdom, but rather makes concrete the coming eschatological reversal. The economic inequities of the present are symptoms of the need of redemption, as are sickness, demon possession, or self-righteousness. Jesus did not romanticize the goodness of the poor, idealize poverty, nor regard wealth as inherently evil. His warnings against its dangers apply to both rich and poor, and assume that his hearers had at least enough wealth to need warning (Q: Matt. 6:24; Luke 16:13; Matt. 6:25-34; Luke 12:22-31). There is nothing in the whole Jesus tradition comparable to the bitter hatred of the rich found in Jas. 5:1-6. The call to sell possessions and distribute the proceeds to the poor (Luke 12:33; *see also* Mark 10:17-22; Matt. 19:16-22; Luke 18:18-23) is not programmatic but a summons to emancipation from security in order to rely wholly on God's kingdom in the company of Jesus.

Mark's compilation of materials in 10:17-31 reveals his awareness that following Jesus has in fact cost many Christians their economic security. The recompense (with persecution!) mentioned here is doubtless metaphorical, and probably refers to Christian mutual concern.

Matthew is often accused of "spiritualizing" the Beatitudes, especially in changing "Blessed are you poor" to "Blessed are the poor in spirit" (Luke 6:20; Matt. 5:3). The exact meaning of "poor in spirit" continues to be debated. The Qumran parallel (1QM 14.7) does not permit the translation, "Blessed are they who voluntarily became poor." Rather, the phrase refers to those whose spirit is impoverished, downtrodden by circumstances, as the adjacent "mourning" and "meek" (cf. *'ᵃnāwîm*) make clear. (At Qumran the antonym occurs also: the haughty of spirit, 1QS 11.1.) In his own way, Matthew has preserved the note of eschatological reversal, and has prevented a strictly economic interpretation of the Beatitudes as well. It is doubtful that he omitted Q's woes (Luke 6:24-26) simply because he was writing for a wealthier church.

Luke strengthened Q's emphasis on Jesus' concern for the poor. The Magnificat (Luke 1:46-55), the story of the rich man and Lazarus (Luke 16:19-31), and Jesus' refusal to be concerned with equitable division of an inheritance, followed by the parable of the rich fool (Luke 12:13-21), are all peculiarly Lukan. The degree to which Luke's portrait of Jesus both incorporates authentic tradition and/or reflects his own concern to show Jesus as a wandering teacher of the Cynic-Stoic type is unclear (*see* CYNICS[S]). His picture of Jesus does not simply reflect the increasing proportion of wealthy persons in the church but confronts it with a Jesus who was poor and concerned especially for the poor, as the opening scene of the ministry makes clear (Luke 4:16-30, using Isa. 61:1-2).

4. Early Christianity. Though the early Christians were generally poor, evidence does not indicate that they were destitute or that they deliberately impoverished themselves to become "the Poor" of God. The earliest Jerusalem church apparently did share wealth among its members. However, one must be cautious in painting too clear a picture. Our knowledge rests solely on Acts, which reports only two actual cases (Acts 4:36-37; 5:1-11); the other evidence is in the generalizing summaries written fifty years later, and probably outside of Palestine. Indeed, these summaries are somewhat inconsistent, for according to Acts 2:45 and 4:34-35, Christians shared wealth to meet actual need, while Acts 2:44 and 4:32 imply total abolition of private property. Moreover, some property appears to have been retained, for the community met in private homes (Acts 2:46; 12:12). In any case, whereas the Qumranians were required to share wealth upon entering the community and then generated wealth by common work, the Jerusalem church seems only to have pooled resources already owned. The reasons for the development and demise of the practice are obscure; both a sense of mutuality and the conviction of the impending return of the Lord (when private possessions would be irrelevant) might have been involved. Possibly the famine reported in Acts 11:28-30 was a factor in the demise of the practice. In any case, there is no evidence that Christians elsewhere took up the practice.

Epiphanius (fourth century) reports that the Ebionites ("the poor"), a Jewish Christian sect of the second century, traced themselves back to the earliest Jerusalem church. But this cannot be substantiated. The first reference to this group is in Irenaeus, who classifies them as heretics; the fragment of the Ebionite Gospel (*see* EBIONITES, GOSPEL OF THE) is of no help in understanding the group's claims. It has been argued that early Ebionite texts and traditions are embedded in the Pseudo-Clementine literature, but this remains hypothetical.

In the Hellenistic cities Christianity only gradually attracted wealthier persons. Yet I Cor. 1:26 should not be pressed to mean that the earliest Christians were only the destitute and the slaves. Acts mentions converts who apparently had some means (Acts 16:14-15; 17:4, 12; 18:3, 8). The diverse economic status of Paul's churches is reflected in I Cor. 11:22; II Cor. 8:2; 9:2. Still, Paul apparently did not find it necessary to warn against the moral dangers of wealth, as did a successor (I Tim. 2:9; 3:8; 6:5-10, 17-19). "Love of money" comes to be a standard element in later Christian moral counsel (e.g., Heb. 13:5; Did. 3:5; Polyc. Phil. 2:2; II Clem. 4:3). Likewise the Markan interpretation of the parable of the soils is sensitive to the issue (Mark 4:19), and the Seer of Patmos warns the church at Laodicea not to be proud of its wealth (Rev. 3:17). Nowhere is the antipathy toward wealth sharper than in the Epistle of James (esp. 2:1-7; 5:1-6).

5. Concern for the poor. Care for the needy became a standard theme of early Christian PARENESIS (I Thess. 4:12; Eph. 4:28; I Tim. 6:17-19; Jas. 1:27; 2:14-17; I John 3:17; I Clem. 38:2; Did. 4:8). The most eloquent statement of this motif is the parable of the last judgment (Matt. 25:31-46).

In addition to support for the needy within the Jerusalem church, Acts reports that the Antioch church sent Paul and Barnabas with money to Jerusalem during a famine (Acts 11:27-30). This "famine visit" poses many historical problems, largely because it cannot be fitted into Paul's own report of his visits to Jerusalem (Gal. 1:18–2:10). Paul reports that, at the Jerusalem Council, he agreed to "remember the poor" (Gal. 2:10). K. Holl proposed that here "the poor" was actually a technical self-designation of the early church (the Poor), and that Rom. 15:26 supported this: "the poor, the saints" (RSV "the poor among the saints"). Thus, Paul is said to have submitted to a juridical claim that his churches support the Jerusalem church (somewhat analogous to the annual temple tax required of Diaspora Jews), and Rom. 15 is somewhat obscure because Paul is concealing this in order to affirm his independence. Although the proposal did not gain acceptance when first advanced, it was revived after the discovery of the Qumran texts. If valid, it would help to substantiate the claims of the Ebionites (*see* §4 *above*).

However, the hypothesis, including its revived form, must be rejected. (1) There was but one offering, not an annual subvention. (2) Paul clearly does not regard himself or his churches as subject to such claims by the Jerusalem church. (3) He regarded the offering as a concrete gesture of the solidarity of the whole church and of thanksgiving for the gospel (Rom. 15:27). (4) The poor Macedonian churches insisted on participating, and clearly were not obligated to do so (II Cor. 8:3-4). (5) Paul was not even sure that the money would be accepted (Rom. 15:31).

Acts ignores the collection, even though it emphasizes the role of Jerusalem, and despite the fact that it was so important to Paul that he insisted on taking the money personally to Jerusalem before going to Spain. Not until Paul stands before Felix (Acts 24:17 ff.) do we learn that he had brought money to Jerusalem, and then it is said to be "alms and offerings" for the Jews. Perhaps the offering was unknown to the author of Acts (he does not mention it in his account of the council, ch. 15); perhaps Paul's hunch was right—the money was not acceptable, and the author of Acts did not want to mar his account by saying so.

Bibliography. H. Birkeland, *'Ani und 'Anaw in den Psalmen* (1933), conclusions modified in *Die Feinde des Individuums in der israelitischen Psalmenliteratur* (1933); A. Causse, *Les "pauvres d'Israel"* (1922); J. Van der Ploeg, "Les pauvres d'Israel et leur piété," *OTS,* VII (1950), 236-70; A. Gelin, *The Poor of Yahweh* (1953 [ET 1964]); S. Legasse, "Les pauvres en esprit et les 'volontaires' de Qumran," *NTS,* VIII (1962), 336-45; H.-J. Kandler, "Die Bedeutung der Armut im Schrifttum von Chirbet Qumran," *Jud,* XIII (1957), 193-209; J. Dupont, "Les πτωχοὶ τῷ πνεύματι de Matthieu 5[3] et les עניי רוח de Qumran," *Neutestamentliche Aufsätze,* J. Schmid Festschrift (1963), pp. 53-64; L. Keck, "The Poor Among the Saints in Jewish Christianity and Qumran," *ZNW,* LVII (1966), 54-78; J. Dupont, *Les Beatitudes,* 2 vols. (1954, 1958); H.-J. Degenhardt, *Lukas —Evangelist der Armen* (1965); E. Percy, *Die Botschaft Jesu,* LUA, XLIX (1953), 40-108; E. Bammel, "πτωχός," *TDNT,* VI (1959), 885-915; D. Flusser, "Blessed are the Poor in Spirit," *IEJ,* X (1960), 1-13; M. Dibelius "Poor and Rich," *The Epistle of James,* Hermeneia (1964 [ET 1976]); M. Hengel, *Property and Riches in the Early Church* (1974); J. Fitzmyer, "The Qumran Scrolls, the Ebionites and Their Literature," in *The Scrolls and the NT,* ed. K. Stendahl (1957), pp. 208-31; K. Holl, "Der Kirchenbegriff des Paulus in seinem Verhältniss zu dem der Urgemeinde," in *Gesammelte Aufsätze zur Kirchengeschichte,* II (1928), 44-67; G. Theissen, "Soziale Integration und sakramentales Handeln: Eine Analyse von I Cor. XI, 17-34," *NovT,* XVI (1974), 179-206; L. Keck, "The Poor Among the Saints in the NT," *ZNW,* LVI (1965), 100-129; K. Nickle, *The Collection,* SBT, XLVIII (1966); D. Georgi, *Die Geschichte der Kollekte des Paulus für Jerusalem,* Theologische Forschung, XXXVIII (1965).

L. E. KECK

***POTTERY.** Excavations in Palestine during the 1960s and early 1970s have considerably refined the knowledge of the pottery of biblical lands.

1. Significance of pottery for dating ancient remains. The chief value of pottery to the archaeologist and historian is its contribution to a chronological framework. It has had a particular importance in Palestinian archaeology because the land is not rich in cultural or architectural finds, and because written material is lacking for many periods (although the corpus of inscriptional material is gradually increasing: *see* INSCRIPTIONS, SEMITIC[S]).

Pottery's importance for chronology is due to its cheapness and abundance rather than its value or rarity. It breaks fairly easily, and had to be continually replaced. But it does not disintegrate, and thus the fragments or "potsherds" remain for the archaeologist to study. Design and form were adapted to needs, and for any period a certain amount of standardization resulted. Yet, over the years styles and methods of manufacture changed.

From these changes is derived pottery's chronological importance. Preparation of the clay depended upon the clay beds and the function the vessel would have. The pots were formed by hand, on a slow or fast wheel, or in a mold. The firing of the vessel in the kiln could be at a high or low temperature, with or without reduction or stacking. The pots may have been decorated by incision or puncturing, slip, paint, or glaze. They may have been burnished before or incised after firing. *See* POTTERY §1.

Nearly all these features are of potential chronological significance (*see* POTTERY §2). Pottery makers from one era of a town's history may have used different clay beds than their predecessors, used different inclusions, preferred incision to painted decoration, or fired their kilns higher. Some features offer rather precise chronological indications. For instance, pattern burnishing was in vogue only a few brief periods of Palestine's history, and overfiring of pots was common in the later Late Bronze Age (*ca.* 1300-1200 B.C.) and the Early Hellenistic period (*ca.* 330-200 B.C.). While these characteristics offer some chronological data, the same clay beds, potters' wheels, and painted traditions often lasted for centuries. The only feature of ceramic vessels that undergoes a continuous process of change is shape. Bases may become more pointed, rounded, flattened, or elongated. Handles may shift their point of attachment, change their manner of attachment, or develop from round to oval or flat. Most often rims are the best chronological indicators. Possible rim shapes are almost infinite, and a particular rim shape tends to develop persistently and rapidly.

Some shapes tend to change much more rapidly than others. While some forms seem to persist for centuries with little or no change, other types disappear after flourishing for only a few years or decades. A few simple types tend to persist or recur century after century. Lamps, for example, change very slowly over a period of 2500 years (*see* LAMP Fig. 8). Some exotic shapes have a very short life and can be immediately identified and closely dated. The evolutionary trend of ancient pottery is commonly downward. Finely made examples of a new and pleasing shape appear. Soon there is a decline in quality: the shape may sag or bulge; the elaborate decoration may disappear. The poorer form may be typical until a new shape takes its place.

Sir Flinders Petrie excavated the first TELL in the Holy Land in 1890 and recognized the chronological value of sherds in stratigraphical excavation. Stratigraphical excavation involves careful separation of each layer of dirt as it is removed, recording where the artifacts are found in each layer (*see* ARCHAEOLOGY §B2*a*; ARCHAEOLOGY[S] §3*bi*). By noting the stratigraphical relationship of potsherds, Petrie was able to develop a relative chronology of pottery types. When he related certain wares to similar wares found in datable Egyptian tombs, he had a peg for determining absolute chronology for Palestine. All stratigraphical excavation since then has contributed to the development of a typological corpus of Palestinian pottery, relatively by means of stratigraphical digging, absolutely by means of inscriptional material or foreign imports.

The knowledge of pottery chronology grew in the first decades of the twentieth century as leading excavators such as Petrie, L. H. Vincent, and C. S. Fisher shared their field observations (*see* ARCHAEOLOGY §E for a summary of excavation in Palestine). The publication of normative ceramic groups issued from Albright's excavation at Tell Beit Mirsim. In the final reports of that excavation, published between 1932 and 1943, Albright was able to provide a fairly complete picture of the changes in pottery shapes from the late third millennium down to the early sixth century B.C. (*see* POTTERY Fig. 65). Pottery chronology for the periods preceding Tell Beit Mirsim was systematized by Wright in 1937.

Since World War II Albright's framework has been considerably expanded. Kenyon's excavations at JERICHO and the ongoing excavations at Bab edh-Dhra' on the SE shore of the Dead Sea throw considerable light on the pottery of the Neolithic, Chalcolithic, and Early Bronze Ages. When the major excavations at SHECHEM, TAANACH, HAZOR, and GEZER, as well as a host of smaller excavations (*see* ARCHAEOLOGY[S] §1), are fully published, the pottery of the Middle and Late Bronze Ages, Iron I, and Iron II, will be better known. Tell Beit Mirism's history ended with the fall of the southern kingdom, about 587 B.C., and there the stratigraphical presentation of pottery ended until the publication of a corpus of Late Hellenistic and Early Roman pottery (200 B.C.–A.D. 70) by Lapp in 1961. The gap in knowledge of ceramics in the period between 587 and 200 B.C. is being filled in by the excavations at GIBEAH, Shechem, Taanach, Tell el-Hesi (*see* EGLON[S] §2), Wadi Daliyeh (*see* SAMARIA PAPYRI[S]), and En-gedi. Stratigraphically important pottery from the Late Roman and Byzantine periods has been published from HESHBON, and, as the results of the excavations at such sites as Araq el-Emir and CAESAREA become known, corpora of pottery of later Palestinian history should appear.

2. Some significant characteristics of Palestinian pottery. (*See* POTTERY §2, Fig. 63; Vol. K-Q Pls. XIX-XXII.)

a. Neolithic (ca. 8000-4300 B.C.). Pottery first appears toward the end of this period. Simple, primitive, handmade. Usual forms: saucers and bowls with splaying or gently curving walls; globular jars with flat bases, high necks contracting inward, and plain rims; small lug, ledge, or knob handles on jars and bowls. Coarse ware: many grits, much straw for cohesion, soft and crumbly resulting from firing at low temperature. Finer ware: better fired, cleaner clay, attractive finish—smoothed over, cream-colored slip with finely burnished red slip over parts forming a design usually of chevrons or triangles.

b. Chalcolithic (ca. 4300-3200 B.C.). The transition from Neolithic to Chalcolithic is still uncertain, but Yarmukian and Jericho Pottery Neolithic B cultures appeared at the end of the fifth millennium and into the fourth. Better fired, thinner, less straw, forms more advanced. Jar rims have concave interior. Dark red slip common, sometimes burnished. Incised herring-bone design. Ghassulian culture widespread in Late Chalcolithic. Ware is hard, thin, and well-fired. Some vessels of elaborate form; characteristic are "churns" (*see* Vol. K-Q Pl. XXII) and "cornets." Decoration includes applied bands and dark painted designs.

c. Early Bronze (ca. 3200-2050 B.C.). Handmade until late in the period. Typical are ledge handles, high loop handles on juglets, vertical pierced lug handles on jars and juglets, flat bases, shallow bowls. Characteristic EB I finishes: red-burnished slip, "grain wash," "line-group" painting. In EB II metallic ware and "Abydos" jugs appear. Khirbet Kerak ware (*see* Vol. K-Q Pl. XXII) appears in EB III. EB IV–MB I is an intermediate period, closer in many respects to the Early Bronze Age. "Teapots" are common.

d. Middle Bronze (ca. 2050-1550 B.C.). Caliciform jar and bowl lamps with four pinched spouts in MB I. In MB II, wheel-made, homogeneous, pleasing forms. Carinated bowls often continuously burnished over rich dark or cream slip, sometimes with trumpet foot. Piriform and cylindrical juglets sometimes with double handles, button bases. Elongated dipper juglets. Graceful large jar and bowl forms. Richer burnishing and elaborate forms in MB IIA and B with some deterioration in MB IIC.

e. Late Bronze (ca. 1550-1200 B.C.). LB I: Bichrome painted ware—friezes of birds, fish, and geometric designs (*see* ART §2*d*, Figs. 72-74; Vol. K-Q Pl. XX). LB II: imported pottery from Mycenae (stirrup jars, piriform jugs, pyxides) and Cyprus ("bilbils," "milk bowls"); local imitations and some very poor wares. Astarte molded plaques (cf. POTTERY §5; Vol. K-Q Pl. XXIII*b*).

f. Iron I (ca. 1200-918 B.C.). Philistine pottery: red and black geometric designs and swans on craters and beer mugs (*see* PHILISTINES Fig. 50;

ART §2*d*, Fig. 75; Vol. K-Q Pl. XX*f*). Local forms: large jars with collared rims, vertically burnished juglets with trefoil mouths, black-burnished juglets, chalices, bowls with chordal hand burnishing. Imported Cypro-Phoenician juglets.

g. Iron II (ca. 918-587 B.C.). Standardization of ware through mass production, varying sizes of wheel-burnished bowls, red and black burnished oil juglets, vertically burnished elongated juglets, cups, pitchers, cooking pots, decanters. "Snowman" figurines. *See* POTTERY §§3, 5; Vol. K-Q Pl. XXI.

h. Exilic-Persian (ca. 587-332 B.C.). Elongated bottles, sausage jars with sharp shoulders and bases tapering to a point, "basket" handle jars with stump bases, flat, wide-rimmed lamps. Chalky orange ware, ware with greenish cast, impressed chevron designs.

i. Hellenistic (ca. 332-63 B.C.). Imported black-glazed pottery, especially small bowls and plates; imitated locally by painting or wash, then without painting and with deterioration in form. Rhodian jars with inscribed handles imported. Closed lamps: wheel-made, small, folded, and in the second century—molded. Bottles: globular and fusiform unguentaria.

j. Roman (63 B.C.–A.D. 324). *Terra sigillata* (red-glazed bowls and plates with rouletting on interior and rim) imported. Thin and delicate Nabatean ware with elaborate painted floral designs in Transjordan and the Negev. (*See* NABATEANS for a history of these people.) Locally made globular juglets, small bowls, flasks with twisted handles, Herodian bow-spouted lamps; ribbed ware. In first and second centuries A.D. molded lamps with elaborate designs and figures were imported from Italy and imitated in Palestine. *See* LAMP Fig. 8, no. 8; the identification in IDB is in error; it is Roman.

k. Byzantine (A.D. 324-630). Ribbing quite pronounced on jars and cooking pots. Jugs and bowls with incised lines—straight and wavy combed patterns; long-necked juglets with angular handles. Late Byzantine: slashes and nicks on shoulders of juglets; single wavy lines on bowls. Slipper, high-bowl, and candlestick lamps. *See* MENORAH[S].

3. New methods in pottery study. Descriptions of clay and ware have become more standardized in recent years in an attempt to make the descriptions more objective. The Munsell Soil Color Charts are now commonly used in order to describe accurately the hue, lightness value, and chroma of a sherd—both its surfaces and its core. Such data can now be analyzed by a computer, and this has been done by some excavators.

Various scientific tests are undertaken to determine the composition of clays and fired wares. In petrographic analysis thin sections of potsherds are studied to determine the mineral content of a ware. In spectographic analysis the composition of clays is investigated. Chemical analysis aids in the identification of clay constituents. Kiln tests try to re-enact the methods of ancient pottery firing. These studies make it possible to trace the source of clay beds, discover ancient cultural ties and trade routes, and to learn what people of the past considered the best clay for their purposes. Studies have been undertaken to consider possible chronological implications of clay density and to discover whether a particular type of clay was considered best for a certain kind of vessel. *See* ARCHAEOLOGY §C6.

A method known as thermoluminescence has been developed to determine the date pottery was fired and thus the time a vessel was in use. As carbon 14 measures the amount of carbon in organic material, thermoluminescence measures the change heat has made in texture and the amount of degradation which has taken place in ceramic material. If such a method were perfected it could be correlated with the archaeologist's knowledge of pottery forms and types for chronological purposes. As yet the tests are not foolproof, and as with carbon 14, a knowledge of pottery form can refine thermoluminescence dates. *See* ARCHAEOLOGY [S] §3*c*; CHRONOLOGY, MESOPOTAMIAN (METHOD) [S].

See also ASHDOD[S].

Bibliography. R. Amiran, *Ancient Pottery of the Holy Land* (1969), most comprehensive corpus of pottery from the Neolithic period to the end of Iron II, presented chronologically and regionally; W. F. Albright, *The Archaeology of Palestine* (1960), latest edition of this authoritative work; G. E. Wright, "The Archaeology of Palestine," in *The Bible and the Ancient Near East*, ed. G. E. Wright (1961), pp. 73-112, discussion of excavations by periods with charts and particular attention to stratigraphical significance; K. M. Kenyon, *Archaeology in the Holy Land* (1970), especially good concerning methodology, the excavation of Jericho, and its contribution to the early periods of Palestine's history; P. W. Lapp, *Palestinian Ceramic Chronology, 200 B.C.–A.D. 70* (1961), gives discussion and corpus of pottery for Late Hellenistic and Early Roman times, "The Pottery of Palestine in the Persian Period," *Archäologie und AT*, ed. A. Kuschke and E. Kutsch (1970), pp. 179-97, and *The Tale of the Tell* (1975), popularly written short dig reports and introduction to methodology; J. A. Sauer, *Heshbon Pottery 1971* (1973), first stratigraphical study of some pottery of the Byzantine and Arabic periods. *Archaeometry*, periodical reporting recent research in scientific methods, such as thermoluminescence, and archaeology. *Munsell Soil Color Charts* (1971), the charts now used by most excavators for ware descriptions of pottery.

N. L. LAPP

***POVERTY.** *See* POOR[S].

***PREHISTORY IN THE ANCIENT NEAR EAST.** This summary discussion is organized under headings which show the chronological order of the major features of human development in the Near East prior to written history.

1. Paleolithic food collectors. Man's history as a toolmaker is now known to extend back over two million years. For more than 99.5 per cent of this time, man and his antecedents survived by hunting and collecting wild resources. Virtually all the evidence of the earliest phases of tool manufacture is presently confined to Africa, with the earliest evidence from Europe suggesting an arrival of toolmaking hominids there by about one million years ago. While this implies that such creatures were present in the Near East before that time, no substantiating evidence is yet at hand.

a. The earliest sites in the Near East. Our earliest evidence of a toolmaking hominid in the Near East comes from the site of Ubeidiya, a short distance S of the Sea of Galilee. Here primitive pebble chopper tools and crude hand axes have been found associated with the bones of hippopotamuses, crocodiles, and various animals now extinct, in geological deposits whose age is estimated at about 600,000 years. Fragmentary hominid remains from the site suggest the presence of *Homo erectus* ("Pithecanthropus") as the toolmaker. The hand axes are deeply flaked pointed pebbles, characteristic of the early stages of manufacture of this type of tool in other areas of the Old World, and thus seem to fit the early Middle Pleistocene date assigned to the deposits. The site is an archaeological curiosity, in that the geological layers have been tilted into vertical positions and even overturned by the active geological forces at this extremity of the Great Rift system.

Another very early site, dating somewhat later in the Middle Pleistocene, is Latamne, near the Orontes River in NW Syria. Here a heavy concentration of hand axes and other stone tools of somewhat more refined manufacturing technique than those of Ubeidiya has been discovered. Unfortunately, animal bones were not well preserved at the site, so that specific activities other than stone-tool manufacture are difficult to interpret. The presence of large stone blocks may be evidence of windbreaks or other crude structures.

Surface finds of hand axes occur throughout the Near East, but mostly in the Levant and Egypt, and suggest the presence of man (presumably in the form of *Homo erectus*) through the whole of the Middle Pleistocene. On the basis of the kinds of animals butchered at Ubeidiya we can conclude that these hominids occasionally engaged in cooperative hunts involving at least several adult males, although most of their subsistence was probably derived from plant foods and smaller animals.

b. The appearance of modern man. A major problem in Paleolithic studies throughout the Old World concerns the appearance of anatomically modern *Homo sapiens,* as distinct from earlier Neanderthal forms. The circumstances under which modern man appeared in the Near East, as well as in the rest of the Old World, are still relatively little understood. Throughout the Near East hominid fossils dating to the earlier part of the Late Pleistocene (i.e., earlier than about forty thousand years ago) are either quite similar to Neanderthal man, as known elsewhere, or differ significantly from modern man in their possession of features suggesting Neanderthal affinities. Sites yielding Near Eastern Neanderthals include Shanidar in N Iraq, and Amud, Zuttiyeh, and Tabun in Palestine. All are cave or rock-shelter deposits. The site of Skhul, a shallow shelter in the Wadi el-MUGHARAH only a few hundred meters from Tabun, has yielded the remains of perhaps eleven individuals which share features of both Neanderthal and modern man. While the cultural remains found with all of these fossils in the Levant are generally similar, recent evidence from Tabun suggests that the Skhul hominids are significantly later in time than the Tabun Neanderthal. Another site which is important in this regard is the cave of Qafzeh, near Nazareth in Palestine. Here excavations in the 1930s and the 1960s yielded the remains of over a dozen individuals of anatomically modern man in association with an industry resembling that from the other Levantine fossil-man sites. It is hoped that future dating of this site relative to Tabun and Skhul will help to resolve the question of whether modern man and Neanderthal man were contemporaries in the Near East in the middle Late Pleistocene, or whether a chronological ordering exists suggesting the development of modern man from a Neanderthal ancestor. The stone-tool industries associated with these fossil men are generally termed "Middle Paleolithic" (or "Mousterian") to contrast them with those of the earlier Lower Paleolithic hand-ax industries. They show a complex use of manufactured flakes of stone in the fabrication of many specialized implements, some of which suggest the hafting of stone to spear shafts or handles. Other evidence of the increasing complexity of human culture is seen in the deliberate burials of the Neanderthals, occasionally accompanied by foreign objects (most frequently animal bones) which have been interpreted as grave offerings to accompany the deceased in a future existence. If this interpretation is correct, the concept of an after-life dates back at least as far as the Late Pleistocene world of Neanderthal man.

c. The intensive collectors of the terminal Pleistocene. By the end of the Late Pleistocene (coincident with the final retreat of the great continental and alpine glaciers ten thousand years ago), man's activities in the Near East reflect a more intensive utilization of wild resources than previously. This intensive exploitation can be seen in the development of new items in the technology such as sickles for the harvesting of tough-stemmed plants and milling stones for grinding seeds or nuts, and by the presence of food remains not previously represented in significant quantities, such as snails. Although the use of sickles and milling stones appears first in the Upper Nile Valley at about 10,000 B.C., this kind of activity seems not to have persisted there, and is best known from several sites in Palestine assigned to the Natufian culture (named after the site of Shukbah in the Wadi Natuf, NW of Jerusalem). Several Natufian sites, including El Wad in the Wadi el-Mugharah between Skhul and Tabun, Ein Mallaha N of the Sea of Galilee, and the basal levels at Jericho (*see* JERICHO[S] §2), suggest the presence of at least semipermanent communities characterized by substantial architecture. Each of these sites is postulated to have been in the immediate vicinity of abundant resources of plant and animal food at 8000-9000 B.C. Perhaps these resources were sufficient, given the development of a system of storage (e.g., for wild grains), for the development of permanent settlements. Such settlements outside Palestine are suggested by the impressive deposits at Mureybit on the Euphrates and perhaps by the lower levels of Ganj Dareh in the Kermanshah region of Iran, both of which appear to date to the ninth millennium B.C.

2. The early food producers. How and under what circumstances human beings began to cultivate plants and raise animals has been a major focus of research since the pioneering work of

Braidwood at Jarmo shortly after World War II. The earliest known example of domestication anywhere is the dog from the Late Pleistocene site of Palegawra in N Iraq, dating to approximately 10,000 B.C. Based upon the evidence of disproportionately high quantities of the bones of young animals, it is now believed that domestic sheep were present at the site of Zawi Chemi Shanidar in the same area by the first half of the ninth millennium B.C. At all other sites showing evidence of early food production, however, goats either predominate (as at Ali Kosh in the Deh Luran plain of SW Iran), or are the exclusive domesticated herbivore (as at Beidha near Petra in SW Jordan). Throughout the Near East early sites of food producers show heavy reliance on domesticated grains (wheat and barley) as well as a continuing dependence on wild resources.

a. The Levant and Anatolia. The classification of sites of early food producers in this area is largely based on the sequence in the early levels of Jericho, where two sequent aceramic cultures were described: Prepottery Neolithic A (PPNA) and B (PPNB). PPNA, as known only from Jericho and the Nahal Oren site on Mount Carmel, is characterized by relatively large circular house structures, a lithic industry suggesting Natufian antecedents, and possible early phases of domestication of wheat and barley. Radiocarbon determinations suggest that the PPNA levels span most of the eighth millennium B.C. In contrast to PPNA, PPNB culture (late eighth to early seventh millennium B.C.) is known from over half-a-dozen sites in Palestine and adjacent areas. It is characterized by well-established domestication of wheat and barley, domestic goats, rectangular-roomed architecture incorporating lime or gypsum plaster, and a curious mortuary complex involving the removal and treatment of selected skulls (*see* JERICHO Fig. 15). It appears that the PPNB culture represents the first widespread pattern of successful food production in the Levant, with sites now known from virtually all areas of Palestine. Patterns of contact between the PPNB settlements of the Levant and contemporary peoples in Anatolia are indicated by Turkish obsidian in the PPNB sites and, perhaps, by the use of plastered floors and subfloor structures at Çanyönü Tepesi near Diyarbekir, and the retention of human skulls in rooms with plastered floors in the aceramic levels at Hacilar in SW Anatolia. These widespread similarities suggest a rapid and unified spread of early food production through the W portion of the Near East at the close of the eighth millennium B.C.

b. The Zagros foothills of Mesopotamia. The earliest stages of food production in this area are represented by Zawi Chemi Shanidar and Karim Shahir in the N and by Ganj Dareh and the Bus Mordeh phase at the Ali Kosh site in the S. Of these, only Ali Kosh has been completely reported. In this eastern area it appears that fully efficient food production was not effective until after 7000 B.C. Such sites as Jarmo in N Iraq, and the Ali Kosh phase at Ali Kosh in SW Iran are good examples of early food-producing villages in this region. This complex of food production relies on both sheep and goats, and in some instances domestic pigs, as well as wheat, barley, and perhaps a somewhat wider range of other cultigens. There seem to be fewer unifying features between the early villages in these eastern areas than in the W. Several sites in both E and W have yielded small, highly stylized female figurines which may be evidence of a shared ideology, but evidence for this remains sketchy. On the basis of limited architectural exposures in the E it appears that ritual activity at this time was probably based in the household, while in the W there is more evidence for communal centralization of religion.

3. The late food producers and the appearance of complex societies. During the last half of the seventh millennium B.C., well established farming communities are found from central Anatolia to the Levant and around the Taurus-Zagros arc along the margins of the Mesopotamian plain. It is during this period that ceramics first appear (aside from occasional, probably accidentally fired clay containers at some earlier sites), and by 6000 B.C. pottery occurs wherever villages are found. The most impressive settlement described for this period is Çatal Hüyük, on the Konya plain of S central Anatolia. The site consists of a tell covering an area of some thirty-two acres, a sizable portion of which was probably under continual occupation. The architecture, consisting of contiguous rectangular-roomed structures of mud brick, incorporates numerous rooms apparently used for ritual purposes and decorated with painted murals, low-relief sculpture in clay, and frequently with the reconstructed craniums and horn cores of large bulls, as well as the jaws and skulls of sheep, goats, and pigs. The number of these "shrines" (as they are termed by the excavator, Mellaart) in relation to domestic structures suggests a lineage-based ritual structure, or perhaps small cross-lineage ritual societies. The factors which brought and held together a community of this size in this period have yet to be explained. By the early sixth millennium, the cultural traditions which were to lead to complex societies and ultimately civilization are fully in evidence along the eastern edges of the Mesopotamian plain. By the late sixth millennium B.C. such sites as Tel Es-Sawwan on the Tigris near Baghdad show the beginnings of irrigation agriculture and complex architectural features suggesting an early central temple structure, two basic elements in later Mesopotamian civilizations. Ultimately, a concentration on sheep and fish as sources of protein, and salt-resistant barley as the basic crop for irrigation agriculture, allowed man to take full advantage of the rich potential of the S Mesopotamian plain to achieve urban settlements and literate civilization in that area.

In contrast, the promise of the early settlements in the Palestinian area was never realized in terms of an independent development of civilization. The cultural antecedents of the cities of the biblical period remain little understood, largely because of the concentration of archaeological interest in earlier and later periods and the physical difficulties of exposing significant areas of the deepest levels of the more important sites. The picture at present suggests small agricultural settlements in favorable areas, with greater concentration on pastoralism in marginal regions, as was the case at the beginning of recorded history. The early importance of Palestine with regard to economic and cultural exchange between the Near East and Egypt is evident in the fourth-millennium sites near BEER-SHEBA in the N Negeb, which have yielded ivory objects similar to those of predynastic Egypt, in association with copper implements of probable local manufacture, but indicating a diffusion of metallurgic techniques from the N. There can be little doubt that the growth of such strategically located historical cities as Gezer, Beth-shan, and Megiddo owed much to these prehistoric patterns of trade as well as to the long agricultural heritage of the Levant. *See also* AGRICULTURE[S].

Bibliography. R. J. Braidwood, *Prehistoric Men* (8th ed., 1975); F. Hole, K. V. Flannery, and J. A. Neely, "Prehistory and Human Ecology of the Deh Luran Plain," *Memoirs, Museum of Anthropology, University of Michigan,* I (1969); J. Perrot, "Préhistoire palestinienne," *DBSup,* VIII (1972), cols. 286-446; P. Singh, *Neolithic Cultures of Western Asia* (1974); G. A. Wright, "Origins of Food Production in Southwestern Asia: A Survey of Ideas," *Current Anthropology,* XII (1971), 447-77.

A. J. JELINEK

***PRESENCE OF GOD, CULTIC.** How Yahweh, the God of Israel, is present constitutes a major concern to both ancient Israel and the early church. There is no clear or single resolution of the question, but only a variety of explorations of it. Israel's struggle can be articulated in concerns which are in tension but which must be held together. The central polarity concerns the freedom of Yahweh and his accessibility. It was of primary importance to have regular, reliable access to the HOLY ONE around which the community gathers and focuses. It is the responsibility of cult to regularize such access through holy times (Deut. 16:16-17), holy actions (Exod. 16:32-33), and holy words (*see* WORSHIP IN THE OT; WORSHIP IN NT TIMES, JEWISH), so that approach to the Holy God is done without inordinate anxiety (*see* HOLINESS §A2*d*). At the same time, Yahweh had shown himself to be free and sovereign, captured in no cultic theory or practice, but abroad in the land according to his inscrutable purposes.

This polarity runs throughout the history of Israel. Yahweh is the utterly free one who goes to and fro as he chooses (II Sam. 7:6), and yet who faithfully accompanies his people (Exod. 33:14; Isa. 43:2) and answers them when they call (Exod. 2:24–3:10). So Israel knows that its life is characterized by his presence (Exod. 33:16), but also it has experienced his absence (Ps. 22:1 [H 2]; Isa. 49:14).

This polarity is evident in two crises which Israel sought to resolve in favor of accessibility. In the first, David proposed a "house" for Yahweh which would end his freedom, and therefore end Israel's precariousness, but Yahweh prohibited it (II Sam. 7:1-7). The second, the dedication of the temple, gives us the central text on cultic presence (I Kings 8). The statement of his accessibility is expressed in the early poem of 8:12-13 which situates Yahweh securely in the "house": "The Lord . . . has said that he would dwell in thick darkness. I have built thee an exalted house, a place for thee to dwell in for ever." But subtle protest is expressed in vs. 9 (the ark is empty), and formal protest in vs. 27 which denies that Yahweh is contained in the cult place: "But will God indeed dwell on the earth? Behold, heaven and the highest heaven cannot contain thee; how much less this house which I have built!" The resolution in vss. 28-30 as "name" theology indicates the delicacy of the issue (*see* NAME §B4*e*). He is the Holy One, unapproachable in his awesomeness, but he is also in our midst, sustaining and defending. It is this bold affirmation, "The Holy One in our midst" (cf. Hos. 11:9; Isa. 12:6), which cultic arrangements seek to express and protect. The concern is twofold: (*a*) that Yahweh not abandon Israel, and (*b*) that his presence not destroy Israel or cause Yahweh to lose his sovereign freedom.

1. The coming God
2. The God who leads
3. The abiding God
4. The God who hides himself
5. Resolutions of the issue
6. NT utilization of themes
7. Conclusion

Bibliography

1. The coming God. Yahweh is experienced and described as the one who comes, unexpectedly and irresistibly, and when he comes, the situation is decisively changed. The coming God dwells in remoteness, parallel to other high gods in Israel's religious environment, who dwell in numinal mystery in some remote mountain. *See* MOUNT, MOUNTAIN[S]; ZION TRADITION[S].

For Israel the theophany at Sinai is the paradigm of his coming (Exod. 19), and that narrative report is undoubtedly stylized as a cultic rubric (*see* THEOPHANY IN THE OT[S]). The language describing his presence is dominated by verbs: he comes, he comes down, he appears. There is no doubt that the language appeals to (*a*) traditions of a storm god who appears in the upheaval of the storm, and (*b*) traditions of a war god who comes as an invader or conqueror to establish his rule and to crush resisters.

These overwhelming experiences stand at the beginning of Israel's sense of Yahweh's presence. They witness to the primitive experience of holiness intruding in the people's life (Exod. 3:1-6; Josh. 5:13-15) and are concerned, not with the manner of his being present, but with the sense of Yahweh's unquestioned freedom, power, and sovereignty. For Israel, religious experience meant coming to terms with that freedom and sovereignty which may be termed "precultic."

2. The God who leads. Yahweh is not regarded as attached to a place but is committed to persons and community. He is not located in space but is a presence in dialogue with, but also in tension with, his partner in dialogue. He comes to individuals unexpectedly even as he did to the nation at Sinai, but the events are less public (Judg. 6:11-18).

Israel is reticent in commenting upon the ways God is with his partners. Visual elements are minimized so that the meeting involves essentially speaking or hearing. Thus even in the overwhelming encounters of Moses (Exod. 3:1-6) and Joshua (Josh. 5:15), the encounter moves immediately to speech. There is no interest in any form of appearance. They were content to hear; this was the way in which they experienced God's presence. And when he speaks he may issue commands (Gen. 12:1-3) or give assurances (Gen. 15:1), but both are in the context of his promise that he will be with his people. This issue is succinctly stated in Exod. 33:14-16:

Yahweh to Moses:	My presence will go with you, and I will give you rest.
Moses to Yahweh:	If thy presence will not go with me, do not carry us up from here. . . . Is it not in thy going with us, so that we are distinct . . . from all other people that are upon the face of the earth?

Israel is a pilgrim people, and Yahweh moves with her (cf. Num. 10:35-36, on the ark as his form of movement).

This conviction constituted for Israel a foundation of faith as well as a central problem. Exod. 33:17-23 indicates the problem: when the assurance of God's presence is given, Israel through Moses wants to know the manner of that presence. The narrative concludes with Yahweh's assertion of his freedom and his refusal to disclose what they want to know: "You shall see my back; but my face shall not be seen" (Exod. 33:23). His assurance is also a warning. He will be present to Israel, but he will not put himself at her disposal. God would be known by Israel, but he would not be seen, for to be seen limits his freedom and subdues the mystery which must be preserved (cf. Exod. 6:3).

Israel's peculiar way through history is with this "Yes-No" of God. The entire period of sojourn in the wilderness is under his leadership which sustains, but that same leadership always leaves her precariously dependent.

His presence is sometimes reported in the form of an angel (Exod. 14:19), or in relation to the ark (Num. 10:35-36), or as a pillar of cloud or fire (Num. 14:14): "Thou, O Lord, art in the midst of this people; for thou, O Lord, art seen face to face, and thy cloud stands over them and thou goest before them, in a pillar of cloud by day and in a pillar of fire by night." This verse is evidence of the problem, because the narrator wants to speak of "face-to-face" presence but must settle for another image. Clearly the linguistic expression of Israel is problematical and ambiguous because her experience of God is problematical and ambiguous. Israel always had to speak about one who was fully present, but whose presence might be withdrawn at any time.

In quite another form his leading, sustaining presence is articulated in the formula "I am with you; I will be with you." It is a bald statement without evidence, without religious explanation or implementation. He is there, as promise on the way to fulfillment (Gen. 39:2-3, 23), as the one who supports in trials (Isa. 43:2), as the eternal "Yes" which all the dangers and threats of historical existence cannot overcome. This simple assurance becomes the bedrock of Israel's confidence and trust (Ps. 23:4; cf. Gen. 26:3, 24; 28:15; 31:3; Deut. 31:6).

But even here, Israel has not given expression to a notion of cultic presence. In her more primitive memory, he is a God known in situations of distress and danger as the guarantor who came where his people were.

3. The abiding God. Religion presses toward organization and regularization. No community, including Israel, could live with the raw, intruding holiness of Yahweh as the coming God nor with the quiet, invisible assurance of his leadership. Therefore Israel evolved a complex cultic apparatus to respond to the question "How is Yahweh present?" As the coming God may be peculiarly linked to the primitive beginnings of Israel in Exodus and Sinai, and as the leading, accompanying God is especially appropriate to the sojourn period of precarious dependence, the articulation of the abiding God is pertinent to the period of the monarchs who sought to bring Israel's various traditions of cult into a coherent pattern. A great political establishment relies on overarching religious symbols with a powerful sense of transcendence, but it cannot tolerate the unpredictable freedom of a coming God who tends to act for the disestablishment of every arrangement. Thus there was an effort to honor Yahweh's majestic sovereignty, but at the same time to conceptualize his presence as amenable to the regime of the period. Such efforts included several features.

a) The utilization of old ark traditions (II Sam. 6). The ark apparently had been a seat for the journeying king-god from very early days. Now he is seated on his throne in the Jerusalem temple (I Kings 8), guest and patron of the regime.

b) The old tent-of-meeting tradition (*see* TENT) was an effort to speak about Yahweh's meeting with rather than dwelling in Israel, but this tradition seems to have evolved into a tradition of the TABERNACLE, which moves closer to affirming that Yahweh is actually there, not simply that he meets there with his people.

c) The GLORY of Yahweh, a symbol of his unapproachability, perhaps derived from solar worship, tended to become a cultic property so that Yahweh in his glory was located in the shrine (Exod. 40:34-38; Isa. 6:3).

d) Aware that such presence tends crudely to deny Yahweh his freedom, the tradition of Deuteronomy (reflected in I Kings 8) articulated a "theology of name" which suggested that, while the temple is a place of his special attention, he is not fully committed to it, and therefore his freedom and power are not domesticated for the royal-urban regime which controls the shrine.

e) The Solomonic temple is based upon Canaanite-Phoenician models and therefore upon non-Israelite theology, which lacked the tension of which we have spoken. Clearly the God who abides in the dark holy of holies is not one who any longer acts in history, not one who sojourns with his people, not one who exercises transcendence over his realm, either as assurance or as judgment. The temple is Israel's supreme attempt to maintain the delicate balance of presence to Israel and freedom from Israel. A high theology of cultic presence suggests that Yahweh sits as a royal ruler on his throne. The emphasis is on his enduring presence, lending stability and legitimacy both to the cult and to the regime which sustains it. Alternatively he is said to sojourn there; i.e., to regard it as his field of action from which he moves about as he chooses. This theology which speaks of tabernacling or tenting (cf. Rev. 21:3) affirms God's presence, but seeks to safeguard the divine freedom. It acknowledges the precariousness of his presence and faces the real possibility of his absence.

Israel's temple and all her expressions of Yahweh's cultic presence are bold efforts to address an insoluble problem. There is no way that Yahweh's holy freedom can be fully honored and yet the certainty of his presence be maintained. Israel's impressions and images ran the gamut from *full presence,* which denied his freedom, to *full freedom,* which made his presence quite uncertain.

The royal-priestly-urban establishment in Jerusalem fostered a notion of cultic presence which promised too much and destroyed the tension of freedom and accessibility. It received expression in the hymnody of Zion: "There is a river whose streams make glad the city of God, the holy habitation of the Most High. God is in the midst of her, she shall not be moved" (Ps. 46:4-5 [H 5-6]; cf. 48:1-3, 8 [H 2-4, 9]). This same royal-priestly theology evoked popular ideology which presumed upon Yahweh: "They lean upon the Lord and say, 'Is not the Lord in the midst of us? No evil shall come upon us' " (Mic. 3:11); "Do not trust in these deceptive words: 'This is the temple of the Lord, the temple of the Lord, the temple of the Lord' " (Jer. 7:4).

Against such popular religion fed by establishment propaganda, prophetic protest rejected a tension-free notion of cultic presence. The prophets reasserted the freedom of Yahweh at the expense of his accessibility. They reasserted that he will be found, not in the domesticated regularity of the shrine, but in the ragged discontinuity of history.

Neither popular royal-priestly religion nor prophetic protest could settle the issue. Israel's cult sought simply to give visible, institutional expression to the tension. The one who causes his face to shine (Num. 6:24-26; Ps. 27:1) and who plants and builds also tears down and plucks up (Jer. 1:10). The affirmation is Israel's fundamental problem and her central conviction.

4. The God who hides himself. Israel discovered that the one who shows himself is the one who also hides himself. The Psalms give expression to a repeated experience in Israel's life—that prayers go unanswered; covenant seems voided; and life is reduced to an unrelieved monologue without response.

It was the Exile that led Israel most deeply to an awareness of God's overwhelming absence. Ezekiel had expressed it powerfully in the image of the departure of the glory of God (10:18-19; 11:22-23). The abiding one can only abide, and royal theology counted on that. But the coming one can leave. And he leaves Israel and its cultic arrangements because his holiness presumes a holy people, committed to his purposes. So as early as Isa. 1:12-15 Yahweh declared: "I cannot endure. . . . My soul hates. . . . I am weary. . . . I will hide my eyes. . . . I will not listen."

The eloquent poetry of Lamentations is replete with expressions of helplessness and despair because of his absence (1:2, 3, 7, 21). And the poetry ends with the recognition of the full weight of the problem: "Restore us to thyself, O Lord, that we may be restored! Renew our days as of old! Or hast thou utterly rejected us? Art thou exceedingly angry with us?" (Lam. 5:21-22). The silence of God is a central theme of the poem of Job, probably also from the Exile. Job cries and demands and insists, but there is no answer. And when there is no answer, the cult is abandoned; life is ended, and hope is gone.

5. Resolutions of the issue. Israel was aware of the complexity of the issue and of a plurality of possible answers.

a) Looking to the end of the Exile, Ezekiel and Second Isaiah together keep the tension alive. Ezekiel affirms the powerful, reliable presence of Yahweh in the temple (43:1-5; 44:4); and, the most powerful establishment form, he describes Jerusalem in 48:35 as the place of the presence: "And the name of the city henceforth shall be, The Lord is there." The tension has been overcome, and both God and people have found a place of safety beyond the disruptions of history.

Second Isaiah announces the promises to Abraham (54:1-4), Noah (54:9-10), and David (55:1-5) as promises now being actualized just when God seemed hidden. But the overpowering presence of Yahweh at the end of the Exile is not in cult; it is in the transformation of historical experience which shatters every presupposition and makes all things new (Isa. 43:18-19). Whereas the God of Ezekiel is one of abiding presence, Second Isaiah is concerned with the God of upheaval and disruption.

b) The Psalms comment upon God's presence. Hymns celebrate his coming to transform (especially the enthronement hymns, 47, 93, 96–99); laments discern his absence and then move to thanksgiving because of new assurances of his abiding concern.

c) Two developments after the Exile provided Israel and the early church with resources for the problem of God's presence. Scribalism (*see* Scribe §3; Pharisees[S]) affirmed his presence in the Torah, in reflection on its demands, in recitation of its memories. The people gathered around the reading and hearing of Torah as a way of being in his presence (Neh. 8:1-8). Apocalypticism reverted to a primitive theology of the war-storm God who comes to transform the world. Scribalism called God's people to reflective listening and acting. Apocalypticism called for waiting and preparation. Both drove Israel to obedience, and it was in her obedience, joyous and confident, waiting and hopeful, that Israel knew herself to be a people in covenant with this one who is accessible, yet free. *See* Torah[S].

The issue of presence is problematical when the temple is destroyed. In such a situation, there was a stress on the remoteness of God and perhaps disdain for the temple (Isa. 66:1-2), or a fresh vision of the re-establishment of Zion and the temple as the center of the world and the locus of pilgrimage for all peoples (Isa. 2:2-6; 25:6-12). The latter suggests the old tradition of the abode of God in the numinous mountain. But alongside such a notion is a countertheme with an ethical stress, that God dwells with the needy and weak and that his earthly place is where he is attentive to prayer (Isa. 65:6-8). Thus the polarity of mythical-ethical becomes yet another expression of the freedom/accessibility theme.

6. NT utilization of themes. The theme of cultic presence is transformed in the NT, and the focus is upon the meaning of Jesus for the church.

a) He will come again; thus the ancient theme of the coming God (Mark 13:14-37; John 14:18; I Cor. 15:22-28; Rev. 22:20).

b) He is the leading one who calls and sends his church (Mark 6:7-13; Luke 10:1-12; Matt. 28:16-19).

c) He is the abiding one who promises presence among his people (Matt. 28:20; John 15:7-11).

d) He is the absent one who leaves his people (John 14:18-19; Luke 24:51).

But consistently the focus is upon the Lord-Servant relation, or communion which is not seriously interested in cultic forms. Presumably this is because the early church utilized the forms already affirmed by Israel. Its fresh articulations were in other areas.

Older ideas about cultic presence were adapted and subordinated to the confession that "Jesus is Lord." Nowhere is this more evident than in Jesus' cleansing of the temple (Matt. 21:12-13; John 2:13-19), by which he establishes his rule over cultic practice and purges it of presumption upon the presence of God (cf. Mark 13:2; 14:58; 15:29). In the Fourth Gospel, it is clear that the destroyed cultic place is displaced by Jesus: "He spoke of the temple of his body" (2:21). The theme of cultic presence is transformed so that an orientation to place is now set aside by the presence of the living Lord. "Presence" now means being in fellowship with him, expressed especially in the Eucharist (cf. Luke 24:35).

Fellowship in his church is the way in which his body, the temple, is acknowledged. Now, cultic presence has become participation in the fellowship of believers. He is with them and accessible; but he is with them as sovereign and therefore free from them if he so chooses. The relation of the church to Jesus is wholly consistent with Israel's relation to Yahweh. Both are in promise of the time when the problem of accessibility and freedom will be fully resolved, and his lordship will be completely in their presence.

It is in the LORD'S SUPPER that the early church made its characteristic affirmation about divine presence. In this activity he was remembered for his historical presence among them and was anticipated in his promise that he would come again. In the meanwhile the church is his body and the temple where he dwells. Clearly the early church perceived his continuing power and transforming work in the communion and witness of his followers. But he is not confined to the cult he authorizes, even that of the church. "Spiritual worship" means to be transformed by the renewal of one's mind (Rom. 12:1-2).

7. Conclusion. The problem of cultic presence is acute because he is "the Holy One . . . in the midst" of his people, and there is tension between the two parts of the affirmation. Each period expressed his presence in a characteristic way: (*a*) the primitive period of origins (Exodus-Sinai): the powerful, coming one; (*b*) the period of wandering: the leading, nourishing one; (*c*) the royal period: the abiding one; (*d*) the Exile: the hidden one. But it must be affirmed that in every period and circumstance, he is always coming and abiding, always leading and hidden, because he will be with his people but free from them. It is the destiny of his people to live with the promise and the precariousness of his free coming and going. The issue is unresolved. It is nowhere better stated than by Jeremiah, when the present is being dismantled and the future is both opening and threatening: "Am I a God at hand, says the Lord, and not a God afar off? Can a man hide himself in secret places so that I cannot see him? says the Lord. Do I not fill heaven and earth?" (Jer. 23:23-24).

Bibliography. J. Barr, "Theophany and Anthropomorphism in the OT," VTSup, VII (1960), 31-38; P. Benoit, R. Murphy, B. van Iersel, *The Presence of God* (1969); R. E. Clements, *God and Temple* (1965); Y. M. J. Congar, *The Mystery of the Temple* (1962); O. Cullmann, *Early Christian Worship* (1953); G. Delling, *Worship in the NT* (1962); M. Görg, *Das Zelt der Begegnung* (1967), excellent bibliog.; D. J. Hänel, *Die Religion der Heiligkeit* (1931); W. Harrelson, *From Fertility Cult to Worship* (1969); A. S. Herbert, *Worship in Ancient Israel* (1959); Jörg Jeremias, *Theophanie* (1965), "Lade und Zion," *Probleme Biblischer Theologie*, ed. H. W. Wolff (1971), pp. 183-98; R. Knierim, "Offenbarung im Alten Testament," *Probleme Biblischer Theologie*, pp. 206-35; H.-J. Kraus, *Worship in Israel* (1965); J. K. Kuntz, *The Self-Revelation of God* (1967); J. Lindblom, "Theophanies in Holy Places in Hebrew Religion," *HUCA*, XXXII (1961), 91-106; E. Lohmeyer, *Lord of the Temple* (1961); C. F. D. Moule, *Worship in the New Testament* (1961); J. Muilenburg, "The Speech of Theophany," *Harvard Divinity Bulletin*, XXVIII (1964), 35-47; R. Niebuhr, "The Ark and the Temple," *Beyond Tragedy* (1937), pp. 47-48; L. Perlitt, "Die Verborgenheit Gottes," *Probleme Biblische Theologie*, pp. 367-82; H. D. Preuss, "Ich will mit dir sein!" *ZAW*, LXXX (1968), 139-73; G. von Rad, *Old Testament Theology*, I (1962), 212-19, 232-79, *Studies in Deuteronomy* (1953), ch. 3; H. H. Rowley, *Worship in Ancient Israel* (1967); R. de Vaux, "The Presence and Absence of God in History According to the Old Testament," in *The Presence of God* (1969), pp. 7-20; G. Westphal, *Jahwes Wohnstätten nach den Anschauungen der alten Hebräer*, *BZAW*, XV (1908); W. Zimmerli, *Grundriss der alttestamentliche Theologie* (1972), pp. 58-68.

W. BRUEGGEMANN

PRIESTLY WRITERS. There are differing views on the origin and development of the Priestly source in the OT (henceforth P), but few remaining disagreements of consequence as to its boundaries, except for some material in the book of Joshua (mainly in chs. 13–22), whose source-critical status has been heatedly debated as part of the HEXATEUCH question (*see* PENTATEUCH §A5). Analyses of the Pentateuch and Joshua on the basis of source criticism are readily available in a number of recent introductions to OT literature, in critical commentaries, and in specific studies of P (*see bibliog.*).

In Genesis, the major contributions of P to the primeval history (chs. 1–11) are versions of the creation story (1:1–2:4*a*), and of the FLOOD epic (in chs. 6, 7, 8). P also concerned itself with covenants, presenting its versions of the covenant with Noah after the Flood (Gen. 9:1-17, 28) and of the covenant with Abram (ch. 17). Along the way, the Priestly writers inserted genealogies, and otherwise showed a distinct interest in the continuity of Abraham's family line (Gen. 21:2*b*-5; 25:7-17 [minus vs. 11*b*]; 27:46–28:9; 35:9-13, 22*b*-29; 46:6-27). *See* GENESIS §B1*e*, 2*d*, 3*c*.

In Exodus, the Priestly writers, in addition to providing the customary genealogical data, amplified earlier sources and added themes of their own, especially as regards the wilderness TABERNACLE. Thus Exod. 6:2–7:13 represents a Priestly version of Yahweh's charge to Moses in Egypt, and introduces AARON as a major participant in the encounter with Pharaoh. Exod. 11:9–12:20; 12:28, 40-51 present a Priestly code on the Passover festival, superimposed on the earlier sources (*see* PASSOVER). In Exod. 16:1-3, 6-27, 32-36, the earlier versions of the Exodus saga are circumscribed by P, which accentuates the role of Aaron, and links the manna account to the observance of the sabbath. Finally, Exod. 24:15*b*–31:17 and 35–40 introduce several strata of Priestly traditions on the initiation of the Yahwistic cult in the days of Moses, in the context of the tabernacle project. *See* EXODUS, BOOK OF §3.

The contents of Leviticus derive entirely from Priestly sources, notwithstanding considerable internal stratification (*see below,* and LEVITICUS §1).

Numbers preserves a small core of early narrative and ancient Hebrew poetry, around which Priestly writers built an elaborate fabric of codes, rituals, and narratives, primarily on the theme of the Sinai experience. *See* NUMBERS, BOOK OF[S] §4.

Vink suggests relating Josh. 8:30-35 to the Priestly school in some way. Generally, Josh. 13–22 take their cue from themes prominent in Numbers, especially the apportionment of the land of Canaan to the Israelite tribes, under priestly direction. Both Vink and Haran have called attention to the importance of Josh. 18:1-10, a passage which has the tent of meeting (אהל מועד) situated at Shiloh during the period of Joshua, thus bridging a gap in the Priestly historiography from the pre-Conquest days of Moses to the time of David when the ark was brought to Jerusalem. *See* JOSHUA, BOOK OF §B1; JOSHUA, BOOK OF[S] §1; DEUTERONOMIC HISTORY, THE[S].

1. The origin and development of P. It is clear that all the texts assigned to P were not composed in the same period. Definitive conclusions as to the origin of the various sections would require evidence presently unavailable, particularly on the history of the priesthood and the Levites, and on the administration of the public cult (*see* PRIESTS [S]). With this caveat, the following observations are relevant:

a) The attempt by Y. Kaufmann to realign the chronology of the sources in the order: J, E, P, D is questionable in many respects (*see* DOCUMENTS). He rejects the idea that Lev. 17, the introduction to the Holiness Code (henceforth H; *see* LEVITICUS §3*e*), was predicated on D's doctrine of a central temple (*see* DEUTERONOMY §4; PENTATEUCH §A4). Rather he claims that Lev. 17 was a response to an earlier set of circumstances, i.e., the religious climate of the period of Israelite settlement, when the issue was the status of sacred stones and altars in the open field. In such terms, Lev. 17 was stating the requirement that sacrifices be offered on a properly consecrated Yahwistic altar. Kaufmann goes on to draw a contrast between the perceptions of D, which speaks of pilgrimages to a central cult site (מקום), and the impermanence clearly evident in H and P, which refer not to a chosen, permanent site, but rather to a portable sanctuary. A corollary to this view is Kaufmann's contention that H and P describe the Passover festival as a clan-oriented celebration, whereas in D the festivals, including Passover, emerge as public celebrations of a national character. It is also relevant for him that Lev. 17 makes no allowance for the "profane" slaughter of animals in order to facilitate meat consumption in local communities which, in view of Deuteronomic legislation on centralization (12:15-16, 20-25), would be without benefit of a sacrificial altar. If, as usually alleged, H is predicated on D's cultic program, how is it that Lev. 17:2-4 appears to stipulate that all slaughter must be sacrificial?

This analysis must be re-examined along the lines now suggested by Haran. P's perceptions of an impermanent environment may be reasonably accounted for as a projection into the past, as has usually been maintained. It does not necessarily follow, however, that this projection was fabricated, without historical basis, in the postexilic, Persian period. Nor does it follow that the Priestly projection was intended to legitimize the postexilic cult of Jerusalem or to serve as a program for it. Accepting P as a projection into the past may just as well be interpreted to mean that many of its codes and narratives were intended to lend sanction to the cult of Jerusalem before the Exile. This would explain the antiquity which P attributes to the cult, with its attendant regimen of duties and rites, as an institutional complex ordained in detail at the outset of Israelite history, in the Mosaic period. In so doing, the Priestly writers composed what they thought was a plausible portrayal of the pre-Conquest period, at times employing ancient materials to accomplish this effect. By and large, they drew on traditions of the earliest period of settlement, which refer to sacred stones (cf. Judg. 13:19). Pilgrimages undoubtedly represented to them a subsequent stage after the Israelite settlement. Kaufmann noticed the reliance of Lev. 17 and other early sections of P on premonarchic traditions, but he took this factor too literally. As noted by Haran, mere usage of the term חג (RSV "feast") to characterize the Passover and other festivals (cf. Exod. 12:14; Lev. 23:34, 39, 41) implies an awareness of the pilgrimage as an aspect of festival celebrations, because that is what חג connotes.

The early perceptions in H and P do mean, not that sacred stones and the worship of wilderness deities, called שעירים, presented a real issue for the Priestly writers, but only that such portrayals lent realism to their account. Similarly, the matter of "profane" slaughter should be seen in perspective. The Priestly writer, in seeking to portray an era before there were stockyards in or near permanent settlements, provided for the consumption of animals or fowl taken in the hunt (Lev. 17:13 ff.). Thus, one does find in H a possible echo of Deut. 12:15, which compares the consumption of domesticated animals profanely slaughtered to the consumption of objects of the hunt. It is also questionable whether, in Lev. 17:2-4, the verb שחט connotes "slaughter" of all types. It may be used in a technical sense to connote only ritual slaughter (cf. Exod. 12:21; Lev. 1:5; etc.), and thus these verses would mean that all *sacrificial* slaughter must take place on the sanctuary altar, in precise agreement with D.

b) Once we accept the over-all dependence of H and P on D and on other earlier sources (allowing of course for instances where the Priestly writers reached back to early, independent materials unaffected by D), the critical question becomes the determination of the date and origin of Deuteronomy itself (*see* DEUTERONOMY; DEUTERONOMY[S]; DEUTERONOMIC HISTORY, THE[S]). If what is original to D is Josianic (621 B.C.), then the argument for dating P in the postexilic period would be strengthened (*see* JOSIAH). However, there is growing evidence for dating essential D in the late eighth century B.C., and for considering it a north Israelite creation, transmitted to Judea during the reign of HEZEKIAH, sometime before 686 B.C. Hezekiah's awareness of D's doctrine might explain his attempt to remove the *bāmôt* ("high places"), for the Judeans would have interpreted D's central sanctuary as Jerusalem and not some unnamed place in the northern kingdom (II Kings 18:1-8; II Chr. 29–31).

Such an origin for essential D has recently been argued, with new evidence, by Ginsberg. He has demonstrated that Hosea, whose prophecies antedate the fall of Samaria (722 B.C.), had influence on the diction of essential D. On the other hand, there is a striking absence of Isaianic influence on essential D. This would hardly be conceivable if it were a product of late seventh-century Judea, since Isaiah's ministry, ending *ca.* 700 B.C., was well known there. As though to clinch the argument, Ginsberg has identified Isaianic influence precisely in those secondary passages in D which are clearly the work of a Judean of Josiah's day, or thereafter. This proposed chronology would point to a *terminus a quo* for the earliest components of H and P in the age of Hezekiah, or thereabouts.

2. The completion of P. It is not yet clear just how late certain sections of P are. Linguistic criteria have been applied to this question with interesting but inconclusive results. Hurvitz has presented arguments for the pre-exilic dating of P. He notes, for instance, that P uses the word שש to designate "fine linen" (a word attested in early biblical usage) but never בוץ (cf. Gr. *bussos*), the term used by the Chronicler. He further notes certain late usages, common to Chronicles and Ezra-Nehemiah, which are absent from P. These include התיחש, "to be enrolled by genealogy" (contrast forms of the verb פקד for the same sense in P). Similarly, Chronicles employs the *hithpa'ēl* התנדב, "to volunteer, offer generously," whereas P uses forms of the *qal*, נדב but never the *hithpa'ēl*. This is, of course, merely oblique evidence, documenting the absence from P of late usage which one might expect if it were a product of the period of the Chronicler.

Ginsberg has noted a stylistic similarity between P's narratives and the Aramaic Bauer-Meissner papyrus, dated 515 B.C.: the frequent repetition of a phrase from a preceding clause, in a slightly modified form with more detail added. Ginsberg admits that this stylistic feature is also attested elsewhere, e.g., in Deut. 16:9. Another bit of evidence has been noted by Vink: in Num. 34:25 we find the patronymic פרנך. This has been identified as a Persian name and is not likely to have been in use before the Achaemenid period.

Aramaisms have been considered evidence for dating P to the Persian period (when ARAMAIC was widely used). Thus, the term משחה (measure, measurement) in Lev. 7:35 (cf. למשחה in Num. 18:8) occurs in the Aramaic papyri from ELEPHANTINE (Kraeling 4:12; 9:11; 12:28), dated to the fifth century B.C. According to S. Kaufman, this word is native to Aramaic, despite its occurrence in Akkadian as *mišiḫtu*. Another possible indication of a Persian environment is the mustering of the Israelite camp according to the unit known as דגל (Num. 2, etc.), usually rendered "standard." This was also the unit of organization in the Jewish military colony at Elephantine, and Porten considers this feature distinctively Persian. Such a conclusion is further suggested by the occurrence, in a Persian-period Aramaic ostracon from Arad, of the personal name *ldgl 'bdḥy,* "of the unit of *'Abdîḥai.*" *See* NUMBERS, BOOK OF[S] §4*bi*.

In conclusion, we must allow for the likelihood that certain sections of P derive from the Persian period. Perhaps the possibilities may be narrowed down through a study of literary development within P, pointing to relatively early, intermediate, and late strata within that source.

3. The literary development of P. ***a. H and the Priestly Passover ritual (Exod. 11:9–12:20, 28, 40-51).*** H and the Passover ritual may rightly be considered the earliest sections of the Priestly tradition, although the customary assignment of Lev. 26:3-46 to H must be questioned. This section conveys a reaction to the destruction of temple and land, and a yearning for restoration (vs. 13). It speaks of the departure of Yahweh's presence (vss. 9, 11-12, 24), and a renewed interest in the covenant with the patriarchs (vss. 42, 45). This suggests that Lev. 26:3-46 was composed soon after the destruction of Judea.

The Passover ritual in Exod. 11:9–12:20, 28, 40-51, although put into final form by a Priestly writer, goes back to early records (Noth). It projects the performance of a Yahwistic ritual into Egypt, prior to Sinai, elsewhere the consistent starting point for the cult of Yahweh in the Priestly source. The disposition of the sacrifice is distinctive in three respects: the זבח (slain offering) was not to be boiled in pots, as usual, but roasted over the fire, an early practice rescinded by D (Deut. 16:7); no altar was used; and the victim was not sectioned but roasted whole.

b. Primary Priestly codification. What constitutes the next identifiable stratum in P? It is reasonable to posit that the actual cult served as the basis for the Priestly narrative. This implies that the process of codification antedated the narrative movement, and that the next stratum is to be sought in codes rather than in the mythic narratives. In the category of primary codes may be included the following sections: Lev. 1–7; 11–16 (minus 16:1-2, an introduction linking the rite of ch. 16 with an event); 27; Num. 5:11-31; 6; 15:37-41; 19; and perhaps the codified materials in 30:2-17 and 35:9-34 (incorporated into a relatively late account on the apportionment of the land).

The above sections generated secondary restatements within P, most of which occur in Numbers. Thus Num. 5:1-10 reflects Lev. 5 and 12–15. Num. 9:1-14 is a reflex of the ancient material in Exod. 11–12. Num. 15:1-36 reflects Lev. 1–7, especially 4; and Num. 18 is largely dependent on Lev. 1-7, as well as 27. Finally, the catalogue of prescribed sacrifices in Num. 28:1–30:1 represents a development subsequent to Lev. 23. To carry the stratification one step further, it is likely that Exod. 29:38-46 is a secondary restatement of Num. 28:1-8, the praxis prescribed for the תמיד (daily offering).

There is a chronological overlapping of code and narrative in P. Some of the secondary codes postdate the primary Priestly narratives, whereas narrative creativity was stimulated, in the first instance, by the codification of cultic practice. Clear stratification in the narrative sections of P is difficult to trace. A basic question is the place of the tabernacle traditions. They relate to a primary concern of P, the origin of the cult of Yahweh in the days of Moses, and one would expect to find early statements on this subject. It appears, nevertheless, that this area accounts for some of the latest sections of P, especially in Num. 1–4. A degree of internal stratification is discernible, nonetheless. The tabernacle project prescribed in Exod. 25–28, 30–31 is restated as a *fait accompli* in Exod. 35–40, with some additions. Lev. 8–9 produced a secondary response in Exod. 29:1-37, relevant to the investiture of the priests. Num. 7 is, for the most part, formulated in a manner close to original temple records, and Num. 8:5-26 is the primary text on the role of the Levites, serving as a basis for further discussion of their role.

The special problem of the half-shekel head tax (Exod. 30:11-16) has been studied by Speiser and Liver. Liver attempts to dissociate this section from Neh. 10:32-33 [H 33-34], and from references to an annual temple tax in Chronicles (II Chr. 24:4-14), insisting on its early provenance. A related problem is the possible connection between the voluntary offering for the tabernacle (Exod. 25:1-2) and the נדבה (voluntary offering) given by the Jews in Babylonia to the Jerusalem temple (Ezra 1:4, etc.). The entire question of temple funding and administration must be studied further for additional data for the dating of P.

4. Notions distinctive to P. Driver has provided a concise summary of the features of P, to which the following observations may be appended.

a) The problems and uncertainty elsewhere evident in statements on the human-divine relationship are muted in P's narratives. Perceptions of good and evil, of divine justice and retribution, are clear. Even the handling of the theme of the hardening of Pharaoh's heart (Exod. 7:3-4, 22, etc.), classically seen as a major theological problem, is a matter of cause and effect. As noted by Childs, in his recent commentary, P is unambiguous in rationalizing the hardening of Pharaoh's heart. It is for the purpose of guaranteeing that he will not harken, thus allowing for more plagues and signs, eventually leading up to the recognition of Yahweh's supremacy at the crossing of the sea. Though such an outlook may leave the reader with problems of an ethical or theological nature, the Priestly writer makes no apology for it, and presents it without complication. *See* THEODICY[S].

b) The Priestly narratives serve to rationalize cultic practice. We see this clearly in the primeval history, where God rests on the sabbath (Gen. 2:1-3; cf. Exod. 20:8-11). The Noahic covenant emphasizes the central importance of blood as the life force, a notion basic to the cultic legislation of H (cf. the formulation in Lev. 17:10-14, esp. vs. 14, with Gen. 9:1-6, esp. vs. 4). Similarly, the Priestly version of the Abrahamic covenant (Gen. 17:1-27) emphasizes the rite of circumcision, a requirement for participation in the Yahwistic cult, epitomized in the Passover ritual (Exod. 12:44, 48, etc.).

In addition to stressing the importance of the cult per se, the Priestly narratives conveyed to the contemporary audience as well as to subsequent readers that adherence to the sabbath and to the rite of circumcision, as well as general obedience to the Priestly regimen of ritual duties, were indispensable to their collective existence and to the fulfillment of their destiny under the covenant. This message undoubtedly held poignant meaning for the Judean exiles and for those who returned. It is during the periods of exile and restoration that we encounter prophetic statements on the importance of the sabbath (Isa. 56:2, 6; 58:13, 66:23; Jer. 17:21-27), and concerning other ritual duties, including fasting (Isa. 65:4-5; 66:3, 17; Hag. 2:10-11; Zech. 7:1-7; 8:18-19; Mal. 3:1-12). It is Ezekiel who refers to the ancient Gentiles as "the uncircumcised" (Ezek. 32:17-32), and who prohibited their presence in the temple in explicit terms (Ezek. 44:7; cf. Isa. 52:1).

What started out as a projection, intended to confirm the temple cult as integral, became, as circumstances changed, a future-oriented theology in which ritual gave expression to group identity and meaning to collective existence.

5. Summary. The principal unanswered question regarding both the origin and meaning of P is a sociohistorical one. What were the societal conditions obtaining at various periods of Israelite and later Jewish history (pre-exilic, exilic, and postexilic) which can account for the central concerns manifest in P? Source-critical analysis, the relation of P to other biblical traditions, the tracing of literary strata within P itself, and the evidence of language—all these methods can lead us only to the threshold of historical conclusions. Further study is required in the history of the priesthood and the Levites and the means of temple administration. Certain critical junctures of Israelite and Jewish history must be isolated and their circumstances examined for clues to cultic and religious problems. Because so much attention has been given to the postexilic period in the study of P, on the *a priori* assumption that its content must somehow refer to the restored Jerusalem temple, it is now time to probe pre-exilic history, especially the period of Josiah.

Bibliography. Introductions and general studies on the Priestly literature of the OT: S. R. Driver, *Introduction to the Literature of the OT* (rev. ed., 1913), pp. 126-50; O. Eissfeldt, *The OT, an Introduction* (1965), pp. 158-212, 233-57; G. B. Gray, *Sacrifice in the OT,* with a Prolegomenon by B. A. Levine (1925 [repr. 1971]); Y. Kaufmann, *The Religion of Israel* (1960); J. G. Vink, "The Date and Origin of the Priestly Code in the OT," *OTS,* XV (1969), 1-144.

Recent commentaries: E. A. Speiser, *Genesis* (1964); M. Noth, *Exodus* (1962); B. S. Childs, *The Book of Exodus* (1974); N. H. Snaith, *Leviticus and Numbers* (1967).

Bibliog. specific to this article: Y. Aharoni, "Arad: Its Inscriptions and Temple," *BA,* XXXI (1968), 11; H. L. Ginsberg, "Aramaic Studies Today," *JAOS,* LXII (1942), 229-30, and "Hosea, Book of," *Encyclopaedia Judaica,* VIII (1971), 1010-24; M. Haran, "Shiloh and Jerusalem: The Origin of the Priestly Tradition in the Pentateuch," *JBL,* LXXXI (1962), 14-24, "Holiness Code," *Encyclopaedia Judaica,* VIII (1971), 820-25, and "Studies in the Bible: The Idea of Centralization of the Cult in the Priestly Apprehension," *Beer-Sheva,* I (1973), 114-21, Hebrew; A. Hurvitz, "The Usage of *šēš* and *bûṣ* in the Bible and Its Implication for the Date of P," *HTR,* LX (1967), 117-21, "The Chronological Significance of 'Aramaisms' in Biblical Hebrew," *IEJ,* XVIII (1968), 234-40, and "The Evidence of Language in Dating the Priestly Code," *RB,* LXXXI (1974), 24-56; S. Kaufman, "The Akkadian Influences on Aramaic" (diss., Yale, 1970), University Microfilms (1973), p. 110, *see "mašāḫu,"* and p. 279, n. 69; E. G. Kraeling, *The Brooklyn Museum Aramaic Papyri* (1953); B. A. Levine, "The Descriptive Tabernacle Texts of the Pentateuch," *JAOS,* LXXXV (1965), 307-18, "On the Presence of God in Biblical Religion," in *Religions in Antiquity,* ed. J. Neusner (1968), pp. 71-87, and *In the Presence of the Lord, A Study of Cult and Some Cultic Terms in Ancient Israel* (1974), pp. 45-52, 67-91; J. Liver, "The Ransom of the Half-Shekel" in *Yehezkel Kaufmann Jubilee Volume,* ed. M. Haran (1960), pp. 54-67, Hebrew; J. Milgrom, "Leviticus, Book of," *Encyclopaedia Judaica,* XI (1971), 138-47; B. Porten, *Archives From Elephantine* (1968) pp. 29-30; V. W. Rabe, "The Identity of the Priestly Tabernacle," *JNES,* XXV (1966), 132-34; E. A. Speiser, "Census and Ritual Expiation," *BASOR,* 149 (1958), 17-25, "Leviticus and the Critics," in *Yehezkel Kaufmann Jubilee Volume,* ed. M. Haran (1960), pp. 29-45; R. de Vaux, *Le sacrifice sans l'AT* (1964), pp. 35-36; R. H. Dornemann, "The Cultural and Archaeological History of the Transjordan in the Bronze and Iron Ages" (diss., Univ. of Chicago, 1970), pp. 9 ff.

B. A. LEVINE

***PRIESTS.** The comments which follow are intended as a supplement to PRIESTS AND LEVITES and will focus on terminology and on the administrative functions of the Israelite and Jewish priesthood.

A complete history of the Israelite priesthood cannot yet be written, primarily because the precise date of the Priestly source (henceforth P) remains elusive (*see* PRIESTLY WRITERS[S]). In line with the view that, in large part, P reflects the cultic practice of the pre-exilic period, evidence from P may, within careful limits, be utilized for studying the pre-exilic priesthood, along with the evidence of the historical books, the early narrative sources J and E (*see* DOCUMENTS; YAHWIST[S]; ELOHIST[S]), and the Psalter and prophetic writings. There is, thus, a considerable body of material which informs us of the functions of the priests while remaining less clear on their detailed history and origin.

The postexilic periods are also problematical, but here the possibilities for reconstructing the history of the priesthood seem to be more promising than for earlier times. Cross has attempted to establish the succession of the high priesthood from the destruction of the temple (587 B.C.) to 320 B.C., the beginning of the Hellenistic domination of Palestine. Using the principle of papponymy, whereby high priests would have occasionally been named for their grandfathers, Cross was able to bridge gaps in the succession, especially during the fifth century B.C. He used newly found Aramaic papyri from Daliyeh, dated to the fourth century B.C., which provide data on the synchronous chronology of the Sanballatids in Samaria (*see* SAMARIA PAPYRI[S]). He also found corollary indications from Greek versions of Ezra, from Josephus, and from contemporary epigraphy, and ventured to suggest a fixed date for Ezra's mission (458 B.C.) and a *Sitz im Leben* for certain sections of Ezra, Nehemiah, and Chronicles. *See* EZRA AND NEHEMIAH[S].

1. Terminology
2. The position and administrative functions of the priesthood
3. The position of the priesthood in the postexilic period

Bibliography

1. Terminology. The normal biblical term for "priest" is כהן, pl. כהנים, a term also attested in Ugaritic, Phoenician-Punic, and in several dialects of Aramaic. Arabic *kâhin,* "seer, soothsayer," clearly reflects older usage but represents a specialized connotation, not the basic meaning of the word. As a West Semitic term of wide distribution, *kōhēn* would logically designate all types of priests, and not necessarily Israelite and/or Yahwistic priests. Thus, Melchizedek, a Canaanite priest, is so designated (Gen. 14:18), as is an Egyptian priest

(Gen. 41:45), Jethro, a Midianite (Exod. 18:1), and the priests of Dagon (I Sam. 5:5).

There is no feminine of כהן in biblical Hebrew. The term בת כהן merely designates a woman of a priestly family (Lev. 21:9; 22:12-13; etc.), just as does Mishnaic כוהנת.

A less frequent term, כמר (priest), has cognates in Phoenician-Punic, several Aramaic dialects, and some varieties of Akkadian. It is used for Baal priests (Zeph. 1:4) and for those priests considered idolatrous or Baalistic by the biblical writers. Thus, II Kings 23:5 uses this term to designate the priests who officiated at "high places," and who were dismissed by Josiah. Hos. 10:5 uses the same term for the royally appointed priests who served the cult of the bull calves in Samaria.

The term קדש, fem. קדשה, is also relevant, by contrast with כהן. In Ugaritic, the masc. pl. *qdšm* is a term for "priests," occurring alongside *khnm*. We have no way of ascertaining what if any institutional differentiation was intended between these two terms. Akkadian attests the fem. *qadištu,* a term often employed to designate temple priestesses, although having other connotations, including "harlot," which are not directly connected to the cultic establishment. *See* WOMAN IN THE ANE [S] §5.

In biblical sources, there is only one possible case where קדשה might mean "harlot" and be synonymous with זונה, "prostitute," and that is in the Tamar episode (Gen. 38:21-22; cf. vs. 15). Job 36:14 may represent a correspondingly unique instance of similar noncultic usage for masc. קדש, meaning simply "male prostitute." Elsewhere in the OT there is always a clear, cultic connection, at least by force of immediate context. It is likely, therefore, that קדש and קדשה primarily designate priestly personnel, and the fact that such were thought to engage in orgiastic activities, either in connection with their official functions or independently of them, does not account for their titles.

Terminology also sheds light on the hierarchy, at least for the late Judean monarchy and thereafter. II Kings 19:2 mentions "senior" priests (זקני הכהנים). In II Kings 25:18 (parallel in Jer. 52:24), the designation for the chief priest is כהן הראש, and the second in charge is כהן המשנה. The former term enters the official and administrative vocabulary at the time of the Babylonian conquest of Judea, whereas just prior to that time, the writer of II Kings still uses the traditional term כהן גדול, "High Priest" (II Kings 23:4). This term is used in the Holiness Code (Lev. 21:10) as well as elsewhere in Kings (II Kings 12:11; 22:4, 8), and, of course, in exilic and postexilic sources (Hag. 1:1, 12; Zech. 3:1, 8; and in Ezra-Nehemiah-Chronicles). In comparative terms, note Elephantine Aramaic *khn' rb'=hakkōhēn haggādhôl*. Ugaritic attests the term *rb khnm,* "chief of the priests," and points to the fact that the office of a chief priest goes far back into Near Eastern antiquity.

The fact that the term for high priest in preexilic non-P sources is also כהן גדול strengthens the view that we have in the Holiness Code a reflection of pre-exilic institutions. Furthermore, the construction title + הראש (or המשנה) occurs with increasing frequency in the postexilic literature and is characteristic of the Chronicler (cf. Ezra 7:5; I Chr. 16:5; II Chr. 19:11). It is probable, therefore, that the high priesthood did not represent a late development in Israelite or Jewish religion, as some have claimed.

The term הכהן המשיח, "the anointed priest," i.e., the high priest (Lev. 4:3, 5), was undoubtedly coined by the Priestly author in order to convey his doctrine that only the high priest was to receive "anointing oil," a doctrine basic to the Holiness Code (Lev. 21:10; and cf. 8:12). It has no attestations outside these limited sections of Leviticus.

The noun כהנה, "priestship," usually refers to the priestly office (Exod. 29:9; Num. 16:10), but in one relatively early source, I Sam. 2:36, it seems to connote the priestly order or a group of priests (cf. Neh. 13:29, and possibly Ezra 2:62=Neh. 7:64). This connotation is prominent in postbiblical Hebrew (cf. M. Ḥag. 2.27; Yom. 1.5, 7; etc.), although the more abstract sense also survives. Denominative of כהן is the *Pi'el* (*kihhēn*), "to serve as a priest" (Exod. 29:1; 30:30; Ezek. 44:13).

2. The position and administrative functions of the priesthood. From the historical books of the OT, essentially Judges through Kings, it becomes evident that the chief priest of a major temple or cult site served in the capacity of a royal official; he was accountable to the king for the handling of temple funds, and was in charge of temple operations. He was assisted by a second in rank and perhaps consulted with a council of senior priests (II Kings 19:2; 23:4; 25:18; Jer. 52:24). The chief priest may be referred to simply as "the priest" (Deut. 17:12; 20:2; 26:4, and frequently in Samuel and Kings), or as the כהן of a named temple (I Sam. 14:3; Amos 7:10). In many such instances it is clear from context that reference is to the priest in charge.

It is also clear that in the premonarchic period priests were appointed by leaders of tribes and clans and served at their pleasure. This is epitomized in the account of the Danite migration, where we are told that a priest previously invested as priest for a family was persuaded to become "priest to a tribe" (Judg. 18:19). Similarly, David had a resident priest, Abiathar, even before becoming king, mostly for oracular assistance when he was leader of a paramilitary band (I Sam. 22:20-23; 23:6-12).

As a royal official, the chief priest and his associates were expected to remain loyal to their sovereign. Amaziah, the priest in charge of the royal temple at Bethel, reports to Jeroboam II on Amos' allegedly seditious activities there, and has him expelled, probably on the king's orders (Amos 7:10-17). The loyalty required of the priesthood in situations of political conflict is dramatized in the account of the massacre of the priests at Nob who gave aid and comfort to David, then considered the king's enemy (I Sam. 22:1-19). It is worthy of note that David rewarded Abiathar, one of the Nob priests, by appointing him to his staff, but Solomon later dismissed him and placed him under house arrest for his role in Adonijah's abortive bid for the royal succession (I Kings 1:7; 2:27-35). The normally hereditary character of the priestly office was subject to a more decisive factor, the authority of the king. Note that Abiathar's son had already been installed as a priest before his father was dismissed (I Kings 1:42). But by appointing ZADOK as chief priest, David initiated a high-priestly dynasty which continued until Maccabean times.

Glimpses into the administrative functioning of the Israelite priesthood are afforded by two parallel accounts in II Kings (chs. 12 and 22). In II Kings 12, the more detailed of the two accounts, we read that Jehoash instructed the chief priest Jehoiada to use donations and other deposits for repairing the temple. When the chief priest failed to act on these instructions, the king intervened and commanded the royal scribe to have the silver melted into ingots, and to use those funds to pay the temple craftsmen. The high priest and his associates were thus subject to the will of the king, who could circumvent priestly channels and determine just how the temple funds were to be disbursed, even suspending manufacture of cultic vessels.

From II Kings 12:5 [H 6] it may be deduced that certain priests actively solicited various types of contributions to the temple from their contacts (RSV "acquaintance"). According to II Kings 16, Ahaz had a new altar fashioned after a Damascene model. He installed it in the Jerusalem temple and gave the chief priest explicit instructions as to its use.

The realities reflected in the royal chronicles are mirrored in the Priestly version of the history of the Israelite cult. It was Gray who most clearly discussed the traditions concerning the priesthood of Moses, who invested the first Israelite priests (Lev. 8–9; Exod. 29:1-37; etc.). The technical term *millē' yādh,* literally, "to fill the hand," cognate to Akkadian *mullû qātē,* denotes investiture (e.g., Lev. 8:33; Ezek. 43:26). Thus, Micah "invests" one of his own sons as a priest in his family chapel, but later appoints a more professional practitioner (Judg. 17:5, 12), and it is said of Jeroboam that he invested priests from whatever family origin, at Bethel and elsewhere in the northern kingdom (I Kings 13:33). In the Priestly traditions Moses, as the leader of the people, is thus acting *in loco regis,* one might say. This undoubtedly represents a projection of later notions of the position of the priesthood under the monarchy back into the early period of Israelite history, a projection typical of P. *See* PRIESTLY WRITERS[S] §1.

As regards the administrative role of the priesthood, Lev. 27 reflects historical realities. "The priest" administers votive funds and assesses the value of different forms of property and goods. He determines the ability of persons to remit standard equivalents established by the cultic administration. In a similar way, "the priest" determines the ability of persons to afford certain obligatory sacrifices, which could be reduced in cases of need (Lev. 5:1-13; 12:8; 14:21-22; etc.).

Among the administrative duties of the priesthood was the handling of tithes and their allocation (*see* SACRIFICES AND OFFERINGS, OT[S]; TITHE). A further indication of the fiscal role of the priesthood is the adoption of a special standard of weights and measures. In the Priestly sources, and only there, we encounter the term שקל-הקדש "sanctuary weight." Remittances to the temple were to be imputed according to that standard (Lev. 5:15; 27:3, 25). There can be little doubt that this is an ancient custom, perhaps even harking back to the administration of the premonarchic cult centers such as Shiloh. It is worthy of note that nowhere in the OT do we find a term for "royal weight," even though there are references to the royal treasury (I Kings 14:26; 15:18; etc.) alongside the temple treasury. All we have is a term for negotiable silver, "according to the rates current among the merchants" (Gen. 23:16). It is at least possible, therefore, that under the monarchy, and in the postexilic periods as well, an ancient standard was preserved, i.e., "sanctuary weight."

Ezekiel, whose plans for the restored Jerusalem contain many features representative of the Jerusalem temple cult during the late Judean monarchy, specifies that the shekel shall contain twenty gerahs (Ezek. 45:12), the same as "the sanctuary weight" according to the Priestly codes (Lev. 27:25; and cf. Exod. 30:13).

The terminology of II Kings 12 and 22 holds even further implications for the administrative role of the priesthood. Hebrew *ḥizzēq bedheq,* literally: "to fasten the breach," i.e., to effect "repairs" (II Kings 12:5 [H 6]; 22:5), carries the extended sense of "inspection, maintenance," as is evidenced by the cognate Akkadian formula *batqa ṣabātu* which can refer to all sorts of functions associated with maintenance, caretaking, etc. It was during such an inspection that the high priest Hilkiah discovered the TORAH document in the time of JOSIAH (II Kings 22:4-8). In Tam. 1.3, we have the requirement of the daily inspection of the temple by two groups of priests, who each morning circled the temple to ascertain that all was in order. It is likely that similar tasks were performed by priests in the Solomonic temple and at other cult sites in the pre-exilic period.

3. The position of the priesthood in the postexilic period. One may assume that earlier functions of the priesthood continued to apply in the restored temple of Jerusalem. The high priest gained in power as the dominance of the Davidide kings diminished under Persian imperial domination. Smith has observed that in the vision of Zech. 6:9-15 we have evidence of friction and unresolved issues between the high priest and king over their respective jurisdictions. By depositing two crowns in the temple as a memorial, the peaceful co-existence of the two authorities was to be symbolized. The king is clearly viewed by the prophet as builder of the temple and as temporal ruler (Zech. 6:12-13); and the high priest, although reassured, does not have his authority as clearly delimited as does the king. The mere fact, however, that the king and the high priest are repeatedly addressed together, as co-leaders of the people in the literature of the restoration period, is significant (Hag. 1:1, 12, 14; 2:2; Zech. 3–4). This undoubtedly indicates that in this period the high priest was not merely a royal appointee or the descendant of one, but a leader of intrinsic authority, autonomous, and directly responsible to the people, in his own right. This development set the stage for the hierocracy which was to follow. *See* AARON, AARONIDES[S].

Bibliography. *Terminology: Batqa ṣabātu* (=Heb. *ḥizzēq bedheq*), "to fasten the breach, repair": *CAD,* XVI (Ṣ), 25-26 (under *"ṣabātu,* 8, *batqu"*); B. A. Levine, "Comments on Some Technical Terms of the Biblical Cult," *Leš,* XXX (1965-66), 3-11, Hebrew.

Khn, rb khnm, "priest, chief priest" (Ugar.): C. H. Gordon, *UT* (1965), glossary, nos. 1209, 2297; R. E. Whittaker, *A Concordance of the Ugaritic Literature* (1972), p. 562, under *"rb."*

Khn, "priest" (Phoen.-Punic): C. F. Jean and J. Hoftijzer, *DISO* (1965-), p. 116, under *"khn."*

Khn' rb', "the chief priest" (Aram.): A. E. Cowley, *Aramaic Papyri of the Fifth Century B.C.* (1923), p. 112, under 30:18; B. Porten, *Archives from Elephantine* (1968), p. 201.

Kmr, "priest" (West Semitic): *DISO,* p. 122, under *"kmr"*; W. Baumgartner, *HALAT,* II (1974), 459, under *"kômer"; CAD,* VIII (K), 534-35, under *"kumru"*; B. Porten, *op. cit.,* p. 201; W. F. Albright, *Yahweh and the Gods of Canaan* (1968), 185, n. 13.

Mullû qātē, "to fill the hand(s), invest," (Akkad.): W. von Soden, *AHW,* p. 598, under *"malû,* D, 8, d."

Qdšm, "priests" (Ugar.): *UT,* glossary, no. 2210; R. E. Whittaker, *op. cit.,* p. 546, under *"qdš"*; M. H. Pope, *Job,* ABi (3rd ed., 1973), pp. 269-70, comment on Job 36:14*b* (Heb. *qedēšîm*).

Qadištu, "priestess," etc. (Akkad.): *AHW,* p. 891, under *"qadištu"*; J. Renger, "Untersuchungen zum Priestertum in der altbabylonischen Zeit," *ZA,* LVIII (1967), 110-18; B. A. Levine, *"Kedushah"* (with bibliog.), *Encyclopaedia Judaica,* X (1970), 869-71.

Tkwnh, "cash, measured silver" (Aram.=Heb. *tekûnâ*): A. E. Cowley, *Aramaic Papyri . . .* (1923), on 15:6.

General bibliog.: A. Cody, *A History of the OT Priesthood* (1969), extensive bibliog.; F. M. Cross, "A Reconstruction of the Judean Restoration," *JBL,* XCIV (1975), 4-18; G. B. Gray, *Sacrifice in the OT,* with a prolegomenon by B. A. Levine (1971), pp. 179-270; M. Haran *et al.,* "Priests and Priesthood," *Encyclopaedia Judaica,* XIII (1970), 1069-88, extensive bibliog.; J. H. Montgomery, H. Gehman, *Kings,* ICC (1951), pp. 426-33, 456-64, 523-24; M. Smith, *Palestinian Parties and Politics that Shaped the OT* (1971), pp. 108-13.

B. A. LEVINE

*PROMISES TO THE PATRIARCHS.

1. Recent research
2. The nature and structure of the promises
3. The separate promises
4. The theological significance of the promises
5. Subsequent history of the promises

Bibliography

1. Recent research. Study of the promises to the patriarchs began with Alt's investigation of them as phenomena of the patriarchal period. Among his concerns was a more precise identification of the individual promises. In the work of von Rad, Noth, Zimmerli, and Wolff, however, emphasis was placed on their earliest documentary form, that is, their significance for J or for the development of the PENTATEUCH (*see* YAHWIST[S]; ELOHIST[S]; PRIESTLY WRITERS[S]). Von Rad distinguished between promises of land, posterity, and blessing on the one hand, and the promise of a new relationship to God on the other. Wolff isolated the characteristic features of the promise of blessing, while Maag contrasted the promise of the land with the promise of new territory in which to live or to pasture herds and flocks, and stressed the distinctive nature of the promise of God's presence. Westermann stressed the difference between the promise of a son and that of posterity; and Seebass distinguished the general promise of the land from the specific promise of the Bethel district. Lohfink saw the promise of the land as an oath, and Koch found in the Ugaritic texts parallels to the promise of a son.

The dates suggested for the promises vary greatly. Maag regarded Gen. 12:1-3, generally considered the work of J, as belonging to the pre-Israelite patriarchal period. But Hoftijzer and van Seters place J around the time of the Exile (*see* PATRIARCHS[S]). Gradually, however, scholars have come to explain each of the promises in terms of a specific background, and to ask if it fits what is known of the patriarchal period and thus could belong there, or if it must be explained as having originated during the written stages of the tradition. *See* TRADITION, ORAL[S].

2. The nature and structure of the promises. ***a. Characteristics.*** The promises to the patriarchs are the most frequent motif in Gen. 12–50. References to them are frequent in other books, especially Deuteronomy, and are found as late as Nehemiah.

These promises are a part of the total complex of OT oracles of blessing, but are different from the others in not having been delivered by a cultic or other type of mediator; they are depicted as having been given directly by God to the patriarchs. This means that some of them may have actually originated in the patriarchal period, because a distinctive feature of the religion of the fathers is the lack of any sort of mediator between God and man (*see* HEBREW RELIGION §A; PATRIARCHS[S] §2*b*). It is, however, possible that they were colored by later oracles and literary forms. In Gen. 15:1-6 there are echos of oracles of blessing and signs of prophetic speech forms; in ch. 17, P has constructed a promise using the later covenant formula, which promises that Abraham's posterity will include nations and kings.

A further hallmark of the promises to the patriarchs is that they are unconditional. What God proclaims does not depend on the fulfillment of any conditions. (Gen. 22:16-18 therefore apparently contains a late interpretation.) *See* COVENANT, DAVIDIC[S] §3.

b. Relation to the narrative framework. Formerly the promises were considered to be merely one of the motifs of the patriarchal narratives (Galling, von Rad, Zimmerli); for Noth they constitute the theme of these narratives. But Hoftijzer has raised the question of whether the promises are an essential or secondary component of the individual narratives. He concluded that the former is the case only in Gen. 15 and 17. Westermann and Lohfink distinguished between accounts such as chs. 15 and 17 that were built around the promises, and others such as chs. 16 and 18, in which the promise is an integral part. In all other cases the promises are in some way or other inserted into the narrative or added to it at the beginning or end: (1) a specific scene in the account: 13:14-17;

(2) a secondary addition: 22:15-18; 28:3-4; 28:13-15; 35:9-13; 46:3-4; (3) a brief added word of promise: 16:10; 21:13; (4) the opening of a cycle of stories: 12:1-3; 26:2-5; (5) a reference to a previous promise: 18:17-19; 24:7; 32:10-13; 48:3-4.

This indicates that the promise motif was originally a part of only a few of the patriarchal narratives, and that it generally belongs to the stage of their convergence and further development.

c. Analysis of the promises. The accounts can be arranged according to literary-critical criteria, in order to trace a development from the earliest to the latest literary sources (Galling). This arrangement, however, is not satisfactory, because the transmission of the various promises is too complicated. Or, they can be arranged on the basis of their importance. Von Rad and Lohfink regard the promise of the land as the most important, while Wolff holds it is the promise of blessing. Others ask, Which God makes the promise? Alt felt they were all made by the "God of the Fathers," but Eissfeldt proposes the Canaanite El.

Two of the most significant criteria for dating are: (1) Is the fulfillment to be soon, or in the distant future? The former is more likely to be a genuine patriarchal expectation. (2) Does the fulfillment point to a way of life similar to, or different from, that of the patriarchal period? The promise to give Israel a territory that was under cultivation (Canaan) may already indicate a settled way of life (*see, however,* NOMADISM[S]). The promise of increased posterity, using such similies as "like the stars of the sky," may reflect knowledge of the size of the nation Israel. The promise "I will be your God," found only in P, presupposes the new relation that was only established much later at Sinai. By contrast, in the promises of a son and of divine aid ("I will be with you") the promise and the fulfillment are close together in time, and it is thus more likely that they date from the age of the patriarchs.

A more important factor is whether a passage contains a single promise or several. Seldom is one found alone, and there is a great variety of combinations. The following occur alone: a son, 18:1-16; the land, 12:7; 15:7-21; 24:7; God's presence, 31:3. The promise of numerous posterity and of blessing are found only in combination with other promises: (1) son and posterity: 15:1-6; 16:7-12; 21:12-13, 17-18; (2) land and posterity: 13:14-17; 35:11-13; 48:3-4; (3) land, posterity, and blessing: 26:4-5; 28:3-4; 28:13-14; (4) posterity and blessing: 12:1-3; 18:18-19; 22:15-18; (5) posterity, blessing, and God's presence: 26:24-25; (6) posterity and God's presence: 46:3-4; (7) God's presence, blessing, and land: 26:2-3; (8) posterity, God's presence, blessing, and land: 26:2-6; 28:13-15. Ch. 17 contains all the promises, except that, instead of the promise of God's presence, we find his promise that he will be their God—the covenant promise.

This survey shows that the most frequent promise in Gen. 12–50 is that of posterity, with that of the land a distant second. The promise of a son is found only in the Abraham stories, and that of God's presence only in the Jacob-Esau stories. The promises usually occur in groups of two, three, or more, with the greatest concentration occurring in P. Such a concentration is a sure sign of late origin.

3. The separate promises. ***a. Promise of a son*** (15:2-4; 16:11; 17:15, 16, 19, 21; 18:10, 14; [21:3]). This is quite independent of the promise of posterity. In ch. 18 it is the central feature of the story, a promise made to a childless person in order to solve the problem he faced. The promise of a son is found elsewhere in the OT (Judg. 13:2-5; I Sam. 1; II Kings 4:8-17) and in the NT (Luke 1, 2). It occurs in Ugaritic texts (Keret and Aqhat: *see ANET*) in the same sequence of motifs: the plight of being childless, promise of a son, birth of a son. In Gen. 12–50 the promise of a son is confined to the Abraham stories, where it dominates the accounts.

A messenger from God may announce the birth of a child (Gen. 16:11; 18:10, 14; Judg. 13:2-5; II Kings 4:16; Isa. 7:14). The announcement to Hagar (Gen. 16:11) is in three parts, as are those in Isa. 7:14 and Luke 1:31. They preserve an old form for the announcement of a birth: announcement of pregnancy and of the birth, and telling what the child's name is to be. Such announcements are made to the mother. A late form of the promise can be seen in Gen. 15:1-6, where it is closely connected with the promise of posterity, and in 17:15-21, where, in addition, the covenant promise states that Isaac will be preferred above Ishmael.

The birth of a son is recounted in 21:1-3, a short time after it had been promised. It is highly probable that the promise of a son belongs to the oldest strand of the patriarchal stories.

b. Promise of God's presence (Gen. 26:3, 24; 28:15 [20]; 31:3; 46:3; [48:15, 21; 50:24]). This promise is found only in chs. 26–50. In 26:3, 24 it is made to Isaac, and elsewhere to Jacob. Just as the promise of a son is the dominant motif in chs. 12–25, this promise is dominant in chs. 26–50. Maag was the first to draw attention to this promise, seeing it as loosely connected with the wanderings of the patriarchs. In each instance, God promises to be with them on a journey. It is given as part of the command to move (46:1-3), or to remain (26:1-3), or to return (31:3). This indicates that the promise goes back to the patriarchal period. It should be observed, however, that this promise is not restricted to descriptions of that period, but is found throughout the OT. Preuss investigated the approximately one hundred passages and noted that the oldest texts deal with a situation before or during a migration. He concluded that it is in the patriarchal narratives that the expression had its earliest significance.

c. Promise of the land. i. *Promise of a new home and new pasture.* Such a promise was probably older than that of the land, the latter being a consequence of transition to a settled life. The former belonged to the migratory life, and Maag felt he could discern it even in Gen. 12:1-3, which contains the command to break camp and instruction about where to go. Maag distinguished between the promise of new pasture, which for nomads meant escape from the threat of starvation, and the promise of land already under cultivation, which belongs to a later stage. In the patriarchal stories, however, there is no account of transhumance, and a promise implying it can only be surmised from 12:1-3 (*see, however,* NOMADISM[S] §2). It is clear that the two promises are quite different and that the promise of new pasture corresponds more closely with the nomadic life of the patriarchs.

ii. *Promise of a land under cultivation* (12:7; 13:14-15; 13:17; 15:7-21; 17:8; 24:7; 26:3, 4; 28:4, 13; 35:12; 48:4; 50:24; outside of Gen. 12–50: Exod. 13:5, 11; 32:13; 33:1; Num. 11:12; 14:16, 23; 32:11; Deut. 1:8, 35; 4:31; 6:10, 18, 23, and thirteen other passages). As can be seen from Gen. 15:7-21 and 13:14-17, the emphasis lies on the promise made to Abraham. The promise that Jacob would gain possession of the land is seen as a renewal of the promise to Abraham (Gen. 26:3, 4; 28:4; 35:12; 50:24). The story in Gen. 15:7-21 concerns only the promise of the land; in fact, the story developed out of the promise. Apart from P, this promise usually is found in a story or a scene; it is found in a promise speech only in late texts.

The language varies so little that we can assume a fixed form, utilizing the verb נתן (give). The promise is probably the basis for an accepted formula for the legal transfer of land (cf. Gen. 48:22). Such an adaptation is suggested by 13:14-17. In the formula "to your descendants I will give this land" Abraham received a promise that would be fulfilled only for his descendants, and so this presupposes a period later than those of the patriarchs. This promise probably was formulated when possession of the land was a life-and-death matter for the tribes that had settled in Canaan. At the end of the patriarchal stories (50:24) it is stated that the promise to Abraham, Isaac, and Jacob refers to the gift of the land of Canaan to the Israelites who leave Egypt. Here the promise functions to tie the history of Israel to the patriarchal narratives. *See* GENESIS[S] §A3.

In twenty-one passages in Deuteronomy the promise of the land is formulated as an oath and has the function of legitimizing the occupation of the land by the tribes.

d. Promise of posterity (12:1-3; 13:16; 15:5; 16:10; 17:2, 5, 6, 16, 20; 18:18; 22:17, 18; 26:2-5, 24-25; 28:3, 14; 32:12 [H 13]; 35:11; 46:3; [47:27]; 48:4, 16, 19; outside of Gen. 12–50: [Exod. 1]; Exod. 32:10; Num. 14:12; Deut. 1:10, 11; 6:3; 13:17 [H 18]; 15:6; Isa. 51:2; Neh. 9:23).

i. *Promise of a son and posterity.* The combination of these two promises is found, like the promise of a son, only in the Abraham cycle. That they were originally separate can be seen in 16:10-12 (cf. 21:12-13, 17-18). Their interrelationship is made completely clear in 15:4-5, where the opening of a new scene in vs. 5 shows that the writer was aware of the independence of the two promises. The sequence also shows that the writer regarded the promise of posterity too numerous to count as an intensification of the promise of a son. It is this intensification that was significant for Israel in the Promised Land, as is shown by the late echo in Isa. 51:2.

ii. *The language and form of the promise.* Of all the promises this one most often had a fixed form and is found exactly or almost word-for-word the same in many passages. Characteristic also is the poetic comparison with the stars of the sky (Gen. 15:5; 22:17; 26:4; Exod. 32:13; Deut. 1:10; 10:22; 28:62; Neh. 9:23), the sand by the sea (Gen. 22:17; 32:12 [H 13]; Isa. 10:22; 48:19), and the dust of the earth (Gen. 13:16; 28:14). A variant form of the promise indicates the transition of the family to the nation, "I will make of you a great nation" (12:2; 17:20; 18:18; 21:13, 18; 46:3; Exod. 32:10; Num. 14:12). In the introduction to the patriarchal narrative this promise is applied in a general way to the future greatness of Israel. This greatness is stressed even more in P. Abraham will be the ancestor of nations (17:16), of a "company of nations" (28:3; 35:11; 48:4), and the "father of a multitude of nations" (17:5). Kings will be his descendants (17:6, 16, 20; 35:11). It is clear that all this refers to (and presupposes) the future greatness of the nation Israel; such promises could hardly have originated in the age of the patriarchs.

iii. *The origin of the promise of posterity.* In many passages it is combined with the promise of blessing (12:2; 17:16, 20; 22:17; 26:4; 26:24; 28:3; 32:12 [H 13]; 35:9-11; 48:3-4 [16]; Isa. 51:2). Most of these passages are probably of late origin, but the same combination is found in the blessing that Jacob pronounces on Ephraim and Manasseh (48:16). Here, in a blessing bestowed by a human being, the numerical increase of posterity is depicted as the unfolding of the blessing. There are also other indications that the origin of this promise is in the bestowal of a blessing. Most of the fixed terminology of the promise of blessing occurs also in blessings. This is seen especially in the blessing of a marriage (Gen. 24:60) and in the Legend of King Keret (*ANET* [2nd ed.], KRT B [ii]). This origin explains a distinctive feature of the promise of posterity. The desire for many descendants cannot be fulfilled in one event, like the birth of a son, but must extend over generations of steady growth.

e. Promise of blessing. i. *The distinctive nature of the promise.* An independent pronouncement of blessing has been preserved only in Gen. 12:1-3. Here all the other promises are subordinated to that of blessing, while in all other passages the promise of blessing is made specific in, or is more fully developed by, the promise of posterity. Gen. 12:1-3 is a literary formulation of J intended to serve as introduction to the stories of the patriarchs and also as transition from the primeval history to that of the patriarchs. In this way J created a formula of far-reaching significance, by making an originally nonhistorical blessing into a historical concept (Wolff; Westermann). While this formulation cannot be earlier than J, the basic blessing may well be from the time of the patriarchs.

ii. *Expansion of the promise.* In Gen. 12:1-3 we find, in addition to the promise of many descendants (vs. 2*a*) and future greatness (2*b*), two expansions. Vs. 3*a* has close parallels in Gen. 27:29 ("Cursed be every one who curses you, and blessed be every one who blesses you!") and in Num. 24:9. So, then, this expansion also is derived from blessings such as human beings bestow. The transformation into a promise is secondary. J took the statement and, in the introduction to the patriarchal history, applied it to Israel. Israel's friends are God's friends, and her enemies are his.

The second expansion, "All the families on earth will pray to be blessed (*niph'al*) as you are blessed" (Gen. 12:3*b* [NEB; contrast KJV]), occurs frequently (*niph'al:* 18:18; 28:14; *hithpa'ēl:* 22:18; 26:4). It is also found in a blessing bestowed by a human, Jacob (48:20 *pi'el*), and in the praise of the king, "May men bless themselves by him, all nations call him blessed" (Ps. 72:17*b, hithpa'ēl*). These two passages made the meaning of the sentence clear. The blessings wished for or promised to the person are to work out for him or her so that these blessings will find an echo over long periods of time and throughout vast areas.

f. The covenant promise ("I will be your God"). In the patriarchal histories it is found only in P (Gen. 17:7-8), and is characterized as a covenant (ברית). Elsewhere in P it occurs in Lev. 11:45; 22:33; 25:38; 26:45; Num. 15:41; *see also* Exod. 29:45; and Ezek. 34:24. In all these passages Israel is the recipient of the promise. In Deut. 29:10-13 it occurs as promise to the patriarchs and is characterized again as ברית. It also occurs as a part of the covenant formula, which also says "and you will be my people." By citing this promise in the middle of ch. 17, P builds a connection between patriarchal history and that of the nation. Israel's existence rests on this promise. Israel lives because God promised Abraham that he would be his God. Although in ch. 17 the basic meaning of the "covenant" is a binding commitment, vs. 7 expands the concept in the direction of the ceremonial conclusion of a covenant which will remain in force forever between God and Abraham's descendants. The binding assurance produces an abiding relationship, the covenant.

4. The theological significance of the promises. It can be seen that while the promises to the patriarchs have various features in common, each of them was originally independent and must be investigated separately. This means that all generalizing conclusions about the promises are problematic. The history of their transmission stretches from the patriarchal period to the postexilic period, and we cannot say that as a group they are either early or late.

We can say with confidence that three of them have their origin in the age of the patriarchs: the promise of a son; the promise of God's presence as the people move on; and the promise of new pastures and a new place to live (this promise is assumed from hints in 12:1-3; *see* §3*c above*). The others function to tie the patriarchs to the history of the nation and arose only after Israel was settled in the land. In part, they were reworked out of older materials and expressed as promises.

The theological meaning of each group must be determined separately. The significance of the first group lies in the fact that they are a component of patriarchal religion as it existed before any contact with the history or religion of Israel. They are witnesses to the earliest connection between what God says (the promise) and what he does (the fulfillment). When the people later were rescued or protected they saw this as the fulfillment of what God had said, and thus we can understand why the patriarchal traditions became a basic part of Israel's traditions.

For the second group, the significance lies in their nature as conscious theological reflection. This is seen clearly at an early stage in Gen. 12:1-3, and at a later stage in Gen. 17. These promises were formulated after Israel's encounter with Yahweh as the God who saves, as he is presented in the Exodus tradition. The promises thus have the function of connecting God's ancient word with what he has more recently done for his people. They give the assurance that God stands by his word, and that he can be trusted for the future.

5. Subsequent history of the promises. The promises to the patriarchs had an amazingly long history. In the prophetic books they are not found outside of Jeremiah, Ezekiel, and Second Isaiah; in Psalms they are seldom referred to. In all passages outside Gen. 12–50 where the promises are mentioned they are related, not to the patriarchs, but to Israel. Those that were fulfilled in the time of the patriarchs are no longer important. For this reason we must reckon with a subsequent history of the promises within Gen. 12–50 in the form of insertions and supplements. For example, when in Gen. 22:15-18 a reason is twice added to a promise (vss. 16, 18), presenting the promise as a reward for Abraham's obedience, we may see in this the concern of a later age, for which Abraham's obedience served as a living example.

Bibliography. K. Galling, *Die Erwählungstraditionen Israels, BZAW,* XLVIII (1928); A. Alt, *Der Gott der Väter* (1929); G. von Rad, "Verheissenes Land und Jahwes Land im Hexateuch," *Gesammelte Studien zum AT,* Theologische Bücherei, VIII (1958 [3rd ed., 1965]), 87-100; W. Zimmerli, "Verheissung und Erfüllung," *Probleme alttestamentlicher Hermeneutik,* ed. C. Westermann, Theologische Bücherei, XI (1960), 69-101; J. Hoftijzer, *Die Verheissungen an die drei Erzväter* (1956); V. Maag, "Der Hirte Israels. Eine Skizze von Wesen und Bedeutung der Väterreligion," *Schweizer Theologische Umschaw,* XXVIII (1958), 2-28; V. Maag, "Malkût Jhwh," *Congress Volume,* VTSup, VII (1960), 129-53; C. Sant, "The Promise Narratives in Genesis," *Melit Theologica* (1959), 1-13; H. W. Wolff, "Das Kerygma des Jahwisten," *Gesammelte Studien zum AT,* Theologische Bücherei, XXII (1964 [2nd ed., 1973]), 345-73; C. Westermann, "Arten der Erzählung in der Genesis," *Forschung am Alten Testament,* Theologische Bücherei, XXIV (1964); W. M. Clark, "The Origin and Development of the Land Promise Theme in the OT" (diss., Yale, 1964); K. Koch, "Die Sohnesverheissung an den ugaritischen Daniel," *ZA,* LVIII (1967), 211-21; N. Lohfink, *Die Landverheissung als Eid* (1967); I. Blythin, "The Patriarchs and the Promise," *SJT,* XXI (1968), 56-73; O. Eissfeldt, "Der kanaanäische El als Geber der den israelitischen Erzvatern geltenden Nachkommenschaft- und Land besitzverheissungen," *Kleine Schriften,* V (1973), 50-62; H. D. Preuss, "Ich will mit dir sein!" *ZAW,* LXXX (1968), 139-73; S. E. Lowenstamm, "The Divine Grants of Land to the Patriarchs," *JAOS,* XCI (1971), 509-10; H. C. White, "The Divine Oath in Genesis," *JBL,* XCII (1973), 165-79; M. Noth, *Die Überlieferungsgeschichte des Pentateuch* (1948); H. Seebass, *Der Erzväter Israel, BZAW,* XCVIII (1966); J. van Seters, "Confessional Reformulation in the Exilic Period," *VT,* XXII (1972), 448-95.

C. Westermann

PRONOUNCEMENT STORY. *See* SAYINGS OF JESUS, FORM OF[S] §6.

*PROPHECY IN ANCIENT ISRAEL.

1. The role of prophecy
2. The prophet as a person
3. The audience
4. Fundamental concerns

Bibliography

1. The role of prophecy. Israelite prophecy served a definite function in the life of a larger whole, contributing to a dynamic process. It complemented two other major aspects of Israelite culture: priestly tradition and wisdom. Each of these eventually became crystallized in one of the three major divisions of the Hebrew canon (*see* CANON OF THE OT §§2-4). The different aspects were by no means always isolated, but could be combined in a single person's life and often in single utterances. A prophetic utterance could (and usually did) include elements more characteristic of priesthood or wisdom. In fact, the combination of functions is older than their separation since societal development has generally been in the direction of increasing specialization. Speculations regarding an originally pure form, to which elements of other traditions have been added secondarily, run contrary to data from the history of religion. Prophecy is distinct but not separate from the rest of Israelite existence. *See* WISDOM IN THE OT[S].

Prophecy shares with priestly tradition a heavy emphasis on divine revelation, expressed stylistically by Yahweh's speaking in the first person. It differs from priestly word in that the priest presents above all the traditions of the sacred past which are believed to have general significance for Israelite life, while the prophet responds basically to particular situations. Since the priestly tradition is foundational, it forms the framework within which the prophet operates; in this sense, the content of the priest's word stands normally above the prophet's. (In Jewish tradition, the Pentateuch is more sacred than the prophetic corpus.) The general applicability of priestly speech implies that it does not require for itself constantly new revelation; it relies on a message received earlier by a mediator of revelation, who may be called a prophet or more than a prophet (especially, Moses). *See* PRIESTS[S]; PRIESTLY WRITERS[S].

While the symbol of divine speech is strongly represented in prophecy, it is by no means the exclusive form employed. Often Yahweh is spoken about in the third person—as in wisdom or lay style—sometimes in rapid alternation with first-person speech by Yahweh. It is possible (although by no means certain) that the third-person form reflects the tradition of the relatively rational diviner as distinguished from the possessed shaman. In some prophetic books the content presented in the form of nondivine speech is relatively similar to that of wisdom literature. In any case, Israelite faith did not bypass human reasoning.

Prophets could speak unasked, but often they responded to the declaration of a problem by presenting an answer. Problems might be expressed in individual and collective laments, confronting deity with the present tension-filled situation. To these a mechanical or inspired oracle could give a response. Many biblical prophecies allude, or directly refer to, actual or imagined complaints set before Yahweh (e.g., Isa. 49:14). Since complaints typically include an accusation directed against divine action or inaction, the responses defend Yahweh (Mic. 6:3). The employment of judicial form in these instances is not at all unusual, for in Israel, as in neighboring countries, such style pervaded life in general, including private conflict, warfare, ritual, and prognostication; also, controversies of any kind are presented thus (e.g., Isa. 41:1, 21; 44:8). In some cases the prophet presented the complaint on behalf of the people. Habakkuk, who does so, is a seer relatively close to wisdom or to the human side of the cult; if he were simply a wise man he might have to leave the question open, but as a prophet he obtains a word from Yahweh (2:1-3).

As already pointed out, the heart of prophecy lies in divine revelation in response to actual situations. Since Israelite (like much of) religion is strongly dynamic in outlook, an important aspect of such speech involves the disclosure of the future. "Future" means the tendency of events, the direction in which they move. A major reason for ancient DIVINATION is to discover the tendency, so that unfavorable actions may be avoided. In Israelite narration, a clear example is given in I Sam. 23:12-13; when the oracle says "yes" to David's question, "Will the men of Keilah surrender me [to Saul]?" David simply leaves the city of Keilah. The understanding that an announcement is subject to revocation—perhaps precisely as a result of the announcement—underlies the story of Jonah; that is a feature of the genre. Of course, there may be some immutable promises (such as are based on a divine decision regarding mankind, Israel, or David's dynasty), providing a framework for the recipient's orientation.

To say that prophecy deals with the future is roughly true, but is in some ways both too broad and too narrow a characterization. Legal literature and wisdom deal with a hypothetical future in the sense of declaring the consequences of certain types of action; precisely for that reason, prophets can interpret particular occasions in terms of such directional structure. Otherwise, reality would lose coherence and significance—a possibility raised in skeptical wisdom. On the other hand, oracles are not limited to declarations concerning coming events. Already quite commonly in primitive societies and in the ancient Near East (e.g., *ANET*, pp. 26, 394-96, 497-98), diviners and shamans had as major tasks the identification of causes of present evil and of an appropriate remedy, the detection of lost objects (cf. I Sam. 9:20), and the transmission of a god's or spirit's will for an occasion. These involve the "future" only in a very broad sense—that of an assessment of, or a reaction to, events. *See* PROPHET, PROPHETISM §D.

2. The prophet as a person. The insight of the prophet was expected to come as a gift. This could mean a dream or a vision (especially in the case of a "seer"); sometimes as a part of, or instead of, such an experience one could receive a message aurally (e.g., Amos 7:7-9; Isa. 40:6). Then the prophet can report the content. Some oracles outside of Israel are described as being delivered while the person is possessed by a "spirit," so that the latter speaks directly to the audience—bypassing, in form at least, the ego of the prophet. Whether such a situation is implied by numerous Israelite oracles, we simply do not know. In some manner, however, the prophet transcends normal self-assertive consciousness and participates in a highly receptive state.

The call to prophesy was experienced typically as an overwhelming external force. At the very least, that is the way recipients spoke about it; numerous parallels from various parts of the world show that as a rule the prophet indeed bowed to a consciously unsought experience. This was often done quite reluctantly, since hardship was entailed in being directly exposed to the will of invisible powers and inadequacy was felt and expressed, both in Israel and elsewhere. A call, or report of a call, was not peculiar to the prophetic task, but it was especially relevant for this the most sacred and perhaps most important role in society.

The prophet's person is of extreme importance and receives considerable attention in the relevant literature. Not only the initial election, but also subsequent commissions are reported in autobiographical style. Such commissions include symbolic actions, carried out literally or in imagination (especially by Hosea, Isaiah, Jeremiah, Ezekiel, Zechariah); those that are literally executed can also be reported by others (e.g., I Kings 22:11). Stories stress the power of the divine word and the conflicts encountered (above all for Elijah, Elisha, Amos, Isaiah, Jeremiah). Neither first-person nor third-person narratives have a strictly biographical purpose, since they legitimize the message and give it dramatic form; but they presuppose the significance of the agent, who is not merely a mechanical tool. Just like a "wise" person, a prophet can be either male or female (Exod. 15:20; Judg. 4:4; Isa. 8:3; II Kings 22:14; Ezek 13:17; Neh. 6:14).

It was inevitable that prophets would differ with each other. A contrary oracle could lead one to doubt one's own revelation, but disobedience to the orders received could be fatal (I Kings 13; cf. Jer. 28). Divergences in message were usually explained in terms of a charge that opponents failed to receive a divine word because they were morally or spiritually corrupt—presenting their own imagination (Jer. 23:16, 26; in a drunken state: Isa. 28:7), yielding to popularity or material reward (Mic. 3:5; cf. Jer. 23:17 and Ezek. 13:10) or, on the other hand, to impulses toward blasphemy or misanthropy (I Kings 22:18; Jer. 26:11; cf. Jonah), or following Baal instead of Yahweh (Deut. 13:2-3; Jer. 2:8). It was also possible to claim that Yahweh deliberately misled someone for purposes of punishment (I Kings 22:19-23; cf. Ezek. 20:25 and *Iliad* II, 1-34). In hindsight an oracle could be verified, if it was fulfilled (I Kings 22:28; Jer. 28:9). Yet it was difficult to prove a forecast false (despite Deut. 18:22), since changed conditions might legitimately bring about a different course of events; indeed, a number of unfulfilled prophecies are left standing in biblical tradition, are slightly adjusted, or are held delayed (e.g., Hag. 2:20-23; Zech. 6:11—among those not expressly withdrawn). *See* PROPHETS, FALSE[S].

Because of their close relation to deity, the prophets' words were considered highly powerful and thus able to affect the future as well as to describe it. In fact, it is often difficult to tell the precise boundary line between determining and announcing (*see* WORD, THE §2). Persons believed to be near God were called upon to engage in intercession to remove or ward off evil, but such prayer was not necessarily successful and could be forestalled or forbidden by deity (Amos 7:8; Jer. 7:16; 11:14). *See* REPENTANCE IN THE OT[S].

3. The audience. Prophets operated under a wide range of circumstances. Individuals could turn to them for concrete problems (I Sam. 9:6-9; implied in I Kings 14:2). Kings and military leaders of Israel, as of neighboring countries, inquired of them before and during warfare (e.g., I Sam. 23:2-4; II Kings 3:11). However, such consultation was apparently not routine (*see,* e.g., I Kings 22:5); often, for political decisions, reliance was placed instead on the advice of a "wise" man (II Sam. 16:23; cf. Isa. 19:11)—a fact which could lead to rivalry between the two professions (Isa. 29:14-15; cf. Mari Texts A 15). Not infrequently, a direction for warfare or politics was presented unasked (I Kings 20:28, 39-42; Isa. 7:3-4; as in MARI, etc.). In relation to the community at large, a prophetic word came in response to a collective fast during a calamity (Jer. 36:6; cf. Isa. 58:1-9), or it could bring about such a fast by a word of judgment (Jonah 3:3-9).

One can ask whether prophets participated in regular cultic ceremonies. As private persons, and especially as representatives of God, undoubtedly they did. Ancient ritual was loose enough in organization to provide opportunity for various kinds of persons to speak to any audience willing to listen; in fact, there was expectation and hope for special divine revelations. Perhaps some prophecies, such as those of Amos, were delivered at festivals. The psalms contain a number of oracular expressions which are general in application, addressed to the "wicked" (Pss. 50:16; 75:4 [H 75:5]) or to those who trust in Yahweh (Ps. 91). Such general oracles belong to the sphere of the liturgist or cultic singer (as specified in the titles of Pss. 50, etc., containing such words). These are close to, but not identical with, prophetic words dealing with specific solutions. In addition, a number of divine declarations are quoted in psalms, as in other types of literature (e.g., in Pss. 2; 60; 68; 87; 89). *See* PROPHET, PROPHETISM §B3.

Although prophets were no match for the king in terms of brute force, in Israelite theory they stood above the king on behalf of Yahweh. As told in biblical narratives, an oracle normally announced the next king (Saul, David, Jeroboam I, Jehu; cf. *ANET,* pp. 289, 446-49) and the end of a royal dynasty or "house" (I Sam. 13:14; 15:28; I Kings 14:7-14). Prophets possessed and exercised the right to criticize a king, who was the chief judicial officer and thus not subject to any other form of prosecution. As elsewhere in the Near East, a divine word could authorize or forbid the building of a temple (II Sam. 7).

Regularly, Israelite prophets condemned the leaders of the country, individually or collectively. Priests were charged with failing to mediate and follow divine instruction and being eager to receive expiatory sacrifices and other remuneration (Hos. 4:6-8; Mic. 3:11; Zeph. 3:4). Prophets were accused of violating the norms of their profession (*see* §2 *above*). The "heads," "princes," or members of government, were criticized for ignoring basic morality, accepting bribes, disinterest in the lot of the weak, and exploitation (Amos 6:1-6; Hos. 5:10; 7:3; Isa. 1:23; 3:14; Mic. 3:1-3, 9-11). For most of such transgressions there was no humanly executed penalty in the system of Israelite society.

Other groups attacked are merchants, for cheating and insensitive rapacity (Amos 8:4-6; Hos. 12:7-8 [H 12:8-9]; Mic. 6:10-12), and city women, for selfish or haughty luxury (Amos 4:1; Isa. 3:16-17). Sometimes there occur laments over pervasive immorality, in a style that was apparently standardized (cf. Ps. 53:3 [H 53:4]; in Egypt, *ANET*, pp. 406, 443-45). Quite frequently accusations are couched in general expressions for "evil," "wickedness," "falsehood," "iniquity," "rebellion," etc. The list of specific sins castigated is largely the same as that which appears in legal and wisdom literature: worship of gods other than Yahweh, idolatry, sacred prostitution (Hos. 4:14), sabbath violation, disrespect to parents (Mic. 7:6), murder, adultery, theft, falsehood, disloyalty to associates (Jer. 9:4 [H 9:3]), covetousness (i.e., aggrandizement: Mic. 2:2), drunkenness, interest on loans (Ezek. 22:12), and incest (Amos 2:7), in addition to others already mentioned. *See* LAW IN THE OT[S] §13.

Of special concern to prophets is the placing of trust in military or other human operations (e.g., Hos. 10:13; Isa. 30:15-17; 31:1; Jer. 17:5). Both idolatry and oppression are seen as instances of misdirected trust (Isa. 30:12; 42:17; Hab. 2:18). The downfall of foreign nations is sometimes grounded in their prideful self-confidence (Isa. 10:12-16; Jer. 50:31; Obad. 3). As a rule, the nation opposed is held guilty more specifically of international "oppression" (Isa. 14:4), i.e., of destructive activity toward Israel or others (Amos 1:3–2:3; Nah. 3:1; Obad. 10-14; Jer. 51:25, 49). For the Israelite audience, the thrust of oracles against enemy countries is to create or support confidence in Yahweh; in fact, the difference between critical and promising words lies largely in the situation of the hearers in terms of whether they inflict or need rescue from oppression or other forms of evil.

4. Fundamental concerns. It would be an error to think that the prophets dealt only with finite and superficial concerns. It is true that primitive divination gives fairly narrow answers to concrete problems; Israelite prophecies, too, were generally quite practical in their point. Yet there are two ways, somewhat interrelated, in which prophetic words went beyond a limited application. First of all, the highly symbolic nature of their expression points to a deeply emotional confrontation with reality. Israelite prophets did not present much precise information to their hearers; however, their words possessed great personal and religious power, which made them resound over centuries and millennia. Second, they declare fundamental trends in existence. Israelite prophets saw deep divergencies and clashes in life. These tensions, some of them said, would be overcome in an ultimate resolution, to arrive soon. It is often difficult to determine how literally they understood the coming of perfect reality; yet the very vagueness in this regard shows how Israelites, like other human beings, lived not just by pragmatic considerations, but in terms of a basic orientation. *See* PROPHET, PROPHETISM §D6-7.

The great Israelite prophets believed that human existence was in severe trouble. Their word, if accepted, leads toward self-transcendence with acknowledgment of guilt. If a "turning" (or "returning") takes place, one might express one's hope for graciousness, without presumption, by use of the phrase "who knows" (II Sam. 12:22; Jonah 3:9; cf. similarly "perhaps" in Zeph. 2:3; Exod. 32:30). A number of major voices declared that only after a downfall would reconstitution be possible. (These included—at least part of the time—Hosea, Isaiah, Jeremiah, Ezekiel: *see* REMNANT; REMNANT[S]; DISCIPLINE, DIVINE[S].) Since the envisioned fulfillment is in line with the divine will seen in the "origin" of human and national reality, various prophets drew upon the protological elements of their tradition for the shape in which they present an eschatological resolution: a new exodus, a new covenant, a new Zion, or a new creation. In these forms a state of perfection is announced (Jer. 31:31-34; etc.; *see* NEW COVENANT, THE[S]). When Israelites lost control of political power, classical prophecy ended; the emphasis shifted from guilt over social evil toward the confident perseverance inculcated by apocalyptic with an announcement of a new world. *See* APOCALYPTICISM; APOCALYPTICISM[S].

The orientation toward an ultimate fulfillment is shared with a number of movements which belong roughly to the same historical period, arising in social situations basically similar to each other. Societies in the Near East and in neighboring areas from India to Greece were reaching a level of complexity which permitted considerable specialization, extensive contemplation, and the high degree of self-consciousness presupposed by acknowledgment of guilt, as well as the social stratification and warlike subjugation which became the object of criticism. Traditional priestly rituals of an impersonal sort became widely questioned; the use of writing enhanced the impact of unusual "great" prophets in Israel as well as of mystics in India (as it supported the dominions opposed). While there are important differences between mysticism and major Hebrew prophecy, they share an orientation toward transcending finite (and especially destructive) self-projections of an individual or of a nation. Representatives of the more extreme points of view necessarily remained a minority in a continuing society, which largely required moderate approaches.

See also PROPHECY IN THE ANCIENT NEAR EAST[S]; PROPHETS, FALSE[S].

Bibliography. V. Elwin, *The Religion of an Indian Tribe* (1955), with parallels, e.g., for the objection to a prophetic call; A. Heschel, *The Prophets* (1962); J. Lindblom, *Prophecy in Ancient Israel* (1962); B. W. Anderson and W. Harrelson, eds., *Israel's Prophetic Heritage* (1962); C. F. Whitley, *The Prophetic Achievement* (1963); E. Würthwein and Otto Kaiser, eds., *Tradition und Situation* (1963); E. von Waldow, *Der traditionsgeschichtliche Hintergrund der prophetischen Gerichtsreden* (1963); N. Gottwald, *All the Kingdoms of the Earth: Israelite Prophecy and International Relations in the Ancient Near East* (1964); W. McKane, *Prophets and Wise Men* (1965); R. E. Clements, *Prophecy and Covenant* (1965); S. Herrmann, *Die prophetischen Heilserwartungen im AT* (1965); N. Habel, "The Form and Significance of the Call Narratives," *ZAW*, LXXVII (1965), 297-323; W. Zimmerli, *The Law and the Prophets* (1965); E. Hammershaimb, *Some Aspects of OT Prophecy from Isaiah to Malachi* (1966); J. G. Williams, "The Prophetic 'Father,'" *JBL*, LXXXV (1966), 344-48; C. Westermann, *Basic Forms of Prophetic Speech* (1967); G. Fohrer, *Studien zur alttestamentlichen Prophetie* (1967); M. Eliade, *From Primitives to Zen* (1967), comparative materials; F. Ellermeier, *Prophetie in Mari und Israel* (1968); G. von Rad, *The Message of the Prophets* (1968); J. Hayes, "The Usage of Oracles Against Foreign Nations in Ancient Israel," *JBL*, LXXXVII (1968), 81-92; A. Neher, *The Prophetic Existence* (1969); M. Buss, *The Prophetic Word of Hosea* (1969), with additional discussion and detailed support; V. Eppstein, "Was Saul also among the Prophets?" *ZAW*, LXXXI (1969), 287-304; M. L. Henry, *Prophet und Tradition* (1969); H. Orlinsky, ed., *Interpreting the Prophetic Tradition* (1969); J. Jeremias, *Kultprophetie und Gerichtsverkündigung in der späten Königszeit Israels* (1970), somewhat speculative; L. Ramlot, "Prophétisme," *Supplément au Dictionnaire de la Bible*, VIII (1970), cols. 811-1222, for a full survey; F. Hecht, *Eschatologie und Ritus bei den "Reformpropheten"* (1971); T. Raitt, "The Prophetic Summons to Repentance," *ZAW*, LXXXIII (1971), 30-49; B. Long, "Two Question and Answer Schemata in the Prophets," *JBL*, XC (1971), 129-39; J. Crenshaw, *Prophetic Conflict* (1971); K. Seybold, *Das davidische Königtum im Zeugnis der Propheten* (1972); W. Janzen, *Mourning Cry and Woe Oracle* (1972); O. H. Steck, *Friedensvorstellungen im alten Jerusalem* (1972); W. Schmidt, *Zukunftsgewissheit und Gegenwartskritik* (1973); H. P. Müller, *Mythos, Tradition, Revolution* (1973); *Studies on Prophecy*, VTSup, XXVI (1974); M. Ota, "A Note on 2 Samuel 7," in *OT Studies in Honor of Jacob M. Myers* (1974), pp. 403-7; B. Gladigow, "Jenseitsvorstellungen und Kulturkritik," *Zeitschrift für Religions- und Geistesgeschichte*, XXVI (1974), 289-309; W. E. March, "Prophecy," in *OT Form Criticism*, ed. J. Hayes (1974), pp. 141-77.

M. J. Buss

***PROPHECY IN THE ANCIENT NEAR EAST.** Various materials from the ancient Near East—inspired messages transmitted from a deity, predictions, eschatological or apocalyptic texts, and social criticism—have all been called "prophetic." Although many of these materials are mentioned below, the focus is on the prophet as an inspired speaker, under divine constraint or commission, who publicly announces an immediate revelation. The speaker may or may not be associated with the cult.

1. Egypt
2. Anatolia
3. Canaan
4. Syria
5. Mesopotamia
    a. Akkadian "prophecies"
    b. The Uruk oracle
    c. Prophecy in the Mari texts
    d. Prophecy in the Neo-Assyrian period

Bibliography

1. Egypt. Based upon the Greek rendering of the title of a class of Egyptian priests, modern scholars often speak of priestly "prophets." The Egyptian title means merely "servant of God." The Greek rendering apparently derived from the fact that these priests had a primary role in formulating questions put to divine oracles and in expounding the divine response. Thus they are not prophets in the sense defined above.

The term "prophecy" is also used to describe a type of Egyptian literature. For example, the composition known as "The Prophecy of Neferti" purports to contain predictions made in the Fourth Dynasty of a future great king, Ameny, whereas the text is generally regarded as a literary fiction composed in the reign of Amen-em-het I of the Twelfth Dynasty. The "predictions," moreover, are not presented as divine revelation. Another composition, "The Admonitions of Ipu-wer" (or "The Admonitions of an Egyptian Sage/of a Prophet"), has been called "'prophetic' in a biblical sense" because of the critique that it contains of the past and present administration in Egypt. But the critique is not based on divine revelation.

2. Anatolia. The "Plague Prayers of Mursilis," which date from the latter part of the fourteenth century B.C., refer to various means by which the king hoped to learn the reason for the plague which was killing off the people. One of the means was through an inspired speaker: "Let a prophet (literally, man of the god) declare it," or "Let a prophet rise and declare it." This means of revelation was distinguished from omens and dreams. Some kind of inspired speaking was therefore known in Anatolia, though there is no further information about the circumstances and no further direct evidence for such activity in the early periods. A number of revelatory dreams are known, particularly in connection with King Ḫattusilis (early thirteenth century B.C.), but the dreams do not contain any specific commissioning of the recipient to convey the message to another party.

3. Canaan. The Bible refers to prophets of Baal and of Asherah (I Kings 18:19), though very little is said about these prophets. Since the same term is used for them as for Israelite prophets, viz., *nābhî'*, the Israelite writers saw some similarity. The Baal prophets are not associated with spoken oracles, but are described as supported by the crown and as engaging in ritual dance and self-wounding. Presumably their wild behavior formed a comparison with the ecstatic, "mad" aspect of Israelite prophecy. *See* PROPHET §B2.

Canaanite sources themselves do not yield any references to prophets. The texts from Ugarit that have been connected with prophecy (in the wide sense) either refer to technical divination or are so unclear that no conclusions can be drawn. What little additional knowledge we have comes from an Egyptian text, a report on "The Journey of Wen-Amon to Phoenicia." Wen-Amon, who visited

Byblos in the first half of the eleventh century B.C., reports that, while the local prince was presenting offerings to his gods, one of his young men became possessed and delivered an oracle authenticating Wen-Amon as a messenger sent by the god Amon and demanding respect for the god and his servant.

4. Syria. One of the few texts from Syria, the stele of Zakir, king of Hamath and Lu'ash in central Syria during the early eighth century B.C., reports prophetic activity. While under siege, Zakir relates that "I lifted up my hands to Baal-Sha[may]n and Baal-Shamay[n] answered me [and spoke] to me by means of visionaries (*ḥzyn*) and . . . (*'ddn*). Baal-Shamayn [said] to me, 'Fear not, for I have made [you kin]g [and I will st]ay with you and rescue you." Although it does not say how the speakers received the message, the text seems to represent prophecy in response to prayer. One of the Aramaic terms used is the analogue of the Hebrew word *ḥôzeh,* which occurs in reference to some of the prophets in Israel. *See* PROPHET §B1.

5. Mesopotamia. As is the case with the Egyptian texts, a variety of materials from Mesopotamia have been labeled prophetic from one point of view or another.

a. Akkadian "prophecies." Some texts have been called prophecies because they contain predictions of coming events, although these predictions at least in part are written after the fact. In form some of the texts resemble the apodoses of omen texts; in some instances the protases are even preserved: "if a meteorite flashes . . . (protasis) Elam will lie waste; its sanctuaries will be destroyed . . . (apodosis)" (Biggs, pp. 122-25; *see also* METEORITES[S]). There are differences from standard omen texts, nevertheless, and the content may be classified as more like apocalyptic literature, in the sense that there is a general description of future events (*see* APOCALYPTICISM; APOCALYPTICISM[S]). One of these texts has turned out to be a speech by the god Marduk which tells the god's history and refers to future conditions of political and natural prosperity. Another is a speech by the deified king, Shulgi, who conveys a divine revelation. The text purports to foretell a period of trouble to be followed by a period of order and cultic reconstruction. Both these texts contain in part predictions after the events (twelfth century B.C.) and statements about future prosperity and order, somewhat after the fashion of apocalypticism rather than prophecy.

b. The Uruk oracle. This text dates from the nineteenth century B.C. and is somewhat unusual; unfortunately it is not fully preserved. A deity visits a man in an unspecified fashion and converses with him concerning Uruk and the establishment of a faithful ruler. The meaning of the message is contained in a damaged portion of the tablet and is therefore unclear. The man considered it important enough, however, to report to the king. The text may be an example of inspired speaking, but much of the desired information is lacking.

c. Prophecy in the Mari texts. The mixed cultural milieu of the Mari texts (*see* MARI; MARI[S]) has many ties with the Hebrew patriarchs and with early Israel. One of the most striking ties is the increasing evidence in the Mari texts (eighteenth century B.C.) for prophetic activity. The geographical range of the activity extends at least from Mari as far west as Aleppo.

i. *Speakers with titles.* The title *āpilu/āpiltu* is found with both men and women. It occurs only in the Mari texts and, apparently, in learned lexical lists. The title was presumably understood by the Mari scribes as an Akkadian designation, "answerer." One indication of the official status of these persons is an administrative text listing distributions from the royal stores to various persons—agricultural, commercial, and ship workers—including a certain *āpilu,* who receives a garment. The "answerers" are often described as related to a specific deity, such as Addu (Hadad), Lord of Halab (Aleppo); Shamash (of Sippar); Diritum; and Dagan (Dagon) of Tuttul. At times the "answerers" seem to operate as a group.

Another title is *assinnu.* At a later time this title becomes well known; it refers to a member of the cultic staff of the goddess Ishtar, associated especially with singing. Also, the *assinnu* may have been a eunuch. At Mari the *assinnu* is connected with Annunitum, a form of Ishtar.

The third title is *muḫḫû/muḫḫûtu,* "ecstatic," found with both men and women. The title is known from other Akkadian texts of this period, but not in connection with oracular speaking. The form cannot be separated from the later title, *maḫḫû/maḫḫûtu,* "ecstatic," which, perhaps by accident of discovery, is not specifically associated with oracular speaking. It is clear from both the older and the later texts that the "ecstatic" had an official role in the cult. A Mari text describing the cult of Ishtar (who is not specifically involved in any of the Mari prophecies) says, following reference to cult singers, "If during the monthly festival the 'ecstatic' has come (!) (but) he is not [. . .] to become ecstatic . . . (mention of a cage)." At the end the text says, "the watered-down beer (?) and the four . . . utensils that have been properly placed, they shall hold for the needs of the 'ecstatics'" (*RA,* XXXV [1938], 1-13). A text from Ugarit, dating toward the middle of the second millennium B.C., says that "my brothers bathe with their own blood, like *maḫḫû* (pl.)," which is reminiscent of the activities of the Baal prophets in I Kings 18. *See* PROPHET §B2.

Another possible title, **qabbātu,* which would mean "(female) speaker," is probably to be understood as a personal name.

ii. *Speakers without titles.* Many of the persons who transmit messages from a deity are not given any special designation. It seems clear that these persons, some of whom are well known, were of private or lay status.

iii. *The setting of the oracles.* It is fortunate that the letters about prophetic activity often indicate something of the circumstances of the message. On occasion the oracle seems to be a response to a previous inquiry, as when a female "ecstatic" says, "O Zimri-Lim, do not go on a campaign. Stay in Mari and I will continue to answer" (ARM X:50).

The oracle may also be in response to a sacrificial offering. One royal correspondent reported to the king that "(when) I offered a sacrifice to the god Dagan for the life of my lord, the 'answerer' of Dagan of Tuttul got up and spoke as follows, saying, 'O Babylon, . . . (an oracle against Babylon)'" (ARM XIII:23). Although this seems to be a favorable response to the offering, on another occasion the king is informed that his sacrifice has arrived and has been presented, cheering the whole country, but "the (male) 'ecstatic' got up before Dagan and spoke as follows, 'I (Dagan) am not given pure water to drink. Write to your lord so that he may give me pure water to drink" (A.455, *see* Huffmon, pp. 211-12).

A number of oracles were delivered in the temple, but without any specific indication of a cultic impetus. In one report a certain Shelibum, an *assinnu,* "in the temple of the goddess Annunitum, on the third day, . . . became ecstatic. 'Thus says Annunitum, "O Zimri-Lim, . . . (warning and assurance)"'" (ARM X:7). In another report the temple administrator supplied information that "in the temple of Annunitum of the inner city, Ahatum, the young woman of the man Daganmalik, became ecstatic and spoke as follows, saying, 'O Zimri-Lim, even if you despise me I will make sweet noises over you'" (ARM X:8). The temple administrator seems to have had some jurisdiction over such activity in the temple (cf. Jer. 29:26).

Revelation by dream, especially associated with private persons, tends either to take place in the temple or to involve a dream visit to a temple. Dream revelations have many parallels in Mesopotamian literature.

Some oracles seem to have a profane setting, even though they may concern cultic affairs, in that the speaker seeks out the king's representative in order to transmit a message for the king. For example, the governor of Terqa writes that "the (male) 'ecstatic' of Dagan came and spoke a word [to me] as follows, saying, 'The god sent me. Hurry, write to the ki[ng] that they dedicate (?) the funerary offerings to the spirit of Yahdun-Lim'" (ARM III:40).

iv. *The content of the oracles.* As illustrated above, the oracles may be either favorable or unfavorable to the king, the recipient of the overwhelming majority of the oracles (because perhaps of the nature of the evidence). The speaker identifies with the deity, speaking in the first person. Use is often made of the messenger form, "thus says the god so-and-so," and there are also references to being "sent" by the deity.

Most of the oracles are oracles of assurance, relating to the varied circumstances of the king. When the god expresses anger against the king's enemy, the king himself is indirectly assured. A variation on assurance is an oracle warning the king, e.g., about a coming revolt. Some oracles contain explicit complaints; e.g., note the "pure water" mentioned above. There may even be a veiled threat, as when the deity says "that which I have given I can take away" (A.1121, *see* HUFFMON, pp. 204-5). Similar to these are the gentle reminders: "Send [to] me quickly at Sippar, [fo]r (your) life, the throne intended for my splendid residence as well as your daughter whom I [Shamash] had requested of you" (A.4260, *see* HUFFMON, pp. 206-7).

Not all of the oracles are directed to the king. One is a warning oracle for the citizens of Terqa. A young man had a dream in which he "saw" as follows: "[The god (said)], 'Do not rebuild (pl.) this temple. (If) you (pl.) rebuild it, I will make it fall into the river'" (ARM XIII:112).

v. *The acceptability of the oracles.* That these oracles represent a departure from proper practice in an outpost of Mesopotamian culture is indicated by the activity in response to them by the king's officials. They often acquire a lock of the HAIR and a snip of the HEM of the speaker and send them on together with their report, presumably for some kind of technical divination. Also, the king is frequently advised to check the message by means of the usual technical divination practice. Sometimes the reliability of the speaker was tested before reporting to the king.

d. Prophecy in the Neo-Assyrian period. In the seventh century, during the reigns of Esarhaddon and Ashurbanipal, there seems to have been an unusual degree of interest in a variety of types of communication with the divine world. In this period at least, Assyrian culture, which was somewhat provincial and which had a strong Aramean element, seems to have been receptive to prophetic oracular speakers.

i. *Speakers with titles.* None of the titles used for oracular speakers in the Mari texts recur in connection with such activity in the Neo-Assyrian period. The most common title, *raggimu/raggintu,* "proclaimer, announcer," borne by both men and women, does occur in texts from the latter half of the second millennium, but not in association with oracles. There are various indications that the "proclaimer" had a cultic role, although the evidence is not decisive. It is clear that the "proclaimer" might play a role in the substitute-king ritual.

Another title, *šabrû/šabrātu,* apparently "revealer," is equated with *raggimu* in one lexical text. This title occurs primarily in texts of Ashurbanipal. Again, there are indications that the "revealer" had a cultic role.

A third title, *šēlûtu,* "(female) votary," is used to identify one of the speakers in a long collection of oracles for Esarhaddon as a "votary of the king." Some dedicatory contracts make it clear that the "votary of the king" is someone dedicated by the king to the service of a deity. The nature of that service, however, is not known.

ii. *Speakers without titles.* Some collections identify the oracles as "from the mouth of so-and-so from such-and-such a city." The absence of a title in connection with these persons allows for the possibility that they had no official position that involved giving oracles. Unlike the situation in the Mari texts, however, there is no further information about these speakers and their status. They may have had some official position that was not mentioned. The speakers are both men and women in roughly equal proportion regardless of status.

iii. *The setting of the oracles.* The texts often point to some of the circumstances of the oracle. That the oracle may be in response to an inquiry, for example, is indicated by an oracle that seems to begin by quoting a question put to Ishtar: "How does she answer the disloyal ones? The word of Ishtar of Arbela, the word of the Queen of Heaven and Earth. 'I will look about and keep on listening, and I will search out the disloyal ones. I will put [them ?] into the hands of my king" (Langdon, pl. II).

Another oracle includes in itself a summary of the occasion, viz., crisis, complaint, divine reassurance, deposit of the written oracle, and presentation of the written oracle to the king to the accompaniment of ritual acts: "Now these rebels have incited against you, they have made you come out, they have surrounded you. You (Esarhaddon) opened your mouth. Now I, Asshur, have heard your distress cry. From the gate of heaven I soar down (?). I will surely overthrow (them); I will surely have fire consume them. You can stand securely among them. From your presence I removed (them). I made them go up to the mountain(s). I rain(ed) down hot stones upon them. I slaughtered your enemies. I filled the river with their blood. Let them see, let them praise me, for I am Asshur, lord of the gods. This is the (oracle of) well-being which is (placed ?) before the (divine) statue. This is the sworn tablet of Asshur. It comes in before the king upon a. . . . They sprinkle special oil, they make sacrifices, the incense burns, (and) they read out (the tablet) before the king" (Strong, pp. 637-39). Ashurbanipal's annals report a similar sequence (Streck, pp. 112-19).

Another oracle, not fully preserved, seems to have a treaty ceremony as its setting: "The word of Ishtar of Arbela to Esarhaddon, king of Assyria. The gods my fathers . . . (break) . . . You (Esarhaddon)/she (Ishtar) gave them water from a special jar to drink. You/she filled a beaker . . . with water from the special jar and gave (it) to them. 'You (pl.) say in your heart: "Ishtar is . . ." Should you (pl.) go to your cities and your districts, eat food and forget these oaths. (then) when you drink from this water you will remember me and keep this sworn agreement which I (Ishtar) made concerning (your obligations to) Esarhaddon'" (Strong, pp. 639-41).

Two letters to Esarhaddon that mention the substitute-king ritual refer to activities of a female "proclaimer" in connection with the rites, but whether the activities were by design or by special (divine) initiative is unclear.

iv. *The content of the oracles.* The Neo-Assyrian oracles mostly represent direct address by a deity through the speaker, though they lack an explicit reference to commissioning. The oracles may begin with a divine self-description such as "I am Ishtar of Arbela." The vast majority of the oracles express assurance to the king (or to the queen mother) in regard to domestic or external trouble, and feature phrases such as "fear not." The kind of criticism that is made of the king seems restricted to modest scolding for such behavior as failure to pay attention to the deity's former utterance. Perhaps this is why the oracles seem to be more readily accepted than those in the Mari texts.

Most of the identifiable oracles derive from Ishtar of Arbela, from whom there apparently were special expectations of divine communication.

v. *Oracle collections.* Most of the oracles are preserved in collections, arranged with reference to the deity involved or, in the Ishtar collections, listed by the individual speaker. One speaker is even represented by two oracles, one in each of two collections. Although these oracles, as with the Mari activity, were delivered orally, at least some were written down almost immediately. There is evidence also for the transmission of oracle collections.

Bibliography. Most of the texts discussed can be found in trans. in J. B. Pritchard, ed., *Ancient Near Eastern Texts* (3rd. ed., with Supplement; 1969), often in rev. form. *See also* S. Herrmann, "Prophetie in Israel und Ägypten," VTSup, IX (1963), 47-65, Egypt; A. L. Oppenheim, *The Interpretation of Dreams in the Ancient Near East,* (1956), pp. 179-255, Anatolia and general; J. C. Greenfield, "The Zakir Inscription and the Danklied," in *Proceedings, Fifth World Congress of Jewish Studies,* I (1971), 174-91, Syria; A. K. Grayson and W. G. Lambert, "Akkadian Prophecies," *JCS,* XVIII (1964), 7-30; R. D. Biggs, "More Babylonian 'Prophecies,'" *Iraq,* XXIX (1967), 117-32; R. Borger, "Gott Marduk und Gott-König Šulgi als Propheten," *BO,* XXVIII (1971), 3-24; G. Dossin, "Sur le prophétisme a Mari," in *La divination en Mésopotamie ancienne* (1966), pp. 77-86; H. B. Huffmon, "Prophecy in the Mari Letters," in *BAR,* III (1970), 199-224; T. Bauer, *Das Inschriftwerk Assurbanipals,* 2 vols. (1933), II, 79-82; S. Langdon, *Tammuz and Ishtar* (1914), 133-40, pls. II-IV; S. Parpola, *Letters from Assyrian Scholars, AOAT,* V, no. 1 (1970), 228-30, 270-71; M. Streck, *Assurbanipal,* II (1916), 32-33, 112-19, 343-51; S. A. Strong, "On some Oracles to Esarhaddon and Ašurbanipal," *Beiträge zur Assyriologie,* II (1891-94), 627-45.

H. B. Huffmon

***PROPHECY IN THE EARLY CHURCH.** Since prophecy was rooted in Israel's experience of the revelation of God's mind to his people through divinely chosen individuals (*see* Holy Spirit §1), the early church understood it as a gift received at God's pleasure and for his purposes. It was not at one's own disposal.

1. Antecedents to Christian prophecy. Although some Jewish sources assert that prophecy had ceased in Judaism, others witness to its continuation. There were, however, certain modifications of the classical forms of OT prophecy.

In the later writings of the OT and in intertestamental literature prophecy manifests an increasing affinity with Wisdom. For example, wisdom is said to reside in the "holy prophet" (Wisd. Sol. 11:1, meaning Moses; cf. 7:27), and Daniel the wise man is regarded as a prophet (4QFlor 2.3). This development is especially pronounced in apocalyptic writings, a genre that is perhaps to be viewed as the child of both prophecy and wisdom. The apocalyptic seers combine, within the context of a revelation of final and cosmic dimension, the prophetic vision and word of knowledge with the wise discernment of its meaning. As forerunners of Christian prophecy such apocalyptic writers are best represented in the book of Daniel and in the

Qumran scrolls. *See* APOCALYPSE, GENRE[S]; APOCALYPTICISM[S].

Prophecy and wisdom manifest a growing affinity because of, among other factors, the increasing association or the identification of both with Israel's Scriptures. From this standpoint prophecy can be understood not only as a word or vision or discernment from God, but also as the inspired exposition and application to the current scene of earlier prophecies (e.g., Dan. 9:2; 1QpHab). In rabbinic tradition also the prophets were the earliest expositors of the law. But it is Daniel and the wise teachers of Qumran, the *maskilim,* who are the direct predecessors of the Pauline pneumatics (*see* SPIRITUAL GIFTS[S]) and, in important respects, of Jesus as well.

According to Matthew (1:20) and Luke (1:30-31, 67; 2:25-26, 36) a number of prophecies, by men and by angels, heralded the birth of Jesus. The testimony of JOHN THE BAPTIST, who was recognized as a prophet, signaled the beginning of Jesus' ministry (Matt. 11:9; 14:5; Mark 1:7-8; John 1:29-34).

2. Jesus as prophet. Jesus is identified in the gospels as a prophet, usually because of his miraculous powers, but also in connection with his crucifixion (Luke 13:33-34), his discernment (Luke 7:39; John 4:19), and his teaching in the synagogue (Luke 4:24). This teaching, which in the custom of the day included the exposition of scripture, was characterized by authority (ἐξουσία, Mark 1:22) and wisdom (σοφία, Mark 6:2). Since such exposition was recognized to be within the prophet's role, it may have contributed to the conviction that Jesus was a prophet.

3. Early Christian prophecy. This follows the model given by Jesus, and one of the tests of its genuineness is its witness to Jesus (I Cor. 12:3; Rev. 19:10). Prophecy appears as a gift from the exalted Lord and reflects the forms of prophetic utterance that characterized his earthly ministry—predictive oracle (Acts 11:27-28), inspired teaching and discernment (Rom. 12:6), and exposition of scripture. The "faithful sayings" of the Pastoral epistles (e.g., I Tim. 1:15, πιστὸς ὁ λόγος) may represent the teaching of a circle of prophets; "the Lord says" (λέγει κύριος) quotations of the OT very probably do (e.g., II Cor. 6:14-18). The latter contain within them a commentary-elaboration and application of the passage to the current situation. OT expositions like that in I Cor. 2:6-16, which appears to be the work of the pneumatics, follow a pattern well-known in Judaism, a pattern that is used also by Jesus (Matt. 21:33-44; Mark 12:1-11; Luke 20:9-17). In this area there appears to be a certain overlapping of the gifts of prophecy and of teaching.

Prophecy appears in the church as both the occasional utterance of various members of the community and the activity of some who are recognized to "have prophecy" (I Cor. 13:2) as a continuing ministry. Apparently only the latter are given the title "prophet" or, in the Pauline literature, the broader designation "pneumatic" (I Cor. 14:37; RSV "spiritual"). They may conduct their ministry in one congregation or throughout a region (Acts 15:22, 32; Did. 11:3 ff.), singly or more often in groups (Acts 11:27; 13:1; cf. John 21:24; Rev. 22:9). Their message is to be "tested" by other prophets and only then to be received as the word of the Lord (I Cor. 14:29; I Thess. 5:19 ff.; I John 4:1; contrast Did. 11:7). The "testing" is not only to distinguish the Spirit's word from the speaker's natural impulses but also to identify and exclude false prophecy.

4. False prophecy. False prophets appear, implicitly or explicitly, in virtually all strata of the NT and in other early Christian literature. They emerge as opponents of Christ's true apostles and prophets (cf. Matt. 7:15; Mark 13:22; Acts 13:6; Did. 11:5 ff.; Herm. Mand. 11:7). They have a different spirit, marked by the proclamation of a different Jesus and a different gospel (II Cor. 11:4, 13 ff.; Gal. 1:6). They convey a teaching of demons (I Tim. 4:1; cf. Jas. 3:15), characterized by greed (Phil. 3:19; Rom. 16:18), by asceticism or sexual licentiousness (II Tim. 3:6; Jude 7-8; Rev. 2:20), and by a disparagement of Jesus (I Cor. 12:3; II Pet. 2:1-3; I John 4:1-3).

Because of the presence of false prophecy and the uncertainties involved in discerning it, the gift of prophecy itself, in spite of occasional revivals, gradually fell into disuse and in some measure into disrepute.

See TONGUES, GIFT OF; TONGUES, GIFT OF[S].

Bibliography. E. Cothenet, "Prophétisme dans le NT," *DBSup,* VIII (1972), cols. 1222-1337; G. Dautzenberg, *Urchristliche Prophetie: ihre Erforschung, ihre Voraussetzungen im Judentum und ihre Struktur im ersten Korintherbrief,* BWANT, CIV (1975); E. E. Ellis, "The Role of the Christian Prophet in Acts," *Apostolic History and the Gospel,* ed. W. W. Gasque (1970), pp. 55-67, "'Wisdom' and 'Knowledge' in I Corinthians," *Tyndale Bulletin,* XXV (1974), 82-98, "Paul and his Opponents," *Christianity, Judaism and other Greco-Roman Cults,* ed. J. Neusner (1975), I, 264-98, and "How the NT Uses the Old," *NT Interpretation,* ed. I. H. Marshall (1976); R. Meyer and G. Friedrich, "προφήτης," *TDNT,* VI (1959), 815-61; U. B. Müller, *Prophetie und Predigt im NT,* StNT, X (1975); J. Panagopoulos, ed., *Prophetic Vocation in the NT and Today,* NovTSup (1976); J. Reiling, *Hermas and Christian Prophecy,* NovTSup, XXXVII (1973); H. B. Swete, *The Holy Spirit in the NT* (1910). E. E. ELLIS

PROPHECY, FALSE. The canonical prophets often found themselves in conflict with other prophets who proclaimed messages fundamentally different from their own. In their view these opposition prophets, both male and female, were guilty of idolatry, immorality, or self-delusion. Jeremiah's accusations are particularly harsh: some prophets are drunken, adulterous, greedy liars. They have not stood in God's council or received a divine call (*see* COUNCIL, HEAVENLY[S]). Consequently, they prophesy lies and lying dreams, encouraging the sins of Israel. Despite this extreme language, the MT does not label these objects of prophetic scorn "false prophets." The LXX takes that step, using *pseudoprophētes* ten times (Jer. 6:13; 26[LXX 33]:7, 8, 11, 16; 27[LXX 34]:9; 28[LXX 35]:1; 29 [LXX 36]:1, 8; Zech. 13:2).

Contradictory prophetic messages derive from the nature of prophecy itself. The twofold task—reception and articulation of the divine word—introduced various possibilities for conflict. Either the authenticity of the revelatory experience could be denied, or the prophet's interpretation of the divine word in terms of his own faith could be challenged. Diverse traditions within Israel produced their champions, and interpretations of divine activity differed from time to time depending upon sacral traditions deemed normative.

Opposing prophetic words may indeed derive from Yahweh, according to canonical testimony. Sometimes contradictory messages are described as divine testing. At other times they approach the demonic, divine purpose being achieved regardless of the effect upon those who are deceived. Noteworthy examples of divine causality in regard to prophetic conflict appear in I Kings 13 and 22:1-40. Ezekiel states the matter boldly: "And if the prophet be deceived and speak a word, I, the Lord, have deceived that prophet" (14:9).

The presence of contradictory prophetic words, whether arising from the nature of prophecy or attributed to divine causality in a monistic universe, forced a decision upon those who heard both messages. Which word is authentic? The struggle to resolve this issue produced criteria for distinguishing bogus words from authentic ones. One set of criteria concentrated on the quality of the message: does it come true? (Deuteronomy); does it offer false hope? (Jeremiah); was it mediated through dreams or visions? (Jeremiah); is it given in service of Yahweh rather than Baal? (Deuteronomy). Another set focused on the prophet: has he stood in the divine council? (Jeremiah); has he been called by God? (Jeremiah); does he behave in an exemplary fashion? (Jeremiah). In time a different sort of criterion arose: did the prophet live during the period from Moses to Ezra? A similar one, the chronological, functioned in early Christian literature as well (Did. 11:3-12). Though useful, these criteria ultimately failed to distinguish authentic prophecy from its opposite. Several factors exacerbated the struggle among prophets: a desire for popularity and success (Jonah), royal wishes, tradition, and individualism. Small wonder prophecy fell into disrepute (Zech. 13:2-6) and was relegated to the remote past or anticipated future.

Modern scholars have made significant progress toward understanding "false prophecy." The criterion of fulfillment is inadequate (Hempel), leaving us with a pneumatic one (Quell) that stresses immediacy of the revelatory experience (Kraus) and a correct interpretation of the historical moment (Buber, Osswald; *see* HERMENEUTICS[S] §§5-6). Although prophets appeal to a number of credentials, in the last resort their call and simple affirmation suffice (Blank). "False prophets" are cultic functionaries, and Deuteronomy is a product of their work (von Rad). Still, fluidity prevails, for a true prophet can become false and vice versa (Harms).

Recent studies have opened up entirely new ways of looking at "false prophets." Disputes recorded in prophetic literature have yielded insights into the theology of so-called false prophets (van der Woude, Crenshaw), and quotations have illuminated their thought, leading to a positive assessment of opposition prophets (Crenshaw). A neutral reading of prophetic argumentation has suggested that the opponents of Isaiah and Jeremiah were engaged in the interpretation of (1) their call and (2) Israel's Torah, Mosaic or Davidic (Sanders), *See* TORAH[S].

Bibliography. S. H. Blank, *Of a Truth the Lord Hath Sent Me: An Inquiry into the Source of the Prophet's Authority* (1955); M. Buber, "Falsche Propheten," *Die Wandlung,* II (1947), 277-83, and "False Prophets (Jeremiah 28)," *On the Bible,* ed. N. Glatzer (1968), pp. 166-71; J. L. Crenshaw, *Prophetic Conflict* (1971); K. Harms, *Die falschen Propheten: Eine biblische Untersuchung* (1947); J. Hempel, "Vom irrenden Glauben," *ZST,* VII (1930), 631-60; F. L. Hossfeld and I. Meyer, *Prophet gegen Prophet* (1973); E. Jacob, "Quelques remarques sur les faux prophètes," *TZ,* XIII (1957), 479-86; H.-J. Kraus, *Prophetie in der Krisis* (1964); E. Osswald, *Falsche Prophetie im Alten Testament* (1962); T. W. Overholt, "Jeremiah 27–29: The Question of False Prophecy," *JAAR,* XXXV (1967), 241-49, and *The Threat of Falsehood* (1970); G. Quell, *Wahre und falsche Propheten. Versuch einer Interpretation* (1952); J. A. Sanders, "Jeremiah and the Future of Theological Scholarship," *ANQ,* XIII (1972-73), 133-45; E. F. Siegman, *The False Prophets of the OT* (1939); E. Tilson, "False Prophets in the OT" (diss., Vanderbilt, 1952); G. von Rad, "Die falschen Propheten," *ZAW,* LI (1933), 109-20; A. S. van der Woude, "Micah in Dispute with the Pseudo-Prophets," *VT,* XIX (1969), 244-60.

J. CRENSHAW

***PROVERBS, BOOK OF.** A collection of "wisdom literature" composed perhaps from the tenth to the fifth or fourth century B.C. The variety of the material it contains has made it the center of recent discussion about the nature and history of Israel's wisdom tradition (*see* WISDOM IN THE OT [S]). While some sections show the influence of non-Israelite didactic literature mediated through scribal education and the international relations of the royal court, much of the book seems to have been written to meet the intellectual demands of a wider circle of readers. The book reflects developments within the religion and theology of Israel which culminated in the elevation of "wisdom" into a theological concept of major importance.

1. Literary forms. Recent discussion has mainly concentrated on those forms likely to provide clues about the origin of Israelite wisdom literature and the milieus in which the various parts of the book were composed. The most evident formal distinction is that between the short, mainly one-line (i.e., single-verse) sayings which comprise the bulk of the book and the longer, connected poems, especially those in chs. 1–9. The view that the longer form developed from the shorter and marks an advance in literary skill has been abandoned. The longer wisdom poem has a long prehistory in the literatures of Egypt and Mesopotamia, where it lay ready at hand as a model for Hebrew authors. Many of the shorter sayings are masterpieces of compression, manifesting as great a degree of literary maturity as the longer poems. Length can therefore no longer be regarded as a criterion for dating the various parts of the book. It is also generally agreed that Proverbs is in no sense a collection of popular sayings. Although popular material may sometimes have been utilized, the literary and poetical forms in the book are quite different from those of popular sayings which occur in the narrative and prophetical books.

Among the shorter sayings the most evident formal distinction is that between the "sentence" or statement (*Aussagewort*) and the "admonition" or precept (*Mahnwort*). The statement points to a fact drawn from experience and extracts from this no explicit conclusion or moral, e.g., 14:10:

> The heart knows its own bitterness,
> and no stranger shares its joy.

Such statements are frequently open to more than one interpretation. Although it may be possible to draw practical advice from them, their purpose is to stimulate further thought.

The admonition, on the other hand, offers clear-cut, practical advice and is expressed in the imperative mood, e.g., 14:7:

> Leave the presence of a fool,
> for there you do not meet words of knowledge.

Although it is not always possible to distinguish between the functions of these two types of saying, it is reasonable to seek the origin of the latter in some kind of educational setting, and it is commonly held that its imperative form points to the influence of the Egyptian type of wisdom book known as the "Instruction," which was essentially educational literature. Recently, however, it has been argued that it originated in a native Israelite "clan wisdom" (*see* §2*c*).

Whatever may be the origin of the shorter admonitions, the existence of Egyptian influence on the longer poems of chs. 1–9 can hardly be doubted, since their resemblance to the Egyptian instruction literature extends to many details of style and vocabulary, and also of thought (*see* §3*a*).

2. Milieu. There is no general agreement concerning the circles in which the book of Proverbs was composed. Four theories merit discussion.

a. The court. From the time of David onward, learned scribes or secretaries were employed at the royal court in Jerusalem. The ascription of literary wisdom to Solomon (I Kings 4:29-34 [H 5:9-14]), the attribution of all or part of the book to him (Prov. 1:1; 10:1; 25:1), and the mention of the literary or editorial activity of the "men of Hezekiah" (25:1) all testify to a tradition of a connection between the court and the book of Proverbs which can hardly be entirely without foundation, although the use of Solomon's name does not prove that he himself composed any part of it. The fact that there was a concentration of educated men at court makes court authorship of some parts of the book a possibility, although there is no uncontrovertible, direct evidence of this in the book itself. The difficult word העתיקו (RSV "copied") in 25:1 cannot be shown to refer to authorship; nor can it be demonstrated that the "wise" or clever men of 22:17; 24:23 are to be identified with these court scribes. The headings of 30:1; 31:1 clearly rule out Israelite court authorship for those sections of the book.

b. Schools. The theory that Israelite schools were the milieu in which Proverbs was written is not a simple alternative to court authorship, since such schools might well have had a close connection with the court. It has been argued that it was through such schools that Egyptian influence on Proverbs was mediated. In fact there is not a single unambiguous reference in the OT to the existence of a formal system of education. Nevertheless, it has been argued on the analogy of the well-documented educational systems of Egypt and Mesopotamia that the establishment under David and Solomon of an organized state with international contacts must necessarily have entailed the adoption of similar educational institutions, and that Proverbs is mainly textbook literature written for the training of scribes. The existence of schools in ancient Israel can neither be proved nor disproved; but it should be remembered that Israel even at the height of its power under the united monarchy was never really comparable to the great empires. The supply of scribes needed for the business of the court and for other purposes may have been adequately assured by the training of boys by their own fathers within a relatively small number of hereditary scribal families, as was the case with other professions. Such scribal families could well have been familiar with foreign wisdom literature. Such domestic education, however, would have been a very different thing from the institutional school.

c. Clan wisdom. It has recently been argued that the admonitions in Proverbs are ultimately derived from a premonarchial institution in which the heads or "fathers" of individual clans formulated ethical rules to be observed by the members of the clan. However, the existence of such an institution has yet to be proved, and the evidence so far offered for it is precarious.

d. An educated class. Most recently there has been an increasing tendency to take a broader view of the context within which Proverbs was composed. It is now recognized that the book is not purely educational in character, and also that there was an educated class in Israel whose interests some parts of the book may have been especially written to serve. Such people were seeking intellectual stimulation and entertainment rather than education in any narrow sense. While some parts of Proverbs undoubtedly bear the marks of the textbook, there is a substantial amount of material which could have been fully appreciated only by an adult, mature readership.

3. Standpoint and purpose. The composition of the book represents a continuing tradition, but one which underwent considerable modification in the course of time. Its authors were not immune from the religious developments which took place in Israel as a whole. The form of the book and the absence of explicit reference to Israel's history and religious traditions make the task of identifying earlier and later material an exceptionally difficult one. But it is perhaps possible to trace very broadly three stages of development.

a) Whatever may be the extent of the contribution made by a premonarchial Israelite "wisdom," foreign wisdom literature, especially that of

Egypt, exercised considerable influence on the early stages of the composition of the book. This is particularly noticeable in the section dependent on the Egyptian *Wisdom of Amen-em-opet* and in the long poems or "discourses" which form a substantial part of chs. 1–9. *See* PROVERBS, BOOK OF §8.

Egyptian wisdom was not irreligious, but it was more concerned with the overarching order of the universe—*maat*—than with the cult of particular gods. The ideal was conformity to this divine order, which would confer "life" in the sense of well-being and prosperity. This point of view is reflected in the earlier material in Proverbs, although there is no equivalent here to the Egyptian *maat*. Wherever a supernatural power is mentioned it is Yahweh, who is regarded as the observer and supreme arbiter of human destiny. The other aspects of Yahweh's character which loom so large in the rest of the OT are, however, noticeably absent. It is assumed that it is within man's own power to adjust his conduct successfully to the demands of the world in which he lives, although in both literatures the limits of this freedom are also recognized (cf. Prov. 16:1-7, 9, 33).

b) This confidence in man's ability to solve his own problems expresses an attitude to life very different from that of traditional Yahwism with its insistence on the total commitment of Israel as a people to the will of Yahweh. The second stage in the development of Israelite wisdom was an attempt to reconcile the two traditions through the recognition that Yahweh himself is the source of true wisdom: hence there can be no contradiction between truths learned through human experience and Yahweh's commands revealed through priest or prophet. Phrases like "the fear of the Lord," which were broad enough to embrace all aspects of moral and religious conduct, played an important part in this synthesis: thus the statement in 13:14 that

> The teaching of the wise is a fountain of life,
> that one may avoid the snares of death

is, as it were, glossed in 14:27, which asserts that

> The fear of the Lord is a fountain of life,
> that one may avoid the snares of death.

9:10 is even more explicit:

> The fear of the Lord is the beginning of wisdom,
> and the knowledge of the Holy One is insight.

This bringing together of traditional wisdom and the Yahwistic tradition led to some modification of the pragmatic and to some extent morally neutral character of the former. This can be seen, for example, in the way in which certain words characteristic of wisdom teaching have acquired new meanings which reflect Yahweh's condemnation of self-confidence and self-interest, which had previously been regarded as virtues. Thus מזמה, which in most passages (e.g., 5:2) is regarded as a desirable quality (translated in RSV by "discretion" or "prudence"), clearly has a bad sense in 12:2 (RSV "evil device"), where Yahweh condemns the man who is given to such self-interested and self-centered calculations. Through such evidence it is possible to conclude that Proverbs gradually received a new theological orientation despite the fact that its characteristic wisdom forms remained unchanged. This process is easiest to detect in chs. 1–9, but undoubtedly affected chs. 10–29 as well.

c) A further theological development is to be found in chs. 1–9, especially in 8:22-31. In these chapters "wisdom" is frequently personified as a woman. Originally this personification, perhaps partly modeled on the Egyptian *maat,* was probably simply a literary device to dramatize the importance of the father's instruction to his son. In 8:22-31, however, wisdom is represented as a being closely associated with Yahweh himself, created before the world and present when that act of creation was performed; and as subsequently (vs. 31)

> rejoicing in his inhabited world
> and delighting in the sons of men.

This new theological insight provided the basis for an entire theology of creation which put human skill and endeavor in their proper place: on the one hand, man's intelligence and his enterprise are recognized as God-given and so legitimate; on the other, their subordination to God in his service provides a framework within which all human activity must operate. With this insight the wisdom tradition ceased to be anthropocentric and found its proper place in the theological world of Judaism.

Bibliography. Commentaries: B. Gemser, *HAT* (2nd. ed., 1963); A. Barucq, *Le Livre des Proverbes,* SB (1964); R. B. Y. Scott, ABi (1965); W. McKane, OTL (1970); R. N. Whybray, CBC (1972).

Other works: U. Skladny, *Die ältesten Spruchsammlungen in Israel* (1962); E. Gerstenberger, *Wesen und Herkunft des "apodiktischen Rechts"* (1965); R. N. Whybray, *Wisdom in Proverbs,* SBT, 1st. ser. XLV (1965); C. Kayatz, *Studien zu Proverbien 1-9* (1966); R. E. Murphy, "The Kerygma of the Book of Proverbs," *Int.,* XX (1966), 3-14; W. Richter, *Recht und Ethos* (1966); R. E. Murphy, "Assumptions and Problems in Old Testament Wisdom Research," *CBQ,* XXIX (1967), 101-12; H.-J. Hermisson, *Studien zur israelitischen Spruchweisheit,* WMANT, XXVIII (1968); R. B. Y. Scott, *The Way of Wisdom in the Old Testament* (1971); G. von Rad, *Wisdom in Israel* (1972); R. N. Whybray, *The Intellectual Tradition in the Old Testament, BZAW,* CXXXV (1974). R. N. WHYBRAY

***PROVINCIAL SYSTEMS IN THE ANCIENT NEAR EAST.** For literature on this subject *see* E. Fohrer, *Die Provinzeinteilung des assyrischen Reiches* (1921); O. Leuze, *Die Satrapieeinteilung im Syrian und im Zweistromlande von 520-320* (1935); A. Alt, "Das System der assyrischen Provinzen auf dem Boden der Reiches Israel," *Kleine Schriften,* II (1953), 188-205; Y. Aharoni, *The Land of the Bible* (1967), pp. 327-35, 353-65 (and esp. map 31); J. Postgate, *Taxation and Conscription in the Assyrian Empire* (1974). For the Assyrian provinces in Syro-Palestine, *see* map 1; for those of the Persian Empire, *see* map 2. The latter is based upon Herodotus, *Histories,* III:89-95 and upon the Scylax papyrus (*see* K. Galling, "Die syrisch-palästinische Küste nach der Beschreibung bei Pseudo-Skylax," *ZDPV,* LXI (1938), 66-96).

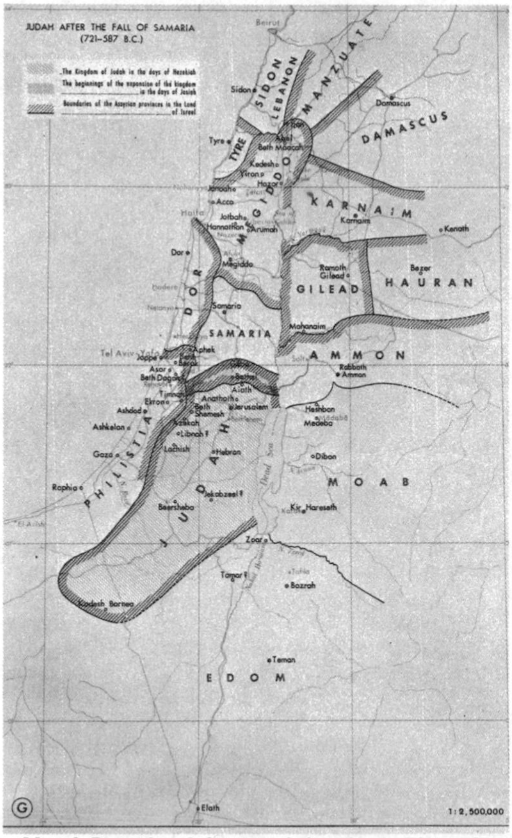

Map 1 Reproduced by permission from *The Atlas of Israel*

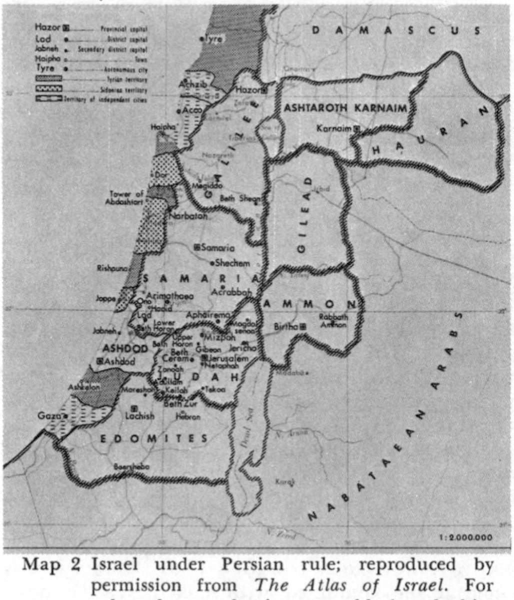

Map 2 Israel under Persian rule; reproduced by permission from *The Atlas of Israel.* For enlarged reproduction see black-and-white map section.

*PSALMS, BOOK OF.

1. The categories of the Psalms and their origin in worship
   - *a.* Psalms of lament
   - *b.* Psalms of praise
   - *c.* Liturgical psalms
   - *d.* Royal psalms
   - *e.* Psalms of Yahweh's kingship
   - *f.* Wisdom or didactic psalms
2. Psalms in the ancient Near East
3. Poetic form of the Psalms
4. The significance of the Psalms

Bibliography

1. The categories of the Psalms and their origin in worship. Gunkel perceived that the Psalms did not originate as literary works, but arose in worship; they were spoken or sung in various ways and on various occasions of worship and were transmitted orally before they acquired written form in small collections (*see* PSALMS, BOOK OF §A2). Gunkel assumed that they were used in a number of quite different worship situations, but his pupil Mowinckel equated worship almost entirely with the major feasts (cult=festival cult) and tried to demonstrate that the vast majority of the Psalms belonged to the Throne Ascension Festival, which was analogous to the Babylonian New Year's Festival (*Psalmenstudien II,* 1921-24; *see* NEW YEAR[S]). In a later work, *The Psalms in Israel's Worship* (1951 [ET 1962]), Mowinckel modified his position and came closer to Gunkel's view.

There is still disagreement as to how closely Israel's psalms were related to the cult of neighboring civilizations, especially to the fertility cult (which was concentrated in cyclical annual festivals) and to the cult of sacred kingship. The extreme position, advocated by the Scandanavian and British "Myth and Ritual School" (especially Engnell and Hooke), that the OT psalms were all or almost all derived from a common Near Eastern cultic ideology, is no longer widely held. It cannot be denied that the cultic practices of Israel's neighbors had considerable influence on Israelite worship, as can be seen in the cult as practiced in Jerusalem. Nevertheless, we must assume that Israelite worship, as reflected in the Psalms, was closely related to the life of the local people in all its variety. This is shown by the prominent role which Israel's history plays in the Psalms (in this respect they are distinctly different from the psalms in other ancient Near Eastern nations); by the presence in the narrative and historical books of components that make up the Psalms (e.g., the shout of praise, the vow, the brief lament, the petition); and by the distinction between the psalms of lament and praise of the individual and those of the community. The experiences of the individual's personal life are different from those of the nation, and therefore each has its own language. As a result, Israel's worship came to include procedures concerned with the individual as well as with the entire nation.

a. Psalms of lament. In contrast to a lament for the dead, which looks backward, the lament in the Psalms is voiced in order to alter a threatening situation, and looks forward. The laments by the people (approximately 10 in number) and by the individual (approximately 50) comprise a major part of the Psalter. Laments by the people: Pss. 44; (60); 74; 79; 80; 83; 89; (90); Lam. 1–5 (esp. ch. 5); Isa. 63–64; Jer. 14–15; Hab. 1; the motif of this category is found in many other passages. Laments by the individual: Pss. 3–17 (except 8, 9, 15); 22–28 (except 24); 35–43 (except 37; 40A); 51–64 (except 60); 140–143; ten scattered psalms; Lam. 3; the laments of Jeremiah; the laments of Job.

Laments are connected to a specific cause, a threat to the people or an individual. A fast is proclaimed (I Kings 21:9, 12; Jer. 36:9), and all the people, including women and children, are summoned (Joel 2:16; Jonah 3:5). The community is sanctified (Joel 1:14) and enjoined to continence, the wearing of sackcloth, and expressions of humility, pleading, and weeping before Yahweh (Judg. 20:23, 26; Jer. 14:12). After the Exile, lamentation was replaced by public confession (Ezra 9).

From I Sam. 1:9-18 and Isa. 38:1-8 we can only guess at the form of worship in which the individual lament was used, and we have no further information. A part of the procedure is God's answer, which indicates that God has heard the lament. This "oracle of salvation" is mentioned in Lam. 3:57: "Thou didst come near when I called on thee; thou didst say, 'Do not fear!' " (cf. II Chr. 20:14-15). This oracle of salvation is not included in the lament itself, but it is often indicated by the sudden change in what the one making the lament says (Pss. 22:19-24 [H 20-25]; 28:4-7; 6:7-9 [H 8-10]). God's answer is seen more clearly in the lament by the people (Pss. 60:6-9 [H 8-11]; 85:8 [H 9]; Isa. 33:10-13; Jer. 4:1-2). God gives a negative answer in Amos 7:8; 8:2; Jer. 14:10; 15:1-4. In the laments by the people the answer is often given by a prophet, and in the individual laments, by a priest.

The psalm of lament has a regular structure, but it never becomes stereotyped. The major parts are address to God, lament, confession of confidence, petition, and vow of praise. God is addressed by name only, in contrast to the Babylonian psalms, where a large number of divine attributes are mentioned. Often the address is followed directly by an introductory cry for help. The lament is in three parts: (1) lament over one's personal suffering (in first person singular or plural); (2) complaint about the foes; and (3) complaint against God, especially with the questions "why?" and "how long?" This threefold division corresponds to the belief that mankind was created in these three relationships. These divisions are expressed in a variety of ways. The first person plural lament can be expanded into an impressive description of the threat to the nation, as in Lam. 5. The complaint against the foes is expanded in one part of the lament of the individual to a description of the foes, or of the godless. The complaint against God found its greatest expression in the book of Job.

The lament leads to the petition, the most regular part of the psalm of lament. The transitive petition, which asks for something specific ("give us . . .") can be distinguished from the intransitive petition, which does not request some favor but pleads for deliverance from danger. This second type of petition is in two parts: (1) the request for God to be attentive ("Come!" "Rise up!" "Hear!" "Turn to us!") and (2) the subsequent request for God to intervene ("Help us!" "Deliver me!"). Various motifs may be combined with the petition in order to move God to intervene. They may refer to God (Ps. 79:9), to the foes (79:10), or to the one making the prayer. One of those motifs is the confession of sin, and where confession is especially stressed we may speak of a "psalm of confession" (Pss. 6; 32; 38; 51; 102; 130; 143). Instead of a confession, however, the insistence on one's innocence may provide the motif (Pss. 5; 7; 26). Schmidt assumes that there was a whole collection of prayers of those who were unjustly accused.

In the individual lament the confession of confidence usually comes between the lament and the petition. The one praying balances the lament by an expression of trust in God (Pss. 3:3 [H 4]; 13:5 [H 6]; 13:14 [H 15]; 52:8 [H 10]; 71:14), and often also the assurance of being heard (Ps. 31:3-5 [H 4-6]; Lam. 3:25-30). The psalms of lament never end with lament but always move on in some way to express the confidence that God will send help. In many psalms the expression of confidence is already contained in the initial address to God (Ps. 80:1-2*a*).

In the lament by the people there is often a reminder of God's earlier saving deeds instead of the confession of confidence (Ps. 80, in the metaphor of the vine; Pss. 44:1-8 [H 2-9]; 74:12-17; 85:1-3 [H 2-4]; Isa. 63, 64). It is here that the historical traditions of Israel are expressed most clearly in the Psalms.

Many of the individual laments conclude with a vow to praise God (Pss. 13:6 [H 7]; 22:22 [H 23]), but this is seldom the case in laments by the people. The vow is often followed by praise of God (13:6 [H 7]; 22:23-31 [H 24-32]), the same form that begins the individual psalm of praise (cf. 13:6 and 30:1). The vow to praise expresses the process, found in many religions, by which the one who cries out enters a permanent relationship with God (50:15).

The structure of the individual lament is shown clearly by a comparison of the short Ps. 13 with the long Ps. 22; for all their differences they have the same structure. Through the centuries this structure underwent many changes, producing various mixed forms, for example, mixtures of parts of individual laments with laments by the people. Certain parts gained prominence (e.g., the description of the foes); others disappeared, including the accusations against God. The petition came to overshadow the lament, and the confession of confidence developed into independent psalms (e.g., 23; 123). The first person singular lament became the lament of human mortality (Pss. 39; 49; 90). Conscious reflection and wisdom motifs came to be combined with lament. *See* PSALMS, BOOK OF §B2*e*.

b. Psalms of praise. In the OT praise is the most frequent expression of a positive relationship to God. The OT has many lexemes for praise (הלל; ידה; ברך; גדל; רמם, and others), whose meaning is difficult to express in modern languages.

They include semantic components such as adoration, awe, and thanks, which later were expressed in separate lexemes. To praise God is really to affirm him, to acknowledge him in his work and in his being. The OT psalms of praise, which are both prayers and songs, take two forms, declarative (תודה) and descriptive (תהלה), commonly called "psalms of thanksgiving" and "hymns." The verb הדה is usually translated as "give thanks," but its basic meaning is "praise." In the OT it is never used of one human being "thanking" another. Our word "thank" is included in the meaning, but does not fully express it. Declarative praise (תודה) is the recounting in praise of God's saving acts for his people and for individuals. Descriptive praise (תהלה) is the praise of God in his being and his activity as a whole. *See* PSALMS, BOOK OF §B2*c-d*.

i. *Declarative praise by the people* is found in the Psalter only in Pss. 124; 129; 66:8-12, and isolated motifs. Miriam's song in Exod. 15:21 is probably the oldest such song in the OT. It consists only of an exhortation to sing and a two-sentence report of what God had done. The context of Exod. 14–15 shows that declarative praise is the immediate reaction to what God does. After the Conquest, its place was taken by the song of victory (Judg. 5, the song of Deborah; Judg. 16:23-24, the Philistine song of victory; and a late imitation, Jth. 16). In the Psalter we encounter it only in isolated motifs (118:15-16; 18; 68; 149). The motif of God's epiphany is a part of the song of victory (Judg. 5:4-5; Pss. 18:7-15 [H 8-16]; 68:7-8 [H 8-9]). The epiphany is found in other contexts in Pss. 50:2-4; 77:16-19 [H 17-20]; 97:2-5; 114; Deut. 33:2-3; Mic. 1:3-4; Nah. 1:3*b*-5; Hab. 3:3-15. God's coming down is depicted in mythopoeic images reminiscent of Egyptian and Babylonian psalms. But in the OT the mythical action is replaced by Yahweh's shaking heaven and earth as he comes to the aid of his people. *See* THEOPHANY IN THE OT[S].

ii. *Declarative praise (or thanks) by the individual* (Pss. 9; 18; 22:22-31 [H 23-32]; 31B; 32; 34; 40A; 66B; 92; (107); 116; 138; Jonah 2; Lam. 3:52-57; Ecclus. 51; Pss. Sol. 15:1-6; 16:1-15; Odes Sol. 25; 29; the THANKSGIVING PSALMS from Qumran). Declarative praise (Ps. 66:16-19) is connected with the presenting of a sacrifice (or vow) of praise (66:13-15). In Hebrew both are called תודה. Pss. 22:26 [H 27] and 116:13 allude to an accompanying sacrificial meal. The occasion is the fulfillment of a vow made in a time of great danger (116:14). Similar practices are known in other religions. The one who has been rescued recounts to a circle of hearers what God has done for him, and they are often exhorted to join in the expressions of praise (Pss. 30:4 [H 5]; 34:3 [H 4]). This might be the origin of the imperative call to praise. Praise was gradually separated from sacrifice. Its permanent significance is shown by the liturgy in Ps. 107, in which four such psalms of praise are woven into a hymn of praise of the community. Some psalms of this category contain wisdom motifs combined with praise. The further movement away from sacrifice is seen in the apocryphal psalms and 1QH, where instruction and reflection are the dominant features.

The structure of this category is remarkably constant. The vow to praise from the end of the lament reappears at the beginning of the psalm of praise as an introduction (Ps. 34:1 [H 2]). This is often followed by an introductory summary (116:1). The main part tells what God has done and includes a looking back to the time of need and a recounting of the rescue ("I cried to him"; "he heard"; "he drew me out"). The danger is often described as being bound or being near to death, and rescue as deliverance from death (Barth). At the end, declarative praise often passes into descriptive praise, as the one who is recounting his rescue broadens his view to include the whole of God's activity (Jonah 2:9 [H 10]; Pss. 18:30 [H 31]; 22:28 [H 29]; 118:5, 8). The life that has been bestowed anew derives its meaning from the praise of God (Pss. 40:3-5 [H 4-6]; 92:15 [H 16]; 118:17).

iii. *Descriptive praise (hymn)* (Pss. 8:19A; 29; 33; (47); 57:7-11 [H 8-12]; 65; 66; 89:5-18 [H 6-19]; 93–99 [except 94]; 100; 103; 104; (107); 111; 113; 117; 134–136; 139; 145–150). See also the doxologies closing groups of Psalms (41:13 [H 14]; 72:18-19; 89:52 [H 53]; 106:48; 150), and in Micah and Amos; Isa. 6:3; 12; Jer. 10:6-16; and isolated statements in various psalms of other categories. Outside the Psalter the category is most fully developed in Second Isaiah and in Job, and it is encountered again in Chronicles, in psalms of the Apocrypha, 1QH, and in the NT, especially in Luke 1–2 and in Revelation.

Descriptive praise is not restricted to a single cultic occasion. It can be sung on any occasion on which the community wants to honor God—the great festivals, the offering of various sacrifices, and on occasions in the temple or in the family, such as Passover or sabbath. The books of Chronicles indicate the great significance of praise for the postexilic community, and the book of Tobit shows how the pious Jew of the Diaspora took part in worship which utilized the words of the psalms of praise.

The structure of psalms of this category is seen most clearly in Ps. 113. It is introduced by an imperative call to praise, a characteristic of the category and a feature that distinguishes it from the Babylonian hymns. The imperative (vs. 1) is carried forward by jussives (vss. 2-3). The main body of the psalm praises God's majesty (4-5) and his goodness (6*b*-9). Between these two affirmations ("who is seated on high, who looks far down," 5*b*-6*a*) there is a tension which can be developed in various ways, and consequently the structure is not so fixed as in other categories. Ps. 33 is an example of how the themes are developed. God's majesty is depicted as that of the Creator (vss. 6-9) and the Lord of history (vss. 10-12). His goodness is seen in his helping his people (vss. 13-19*a*) and his mercy toward all creation (19*b*). The structure of Ps. 136, among others, is similar.

Prominent in this category are groups of psalms which indicate several different occasions of worship. Praise is a component of most liturgical psalms (*see* §*c below*), especially the festival psalms (24; 118; 93–99). One group can be designated as "creation Psalms" (8; 19A; 104; 139; 148; *see*

Albertz). In a psalm like 139 we can observe an abandonment of the worship context and a movement to religious reflection, as in Ps. 19, where the praise of the Creator is combined with praise of the Torah (cf. also Ps. 119). In Ecclus. 39 praise of the Creator has become contemplation of nature. Praise of the Lord of history develops into history psalms, as can be seen in the contrast of Ps. 33:10-12 with 136:10-22 and Ps. 78 with 105.

c. Liturgical psalms. To this category only those psalms should be assigned which give clear indication that they were used on cultic occasions. It is futile to try to construct a festival liturgy out of a combination of separate psalms. Various liturgical procedures are hinted at in the psalms, but the psalms are not liturgies, and the Psalter is not the agenda for a festival.

i. *In Ps. 66, an individual psalm of praise* is combined with the "sacrifice" by means of praise, which is expressed in vss. 13-15. In the same context a sacrificial meal is mentioned in Pss. 22:26 [H 27] and 116:13. In Ps. 118 the sacrifice is in connection with a procession, which marches through the gates of the temple while the choir sings antiphonally. In stately procession, the worshipers move around the altar, carrying branches in their hands (vs. 27). From the temple the priests pronounce a blessing on the procession. Ps. 107 is a composite of four songs of praise for deliverance, combined for use in worship. It begins with a general call to give praise (vs. 1) and ends with praise that describes God's work (vss. 33-43).

ii. *The songs of pilgrimage* (only Ps. 122; allusions to pilgrimage in Ps. 132:7; Isa. 2:3 [=Mic. 4:2]; Isa. 30:29; Jer. 31:6; Gen. 35:3) move between the beginning of the journey and the arrival at the sanctuary. Pss. 120–134 have the superscription "Song of Pilgrimage," but in the strict sense it applies only to Ps. 122. Traveling to the sanctuary was counted as a part of the act of worship. Ps. 122:1-2 tells of starting out and arriving at the temple; vss. 6-9 hail the city of Jerusalem by wishing blessings on her.

iii. *The songs of Zion* (Pss. 46; 48; 76; 84; 87; 132) have much in common with the pilgrimage songs. Here the originally mythical motif of the mountain of the gods in the north is joined with the choice of Zion as the mountain of God, with temple and holy city, and the protection of the city of God from the attacks of the enemy is joined with the battle of the nations outside the gates of the city. God's victory is celebrated in a procession (Ps. 48:12-14 [H 13-15]). These "Zion traditions" go back to pre-Israelite, Canaanite cultic tradition about Jerusalem. Ps. 76 looks forward to a future victory of God in his judgment of the nations.

iv. *Psalms of blessing.* As the worshipers leave the sanctuary, a blessing is bestowed on them; this is one of the most important parts of Israelite worship. In Ps. 118 the priests respond to the request of the worshipers (vs. 25) with the words, "Blessed be he who enters in the name of the Lord! We bless you from the house of the Lord" (vs. 26). The conclusion of Ps. 129 and Ps. 134:3 are similar. The goal of the procession in Ps. 24 is to receive a blessing (vs. 5). The whole of Ps. 67 is a psalm of blessing, in which the congregation receives the blessing in response to its request (cf. Ps. 115:9-15). In the collection Pss. 120–134 more is said about blessing than is usual in the Psalter, because the goal of a pilgrimage is to receive a blessing. By contrast, in Pss. 91 and 121 (cf. Job 5:19-26) the blessing is bestowed on an individual. The priest addresses the petitioner, and, in response to the confession of trust (Pss. 91:2; 121:2), bestows the blessing.

v. Ps. 24:7-10 apparently reflects *a procession* in which the ark is carried into the temple. In antiphonal form, entrance is demanded for the "King of glory." Some scholars hold that Ps. 132 is also part of a procession with the ark, and that the description in Josh. 3–4 of the crossing of the Jordan reflects such a procession.

vi. Those who ask what are the conditions for entry into the temple are given *instruction* in Ps. 15 and Isa. 33:14-16 (cf. the instruction in Mic. 6:6-8). This type of instruction has extensive affinities in the history of religions, and similar phenomena are common. A distinctive development is found in the Egyptian Book of the Dead, with its instruction for entering the land of the dead.

d. Royal psalms (Pss. 2; 18; 20; 21; 45; 72; (89); 101; 110; (132); 144:A). All the surviving royal psalms refer to historical kings of Israel and Judah. They were admitted to the postexilic Psalter because they were applied to the expected future king. This interpretation has its roots in the royal psalms themselves, where the honor and glory ascribed to the king far surpass the reality of the kingdoms of Israel and Judah. He sits at God's right hand (110:1) and is addressed as "God" (45:6 [H 7]). Such exaltation of the king stems from the language of the ancient Near Eastern sacral kingship (*see* KING, KINGSHIP §2). Ps. 89 is based on the Nathan oracle (II Sam. 7), and Ps. 45, a thoroughly secular song, was designated as the wedding hymn of the king. Petitions and thanksgiving on the king's behalf are prominent in Pss. 20; 21; 72; 132. The royal psalms are too diverse, however, to form a category. *See* PSALMS, BOOK OF §B2*b*.

e. Psalms of Yahweh's kingship (throne ascension psalms: Pss. 47; 93; 95–99). These psalms led Mowinckel to assume the existence of a festival for the ascension of Yahweh to the throne, analogous to the Babylonian New Year's Festival. This thesis was widely accepted, and other scholars proposed variations of it. Weiser advanced the idea of a "Covenant Festival" and H.-J. Kraus a "Covenant Renewal Festival" and a "Royal Zion Festival." More recently reservations have been expressed by Kraus, Westermann, and others. It is clear that these psalms were used in worship, perhaps at festivals, and that they honor God as king (*see* KING, GOD AS[S]). They are, however, not a separate category, but are descriptive praise of God (hymns). Only Ps. 47 depicts God's assumption of royal power, in imitation of the ceremony of an early king. Pss. 96:13 and 98:9 proclaim God as judge of the world. As hymns they do not have any form in common, and only the shout "Yahweh is (has become) king!" is shared by them all. (On the translation of this expression, *see* Michel.)

By borrowing the practices of the coronation of an earthly king, the congregation celebrates in these psalms the awaited future kingship of God over all the world. These psalms are significant background for the NT concept KINGDOM OF GOD.

f. Wisdom or didactic psalms. In the Psalter wisdom sayings are found isolated (127:1-2, 3-5; 133) or as the conclusion of a psalm (111:10) or as parts of a psalm (37:5, 8, 16, 22, 27). This shows that in later times psalm traditions and the wisdom traditions converged. Identity of content is seen in the contrast of the ungodly and the pious. Ps. 37 is a wisdom poem with this theme, as is Ps. 1, placed as prologue to the Psalter. The contrast in Pss. 112 and 128 is similar. For the declaration of the blessedness of the godly, as in Proverbs, see Pss. 34:8 [H 9]; 40:4 [H 5]; 41:1-2 [H 2-3]; 84:12 [H 13]; 119:1-3.

The sufferings of the pious caused by the success of the ungodly lead to reflections that resemble wisdom material (Pss. 39; 49; 73). The starting point of Ps. 73 is the consideration of the happiness of the ungodly. The mood changes with the realization that the wicked will be destroyed, but the one offering the prayer can rely on God's help, even to the point of death. In this context the lament by the individual evolves into a lament over human mortality in Pss. 39; 49; 90 (cf. Job 7; 9–10; 14).

Reflective thought that resembles wisdom literature is also found in psalms of praise, especially Ps. 34, where the one who is describing his deliverance begins to urge his hearers to fear God. Compare also Ps. 92:9-15 [H 10-16] and the conclusions of Pss. 107; 111. How such reflections were combined with praise of God can be seen with striking clarity in Ps. 139. In the postcanonical psalms, wisdom language becomes more prominent (Ecclus. 39; 42; Pss. Sol. 3). *See* PSALMS, BOOK OF §B3; WISDOM IN THE ANE[S]; WISDOM IN THE OT [S].

2. Psalms in the ancient Near East. In many religions the two basic forms of calling out to God, praise and thanksgiving at one pole, and lament and petition at the other, have taken form in spiritual songs similar to the Psalms. This is especially true of the Mesopotamian psalm literature (*see* Widengren, Falkenstein, and von Soden). In the Akkadian psalms the same major motifs of praise of God, lament, petition, and vow of praise appear. There is close correspondence even in the use of figurative language, such as the description of foes as dangerous wild beasts and their threats as the setting of traps and snares. In both cultures the concluding vow of praise is similar, often word-for-word the same.

There are, however, significant differences. In the Babylonian psalms, lament is merged with praise, so that a psalm of lament may be introduced with wide-ranging praise of God. In Israel the two modes remained distinct. A piling up of attributes of God in the psalm introduction is typical of Akkadian psalms, but in Israel this is virtually unknown, as is the combining of a psalm of lament with the swearing of an oath, found in many groups of Akkadian psalms.

Egyptian psalms are even further removed from those of the OT, but even here there are frequent affinities in the praise of God. The most striking is the similarity of Ps. 104 to Akh-en-aton's hymn to Aton (*ANET* [2nd ed.], pp. 369-71).

Ugaritic influence on the psalms of the OT has been particularly stressed by Dahood (*see* POETRY, HEBREW[S]; cf. Donner). Many scholars hold that Ps. 29 was originally a Canaanite psalm, and Canaanite motifs may be found in Pss. 19:1-6 [H 2-7]; 68; 82; 93–99. There are also many correspondences in grammar and in poetic form, as, for example, the threefold parallelism in Ps. 93.

3. Poetic form of the Psalms. *See* PSALMS, BOOK OF §B1; POETRY, HEBREW[S].

4. The significance of the Psalms. The relation of men and women to God clearly is expressed in the form of dialogue throughout the OT. For this reason the human response to what God says and does serves to provide cohesiveness to the religion of Israel. The polarity of lament and praise encompasses the whole of human existence in its dependence on God, both in the life of the community and in that of the individual. The swing of the pendulum from lament to praise is more sudden and more thorough than is usually the case with the alternation between petition and thanksgiving in our prayers.

Israel's response to God in lament and praise was expressed as a cry from the depths, and pleading, as clinging to God, as praise voiced by the one rescued, as comprehensive praise of the majesty and the goodness of God, and as such it accompanied the individual as well as the nation through the centuries, changing, yet remaining fundamentally the same. The great significance of the Psalms for the life of the nation is seen in Second Isaiah, and for the life of the individual in Job. In both writings the language and the motifs of the Psalms are a major constituent. It is seen also in the continuing history of psalm writing in the postcanonical literature, especially in 1QH, in Luke 1–2, and in Revelation. It is seen also in the way that the Psalms have lived on in Jewish and Christian worship down to the present.

Bibliography. Studies on the psalm form: A. S. Kapelrud, "Scandanavian Research in the Psalms after Mowinckel," *Annual of the Swedish Theological Institute,* IV (1965), 74-90; O. Kaiser, *Einleitung in das AT* (2nd ed., 1970), pp. 268-76; A. Weiser, *The Psalms* (1962); H.-J. Kraus, *Psalmen* (3rd ed., 1966); M. J. Dahood, *Psalms,* I (1966), II (1968), III (1970).

Articles and monographs: S. Mowinckel, *The Psalms in Israel's Worship* (1962); H. Gunkel and J. Begrich, *Einleitung in die Psalmen* (1935 [2nd ed., 1966]); I. Engnell, *Studies in Divine Kingship in the Ancient Near East* (1943 [2nd ed., 1967]); C. Westermann, *The Praise of God in the Psalms* (1965), "Struktur und Geschichte der Klage im AT," *Forschung am AT. Gesammelte Studien,* Theologische Bücherei, XXIV (1964), 266-305, and "Zur Sammlung des Psalters," *ibid.,* 336-43; D. Michel, *Tempora und Satzstellung in den Psalmen* (1960); R. de Langhe, ed., *Le Psautier: Ses origines. Ses problemes litteraires. Son influence* (1962); H. H. Rowley, "Psalmody and Music," *Worship in Ancient Israel* (1967), pp. 176-212; F. Crüsemann, *Studien zur Formgeschichte von Hymnus und Danklied in Israel* (1969); J. Kuhlewein, *Geschichte in den Psalmen* (1973); R. Albertz, *Weltschöpfung und Menschenchöpfung* (1974), pp. 90-131; H. Donner, "Ugaritismen in der Psalmenforschung," *ZAW*, LXXIX (1967), 322-50; C. Barth, *Die Errettung vom Tode* (1947); G. Widengren, *The Akkadian and Hebrew Psalms of Lamentation* (1937); A. Falkenstein and W. von Soden, *Sumerische und Akkadische Hymnen und Gebete* (1953).

C. WESTERMANN

***PSEUDEPIGRAPHA** [ψευδεπίγραφα, with false superscription, Gr.]. Jewish writings of the second temple period resembling the Apoc. in general character, yet not included in the Bible, Apoc., or rabbinic literature. The use of the term "Pseudepigrapha," however unfortunate in the confusion it engenders, has become firmly entrenched. It seems likely to remain current, although the inherent unclarity about the scope or range of literature denoted by it also seems likely to persist.

1. New directions in the study of the Pseudep. There has been a growing recognition of the intrinsic interest and importance of this literature. Scholarly work has centered chiefly on the investigation of the textual traditions, the establishment of critical editions, and translations. Attempts have been made to apply methods of form and redaction criticism as developed in biblical studies, and also structural principles, to the study of the books, although there is a growing awareness of inherent characteristics of the Pseudep. which differentiate them from biblical writings.

2. The scope of the Pseudep. and the individual books. Advance in the study of the books themselves has been uneven, with those represented among the DEAD SEA SCROLLS receiving most attention. The range of works actively being considered by scholars has increased. In addition to the works noted below, see the separate articles on: ENOCH, BOOK OF; ENOCH, BOOK OF[S]; TESTAMENTS OF THE TWELVE PATRIARCHS, THE, and supplementary article; MACCABEES, BOOKS OF §E; JUBILEES, BOOK OF; ARISTEAS; ODES OF SOLOMON[S]; PSALMS OF SOLOMON.

a) The Syriac Apocalypse of Baruch (*see* BARUCH, APOCALYPSE OF). Chief issues remain the question of sources and the dependence on *LAB* and II Esdras (*see* ESDRAS, BOOK OF §3). The concept of history of the Baruch and Ezra Apocalypses has been fruitfully studied.

b) The Greek Apocalypse of Baruch. A new edition of the Greek text has appeared, and there has been some preliminary interest in the Slavonic version. Recent studies have limited the extent of Christian revision, and try to define the function of the book as a response to certain issues of theodicy. Its lack of eschatological tension is noteworthy.

c) The Apocalypse of Abraham (*see* ABRAHAM, APOCALYPSE OF), extant only in Church Slavonic, is composed of two parts. It relates Abraham's discovery of God (chs. 1–14) and his vision of the heavens, of the divine throne, and of human history (chs. 15–32). Like II Esdras and Syriac Baruch there is a concern for theodicy. In many features of the vision experience, it forms a link between the apocalypses and the Merkabah mystical books, which claim to record visions concerning a heavenly chariot, and are generally dated to the fourth and fifth centuries A.D. A Christian interpolation of unusual character occurs in ch. 29.

d) The Slavonic Apocalypse of Enoch. The origins of the book remain problematical. It seems to reflect sectarian sacrificial practice and Zoroastrian cosmogony. The Melchizedek traditions should be regarded as Jewish. *See* MELCHIZEDEK[S].

e) The Greek Apocalypses of Esdras and Sedrach are now regarded as at least marginally related to the Pseudep. and are included in some collections.

f) The Testament (or Assumption) of Moses is now viewed as a first-century A.D. revision of a work from the period of the Maccabean revolt.

g) The Testament of Abraham (*see* ABRAHAM, TESTAMENT OF) is now recognized as a Jewish work, although it may contain some traces of Christian revision. It relates Abraham's heavenly travels before his death and his conflict with Death in the attempt to retain his soul. It is extant in two recensions, of which the longer seems more original. With it are associated, in the Arabic, Ethiopic, and Coptic versions, the less certainly Jewish Testaments of Isaac and Jacob.

h) The Testament of Job. Recent studies reflect a certain aporia as to the possible circles of origin. Two new editions have appeared, and the relationship with the Abrahamic traditions has been stressed. An Aramaic origin, proposed earlier, seems unlikely.

i) The Testament of Solomon, which is Christian in its present form, remains marginal to the Jewish pseudepigraphic testaments.

j) The SIBYLLINE ORACLES. The place within Egyptian Judaism as well as their common points with the political oracles of the Hellenistic world are to be stressed.

k) The Story of Joseph and Asenath is extant in a Greek version which may be the original. Probably written in Egypt, perhaps as a missionary document, it tells of the conversion and marriage of Asenath to Joseph. It has been proposed that the book originated in Jewish mysteries in Egypt.

l) The Paralipomena of Jeremiah has been re-edited in Greek, and its relationship to Syriac Baruch and to the Coptic Jeremiah Apocryphon has been examined.

m) The Martyrdom of Isaiah. No new evidence has come forward either to prove or disprove the independent existence of this book. The idea that it was produced by the Qumran sect and refers to the TEACHER OF RIGHTEOUSNESS has been revived in a more extreme form.

n) The Lives of the Prophets deals with each of the chief prophets of the Bible in a brief fashion, occasionally incorporating traditions additional to those relating to his tribal origins, birthplace, and mode of death and burial. The work reflects ancient traditions (cf. II Chr. 24:19; Ethio. Enoch 89:51-53; Jub. 1:12; 4QpHos^b 2:4-6; Luke 11:51) and seems to be of Jewish origin. The textual history and transmission are complex, and the book has undergone a number of recensions, some clearly Christian. Various forms of the Lives were popular in Christian hagiographic literature. It shows, on occasion, intimate knowledge of the geography of the land of Israel.

o) The Life of Adam and Eve. The Greek version of this work has been intensively studied with the utilization of many more MSS than were employed in previous editions. There are also Latin and Slavonic versions, as well as a recently published Georgian text and an unpublished Armenian version. The relationship of these texts to each other remains uncertain, in spite of recent studies. Interest in the Adam literature has increased as a result of the renewed research into GNOSTICISM and the Cairo Coptic codices (*see* ADAM, APOCALYPSE OF[S]). Identification of the circles in which this literature originated and its original language and function is uncertain. Adam traditions were significant in medieval Christian culture, and numerous Adam works exist in Syriac, Arabic, Ethiopic, Georgian, Armenian, and other tongues.

p) Pseudo-Phocylides. A collection of gnomic verses attributed to the sixth-century B.C. Milesian Phocylides, generally recognized as having numerous points of contact with biblical literature. It is attributed to Jewish or Judaizing authorship.

q) The body of apocryphal psalms has increased to include a group of five psalms found in certain Syriac MSS of the Psalter. Some of these, together with other apocryphal compositions, were included in 11QPs[a]. This corpus may be further expanded by inclusion of certain pseudo-Davidic poems found in *LAB*.

r) *Liber Antiquitatum Biblicarum,* falsely attributed to Philo in some MSS, is a paraphrase of biblical history from the Creation down to a point corresponding to the beginning of II Kings. The original language was Hebrew, and the book utilized a non-Masoretic biblical text, certainly of (Proto-) Lucianic type in Joshua–I Samuel. A new Latin edition has been announced, and fragments of a medieval Hebrew translation, preserved in the Chronicle of Jeraḥmeel, have been published. Since *LAB* was a source for Syr. Bar. and II Esdras, a first century A.D. date, at the latest, is indicated.

s) The History of Zosimus remains largely unstudied.

t) The Ladder of Jacob is preserved in two Slavonic recensions. The oldest of these contains no Christian elements and is a narrative of Jacob's vision at Luz, of the ladder, of his prayer for its interpretation which is given as an eschatological vision. Sec. 5 appears to refer to the Romans. The prayer has certain characteristics in common with the Apocalypse of Abraham.

u) The Questions Addressed by the Queen and the Answers Given by Solomon is a supplement to the biblical stories of Solomon and the Queen of Sheba. The work contains no clearly Christian elements and may well be of Jewish origin. It is preserved in Armenian, apparently a translation from Syriac, dated by some to the seventh or eighth century. Such riddle literature was known to Josephus (Antiq. VIII.v.3), and medieval works of similar character exist. This writing adds another dimension to the preserved wisdom traditions associated with Solomon.

v) There is a large body of quotations from lost works preserved in patristic and other ancient and medieval sources. The chief information on such fragments was published many years ago, but it can be augmented from time to time as new publications appear. None of the fragmentary works from Qumran as yet coincide with fragments preserved in patristic sources. Finally, it seems unlikely that the Coptic Elijah Apocalypse is of Jewish authorship, although it contains much of interest. The fourth and seventh Epistles of Heraclitus are no longer considered Jewish.

3. Pseudep. and Qumran. (*See also* DEAD SEA SCROLLS and supplementary article.) The relationship between the scrolls from Qumran and the Pseudep. is complex. First, when they exist, the Qumran MSS are most important for the study of books which were already known before the Judean desert find. The best examples of this published so far are the MSS of the Testament of Levi and of the book of Enoch. The literary history of these works has been rewritten as a result.

It is difficult to determine whether nonbiblical works from Qumran, unknown from elsewhere, can be considered part of the collection of Pseudep. A number of these works are certainly analogous to the Pseudep. in general character and literary type. Such writings as 1Q16, the Book of Giants, 1QGen Apoc, 4Qpseudo-Ezekiel, and others should, on such grounds, be included in the collection. It may seriously be questioned, however, whether the works of peculiar sectarian character, the *Pesher* commentaries, the Manual of Discipline, etc. will come to be regarded as Pseudep. They have a distinct stamp of their own. In any case, this matter will be determined both by scholarly practice and by tradition of transmission. A final conclusion cannot be expected to emerge before the full publication of the Cave IV MSS. Meanwhile, the study of the Qumran scrolls is extraordinarily important and enlightening for students of the Pseudep.

Bibliography. Introductions, translations, and general studies: O. Eissfeldt, *The OT: An Introduction* (3rd ed., 1964), pp. 571-637; G. Delling, ed., *Bibliographie zur jüdisch-hellenistischen und intertestamentarischen Literatur 1900-1965, TU,* CVI (1969); A. M. Denis, *Introduction aux Pseudépigraphes grecs de l'ancien testament,* Studia in Veteris Testamenti Pseudepigrapha, I (1970); L. Rost, *Einleitung in die alttestl. Apok. und Pseudepig.* (1971); *Mveli Āḡt'kxmis Ap'okrip'ebis Kart'uli Versiebi,* 2 vols. (1970, 1973), Georgian version; M. E. Stone, "The Apocryphal Literature in the Armenian Tradition," *Proceedings of the Israel Academy of Sciences and Humanities,* IV (1969), 59-77; J. H. Charlesworth, "The Renaissance of Pseudepigrapha Studies," *JSJ,* II (1971), 106-14, survey of scholarship.

Special studies and editions: Syriac Baruch: P. Bogaert, *L'Apocalypse syriaque de Baruch,* 2 vols., Sources chrétiennes, CXLIV, CXLV (1969); A. F. J. Klijn, "The Sources and the Redaction of the Syriac Apocalypse of Baruch," *JSJ,* I (1970), 65-76; W. Harnisch, *Verhängnis und Verheissung der Geschichte, FRLANT,* XCVII (1969). Greek Baruch: J. C. Picard, *Apocalypsis Baruchi Graece,* Pseudepigrapha Veteris Testamenti Graece, II (1967); E. Turdeanu, "Apocryphes bogomiles et apocryphes pseudo-bogomiles," *RHR,* CXXXVIII (1950), 177-81. Apocalypse of Abraham: G. Scholem, *Major Trends in Jewish Mysticism* (1941), pp. 68-72, and *Jewish Gnosticism, Merkabah Mysticism, and Talmudic Tradition* (1965), pp. 20-30; E. Turdeanu, "L'Apocalypse d'Abraham en Slave," *JSJ,* III (1972), 153-80. Ethiopic Enoch: J. T. Milik, "Problèmes de la littérature Hénochique à la lumière des fragments araméens de Qumrân," *HTR,* LXIV (1971), 333-78, "Turfan et Qumrân, Livre de Géants juif et manichéen," *Tradition und Glaube,* ed. G. Jeremias *et al.* (1971), pp. 117-27, and "Milki-ṣedeq et Milki-reša' dans les anciens écrits juifs et chrétiens," *JJS,* XXIII (1972),

95-144. Slavonic Enoch: S. Pines, "Eschatology and the Concept of Time in the Slavonic Book of Enoch," *Types of Redemption,* Studies in the History of Religions, XVIII, ed. R. J. Z. Werblowsky and C. J. Bleeker (1970), 72-87; J. A. Fitzmyer, "Further Light on Melkizedek from Qumran Cave 11," *Essays in the Semitic Background of the NT* (1971), pp. 215-67. Testament of Moses: E. M. Laperrousaz, *Le Testament de Moïse,* Semitica, XIX (1969); G. W. E. Nickelsburg, ed., *Studies on the Testament of Moses,* SBL Septuagint and Cognate Studies, IV (1973). Testament of Abraham: M. E. Stone, *The Testament of Abraham,* SBL Texts and Translations, II, Pseudepigrapha Series 2 (1972); G. W. E. Nickelsburg, "Eschatology in the Testament of Abraham," *1972 Proceedings,* SBL Septuagint and Cognate Studies, II, ed. R. A. Kraft (1972), pp. 180-227. Sibylline Oracles: V. Nikiprowetzsky, *La troisième Sibylle* (1970); J. J. Collins, *The Sibylline Oracles of Egyptian Judaism,* SBLDS, XIII (1974). Testament of Job: S. P. Brock, *Testamentum Iobi,* Pseudepigrapha Veteris Testamenti Graece, II (1967); R. A. Kraft, *The Testament of Job,* SBL Texts and Translations, V, Pseudepigrapha Series 4 (1974). Joseph and Asenath: M. Philonenko, *Joseph et Asénath,* SPB, XIII (1968); C. Burchard, *Untersuchungen zu Joseph und Asenath,* WUNT, VIII (1965). Paralipomena of Jeremiah: R. A. Kraft and A.-E. Purintun, *Paraleipomena Jeremiou,* SBL Texts and Translations, I, Pseudepigrapha Series 1 (1972); G. Delling, *Jüdische Lehre und Frömmigkeit in den Paralipomena Jeremiae, BZAW,* C (1967); G. W. E. Nickelsburg, "Narrative Traditions in the Paralipomena of Jeremiah," *CBQ,* XXXV (1973), 60-68; M. E. Stone, "Some Observations on the Armenian Version of the Paralipomena of Jeremiah," *CBQ,* XXXV (1973), 47-59. Martyrdom of Isaiah: M. Philonenko, *Le Martyre d'Esaïe et l'histoire de la secte de Qoumran,* Cahiers de la RHPR, XLI (1967), 1-10. Life of Adam and Eve: M. Nagel, "La Vie greque d'Adam et d'Ève," 3 vols. (diss., Strassbourg, 1972). Apocryphal Psalms: J. A. Sanders, "The Psalms Scroll of Qumran Cave 11," *DJD,* IV (1965); J. Strugnell, "More Psalms of David," *CBQ,* XXVII (1965), 207-16. *Liber Antiquitatum Biblicarum:* D. J. Harrington, *The Hebrew Fragments of Pseudo-Philo,* SBL Texts and Translations III, Pseudepigrapha Series 3 (1974), "The Original Language of Pseudo-Philo's *LAB,*" *HTR,* LXIII (1970), 503-14, and "The Biblical Text of Pseudo-Philo's *LAB,*" *CBQ,* XXXIII (1971), 1-17. Odes of Solomon: J. H. Charlesworth, *The Odes of Solomon* (1973). The Ladder of Jacob: M. R. James, *Lost Apocrypha of the OT* (1920), pp. 96-103. Questions of the Queen: J. Issaverdens, *The Uncanonical Writings of the OT* (2nd ed., 1934), pp. 163-66. *See also* J. Strugnell and H. Attridge, "The Epistles of Heraclitus and the Jewish Pseudepigrapha," *HTR,* LXIV (1971), 411-13. M. E. STONE

PSEUDONYMOUS WRITING sū dŏn'ĭ mŭs. A text is pseudonymous when the author is deliberately identified by a name other than his own. In contrast to our culture, where the assumed name is often freely invented (e.g., Mark Twain), pseudonymous writings in the Bible and other ancient literatures borrow the name of a well-known person of the past; thus, pseudonymous writing is also pseudepigraphic. For modern consciousness, publishing your work under someone else's name can be explained only by an intent to forge or by pathological transformation of the ego (insanity, trance). Neither interpretation adequately explains the pseudonymous writings of antiquity.

1. Primary and secondary pseudonymity. In both the OT and NT there are a number of books which, at the time they were written, were deliberately ascribed to someone other than the author. Deuteronomy (the first book in the Bible which is definitely pseudonymous) is attributed to MOSES, Ecclesiastes to a king of Jerusalem, DANIEL to a man from the time of the Exile, the PASTORAL LETTERS to Paul, and II Peter to Jesus' disciple. Pseudonymity is even more common in the APOCRYPHA (I Baruch; Epistle of Jeremy; Wisdom of Solomon), in the PSEUDEPIGRAPHA, and in many Gnostic writings (*see* NAG HAMMADI[S]). In these cases one may speak of "primary" pseudonymity.

"Secondary" pseudonymity appears where originally anonymous writings are later attributed to well-known biblical figures, as the Pentateuch is attributed to Moses, the Psalms to David, Lamentations to Jeremiah, the first gospel to Matthew, and the Letter to the Hebrews to Paul. In some cases it is unclear whether the pseudonymity is primary or secondary (Malachi, the Gospel of Mark).

2. Cultural explanations of the phenomenon. While some exegetes transfer modern categories to biblical times and assume deliberate forgery in pseudonymous writings, others attempt to find possible explanations which fit a culture which does not yet know the concept of intellectual property. Four such explanations are:

a) Pseudonymity could be recognized by the reader of that time; it is a stylistic device, not a strict statement of authorship (Rowley).

b) Since the epoch of canonical revelation was viewed as closed, new religious works had to borrow canonical names (Osswald, Balz).

c) A mystical feeling unites the anonymous author of a later time with the pious people of an earlier age, who are now in heaven, inspiring the later author (Speyer), or giving the author an understanding of himself as an "extended personality" of an earlier man of God (Russell). For the NT era the connection may be ascribed to the continuing effects of the Holy Spirit (Aland). In this interpretation the psychological category of "authenticity of experience" usually becomes the criterion for differentiating between legitimate and illegitimate pseudonymity.

d) A long period of oral tradition precedes the pseudonymous writings; threfore, when they are written down, the supposed initiator of the tradition is given (Oesterley).

These explanations are so far inadequate, as they do not take into account the circumstances surrounding the origin of writings in cultures without a literary market, and therefore without copyright or a corresponding ethical criterion of authenticity. More adequate explanations would be:

a) Written works of the ancient Near East are typically anonymous (cf. the historical books of the OT). In more developed situations colophons are usual, which name those persons responsible for the submitted version of the text (as in Babylon and Ugarit), although the question remains open how much they copied and how much they themselves formulated. Only in Greece (beginning in the sixth century B.C.?) did there develop a literary market that encouraged a distinct consciousness of authorship in those who wrote for that market.

b) Only inscriptions or certain kinds of books (Mesopotamian law books, Egyptian wisdom literature, OT prophets) named the author; however, since those writers did not shrink from plagiarizing older texts (even in Egyptian royal inscriptions), they are as much collectors as authors. There is no fundamental difference between this practice and the listing of names in colophons.

c) It is also taken for granted in books bearing authentic names that the author will reformulate the words of a person in the story and so use him as a pseudonymous vehicle for his own thought (cf. the Platonic Socrates or the Johannine Jesus).

3. Oral and written tradition. In biblical times, oral and written tradition were not fundamentally distinguished, but stood in a reciprocal relationship (*see* TRADITION, ORAL[S]). The following points are significant for religious tradition:

a) The attribution of anonymously circulating traditions to famous figures of the past. Thus, sayings of the tribes are attributed to Jacob (Gen. 49) or Moses (Deut. 33); psalms are put in the context of historical situations (Exod. 15; I Sam. 12); and wisdom sayings are attributed to respected rabbis (Pirke Aboth), or to Jesus. Since there is no intention of claiming a false author, such attribution is not pseudonymous. Even for trained historians it is often difficult to ascertain whether the statement of authorship is accurate or not (e.g., Exod. 15:21, Miriam; Judg. 5, Deborah).

b) Writings ascribed to God, angels, or Christ. The people of antiquity were convinced that ethereal beings also write, that there are books in heaven which chosen people see and copy, or write down at the dictation of an angel. Authorized words of the gods are different from oracles and magical sayings; they are transferred by inspiration to certain people to be passed down orally or in writing. The Decalogue belongs to this category (Exod. 34:1); but also in the superscription "the Word of Yahweh," most of the books of the prophets name God himself as the author and the prophet as mediator. In the same way, in the NT the exalted *Kyrios* is identified as the author (Revelation to John; cf. the Didache). Outside the Bible there are many theonymous writings (Avesta, Hermetic books, Koran). For the majority of such cases it would have been presumptuous to indicate a human rather than a divine author.

Even writings attributed to God or Christ were not considered unchangeable. As tradition criticism shows, commands or prophecies formulated by God are again and again reformulated by editors in the course of time (*see* TRADITION CRITICISM, OT[S]). This is done in good conscience, probably as a holy duty.

That writers deliberately presented a purely human word as divine cannot be proved with certainty in either the ancient Near East or the Bible (only Herodotus assumes this for some—by no means all—Greek oracles).

c) Legitimizing association of traditions. Mowinckel explains the editorial expansion of the prophetic books as the work of schools which considered themselves true to the master prophet, so that even after his death they prophesied in his name and sometimes fixed those prophecies in writing. There was an analogous situation in the Greek schools of philosophy, where the ideal of imitation of the master led to pseudo-Socratic and pseudo-Platonic writings. Apocalyptic literature may have been written in synagogues that bore the names of earlier figures (cf. the Elijah Synagogue in ancient Rome). Could something similar hold true for the Deutero-Pauline letters or the letters of Peter?

It is probable that consciousness of an association with an ancient personage arises even when that personage never actually lived. Above all, this can be assumed for apocalyptic literature, in which a long period of growth may be recognized, and in which the process of tradition is never definitively concluded (e.g., Enoch literature; Aramaic, then Hebrew Daniel, finally apocryphal additions; Sibyllines). *See* APOCALYPTICISM[S].

Famous names are capable of attracting entire genres of literature. Therefore, all divine law comes from Moses (even the oral Torah of the rabbis), all wisdom from Solomon, and every church regulation from the apostles.

No matter whether the existence of prophetic schools is assumed or not, a consciousness that association with a tradition confers legitimacy (a concept that is foreign to us today) may be presupposed; otherwise the amount of pseudonymous writing in the Bible and in the ancient Near East would be inexplicable. In many cases the authors to whom the writings are ascribed are considered as alive in heaven and therefore still effective in the present. To this extent attribution of authorship to men of God is similar to ascribing it to God, Christ, or angels. Since what is involved is not the conscious use of an inaccurate name, the designation "pseudonymous" should be used only with reservations.

4. Pseudepigraphy and pseudonymity. Since not much light has yet been shed on the relationships of oral and written tradition in ancient literature outside the Bible, we must be careful in making judgments about whether a pseudepigraphic document was consciously forged. Only in the writings of the Hellenistic diaspora (Aristeas, Pseudo-Phocylides) should such forgery be taken into consideration. In the Christian area, consciousness of the possibility of pseudonymous writings probably arose only with the formation of the canon in the second century.

Bibliography. W. O. E. Oesterley, *The Jews and Judaism During the Greek Period* (1941), pp. 74-77; H. H. Rowley, *The Relevance of Apocalyptic* (1944), pp. 39-42; S. Mowinckel, *Prophecy and Tradition* (1946); L. H. Brockington, "The Problem of Pseudonymity," *JTS,* NS IV (1953), 15-22; J. A. Sint, "Pseudonymität im Altertum," *Commentationes Aenipontanae,* XV (1960); K. Aland, "The Problem of Anonymity and Pseudonymity in Christian Literature of the First Two Centuries," *JTS,* NS XII (1961), 39-49; E. Osswald, "Zum Problem der *vaticinia ex eventu,*" *ZAW,* LXXV (1963), 27-44; D. S. Russell,

The Method and Message of Jewish Apocalyptic (1964), pp. 127-39; H. R. Balz, "Anonymität und Pseudepigraphie im Urchristentum," *ZThK,* LXVI (1969), 403-36; *Pseudepigrapha I,* Entretiens sur l'antiquité classique, XVIII (1972), esp. the articles by M. Smith, M. Hengel, and W. Speyer; W. Speyer, "Religiöse Pseudepigraphie und literarische Fälschung im Altertum," *Jahrbuch für Antike und Christentum,* VIII/IX (1965/1966), 88-125; J. C. Fenton, "Pseudonymity in the NT," *Theol.,* LVIII (1955), 51-56.

K. Koch

*Q. According to the two-document hypothesis (*see* SYNOPTIC PROBLEM; SYNOPTIC PROBLEM[S]), Matthew and Luke borrowed from the Gospel of Mark the Markan material which they have in common, while the non-Markan material they have in common is from a second source, the hypothetical Logia or sayings source, Q. Some who hold to the priority of Mark defend alternative solutions: the influence of oral tradition (Jeremias, Wrege) or Luke's direct dependence upon Matthew (Farrer). On the other hand, in the "Primitive Gospel" theory the hypothetical common source is a real gospel, including both the Markan and the non-Markan material.

1. The existence of Q. The Q hypothesis was developed in connection with the hypothesis of the priority of Mark (C. H. Weisse, 1838). Three observations gave rise to the assumption of a second common source beside Mark: the verbal agreements of the double tradition texts (non-Markan material common to Matthew and Luke), the presence of doublets (i.e., the same saying in a Markan form and in a "Q" form), and the common order in Matthew and Luke.

The phenomenon of order deserves special consideration. The double tradition passages are in a different Markan context in Matthew and Luke, with the exception of the first two sections—the preaching of John the Baptist and the temptation (Mark 1:7-8, 12-13). In Luke the material is presented together with peculiar texts in the three insertions between Mark 3:19/4:1 (Luke 6:20–7:35), Mark 9:40/10:13 (Luke 9:51–18:14), and Mark 10/11 (Luke 19:1-17; *see also* 22:28-30). In Matthew the situation is quite different. There the evangelist combines the parallel Q traditions not only with Mark 1:7-8 and 12-13 but also with Mark 3:22-29; 4:30-32; 6:7-11; 8:11-12; 12:38-39, and assembles the sayings in the great discourse complexes of Matt. 5–7, 10, (11–12), 13, 18 and 23, 24–25. Still, in both Matthew and Luke a common order can be seen in the following sections:

Matthew	Luke
3:7-12	3:7-9, 16-17
4:2-11	4:2-13
5:3-6, 11-12, 39-42, 45-48	6:20-23, 27-30, 32-36
7:1-5, 16-21, 24-27	6:37-38, 41-49
8:5-10, 13	7:1-10
11:2-19	7:18-35
[8:19-22]	9:57-60
[9:37-38; 10:7-16]	10:2-12
11:21-23	10:13-15
11:25-26	10:21-22
12:22-30	11:14-23
12:43-45	11:24-26
[12:38-42]	11:29-32
23:4, 23-25, 29-36	11:39-52
23:37-39	13:34-35
24:26-27, 37-39, 40-41	17:23-27, 34-35
25:14-30	19:11-27

The bracketed passages differ in order, but Matthew may be responsible for these inversions.

Within the Matthean discourses, too, the common sequence is broken by editorial rearrangement (e.g., 7:12, cf. Luke 6:31; 10:16, cf. Luke 10:3) and by a number of insertions not referred to in the list above. When compared with Luke, this series of passages sometimes shows the same order in both gospels (Taylor); e.g.,

Matthew	Luke
6:9-13	11:2-4
6:20-21	12:33-34
6:22-23	11:34-35
6:25-33	12:22-31
7:7-11	11:9-13
7:13-14	13:23-24
7:22-23	13:26-27
8:11-12	13:28-29

It is generally held that the original order of Q is preserved more faithfully in Luke.

The common order is hardly conceivable as a result of Luke's dependence upon Matthew, not only in view of the absence in Luke of typically Matthean characteristics, but also because of Matthew's conflations with Mark and the placement of the sayings in different Markan contexts. On the other hand, the evidence of order is unduly neglected by those who suggest that several traditions or groups of sayings, instead of a single document, formed the basis of the double tradition in Matthew and Luke.

2. The contents of Q. Although the variety of reconstructions is frequently cited as an objection to the Q hypothesis, there is a consensus regarding the double tradition passages. In the order of Luke these are: 3:7-9, 16-17; 4:2-13; 6:20-23, 27-49; 7:1-10, 18-35; 9:57-60; 10:2-16, 21-24; 11:2-4, 9-26, 29-35, 39-44, 46-52; 12:2-12, 22-31, 33-34, 39-40, 42-46, 51-56, 58-59; 13:18-21, 24-30, 34-35; 14:16-23, 26-27, 34-35; 15:4-7; 16:13, 16-18; 17:1, 3-4, 6, 23-24, 26-27, 30, 33, 34-35, 37; 19:12-27; 22:18-30.

Some scholars have reservations about Luke 7:29-30; 14:16-23; 19:12-27, because of the verbal dissimilarities in the Matthean parallels. It is more doubtful whether texts peculiar to Luke (e.g., 6:24-26; 9:61-62) or Matthew (e.g., 10:23) can be assigned to Q. In these instances the editorial activity of the evangelists deserves careful examination. Some overlappings with Mark cannot be denied (Luke 3:16; 11:15-18; 13:18-19; 14:34-35; cf. the doublets 10:4, 5, 7*a*, 10, 11*a;* 10:16; 11:33, 43; 12:2, 9, 11-12; 14:27; 17:33; 19:26; and, with a doublet in Matthew, 11:29*b;* 13:30; 16:18), but an origin in Q is not demonstrated by the presence of minor agreements between Matthew and Luke against Mark in Luke 3:1-6; 3:21-22; 4:1-2; 6:12-16; 10:25-28, and some other passages of the triple tradition.

The overlapping of double and triple tradition sayings may be due to the common dependence of Mark and Q on oral tradition. The hypothesis of a literary relationship between Mark and Q is hardly acceptable, either in the form put forward by Wellhausen (Q depends on Mark) or in the form proposed by more recent writers: Mark borrowed from Q or from a recension or revision of Q (Brown; *see* Synoptic Problem[S] §1*a*).

The reconstruction of the original Q text is an easy task for those sections where the wording in Matthew and Luke is almost identical: Luke 3:7*b*-9; 7:22-23, 24*b*-28; 10:13-15, 21-22, 24-25; 13:34-35. In other instances the verbal disagreements are so important that attempts at reconstruction necessarily involve differing opinions. However, this difficulty should not lead us to doubt the existence of a written "Q" source. The difficulty stems from the editorial intervention of the evangelists, and the problem is therefore to give a fair description of what they have done.

3. The literary genre. The "gospel" genre as it is known from Mark and the other gospels (*see* Gospel, Genre[S]) cannot be applied to Q because there is no Passion Narrative in Q, and the narrative portions are almost exclusively introductions to sayings material. Thus, the two miracles in Luke 7:1-10 and 11:14 serve more as a setting for the words of Jesus than as a proper story. Manson has described Q as a collection of parenetical sayings made by the primitive church, and different from the "kerygma" of the gospel compositions. Analogies have been drawn to the OT prophetic books, wisdom collections, Jewish haggadah (especially Pirke Aboth), and the Didache. The Gospel of Thomas, a collection of 114 sayings ascribed to Jesus, with no other introduction than "Jesus said," has been proposed as a closer analogy. According to Robinson, the literary genre of Q, before its incorporation in the Gospels of Matthew and Luke, was that of λόγοι σοφῶν (sayings of wise men) as preserved in the Gospel of Thomas. This is, however, a Gnostic composition which borrows from the canonical gospels, and its literary genre is most probably of a later origin. The Q source may represent a primitive Christian genre *sui generis.* Since it is not a mere "collection of sayings" (*Logienquelle*), Schürmann prefers to call it a "discourse source" (*Redequelle*).

4. The redaction and the theology of Q. Because of the hypothetical character of the reconstruction, together with the possibility of successive redactions of Q, it is difficult to establish criteria for the study of the redaction and its separation from tradition. The selection of the materials and the composition and structure of the source can be examined, and the Q passages can be compared with Mark for overlappings. Although the conclusions of recent Redaction Criticism are diverse, there is at least a general trend to concentrate on the christological implications. There is likewise much divergence about Q's place of origin: (1) a Palestinian community of Christians in lively confrontation with the Jews; (2) a Hellenistic milieu which continued the preaching of Jesus by announcing the eschatological judgment; (3) a missionary community.

Bibliography. J. Jeremias, "Zur Hypothese einer schriftlichen Logienquelle Q," *ZNW,* XXIX (1930), 147-49; T. W. Manson, *The Teaching of Jesus* (2nd ed., 1935), pp. 27-34; V. Taylor, "The Original Order of Q," *NT Essays,* ed. A. J. B. Higgins (1959), pp. 246-69; H. E. Tödt, *The Son of Man in the Synoptic Tradition* (1959 [ET 1965]), Son of man Christology; W. D. Davies, *The Setting of the Sermon on the Mount* (1964), crisis Christology; J. M. Robinson and H. Koester, *Trajectories through Early Christianity* (1971), esp. Robinson's article, "*Logoi Sophon:* On the Gattung of Q," pp. 71-113; J. M. Robinson, "Kerygma and History in the NT," *The Bible in Modern Scholarship,* ed. J. P. Hyatt (1965), pp. 114-50; P. D. Meyer, "The Community of Q" (diss., Univ. of Iowa, 1967); H. Schürmann, *Traditionsgeschichtliche Untersuchungen zu den synoptischen Evangelien* (1968), pp. 111-25; H. Wrege, *Die Überlieferungsgeschichte der Bergpredigt,* WUNT, IX (1968); A. Polag, "Die Christologie der Logienquelle" (diss., Univ. Trier, 1968); P. Hoffmann, *Studien zur Theologie der Logienquelle,* NTAbh, NF VIII (1972); S. Schulz, *Q. Die Spruchquelle der Evangelisten* (1972), and *Griechisch-deutsche Synopse der Q-Überlieferungen* (1972); M. Devisch, "De geschiedenis van de Quelle-hypothese" (diss., Leuven, 1975), history of the hypothesis; "Le document Q, source de Matthieu," *L'évangile selon Matthieu,* ed. M. Didier, BETL, XXIX (1972), 71-97, and "La relation entre l'évangile de Marc et le document Q," *L'évangile selon Marc,* ed. M. Sabbe, BETL, XXXIV (1974), 59-91.

F. Neirynck

***QERE-KETHIBH** (QK). The most important notes in the Masora *parva* (*see* Text, OT §A4*a*). A word (*kethibh,* "that which is written") in MSS and printed editions of the Hebrew Bible is often marked by a small circle above, which refers to another word in the margin which must be "read" (*qere*) in its stead. The traditional Jewish pronunciation (*q^{e}ri-k^{e}thibh*) arose through a faulty reading of the nonvocalized consonantal word קרי. The *yōdh* in this *scriptio plena* was taken as the *mater lectionis* of *ḥireq,* on analogy of the *yōdh* of the expression כתיב, whereas the word should be read with a *ṣērê* (Aramaic imperative or passive participle). Logically, the order of the phrase should read *kethibh-qere,* "what is written and what is read."

The QK notes were designed to ensure, whether for synagogal reading or for sacred study, that the consonantal Textus Receptus be transmitted unaltered, and that the traditional enunciation be preserved. They form part of the oldest and most important teachings of the Masoretic scribes. At first they were handed down orally, and not written in the margin of the MSS, as is shown by the examples of *qere perpetuum,* which were rarely indicated in the MSS or printed editions. Later, the bulk of the notes that bear the title *qere-kethibh* were written in the margin of the MSS by the Masoretic scribes, at the same time as the earliest texts of the qualitative *Masora parva* appeared. Subsequently, a certain number were incorporated in the lists of the *Masora magna,* the quantitative character of which marks the ultimate form of the work of conservation effected by the scribes and Masoretes. However, the question may legitimately be asked, What was the most ancient form of the *qere-kethibh*?

1. *Qere perpetuum*
2. *Tiqqune Sopherim*
3. The oldest Talmudic statement
   a. *Miqra' Sopherim*
   b. *'Iṭṭure Sopherim*
   c. *Qeriyyan we-la' Kethibhan*
   d. *Kethibhan we-la' Qeriyyan*
4. Other Talmudic statements
5. Symbols, terminology, and form of the QK
6. Purpose of the QK
   a. Guide against blasphemy
   b. Guide against obscenity
   c. Guide against erroneous reading
7. The seven classes of QK according to Elias Levita
8. Theories on the supposed origin of the *qere-kethibh*
   a. Source of the theories
   b. Early Jewish opinions
   c. The synthesis of Elias Levita and the first indications of the Masoretic origin of the QK
   d. Modern theories

Bibliography.

1. Qere perpetuum. The earliest instance where a word in the biblical text was not read, but another was pronounced in its stead, is that of the TETRAGRAMMATON (YHWH). The prohibition of pronouncing "The Name," and the obligation of substituting in perpetuity a term that expresses the divine majesty, are explicitly recognized in the Babylonian Talmud (Pes. 50a): "Said the Holy One, blessed be He: not as I am written, am I read. I am written י״ה (*yōdh-hē'*, i.e., the Tetragrammaton), but I am read א״ד (*'āleph-dāleth*, i.e., Adonai)." The antiquity of this prohibition is evident from the fact that the Hebrew Tetragrammaton was not translated in the most ancient recensions of the LXX, where it appears only in Hebrew script. Later it was rendered into Greek by κύριος (Lord), which conveys the sense of the Hebrew Adonai. In the Greek text, at the beginning, the same procedure was followed as in the Hebrew, namely, the equivalent of the divine name was first abbreviated, through reverence, into the form κ̱ς, then, in later texts and under Christian influence, it came to be written out fully. In the same way, the Babylonian Targ. on the Pentateuch (Targ. Onkelos) systematically renders the Tetragrammaton into Aramaic by the abbreviation ייי (the arithmetic equivalent of which—26—is the same as that of the Tetragrammaton fully written in its Hebrew form). *See* WORDPLAY IN THE OT[S] §1; ABBREVIATIONS, HEBREW TEXTS[S] §2.

This ancient prohibition of pronouncing the divine name persisted orally until the introduction of the Hebrew vocalic system, where the vowels written under the Tetragrammaton are those of the substitute word Adonai. Its antiquity clearly shows that it originated in the oldest Jewish oral traditions that accompanied the transmission (*masora*) of the sacred text from the beginning. In contrast to the *qere perpetuum*, substituted orally for the Tetragrammaton, the Masoretic tradition, as a precautionary measure, indicated in the margin of later MSS, in the form of a statistical note (קֹלֹד = 134), the number of times in the text where God is explicitly designated by the title אֲדֹנָי (cf. Gen. 18:3 and *passim*). In this way, they sought to forestall any change in the form of the sacred text that might be made by an overhasty scribe. Apart from the Tetragrammaton, there are some other instances of *qere perpetuum* in the Pentateuch, e.g., הוא (*hû'*), read as היא (*hî'*), Gen. 3:12 and *passim*. These were noted sporadically in the margins of the MSS, but without any definite system as regards the form of their transmission. Thus, in MS B 19a from Leningrad, used as the basic text for the third edition of Kittel's *Biblia Hebraica* (BHK) and for the *Biblia Hebraica Stuttgartensia* (BHS), this *qere perpetuum* is indicated only in the margin of Lev. 6:18 and 22. The *Masora parva* (MP) of the same MS, however, in the case of הִיא in Gen. 14:2 and Lev. 11:39, scrupulously inserted the statistical note: יֹא כתֹ י בתורֹ, i.e., "eleven instances in the Torah where היא is expressly written with a *yōdh*." From this example it may be inferred that the differences discernible in the transmission of these marginal notes are not due to divergences between schools, nor to the relative antiquity of the variants, but simply to lack of system in handing down both the notes and the archetypes on which the codices were based. Proof of this is found in the *qere perpetuum* נַעֲרָ, read נַעֲרָה—nowhere noted in the margin of the book of Genesis (24:14 and *passim*) in the Leningrad MS, whereas it is regularly indicated in the margin of Deuteronomy (22:15 and *passim*) in the same MS. From the above examples we can deduce the basic *raison d'être* of the QK formulas. They served, first, to guarantee the written form of the text, as it had been received at a particular period. Second, they ensured correct reading of the text, according to the traditional principles developed in the schools of the first scribe-grammarians, who were also the first exegetes. However, this stage where, thanks to the QK, reading of the consonantal text had been standardized, was preceded by at least one type of scribal tradition involving a more drastic form of activity, the *tiqqune sopherim*.

2. Tiqqune Sopherim. The Masoretic tradition has preserved a list of eighteen of the most ancient scribal corrections, with the note: יֹחֹ מלין תקן עזרא, "Ezra corrected eighteen words [of the Bible]" (*Ochlah*, no. 108), or again: יֹחֹ מלין כנויי סופרים, "Eighteen words are euphemisms due to the Scribes" (*Diqduqe ha-Ṭe'amim*, no. 57), or, in more general and more usual form: יֹחֹ מלין תקוני סופרים, "Eighteen words have been emended by the Scribes" (*see* EMENDATIONS OF THE SCRIBES[S]). Geiger and Barthélemy have proved that in eighteen instances recorded by tradition, the scribes, otherwise so scrupulous, have corrected the sacred text. This took place at a period when Pharisaic influence had not yet declared the sacred text unchangeable; and we may well believe that the list of eighteen scribal corrections is not exhaustive. Only with the appearance of the school of Rabbi Akiba do we find a clear perception of the form and character of the canon, together with a theological affirmation of the inviolability of the text itself (*see* TEXT, HEBREW, HISTORY OF[S] §1). Any variants which arose subsequently would not be inserted in the graphic structure of the text, but only its reading, according to different opinions held by one or other of the Masoretic schools. At the same time, it is remarkable that the strictest Jewish tradition never sought to eliminate ancient textual corrections, such as the *Tiqqune Sopherim* or the *'Iṭṭure Sopherim.* On the contrary, this tradition conscientiously detailed the corrections of which it was aware, or of which some trace had been preserved, as a precautionary measure. The question that now arises is this: Is it possible to recover the most ancient scriptural examples of these critical marginal notes, destined to secure normative reading of the text, and so trace their origin?

3. The oldest Talmudic statement. The first reference to the terms קרי and כתיב is found in the Babylonian Talmud (Ned. 37b): אמר רב יצחק: מקרא סופרים ועיטור סופרים וקריין ולא כתיבן וכתיבן ולא קריין הלכה למשה מסני, "Rab Isaac said: 'The pronunciation fixed by the sopherim, the omissions of the scribes, words read which are not written in the text, and words written in the text which are cancelled in reading, are a law of Moses on Sinai'." The text then proceeds to give examples of each one of the categories mentioned.

a. Miqra' Sopherim, "the pronunciation of the scribes." This teaching relates to words whose consonantal form is not in doubt (e.g., ארץ, שמים and מצרים, subsequently mentioned in the Talmud). Hence we are clearly dealing with rules touching the traditional enunciation of the sacred text, not its transmission in consonantal form. The examples quoted show that this rule was formulated before any system of vocalic notation existed. The words in question may be read indifferently as אֶרֶץ or אָרֶץ, שָׁמַיִם or שָׁמָיִם, and מִצְרַיִם or מִצְרָיִם, according to where they are placed—at the beginning, or in the course of the verse, or at the pause. This teaching, then, is related to the traditional division of the text into verses—the great work of the teachers of this period, based on an oral tradition peculiar to the reading of sacred texts.

In order to grasp the importance attached to the traditional enunciation of the text, before the establishment of written systems of vocalization, we must examine another statement of the Babylonian Talmud (Sanh. 4a) that sheds special light on the subject. The text first mentions the controversy: "יש אם למקרא—whether our guide in exposition must be the pronunciation of the rabbis (*qere*) or יש אם למסורת—the spelling of a given word (*kethibh*)." The problem is then illustrated by the following examples: "Rabbi and R. Jehudah b. Ro'eṣ, the school of Shammai, R. Shime'on and R. Akiba, all hold that the pronunciation (מקרא) of the word is the determinant in biblical exposition . . . and R. Hunah said: What is the reason found in the Bible for the Shammaites' opinion? [The answer is]: the word קרנות (horns of the altar) occurs three times in the context (Lev. 4:25, 30, 34), and, when it is pronounced *qarnot,* as a plural, each occurrence implies two sprinklings, which makes six altogether. . . . But the school of Hillel argues that, since the word in question is twice written defectively, (קרנת), and can be read *qarnat,* as a singular (giving only one sprinkling in each case), and only once written *plene,* קרנות (*qarnot*), this makes four sprinklings in all." This orthographical example is in complete contradiction to our *textus receptus,* where, in each of the three instances, the word appears with defective spelling. Once again, it is clear that the examples of *Miqra' Sopherim* given by the Talmud are not exhaustive. They are but a sample of the problems involved in reading the text before its vocalization was fixed in writing.

b. 'Iṭṭure Sopherim. The instances of "omissions of the scribes" given in the Talmud relate to the suppression of the conjunction *wāw* before the word אחר, "after," e.g., Gen. 18:5; 24:55; Num. 31:2; Ps. 68:25 [H 26], and before משפטך, "thy righteousness" (Ps. 36:6 [H 7]). Once more, these examples cannot be regarded as the only cases where the early scribes exercised their skill in this fashion. They were recorded by Rabbi Isaac by the way of excursus in the course of a more general exposition of the normative and philological work of the scribes of the Talmudic era. Nonetheless, his information is important for an understanding of the transmission of the biblical text, and, in particular, for an appreciation of the work of textual criticism achieved by these teachers. The teaching of this Talmudic master bears witness to a most ancient tradition, long transmitted orally, and finally written down as a testimony of inestimable worth.

It has been necessary to examine the different aspects of scribal transmission expounded by the Talmudic masters, in order to understand how we can at last approach the problem posed by marginal corrections. The two lists given in the Talmud are the first and oldest scriptural testimonies to the traditional marginal corrections. These would subsequently develop in systematic fashion and be written down in the margins of the texts.

c. Qeriyyan we-la' Kethibhan. "Words which are to be read, but are not written" comprise the following: פרת, "Euphrates" (II Sam. 8:3); איש, "man" (II Sam. 16:23); באים, "come" (Jer. 31:38); לה, "thereof" (Jer. 50:29); את (accusative particle, Ruth 2:11); אלי, "unto me" (Ruth 3:5, 17). R. Isaac's statement quotes these seven cases where a word which does not appear in the biblical text is added in reading. In the text of our Bibles, following the Western tradition, no marginal note indicates the reading את כל for Ruth 2:11, whereas this reading is required by the Eastern tradition, which is not surprising, seeing that this reading is given in the Babylonian Talmud. Besides, we must remember that the qualitative list found in the Talmud is incomplete, and differs from other versions of the same list to be found in *Massekhet Sopherim* VI, 8; *Ochlah we Ochlah* no. 97; and *Massorah Gedolah* no. 2745, where the list is quantitative, and bears the precise title י׳ מלין דקריין ולא כתיבן (ten words which are to be read . . .). In the final form of these lists, there is no reference to Ruth 2:11, but the following examples are added: בני, "sons of" (Judg. 20:13); כן, "therefore," "because" (II Sam. 18:20); צבאות, "of hosts (II Kings 19:31); בניו, "his sons" (II Kings 19:37).

d. Kethibhan we-la' Qeriyyan. The "words written in the text, but cancelled in reading" are enumerated as follows by the Talmud: נא, "now" (II Kings 5:18); זאת (demonstrative pronoun, Deut. 6:25); ידרך, "he shall bend" (Jer. 51:3); חמש, "five" (Ezek. 48:16); אם, "if" (Ruth 3:12). Comparison with the other recensions found in *Massekhet Sopherim* VI, 9, and in quantitative form in *Ochlah, no.* 98 and *Massorah Gedolah,* no. 2752, shows that the Masoretic tradition has maintained the title ח׳ כתיב׳ ולא קרי׳, "eight words written, but cancelled in reading," by suppressing the case of Deut. 6:25 (the only one relating to the Torah) and adding the following אם in II Sam. 13:33 and 15:21; את in Jer. 38:16 (substituting for Deut. 6:25) and אם in Jer. 39:12. These differences between the traditions of the Talmud and those of the Masora should not be taken too literally, as if they represented opposing schools. R. Isaac, in the Talmud, presents a general exposition of scribal methodology and does not claim to be exhaustive. The case is different for the latter lists, first in *Massekhet Sopherim,* and subsequently in Masoretic works such as the *Diqduqe ha-Ṭe'amim* or the *Massorah Magna.* It is important to bear in mind that R. Isaac, who belonged to the third generation of Talmudic masters (*'Amora'im*), taught at Babylon toward the close of the third century A.D., whereas the rules in *Massekhet Sopherim* concerning the Bible were compiled anonymously only about the eighth century, and summarized in the tenth by Aaron ben Asher in his *Diqduqe ha-Ṭe'amim.*

4. Other Talmudic statements. The Masora cites a considerable number of QK; authors who have endeavored to reckon up the exact number vary considerably in their estimates. That the practice of QK, the antiquity of which has already been shown, was very widespread is seen in the numerous examples quoted by the Mishna, the Talmud, and the oldest Midrashim (Men. 89b; Bereshit Rabbah XXXIV, etc.). Systematic and carefully argued lists are found for the first time in *Massekhet Sopherim* VII, etc. Eventually these lists would be methodically revised in Masoretic treatises such as the *Ochlah,* so as to ensure their transmission in the statistical form that we know today (cf. nos. 112-13; 119-20). Ch. VIII of *Massekhet Sopherim,* while detailing the systematic variants between the Psalter text of Ps. 18 and the version found in II Sam. 22, offers by implication a possible solution to the problem of the origin of the marginal variants. This solution has been taken up by Sperber and integrated into one of the most interesting theories on this question (cf. §8eiii *below*).

5. Symbols, terminology, and form of the QK. *a*) It is easy to understand how the terms *qere* and *kethibh* originated. We have already seen the use of the Aramaic formula in plural form, as employed by R. Isaac in T.B. Ned. 37b: קריין ולא כתיבן. The same terminology is taken up again in *Massekhet Sopherim* VI, 4 by the anonymous author who compiled the first lists of QK: שלשה לא כתובים בלמ״ד אל״ף וקרואים לו, "three instances of *lō'* [viz., Exod. 21:8; Lev. 11:21 and 25:30] are written *lāmedh-'āleph,* but read as *lāmedh-wāw* (*lô*)." This terminology is related to another usage of the Talmudic masters. For example, in T.B. Ber. 64a and *passim,* R. Eleazar, in the name of R. Ḥanina, declares: "The wise men increase peace in this world, as it is said (Isa. 54:13): 'All thy children (*bānāyikh*) are taught by God and their peace is great,' אל תקרי בָּנָיִךְ אלא בוניךְ—do not read *bānāyikh* (thy children), but *bônāyikh* (thy builders, i.e., the scholars)." Hence the formula אַל תִּקְרֵי. . . אֶלָּא (or תִּקְרִי, Aramaic form), "do not read . . . but," means "change the traditional Masoretic reading for homiletical purposes." The expression, then, originated in a learned, homiletic play on words, of which the Talmud and the Midrash give numerous and frequent examples. From this original connotation of an oral correction of homiletic character, the phrase gradually came to be used to denote the requirements of oral standardization, systematic or sporadic, which would eventually be laid down definitively by the Masoretic tradition.

b) The QK formulas, in their permanent form, were hardly ever noted in the margins. The most ancient indication of the existence of an oral variant was the presence of a sign or symbol in the margin. Many examples are to be found in the oldest and most celebrated MSS (Petropolitanus B 3 and B 19a from Leningrad, C from Cairo, etc.). This sign, thick and elongated in character——has been likened to an archaic, final ן (*nûn*), though this does not explain its origin. From the oldest MSS, however, we know that, between the tenth and eleventh centuries, the scribes had already forgotten its meaning. In fact, both this sign and the QK, in the form known today, are noted in the margin in the following cases: Ezek. 40 *in toto* in Petropolitanus (*see* Fig. Q1); Jer. 2:33; 3:2, 4, 7 in the Qaraite MS of the Prophets from Cairo; and Job 39:30 in MS B 19a from Leningrad.

c) A number of stages preceded the final, marginal form of the *qere* that was ultimately adopted unanimously by the scribes. In rare cases—those of very ancient and worn MSS with supralinear Palestinian vocalization—what is noted in the margin is not the whole word, as is done now, but only the particular letter in its proposed corrected form. In the oldest MSS with supralinear Babylonian, or with Tiberian vocalization, rather than the sign  one finds the letter קׄ, abbreviation for קרי, above which is written the new letter proposed by the marginal reading. E.g., in MS L, at Lev. 13:20, הוא (*hû'*) is noted in the margin by קׄ, to warn the reader to read היא (*hî'*). Similarly, in the margin of the same MS, another abbreviated form of QK is found in abundance in Ezek. 40, for example vs. 25, where the word וְאֵילַמָּו has the note למיו קׄ in the margin. *See* Fig. Q1.

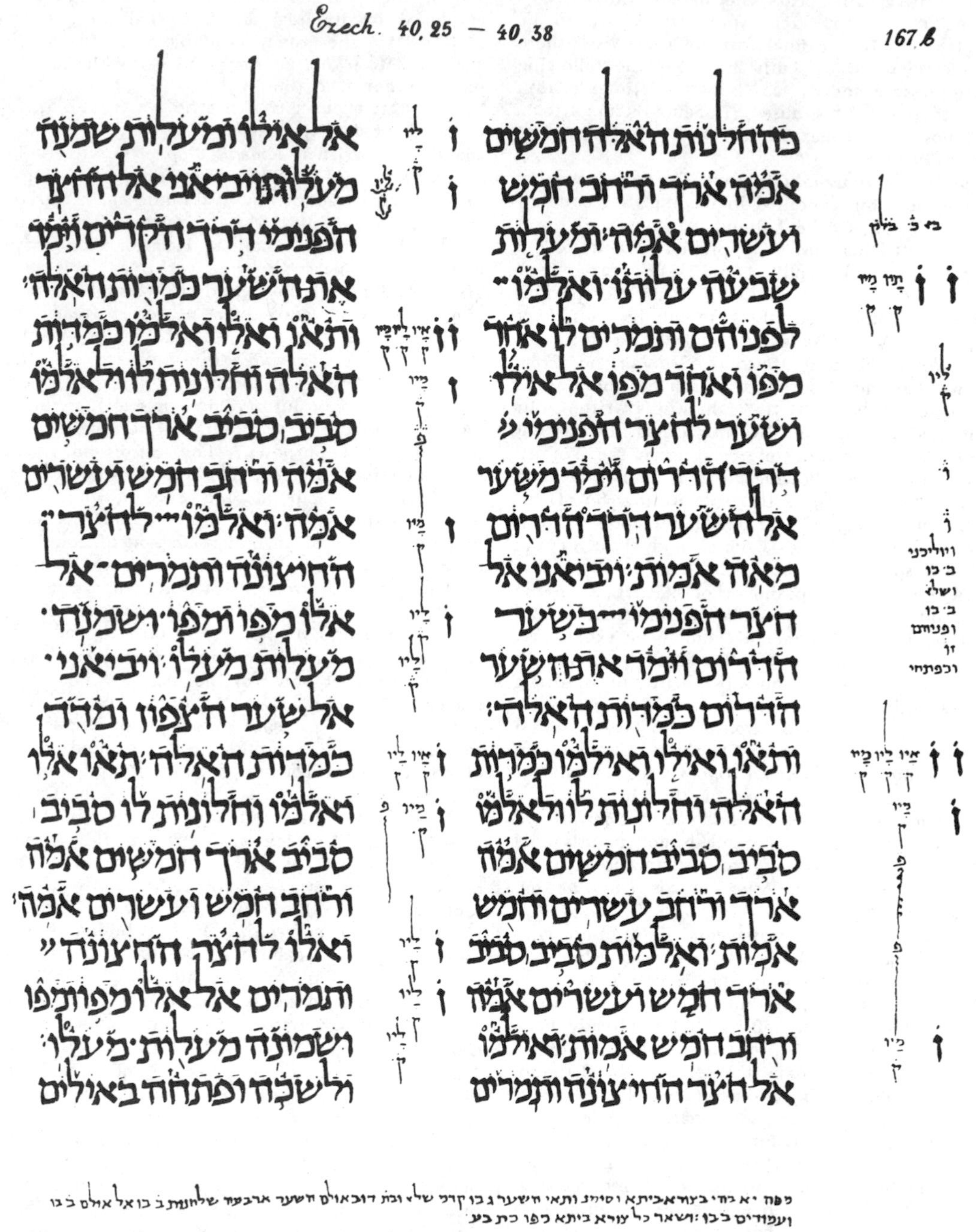

Courtesy G. E. Weil

1. A page from Codex Petropolitanus, displaying archaic and more recent *qere* notations

d) In their normal form, the QK of good Masoretic MSS are written out in full in the margin, e.g., הַיְצֵא of Gen. 8:17 has the marginal annotation היצא ק. When the Masoretes fixed the traditional enunciation of the sacred text, they pointed the word in the consonantal text with the vowels of the word to be read orally. This is the case with the preceding example, where, instead of הוצא we are to read the surprising הַיְצֵא, a form which occurs nowhere else in the Bible. Editors of the Hebrew Bible since Bomberg have felt obligated to follow this model in their editions. However, recent editors, such as C. D. Ginsburg and A. S. Hartom, have tried to facilitate the reader's task by printing the *kethibh* without any vowels, and then vocalizing the proposed word (*qere*) in the margin.

e) Besides these classic forms of QK, there are other marginal notes which, in fact, have the same function. For instance, at Ezra 4:11, ארתחששתא is annotated in MS L with יתיר א לא קר, "'*āleph* superfluous (not rendered audibly) in reading," while other MSS have ארתחששת ק, written without '*āleph*, as is found a few verses earlier at Ezra 4:7. Also in MS L, in connection with אָהֳלֹה (Gen. 9:21; 12:8; 13:3; 35:21; cf. *Massorah Gedolah,* no. 83), there occurs three times the Masoretic note ד׳ כת׳ ה, "four times written fully with a *hē'*," and only once, at Gen. 13:3, the *qere* ו ק for אהלו ק. It is not difficult to see that this *qere* is a needless repetition of the note of the MP, and points to two recensions of the same Masoretic teaching (cf. also *Massorah Gedolah,* nos. 598, 2917, etc.).

f) In sum, then, the *qere* tradition has been transmitted in various ways. Some MSS offer a simple reminder without explicit annotation (the above-mentioned archaic sign). Others have an explicit marginal note. Others again qualify their marginal corrections with the words יתיר, "superfluous," מלא or שלם, *"plene,"* and חסיר, "defective." In some cases the Masoretes have also used the qualifications סבירין, "conjectures," and משתבשין, "erroneous," in the case of doubtful or difficult readings. Since no explicit rule was ever promulgated with regard to the QK formulas, scholars differ notably in the number they find in the margins of the MSS. Levita numbered 848, Cappellus found 1,548 in the Bomberg Bible and 1,566 in that of Plantin. Gordis found 1,350, and the recent edition of the *Masora parva* of the BHS reckons 1,272, excluding the *qere perpetuum.* No estimate can be considered final if we bear in mind the minimal figure given by Levita, and the much larger number proposed by Ginsburg (in *The Massorah,* under letter *kaph,* nos. 488 ff.).

6. Purpose of the QK. Systematic study of the *qere* tends to show that they concern basically three kinds of corrections. The following general classification by Gordis may be accepted.

a. Guide against blasphemy: cases where the Tetragrammaton is not pronounced, and the word "Lord" or "God" is substituted in reading.

b. Guide against obscenity: cases where the text has a word which might sound too coarse when read in the synagogue, and the reader is enjoined to substitute a euphemism.

c. Guide against erroneous reading. With regard to this extensive class—which may be further divided into nine subsections—it must be borne in mind that discrepancies of this kind between the *kethibh* and the *qere,* when traced to their sources, are not simply a means of preserving MS variants. They may also be closely linked with the ultimate goal of Masoretic activity: textual standardization, specifically between passages transmitted in parallel recensions, as Sperber has shown (*see* §8diii *below; see also* Text, Hebrew, History of[S] §2). These notes, then, directed as they were to the standardization of the sacred text, were introduced at the same time as vocalization was inserted into the text. As guideposts for the reader, they warn against faulty enunciation in consequence of: (1) difference in the division of words; (2) pronunciation of the archaic diphthong *ay;* (3) other archaic forms; (4) phonetic variants in the light of the new philological system just elaborated by the Tiberian school; (5) fluctuation in the morphology of nouns; (6) fluctuation in the morphology of verbs; (7) variations in agreement; (8) variations in the use of particles; (9) other nonclassifiable Masoretic options.

7. The seven classes of QK according to Elias Levita. In the first section of the second table of his celebrated *Massoret ha-Massoret,* Levita divided the QK, on the basis of external resemblances, into "seven classes, corresponding to the seven kinds of fruit for which the Holy Land was famed (Deut. 8:8)."

a) Letters of words which are read from the margin, but not written in the text, and vice versa. This affects principally the letters *yōdh, hē', wāw,* and '*āleph,* occurring at the beginning, end, or middle of a word.

b) Letters which are interchanged in the *qere* and the *kethibh.* This, too, occurs principally with the letters *yōdh, hē', wāw,* and '*āleph.*

c) Transpositions of letters: In the text, the letter is placed later in the word than it should be, while the marginal reading restores it to its correct, earlier position.

d) When two words are in sequence and the first has taken a letter which belongs to the second. This happens only with the preformative letter *hē'*, erroneously placed at the end of the first word instead of at the beginning of the second. Accordingly, the Masoretes pointed it in the text with the vowel *pathaḥ* (a), while in the marginal reading it is made the definite article of the next word.

e) Entire words written in the text, but not read, as well as words read from the margin but not found in the text.

f) Expressions written as one word in the text, but read in the margin as two, and vice versa.

g) The substitution of euphemisms for ill-sounding phrases (*see* §6*b above*).

8. Theories on the supposed origin of the qere-kethibh. *a. Source of the theories.* In general, theories that have arisen since the Middle Ages and place the origin of the QK at the time of Ezra have their source in a celebrated passage of classical Jewish literature (J.T. Ta'an. IV.2; *Abot de-Rabbi Natan B* XLVI; *Sifre* Deut. 356; *Massekhet Sopherim* VI.4): "R. Shime'on b. Laqish said: 'three scrolls of the Law were found in the Temple court (עזרה).... In one they found written מעון, and in the other two was written מעונה אלהי קדם (Deut. 33:27); they adopted the two and discarded the one. In the one they found written וישלח את זאטוטי (Exod. 24:5), and in the two was written וישלח את נערי; they adopted the two and discarded the one. In the one they found הוא written eleven times, and in the two היא was written eleven times; they adopted the two and discarded the one.'" This passage was a source of confusion because of the similarity between the words עזרה ('*azarah*), "the Temple court," and עזרא, "Ezra [the scribe]." For it was to Ezra and to the teachers of his time that tradition ascribed not only the collecting of the canonical books of the Bible, but also the invention of vocalic signs in the text and of signs for cantillation. The text we have just quoted, however, simply speaks of the presence, in the buildings of the temple court, of texts which were used periodically to standardize the Sacred Scriptures; there is no reference, even implied, to Ezra the scribe.

b. Early Jewish opinions. Both the Fathers of the church and the Jewish medieval writers held that the compilation of the QK was the work of Ezra and his colleagues. However, these authors already differed as to the fundamental norms that necessitated these marginal variants. David Qimḥi (*ca.* 1160?-1235?), in his introduction to the Former Prophets, traces the origin of the QK to the Babylonian exile and its detrimental effect on sacred MSS, in consequence of which many variants made their appearance in the texts. The *qere* is thus a variant encountered and preserved by Ezra and his successors.

Abrabanel (b. Lisbon 1437, d. Venice 1508), in the introduction to his commentary on the book of Jeremiah, refutes the opinion of his predecessors: "For how can I believe with my heart, and speak with my lips, that Ezra the scribe found the book of the Law of God and the books of his holy Prophets in a disordered state, due to deletions and mistakes? Is not that scroll of the Law illegal in which one letter is omitted?" He proposes that a *qere* is Ezra's observation about or correction of an unusual form in the text, a form which goes back to the biblical author.

c. The synthesis of Elias Levita and the first indications of the Masoretic origin of the QK. For Qimḥi, the QK originated in the misfortunes undergone by the Sacred Writings during the Babylonian exile. This view was followed by the Buxtorfs, Matthew Hiller, and J. G. Carpzov, and underlay the thinking of those schools which saw in the QK the result of divergences between the ancient MSS. In opposition to this was another school, first represented by the opinion of Abrabanel, which viewed the QK as the product of an effort to suppress erroneous readings. Elias Levita took into account both theories. Though he acknowledged that Ezra was the initiator of the work of scribal criticism, he endeavored, however imperfectly, to seek the reasons for the QK in the process of standardization of the consonantal text, a process which would attain its apogee after the completion of the Talmud, thanks to the philological work of the Masoretic schools at Tiberias. It is to Levita's critical analysis that we owe the first attempt to date the schools of Masoretic vocalization.

d. Modern theories. J. G. Eichhorn, H. F. W. Gesenius, W. M. L. de Wette, A. Dillmann, J. Koenig, and Z. Frankel upheld the view that the QK originated in the variants between the most ancient MSS. On the other hand, in support of the view that the QK were the result of critical work on erroneous readings, we have, first, J. Morinus and R. Simon, and later, H. Strack, C. D. Ginsburg, and J. Wellhausen. In favor of Levita's synthesis of the two theories, we have Cappellus, and later, J. Derenbourg. In our own day, three authors have re-examined the problem.

i. Orlinsky, on the basis of his study of the LXX, attempts to reformulate the problem of the origin of the QK. The Masoretes, he holds, "were neither correctors nor selectors; i.e., they did not deal with the Hebrew text of the Bible subjectively, *ad hoc,* deciding each reading within its own context." As Levita, by implication, had already done, he assigns to the same time period the invention of vocalic signs and the establishment of the QK. "The chronology," he continues, "is certain enough: neither the Babylonian nor the Palestinian Talmud makes any mention at all of either of these two phenomena, or contains any reference to their technical terminology; and St. Jerome, who evinced an especial interest in the Hebrew text . . . knows nothing about vowel symbols or the QK system." Referring to the above-quoted text on the three scrolls of the Law in the temple court, Orlinsky claims that the Masoretes first selected the three best MSS available to them. Where the three MSS had no variant readings, no difficulty was experienced in vocalizing the text. Where, however, the MSS differed, the Masoretes accepted the reading of the majority and vocalized it, and the reading became the *qere.*

ii. In one of the longest and best studies devoted to the problem (*The Biblical Text in the Making*), Gordis adduces evidence for the division of the QK into several groups, belonging to different periods, and so, for the first time since Levita, offers an attempt at dating to resolve the problem. The most ancient group was meant to guide the reader by supplying *matres lectionis,* and by removing readings which seemed blasphemous or unbecoming. The second and more recent group consists of variants bearing on one word or on a group of words. This second group includes the greater part of the QK, and its acceptance—as with Orlinsky—would be due to the adoption, toward the end of the period of the second temple, of readings resulting from the collation of the three MSS mentioned in rabbinic tradition. For this second group, however, Gordis proposes a theory closely related to the theory of textual variants. An obvious objection presents itself: Why were there never more than two variants? In the case where the three MSS presented three varying readings, the final reading would have been chosen on the basis of the context and of those philological rules which were already being used for the insertion into the consonantal text of the new vocalization.

iii. One last author has dealt more amply with the problem, and, together with the two preceding scholars, has furnished material for a new in-depth analysis of this question. Sperber has set in clear light the composite nature of much of the Hebrew Bible, resulting from two ancient recensions. The scribes, seeking to standardize the MT, preserved variants from both recensions by means of the QK. This work of standardization, Sperber believes, began very early; the first indications of it are found in the statement of R. Isaac in T.B. Ned. 37b (cf. §3 *above*).

Bibliography. (BHS) *Biblia Hebraica Stuttgartensia,* ed. K. Elliger and W. Rudolph, Masoram elaboravit G. E. Weil (1968-76).

On the Masora: S. Frensdorff, *Das Buch Ochlah*

W'Ochlah (1864), and *Die Massorah Magna* (1876 [rev. ed., 1968, with a prolegomenon by G. E. Weil]); C. D. Ginsburg, *Introduction to the Massoretico-Critical Edition of the Hebrew Bible* (1897), and *The Massorah compiled from Mss. alphabetically arranged,* 4 vols. (1887-1907); G. E. Weil, *Massorah Gedolah, juxta codicem Leningradensem B 19a* (1971).

On §2: A. Geiger, *Urschrift und Übersetzungen der Bibel in ihrer Abhängigkeit von der innern Entwicklung des Judentums* (2nd ed., 1928); D. Barthélemy, "Les Tiqquné Sopherim et la Critique Textuelle de l'Ancien Testament," VTSup, IX (1963), 285-304.

On §7: E. Levita, *Massoret ha-Massoret* (1539); C. D. Ginsburg, *The Massoreth ha-Massoreth of Elias Levita* (Hebrew with ET 1867 [2nd ed., 1968]); G. E. Weil, *Elie Lévita, Humaniste et Massorète* (1963).

On §8*a*: J. Z. Lauterbach, "The three books found in the Temple at Jerusalem," *JQR,* VIII (1917-18), 385-423; S. Talmon, "The three scrolls of the Law that were found in the Temple court," *Textus,* II (1962), 14-27.

On §8*d*: J. G. Eichhorn, *Einleitung in das AT,* 5 vols. (4th ed., 1923); S. Bamberger, "Die Bedeutung des Qeri-Kethib, ein Beitrag zur Geschichte der Exegese," in *Jahrbuch der Jüdisch-literarischen Gesellschaft,* XV (1923), with fairly complete bibliog. on the history of the QK; J. Morinus, *Exercitationes biblicae de hebraici graecique textus sinceritate* (1633); R. Simon, *Histoire Critique du Vieux Testament* (1678); H. L. Strack, *Prolegomena Critica in VT hebraicum* (1873); F. Bleek, J. Wellhausen, *Einleitung in das AT* (6th ed., 1893); L. Cappellus, *Arcanum punctuationis revelatum* (1624); *Critica Sacra* (1605); J. Derenbourg, "Manuel du Lecteur d'un auteur inconnu," *JA,* 6th ser. XV (1870), 309-550.

On §8*di*: H. M. Orlinsky, "The import of the Kethib-Qere and the Massoretic Note on Lekah, Judges 19, 13," *JQR,* XXXI (1940-41), 59 ff., and "The origin of the Kethib-Qere system: A new approach," VTSup, VII (1959).

On §8*dii*: R. Gordis, *The Biblical Text in the Making: a Study of the Kethib-Qere* (1937 [rev. ed., with a prolegomenon by the author, "The Origin of the Massoretic Text in the Light of Rabbinic Literature and the Qumran Scrolls," 1971]).

On §8*diii*: A. Sperber, *A Historical Grammar of Biblical Hebrew* (1968), "Hebrew based upon Biblical Passages in Parallel Transmission," *HUCA,* XIV (1939), 153-249, and "Problems of the Masora," *HUCA,* XVII (1942-43), 293-394; G. E. Weil, "La Massorah," *REJ,* CXXXI (1972), 5-104.

G. E. Weil

QUADRATUS. *See* Apostolic Fathers[S] §10.

*__QUMRAN, KHIRBET.__ *See* Dead Sea Scrolls[S].

R

***RABBAH. 1. Bronze Age occupation.** Though the recovery of flint implements from the hills surrounding Jebel el-Kal'ah (the citadel hill of the ancient Ammonite capital) indicates a prehistoric habitation of the area from Paleolithic to Chalcolithic times, sedentary occupation is not attested until the Early Bronze Age (*ca.* 2900-2300 B.C.). While archaeological investigation of Jebel el-Kal'ah has turned up unstratified pottery from most of the major ceramic horizons of Early Bronze, Middle Bronze, and Late Bronze Ages, none so far has been found associated with clearly defined occupation levels, except for MB IIB. N of the Hellenistic-Roman wall in the citadel area has been uncovered what seems to be a section of an MB IIB Hyksos-type glacis with associated walls, suggesting a rather heavily fortified settlement from this period (*ca.* 1750-1550 B.C.). Four tomb groups from the surrounding area have produced pottery, scarabs, and cylinder seals dating from the whole span of MB II B-C (1750-1550). All the evidence suggests a rather significant occupation on and around the site of Rabbah, particularly during MB II. The few LB sherds recovered from unstratified contexts on the citadel point to a continuing occupation during the LB period, an occupation which perhaps should be associated with the so-called LB temple discovered on the edge of the Amman airport in 1955 and most extensively excavated in 1966. Though its function as a temple has been disputed, both its form and content agree better with a cultic than a military or domestic interpretation. However, during the period before its abandonment in the early thirteenth century B.C., certain architectural changes removed the building's presumed cultic feature so that at the end it could well have been only a lookout tower or dwelling, though overwhelming support for this is not present. That, as recently proposed, the temple may have been built to serve as a tribal league shrine for the early Ammonite and/or related tribes is very problematical in the absence of any historical references to such a confederation in this period.

2. The Iron Age city. Small-scale excavations carried out sporadically since 1957, under the auspices of the Department of Antiquities of the Hashemite kingdom of Jordan, have produced the first stratified remains of Rabbah from the Iron I and Iron II periods (*ca.* 1200-580 B.C.). Especially noteworthy was the uncovering of phases of the tenth-ninth-century Iron Age defense wall. The first rebuilding of this wall dates to the early tenth century B.C., and perhaps can be associated with the reconstruction of Rabbah after its capture by David *ca.* 980 B.C. The pottery recovered from this stratum shows a basic Palestinian orientation, as one might expect on the basis of the biblical historical account. A portion of a fine plaster-floored building dating from the eighth century B.C. was the most significant architectural find belonging to the first phase of the Iron II period. It gave evidence of having been destroyed by fire, perhaps as a result of one of the Assyrian incursions against the capital. The final phase of Iron II (seventh-sixth centuries) was illustrated by a few walls too fragmentary for discerning their relation to house or building plans. For recently discovered Ammonite inscriptions, *see* INSCRIPTIONS, SEMITIC[S] §3*c*; AMMON, AMMONITES[S] §5.

Among the more impressive discoveries dating from the Iron II period are a number of fine examples of native sculpture art, including several full representations of what would appear to be kings of Ammon (*see* AMMON, AMMONITES[S] §4). It has been suggested that they were part of a royal shrine or treasury. Augmenting the sculpture collection is the recent discovery of four female double-faced heads, found outside their original architectural context, built into a Hellenistic drain. Based upon parallels with Egyptian multiple-headed Hathor capitals, it would seem that these heads initially served as ornamentation on capitals supporting the roof of an important public building dating from the end of the seventh century B.C.

Bibliography. R. Dornemann, "The Cultural and Archaeological History of the Transjordan in the Bronze and Iron Age" (diss., U. of Chicago, 1971); G. L. Harding, *The Antiquities of Jordan* (rev. ed., 1967), pp. 61-70; J. B. Hennessy, "Excavation of a Late Bronze Age Temple at Amman," *PEQ*, XCVIII (1966), 155-62; W. A. Ward, "Cylinders and Scarabs from a Late Bronze Temple at 'Amman," *ADAJ*, VIII-IX (1964), 47-55; "Scarabs, Seals and Cylinders from Two Tombs at Amman," *ADAJ*, XI (1966), 5-18; F. Zayadine, "Recent Excavations on the Citadel of Amman," *ADAJ*, XVIII (1973), 17-35.

G. M. LANDES

***RABBAH (OF JUDAH).** Aharoni proposes to identify this town with Khirbet Ḥamîdeh (which he called Khirbet Bîr el-Ḥilū), two miles W of Bâb el-Wâd beside the road to Laṭrûn. Josh. 15:60 indicates that Rabbah and Kiriath-baal (-jearim) were the W and E anchor points respectively in a narrow district comprising the corridor from the plain to Jerusalem. Besides the Rubutu of the el-Amarna letters, other references to this town are No. 105, *r-b-t*, in Thut-mose III's topographical list, and No. 13, *r-b-t*, in Shishak's list.

Bibliography. Y. Aharoni, "Rubute and Ginti-kirmil," *VT*, XIX (1969), 137-45.

A. F. RAINEY

***RACHEL'S TOMB.** The oldest tradition concerning the location of Rachel's tomb placed it near

Kiriath-jearim (Deir al-'Azar), *ca.* eight miles W of the Old City of Jerusalem. Two other places also claim connection with the tomb, Bethlehem and Ramah.

The earliest attestation for Ramah (er-Ram, five miles N of Jerusalem) is uncertain; some LXX readings of Jer. 38:15 [H 31:15], quoted in Matt. 2:18, are a remote possibility; Midrash Gen. Rabbah 82:5 (perhaps fourth century, and parallels) is another, if the passage plays on *'prty* (N of Jerusalem!) and *ṣwpym* (both I Sam. 1:1). The connection with Ramah is based on Jer. 31:15 with the translation "A voice is heard in Ramah, lamentation and bitter weeping. Rachel is weeping for her children." It enjoys wide acceptance today, but it is wrong. (1) Burials, graves, or the like do not figure in the text. (2) This location conflicts with Gen. 35:19-20; 48:7; and I Sam. 10:2. (3) It presupposes a change of vocalization (*bᵉrāmâ* into *bārāmâ*), not required otherwise. (4) It disregards the great similarity of its text with Jer. 3:21. In the light of (3) and (4), Jer. 31:15 is to be translated "A voice is heard on a height." Elevations are places for crying and mourning (Jer. 3:21; Judg. 11:37).

The location of the tomb near Bethlehem rests on the identification of Ephrath(ah) with Bethlehem: "Rachel . . . was buried on the road to Ephrath (that is, Bethlehem)" (Gen. 35:19; similarly 48:7). Though early, this location must also be rejected because the identifying clause is generally and for good reasons taken as an erroneous gloss.

The most probable location is in the vicinity of Kiriath-jearim, based on "Rachel's tomb in the territory of Benjamin at Zelzah" (I Sam. 10:2). (1) It is compatible with the information in Genesis, without the gloss. (2) Kiriath-jearim is one of three towns, another being Bethlehem, whose populations related themselves to Ephrath(ah) (I Chr. 2:50-51; cf. Ps. 132:6, which has a poetic substitution, "Jaar"). (3) The town was at the "border (RSV "territory") of Benjamin" of the probable pre-Davidic extent of the tribal area. (4) For Zelzah (*ṣelṣaḥ*), the precise though unknown location, the LXX has five different renderings. While three agree with the Hebrew in various ways, two point to the neighborhood of Kiriath-jearim (Tsevat, pp. 112-13). (5) The part of the LXX that agrees with the Hebrew (and has so far not been related onomastically to Kiriath-jearim) suggests the emendation Ze/iloh (*ṣē/ īloaḥ*) for Zelzah. Ze/iloh is very close to the name *silona* used for Kiriath-jearim by the seventh-century pilgrim Theodosius. Thus this location is consistent with all extant information (excluding the gloss of Genesis), and shows that the divergent LXX renderings in reality converge on one place and its immediate vinicity.

The gloss of Genesis, "(that is, Bethlehem)," reflects the situation of a later time when, possibly, the area of Ephrath(ah) did not extend as far as Kiriath-jearim any more, and when the matriarchs were no longer connected exclusively with the tribes of their genealogies (Gen. 29; 30) but had become mothers of the whole nation. At that time the tomb of the "mother" of Joseph and Benjamin could be shown anywhere in the land of Israel, Judean Bethlehem not excepted.

Bibliography. Theodosius, "De situ terrae sanctae," in P. Geyer, *Itinera hierosolymitana saeculi IIII-VIII* (1898), pp. 138-50; R. A. S. Macalister, "The Topography of Rachel's Tomb," *PEFQS* (1912), pp. 74-82; M. Tsevat, "Interpretation of I Sam. 10:2," *HUCA*, XXXIII (1962), 107-18; E. Vogt, "Benjamin geboren 'eine Meile' von Ephrata," *Bibl.*, LVI (1975), 30-36.

M. Tsevat

*__RAINBOW.__ Bow and Arrow and Rainbow (the Hebrew and Greek terms being the same, except for use of ἶρις instead of τόξον in Rev. 4:3; 10:1) omitted reference to sexual symbolism. Both bow and arrow are potent masculine symbols, as the quiver is understandably a feminine symbol. Job, harking back to the days of his youthful vigor, says:

> My root spread out to the waters,
> with the dew all night on my branches,
> my glory fresh with me,
> and my bow ever new in my hand (Job 29:19-20).

Failure to apprehend the sexual symbolism of the bow has been a cause of confusion in the renderings of Gen. 49:22-25, from ancient versions to the modern. The characterization of Joseph as a "wild colt" (ABi and NAB) or a "wild ass" (NJV) seems more likely than the traditional "fruitful bough." The male ass is notorious for sexual power, but the possible sexual implications of the bow symbolism appear to have been missed:

> Yet each one's bow stayed rigid,
> and their arms were unsteady (Gen. 49:24, ABi).

> But each one's bow remained stiff,
> as their arms were unsteady (NAB).

The suggestion of phallic symbolism is plainer in NJV:

> Yet his bow stayed taut,
> And his arms were made firm.

The possessive pronominal suffix, "his," certainly refers to Joseph, rather than to his assailants.

Ps. 127:4-5 likens sons sired in a man's youth to arrows in a warrior's quiver. Elsewhere (Ecclus. 26:12) the arrow figures the phallus and the quiver the vulva in the complaint about the "headstrong" daughter who, like the thirsty wayfarer who will drink any water, will "squat before any post and open her quiver to the arrow."

Both the quiver (full of arrows) and the tensile bow are symbols of virility in Mesopotamian literature. An incantation for male potency petitions, "May the [qu]iver not become e[mpt]y, may the bow not be slack" and in the accompanying ritual are instructions for making of model bows to be used in the rites (R. D. Biggs, *ŠÀ.ZI.GA, Ancient Mesopotamian Potency Incantations* [1967], p. 37, No. 18, lines 3-4). In a curse sanctioning a treaty we have the imprecation: "As for the men, may the Mistress of Women take away their bow." The Hittites, wishing to destroy the prowess of their enemies, prayed to Ishtar of Nineveh: "Take from [their] men masculinity, prowess, robust health, swords (?), battle axes, bows, arrows, and dagger[s]! And bring them to Hatti! Place in their hand the spindle and mirror of a woman! Dress them as women!" The removal of a warrior's bow or other weapon was thus more than mere disarmament; it was also a humiliation and ceremonial emasculation, making the warrior a woman.

Some interpreters find bow symbolism in the phallic imagery of lines 37, 40, 43-44, 46-47 of the Ugaritic *hieros gamos* text 23 [52]. F. M. Cross, e.g. (*Canaanite Myth and Hebrew Legend,* p. 23), rendered line 37 thus:

il. ḫṭh. nḥt	El bends his bowstave,
il. ymnn, mṭ ydh	He drew his mighty shaft.

The noun *ḫṭ* (=Akkad. *ḫaṭṭu,* "scepter, staff, stick, branch") is alleged to mean "bowstave" here while the verb *nḥt,* "descend," is given the sense "bend [a bow]" on the basis of II Sam. 22:35 (=Ps. 18:34 [H 35]), an obscure and probably corrupt passage which none of the ancient versions understood to refer to the bending of a bow. Many interpreters, including the present writer, have taken *ḫṭ* in the established sense of "rod" or "staff" and the verb *nḥt* also in the usual sense "be low," thus making the divine member a drooping rod rather than a taut bow. In any case, whether the *yd,* "hand" (i.e., *membrum virile*) of El is represented as a staff or a bow, or as drooping or taut, the passage is concerned with male potency or the lack of it.

In the Ugaritic epic of Aqhat a crucial episode involves the masculine symbolism of the bow (Hillers) and a conflict with the Virgin Anath, goddess of love and war, who covets the bow of the young hero and tries to get it from him with offers of silver and gold, immortality, and perhaps love (*ANET* [2nd ed.], p. 151). The brash young hero spurns all offers and (apparently) suggests that the goddess as a female has no business with a bow. The goddess is incensed and begins a series of actions which culminate in the assassination of Aqhat in order to get his bow.

The bow in the clouds as a reminder of the covenant (Gen. 9:12-13) takes on new significance with the appreciation of possible sexual symbolism. As a sign that God's wrath had ceased, it was explained (Nachmanides on Gen. 9:12) that the end of the bow pointed downward, as the warrior lowers his bow in declaring peace. It is at the same time a sign that the divine glory and potency persists. Ezekiel's vision of the gleaming loins of the anthropoid rider of the marvelous vehicle evoked comparison with the rainbow (Ezek. 1:26-28). Whether the attention to the loins (Ezek. 1:27) is connected with the figure of the bow is moot. The rabbis generally disapproved of bowing down at the sight of the rainbow, which might appear to be worship of rain, but there is a blessing to be recited on seeing it (T.B. Ber. 59a).

Bibliography. H. A. Hoffner, Jr., "Symbols for Masculinity and Femininity: Their Use in Ancient Near Eastern Sympathetic Magic Rituals," *JBL,* LXXXV (1966), 326-34; D. R. Hillers, "The Bow of Aqhat: The Meaning of a Mythological Theme," in *Occident and Orient,* ed. H. Hoffner (1973), pp. 71-80, *Treaty-Curses and the OT Prophets* (1964), pp. 66-68, on the theme "Warriors become women."

M. H. POPE

*__RAMOTH-GILEAD.__ An important administrative center and fortress E of the Sea of Galilee, located in the E part of the territory of Gad.

1. History. Ramoth-gilead was one of the three cities of refuge located E of the Jordan (Deut. 4:43; Josh. 20:8). It was assigned to the sons of Merari, of the tribe of Levi (Josh. 21:38; I Chr. 6:80). Solomon made the city the administrative center of his sixth province, which included Bashan and upper Gilead, and contained sixty fortified towns, "with gate-bars of bronze" (I Kings 4:13 NEB). Before the death of Solomon in 922 B.C., Rezon established the independence of the Aramean kingdom of Damascus from Israel (I Kings 11:23-25), and Ramoth-gilead, located on the constantly shifting border between the two kingdoms, was caught in their struggles over the next two hundred years.

2. Location. The precise location of Ramoth-gilead has not been established with certainty. In the *Onomasticon* the site is placed fifteen miles W of Philadelphia (Amman). But both the references to the united kingdom's administrative centers and the descriptions of the conflicts with Aram demand a site farther N. At least three sites have been rivals for identification as Ramoth-gilead: Ramtha, Tell el-Husn, and Tell er-Ramith. Surface surveys failed to produce ceramic evidence supporting the claim of either Tell el-Husn or Ramtha, but, while not conclusive, the material from excavations at Tell er-Ramith supports Nelson Glueck's early identification of that site as Ramoth-gilead. The continuity of the name also supports the identification, as does the geographical location. It is a tell seventy miles S of Damascus on the Wadi Shomer, in the middle of a rich valley fifteen miles E of Irbid. Most important of all is the occupational history of the site as determined by ceramic and architectural evidence. The ceramic groups contain Iron Age pottery from Israel and from Syria. The stratigraphic evidence for the construction and destruction of the defenses and buildings on Ramith was precise. All the evidence conforms to the history of Ramoth-gilead as presented in the OT from the time of Solomon to the destructive campaign of Tiglath-pileser III in 733 B.C. The lack of evidence for the occupation of Ramith from the period before Solomon provides a problem in interpretation. However, this lack supports the critical view of R. de Vaux and others that the institution of refuge cities is not related to tribal organization and does not antedate the reign of Solomon.

Bibliography. P. Lapp, "Tell er-Rumeith," *ASOR,* No. 6, October, 1967; R. de Vaux, *Ancient Israel* (1961).

H. M. JAMIESON

*__RECHABITES__ [בית רכבים, probably house of (chariot) riders; LXX οἶκος Αρχαβιν]. A group of metallurgists or smiths whose peculiar life-style was derived from their occupational pattern.

The Rechabites are typically described as a puritanical, clan-like association which lived in a nomadic setting and proscribed wine-drinking, house-building, and vineyard husbandry as a religiously based protest against the prevalent way of life in the cities of the divided monarchy. This interpretation views them as extreme examples of the ideal toward which the prophets tended and maintains that both operated out of an ideology in which anti-urbanism was the negative pole of a position which had a nomadic ideal as its positive pole.

Recent studies have challenged both the importance of a nomadic ideal in Israel and the assumption that the Rechabites' regulations derived from nomadism and sought to raise the nomadic life to the level of religious principle. A group such as the Rechabites have been purported to be has no social parallel in the ancient Near East. An often-cited Nabatean group, mentioned by Diodorus of Sicily (XIX.xciv.2-4) is not a genuine parallel, owing to historical distance, the disparate function of the two disciplines, and the general cautions applicable in the use of sources concerning the NABATEANS.

Since the Rechabites of Jeremiah's day looked upon J(eh)onadab-ben-Rechab as their "father," II Kings 10:15-17 was regarded as the account of the origin of their sect. This passage, however, gives no indication that J(eh)onadab represented a nomadic ideal or that he lived a nomadic existence. Evidence for the social location of J(eh)onadab is perhaps found in his name, which combines the theophoric element J(eh)o with the root *n-d-b*. The noun *nādhîbh* denotes a member of the ruling nobility. All names in the OT containing the root *n-d-b* belong to members of this class (Exod. 6:23; I Sam. 31:2; I Kings 4:14; 14:20; I Chr. 3:18), and there is no reason to consider J(eh)onadab an exception.

In considering the second element in the name (ben-Rechab), one cannot say whether *ben* implies a father-son relationship or a descendant of Rechab (possibly the one mentioned in II Sam. 4:2 ff.) or whether, like the Akkadian *māru* and *aplu,* it indicates membership in an occupational group or guild. The guild head was called "father"; apprentices were called "sons." In Ugaritic texts, there is a specialty group in royal service called *ḥrš-mrkbt,* "chariot-makers" or "wainwrights" (*UT* 114:8; 308:6; 1024:24; 1039:13), and the designation ben-Rechab might indicate that J(eh)onadab belonged to a similar occupational group. A cognate of ben-Rechab appears on an Aramaic seal impression from Zenjirli-Samal, belonging to *br rkb* (Bar-Rakkab), son of Panammu II (733-727 B.C.). The principal god of Bar-Rakkab was Rakkab-El, and it is generally agreed that Rakkab-El means "Charioteer of El," whose symbol on the Kilamu Orthostat and elsewhere is a chariot yoke (=Rakkab) and a winged disc (=El). This deity is related to the [d] *Bé-ʿ-li-ra-kab-bi* (*ša URUSa-ma-al-la*), "Lord of the Chariot," of cuneiform sources. Such parallels, as well as the employment of hypocorisms in the OT, suggest that *bn rkb* may be equivalent to *br rkb* (*'l*) and thus mean "son of the charioteer of El (or God)." It is perhaps significant that the alliance mentioned in II Kings 10 is made in Jehu's chariot, possibly presupposing prior association of the men in the royal chariotry, J(eh)onadab being either chariot maker and/or chariot driver. *See* YA'UDI[S].

Probably the most that can be said is that J(eh)onadab was a supporter of Yahwism in the face of the threat of Baalism under the Omrides. It is fanciful to assert that he was a naïve man of the wilderness, or to assume that there existed a group of "Proto-Rechabites" who were ready to follow the lead of a champion of the nomadic ideal.

Seeing the Rechabites in Jer. 35 as defenders of a nomadic ideal depends upon the assumption that abstention from intoxicants is a distinctive trait of nomadic society, that tent-dwelling necessarily indicates nomadism, and that refraining from agriculture implies nomadism. It is questionable whether these cultural traits should be interpreted as exclusive indicators of nomadism, and it has been suggested that the Rechabites were craftsmen, probably a guild of metalworkers involved in the manufacture of chariots and weaponry, among other things.

The smith commanded technical lore which was jealously guarded and handed down from generation to generation. Thus metallurgists in antiquity formed endogamous lines with long genealogies, a fact accounting for the lengthy existence of the Rechabites. The smith moved from one location to another in search of ore and/or fuel, thus precluding establishment of a fixed domicile and agriculture. The teetotalism of the Rechabites is not a distinctive trait of nomadism and can just as well be seen as another measure for guarding trade secrets.

Jeremiah's praise of the Rechabites is not a positive valuation of their discipline's content, but rather of their obedience to a command. Thus Jer. 35 does not support a nomadic ideal on the part of Jeremiah or the other prophets.

The supposition that the Rechabites were a guild of craftsmen is further supported by genealogies in I Chr. 2 and 4. A genealogy reconstructed by combining references from these chs. lists the sons of various clans (or guild members) in such a way that clansman "X" becomes the father of place "Y," e.g., 4:12 may be translated: "Eshton begot Beth-rapha and Paseah, and Tehinnah the father of Ir-nahash. These are the men of Rechab." Ir-nahash can mean "City of Copper" or "City of Smiths" and is identified with Khirbet Nahas in the northern Arabah. Ch. 4 includes references to other groups of craftsmen (4:14, 21, 23). In I Chr. 2:55 the Rechabites are associated with the Kenites: "These are the Kenites [or smiths] who came from Hammath, the father of the house of Rechab." This reference is significant in that the house of Rechab is again connected with a site and Kenites, who appear to have made their livelihood as metal craftsmen and may have introduced metallurgy to the Israelites. It has been suggested that the Kenites were a group of ironsmiths who migrated from the Hittite Empire after its destruction.

In rabbinic literature there are references to the Rechabites which allow the inference that they continued to exist during the second commonwealth, but whether they continued to exercise their craft during the period of the second temple and later is subject to doubt.

Bibliography. S. Abramsky, "The House of Rechab," *Eretz Israel,* VIII (1967), 255-64 (Heb. with Eng. summary, p. 76*); M. Eliade, *The Forge and the Crucible* (1962); R. J. Forbes, *Studies in Ancient Technology,* VIII (1964); F. S. Frick, "The Rechabites Reconsidered," *JBL,* XC (1971), 279-87; G. Mendenhall, *The Tenth Generation* (1973); P. A. Riemann, "Desert and Return to Desert in the Pre-exilic Prophets" (diss., Harvard, 1963-64); S. Talmon, "The Desert Motif in the Bible and in Qumran Literature," in *Biblical Motifs: Origins and Transformations* (1966), pp. 33 ff.

F. S. FRICK

The Rechabites became associated in Jewish legends and rabbinic literature with the lost tribes of Israel, said to have been taken by God to a safe and paradise-like refuge until they could return and claim the land of Palestine. The Christian apocalypse of Zosimus portrays the blessed inhabitants of an island as descendants of the Rechabites. Their ascetic practices follow the commandments given in Jer. 35: they wear no clothing, they eat only the fruit provided for them or the manna which drops from the sky at specific times of the year, drink only the water from a special stream, and have intercourse only once in their lives, following which the woman bears two children, one of whom remains forever chaste.

Bibliography. L. Ginzberg, *The Legends of the Jews* (1938), vol. III, 76-77, 380; vol. V, 96; vol. VI, 29, 134, 409; M. R. James, "Story of Zosimus," *Apocrypha Anecdota,* Text and Studies, II (1893), 96-108; A. Craigie, "The Narrative of Zosimus," *The Ante-Nicene Fathers,* (1893 [repr. 1969]), pp. 219-24; forthcoming ed., trans., and intro. by J. H. Charlesworth and E. G. Martin.

E. G. MARTIN

***RECONCILIATION.** The act of establishing friendship and peace by removing enmity, and the resulting state of oneness. Since in the NT relationship to God primarily is involved, reconciliation, which comes through Christ's cross, is closely related to "at-one-ment" (cf. Rom. 5:11 KJV). (*See* ATONEMENT; DEATH OF CHRIST; FORGIVENESS; MEDIATOR esp. §C3*d*.) The whole of biblical theology may be drawn in as background.

"The NT doctrine of reconciliation" has, in the last century, become a catchword under which all soteriology has been subsumed (cf. SALVATION §5*b*). From A. Ritschl's *Rechtfertigung und Versöhnung* (1870) to the Presbyterian Confession of 1967 it has been used especially of interpersonal, racial, social, and political relationships. Yet the term itself is rare in the Bible (sixteen times in RSV, only once in the OT). It seems to originate in Hellenistic Christianity. Only the Pauline corpus contains the theme, and Paul did not stress reconciliation as much as earlier traditions and his later disciples did.

1. Backgrounds. Reconciliation has to do with personal relationships. The Philistines feared David would betray them to "reconcile (*hithpael* רצה, make pleasing; LXX διαλλάσσω) himself" to Saul (I Sam. 29:4). Moses "would have reconciled" two quarreling Israelites (συνήλλασεν αὐτοὺς εἰς εἰρήνην, Acts 7:26). A wife separated from her husband should "remain single or else be reconciled (καταλλαγήτω)" to him (I Cor. 7:11). Jesus enjoined readiness to reconciliation: "If . . . at the altar . . . [you] remember that your brother has something against you, . . . first be reconciled to your brother" (διαλλάγηθι, Matt. 5:23-24; cf. 6:12—the forgiven disciple must forgive when seeking God's forgiveness—even when the grievance is on the other person's part).

In the OT, cult, law, and prayer are means for reconciling God and people, or person with person, in light of understandings of COVENANT and SIN, especially after the Exile (*see* RECONCILIATION §1). Even so, reconciliation is not an OT term. It begins to appear in II MACCABEES, *ca.* 100 B.C. (it is hoped and prayed God will be "reconciled" to his people [1:5; 5:20; 7:33; 8:29]), in Josephus (Antiq. VI.vii.4, Samuel entreated "God to be reconciled to Saul"), and the rabbis (Str-B, III, 519-20).

In the Greek world, terms from ἀλλάσσω were common for the reconciliation of one person with another, but rare in religion (exception: Sophocles, *Ajax* 744, the chorus hopes Ajax might be "reconciled to the gods from anger").

2. In the Pauline letters. Reconciliation terms occur a dozen times, mostly in passages shaped by hymnic, liturgical, and doxological traditions from the Hellenistic community (Käsemann).

a) Pre-Pauline tradition can be seen in (1) the "Christ hymn" of Col. 1:15-20, which concludes, "through him [Christ] to reconcile [ἀπο-καταλλάξει, the double compound verb unattested prior to its three NT occurrences] to himself [God] all things, whether on earth or in heaven, making peace." The hymn proclaims Christ the cosmocrator who unites what had been separated within the All. The vision is of cosmic peace, like that in Vergil's Fourth Eclogue of the *Pax Romana.* (2) In the hymnic, christological insert in Eph. 2:14-18, based on Isa. 57:19, about "preaching peace," vss. 15*b*-16 speak of Christ's work "making peace" between Jew and Gentile, that he "might reconcile (ἀπο-καταλλάξῃ) us both to God in one body through the cross, thereby bringing the hostility to an end." Here alone is Christ, not God, the subject of "reconcile." (3) Rom. 11:15, if rejection of the Jews "means the reconciliation of the world, what will their acceptance mean but life from the dead?" The abrupt phrase καταλλαγὴ κόσμου seems a formula, akin to (4) II Cor. 5:19-21, "in Christ God was reconciling (καταλλάσσων) the world to himself, not counting their trespasses against them [cf. Rom. 3:25*b,* another pre-Pauline fragment], and entrusting to us the message of reconciliation (τὸν λόγον τῆς καταλλαγῆς) . . . . Be reconciled to God (καταλλάγητε)." Vs. 21 then provides the vicarious, christological base with references, unusual for Paul, to Jesus' sinlessness and to believers as "the righteousness of God." Examples (1) and (2) deal with reconciliation *within* the cosmos, (3) and (4) reconciliation *of* the cosmos with God. (1) is cosmological, (2) ecclesiological, (3) and (4) more anthropological, as is (5) Rom. 5:10-11, "If while we were enemies we were reconciled (κατηλλάγημεν) to God by the death of his Son, much more, now that we are reconciled (καταλλαγέντες), shall we be saved . . . through . . . Christ, through whom we have now received our reconciliation (καταλλαγήν; KJV "atonement")." Only a community which has experienced God's transforming power in Christ, eschatologically realized, can say such things.

b) Paul uses such material to emphasize the justification of "the ungodly" (Rom. 4:5) as the justification of God's "enemies" (5:9-10), but he is aware of dangers from such enthusiast language: individual Christians may see themselves as beyond sin, already fully saved, without need to give themselves in the service of others. Hence Paul welcomes identification with the pre-Pauline theme of "righteousness" (II Cor. 5:21) which he developed as "justification" (*see* RIGHTEOUSNESS IN THE NT and supplementary article). "Righteousness" means we are at "peace with God" (Rom. 5:1) *"without* our doing anything"; reconciliation, that God ended enmity *"before* any effort of man" (Rom. 5:10) (Bultmann). Paul also welcomes the parenetic implications of the imperative "Be reconciled," i.e., live as reconciled persons. He balances "realized eschatology" ("now reconciled") with future hope, and stresses the anthropological rather than the cosmological: II Cor. 5:18, "God . . . reconciled (καταλλάξαντος) *us,"* interprets 5:19, "God was reconciling *the world."* Stressed above all is "the ministry of reconciliation" given in Christ (5:18, parallel to the "ministry of righteousness," II Cor. 3:9, author's trans.).

c) The Deutero-Pauline epistles take a similar line. What Christ "has now reconciled (ἀποκατήλλαξεν) . . . by his death" (Col. 1:22) is designated, not as—in the hymn—"all things," but as "you, who were once estranged and hostile in mind" (1:21), i.e., the Colossians who have believed the gospel Paul preached (1:23). Further, "the body" of Christ, the church, is to be the missionary force extending Christ's lordship in the world (1:21 ff.; cf. Schweizer). Similarly, Eph. 2:15-16 sees the church as the place of reconciliation. Here we may add Heb. 2:15, Christ's death was to "deliver (ἀπαλλάξῃ, NEB "liberate")" those in bondage to death and the devil.

d) An alternative to the traditio-historical view offered above is suggested by Goppelt: Paul himself first designated Christ's work as reconciliation, against a Jewish background (II Maccabees, Josephus, rabbis) and in light of the historical Jesus who taught and practiced love even for enemies and who "died for all" (II Cor. 5:14). But a locus for language about *God* "reconciling" the *world* does not seem to be demonstrable here, as in Hellenistic (-Jewish?) Christianity.

3. Conclusion. Reconciliation, then, is one soteriological concept among many in the Pauline school: God, through Christ's cross, reconciles hostile humans who are to receive the proferred reconciliation/expiation/new-life situation. They are to respond by proclaiming the message of reconciliation about Christ crucified, for God "has enlisted us in this service of reconciliation" (II Cor. 5:18 NEB). From God's side the work of reconcilement is complete; the task of setting it forth in the world goes on. Occasionally in the NT there are hints about reconciliation between persons or parties (Eph. 2:16; cf. Matt. 5:24; I Cor. 7:11), but even in these places the arena is the believing community, and in Eph. 2 reconciliation is primarily "to God through the cross." There are also hints about reconciliation as cosmic harmony, but in Colossians this is interpreted as reconciliation of estranged people to God through missionary proclamation (1:20 ff.). It remained for later theology to expand the theme into a comprehensive doctrine, rich in potential but not without dangers.

Bibliography. F. Büchsel, "αλλάσσω, κτλ.," *TDNT,* I (1933 [ET 1964]), 251-59; L. Morris, *The Apostolic Preaching of the Cross* (1955), pp. 186-223; H.-G. Link and H. Vorländer, "Versöhnung," *Theologisches Begriffslexikon zum NT,* II (1971), cols. 1302-13, covers ἀποκατάστασις (cf. Acts 3:21; *see* RESTORATION), ἱλάσκομαι (*see* EXPIATION; PROPITIATION), and καταλλάσσω; R. Bultmann, *Theology of the NT,* I (1948), 285-87; E. Schweizer, "The Church as the Missionary Body of Christ," *NTS,* VIII (1961), 1-11; E. Käsemann, "Some Thoughts on the Theme 'The Doctrine of Reconciliation in the NT,'" in *The Future of Our Religious Past,* ed. J. M. Robinson (1964 [ET 1971]), pp. 49-64; L. Goppelt, "Versöhnung durch Christus," *Christologie und Ethik* (1968), pp. 147-64; R. Banks, ed., *Reconciliation and Hope* (1975).

J. REUMANN

REDACTION CRITICISM, OT. A special branch of OT research devoted to the study of the way older elements of tradition were compiled, edited, and re-edited to produce the final form of the text. It is related to LITERARY CRITICISM and SOURCE CRITICISM in its concern to distinguish between older source materials and to separate them from editorial modifications introduced by later hands. It is related to TRADITION CRITICISM in its concern to show how each stage of redaction gives a new shape to the traditions it preserves. Ordinarily the term "redaction" is used to refer to the work of a later writer who deliberately selects, combines, and arranges already existing materials to create a new literary entity. From the way in which the material is ordered, as well as from discernible editorial links and interpretive comments, we can form an opinion as to the circumstances under which the redaction may have taken place and the special concerns that may have motivated the redactors. The terms "redaction" and "editing" are often used interchangeably, and it is perhaps unwise to press a distinction between them. Nevertheless, a redaction may employ materials that have previously been edited, often for purposes different from those to which the redactor now puts them. The term must therefore be broad enough to include the idea of "re-editing" as well as "editing."

1. Origins of the discipline
2. Examples of redaction critical problems
3. Priorities for redaction criticism

Bibliography

1. Origins of the discipline. A clear statement of the view that certain OT books may have been formed by a process of compiling, ordering, and editing can be found as early as the sixteenth century. The Roman Catholic scholar Andreas

Masius used such language to describe the formation of Joshua, Judges, and Kings, in his commentary on Joshua published in 1574 (and promptly placed on the Index). It is instructive that he uses the Latin verb from which "redaction" is derived, in a sense conformable to modern critical understanding of the process. Striking also is the fact that he is willing to conjecture that Ezra, or a person of comparable piety and erudition, may have carried out the work.

Evidence of the sort that led Masius to this conclusion is abundant in the OT, and it had been duly noted long before his time. Even the great rabbis of the eleventh and twelfth centuries, such as Rashi and Ibn Ezra, perceived with remarkable clarity that certain anachronisms in the Torah betrayed the viewpoint of an author who lived long after the events he recorded.

Use of evidence from the text itself to determine the origins and dating of biblical material began to be championed in the seventeenth and eighteenth centuries by persons as diverse as Hobbes, Spinoza, Simon, and Selmer. In their work the characteristic views of the Enlightenment and rationalism began to prevail. Common human reason, freed from the claims of ecclesiastical tradition and authority, was the appropriate instrument for discerning what could be known about the origins and development of the text, based on its own indications. *See* Biblical Criticism §§1-3; Biblical Criticism, History of §1.

While this movement uncovered many of the phenomena underlying redaction criticism, it was not until the nineteenth century that terms such as "redactor" and "redaction" (often abbreviated "R") became commonplace in critical biblical scholarship. Pentateuchal analysis particularly demanded a distinction between the "fragments" or "Documents" and the redactional framework in which they had been preserved.

Against the background of traditional views about the authorship and origins of various parts of the Bible, it is understandable that nineteenth-century scholarship developed special enthusiasm for recovering the work of the "original authors." For this and other reasons rooted in the temper of the times, any material that could be identified as secondary, or redactional, tended to be regarded as less valuable. At worst, it was scorned as an unworthy or tendentious distortion of the original. Redaction criticism was therefore most often undertaken in the interest of liberating earlier material from its later redactional trappings.

Deeper understanding, which also had its beginnings in the nineteenth century, eventually led in the twentieth century to a vastly different evaluation of the work of the redactors. Recognition that a wealth of oral tradition underlay much OT material began to alter conceptions of "authorship" (*see* Tradition, Oral[S]). In the case of the Pentateuch, for instance, it became clear that the earliest discernible "document" (J) was itself the product of a kind of "redaction," or selective compilation and ordering of material which already had a long history of oral transmission (*see* Yahwist[S] §§2-3). Even the Priestly stratum, long regarded as the latest of the Pentateuchal sources, came to be seen as a crystallization of ancient oral tradition. *See* Priestly Writers[S] §1.

Such insights opened the way for an integrated analysis of the entire process by which tradition moved through various stages in oral and written forms until it issued in the present state of the text. One might still make value judgments about the relative merits of various levels of tradition, on aesthetic or intellectual or religious grounds, but judgments of this kind were no longer regarded as inherent in the analysis itself. Attention could now be turned away from the question of whether a given redaction had obscured its source materials. As a new literary achievement, a new stage in the history of tradition, it could be described and evaluated in terms appropriate to its own character and design.

Redaction criticism remains useful as a tool for discerning the earlier materials with which the redactor may have worked. But it is also a constructive tool for assessing the special new shape of the tradition as it leaves the redactor's hand. One must take into account, not only such editorial biases and tendencies as we can discern, but also the inner character of the new constellation of traditions achieved by the redactor. Every combination of earlier traditions, whether written or oral, achieves a life of its own which can never be wholly circumscribed by the special intentions of those who combined them. Within the new literary entity achieved by a redactor, one must attempt to discern the way in which the received traditions modify and condition each other when perceived in the intended unity.

2. Examples of redaction critical problems. Several instances of redaction can be readily identified by the ordinary reader, working only with the text in translation. Perhaps the clearest examples occur in the books of Judges and I and II Kings. Judg. 2:11-19 leaves no doubt in the reader's mind that the author of these words is reviewing the entire period of the Judges from the perspective of a time long after it was over. He shows that he is not so much interested in recording the history of the period as he is in giving his readers a theological or religious explanation of why the history unfolded as it did. Before a single episode of the story is narrated, we are told in advance why Israel was ravaged and oppressed by its enemies. Every such instance was the result of an outbreak of "the anger of the Lord" (vs. 14), because "the people of Israel did what was evil in the sight of the Lord and served the Baals" (vs. 11). Every instance of successful resistance to, and victory over, the enemy occurred because "the Lord raised up judges, who saved them out of the power of those who plundered them" (vs. 16), in response to their cries of distress (vs. 18). Periods of security and well-being were granted to Israel during the lifetime of each judge (vs. 18), but with the death of the judge, Israel quickly relapsed into idolatry (vss. 17, 19). This produced a new outburst of divine anger, and the cycle of oppression and deliverance began again.

The redactor is now ready to illustrate his point by retelling a series of ancient stories about the times when deliverers arose among the people and won great victories. In each case the episode is introduced by a brief statement of the theological reason for the oppression (3:7, 12; 4:1; 6:1; 10:6; 13:1; note the exception in 3:31), usually including notice of Israel's cry for deliverance (3:9, 15; 4:3; 6:6; 10:10). Twice there is an explicit statement that the Lord raised up the deliverer (3:9, 15). The stories themselves are clearly derived from much earlier traditions that were originally told and preserved for reasons quite different from that of illustrating the redactor's overarching interpretation of the entire period.

As clear as this editorial scheme appears to be, the work of redaction criticism in the book of Judges has only begun when such observations have been made. Many questions about the editorial process confront us in the text, some of which can probably never be answered conclusively in the light of available evidence. Leaving aside the question of how the material in Judg. 1 (and perhaps also 2:1-5) may have come to be included in its present place, the redaction critic is confronted by an abrupt change—both in editorial policy and in content—in Judg. 17–21 (note the editorial comments in 17:6; 18:1; 19:1; 21:25). Can these chapters be seen as having served the purposes of the redactor whose hand is disclosed in Judg. 2:11-19? If so, how is the change to be accounted for? If not, how is the redactional process to be viewed by which chs. 17–21 were included in their present place?

Even within the more-or-less unified section 2:6–16:31, the redaction critic notices material that may well not have been included by the redactor of 2:11-19. It is widely assumed, for instance, that the Samson stories of Judg. 13–16 were not part of the collection of deliverer stories from which this redactor worked. This points toward the possibility of two or more redactions, by people who were concerned to augment and extend essentially the same theological program (*see* 13:1). Apparent elaborations such as those in 2:20-23 (cf. 2:1-5); 6:7-10; and 10:10-16 could perhaps also be accounted for in this way.

In another direction, questions must be raised about the form and content of the source material employed by the redactor of 2:11-19. Did he have at his disposal a "book of deliverers" previously edited in a unified way? Was it already furnished with a chronological apparatus? Were the duplicated traditions of Judg. 4 and 5 present to the redactor in this form? Was the material dealing with figures not characterized as deliverers (*see* chs. 9; 10:1-5; 12:8-15) already fused together with the deliverer stories? Were the several episodes already furnished with interpretive introductions, as divergences between the program of 2:11-19 and the several introductory formulas might suggest?

In the light of such questions, the redactional history of the book of Judges is seen to be much more complex than the editorial comment of 2:11-19 and the arrangement of chs. 3–16 initially indicate. Further attempts at clarification demand, not only careful consideration of the history of the traditions underlying Judges, but also renewed attention to details in the text of the sort isolated and analyzed by the older literary critics. *See* JUDGES, BOOK OF §D and supplementary article.

In some respects the redactional history of I and II Kings is both more clearly attested and more complex than that of Judges. The redactors inform us that the basic historical sequence as well as much of the substance of their work are derived from scrolls that were at their disposal. Underlying the account of Solomon's reign was the "book of the acts of Solomon" (*see* I Kings 11:41). "The Book of the Chronicles of the Kings of Israel" (I Kings 14:19) and "the Book of the Chronicles of the Kings of Judah" (I Kings 14:29) are cited as source materials. These citations compel us to envision the work of redaction, in this instance at least, as a scholarly literary undertaking of rather astonishing magnitude. The diverse kinds of information abstracted from these sources have been forged into a new unity and given an overarching theological coherence quite different from their original purpose. Moreover, the redactors have woven into this historical sequence a large body of material of a strikingly different sort: story after story involving prophetic figures who often stand in unqualified opposition to this or that monarch (*see* I Kings 11:29-39; 13:1-32; 14:1-18; 17–19; 20:13-16; 21; 22:1-40; II Kings 1–9; 13:14-21; 19; 20). Some of this prophetic material is preserved by the redactors in forms that clearly betray a much earlier time than their own. One must therefore ask whether scrolls containing such material did not exist independently before the redactors, alongside the royal scrolls explicitly cited. In any case, the redactors must be credited with having preserved and fused two streams of tradition from widely different communities in the life of Israel. *See* KINGS, I AND II §C; KINGS, I AND II[S] §§2-3.

The magnitude of this achievement was largely overlooked when scholars first isolated the evidence for redaction and identified it with the ideology of the Deuteronomic reformation in the days of King Josiah. Emphasis was placed on the hopelessly simplistic theology of the redactors, which reduced four hundred years of history to a series of illustrations of mechanically operating religious principles. Such an assessment underestimates not only the passionate exigencies of the religious crisis in the last days of the Judahite monarchy, but also the remarkable fidelity of the redactors to their source materials. Heavy-handed as the interpretation is at many points, ancient material is often preserved in ways that both challenge and enrich the redactors' own points of view. Thus the redaction is to be evaluated, not only in terms of the special interpretations of the redactors, but also in terms of the full implications of their achievement viewed as a new literary whole.

Through their activity, two enormously significant themes in OT tradition are brought into fruitful conversation. The first is the theme of God's covenant claim upon Israel, demanding radical obedience to God's clearly expressed will as a matter of life or death. In the course of time, this reached special focus in the traditions of Moses, Exodus, and Sinai, with central emphasis upon a discrete body of divine statutes delivered through Moses. *See* Covenant; Covenant, Mosaic[S].

The second is the theme of God's irrevocable commitment to Israel, fundamentally unmerited. In the course of time this theme reached peculiar focus in the traditions of the election of David and Zion. The dynasty was understood to be grounded upon God's irrevocable promise to establish through David an everlasting kingdom, whose authority was intended to extend to all peoples in paradise-like peace. The temple on Zion was conceived as God's eternal dwelling place, the sign of his commitment to dwell forever in the midst of his people. *See* Covenant, Davidic[S]; Zion Tradition[S].

The redactors of Kings have achieved an account of the history of Israel and Judah in which each of these themes intrudes upon the other. Irrevocable command and irrevocable grace confront each other, with the result that each is decisively modified. The older judgment that legalism ultimately dominates in the work of these redactors no longer stands unchallenged. The ideal picture of David with which the redactors operate, mirrored in good King Josiah, as well as their inordinate concern for true worship in the Jerusalem temple, betray an enormous positive investment in the traditions of David and Zion. Even though they affirm that the inner character of the David promise and the Zion promise were always conditioned upon radical obedience to Mosaic Torah (*see* I Kings 9:1-9), the redactors never surrender their confidence in God's fidelity to these promises. In various ways the redactors prepare Israel to distinguish between God's purpose in choosing David and the wholly justified act of bringing the Davidic dynasty under divine judgment, to distinguish between God's commitment to dwell forever in Zion and the wholly justified act of destroying the temple of Solomon. It is unlikely that the Davidic hope and the Zion hope could have survived without this achievement by the redactors of Kings.

It seems increasingly certain that this massive work was not achieved in a single burst of redactional activity. The question is still lively as to whether an early stage of the redaction was not already completed before the Exile, perhaps during the reign of Josiah himself, even though the process obviously extended into the exilic period. II Kings 17:24-41 (perhaps reflecting the Samaritan schism?) raises the question of postexilic elaborations of the text. It must be stressed that attempts to evaluate the over-all achievement of the redaction, such as the one sketched out above, must remain subject to serious challenge and modification.

The general theological viewpoint of the dominant redactional material in Joshua, as well as in Judges and Kings, has long been recognized as "Deuteronomic." Detailed congruence in language and style leaves no doubt that a profound relationship exists between Deuteronomy and the present redactions of these historical works. The most ambitious hypothesis based on these observations envisions a deliberate redactional effort to integrate Deuteronomy, Joshua, Judges, I and II Samuel, and I and II Kings into a single "Deuteronomic historical complex." On this view, the opening chapters of Deuteronomy are understood as a redactional introduction, not to Deuteronomy alone, but to the entire complex (*see* Deuteronomic History [S]). Similarly, the books of Genesis, Exodus, Leviticus, and Numbers are viewed as a "Priestly historical complex" which reached its completed form through a work of Priestly redaction (*see* Canon of the OT[S] §1*c*). I and II Chronicles, Ezra, and Nehemiah, by similar reasoning, constitute the "Chronicler's historical complex" which underwent its decisive redaction perhaps as much as two hundred years after the reforms of Ezra and Nehemiah.

3. Priorities for redaction criticism. Useful as these and other theoretical constructions have proven to be, they will serve redaction criticism best as challenges to re-examine the evidence with appropriate reserve and with openness to new possibilities. Given the complexity of redaction history, it is to be expected that modification and perhaps alternative theoretical constructions will be required to account better for the phenomena of the text.

Often the text supplies us with little more than a strong suspicion that a given composite unit may have resulted from a deliberate redaction of previously disparate material. In such cases the redaction critic must test this possibility against other ways of accounting for the state of the text, such as confluences in the oral tradition, or unsystematic omissions, alterations, and elaborations that occurred in the transmission of the text. The reformulation, testing, and refining of criteria remains an important frontier for the discipline.

Both historians of tradition and redaction critics will be well served by renewed attention to the astonishingly assiduous and ingenious work of the great literary critics of the nineteenth and early twentieth centuries. Their analyses must be accounted for—if no longer on purely literary-critical grounds, then in other ways that are responsive to the same evidence. Redaction is still best understood as a literary undertaking, and redaction criticism is therefore peculiarly dependent upon solid literary-critical methods.

Obviously it is possible that combinations and elaborations of diverse traditional materials occurred without the intervention of a literary redactor. Solid attempts at redaction criticism may serve to confirm this, in a given instance, rather than to disprove it. In other instances, however, stages of reordering and reinterpretation may be uncovered that can only be understood as deliberate pieces of redaction. In either case, redaction criticism provides an indispensable tool for assessing the total process by which the biblical text achieved its present form.

Bibliography. O. Eissfeldt, *The Old Testament: An Introduction* (1965); K. Koch, *The Growth of the Biblical Tradition* (1969); H. J. Kraus, *Geschichte der historisch-kritischen Erforschung des Alten Testaments* (2nd ed., 1969); M. Noth, *A History of Pentateuchal Traditions* (1972), and *Überlierferungsgeschichtliche Studien I* (2nd ed., 1957); E. Sellin–G. Fohrer, *Introduction to the Old Testament* (1968); G. von Rad, *Old Testament Theology,* I (1962).

J. A. Wharton

REDACTION CRITICISM, NT. A method of studying the NT that concentrates on the way the principal author of a work has adapted ("redacted") earlier materials to his own theological ends. Also called redaction history, from the German *Redaktionsgeschichte* (literally, [a study of] the history of redaction), and composition criticism (*Kompositionsgeschichte*).

1. What is redaction? Redaction is the conscious reworking of older materials in such a way as to meet new needs. It is editing that does not simply compile or retouch but creatively transforms.

The term applies most obviously to the work of each EVANGELIST in producing the GOSPELS. As long as the evangelists were regarded as eyewitnesses of the events they recorded, their authorship was assumed to be minimal, though the many differences among the four canonical gospels were not easily accounted for in this way. When the apostolic authorship of the gospels was no longer maintained and their dependence on earlier sources was recognized, the opportunity arose to focus on the way those sources were edited. But in fact the source criticism of the Synoptic gospels (*see* SYNOPTIC PROBLEM; SYNOPTIC PROBLEM[S]) tended for a long while to treat those sources in a way that emphasized their historical accuracy, to assume that they were so regarded by the evangelists, and so to minimize the latters' contribution, held to be little more than "scissors-and-paste" editing.

The emergence of FORM CRITICISM revealed that between the historical Jesus and any written documents such as our gospels or their sources there stands a long and complex period of oral tradition that reflects for each individual story or saying a historical context, a life setting (*Sitz im Leben*), of its own, not necessarily like the *Sitz im Leben* of Jesus.

Redaction criticism, in turn, is based on the recognition that the production of the gospels, and probably of their written sources as well, represents a third life setting, distinct from that of Jesus and the intermediate period of unwritten tradition, and that consequently the activity of the authors who produced these documents demands investigation. Both in their rewriting of earlier works and in their interpretation of the still fluid tradition they may display imagination and innovative freedom, while at the same time paying considerable respect to the material they start with.

2. The method at work. When we possess a document which an author has used as source, the task of redaction criticism is simplest; we are able as it were to look over his shoulder as he rewrites, and the only question is why he adapts it as he does. The more precisely, then, we can reconstruct the text lying before the author as he worked, the more confidently we can understand his redaction. But often such a written text either is not accessible to us or never existed, so that we cannot perceive the hand of the author by working forward from an earlier document; rather, we must go backward from his finished work, using as far as possible the insights of form criticism. Thus, if the author of Matthew has used Mark as a principal source, his detailed handling of the Markan material will be quite clear; on the other hand, since we have reason to believe that the author of Mark began only with more or less independent traditions whose pre-Markan form is not directly knowable, his adaptation of them will be harder to identify and must emerge cumulatively as we work through his gospel, noting recurring phrases, themes, and emphases that appear to have been added by him to the tradition. But in either case the separation of redaction from source or tradition is an essential step toward perceiving the author's meaning.

The redaction critic, then, pays closest attention to what distinguishes the work before him from the earlier material on which it is based. He observes how that material has been arranged or rearranged, how a new setting for a traditional unit gives it new meaning, in what ways the author both emphasizes ideas not originally prominent and inserts new themes, how he comments on the older material in editorial asides and transitional passages, and so forth. In ways such as these the particular interests of the author are allowed to stand out and to be seen as functions of his own historical situation, illuminating how his *Sitz im Leben* has changed from that of the earlier source or tradition. If more attention is given to the distinctiveness of the work than to its total content, this is done only so as to set in sharper focus the way the author intends the older content to be understood. Redaction criticism is no substitute for comprehensive EXEGESIS but contributes importantly to it.

3. The Synoptic gospels and Acts. While it is true that the first three gospels in the NT canon are interrelated in a very close way, so that they can be grouped together as the Synoptic gospels and their more or less common body of material known as the synoptic tradition, this fact has tended to obscure the many subtle differences among the three gospels and even some more obvious ones. Redaction criticism, which from the beginning has chiefly applied itself to these gospels, has served to correct this shortcoming. Each of the evangelists is seen as a distinctive author and a theologian in his own right, as formerly only the Fourth Evangelist was viewed.

On the broadest scale this means that the overall literary form or genre of each of the three gospels is distinctive. Although we usually refer to all three as versions of the *gospel* (i.e., the good news), it is to Mark that this term best applies, as its use in the opening verse and throughout the work indicates. Neither Matthew nor Luke would deny that his own work too is a presentation of the good news and so, according to later usage, a gospel; but the format and purpose of their respective books are more aptly described in other terms. Matthew is not so much a theological proclamation, like Mark, as a manual of belief and action for a particular Christian community; and Luke comes closest of all the evangelists to producing a history, if we understand that term in a theological, not a factual, sense. *See* GOSPEL, GENRE, [S].

The detailed redaction criticism of the Synoptic gospels (*see bibliog.*) has tended to rely heavily on the widely accepted solution of the synoptic problem, the so-called two-document hypothesis, according to which Matthew and Luke have independently used both Mark and the hypothetical source Q (*see* Q and Q[S]). Although this solution has been challenged from time to time, the success of redaction critics in explicating the Synoptics by means of it lends it considerable support. Mark too, whose sources on this theory are not available to us, has been illuminated by comparison with the later gospels dependent on it. In short, the theological movement from one document to another sheds light on both. Even Q, uncertain as are its exact content and text, can be better understood by examining what Matthew and Luke have done with it. *See* SYNOPTIC PROBLEM[S].

On the other hand, redaction criticism of the Synoptics does not rest solely on a source-critical solution of the synoptic problem, for whatever their literary relationships, it may be presumed that each of the three gospels is also directly dependent on tradition. As we saw in §2, it is possible to examine the redaction not only of sources but also of tradition, i.e., to perceive what was accomplished by the fixing of a tradition in written form and its combination with other traditions. The redaction-critical treatment of Mark, whose sources are unknown, has flourished no less than that of Matthew and Luke. And because the method can thus be applied when only one document is involved, it has begun to deal also with Acts, unique among first-century Christian writings. This is possible not because Acts was probably written by the author of Luke—though that undoubtedly suggested the possibility—but because it appears to be dependent on its own body of traditions. The fact that those traditions are otherwise almost unknown to us—except as their *Sitz im Leben* may correspond to that of the epistles or the pregospel traditions—makes their redaction-critical investigation more difficult but not impossible. *See also* ACTS OF THE APOSTLES and supplementary article; articles on the gospels of MARK, MATTHEW, LUKE.

4. The Fourth Gospel. Because of its considerable differences from the Synoptics, the Gospel of John has always been assumed to be the work of a theologically creative author, but as long as he was held to be either an eyewitness of the events he describes or dependent on one or more of the other gospels, there was no way of adequately accounting for the independence of his gospel. Once it is recognized that he did not use the Synoptics as sources, although sharing a good deal of traditional material with them and possibly having some acquaintance with one or more of them, the possibility of exploring his relation to no longer extant materials by means of redaction criticism is raised. Analysis of his interpretation of a unique oral tradition, especially as it appears in the discourses of Jesus, has been limited by the relative lack of form-critical treatment of that material. But in the case of the gospel's narrative material the evangelist is in a situation analogous to that of Mark, except that John is increasingly believed to have begun with a far more fixed body of narratives: the so-called Signs Source (SQ) and an account of the Passion (*see* JOHN, GOSPEL OF[S] §1; SIGN IN THE NT[S] §4).

Considerable attention has been given to the movement from SQ to present gospel as that movement sheds light in particular on John's Christology and on his understanding of Jesus' miracles ("signs"). In the former connection, the strong possibility that the evangelist has adapted a christological hymn in producing the gospel's prologue (1:1-18) has opened the way to redaction-critical study of that passage. Along with such detailed examination of the text, the broader questions of the gospel's genre, historical setting, and relation to first-century Jewish and Christian thought have been reopened.

5. The epistles. The various letters in the NT are primarily *ad hoc* writings, produced more or less spontaneously in response to specific situations (*see* LETTER §4, LETTER[S]). To that extent they do not immediately suggest themselves for redaction-critical analysis as it focuses on the reworking of older material. But at least the earliest letters (those of PAUL) were produced at the same time as the traditions behind the gospels and Acts were developing and can be expected at points to reflect a similar tradition. It is widely held that Paul occasionally uses even relatively fixed traditional material in the course of his correspondence (e.g., the christological hymn in Phil. 2:6-11), so that his redaction of it can be explored. The growing field of form-critical investigation of the epistles (*see* FORM CRITICISM, NT[S]) will undoubtedly yield other traditional data for the redaction critic. When more than one letter from an author (Paul, "John") exists, in which similar theological material is variously handled, or when successors have reused his ideas, further possibilities are presented for a kind of redaction criticism.

Bibliography. N. Perrin, *What is Redaction Criticism?* Studies in Creative Criticism, I (1969); R. H. Stein, "What is Redaktionsgeschichte?" *JBL,* LXXXVIII (1969), 45-56, and "The Proper Methodology for Ascertaining a Markan Redaction History," *NovT,* XIII (1971), 181-98; *see also* introductions in works by Marxsen and Bornkamm cited below. J. Rohde, *Rediscovering the Teaching of the Evangelists,* NTL (1966), discusses the method and its background (pp. 1-46), then summarizes many Ger. examples of its application to the Synoptic gospels and acts.

Two scholars anticipated the rise of redaction criticism: K. L. Schmidt, *Der Rahmen der Geschichte Jesu* (1919); R. H. Lightfoot, *History and Interpretation in the Gospels* (1934), and *The Gospel Message of St. Mark* (1950).

Of the innumerable examples of redaction-critical work on the NT, esp. journal articles, only a representative selection can be listed. J. M. Robinson, *The Problem of History in Mark,* SBT, XXI (1957); W. Marxsen, *Mark the Evangelist* (1956 [ET 1969]), also extends the studies to include Matthew and Luke; H. Conzelmann, *The Theology of St. Luke* (2nd ed., 1957 [ET 1960]); Günther Bornkamm *et al., Tradition and Interpretation in Matthew* (1960); C. E. Carlston, *The Parables of the Triple Tradition* (1975); R. A. Edwards, "An Approach to a Theology of Q," *JR,* LI (1971), 247-69; J. T. Lienhard, "Acts 6:1-6: A Redactional View," *CBQ,* XXXVII (1975), 228-36.

J. Louis Martyn, *History and Theology in the Fourth Gospel* (1968); W. Wilkens, *Zeichen und Werke* (1969); J. Becker, "Wunder und Christologie," *NTS,* XVI

(1970), 130-48; F. Schnider, and W. Stenger, *Johannes und die Synoptiker,* Biblische Handbibliothek, IX (1971); W. Nicol, *The Sēmeia in the Fourth Gospel,* NovTSup, XXXII (1972); R. T. Fortna, "From Christology to Soteriology: A Redaction-Critical Study of Salvation in the Fourth Gospel," *Int.,* XXVII (1973), 31-47; R. Kysar, *The Fourth Evangelist and His Gospel* (1975).

G. Strecker, "Redaktion und Tradition im Christushymnus Phil. 2:6-11," *ZNW,* LV (1964), 63-78; C. Buck and G. Taylor, *Saint Paul: A Study in the Development of his Thought* (1969); C. H. Talbert, "Tradition and Redaction in Rom. 12:9-21," *NTS,* XVI (1969), 83-93; B. Rigaux, "Tradition et rédaction dans I Th. v.1-10," *NTS,* XXI (1975), 318-40.

R. T. Fortna

***REFINING.** *See* Tell el-Kheleifeh[S].

***REMNANT.** The remnant is a key motif in eschatology and the hope for the future. Hebrew, Aramaic, and Greek terms reveal a variety of remnant ideas, and the theme is also present in words that belong to a larger semantic range.

1. Terminology in the OT. Derivatives of six Heb. roots, which are employed over 540 times, express the OT remnant theme.

***a. Derivatives of* שׁאר.** This root (266 Heb. usages, 10 in Aram.) is attested also in cognate languages. Verbal forms in Heb. denote "to remain" (*qal*), "to be left over, remain (over, behind)" (*niph'al*), and "to leave (over, behind), have left" (*hiph'il*). The nouns שְׁאָר and שְׁאֵרִית denote "remnant, remainder, rest, residue." Basically the various forms designate the part which is left over (Gen. 7:23; Isa. 11:11; Dan. 10:8) or remains (Exod. 10:5; Isa. 4:3; 17:6) after the removal of a small part, half, or the larger balance. שְׁאֵרִית, "remnant," may even designate the whole without the loss of any part (Gen. 45:7). שְׁאָר is Isaiah's favorite word of his remnant theology with twelve of twenty-six usages in the OT (10:19-21; 11:11, 16). At times derivatives of the root שׁאר express the insignificance (Deut. 3:11), smallness (Deut. 4:27; Jer. 8:3), and meaninglessness or total loss of the remnant (Gen. 47:18; Exod. 8:31), but normally an intense, future-directed aspect is present, which underlines the inherent potentiality of renewal of the remnant, no matter what its size.

***b. Derivatives of* פלט.** This Heb. root (80 usages) also appears in a number of cognate Semitic languages. Heb. derivatives of the root appear in verbal forms with the meanings "to escape, get away" (*qal*), "to deliver, bring to safety" (*pi'el, hiph'il*), and as nouns פליט (*pālîṭ* and *pālêṭ*), "escapee, fugitive," and פליטה (often parallel to nouns of the root שׁאר), "escape, deliverance" (Gen. 45:7; II Sam. 15:14). With human entities, forms of פלט refer mostly to an "*escaped* remnant" (Gen. 32:8 [H 9]; Judg. 21:17; Isa. 4:2-3). Sometimes the purely negative aspect of decimation or total loss comes to expression (Amos 9:1; Jer. 42:17), but usually Israel's "*escaped* remnant" experienced deliverance from a divinely caused threat to life and continual existence (Isa. 37:31-32=II Kings 19:30-31; Ezek. 6:8-10). Some of God's people will escape Yahweh's final judgment (Isa. 4:2; Joel 2:32), from which even the believing Gentile can be delivered (Isa. 66:19).

***c. Derivatives of* מלט.** This root (89 usages), which developed from פלט, appears only in verbal forms and denotes "to escape, get oneself to safety, make for safety" (*niph'al*) and "to deliver, save, let escape" (*pi'el*). Some contexts indicate that it is impossible to escape to safety (Isa. 20:6), and so total destruction results (Judg. 3:29; Jer. 32:3-4). However in most contexts the escape was successful (Gen. 19:17-22; Jer. 51:6) and life was saved (I Kings 1:12; Jer. 51:45). In the end time, Yahweh will save those who have escaped (Isa. 49:24-25) and who call upon his name (Joel 2:32), all those whose names are written in the book of life (Dan. 12:1; cf. Isa. 4:2-3).

***d. Derivatives of* יתר.** At least 110 usages of 248 forms of derivatives of this root (attested in cognate languages) contain the remnant idea. They contain the meanings "to be left over, remain over" (*niph'al*), "to leave over (behind), have remaining, have left" (*hiph'il*) in verbal forms, and in nominal forms "remainder, rest, remnant." Various forms denote either a small part (Judg. 8:10; II Sam. 8:4), one half (Exod. 28:10; Isa. 44:19), or the larger balance (Lev. 14:18; II Chr. 31:10; Judg. 7:6; I Sam. 15:15). The phrase "the rest of the people" (שׁאר העם=יתר העם, Neh. 10:28 [H 29]; 11:1, and שׁארית העם, Hag. 1:12; Neh. 7:72 [H 71]) refers to the remnant in Jerusalem and a victorious future remnant (Zeph. 2:9; Zech. 14:2). The "remainder" possesses the full potentiality of future existence for clan (Gen. 44:20), dynasty (Judg. 9:5), or the faithful (I Kings 19:10, 14) and consists of a new whole in which resides the seed for regeneration and continued, abundant life.

***e.* שׂריד *and* אחרית.** The Heb. noun שׂריד (28 usages) describes the "survivor" from military disaster (Josh. 10:20; Deut. 3:3).

Finally, the Heb. noun אחרית has clearly the meaning "remnant" in Num. 24:20 (RSV "in the end"); Amos 4:2; 9:1; and Ezek. 23:25 and possibly in Jer. 31:17.

2. Terminology in the NT. Substantival usages of the adjective λοιπός designate "the rest" (Luke 24:9; Rom. 1:13) and can be employed in a critical sense to denote those who hardened their hearts (Luke 8:10), disbelieve (Mark 16:13), act insincerely (Gal. 2:13), and refuse to repent (Rev. 9:20). In Acts 15:17 (=Amos 9:12 from LXX) the term κατάλοιποι denotes the "remnant"; in Rom. 11:3 (=I Kings 19:10), ὑπολείπω refers to the one who alone "is left (remaining)"; and in Rom. 9:27 (=Isa. 10:22 from LXX) the noun ὑπόλειμμα designates the "remnant." The noun λεῖμμα denotes "remnant" in Rom. 11:5. *See* §4ciii *below*.

3. The origin of the remnant idea. *a. In the ancient Near East.* The remnant idea is present in Sumerian, Akkadian, Hittite, Ugaritic, and Egyptian cultures in a large variety of genres, such as myth, legend, epic, prophecy, prayer, hymn, letter, and annal. It appears with such human entities as individual, family, clan, tribe, army, nation, and mankind as a whole. The large variety of mortal threats in the natural, social, and political spheres emphasizes the common denominator of the respective remnant notions, namely man's existential concern to preserve life when endangered by mortal threats. A remnant means life and continued existence through innate potentialities of renewal and restoration.

The remnant concept finds its first explicit expression in stories of a universal flood. The Sumerian and Babylonian flood traditions testify that in a small surviving remnant all future for mankind resides. *See* FLOOD (GENESIS) §3.

b. In the OT. The earliest explicit reference is in the flood story: "Only Noah was left, and those that were with him in the ark" (Gen. 7:23). Other early traditions in Genesis speak of mortal threats to life by means of fire (18:17-33; 19:16-24), family feud (32:8-12), and famine (Joseph cycle, 43:1-8). Whereas the earliest biblical traditions place the remnant idea in the midst of mortal threats and thus testify to the origin of the concept in the concern to preserve life, they also put the concept from its beginning into a theological framework with a strong salvation-historical emphasis. The OT has an overarching correlation between the salvation of a remnant and the nucleus of the true people of God, where the initiative of God succeeds in spite of all threats, obstacles, and fears. The remnant theme is an essential part of biblical hope and eschatology. *See* HOPE IN THE OT[S].

4. History of the remnant idea. *a. In the OT.* *See* REMNANT.

b. In late Judaism. The Qumran covenanters believed that they were "the remnant of thy people [Israel]" (1QM 14.8-9) spared by God's mercy as the only true remnant (CD 2.11; 1QH 6.8; 1QM 14.9) when Israel came to an end (CD 3.13; cf. 1QM 13.8). They were now the sole bearers of the covenant promises (1QM 14.9; CD 1.4) and were alone the "new covenant community" (CD 6.19; 19.33-34). God spared them because they kept the divine "commandments" (CD 3.12), even the "whole *torah*" (4QFlor 2.2). They alone will "fill the earth with their seed" (CD 2.12). Those who fall away from them "shall have no remnant or survivor" (CD 2.6-7; cf. 19.10; 1QS 5.13; 1QH 6.32), sharing the fate of the "sons of darkness" (1QM 1.6; 4.2; 14.5; 1QS 4.14; 1QpHab 9.7; cf. 1QM 2.11; 11.15).

Apocryphal Jewish apocalypses reveal a distinct remnant theology (*see* REMNANT). In rabbinic thought the remnant idea recedes, and all Israel has part in the future world (M. Sanh. 10.1).

c. In the NT. i. *John the Baptist.* The cry of judgment and repentance by John the Baptist led to the gathering of a faithful, penitent remnant (Matt. 3:1-12). Yet, his preaching was universalistic and his invitation for baptism was addressed to all who would "bear fruit that befits repentance" (Matt. 3:8).

ii. *Jesus.* The message of Jesus, salvation for all who repent and believe in the gospel (Mark 1:15), was never intended to create a remnant that was exclusive and narrow. Although Jesus' call was universalist, he was conscious that his work was for "the lost sheep" (Matt. 10:6) and that only "few" (Matt. 7:14) would accept the invitation. Those "few" made up of the "poor" (πτωχοί, Matt. 11:5) and "little ones" (μικροί, Matt. 10:42) were the "chosen" (ἐκλεκτοί, Matt. 22:14), who must be considered a remnant of faith. Nowhere in the gospels is the designation "remnant" employed for this new community. The ones who remained outside the group are polemically designated as the "others" (λοιποί) who act wickedly (Matt. 22:6; Luke 8:10). Contrariwise, those who have accepted Jesus Christ are the remnant of faith. The angelic reapers will carry out a process of sifting at the end of time (Matt. 13:24-30).

iii. *Paul.* Paul addresses himself explicitly to the question of the remnant in Rom. 9–11. By citing OT passages (Isa. 10:22-23; 1:9=Rom. 9:27-29) the apostle teaches that only a remnant of the Israel of the "flesh" (Rom. 9:8; 11:13-24) is saved and that believing Gentiles are grafted into the new community of faith. This "remnant" (λεῖμμα, Rom. 11:5) is a present reality made up of both Jews and Gentiles (Rom. 9:24), the "elect" (Rom. 11:7) who are "chosen by grace" (Rom. 11:5). As such, the remnant is the Israel of the promise (Rom. 9:8), the true spiritual Israel of faith.

iv. *Revelation.* In the NT apocalypse the adjective λοιπός applies to the remnant in the church of Thyatira who hold fast to love, faith, and service (Rev. 2:24). The church in Sardis is virtually dead, but "what remains" is to be strengthened (Rev. 3:2), because there are "a few names" who have unsoiled garments (vs. 4). Rev. 11:13 speaks of the remnant which survived the earthquake and glorified God. Finally, the dragon makes war against the "rest" of the woman's offspring "who keep the commandments of God and bear testimony to Jesus" (Rev. 12:17). This last faithful remnant withstands the fiercest persecution by the lamb-like beast (Rev. 13:11-18) and is saved by the rider on the horse, while the others are slain in the apocalyptic battle (Rev. 19:21). Victory belongs to the last faithful remnant.

Bibliography. J. Meinhold, *Studien zur israelitischen Religionsgeschichte. Band I: Der heilige Rest* (1903); C. Müller, *Gottes Gerechtigkeit und Gottes Volk. Eine Untersuchung zu Römer 9-11* (1964); J. Jeremias, "Der Gedanke des 'heiligen Restes' im Spätjudentum und in der Verkündigung Jesu," *Abba* (1966), pp. 121-32; B. F. Meyer, "Jesus and the Remnant of Israel," *JBL*, LXXXIV (1965), 123-30; V. Herntrich and G. Schrenk, "λεῖμμα ητλ," *TDNT*, IV (1967), 194-214; J. Munck, *Christ and Israel* (1967); U. Stegemann, "Der Restgedanke bei Isaias," *BZ*, XIII (1969), 161-86; P. Richardson, *Israel in the Apostolic Church* (1969); G. Fohrer, "The Stems of פלט and מלט in the OT," *TDNT*, VII (1971), 978-80; G. F. Hasel, "Linguistic Considerations Regarding the Translation of Isaiah's *Shear-Jashub:* A Reassessment," *AUSS*, IX (1971), 36-46, "Semantic Values of Derivatives of the Hebrew Root *š'r*," *AUSS*, XI (1973), 152-69; W. E. Müller and H. D. Preuss, *Die Vorstellung vom Rest im AT* (2nd ed., 1973), contains a rich bibliography of studies which reflect Müller's influence; G. F. Hasel, *The Remnant. The History and Theology of the Remnant Idea from Genesis to Isaiah* (2nd ed., 1974), has complete lit. on the subject. G. F. HASEL

***REPENTANCE IN THE OT.** In the religion of ancient Israel, in distinction to its neighbors, rituals were not inherently efficacious. This point is underscored by the sacrificial formula of forgiveness; the required ritual is carried out by the priest, but its desired end, forgiveness, is granted solely by God: "The priest shall make atonement for him for his sin, and he shall be forgiven" (Lev. 4:26, and *passim*). Moreover, contrition and confession are indispensable elements of all rituals of forgiveness, whether they are expiatory sacrifices (Lev. 5:5-6) or litanies for fasting (Joel 2:12-14; I Sam. 7:5-9).

Indeed, man's involvement, both in conscience and deed, is a *sine qua non* for securing divine forgiveness. It is not enough to hope and pray for pardon; man must humble himself, acknowledge his wrong, and resolve to depart from sin (e.g., David, II Sam. 12:13 ff.; Ahab, I Kings 21:27-29). The Psalms provide ample evidence that penitence and confession must be integral components of all prayers for forgiveness (Pss. 32:5; 38:18 [H 19]; 41:4 [H 5]; Lam. 3:40-42). The many synonyms for contrition testify to its primacy in the human effort to restore the desired relationship with God; e.g., seek the Lord (II Sam. 12:16; 21:1); search for him (Amos 5:4); humble oneself before him (Lev. 26:41); and direct the heart to him (I Sam. 7:3). The rituals of penitence, such as weeping, fasting, rending clothes, and donning sackcloth and ashes, are unqualifiedly condemned by the prophets if the heart is not involved (Isa. 1:10 ff.; 29:13; Hos. 7:14; Joel 2:12-13).

At the same time, inner contrition must be followed by outward acts; remorse must be translated into deeds. Two substages are involved in this process: first, the negative one of ceasing to do evil (Isa. 33:15; Ps. 15), and then the positive, active step of doing good (Isa. 1:17; Jer. 26:13; Amos 5:14-15). Again, the language used to describe man's active role in the process testifies to its centrality; e.g., incline the heart to the Lord (Josh. 24:23); make oneself a new heart (Ezek. 18:31); circumcise the heart (Jer. 4:4); wash the heart (Jer. 4:14); and break one's fallow ground (Hos. 10:12). However, all these expressions are subsumed and encapsulated by one verb which dominates the penitential literature of the Bible, שוב, "turn, return." This root combines in itself both requisites of repentance: to turn from evil and to turn to good. The motion of turning implies that sin is not an eradicable stain but a straying from the right path, and that by the effort of turning, a power God has given all men, the sinner can redirect his destiny.

That the term for repentance is not a prophetic innovation but goes back to Israel's ancient traditions is clear from the fact that Amos, the first writing prophet, uses it without bothering to explain it (Amos 4:6-11). Moreover, the concept of repentance (though not the term שוב) is also assumed in the early narratives about Pharaoh (Exod. 7:3-4; 10:1; 11:10) and the sons of Eli (I Sam. 2:25); these accounts say that God deliberately blocks their repentance. Finally, the motif of repentance occurs in the tales of the early heroes: David (II Sam. 12:13-14; 24:10-14), Ahab (I Kings 21:27-29), and Josiah (II Kings 22:18-20).

Nonetheless it must be noted that the repentance of these early narratives is not the same as that taught by the prophets. First, repentance in the narratives is ineffectual. At best it mitigates retribution (e.g., David) or postpones it (Ahab, Josiah). And on occasion it is of no avail (e.g., to Moses himself; Deut. 3:23-26). Repentance, it is true, is found in the admonitions of P and D (*see* DOCUMENTS; Lev. 26:40-42; Deut. 4:29-31; 30:1-10), but here, contrary to the prophets, repentance can only terminate the punishment but cannot prevent its onset. The limited scope of repentance in these stories can best be appraised by contrasting it with the success of the people of Nineveh in averting their doom (Jonah 3:1-10).

Secondly, wherever repentance occurs in the early narratives, it is a human virtue. God does not call upon man to repent or upon his prophet to rouse him to repentance. The role of Moses is to intercede for Israel so that God will annul his evil decree (e.g., Exod. 32:11-13, 31-34; 34:9; Num. 12:11-13; 14:13-19; Deut. 9:16-29), but not once is he expected to bring his people to repentance so that they might merit divine forgiveness. Other intercessors are also recorded in the early narratives, e.g., Abraham (Gen. 18:23-33), Samuel (I Sam. 7:5-9; 12:19-25), Elijah (I Kings 17:17-23), Elisha (II Kings 4:33; 6:15-20), and Job (Job 42:7-9). These righteous leaders, just like Moses, turn to God to ask for pardon but not to man to urge repentance.

It is against this backdrop that the innovation of the Priestly legislation can be measured (*see* PRIESTLY WRITERS[S]). Repentance is operative in sacrificial expiation, as indicated by the terms התודה, "confess" (Lev. 5:5; Num. 5:7) and אשם, "feel guilt" (*see* SACRIFICES AND OFFERINGS, OT[S] §2*b*). However, the term שוב, meaning "repent," never appears in P. Neither does it appear in the Tetrateuch and early narratives. In this literature, שוב does occur in four passages but in the opposite sense (apostasy), turn away from the Lord (Num. 14:43 [JE]; 32:15 [JEP]; Josh. 22:16, 18, 23, 29 [P]; I Sam. 15:11). This is as expected, since in the early sources, though Israel is guilty of apostasy, it is never expected to repent.

שוב as "repent" exhibits the following distribution pattern: twenty-three times in the eighth-century prophets, Amos, Hosea, and Isaiah; fifty times in Jeremiah and Ezekiel; and twenty-eight times in nine postexilic books. Conversely, the use of אשם, "feel guilt," which approximates the notion "repent," is only found in the Priestly Code. Thus it may be concluded that P derived its penitential terminology at a time when שוב had not become the standard idiom for repentance. However, under the influence of the prophets, especially Jeremiah and Ezekiel, the root שוב overwhelmed all of its competitors. That the Priestly doctrine of repentance is pre-exilic is supported by an additional consideration. Though the power of repentance in P is such that it can reduce a deliberate sin to an unintentional one, P insists that for the complete annulment of sin sacrificial expiation (כפר) is mandatory. It does not know the prophetic teaching that repentance suffices in itself to nullify sin.

The prophets differ among themselves on the function of repentance, especially in their eschatological prophecies. Isaiah, for example, withdraws the offer of repentance at an early point in his career (cf. 1:16-20 with 6:9-13). He insists that only the few survivors of God's purge will be allowed to engage in a program of repentance that will qualify them for the new Zion (e.g., 32:1-8, 15-17; 33:5-6). Indeed, he even gives his first-born a name that carries the message: "[Only] A Remnant Will Repent" (Isa. 7:3n.; *see* REMNANT; REMNANT[S]). In the teaching of Jeremiah, on the other hand, the call to repent is never abandoned. When Jeremiah despairs of men's capability of self-renewal, he postulates that God will provide a "new heart" which will overcome sin and merit eternal forgiveness (31:33; Deut. 30:6; Ezek. 36:26-27). *See* NEW COVENANT[S] §§1, 2.

Bibliography. C. R. Smith, *The Biblical Doctrine of Sin* (1953); E. F. Sutcliffe, *Providence and Suffering in the Old and New Testaments* (1953); W. L. Holladay, *The Root Šûbh in the OT* (1958); W. Eichrodt, *Theology of the OT*, II (1967), 380-495; J. Milgrom, *Cult and Conscience* (1966) and "The Cultic שגגה and its Influence in Psalms and Job," *JQR*, LVIII (1967), 115-25.

J. MILGROM

***REPENTANCE IN THE NT.** The English word "repentance," which means primarily regret, remorse, or sorrow regarding an action, attitude, or thought, has been used in the NT to translate the Greek noun μετάνοια, and the verb "repent" to translate μετανοέω. In the LXX the verb, and its synonym μεταμέλομαι, translated primarily the Hebrew term נחם, which meant to be sorry in the sense of ruing one's prior decisions or deeds (Jer. 8:6; *see* REPENTANCE IN THE OT[S]). Generally speaking, in the Greco-Roman world μετάνοια meant a "change of mind" (Plato, *Euthydemus* 279C; Prov. 14:15, LXX), though that frequently implied dissatisfaction with one's previous decision and therefore "regret" (Matt. 27:3). However, in Jewish intertestamental literature, μετανοέω became synonymous with ἐπιστρέφω, a Greek term used to translate the Hebrew שוב, which meant a "turning (or returning) to God," i.e., conversion in the religious and moral sense of the word (Test. Zeb. 9:7). Among the Jews such a turning or returning to God was often accompanied by some public act, such as fasting (Test. Simeon 3:4; Test. Reuben 1:9; Sanhedrin 25b; Luke 19:8; Acts 26:20). With this development in Judaism it comes as no surprise that the NT term μετανοέω was translated *poenitentiam agite* (do penance, Acts 2:38, Wycliffe) in the Vulg.

1. The message of Jesus and John the Baptist. The Jewish understanding of repentance as a turning from sin to God paved the way for the basic proclamation of Jesus in the gospels: "the kingdom of God is at hand; repent" (Mark 1:15; cf. Matt. 4:17). The early church understood the call to repentance as an imperative to "turn and become like children" (Matt. 18:3). Parables such as that of the prodigal son illustrated this "turning back" to the Father. While the eschatological saying which accompanied the call for repentance stressed the urgency of the matter (for the Lord would come as a thief in the night: Matt. 24:42-44; Luke 12:39-40; cf. I Thess. 5:4; Rev. 3:3), the over-all function of Jesus' ministry was to allow time (the delay motif) for repentance to occur (Luke 13:6-9). Jesus' sharpest threats were reserved for those who counted on that delay for their own purposes, or who failed to repent when offered the delay (Matt. 11:20-24; 12:38-42; 24:48-51; 25:1-13; Luke 10:13-15; 11:29-32). *See* TEACHING OF JESUS §4; TEACHING OF JESUS[S] §*3a, b*.

JOHN THE BAPTIST also preached a call to repentance before the coming kingdom (Matt. 3:2), but in addition he offered a baptism of repentance for forgiveness of sins (Matt. 3:11; Mark 1:4; Luke 3:3; Acts 13:24; 19:4) which would lead to acts of righteousness (Luke 3:8; Matt. 3:8). The connection between human repentance and divine forgiveness had already been made in intertestamental Judaism (Prayer Man. 7; Test. Gad 7:5), but a "baptism of repentance for the forgiveness of sins" had no prototype. The lustrations of the Qumran community (*see* DEAD SEA SCROLLS §5*b*; DEAD SEA SCROLLS[S] §7) did entail a repentance and a cleansing (1QS 3.4, 9; 4.21; 5.13-14), but the washing was neither a baptism nor an eschatological act. Whatever its origin, the anarthrous (lack of definite article in the Greek) nature of the phrase in the NT and its continued usage in the early church (Acts 2:38; Barn. 11:1; Herm. Man. IV.3.1) indicate its confessional importance for the first Christians.

2. Repentance and conversion. As in contemporary Hellenism and Hellenistic Judaism, the term "turn" was used to describe the shift of religious loyalty or philosophical insight (Epictetus, *Discourses* I.iv.18; Test. Iss. 6:3), so in early Christianity the term for conversion to the new religion was ἐπιστρέφω. In I Thess. 1:9 Paul used conversion language to describe how the Thessalonians "turned to God," and he feared the Galatians might "turn back" to their former conviction (Gal. 4:9; cf. 1:6). Paul's use of the word "repentance" was not conversionary but signified a change of attitude (II Cor. 7:9-10) or a moral change (II Cor. 12:21; Rom. 2:4). In Acts we find the same "turning" terminology to describe conversion (9:35; 11:21; 14:15; 15:3, 19; 26:18), except that now μετανοέω has been added as a synonym ("repent and turn to God," 3:19; 26:20). The language of repentance gradually displaced the language of turning, both in Hellenism and Christianity (Poimandres I, 28; ApocryJn II 9, 20-22; 13, 23–14, 2). Within the NT itself repentance began to shift from a radical turning to God in face of the end time to a remorse over one's pagan ways and an adoption of the Christian gospel (II Pet. 3:9). It was in this context of conversion that the baptism of repentance became so important (Acts 2:38).

3. Church renewal and personal recommitment. The author of the book of Revelation (*see* REVELATION, BOOK OF) shared the early church's idea of repentance as conversion from pagan ways to the Christian faith (9:20-21; 16:9-11), but he also understood it as the reaffirmation of faith. So in the letters to the seven churches he appealed for repentance, i.e., the renewal of Christian commitment (2:5, 16, 21-22; 3:3, 19). The author of II Timothy had a similar concern for wayward persons in the congregation (2:25), though the context is more that of schism than of apathy (*see* PASTORAL EPISTLES).

The authors of the gospel of John, the letters of John (*see* JOHN, GOSPEL OF; JOHN, LETTERS OF), and Hebrews (*see* HEBREWS, LETTER TO THE) saw in Jesus Christ the ultimate manifestation of the heavenly truth. Because repentance (conversion) was the acceptance of ultimate truth, falling away from the faith could only occur to those who did not or could not appropriate it. Thus, the author of I John believed that persons who left the faith had never been a part of it (2:19). And the author of Hebrews declared that for such there was no further possibility of repentance (6:4-6; cf. 12:17).

Postapostolic writers continued to call for repentance from apathy much as the prophets had exhorted Israel (I Clem. 7). But repentance became primarily the return of errorists to the unity of the church (Ign. Phila. 3:2), described theologically by Ignatius as unity with God (Ign. Phila. 8:1; Ign. Smyr. 9:1). Apparently some teachers or leaders interpreted Heb. 6:4-6 in a legal sense rather than a philosophical one, so that they decried the laxity of a "second repentance" (Herm. Mand. IV.3.1). Writing in a pastoral way, the author of the Shepherd of Hermas (*see* HERMAS, SHEPHERD OF) agreed with their intent that conversion should be complete, but he also insisted on God's mercy if the Christian failed (Herm. Mand. IV.3.5).

See BAPTISM[S] §2.

Bibliography. J. Behm, "μετανοέω," *TDNT,* IV (1942 [ET 1967]), 989-1008; G. Bertram, "ἐπιστρέφω," *TDNT,* VII (1964), 722-29; B. Poschmann, "Busse," *RAC,* II (1954), cols. 802-12, and *Penance and the Anointing of the Sick* (1951 [ET 1964]), pp. 5-35; A. D. Nock, *Conversion* (1933); J. B. Bauer, "Conversion," *Sacramentum Verbi,* I, 138-40; H. Pohlmann, *Die Metanoia als Zentralbegriff der christlichen Frömmigkeit,* Untersuchungen zum NT, XXV (1938); E. F. Thompson, Μετανοέω *and* Μεταμέλει *in Greek Literature until 100* A.D., Historical and Linguistic Studies in Literature Related to the NT (1909); G. F. Snyder, *The Shepherd of Hermas,* The Apostolic Fathers, VI, (1968), 69-72; W. D. Chamberlain, *The Meaning of Repentance* (1943); K. Barth, *Church Dogmatics,* IV/2 (1955), 566-70; W. Barclay, *Turning to God* (1964); S. Richter, *Metanoia* (1966), pp. 11-37.

G. F. SNYDER

***REPHAIM.** While the basic understanding of the two usages of the term in the OT has not changed since 1962 (*see* REPHAIM), the Ugaritic evidence has been much discussed, particularly since the publication of new texts in *Ugaritica* V. Recent attempts at synthesis entail different explanations of the origins of and the relation between the two Hebrew usages.

1. The Ugaritic evidence. At the end of the major BAAL myth, the sun-goddess Shapsh is described as ruling over the *rpum* and consorting with the dead. On the occasion of Keret's marriage, El blesses him with the promise that he will be great "among the *rpum* of the earth/underworld, in the assembly of the gathering of Ditana"—the latter an old tribal name. The so-called "Rephaim texts" (*see* REPHAIM 1) still have many obscure features. An individual divine name of the same root has been identified in personal names, and in the title of Danel: "Man of Rapi'." This deity is the main subject of a recently published text (Gordon 602) in which he is called "everlasting king"; on the obverse he drinks at a banquet with certain high gods; on the reverse is a prayer that his power may be in Ugarit forever—here he is addressed as "Rapi' of the earth/underworld."

2. Recent interpretations. There are two alternative views. According to one, the Ugaritic *rpum* refers to the dead, deified in some sense (cf. the parallelism: "*rpum* . . . divine ones"), and possessing healing and quickening powers. Their name is taken as a present participle: "Healers." Thus it is among his dead ancestors that Keret will be reckoned to be great, and it is over the dead that Shapsh exercises authority during her nocturnal journey through the underworld. The "Rephaim texts" have been interpreted as dealing with Danel's invocation of his dead ancestors. The primary use of the Hebrew term would then be also in reference to the dead, though they are deprived of their special powers. The ethnic use would be a secondary application to those now among the dead who were believed to have once lived in the land as a race of giants. Ugarit also knew a deity with the cognate name Rapi', "Healer," who may originally have had nothing to do with the dead, but may have come to be regarded as the head of the *rpum.* He was Danel's patron, as El was Keret's. *See* DEITIES, UNDERWORLD[S] §1*d.*

According to the other view, the *rpum* represent both a mythological and a social group. The former ("divine ones") were headed by the god Rapi', and were patrons of the latter, an aristocratic warrior guild headed by the king (Keret or Danel in legend), and dedicated to the service of the former. Both OT usages would derive from this situation at Ugarit: the reference to the specialized guild would be the source of the ethnic sense; application of the term to the guild's deceased members would have been generalized to apply to all the dead. In one development of this view the name is interpreted as a stative: "healthy, whole." The mythological *rpum* are taken to be the pantheon in general, and Rapi' is identified with EL. The "Rephaim texts" and two of the newer texts are read as mythological accounts of a banquet (*mrz'*) corresponding to a feast celebrated by the guild.

Bibliography. A. Caquot, "Les Rephaim ougaritiques," *Syria,* XXXVII (1960), 75-93; A. Jirku, "Rapa'u, der Fürst der Rapa'uma-Rephaim," *ZAW,* LXXVII (1965), 82-83; B. Margulis, "A Ugaritic Psalm (RŠ 24.252)," *JBL,* LXXXIX (1970), 292-304, esp. 299-302; S. B. Parker, "The Ugaritic Deity Rāpi'u," *UF,* IV (1972), 97-104; C. E. L'Heureux, "The Ugaritic and Biblical Rephaim," *HTR,* LXVII (1974), 265-74.

S. B. PARKER

RESURRECTION IN INTERTESTAMENTAL LITERATURE. *See* FUTURE LIFE IN INTERTESTAMENTAL LITERATURE[S].

***RESURRECTION IN THE NT.** The primary reference of resurrection in the NT (ἀνάστασις; once only ἔγερσις, Matt. 27:53) is to the action of God in raising Jesus from the dead to life and enthroning him at his right hand. Only once in the NT is Jesus said to have raised himself (John 2:19, cf. 10:17-18); elsewhere it is always God's act. But resurrection as such is inadequate to convey the fullness of Easter faith that infuses the NT writings. It is not raising to life as a resuscitation, but a raising of Jesus from the underworld of the dead to a position of sovereignty by the defeat of death to make life available and to exercise judgment at the end. Prior to faith in the Risen One is the experience of the crucified Jesus as the Living One (a title in Rev. 1:18 and perhaps Luke 24:5; cf. the prologue to the GOSPEL OF THOMAS) in which the latter is understood in the sense of the Exalted or Glorified One.

1. The resurrection tradition in the gospels. The gospels contain a variety of traditions and theological reflections which were derived from the one common affirmation that Jesus' disciples had encountered him in such a way that they were convinced that he was the living LORD, commissioning them to continued service.

a. The empty tomb. It is generally recognized that Mark 16:1-8 is the full account this gospel originally had of the resurrection story (*see* MARK, GOSPEL OF §10, and MARK, GOSPEL OF[S]) . For Mark the discovery of the empty tomb by the women is the form by which the Resurrection is proclaimed. The meaning of the tomb is interpreted to the women and Mark's readers in the words, "He has risen, he is not here" and the promise of reunion in Galilee (vss. 6-7) .

A tradition reported in John's gospel and interpolated into some MSS of Luke tells that Peter visited the tomb to convince himself of the women's story, but that he remained uncertain (Luke 24:12) . In John it is the BELOVED DISCIPLE, the companion of Peter at the tomb, who is brought to belief (John 20:2-9) . Tradition analysis has not yet resulted in common agreement as to whether we have in this story an early Easter testimony or a later development of the kerygma.

b. The appearances. The concept of resurrection from the dead is an interpretative statement explaining in Jewish apocalyptic and anthropological categories the basic Easter event, viz., the appearances of Jesus to his disciples. Resurrection is a reflective interpretation of encounters with the Living One which had the power to convince, to generate a new community, to establish an authorized leadership, and to commit to mission. The key word is ὤφθη, which is probably to be translated in an active sense, "he (Christ) appeared" or "he showed himself."

For Matthew and his community the significance of the Resurrection was the authentication by the enthroned Messiah of the church's role in making disciples, baptizing converts, and giving guidance in the way of discipleship (Matt. 28:18-20) . To Mark it confirmed the way of the SON OF MAN in humiliation and exaltation, which is the true way for each disciple. Luke recognized the risen Jesus as the sovereign Lord who is the source of repentance, forgiveness, and final redemption, and for John resurrection found expression in the offer of forgiveness of sins and the interpretation of the truth of Christ through the Spirit (John 16:13-15; 20:23) .

c. The pregospel tradition. Behind the traditions presented in the gospels are hints of an earlier witness to an appearance of the risen Jesus to Peter and the disciples in Galilee (Luke 22:31-32; 24:34, perhaps 5:1-10; Mark 16:7; cf. I Cor. 15:5 and John 21) , but nowhere in the NT is there any story of that formative experience. Many interpreters believe that the oldest report of the Easter appearances made no distinction between the resurrection of Jesus and his elevation to share the rule with the Father. Cf. Mark 14:25, 62; Luke 23:43; John 12:32; 7:39; 12:16; 13:31; Acts 2:32-33; 3:13; 5:30-31; Rom. 8:34; Eph. 1:19 ff.; Phil. 2:8-9; Col. 3:1; Heb. 1:3; 8:1; I Pet. 1:21. Raising already carries the idea of elevation, but exaltation conveys more graphically the affirmation of the lordship of Jesus. The earliest form of the Easter event may have been the experience of Peter and his brethren in coming to faith, "seeing" that Jesus was not a martyred prophet but in very fact Lord and Christ enthroned in glory. The mystery of that conviction is the mystery of faith.

2. The Pauline tradition. It is generally agreed that in I Cor. 15:3-5 Paul has used an early creedal or catechetical formulation, perhaps dating back to the Damascus community *ca.* A.D. 40. The list of witnesses—perhaps a combination of two groupings —contains a series of statements each introduced by ὤφθη, followed by the names of witnesses, six in all if we include those Paul added to the traditional statement (vss. 6-8) . The emphasis falls upon the direct experience of seeing as also in I Cor. 9:1 or in the equivalent phrase "reveal" (ἀποκαλύπτω) in Gal. 1:16. Probably the traditional form is a legitimation formula basing the community and the authority of its leaders on an appearance of the risen Christ. It is certain that Paul's references to his own vision of the Lord, the only primary testimony we have from an eyewitness, are presented as the credentials of his apostleship.

For Paul, the eschatological act of God in raising Jesus from the dead gives assurance of the believer's future transformation into a new existence as a complete and restored person or, in Paul's own term, a body-spiritual (σῶμα πνευματικόν) (I Cor. 15:42-50, 51-57; II Cor. 5:1-5; Phil. 3:21) . *See* BODY §B2*d*; BODY[S]; IMMORTALITY; IMMORTALITY[S]; FUTURE LIFE IN INTERTESTAMENTAL LITERATURE[S] §3.

3. Derivative meanings. The *raising* of Jesus is not the fundamental datum of Christianity; more accurately it is that the *living* and *sovereign* Lord is identified with Jesus of Nazareth. The concept of resurrection recalls the historical personage and ministry; exaltation declares the heavenly power and glory of the same person.

Each of the gospels and Paul's own word interpret the Resurrection as a call to preach the gospel to everyone. Jesus had risen in the world and not out of it, and this meant the continuation of his program of action. The events of Good Friday and Easter were determinative for this preaching, but so was Jesus' own announcement of the nearness of God's rule and his teaching about discipleship that went with it. *See* Matt. 28:16-20; John 20:19-23; 21; Acts 10:40-42; I Cor. 9:1; Gal. 1:15-16; II Cor. 4:6.

In Paul's understanding, the fact that God raised Jesus from the dead became the model for the new life of the believer now and the promise of the ultimate outcome of redemption. Thus he began the disassociation of Resurrection from its unity with the final events of PAROUSIA and Judgment and made it interpretative also of the basic nature of Christian living from start to finish.

See also THEOPHANY IN THE NT[S] §3*a*.

Bibliography. For literature prior to 1960, see the bibliog. to original art. Of extensive recent studies, the following are representative. M. Barth and V. H. Fletcher, *Acquittal by Resurrection* (1964); D. P. Fuller, *Easter Faith and History* (1965); W. Künneth, *The Theology of the Resurrection* (rev. ed., 1951 [ET 1965]); H. Conzelmann, "On the Analysis of the Confessional Formula in I Cor. 15:3-5," *Int.*, XX (1966), 15-25; S. H. Hooke, *The Resurrection of Christ as History and Experience* (1967); C. F. D. Moule, ed., *The Significance of the Message of the Resurrection for Faith in Jesus Christ,* SBT, 2nd ser. VIII (1968); F. Mussner, *Die Auferstehung Jesu,* Biblische Handbibliothek, VII (1969), new Ger. research; P. de Surgy, ed., *La résurrection du Christ et l'exégèse moderne* (1969); C. F. Evans, *Resurrection and the NT,* SBT, 2nd ser., XII (1970); W. Marxsen, *The Resurrection of Jesus of Nazareth* (1968); R. H. Fuller, *The Formation of the Resurrection Narratives* (1971).

E. W. SAUNDERS

RESURRECTION, THE TREATISE ON. A brief, didactic letter written by a Christian-Gnostic teacher to his pupil Rheginos in response to the latter's questions concerning the resurrection of individual believers. Found at NAG HAMMADI and known also as "The Epistle to Rheginos," this letter is of singular importance for illuminating the type of heretical teaching combatted in II Tim. 2:18, "that the resurrection is past already."

1. Nature of the document. The text, which is generally well-preserved, is one of five writings in Codex I (the Jung Codex). It is written in the Subachmimic dialect of the COPTIC LANGUAGE, but the original text was composed in Greek. The same scribe who copied the text of OnRes was responsible for the first two writings of Codex XI.

The title, like those of twenty-one other tractates from Nag Hammadi, appears only at the end of the document and describes only in part its literary genre. This title was probably formulated out of the allusion to Rheginos' questions "concerning the resurrection" (*etbe tanastasis*) in 44:6 and the teacher's offer "to discuss (*mareplogos*) the matter" in 44:11-12: thus, *plogos etbe tanastasis,* "The Treatise/Discourse on the Resurrection." In fact, it is a letter whose structure reflects that of epistolary literature of the first centuries A.D. Opinion differs, however, over whether OnRes has a general address and is highly conventional in tone; or whether it is more personal in nature, even though lacking a *praescriptio* naming sender and receiver (cf. Ptolemy's *Letter to Flora*).

2. Major themes. ***a. Individual resurrection.*** Although resurrection of the individual is not philosophically demonstrable and seems to be fantasy, it is, because of Christ's resurrection, an assured reality for the elect (46:3–47:10; 48:3-38). Appropriating some of the phrases of Pauline mysticism, the author tells Rheginos: "We suffered with him (Christ), and we arose with him, and we went to heaven with him" (45:24-28; cf. Rom. 8:17 and Eph. 2:5-6). Although some have found here a mystical union of the believer with Christ rooted in baptismal experience (cf. Rom. 6:3-11), the author's emphasis is not sacramental but is rather on the need for the elect through "knowledge" (γνῶσις) *and* "faith" (πίστις) to identify with and experience proleptically Christ's own death, resurrection, and ascension (44:27-29; 46: 14-19). This may be a case of "over-realized eschatology" built tendentiously on such Pauline teachings as Col. 1:13-14 and Eph. 2:4-6.

b. The spiritual body. The resurrection of the elect will entail, immediately at death, the ascension to heaven of a spiritual body constituted of inward, invisible "members" covered with a new, spiritual "flesh" (47:4-8; 47:38–48:3). The usual Gnostic belief (e.g., in II ApocJas 59:9-14; ApocPaul 20:22-23; 21:17-20; Iren. Her. I.xxv.4) in the ascent and ultimate reabsorption into the spiritual godhead of the bare "spirit-self" is not present here. Instead, in a manner remarkably like that of Paul (cf. I Cor. 15:35-38), the author posits a radical discontinuity of form between the earthly and the resurrection bodies, but continuity of identification (e.g., Moses and Elijah are introduced from Mark's transfiguration story as proofs of the Resurrection, 48:3-11).

c. Resurrection life. The believer should live in the present as though his resurrection had already occurred (49:16-36). The cessation of life on this earth (the "not yet" of eschatological hope) is inevitable; but having participated in the resurrection and ascension of Christ (the "already" of eschatology), the believer ought to live as one already dead and thus already raised (49:24-36). Doing so involves continual "practice" (ἀσκεῖν) in freeing oneself from the "divisions," the "bonds," and the inimical "Element" who rules this life and world (49:11-16, 29-35). Such a view differs from Paul's eschatological reservation, the "not yet" of Christ's PAROUSIA (I Cor. 15:51-55; II Thess. 2; *see* PAUL THE APOSTLE §10).

3. Authorship, provenance, date. The first editors of OnRes argued that it was written by the Gnostic teacher Valentinus (*see* GNOSTICISM §2*c*; GNOSTICISM[S] §4*b*), following his composition of the Gospel of Truth and his break with the church at Rome, i.e., between 140-45 and *ca.* 165. Most scholars acknowledge that it contains the fragment of a Valentinian cosmogonic hymn (46:35–47:1), uses Valentinian symbolism (48:34–49:5), and shows familiarity with Valentinian aeon speculation (45:11-13). But a majority reject Valentinus himself as the author. Because of a developed sense of a scriptural "canon," the affinities of the letter's arguments with second-century debates about resurrection, and the similarity of its secondary usage of Gnostic motifs to the practices of some of the Alexandrian Fathers, most now hold OnRes was written late in the second century by an anonymous Christian-Gnostic teacher who was familiar with Valentinian teaching.

See also NAG HAMMADI[S]; GNOSTICISM; GNOSTICISM[S] §4*b*; RESURRECTION IN THE NT and supplementary article.

Bibliography. M. Malinine, H.-Ch. Puech, G. Quispel *et al.*, *De Resurrectione* (*Epistula ad Rheginum*) (1963), the first critical ed.; M. L. Peel, *The Epistle to Rheginos: A Valentinian Letter on the Resurrection* (1969; rev. Ger. ed., 1974), a full study of the letter's teaching and of responses to the first critical ed. The most important articles include: R. Haardt, "Die Abhandlung über die Auferstehung des Codex Jung, I und II," *Kairos,* XI-XII (1969/70), 1-5, 241-69; H. M. Schenke, "Auferstehungsglaube und Gnosis," *ZNW,* LIX (1968), 123-26, denies the letter's Valentinian provenance; W. C. van Unnik, "The Newly Discovered 'Epistle to Rheginos' on the Resurrection, I and II," *Journal of Ecclesiastical History*, XV (1964), 141-52, 153-67. M. L. PEEL

RETRIBUTION. In English usage, the term continues to carry the reciprocal sense of its Latin antecedent, *retribuere* (to give again, to give as due). Broader than VENGEANCE, which refers only to punishment inflicted in return for a specific injury, retribution means the repayment of someone according to that person's just merits or deserts. In religious literature, the term usually refers to the rewards and punishments meted out to persons by God—especially to the dead who are resurrected on the judgment day (sometimes called the day of retribution).

1. Terminology. For all of its importance in theological discussion, the English term "retribution" has no exact biblical equivalent. KJV never employs it, and RSV uses it only twice (Rom. 11:9; Heb. 2:2). Yet the conviction to which the term points—e.g., that God rewards the righteous and punishes the wicked—must surely be regarded as one of the most fundamental motifs of Scripture. Where that motif is present in the OT, such verbs as שכר, "hire"; the *piel* of שלם, "reward, requite"; גמל, "recompense"; נקם, "avenge"; or their derived nouns may occur. Similarly, the terms μισθός, "wages, reward"; ἀποδίδωμι and ἀνταποδίδωμι, "repay, recompense"; ἐκδικέω, "avenge"; and their related forms may occur in NT discussions. However, a study of terminology is not the best way to approach a biblical theme such as this. Key passages dealing with the image of God as judge, the relation of sin to misfortune, and eternal reward and punishment often contain none of the terms mentioned above. A more satisfactory approach is to examine treatments of the idea of retribution in their larger biblical contexts and, without creating an artificial synthesis, to attempt to relate these discussions to one another.

2. The evolution of biblical notions of retribution. The classic OT embodiment of the ancient Near Eastern principle of retribution is the so-called *lex talionis* (Exod. 21:23-25; cf. Lev. 24:19-20; Deut. 19:21). According to this "law of retaliation," a willfully injured party can claim the right to exact from the offender "life for life, eye for eye, tooth for tooth." *See* CRIMES AND PUNISHMENTS §A2; LEX TALIONIS[S].

a. Retribution in civil law. Although a broad principle of retribution underlies the OT laws of injuries (e.g., Deut. 25:11-12), Israel's tradition of civil law in fact has seldom demanded literal in-kind retaliation against offenders. The literature is rich with laws providing for the punishment of crimes, including capital punishment; however, by insisting on strict tests of intentionality and providing monetary substitutes for "life," "eye," etc. (cf. Mekilta at Exod. 21:23-24), rabbinic interpreters acknowledged the inadequacy of a rigid and exact application of the law of retaliation to the task of regulating interpersonal affairs. Jesus also denied its validity in moral behavior by opposing to it an ethic of radical nonviolence (Matt. 5:38-42). Paul echoes this rejection of the *lex talionis* in his admonition, "Repay no one evil for evil" (Rom. 12:17). When understood in its strictest sense as recompense in kind, retribution seems to biblical writers to be a prerogative more of God than of man (Rom. 12:19-21; cf. Heb. 10:30; Deut. 32:35).

b. Divine retribution. i. *OT.* The older Pentateuchal narrative sources drew upon the theme of retribution in accounting for specific episodes in the history of Yahweh's dealing with his creation generally (e.g., the punishment of Adam, Eve, and the serpent, Gen. 3:14-19; cf. 4:11-12; 6:5-7; 11:6-9), and with Israel in particular (e.g., Korah's rebellion and consequent punishment, Num. 16; cf. 11:31-35; 12:1-16; 21:4-9). However, it remained for the eighth-century B.C. prophets Amos, Hosea, Isaiah, and Micah to identify the idea of retribution almost solely with the activity of God, and to elevate the principle of divine retribution into a thoroughgoing basis for historical understanding. Amos' frequent indictment-threat sequences assert that the historical disasters which afflict the covenant people are in fact Yahweh's retributive acts (e.g., Amos 2:4-5; cf. 4:1-3; 6:4-7; Isa. 28:14-22; Mic. 3:9-12). Under the influence of the preaching of the prophets, the school of theologians who produced the Deuteronomic writings (*see* DEUTERONOMY; DEUTERONOMY[S]; *also* DEUTERONOMIC HISTORY, THE[S]) expanded the concept of divine retribution in two ways. First, they greatly amplified the contingent nature of divine rewards and punishments within the covenant relationship, characteristically employing conditional formulations in their sustained exhortations: "If you obey the voice of the Lord your God, being careful to do all his commandments . . . , all these blessings shall come upon you and overtake you" (Deut. 28:1-2). Second, by undertaking to reinterpret Israel's experience from its beginning as a legal relationship enforced by specified sanctions, they and the author of the CHRONICLES after them established the retributional scheme as the normative OT way of looking at Israel's history.

The effect of God's retributive justice on individuals rather than the nation as a whole is the concern of the OT wisdom literature (*see* WISDOM IN THE OT[S]). From very early times peasant and king alike had sought the counsel of the sage on how best to attain blessing and avoid God's anger. Much of the book of Proverbs is given over to contrasting the destinies of the godly and the ungodly (*see* PROVERBS, BOOK OF §12). Loss of wealth, progeny, even life itself, lie in store for the wicked; the righteous can hope for the opposite fate (13:21; cf. 15:24). Such suffering as good men do experience can be put down as evidence of Yahweh's favor. "My son, do not despise the Lord's discipline or be weary of his reproof, for the Lord reproves him whom he loves, as a father the son in whom he delights" (3:11-12). The same theme is carried on in the PSALMS, particularly in the seventeen wisdom-based "Psalms of the Two Ways" (e.g., Pss. 1; 37; 73), and in the deuterocanonical wisdom book of ECCLESIASTICUS. In each of these collections, the retribution which falls on transgressors is often seen as the consequence inherent in the evil deed, and therefore inevitably to be expected. "Behold, the wicked man conceives evil," writes a psalmist. "He makes a pit, digging it out, and falls into the hole which he has made" (Ps.

7:14-15 [H 15-16]; cf. Prov. 26:27; Ecclus. 27:25-26). This insight has led some scholars to assert that OT writers regarded retribution as the automatic result of "fate-producing deeds" rather than a direct act of God (Koch).

The last major OT refinement in the notion of divine retribution answers the objection of those who, particularly in times of oppression, failed to see any reward for the righteous in the events taking place around them. As if in answer to the psalmist's question, "O Lord, . . . how long shall the wicked exult?" (Ps. 94:3), the apocalyptic writers of the late OT period posit for the first time a judgment day at the end of the age. On that day of retribution, all resurrected persons will be judged according to their records in the heavenly book, and some will be sent "to everlasting life, and some to shame and everlasting contempt" (Dan. 12:2). *See* APOCALYPTICISM; APOCALYPTICISM[S]; IMMORTALITY[S]; FUTURE LIFE IN INTERTESTAMENTAL LITERATURE[S].

ii. *NT*. The idea of divine retribution is mediated to early Christianity principally in its eschatological form. Jesus frequently asserts that those who love their enemies and do good will receive God's forgiveness and reward at the end—with the clear expectation that the opposite is also true (Luke 6:35-38; cf. Matt. 18:35). In such gospel passages as Matt. 25, the Son of man is the eschatological judge who sends the unrighteous "into eternal punishment, but the righteous into eternal life" (vs. 46). The concept permeates the thought of Paul, the catholic epistles, and the Epistle to the Hebrews. Although Paul does not dwell in detail on the picture of the judgment day, he exhibits the faith that, at the end of time, God will "render to every man according to his works" (Rom. 2:6; cf. 13:12; 14:10-12; I Cor. 15:32; II Cor. 5:10). As for the book of Revelation (*see* REVELATION, BOOK OF and supplementary article), it seeks to inculcate confidence in God's final act of reward and punishment. "Behold, I am coming soon, bringing my recompense, to repay every one for what he has done" (Rev. 22:12).

3. The biblical context of divine retribution. Contemporary believers and theologians generally find the concept of divine retribution repugnant, at least in its most explicit biblical versions. Inconsistently and unsystematically expressed though it is, however, the motif is deeply rooted in OT and NT and cannot be explained away. The theme stands as a constant reminder of the seriousness with which the biblical writers understood God's hatred of evil and injustice and his will to overcome them. However, the Bible also records dissent to the image of God the requiter. This critique, although no more consistent and systematic than the retribution scheme itself, forms a broad theological context within which the notion of divine retribution can be seen.

The Pentateuchal writers J and E (*see* DOCUMENTS; YAHWIST[S]; ELOHIST[S]) understand the operative principle in history to be, not the *lex talionis,* but rather a divine plan of national and human salvation. Beginning with the unconditional promise to Abram (Gen. 12:1-3), they trace the journey of the chosen people toward a renewed state of unbroken relationship with God in a new Eden, the Promised Land. In various ways the prophetic writers, too, encompass the theme of divine retribution within this larger vision, stressing God's redemptive purpose (*see* DISCIPLINE, DIVINE [S]). Later writers, particularly Deutero- and Trito-Isaiah (Isa. 40–55; 56–66), see the possibility of a relationship between God and humanity that transcends reward and punishment, and which they describe in the figures of "new heavens and a new earth" (Isa. 65:17) and "a new covenant" (Jer. 31:31; *see* GRACE IN THE OT[S]). On empirical, existential grounds Job rejects the retributional scheme advanced by his "friends," and goes so far as to accuse God of inexplicably slaying both the wicked and the righteous (Job 9:22-24; cf. Eccl. 8:14). Yet, in the last analysis, Job discovers that the reality of God's unfailing presence supersedes all questions arising from the apparent failure of his absolute justice and righteousness. *See* JOB, BOOK OF §11 and supplementary article §5.

Challenges to the theme of retribution from the side of God's redemptive purpose also run through the gospels and the teachings of Paul. In the parable of the prodigal son (Luke 15:11-32), Jesus shows that God's will to redeem far outweighs his need to pay exact recompense for sins (cf. Matt. 20:1-16; Luke 18:9-14). John's gospel in particular reveals the tension between the retributional scheme and the theme of God's larger saving purpose. John affirms the tradition that the Son of man will judge the dead at the general resurrection (John 5:25-29), and he asserts the impossibility of salvation outside of belief in the Christ (3:18). Yet in the same context, his gospel affirms, "God sent the Son into the world, not to condemn the world, but that the world might be saved through him" (3:17).

Although Paul is deeply committed to the absolute demands of God's righteousness (cf. I Cor. 6:9), like other Jewish writers of his time he sees that a strictly conceived retributional theology would provide no grounds for hope (cf. IV Ezra 7:119). All have sinned and fallen short of the glory of God, and therefore all are justified by his grace only as a gift and not because of merit (Rom. 3:23-24). In fact, the apostle goes well beyond the retributional scheme to speak of a judgment which destroys evil works but spares the doers of those deeds (I Cor. 3:15). In his several affirmations that the entire universe can look forward to the day of redemption (e.g., Rom. 8:21), Paul articulates a divine plan of universal salvation which is the larger context within which his teachings regarding divine retribution should be placed. "Then comes the end," he writes, "when he delivers the kingdom to God the Father after destroying every rule and every authority and power. . . . When all things are subjected to him, then the Son himself will also be subjected to him who put all things under him, that God may be everything to every one" (I Cor. 15:24, 28).

Only the apocalyptic books of the Bible appear to admit no exception to the conviction that God's purpose for his creation cannot be completed until his retributive justice has run its full course, and all evil forces and persons have been extirpated. But even in this literature it seems arguable, in the book of Daniel at least, that the primary purpose of the author(s) is not to revel in the bloodshed and misery of those condemned to everlasting contempt, but rather to show that God's purpose will be vindicated precisely at that moment when the principalities and powers of this world confess him "God of gods and Lord of kings" (Dan. 2:47; cf. Phil. 2:9-11).

4. Summary: retribution within redemption. The retributional approach to understanding God's way of dealing with evil in the world, though frequently adopted by biblical writers, is also qualified and perhaps finally overcome within the Bible itself. The often-expressed faith that God's redemptive purpose is greater than the literal requirements of his justice is neither a denial of the seriousness of God's opposition to evil in every form, nor failure to recognize the moral relationship of human deeds to their consequences. But it is a powerful countermotif to the notion that God is bound to exact payment in kind from sinners. In their confrontation with God's holiness and mercy, biblical figures repeatedly discover, not only their own unworthiness and culpability, but also his determination to redeem and restore them.

Bibliography. K. Koch, "Gibt es ein Vergeltungsdogma im AT?" *ZThK,* LII (1955), 1-42, argues that biblical writers understood retribution to consist of the automatic consequences of "fate-producing deeds," rather than of any direct divine activity. This article, critical response to it, and other relevant essays have been collected by Koch in his *Um das Prinzip der Vergeltung in Religion und Recht des AT* (1972). *See also* J. G. Gammie, "The Theology of Retribution in the Book of Deuteronomy," *CBQ,* XXXII (1970), 1-12, which also lists other participants in the debate. Relevant dictionary articles on retribution include: G. Lanczkowski, F. Horst *et al.,* "Vergeltung," *RGG,* VI (3rd ed., 1962), cols. 1341-55; H. Preisker and E. Würthwein, "μισθός κτλ," *TDNT,* IV (1967), 695-728. Recent longer studies include: J. P. Martin, *The Last Judgment in Protestant Theology from Orthodoxy to Ritschl* (1963), which documents the increasing unacceptability of retribution ideology to dogmatic theology; L. Morris, *The Biblical Doctrine of Judgment* (1960), largely a semantic study written from a conservative standpoint. *See also* W. S. Towner, "Retributional Theology in the Apocalyptic Setting," *USQR,* XXVI (1971), 203-14; B. S. Jackson, "The Problem of Exod. XXI 22-5 (*Ius talionis*)," *VT,* XXIII (1973), 273-304.

W. S. TOWNER

***REVELATION, BOOK OF.** The variety of proposals and solutions that continue to be offered by scholarly research on Revelation substantiates the judgment that few primitive Christian writings have received so much attention and yet have remained so elusive.

The current progress in understanding Revelation moves in a way parallel to that of other NT writings. Just as in the study of the Synoptic gospels, the emphasis on source criticism and FORM CRITICISM has been replaced by stress on REDACTION CRITICISM. The source theories of the last century gave way to a scholarly consensus that Revelation is the theological work of one author. Whereas the different source hypotheses assumed that Revelation is a more-or-less mechanical compilation of sources, recent studies have established the unity of the book by analyzing its style and language, and by showing its careful composition and its compelling theological conception. For example, since linguistic analyses show that the seven letters form an integral part of the book, Revelation as a whole can no longer be seen as a Jewish writing to which minor Christian corrections have been added. Instead it must be evaluated as an authentic Christian work addressed to the situation and problems of the Christian communities in Asia Minor. Recent studies of its Christology have amply demonstrated its genuinely Christian outlook. But the author did not develop his Christian vision of reality in abstract theological sentences. Instead he used the language of symbol and myth.

1. Literary composition. In form Revelation is a literary creation in which a vision or myth has been set within an epistolary framework. The author has arranged the visions and auditions according to a definite plan, in which the number seven has a key role.

a) Although Revelation contains diverse images and visions, its over-all organization reveals careful composition and startling coherence. The repetition of stereotyped formulas and the archaizing, Hebraizing style of the book are a primary means for achieving this effect. Further features of composition are: cross references (e.g., the characterizations of Christ in the inaugural vision all recur in chs. 2–3, and all the promises to the victor in chs. 2–3 are repeated in chs. 21–22); pre-announcements (e.g., the announcement of the final judgment in 14:6-10 refers to chs. 17–20); contrasts (e.g., the great harlot in ch. 17 is a contrasting image to the woman in ch. 12 as well as to the bride of the Lamb in ch. 19). A basic device is simple repetition. One vision is set after another, linked together by a common stock of images and symbols, the repetition of which gives unity to the whole and creates a cumulative effect (e.g., the color "white" occurs throughout the book). Whereas in Daniel each vision has its own set of symbols, in Revelation they are distributed over the whole book.

The use of numbers and numerical structures (e.g., seven churches, seven stars, seven candelabra, seven messages, seven seals, trumpets, and bowls; two book visions, two witnesses, two beasts, etc.) is another means chosen by the author to achieve an interwoven texture and unitary composition. This interweaving of the visions in a numerical way has the effect of combining a cyclic sense of repetition with a continuing forward movement. This forward thrust of the narrative is interrupted by interludes (e.g., eschatological announcements, visions, or hymns) which proclaim the final salvation. By repeatedly breaking through the successive visions of cosmological plagues and historical struggles, the author is able to show the final sense of all these struggles and sufferings in the present. This double pattern of forward-moving narrative and anticipatory depiction in the interludes is a structural expression of the tension between the present reality and the hope for the future.

b) Since the author does not employ discursive, logical patterns but speaks in the language of symbol and myth, his images are "open ended" and cannot be nailed down to one single, definite interpretation. The difficulty of interpretation, moreover, is greatly increased because the author did not freely create his materials. Instead he used traditional materials, especially from the OT, Jewish apocalypticism, pagan and Jewish mythologies, and early Christian traditions. To express his own theological vision he reworked them into a new and unique composition. Revelation therefore appears on the one hand as an artificial construction of materials derived from traditions which are heterogeneous in origin and theology, and on the other hand as an artistic mosaic of poetic conciseness. The author does not quote his materials verbatim or copy them, but reworks them to present his own message, as can be clearly seen from his use of the OT. It is therefore very difficult to separate tradition from redaction and to give the imagery of Revelation a definite and clear meaning. This multivalent character of the imagery and the visions makes it necessary to interpret each symbol and image of Revelation in the context of the theological perspective and meaning of the whole book.

2. Theological perspective. One of the most significant features distinguishing Revelation from Jewish apocalyptic literature is that it is not pseudonymous (*see* PSEUDONYMOUS WRITING[S]). The author does not take a fictitious standpoint in the past in order to present surveys of world history in the form of predictions. What he writes is not esoteric knowledge but an unsealed, open, and clear theological message and exhortation, related not to the past but to the present and to the immediate future. Revelation therefore gives neither an interpretation of history nor an interpretation of the OT but a prophetic interpretation of the situation of the Christian community in the time before the end.

a) Although Revelation is full of eschatological language, scholars have nevertheless considered history rather than eschatology as the main theme and formal structural principle of the book. The different historical interpretations of Revelation maintain that it describes the sequence of real events that will take place in the course of the history of the church or in the final times before the end of the world. The historical-theological interpretations, on the other hand, seek to show that enduring, valid truth concerning history, especially salvation history, is revealed in the visions of the book. These interpretations have also presupposed that the author's concern with history has determined the structure of Revelation. The proponents of the historical interpretation seek to trace in the sequence of images a continuous or dialectic line of history. Previous attempts to explain the sequence of the visions by a linear or cyclic understanding of time have not succeeded in presenting a convincing interpretation, however. The central apocalyptic section creates special difficulties for these interpretations. The author mixes elements of past, present, and future, just as he mixes his verb tenses. Revelation therefore does not appear to be structured according to a temporal, historical sequence. Instead, its contents seem to be ordered thematically.

The main concern of the author is not the course of history but the particular power struggle between the divine and antidivine forces which are represented on earth by the Christian community and the ROMAN EMPIRE. In contrast to Jewish apocalypticism, Revelation attempts to give meaning to the suffering of the Christian communities, not by reference to the divine plan of history, but by an understanding of the present from the horizon of the future. The imminent expectation of the author is not based, as in Jewish apocalypticism, on the belief that the world is growing old and reaching its end. It is based on the understanding that the Christian community is the "sign" that through the death and resurrection of Jesus Christ the reign of the satanic powers on earth is limited. In Revelation the focal point of the "already" and "not yet" is not history but the KINGDOM OF GOD and the rule of Christ. The main theological symbol of Revelation therefore is the throne.

b) The apocalyptic question, who is Lord over the world, is central for the theology of Revelation and is formulated here in mythological categories. Whereas Paul understood the question in terms of the alternative between the lordship of Christ and that of the cosmic powers, the author of Revelation interprets this alternative in political terms. The question, God or Satan, is now posed as the question of the kingship of God and Christ or the dominion of the Roman Caesar and the goddess Roma. This cosmic-mythological and political alternative is reflected in the lives of the Christians who represent the kingdom of God on earth (1:6; 5:10), but are still in danger of losing their right to participate in the eschatological kingdom by becoming followers of the beast. Those rejecting the beast and its cult are excluded from the economic and social life of the earth (13:15) and have to accept captivity and death (13:10). Revelation demands unfaltering resistance to the Roman imperial cult, because to give divine honors to the emperor would mean to ratify his claim of dominion over all people.

The author of Revelation appears to formulate his theology in opposition to an enthusiastic, Gnosticizing position which advocated accommodation to the syncretistic Roman religion and its cultic practices. Since loyalty to the Roman civil religion did not necessarily involve creedal statements, but mainly required participation in certain cultic acts and ceremonies, enthusiastic theology made it possible to conform to the imperial cult without giving up faith in the one true God and Jesus Christ. It was an attractive solution for Christians in Asia Minor, since it allowed Christian citizens to participate actively in the social, commercial, and political life of their society. This theology, probably represented by the Nicolaitans, had many followers in the Christian communities of Asia Minor, precisely because it advocated such a policy of accommodation. In this polemic context the theology of Revelation took shape.

The author gives an alternative theological interpretation of the situation of the Christian community in Roman society. His sharp rejection of the Nicolaitans in the seven letters and his total rejection of the imperial cult in the main part of the book are interrelated. The letters and the apocalyptic part of the book polemicize against the same theology and address the same situation. The author of Revelation can advocate such a sharp rejection of the Roman Empire and its cult because he is convinced that the power and dominion of God and Christ will prevail over the antidivine forces. His prophetic interpretation of the situation presupposes that a victory of God and Christ in this power struggle is at hand, and that God's kingship will soon be exercised on earth as it is now in heaven.

The author describes in three steps how the dominion of God and Christ extends over the world. It is established first in heaven; then it extends to the earth; and finally it destroys the underworld. Through his death and enthronement in heaven, Christ receives the kingship (ch. 5), whereas Satan is thrown down to earth (ch. 12). The representatives of Christ and Satan are therefore pitted against each other on earth in the end time. With the parousia of Christ the second step is taken (19:11–20:6): Christ and the victorious Christians assume the kingship on earth; the two beasts are imprisoned; and Satan is thrown into the abyss. Finally, Satan, death, and Hades are destroyed (20:7-15) in the last judgment, and a new heaven and earth appear (21:1–22:5). Then the victorious Christians will serve God and Christ on their thrones, and they will exercise their kingship forever.

See also Apocalypse, Genre[S]; Apocalypticism; Apocalypticism[S]; Eschatology of the NT[S] §1*c*; Prophet in the NT; Rome, Early Christian Attitudes Toward[S] §6.

Bibliography. G. B. Caird, HNTC (1966); J. Comblin, *Le Christ dans l'Apocalypse* (1965); A. Feuillet, *The Apocalypse* (1962); E. Schüssler Fiorenza, *Priester für Gott. Studien zum Herrschafts-und Priestermotiv in der Apokalypse,* NTAbh, NS VII (1972), "The Eschatology and Composition of the Apocalypse," *CBQ,* XXX (1968), 537-69, and "Apocalyptic and Gnosis in the Book of Revelation and Paul," *JBL,* XCII (1973), 565-81; T. Holtz, *Die Christologie der Apokalypse des Johannes, TU,* LXXXV (2nd ed., 1971); H. Kraft, HNT (1974); K. P. Jörns, *Das hymnische Evangelium,* StNT, V (1971); P. S. Minear, *I Saw a New Earth* (1968); U. Vanni, *La Struttura Letteraria dell' Apocalisse,* Aloisiana, VIII (1971).

E. Shüssler Fiorenza

***REVELATION IN HISTORY.** The formula "revelation in history" rose to prominence largely in reaction against the biblical interpretation of the "liberal" period in theology. It had then been common to depict a process whereby biblical man moved from a more "physical," "natural," and "tribal" view of God to conceptions increasingly more spiritual, elevated, ethical, and universal. Even if degenerations also occurred, the positive side of biblical religion lay in this progress to higher forms.

Against this the later biblical theology (*see* Biblical Theology[S] §8) reacted strongly. The core of the Bible, it argued, was not a process of discovery or an advance toward higher conceptions; it was not an increasingly spiritual religion, but a revelation, through which God had made himself known to man. The medium through which he did so was not ideas or conceptions, however lofty, but historical acts, earthly, timebound, and contingent. The Bible was not the document of man's religion in its progressive refinement: rather, revelation came to man from without; it was different from his religion and cut across its lines and patterns.

The argument thus directed against liberal theology was used also against old-fashioned conservative theology: the revelation of God was not in statements or propositions, whether those of the Bible or of traditional theological documents, but in acts of history. The Bible witnessed to these acts and was in this sense a book of history, but its narratives were not intended as exact and objective history. Rather, they were theologically informed history, and it was wrong to make faith depend on their historical accuracy.

1. Problems about revelation in history
2. Cullmann
3. Bultmann
4. Wright
5. Von Rad
6. Pannenberg
7. Albrektson
8. A possible alternative
Bibliography

1. Problems about revelation in history. As a reaction against the older liberal and conservative positions, the emphasis on revelation in history was right and proper. Positively, on the other hand, it was much less helpful. The formula "revelation in history" has proved to be a highly ambiguous one.

a. Ambiguity about the nature of the revelatory events. Are these events which seem to involve transcendent causation, like the raising of someone from the dead? May they equally be events that follow normal patterns of historical causation, like the campaigns of Nebuchadrezzar? And what about non-events, events that are solemnly related by the Bible but probably never took place at all, like the Flood? Again, what of events that, if they took place at all, took place in a form so far different from the biblical narrative of the incident as to be scarcely recognizable, such as the capture of Jericho by Joshua (or indeed, on some theories, the entire story of the conquest of Canaan)?

Again, does an event, in order to be revelatory, have to be an "outward" event and in that sense historical, or can it also be a mental event, perhaps the perception of problems by a teacher or writer in a particular way in his own historical situation, and thus a perception that starts a new train of thought and a new direction in biblical tradition? But if events of this latter kind are admitted, does this not mean that "revelation" is not absolutely different from normal processes of cultural or literary development?

b. Ambiguity about the sense of "history." Is the character of the revelatory event accessible to critical historical investigation in the same way as any other historical event? If it is not, then in what sense is it history? If it is, then can critical investigation confirm that the event was revelatory in the sense of being different from any other event? If critical investigation cannot determine this, then it means that the event, as seen by critical history, is a quite normal event, and that the revelation aspect is hidden from historical study. If this is so, is it not disingenuous to claim that the revelation is "in" history? Again, since it is agreed that the Bible must be read with the methods of historical criticism, did the revelation occur in the story as the Bible tells it or in the history reconstructed by critical study which we believe to have been the actual history?

c. Ambiguity about the relation between revelation and history. Is history itself equivalent to revelation? Or is revelation a special historical process clearly different from the remainder of history? Is it a series of momentary vertical irruptions into history? Does it infiltrate into all history, or only into those segments of history which are described or interpreted in the Bible? And why should revelation in history stop at the end of the biblical canon—and indeed in the middle of it, since (to judge from most works on the subject) remarkably little revelation in history took place between the Babylonian exile and the coming of Jesus?

One unclarity has been particularly damaging: many writers, while emphasizing that revelation took place in history, effectively said no more than that ancient Israel and the early church *thought in terms of* a historical revelation. There is all the difference in the world between a claim to revelation in history and an observation about the thought patterns of ancient Israel. The latter, even if correctly so stated, might be no more than a striking feature of the thought or religion of the time, and is quite different from an actual affirmation of revelation in history. The more scholars have emphasized the biblical thought patterns, the more they have left themselves open to the supposition that these thought patterns, rather than the claimed revelatory events, were the true foundation for biblical theology.

d. Difficulties in the relation between revelation and the biblical text itself. Does everything in the Bible derive from, or point to, revelation, or is this true only of certain elements within the Bible? Are there elements which, far from being revelatory, are only evidence of the religious traditions of the time? But, if so, is it possible for scholarship to treat its material on two quite separate levels? Does not all of the Bible then require interpretation as the religion of the Israelites, of Paul, of John? If historical events are revelatory only as interpreted within the perspective of biblical faith, is it not the religion of Israel that provided the basis for this interpretation? But, since the term "revelation" has been largely used in express opposition to religion, does this not deprive the term itself of its *raison d'être*?

Again, the Bible seems to include substantial bodies of material which do not emphasize a revelation in history: e.g., in the OT, the wisdom literature, and much of the Psalms. More serious still, there are difficulties even with central and favorite texts like the story of the Exodus. The text does not depict a divine act, which is the basis of all knowledge of God; rather, it represents God as communicating freely with men before, during, and after the events. Only God's previous communication with Moses made the exodus event intelligible or even possible. The conversation at the burning bush, far from being an "interpretation" of the divine acts, is a precondition of those acts. It seems impossible to consider the events as a separate and prior source from which the form of the entire biblical text necessarily derived.

2. Cullmann. In the postwar period his *Christ and Time* provided a very powerful advocacy of a salvation history (*Heilsgeschichte*) approach. The early Christian conception of time, he argued, was that of a straight line, formed by the joining together of decisive moments (this he took to be the sense of καιροί). Contrary to Greek views, eternity was not something different from time, nor a negation of time; rather, it was identical with the totality of time. The effect was to separate out from the totality of history the special period of revelation; this in turn lent authority to the Bible as the witness deriving from that time. Cullmann met severe criticism for his general exegetical and theological position (Bultmann, Conzelmann) and also for his linguistic arguments (Barr). His later *Salvation in History* seeks to restate the same position, but uses a rather different set of arguments.

3. Bultmann. Bultmann's position was far different. To him also the term "history" was of great importance. He was critical of mere "historicism" and had some other points in common with those who emphasized revelation in history; but on the whole his views led in another direction. The great "event" of Jesus is in a sense a historical event, but in a more important sense it is an eschatological event, and this means a proleptic anticipation of the end of history, which thus takes the believer "out of" history. The emphasis thus falls rather on the "historicity" of human existence, which is given and confirmed by the event of faith. Thus while revelation is a significant term, it is less important that it should be "in history"; rather, it must be here and now, and have an effect that takes one out of history. Many of the events narrated in the Bible are miraculous and thus mythical; such narrations may indeed serve as a vehicle of revelation, but this does not mean that the events are a locus of revelation in history. Moreover, though Bultmann is not so completely negative toward the OT as has been supposed, he does make it clear that "to the Christian faith the OT is no longer revelation" and thus "to us the history of Israel is not history of revelation." When the locus of revelation is thus restricted to the NT, the meaningfulness of any emphasis upon revelation in history is reduced.

4. Wright. Wright's position was typical of those in the English-speaking world that were based on the OT. He laid a heavy emphasis on revelation in history, contrasting this drastically with the environing religions, in which history had little or no role. The viewpoint, however, was more associated with archaeology than with exegesis of the OT text, and the events were more emphasized than the transmission of tradition. But what was the character of these events? The terminology of the "God who acts" was taken over from the realism of the biblical narrative, but the scholar himself looked on the events in a quite immanent and naturalistic way. The events were thus emptied of all the precise features (dividing of the sea, wall of water, etc.) which alone gave special content to the terminology of "God who acts," and the acts of God became only an abstraction. Wright was thus open to the charge of equivocation, pressed especially by Gilkey. Wright's later thought moved away from the supposed events to characteristic Israelite mental patterns, such as the covenant idea; it seemed as if the whole emphasis on "God who acts" had never been meant at face value. The actual narrative form of the text had little impact upon Wright's thinking.

5. Von Rad. Von Rad's theology also takes salvation history as a central category. By contrast with a man like Wright, the association is with literary analysis, form criticism, and tradition-history, and the approach is exegetically fertile. The stress is laid on the specific *kerygma* of the various strata within texts. Israel's "confession" was to historical events, and the mainstream of its traditions consisted in the kerygmatic reinterpretation of the tradition of these events. The OT is thus in principle a book of history. But von Rad is well aware of a difference between history as the OT tells it and history as critical scholars perceive it. There are "two histories" in question, and it is with the history as "confessed" by the OT that OT theology has to deal. But in what sense is it revelation in history if the confession is not to events as they took place? Von Rad replies that, though the two histories are different, the difference should not be exaggerated, and the history as confessed has its roots and basis in the actual history, though it is not identical with it.

His definitions of what constituted the salvation history seem artificial; they fit with the Deuteronomic point of view, rather than (say) with that of P. Von Rad strikingly fails to identify this history with all the history related in the OT. It does not include the story of David; and the entire late OT tradition, because of changes in the views of history and of law, does not count as salvation history either. Thus his work, in spite of the stimulus it afforded, left an enormous range of problems open.

6. Pannenberg. The systematic theologian Pannenberg, working within the heritage of von Rad, put forward proposals intended to obviate some of these difficulties. He abandoned the idea of "two histories," one of them known to critical investigation and the other the subject of "confession." If revelation is in history, it must be in a history accessible to critical study—though Pannenberg interprets this in a wide sense. Moreover, revelation, because it was revelation of God himself, could not be partial and therefore could not be commensurate with less than the totality of history; it thus took place at the end of history. Here he takes up apocalyptic—an aspect which fitted rather badly into the von Rad theology—and makes it central to his theological scheme. Pannenberg's position, though restating a view of revelation in history, contains many innovations as against earlier views and must be judged to be only partly in continuity with them.

7. Albrektson. It has generally been assumed that the view of history as the milieu of divine activity was distinctive to Israel and lacking from its environment. Ancient religions, with the sole exception of that of Israel, were built not upon history but upon nature, or upon a cyclic view of time. These beliefs rest on no close and competent analysis of the facts of ancient religion; rather, they are a transcript of outdated philosophical views coming from the mid-nineteenth century before good sources for ancient religion were available. G. E. Wright, indeed, built much upon the studies of the Frankforts and Jacobsen, but they connected Mesopotamian religion with society and social organization rather than with nature. Albrektson's recent work, in spite of any corrections in emphasis that may be needed, shows that the entire picture of ancient religion assumed in much theology is false: "The OT idea of historical events as divine revelation must be counted among the similarities, not among the distinctive traits; it is part of the common theology of the ancient Near East."

If we extend this into a later period, we must recognize that theology has been equally misguided in minimizing the sense for history among the Greeks. Within the total construct "history" only some elements can be ascribed to the OT; others come primarily from Greek sources. Moreover, the OT in its later stages fixed the canonical history in a past time and bequeathed little historiographical stimulus to a later age; in Hellenistic times it was where Jewish life came into contact with the Greek world that it was historically creative.

8. A possible alternative. The character of the OT is story rather than history: over large portions its form is narrative, though there also are large areas which are not narrative at all. This narrative spirals back and forward across what we would call history, sometimes coming closer to it and sometimes going far away from it. The story is cumulative: each stage provides material that is essential for what follows. This happens on different levels. In one way it happens in the reading of the text as a text, with its sequence from the beginning onward; it also happens, in another way reconstructed by critical study and not visible on the surface of the text, in the actual growth of the tradition. The sequence is not a development in an evolutionary sense, since it does not necessarily rise to ever higher forms; but it is a cumulative story in which new elements are made meaningful through that which has gone before, while tensions in the existing tradition lead to changes and the formation of new tradition. Each stage of tradition has an influence on the religion of the following stage, and it is through the religion that the older tradition is mediated to later stages.

The term "revelation," as it has come to function within theology, does not fit with the structure of communication through cumulative tradition within the Bible. In theology, revelation indicates the basic possibility of communication from God to man, but in the Bible this is assumed rather than stated; it does not constitute a problem, for it is assumed from the beginning of the story that God freely communicates with man. All that is said or done thereafter is *further* communication and not a primal initiation of communication. Further, as we have seen, though in theology revelation is sharply distinguished from religion, within biblical study this distinction cannot be usefully made.

It may be expected therefore that the clear thematic guide, which revelation in history appeared for a time to furnish for biblical theology, will in the future be cut across by many other considerations, and that the formula in itself will cease to be either clear or useful. Historically, however, it will be seen to have played an important part in biblical study over several decades.

Bibliography. B. Albrektson, *History and the Gods* (1967); J. Barr, *Old and New in Interpretation* (1966), *Biblical Words for Time* (2nd. ed., 1969), and "Some Aspects of Berkhof's 'Christelijk Geloof," in H. Berkhof, *Weerwoord* (1974); R. Bultmann, *History and Eschatology* (1957), "The Concept of Revelation in the NT," *Existence and Faith* (1960), and "The Significance of the OT for Christian Faith," in *The OT and Christian Faith,* ed. B. W. Anderson (1963); H. Conzelmann, *The Theology of St. Luke* (1960); O. Cullmann, *Christ and Time* (1951 [2nd ed., 1962]), *Salvation in History* (1967); H. and H. A. Frankfort, J. A. Wilson and T. Jacobsen, *Before Philosophy* (1946); L. Gilkey, "Cosmology, Ontology, and the Travail of Biblical Language," *Journal of Religion,* XLI (1961), 194-205, and *Naming the Whirlwind* (1969); W. Pannenberg, *Revelation as History* (1968); G. von Rad, *OT Theology,* 2 vols. (1957, 1960); G. E. Wright, *The OT against its Environment* (1950), *God Who Acts* (1952), and *The OT and Theology* (1969). J. BARR

***RIDDLE.** A saying that both puzzles the hearers and communicates to them. Riddles can only arise where language is ambiguous, for they employ common vocabulary to dispense privileged information to those worthy of receiving it. In antiquity riddles tread on perimeters of myth and divination, particularly in rites of passage. Often constituting a judgment situation, they generate anxiety on the part of riddler and opponent. Tests of worthiness more than intelligence, riddles endeavor to drain opponents of strength (I Kings 10:1-5).

The form of riddles includes interrogative and statement, poetry and prose. When couched in poetic language, they employ the full repertoire of ancient rhetoric—parallelism, strophic arrangement, paronomasia (*see* WORDPLAY IN THE OT[S]), onomatopoeia, description, personification, narrative debate, and so forth. A special prose category is the "neck riddle," in which the hero must pose a riddle that cannot be solved, or unravel one given him on penalty of death should he fail (cf. contest literature and controversy dialogues).

The content of riddles ranges widely, but sex and religion stand out above all other topics. Once the mythical and demonic background gives way, riddles come to function as teaching devices and entertainment. Their place in life includes initiation ceremonies, courtship and marriage, political contests between kings or courtiers (I Esd. 3:1–4:47), ritual questions in catechetical form, banquets, and schools.

In Israel *ḥîdhâ,* "riddle" (=*meliṣâ* and *māshāl*) serves as an umbrella term, referring to enigmatic proverbs and allegories, impossible questions, contest literature, question and answer dialogue, and embryonic catechisms. A bond between numerical proverb and riddle is probable. Still, differences suggest caution. These include the attitude toward paradox, the nature of the solution, and the specificity of the answer. While allegory and parable/simile use ciphers, they differ from the riddle in that they do not attempt to mislead.

The classical riddle in the OT occurs in the Samson narrative (Judg. 14), itself a "neck riddle." Actually three riddles lie concealed within the story, each resplendent with *double entendre* and ornate poetic clothing. Samson's riddle ("Out of the eater came something to eat. Out of the strong came something sweet") probably antedates its context. The Philistines respond with a riddle whose answer is love ("What is sweeter than honey? What is stronger than a lion?"), and Samson retaliates with an allusion to cohabitation ("If you had not plowed with my heifer, you would not have found out my riddle"). The attempt to explain Samson's riddle as one of consonance is entirely unnecessary and depends on a questionable Ugaritic and Arabic parallel and an assumption that *dbsh* has replaced a hypothetical, rare Hebrew word for honey, *'ary.*

Attempts to discover riddles in Pss. 19 and 49 have produced interesting results. In both instances the riddle form has been altered, but can be restored with minimal textual disturbance. Two possible riddles in Ps. 19 describe the sun as a bridegroom making a journey to the ends of the earth and allude to mute divine messengers, day and night. Similarly Ps. 49 may preserve two riddles. The first asks how man and beast are alike, providing the misleading answer that they are both stupid. The real solution, however, is that both die. The second picks up the theme of death's sovereignty and asserts victory over it, presumably for the wise person who solves the "neck riddle." Even the pessimistic Sayings of Agur (Prov. 30:1-4) may conceal an ancient riddle reminiscent of the first one in Ps. 49.

Riddles in disintegrated form may lurk beneath the biblical text in far more places than has so far been ascertained. The suggestion in Num. 12:8 that normal prophetic utterance was in riddles and the legend about Solomon's riddling (I Kings 10:1-5; II Chr. 9:1-4) support such an assumption. For example, does the proverb cited in Eccl. 9:4 ("A living dog is better than a dead lion") conceal a riddle that justifies remarriage by a woman who, once the wife of an important citizen, now joins herself to a nobody? Many ciphers within the OT can easily be transformed into riddle; the crucial question is whether or not they ever existed in riddle form. While a final decision cannot be made at present, the following texts may conceal disintegrated riddles: Prov. 5:1-6, 15-23; 6:23-24; 16:15; 20:27; 23:27, 29-35; 25:2-3; 27:20; 30:15-33; Song of

S. 4:12. Perhaps, too, the enigmatic revelations to Moses (Exod. 3:13-15) and Manoah (Judg. 13:17-19) were once riddles seeking to determine worthiness.

Bibliography. J. L. Crenshaw, "The Samson Saga: Filial Devotion or Erotic Attachment?" *ZAW,* LXXXVII (1974), 470-504, and "Wisdom," *OT Form Criticism,* ed. J. H. Hayes (1974), pp. 225-64 (esp. pp. 239-45); M. Hain, *Rätsel* (1966); A. Jolles, *Einfache Formen* (2nd ed., 1956); H. P. Müller, "Der Begriff 'Rätsel' im AT," *VT,* XX (1970), 465-89; L. G. Perdue, "The Riddles of Psalm 49," *JBL,* XCIII (1974), 533-42; J. R. Porter, "Samson's Riddle: Judges XIV, 14, 18," *JTS,* NS XIII (1962), 106-9; S. Schechter, "The Riddles of Solomon in Rabbinic Literature," *Folklore,* I (1890), 349-58; A. Taylor, *A Bibliography of Riddles* (1939), and *The Literary Riddle Before 1600* (1948); A. Wünsche, *Die Räthselweisheit bei den Hebräern mit hinblick auf andere alte Völker* (1883).

J. L. CRENSHAW

***RIGHTEOUSNESS IN THE NT.** Recent discussion of terms pertaining to "righteousness" focuses essentially on the Pauline material.

1. Käsemann's thesis, prompted by Schlatter, is that it is philologically impermissible and theologically fatal to absolutize the meaning of "righteousness of God" as a divine gift. Käsemann especially criticizes the trend in interpretation since Bultmann and warns against isolating the gift from its giver, thus allowing it to be subject to human disposal. This, he believes, tends improperly to set both ecclesiology and anthropology above Christology, and fails to recognize that "the indissoluble connection between power and gift" represents a "fundamental phenomenon" of Pauline theology. Even though Paul regards God's righteousness primarily as a gift, still the traditional meaning of "a power which brings salvation to pass" continues to play a major role, and it modifies the motif of gift in such a way that a distinction must be made between the justification that is vouchsafed to the individual on the one hand, and, on the other, the power, asserted in it, of the divine righteousness as the claim to lordship over creation. God's righteousness is therefore to be defined as "the rightful power with which God makes his cause to triumph in a world which has fallen away from him and which yet, as his creation, is his inviolable possession."

While Käsemann strives to avoid suggesting that the two aspects of gift and power are mutually exclusive, his followers have largely neglected the character of gift. Müller explicitly eliminates the motif of "the effect of a judicial decision" from the concept and defines it one-sidedly as eschatologically making God's rightful power real in the world. Stuhlmacher fully absolutizes the concept of power, seeing in God's righteousness a "judicial and creative process that concerns the world," "God's governance that spans the eons," which is personified in Christ and is manifested as "the creator's liberating right to his creation."

This position appeals first of all to the religio-historical roots of the idea of righteousness. Käsemann interprets "righteousness of God" as a fixed Jewish formula, particularly significant in Qumran literature, but to be traced back all the way to Deut. 33:21. Stuhlmacher regards it as a technical term and attempts to demonstrate that it is a basic theme in apocalyptic, "the creator's demonstration of power that establishes justice." The continuing function of the formula in earliest Christianity is said to be evident in Matt. 6:33 and Jas. 1:20, as is Paul's familiarity with this tradition in Rom. 3:5, 25. It is conceded that Paul does not appropriate it unaltered, yet because of the analogous usages in Qumran literature, neither the righteousness of God as present fact nor the *sola gratia* can be regarded as peculiar to Paul; what Paul did was to expand the motif of covenant-faithfulness into that of faithfulness to the creation (Müller), or to provide a "christological orientation," understood as a "radicalization and universalization of the promise in the doctrine of the justification of the ungodly" (Käsemann).

The strongest exegetical support for this interpretation is provided by those passages which, in Käsemann's view, treat the righteousness of God "not primarily as a gift, but as power" (II Cor. 3:9; Rom. 10:3; 6:13 ff.), employ it as a designation for Christ (I Cor. 1:30), use it as a synonym for "God's glory" (Rom. 3:21 ff.), and, like Rom. 3:5—which Käsemann describes as a key passage—treat of God's covenant faithfulness. Such an interpretation claims to offer the theological advantage of joining the gift to the divine Giver and of overcoming the old alternatives of imputed and effectual righteousness and of justification and sanctification. Only thus, it is said, can we avoid an individualistic narrowing of the concept and give due regard to the worldwide import of God's righteousness.

2. The question of the religio-historical background. The view that "the righteousness of God" is a Jewish formula has been contested on the grounds that the documentation is sparse (Lohse). Thyen accepts only the evidence of Deut. 33:21; 1QS 10.25; 11.12; 1QM 4.6; Test. Dan. 6:10. In addition, Bultmann has noted that there is a breadth of meaning impossible for technical terminology. Against Stuhlmacher's soteriological interpretation of Deut. 33:31, Thyen sees here the sense of the "righteousness of God as punishing judge." Independent of the controversy, Becker had already shown that, while God's righteousness appears in the Qumran materials as the "sphere of salvation," it also appears there as a gift (so also Kertelge), and Lohse finds that throughout the literature of postbiblical Judaism the concept has the sense of a genitive of origin. Finally, it is impossible to speak of an influence of a formal concept of power in Matthew, because there "righteousness" (δικαιοσύνη) is always used in an ethical sense (Strecker).

The question of the relevance of Jewish documentation for the understanding of Paul is also raised by recent fundamental reflections on linguistics (e.g., Barr). The history of concepts does not unfold according to evident necessity. Whenever a concept is used, previous semantic contents are open to modification. That is to say, the origin of the concept "righteousness of God" does not automatically determine its function in a new context; the priority of the synchronic interpretation over the diachronic must be unconditionally maintained (Klein).

Rom. 3:25-26 offers striking proof of the way Paul adapted and changed the term "righteousness of God." In the fragment of Jewish-Christian tradition which underlies vs. 25, δικαιοσύνη θεοῦ is clearly to be read as a subjective genitive, meaning God's redemptive faithfulness in forgiving sins. But after the formulation of vs. 26*a*, deliberately parallel to that of vs. 25*b*, Paul's own interpretation appears in vs. 26*b*, whereby it is clear how far for him the tradition is at the same time acceptable and in need of revision. Paul's essential concern is not to universalize the particularist motif of covenant-faithfulness into that of faithfulness to the creation (contra Käsemann, Müller, Stuhlmacher). The material from the tradition does not even sound the covenant theme, at least explicitly. Moreover, the category of "faithfulness to the creation" is far from adequate for an apostle who understands the Christ event precisely as the bringing about of a *new* creation (Kertelge). Käsemann's thesis that Paul's correction is motivated by his dissatisfaction with the catchword of the forgiveness of past guilt is not wrong, but too limited. Rather, Paul (with some support from earlier confessional formulations, Rom. 4:25; I Cor. 6:11) goes beyond the traditional expression, because he wishes to transpose its concept of God's righteousness as the definition of God's nature ("that he himself is righteous," εἰς τὸ εἶναι αὐτὸν δίκαιον) into a definition of God's way of working ("that he justifies him who has faith in Jesus," καὶ δικαιοῦντα τὸν ἐκ πίστεως Ἰησοῦ). His interest is obviously focused on anthropology. The specifically Pauline tendency is shown by the transposition of substantives into verbs (Conzelmann). That the noun "righteousness" is used with reference to human beings is clear from the fact that Paul describes it as "the righteousness of God through faith" (Rom. 3:22; cf. Phil. 3:9 and the parallelism of Rom. 10:4 and 10:6), thus the result of God's justifying action.

3. **Romans 3:5,** the only passage in which Paul himself speaks of God's righteousness using a subjective genitive, is not really the "key passage" for Käsemann's thesis. Instead, it is a further argument against it. Käsemann sees a parallel between the phrase in 3:5 and "the faithfulness of God" (πίστις τοῦ θεοῦ) in vs. 3. But this is misleading, because it disregards the connection between verb and substantive which is constitutive for the immediate context. In keeping with the setting of a trial, God's righteousness results from his having been justified (note the passive, δικαιωθῆναι, in vs. 4). God's righteousness is therefore the judgment, wrested from his human adversaries in the judicial process (κρίνεσθαι) which they have plotted. It means neither the judicial *justitia distributiva* (contra Bultmann, Bornkamm, Kertelge) nor the divine faithfulness to the covenant which will prevail in accordance with the apocalyptic expectations (contra Käsemann). It has rather an unequivocally forensic structure stating an essential characteristic of a relationship. It is true that in the context of Pauline usage this passage forms an exception. The irregularity, however, is due to the fact that, rather than God, humans pronounce judgment and are the "source" of the righteousness (Klein); it is not due to the fact that righteousness denotes a relationship established by the pronouncement of the judgment.

4. **Other passages** to which Käsemann has appealed also need to be reviewed.

i. *Rom. 6:13-23.* Whatever the precise meaning of "righteousness" here (commentators differ), in vs. 16 the accent is clearly placed, by means of the contrast ("death"), on the lot one is assigned —thus on the idea of gift. Moreover, Paul does not speak here of "the righteousness of God" but in nonspecific terms of "righteousness."

ii. *II Cor. 3:9.* Contrary to Käsemann's view, "righteousness" here should not be interpreted with reference to 1QH 6.19 but in light of "condemnation" (κατάκρισις), the concept with which it is contrasted. Thus, righteousness is here the gift of divine aquittal.

iii. *Rom. 10:3.* It is not the catchword "submission," but the contrast with "righteousness of their own" that determines the meaning of righteousness here. The latter is not a power but the product of human conduct, blasphemous self-confirmation.

iv. *I Cor. 1:30 and II Cor. 5:21.* These by no means document a "sphere of radiance" of righteousness conceived in terms of Jewish thought (Käsemann); rather, the parallelism with "sanctification" and "redemption" (I Cor. 1:30), like that of II Cor. 5:21*b* with vs. 19 ("not counting . . . trespasses"), shows that the gift of salvation is meant.

5. **Conclusion.** The consistent association of the substantive "righteousness of God" with the verb "justify" and the adjective "righteous" (cf. Rom. 1:17; 3:22-31; Gal. 3:11 with vs. 21) is important. Stuhlmacher's neglect of this is a serious error in method (Lohse), and conversely, Ziesler's differentiation between a forensically determined verb and an ethically determined substantive/adjective does not at all do justice to that association. Where a differentiation is made between the "fact" of justification and the "possibility" of moral renewal (Watson), provision is made anew for human autonomy, and the Pauline unity of justification and sanctification is shattered.

Käsemann's deepest concern is to ensure this unity and thus to emphasize the motif of the divine claim to dominion over the world as the center of Pauline theology. His concern is threatened, however, when the cosmological and anthropological dimensions are explained conceptually with the motifs of power and gift, or are set in opposition to each other. If we recognize that the righteousness of God is for Paul a relational concept which, in the genitive of origin, identifies the initiator and continuing Lord of this relationship and understands it as a miracle—as a new orientation of existence that is established by grace—then the gift is consistently regarded *as* power. It is no longer necessary to cast sideward glances at those dimensions which lie beyond anthropology, because it is certain that the divine action of justification does not occur except in the context of faith, and that God conquers the world by pacifying those who rebel against him.

Bibliography. E. Käsemann, "'The Righteousness of God' in Paul" (1964), *NT Questions of Today* (1969), pp. 168-82, "Justification and Salvation History in the Epistle to the Romans" (1969), *Perspectives on Paul* (1971), pp. 60-78, and *An die Römer,* HNT, VIIIa (1973); R. Bultmann, "ΔΙΚΑΙΟΣΥΝΗ ΘΕΟΥ," *JBL,* LXXXIII (1964), 12-16; J. Becker, *Das Heil Gottes. Heils- und Sündenbegriffe in den Qumrantexten und im NT,* SUNT, III (1964); C. Müller, *Gottes Gerechtigkeit und Gottes Volk. Eine Untersuchung zu Römer 9-11, FRLANT,* LXXXVI (1964); P. Stuhlmacher, *Gerechtigkeit Gottes bei Paulus, FRLANT,* LXXXVII (1965); G. Strecker, *Der Weg der Gerechtigkeit. Untersuchung zur Theologie des Matthäus, FRLANT,* LXXXII (2nd ed., 1966); K. Kertelge, *"Rechtfertigung" bei Paulus. Studien zur Struktur und zum Bedeutungsgehalt des paulinischen Rechtfertigungsbegriffs,* NTAbh, NF III (1967); G. Klein, "Gottes Gerechtigkeit als Thema der neuesten Paulus-Forschung," *Rekonstruktion und Interpretation,* BEvT, L (1969), 225-36; H. Conzelmann, "Paul's Doctrine of Justification: Theology or Anthropology?" (1968), *Theology of the Liberating Word,* ed. F. Herzog (1971), pp. 108-23; N. Gäumann, *Taufe und Ethik. Studien zu Römer 6,* BEvT, XLVII (1967); H. Thyen, *Studien zur Sündenvergebung im NT und seinen alttestamentlichen und jüdischen Voraussetzungen, FRLANT,* XCVI (1970), 56-60; G. Bornkamm, "Theologie als Teufelskunst, Römer 3, 1-9," *Geschichte und Glaube,* II, BEvT, LIII (1971), 140-48; C. J. Roetzel, *Judgement in the Community. A Study of the Relationship Between Eschatology and Ecclesiology in Paul* (1972); J. A. Ziesler, *The Meaning of Righteousness in Paul: A Linguistic and Theological Inquiry,* NTSMS, XX (1972), reviewed by N. M. Watson, *NTS,* XX (1974), 217-28; E. Lohse, "Die Gerechtigkeit Gottes in der paulinischen Theologie," *Die Einheit des NTs* (1973), pp. 209-27; J. Barr, *The Semantics of Biblical Language* (1962).

G. KLEIN

ROBINSON'S ARCH. *See* JERUSALEM Fig. 21; TEMPLE OF HEROD[S].

***ROMANS, LETTER TO THE.** Recent discussions of Romans have focused on certain problems of LITERARY CRITICISM, the structure of the letter, and its purpose (*see bibliog.*).

1. Literary criticism. ***a. Glosses.*** According to Bultmann's analysis, many verses are suspect. (i) 2:1 because of a break in context, which Schmithals believes is perhaps a marginal note by Paul to explain the sudden change of theme in vs. 3. But is there anything unclear about the transition? (ii) 2:16 because of the apocalyptic reference. Käsemann holds that this is indispensable. But in context it merely demonstrates the present application of the Law even among the Gentiles. Schmithals believes that vs. 16 has been separated from vs. 13 by a copier. But is such a misleading correction by a copier plausible? (iii) 6:17*b* because it breaks up an antithesis and uses non-Pauline terminology. Käsemann says that vs. 16*b* could not be continued without 17*b*. But 16*b* formulates the basic alternative, while 17*a* and 18 show the actual situation of the readers. (iv) 7:25*b* and 8:1 because of the psychological shift from the conflict previously described and because of a break in the train of thought. Käsemann agrees. (v) 10:17 because of a tendency toward generalization that does not fit the context. Käsemann believes that it is a christologically more precise variation of vs. 15. (vi) 13:5 because of a logical tension with vs. 6. Käsemann points out that this argument is circular. In addition, Schmithals excludes 5:6-7 on the basis of contextual analysis.

b. Chapter 16. Donfried does not find the arguments for the Ephesian note hypothesis convincing. According to him the textual evidence that Romans originally ended with 15:33 is too weak, considering the placement of the doxology in P⁴⁶. He suggests that the polemic of 16:17-20 is a concluding summary of ch. 14, that the people greeted as Paul's personal acquaintances are Jewish Christians who have returned to their homes in Rome after the revoking of the edict of CLAUDIUS, and that his acquaintance with them makes it possible for Paul to begin work in a previously unknown congregation. However, the evidence of P⁴⁶ can only be neutralized by the desperate postulate of an archetype whose author had to omit 16:1-23 for lack of space (Schmithals); 16:17-20 has an antiheretical character because it does not admonish peace between two groups in the church as does ch. 14, but rather separation from the pseudo-Christians; and the hypothesis of the returning exiles is inadequate, because Romans addresses the congregation as a whole as Gentile Christians (1:5-6, 13-15; 11:13; 15:15 ff.). On the other hand, 15:33 marks an ending just as clearly as does 16:20*b*; the final greeting missing there may have been included in 16:21-23, which competes with 16:16*b* and is misplaced after 16:20*b*—therefore difficult to explain (with McDonald) as a postscript. It is hardly conceivable that a letter addressed, like Romans, to a whole congregation would include such a list of greetings to individuals. This would be more appropriate in a letter to a prominent address in Ephesus (the household of ONESIPHOROS?), if the whole congregation is included and the warning against heresy applies to them all (Schmithals). The Ephesian destination of 16:1-20 can therefore hardly be disputed, whether this letter was sent to its recipients together with a copy of Romans (Manson), or whether it was first joined with Romans in the course of publishing the earliest Pauline corpus (Schmithals).

c. Integrity. Schmithals argues that we must reckon with two different letters, "Romans A" (1:1–4:25; 5:12–11:36; 15:8-13) and "Roman B" (12:1-21; 13:8-10; 14:1–15:4*a*, 7, 5-6; 15:14-32; 16:21-23; 15:33). He holds further, that 5:2-11 and 13:11-14 are Pauline, yet not originally part of the Roman correspondence; that 13:1-7 is traditional Jewish material added by an editor; and that 15:4*b* and perhaps 5:1 are attributable to an editor. Romans A and B are said to differ as to situation and theme: in A Paul has been hindered in his planned visit to Rome (1:13) and has no plans to visit Spain, whereas in B this visit is clearly seen as a step on the way to Spain; A deals with the universality of justification by faith, while B is concerned exclusively with peace between the strong and the weak; A attempts to win over the Romans to the Pauline gospel (1:15), while B treats them as a Pauline congregation. But just as it is methodologically precarious to resolve by literary criticism the undeniable tension between the earlier and later parts of the letter, so, on this hypothesis, the function of 5:1 and 12:1-2 as significant transitional markers would not be taken into account.

2. Structure. ***a. Compositional unity.*** Romans has no equal among the authentic letters of Paul for uniformity of composition. Leading the way among the numerous proposals for dividing Romans (overview in Zeller) is Bultmann's insight that chs. 1–8 successively treat the universal necessity of God's righteousness (δικαιοσύνη θεοῦ) (1:18–3:20), its christological manifestation as justification by faith (3:21–4:25), and its anthropological effect (5:1–8:39). This conception of God's righteousness is by no means lacking in 6:1 ff. (contrary to Luz's opinion); nor can it be reduced to a secondary theme in chs. 9–11 (Dinkler); rather, it provides the normative interpretation of the history of Israel and the basis of the concrete PARENESIS in 12:1–15:13 (Käsemann).

b. Arrangement. The compositional unity corresponds to the precise arrangement. Sections with a transitional function hold the entire work together: 3:9-20 sums up 1:18–3:8; 5:1 restates 3:21-31 and lays the basis for chs. 5–8; ch. 8 is a pneumatological variation of chs. 5–7; 12:1-2 is a transition from indicative to imperative; 13:11-14 concludes the general parenesis and leads to the special appeals to different groups. Moreover, calculated stylistic effects accentuate the conclusion of larger sections: e.g., a rhythmic Christ-formula, 4:25; the hymn-like passage, 8:38-39; the doxological praise, 11:33-36. There is also a purposeful use of traditional materials at key theological points: christological formulas, 1:3-4 and 4:25; a liturgical fragment, 3:25; the combination of a faith-formula and a confession, 10:9. Even though it may be extreme to conceive broad segments of Romans as a commentary on faith formulas which Paul has taken over (Conzelmann), nevertheless the consistent orientation of the argument to the church's credo is clear.

c. Themes. Most of the letter takes up themes of earlier Pauline epistles (especially of Galatians, Philippians, I and II Corinthians) (Bornkamm). Examples are: justification (cf. Gal. 3–4; Phil. 3; II Cor. 3); natural revelation (cf. I Cor. 1:21); Abraham (cf. Gal. 3–4); Adam and Christ (cf. I Cor. 15:22, 45 ff.); freedom of the children of God (cf. Gal. 4:4 ff.); the church as the body of Christ (cf. I Cor. 12); the strong and the weak (cf. I Cor. 8–10). It is not a question of simple restatement in Romans. Many themes reappear in modified form (e.g., in Rom. 5:12 Adam's fate is no longer, as in I Cor. 15:45 ff., a physical one, but rather one to be understood as a result of sin), and most themes are taken out of specific controversies, raised to a generalized level, and integrated into the leitmotif of God's righteousness. This fundamental characteristic makes Romans unique among Paul's writings, and allows it to be seen, to a considerable extent, as a résumé of Pauline theology. Its uniqueness marks it as a "letter-essay" in form (Donfried) and points to the historical puzzle of Romans.

3. Purpose. The peculiar literary structure of Romans makes it extremely difficult to see the relation between content and purpose. The question is not only why Paul writes to Rome at all, but why he writes the way he does. The question is not resolved by the supposition, based on a variation of the older circular letter thesis, that Paul is not only directing his words to the Romans, but that he has "all the Christian churches in mind" (Donfried).

a. The traditional view of the letter traces it back to Paul's interest in winning the support of the congregation for his Spanish mission, establishing himself in Rome for this purpose, and protecting his mission from possible Jewish or Jewish-Christian disparagement. But against this are the following: (i) plans to visit Spain are only casually mentioned (15:24, 28); (ii) the anti-Judaistic passages are few (only 3:8; 6:1, 15 are unequivocal); (iii) Paul's most dangerous opponents were not Judaizers but Gnostics; and, above all (iv), the indication in 1:5-6, 15 that Paul's main intention is to preach the gospel to the Romans, an intention already given impetus by this letter (15:15-16).

b. Alternative views. The same objections (*see* §3*a*) apply to explanations based on events in Paul's life (Suggs, Bornkamm, Jervell, Wilckens). Paul's past history with his congregations and his impending visit to Jerusalem partially explain what he writes, as well as his choice and arrangement of themes—which almost give the letter the appearance of a last will and testament. But they do not explain his reason for writing. The reason is not that Paul was seeking to acquire support from the Romans in the expected conflicts in Jerusalem. How could such an alliance have been established so quickly? Or how could the plea for intercession (15:30) as a "political, diplomatic act of the Church" (Wilckens) be a key to the whole letter?

Some suggest that Paul is intervening in a dispute within the Roman congregation itself—by deciding against a Gentile-Christian (Donfried) or Jewish-Christian group, or by trying to reconcile two groups (Minear). But the Gentile-Christian origin of the community contradicts such an interpretation; the conflict dealt with in chs. 14–15 cannot be identified with such a contrast; and chs. 1–13 are in no sense a prelude to chs. 14–15.

c. Another solution. Any adequate resolution of the problem must begin with an often neglected difficulty. Although Paul wants to carry the gospel to Rome and does so with this letter, he is aware of his principle of "nonintervention" (15:20; cf. II Cor. 10:15), which constrains him from promulgating it where a congregation already exists. Both points have to be taken into account. His intention to preach the gospel is not directed toward "unconquered territory" in the world capital (Käsemann), nor can it be relegated to the past (Zeller), or reduced to an intention merely to visit (Wilckens). Even if the principle of nonintervention has motivated Paul's previous hesitation about visiting Rome (Bornkamm), this does not diminish its implicit validity, which is rooted in Paul's conviction that the "foundation" of a community (15:20*b*)—the realization of Christ's gospel as a force for establishing a church (I Cor. 3:11)—can be laid only once (I Cor. 3:10). This fact creates a special relationship between the congregation and the apostle who is entrusted with the gospel (cf. I Cor. 3:10-15 with 4:15). It has been concluded from this (Klein) that in the course of turning his missionary work toward the West, Paul would have sought to evangelize Rome because of its lack of a "foundation." It may be misleading to describe its shortcomings as a lack of *apostolicity*. But it is clear that on Paul's definition, no consolidated congregation yet existed in Rome, i.e., no congregation solidly bound to the one true gospel (Gal. 1:6 ff.). This view corresponds to known historical data. Related to this is the unique absence of a cowriter and the unusual appearance of the gospel motif in the salutation (1:1-7), as well as the surprising absence of the "church" (ἐκκλησία) concept in the letter. Schmithals also believes Paul wanted to proclaim his gospel in Rome and thus establish Christianity there as a *church* (ἐκκλησία), but he ascribes this to the fact that the Roman Christians, formerly "God-fearers," remained susceptible to Jewish influences. Thus he does not consider "Romans A" a summary of the Pauline gospel, but its application to the equality of Jew and Gentile. But one must ask whether this concrete anthropological issue is not in fact fundamental for the Pauline message of justification, and conversely, whether the assessment of 7:17–8:39 as a dogmatic section independent of the theme is correct. In any case, recent debate shows that Romans can be adequately interpreted only by seriously viewing it as an occasional letter in the form of an essay that goes beyond the occasion, by investigating the circumstances that make such a literary genre necessary, and by reflecting appropriately on the fact that on this occasion Paul places the theme of God's righteousness at the center of the discussion.

Bibliography. T. W. Manson, "St. Paul's Letter to the Romans—and Others," *Studies in the Gospels and Epistles*, ed. M. Black (1962), pp. 225-41; R. Bultmann, "Glossen im Römerbrief," *Exegetica: Aufsätze zur Erforschung des NT*, ed. E. Dinkler (1967), pp. 278-84, and *Theology of the NT*, I (1948); E. Dinkler, "Prädestination bei Paulus," *Signum crucis* (1967), pp. 241-69; H. Conzelmann, "Paulus und die Weisheit," *Theologie als Schriftauslegung*, BEvT, LXV (1974), 177-90; M. J. Suggs, "The Word is Near You," *Christian History and Interpretation*, ed. W. R. Farmer, C. F. D. Moule, R. R. Niebuhr (1967), pp. 289-312; U. Luz, "Zum Aufbau von Röm. 1-8," *TZ*, XXV (1969), 161-81; G. Klein, "Der Abfassungszweck des Römerbriefes," *Rekonstruktion und Interpretation*, BEvT, L (1969), 129-44; J. I. H. McDonald, "Was Romans XVI a Separate Letter?" *NTS*, XVI (1970), 369-72; P. S. Minear, *The Obedience of Faith*, SBT, 2nd Ser., XIX (1971); G. Bornkamm, "Der Römerbrief als Testament des Paulus," *Geschichte und Glaube*, I, BEvT, LIII (1971), 120-39; J. Jervell, "Der Brief nach Jerusalem," *ST*, XXV (1971), 61-73; K. P. Donfried, "A Short Note on Romans 16," *JBL*, LXXXIX (1970), 441-49, and "False Presuppositions in the Study of Romans," *CBQ*, XXXVI (1974), 332-55; E. Käsemann, HNT (1973); D. Zeller, *Juden und Heiden in der Mission des Paulus*, Forschung zur Bibel, I (1973), with bibliog.; U. Wilckens, "Über Abfassungszweck und Aufbau des Römerbriefes," *Rechtfertigung als Freiheit: Paulusstudien* (1974), pp. 110-70; W. Schmithals, *Der Römerbrief als historisches Problem*, StNT, IX (1975), with bibliog.; C. E. B. Cranfield, ICC (rev. ed., I, 1975).

G. Klein

***ROME, CHRISTIAN MONUMENTS. 1. The early Christian catacombs.** Until the end of the second century Christians were buried in pagan cemeteries, but as the Roman church became more organized and gave more attention to the cult of the martyrs, Christian cemeteries came into being, especially after the accession of Callistus in A.D. 217. The cemetery of Domitilla is dated to the second half of the second century and its decoration to the end of the century. The *Memoria Apostolorum* (St. Sebastian), of comparable date, is centered around three family tombs, and the two-galleried cemetery of Praetextatus dates from the second half of the third century. Callistus has two important centers, the area of Lucina (A.D. 190-200) and the crypt of the popes (from the late second to the early third century). The first pope to be buried outside the Vatican was Zephyrinus near the area of Callistus in 217. Callistus himself was buried in the cemetery of Calepodius in 222.

The newly discovered catacomb of the Via Dino Campagni has a mixture of pagan and Christian elements, and in the catacomb of the Aurelii (first half of the third century) Gnostic cosmogonic themes are present along with Christian figures, including the city's oldest representation of the cross. This mixture of subjects indicates the coexistence of orthodox and heretical Christian views before the Constantinian era. There are several Jewish catacombs which, however, do not predate the Christian catacombs. *See also* ART, EARLY CHRISTIAN[S] §§3*a*, *b*, 4*b*ii.

2. Vatican excavations. Explorations beneath the main altar of St. Peter's (1939-50, 1953-57) uncovered an ancient cemetery along the Via Cornelia running from the Tiber to the Vatican Hill under the nave of the present basilica. Both St. Peter's and its Constantinian predecessor are centered over an open area among some pagan mausoleums on the Roman road. In a wall of this area is a niche with two small columns supporting a cover that protected it from rain. The edifice is dated from the wall in which it rests to *ca.* A.D. 150; between 150 and 320 some twenty-six inhumations were made in the immediate area. Since this monument, thought to be the trophy of Gaius from *ca.* 190 mentioned in Eusebius (Hist. II.xxv.7), determined the architectural evolution of the later buildings, it appears that when the Basilica of Constantine was built in the fourth century, the church had no doubt that this was Peter's grave. No bones were found in the cavity beneath the niche, although human remains were found nearby. It is usually said, therefore, that the site of the apostle's tomb has been demonstrated to be here, rather than specifically found here. *See also* PETER §11; PETER[S] §6.

3. Early Roman churches. ***a. Pre-Constantinian.*** These were close to the wall of Servius Tullius with a few exceptions, e.g., St. Marcellus on the Corso. Most were in poor and populous parts of the city. Excavations beneath churches such as John and Paul, Pudentiana, Caecilia, Chrysogonus, etc., have shown that houses of the late second and early third centuries were transformed into places of Christian meeting and worship. The complex beneath John and Paul was a series of private houses dating from the beginning of the third century and was used as a burial site until the sixth century. The house under Caecilia shows Christian use from the beginning of the third century, while that under Pudentiana dates from *ca.* 129, and its remodeling from *ca.* 387. Beneath the church of S. Martino ai Monti Christian paintings have been found dating to the period of the Severi (*ca.* 195-235). Evidence of Christian meeting places has been found, too, under and in the environs of the churches of St. Clement and St. Prisca. At these sites excavators have also uncovered Mithraic temples (*see* GREEK RELIGION AND PHILOSOPHY §4*d*) dating from the time of TRAJAN. *See* Fig. R1.

b. Constantinian. In the period between Constantine and Charlemagne, Rome was transformed from the capital of the Empire into a Christian city. Churches were built by Constantine in the area outside the Aurelian walls in honor of the martyrs. Resistance to Constantine was strong at Rome, and this appears to be the reason why his church buildings are at the periphery of the city,

J. M. Ward

1. The Mithraeum, San Clemente, Rome

and why the cathedral itself was built just at the walls. These buildings were mainly on imperial property and financed with imperial monies. The following are the principal churches built by Constantine in the fourth century: the Basilica Constantiniana begun shortly after 312 on imperial property which formerly belonged to the Laterani; nearby, the Basilica Sessoriana of the Holy Cross in Jerusalem; the basilica of St. Peter, or the Basilica Vaticana, whose atrium and precinct were laid out around 333; a small martyrium above the pagan cemetery on the Ostian Way where St. Paul was buried; the Basilica Apostolorum (St. Sebastian) on the Appian Way over a third-century martyrium in which the relics of Peter and Paul were kept during the persecution of Decius; a funeral basilica dedicated to St. Lawrence at the base of the Verano hill; on the Via Labicana a basilica in honor of Sts. Peter and Marcellinus. Joined to this last was a mausoleum which Constantine built for himself and in which his mother Helena was buried. Constantine's daughter, Constantina, built a funeral basilica on the Via Nomentana near the basilica of St. Agnes. *See also* ART, EARLY CHRISTIAN[S] §§3*a*, 4*a*.

4. Christian remains in the Forum and Palatine. ***a. Sta. Maria Antiqua.*** This church occupies a situation on the S side of the Forum between the W escarpment of the Palatine and the library of Augustus. A Roman building was transformed into a church at the beginning of the sixth century, and in the second half of the century an apse and ambulacri were created. Almost the entire church was frescoed; its layers date from Popes Zacharias (741-752), Stephen (752-757), and Paul I (757-767). A chapel to the left of the apse has the famous fresco of the Crucifixion painted shortly after 741, showing Christ clothed and in a style reminiscent of that of refugees from Iconoclasm. In the left aisle is a sarcophagus from the middle of the third century showing the JONAH cycle of the stages of Christian initiation. The appellation "antiqua" may come from the church's having possessed the city's oldest icon of the Virgin Mary (now in Sta. Maria Nova).

b. The altar of victory. On the wall opposite the entrance to the *curia* stood the statue of Victory brought by Augustus to Rome. To this the senators paid their respects upon entering the chamber. It was removed by Gratian in 382, but after his death an attempt was made by the pagan aristocracy led by Symmachus to have it replaced, a last effort of a dying paganism. The attempt failed because of the pressure which St. Ambrose of Milan brought on Valentinian II.

c. Graffito of the Palatine. In 1857 a series of graffiti were discovered in the *domus Gelotiana* or Paedagogium of the Palatine. One of these, dated to the time of the Severi, represents the Crucifixion seen from behind. Christ is clothed in the robe of a slave and has a donkey's head. Below and to the left is the figure of a young man in prayer with his right hand raised in the gesture of *jactare basia* toward the cross, and the inscription: Alexamenos worships his god. The pagan belief that Christians worshiped an ass is referred to by Tertullian (Apol. xvi), and Minucius Felix (ix.3; xxviii.7).

Bibliography. S. Alexander, "Studies in Constantinian Church Architecture," *Rivista di Archeologia Cristiana,* XLVII (1971), 281-330; C. Cecchelli, *Monumenti cristiano-eretici di Roma* (1944); W. De Grüneisen, *Sainte Marie Antique* (1911); M. Grant, *The Roman Forum* (1970); M. Guarducci, *Le Reliquie di Pietro* (1965); R. Krautheimer, *Corpus basilicarum christianarum Romae,* several vols. [English] (1937-67); G. Lugli, *Itinerario di Roma antica* (1970); A. Nestori, "La Catacomba di Calepodio," *Rivista di Archeologia Cristiana,* XLVII (1971), 199-278; J. Ruysschaert, "Nouvelles recherches concernant la tombe de Pierre au Vatican," *Revue d'Histoire Ecclésiastique,* LX (1965), 822-32; P. Romanelli and P. Nordhagen, *S. Maria Antiqua* (1964); P. Testini, *Le Catacombe e Gli Antichi Cimiteri Cristiani in Roma,* Roma christiana, II (1966); V. Väänänen, *Graffiti del Palatino,* 2 vols. (1966).

R. L. FOLEY

ROME, EARLY CHRISTIAN ATTITUDES TOWARD. 1. Palestinian Christianity. Christians were affected by the various Jewish attitudes toward foreign powers. Zealots advocated open rebellion as the means of establishing God's kingdom in history (*see* ZEALOT; ZEALOT[S]). Others, hoping for Rome's destruction by the Messiah (Pss. Sol. 17:39), taught that the pious should wait in resignation and in obedience to the law until God raised up this king. Still others believed that deliverance from Rome could be found only beyond history in the great apocalyptic upheaval. But there were also Jews, especially in the Diaspora (*see* DISPERSION), who expressed loyalty to Rome, not merely out of political opportunism, but out of a theologically grounded realism which believed that even pagan empires were ordained of God. Many first-century Jews offered sacrifices and prayers for Rome's welfare in Jerusalem's temple (AB. 3:2; Jos. War II.x.4; cf. Jer. 29:7; Ecclus. 4:27 [Heb.]; Prov. 8:15; 24:21; Philo, *On the Embassy to Gaius* (236, 280, 305). Yet Jewish loyalty to the Empire always depended on Rome's religious toleration of Judaism.

The condemnation and CRUCIFIXION of Jesus by the Roman prefect could hardly endear imperial authority to early Christianity. The belief that God had vindicated Christ on Easter implied that the apocalyptic reversal had already begun and that Christ's earthly judges would encounter him as their heavenly judge. Some Christian groups even concluded that "the kingdoms of the world" and "their glory" belonged to the devil (Luke 4:5-6 [Q]). Therefore, they expected that these kingdoms would be destroyed by the one who resisted the temptation to establish an earthly kingdom.

In general, the early Christians did not join the struggle of the Zealots; they had come to understand that the KINGDOM OF GOD could no more be established through violence than could the resurrection of Jesus have been accomplished by human co-operation and piety. But neither did they side with the quietists and withdraw into the desert to wait. On the contrary, they went to Jerusalem, shared in the general stability which Rome's presence ensured, and in accord with a word of Jesus, rendered "to Caesar the things which are Caesar's"—namely, taxes (Mark 12:17). This saying does not declare the Empire to be a divine institution but merely states that Christians are obliged to honor certain of the emperor's claims. The second part of the saying goes beyond the original question of Mark 12:14, and therefore contains its climax: "(render) to God the things that are God's." The contrast between Caesar and God in this saying desacralizes the Empire and relativizes its claims without declaring it to be demonic. The church can be politically loyal because the kingdom of God is not of this world and because the Messiah is not a political revolutionist or social reformer. All important is understanding oneself as the property of God and surrendering to his claims (cf. Luke 13:1-3). Such obedience will result in the right attitude toward Caesar.

When the flames of Zealot fanaticism engulfed the nation in a messianic war against Rome (Jos. War VI.v.4) some segments of Palestinian Christianity were probably swept along by the religious hysteria and by the assertion of Christian prophets that they represented the presence of Jesus (Mark 13:6). The tradition behind Luke 22:35-36 distinguishes two periods, one calling for armed resistance in the present opposed to one which had enjoined powerlessness upon Jesus' followers in the past. This saying, which contradicts traditions like Matt. 5:39-42, would at the very least facilitate Christian participation in the war against Rome. The desecration and destruction of the Jerusalem temple by the Romans was viewed by some Christians as an apocalyptic manifestation of the power of Satan immediately before the End, present in the person and actions of the Roman general Titus (Mark 13:14; cf. Jos. War VI.vi.1.). But others interpreted this disaster as divine judgment for Israel's disobedience toward its prophets and the Messiah who had taught them to love their enemies (Matt. 23:37-38; 5:44). Palestinian Christians around A.D. 70 felt "hated by *all*" (Mark 13:13), by the Romans for whom they were Jews, and by Jews because faith in the Messiah Jesus prompted most of them to reject participation in the war against Rome (Euseb. Hist. III.v.2-3).

2. Paul. The most important text for understanding the attitude toward Rome of early Hellenistic Christianity is Rom. 13:1-7. Even though Paul himself had suffered at the hands of Roman officials (II Cor. 11:25) and knew that Caesar's representatives had brought Jesus to the cross, he wrote of the necessity of submission to NERO and the imperial authorities. Here he stood in the tradition of loyalty as advocated in HELLENISTIC JUDAISM, used concepts from the Roman bureaucracy, and based his exhortation upon the belief that the political authorities are part of God's order within this world. Hence he can say that there is no authority except from God, that the authorities are instituted by God (Rom. 13:1), and that they function as *diakonoi* and *leitourgoi* of God "for your good" (13:4, 6). The "good" here is not eschatological salvation but the benefit of earthly security and well-being. The exhortation to submit to imperial powers is placed within the context of the Christian's service in the world (12:1-2). Such service is qualified by the apocalyptic view that this old aeon, and with it the Empire, passes away (13:11-12), and it is performed in response to the command to love one's neighbor, including the enemy (12:19-21). Hence governmental structures and demands cannot be absolutized. Paul himself, for instance, did not submit to the order given for his arrest by the ethnarch ARETAS, but rather fled the city (II Cor. 11:32-33). He did not delineate the limits of Christian obedience in Rom. 13 because he was not addressing a situation where the state made demands contrary to the Christian conscience.

While Paul himself viewed the imperial power primarily as God's order within the world which passes away, the pseudonymous letter of II Thessalonians (2:3-10) assigned an apocalyptic role to a particular Caesar and his empire (cf. Dan. 9:24-26). He functions as the force which for a while "restrains" the counter-Messiah. But Caesar and his empire will disappear with the parousia of "the lawless one" who "is already at work" and who is described in terms of a self-deifying ruler (II Thess. 2:3-4, 7, 9; cf. Dan. 11:31, 36-37).

3. I Peter. The exhortation to submit to imperial authorities is also contained in I Pet. 2:13, but with persecution in view (4:12, 14, 16). Contrary to the RSV, 2:13 should be translated "be subject to every human *creature*," be it emperor, governor, or pagan neighbor. Hence, "Honor all men. . . . Honor the emperor" (2:17). I Peter speaks of the emperor as fellow creature, not as representative of a divine ordinance. Civic duties and submission to Caesar are only one instance of the general duties which believers have toward their fellow human beings. Alongside the admonition of 2:13-17 is an apocalyptic interpretation of the persecution of Christians within the Empire as satanic action. The call is not for rebellion, but for spiritual resistance (5:8-9; cf. Eph. 6:10 ff.) in the form of faith and hope (1:3-9) and the willingness to share in Christ's suffering (4:13). The author of I Peter still hoped that the exemplary moral conduct of Christians might eliminate further persecutions, or at least counteract pagan defamations. Like IGNATIUS and I Clement (*see* CLEMENT, EPISTLES OF), he was aware of persecutions and martyrdoms inflicted by the state since Nero's time. But since these writers sought to avoid confrontation with the state, they did not denounce the injustices of the authorities.

4. Other epistles. An exhortation for prayer on behalf of emperors and magistrates is embedded within the general exhortation to pray "for all men" in I Tim. 2:1, yet other writers make it clear that Christians do not pray for the emperor's conversion but for his well-being and the peace of the Empire (I Clem. 60:4–61:2; Polyc. Phil. 12:3). Readiness for suffering and persecution did not preclude praying for earthly peace, because martyrdom was not to be sought out. Explicit warnings against recklessly provoking Roman authorities and seeking martyrdom (typical of certain Montanists) are found in the Martyrdom of Polycarp (1:2). The antecedents to these warnings lie in the synoptic command "to flee" in the face of persecution (Matt. 10:23; Mark 13:14).

5. Luke-Acts. Although the author of Luke-Acts was aware of Paul's martyrdom, he hoped for toleration by the Empire, whose representatives must testify to the political innocence of Jesus and

Paul. Difficulties which Christians experienced were usually attributed to Jews and to Roman officials who failed to perform their duty. Luke wished that the Roman government would become cognizant of its incompetence to judge Christians in religious matters (Acts 18:12-17). He not only stressed Paul's pride in his Roman citizenship (e.g., Acts 22:25), his loyalty toward Caesar (25:8), and the social importance of many believers (10:1; 13:1; 17:12, etc.), but he also told of Roman officers rescuing Paul on various occasions (Acts 21:32 ff., etc.). Luke's reference to the ASIARCHS as friends of Paul (19:31) may indicate he was unaware that, as representatives of the emperor cult, they posed a threat to the churches of Asia in his own time. Or else he may be appealing to the time when the emperor cult had not yet become a threat to the church. In the past, Luke would be suggesting, Asiarchs could even be friends and, in the person of the town clerk, defend Christians before a mob, demanding proper legal procedure for them (19:34-41). Luke hoped that Empire and church could co-exist because the latter was loyal and the former could be just. But he also knew that "through many tribulations we must enter the kingdom of God" (14:22), and that in case of conflict between church and state, the normative principle remained: "We must obey God rather than men" (5:29). Above all, he believed that "the times of the Gentiles" will come to an end with Christ's PAROUSIA (Luke 21:24 ff.). In the meantime, Rome cannot hinder the word of God, even as Jerusalem could not destroy Jesus. *See also* LUKE, GOSPEL OF §2; ACTS OF THE APOSTLES §9, and supplementary articles.

6. The book of Revelation. The apocalyptic prophet John saw Rome exclusively in terms of its imperial cult. Instead of loyalty toward Rome, praying for, submitting to, and honoring the emperor, the Apocalypse calls for endurance in faith, for suffering, and for fleeing into the wilderness (13:10; 14:12; 12:6, 14). But Rome, the beast and great harlot (Rev. 13; 17), will fall (18:2), and God will avenge the blood of his servants. The judgment, however, remains strictly the action of God, and no call is issued for believers to take vengeance against Rome. The apocalyptic tradition of hatred against Rome remained alive during the second century ([Christian] SIBYLLINE ORACLES Book VIII), especially among Montanists and in modified form also in early catholic churches (cf. HERMAS Vision IV; Similtude I). It did not, however, constitute the dominant attitude of second-century Christianity or determine the further development of the church's relation to the Empire (cf. Just. Apol. I, xii; Melito in Euseb. Hist. IV.xxvi.5-11). *See also* REVELATION, BOOK OF §E4 and REVELATION, BOOK OF[S]; ETHICS IN THE NT[S] §§1*e*iii, 3*d*iv, 5*a*, 7.

Bibliography. G. Kretschmar, "Der Weg zur Reichskirche," *Verkündigung und Forschung,* XIII (1968), 3-43, discusses the lit. *See also* S. Benko and J. J. O'Rourke, eds., *The Catacombs and the Colosseum: The Roman Empire as the Setting of Primitive Christianity* (1971); B. Reicke, *The New Testament Era* (1964); H. Lietzmann, *The Beginnings of the Christian Church* (2nd ed., 1937 [ET 2nd ed., 1949]); G. F. Moore, *Judaism in the First Centuries of the Christian Era,* II (1927), 112-18.

G. KRODEL

*__RUTH, BOOK OF. 1. Form.__ The most distinctive feature of the book of Ruth is its literary genre. It is a short story or *novella,* one of very few in the OT. While its content deals in general with historical matters, it is form rather than content which is of decisive influence, for the historical information is clearly subordinated to and employed for the sake of the desire to entertain. This is most evident in the story's plot, which is developed so as to maximize the element of suspense. Because the historical facts about David's ancestry must have been generally known, the suspense involved is not the kind achieved by the concealing of information, but rather the subtler sort in which what everyone already knows is delicately hinted at and patiently traced through all its complexities.

The analysis of the book's structure demonstrates the focus on subtle suspense. The decisive point about the ancestry of David is not mentioned until the fade-out ending (4:17) after the climax. The four scenes (1:6-18, the road to Bethlehem; 2:1-17, the field of Boaz; 3:6-15, the threshing floor of Boaz; and 4:1-12, the gate of Bethlehem) are held tightly together, not only by a series of brief transitions (1:1-5, introduction; 1:19-22; 2:18-23; 3:1-5; and 3:16-18, interludes; and 4:13-17 conclusion), but also by a series of carefully staged, potential wrong endings and signposts of dramatic irony. When Naomi so effectively insists that her daughters-in-law return to Moab (1:11-15), when the existence of the nearer kinsman is revealed (3:12-13), and when he indeed agrees to serve as redeemer (4:4), a lump rises in one's throat at the thought that the entire plot will collapse. And yet all along delicate hints point to the successful achievement of the desired outcome. When Naomi raises the question of levirate marriage (1:11; *see* LEVIRATE LAW), when Ruth "happens" to glean in the field of Boaz (2:3), when Boaz prays for a recompense for Ruth's fidelity (2:12), when the word "redeemer" (RSV "nearest kin") is mentioned by Naomi (2:20), and when the neighbors pray the Lord's blessing on the house of Boaz (4:11-12), the knowing reader smiles at the way the outcome is being subtly foreshadowed.

2. Theology. Although depicting the complexities of ordinary human existence, the story is by no means a secular one. Any writing which traces the way God's purposes are worked out in human affairs deals with God's providence, but instead of straightforward affirmation, the writer chooses the most indirect ways imaginable. He even speaks of "chance" in 2:3—the exact opposite of what he is actually affirming, namely, total divine causality. This perspective is evident in the statements of the narrator himself (1:6; 4:13) and in the words of his characters (1:13; 1:20-21; 2:20; 4:14). The stress on absolute causality becomes even more apparent when it is noted that every prayer in the book finds an answer in the course of the plot (1:8-9; 2:12; 2:19-20; 3:10; 4:11-12; 4:14). Here is an affirmation of causality which doesn't miss a chance!

The subtlety of these points is clear evidence that the author understands God's control of human events to be not only complete, but also, by its very nature, hidden. The theology which the book affirms is one of hidden but absolute causality.

3. Purpose and date. In what historical context is an affirmation of Yahweh's hidden causality understandable? The succession history of David (II Sam. 9–20) and the JOSEPH STORY (Gen. 37–50) are the writings most closely akin to the book of Ruth in both theology and style. The three works are united by the over-all theme of the God who is totally and continuously, though in an unperceived way, in control of all human events. Even more impressive is the manner in which the three authors employ the same short-story techniques of potential wrong endings, subtle signposts, and even answered prayers. In each case the same "profane" and "humanistic" presentation of "nothing but the facts" is utilized to express an amazingly profound theological conviction.

The succession history and the Joseph story are products of the Solomonic era. As holy war, charismatic leaders, and local shrines in which Yahweh's presence had been so close and easily discernible began to vanish in the new era of the empire, with its mercenary army, established dynasty, and royally controlled temple, the question was bound to arise: Where is Yahweh now? (*See* YAHWIST[S] §§2–3; PRESENCE OF GOD, CULTIC[S] §3.) The literature of the Solomonic enlightenment returned the penetrating answer which is the message of the book of Ruth: He is everywhere—but totally hidden in purely human coincidences and schemes, such as a young girl's accidental steps and an old woman's risky plan.

4. Other factors bearing on the date. Inasmuch as the era of the Solomonic enlightenment covered a span from the mid-tenth century to perhaps the mid-eighth century, it is desirable to fix upon hard evidence to pinpoint a date. Unfortunately, the net result of recent study of the book of Ruth has been to weaken the force of all the criteria previously used. Linguistic evidence now leads to the conclusion that late idioms do not occur, but many archaic forms do. Legal customs can no longer be seen as pointing to any particular time. Although they are related to somewhat different situations, the same legal principles underlie both the redemption of Elimelech's property by Boaz and the levirate law of Deut. 25:5-10. It has also been almost universally accepted that the laws about gleaning, though preserved in late material (Deut. 24:19; Lev. 19:9-10; 23:22), reflect old practices of the tribal league which this later legislation sought to restore. The whole idea of a postexilic date reflecting a *Tendenz* opposing the hostility to foreign wives in Ezra-Nehemiah (*see* RUTH §3) is best given up as unfounded. In view of the antiquity of many psalms and proverbs, Ruth's place in the canon of the Writings (*see* CANON OF THE OT §4) cannot be seen as indicative of a late date. In the light of our knowledge of the Deuteronomic historian's use of old source material, the bare reference to "the judges" in 1:1 scarcely suggests a dependence on the completed DEUTERONOMIC HISTORY. On the other hand, the genealogy in 4:18-22 does seem to reflect dependence on both P (*see* PRIESTLY WRITERS[S]) and Chronicles. However, this merely argues for what was already obvious, that the genealogy is a secondary appendix to the original story, whose ending came in 4:17*b*. Thus all the old "evidence" has shown itself to be quite indecisive. The only new argument is that of Gerleman, who contends that a story of a Moabite background for David must antedate the "transfigured" picture of David in the days of the Chronicler and even the era of the royal psalms. Accordingly, perhaps all that can be said is that such evidence as does exist points to a date in the monarchic period, and more likely the earlier part of it.

Bibliography. Commentaries: P. Joüon, *Ruth* (1952); G. Gerleman, BKAT, XVIII (1960); W. Rudolph, *KAT*, XVII (1962).

Special studies: J. M. Myers, *The Linguistic and Literary Form of the Book of Ruth* (1955); P. Humbert, "Art et leçon de l'histoire de Ruth," *Opuscules d'un Hébraïsant* (1958), pp. 83-110; T. and D. Thompson, "Some Legal Problems in the Book of Ruth," *VT*, XVIII (1968), 79-99; R. Hals, *The Theology of the Book of Ruth* (1969); D. Leggett, *The Levirate and Goel Institutions in the OT* (1974).

R. M. HALS

S

***SABBATH.** The seventh day of the seven-day week, distinguished from the other six days throughout Israelite and Jewish history by special observance. The noun is probably derived from the verb שׁבת, "to cease, come to an end, finish," and the most fundamental form of observance has been the cessation of certain types of work (e.g., Exod. 34:21; 20:8-11; Amos 8:5; Jer. 17:19-27; Neh. 13:15-22; Jub. 50:9; I Macc. 2:31-41; M. Shab. 7.1-2).

The NT records many disputes between Jesus and the Pharisees over proper sabbath-keeping (*see* PHARISEES[S]). On sabbaths Jesus' disciples plucked ears of grain without being in mortal danger, and Jesus continually healed people who were not mortally ill. These acts violated Pharisaic norms. In the Synoptic and Johannine traditions Jesus often called attention to the exceptions to sabbath-keeping which the Pharisees themselves allowed. For example, the sabbath could be "broken" by priests making sabbath or Passover offerings (cf. Matt. 12:5), people in mortal danger (such as David—Mark 2:25-26), people aiding others in mortal danger (cf. Mark 3:4), people aiding animals (cf. Matt. 12:11; Luke 13:15; 14:5), and people circumcising a child on the eighth day (cf. John 7:22). The Pharisees also believed that God did not cease work on the sabbath. He continued to give life and to judge the dead (cf. John 5:17). Having noted such exceptions Jesus often went on to apply a traditional form of rabbinic logic: If you allow work in such lesser matters, how much more ought you to allow my work in these greater matters (Matt. 12:5-6, 11-12; Luke 13:15-16; John 7:22-23). Jesus apparently saw his healings as fulfillments of the redemptive purpose of the law. Despite the traditional form of the argument, Jesus' evaluation of the "lesser" and the "greater" seemed to be based on an altogether untraditional assertion of personal authority, which provoked the Pharisees' anger.

Early Gentile Christianity understood traditional sabbath observance to be part of the law which had been annulled in Christ. *See* LORD'S DAY §2.

1. Origin. There is no consensus on the origin of the sabbath or of the seven-day week. However, the hypothesis found in SABBATH and WEEK is among the least likely to be correct and has few supporters. It is based on a supposed early Semitic pentecontad calendar, for which there is no generally accepted evidence.

A calendar has three natural units: the day (24 hours); the synodic (or lunar) month (the time between consecutive conjunctions of earth, sun, and moon—on the average, 29 days, 12 hours, 44 minutes, 2.78 seconds); and the tropical year (the time between two crossings of the sun at the vernal equinox—365 days, 5 hours, 48 minutes, 46 seconds). Many ancient societies felt the need for an additional unit of time intermediate between the day and the lunar month. In a general way Mesopotamian societies divided the lunar month into halves separated by the fifteenth day, the day of the full moon (*šabattu* or *šapattu*). Greece divided the month into three decades related to phases of the moon (increase, culmination, and decrease). In Rome an eight-day cycle (*nundinae*) ran independently of lunar phases and the calendar month. The eighth day was a market day on which agricultural work ceased. The trading colonies of Assyria (*ca.* 1950-1800 B.C.) had a five- (or six-?) day unit of time (*ḫamuštu*), which was used frequently in loan contracts.

In addition to such units of time, ancient Near Eastern texts commonly speak of a seven-day, noncalendrical period of time. For example, Gudea of Lagash celebrates the building of the temple E-Ninnu with a seven-day feast. In the Gilgamesh Epic, Gilgamesh laments Enkidu's death for seven days; Utnapishtim completes his ship on the seventh day; the flood wind blows for six days and subsides on the seventh; and, after resting atop Mount Nisir for six days, on the seventh Utnapishtim sends forth the dove, swallow, and raven. In the Baal and Anath cycle fire purges the house for six days and dies out on the seventh, its work having been concluded. In the Legend of King Keret six days of marching culminate in a seventh-day attack, and six days of tarrying culminate in a seventh-day victory. In the Tale of Aqhat, Danel offers oblation for seven days, and on the seventh Baal intercedes for him. Thus, "seven days" functioned as a literary and cultic symbol for a fullness in time, and the events of the seventh day were often explicitly climactic. Perhaps the key to understanding this symbol lies in the Sumerian-Akkadian lexical equation "7=*kiššatu*" (the whole, totality). *See* SEVEN, SEVENTH, SEVENTY.

What then can one say about the origins of the seven-day week and sabbath? Was the sabbath related to the Mesopotamian *šapattu* (day of the full moon), and was the seven-day week, like the Greek decade, linked to phases of the moon? Or was the seven-day week, culminating in cessation from agricultural work, a market-day cycle like the Roman *nundinae*? Or did Israel convert a literary and cultic symbol—the seven-day period as significantly complete time—into a formal calendrical unit? *See also* WEEK[S].

The appearance of the new moon marks the first day of a lunar month. The full moon usually occurs on the fourteenth or fifteenth day, and the dark of the moon follows on the twenty-eighth or twenty-ninth. Thus, seven-day intervals such as the first, eighth, fifteenth, twenty-second, and twenty-ninth of the month or the first, seventh, fourteenth, twenty-first, and twenty-eighth of the month can be correlated with lunar phases. However, if the sabbath originated as a seven-day interval fixed by the appearance of the new moon, it could not have recurred every seventh day. A "lunar" sabbath would have been recycled each month, because a lunar month is not evenly divisible by seven days. Yet the oldest biblical traditions suggest that the sabbath did occur every seven days (Exod. 23:12; 34:21). Thus, the sabbath was ordinarily out of phase with the moon.

This difficulty with a lunar hypothesis has led many scholars to limit the search for a cultural parallel to days of cessation from work recurring at intervals unrelated to the moon. Some believe that the best parallel is the market day—which recurred at intervals of four, five, six, or eight days in many cultures, including Rome's. Although a market-day cycle apparently existed nowhere else in the ancient Near East, the custom could have developed independently in Israel, just as it has in many cultures. On market day farmers rest from their fields and engage in bartering, trading, games, and convocations. Of course those who trade must work by bearing goods, and therein lies a serious difficulty with the hypothesis. A number of biblical passages deplore or forbid trade on the sabbath (Amos 8:5; Jer. 17:19-27; Neh. 13:15-22). Nonetheless, it is possible that the sabbath originated as a market day, but that powerful groups subsequently theologized its observance in such a way as to discourage or forbid the very activity which had given rise to it.

Another hypothesis focuses on the power of the symbol "seven days" in Akkadian, Ugaritic, and Hebrew literature. Just as the symbol figured in the Mesopotamian flood epic, so it did in the Hebrew (Gen. 7:4; 8:10-12). Just as Gilgamesh lamented seven days, so did Joseph, Job's friends, and the people of Jabesh-gilead (Gen. 50:10; Job 2:12-13; I Sam. 31:13). Just as Keret's seven-day encampment culminated in victory, so did Joshua's and Ahab's (Josh. 6:1-21; I Kings 20:26-30). Just as seven-day feasts were celebrated in Mesopotamia, so they were in Israel (the Feasts of Unleavened Bread and Booths and wedding festivals—Exod. 23:15; Deut. 16:13-15; Judg. 14:10-18). "Seven days" was a powerful symbol of significantly complete time. It is possible that the symbol somehow conditioned Israel's choice of an intermediate unit of time and its designation of the seventh day as climactic and holy. (The verb שבת can mean "to come to an end, finish.") Yet this hypothesis, too, must share the weakness of conjecture.

2. History. Greater agreement exists on the historical development of the sabbath institution than on its origin. However, here too attempts at a systematic exposition are vexed by disagreements on the date and authenticity of crucial OT texts and on the extent to which later texts may preserve ancient traditions. The following reconstruction must be considered tentative.

Premonarchic Israel observed the seventh day by cessation of work rather than by cultic celebration (Exod. 34:21). The oldest recorded rationale for such observance is "that your ox and your ass may have rest, and the son of your bondmaid, and the alien, may be refreshed" (Exod. 23:12). Although the legal traditions from this period reflect the situation of an agricultural society, it is possible that the basic commandment—"Six days you shall work, but on the seventh day you shall cease" (author's trans.)—originated earlier in seminomadic society. Flocks do require care every day; however, contemporary Moslem nomads are able on Fridays to bring their work to an end and to observe a half-day of rest. Whether or not the sabbath had a pre-agricultural history, the oldest form of the fourth commandment—"Remember the sabbath day" (Exod. 20:8*a*)—demonstrates the centrality of seventh-day observance to the covenant life of premonarchic Israel.

During the monarchy the royal and priestly cult gradually attracted the seventh day to itself, and cultic celebration became an additional feature of sabbath observance (II Kings 11:4-12; 16:18; Lev. 19:30; Num. 28:9-10). Accordingly the rationale for sabbath observance came to be linked with the Priestly creation traditions (Exod. 20:11; 31:17; cf. Gen. 2:2-3). The prophets and others who venerated the Sinai covenant tradition did not particularly welcome the cultic development (Hos. 2:11 [H 13]; Isa. 1:13); and the Deuteronomic tradition of the Decalogue, far from grounding the fourth commandment in Creation, grounded it in the prologue of the Sinai covenant (Deut. 5:15; cf. 5:6 and Exod. 20:2). For Jeremiah the proper sabbath observance continued to be cessation of work. If this covenant stipulation were disobeyed, Judah would cease to exist (17:19-27). Jeremiah emphasized the sabbath tradition as a bulwark against self-destructive assimilation to the alien culture and cult.

Ezekiel, the priest-prophet of the Exile, shared both the prophetic view that sabbath-breaking would bring on Judah's destruction (22:8, 15) and the Priestly view that cultic activity was a primary feature of sabbath-keeping which would be restored after the Exile (45:17; 46:1-5). For Ezekiel the sabbath was not so much the focus of a covenantal stipulation as it was a distinctive mark given to Israel as a sign of its sanctity (20:12). Throughout the Exile the sabbath remained a symbol of Israel's distinctive culture.

In the postexilic period the followers of Second Isaiah re-emphasized the association between sabbath-keeping and covenant (Isa. 58:13-14; 56:4, 6). Their universalism found expression in the affirmation that even foreigners and eunuchs who kept sabbath could be members of Yahweh's community (56:1-8). However, some eighty-five years later Nehemiah found sabbath-keeping in Jerusalem shockingly lax. He forbade trading on the sabbath (Neh. 13:15-22), and the citizens pledged both to refrain from trade on the sabbath and to support the sabbath offerings (10:31-33 [H 32-34]). Thus were reaffirmed both aspects of priestly sabbath-keeping—cessation of work and cultic offerings.

In the five hundred years between Nehemiah and the destruction of the second temple in A.D. 70, sabbath observance became an ever more important bulwark of Jewish identity against alien, imperial cultures. A considerable elaboration and refinement of the previously uncomplicated sabbath legislation began to occur, and serious differences in interpretation became characteristic of the various parties and sects. For details on this process, *see also* SABBATH §2; SABBATICAL YEAR[S].

Bibliography. N.-E. A. Andreasen, *The OT Sabbath* (1972), with full bibliog.; R. de Vaux, *Ancient Israel* (1961), pp. 475-83; H.-J. Kraus, *Worship in Israel* (1966), pp. 76-88; E. J. Bickerman, *Chronology of the Ancient World* (1968); S. Talmon, "The Calendar Reckoning of the Sect from the Judaean Desert," *Scripta Hierosolymitana,* IV (1958), 162-99. For the sabbath in Judaism, the NT, and early Christianity, E. Lohse, "σάββατον," *TDNT,* VII (1971), 1-35. For the sabbath in Jewish history to the present day, M. Greenberg *et al.,* "Sabbath," *Encyclopaedia Judaica,* XIV (1971), 557-72; A. E. Millgram, *Sabbath: The Day of Delight* (1944).

B. E. SHAFER

***SABBATICAL YEAR.** The sabbatical year, like its counterpart the weekly sabbath, was a uniquely Israelite institution. Despite repeated claims that the sabbatical reckoning had its origin in the calendars of ancient Babylonia, no parallel to it has been found. This institution apears to be derived from the Israelite's concept of time as having been created by God, who gave six years (days) of it to man, but retained the seventh for himself. God is seen as the owner of the land during the seventh year, when time is, so to speak, suspended. The human owner is not allowed to plow or harvest his fields, for this would give him a claim to the produce that in fact belonged to God and must be shared with other humans. Since the slave and owner have the same rights to the land, the Hebrew slave was to have a chance of regaining his freedom. Morgenstern (*see* SABBATICAL YEAR) posits that the sabbatical year originated in the northern kingdom, whose population consisted of peasants. However, such utopian legislation is unlikely among a people living from agriculture. An analysis of the sources suggests that both the yearly and weekly sabbaths probably go back to the earliest stage of Israelite history, if not to Moses himself. The legislation makes sense among wandering tribes who were fearful of the impending change to a sedentary way of life. *See also* SABBATH[S]; WEEK[S].

Exod. 23:10-11 offers the first, and evidently the oldest, practice of the sabbatical year. The two sabbatical institutions appear to serve as a bridge between the social commandments to protect the poor and stranger (vss. 1-9) and the commandments pertaining to the cult, such as the ritual of the pilgrim festivals (vss. 14-17).

Related to the social aspects of sabbatical legislation is the provision (Exod. 21:1-11; Deut. 15:12-18) that the Hebrew bondsman or maid is to be freed in the seventh year. Ancient as well as modern exegesis differs as to whether freedom was to be granted after seven years of servitude or at the sabbatical year. The former meaning seems to be implied in Isa. 61:1-3 and in Jer. 34:8-22. The Book of the Covenant contains the concept, if not the wording, that the sabbatical year was to be the time of freedom (Exod. 21:1-11).

The Holiness Code (at Lev. 25:1-7) stresses the cultic aspects of the sabbatical year. The Lord, not the poor, becomes the owner of the land, symbolized by its fallowness; what grows of itself should be shared by the landlord with the slaves, strangers, and animals. The radical social legislation ordained in Exod. 21:1-11; 23:10-11, is relegated in Lev. 25:8-55 to the JUBILEE, which is to be solemnly proclaimed at the end of the seventh sabbatical year.

Deut. 15:1-18 appears nearer to the views recorded in the Book of the Covenant than to those of the Holiness Code. The Deuteronomist (15:1-11) radically extends the social legislation by ordaining that in the seventh year the creditors release the debtors from obligations. The passage could be interpreted as meaning that this release was either a suspension of payment or an absolute cancellation. But ancient exegesis (Josephus, the rabbis) is unanimous that it meant the latter. If so, lending money could never be a business transaction in Israel, but only an offer of assistance to the needy. The sabbatical year laws appear to be the most radical social legislation prior to the twentieth century.

Contrary to the view expressed since Wellhausen, biblical passages suggest the actual observance of the sabbatical year during the pre-exilic period. The tithing cycles (Deut. 14:28; 26:12) divided the sabbatical cycle into two three-year periods plus the sabbatical year, which presupposed the existence of the year of release. The same is true of Deut. 31:10, which prescribes the reading of Scripture at the end of the sabbatical year. Lev. 26:34, 43 (cited in II Chr. 36:21) accounts for the Babylonian exile as retribution for backsliding in the observance of sabbatical legislation. The prophecies of a seventy-year exile (Isa. 23:15 referring to Tyre; Jer. 25:12; 29:10; Zech. 1:12; Dan. 9:2) take for granted the existence of sabbatical cycles. Nehemiah's pledge to let the land stay fallow and to remit all debts in the sabbatical year (Neh. 10:31) is a renewal rather than an innovation of sabbatical observance. But although the existence of sabbatical institutions during the period of the monarchy need not be doubted, the precise calendar and mode of observance remain open questions.

I Macc. 6:49, 53-54 records that Judas Maccabeus was forced to yield the fortress of Beth-zur to the Syrians on account of a famine which occurred during a sabbatical year. This reference furnishes not only the earliest dated sabbatical year but also offers the first direct testimony that sabbatical observance influenced military and political events. Josephus excuses John Hyrcanus' failure to avenge the murder of his father on account of the sabbatical season (Antiq. XIII.viii.1). It also facilitated Herod's capture of Jerusalem (Antiq. XIV.xvi.2). King Agrippa, presumably Agrippa I, recited from Deuteronomy during the Festival of Booths of a year beginning a new sabbatical cycle (M. Soṭ. 7.8). Finally, a contemporary Aramaic papyrus, dated in the second year of Nero, records that the note of indebtedness was written during a sabbatical year (*DJD* II, 101). The Julian dates of these sabbatical years, which ran from Tishri to Elul 29, are as follows: 163/162 B.C. (capture of Beth-zur); 135/134 B.C. (murder of Simon); 37/36 B.C. (Herod's capture of Jerusalem); A.D. 41/42 (Agrippa I's recitation of Scripture); 55/56 (Nero's second year). These and other attested dates permit us to construct a calendar of sabbatical cycles from postexilic times to the fifth Christian century, at least.

The Mishna (*Shebi'ith,* "seventh [year]") and the Tosefta give details of sabbatical legislation. In the Babylonian Talmud, the commentary on the Mishna is scattered throughout various tractates, i.e., there is no specific tractate *Shebi'ith.* These talmudic texts deal almost exclusively with agricultural aspects, and only marginally with the cancellation of indebtedness. The Mishna extends the prohibition of plowing or planting to the Pentecost preceding Tishri 1 of the sabbatical year (1.1) and postpones permission to work the fields to the end of the Festival of Booths. We may conclude from the Tosefta (I.1) that these extensions were abolished at the end of the first Christian century. Rabbinic tradition assumes that strict sabbatical legislation was limited to Judea and other regions under direct Jewish jurisdiction in postexilic times; only leniently applied to the regions which were Jewish under the former Davidic empire; while foreign lands were entirely exempt from sabbatical laws. This meant that produce from abroad could be imported during the sabbatical year, frequently averting famine. In view of these difficulties, the observance of the sabbatical laws exemplifies the characteristic piety of the Jewish people, who viewed the commandment not as a burden but a joy. Perhaps under Roman or Herodian pressure, Hillel is said to have instituted the *prozbul,* which suspended the cancellation of debts at the end of the sabbatical year (M. Sheb. 10.3). But the documents of Bar Kochba suggest either that no such abrogation was recognized by the rebel authorities or that it did not extend to rentals. The contracts of renting lands signed by the rebel leader contained a stipulation that was valid only to the end of presabbatical year (*DJD* II, 121-32). The occupying powers, under Alexander the Great and Julius Caesar, exempted Judea from tribute during the seventh year. The sabbatical year remained a living institution in Palestine until the period of the Crusades.

The economic sacrifices involved were so large that texts frequently associated rewards and retribution with the observance or violations of this commandment (Lev. 25:21; Deut. 15:10; Jer. 34:12-22). But it was only with the book of Daniel that national and cosmic significance was ascribed to the sabbatical year. Daniel studied the secret number mentioned in Jer. 25:11-12; 29:10, the seventy years of exile. Dan. 9:24-27 suggests that this period referred in fact to seventy sabbatical cycles or 490 years, the time from the fall of Jerusalem until the messianic age.

Vs. 25 divides the 70 sabbatical cycles into 7 plus 62, with a remainder of 1 [$(7 \times 7) + (62 \times 7) + (1 \times 7) = (70 \times 7) = 490$]. According to this interpretation the persecution (apparently of Antiochus IV) would occur in the seventieth sabbatical cycle.

Daniel's sabbatical messianism became the mysterious text, whose key was sought by ancient exegetes, which would yield the timing of the messianic age. Enoch 93 presents an apocalypse based on the seven sabbatical ages, to which 91:12-17 adds three more, making a total of ten sabbatical ages. Jub. 1:27-29 presumes that at creation God divided time into sabbatical and jubilee cycles. The births of Adam, Noah, Abraham, and other patriarchs were timed to coincide with the sabbatical division epochs (4Q181, fragments 1-2). Qumran writers also projected the future reigns of the Kings of Wickedness and Righteousness in light of a sabbatical calendar, envisioning the last year of the cycle to be the beginning of the messianic age (11QMelch 3.2). In the rabbinic tradition, too, the prayer for the redemption of Israel in the Eighteen Blessings is said to have been placed seventh to show the link with the redeeming features of the seventh year (T.B. Meg. 17b). Although the Jew could expect the coming of the Messiah at any time, certain periods were more propitious than others. The cyclic nature of redemption is illustrated in the rabbinic statement: "During the month of Nisan they were redeemed and in the month of Nisan they will be redeemed again" (T.B. R.H. 11a). Passover of the sabbatical year thus became the period when the redeemer's coming was expected most.

Politically, on account of the messianic stirrings, the sabbatical year was a restless time. John's ministry (A.D. 28-29), the Egyptian Messiah (A.D. 55-56), and the Bar Kochba uprising (A.D. 132-133) occurred in years which had been dedicated to the Lord as his sabbath. It is possible that the sabbatical date was only accidental, but in light of the apocalyptic writings which link the two, it is probable that John timed his ministry to synchronize with the season when the land belonged to the Lord, the Hebrew slaves were to be set free, and all indebtedness cancelled.

Bibliography. N. Sarna, "Zedekiah's Emancipation of the Slaves and the Sabbatical Year," *Orient and Occident* (1973), pp. 143 ff.; B. Z. Wacholder, "The Calendar of Sabbatical Cycles during the Second Temple and Early Rabbinic Period," *HUCA,* XLIV (1973), 153-96, and "Sabbatical Chronomessianism and the Timing of Messianic Movements," *HUCA,* XLVI (1975); J. T. Milik, "Milkî-ṣedeq et Milkî-reša'," *JJS,* XXIII (1972), 95-144.

B. Z. WACHOLDER

*SACRIFICES AND OFFERINGS, OT.

1. Introduction
   a. Origins
   b. Principal laws
   c. Graded holiness of the sanctuary
   d. Priests and laymen
   e. Role of the layman
   f. Role of the priest
2. Expiatory sacrifices
   a. *Ḥaṭṭā'th*
      i. Theory
      ii. Theology

iii. Laws
iv. Scaled *ḥaṭṭā'th*
b. *'Āšām*
c. *'Ōlâ* in expiation
d. *Minḥâ*
3. *Šᵉlāmîm*
a. Etymology
b. Lev. 17:11
c. Other functions
4. The people's evaluation
Bibliography

1. Introduction. ***a. Origins.*** Researchers in primitive and comparative religion distinguish four possible purposes behind the institution of sacrifices: (1) to provide food for the god (Eichrodt); (2) to assimilate the life force of the sacrificial animal (James); (3) to effect union with the deity (Smith); (4) a gift to induce the aid of the deity (Taylor). The first three purposes are not to be found in the Bible. True, the first one is still ensconced in some sacrificial idioms, e.g., "my table" (Ezek. 44:16); "the food of his God" (Lev. 21:22; cf. vs. 17); "my food, . . . my pleasant odor" (Num. 28:2; author's trans. throughout). The original aim of the sacred furniture of the tabernacle/temple (the table for the bread of presence, the candelabrum, and the incense altar) probably was to provide food, light, and pleasant aroma for the divine residence. Even the sacrificial procedure betrays this anthropomorphic background; e.g., God must receive his share of the sacrifice before man (cf. I Sam. 2:29). Nonetheless, these words and mores are only fossilized vestiges from a dim past, which show no signs of life in the Bible. The second purpose is found in animistic religions but not in ancient Israel. Even its derivative—the animal dies on the altar instead of the offerer (Médebielle, cols. 48-81)—can find no support in Scripture. Lev. 17:11, which usually has been so interpreted, is subject to another interpretation (*see* §3*b below*). The same is true for the third purpose: the verses allegedly proving that the *šᵉlāmîm* creates a mystic union between God and the offerer should be interpreted in a totally different way (Gray; *see* §3 *below*).

Only the fourth purpose remains valid for Israel: a gift to God to induce his aid. Support derives from sacrificial terms connoting a gift (e.g., קרבן, מנחה, נדבה, משאת, and perhaps אשה, *'iššê*) and from unequivocal attestations of the text—e.g., "Offer to God a thanksgiving offering and pay your vows to the Most High; . . . I will deliver you, and you shall glorify me" (Ps. 50:14-15). This motivation, to secure divine aid, can be subdivided: (1) external aid to secure fertility or victory, i.e., for blessing; and (2) internal aid, to ward off or forgive sin and impurity, i.e., for expiation. Thus the *'ōlâ* is a gift to God to obtain his blessing or for expiation (*see* §2*c below*). The *šᵉlāmîm* also reveals this two-function gift, since its blood ransoms the life of the slaughterer, and its fat gives thanks to the Deity for the meat (*see* §3 *below*).

b. Principal laws. Most of the details of the priestly sacrificial system are found in Lev. 1–16 (*see* LEVITICUS[S]). The sacrifices are enumerated in chs. 1–7 in two overlapping series. The first series (chs. 1–5) is addressed to the offerer (cf. 1:1-2) and is ordered according to his perspective: voluntary offerings (*'ōlâ, minḥâ šᵉlāmîm*) and mandatory offerings (*ḥaṭṭā'th, 'āšām*). The second series (chs. 6–7) is addressed to the priests (6:9 [H 2]), emphasizing their duties (e.g., 6:10-11 [H 3-4]) and privileges (6:26 [H 19]), and listing the sacrifices according to their sanctity: *'ōlâ, minḥâ, ḥaṭṭā'th, 'āšām,* which are most-sacred, i.e., consumed on the altar or by the priest, followed by the *šᵉlāmîm,* which is less sacred, i.e., consumed by the laity. Thereupon follow the sacrificial rites that set the pattern for the cultic service: the consecration of the priests (ch. 8) and of the tabernacle (ch. 9). Individuals bearing severe impurities are required to bring a purgation offering (*ḥaṭṭā'th, see* §2*a below*): the parturient woman (ch. 12), the leper (ch. 14) and the gonorrheic (ch. 15). The sacrificial corpus closes with the ritual for the Day of Atonement, ch. 16 (*see* ATONEMENT, DAY OF[S]). Miscellaneous sacrificial rites are: holy days (Lev. 23; Num. 28-29), the ordination of the Levites (Num. 8:5-22), the suspected adulteress (Num. 5:12 ff.; *see* ORDEAL, JUDICIAL[S]), and the NAZIRITE (Num. 6). For the schedule and materials of the offerings, *see* SACRIFICES AND OFFERINGS, OT §§A2*b*ii, D.

c. Graded holiness of the sanctuary. According to the P Code, the layman participates alongside the priest in the preliminary stages of the sacrifice at "the entrance to the Tent of Meeting," i.e., in the forecourt between the entrance and the altar. The court is accessible to the laity because it is less sacred than are the tabernacle and its appurtenances, which are ranked as most-sacred (Exod. 30:26-29; 40:9-11), and hence are off limits to the laity. The lesser sanctity of the court is evidenced by the Day of Atonement ritual. The purificatory blood is applied within the tent and to the outer altar, but not one drop is sprinkled on the court or its curtains. In theory, therefore, the entire court is open to laymen, and the circumambulation of the altar by worshipers during the Feast of Booths (M. Suk. 4.5) indicates that in the second temple this was also the practice—perhaps in the first temple, too (cf. Ps. 26:6).

Though the cult furniture is most-sacred and barred to the laity, its holiness is not contagious to persons as the following evidence demonstrates: (1) The formula "everything which touches is sanctified (Exod. 29:37; 30:26-29; Lev. 6:18 [RSV "whoever"], 27 [H 11, 20]) applies only to objects, not humans. (2) The most-sacred curtains of the tabernacle are handled by Levites, though they have the status of laymen (Num. 4:24-26). (3) Though the inadvertent trespasser (*m'l*) upon the sanctums must make momentary sacrificial amends (*see* §2*b below*), he does not have to undergo a desanctification ritual. (4) The formula "everything which touches is sanctified" (Exod. 30:29) lies between the prescription to anoint the cultic objects (vss. 26-28) and the priests (vs. 30), indicating that the priestly clothing is not contagious. True, the Kohathite Levites are expressly warned not to touch or even view the sanctums while they are dismantled (Num. 4:15,

17-20). However, that passage probably stems from an older Priestly source in which the sanctums possess lethally contagious power, just as they do in the nonpriestly narratives (e.g., I Sam. 6:19; II Sam. 6:6-8). Thus the Priestly Code shows inner development, an attempt to eliminate the contagious power of the sanctums.

The book of Ezekiel, on the other hand, is governed by older taboos. Its sanctums are contagious to persons as well as to objects. This postulate underlies the radical departure of Ezekiel's blueprints of the future temple from its Solomonic predecessor. The inner court, containing the altar, is entirely off limits to the laity. Even the chief of state (*nāśî'*) can enter only as far as the gateway and is barred from the court itself (Ezek. 46:1-3). The priests are forbidden to bring most-sacred meat into the outer court (46:20) or to enter it wearing their priestly clothing (44:19) lest "they sanctify the people." Thus Ezekiel requires two courts instead of the one of the tabernacle/temple: the outer to accommodate the laity, and the inner to conceal the contagious sanctums.

d. Priests and laymen. Throughout the ancient Near East, the temple was usually regarded as the private preserve of the priests. Only the Hittites permitted laymen access to the sacred precincts, and then only under priestly escort (*ANET* [2nd ed.], p. 208). In general, the laymen could glimpse the images of the gods only on festival days, when they were paraded in religious processions. It was forbidden to show ritual instructions to nonpriests. In this respect, Israel was radically different. The tabernacle/temple—at least its forecourt—was accessible to the laity (*see* §1*c above*). More significantly, the sacrificial laws were incorporated into the Pentateuch as "a heritage of the congregation of Jacob" (Deut. 33:4). As the editorial headings indicate (Lev. 1:2; 4:2; 7:38; 12:2; 15:2; 16:29-31; etc.), these laws were made available to the people at large. The only clear exceptions are the instructions concerning the inebriated priest (10:8) and leprosy (chs. 13–14), but even these fall under the fundamental definition of the priest's job: "to make a distinction between sacred and profane, between clean and unclean, and to teach the Israelites all the decrees" (Lev. 10:10-11 NEB).

e. Role of the layman. The offerer participated in the following rituals involving his animal: laying of the hands, *t^{e}nûphâ* (*see* WAVE OFFERING [S]), slaughter, skinning, dissecting, and washing. All these acts are performed in the forecourt. The rituals reserved for the priests are: *t^{e}nûphâ* (jointly with the offerer), blood manipulation, arrangement of the wood and sacrifice on the altar, and incineration. The division follows this rule: anything to do with the altar is the exclusive domain of the priest. This rule is clearly evident in the *'ōlâ* procedure (Lev. 1): the anonymous subject is always the offerer, but when the action switches to the priest he is mentioned by name. In the case of the *'ōlâ* bird, however, the offerer is omitted from the procedure (1:14-17), because there is no place for lay participation. Even the "slaughter" is performed by pinching off the head at the altar, an act of necessity done by the priest.

The purpose of the laying of hands (סמך יד) has yet to be clarified. Perhaps there are two discrete acts, with two hands and with one. The former might be a transference rite, transferring the performer's authority (Num. 27:18 [LXX], 23) or impurity (Lev. 16:21; 24:14) to the animal/person, whereas the latter, used exclusively with sacrifices (e.g., Lev. 1:4; 3:2, 8, 13; 4:4, 24, 29, 33), could be an identification rite, identifying both the owner of the sacrifice and its type. Laying hands on a sacrifice seems to be unique to Israel, since elsewhere this rite is only of the former category, an exorcism of demonic evil and its transference to a surrogate (e.g., Mastiggas, the Hittite sorceress I, line 18; III, line 50, *ANET,* pp. 350-51). The rabbis claim that the laying of hands is always accompanied by a confession (Tosef. Men. X.12), but this is unlikely, since the confession generally preceded the actual bringing of the animal to the sanctuary (e.g., Lev. 5:5-6). Apparently every sacrificial animal required that hands be laid on it except the *'āšām* (omitted in Lev. 7:1-7) since it, alone among the sacrifices, is commutable to currency (*see* §2*b below*).

That ritual slaughter could be performed by anyone, not just the priest (as claimed by Philo, *On the Special Laws,* I, 199; cf. Lev. Rabbah 22.7), is shown by the alternation of subjects in Lev. 1 (*above*; cf. also I Sam. 1:25 [LXX and 4QSam]; Jos. Antiq. III.ix.1-4). The priests customarily slaughtered their personal sacrifices (Lev. 9:8, 12; 16:11) and the public sacrifices (Lev. 9:15, 18; II Chr. 29:24), occasionally assisted by the Levites (Ezra 6:20; II Chr. 30:17; 35:6, 11; cf. Ezek. 44:11). Most-sacred cattle were slaughtered "before the Lord" (e.g., Lev. 1:5), i.e., anywhere in the forecourt, whereas most-sacred sheep and goats were slaughtered "on the north side of the altar" (Lev. 1:11; cf. 4:4, 15, with 4:24, 29, 33). Certain texts indicate that slaughtering also took place on the altar itself (Gen. 22:9; Exod. 20:24), but here private altars are meant, not that of the tabernacle/temple.

The *t^{e}nûphâ* (RSV "wave offering") was performed by the priest but, on occasion, in partnership with the offerer (e.g., Exod. 29:24; Lev. 8:27). It is a dedicatory rite for less sacred offerings, which remain the property of the owner up to the time he brings them to the sanctuary, in which case the *t^{e}nûphâ* enacts the transfer of the offering from the owner to the Deity. It is also ordained for most-sacred offerings whose ingredients or procedure vary from the norm and is intended to focus the attention of the Deity to the offering's purpose. In the case of the *š^{e}lāmîm* it is incumbent upon the offerer to hand the breast and fat to the officiating priest, the former for *t^{e}nûphâ,* and the latter for incineration on the altar (Lev. 7:30-31).

f. Role of the priest. The priest's principal functions are the manipulation of the blood and the incineration of the sacrifice, both performed on the altar. The centrality of the blood in the sacrificial ritual is evidenced by the rule that the priestly portions of the sacrifice are assigned to one who manipulates the blood (Lev. 6:26 [H 19]; 7:7). The verbs *ḥiṭṭē'* and *kippēr* underscore its importance (Lev. 6:26 [H 19]; 7:7; 16:16-18; 17:11;

Ezek. 43:26). The rabbis concur on its centrality (M. Zeb. 5.1-4), as emphasized by their rule: "There is no expiation without blood" (T.B. Yom. 5a; Sifra, Nedaba 4.9; cf. Jub. 6:2). The blood of the *'ōlâ, 'āšām,* and *š^elāmîm* is dashed on all sides of the altar (Lev. 1:5; 3:2; 7:2), whereas the blood of the *ḥaṭṭā'th* is daubed on the horns of the outer altar if the sacrifice is brought by a tribal chief or commoner (4:25, 30, 34); if it is brought by the high priest or community, it is sprinkled seven times before the veil and daubed on the horns of the inner altar (4:6-7, 17-18). The blood of the *'ōlâ* bird is drained against the side of the outer altar (1:15), and that of the *ḥaṭṭā'th* bird is partially sprinkled on the side of the altar (5:9). The remainder of the blood is always drained at the base of the altar. For the special significance of the *ḥaṭṭā'th* blood, *see* §2*a below.*

The incineration on the altar is designated by הקטיר, to distinguish it from normal burning, שרף. The latter implies elimination, riddance, whereas the function of altar incineration is to provide "sweet savor to the Lord" (e.g., Lev. 1:9; 3:5). The *'ōlâ* is incinerated in its entirety (1:9), except for its skin, which becomes the emolument for the officiating priest (7:8). Of the remaining sacrifices, only their fat is incinerated (3:9-10; 4:26, 31, 35; 7:3-4). Sacrificial portions may not be eaten prior to the incineration of the altar portions, since God is given his share before man. For example, the breast is given to the officiant (Moses) only after the incineration of the fat and thigh (8:28-29). This rule is confirmed by the condemnation of Eli's sons: "Why then treat with scorn my sacrifices by fattening yourselves upon the choicest parts of every offering ahead of me?" (I Sam. 2:29 LXX).

The eating of the sacrificial meat is governed by special rules. The most-sacred offerings, the *ḥaṭṭā'th* and *'āšām,* must be eaten by the priests within the sacred precincts before the following morning. The *š^elāmîm,* being less sacred, may be eaten over a two-day period by anyone who is neither impure nor in an impure place. The thank offering (תודה) and paschal offering (פסח), as *š^elāmîm* types, must be eaten before morning (Exod. 12:10; Lev. 7:11-15; cf. §3 *below*). The rabbis claim that priests' eating of the sacrifices is an integral part of the expiation process (Sifra, Shemini 2.4), which they derive from this verse: "He has given it to you to remove the guilt of the community and to make expiation for them before the Lord" (Lev. 10:17). However, this interpretation is unlikely, since expiation is not the function of all sacrifices (*see* §3 *below*), and the verse is best rendered with A. Ehrlich: "He has given it to you [as a reward] for removing the guilt of the community by making expiation for them before the Lord." In this respect, the Levites are similar to the priests, for they too receive a reward, i.e., the tithe, for replacing the Israelites in the sanctuary, thereby bearing their guilt (Num. 18:22-23; Milgrom, *Studies,* pp. 22-25).

2. Expiatory sacrifices. The expiatory sacrifices are the *ḥaṭṭā'th* and the *'āšām,* at times the *'ōlâ* and *minḥâ,* and, in one case, the *š^elāmîm.* Expiation is expressed by the verb *kippēr* (RSV "make atonement"; Lev. 1:4; 4:31; 5:16; 14:20; 17:11), but its meaning is not the same for every sacrifice (*see* ATONEMENT IN THE OT[S]). The original meaning is probably preserved in the *ḥaṭṭā'th. See* LEVITICUS §1, for §§2*a-d,* 3 *below.*

a. Ḥaṭṭā'th (חטאת). The name of the sacrifice is derived from the *piel* (*ḥiṭṭē'*), which is synonymous with *ṭihar,* "purify" (e.g., Ezek. 43:23-26) and *kippēr,* "purge" (Ezek. 43:20, 26). The *ḥaṭṭā'th,* therefore, is to be rendered "purgation offering." Its purpose, however, is not to purge the offerer but the sanctuary. That the *ḥaṭṭā'th* blood functions only as a ritual detergent for purging the sanctuary is demonstrated by the following: (1) The *ḥaṭṭā'th* blood is never used on a person. The rites for the healed leper (Lev. 14) and the priests' consecration (Exod. 29; Lev. 8) do call for a *ḥaṭṭā'th* and a blood daubing, but the blood is taken from a different sacrifice. (2) The vexing problem of the prepositions that follow *kippēr* can now be resolved. In the Priestly writings, when the object is nonhuman, *kippēr* takes a direct object or the prepositions *'al* or *b^e*. The direct object is that which is purged, and the prepositional object is that "on" or "in" which purgation takes place. However, when the object is a person, a preposition must follow, for *kippēr* can never have a personal direct object. The preposition is usually *'al,* rarely *b^e'adh,* both meaning "on behalf of, for." They signify agency, i.e., the person has the purgation done by an agent who, in P, is always the priest. Thus the priest purges the sanctuary by means of the *ḥaṭṭā'th* on behalf of the person (or group) who has polluted it either by physical impurity (e.g., Lev. 12–15) or inadvertent offense to God (e.g., Lev. 4). Unrepented impurities, however, cannot be purged by the offender's *ḥaṭṭā'th* (cf. Num. 15:27-31) but must await the annual purgation of the sanctuary and nation on the Day of Atonement.

i. *Theory.* The *ḥaṭṭā'th* presumes that impurity is a dynamic (but not demonic) force that attacks the sanctuary. This is Israel's transformation of the universal belief that impurity is a demonic force that attacks both men and gods, the latter in their sanctuaries. Whereas pagans must constantly purify their sanctuaries against unrelenting demonic invasions, Israel recognizes only one source of evil—man. He alone can pollute the sanctuary by his physical and moral impurity and thereby drive out God from his midst. This assumption of dynamic, real impurity is confirmed by the biblical texts. Molech worship is forbidden because it pollutes the sanctuary (Lev. 20:3). The gonorrheic and menstruant are commended to purify themselves "lest they die through their impurity by polluting my tabernacle which is among them" (Lev. 15:31). The corpse-contaminated person who "does not purify himself pollutes the Lord's tabernacle" (Num. 19:13). The rabbis claim that these impure persons are not liable unless they have entered the sanctuary or eaten sacred food (cf. Sifra, Hoba 12.10). However, their premise is nowhere expressed in the text.

ii. *Theology.* This view of the *ḥaṭṭā'th* also

discloses the priestly doctrine of THEODICY. Since the *ḥaṭṭā'th* blood removes the impurities of the sanctuary through absorption, it contaminates any object it is spilled upon or touches (Lev. 6:27 [H 20]). Hence the laws of impurities prevail in the cleansing of objects contacted by the *ḥaṭṭā'th*: earthenware is broken (cf. 6:28*a* [H 21*a*] with 11:33, 35; 15:12*a*), and metalware is scoured (cf. 6:28*b* [H 21*b*] with Num. 31:22-23). Again, because the *ḥaṭṭā'th* cleanses by absorbing impurity, it contaminates those who handle it. Thus whoever burns the *ḥaṭṭā'th* after it has purged the sanctuary (e.g., 16:16) must submit to ablutions (16:28). Similarly, he who prepares or uses the ashes of the red heifer (called *ḥaṭṭā'th,* Num. 19:9), e.g., by burning it (Num. 19:8), gathering its ashes (19:10), or applying it (19:21), is thereby rendered impure and requires purification. The rabbis regarded the effect of these ashes as a paradox: they purify the contaminated and contaminate the pure (Tanḥ. Hukkot 4.26; cf. M. Par. 4.4). However, this view of the *ḥaṭṭā'th* resolves the paradox. The ashes of the red heifer are no different than any other *ḥaṭṭā'th*: they absorb the impurities of the object upon which they are sprinkled, and, conversely, they transmit impurity to the one who prepares or administers them. The principle that purificatory materials become the carriers of the very impurity they remove is also found in the Hittite Code §44 (*ANET,* p. 191). *See also* ATONEMENT IN THE OT[S] §2*a*.

The polaric nature of the *ḥaṭṭā'th* as a most-sacred yet impurity-bearing sacrifice, i.e., a carrier of the impurity it absorbs, also explains the peculiarity that, on occasion, the *ḥaṭṭā'th* flesh is burned outside the camp (e.g., Lev. 4:11-12, 21) instead of being eaten by the officiating priest (6:26 [H 19]), as expressed in the law: "No *ḥaṭṭā'th* may be eaten from which any blood is brought into the tent of meeting for purgation within the sanctuary: it shall be consumed by fire" (6:30 [H 23]; cf. 10:17-18). As will be shown below, the impurities inside the sanctuary represent Israel's gravest sins. Since they are especially malefic, the *ḥaṭṭā'th* to which they are transferred is lethal and inedible. It must be destroyed by fire; and, so that it will not work havoc on its surroundings, it is burned outside the camp. Of course, the one who is charged with burning it must purify himself before he returns (16:28).

The purging of the sanctuary takes place in three stages: (1) When an individual commits an inadvertency or contracts a severe impurity, the *ḥaṭṭā'th* blood is daubed on the horns of the outer altar (e.g., Lev. 4:25; 9:9; 14:19). (2) When the entire community (even through its anointed priest: 4:3) commits an inadvertency, the blood is brought inside the shrine where it is sprinkled before the veil and daubed on the horns of the inner altar (Lev. 4:5-7, 16-18). (3) For presumptuous sins, of the individual or the group, the blood is brought inside the adytum where it is sprinkled before and upon the ark, followed by the ritual of the previous two stages in reverse order. Only one postulate explains these data: the greater the offender and the graver the offense, the more the resultant impurity penetrates into the sanctuary. Inadvertences of the individual pollute the outer altar; inadvertences of the group pollute the shrine; but presumptuous sins penetrate into the adytum and only the rites of the Day of Atonement can purge them. That the Day of Atonement is concerned with presumptuous sins is indicated by the unique occurrence of *peša'* (RSV "transgressions"; Lev. 16:16, 21), a term borrowed by P from political terminology denoting rebellion (e.g., II Kings 3:5; Ezek. 20:38). The congruence of the impurity stages and the blood placements can be clarified by the following sketch:

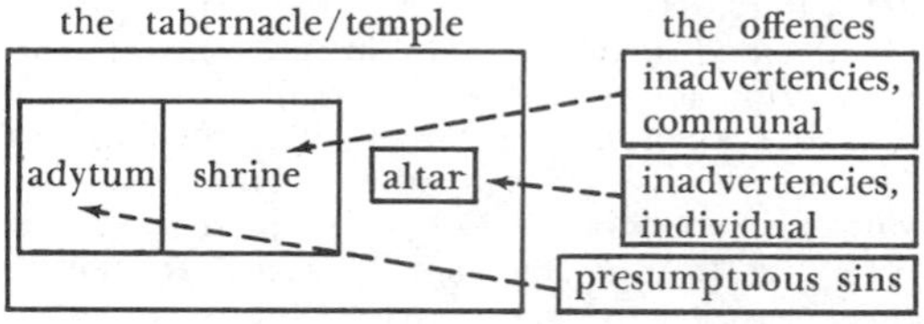

iii. *Laws.* The *ḥaṭṭā'th* laws are based on the assumption that the inadvertent offender becomes aware of his act and feels remorse for it. Awareness and remorse are predicated by the verb אשם (*'āšam*). Consequently, the protasis of the *ḥaṭṭā'th* laws must be rendered: "When he feels guilty (RSV "is guilty") or is informed by his wrongdoing, he shall bring . . ." (Lev. 4:22-23, 27-28). Repentance is thus a precondition for the *ḥaṭṭā'th*. Moreover, only the inadvertent violation of prohibitive commandments is subject to this sacrifice (Lev. 4:2, 13, 22, 27), not the neglect or omission of performative commandments. This is so because impurity can result only from a violation, not an act of omission.

The *ḥaṭṭā'th* for inadvertences are graded according to the socioeconomic position of the offender: a bull for the high priest and community, a he-goat for the tribal chieftain, and a female of the flock for the commoner. The cases of the high priest and community form one law: the inadvertence of the high priest causing the people to err (Lev. 4:2-21; cf. T.B. Hor. 7a, 13a). This follows textually from (1) the absence of the conclusion "and he shall expiate . . . , be forgiven" in vs. 11 (cf. vs. 20*b*); (2) the similar procedure for both (emphasized in vs. 20*a*); (3) the communal *ḥaṭṭā'th,* elsewhere a he-goat (Lev. 9:3, 15; 16:5; Num. 15:24), only here is a bull, since the high priest is among the offenders, and only a bull can expiate for his inadvertences (Lev. 4:3; 9:2 [RSV "calf"]; 16:11). A variant in the procedure for communal inadvertences is found in Num. 15:22-26, i.e., an *'ōlâ* bull and a *ḥaṭṭā'th* he-goat. The discrepancy is probably due to two extant techniques of purging the sanctuary. Ezekiel fuses them in his altar consecration (43:18-27).

Not all the ritually impure bring the *ḥaṭṭā'th,* only those whose impurity lasts a minimum of one week. The gonorrheic brings a bird, and the leper brings a female sheep or, if poor, a bird. Whoever brings a bird (turtledove or pigeon) brings another of the same kind as an *'ōlâ* to provide an adequate gift to the altar (Ibn Ezra on Lev. 5:7). The *ḥaṭṭā'th* for impurity, no differently than for inadvertences, purges sanctuary pollution (T.B. Ker. 26a). Contamination by a corpse does not require a *ḥaṭṭā'th,* since it is of lesser impurity than the leper or gonorrheic (M. Kel. 1.1-4). Instead, the person contaminated by the corpse is sprinkled with the purificatory waters containing the ashes of a red heifer on the third and seventh day (Num. 19). Ezekiel, however, holds that a priest contaminated by a corpse must undergo purification for a second week and sacrifice a *ḥaṭṭā'th.*

In a sacrificial series, the *ḥaṭṭā'th* is always the first to be offered (Lev. 5:8; cf. M. Naz. 6.7; M. Zeb. 10.12; Tosef. Par. I.1). True, the *'ōlâ* is often found first but only in prescriptive lists; in descriptive lists, the priority goes to the *ḥaṭṭā'th.* The two kinds of lists can be illustrated by the following example: the Nazirite who fulfills his vow is commanded, "And he shall present" (Num. 6:14); in this list the *'ōlâ* appears first. But in the execution of the ritual: "the priest shall offer" (vs. 16), the *ḥaṭṭā'th* is listed first. The priority of the *ḥaṭṭā'th* is clear from its function: the altar need be purged before it is fit for sacrificial gifts to the Lord.

iv. *Scaled ḥaṭṭā'th.* An appendix to the *ḥaṭṭā'th* laws (Lev. 5:1-13) gives four marginal cases where the *ḥaṭṭā'th* is scaled, not according to the social position of the offender, but according to his economic status. The commoner who cannot afford a female of the flock is given the option of offering two birds (turtledoves or pigeons) or a tenth of an ephah of flour. This pericope constitutes a new law and is not a continuation of the previous passage on the commoner's *ḥaṭṭā'th* (4:27 ff.) because: (1) The opening phrase ונפש כי (5:1) usually begins a new law. (2) The text expressly states that the sacrifice is for "one of these" offenses of 5:1-4 (5:13; cf. vs. 5). (3) The prerequisite for the *ḥaṭṭā'th,* inadvertency in connection with a prohibitive commandment, is missing, as a closer examination of the four cases reveals. In the first case (5:1) a witness refuses to testify in spite of an imprecation to do so, and in the fourth case (5:4) a person violates an oath he has forgotten. The second and third cases (5:2-3) deal with a person who forgets he is impure, but his offense is not clear. The rabbis hold that his offense consists of making contact with sanctums during his impurity, but this is nowhere stated. The theory of a real, dynamic impurity affords a simpler explanation: amnesia caused the prolongation of his impurity. According to P, he who deliberately delays his required purification will be punished by God (e.g., Lev. 17:16; Num. 19:13, 20; cf. M. 'Er. 10.15; Jos. Antiq. III.xi.3). However, since Lev. 5:2-3 deals with one who forgot he was impure, the prolongation of his impurity was not deliberate and is expiable by a *ḥaṭṭā'th.*

b. 'Āšām (אשם). The main *'āšām* cases are cited in Lev. 5:14 ff. and its sacrificial procedure in Lev. 7:1-7. The root אשם has four cultic meanings: as a noun, "reparation" (e.g., Lev. 5:6) and "reparation offering" (RSV "guilt offering"); and as a verb, "incur liability" to someone (e.g., 5:19); and, if it has no personal object, "to feel guilty" (e.g., 5:5, 17; 6:4 [5:23]). The meaning "reparation offering" can be adduced from the unique accompanying verbs *hēšîbh,* "restore" (RSV "make restitution"; Num. 5:7-8; 18:9; I Sam. 6:3-4, 17), and *šillēm,* "repay" (RSV "restore"; Lev. 6:5 [H 5:24]), implying indemnities, as well as from the fact that the *'āšām* is the only sacrifice that is commutable into currency (Lev. 5:15, 18; 6:6 [H 5:25]).

The first *'āšām* case (5:14-16) deals with inadvertent trespass (*ma'al*) upon sanctums. The trespasser must restore the value of the desecrated sanctums, pay a one-fifth fine, and bring a ram or its monetary equivalent as a reparation offering. The sanctums subject to this law are not clarified, but from Hittite documents (e.g., *ANET,* p. 208) and tannaitic sources (M. Me'il. 3.7-8; 4.1; 5.1; 6.6; Sifra, Hoba 20.3-5) it is clear that all sanctums are included, animate and inanimate alike. Further clarification of the *'āšām* is gained from a comparison with the redemption of sanctums described in Lev. 27. Both the desecration and redemption of sanctums require a one-fifth penalty, but in Lev. 27 it is a surcharge for legitimate desanctification (redemption), whereas in Lev. 5 it is a penalty for illegitimate desanctification (desecration), which also requires a reparation offering to God. Additional cases in which desecration of sanctums is expiated by the *'āšām* are: (1) the contaminated Nazirite (Num. 6:1-12), who must make reparation for his desecrated hair and vow; (2) Jeremiah's haggadic MIDRASH (2:3), calling for divine retribution upon the nations who have desecrated the sanctum of Israel; and (3) Ezra's legal midrash (10:19), whereby those who have intermarried with foreigners must make reparation for their desecration of Israel's holy seed.

The *'āšām* case of Lev. 5:17-19 deals with suspected trespass on sanctums. He who suffers in body or conscience without knowing the cause suspects that he is being punished by God for trespassing on his sanctums. In this respect, ancient Israel is no different from its environment, where unconscious sanctum trespass was identified as a prime cause for divine retribution (e.g., *ANET,* pp. 34-36, 391-92). Lev. 5:17-19, then, is a continuation of vss. 14-16—the first case dealing with known trespass, the second with suspected trespass (cf. M. Ker. 5.2-8; T.B. Ker. 22b; Sifra, Hoba 12.1). In the ancient Near East, leprosy was frequently attributed to sanctum trespass, and it may explain why an *'āšām* is included in the sacrificial ritual for the healed leper (Lev. 14:10-32).

The third case (Lev. 6:1-7 [H 5:20-26]) concerns the defrauding of man, compounded by a false oath to God. It presumes that the false oath follows all the previously enumerated crimes, i.e., that the fraudulent act was followed by a lying oath (cf. M. B.M. 1.4, 7; Sifra, Hoba 13.8; 23; Philo, *On the Special Laws,* I, 255; IV, 31-32). This case states that, if the offender repents of his deed (אשם) before he is apprehended, he need only restore the value of the property to the owner, add a one-fifth fine, and bring a reparation offering to God. A parallel law in Num. 5:6-8 adds two more stipulations: (1) if the owner dies without heirs, the total reparation belongs to the sanctuary; and (2) the defrauder must articulate his repentance in a confession. The latter stipulation points to a basic postulate of the Priestly Code: voluntary confession reduces deliberate sins to inadvertences, thereby rendering them eligible for sacrificial expiation (cf. Sifra, Aharei 2.4, 6).

c. 'Ōlâ* (עלה) *in expiation. That the *'ōlâ* (RSV "whole offering," Lev. 1) expiates (*kpr,* RSV "make atonement") is expressly stated in its prescription (Lev. 1:4), in certain rituals (Lev. 9:7; 14:20), and in nonpriestly sources (Job 1:5; 42:8; cf. *UT* 9.1). Since it is entirely consumed on the altar (the skin excepted, Lev. 7:8) it is called *'ōlâ* or *kālîl,* i.e., "holocaust" (RSV "burnt offering"; Deut. 33:10; I Sam. 7:9; *UT* 1015.14, and *KAI* 69.3, 5, 7, 9; 74.5). The *'ōlâ* has thus far been evidenced in Greece, Anatolia, and Canaan, but not in Egypt or Mesopotamia.

The offenses expiated by the *'ōlâ* are not cited in the Bible, but it is reasonable to assume that since the *ḥaṭṭā'th* and *'āšām* expiate for the limited sins of the pollution and desecration of sanctums, the *'ōlâ* expiates for the remaining, much broader scope of sins, such as the neglect of the performative commandments (cf. Tosef. Men. X.12; Lev. Rabbah 7:2). The *'ōlâ* serves other functions, e.g., petition (I Sam. 13:12) and thanksgiving (Lev. 22:17-19; Num. 15:1-16). The *'ōlâ,* then, is all-encompassing; it answers to all the emotional needs of the worshiper.

The development of the expiatory sacrifices is seen in three stages: (1) Originally, the *'ōlâ* was the sole expiatory sacrifice. The earliest sources do not mention the *ḥaṭṭā'th* and *'āšām,* but they tell of the expiatory *'ōlâ* on behalf of the individual (Job 1:5; 42:8) and community (Judg. 20:26; II Sam. 24:25). The rabbis express a similar view: Originally "the open altars (*bamoth*) were permitted, and only the *'ōlâ* was offered" (Tosef. Zeb. XIII.1). (2) In contrast to open altars, sanctuary residences of the deity required purgation of and protection from pollution and desecration, giving rise to the *ḥaṭṭā'th* and *'āšām,* respectively. (3) That all public sacrifices are limited to male animals—the requirement for the *'ōlâ*—probably means that originally the *'ōlâ* was the only public sacrifice, and when other sacrifices were added to the cultic calendar, they were made to conform to the *'ōlâ.*

d. Minḥâ (מנחה). Since the *minḥâ* (RSV "tribute offering") is a cereal offering in P, it is likely that it served as a cheap *'ōlâ* for those who could not afford an animal (T.B. Men. 104b; Lev. Rabbah 1:5; 8:4). In Mesopotamia too, the cereal offering was a concession to the poor: "they approach you, the widow, with an *upuntu* (inexpensive flour), and the rich with a sheep" (*KAR* 25, II, 29). The procedure for the *minḥâ* (Lev. 2) was probably inserted between the procedures for the *'ōlâ* (ch. 1) and the *šelāmîm* (ch. 3; 3:1 is a subsection of 1:2; cf. 1:3), because the *minḥâ* became the regular accompaniment to the *'ōlâ* (e.g., Lev. 14:20; Num. 28–29), and especially because it was the *'ōlâ* of the indigent, serving the same wide-ranging functions, including expiation (T.B. Men. 110a; Philo, *On the Special Laws,* I, 271; cf. *KAR,* 25, II, 19).

3. Šelāmîm (שלמים). In P, the *šelāmîm* offering is often coupled with or replaced by the noun זבח (*zebhaḥ*). In Ugaritic, Punic, and rabbinic Hebrew, the root *zbḥ* can refer to all blood sacrifices, but this is not the case in the Bible, except possibly II Chr. 7:12. It is reserved for those sacrifices whose flesh is eaten, e.g., feasts at altars (I Sam. 2:13), the yearly *zebhaḥ* (I Sam. 1:21), the family *zebhaḥ* (I Sam. 20:29). The root *zbḥ* itself means "slaughter" (for food). In P, *zebhaḥ* often occurs in construct with other sacrifices, e.g., *zebhaḥ pesaḥ* (paschal offering), *zebhaḥ tôdhâ* (thank offering), and *zebhaḥ šelāmîm* (which because of its frequency is occasionally abbreviated to *zebhaḥ* or *šelāmîm*).

a. Etymology. *Šelāmîm* is plural formation. The singular is found once in the Bible (Amos 5:22) but frequently in Ugaritic (*UT* 1:4; 3:17, 52, etc.). The following etymologies have been suggested: (1) *šālôm* (peace), since "it effects peace between the altar, the priests, and the offerer," i.e., those who share in the offering (Tosef. Zeb. XI.1). Support is adduced from the early sources which hold that this sacrifice was eaten "before the Lord" (e.g., Deut. 27:7; I Sam. 2:13-16) as a shared meal (e.g., Gen. 31:54). W. R. Smith further held that the *šelāmîm* effected a mystic union between the deity and offerer, a meaning which, however, the Bible seems to reject (Judg. 6:18-21; 13:16; Ps. 50:12-13). Moreover, as Ehrlich pointed out, the sacrifice is eaten "before (*liphnê*) the Lord," not "with" him. (2) The Akkadian cognates *salimu,* "covenant," or (3) *šulmānu,* "gift" (Levine) have been proposed as well as a derivative from (4) *šālēm,* "whole, sound," i.e., the offerer gives thanks for his well-being (Tosef. Zeb. XI.1; Sifra, Nedaba 16.2; Philo, *On the Special Laws,* I, 212), and (5) *šillēm,* "repay", i.e., the sacrifice repays God for his blessings (Rashbam on Lev. 3:1; cf. Prov. 7:14). (6) The LXX provides three translations, two corresponding to (1) and (4) above, and σωτήριος, "save, preserve." However, all these etymologies remain conjectural. The rendering "offering of well-being" is tentatively adopted here.

Originally, the *šelāmîm* was eaten close by the altar (I Sam. 2:13; 9:24; cf. Ezek. 46:24), reflexes of which are found in the Nazirite's "boiled shoulder" and "fire under the *šelāmîm*" (Num. 6:18-19) and in the special room in the second temple where the Nazirites cooked their *šelāmîm* (M. Middot 2.5).

The absence of birds from the eligible *šelāmîm* animals bespeaks its antiquity. In the wilderness period all birds were considered game; their blood was not dashed on the altar but buried (cf. Lev. 17:13-14). This rule continued to prevail in Canaan, even after birds were entered into the sacrificial lists of the *'ōlâ* and *ḥaṭṭā'th.*

b. Lev. 17:11. That the (*zebhaḥ*) *šelāmîm* is not expiatory is evidenced by its avoidance of the verb *kippēr.* There are three ostensible exceptions: (1) Ezek. 45:15, 17, where, however, *kippēr* may refer to the *'ōlâ* and *ḥaṭṭā'th* in the list and not to the *šelāmîm.* (2) I Sam. 3:14, where, however, the term *zebhaḥ ûminḥâ* is a synecdoche referring to all the sacrifices (for *minḥâ* as a blood offering, cf. I Sam. 2:17, 29). (3) Lev. 17:11, which translates as follows: "For the life of flesh is the blood and I have assigned it to you upon the altar to ransom (*kpr*) your lives, for it is the blood as life that ransoms (*kpr*)" (*see* ATONEMENT IN THE OT[S] §2*c*). It can be demonstrated that the context of this verse is concerned exclusively with the *šᵉlāmîm*: (1) Vss. 10-14 form a bipartite law, the second referring to game for the table "that may be eaten" (vs. 13), the first to edible domesticated species (cf. 17:3). (2) The same chapter rules that domesticated, pure animals must be sacrificed at the authorized altar before they may be eaten (vss. 3-5). (3) The prohibition against eating blood (repeated five times in vss. 10-14) implies that the blood is ingested while eating meat. This prohibition occurs elsewhere only in connection with eating meat (Deut. 12:15-16, 23-25; 15:23). Thus Lev. 17:11 refers to the *šᵉlāmîm*, the only sacrifice eaten by the offerer. Yet this nonexpiatory sacrifice bears in this context a strictly expiatory (*kpr*) function. This paradox is resolved by 17:3-4: if one does not slaughter his animal at the altar, "bloodguilt shall be imputed to that man; he has shed blood." The animal slayer is a murderer unless he offers its blood on the altar to ransom his life (vs. 11).

This doctrine is related to the Priestly account of Creation, whereby man was meant to be a vegetarian (Gen. 1:29). Beginning with Noah, God concedes to man's carnivorous desires, provided he abstains from ingesting the blood (Gen. 9:3-4). Thus all men are enjoined to avoid the lifeblood of the animal by draining it and thereby returning it to its Creator (Gen. 9:3-4; Lev. 17:13-14). Israel, as part of its discipline to achieve holiness (cf. Lev. 19:2; 20:26), must observe an additional safeguard: the blood of sacrificial animals must be drained on the authorized altar, thereby ransoming the life of the one who slays the animal (Lev. 17:11).

c. Other functions. The motivations for bringing the *šᵉlāmîm* as a special sacrifice are adduced in Lev. 7:11-16, i.e., thanksgiving (*tôdhâ*), fulfillment of a vow (*nedher*; RSV "votive"), or freewill offering (*nᵉdhābhâ*; cf. Philo, *On the Special Laws*, I, 224; so also among the Greeks, cf. Plato, *Laws*, 909-10). The common denominator to all these motivations is rejoicing: "You shall sacrifice these *šᵉlāmîm* and eat them, rejoicing before the Lord your God" (Deut. 27:7). According to the rabbis, the *tôdhâ* offering is not subsumed under the *šᵉlāmîm* (M. Zeb. 5.6-7; cf. I Macc. 4:54-56). Its discreteness has a scriptural basis (Lev. 19:5-7, cf. 22:29; Jer. 17:26; II Chr. 29:31-33; 33:16). Moreover, it is coupled with a bread offering and eaten on the same day (Lev. 7:11-16), whereas the *nedher* and *nᵉdhābhâ* are unaccompanied by a bread offering and eaten over a two-day period (cf. Lev. 19:5-6). Also the *nedher* or *nᵉdhābhâ* may be brought as an *'ōlâ* as well as a *šᵉlāmîm* (Num. 15:3, 8; Ezek. 46:2, 12), but apparently not the *tôdhâ* (cf. II Chr. 29:31).

Other less sacred altar offerings are the *pesaḥ* (*see* PASSOVER), the *bᵉkhôr* (*see* FIRST-BORN[S]), and the animal tithe (*see* TITHE). Non-altar sacrifices include the *ma'ᵃśēr* (*see* TITHE), *bikkûrîm* and *rē'šîth* (*see* FIRST FRUITS, OT[S]), *ḥērem* (*see* DEVOTED) and *heqdēš* (*see* SANCTIFICATION[S]). For the sacrificial schedule and procedure, and for the conditions of purity of the officiant and offerer, *see* SACRIFICES AND OFFERINGS, OT §§A2*b*, C, E.

4. The people's evaluation. The sacrifices filled a wide range of spiritual and emotional needs. True, the prophets jeered at their ineffectiveness in refining ethical behavior. But this cannot negate the clear evidence that the masses participated in the sacrificial services from inner initiative, reverence, and love; "I will go to the altar of God, to God my exceeding joy" (Ps. 43:4). "Blessed is he whom thou dost choose and bring near, to dwell in thy courts! We shall be satisfied with the goodness of thy house, thy holy temple!" (Ps. 65:4). "My soul longs, yea, faints for the courts of the Lord. . . . For a day in thy courts is better than a thousand elsewhere" (Ps. 84:2, 10).

The attachment of the masses to the sacrifices did not diminish during the days of the second temple, as indicated by the praise which Ben Sirach lavishes upon his high priest Simeon (Ecclus. 50:1-21; *see* AARON, AARONIDES[S]). The many prayers recorded in the rabbinic literature for the reconstruction of the temple (Mishna Aboth and Aboth de Rabbi Nathan, end of ch. 5; Mishna Pesahim, end of Jerusalem version; Gen. Rabbah 13:2, etc.), plus the plethora of laws and entire tractates on the sacrifices, testify that even when the conviction began to take hold that the synagogue had transcended the temple, there were many who maintained that without the sacrificial service Israel's spiritual life would remain impaired.

Bibliography. General: H. Hubert and M. Mauss, *Sacrifice: Its Nature and Function* (1898 [ET 1964]); F. B. Jevons, *An Introduction to the History of Religion* (9th ed., 1927); E. B. Tylor, *Primitive Culture* (7th ed., 1924); G. van der Leeuw, *Phänomenologie der Religion* (2nd ed., 1956), pp. 393-406; A. Schimmel, "Opfer," *RGG*, IV (3rd ed., 1960), at 1637-41.

Biblical sacrifice: D. Hoffmann, *Das Buch Leviticus* (1956); Y. Kaufmann, *History of Israelite Religion*, I (1938), pp. 113-84, 532-88, Hebrew, trans. and abridged; M. Greenberg, *The Religion of Israel* (1960), pp. 53-57, 101-21; O. E. James, "Aspects of Sacrifice in the OT," *ET*, L (1938-39), 151-55; A. Metzinger, "Die Substitutions-theorie," *Bibl.*, XXI (1940), 159-87, 247-72, 353-77; S. Belkin, *Philo and the Oral Law* (1940), pp. 49-66; H. W. Robinson, "Hebrew Sacrifice and Prophetic Symbolism," *JTS*, XLIII (1942), 129-39; L. Moraldi, "Terminologia Cultuale Israelitica," *RSO*, XXXII, 1 (1957), 321-37; R. Hentschke, "Opfer," *RGG*, IV (3rd ed., 1960), 1641-47; I. Fransen, "La Loi du Sacrifice," *Bible et vie chrétienne*, XXX (1959), 21-30; M. Haran, "The Complex of Ritual Acts Performed Inside the Tabernacle," *Scripta Hierosolymitana*, VIII *Studies in the Bible*, ed. C. Rabin (1961), 272-301, and "The Priestly Image of the Tabernacle, *HUCA*, XXXVI (1965), 191-226; W. Eichrodt, *Theology of the OT*, I (1961), 141-72; R. de Vaux, *Studies in OT Sacrifice* (1964); B. A. Levine, "The Descriptive Tabernacle Texts of the Pentateuch," *JAOS*, XXCV (1965), 307-18; R. B. Wright, "Sacrifice in the Intertestamental Literature" (diss., Hartford Seminary, 1966); S. Daniel, *Recherches sur le vocabulaire du culte dans la Septante*

(1966); R. Rendtorff, *Studien zur Geschichte des Opfers im Alten Israel* (1967); H. H. Rowley, *Worship in Ancient Israel* (1967), pp. 111-43; A. Rainey, "The Order of Sacrifices in OT Ritual Texts," *Bibl.*, LI (1970), 485-98; J. Milgrom, *Studies in Levitical Terminology,* I (1970), 1-43.

Comparative: S. Sauneron, *The Priests of Ancient Egypt* (1960); A. L. Oppenheim, *Ancient Mesopotamia* (1964), pp. 172-97; L. Rost, "Ein hetitisches Ritual gegen Familienzwist," *MIO,* I (1953), 345-80.

Expiatory Sacrifices: S. Landersdorfer, *Studien zum biblischen Versöhnungstag* (1924); P. Saydon, "Sin-Offering and Trespass-Offering," *CBQ,* VIII (1946), 393-98; L. Morris, "'Asham," *EvQ,* XXI (1958), 196-210; K. Elliger, "Zur Analyse des Sündopfergesetzes," in *Verbannung und Heimkehr,* ed. A. Kuschke (1961), pp. 39-50; R. J. Thompson, *Penitence and Sacrifice in Early Israel Outside the Levitical Law* (1963); N. H. Snaith, "The Sin-Offering and the Guilt-Offering," *VT,* XV (1965), 73-80; K. Elliger, *Leviticus* (1966), pp. 53-79; J. Milgrom, *Cult and Conscience* (1976), "The Function of the Ḥaṭṭā't Sacrifice," *Tarbiz,* XL (1970), 1-8, Hebrew, "Sin-Offering or Purification-Offering," *VT,* XXI (1971), 237-39, "Two Kinds of ḥaṭṭā't," *VT* (forthcoming), "Israel's Sanctuary," *RB* (forthcoming), and *Encyclopaedia Judaica* articles, "Day of Atonement," V (1971), cols. 1384-87, "Kipper," X, cols. 1039-44, and "Leviticus, Book of," XI, 138-47; D. Kellermann, אשׁם, *TWAT,* I (1971), 463-72; B. A. Levine, *In the Presence of the Lord* (1974), pp. 53-114; A. Médebielle, "Expiation," *DBSup,* III (1938), cols. 48-112.

Other animal sacrifices: W. B. Stevenson, "Hebrew 'Olah and Zebach Sacrifices," *Festschrift Alfred Bertholet* (1950), pp. 488-97; N. H. Snaith, "Sacrifices in the OT," *VT,* VII (1957), 308-17; A. Charbel, "Virtus Sanguinis non Expiatoria in Sacrificio Šelāmîm," *Sacra Pagina,* I (1959), 366-76; N. M. Loss, "La Partecipazione Dei Laici al Rito Dell' Olocausto," and "Olocausto e Sacrificio Pacifico," *Salesianum,* XXIII (1961), 353-62, XXIV (1962), 525-33; R. Schmid, *Das Bundesopfer in Israel* (1964); J. Hoftijzer, "Das Sogenannte Feueropfer," VTSup, XVI (1967), 114-34; M. Haran, "Zebah Hayyamîm," *VT,* XIX (1969), 11-22; J. Milgrom, "A Prolegomenon to Leviticus 17:11," *JBL,* XC (1971), 149-56, and *Encyclopaedia Judaica* articles, "Anointing," III (1971), cols. 27-28, "Bloodguilt," IV, cols. 1118-19, "Desecration," V, cols. 1559-60, "Leprosy," XI, cols. 33-36, and "Nazirite," XII, cols. 907-9; G. Gerleman, "Das Wurzel *šlm*," *ZAW,* LXXXV (1973), 1-14; B. A. Levine, *In the Presence of the Lord* (1974), pp. 1-52.

J. MILGROM

***SAMARIA.** In recent years the site of Samaria has been the subject of two excavations, one by the Department of Antiquities of Jordan during 1965, the other a season in 1968 by the British School of Archaeology in Jerusalem.

The 1965 excavations were primarily concerned with the improvement of tourist facilities at the site—the reopening of the theater and a new pathway from the Streets of the Columns to the main monuments on the Acropolis. This necessitated the re-excavation of many of the trenches of earlier expeditions, but at the same time the opportunity was taken to excavate new control trenches which have produced important stratigraphic evidence.

The Hellenistic rampart was based on the rubble foundations of an earlier Iron Age II wall, since the foundation trench immediately beneath the Hellenistic rampart produced only sherds of Iron II. Fragments of earlier Iron II walls and parts of a new Hellenistic tower were also uncovered. The destruction of the latter can be linked either with the retreat of Ptolemy I (Soter) in 312 B.C., or with Demetrius Poliocretus in 296 B.C. Within the theater six separate staircases ranging through a flight of fourteen steps were uncovered.

The excavations in the area of the colonnade confirmed the results of the earlier expeditions, with the initial foundation of the road and shop system dating to the second century A.D. The area appears to have remained commercially important during the early Byzantine period. Its destruction may be associated with either the revolt of the Samaritans under Justinian in A.D. 529 or the earthquake of A.D. 551. After a brief period of abandonment, the area appears to have been walled and terraced for cultivation.

The 1968 excavations were designed to establish the sequence and geographical limits of the domestic quarters of the Iron Age, Hellenistic, and Roman settlements (which, at present, remain a complete blank in our knowledge of this important town).

Five trenches were opened N and NW; four of them immediately below the summit and citadel area. All were within the supposed limits of the town walls of the successive occupations. The four trenches above the 448-yard line all reached bedrock at an average depth of 25 to 26 feet.

A major feature of these trenches was an overburden of about 10 to 12 feet completely lacking in constructions of any kind and appearing to represent a deliberate fill or throw-out—part of a single operation possibly associated with work on the nearby citadel area. The pottery from the overburden in all four trenches was consistent and suggests that the operation took place late in the first or early in the second century A.D. The overburden sealed the shaft of a rock-cut water system, which had remained in use until well into the first century A.D. The system neck had been built up to keep pace with accumulating soil and silt washes which lay directly under the overburden. No buildings appear to have been associated with the final use of the system, but it had obviously remained a source of water for some time after the domestic desertion of the immediately surrounding area. Beneath the wash lines in all four trenches, there was evidence of widespread and thorough robbing of earlier walls; the pottery and coins of the robber trenches suggest Herod I. These trenches were cut through a series of poor house floors and destruction levels of the late Hellenistic period. Unfortunately, the finds were too scanty to give a precise date. The pottery suggests a date late in the first or early in the second century B.C., while the latest coins (Akko Ptolemais) of the second century B.C. tempt one to suggest that this final occupation was that brought to an end by John Hyrcanus and his sons in 107 B.C. An alternative suggestion and, perhaps more likely, is that the final desertion of the area was due to Pompey (63 B.C.), and that the evidence for the destruction of Samaria by Hyrcanus lies in the deep wash and destruction lines beneath these late house floors.

By far the greater part of the remaining deposit in the upper trenches belongs to the Hellenistic period. A surprising feature of the 1968 excavations was the complete lack of Iron Age deposits. In all four trenches which reached bedrock, the only remains earlier than Hellenistic were in two small pits cut into bedrock and containing pottery of the Persian period. This suggests that the western city wall of the Iron Age settlement lay between this area and the citadel with a concentration of settlement to the E and S of the hill nearer to the water supply.

Bibliography. F. Zayadine, "Une Tombe der Fer IIA Samarie-Sébaste," *RB,* LXXV (1968), 562-85; J. B. Hennessy, "Excavations at Samaria-Sebaste, 1968," *Levant,* II (1970), 1-21; K. M. Kenyon, *Royal Cities of the OT* (1971). J. B. HENNESSY

SAMARIA PAPYRI. The Samaria Papyri are a collection of extremely fragmentary Aramaic documents that were acquired in 1962-64. Discovered primarily by the Ta'amireh Bedouin, they shed important light on the fourth century B.C., one of the least known eras in Palestinian history.

Because of references in the papyri to Artaxerxes II (404-359) and Darius III (335-330), it has been possible to place these documents in the period between 375 and 335 B.C., a dating corroborated by the coins discovered by archaeologists, all of them dating shortly before Alexander's invasion in 332 B.C. According to the Bedouin, the MSS were discovered in a cave of the Wadi Daliyeh, 490 yards above the river Jordan, and about 9 miles N of ancient Jericho. The discovery of a few additional fragments during the course of two archaeological expeditions in 1963 and 1964 confirmed that this cave was indeed the site where the documents had rested. The cache seems to consist of some twenty documents, all of a legal or administrative nature. In the cave were discovered approximately two hundred skeletons of people who were quite affluent, judging from the papyri themselves and the exquisite seal rings, jewelry, and other artifacts that were recovered. Presumably all the inhabitants of the cave were killed at the same time. The excavator conjectured that a fire had been set outside, and it suffocated the men, women, and children.

This evidence of a massacre of upper-class people and frequent references in the papyri to Samaria and its governors have led scholars to co-ordinate these finds with various references in ancient historians, particularly Josephus. According to this reconstruction, the city of Samaria was at first favorable toward Alexander, but later burned Andromachus, his prefect over Syria, while Alexander himself was occupied with his Egyptian campaign. Alexander returned to Samaria and destroyed it, but the leaders, hearing of his approach, fled to the cave where the Macedonian soldiers eventually discovered them and annihilated them. Samaria was then resettled by Alexander with Macedonians who were responsible for the erection of its Hellenistic towers. The remnants of the Samaritan community moved on to Shechem and established it as their new capital, thus accounting for the sudden and rapid reconstruction of that city noted in the recent excavations.

Because of the paucity of information from the time preceding Alexander's invasion, the Samaria Papyri assume an importance beyond first expectations. They are prized by palaeographers for helping to establish a set of absolute dates for fourth-century Aramaic cursive script and this, in turn, has confirmed the third-century dating of the earliest Qumran documents. *See* ALPHABET §1*c*; ALPHABET[S] §2.

The papyri have also been useful in reconstructing the lists of Samaritan governors (*see* SANBALLAT[S]) and in restoring names to our records of Jerusalem high priests, lost up to now by ancient haplography. They have tended to confirm some of the controversial data presented by Josephus, although not without exposing certain confusions he perpetrated concerning the period between the fifth and fourth centuries. His account of a marriage between Manasseh, brother of the Jerusalem high priest Jaddua III, and Nicaso, daughter of Sanballat III, can now be considered plausible, even probable. That such a relationship could exist between Judah and Samaria in the fourth century has tended to confirm the hypothesis of a late date, at the end of the second or the beginning of the first century B.C., for the definitive split between the two communities. *See also* SAMARITANS §B; SAMARITANS[S].

Bibliography. F. M. Cross, "Papyri of the Fourth Century B.C. from Dâliyeh: A Preliminary Report on Their Discovery and Significance," in *New Directions in Biblical Archaeology,* ed. D. Freedman, M. Greenfield (1969), pp. 41-62. A first volume of the final report of the archaeological expeditions, led by the late Paul W. Lapp, is forthcoming. R. W. KLEIN

***SAMARITAN PENTATEUCH.**

1. Character of SP. SP may be described as a full text. That is, its distinctive readings are usually fuller or longer than the corresponding passages of MT. This characteristic is reflected in such features as the addition of particles and prepositions for clarification, smoother or otherwise distinctive grammatical constructions, and the addition of words for explication or harmonization. The most striking feature is the occurrence of expansions (sometimes several paragraphs in length) based on parallel passages. The orthography is characterized by full use of the internal *matres* (consonantal vowel indicators), in contrast to the more restrictive orthography of the Masoretic tradition (*see* HEBREW LANGUAGE §4). Readings of a distinctively sectarian nature are of a type consistent with the general character of the text.

a. Expansions and pleonasms. There are approximately thirty-four instances in which SP includes significant expansions designed to accommodate parallel or synoptic readings from other parts of the Pentateuchal narrative. These are sometimes of considerable length, but may include only a line or two of additional material. They serve the purpose of reconstructing conversations or recording events which are alluded to elsewhere in the narrative. The following are examples of this characteristic. (1) Following Gen. 30:36, an addition paralleling Gen. 31:11-13. The latter passage refers to a previous event in which the angel of God was said to have visited Jacob; the addition—lacking in MT—records this event. (2) Additions to the story of the contest with Pharaoh, following or within Exod. 7:18; 8:4 [H 7:29]; 8:5 [H 1], 23 [H 19]; 9:5, 19; 10:2; 11:3. The narrative is filled out by the repetition of speeches given by God to Moses for Pharaoh—indicating that they were delivered as commanded (so the additions to 7:18; 8:4 [H 7:29], 23 [H 19]; 9:5, 19), or that the delivery corresponded to the speech as given by God (so the additions to 10:2; 11:3). In one instance, a message given by God to Moses for Aaron is repeated verbatim in the text (addition to 8:5 [H 1]). (3) Additions to the Decalogue in Exodus, following 20:17, within 20:19; and following 20:21. The first of these additions is discussed below under sectarian readings (*see* §1*b below*). The addition within Exod. 20:19 is based on Deut. 5:24-27, and includes the response of the people to Moses which was alleged to have been offered at Sinai (*see* Deut. 5:24). Similarly, the addition to Exod. 20:21 is based on Deut. 5:28-31, interrupted by an addition paralleling Deut. 18:18-22, and includes the response which God allegedly made on that occasion (*see* Deut. 5:28; 18:17). (4) Additions to Numbers paralleling Deut. 1–3. The address of Moses in Deut. 1–3 contains references to previous events and to speeches supposedly given on previous occasions. These are not contained in the earlier narrative of MT, but are so noted in expansions in the Samaritan text (Deut. 1:6-8 preceding Num. 10:11; Deut. 1:20-23 preceding Num. 13:1; Deut. 1:27-33 following Num. 13:33; Deut. 1:42 preceding Num. 14:41; Deut. 2:2-6 following Num. 20:13*b*; Deut. 2:9 following Num. 21:11; Deut. 2:17-19 following Num. 21:12; Deut. 2:24-29, 31 following Num. 21:20 and included in 21:21-23; Deut. 3:21-22 following Num. 27:23; Deut. 3:24-28 following Num. 20:13). Similarly, the narrative in Deuteronomy has been filled out by the addition of parallel materials from Numbers (so Deut. 2:8, based on Num. 20:17-18; Deut. 10:6-7, based on Num. 33:31-38*a*). Parallel or synoptic readings in the Samaritan text consistently result in longer texts. An exception is Deut. 34:2-3, where the text has been reduced by the use of materials from Gen. 15:18, in place of the longer text preserved in the Masoretic tradition (the same reading is found in Gen. 10:19 of SP).

In addition to expansions based on parallel materials, the Samaritan text exhibits a pleonastic tendency, with additions for clarification and explication. These include such additions as subjects, appositives, prepositions, and particles, and sometimes the repetition of words and phrases which render the texts somewhat redundant.

b. Sectarian readings. Several distinctive readings in SP support the theological position of Samaritanism on the priority of Mount Gerizim/Shechem as the chosen place of Israelite worship. These are frequently referred to by scholars as egregious tamperings with the biblical text, but they are less blatant than might first appear, given the character of the textual tradition (expansionist and harmonizing) in which they are preserved. Included in the expansions to the Decalogue, as noted above, is an addition following Exod. 20:17 (also following Deut. 5:18) based on Deut. 27:2-3*a*, 4-7, and 11:30 of the Samaritan text. These passages underscore the command of God to build an altar on Mount Gerizim (SP reads "Gerizim" rather than "Ebal" in Deut. 27:4) by making this part of the Ten Commandments. The Samaritan text of Deut. 11:30 reads "beside the oak of More' in front of Shechem" (MT="beside the terebinths of Moreh"). This latter reading may be understood as an explicating pleonasm. The reading "Gerizim" rather than "Ebal" in Deut. 27:4 is probably a sectarian alteration, although it may be argued that the Samaritans chose an alternate, ancient nonsectarian (or presectarian) reading. The sectarian apologetic was, however, clearly served by the inclusion of Deut. 27:2-3*a*, 4-7; 11:30 in the Decalogue, a pericope which was otherwise expanded by the use of materials from Deut. 5:24-27, 28-31, and 18:18-22. Some scholars have regarded the inclusion of Deut. 18:18-22 in the Decalogue as a sectarian reading based on the eschatology of the sect (allegedly, the belief in a Mosaic eschatological prophet). The addition may be understood, however, as an expansionist harmonization based on Deut. 18:16.

In addition to the readings in the expanded Decalogue, sectarian claims are supported in twenty-one instances in Deuteronomy in which worship is commanded at the particular site of God's choice. The MT reads, "the place which the Lord your God will choose (*yibhḥar*)" (e.g., 12:5). The Samaritan text omits the *yod* prefix of the verb, rendering it as a perfect (*bāḥar*), "the place which the Lord thy God has chosen." The place already chosen was, according to the Samaritans, Shechem/Gerizim—which they identify as Bethel of the patriarchal narrative, as well as Salem (Gen. 14) and Moriah (Gen. 22). Although this reading is more subtle than the expanded Decalogue passages, it may actually have involved a more overt tampering with the biblical text.

There are also readings in SP which either reflect emphases in Samaritan theology, or which have been used by the Samaritans in the development of their doctrines. These include "unto *your* dust you shall return," in Gen. 3:19 (a textual basis for resurrection); "the *day of* vengeance and recompense," in Deut. 32:35, also attested in LXX (a textual basis for the day of judgment); "there shall not rise again in Israel a prophet like Moses," in Deut. 34:10 (a textual basis on the unique superiority of Moses as God's prophet); and distinctive readings in several legal texts through which Samaritan halachic observances have come to differ from Jewish practice.

c. Other characteristics. In SP the preposition *'al* frequently appears where MT has *'el,* and there are also other interchanges of laryngals. The third-person singular pronouns are given the appropriate gender in SP, in agreement with the *qere* of MT (but not the consonantal text). The syndetic use of *wāw* is preferred in SP, in contrast to the more archaic asyndetic constructions in the Pentateuch of MT (the LXX frequently agrees with SP in this characteristic). The *hiph'il* stem of the verb is frequently preferred to the *qal*; there is a tendency to disregard collective forms in favor of plurals, or to combine collective forms with plural verbs; there is a diminished frequency of the absolute infinitive for the imperative and adverbial qualifications; the apocopated forms of *lamed he* verbs are sometimes rejected in favor of longer forms; frequent use is made of the *imperfectum consectivum*, or pseudo-cohortative, with the addition of the *he* to the imperative as well as the imperfect; and the syntax of SP usually represents agreement in gender and number between verbs and nouns, or verbs and other verbs, in instances in which MT displays discrepancies.

d. Orthography and script. Samaritan Pentateuchal MSS in general show a preference for the *plene* or full orthography. The internal *matres lectionis yōdh* and *wāw* are used extensively, and the *'āleph* is also sometimes employed as an internal *mater*. By comparison, the orthography of the Pentateuch of the MT is more restrictive and less consistent. It was assumed for some time that this orthographic tradition was a product of the Middle Ages (Gesenius). On the other hand, it has been suggested that the Samaritan orthography was related to an ancient textual tradition (Kahle). The discovery of biblical texts from Qumran with full orthography (including Pentateuchal texts agreeing in other respects with SP) indicates that the Samaritan orthography is indeed ancient: it reflects the full orthography of Hebrew writing during the Hasmonean period.

The script which has been employed by the Samaritans in Pentateuchal MSS exhibits a general uniformity, with only minor modifications and developments from medieval to modern times. The evolution of this script may be traced to an earlier time, however, by the use of Samaritan inscriptions of the Byzantine and Roman periods. A comparison of the archetypal forms of the Samaritan letters with the late history of Paleo-Hebrew writing indicates that the Samaritan script began to diverge from Paleo-Hebrew as it was used among Jews at a comparatively late date (late Hasmonean and early Roman times). This necessitates a re-evaluation of the popular opinion that the Samaritan script developed from Paleo-Hebrew writing at the time of Ezra. The Samaritans, who claimed to be the ethnic and spiritual descendents of old Israel continued to use and develop the Paleo-Hebrew script. *See* ALPHABET; ALPHABET[S]; INSCRIPTIONS, SEMITIC[S] §2*a*.

e. Comparison with MT and LXX. Approximately six thousand instances of SP variations from MT have been noted based on the edition of SP published in the London Polyglot. Most of the variations are, however, orthographic, and figures vary according to the manuscript on which the collation is based. There are about nineteen hundred instances in which SP agrees with LXX against MT. Some of these are significant textual variants, but many are slight, such as the syndetic use of the *wāw* in about two hundred cases in SP and LXX against MT asyndetic construction. SP differs from both MT and LXX in the ages of the antediluvians given in Gen. 5:19-20 (Jared); 5:25-27 (Methuselah); 5:28, 30-31 (Lamech); and in the ages of the line of Shem given in Gen. 11:10-26. On the whole, however, SP is in greater agreement with MT than with LXX. It has been noted that textually SP bears a relationship to the Pentateuch of the MT which is similar to the relationship of Chronicles to Samuel-Kings. *See* SEPTUAGINT[S] §1*c*; TEXTUAL CRITICISM, OT[S].

2. Assessments of importance. ***a. Early history.*** SP did not come to the attention of Western scholars until 1616, when the learned traveler Pietro della Valle secured a còpy in Damascus. The initial enthusiasm for this text is indicated in the fact that it was published in the Paris (1645) and London (1657) Polyglots. Unfortunately, the discussion of its merits was less than critical, and many who spoke for or against it did so out of doctrinal considerations. Protestant scholars at that time were intent on defending the value and authority of the MT. Morinus, a Roman Catholic, noted that SP sometimes agreed with the LXX and the Vulg. A complete reading of SP would have revealed a stronger agreement with MT, but once the discussion centered on textual agreements of SP with LXX, it had a tendency to remain there. Consequently, the Protestant scholars S. de Muis and J. Hottinger sought to demonstrate that SP was a faulty revision of MT, and even claimed that it contained mistakes of copyists derived from misreadings of the square Jewish script. On the whole little was accomplished in SP research during the seventeenth and eighteenth centuries, with attention focused on variant readings rather than on the character of the text as a whole.

b. From Gesenius to Kahle. In 1815 Gesenius published what was to become a classic study on SP, *De pentateuchi samaritani origine*. For the first time, the Samaritan text was examined in its totality. Out of this, Gesenius classified Samaritan readings into eight categories: (1) emendations of a grammatical nature, (2) glosses in the text, (3) conjectural emendations, (4) corrections based upon parallel passages, (5) expansions based upon parallel passages, (6) adjustments of chronologies, (7) Samaritan forms of words (including the unusual behavior of laryngals, and (8) sectarian readings based upon the theology and worship of the Samaritans. Although Gesenius maintained that the greater number of Samaritan variants were due to corruptions, corrections, and interpolations of a late date, his research led him to conclude that SP might have some limited text-critical value, inasmuch as it appeared to be derived from Jewish codices which differed from those upon which the texts of both LXX and MT were based. He also noted that the origin of the Samaritan text went back to the pre-Christian era and that there were some similarities between the text traditions of LXX and SP. The major thrust of his work, however, was toward a negative evaluation of SP, and the refutation of scholars who had made uncritical judgments on the text. Consequently, the question of the value of SP ceased to be a live issue for some time. About forty years later, however, Geiger took issue with Gesenius, noting that rabbinic traditions point to the existence of variant textual traditions which were rejected in the stabilization of the biblical text, and suggesting that the Samaritan text was the survival of an ancient textual tradition, rather than a late and corrupt development of a Jewish text. So too, the work of Paul de Lagarde, in the late nineteenth century, led to a greater appreciation of both the LXX and SP as witnesses to the early state of the Hebrew text prior to its stabilization. Most of the research which followed upon de Lagarde's work tended to concentrate on the original form of LXX, resulting in the classification of Greek manuscripts into families and the establishment of criteria in reconstructing the Proto-LXX. SP remained, however, a problem; for, while it agreed in some respects with LXX, it was closer to MT and presented its own deviations from the received Hebrew text. This problem was attacked early in the nineteenth century by Paul Kahle, who took his lead from Geiger rather than Gesenius, and who attempted to move beyond de Lagarde. Kahle suggested that SP is a witness to an ancient popular or "vulgar" textual tradition which survived independently of the rabbinic revision which led to MT. He found attestations of comparable vulgar texts in citations in the NT, in Philo, in rabbinic and pseudepigraphic literature, and in texts from the Cairo Genizah. Kahle explained the similarities of SP to LXX by suggesting that the earliest Greek translations were based upon popular texts like that preserved in SP, and explained the greater agreement of SP to MT by the suggestion that the Samaritan text was revised at some time to bring it into general agreement with the received Jewish text.

c. Recent assessments. The discovery of the Proto-Samaritan textual tradition in biblical fragments at Qumran indicates that Kahle was certainly correct in at least one respect: the text preserved in SP does represent an ancient, pre-Masoretic textual tradition. Several attempts have been made to clarify the relationship of Proto-SP to Proto-LXX and Proto-MT. Of these, the position of Kahle (official/vulgar texts) has been followed by some (notably, Greenberg). The development of the theory of local texts (principally by Cross and his students) has, however, provided a fresh context in which to view Proto-SP. Accordingly, SP may be seen as bearing witness to an ancient Palestinian textual tradition (known also from nonsectarian, Proto-SP fragments at Qumran). The LXX may be seen as bearing witness to a textual tradition (Proto-LXX) which branched off from the Palestinian tradition at an early time to undergo its own development (the Egyptian local text). This would explain certain similarities between LXX and SP (in the common origin of the two local traditions) as well as dissimilarities (the result of independent development of the traditions). MT represents a different textual family, at least for the Pentateuch, which Cross has suggested emanated from a Babylonian tradition. This tradition shows no influence of the local traits which marked the development of the Palestinian text (additions of explication and clarification) in the Pentateuch, and must have developed in isolation from it. In the stabilization of the biblical text in the Jewish community, the shorter, more austere (orthographically as well as textually) tradition was chosen for the received Pentateuchal text *(see* TEXT, HEBREW, HISTORY OF[S]). The Samaritan community, however, retained a fuller text derived from the old, local Palestinian tradition. But the agreement of SP with MT would suggest that at some time the Samaritan text underwent editorial work utilizing the Babylonian local tradition (Proto-MT). The activity must have occurred prior to the theological breach between Samaritans and Jews *(see* SAMARITANS §B; SAMARITANS[S]). Also the promulgation of the distinctively sectarian redaction of SP (based on the Proto-SP text) appears to have occurred rather late in the history of Jewish-Samaritan relations, most likely in the late Hasmonean/early Roman periods—judging from the textual, orthographic, and paleographic evidence.

Bibliography. Printed editions: Early studies were based on the della Valle text published in the Paris and London Polyglots. See G. M. LeJay, *Biblica* (1629-45); B. Walton and E. Castell, *Biblia sacra polyglotta,* vol. VI, Pts. IV, V (1957). *See also* B. Blayney, *Pentateuchus Hebraeo-Samaritanus* (1790); J. H. Petermann and K. Vollers, *Pentateuchus Samaritanus* (1872-91). The standard critical edition is A. F. von Gall, *Der Hebräische Pentateuch der Samaritaner* (1918 [1966]). The oldest portion of the Abisha scroll, the most revered of Samaritan texts, has been published by F. Pérez Castro, *Séfer Abiša* (1959). Printed editions prepared by modern Samaritan scholars include A. Sadaqa, *ḥamiššâh ḥûmšê tôrâh, nôsaḥ šāmrî (šômrôni),* in Samaritan script (1959), and A. Sadaqa and R. Sadaqa, *ḥamiššâh ḥûmšê tôrâh, nôsaḥ yehûdî, nôsaḥ šômrôni,* SP and MT in parallel columns, in the Jewish script (1962).

Critical studies: F. M. Cross, "The Contribution of the Qumrân Discoveries to the Study of the Biblical Text," *IEJ,* XVI (1966), 81-95; "The Evolution of a Theory of Local Texts," *Septuagint and Cognate Studies 2,* ed. R. Kraft (1972), 108-26; A. Geiger, "Einleitung in die biblischen Schriften," in *Nachgelassene Schriften,* IV (1876), 54-67, 121-32, and *Urschrift und Übersetzungen der Bibel* (1857); G. Gerleman, *Synoptic Studies in the Old Testament,* in *Lunds Universitets Årsskrift,* NS XLIV, no. 5 (1948); W. Gesenius, *De pentateuchi samaritani origine, indole et auctoritate commentatio philologica-critica* (1815); M. Greenberg, "The Stabilization of the Text of the Hebrew Bible Reviewed in the Light of the Biblical Materials from the Judean Desert," *JAOS,* LXXVI (1956), 157-67; P. Kahle, "Untersuchungen zur Geschichte des Pentateuchtextes," *TSK,* LXXXVIII (1915), 399-439; *The Cairo Geniza* (1947; 2nd ed., 1959); H. G. Kippenberg, *Garizim und Synagoge* (1971), pp. 68-74; J. D. Purvis, *The Samaritan Pentateuch and the Origin of the Samaritan Sect* (1968); P. W. Skehan, "Exodus in the Samaritan Recension from Qumran," *JBL,* LXXIV (1955), 182-87, "The Biblical Scrolls from Qumran and the Text of the Old Testament," *BA,* XXVIII (1965), 87-100; B. K. Waltke, "Prolegomena to the Samaritan Pentateuch" (diss. Harvard, 1965), "The Samaritan Pentateuch and the Text of the Old Testament," in *New Perspectives on the Old Testament,* ed. J. B. Payne (1970), pp. 212-39.

J. D. PURVIS

***SAMARITANS.** Research on the history, literature, and religion of the Samaritans has advanced considerably in the last decade. Studies on the early history of the sect have profited from recent archaeological discoveries, and investigations of Samaritan literary and religious traditions have been abetted by publications of texts and translations. Also, Samaritan traditions have been examined in relation to the expanded knowledge of the religious complex of Judaism in late antiquity, including sectarianism in general and Christian origins in particular.

1. Early history and sectarian origins. A clearer evaluation of Josephus' account of early Samaritan history (and especially of the building of the Samaritan temple) has become possible due to archaeological discoveries relating to the Samaritans, SHECHEM, and Mount Gerizim (*see* GEREZIM, MOUNT[S]), specifically: the Aramaic papyri from Wadi Daliyeh (*see* SAMARIA PAPYRI[S]); the excavations of Tell Balata; and the excavations at Tell er-Râs. The papyri from Wadi Daliyeh provide important data relating to the Samaritan uprising against the Macedonians (fourth century B.C.) as well as evidence of the existence of a grandson of Sanballat the Horonite, who bore the same name. This Sanballat (II) was neither the contemporary of Nehemiah, known from the Bible, nor the contemporary of Alexander the Great, known from Josephus' account of the building of the Samaritan temple. He was most likely the grandfather of the latter. The excavations at Tell Balata indicate that the city of Shechem was rebuilt in the early Hellenistic period (evidently by the disenfranchised Yahwists of Samaria) after having been virtually abandoned during the Persian period. The excavations of the Hadrianic temple at Tell er-Râs on Mount Gerizim have uncovered the foundations of an earlier temple of the Hellenistic period. This is most likely the temple which served the cultic needs of the Samaritan community from the time of Alexander the Great to its destruction in the time of John Hyrcanus (following Josephus). Considered together, these data indicate that Josephus was correct in his contention that the Samaritans built their shrine in the early Hellenistic period. This was a major step in the life of that community, leading to its eventual estrangement from Judaism and its traditions. It now seems virtually certain that this important move was not made earlier, in the Persian period (which had been conjectured from a conflation of Josephus' account with Neh. 13:28). Recent research on the SAMARITAN PENTATEUCH indicates that it may have undergone sectarian redaction in late Hasmonean period, roughly contemporaneous with the destruction of the Samaritan temple, *ca.* 128 B.C., by John Hyrcanus. It seems unwise to view the separation of Samaritanism from Judaism as a schism which occurred at a particular point in time. The separation between the two was certainly complete, however, by the time of John Hyrcanus.

2. Literature and religion. A clearer understanding of Samaritan Hebrew and Aramaic has emerged from recent Samaritan linguistic studies, especially from the research of Ben-Ḥayyim of the Hebrew University, but also from scholars pursuing some lines of inquiry opened by Kahle. In the field of Samaritan literature, the publication of the catalogue of the Gaster MSS of the John Rylands Library by Robertson has been a major contribution. Also, the publication of new texts and translations of the *Memar Marqah* and a major Samaritan chronicle tradition by Bowman of Leeds University have been important additions to the corpus of Samaritan literature available for scholars. In addition to these texts, a significant number of Samaritan liturgical works and religious treatises have been edited and translated as dissertations by Leeds University scholars. In the field of Samaritan religious studies, Macdonald's *Theology of the Samaritans* should serve as a major reference work. Although Samaritan religious thought has displayed a general uniformity from late medieval to modern times, it is evident that its earlier religious history was more complex, and that the various Samaritan religious traditions reflect a diversity of religious opinion which had once existed within the community. An attempt to identify distinct traditions by reference to a priestly orthodoxy and lay, heterodox sectarian movements (especially Dosithean) has been made by Bowman and Crown. Similarly, Kippenberg has applied the *traditionsgeschichtliche* methodology (*see* TRADITION CRITICISM[S]) to the study of early Samaritan traditions, an approach which should prove extremely helpful for the critical use of Samaritan traditions in the study of Judaism in late antiquity. In the latter regard, Samaritan traditions have recently been examined in studies on Jewish apocryphal literature and the NT (notably, the Gospel of John).

Bibliography. Early history: R. J. Bull, "The Excavation of Tell er-Ras on Mt. Gerizim," *BA,* XXXI (1968), 58-72; F. M. Cross, "Aspects of Samaritan and Jewish History in Late Persian and Hellenistic Times," *HTR,* LIX (1966), 201-11, and "Papyri of the Fourth Century B.C. from Dâliyeh," in *New Directions in Biblical Archaeology,* ed. D. N. Freedman and J. Greenfield (1969), pp. 45-69; H. G. Kippenberg, *Garizim und Synagogue: Traditionsgeschichtliche Untersuchungen zur samaritanischen Religion der aramäischen Periode* (1971), pp. 33-171; J. D. Purvis, *The Samaritan Pentateuch and the Origin of the Samaritan Sect* (1968); G. E. Wright, "The Samaritans at Shechem," in *Shechem* (1965), pp. 170-84.

Literature and religion: Z. Ben-Ḥayyim, *The Literary and Oral Tradition of Hebrew and Aramaic amongst the Samaritans,* 3 vols. (1957-67), Hebrew; J. Bowman, "Early Samaritan Eschatology," *JJS,* VI (1955), 63-72, "The Importance of Samaritan Researches," *ALUOS,* I (1958-59), 43-54, "Pilgrimage to Mt. Gerizim," *Eretz Israel,* VII (1964), 17-28, and *Samaritanische Probleme: Studien zum Verhältnis von Samaritanertum, Judentum, und Urchristentum* (1967); M. F. Collins, "The Hidden Vessels in Samaritan Traditions," *JSJ,* III (1972), 97-116; A. D. Crown, "Some Traces of Heterodox Theology in the Samaritan Book of Joshua," *BJRL,* L (1967-68), 178-98; T. H. Gaster, "A Samaritan Poem About Moses," in A. Berger *et al.,* eds., *Joshua Bloch Memorial Volume* (1960), pp. 115-39; J. C. Greenfield, "Samaritan Hebrew and Aramaic in the Work of Prof. Zev Ben-Ḥayyim," *Bibl.,* XLV (1964), 261-68; P. Kahle, "Die zwölf Marka-Hymnen aus dem 'Defter' der samaritanischen Liturgie," in *Opera Minora* (1965), pp. 186-212; H. G. Kippenberg, *Garizim und Synagoge* (1971), pp. 175-349; J. Macdonald, "The Leeds School of Samaritan Studies," *ALUOS,* III (1963), 115-18, *Memar Marqah: The Teaching of Marqah,* 2 vols., *BZAW,* LXXXIV (1963),

Samaritan Chronicle No. II, BZAW, CVII (1969), "The Theological Hymns of Amram Darah," *ALUOS,* II (1959-61), 54-73, and *The Theology of the Samaritans* (1964); R. Macuch, *Grammatik des samaritanischen Hebräish* (1969); A. Murtonen, *Materials for a Non-Masoretic Hebrew Grammar,* vol. II: *An Etymological Vocabulary of the Samaritan Pentateuch, Studia Orientalia,* XXIV (1960), vol. III: *A Grammar of the Samaritan Dialect of Hebrew, Studia Orientalia,* XXIX (1964); J. D. Purvis, "Samaritan Traditions on the Death of Moses," in G. W. E. Nickelsburg, Jr., ed., *Studies on the Testament of Moses, Septuagint and Cognate Studies,* IV (1973), pp. 93-117; J. Ramon Diaz, "Arameo Samaritano," *Biblicos,* XVIII (1959), 171-82; E. Robertson, *Catalogue of the Samaritan Manuscripts in the John Rylands Library,* 2 vols. (1938-62).

Samaritans and the NT: J. Bowman, "The Fourth Gospel and the Samaritans," *BJRL,* XL (1957-58), 298-308; G. W. Buchanan, "The Samaritan Origins of the Gospel of John," in J. Neusner, ed., *Religions in Antiquity* (1968), pp. 149-75; W. Meeks, *The Prophet-King: Moses Traditions in the Johannine Christology* (1967), pp. 216-57, 286-319; J. D. Purvis, "The Fourth Gospel and the Samaritans," *NovT,* XVII (1975), 161-98; C. H. H. Scobie, "The Origins and Development of Samaritan Christianity," *NTS,* XIX (1972-73), 390-414; A. Spiro, "Stephen's Samaritan Background," in J. Munck, *The Acts of the Apostles,* ABi, XXXI (1967), 285-300.

J. D. PURVIS

***SAMUEL, I AND II.** In the English Bible the ninth and tenth books; in the Hebrew Bible, where they count as one book, the eighth.

1. Title
2. Text
   a. I Chronicles and Psalms
   b. Judean Desert Hebrew texts
   c. LXX
3. Composition
   a. Four current hypotheses
   b. A hypothesis proposed
4. The leading idea and the essence of Samuel
Bibliography

1. Title. The name [book of] Samuel is attested in a tannaitic source (second or early third century, quoted in an undated amoraic text) and a little later by Origen (first half of the third century, as quoted by Eusebius; *see* Sweete; Schulz). The former is found in T.B. Baba Batra 14b, giving the order of the "prophetic" books as Joshua, Judges, Samuel, Kings. I Chr. 29:29 contains a statement that the first and last Chronicles of King David are "written in the Chronicles of Samuel the seer, and in the Chronicles of Nathan the prophet, and in the Chronicles of Gad the seer." Since the last two works are not extant books, the first cannot be presumed to be one either (namely, our book of Samuel); in other words, I Chr. 29 is not the earliest witness to the name [book of] Samuel. In the LXX, Samuel goes together with Kings as (τῶν) βασιλειῶν (βίβλος) or similarly, i.e., "[Book of the] Kingdoms/Reigns," again first attested by Origen. Jerome uses both names, "Samuel" and *(Liber) Regum/Regnorum,* "The Book of Kings/Kingdoms" (together with our Book of Kings). The Peshitta editions call it "The Book of the Prophet Samuel."

The position of Samuel in the Hebrew Bible, at least since tannaitic times, is between Judges and Kings. The LXX, Peshitta, and Vulg. MSS overwhelmingly place Ruth between Judges and Samuel (hence the order in the English Bible), but there are also other orders.

The question as to which arrangement is authentic, that of the Hebrew (and English) Bible (two books, Samuel and Kings) or that of the Greek Bible (one long book, Reigns), loses part of its possible interest to students who are impressed by Noth's opinion that the books Deuteronomy-Kings originally formed one unit *(see* §3*ai*; *see also* DEUTERONOMIC HISTORY, THE[S] §§1-2). As to the mutually independent existence, original or eventual, of Samuel and Kings, different points of division exist or have been proposed: after II Sam. 24 (the common division), after I Kings 2:12 (according to the Lucian group of the LXX), after I Kings 2 (the preference of many modern scholars). The division of Samuel into two books is mentioned first by Origen in a commentary on the LXX ("Reigns 1, 2, [3, 4]"). The Masoretes do not mention it. In the colophon to II Samuel, they give the number of verses "of the Book of Samuel," i.e., of one unified book. The split was introduced into the Hebrew Bible under the influence of the LXX and the Vulg. in a Spanish MS of 1448 *(see* Ginsburg). It spread with the printed rabbinic Bibles (Venice) from 1517 on, again under the influence of the translations. In a similar fashion, Kings, Ezra [-Nehemiah], and Chronicles were divided.

2. Text. Although Samuel has the reputation that its text is among the worst of the OT books, this is not evident to the ordinary reader. Whereas innumerable textual difficulties, commonly traced to corruptions and expansions, often frustrate the simple understanding of Ezekiel and some other books, the reader of Samuel advances through chapter after chapter without being arrested by significant difficulties traceable to deterioration of text. This is not to deny that Samuel has its share of obstacles to understanding because of textual corruption. A sampling may comprise II Sam. 1:18-27; 23:1-7 (both poetry); 5:8; 23:8 (both prose). But the generalizing condemnation of the Received Text (TR; *see* TEXTUS RECEPTUS [S]) is probably occasioned by the existence of a relatively great variety of different text forms rather than by its obscurity.

The following main groups of text are available for comparison with the TR.

a. I Chronicles and Psalms: (i) A list of major parallels between Samuel and I Chronicles: I Sam. 31=I Chr. 10:1-12; II Sam. 3:2-5=I Chr. 3:1-3; II Sam. 5:1-10=I Chr. 11:1-9; II Sam. 5:11-25=I Chr. 14:1-16; II Sam. 6:2-11=I Chr. 13:6-14; II Sam. 6:12-19=I Chr. 15:25–16:3; II Sam. 7=I Chr. 17; II Sam. 8=I Chr. 18; II Sam. 10:1–11:1=I Chr. 19:1–20:1; II Sam. 12:30-31=I Chr. 20:2-3; II Sam. 21:18-22=I Chr. 20:4-8; II Sam. 23:8-9, 11-39=I Chr. 11:11-40; II Sam. 24:1-4, 8-9=I Chr. 21:1-5; II Sam. 24:10-25=I Chr. 21:8-26. (ii) II Sam. 22=Ps. 18.

b. Judean Desert Hebrew texts. The following passages, many quite fragmentary, have been published; they are from the later part of the Second Commonwealth period: I Sam. 1:22–2:6, 16-25 (Cross, *BASOR,* 132 [1953], 15-26, 4QSam[a]) ; 16:1-11; 19:10-17; 21:5-10; 23:9-17 (Cross, *JBL,* LXXIV [1955], 147-72, 4QSam[b]; inconsequential fragments in *DJD,* I [1955], 64-65) . In the *Textual Notes on the NEB* (St. Anthony's Guild, 1970, pp. 342-51) , additional, unpublished Judean Desert material (4QSam[c]) has selectively been incorporated. *See* DEAD SEA SCROLLS; DEAD SEA SCROLLS[S].

c. LXX. Within the LXX three groups are commonly recognized (*see* SEPTUAGINT; SEPTUAGINT[S]; VERSIONS, ANCIENT §2*a*; TEXT, OT §C) . (i) The Vaticanus group. Its chief representative is MS B (the letter symbols are those of the Cambridge editions) . To it belong primarily B, y, a_2 and in various ways most LXX MSS. This group underwent a notable change in II Sam. 11:2 (or 10:1) – I Kings 2:11 toward a literal rendition of a Hebrew text (Proto-TR?), to the point of disregarding canons of Greek style; its outstanding example is καίγε, a combination translating גם, "also" (καίγε does not exist in common Greek) . Often dubbed the *Kaige* group, it is not limited to Samuel, and the sixth column of the Hexapla (Theodotion) is connected with it (*see* GREEK VERSIONS, MINOR [S] §§1-2) (ii) The (Proto-) Lucianic group. ("Lucianic" serves here as a conventional appellation comparable to "Septuaginta," Seventy [Translators].) It is represented by MSS b, o, c_2, e_2, and it shows relations of varied nature to the Hebrew text of Chronicles, (some?) Judean Desert fragments, and the *Antiquities* of Josephus. (iii) The Alexandrian group, represented by MSS A, c, x. It is said to be the LXX of Origen (the fifth column of the Hexapla) .

The discussion about these groupings, the relation of the groups to non-LXX witnesses, and related questions is very much in flux (*see* Kraft) . The present survey would be inadequate, however, were it not followed by a few observations—facts and principles. The principles are not new to philology, but they are submitted here because they have not always been accorded due consideration. *See* TEXTUAL CRITICISM, OT[S].

(i) Studies on the LXX of Samuel are always squarely based on Lagarde's *Urseptuaginta* theory as opposed to Kahle's so-called Targum theory (*see* GREEK VERSIONS, MINOR[S] §1*c*; TEXT, OT §C1*a*) . Today, Kahle is not widely followed. But the problem of OT quotations (not from Samuel) in the NT, a basic element of Kahle's theory, is only ignored, not solved. (ii) The number of witnesses to a reading or type of reading has no bearing on the value of the testimony. (iii) In OT textual criticism the age of a witness ordinarily has no bearing on the value of the testimony. (iv) In OT study, textual criticism is practiced by and large from the vantage point of the Hebrew text, the TR. This means that authors of commentaries and other scholarly works read the Hebrew until they come to a difficult or suspect passage. Then they consult the versions in the hope of finding a better reading or to substantiate their suspicion of a corruption. It is then only natural that the sum total of preferred versional readings obtained this way tends to impress the exegete with the superiority of a given version to the Hebrew text. Had he proceeded contrariwise, taking that version as his basic text and consulting the Hebrew whenever he experienced a difficulty in his chosen text, he might well have had the contrary impression and extolled the Hebrew Bible. (v) Scholars are sometimes inclined to view difficult or multiple readings as problems to be recognized and decided, wherever possible, primarily by rules of textual criticism (e.g., haplography, homoeoteleuton, and their remedies; *see* TEXT, OT §D; TEXTUAL CRITICISM, OT[S] §4) . Now these rules are nothing but standardized genetic explanations accounting for one reading, which one would emend or reject in favor of another reading. Assuming deteriorations and explaining them should be secondary, however, to maintaining extant texts and explaining their difficulties and conflicts in terms of literary, historical, or similar considerations. One example: The question in I Sam. 14:37 ff. is whether a sin has been committed by Saul or his son on the one hand or by the people on the other hand. The TR of vs. 41 translates approximately: "Saul said to the Lord, 'O God of Israel, let there be a clear oracle.' " The LXX has: "Saul said, O Lord God of Israel, why have you not answered your servant today? If the guilt is mine or my son Jonathan's, O Lord God of Israel, let there be *urim*; but if the guilt is your people Israel's, let there be *thummim*." Both readings make sense and both can be supported by known oracular models. The request of the TR is of the kind encountered in Assyro-Babylonian omen prayers; that of the LXX corresponds to Hittite practice. Which reading, if any, is to be preferred is to be decided by the history of religion or the history of tradition; techniques of textual criticism are to be employed where the readings yield poor sense or nonsense.

3. Composition. Samuel stands in the sequence of the narrative books, consisting of the Pentateuch and the Former Prophets. It is therefore no surprise that some scholars approach the question of its composition in a manner similar to their approach to the books of Genesis through Judges (*see* DOCUMENTS) . Most critics, however, do not apply to Samuel the methods they apply to the higher criticism of the Pentateuch, but this majority is internally diversified. McKenzie said in 1971 that it was his impression "that literary criticism on Samuel is about as far advanced as the criticism of the Pentateuch was when de Wette [1780-1849] wrote."

a. Four current hypotheses. i. The books of Samuel are a braid of two or three strands, into which a few individual short threads have been woven in random fashion (*see* SAMUEL, I AND II §C1*b*, 2) . This hypothesis was fully developed first by Budde, then by Eissfeldt. Budde holds that Samuel is made up of two parallel components (J and E) , continuing the components of the HEXATEUCH (Heptateuch) , which were intertwined in a first redactorial process (RJE) . The resulting narrative was then shortened in the redactorial operation, that of the Deuteronomist(s) (R^D), but later its original length was partly restored. Eissfeldt recognizes three basic constituents (in his reconstruction, redactors play a relatively minor role). In I Samuel the narrative lines of the constituents, for the most part, run parallel, as it were, whereas in II Samuel the consecutive order prevails. When he first proposed his view, Eissfeldt assigned the constituents plain numbers, implying thereby nothing more than their assumed chronological order ("I" is the earliest constituent, and so forth). In his introduction to the OT he relates these constituents to those he proposes for the Hexateuch (I=L, II=J, III=E), thus moving toward the position of Budde. The following is a slightly condensed summary of his analysis of 1931. (A verse listed in two components is either divided between them or cannot definitely be assigned to either.)

(I) I Sam. 4:1-10, 15-16, 21; 5:2-5; 6:1-2, 5-12, 14-15, 18-21; 7:1-2; 10:21-27; 11:1-15; 13:1-4, 6-7, 16-22; 14:1-52; 16:18, 21; 18:5-9, 20-29; 19:8, 11-17; 21:2-10; 22:1-2, 6-23; 23:1-13; 25:2-44; 26; 27:1-7; 29:1-2, 4-8, 10-11; 30; 31; II Sam. 1:1-2, 5-10, 13-16; 2; 3; 4:1-3, 5-12; 5; 6; 8. (II) I Sam. 1:3; 2:12-17, 22-25, 27-36; 3:2; 4:11-14, 16-22; 5:1, 6-12; 6:2-4, 12-14, 16-20; 9; 10:1-16; 11:6; 13:3-5, 7-15; 17:1-31, 40-58; 18:1-4, 17-19, 30; 20:1-42; 21:1-10; 22:1-2, 6-23; 23:14, 19-28; 24; 27:1-4, 8-12; 28:1-2; 29:3-5, 9-10; II Sam. 1:1-4, 11-12, 17-27; 4:4; 21:1-14; 9; 24:1-9, 15-16, 19-25; 10; 11; 12:15-31; 13; 14:1-24, 28-33; 15:7-15, 17-26, 29, 31-37; 16:1-20, 23; 17:1-26; 18; 19; 20:1-2, 4-26; [I Kings 1; 2:13-31, 34-43, 46]. (III) I Sam. 1; 2:1-11, 18-21, 26; 3; 7:2-17; 8; 10:17-21; 12; 15; 16; 17:1-11, 32-54; 18:10-16; 19:1-7, 9-10, 18-24; 20:1; 21:11-16; 22:3-5; 23:14-18; 25:1; 28:3-25; II Sam. 7; 24:10-14, 17-18, 21, 25; 12:1-15; 14:25-27; 15:1-6, 16, 23, 27-28, 30; 16:21-22; 17:27-29; 20:3; [I Kings 2:1-12, 31-33, 44-45]. (II Sam. 21:15–23:39 does not belong to any of these components.)

The number of critics who follow Budde or Eissfeldt or hold similar positions is relatively small; the probable reason is the difference between the Pentateuch and Samuel. According to the corresponding Pentateuchal hypothesis, the constituents (or "documents" or "sources") of the Tetrateuch/Pentateuch/Hexateuch are identified by five criteria: different divine names, differences of lexicon and grammar, different religious and ethical outlooks, duplication of substance, contradictions (*see* Source Criticism, OT[S]). In Samuel their number and usability are reduced. The first does not exist, and the second and third are doubtful or blurred. Duplication and contradiction occur. For example, twice or three times David is introduced to Saul (I Sam. 16:14-23; 17:31-33; 17:55-58); twice David has the opportunity to kill Saul but he spares his life, and the two talk about it (24:3-22 [H 4-23]; 26:5-25); twice David flees to Achish king of Gath (21:10-15 [H 11-16]; 27:1-3); twice Goliath is killed and by different men (17; 19:5; 21:9 [H 10], as against II Sam. 21:19). But this collection is made up of quite motley items and is too scanty for a foundation of a hypothesis about the composition of the book. Weiser and Fohrer add that the postulated constituents of Samuel are devoid of a distinct and distinguishing character, and that the parts of each constituent cannot be combined to form consecutive narratives.

ii. Gressmann rejects hypothesis (i) because its concept of a literary constitutent is too general. Its authors postulate constituents, but it is not possible to distinguish in Samuel two or three trains of narratives that relate largely the same sequels of happenings or circumstances, each one in its own peculiar way. Only elements that lend themselves to such ordering deserve the name literary "sources" that can be integrated into a hypothesis like the one proposed by Budde or Eissfeldt. Gressmann's answer to the problem of the literary prehistory of Samuel is that the book represents one narrative stock, expanded by isolated duplications and accretions, many of which derive from widely deviating MS variants. He also reckons with a Deuteronomic redaction to which he ascribes several pieces in a manner distantly reminiscent of Noth.

iii. Noth deals with Samuel in his study of the Deuteronomic history (DH) which runs from Deuteronomy through Kings. Its composers used literary material of various provenance and worked it into one narrative by selection, concatenation, and addition of connecting links and summaries. These men were authors of a history, not redactors; prior to them there existed no history of Israel in its land. But Samuel, unlike Judges or Kings, contains only a few such additions, the visible mark of the activity of the Deuteronomists. They are: I Sam. 7:2–8:22; 10:7-21*abα*; 12:1–13:1; II Sam. 2:10*a*, 11; 5:4-5; 7:1*b*, 7*a*, 11*a*, 12*b*, 13*a*, 22-24; 8:1*aα*, 14*b*. When allowance is made for glosses, we should say that the Deuteronomists took everything else from their sources.

Noth's opinion on the composition of Samuel is part of his comprehensive hypothesis and cannot, therefore, be fully evaluated here. The following refers only to a specific issue in Samuel. I Sam. 7–12, which Noth, following Wellhausen, assigns to DH, has virtually nothing in common with the DH passages of Judges and Kings as these are commonly identified, either in language, manner of literary presentation, contents, or structural function. But Noth has an additional criterion: from Deuteronomy through Kings the Deuteronomists have set up markers to emphasize caesuras in the flow of history, usually in the form of speeches that summarize the preceding periods and culminate in exhortations. To his mind, I Sam. 12 is such a speech, and having confirmed it as such by its literary form, content, and place, he uses it as a means to confirm as Deuteronomic those parts of chs. 7–10 that, in his opinion, resemble it in historical outlook. This is to say that here Noth recognizes literary constituents of composite texts by their function and philosophy, criteria which later he rejected for the analysis of the Pentateuch (*see bibliog.*). True, he builds on Wellhausen, who had assigned those sections to DH, but Wellhausen himself argues largely from the historical and religious outlook of the sections. The governing principle of Noth's critical analysis is, directly or indirectly, the philosophy of the purported constituents of the literature so analyzed.

iv. Weiser and, similarly, Fohrer hold that the basic elements of Samuel are single stories. Yet the stories reached the author, not in their first stage, individually and disjointly, but in distinct collections or groupings which bore their own individual stamps. The main collections, the constituents (following Weiser), are: (1) the story of the ark (I Sam. 4–6; II Sam. 6); (2) the rise of Saul (I Sam. 9:1–10:16; 11; 13–14); (3) the rise of David (I Sam. 16:14–II Sam. 5:12); (4) the story of the dynastic succession (II Sam. 9–20; I Kings 1–2). The difference between the constituents of Budde and Eissfeldt (§i *above*) and those of Weiser and Fohrer is this: Budde's constituents are narratives which cover extended spans of time in most cases and tell approximately the same happenings (II Sam. 9–20 is the exception). Weiser's constituents, likewise narratives, tell about shorter segments of time; each one is concerned with one historical theme which it does not share with the others, and all are arranged in the book not in quasi-parallel fashion but successively. The constituents, themselves collections, represent the second stage of literary development; during this stage they existed independently. In a third stage they were arranged chronologically and formed one consecutive narrative from Eli to the death of David. A fourth stage saw the infusion of the narrative with prophetic ideas. The fifth stage is marked by a modicum of Deuteronomic editing. The process was completed by adding sundry pieces, among them poems. A fair number of scholars follow the general approach of Weiser and Fohrer.

The assumption of independent collections of stories at a certain stage of the development of the book is the distinctive feature of this hypothesis. The assumption is neither probable nor improbable, which is to say, it has no scientific value. In its support two arguments have been put forth: (1) The stories that make up each hypothetical collection have a special style and point of view in common. (2) There are portions or apparent fragments in the book which seem to be there to supply what is missing in the collections. These arguments, however, carry no conviction. First, every good story has a character all its own, but several such stories from similar milieus about similar themes tend to have similar characteristics. For example, stories about the wanderings of an outlaw and his men are typically different in style, thrust, and bias from stories about competition and intrigue at a royal court; and it would occur to no one, much less can it be demonstrated, that the stories acquired these features when they were integrated in the collections. Second, by definition, a supplement supplies what is missing, and in the development of a document there is no preferred stage for filling gaps.

Except for a Deuteronomic edition, no edition or revision, prophetic or other, is recognizable. Its nature is not sufficiently defined, and its traces are not specified or identified. Hardly any effort has been made to show a connection between the prophetic edition and any historical prophetic activity, or between other editions and other historical phenomena. As to post-Deuteronomic additions, this is not an unlikely assumption, but the additions cannot be identified.

The hypothesis has another shortcoming: the difficulty of determining the extents and meanings of the collections. The question is basic, but the answers are, for the most part, unsettled. This is even the case with what is considered the most easily identifiable collection, the stories about the controversies at David's court in II Samuel. First, its extent—does it begin with ch. 9 or 11 (or 13), and end with ch. 20 or I Kings 2? One question only can be selected here, and its answers will be limited to one pair of alternatives: Does the collection begin with ch. 9 or 11? The answer depends on the answer to another question: What is the governing idea and the intent of the cycle of stories (the collection)—the vicissitudes of establishing the succession to David's throne, the legitimization of Solomon, the sin and punishment of David in a measure-for-measure fashion? Is it pro-David or anti-David, southern or northern, monarchic or amphictyonic, composed by an insider or an outsider? (For each of these and the above pairs of questions, pairs of opposite answers have been proposed.) If the theme is succession narrative, chs. 9 and 10 may perhaps be seen as an introduction, though with difficulty; if it is sin and punishment, they cannot. There is no need to continue in this vein. If fundamental uncertainties loom so large about this particularly well-written collection, then material for constructing a hypothesis such as Weiser's cannot be said to be contained in Samuel.

b. A hypothesis proposed. The position on the composition of Samuel put forth in this article is distantly related to the position of Weiser and Fohrer. Samuel was composed from individual narratives—the bulk of the material—and some lists and (semi-) official records, as well as a few poems. Deuteronomic editing is recognizable in I Sam. 4:18*b*; 13:1; II Sam. 2:10*a*, 11; 5:4-5 (*see* Bentzen). This position is not only tentative but also minimal. Regarding the literary prehistory of Samuel, it allows for pregrouping of narratives but recognizes no valid criteria for postulating it. And it would leave to further investigation the determination of the extent of each primary component, its prehistory, and its bonds with adjacent or nearby components (*see* TRADITION CRITICISM, OT[S]; REDACTION CRITICISM, OT[S]). On this hypothesis the book of Samuel originated in the act (or at the moment, whenever it occurred) by which (or at which time) material was assembled and brought to the present stage of integration in narration, as well as in character, purpose, and idea.

4. The leading idea and the essence of Samuel. Samuel is part of the history that stretches from the creation of the world to the Babylonian exile (*see* CANON OF THE OT[S] §1*c*). Many of the individual stories of this history can exist as independent narratives, but the totality of the composition is sustained and in turn sustains its parts by the idea of God who obligates, man who is obligated (first all mankind, then chiefly the Israelites and all Israel), their mutual nearness and remoteness, and the changing forms of the obligation. In recounting the events, the book describes one of the most severe crises in biblical history, the crisis of the relation of God and Israel, the people's failure in its obligation, and the transformation and reformulation of the obligation. From the time of Abraham's exodus from Chaldean Ur to the end of the period of the "Judges," Israel "followed the Lord," who led them in a pillar of cloud and by his Word which he revealed to his servants, men who had no more power or permanence than the pillar of cloud. In that period Israel was certainly not always virtuous, but it always returned to God, and the mutual relationship was re-established (*see* JUDGES, BOOK OF[S] §1*b*). But with the growing pressure of the Philistines, Israel found that the existing religio-political order of divine leadership fell short of the new exigency, and it demanded a political order of greater substance and stability, a secular, that is, self-sufficient, independent monarchy (*see* KING §3). Some modern scholars say that the difference between the political organization under the Judges and under the incipient monarchy was insignificant, but Scripture does not see it this way; in the biblical view the difference was one of a paramount principle, and the change of order placed in jeopardy the religious and national identity of Israel. *See* GOVERNMENT, ISRAELITE[S].

The book tells of the strain in the relationship between God and Israel that sprang up at that juncture, but its story contains more than is explicitly reported in I Sam. 8:4–12:25. The following points merit mention. (i) What gives the story its classical dimension is its perspective. The crisis is not a fleeting, one-time situation; from its breaking out in the time of Samuel and Saul to the end of the kingdom of Judah the crisis fluctuated between acute and dormant stages but it never went away. (ii) The crisis between God and Israel is reflected in the relation between prophet and king (*see* PROPHET §C4). Also in this respect the book marks the beginning of a development (Samuel and Saul, Nathan [Gad] and David) which continued to the fall of Jerusalem (Jeremiah and Zedekiah). (iii) The biblical judgment of the crisis is clear from the outset: In demanding a king, Israel rejects (מאס, despises) God (I Sam. 8:7; 10:19). The Bible never takes this statement back; quite the contrary, it is preserved and reflected in the prophets: turning for help to national or foreign power is rejection of God (Isa. 8:6).

Another evaluation of the monarchy is also recorded in the OT and it too dates back to the foundation of the monarchy: the institution of kingship is good, it is a gift of God to his people (I Sam. 10:24-27; 11:14-15; and elsewhere). God shows grace to the king, so the book continues, and makes a ברית (covenant/commitment) with/to him (II Sam. 7:8-9, 11; 23:5; and elsewhere). Also this conception can be traced on to the prophets (Isa. 55:3). *See* COVENANT, DAVIDIC[S].

Both judgments are found in close proximity in Samuel (e.g., I Sam. 10:17-27). Critics have responded to this fact with hypotheses that separate the judgments and locate them in different literary constituents of the pericope or pericopes; their presupposition is a one-to-one scheme: one constituent—one judgment. This presupposition, which is made as if it did not require justification, ought to be rejected. The problem is to be resolved differently; the literary tension between the two views of the monarchy corresponds to a similar tension in the historical reality. The reality is attested in numerous passages in different books; taken together they express similarly conflicting positions about the monarchy current in Israel, but the passages cannot meaningfully (in terms of the totality of their contexts) be sorted out and traced to different assumed sources according to praise or denunciation which they have for the monarchy and its organs. How complicated the problem is on the literary level a synopsis of interpretations of the Deuteronomic contribution shows. There is far-reaching scholarly agreement about the Deuteronomic minimum in Samuel, but it co-exists with scholarly disagreement as to whether the Deuteronomists are for or against the monarchy. The historical reality cannot have been less complicated, and the pros and cons of a question of such gravity must have been fought over bitterly for a long time. The literary crystallization, in Samuel, of this reality with its conflicts leads to the fundamental question: Is the monarchy a scion unrelated to the Israelite stock? And if it is, what is the prospect of a successful graft? The book of Samuel raised the question and made it a theme for many other biblical books.

The reason that these issues are expressed in Samuel with such vigor is that they first arose, with vigor and urgency, in the period reported there. Seen this way, Samuel is a history of the first order. Furthermore, it is likely that the book contains some of the earliest expressions concerning these issues, expressions that may go back to a period which is close to the narrated time. But it is almost as likely that late voices, originating centuries after the narrated time, are also recorded in Samuel. Their authors were probably neither able nor motivated to tell the story of the relatively distant past without reflecting in their writings on the later developments and their results. The early elements and the late elements are not always identifiable, but their combination gives the book a depth which adds to its significance among the books of the OT.

Bibliography. Commentaries: K. Budde, *KHC* (1902); H. W. Hertzberg, OTL (1964); H. J. Stoebe, *KAT*, NS VIII, 1 (1973), I Samuel only, with bibliog.

Studies: M. Buber, "Der Gesalbte," *Werke*, II (1964); Ou-Testamentiese Werkgemeenskap in Suid-Afrika, *Studies in the Books of Samuel* (1960); M. Tsevat, "Studies in the Book of Samuel," Pts. 1-5, *HUCA*, XXXII-XLVI (1961-75). M. TSEVAT

***SANBALLAT.** The discovery of the fourth-century SAMARIA PAPYRI and a re-evaluation of information previously known from Jos. Antiq. (XI.vii.7–viii.6) and Quintius Curtius' *History of Alexander* permit the reconstruction of a line of governors named after or descended from the Sanballat who clashed sharply with Nehemiah over the rebuilding of the walls of Jerusalem. *See* SANBALLAT.

Nehemiah's Sanballat may have been the first of the line since he is identified by a gentilic, the Horonite (that is, from Beth-horon), rather than by a patronymic or father's name (Neh. 13:28). He was in office by 445 B.C. when Nehemiah arrived in Jerusalem and seems to have been replaced by his son Delaiah no later than 410, as we learn from a letter in the ELEPHANTINE PAPYRI (Cowley 30.29). Another papyrus reports that Delaiah and Bagohi (=Bagoas), governors of Samaria and Judah respectively, authorized the Jews to petition the satrap Arsames about rebuilding the Jewish temple at Elephantine (Cowley 32; *ANET* [2nd. ed.], p. 492).

Evidence for additional Sanballats comes from a sealing attached to Samaria Papyrus #5, mentioning a Yᵉšaʿyāhû, son of Sanballat, governor of Samaria, and from Papyrus #14, which refers to Yēšūᵃᶜ, son of Sanballat, and a certain Hanan the prefect. A third papyrus, #8, which can be precisely dated to March 4, 354 B.C., helps to locate this Hanan[iah] by its reading, "before Hananiah, governor of Samaria." Because none of these papyri can be dated earlier than 375 B.C., the Sanballat to whom they refer is not identical with the one known from the Bible; hence he must be called Sanballat II.

Building on references in Josephus, it is possible now to identify a third Sanballat, appointed by Darius III (335-330), who gave his daughter Nicaso in marriage to Manasseh, the brother of the high priest Jaddua in Jerusalem. Sanballat III received Manasseh when he was expelled from the priesthood by the elders of Jerusalem, offered him the high priesthood over the Samaritans, and built for him a temple on Mount Gerizim by the permission, first, of Darius III, and later of Alexander himself. After Darius III lost to Alexander, contrary to Sanballat's expectations, Sanballat offered eight thousand Samaritan troops to Alexander to assist with the siege of Tyre, but he died after Alexander had besieged Tyre for seven months and Gaza for two.

Thus Delaiah, son of Sanballat I, was succeeded by Sanballat II, mentioned in the Samaria Papyri. Sanballat II was followed successively by his two sons Yᵉšaᶜyāhû (=Yēšûᵃᶜ) and Hananiah (= Hanan), the latter being in office in 354. The last of this line known to us is Sanballat III, attested so far only in Josephus. The following line of Sanballatids, therefore, can be reconstructed: Sanballat I, born about 485; Delaiah, his son, born about 460; Sanballat II, son of Delaiah, born about 435; Yēšūᵃᶜ (spelling of name somewhat uncertain), son of Sanballat II, born about 410; Hananiah (Hanan), son of Sanballat II and brother of Yēšūᵃᶜ also born about 410; Sanballat III, son of Hananiah, born about 385.

The discovery of a second and third Sanballat and the principle of papponomy in this family (that is, the naming of a man after his grandfather) have led to several suggested additions, indicated by brackets, in the following list of Jerusalem high priests: Jozadak (taken into exile); Jeshua (cf. Haggai-Zechariah); Joiakim (Neh. 12:10, 12, 26); [Eliashib I]; [Johanan I] (contemporary of Ezra); Eliashib II (contemporary of Nehemiah); Joiada I (Neh. 12:10-11, 22; 13:28); Johanan II (Cowley 30.18); Jaddua (caritative for Joiada) II; [Johanan III]; [Jaddua III].

The marriage between Nicaso, daughter of Sanballat III, and Manasseh, brother of Jaddua III, is similar to but not identical with the marriage of a son of Joiada I and a daughter of Sanballat I (Neh. 13:28). Not only was the high priest's relative in one case a brother and in the other a son, but the expulsion was handled quite differently; Manasseh was given an ultimatum by the elders of Jerusalem to get a divorce or to resign the priesthood, whereas Nehemiah himself chased the married couple out of the city. The intermarriage between a priest of Jerusalem and a governor's daughter from Samaria in the late fourth century supports the notion that the total breach between Judah and Samaria came much later than formerly thought, perhaps late in the second or early in the first century B.C. *See* SAMARITANS; SAMARITANS[S].

While vindicated in general, Josephus seems to have been confused by the repetitious names in the high priestly and Sanballatid lines. Manasseh, who married Sanballat III's daughter Nicaso, was the brother of Jaddua III, the high priest. Josephus incorrectly identified Jaddua III with Jaddua II, just as he coalesced Sanballat I and Sanballat III. Since Jaddua II became high priest in the time of Darius II (423-404), thus no later than 404, it is not likely that he would still be serving as high priest in the 330s, nor is he likely to have had a brother of marriageable age, as the Josephus account would have it. Josephus also identifies Bagoas, the Persian governor of Judah, who imposed tribute on the Jews after Johanan I had killed his own brother Jesus in the temple, with Bagoas, the notorious eunuch and general who served under Artaxerxes III (358-338). Some identify the Bagoas who imposed tribute as a general of Artaxerxes II.

Bibliography. F. M. Cross, "Papyri of the Fourth Century B.C. from Dâliyeh: A Preliminary Report on Their Discovery and Significance," *New Directions in Biblical Archaeology,* ed. D. Freedman and M. Greenfield (1969), pp. 41-62, and "A Reconstruction of the Judean Restoration," *JBL,* XCIV (1975), 4-18. For the Elephantine material consult Bezalel Porten, *Archives from Elephantine* (1968).

R. W. KLEIN

***SANCTIFICATION.** Sanctification means the transition from the realm of the profane to that of the holy. It is invariably expressed by the root קדש in all its conjugations. There is sanctification of time, space, persons, and things.

1. Of time. Certain time is inherently holy because it was sanctified by God, e.g., the SABBATH (Gen. 2:3), the festivals (Lev. 23:4 ff.; Neh. 8:9-11), the JUBILEE (Lev. 25:12). Israel is enjoined to sanctify these holy periods by adhering to the special rules which govern them.

2. Of space. The land of Canaan is the Lord's land, and therefore holy (Exod. 15:13; Isa. 11:9). This is the premise of the Holiness Source, which states that offenses against God pollute the land (cf. Lev. 18:27-28), and hence all its inhabitants, including the resident alien, must observe God's prohibitions (Lev. 17:8-12; 18:26; 20:2; 24:16). All other land is impure (Josh. 22:19; Amos 7:17), except where a THEOPHANY has occurred (Exod. 3:5; Josh. 5:15).

The doctrine that Jerusalem is the holy city

par excellence has its origins in the First Isaiah, who proclaims Jerusalem as the divine residence (Isa. 8:18; 18:7; 30:29; *see* ZION TRADITION[S]). Its future inhabitants will *eo ipso* be sanctified (Isa. 4:3). Jeremiah predicts that the future Jerusalem will extend beyond its former limits, and will be "holy to the Lord" despite the inclusion of burial ground (31:37-39). Since recent excavations in the old Jewish quarter have unearthed a city wall dating to the time of Hezekiah or Manasseh, and excavations in the nearby TYROPOEON VALLEY have divulged empty tombs of approximately the same period (*see* JERUSALEM[S] §1), it seems safe to conclude that Jerusalem had expanded to three or four times its former size. It was by then conceived of as a holy city, for its dead were apparently disinterred and removed beyond its new walls (the kings excepted, Ezek. 43:7*b*-9; cf. AB. R. Nathan, B. 39). By the time of the Exile it received the appellation "the holy city" (Isa. 48:2; 52:1).

3. Of persons. Certain persons become holy when they undergo consecration. Priests are holy, according to P, because they received the most-sacred oil of anointment (Exod. 30:30-32; 40:13 ff.) in conjunction with a sacrificial service. The high priest Aaron's head is doused (יצק) with the oil before the service, and his sons are sprinkled (נזה) with the oil after the service (Exod. 29:7, 21; Lev. 8:12, 30).

In the person of the NAZIRITE, the layman attains quasi-priestly status, for he is "holy to the Lord" (Num. 6:8; cf. Philo, *On the Special Laws,* I, 249). Indeed, by his taboos, the Nazirite approximates the higher sanctity of the high priest, since he may not contaminate himself by contact with the dead, even of his immediate family (Num. 6:7; cf. Lev. 21:11), and, like the high priest, the head is the focus of his sanctity (Num. 6:11*b*; cf. Exod. 29:7). Since, however, the Nazirite period (in P) is only for a fixed term, the parallel to sanctified land (*see below*) is more instructive: both terms are limited, the land reverting to its owner at the Jubilee (Num. 6:13; cf. Lev. 27:21). Both periods can be terminated earlier, the Nazirite's by contamination (Num. 6:9-12) and the land's by redemption (Lev. 27:16-19). In such cases a penalty is exacted: the Nazirite pays a reparation offering (אשם) to the sanctuary (*see* SACRIFICES AND OFFERINGS, OT[S] §2*b*), and the land owner pays a one-fifth surcharge to the sanctuary.

All Pentateuchal sources (*see* DOCUMENTS) agree that the people Israel is enjoined to holiness. In JE, all that is involved is refraining from flesh torn by a beast (Exod. 22:31 [H 30]), whereas in P, Israel's sanctification can be achieved through a comprehensive behavior pattern which embraces fine points of ethics as well as ritual (e.g., Lev. 19). D, however, mentions Israel's sanctification only in connection with ritual prohibitions (idolatry, Deut. 7:5-6; certain mourning rites, 14:1-2; and forbidden foods, 14:3-21). Jeremiah uses Israel's sanctity to weave a haggadic MIDRASH to condemn their enemies (2:3), whereas Ezra fashions a halachic midrash to condemn intermarriages (9:2). The term "consecrate" is also used of a prophet (Jer. 1:5), but its use is metaphorical.

4. Of objects. ***a. The sanctuary.*** The tabernacle, its sanctums, and the priestly clothing are sanctified with the anointment oil (Exod. 30:25-29; 40:9-11; Lev. 8:10 ff.). If the polluted altar needs be resanctified, the blood of the purgation offering (חטאת) is sprinkled upon it seven times (Lev. 16:19). The tabernacle sanctums, being "most-sacred," sanctify other objects upon contact (Exod. 29:37; 30:29), but they are not contagious to persons. This also holds true for the most-sacred offerings: the מנחה and the חטאת (Lev. 6:18, 27 [H 11, 20]), and probably the אשם and עלה. Ezekiel, however, affirms that the sanctums—including the priestly clothing—are contagious even to persons (44:19; 46:20). The temple of Solomon was probably consecrated upon its completion, though the verb קדש is used only in connection with the extension of the sanctity of the altar into the court in order to accommodate the overwhelming number of offerings (I Kings 8:64=II Chr. 7:7).

b. The sacred gifts. The objects which become sanctuary property by virtue of sanctification can be categorized as follows: (i) Objects whose sanctity is inherent, i.e., first-born males of female animals and human beings (Exod. 13:2, 12 ff.; Lev. 27:26; *see* FIRST-BORN[S]), first-ripe fruits (e.g., Neh. 10:36 [H 37]) and first-processed fruits (Num. 15:20; 18:12; *see* FIRST FRUITS, OT[S]), and the fourth-year yield of fruit trees (Lev. 19:24). (ii) Objects whose sanctification is required, i.e., tithes of crops and pure animals (Lev. 27:30-33; Deut. 26:13). (iii) Objects whose sanctification is voluntary, partially listed in Lev. 27: votive dedications of persons (rather, their fixed value; vss. 1-8) and animals (vss. 9-13), dedications (הקדיש) of houses (vss. 14 ff.) and fields (vss. 16-25), and proscriptions (חרם) of persons, animals, and property (vss. 28 ff.). The underlying postulate is that, if the object is permissible as an offering on the altar, it is irredeemable; if it is not permissible, it is redeemable, except for חרם (something to be "utterly destroyed"), which may never be redeemed. The sanctifications recorded in Lev. 27 are the result of individual initiative, but more likely the sanctuary received most of them as spoils of war (e.g., Num. 31). Historical sources also attest that captured vessels were dedicated to the temple (II Sam. 8:10 ff.; I Kings 7:51, 15:15; I Chr. 26:27-28), including precious weapons (II Sam. 8:7; I Kings 14:26 ff.; II Kings 11:10).

5. Inception. When did the sanctification of an object take effect? It took effect not when it was brought to the sanctuary, as might be expected, but when a declaration of dedication was made. This is the only possible deduction from the dedication (חרם) of Jericho (Josh. 6:17-19) and the story of the dedicated silver (Judg. 17:3). Also the wording of the following sacred gifts indicates that they were sanctified before they were brought to the sanctuary: first-ripe/processed fruits (Num. 18:12-13), tithes (Lev. 27:30-33), and most-sacred offerings (Lev. 6:25 [H 18]; 7:1 ff.). The tannaitic dictum: "Oral dedication is equivalent to transfer" (M. Ḳid. 1.6; Tosef. Ḳid. I.9) prevails in the Bible as well. Within the sanctuary, sanctification could take place by means of the התנופה. *See* WAVE OFFERING[S].

6. Purification as sanctification. The ablutions prescribed before a theophany effect sanctification, e.g., Exod. 19:10 ff.; Num. 11:8; Josh. 3:5; 7:13 ff. In these cases, the ablutions take place the day before God appears, except for the theophany at Sinai, whose uniqueness requires two days of prior sanctification. The Priestly Code always enjoins severely contaminated persons to undergo ablutions the day before they appear in the sanctuary with their required offerings (the gonorrheic, Lev. 15:13 ff.; the leper, Lev. 14:9 ff.; etc.). However, P never designates this process by the root קדש, which it reserves exclusively for the sanctification of objects and persons (*see above*). The historical and prophetic books attest that solemn gatherings and fasts are also designated by קדש (e.g., II Kings 10:20; Joel 1:14; 2:15-17), as is the call to war (e.g., Jer. 6:4, "prepare"; Joel 3:9 [H 4:9]; Mic. 3:5, "declare"), originating in the sanctity of the war camp so that God would abide within (cf. Deut. 23:10-14 [H 11-15]).

Bibliography. J. Milgrom, *Cult and Conscience* (1975), §§19-32; M. Broshi, "The Expansion of Jerusalem in the Reigns of Hezekiah and Manasseh," *IEJ*, XXIV (1974), 21-26, "La population de l'ancienne Jerusalem," *RB*, XCII (1975), 5-14; N. Avigad, "Excavations in the Jewish Quarter of the Old City of Jerusalem, 1970," *IEJ*, XX (1970), 129-40; B. Mazar, "Finds . . . Near the Temple Mount," *Qadmoniot*, V (1972), at 88-90, Hebrew.

J. Milgrom

***SANCTUARY.** *See* Sites, Sacred[S].

***SANHEDRIN.** From the Greek συνέδριον, literally "council," but the Jewish Hellenistic and rabbinic accounts differ as to its nature. (1) In Hellenistic sources it appears as a supreme political and judicial council, presided over by the king (according to Josephus) or by the high priest in the period of the procurators (according to the NT). (2) The rabbinic sources speak of two sanhedrins, both consisting of religious scholars: (*a*) the Great Sanhedrin of seventy-one members, which met in the Hall of Gazit ("hewn stones") in the temple; and (*b*) the small sanhedrins of twenty-three members each, which met in the various cities (Mishna and Tosefta).

1. Various theories. The divergence in the usage of "sanhedrin" has given rise to three types of solutions:

a) One group of scholars believes that there was only one sanhedrin and that it was in Jerusalem. Some of them accept only the Hellenistic sources, while others rely only on rabbinic materials. The argument of the former is that the Mishna's description is anachronistic, describing the sanhedrin of the temple era in terms of the situation after its destruction. But these scholars overlook the fact that all the functions ascribed to the sanhedrin in the Mishna, such as judging the tribes, the false prophet, the high priest, etc. (M. Sanh. 1.5), had no relevance after the destruction of the temple. In fact, the avowed aim of the tannaim was to preserve the tradition, so that it not be forgotten because of the changes after the destruction (M. R. H. 4.3).

b) The second group regard the Great Sanhedrin of the rabbinic sources as a joint meeting of the three small sanhedrins, which were situated in various parts of the temple mount, each consisting of twenty-three members. Together with the president (*nāśî'*) and the vice-president (*'ābh bêth dîn*), they constituted seventy-one members. This theory flounders on the fact that it is based on a Baraita in the Babylonian Talmud (Sanh. 88b), whereas the Palestinian sources (whose traditions concerning Palestinian events are of course more reliable) assign only three members to each of the courts (*battê dîn*) which met on the temple mount (J.T. Sanh. I.7; Tosef. Ḥag. II.9; Tosef. Sanh. VII.1). Besides, there is no evidence that the three bodies ever held joint meetings.

c) The third group regard both the Hellenistic and tannaitic sources as authentic. They do not contradict each other, since each refers to a different institution, one to a political authority and the other to a religious one. This approach is no doubt the correct one, since the term συνέδριον applies to various types of councils. In Greek historical writings the term describes a council of federated states, or of chiefs of allied armies, or of a board of trade; in Hellenistic Egypt it designated a council of high officials; and in papyri, a council of a private association. There is no reason, therefore, why in Jerusalem the term "sanhedrin" could not have been applied to both the highest governmental council and to the supreme religious body.

In general, it may be argued that, since the sanhedrins in the Hellenistic sources were presided over by the head of the state, whether king or high priest, they could not have dealt with halachic questions as would a religious sanhedrin. Not only the Herodians, but some of the high priests were not versed in interpreting the Scriptures (M. Yoma 1.6). Josephus boasts that, when he was a boy of fourteen, the chief priests used to come to him constantly "for precise information on some particular in our ordinances" (Jos. Life 2.8). More than that, many, if not most, of them, were Sadducees who rejected the Halachah altogether. It is inconceivable, therefore, that they presided over halachic discussions.

2. The sources. A closer look at the context in which the terms *synedrion* (Gr.) and *sanhedrin* (Heb.) occur will confirm that there were two types.

a) The first time the term *synedrion* is mentioned in Jewish historical sources is in connection with the Roman general Gabinius. Josephus reports that in the year 57 B.C. he divided the country into five regional synods (σύνοδοι; Jos. War I.viii.5) or *synedria* (συνέδρια; Antiq. XIV.v.4). As the Romans did not customarily interfere in the religious life of conquered peoples, it may be assumed that the reference is not to religious bodies, but to political councils or financial agencies charged with the collection of taxes. All trials by a *synedrion* which Josephus relates deal with political cases. Hyrcanus, as ethnarch, presided over the *synedrion* which tried Herod for political murder (Antiq. XIV.ix.4-5). Herod, as king, had a *synedrion* condemn Hyrcanus for plotting against him (Antiq. XV.vi.2), though elsewhere Josephus reports that he did so without benefit of a *synedrion*. The versions are easily reconcilable if the *synedrion* was Herod's royal council. Herod's sons, charged with rebellion against their father, were tried before a *synedrion* consisting of Roman officials (Antiq. XVI.xi.1-3) or, according to another version, by Herod's "own relatives and the provincial governors" (Jos. War L.xxvii.1).

It would seem on the surface that the condemnation of James, the brother of Jesus, by a *synedrion* was for religious reasons. But then why was it precisely those "who were strict in observance of the law" (Antiq. XX.ix.1) who protested most vigorously against the judgment? The claim that he was condemned for practicing the Pharisaic view is farfetched, since most people followed Pharisaic religious practice. We must conclude that the condemnation was due to a flimsy political reason, namely, that he preached the imminent coming of the Messiah, who was to redeem the people from Roman oppression.

At first sight it would appear as if the *synedrion* which Agrippa II convened to permit the Levitical singers to wear priestly garments (Jos. Antiq. XX.ix.6) was a religious and Pharisaic one, especially since this body's judgment accords with Pharisaic principles (T.B. 'Arak. 2a-b). Actually, matters pertaining to temple procedure were not in the hands of either sanhedrin, but in those of the priestly court (*bêth dîn shel kōhănîm*). Toward the end of the temple era, this court came under the influence of the Pharisaic outlook, as evidenced by the report of the Megillath Ta'anith. This would explain their pro-Pharisaic decision. It is likely that Josephus used the term *synedrion* here merely for convenience' sake. As evidence that this was a *bêth dîn shel kōhănîm* may be cited the fact that Agrippa II had no political authority in Jerusalem; his appointment was solely as curator of the temple (Jos. Antiq. XX.ix.7).

b) As for the *synedrion* mentioned in the NT accounts, scholars are divided on whether it was a political or religious one. Our argument is that it was political.

The accusation for which Pilate crucified Jesus was inscribed on the cross: "The King of the Jews" (Mark 15:26; Matt. 27:37; Luke 23:38). The high priest's concern was similarly political: "If we let him go on thus, every one will believe in him, and the Romans will come and destroy both our holy place and our nation" (John 11:48).

Various arguments have been put forth to show that Jesus violated religious rules for which a religious sanhedrin would impose capital punishment:

i. He deserved death for prophesying the destruction of the temple. But such prophesies were made, not only by the prophets Jeremiah (7:14), Micah (3:12), and Ezekiel (24:21), but also by R. Johanan ben Zakkai (T.B. Yom. 39b) and R. Ẓadok (T.B. Giṭ. 56a) toward the end of the second temple. In general such prophecy is nothing but the application of Scripture (Lev. 26:31).

ii. Another religious reason claimed for Jesus' death penalty is the various violations of the Torah attributed to him or to his disciples (Mark 7:2-5; Matt. 15:2; Luke 11:38; Mark 3:1-6; Matt. 12:9-14; Luke 6:6-11; Matt. 12:1-2; Mark 2:23-24; etc.). But none of these acts call for any kind of punishment. At any rate, it has been argued well that the antinomian passages in the NT were written with a missionary intention in Antioch, Alexandria, and Rome.

iii. Talmudic haggadah has also been cited as evidence. T.B. Sanh. 43a relates:

> It was taught: On the eve of Passover Yeshu [the Nazarene] was hanged. For forty days before the execution took place, a herald went forth and cried, "He is going forth to be stoned because he has practiced sorcery and deceived and led astray Israel. Any one who knoweth aught in his favor, let him come and plead in his behalf." But since nothing was brought forward in his favor, he was hanged on the eve of Passover.

This haggadah bears the mark of the postschismic period, when it would have been invented to justify the separation of the Jews from the Christians. That this tradition is not genuine is proved by the fact that Jesus was said to be a contemporary of Joshua ben Peraḥya (*ca.* 80 B.C.), and that his punishment was by hanging. According to some versions, he is called Ben Stada (T.B. Shab. 104b; Tosef. Sanh. X.2), while in another haggadah, his name was Ben Pandera (J.T. 'A.Z. 2.2), or Pantera (Tosef. Ḥullin II.22). Elsewhere it is said that he was stoned for being a deceiver (Tosef. Sanh. X.11; J.T. Sanh. 7.16; T.B. Sanh. 67a).

Besides, to "deceive" or to "lead astray" (*mēsîth*), the term used in the haggadah, is a technical term that refers specifically to idolatry, of which Jesus was not accused. The title "Son of God," which he may have assumed, is elsewhere applied not only to all Israel (Exod. 4:22) and to righteous people (Wisd. Sol. 2:13, 16, 18, etc.), but also especially to the Messiah (Ps. 2:7), on which basis Jesus claimed the title for himself (Mark 14:61-62). Nor is the claim of messiahship a punishable crime in Judaism. A hundred years after Jesus, R. Akiba hailed BAR KOCHBA as "King Messiah" (J.T. Ta'an. 4.2). *See* TRIAL OF JESUS[S] §3*d* (4).

The claim that the Jews forced Pilate to crucify Jesus because "it is not lawful for us to put any man to death" (John 18:31) is no doubt the result of polemic necessity in the Roman Empire, rather than a historical record. We have a number of instances which contradict this claim (*see* TRIAL OF JESUS[S] §1). A sanhedrin condemned Stephen for blasphemy, by stoning (Acts 6:12; 7:58). James, the brother of Jesus, was condemned to stoning by a sanhedrin. The Jews even had the right to execute a Gentile who trespassed on the second enclosure of the temple (Jos. Antiq. XV.xi.5; cf. War V.v.2). The Mishna, too, records R. Ẓadok's eyewitness account of the execution of the adulterous daughter of a priest (M. Sanh. 7.2). In sum, sanhedrin in Hellenistic sources (Josephus and NT) refers to a political body.

c) On the other hand, the Mishna's list of the Great Sanhedrin's functions cannot be said to include a single case that applied to the sanhedrins in the postdestruction era, in Jamnia (Jabneel), Usha, Tiberias, etc. It could judge a tribe, a false prophet, or the high priest; send forth (the people) to a battle waged of free choice; extend the boundaries of the city (Jerusalem), and of the courts of the temple; set up sanhedrins for the several tribes; proclaim a city apostate (M. Sanh. 1.5). Other functions were the administration of Water of Ordeals (M. Soṭ. 1.4; *See* ORDEAL, JUDICIAL[S]) and the breaking of the heifer's neck (M. Soṭ. 9.1). It also examined the genealogy of the priests (M. Middot 5.4). The Tosefta adds four more activities: to burn the red heifer, to declare an elder rebellious, to set up a king or to set up a high priest (Tosef. Sanh. III.4). Several of these acts have been substantiated by I and II Maccabees. Thus the description of the Great Sanhedrin's activities in rabbinic literature is historically correct. While its political functions go back to early days, those of a religious nature are applicable to the Roman period.

The only prerogative ascribed by the rabbis to the Great Sanhedrin which was also practiced by the sanhedrins in the postdestruction era was the authority to fix the halachah for all Israel (Tosef. Ḥag. II.9; Tosef. Sanh. VII.1). However, we have the record of two instances where questions of halachah were submitted for final decision to the sages in the Hall of Gazit (M. Pe'ah 2.6; M. 'Eduyot 7.4) in the temple.

3. Sanhedrin, bêth dîn, and kenishta. It is generally assumed that these terms are different names for the same body. An analysis of the texts in which they appear will show that they are not synonymous, though a sanhedrin may occasionally act as a *bêth dîn* (court).

a) That the small sanhedrins (of twenty-three) were not permanent courts is suggested by the fact that each contained only one ordained scholar (*Muphlā'*) without whose consent no halachic decision was valid (T.B. Sanh. 17b; M. Hor. 1.4). It would seem strange for a permanent court of this size to contain only one jurist. Further, another member, the counselor (*Yô'ēṣ*), is designated by the Greek βουλευτής, "member of the city council" (T.B. Sanh. 86b-87a; J.T. Sanh. 2.3; Sifre Deut. 152). Hence, these sanhedrins were city councils, acting only incidentally as courts.

Concomitantly, the Great Sanhedrin was the national council, the supreme political body, with judicial competence limited to a few rare cases. But the late Hasmonean princes, along with the Herodians and Roman procurators, refused to share political hegemony. However, they granted the PHARISEES full religious authority, leading to the separation of the Great Sanhedrin into a political and a religious one. It is chiefly this latter sanhedrin which is described in the rabbinic literature, along with a few of the prerogatives of the national council of early Hasmonean days.

A *bêth dîn,* on the other hand, was a court of justice. Such were the bodies of "seven individuals in each city to adjudicate petty disputes" (Jos. War II.xx.5) and the courts of three which dealt with cases of property, theft, personal injury, etc. (M. Sanh. 1.1-3).

b) The *kenishta* (כנישתא) is identified with a sanhedrin only once, in the *scholium* (*ca.* A.D. tenth century) to Meg. Ta'an. 10. This identification is part of a late fiction which scholars have almost universally accepted as fact. It is safer to assume that the term *kenishta* here retains its usual meaning, as in בי כנישתא, "the House of the Keneset," namely, the Pharisaic party. This corresponds to the Greek οἶκος, "House [of the Hellenistic associations]." Meg. Ta'an. therefore discusses the legitimization of the Pharisaic party in the days of Simeon ben Shetah.

4. An antecedent for the religious sanhedrin. The exclusively religious sanhedrin was not a *creatio ex nihilo.* The citations in the name of the "men of the Great Synagogue," who flourished in the pre-Maccabean era (M. AB. 1.1-2), are exclusively religious (T.B. Ber. 33a). In contrast to the high priests, who represented the government and the cult, they headed a movement for private piety and study. Thus they were the forerunners, not only of the Pharisees, but also of the Great Sanhedrin in the temple. *See* SYNAGOGUE, THE GREAT[S].

5. The origin of the term "sanhedrin" in Judaism. Those who trace its origin to Herod's *synedrion* overlook the earlier reference to it in connection with Gabinius (57 B.C.). Others who see it as an imitation of the Athenian Areopagos (also called a *synedrion*) or the Greek *synedria* (councils or courts) neglect the chronological problems and the absence of direct cultural contact.

More likely, the term came from Hellenized Egypt, where it signified a council of high officials who occasionally acted as a court. Judah in the third century B.C. was subject to the Ptolemaic dynasty, and religious and social contacts continued for centuries thereafter. Thus the LXX uses the term *synedrion* (Prov. 15:22; 22:10) in the sense of deliberative assembly and court of justice.

Bibliography. General: H. Mantel, *Studies in the History of the Sanhedrin* (1965). On the small sanhedrins: H. Mantel, "Ordination and Appointment in the Period of the Temple," *HTR,* LVII (1964), 325-46. On the trial of Jesus: D. R. Catchpole, *The Trial of Jesus* (1971), differs from several of my own conclusions, TRIAL OF JESUS[S]. On the term "sanhedrin" in Judaism: H. Mantel, *Meḥkarim be-Toledot ha-Sanhedrin* (1969), pp. 117-21. On the term *kenishta:* H. Mantel, "The Megillat Ta'anit and the Sects," *Studies in the History of the Jewish People and the Land of Israel,* ed. A. Gilboa, Memorial Vol. for Zvi Avneri (1970), pp. 51-70, Hebrew.

H. MANTEL

***SARDIS.** Excavations since 1958 and attendant research into the sources have added extensively to knowledge of Sardis.

1. Acropolis. Two series of pre-Hellenistic walls have been uncovered: on the N side are segments of two concentric terracing walls of evenly trimmed ashlar blocks; on the S are walls of irregular limestone and sandstone blocks (cf. Arrian, *Anabasis of Alexander* I.xvii.3-6, a triple-fortification wall seen by Alexander in *ca.* 334 B.C.).

2. Temple of Artemis. Excavation has produced no evidence of the Archaic temple but shows the area in use from *ca.* 600 B.C. The temple is a two-cella dipteral structure oriented to the E. The remains are largely Roman. At the W end is a freestanding altar first built during the sixth-fifth centuries B.C.

3. Churches. On the E bank of the Pactolus are remains of a Middle Byzantine church (Church E) of a five-dome type known in Serbia, Bulgaria, Greece, and Calabria but otherwise unknown in

Constantinople and Asia Minor. The exterior was embellished with decorative brickwork, the interior with mosaics, frescoes, and stained glass.

Church E was built over a large, fourth-century basilica (EA) having two aisles and an apse. There is evidence that an entire city quarter was transformed into a Christian complex. The period of construction as indicated by coins was mid-fourth to early fifth century.

4. Cemeteries and tombs. An extensive burial area has been excavated around Churches E and EA, which was in use until *ca.* 1400. The shallow graves were lined with tiles or stone slabs and were poor in burial accouterments.

Two chamber tombs having frescoes depicting garlands, Christogram, peacocks, and bread basket (generally accepted symbols of the Eucharist) which date to the fifth and sixth centuries have been excavated. The paintings from one, the "Peacock Tomb," are in the Archaeological Museum, Manisa.

The largest of the Lydian tumuli, believed to be that of Alyattes, has a chamber of carefully fitted limestone masonry. Further W a mound, second in size, is believed to be that of Gyges. An attempt to locate the chamber failed, but the circular wall at the base of a smaller, inner mound was discovered. The wall is of limestone blocks, many of which have drafted borders similar to those of the walls on the S side of the acropolis; the top course has a rounded bolster.

5. The Lydian sectors. The Lydian city was an irregular agglomeration (cf. Herodotus V.101, 499 B.C.) with an extension southward along a sacred road to the Artemis precinct. Buildings were of mud brick, many with thatched roofs. Some were brightly decorated with painted tiles and in some cases the roof tiles were painted red and white to form diamond patterns. The industrial and commercial center was enclosed by an irregular stone wall abutted by single room houses or shops (designated HoB in site plans). Further S on the E bank of the Pactolus (designated PN) are Lydian units attached in complexes forming court-like spaces. In this sector are remains of an Archaic altar to Cybele and sacral precinct. S and W of the altar conclusive evidence has been found for gold-refining processes, cupellation, and cementation, dating *ca.* 600-547 B.C.

6. Gymnasium and synagogue. The gymnasium (N of the modern highway) is supported on artificial terracing created after an earthquake destroyed the Hellenistic city in A.D. 17. Symmetrical to the E-W axis the gymnasium had a palaestra on the E and large baths of "Imperial" type on the W. The central unit, comprised of a pair of double-apsed halls flanking a rectangular room, was completed *ca.* 166 when a base bonded into the podium was inscribed in honor of Lucius Verus. The eastern section centered around a monumental marble court, which has been restored to the top of the second story. A dedicatory inscription to Caracalla, Geta, and Julia Domna dates the façade to 211. An ornate gate leads W into a barrel-vaulted hall with pool and fountains; to the E is a screen colonnade opening into the palaestra.

An integral part of the complex is a large basilican building on the S side of the palaestra, oriented E-W, which was used as a synagogue from *ca.* A.D. 200 to 616. Partly restored by the Harvard-Cornell expedition, the building comprises three parts: the entrance porch, which fronted on a colonnaded road, a peristyle forecourt having a central krater-fountain, a long main hall ending in an apse. On the N wall of the forecourt above a marble dado is a restored sample of wall decoration belonging to a fifth- or sixth-century redecoration: short pilasters support arcades with a pattern of doves and kraters against a recessed background filled with red mortar. At the E end of the main hall are two small shrines, one Doric and the other Corinthian in style. The hall was divided into seven bays by six pairs of piers; at the W end is an apse lined by three marble benches. The ritual furnishings include a massive marble table supported by eagles in relief and flanked by two pairs of back-to-back lions. Among the finds was a large stone menorah. The floors of both the forecourt and hall were covered with geometric mosaics of the fourth century A.D. On the apse floor is a mosaic showing a water-filled urn from which twine two vines. Above is a dedicatory inscription within a wreath. On either side were peacocks. The walls were revetted with polychrome marble in a framework of Corinthian pilasters. Inscriptions, most in Greek dedicating aspects of the building, attest the status of members of the congregation: many are "citizens of Sardis," nine are city councilors, one a former procurator, and one a count. *See* Fig S1.

Along the S side of the building runs a row of shops (*ca.* A.D. 400-600) which opened onto the main E-W colonnaded avenue. One has a marble tank with crosses on it, fed by water pipes. Inscriptions, carved menorahs and crosses, and other finds indicate that both Christians and Jews traded in the shops.

Bibliography. See, in the series Archaeological Exploration of Sardis, ed. G. M. A. Hanfmann and S. W. Jacobs: G. E. Bates, *Byzantine Coins,* Monograph 1 (1971); J. G. Pedley, *Ancient Literary Sources on Sardis,* Monograph 2 (1972); R. Gusmani, *Neue epichorische Schriftzeugnisse aus Sardis (1958-1971),* Monograph 3 (1975); C. Foss, *Byzantine and Turkish Sardis,* Monograph 4 (1976); G. M. A. Hanfmann, J. C. Waldbaum, *A Survey of Sardis and Major Monuments Outside the City Wall,* Report 1 (1975). Preliminary reports by G. M. A. Hanfmann and others have appeared annually in *BASOR*. G. M. A. Hanfmann, *Letters from Sardis* (1972) includes earlier bibliography.

J. A. SCOTT

SAYINGS OF JESUS, FORM OF. The various forms of the sayings of Jesus correspond to forms familiar from the OT and from the intertestamental literature, above all from the prophetic and wisdom writings. The juxtaposition of independent sayings in larger compositions and in brief scenes also follows from these writings.

Any classification of the sayings must take into consideration formal criteria as well as criteria based on content. It is not enough to try to identify pure forms, for often forms that are quite old have been modified or expanded.

Courtesy Sardis Expedition

1. Forecourt of the synagogue at Sardis with krater fountain and frieze of doves and kraters. The marble court is in the background.

1. Wisdom sayings. Large portions of the sayings are reminiscent of the various forms found in wisdom literature. Many of them give the impression of being proverbs, even if they do not all have parallels in the extant Jewish literature (*see* WISDOM IN THE NT[S] §§1*b*, 3*a*). One group formulates observations from experience in pronouncements immediately obvious to every hearer (Matt. 6:24; Luke 16:13). The hearer can only agree with what has been said, and is then expected to draw new conclusions from it. The rhetorical question is a variant of the pronouncement which forces the hearer much more directly to take a stand (Mark 4:21). Whereas in wisdom literature formulated experience is frequently clothed in the form of a beatitude, of the beatitudes in the Jesus tradition only Luke 11:28 is of this type. Admonitions in the imperative summon the hearer, as in the wisdom literature, to wise behavior and right action (Luke 6:31; Matt. 7:12). Such admonitions often result directly from a proverbially formulated pronouncement but may also occur in eschatological contexts. Finally, conditional sentences also belong in this category (Matt. 6:22-23; Luke 11:34-36). They assert a relationship between an act and its consequence which always holds good in the field of experience. *See also* LITERATURE, EARLY CHRISTIAN[S] §5.

2. Prophetic and apocalyptic sayings. These have essentially the same sentence structure as the wisdom sayings, but the content is different. BEATITUDES and woes, both familiar from the apocalyptic tradition, also occur in the sayings of Jesus. In both traditions they have been brought together in small groups (beatitudes, Luke 6:20-23; Matt. 5:3 ff.; woes, Luke 11:37-52; Matt. 23:13 ff.). The clauses which form the second part of the sayings give the reason for blessedness or woe; the exclamations have eschatological significance. In Luke 10:13-15; Matt. 11:21-23 we have a parallel to the OT form of the oracles against foreign nations, and the series of woes in Luke 11:37-52 concluding with the announcement of judgment reminds one of Isa. 5:8-24. Related to the beatitudes are the general descriptions of wholeness which fulfill ancient expectations (Luke 7:22-23; Matt. 11:4-6). Sentences formulated according to the law of retaliation, although similar to casuistic law, really correspond to the conditional sentences of the wisdom sayings. Here a relationship is established between one's activity on earth and one's reward or punishment at the final judgment (Luke 12:8-9; Matt. 10:32-33). The announcement of judgment in the form of a threat is especially typical of Q (*see* Q and Q[S]). As Luke 11:49 shows, Jewish prophecies have most likely been taken up here. Extended announcements of judgment occur at the end of the SERMON ON THE MOUNT and its parallel, the Sermon on the Plain in Luke; evidently such judgments already occurred in the document underlying both in Q. They usually appear in the form of parables (*see* PARABLE;

PARABLE[S]). Apocalypses (*see* APOCALYPSE, GENRE [S]) are found in the Markan and in the Q tradition (Mark 13; Luke 17:22-37; Matt. 24:26 ff.) and also in Paul (I Thess. 4:15-17), probably as sayings of the Lord.

3. Laws and community rules. The antitheses in the Sermon on the Mount place commands that have been handed down from the OT along with their Jewish interpretation in contrast to their abrogation or expansion by Jesus. Legal statements are formulated in apodictic as well as in casuistic form, and are regarded as binding on the community. Similar material can also be found in the conflict stories where Jesus opposes a Jewish halachah by giving a new one. There are also sayings in which Jesus replaces the Jewish religious practice with new religious rules (Matt. 6:1-18). Early Christian missionary practices are reflected in the accounts of the commissioning of the disciples, where instructions are given for how the missionaries are to be equipped, how they are to conduct themselves, and how they are to proclaim their message (Mark 6:7-13; Luke 10:2-16). The beginnings of discipline within the community can be seen in the new interpretation of Luke 17:3-4 in Matt. 18:15-17, to which close parallels both in content and in form occur in 1QS 6.1 and CD 9.2-4. A large portion of this material can be attributed to the community which handed on the sayings. Where Paul explicitly quotes sayings of the Lord in I Corinthians, he develops instructions from them concerning behavior in the community.

4. Christological sayings. Sayings in the first person belong in this category. Words which in the tradition spoke about the SON OF MAN in the third person could be transformed into the first person (Matt. 10:32-33; Luke 12:8-9). Other sayings speak about the purpose of Jesus' coming (Mark 2:17), of his peculiar relationship to the Father (Matt. 11:25-27; Luke 10:21-22) or of his approaching suffering and resurrection (Mark 8:31). Evidently the Christology of the early community is here formulated as utterances of Jesus himself. *See also* CHRISTOLOGY OF THE NT[S] esp. §3*a*.

5. Parables. *See* PARABLE; PARABLE[S].

6. Scenes. Some of the sayings are placed in brief scenes, where a question, either from Jesus' disciples or his opponents, or the conduct of Jesus or of his disciples, occasions a question which the saying of Jesus then answers. This corresponds to the "apophthegm" form familiar from Greek literature; the classification of such material as "pronouncement story" expresses more emphatically the fact that Jesus is here portrayed more as a preacher than as a teacher. The introductory scene can also be a miracle story (*see* MIRACLE STORIES, NT[S]). A subcategory is that of the conflict story, where discussion centers about the correct interpretation of an OT command after the manner of rabbinic teaching sessions.

7. Collections. Sometimes several sayings are juxtaposed in larger compositions, partly according to formal and partly according to material aspects, e.g., a small collection of parables similar in content (Luke 15). Material of similar content but containing different forms has been put together in the early Christian apocalypses (Mark 13; Matt. 24; Luke 21) and in Luke 7:18-35; Matt. 11:2-19 with the three pericopes concerning John the Baptist. Similar collections are also found in compositions such as the discourse in Q, which lies behind the Sermon on the Mount in Matthew and the Sermon on the Plain in Luke, and in the collections of sayings found in the APOSTOLIC FATHERS. The GTh (*see* THOMAS, GOSPEL OF[S]) presents one saying after another, introduced by the stereotyped, "Jesus said," and only occasionally expanded into an apophthegm. Q shows how soon biographical interest arose, even though the sayings predominate. By connecting the Q tradition with the Markan tradition, Matthew produced summaries of the sayings tradition in longer discourses.

8. Transmission. FORM CRITICISM offers no specific criteria for determining the authenticity of a saying; such criteria result only from a combination of observations concerning form, language, and content. Although form criticism has demonstrated that it was not larger compositions, but small units, rarely consisting of more than two or three sentences, that stood at the beginning of the tradition, these small units are only excerpts from the more comprehensive preaching of Jesus. They may either be fundamental principles formulated by Jesus himself or compressed summaries of his preaching formulated by the first transmitters.

The proclamation of Jesus was handed on by the primitive community, because for certain groups salvation was connected with what the pre-Easter Jesus had said. This type of early Christian theology must be distinguished from the type represented by Paul, where the question of salvation centered on the events of Jesus' death and resurrection. Here the sayings of Jesus are used only in PARENESIS. But the interests of those who transmitted Jesus' words cannot be defined as only parenetic or catechetic. In Q and GTh, Jesus is the one whose teaching signifies salvation. Theology here stands in continuity with the teaching of the pre-Easter Jesus by handing on his words; it does not involve that discontinuity with the pre-Easter Jesus which was produced by the interpretation of his death and resurrection.

Bibliography. R. Bultmann, *History of the Synoptic Tradition* (2nd ed., 1931 [ET 1968]); M. Dibelius, *From Tradition to Gospel* (2nd ed., 1933); N. Perrin, *Rediscovering the Teaching of Jesus* (1967); J. M. Robinson, H. Koester, *Trajectories through Early Christianity* (1971); V. Taylor, *The Formation of the Gospel Tradition* (2nd ed., 1935). D. LÜHRMANN

SCIENCE AND THE BIBLE. During the millennium in which the written Bible was produced, SCIENCE was limited and fragmentary; it originated outside of Israel, largely in Babylonia, Egypt, and (later) Greece. As a result the Bible reflects the perspectives of a pre-scientific age. Since the time of Copernicus and Galileo, what we know as modern science has been slowly changing our entire view of ourselves and the universe. The contrast between the world view of the Bible and that of science has in the past resulted in much stress and conflict. Science, however, has in the last half century changed greatly, both in its view of itself and in its understanding of the world it investigates. At the same time, our understanding of the Bible has also greatly changed, in terms of the complexity of the history of its production, and of the cultural context within which its witness was borne. The conflicts and tensions of the past are being replaced by a new perspective, in which the aspects of reality which each illuminates may be seen to be complementary and mutually enriching. These aspects are discussed here under the following:

1. The universe and man
2. Mystery and transcendence
3. Cosmology and creation
   a. Creation out of nothing
   b. Primordial chaos
   c. Creation by process
4. Biological evolution
5. Miracle

Bibliography

1. The universe and man. The universe known to those who wrote the Bible was a compact and well-arranged home for man. At its center was the earth, with its abundant resources for all human needs. Above the earth moved the sun, moon, and stars, and beneath it were mysterious forces shrouded in darkness (*see* EARTH; HEAVEN). It had been created only some four thousand years ago, or not much more than a hundred life spans of an individual.

The progress of science has changed all this. First, the earth was removed from the center and given the same status as the other planets around the sun. Then the sun was removed from the center and became only one of a hundred billion other stars making up our galaxy, the Milky Way. Finally, the Milky Way was seen to be just one of billions of similar galaxies in an expanding universe of unimaginable vastness extending out to billions of light-years. The contrast between this universe and that of the Bible seems stark and irreconcilable. Where could the God of the Bible and the creature, man, created in his image find a place in such a universe?

Cosmology and astrophysics have in the last few decades been leading to some new and unexpected thoughts about the universe. For one thing, the contingency and mutability of the universe have emerged as essential elements of it. Everything in the universe, and the universe itself, has a history. Everything is born, has its own pilgrimage through time, and dies. Even space and time and the laws of physics describing behavior in space and time have a beginning and an end. The history of stars from birth to death has become a commonplace. Histories of atoms from hydrogen to uranium and beyond are now being intensively investigated, and the history of galaxies is beginning to be studied. Nothing in nature has permanence any more. The universe as a whole and everything in it appears to be radically contingent on forces beyond itself.

In a chapter in a recent book devoted to Copernicus, Wheeler raised speculations about the universe as a home for man. If the universe had been much smaller than it is, and had it contained correspondingly less matter, it would not have had a sufficient life span to have produced man anywhere within it. Before life could be possible, carbon, nitrogen, oxygen, and phosphorus atoms had to evolve in quantity, and that required several billion years. Once they were available, several more billion years were needed for life to begin and then evolve up to man. So the universe, if it was to produce mankind, had to last at least about eight billion years. But in order to last that long, the universe, according to Einstein's general theory of relativity, had to be about that many billion light-years in size. This can lead to the speculation that man, after all, may be the real reason why the universe is as big as it is. Wheeler raised a second point. Three fundamental constants, the velocity of light, the quantum of angular momentum, and the electric charge on the electron, have precise values in our universe which are independent of each other. The product of the first two divided by the square of the third is a pure number whose value is slightly over 137. If this number had a smaller or a larger value of say 130 or 145, a star like the sun would not be possible, and under those circumstances it does not seem that life could have developed anywhere within the universe. Could it be that God chose the values of these three fundamental constants at the outset when he first created the universe in order eventually to have the opportunity of creating man? Such questions are admittedly highly speculative, but they do suggest that the universe may not be as alien to man as was believed just a short time ago.

2. Mystery and transcendence. Until recently, science looked upon its mission as one of clearing up and dispelling one long-established mystery after another. The secrets of nature were believed to lie just below the surface of things. It was felt that when science finished its task, the world would be laid bare and revealed as completely intelligible and nonmysterious. The Bible, on the other hand, is permeated with a profound sense of the mystery of existence. Here again modern science is strongly reviving a sense of mystery, but now it is not the mystery of a problem to be solved, but rather the mysterious quality of the known. The quest for the secret of matter has led into unsuspected depths where strangely beautiful patterns and symmetries emerge. Every particle of matter has a mirror image of itself in a particle of antimatter. Particles and antiparticles are materialized out of radiation, and when they come back together are annihilated. Neutrons and protons seem to be made on an unbreakable "trinity" of very odd particles called "quarks." They do not exist by themselves; but apart from quarks in combinations of three, matter itself cannot exist.

Science is in the process of discovering that mystery is not so much a puzzle to be cleared up as an essential quality of reality by which what is known presents itself to us as strange, amazing, and yet fascinating. Even more compelling is the encounter with mystery in the macrocosm in the death of stars. The final stage of stars approximately the size of our sun is a "white dwarf." In this stage the star is compressed to a density of several million tons per cubic inch, is about the size of the earth, and behaves physically like a single superatom. Stars somewhat larger than the sun have such strong gravity that their final collapse takes them through the white-dwarf stage into that of a "neutron star" or "pulsar" with a diameter of only ten to thirty miles and a density of billions of tons per cubic inch. The state of matter in them is like that inside the nucleus of an atom, and they rotate extremely rapidly and possess unimaginably powerful magnetic fields. Still more massive stars cannot even stop at this stage. They must collapse through it to such a high density that not even light can escape from their powerful gravity. At this stage, what had been a star becomes an unobservable "black hole." Thereafter nothing can be known about what goes on inside it; the laws of physics discovered here on earth are cancelled and no longer apply. It now seems that the entire universe was born in a black hole and may well end in one. A black hole is by all odds the most mysterious phenomenon in the universe, and its mystery is ineradicable in principle. In the category of mystery, the scientific and biblical perspectives are again beginning to complement and reinforce each other.

Another way in which science has seemed to conflict with the Bible in the past has been in its apparent denial of any reality transcendent to the natural order. By definition, science is the study of nature. In the fulfillment of its mission, it has staunchly resisted all supernatural explanations. The basic faith for science has been that ultimately all objects and events in space and time would be explained in terms of other objects and events in space and time. A corollary of this faith has been the conviction that the success of science would remove any need of appeal to a transcendent order

NASA

2. The sphere of the earth as photographed from the Apollo 17 spacecraft—from the Mediterranean Sea to the Antarctica south polar ice cap. The Arabian Peninsula can be seen at the NE edge of Africa; the Asian mainland is on the horizon toward the NE.

for such explanations, and that even if such an order existed, it would not affect anything happening in nature. In contrast to this conviction of science, the Bible manifests a lively conviction in the reality of a world transcendent to the natural order, of the heavenly as opposed to the earthly, of the reality of an invisible and unseen world. Moreover this transcendent order is living and active, and powerfully affects events taking place in the natural order. It is, in the NT, the domain of dark and demonic powers capable of destroying man (e.g., Eph. 6:10-16). But most important, it is the domain of the holy and transcendent God whose creative energy and power is immanently at work in nature toward the achievement of his purpose for it.

In this respect also, however, science has been changing greatly in the last few decades. There are numerous and growing hints of a reality transcendent to the natural order. The most complete and accurate theory achieved in physics to date is quantum mechanics. The impressive achievements of this theory all require that particles and atoms be represented by waves which, however, are not waves in our space but probability waves in a shadow realm called "configuration space." The deeper the quest for the secret of matter is pushed, the more it seems to be leading beyond space and time into other dimensions where the ground of existence in space and time is to be found. Physicists studying the properties of our four-dimensional space-time universe do so by "embedding" it in larger spaces of up to ten dimensions. Others work out the mathematics of "white holes," through which matter disappearing from our universe under gravitational collapse into black holes emerges through a narrow passage into some other universe with perhaps different dimensions and properties from ours. Thus some areas of modern science involve an unobservable reality transcendent to our three-dimensional universe, a reality in which our universe is immersed and with which it is in intimate contact at every point.

The contrast between discovery and revelation will always mark the relationship between science and the Bible. It is, however, significant that a growing segment of modern science believes, like the Bible, that a transcendent order of reality does exist. This means that the great revelatory insights of the Bible may again come to illuminate the nature of that part of reality to which science is inexorably being led, but which it finds itself unable to explore.

3. Cosmology and creation. The Bible has no single doctrine of creation. In one view, creation does not refer to the origin of things, but refers to a continuous process in which God is always creating "from beginning to end." This "process" creativity is expressed in many biblical passages (cf. Deut. 4:32-39; 26:5-10; Ezek. 16:1-14), and this mode of creation is inherent in the recognition of the God of Israel as the God of history.

In another biblical strand, God creates by bringing order out of CHAOS. This is the case with the two creation stories in Genesis. In the earlier (Gen. 2:4*b*-23), the account may originally have begun with a story similar to the myth in which the earth was formed out of the remains of the dragon Rahab, but in the Bible all that remains of that myth are references in other biblical authors (Job 9:13; Ps. 89:10; Isa. 51:9). In the later P account, the primordial chaos is water (Gen. 1:2). In either case, passages in the Bible indicate that chaos continues to lurk in the outlying regions, always ready to return and inundate the creative achievement of God. At a much later stage, the idea of *creatio ex nihilo,* creation out of nothing, arose in order to emphasize that everything which exists in the created order owes its existence to God, and that nothing can exist and participate in being apart from God (Rom. 4:17; Heb. 11:3). For a complete discussion of these several strands in the biblical idea of creation, *see* COSMOGONY and CREATION.

The current scientific account of creation includes all three of these biblical concepts, as may be seen in the following outline in reverse order:

a. Creation out of nothing. A mounting mass of evidence is leading to the conclusion that the present vast universe of galaxies and stars, along with space, time, and matter, was born around ten to twelve billion years ago. In this view of its history, the whole universe would appear to have been born in a black hole, and if so what it contained at birth must, in principle, remain forever hidden and unknown. Such an event can truly be described as a "creation out of nothing." The universe at this point, however, was rapidly expanding as from an immense primordial explosion, and in a very short time it passed out of the black-hole stage and emerged as a visible universe.

b. Primordial chaos. A few hours after the beginning of the universe, the expanding space had become filled with a mixture of hydrogen and helium gases formed by nuclear condensation of the neutrons and protons which emerged from the black hole. The temperature was extremely high, and as a result space was also filled with intense light, making the whole universe one vast fireball. For over a billion years, the expanding and cooling mixture of hydrogen and helium was all that existed and so constituted a true "primordial chaos." The immense variety of things now represented in the universe had to take form out of it step by step, in a process of ever-increasing complexity.

c. Creation by process. The expanding hydrogen and helium cooled and slowly segregated under gravity into large masses which became our present galaxies, and which the expansion of the universe has carried farther and farther apart ever since. After a few billion more years, smaller masses of hydrogen and helium within each protogalaxy underwent gravitational collapse and became stars. In the hot interiors of the larger stars, heavier atoms from carbon to iron were formed. When these stars exploded, even heavier atoms up to uranium and beyond were formed and then mixed with the surrounding hydrogen and helium. Out of such a mixture, our sun and planets were produced in another gravitational collapse 4.6 billion years ago. In the earth's early oceans, life began and was then carried forward in an amazing process all the way to man.

It is evident from this brief synopsis that, although the size, time span, and details are totally different from those in the world views which prevailed when the Bible was written, all the biblical insights into the nature of God's creative activity are applicable to our present understanding, and that understanding is compatible with the creator God revealed in the Bible. The majesty and religious purity of Genesis 1 stand in sharp contrast to the Babylonian sources from which it was drawn during the Exile. The proper use of the Bible today is not to attempt to make twentieth-century A.D. cosmology conform with sixth-century B.C. Babylonian cosmology, but rather to perform the same interpretive and revelatory function on the former which the Priestly authors performed on the latter.

4. Biological evolution. The history of life on earth began 4.6 billion years ago when the sun and planets were formed. The composition of the earth's early atmosphere in conjunction with energetic radiation from the sun was essential for producing the molecules necessary for life. Also essential was liquid water made possible by the precise location of the earth's orbit around the sun. During the first billion years of the earth's history, such molecules combined into long spiral filaments called "nucleic acids" capable of storing information in a very ingenious but simple coding scheme. The code directed the sequence of letters in a twenty-letter alphabet of amino acids to form words of specific spelling called "proteins." By 3.2 billion years ago, this "language of life" had been perfected and elaborated to the point of producing complex organisms similar to modern bacteria.

By 2.5 billion years ago, an auxiliary system, chlorophyll, had evolved which could manufacture nucleic acids and amino acids from sunlight and carbon dioxide, with oxygen as the waste product. Another very similar auxiliary system, cytochromes, also evolved which could manufacture the same components by reacting sugar with oxygen. By 1.9 billion years ago, these systems had become incorporated into many species of organisms like modern algae. By .6 billion years ago, the earth had acquired sufficient oxygen in its atmosphere to shield its surface from lethal ultraviolet radiation from the sun, and life was able to rise to the surface of the sea and, eventually, begin to cover land areas. Visible creatures made up of millions of cells evolved. By .3 billion years ago, the seas swarmed with a wide variety of creatures, and the land was covered with verdure, together with a diversity of insects and oxygen-breathing animals. A major ecological crisis came seventy million years ago, in which many species of marine animals and land reptiles, including the giant dinosaurs, became extinct. There followed a rapid evolution of mammals and of grasses and flowering trees and shrubs. The history of this exciting development culminated just a few million years ago in the evolution of an erect species of primates with ever-enlarging brains, which finally led some forty thousand years ago to the achievement of modern man, when homo sapiens replaced the Neanderthals.

Energetic radiation, chemicals, temperature, and other agents can cause changes in the elaborate codes carried in nucleic acid. The modified code directs changed sequences of amino acids in proteins which may lead to detectable changes in the organism called "mutations." A large population of any species exhibits a number of mutant forms which appear with varying frequencies. In an ever-changing environment, the genetic character of the population will slowly drift, as some mutations are favored and others suppressed. This process is called "natural selection." Selective pressures exerted on mutation patterns of populations in an ever-changing environment led, over long periods of time, to the evolution of species. This is the scientific theory of evolution.

Science can provide increasingly lucid explanations of how the molecular structure of life has operated in evolutionary development, but it cannot account for the particular course which evolution has taken. The reason for this is the statistical character of scientific laws governing the course of events in time. At every moment in the evolution of life, valid alternatives governed by probabilities are open. Science can specify and predict the probability of each alternative, but it has no way of knowing which alternative will be taken in any particular instance. Indeed, the introduction of probability in the formulation of a scientific law constitutes an explicit renunciation of any causal explanation for the alternatives governed by it.

From a strictly scientific standpoint, the history of life on earth, like all other history, could just as well have followed many other paths than the one it took. A number of these would not have led to any notable achievements, and some would seem regressive by our standards. The nature of science and of probability prohibits any evaluative judgments in purely scientific terms among possible courses for the evolution of life. Yet the one course which evolution actually took constitutes an immense creative achievement, an achievement which suggests the patient working out of a transcendent purpose through the hidden operation of an immanent creative energy working through the chances and accidents of history. This is the biblical perspective on the evolution of life and of man.

5. Miracle. Historically one of the sharpest lines of division between science and the Bible has been over miracles. This controversy has been sustained by the tacit agreement of both parties that the essence of MIRACLE is the intervention in, and violation of, a law of nature as formulated in science. A careful examination of the concept of miracle in the Bible does not, however, support this assumption. Briefly stated, a miracle in the Bible is an extraordinary event which, for the believer, is clear and certain evidence of the presence and action of God in all events. Whether or not it violates a scientific law is irrelevant. Nevertheless, the majority of the miracles in the Bible, when evaluated in their historical context, do not violate any law of science as such laws are presently understood.

As noted in the preceding section, scientific laws which govern the course of events in time are probabilistic in character. They do not predict what must happen, but only the probability that one of several alternatives will occur (e.g., the probability of rain in weather forecasting). Moreover events in history (as opposed to controlled conditions in scientific laboratories) are made up of the accidental coming together of elements having no causal relationship with each other (e.g., a sudden fog hides an escaping ship). It is true that most of the time the most probable is what actually happens, and accidents are either avoided or are not crucial. Then history follows the smooth course it is expected to follow, and God's activity in it is not evident. But the great creative turning points in history are formed when several extremely improbable happenings accidentally combine with other improbable happenings to produce some great achievement. In the Bible such an event is a miracle. Many miracles of this character were crucial in the evolution of life and of man. For those, however, who acknowledge no source of truth or understanding beyond science, the same event is not a miracle. For them it must remain an extremely odd and unpredictable occurrence without meaning or explanation. Science has no operational means of probing behind probability and accident. For the believer, however, such a turning-point event decisively reveals the presence and action of God, either in redemption or judgment, in the shaping of all history. It is only through biblical faith that the event can be recognized and responded to as a purposeful action of God and, therefore, as a miracle. The categories of faith and miracle are inextricably and necessarily bound together.

Bibliography. General: A. Richardson, *The Bible and Modern Science* (1971); E. C. Rust, *Science and Faith* (1967); L. Gilkey, *Religion and the Scientific Future* (1970). The universe and man: O. Gingerich, ed., *The Nature of Scientific Discovery* (1975), esp. J. A. Wheeler, "The Universe as Home for Man"; J. Neyman, *The Heritage of Copernicus* (1974); L. Eiseley, *The Unexpected Universe* (1969). Mystery and transcendence: E. A. Abbott, *Flatland* (1880 [repr., 1952, 1963]); W. G. Pollard, *Physicist and Christian* (1961). Cosmology and creation: W. J. Kaufmann, *Relativity and Cosmology* (1973); L. Gilkey, *Creator of Heaven and Earth* (1959); W. G. Pollard, *Science and Faith—Twin Mysteries* (1970). Evolution: A. V. Knight, *The Meaning of Teilhard de Chardin* (1974); P. Teilhard de Chardin, *The Phenomenon of Man* (1959); L. Eiseley, *The Immense Journey* (1946); E. C. Rust, *Nature—Garden or Desert?* (1971). Miracle: W. G. Pollard, *Chance and Providence* (1958); O. Handlin, *Chance or Destiny* (1955).
W. G. Pollard

SCRIPTURE, AUTHORITY OF. The question of the authority of Scripture underlies many of the problems within modern biblical study, even where it is not expressly mentioned. Most interpreters stand within some tradition in which it has been understood for centuries that the Bible is studied not just for its antiquarian interest, nor for the aesthetic beauty of its imagery, nor as the opinions that this person or that happened to hold, but because it has and should have some commanding influence over what is to be believed, said, and done. In other words, the Bible is worthy to be called Holy Scripture because it conveys, mirrors, or reflects something authentic or valid about God and his works. Even those who seek to practice an exegesis that is theologically neutral will often tend to find in the Bible some indication of a principle or a process which they believe to be dominant in human existence or supremely important for it; and, in any case, they find it hard to free themselves entirely from the influence of the long tradition which has interpreted the Bible as a book having authority. But the term "authority" and the term "Scripture" both direct us toward the theological and religious use of the Bible, rather than the strictly scientific study of it.

1. The terminology
   a. Inspiration
   b. Word of God
   c. Authority
2. Sources of the Bible's authority
   a. Its character as the classical literature of the people of God
   b. Its relation to the events which it narrates and from which it derives
   c. Its theology
   d. Cumulative tradition
3. Problems about the authority of Scripture
   a. The canon
   b. The "center"
   c. Applicability and relevance

Bibliography

1. The terminology. ***a. Inspiration.*** This is a classical term in theology, but in modern times it has come to be used mainly in conservative circles, both Protestant and Roman Catholic. The word lays emphasis on the origin of Scripture: it suggests that Scripture in some way comes from God. The question then is, How? In what way is it intelligible to us today to affirm that the Bible, a human book, of known historical origins, came from God? The historical-critical exegete explains the Bible through its derivation from the thought of the writers and the tradition behind them, the thought of ancient Israel and of the leaders of the early church; and he does not find any element which in principle is not so explicable. Thus, even if the Bible is thought of as "coming from" God, it does not seem to make any decisive difference to exegesis.

Among conservatives inspiration has commonly been linked with ideas of inerrancy and infallibility. Because the Bible comes from God, it is supposed, there cannot be any error in it, whether theological or historical. At the present time there are signs of a fresh interest in the idea of inspiration in a form which would be dissociated from these conservative suggestions. It is felt that, in spite of the human character and derivation of the Bible, there must be some sense in which it is meaningful to say that it comes from God; but this would have to be so framed as to accept the historical inaccuracies and even contradictions of the Bible. Indeed, inspiration might have to be so thought of as to admit even theological imperfection.

b. Word of God. In some modern theology, and especially in the current which is best represented by Karl Barth, the term "Word of God" has been much more prominent than the term "inspiration." Barth emphasized the Word of God but did not identify it with the Bible. The primary form of the Word of God was Christ himself; the secondary was Scripture; and the tertiary was the preaching of Christ by the church on the basis of the scriptural witness. The Bible is thus not revelation, but is human witness to revelation. Yet it is a necessary witness to revelation, and because of this it has authority. It is the given criterion for what is to be said in the preaching of the church. If Scripture on one side is entirely the word of man, on another side it is entirely the Word of God.

This scheme, for all its fine balance, has received less attention in recent years. Though theologically impressive, it has seemed to offer little help in solving actual interpretative problems within biblical scholarship; also, the focus of study has moved from the difference between divine and human to the difference between ancient and modern, between biblical times and our own.

c. Authority. This is the term that has been most generally used in modern discussions of the status of the Bible in church and theology. It is a term that defines relations, in particular, the relation between the Bible and ourselves, implying that the Bible is something binding upon us, something to which we have to submit ourselves. It is also used to define the relation between the Bible and other documents or sources of knowledge which might influence us in a similar way. It implies that these other sources are important and proper, but that the Bible has a higher order of authority than they.

The term "authority" is thus flexible. It can be used of the Bible without absolutizing it, without implying that it has some kind of perfection. It can take the Bible just as it is. Whatever the matter of its origin, and whether it contains historical inaccuracies or not—even whether it contains theological errors or not—it can still be ranged in terms of authority as against all other factors that might influence the faith and life of the church.

In the last years, nevertheless, there has been some difficulty about the idea of authority also. In earlier centuries it seemed obvious that religion involved authority and that it worked through an authority which was imposed upon people and had to be simply accepted by them. Modern trends of thought resist this. Not only is general opinion critical of claims to authority, but even theology itself is no longer necessarily, or ordinarily, an authority structure.

Moreover, the idea of the authority of Scripture has been associated with the search for one overarching principle which might justify and support that authority in all the diverse applications of Scripture. In contrast with this, some recent thought has tried to distinguish between the various *functions* of Scripture, suggesting that the Bible had no single form of authority but that its influence and importance varied from one to another of its functions.

2. Sources of the Bible's authority. If the Bible has some sort of special status, then this is not simply because it is the Bible. It is usual to point to something, other than just the Bible itself, as the ground upon which this status rests. Different views of the authority of Scripture rest upon different views of this basis.

a. Its character as the classical literature of the people of God. The Bible may be thought of as the classical literature of the people of God in ancient times, the Israelites of the OT and the early Christian community. This people, like other societies, has a kind of foundation myth or story, which has been inherited by subsequent generations of the same community, and which is solemnly read and expounded when the people come together. This myth informs the minds of the members of the community, providing them with pictures, types, and categories through which they organize their experience. Though the community has added later tradition and experience, this later tradition has itself acknowledged the Bible as its own authority. Thus Christian or Jewish experience quite factually means experience within a tradition for which the Bible has always been the basic literary paradigm. The effectiveness of the Bible as the basic literary paradigm is not dependent on whether the stories contained in it are historically true. The Bible contains materials, like the stories of Job or of Jonah or the parables of the NT, which are more or less fictional in character.

Most scholars hold that this, even if part of the truth, is not the whole truth. Many of the main theological issues concerning the Bible do not find expression at all in a purely literary approach to its authority.

b. Its relation to the events which it narrates and from which it derives. A much more prevalent and influential view has based the authority of Scripture on the events that lie behind it, the history that it narrates. Revelation is in historical events (*see* REVELATION IN HISTORY[S]), and it is upon these events that faith is based. Scripture is not itself revelation, but is a supreme witness to certain events, which it interprets theologically. Purely descriptively, it is said, this is a characteristic feature of the Bible. In comparison with other sacred and religious books, it is distinctively a work concerned with history. If the Bible has authority, then, it is not because of its intrinsic character as an inspired book, but because of the events which it narrates and from which it derives.

This view has the advantage that it can allow that the biblical reports of events are imperfect. There were indeed events, and these events are the media of revelation; but the events were not exactly as they are depicted in the Bible. This distinction between the real events and the biblical depictions of them has seemed to be an advantage. The biblical reporting of events is never mere objective reporting; rather, it is testimony in faith, a record of events as seen through the screen of that faith which these same events generated. That differing accounts of the same event should arise is natural: these depend on different faith interpretations, but all are alike valid testimonies to the events.

A position of this kind has been the dominant one in mid-twentieth-century biblical theology (*see* BIBLICAL THEOLOGY[S]), but it suffers from several weaknesses. First, there is much obscurity about the nature of the "events" which lie behind Scripture and to which a revelational function is ascribed. Are they accessible to historical investigation or not? Are they special events which break the chain of normal historical causation, or are they events on a normal historical level which nevertheless somehow bear the imprint of a divine hand in a way in which other historical events do not? Again, some of the "events" registered in the Bible were not events at all (Noah's flood, Jonah's voyage in the belly of the whale); or, if they took place at all, the actuality was so far removed from the biblical depiction as to mean that this depiction was not a fair representation of this event (e.g., the Israelite capture of Jericho).

Thus, secondly, the emphasis on the events has often in effect been an emphasis on the history-centered way of thinking characteristic of the Bible; in other words, it has been an emphasis on a feature of the *religion* of the Bible, rather than on events as factual occurrences. The scheme of revelation in history, event and interpretation, took its departure from the realistic idiom of the "mighty acts of God." God is depicted as speaking in normal human sentences, sending thunder, fire, and plagues, submerging the world in water, and dividing the sea so that its water stands up like a wall. But the emphasis passed quickly from these acts to the mental structure of Israel's response, and the resultant picture of a revelation through history has had no close fit with the biblical depiction from which it started and from which it drew its theological and emotional values.

Thirdly, the argument from events does not satisfactorily demonstrate the authority of Scripture, of this group of books in particular. It might equally well lead to some kind of creed, a list of major events with an interpretation attached. To those who in any case believed passionately in the authority of Scripture it seemed easy enough to say that it has authority because of the events that lie behind it. But to the modern person, to whom it is really doubtful in what sense, if any, the Bible has authority, this argument does not work. Starting from the events, he does not necessarily arrive at the authority of this mixed collection of books. For not all that is in the Bible can reasonably be classed as reportage or interpretation of events. It includes all kinds of information—historical, geographical, cosmological, social, anthropological, legal, and religious. And certain sections—notably the wisdom literature of the OT and many psalms—do not have narrative form and do not concern themselves with the interpretation of past events.

c. Its theology. It is probable that most views of scriptural authority have really depended on another basis, which has not been articulated clearly: it is the theology of Scripture that gives it authority. It was at one time unfashionable to speak of Scripture as containing theology, but this feeling has now largely passed away, and many detailed studies are evidence of the sense among scholars that the Bible contains theology, although its theology takes forms different from those of most later theological writing. A current of theological development, conflict, and reconstruction forms the center of intellectual history within Scripture. To say then that Scripture has authority means that the theology within Scripture is normative for the theology of later times. Theology has continued after scriptural times and will always continue, but it can be wholesome for the church only insofar as it seeks to relate itself to, or to accept as a criterion, the theology of Scripture itself.

This position, however, has two weak points: the existence of theological differences within Scripture and the existence of theological continuity between Scripture and postscriptural theology. How then can a clear difference between scriptural and other theology be maintained?

d. Cumulative tradition. The Bible is not so much history as it is history-like. Much of it has narrative character, and this narrative spirals back and forth across the line of history. Sometimes it is nearer to history, sometimes farther from it. The relation to history is thus important but cannot be made into the absolute mark of biblical style and the source of its authority. The story is cumulative; we do not begin with a great revelatory event, from which a definitive set of interpretations are then drawn. Rather, we begin with small events, the tradition of which generates a religious and theological framework within which later events may be understood. It is often unclear to us whether the "events" narrated are external historical events or rather the symbols of intellectual crises within the tradition. At any one stage the tradition has within it a model for the understanding of God, which model forms the basis for conflicts and discussions which in turn lead on to another stage. Christian faith, like Jewish faith, is faith structured upon such a basic model. This model was worked out in Scripture; Scripture contains not only the finished product but elements of the stages through which the tradition passed. The fixation of tradition in the form of Scripture altered the character of the tradition. Tradition ran on into postbiblical times (which actually overlapped with Scripture) but increasingly became a tradition that interpreted an already existing Scripture. Thus the existence of a "Holy Scripture" is something built into the structure of Jewish and Christian faith and tradition; it played its part in the events of the origin of Christianity and in the relating and interpreting of these events. The existence of this model in a fixed, written source enables us today to look critically at our own tradition in the light of that earlier source; it also provides a means by which we, looking at the present and future, can orient ourselves in relation to our problems.

But must modern theology be "biblical" in its form? If Scripture is built into the structure of tradition and religion, then theology, if it understands itself as an explication of faith, must at some point meet with the Bible and express its own relation to it. But whether theology takes a more or a less scriptural form and style is a question decided not by external authority, but by theology itself in its expression of that relation.

3. Problems about the authority of Scripture. ***a. The canon.*** The fact of the canon of Scripture is often felt to be irrational: Why should some books be included and others not? Is there any clear difference of value between those books which lie within our Bible and those which do not? In brief, one would have to say that the canon is something inherited from a particular time in the past when canon formation was an active process. The reasons why this or that book was received or rejected are imperfectly known, and if they were known it is doubtful whether they could be reconciled with the findings of modern exegesis. It is certainly not possible to draw absolute distinctions of value between books that have become canonical and others which have not. Where such distinctions can be made, one can point to similar distinctions within the canonical literature itself. Thus one may doubt if there is much difference between Ecclesiastes and Ecclesiasticus, but there is a big difference between either of them and Deuteronomy or Isaiah. The distinction is a relative one, but that does not mean it is unimportant. There is a real historical and theological distinction between books that came close to the same tradition from which the canonical Scripture came, such as Ecclesiasticus or Wisdom, and books that came from a substantially differing current of tradition, such as some Gnostic documents. *See* CANON OF THE OT §9 and supplementary article; CANON OF THE NT §§B, C and supplementary article.

b. The "center." Interpreters of Scripture seldom find themselves able to take all of it as one piece. Certain elements seem to be peripheral for many purposes while others are central. But it is hard to find a definition of the "center" which will satisfy everyone. For the OT a good example is the formula "Yahweh the God of Israel, Israel the people of Yahweh" (R. Smend, after Wellhausen). Some, by contrast, and notably von Rad, have denied that any such center is to be found. After a period in which the "unity of the Bible" was stressed (*see* BIBLICAL THEOLOGY[S]), there came a tendency to admit severe theological conflicts within Scripture. Yet most theologies of OT and NT continue to work with some idea of a center.

The identification of such a center means the granting of priority to certain parts of Scripture or certain themes within it. Sometimes such priorities are spoken of as a "canon within the canon." This is unfortunate, since "canon" suggests something public, fixed, and permanent. Instead, the priorities are individual to various currents of exegesis; they are (or should be) fluid and liable to change. It is unlikely that interpretation can work without such priorities, in spite of their tentative and impermanent character. They are valid because they derive from a characteristic of the scriptural material itself, which is not homogeneous but has points of greater and lesser explicitness and clarity. The less explicit areas may be survivals from earlier stages of the tradition or background rather than central material for its current movement. But even that which is peripheral has importance for the picture as a whole, and that which has in the past been taken as peripheral may become much more central than was expected.

c. Applicability and relevance. To many the authority of Scripture now seems less important than its relevance. Cultural conditions have changed since biblical times, and how can biblical thoughts, whether authoritative or not, decide what we should do or think under our very different cultural and social conditions? The range of applicability of the Bible has in fact been suffering reduction over a long period. At one time it was thought to have authority even in matters of natural science, but this is no longer believed. This process has been a gain, in that it has concentrated attention on the function of Scripture as a theological and religious document. But will even this be lost, if it is felt that Scripture, though truly theological in character, cannot speak relevantly to us today?

Only one brief suggestion can be offered here. Scripture is an ancient book and cannot be made into anything else. The task of interpretation is not to drag the texts out of their original situation and "apply" them to the modern world. Rather, Scripture, as a work of the past and so understood, feeds and illuminates the understanding of modern men and women in their situation. It does not usually apply directly to the modern situation, but within the church and the situation of faith it builds and enriches the faith in which people are able to see their own situation more clearly and to judge their actions more rightly. On the other hand, it is wrong to absolutize the differences between biblical society and modern society, as if no bridge could be built between them. Cultures are not completely closed entities —biblical culture in particular was not—and the ability to receive and absorb from other cultures is a mark of modern culture in particular.

Bibliography. Older works: C. H. Dodd, *The Authority of the Bible* (1929); H. Cunliffe-Jones, *The Authority of the Biblical Revelation* (1945); J. K. S. Reid, *The Authority of Scripture* (1957); A. Richardson and W. Schweitzer, *Biblical Authority for Today* (1951).

More recent discussions: study outline with questions, J. Barr *et al.*, "The Authority of the Bible," *Ecumenical Review,* XXI (1969), 135-66; J. Barr, *The Bible in the Modern World* (1973); C. F. Evans, *Is 'Holy Scripture' Christian? & Other Questions* (1971); J. D. Smart, *The Strange Silence of the Bible in the Church* (1970).

On "history-like" narrative in Scripture: H. W. Frei, *The Eclipse of Biblical Narrative* (1974); on the "center" of Scripture, R. Smend, *Die Mitte des Alten Testaments* (1970).

J. BARR

*__SCYTHIANS__ [Σκύθαι]. The name given by Greeks to tribes ruling southern Russia after the eighth century B.C., and by extension applied to all similar inhabitants of the Russian steppe. Iranian by language and origin, the Scythians were horse nomads in central Asia who, pressured by tribes further east, invaded southern Russia. Among the opposed to using chariots), they drove out or subjugated the earlier inhabitants, the Cimmerians (*see* GOMER §1). Forced southward, the Cimmerians entered the Near East through Urartu (*see* ARARAT §1) during the reign of the Assyrian King Sargon II (722-705 B.C.), but were driven into Asia Minor, where they destroyed the kingdom of Phrygia.

The Scythians (Akkad. *Ašguzai, Iškuzai*) first appear in Assyrian records under Esarhaddon (681-670 B.C.), led by their king, Ishpaka. Another of their chiefs, Bartatua, concluded a treaty with Esarhaddon and asked for one of his daughters in marriage. During the final years of the Assyrian Empire, they extended their hegemony over much of northern Mesopotamia E of the Halys river as far as Media, and according to Herodotus (I.104, 106; IV.1; VII.20) ruled almost all of this area for twenty-eight years, raiding the surrounding countries. Herodotus (I.105) records a raid to the borders of Egypt, where they were bought off by Pharaoh Psammetichus (presumably I, 663-609 B.C.). On their return they are said to have destroyed the temple of the "Heavenly Aphrodite" at ASHKELON.

The part played by the Scythians as Assyrian allies in the years leading up to the fall of Nineveh (612 B.C.) and the chronology of their movements is much debated, and no scholarly consensus has yet been achieved. This uncertainty makes it difficult to assess their precise influence on the OT. The Scythian raid into Palestine has been cited as the occasion for the book of ZEPHANIAH and the so-called "foe from the north" oracles in JEREMIAH (*see* §B1). The identification is based in part on the assumption of a massive Scythian presence in Palestine—an assumption founded on a misinterpretation of Herodotus, who portrays the Palestinian raid as secondary to the main Scythian activity in the N. The Hellenistic name of BETH-SHAN (*see* §4), Scythopolis, can no longer be used as evidence of permanent Scythian settlement in Palestine. Thus the influence of the Scythians on these passages was apparently less direct than allowed by older scholarship.

The Scythians are referred to as ASHKENAZ in Gen. 10:3; I Chr. 1:6; and Jer. 51:27, where they are associated with peoples of Asia Minor and northern Mesopotamia. After their period of domination, they were pushed back into southern Russia by the Medes, where they were the ruling power until the third century B.C., after which they were gradually conquered by the Sarmatians, another nomadic Indo-Iranian people.

Almost all that is known of the Scythians' life and beliefs is derived from references in ancient literature, notably Book IV of Herodotus' *History* and the Pseudo-Hippocratic *De Aeris, Aquis, Locis*. As nomads, the Scythians had no permanent settlements and, with one notable exception, left no permanent monuments. In their movements the men rode on horseback, while the women and children were carried in tent-like covered wagons. Little is known of their religion, except the names of some members of their pantheon and that they earliest peoples to master the art of riding (as apparently believed in a life after death not too different from that on earth. This last is deduced from the extensive burial mounds erected over the tombs of their kings, the excavation of which has provided us with our other great source of information about the Scythians. The Scythian rulers were embalmed and buried together with their horses, concubines, and retainers, and a considerable number of personal ornaments and effects, often in gold. These ornaments were spectacularly decorated in the so-called "animal style" and are the Scythians' chief surviving cultural legacy. The origin and affinities of this style are disputed, but it does show a relationship with some ancient Near Eastern and Iranian art.

Despite the skill displayed in their art, the Scythians were regarded by other peoples as the epitome of barbarism, and their name became proverbial for extreme savagery. In this sense they are mentioned in the Apocrypha and Pseudepigrapha (II Macc. 4:47; III Macc. 7:5; IV Macc. 10:7) as well as the NT (Col. 3:11), where Paul teaches that the Christian dispensation is for all men, including the Scythians.

Bibliography. E. H. Minns, *Scythians and Greeks* (1913); T. T. Rice, *The Scythians* (1957) and J. A. H. Potratz, *Die Skythen in Südrussland* (1963) contain good general bibliographies; E. D. Phillips, *The Royal Hordes* (1965); M. Avi-Yonah, "Skythopolis," *IEJ*, XII (1962), 123-34; H. Cazelles, "Sophonie, Jérémie, et les Scythes en Palestine," *RB*, LXXIV (1967), 24-44; R. P. Vaggione, "Over All Asia? The Extent of the Scythian Domination in Herodotus," *JBL*, XCII (1973), 523-30 (notes in two last give bibliographies of treatment by biblical scholars); for Scythian art and the animal style see M. I. Artamonov, *Treasures from Scythian Tombs* (1969) and especially K. Jettmar, *Art of the Steppes* (1967).

R. P. VAGGIONE

***SEA, MOLTEN.** The largest of the bronze objects standing in the courtyard of Solomon's temple. There are no clear archaeological parallels. Parrot, however, has compared it with a huge basin, made of limestone, that was found in Cyprus. Four imitation handles carved in relief near the edge of the basin encircle representations of bulls, a motif which figures prominently in the biblical description of the Sea.

Bibliography. A. Parrot, *Le Temple de Jérusalem* (1954), pp. 32-34; G. Bagnani, "The Molten Sea" in *The Seed Of Wisdom*, ed. W. S. McCullough (1964), pp. 114-17; L. A. Snijders, "L'Orientation du Temple de Jérusalem," *OTS*, XIX (1965), 220-22; Th. A. Busink, *Der Tempel von Jerusalem* (1970), pp. 326-36.

J. OUELLETTE

SEA PEOPLES. *See* PHILISTINES; PHILISTINES[S].

***SECRET, MESSIANIC.** A major theme in the Gospel of Mark, first identified by Wrede, who pointed out Jesus' frequent commands to secrecy in the gospel: the commands to demons to be silent about his messianic status (1:25, 34; 3:12); the prohibitions against speaking of the miracles (1:43-45; 5:43; 7:36; 8:26); the commands to the disciples to be silent about Peter's confession (8:30) and the transfiguration (9:9). In addition to these specific commands to secrecy there are general attempts by Jesus to remain incognito (7:24; 9:30-31), and in the account of the healing of the blind man at Jericho "many" command him to secrecy (10:48).

1. Wrede's thesis. Wrede attempted to explain the secrecy theme in Mark by arguing that Jesus had not claimed messiahship during his lifetime and that messianic status was first attributed to him after his death by the early Christians. As they came to believe in Jesus as the Messiah, the early Christians created traditions about him which showed him being accepted as Messiah during his lifetime. Such traditions are to be found in the Gospel of Mark, and so far as it presents this understanding of Jesus as Messiah the gospel is the first chapter of a history of Christian doctrine: it depicts Jesus according to an understanding of his person reached by theological reflection in the early Christian communities. But, Wrede held, such an understanding of Jesus and his ministry would necessarily stand in tension with actual historical reminiscence of that ministry as having been nonmessianic. Thus, the idea of the messianic secret developed in the early Christian communities as a literary device for resolving this tension. Jesus was depicted as exhibiting during his lifetime the qualities which Christian piety had come to attribute to him, but as commanding secrecy about them until after his death and resurrection. In this way the Christian scribes were able to develop their essentially dogmatic traditions of Jesus as the Messiah–Son of God, and to reconcile them with the nonmessianic traditions concerning his actual life and death.

2. Discussion since Wrede. Wrede's thesis was propounded at a time when the Gospel of Mark was considered essentially a historical chronicle of the ministry of Jesus, and it proved to be a bombshell in the scholarly discussion. But support for the thesis grew, especially after 1919 when FORM CRITICISM undermined the older historicizing view of the gospel (*see* MARK, GOSPEL OF[S] §1). As it gathered support, however, the thesis underwent significant modification. The monolithic character of Wrede's hypothesis was given up, and so was the attempt to make the one hypothesis explain all the elements in the gospel to which Wrede called attention. Moreover, it came to be recognized that the most important elements were those connected with the messianic status of Jesus; not the general commands to silence, but the specific commands to secrecy about his person. It was recognized, further, that this christological element in the messianic secret was a theme developed by the evangelist, rather than by anonymous scribes in the pre-Markan tradition. But before 1950 scholars lacked the methodological resources to investigate a literary concern of the evangelist himself, so further progress was difficult. After 1950 this situation changed as REDACTION CRITICISM developed and provided the methodological basis for such an investigation. Subsequently, the discussion has moved to firmer ground.

A current understanding of the messianic secret would be that it is a theme pursued by the evangelist Mark, not in order to introduce a christological motif into the tradition, but rather to correct one already present. Mark inherited a tradition in which Jesus was depicted as a wonder-working Son of God, and he is concerned to supplement this christological understanding by interpreting Jesus also as the Son of man who must necessarily suffer.

Such an understanding would distinguish between commands to secrecy already present in the tradition and their purpose, and commands introduced redactionally by the evangelist and their purpose. So, for example, 1:25 would be understood as traditional, a typical element in an EXORCISM story, while 1:34; 3:12; 8:30; 9:9 would all be seen as redactional and as serving a Markan redactional purpose. To these latter 14:62 would be added. There Jesus formally discloses the messianic secret by means of his formula-like acceptance of the titles "Christ" (=Messiah) and "Son of the Blessed" (i.e., of God): "I am." (Compare 13:6 where RSV, "I am he!" translates the same formula-like phrase translated "I am" at 14:62.)

The redactional commands, therefore, are to be understood as a literary device whereby the evangelist emphasizes that the titles are not to be used unless they can be properly interpreted. This meaning is taught by the use of Son of man in 8:27–10:45, and only after this can the titles be properly used, as they are in 14:61 (ironically by the high priest) and 15:39 (by the centurion symbolizing the Gentile mission). These two are the only instances in the gospel of a public testimonial or confessional use of Christ/Messiah or Son of God which is not followed by a command to secrecy (as at 1:34; 3:12; 8:30; 9:9 [secrecy concerning the Transfiguration testimony; the Baptismal testimony, 1:11, is not public but private —only Jesus hears the voice]) or by an interpretation using Son of man (8:31; 9:31; 10:32-34 all interpret the confession of 8:29). The apparent exception, 5:7, is not testimony or confession but recognition, a traditional element in exorcism stories. 14:61 and 15:39 both come after the true meaning of the titles has been established: the former provides the occasion for the formal disclosure of the secret; the latter symbolizes the Gentile acceptance of "the gospel of Jesus Christ, the Son of God" (1:1).

Bibliography. W. Wrede, *The Messianic Secret* (1901 [ET 1971]). Reviews of the discussion: H. J. Ebeling, *Das Messiasgeheimnis und die Botschaft des Marcusevangelisten,* BZNW, XIX (1939); G. H. Boobyer, "The Secrecy Motif in St. Mark's Gospel," *NTS,* VI (1959/60), 225-35; H. G. Minette de Tillesse, *Le Secret messianique dans l'Évangile de Marc,* LD, XLVII (1968); W. C. Robinson, Jr., "The Quest for Wrede's Secret Messiah," *Int.,* XXVII (1973), 10-30.

Other studies: T. A. Burkill, *Mysterious Revelation* (1963); G. Strecker, "Zur Messiasgeheimnistheorie im Markusevangelium," *Studia Evangelica,* III, *TU,* LXXXVIII (1964), 87-104; E. Schweizer, "Zur Frage des Messiasgeheimnisses bei Markus," and U. Luz, "Das Geheimnismotiv und die markinische Christologie," *ZNW,* LVI (1965), 1-8, 9-29; N. Perrin, "Towards an Interpretation of the Gospel of Mark," *Christology and a Modern Pilgrimage,* ed. H. D. Betz (rev. ed., 1974), pp. 1-52.

N. PERRIN

SEDHEQ (GOD) sĕ'dĕk [צדק, "propriety" or "justice"]. Ṣedheq was worshiped by western Semites as the personification of cosmic order, that which vindicated the innocent and brought the guilty to punishment. The root *ṣdq* appears as a theophoric element in personal names throughout the Semitic world. The deity was prominent in the pre-Judean cult of Jerusalem and in the development of biblical religion came to be merged into the person of Yahweh. In the Bible, *ṣedheq* and *mîšôr* (justice and right) often appear together (Isa. 11:4; 45:19; Pss. 9:8; 45:7; 58:1 [H 2]; 98:9), corresponding to the divine pair *ṣdq* and *mšr* in the Ugaritic texts and to Suduk and Misor in Sanchuniathon's account of Phoenician religion preserved by Philo of Byblos.

Ṣedheq and Mishor correspond to Kittu and Mesharu in the Babylonian solar cult. These deities are attendants of Shamash, the sun god, and are described as "seated before Shamash," or "the minister of his right hand." That Kittu ("justice," from Akkad. *kānu*) is to be equated with Ṣedheq is confirmed by the name of King Ammisaduqa of the First Dynasty of Babylon. One of the king lists renders this West Semitic name into Akkadian as Kim-tum-kit-tum ("the Kinsman is Kittu").

It is quite likely that Ṣedheq of Jerusalem was likewise associated with the sun, and that even in biblical religion this association did not die out (note the expression *šemeš ṣᵉdhāqâ,* "sun of righteousness," in Mal. 4:2). The association of Ṣedheq with Canaanite Jerusalem is demonstrated by the royal names Melchizedek ("My King is Ṣedheq," Gen. 14:18) and Adonizedek ("My Lord is Ṣedheq," Josh. 10:1). The name of Zadok, whom Solomon appointed as his chief priest (I Kings 2:35), is linked to the cult of Ṣedheq. The displacement of the old priesthood of Yahweh by the line of Ṣadhoq no doubt resulted in the merging of some of the indigenous cultic traditions of Jerusalem into Yahwism. The persistence into Judean times of the influence of Ṣedheq is shown by Isaiah's reference to Jerusalem as "the city of Ṣedheq" (Isa. 1:26; cf. vs. 21), and Jeremiah's description of the city as "the habitation of Ṣedheq" (31:23).

Deutero-Isaiah uses Ṣedheq as a synonym for Yahweh (Isa. 51:1; 61:3). It is likely that, even before the Babylonian exile, Ṣedheq had come to be regarded as a hypostasis of Yahweh, a divine entity in its own right but basically a manifestation or personification of a quality or component part of the superior divinity. Ṣedheq seems to have been venerated as the "right hand" of Yahweh (Isa. 41:10; cf. Ps. 48:10 [H 11]). Ṣedheq as attendant upon Yahweh is also known: Ps. 85:13 [H 14] states that Ṣedheq "will go before him, and make his footsteps a way," while 85:11 relates that Ṣedheq "will look down from the sky." Ṣedheq as a heavenly being appears in the Dead Sea Scrolls (1QM, col. 17, lines 6-8: "Ṣedheq will rejoice in the heavenly heights"), and in the Jewish mystical tradition Ṣedheq becomes a term for the Shekinah, the feminine aspect of Deity that executes judgment.

The idea of Ṣedheq as the right hand of Yahweh caused him to be linked to the figure of the Messiah, the King who sits at Yahweh's right hand. He is called the *ṣemaḥ ṣedheq* or *ṣemaḥ ṣᵉdhāqâ* ("the Shoot of Ṣedheq"; cf. Jer. 23:5). The Priestly Messiah is called the *môrê ṣedheq* ("the Teacher," or "Rain, of Sedeq"). Behind these titles is the ancient concept that the king embodies the principle of cosmic order, and will vindicate the innocent and punish the guilty.

Because Ṣedheq is the personification of divine justice, the name is applied to the planet Jupiter (T.B. Shab. 156a, b; 'Er. 56a, b). In late Babylonian times, the god Marduk, associated with the sun and the planet Jupiter, was the patron of justice. Hence Jewish astrology, derived from Babylonian traditions, calls the planet Jupiter "Ṣedheq," and the "star of the Messiah."

Bibliography. M. C. Astour, "Some New Divine Names from Ugarit," *JAOS,* LXXXVI (1966), 282-83; P. Clemen, *Die Phoenikische Religion nach Philo von Byblos* (1939); R. A. Rosenberg, "The God Ṣedeq," *HUCA,* XXXVI (1965), 161-77, "Who Is the Moreh hasṢedeq?" *JAAR,* XXXVI (1968), 118-22, review of H. H. Schmid, *Gerechtigkeit als Weltordnung,* in *Biblica,* L (1969), 565-68.

R. A. Rosenberg

***SELA (OF EDOM).** The biblical and postbiblical evidence favors an identification with es-Sela', 2½ miles NW of Bozrah (Buseira). The identification with Petra dates back to the LXX (e.g., II Kings 14:7; Obad. 3; cf. also Judg. 1:36), which influenced Eusebius (Euseb. Onom. 142:7-8; 144:7-9). Eusebius also admits that the Syrians called Petra "Rekem." Josephus knows only Rekeme (Jos. Antiq. IV.vii.1); corrupt variant Arkē (Jos Antiq. IV.iv.7; cf. Euseb. Onom. 36:13-14, who gives Arkem), which he derives from Rekem, the name of a Midianite ruler (Num. 31:8; Josh. 13:21). Rabbinic literature knows it by the name Rᵉqām dᵉḥagrâ (Targ. Gen. 14:7; 20:1, etc.), "Rekam of the Hagra (=Limes)," or Rᵉqam Gê'â, "Rekam of Geia" (Targ. Num. 34:4, etc.) but also reflects the belief that the place was identical with Kadesh-Barnea. The Nabateans themselves called Petra by the name Raqmu (written *rqmw*) as demonstrated conclusively by a new memorial inscription found near the mouth of the Wadi Musa.

Bibliography. R. Hartmann, "Die Namen von Petra," *ZAW,* XXX (1910), 143-51; J. Starcky, "Nouvelle épitaphe nabatéenne donnant le nom sémitique de Pétra," *RB,* LXXII (1965), 95-97, "Nouvelles steles funeraires à Pétra," *Annual of the Department of Antiquities of Jordan,* X (1965), 44-47, and "Pétra et la Nabatène," *Supplément au Dictionnaire de la Bible,* VII (1966), cols. 886-900; B. Mazar, "Sela'," *Encyclopaedia Biblica* (Hebrew), V (1968), cols. 1050-51.

A. F. Rainey

SEMANTICS. The study of the ways in which linguistic messages, both oral (utterances) and written (texts), convey meanings from their sources (speakers or writers) to their receptors (hearers or readers). It is part of the larger study of semiotics, which is concerned with the functioning of all signaling and symbolic systems, whether human, animal, or mechanical. More specifically, semantics deals with those aspects of meaning which derive from the internal structure of language, and leaves to other disciplines (history, anthropology, psychology, etc.) the task of discovering the way in which pragmatic, extralinguistic factors contribute to the total meaning of a message.

Semantics in this sense is a recent phenomenon, though speculation on language and meaning is very ancient. The Hebrews thought of words as creative, dynamic forces, bringing into being their referents and constituting an essential part of their being. Plato believed that the relationship of "names" to their referents was natural, intrinsic, and necessary. Such a view, of course, could arise only in a totally monolingual universe of thought. One of the earliest empirical observations arising from the diversity of human languages was that, apart from a tiny part of any language's vocabulary, the relationship between form and meaning is purely arbitrary and conventional. This is a crucial property of language, which contributes greatly to its flexibility and open-endedness. Later both sophists and rhetoricians made useful studies of stylistic devices and their impact. Thinkers in the Middle Ages, the Renaissance, and the Enlightenment, though they gave much thought to language, did not advance semantics.

Progress was impossible, in fact, until a clear distinction was made between *reference* (the use of a word to refer to something) and *denotation* (the abstract representation of the "meaning" of a word). Reference, like mental image, is highly specific, concrete, and idiosyncratic; it is not accessible to systematic study in linguistic terms. Denotation, on the other hand, is related to concept: it is abstract, general, and common to all speakers of a language. When I refer to a specific house, or when I conjure up a mental image of a house, it is highly particularized. But the denotation of *house* (in its ordinary sense) is "building used for human habitation." This precisely defines the domain of all particular houses; it specifies what an object must be in order to be a house, and how we can recognize a house when we see one, but it ignores all the details that distinguish one house from another. Denotation is thus quite accessible to rigorous linguistic analysis; we can work at specifying as parsimoniously as possible the necessary and sufficient conceptual conditions for the appropriate use of a word.

1. Semantics and etymology. In the nineteenth century, progress was made as historical and comparative linguistics began to provide for the first time reliable reconstructions of the development through time of linguistic *forms,* so that studies of the development through time of their *meanings* could be based on a solid foundation. Scholars were able to trace with considerable accuracy a number of conceptual paths which the senses of words tend to follow throughout their history. This finally put etymology on a more scientific basis.

a. Etymology and exegesis. The result of historical-semantic studies for biblical studies (and for the exegesis of texts in general) is largely negative. It underlines certain empirical facts about language. (1) Semantic change is a universal process, so that virtually all words in all languages change their meanings through time. (2) Though it is possible in retrospect to describe the semantic evolution of words, it is not possible to predict or to control this evolution. (3) Because languages evolve continuously, it is impossible to fix a "time of origin" for a given language or for its vocabulary, except in the relatively rare case of words for whose origin we have documentation; thus, the notion of an "original" meaning is a chimera. (4) Therefore, what a word meant at some past moment, even the moment when it first entered the language, is not determinative of its meaning at a later moment; resemblance between earlier and later meanings of words is a matter to be empirically discovered, not assumed at the outset. (5) Therefore again, it is not legitimate to say that the "original" meaning of a word is its "real" meaning; the "real" meaning of a word must be inferred from its usage in messages of a contemporary period.

It is clear that this negative finding is of importance for biblical studies, since some scholars still work today as if "original" meanings of Greek and Hebrew words have a privileged position in exegesis. But given the above facts, this is an illusion.

b. The use of cognates. Though far less work has been done on shifts of meaning which occur when words pass from one language to another (loanwords) or on the independent evolution of cognate words in related languages, enough has been done to show that the comparison of cognates is also a highly erratic and unreliable guide to meaning. It can be used only with great caution; where it is not possible, as with a *hapax,* to control the results by reference to contemporary texts in the same language, it must be admitted that reconstructions are purely speculative. No service is rendered to responsible exegesis by exaggerating the reliability of available evidence.

2. Synchronic semantic analysis. In this century, semantics is for most scholars a synchronic study of how linguistic messages convey meanings. Contributions to this study come from linguistics, cultural anthropology, information theory, formal logic, and linguistic philosophy. Differences in focus and terminology will be minimized in this article by taking linguistics as the basic approach.

a. Words with several meanings. It has become evident that each word in every language typically has not one but several meanings or senses. This insight is a real advance over the naïve earlier view that each word had "a" meaning, but that "the" meaning of some words was very broad and required multiple or complex definitions. At first, efforts continued to be made to preserve a sense of unity among these several meanings by discovering a core or common meaning of which specific senses were extensions. But, though conceptual links can in fact often be established between such senses, it has become increasingly evident that not all senses of a given form could be so related; today, the emphasis is on the discreteness of senses. It is this fact that gives point to critiques in recent decades of that approach to biblical lexicography that sees all of the "wealth of meaning" of certain important words in each of their occurrences. It seems to be a fact of the way people use language that in all but exceptional cases (puns and poetry, for instance), any word has in each of its occurrences one and only one of its several discrete senses.

i. *Polysemy and concordant (literal) translation.* It is the fact that words have several senses that makes concordant translation such a futile exercise, not only because it results in highly bizarre usage in the receptor language, but also because it cannot achieve fidelity to the original. This approach is based on two erroneous assumptions: that each word has *a* meaning, and that *the* meaning of a word has a single precise equivalent meaning in *a* word of the receptor language.

ii. *Polysemy and homonymy.* Attempts have been made to differentiate between polysemy (multiple meanings of the "same" word) and homonymy (meanings of "different" words accidentally sharing the same form). The usual understanding of what makes different specimens of a form the "same" word or "different" words is based on history: thus, *corn*$_1$, "grain," and *corn*$_2$, "specific types of grain: maize" are the "same" because they are etymologically related, whereas *corn*$_3$, "horny node on the toe" is a homonym because it is etymologically unrelated. But these attempts are futile, because historical approaches are not adequate to the task of determining contemporary meanings. On the one hand, people in general are ignorant of the history of their language, so all they can relate are contemporary concepts; on the other hand, it turns out that the different senses of a polysemous form can be just as different as the senses of homonyms, while the senses of homonyms can converge under a popular impression that they are related. Thus, for the understanding of messages, the distinction between polysemous words and homonyms becomes moot.

iii. *Functional value of discreteness.* It is important for purely functional reasons that the senses of a form (whether polysemous or homonymous) be sufficiently different to avoid ambiguity in communication. If senses were conceptually very close, communication would break down in a confusion of misunderstood messages. To use an analogy, there are a number of towns in the United States called Dayton, but they are unambiguously distinguished by being in different states; if there were two Daytons five miles apart, confusion would be total.

iv. *The use of context.* The mechanisms used by receptors to select the right sense for each word all involve the use of context at a number of levels. There is first the immediate *linguistic* context within the message itself. This involves both grammar (as when a verb has different senses when it is transitive and intransitive, or when a preposition has different senses when followed by different cases) and lexical context (as when *hand* has different meanings in "hand of bananas," "hand of bridge," and "minute hand"). A given sense is either compatible or incompatible with the context. Second, there is, in the case of extended messages and corpuses of messages from the same source, a broader context, in which we must consider the *usage* of the source; here we can assume a high degree of consistency within analogous linguistic contexts (though this must not be allowed to lead to concordant exegesis). Third, there is the specific *situational* context in which the message is formulated and understood. Thus, the sentence "He watered the stock" has different meanings when used on a ranch, in a corporation board room, and in a kitchen. Finally, there is the broader situational context of place, historical period, society, language, and culture. From the last three types of context, one can often infer information about the source's attitudes, beliefs, and intentions, and about the relationships between him and his receptors. In actual communication, all types of context are used simultaneously by receptors to understand messages and to select for each form one meaning only. In other words, true ambiguity (as distinguished from vagueness) is rare. When it does occur, it results either from failure of the source to specify context sufficiently, or from failure of the receptor to operate in the same context as the source. But even here, the subjective experience of ambiguity (in which the receptor consciously is led to ask "Do you mean A or B?") is infrequent; more often, a receptor will clearly understand a single meaning, but one different from the intended one.

In terms of information theory, the sense to be selected is the one which is most predictable from context; or, to put it another way, the one which adds least information to the context. Thus, in "He threw the ball to his sister," one understands *ball* as "spherical toy," not "dance," because "dance" would introduce too much extraneous information, whereas "spherical toy" is just what one would expect a boy to throw to his sister.

The implications of this for exegesis are clear:

to understand a word in a passage, one determines first what are its potential senses; then one uses all available contextual clues to select the one that fits the context. All others are irrelevant.

v. *Exceptions.* Exceptions to this rule do occur, especially in puns and poetry, where for special reasons people intentionally exploit two or more meanings of a form. But such cases are striking precisely because they are scarce; and they are almost invariably marked in some way by context as intentional ambiguities.

In the case of ancient documents, we do encounter irreduceable ambiguities. But from what we know of the way people use language, it is sounder to assume that the ambiguity results from our ignorance of some part of the original context than from the intention of the authors.

vi. *Central and peripheral senses.* Attempts are sometimes made to distinguish between "central" and "peripheral" (or "extended" or "secondary") senses. This contrast suggests that among the senses of a form, there is one that may in some sense be most important. This is true in some cases, but not always. Nor has the contrast always been understood in the same way. We have already seen that the "etymological" meaning cannot be taken to be "central," since not all etymological meanings are even in current use. Others have understood "central" as meaning the sense from which it is easiest to trace the others by a chain of conceptual links; but it is not always possible to find such links. Probably the best use of this concept is to define as "central" the sense which is least marked; that is, the sense which is spontaneously thought of when the word is given without any context. Thus, "table" for most native speakers of English evokes the notion of a piece of furniture with a flat top; contexts must be added to lead hearers to the other senses. Once again, the effort to show how senses may be derived from each other may be interesting, but it is of no help in understanding messages.

vii. *Literal and figurative meanings.* The trouble with the distinction between literal and figurative senses is that it is easier to discern intuitively that we are dealing with a figure than to specify what makes it a figure. The ancient rhetoricians provided an analysis of types of figures, whether based on association of ideas (metonyms, synecdoches) or on similarities (similes, metaphors), which has scarcely been improved on in our day. The difficulty is that many extended meanings which are not today perceived as figures clearly originated as figures. They have apparently lost their freshness and hence their impact, and are felt as extended "literal" senses rather than as figures. It may be the case that a sense remains figurative as long as people still think actively of the primary sense on which the figure is based, but loses its figurative quality when it becomes so mundane as to stand on its own. It has also been pointed out that many figures are based on supplementary components of meaning, that is, components not central to the primary meaning of a word. But this is equally true of many "dead" figures, and is by no means true of all still live figures.

One thing is clear, however; when we are dealing with a dead figure, appeal to the literal sense is not helpful to understanding messages. With figurative as with other senses, either a sense is present or it is not. If the literal sense is not the one intended in a given passage, then it is simply not present. Mention of it only confuses the issue of understanding. A good example is provided by Greek σάρξ, of which the unmarked sense was "soft tissue of a living thing." In this sense, and in no other, the English equivalent is "flesh," which has the same unmarked meaning. But when σάρξ is used to mean "race" (Rom. 9:2), or when it means "human nature" (Rom. 8:3), it should not be translated "flesh," nor should a note giving the "literal" meaning be appended, since it would only confuse the ordinary reader.

To summarize: if the senses of a single form are so different as to be readily distinguished by use of the context, then the resolution of ambiguity is not the central problem of semantics, especially insofar as semantics aims to help a reader understand a text.

b. Related senses of different forms. A far more important issue is the study of closely related senses of different forms, since these are in fact often quite close, and thus do give rise in the mind of the source to choice, and in the mind of the receptor to understanding the reason for the choice. It must be said here that we are concerned with sets of similar senses, not similar words; we can deal with only one sense per form, since the other senses by definition do not belong to the same set (recall the different Daytons in different states). Thus, *chair, stool,* and *bench* all have senses specifiable as "manufactured object used for sitting," and these senses constitute, along with a number of others, a set which is so defined. But each of these words also has senses which do not belong to this set: *chair* as "faculty position," *stool* as "feces," *bench* as "judiciary," etc.

Types of conceptual relationships between the senses of such a set include synonymy and similarity (overlap), inclusion (including the multilayered inclusion called taxonomy), antonymy, and polarity.

i. *Synonymy and similarity.* Synonymy and similarity are discussed together because there is no sharp cut-off point between them. Synonymy is no more than a high degree of similarity, such that certain terms can substitute for each other in certain contexts with no change in meaning. The more different contexts a pair of terms can be used in interchangeably, the more nearly they are synonymous; but absolute synonymy, which would involve interchangeability in all contexts, seems not to exist. A more rigorous approach to the specification of degrees of similarity of meaning is to analyze senses in terms of semantic components. That is, by decomposing senses into more elementary concepts, one can see which components are shared by a pair of senses and which distinguish them. For example, let us analyze the unmarked sense of *nail, screw,* and *bolt.* The components they all share, and which make them a set, are "metal fastener" and "head wider than shaft." The components which distinguish them can best be shown in a matrix:

	nail	*screw*	*bolt*
shaft shape:	straight	tapered	straight
shaft surface:	smooth	threaded	threaded
tip:	pointed	pointed	blunt
grips by:	friction in hole	threads in hole	threads in nut

It will be noted that there is a certain amount of redundancy here, in that more components are specified than are absolutely necessary. This is often the case in ordinary language; it gives rise to a range of possible definitions of the necessary and sufficient sort.

To take a biblical example, various views have been held of the relationship between the meanings of ἀγαπάω and φιλέω in contexts where both subject and object are persons (either human or divine). In such contexts, in which both verbs appear often, they both have components of affection, concern, appreciation, and so on; in other words, in the context God/human——God/human, they are almost synonymous. Closer examination shows in addition that φιλέω is always used of a love which is based on a pre-existing relationship and is motivated by that relationship; ἀγαπάω is not so specified. But because ἀγαπάω is a more general term which need not be motivated by an existing relationship, it is uniquely appropriate to express the love of God for sinners who are still alienated from him. It is only after such sinners have been justified that φιλέω can be used of God's love for them. In other words, wherever an existing relationship is involved, either verb can be used, as in John 21:15-17, with no difference in meaning. But where a relationship is absent, only ἀγαπάω can be used.

ii. *Inclusion.* Consideration of ἀγαπάω and φιλέω leads naturally to the relationship of inclusion. In this relationship, one sense completely includes the other. Another way of saying the same thing is to say that one sense is more specific, the other more generic. The more generic senses are defined by the fewest components, while more specific senses require more components to define their greater specificity. Incidentally, this relationship *may* obtain between different senses of a single form as well as between senses of different forms. Often, a single generic sense includes a set of more specific senses, which share all of the generic components but which are distinguished by their specific components. In such cases, we have a taxonomy. For instance, under the term "bolt" mentioned above, one may distinguish stove bolts, carriage bolts, machine bolts, and so on. Similarly, the unmarked sense of "walk" can be made more specific in the senses of "stroll," "march," "shuffle," and so forth. In general, it is possible to substitute a generic sense for a specific one (with loss of the components of specificity); but it is not possible to substitute a specific sense for a generic one in any context where the specific components would be inappropriate (see the discussion of ἀγαπάω and φιλέω above).

As an illustration of inclusion between senses of the same term, we may use *animal,* which in ordinary language has at least three senses: *animal*$_1$, the most generic, in contrast with vegetable and mineral; *animal*$_2$, one type of *animal*$_1$, in contrast with man, which is another type of *animal*$_1$; *animal*$_3$ (roughly synonymous with scientific *mammal*), a type of *animal*$_2$, in contrast with other types of *animal*$_2$, such as birds, fish, and so forth. It will be noted that ordinary language taxonomies, in contrast with scientific ones which elaborate and correct them, have fewer levels, and display at times gaps, overlappings, and ambiguities.

iii. *Antonymy.* Antonymy exists between senses of two terms when they share all components except one, for which they have opposite values. For example, *mother* and *father* share the components "kin," "lineal," and "first ascending generation," but are opposites on the sex component. *Father* and *son* share "kin," "lineal," and "male," but are opposite on the generation component.

iv. *Polar oppositions.* Polar opposites can be viewed as a special case of antonymy, in which the set comprises only two senses, there is only one crucial component to define the set, and the two senses have opposite values on the one component. Thus, *good* and *bad* are the only terms in their set, which is defined by the component "general evaluation"; they are respectively at the positive and negative poles on that dimension. The fact that such senses occur only in pairs can be illustrated by the pairs *big–little, large–small*: though the first terms of each pair are synonymous, and also the second terms of each pair, they do not interchange in the polar relationship.

3. Structural meanings. So far we have been considering the meanings of terms and sets of terms. But words do not convey meaning in isolation; they are normally constituent parts of phrases, clauses, sentences, and whole messages, and the ways in which these are constructed are as important as the words in carrying meaning.

The rules which control these constructions are highly complex and variable. They include the rules of syntax (which for the most part operate within sentence boundaries), rules for the smooth flow of information, rules for connecting up successive references to the same bit of reality throughout a whole message, rules of transition, and so on. Once again, as with individual words, there is no simple one-to-one relationship between a feature of structure and a feature of meaning; the links are in fact extremely complex and subtle.

To illustrate the importance of such structural meaning, it suffices to note the very different meanings of "Bill hit Jim" and "Jim hit Bill," and of "Bill went for a walk after eating" and "After he went for a walk, Bill ate."

a. Surface structure and deep structure. It is tempting to think of syntactic structure as conveying meaning directly. Thus, grammarians long defined the syntactic relation "subject of the verb" as if it were synonymous with the semantic relation "actor of the event." A quick glance at the realities, however, dispels such a notion; in "Jim was hit by Bill," *Jim* is the subject, and *Bill* a kind of complement; but the semantic relations are identical with those in "Bill hit Jim." Of course, what signals the difference is the use of a different verbal form, the passive. But consider the set of sentences

(1) "Bill broke the window with a stone"; (2) "The stone broke the window"; (3) "The window broke." In the first instance, with all the roles (actor, victim, instrument) explicit, the actor is indeed the subject. But in the second sentence, making *stone* the subject hardly makes it an actor in the semantic sense: it cannot have intentions and self-propulsion, but must be moved by someone (here left implicit). In the third sentence, it would be absurd to consider *window* an actor. In these cases, the inherent meanings of the words override the apparent significance of the syntactic relation, and no one is fooled into visualizing either a stone or a window as taking an active role in the active verb *broke*. In other words, there are wide discrepancies between the surface appearances and the deep meaning; linguists formalize these discrepancies by talking about surface structure and deep structure. Though many linguists still consider the deep structure to be a part of the syntax, a growing number consider it more economical and intuitively more correct to see it as being strictly semantic.

b. Parts of speech and semantic categories. Besides the differences between deep (semantic) structure roles (actor, victim, etc.) and the surface structure syntactic functions (subject, object, etc.), there is in all languages another important type of discrepancy: that between grammatical parts of speech and the semantic nature of the denotata. Traditional grammar ignored this kind of discrepancy also, defining the parts of speech in semantic terms. Nouns, for instance, were often defined as names of persons, places, and things. Nouns which did not fit this definition (*freedom, redness, redemption,* etc.) were lumped in a residual category called "abstract nouns." Once linguists began to see the differences between deep and surface structures, however, a number of them applied this difference to individual terms. They then defined the parts of speech strictly in terms of their potential syntactic functions, and applied semantic definitions to strictly semantic categories of units. Thus, nouns are words which can be potentially subjects and objects of verbs, among other things. It is *objects* (O's—in some recent work called entities) which are persons, animals, inanimate things, etc. Similarly, verb is a strictly syntactic term, while *events* (E's) are defined semantically as actions, processes, etc. This is very useful, as it permits us to recognize as syntactic verbs units which have nothing to do with actions (*be, have*), and which in traditional grammar constituted just as awkward a residual class as abstract nouns. Now it becomes possible to notice that a number of the old abstract nouns (*redemption, baptism, sin,* etc.) are in fact semantically events (many of them in fact derived from verbs) which are syntactically nouns in order to permit the construction of various types of complex surface structures. A third category of semantic units are the *abstracts* (A's—concepts of quality or quantity abstracted from the objects and events in which they inhere). Most of the "abstract nouns" of traditional grammar which are not events are semantically abstracts (*free-dom, red-ness,* etc.). Indo-European languages typically have parts of speech called adjectives and adverbs which often express these abstracts; they do not in the least change their semantic nature when they are nominalized.

One of the side benefits of the important insight into the difference between nouns, verbs, adjectives, and so forth on the one hand, and the O, E, and A categories on the other, is that we can be liberated from the danger of reifying units which happen to be expressed by "abstract nouns." We can discern, under their superficial noun-ness, their deep nature as E's or A's.

A second bonus, especially precious in translation, is that the translator is liberated from the burden of finding nouns to translate nouns, verbs for verbs, and so on. He recognizes that while the O, E, and A categories are universal, the parts of speech each language makes available for their surface expression are highly variable, both in number and in their specific potential for encoding the categories. Thus, the translator who works in a language where "abstract nouns" do not exist, or are stylistically awkward, is perfectly free to translate a Greek abstract noun by the appropriate verb or other part of speech in another language.

c. Semantic relations. The O's, E's, and A's do not occur in isolation, any more than nouns and verbs do in surface structure; they are linked by a great number of semantic *relations* (R's). A number of relations may link objects and events (actor, victim, product, beneficiary, instrument, etc.); these can be usefully labeled roles (some linguists call them cases, but this is too easily confused with a surface phenomenon of the same name). There are also R's that express relations between two O's (location, part-whole, possession, kinship, etc.). Finally, there are R's that obtain between two or more E's (time R's, such as simultaneous and sequential; logical R's such as cause-effect, conditions, and many others). The surface devices used by different languages to encode the different types of R's are extremely varied: word order, affixes, particles, other lexical devices, and many others. The lack of the same device in a receptor language as is found in a source language need not discourage the translator: he needs first to discover exactly what kind of R he is dealing with, and then to find what device the receptor language uses to encode that kind of R.

The same kinds of R's which obtain within clauses and sentences can often structure (in part) whole messages; that is, they can relate not only single units but large clusters of units in a successive hierarchy of units all the way up to the whole message.

d. Transformations. Though the relationships between deep and surface structures are complex, they are not chaotic. Linguists call the rules which formalize the links from deep structure to surface structure (and which can be understood as directions for making appropriate surface structures to match deep structures) *transformations*. Typical transformations which are used in English include the passive transformation: "Bill hit Jim" → "Jim was hit by Bill"; various kinds of highlighting transformations, e.g., "It was Bill who hit Jim";

nominalizations that permit embedding one construction in another, e.g., "Bill's hitting Jim," "The fact that Bill hit Jim," and so on.

Two facts must be pointed out concerning transformations. The first is that any two languages, even if they are closely related, need not have exactly the same kinds of transformations, in terms of surface structure effects. For example, many languages lack a passive transformation. The second is that even when two languages have the "same" transformation, it by no means follows that it is used in the same way, either semantically or stylistically. Thus, English, French, Koine Greek, and Modern Arabic all have passives; but no two of them use passives in the same way. It is thus an error to translate automatically; one must determine the significance of the form in the source text, and translate that.

e. Kernels. One way of thinking of deep structures is to visualize them in terms of very simple, very explicit, elementary sentence-types called kernels. English, for instance, has about eight basic kernel types: "John ran"; "John hit Bill"; "John gave Bill an orange"; "John is sick"; "John is in the house"; "John is a boy"; "John is the boy"; and "John has a hat." It will be noted that each encodes in the form of a predication one set of relations between units: three are R's between O's and E's, three are R's between O's (location, identity, "possession"), one is descriptive, and one is classificatory. By the application of various transformations, alone or in combination, all the multitude of surface structures of English can be generated from these types of kernels.

A highly significant fact, especially for translation, is that languages which differ in all possible dimensions when it comes to surface structure are relatively similar when it comes to kernels. The implication for translation is that if one can discover in the source text the kernels underlying the surface structure, one is in a much better position to translate both accurately and idiomatically.

4. Connotation. Messages by no means convey only conceptual information; they also typically convey information about the feelings and the attitudes of the source, and the feelings and attitudes that person wants to evoke in the receptors of the message. This is connotation (some call it emotive meaning). Though approaches to the study of connotation remain almost as impressionistic as their subject matter, it seems to be the case that sources convey connotations by their selection of linguistic forms (words, idioms, styles of speech, etc.) which conventionally bear for native speakers of a language a positive or negative emotive content.

Some forms are so strongly charged that they are taboo: people avoid using forms which refer to things they are very much afraid of, or which disgust them, and they develop veiled ways of referring to them (euphemisms). Other forms, while not so potent as to be taboo, give rise to strong feelings, which may run the whole gamut of human emotions.

In addition to the inherent feelings people have about the referents of terms, connotations may arise from associations with the people who typically use a given form (as when we identify people we admire or despise by their speech), the circumstances in which they are typically used, and the kinds of messages in which they are usually found.

5. Explicit and implicit information. Normally messages are used in communication between persons who share some common background of belief, knowledge, attitude, and so on; in such cases, it is rarely necessary or even desirable for the source to spell out explicitly all that she or he intends the receptor to understand by the message. He selects some of the information he wants to convey and makes it explicit; other information he will leave implicit, trusting the receptor to supply it to complete the message. What must be emphasized is that implicit information is not the same as omitted information: it is information which is crucial to a right understanding of the message, but which is not explicit because the source knows that the receptor already knows it. The difference becomes clear when a second receptor, not privy to the information shared by source and first receptor, tries to understand the message: he will often be puzzled and will fail to understand or will misunderstand, simply because he cannot supply the implicit information.

The significance of this is that in translation it is under certain circumstances legitimate and necessary to make explicit for a second receptor information which was clearly available to the original receptor and without which the message is actually mutilated. The constraints under which the translator must work here are: (1) that the information is truly implicit, not omitted; (2) that it is necessary for understanding; and (3) that it is not so bulky as to distend the message. Implicit information which fails to meet criterion (3) can be supplied in footnotes or in a glossary.

6. Implications for exegesis and translation. We have already mentioned a number of implications of this view of semantics for exegesis and translation, so that we can briefly summarize. First, a careful semantic analysis of a text will include the following steps: (1) analysis of the deep structure, in terms of the kernels underlying the surface structure and the semantic nature of the units (O's, E's, A's, R's) with notation of the significance of the transformations used in the original; (2) componential analysis of the senses of terms; and (3) analysis of connotations. Though this is no guarantee of sound exegesis, it is a powerful tool which will help in eliminating some superficially plausible interpretations and in forcing the exegete to face up to all the linguistic evidence.

With respect to translation, this view has led to a theory which reconciles the otherwise irreconcilable aims of translation: idiomaticity and faithfulness. Translation is broken down into three steps: (1) analysis, which corresponds to the thorough exegesis mentioned above; (2) transfer, at the level of kernels and components, into the receptor language; and (3) restructuring, through which the raw materials are made into an appropriate surface structure in the receptor language. In other words, this theory leads to a dynamic equivalent translation, one that conveys to its receptors the same total meaning and impact as the original text did to its receptors.

Bibliography. W. L. Chafe, *Meaning and the Structure of Language* (1970); the following works by E. A. Nida: *Toward a Science of Translating* (1964); *Componential Analysis of Meaning* (1974); and *Exploring Semantic Structures* (1975); E. A. Nida and C. R. Taber, *Theory and Practice of Translation* (1969); and the following articles by C. R. Taber: "The Identification of Participants in a Narrative," *The Bible Translator,* XX (1969), 93-98; "Exegesis and Linguistics," *The Bible Translator,* XX (1969), 150-53; "Explicit and Implicit Information in Translation," *The Bible Translator,* XXI (1970), 1-9.

C. R. TABER

***SEPHARAD.** A country of Israelite exile, mentioned in a very corrupt passage, Obad. 20, which should be emended thus: "The exiles who are in Halah and Gozan shall possess the land of the Canaanites as far as Zarephath; and the exiles who are in Sepharad shall possess the cities of the Negeb." Sepharad is usually identified with Sardis in Lydia (*see* SEPHARAD), but the historical and geographical context of the prophecy makes it much more probable that it corresponds to Saparda, a territory in Media, conquered by Sargon II in 716 B.C. and turned into an Assyrian province, in which he settled prisoners from Ḫatti-lands (Syria-Palestine). *See also* SEPHARVAIM[S].

Bibliography. *DPaR* (1920), pp. 92-93; I. M. Diakonoff, *Istorija Midii* (1956), pp. 208-9, 212-13, 255-56, 260; S. Parpola, *Saparda* in *Neo-Assyrian Toponyms* (1970), for Assyrian occurrences.

M. C. ASTOUR

***SEPHARVAIM.** Hitherto suggested identifications are unacceptable: (1) the Babylonian city of Sippar has never been a political entity and had no king of its own; (2) the alleged URU*Ša-ba-ra-'-in,* conquered by Shalmaneser V in 722 according to the Babylonian Chronicle I:28, is to be read URU*Ša-ma-ra-'-in*=Samaria (cf. II Kings 17:3, 6); (3) Sibraim, according to its only mention (Ezek. 47:16), was located on the border between the territory of Damascus and that of Hamath and thus did not form a separate kingdom. One must look among the Assyrian conquests in the latter part of the eighth century for a state whose name would correspond to ספרוים. Since cases of graphic confusion between the letters ד, ר, and ו are attested in the OT, one should read ספרדים, the people of Sepharad=Saparda in Media, conquered by Sargon II in 716 and again, after a rebellion, in 714 (*see* SEPHARAD[S]). In Isa. 37:13 (=II Kings 19:13), מלך ספרוים is followed by הנע ועוה, but there are no traces of toponyms "Hena" and "Ivvah" anywhere in the Near East; they are due to a dittography in the original phrase איה מלך ספרדים הנעוה, "where is the perverse King of the Sapardians?" As for the people of Sepharvaim in the anti-Samaritan story II Kings 17:24-41, its author found the already misspelled Sepharvaim and Avvah (Ivvah), as well as Hamath, in the narrative of Hezekiah and Sennacherib, and utilized these names in his attempt to trace back the heathen antecedents of the Samaritans.

Bibliography. H. Tadmor, "The Campaigns of Sargon II. . . ," *JCS,* XII (1958), 40, reading *Ša-ma-ra-'-in;* H. H. Rowley, "The Samaritan Schism in Legend and History," in *Israel's Prophetic Heritage: Essays in Honor of James Muilenburg* (1962), pp. 208-9, 222, on the unhistorical character of II Kings 17.

M. C. ASTOUR

***SEPTUAGINT.**

A. Contribution to OT scholarship
- 1. The Hebrew (Aramaic) *Vorlage* of the LXX
  - *a.* General
  - *b.* Reconstructing the *Vorlage*
  - *c.* The character of the *Vorlage*
  - *d.* The LXX and textual criticism
  - *e.* The LXX and the Hebrew scrolls from Qumran
  - *f.* The LXX and literary criticism
- 2. Exegesis of the translators
  - *a.* Contextual exegesis
  - *b.* Tendentious exegesis
- 3. Linguistic knowledge of the translators
  - *a.* Exegetical traditions
  - *b.* Context
  - *c.* Etymology
  - *d.* Postbiblical Hebrew
  - *e.* Aramaic
  - *f.* Translation of the Pentateuch

Bibliography

B. Earliest Greek versions ("Old Greek")
- 1. Terminology, technology, and text
  - *a.* The term "Septuagint"
  - *b.* Ancient technology and modern OG study
  - *c.* Canon, order of contents
  - *d.* Textual complications
- 2. Working backward toward the earliest accessible stages
  - *a.* Grouping the witnesses by families
  - *b.* Identifying lost archetypes
  - *c.* Moving behind the archetypes, attested recensions, and unaligned witnesses
  - *d.* The earliest preserved OG materials
- 3. Reconstructing OG origins
  - *a.* Tradition, theory, and data
  - *b.* Sections of Scripture with a relatively narrow textual base
  - *c.* Sections with a problematical textual base
  - *d.* Classifying translation types and techniques
  - *e.* Synthesis of results
- 4. Influence of OG on later developments
  - *a.* On Greek vocabulary and syntax
  - *b.* Quotations/allusions drawn from OG

Bibliography

A. CONTRIBUTION TO OT SCHOLARSHIP. With the exception of the MT, the LXX is the most important source for the text of the Bible. Its "rival," the Hebrew scrolls from Qumran, important though they are, are fragmentary and of a special nature. In addition, the LXX can yield much information about the translators themselves: the translation techniques employed, the Greek language of their world (especially Egypt), and their cultural and intellectual settings.

1. The Hebrew (Aramaic) *Vorlage* of the LXX. ***a. General.*** At times the LXX reflects a Hebrew or Aramaic source (*Vorlage*) different from the MT. Ever since scholars began to recognize this possibility, there have been tendencies toward an extreme acceptance of the LXX, which resulted at times in a negative judgment on the value of the MT. On the other hand, there has also been a tendency to depreciate the LXX by those who viewed the majority of its deviations from the MT as merely results of the translators' techniques. Both trends were partly influenced by the religious prejudices of those accustomed to viewing either MT or the LXX as the sacred text of the synagogue or church.

A more adequate understanding of the LXX as a tool in OT criticism was advanced in the middle of the twentieth century by the finds at Qumran (*see* DEAD SEA SCROLLS; DEAD SEA SCROLLS[S]). Many of the scrolls contain variants reflected in the LXX (*see* §1*e below*). This enhanced the credibility of the LXX as a whole, although much discussion has continued with regard to matters of detail.

b. Reconstructing the Vorlage. Opinions differ among scholars regarding the reconstruction of the *Vorlage* of the LXX. Criteria have never been outlined systematically; however, aspects of the problem have been discussed especially by Margolis, Ziegler, Goshen-Gottstein, and Barr.

While the rules for reconstruction are in principle identical for all sections of the LXX, in practice they differ because of the translational character of each section. If a book has been rendered with relative consistency, i.e., if Hebrew words are usually reflected by the same Greek translation equivalents, the reconstruction of the Hebrew *Vorlage* is facilitated. But, if a book has been rendered freely, this reconstruction is far more difficult. Most of the books contained in the LXX lie somewhere between these two types. *See* §B3*d below*.

When the Greek text differs from the MT, one need not immediately assume that its *Vorlage* was different, for such "deviation" could have resulted from one of many translational factors, such as free translation, tendentious changes, harmonization with parallel passages, and inability to solve a linguistic difficulty in the Hebrew text. The deviation could also have resulted from error in the transmission of the Greek MSS. *See* TEXTUAL CRITICISM, OT[S].

If the deviation from the MT has not resulted from such translational factors, one might consider the possibility that the Greek is based on a *Vorlage* different from the MT. This can be reconstructed, with various degrees of probability, with the aid of various tools for study. (Foremost among these is Hatch and Redpath, *A Concordance to the Septuagint,* which lists MT equivalents of LXX Greek words.) For example, in Deut. 31:1 the LXX reads, συνετέλεσε Μωυσῆς λαλῶν (Moses finished speaking) for the MT, וילך משה וידבר (and Moses went and spoke). The concordance informs us that the verb συντελέω usually renders the Hebrew verb כלה. Since the LXX deviation cannot easily be attributed to any other factor, it seems likely that it reflects a variant ויכל from which the reading of the MT developed by metathesis (location exchange of consonants): ויכל→וילכ; the opposite assumption seems unlikely. The reconstructed variant is supported by a Hebrew fragment from Qumran, as well as by the similar clause in MT Deut. 32:45 (ויכל משה לדבר).

As a rule, the criteria for recovering possible Hebrew variants underlying the LXX are subjective. However, a few less subjective criteria may be recognized:

(1) If the proposed variant has developed from the MT (or vice versa) by confusion of similar-looking letters, and if the two Hebrew words are remote from one another in meaning, the assumption of a variant is well-based. E.g., in Jer. 23:9, שכור (drunken) is reflected in the LXX as שבור (συντετριμμένος, broken). *See also* the above-mentioned example from Deut. 31:1.

(2) Some reconstructions are supported by Hebrew evidence, direct or indirect. E.g., in Isa. 36:11 the Greek τῶν ἀνθρώπων reflects האנשים as opposed to the MT העם. That LXX is not an interpretation of MT is suggested by 1QIs[a], which reads האנשים. In I Sam. 2:20 the Greek reflects ישלם (ἀποτείσαι), as does 4QSam[a] (MT ישם). In I Sam. 2:17 both the LXX and 4QSam[a] lack MT האנשים.

(3) Hebraisms in LXX phrases which deviate from the MT make the assumption of a Hebrew variant probable; e.g., Jer. 38:33 [H 31:33], διδοὺς δώσω=נתן נתתי, as against נתתי in the MT; Jer. 49:19 [H 42:19], ידע תדעו in MT, but καὶ νῦν γνόντες γνώσεσθε=ועתה ידע תדעו in the LXX (cf. vs. 22).

Very few Greek words can be retroverted with certainty as Hebrew variants. In general one does not know whether the deviation resulted from a Hebrew variant or from, e.g., a free translation. Furthermore, even if the assumption of a variant seems a certainty, it may never have existed in reality: the translator may have misread the Hebrew text. An obvious error, for example, is found in I Sam. 21:7 [H 8], where the LXX calls Doeg ὁ Σύρος, reconstructed as הארמי (the Aramean) as against the MT האדמי (the Edomite), which is found elsewhere in the OT. It cannot be determined, however, whether the *Vorlage* of the Greek actually read הארמי, or whether the translator incorrectly read האדמי as הארמי. In either case it will be said that the LXX reflects a "variant," הארמי, although possibly such a reading never existed in an actual Hebrew text.

Since scholars differ in their approach to reconstructing the *Vorlage* of the LXX, deviations from the MT in the LXX may be retroverted by some scholars as Hebrew variants, while others may regard them as inner-Greek changes. Furthermore, once a deviating translation equivalent is recognized as a variant, the number of possible retroversions seems boundless. Many of them have been collected in the *Biblia Hebraica* (*BH*), edited by R. Kittel and P. Kahle. *BH* has rightly been criticized as containing too many uncautious reconstructions of Hebrew variants. However, some improvement may be detected in its fourth edition (*BHS*). Much more cautious are the reconstructions in the *Hebrew University Bible* (ed. M. Goshen-Gottstein), where every possibility of an inner-Greek change is carefully weighed against the assumption of an underlying Hebrew variant.

c. The character of the Vorlage. Because the Greek translation is believed to have been made in Egypt, its *Vorlage* has generally been described as "Egyptian." This position has been emphasized particularly by scholars who support a theory of "local texts." According to this theory, which originated with Albright and has been further developed by Cross, the textual witnesses of the OT may be divided into textual traditions which originated in either Palestine, Babylon, or Egypt. *See* TEXT, HEBREW, HISTORY OF[S].

While the theory of local texts cannot be sustained in its present rigid form, the LXX contains some evidence which could be understood in terms of its local background. E.g., the *Vorlage* of the LXX of Jeremiah, which differs recensionally from the MT (*see* §*f below*), could have survived only in comparative isolation from the MT.

Scholars often mention a close relationship between the LXX and the Samaritan Pentateuch. Indeed, of the six thousand differences between the MT and the Samar., some nineteen hundred are common to the LXX. However, most of the agreements are in minor points such as omissions/additions of *wāw,* and the real nature of their relationship has yet to be investigated. *See* SAMARITAN PENTATEUCH §§1*e*, 2*a*.

The relationship between the LXX and the Peshitta is also in need of reinvestigation (*see* SYRIAC VERSIONS[S]). Despite statements to the contrary, there are not many agreements between the two except for Isaiah and a few other books. In Isaiah, however, the Peshitta translator did not rely on the LXX, as has often been assumed, but rather the LXX is based upon the same exegetical traditions which appeared later in written form in the Peshitta and the Targum.

d. The LXX and textual criticism. Of all the ancient translations, the LXX reflects the largest number of significant variants. The importance of these assumed variants differs from book to book; e.g., many important variants are reflected in the LXX of I–II Samuel, whose Hebrew text has been poorly transmitted in several parts.

Once a variant reflected in the LXX has been isolated, it is the concern of textual criticism to decide between the MT and LXX readings. Such varying disciplines as the linguistics of biblical Hebrew, vocabulary and style of the unit or book under discussion, biblical exegesis, and literary criticism are useful criteria for decision. Decisions of this kind are necessarily subjective, more so than the decision as to whether or not a given Greek expression reflects a Hebrew variant. *See* TEXTUAL CRITICISM, OT[S].

For example, את-מה-משא in Jer. 23:33 is very difficult in its context; and אתם המשא, reflected in the LXX ὑμεῖς ἐστε τὸ λῆμμα, is preferable. For contextual reasons, too, in Gen. 49:19-20, עקבם: אשר of the LXX (κατὰ πόδας. Ασηρ . . .) must be preferred to MT עקב: מאשר. The MT text of Judg. 16:13 and I Sam. 14:41 cannot be well understood without restoring erroneously omitted words which are still preserved in the LXX. The vocalization of the MT in Jer. 23:17, לְמנאֲצַי דִּבֶּר יהוה (to those who despise me, the Lord has said), has to be corrected to לְמנאֲצֵי דְבַר יהוה (to those who despise the word of the Lord), as reflected in the LXX.

Especially noteworthy for their treatment of textual issues are the commentaries of G. A. Cooke on Joshua, J. Wellhausen and S. R. Driver on Samuel, G. A. Cooke and C. H. Cornill on Ezekiel, J. A. Montgomery on Kings and Daniel, and E. Dhorme on Job.

e. The LXX and the Hebrew scrolls from Qumran. Some of the Hebrew scrolls from Qumran often coincide with a textual tradition of the LXX. But no scroll has yet been found which coincides in most of its deviations from MT with a single Greek tradition, and no single Greek tradition agrees in most of its deviations from MT with a Hebrew scroll from Qumran.

Close relationships have been recognized between the LXX of Deuteronomy and 4QDeut (Skehan), of Samuel and 4QSam[a] and 4QSam[b] (Cross), and Jeremiah and 4QJer[b] (Cross). The agreements between the LXX of Isaiah and 1QIs[a] as pointed out by Ziegler are not especially significant.

Some scholars describe the relationship between the LXX and some of the above-mentioned Hebrew scrolls as if they belong to one textual family. However, the Hebrew and Greek sources both contain a large number of independent readings, and should therefore be regarded as related, but nevertheless independent, textual traditions.

Cross has drawn attention to the frequent agreement between 4QSam[a,b] and the "Lucianic" tradition in Samuel. According to him, this resulted from the fact that the substratum of the Lucianic tradition contained a revision of the Old Greek translation on the basis of a Hebrew text like 4QSam[a,b]. Barthélemy and Tov regard this substratum as the Old Greek translation of Samuel-Kings, now lost, which often agreed with 4QSam[a,b]. However, the precise relationship between 4QSam[a,b] and the textual traditions of the LXX can be determined only after the complete publication of the texts, when the agreements between the Hebrew and Greek traditions can be analyzed statistically.

f. The LXX and literary criticism. More than the other witnesses to the text of the OT, the LXX contributes to its literary criticism. The LXX of Jeremiah is a salient example. It has been suggested by Tov that the LXX reflects a first edition of the book which was expanded in all its literary layers into a second edition, now found in the MT. The differences between the two editions are visible in their respective lengths (the *Vorlage* of the LXX is one eighth shorter than the MT) and text arrangements (the most striking example is the different location of the prophecies against the foreign nations). The Hebrew tradition behind the LXX is now evidenced in 4QJer[b], both in the matter of length and in the arrangement of the text.

Contributions to literary criticism also come from the LXX's short version of I Sam. 17–18, its different arrangement of chapters in Proverbs and Psalms, from various differences (omissions, additions, and changes) between the MT and the LXX in Joshua, and from the chronological system of the LXX in I-II Kings. All these texts as well as additional ones were discussed by W. R. Smith.

The contribution of the LXX (as well as of other textual witnesses) to the field of Hebrew stylistics has been discussed by S. Talmon.

2. Exegesis of the translators. The LXX reflects both contextual and tendentious exegesis. Both are of interest to OT scholarship, but the latter is more relevant for identifying the nature of the translators and their settings.

a. Contextual exegesis. Contextual exegesis reveals itself especially in the choice of unusual translation equivalents, in the connections made between words, and in the adaptation of Hebrew to Greek diction (for example, when idiomatic Hebrew phrases are translated into Greek). E.g., Exod. 6:12, ערל שפתים (of uncircumcised lips), is translated by ἄλογος (speechless). Several deviating translations result from a translator's legitimate exegesis of certain words or phrases. E.g., Gen. 1:1, תהו ובהו, is rendered by ἀόρατος καὶ ἀκατασκεύαστος (invisible and shapeless); and in Isa. 9:14 [H 13], כפה ואגמון (RSV, palm branch and reed), is rendered by μέγαν καὶ μικρόν (great and small).

b. Tendentious exegesis. The LXX contains various types of exegesis not necessitated by the context but inserted extraneously by the translators. Apparently religious motivations, adherence to certain exegetical traditions, and didactic considerations allowed them to translate in a manner often similar to the Targumists (*see* Targums[S]). The following sections briefly discuss two types of such exegesis:

i. *Theological exegesis.* Theological exegesis may relate to the description of God and his acts, the Messiah, Zion, and the Exile, as well as various religious feelings. It may be expressed through theologically motivated choices of translation equivalents, as well as through additions or omissions of ideas considered offensive. Theological tendencies are apparent throughout the LXX, but they are more frequent in "free" translation sections such as the book of Isaiah. For example, the idea that God brings σωτήριον (salvation, referring particularly to salvation from the Exile) has often been inserted in the LXX. E.g., Isa. 38:11, "I shall not see the Lord, the Lord," has been rendered as, "I shall no more see at all the salvation of God"; 40:5, "[And the glory of the Lord shall be revealed], and all flesh shall see it together," has been rendered as "and all flesh shall see the salvation of God."

Other theological trends reveal themselves in the addition of religious color to secular descriptions, and in anti-anthropomorphic renditions.

ii. *Midrashic renderings.* Some of the freely translated books reflect midrashic elements (some of them are found in extant rabbinic sources) which, by their very nature, add to the plain meaning of Scripture. *See* Midrash; Midrash[S].

Several midrashic elements clarify the Pentateuchal laws. To Exod. 22:8 [H 7], "the owner of the house shall come near to God," the translator added, "and shall swear" (cf. T.B. B.Ḳ. 63b). מלאתך ודמעך, "your abundance and your juice," in Exod. 22:29 [H 28], has been exegetically rendered as "the first-fruits of your threshing floor and wine-press."

Other midrashic elements are of haggadic nature. Thus, "the tree" in Isa. 65:22 has been explained in the LXX as "the tree of life." In Isa. 1:13, קרא מקרא (the calling of the assembly) has been explained as ἡμέραν μεγάλην, i.e., "the great day," one of the appellations of the Day of Atonement in the Talmud. חרבות צרים (flint knives) in Josh. 5:2 has been translated by μαχαίρας πετρίνας ἐκ πέτρας ἀκροτόμου (stone knives of flinty rock); the second element of this doublet reflects a midrashic translation of the Hebrew phrase based upon Deut. 8:15, (מ)צור החלמיש, (ἐκ) πέτρας ἀκροτόμου, and similar phrases.

As a rule, the midrashic deviations of the LXX are not as extensive as those of the Palestinian Targs., but there are some exceptions. Thus the LXX translation of Proverbs is frequently more a Jewish-Hellenistic midrash than a Greek translation.

3. Linguistic knowledge of the translators. There is no concrete evidence that the translators possessed either dictionaries or word lists. Thus, when attempting to determine the meaning of a word, they resorted to various sources of information.

a. Exegetical traditions. The exegesis reflected in the LXX is often paralleled elsewhere. The translators must therefore have known several exegetical traditions. For example, in Exod. 12:13, 27, פסח has been rendered by σκεπάζειν (to pity), similar to the tradition found in rabbinic sources, Targ. Onkelos, and some Jewish grammarians.

In Gen. 33:19, Josh. 24:32, and Job 42:11, קשיטה (a unit of unknown value) has been rendered as "lamb" in the LXX, Targ. Onkelos, and the Vulg. In Genesis Rabbah it has been similarly explained.

b. Context. Translators frequently inferred the meaning of an unknown word from the context. Often this procedure was little more than guesswork, and the number of guesses of this kind is larger than is generally thought. This applies especially to rare or unique words. Thus the translator of Isaiah rendered the rare word נשף (twilight) three times according to its context, each time differently: 5:11, τὸ ὀψέ (late); 21:4, ψυχή (soul); 59:10, μεσονύκτιον (midnight). In the book of Jeremiah, four different verbs which were understandably difficult for the translator have been rendered by the general verb παρασκευάζω (to prepare): 6:4; 12:5; 46:9 [LXX 26:9]; 51:11 [LXX 28:11].

c. Etymology. Often the translators were guided by etymological considerations. Thus the word מועד in the phrase אהל מועד (tent of meeting) has always been rendered as μαρτύριον (witness) as if it were derived from עוד, rather than יעד; and ערבה (desert plain) has sometimes been rendered as if connected with מערב (west).

d. Postbiblical Hebrew. Most of the translators seem to have been well-acquainted with postbiblical Hebrew, more so than with biblical, and at times their translation equivalents are better understood against this background. For example, the word ארמון (palace, citadel), occurring frequently in the OT, is rare in later Hebrew. This may account for a variety of guess-translations in the LXX (house, city, land, cave, fundaments, tower, etc.).

At times the translators rendered a certain word according to its meaning in postbiblical Hebrew even though in the OT the word occurred in a different sense. Thus ונפצתי (and I will break), in Jer. 51:20-23 [LXX 28:20-23], has been rendered as καὶ διασκορπιῶ (and I will scatter) in accordance with the meaning of the verb in later Hebrew. *See* HEBREW LANGUAGE[S] §2*b*.

e. Aramaic. When the Greek translations were made, Aramaic was the lingua franca of many of the inhabitants of Egypt and Palestine. Within the LXX this becomes evident, e.g., from transliterations reflecting Aramaic rather than Hebrew forms of words: γιώρας (גיורא), representing OT גר; πασχα (פסחא) =OT פסח; μαννα (מנא) =OT מן.

At times the translators' knowledge of Aramaic misled them when the meaning of a Hebrew root differed from its Aramaic counterpart. E.g., in Pss. 60:8 [H 10; LXX 59:8] and 108:9 [H 10; LXX 107:9], סיר רחצי (my wash basin) has been rendered as λέβης τῆς ἐλπίδος μου (basin of my hope) according to the meaning of the root רחץ in Aramaic.

f. Translation of the Pentateuch. Translators of the later books were sometimes guided by that of the Pentateuch. Thus the word זועה/זעוה (terror) has been rendered in Jer. 34:17 [LXX 41:17] by διασπορά (diaspora) according to the LXX of Deut. 28:25. On four occasions in Jeremiah אהה (alas) has been translated by ὁ ὤν (he who is) following the LXX of Exod. 3:14 (אהיה אשר אהיה), ἐγώ εἰμι ὁ ὤν.

Bibliography. For the general problems discussed, *see* H. M. Orlinsky, "Current Progress and Problems in LXX Research," in *The Study of the Bible Today and Tomorrow*, ed. H. R. Willoughby (1947), pp. 144-61; P. Katz, "Septuagintal Studies in the Mid-Century," in *The Background of the NT and its Eschatology* (1964), pp. 176-208.

For §1*a-d*, *see* H. S. Nyberg, *Studien zum Hoseabuche* (1933); M. L. Margolis, "Complete Induction for the Identification of the Vocabulary in the Greek Versions of the OT," *JAOS*, XXX (1910), 301-12; J. Ziegler, *Untersuchungen zur Septuaginta des Buches Isaias*, III (1934); M. H. Goshen-Gottstein, "Theory and Practice of Textual Criticism—the Text-Critical Use of the LXX," *Textus*, III (1963), 130-58; J. Barr, *Comparative Philology and the Text of the OT* (1968).

For §1*c, e, see* the papers by F. M. Cross, D. Barthélemy, and E. Tov in *Septuagint and Cognate Studies*, II, ed. R. A. Kraft (1972), pp. 3-126.

For §1*e, see* H. M. Orlinsky, "Qumran and the Present State of OT Text Studies," *JBL*, LXXVIII (1959), 26-33; F. M. Cross, Jr., and S. Talmon, eds., *Qumran and the History of the Biblical Text* (1975); P. W. Skehan, VTSup, IV (1957), 148-60; J. Ziegler, "Die Vorlage der Isaias-Septuaginta," *JBL*, LXXVIII (1959), 34-59.

For §1*f*, see W. R. Smith, *The OT in the Jewish Church* (2nd ed., 1908), pp. 108 ff.; A. T. Olmstead, "Source Study and the Biblical Text," *AJSL*, XXX (1913), 1-35; E. Tov, "L'Incidence de la critique textuelle sur la critique littéraire dans le livre de Jérémie," *RB*, LXXIX (1972), 189-99, and the literature mentioned there; S. Talmon, "The Textual Study of the Bible—A New Outlook" in F. M. Cross and S. Talmon, *op. cit.*

For §§2 and 3, see the monographs on the various books of the LXX. On midrashic exegesis *see* L. Prijs, *Jüdische Tradition in der Septuaginta* (1948).

E. TOV

B. EARLIEST GREEK VERSIONS ("Old Greek"). Questions concerning the history and significance of the Greek text have received relatively less attention than those concerning the relation of the Greek to its Semitic parent. *See* TEXT, OT §C; §A *above*.

1. Terminology, technology, and text. Several closely interrelated problems have sometimes interfered with fruitful scholarly discussion of the Greek materials.

a. The term "Septuagint." As early as the second century A.D., "Septuagint" was used as an umbrella term for the Christian collection[s] of Jewish scriptures in Greek translation, which were believed to be inspired *(see* SEPTUAGINT §2) and thus superior to the "later" translations *(see* GREEK VERSIONS, MINOR[S]). This convenient but potentially misleading use of the term still prevails (e.g., "LXX" is sometimes used for Rahlfs' 1935 edition and its eclectic text; *see* SEPTUAGINT §9*b*). Since there is no homogeneity among the various translation units of this collection *(see* §3*d below)*, it is more accurate to speak of the oldest recoverable Greek form of each section/book (OG= "Old Greek"), which in the Pentateuch is the LXX proper *(see* ARISTEAS). Discussion must proceed section by section, or book by book, according to identifiable translation units.

b. Ancient technology and modern OG study. The possibility of including the entire Jewish Scriptures in a single volume did not exist until the development of the large-scale CODEX format in the fourth century. Prior to that, small-scale codices (second-third centuries) and rolls were used, which could hold only one or two major writings (e.g., Numbers-Deuteronomy). Even during the Middle Ages the practice of including the entire Greek OT under one cover was not widespread—only about one percent of the approximately twelve hundred known MSS of portions of OG contain a majority of the OT writings.

c. Canon, order of contents. Identification of "canonical" writings *(see* CANON OF THE OT) must have depended less on comprehensive OT MSS than on traditional lists of canonical literature. (Perhaps repositories for storing the various individual scripture rolls together were used in early times.) The relative imprecision of the early lists, the varying order in the later lists, and the fluidity with which the term "scripture" is applied by certain early authors may to some extent be due to the developing technological situation.

d. Textual complications. Technical considerations must also have contributed to the complexity of the text itself. If alternative text types existed in a given locale, it would have been extremely difficult to preserve a homogeneous text type in a section of material requiring multiple scrolls or small codices. The process of copying the smaller units in order to construct larger codices would tend to encourage the intermixing of materials with diverse textual histories. Relatively mechanical textual confusion of this sort may be reflected in the widespread appearance of "Theodotionic" Daniel texts (*see* DANIEL[S]), and doubtless helps explain other textual problems in presumably homogeneous OG sections (*see* §3*b-c below,* especially Samuel-Kings), including the fact that certain Greek MSS even change their textual affinities within a given book. In addition, all of the usual problems relating to the transmission of texts in antiquity apply as well to the history of OG materials (*see* TEXT, OT §D; TEXT, NT §A), along with the special problems relating to translated literature (*see* §3*e below*) and to Hexaplaric influence. *See* VERSIONS, ANCIENT §2*a*.

2. Working backward toward the earliest accessible stages. Including commentary MSS, lectionaries, and catenae, over two thousand direct witnesses to the Greek text of Jewish Scriptures are extant, dating from the sixteenth century or earlier. About ninety per cent of the actual OG MSS contain only a single book or a discrete, relatively small section—e.g., the text of Psalms or of Psalms plus Odes is found by itself in more than 750 MSS! By means of TEXTUAL CRITICISM, scholars attempt to reconstruct as accurately as possible the form of the text as it first appeared. One of the first steps in that direction involves a careful comparison of the preserved witnesses, including versions and quotations as well as the aforementioned Greek materials.

a. Grouping the witnesses by families. The witnesses frequently show textual relationships among themselves that encourage the construction of textual "family trees" which theoretically provide a route back to MS ancestors no longer extant. Sometimes the lost ancestor of a textual family might even be a conscious revision of the text (e.g., "Lucianic," "Hexaplaric"). Unfortunately, the incomplete nature of the preserved evidence (missing links) and the presence of cross-fertilization between MSS and families (e.g., through conscious "correction" and harmonization) seriously complicates this endeavor. *See* SEPTUAGINT §4.

b. Identifying lost archetypes. Prior to the tenth century A.D. MSS seldom provide explicit information regarding their own transcriber, location, date, or the MS from which they were copied. Occasionally it is possible to assign a given type of handwriting or format or system of notation to a precise locale and/or date, but the earlier the materials the more difficult such identification becomes. Sometimes the text reflected in one of the "daughter versions" made from the Greek or in quotations made by an identifiable author may provide clues to the origin of a MS or to a lost archetype—e.g., a text displaying strong affinities with the Coptic-Sahidic version might have a middle Egyptian provenance, or affinities with quotations in Antioch-related church Fathers often receive the label "Lucianic." Other clues to a family's background are sometimes provided by the use of Origen's Hexaplaric signs within the text (*see* SEPTUAGINT §4*a*), or by the appearance of a variety of marginal notations attempting to identify particular readings (e.g., "from the Samaritikon," "from Aquila," etc.).

c. Moving behind the archetypes, attested recensions, and unaligned witnesses. Unfortunately, very little concrete evidence is available for tracing the history and development of Greek scriptural texts in the centuries prior to Origen (*ca.* A.D. 250) and the so-called Hesychian and Lucianic recensions (*ca.* 300; *see* SEPTUAGINT §4). While it is sometimes possible to detect the influence of Origen's Hexapla on later MSS, identification of the supposed "Lucianic" recension (and its background) is still widely debated (*see* GREEK VERSIONS MINOR[S] §§1*c*, 4), and there has been little success in isolating a specific "Hesychian" recension. Furthermore, the few preserved MSS and fragments that antedate Origen seem to defy classification by post-Origen criteria. With the exception of materials used to posit a "Proto-Lucianic" textual stream going back at least to Josephus, the earliest witnesses have sometimes been termed "prerecensional" or "mixed texts" (i.e., not aligned with established recensions or families). But such terminology should not be allowed to obscure the probability that conscious revisional activity in Greek texts took place almost from the very beginning, both by way of refinement of style and vocabulary and through attempts to keep the Greek text in close conformity to the (changing) Hebrew/Aramaic textual situation (*see* TEXT, HEBREW, HISTORY OF[S] §1). Indeed, the traditions about later translation activity (*see* GREEK VERSIONS, MINOR[S]) support such suspicions. Furthermore, unintentional changes that also create family relationships among MSS were inevitable at every stage of copying. Thus in principle, the pre-Origen situation in OG texts should not be expected to differ from the post-Origen situation; there certainly were MS families and probably also conscious revisional activities of various sorts.

d. The earliest preserved OG materials. The growing body of relevant materials that antedate the Second Jewish Revolt (A.D. 135) permits a glimpse of early OG textual developments. Actual Greek fragments include:

Approximate Date	*Siglum*	*Identification*	
2nd B.C.	801	4 QLXX	Lev[a]
2nd/1st B.C.	957	P. Rylands 458	Deut
	805	7 QLXX	Exod
	804	7 QLXX	Epist. Jer.
1st B.C.	942	P. Fouad 266	Gen
	848	P. Fouad 266	Deut #1
1st B.C./1st A.D.	802	4 QLXX	Lev[b]
	803	4 QLXX	Num
1st A.D.	847	P. Fouad 266	Deut #2
1st/2nd A.D.	814	P. Yale 1	Gen (codex)
Early 2nd A.D.	963	Chester Beatty	Num-Deut (codex)

Extensive quotations and allusions in Greek are also preserved in Philo (*ca.* A.D. 30), Paul (*ca.* 50), Josephus (*ca.* 80), I Clement (*ca.* 95), and a number of other Christian texts from the early period. Determination of the exact wording of a quotation often must remain problematical, however, since the original text of the document in which it occurs must itself be reconstructed by careful text-critical methods. Finally, some later non-Greek versions and quotations (especially OL) can also be used, since they are clearly based upon Greek texts of an early date (*see* LATIN VERSIONS [S]). The general conclusion to be drawn is that considerable textual variety is present at every stage for which sufficient evidence is preserved. Any hopes to reconstruct with precision the original form of each OG translation by a relatively mechanical use of the preserved witnesses seems doomed to falter on the stormy sea of textual variations.

3. Reconstructing OG origins. Although ultimately the available evidence is inadequate for the task, there is some value in attempting to indicate fruitful avenues of approach to the problems of OG origins.

a. Tradition, theory, and data. First, it is hoped that current discussion can move beyond the heated dispute carried on in the names of Lagarde (one original OG existed from which the textual families, recensions, etc. developed) and Kahle (from independent competing Greek translations, a Christian Greek OT was formed by various selective processes; *see* SEPTUAGINT §5). The generalized polemic positions are too simple to do justice to the evidence; what may be true for the OG Pentateuch is not necessarily true for OG Judges or Tobit and vice versa. Secondly, the relation between the ARISTEAS legend of Pentateuchal LXX origins and the question of the origin of the other OG sections calls for careful re-examination. The frequent assumption that virtually every OG section was translated in Alexandria, although not at the same early date as the Pentateuch, requires careful evaluation in light of the full range of alternative possibilities (including Palestine itself; *see* Barthélemy). While more satisfactory criteria are being developed for identifying place of origin and date of Greek translations from Semitic originals, Alexandria should not be allowed to dominate by default.

b. Sections of Scripture with a relatively narrow textual base. The extant witnesses to several OG sections attest a relatively small range of textual variation, which suggests that a single OG translation may underlie each (unless evidence of ancient alternative translations has disappeared, as almost happened in Daniel): the Pentateuch (with some special problems in Exodus and Deuteronomy), Joshua, Ruth, Isaiah, Job (later supplemented from Theodotion), Psalms, Proverbs, Koheleth (probably in Aquila's version), Chronicles, I Maccabees. A few other books have a relatively narrow base because they were probably written originally in Greek: II–IV Maccabees, Wisdom of Solomon.

c. Sections with a problematical textual base. The extant witnesses to other portions of the Greek OT show such a wide range of divergence that it is difficult to determine whether a single original OG translation (which later underwent corruption and revision) lies behind them, or whether two or more relatively independent Greek translations of the same section should be posited. Especially noteworthy are Sirach (complex Hebrew and Greek textual situations), Daniel ("Theodotion" versus non-Theodotionic text), Tobit (text preserved by most MSS versus that of Sinaiticus and OL; perhaps a third version in a few witnesses), Judges (majority text versus that of Vaticanus and a few allies), Ode of Habakkuk (Hab. 3; majority text versus "Barberini" version). Samuel-Kings also deserves mention here, with at least two different translation techniques (*kaige* and non-*kaige*) interwoven in the preserved witnesses (*see* SAMUEL, I AND II[S] §2*c*). The probable translation block encompassing Jeremiah-Baruch + Ezekiel + Minor Prophets also exhibits some textual problems requiring thorough analysis—possibly extensive recensional activity on a single OG translation produced the situation. Similar textual problems occur also in Ezra-Nehemiah (*see* OG "I Esdras"), Esther, and Judith.

d. Classifying translation types and techniques. More precise features of the respective OG versions in each translation section are sometimes ascertainable with a high degree of probability, if the investigator moves beyond mere eclectic use of preserved textual witnesses to cautious, controlled conjectural restorations. If it can be assumed that (1) the OG translator(s) usually followed specific patterns, and (2) used a Hebrew/Aramaic text roughly similar to (or reconstructable from) available witnesses; and, if significant evidence of such patterns is still embedded in the extant witnesses to the Greek, it is often possible to identify other passages in which the pattern is expected but has now disappeared. The more self-consciously consistent the translator, the easier the task of conjectural reconstruction. Conversely, inconsistent or extremely free translation efforts are less susceptible to this sort of controlled conjecture. The science of identifying translation patterns in this literature is still in its infancy (*see* Barthélemy, Tov, Wevers, Martin; *see also* GREEK VERSIONS, MINOR[S]). The following tentative classifications of types of translations, according to the translator's relative skills in representing the Semitic parent language and producing an acceptable Greek version, may provide some impression of the relationship between the identifiable translation blocks in Jewish Greek Scriptures:

1. Literal translation reflecting closely the Semitic text:
   a. Relatively more focus on parent text:
      (1) mechanical: Aquila, OG Koheleth (=? Aquila);
      (2) relatively wooden/stilted: *"Kaige,"* Vaticanus text of Judges.
   b. Relatively more focus on producing acceptable Greek:
      (1) relatively stilted: Psalms, Jeremiah-Baruch+Ezekiel+Minor Prophets, text A of Judges (-Ruth), Chronicles, Canticles (?), Ezra-Nehemiah (?), Joshua (?), "Theodotionic" Daniel (?);

(2) more idiomatic Greek: the Pentateuch, Symmachus, Esther (part), "Theodotionic" Job and Daniel texts (?), I Maccabees (?).

2. Free translation less concerned with the parent language/text:
   a. nonparaphrastic free renderings: Isaiah, non-"Theodotionic" Daniel, Barberini Ode of Habakkuk, I Esdras (?);
   b. free paraphrase: Job, Proverbs.

e. Synthesis of results. It is not always possible to make absolute distinctions between OG and "later translators" (revisors?), or to distinguish with any confidence between an independent translation (prepared *de novo* from an available Hebrew/Aramaic base text), a recension (conscious large-scale revision of an existing Greek translation), and sporadic revision/interpolation/glossing (conscious spot "correction" of existing Greek texts). There is abundant evidence of various conscious editorial efforts prior to Origen's Hexapla—sometimes bringing a Greek text closer to a known Semitic base, sometimes incorporating (or substituting) material from other known Greek renderings or smoothing apparent problems. Special text-critical criteria are necessary for dealing with translation Greek, especially since the Hebrew/Aramaic materials were also undergoing textual modification over a long period in which Greek translations already were available. The old text-critical "rule" to prefer a "freer" reading to a more literal one is only of limited use. With relatively free OG renderings, the expected revisional tendency would often be toward literalistic correction rather than away from it. But with originally hyperliteral versions, the tendency could be just the opposite. The more general question about whether the development went from relatively free translations toward more literal ones as concepts of inspired text (and canon) became self-conscious is oversimple and not always applicable. Until it can be determined more precisely who made which translations for what purposes (e.g., private use versus public liturgy; *see* Brock), speculation about unilinear development in translation types and techniques must remain highly tentative. Even with our present state of knowledge, both Aquila (hyperliteral) and Symmachus (much more idiomatic) stand relatively near each other chronologically. The situation might have been similar for the earliest translations.

4. Influence of OG on later developments. In a variety of ways, OG materials have influenced subsequent language and literature, both in Greek and in translation.

a. On Greek vocabulary and syntax. The OG translations not only introduced some new words into Greek but also often modified the meanings of extant vocabulary. The extent to which they reflect spoken (Jewish) Greek dialects remains an open question. Sometimes it is impossible to determine whether a preserved Greek writing (or section thereof) was composed in Greek strongly influenced (consciously or unconsciously) by the available translation idiom, or was itself translated from Semitic. Criteria for judging this sort of problem are being developed (*see* R. A. Martin, *Syntactical Evidence of Semitic Sources in Greek Documents* [1974]), and should receive a strong assist from contemporary computer technology.

b. Quotations/allusions drawn from OG. Knowledge of Jewish Scriptures and scriptural tradition in the Greek-speaking world usually was mediated through OG and related translations. Quotations/allusions not only provide a potentially valuable indication of textual developments (*see* §2*b above*), but also often indicate how particular passages were interpreted and applied at various times and places (*see* EXEGESIS[S]). The "Centre d' Analyse et de Documentation Patristiques" at Strasbourg is building a central file of patristic biblical quotations: *see* J. Allenbach *et al., Biblia Patristica: Index des citations et allusions bibliques dans la littérature patristique,* 1 (1975).

Bibliography. A period of renewed activity in the study of OG and related materials began in 1968 with the founding of the International Organization for Septuagint and Cognate Studies (IOSCS). Its annual *Bulletin* chronicles current work, and detailed listings of literature published through 1969 appear in *A Classified Bibliography of the LXX,* compiled by S. P. Brock, C. T. Fritsch, and S. Jellicoe (1973).

Text-critical materials, editions, studies: The main center of text-critical activity on OG remains the Göttingen "Septuaginta-Unternehmens"; especially noteworthy among related projects is the continuing work on OL biblical material by the Beuron Institute. The latest Göttingen eds. are IX.2-3=*Maccabacorum liber II* (1959) and *III* (1960), ed. R. Hanhart; XII.1-2=*Sapientia Salomonis* (1962) and *Sapientia Iesu Filii Sirach* (1965), ed. J. Ziegler; VIII.3=*Esther* (1966), and VIII.1=*Esdrae liber I* (1974), ed. R. Hanhart; and I=*Genesis* (1974), ed. J. Wevers. Corrected reprints of several earlier volumes have also been issued. New MSS and fragments (esp. papyri) continue to appear—*see* esp. K. Treu, "Christliche Papyri I-IV," *Archiv für Papyrusforschung,* 19-22 (1969-73). Important recent studies of text-critical importance include: D. Barthélemy, *Les Devanciers d'Aquila* (1963); *Proceedings* of IOSCS Symposium on Samuel-Kings, ed. R. A. Kraft, *LXX and Cognate Studies,* II (1972); P. Walters [Katz], *The Text of the LXX: Its Corruptions and Their Emendation,* ed. D. W. Gooding (1973); E. Tov, *The LXX Translation of Jeremiah and Baruch* (1975); J. W. Wevers, *Text History of the Greek Genesis* (1974); D. W. Gooding, *Relics of Ancient Exegesis: A Study of the Miscellanies in 3 Reigns 2* (1975); R. Klein, *Textual Criticism of the OT* (1974). A new ed. of the Letters of Aristeas, by A. Pelletier, has appeared as *Sources Chrétiennes,* 89 (1962).

Lexicography, tools, and studies: J. Reider's long awaited *An Index to Aquila* is finally available (ed. N. Turner, 1966), and various efforts to enhance the usefulness of the Hatch-Redpath concordance and its Hebrew-Greek index have appeared: e.g., X. Jacques, *List of LXX Words Sharing Common Elements: Supplement to Concordance or Dictionary* (1972); E. C. Dos Santos, *An Expanded Hebrew Index* (1973).

Plans for a special "LXX Lexicon" are under way through IOSCS auspices: *see* R. A. Kraft, ed., *Septuagintal Lexicography* (1972), for background work. Specific investigations of vocabulary include S. Daniel, *Recherches sur le vocabulaire du culte dans la Septante* (1966); D. Hill, *Greek Words and Hebrew Meanings* (1967).

General works, collected essays, etc.: Swete's invaluable *Introduction to the OT in Greek* (1900 [2nd ed., 1902]) has been updated by S. Jellicoe, *The LXX and Modern Studies* (1968). On ancient translation activities, *see* S. P. Brock, "The Phenomenon of the LXX," *OTS*, XVII (1972), 11-36. Pertinent essay collections include J. Ziegler, *Sylloge: Gesammelte Aufsätze Zur LXX* (1971); J. Schreiner, ed., *Wort, Lied und Gottesspruch* (1972); S. Jellicoe, ed., *Studies in the LXX: . . . Selected Essays* (1974). R. A. KRAFT

SEPULCHRE. *See* HOLY SEPULCHRE, CHURCH OF THE[S].

***SERMON ON THE MOUNT.** Under the influence of redaction criticism, discussion of the Sermon on the Mount has emphasized the role it plays in Matthew's theological statement. There have been new insights into the original matrix of some of the sayings. There is also a renewed interest in the relationship between the historical forces that shaped the Sermon on the Mount and those which molded the sectarian Judaism of Qumran prior to A.D. 70 and the rabbinic Judaism of Jamnia in the period immediately following the destruction of Jerusalem (A.D. 70).

1. The Sermon on the Mount in Matthew's theology. Matthew's Gospel is a threefold christological statement expounding (*a*) The Person of Jesus the Messiah (1:1–4:16); (*b*) The Proclamation of Jesus the Messiah (4:17–16:20); and (*c*) The Suffering, Death, and Resurrection of Jesus the Messiah (16:21–28:20). (*See* MATTHEW, GOSPEL OF[S] §2.) The Sermon on the Mount opens (*b*); it is the initial expression of the Messiah's proclamation. In 4:17 we are told that Jesus began to proclaim, "Repent, for the kingdom of Heaven is at hand." Then he appointed his disciples (4:18-22). In 4:23, the content of the proclamation is summarized: "And he went about all Galilee, teaching in their synagogues and preaching the gospel of the kingdom and healing every disease and every infirmity among the people." Virtually the same words occur at 9:35, and this suggests that the material bracketed by these two summaries should be considered as a single theological statement. The Sermon on the Mount (chs. 5–7) is described, therefore, as the "teaching in their synagogues" which announces "the gospel of the kingdom," while chs. 8 and 9 recount the "healing [of] every disease and every infirmity." Together the teaching and healing constitute "the gospel of the kingdom." The distinction between chs. 5–7 and 8–9 is not rigid, since 8 and 9 do contain material other than miracles (two pericopes on following Jesus, 8:18-22; 9:9-13; one pericope on the newness of the event of his presence, 9:14-17).

That the Sermon on the Mount is viewed by Matthew as the proclamation of the gospel of the kingdom should warn us against too hasty an assumption that we have in it a new law. Jesus is not a counterpart to Moses, giving a new Torah from a new Sinai. Although the motif of a new Moses is present in Matthew, it is not predominant. The parallelism between Moses and Jesus which is sometimes present in this gospel is only one aspect of Matthew's Christology. In Matthew, Jesus the Messiah has "absorbed the Mosaic function" so that, while suggesting the law of a new Moses, the Sermon on the Mount is in fact the "messianic Torah" (Davies).

The key to understanding the theological import which the Sermon on the Mount had for Matthew is that it is a proclamation of the kingdom by the Messiah. As moral teaching, therefore, it is as much a part of the event of grace as are the healing miracles. It represents the demand implied in the offer, the task entailed by the gift. The Beatitudes (5:3-12), which are in form prophetic-apocalyptic utterances (*see* BEATITUDES §4), strike the note of eschatological proclamation clearly and forcefully; and as the Sermon on the Mount begins with the announcement of the long-awaited coming of God to his people in the Beatitudes, so it ends with the theme of the judgment, presented by means of the wisdom imagery of the two ways and the parable of the two houses (7:13-29), PARABLE being a device characteristic of the wisdom tradition.

Indeed, throughout the Sermon on the Mount there is a mixing of apocalyptic and wisdom forms. The Beatitudes themselves were earlier identified as wisdom forms, but now the consensus is that they are from the apocalyptic tradition. The phenomenon of this mixture shows that sayings were assembled from various contexts and presented by Matthew as part of the eschatological event. Thus, seemingly prudential maxims like "No one can serve two masters" (6:24), or "Judge not, that you be not judged" (7:1), take on a dimension of urgency and religious depth; wisdom sayings become eschatological revelations and call the hearers to make a decision.

The famous "antitheses" (5:21-48) as well as the notoriously difficult saying on the continued validity of the law and its fulfillment (5:17-20), which precedes the antitheses, are to be understood on the same basis. They set forth the eschatological depth of the TORAH, which is more demanding because it belongs to the new age. The difficult ambiguity of the presence of the new age, its appearance "already but not yet," is acknowledged in the phrase "until all is accomplished" (5:18).

In sum, the Sermon on the Mount is for Matthew the messianic Torah proclaimed by Emmanuel, "God with us." This Torah finds its epitome in the GOLDEN RULE (7:12), understood as a summary of all that has gone before and as the fulfillment of the Law and the prophets.

2. The historical matrix of the Sermon on the Mount. Given that the Sermon on the Mount is a collection of teachings and not an actual "sermon" of Jesus', one might inquire what historical circumstances in the early church caused such a collection to be made. There are two such influences that warrant consideration, but neither of them alone is sufficient to explain the phenomenon.

The first to be considered is the sectarian Judaism we know from Qumran and the DEAD SEA SCROLLS. In 1QM 14.7 (and possibly also 14.3) the phrase "poor in spirit" occurs, indicating the possibility that the longer Matthean version of the first beatitude (Matt. 5:3; Luke 6:20) shows that the folk who formed the Sermon on the Mount understood themselves to be the "religious poor," a special group of the pious, dedicated to the teaching given to them by their authoritative interpreter of the Law, like the Qumran community and its dedication to the TEACHER OF RIGHTEOUSNESS (*see* POOR[S] §2). The concurrence of blessing and cursing in Luke's version (Luke 6:20-26) recalls 1QS 2.2*b*-4, 5*b*-9; and 1QS 1.18 ff. suggests that Luke's "sermon" might, like the similar material in 1QS, have been part of the rite of admission to the community—in this case, baptism.

It is also significant that only in 1QS 1.3-4, 9-10; 9.16, 21-22; 10.20-21 and CD 2.14 ff. is anything like a command to hate one's enemies to be found in ancient Jewish literature. This may be a genuine point of contact between Qumran and the Sermon on the Mount, since such a command is specifically rejected in Matt. 5:43-44. Nevertheless, in 1QS and CD the obligation of hostility is generalized to apply to all outsiders, whereas Matthew presumes a strict pattern of reciprocity, "Hate those who hate you." The parallel at this point is loose at best.

These and other similarities between the Sermon on the Mount and the Dead Sea Scrolls, however, establish beyond doubt that the Matthean church and the Qumran sectarians at least shared a common world of thought. Both understood themselves to be true expressions of Jewish religion.

Besides sectarian affinities, the gospel in general and the Sermon on the Mount in particular show the influence of rabbinic Judaism. That the Matthean church practiced a sort of scriptural commentary similar to rabbinic midrash has been established, although even in this regard Qumran influence is conspicuous (*see* MATTHEW, GOSPEL OF[S] §1). There is, however, in addition, an intriguing similarity to be observed between the structure of the Sermon on the Mount and that of the Mishna as it took shape in the rabbinic school of Jamnia. Davies has argued ingeniously that the Sermon represents a Christian counterpart of the rabbinic codification of the oral law at Jamnia, which formed the basis of the later Mishna. For instance, the three pillars of Judaism as expressed in AB. 1.2 by Simon the Just: "Torah, Temple service, and deeds of loving kindness," might be seen as roughly paralleled in Matt. 5:17-48 (Torah), 6:1-6 (worship), and 6:19–7:12 (deeds of loving kindness). Furthermore, the six antitheses (6:17-48) recall the six Sedarim of the Mishna. Davies wisely characterizes these suggestions as "very tentative" and "merely exploratory"; but, although they probably cannot be shown to pertain beyond reasonable doubt, they do point in the right direction. The Sermon on the Mount was formed in the conversation between the Matthean church and post-Jamnian Judaism, and this process represents a development of an element in the teaching of the historical Jesus. His proclamation of the kingdom included a moral demand as well as a promise. *See* ETHICS IN THE NT §A; ETHICS IN THE NT[S] §1*a*.

Other possible formative elements, like the influence of incipient GNOSTICISM, transforming Jesus into a Gnostic revealer (which some see behind the formation of Q), or the need to counteract Pauline antinomianism, are less probable in a gospel so patently involved with Jewish "school" activity.

Bibliography. W. D. Davies, *The Setting of the Sermon on the Mount* (1964); E. Schweizer, "Formgeschichtliches zu den Seligpreisungen Jesu," *NTS,* XIX (1972-73), 121-26; G. Strecker, review of W. D. Davies, *The Setting of the Sermon on the Mount, NTS,* XIII (1966-67), 105-12; H. T. Wrege, *Die Überlieferungsgeschichte der Bergpredigt,* WUNT, IX (1968).

R. G. HAMERTON-KELLY

***SERPENT.** The serpent is widely attested in the history of religions as a symbol used to represent both beneficent and hostile sacred powers. Among the Canaanites, the primeval chaotic power is portrayed as a serpentine figure, Lothan (cf. LEVIATHAN; RAHAB [DRAGON]), but archaeologists have also uncovered Canaanite serpent-entwined goddesses, which clearly represent friendlier powers (Fig. S3), as well as independent serpent figurines (Bodenheimer, pp. 186-87), which may have served as charms or talismans.

Within the Bible, however, the serpent is rarely viewed in a positive manner, although traces of an archaic reverence may be concealed in the persistent traditions about the serpents of Moses (i.e.,

© Y. Yadin

3. Silver-plated bronze cult standard from Hazor. Above, crescent and stylized snake. Two snakes flank figure of the deity. Stylized snake at bottom.

the serpent rod, the bronze serpent, NEHUSHTAN). II Kings 18:4 suggests as much when it informs us that a serpent image attributed to Moses was still part of the Judean cult at the time of Hezekiah, who destroyed it together with other symbols of Canaanite influence: high places, pillars, and Asherah. The wisdom tradition, which directed its concern to the natural features of snakes, contains a few respectful references to their wondrous mode of locomotion (Prov. 30:19) and their reputed wisdom (Matt. 10:16). Elsewhere, however, the poisonous, threatening, negative qualities of snakes are most frequently noted.

The author of Gen. 3 made a significant contribution to the serpent's evil reputation. When his story is read against the background of ancient Near Eastern legend or myth (*see* Gaster), one recalls the wise, bearded, friendly, talking serpent encountered in the Egyptian tale of The Shipwrecked Sailor or the Akkadian serpent who robbed the hero of a chance for immortality in the Gilgamesh Epic (*ANET* [2nd ed.], pp. 72-99). But the biblical account remains distinct. From all the animals created by God it has singled out the serpent to receive a special curse. Although the focus of the story of Eden is properly the sin of man, the serpent's tale (Gen. 3:1-15) has its own symmetrical form. It begins with the observation that "the serpent was more subtle than any other wild creature" (vs. 1), and it ends when the serpent is cursed "above all wild animals" (vs. 14). The use of the comparative construction in vs. 14 heightens the contrast with the beginning of the story; it does not imply that the other animals were cursed. In vs. 1 the friendly serpent speaks freely with the woman, but in vs. 15 continual enmity is set between them. The story begins with a positive appraisal of the wise serpent, wise enough to know the source of total knowledge, i.e., everything "good and evil." It ends with a negative appraisal of that cursed beast which crawls on its belly and eats dust, the prototype of all of the subdued enemies of God's people (Mic. 7:17, cf. Ps. 72:9). The etiological details in the curse, which explain the strange habits of snakes and the natural aversion that women feel to them, should not obscure the author's intent to show the totally negative consequences of God's curse. In the first verse the author chose the word "subtle" (ערום) to describe the serpent's wisdom in order to create a pun with the word "naked" (ערומים), which was used to describe the human couple in 2:25. In ch. 3, the "subtleness" of the serpent subsequently led the man and woman who tended the Garden to discover their own "nakedness." The reader of the story is clearly intended to understand that the serpent is a cursed beast whose wiles lead to no good.

The role of the serpent in the Genesis account provided the starting point for a considerable amount of exegetical expansion. The descriptions of an eschatological age in which enmity between man and snake will no longer prevail, so that even poisonous serpents will be rendered harmless (Isa. 11:8; 62:25), suggest a return to conditions prior to the Fall. The author of the book of Jubilees dealt with the problem of a talking serpent by assuming that all the animals in Eden spoke a single intelligible language (i.e., Hebrew) until the day that Adam was expelled from the Garden (3:28; 12:26). The postexilic preoccupation with THEODICY, which was resolved in certain circles by making SATAN responsible for all evil, also contributed to the exegesis of Genesis by making the serpent either an agent of Satan or Satan himself (Wisd. Sol. 2:24; Apoc. Sedrach 4; II Enoch 31; Vita Adae 16). That exegetical tradition was so widespread and firmly held by NT times that it was reflected in Rev. 12:9.

The exegetical expansion did not cease with the NT. The story of the Fall was a favorite with the Gnostics, who transformed it so that the God of the OT became an ignorant or evil god who sought to prevent man from gaining wisdom. One group of Gnostics who were known as Ophites (from ὄφις, serpent) claimed the serpent as their patron. The NAG HAMMADI tractate which has been designated "On the Origin of the World" contains a passage which reflects very early (before second century A.D.) exegesis based on the meaning of the name for serpent in Aramaic. In Aramaic the words "Eve," "life," "instructor," and "serpent" all appear to be derived from the same root and may be written with similar consonants. Therefore this text explains that a heavenly Eve, whose name means "life," appeared in the form of the serpent (i.e., instructor) in order to persuade the earthly Eve to eat the fruit and gain its Gnostic wisdom.

Bibliography. F. S. Bodenheimer, *Animal and Man in Bible Lands* (1960); U. Cassuto, *A Commentary on the Book of Genesis,* Pt. I, (1961); T. H. Gaster, *Myth, Legend, and Custom in the OT* (1969); B. Pearson, "Jewish Haggadic Traditions in *The Testimony of Truth from Nag Hammadi* (CG IX, 3)," *Ex Orbe Religionum* (1972), pp. 457-70; J. B. Pritchard, *The Ancient Near East in Pictures Relating to the OT* (1954); G. von Rad, *Genesis* (1961); B. Renz, *Der Orientalische Schlangendrache* (1930); H. Wohlstein, "Zur Tier-Dämonologie der Bibel," *ZDMG,* CXIII (1963), 483-92.

O. WINTERMUTE

SEVEN. *See* SEVEN, SEVENTH, SEVENTY; GENERATION, SEVENTH[S]; EZEKIEL[S] §1.

*** SEX, SEXUAL BEHAVIOR.** Since sex is both a powerful physiological-psychological drive and a crucial aspect of the reproduction of populations, no society leaves the matter unregulated. Some societies take a very positive view of sex and are permissive, while others take a negative view and are restrictive. In general, societies of the Mediterranean area are of the second type. There is also a strong statistical correlation between restrictions on premarital sex, the placing of a high value on virginity in brides, the existence of a double standard, and the existence of prostitution.

The ancient Hebrews, however, do not fit neatly into this scheme; their attitude toward sex is ambivalent. On the one hand, they valued it and celebrated it joyously; on the other, they feared and depreciated it. And while they believed (Gen. 2) that the primordial relation between the sexes was one of complementarity between equals, they in fact practiced a marked double standard.

1. Fundamental attitudes. ***a. Ambivalence.*** On the one hand, sex is good; it is regarded almost with awe as representing divinely given power, and is celebrated with joy and abandon. On the other hand, it is bad, to be feared and hushed up.

i. *Sex is good.* The assumption that sex for reproduction is good can be seen from the tone of the creation narrative. God creates a heterosexual humankind and commands and blesses the reproductive function (Gen. 1:26-31). In many passages fertility of women is seen as a sign of God's favor and barrenness as a sign of his disfavor (e.g., Gen. 29:31–30:24; I Sam. 1:5-20). As for virile potency, no better indication of its value can be found than in the fact that Abraham required his servant to swear by it ("under my thigh," Gen. 24:2, meaning the genitals). Furthermore, sex does not exist only for reproduction: companionship between spouses is a part of the creation account (Gen. 2:18-25). And at a much later period, there is in all literature no more innocently frank celebration of erotic love than in the Song of Solomon.

This might be compared with the Canaanite cult of fertility and sexuality, centering in the worship of the Baalim and the ASHTAROTH, and characterized by the practice of cult prostitution (*see* BAAL). Indeed, the Hebrews up to the time of the return from Babylon were often involved in this cult. But it was at all times strongly condemned by the leaders and prophets. The "official" view in the OT is that sex is good because God gave it, but sex mistaken for God is an idolatrous abomination.

ii. *Sex is bad.* That the OT frequently takes a negative view of sex can be seen from the following examples.

First, there is a strong negative feeling associated with nudity. Although nudity was a part of the innocent original estate of man (Gen. 2:25), after the FALL, to be human is to be clothed (Gen. 3:21; cf. Luke 8:27, 35); to be naked is shameful (Gen. 3:7, 10, 21). Priests had to wear shorts under their robes when carrying out their duties on platforms to avoid exposure (Exod. 20:26). To strip another was to attack his human dignity (Isa. 3:17). That this is related to sex can be seen from the explicit references in these verses to the genitals. "To uncover someone's nakedness" is the euphemism often used for the sex act, especially a deviant one (Lev. 18:6 ff.). Thus, the horror of seeing another's genitals can be related, in the case of kin, to the incest taboo; and, in the case of males, to the taboo on homosexuality (Gen. 9:22-27).

Second, we must note the poverty of the biblical languages in terms for genitals and the sex act and the frequent use of euphemisms such as "to know" for the sex act and "thigh" for the male genitals. This is so well-known that it requires no further elaboration here.

Third, there are frequent cautions against a man's spending his energies on sex (Prov. 31:3). More specifically, there are taboos on sexual contact under certain circumstances: during a woman's menstrual period or when she was having a vaginal discharge (Lev. 15:19-30); before or during battle (I Sam. 21:4-5; it was this rule that frustrated David's effort to hide his adultery with Bathsheba, II Sam. 11:6-13), which explains the exemption of newlywed men from military service (Deut. 24:5); and especially in preparation for religious rituals (Exod. 19:15-16).

b. Double standard. The Hebrew double standard can be seen from a number of indications.

Women were subordinated to men, whether their fathers and brothers or their husbands (Num. 30:3-15). Men are shown to be active, taking initiative, and women are (supposed to be) passive. The woman who makes advances is both evil and dangerous (Prov. 6:23-28).

A high value was placed on premarital virginity in women (Gen. 19:8; Song of S. 4:12; Matt. 1:18-25); discovery that a bride was not a virgin was grounds for punishment, whether by stoning (Deut. 22:20-21) or divorce (Matt. 1:18-19). In contrast, the question of male virginity at marriage is not mentioned.

There are sharply divergent standards of fidelity in marriage. The adulterous wife is liable to the death penalty (Num. 5:11-31; Deut. 22:22-27). The unfaithful husband, on the other hand, though he is warned that his conduct is reprehensible and leads to moral perdition (Prov. 2:16-19; 7:26-27), is subject to no legal sanction unless he has violated the rights of some other man in the woman in question and incurred either his revenge or his demand for damages (Prov. 6:27-35). A man has also the right to take additional wives and concubines, and has the recognized right of access, with some restrictions, to slave and captive women (Num. 31:18-19; *see* SLAVERY IN THE OT §4*b*) and to prostitutes (Gen. 38:12-19; Josh. 2:1-7); it is even suggested (Prov. 6:26) that it is both cheaper and less dangerous to resort to a prostitute than to commit adultery.

The double standard required that men and women be distinguished in every way: in dress, so that transvestism was an abomination (Deut. 22:5); in economic roles; and in every area of life. It must not be thought, however, that all of the advantages of the double standard accrued to the men. Anthropologists have come to realize that the customary division of roles between the sexes gives to each certain prerogatives, which is to say leverage. There is a mutual dependency, such that men without women are about as helpless as women without men.

c. The rationale. What is the source of the ambivalence and the double standard? At the ideological level, the most plausible explanation derives from the Hebrew view of the Fall. In other words, what God created perfect was warped and spoiled by man's—and even more, by woman's—foolish willfulness. What was in the Creation perfect companionship became a hierarchy of dominance and submissiveness (Gen. 3:16), and what was designed to be pure bliss became, on its underside, disruptive and dangerous. Thus the Hebrew view is not like that of the Neoplatonists, who totally despised the body and its functions; it is more like the gingerly caution with which one handles a dangerous explosive.

2. Restrictions and deviations. In light of the ambivalent view the Hebrews had of sex, it is not surprising that they hedged it in with a complex set of rules. We will discuss these in terms of a successive narrowing of the scope of a man's legitimate sexual contacts.

a. Bestiality and homosexuality (*see* BESTIALITY [S]; HOMOSEXUALITY[S]). Throughout the biblical era, it was the uniform conviction of the Hebrews that coitus should be restricted to human heterosexual contacts. This was part of the order of creation (Gen. 1, 2). Contact between persons and animals was known but condemned and subject to the death penalty (Exod. 22:19). The same was true of male homosexuality (Lev. 18:22). In the story of Lot (Gen. 19:5) and in that of the Levite and his concubine (Judg. 19:22-25), it is not clear which motif predominates in the host's refusal to allow the townspeople to abuse his guest sexually, the horror of homosexuality or the sacred duty of hospitality. In each case, the host offered his virgin daughter(s) as a substitute. Lesbianism is not mentioned in the OT, but is condemned with male homosexuality in the NT (Rom. 1:26-27; Gal. 5:19-20); it may have been learned from the Greeks.

b. Incest. A taboo on INCEST is a universal trait of human societies. But both the form it takes and the apparent underlying motives vary greatly. Incest taboos should not be confused with rules of exogamy, though they may largely coincide; the former relate to sexual contact, the latter to marriage. In the OT, the list of prohibited women is given in full (Lev. 18:6-18). It includes a man's mother and stepmother, sister and half sister, granddaughter, father's and mother's sisters, father's brother's wife, brother's wife, and son's wife. It is not clear why daughter should be omitted, for the story of Lot and his daughters shows that this was also taboo. Grandmother is not mentioned, possibly because a much older woman would not represent a genuine temptation. What is clear is that the basis of this list is social, not genetic. First cousins are not taboo, though closely related biologically; but a number of wives of kin are taboo, though unrelated biologically. A much more plausible explanation is that in all the specified relationships, sexual contact would be potentially disruptive of extended family relations by creating competition between related men for the same women. It is not an accident that in almost every case, a woman is specified in terms of the man whose rights in her would be violated by an act of incest.

It is intriguing that penalties for incest are apparently left up to God; whereas for many offenses penalties are spelled out, in the case of incest offenders are cursed, the curse including childlessness (Deut. 27:20-23).

Infractions of this taboo are mentioned in the OT. The incest of Lot's daughters was justified by them on grounds of the necessity of keeping the family line alive, but was condemned by the Hebrews. Reuben's incest with his father's concubine (Gen. 35:22) was at the time overlooked by Jacob, but was mentioned at the time of the paternal "blessing" (Gen. 49:4). The case of Abraham's marriage with Sarah, whom he presents as his half sister (Gen. 20:12) may be explained as representing an earlier custom, though it does not conform to any explicit permission. A similar puzzle is presented by the case of Amnon's incest with his half sister Tamar (II Sam. 13). The problem is not the rape itself, but Tamar's statement (vs. 13) that David could have given Amnon permission to take her legitimately. The brother-sister marriage of Egyptian divine royalty would have been known, but could not have been transferred, at least with the same rationale, to Israel. It may represent a survival of the earlier custom in spite of, or before, the explicit formulation of the law.

c. Rape. If a man raped a virgin not already engaged, he paid her father the bride price, whether or not he married her (Exod. 22:16-17). Elsewhere (Deut. 22:28-29), it is said that he had to marry her and could never divorce her. If a man raped an engaged virgin in circumstances where she could not get help, he was stoned, but she was not punished; but if she could have called for help, she too was stoned (Deut. 22:23-27).

d. Adultery. Adultery was viewed on the one hand as an offense against the rights of the husband, and on the other as an offense against God (Prov. 6:27-35; Ps. 51:4). It is not clear whether both views were held simultaneously, or whether the former was earlier and the latter a subsequent development. In either instance, the penalty for both adulterers was death (Deut. 22:22).

e. Prostitution. Since prostitution was a recognized social institution, it may be anomalous to deal with it under the rubric of deviations. However, there seems to have been a gradual development of the view that it was bad not only for the women involved, but for the men who resorted to them. In the patriarchal period, the only fault that was held against Judah (Gen. 38) was his failure to honor the levirate rule; his use of Tamar as a prostitute passes without comment. But later, consorting with prostitutes is condemned as foolish, dangerous, and wrong (Prov. 29:3; 31:3; 2:16-22).

f. The "sons of God" and the "daughters of men." The much-discussed case (Gen. 6:1-4) in which, in antediluvian times, beings called "SONS OF GOD" consorted with "daughters of men" should probably be understood as representing relations between heavenly, divine, angelic beings and human women. This is in keeping with the general use of the phrase "sons of God" (Job 1:6), and no other convincing explanation of the phrase which would make it different in meaning in Genesis has been presented.

3. Techniques. Little if anything is said directly about the positions and techniques of the sex act. From passing details in the Song of Solomon, one may infer that the usual position was front-to-front, with the man on top. Erotic caresses were used (Song of S. 2:6 and *passim*). Various body parts of a woman are listed in the Song of Solomon as being erotically stimulating to a man, and body parts of a man which are stimulating to a woman. Scent is an important stimulus, including perfume (Song of S. 1:3, 12-14), and cosmetics are used for the same purpose (Jer. 4:30).

4. Summary. In summary, the ancient Hebrews considered sex to be a gift of God, to be used both for procreation and for erotic pleasure. But as a result of the Fall, it was felt to have become, because of its enormous power, a potentially explosive and disruptive force, destroying the individual, the family, and society; it therefore had to be guarded by a host of restrictions. These restrictions, in association with the polar view of the relations between active men and passive women, and because of woman's special role in bringing about the Fall, brought into being the double standard described above. This was reinforced by the example of many of the other societies with which Israel was acquainted, and by the type of social structure which characterized Israel for most of its history. It would seem that in the intertestamental period, there was both an elaboration and rigidification of the ideological basis for the double standard and an alleviation of its cruder applications. But in the context of such a system, the NT teaching, mild as it may seem to modern readers—or even reactionary to some—came with revolutionary impact. Even though the social inequality of the sexes was not eradicated in NT thought, and in some ways was actually reinforced, the gist of the example of Jesus and of the teachings of Paul was that it was a temporary and pragmatic matter, relative and conditioned by social circumstances; but in terms of the unconditioned rule of God, who in Christ made all things new, there is again a complementarity of equals (Gal. 3:28). *See also* DIVORCE[S]; MARRIAGE[S].

Bibliography. *See bibliog.* for MARRIAGE[S].

C. R. TABER

SHALAH (GOD) shä läh′. The (Canaanite?) god Shalah (*šelaḥ*) is not directly attested, but his indirect attestation is manifold. He is the god of watercourses, and, in particular, of the netherworld river which the dead must cross. Crossing seems to be the occasion of their judgment, and Shalah might play an important role in it. Indirect attestations include the following.

(1) The personal name Methuselah (Gen. 5:21-27) translates "man of *šelaḥ*," where *šelaḥ*, in accordance with the pattern of Semitic name formation, occupies the place of a divine name. *See* NAMES, RELIGIOUS SIGNIFICANCE OF[S] §2*a*.

(2) Job 33:18 reads: "He keeps back his soul from the Pit, his spirit from [the] *šelaḥ*" (Tsevat); *see also* 36:12 (RSV "sword") and compare 33:28, which substitutes "the Pit" for "[the] *šelaḥ*" of vs. 18. These passages refer to the underworld; "Pit" is one aspect of it and *šelaḥ* another. Several appellatives and topographical names show that the latter word means "current" (Neh. 3:15; Isa. 8:6; and Song of S. 4:13 [RSV "shoots"] further substantiate this). This is to say that *šelaḥ* corresponds to the River Ḫubur of Mesopotamian mythology, over which the dead pass as they enter the underworld. Furthermore, Mesopotamian texts make the crossing the occasion of judgment. In Palestine the idea of judgment at bodies of water is traceable in the bynames of Kadesh: (Me-)-meribah, "[water of] contention/litigation" (Num. 20:13; 27:14) and En-mishpat, "spring of judgment" (Gen. 14:7). The rite of Deut. 21:1-9 is probably an act of purification by sacrifice to the deity who is present in or represented by the brook. Being quite dissimilar to all other biblical rites, it is reinterpreted by the prayer of vs. 8, but the contours of a distorted, non-Yahwistic sacrifice loom behind it.

(3) The Middle Hebrew terms for irrigated and nonirrigated fields are respectively, [*śᵉdhê*] *bêth haššᵉlāḥîn* and [*śᵉdhê*] *bêth habbaʿal.* The second is clearly "[field of] Baal's ground," i.e., watered by rain, the gift of Baal. The first is apparently "[field of] the currents' ground," but since the word is quite rare in Middle Hebrew outside this compound, the interpretation "[field of] the *šelaḥs*' ground" is suggestive (the plural stands for the plurality of irrigation ditches); one kind of field is called after the god of the celestial water, the other after the god of the subterranean water.

(4) The afore-mentioned Methuselah is a member of one of two parallel genealogies, Gen. 5:1-32 and 4:1, 17-22. The corresponding member of the other genealogy is Methushael (4:18). As it stands, the name has no linguistically acceptable meaning. A change of vocalization from *mᵉthûšāʾēl* to *mᵉthûšᵉʾôl,* however, yields "Man of Sheol" (*see* DEITIES, UNDERWORLD[S] §2*b*ii). This corresponds perfectly to "man of *šelaḥ* (Shalah)" of the other genealogy. Both names designate their bearers as devotees of a god of the netherworld.

Bibliography. M. Tsevat, "The Canaanite God Šälaḥ," *VT,* IV (1954), 41-49, 322; D. Leibel, "*ʿbr bšlḥ,*" *Tarbiz,* XXXIII (1964), 225-27, 405, Hebrew.

M. TSEVAT

***SHALEM (GOD)** shä′lĕm [שלם, "the stable one"]. The West Semitic deity Shalem or Shulmân is the god whose name is perpetuated in that of the city of Jerusalem, "the foundation of Shalem." In the Assyrian vocabulary K.4339 he is identified with Ninurta, the Assyro-Babylonian deity manifested in the planet Saturn, which was, in the thinking of the ancient Semites, the "stable" planet. The root *šlm* in most of the Semitic languages signifies "perfect, true, faithful, whole, healthy," ideas summarized in the concept of stability. Just as Ninurta in Assyria and Babylonia was looked upon as the founder of a number of cities, and El or Kronos, the Saturn deity of the Canaanites, was deemed the founder of Byblos in Phoenicia (according to Sanchuniathon's account of Phoenician religion preserved by Philo of Byblos), so too was the Saturn deity of Jerusalem regarded as the city's founder. His city, particularly the sacred precinct within it, restrained the waters of chaos beneath, and was considered the center of the earth. *See* NAVEL OF THE EARTH[S].

In Middle Assyrian lists, the consort of Shalem or Shulmân is called Shulmitu or Shulmanitu, and is defined as "the Ishtar of Jerusalem." Shalem and Shulmanitu probably underlie the "shᵉlōmô" and "shûlammîth" (Solomon and the Shulamite) of the Song of Songs. The names *shᵉlōmô* ("belonging to Shalem") and Absalom ("the Father is Shalem"), bestowed by David upon his sons, highlight David's desire to pay his respects to the god of Jerusalem.

It is likely that in the cult of Jerusalem, *ʿelyôn* ("the most high") was another name for Shalem.

Gen. 14:18-20 indicates that the god of the city was invoked as *'ēl 'elyôn* ("God Most High"), maker of heaven and earth (perhaps read, rather, "possessor" or "parent" of heaven and earth). Saturn was the most distant of the planets known to the ancients, and it was quite natural that it be called "the most high." Sanchuniathon names Elioun as the father of the deities Heaven and Earth, from whom El or Kronos (Saturn) was born. Elioun and Saturn thus constitute different generations of gods; in Jerusalem, however, they were probably invoked as the same divinity.

In like manner, while Shahar and Shalem are twin sons of El in Ugaritic myth, in Jerusalem Shalem was another name applied to the great god El or Elyon. This reflects the tendency toward syncretistic monotheism among the ancient Semites, whereby the god of a particular locality was regarded as absorbing other divinities into his person.

Shahar (Dawn) and Shalem in Ugaritic myth are likely the morning and evening stars, the two aspects of the planets Venus or Mercury. (Shahar in Isa. 14:12 is Mercury, since the king of Babylon taunted by the prophet is Nabonidus, who bears the name of the god Nabu, the Assyro-Babylonian Mercury.) Shalem, at Ugarit the evening star, came in the cult of Jerusalem to be one of the names of Saturn because of the widespread association of Saturn with the sun. After sunset (Akkad. *šalâm šamši*), the representative of the sun in the nocturnal sky was thought to be the planet Saturn because of the slowness and regularity of its movement. Saturn is repeatedly called "the sun-star" in Assyro-Babylonian astrological literature. It is known that the sun played a prominent role in the cult of Jerusalem far into Judean times. It is likely that in pre-Judean times, the god and founder of the city was venerated during the day as the sun and by night as Saturn, "the stable one, the most high."

Bibliography. P. Clemen, *Die Phoenikische Religion nach Philo von Byblos* (1939); C. H. Gordon, *Ugaritic Literature* (1949), pp. 59 ff. (trans. of myth of Shahar and Shalem); J. Gray, "The Desert God 'Aṯtar in the Literature and Religion of Canaan," *JNES*, VIII (1949), 72-83, maintains Shalem is Venus as evening star; M. Jastrow, "Sun and Saturn," *RA*, VII (1910), 163 ff.; H. Lewy, "Origin and Significance of the *Mâgên Dâwid*," *ArOr*, XVIII, Pt. 3 (1950), 330-65, maintains Shalem is Saturn.

R. A. ROSENBERG

***SHALMAN.** Hosea, foretelling the imminent destruction of Israel by the Assyrians, cited a historical precedent (10:14): "All your fortresses shall be destroyed, as Shalman destroyed Beth-arbel on the day of battle." Hosea had in mind the first Assyrian invasion of Israel in 841 B.C., by Shalmaneser III, of whose name "Shalman" is a hypocorism (*see* CARMEL, MOUNT[S]). Beth-arbel (now Irbid in Jordan) lay near the border; it follows from Hosea's words that it was taken and destroyed and its population massacred by the Assyrians as a grim warning to Israel. King Joram's murder by Jehu, who immediately did homage and paid tribute to Shalmaneser III, must be seen as a propitiatory measure to stop further Assyrian retaliation.

Bibliography. M. C. Astour, "841 B.C.: The First Assyrian Invasion of Israel," *JAOS*, XCI (1971), 383-89, with further references.

M. C. ASTOUR

***SHAREZER.** *See* BETHEL-SHAREZER[S].

***SHECHEM (CITY)** shĕk'əm *or* shə kĕm'. The original IDB article covers the biblical data thoroughly; what follows describes archaeological results since 1960.

Excavation ended in 1973 after eighteen years. Twenty-four periods of occupation have been traced on the roughly sixteen-acre tell. Gaps in occupation divide the city's history into five eras:

(a) Two periods of small village settlement within the Chalcolithic Age, falling roughly 3600-3200 B.C. (strata XXIV-XXIII).

(b) The Middle Bronze Age city-state, from about 1900 B.C. to about 1540 B.C., when Egyptians destroyed towns throughout Canaan as they drove out the HYKSOS (strata XXII-XV).

(c) The Late Bronze Age city-state, starting about 1450 and extending past the time of the Hebrew conquest to about 1125, when destruction came (Judg. 9) (strata XIV-XI).

(d) After a gap of more than a century, continuous occupation as a city through the time of the northern kingdom, with a major destruction in 724 B.C., and as a village among ruins down to about 475 B.C. (strata X-V).

(e) A flourishing, fortified Hellenistic city from about 330 to 107 B.C. (strata IV-I), relating to the Samaritan temple on Mount GERIZIM high above the city.

Shechem's history is closely related to a succession of sanctuaries mentioned or implied in the OT and attested archaeologically. At the western edge of the city, a walled precinct contained sacred buildings covering a time span of more than six hundred years. Beginning about 1750 the precinct contained courtyard temples made up of small rooms and a plaza surrounding a central court open to the sky, in which a free-standing pillar probably rested on a rock base. About 1650, a massive fortress-temple, with walls seventeen feet thick, replaced the courtyard temples. An altar in front of the fortress-temple sat on a thick layer of fill (note the Beth-millo, house of the filling, in Judg. 9:6), directly over the central court of the series of courtyard temples. The fortress-temple first had a stone pillar standing in the center of its entrance; in a second phase, shaped slabs of rock standing in sockets flanked the entrance. Continuing the sanctuary tradition in this one spot was a less massive one-room temple built on the foundations of the fortress-temple. This structure's two phases cover the period 1450-1125; in front of it, next to an altar above the earlier altar, stood a huge slab of shaped limestone in a stone socket. In short, a sanctuary tradition carried through two major shifts of political allegiance (Hyksos to Egyptian-vassal Canaanites about 1540, Canaanite to Israelite around 1200). Characteristic of the tradition was the sanctity of a specific spot and a continuing use of standing stones, Hebrew masseboth (*see* PILLAR; PILLAR[S]). When the archaeological data is compared with passages such as Gen. 12:6; Josh. 24:1-28; and Judg. 9:1-49, a group of constants emerges: sanctuary, famous tree (*see* DIVINERS' OAK[S]), standing stone, and covenant making at Shechem. It is quite likely that all the structures mentioned in Judg. 9:4, 6, and 46 are part of the complex in Shechem's sacred precinct.

Other sanctuaries have been found within the city and nearby. Between the fortress-temple and the great fortification wall at the W perimeter of the city, salvage excavation in 1973 identified a royal "chapel" of three rooms on a single axis, with an altar along the center of the inmost wall; it was contemporary with the fortress-temple and the outermost city wall (1650-1540). Also contemporary was a square sanctuary built around an open central court with a base for a central pillar, located on a low hillock on the flanks of Mount Gerizim, above and just S of Shechem. Contemporary with the 1450-1125 period sanctuary in the sacred precinct was what appears to be another sacred building among the houses near the heart of the city, again with a large, shaped slab of rock lying on its floor.

The existence of these sanctuaries outside the sacred precinct, and in one case outside the city altogether, throws indirect light on the Deuteronomic traditions of sacred places in the Shechem pass between Mount Gerizim and Mount Ebal (Deut. 11:29-32; 27:1-26; Josh. 8:30-35), as well as on the patriarchal traditions in Gen. 12:6; 33:18-20; and 35:4. *See* JOSHUA, BOOK OF[S] §5*d*.

From the Hellenistic period comes one more important sanctuary near Shechem, represented by a solid block of masonry sixty-five feet on a side and thirty-two feet high, poised on Tell er-Râs, 1100 feet above the floor of the valley. Visible from everywhere in the Shechem pass and adjacent plain, including from the mouth of the traditional Jacob's Well (John 4:6; cf. vs. 20), it is almost certainly the base of the altar or even the podium of the Samaritan worship center on Mount Gerizim (*see* SAMARITANS; SAMARITANS[S]). The emperor HADRIAN built a temple of Zeus on top of the ruin about A.D. 130.

Bibliography. For reports of the excavations season by season, consult *BASOR,* 144 (1956), 9-20; 148 (1957), 11-28; 161 (1961), 11-54; 169 (1963), 1-60; 180 (1965), 7-41; 190 (1968), 2-41; 204 (1971), 2-17; 205 (1972), 20-35; 216 (1974), 31-52. A lucid synthesis (through 1962) is G. E. Wright, *Shechem: The Biography of a Biblical City* (1965); a new ed. covering the entire expedition is in preparation. More popular and synthetic articles include E. F. Campbell, Jr., and J. F. Ross, "The Excavation of Shechem and the Biblical Tradition," *BA,* XXVI (1963), 2-27; R. J. Bull, "The Excavation of Tell er-Ras on Mt. Gerizim," *BA,* XXXI (1968), 58-72; R. G. Boling, "Bronze Age Buildings at the Shechem High Place: ASOR Excavations at Tananir," *BA,* XXXII (1969), 82-103; E. F. Campbell, Jr., and G. E. Wright, "Tribal League Shrines in Amman and Shechem," *BA,* XXXII (1969), 104-16. Full description of the archaeology, stratum by stratum, is given by L. E. Toombs, "The Stratigraphy of Tell Balaṭah (Ancient Shechem)," *ADAJ* (forthcoming).

E. F. CAMPBELL

*__SHILOH (CITY).__ In the beginning of the eleventh century B.C. Shiloh was Israelite property, but there is no evidence in the OT of when it came to be so, and no information is given of an Israelite conquest of the town.

After the Israelite defeat when the ark was taken by the Philistines as a war trophy (I Sam. 4:1-11), Shiloh disappears from the traditions in I Samuel. When the ark is later returned to Israel it is placed in Kiriath-jearim in Judah, not in Shiloh as might be expected. This has led to the conclusion that Shiloh had been destroyed by the Philistines *ca.* 1050 B.C., and that it is this destruction that Jeremiah alludes to: "Go now to my place that was in Shiloh, . . . and see what I did to it" (Jer. 7:12; cf. 26:6). However, it seems unlikely that Jeremiah (*ca.* 600 B.C.) would refer to a destruction that had taken place roughly 450 years earlier. Further, Shiloh seems to have been still in existence at the time of King Jeroboam I (*ca.* 925 B.C.) (I Kings 11:29; 12:15; 14:2-4), though it cannot be taken for granted that because the prophet Ahijah lived in Shiloh, there was also a sanctuary there. Jer. 41:5, dating from *ca.* 585 B.C., talks of "men from Shiloh," which could mean that Shiloh was still inhabited then, but it may also be understood as men from that district. In this case, however, the LXX (48:5) reads Σαλημ instead of the normal transcription Σηλω (μ). Shiloh thus seems to have been in existence as a town through most of the monarchic period, though it may have suffered devastation in connection with the fall of the northern kingdom in the year 722 B.C. The passages from Jeremiah may be understood as referring to the sanctuary alone, not to the town proper; Ps. 78:60 only says that God gave up his abode at Shiloh. It may therefore well be that Shiloh was a living town, whereas at a certain time its sanctuary had been destroyed and abandoned.

The Danish excavations at Seilun, carried out in the years 1926 and 1929, were interrupted in 1932 by the sudden death of H. Kjaer, the director. Only preliminary reports appeared. According to these, Seilun had suffered heavy destruction some time during the Iron I period and never recovered completely. Most scholars took this as a proof of the theory that Shiloh had been destroyed in the Philistine war, *ca.* 1050 B.C.

A closer examination of the finds, combined with a short supplementary excavation carried out in 1963 by the present writer, has necessitated a revision of the earlier conclusions. There is no evidence of a regular destruction in the Iron I period, and ceramics from Iron II are abundant. The first flourishing period of Seilun was Middle Bronze II (*ca.* 1800-1550), when the town was surrounded by a heavy wall. At the end of this period Seilun seems to have been destroyed like many other Palestinian towns, possibly in connection with the Egyptian campaigns. In Late Bronze I Seilun seems not to have been inhabited, but LB II as well as Iron I are represented, though on a lesser scale. Iron II—mainly the time of the divided monarchy—was a flourishing period, whereas the sudden scarcity of ceramics from Iron III points to a final destruction of Seilun *ca.* 600 B.C. The town did not come into existence again until

Late Hellenistic or Early Roman days. During the Roman and Byzantine periods it seems to have been a prosperous town, but after the Islamic conquest it lost much in importance. During recent centuries Seilun has no longer been inhabited.

The excavations have shown no traces of a sanctuary on the summit of the mound where one would have expected it. This may be due to the summit having been almost completely denuded, partly by erosion, partly by an artificial leveling right down to the bedrock when the town was rebuilt during the Roman period. The ritual dancing in the vineyards (Judg. 21:19-24) may, however, mean that the sanctuary was outside the town itself.

Bibliography. A. T. Richardson, "The Site of Shiloh," *PEQ*, XXIX (1927), 85-88; W. F. Albright, "The Danish Excavations at Seilun: A Correction," *PEQ*, XXIX (1927), 157-58; H. Kjaer, "The Danish Excavation of Shiloh," *PEQ*, XXIX (1927), 202-13, "The Excavation of Shiloh 1929," *JPOS*, X (1930), 87-174, "Shiloh. A Summary Report of the Second Danish Expedition, 1929," *PEQ*, XXXI (1931), 71-88; M.-L Buhl and S. Holm-Nielsen, *Shiloh. The Danish Excavations at Tell Sailûn, Palestine, in 1926, 1929, 1932 and 1963* (1969).

S. Holm-Nielsen

***SHIPS AND SHIPPING.** New discoveries have shed fresh light on ships of the Bronze Age and of the Greek and Roman periods.

1. The Bronze Age. Until recently we knew the ships in use in the Mediterranean during the Bronze Age (roughly 2000 to 1200 B.C.) solely through small, often crude, representations on pottery and seals and a few rough clay models. In 1972 there was uncovered at Akrotiri on the Greek island of Thera (Santorini) a painted frieze from about 1500 B.C. that includes a marine scene in which half a dozen ships are carefully drawn in large scale (Fig. S4). The new pictures confirm much that had hitherto been suggested but was not certain: that the sailors of Crete and the

Courtesy L. Casson
4. The Thera frieze

nearby islands used long, slender galleys rounded at both ends and rigged like contemporary Egyptian craft, with a broad square sail stiffened by a boom along the foot (not loose footed, as sails were to be from the close of the Bronze Age on). Even more important, the pictures settle an argument of long standing. On many of the vessels portrayed on seals and ceramics, one end terminates in a lofty post while the other is lower and has a distinctive projection at the water line. The point at issue has been: which is prow and which stern? Most have held that the lower end is the prow, and that the projection is the earliest example of that naval weapon par excellence, the ram. This theory must now be abandoned once and for all, for the new pictures, although they do not make clear what the projection is, show that it is unquestionably at the stern. It seems to be removable; perhaps it served as a balancing platform attached on ceremonial occasions when the vessels, as in the frieze, carried a heavy concentration of passengers aft.

2. Merchantmen. Until World War II our knowledge of the sailing ships which the ancients used for carrying cargo was limited to what could be gleaned from casual references in literature and from representations in painting and sculpture. Few of these showed any detail, and none were to scale. The development of scuba diving after the war and the new field of underwater archaeology to which it gave rise have totally changed the picture. Hundreds of wrecks of ancient sailing vessels have since been located, ranging in date from the seventh century B.C. to the seventh A.D., and in type from small coasting craft to freighters of respectable size. In all cases there are remains of cargo; in many, remains of the ship's equipment; in a precious few, remains of the bottom of the hull, protected from disintegration by the cargo lying over it. As a result, for the first time we know how Greek and Roman sailing craft were constructed.

a. Construction. There are fundamentally two ways of building a wooden vessel. One, familiar to us since it has been standard in the West, is to start with a skeleton of keel and frames (ribs) and then fasten to this a skin of planks. The other, favored by most of Asia but also some parts of Europe, reverses the procedure. First a shell of planks is made by pinning each plank to its neighbors, and then a certain number of frames are inserted to stiffen the shell.

Ancient wrecks reveal that the Greek and Roman shipwright consistently used the second method—but with such care that the results more resemble cabinet work than carpentry. He built up a shell of planks, pinning them to each other with close-set mortises and tenons—they are almost always less than ten inches apart, most often two to eight, and sometimes with hardly any space at all between—and to make sure they would never separate, he transfixed each with a dowel. Then, into this sturdy shell he inserted a powerful and complete set of frames made fast to the planking by long wooden dowels (treenails). The frames were rarely more than ten inches apart and usually much closer. Hulls so built must have been immensely durable and resistant.

Since the only wood to survive was that protected by an overlay of cargo, in almost all cases merely the bottom of the hull has been preserved (Fig. S5), and only in a very few is there planking or structural material from higher up. For the superstructure we must still depend on ancient pictures (e.g., Ships and Sailing in the OT Figs. 48, 51, both standard two-masters of the Roman period). The remains of a small coasting vessel of late date (seventh century A.D.) include parts that

Michael L. Katzer, courtesy of the American Institute of Nautical Archaeology

5. Wooden timbers of the Kyrenia ship preserved and reassembled (photo taken from the stern)

permit the reconstruction of the kitchen it carried at deck level aft, a roomy affair with a sizable hearth for preparing hot food; such facilities were far more elaborate than those which Columbus' ships boasted.

b. Size. The largest wreck uncovered so far was about 140 feet long. Quite a few were 100 feet or somewhat more. The beam runs between one third and one quarter the length, ratios common in sailing ships of all ages.

c. Materials. Most hulls were made of fir, cedar, or pine, woods traditionally favored by shipwrights. But cypress, elm, alder, and other woods have been identified, indicating that builders turned to locally available materials. Oak was commonly used for tenons and dowels, and occasionally for framing.

d. Equipment. Anchors are the piece of equipment most often found. The many hundreds that have been recovered enable us to reconstruct in some detail the various types and their development. The simplest anchors were of stone, including certain kinds still in use today. More sophisticated types had a stone or lead stock and wooden shank and arms. According to Acts 27:29-30 Paul's ship dropped four anchors astern and had others ready forward; underwater finds confirm that it was standard practice to carry multiple anchors fore and aft. Anchors were big as well as numerous. The 140-foot ship mentioned above had one with a lead stock 8 feet long that weighed over 1,500 pounds.

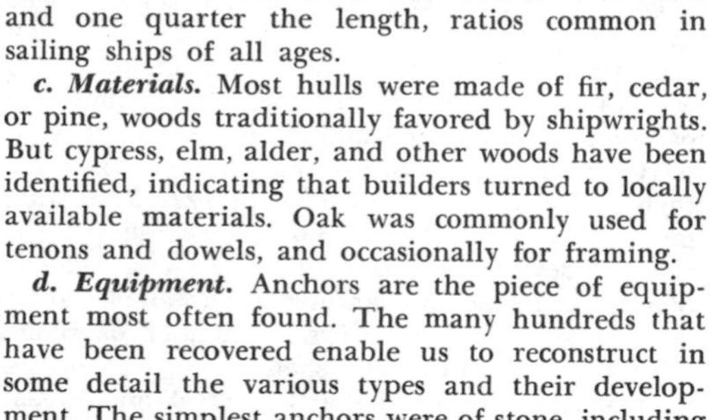

John Veltri, courtesy of the American Institute of Nautical Archaeology

6. Divers excavating the Kyrenia ship (photo taken from the stern)

Other items of equipment commonly recovered include lead and bronze rings in various sizes, tools, and vessels from the ship's kitchen.

e. Cargoes. The commodities that figured largest in ancient overseas commerce were grain, wine, and olive oil. Since grain was shipped in sacks or bulk, no cargoes of it have survived. Wine and oil, as well as certain other products (dried fish, olives, nuts, pitch), were shipped in amphorae (clay jars generally holding from five to ten gallons); since these are unaffected by sea water, cargoes of amphorae are what the divers most frequently come across. Each city tended to use distinctive types of jars whose features changed over the years, so amphorae have become an invaluable index to the date of a wreck and the ports where it took on cargo.

Divers have also found cargoes of building stone (both rough blocks and finished members such as column drums), roof tiles, lead and copper ingots, and even of works of art such as marble and bronze sculptures.

Bibliography. L. Casson, "Bronze Age Ships," *International Journal of Nautical Archaeology*, IV (1975), 3-10, and *Ships and Seamanship in the Ancient World* (1971); G. Bass, ed., *A History of Seafaring Based on Underwater Archaeology* (1972). L. CASSON

***SHISHAK.** On possible relationship to Solomon, *see* EGYPT, CHRONOLOGY OF[S] §4.

***SIGN IN THE NT.** The Greek word σημεῖον, meaning "sign," occurs about seventy-five times in the NT, sixteen times together with τέρας (wonder) (*see* SIGNS AND WONDERS). The term "sign" may refer to a natural event or circumstance (Luke 2:12; II Thess. 3:17), to a miraculous authenticating deed (Mark 8:11; John 2:11), or to an apocalyptic portent (Mark 13:4; Rev. 13:13). The last two NT usages are of more direct theological significance.

1. Jesus' attitude toward miraculous signs. In Mark and the Synoptics generally, Jesus rejects the demand for an authenticating "sign from heaven" made by hostile or unbelieving persons (Mark 8:11-13; Matt. 12:38-39; cf. John 2:18), and Jesus' miracles are not presented as signs. This rejection of signs is taken to reflect the attitude of Jesus himself, since the contents of the gospels, as well as the book of Acts, indicate that early Christians were impressed with the miraculous deeds of Jesus and others, seeing in them tokens of God-given power and authority. Quite possibly Jesus viewed his own deeds more as signs of God's inbreaking kingdom than as indications of his own status and authority (Matt. 12:28).

2. Signs as authenticating miracles in Paul. Paul never mentions Jesus' miracles but speaks of his own performance of apostolic signs and wonders (II Cor. 12:12; Rom. 15:19). The context of II Corinthians makes two important facts clear: the opponents of Paul had performed such signs (12:11), and the signs in question were understood to be miraculous—"signs and wonders and mighty works" (12:12; cf. Rom. 15:19). Paul himself refused to exult in these manifestations as his opponents apparently did, but placed them under the rubric of foolishness and boasting (12:1, 11). He himself would boast only in weakness (12:9-10), however, as befitted his understanding of Christ. Possibly Paul's opponents in Corinth also placed great store in the miracles of Jesus, whom they viewed as a DIVINE MAN (θεῖος ἀνήρ), but the evidence is scarcely sufficient to warrant a firm conclusion. Significantly, in referring to miraculous spiritual gifts (I Cor. 12:9-10, 28-30) Paul does not speak of signs, but seems to reserve that term for deeds authenticating an apostle.

3. Signs in Acts and John. Jesus' miracles of healing are mentioned in the speeches of Acts (10:38), and he is said to have been attested by miraculous signs (2:22). Moreover, the miracles performed by Moses in Egypt (7:36), as well as those performed in the church, are called signs and wonders (2:43; 5:12; cf. Heb. 2:4). Such references to signs and wonders provide an additional context in which to interpret the data of II Cor. 12, for they give further indication of the role played by signs in the missionary preaching and life of the church.

It is therefore not entirely surprising that in the Gospel of John, Jesus' miracles are regularly called signs. As such they are clearly intended to point to his God-given role and dignity, although the evangelist does not view them naïvely or uncritically. In this gospel Jesus himself does not characteristically use the word "sign," speaking instead of his works (ἔργα), but he does not refuse to do signs. Here, in sharp contrast with the Synoptics, he takes the initiative in performing them, with the apparent intention of eliciting faith in himself. The signs then provide occasion for Jesus' discourses and discussions with his opponents in which the Johannine theology finds expression (John 5 and 9 esp.).

John's somewhat ambivalent attitude toward signs may result from his appropriation and editing of a collection of stories (a σημεῖα source) designed to persuade the reader of Jesus' divine power and dignity simply by recounting his miracles (*see* JOHN, GOSPEL OF[S] §2). Such a source corresponds to the situation we find in the book of Acts and with Paul's Corinthian opponents, for in each case authentication by signs plays a role. In this connection, Paul's statement that "Jews demand signs" (I Cor. 1:22) is also noteworthy. If the Johannine signs were drawn from some such traditional source or sources, it is unlikely that the evangelist took over so much of this material only to criticize it. The gospel leaves the unmistakable impression of a powerful and nearly omniscient Jesus, despite a recognition of his humanity (1:14) and the ambiguity of miracles as tokens of divine revelation (12:37). Although the Johannine Jesus takes on some of the traits of the Hellenistic-Jewish divine man, the ultimate background of this understanding of signs is likely the σημεῖα (אותות) attributed to Moses in the Exodus tradition, which validate his role as God's messenger.

4. Signs as eschatological portents. In Hellenistic as well as Jewish and Christian sources, signs sometimes appear as portents of the future. This usage is found both in the apocalyptic discourses of the gospels (Mark 13:4, 22) and in the book of Revelation (12:1, 3). The description of apocalyptic wonders in the OT book of Joel (2:30), cited in Acts 2:19, has been supplemented to include a reference to signs. Miraculous or otherwise astonishing apocalyptic signs were expected to signal and usher in the final crisis of God's redemption. Quite possibly the term first entered the Christian tradition in this sense. Such signs were not, however, the sole prerogative of God's emissaries. The final hour was to be marked by the appearance of false Christs and prophets performing signs (Mark 13: 22; Rev. 19:20).

The movement from eschatology to Christology, which can be seen in the case of signs, is typical of the transition in early Christianity from an eager expectation of the return of Jesus in apocalyptic glory to a perception of God's glory in or behind his earthly ministry.

Bibliography. On signs in the Bible and NT generally: K. H. Rengstorf, "σημεῖον," *TDNT,* VII (1964), 200-261.

On signs in the Gospel of John: R. Formesyn, *Le sèmeion johannique et le sèmeion hellénistique,* ALBO, sér. 4, fasc. 7 (1962); R. T. Fortna, *The Gospel of Signs,* NTSMS, XI (1970); W. Nicol, *The Semeia in the Fourth Gospel,* NovTSup, XXXII (1972).

On the "sign of Jonah": R. A. Edwards, *The Sign of Jonah,* SBT, 2nd ser., XVIII (1971).

D. M. SMITH

***SINITES** [ethnic הסיני, LXX Ασενναῖος, Ugar. *Syn,* ethnic sing. *syny,* pl. *synym,* second-millennium Akkad. *Siyan(n)i,* Neo-Assyr. *Sian(n)nu,* ethnic *Šian-aya*]. A northern Canaanite people, listed Gen. 10:17. It has long been recognized that the ethnic should be vocalized *has-siyānî* (instead of *has-sînî*) and identified with the N Phoenician city-state of Siyan(n)u. Documents unearthed at UGARIT added much to our knowledge of it and established its location at the large mound near the village still called Siyānū (*see* HITTITES[S] map). In the Late Bronze Age, the dual state of Siyan(n)u-Ushnatu was under the overlordship of Ugarit, till the Hittite king Mursilis II, *ca.* 1330 B.C., subordinated it directly to the king of CARCHEMISH, who was the Hittite viceroy for northern Syria. Both cities survived the collapse of Ugarit. In the ninth century, they formed two independent states which participated in the Battle of Qarqar (*see* AHAB 1; SHALMANESER 3). Tiglath-pileser III, in 738, incorporated them into the newly established Assyrian province of Ṣimirra (*see* ZEMARITES).

Bibliography. *DPaR* (1920), p. 58; J. Nougayrol, *PRU,* IV (1956), 16-17, 71-83, 281-91; M. Liverani, *Storia di Ugarit . . .* (1962), pp. 72-77, 118-20, 150-52; H. Klengel, *Geschichte Syriens im 2. Jahrtausend v. u. Z.,* II (1969), 355, 367-68, 380-83. M. C. ASTOUR

SIROCCO. *See* PALESTINE, CLIMATE OF §6.

SITES, ANCIENT, IDENTIFICATION OF. Modern research in historical geography requires the co-ordination of four major disciplines, philology, linguistics, geography, and archaeology, each with its own rules of evidence and frames of reference.

1. **Historical source analysis.** Since the goal of historical (as opposed to physical) geography is the understanding of ancient peoples in their environment, a philological analysis of all written sources is mandatory. Geographical annotations occur in the Bible to facilitate the reader's orientation (e.g., Gen. 14:2, 3, 7). Much of Jewish law is predicated upon conditions prevailing "when you come into the land" (Lev. 25:2; Num. 15:2; cf. 34:2; Deut. 12:1, etc.); thus it was necessary to know the nature and extent of the land of Israel, and the rabbinic authors show a lively interest in biblical geography. Christians were also concerned with identifying the scenes of scriptural events. Biblical scholars who lived in the land, such as Origen, Eusebius, Jerome, and Epiphanius, knew the country intimately and had frequent contacts with Jewish scholars and documents. Eusebius' *Onomasticon* was the most important composition to emerge from this age, but many others, including the mosaic map of Medeba, record the Byzantine locations of numerous sites.

During the subsequent periods, the works of Arab geographers are usually superior in value to the pilgrim itineraries because they had direct access to the local populace. One neglected scholar of the fourteenth century A.D. is Eshtori Haparhi, a Jew from Spain who studied the countryside and identified many biblical and talmudic sites. The most lasting contributions were made by E. Robinson, C. Clermont-Ganneau, and others, who combined field work with deep knowledge of, and constant reference to, the written sources.

Today the corpus of available materials as well as geographical research tools (concordances, geographical glossaries, etc.) encompasses not only the Bible but also extrabiblical texts. The postbiblical sources, Jewish, Christian, and Moslem, have lost none of their value; on the contrary, many sites known heretofore only in these late texts are now documented in extrabiblical inscriptions from the second millennium B.C.

The serious historical geographer must be thoroughly equipped to handle at least some of these written sources in the original language. Of special importance is sound philological method, well seasoned with common sense. Texts must be analyzed for their geographical information: place names and topographic features. Biblical texts must be critically evaluated and their literary genre defined; internal evidence such as possible geographical order within lists and narratives must be established. When seeking to locate a particular ancient settlement, all known references to the place from every written source available must be collected and studied in their contexts, preferably in the original. Distinction should be made between explicit and general references. Sociological and geopolitical details may have special significance; e.g., was the settlement a village, was it fortified, did it belong to a known political league or administrative district? Did it play a role in military events? The correct linguistic form of the name must also be established by means of text criticism and the comparison of epigraphic evidence.

2. **Toponymic investigation.** The linguistic link between the historical records and the landscape is the preservation of numerous ancient names in Arabic form. Eshtori Haparhi was the unheralded pioneer in rediscovering Hebrew and Aramaic names among local toponyms, but in modern times it was Eli Smith, Edward Robinson's traveling companion, who assembled and analyzed this material for the first time. Many factors, mainly psychological and sociological, have complicated the picture. Some ancient names have been transformed into a similar sounding name with an entirely different Arabic meaning; a few have been translated into Arabic. Names resembling the Arabic word for demon (*'ifrît*) have been euphemistically converted to *eṭ-Ṭaiyibeh,* "the favored," or the like. Where some Moslem clan or tribe has supplanted an older place name, the latter may have been transferred to the tomb of a local saint or sheikh. Rocks, water sources, and other prominent topographical features may also inherit some truly ancient name. Where the original name has disappeared, a TELL may come to be named after a nearby village, e.g., Tell Beit Mirsim.

Semitic names frequently survived the imposition of Roman-Byzantine titles; OT Lod (NT Lydda) was called Diospolis but with the Arab conquest the name Ludd/Lod came to the surface from among the Semitic peasantry. But in contrast is the modern village of Sebastiyeh, where the Semitic-speaking Samaritans were ousted and replaced by Greeks and Macedonians, thus paving the way for Herod's new Sebaste (in honor of Augustus) to replace permanently the ancient Shōmerôn (Samaria).

3. **Physical topography.** Modern research in historical geography must reckon with the ecological environment: types of rock and soil, water resources, rainfall, agricultural potentialities, and their effects upon the pattern of human settlement (as well as man's effect on them). Such research may contribute to the elucidation of certain passages in the ancient texts, but the investigator must first define carefully the content of the written source in accordance with sound rules of linguistics and philology before trying to impose a new interpretation in the light of the physical sciences.

4. **Archaeological research.** A century ago, the term archaeology could still be applied to details of *realia* gleaned from ancient texts, e.g., the Bible, the Talmud, etc. Most explorers thought only of visible remains, columns, foundations, carved-out tombs, etc., as archaeological. J. L. Porter and perhaps a very few others realized almost instinctively that the truncated, conical-shaped mounds near most villages bearing biblical names were actually the sites of the really ancient settlements; but they were in the minority. C. R. Conder even argued that these tells, or mounds, were the sites of ancient brick factories. Flinders-Petrie proved in 1890 that Tell el-Hesī contained the stratified remains of ruined cities, always rebuilt on the same site. By the First World War numerous excavations had been conducted. In the 1920s and 1930s a kind of positivism developed in which subjective impres-

sions gained during field excursions were elevated to the authority of objective archaeological facts. Theories based on insufficient evidence were accepted in the textbooks as axiomatic; since World War II many of these have been disproved by more intensive research. Especially has that been true when older proposals conflicted with clear statements in the texts; e.g., the supposition that Debir was not really in the hill country, or that Philistine Gath could be sought in the S. Hastily drawn conclusions, founded on incomplete archaeological findings, have had to be revised in numerous cases. Tell Abū Hureireh (Tel Haror) was formerly pronounced of no significance until meticulous survey revealed an extensive "lower city" with Bronze Age remains; Tell en-Nejîleh produced abundant surface pottery from the Iron Age, but excavation showed that no substantial town from the Israelite period ever stood there. The excavator at Deir'alla denied the identification with Succoth on the basis of early results in a very limited digging area; the later discovery of an Aramaic inscription showed that the site was occupied much longer than he had originally supposed.

Excavations have seldom produced epigraphic material confirming the name of a site. In only one case, Tell ed-Duweir, was an identification proved by such a find (Lachish, mentioned in an ostracon); elsewhere, e.g., at Gezer, Gibeon, Bethshan, Arad, and Dibon, the Arabic name was already clear evidence for the name of the ancient site.

Even the presence of stratified remains corresponding to the historical periods of a town is not valid evidence for identification unless the locale and other factors harmonize with the texts. Conversely, the absence of material from some documented period is not conclusive if the other demands of the written records are clearly met. Extensive building activity in one period may have obliterated some previous occupation level(s). The ancient name may have moved from the original tell when its surface became too small to support a town. The present-day village may be some distance away from the biblical site. This fact, often hidden from the nineteenth-century explorers, is discernible by the proper archaeological criteria.

The historical evaluation of archaeological evidence is fraught with pitfalls. Though artifacts discovered during excavation are quite objective in themselves, they are no more so than the clear statement of an ancient text. In both instances the interpretation of the facts, archaeological as well as philological, is bound to be highly subjective, reflecting the personal bias of the individual scholar. Just as many passages are ambiguous, so are the supposed results of excavated areas. Therefore, one must be cautious of accepting historical interpretations based on limited results in a probe or narrow trench.

The connection between particular strata in an excavation and the general historical framework is often determined by the ceramic and other artifactual evidence found *in situ*. Datable inscriptions in stratified contexts are rare, and the pottery chronology, though well defined for broad periods (Bronze Age, Iron Age, Hellenistic, Roman, etc.), is seldom perfected for periods of less than a century. Especially is this true with regard to the historical periods such as the Israelite monarchy. Furthermore, it is well known that older sherds work their way up in a mound and later sherds work their way down. A valid topological sequence must be based on whole vessels from stratified contexts (not just from tombs). Thus, baulks must be removed to uncover entire rooms or other living contexts in order to permit restoration of broken vessels. For historical research, one must correlate the over-all type of settlement present at a site during specific periods. The picture that emerges may then be compared with the textual evidence.

The real service rendered by an archaeological survey is the establishment of the general character of specific sites. A trained investigating team can discern such typical features as over-all configuration, location, distance from water sources, fortified slopes, etc.

Similar principles govern the study of geographic regions. First, one must determine from the texts what a particular geographic term seems to mean. Classic examples of misused terminology are the alleged difference between Esdraelon and Jezreel (the former is simply the Greek reflex of the latter; both refer to the same valley) and the modern extension of the term Negeb to include all of southern Israel (=Mandated Palestine) down to Elath. Current books on geography, even those designed for use as biblical reference books, fail to observe that the biblical Negeb is basically the E-W zone from Gaza to the Dead Sea (with Beersheba as the focal point), what is popularly called today "the northern Negeb." Neither the Middle Bronze Age I settlements made famous by Nelson Glueck nor the Nabatean/Byzantine cities of 'Avdat and Shivta were in the Negeb of Israelite times. In all such cases, the geographer must establish the textual evidence first, and then he can attempt to correlate features of the terrain with historical nomenclature.

5. Correlation and synthesis. When seeking to locate a biblical settlement or, conversely, to find a historical identification for an archaeological site, the evidence from all the relevant disciplines must be compared. In rare instances, the facts in one sphere serve to resolve a problem in another, but great caution must be exercised. Any new site identification should be tested by a team of scholars from the various disciplines.

Bibliography. For detailed references, cf. Y. Aharoni, *The Land of the Bible* (1967), pp. 73-117; Y. Ben-Arieh, "The Geographical Exploration of the Holy Land," *PEQ*, CIV (1972), 81-92; D. Baly, *The Geography of the Bible* (rev. ed., 1974).

A. F. RAINEY

SITES, SACRED. The fact that the biblical account describes both the patriarchs and the followers of Moses as entering a land which was already occupied is an important datum for the consideration of sacred sites. In many cases, the holy places of the previous inhabitants were maintained by the newcomers, who sanctioned their use by describing theophanies of the God of

Israel which occurred there (*see* THEOPHANY IN THE OT[S] esp. §1*ai*). For example, Gen. 12:6-7 reports that Yahweh appeared to Abraham at the מקום (i.e., [holy] "place") in Shechem. The fact that the מקום was then under Canaanite control is made clear by the notice that "the Canaanites were [then] in the land." This patriarchal story explains why the site was subsequently regarded as sacred by Israel.

The modern reader, who tends to view all space as homogeneous, might wonder why Yahweh would be thought to reveal himself in a Canaanite holy site. In the consciousness of ancient man, however, there was a radical distinction between sacred and profane space. Sacred space was awesome, filled with a terrifying holiness (Gen. 28:17; Exod. 3:5). Places known to possess such qualities had been isolated by successive generations, and it seemed reasonable to worship the God of Israel at them and assume that he was the patron of the holiness attested there. *See* SANCTIFICATION IN THE OT[S] §2.

The men of Israel shared with the ancient inhabitants of Canaan a general understanding of the type of location which would be most suitable for cultic purposes. That typology is illustrated by the location of pre-Israelite sanctuaries: (1) temples in major urban centers, and (2) numerous sacred places which were more frequently located outside the cities, often in open spaces near sacred trees, by springs, on hills, or in the valleys.

In the major urban centers the temple was conceived of as a house (בית) or a palace (היכל) for the god whose presence was acknowledged by gifts, sacrifices, and other cultic acts. The god was symbolically represented by an icon or sacred symbol, which was housed in the inner *cella* (דביר). (*See* GRAVEN IMAGE; MOLTEN IMAGE; IDOL.) Architecturally, Israelite temples were quite similar to those of their neighbors (*see* TEMPLE, JERUSALEM; TEMPLE OF SOLOMON[S]), but the rigid aniconism of Yahwehism prohibited the construction of any divine image. It may be assumed that most of the major cities of Canaan contained pre-Israelite temples. Archaeologists have provided us with evidence for many (*see* TEMPLES; TEMPLES, SEMITIC[S] §1). Further evidence is supplied by the names of Canaanite cities. Many of the names compounded with *beth* (house of) indicate the presence of a temple, e.g., Bethel (House of El); Beth-shemesh (House of Shamash, i.e., a sun god). Other cities containing a theophorous element in their name provide similar evidence, e.g., Baal-hazor, Ashtaroth.

Evidence for temples of Yahweh in major urban centers has been obscured by a later orthodoxy which insisted that the cult of Yahweh be restricted to a single sanctuary (Deut. 12:5). Nevertheless, traditions about the house of Yahweh at Shiloh have been preserved (I Sam. 1:7, 24; 3:15) as well as notice of Jeroboam's schismatic temple at Bethel, where Amos spoke (Amos 7:13). Amos' condemnation of cultic practices at Gilgal, Beer-sheba (5:5), Dan, and Samaria (8:14) has led to the suggestion that royal sanctuaries were also located in those cities. (Aharoni; *see* TEMPLES, SEMITIC[S] §2*a*.)

The association of sacred sites with springs, trees, and heights has generally been interpreted as an expression of the nature religions of Canaan. Farmers, who were dependent upon a sufficient amount of annual rain, looked upon the heights where storm clouds gather as most appropriate sites to petition the storm-gods, a situation which the story of Elijah's rain-making on Mount Carmel illustrates (*see also* MOUNT, MOUNTAIN[S]; CLOUD [S]). Springs and wells are likewise sources of life-giving water, while flourishing trees provide apt and living witness to fertile powers within a sacred area. The worship of chthonic deities, which would be most appropriately conducted in caves or low places, may also be related to the fertility of the land, since fertility depends upon powers which arise from within the earth and are under control of the deities who live there. *See* DEITIES, UNDERWORLD[S].

Many of the sites accepted as sacred by the people of Israel were also associated with trees, springs, or mountains. At Gen. 12:6 there is mention of the "oak of Moreh" at Shechem, and at Gen. 13:18 the "oaks of Mamre" in Hebron are mentioned (*see* DIVINERS' OAK[S]). At both sites Abraham is reported to have built an altar to Yahweh. In Gen. 21:33 Abraham is described as planting a tree at Beer-sheba and calling on the name of Yahweh (*see also* Gen. 23:17; Judg. 4:5). However, the continuous association of sacred groves with the Baal cult subsequently called forth vigorous prophetic denunciations (e.g., Hos. 4:12-13; Jer. 2:20; Ezek. 6:13). The kings who frequented such sacred places were judged disloyal to Yahweh by the editors of the historical books (e.g., II Kings 16:2-4).

It is obvious from Abraham's sacrifice on a mountain in Moriah (Gen. 22:2) or Elijah's sacrifice on Carmel (I Kings 18) that mountains provided appropriate sites for the worship of God. Two mountains maintain their sacred status throughout the history of Israel: Sinai-Horeb, where Yahweh spoke to Moses (Exod. 3:12) and Zion, which was chosen for his holy habitation (Ps. 68:15-16 [H 16-17]; 132:13-14; *see also* ZION TRADITION[S] §§1*a*, 2, 3; ZAPHON, MOUNT[S]). Other mountains, however, were subjected to prophetic censure because of their continued association with Canaanite cults (Ezek. 18:6, 11, 15; Jer. 3:2, 6; Hos. 4:13). Mountain heights frequently served as the site for a type of Canaanite sanctuary called a "high place" (במה). The name is slightly misleading because the במה could be constructed at any altitude, including a famous "high place" in the valley of HINNOM (Jer. 7:31; *see* BAMAH; HIGH PLACE).

Sacred springs and wells also played a role in the history of Israel. According to the account in Num. 20, Israel camped at a sacred district named Kadesh (i.e., "holy"). It was there that Moses struck a rock from whence the waters of Meribah flowed. Elsewhere (Gen. 14:7) Kadesh is referred to as En-mishpat (i.e., "the spring of judgment"). In the patriarchal traditions, the well at Beer-sheba (Gen. 21:30-31; 26:31-33) is located in the vicinity of the altar which Isaac built when Yahweh appeared to him there (Gen. 26:23-25). The naming of Beer-lahai-roi, "well of one who sees," at Gen. 16:14 is explained on the basis of Hagar's encounter with the angel of Yahweh. When David's son Adonijah sought to set himself up as king he first offered sacrifice "by the Serpent's Stone, which is beside En-rogel," a spring in the Valley Kidron (I Kings 1:9). Solomon, however, was anointed by the spring Gihon. Sacred springs do not receive the same intensive prophetic denunciation as sacred groves or mountains. In fact, eschatological prophecies include notice of a sacred spring within the Jerusalem temple itself (Joel 3:18 [H 4:18]; Ezek. 47:1; Zech. 14:8; Rev. 22:1).

In contrast to sacred springs, sacred sites associated with chthonic deities and cults of the dead were unanimously rejected by the biblical editors. The most notorious site was TOPHETH in the Valley of Hinnom, where "the sons of Judah . . . built the high place . . . to burn their sons and their daughters in the fire" (Jer. 7:30-31; cf. 19:5; 32:35). In the light of Ugaritic parallels, Lehmann has reidentified the "fields" (שדמות) of the Kidron Valley at II Kings 23:4 and elsewhere as the "field of Mot," the Canaanite god of death, thereby extending the sacred chthonic area from Hinnom down into the Kidron (*see* MOT, DEITY[S]). The site is singularly appropriate for a cult of the dead because it has the lowest altitude of any point in the general area and lacked the fertility which the rains of Baal were believed to bestow. *See also* GEHENNA.

Within a sacred precinct certain areas could be designated as more sacred than others. It was also possible for the sacredness to extend outward from its central altar or sacred object to include much of the surrounding area (*see* SANCTIFICATION[S] §4*a*; SACRIFICES AND OFFERINGS, OT[S] §§1*c*, 2*a*ii). In Exod. 19:12 the whole of Mount Sinai was marked off as sacred. A specialized extension of sanctity is probably to be seen in the establishment of the CITY OF REFUGE. The right of sanctuary for involuntary homocide, traditionally provided only at the altar, was extended to anyone permitted to enter the city.

In addition to local sanctuaries, the OT contains traditions concerning a portable shrine (or TABERNACLE) and various "central sanctuaries" (e.g., SHECHEM, SHILOH) of tribal leagues which preceded the monarchy (*see* AMPHICTYONY[S]). Both were conceived of by later writers as cultic centers for "all Israel" (Exod. 25:1-8; Josh. 18:1; 8:33). When Solomon built the temple of Yahweh in Jerusalem, he claimed for it the status of central sanctuary (I Kings 8). The influence of this central sanctuary increased under the Davidic dynasty of Judah until it was finally able to support claims that it was the only legitimate sanctuary. The first notice of such claims dates from the reign of Hezekiah (II Kings 18:4, 22). Nearly a century later, Josiah attempted a similar reform (II Kings 23:1-20) supported by Deuteronomy (Deut. 12:5, 11, 18, etc.), which spoke of a single place which God would choose. In the postexilic period the centralization of cult in Jerusalem became the normative biblical view, despite the fact that temples to Yahweh actually existed in Samaria (II Macc. 6:2), Leontopolis (Jos. Antiq. XIII.iii.1), and an island in Egypt, Elephantine (*see* ELEPHANTINE PAPYRI).

Bibliography. Y. Aharoni, "The Israelite Sanctuary at Arad," in *New Directions in Biblical Archaeology*, ed. D. N. Freedman and J. C. Greenfield (1969), pp. 25-39; M. R. Lehmann, "A New Interpretation of שדמות," *VT*, III (1953), 361-71; H. H. Nelson, L. Oppenheim, G. E. Wright, "The Significance of the Temple in the Ancient Near East," *BA*, VII (1944), 41-63, 65-77; R. de Vaux, *Ancient Israel* (1961), Pt. IV, chs. 1-4.

O. WINTERMUTE

***SLAVERY IN THE OT.** A comparison of Israelite slave laws with those of neighboring countries shows that in Israel there were tendencies to humanize this institution, even though slavery itself was in no way questioned.

This fact can be explained on the basis of Israel's knowledge of the one Creator, the belief in this one God, and the conviction that all humans, including slaves, were made in the image and likeness of God. There are, however, only a few statements which support such a view. The wisdom literature, which assumes a theology of creation, is clearest in this regard. Job confesses: "If I have rejected the cause of my manservant or my maidservant, when they brought a complaint against me; what then shall I do when God rises up? When he makes inquiry, what shall I answer him? Did not he who made me in the womb make him? And did not one fashion us in the womb?" (31:13-15). The writer of Ecclesiastes urges indulgence toward a slave who curses his master: "Do not give heed to all the things that men say, lest you hear your servant cursing you; your heart knows that many times you have yourself cursed others" (Eccl. 7:21-22). We know today that the specific theological concept of man's being made in God's image is not without analogy in other cultures (cf. the Egyptian "Teaching of Merikare," *ANET* [2nd ed.], pp. 414-18). In Gen. 9:6, this concept is used to substantiate the order which God established: "Whoever sheds the blood of man, by man shall his blood be shed; for God made man in his own image." In this context the command of the Book of the Covenant should be mentioned, whereby the killing of a slave must be atoned for (Exod. 21:20). The slave is valued not only as the property of the master, but also as a human being.

The characteristic statements on the humanization of slave treatment stem from another area, Israel's acknowledgment that Yahweh, Israel's God, has led his people out of bondage in Egypt. This thought is expressed most clearly in the Deuteronomic version of the Ten Commandments: "You shall remember that you were a servant in the land of Egypt, and the Lord your God brought you out thence with a mighty hand and an outstretched arm" (5:15*a*). This thought is expressed further in the admonition to supply the slave with the means of life in the year of his emancipation, so that he can participate fully in the life of a free man or woman (Deut. 15:13-14). The whole concept of brotherhood in Deuteronomy is to be understood in this framework. This relationship among God's people includes both king (17:15)

Scala

7. Relief with Negro slaves, from the tomb of Hor-em-heb, 18th Dynasty

and slave (15:12). All who have been joined together in this way are descended from the Israel which Yahweh originally freed. Since Yahweh has laid claim to all of them as his slaves (servants), it is unnatural for any one of them to become the slave of another. This concept is formulated within the ordinance of the year of emancipation (Lev. 25:42-43; *see* JUBILEE, YEAR OF[S]). In this light it is possible to understand the general rule, unusual in ancient Near Eastern law, that a fugitive slave should not be returned to his master (Deut. 23:15-16). The humane rule of the Book of the Covenant, that a slave wounded by his master should be freed (Exod. 21:26-27), can be interpreted only in the light of Israel's recognizing that they were a people whom Yahweh had freed from slavery. This fact is clear in the eschatological perspective of Joel 2:29 [H 3:2], where the pouring out of the Spirit is expanded (possibly in a later addition) to "the manservants and maidservants." "There is neither slave nor free . . . for you are all one in Christ Jesus" (Gal. 3:28-29), Paul would say in the light of the eschatological Christ-event. Something of the revolutionary explosiveness that would later bring the entire institution of slavery into question and finally destroy it was already at work in the development of the OT belief in Yahweh.

Bibliography. G. von Rad, *Das Gottesvolk im Deuteronomium, BWANT* (1929); H. W. Wolff, "Masters and Slaves," *Int.*, XXVII (1973), 259-72. W. ZIMMERLI

SLAVERY IN THE NT. Slavery, the legal ownership of one person by another, is a conspicuous feature of the world in which the NT emerges. An examination of the terminology and practices associated with slavery in the Greco-Roman world indicates its importance for understanding the social, literary, and theological history of the early church.

1. Terminology
2. Procurement, sale, and distribution
3. Legal status and servile occupations
4. Manumission
5. Servile names
6. Slaves in the early church
7. Servile imagery in the NT

Bibliography

1. Terminology. The primary term for slave in the literature of the period is δοῦλος (masc.), δούλη (fem.), indicating a person who is the property of another person. Legally the slave is distinguished both from the free person (cf. ἐλεύθερος, γνήσιος; L. *ingenuus, līber*) and the freed slave (cf. ἀπελεύθερος, ἐξελεύθερος; Lat. *lībertus, lībertīnus,* Acts 6:9).

Additional terms are used to denote slaves, indicating special servile types or functions: (*a*) ἀνδράποδον (a person taken in war and sold as a slave; cf. ἀνδραποδιστής, "slave-dealer," or "kidnaper," I Tim. 1:10); (*b*) ἐνδογενής, οἰκογενής (masc. or fem.), οἰκότριψ (home-bred slave); (*c*) οἰκέτης (masc.), οἰκέτις (fem.) (domestic slave; cf. οἰκετεία, the staff of household slaves, Matt. 24:45); (*d*) θεράπων (masc.), θεράπαινα (fem.) (personal slave; cf. θεραπεία, group of slaves, Luke 12:42); (*e*) παῖς, παιδάριον ("boy" or "girl" slave) and παιδίσκη (servant girl); (*f*) οἰκονόμος (slave in charge of household or estate); (*g*) σῶμα (a "body," female [σῶμα γυναικεῖον] or male [σῶμα ἀνδρεῖον]; a term used in servile inventory lists; cf. Rev. 18:13).

2. Procurement, sale, and distribution. The slave supply derived from various sources: (*a*) kidnaping (I Tim. 1:10), (*b*) debt-enslavement, (*c*) self-sale (I Clem. 55:2), (*d*) home-bred slavery (offspring of female slaves; cf. Gal. 4:21-31), and (*e*) military captivity and enslavement (cf. II Macc. 8:10-11). In the post-Augustan period, Rome turned increasingly toward home-bred slaves to sustain the labor pool. Earlier it had depended heavily on mass enslavements during war, which often produced as many as 30,000 slaves in a single battle.

Slaves were sold at public auction, Eastern slaves (e.g., Greek, Egyptian, Syrian, Judean) generally bringing higher prices than those from the W (e.g., German, Gallic, Sardinian, Britannic). Racially, the majority were Caucasian, though the presence of Negroid slaves is also attested, e.g., in paintings and art objects as well as in names using the cognomen *Afer* (*Afra*) and in the use of the adjective *nigra* (*see also* BLACKS, EARLY CHRISTIANITY AND[S] §1). The prodigious influx of foreign slaves into Rome inspired Juvenal's quip that "the Syrian Orontes has . . . poured into the Tiber" (Satire III, 60).

Population statistics indicate a slave-freedman ratio of one to five throughout the Empire, and probably one to three in Rome, with the number of slaves (male and female) in individual households ranging from 20,000 in the *familia Caesaris* (cf. Phil. 4:22; *see* CAESAR'S HOUSEHOLD) to a squad of eight among the lower middle class. Extravagant manumissions of slaves in the Republic and subsequent intermarriage produced a Roman society of which five-sixths were either servile or of servile background by the end of the first century. Roman legislation near the beginning of the century had attempted to avoid this by decreeing that no master would be allowed to manumit more than one hundred slaves at the time of his death (*Lex Fufia Caninia,* 2 B.C.).

3. Legal status and servile occupations. The slave had few rights before the law. Though entitled to a common-law marriage (*contubernium*), slaves were not allowed legal marriage (*connubium*) and exercised no legal right over their spouses or children. The slave was denied participation in municipal government and in state religion, but was permitted to join a governmentally licensed "association" (*collegium, corpus, sodalicium,* ἑταιρεία; cf. the Julian Law of Associations, A.D. 7) to meet social and religious needs and frequently to provide burial and commemorative services (*collegium funeraticum*). Immunity from military conscription and from direct taxation were two of the very few benefits the slave enjoyed before the law.

Servile occupations ranged from gang labor on farms and in the mines to seats in the imperial cabinet. Between these extremes lay the vast majority who served in homes as personal maids or servants, or engaged in crafts, or managed houses, estates, inns, and businesses for their masters. Not infrequently slaves owned slaves of their own. Philo observes that many slaves "pursue the occupations of the free" (*Every Good Man is Free* vi.35).

Slaves and freedmen who rose to some historical prominence include Helicon, chief of CALIGULA's household (cf. Philo, *On the Embassy to Gaius* XXVI–XXVII; XXX, 203-6); Publius Terentius Afer (Terence), the black author of Roman comedy (*ca.* 190-159 B.C.); Phaedrus (15 B.C.-A.D. 50), the fabulist; the Stoic philosopher EPICTETUS (A.D. 55-135); Marcus Antonius FELIX, procurator of Judea, *ca.* A.D. 52 (cf. Acts 23:24 ff.); and the early Christian author HERMAS (Vis. I.1.1).

4. Manumission. Manumission was of two types, "formal" (*iusta*) and "informal" (*minus iusta*). Of the "formal" type, the most common was the manumission *per testamentum* ("by will"), by which the master designated certain slaves to be freed at the time of his death. Massive manumissions during the Julian period, however, led to Roman policy that favored the manumission *per vindictam* ("with a rod"), requiring a slave's eligibility for manumission to be assessed before a magistrate prior to touching him "with the rod" of manumission.

"Informal" manumission was executed either through the writing of a letter (*per epistulam*), by invitation to sit at table with one's master (*per mensam*), by the gathering of friends as witnesses (*inter amicos*), or by a request "in faith" that one's prospective heir release certain slaves at the time of one's death (*fidei commissum*). "Informal" manumission had the advantage of exempting the master from a five per cent manumission tax, but the disadvantage of leaving the freedman without legal proof of his new status.

The manumitted slave or freedman received full civil rights with the opportunity of obtaining full Roman citizenship in time; he was exempted from unwarranted seizure and was at liberty to go where he pleased. At the same time his ties with his former master or patron were sustained through customary obligations (*obsequia, officia*) which required him to work for his patron or perform professional services (*operae*) under certain conditions. *See also* FREEDMEN, SYNAGOGUE OF THE.

5. Servile names. Servile status or background was often apparent in personal names. In the Roman West, Greek names in themselves had a servile taint, the most common of which were names of prominent Greeks in the past (cf. "Alexander" in Mark 15:21), names of Greek Gods (cf. "Hermes" in Rom. 16:14), and Greek nicknames, e.g., Eutychus ("lucky," Acts 20:9), Epaphroditus ("lovely," Phil. 2:25), Philologus ("talkative," Rom. 16:15), Phoebe ("radiant," Rom. 16:1), Epaenetus ("praiseworthy," Rom. 16:5), Erastus ("beloved," Rom. 16:23), ONESIMUS ("useful," Col. 4:9), Onesiphorus ("profit-bearing," II Tim. 1:16), Tychicus ("fortunate," Col. 4:7).

Latin servile names include those which indicate national origin, real or assumed, e.g., Persis ("Persian," Rom. 16:12) or Achaicus ("Achaean," i.e., Greek, I Cor. 16:17), as well as nicknames, e.g., Fortunatus ("lucky," I Cor. 16:17), Ampliatus ("magnificent," Rom. 16:8), Tryphaena ("dainty," Rom. 16:12), Urbanus ("refined," Rom. 16:9), Rufus ("red-headed," Rom. 16:13), and Primus, Secundus, Tertius (Rom. 16:22), and Quartus (Rom. 16:23) ("first," "second," "third," "fourth," in order of birth).

The servile background of a person might be rendered even more visible after manumission. Some followed the custom of adopting a name that incorporated that of their master, along with the letter "l." (*lībertus*), indicating their relationship as "patron" and "freedman." For example, a slave named Tiro, manumitted by his master, Marcus Tullius, adopted the freedman's name of M. Tullius l. Tiro.

6. Slaves in the early church. The presence of slaves in the early church receives no special notice in the NT except when servile status presents a problem, e.g., in the case of a runaway slave (*see* PHILEMON, LETTER TO §3; PHILEMON, LETTER TO[S]) or of difficulty between slave and master (Eph. 6:5-9; Col. 3:22–4:1; I Tim. 6:1-2; Tit. 2:9-10; I Pet. 2:18-25; cf. Barn. 19:7; Did. 4:10-11; *see* LISTS, ETHICAL §3; LISTS, ETHICAL[S] §2*ai,'* iii). Otherwise the presence of slaves in the church is taken for granted.

The attitude of the early church toward slaves echoes in large part the growing egalitarianism voiced by the Stoics and gradually reflected in Roman legislation (cf. Seneca, Moral Epistles XLVII; Justinian, Digest I.v.4). The NT urges the acceptance of the slave as a brother (Philem. 16), recognizing that "in Christ" slave and free are one (I Cor. 12:13; Gal. 3:28; Col. 3:11). Slaves are not to be abused (Eph. 6:9; cf. Did. 4:10; Barn. 19:7), but to be treated with equality and fairness (Col. 4:1).

By the same token, the slave is to perform his duties conscientiously, not fawning (Col. 3:22) or acting in an insubordinate or thieving manner (Tit. 2:9, 10), and not using his "brotherly" relationship with his master as an occasion for disrespect (I Tim. 6:2).

Though maltreatment of slaves is repudiated in the NT, the existence of the institution of slavery itself is not. The only first-century group known to issue a programmatic denunciation of institutionalized slavery by refusing to own slaves and condemning those who do, are the ESSENES (cf. Philo, *Every Good Man is Free* xii.79), and possibly the Therapeutae (Philo, *On the Contemplative Life* ix.70). At most, individual authors of the NT score aspects of institutional slavery, e.g., the author of Revelation, who decries the inhumanity of the slave trade (18:13) and the author of I Timothy who classifies slave-kidnapers among the "unholy and profane" (1:9-10). According to one theory, Paul urges a master to free his slave for Christian service (*see* PHILEMON, LETTER TO §3), but beyond this the NT authors simply seem to recognize the desirability of free status and to encourage the slave faced with the opportunity of manumission to take it (I Cor. 7:21). However, in later decades, certain church communities engaged in the practice of financing manumissions (Herm. Sim. I.8; Herm. Mand. VIII.10) and in some instances redeemed slaves at the price of the self-enslavement of some of the members (I Clem. 55:2), though not without criticism from other quarters of the church (Ign. Polyc. 4:3). *See also* ETHICS IN THE NT[S] §3*d*iii.

7. Servile imagery in the NT. The widespread presence of slaves in Hellenistic culture and the presence of slaves in the early church account in large part for the frequent use of servile imagery in the NT.

(*a*) In the gospels slaves appear as stock figures, much as they do in plays and essays of the period. The gospel narrative and the parables and teachings of Jesus portray slaves in typical roles and situations, e.g., the slave of a centurion (Luke 7:1-10; Matt. 8:5-13); the slave of a high priest (Matt. 26:51; Mark 14:47; Luke 22:50; John 18:10, 18, 26); slaves who plow, keep sheep, serve at table (Luke 17:7), care for the wardrobe (Luke 15:22), and carry messages for their masters (Matt. 22:3-10; Luke 14:17-24); slaves in charge of estates (Matt. 24:45-51; Luke 12:42-46) or who are provided with investment capital by their masters (Matt. 25:14-30; Luke 19:12-27); conscientious slaves (Luke 12:37-39) and those who are not (Luke 12:41-46; Matt. 24:45-51); slaves of mean character who maltreat the slaves in their charge (Luke 12:45), who refuse to show their fellow slaves the generosity they have known from their master (Matt. 18:23-35), and who alter business records to their own advantage (Luke 16:1-7). In addition, three epigrammatic sayings of Jesus employ servile metaphors: "the slave is not above his master" (Matt. 10:24); "no one can serve two masters" (Matt. 6:24; Luke 16:13); and "whoever would be great among you must be your servant" (Mark 10:43; Matt. 20:26).

(*b*) In the epistles and Revelation, servile metaphors are also used to describe (1) the status of the sinner; (2) the status of the Christian; and (3) the role of Christ.

(1) The status of the sinner is described in terms that are commonplace in Hellenistic literature, which employs servile imagery to describe an attitude of mind (cf. Philo, *Every Good Man is Free* viii.45 and *Allegorical Interpretation* III. 193; Test. Judah 18:6). Though one may be legally free, one may be attitudinally a slave, e.g., a slave to sin (Rom. 6:6, etc.), to the passions and pleasures (Tit. 3:3), to the "elements" (Gal. 4:3, 9), or to corruption (II Pet. 2:19*a*). "Whatever overcomes a man, to that he is enslaved" (II Pet. 2:19*b*).

(2) The status of the Christian is described with a variety of servile metaphors. On the one hand, the Christian is portrayed as the slave of God (e.g., Rom. 6:22; I Pet. 2:16; Rev. 1:1; Herm. Sim. II.2), the slave of righteousness (Rom. 6:18), or as the slave of Christ (e.g., Rom. 1:1; Eph. 6:6; Phil. 1:1) or the Lord Jesus Christ (Jas. 1:1). On the other, the Christian is depicted as Christ's freedman who has been purchased (ἐξαγοράσῃ) by Christ and awarded the status of adopted son (*see* ADOPTION §2) and heir (*see* INHERITANCE IN THE NT[S]; cf. Gal. 4:1-7). Again, Paul describes the Christian in eschatological terms, comparing him with the slave who waits in hope for adoption and manumission (*see* REDEEM §3) of his BODY, just as every created thing longs for the time when it will be set free from its bondage to decay and obtain the LIBERTY of the children of God (Rom. 8:19-25).

(3) The role of Christ is described in servile imagery that expresses a christological paradox common to the gospels and epistles, namely that Christ, though Lord, condescends to the role of a slave (Luke 22:27), coming among men not to be ministered to but to minister and to give his life as the redemption price (λύτρον) for others (Mark 10:45).

The paradox is elaborated in several key passages: (*a*) in the Johannine portrait of Christ washing the feet of his disciples in the manner of a domestic slave (John 13:1 ff.); (*b*) in the PARENESIS of I Pet. 2:18-25 which sets Christ forth as a model of endurance for slaves suffering harsh masters; and (*c*) in the hymn of Phil. 2:6-11, which extols Christ as one who was "in the form of God" but "emptied himself, taking the form of a slave."

Bibliography. For general bibliog. prior to 1967, cf. M. I. Finley, ed., "Bibliographical Essay," *Slavery in Classical Antiquity* (1968), pp. 229-36. Also valuable: S. Bartchy, *First Century Slavery and the Interpretation of 1 Corinthians 7:21,* SBLDS, XI (1973); S. Benko and J. O'Rourke, eds., *The Catacombs and the Colosseum* (1971), see Index; J. A. Crook, *Law and Life of Rome* (1967), pp. 179-205; H. Guelzow, *Christentum und Sklaverei in den ersten drei Jahrhunderten* (1969); J. B. Lightfoot, *St. Paul's Epistle to the Philippians* (rev. ed., 1885), pp. 171-78; F. Lyall, "Roman Law in the Writings of Paul: The Slave and the Freedman," *NTS,* XVII (1970), 73-79, and "Roman Law in the Writings of Paul: Adoption," *JBL,* LXXXVIII (1969), 458-66; K. H. Rengstorf, "δοῦλος, κτλ." *TDNT,* II (1935 [ET 1966]), 261-80; K. C. Russell, *Slavery as Reality and Metaphor in the Pauline Letters* (diss., Pontifical Univ., 1968); F. Snowden, *De Servis Libertisque Pompeianis* (diss., Harvard, 1947); G. Taylor, "The Function of ΠΙΣΤΙΣ ΧΡΙΣΤΟΥ in Galatians," *JBL,* LXXXV (1966), 58-76; A. Weiser, *Die Knechtsgleichnisse der synoptischen Evangelien,* StANT, XXIX (1971); D. B. Davis, *The Problem of Slavery in Western Civilization* (1966); J. Vogt, *Ancient Slavery and the Ideal of Man* (2nd ed., 1972). *See also bibliog. for* PHILEMON, LETTER TO[S].

W. G. ROLLINS

***SOLOMON.** For re-evaluation of building complexes formerly assigned to the Solomonic era, *see* HAZOR[S]; MEGIDDO[S]; TELL EL-KHELEIFEH[S].

***SON OF GOD.** *See* CHRISTOLOGY IN THE NT[S].

***SON OF MAN.** The question about the Son-of-man figure in Jewish apocalyptic, in the message of Jesus, and in the gospels is still widely and vigorously debated. The following points continue to be most at issue.

1. The scholarly debate
2. The Son of man in Jewish apocalyptic
   a. Dan. 7
   b. II Esd. 13
   c. The Similitudes of Enoch
3. The origin of the Christian conception
4. The use of the title in earliest Christianity
   a. The Gospel of Mark
   b. Other NT writers
Bibliography

1. The scholarly debate. The debate about the figure of the Son of man was reopened by Tödt, who argued that Jesus proclaimed the coming of the Son of man but did not identify himself with this figure, and that earliest Christianity took the step of identifying Jesus as the Son of man. But there are two problems with this view. First, it projects a role for the Son of man which is rather different from the elaborate conception met in the Similitudes of Enoch (*see* §2*c below*), and for which there is absolutely no evidence elsewhere in ancient Judaism. Second, it implies the authenticity of some of the apocalyptic Son-of-man sayings, a conclusion for which it is increasingly difficult to argue.

There are also scholarly exponents of the view that Jesus used the title "Son of man" as an enigmatic self-designation, to which he gave his own particular content (Schweizer, Hooker, and Borsch). There are also difficulties with this view, however. It, too, implies the authenticity of many of the Son-of-man sayings, and it assumes the possibility of such a use of the title in colloquial Aramaic at the time of Jesus, a possibility not supported by our current knowledge of that language.

The linguistic possibilities for the use of the title "Son of man" in Aramaic have been carefully discussed by Vermes, who has also provided a full-scale discussion of the figure of the Son of man in ancient Judaism. His findings agree essentially with those summarized below.

2. The Son of man in Jewish apocalyptic (*see also* Apocalypticism §2*c*). The expression "son of man" is found in three Jewish apocalyptic works, the earliest of which is ch. 7 of the book of Daniel. Conscious use of this chapter is made in II Esdras and the Similitudes of Enoch.

a. Dan. 7. It is a characteristic of apocalyptic writers that they constantly use and reinterpret the texts available to them; and in Dan. 7 the author takes up what is apparently an ancient Canaanite mythological text describing the taking of power by a younger god, described as "one like a son of man," from an older god, described as "one that was ancient of days" (Dan. 7:9-10, 13-14). The author is particularly interested in one part of this text:

> And behold, with the clouds of heaven
> there came one like a son of man,
> And he came to the Ancient of Days
> and was presented before him.
> And to him was given dominion
> and glory and kingdom. (7:13-14)

This description of the taking of power by the younger god is interpreted by the author of Daniel as the giving of glory by God to a symbolic figure, the "one like a son of man," and he further interprets this cryptically designated figure as representing the Maccabean martyrs.

> And the kingdom and the dominion
> and the greatness of the kingdoms
> under the whole heaven
> shall be given to the people of the
> saints of the Most High;
> their kingdom shall be an everlasting kingdom,
> and all dominions shall serve and obey them. (7:27)

b. II Esd. 13. In II Esdras and the Similitudes of Enoch, the cryptic reference to "one like a son of man" in Dan. 7 is taken up and used in connection with the development of conceptions of apocalyptic redeemer figures. The author of II Esd. 13 conceives of God redeeming his people through a supernatural figure who is, however, man-like in appearance: "After seven days I dreamed a dream in the night; and behold, a wind arose from the sea and stirred up all its waves. And I looked, and behold, this wind made something like the figure of a man come up out of the heart of the sea. And I looked, and behold that man flew with the clouds of heaven; and wherever he turned his face to look, everything under his gaze trembled, and whenever his voice issued from his mouth, all who heard his voice melted as wax melts when it feels the fire," (13:1-4). This description of the redeemer as "something like the figure of a man," and of his movement as flying "with the clouds of heaven," is inspired by Dan. 7:13, just as the description of the supernatural power of his voice is inspired by Isa. 11:4: "He shall smite the earth with the rod of his mouth, and with the breath of his lips he shall slay the wicked." In his account of his vision the author continues in this vein. He refers to the redeemer as "the man who came up out of the sea," and "the same man" (II Esd. 13:5, 12), and to his supernatural powers as "a stream of fire" from his mouth, "a flaming breath" from his lips, and "a storm of sparks" from his tongue (vs. 10). The author builds major aspects of his conception of the redeemer on the two OT texts, Dan. 7:13 and Isa. 11:4.

c. The Similitudes of Enoch. The Similitudes represent a large unit now incorporated in the book of Enoch (chs. 37–71), but apparently originally independent of the remainder of the book. The Qumran community, which knows the rest of the book, apparently did not know the Similitudes, because fragments of Enoch 37–71 are conspicuous by their absence from the Qumran caves. We have no clear idea of the date of the Similitudes, but they and the NT texts do appear to be completely independent of one another, and this brings into sharp focus a remarkable parallelism between them. Both have a hero figure they regard as being with God in the heavens, Enoch and Jesus respectively; both develop the phrase "Son of man" as a designation for these figures; and both develop conceptions of their heroes as about to appear from heaven as apocalyptic redeemers. *See* ENOCH, BOOK OF §4*c*; ENOCH, BOOK OF[S] §2*c*.

The Similitudes take their point of departure from Gen. 5:24. "Enoch walked with God; and he was not, for God took him," which is interpreted as referring to the translation of Enoch.

And it come to pass after this that my spirit was translated
And it ascended into the heavens:
And I saw the holy sons of God. . . .
And they came forth . . . ,
And with them the Head of Days, . . .
And [the angel] came to me . . . and said unto me
"Thou art the Son of Man, who art born
unto righteousness." (71:1, 9, 10, 14)

The details of this vision are taken from Gen. 6, Ezek. 1, and Dan. 7; the use of "Son of man" is a development from Dan. 7:13.

This understanding of Enoch being translated to heaven and then identified there as the Son of man of Dan. 7:13 is fundamental to the Similitudes. With this as the starting point, they go on to develop a concept of Enoch as a heavenly redeemer. In this process they use many OT texts, including Dan. 7:13 and Isa. 11:4, two also used in II Esd. 13.

And the Lord of Spirits seated him on the throne of His glory,
And the spirit of righteousness was poured out upon him,
And the word of his mouth slays all
the sinners, . . .
And they shall be downcast of countenance,
And pain shall seize them,
When they see that Son of Man
Sitting on the throne of his glory. (Enoch 62:2, 5)

It should be noted that "Son of man" is only one of several designations for Enoch in the Similitudes; he can also be called "the [Lord's] Anointed" (a reference to Ps. 2:2), "the Elect One," "the Righteous and Elect One," and so on. He is the apocalyptic redeemer expected by the scribes of the Similitudes, and those scribes develop various designations for him, as they use various OT passages to develop their understanding of aspects of his work.

3. The origin of the Christian conception. The Similitudes of Enoch begin with the conviction that God had translated Enoch to heaven; earliest Christianity begins with the conviction that, although he had died, Jesus had nonetheless been exalted to the presence of God, that God had "raised him up, having loosed the pangs of death, because it was not possible for him to be held by it" (Acts 2:24). In the NT this conviction is expressed in terms of the resurrection of Jesus, but the idea of the RESURRECTION of an individual while history itself continued—as distinct from that of a general resurrection as part of the eschatological events which would bring history itself to an end—is so new and revolutionary a concept in ancient Judaism that there must have been considerable preparation for it in early Christian experience and reflection. Ancient Jewish apocalyptic could think of an individual translated to be with God in the heavens, as in the case of the Similitudes of Enoch; and this fact, together with the general parallelism between the Similitudes and the NT, make it most probable that their first experiences of Jesus after his death convinced his followers that God had "raised him up" to be with him in the heavens, having in this way "loosed the pangs of death." From this point the early Christian communities moved in two directions. On the one hand they developed their understanding of the process by means of which Jesus had been "raised up," moving in the direction of empty-tomb narratives, appearances of the Lord as "risen" and appearance stories, and ultimately to the conception of a resurrection and of an ascension as an event separate from the Resurrection, first appearing in Luke-Acts. On the other hand early Christianity moved also in the direction of developing the conviction that Jesus was now in heaven at the right hand of God, and that he would soon return from heaven as apocalyptic redeemer, the Son of man. In other words, the earliest conviction of all was that God had vindicated Jesus by raising him from death to be with him in the heavens. From that point the early Christians moved in one direction to fill out their understanding of how this took place, and in another direction to fill out what was now to be expected since it had taken place. It was in the service of this second objective that the early Christians first applied to Jesus the title "Son of man."

As the early Christian scribes searched the scriptures in an effort to understand how God had vindicated Jesus by raising him from death, they found help particularly in texts from those Psalms which use the Hebrew word *ḥᵃbalîm*. The term is employed frequently in connection with the word for death, and it can mean both "pain, pangs" and "lines, cords, bonds." That early Christian scribes wrestled with this word and its ambiguities can be seen from Acts 2:24, quoted above, where "having loosed the pangs of death" uses a verb appropriate to the meaning "cords, bonds," but gives the noun the other meaning.

Early Christian scribes turned particularly to Ps. 18:4, 5 [H 5, 6], "The cords of death encompassed me . . .; the cords of Sheol entangled me." This they understood as referring to the death of Jesus. But in Ps. 16:6, the same word is used of "lines," not in the bad sense of "bonds," but in the metaphorical sense of "fate, destiny": "The lines have fallen for me in pleasant places. . . . Thou didst not give me up to Sheol." The context here speaks of the overcoming of Sheol (vs. 10), and the early Christian scribes interpreted the passage to mean that God had delivered Jesus from the cords of Sheol, from the pangs of death. In this way, by meditating on Ps. 16:6, 10, Christian scribes reached the conviction expressed in Acts 2:24. But Ps. 16:8-11 can be interpreted as describing in some detail a presence of Jesus with God in heaven, and that the Christian scribes understood it in this way can be seen from Acts 2:25-32, which quotes it at length in such a connection. These interpreters then turned to further texts, especially Ps. 110:1: "The Lord says to my lord: 'Sit at my right hand, till I make your enemies your footstool' "; and Ps. 2:7, "I will tell of the decree of the Lord: He said to me, 'You are my son, today I have begotten you.' " These texts convinced them further that Jesus was exalted as heir to the promises to David. Ps. 110:1, "till I make your enemies your footstool," led the Christian scribes to Ps. 8:6, "Thou hast put all things under his feet"; and Ps. 8:6 led them to Ps. 8:4, "What is man that thou art mindful of him, and the son of man that thou dost care for him?" This exegetical process established the early Christian conviction that Jesus had been exalted to God's right hand as Son of man, and from that point the Christian scribes turned not only to Dan. 7:13 but also to Zech. 12:10, "They [shall] look on him whom they have pierced, they shall mourn." By means of these texts, they developed the expectation that Jesus, exalted to God's right hand as heir to the promises to David and as Son of man, would return "on the clouds of heaven" as Son of man to judge the world and to redeem the faithful.

Given the concept of Jesus returning to earth as Son of man and apocalyptic redeemer, early Christianity then endowed it with a particular form and content in two ways. One way was to employ the ideas and texts traditionally used in this connection in Jewish apocalyptic, and one result of this process is Mark 13:24-27. "But in those days, after that tribulation, the sun will be darkened, and the moon will not give its light [cf. Isa. 13:10], and the stars will be falling from heaven [cf. Isa. 34:4], and the powers in the heavens will be shaken [cf. Hag. 2:6]. And then they will see the Son of man coming. . . . And then he will send out the angels, and gather his elect from the four winds, from the ends of the earth to the ends of heaven [cf. Deut. 30:4]." Another way was to search the Scriptures for analogous judgmental catastrophes, and natural phenomena for suitable metaphors. The Son-of-man sayings in Q are a result of this process: Luke 12:8-9 (=Matt. 10:32-33), emphasizing judgment; Luke 17:24 (=Matt. 24:27), comparison with lightning; Luke 17:26 (=Matt. 24:37), comparison with days of Noah; Luke 12:40 (=Matt. 24:44), unexpectedness of the Son of man's coming; Luke 17:28-30 (cf. Matt. 24:37-41), comparison with Lot; Luke 11:30 (cf. Matt. 12:40), comparison with Jonah.

4. The use of the title in earliest Christianity. "Son of man" is much the most-used designation of Jesus in earliest Christianity. After it was developed in connection with the convictions that Jesus was in heaven at God's right hand, and that he was about to come from heaven as apocalyptic redeemer, it came to be used of Jesus in two further contexts: in passion apologetic, and in reflection on the meaning of the earthly ministry of Jesus. In passion apologetic, Christians sought to find a defense for, and positive meaning in, the passion of Jesus as God's Messiah. One way of doing this was to use the verb "to deliver up, betray" (παραδιδόναι) in connection with the fate of Jesus, a verb deemed particularly appropriate to describe the traditionally unhappy fate of godly men in ancient Judaism. When this verb was used of Jesus, he was spoken of as Son of man, as in the Gethsemane pericope: "The Son of man is betrayed into the hands of sinners" (Mark 14:41). As they celebrated their sacred meal (the LORD'S SUPPER) early Christians both anticipated the coming of Jesus as redeemer and also looked back over his past ministry on earth, especially of course his passion. In this reflection on the earthly ministry of Jesus they developed sayings using the title: "The Son of man . . . came not to be served but to serve, and to give his life as a ransom for many" (Mark 10:45); "The Son of man came to seek and to save the lost" (Luke 19:10); "He who sows the good seed is the Son of man" (Matt. 13:37). The last saying is probably a comparatively late imitation of this early practice, but the first two fit an early eucharistic context.

The Son-of-man title is not carried over into the Pauline or Deutero-Pauline letters. Indeed it is conspicuously absent where we would expect to find it. I Thess. 1:10 speaks of Christian faith in terms of waiting "for his [God's] Son from heaven"; in Q or the gospel traditions one would find Son of man in such a context. The saying found in Mark 10:45 is also found in the Pastorals, but in I Tim. 2:6 it is not the Son of man but "the man Christ Jesus, who gave himself as a ransom for all," and in Tit. 2:13-14 it is "Jesus Christ who gave himself for us."

a. The Gospel of Mark. The major development in the use of Son of man of Jesus in the NT comes in the Gospel of Mark (*see* MARK, GOSPEL OF). One of the evangelist's major purposes is christological: he seeks to combat a false Christology which unduly emphasizes the power and glory of Jesus, and which sees his passion and death only as a prelude to glory; i.e., the passion became an apotheosis. In deliberate contrast to this, Mark develops and emphasizes the theme that a true Christology must see not only the power and glory of the Christ but also the necessity for his suffering. He emphasizes, further, the fact that true Christian DISCIPLESHIP must accept the necessity to follow in the "way" of the Master, through suffering and death to glory. In his gospel the evangelist accepts CHRIST (MESSIAH) and SON OF GOD as proper confessional designations of Jesus (1:1, reading "the Son of God" with RSV; 8:29; 14:61-62), but he constantly interprets them by using Son of man (8:31; 14:62), and he uses Son of man as the vehicle for the expression of his own Christology.

In his references to the Son of man, Mark develops further the three uses of the title we noted as characteristic of earliest Christianity. First, he echoes the apocalyptic use; indeed, he does so with enthusiasm. "When he comes in the glory of his Father," in 8:38, is characteristic of Mark himself, as is "with great power and glory," of 13:26. But he only has to add characteristic touches to the conception of Jesus as Son of man and apocalyptic redeemer, because that christological emphasis was already fully developed in the community or communities for which he wrote. It is otherwise, however, in the case of his second use of Son of man applied to Jesus in passion apologetic, and of his third use of the title in reflection upon his earthly ministry. In these cases the evangelist develops into major christological emphases what were previously only tentative uses of the Son-of-man concept.

From the use of Son of man in passion apologetic, Mark creates the three passion predictions which form the core of the central interpretive section of his gospel, 8:27–10:45. These are 8:31, "The Son of man must suffer many things, and be rejected . . . , and be killed, and after three days rise again"; 9:31, "The Son of man will be delivered (παραδίδοται) into the hands of men, and they will kill him; and . . . after three days he will rise"; 10:33-34, "The Son of man will be delivered (παραδοθήσεται) to the chief priests and the scribes, and they will . . . deliver (παραδώσουσιν) him to the Gentiles; and they will . . . kill him; and after three days he will rise." As they stand in the gospel, these sayings have been composed by Mark, and they represent a major development in NT Christology.

From the use of Son of man in reflection upon the earthly ministry of Jesus, Mark takes the ransom saying (10:45) and gives it a major place in the literary structure of his gospel; it is the climax of the central interpretive section, 8:27–10:45. But he also develops a new emphasis: he uses Son of man in sayings which emphasize the proleptic authority of Jesus as Son of man in his earthly ministry. These sayings are 2:10, "The Son of man has authority on earth to forgive sins"; and 2:28, "The Son of man is lord even of the sabbath." In this way Mark establishes the authority of Jesus on earth as already his authority as Son of man.

b. Other NT writers. Of all the NT writers, the evangelist Mark made the most significant use of the title "Son of man." Subsequently the title gradually fell into disuse.

The evangelist Matthew is mainly concerned with Jesus as the authoritative revealer of God and his will. Since he believes that this revelation supersedes the revelation to the Jews, he has no particular reason to echo the Markan Christology. He reproduces the Markan emphases, but his restructuring of the outline of Mark's gospel destroys the particular impact of the Markan presentation. Matthew, however, has strong links with early Palestinian Christianity, with its emphasis upon Jesus as apocalyptic Son of man, and he in turn echoes this emphasis; e.g., 10:23; 13:41; 25:31. Matthew is also the first to use PAROUSIA as a technical term for the coming of Jesus as Son of man: 24:27, 37, 39, where the word translated "coming" is always παρουσία. *See also* MATTHEW, GOSPEL OF[S] §3.

The author of Luke-Acts is concerned to deemphasize the eschatological hope of early Christianity, and he has therefore no particular interest in the use of Son of man concerning Jesus, with its natural emphasis upon apocalyptic expectation. He tends to see Jesus particularly in prophetic terms, so he also has no interest in maintaining the emphases Mark developed in his use of Son of man. He seems never to use Son of man except when he is following a source. Perhaps the most interesting reference to Son of man in Luke-Acts is Acts 7:56, where STEPHEN, the proto-martyr, sees "the heavens opened, and the Son of man standing at the right hand of God." This is a reflection of the early Christian conception of Jesus' exaltation as Son of man. *See also* LUKE, GOSPEL OF §4g and supplementary article.

The evangelist John goes his own way in Christology, as he does in most things. He is concerned to express a Christology in which Jesus is understood as a descending-ascending heavenly redeemer. This has its nearest counterpart in the NT christological hymns (Phil. 2:6-11; Col. 1:15-20; I Pet. 3:18-19, 22; I Tim. 3:16; Eph. 2:14-16), and seems to have been Hellenistic in ultimate derivation. Insofar as he uses Son of man, he tends to do so in the service of this Christology (e.g., John 3:13; 6:62), and this kind of use is peculiar to him among the NT writers. *See also* JOHN, GOSPEL OF §D1 and supplementary article.

The author of the book of Revelation (*see* REVELATION, BOOK OF), John of Patmos, uses Dan. 7:13, as does the author of II Esdras, i.e., in the service of his own particular vision. This is how we should understand the references to "one like a son of man," who is "in the midst of the lampstands" in Rev. 1:13, and "seated on the [white] cloud" in 14:14. Very interesting from our point of view is 1:7, "Behold, he is coming with the clouds, and every eye will see him, every one who pierced him; and all tribes of the earth will wail on account of him." This text is evidence for the bringing together of Dan. 7:13 and Zech. 12:10, 11, which was claimed to be a part of the development of the use of Son of man of Jesus in early Christianity (§3 *above*).

Bibliography. N. Perrin, *A Modern Pilgrimage in NT Christology* (1974), gives a comprehensive bibliog. of the discussion since 1959, and *The NT: An Introduction* (1974), gives in more detail the interpretations of the NT writers offered above; R. A. Edwards, *The Sign of Jonah in the Theology of the Evangelists and Q,* SBT, 2nd series, XVIII (1971), discusses the Son of man in Q; J. R. Donahue, *Are You the Christ? The Trial Narrative in the Gospel of Mark,* SBLDS, X (1973), discusses particular Markan apocalyptic emphases; G. Vermes, *Jesus the Jew* (1973).

For other approaches and points of view see: H. E. Tödt, *The Son of Man in the Synoptic Tradition* (1959); R. H. Fuller, *The Foundations of NT Christology* (1965); E. Schweizer, "The Son of Man," *JBL,* LXXIX (1960), 119-29, and "The Son of Man," *NTS,* III (1962-63), 256-61; M. D. Hooker, *The Son of Man in Mark* (1967); F. H. Borsch, *The Son of Man in Myth and History* (1967).

N. PERRIN

***SONG OF SONGS.** Research on the Song of Songs since 1962 has borne out the main conclusions of Gottwald's balanced article (*see* SONG OF SONGS). However, there have been some new emphases and new efforts at solving old problems.

1. Extrabiblical parallels. While the cultic interpretation (Meek *et al.*) had always utilized

Mesopotamian sources concerning sacred marriage, there was little evidence available about simple love between the sexes. Thus far, only two such texts have been published (by Cooper and Held). Although Kramer has furthered the cultic interpretation, this view is not widely held. It is reasonable to suppose that there was mutual influence between the language of Hebrew love poetry and that of the pagan fertility rites, but there is no evidence that portions of the Song were originally composed for, or modeled upon, these rites.

The most extraordinary parallels are to be derived from Egypt. The work of Hermann is of fundamental importance. He has singled out several topoi of Egyptian love poetry which appear also in the Song: the brother-sister style of address, the expression of the love relationship in terms of uniqueness and the exclusion of others, love under the trees, the beloved's hair as a love charm, etc. The approach is concrete and sensible, not abstract: by way of seeing, hearing (the voice), touching, smelling, and tasting. There is lovesickness, and there are friends (messenger, mother, etc.) of the lovers. Quite striking are the literary fictions by which the beloved is portrayed as a shepherd or a servant (gardener). Like the Song of Songs, the Egyptian poems are dialogues, and the *waṣf,* or description of the physical charms of the beloved, is frequently employed. One receives the clear impression that the Egyptian songs and the Song of Songs move in the same atmosphere: gardens, animals, fruits, flowers, perfumes, trees. This is the make-believe language of love. The texts of four substantial collections (Chester Beatty I Papyri, Papyrus Harris 500, Turin Papyrus, Cairo Ostracon 25218) are available in the translations by Schott and Simpson (partially in Pritchard, *ANET*).

2. Structure. The structure of the Song still remains a problem, as one can see from the wide variety of views put forth on this topic. There are two general tendencies (apart from the so-called dramatic theory): the recognition of more or less a half-dozen unitary poems, or the recognition of several disparate poems (thirty–forty), even of a verse in length, which have been collected into a tenuous unity. There is no denying the existence of refrains and repetitions within the eight chapters of the Song. The most striking (cf. Angénieux, Exum) are the refrain of awakening (2:7; 3:5; 8:4), the refrain of movement (2:17; 4:6), the refrain of possession (2:16; 6:3), the refrain of embrace (2:6; 8:3). But as yet there is no compelling argument to show how these refrains and repetitions contribute to the structure of the whole.

3. Setting. There has been a trend among recent commentators to ascribe the songs to a wedding celebration, or at least to a betrothal. This view is not new, but it seems to be gaining ground. Thus, Würthwein finds a "clear" reference to marriage in twenty-four of the twenty-nine units which he recognizes in the Song. Rudolph and Krinetzki likewise acknowledge wedding and love songs. It should be emphasized, however, that the only clear reference to marriage is in 3:6-11. Although many sections may have been used in a wedding feast, we have no evidence for the claim that they originated in a wedding feast. Audet distinguished between a preliterary stage (a betrothal song) and the literary stage (when the Jewish sages put the work forth as the "Song of Songs"), but he found both levels at one as far as the meaning is concerned: an exchange of love between the betrothed, equivalent to a mutual promise of fidelity. Würthwein agrees with Audet that the work stems from "the circle of post-exilic sages of Jerusalem." This does not mean that the Song of Songs belongs to wisdom literature; rather, it was the sage who recognized the value of these songs, preserved and published them.

4. Specific literary features. As opposed to or, better, in addition to, traditional form-critical analysis (genre, setting, etc.), greater attention is being given to the poetic qualities of the Song of Songs in the light of modern understanding of poetry. Krinetzki's commentary (esp. pp. 42-82) is particularly valuable in this regard. He points out not only the usual parallelism of verses (*see* POETRY, HEBREW) but even the rhythmic sounds (consonantal and vocalic), alliteration, assonance, the contrast between nominal and verbal sentences, CHIASMUS, and rhetorical figures such as paronomasia, catchwords (uniting two separate units), etc. This is an important contribution to appreciating the work, one that goes beyond the customary attention that had always been given to the extraordinary range of proper names and of animals, plants, etc., that are to be found in the book.

5. Meaning. There is a practical consensus (cf. the survey by Würthwein) that the Song of Songs has to do with human love in the literal historical sense, as opposed to the allegorical view still represented in the valuable commentary by Robert-Feuillet-Tournay. However, one may legitimately ask if modern hermeneutical concerns have not moved away from the old literal-allegorical polarization. It would be a bold claim to say that the literal historical sense exhausts the meaning of the Song of Songs. The history of its interpretation in both the Jewish and Christian tradition shows that the communities in which the book was received found other levels of meaning.

Bibliography. History of interpretation: E. Würthwein, "Zum Verständnis des Hohenliedes," *Theol. Rundschau,* XXXII (1967), 177-212.

Commentaries and special studies: *a*) Allegorical: A. Robert, A. Feuillet, R. Tournay, *Le Cantique des Cantiques* (1963).

b) Cultic: H. Schmökel, *Heilige Hochzeit und Hoheslied* (1956); S. N. Kramer, *The Sacred Marriage Rite* (1969).

c) Lyric: J. Angénieux, "Structure du Cantique des Cantiques," *ETL,* XLI (1965), 96-142; J.-P. Audet, "Le sens du Cantique des Cantiques," *RB,* LXII (1955), 197-221; J. C. Exum, "A Literary and Structural Analysis of the Song of Songs," *ZAW,* LXXXV (1973), 47-79; G. Gerlemann, *Das Hohelied* (1965); L. Krinetzki, *Das Hohe Lied* (1964); O. Loretz, *Das althebräische Liebeslied* (1971); R. Murphy, "Canticle of Canticles," *JBC,* I (1968), 506-10; W. Rudolph, *Das Hohe Lied* (1962); E. Würthwein, *Das Hohelied* (1969).

d) Extrabiblical parallels: (Mesopotamia) J. Cooper,

"New Cuneiform Parallels to the Song of Songs," *JBL*, XC (1971), 157-62; M. Held, "A Faithful Lover in an Old Babylonian Dialogue," *JCS*, XV (1961), 1-26; (Egypt) A. Hermann, *Altägyptische Liebesdichtung* (1959); S. Schott, *Altägyptische Liebeslieder* (1950); W. K. Simpson, *The Literature of Ancient Egypt* (1972).

R. E. MURPHY

SOURCE CRITICISM, OT. The analysis of the features of a literary piece in order to delineate authorship, historical setting, and compositional character. It is especially concerned to determine whether a document is a unity or composite and, if the latter, the nature of the sources used and the stages of composition.

It has been common to identify source criticism and LITERARY CRITICISM. The latter, however, is now considered a more general designation, including source criticism as well as analysis of style and other features.

Source criticism has been applied to all biblical writings; the results to date, however, have varied considerably in precision and certainty. It has demonstrated with some exactness the compositional character of books such as Isaiah and Zechariah, but has achieved less definitive results with other texts, e.g., Jeremiah and Micah. It has greatly illuminated the editorial processes at work in the histories of the Deuteronomist and the Chronicler, while shedding little light on the study of Psalms and Proverbs. It has been especially fruitful in delineating the compositeness of the Pentateuch, but much uncertainty remains regarding the details of this analysis. *See* BIBLICAL CRITICISM; BIBLICAL CRITICISM, OT[S]; BIBLICAL CRITICISM, HISTORY OF.

1. Assumptions and guidelines. Source criticism has sometimes been improperly used, often with unfortunate results. The following matters need careful consideration:

a) It has been suggested that source criticism presupposes a modern conception of literary composition and is thus inappropriately applied to the biblical writings. It has clearly been shown, however, that ancient Semitic texts do contain evidence of such a compositional mode, both within the OT (e.g., Num. 21:14; Josh. 10:13) and outside it (e.g., the Gilgamesh Epic). This is sufficient justification for the use of source criticism. Yet there are differences between ancient and modern modes of composition that need to be kept in mind in source-critical analysis (e.g., literary originality, firmness in logical construction).

b) The theory and practice of the historical-critical method is not bound to an understanding which views history as a closed continuum in which there is no room for divine activity. Source criticism must recognize that the biblical literature emanated from a religious community. The intention of its authors was never merely literary or historical, and due consideration must be given to theological intentions, which inevitably affected literary composition. Moreover, this means that source criticism cannot be an end in itself, but must stand in the service of the explication of the full meaning of the biblical text.

c) Source criticism cannot be distinguished entirely from other methods such as FORM CRITICISM, tradition criticism, and redaction criticism, nor used in isolation from them. The source critic's work must be informed in significant ways by these approaches to the text, as the following examples from Pentateuchal studies show. *See* PENTATEUCH.

Much of the Pentateuchal material was transmitted orally for generations before being incorporated into written sources (*see* TRADITION, ORAL and TRADITION, ORAL[S]). At the same time, distinctions within the oral tradition need to be made, e.g., between relatively independent traditions and more firmly fixed collections of material ("oral literature"). The latter must be considered just as legitimate a subject of source-critical analysis as written sources. This applies, for example, to the assumption of a G (*Grundschrift*) source upon which both J and E are dependent. *See* DOCUMENTS; YAHWIST[S] §2; ELOHIST[S].

Moreover, the tradition did not remain unaltered once it had assumed written form. In response to changing situations in the Israelite community, written forms of the tradition were adapted and supplemented over the centuries by means of oral and written materials, as well as by kerygmatic and haggadic usage of the tradition (*see* TRADITION CRITICISM, OT[S]). This means that one cannot propose dates for all of the material within a source with the confidence characteristic of earlier scholarship. One can, however, still speak of the time when the source was given its essential shape by an author or creative compiler. Thus, for example, it is in order to speak of an exilic date for the P source, even though many of the traditions originated in previous centuries and other materials were subsequently attracted to it (e.g., Lev. 17–26). *See* PRIESTLY WRITERS[S].

It also needs to be remembered that breaks in the coherence of a text need not point to the use of already formed sources. A lack of clear continuity in a work may indicate a relatively haphazard growth of the tradition in its preliterary (or redactional) stages. On the other hand, the observed diversity may be ascribed to the interweaving of sources already formed, if there is evidence of unity (at the level of style, vocabulary, and especially viewpoint) throughout the larger context to which the various units may be related. Crucial here is the isolation of characteristics which, by giving literary cohesion and unity of perspective to separated units, produce a distinctive source profile.

Moreover, in contrast to earlier source-critical studies which tended to depreciate secondary elements introduced by editors, there is now increased recognition of the importance of the redactors' art. Their endeavors, far from being merely additive in character, resulted in new wholes with a meaning greater than that of the sum of the parts with which they worked. On the other hand, the results of the redactors ought not be extolled at the expense of their sources. *See* REDACTION CRITICISM, OT[S].

d) Structural and/or stylistic analysis of the final redaction in itself cannot be used as evidence for the unity of a literary piece. A redactor can create a structure that brings divergent sources into a functionally unified whole. For example, it is not at all inconsistent to consider the JOSEPH STORY both a literary masterpiece in every way and also an interweaving of different sources.

e) Diversity of style and vocabulary should not necessarily be considered evidence for compositeness; a single author can employ variations. It is important to observe the distribution of such variations. A text is most likely to be composite when instances of diversity are undistributed, i.e., appearing, disappearing, and reappearing as one moves from one unit of material to another. An example of this would be the alternation of the divine names Yahweh and Elohim in the Pentateuch, especially prior to the revelation of the name Yahweh in Exod. 3.

Yet, an analysis based upon such variations cannot be applied mechanically. Such a procedure has commonly led to an overly minute dissection of the text. It needs to be kept in mind that redactors have certainly blurred the distinguishing traits of a source at points (cf. the use of the name Yahweh in Gen. 17:1; 22:14).

f) The strength of source-critical conclusions is relative, depending chiefly upon the variety of types of criteria that can be successfully applied in conjunction with each other (*see* §2 *below*). Compositeness may be determined even where sufficient criteria are not available for a precise delineation of sources. In such instances, there will be greater difficulty in achieving scholarly consensus (e.g., Gen. 15; Exod. 19), but isolated instances of difficulty should not prejudice the larger case; source criticism must be pursued and its results evaluated on the basis of the study of the entire literary piece (e.g., the Pentateuch).

g) The use of the method must not be controlled by philosophical or dogmatic preconceptions of historical or religious developments in Israel (e.g., Wellhausen, or fundamentalism). For example, it ought not be assumed that fewer anthropomorphic references to God represent a later or more sophisticated stage in the history of the tradition.

2. The method outlined. The source critic begins by determining the natural units into which the text under study falls (e.g., Gen. 11:1-9). One first studies these units in isolation, and then in relationship to one another, watching for:

a) Changes in literary style (cf. the book of DEUTERONOMY with what precedes).

b) Shifts in vocabulary and phrasing (cf. Gen. 1:1–2:4*a* with what follows).

c) Breaks in continuity and the nature of the connections within and between units (cf. Gen. 6–8).

d) Changes in viewpoint, especially theological perspective (cf. Isa. 1–12 with 40–55). *See* ISAIAH; ISAIAH[S].

e) Duplications (cf. Gen. 12:10-20 with Gen. 20; Exod. 21:1 ff. with Deut. 15:1 ff.).

f) Logical, thematic, chronological, or factual inconsistencies (cf. Gen. 4:26 with Exod. 6:2-3).

If on the basis of the analysis it is determined that the text is a unity, then the following questions must be considered: authorship, dating, provenance, intended audience, purpose.

If, on the other hand, the analysis suggests a composite work, then a somewhat more complex task presents itself. One must lay out the results of the initial analysis and seek to determine relationships among the isolated parts. Of special significance here are possible duplications. If present (as in the Pentateuch), they constitute a control grouping. After a full description of these materials, other units of the text are sought out which have the same or similar characteristics. In this way distinctive sources with peculiarities of language and perspective may begin to emerge.

Essentially two aspects of the task then remain. The compositional stages through which the document has gone will need to be determined, from the first combination of sources to the final redaction. Thus, for example, it will need to be determined if the P tradition was originally an independent narrative or simply a new edition of the JE redaction.

Finally, the aforementioned questions of authorship, dating, provenance, intended audience, and purpose must be posed for each of the sources and redactions which have been distinguished.

The end product should consist of as full a description as possible of each of the sources, as well as the nature of each stage of the editorial process.

Bibliography. J. Wellhausen, *Prolegomena to the History of Israel* (1885); J. E. Carpenter and G. Harford-Battersby, *The Hexateuch According to the Revised Version,* 2 vols. (1900); H. H. Rowley, ed., *The OT and Modern Study* (1951); H. F. Hahn, *The OT in Modern Research* (1954); E. Nielsen, *Oral Tradition* (1954); A Bentzen, *Introduction to the OT* (5th ed., 1959); O. Eissfeldt, *The OT: An Introduction* (1965); G. von Rad, *The Problem of the Hexateuch and Other Essays* (1966), pp. 1-78; I. Engnell, *A Rigid Scrutiny* (1969); K. Koch, *The Growth of the Biblical Tradition* (1969); H.-J. Kraus, *Geschichte der historisch-kritischen Erforschung des Alten Testaments* (2nd ed., 1969); N. C. Habel, *Literary Criticism of the OT* (1971); W. Richter, *Exegese als Literaturwissenschaft: Entwurf einer alttestamentlichen Literaturtheorie und Methodologie* (1971); R. de Vaux, *The Bible and the Ancient Near East* (1971), pp. 31-48; M. Noth, *A History of Pentateuchal Traditions* (1972).

T. E. FRETHEIM

***SPIRIT. 1. In the OT and Judaism.** Early references in the OT denote God's power manifest in prophecy and mighty deeds (Judg. 13:25; 14:6; 15:14; I Sam. 10:6, 10). The same premise is operative in Gen. 2:7, that the source of life and power is God. The connection of these themes to the root meaning of breeze or breath is not only that the latter is essential to life but also that Yahweh uniquely uses WIND as a tool for his creative and redemptive activity (Gen. 1:2; Exod. 10:13, 19; 14:21; Ezek. 13:13). The connection between spirit and the creative word is visible in Ps. 33:6.

Since spirit is the enlivening element in human beings, it is frequently used to depict particular moods or impulses (I Kings 10:5; 21:5; Josh. 5:1). Hence disposition comes to be described in terms of spirit (Prov. 18:14), without recourse to the alien notion of a divine element intrinsic to humankind.

The OT was conscious of alien (I Kings 22:21-23), perverted (Hos. 4:12; 5:4), and demonic (I

Sam. 16:15-16) spirits which overpower persons. The need to distinguish among prophetic spirits was present long before the NT era. The idea of Yahweh's righteous purposes in history gave the OT statements about his Spirit a distinctively dynamic, moral, yet finally inscrutable quality.

The association of Spirit with the messianic king (Isa. 11:2; 42:1) and the expectation of widespread manifestations of the Spirit in the messianic age (Joel 2:28-29) contributed to the conviction in the intertestamental period that the Spirit would be silent until the new age dawned (cf. I Macc. 4:46; 9:27). New prophetic writings appeared under pseudonyms (*see* PSEUDONYMOUS WRITING[S]), and ecstatic manifestations were discouraged by the prevailing legalism of postexilic Judaism.

2. In the gospels and Acts. According to Luke 4:18 Jesus announced the beginning of the era of the Spirit in the Nazareth sermon. His authority was charismatic rather than legal (Mark 1:22; 6:15; Matt. 21:11, 46; Luke 7:16). In a unique way Jesus associated EXORCISM with Spirit and kingdom (Matt. 12:28). The saying in Mark 13:11 presupposes that the disciples are likewise recipients of the Spirit (cf. Matt. 10:7-8; Luke 9:2; 10:17-20).

Redaction critics (*see* REDACTION CRITICISM, NT [S]) have noted the reticence of Matthew and Mark to read back into the life of Jesus the spiritual enthusiasm of early Christianity. Most of the references to Spirit are heavily influenced by OT assumptions and deal with aspects of Jesus' life about which direct statements by Jesus himself were unavailable, such as the baptism and the birth stories. The aim of most of the references to Spirit is to affirm Jesus' messianic uniqueness.

Luke and Acts betray a stronger interest in the Spirit as a sign of the age of the church. Jesus is pictured as conveying the Spirit to the church rather than himself being subject to the Spirit (cf. Mark 1:12 with Luke 4:1). The abiding presence of the Spirit in Christ and his community is emphasized (Acts 4:31; 6:3; 11:24), openly manifested in prophecy and triumphant mission (Luke 3:22; Acts 2:3-6; 8:9-24). Luke's emendation of a saying about the "good gifts" of the kingdom (Matt. 7:11) into a promise of the "Holy Spirit" (Luke 11:13) is consistent with the picture of a spirit-filled church in Acts. That those who were baptized had a visible gift of the Spirit is stressed (Acts 2:38-39; 19:2-6), but Acts refrains from a binding of sacramental act to spiritual gift, as this would restrict the freedom of God.

3. In the Pauline letters. Paul's letters reflect a dialogue with Hellenistic assumptions about the Spirit as a divine, material substance whose impartation produces transhistorical salvation. This Hellenistic notion surfaced in the mistaken prophecy that the end of the world had come (II Thess. 2:2), rendering normal work and family ethics superfluous. It also appeared in the ecstatic cursing of the historical Jesus by the enthusiasts in Corinth who opposed the ethic of responsible love (I Cor. 12:1-3). Paul countered by associating the ecstatic spirit they had experienced with holiness and its ethical imperatives (I Thess. 1:5-6; 4:8; II Thess. 2:13). In so doing he refrained from authoritarian suppression of ecstatic phenomena, insisting only that every charismatic manifestation be evaluated (I Thess. 5:19-21). He opposed the Hellenistic tendency to absolutize the spirit while disparaging the soul and body by including all three in a benediction which insists that the unity of one's personhood remains intact until the PAROUSIA (I Thess. 5:23). Here Paul was thinking of the apportionment of the divine Spirit which enters into the possession of the Christian; thus, "your spirit" (cf. Gal. 6:18; Phil. 4:23; Philem. 25). To counter the misunderstanding of such early Christian usage, Paul distinguished between the divine and human spirit (I Cor. 2:11) and insisted in I Cor. 12:1-3 that not every ecstatic manifestation is from God. The criterion "Jesus is Lord" (I Cor. 12:3) is elaborated with reference to loving service to the community (I Cor. 12:4 ff.), and this leads to his instructions about the necessity of expressing spiritual gifts in rationally comprehensible ways (I Cor. 14:13 ff.).

The premise for Paul's doctrine is set forth in II Cor. 3:17, "Now the Lord is the Spirit." This implies that ecstatic experience is not to be regarded as impersonal or amoral; the gift of Spirit establishes moral lordship. Since the gift and the giver are identical, ecstatic experience is ethicized and personalized; implacable compulsion is replaced by free responsibility. The same idea is present where Paul associates the ecstatic experience of faith with the cry, "Abba! Father!" (Gal. 4:6; Rom. 8:13-16). The gift impels an intimate relation with the giver, personalizing the love of God as revealed in Christ. But despite the emphasis on present experience in the Spirit, the eschatological proviso remains intact as a hedge against enthusiastic misunderstandings, with Spirit as the first fruits (Rom. 8:23) or pledge (II Cor. 5:5; 1:22) of the coming fulfillment. *See* SPIRITUAL GIFTS; SPIRITUAL GIFTS[S].

4. In the Johannine literature. In view of the need to "test the spirits" in face of heretical ecstasy, the Johannine tradition develops an incarnational criterion (I John 4:1-2). Since believers and heretics both claim ecstatic experience (I John 3:24; 4:13), the decisive step is to identify the Spirit with God as revealed in Christ. John's gospel carries out this effort by naming the Spirit the "Counselor" (14:26), further defined as the "Spirit of truth" (14:16-17; 15:26; 16:13; *see* PARACLETE; PARACLETE [S]). His role is to "bear witness" to Christ (15:26), to "bring to your remembrance" all that he taught (14:26), and thus in effect to call forth faith (6:63-64). Since full knowledge includes acknowledgment of the command to love (John 15; I John 4:21–5:4), the ethical consequences of this view of the Spirit resemble those of Paul.

In this literature "spirit" is used anthropologically only with reference to Jesus (John 1:32-33; 11:33; 13:21; 19:30). The relation of the ecstatic, apportioned Spirit to the enlivening spirit in the believer remains unclarified.

5. Elsewhere in the NT. In the rest of the NT the use of πνεῦμα is traditional and nonpolemical, with the exception of Hebrews where the apportioned Spirit (2:4; 4:12; 6:4-5) is the "Spirit of grace" (10:29) which this author relates to Christ (9:14). But the traditional Jewish usage is visible in the references to angels and departed saints as "spirits" (1:14; 12:23), and to God as the "Father of spirits" (12:9).

See also FLESH; FLESH[S]; BODY; BODY[S]; MAN, NATURE OF, IN THE NT; MAN, NATURE OF, IN THE NT[S].

Bibliography. E. Käsemann, "Geist und Geistesgaben im NT," *RGG,* II (3rd ed., 1958), cols. 1272-79; H. Kleinknecht *et al.,* "πνεῦμα," *TDNT,* VI (1959 [ET 1968]), 332-451; R. Jewett, *Paul's Anthropological Terms,* AGJU, X (1971); K. Kertelge, "Heiliger Geist und Geisterfahrung im Urchristentum," *Lebendiges Zeugnis,* III (1971), 24-36; J. Jeremias, *NT Theology: The Proclamation of Jesus* (1971); H. W. Wolff, *Anthropology of the OT* (1973); F. B. Craddock, "The Gift of the Holy Spirit and the Nature of Man," *Encounter,* XXXV (1974), 23-35.

R. JEWETT

***SPIRITUAL GIFTS.** The gifts (χαρίσματα) of the HOLY SPIRIT were regarded by the early church as the fulfillment of prophecies made by John the Baptist (Mark 1:8) and by Jesus (Luke 24:49; Acts 1:4-5; John 7:38-39). As such, they are realities of the age to come (Matt. 12:28), imparted by God (I Cor. 12:28), by the Spirit (I Cor. 12:11), or by the exalted Lord (Acts 2:33; Eph. 4:7-8; cf. I Cor. 12:4-6). They are not the activity of a different Spirit but a different role of the same Spirit who is manifest in the present creation (Gen. 1:2) and in the OT prophets. Thus, they can be described as fulfillments of OT promises (Acts 2:16 ff.; Eph. 4:7-8) and, alternatively, OT acts of the Spirit can be associated with the new-age realities (Rom. 7:14; I Cor. 10:3, RSV n.). Apart from I Pet. 2:5; 4:10 the terms "gifts" (χαρίσματα) and "spiritual gifts" (πνευματικά) are limited in the NT to the Pauline literature, but the endowments expressed by the terms are widely evident throughout early Christianity.

1. The classification and characteristics of gifts. Singularly, the gift from the risen Lord is the Holy Spirit (Acts 2:38) or SALVATION (Rom. 6:23). Distributively, different gifts are enumerated in several Pauline passages (Rom. 12:6-8; I Cor. 12:8-10, 28-30; Eph. 4:11) and inferentially detailed in Acts 2:17-18. They are designated variously in each passage, suggesting that they were of no fixed number or kind. However, they are subject to some classification; and "spiritual gifts" (*see* §5 *below*), including those of prophecy (*see* PROPHECY IN THE EARLY CHURCH[S]) and tongues (*see* TONGUES, GIFT OF[S]), appear to be of particular significance.

The gifts emanate from the exalted Jesus and will, if they are genuine, issue in a confession of him (I Cor. 12:3; I John 4:2; cf. Rev. 19:10). They may be sought by prayer (I Cor. 12:31; Jas. 1:5) and may be imparted in the laying on of hands by gifted persons (Acts 19:6; cf. 13:3; I Tim. 4:14). But they are at the disposal of the sovereign Spirit, who dispenses them as he wills, diversely and for the common good of the church (I Cor. 12:7, 11). Thus, no one gift is imparted to all (I Cor. 12:29-30). And apparently no one person is given all gifts, although certain gifts, e.g., apostleship, may implicitly include others (Acts 5:12; II Cor. 12:12).

2. Spiritual gifts and baptism. The "baptism in Holy Spirit" or equivalent imagery apparently is used only of the initial giving of the Spirit. It is often associated with BAPTISM in water, both in the case of Jesus (Mark 1:9-10) and in the early church (Acts 2:38; 9:17-18; I Cor. 12:13; Gal. 3:27). But it is not necessarily conterminous with the baptismal rite and, at least in Acts, may occur before (Acts 10:44-48; 11:15) or after it (Acts 8:15-18; 19:5-6; perhaps Tit. 3:5-6). In either case it may be accompanied by the laying on of hands and may be the occasion for the impartation of specific gifts; or the gifts may be imparted or manifested only at a subsequent time (Acts 6:3, 6, 8, 10; I Cor. 12:31; 14:1; I Tim. 4:14; II Tim. 1:6). For Paul, baptism in the Spirit incorporates one into the body of Christ (I Cor. 12:13). Baptism means to "have the Spirit" (Rom. 8:9) and is an essential characteristic of all Christians; the possession of certain spiritual gifts means to be a "pneumatic" (I Cor. 14:37; RSV "spiritual") and is characteristic only of a select group of Christians.

3. The gifts and ministry. The ministry of the NT church rests solely upon the gifts from the exalted Lord and, thus viewed, is the continuation of the ministry of Jesus: he is the apostle (Heb. 3:1), the prophet (John 7:40; Acts 3:22), the teacher, the miracle worker (Acts 2:22), the healer, the bishop (ἐπίσκοπος, RSV "Guardian," I Pet. 2:25), the mediator of divine wisdom (Mark 6:2; *see* WISDOM IN THE NT[S] §3*a, b*) who manifests his powers through his followers (I Cor. 12:8, 28 ff.). The manifestation of gifts does not itself constitute such believers a ministerial class. But some gifted persons appear to have been recognized or appointed from the first as an ordered ministry, i.e., worthy of the community's esteem, submission, and financial support (Luke 10:7; Acts 6:3; 14:23; I Cor. 9:6-14; 16:15-18; Gal. 6:6; I Thess. 5:12). However, ordered ministries are no less charismatically determined and are equally dependent on the constantly recurring miracle of God's grace (Schweizer; *see bibliog.*).

4. The gifts and the fruit of the Spirit. Several distinctions between the gifts and the fruit (Gal. 5:22-23) of the Spirit may be noted. The gifts are diverse, the fruit is the same for all; the gifts manifest the work of Christ, the fruit demonstrates the character of Christ.

The fruit and the gifts complement one another: "Make love your aim, and earnestly desire the spiritual gifts" (I Cor. 14:1). The absence of the fruit makes the gifts at best ineffective (I Cor. 13:1 ff.). It may indicate that they also are absent or spurious, the product of human, "fleshly" powers (I Cor. 3:1-4; Jas. 3:13-18) or of a demonic spirit (II Cor. 11). Like the christological confession, the fruit of the Spirit in the charismatic person provides a test of the genuineness of the gift.

5. Spiritual gifts (πνευματικά). In Rom. 1:11 a "spiritual" (πνευματικόν) gift (χάρισμα) is to be distinguished from others. Spiritual gifts are identified elsewhere as gifts of inspired speech or discernment (I Cor. 2:13; 12:1 ff.) and appear to be equated with the "higher gifts" that believers are urged to seek (I Cor. 12:31; 14:1). In a word they are prophetic-type gifts (I Cor. 14:37). They bring to their possessors, the pneumatics, a certain prominence in the worship and teaching of the church (Acts 13:1; 15:32; I Cor. 14; Gal. 6:1; I Thess. 5:19-20; Jas. 3:1; Rev. 1:3) just as gifts, e.g., of oversight, bring corresponding responsibilities in other aspects of the church's life (Acts 14:23; 20:17, 28; Phil. 1:1; I Tim. 3:5; Jas. 5:14; III John 1, 9).

Bibliography. H. Conzelmann, "χάρισμα," *TDNT,* IX (1973), 402-6; E. E. Ellis, "Christ and Spirit in I Corinthians," *Christ and Spirit in the NT,* ed. B. Lindars and S. S. Smalley (1973), pp. 269-77, and "'Spiritual' Gifts in the Pauline Community," *NTS,* XX (1973-74), 128-44; E. Schweizer, *Church Order in the NT,* SBT, XXXII (1959), 171-210 (§§21-25).

E. E. Ellis

STAR OF BETHLEHEM. The celestial phenomenon that brought the wise men from the East to seek the newborn "king of the Jews" (Matt. 2:2) has not been definitively identified. It has been suggested that it was the planet Venus, but the phases of Venus are too common and well known for that star to have been taken as a harbinger of the Messiah's birth. Likewise the notion that it was a shower of shooting stars or a brilliant meteor does not commend itself, for these events are much too transient. Chinese astronomical records mention the appearance in 12 B.C. of what later came to be called Halley's Comet, but it is extremely unlikely that the "star" was a comet, for the ancients interpreted the latter as omens of disaster.

The Chinese also recorded the appearance of a nova in 5 B.C. This was a stellar explosion or eruption near the star Alpha Aquilae that remained visible to the naked eye for about seventy days. This could have been the "star of Bethlehem," but since a nova is rather unimpressive, it is not likely that one would have been interpreted as a herald of the Messiah. A supernova is a vast explosion in which a star sheds its outer layers and increases in brightness by a factor of about one billion. One was recorded by the Chinese in the constellation Taurus in A.D. 1054 (the Crab Nebula is its result to the present day), and others appeared in 1572 and 1604. There is no record of one, however, in the late first century B.C.

It was the great astronomer Johannes Kepler who suggested in the early seventeenth century that the "star of Bethlehem" may have had something to do with the conjunction of the planets Jupiter and Saturn. A conjunction is said to occur when two or more heavenly bodies occupy the same celestial longitude. Kepler noted that a conjunction of Jupiter with Saturn shortly preceded the appearance of the supernova of 1604, and surmised that something similarly miraculous may have occurred in 7 B.C. when three conjunctions of these two planets took place in the constellation Pisces—on May 29, September 29, and December 4. In 1821 Bishop Münter of the Lutheran Church of Denmark went a step further and suggested that there was no need for a "miracle," for the thrice repeated conjunction of Jupiter with Saturn in 7 B.C. could itself have been the "star of Bethlehem." This seems quite likely, for a Jewish astrologic tradition connects the appearance of the Messiah with the conjunction of Jupiter and Saturn that occurs in Pisces. (Conjunctions of these two planets occur roughly every twenty years, but astrology developed the ability to see in them portents of ever-growing significance over the larger cycles of time in which they occurred.) Pisces was regarded as the constellation of the Jews and of the month Adar, immediately preceding the month Nisan when the redemption (Passover) was to occur. Saturn was the planet of the Jews because of its association with Saturday and because it was the "most high," the most distant of the planets known to the ancients and hence a manifestation of the Most High God of the Jews. Jupiter was the planet of royalty, based upon its ancient identification with Marduk, the god of Babylon who ruled a universal empire. Jupiter was thus regarded as the star of the Messiah, and its conjunction with Saturn symbolized the transfer of royal power from the Most High to his messianic king. *See* SHALEM, GOD[S].

When the wise men said, in Matt. 2:2, "We have seen his star in the East," the star to which they referred was probably Jupiter. In Hebrew the planet's name is *Ṣedheq* ("justice" or "vindication"), an epithet applied frequently to the Messiah (*see* ṢEDHEQ, GOD[S]). The OT basis for regarding Jupiter as the messianic star was Isa. 41:2, the first part of which can be translated, "Whom has *Ṣedheq* stirred up from the east?" Hence the gospel spoke of the wise men as coming from the East for it was there that the messianic star was made manifest. (The phrase "in the East," used in Matt. 2:2 and 2:9, referred to the location of the wise men, not of the star. One Syriac MS, Sinaiticus, in Matt. 2:2 reads instead "from the east," but this is probably a copyist's error influenced by the language of 2:1.)

Bibliography. W. Burke-Gaffney, "Kepler and the Star of Bethlehem," *Journal of the Royal Astronomical Society of Canada,* XXXI (1937), 417-25; W. Keller, *The Bible as History* (1964), 345-54; H. C. King, *The Christmas Star,* Royal Ontario Museum (1970); R. K. Marshall, *The Star of Bethlehem,* Morehead Planetarium (1949); R. A. Rosenberg, "The 'Star of the Messiah' Reconsidered," *Bibl.,* LIII (1972), 105-9.

R. A. Rosenberg

***STOICS.** *See* CYNICS[S]; EPICTETUS[S].

STRUCTURALISM. *See* LITERATURE, BIBLE AS[S] §4.

***SUCCOTH-BENOTH.** In II Kings 17:30 this looks like a divine name (*see* SUCCOTH-BENOTH), but attempts to identify it with some Babylonian deity are tenuous. The simplest solution is to take the words in their literal meaning: "booths for girls," i.e., quarters for sacred prostitution, which was so widespread in late Babylon that Herodotus (I.199) erroneously thought that each Babylonian woman had to perform this duty once in her life.

Bibliography. B. Meissner, *Babylonien und Assyrien,* II (1925), 68-70, 435-37, concerning prostitution.

M. C. Astour

***SYNAGOGUE, ARCHITECTURE. 1. Dating.** While previous research had tended to date the major period of synagogue building to the late second century A.D. onward, current scholarship has produced abundant evidence for this activity some time in the third century and at the beginning of the fourth century A.D. Dramatic new discoveries make it possible to follow the development of a variety of synagogue types with great clarity. The remains of more than one hundred synagogues of ancient Palestine have been identified, and there are at least twenty known synagogue sites in the Diaspora. In recent years, the issue of chronology has centered about the synagogue of Capernaum (*see* CAPERNAUM[S] §3).

Though often a very complicated matter, the archaeological dating of synagogues is a much greater possibility today than ever before. Sealed materials from underneath the synagogue floor at Khirbet Shema have enabled the excavators to argue for a third-century date for the erection of a first synagogue there. A second synagogue was built on the ruins of the first one in the fourth century and was destroyed in an earthquake at the beginning of the fifth century.

The earliest Palestinian synagogues are those discovered at Masada and Herodium, which date to the first century. An early dating (first or second century A.D.) has also been proposed for a building at Chorazin discovered in 1926; however, this proposal has not won broad acceptance. Of the later Palestinian synagogues, Gerasa in Transjordan dates prior to A.D. 530, since a church is erected over its ruins at that time. Gaza is dated by an inscription to A.D. 508-509, and Beth Alpha is dated to the reign of Emperor Justin I, who ruled from 518 to 527.

Therefore, the reality of the situation is that the vast majority of ancient synagogues belong to the late Roman and early Byzantine period. While the art of the synagogue has often been thought to contribute to an understanding of Judaism at the time of Jesus, extreme caution is called for in interpreting material that primarily derives from the period of roughly A.D. 300-600. The very fact that few "early" synagogues have been found in Palestine raises fundamental questions about the very nature of the synagogue in the first centuries A.D.

2. Types of synagogues. ***a. The basilical synagogue,*** often referred to as the "early" or "Galilean" type. Rectangular in plan, it has two rows of columns running lengthwise and a short row running crossways opposite the main entrance, dividing its space into a central nave and two side aisles. The main façade usually consists of three entrances and is always oriented toward Jerusalem. The sanctuary is often flanked by a courtyard or adjoining building such as is found at Capernaum. A gallery often runs along three sides, and while most scholars view it as functioning for women only, at least one scholar has argued convincingly that women were not excluded from participating with men in worship during the Talmudic period. Access to this gallery, in any case, was usually gained from outside. *See* SYNAGOGUE Figs. 95-98.

The awkward feature in the basilical synagogue is that it requires those who enter it to make a complete about-face in order to worship facing Jerusalem. Hence, it is usually thought that a Torah shrine was movable in these synagogues and was wheeled out during the services. However, no trace of any such shrine, movable or fixed, has been found in this type of building, with the possible exception of the niche on the wall facing the façade at Arbel (Irbid), if that can be assigned to the early building there.

The floors of these basilical buildings are often paved with ashlars (as at Baram and Capernaum) or sometimes with simple black/gray and white tesserae, though no such mosaic floor has survived intact. Stone benches frequently run along the sides to provide seating.

The origin of this type of building is generally thought to be the typical basilica of the Greco-Roman world mediated to Palestine through Syro-Roman and Nabatean prototypes. Examples from Galilee number around fifteen, with a like number now identified in the Golan Heights. Although few new excavations have been conducted, the general dating ranges for these buildings can be said to be third and fourth century A.D.

b. The broad-house synagogue. The appearance of this type is usually thought to coincide with the time when a fixed receptacle for the Torah was adopted. The earliest example comes from the Diasporan site of Dura-Europos in the third century A.D. (*see* ART, EARLY JEWISH[S] §2). From the S of Palestine came the exciting new synagogue finds at Eshtemoa and Susiya. In both these buildings, the focus of worship is located on the long wall facing Jerusalem, neither of them containing internal columnation. Standing before the entrance of these synagogues, which consists of a monumental, three-portal façade on the short wall, was a pillared porch. In addition, both have a bema, or podium, and an *aediculum,* or Torah shrine, on the long wall. The broad house thus represents another means of resolving the difficulties, posed by the basilica, or worshiping toward Jerusalem; this would explain why the entrance remained on the short wall and not on the long wall opposite the bema as one might expect in a broad house. *See* SYNAGOGUE Figs. 99D, H.

At Susiya we find fourth-century mosaics, the earliest decorated mosaics thus far preserved. At Caesarea, the earlier of two superimposed synagogues belongs to this type also.

At Khirbet Shema near Meiron, the first broad house in Galilee was uncovered. It differs from the ones in the south by adapting the basilical plan to the broad house. In other words, it has internal columnation oriented E-W, but the bema on the long S wall indicates that the focus of worship was located on the long wall from the beginning. Only black and white tesserae were found there, indicating a simple mosaic floor. Two major entrances were found, the one on the N wall opposite the bema having a menorah incised on the lintel, and the one on the west having an eagle incised on one of the doorjambs. *See* Fig. 8.

While the origin of this type of building is not certain, the basic Syro-Palestinian temple type—the broad house—could well have influenced it (*see* TEMPLES, SEMITIC[S]). Palestinian broad-house synagogues are referred to as the "transitional" type, but recent excavations have shown that such

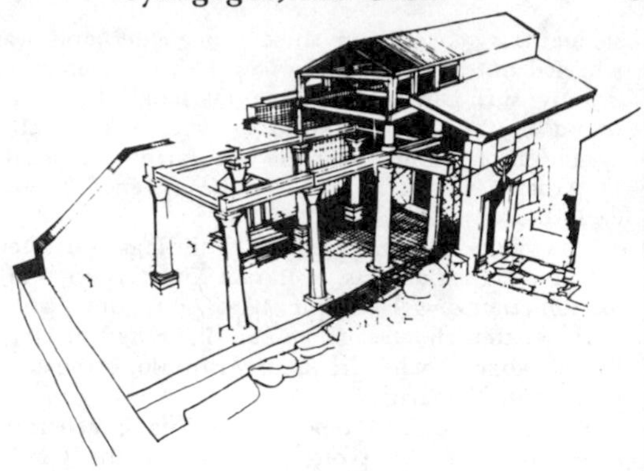

John F. Thompson, architect; by permission of E. M. Meyers

8. Architect's reconstruction of Khirbet Shema Synagogue I. Note aediculum on S wall and menorah lintel in N portal.

a designation is erroneous because some broad houses antedate the so-called "early" basilica-type synagogues which consist of a broad room with an elaboration in portico.

c. The apsidal synagogue. The beginnings of a new type of building can be dated to the fifth century A.D. On the basis of the synagogue at Gerasa, which was rebuilt as a church in A.D. 530, this form continues until the eighth century. It is based on the basilica plan; the novelty is the fact that the apse points in the direction of Jerusalem and does not force the worshiper to do the awkward about-face after entering through the main façade. It very often was built with a court and forecourt. In this type the apse, separated by a screen from the rest of the sanctuary, served as the repository for the Torah shrine and often as a place for storing old scrolls.

Since the Byzantines laid strictures against the building of new synagogues, the ornament of this later type was concentrated within. Hence, most are characterized by lively and colorful mosaics, beautifully carved chancel screens, and elaborate capitals. Parade examples of this type are Gaza, Maon, Beth Alpha, Hammath Gader, etc. *See* ART, EARLY JEWISH[S] §3.

3. Outstanding problems. Given the fact that the current work has been published in such fragmentary fashion, the time has not yet come to speak with certainty on the development of synagogue architecture. In the Diaspora, in addition to Dura, major works are due on SARDIS, Stobi (Yugoslavia), and Ostia (Italy). In Palestine, full reports are not yet available on any of the newly excavated or recently discovered sites. What can be said is that local traditions have apparently a good deal more to do with the development of synagogal plans than was heretofore recognized. Hence, rigid typological arguments tied to a fixed chronology can no longer be accepted at face value. New discoveries will doubtless raise new questions. Nonetheless, a study of synagogue remains, including artistic and architectural features, will continue to provide fresh insights into the religious and aesthetic sensibilities of Jews in antiquity.

Bibliography. M. Avi-Yonah, "Ancient Synagogues," *Ariel,* XXXII (1973), 29-43, "Editor's Note," *IEJ,* XXIII (1973), 43-45, "Synagogue," *Encyclopaedia Judaica,* XV, 595-600, and "Synagogue Architecture in the Classical Period," in *Jewish Art* (1961), 157-90; D. Bahat, "The Synagogue at Beth-Shean: Preliminary Report," *Qadmoniot,* V (1972), 55-58, Hebrew; D. Barag, Y. Porat, and E. Netzer, "The Second Season of Excavations in the Synagogue at En-Gedi," *Qadmoniot,* V (1972), 52-54, Hebrew; G. Foerster, "Ancient Synagogues in Eretz Israel," *Qadmoniot,* V (1972), 38-42, Hebrew, "Les Synagogues de Galilée," *Bible et Terre Sainte,* CXXX (1971), 8-15, and "The Synagogues at Masada and Herodium," *Eretz Israel,* XI (1973), 224-28, Hebrew; E. Meyers, "The Ancient Synagogue of Khirbet Shema," in *Perspectives in Jewish Learning,* V (1973), 28-40; "Ḥurvat Shema'—The Settlement and the Synagogue," *Qadmoniot,* V (1972), 58-61; E. Meyers with A. T. Kraabel and J. F. Strange, "Archaeology and Rabbinic Tradition at Khirbet Shema: 1970 and 1971 Campaigns," *BA,* XXXV (1972), 2-31; S. Safrai, "Was There a Women's Gallery in the Synagogue?" *Tarbiẓ,* XXXII (1963), 329-38, Hebrew; S. Saller, *Second Revised Catalogue of the Ancient Synagogues of the Holy Land* (1972); N. Tsori, "The Ancient Synagogue at Beth-Shean," *Eretz Israel,* VIII (1967), 149-67, Hebrew; Z. Yeivin, "Excavations at Khorazin," *Eretz Israel,* XI (1973), 144-57, Hebrew, "The Synagogue at Eshtemoa," *Qadmoniot,* V (1972), 43-45, Hebrew, and with S. Guttman and E. Netzer, "Excavation in the Synagogue at Khirbet Susiya," *Qadmoniot,* V (1972), 47-51, Hebrew.

E. M. MEYERS

***SYNAGOGUE, THE GREAT** [כנסת הגדולה, variously translated Great Synagogue, Great Assembly, Great Synod, Great Community]. Rabbinic tradition seems to associate it with the period of Ezra and Nehemiah and with the religious assemblage of Neh. 8–10. Because M. AB. 1.2 lists Simon the Just as among the remnants of, or survivors of, the Great Synagogue, the institution was considered to have been dissolved during his lifetime (third century B.C.). Sources disagree as to whether there were 85 or 120 members.

Traditions attribute to this assemblage the establishment of the festival of Purim; the writing (i.e., codification) of Ezekiel, Daniel, Esther, and the twelve minor prophets; the classification of rabbinic tradition into Midrash, halachoth and haggadoth; the determination of biblical characters who have no portion in the "world to come"; the maxims listed in M. AB. 1.1; and many other enactments.

While tradition does not yield much reliable information about this institution, it does project back to it the origin of some of the most essential features and conceptions of Judaism: its prayers, its divisions of the oral Law, its festivals. This process of anachronization, reading back into the distant past the beginnings of contemporary institutions, laws, and beliefs, is typical of rabbinic Judaism and should be understood for what it tells of the later period rather than the earlier one.

Modern scholars disagree on nearly every issue regarding the Great Synagogue. Some reject its historical existence. Others attribute its origin to the assembly mentioned in Neh. 8–10, or to an assembly convened about 198 B.C. to determine whether to give political support to either Antiochus III of Syria or Ptolemy V of Egypt, or to the "large assembly" (συναγωγῆς μεγάλης) mentioned in I Macc. 14:28 ff. Scholars also argue that each of the above was a Great Synagogue

(Assembly), or that one or the other was the only Great Synagogue. Thus the institution has been variously dated in the fifth, fourth, third, and second centuries B.C., and its duration conceived as spanning from three hundred years to one generation. Further, this institution has been seen as identical with, a precursor of, or unrelated to, the *Bêth Dîn HagGādhôl,* the γερουσία, or the Great SANHEDRIN. Its function is considered to have been purely religious or a mixture of religions, secular and political; either view is shaped by notions regarding the composition of the Great Synagogue. Scholars argue that the following groups were represented simultaneously, successively, or exclusively: prophets, priests, sages, scribes, aristocrats, and members of the *Ma'ᵃmādhôth,* or watches representing all Israel at the sacrifice of the communal offering. Most recently, the Great Synagogue has been tied to Pharisaic Judaism. One view conceives of the assembly in I Macc. 14:28 as a revolutionary one-day gathering at which the Pharisaic leaders and the people rejected the Zadokite-Sadducean priesthood; another sees the institution as a federation of various branches of Pharisaic associations or clubs.

Bibliography. W. Bacher, "Synagogue, the Great," *Jewish Encyclopedia,* XI, 640-43; H. Englander, "The Men of the Great Synagogue," *Hebrew Union College Jubilee Volume* (1925), pp. 145-69; L. Finkelstein, "The Maxim of the Anshe Keneset Ha-Gedolah," *JBL,* LIX (1940), 455-69, and *Ha-Perushim ve-Anshe Keneset Ha-Gedolah* (1950), contains English summary, and ch. 4 lists all passages in rabbinic literature where the Great Synagogue is mentioned; S. Krauss, "The Great Synod," *JQR,* X (1898), 347-77; H. Mantel, "The Nature of the Great Synagogue," *HTR,* LX (1967), 69-91; G. F. Moore, *Judaism,* III (1930), 7-11; D. Sperber, "Synagogue, the Great," *Encyclopaedia Judaica* (1971), XV, 629-31; C. Tchernowitz, *Toledoth Ha-Halakah,* III (1943), 60-81, contains simple summaries and evaluation of nineteenth-century scholarship on this subject; I. H. Weiss, *Dor Dor Ve-Dorshav,* I (1924), 48-94.

L. M. BARTH

***SYNOPTIC PROBLEM.** The two-document hypothesis is undoubtedly the most widely accepted source-critical hypothesis in NT introductions, gospel commentaries, and monographs. It is presupposed in a considerable number of redaction-critical investigations, and, in particular, the recent study of the Matthean as well as the Lukan redaction and theology has shown the practicability of the theory (*see* REDACTION CRITICISM, NT[S]). Nevertheless, the existence of the hypothetical "Q" source is still contested (*see* Q[S]), and objections raised against the priority of Mark have tended to call the two-document hypothesis into question and, in some quarters, have led to other theories (oral tradition, gospel fragments, primitive gospel, priority of Matthew).

The recent discussion has concentrated upon three problems: the minor agreements, the argument from order, and the style of Mark.

1. The minor agreements. On the hypothesis of the independent editing of Mark by Matthew and Luke the minor agreements of these gospels against Mark (in the triple tradition) are the most serious stumbling block. Occasionally, textual corruption and harmonization can be the cause of the agreement, but only on a more limited scale than was proposed by Streeter. Because of the great number of these coincidences in content, vocabulary, style, and grammar, the concatenation of agreements in certain sections, and the combination of positive and negative agreements, many authors do not accept accidental coincidence as a satisfactory explanation for the whole of the phenomenon. Without abandoning the priority of Mark, several solutions have been proposed.

(*a*) Proto-Mark or Deutero-Mark. Matthew and Luke used a Markan text which is slightly different from our Mark, either a Proto-Mark (Boismard) or a Deutero-Mark, due to textual corruption (Glasson: cf. Western text), revision (Brown: cf. Caesarean text), or edition (West: Primitive Luke; Fuchs: Mark already combined with Q).

(*b*) Luke's subsidiary dependence on Matthew. Luke, who follows Mark as his basic source in the triple tradition, is also acquainted with and influenced by Matthew. According to some authors the double tradition, too, is borrowed from Matthew (Farrer), but others suggest that the minor agreements (in the triple tradition) and the double tradition or Q sections are to be explained differently (Morgenthaler).

(*c*) Common source. Both Matthew and Luke depend on another source besides Mark: a primitive gospel, Proto-Matthew (Vaganay, Boismard), gospel fragments (Léon-Dufour), or oral tradition (Dahl; Schramm: "tradition variants").

In the two-document hypothesis it is a common assumption that some of the agreements should be assigned to Q (especially the *major* agreements in the sections parallel to Mark 1:7-8, 12-13; 3:22-30; 4:30-32; 6:7-11, and, less convincingly, 12:28-34). The great bulk of minor agreements, however, can be explained by coincident correction and the common tendencies of the independent editors, Matthew and Luke, and are therefore highly significant for the redactional study of the gospels (Neirynck). Only a small number of residual cases are attributed to the influence of oral tradition (Kümmel) or to textual corruption (Schmid; cf. de Solages, McLoughlin).

On the GRIESBACH HYPOTHESIS, with the assumption of some direct literary relationship between Matthew and Luke, the minor agreements are explained by Mark's "own peculiar stylistic preferences" as he conflated the two earlier gospels (Farmer).

2. The argument from order. The relative order of sections in Mark is in general supported by both Matthew and Luke; where Matthew diverges from Mark, Mark's order is supported by Luke, and where Luke differs from Mark, Mark's order is supported by Matthew. From this statement of the absence of agreement in order between Matthew and Luke against Mark (in the triple tradition), proponents of the two-document hypothesis draw the conclusion that Mark is the common source, independently edited by Matthew and Luke.

a. The validity of the argument. B. C. Butler has contended that there is a logical error in the traditional argument from order. A number of scholars, among them some who continue to espouse the two-document hypothesis on other grounds (Styler, Fuller), have in fact dismissed the argument as useless. It is allowed that the argument has probative force on the assumption of a common gospel source:

Mark's order

Matthew   Mark   Luke

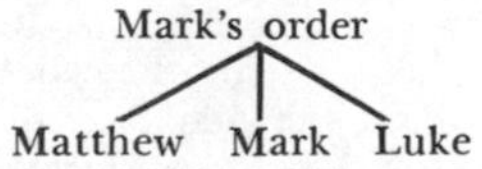

but, it is claimed, once this solution is abandoned the phenomena of order are satisfactorily explained not only on the hypothesis of Markan priority, but also on any other hypothesis which proposes Mark as the middle term:

Mk		Mt	Lk	Mt	Lk
Mt	Lk	Mk		Mk	Mk
				Lk	Mk

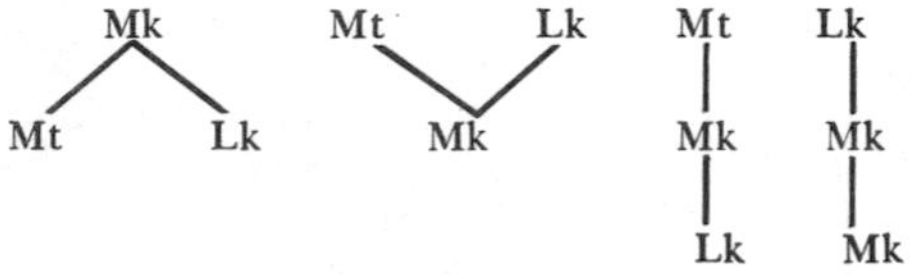

However, some other observations need to be made.

i. If the relative order of the gospel *episodes* is studied as a specific literary phenomenon, it becomes clear that there are virtually no places where Matthew and Luke agree against Mark. (Sanders, however, also considers individual sentences or phrases where there is agreement in order and regards this as indicative of Luke's dependence on Matthew.)

ii. The description of the evidence as "alternating support" (i.e., when Matthew diverges from Mark, Mark's order is supported by Luke, and when Luke diverges from Mark, Mark's order is supported by Matthew) should be corrected by a more concrete approach. In fact, the basic phenomenon to be reckoned with is the common order between Mark and Matthew and between Mark and Luke. The changes of order are exceptional: in Luke the alterations of the Markan order are limited in number, and in Matthew the transpositions are confined to 4:23–11:1. (In the Griesbach hypothesis, too, the argument from order is based on the so-called "alternating support," explicable only by the deliberate intention of a writer, on this hypothesis, by Mark's decision to remain close to at least one of his sources, Matthew and Luke.)

iii. The evidence of the relative order excludes the oral tradition hypothesis and the fragments theory.

iv. The appellation "Lachmann fallacy" (Butler) is misleading, not only because Lachmann's observations (1835) were made within the primitive gospel hypothesis, but also because he did not use the formulation of "Mark's order supported either by one or the other," which originated in the Griesbach hypothesis and was first employed in the Markan hypothesis by Weisse (1838).

v. Lachmann's concern was to determine the reasons which could have influenced the evangelists in altering the sequence of the gospel sections in some *Urgospel*. His argument for the priority of Mark's order is still a valuable one insofar as an acceptable explanation can be given for Matthew's

and Luke's transpositions, and no good reason has been found why Mark would change the order of Matthew or Luke.

b. Matthew and Mark. The disagreements in order are found in the first part of Matthew. From 14:1 on, Matthew follows faithfully the Markan sequence (Mark 6:14–16:8): there are only a few omissions (Mark 8:22-26; 12:41-44; 14:51-52), and the alterations of order in Matthew 15:3-6; 19:4-6; and 21:12-13 are merely inversions within the same context; the discourse fragment of Matt. 10:17-22 (cf. Mark 13:9-13), which is sometimes quoted as the only transposition in the gospel, is a redactional duplication (cf. 24:9, 13-14; Mark 13:9-10, 12c-13). The presence of transpositions in the first part of Matthew does not necessarily point to a different tradition (Gaboury: multiple sources in a less advanced state). Matthean editorial concentration is a much more plausible explanation. In the discourses of Matt. 5–7 and 9:37 ff. Matthew combined the double tradition parallels with other Q sections. If we can admit, as most authors do, that the original order of Q is better preserved in Luke, then Matthew not only anticipated these sections but also reversed the order of the Baptist and the mission sections:

Matthew	Luke
5:3–7:27	6:20-49
8:5-13	7:1-10
8:19-22	
9:37–10:16	
11:2-19	7:18-35
	9:57-62
	10:2-12
11:20-24, 25-27	10:13-15, 21-22

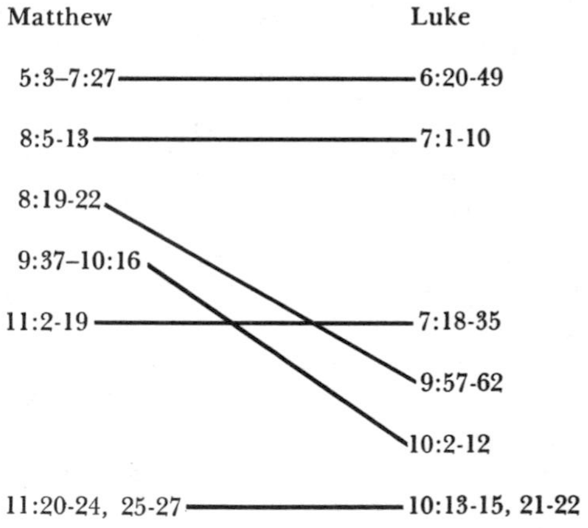

A similar observation is to be made regarding the triple tradition: the transpositions are found in the great complex of 4:23–11:1, from the Sermon on the Mount to Jesus' answer to John the Baptist. The section opens with a solemn introduction in which Matthew combined several motifs from Mark's "Day at Capernaum" (Mark 1:21-39), and also from other summaries in Mark:

Matthew	Mark
4:23a	1:39a; 6:6b
23b	1:14-15
23c	1:39b
24a	1:28
24b	1:32, 34

Matthew	Mark
25	3:7-8
5:1*a*	3:13
2	1:21

The Sermon on the Mount is the only one of the five great discourses in Matthew (5–7; 10; 13; 18; 24–25) for which the occasion is not provided by a rudimentary discourse in Mark (cf. Mark 6:7-11; 4:31-34; 9:33-50; 13). Perhaps the first mention of Jesus' *teaching* in Mark 1:21 explains why Matthew placed the first sermon here and used Mark 1:22 in his description of the reactions of the multitude: Matt. 8:1-17 combines the miracle story which followed the sermon in Q (Luke 7:1-10) with miracle stories from Mark 1. The first place is given to the cleansing of the leper (8:2-4, with the *inclusio* in 9:30*b*-31; cf. Mark 1:43, 45). The inversion of the order has to do with Matthew's interest in the composition of 8:1–9:34. At the same time Mark 1:40-45 is introduced within the "First Day" of Jesus' ministry, Matthew's replacement of the "Day at Capernaum" in Mark (5:1–8:17):

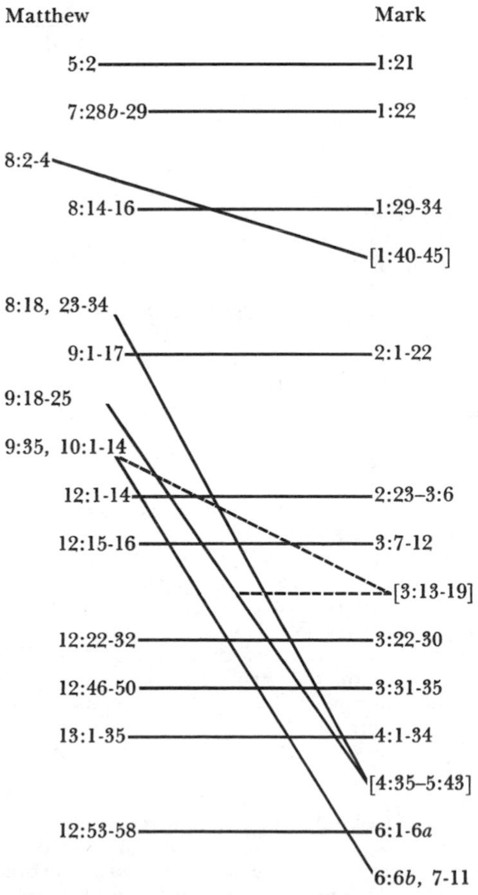

In the second section of miracles (8:18–9:34) Matthew anticipated Mark 4:35–5:43 and duplicated other miracle stories in 9:27-34. However, the insertion of the Q passage in 8:19-22 clearly shows that the editorial interest is not merely in the miracles of Jesus. The summary of Jesus' ministry is echoed in 10:1, 7-8 and unites the activity of Jesus and the mission of the disciples. Thus, Matthew's editing can be seen in a double anticipation: that of the miracles from Mark 4:35–5:43, and that of the disciples sections from Mark 6:6*b*-11 (combined with 3:13-19), and from Q (cf. Luke 9:57–10:12). Matt. 8:18–9:34 is the evangelist's own composition around the Markan sequence of 2:1-22. In 12:1 he comes back to Mark 2:23 and from there on follows the order of Mark, with the exception only of the anticipated pericopes.

c. Luke and Mark. The situation in Luke is quite different. There is no such rearrangement as we have in Matt. 4:23–11:1. Luke normally follows the order of Mark. It has been argued that Luke, where he borrowed from Mark, *always* follows the Markan order and that the few instances of divergence in the ministry, and the more frequent alterations of order in the PASSION NARRATIVE, are explainable only by the influence of non-Markan sources (Proto-Luke). However, for each transposition a valuable redactional explanation can be adduced, although many exegetes admit a non-Markan tradition behind pericopes such as:

Luke 4:16:30	from Mark 6:1-6*a*
5:1-11	1:16-20
6:12-16, 17-19	3:13-19, 7-12
7:36-50	14:3-9
8:19-21 (after 8:4-18)	3:31-35 (before 4:1-34)
10:25-28 (cf. 20:39-40)	12:28-34
22:21-23	14:19-21
22:24-27	10:42-45
22:31-34	14:29-30.

3. The style of Mark. The roughness of Mark's style is a well-known argument for the gospel's early dating (*see* MARK, GOSPEL OF §5; GOSPELS). The evidence of stylistic improvements and christological corrections in Matthew and Luke is impressive, although those who question Mark's priority dismiss it as unconvincing and argue, to the contrary, that there are passages in Mark which suggest that Mark is secondary to Matthew and Luke (Farmer).

The new defense of the Griesbach hypothesis holds that duplicate expressions, of which one element has a parallel in Matthew and the other in Luke, are the result of conflation. According to Boismard and some other exegetes, the sources combined by Mark are not the gospels of Matthew and Luke but Proto-Mark and Proto-Matthew, or other gospel sources. However, a re-examination of the evidence shows that duplicate expressions and other forms of duality form a characteristic feature of Mark's style. The two-step expressions, in which the second statement adds precision to the first, is typical. It points to the originality of

Mark rather than to conflation and combination of sources.

Bibliography. Tools for study: K. Aland, *Synopsis of the Four Gospels,* Greek-English ed. of the *Synopsis Quattuor Evangeliorum,* using text of the RSV (1972); W. R. Farmer, *Synopticon* (1969); R. Morgenthaler, *Statistische Synopse* (1971).

Alternatives to the two-document theory: W. R. Farmer, *The Synoptic Problem* (1964), argues for Mark's dependence on Matthew and Luke (*see also* bibliog. for GRIESBACH HYPOTHESIS[S]); R. H. Fuller, E. P. Sanders, T. R. W. Longstaff, "The Synoptic Problem: After Ten Years," *PSTJ,* XXVIII, 2 (1975), 63-74, assesses Farmer's position and the discussion of it to date, with bibliog.; A. Gaboury, *La structure des évangiles synoptiques,* NovTSup, XXII (1970), proposes multiple sources for Matt. 4–13, but adheres otherwise to a common gospel source; M.-E. Boismard, *Synopse des quatre évangiles en français,* II: *Commentaire* (1972), admits that the final redactions of Matthew and Luke depend on Mark, but also accepts a final redaction of Mark depending upon both Matthew and Luke, i.e., Proto-Luke (cf. F. Neirynck, "Urmarcus redivivus? Examen critique de l'hypothèse des insertions matthéennes dans Marc," in *L'évangile selon Marc,* ed. M. Sabbe, BETL, XXXIV [1974], 103-45).

Minor agreements: F. Neirynck in collaboration with T. Hansen and F. Van Segbroeck, *The Minor Agreements of Matthew and Luke against Mark with a Cumulative List* (1974), historical survey, cumulative list and classification; W. R. Farmer, *The Synoptic Problem,* pp. 94-152, reacts against Streeter; M.-E. Boismard, *Synopse des quatre évangiles en français,* II: *Commentaire,* Proto-Mark and Proto-Matthew; T. F. Glasson, "Did Matthew Use a 'Western' Text of Mark?" *ET,* LV (1943-44), cols. 180-84, and "An Early Revision of the Gospel of Mark," *JBL,* LXXXV (1966), 231-33; J. P. Brown, "An Early Revision of the Gospel of Mark," *JBL,* LXXVIII (1959), 215-27; H. P. West, "A Primitive Version of Luke in the Composition of Matthew," *NTS,* XIV (1967), 75-95; A. Fuchs, *Sprachliche Untersuchungen zu Matthäus und Lukas,* AnBib, XLIX (1971); A. Farrer, "On Dispensing with Q," *Studies in the Gospels,* ed. D. E. Nineham (1955), pp. 55-86; M. D. Goulder, *Midrash and Lection in Matthew* (1974), Farrer's hypothesis; R. Morgenthaler, *Statistische Synopse,* pp. 301-5; L. Vaganay, *Le problème synoptique* (1954), pp. 69-74, 293, 319, 423-25; X. Léon-Dufour, "Les évangiles synoptiques," *Introduction à la Bible,* II (1959), 291-95, and "Passion," *DBSup,* VI (1960), cols. 1444-47; N. A. Dahl, "Die Passionsgeschichte bei Matthäus," *NTS,* II (1956), 17 ff.; T. Schramm, *Der Markus-Stoff bei Lukas,* NTSMS, XIV (1971), 72-77; W. G. Kümmel, *Introduction to the NT* (rev. ed., 1975); J. Schmid, *Einleitung in das NT* (1973), revision of A. Wikenhauser's introduction; B. de Solages, *A Greek Synopsis of the Gospels* (1959), and *La composition des évangiles de Luc et de Matthieu et leur sources* (1973); S. McLoughlin, "Le problème synoptique," in *De Jésus aux évangiles: Tradition et rédaction dans les évangiles synoptiques,* BETL, XXV (1967), 17-40.

Argument from order: F. Neirynck, "The Argument from Order and St. Luke's Transpositions," *The Minor Agreements,* pp. 291-322; A. Gaboury, *La structure des évangiles synoptiques;* F. Neirynck, "The Gospel of Matthew and Literary Criticism. A Critical Analysis of A. Gaboury's Hypothesis," *L'évangile selon Matthieu,* ed. M. Didier, BETL, XXIX (1972), 37-69; E. P. Sanders, "The Argument from Order and the Relationship between Matthew and Luke," *NTS,* XV (1969), 249-61; G. M. Styler, "The Priority of Mark," in C. F. D. Moule, *The Birth of the NT* (1962), pp. 223-32; N. H. Palmer, "Lachmann's Argument," *NTS,* XIII (1967), 368-78, and *The Logic of Gospel Criticism* (1968); B. C. Butler, *The Originality of St. Matthew* (1951).

Style of Mark: F. Neirynck, *Duality in Mark. Contributions to the Study of the Markan Redaction* (1972); W. R. Farmer, *The Synoptic Problem.*

See also bibliog. with original article and with the article Q[S]. F. NEIRYNCK

SYRIAC LANGUAGE. *See* ARAMAIC[S] §C2*a*.

***SYRIAC VERSIONS** (*see* VERSIONS, ANCIENT §4).

1. Versions of the OT
   a. The Old Syriac Version
   b. The Peshitta
   c. The Philoxenian Version
   d. The Palestinian Syriac Version
   e. The Syro-Hexaplar Version
   f. The version of Jaqob of Edessa
   g. The Syriac Masora
2. Versions of the NT
   a. The Diatessaron
   b. The Old Syriac Version
   c. The Peshitta
   d. The Philoxenian Version
   e. The Harclean Version
   f. The Palestinian Syriac Version
   Bibliography

1. Versions of the OT. A close examination of the text of the Peshitta, the standard Syriac version, reveals that the Syriac OT underwent a long period of development. This became clear from the early studies of Perles; later Baumstark established that the *Vorlage* can be traced back to the traditions of the Palestinian Targ. (*see* TARGUMS[S]). More recently, research on patristic and liturgical sources found in previously unknown MSS has opened new avenues for the illumination of the history of the Syriac Pentateuch, and has enabled us to see more of the profile of the Old Syriac (*Vetus Syra*). Other parts of the OT still need similar investigation, but it is already clear that the same archaic layer is present in the Psalter and the prophetic books as well, reflecting the pattern of the ancient Palestinian Targumic traditions.

a. The Old Syriac Version. There is no agreement as to whether this version had a Jewish or a Christian origin. It has been suggested that a historically suitable situation for its creation was the conversion to Judaism (*ca.* A.D. 40) of the royal house of Adiabene, a kingdom situated between the two rivers Zab, E of the Tigris. It then became necessary to make the Scripture available in Syriac, the vernacular of the area. The Bible, beginning with the Pentateuch, was introduced into the kingdom in the middle of the first century (Kahle). This could have been accomplished by adapting the West Aramaic Targ. into the Syriac of Adiabene.

However it is equally possible that the Old Syr. originated with the beginnings of Christianity in Mesopotamia. According to ancient records the gospel reached Adiabene through Jewish Christian emissaries. Against this background the first translation of the Scriptures would have been made, not from the MT nor from the LXX, but from the ancient Palestinian Targ. Not only did this Syriac version serve as the basis for a revision which produced the Peshitta, but some MSS escaped revision and continued to circulate. One such text became the base for the Palestinian Syriac version of the OT (*see* §1*d below*) and for an Arabic version.

b. The Peshitta. The revised form of the Syriac Bible, the Scripture of Syrian Christianity, is called the "Peshitta," a term meaning "the simple [version]," i.e., easy to understand. It seems that this designation resulted from the contrast with other, more elaborate and scholarly versions equipped with textual-critical apparatus (*see* §1*e*). Confirmation of this hypothesis can be seen in the fact that this designation does not appear in any Syriac author earlier than the ninth century. The transmission of the version is well attested by extant MSS. The most ancient codex is MS British Museum Add. 14425, containing Genesis, Exodus, Numbers, and Deuteronomy. It was copied in the year 463/64. MS Br. Mus. Add. 14427, containing Leviticus, Numbers, and Deuteronomy with gaps, is of the sixth century, and MS Ambr. B 21 inf., containing the whole OT (*Translatio Syra Pescitto VT,* ed. A. M. Ceriani [1876]) is of the sixth or the seventh century.

The Peshitta was not a new translation but a revision. Internal evidence indicates that it cannot be of one cast, but must have had behind it a history of gradual growth in different epochs. This is suggested not only by variations in style but also by its text, which displays evidence of revision and exposure to Targumic and LXX influences, in varying degree from book to book. Certain books render the *Vorlage* quite literally (Song of Songs); some even servilely (Job); others show more freedom (Psalms and especially Isaiah and the Minor Prophets); some display a surprising paraphrastic freedom (Ruth); others unfold Targumic pattern in textual formation (Pentateuch, Ezekiel, Proverbs), and some have an even fuller degree of paraphrastic renderings derived from the Midrashic and Targumic traditions (Chronicles). Disparate elements appear even in the fabric of the individual books. These phenomena indicate that different parts of the Peshitta go back to different textual bases, and that they originated in different periods.

Since the Peshitta is one of the oldest and most important witnesses, it occupies an important place in textual criticism (*see* Textual Criticism, OT[S]); Textual Criticism, NT[S]). The Isaiah scroll from the caves at the Dead Sea reveals close affinities with the Peshitta and confirms its value as a witness to the text (cf. Text, OT §A1). On the other hand, the Greek Bible in all its forms has also left its impact on the Peshitta. The problem of the influence of the LXX is complicated; whether it originally influenced the process of revision or only came on the scene later is not yet clarified. In any case its influence is reflected in the most ancient MSS extant.

The literary and historical problems of the Peshitta are extremely intricate. Its date and the identity of the revisers and translators are unknown. Advocates of a Jewish origin have been challenged by those who claim Christian provenance. The latter position is probably correct.

There is no critical edition of this version, except for the Song of Songs, Tobit, and IV Esdras (Leiden, 1966), and Canticles and Apocryphal Psalms (Leiden, 1972). Adequate editions exist for the Pentateuch (*Pentateuchus syriace,* ed. W. E. Barnes [1914]) and the Psalter (*The Peshitta Psalter,* ed. W. E. Barnes [1904]). The London edition (*VT syriace,* ed. S. Lee [1823]) is essentially a reprint of the texts of the Paris and Walton polyglots. The Urmia edition (1852) is different in character, since it follows the East Syrian traditions. That of Mosul (1887-91) also depends upon the East Syrian tradition but is limited in value, and that of Beirut (1951) rests on a very narrow MS basis.

c. The Philoxenian Version. Syrians are well-known for their ongoing attempts to improve the translations of the Bible. According to the testimony of Moshe of Aggel, Philoxenus, bishop of Mabbug, sponsored a translation of the NT and the Psalter. Ceriani has proposed that the actual work was produced by Polycarp, chorepiscopus of Philoxenus, and this view has much in its favor. Some vestiges of the work have been identified which are of sufficient significance to require careful examination. A scholion in the codex of the Syro-Hexaplar MS Mil. C 313 inf., which quotes from the version of Philoxenus, seems to deserve credence. In MS Br. Mus. Add. 17106 a segment of this version has apparently survived in a fragment of Isaiah (*Esaiae fragmenta syriaca versionis anonymae,* ed. A. M. Ceriani [1868]). The version was based not on the Peshitta but on a more archaic form of the text, and the Greek text used for its revision was not the Alexandrian LXX but the Lucianic. The same type of text appears in the quotations of Isaiah in the Syriac translation of Cyril's *Glaphyra* prepared by Moshe of Aggel not long after Philoxenus.

d. The Palestinian Syriac Version. While the versions described above originated in an area where Syriac was spoken, centering around Edessa in Mesopotamia, this version is entirely different. It is written in an idiom with linguistic features that deviate considerably from Syriac and represents a dialect that belongs to the Western Aramaic spoken in Palestine and neighboring regions (*see* Aramaic[S] §C1). Its script is also distinctive, representing a rigid and archaic form of the Estrangela, a script that resembles the Hebrew and early Syriac scripts. This version is extant mainly in lectionaries, the most important being a MS found in Cairo, which contains selections from the Pentateuch, Job, and Proverbs (*A Palestinian Syriac Lectionary,* ed. A. S. Lewis [1897]). In the extant material the best represented book is the Psalter, with forty-two psalms complete, plus fragments. This form of the lectionary texts does not preclude the possibility that the pericopes rest on a more ample Syro-Palestinian Bible.

The text of this version, which is quite independent of other Syriac versions, reveals archaic features. Among them the Targumic influence is most conspicuous, but the underlying Greek text also had many peculiarities. Therefore it is the more regrettable that the historical problems connected with this unique version are shrouded in darkness. The evidence from paleography gives little help. The script used in the palimpsest MS, which is the oldest witness, leads to the ninth century, but the version itself must be older. An Arab author, Ibn Ishaq, used this version about the year 700. The Christians in Palestine, who were provided with oral translation when the Greek Scriptures were read in the worship services, must have soon felt the need for a written version of their own. It is possible that a reference by Jerome to the burial of St. Paula (d. 404) in Bethlehem, "Graeco Latino Syroque sermone psalmos in ordine personabant" (*Epistulae* CVIII. 29), may be the earliest hint of the beginnings of this version. The reference is the more interesting since, in connection with the discussion regarding whether the version originated in Antioch (Burkitt), in Egypt (Marshall), or in Palestine (Lagrange), new discoveries now point to Palestine. These discoveries are an inscription from the sixth or seventh century (Milik) and a letter.

e. The Syro-Hexaplar Version. This version has re-emerged very slowly. Until recently little material was available for the first part of the OT, particularly the Pentateuch. Since there were only some individual books extant, most with gaps or even in fragments, and some were completely unknown, the discovery of the Pentateuch in MS Midyat (*The Pentateuch in the Version of the Syro-Hexapla*) is highly significant. This MS belongs to the eleventh or twelfth century. MS Ambr. C 313 inf., which contains Job, the wisdom literature, the Prophets, and other material (*Codex Syro-Hexaplaris Ambrosianus,* ed. A. M. Ceriani [1874]) is of the ninth century. New discoveries, among them a book of Isaiah in MS Jerusalem St. Mark 1, written on parchment, have increased the amount of evidence (*The Book of Isaiah,* ed. A. Vööbus [1976]). The history of the version is unfolded in the colophons added to the individual books. The man who undertook to produce this new and scholarly version of the OT was Paul, bishop of Tella de-Mauzelath, in Mesopotamia. Forced to flee the invading Persians, he found a place of refuge in Egypt and devoted his life in exile to this undertaking. It must have been accomplished between the years 615 and 619—in any case before the summer of 619—in a Syrian monastery at the ninth milestone near Alexandria. A team of co-workers assisted Paul, and in a colophon Tuma is mentioned as the most outstanding among them. However, the unity of style through the entire translation can be interpreted in only one way—one man has impressed his stamp upon the entire Syro-Hexaplar.

The importance of the version is due to the fact that it is based on the fifth column of the Hexapla of Origen, the disappearance of which was a great loss. This translation, inspired by scholarly considerations to produce an exact rendering of the LXX column, reproduces the Greek text word by word. Everywhere it displays a painful concern to present the Greek as accurately as possible, indeed, even to mold the Syriac to the Greek original by imposing an unnatural order of words and by enforcing strange and unnatural grammatical forms, resulting in curious idiosyncrasies in syntax. Because of the strictness of the method of translation, and the care and accuracy exercised, the Syro-Hexaplar is of the greatest value as a means of restoring the lost Hexapla of the LXX (*see* SEPTUAGINT §4*a*). The importance of the version is increased by the fact that it is not only an early witness to the text of the Hexapla, but it has also preserved the text-critical sigla of the Hexapla (*see* VERSIONS, ANCIENT §2*a*), which have rarely survived in Greek. Their value is enhanced by the margin, which includes numerous variant readings from Aquila, Symmachus, and Theodotion (*see* SEPTUAGINT §3; GREEK VERSIONS, MINOR[S]), and, in the Psalter, also from the Quinta and the Sexta, both otherwise almost unknown ancient versions. It is surprising that this scholarly version found its way into the precincts of cult and liturgy. The discovery of two new lectionaries preserved in MS Mardin Orth. 47 and 48 provides additional evidence of its use in this way.

f. The version of Jaqob of Edessa. A new recension of the OT was produced by Jaqob of Edessa (d. *ca.* 708), celebrated as one of the greatest Syriac scholars. His work marks the end of the long history of Bible translation among the Syrians. The version has survived only in part. MS Br. Mus. Add. 14429, copied in 719, very soon after the death of Jaqob, is the earliest witness; it contains I and II Samuel and the beginning of Kings. MS Par. Syr. 26 has preserved the Pentateuch; MS Par. Syr. 27 contains Daniel, and MS Vat. Syr. 5, Ezekiel, all with some gaps. From other parts of the Bible there are only fragments (*Daniel sec. ed. LXX interpr.,* ed. G. Bugati [1788]; *Monumenta sacra et profana II,* ed. A. M. Ceriani [1863]; M. Ugolini, *Or Chr.* 2 [1902], 409-20). Jaqob's version was a revision. Working with the Peshitta and the Syro-Hexaplar, he tried to improve the Peshitta on the one hand and on the other to give to the Syro-Hexaplar a shape which would bring it back to a more normal Syriac idiom. Jaqob's undertaking introduces the first systematic work in the Syriac Masora, furnished with marginal glosses regarding pronunciation and variants. It also introduces chapter divisions and summaries of content. This work was produced during the last years of Jaqob's life, when he lived in the monastery of Tell'ada. A colophon helps to establish chronology for the revision of I Samuel and Daniel, which were completed in the year 705. Some other parts originated before, and some after this date.

g. The Syriac Masora. This parallels the Jewish practice of supplying vowels for texts written in the consonantal script. The West Syrian Masora is related to the traditions cultivated in the monastery of Qarqaphta, near Ris'aina, by the monk Tubana Santa and the scribe and deacon Saba, a native of Ris'aina. MS Br. Mus. Add. 14428, 14430 and 19135 were copied by him; the second is dated in the year 723/24 and the third in 726, helping to fix the chronology of Saba's life. Almost nothing is known of Tubana, but he was probably older than Saba, who corrected his textual readings. In contrast to the Greek vowels used in the West Syrian Masora, the East Syrian Masora employed a special system of points. This work has a complicated history. The only codex which contains the OT and NT is preserved in MS Br. Mus. Add. 12138, written in the year 899. This MS, which is furnished with marginalia about the pronunciation and special characteristics of the Nestorian traditions, ascribes the introduction of the system to Joseph Huzzaya. In this connection, tradition has preserved the memory of the work of Ramisho, and of a still-older stratum in the tradition that is connected with the work of Abraham and Johannan in the School of Nisibis. *See also* TEXT, HEBREW, HISTORY OF[S] §2*a*.

2. Versions of the NT. ***a. The Diatessaron.*** In the development of the versions, as well as in the early phase of the history of the NT text, there is no greater name than Tatian (Euseb. Hist. IV. 29.6), a native of the Euphrates Valley who shortly after the middle of the second century composed the *Evangelion da-mehallete,* "the Gospel which is a composite," known to the Greek-speaking Christians as the Diatessaron (literally "through the four [gospels]"). No MS of it has survived; its text is known only through citations. The study of this unique monument of ancient Christian literature is beset with numerous complicated problems which have made it one of the most difficult topics in the field of NT textual criticism. Many have argued that its original language was Greek. Internal evidence, however, has inspired students to regard Syriac as the original language. Two small fragments in Greek, one found in Dura-Europos and the other in Egypt, have strengthened this view, since both bear unmistakable signs of a Syriac original.

The Diatessaron possessed several characteristics which ensured its appeal and its widespread use. It is not a synopsis in the modern sense, but is a composition in which the threads of the narrative are dexterously interwoven into a continuous life of Jesus. This composition was guided by meticulous care to include everything possible; hardly a word was dropped. The composition also included some readings of extracanonical provenance, readings which were precious to the Syrians. The work has literary qualities that give it a peculiar charm. Tatian's hand becomes visible again and again as he smoothed and filed the text into conformity with his fine taste. This scholar, who in his Apology reveals himself as a master of the Greek language, also shows himself a master of the language of his home country. In addition to its intrinsic beauty and its missionary use, national pride was also a factor in the rapid dissemination of the Diatessaron. It was a Syrian gospel, created by a Syrian, and composed in their own tongue. No other Christian community could claim such a gospel text as its own. Also its vigorous interpretation of the Christian faith must have been particularly appealing in the early phase of the development of Syrian Christianity.

Tatian's work continued to serve the spiritual needs of Syrian Christians for several generations. We have clear evidence that in the fourth century it was still used in many circles. Ephrem of Edessa (d. 373) wrote a commentary on it, which formerly was available only in Armenian translation, but recently has come to light in a unique Syriac MS. In his diocese of Cyrrhus, Theodoret (d. *ca.* 460) found more than two hundred copies still in use in the churches and had them destroyed (PG 83,372). The fact that no copy in Syriac has survived indicates what drastic measures were employed to eradicate it.

As to whether Tatian also translated Acts and the letters of Paul, it must be said that it does not seem probable that he would have been satisfied with giving Syrian Christians only the gospel harmony. Historiographic sources leave us in the dark on this question, except for one cryptic remark in Eusebius (Euseb. Hist. IV.xxix.6), who mentions that Tatian dared to paraphrase and to correct certain words of the Apostle. Nevertheless we have evidence in the remains of ancient Syriac literature that an archaic text of the Acts and the Pauline epistles existed and circulated among Syrian Christians. Ephrem the Syrian composed a commentary on this text of the Acts as well as on the epistles, but unfortunately the works in their original form have perished, and only translations in Armenian have saved them from complete destruction. Many features of this text arrest one's attention, because they have the same ring which characterizes Tatian's work on the gospels, and the style echoes an archaic form of the material, which must have circulated in Mesopotamia.

Tatian produced a work of unparalleled significance for the whole of Christianity. The Diatessaron enjoyed such popularity that it spread E and W, far beyond the confines of the Syriac language area. Its success from Armenia to Abyssinia and from Persia to the British Isles indicates the striking influence of this document. It was translated into many languages, and these versions constitute the material for a modern reconstruction of the lost original. From the East we have several Arabic MSS and one in Persian; from the West, MSS in Latin, the Tuscan and Venetian dialects of medieval Italian, Old High German, Middle High German, medieval Dutch, medieval French, and Middle English. That these versions are in many cases adaptations rather than straight translations makes their evaluation difficult. The reconstruction of the Diatessaron would be of great value to textual criticism. Not only does it constitute the beginning of the Syrian textual tradition for the gospels; it was a factor in the transmission of the Greek text itself, for according to all indications Tatian used a form which was current in Rome about the middle of the second century.

b. The Old Syriac Version. Initial evidence for the existence of an early Syriac form of the four gospels emerged with the discovery of the Codex Syrus Curetonianus (Syr-Cur) among the MSS from the Syrian monastery of St. Maria Deipara in the Nitrian desert in Egypt. This is MS Br. Mus. Add. 14451, first published in 1858 (*Remains of a Very Ancient Recension of the Four Gospels* [1858]) and later republished by Burkitt. It contains the four gospels in an unusual order: Matthew, Mark, John, Luke. The major MS of the Old Syriac Version, MS Sinai Syr. 30, which became known as the Codex Syrus Sinaiticus (Syr-Sin), a palimpsest codex, was unearthed fifty years later by Mrs. A. Smith in the monastery of St. Catherine on Mount Sinai. Great effort was required to decipher it (*The Old Syriac Gospels,* ed. A. S. Lewis [1910]; *Syrus Sinaiticus,* ed. A. Hjelt [1930]). Both MSS date from the first part of the fifth century, and both have gaps.

The importance of the MSS was not at first understood, and the version was regarded as a library copy that had no part in the history of the gospel text in Syriac. Systematic research has since opened new vistas for the role of this version. New and rich materials have emerged in the patristic sources. Scrutiny of the entire MS tradition has uncovered evidence previously unknown from the gospel MSS and lectionaries.

The Syriac name of the version, *Evangelion da-Mepharreshe,* "the gospel of the separated," contrasts with the "mixed" Diatessaron (*above* §2*a*) and tells us that this version is related to Tatian's Diatessaron; moreover, it exhibits archaic characteristics. The relationship of these two text forms, the Diatessaron and the Old Syr., has been the subject of a long controversy. However, new textual evidence leads to the conclusion that the Old Syr. was developed from the harmonistic pattern of the Diatessaron. In the new evidence this pattern has occasionally been preserved far better than in the Old Syr. MSS. Thus the Old Syr. constitutes a synthesis in which the ancient textual material of the Diatessaron has been adapted to the four-gospel form.

The text of the Old Syr. generally sides with the Western witnesses, although some have seen in it a witness to an Antiochian text type. A further characteristic is the surprising flexibility of the text. We find that Syr-Cur frequently has a more archaic form than Syr-Sin, and vice versa. The differences between these two witnesses have created a puzzle. Some have explained it to mean that Syr-Cur is simply a recension of Syr-Sin; others have supposed the existence of two different translations. Examination shows that the Syr-Cur and Syr-Sin were not mutually dependent, and were not two different translations, but represent independent textual traditions of the same version. Each text has lived a life of its own. These phenomena fit in the total textual picture as filled out by newly discovered sources.

Besides its importance as a textual witness, the Old Syr. offers other interesting features. Words and phrases reflect knowledge of Palestinian topography, and local customs. There are also specific terms, idioms, and grammatical forms of Palestinian Aramaic provenance, preserved here, but unknown in classical Syriac. In addition, there are features which show that idiomatic Syriac has been preserved. These linguistic elements are present in this material but not in the later versions.

Although the origin of the Old Syr. is not definitely known, the use of the *Evangelion da-Mepharreshe* as an official gospel text under Aitallaha, bishop of Edessa, indicates that it originated in the third century. The version had a long history in which the archaic features were exposed to adaptation and revision, a process reflected in the earliest sources. The Old Syr. was subjected to a gradual revision, which complicated its transmission. As the new textual materials demonstrate, this version, because of the charm and power of the original Syriac readings, played an important role in the history of the gospel text. Its hybrid forms continued to circulate for centuries, and it became the basis for a number of other Oriental versions of the gospels: the Old Armenian, Old Ethiopic, and Old Arabic. Of the Old Syr. NT only the gospels have survived, but there are traces of other books. A portion of Acts has survived in a commentary by Moshe bar Kepha, but the Pauline letters appear only in citations.

*c. **The Peshitta.*** The standard version, the Peshitta (on the name, *see* §1*b above*), has come down to us in a number of codices that are quite old. MS Par. Syr. 296 (Luke) was written probably in 463/64; MS Br. Mus. Add. 14459 (Matthew and Mark) and MS Br. Mus. Add. 17117 (Matthew and Mark) are both of the fifth century. MS Br. Mus. Add. 14453, which contains all the gospels, is of the fifth or the sixth century. Acts and the letters of Paul survive in MS Br. Mus. Add. 14476 and Add. 14480, which are of the fifth or sixth century. A critical edition exists only for the gospels (*Tetraevangelium sanctum,* ed. P. E. Pusey and H. C. Gwilliam [1901]), in which the text of the gospels has been supplemented by Acts and the epistles, including books which the Peshitta did not contain (*see* §2*d below*). The Peshitta was the result of a redaction of the Old Syr. to make it conform to the vulgar Greek text used in the patriarchate of Antioch. In this process, digressions and additions were removed; omitted material restored; and archaic peculiarities retouched, giving the text a wholly new complexion that conformed more or less to the Greek original. However, a considerable amount of the Old Syr. base remains in the new version. Many idiomatic expressions found in the Old Syr., particularly the conjunctive construction instead of the infinitive and the predilection for nominal sentences, have been modified and adapted to the Greek model, but a sense of balance and of faithfulness to the genius of the idiom guided the process of revision and kept it from servility to the Greek text. In this way much of the idiomatic phraseology and even the paraphrastic renderings have been retained. Many older syntactic constructions were retained, but the later development of Syriac is also reflected, resulting in a smooth, readable style.

New evidence on the circumstances of the origin of the Peshitta has emerged. The view that Rabbula, bishop of Edessa (411-35), is its author (Burkitt) must now be discarded. First, this view is definitely refuted by the discovery of remnants of the text which Rabbula himself employed near the end of his life—a type of the Old Syr. Version. Moreover, the Peshitta was adopted by both the Monophysite and Nestorian branches of Syrian Christianity; it is unlikely that they would have accepted a sacred text revised by a man who had mortally insulted the adherents of the Antiochian party, as Rabbula had. There are also reasons which compel us to place the origin of the version in an earlier period. The canon of the Peshitta does not include II Peter, II and III John, Jude, and the Apocalypse, and so represents the ancient canon used in the patriarchate of Antioch in the fourth century. Furthermore, some remnants of the Peshitta have emerged in MS Br. Mus. Add. 12150, copied in 411 in Edessa. In view of these facts the last decades of the fourth century appear to be the most probable date for the origin of the Peshitta. Further evidence regarding its origin can come only from the version itself. The textual character of the version is uneven. Sometimes it surprises us with early Western readings (particularly in Acts). There is also a lack of consistency in the use of vocabulary, together with varying mannerisms and techniques of revision. All these phenomena suggest that several hands must have been at work, and point to the bilingual centers of Greco-Syrian translation studies as the most likely places for its origin. This agrees with the tradition of the Syrians themselves, according to which the version was produced anonymously.

The critical edition by Gwilliam rests on forty-two MSS of different periods, the oldest of these dating from the fifth century. The results obtained through use of his critical apparatus confront us with the astonishing fact that his edition does not materially differ from that of the first printed edition (*Liber sacrosancti Evangelii,* ed. J. A. Widmanstadt [1555]). This is because the number of variants in the Peshitta is very small. That forty-two MSS agree so closely demonstrates the constancy of its text. The text was obviously copied with great circumspection and carefully handed down from generation to generation.

d. The Philoxenian Version. A colophon provides us with the following information regarding the origin of this version: "In the town of Mabbug in the year 819 of Alexander of Macedonia, in the days of holy Mar Philoxenus, confessor, bishop of this town." According to this evidence the version was prepared in 507/8 and sponsored by Philoxenus (or Aksenaya), bishop of Mabbug (Hierapolis), in Euphratesia. According to other sources, it included the OT or parts of it (*see* §1*c above*). The text in the colophon does not give the name of the man who actually prepared the version. Moshe of Aggel, who was almost a contemporary of Philoxenus, identifies him as the chorepiscopus Polycarp. Two centuries ago White published the *Sacrorum evangeliorum versio syriace Philoxeniana* I-II (Oxonii, 1778), and thereby started a debate regarding the provenance of this text. Did Polycarp prepare the "Philoxeniana," which was later taken over by Thomas of Harkel (*see* §2*e below*) and furnished with a text-critical apparatus, or does the version edited by White really belong to Thomas? If the latter is true, the version of Philoxenus is lost. The problem created by the ambiguity of the colophon has haunted scholars for two centuries. Until 1953 this version existed only in name, but remnants have now finally come into our possession. MS Br. Mus. Add. 14534, a codex of the first quarter of the sixth century, has preserved the commentary of Philoxenus, who used the recently prepared version as a basis for his exegetical work. Now for the first time we are allowed to see the nature of this version. The remnants reveal that it was not a new translation but a revision. Polycarp's work was intended to bring the text of the Peshitta into conformity with the Greek original. For this purpose he tried to remove all traces of its past, and to expunge from the text any elements not legitimate when measured by Greek textual standards. Not only were variant readings removed, but he extended his revision to particles as well. Even minor matters which had helped to improve the fluency of the Peshitta were changed. His determination to achieve conformity can be seen in those places where in general the Peshitta already agreed with the Greek, and yet efforts were made to attain still greater conformity. So far no MS has been discovered of the gospels, Acts, or those epistles contained in the Peshitta.

With this revision the minor Catholic epistles and the Apocalypse were included in a Syriac Bible for the first time. It has been assumed that those parts of the NT which did not exist in the ancient canon but were added later, namely II Peter, II and III John, and Jude, were first translated for this version, and the same assumption has been made in regard to the Apocalypse. Printed editions of the Peshitta frequently include these books in order to fill out the gap.

e. The Harclean Version. This is parallel to the production of the Syro-Hexaplar (*see* §1*e above*), since it is a scholarly version. It is well attested by MS evidence. MS Vat. Syr. 268, which once was regarded as the autograph, but which more probably belongs to the seventh century, is the earliest witness. It includes also a text-critical apparatus. Another branch in the tradition has left the apparatus out; its oldest representative appears in MS Laur. I, 40 of the year 757. The MS evidence includes a number of ancient MSS belonging to the seventh and eighth centuries. The only edition available is the first (*Sacrorum evangeliorum versio syriace Philoxeniana,* ed. J. White [1778]; *Actum apostolorum et epistolarum* [1799-1803]). The section on Hebrews was edited later (*The Harclean Version of the Epistle to the Hebrews, Chap. XI, 28-XIII, 25,* ed. R. L. Bensly [1889]). The Apocalypse was discovered recently and published in a facsimile edition (*see bibliog.*). The discoveries of remnants of the Philoxeniana settle a very old problem, so that the way finally is open for understanding what the colophons in the MS tell about the work of Thomas. Since much of the preparatory work had been done by Polycarp, his version was taken as a base for the comparison with two (some MSS read "three") Greek MSS in preparing a new text. Many features which Polycarp introduced were approved by Thomas, who carried them out with greater consistency and precision. It is strange how little respect this revision shows for Syriac idiom and linguistic taste. It follows the Greek to such an extent that clarity is sacrificed. This version is equipped with a text-critical apparatus using a system of obelus, asterisk, and metobelus in the text; the margin is reserved for variant readings and notes. In Acts the version is the most important witness to the Western form of the text, second in importance only to that of Codex Bezae itself. For this scholarship we are indebted to the labors of Thomas (Tuma) of Harkel (Heraclea) in Mesopotamia. When masses of refugees were set on the move by the Persian armies, Thomas found safety at the Enaton, a Syrian monastic community near Alexandria. Here in exile with his co-workers he accomplished his project, completing it in the year 616, as we know from the colophon which Thomas added to the text. Like the Syro-Hexaplar (*see* §1*e above*), this scholarly version found its way into the liturgy. For this privilege it had to pay a price in alterations and changes that produced a strange, Hellenized text. MS Chester Beatty Syr. 3 includes a colophon, according to which a need was felt to restore the text to its original purity.

f. The Palestinian Syriac Version. This has survived only in lectionaries. The oldest of these is MS Vat. Syr. 29 of the year 1029, which has preserved the texts of the gospels (*The Palestinian Syriac Lectionary of the Gospels,* ed. A. S. Lewis, M. D. Gibson [1899]). Lessons from Acts and the epistles were found in a MS in the monastery of St. Catherine of Mount Sinai (*A Palestinian Syriac Lectionary*) and in a palimpsest (*Codex Climaci rescriptus,* ed. A. S. Lewis [1901]). The rest exists only in fragments. Its dialect is Western Aramaic, as is that of the Palestinian Syr. Version of the OT. Of the several Syriac NT versions, this one is closest to the standard Byzantine text. Yet it does not conform completely with this text, but has affinities with the text of Origen and the Old Syr. Version. Regarding its time and place of origin, *see* §1*d above.*

Bibliography. Old Syr. OT: F. Perles, *Meletemata Peschittoniana* (1859); C. Peters, "Peschitta und Targumim," *Museon,* XLVI (1933), 275-96; A. Vööbus, *Peschitta und Targumim des Pentateuchs* (1958). Peshitta: L. Haefeli, *Die Peschitta des AT* (1927); B. J. Roberts, *The OT Text and Versions* (1951), pp. 214-27; P. Kahle, *The Cairo Geniza* (2nd ed., 1959), pp. 265-74; A. Vööbus, *Peschitta und Targumim,* pp. 37-112; M. H. Gottstein, *Text and Language in Bible and Qumran* (1960), pp. 65-85, 163-204.

Philoxenian Version: A. Baumstark, *Geschichte der syrischen Literatur* (1922), pp. 144-45; L. Delekat, "Die syrolukianische Übersetzung des Buches Jesaja," *ZAW,* LXIX (1957), 21-54.

Syro-Hexaplar: A. M. Ceriani, ed., *Codex Syro-Hexaplaris Ambrosianus* (1874); S. Jellicoe, *The LXX and Modern Study* (1968), pp. 246-49; A. Vööbus, *Discovery of Very Important MS Sources for the Syro-Hexapla* (1970), *The Hexapla and the Syro-Hexapla* (1971), *The Pentateuch in the Version of the Syro-Hexapla,* A. Vööbus, ed., *Discovery of a Unique MS* (1975), introduction, *The Book of Isaiah* (1975).

The version of Jaqob of Edessa: M. Ugolini, "Il ms. Vat. sir. 5," *Oriens Christianus,* II (1902), 409-20; A. Baumstark, *Geschichte der syrischen Literatur,* pp. 251-52.

The Palestinian Syr.: A. S. Lewis, ed., *A Palestinian Syriac Lectionary* (1897); F. Rosenthal, *Die aramäistische Forschung seit Th. Nöldeke's Veröffentlichungen* (1930), pp. 144-59; J. T. Milik, "Une inscription et une lettre en araméen christo-palestinien," *RB,* LX (1953), 526-39; L. Delekat, "Die syropalästinische Jesaja-Übersetzung," *ZAW,* LXXI (1959), 165-201.

The Diatessaron: H. Vogels, *Beiträge zur Geschichte des Diatessaron im Abendland* (1919); C. Peters, *Das Diatessaron Tatians* (1939), pp. 29-48; A. Vööbus, *Early Versions of the NT* (1954), pp. 1-31.

The Old Syr. NT: F. C. Burkitt, *Evangelion da-Mepharreshe,* I-II (1904); A. Vööbus, *Neue Ergebnisse in der Erforschung der Geschichte der Evangelientexte im Syrischen* (1948); *Studies in the History of the Gospel Text in Syriac I* (1951).

The Peshitta: P. E. Pusey and H. C. Gwilliam, eds., *Tetraevangelium Sanctum* (1901); M. J. Lagrange, *Critique textuelle* (1935), pp. 218-23; A. Vööbus, *Investigations into the Text of the NT Used by Rabbula* (1947); *Early Versions of the NT* (1954), pp. 88-103.

The Philoxenian Version: J. Gwynn, *Remnants of the Later Syriac Versions* (1909); G. Zuntz, *The Ancestry of the Harklean NT* (1945); A. Vööbus, "New Data Concerning the Philoxenian Version," *Festschrift K. Kunzins* (1953), pp. 169-86, and *Early Versions of the NT* (1954), pp. 103-21.

The Harclean Version: G. Zuntz, *The Ancestry of the Harklean NT;* A. Vööbus, *Early Versions of the NT* (1954), pp. 103-21; A. Vööbus, ed., *The Apocalypse in the Harclean Version* (1976), introduction.

The Palestinian Syr.: M. J. Lagrange, "L'origine de la version syro-palestinienne des Évangiles," *RB,* XXXIV (1925), 481-504; A. Vööbus, *Early Versions of the NT* (1954), pp. 121-313.

A. Vööbus

T

*TAANACH. 1. **Nonbiblical sources.** Both Thutmose III in 1468 B.C. and Shishak I in 918 B.C. list Taanach as a city captured by their forces. Knudtzon's restoration of "Taanach" (ta-aḫ-[nu-k]a) in the early fourteenth-century Amarna Letter (248:14) is unlikely on archaeological and paleographic grounds. Eusebius' *Onomasticon* (Klostermann ed., 1914, 100:7-10) indicates that in the third century A.D. θαανάχ (Thaanach) was a "very large village."

2. **Biblical references.** Taanach achieved eminence first in biblical tradition as the site of the battle between Israel, mustered by Deborah and Barak, and the Canaanites, led by Sisera (Judg. 5:19). Though its king was reported taken by Joshua (Josh. 12:21), and the city was assigned to Issachar and Asher, Taanach was later given to Manasseh (Josh. 17:11; I Chr. 7:29), who, however, was not able to occupy it because the Canaanites were too powerful (Judg. 1:27). In time, probably not before the tenth century B.C., "when Israel grew strong, they put the Canaanites to forced labor" (Judg. 1:28) and occupied (ruled) the site. In the same century Taanach seems to have become a Levitical city (Josh. 21:25) as well as the headquarters of Baana, administrator of Solomon's Fifth District, which included all of the Jezreel Plain to just beyond the Jordan River (I Kings 4:12).

3. **First excavation.** The first excavator of Taanach, 1902-4, was Ernst Sellin of Vienna. In three campaigns he extensively trenched the tell. He found no city walls and concluded that the site was defended by a series of forts of which a modest structure with subterranean rooms in the N center of the tell was thought to be the earliest. Albright later interpreted the structure as an Early Bronze funerary chamber similar in construction to Third-Dynasty Egyptian tombs.

In the debris above the upper level of this building Sellin discovered an archive of twelve Akkadian cuneiform tablets. At the S end of a long central trench he uncovered fragments of a cult stand. When restored it stood three feet high, showing four tiers of modeled lions on each side of a windowed façade capped by a basin. On the upper-left side panel, a youth strangles a serpent, and on the front of the lowest is a tree of life with ibexes on either side. Both tablets and cult stand are now in museums in Istanbul. Sellin identified four major strata of occupation, each with two phases: (1) fifteenth-fourteenth centuries B.C., including the cuneiform archive, its related structure, and the W Building; (2) thirteenth-ninth centuries B.C.; (3) eighth-sixth centuries B.C., when the Solomonic NE Building founded in period 2 and the "incense altar" were destroyed; (4) eleventh-twelfth centuries A.D. marked by an Arab fortress palace.

The Akkadian tablets (including the new TT 950) are either letters to the local king or administrative name lists. Two of the four readable letters (four more are in fragments) are from Amanḫatpa, an Egyptian administrator posted in Gaza but probably writing from Megiddo. He requests chariots and men for his garrison, and that prisoners of war be sent to him, as well as tribute. Aḫiyami orders a bow, bowstrings, chariot wheels, and a copper javelin. Also, wishing to be married, he seeks a suitable brother-in-law. A third writer is Eḫli-Tešub, who promises to repay fifty shekels of silver, asks for wood and myrrh, and advises that a servant girl be sold or married. Though written in Akkadian, the syntax and morphology of these letters have many Semitic features. Five tablets, TT 950 included, are name lists. Letters and lists contain some ninety names. About 60 per cent are Northwest Semitic, and 20 per cent each Indo-Aryan and Hurrian-Anatolian.

4. **Second excavation.** The second expedition was conducted between 1963 and 1968. The results correct and elaborate Sellin's excavation at many points. While the new excavations were limited largely to the SW quadrant of the tell, the general impression from Sellin was confirmed, that in no period was the city occupied wall to wall with buildings as at other important sites. However, the discovery of massive defenses on both the S and W shows, not only that the site was defended by city walls in all major periods, but also that the earliest city dates to EB II-III (*ca.* 2700-2400 B.C.), both contra Sellin. An EB occupation had already been suggested by Albright on the basis of published pottery.

After a long hiatus, the Middle Bronze Age began with camps (*ca.* 1700 B.C.) followed by somewhat extensive but poorly constructed domestic and defense architecture. The W Building excavated by Sellin has been redated to *ca.* 1600 B.C.; it was a patrician dwelling that formed part of a substantial rebuilding of the MB IIC city. Associated with MB IIC was a casemate wall, indicating that this style of city wall construction predated the Israelite monarchy. Selective destruction marked the end of MB IIC. Taanach continues a substantial city into LB I, suffering a major catastrophe at the hands of Thut-mose III *ca.* 1468 B.C. In the modest occupation that followed, an Akkadian cuneiform tablet (TT 950) name list appeared. A date *ca.* 1450 B.C. is satisfactory for the new tablet as well as the entire archive. Almost 90 per cent of sixty-four MB IIC subfloor and intramural cist burials were children entombed in store jars.

Though most of the limited quantity of Late Helladic pottery dates to the Mycenaean IIIA2 period (fourteenth century) there is no significant occupation between the mid-fifteenth century and the late thirteenth. Substantial houses which date to the twelfth century were completely destroyed *ca.* 1125 B.C. Where Iron Age defenses were detected on the W, they dated also to the twelfth century. In the N center of the SW quadrant a Canaanite cuneiform tablet (TT 433) turned up in the early twelfth-century destruction of a large building. The two-line inscription registers the receipt of a shipment of grain. A slight eleventh-century occupation is followed by a greater tenth-century presence, destroyed by Shishak *ca.* 918 B.C. To this period belongs a structure related to the local cult. The heavy ash covering the floors contained 9 iron knife blades, 140 pig astragali, some 80 restorable vessels, 58 loom weights, many querns, rubbing stones, pestles, 3 small stelae, and a figurine mold. In an associated cistern an elaborate cult stand (Fig. T1) emerged not far from where

David Harris
1. Cult stand from Taanach

Sellin found the "incense altar." Standing less than two feet high, the cult stand is built up of four superimposed hollow clay squares topped by a ridged basin. The lion and human faces protruding above animal legs on the corners of the three panels are each accompanied by winged leonine bodies in relief along the side panels. These animals represent demons protecting the deity, symbolized by the stylized winged sun disc between volutes and above an equine in the top panel.

Evidence for later occupation is limited to a tower dating to the ninth century B.C. and some fifth-century B.C. Persian pits plus two rooms. In Late Abassid times (tenth-eleventh centuries A.D.), an elaborate palace was constructed at the highest point of the tell. A cemetery on the S slope over the EB defenses seems to date from the early seventeenth century A.D.

Bibliography. In addition to bibliog. at TAANACH: H. Thiersch, "Die neueren Ausgrabungen in Palästina," *Archäologischer Anzeiger, Beiblatt zum Jahrbuch des kaiserlich deutschen archaeologischen Instituts,* XXII (1907), cols. 311-57; A. Gustavs, "Die Personennamen in den Tontafeln von Tell Ta'annek," *ZDPV,* L (1927), 1-18 and LI (1928), 169-218; M. Lods, "Autel du réchaud? À propos du 'brûle-parfums' de Taanak," *RHR,* CIX (1934), 129-47; B. Maisler (Mazar), "The Taanach Tablets," *Klausner Festschrift,* ed. N. H. Tur-Sinai (1937), pp. 44-66, Hebrew; P. Lapp, "The 1963 Excavation at Ta'annek," *BASOR,* 173 (1964), 4-44; D. Hillers, "An Alphabetic Cuneiform Tablet from Taanach (TT 433)," *BASOR,* 173 (1964), 45-50; C. Graesser, "Taanach," *The Biblical World,* ed. C. F. Pfeiffer (1966), pp. 556-63; P. Lapp, "The 1966 Excavations at Tell Ta'annek," *BASOR,* 185 (1967), 2-39, "The 1968 Excavations at Tell Ta'annek," *BASOR,* 195 (1969), 2-49; D. Hillers, "The Goddess with the Tambourine," *CTM,* XLI (1970), 606-19; A. E. Glock, "A New Taanach Tablet, *BASOR,* 204 (1971), 17-30.

A. E. GLOCK

***TARGUMS.** It is almost universally assumed that Targs., i.e., Aramaic translations of the OT, existed by NT times, and that the Hebrew texts read in the synagogues on the sabbath were orally translated into Aramaic, the vernacular of at least a good part of Palestine. And yet, apart from fragments of the Targ. of Job (11QtgJob; 4QtgJob) and of a single chapter (16) of Leviticus (4QtgLev) from Qumran, the Targ. texts which we now possess were transcribed well after the NT period. The earliest texts may be dated to the seventh century, with the majority much later, even as late as the sixteenth century. As a consequence, scholars have been divided on the advisability of using the Targs. as a witness to early Jewish belief and as sources for an understanding of NT writings. The question at issue was whether the Targs. in general, or any one of them in particular, were basically pre-Christian.

Kahle's publication of portions of the Palestinian Targs. on the Pentateuch (*Masoreten des Westens* II, 1930) aroused new interest, and subsequent research in Jewish MIDRASH led some scholars to regard these Targs. as basically very old, even pre-Christian, even though they contain some later elements. A further impetus was given to Targ. study in 1956 when Díez Macho identified an almost complete text of the Palestinian Targ. on the Pentateuch in Codex Neofiti I of the Vatican Library. After some years of preliminary studies, Kahle could write in his second edition of *The Cairo Geniza* (1959, p. 208): "In the Palestinian Targum of the Pentateuch we have in the main material coming down from pre-Christian times which must be studied by everyone who wishes to understand the state of Judaism at the time of the birth of Christianity. And we possess this material in a language of which we can say that it is very similar to that spoken by the earliest Christians. It is material the importance of which can scarcely be exaggerated." This twofold assumption concerning the early date of both the tradition and the language of the Palestinian Targs. of the Pentateuch played a central role in Targ. research from 1963 onward. Both assumptions, however, were called into question toward the end of the decade.

1. A decade of Targ. study
   a. Edition of texts
   b. Interrelationship of Targs.
   c. Targumic Aramaic
   d. Targ. and midrash
   e. Targ. and NT
   f. Dating the Targs.
   g. Early date of Targs. queried
2. Observations on the nature and utility of Targs.
   a. Aramaic of Targs.
   b. Special importance of Palestinian Targs.
   c. Formation of targumic tradition
   d. Date of Palestinian Targ.
   e. Targ. and NT
3. Conclusion

Bibliography

1. A decade of Targ. study. The extent of the research in targumic studies since the publication of IDB in 1962 has been phenomenal. Practically every aspect of targumic study has been treated.

a. Edition of texts. (*See* VERSIONS, ANCIENT §1.) The first volume of the *editio princeps* of Codex Neofiti I appeared in 1968, others following later. The lengthy introductions prefixed to the various volumes treat such questions as the nature of the Targ., its language, its relevance for NT studies. The date of transcription, expressed in the colophon by a Hebrew word intended to be deciphered numerically, is now generally accepted to have been A.D. 1504.

The *editio princeps* of Neofiti is being published in Madrid-Barcelona. Another project currently in progress in Spain is the Madrid Polyglot—*Biblia Polyglotta Matritensia*—which will have new editions of all the Targs., including those on the Pentateuch. The edition of Onkelos will be based on Babylonian MSS. Until recently the Fragment Targ. was known to have been preserved in four MSS: Ebr. Vat. 440, Nüremberg 1, Leipzig 1, and Paris, Bibliotèque Nationale 110 published by Ginsburger in 1899. Two further MSS of the work are now known: 264 of the Sassoon Collection (Lechworth, England) and No. 6684 of the Microfilm Institute of the National Library, Jerusalem (MS belonging to the Gunzburg Collection, Public Library, Moscow). A study of the nature and character of the Targ. of the Samaritan Pentateuch has been made, and a critical edition is being prepared. New editions of all the Targs. (with the exception of the Palestinian Targ. on the Pentateuch) have been made by Sperber and of some of the Targs. of the Hagiographa by other scholars. There have also been reprints of earlier editions of the Targums: of Onkelos by Berliner, of the Fragment Targ. and Pseudo-Jonathan by Ginsburger, of the Prophets and Hagiographa by De Lagarde. Walton's London Polyglot, containing the Targs. known in the seventeenth century, has also been reprinted. Earlier translations of the Targs. on the Pentateuch and the Five Megilloth have also been reprinted. A new dimension was added by the publication of the extensive fragments of the Qumran Targ. of Job (11QtgJob) in 1971. It may be the same text as that known to Gamaliel I (*ca.* A.D. 25-50) and used by his grandson Gamaliel II (A.D. 90-110) according to rabbinic sources (Tosef. Shab. XIII.2; T.B. Shab. 115a). It is, by and large, a literal rendering of the Hebrew. In this respect and in the character of its Aramaic it differs from the "rabbinic" Targ. of Job and also from the Palestinian Targ. on the Pentateuch. It is uncertain whether the Qumran fragments of Targ. Lev. ch. 16 (vss. 12-15, 18-21) are from an entire Targ. of this book or merely from a separate ritual text for the Day of Atonement. Though brief, the fragments represent a literal rendering and are seen by some to have an affinity with the Targ. of Onkelos. Why the Qumran community, apparently quite conversant with Hebrew, should need an Aramaic rendering at all has received no satisfactory answer.

b. Interrelationship of Targs. Even where they are not verbally identical, there is a close relationship between Neofiti, the Fragment Targ., and Pesudo-Jonathan. It was this fact that led earlier writers to speak of the Palestinian Targ. (rather than Palestinian Targs.) on the Pentateuch. The differences have since been emphasized and exception taken to the designation "Palestinian Targ." As a result, modern writers tend to use the plural, "Targums," rather than the singular. No small amount of attention has been devoted to these similarities and differences, but no generally accepted solution has been put forward as yet. In part, as we shall see, they may be due to a rather fluid tradition variously formulated and preserved. The origin of the Fragment Targ. is still debated. It probably arose as excerpts from a Palestinian Targ. which were intended as a supplement to the more literal rendering of Onkelos or as variants to some other text of the Palestinian Targ. Were the lengthier glosses of Neofiti put together, we would have a further Fragmentary Targ. More recent study has revealed that the Paris MS of the Fragment Targ. represents a different recension from that of the other MSS. Pseudo-Jonathan differs from the other texts of the Palestinian Targ., both in the extent of its extra midrash and in its language (which usually approximates to that of Onkelos). Its exact relation to the latter text remains to be clarified, as do its origins. Although Onkelos became the official text of Babylonian Judaism, it is now generally recognized that it originated in Palestine. Although generally quite literal, it contains an extensive amount of HAGGADAH. It can be presumed to have contained still more before being edited in Babylonia.

The Targ. of Chronicles seems to be related to the Palestinian Targs. both in vocabulary and exegetical method. It also appears to be related to Targ. Jonathan on the Prophets. The author may also have used the Palestinian Targ. of the Prophets (only small fragments of which survive) and a Targ. on the Psalms different from the texts now known to us.

*c. **Targumic Aramaic.*** The problem of the ARAMAIC of the Targs. is part of the larger question of the Aramaic written and spoken in Palestine from the first century B.C. to the sixth century A.D. For the earlier period we have ample evidence in the texts of Qumran, Murabba'at, the letters of BAR KOCHBA, and ossuary inscriptions (*see* MANUSCRIPTS FROM THE JUDEAN DESERT[S]). The Palestinian Targs. on the Pentateuch (and the greater part of those on the Hagiographa) are written in a form of Aramaic almost identical with that of the Aramaic sections of the Palestinian TALMUD and Midrashim, a dialect generally designated "Galilean." For this reason some authors refer to them as Galilean Targs. The so-called "Babylonian" Targs. are written not in Jewish Babylonian Aramaic but in a language that either is a form of literary Aramaic or is another dialect of Palestinian Aramaic. The Aramaic of all these Targs. differs from that of Qumran and the other early texts just noted. Some scholars wish to class the language of the Palestinian Targs. as "Late Aramaic," i.e., post–A.D. 200. However, a number of Targ. scholars defend an early date for the Aramaic of the Palestinian Targ., regarding the Aramaic of Qumran as a literary rather than a spoken language.

It is recognized that progress in this debate cannot really be made until we have grammars of each of the Palestinian and other Targs. Work is already under way in this field, particularly with regard to the language of Neofiti. Grammars of Neofiti Exodus and Deuteronomy have already been made at the University of Barcelona. The tendency of the Barcelona school is to regard the Aramaic of Neofiti as that of first-century Palestine. Other scholars have reached quite different conclusions, dating it to the third century A.D. and believing that the text of Neofiti represents a rendering from a Greek rather than a Hebrew original. Foster believes that while it may be granted that there was an oral tradition and interpretation of the Scriptures in the synagogues before the Christian era, it was not in the form of Aramaic now found in the Palestinian Targs. The Aramaic of the original paraphrase would have been constantly updated to the conditions of later times, and our present texts would be from a Greek form of the tradition.

On the other hand, after a detailed study of the Aramaic of the Former Prophets (in Targ. Jonathan), A. Tal has reached the conclusion that the language of the Targ. cannot be dated later than A.D. 70. After a study of the language of the Qumran Targ. of Job, S. A. Kaufman concluded that the final forms of Onkelos and Jonathan on the Prophets date from between A.D. 70 and 135, whereas the Palestinian Targs. must be post–A.D. 135.

*d. **Targ. and midrash.*** Midrash is the manner in which the Jewish mind approaches Scripture as the word of God which addresses each successive generation. Both the written word and personal experience are involved in it. Midrash seeks to make the message of Scripture relevant, understandable, and acceptable to later generations. It is generally accepted that midrash is already present in the later books of the Hebrew canon and in pre-Christian Jewish books outside this canon, e.g., Wisdom of Solomon. The entire question of the development of pre-Christian Jewish tradition has recently been studied and certain laws governing it isolated. *See* INTERPRETATION, HISTORY OF[S] §D; MIDRASH[S].

That the midrashic process is present in the Targs., and indeed central to most of them, is clear. A problem that arises in this connection is that much of the midrash found in the Targs. is also attested in other Jewish sources, particularly in rabbinic texts. This gives rise to the question of priority: Do the Targs. depend on the other sources, or vice versa? Or are both tributaries to a common source? The Targs. contain items of HALACHAH which run counter to official decisions found in the MISHNA, and some scholars accept as an axiom that what is anti-Mishnaic is pre-Mishnaic. This is contested by other scholars, who maintain that there was no objection to the presence of antihalachic teaching in private, nonofficial Targs. A detailed study of the interpretation of Scripture in Neofiti and Pseudo-Jonathan has led one specialist to conclude that, while these Targs. contain later elements, their origins go back to the early days of the second temple, and they contain material which served as a source for the Mishna and the halachic Midrashim. The differences between the schools of Hillel and Shammai, in fact, are seen to derive from these two Targs., the former in general following Pseudo-Jonathan, the latter, the Palestinian Targ. (more specifically Neofiti). The central contention of this view, we may note, is similar to that of Renée Bloch (an earlier specialist in midrash) who believed that the Palestinian Targ. was the articulation joint between the Bible and later midrash.

*e. **Targ. and NT.*** Scholars are turning increasingly to the Targs. in their efforts to understand the NT writings and to explain the development and formulation of early Christian tradition. In fact, this presumed influence explains much of the interest in the Targs. themselves. Monographs and special essays have been devoted to certain targumic themes related to the NT: the TORAH, the *Mēmrā* (*Logos*) of the Lord, the Holy Spirit, the Shekinah (Divine Presence with Israel), the glory of the Lord, the Palestinian manna tradition, the feasts of Passover and Pentecost, the Lamb of God, traditions concerning Abraham, Isaac, Abel, Moses. Jacob's Ladder, Jacob's Well, the well following Israel in the wilderness, etc. Targumic expressions (such as "Father in heaven," merit, good works) have also been studied. The gospels, Acts, and the Pauline and Johannine writings have been studied in relation to targumic tradition, in particular to the Palestinian Targ. on the Pentateuch. Agreements and divergences in the formulation of basically the same paraphrase have been regarded as constituting a targumic "synoptic problem," which may have a valid contribution to make toward the understanding, and possibly the solution, of its NT counterpart. One reason for the importance attached to the Targs. in NT studies is that they represent liturgical Judaism, and as such stood at the very center of everyday Jewish life. It was probably through them that the interpreted message of the Law and the Prophets was transmitted to the mass of the Jewish people.

f. Dating the Targs. No general claim for an early date for the Targs. on the Hagiographa (not used in the liturgy) has been made. Interest has centered rather on the date to be assigned to the Palestinian Targs. on the Pentateuch, particularly on the date of origin of Neofiti. Although Pseudo-Jonathan contains some late references, e.g., mention of the wife and daughter of Mohammed and of the six orders of the Mishna (Gen. 21:21; 26:9), sections of it are regarded as very old and pre-Christian. We have already noted some individual views on the date of the Palestinian Targ. The chief arguments are as follows: (1) the principles underlying the paraphrase are already attested in the OT and pre-Christian Jewish writings; (2) the paraphrase is related to early Jewish non-halachic midrash; (3) some of its halachah are anti-Mishnaic in character (anti-Mishnaic being accepted as pre-Mishnaic); (4) in rabbinic texts from the second century A.D. onward there are Aramaic renderings which coincide with those found in the Palestinian Targs.; (5) some geographical names do not require a date later than the second century A.D.; (6) Greek loanwords are found in the Aramaic, indicating a Hellenistic environment; (7) the Palestinian Targs. have a manifold relationship to the NT.

Apart from these arguments for an early date for the main body of targumic tradition, individual sections of the Targs. can be dated with more or less probability by comparison with Jewish traditions which are themselves datable. And apart from these arguments, the view has been put forward that the main body of Jewish midrashic and interpretative tradition had been formed by A.D. 132. As a result, the following rule of thumb for the date of the Palestinian Targs. has been proposed: Unless there is specific proof to the contrary, the haggadah of the Palestinian Targs. is likely to be tannaitic and to antedate the outbreak of the Second Jewish Revolt in A.D. 132.

g. Early date of Targs. queried. The early date assigned to the Palestinian Targs. on the Pentateuch and their relevance for NT studies have not gone unchallenged, especially by students of Qumran Aramaic literature. The chief arguments are the following:

i. *Language.* The Galilean Aramaic of the Palestinian Targs. is not earlier than A.D. 200. The presence of Greek loanwords argues for a later rather than an early date, since such loanwords are absent from Qumran Aramaic but present in later Syriac. If presumed late, the use of targumic Aramaic would be illegitimate in the consideration of the Aramaic substratum of the gospels.

ii. *Targs. from Qumran.* Both in language and style of translation the pre-Christian Targs. from Qumran differ from those under discussion. If the Qumran Targs. are of the type current in early times, then the other must be presumed late. Furthermore, the term *Mēmrā* (written מאמר, always with a suffix) occurs twice in 11QtgJob (col. 28, 9: Job 36:2; col. 33, 8: Job 39:27); in the second instance (and possibly also in the first) in the sense of "word," or "command," not as a surrogate for God, a "buffer" word to avoid mention of the divine name, as in the other Targs.

iii. *Circular reasoning.* Scholars using the Targs. in NT studies have been accused of circular reasoning; i.e., they tend to assign an early date to targumic texts because of the relation they bear to the NT, and then to use these same texts for their studies because they are presumed to be pre-Christian.

iv. *Criteria for dating insufficient.* The proposed criteria (*see* §*f above*) for establishing an early date for the Palestinian Targ. have been regarded as insufficient and unconvincing. A caveat has been entered against "parallelomania"; the presence of individual parallels or traditions in the NT and Targs. does not prove that the entire Targ. or even the greater part of it is pre-Christian.

v. *Other objections.* As already noted, strong exception has been taken to the persistent habit of referring to *the* Palestinian Targ. on the Pentateuch, whereas in reality we have more than one such Targ.: Neofiti, Fragment Targ., etc. The emphasis on the Palestinian Targs. on the Pentateuch to the neglect, or even disparagement, of the other Targs. has also received criticism.

2. Observations on the nature and utility of Targs. In a reassessment of the situation it is necessary to examine the value of the objections we have listed above and also to bear in mind the nature of targumic tradition and the differences between targumic studies and other branches of science, such as Qumran studies.

a. Aramaic of Targs. That Qumran Aramaic was a literary language in Palestine in NT times and for some time previously is beyond question. It is also to be granted that the Qumran texts contain Aramaic of a transitional type, standing between the Aramaic of Daniel and that of the Targs. and Christian Palestinian Aramaic. What is in no way certain is that Qumran Aramaic represents, or was very similar to, the language then currently spoken in Palestine or in part of it. More than one dialect may have been spoken, and thus there is no convincing reason why we should come down to the third century of our era for the emergence of Galilean Aramaic. Typical forms of Eastern Jewish Aramaic are attested in a document from Dura-Europos dated A.D. 200, and Galilean Aramaic could have emerged just as early, if not earlier. We must also reckon with the possibility, indeed the probability, of an undercurrent of words and grammatical forms from earlier times which are attested only in later writings. The "Late Hebrew" of the Mishna contains a number of words without biblical equivalents which are found in

Ugaritic texts (*see* Hebrew Language[S] §2*b*). The common use of ית as the sign of the accusative has its equivalent in אית='*iyyat* of Old Aramaic. The occurrence of the form ארי, equivalent to the Hebrew כי, was once restricted to the "Babylonian" Targs.; it has now turned up in Qumran Aramaic. The form corresponding to it in the Palestinian Targs. is ארום, formerly unattested outside them. It now occurs in 11QtgJob as ארו. Forms from the verb הוה in the Murabba'at documents correspond to those found in Onkelos and later Galilean inscriptions, e.g., יהי, להוה. For the former word, Neofiti has the classical orthography יהוה, evidence of its conservative nature. Careful and painstaking research will thus be required before we can speak authoritatively concerning the Aramaic of first-century Palestine. *See* Aramaic; Aramaic[S].

To show that Galilean Aramaic existed, or may have existed, in first-century Palestine, is not to prove that the Palestinian Targs. or other texts in Galilean Aramaic are early, since this dialect was also used in later centuries. Neither would proof of the later emergence of the Galilean dialect prove of itself a later origin for the tradition enshrined in the Palestinian Targs., since both the tradition and phraseology could easily have been recast in a later form of the language. Certain scholars believe that this is what really happened.

The Aramaic substratum of the gospels presents a number of problems, as we must reckon with the possibility of both a literary and popular Aramaic background. Written texts would probably have been in literary Aramaic, while oral tradition might have been handed on in the spoken language.

b. Special importance of Palestinian Targs. The special interest shown in the Palestinian Targ. on the Pentateuch is due to the special position we know that the Pentateuch had in Jewish life and liturgy, to the paraphrastic nature of these Targs., and to their presumed early date. Onkelos and Jonathan on the Prophets may be important from the philological point of view; but, being more literal than the Palestinian Targs. they may have less to offer on Jewish concepts of the NT period.

c. Formation of targumic tradition. Jewish tradition traces the origin of Targs. back to Ezra (T.B. Meg. 3a; J.T. Meg. IV.1; T.B. Ned. 37b; cf. Neh. 8:1-8). It seems reasonably certain that the Torah and the Prophets, read in Hebrew in the synagogues, were translated into Aramaic before the Christian era. The nature of this translation is a question that immediately arises. Was it literal or paraphrastic? To which tradition of interpretation did it belong? Since the synagogue stood in the mainstream of Jewish life, and by NT times seems in the main to have come within the ambit of Pharisaic Judaism, the translation can be presumed to have belonged to this tradition.

A central function of the synagogue service was to teach the Torah of Moses, a concern going back at least to the days of Ezra (Ezra 7:25-26; Neh. 8:1-8; Acts 15:21; Jos. Apion II.18). But explanation of the Torah as God's word and Israel's guide called for an entire interpretative tradition. Apparent contradictions had to be explained, or explained away, through midrash; anthropomorphisms and expressions offensive to the religious sensibilities of a later generation had to be avoided (*see* Emendations of the Scribes[S]); the text had to be made relevant to later generations (*see* Hermeneutics[S] §§3-5). It is extremely likely that the Targs. would draw heavily on such traditions of interpretation.

Rather than postulate the existence of a fixed primitive Palestinian Targ., it seems better to regard the early synagogue Aramaic renderings as expressions of a relatively fixed tradition of interpretation. What evidence we have indicates that the vernacular rendering was given orally. A fixed text is less easily understandable in such a situation. Dependence on a relatively fixed tradition would ensure that the different oral renderings would be basically the same. While differing among themselves, such texts as Neofiti, the Fragment Targ. and sections of Pseudo-Jonathan have basically the same paraphrase, which seems to argue for the existence of a common tradition which was not fixed verbally. An illustration can be seen in the way the Hebrew word מאד of Deut. 6:5 and II Kings 23:25 is understood in the Targs. and Peshitta. All of them understand the word—rendered as δύναμις, ἰσχύς, in the LXX; RSV, "might"; JB, NEB, "strength"—as "riches" or "abundance," but use different terms to express it: "wealth" (ממון) in Neofiti, Fragment Targ. and Pseudo-Jonathan; "property" (נכסים) in Onkelos and Jonathan; "possessions" (*qnyn*) in the Peshitta.

It may well be that interpretive tradition was expressed in Greek as well as in Aramaic in third- or fourth-century Palestine. Jerome (*Quaestiones hebraicae in Genesin* 25:3) gives us a current Jewish rendering of Gen. 25:3 which coincides with that of the Palestinian Targ. Since his paraphrase contains a Greek word, Jerome may have come to know it in Greek.

d. Date of Palestinian Targ. If we grant the existence of an early Aramaic paraphrase, can we prove or presume that it has basically been preserved in Neofiti, the Fragment Targ., or Pseudo-Jonathan? The arguments in favor of an early and basically pre-Christian date for the tradition found in these texts have not been invalidated by the objections advanced against them. It can scarcely be an accident that, in rabbinic texts from the third century onward, we have Aramaic renderings of texts of the Pentateuch coinciding with those of the Palestinian Targ. The manifold relationship of the Palestinian Targ. with the NT is still a valid argument for the antiquity of the Targumic tradition. The reasoning at this point may be regarded as convergence of evidence rather than a circular argument. *See* §1giii *above*.

Arguments have been advanced in favor of Neofiti as the best representative of the early Palestinian targumic tradition. It is too early to be confident in this assertion.

e. Targ. and NT. The value of the Targs. at this point, and in particular of the Palestinian Targ. on the Pentateuch, lies not so much in individual parallels as in the likelihood that we have a body of literature which was central to the life of the Jewish people in NT times, a literature which contains their religious concepts, and which illustrates the manner in which they expressed their traditions. As such it can help us understand the original expression, the development, and final formulation of the NT message. This is not to deny the importance of the other texts for understanding aspects of Jewish life and thought in NT times, nor to suggest that the NT writers knew the OT only through the Targs. We have evidence that both Jesus and the early Christian community went beyond traditional interpretations to the text of the OT itself, interpreting it in the light of new events. This reinterpretation is occasionally referred to as Christian midrash. Thus future research must isolate the differences as well as the relationships between Targs. and the NT.

3. Conclusion. Over the centuries, scholars have been attracted to the Targs. because of the importance these were believed to have for a better understanding of the NT. Research has now passed beyond this stage, and Targ. study has become a science in its own right. A number of problems still remain, but the renewed interest and the work currently in progress augur well for the future.

Bibliography. Introductions and studies: A. Diez Macho, "Targs.," *Enciclopedia de la Biblia,* VI (1965), 865-81: R. Le Déaut, *Introduction à la littérature targumique,* I (1966); M. McNamara, *The NT and the Palestinian Targ. to the Pentateuch* (1966), pp. 1-66; J. Bowker, *The Targs. and Rabbinic Literature* (1969), contains a translation of much of Targ. Pseudo-Jonathan on Genesis; M. McNamara, *Targ. and Testament* (1972), pp. 173-205; G. Vermes and F. Miller in "Introduction" to *A History of the Jewish People in the Time of Jesus Christ,* E. Schürer, I (rev. ET 1973), 99-114, has an extensive bibliog.; A. Díez Macho, *El Targ.* (1972), "Le Targ. Palestinien," *RevScRel,* XLVII (1973), 169-231, and "Un nuevo manuscrito del Targ. Fragmentario," *Homenaje a Juan Prado* (1975), pp. 533-51, a study of MS 6684 of the National Library, Jerusalem; G. Vermes, "Haggadah in Targ. Onkelos," *JSS,* VIII (1963), 159-69; J. W. Bowker, "Haggadah in Targ. Onqelos," *JSS,* XII (1967), 51-65; R. Bloch, "Midrash," *DBSup,* V (1957), 1263-81.

Bulletins, bibliographies, etc.: R. Le Déaut, "The Current State of Targumic Studies," *Biblical Theology Bulletin,* IV (1974), 3-32; P. Nickels, *Targ. and NT. A Bibliography Together with a NT Index* (1967); B. Grossfeld, *A Bibliography of Targ. Literature* (1972), a supplement in preparation; omissions noted by A. Díez Macho in *Neophyti I,* Pt. IV, Números (1974), 11*-16*; *Newsletter for Targ. Studies* (1974—), lists works not in Grossfeld and notes work in progress; A. D. York, "The Dating of Targumic Literature," *JSJ,* V (1974), 49-62.

Editions of texts, reprints, and translations: A. Berliner, *Targ. Onkelos* (1884 [repr. 1968]); A. Sperber, *The Bible in Aramaic. I. The Pentateuch according the Targ. Onkelos* (1959); M. Ginsburger, *Das Fragmententhargum* (1899 [repr. 1966]), and *Pseudo-Jonathan* (1903 [repr. 1971]); A. Díez Macho, *Neophyti I,* Pts. I-IV, Génesis-Números (1968, 1970, 1971, 1974), Aram. text with Sp., Fr., and Eng. trans.; *The Palestinian Targ. to the Pentateuch,* photocopy of MS Neofiti I, 2 vols. (1970); J. W. Etheridge, *The Targ. of Onkelos and Jonathan Ben Uzziel on the Pentateuch,* 2 vols. (1862, 1865 [repr. in single vol., 1968]); P. De Lagarde, *Prophetae Chaldaice* (1872); A. Sperber, *The Bible in Aramaic,* II (1959), III (1962), *Targ. to the Former Prophets: Codex New York 229,* Heb. "Introduction" by A. Díez Macho, pp. 7-34 (limited facsimile ed., 1974); P. Churgin, *Targ. Jonathan to the Prophets* (1907 [repr. 1971 with a new intro.]); P. De Lagarde, *Hagiographa Chaldaice* (1873); A Sperber, *The Bible in Aramaic,* IVA (1969); R. Le Déaut and J. Robert, *Targ. des Chroniques* (1971), edition of Codex Vat. Urb. Ebr. 1, text, Fr. trans., and glossary; É. Levine, *The Aramaic Version of Ruth* (1973), Codex Vat. Urb. Ebr. 1, Eng. trans., apparatus, and notes; B. Grossfeld, *The Targ. of the Five Megilloth* (1973), intro. and reprints of English trans. of Targs. to the Pentateuch and the Second Targ. to Esther; J. M. P. van der Ploeg *et al.,* eds., *Le Targ. de Job de la grotte XI de Qumrân* (1971). A critical ed. of the Samaritan Targ. is being prepared by A. Tal; *see his art.,* "The Samaritan Targ. to the Pentateuch," *Proceedings of the Sixth World Congress of Jewish Studies* (1975), and *Newsletter for Targ. Studies,* I, no. 3 (1974), 4.

Language: J. A. Fitzmyer, "The Languages of Palestine in the First Century A.D.," *CBQ,* XXXII (1970), 501-31; A. Tal, *The Language of Former Prophets and its Position within the Aramaic Dialects* (1975), Heb.; E. Y. Kutscher, "Studies in Galilean Aramaic, *Tarbiz,* XXI (1950), 192-205, XXII (1951), 53-63, 185-192, XXIII (1952), 36-60, in Heb. with Eng. summary; A. Díez Macho, "The Recently Discovered Palestinian Targ.," VTSup, VII (1959), 222-45, and *Neophyti I,* Pt. 1, pp. 133-36, Pt. 2, pp. 63-69, Pt. 3, pp. 56-69, with summaries of dissertations on the trans. of the Palestinian Targ. from Greek, a grammar of Neophiti, Exodus; J. Fitzmyer's review of M. Black, "An Aramaic Approach to the Gospels," in *CBQ,* XXX (1968), 417-28; M. McNamara's review of J. Fitzmyer, "The Genesis Apocryphon of Qumran Cave I," in *The Irish Theological Quarterly,* XL (1973), 283-85. A study of the phases of the Aramaic language has been announced by J. Fitzmyer: *see Newsletter of Targ. Studies, II,* 1 (1975), 3; G. Lasry, "Some Remarks on the Jewish Dialectical Aramaic of Palestine . . . ," *Augustinianum,* VIII (1968), 468-76; J. G. Cowling, "New Light on the New Testament?" *The Theological Students' Fellowship Bulletin,* LI (1968), 6-14; S. A. Kaufman, "The Job Targum from Qumran," *JAOS,* XCIII (1973), 317-27.

Targ. and NT: R. Le Deaut, *La Nuit Pascale* (1963), and *Liturgie juive et NT* (1965); M. McNamara, *The NT and the Palestinian Targ. to the Pentateuch* (1966), and *Targ. and Testament* (1972); B. J. Malina, *The Palestinian Manna Tradition* (1968); J. Potin, *La fete juive de la Pentecote* (1971); D. Munoz León, "Dios-Palabra, Empleo del apelativo 'Memra de YY' en los targumim del Pentateuco y su relacion con el Logos de Juan" (diss., Pontifical Biblical Institute, 1968), summarized in *Neophyti I,* Pt. 3, pp. 70-83; R. Le Deaut, "Targumic Literature and NT Interpretation," BThB, IV (1974), 243-89, with bibliog.; M. P. Miller, "Targ., Midrash, and the Use of the OT in the NT," *JSJ,* II (1971), 29-82, esp. pp. 29-64; J. A. Fitzmyer, "Methodology in the Study of the Aramaic Substratum of Jesus' Sayings in the NT," in *Jésus aux origines de la Christologie,* ed. J. Dupont (1975), pp. 73-102.

M. McNamara

TEACHER OF RIGHTEOUSNESS [מורה הצדק]. A phrase used to describe the dominant and guiding personality in the Qumran community, the only individual figure who was emphasized. He shaped the history and theology of the community, and his preaching remained normative even for the time after his death.

1. The title "Teacher of Righteousness." The title stems from Joel 2:23 or Hos. 10:12, where, however, מורה and יורה mean, respectively, "rain" ("the early rain for your vindication") and "to rain" ("and rain salvation"). The teacher's adversary is given the opposite title, "preacher of lies" (מטיף הכזב), and here too the use of water as an image for teaching is apparent (מטיף is from the root נטף, "to cause to sprinkle"); cf. CD 1.14-15, the preacher of lies "sheds upon Israel the water of lies." This passage shows, moreover, that falsehood characterizes the content of the teaching. Therefore, the genitive in the title "Teacher of Righteousness" is also to be taken as objective, referring to the content of the teaching. The alternative, frequently adopted, would be to regard it as qualitative, characterizing the person of the teacher (e.g., "Right-Teacher," as in Dead Sea Scrolls §5).

2. Date. The texts, which contain few biographical notes about the Teacher of Righteousness, presume he is sufficiently well known to all. Even his death is mentioned only in passing (CD 19.35–20.1). Therefore any attempt to identify him with a person otherwise known or to find him in other than the Qumran texts is doomed to failure. Similarly, attempts to assign the utterances about the teacher to several different persons or to see behind his title an office have failed. A precise placing of the teacher in history is possible, however, with reference to one of his direct opponents. The texts name two such opponents, both of them with cover names: the "preacher of lies" (מטיף הכזב) and the "priest of wickedness" (הכוהן הרשע). The latter is evidently the ruling high priest in Jerusalem, since he is also simply called "the priest" (his epithet may be a deliberate distortion of his official title), and since he exercised political power over Israel (1QpHab 8.9-10). Of this priest of wickedness, who personally took action against the teacher (an especially grievous instance occurred on the Day of Atonement, which was celebrated by the community according to its own calendar; 1QpHab 11.4 ff.), it is frequently related that God punished him by letting him fall into the hands of Gentiles who frightfully tortured and killed him (cf. esp. 1QpHab 8.13–9.2; 9.9-12; 4QpPs37 4.8-10). This can only have been Jonathan, who became high priest in 152 B.C. In 143 he was taken prisoner by the Syrians and, after an extended imprisonment, executed. Thus, Jonathan must have been the teacher's opponent between 152 and 143. *See also* Dead Sea Scrolls[S] §5.

3. The teacher as founder of the community. Was the teacher the founder of an organized community, or was he simply the first to give to an already existing organization the imprint that was decisive for its later self-understanding? The summary outlines of the history of the Qumran community (particularly CD 1.3-11: the numbers given are symbolic; cf. the allegorical portrayal in 1QH 8.4 ff.) show that the divine "planting" had a "root" before the teacher appeared. But without the teacher the pious ones were like "blind men" and "people only feeling their way along." It was the teacher who first led them "on the way of the divine heart." Of crucial importance is 4QpPs37 3.14-16, where the commentary on Ps. 37:23 declares, "The meaning refers to the priest, the Teacher of Righteousness [. . .] has set him, that he might build for him a community of [. . .]." Thus the community saw in the teacher, not only the figure that gave it its decisive imprint, but also its founder. Whether this is considered historically accurate depends on how one evaluates the crisis which occurred during the teacher's lifetime, when the community of the "preacher of lies" apparently separated from the teacher's community.

4. The function of the teacher. For the Qumran community the teacher was the definitive authority. As the great teacher of the Torah, sent from God, he led the community in accordance with God's will. To what extent the regulations of the community derive from him is unclear. The texts speak of him as the normative interpreter of Scripture (*see esp.* 1QpHab 7.1 ff.), but not as the lawgiver. To the Teacher of Righteousness "God has made known all the mysteries of the words of his servants the prophets." Here, as in the NT (I Pet. 1:10-12), the view is held that all the prophetic sayings have reference to the endtime. Only for the teacher has God decoded the mysteries of the prophetic sayings, and in the final judgment deliverance will come to those who actually do the will of God by following the teacher's interpretation of the Law (1QpHab 8.1-3).

5. The teacher's utterances about himself. IQH 2.(1)-19; 2.31-(39); 3.(1)-18; 4.5–5.4 (perhaps only to 4.29*a*); 5.5-19; 5.20–7.5; 7.6-25; 8.4-(40) in the large Psalm scroll are distinctive in language, form, and content. They radiate great religious vigor, and in them the psalmist stands out from the community to which he brings deliverance. They evidently come from the teacher himself. They all stress the mercy of God, who grants the divinely ordained community the ability to fulfill his will. The righteous and the unrighteous are distinguished by their attitude toward the teacher, to whom God has revealed his will (2:8-11, 13-15, 18-19; 4:23-25, 27-29; 5:9). The community is utterly dependent upon this teacher (7.20-22; 8.22-24), who, even when he is opposed, knows that God will keep him safe (5.22-25; 7.12). When he looks at himself, he is able to speak only of being lost and guilty; but God's great mercy and the abundance of his grace save him from doubt and despair (7:16-18). All of the psalms from the teacher are pervaded by this deep trust in God. Along with thanksgiving for the saying act, this is their central content.

6. The teacher is not an eschatological figure of salvation. Immediately upon publication of the Qumran texts, the question arose whether the Teacher of Righteousness was a forerunner of Jesus, indeed, whether Jesus was not merely a pale imitation of the teacher. Some interpreters found in the texts references to the teacher's crucifixion and resurrection, his designation as Messiah, the expectation of his return, belief in the teacher as a saving figure, and even the teacher as a cultic figure. But subsequent study has demonstrated that such theses are untenable. Only one text appears at first to argue that people expected the teacher to return in the end time: "Outside these [prescriptions] they shall accept nothing until that one comes who shall teach righteousness at the end of time" (CD 6.10-11). Yet a comparison of this passage with others which speak of the expectation of the saving figures of the end time shows that the language here is cast in a sort of formula. In this the appended "at the end of time" is to be connected with the verb "teach," and is meant to distinguish the future teacher from the teacher previously mentioned. The laws of the community will retain their validity until a new teacher appears at the end of time. This expectation of one who will solve all the controversial questions about the Torah is shared by this community with contemporary Judaism. This teacher was frequently identified as the returning Elijah.

7. Concluding evaluation. The Teacher of Righteousness is one of the most significant religious figures known to us from the Judaism of late antiquity. He embodies the most radical attempt to achieve salvation in faithful obedience to God. God's demand upon man is total; the grace of God, for which the teacher never wearies of giving thanks, consists in God's having revealed to him the correct interpretation of the Torah, which now makes it possible for the first time actually to keep the Law. The teacher's claim that he, the recipient of the one correct interpretation of the Torah, is the only one who can point the way to salvation, and that salvation or perdition is determined by acceptance or rejection of his teaching, is without parallel in the Judaism of late antiquity.

Bibliography. G. Jeremias, *Der Lehrer der Gerechtigkeit,* SUNT, II (1963), for details and bibliog.; and H. Stegemann, *Die Entstehung der Qumrangemeinde* (1971), for an important subsequent discussion. *See also* bibliographies for DEAD SEA SCROLLS; DEAD SEA SCROLLS[S].

G. JEREMIAS

***TEACHING OF JESUS.** Discussion continues about the extent to which the authentic teachings of Jesus may be recovered, as well as about the interpretation of special materials like the parables, the place such concepts as the KINGDOM OF GOD played in Jesus' teaching, and the over-all meaning of his ministry within the environment of first-century Palestine.

1. Methodology
   a. Criteria for determining authentic teachings
   b. Special significance of the parables
2. The Palestinian setting of Jesus' ministry and teaching
3. The career of Jesus
   a. Jesus and John the Baptist
   b. Jesus and the religious establishment
   c. Difficulties internal to his own fellowship
   d. Jesus' ethical teachings
4. Problems outstanding
   a. Jesus' relation to the Zealots and his teaching about the kingdom
   b. Messianic consciousness

Bibliography

1. Methodology. ***a. Criteria for determining authentic teachings.*** The environment of Jesus was geographically and politically Palestinian, culturally Jewish, and chronologically pre-Pauline. What he did and said was accommodated to those who shared this environment. Tradition concerning Jesus' words and actions which achieved a stable form at an early date reflects this environment, both conceptually and pictorially. The environment of the evangelists, however, is non-Palestinian, predominantly Gentile, and post-Pauline. What the evangelists wrote was accommodated accordingly. Other NT writings make clear that social and theological forces set in motion by Jesus and his disciples spread outside the original Jewish-Palestinian environment at an early period. This transition is viewed in retrospect in the book of the Acts of the Apostles. It is seen first-hand in the letters of the apostle Paul.

The historian is not limited in some circular fashion to the writings of the NT in the effort to delineate the environment of Jesus. The DEAD SEA SCROLLS as well as other Jewish writings from the intertestamental period, and some rabbinic materials, taken together with the works of JOSEPHUS, and modern archaeological and topographical study provide reliable controls in determining the nature of the religious, social, economic, and political environment of Jesus. When a tradition concerning Jesus comes alive against the background of his environment, it may be presumed to be early. When this tradition would be unintelligible outside Palestine, or unfamiliar in circles primarily oriented to Gentile culture, then the probabilities are increased that such a saying or story is early. Material in the gospels which presupposes the death and resurrection of Jesus, and reflects a situation where he is not only remembered but also worshiped as a transcendent being, represents tradition which originated in some post-Easter Christian community. How one can move with confidence from the general category "early Jesus tradition" to speak in specific terms about Jesus is best understood from a consideration of his parables.

b. Special significance of the parables. Within the corpus of the tradition which originated with Jesus, it is his parables form-critically analyzed which afford the key for understanding his teaching and ministry. FORM CRITICISM enables the critic to identify these as belonging to the genre of rabbinic parables, while as a whole presenting theologically distinctive content. Form criticism also enables the critic to distinguish the original form of Jesus' parables from the additions that were made in the early church. *See* PARABLE; PARABLE[S].

One of the aspects of Jesus' career most firmly established by historical research is the opposition he met from the religious authorities. The centrality of this crisis, considered in relation to the teachings of the parables, makes it possible to reconstruct the probable course of his earthly career. It must be assumed that Jesus' parables, like Paul's letters, were occasioned by particular situations. Thus, parables in which Jesus rebukes the self-righteousness of those who resent God's mercy toward repentant sinners were probably occasioned by Jesus' defense of his eating with tax collectors and sinners. Behind this lay the criticism of the PHARISEES and behind that, Jesus' decision to invite repentant tax collectors and sinners into his table fellowship. This invitation, in turn, would be directly related to Jesus' initial decision to leave the Judean wilderness and carry his gracious call to REPENTANCE to the more populated areas of the land.

2. The Palestinian setting of Jesus' ministry and teaching. Jesus was a Jew who lived in Palestine during the period of Roman occupation. The climax of his ministry came while the procurator of Judea was Pontius Pilate, whose responsibilities included procuring supplies and funds from the local populace to defray the costs of military occupation. Jewish tax collectors were engaged to gather these funds, and PILATE had at his disposal sufficient forces to support the incumbent Jewish regime, to see that taxes were collected, and to police the normal rash of political discontent. It was seldom necessary to call for the help of the Roman provincial governor who resided in Syria, and in whose hands rested ultimate military power.

Key figures in the established world of Jewish piety were the Pharisees who sat in "Moses' seat" (Matt. 23:2) and were recognized by the Romans as interpreters of the Law (HALACHAH), whose influence over the people in the cities and towns of Galilee was their best hope for maintaining social stability in that area. It is important in understanding the life situation of Jesus to realize that though the Pharisees sat in Moses' seat, it was their passive acceptance of Roman rule that assured their standing with the civil authorities.

The Romans found their most direct key to effective control over the Jewish population as a whole through influence within high priestly families in Jerusalem. Because of the strong place of the temple cultus in Jewish law and piety, Rome found it possible, by offering security to the temple authorities, to maintain its control over the nation. Only such Jewish groups as rejected the authority of the incumbent high priestly families were free from some measure of effective co-operation with Rome, and the price required for complete freedom was withdrawal from public life. Only a relatively small percentage of the population was either willing or able to pay this price. This included such groups living in the wilderness of Judea as the Qumran community (*see* ESSENES; ESSENES[S]), and such paramilitary resistance elements as the Zealots. The Pharisees by way of contrast co-operated with the Jerusalem oligarchy, and thus at least indirectly co-operated with Rome.

The benefits of the Pax Romana were felt not only by the educated and privileged classes, but by the general populace. But these benefits could not be enjoyed by the Jews with as little internal disruption as may have been possible for some other ethnic groups within the Empire. This was because of a peculiar heritage of the Jews, many of whose customs and laws needed to be liberally interpreted wherever and whenever the inevitable need for close contact with Gentiles arose. Alongside the laws governing Jewish life and practice, and inextricably bound up with them in the scriptures of the Jews, were certain promises of God bearing upon the welfare of his covenanted people. These promises were conditional upon obedience to the Law, so the less privileged classes, on the basis of these promises, were always capable of envisioning a relative improvement in their welfare, if only more effective ways could be found to keep the Law.

Elements of the Jewish populace whose close co-operation was essential to the effectiveness of the Roman occupation and thereby to the prosperity and security of the Jewish people as a whole included those like the Pharisees who sought conscientiously to be observant of the Mosaic law, as well as those who in this respect were more or less lax. Those willing at times to be somewhat lax, especially in their attitude toward the dietary regulations and other Levitical rules for ceremonial cleanliness, were occasionally preferred by persons in authority for some of the more important and lucrative positions in the complex fabric of Roman hegemony over Jewish life. In the parlance of those Jews who were strictly observant of the laws of Moses, these nonobservant compatriots were sometimes referred to derogatively as "tax collectors and sinners." To the degree that they were not observant, these Jews were regarded by observant Jews as having abandoned the covenant. Observant Jews, on the other hand, were dependent upon the guidance and support of legal experts like the scribes and the Pharisees, who could tell them what the Law did and did not require under ever-varying circumstances.

3. The career of Jesus. ***a. Jesus and John the Baptist.*** Parables of Jesus which dramatically illustrate the folly of postponing repentance (Matt. 22:1-10; Luke 13:6-9) and teach the wisdom of living in ready expectation of God's gracious judgment (Luke 12:35-38) would probably have originated in situations where such expectations had been enlivened and heightened, i.e., in the period of Jesus' active ministry following his baptism into the movement of JOHN THE BAPTIST and his decision to continue to proclaim the imminence of the kingdom following John's arrest and death.

When certain parables of Jesus are interpreted within the context of his gracious call for repentance, they serve like mirrors in which it is possible to delineate the mind of Jesus as he responded to the exigencies and difficulties he encountered. How was one to understand the delay in the coming of the kingdom which John had pronounced to be at hand—especially after John's arrest and execution? And if one were to continue to proclaim the coming of the kingdom, how should this ministry be perceived? Was the work of God to be carried out during an extension of the period of grace before the coming judgment? If so, was it not reasonable to expect that in due season, if there were no fruits of repentance, this period of grace would come to a sudden and just end (Luke 13:6-9)?

As for those who would mistakenly hold back because of their fear that the cost of repentance might be too great, was it not important for their sake to emphasize the joy of the kingdom (Matt. 13:44, 45)? And should not those who were hesitant about setting their house in order be reminded of the inevitability of judgment (Matt. 21:33-41; Luke 20:9-16); the appropriateness of radical action in the face of certain change (Luke 16:1-8*a*); the folly of not trusting God (Matt. 25:14-30; Luke 19:11-27); and the suddenness and unexpectedness of God's judgment (Matt. 24:45-51; Luke 12:42-46; 13:1-5)?

Even within this initial period of Jesus' ministry it is possible to delineate development. Presumably Jesus would have understood the lesson the authorities intended by John's execution. "A disciple is not above his teacher" (Matt. 10:24). Jesus' decision to carry on would have been realistic only if he understood that he did so at great risk. While John had been beheaded, a more usual form of execution was CRUCIFIXION. When Jesus said, "Take up [your] cross and follow me" (Matt. 16:24), he made it clear that he had placed himself outside the discipline and protection of the established world of Jewish piety and was calling upon others to do the same. Since this world derived its earthly jurisdiction from Rome, in coming into conflict with the religious authorities Jesus was risking the ultimate wrath of Roman power. To speak in this way was a determined response to a policy of oppression which had been calculated to discourage dangerous rhetoric associated with messianic activity. But Jesus was not intimidated by what the authorities did to John. Jesus continued to preach: "No one can serve two masters. . . . You cannot serve God and mammon" (Matt. 6:24); "Repent, for the kingdom of heaven is at hand" (Matt. 4:17).

In uttering such sayings as, "If any man would come after me, let him deny himself and take up his cross and follow me" (Matt. 16:24) and "Follow me, and leave the dead to bury their own dead" (Matt. 8:22), Jesus took upon himself the full measure of messianic leadership. In such startling statements he challenged others to free themselves from a paralyzing fear of human authorities, even those who sat in Moses' seat and those who represented the emperor. In the former saying, Jesus unobtrusively clarified the all-important question whether he was naïvely calling people into a course of action where the sacrifices being risked might be greater than he himself was prepared to bear. With such words Jesus staved off temptation to abandon hope for the kingdom's coming, once news of John's arrest and imprisonment was followed by confirmation of his death. Even so, such sayings do not carry one to the heart of Jesus' message. They simply show that Jesus gave expression to qualities of leadership that help account for his emergence as a contender for the mantle of John.

Jesus stood in prophetic continuity with John in his commitment to the call for national repentance in the face of the imminent coming of the kingdom (Matt. 11:7*b*-19). But Jesus differed from John in regard to the basis for admission into the kingdom (Matt. 11:18-19). John came in the way of righteousness according to the Law (Matt. 21:28-32) and his strictures against the moral laxities of the people were uncompromising. The ostensible cause for his death was his denunciation of immorality in high places. While Jesus was not unmindful of the precarious situation of the rich (Matt. 19:23-24; Luke 16:19-31), the misdeeds of the wealthy and powerful did not seem to preoccupy him. He came to save sinners, not to condemn them. As sons of their Father in heaven, they in turn were counseled to love their enemies even as God loved his (Matt. 5:43-48). They were admonished not to put forgiveness on any calculating basis, but to forgive freely, boldly, unconditionally, from the heart—"Not . . . seven times, but seventy times seven" (Matt. 18:22).

Jesus taught, "There will be more joy in heaven over one sinner who repents than over ninety-nine righteous persons who need no repentance" (Luke 15:7). Therefore, he ate with sinners and celebrated their repentance (Luke 15:1-10). Such practice was difficult to justify by any precedent from Jewish scriptures. This revolutionary behavior offended the sensibilities of authorities whose well-being rested upon communal recognition of their mastery of the intricacies of a life-encompassing religious system. John the Baptist, coming to show the way of righteousness, had followed the normative practice of righteous Jews and had not eaten with sinners. But Jesus did. This marks a profound theological difference between the two (Matt. 11:16-19*b*).

b. Jesus and the religious establishment. The opposition of the scribes and Pharisees to Jesus' practice of eating with tax collectors and sinners created a major crisis. Jesus himself came from a religious background so akin to Pharisaism as to command the respect of the Pharisees, so their anxiety over what he was doing was rooted in a perception that one of their own was endangering their interests. Jesus openly said that he did not come to call the righteous (Matt. 9:1-13), but he himself was known as a righteous man. And, in eating with sinners, he was breaking down the barriers by which many of his righteous contemporaries maintained the strength of the inner group so that they could withstand external pressures to compromise religious scruples in the interests of achieving economic prosperity and a more cosmopolitan society. To abandon this practice of eating with sinners might have brought Jesus favor, but, instead, he struck at an important root of the problem, the self-righteousness of a scrupulous religious establishment. And when these legal authorities, emphasizing minutiae of the Law, neglected justice, mercy, and faith, Jesus caricatured them as "blind guides" (Matt. 23:23-24).

Jesus' table fellowship with tax collectors and sinners was based upon the recognition that God is the Father of all. Indeed, if a man has a hundred sheep and one goes astray, he will leave the ninety-nine and go in search of the one that is lost, and having found it, he will put it on his shoulder and bring it back rejoicing, and call to his friends, "Rejoice with me, for I have found my sheep which was lost" (Luke 15:3-6; cf. Matt. 18:10-14). How much more will our heavenly Father rejoice over the return of a lost son (Luke 15:11-23), and, therefore, how appropriate that we celebrate the repentance of those lost who, once dead in trespasses, are now alive through God's merciful judgment (Luke 15:25-32; 19:1-10).

By such forceful imagery as this, Jesus defended his practice of table fellowship with tax collectors and sinners. Such parables as "the lost son and his elder brother" (Luke 15:11-32), and "the laborers in the vineyard" (Matt. 20:1-15), were first created in response to this crisis in Jesus' ministry. They were used to defend the gospel of God's unmerited and unconditional acceptance of the repentant sinner. Similarly, the parable of "the great banquet" (Matt. 22:1-10; Luke 14:16-24) serves to remind the righteous that they have no ground for complaint over the eschatological acceptance of sinners, since they themselves have turned their back on the kingdom (cf. Matt. 23:13). Such parables were not intended to alienate the religious authorities, but to forestall their inquisitorial activity among the disciples. Nor is a parable like that of the Pharisee and the tax collector in the temple (Luke 18:9-14) aimed to hurt the Pharisees. That particular Pharisee does not represent all Pharisees, and certainly not the ideal Pharisee. But in order to make his point that goodness can become demonic and destructive when it leads righteous people to isolate themselves from and look down on others, Jesus chose a man from a highly virtuous circle of Jewish society. Such a man, no matter how moral, goes down from the house of God to his own house in a wrong relationship to God. Instead of placing his trust in the mercy of God, like this sinner, he has placed it in his own righteousness and has despised others.

God's love for the sinner shows no lack of love for the righteous. "All that is mine is yours," says the father to his elder son. "It was fitting to make merry and be glad, for this your brother was dead, and is alive; he was lost, and is found" (Luke 15:31-32). In spite of the cogency and charm of this parable, the implications for the righteous could be perceived as grossly unfair. As opposition from the religious establishment stiffened, Jesus formulated woes against the "scribes and Pharisees." These utterances are uncompromising. Either the people of Israel followed those whom Jesus characterized as "blind guides," who held in their hands the keys of the kingdom, but who hypocritically neither entered themselves nor allowed others to enter (Matt. 23:13), or they could follow him. Irony turns to bitter sarcasm in the judgment: "Woe to you, scribes and Pharisees, hypocrites! for you build the tombs of the prophets and adorn the monuments of the righteous, saying, 'If we had lived in the days of our fathers, we would not have taken part with them in shedding the blood of the prophets.' Thus you witness against yourselves, that you are sons of those who murdered the prophets" (Matt. 23:29-31).

By using hard words like these Jesus further alienated himself from the religious authorities, for he was unmasking what many in positions of privilege and power could not bear to have unmasked. Jesus penetrated the façade of goodness behind which those with authority over the people were hiding their lust for power and he likened them to "whitewashed tombs, which outwardly appear beautiful, but within . . . are full of dead men's bones" (Matt. 23:27). After invective like this, the authorities were naturally interested in seeing the activity and influence of Jesus curtailed. Opposition to Jesus within high priestly circles in Jerusalem was assured once Jesus entered the city and cleansed the temple. For by such bold action Jesus made clear that a thirst for righteousness called for changes not only in the hearts of people, but in the institutions of Zion (Matt. 21:12-13).

After Jesus had alienated the authorities in Galilee and challenged the Roman-supported priesthood in Jerusalem, his death at the hands of the Romans followed almost inevitably as a consequence of the political co-operation that was required in order for Rome to maintain viable control over a key sector on the defensive perimeter of its eastern frontier with the Parthians.

Jesus ran afoul of religious authorities not only when he ate with tax collectors and sinners, but in other matters as well, e.g., the question of Sabbath observance (Matt. 12:1 ff.; Luke 14:5). It is true that he insisted that he came not "to abolish the law and the prophets . . . but to fulfil them" (Matt. 5:17), but at the same time he taught his disciples that unless their righteousness exceed that of the scribes and Pharisees they would never enter the kingdom of heaven (Matt. 5:20).

While according to the view of his followers Jesus died a righteous man, he did not go to his cross innocent of breaking the Law as that was represented by the mores of the Jewish populace in Galilee, nor was he innocent of disturbing the peace in Jerusalem as that was maintained through Roman order.

When Jesus was pressed to declare himself on the legitimacy of Roman order he asked that the coin be brought to him that was used by Jews to pay taxes to Rome. Noting that this coin bore Caesar's image, he said, "Render therefore to Caesar the things that are Caesar's, and to God the things that are God's." His hearers, having been taught that they bore the image of God, were left in no doubt as to whose authority Jesus believed they should render themselves (Matt. 22:15-22). This essentially religious attitude could hardly be disputed by the Pharisees, but it entailed radical political implications that those in positions of authority could not support without placing their power in jeopardy. It was Jesus' uncompromising obedience to the will of God that caused him difficulty, because it put him in conflict with all human authority which posed as being ultimate, especially human authority which he perceived as clothing itself in religious garb (Matt. 15:1-9). For somewhat different views of Jesus' death *see* SANHEDRIN[S] §2*b*; TRIAL OF JESUS [S] §§2, 3.

c. Difficulties internal to his own fellowship. There is evidence that even within Jesus' own circle of followers there was uneasiness and frustration. For instance, invidious comparisons arose where disciples experienced different degrees of success and failure. In response, Jesus admonished them to think of their work in relation to that of a sower who scatters the seed indiscriminately. Those who sow in that fashion will neither be elated because of good results, nor discouraged because of poor results (Matt. 13:3-9).

Another problem was the uncertainty which arose as weeks and months passed without the full restoration of God's sovereign rule over Israel. To meet the frustration which this delay produced, Jesus compared the kingdom of heaven with mustard seed and leaven to remind the disciples that great things come from small beginnings (Matt. 13:31-33), the corollary of which would be that what is impressive and grand can be deceptive (cf. Matt. 24:1-2). Jesus argued repeatedly from everyday examples that it is reasonable to be hopeful and to believe that the inbreaking of God's sovereign love into the lives of the disciples would be followed by the coming of his kingdom. If a judge who is bound by oath to render justice, even though he is dishonest and subject to the influence of important people, will nonetheless hear the cry of a helpless widow who faithfully persists in calling out to him for justice, how much more will our heavenly Father hear the faithful when they cry to him for full vindication. Therefore, do not give up petitioning God: that which God holds for the faithful in promise he will fulfill, and that which he has begun he will complete (cf. Luke 18:1-8; 11:5 ff.; 14:28-32). "Or what man of you, if his son asks him for bread, will give him a stone? Or if he asks for a fish, will give him a serpent? If you then, who are evil, know how to give good gifts to your children, how much more will your Father who is in heaven give good things to those who ask him!" (Matt. 7:9-11). Therefore, pray expectantly and with belief in your hearts: "Thy kingdom come. They will be done, On earth as it is in heaven. Give us this day . . ." (Matt. 6:10).

Again, some of Jesus' disciples apparently expressed their uneasiness over the presence of persons of questionable character within their fellowship, perhaps agreeing with the scribes and Pharisees on this point. Jesus' parable of the wheat and the tares may be interpreted as a response to this uncertainty (Matt. 13:24-30). Here Jesus teaches that God, not man, in due season will separate the just from the unjust. A similar teaching is given in the parable of the dragnet (Matt. 13:47-52).

d. Jesus' ethical teachings. Jesus' ethical teachings must have left a deep impression upon his disciples, since these sayings have an important place in the earliest Jesus tradition. Jesus' teaching on love of enemies (Matt. 5:43-48) seems to penetrate to the heart of his message and carries the hearer to the very center of the gospel. The ethical doctrine that we should love our enemies cuts sharply against the grain of human instinct. It has no other ground than the character of God. Because God loves his enemies, we should love our enemies. *See also* LOVE IN THE NT §2 and LOVE IN THE NT[S] §1.

Other counsels that have a strong claim to being authentic include the teachings on being angry with the brother (Matt. 5:21-24), the appropriateness of radical ethical surgery (Matt. 5:29-30 and 18:8-9), retaliation (Matt. 5:38-42), and on serving two masters (Matt. 6:24). With serious claims to authenticity are such additional sayings as that on doing good works to be seen by others (Matt. 6:2-4, 5-6, 16-18); on laying up treasures (Matt. 6:19-21); on the eye being the lamp of the body (Matt. 6:22-23); on not casting pearls before swine (Matt. 7:6); on being wise as serpents and innocent as doves (Matt. 10:16); on not fearing those who can kill the body but cannot kill the soul (Matt. 10:28-31); on whoever would be greatest becoming the servant of all (Matt. 20:26*b*-27); on not presuming in matters of honor (Luke 14:8-10); on inviting as guests the poor and disadvantaged who cannot repay (Luke 14:12*b*-14*a*); and on identifying with the disadvantaged and taking responsibility for their welfare even in the absence of ethnic obligation and at the risk of one's own security (Luke 10:30-35). *See also* ETHICS IN THE NT §A; ETHICS IN THE NT[S] §1.

4. Problems outstanding. This approach to the teachings of Jesus can help in dealing with certain special problems that continue to plague historical study.

a. Jesus' relation to the Zealots and his teaching about the kingdom. The question of Jesus and the Zealots (*see* ZEALOT; ZEALOT[S]) cannot be settled by an appeal to problematic details in the gospel narratives. It can be better approached from a form-critical study of Jesus' teachings. The basic problem can be stated in terms of the confluence and conflict of a theology of zeal for God defined in terms of strict obedience to the Law and a theology of obedience to God defined in terms of love of enemies. Adherents of both theologies could unite against injustice and corruption within the established world of Jewish piety—but on quite different grounds. One makes God's jealousy and his consequent opposition to the sinner the normative first cause of theology, while the other makes God's unbounded redeeming, forgiving love for the sinner that primal ground.

Jesus was neither a Zealot nor, as a critic of their opponents, would he have been an open object of Zealot hatred. The Zealot's righteous passion for the sovereign reign of God was something with which Jesus and all Jews could identify. This national passion made the question of God's kingdom the central and popular concern. Jesus adopted the kingdom of God as the basic theme of his discourse as much to juxtapose his theology to that of the Zealots as for any other reason. Jesus' expectation of the kingdom's coming was derived from John the Baptist, but his explication of the kingdom's meaning was original. Whereas most rabbinic parables were used to bring out and make clear something perceived to be present in the text of scripture, Jesus used parables to explicate on his own authority that the kingdom prevailed where God's will prevails. Some of Jesus' parables may also have originated in his pondering the meaning of one or another scriptural text. But most of the parables appear to have been created to clarify his vision of how it is in the kingdom of God. In this way Jesus' prophetic consciousness became the immediate source of his authoritative revelation. This prophetic consciousness was prepared by his study of scripture, but also affected by the exigencies of his historical ministry. God's action in history prophetically interpreted is thus the foundation of Jesus' theology and ethics. What Jesus has to say about the kingdom makes it clear that he was not preoccupied with eschatological speculation but concerned to clarify the essentials of one's true relationship to God and one's right relationship to the neighbor. Why the Zealots (and for that matter the Essenes) are not addressed by name in Jesus' teaching remains an unresolved question.

b. Messianic consciousness. The question of the messianic consciousness of Jesus has been dominated since the late nineteenth century by a preoccupation with Peter's confession at Caesarea Philippi that Jesus is the Christ (Matt. 16:13-23; Mark 8:27-33; Luke 9:18-22). According to nineteenth-century reconstructions, it was at Caesarea Philippi that Jesus' career in Galilee reached its climax, and it was Caesarea Philippi that marked the turning point in Jesus' decision to go to Jerusalem and to his death. But this approach presupposed both the historicity of this event and the possibility of reconstructing the outline of Jesus' life from the chronological framework provided by Mark. On both these counts, form criticism has led to skeptical conclusions while, at the same time, applied to Jesus' teachings, it has opened up the question of messianic consciousness in a new way. For example, the formula repeated in Matthew 5:21-48, "You have heard that it was said to the men of old . . . But I say to you . . . ," sets Jesus in a special relationship to God, because what was said "to those of old" was invariably taken from the Jewish scripture. Thus, Jesus stands as a reformer within the established world of Jewish piety, acknowledging the givenness of the Mosaic tradition, but not its finality or perfection. The freedom of Jesus in relationship to scripture in these sayings is as remarkable as it is radical. The hearer is called upon to acknowledge the limitation of the Mosaic revelation if he or she accepts the authority of Jesus. This means that these sayings call for a decision about the person of Jesus.

The words that conclude the SERMON ON THE MOUNT, "the crowds were astonished at his teaching, for he taught them as one who had authority, and not as their scribes" (Matt. 7:28-29), apply to none of Jesus' sayings more appropriately than to those which begin with the arresting formula, "You have heard . . . But I say . . ." Those who accepted his authority were implicitly acknowledging him to have a status at least equal to if not above that of Moses. In this sense messianic claims were inherent in Jesus' teaching and preaching.

Jesus was conscious of the radical implications in his message and the style of its presentation. "Think not that I have come to abolish the law and the prophets; I have come not to abolish them but to fulfil them" (Matt. 5:17). "Do not think that I have come to bring peace on earth; I have not come to bring peace, but a sword" (Matt. 10:34). Jesus thus copes with misconceptions of his purpose and gives shape to his public image as a self-conscious authority on the kingdom of heaven. He was desirous of making clear the radical character of his message, and was also concerned to have others perceive his teaching in continuity with the Law and the Prophets and as the fulfillment of their divine purpose.

Bibliography. N. Perrin, *Rediscovering the Teaching of Jesus* (1967), while continuing to assume Markan priority, updates the form-critical results of Bultmann and Dibelius by taking account of subsequent developments, especially progress achieved in parable research; includes annotated bibliographies. G. N. Stanton, *Jesus of Nazareth in NT Preaching,* NTSMS, XXVII (1974), develops a comprehensive argument for the view that the missionary preaching of the earliest Christian communities was characterized not only by a concern for the present and future of Jesus, but also for his past, including his teaching. J. Bowker, *Jesus and the Pharisees* (1973), is valuable for showing the grounds for and consequences of the Pharisees' opposition to Jesus; provides Eng. trans. of the most important Gr., Heb., and Aram. texts. J. Neusner, "The Fellowship (Haburah) in the Second Jewish Commonwealth," *HTR,* LIII (1960), 125-42, illuminates the way in which the concern over the observance or nonobservance of Levitical purity laws and the laws governing the tithing of food affected the social life of some Pharisees during the time of Jesus. For fuller treatment of the issues discussed in the present article, and for some of the historical and literary presuppositions of the approach taken here, see W. R. Farmer, "The Problem of Christian Origins: A Programmatic Essay," *Studies in the History and Text of the NT,* ed. B. L. Daniels and M. J. Suggs, Studies and Documents, XXIX (1967), 81-88, "An Historical Essay on the Humanity of Jesus Christ," *Christian History and Interpretation,* ed. W. R. Farmer *et al.* (1967), pp. 101-26, and "Jesus and the Gospels: A Form-critical and Theological Essay," *Perkins School of Theology Journal,* XXVIII (1975), 1-74, all with citations of other literature.

W. R. FARMER

***TEL-ASSAR.** In Isa. 37:12 (=II Kings 19:12), "the people of Eden who were in Telassar" are listed among peoples conquered by the predecessors of Sennacherib. *Tᵉla(')ššār* is a correct transcription of Assyr. *Til-Aššuri.* In 737 B.C., Tiglath-pileser III conquered and annexed to Assyria "Til-Aššuri, which is a fortress of the Babylonians," also called Silḫazi. It was located in Media, apparently not far from Ecbatana, but was inhabited by Babylonians and had a temple of Marduk. Esarhaddon also mentioned *Til-Ašurri* as being in Media. Perhaps its settlers belonged to the Babylonian-Aramean tribe of Bit-adini. *See* EDEN[S] §3.

Bibliography. *ARAB,* I, §§768, 774, 775, 795; II. §§517, 532; E. Kraeling, *Aram and Israel* (1918), pp. 63-64, gives a wrong location; I. M. Diakonoff, *Istorija Midii* (1956), pp. 201, 267.

M. C. ASTOUR

TELL [Akkad. *tillu,* "ruin-heap"; Arab. *tell,* "artificial hill"; Heb. תל (*tel;* final consonants in Heb. cannot be doubled)]. A term used by local Arabic- and Hebrew-speaking populations and by Near Eastern archaeologists to describe mounds containing the remains of ancient cities. Equivalent terms are Turkish *hüyük* and *tepe;* contrast Arab. *khirba(t),* "ruin."

A *tell* results when debris accumulates within city walls (often situated atop a natural hill), thus slowly elevating the ground level. Successive destructions and rebuildings add to the accumulation until the city may be situated atop a deposit more than one hundred feet high. This may help explain the discouraging report of the Israelite spies that the cities of Canaan had "fortifications towering to the sky" (Deut. 1:28 NEB; cf. Num. 13:25-28).

For a representative cross section, *see* ARCHAEOLOGY Fig. 45; for a photo, *see* MEGIDDO Figs. 22-25; for the methodologies for discovering the ancient identity of a tell, *see* SITES, ANCIENT, IDENTIFICATION OF[S]. L. R. BAILEY

***TELL EL-AMARNA. 1. Historical context.** An attempt by Campbell to cast serious doubts on the coregency of Amen-hotep III and Amen-hotep IV has been countered by incisive arguments on the part of Kitchen. The likelihood of a coregency still prevails.

2. Historical significance of the Amarna Letters (*see* TELL EL-AMARNA §2*b*). The main Egyptian administrative center in Canaan was at Gaza with two other district capitals at Ṣumur (Zemer, home of the Zemarites), N of the Nahr el-Kebîr for the Phoenician coastal region, and at Kumidi (Kâmed el-Lôz) for the Lebanese Beqaʻ (the "land of Amqi") and the Damascene. The districts were supervised by commissioners (*rābiṣū*). The city-state rulers, called kings by their own subjects, ranked as "city managers" (*ḫazānūtu*). They were supported by councils of the oligarchs in each city who managed affairs when no prince was in office.

Two major city-states are known in the hill country (of later Ephraim and Judah), Shechem and Jerusalem. The ruler of the former, Lab'ayu, was supported by Habiru troops (*see* HABIRU, HABIRU[S]) in his attempt to seize control of the major arteries of communication. He made common cause with Milkilu of Gezer and Tagu of Gath-carmel; then he pressured Baʻlu-meher of Gath-padalla to accept his suzerainty over the Sharon Plain. By force he occupied ʻArabu and Burquna (towns in the Valley of Dothan) and he destroyed Shunem (in the Valley of Jezreel). The elders of Taanach ousted Yashdata, their ruler, who found asylum with Biridiya of Megiddo. Megiddo had been rendered more vulnerable since the Egyptian garrison had been withdrawn, so Lab'ayu placed it under virtual siege. An order was finally issued for Lab'ayu's arrest. The local rulers captured him, and Suratu, king of Acco, agreed to send the culprit to Egypt by ship. Instead he accepted a bribe and released Lab'ayu (also Baʻlu-meher) at Hannathon. Lab'ayu was evidently slain by the men of Gina (modern Jenîn) while fleeing homeward to Shechem.

Lab'ayu's sons took up the cause, encouraged by Milkilu of Gezer, who had joined Shuwardata (of Gath?) and Tagu in a dispute with ʻAbdu-Khepa of Jerusalem. Friction had already occurred between Shuwardata and ʻAbdu-Khepa over possession of Qila (Keilah); now the strife centered around Rubutu (Rabbah in Judah) and Beth-NINIB (perhaps Beth-horon?).

To the N, ʻAbdi-Ashirta, ruler of Amurru, embarked on a campaign of subversion and conquest among the cities along the coast. He even took over the provincial capital at Ṣumur and threatened Rib-Addi at Gebal (Byblos). The latter finally persuaded the Egyptians to intervene by force; ʻAbdi-Ashirta was arrested and probably released only to be slain by his own countrymen. His sons, particularly Aziru, renewed the program of expansionism and regained control not only of Ṣumur but eventually of Gebal and other towns on the Phoenician coast. His rise to power and the demise of poor Rib-Addi (who fled to Beirut, tried to make a deal with Aziru, and was assassinated at Sidon) must have had the tacit support of some Egyptian official(s), probably Tutu at the royal court. Aziru was ordered to Egypt where he spent nearly two years, apparently convincing Pharaoh of his loyalty. Immediately upon his return to Amurru, he betrayed Egypt and became a vassal of the Hittites.

Aziru's activities and/or the troubles with Lab'ayu's sons in the S may have been the occasion for a planned expedition to Canaan. Orders were sent out to the local rulers to prepare provisions and to place their local troops on the alert. Whether the Egyptian army actually marched forth or not is unknown; it is clear, however, that the government of Akh-en-Aton was not neglectful of the province as scholars have often assumed.

Bibliography. A. R. Schulman, "Some Observations on the Military Background of the Amarna Period," *Journal of the American Research Center in Egypt,* III (1964), 51-69; E. F. Campbell, Jr., *The Chronology of the Amarna Letters* (1964), and "Shechem in the Amarna Archive," in G. E. Wright, *Shechem* (1965), pp. 191-207; H. Reviv, "The Planning of an Egyptian Campaign in Canaan in the Days of Amenhotep IV," *Yediot,* XXX (1966), 45-51, Hebrew; J. F. Ross, "Gezer in the Tell el-Amarna Letters," *Museum Haaretz, Bulletin 8* (1966), 45-54 (abridged in *BA,* XXX [1967], 62-70); K. A. Kitchen, review of Campbell, *Chronology of the Amarna Letters, JEA,* LIII (1967), 178-82; A. F. Rainey, "Gath-padalla," *IEJ,* XVIII (1968), 1-14, and *El Amarna Tablets 359-379* (1970 [rev. ed. 1975]); W. L. Moran, "The Death of ʻAbdi-Aširta," *Eretz Israel,* IX (1969), 94-99; P. Kyle McCarter, "Rib-Adda's Appeal to Aziru (*EA* 162, 1-21)," *Oriens Antiquus,* XII (1973), 15-18. A. F. RAINEY

TELL EL-KHELEIFEH. 1. Location. Tell el-Kheleifeh is situated near the center of the N shore of the Gulf of Aqabah, W of the city of Aqabah, Jordan, about 1/3 mile N of the shore line.

2. Excavation. Tell el-Kheleifeh was excavated during three seasons, 1938-40, under the direction of Nelson Glueck, for the American Schools of Oriental Research, with the assistance of the Department of Antiquities, Transjordan, the American Philosophical Society, and the Smithsonian Institution. The excavation lacked proper stratification, and dating is therefore difficult.

At the NW corner of the tell was found a large mud brick building with three small square rooms and three long rectangular ones. The excavator theorized that it was a fortified Solomonic copper smelter. In 1965 he modified his views and said that the structure was a storehouse and granary. In its walls were rows of apertures, left by the destruction of wooden beams. On three sides was an open court, protected by a casemate wall. Beyond it was a larger courtyard and a wall surrounding the whole enclosure, with salients, recesses, towers, and a gateway with two pairs of guard rooms. The plan of this fortress is reminiscent of the Iron Age II Assyrian open court style.

Some of the Kheleifeh pottery is like the eighth- and seventh-century B.C. ware found by M. E. L. Mallowan at Nimrud, and by C.-M. Bennett at Umm el-Biyara, Tawilan and Buseira, in Jordan.

A seal was discovered with the letters *l y t m* (belonging to Jotam, Yitm ?) engraved over a horned ram. It is enclosed in a copper holder, similar in style to a seventh-century gold one found at Nimrud. The theophoric name Qaus occurs in some seal impressions stamped *Qaus'nl* on jars. Among those who paid tribute to Tiglath-pileser III (745-727 B.C.) was Qauš-malaku of Edom. The prism of Esarhaddon (681-669 B.C.) mentions Qauš-gabri, King of Edom.

3. Identification. Whether Tell el-Kheleifeh is the location of either ELATH or EZION-GEBER continues to be debated.

Bibliography. M. E. L. Mallowan, *Nimrud and Its Remains* (1966), p. 114; E. K. Vogel, "Bibliography of Holy Land Sites," *HUCA,* XLII (1971), 85-86; C.-M. Bennett, "Buseirah," *Levant,* VI (1974), 4, 19; *ANET* (2nd ed.), pp. 282, 291. E. K. VOGEL

TEMAN. *See* EDOM[S].

*__TEMPLE OF HEROD.__ Excavations on a large scale have been taking place around the temple mount since 1968. The extensive finds of buildings and objects have stimulated renewed study of the city, especially of the Herodian period.

The temple mount is bounded by four giant retainer walls designed to hold the huge, paved platform which surrounded the temple building. The area of this platform, one of the largest known temple areas in the ancient and classical world, is about 35 acres. The walls measure on the W 1,595 feet, on the N 1,020 feet, on the E 1,562 feet and on the S 921 feet. *See* TEMPLE, JERUSALEM Fig. 12.

A paved street ran all along the western wall and continued from the SW corner to the Pool of Siloam, another 1,645 feet. The slabs of the pavement are of local Jerusalem limestone, up to 47x79 inches in size. The street is about 32 feet wide, and on both sides of it there were small structures. This was apparently the central market place of Jerusalem in the Herodian period. Under the street, at a depth of about 20 feet, ran a water conduit, partly cut into the natural rock. Many channels in the area run into this conduit, which also drains the rain water from the street itself. A large quantity of water was thus directed to the Pool of Siloam, which served as a reservoir. The foundations of the temple mount wall descend in this area to a depth of between 23 and 72 feet below the street level. The height of the wall was more than 98 feet above the street level, and there may have been towers on the corners, reaching even higher.

The retaining part of the walls was smooth, but the upper parts, which surrounded the sacred area, were built with pilasters at regular intervals. These were also the outer walls for the colonnades of the temple mount.

According to the description given by Flavius Josephus there were four gates in the western wall (*see* TEMPLE, JERUSALEM §C2). The two upper ones, over arches, are now known as Robinson's Arch and Wilson's Arch, and the two at street level are known as Warren's Gate and Barklay's Gate (*see* TEMPLE, JERUSALEM §C4 and Fig. 34). It was thought previously that Robinson's Arch was one of seven arches forming a bridge across the TYROPOEON VALLEY from the Royal Portico on the temple mount to the upper city in the W. This reconstruction must now be rejected, since no more arches crossing the valley to the W have been discovered. Instead, a series of arches, perpendicular to Robinson's Arch, go from N to S, each one lower than the other. Dozens of stair stones were found in the area, and on one of the lower arches a few stones were still in place. The whole structure seems, therefore, to be a large staircase, over the arches, leading from the street up to the Royal Portico (*see* Fig. T2). This fits with Josephus' description: "From the fourth gate [southern-most in the west wall] one descends over many stairs to the valley whence one ascends again to the upper city by many more stairs" (Antiq. XV.xi.5).

Over the SW corner of the temple mount

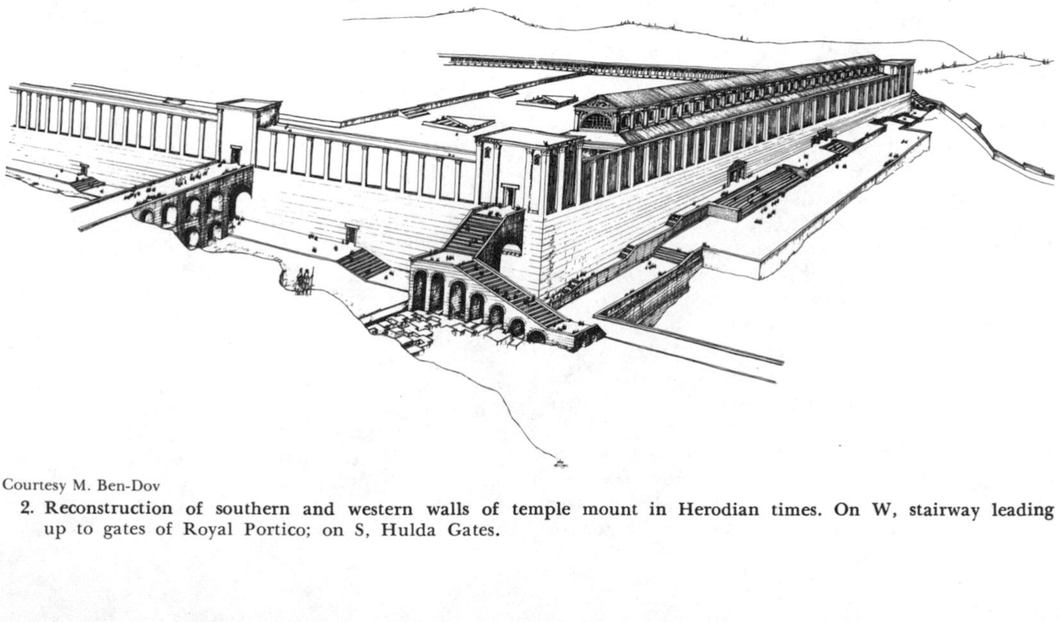

Courtesy M. Ben-Dov

2. **Reconstruction of southern and western walls of temple mount in Herodian times. On W, stairway leading up to gates of Royal Portico; on S, Hulda Gates.**

courtyard stood a tower, atop which one of the priests stood on Friday afternoons and blew the trumpet to announce the beginning of the sabbath and the closing of business. A stone with a Hebrew inscription confirming this fact was found in the debris at the SW corner. *See* Fig. T3.

Inside the temple mount courtyard, along its southern wall stood the magnificent Royal Portico. It was built in a basilical plan, with one central aisle and two side ones divided by rows of columns, 160 in all, that supported the roof. Many architectural remains of this building were found in the excavations, decorated in relief with floral and geometrical designs. Out of many dozens of fragments found, not one had a human or animal figure. Many fragments of columns were also found, the diameter of which can be calculated to be 5 feet, which agrees with Josephus' report that three people were required to encircle them. All stones are local Jerusalem limestone. Some gold-painted fragments found in the debris confirm Josephus' descriptions. The Royal Portico evidently served as a center for business, money changing, etc. Later it might even have housed the SANHEDRIN, the main legal court of Jerusalem. Being on the temple mount and out of the sacred area enhanced civil and economical activities and also the resolution of complaints aroused by this location. It is possible that this is the place where Christ overturned the tables of the money-changers as told in the gospels.

Intensive excavation work was carried out along the entire length of the southern wall, which, during the second temple period, contained the two main entrance gates to the temple mount. This was, therefore, its façade. The strength of this wall is emphasized by the gigantic ashlars in the corners, stones weighing up to seventy tons each.

In this wall were the two Hulda Gates through which pilgrims entered the temple mount (M. Middot 1.3). The pilgrims entered by the eastern gate, passed through an underground passageway under the floor of the Royal Portico, emerged to the courtyard, walked around the temple, and went out through the western gate by means of another underground passageway. Jews who were mourning the death of a relative would reverse the order, entering the western gate and going in the opposite direction. When they passed by the rest of the pilgrims they would be recognized and comforted.

While the remains of the eastern gate are few, the western gate survives almost in its entirety and a new survey of it has recently been conducted in co-operation with the Moslem authorities of the temple mount. This survey shows that almost eighty-five per cent of the gate is originally of the second temple period. Especially interesting are the decorations carved in its domes.

In front of the gates there were large stairways. The western one, of thirty steps, is one of the widest known in any temple (*ca.* 214 feet). The stairs, descending from N to S, brought the pilgrims to a street 23 feet wide, running all along the southern wall.

On descending the stairs, one came to a platform paved with huge slabs similar to those used in the streets, whose southern edge has not yet been found. By what way one continued from the platform further S is not known. In this area, fragments of inscriptions in Hebrew have been found, testifying to the existence of carved signs in various public buildings nearby.

An interesting discovery is that of tunnels cut in the natural rock under the main stairways (*see* Fig. T4). In the walls are niches for housing oil lamps, alternating on the right and left. Such tunnels are mentioned in the Mishna as winding passages (*mesibot*) for quick and isolated exit of priests and other people and objects which had become defiled during the ritual in the temple. They would go out to a nearby bathhouse, be purified, and return to their regular chores through the gates.

A little further to the S of the gates large cisterns were found, over which were remains of mosaic floors. These may be connected to various water-supply systems in front of the temple mount that served the large crowds of pilgrims.

Two important discoveries are connected with the fortifications of the city. It is now clear beyond doubt that the city wall was further E of the temple mount wall and did not come out of its SE corner. The entire corner of the latter was thus inside the city walls.

It is also clear that W of the temple mount, on the eastern slope of the western hill where the upper city was located, there are no traces of any wall whatsoever, at either the foot of the hill or higher up the slope. One should remember that Josephus does not mention a wall there, and it must now be considered an invention of various scholars.

Courtesy M. Ben-Dov

3. Hebrew inscription on stone from walls of temple mount: "To the place of trumpeting . . ."

Courtesy M. Ben-Dov

4. Rock-hewn tunnel outside Triple Gate

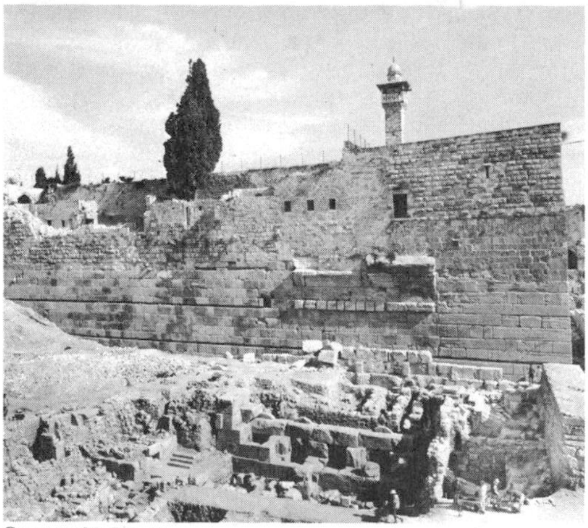

Courtesy M. Ben-Dov

5. Southwestern corner of temple mount

Small finds of the second temple period include pottery, coins, bone and bronze objects, stone weights and vessels, and installations made of stone (some for pressing oil, etc.). Commercial activity is well expressed by the finds, as well as social and religious customs known from various literary sources.

Bibliography. B. Mazar, "The Excavations in the Old City of Jerusalem," *Eretz Israel,* IX (1969), 161-74, Hebrew, "The Excavation South and West of the Temple Mount in Jerusalem," *BA,* XXXIII (1970), 47-60 (*see also Ariel, Israel,* XXII [1971], 11-19), "The Excavations . . . Second Preliminary Report," *Eretz Israel,* X (1971), 1-34, Hebrew, and "Finds from the Archaeological Excavations near the Temple Mount," *Qadmoniot,* V (1972), 74-90, Hebrew; M. Ben-Dov, "Archaeological Excavation near the Temple Mount," *Christian News From Israel,* XXII (1972), 135-42; A. Friendly, "Recent Excavations in Jerusalem," Expedition, XV, no. 3 (1973), 15-24.

M. Ben-Dov

***TEMPLE OF SOLOMON. 1. The site.** It is still commonly agreed among scholars that the temple of Solomon stood on the middle part of the ridge now occupied by the Haram esh-Sharif (*see* Temple, Jerusalem Figs. 12-13). More precisely, the site is identified with that of the Moslem shrine known as Qubbet es-Sakhra, the "Dome of the Rock." In recent years, however, archaeological excavations have shed new light on what could have been the S boundary of the Solomonic platform. A straight joint, previously observed by Warren in 1887 in the masonry of the SE corner of the temple platform, points to a clear demarcation between the Herodian and the Persian masonry. According to Kenyon, this joint may represent the SE corner of the original temple precinct.

2. Basic structure and archaeological parallels. The archaeological parallels that are most frequently quoted by scholars include the small sanctuary found at Tell Tainat in Syria, the temple of stratum 1B (LB II) at Hazor, and the Iron Age temple of Tell 'Arad. In each case, scholars justify the comparison by stressing the tripartite division of all the structures considered. However, even a superficial look at the ground plans of the three temples reveals how basically different they were from Solomon's temple. The description contained in I Kings 6:1-6 makes it clear that the Solomonic temple conformed to the "long house" type of building, rectangular, with the entrance in one of the short sides (*see* Temple, Jerusalem Fig. 19), a feature that sets it immediately apart from the Hazor and Arad temples. Its plan included a vestibule of the "broad room" type (entrance in one of its long sides), a nave that was a "long room" with an axial entrance in one of its short sides, and finally an inner sanctuary described in I Kings 6:16-20 as a perfectly square room. *See* Temple, Jerusalem Fig. 17.

a. Tell Tainat. Given the basic structure of the temple, as outlined above, the general plan of the sanctuary at Tell Tainat (*see* Temple, Jerusalem Fig. 20) may offer the best archaeological parallel. The similarities, however, should not mask differences that are equally obvious. Thus the inner sanctuary at Tell Tainat, unlike that at Jerusalem, was not square. Also, the contention that the Jerusalem inner sanctuary, unlike its counterpart at Tell Tainat, was architecturally distinct from the nave, appears to be baseless, since one can easily show, on the strength of I Kings 6:16-20, that the inner sanctuary was obtained by the mere partitioning of the main room of the temple (Fig. T6).

b. Tell 'Arad. Of the Iron Age temple (Fig. T7) excavated at Tell 'Arad (*see* Temple, Semitic[S] §2*a*), Aharoni has said that it preserves the "essential plan of the Jerusalem temple." This claim does not seem to be warranted, although scholars have been impressed by features common to both temples. For example, it has been correctly observed that the sacrificial altar stood in each case in the courtyard of the temples. But the differences in ground plan are no less striking. First, the temple

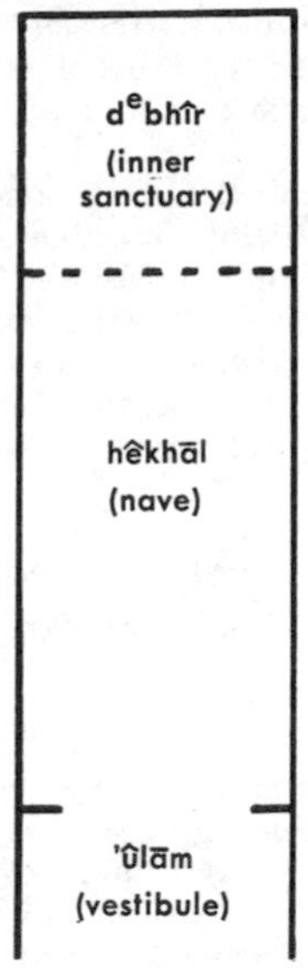

6. Ground plan of Solomon's temple

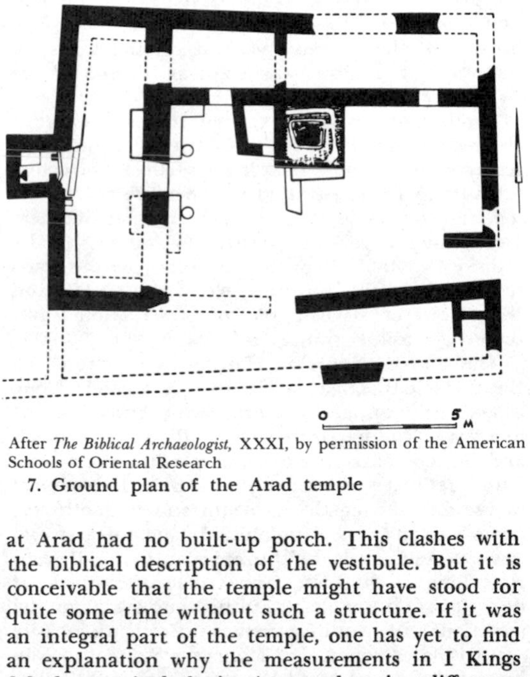

After *The Biblical Archaeologist*, XXXI, by permission of the American Schools of Oriental Research

7. Ground plan of the Arad temple

at Arad had no built-up porch. This clashes with the biblical description of the vestibule. But it is conceivable that the temple might have stood for quite some time without such a structure. If it was an integral part of the temple, one has yet to find an explanation why the measurements in I Kings 6:2 do not include it. A second major difference between the two buildings lies in the basic plan of their main room. In Jerusalem, the nave conformed to the "long room" type of construction, but at Arad the corresponding room was a distinct "broad room," with a rectangular court in front of it. And, finally, the inner sanctuary at Arad is represented only by a niche formed by a recess in the long wall of the nave, whereas in Jerusalem the inner sanctuary was built as an extension of the long walls of the nave.

c. ***Hazor.*** In the fourteenth-century B.C. temple found at Hazor, Yadin has urged scholars to see a prototype of Solomon's temple. The tripartite division of the Hazor temple (Fig. T8), with its doorways on a single axis, is an obvious basis for comparison. The entrance hall, like the vestibule, was a broad room. But it was narrower than the front of the temple, in contrast with the Solomonic porch, which occupied the full width of the nave. As to the middle hall, it was almost square and thus can hardly be compared with the main room of Solo-

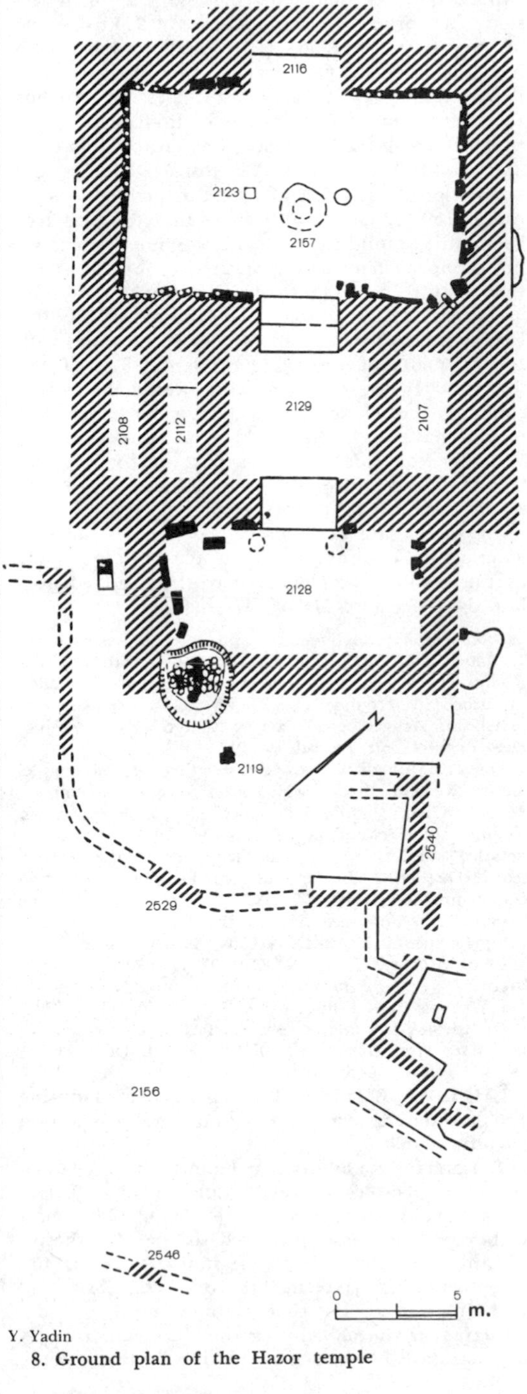

Y. Yadin

8. Ground plan of the Hazor temple

mon's temple. At Hazor, there was also a rear hall with a niche appended to it. This feature alone accentuates the differences that existed between the two sanctuaries.

3. The side wing. The intricate text of I Kings 6:5-10 contains a rather obscure description of two mysterious structures called respectively יצוע (JB "annex"; RSV "structure") and צלעות (RSV "side chambers"). Scholars usually regard the former structure as a part of the latter. There are difficulties, however, in identifying the יצוע with the side wing, properly designated as צלעות. First, some of the ancient versions (LXX and Syr.) seem to have imagined the יצוע near the roof of the temple, if not on the roof itself. The MT does not bear out this interpretation unless one understands the preposition על in vss. 5 and 10 as meaning "on" or "on top of" instead of "against," which is the translation usually accepted for this passage. Also, a comparison of vss. 5 and 8 shows that the יצוע had been built around the nave and the inner sanctuary, but stopped short of the vestibule. But the structure known as צלעות had its entrance near the "shoulder" of the temple. The shoulder of a building, as shown by Exod. 27:14, clearly coincides with the segments of its façade on both sides of the doorway. If so, the side wing would have surrounded the whole temple like a horseshoe and would have extended as far as the vestibule. Whether the side wing was part of the original Solomonic structure has been doubted by a few scholars, mainly on literary grounds. If the vestibule itself was a late addition to the temple, the side wing, which encompassed the whole building as far as the vestibule, could also have been added at a late date. *See also* HAZOR; HAZOR[S].

Bibliography. Commentaries: on relevant passages, see J. Gray, *I and II Kings* (1963), pp. 150 ff. and M. Noth, *Könige*, I (1968), 95 ff. The most comprehensive study published in recent years, with an almost exclusive emphasis on archaeological data, is that of T. A. Busink, *Der Tempel von Jerusalem* (1970).

For archaeological discoveries relating to the temple, see K. Kenyon, "New Evidence on Solomon's Temple," *MUSJ*, XLVI (1970), 139-49; cf. also E. Vogt, "Vom Tempel zum Felsendom," *Bibl.*, LV (1974), 23-64. For detailed studies on the basic structure of the temple, see J. Ouellette, "Le vestibule du Temple de Salomon était-il un bît ḫilâni?" *RB*, LXXVI (1969), 365-78, "The Solomonic *Debîr* According to the Hebrew Text of I Kings 6," *JBL*, LXXXIX (1970), 338-43, "The Yāṣīaʿ and the Ṣelāʿōt," *JNES*, XXXI (1972), 187-91; K. Rupprecht, "Nachrichten von Erweiterung und Renovierung des Tempels in J. Könige 6," *ZDPV*, LXXXVIII (1972).

On the Tainat temple, see C. Haines, *Excavations in the Plain of Antioch*, II (1971). J. QUELLETTE

***TEMPLES, SEMITIC.** Temples discovered during the last decade constitute a considerable addition to our knowledge.

1. Canaanite and foreign temples. ***a. Pre-Israelite.*** Four temples of the Middle to Late Bronze Ages have been discovered at HAZOR. The most elaborate and best preserved is the "Orthostat Temple" of area H. Its beginnings are in the seventeenth or sixteenth century B.C. (MB II), and it was several times rebuilt until the destruction of the city during the thirteenth century B.C. (strata 3-1A). Its name derives from smoothly dressed basalt orthostats (reused from earlier structures), which lined the walls of the outer and inner rooms during the latest phase of the temple (stratum 1A).

On the floor of the latest temple were found incense altars and libation tables, the basalt statue of a seated king, and the broken statue of a deity standing on a bull. On the deity's breast is a four-pointed star surrounded by a circle, which appears also on one of the incense altars. The emblem and the bull are symbols of the storm-god Hadad.

The cella of all four phases was a large "broad room" with a central niche for the main cult object. In the two early phases (strata 3 and 2) the cella was fronted by a small porch with two tower-like side rooms. In the two later phases (strata 1B and 1A) another outer porch was added. At the entrance to the original porch the bases of two freestanding pillars were found, resembling JACHIN AND BOAZ of the Solomonic temple. Striking comparisons to the plan of the temple and its orthostats have been found at ALALAKH in N Syria.

The small "Stelae Temple" was discovered at the foot of the rampart of the lower city (area C). Its two phases belong to the fourteenth-thirteenth centuries B.C. (strata 1B and 1A). Yadin supposes that the shrine was dedicated to the moon-god, because of the crescent pendant on the breast of the seated figure and the emblem on one of the stelae. *See* TEMPLES §2*a*.

Another, much larger temple complex was discovered in the SE part of the lower city (area F). It began as a double temple with two inner courtyards in MB II (stratum 3), became a "square temple" similar to those of Amman and Shechem (*see below*) in LB I (stratum 2), and was finally transformed into an open high place in the fourteenth-thirteenth centuries B.C. (strata 1B and 1A). However, its bad state of preservation leaves these conclusions conjectural.

The fourth temple at Hazor was discovered in the upper city (area A). Its plan is a single "long room," in contrast to the two "broad room" temples of the lower city. Other than votive bowls and pottery beakers, no distinct cult objects were found. Its first phase belongs to MB II. It remained in use only during the sixteenth and fifteenth centuries B.C. and was abandoned during the last two Bronze Age levels, with some cult installations remaining around it. This curious manner of desertion and the date of the temple's final destruction still requires further investigation.

An isolated square building near Amman (Rabbah of the Ammonites) has raised again the question of the function of a similar structure near Shechem. In the center of each is the base of a round pillar, thought to be an altar. The function of these "square temples" as central tribal league shrines has been suggested by Campbell and Wright, because of their unique architecture and their location outside of the cities. However, the Shechem building has been interpreted by Albright as a villa and that of Amman by Fritz as a tower fortress. Their dates are different: seventeenth-sixteenth century B.C. at Shechem and fourteenth-thirteenth century B.C. at Amman. No special cult objects have been found in them and the central pillar might well have served a structural purpose.

A temple dated approximately to the period of the desert wanderings has been discovered at the Timna' copper mines in the southern Arabah. It was erected by the Egyptians and dedicated to Hathor, the patron of mining enterprises. Its plan is a small *naos* with a central niche, surrounded by a square courtyard. The votive objects bear cartouches of Sethos I, Ramses II, Mer-ne-Ptah, Sethos II, and Queen Tawosre of the Nineteenth Dynasty, and Ramses III, IV, and V of the Twentieth Dynasty, i.e., from *ca.* 1300 to *ca.* 1150 B.C. In its later phase a row of standing stones (*masseboth*) occupied the left side of the courtyard. Decorated "Midianite pottery" led Rothenberg to see in the last phase a Midianite tented shrine. Among the votive objects is a crude male copper figurine and a copper serpent (4½ inches long) with a gilded head.

b. After the Israelite conquest. Philistine cult places have been discovered at ASHDOD and Tell Qasile. A small shrine at Ashdod belongs to the twelfth and eleventh centuries B.C. Its plan is fragmentary. Of much interest is a clay figurine of a seated goddess whose lower part is in the form of a couch or offering table (*see* ASHDOD[S] Fig. 24). Another shrine of the eighth century B.C. was discovered in the lower city. In it were found mainly male figurines, according to Dothan, possibly representing Dagon.

At Tell Qasile the main cult room is a "long room" with two wooden pillars standing on round stone bases (cf. the "two middle pillars" of the Dagon temple at Gaza which were tumbled by Samson: Judg. 16:29).

Pottery and cult objects show the Philistine character of the temple. It belongs to the twelfth-eleventh century B.C. but seems to have remained in use even later. A Hebrew-Phoenician ostracon found on the tell mentions the "House of Horon": בית חרן; possibly this means that the temple was dedicated to the Canaanite god Horon. *See* BETH-HORON.

2. Israelite sanctuaries and temples. *a. Pre-exilic.* The only unquestionably Israelite temple discovered by archaeologists is at ARAD. Constructed in the period of the united monarchy as part of a royal border fortress, it was preceded by an open high place, erected during the twelfth-eleventh century B.C. In the vicinity of the high place were many burned animal bones, including the skeleton of a lamb with only the head missing (a "whole burnt offering").

The temple consisted of one main room, the *hêkhāl,* six by twenty cubits. This distinct "broad room" was enlarged in the ninth century by another five feet, which fits exactly the difference between twenty Egyptian common and royal (large) cubits (cf. II Chr. 3:3, "in cubits of the old standard"). To the W of the *hêkhāl* was a raised cella, the holy of holies or *d^ebhîr.* Flanking the entrance of the latter were two incense altars, and it contained a small *bamah* and a *massebah.* Flank- the entrance to the main building were two stone slabs, probably bases of pillars, like JACHIN AND BOAZ in Jerusalem. Near the center of the court was the altar of burnt offering. It was built of earth and unhewn stones (cf. Exod. 20:24-25) and its measurements were five cubits square, three cubits high, like the altar of the tabernacle (Exod. 27:1; cf. II Chr. 6:13). The altar went out of use at the end of the eighth century and the temple was destroyed with the erection of the last Israelite citadel at the end of the seventh century. The two phases of its abolishment probably belong to the days of Hezekiah and Josiah, the two kings who concentrated worship in Jerusalem. Hebrew ostraca found in the temple contain names of priestly families known from the Bible, i.e., Meremoth, Pashhur, and the sons of Korah.

The importance of the temple may stem from its function as a royal border sanctuary, like Dan and Bethel in Israel and Beer-sheba in Judah. The Bible, speaking about cult places outside of Jerusalem, may be referring to such border temples of the kingdom.

For the parallels between the Arad temple and the temple in Jerusalem, *see* TEMPLE OF SOLOMON [S] §2*b;* for ground plans of the Arad and Hazor temples, *see* TEMPLE OF SOLOMON[S] Figs. 7, 8.

For other pre-exilic Israelite temples, *see* BEER-SHEBA[S] and LACHISH[S].

b. Postexilic. Postexilic temples which seem to go back to pre-exilic traditions have been discovered at Lachish and Beer-sheba. All have an E-W orientation and the same basic plan as the Arad temple: a large courtyard leading to a definite "broad room" cella with an inner sanctuary (*adyton*) at its center. The similarity of the Lachish temples to the Israelite temple of Arad, the absence of pagan objects, and the information that Jews still dwelt at Lachish in the postexilic period (Neh. 11:30), all support the assumption that these were Jewish temples.

The Hellenistic temple at Beer-sheba was erected in the third or second century B.C. A wealth of pagan figurines and votive objects shows its cosmopolitan nature.

Bibliography. Hazor: Y. Yadin, *Hazor* (1972), pp. 67-105. Amman and Shechem: J. B. Hennessy, "Excavations of a Late Bronze Age Temple at Amman," *PEQ,* XCVIII (1966), 155-62; G. R. H. Wright, "The Bronze Age Temple at Amman," *ZAW,* LXXVIII (1966), 351-57, and "Temples at Shechem," *ZAW,* LXXX (1968), 1-35; E. F. Campbell, Jr. and G. E. Wright, "Tribal League Shrines in Amman and Shechem," *BA,* XXXII (1969), 104-16; W. F. Albright, *The Archaeology of Palestine* (1963), p. 92; V. Fritz, "Erwägungen zu dem Spätbronzezeitlichen Quadratbau bei Amman," *ZDPV,* LXXXVII (1971), 140-52. Timna': B. Rothenberg, *Timna* (1972), pp. 125-201. Ashdod: M. Dothan and D. N. Freedman, "Ashdod I," *Atiqot,* VII (1967), 130-44; M. Dothan, "Ashdod, " *Qadmoniot,* V (1972), 6-10. Tell Qasile: A. Mazar, "A Philistine Temple at Tell Qasile," *Qadmoniot,* VI (1973) 20-23, Arad: *see* ARAD [S]. Beer-sheba: *see* BEER-SHEBA[S]. Lachish: *see* LACHISH [S].

Y. AHARONI

***TEN COMMANDMENTS.** The English equivalent of the Hebrew expression "ten words" (Exod. 34:28 and Deut. 4:13; 10:4). Since Irenaeus they have been known as the Decalogue. The passages in Deuteronomy say they were written on "two tables of stone," and consequently the term refers to the commandments found in Deut. 5:7-21, described in vs. 22 as having been written on two tables. Exod. 34:28 might be taken to mean the commandments in Exod. 34:14-26, but the editorial process has created problems in vss. 27-28, and it is not possible to identify a precise list of ten commandments in this text. Traditionally the expression is also applied to the commandments found in Exod. 20:3-17. This text is found in separate documents such as the Nash Papyrus, in phylacteries, and in fragments from Qumran. *See* DEAD SEA SCROLLS[S] §2.

1. Text. All these materials contain variant readings, which resulted from the work of scribes and redactors (*see* SCRIBE §§1-2; TEXT, OT §A3). This is not surprising, because in the Bible itself there are incomplete texts or summaries of the Decalogue, e.g., Lev. 19:3-4, 11-13; Hosea 4:2; Jer. 7:9; Pss. 15:2-5 [H 3-6]; 24:4. Stamm has listed at least twenty variants between Exod. 20 and Deut. 5. Seven cases involve merely the addition of the conjunction (*wāw*), but in Exod. 20:4 this is of significance, for it changes the meaning of פסל (graven image) by making it synonymous with תמונה (likeness). The following are the most significant variant readings: (*a*) Deut. 5:10 has "his commandments" (*kethibh*); Exod. 20:6, "my commandments." (*b*) Deut. 5:12 says "observe the sabbath day," adding "as the Lord your God commanded you"; Exod. 20:8, "Remember the sabbath day," without the additional clause. (*c*) To the list of those who are not to work on the sabbath, Deut. 5:14-15 adds "your ox, or your ass," and gives a long justification for the commandment. (*d*) Exod. 20:11 has a different justification for observing the sabbath. (*e*) To the command to honor one's parents, Deut. 5:16 adds "as the Lord your God commanded you"; it also adds to the promise of long life, "that it may go well with you." (*f*) Deut. 5:20 speaks of "emptiness" (שוא; RSV "false witness"); Exod. 20:16 speaks of "falsehood" (שקר; RSV "false witness"). (*g*) In both passages the last commandment consists of two propositions, but Deut. 5:21*b* has התאוה for the second verb instead of חמד (both meaning "desire, covet") and inverts the words "wife" and "house."

2. Composition. Two elements can be observed in these two parallel passages. First, a series of prohibitions, and second, an editorial element consisting of justifications, enumerations, and a general statement, "I am the Lord your God." If the editorial material is removed, what remains is a series of eleven prohibitions, the last of which seems to be a doublet to the tenth, since Exod. 20:17 repeats the verb חמד.

3. Lists of prohibitions in the ancient Near East. From the ancient world we have lists analogous to the series of prohibitions in the Decalogue, but they do not consist of ten elements, and they are not in the form of prohibitions.

The best known of these are the lists in ch. 125 of the Egyptian "Book of the Dead" (New Kingdom). Maystre termed them "declarations of innocence." The dead person declared in the first person before the tribunal of Osiris, "I have not stolen . . . etc." Similar lists are found in the stela of Ramses IV at Abydos. The late papyrus of Jumilhac does not contain declarations but a simple list of forbidden acts (ch. xviii). These lists seem originally to have belonged to sanctuaries in various districts and described prohibited actions.

In Babylonia at the New Year Festival the king made a similar protestation of his innocence. We also have lists of wrongs committed. They are in the third person and were pronounced by the priest-exorcist, as, for example in the series of *Šurpu:* "He entered his neighbor's house, had intercourse with his neighbor's wife, shed his neighbor's blood." Some of these lists date from the Old Babylonian period (1800 B.C.), and seem to have been compiled in the Kassite period (sixteenth-twelfth centuries B.C.).

These lists may be compared to stipulations in treaties imposed by a sovereign on a vassal (*see* COVENANT §C; COVENANT, MOSAIC[S] §4). These treaties are of little help in establishing the list of ten commandments, but may cast light on some editions of the Decalogue.

4. The different commandments. There are variations even in the traditional enumerations. Origen and Clement of Alexandria were followed by Augustine and the Catholic and Lutheran churches in distinguishing coveting the neighbor's wife and his house as separate commandments. On the other hand, they place together in one commandment the prohibition of worshiping other Gods and that of making images. The Talmud, however, and Philo, the Eastern churches, and the Reformed Churches separate these two commandments and see the prohibitions of covetousness as constituting only one.

One factor in arriving at a solution is the observation that Exod. 20 contains a number of Deuteronomic expressions, such as "the Lord your God." The dual form of the last commandment is the result of the Deuteronomic recension, or of the anomalous situation in which "house" precedes "wife."

5. The Ten Commandments as contained in the Bible. On this basis it is possible to establish an original list of "ten words" that can all be explained in the cultural milieu of the second millennium B.C.: (*a*) prohibition of images (פסל) set up to assure the presence of the god in the sanctuary; (*b*) prohibition of worshiping idols that represent other gods; (*c*) prohibition of serving them; (*d*) prohibition of taking unnecessary oaths in the name of Yahweh; (*e*) prohibition of working on the sabbath; (*f*) prohibition of committing murder (רצח) under conditions that do not confer the right of asylum; (*g*) prohibition of sexual violence; (*h*) prohibition of stealing (according to Alt, kidnaping, but in other lists the prohibition is general); (*i*) prohibition of accusing a neighbor falsely; (*j*) prohibition of seizing a neighbor's house (חמד dealt originally with an act and not covetousness, cf. Herrmann). This list may have been compiled by Moses and preserved by his Priestly successors. Like the Egyptian lists, it determined the possibility of participating or not participating in cultic activities, as Mowinckel has shown by comparing it with the liturgies used on entering a sanctuary (Pss. 15 and 24). Its originality consists in its having the form of prohibitions, which reminds us of both the wisdom traditions and the covenant formulas.

Inscribed on tables of stone, this list found a place in Solomon's temple (I Kings 8:9). This explains the importance ascribed to it by Deuteronomy, which was dependent on both wisdom literature and covenant formulas. The Deuteronomic edition of the commandments underscored the direct intervention of "the Lord your God, who brought you out of the land of Egypt." It instilled respect for parents and required observance of the sabbath, and not merely a refraining from work. It gave to חמד the meaning "covet," and listed both violence toward the neighbor's house and toward his wife, placing the latter first. It insisted on the prohibition of images and the demands of monotheism, producing thereby the expanded form of the first part of the text.

The Decalogue became the basis of all Israelite legislation. It was placed at Sinai, prior to the covenant regulations and the conclusion of the covenant (Exod. 20:24–24:12), and thus belongs to the central revelation of the Mosaic religion.

Bibliography. J. J. Stamm, with M. E. Andrew, *The Ten Commandments in Recent Research* (1967); R. H. Charles, *The Decalogue* (2nd ed., 1926); G. Reventlow, *Gebot und Predigt im Dekalog* (1962); E. Nielsen, *Die zehn Gebote, eine traditions-geschichtliche Skizze* (1965); H. Cazelles, "Les Origines du Decalogue," *Eretz Israel*, IX (1969), 14-19; J. Herrmann, "Das zehnte Gebot," *Sellin Festschrift* (1927), pp. 69-82; C. Maystre, *Les Déclarations d'innocence* (1937); A. Alt, *Kleine Schriften* (1953) I, 333-40.

H. CAZELLES

TENUPHA. *See* WAVE OFFERING[S].

TERUMA. *See* HEAVE OFFERING[S].

***TESTAMENTS OF THE TWELVE PATRIARCHS, THE.** The interweaving of Jewish and Christian materials, including sections of unquestionable affinity with the literature from Qumran (*see* DEAD SEA SCROLLS; DEAD SEA SCROLLS[S]), has prevented any consensus on questions of original language, date, and provenance. Recent scholarship has directed itself particularly to the establishment of reliable texts and to the criticism of textual transmission.

1. The text. The work has been preserved in Greek, Armenian, and Slavonic versions, and during the last decade the number of available MSS has steadily grown. M. de Jonge's *editio minor* of the Greek text is based on Cambridge MS Ff. 1.24, thus reversing previous evaluations. This MS and those related to it will occupy a prominent place in the full critical edition. A number of newly discovered Greek witnesses will also be used in that edition. The Armenian MSS (over fifty are now known) have also been further investigated, and their importance for the study of the Greek text evaluated. The Slavonic version seems of less significance.

Study of the MSS of the Testament of Levi from Qumran continues, as well as of 4Q Visions of Amram, a work discovered at Qumran which may be associated with the Aramaic Testament of Levi. These works form a body of material in which priestly figures play a central role.

2. Criticism. The character of the Greek text remains a chief question. Are the Christian passages mere interpolations, or is the present form of the Greek work a Christian edition of older Jewish materials? Some have sought to minimize the extent of Christian interpolation by regarding many passages, previously held to be Christian, as ESSENE in origin. Other critics distinguish a Jewish-Christian interpolator at the earliest level, or a very limited Jewish-Hellenistic *Grundschrift* from late pre-Hasmonean days which reached its present shape by a complex process of expansion, interpolation, etc. The relationship between the Aramaic Testament of Levi and the Greek version has also received preliminary investigation.

Bibliography. General: O. Eissfeldt, *The OT: An Introduction* (3rd ed., 1964), pp. 631-36, 775; D. Flusser, "Patriarchs, Testaments of the Twelve," *Encyclopaedia Judaica*, XIII (1971), cols. 184-86; M. de Jonge, "Recent Studies on the Testaments of the Twelve Patriarchs," *SEA*, XXXVI (1971), 77-96, summary of recent literature; C. Burchard, J. Jervell, and J. Thomas, *Studien zu den Testamenten der Zwölf Patriarchen*, BZNW, XXXVI (1969); M. de Jonge, ed., *Studies on the Testaments of the Twelve Patriarchs: Text and Interpretation* (1975).

Text and Versions: Greek: M. de Jonge, ed., *Testamenta XII Patriarcharum*, Pseudepigrapha Veteris Testamenti Graece, I (2nd. ed., 1970); on the future *editio maior*, H. J. de Jonge, "Die Textüberlieferung der Testamente der Zwölf Patriarchen," *ZNW*, LXIII (1972), 27-44. Armenian: Burchard *et al.*, BZNW, XXXVI (*cited above*); M. E. Stone, "The Jerusalem Manuscripts of the Testaments of the Twelve Patriarchs," *Sion*, XLIV (1970), 29-35, *The Testament of Levi* (1969), and "Methodological Issues in the Study of the Text of the Apocrypha and Pseudepigrapha," *Proceedings of the Fifth World Congress of Jewish Studies* (1971), pp. 211-17. Slavonic: E. Turdeanu, "Les Testaments des douze Patriarches en Slave," *JSJ*, I (1970), 148-84. Qumran fragments: J. T. Milik, "Problèmes de la littérature Hénochique à la lumière des fragments araméens de Qumrân," *HTR*, LXIV (1971), 333-78, and "4Q Visions de 'Amram et une citation d' Origène," *RB*, LXXIX (1972), 77-97. On the relationship of Aramaic and Greek: M. de Jonge, "Notes on Test. Levi II–VII," *Travels in the World of the OT*, ed. M. S. H. G. Heerma van Voss *et al.* (1974), 132-45.

Criticism: M. de Jonge, "Christian Influence in the Testaments of the Twelve Patriarchs," *NovT*, IV (1960), 182-235; J. Becker, *Untersuchungen zur Entstehungsgeschichte der Testamente der Zwölf Patriarchen*, AGJU, VIII (1970); D. Haupt, "Das Testament Levi" (diss., Halle-Wittenberg, 1969); A. Hultgård, "Croyances Messianiques des Testaments des XII Patriarches," (diss., Uppsala, 1971); H. J. de Jonge, "La Bibliothèque de Michel Choniates et la tradition occidentale des Test. XII Patr.," *Nederl. Archief voor Kerkgeschiedenis*, LIII (1973), 171-80.

M. E. STONE

TETRAGRAMMATON tĕt' rä grâm'ä tŏn [τετραγράμματον, "(the) four letters"]. The four Hebrew consonants (יהוה) contained in the proper name of Israel's god. For discussion of the ancient pronunciation and earliest form of the name, *see* GOD, NAMES OF §B2; for its meaning, §B3; for the process whereby the epithet אדני, "[the] Lord," was read (*qᵉrê*) as a substitute when the written form (*kᵉthîbh*) was encountered, *see* §C6. *See also* LORD; JEHOVAH; QERE-KETHIBH[S].

TETRATEUCH. *See* CANON OF THE OT[S] §1*c*.

***TEXT, HEBREW, HISTORY OF.** After a period marked by the multiplication of various consonantal text forms, a standardized consonantal Hebrew text of the Bible attained normative status about the end of the first or the beginning of the second century A.D. *See* TEXT, OT §2.

Then, after another period marked by the proliferation of punctuations (vowels and accents), and of various types of Masora, a system of punctuation and of Masora was perfected toward the end of the ninth or the beginning of the tenth century A.D. From that time it acquired virtually normative authority. *See* TEXT, OT §§3-6.

1. Standardizing the consonantal text
   a. Early diversity
      i. The theory of local texts
      ii. Precanonical fluidity
   b. Unification of the consonantal text
      i. Learned preference for archaic text forms
      ii. The Proto-MT
      iii. The process of fixing the consonantal text
2. Standardizing punctuation and Masora
   a. The Babylonian school
   b. The Palestinian school
   c. Supremacy of the school of Tiberias
   d. Survival of other types

Bibliography

1. Standardizing the consonantal text. *a. Early diversity.* Before the discovery of the Qumran MSS, (*see* DEAD SEA SCROLLS and supplementary article) the only important sources of consonantal variants antedating the time of standardization were the SEPTUAGINT and the SAMARITAN PENTATEUCH. We do have other ancient witnesses to the Hebrew text, viz., the Hexaplaric material (Theodotion, Aquila, Symmachus, the Quinta, and transcriptions of the second column; *see* GREEK VERSIONS, MINOR[S]), the VULGATE and SYRIAC, the various TARGUMS, rabbinic citations, the Arabic version of Sa'adya, and the variants in medieval biblical MSS. All this material, however, postdates the period of textual standardization; it can offer only variants that somehow survived the standardizing process. Biblical quotations in the Apocrypha and Pseudepigrapha, in the NT, and in Hellenistic Jewish sources are too sparse to be a helpful source of variants, or simply follow the LXX tradition. Finally, the Samaritikon, i.e., the Greek version of the Samaritans, is known only through a few fragments.

With the Samaritan Pentateuch (*see* TEXTUAL CRITICISM, OT[S] §1*b*; TEXT, OT §B), we possess a witness in Hebrew to the entire TORAH, which bears direct comparison with the MT. Moreover, its textual tradition is remarkably consistent and was carefully maintained by those to whom it was entrusted. Gesenius, however, proved that virtually all the variants in Samar. could be reduced to eight types of retouches, modifying a basic text preserved intact by the MT.

Because it covers the whole OT, the witness of the LXX is particularly valuable (*see* TEXT, OT §C1). Yet because it is a translation, the evidence it affords for its Hebrew *Vorlage* remains ambiguous. It is not surprising, then, that scholars have interpreted the evidence in very different fashions. Wellhausen (1871) drew from the LXX text of Samuel a great number of Hebrew variants, which he considered generally preferable to the MT. On the other hand, Nyberg (1935), basing himself on the text of Hosea, found the LXX full of faulty interpretations, though based on a consonantal *Vorlage* very close to the MT. As often happens, the critical pendulum swung to and fro between the two opinions; but by the time the first Qumran scrolls were discovered (1947), it was Nyberg's view that held the field. Scholars were more and more reluctant to admit that every variant of the LXX was based on a Hebrew *Vorlage* distinct from the MT. Divergencies, they thought, were to be found most often on the level of interpretation.

Following the discovery in Qumran Cave I of the large Isaiah scroll (1QIs[a]), and especially of the thousands of fragments from Cave IV, scholars were faced with an abundance of texts, typologically extremely varied, and covering every book of the Hebrew canon except Esther. Moreover, certain MSS of the same book, through the characteristic variants they contained, seemed to be linked to the textual family of Samar. or of the LXX *Vorlage*. Less frequently, a MS contained a text that was evidently a prototype, more or less direct, of the MT. For fuller description, *see* TEXT, OT §A1; DEAD SEA SCROLLS and supplementary article.

The most striking aspect of these discoveries, then, was a profusion of Hebrew variants of such consequence that the apparent monolithic structure of the MT suddenly disintegrated. In effect, in the period just before A.D. 68, we have a textual situation both varied and fluid in a Jewish community that was well settled and spiritually integrated.

i. *The theory of local texts*. The first preoccupation of scholars was to try to bring some order into this textual chaos. Drawing on his expert knowledge of the unpublished fragments from Cave IV, Cross proposed a theory of "local texts." For the Pentateuch, he distinguished three text forms, which maintained their separate identity only because they developed in different geographical milieus: (*a*) a type marked by expansions, both in text and orthography, attested by several Qumran MSS, and by the Samar. as a late collateral witness; (*b*) the short, relatively pristine text preserved in the MT; (*c*) the LXX *Vorlage*, already clearly distinct from the earliest Qumran exemplars, yet much closer to the first textual type than to the second. The first type originated in Palestine. The Egyptian origin of the LXX points to Egypt as the locale of the third type. The second type must have been located in an area that was, so to speak, a textual refrigerator, i.e., where evolution was very slow. Only thus can we explain the stability of its sober text and the persistence of its archaic orthography. For Cross, a Babylonian milieu meets these requirements. In the case of Samuel, too, Cross rediscovers his three text forms, with their distinct places of origin. The 4Q fragments represent the Palestinian text; the *Vorlage* of the ancient LXX stems from Egypt; and the place of origin of the Proto-MT is probably Babylon. For Jeremiah, there are only two text forms, since the Proto-Masoretic and Palestinian combine here. There is, first, a long text, attested at Qumran by 4QJer[a] (end of the third century B.C.) and 4QJer[c] (no earlier than the end of the first century B.C.). Second, there is a short form, represented by the LXX *Vorlage* and by 4QJer[b] (from the Hasmonean period). Cross holds that this form developed in Egypt. In the case of Isaiah, Cross believes that all the seventeen MSS from 1Q and 4Q are congeners of the archetype of the MT. The LXX *Vorlage,* though belonging to a different textual tradition, is closely allied, and shares the expansionist or "full" attributes of the Proto-Masoretic tradition. *See* SAMARITAN PENTATEUCH[S] §2*c;* SEPTUAGINT[S] §A1*e.*

Cross's theory of local texts has been favorably received by some (e.g., Skehan), but sharply criticized by others (e.g., Goshen-Gottstein and Talmon). Cross was convinced that only geographical isolation could explain the facts, viz., the persistence over some centuries of several clearly distinct textual forms, some of which remained remarkably stable while others developed by way of expansions, i.e., harmonizing parallel passages and modernizing grammar and orthography. To this it may be objected that we know practically nothing about the literary vitality—or lack of it—in Babylonian Judaism during the period from Ezra to Hillel. Neither are we any better informed on any alleged literary competence in Hebrew on the part of Egyptian Jews of the same period. Again, while there are solid reasons for holding that the Greek translations of the Pentateuch and Chronicles were made in Egypt from Hebrew texts (which could have been recently imported), it is equally probable that the Greek translation of the Psalter was made in Palestine. As for the Greek version of Samuel and Kings, there is no difficulty in holding that it was brought from Palestine to Alexandria toward the beginning of the second century B.C. The same was true for the translation of Esther about the beginning of the following century. We cannot, therefore, automatically qualify as Egyptian every Hebrew *Vorlage* of a book of the LXX. A further objection is this: how is one to tell if two MSS belong to the same or to different text types? This is more or less a matter of personal judgment. Thus, Cross assigns to the same textual family the MT of Isaiah, the two Isaiah scrolls from 1Q, and the fifteen fragmentary scrolls from 4Q—though he holds that, in the case of the Pentateuch, three types of text are represented at Qumran. Talmon's opinion is exactly the opposite. He holds that, in the Hebrew tradition of the Pentateuch at Qumran, we can observe the same relative textual compactness and the same relative sparseness of variant readings which have already been pointed out in the LXX Pentateuch. On the other hand, he continues, the extant copies of the book of Isaiah and, above all, the complete 1QIs[a] present us with a great richness of variant readings. Besides, even if agreement were reached on this point, it would seem strange that the same Egyptian environment should lead to diametrically opposite results, i.e., a short and primitive text form in the case of Jeremiah, and a full and conflate text—as Cross puts it—for most of the other books of the Bible. Finally, the most weighty objection to the theory of local texts arises from the content of the Qumran library itself. There, in A.D. 68 (when the settlement was destroyed by Vespasian's armies), we have the library of a community that spiritually was closely knit, since, in all probability, it formed the central monastery of the Essenes. Now, side by side in that library, we have the two textual traditions that are consistently divergent, those of Jeremiah; and—what is still more striking—they had co-existed there for nearly two centuries, since the Proto-Masoretic tradition is represented by a MS copied in the Hasmonean period. Realizing this difficulty, Cross supposed that this MS must have been copied in Egypt and only later introduced into Qumran. *See also* DEAD SEA SCROLLS[S] §4.

ii. *Precanonical fluidity.* The problem must, however, be posed on a broader basis. It is not simply a matter of different text forms, but a matter of a plurality of redactional traditions. Why, in fact, when comparing the Hebrew *Vorlage* of the LXX version of Jeremiah with the Proto-MT, should we imagine that the first must be an abbreviation of the second or, alternatively, the second an expansion of the first? Actually, as Tov points out, the differences between the MT and the LXX in the case of Jeremiah are more striking than would be expected of two text types. First, the two texts diverge broadly in their arrangement of material. Second, both in prose and in poetic sections the MT expansions contain many authentic elements and numerous Deuteronomic additions. It is therefore more accurate to say that the MT and the LXX are witnesses to two distinct, though related, redactional traditions. We must conclude, then, that the two forms of the book of Jeremiah came into being during a precanonical period marked by redactional fluidity. This in no way prevented both of them being used as sacred Scripture at Qumran. This again will occasion no surprise if we recall that—even after the canon was fixed—parallel, though differing, accounts from Kings and Chronicles were read side by side in Pharisaic Judaism.

Furthermore—a point that emerges clearly only in recent studies—we must not impose a post-canonical conception of Scripture on the Qumran community. It appears likely that both their sacred library as a whole and the literary structure of certain of its books were still in a state of openness. This does not mean, however, that all was uncertain, with no distinction between the Word of God and the literary creations of men. The canonization of the Pentateuch was already a thing of the past (*see* CANON OF THE OT §2 and supplementary article §§1, 4*a*). The prophetic writings, too, were read as the Word of God (*see* CANON OF THE OT §3 and supplementary article §2*b*).

However, they had no more reason for eliminating one of the two recensions of Jeremiah than had the early Christians for eliminating three out of the four versions of the gospel of Jesus Christ.

As regards the Psalms, it was their firm belief that David had composed under inspiration 3,600 psalms and 450 canticles (11QPs[a], col. 27). J. A. Sanders is probably correct in maintaining that the various Qumran Psalters—whether normal in order and content, or with a special sequence (4QPs[a,b,d]), or including apocryphal psalms (4QPs[f], 11QPs[a])—were all read as Holy Scripture. It is surely an anachronism to consider these Psalters as just "library editions," or as the earliest examples of Jewish prayer books. Rather, there were two types of MSS at Qumran: one in which the collection of 150 psalms was fixed in structure and content; the other in which, so to speak, it continued to put forth new shoots. On the one hand there was a nucleus—the major part of the collection—firmly embedded in all the MSS, which became the object of the community's *Pesharim* (*see* DEAD SEA SCROLLS §5*a*). On the other hand certain MSS presented a collection that was still open-ended. Somewhat the same can be said about the status of the *Kethûbhîm* as a whole (*see* CANON OF THE OT §4). Together with David's poems, Solomon's wisdom writings were certainly used as Scripture, but what were the precise limits of this collection? There is every reason for thinking that the eleven copies of Jubilees and the ten of Enoch were regarded as bearers of divine revelation to a higher degree than Ezra and Chronicles (one copy of each) or Esther (not represented at all). And what of Tobit, with its four Aramaic and one Hebrew MSS? Who can say? The fact that this book was incorporated into the codices of the LXX makes it probable, though not certain, that the Semitic texts were regarded as Scripture at Qumran. Ecclesiasticus, too, was well known at Qumran. Several rabbis of the Talmudic era were to quote it as Scripture. How sacred was this book considered by the community of the new covenant? Whatever the answer, they must surely have considered even more sacred the Rule of the Community, known from fourteen copies (*see* DEAD SEA SCROLLS §5*b*). Apropos of this document—and the same can be said of the ten copies of the Damascus Document (*see* ZADOKITE FRAGMENTS), the seven copies of the *Hodayoth* (*see* DEAD SEA SCROLLS §5*d*), and the seven of the War Scroll (*see* DEAD SEA SCROLLS §5*c*)—could we not speak of a "reopening" of the canon, analogous to that which took place with the early Christian community? Still, this would be an anachronism in both instances, for we cannot speak formally of a closing of the canon, or even of a canon itself (i.e., a closed list of sacred books) in Judaism prior to the end of the first century A.D.

It would seem, therefore, that the Qumran MSS reflect a list of sacred writings that was still open, i.e., where some books have a well-established and time-honored place, while others—especially from the Apoc. and Pseudep.—were admitted only after their supposed authenticity was accepted by the community. It is altogether likely that certain books remained in a marginal position, as *antilegomena*. Some would have used them as sacred, while others doubted their authenticity. It was likewise to be expected that certain collections, such as the Psalms of David, would remain open; some added certain poems, others excluded them. In any event, it would be a serious misconception to limit the significance of the Qumran library to the question of the history of the biblical text. Rather, this question is part of a larger problem—that of the prehistory of the canon of sacred Scripture—and its true meaning can be appreciated only in this context.

Viewed in this light, the theory of local texts appears much too narrow. The same physical laws do not apply to liquid lava and to the crystalline rocks which it produces on solidifying. The history of the text begins only when a definite literary structure emerges in solid form. In fact, it can be said that the whole process of crystallizing the OT text involves four successive phases. First comes the assured conviction that a certain book is sacred Scripture. This conviction, in turn, leads with greater or less rapidity to a literary crystallizing of the book into one or more traditions, in which no more deliberate redactional additions are permitted. Once assured from the literary angle, the book will then be transmitted by copyists of varying caliber. In the process the text would undergo corruption to a greater or lesser extent, whether by slips in writing, conjectural emendations, harmonizations, concealed theological corrections (*see* TEXT, OT §A3; EMENDATIONS OF THE SCRIBES[S]; QERE-KETHIBH[S]), or by modernization in orthography and grammar. Finally, the community which regards the text as sacred would endeavor to counteract this corruption by a fresh attempt at stabilizing the text. In line with the requirements of Hebrew writing, this attempt would proceed by two stages: first, a fixing of the consonantal text, and second, the invention of supplementary signs to ensure correct reading.

b. Unification of the consonantal text. i. *Learned preference for archaic text forms.* Just as widely divergent literary traditions of the same book (e.g., Jeremiah) are represented at Qumran, so too, we find there several textual forms of the same literary tradition (e.g., the Pentateuch or Isaiah). Roberts (*see* TEXT, OT §A1) has pointed out that the principal contribution of the Qumran discoveries to the history of the text does not consist in the great number of readings that diverge from the MT. Rather, as comparison of 1QIs[a] with 1QIs[b] shows, the major contribution was to show that, alongside popular texts marked by manifold corruptions, there existed some carefully executed MSS. They were restrained and conservative in orthography, and their scribes had scrupulously preserved difficult readings which other MSS had altered or eliminated and incongruities which others had smoothed over. To be sure, the value set at Qumran on a conservative MS such as 1QIs[b] was not so high as to necessitate the correction or elimination of 1QIs[a], which was hidden away in the same cave as a treasure of equal value. Yet it is important to remember that 1QIs[b] is 100 years (Avigad) or 150 years (Birnbaum) more recent than 1QIs[a]. This shows that at the end of the Herodian period some scribes continued to reproduce an archaic and difficult text (1QIs[b]) in preference to one that was easier, more developed, and replete with *matres lectionis*. *See* TEXT, OT §4*b*.

Although 1QIs[b] already exhibits those characteristic readings which the MT of Isaiah would reproduce and therefore fits exactly into the pre-Masoretic line of descent, it would not do to call it Proto-Masoretic, since it does not yet have those distinctive features of consonantal script which are the hallmarks of the MT. It is not surprising that scholarly texts of this kind, recent as regards copying but ancient in respect to their prototypes, should be somewhat rare at Qumran. An analogous situation exists for the biblical fragments of the Cairo Genizah. There we have an abundance of copies made with little care, or pretentious in appearance but poor in quality, while exemplars executed with genuine skill and carefulness are a small minority. *See* TEXT, OT §A5.

ii. *The Proto-MT*. Turning now to the caves of the Second Revolt, those of the Wadi Murabba'at and of Naḥal Ḥever, we find that the only biblical text represented there is one which truly deserves the name Proto-Masoretic (*see* TEXT, OT §A1*b*; MANUSCRIPTS FROM THE JUDEAN DESERT[S] §2). It was for this reason that its discovery aroused so little interest in those who published the fragments. They were content to remark briefly, and somewhat disappointedly, "the text and the spelling are identical with the MT." Yet in reality this was one of the most significant contributions made by the discoveries in the desert of Judea. In the year A.D. 68, archaic and carefully executed biblical texts occupied only a small place in the library of the community of the New Covenant. Yet it was a text of this type that ousted all other text forms and became the Holy Scripture of the refugees of Wadi Murabba'at and Naḥal Ḥever. The same text furnished the consonantal basis for the work of the Masoretes 750 years later.

In spite of some persistent peculiarities of script, the fragments from the Second Revolt exhibit those rare orthographic features and accidental changes that unquestionably identify them with the consonantal text attested by the Masoretes. For example, in the Psalms fragment from the Cave of Letters, we have the defective script *ymr* for the imperfect indicative *Hiph'îl* of the verb *mwr* (Ps. 15:4)—a form which the *Masora parva* was to deem worthy of preservation by noting its unique character. In the fragments of the scroll of the minor prophets from Murabba'at, we find instances of the first-person singular imperfect *Hiph'îl* of the verb *bw'*. Now the final *'āleph* is present in Zeph. 3:20 as in the MT, while it is wanting in Mic. 1:15, a point confirmed by the *Masora parva* (*see* TEXT, OT §4*a*). With regard to *matres lectionis,* it can be established that these MSS were revised so as to conform to a particular prototype. For instance, in another fragment from Murabba'at, the word *'ḥtnw* in Gen. 34:31 is corrected to *'ḥwtnw* (as in MT). In turn, the *Masora parva* will note this *scriptio plena* as a *hapax*. So, too, in the scroll of the minor prophets from the same locality, the corrector adds a *yōdh* at Amos 9:8 to give *hšmyd, scriptio plena* of the infinitive absolute *Hiph'îl*—once again noted subsequently by the *Masora parva* as a *hapax*. In conclusion, all the scribal corrections in the biblical MSS from the caves of the Second Jewish War serve to bring the text closer to the consonantal *Vorlage* of the MT.

Though they have left us no treatise or marginal glosses explaining their working principles, the men we see in action here are the real Proto-Masoretes, contemporary with Akiba (*see* TEXT, OT §A3*b*). Moreover, at this time (the Second Revolt), the successful labor of fixing the consonantal text had already gone beyond the limits of the biblical texts in synagogal usage. The alternation of *scriptio plena* and *scriptio defectiva* in the text of phylacteries had already been clearly determined. The Murabba'at phylactery text illustrates this as follows: *yby'k* (*scriptio plena*) in Exod. 13:5, and *scriptio defectiva* in Exod. 13:11; *ṭwṭpt* (*scriptio plena*) in Exod. 13:16, contrasted with *scriptio defectiva* in Deut. 6:8; *mzwzwt* (*scriptio plena*) in Deut. 11:20, and *scriptio defectiva* in Deut. 6:9; *ydkh* in Exod. 13:16, and *scriptio defectiva* in Exod. 13:9 and Deut. 6:8. Reading these details of orthography is like having the MT before one's eyes.

iii. *The process of fixing the consonantal text.* The existence of 1QIs[b] proves that toward the close of the Herodian era certain qualified scribes were disseminating an archaic text of the kind that would soon be retained by those who finally fixed the consonantal text. So, too, the Greek fragments of the minor prophets found in one of the Naḥal Ḥever caves show that in the first decades of the Christian era certain editors of the Pharisaic tradition were revising the LXX to bring it also into conformity with a text of the type later accepted as the standard consonantal text (*see* GREEK VERSIONS, MINOR[S]). There is no proof that a parallel work of recension took place in the same milieu for the Hebrew text of the Bible. It is probable, however, that before the Second Revolt a vigorous reaction against the current corruption of the Hebrew text had already commenced in Pharisaic circles. Nonetheless, it was the catastrophe of A.D. 70 that had the most decisive effect on the work of standardizing the text. This was but one of the many measures of conservation and defense that were then adopted to save Judaism.

By "text" should we understand a textual family, or a MS? The answer to this question may be found by comparing 1QIs[b] with the biblical fragments or phylacteries of the Second Revolt. 1QIs[b] belongs to the same textual family as the consonantal MT, but is not its direct ancestor, for the latter differs in certain textual options and accidental orthographic variants of long standing. On the other hand, the MSS and phylacteries of the Second Revolt, especially in their scribal corrections, show distinctive peculiarities of script—*plena* or *defectiva* of unusual type and other abnormalities—so distinctive that they betray a conscious effort to disseminate the text of a particular MS. Thus textual standardization must have been effected principally by careful copying of one text chosen as normative. Together with this there surely went the task of correcting existing MSS. A certain number not considered worth correcting must have been consigned to the genizah. For another perspective, *see* QERE-KETHIBH[S] §8*d*.

2. Standardizing punctuation and Masora. We may be sure that even before the Second Revolt the scribes were not satisfied merely with reproducing a text regarded as normative. They also orally transmitted *sîmânim,* i.e., easily remembered catchwords, to denote certain orthographic details of the text. For example, Jehudah ben Bathirah, who taught at Nisibis in Upper Mesopotamia and died *ca.* A.D. 90, used the *sîmân mym* (water) to indicate distinctive features of the text of Num. 29:12-38, which details the sacrifices offered during the eight days of the Feast of Booths. Cf. Sifre Numbers.

a. The Babylonian school. It was surely not by chance that the earliest Masorete whose name has come down to us (*above*) lived in Babylonia. If Babylonia followed Palestinian norms for establishing the standard text of the Pentateuch, it maintained somewhat different traditions for the text of the Prophets and the Writings. For these books, and for them alone, there exist traditional lists of variants that distinguish the Babylonian consonantal text from that of Palestine. This is due to the fact that Babylonia very quickly developed a Masoretic activity that was relatively autonomous. Indeed, the Babylonians did not confine their activities to establishing, by their Masora, a standard biblical text. They revised according to the Hebrew the prolix and disordered Palestinian Targums, and, by means of a special Masora, fixed the text of the so-called Targ. of Onkelos; this, too, was read in the liturgy. The interpretative material attached to the MT—the two Masoroth, together with vocalization and accentuation—was transmitted orally for a long time. It was in fact—as in principle it still is today—forbidden to add the least sign to the consonantal text of the Torah scrolls used in synagogue worship. Hence the scribe had to look outside the text for the information necessary to evaluate its authenticity, and so did the reader. This included matters of vocalization, rhythm, and modulation. The first edition of the Masora in Babylon took the form of running commentaries which followed the text word by word without being incorporated into it. Fragments of these commentaries for the Pentateuch and for the Prophets have come to light. It seems unlikely that such commentaries existed for the Writings, which were not read in the sabbath liturgy. The fact that these commentaries cite the opening word of each verse—whereas the synagogue scrolls do not indicate where the verse begins—tends to show that they were designed to help not only the scribe but also the synagogue lector. At all events, it was for purposes of synagogal reading that the *serûgîn* were composed; i.e., for each verse, only the first word was written completely, followed by each letter in the rest of the verse that had a disjunctive accent (*see* MASORETIC ACCENTS). A restrained MNEMONIC DEVICE of this kind, designed to teach the traditional modulation used in synagogal reading, presupposes that the vocalization of the text has been committed to memory. From the fourth century A.D., Syrian Christians, in order to distinguish words written with the same consonants, began to employ a point above or below a characteristic letter to denote strong or weak vocalization, e.g., to distinguish the first syllable of a *qâṭel* from that of a *qeṭal* (*see* SYRIAC VERSIONS[S] §1*g*). This rather primitive system was further developed about the seventh century by the eastern Nestorian Syrians, who invented a system of indicating vowels by points above or below the consonants. In the next century, the western Jacobite Syrians worked out another system, substituting Greek vowels for points. At the same time or a little later, and very probably under Syrian influence, the Jews of Babylon invented a system of vocalization and accentuation composed of letters or parts of letters and of points placed above the consonants. In Palestine the most ancient Masoroth witness to the use of points both above and below, in a way that seems virtually identical with that followed by the ancient Syrians (*see* HEBREW LANGUAGE §4; TEXT, OT §A4*b*). The presence of such signs on the liturgical scrolls of the Torah and the *Haphtaroth* (synagogal readings from the Prophets) was forbidden, and yet the need was felt for writing down the authentic vocalization of the biblical text. The solution adopted in Babylon was to copy the biblical books on codices. In them the biblical text could be vocalized and accented, for they were not destined for liturgical use. Certain of these volumes, particularly those containing the Writings, had complementary Masoretic notes written in small characters above certain words, indicating peculiarities of script which might cause trouble to copyists. At the foot of various pages other Masoretic notes supplied statistical information. *See* MASORA.

b. The Palestinian school. At the same time or a little later, a complex and poorly organized system of vocalization developed in Palestine (*see* TEXT, OT §A4*b*; HEBREW LANGUAGE §4). In spite of recent intensive studies, the greatest uncertainty still prevails today regarding the relative and absolute dating of the subgroups of this system. Dietrich, with most of the writers who preceded him, held that this system antedated the Tiberian and evolved from a stage in which not all phonemes were differentiated to one in which they were differentiated. Revell, however, holds that the dialect attested by this vocalic system is more advanced than that represented by the Tiberian.

It is certain in any event that this system, like that of Tiberias, is linked to a type of Masora clearly distinct from that which circulated in Babylon. In essence this Masora is composed of extensive lists detailing all the occurrences of a rare phenomenon in the whole Bible or in one of its parts. The collection *Ochlah we Ochlah* codifies the principal data gathered by the Masoretes of Palestine. Frequently this data is not repeated in the Masora of the MSS. Hence the collection remains indispensable, inasmuch as it furnishes the key to the intentions of those who vocalized the MSS.

c. Supremacy of the school at Tiberias. It was at Tiberias that the most complete and exact system of vocalization was established (*see* TEXT, OT §A4*b*; HEBREW LANGUAGE §4). Of the material that has survived, the oldest dated biblical MS is the codex of the Prophets from the Karaite synagogue of Cairo. This was copied and provided with vowel points and Masora in 896 by Moshe ben Asher, whose son Aaron later pointed and supplied with Masora the celebrated Aleppo Codex, containing the whole Bible. The great renown of this MS is due to the fact that it was probably the only complete MS of the Bible produced by this Masorete. Maimonides referred to it as the normative form of the MT. *See* TEXT, OT §A6.

The rediscovery of the Aleppo Codex has made it clear that MS B19a from Leningrad—chosen by Kahle as basic text for the third edition of Kittel's *Biblia Hebraica* (*see* TEXT, OT §A7*c*), and retained for the *Biblia Hebraica Stuttgartensia*—cannot be regarded as a pure witness to the tradition of Aaron ben Asher. Noteworthy discrepancies exist between the Masora of this MS and its text. Its vocalization, in the state in which it was in A.D. 1008, is some distance removed from the norms laid down by Aaron ben Asher. The gap was bridged only by later correctors. Nevertheless, it must not be imagined that the Aleppo Codex itself is a perfect example of the tradition of Aaron ben Asher, as codified by Mishael ben ʿUzziel, or again, of the Masoretic tradition formulated in Aaron's *Diqduqê ha-Ṭeʿamîm*. These discrepancies led Dotan to question the accepted view that Aaron was responsible for the Aleppo Codex. The authentic form of the text of Aaron ben Asher, then, still awaits precise identification.

Perhaps it should be said that there has never existed a complete MS of the Bible that presented an entirely unified Masoretic tradition. The best fruits of the systematic work of the great Tiberian Masoretes are the well-integrated editions of portions of Scripture, e.g., the Cairo Codex of the Prophets, or the British Museum Codex Or 4445 of the Pentateuch. Very likely the Aleppo Codex represents a final, though imperfect, attempt to bring together all these partial undertakings, by providing the whole Bible with a Masora and a consistent vocalic system. It must also be noted that the accepted criteria for distinguishing authentic Ben Asher Masoretic material are not completely reliable. Scholars still argue about the original form of the *Diqduqê ha-Ṭeʿamîm*. As for the list of agreements and disagreements between ben Asher and ben Naphtali drawn up by Mishael ben ʿUzziel, it is very probable—according to Harkavy, Poznanski, Steinschneider, and Mann—that its author lived in the second half of the twelfth century. It is certain that an earlier list of this kind, now lost, was composed by the Karaite Levi ben al-Ḥassan ben Ali al-Baṣrî during the first half of the eleventh century. Furthermore, Mishael ben ʿUzziel specifies on several occasions that the two Masoretes changed their positions on certain points in the course of their careers. This explains why a particular work of Aaron ben Asher does not correspond in every respect with a list which is, perhaps, not a firsthand work, and which could be based on other writings of the same Aaron. *See* TEXT, OT §A6.

According to Jacob ben Ephraim, about the beginning of the tenth century the Babylonian tradition governing the correct reading of the biblical text prevailed from the borders of China to the mouth of the Euphrates and down to Yemen, while the Palestinian tradition was much less widespread. However, Jacob's contemporary, who relates his testimony—Abu Yusuf Yaʿqûb al-Qirqisâni—states that educated Jews of all areas were at one in holding that only the Palestinian scholars had maintained in its purity the authentic pronunciation of biblical Hebrew.

How are we to define the relation between the Palestinian vocalic system and that of Tiberias? Kahle held that the Palestinian system was obviously more ancient, while Revell concluded that the Tiberian system clearly represented a more pristine state of the language. We may concede that the Palestinian system represents the pronunciation current among Palestinian rabbis of the period. On the other hand, there are good reasons for believing that the Tiberian system was invented by the Masoretes and grammarians of Tiberias.

The authors of the lists of disagreements mention as of equal standing Abu Saʿid Aaron ben Moshe ben Asher, and Abu Imrân Moshe ben David ben Naphtali. The differences that separate these two, though extensive, are slight and hardly ever change the interpretation of the text. We know nothing certain of the religious affiliations of ben Naphtali. As regards the ben Asher family, immediately following the rediscovery of the Aleppo Codex, Ben-Zvi tried to show that they were not Karaites; however, recent discoveries by Allony and Yeivin seem to have weighed the balance decisively in favor of the contrary position. Be this as it may, it is certain that it was the Karaites who drew up the lists of agreements and divergencies between the Masoretes of Tiberias. It is also certain that the majority of Jewish scholars soon acknowledged the superiority of those MSS, prototypes of the MT, of which these Karaites were guardians. The Tiberian MT won acceptance as the most accurate and scholarly edition of the consonantal text that had been fixed about the end of the first century A.D., an edition, moreover, which included the most faithful notation of that traditional pronunciation of the text judged most authentic by the learned Jews of the ninth century.

d. Survival of other types. The Tiberian tradition did not entirely supplant its rivals. Yemen has maintained down to the present day the Babylonian vocalic notation, though in reality, under this outward form a Tiberian type of vocalization has gradually crept in. In northern Europe ancient MSS may be encountered which use signs of a Tiberian type to clothe a non-Tiberian phonetic system. Kahle ascribed these MSS to the tradition of ben Naphtali. Morag has proved that it is actually a case of the persistence of Palestinian phonetic in Tiberian dress.

Bibliography. On §1: G. Gesenius, *De pentateuchi samaritani origine, indole et auctoritate commentatio philologico-critica* (1815); J. Wellhausen, *Der Text der Bücher Samuelis* (1871); H. S. Nyberg, *Studien zum Hoseabuche* (1935); F. M. Cross, Jr., "The OT at Qumrân," in *The Ancient Library of Qumran* (2nd ed., 1961), pp. 161-94, "The History of the Biblical Text in the Light of Discoveries in the Judaean Desert," *HTR,* LVII (1964), 281-99, "The Contribution of the Qumrân Discoveries to the Study of the Biblical Text," *IEJ,* XVI (1966), 81-95, and "The Evolution of a Theory of Local Texts," in *Septuagint and Cognate Studies,* II (1972 Proceedings, Society of Biblical Literature), 108-26; P. W. Skehan, "The Biblical Scrolls from Qumran and the Text of the OT," *BA,* XXVIII (1965), 87-100; M. H. Goshen-Gottstein, *The Book of Isaiah, Sample Edition with Introduction* (1965), p. 14, n. 15; S. Talmon, "The OT Text," in *The Cambridge History of the Bible,* I (1970), 194-99; E. Tov, "L'incidence de la critique textuelle sur la critique littéraire dans le livre de Jérémie," *RB,* LXXIX (1972), 189-99; J. A. Sanders, "The Qumran Psalms Scroll (11QPs^a) Reviewed," in *On Language, Culture, and Religion: in Honor of Eugene A. Nida* (1974), pp. 95-99.

On §2: M. H. Goshen-Gottstein, "Hebrew Biblical MSS," *Bibl.,* XLVIII (1967), 243-90; M. Dietrich, *Neue palästinisch punktierte Bibelfragmente* (1968); E. J. Revell, *Hebrew Texts with Palestinian Vocalization* (1970), and "Studies in the Palestinian Vocalization of Hebrew," in *Essays in the Ancient Semitic World,* ed. J. W. Wevers and D. B. Redford (1970), pp. 51-100; A. Dotan, "Was the Aleppo Codex Actually Vocalized by Aharon ben Asher?" *Tarbiz,* XXXIV (1964-65), 136-55, Hebrew; D. S. Loewinger, "The Aleppo Codex or Diqduqe hatteʿamim," *Tarbiz,* XXXVIII (1968-69), 186-204, Hebrew; A. Harkavy, *Ḥadashim gam Yeshenim* (1969-70), pp. 22-25, Hebrew; S. Poznanski, "Miscelle," in *Zeitschrift für hebräische Bibliographie,* IV (1900), 186; M. Steinschneider, *Die arabische Literatur der Juden* (1902), §167; J. Mann, *The Jews in Egypt and in Palestine under the Fâtimid Caliphs,* I (1920), p. 245. The *Kitâb al-Khilaf* of Mishael ben ʿUzziel was published by L. Lipschütz in *Textus,* II (1962), 1-58, Hebrew. On the priority of the list of Levi ben al Ḥassan, *see* L. Lipschütz, "Kitāb al-Khilaf," *Textus,* IV (1964), 3; G. Vajda, "Etudes sur Qirqisâni II," *REJ,* CVII (1946-47), 93, n. 45; P. E. Kahle, *The Cairo Geniza* (2nd ed., 1959), p. 75; N. Allony, ed., *Geniza Fragments of Rabbinic Literature with Palestinian Vocalization* (1973), and " 'Eli ben Yehuda Hannazir and His Treatise 'Kitab 'Uṣul al-Lugha al-'ibranyya'," *Leš,* XXXIV (1969-70), 75-105, 187-209, Hebrew; I. Ben-Zvi, "The Codex of Ben Asher," *Textus,* I (1960), 5-6; N. Allony, "Seder hassimanim," *HUCA,* XXXV (1964), 7-8, Hebrew; I. Yeivin, "The Vocalization of Qere-Kethiv in A," *Textus,* II (1962), 148; P. E. Kahle, *Masoreten des Westens,* II (1930), 45*-68*; S. Morag, "The Vocalization of Codex Reuchlinianus: Is the 'Pre-Masoretic' Bible Pre-Masoretic?" *JSS,* IV (1959), 216-37.

General: To the above-mentioned may be added two recent studies of general interest: Diez Macho, *Manuscritos hebreos y arameos de la Biblia* (1971); G. E. Weil, "La Massorah," *REJ,* CXXXI (1972), 5-104.

D. Barthelemy

***TEXT, NT. 1. Sources.** The most recent information about sources is contained in the official list prepared by Aland in 1963, and regularly brought up to date (*see bibliog.*). For every known document this list contains the officially assigned number, its content, date, material (papyrus, parchment, or paper), number of pages, the number of columns per page, number of lines, its format, and the library where it is preserved. Presently the number of direct witnesses of the Greek text known to us is roughly the following: 86 papyri, 269 uncials, 2,795 minuscles, and 2,207 lectionaries, for a total of 5,357. Actually the true number of witnesses is about 200 less, since some MS fragments preserved in different libraries and designated by different numbers are really a single MS. Of these 5,000-odd witnesses, only 59 contain the whole NT (or once contained it, since some are fragmentary). The major part of the codices contain only a part of the NT, the four gospels, for example.

a. Papyri. Among the more important papyri recently published are:

(i) P^{72} (Cologny-Geneva, Bodmer Library, Papyri Bodmer VII-VIII) contains the letter of Jude and I and II Peter. It has been dated to the third or fourth century, and was published by M. Testuz in 1959.

(ii) P^{75} (Cologny-Geneva, Bodmer Library, Papyri Bodmer XIV-XV) contains much of Luke and John, and was written at the beginning of the third century. Its great importance is in demonstrating the antiquity of the text type contained in Codex Vaticanus B (fourth century). It was published by V. Martin and R. Kasser in 1961.

b. Uncials. The tendency of some recent critics to assign a much earlier date to codex D (05) (Bezae) and D^p (06) (Claromontanus) is noteworthy. The first possibly dates from the fourth century according to E. A. Lowe and H. J. Frede, and the same authors assign the second with certainty to the fifth century.

2. Printed text of the NT. Among recent minor critical editions of the NT, *The Greek NT* (1st ed., 1966) is worthy of note. It presents a critical text prepared by a committee of scholars (presently K. Aland, M. Black, C. M. Martini, B. M. Metzger, A. Wikgren) with a critical apparatus of variants selected for their significance for meaning. For each variant all the representative evidence is listed. A commentary on these variants has been prepared by Metzger.

The International Greek NT Project is still at work on the Gospel of Luke. Another project of *editio critica maior* has in the meantime been undertaken by Aland, Duplacy, and Fischer, who are preparing material on the Catholic epistles.

3. Theory and method. Developments in research since von Soden concern especially the Western text, the Caesarean text, and the Alexandrian and proto-Alexandrian text.

a. The Western text. Von Soden grouped a series of MSS of various origins under his type I (Jerusalem). It soon became clear that it was impossible to study them together, but that it was necessary to distinguish two groups of variants. One group, found especially in codex D (Bezae), was given the name "Western." The other, found in P^{45} and many later MSS (in particular in codex Θ [Koridethi]), had a different origin and history, and was given the name "Caesarean."

Studies of the Western text have not as yet succeeded in discovering the precise origin and development of this text type. B. H. Streeter considered it a local text; Blass suggested that it derived from two different editions of Luke-Acts produced by the original author; J. R. Harris and D. Ploij proposed its derivation (for the gospels) from an ancient gospel harmony, while Epp sought to demonstrate that many of the variants of D in Acts are due to an anti-Judaizing tendency.

Among recent hypotheses it is helpful to recall that of E. Haenchen, who claims to have distinguished several strata in the text of codex D of Acts.

There are, as a matter of fact, many minor variants which seem to be conscious corrections meant to improve the text: e.g., indicating more clearly the subject and object of a clause, expanding the expression, etc. These might be the result of a very ancient revision of the text; they appear also in the gospels, especially in Matthew and Mark, and are documented by Tatian, Justin, Irenaeus, etc.

Other variants appear due to a very diligent reader of the text, who still knew well the situation and traditions of the ancient church. For example, in Acts 3:11 D clarifies that Peter and John leave the temple (understood as the interior part of the sacred precinct) to go to Solomon's gate; in Acts 16:30 D adds the detail that after the earthquake the prisoners who were with Paul and Silas were returned to prison, etc. Haenchen suggests that likewise some "Western noninterpolations" (omissions characteristic of the Western text which Westcott and Hort considered original) belong to this type of variant.

Finally, there are in D (but without support in Syr. or the Fathers) variants which on close examination appear to be either scribal errors or the result of influence of the Latin on the Greek text. Haenchen tends thus to interpret certain expressions characteristic of D which others explain as "Aramaisms." The problem is far from solution.

b. The Caesarean text. It was stated above (§3*a*) that many MSS which von Soden put under group I actually had origins quite different from those of the Western text. The text type evidenced by these readings came, by the 1920s, to be called the Caesarean text.

Already in the nineteenth century W. H. Ferrar had noted the affinity of certain minuscles (13, 69, 124, 346). At the turn of the century K. Lake discovered another group of related MSS (1, 118, 131, 209). After the text of codex Θ (ninth century) became known in 1913, and that of W (fifth century) in 1912 and 1918, Lake and R. P. Blake noted the similarity of text in all these codices. Streeter demonstrated the relation between this text type and that used by Origen and Eusebius, thus tracing its origin to the church of Caesarea in the third century.

After the publication of P^{45}, readings subsequently assumed by the Caesarean text were recognized in it. Accordingly, Ayuso proposed a distinction between a "pre-Caesarean" text (found in P^{45}, W in Mark 5:31–16:20, family 1, family 13) originating probably in Egypt, and perhaps carried to Caesarea by Origen, and a recensional Caesarean form (found in 565, 700, as well as Origen and Eusebius).

These studies, carried out so far only on portions of the Gospel of Mark, must be extended and deepened. The existence of a Caesarean text as a text type really distinct from all the others and clearly defined awaits the confirmation of further research.

c. The Alexandrian and proto-Alexandrian text. Since von Soden it had become customary to call the text type principally represented by codices Vaticanus B and Sinaiticus א the Hesychian recension. Many held that this text type represented the result of a recension at the beginning of the fourth century by Greek scholars in Alexandria, an important center of exegetical activity. But a comparison of B, written toward the mid-fourth century, with P^{75}, written around the beginning of the third century, and published in 1961, has shown that, at least for the gospels of Luke and John, nearly all the characteristic readings of B, in particular those considered the result of learned recension, were already present in P^{75}, and probably also in the common tradition earlier than P^{75} and B. Thus the text at the basis of P^{75} and B could be called "proto-Alexandrian," leaving the name "Alexandrian" for the text found in L, T, 33, and others. It is not denied that the proto-Alexandrian text underwent the influence of some recensional setting, such as Alexandria: that is apparent especially in its aversion to long readings, and for whatever gives suspicion of a gloss of the text—an aversion which could have led in some cases to dropping some traditional reading. But on the whole the proto-Alexandrian text claims a very ancient tradition, which, while it is not exempt from errors and some conscious emendations, has been transmitted by scribes with care and respect for the text.

4. Conclusion. From what has been said, it should be obvious that textual criticism of the NT cannot yet claim to have achieved a clear and detailed history of the text. That does not mean, however, that the critic should indulge in a certain skepticism and be content with an eclectic method which would choose from here or there the proper reading, without averting to the MSS from which it comes, nor to the textual types to which it could be reduced.

There are some facts of the history of the text which seem beyond dispute. It is clear, for example, that the distinctive readings of the Byzantine text are usually secondary. On the other hand, proto-Alexandrian readings cannot be definitively considered recensional; on the contrary, in many cases they have a solid probability of representing a reading current in the second century. Further, systematic study of the character of the typically Western and Caesarean readings in ternary variants seems to show consistently that the Western reading is usually inferior to the alternative reading, and suspect of emendation, while the Caesarean reading (which really offers a genuine alternative only rarely) often appears to be an attempt to emend the text or at least to reconcile earlier readings. A reading that upon examination of the witnesses can be defined as *not* Western, *not*

Caesarean, *not* Byzantine (it was in this negative sense that Westcott and Hort spoke of "neutral" readings) usually appears, to internal criticism as well, closer to the original reading than the alternative readings. Even if these criteria do not offer a general solution for all the problems of the text, they are nonetheless to be kept in mind if the goal is a considered reconstruction of the original which takes into account our present knowledge of the history of the textual tradition. *See also* TEXTUAL CRITICISM, NT[S]; VERSIONS, ANCIENT; LATIN VERSIONS[S].

Bibliography. Information on current problems of textual criticism is published regularly by J. Duplacy in "Bulletin de critique textuelle du NT"; from 1962 to 1966 in *Recherches de science religieuse,* then in *Biblica* since 1968. For the earlier years, see J. Duplacy, *Où en est la critique textuelle du NT?* (1959).

For the sources: K. Aland, *Kurzgefasste Liste der griechischen Handschriften des NT,* ANT, I (1963), corrections and additions in *Materialien zur neutestamentlichen Handschriftenkunde,* I (1969), 1-37, and *Bericht der Stiftung zur Förderung der neutestamentlichen Textforschung* (1974), pp. 11-13.

For the most recent developments in the history of the text see: K. Aland, "Die Bedeutung des P^{75} für den Text des NT. Ein Beitrag zur Frage des 'Western non-interpolations,'" and "Die Konsequenzen der neueren Handschriften für die neutestamentliche Textkritik," *Studien zur Überlieferung des NT und seines Textes,* ANT, II (1967), 155-72, 180-201; B. M. Metzger, *Chapters in the History of NT Textual Criticism,* NTTS, IV (1963), *The Text of the NT: Its Transmission, Corruption and Restoration* (2nd ed., 1968), and *A Textual Commentary on the Greek NT* (1971).

On the Western text: A. F. Klijn, *A Survey of the Researches into the Western Text of the Gospels and Acts* (1949), with a supplement, *Part II: 1949-1969,* NovTSup, XXI (1969); E. J. Epp, *The Theological Tendency of Codex Bezae Cantabrigiensis in Acts,* NTSMS, III (1966); E. Haenchen, *The Acts of the Apostles: A Commentary* (1961 [ET 1971]), pp. 56-60; B. H. Streeter, *The Four Gospels* (4th ed., 1930), pp. 53-127.

On the Caesarean text: T. Ayuso, "Texto cesariense o precesariense?" *Bibl.,* XVI (1935), 369-415.

On the Alexandrian text and codex B: C. M. Martini, *Il problema della recensionalità del codice B alla luce del papiro Bodmer XIV* (1966).

On the versions: M. Black, B. Fischer *et al.,* K. Aland, ed., *Die alten Übersetzungen des NT, die Kirchenväterzitate und Lektionare. Der gegenwärtige Stand ihrer Erforschung und ihre Bedeutung für die griechische Textgeschichte,* ANT, V (1972).

On patristic citations: G. D. Fee, "The Text of John in Origen and Cyril of Alexandria: A Contribution to Methodology in the Reconstruction and Analysis of Patristic Citations," *Bibl.,* LII (1971), 357-94.

On methodology: in addition to the bibliog. for TEXTUAL CRITICISM, NT[S], J. Froger, *La critique des textes et son automatisation* (1968).

C. M. MARTINI

TEXTUAL CRITICISM, OT. The work of determining the Hebrew or Aramaic biblical text in its earliest attested form; that is, the form best supported by Hebrew MSS and ancient versions as evaluated by proven principles. Textual criticism is sometimes called LOWER CRITICISM, in contrast to higher criticism, which deals with the date, unity, and authorship of the biblical writings.

1. Materials and aids
   - *a.* Hebrew and Aramaic biblical texts
   - *b.* Samaritan Pentateuch
   - *c.* Translations
   - *d.* Quotations
2. Literary features and textual criticism
   - *a.* Parallels
   - *b.* Parallelism in poetry
   - *c.* Poetic meter
   - *d.* Acrostics
   - *e.* Characteristics of MSS and redactions
3. Principles of OT textual criticism
   - *a.* Best Hebrew text
   - *b.* Use of ancient versions
   - *c.* Readings
   - *d.* Shorter reading
   - *e.* More difficult reading
   - *f.* Unassimilated, disharmonious reading
   - *g.* Limited use of conjecture
   - *h.* Comparative philology
4. Scribal errors and their correction
   - *a.* Unintentional errors
   - *b.* Intentional changes
5. Conclusions

Bibliography

1. Materials and aids. ***a. Hebrew and Aramaic biblical texts.*** i. *Pre-Masoretic.* The discovery of ancient MSS in the Judean Desert has changed the picture of OT textual criticism. Fragments of every OT book except Esther have been discovered near Qumran, ranging in date from the third century B.C. to the first century A.D. (*see* DEAD SEA SCROLLS and supplementary article). Many of these texts support the traditional MT, but some support the LXX, particularly in the books of Samuel and Jeremiah. Thus the validity and antiquity of both these textual traditions have been affirmed. *See* SEPTUAGINT[S]; TEXT, HEBREW, HISTORY OF[S] §1.

ii. *Masoretic.* The Masoretes (*ca.* A.D. 500-1200) tried to ensure the correct understanding and transmission of the text by developing systems for writing vowels, by compiling statistics about the occurrence of various phenomena in the text, and by notes on the text. *See* TEXT, OT §A4; TEXT, HEBREW, HISTORY OF[S] §2; MASORETIC ACCENTS; QERE-KETHIBH[S].

The work of the Masoretes has important implications for textual criticism. (*a*) The vocalization of the text is usually that implied in the ancient versions, but sometimes the versions imply another vocalization. For example, in Isa. 7:11 the MT vocalization is *sh^{e}'ālâ* (ask) but Targ., Peshitta (the Peshitta Syriac), Vulg., and the Greek translations of Aquila, Symmachus, and Theodotion all imply a vocalization *sh^{e}ōlâ* (to Sheol) which fits the context better and is followed by RSV, NEB, and NAB.

(*b*) Over a thousand times the Masoretes have one reading in the text (the *kethibh,* "written") and another reading in the margin (the *qere,* "to be read"). In effect the *kethibh* and the *qere* give two variant readings, between which the textual critic must choose. *See* QERE-KETHIBH[S].

(*c*) The Masoretes also collected a list of eighteen places (called *Tiqqune Sopherim*) where the scribes were said to have changed the text, mostly to avoid dishonoring God. *See* EMENDATIONS OF THE SCRIBES[S]; QERE-KETHIBH[S] §2.

(*d*) Sometimes the scribes wrote letters in peculiar ways to call attention to textual changes or problems. In Judg. 18:30 the scribes inserted a raised *n* to make the name "Manasseh" (*mnšh*) where the original was certainly "Moses" (*mšh*), attested by the LXX and the Vulg., followed by RSV, NEB, and NAB. The scribes evidently thought it demeaning to Moses to write that the idolatrous Jonathan was his grandson.

(*e*) The Masoretes noted places where material not written was to be added in reading. For example, in Jer. 31:38 the standard MT has "behold the days," but the marginal note indicates that "are coming" is to be added in reading. This addition is in the text of some Hebrew MSS and in LXX, Targ., Peshitta, Vulg., followed by RSV, NEB, and NAB. Conversely, places were noted where material written was not to be read, e.g., in Ezek. 48:16, where the MT has "five five hundred," the Masoretic note indicates that the second "five" is not to be read. LXX, Peshitta, Targ., Vulg., RSV, NAB, and NEB also omit this second "five," which is a dittography. *See* §4*a*viii *below;* QERE-KETHIBH[S] §3*c*.

(*f*) In 350 cases Masoretic margins have variants called *sebirin,* "conjectures," and in some cases these variants are clearly right, as in I Sam. 12:5 where the standard MT has "and he said, 'He is witness,'" but the *sebir* reads "and they said, 'He is witness.'" This plural reading is supported by the context, some Hebrew MSS, LXX, Targ., Peshitta, Vulg., and is reflected in RSV, NEB, and NAB. *See* TEXT, OT §A3*a* (*f*).

The work of Masoretes in establishing and preserving a standard text was so effective that all medieval Hebrew MSS have essentially the same text. Most of the variants are minor and do not affect the meaning, and most of them can be explained as scribal errors or harmonizations. Some of the earliest Masoretic texts, some with Tiberian and some with Babylonian vowels, have been found in the Genizah, or storeroom, of the Ben-Ezra Synagogue in Old Cairo, Egypt (*see* TEXT, OT §A5). The oldest of these biblical fragments come from the sixth century A.D.

iii. *Printed texts*. Questions about the validity of some of the references to ancient versions and of many of the proposed emendations in *Biblia Hebraica* (1937) have led to a new edition, *Biblia Hebraica Stuttgartensia* (beginning in 1968). It also is based on Codex Leningradensis (A.D. 1008), but with revised and reduced textual notes. *See* TEXT, OT §A7*c*.

The Aleppo Codex, from the first half of the tenth century, was provided with vowels by Aaron ben Moshe ben Asher. Unfortunately, about one fourth of this MS has been destroyed. It is the main basis for the edition of the Hebrew University Bible Project (beginning with a sample of Isaiah in 1965). This edition has references to readings of Hebrew MSS, ancient versions, and quotations in rabbinic literature.

b. Samaritan Pentateuch. The Samar. is really the Hebrew text of the Pentateuch written in Samaritan script. It differs from the MT in about six thousand cases, most of them minor. Since the Samar. agrees with the LXX against the MT in about nineteen hundred places, it appears to be based on a recension similar in many cases to the Hebrew basis for the LXX. *See* SAMARITAN PENTATEUCH[S].

c. Translations. i. *Greek*. Since the translation of the Pentateuch goes back to the third century B.C. (the rest was completed by the second century B.C.), the LXX remains, even after the Qumran discoveries, the earliest complete witness to the OT text. It differs markedly from the MT in Samuel, Job, and especially in Jeremiah, where it is about one eighth shorter. Now some Qumran Hebrew fragments show that there was a Hebrew basis for the LXX in at least some of these large differences from the MT. *See* SEPTUAGINT[S].

Other ancient Greek translations include those by Aquila (very literal), by Symmachus, and by Theodotion. These translations survive only in quotations and fragments. *See* GREEK VERSIONS, MINOR[S].

ii. *Aramaic (Targs.)*. Targ. Onkelos on the Pentateuch, going back in its present form to the second or third century A.D., is quite literal, except that it modifies anthropomorphisms. Targ. Neofiti and the Jerusalem Targs. of the Pentateuch are more expansionist. Targ. Jonathan covers the Former and Later Prophets and is more paraphrastic than Onkelos. There are later Targs. on the Writings, except for Ezra, Nehemiah, and Daniel. The Samaritans also made translations of the Pentateuch into their Aramaic dialect. *See* TARGUMS[S].

iii. *Syriac*. The most ancient Syriac translation, perhaps going back to the second century A.D., is called the Peshitta, meaning "simple." It follows the Hebrew quite closely, especially in the Pentateuch. There has also been some influence from the LXX. Later Syriac translations were based on the LXX. Paul of Tella's seventh-century version, the Syro-Hexapla, is important because it preserves Origen's editorial markings used in the Hexapla edition of the LXX. *See* SYRIAC VERSIONS[S] §1.

iv. *Latin*. The OL translations, beginning in the second century A.D., were based on the LXX. The surviving fragments of these translations differ according to geographical area and MS, but they are important witnesses to the LXX text before the time of the great fourth-century Greek MSS, Vaticanus and Sinaiticus.

Jerome's OT, known as the Vulgate (completed in 405), was supposed to be based on the Hebrew. This is largely true for the historical books, but in the prophets Jerome was much influenced by the OL, LXX, Aq., Symm., and Theod. For the Psalms Jerome made three translations, two from the LXX—the Roman Psalter and the Gallican Psalter (which is found in the Vulg.)—and one from the Hebrew. Therefore the Vulg. usually, but not always, represents the Hebrew text of the later fourth century. *See* LATIN VERSIONS[S] §2.

v. *Other ancient translations*. The other ancient translations are mostly translations of translations and are only occasionally valuable for textual criticism. *See* VERSIONS, ANCIENT §§5-11.

d. Quotations. Quotations may also witness to the OT text. The limitations are that quotations were often made from memory, not word for word, and that quotations were sometimes adapted to later forms of the biblical text as the quoting document was recopied. Deviations from the MT are found in quotations in the MISHNA, the Talmud, and the Midrashim (early Jewish commentaries; *see* MIDRASH[S]). Writings of Syriac, Greek, and Latin church Fathers also have quotations from the OT. The quotations of Jerome are especially important because he sometimes refers to the Hebrew text specifically and even transliterates it.

2. Literary features and textual criticism. ***a. Parallels.*** Some passages have parallels or almost exact duplicates, called deuterographs, elsewhere in the OT. Some noteworthy examples are II Sam. 22 and Ps. 18; II Kings 18:13–20:19 and Isa. 36–39; II Kings 24:18–25:21; 25:27-30; and Jer. 52; Ps. 14 and Ps. 53. A parallel can sometimes help to correct a text. For example, in Gen. 10:4, MT "Dodanim" can be corrected to "Rodanim" in the light of the parallel in I Chr. 1:7. Furthermore, at Gen. 10:4, Samar. and LXX (reflected in NEB and NAB) read "Rodanim." ר (*r*) and ד (*d*) were easily confused, and the Dodanim have not been identified in extrabiblical sources, whereas the Rodanim are the people of Rhodes. Yet parallels do not always justify complete harmonization, since each text has its own history. Scribes are likely to harmonize, and so disparate parallel texts are more likely to be original than identical ones.

b. Parallelism in poetry. Hebrew poetry is marked by parallelism between elements in one line with corresponding elements in the following line. In the MT of Isa. 60:19, the element "by day" in the first line has no corresponding parallel in the second line. A Qumran text (1QIs[a]) supplies the missing parallel, "by night," and it is also attested in LXX, OL, Targ., and followed by RSV, NEB, and NAB. *See* POETRY, HEBREW §C.

c. Poetic meter. Many scholars think that Hebrew poetic meter was based on certain patterns of accented syllables, such as three accents followed by a parallel line with two accents (3+2) or three accents followed by three accents (3+3). On the basis of meter some scholars wish to eliminate "to Cyrus" in Isa. 45:1, claiming that this overburdens the poetic line. But other scholars, using another method of counting accented syllables, find that "to Cyrus" fits the 3+3 meter which is used in the context together with 3+2. Since Hebrew rhythms are varied, meter should be used only to support other evidence in textual criticism, and not as decisive evidence when standing alone. *See* POETRY, HEBREW §D.

d. Acrostics. Some Hebrew poems have their lines beginning with the successive letters of the alphabet. The fact that the acrostic in Nah. 1:2-14 is mutilated and incomplete indicates that some textual corruption has taken place. The verses of Ps. 145 form an alphabetic acrostic, but the standard MT lacks a verse beginning with נ (*n*). A verse beginning with נ (*n*) is found in a Qumran Psalms scroll and in the margin of a medieval Hebrew MS (Kennicott 142), and is implied by LXX and Jerome's translation of the Hebrew (followed by RSV, NEB, and NAB). *See* MNEMONIC DEVICES[S] §1.

e. Characteristics of MSS and redactions. The over-all carefulness or carelessness of a MS has a bearing on assessing the value of an individual reading of that MS. For example, the MT of the books of Samuel has suffered obvious corruption, and this must be taken into account in evaluating MT's readings in these books.

3. Principles of OT textual criticism. ***a. Best Hebrew text, usually the MT, is basic.*** Most scholars take the MT as a point of departure in textual criticism, because it is a complete, standard text which has been carefully copied. Sometimes the readings of the Qumran Hebrew MSS are shown by the context and by agreement with ancient versions to be superior to the MT, but the Qumran MSS are incomplete, and some were carelessly copied.

b. Use of ancient versions. The ancient versions can be used to correct errors in the MT. The age, quality, and relation to the Hebrew must be taken into consideration in weighing the value of the reading of a version. Its general tendency must be determined: whether it is usually accurate or full of errors, whether it is literal or paraphrastic, whether it is brief or expansionist, whether it preserves disharmonious readings or harmonizes. Since the LXX is the oldest translation, since it is in most books fairly literal, and since it is based on a Hebrew original (*Vorlage*), it is the most important version for textual criticism. The Targs. are also old and based on Hebrew, but they are paraphrastic and expansionist. The Peshitta to a greater extent and the Vulg. to a lesser extent are based on Hebrew, but they have both been influenced by the LXX. The Coptic and OL are old, but are based on the LXX and therefore are only indirect witnesses to the Hebrew text. The Arabic of Sa'adya is based on Hebrew of the tenth century A.D.

c. Reading which explains other readings usually best. In I Sam. 2:11, MT, Targ., Peshitta, Vulg. (followed by RSV, NEB, and NAB) state "Elkanah returned," and in a patriarchal society it would be understood that his wives went with him. To make this clear Codex Alexandrinus of the LXX says "they returned." Since the speaker in vss. 1-10 is Hannah, Codex Vaticanus of the LXX says "she returned." These latter two different readings seem to be derived from the more original MT reading.

d. Shorter reading usually best. The tendency of scribes is to add explanations or material from parallel passages, rather than to condense their material. For example, in Gen. 15:21 the reading of MT, Targs., Peshitta, Vulg. (followed by RSV and NAB) is "and the Girgashites," but LXX and Samar. add "and the Hivites," followed by NEB. The longer reading is probably an assimilation to such passages as Deut. 7:1, where the Hivites are included, and for this reason the shorter reading is probably better.

e. More difficult reading usually best. In Gen. 25:18, MT, Targs., and Peshitta read the more difficult plural "they dwelt," followed by RSV, NEB, and NAB. The easier reading, "he dwelt," is found in LXX and Vulg. The MT reading is more difficult because of the singulars in vs. 17 and in the end of vs. 18, but the plural makes sense because it refers to the sons of Ishmael mentioned in vss. 12-16.

f. Unassimilated, disharmonious reading usually best. A scribe will often assimilate to a parallel passage or harmonize with data elsewhere. For example, in II Sam. 22:33, LXX, Peshitta, and Targ. support MT "my strong refuge" (followed by RSV), but the Lucianic LXX and Vulg. support the reading of the parallel Ps. 18:32 [H 33], "who girded me with strength" (followed by NEB and NAB). The MT probably has the correct (unassimilated) reading in the Samuel setting.

g. Limited use of conjecture. Many modern scholars accept a limited use of conjectural emendation when neither the Hebrew nor the ancient versions make good sense. Such conjectures should reflect good Hebrew usage and should be forms which could easily give rise by scribal error to the present Hebrew text. In Amos 6:12, MT reads *babbeqārîm,* "with oxen," but RSV, NEB, and NAB are based upon a conjectural emendation of the word division and of the vowels: *bebhāqār yām,* "the sea with oxen." This emendation provides "sea" as a parallel to "rock" of the first line of the verse. The resultant collective singular, *bāqār,* "oxen," is usual, whereas the plural of MT is late and rare, only elsewhere in II Chr. 4:3; Neh. 10:36 [H 37]. Some scholars classify conjectural emendations, not under textual criticism, since they are not based on textual evidence, but under literary criticism.

h. Comparative philology makes some conjecture unnecessary. In Prov. 14:24, MT has *'ošrām* usually translated "their riches." The LXX *panourgos,* "clever," makes a better parallelism with the following line, where the corresponding word is "folly." Following the meaning of the LXX, RSV assumes that MT is to be emended to *'ormāthām,* "their wisdom"; and NAB assumes *'ormâ,* "resourcefulness." But NEB follows the MT without emendation and translates "insight," following the meaning of an Arabic cognate, *'athr.* Ugaritic cognates are especially useful because of the nearness of this language to biblical Hebrew in time, place, and linguistic affiliation. Such importations of new meanings for Hebrew roots must be done with restraint and caution.

4. Scribal errors and their correction. In the process of copying, scribes made mistakes of omission, addition, and of other changes unintentional and intentional. Some of these can be corrected by better Hebrew MSS or by the ancient versions.

a. Unintentional errors. i. *Incorrect word division.* According to the MT, Samar., and Aq., the last word of Gen. 49:19 and the first word of vs. 20 is *'āqēbh/mē'āshēr,* "heel/From Asher." According to LXX, Targs., Peshitta, Vulg. (followed by RSV, NEB, and NAB), these words should be divided *'aqēbhām/'āshēr,* "their heels/Asher," which makes better sense and is surely correct. *See* Text, OT §D2*b*.

ii. *Transposition of letters and words (metathesis).* In Ps. 49:11 [H 12] MT, the Hexaplaric Hebrew in Greek letters, Aq., Symm., and Jerome's translation of the Hebrew read *qirbām,* "their inward thought." On the other hand, LXX, Targ., Peshitta, and Vulg. read *qibhrām,* "their graves," which suits the context better. Evidently some scribe transposed ב (*b*) and ר (*r*), resulting in the faulty MT. In II Chr. 3:1, MT has the order *'asher hēqîn bimqôm dāwîdh,* "which he had appointed in the place of David." But LXX, Peshitta, Vulg. (followed by NEB and NAB) imply another order of words, *bammāqôm 'asher hēqîn dāwîdh,* "in the place which David has appointed," which fits the context better and is probably original.

iii. *Confusion of letters.* The Hebrew letters which scribes most frequently confused are ד (*d*) and ר (*r*). For example, in Isa. 33:8, MT, Targ., Peshitta, and Vulg. support the reading *'rym,* "cities," but a Qumran MS (1QIs[a]) has *'dym,* "witnesses," followed by RSV, NEB, and NAB. The latter reading fits the context better and was suggested by Bernhard Duhm in 1892, long before the discovery of the Qumran MSS. *See* Text, OT §D2*a*.

iv. *Confusion of words which sound alike.* Hebrew *lô,* "to him," and *lō',* "not," are pronounced alike. In Ps. 100:3, the MT has *lō',* "not," followed by LXX, Peshitta, Symm., and Vulg. (so KJV); while the *qere* reading in the margin of the MT is *lô,* "his," followed by many Hebrew MSS, Aq., and Jerome's translation of the Hebrew (so RSV, NEB, and NAB). The latter fits the context better because it makes a better transition to the following phrase, and this reading is closer in meaning to the similar verses Ps. 95:7 and Isa. 43:1. *See* Text, OT §D2*f*.

v. *Omission because of homoeoteleuton,* that is, similar ending of successive phrases. In I Sam. 13:15, MT, Peshitta, Targ., Vulg. (so RSV) read "from Gilgal to Gibeah." But after "Gilgal," LXX, Symm., NEB, and NAB insert the reading "and went on his way, but the rest of the people went up after Saul to meet the soldiers. And they came from Gilgal." A scribe, by a slip of the eye, omitted the material between the two occurrences of "from Gilgal" resulting in the present MT. *See* Text, OT §D2*e*.

vi. *Omission because of homoeoarchton,* that is, similar beginning of successive phrases. In I Sam. 10:1, MT, Peshitta, Targ., Vulg. (so KJV) read, "Is it not that the Lord anointed you to be prince over his heritage?" But after "not," LXX, Vulg. (so RSV, NEB, and NAB) add, "the Lord anointed you to be prince over his people Israel? And you shall reign over the people of the Lord and you shall save them from the hand of their enemies round about. And this shall be the sign to you," and then continue with MT, "that the Lord anointed you to be prince over his heritage." A scribe's eye evidently jumped from one, "the Lord anointed you to be prince over," to another, leaving out what was between.

vii. *Omission because of haplography,* writing once two identical adjacent letters or two similar words or phrases. In Hos. 4:19, MT, Vulg. (so NEB) read *mizzibhḥôthām,* "because of their sacrifices." But in LXX, Targ., Peshitta, OL (so RSV and NAB) read *mimmizbeḥôthām,* "because of their altars," retaining the original double writing of *m.* (The possibility must be recognized, however, that biblical scribes, like those of the Lachish Letters, may have occasionally deliberately written a single consonant which was intended to be pronounced twice—double duty consonants.) In I Sam. 9:16, MT, Peshitta, and Vulg. read *'ammî,* "my people" (third occurrence in verse). But LXX, Targ. (so RSV, NEB, and NAB) read *'ᵒnî 'ammî,* "the affliction of my people," perhaps retaining the original two similar words. The latter expression occurs also in Exod. 3:7 and II Kings 14:26. Some scholars have argued that, because the expression "I have seen the affliction of my people" is used elsewhere, the unusual "I have seen my people" is more original (*see* §3*f*). This case illustrates the difficulty of principles pointing in opposite directions. *See* TEXT, OT §D2*d*.

viii. *Addition because of dittography,* writing twice what should be written once. In II Kings 7:13, MT and Targ. read twice, "seeing that those who are left here will fare like the whole multitude of Israel." On the other hand, about forty-five Hebrew MSS, LXX, Peshitta, Vulg. (so RSV and NAB) omit the second occurrence of this clause. *See* TEXT, OT §D2*d*.

b. Intentional changes. i. *Assimilation to parallel passages.* This was one of the most common reasons for scribal changes. For example, in Lev. 6:6 [H 5:25], MT, the Targs., some later LXX MSS, Peshitta, (so RSV and NAB) read "to the priest." This phrase seems to be an assimilation to Lev. 5:18, and is not found in Samar. or Codex Vaticanus of the LXX (so NEB), and is not quoted in Sifra, the early rabbinic commentary on Leviticus. For a case where some of the versions assimilate to a parallel passage, *see* §3*f above.*

ii. *Adding epithets,* or qualities. In Jeremiah the phrase "thus says Yahweh" occurs many times, and in sixty-nine cases the MT contains additional epithets: "of hosts, the God of Israel" (thirty-one times), "of hosts" (nineteen times), "God of Israel" (fourteen times), "the God of Israel" (three times), "the God of hosts" (one time), "Lord" (one time). The LXX contains additional epithets only nineteen times: "God of Israel" (fourteen times), "of hosts" (four times), "God" (one time). For example, 6:6 MT contains the epithet "of hosts," but the LXX lacks it. It is possible that in this verse and in many others, MT has added epithets after "the Lord."

iii. *Adding names of subjects and objects.* In eight cases in Jeremiah (27:6, 8, 20; 28:3, 11, 14; 29:1, 3) MT has the name "Nebuchadnezzar." In all these cases LXX omits the name and in 27:8; 28:3; and 29:1 omits the entire clause. An indication that the name is a later addition in MT is that elsewhere in Jeremiah this name is spelled "Nebuchadrezzar."

iv. *Conflation,* or combination of readings. In the MT of Ezek. 1:20 there are two similar phrases with the same meaning, "wherever the spirit wanted to go." The only difference is that the word for "wherever" in the first phrase is *shām* and in the second phrase *shāmmâ.* Some call this a case of dittography, but the phrases are slightly different and not adjacent, and therefore it is possible that a scribe found these two readings and combined them. Some Hebrew MSS, LXX, Peshitta, (so JB and NAB) omit the second phrase, which may have been added by conflation. *See* CONFLATE READINGS, OT[S].

v. *Substitution of synonyms.* In I Sam. 20:34, MT, Targ., Peshitta, Vulg. (so RSV and NEB) read *wayyāqom,* "and he rose," while a Qumran fragment (4QSam[b]), LXX (so NAB) read the almost synonymous *wayyiphḥaz,* "and he jumped up." Since the second verb is not common, it is probable that MT substituted a more common word. The rare reading more fitly expresses Jonathan's anger, which is mentioned in the context.

vi. *Harmonization.* Sometimes a scribe made a change to create better agreement with some statement in the immediate context or elsewhere in the OT. In Gen. 2:2, MT, Targ. Onkelos, the two Jerusalem Targs., Targ. Neofiti, Vulg. (so RSV and NAB) read "on the seventh day God finished his work." Some scribe evidently thought that this did not harmonize with the following statement that God rested on the seventh day, and therefore he changed the first "seventh" in this verse to "sixth," which is reflected in Samar., LXX, Peshitta, Jub. 2:16 (so NEB). Of course, the reading of MT is not necessarily disharmonious, for MT can be interpreted, "By the seventh day God had finished his work."

vii. *Removal of objectionable expressions.* Some original expressions in the OT were considered objectionable because they were thought to dishonor God. In Job 7:20, MT, Peshitta, Targ., and Vulg. read "to myself" (referring to Job). But LXX (so RSV, NEB, and NAB) reads "to thee" (referring to God). This passage is in the Masoretic list of places where the scribes changed the text (*Tiqqune Sopherim; see* §1*a*ii above). Evidently it was thought demeaning to God's honor to write that a human being was a burden to him, and therefore a scribe changed the pronoun to refer to Job, producing the MT reading.

Some statements were considered objectionable because they were thought to dishonor national leaders. In I Sam. 25:22, MT, Targ., and Vulg. read "to the enemies of David." On the other hand, LXX, Peshitta (so RSV, NEB, and NAB) read "to David." Some scribe, wishing to avoid writing about a possible curse on David, introduced "enemies" as objects of the curse. The LXX and Peshitta reading agrees with the usual formula whereby a speaker wishes a curse on himself if he does not do a certain thing (e.g., I Sam. 20:13).

5. Conclusions. Future projects in OT textual criticism should include a fuller assessment of the Qumran material, the preparation of critical editions of the ancient versions, further study of ancient Jewish and Christian quotations of the OT, and the application of the study of various redactions to the determination of the best text.

Bibliography. D. Ap-Thomas, *A Primer of OT Text Criticism* (2nd ed., 1966), a clear intro. with examples; V. Aptowitzer, *Das Schriftwort in der rabbinischen Literatur* (1906 [repr. 1970]), variants from MT in I and II Samuel, Joshua, and Judges; J. Barr, *Comparative Philology and the Text of the OT* (1968), criticism of overuse of cognates in Semitic languages; D. Barthélemy *et al., Preliminary and Interim Report on* *the Hebrew OT Project* (1973), a condensed treatment of text problems in the Pentateuch; L. H. Brockington, ed., *The Hebrew Text of the OT: The Readings Adopted by the Translators of the New English Bible* (1973); F. M. Cross, *The Ancient Library of Qumran and Modern Biblical Studies* (rev. ed., 1961), and, "The Contribution of the Qumrân Discoveries to the Study of the Biblical Text," *IEJ*, XVI (1966), 81-95; F. M. Cross, D. N. Freedman, "Some Observations on Early Hebrew," *Bibl.*, LIII (1972), 413-20, justifying principles used in textual reconstructions in answer to D. W. Goodwin; M. J. Dahood, "The Value of Ugaritic for Textual Criticism," *Bibl.*, XL (1959), 160-70; F. Delitzsch, *Die Lese- und Schreibfehler im AT* (1920), based on principles, but overuses emendation; S. R. Driver, *Notes on the Hebrew Text and the Topography of the Books of Samuel* (2nd ed., 1913), the intro. is a masterful survey of the materials of textual criticism, and the commentary is a model of judicious text-critical work; O. Eissfeldt, *The OT, an Introduction* (1965), pp. 669-721, 778-85, good survey and bibliog.; K. Elliger, W. Rudolph, eds., *Biblia Hebraica Stuttgartensia* (beginning in 1968), same text as *Biblia Hebraica*, but text-critical notes are fewer and more sober; C. D. Ginsburg, *Introduction to the Massoretico-Critical Edition of the Hebrew Bible* (1966), with Prolegomenon by H. M. Orlinsky, "The Masoretic Text: A Critical Evaluation," pp. i-xlv; C. D. Ginsburg, ed., *The Pentateuch, The Earlier Prophets, The Later Prophets, The Writings*, diligently revised according to the Masora and the early editions with the various readings from MSS and the ancient versions (1926); D. W. Goodwin, *Text-Restoration Methods in Contemporary U.S.A. Biblical Scholarship* (1969), criticism of reconstructions of Albright, Cross, Freedman; R. Gordis, *The Biblical Text in the Making: A Study of the Kethib-Qere* (2nd ed., 1972); M. H. Goshen-Gottstein, ed., *The Book of Isaiah, Sample Edition with Introduction* (1965), "Hebrew Biblical MSS: Their History and Their Place in the HUBP Edition," *Bibl.*, XLVIII (1967), 243-90, and "Theory and Practice of Textual Criticism, the Text-Critical Use of the Septuagint," *Textus*, III (1963), 130-58; P. Kahle, *The Cairo Geniza* (2nd ed., 1959), covers not only the Genizah material but many other aspects of OT text; J. Kennedy, *An Aid to the Textual Amendment of the OT* (1928), based on principles, but overuses emendation; B. Kennicott, *Vetus Testamentum Hebraicum cum variis lectionibus*, 2 vols. (1776-80), consonantal variants in medieval Hebrew MSS; R. Kittel, ed., *Biblia Hebraica* (16th ed., 1973), a good edition of the MT, but the text-critical notes must be used with discrimination; R. W. Klein, *Textual Criticism of the OT* (1974), good examples of textual criticism, using LXX and Qumran evidence; J. H. Marks, *Der textkritische Wert des Psalterium Hieronymi juxta Hebraeos* (1956); M. Noth, *The OT World* (1966), 301-63; W. Nowack, *Die Bedeutung des Hieronymus für die alttestamentliche Textkritik untersucht* (1875); H. S. Nyberg, *Studien zum Hoseabuche, zugleich ein Beitrag zur Klärung des Problems der alttestamentlichen Textkritik* (1935), uses LXX and Peshitta; H. M. Orlinsky, "The Textual Criticism of the OT," in *The Bible and the Ancient Near East*, ed. G. E. Wright (1961), pp. 113-32, criticism of notes in *Biblia Hebraica;* B. Pick, "Die Tosefta-Citate und der hebräishe Text," and "Text-Varianten aus Mechilta und Sifré," *ZAW*, VI (1886), 23-29, 101-21; R. H. Pfeiffer, *Introduction to the OT* (rev. ed., 1948), pp. 71-126, a good survey with examples; B. J. Roberts, *The OT Text and Versions* (1951), still the fullest treatment in English, good bibliog.; G. B. de Rossi, *Variae lectiones Veteris Testamenti*, 4 vols. (1784-98), consonantal and vocalic variants in medieval Hebrew MSS; P. W. Skehan, "The Qumran MSS and Textual Criticism," VTSup, IV (1957), 148-58; B. Walton, *Biblia sacra polyglotta*, 6 vols. (1655-57), still the most convenient assemblage of the ancient versions; *Textus*, Annual of the Hebrew University Bible Project (beginning 1960), many valuable articles on OT text; D. W. Thomas, "The Textual Criticism of the OT," in *The OT and Modern Study*, ed. H. H. Rowley (1951), pp. 238-63, a judicious survey; E. Würthwein, *The Text of the OT* (1957), a good introduction to the Hebrew text and the ancient versions, geared to the apparatus of *Biblia Hebraica*.

J. A. Thompson

TEXTUAL CRITICISM, NT. Textual criticism of ancient writings, such as those comprising the NT, is understood only partially from descriptions of the primary sources and from the history of the printed text (*see* Text, NT §§B, D); a more adequate understanding comes only through a grasp of the text-critical theories and methods that are applied to the sources and are reflected in the printed texts. Both the sources and the printed texts increase in number as time passes; similarly, theories of the text and methodologies employed in analyzing it also continue to develop and are subject to perennial refinement, expansion, and alteration. Sometimes newly discovered sources will have striking effects upon theory and will lead immediately to new methodologies appropriate both to such discoveries and to older materials, but more often methodology lags behind discoveries of primary materials, and—at least in the NT field—methods have yet to catch up in an adequate way to materials known for generations.

1. Criteria for choosing among readings
2. Synergism of internal and external evidence
3. Polarity of internal and external evidence
4. Eclecticism
5. Historical-development and documentary emphases
6. Conclusion
Bibliography

1. Criteria for choosing among readings. Text-critical methodology is concerned essentially and primarily with the *criteria* used in the selection of the most likely original reading when, at a given point in the NT text, two or more readings are extant in the MS tradition. Historically, the choice of the "original" reading has been based on one or more of a number of criteria or "canons of criticism," including a reading's support (*a*) by the most MSS, (*b*) by the earliest MSS, (*c*) by the "best" MSS, (*d*) by MSS with the widest geographical distribution, or (*e*) by established groups of MSS of specifiable age, character, and perhaps location; and a reading's conformity (*f*) to the author's style, (*g*) to Koine (as opposed to Attic) Greek, or (*h*) to Semitic forms of expression; or a reading's lack of conformity (*i*) to its context, to parallel passages, or to OT passages, or (*j*) to extrinsic doctrinal views; and whether a reading is (*k*) the shortest reading, (*l*) the "hardest" reading, and (*m*) is not a demonstrable scribal error; and finally (*n*) whether a reading most adequately accounts for the presence of all other readings.

Not all these criteria can be applied at once, nor will all be applicable to each instance of variation; in fact, if they were so applied, they often would conflict and exclude one another.

Ambiguities may abound even when only a few criteria are applied to a given set of variants, for in a gospel passage the "hardest" reading from the scribe's standpoint may also be the least Semitic or be attested only in a late and "inferior" MS, or the shortest reading may be out of harmony with the author's usual style, or the reading of the "best" MSS may show evidence of assimilation to a parallel passage. It is understandable, then, why the matter of text-critical criteria is both a complex and difficult problem of long standing and also a crucial issue methodologically. Naturally, many further questions of text-critical method—often more difficult still—are veiled by the phrases "earliest MSS," "best MSS," "author's style," "hardest reading," and "demonstrable scribal error," to mention only a few. Such prior questions must be settled before the criteria have much utility at all.

2. Synergism of internal and external evidence. The criteria listed above fall roughly into two groups or classes: one class emphasizes "external" evidence—the age, quantity, quality, grouping, and distribution of MSS (items *a* through *e above*), while the second class emphasizes "internal" considerations—scribal habits and the literary and ideological peculiarities of the author (items *f* through *n above*). In Hort's classical 1882 formulation of NT text-critical procedures (*see* TEXT, NT §E5), these two general kinds of criteria co-operated to produce a particular theory of the text: internal evidence separated the "inferior" readings from the "superior" and led to a similar judgment on the inferiority or superiority of the principal groups of MSS, resulting (as chance would have it) in a clear preference for the early, so-called Neutral group or text type, whose chief representatives were codices B and, secondarily, ℵ, which (as it happened) were the oldest extensive NT MSS known to Westcott and Hort. Hence, for Hort, B assumed "a unique position," for it, along with ℵ, was superior to all other MSS on the grounds both of internal and external considerations. Once the synergism of internal and external evidence (the best readings→the best group of documents→the best documents) had isolated B and ℵ as those least mixed MSS that represented the purest NT text type, then an "objective" criterion of an "external" kind (isolation of the best *documents,* rather than merely the best *readings*) had been established. This presumably objective and apparently external criterion—the best text type composed of the best MSS—then was utilized by Westcott and Hort, and by perhaps most scholars since, as the divining rod for locating the original vein of the NT text. Critics of this approach have called it the "cult of the best MS."

3. Polarity of internal and external evidence. Critical reflection on Westcott and Hort's scheme, particularly on their other major and early textual tradition, the so-called Western text (*see* TEXT, NT §E5*d*), disclosed a tension between the external evidence pole and the internal evidence pole of their theory. This was the case because the Western text, as Hort admitted, was both early and widespread in primitive Christianity, perhaps even earlier and more widespread than the Neutral. Hence, to judge B as the best NT MS both on internal grounds and external (as a text unaffected by corruption in the process of transmission) proved to be a strain on logic; to accredit its readings in almost all cases as virtually identical with the original text simply because they are present in this most excellent MS with presumably the most ancient NT text, and yet reject possibly older readings (in terms of demonstrable evidence) because they happen to occur in a "corrupt" MS like codex D (when judged on internal grounds) pointed to the ambiguity of both the external criteria and the internal criteria. The two emphases, internal and external evidence, may have co-operated in the coronation of B by Westcott and Hort, but they did not with consistency make the case for the dethronement of D that Hort claimed. The internal evidence appeared to involve some ambiguous, certainly subjective, and at times quite arbitrary considerations of "purity" and "corruption," while external evidence seemed to issue in contradictory conclusions in otherwise similar situations. The two kinds of evidence were pushed apart to the extent of assuming a dualistic stance. This emerging polarity displaced Westcott and Hort's felicitous synergism of internal and external evidence and had far-reaching effects on NT textual criticism; in large measure, it is the cause for the uncertainty and confusion in recent and current text-critical theory, as will be evident from what follows.

4. Eclecticism. During the twentieth century eclecticism has emerged as the mainstream of NT text-critical method. In an effort to identify the most likely original reading, eclecticism employs in various ways the bevy of criteria surrounding each pole of the internal/external evidence tension. Two schools of thought can be distinguished among the practitioners of the eclectic method.

a. Moderate eclecticism. A moderate eclecticism, though sometimes oblivious to the dualistic emphases and to the ambiguities inherent in the criteria attached to each, is currently the dominant text-critical method. This method weighs against one another the relative merits of applicable criteria from the historical-development and documentary side (external evidence) and those from the scribal and stylistic side (internal evidence). E.g., should one reading among several be the hardest reading from the standpoint of scribal habits, comport with the author's ascertained style or vocabulary, and have the support of "excellent" MSS with wide geographical distribution, it would be chosen as the most likely original reading. In another case, if one of two or more readings should share the first two characteristics listed in the preceding example, but should be attested only by a group of late Byzantine MSS (considered inferior by most textual critics), the decision would be more difficult, though not as difficult as when several internal considerations favor a reading supported solely or mainly by Western MSS. Most difficult of all for most moderate eclectics would be those cases where B and ℵ support different readings. In all cases where some criteria decidedly favor one reading and others decidedly favor another—a not uncommon situation—the ambiguity and mutual exclusiveness of these text-critical criteria are brought fully into view, and when certain internal criteria side with one another over against certain external criteria, as is so often the case, the polarity and tension described earlier become painfully evident. Consideration of any extended series of variation-units (*see,* e.g., Metzger's *A Textual Commentary on the Greek New Testament,* 1971) will illustrate the point and show, furthermore, that very often the balance of criteria for and against a given reading is at best an uncertain one and that decisions in these cases will tend to be made according to a predisposition for one or the other of the two dichotomous poles. Either a prepossession as to what are the "best" MSS will assume the decisive role or a predilection for the importance of author's tendencies or scribal probabilities will dominate the decision process. A moderate eclecticism, one that attempts to utilize the whole range of possible text-critical criteria, lives within and tries to live with the internal/external tension, drawing its criteria almost randomly from one pole or the other as they seem appropriate to the set of readings under consideration. It is evident from this state of affairs that definitive principles for NT textual criticism have not been formulated as yet, for on the one hand there is neither consensus on the earliest history of the NT text nor an acceptable reconstruction of that history, while on the other hand there is no set of criteria for selecting the most likely original reading that can be applied uniformly, consistently, and without risk of mutual conflict. This is what makes textual criticism, as currently practiced, an art as well as (or is it rather than?) a science, and, moreover, this is what behooves textual critics to continue their scrutiny and to press their analysis of both poles of the current methodological tension in NT textual criticism.

b. Thoroughgoing eclecticism. One way out of the dilemma of internal evidence versus external evidence is to opt for one of them and largely to ignore the other. A school of thought within eclecticism that has become known, justifiably or not, as rigorous or thoroughgoing eclecticism (identified in recent decades primarily with Kilpatrick, *see bibliog.*) emphasizes in a thorough fashion the various internal criteria and deemphasizes, in a similarly thorough way, the historical-development and documentary criteria (external evidence). This approach, which eschews the notion that any MS or group of MSS is "best" or is "right" as a whole, treats readings—and accepts or rejects them—entirely on their individual and intrinsic merits. Whether a reading is found in an early MS or a late one or whether it is a component of a presumed text type that is ancient or more recent is immaterial, for the stylistic, linguistic, and scribal factors are the decisive determinants of whether any reading is original or secondary. Thus, each reading at any given point in the NT text has an equal opportunity to be recognized as the most likely original text and will be so designated if it stands up to the requisite internal tests of originality. Thoroughgoing eclecticism, then, affirms that decisions on readings—and this means decisions on practically all readings—must precede decisions on the quality or weight of MSS, precisely the opposite emphasis from Hort's famous dictum: "Knowledge of documents should precede final judgement upon readings."

The rigorous application of internal criteria by the advocates of thoroughgoing eclecticism has been beneficial for NT textual criticism in that (*a*) older criteria have been exploited extensively and have been refined in the process, (*b*) some new criteria or fresh applications have come to light and have been tested, and (*c*) both the obvious strengths and the recognized limitations of internal criteria are open to scrutiny as never before.

5. Historical-development and documentary emphases. Judging from the past fifty years or so, most textual critics, while willing to learn from the thoroughgoing eclectics, are reluctant to emphasize internal considerations to the virtual exclusion of external factors. Most, therefore, follow a moderate form of the eclectic method, apparently clinging to the still unfulfilled hope that a definitive reconstruction of the history of the earliest NT text can be formulated and that such a formulation will point to *one* demonstrably superior text type or MS tradition, which then could be given the deciding voice in instances of disputed text. Furthermore, most textual critics reveal a predisposition for the B-א (Hort's "Neutral") text type in this decisive role, despite the lack of a clear rationale for such a view. This predisposition is attested also by the most widely used hand-editions of the Greek NT in the twentieth century, because editions such as those of Nestle-Aland (1898, 1963[25]), Merk (1933, 1965[9]), Bover (1943, 1968[5]), and the *United Bible Societies' Greek New Testament* (1966, 1968[2]) all have a text relatively close to the NT text of Westcott-Hort and close, therefore, to their best MSS, B and א. (This same kind of Greek text, incidentally, underlies virtually all recent English translations of the NT; *see* VERSIONS, ENGLISH[S].) Both the longing for such a demonstrably "best" text type or "best" MS and particularly the conviction that a tracing and reconstruction of the history of the earliest NT text would permit the identification of such superior documents have pushed some textual critics toward the external evidence pole of the current text-critical dilemma. No one today, however, relies exclusively on external evidence in making NT text-critical decisions, with the rare exception of a genealogical textual critic (*see bibliog.* under Textual Analysis; also cf. TEXT, NT §E5*d*). Much scholarly effort has been expended, though, on the history of the earliest NT text and on ways to measure MS relationships quantitatively. Both endeavors emphasize external evidence and the historical-development and documentary factors involved in textual decisions.

a. Reconstruction of the earliest history of the NT text. Attempts to plot the history of the NT text in its early stages of development usually have gone hand in glove with attempts to classify the NT MSS into groups and to identify early recensions; the goal, naturally, is to trace the lines of development back to the earliest possible stage and to isolate thereby that primitive form of the text closest to the original. Modern studies of this kind began with J. A. Bengel in 1725 and reached their most notable—though still unsatisfactory—formulations in the work of Westcott and Hort (1881-82) and H. Von Soden (1902-13) (*see* TEXT, NT §§E3-6). The net result of the past century of scholarship is adherence still to the basic scheme of Westcott-Hort: two early textual streams, with roots traceable to the second century, can be identified, the Alexandrian or Egyptian text type (Hort's "Neutral") and the so-called Western text type. Elaborate attempts have been made to isolate a third early stream, a Caesarean text type, but there is now considerable uncertainty about its reality. In addition, the Byzantine text type, which issued eventually in the TEXTUS RECEPTUS, was identified by Westcott and Hort as a late fourth- or early fifth-century coalescence of the Neutral and Western streams, thus removing this text type from the earliest formulative stages of the NT text. Whether further progress, aided perhaps by the striking discoveries of early and extensive NT papyri (such as P^{45}, P^{46}, P^{66}, and P^{75}), can be made toward the clarification of the textual situation in the first two centuries of NT textual transmission remains to be seen; that is the crucial period and also the most enigmatic, but to discover its secrets, if only about the formation and interrelationship of the Alexandrian and Western textual streams, would clarify matters immeasurably and add substantively to our understanding of the original text of the NT, and this remains one of the most urgent tasks in the field.

b. Quantitative measurement of MS relationships. The attempt to measure and to establish relationships between and among NT MSS has a long history in modern textual criticism, but throughout much of that history measurements have been made on too narrow a base, with inadequate data or controls, or with insufficient exactness, and, not surprisingly, with inconclusive or questionable results. Too often, e.g., MS relationships were calculated from random samplings, or by a mere comparison of the quantity of separate agreements of two or more MSS with an arbitrary standard, or by measuring two or three MSS against one another but without reference to the larger MS tradition. Recently, more adequate methods have issued from proposals by Colwell and Tune (*see bibliog.*). Ideally, of course, a NT MS should be compared with all other NT MSS to determine its place in the MS tradition; though this ideal is still out of reach, Colwell and Tune's method requires that MS relationships must be determined by *direct* and *mutual* comparison of an adequate number and a representative selection of MSS (and not merely by independent comparisons with an external standard) and, furthermore, that the total amount of variation—both agreements and disagreements—among all MSS treated must be calculated if a sound and usable result is to be obtained. Fee's work (*see bibliog.*) exemplifies so far the most extensive use and refinement of this new method of quantitative measurement of NT MS relationships.

The so-called Claremont Profile Method for grouping NT minuscule MSS (*see bibliog.*) is another recent development in quantitative method; for the present, at least until computers can be utilized extensively in NT textual criticism, it is a sampling method that employs carefully selected test readings to isolate characteristic profiles of readings in various groups of MSS and thereby to distinguish the groups from one another. Since the method is designed for and applicable primarily to Byzantine MSS, it does not rely, as older methods did, on "unique group readings" (which are rare in Byzantine groups) but on "characteristic group readings" that constitute a distinctive group profile. Built upon but also correcting the extensive classification system of Von Soden and incorporating Colwell's methodological insights, the method not only allows for the quick classification of a minuscule MS, but also identifies those subgroups and individual MSS worthy of more detailed study.

Determining NT MS relationships with the aid of computers is most promising under the procedures employed at the Münster Institute for New Testament Textual Research (K. Aland. chairman), where Ott utilizes the computer to classify MSS and to define the relationships among them (*see bibliog.*)

These developments represent only a beginning in the disciplined measurement of MS relationships, but they and similar methods are essential if the thousands of NT MSS are to be sorted and classified and if the resulting groups are to be useful in reconstructing the history of the NT text—tasks still considered by most textual critics to be basic to the recovery of the original NT text.

6. Conclusion. NT text-critical methodology faces substantial challenges on each of its fronts. The whole range of criteria for choosing among readings awaits further definition and precision, sophisticated methods for determining MS groupings have developed only recently; and both a definitive history and a definitive theory of the text are lacking. Newly discovered MSS have enriched the already abundant storehouse of NT source materials, but text-critical theory still lags behind. Yet the current, though recent, recognition by textual critics that they face a crisis of theory may itself be a significant step forward in the solution of that crisis.

Bibliography. On methodology in general: B. F. Westcott and F. J. A. Hort, *The NT in the Original Greek,* 2 vols. (1881-82); E. C. Colwell, *Studies in Methodology in Textual Criticism of the NT,* NTTS, IX (1969); K. W. Clark, "The Textual Criticism of the NT," *Peake's Commentary on the Bible,* eds. M. Black and H. H. Rowley (1962), 663-70; B. M. Metzger, *The Text of the NT: Its Transmission, Corruption, and Restoration* (2nd ed., 1968); *A Textual Commentary on the Greek NT: A Companion Volume to the United Bible Societies' Greek NT* (1971); K. Aland, *Studien zur Überlieferung des NT und seines Textes,* Arbeiten zur NT Textforschung, II (1967); J. N. Birdsall, "The NT Text," *The Cambridge History of the Bible,* I (1970), 308-77; E. J. Epp, "The Twentieth Century Interlude in NT Textual Criticism," *JBL,* XCIII (1974), 386-414.

On eclecticism (also called rational criticism): M.-J. Lagrange, *Critique textuelle, II: La critique rationnelle* (1935); G. D. Kilpatrick, "Western Text and Original

Text in the Gospels and Acts," *JTS,* XLIV (1943), 24-36, ". . . in the Epistles," *JTS,* XLV (1944), 60-65, "Atticism and the Text of the Greek NT," *NT Aufsätze: Festschrift für J. Schmid,* ed. J. Blinzler, O. Kuss, and F. Mussner (1963), pp. 125-37, and "The Greek NT Text of Today and the *Textus Receptus,*" *The NT in Historical and Contemporary Perspective: Essays in Memory of G. H. C. Macgregor,* ed. H. Anderson and W. Barclay (1965), pp. 189-206; J. K. Elliott, "Rational Criticism and the Text of the NT," *Theology,* LXXV (1972), 338-43, "Can We Recover the Original NT?" *ibid.,* LXXVII (1974), 338-53.

On textual analysis: V. Dearing (who follows genealogical method, forming a stemma of the "states" of the text), *A Manual of Textual Analysis* (1959); *Principles and Practice of Textual Analysis* (1974).

On quantitative methods: E. C. Colwell and E. W. Tune, "Method in Establishing Quantitative Relationships between Text-Types of NT Manuscripts," in Colwell, *Studies . . . ,* 56-62; G. D. Fee, *Papyrus Bodmer II (P66): Its Textual Relationships and Scribal Characteristics,* Studies and Documents, XXXIV (1968), "Codex Sinaiticus in the Gospel of John: A Contribution to Methodology in Establishing Textual Relationships," *NTS,* XV (1968/69), 23-44; on the Claremont Profile Method: F. Wisse and P. R. McReynolds, *JBL,* LXXXVII (1968), 191-97; "Family E and the Profile Method," *Bibl.,* LI (1970), 65-75; on computers in textual criticism: K. Aland, "Novi Testamenti graeci editio maior critica," *NTS,* XVI (1969/70), 163-77; W. Ott, "Computer Applications in Textual Criticism," *Computer and Literary Studies,* ed. A. J. Aitken, R. W. Bailey, and N. Hamilton-Smith (1973), pp. 199-223.

E. J. Epp

***TEXTUS RECEPTUS.** Although this technical term and its English equivalent, "received (accepted) text," are most often used by NT scholars, they are sometimes applied, with resultant ambiguity, to one or more of the following stages in the development of the Hebrew OT text: (1) the standardized consonantal text which replaced multiple textual traditions, perhaps in the first century A.D. (*see* TEXT, OT §A2; TEXT, HEBREW, HISTORY OF[S] §1); (2) the text as vocalized by the Tiberian Masoretes of the ben Asher family, completed perhaps in the eighth-ninth centuries A.D. (*see* TEXT, HEBREW, HISTORY OF[S] §2); (3) the text as edited by Jacob ben Hayyim and printed with rabbinic commentaries by Daniel Bomberg in 1524/5 A.D. (the Second Rabbinic Bible, sometimes called Bombergiana).

L. R. Bailey

THANKSGIVING PSALMS. (1QH). A scroll from Cave I at Wadi Qumran, containing a collection of noncanonical hymns in praise of God (*hôdāyôth*). *See* DEAD SEA SCROLLS §5*d;* PSALMS, BOOK OF[S] §1*b*ii.

THEODICY [θεός "god" plus δίκη "justice"]. Perhaps the most difficult question asked by ancient Israel was: Why do the innocent suffer and the wicked prosper (Jer. 12:1)? The question attempts to reconcile evil's existence with a world governed by a benevolent God.

The problem was acute in Israel and Mesopotamia, but less so in Egypt, perhaps because of prevailing belief in a future life and the absence of a concept of justice as one's right rather than a gift. In Egypt, "The Protests of the Eloquent Peasant" (*ANET* [2nd ed.], pp. 407-10), "The Admonitions of Ipūwer" (pp. 441-44), "A Dispute over Suicide" (pp. 405-7), and "The Instruction of Amen-em-het" (pp. 418-19) wrestle with the problem of unjust suffering. Such literature struggles to understand why social turmoil invades a society ruled by god in the person of Pharaoh. Here, human shoulders bear the blame. Not so in Mesopotamia and Israel, for there one encounters direct attack against the gods. Mesopotamian literature consists of a Sumerian "Job" ("Man and His God," pp. 589-91) and three later texts which directly or indirectly attack the gods: "A Babylonian Theodicy" (pp. 601-04), "I Will Praise the Lord of Wisdom" (pp. 434-37), and "A Pessimistic Dialogue between Master and Servant" (pp. 437-38). Israelite dissent gives birth to Job and Ecclesiastes and haunts various authors, particularly Sirach, Jeremiah, and the poet responsible for Ps. 73. In Israel (and Egypt) a literary genre of debate occurs in texts dealing with divine injustice. The form consists of an initial prohibition formula, "Say not," a direct quotation, and a refutation (usually introduced by *kî*).

In essence the theodicy problem concerns three types of evil: primary (or natural), religious, and moral. Israel probes the first in the Yahwistic narrative (*see* YAHWIST[S]). Moral evil exercises its energies constantly. Religious evil surfaces quite late, specifically in II Esdras. None of these issues receives adequate answer, although many avenues are explored.

A number of texts bear witness to the ubiquity of man's struggle to justify God's ways. Abraham's protestations against the intended destruction of Sodom and Gomorrah (Gen. 18) lay bare the decisive issue: "Shall not the Judge of the whole earth do justice?" (author's trans.). In Exod. 32 Moses rebukes God for his merciless decision to destroy the sinful Israelites who reverted to idolatry. Within prophetic literature numerous popular attacks on God's justice are cited for the sake of refutation; presumably the essential message of these quotations represents authentic responses to the problem of theodicy. Israel's prophets wrestled with a God who appeared to seduce men to their destruction (I Kings 22; Isa. 6) and who, at times, resembled a deceitful brook (Jer. 15:18).

Various solutions are proffered. Human sinfulness was perhaps the most common explanation. Since sin bears within itself the seed of punishment, a dogma of RETRIBUTION arises early. It is strengthened by a concept of solidarity, in which a man's descendants can suffer for his sins. Such an understanding pervades the Yahwistic narrative, the DEUTERONOMIC HISTORY, and the work of the Chronicler. Job's friends argue from such a position, as do Pss. 37 and 49. Even unwitting sins fall under this theory, which survives despite clear instances of innocent suffering (Abel). But the moral theory is torn from its corporate moorings by Ezekiel, who insists that God judges each generation on its own merits (Ezek. 18).

In cases of execution, men are admonished to give glory to God (Josh. 7:19). Such doxologies of judgment and formulaic expressions as "Righteous art thou, O Lord" (Jer. 12:1) reveal the necessity of maintaining divine justice despite overwhelming contradictory evidence.

Another solution focuses upon suffering as an instrument of divine pedagogy; this educational or disciplinary theory is advanced by Elihu, Job's younger critic. Suffering teaches essential facts about one's self and God; it leads from second-hand to primary knowledge. Nor is suffering's lesson restricted to the victim of divine wrath or test; the story of innocent suffering offers a model of conduct for others facing difficulty. *See* DISCIPLINE, DIVINE[S].

A third answer is divine presence, theophany. Such a spiritual response appears in Job 38–41, Hab. 3, and Ps. 73. God's majestic presence gives rise to hymnic praise or profound silence; all previous questions vanish when God manifests himself to the suffering one, who knows that a sinner cannot stand before God. *See* THEOPHANY IN THE OT[S].

An eschatological response is also found in a number of texts. The messianic age will rectify all injustice. In late, primarily deuterocanonical literature, belief in a FUTURE LIFE provides a powerful answer to the question of theodicy. Still, the agonizing question in II Esdras derives little comfort from a promised IMMORTALITY, for Ezra cannot forget the masses of mankind suffering in perdition. *See* APOCALYPTICISM §2*c*; APOCALYPTICISM[S].

Sirach introduces two additional solutions. He argues that one must distinguish appearance from reality. Sirach thus combines metaphysical and psychological arguments, the latter of which appeals to excessive anxiety as punishment for sin. The author of Wisdom of Solomon uses both arguments to buttress his relatively new and foreign idea of immortality.

Still another answer is far more radical. In it God is viewed as unjust. Such a skeptical stance underlies Ecclesiastes, parts of Job, the sayings of Agur (Prov. 30:1-4), and the popular criticisms recorded in several prophetic books. The flippant question "Who knows?" (Eccl. 3:21) scarcely conceals the author's dismay over a world gone awry, an existence *in tormentis.*

Perhaps a final response, the redemptive, should be separated from the aforementioned educational theory. According to the Servant Poems in Second Isaiah, suffering can be vicarious, bringing redemption to sufferer and others alike.

In a sense, one may even speak of a tendency toward antitheodicy in ancient Israel. The insistence upon divine freedom (*see* PRESENCE OF GOD, CULTIC[S]) and human limitations of knowledge persists in spite of quests for rational solutions. The sage knows pride's folly, the arrogant insistence upon judging God at the bar of reason. Such intuition leads Job to an answer within revelation rather than wisdom.

The COVENANT relationship intensified the problem of theodicy, for Israel knew which God was punishing her. History exacerbates the issue: the fortunes of ancient Israel often did not justify belief in divine providence (Josiah's fate in particular). The consequent crisis of faith spawns a transcending of the ethical principle and a universalization of providence; reasons for such beliefs are rooted in Israel's creation faith. The Creator of the universe alone can be declared just, for he has both power and will to reward virtue or punish vice. Confronted with the Maker who alone has full knowledge, the questioning soul has one of two resorts: repentance or despair. *See* SUFFERING AND EVIL.

Bibliography. P. L. Berger, *The Sacred Canopy* (1967), pp. 53-80; J. L. Crenshaw, "Popular Questioning of the Justice of God in Ancient Israel," *ZAW,* LXXXII (1970), 380-95, "The Problem of Theodicy in Sirach," *JBL,* XCIV (1975), 47-64, *Prophetic Conflict* (1971), pp. 23-38, and *Studies in Ancient Israelite Wisdom* (1975); W. Eichrodt, "Vorsehungsglaube und Theodizee im AT," *Festschrift Otto Procksch* (1934), pp. 45-70; A. Kuschke, "Altbabylonische Texte zum Thema 'Der leidende Gerechte,'" *TLZ,* LXXXI (1956), 69-76; J. A. Sanders, *Suffering as Divine Discipline in the OT and Post-Biblical Judaism* (1955); H. H. Schmid, *Wesen und Geschichte der Weisheit* (1966), *Gerechtigkeit als Weltordnung* (1968); J. J. Stamm, "Die Theodizee in Babylon und Israel," *JEOL,* IX (1944), 99-107; R. J. Williams, "Theodicy in the Ancient Near East," *CJT,* II (1956), 14-26.

J. L. CRENSHAW

***THEOPHANY IN THE OT.** (For the meaning of the term, *see* THEOPHANY IN THE NT[S]). The OT contains a great variety of accounts of an appearance of God, which are not always clearly distinguishable from visions. Two types may be differentiated: (1) a theophany which is intended generally for individuals and represents for them a special demonstration of favor, and (2) a manifestation of God through the powers of nature which causes alarm among his enemies (theophanies of Yahweh as warrior). Within the first group, it is possible to distinguish between an appearance which serves to legitimate a cult center or person and occurs only once, and one which occurs under prescribed circumstances and can be repeated (theophanies within the cult).

1. Theophanies as a demonstration of favor. ***a. Noncultic legitimations.*** The following categories or instances may be noted.

i. In the patriarchal stories appearances of Yahweh are the occasion for an announcement of divine promises, in response to which the person concerned erects an altar (Gen. 12:7; 26:24-25; 28:12-19; 35:1-15). Such appearance stories originally served to legitimate a particular cult center (sanctuary ETIOLOGY[S]) and did so without the element of promise (*see* PROMISES TO THE PATRIARCHS[S]). The manner of the divine appearance is never portrayed in any detail. It is mentioned only as an introduction to the essential element: God's verbal communication (Gen. 22:1 ff.; 26:1 ff.). *See* PRESENCE OF GOD, CULTIC[S] §2.

ii. Stories about appearances of divine beings in human form and their reception as guests are generally associated with the appearance of the angel of Yahweh (Judg. 6:11, 18 ff.; 13:2 ff.; note however Gen. 18:1 ff.; cf. 19:1). Quite often the point of such stories is the announcement to a barren woman that she will have a child (cf. also Gen. 16:7 ff.). Only in Judg. 6 (cf. Gen. 16:13-14) is a sanctuary etiology found; it, however, has been recast during its transmission into a story of a divine call at a sacred site—(also recast are Exod.

3:1 ff.; cf. Gen. 28:20-21; and Josh. 5:13-15). Instead of legitimating the sacred site, the theophany now serves to legitimate the person who is the chosen instrument of Yahweh.

iii. Moses (Exod. 3:1 ff.), Samuel (I Sam. 3:10; cf. vs. 21), and Solomon (I Kings 3:5; 9:2) were called and commissioned through appearances of God at a holy place. While Isaiah was in the temple, he saw God as the heavenly king (Isa. 6).

iv. Also serving as legitimations are the accounts of the theophany at Mount Sinai (Exod. 19 ff.), since they describe the establishment of Israel's relationship to God. These accounts are not the source of descriptions of other theophanies but rather have been influenced by them (*see* §2). According to J, Yahweh descends from the heavens as the awesome destroyer accompanied by volcanic manifestations, permits Moses to draw near, and confers on him the promise to Israel. According to E, God resides on the mountain peak and appears in the midst of a cultic festival accompanied by a thunderstorm. The people in their alarm ask Moses to mediate, and bind themselves to God through a blood rite. In subsequent layers of the tradition, the theophany culminates (through inclusion of the TEN COMMANDMENTS, the cultic Decalogue, and the Book of the Covenant) in the communication of Yahweh's will, reconciliation after apostasy (Exod. 32–34), and the covenantal accord with its obligations. In P the appearance on the mountain top of Yahweh's glory (כבוד) leads to the construction of the sanctuary and the inauguration of the legitimate cult in Israel. *See* DOCUMENTS.

v. As the God of Sinai, Yahweh accompanies Israel through the wilderness in the form of a pillar of fire and cloud (Exod. 13:21-22; 14:19-20, 24). The God who gives his promise to Abraham is portrayed in J with the characteristics of Yahweh on Sinai: he passes in fire and smoke between the parts of the animals (Gen 15:17-18*a*). Correspondingly, in P, during Israel's march through the desert Yahweh manifests himself and speaks in the same form—his כבוד—as he did during his revelation at Sinai (Num. 14:10; 16:19).

vi. The account of Elijah at Horeb (I Kings 19) contains strong reminiscence from the Sinai tradition (especially from Exod. 33:18 ff.; 34:5-6). The theophany is filled with anti-Canaanite polemic (storm, fire, and earthquake as mere accompanying manifestations; Yahweh is present only in the audible voice) and legitimates Elijah's new commission.

vii. Normative for the OT are the words: "Man shall not see me and live" (Exod. 33:20; cf. 19:21; Judg. 13:22; etc.). The extraordinary character of all theophanies is, therefore, set off with special emphasis (Gen. 16:13; Exod. 3:6; 33:22).

viii. In Exod. 33, an advanced stage of development is reflected in the question of how God can be present among a guilty people. Here we find almost all the substantive terms for the manifestation of God: angel (מלאך), face (פנים), glory (כבוד), beauty (טוב), and name (שם). It is all placed in the context of concern for the protection of people from the danger of the Holy One (vss. 2-3: Yahweh's angel will act only benevolently; vss. 21 ff.: Moses is sheltered by God's hand and may see Yahweh only from the back; in P similarly the cloud protects men from the fiery כבוד). *See* PRESENCE OF GOD, CULTIC[S] §§2-3.

b. Theophanies within the cult. That E describes the Sinai theophany within the framework of a cultic festival (note the sound of the trumpet and the purification rites in Exod. 19:10 ff.) suggests that Israel was familiar with theophanies in the worship service. The following situations may be cited.

i. The tradition of the tent of meeting probably goes back to an ancient oracular practice (Exod. 33:7). Yahweh is depicted as descending to the entrance to the tent in order to commission someone (Exod. 33:7 ff.; Num. 11:24-25; Deut. 31:14-15) or to carry out judgment (Num. 12).

ii. In the festive worship service, the priest utters Yahweh's self-introduction: "I am Yahweh" (Pss. 50:7; 81:10 [H 11]).

iii. Divine verdicts in behalf of refugees seeking sanctuary, or of the innocent accused of crimes, are pronounced in the cult (Pss. 11:4 ff.; 17:15; cf. Job 19:26-27; for the technical term "seeing God" [*ḥāzâ*], *see* Beyerlin).

iv. The custom of burning incense at the sanctuary, the blowing of the trumpet, and the processions of the ark may represent Yahweh's theophany (Weiser, Beyerlin, Müller).

To be distinguished from all of this is the fact that some texts of the *Gattung* (cf. §2 *below*), especially in postexilic times, found their application in cultic contexts (e.g., Pss. 50 and 97) to which they did not originally belong.

2. Theophanies of Yahweh as warrior. *a*) In the OT we very often hear about a "coming" of Yahweh which produces a reaction of terror. The description follows a fixed pattern: the first part refers to the "going forth" or descent of Yahweh; the second refers to the resultant agitation of nature (mountains quake, and heaven and earth fall into confusion). This pattern is documented in the oldest poetry of Israel (Judg. 5:4-5; cf. Deut. 33:2), and was still in use in post-OT times (Ecclus. 16:18-19; 43:16-17; Jth. 16:15; Wisd. Sol. 5:21-23; Asmp. Moses 10:3-6; IQH 3:32-36). It may encompass one or two verses (Amos 1:2) or extensive compositions (Ps. 18:7-15 [H 8-16]; Hab. 3:3-15; etc.). With the passage of time, both parts were able to establish themselves independently (this is especially true of the first part, in prophetic material: Isa. 30:27-28; Jer. 25:30-31; Ps. 50:2-3; etc.; for the second part, cf., e.g., Ps. 114:3-8; Job 26:5).

b) Such theophanic descriptions are not uniquely Israelite. Sumerian and Akkadian hymns and Hittite and Ugaritic myths describe the storm-god (Ishkur, Teshub, Adad, Baal, and other deities) as a "divine warrior" (Cross, Miller) surrounded by dazzling radiance (Akkad. *melammū*), who rides the storm and travels on cloudy chariots, and who hurls bolts of lightning as arrows. In response the earth quakes; mountains stagger; and the ocean trembles (Jeremias, Lipiński).

c) Such warrior imagery characterizes many of the hymns that describe theophanies in Israel, epecially in the period of the monarchy (Pss.

18:7-15 [H 8-16]; Nah. 1:2*a*, 3*b*-6; Hab. 3:8-15; Jer. 10:13). Archaic texts speak, however, about Yahweh's coming, his descent, and especially his "going forth" (יצא, technical term for the war of Yahweh; cf. Judg. 4:14; II Sam. 5:24) from his abode, an emphasis which is not found in similar texts in other nations of the ancient Near East. His abode may be heaven, Zion, or Sinai, the last giving the impression of being the most ancient. Yahweh is called in Judg. 5:5 (cf. Ps. 68:8 [H 9]), "the One from Sinai (זה סיני)." In its early history, therefore, Israel substantially altered the pattern in use among its neighbors, a process which was influenced by the unique Sinai tradition, which had not yet assumed the form it has in Exod. 19 ff. (cf. §1*a* iv). The differences between the pattern that was influenced by Israelite thought and the one that was more influenced by non-Israelite cultic patterns are clearly recognizable in Hab. 3:3-7.

d) During the process of transmission, the theophany descriptions were influenced by mythical and historical traditions, e.g., the struggle with chaos (Nah. 1:4; Hab. 3:8; Ps. 18:15 [H 16]), the crossing of the Red Sea (Pss. 77:19 [H 20]; 114:3, 5), the Day of the Lord (Hab. 3:10-12; Amos 1:2*b*; Nah. 1:4*b*, 5*b*), and particularly the concept of divine rule (Deut. 33:5; cf. the contexts of Pss. 29; 97; Zech. 9; 14).

e) Essentially the pattern of the theophanic descriptions belongs in the category of hymn. Originally it was part of the hymn of triumph sung upon the successful completion of Yahweh's wars (Judg. 5:4-5; cf. Deut. 33:2-5, 26-29; however, Lipiński judges its most ancient situation to be a ritual prior to the war of Yahweh). In the monarchic period we meet the pattern in hymns which celebrate the defeat of the nations attacking Zion (Ps. 46:6 [H 7]), the protection and blessing of Israel in the wilderness (Ps. 68:7-8 [H 8-9]), the triumph over the waters of chaos at the Red Sea and the Jordan (Pss. 77:16-19 [H 17-20]; 114:3-6), the defeat of Israel's enemies (Nah. 1:2 ff.; Hab. 3:3-15), the deliverance of the king from affliction (Pss. 18:7-15 [H 8-16]; 144:5-6), or, more generally, Yahweh's supremacy as the king of the world (Pss. 29; 99:1; etc.). In postexilic times the theophany representations celebrated Yahweh's power over the gods (Ps. 97:6-7; Jer. 10:10) and over the universe (Amos 9:5; Job 9:5-6; 26:5-6, 11). In prayers the people can supplicate Yahweh to intervene in this way (Ps. 80:1-2 [H 2-3]; Hab. 3:2).

f) Within the older prophetic writings the direction of the pattern was completely changed: Yahweh's coming is now a future event which will bring judgment upon Israel (Mic. 1:2-7; Amos 1:2)! In exilic and postexilic times the prophets often announced the coming of Yahweh as the warrior to free Israel (Isa. 40:10-11; 42:13); to do battle against foreign nations (Isa. 19:1; cf. Zech. 9:14 and 14:3-4); and to fight against the wicked in Israel (Isa. 59:15-19; 66:15-16; Mal. 3:1-5). Finally, in the beginnings of APOCALYPTICISM, the Warrior comes to bring judgment upon the world (Jer. 25:30-31; Isa. 26:21; IQH 3:32 ff.; etc.).

Bibliography. For §1*a*: J. Morgenstern, "Biblical Theophanies," *ZA*, XXV (1911), 139-93, XXVIII (1913-14), 15-60; F. Nötscher, *"Das Angesicht Gottes schauen" nach biblischer und babylonischer Auffassung* (1924 [2nd ed., 1969]), pp. 20-53, 147-70; J. Barr, "Theophany and Anthropomorphism in the OT," VTSup, VII (1960), 31-38; J. Lindblom, "Theophanies in Holy Places in Hebrew Religion," *HUCA*, XXXII (1961), 91-106; R. Rendtorff, "Die Offenbarungsvorstellungen im Alten Israel," in *Offenbarung als Geschichte*, ed. W. Pannenberg, Kerygma und Dogma, Beiheft I (1961), 21-41; W. Beyerlin, *Origins and History of the Oldest Sinaitic Traditions* (1965); J. K. Kuntz, *The Self-Revelation of God* (1967); C. Westermann, "Die Herrlichkeit Gottes in der Priesterschrift," in *Wort-Gebot-Glaube*, ed. H.-J. Stöbe *et al.*, ATANT, LIX (1970), 227-49; E. Zenger, *Die Sinaitheophanie* (1971); H. Mölle, *Das "Erscheinen" Gottes im Pentateuch* (1973).

For §1*b*: G. von Rad, "'Gerechtigkeit' und 'Leben' in der Kultsprache der Psalmen," *Gesammelte Studien zum AT*, I, (1958), 225-47; W. Zimmerli, *Gottes Offenbarung* (1963), pp. 11-40; J. Muilenburg, "The Speech of Theophany," *HDSB*, XXVIII (1964), 35-47; H.-P. Müller, "Die kultische Darstellung der Theophanie," *VT*, XIV (1964), 183-91; W. Beyerlin, *Die Rettung der Bedrängten in den Feindpsalmen der Einzelnen* (1970), pp. 141-46; A. Weiser, "Zur Frage nach den Beziehungen der Psalmen zum Kult," in *Festschrift A. Bertholet* (1950), pp. 513-31.

For §2: W. F. Albright, "The Psalm of Habakkuk," in *Studies in OT Prophecy Presented to T. H. Robinson*, ed. H. H. Rowley (1950), pp. 1-18; F. Schnutenhaus, "Das Kommen und Erscheinen Jahwes im AT," *ZAW*, LXXVI (1964), 1-21; J. Jeremias, *Theophanie. Die Geschichte einer alttestamentlichen Gattung* (1965); M. Weiss, "The Origin of the Day of the Lord Reconsidered," *HUCA*, XXXVII (1966), 29-71; C. Westermann, *The Praise of God in the Psalms* (1965 [4th Ger. ed., 1968]), pp. 69-76; W. H. Schmidt, *Alttestamentlicher Glaube und seine Umwelt* (1968), pp. 40-42, 47-48, 148-52; E. Lipiński, *La Royauté de Yahwé dans la poésie et le culte de l'Ancien Israël* (2nd ed., 1968), pp. 187-256, and "Les Psaumes," *DBSup*, IX (1974), 16-23; E. Jenni, "'Kommen' im theologischen Sprachgebrauch des AT," in *Wort-Gebot-Glaube*, ed. H.-J. Stöbe *et al.* (1970), 251-61; P. D. Miller, *The Divine Warrior in Early Israel* (1973); F. M. Cross, *Canaanite Myth and Hebrew Epic* (1973), 91 ff., 147 ff.

J. JEREMIAS

***THEOPHANY IN THE NT.** The word theophany [Gr. θεοφάνεια] does not itself appear in the NT, where the fundamental affirmation is that God's decisive self-disclosure occurred in Jesus (e.g., John 1:14, 18; Col. 1:15; Heb. 1:1-3; *see* CHRISTOLOGY IN THE NT[S]). Nevertheless, theophanic backgrounds are discernible in certain layers of tradition within the NT.

1. Meaning and method. "Theophany" is a compound of the Greek word for God (Θεός) and the verb φαίνω, which means to appear, become visible, make manifest or show oneself (for philological studies, *see bibliog.*). While the word θεοφάνεια and related ones such as ἐπιφάνεια often connote a sudden, unexpected manifestation of divine activity, the primary idea is of "helping intervention," a picture borrowed perhaps from military terminology. The NT uses such language in speaking of the eschatological appearance of Jesus in his earthly ministry (cf. II Tim. 1:9-10; 4:8; Tit. 2:11; 3:4; also Luke 1:79; John 1:5; I John 2:8), and of his future appearance at the Parousia (cf. II Thess. 2:8; I Tim. 6:14; II Tim.

4:1, 8; Tit. 2:13). Other verbs of seeing (e.g., βλέπω, ὀπτάνομαι θεάομαι, θεωρέω, φανερόω, and ὁράω>ὤφθη, a key word in theophanies), as well as verbs of hearing (or of other sense perception) are also used in narratives which may be called theophanic in the strictest sense.

The history of religion school (*see bibliog.*) emphasized the common features of theophany texts. But these scholars tended to neglect points of contrast and distinctiveness, to draw analogies too quickly, and to assume too readily that material had been carried over from one culture to another. Therefore, investigation of theophanies in the literature of classical antiquity as well as in the Bible has been renewed with special concern for a more precise methodology. Recent scholarship has shown that, when theophany texts from various religious traditions are analyzed form-critically, and their religious ideas are subjected to careful comparative study, much can be learned about the meaning of theophany, the structural forms in which a theophany was recounted, and the place of theophany within earliest Christianity, including the NT.

2. Hellenistic backgrounds. OT and Jewish sources provide important materials for comparison (*see* THEOPHANY IN THE OT[S]), but Hellenistic sources must also be considered. From the earliest times, the belief in the everyday reality of divine intervention, the self-disclosure of deities, and the imposition of their will was basic to the Greek understanding of life and the universe (e.g., Homer, *Odyssey* XVII, 483-87). Special importance accrues to divine appearances in human likeness. In Lystra, Paul and Barnabas are held to be Hermes and Zeus as the people cry out: "The gods have come down to us in the likeness of men!" (Acts 14:8 ff.; cf. the appearance of Zeus and Hermes to Philemon and Baucis, Ovid, *Metamorphosis* VIII, 611-724). The resistance of the apostles is characteristic of the tensions expressed in such encounters (cf. Acts 10:26 and 28:6).

The classical example of theophany in the Greek world was the festival celebration at Delphi (and elsewhere) for Apollo, the "Theophania," where his image and those of other deities were paraded about for the worshipers (e.g., Herodotus, *History* I.51; and Philostratus, *Life of Apollonius of Tyana* IV, 31). Representations cast in the form of dreams and visions abound in this literature (e.g., Apuleius, *Metamorphosis* XI). Nevertheless, a conscientious effort was frequently made to distinguish between these and "actual" appearances in a waking state (e.g., the story of the Asclepius supplicant who was visited and cured, not during her sanctuary vigil ["incubation"], but during her journey home; or the lifesaving visit to Simonides of Castor and Pollux; *see bibliog.*). In the Hellenistic period, heroic tradition influenced the theophany concept, and this cultural and religious fusion spawned cults which hailed the deification of past figures (especially rulers), stories of the "translation" of famous persons, and novelistic lives of certain "divine men." *See* ARETALOGY[S].

3. Theophany and the NT. ***a. The Easter appearance traditions.*** A number of scholars hold that the earliest church accommodated its teaching about Jesus (e.g., his birth, career, resurrection) to the model of the DIVINE MAN. In the Hellenistic world, certain famous persons were popularly accorded this status and were revered for their possession of supernatural wisdom and powers (e.g., Moses, Elijah, Romulus, Apollonius, Peregrinus). Thus, the question must be raised whether the Easter appearance stories in the NT have been influenced by stories told about such divine men.

Form-critical analysis of early Christian appearance traditions (Matt. 28:16-20; Luke 24:13-35, 36-49; John 20:14-18; 19–29; 21:1-14; perhaps also Mark 6:45-52; Matt. 14:22-23; John 6:15-21; Gos. Pet. 9 (35)-14 (60); Gos. Heb. [Jerome, *De viris illustribus* 2]) demonstrates that at the preredactional level they share a remarkably similar pattern of motifs and themes: (1) the disciples are bereft of their Lord; (2) Jesus suddenly and unexpectedly comes into their presence and addresses them; (3) their reaction is in part doubt and lack of recognition and/or belief and joy; (4) their eyes of understanding are opened; and (5) he sends them forth.

Hellenistic stories about how divine men died or were translated to another sphere are in some ways parallel with the NT traditions, but such parallels are in fact limited to matters of form, diction, and imagery. If intention and function are considered as well, the traditions about Jesus' appearances stand closer to the anthropomorphic theophanies of the OT (e.g., LXX Gen. 18; Exod. 3–4; Judg. 6 and 13; I Sam. 3; also Tob. 5 and 12; Test. Abraham). The Hellenistic stories served to confirm the apotheosis of the divine men whose death and subsequent reappearance they recounted. The NT appearance stories, however, seem to have been deliberately anchored within the OT theological tradition in order to function as explicit theological statements about the continuing history of God's self-disclosure.

b. Other traditions. Similar perhaps in content, but radically different in form, are the "heavenly radiance" theophanies of Acts 7:54-60 and, especially, the accounts in Acts 9, 22, and 26 of Paul's vision on the Damascus Road. Their origin and relationship to the anthropomorphic appearance form must be settled through further research. Theophany motifs have probably also entered into the formulation of the traditions in Matt. 27:51; Acts 8:26-40; 10:1-33; John 12:27-32. Stories about the visitation and declarations of angels, both in canonical and extracanonical sources, represent an appearance type categorically distinct from theophanies, although they can approach the anthropomorphic form (e.g., Heb. 13:2, and perhaps the empty tomb tradition).

Bibliography. Meaning and method: R. Bultmann and D. Lührmann, "φαίνω," *TDNT*, IX, 1-10; S. Morenz and J. Hempel, *RGG*, VI (3rd ed., 1962), cols. 840-43; D. Lührmann, "Epiphaneia," *Tradition und Glaube: Das frûhe Christentum in Seiner Umwelt*, ed. G. Jeremias, H.-W. Kuhn, H. Stegemann (1971), pp. 185-99; W. Michaelis, "ὁράω," *TDNT*, V (1954 [ET 1968]), 315-82; C. Clemen, *Religionsgeschichtliche Erklärung des NT* (2nd ed., 1924); C. Colpe, *Die religionsgeschichtliche Schule, FRLANT*, LXXVIII (1961); J. Robinson and H. Koester, *Trajectories through Early Christianity* (1971).

Hellenistic backgrounds: On Acts 14: E. Haenchen, *The Acts of the Apostles* (1971), pp. 367-68; H. Conzelmann, *Die Apostelgeschichte,* HNT, VII (2nd ed., rev., 1972), pp. 87-90; S. Lösch, *Deitas Jesu und antike Apotheose* (1933), pp. 38-46; E. Plümacher, *Lukas als hellenistischer Schriftsteller,* SUNT, IX (1972), 92-95. On the Asclepius supplicant and Simonides: R. Pfister, "Epiphanie," PWSup, IV, cols. 295-96; O. Weinreich, *Antike Heilungswunder,* Religionsgeschichtliche Versuche und Vorarbeiten, VIII/1 (1909), 171-74; C. M. Bowra, "Simonides," *Oxford Classical Dictionary,* p. 840. On divine men: C. Habicht, *Gottmenschentum und griechische Städte,* Zetemata, XVI (2nd ed., 1970), esp. 200-205; D. L. Tiede, *The Charismatic Figure as Miracle Worker,* SBLDS, I (1972); J. Alsup, *The Post-Resurrection Appearance Stories of the Gospel Tradition,* Calwer Theologische Monographien, A/V (1975), esp. 215-39.

In general: E. Pax, "Epiphanie," *RAC,* V, cols. 832-909, and ΕΠΙΦΑΝΕΙΑ, Münchener Theologische Studien, I (1955); J. Leipoldt and W. Grundmann, eds., *Die Umwelt des Urchristentums,* 3 vols. (1967).

Theophany and the NT: A. R. C. Leaney, "Theophany, Resurrection and History," *Studia Evangelica,* V, *TU,* CIII (1968), 101-13; H. Koester, "One Jesus and Four Primitive Gospels," *Trajectories,* pp. 193-98; Alsup, *op. cit.,* pp. 239-65. J. E. ALSUP

***THESSALONIANS, FIRST LETTER TO THE.** Recent study has continued to build on the insights of previous interpreters. Authorship by the apostle Paul is almost universally accepted despite some statistical argument to the contrary (*see* PAUL THE APOSTLE[S] §1*a*). Similarly, suggestions that the canonical letter was compiled by an editor from Pauline fragments have attracted scant following. While it is true that Paul's letters were edited into a collection prior to any surviving MS, partition theories for I Thessalonians have seemed arbitrary and are certainly contradictory. Somewhat more weight, however, has been given to the thesis that 2:13-16 is a non-Pauline interpolation. The anti-Jewish polemic is unusual for Paul, and reference to the final expression of God's wrath could well look back to the capture of Jerusalem and the destruction of the temple in A.D. 70. However, structural study (*see* PAUL THE APOSTLE[S] §1*b*), makes even this suggestion unlikely. The letter illustrates Paul's fondness for triptychs, i.e., A-B-A patterns (cf. I Cor. 8-9-10 and 12-13-14). Thus 1:2-10 closely parallels 2:13-16 with 2:1-12 as the middle member. So, too, 2:17-20 is parallel to 3:9-13 with 3:1-8 as the central section. Accordingly the similarity of 2:13-16 to 1:2-10 is evidence of genuineness, not imitation.

In general I Thessalonians has the normal structure of a Pauline letter (*see* LETTER[S] §4): sender(s), recipient(s), greeting (1:1), thanksgiving (1:2-10), body (with renewed thanksgiving, 2:1-16), apostolic visitation (2:17–3:13), PARENESIS (4:1–5:22), blessing (5:23-24), and autograph coda (5:25-28). As a subtype, however, it can be classed with I Corinthians as a "response letter." In both letters Paul devoted the first major section to binding more firmly the ties between himself and his congregation (2:1–3:10; cf. I Cor. 1:10–6:11). Then after a brief transition (3:11-13; cf. I Cor. 6:12-20) he turned to answer specific questions from his congregation (4:1–5:11; cf. I Cor. 7:1–16:12). In I Corinthians Paul tells us that the questions had arrived by letter (7:1). It is entirely possible that I Thessalonians also was written in response to a letter. The questions concerned sexual morality (4:1-8), brotherly love (4:9-12), the fate of Christians who died before the Lord's coming (4:13-18), and the date of that great event (5:1-11).

A second area in which new progress has been made is historical. There is now some hesitation about using Acts to provide the setting for this letter (*see* PAUL THE APOSTLE[S] §1*c*). Traditionally the letter is dated by connecting I Thess. 3:6 (arrival of Timothy) with Acts 18:5 (Paul in Corinth shortly after founding the church in Thessalonica). However, the letter itself implies the passage of several years. Since Paul's original mission the Thessalonian Christians have themselves worked as missionaries in both Macedonia and Achaia (1:7-8). News of their work has spread beyond this region. Paul (apparently as he traveled outside Greece) continually met those who knew of their conversion (1:9). Some time later the Thessalonians were subjected to persecution so severe that Paul feared they might abandon their faith. He had tried repeatedly to revisit them. Since he was "at present" (2:17; "short time" in the RSV is misleading) still absent from them (he was in Athens), he sent Timothy in his stead, and Timothy has now returned with good news. In the course of these events one or more of the Thessalonians have died. This interval may also include the writing of II Thessalonians (*see* THESSALONIANS, SECOND LETTER TO THE[S]).

For the theory that Paul wrote to combat a group of opponents variously described as "Gnostics," "radicals," or "libertines," *see bibliog.*

Bibliography. Commentaries: E. Best, HNTC (1972), the most comprehensive since Rigaux. Also A. L. Moore, Century Bible (1969); D. E. H. Whiteley, New Clarendon Bible (1969); L. Morris, NICNT (1959).

Studies: R. Jewett, "Enthusiastic Radicalism and the Thessalonian Correspondence," *Proceedings of the Society of Biblical Literature,* I (1972), 181-232; contrast A. J. Malherbe, "Gentle As a Nurse," *NovT,* XII (1970), 203-17, and F. Laub, *Eschatologische Verkündigung und Lebensgestaltung nach Paulus,* Biblische Untersuchungen, X (1973). J. C. HURD

***THESSALONIANS, SECOND LETTER TO THE.** An enigmatic letter, most probably written by the apostle Paul, which presents a number of problems to the modern interpreter. It may well be the earliest surviving piece of Christian writing.

The traditional interpretation supports the genuineness of the letter but leaves a number of questions almost completely unanswered. Why should Paul need to write the Thessalonians so soon after writing I Thessalonians? Why are the two letters so different in spirit and content although so similar in outline and phraseology? Why should Paul have to guard against the possibility of letters forged in his name (2:2; 3:17)?

In considerable measure these problems spring not from the letter itself but from the way in which it is usually related to other evidence about Paul. Specifically, the Acts narrative makes it appear that there was not sufficient time for Paul to have written to the Thessalonians prior to I

Thessalonians. However, the abrupt sequence of events in Acts does not form a natural background for I Thessalonians (*see* THESSALONIANS, FIRST LETTER TO THE[S]) and is awkward for II Thessalonians: those who reject the letter's authenticity do so mainly because it seems so pointless as a sequel to I Thessalonians.

However, a number of interpreters today begin with the letters rather than Acts (*see* PAUL THE APOSTLE[S] §1*c*). When the Thessalonian letters themselves are compared, several reasons emerge for choosing II Thessalonians as the earlier. *(a)* The problem of those who do not work because of their belief in the imminent end of the age sounds new in II Thess. 3:6-12 but old in I Thess. 4:11; 5:14. *(b)* Thessalonian persecution is an immediate reality in II Thess. 1:6-7. It is both past and present in I Thess. 1:6; 2:14; 3:3-5. Moreover, in the latter, Paul has conceived the idea of revisiting the Thessalonians and has in fact sent Timothy. *(c)* The gathering of (living) Christians to meet the Lord is the topic of II Thess. 2 (*see* vs. 1). When I Thess. 4:13-18 speaks of both the living and the dead, the death of Christians seems to be a new problem. *(d)* The Thessalonians' disillusionment in II Thess. 2:2 appears to stem from the failure of the "Lord Jesus Christ" to appear after a sequence of events which they have invested with apocalyptic significance. Paul countered with his own sequence, as yet in progress. (Some refer belief that the Day was present to Gnostic radicals; *see bibliog.*) I Thess. 5:1-11, however, is more timeless and less apocalyptic. As in his later letters, Paul speaks of the Day as coming at an indefinite time. *(e)* The problem of indicating that his dictated letters represented his own presence would presumably concern Paul more at the beginning of his letter-writing career than later (II Thess. 2:2; 3:17).

The identity of the restrainer (II Thess. 2:6-7) remains a problem, for Paul spoke with intentional obscurity. However, CALIGULA's attempt to have his statue erected in the temple in Jerusalem (A.D. 40) comes closer than any other event in the period A.D. 30-70 to fulfilling Daniel 11:31 (the setting up of the abomination in the temple, cf. Mark 13:14), which had been part of Paul's original apocalyptic preaching (II Thess. 2:5).

The resemblances between the two Thessalonian letters which go beyond the common stock of eschatological terms seem mainly concentrated in the structural conventions Paul inherited and developed as a letter writer (*see* LETTER[S] §4). The sender, addressee, and greeting are stereotyped. Each letter has Paul's customary thanksgiving section (II Thess. 1:3-12; I Thess. 1:2-10), though in each it is renewed (II Thess. 2:13-17; I Thess. 2:13-16), which is unusual. The bodies of the two letters concern different subjects. As with most of Paul's letters the body section is followed by moral instruction (II Thess. 3:1-15; I Thess. 4:1–5:22). Both letters include a number of prayers and blessings which contain similar liturgical phrases. It appears that as Paul's career progressed he became more varied in his letter style.

Bibliography. In addition to bibliog. for THESSALONIANS, FIRST LETTER TO THE[S]: C. H. Giblin, *The Threat to Faith,* AnBib, XXXI (1967), on ch. 2; C. H. Buck and G. Taylor, *St. Paul: A Study in the Development of His Thought* (1969), on date; W. Trilling, *Untersuchungen zum 2. Thessalonicherbrief,* Erfurter Theologische Studien, XXVII (1972), argues for the letter's pseudonymity.

J. C. HURD

***THESSALONICA.** Archaeological investigation has brought to light the Roman forum, with a large, open, paved area at least 70 by 110 yards. To the E

H. G. May

9. The Agora, Thessalonica

it is defined by a double stoa which has Corinthian columns and well-preserved floor mosaics of geometric design. To the S the forum is bounded by a stoa supported by a *cryptoporticus,* which shelters a number of rooms where Christian wall painting was added. The forum buildings are dated to the first or early second century A.D. Later, about the end of the third century, a Roman odeum was built adjoining the E stoa of the forum. Six semicircular rows of seats are preserved, and under them are vaulted lobbies approached from the odeum through monumental doorways.

Farther E the palace of Galerius, who shared in imperial power A.D. 293-311, has been cleared, revealing a large peristyle courtyard and an octagonal building adjoining it. The octagon, with apses on each of the sides, soon became a church, with an associated baptistery.

Other discoveries have come from ancient cemeteries on the outskirts of the city and various construction sites in the center. A recently studied inscription with a Greek translation from the OT (Num. 6:22-27) and Hebrew phrases is said to show the presence of a Samaritan diaspora community in Thessalonica.

Bibliography. Surveys: "Archaeology in Greece," *AR,* IV (1957)–XIX (1972-73); "Χρονικά," *AD,* XVIII (1963)–XXV (1970).

Inscriptions: *IG,* X.2, ed. C. Edson (1972).

Other: A. Vacalopoulos, *History of Thessaloniki* (1963); B. Lifshitz and J. Schiby, "Une Synagogue samaritaine à Thessalonique," *RB,* LXXV (1968), 368-78; Φ. Πέτσας, "Ἡ Ἀγορὰ τῆς Θεσσαλονίκης," *Athens Annals of Archaeology,* I (1968), 156-62; *Ancient Macedonia,* ed. B. Laourdas and C. Makaronas (1970), pp. 224-27, 239-51; H. J. Vickers, "Hellenistic Thessaloniki," *JHS,* XCII (1972), 156-70.

C. L. THOMPSON

***THOMAS, GOSPEL OF.** A collection of 114 sayings of Jesus discovered in a Coptic version in the years 1945-46 (*see* NAG HAMMADI[S]) in Upper Egypt, and not to be confused with the infancy gospel of Thomas (*see* APOCRYPHA, NT[S] §4). In 1897 and 1903 Greek fragments of a similar writing were found at Oxyrhynchus (*see* OXYRHYNCUS SAYINGS OF JESUS) in Egypt; the Coptic text could therefore be a translation of a Greek original. The MS of the Coptic version probably dates from the fourth century A.D. The Greek original, however, has always been dated about A.D. 140, and there are so far no reasons to modify that conclusion. The contents of the newly discovered Gospel of Thomas are Jewish Christian, Encratitic, and Gnostic.

1. GTh and Jewish Christianity
   a. Logion 65
   b. Logion 8
   c. Other evidence
2. Encratitic influences
3. GTh as a Gnostic gospel
Bibliography

1. GTh and Jewish Christianity. The author of GTh seems to have used a Jewish Christian source. He believes, for instance, that James the Righteous (*see* JAMES §5), and not Simon Peter, shall be great among the Christians after the death of Jesus (Logion 12); that the sabbath, and not Sunday, should be observed (Logion 27); and that the PHARISEES have received the keys of knowledge, that is, the oral part of the Jewish Law which makes possible the interpretation and application of the written Law in daily life (Logion 39). Edessa (now Urfa in Turkey) became the permanent center of Syriac, Aramaic-speaking Christianity, and it would not be surprising if GTh originated there. Even if the story of the conversion of King Abgar by the Palestinian Jewish-Christian Addai is a legend (*see* ABGARUS, EPISTLES OF CHRIST AND), the possibility remains that Addai was a historical figure, and that the foundations of Syriac Christianity were Jewish Christian.

The main issue, however, is whether GTh is independent of our canonical gospels, and if so whether the sayings have any claim to authenticity. This would seem to be the case for about half the sayings that are of synoptic type or similar to the canonical text. This can be illustrated by examination of two familiar parables as they are presented in GTh. In each case it can be seen that this author transmitted an independent tradition.

a. Logion 65. The parable of the wicked husbandmen (Matt. 21:33-41; Mark 12:1-9; Luke 20:9-16). The GTh version is as follows:

> He said: A good man had a vineyard. He gave it to husbandmen so that they would work it, and he would receive its fruits from them. He sent his servant so that the husbandmen would give him the fruit of the vineyard. They seized his servant, and beat him, a little more and they would have killed him. The servant came and told it to his master. His master said: "Perhaps they did not know him." He sent another servant; the husbandmen beat him as well. Then the owner sent his son. He said: "Perhaps they will respect my son." Since those husbandmen knew that he was the heir of the vineyard, they seized him and killed him. Whoever has ears, let him hear.

Three different people are mentioned here, with the emphasis on the third. This is a device of popular narrative all over the world and is characteristic of Jesus' teaching, e.g., in the parable of the Good Samaritan: a priest, a Levite, a Samaritan. The same is found in Logion 65: "his servant," "another servant," "his son." This pattern distinguishes the parable as it appears in GTh from the Synoptic gospels. Moreover, other features from the Synoptics are absent: the "son" is not called "beloved" (Mark, Luke); "[Come,] let us kill him" (an allusion to the story of Joseph; cf. LXX Gen. 37:20) is omitted; there is no hint of the murder of the prophets (Mark 12:5), of the earlier and later prophets (Matt. 21:35-36), of the crucifixion outside the town (Matthew, Luke), or of the mission among the Gentiles and the rejection of Israel (Matt. 21:41). GTh has, therefore, no allegorical features at all. Rather, the parable describes a scene from daily life, namely, the revolutionary situation in Galilee, where tenants refused to pay their absentee landlord the rent. The point is, not what is said about the son, but what is said about the farmers. Every Jew would have understood that Jesus was speaking about Israel and its survival, threatened at the time by the adventurous plans of the Zealots (*see* ZEALOT; ZEALOT[S]). The vineyard was a symbol of Israel (Isa. 5:1). GTh does not presuppose, like all three Synoptics, the LXX version, "he planted a vineyard," or, like Mark, the LXX reading, "set a hedge about it" (Isa. 5:2). Neither of these readings is found in the Hebrew Bible. Thomas speaks also of the "heir of the vineyard," an expression which the NT does not have. In GTh, as in the OT and the rabbinic writings, the idea of INHERITANCE is concrete: the vineyard is the land of Israel, and the heir of the vineyard is the Messiah (*see* MESSIAH, JEWISH) of Israel, not necessarily the savior of the world.

This author, therefore, remains more faithful to his Jewish Christian source, and he has none of the editorial motifs of the synoptic writers. His understanding of the parable is traceable to an independent tradition which is closer to the Jewish Christian mentality.

b. Logion 8. This logion is parallel to Matt. 13:47-50, the parable of the net.

> And he said: Man is like a wise fisherman who cast his net into the sea and drew it up from the sea full of small fish; among them he found a large [and] good fish, that wise man. He threw all the small fish back into the sea and chose the large fish without pain. Whoever has ears to hear, let him hear.

In Matt. 13:47-50 the parable has become an allegory of the last judgment, but this is not the case in GTh. Here it is, not a parable of the fishing net, but a parable of the fisherman. He does not fish from a boat with a trawling net (Matthew), but stands in the water near the shore and uses a casting net. Both ways of fishing can still be observed at the Sea of Tiberias, and both could depict a fisherman's daily life in Palestine (*see* FISHING; FISHERMEN, NT[S]). A Syriac author of the sixth century, Philoxenos of Mabbug, gives a similar description of the fisherman (*Homilies,* I.9):

> Then one will see the fisherman cast his net into the sea of the world and fill it with fish, small and great. . . . At that time he will draw his net and bring it up to the shore of the sea, as he set it, and he will choose the good fish and will put them in his vessels, . . . and he will throw away the wicked ones into utter darkness, where there shall be wailing and gnashing of teeth.

Here, as in GTh, an eschatological motif is lacking. As it appears in GTh, the parable merely teaches eternal wisdom, and thus shares the unhistorical, international, and humane characteristics of wisdom literature. According to scholars such as Quispel (*see bibliog.*), this is a strong argument in favor of Thomas' independence, in light of the results of REDACTION CRITICISM and of research into the theology of the evangelists.

c. Other evidence. Many other examples of the independence of traditions in GTh could be adduced. For instance, some of the figures of speech it contains are completely new, like the one on fire in Logion 82: "He who is close to me is close to fire, and he who is far from me is far from the kingdom." Whether or not these sayings are parables, and whether they are contained in the canonical gospels or not, all of them could perhaps be traced back to Jesus himself and may be authentic. In GTh allegorical additions to the parables are rare. Where small additions can be discerned, they merely make explicit what is already implicit in Jesus' proclamation: that one should look neither to the future nor to the past, but should believe in the kingdom of God which is already present here and now in his inspired and wise words. The remarkable feature of these parables in GTh is that they are never understood as eschatological, but rather as admonitions to find the mysterious treasure in Jesus' words or, as Logion 3 puts it, in one's own self.

2. Encratitic influences. Related as it is to Syriac literature, GTh could also be Encratitic, since the main representatives of Encratism are Syriac works which originated in Edessa, e.g., the *Homilies* of Macarius and the *Libri Graduum.* This movement was a Christian approach to the problem of love, sex, and wholeness. According to the Encratites, the male is only half of the human being. Adam has been created as an androgynous being (*see* ANDROGYNY[S]); but while he slept, Eve was taken out of him, and so he lost his completeness. The fall is therefore the differentiation of sexes. But Christ, the whole person, has come to restore the primitive unity (the main theme of the Gospel of Philip (*see* PHILIP, GOSPEL OF[S]), also from Nag Hammadi. This view, however, was not exclusively Encratitic. In Plato's *Symposium,* Aristophanes tells a myth, according to which man was originally both male and female. Split by the ire of Jove they seek reunion, and this is love. Many others, e.g., Johannes Scotus Erigena, León Ebreo, and Jakob Böhme, adopted similar ideas. Characteristic of all these thinkers was their veneration of Sophia (Wisdom), the female aspect of deity.

GTh exhibits practically the same views. Here, too, the Holy Spirit is a mother, and as the true mother who gives life she is contrasted with the carnal mother who brings death, because whoever is born is bound to die (Logion 101). When Adam lived in the heavenly Paradise he was one, but through the separation of Eve from his side he has become two (Logion 11). But Christ has come to restore by his teaching the original unity and to make man a *monachos,* i.e., a person who is both unmarried and whole. Logion 22 is symptomatic of such Encratitic (or Greek; cf. Plato, *Symposium* 191 CD) influence:

> Jesus saw children who were being suckled. He said to his disciples: These children who are being suckled are like those who enter the kingdom. They said to him: Therefore, if we become children, will we enter the kingdom? Jesus said to them: When you make the two one, and when you make the inner as the outer, and the outer as the inner, and the above as the below, and when you make the male and the female into a single one, so that the male will not be male and the female not be female, when you make eyes in the place of an eye, and a hand in the place of a

hand, and a foot in the place of a foot, an image in the place of an image, then shall you enter the [kingdom].

Part of this saying is to be found in the Gospel According to the Egyptians (*see* EGYPTIANS, GOSPEL ACCORDING TO THE), probably written in Alexandria in the second century: "When the two become one . . . and the male with the female [become] neither male nor female" (Clem. Misc. III.xiii.92). One could reasonably suppose that the author of GTh used this GEgypt as a source, here and elsewhere. Thus, Encratitic ideas would not have been indigenous in Edessa, but would have been imported from Alexandria, where Jews, like Philo, identified the biblical Adam with the androgynous Anthropos of Plato or the Greek HERMETIC LITERATURE (cf. *Corpus Hermeticum* I.15). Compare Philo, *On the Creation of the World,* 151-52:

> For so long as he [Adam] was by himself, as accorded with such solitude, he went on growing like to the world and like God. . . . But when woman too had been made, beholding a figure like his own and a kindred form, he was gladdened by the sight, and approached and greeted her. . . . Love supervenes, brings together, and fits into one the divided halves, as it were, of a single living creature, and sets up in each of them a desire for fellowship with the other with a view to the production of their like.

3. GTh as a Gnostic gospel. It is not necessary to go back to Philo to understand Thomas' views on the androgynous man. Writings closer to Thomas, like those of the Naassenes (cf. Hippolytus, *Elenchos* V.vi.3–xi.1), reinterpreted the myth of the androgynous man as a symbol of the primeval oneness at which Gnostics must aim. The essential doctrine of GNOSTICISM, particularly well outlined by the Gospel of Truth (*see* TRUTH, GOSPEL OF[S]), is its knowledge of the "self" realized by the soul putting aside the scatteredness of the senses and being reunited to its other self, the spirit or pneuma. Two other Nag Hammadi tractates (GPh and Exegesis on the Soul) describe this union of soul and spirit as being a sacred wedding (ἱερὸς γάμος). Therefore, it is also appropriate to look at GTh from a Gnostic point of view.

Gnosticism was mainly the search for one's nature, a nature which had been lost in the fall from the heavenly Paradise into matter. This idea is present in the various types of Gnosticism: (*a*) Greek, as in Valentinianism (the Gospel of Truth, the Treatise on the Resurrection, the Tripartite Tractate, tractates of Codex I of Nag Hammadi); (*b*) the more or less Syriacized type (GPh and GTh); (*c*) the type influenced by the Bible: ExSoul, some tractates of Codex II (The Nature of the Archons, On the Origin of the World), the various versions of the Apocryphon of John (*see* JOHN, APOCRYPHON OF[S]), the apocalypses of Codex V (the First Apocalypse of James, 2 ApocJas, the Apocalypse of Adam); (*d*) and the genuinely non-Christian type, like Eugnostos the Blessed, of which the Sophia of Jesus Christ is nothing else but a Christianized version.

Logion 3 of GTh, where biblical wisdom is being replaced by Greek wisdom, exemplifies this same kind of Gnostic teaching. Based on the well-known Delphic axiom, "Know thyself," this logion teaches one how to recognize one's own ontological "ego":

> Jesus said: If they who lead you say to you, Behold, the kingdom is in heaven, then the birds of heaven will precede you. If they say to you, It is in the sea, then the fish will precede you. But the kingdom is within you and it is outside you. When you know yourselves, then shall you be known, and you shall know that you are the children of the living Father. But if you do not know yourselves, then you are in poverty, and you are poverty.

If the soul does not come to know itself anew, it lives in the poverty of ignorance instead of being mystically identified with the Father from whom it has emanated. In spite of the influence here of Paul's "to know" and "to be known" (I Cor. 8:1-3; 13:12*b*; Gal. 4:8-9: God knows man first in order to be known by him afterward), "Thomas" intends to say that the primeval unity cannot be reached except through self-knowledge, and that oppositions like "the inner and the outer," "the higher and the lower," are then abolished. When the soul refrains from being scattered and puts aside all these dualisms characteristic of an earthly world, it rediscovers its fundamental oneness. This is highly Gnostic (cf. GEgypt and Clem. Misc. III.xiii.92; Hippolytus, *Elenchos* V.vii.13-15 and the Naassene interpretation of the myth of Attis).

The notion of the kingdom of God in GTh also differs essentially from Paul's. No mention is made of a future advent of Christ, and the eschatological kingdom is now being actualized (Logion 113). This is not surprising, because Gnosis and Gnosticism belong to the wisdom tradition rather than to the kind of prophetic religion which forecasts the coming of a savior or redeemer. God's presence within the soul is assured through a divine spark, the πνεῦμα, which is called here the "pearl" (Logion 76) or the "leaven" (Logion 96).

In one of the most beautiful poems of the Syriac literature, the "Song of the Pearl" (Acts of Thomas 108-13), the individual soul is the pearl which has been lost in Egypt, the realm of matter. The coming of the young prince from his Parthian kingdom to look after the pearl and to save it is interpreted as the fall of a universal soul into the world. In the end the prince saves himself when he discovers the pearl which is part of himself and carries it back to its homeland.

The discovery of GTh has supplied the missing link between the various Gnostic trends of thought of the second century and the great Gnostic ideology of the third, MANICHEISM. Thomas was a popular figure in Manichean communities, as we already knew from the Acts of Thomas (*see* THOMAS, ACTS OF) which are pre-Manichean, and from the Psalms of Thomas of the Manichean Psalter. Like GTh, Mani and Manicheism hold the theory of a primeval man who has fallen into the realm of matter. Another common theory shared by GTh, the Acts of Thomas, and Manicheism deals with the five trees of light (Logion 19).

These trees are the spiritual members of the soul which enable it to rediscover its own "self."

Even though GTh lacks the usual Gnostic portrayal of the Archons asking the soul for a key word or preventing it from climbing to heaven, this should not be an argument against the Gnostic character of the gospel. Such portrayals belong to a mythical rather than to a philosophical type of Gnosticism.

Bibliography. The best Eng. trans. is in A. Guillaumont, H. C. Puech, W. Till, and Yassah 'Abd-al-Masīḥ, *The Gospel According to Thomas* (1959).

Special studies: C. R. C. Allberry, *A Manichaean Psalm-Book* (1938); A. Baker, "Pseudo-Macarius and the Gospel of Thomas," *VC,* XVIII (1964), 215-25; "The Gospel of Thomas and the Diatessaron," *JTS,* XVI (1965), 449-54; "The 'Gospel of Thomas' and the Syriac 'Liber Graduum,'" *NTS,* XII (1965), 49-55, all of which are valuable for the Syriac influence on GTh; G. Bornkamm, *Mythos und Legende in den apokryphen Thomas-Akten, FRLANT,* XXXI (1933), a classical study of the Acts of Thomas; B. Gärtner, *The Theology of the Gospel of Thomas* (1960), the best study of the theology of the gospel; R. M. Grant, D. N. Freedman, *The Secret Sayings of Jesus* (1960), includes an interesting analysis of the gospel's main themes; H. Jonas, *The Gnostic Religion* (2nd ed., 1963), a clear and complete essay based on the author's well-known work, *Gnosis und Spätantiker Geist* (1934-54); H. C. Kee, "Becoming a Child in the Gospel of Thomas," *JBL,* LXXXII (1963), 307-14; A. F. J. Klijn, "The So-called Hymn of the Pearl," *VC,* XIV (1960), 154-64; "The 'Single One' in the Gospel of Thomas," *JBL,* LXXXI (1962), 271-78; J. E. Ménard, *L'Evangile selon Thomas* (1975); H. C. Puech, "Gnostic Gospels and Related Documents," *NT Apocrypha,* I: *Gospels and Related Writings,* ed. E. Hennecke, W. Schneemelcher, Eng. trans. ed. R. M. Wilson (1959; 2nd ed., 1968), pp. 231-362; G. Quispel, "The Gospel of Thomas and the NT," *VC,* XI (1957), 189-207, "The Syrian Thomas and the Syrian Macarius," *VC,* XVIII (1964), 226-35, "The 'Gospel of Thomas' and the 'Gospel of the Hebrews,'" *NTS,* XII (1965-66), 371-82, and *Makarius, das Thomasevangelium und das Lied von der Perle,* NovTSup, XV (1967); A. Resch, *Agrapha, TU,* XV (2nd ed., 1906); W. R. Schoedel, "Naassene Themes in the Coptic Gospel of Thomas," *VC,* XIV (1960), 225-34; W. Schrage, *Das Verhältnis des Thomas-Evangeliums zur synoptischen Tradition und zu den koptischen Evangelien-übersetzungen,* BZNW, XXIX (1964); R. M. Wilson, *Studies in the Gospel of Thomas* (1960).

For other texts, translations, and special studies see, in addition to the bibliographies for related articles, D. M. Scholer, *Nag Hammadi Bibliography 1948-1969* (1971), with supplements in *NovT* (1971 ff.).

J. E. Ménard

***THRESHOLD.** Two Hebrew words are used to designate "threshold." The more frequent term is *saph,* which is related to Akkad. *sippu,* a word that clearly means "threshold." The meaning of the second term, *miphtān,* has recently been debated. In the first edition of the Koehler-Baumgartner *Lexicon* (1953) the editors followed a suggestion attributed to H. Winkler and defined the word as "podium of idol." More recently Donner has carefully re-examined the word in context and demonstrated that the location and activities associated with *miphtān* strongly suggest "threshold."

The sanctity of thresholds is widely attested. In various cultures, it is the object of a wide range of taboos which prohibit sitting, working, treading (I Sam. 5:5), or disciplining children upon it. As part of the entrance to a household it may be the scene of ritual acts initiating new relationships with those entering the household (Exod. 21:6; Deut. 15:17) or sacrifices for those returning after an extended absence. The household's relationship to numinous powers may be symbolized by icons or other protective symbols buried beneath the threshold, attached to the threshold, or affixed to the doorway above it (Deut. 6:9). The household's security is preserved by keeping demonic powers from crossing the threshold. This may be done by setting up awesome monsters outside the entrance or attaching apotropaic devices to the door (Exod. 12:7). All these attitudes have been attested among Israel's neighbors.

The Israelite perspective differs somewhat from that of surrounding cultures. Given religious laws that prohibit the making of icons, there was no justification for burying protective deities beneath their thresholds. Consequently there appears to have been no requirement to avoid stepping on them. Where such practices were noted, they were treated as either the strange custom of a foreign people, for which biblical writers provided a likely Etiology (I Sam. 5:2-5), or as a dangerous affectation of alien manners (Zeph. 1:9). Elsewhere, however, the mention of thresholds sometimes reflects their special significance. Two passages make note of death at a threshold (Judg. 19:27; I Kings 14:17). Within the temple area, the keepers of the threshold are men of considerable importance (II Kings 22:4; 25:18; II Chr. 34:9; cf. Esth. 2:21; 6:2). A shaking threshold is a feature of the theophanies in Isa. 6:4 and Amos 9:1. Ezekiel heard the glory of God speak from the threshold (Ezek. 9:3; cf. 10:18). He also reports that God's holy name was defiled by those who set their threshold adjoining his (43:8), and in 47:1 he describes life-giving waters which flow from beneath the threshold.

Bibliography. H. Donner, "Die Schwellenhüpfer: Beobachtungen zu Zephanja 1, 8 f.," *JSS,* XV (1970), 42-55; L. Koehler and W. Baumgartner, *Lexicon in Veteris Testamenti Libros* (1953); H. Clay Trumbull, *The Threshold Covenant* (1896).

O. Wintermute

TIQQUNE SOPHERIM. *See* Emendations of the Scribes[S]; Qere-kethibh[S] §2.

***TOMB.** Recent discoveries have substantially heightened our understanding of Palestinian burial customs and tomb architecture. Chief among the new sites are: Bab edh-Dhra', Dhahr Mirzbaneh, Jebel Qa'aqir, Jerusalem and environs, Qumran, Beth She'arim, Khirbet Shema', and Gush Halav.

While none of these sites individually has revolutionized our understanding, collectively they provide an overview of the kinds of new data available.

Recent advances in archaeological reporting, field techniques, and science, as it relates to the interpretation of archaeological data, also have contributed greatly to our understanding. Moreover, the rapidly developing discipline of ceramic typology enhances the possibility of achieving a highly accurate dating schema. Since most of the older excavation reports have not undergone such critical scrutiny, the reader is urged to consult the standard works on POTTERY chronology in determining the accuracy of earlier conclusions.

1. Mode of inhumation. From earliest times two types of burial procedures were in use: primary and secondary interment. A primary interment is one in which the corpse remains in the original position in which it was buried. A secondary burial is one in which skeletal remains are reburied in a pit or OSSUARY, either within the precincts of the same tomb cave or at a new locus. This custom appears to be widespread in ancient Palestine, especially from the Iron Age onward. By the Roman period secondary burial in wood or stone ossuaries, along with more simple forms of secondary interment, came to dominate at the important necropolises of Beth She'arim and Khirbet Shema'.

2. Idioms for death and burial. Since ancient custom and law as well as climate dictated the need for rapid BURIAL, interment in the family tomb was not always possible. Hence there was a need, especially in a nomadic culture, for secondary burial, whereby the deceased could be "gathered to the people" or could "sleep with the fathers." These idioms could indicate burial or reburial in the family tomb (II Sam. 21:12-14) but were broadened to include descent to SHEOL (Gen. 25:8; 35:29; Num. 20:23-28). In this way the biblical writers conveyed the idea of a peaceful death (*see* DEATH, THEOLOGY OF[S]). Only violent death in battle or by suicide was described in other terms.

These idioms, viewed with the biblical preoccupation for proper burial, give special poignancy to the acute fear of exhumation and nonburial (Jer. 8:1-2; 25:33). Moreover, subterranean tomb chambers doubtless influenced Israelite beliefs about Sheol. It was located beneath the earth (Gen. 37:35), dark (Job 10:21-22), dusty (Job 17:16), and silent (Ps. 94:17).

3. Tomb types and special features. Many tomb types as well as burial customs continued in use over a long period of time, albeit in highly modified forms. Conservatism runs deep where death is concerned. Shaft tombs, common in the Early Bronze Age (Proto-Urban phase), reappear in the Middle Bronze Age for single and multiple burial (*see* Fig. T10:1, 2). In the Early Bronze Age charnel houses at Bab edh-Dhra', S of the Dead Sea, replace shaft tombs in the second burial phase and function as a common burial ground. Recent excavation of DOLMENS has confirmed that they originated in the Middle Bronze Age and were used for secondary burials.

In the Late Bronze Age and especially in the Iron Age, tombs conform to established typological patterns. The introduction of the rectangular bench-type tomb, however, is an innovation which coincides with the coming of the Sea Peoples and Philistines to Palestine (*see* Fig. T10:6). The elaborate anthropoid sarcophagi used in Philistine burials are notable (*see* BETH-SHAN Fig. 38). Multiple-chambered tombs continue alongside the shaft type from which they are derived, and are often a converted natural cave or an older tomb re-used. They are usually entered by a stepped entryway or *dromos* (*see* Fig. T10:3, 3*a*, 4).

Coincident with these features is the appearance

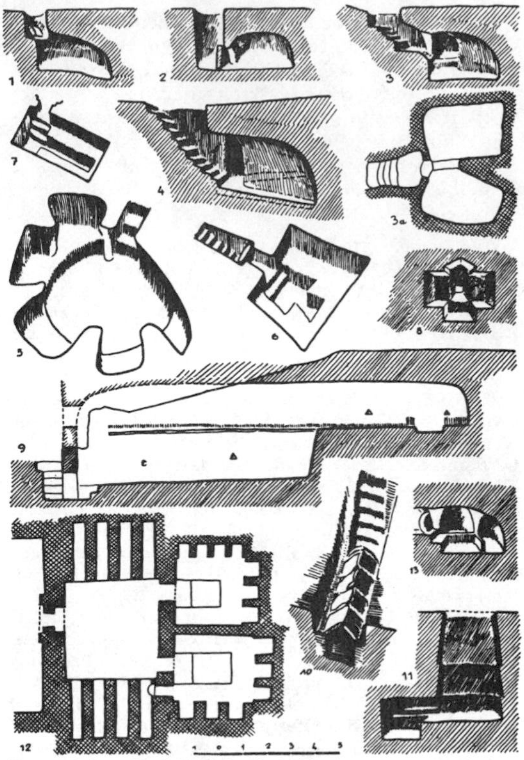

By permission of J. C. B. Mohr (Paul Siebeck)
10. Various types of tombs

of the repository for the collection of bones. Primary burial would occur on the bench or ledge, and at some later time the skeletal remains would be cleared or reburied in a central repository (depression), communal ossuary, or sometimes in a separate bone chamber. All these features continue in some form or other into the Hellenistic and Roman periods. Excellent examples of this type of arrangement are to be found at the 900 and 500 cemetery at Tell el-Far'ah (Sharuhen), and Lachish Tombs 106, 213, and 223. Disc-shaped recessed depositories are found in Tomb 1 at Beth-shemesh or Tomb 54 at Tell en-Nasbeh. *See* Fig. T10:5.

Single graves are found in the Iron Age, continuing a popular form of interment. Prime examples come from Lachish, where N-S graves were simple trenches, sometimes with a step in each side, and burials oriented E-W were in the shape of a trench with an undercut chamber along the bottom of one side. The body was always stretched out on its back. While the use of the coffin is not well-attested in the Iron Age, several examples have come to light. *See* BURIAL Fig. 59.

Familiarity with Iron Age tombs and burial practices greatly facilitates understanding the data from later periods. While in general there came to be a much greater emphasis on external features, the internal arrangement is remarkably similar. The introduction of the individual loculus or *kôkh* (a burial shaft which is cut perpendicularly back into the wall of the tomb chamber) and the "kline" or arcosolium tomb (the roof of the shelf niche made into an arch) are the most distinctive innovations in Hellenistic tombs and can be associated with both primary and secondary burials. *See* Figs. T10:13, T11.

The individual receptacle or ossuary for secondary burials became commonplace by late Hellenistic times and continued well into the Roman period. Only scattered evidences of individual wood or stone ossuaries, however, are found after the Bar Kochba period. The dominance of the loculus arrangement (with ossuaries and/or secondary burials in pits—*see* Fig. TOM 10:12—repositories and charnel rooms) continued into the Byzantine period, as evidenced at Meiron and Khirbet Shema'. Sarcophagi (for single interments but sometimes used for multiple burials) also are much more prevalent in Hellenistic and Roman times and often are highly decorated.

Courtesy E. M. Meyers
11. Arcosolium tomb at Khirbet Shema'

The vast material uncovered in the Jerusalem area is inadequately reflected in the published literature. The monumental tomb of Jason provides a glimpse into the world of a family of high social standing in the first century of the Hellenistic era. This family may have been involved in naval exploits along the E Mediterranean, judging from the drawings of ships on the porch wall. Corpses were interred in ten loculi (Fig. T12 room A), and there was a charnel room (B) for the final storage of disarticulated remains.

At Qumran the vast majority of burials thus far excavated have been primary inhumations in shaft graves with a recess at the bottom. Since by this time most Palestinian tombs were employing the loculus grave arrangement, the method used by the Qumran community would seem to be a conscious effort at setting themselves apart. Some secondary burials have been noted, possibly reflecting a desire to be reburied in the family cemetery.

The most important necropolis thus far excavated in Roman Palestine is Beth She'arim in W

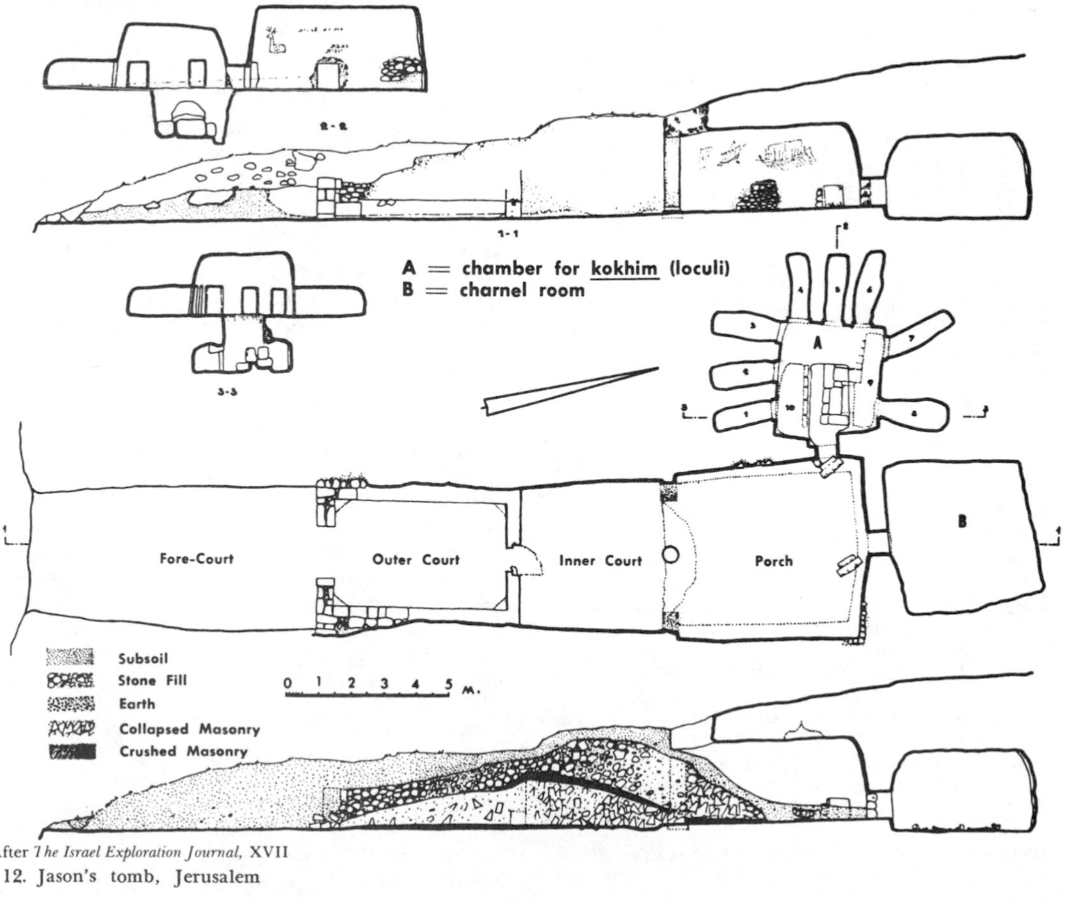

After *The Israel Exploration Journal*, XVII
12. Jason's tomb, Jerusalem

lower Galilee. Here the full variety of methods of interment is to be found, with secondary burial (in a variety of ways) as the dominant form. Tombs include those of Jewish families of the Diaspora as well as the family of Rabbi Judah himself. An extensive collection of inscriptions in Greek, Hebrew, and Aramaic provides data for evaluating the significance of these tombs and burials. The abundant art found on tomb portals, on coffins, and on the walls of catacombs provides an array of material relevant to the study of Oriental art in general and Jewish funerary art in particular. *See* ART, EARLY JEWISH[S] §4.

Jewish tombs of the second temple period provide the proper setting for considering burial practices alluded to in the NT. Rabbinic sources which discuss details concerning tombs and burial are preserved in the late tractate on mourning, *Semaḥot,* as well as in a host of other Jewish sources. *See* MOURNING.

4. Summary. The tradition of the family tomb would seem to be the most important factor in the data which pertain to burial and tombs in both OT and NT times. The need to be joined to one's fathers in death is an overriding factor which contributes to the interrelationship between primary and secondary burial. While a doctrine of life after death appeared only at the end of the OT period, during Hellenistic times a variety of such beliefs developed. Whether or not the modes of burial and construction of tombs reflect this variety is a matter for further study. *See* IMMORTALITY; IMMORTALITY[S]; RESURRECTION; FUTURE LIFE IN INTERTESTAMENTAL LITERATURE[S]; JUDAISM, HELLENISTIC[S].

Bibliography. B. Alfrink, "L'Espression נאסף אל עמיו," *OTS,* V (1948), 118-31; N. Avigad, *Ancient Momuments in the Kidron Valley* (1954), Hebrew; A. P. Bender, "Beliefs, Rites, and Customs of the Jews Connected with Death, Burial, and Mourning," *JQR,* VI (1893-94), 317-47, 664-71, and VII (1894-95), 101-18, 259-69; J. Callaway, "Burials in Ancient Palestine: From the Stone Age to Abraham," *BA,* XXVI (1963), 74-91; J. Finegan, *The Archaeology of the New Testament* (1969); K. Galling, *Biblisches Reallexikon* (1937), cols. 237-52; E. R. Goodenough, *Jewish Symbols in the Greco-Roman Period,* I (1953); S. Klein, *Tod und Begräbnis in Palästina zur Zeit der Tannaiten* (1908); P. Lapp, "The Cemetery at Bab edh-Dhra' Jordan," *Archaeology,* XIX (1966), 104-11, and *The Dhahr Mirzbâneh Tombs* (1966); B. Mazar, *Beth She'arim,* I (1973), and "On the Practice of Cremation," *Qedem,* II (1945), 126-28, Hebrew; E. Myers, *Jewish Ossuaries: Reburial and Rebirth* (1971), and "Secondary Burials in Palestine," *BA,* XXXIII (1970), 2-29; J. Perles, "On Interment of the Dead in Post-Biblical Judaism," *Hebrew Characteristics* (1875); L. Y. Rahmani, "Jason's Tomb," *IEJ,* XVII (1967), 61-100, and "Jewish Rock-Cut Tombs in Jerusalem," *Atiqot,* III (1961), 93-120; E. L. Sukenik, *Jüdische Gräber Jerusalems um Christi Geburt* (1931); J. Waldbaum, "Philistine Tombs at Tell Fara and Their Aegean Prototypes," *AJA,* LXX (1966), 331-40; C. Watzinger, *Denkmäler Palästinas,* 2 vols. (1933-35); D. Zlotnick, ed., *The Tractate "Mourning"* (1966).

E. MEYERS

TOMB OF JESUS. *See* HOLY SEPULCHRE, CHURCH OF THE[S].

***TONGUES, GIFT OF.** Speaking in tongues or languages (λαλεῖν γλώσσαις), glossolalia, is used in a technical sense in the NT for a gift from the exalted Lord. As such it is found almost exclusively in Acts and in I Corinthians. However, the phenomenon was not uncommon in early Christianity (cf. Mark 16:17; perhaps Rom. 8:26; Iren. Her. V.vi.1; Tert. Marcion V.viii; Origen, *Against Celsus* VII.ix) and has appeared from time to time throughout the history of the church.

1. Tongues and prophecy. Tongues are in the class of "spiritual" gifts (πνευματικά) and thus are a "higher gift" that Paul himself manifests and urges other believers to seek zealously (I Cor. 14:1, 18; cf. 12:31). As a gift of inspired speech they have a number of affinities with prophecy and can be regarded as a kind of prophecy. Perhaps experienced earlier by OT prophets (cf. Isa. 28:9 ff.), they are the same phenomenon that is associated or identified with prophecy in Acts (2:17-18; cf. 19:6). Like prophecy and other πνευματικά, tongues can be manifested in an ecstatic or nonecstatic manner. Like prophecy, they are spoken "in the Spirit" and therefore, when interpreted, mediate the mind of God (I Cor. 14:2; 2:6-16).

Unlike prophecy, tongues are manifested with the speaker's mind (νοῦς) held in abeyance. While they edify a person, they do not instruct the mind or the minds of the hearers. Consequently, as a public manifestation of the HOLY SPIRIT in church, tongues are less desirable than prophecy and are to be restricted or, when no one gifted to interpret is present, to be abstained from (I Cor. 14:5, 13-19, 27-28).

2. Tongues and language. As the term presupposes, tongues are meaningful language, of men or of angels, that speak "to God" and that may be "interpreted" (I Cor. 13:1; 14:2, 5). If a human language, they may be understood (Acts 2) and linguistically analyzed. If a heavenly language, they are presumably beyond the scope of the linguist's tools or talents. Tongues are the Spirit's language being mediated to and through the speaker (Acts 2:4, "gave" [ἐδίδου]) and are not to be understood as a miraculous ability to speak via one's own mind in a foreign tongue.

3. Tongues and ecstasy. Ecstatic manifestations of the πνευματικά are to be distinguished both in origin and, ultimately, in effect from ecstasies that are emotional, pathological, or demonic in origin. Even when similarities are present, they do not necessarily imply similar stimuli, for what is sometimes a natural or even pathological phenomenon may at other times be an instrument of the Holy Spirit (Lewis). For example, Paul's Damascus vision may be distinguished from a mental illness or an emotional reverie by the effects that it produced.

One must resist the temptation to "psychologize" the manifestations of the Holy Spirit. At the same time one must seek criteria by which the manifestations of the Spirit may be distinguished from similar psychological phenomena. For Paul the criteria are the same for all the spiritual gifts: a christological focus and the fruit of love, the confessional and ethical norms of a healthy Christian life (I Cor. 12:3; 13:1).

Emotion or ecstasy does not produce a gift of the Spirit. But the presence of the Spirit in power may produce emotion that the unknowledgeable observer may mistake for a psychological aberration (Mark 3:21; Acts 2:13; 26:24). Nevertheless, for tongues no less than for prophecy Paul's rule is valid: "The spirits of prophets are subject to prophets" (I Cor. 14:32). Uncontrolled ecstasy ceases to be responsible Christian ecstasy.

4. Tongues and baptism in the Holy Spirit. For Paul tongues are a gift of the Spirit and, like other gifts, they are not imparted to all believers (I Cor. 12:30). In contrast, baptismal imagery is used for the initial coming of the Spirit, which is the characteristic mark of all who are "in Christ" (I Cor. 12:13; cf. Rom. 8:9). In Acts tongues and prophecy often accompany the initial coming of the Spirit (Acts 2:4, 18; 19:6), but this does not always appear to be the case (Acts 8:17; 9:17). The interpretation of the gift of tongues as (the necessary outward sign of) baptism in the Spirit is not justified by the NT evidence. *See* BAPTISM[S] esp. §2*c*.

5. A ministry of tongues is not explicitly mentioned in the NT but, on the analogy of other spiritual gifts, it may be implied. Like prophecy, the gift of tongues may be manifested by some only on occasion; for others it may be a continuing ministry. When it is accompanied by the gift of interpretation (I Cor. 12:10), it may constitute prophetic teaching and exhortation. More often it may be a ministry of prayer, whether of worship or intercession or praise (I Cor. 14:2, 14-15, 28). Thus viewed and practiced, the gift of tongues also has its place in "building up the body of Christ" (Eph. 4:12).

See also SPIRITUAL GIFTS; SPIRITUAL GIFTS[S]; PROPHET IN THE NT; PROPHECY IN THE EARLY CHURCH[S].

Bibliography. General: J. Behm, "γλῶσσα," *TDNT,* I (1933 [ET 1964]), 722-26; P. W. Schmiedel, "Spiritual Gifts," *Encyclopedia Biblica,* IV (1907), cols. 4761-72; F. Stagg, E. G. Hinson, W. E. Oates, *Glossolalia: Tongue Speaking in Biblical, Historical, and Psychological Perspective* (1967), with bibliog. Special studies: F. W. Beare, "Speaking With Tongues," *JBL,* LXXXIII (1964), 229-46; S. D. Currie, "Speaking in Tongues," *Int.,* XIX (1965), 274-94, deals with early Christian evidence outside the NT; J. P. Kildahl, *The Psychology of Speaking in Tongues* (1972); C. S. Lewis, "Transposition," *Weight of Glory and Other Addresses* (1949), pp. 16-29; W. J. Samarin, *Tongues of Men and Angels: The Religious Language of Pentecostalism* (1972); D. M. Smith, "Glossolalia and Other Spiritual Gifts in a NT Perspective," *Int.,* XXVIII (1974), 307-20; J. P. M. Sweet, "A Sign for Unbelievers: Paul's Attitude to Glossolalia," *NTS,* XIII (1967), 240-57; C. G. Williams, "Glossolalia as a Religious Phenomenon: 'Tongues' at Corinth and Pentecost," *Religion,* V (1975), 16-32.

E. E. ELLIS

***TORAH** [תורה, perhaps from ירה, "to throw"; *hiph'îl,* "to point the way" or "to cast lots"; perhaps related to Akkad. *tērtu,* "oracle"]. A word in the Hebrew Bible meaning instruction, guidance, oracle; in Deuteronomy and postexilic literature it also means law or law code. In early Judaism it had a wide range of connotations, from PENTATEUCH (Torah par excellence) to all divine revelation in biblical and postbiblical literature (in some contexts, it is a designation for Judaism itself).

In the OT, Torah can mean a priestly or prophetic oracle, a divine response to a particular question, a directive sign; it can also mean instruction by a parent or wise person. In Isaiah, it seems to designate the prophet's system of teaching. Generally in prophetic speech, it is used as a synonym for Yahweh's Word or Way. In the broadest sense, it designates the divine will for Israel in the covenant relationship—both specific directive and the entire body of tradition which relates God's gracious acts and anticipates Israel's obedient response.

The entire range of meanings is retained in postbiblical Judaism. Torah includes not only HALACHAH (the rules of conduct: commandments, statues, and ordinances) but also HAGGADAH (religious teaching in a more general sense). It thus includes the whole of revelation, preserved in writing or orally—all that God has made known of his character, purpose, and expectation. "Talmud Torah" (study of Torah) includes reading a postbiblical MIDRASH or a medieval commentary. "In a word, Torah in one aspect is the vehicle, in another and deeper view it is the whole content of revelation" (Moore). Whether in the Bible or in Judaism, Torah was clearly viewed as a mixture of two equally essential elements: story and stipulation, haggadah and halachah, mythos and ethos, gospel and law.

How and when was this balance misperceived, so that Torah came to be viewed largely and in essence as halachah (or "law")? One point of view places the blame upon the translators of the LXX: too consistently they rendered the word *torah* by the Greek *nomos* instead of varying the translation according to the contextual demand (e.g., as *didache, didaskalia, dogma,* etc.). In any case, there has been consistent agreement that their rigidity in the use of *nomos* has been misleading, since it conveys only the narrower sense of the word *torah.* But more recent study suggests that they chose precisely the word that they should have chosen. In the Hellenistic world which early Judaism inhabited, *nomos* had at least the same breadth of meaning which *torah* had for Judaism. "*Nomos* in the Pentateuch . . . means divine revelation, considered as a whole, composed of a doctrinal part and of a legislative part" (Pasinya).

However, there is a general recognition that Judaism, in some aspects and expressions, has tended to stress halachah (and the necessity for obedience) as a condition for survival. This would have been a major lesson of history for those who experienced the exile of the sixth century B.C. One view is that it was the priestly writers and editors of the exilic period who began to equate Torah with law and to use the word interchangeably with statute, commandment, etc. (Östborn). A more recent view would place the narrowing of meaning in the book of DEUTERONOMY, especially in its exilic redaction (Lindars). In any case, it would be a mistake to think that Judaism as a whole concentrated on halachah to the neglect of haggadah. In Pharisaic-rabbinic Judaism, as in all Jewish denominations, Torah has always retained the meaning of revelation in a general sense. This observation has led to the view that it was in Hellenistic Judaism that Torah came to be understood primarily as law (Dodd). This view cannot be maintained.

It is becoming increasingly clear that sharp distinctions along such lines between Palestinian and Hellenistic Judaism (or between so-called normative and heterodox Judaism) did not exist (*see* JUDAISM, EARLY RABBINIC[S]; JUDAISM, HELLENISTIC[S]). Early Judaism (i.e., that of the period before A.D. 70, when Jerusalem fell to the Romans) was remarkably diverse, not only in Palestine but also in the Diaspora communities.

An intense struggle took place in Palestine *ca.* 175-164 B.C. as the result of efforts to accommodate Jewish cult and life to "modernization" (Hellenization). The zeal of the reformers was matched and countered by reactionary forces who feared the loss of Jewish identity. The reaction was marked by a distinct zeal for Torah as a countermeasure to assimilation. Out of this crisis arose such traditionalist adherents as the HASIDIM and ESSENES, who, Hippolytus noted, were characterized by zeal for Torah. The reaction led to a successful armed revolt against the Seleucid domination of Palestine (*see* I-II MACCABEES; ISRAEL, HISTORY OF §§13-14). Thereafter, the fortunes of such traditionalists waxed and waned under the political and cultural ambitions of the Hasmoneans and Romans.

The destruction of the first temple (sixth century B.C.) had already necessitated the study of the ancient authoritative traditions for answers to the questions of identity and life-style in that destitute situation. While many exiled Judeans assimilated to the dominant Babylonian and Persian culture, others turned to the old stories for reaffirmation of their ancient identity, and drew from them survival power. This quest resulted, not only in a singling out of the Pentateuch for special emphasis (a Torah within the Torah, a status which it has had ever since) and its final shaping, but also in its receiving the enduring designation ספר חיים the "Book of Life." Torah became stable textually and adaptable canonically. It could be taken anywhere (Palestine or the Diaspora) and made relevant to changing contexts by whatever HERMENEUTICS were necessary to make it so. Of secondary authority were other traditions (Prophets and Writings) which were part of Torah in wider sense.

Such Torah zealotry gave rise to the oral Torah (*see* PHARISEES[S]; MISHNA; TALMUD). When the written Torah no longer seemed relevant to some aspects of the new situation under the challenges of Hellenism, oral traditions were collected and expanded in order to address the question of identity. Emphasis was placed upon recognizable practices in personal and communal life, i.e., upon halachah. An enduring attitude of self-examination and correction arose which sought not only to maintain identity but also to prevent a repetition of past and present catastrophes. The lessons of the past must not go unheeded. No detail of the Torah was so insignificant as to warrant neglect. Out of such desire for obedience and dedication to righteousness arose what, from another point of view, came to be viewed as the pursuit of righteousness based upon works of the Law (Rom. 9:31-32). However, there is no basis for thinking that the more the Pharisees emphasized halachah the more they neglected haggadah. On the contrary, Torah for them always meant both the story of God's gracious acts in creating and preserving a people for himself (*see* GRACE IN THE OT[S]) and also God's will for the way that people should shape their lives in the light of those acts.

The wide spectrum of Jewish belief and practice prior to A.D. 70 included groups who were preoccupied with scenarios of how God would act in their own time. Just as he had acted at the Exodus or at other times in the Torah story, perhaps he would act now for a final settlement of the struggle between right and wrong, between the forces of light and the forces of darkness (*see* APOCALYPTICISM; APOCALYPTICISM[S]). Belief that he could and would do so took precedence for some over the other rightful Jewish concern to reflect God's righteousness in daily life.

Concentration on the traditions of God's free acts to effect righteousness resulted in an apparent emphasis on Torah as precisely that type of story; concentration on the traditions of Israel's proper response to those acts resulted in an emphasis on Torah as precisely a call to response. But Torah itself was always a balance between the two.

In order to understand Paul's attitude toward the "Law" (*nomos*), it is necessary to remember that this term, after all, is used in the LXX to express the full range of meanings which the word *torah* expressed in Hebrew. In some NT passages, and especially in Paul, *nomos* is used in the sense of Torah story as well as Torah stipulations. Paul possibly does not set faith over against works (as is commonly thought), but asks in whose works one should have faith—those of God, or those which humans perform in obedient response to God's works. If the former, argues Paul, then one could recognize in Jesus another climactic work of God (Rom. 10:4). If the latter, then one might fail to recognize the work of God in Christ for what Paul was sure that it was. Thus the early church should be seen as an heir of those denominations in early Judaism which focused on Torah as the story of the free acts of God which he performed in order to establish righteousness on the human scene. Rabbinic Judaism should be seen as an heir of those denominations which focused on Torah as indicative of how one should live in obedient response to those free acts of God. In either case, Torah was the way, the truth, and the life for Israel.

Bibliography. W. D. Davies, *Paul and Rabbinic Judaism* (1948), pp. 147-76, and *Torah in the Messianic Age* (1952); C. H. Dodd, *The Bible and the Greeks* (1935), pp. 25-41; I. Engnell, *Israel and the Law* (1946), pp. 1-16, a review of Östborn; W. Gutbrod and H. Kleinknecht, "Law," *TDNT*, IV (1967), 1022-85; M. Hengel, *Judaism and Hellenism*, I (1974), 58-254; B. Lindars, "Torah in Deuteronomy," in *Words and Meanings*, ed. P. Ackroyd and B. Lindars (1968), pp. 117-36; G. F. Moore, *Judaism*, I (1927), 235-80; L. Monsengwo Pasinya, *La Notion de nomos dans le Pentateuque grec* (1973); J. Neusner, *The Way of Torah* (1970), pp. 1-52; G. Östborn, *Tōrā in the OT* (1945); D. Rössler, *Gesetz und Geschichte* (2nd ed., 1962); J. Sanders, *Torah and Canon* (2nd ed., 1974), "Torah and Paul" (forthcoming in the N. Dahl *Festschrift*, ed. W. Meeks), and "Torah and Christ," *Int.*, XXIX (1975), 372-90; M. Smith, "Palestinian Judaism from Alexander to Pompey," in *Hellenism and the Rise of Rome*, ed. P. Grimal (1968), pp. 250-66; M. Stone, "Judaism at the time of Christ," *Scientific American* (Jan. 1973), pp. 80-87; V. Tcherikover, *Hellenistic Civilization and the Jews* (1974), pp. 1-265; E. Würthwein, "Der Sinn des Gesetzes im AT," *ZThK*, LV (1958), 255-70; P. Hanson, "Jewish Apocalyptic Against its Near Eastern Environment," *RB*, LXXVIII (1971), 31-58.

J. A. Sanders

***TOTEMISM.** Derived from an Ojibwa Indian word which denotes animals and plants associated with a group of blood-related persons who, being of the same totemic group, are prohibited from marriage. The term became generalized in literature and came to denote various traits in the religious and social organization of primitive peoples.

Although no society encompasses all the traits characterized as totemic, one can list the criteria of an ideal totemism. (1) The tribe is divided into limited groups, each having a definite relationship to an animal or plant. (2) Membership in a totemic group is permanent, and is received through inheritance. (3) The group's attitude toward its totem is negatively expressed in terms of fear or danger. (4) One's totem object is surrounded by taboo which may be ritually expressed. (5) The totem is ancestral in some sense, ties its members to one another, and requires exogamy in marriage and sex. (6) The totem is expressed in oral literature, particularly in the form of myths and legends. (7) The totem is represented graphically by designs on objects or on the human body.

1. Distribution. Totemism is by no means a universal cultural phenomenon, but it appears to enjoy world-wide distribution. It is found among the Australian aborigines and in Micronesia, Melanesia, and Polynesia. It is widespread in N and S India, throughout Africa, and in the Americas, but appears to be totally lacking among the Eskimos. Regarding totemism among the Semitic peoples, de Vaux dismisses it, explaining that the only evidence that the ancient Arabs practiced totemism comes from the spurious story of St. Nilus. He adds that it is impossible to discern any traces of totemism among the early Israelites.

2. Variations in practice. As stated above, ideal totemism is a construct, and in practice totemic behavior varies greatly from place to place. The American Indian totem is more of a label for one's clan, and the animal representing one's totem may be killed and eaten. One may be initiated into a society which has a patron animal, but there may be no consequent marriage restriction. Some of the Bantu peoples of West Africa practice strict clan exogamy and will neither kill nor eat their totem, and yet they often lack any legends attributing their descent from the totem animal. Among some of the peoples of the New Hebrides there are no totemic clans, yet they religiously avoid killing or eating certain animals with which they are thought to be related.

3. Theories. This awareness of the great variations in totemic ways did not come from the writers who elaborated theories of religion such as Frazer, Freud, and Durkheim, but rather comes from field anthropologists who study living behavior of folk societies.

The idea that sacrifice was an effort to establish a communion between the members of the sacrificing group and their God was developed by W. R. Smith. He recognized that the Arabian restrictions on the killing of the camel were similar to the classic idea of totemism, and elaborated conjectural statements based on presuppositions regarding primitive mentality to convince himself that the early Semites were totemic.

Freud drew upon Smith, among others, and reconstructed a view of totemism based mainly on psychoanalytic theory. It rests on the assumption of the universality of the Oedipus complex, in which the sons kill their father, then identify him and his strength with some animal. They later feel guilt for their deed and institute sacrifice for him, and the sacrifice of the animal becomes the totemic symbol. By declaring that the killing of the father substitute, the totem, is forbidden, they undo the evil they have committed.

Smith's allegation that blood sacrifice is the core of ancient cult is true only in a very limited geographical area, and even among the Semites at only a certain period during their long cultural history. There is no reason to assume that blood sacrifice goes back to a totemic observance. The basic fault with Freud's theory is that he attempts to deal historically with nonhistorical data. To speak of origins one must deal with place, time, and order. Freud deals rather with intuitive psychobiological assumptions.

In Durkheim's thought all life is divided into the profane and the sacred. The totem becomes the object of the sacred attitude, and in so doing society deifies itself. Durkheim equates society with God. Not only are the members of society sacred, but also its symbols, the totemic plants and animals, are sacred.

These theorists assume that totemism represents the simplest form of primitive religion, an assumption which is open to argument. Conclusions drawn from totemism can hardly apply to societies where totemism does not or has not existed. Finally, totemism continues to receive some interest in current ethnographic studies. However, the theories of the origins of religion which it generated have been largely discarded in the twentieth century.

4. Totemism in Scripture. A careful reading of the Bible indicates that, while there is no totemic society in the biblical record, there are major elements which suggest totemic behavior: food taboos, clan markings, exogamy, animal worship, and animal and plant names.

Lev. 11 offers a list of animals, birds, and insects which are taboo for eating. There is nowhere any suggestion, however, that any one of them is taboo because the Hebrews were descended from them. Rather, certain forms of life were identified with that which was set apart as holy or unholy, and contact with all that was unholy rendered the people unholy and therefore unfit for cultic relationship with a holy God.

Body markings occur for some purpose of identification, probably in the form of tattoo, e.g., the mark of Cain (Gen. 4:15). Body marks are mentioned in Ezek. 9:4; Zech. 13:6; and Isa. 44:5. In none of these references are the marks related to tribal identity. In Ezek. 9:4 the marks are to identify those who stand against the abominations committed in the prophet's vision. Cutting the flesh or tattooing is forbidden in Lev. 19:28.

Regarding marriage and kinship, it was once assumed that the matriarchate was historically a primitive form of social organization and that evidences of it implied totemism. However, there is no correlation established between totemism and matrilineal descent patterns. Exogamy, or obligatory marriage outside one's own kinship group, is a characteristic of totemic societies, and exogamy is found explicitly in Judg. 12:9. Generally, however, the Hebrews were endogamous and, as in many Moslem Arab families today, cousin marriage was common. *See* MARRIAGE[S] §1*b*; KINSHIP AND FAMILY [S] §§4, 5.

The worship of animals appears in Ezekiel's vision (Ezek. 8:7-11), and appears to have been practiced popularly in spite of the second commandment. However, the major role of animals in relation to Hebrew worship was in the sacrificial rituals, and the animal in no case is thought of as representing the ancestor of the people.

The OT contains names of clans, persons, and places which are taken from animals and plants; e.g., among the Israelite clans are the Arodites (ass clan, Num. 26:17), the Tolaites (worm clan, Num. 26:23), the Elonites (oak clan, Num. 26:26) and the Calebites (dog clan, I Sam. 25:3). Only twenty-two OT Hebrew personal names are taken from animals (either clean or unclean), and all are pre-exilic, e.g., Ahiah (vulture), Caleb (dog), Deborah (bee), Jonah (dove), Rachel (ewe), Zibiah (gazelle). The resurgence in the time of Josiah of personal names taken from unclean animals, e.g., Achbor (mouse), Huldah (weasel), Shaphan (rock badger), has suggested to some a revival of totemism. However, the Arabs continue today to give their children such names as Nimir (tiger), Assad (lion), Kalb (dog), and Nakhla (palm tree), and no practice of totemism is involved.

To derive from the above features a historical reconstruction of a totemistic society would require a historical approach, setting out in terms of place and time the necessary features at each period. Such reconstruction is far beyond the reach of the anthropologist and the historian. One must avoid the generalizing that has been done by Smith, Freud, and Durkheim. These generalizations have no basis in an ordered chronological sequence and must be dismissed along with all other speculations about Hebrew totemism.

See also: CLEAN AND UNCLEAN; MAN AND SOCIETY; SACRIFICES AND OFFERINGS, OT; TRIBE.

Bibliography. W. R. Smith, *Lectures on the Religion of the Semites* (1889); S. Freud, *Totem and Taboo* (1913 [ET 1950]); E. Durkheim, *The Elementary Forms of the Religious Life* (1915); W. A. Lessa and E. Z. Vogt, eds., *Reader in Comparative Religion, An Anthropological Approach* (1965), contains a ch. dealing with totemism and is a valuable summary of the problem of totemism; E. E. Evans-Pritchard, *Theories of Primitive Religion* (1965); R. de Vaux, *Ancient Israel: Its Life and Institutions* (1961); A. A. Goldenweiser, "Totemism: An Essay on Religion and Society," in *The Making of Man; An Outline of Anthropology*, ed. V. F. Calverton (1931); "Totemism," *Encyclopaedia Britannica*, XX (1969), p. 103.

W. D. REYBURN

TRADITION CRITICISM, OT. Tradition criticism, also known as tradition history, is a method for analyzing biblical literature in terms of the process by which it moved from stage to stage until it reached its final form. The method is valid for any literature that originated as folk material and was passed down for generations by word of mouth (*see* TRADITION, ORAL; TRADITION, ORAL[S]). The method assumes that folk tradition can reveal the marks of each generation actively involved in its preservation. It presupposes that a tradition has a history, that the history can be traced in some detail, and that to uncover the history will provide insight into the significance of the material.

1. The method in general. As applied to the OT, the method has been focused on two related but distinct questions:

a) The circumstances and manner of transmitting the material. It is important to know whether a text was passed down orally and when or under what circumstances it shifted to written form. Moreover, it is important to know the values, goals, or prejudices of the people involved in the transmission, since those factors would have influenced the shape of a tradition preserved by any particular storyteller or collector. This style of criticism reflects the influence of Nyberg, Engnell, and their colleagues.

b) The characteristic content of the material. Here the methodology can help the investigator deal with at least two distinct subjects. (1) The identity and significance of recurring motifs. A motif is a word or a larger pattern of words, perhaps a concept, a problem that recurs, evoking a mood. It can have its own existence as a stereotyped pattern quite apart from its use in any particular passage. Tradition criticism enables the interpreter to determine the general characteristics as well as the peculiar use of a motif in a given text. An example of this work can be seen in the analysis of the "wise courtier" motif by Humphreys. *See* JOSEPH STORY, THE[S] §3.

(2) The identity and interpretation of larger units of tradition that may carry unique significance for some community. Such units may appear as stories, speeches, poems, or other forms of communication, bound together by common motifs. Koch shows how this may be done in his investigation of the stories about a threat to the ancestral mother. Or the units may appear as a larger construction of tradition, a "theme." In this case, various stories or poems may appear or reappear. The guiding concern, however, is to determine the pattern of construction that holds all of the stories together. The term "theme" is thus not a synonym for motif. Nor does it connote simply a subject of a

discourse or a summary of the content in a unit of material. Its meaning is best clarified by comparing it with a corresponding term, plot, and seeing the theme as a sequence of motifs, episodes, and even significant words. Noth's work on the exodus theme or the wilderness theme illustrates the relevance of this concern.

One caveat must be noted. The procedure works most effectively with literature that has developed through oral transmission in a folk culture. It cannot work as well for something that was, from its inception, a finished work of literary art. The limitation can be seen in the Joseph story, Gen. 37–50. It seems clear that an author created the story, and that it was subsequently expanded and placed in a larger, redactional context between the patriarchs and the Exodus. To ask about the redactional context is, perhaps, the task of REDACTION CRITICISM, although the question cannot be seen as totally different from that raised by tradition criticism. But when one asks about the tradition history of the Joseph story itself, the limitation is apparent. One can appropriately explore the tradition history of a story (Gen. 39–41) within the larger story. One can also explore the tradition history of various motifs employed by the author, such as the wise courtier motif. But in almost all these cases the subject of the analysis is, not the Joseph story itself with evidence produced for reconstructing earlier stages of the story, but distinct sources or motifs used by the author to construct his own, original story. Thus the method demands a text that went through some stages of oral transmission, or at least it is most productive when that kind of material is analyzed.

The methods for investigating the characteristic content of OT material are dependent on the work of Gunkel, Gressmann, and their colleagues. For Gunkel and Gressmann, no less than for Nyberg and Engnell, a history of a tradition is valuable by virtue of its contribution to an understanding of the final text. But the significance of that text can be seen most clearly when the interpreter identifies the process that produced it, along with the interpretative reshaping which the process effected.

2. Procedures for applying the method. In practice the method calls for two distinct stages. The first is an analytic process whose particular steps are dictated by the shape of the texts under examination. The second, built on the foundation provided by the analysis, is a sketch of the history of the tradition.

a) The analysis proceeds by comparison of parallel examples in the tradition field. A good test case is the story about a threat to the ancestral mother (cf. Gen. 12:10-20; 20:1-18; 26:6-11). But others abound: the manna stories, prophetic oracles against the foreign nations, psalms reciting the CREDO traditions, to list but a few. Tradition criticism begins by describing the relationship between the parallels, with a primary concern to determine the significant differences and whether the differences reflect a diachronic relationship. If they do, the next step is to determine how the tradition moved from one stage to another, and what changes occurred as a result of the move.

The process becomes more difficult when the parallels appear as intertwined and even harmonized elements within the structure of a single text. If the text preserves two or more distinct literary sources, each recounting the same subject, the parallels can theoretically be separated. The difficulty increases, however, when the evidence points not so much to a combination of written sources as to a process of growth and change in the tradition before the material became a part of any written document. In that case, parallel written accounts of the tradition cannot be reconstructed. The critic stands under the necessity, moreover, not to be overly hypothetical in reconstructing oral stages. Yet it is just this kind of tradition complex that most readily responds to the procedures of the method.

b) The analytic procedure provides the evidence for the second stage, reconstructing a tradition's history. One can now explore possible causes for changes in the tradition, such as settings in Israel's life that would have promoted the use of the tradition in distinct ways, and the basic intentions or functions that might have been fulfilled in the process. To trace the history of a tradition to the point of its origin is a worthwhile goal only if the effort is based upon evidence provided by the text. The value of the method is greatest when it illumines the final stage in the tradition history.

3. The method in relationship to other methods. The critic cannot open his analytic operation with the round of questions provided by tradition criticism; the method presupposes certain results already established by other basic methods of biblical analysis.

TEXTUAL CRITICISM is an obvious starting point, enabling the critic to recover the wording of a text at earlier stages in its transmission. Beyond that stage, the set of questions provided by FORM CRITICISM come into play. Particularly, the presence or absence of structural unity in the text can be determined. Then, one may ask whether the unity results from a single movement to a written form, or from a combination of two or more previously written forms. If the latter is the case, the methods of SOURCE CRITICISM and redaction criticism can be employed. And the results from these procedures are relevant to the general reconstruction of the tradition's history. In the former case, the comparative operation of tradition criticism proves most useful. The important point is that a critic does not have the choice of working with one method to the exclusion of all others. The methods should not be competing, the private preserve of various schools, but should be complementary stages in a single analytic operation.

Tradition criticism is not designed primarily to evaluate the historical accuracy of traditions. It does not seek to determine, for instance, whether the ancestral mother was, in fact, endangered by being committed to a foreign potentate's harem. The concern is to determine why Israel remembered the story as it did, why the story was changed, and what factors may have been reflected in the changes. But the method may produce evidence that will enable the critic to formulate historical conclusions. A traditio-historical examination of the traditions of the murmuring preserved within the wilderness theme, for example, raises serious questions about the historical accuracy of the tradition that depicts the entire people as rebels during their wilderness life. But the primary goal of the method is not to establish the historicity of the text; it is to recover the various stages in the tradition's history.

4. Conclusions. Practitioners of the method have been justly criticized for reconstructions that are too hypothetical to be convincing. Moreover, they can lose sight of the goal of the methodology, i.e., to interpret the final form of the text. Nonetheless, the method has produced significant results, two of which should be noted.

a) The method has opened up a valuable perspective for understanding how Israel viewed its own history. The past for Israel was not static, limited in its impact to the shape of immediately successive events. Nor was it simply an objective datum, to be reconstructed by subsequent historians. On the contrary, history was in some degree subjective, requiring a particular commitment from each succeeding generation. It is significant, then, that each of those observers might have reshaped the tradition in order to bring the weight of the commitment more fully to bear on the contemporary generation. One might say, in fact, that history for Israel was essentially tradition history, a process that makes the crucial events of the past real and vital for the present. Moreover, a crucial event of the past might have formative influence on an emerging event in the present without being immediately related to it. Indeed, it might facilitate participation in an emerging future by enabling participants to shape the present and to understand what the future might be. *See* YAHWIST[S] §§2-3; ELOHIST[S].

b) This view of history also makes clear the significant focus of Israel's theology. It is in the movement of the tradition, with events gaining new strength by virtue of their influence on new events, that Israel developed her distinctive theology. Moreover, that theology is characteristically moral. It carries God's call for a particular behavior in the future. And Israel explores that call, the significance of that history, in terms of successive reformulations of law. Thus, Israel's view of both history and theology, carried by her preservation of tradition, has a traditio-historical character. The past enables Israel to interpret her present, and it orients her present toward the future. *See* TORAH[S].

Bibliography. Detailed treatment of the method: D. Knight, *Rediscovering the Traditions of Israel,* Dissertation Series, IX (1973), a history of the rise of the method, with a briefer but useful description of the method itself; K. Koch, *The Growth of the Biblical Tradition* (1969), a more detailed description of tradition criticism as a part of the total task of biblical interpretation, with examples; S. Mowinckel, *Prophecy and Tradition* (1946); W. Rast, *Tradition History and the OT* (1972).

Examples of the method at work: I. Engnell, *Gamla Testamentet, En Traditionhistorisk inledning* (1945); H. Gressmann, *Mose und seine Zeit* (1913); H. Gunkel, *Schöpfung und Chaos in Urzeit und Endzeit* (1895); W. L. Humphreys, "The Motif of the Wise Courtier in the OT" (diss., Union, N.Y., 1970); M. Noth, *A History of Pentateuchal Traditions* (1972); H. S. Nyberg, *Studien zum Hoseabuche* (1935). G. W. COATS

***TRADITION, ORAL, OT.** The literature of ancient Israel has many features that are comparable to those of present-day oral traditions which can be observed and studied directly. By analogy the oral hypothesis assumes that Israelite literature is related to a Hebrew oral tradition that flourished independent of any written tradition.

1. Written tradition and oral tradition. The essential characteristic of the written word is fixation; once an utterance is consigned to writing it usually does not change. Oral tradition has as its essential characteristic multiformity, or repetition with variation: each time a composition is performed, it is recomposed from a set of traditional elements whose make-up and relations continually shift. A particular oral composition is a unique manifestation of elements which the composer adopts from his tradition to suit a particular subject, time, and place. There is no fixed text by which the oral composer might evaluate the accuracy of a given performance. What the composer would regard as the identical composition from one performance to another, the literate observer would regard as a constantly changing one.

Concern about the role of oral tradition has often centered on the issue of its reliability judged in terms of a written or memorized text. This issue arises primarily from the effort to establish the original fixed wording of the canonical documents and the desire to determine the facts about historical events. It is assumed there once did exist a single fixed tradition, This, however, may not be the case.

2. Types of oral multiformity. The types of variation found in oral tradition may be seen by comparing multiple versions of the same element of composition, assuming they derive from recomposition rather than literate borrowing or copying. The short utterance that is repeated intact is identified as a formula. There are many line-long formulas in OT poetry, for example: "The cords of death encompassed me" (Ps. 18:4 [H 5]; cf. Ps. 116:3) . If a word or words in a formula vary, but the meaning and, in the case of poetry, the prosodic characteristics of the utterance remain the same, the two utterances are said to be formulaic variants of each other; neither is considered older or superior, though on a given occasion one might be more apt than the other. Note the formulaic variants in Ps. 18:4-5 [H 5-6]; II Sam. 22:5-6; Ps. 116:3. In Hebrew the relationship between formulaic variants is consistently the same as between members of poetic parallelism. The poet, utilizing his version of a tradition of groups of synonymous words, could formulate other variants of this line. These he might use either as parallel members in the same performance or as variants in another performance. Thus to express the threat of death, the poet commanded a system of formulaic variants:

	cords			assail	
	snares		death	confront	
The	torrents	of	Sheol	entangle	me,
	waves		Belial	encompass	
	pangs			lay hold on	

of which still further variations are possible (cf. Ps. 22:12 [H 13], 16 [H 17]). The individual words in these formulaic variants were regarded as synonyms. This is confirmed by formulaic variants whose variant word group is found elsewhere in poetic parallelism (Isa. 37:24; II Kings 19:23; cf. Isa. 44:26), or whose variation consists in reversing such a pair of words (Isa. 2:4; Mic. 4:3).

Formulaic variation in prose also involves the use of synonyms. The expectation that short or especially significant sayings should show the least variation does not always hold.

> In you all the families of the earth [האדמה] shall be blessed (Gen. 12:3 n.).

> By your descendants all the nations of the earth [הארץ] shall bless themselves (Gen. 26:4).

Formulaic variants have been preserved in great numbers in different phases of OT textual transmission: (*a*) double (conflate) readings (Hos. 7:15); (*b*) Qumran MS variants (Isa. 51:9; cf. 1QIs[a]); (*c*) alternate Hebrew traditions (Gen. 19:12; cf. MT and Samar.); (*d*) Qere-kethibh (Jer. 9:22 [H 21]); (*e*) the versions (Exod. 19:3; cf. MT and LXX).

In other traditions changes in meaning evolve within the framework of formulaic systems; the same was probably true for the Hebrew tradition, even though it is unlikely that this process can be reconstructed from the materials available.

The principle of multiformity applies similarly to units of discourse beyond the single line, and the evidence for variation in longer segments is preserved in much the same way as with formulas. Variant sections several lines long may differ mainly on the basis of variants in wording (cf. Ps. 14 with Ps. 53; Ps. 57:7-11 with Ps. 108:1-6), or they may show a difference in length. The relationship between short and long variants is easy to visualize by comparing Job 38:1-3 and 40:6-7. Both express the same essential idea (cf. also Exod. 20:8-12 with Deut. 5:12-16). Variants like these are often evidenced by divergent textual traditions. Compare Job 21:14-16 and 22:17-18 with the variant reflected by the Greek translation of Job 21:14-16.

It is clear that wording, length, and internal order may each vary (cf. Gen. 1:1–4:26 with I Chr. 1:1; Gen. 49:25-26 with Deut. 33:13-16; II Sam. 24 with I Chr. 21:1–22:1; Jer. 6:12-15 with Jer. 8:10-12). Partly on the basis of such variation of smaller units, progressively longer segments and even whole books may be extant in variants which differ considerably in wording and length. In the same way that single terms produce formulaic variants, names of persons and places and other details may change to yield whole narrative variants. In many instances thematic similarity with variation among stories is obvious (cf. Gen. 12:10-20; 20:1-18; and 26:6-11; Gen. 24:1-67 with Tob. 5:1–11:19). In most cases the classification of similarities and differences unavoidably involves subjective judgment. *See* TRADITION CRITICISM, OT[S].

Multiformity refers, not to a plethora of random forms, but to the multiplicity of appearances of a given form. The study of living oral tradition has shown that an oral composer draws on a set of traditional formulas, segments several lines in length, themes, and thematic patterns in order to compose rapidly line after line without the help of writing or memorization. The multiform conventions of OT literature at all levels of discourse are by analogy inferred to be a heritage from oral tradition. It is impossible to say with certainty that any particular phrase is an oral formula, but presumably some OT formulas and formulaic variants are true vestiges of oral tradition. The task of discerning thematic elements and their permutations is shared with form criticism. *See* FORM CRITICISM, OT[S].

3. Capacity of oral tradition. A work that was composed orally may be of virtually any length; the length is not determined by the composer's ability to memorize, nor is it necessarily fixed from performance to performance. There is also no theoretical limit to the aesthetic quality of an orally composed work, although attributes such as unity, complexity, and intensity may be taken as a sign of a tradition's maturity, since they grow with repetition and variation. Moreover, oral tradition is adept at developing intricate word plays, as well as exploiting the assonant features of language in general. The near certainty that Homer was an oral poet nullifies the belief that only what is rhetorically primitive could have been composed orally.

4. Areas of special significance. *a. Textual criticism.* The books of the OT may differ in their relationship to oral tradition, but synonymous variants and related types of variants are attested throughout the OT with sufficient uniformity to indicate that they reflect the process of textual formation and transmission in general, and are not features of the literature of a particular date or type. During the period of the formation of OT literature there seems to have been no great preoccupation with a single original text: the older the evidence of textual transmission of the OT, the greater is the divergence among extant MSS. The precise relationship of oral tradition to the synonymous variants preserved in these MSS has yet to be determined. This problem must be approached by also considering the origin of the same type of variants which pervade the textual evidence of compositions of Sumerian, earlier Akkadian, and Egyptian literature, as well as in medieval vernacular and other literatures. Ultimately they, or their class, go back to the formulaic variation inherent in repeated performances in oral tradition. The oral hypothesis suggests that, rather than reducing and harmonizing such variants, one should retain them side by side, so as to reveal their relation to one another and to their tradition.

b. Oral prosody. The rules governing the composition of oral Hebrew verse may be inferred from the properties of numerous repeated line-long phrases and phrase patterns in written Hebrew verse, if these are taken to be the residue of oral formulaic diction. Since these conventional phrases with their variations contradict principles of strict internal ordering or metrics, the rules appear to have been roughly these: (1) the verse line was not measured in stresses, beats, syllables, or words, but by some nonverbal component of oral performance such as rhythm, musical phrasing, or the poet's feeling of rightness; (2) the meaning of the line was self-contained, so that in oral performance a pause between lines did not disrupt the flow of meaning (absence of enjambment). In oral verse the combination of two or more lines through parallelism or conventional syntactical patterns does not seem to have been governed by predetermined restrictions. The ambiguity of the metrical properties of written Hebrew verse may result from two factors: that prosodic rules were indeterminate at the oral stage, and that poets lost their aural guides as oral performance diminished in significance.

5. Current limitations. The oral hypothesis as it applies to biblical literature will remain a hypothesis for the foreseeable future. The study of the oral composition of genres other than narrative poetry is in its infancy. Biblical poetry is of such a nature as to preclude the use of quantitative tools, developed in other fields, to prove that any part of the Bible is a transcription of an oral composition or directly related to such a composition. Although some parts of the OT may have preserved genuinely oral compositions, biblical literature seems for the most part to belong to a transitional stage during which there developed an interplay among oral tradition, MS tradition, and memory. It is precisely this intermediate stage that is at present least understood.

Bibliography. A. B. Lord, *The Singer of Tales* (1960); R. C. Culley, *Oral Formulaic Language in the Biblical Psalms* (1967); W. J. Urbrock, "Formula and Theme in the Song-Cycle of Job," *Society of Biblical Literature 1972 Proceedings,* II, 459-87; *Semeia* (Spring, 1976).

R. B. COOTE

TRAJAN trā'jən. Marcus Ulpius Traianus, Roman emperor (A.D. 98-117). The first emperor of provincial origin, Trajan was born in 53 at Italica, near Seville, in S Spain. In October, 97, he was adopted as son and successor by Nerva (96-98); he became emperor early in the following year.

Trajan's reign was celebrated in his own time (Pliny the Younger, *Panegyric,* A.D. 100) and remembered in later times (Dio Cassius, *Roman History* LXVIII, *ca.* A.D. 215) for its bright contrast to the tyranny of Domitian; and, in fact, his rule seems to have been marked by effective administration of the Empire and relatively modest claims for the position of the emperor. Domitian allowed himself to be flattered as "lord and god"; Trajan styled himself "best of rulers" (*optimus princeps*), a title which appears on his coins from 103 onward. His period was of great importance in the development of Roman and imperial art, the innovative relief on Trajan's Column being particularly influential upon later narrative art, both Roman and Christian. Perhaps the most noteworthy features of his reign were the conquest of Dacia (modern Rumania) in campaigns of 101-2 and 105-6, extending the Empire's boundaries N of the Danube and bringing Dacian gold into the Roman treasury, and his fleeting victories of 114-17 over the PARTHIANS in the E. The Parthian conquests were abandoned by Hadrian, however, immediately following Trajan's death. The years 115-17 saw also a massive and bloody Jewish uprising which spread from CYRENE to EGYPT, CYPRUS and eastward to MESOPOTAMIA, where the Jews joined a general rebellion in the newly conquered Parthian territory. The revolt was crushed, and one result was the ban of Jews from Cyprus. Trajan died in August, 117, while returning to Rome from the East.

From Trajan's reign comes the earliest non-Christian description of Christianity and the first clear indication of an imperial policy toward the new religion (*ca.* 112). Pliny the Younger, whom Trajan had appointed special governor (*legatus propraetore consulari potestate*) to the province of Bithynia-Pontus, had encountered accusations against the Christians and conducted investigations. He released those who denied that they were Christians and were willing to pray to the Roman gods, to sacrifice before the statue of the emperor, and to curse Christ. Those who persistently maintained their Christianity he condemned to execution for their obstinacy, if for no other crime. Reporting to Trajan (*Epistles* X.96), Pliny described what he had learned of Christian practice and professed himself uncertain both as to the precise nature of the Christians' crime and as to the appropriate punishment. Trajan's reply (Pliny, *Epistles* X.97) notes that the Empire has no settled procedures for dealing with Christians, but confirms Pliny's actions: Christians are not to be sought out; but if accused and convicted, they must be punished; those who deny that they are Christians are to be pardoned; anonymous accusations are not to be admitted. This response leaves the legal character

The Archaeological Museum, Ankara

13. Trajan in old age

of the crime uncertain, but shows that the Empire had no policy of persecution and that Trajan did not establish one. In effect, the Empire would take action against Christianity only when unable to ignore it.

Christian literature probably or possibly from Trajan's reign includes: IGNATIUS of Antioch, I CLEMENT, DIDACHE, POLYCARP's letter to the Philippians. The gospel and letters of John (*see* JOHN, GOSPEL OF; JOHN, LETTERS OF and supplementary articles) are often attributed to this period (*ca.* 98-110), and numerous scholars seek to correlate the Pliny-Trajan correspondence with passages in I Peter (*but see* PETER, FIRST LETTER OF §5). Despite the prominence of suffering and martyrdom as themes in these writings, they show little or no antagonism to the Empire or its authorities.

Trajan passed into Roman lore as a model emperor. In the fourth century, it was recorded that the senate's highest acclamation for an emperor was: *felicior Augusto, melior Traiano,* "more favored than Augustus, better than Trajan."

Bibliography. Sources: Pliny, *Letters, Panegyric,* ed. Radice, LCL; Dio Cassius, *Roman History,* LXVIII, ed. Boissevain, preserved only in Byzantine epitomes. On Pliny: A. N. Sherwin-White, *The Letters of Pliny* (1966). On Dio: F. Miller, *A Study of Cassius Dio* (1964). Selected inscriptions: E. M. Smallwood, *Documents of Nerva, Trajan and Hadrian* (1966).

Studies: B. W. Henderson, *Five Roman Emperors* (1927); *CAH,* XI (1936), with bibliog.; R. Syme, *Tacitus,* 2 vols. (1958). The Jewish Revolt: A. Fuks, "Aspects of the Jewish Revolt of 115-117," *JRS,* XI (1961), 98-104. Pliny and I Peter: J. Knox, "Pliny and 1 Peter: A Note on 1 Peter 4:4-16 and 3:15," *JBL,* LXXII (1953), 187-89. Art: R. Bianchi Bandinelli, *Rome: The Center of Power* (1970). W. S. BABCOCK

***TRIAL OF JESUS.** Mark 15:26 is the necessary starting point for a discussion of Jesus' trial. The superscription on the cross corresponds to the procedure described in Suetonius, *Domitian* 10 and *Caligula* 32.2, Dio Cassius LIV.iii.7, and Eusebius, Hist. V.i.44, while its wording corresponds to Josephus, Antiq. XIV.iii.1. Therefore a Roman CRUCIFIXION of Jesus as an alleged claimant to Jewish kingship is an almost firm datum.

1. The problem of sanhedrin powers. The supreme Jewish legal authority at the time of Jesus was the Great Sanhedrin or συνέδριον (Mark 14:55—RSV "council") in Jerusalem. Most scholars, including the present writer, do not agree with the theory that there were two such bodies, one political and the other religious. (For the latter view *see* SANHEDRIN[S].) If this supreme body still possessed under Roman administration full powers to execute offenders, whether religious or otherwise, then the manner of Jesus' death must indicate minimal proceedings (perhaps even none) against him on the Jewish side. If, on the other hand, such full powers were no longer possessed by the sanhedrin, some sort of Jewish legal proceedings against Jesus become a possibility, though their occurrence has not thereby been demonstrated. Certainty on this question is elusive. The evidence is as follows:

(1) Studies of Roman legal procedures support the view that normal policy in the provinces (except in "free cities," of which Jerusalem was not one) was to keep control of capital punishment in the hands of the Roman authorities.

(2) Tannaitic tradition (J.T. Sanh. 1:1; 7:2; T. B. Sanh. 41a) affirms, with no apparent *Tendenz,* a limitation of Jewish powers which should probably be dated in A.D. 6 (cf. Jos. War II.viii.1).

(3) M. Sanh. 7.2 records the execution by burning of a priest's daughter for adultery, an occurrence which would favor Jewish capital powers except for chronological evidence that this event, like the execution of JAMES (Acts 12:2), occurred during the reign of Agrippa I (A.D. 41-44).

(4) The warning inscription in the temple (Philo, *On the Embassy to Gaius* 307; Jos. War V.v.2; VI.ii.4; Antiq. XV.xi.5) envisages Jewish authority to execute Gentile trespassers on the sacred site. Josephus' interpretation of this inscription points to its being a concession and therefore indicates a normal legal situation which, in the case of Jews as well, was more restricted.

(5) The deposition of ANNAS II from the high priesthood following his summary execution of James (Jos. Antiq. XX.ix.1) may have been simply because he convened the sanhedrin without permission, but the indignant criticism of those who were "strict in observance of the law" is not then adequately explained. More probably two causes of offense were involved: unjust judicial behavior, to which the Pharisaic group objected, and an unauthorized execution which provoked the incoming procurator.

(6) The case of Jesus ben Ananios (Jos. War VI.v.3) involved a Jewish hearing followed by an interrogation by Albinus. Though there is some uncertainty about whether the offense was a capital one, a limitation of Jewish judicial powers may well be involved.

(7) The renewal of the practice of executing criminals, documented in Meg. Ta'an. 6, suggests an earlier curtailment.

(8) The evidence of John 18:31 can only be assessed within a general evaluation of the range of editorial intervention within Johannine passion material (*see* PASSION NARRATIVE[S] §2*d*). Those who favor full Jewish powers incorporate John 18:31 within a promise/fulfillment scheme of the editor's creation (cf. John 18:32); those who decide otherwise point to the existence of historical traces within the theological pattern and dispute the necessary incompatibility of the fulfillment scheme and historicity (cf. the parallel example in John 18:8-9).

(9) The execution of STEPHEN is perhaps the strongest piece of evidence that full Jewish powers remained intact, especially as the suggestion of lynch law is jeopardized by indications of scrupulous legal procedure in Acts 7:57-59. The position is nevertheless confused in that a death lament, withheld normally in the case of a legally executed offender, took place in Stephen's case (Acts 8:2), so the trial may have been brought to a premature end and a hurried execution carried out in defiance of Roman norms.

That there was a Jewish hearing in the case of Jesus is therefore very possible.

2. The Roman proceedings. On any showing the final decision about Jesus was taken by Pilate (on whom, see Philo, *On the Embassy to Gaius* 299-305; Jos. War II.ix.2-4; Antiq. XVIII.ii.2; iii.1-3; iv.1-2; vi.5). As to the details of the hearing before Pilate, little can be said. The charge seems to have been focused on the messianic claim (Mark 15:2), since additional elements presented in Luke alone (23:2: "perverting our nation, and forbidding us to give tribute to Caesar," cf. 23:5) are almost certainly redactional, stemming from Lukan theology and apologetic (*see* LUKE, GOSPEL OF §§2, 4*h*). To the messianic question, which provides background for Mark 15:26, Jesus responded with an affirmation qualified only by strategic reserve (on "You say/have said," cf. Matt. 26:25; 26:64, interpreted by 27:40-43; Mark 15:2, in the light of Mark 15:9; Eccl. Rabbah 7:12; Tosef. Kel. I.6). On this all traditions agree. Other features of the traditions are more problematical: the tendency to shift responsibility in the direction of the Jewish leaders has powerfully affected all accounts, not only in the conspicuous cases like Matt. 27:19, 24-25, and the BARABBAS material lacks independent corroboration (Pes. 8.6 is concerned with a wholly distinct problem). It would, however, be incautious to conclude that Pilate was put under no pressure at all.

3. The Jewish proceedings. ***a. The balance of the evidence.*** Viewed from the perspective of the modern debate about the trial of Jesus, the earliest Christian and Jewish sources are startlingly unanimous in speaking of a Jewish initiative, even though the extent of that initiative varies. Mark 14:55-64 and (following this) Matt. 26:59-66 envisage a full trial. Luke 22:66-71 contains no reference to a defined charge or verdict and is regarded by some scholars as a description of an informal hearing; nevertheless, Luke probably was thinking of a full trial in view of the location (συνέδριον can be translated "council chamber") and the reference to testimony (22:71), supported by statements which he made elsewhere (9:22; Acts 13:27-28). John, while only hinting at a hearing before Caiaphas in 18:24, 28, seems to have incorporated trial traditions earlier in 10:24-25, 36 (cf. Luke 22:67-68, 70), a procedure parallel to his retrojection of other passion material in 2:13-22 and 6:51. On the Jewish side, Josephus' text (Antiq. XVIII. iii.3), at a point where no mark of Christian editing is apparent, mentions Jewish charges against Jesus before Pilate, and subsequent tannaitic tradition (e.g., T.B. Sanh. 43a, 107b) mounts a critique of Jesus and of Christianity by exaggerating, rather than by disputing, sanhedrin participation. Tacitus (*Annals* XV.xliv) indeed refers only to Roman action, though his Roman preoccupations and limited interest in the case of Jesus as such restricts any argument from silence here. This unanimous testimony is reinforced by the strong probability that Jesus' proclamation was theologically radical and unacceptable, especially in relation to the Law, but politically innocuous. This would certainly be disputed by those who detect in Jesus a ZEALOT-like tendency (which is open to severe criticism), and could in principle be weakened if his downfall, like that of JOHN THE BAPTIST (Jos. Antiq. XVIII.v.2), resulted from any widespread popular unrest he caused. But since the sayings tradition (e.g., Luke 10:13-15) and the situation presupposed by many parables attest a pattern of restricted influence, frustration, and failure, this is not likely, and it remains more probable that any legal proceedings against him would relate to what he had said and done rather than to what he had not.

b. Traditio-historical problems. Source- and redaction-critical explorations of the Lukan and Johannine accounts suggest the probable presence of non-Markan material in each, as well as a common scheme, according to which a period in the house of the high priest (Luke 22:54; John 18:15: Annas?) was followed by a move elsewhere in the morning for a hearing before Caiaphas (Luke 22:66; John 18:24). When cognizance is taken of Markan editorial work, which has positioned Mark 14:55-65 within Mark 14:54–15:1, a certain awareness of this scheme can also be traced in pre-Markan material. But more important is the linguistic and redactional evidence that parts of Luke 22:63-71 contain an alternative tradition which, especially in the case of Luke 22:63-64, 67-68, 70 (?), appears more primitive than Mark's version. The latter has long been suspected of reflecting post-Easter Christian convictions, and its over-all coherence with characteristically Markan convictions has recently been argued to some effect. But in principle the possibility remains that pre-Markan tradition existed to be molded into this shape. Equally, the fact that Mark's main trial passage is presented as the central element in an interpolation structure by no means demonstrates the total unhistoricity of this or any other trial tradition, as can be deduced from the analogous cases of Mark 3:22-30; 6:14-29; 11:15-19. So while the presence of post-Easter concerns and convictions within all traditions can hardly be disputed, the consequent traditio-historical pattern draws particular attention to the Lukan evidence. It also means that the relationship between the traditions and current legal norms cannot be decided simply by fastening on Mark.

c. Legal problems. Explicit suggestions of improper legal procedure enter the Christian traditions only at Matt. 26:59. Neither Markan (cf. the rejection of discordant testimony, Mark 14:56, 59) nor Lukan forms of the tradition aim to make this an issue. The modern debate has seen things differently, frequently containing allegations (or denials) of wholesale illegality, though recently the discussion has narrowed to five major problems:

(1) A trial in the high priest's house, rather than in the Hall of Hewn Stones, diverges from M. Sanh. 11.2. But in fact no tradition suggests that Jesus' trial took place there! Neither Mark 14:55-65 nor Mark 15:1 contains a place-note, and to apply the geographical detail of 14:53 to the former passage ignores the interpolation structure of Mark's narrative. Similarly, Luke 22:66 should probably be taken as indicating a movement (cf. "they led him away") to a new location, the council chamber. John (18:24, 28) agrees.

(2) Nocturnal proceedings would infringe M. Sanh. 4.1. But again the suggestion of a nocturnal trial is an impermissible deduction from the present secondary position of Mark 14:55-65 and clashes with Luke 22:66.

(3) A trial on a festival day (synoptic chronology) or on the eve of a festival (Johannine chronology), and indeed on the eve of a sabbath (Mark 15:42; Matt. 27:57; John 19:31) clashes with M. Sanh. 4.1 and Bez. 5:2. This is the most substantial of all the suggested discrepancies, though even this one may not stand since Jos. Antiq. XVI.vi.2 may indicate a progression in the development of this law, and the distinct possibility that its final form, as in the texts cited, was not in operation at the time of Jesus.

(4) The failure to hold a second session to ratify a verdict of "guilty" clashes with M. Sanh. 4.1. But other Jewish legal material (e.g., Jos. Antiq. XIV.ix.5; XV.vii.5; XVI.vi.2; Tosef. Sanh. X.11) shows no awareness of this rule, which may therefore stem from the developing liberal tendency in later Pharisaism.

(5) The introduction of the category of "blasphemy" (Mark 14:64) as a description of anything Jesus had thus far said, fits ill with Lev. 24:16 and M. Sanh. 7.5. But the term "blasphemy" is mentioned only by Mark and cannot, in view of Mark 2:7, be assumed to be more than a general description of what is theologically horrifying.

Specifically legal objections to the trial traditions turn out, therefore, to be somewhat brittle. Moreover, the appeal to them is the more unsatisfactory in view of (*a*) the proven discrepancy between Mishnaic laws codified around A.D. 200 and those operating in Jesus' time; (*b*) uncertainty about whether Sadducean authorities would follow Pharisaic rules (though Jos. Antiq. XVIII.i.4 envisages such acquiescence); (*c*) the irrelevance of all formal rules if the proceedings were only informal.

d. The status of the event. If then the earliest form of the tradition evinces no inherent legal problems, it remains to determine the character of the proceedings—as formal trial or as informal preparatory session—as well as the content and definition of the charge. On all these points opinion is sharply divided. The formality of a trial in the strict sense is favored by explicit Markan and implicit Lukan evidence, with which early Jewish testimony agrees. Against this stands (1) the impression given by the hearing before Pilate that the case was being dealt with *de novo;* (2) the distinct possibility that all Lukan hints of formal procedure are inferences from Mark, who in turn has exaggerated the scale of the event; (3) the difficulty of two trials, one Jewish and one Roman, following consecutively (though see Jos. War VI.v.3); (4) the final penalty of crucifixion, as against a specifically Jewish method of execution. Also, if messiahship was the issue which decided Jesus' case in the Jewish hearing, the fact that a messianic claim was technically inoffensive would also require us to interpret that hearing as informal and preparatory alone. But was messiahship in isolation the issue? Certainly it has been widely favored, and can reasonably be preferred to suggestions which fasten on the temple saying (Mark 14:58) or the words "I am" (Mark 14:62) or the announcement of the Son of man's enthronement (Mark 14:62). But if the Lukan tradition in 22:67-68 is historical—and it coheres exactly with the approach of Jesus in Mark 11:27-33, while at the same time exhibiting none of the typical tendencies of Christian remodeling—it implies that Jesus was asked about messiahship, but that his answer contained insufficient basis for a charge. It may well be, therefore, that the theological issue of divine Sonship (Luke 22:70) intervened and to some extent interrupted the continuity between the events of Luke 22:67-68 and Mark 15:2. This element of divine Sonship, given prominence by all evangelists (cf. in addition to synoptic evidence, John 19:7), would gain in force if the authenticity of Sonship material elsewhere in the gospels (Matt. 11:27; Mark 12:6; 13:32) should prove defensible, and if Luke 22:70 should, as is very probably the case (though this is disputed), prove to stem from the pre-Lukan form of the tradition along with 22:67-68. If so, and if the hearing was in fact a formal trial, it is necessary to look for a definition of Jesus' offense. In the history of the discussion the range of suggestions put forward has included blasphemer, beguiler, false prophet, and rebellious elder, among others, but among them it is almost impossible to choose with confidence. *See also* CRIMES AND PUNISHMENTS §E.

Bibliography. J. Juster, *Les Juifs dans l'Empire Romain,* Sources litteraire, I (1914); S. Zeitlin, *Who Crucified Jesus?* (1942); H. Lietzmann, "Der Prozess Jesu," repr. in *Kleine Schriften* II, ed. K. Aland (1958); A. N. Sherwin-White, *Roman Society and Roman Law in the NT* (1963); S. G. F. Brandon, *The Trial of Jesus of Nazareth,* Historic Trials Series (1968); J. Blinzler, *Der Prozess Jesu* (4th ed., 1969); G. Schneider, *Verleugnung, Verspottung und Verhör Jesu nach Lukas 22,54-71,* StANT, XXII (1969); E. Bammel, ed., *The Trial of Jesus,* SBT, 2nd. ser. XIII (1970); E. Linnemann, *Studien zur Passionsgeschichte, FRLANT,* CII (1970); W. S. Wilson, *The Execution of Jesus* (1970); D. R. Catchpole, *The Trial of Jesus,* SPB, XVIII (1971); E. Lohse, "συνέδριον," *TDNT,* VII (1971), 860-71; H. Cohn, *The Trial and Death of Jesus* (1968); P. Benoit, *Jesus and the Gospel,* I (1961 [ET 1973]); J. R. Donahue, *Are you the Christ?* SBLDS, X (1973); G. Sloyan, *Jesus on Trial* (1973); P. Winter, *On the Trial of Jesus* (2nd ed., 1974).

D. R. CATCHPOLE

***TRIBE.** An association of the real or assumed descendants of a legendary, mythical, or remote ancestor. The biblical groups known as tribes could be more accurately identified as "clans" (*see* KINSHIP AND FAMILY[S] §§2, 8). Since such groups are found in the early stages of urban societies as well as in nomadic and agricultural societies, the presence of "tribes" in the Bible is no indication of a nomadic origin of the Israelites. *See* NOMADISM[S].

A tribe may base its kinship system on a common (eponymous) "ancestor." The questions of whether the ancestor was an actual historical personage and whether the members of the tribe had any plausible historical connection with him are irrelevant to the function of the social symbol that he represents.

Ideologically a tribe seems to be an attempt to transfer the loyalty of kinship ties to a larger social organization. This transference is sometimes motivated by the necessity of forming large economic or political power structures, often as a reaction to a competing structure.

A tribe may be held together by the need to lay claim to and mobilize the defense of territory. Such social coalitions have often been formidable opponents to the ambitions of political empires, but once the opponent is gone, the tribe will often disintegrate as well. For this reason a tribe is weakly bonded socially and thus ephemeral by its very nature. The large number of "tribes" in the biblical texts which come and go may thus not be relevant to larger questions of population and cultural continuity.

It follows that the name, either of a tribe or of a supposed state, has to do only with the particular social organization for which it is attested. The continuity of a name has no necessary correlation with the continuity of any sort of social, cultural, or religious reality.

We have two major bodies of material from which relevant evidence may be gathered.

The first is the extensive body of documents from MARI, in which a "tribe" called Banū-yamīna constitutes a formidable force against the Mari centralization of control. The identification of these "sons of the right [bank?]" with primitive "nomads" is now unacceptable. The foundation deposit inscription of Iaḫdun-Lim suggests that the Banū Yamīna constituted a resistance movement that arose in reaction to his ephemeral conquest of city-states further upstream along the Euphrates.

As at Mari, the primary function of Israelite tribes seems to have been the organization of a large and strongly bonded (on the specifically religious grounds of the Yahwist covenant) society that could ward off the constant attempts of urban rulers to regain economic and political control of villages. With the establishment of the centralized monopoly of force under David, the older tribal organization had no social functions and withered away. The tribal names seem to have survived for a time as genealogical traditions. *See* GOVERNMENT, ISRAELITE[S] §§2-3.

Bibliography. Mendenhall, G. *The Tenth Generation* (1973), ch. VII, and "The Twelve-Tribe Federation of Ancient Israel," in *Magnalia Dei,* Festschrift in honor of G. E. Wright (1976); E. R. Service, *Primitive Social Organization* (1962); E. Wolf, *Peasants* (1966). These latter two works furnish excellent and much needed insights into the nature and functioning of simple village communities. G. MENDENHALL

***TRIBES, TERRITORIES OF.** The sources pertaining to the tribal territories and the proper manner of their interpretation continue to be subjects of discussion.

The distinction between the tribal boundary system (*see* §§1-2 *below*) and the town lists (§3 *below*) should be retained. Together with auxiliary sources and related lists, these discriptions may be analyzed and assigned to periods that provide a probable historical background. The boundary descriptions are sufficiently realistic to refute the assumption that an original, more restricted core was artificially extended according to some visionary ideal. The borderline between the assumed actual boundaries and the theoretical extensions is arbitrary and based on preconceived historical and literary notions. Furthermore, even if earlier historical-territorial phases may be discerned (which is rarely the case), and assuming that these were altered or edited according to a later situation, this final form is to be regarded as historically valuable in its entirety, in contrast to the opinion which relies only on the parts presumed to be original, and either disqualifies the additions or regards them as secondary modifications.

1. The boundary system. The tribal boundary descriptions cover the whole country without interruption. The allotments are contiguous and do not overlap. A controversial instance is the border between Manasseh and the Galilee tribes. Josh. 17:10-11 is to be taken as an enumeration of the peripheral areas of Manasseh along the border that abuts upon Asher and Issachar.

Although it is quite clear that the tribal territories underwent changes, the boundary system is based on one phase in that history. Within that system only ten tribes are explicitly represented. Landless Levi (Josh. 18:7) has been replaced by the division of Joseph into Manasseh and Ephraim, while Simeon and Dan are not part of that descriptive framework.

The form of description varies, ranging from detailed delineations of border features and regions to scant allusive outlines. Considering this diversity of form, the boundary system cannot be restricted only to those tribes whose description is marked by an enumeration of border features, nor can the over-all map be based solely on such border points. Perhaps abbreviated in some instances and amplified in others, the descriptions define the individual territories from within. At times this was done by enumerating various regions at the periphery of the territory, or even by references to neighboring allotments, and at others by describing the border areas in detail. Particular geographical features are sometimes also added. The outer edges of the border regions constitute the boundary lines, which generally are only implied and are rarely defined in detail. Noth's theory of *Grenzfixpunkte* (boundary-fixing points) is thus rendered inapplicable. Instead of points, extended border regions are inferred, and this naturally affects how the map is to be drawn. The results of this method are of particular importance in Transjordan. There the description of the tribal allotments is based on an enumeration of regions only. The territorial units are of different size (some arranged to indicate the N-S extent of the allotments, while others add detail in breadth), or general territorial definitions are explained by an enumeration of minor units, providing internal detail.

E borders in Transjordan are sometimes reconstructed on the basis of some of the territorial centers listed (Josh. 13). Such regional centers, in sequence and marked by the "from . . ." or ". . . to" formula, were erroneously regarded as boundary-fixing points (*see* TRIBES, TERRITORIES OF §8 and map). Most of N Gilead and the entire Bashan were thus omitted, as well as the E parts of Gad and Reuben. The present method thus will materially alter both the over-all picture and the internal picture.

Auxiliary material is generally instructive and particularly decisive for the N borders of East

Manasseh (in Transjordan), Asher, and Naphtali. The N border of East Manasseh is vague; that of Naphtali is not indicated at all; and Asher's territory is defined as extending "as far as Sidon the Great" (Josh. 19:28; however, this phrase is generally regarded as a secondary emendation or understood as excluding this area).

2. The general framework of the boundary system. A number of territorial descriptions and lists are based on the same historical-territorial concept as the boundary system. These include the following: the land of Canaan; the over-all framework of the Conquest combined with "the remaining land," partly allotted and partly unallotted; the "conquest lacunae" (Alt's "negative inventory of possessions," *see below,* and TRIBES, TERRITORIES OF, p. 701*b*); and the list of Levitical cities, which displays a somewhat varied intertribal division, without apparently modifying the external borders.

The over-all extent of the Conquest W of the Jordan is narrated in several instances. There are two cycles of conquest stories, the southern and

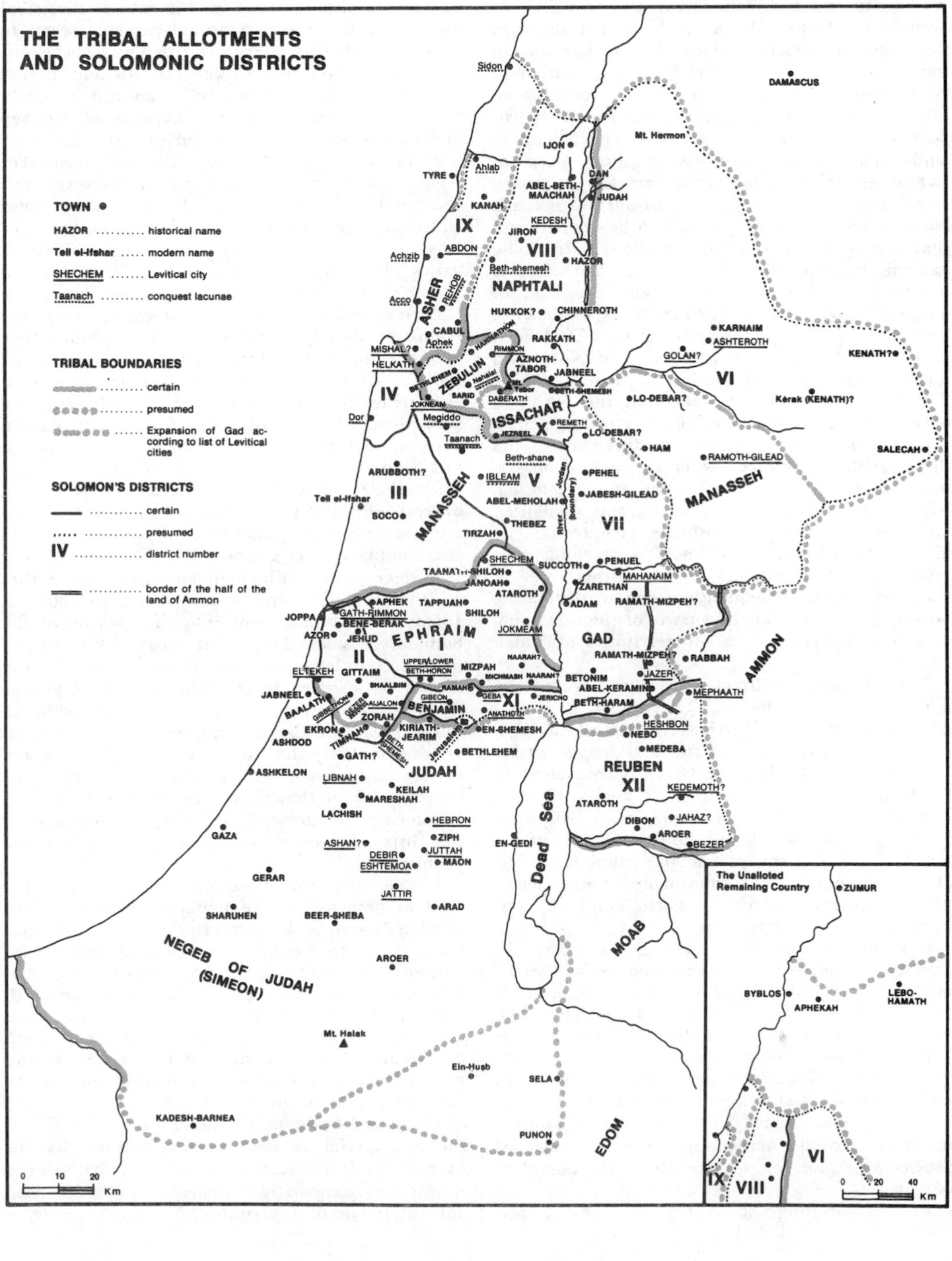

the northern, summarized in Josh. 10:41 and 11:2-3, 8. The entire conquest of W Palestine is then recounted in brief in Josh. 11:17 and 12:7. As part of the complete scheme, the conquest of Transjordan is outlined: Deut. 2:36-37; 3:8, 10, 15-17; Josh. 12:1-5; 13:9-13. Thus the peripheral borders of the complete tribal league are obtained. In Transjordan the area reaches from the River Arnon in the S, up to and including Mount Hermon in the N, and eastward to the desert and the upper (S-N) Jabbok, and in the Bashan as far as Salecah. In W Palestine the area defined extends from Kadesh-barnea and Mount Halak in the S to Baal-gad in the valley of Lebanon below Mount Hermon in the N, and to the sea in the W. The N border in W Palestine is further qualified by resorting to the definition of the remaining land, and particularly to the part that was allotted. The remaining land (Josh. 13:2-6) consists of those parts of Canaan in W Palestine which are as yet unpossessed (cf. Judg. 3:1-3), and a distinction is made between the part which is still to be allotted and that part which will remain unallotted. In doing so, the relative position between the allotted territory (the land of Israel) and the land of Canaan, which extends further N, is established. The S portion of the remaining land is defined in Josh. 13:2-3 (plus "in the south" of vs. 4), and the N in 13:4 (without the initial "in the south"). Vss. 5-6 provide further details in the N. Vs. 5 opens with a *Wāw explicativum* ("to wit"; RSV "and") and recounts those northernmost parts that remain unallotted, whereas vs. 6 defines a more southwestern tract which is to be allotted. The border between the allotted and unallotted areas is Baal-gad of Joshua's conquests. The allotted area is further defined as reaching Misrephoth-maim, mentioned in the northern war of conquest, which consequently seems to denote the northern limit. The allotted parts of the remaining land are incorporated in the territories of Judah and Asher.

Thus the land of Israel is measured against the land of Canaan (Num. 34:2-12; cf. Ezek. 47:15-20). The Transjordanian portions conquered, as narrated in Numbers, are regarded as being outside Canaan. Thus the land of Israel is equivalent to the land of Canaan, excluding the unallotted land, and with the addition of Transjordan. All these sources unanimously depict the over-all area of the tribal league and thus define the external borders of the combined tribal allotments. Consequently the N borders of East-Manasseh, Naphtali, and Asher can also be established.

It should be mentioned that Scripture has still another, earlier, account of the conquest and settlement of Transjordan. This is found in Num. 21:24, 32, 33, 35 (cf. Judg. 11:13, 22) and 32:2-3, 33, 34-38, 39, 40, 41-42. Here most of the area is outside Canaan proper, whereas the larger territories of the Transjordanian tribes in Josh. 13 clearly conflict with the borders of Canaan. However, only these larger Transjordanian allotments integrate into the harmonious over-all scheme of the tribal allotments that constitute the boundary system.

The list of conquest lacunae (*see above*) and the list of Levitical cities provide details regarding the individual tribal allotments. The conquest lacunae (Judg. 1) are drawn up according to the allotments of the boundary system. Therefore, they recount certain aspects of settlement history, as viewed from the completed situation depicted in that system. The document is to be dated, not by possible references to an early situation, but by its comprehensive retrospective view. Judg. 1:31 proves the inclusion of Sidon in the allotment to Asher. The list of Levitical cities (Josh. 21; I Chr. 6) also supplies material for the map of the tribal allotments, but the background depicted seems to indicate a slightly different situation. Shechem is assigned to Ephraim, while Josh. 16 and 17 are unclear in this respect. In Transjordan, Gad's territory is enlarged at the expense of Reuben and East Manasseh, as recorded in Josh. 13.

3. The town lists. The town lists are an element separate from the boundary system. However, this does not automatically imply that they differ chronologically and in their essential nature. The lists are not uniform, and the degree of detail varies. In some instances (e.g., the House of Joseph), the lists are practically nonexistent; in Galilee they are diversely integrated into the boundary description; and in Transjordan they are so scant as to contract into a list of regional centers. It must also be noted that the northern areas, particularly in the list of Naphtali, seem deficient. Only the lists of Judah, Benjamin, Simeon, and Dan are detailed. Of these, Simeon and Dan do not belong to the boundary system, since their territories are covered by those of other tribes, and the lists of Judah and Benjamin are the only ones which are not integrated into the boundary descriptions.

Evidence based on present knowledge shows that all the lists of towns by tribes—except those of Judah and Benjamin—fit into the division of the boundary system. The tribal geography envisaged is therefore based on the same framework and should be assigned to the same period. It follows that lists of towns or regional centers were an integral part of the description of the individual allotments. Only the lists of Judah and Benjamin, which conflict with their respective border descriptions, show that they were amplified according to later developments. The dating and inclusion of the lists of Simeon and Dan pose a separate problem.

4. The historical framework. The extent of the land as depicted in the boundary system and its auxiliary sources restricts the possible historical background to periods of widest territorial expansion: the united monarchy under David and Solomon, or the times of Uzziah and Jeroboam II. The latter period, however, must be ruled out. The territory of Asher cannot be reconciled with conditions of that period, nor can the border between Judah and its northern neighbors or the intertribal borders in Transjordan. For the period of David and Solomon, on the other hand, sufficient source material is available to indicate that its over-all territorial extent served as a basis for a retrospective schematic description of the Conquest and allotment of the country.

The census of David (II Sam. 24) provides the peripheral outline of the national territory of Israel, including subjugated Canaanite areas, and excluding vassal countries. Here too, it is mainly territories that are enumerated. In N Transjordan an unclear definition baffles all commentators, but judging by Solomon's districts (*see below*), Bashan is probably referred to and definitely included. The area thus obtained tallies with that of the boundary system and the conquest framework. Solomon's administrative districts (II Kings 4), though excluding Judah, fit the framework provided by David's census. It is particularly noteworthy that, wherever this administrative division digresses from the tribal boundaries, the common basis of the two systems and the derivation of the one from the other are evident. Particularly in Transjordan, where major territorial changes resulted from David's wars against the Arameans, there seems to be a close dependence of the tribal areas on the administrative districts.

On the basis of this and other historical material, dating of the diverse geographical lists may be suggested.

The boundary system with its integrated town lists reflects the end of David's and particularly the inception of Solomon's reign. The incorporation of Gezer and the subjugation of Philistia must be added to the testimony of David's census. Solomon's districts belong to the same period. While the one system records the tribal-territorial division, the other describes the administrative organization. However, there is yet a third framework: the tribal-clan register based on genealogical affiliation (Exod. 6:14-25; Num. 3:14-37; etc.). Accordingly, Simeon within Judah, or Dan in Naphtali, may retain their separate identities. All these systems co-exist and are not mutually exclusive.

The boundary system reflects a late development. Simeon and Dan have been eliminated, and an expansion of Ephraim at the expense of Manasseh is recorded. Jerusalem has been incorporated, and the peripheral borders are quite extensive. The list of Levitical cities is more schematic on the one hand—by recording cities from Simeon and Dan in its historical S location—and on the other, it displays an even more advanced territorial development, with Shechem in Ephraim and Gad's territory enlarged at the expense of both its neighbors. A date about one generation later than the boundary system, in the second half of Solomon's reign, before the cession to Tyre of the land of Cabul, is indicated.

Simeon's town list in Josh. 19:2-8 seems to reflect the expansion under David, whereas the related list in I Chr. 4:28-33 is slightly earlier "until David reigned" (4:31). Dan's town list is an expansion of its historical area and seems to reflect Solomon's second district.

Only the lists of Benjamin and Judah reflect a later period. Benjamin seems to be based on the expansion under Abijah (II Chr. 13:19), with one district accidentally missing. Judah's list displays characteristics of Hezekiah's reign, perhaps updated under Josiah; one missing district is preserved in LXX.

5. Summary. The territories of the tribes, as recorded in the book of Joshua and Judg. 1, are part of a historiographical composition that describes the conquest and allotment of the country according to formalized traditions reflecting the completion of the process. In order to include all twelve tribes, town lists of Simeon and Dan are also recorded, though with appropriate remarks defining their status. The lists of Judah and Benjamin, which constituted the kingdom of Judah, are preserved in later amplified versions. Town lists of Ephraim and Manasseh are missing for no apparent reason. The growth of the Transjordanian territories breached the borders of Canaan; and since all the tribes there are traditionally regarded as being settled outside Canaan, Josh. 22 blurs the status of East Manasseh.

Bibliography. Y. Kaufmann, *The Biblical Account of the Conquest of Palestine* (1953), a utopian view; Y. Aharoni, *The Land of the Bible* (1967), mainly adhering to the concepts of Alt and Noth; W. F. Albright, *Archaeology and the Religion of Israel* (1956), pp. 121-25, the boundary system reflects David's period; M. H. Segal, *Introduction to the Bible* (1950), pp. 158-61, Hebrew, and "Joshua," in *Tradition and Criticism* (1957), pp. 126-35, Hebrew, assigns the geographical lists to the period of David and Solomon; S. Mowinckel, *Zur Frage nach Dokumentarischen Quellen in Josua 13-19* (1946), and S. Yeivin, *The Israelite Conquest of Canaan* (1971), pp. 247-66, both postulate the descriptions to originate in diverse traditions of different periods; Z. Kallai-Kleinmann, "Note on the Town Lists of Judah, Simeon, Benjamin and Dan," *VT*, XI (1961), 223-27, *The Tribes of Israel* (1967), Hebrew, and "The Boundaries of Canaan and the Land of Israel in the Bible," *Eretz Israel,* XII (1975), 25-34, Hebrew; "Organizational and Administrative Frameworks in the Kingdom of David and Solomon," *Proceedings of the Sixth World Congress of Jewish Studies*, I (1975).

Z. KALLAI

TRUST. *See* BOLDNESS[S]; FAITH, FAITHFULNESS IN THE NT[S].

TRUTH, GOSPEL OF. A Gnostic, perhaps Valentinian, work preserved in COPTIC which discourses in meditative and sometimes homiletic fashion on the person of Christ and his redemptive work. It is completely preserved in a translation in the Subachmimic dialect in Codex I (the Jung Codex) from the NAG HAMMADI library; the official designation is I,*2*:16,31–43,24. Three small but clearly recognizable fragments of a Sahidic version containing parts of six pages are found in the remains of Nag Hammadi Codex XII (XII,*2**:53*,19–60*,30). These represent an independent translation from what was undoubtedly a Greek original, and because they exhibit some notable differences not accounted for merely by the process of translation, they suggest that more than one recension of the Greek may have existed. The Coptic texts may be dated to the mid-fourth century. Attempts to date the Greek original hinge on the identification of the work. The Gospel of Truth was the first of the Nag Hammadi writings to be published. Because two leaves of it had been separated from the Jung Codex, the original *editio princeps* and some earlier translations are missing four pages (33–36).

1. Identification. Since the GTr first became

known, a majority of scholars have associated it with the "Gospel of Truth" mentioned by Irenaeus in Her. III:xi.9: "But the followers of Valentinus, being utterly rash in putting forward their own compositions, pride themselves on having more gospels than there really are. They have even reached such a point of audacity as to entitle their own rather recent writing 'The Gospel of Truth,' though it has nothing in common with the Gospels of the apostles. Thus among them not even the gospel is lacking in blasphemy. For if the one they put forward is the gospel of truth and yet is quite unlike those handed down to us from the apostles, all who wish can learn, as is shown by the Scriptures themselves, that what has been handed down from the apostles is now not the gospel of truth" (author's trans.).

Insofar as it is decidedly different from the canonical gospels, the GTr fits this description, but the remark of Irenaeus is otherwise very unspecific. The evidence for the title "Gospel of Truth" in the case of the Coptic work is only indirect. Unlike most works in the Nag Hammadi library, and indeed in the Jung Codex, it has no title either at the beginning or at the end. The work begins: "The gospel of truth is a joy for those who have received from the Father of truth the gift of knowing him." In accordance with a widespread ancient custom, the *incipit* may be regarded as incorporating the title of the work, hence the modern designation "Gospel of Truth." The possibility must be borne in mind, however, that our document may not itself be the "Gospel of Truth" but a reflection on it.

At first sight, the GTr seems to fail to meet Irenaeus' description in that it lacks the most distinctive elements of Valentinianism, such as the elaborate structure of the heavenly aeons, the fall of Sophia, the role of the demiurge as distinct from the Father, and other features (*see* GNOSTICISM[S] §4*b*). Nevertheless, with its sharp distinction between the perfect world of the pleroma and the earthly world of deception, its notion of the captivity of the spiritual element of persons in this world, its concentration on the primacy of knowledge as knowledge of self, and other features, the GTr is an unmistakably Gnostic work. Much of its technical language reflects the vocabulary of the second-century Valentinians, and its account of the creation of matter by error (Greek πλάνη) seems to reflect a Valentinian myth of the fall of Sophia and the work of the demiurge. Some interpreters have concluded from the absence of highly developed Valentinian myths that the work was an early or transitional composition by Valentinus himself. This would allow it a date in the middle of the second century. Yet because the document seems to rest on a well-developed Valentinian mythology without repeating it, it is safer to conclude simply that it is the work of a member of the Valentinian school. If the document really is the "gospel" mentioned by Irenaeus, it may still be dated in the second half of the second century.

2. Literary character and contents. The GTr is in no respect a "gospel" in the sense in which that term is applied to the four canonical gospels. It is true that it focuses on Jesus and contains a Christology, but it does not narrate anything of the earthly life of Jesus nor record his words. Instead, it uses the term "gospel" (Greek εὐαγγέλιον) in the sense of "good news" (once translated literally so into Coptic, 34,35), much in the manner of Pauline usage in Rom. 1:16, for example. The parallel with Romans may be carried further, for just as the first part of Paul's great epistle first sets forth the world's need for redemption and then reflects on the meaning of God's redemptive act in Christ, so the GTr embodies this structure, though in a less clear manner. Because its reflections on the redemptive act and the person of Christ are occasionally interrupted by direct exhortation to the readers, some have chosen to classify the work as a homily or sermon. It is in any case perhaps best described as a meditation on the gospel (Grobel). Some early interpreters conjectured a setting for the homily in a baptismal or confirmation rite, basing their view on possible sacramental allusions in the text. Generally speaking, however, this suggestion has not been favorably received.

The almost total lack of systematic arrangement makes it impossible to summarize the contents adequately. Instead, one can only list some of the themes in the order in which they occur in the work. After an introductory statement in which the god of salvation is identified with the knowledge that comes through the Savior, the author then establishes the world's need for redemption by narrating its separation from the Father in terms of ignorance and error. Knowledge is communicated to the ignorant by Jesus in his death and his teaching. Then the death of Jesus is reinterpreted in the development of a sustained metaphor, that of the living book in which the names of the elect are eternally inscribed and which was manifested by Jesus. This passage contains some of the classic statements of Gnostic teaching which are frequent in the GTr: "Those whose name he [the Father] knew in advance were called at the end, so that one who has knowledge is the one whose name the Father has uttered. For he whose name has not been spoken is ignorant. . . . If one has knowledge, he is from above. If he is called he hears, he answers, and he turns to him who is calling him, and ascends to him. And he knows in what manner he is called. Having knowledge, he does the will of the one who called him, he wishes to be pleasing to him, he receives rest. Each one's name comes to him. He who is to have knowledge in this manner knows where he comes from and where he is going" (21,25–22,15; here and elsewhere author's trans.).

After a series of somewhat rambling reflections on the saving act as the transformation of deficiency into wholeness and of ignorance into knowledge, there is a description of the work of the Word as the judgment of the world, followed by further reflections on the Father and his plan to save. There is then a vivid passage, possibly inspired by Homer (*Iliad* XXII, 199-201), which depicts ignorance as living in a nightmare and the coming to gnosis as awakening. After describing many of the typical experiences of nightmares such as flight, pursuit, fighting, falling, flying, murder, blood, the passage concludes: "When those who are going through all these things wake up, they see nothing, they who were in the midst of all these disturbances, for they are nothing. Such is the way of those who have cast ignorance aside from them like sleep, not esteeming it as anything, nor do they esteem its works as solid things either, but they leave them behind like a dream in the night. The knowledge of the Father they value as the dawn" (29,26–30,6).

In a further set of christological reflections there is a Gnostic exegesis of the parable of the lost sheep based on number symbolism in which Jesus is the shepherd. This is followed by another series of reflections on the relationship of the knower to the Father, the meaning of the redemption in Gnostic language, and another set of metaphors for redemption. There is then a long christological meditation on the Son as the name of the Father, containing the refrain, "The name of the Father is the Son." After a final set of reflections on the saving work of the Son, the meditation ends with a description of the life and destiny of the true Gnostics in union with the Father. "His children are perfect and worthy of his name, for he is the Father: it is children of this kind that he loves" (43,20-24).

3. Christology and soteriology. A great part of the author's meditation focuses on the person and work of Christ, who is referred to by a variety of titles, often with a conscious play on their meaning. Although he sometimes mentions Jesus by name, the author has no real interest in either the Jesus of history or the history of Jesus. Instead he moves back and forth between the pre-existent and eternal divine Son in the pleroma of the Father and the Logos who reveals the Father to men. It is only the identity of the two that matters. Jesus is once called Savior, in the context of a wordplay on his mission to save, and only twice called Christ, once in a play on Χριστός, "anointed," in the context of the idea of anointing. The most frequent christological titles, however, are Word or Logos, perhaps inherited from the Fourth Gospel, and Son. The latter, along with the elaborate development of name Christology, emphasizes the close relationship with the Father, so close that it is the Father whom the Logos-Son reveals in himself. The GTr does not call the Son Lord (Κύριος), but it seems to be familiar with this title in its references to the Son as the "proper name" (κύριον ὄνομα) of the Father.

Although the issue has been debated by some interpreters, it is clear that the Christology of the GTr is Docetic, as might be expected of a Gnostic document. The problem is the vagueness of its rare references to the incarnation, compounded by the uncertainty of detecting nuances in a Coptic translation. Nevertheless when the document reinterprets the Crucifixion as Jesus' revelation of the living book in which the names of the elect are inscribed, it seems clearly to dwell on the paradox of only apparent death: "O such great teaching! He draws himself down to death though life eternal clothes him!" (20,27-30).

What is at issue in the saving work of Christ is unmistakable: he enters a world that is characterized, not by sin as alienation from God, but by ignorance of the essentially unknown Father. Christ's work is to reveal the Father and thus dispel ignorance with knowledge: "He gave them the means of knowing the knowledge of the Father and the revelation of his Son" (30,24-26). But despite the emphasis on knowledge of the Father, it is essential to realize that the content of gnosis is primarily knowledge of self: "If one has knowledge, he is from above. . . . He knows where he comes from and where he is going" (22,3-15). The Gnostic knows the Father in the sense that he knows his own divine origin and destiny.

In the GTr the emphasis on self-knowledge as redemption is so dominant that ultimately the work is not really concerned with the person of Christ at all despite its apparent Christocentrism. Christ is of interest only as the vehicle of revelation, revealer of the Father in the sense of revealer of the true nature of himself and every Gnostic. Every Gnostic is a son of the Father, and revelation is ultimately an interior phenomenon within the Gnostic himself.

4. The NT in the GTr. Unlike many Gnostic writings, the GTr does not cite or clearly refer to any OT passage, but this limitation may have been dictated by the subject matter. In addition, however, it contains no explicit citation from the NT. Yet a careful comparison shows that the author has borrowed extensively from NT themes and language. There are clear allusions to all the gospels, almost all the Pauline epistles, Hebrews, I John, and Revelation, and probable allusions to other books as well. In almost all cases, the author interprets the NT texts in his own fashion, sometimes completely at cross-purposes with the originals. His use of the parable of the lost sheep (Matt. 18:12-14; Luke 15:4-6), which is remarkably similar to the interpretation which Irenaeus attributes to the Valentinian followers of Marcus (Her. I.xvi.2), furnishes a clear example: "He [the Son] is the shepherd who left behind the ninety-nine sheep which were not lost. He went searching for the one which was lost. He rejoiced when he found it, for 99 is a number that is in the left hand which holds it. But when the one is found, the entire number passes to the right hand. Thus [it is with] him who lacks the one: that is, the entire right which draws what was deficient and takes it from the left-hand side and brings it to the right, and thus the number becomes 100. It is the sign of the one who is in their sound; it is the Father" (31,35–32,17).

The fact that the GTr uses so many of the NT books may, if the work be dated in the middle of the second century, have some significance for the development of the NT canon. In particular, it is significant that the author alludes to both Hebrews and Revelation, for the acceptance of these books was challenged in the West and in the East respectively in the second century, according to the common theories of the development of the canon.

5. Importance. The GTr, as has rightly been recognized by the many scholars who have written on it, may be one of the most important of the Nag Hammadi writings. It is probable that it provides access to an original work of second-century Valentinianism, and one must remain open to the hypothesis that it was written by Valentinus himself. In any event, it is one of the clearest statements of Christian Gnosticism that has survived. It does not lose its force in the maze of mythological speculations for which Irenaeus reproached the followers of Valentinus. Moreover, it expresses the Gnostic experience of salvation in a language intimately related to the traditional language of the NT yet characterized by its own coherent theology. The surviving Gnostic literature, including that of Nag Hammadi, is conspicuously lacking in literary quality. The GTr stands out as an exception; in its own discursive and meditative style, it possesses a certain beauty which is not always obvious, due to the accident of its preservation in a sometimes awkward Coptic translation.

Bibliography. Text: M. Malinine, H.-C. Puech, and G. Quispel, *Evangelium Veritatis: Codex Jung f. VIII^v-XVI^v (p. 16-32)/f. XIX^r-XXII^r (p. 37-43)* (1956) and *Supplementum: f. XVII^r-XVIII^v (p. 33-36)* (1961). Eng. trans.: W. Foerster, ed., *Gnosis: A Selection of Gnostic Texts,* II (1971), 53-70. Commentaries: K. Grobel, *The Gospel of Truth* (1960); J.-É. Ménard, *L'Évangile de Vérité* (1962), with Gr. retroversion, and *L'Évangile de Vérité,* Nag Hammadi Studies, II (1972). Discussion: F. L. Cross, ed., *The Jung Codex* (1955); S. Arai, *Die Christologie des Evangelium Veritatis* (1964); C. I. K. Story, *The Nature of Truth in "The Gospel of Truth" and in the Writings of Justin Martyr,* NovTSup, XXV (1970). Bibliography: D. M. Scholer, *Nag Hammadi Bibliography 1948-1969,* Nag Hammadi Studies, I (1971), with supplements in *NovT* (1971 ff.).

G. MacRae

TWINS. 1. In the OT. The OT speaks of two sets of twins, both fraternal: Esau and Jacob, sons of Isaac and Rebekah; Zerah and Perez, sons of Tamar and Judah. Ward has identified the following patterns that occur frequently in ancient stories about twins. (*a*) Dual paternity. That multiple conceptions are the cause of multiple births is a widely held belief. The elder child is usually thought to be fathered by a deity (cf. Herakles and Iphikles, sons of Zeus and Amphitryon). Such a notion is unlikely in the OT. (*b*) Temperamental differences between twins. "Jacob was a quiet man, dwelling in tents," while "Esau was a skilful hunter, a man of the field" (Gen. 25:27). Typically, this contrast is apparent even before birth. The struggles of the twins in the womb (Gen 25:20-26; 38:27-30) are meant to portend future hostilities between their descendants. (*c*) Treatment of the mother of the twins. The exceptional nature of the birth often promotes hostility toward the mother, due to fear or jealousy. This motif might explain Judah's decision to neglect Tamar (Gen 38:26). (*d*) Twins as symbols of fertility. Produced by a fertile mother, twins display an unusual ability to promote abundance. Jacob not only fathers a large family but, by means of magical tricks, enormously increases his and Laban's flocks (Gen 30:25-43). (*e*) Names of twins. A number of patterns are commonly followed in naming twins. However, none of Ward's typology obtains in the OT. (*f*) Friendship and hostilities of twins. In this motif, twins are shown to display great affection or great hostility toward each other. Initially at each other's throats, Jacob and Esau reunite in an admirable display of brotherly love (Gen 33:1-17). (*g*) Divine status of human twins. A thin line separates the divine from the human. Jacob communes with the deity and, exceptionally, even wrestles with him (Gen 32:22-32).

2. Rabbinic and postrabbinic tradition. Eve's enigmatic statement upon the birth of Cain (Gen. 4:1) was interpreted to mean: "I have gotten a man through an angel of the Lord." Hence Cain, sometimes considered a twin of Abel, was sired by the semidivine serpent Sama'el. Except for Joseph, every one of Jacob's children was said to be a twin. Rabbis supposed Leah and Rachel to be twins, destined to marry Esau and Jacob. Zebulun, in association with Issachar, was identified with the zodiac's Gemini.

3. In the ancient Near East. A number of deities were considered to be twins: Lugalgirra and Meslamta'èa, both of whom were underworld gods; Sîn (Moon) and Nergal (Mars). Other traditions thought Shamash (Sun) to be Sîn's twin. Ugaritic texts speak of El's twin sons, Shahar (Dawn) and Shalem (Dusk). These two manifestations are also known from Palmyra as Arṣu and 'Azizu and from Edessa as Monimus and 'Azizus. The last, as Bailey shows, were replaced in the Christian era by the supposed twins, Jesus and Thomas (the "Twin"). On the human level, omen series list the good and bad effects that the birth of twins will have on Mesopotamian society. Among the Sumerians the following was said: "May you become a household built up by twin sons."

Bibliography. L. Ginsberg, *The Legends of the Jews,* VII (1910-38), 484 (sub "twins"); E. I. Gordon, *Sumerian Proverbs* (1959), p. 282; D. Ward, *The Divine Twins* (1968; contains bibliog.); L. Bailey, "The Cult of the Twins at Edessa," *JAOS,* LXXXVIII (1968), 342-44; E. Leichty, *The Omen Series Summa Izbu* (1970), pp. 47-48.

J. M. Sasson

TYPOLOGY. That form of biblical interpretation which deals with the correspondences between traditions concerning divinely appointed persons, events, and institutions, within the framework of the salvation history.

Renewed interest in typology among biblical interpreters has resulted from a new appreciation of the unity of the Bible and from the work of Tradition Criticism. The latter has shown that there are in fact traditions concerning the acts of God which are analogous to that which had gone before in the biblical history, or which foreshadow that which comes after. The exodus tradition, for example, forms the type for Second Isaiah's understanding of Israel's final redemption (51:10-11; 52:7-12), and the wilderness time serves as a type for Hosea's understanding of God's final relationship with his people (2:14-15). Similarly, the career of Moses foreshadows that of Christ, in Matthew's understanding (cf. the threat to male children, Matt. 2:16-18; the commandments given on the mount, Matt. 5-7), and Paul understood

Christ's crucifixion as analogous to the Passover sacrifice (I Cor. 5:7).

Typology can refer either to the re-employment of traditions or to the fulfillment of prophecy. Where an older tradition is used to express a new act of God, the older is the type that foreshadows the new, the antitype (e.g., the figure of MELCHIZEDEK, Ps. 110, foreshadows that of Christ, in Heb.); where a new situation is analogous to that which has gone before, it is the antitype and fulfillment of the previous situation (e.g., the new covenant in Christ is the antitype of Jer. 31:31-34 and its fulfillment). Where prophecy is fulfilled, the original prophecy is the typological foreshadowing of the fulfillment (e.g., David is the foreshadow of Christ, in whom the promise to David is fulfilled).

Most modern understandings of typological interpretation emphasize the historical nature of types. The biblical traditions are set firmly in the history of Israel and of the church, and only when there are actual correspondences between traditions within that history can typological interpretation legitimately be employed. Types are no longer understood as symbols or pictures of general religious truths, as they were in the seventeenth century, or as allegories, as they were in pre-Reformation times. (*See* INTERPRETATION, HISTORY OF[S].) Consequently, the modern use of the word "typology" is sometimes misleading, conjuring up earlier fanciful interpretations, and it would perhaps be better for scholars to speak of correspondences, analogies, foreshadowing, and fulfillment.

It is also doubtful that individual texts should be interpreted typologically, unless they belong to a larger complex of traditions that have typological significance. For example, some scholars consider Isaac, carrying the wood for his own sacrifice (Gen. 22:6), as a type of Christ, bearing his cross, but such isolation of individual texts borders on allegory, and is, at best, questionable.

Because the NT interprets Jesus Christ as the fulfillment of the major OT traditions (cf. Luke 24:44-45; John 1:45; II Cor. 1:20, etc.), many analogies can be drawn between the testaments. For example, the Deuteronomic stress on the land as Israel's place of rest is applied to Christ, and the promise of the land becomes a foreshadow of the final rest promised to the Christian in Christ (Heb. 3:7–4:13). The ideal Davidic king in the royal psalms (esp. 2 and 110) foreshadows Jesus the Messiah, just as the suffering of Christ on the cross (Mark 15:24, 29, 23; Luke 23:46, 49; John 19:24, 28-30) is analogous to the pious sufferer in the laments in the Psalter (Pss. 22, 69, 38, 31). Deuteronomy's pictures of Moses as a suffering, prophetic mediator (18:15; 9:9, 18-20; 1:37; 3:23-27; 4:21-22) foreshadow Jesus, the Mosaic prophet of Acts 3 and 4. Indeed, there is a sense in which the entire NT story is analogous to the OT history.

The historical analogy between Israel and the church is clear: for example, both are redeemed out of slavery and made sons of God, with no deserving on their part; both are brought to the table of the Lord and enter into covenant with him; both are given a new life of freedom and set on a pilgrimage toward the promised land, their place of rest; both are accompanied on their journey by God. The Christian can therefore read the OT as his own story, as that which foreshadows God's act in Jesus Christ.

Type and antitype are seldom identical in the Bible. For example, a new temple, a new land, a new people, a new covenant, a new David, a new exodus, and a new wilderness wandering, are all promised by the prophets in the OT. But all are embodied in the person of Jesus Christ, and that which was foreshadowed takes on unexpected dimensions in its fulfilled reality.

Typological relationships exist in the Bible, not because God acts the same way in every age, and not because the salvation history is cyclical, but because God is faithful to his word. The biblical tradition-history of salvation is characterized by a series of new words spoken by God to his people and manifested in new acts toward them. Yet the old words are never lost. For example, God promises Israel, "I will be with you" (Exod. 3:12), or, in the covenant formula, "I will take you for my people, and I will be your God" (Exod. 6:7). When Israel breaks the covenant, a new word comes, "You are not my people and I am not your God" (Hos. 1:9). Yet the word of God stands forever (Isa. 40:8), and beyond the judgment, God's former word of promise is gathered up and renewed: "My dwelling place shall be with them" (Ezek. 37:27). This new word finds no fulfillment in the OT, but it is brought to reality in the New (Luke 1:68), and Jesus completes and extends the promise given to Israel from the first: "Lo, I am with you always, to the close of the age" (Matt. 28:20). The first promise of God's presence with Israel foreshadows the final promise of Jesus' presence with his disciples, because in the salvation history, God has kept his word (Isa. 55: 11; Ezek. 12:28).

It is the witness of the NT, then, that the final interpretation of God's words spoken to Israel is given in Jesus Christ, who is the summation and completion of Israel's history with God.

In addition, Christ also spoke new words, and the church, like Israel, lives between promise and the fulfillment of these new words. In the present, "we see in a mirror dimly" (I Cor. 13:12), and have only the first fruits. The Lord's Supper foreshadows the final messianic banquet; Jesus' works foreshadow the final healing in the Kingdom of God; the love in the church foreshadows the final fellowship of the saints; and the decision about Jesus foreshadows the final judgment. In this way, the NT too can be interpreted in typological fashion, as the first fruits of that which will come. Yet, that which will come will be analogous to that which the church now knows, because God is faithful to his word and will bring it to completion. Typological interpretation of the Scriptures rests on the faithfulness of God, and consequently may often be legitimately employed.

Bibliography. G. von Rad, *Old Testament Theology* II (1965); C. Westermann, *Essays on Old Testament Hermeneutics* (1963); G. W. H. Lampe and K. J. Woolcombe, *Essays on Typology,* SBT (1957); E. Achtemeier, *The Old Testament and the Proclamation of the Gospel* (1973).

E. ACHTEMEIER

U

*UGARIT.

1. Excavations
2. New alphabetic texts
3. New syllabic texts
4. Religion
5. Relationship to the OT

Bibliography

1. Excavations. The excavations have continued until 1973 (thirty-fourth campaign). Unfortunately the port Minet el-Beida, which in Ugaritic times was called Ma'ḫadu, is now being transformed into a naval base of the Syrian government, so that the future of the excavations both there and on Tell Ras Shamra itself is uncertain.

Thus far only preliminary reports about the excavations have been published. Therefore it is still difficult to get a comprehensive view of the excavated areas and to establish the exact localizations of the finds. In 1973 Robert North made a praiseworthy attempt at reconstructing a horizontal and vertical grid. Soon afterward this was supplemented and, in some respects, corrected by Jacques-Claude Courtois, one of the excavators (*see* Fig. U1).

At first Schaeffer established only five different levels of occupation, but he modified this in later studies. Today it seems probable that at least fifteen strata must be distinguished, ranging from Roman times to the Pre-Pottery Neolithic period (*ca.* 6500 B.C.).

The upper strata have not been sufficiently studied to date. It seems certain, however, that the tell was not occupied during the early Iron Age. New finds confirm that the later half of the second millennium B.C. was the time of Ugarit's greatest prosperity. Best known are the three Late Bronze strata, to be dated *ca.* 1550-1450, 1450-1365, 1365-1180 B.C. respectively. The last of these yielded a large number of written documents as well as some splendid objects of art. The LB ended with the invasion of the so-called Sea People about 1180 B.C. (*see* PHILISTINES; PHILISTINES[S]). By that time recurrent epidemics, followed by a period of excessive drought, had disrupted the affluent urban civilizations of the Near East.

The excavators claim an occupation lacuna from 1650-1600 (or 1550) B.C., but the archaeological evidence for this is not very convincing. Although it is certainly possible that there was a period of decline about the middle of the second millennium, several arguments may be adduced in favor of an essential continuity of the Ugaritic culture during the Middle and the Late Bronze Ages.

The kingdom was founded at the beginning of the MB I (*ca.* 2100-1900 B.C.), probably by an Amorite tribe which erected the temple of El (Schaeffer's appellation, "Temple of Dagan," is probably a misnomer).

The date of the beginning of the Early Bronze Age at the site is still a matter of dispute (*ca.* 3300 B.C. ?), as is the exact number of strata during this period. The Early Bronze ended *ca.* 2100 in a disastrous conflagration, the cause of which is unknown.

The Chalcolithic period, beginning *ca.* 5000 B.C., may be roughly divided in two strata. In Neolithic times (*ca.* 6500-5000 B.C.) there was a dense population at the tell which built solid brick houses on stone foundations. Toward the end of this period a brittle type of pottery was introduced.

2. New alphabetic texts. Most tablets from the four palace archives have now been published. Important new religious texts were discovered in private houses in the so-called Aegean quarter E of the royal palace (map, B) and in the city S of the acropolis (map, D-E). They greatly advance our understanding of the Ugaritic language. The smaller the number of available texts, the less one is able to base interpretation on a careful comparison of the contexts in which a term occurs. Thus the translator is often compelled to guess at meanings on the basis of etymological parallels in other Semitic languages. It has become clear that this is a dubious method which produces very uneven results. Therefore it is appropriate to note that studies on Ugaritic subjects tend to fall out of date rather rapidly and should be consulted with caution.

The definitive edition of all the tablets excavated between 1929 and 1939 was published by Andrée Herdner in 1963. The edition brings many new readings as compared to its precursors. Also it contains a number of hitherto unpublished texts.

In 1960 a small tablet was published which received much attention because there seemed to be unmistakable parallels between it and the cult of Dionysus, a cult in which classicists had long suspected the existence of Oriental elements. This tablet might become one of the most convincing proofs for their theory. The line stating that Anath ate the flesh of her lover Baal ("She ate his flesh without a knife; she drank his blood without a cup") strongly recalls the omophagia of the Bacchantes.

As many as 172 new texts from the royal palace appeared in 1965. Next to administrative lists and rosters, there were a number of Ugaritic letters, often translations from Babylonian originals. A very fortunate find was an oven containing about thirty intact tablets which had been put into it for baking. Such a collection of demonstrably contemporary tablets is unique.

Among the alphabetic texts published in *Ugaritica,* V, was an Ugaritic myth relating how El, the head of the pantheon, once gave a banquet for the younger gods. Toward the end of the feast El got so drunk that he fell in his own feces and had to be carried off. This unedifying scene might indicate that the story dates from comparatively recent times, when the position of El as the supreme god had already been undermined by the popularity of Baal.

Another tablet contains an Ugaritic psalm which was perhaps sung during the New Year festival. On the reverse the king implores the blessing of Baal (who is called "Savior" here) for the year to come: "May your protection, your guard, your strength, your patronage, your blessing be in the midst of Ugarit during all the days of sun and moon and the happiest of El's years!" The expression "the days of sun and moon" reminds us of Pss. 72:5, 7 and 89:36-37 [H 37-38], whereas the "years of El" may be compared with Ps. 102:24, 27 [H 25, 28]; Job 36:26.

In addition to offering texts and fragments of the already well-known myth of Baal, *Ugaritica,* V,

1. Excavation at Ugarit

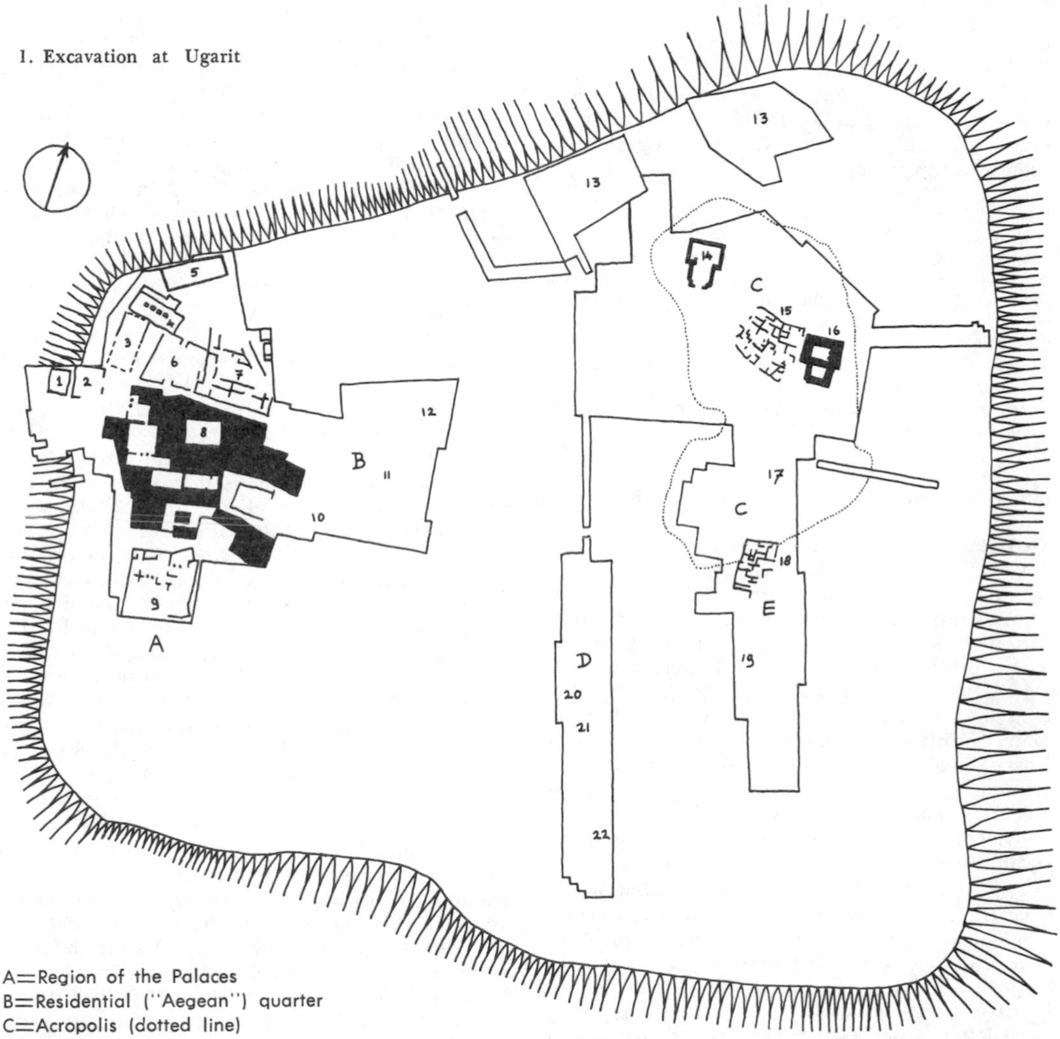

A=Region of the Palaces
B=Residential ("Aegean") quarter
C=Acropolis (dotted line)
D=Southern City
E=Southern slope of Acropolis
1=Tower
2=Fortress
3=Shrine
4=Tetrastyle building
5=Queen Mother's residence
6=Army quarters
7=Northern Palace
8=Royal Palace (in black except for courtyards)
9=Southern Palace
10=Alabaster house
11=Houses of Rašap'abu and the Scholar (private libraries)
12=House of Rap'anu (private library)
13=Lower "Hyksos" Town
14=Temple of Baal
15=Residence of high priest and scriptorium
16=Temple of El (formerly called Temple of Dagan)
17=Patiluwa house
18=Omen house
19=Hoard of gold and electrum bowls
20=Public square
21=House with private library
22=Statuettes of El, Asherah & Baal

contains two Ugaritic incantations against snakebite, a number of Hurrian rituals in alphabetic script, and photographs of a treatise on horse diseases.

In *Ugaritica,* VI, some inscribed clay models of sheep's livers and lungs were published. One of the longer inscriptions, apparently an omen against the plague, runs as follows: "If the town is affected, if Death overpowers a man, the family of that man shall take a goat to read the future."

A small collection of six tablets was procured and published by Loren Fisher. The most interesting of these deals with the cultic society called *mrzḥ,* which continued to play an important role in Canaanite religion until the beginning of the Christian era.

Finally mention should be made of a prayer which was published by Herdner in 1972. It expresses the faith that Baal will rescue Ugarit if an enemy attacks the city:

> If a strong one attacks your gate, a warrior your walls, raise your eyes to Baal [praying]: "O Baal, please drive away the strong one from our gate, the warrior from our walls! The bulls for Baal we will consecrate; the vows for Baal we will fulfill; the firstborn for Baal we will consecrate; the *ḥitpu*-rite for Baal we will fulfill; the tithe for Baal we will pay; to the sanctuary of Baal we will go up, upon the path to the house of Baal we will walk!" Then Baal will hear your prayer. He will drive away the strong one from your gate, the warrior from your walls.

3. New syllabic texts. Since 1962 many new tablets written in Babylonian cuneiform have been published. They confirm that the Ugaritic court used Babylonian, the lingua franca of those days, not only for diplomatic correspondence, but also for purely internal affairs such as contracts and administrative lists. Apparently several Ugaritians had received a thorough education in Babylonia. Their private libraries contained literary texts in Sumerian and Babylonian, among them wisdom texts and a fragment of the story of the deluge. Many multilingual vocabularies were executed in Ugarit. Some of these were furnished with an extra column giving the Ugaritic equivalents of the Sumerian and Akkadian words in syllabic signs. This offers a unique possibility for determining the vocalization of certain Ugaritic words.

The impact of Mesopotamian civilization on Ugaritic culture should not be underestimated. Not only do the Sumerian and Babylonian tablets bear testimony to that influence, but also a number of loanwords and borrowed expressions in the Ugaritic language itself. This is not surprising, since letters from Mari prove that as early as the eighteenth century B.C. Ugarit conducted a lively trade with Mesopotamia.

4. Religion. New lists of deities enable us to gain a clearer insight into the structure of the Semitic pantheon of Ugarit. More than 250 divine names are attested, but the nucleus of the pantheon was formed by only 28 gods of varying importance. The Ugaritic pantheon may be subdivided into an originally Amorite group of older deities around El, and a younger group supporting Baal. The latter's adoption in the Ugaritic pantheon was rationalized by the assumption of a marriage with El's daughter Anath. Baal had doubtlessly become the national god of Ugarit toward the end of the Late Bronze Age.

Some very fine bronze statuettes, as well as a decorated drinking mug, published by Schaeffer in 1966, give us a better idea of how the Ugaritians visualized their more important gods. Two of the statuettes depict El and Asherah as aged, stately deities. Both are enveloped in long robes and raise their hands in a gesture of blessing. In his other hand El holds a cup of wine (cf. *CTA* 15:II:16-18). Both El and Baal wear horns on their head (*see* HORNS OF MOSES[S]). It is possible that one of the statuettes represents El in the form of a bull. Baal is usually depicted as a vigorous young man, swaying a mace (thunder) and a lance (lightning bolt). He is clad in only a loincloth.

The interpretation of the great myth of Baal continues to be a matter of dispute. According to a recent theory, the tablets, if read in the sequence *CTA* 3-1-2-4-5-6, would describe in chronological order the mythological prototypes of the climatologic, agricultural, and cultic events of a normal year at Ugarit. Thus the narrative would be a combination of a nature myth and a cult myth, which should indeed be related to the seasons. It would have played an important role during the Ugaritic New Year festival which was celebrated in autumn (*see* NEW YEAR; NEW YEAR[S] §1*d*). Several aspects of this theory, however, remain hypothetical.

5. Relationship to the OT. The discoveries of Ras Shamra have taught us that Israelite religion and culture did not develop in the splendid isolation which was the ideal of the Deuteronomist and later generations of Bible writers. It is certain that to some extent the Hebrew concept of God was influenced by Canaanite conceptions about EL and BAAL. Yahweh assumed all the roles which were allotted to different deities in Canaanite religion. It is also true that several cultic institutions were taken over by the Israelites, including perhaps the autumnal New Year festival, which later on became the Feast of Booths. However, in almost every case it is possible to demonstrate that the content of these Canaanite terms and ideas underwent a fundamental change in Israelite thought.

The comparison of Hebrew and Ugaritic literature has led to a better understanding of many OT passages. Words which were corrupted or misunderstood in the course of the long scribal tradition of the MT were recovered with the help of Ugaritic. Grammatical rules which are operative in Ugaritic appear to have also existed in Hebrew. This has resulted in new translations for many difficult verses. The structure of Hebrew poetry closely resembles that of the Ugaritic epics. It has been noted that the poets often use the same poetic devices. *See* POETRY, HEBREW[S].

Nevertheless, great caution should be observed in using Ugaritic for the elucidation of the text of the Hebrew Bible. Unfortunately the number of superficial comparative studies in this field is far too great, and there is a deplorable tendency to overestimate the indebtedness of the Israelites to the Canaanites.

Bibliography. General works of major importance: M. Dietrich, O. Loretz, P.-R. Berger, J. Sanmartín, *Ugarit-Bibliographie 1928-1966,* thus far 4 vols. (1973); J. P. Lettinga, "Ugaritic," *A Basic Bibliography for the Study of the Semitic Languages,* ed. J. H. Hospers, I (1973), 127-45; M. Dietrich, O. Loretz, *Konkordanz der ugaritischen Textzählungen* (1972); M. Liverani, *Storia di Ugarit* (1962); H. Klengel, *Geschichte Syriens,* II (1969), 326-421; *Ugaritica,* IV (1962), and VI (1969).

A specialized new annual is *Ugarit-Forschungen,* I (1969).

On the excavations: R. North, "Ugarit Grid, Strata, and Find-Localizations," *ZDPV,* LXXXIX (1973), 113-60; J.-C. Courtois, "Ugarit Grid, Strata, and Find-Localizations—A Re-assessment," *ZDPV,* XC (1974), 97-114.

New alphabetic texts: A. Herdner, *Corpus des tablettes en cunéiformes alphabétiques découvertes à Ras Shamra-Ugarit de 1929 à 1939,* 2 vols. (1963); C. Virolleaud, "Un nouvel épisode du mythe ugaritique de Baal," CRAI (1960), 180-86, *PRU,* V (1965), and in *Ugaritica,* V (1968), 545-606, *see also* the photographs, 625-27, Figs. 16-16*b*; M. Dietrich, O. Loretz, in *Ugaritica,* VI (1969), 165-79; L. R. Fisher, ed., *The Claremont Ras Shamra Tablets* (1972); A. Herdner, "Une prière à Baal des Ugaritiens en danger," CRAI (1972), 693-97 with 698-703.

Some new works on Ugaritic philology: *See above,* Lettinga, "Ugaritic" bibliog. Further: R. E. Whitaker, *A Concordance of the Ugaritic Literature* (1972). An index of the Ugaritic passages treated by Gordon in his *Ugaritic Textbook* was prepared by B. J. Beitzel, *AOAT,* XXII (1973), 235-68. For a general survey *see* J. C. de Moor, "Ugaritic Lexicography," *Studies on Semitic Lexicography,* ed. P. Fronzaroli (1973), pp. 61-102. An important volume of new translations and comments is: A. Caquot, M. Sznycer, A. Herdner, *Textes ougaritiques,* I (1974).

Syllabic texts: In addition to earlier publications by Thureau-Dangin in *Syria,* the most important editions are: J. Nougayrol, *PRU,* III (1955), IV (1956), VI (1970), and in *Ugaritica,* V (1968), 1-446.

Religion: C. F. A. Schaeffer, "Nouveaux témoinages du culte de El et de Baal à Ras Shamra," *Syria,* XLIII (1966), 1-19; A. S. Kapelrud, *The Violent Goddess* (1969); U. Oldenburg, *The Conflict between El and Ba'al in Canaanite Religion* (1969); H. Gese, "Die Religionen Altsyriens," *Die Religionen der Menschheit,* X, 2 (1970), 1-232; J. C. de Moor, "The Semitic Pantheon of Ugarit," *UF,* II (1970), 187-228; U. Cassuto, *The Goddess Anath* (1971); J. C. de Moor, *The Seasonal Pattern in the Ugaritic Myth of Ba'lu* (1971), *New Year with Canaanites and Israelites,* 2 parts (1972); P. J. van Zijl, *Baal* (1972).

Ugarit and the OT: O. Kaiser, *Die mythische Bedeutung des Meeres in Ägypten, Ugarit und Israel* (2nd ed., 1962); J. Gray, *The Legacy of Canaan* (2nd ed., 1965); A. S. Kapelrud, *The Ras Shamra Discoveries and the OT* (1965); W. H. Schmidt, *Königtum Gottes in Ugarit und Israel* (2nd ed., 1966); W. F. Albright, *Yahweh and the Gods of Canaan* (1968); L. R. Fisher, ed., *Ras Shamra Parallels,* I (1972); F. M. Cross, *Canaanite Myth and Hebrew Epic* (1973); J. C. de Moor, P. van der Lugt, "The Spectre of Pan-Ugaritism," *BO,* XXXI (1974), 3-26; S. E. Loewenstamm, "Ugarit and the Bible," *Bibl.,* LVI (1975), 103-19.

For a bibliog. of the writings of M. J. Dahood up to 1966, *see* E. R. Martinez, *Hebrew-Ugaritic Index to the Writings of Mitchell J. Dahood* (1967). Many monographs and articles by Dahood and his pupils have appeared in *Bibl., CBQ, Scripta Pontificii Instituti Biblici* and *BibOR.*

J. C. DE MOOR

V

VALENTINUS. *See* GNOSTICISM §2*c*; GNOSTICISM[S] §4*b*.

***VENGEANCE.** Recent linguistic studies require a radical reassessment of the previous translations of the Hebrew root נקם as "vengeance," "revenge," etc., and of the concepts supporting such translations (Mendenhall). Comparison of biblical and prebiblical sources shows that the root is used in nearly identical constructions in both, with meanings quite contrary to and incompatible with the idea of vengeance or revenge, or with the ancient notion of blood feud with which it was formerly assumed that נקם was associated.

In the Amarna Letters *nqm* is characteristically used in appeals to the legitimate sovereign for "deliverance" or "rescue" from jeopardy at the hands of either rebels or foreign invaders. In any case, what is hoped for is an executive act on the part of the sovereign whereby the sovereignty is secured or vindicated, and faithful subjects are protected or rescued. In cases where the transaction is viewed from the perspective of the interaction between the sovereign and the enemy, a translation such as "defeat" or "punish" may be called for. That is to say, "rescue" of the faithful servant may require "defeat" or "punishment" of the offending party or parties.

Early biblical usage is almost identical, and numerous examples could be cited. For instance, Judg. 11:36 and II Sam. 22:48 are about Yahweh's "deliverance" of his faithful from their enemies and his. Ps. 18:47 certainly refers to Yahweh's "deliverance" and not to "vengeance." Josh. 10:13 is a case of both defensive and punitive vindication, for which Mendenhall suggests, "until he defeated the forces of his enemies," as the proper translation.

Mendenhall argues that all the evidence points to the conclusion that blood vengeance and any similar forms of self-help to obtain redress have been ruled out as socially unacceptable long before the Hebrew settlement in Palestine. Both in Israel and in neighboring societies, power to act for redress or deliverance has been turned over exclusively to the highest authority, and in Israel that is Yahweh alone. Thus in cases of damage or jeopardy for which normal judicial processes do not exist, one's sole source of appeal is to the sovereign. The action requested or hoped for is not revenge or vengeance but deliverance or redress. Moreover, to act on one's own behalf would be a direct challenge to the sovereign's authority.

There are instances, of course, in which men do just that, but such acts are clearly unacceptable. Thus David cannot accept such an act done on his behalf (II Sam. 4:1-12). In this case the RSV may be correct when it has David's would-be benefactors saying of their murderous deed, "The Lord has avenged my lord the king" (vs. 8), for these are clearly the words and view of "wicked men" and not of David or of the author of II Samuel. The confrontation between David and Saul recorded in I Sam. 24:8-15 (cf. 26:10-25) is particularly instructive. David refuses to slay Saul and says, "May the Lord deliver me from you; but my hand shall not be upon you" (24:12; RSV "May the Lord avenge me upon you"). For David and/or for the author of I Samuel, vindication—defensive or punitive—belongs to Yahweh alone (Deut. 32:35; cf. Rom. 12:19). This is clearly reinforced in the story of David, Nabal, and Abigail, although the root נקם does not occur there (I Sam. 25, esp. vs. 33). Provision for the delegation of Yahweh's power in specified situations is illustrated in the ancient law code in Exodus, where a mechanism is provided for "punishing" a slave owner who has beaten his slave to death (Exod. 21:20). This is clearly a case of punitive vindication and redress, but not of vengeance.

Of all known occurrences of the root נקם (both biblical and extrabiblical), in only two places (according to Mendenhall) can it refer to sanctioned vengeance. One of these is a Mari letter with insufficient context for precise determination (Jean). The other is Gen. 4:24. In the Genesis narrative, however, the setting is prior to the Flood, a time for which the biblical writers might have felt that the blood feud was still socially acceptable as a form of redress.

In the time of Jeremiah and Second Isaiah the word נקם was fairly frequently used, but in the period from David to Jeremiah it occurs only three times: II Kings 9:7; Isa. 1:24; and Mic. 5:15 [H 14]. It is used in Jeremiah in two distinct types of situations, those having to do with internal strife and those involving Yahweh's punitive action against external foes. Examples of the former would be Jer. 20:10-12; 11:20; and 15:15. Jer. 20:10-12 is of particular interest, for it manifests the same sort of contrast found in II Sam. 4:1-12. Jeremiah's enemies plotting an action of self-help say, "Perhaps he will be deceived, then we can overcome him, and take our revenge (*nqm*) on him" (vs. 10). Jeremiah's response is an appeal to Yahweh for deliverance: "Let me see thy deliverance (*nqm*) from them, for to you I have entrusted my case" (vs. 12, Mendenhall's translation). In this particular case the word "vengeance" in Jeremiah's mouth would be particularly inappropriate, for the threat or jeopardy is still future. Also included under the first sort of situation would be cases of punitive vindication such as 9:9 and 5:9, in which Yahweh must act against the unfaithful people of the nation. Instances of the second sort, punitive vindication against foreign enemies, are 46:10; 50:15; 51:36. Similar instances are found in Ezek. 24:2-14 and 25:15-17.

It is perhaps in Second Isaiah that the root is used in ways which most completely contrast with the notion of vengeance. The "day of vengeance" of Isa. 61:1-4 is rather a day of relief and salvation having nothing to do with punitive action of any sort. Mendenhall suggests that even in the oracles against Edom and Babylon (Isa. 34:8; 63:4; and 47:3), while there is the aspect of punitive action or punishment, the action is not so much hostility against enemies for Israel's sake, but action aimed at giving redress, relief, and comfort to those who have suffered so long. Isa. 35:4 clearly has nothing to do with vengeance but rather with deliverance.

The Greek word ἐκδικέω, the normal translation of the Hebrew נקם, occurs some fourteen times in the NT. A typical instance is Luke 18:1-8, where the RSV translation, "vindicate," seems adequate, though Mendenhall suggests "deliver." Rom. 12:19 is a reference to Deut. 32:35 and should not be rendered, "Vengeance is mine," but perhaps, "Vindication is mine," or, "Sovereignty is mine" (Gr. ἐκδίκησις).

Bibliography. G. E. Mendenhall, *The Tenth Generation, The Origins of the Biblical Tradition* (1973), ch. 3; C.-F. Jean, "Les noms propres de personnes" in *Studia Mariana,* ed. A. Parrot (1950), p. 87.

J. E. Lindsey, Jr.

*__VERSIONS, ENGLISH.__ The years between 1960 and 1975 were marked by the appearance of a large number of new English versions of the Bible, some of which had been in preparation for two decades or more. All the important ones were new translations, not revisions. This represents a distinctive break with the KJV-RSV tradition. One exception was the New American Standard Version, a revision of the ASV of 1901, sponsored by a private foundation.

Increasing interconfessional co-operation was a natural outgrowth of the common body of scholarship on which the translations drew, and of the abandonment of some time-honored shibboleths. Nevertheless, The Jerusalem Bible was a thoroughly Catholic project, the New Jewish Version thoroughly Jewish, and The New English Bible, The New International Bible, and Today's English Version thoroughly Protestant. Only The New American Bible had active collaboration of Catholic and Protestant scholars. JB and NEB are more British in style and vocabulary, and the others more American.

NEB published the OT Apocrypha as a separate volume, but included it in some editions of the entire Bible, as RSV had done earlier. In NAB and JB these books (known among Catholics as deuterocanonical) appear in their usual places among the books of the OT.

In addition to the bibliography at the end of this article, the reader should consult the prefaces to the various versions, which give valuable information on points which the translators considered significant for an understanding of their work.

1. The New English Bible
2. The New Jewish Version
3. The Jerusalem Bible
4. The New American Bible
5. Today's English Version
6. The New International Bible
7. The Living Bible
Bibliography

1. The New English Bible. The Church of Scotland, at its General Assembly in May, 1946, adopted a resolution "that a translation of the Bible be made in the language of the present day." This initiative found a ready response. Within a few months, delegates from several denominations had met and set in motion the process that culminated in the publication of the NEB in 1970. Other groups promptly joined, making the project fully representative of the non-Roman Catholic Christian bodies in the British Isles.

a. The purpose of the translation. This was to be not a revision but a completely new translation. The translators were therefore free to render the original into contemporary English without having to retain any of the language of the earlier versions. Further, they were free to abandon the grammatical constructions of the original languages and avoid Hebraisms (i.e., literal translations of Hebrew idioms) and other un-English expressions. The resultant translation was to be made even more acceptable by printing prose material in paragraph form and poetical passages in verse form, and by employing modern punctuation, including quotation marks.

Three classes of readers were in mind. The first was the large portion of the population with which the church had no communication, and which found traditional versions unintelligible. The second was the younger generation, and the third the "intelligent people who do attend church," but for whom the traditional language of the Bible had lost its impact through too great familiarity.

b. The organization of the work. The work was done by three translating panels, one each for NT, OT, and Apoc., and by a literary panel, which read all the material and made suggestions to the translating panels. C. H. Dodd served as convener of the NT panel and as general director of the project. T. H. Robinson was the first convener of the OT panel, and after his death in 1957, Sir Godfrey Driver held this post until completion of the translation, becoming in addition a joint director with Dodd. In 1968 W. D. McHardy, a member of the OT panel and convener of the Apoc. panel, became deputy director.

The joint committee, which held final responsibility for the work, was composed of representatives of the participating churches, roughly in proportion to their membership, representatives of the Bible Societies and of the University Presses of Oxford and Cambridge, and the conveners of the panels. Alwyn T. P. Williams was chairman of the joint committee and convener of the literary panel until his death in 1968.

Members of the panels were chosen for scholarly competence, not as representatives of denominations. An individual member of a translating panel would produce a draft of a biblical book and circulate it in typescript among the other members of the panel. Then the panel would meet and discuss the draft sentence by sentence. The amended draft was retyped and passed to the literary panel, which scrutinized it to determine if the tone and level of the language were appropriate to that particular type of biblical writing. Some material traveled back and forth between literary panel and translators before agreement was reached, but on points of interpretation the translating panel's decisions were final.

The NT was completed first and was published in 1961. The Apoc. did not receive high priority, and this panel was completely reorganized during the course of the work. But it was completed in time for publication together with the OT and a second edition of the NT in 1970.

c. Textual basis. Separate publications deal with the textual basis of the OT and NT translations (*see bibliog.*), but departures from the traditional text are noted in the footnotes in the "Library Editions" of NEB, and to a lesser extent in other editions. In most books of the Bible there were numerous emendations. Some were based on the ancient versions, especially the LXX, some on the DEAD SEA SCROLLS, and some on conjectures as to the "probable reading" of the original. In many instances verses were moved from their traditional place to their hypothetical location at a precanonical stage in the transmission of the text.

d. Interpretation. While footnotes call the reader's attention to textual changes, nothing prepares him for the reinterpretation of Hebrew words in terms of derivation from roots preserved in other Semitic languages. Yet this approach led to at least as many departures from traditionally accepted meanings of OT passages as did textual emendation. Some of these derivations are based on Ugaritic, but many more are traced to Arabic roots. A notable example is found in Judg. 1:14 (=Josh. 15:18). In this and other instances, the NEB translators assumed, contrary to the findings of modern linguistics, that cognate words retain identical semantic components in separate languages, when in fact they often are found in totally different semantic domains. *See* SEMANTICS [S].

Two other methods of interpreting the original involve the reassessment of syntax and the attempt to express more fully the original meaning of terminology. Both of these are illustrated in NEB in Gen. 1:1-4, where vs. 1 becomes a prepositional phrase, and רוח אלהים is translated as "a mighty wind." NJV is similar. An example of the second is seen in Rom. 1:17, where δικαιοσύνη θεοῦ is translated "God's way of righting wrong."

e. English usage. The language of NEB is at a high level of complexity in both syntax and vocabulary. See, e.g., Heb. 1:1-3. In some instances, too literal a reproduction of the Hebrew DISCOURSE STRUCTURE results in pronouns without clear antecedents, as in Judg. 3:21. There are numerous words that are more familiar in British English than American, and some archaisms, such as "hark." In all prayer, the archaic second person singular pronouns and the accompanying verb forms were retained. NEB is the only new translation to do this. Dialogue is often natural, but in Gen. 31:35 and elsewhere it is stilted.

In keeping with the original statement of principles, the OT translators reproduced Hebrew poetry as English verse, retaining in most instances the form of the Hebrew poetic line. A startling effect that is not explained in any editions of the NEB is achieved by printing lines of poetry that have four stressed syllables in Hebrew at the first level of indentation, and those with three and two stressed syllables at a second and third level of indentation. The results, e.g., Pss. 8, 19, 30, 37, look like no known form of English poetry.

Taken as a whole, the NEB reflects the main stream of British biblical scholarship in the quarter century after World War II.

2. The New Jewish Version. To replace its English translation of 1917, the Jewish Publication Society began work in 1955 on a totally new translation that would be intelligible in diction and would make full use of older commentaries, especially those of medieval Jewish scholars (*see* INTERPRETATION, HISTORY OF[S] §F). *The Torah* was published in 1962 and was subsequently revised. In 1969 *The Five Megilloth and Jonah* appeared, in 1973 *The Book of Isaiah* and *The Book of Psalms,* and in 1974 *The Book of Jeremiah.*

a. Organization of the work. Translation was begun by a committee of seven: three biblical scholars, one representative of each of the three sections of organized religious Jewish life in America—conservative, reform, and orthodox—and the editor of the Jewish Publication Society. In 1966 an additional committee, organized on the same lines, was set up to translate the *Kethubim,* the third division of the Hebrew canon. Harry M. Orlinsky serves as editor-in-chief.

In producing *The Torah,* the editor-in-chief prepared a draft translation, accompanied by pertinent supporting data: the renderings of older versions and modern translations, the comments of notable exegetes, and some justification for any important new renderings. This material was reproduced chapter by chapter and sent to each member of the committee. They sent in their comments, and on the average of once every two weeks the entire committee met for a full day. Most decisions were made by consensus, but if a vote was necessary, a majority of those voting decided the issue.

b. Textual basis. *The Torah* has the subtitle, "A New Translation of the Holy Scriptures According to the Masoretic Text." By their strict adherence to MT, the translators have demonstrated that in many places where other scholars have emended because they felt the meaning was not clear, MT yields excellent sense, and that no departure from it is justified. Frequent footnotes in NJV take note of the more significant emendations. The evidence of the major ancient versions is also cited in many passages. Difficulties are acknowledged by notes that say "Heb obscure," "Meaning of Heb uncertain," "Exact force of Heb uncertain," etc.

In a few passages, what other versions accomplish by emendation NJV accomplishes by assigning a new meaning to a Hebrew word. For an example, compare Ps. 19:4 [H 5] in the RSV and the NJV.

In most translations, large numbers of problems are solved by changing the Hebrew vowels, while leaving the consonantal text intact. NJV consigns such solutions to footnotes, e.g., Gen. 10:10; Jer. 7:3. In Isaiah, distinctive textual variations in the DEAD SEA SCROLLS are noted. Among modern scholarly translations in English, NJV is the most conservative in its handling of problems of text.

c. Interpretation. Footnotes are used not only to identify textual problems, but also to point out the source of the interpretation of specific passages (Ps. 30:8); to explain metaphors (Isa. 37:3) or customs (Isa. 44:5; 51:18); to indicate that a part of a verse has been transposed (Isa. 8:4, 10:16, 18). Notes also give the literal Hebrew expression in instances where a more accurate English term has been placed in the text, e.g., Ps. 7:10, where "conscience" is chosen over the literal "kidneys," and Gen. 14:22, "I swear," literally, "lift up my hand."

More basic to NJV is the procedure discussed in *Notes on the New Translation of the Torah.* Here Orlinsky illustrates the way the committee followed the principle of contextual consistency and translated in such a way as to bring out the meaning of the Hebrew. Depending on context, בית is rendered as "household" and "palace," as well as "house." In Isa. 7:13, however, NJV translated "House of David" even though "dynasty" might be more appropriate.

A basic but difficult word, צדק, is translated "grace" in Isa. 42:6 and "victory" in Isa. 45:8. In Isa. 45:8 ישע is rendered as "triumph" and in 42:1 משפט as "the true way."

d. English usage. Because the translators chose natural English equivalents for most words and idioms, NJV reads more smoothly than older translations. Modern forms of personal pronouns and verbs are used throughout, and the vocabulary is, in general, contemporary, although some archaisms remain. "Lest" occurs frequently, as do "lo," "hark," and "of yore."

While striving for clarity, the translators did not simplify unduly. NJV is on a high literary level, appropriate for the reading public for which it was designed.

3. The Jerusalem Bible. The great popularity of *La Bible de Jérusalem,* translated by French Dominican scholars (1954-55), prompted similar translations in other European languages, of which this is one. JB bears a complicated relationship to its French counterpart. The introductions and the notes were translated from French; the text of the Bible itself was translated under the direct influence of the French version. Most of the translation was made directly from the original languages. Some portions, however, were originally translated from the French, and the resulting translation was then compared with the Greek or Hebrew original. The English translators followed the textual basis which the French had established, and in most instances they also followed the interpretation found in the French version, although occasional deviation can be noted.

Critics have questioned whether this type of procedure entitles JB to be considered a fresh translation. If JB is judged by the results rather than the procedures that were followed, it is a distinctly new and readable version.

a. Textual basis. *La Bible de Jérusalem* was originally published in fully annotated fascicles, which document the care given to the problems of text. In JB, footnotes indicate the conjectural emendations that have been accepted and the evidence of the ancient versions, where they were followed. In the OT, JB departs frequently from MT and relies in many instances on LXX. The NT is more conservative, with, for example, Mark 16:9-20 and John 7:53–8:11 printed in the text. (It is significant that recent editions of RSV have followed this procedure, in contrast to the earlier RSV practice of printing these passages in footnotes.) JB does omit the "three heavenly witnesses" that crept into the Vulgate text of I John 5:7-8. Passages where the Vulg. differs significantly from the Greek are identified in the footnotes. Ecclesiasticus was translated from the Greek text, because "the Church recognizes the canonicity only of the Greek text"; Hebrew variants are consigned to footnotes.

b. Interpretation. The footnotes and the extended introductions to the separate books of the Bible inform the reader of the way the translators interpreted the message of the Bible. Their point of view represents sober, modern critical study. It also represents a distinctively Christian position, as shown in the notes to Gen. 3:15; Isa. 7:14; but by no means are all traditionally messianic passages taken to refer to Christ, e.g., Zech. 13:6. In Rom. 1:17 δικαιοσύνη is translated as "justice," following the Vulg. tradition (*iustitia*), but a note explains the word as "the saving justice of God, who fulfils his promise to save by giving salvation as a free gift." All in all, JB presents the biblical message in a way that makes it acceptable to a wide audience.

c. English usage. Proper names are spelled according to the RSV tradition and not in the traditional Catholic manner. The divine name is given as "Yahweh." The introduction to the Psalms recognizes that this sounds strange, especially in public worship, and suggests that the reader substitute "the Lord." JB maintains a high literary quality throughout, despite an occasional awkward expression. (Gen. 23:8; 37:22; Matt. 8:27; 9:6; 24:21 have been singled out as examples of unsatisfactory style.) OT passages that are Hebrew poetry are printed as verse in English, and some of them attain a high level of quality as free verse. The diction is contemporary and free of archaisms, and although JB is the work of British scholars it does not sound unduly British.

4. The New American Bible. This translation took shape during a period of more than three decades, during which time the Catholic Church was becoming increasingly concerned to make the Bible available in modern languages. Work began in 1936 on a new American translation from the Vulg. In 1943 the encyclical *Divino Afflante Spiritu* enabled the translators to go directly to the original languages, and the decisions of the Second

Vatican Council in the early 1960s made it possible to add Protestant scholars to the committee and make this a truly ecumenical work. The length of time involved, however, resulted in an unevenness of style and interpretation. Some books were revised thoroughly; others were not. Genesis, for example, appeared in trial versions in 1950 and 1952, and was completely redone for final publication of the entire Bible in 1970. It is one of the most successful parts of NAB.

a. The method of work. The portions of this version that were published early were known as the Confraternity of Christian Doctrine Version, after the name of the sponsoring body. Translation was done by members of the Catholic Biblical Association. Individual scholars prepared the draft of the book or books assigned to them, and some distinctive features of style or interpretation perhaps are due to this procedure, in spite of the final editing. The OT was prepared by an editorial board of which Louis F. Hartman, C.SS.R., was chairman. Myles M. Bourke was chairman of the NT committee, and Gerard Sloyan served as English editor.

b. The textual basis. The OT translators used their best critical judgment in evaluating the textual data, and in many instances preferred the evidence of the ancient versions, especially LXX, to MT. The Dead Sea Scrolls were used extensively, including some scroll material not yet published. Emendations were not identified in footnotes as in most other recent translations, but were collected in an appendix that is found in some, but not all, editions of NAB. The textual changes in Ezekiel alone fill some fifteen pages; those in Sirach (Ecclesiasticus) occupy twelve and a half pages, compared to ten pages on the entire Pentateuch. This indicated the importance of using the Hebrew text of Sirach as a basis for translation. The nature of the changes shows that great care was taken in every instance. The editors felt that there is sufficient agreement on NT text problems, so that no textual notes or appendices were needed.

c. Interpretation. In this area the unevenness of NAB is evident, particularly in the introductions; some are scholarly, but others, such as Joshua, are didactic. Distinctively Catholic views are expressed at Isa. 7:14, both in the note and in the text. A note at John 3:5 informs the reader of the interpretation of this verse accepted by the Council of Trent. NAB has been both criticized and praised for not adopting more hypothetical interpretations of Hebrew vocabulary on the basis of Ugaritic cognates. The translators were cautious in this area, generally preferring to accept the traditional meaning of words, especially in the Psalms.

d. English usage. The style is modern but formal, with an occasional archaism, although archaic pronouns and verb forms have been entirely eliminated. Some biblicisms survived. In Josh. 1:8 the people are told to "keep this book of the law on your lips," and in Judg. 4:21 Sisera "perished in death."

As for larger matters of style, it was a basic principle of the translation to employ the same level of usage found in the Hebrew or Greek of each part of the Bible, and not smooth out features that modern taste finds objectionable, such as Paul's "lapses into anacoluthon." Hebrew poetry was translated as poetry, and large sections of the gospel of John are printed as verse. Taking NAB as a whole, the translators were successful in finding appropriate English equivalents at a formal and solemn level.

5. Today's English Version. The American Bible Society commissioned TEV to be a completely modern translation on a level of language that could be readily understood by any reader of English, regardless of the reader's education. This was the first English translation to make consistent use of advances in general linguistics and in secular translation theory. In 1966 the NT was published in paperback as *Good News for Modern Man.* Portions of the OT appeared between 1970 and 1975, at which time the translation was completed for publication in 1976.

a. Organization of the work. The draft of the entire NT was prepared by Robert G. Bratcher, a professional translator and translations consultant, and was reviewed by a panel of scholars. A second edition appeared in 1968, a third in 1971, and a fourth in the publication of the entire Bible.

Serious work on the OT began in 1969. Bratcher served as chairman of a committee of six, all of whom had professional experience as translators. Each member prepared a draft of the books the committee had agreed that he was to do; the draft, with extensive notes explaining the translation, was circulated to the committee; and finally the committee would meet and go over the translation in detail. Meetings were for one or two weeks at a time, and in the summers of 1972-73, for up to twelve weeks. Translators were chosen not as representatives of any denominational position, but for assent to the principles of the project and professional experience. Where consensus could not be reached, a majority vote of those present decided the question.

The work of the committee, together with revised explanatory notes, was circulated to persons involved in translations into other languages around the world, in order to solicit their comments and to serve as a guide in their own translations. After a final revision, and review by a committee of the Bible Society board, each book was considered ready for publication. Beginning in 1971, the British and Foreign Bible Society was represented in the committee.

b. Textual basis. The NT was based on the Greek text published by the United Bible Societies. The OT committee gave precedence to the readings of MT, but relied on other Hebrew MS evidence where it seemed superior. All instances where there is no Hebrew evidence for a reading that was adopted were indicated in footnotes.

c. Interpretation. From the first, TEV was not intended to present innovative interpretations. Its distinctive feature was to be the phrasing of the generally accepted meaning in idiomatic English, avoiding traditional biblical language wherever possible. Rom. 1:17 illustrates this approach to Pauline language, and Luke 15:11-32 illustrates it in narrative material.

The OT committee tried to determine the meaning which the text had when it was accepted as scripture by the ancient Jewish community, and so avoid reading later interpretations into it. Obviously there is a large subjective element in any such decisions. In keeping with their orientation to linguistics and translation theory, the translators accepted comparatively few "new meanings" based on cognates in other Semitic languages and relied more on archaeological and anthropological data.

d. English usage. The basic principle underlying the choice of vocabulary, sentence structure, DISCOURSE STRUCTURE, and other features of English style was that the translators should find the "closest natural equivalent" in English. The form of the Greek and Hebrew was not to determine the form of the English. For example, participants in actions or dialogue were identified by either nouns or pronouns in accord with English usage, regardless of how they were identified in the original. Metaphors not readily intelligible to the reader might be turned into similes, replaced by other metaphors, or expressed in nonmetaphorical language.

The treatment of poetry depended on the nature of the material. Prophetic oracles whose content was appropriate to English prose were translated as prose, regardless of their form in Hebrew. If the content of a passage was suitable for poetic treatment in English, every effort was made to make the translation rhythmical and poetic. To this end, lines were restructured so that too much parallelism would not produce monotonous English.

Special care was taken to achieve poetic quality in Job and Song of Songs. In Proverbs, chs. 1–7 and 9 were translated into prose, and ch. 8 into verse. Most of the rest of the book appears as short prose maxims.

While there were no strict limits on vocabulary, the translators avoided words the average reader might find difficult, and sentences were structured for clarity and ease of comprehension. Simplicity and readability were considered more important than literary quality, so that the version could be understood by persons outside the church, as well as by those in the church who are not familiar with biblical language.

6. The New International Bible. Conservative Protestants, dissatisfied with existing modern language translations, worked through the New York Bible Society to produce a version whose purpose was "to do for our time what the King James Version did for its day." The translation was to be faithful to the original languages and avoid paraphrasing; to be acceptable to both British and American readers; and to be equally effective for public worship and for private study. A trial version of John appeared in 1970 as "A Contemporary Translation" (ACT), and the complete NT in 1973. Work on the OT is well under way.

a. Organization of the work. A committee on Bible translation, composed of fifteen scholars, organized the work of translation and gave its final approval. Actual translation was done in a more decentralized fashion than that of any other recent project, but supervision was tightly controlled. Twenty teams of five persons each were organized: two co-translators, two translation consultants, and one English stylist. Each team was assigned a specific section of scripture, and their work went to the intermediate editorial committee for OT or NT, respectively. After review at this level, the material went to a general editorial committee, and then to the committee of fifteen. According to the NT, thorough revision was done at each level. A comparison of the two published versions of John, however, indicates that only a few changes were made there, and these were in the direction of greater literalism.

b. Textual basis. The translators indicate in footnotes those instances where they did not follow the TEXTUS RECEPTUS (e.g., Matt. 6:13; Rom. 8:28), or where they were uncertain about the text (Matt. 16:2-3). Mark 16:9-20 and John 7:53–8:11 are set off in the text from the surrounding material, and a line of smaller type says that they are omitted by "the most reliable early MSS." Textual notes are not numerous, but these are typical.

c. Interpretation and English usage. The version is free from eccentricities of interpretation and style. In all instances "you" is used for both singular and plural, and there are few holdovers from the KJV-RSV tradition of language. The style is dignified and somewhat formal and reflects literary rather than spoken English.

7. The Living Bible. This is the most controversial English version of the 1970s and one of the most successful commercially. Essentially the work of one man, Kenneth Taylor, and advertised as a "paraphrase," LB was produced over a period of seventeen years and published a section at a time.

Unable to translate from the original languages, Taylor began to rewrite the NT epistles in modern language, using the ASV of 1901 as his source. As publication of various portions progressed, the ASV was abandoned, and the OT reflects in many passages the use of the LXX as the textual basis.

LB consistently interprets the message of the Bible in messianic terms, with notes which say that the meaning expressed in the text is "implied," or which give a "literal translation" that is often far removed from the text. At Zech. 13:6, however, LB rejects the messianic interpretation and in two footnotes relates the passage to false prophets. Another striking feature is the inclusion of ideas that are not found in that context at all, e.g., Gen. 1:4-5 and Rom. 1:17.

A major reason for the popularity of LB is its readable style, which is often colloquial and even racy (I Sam. 20:30). At other times the style is formal, and occasional archaisms such as "lest" are not hard to find. Even so, long sections of LB can be read privately with ease, and it maintains a high level of interest for the reader.

Bibliography. James Barr, *Comparative Philology and the Text of the OT* (1968); L. H. Brockington, *The Hebrew Text of the OT: the Readings Adopted by the Translators of the NEB* (1973); F. F. Bruce, *The English Bible* (1970); Geoffrey Hunt, *About the NEB* (1970); Alexander di Lella, "The Jerusalem Bible," *CBQ*, XXIX (1967), 148-51; E. A. Nida, *Toward a Science of Translating* (1964); H. M. Orlinsky, *Notes on the New Translation of the Torah* (1969); Gerald S.

Sloyan, *The New American Bible* (1970); R. V. G. Tasker, *The Greek NT: Being the Text Translated in the NEB, 1961* (1964). K. R. Crim

VERSIONS, LATIN. *See* Latin Versions.

*__VERSIONS, MODERN (NON-ENGLISH).__ According to the records of the United Bible Societies, by the end of 1974 the complete Bible had been translated into 257 languages. In addition, one of the Testaments (usually NT) had been translated into another 368 languages, and at least one complete book into an additional 924 languages, making a total of 1,549 different languages and dialects into which part or all of the Bible has been translated so far. It is estimated that this total encompasses well over ninety-seven per cent of the world's population. There still remain, however, over 1,000 mutually unintelligible languages and dialects into which no part of Scripture has ever been translated.

1. **First translations.** These are made for the two to three per cent of the world's population which as yet have no written Scriptures. In many instances these languages have not been reduced to writing, and so the translator must also be a trained linguist who is able to detect all the phonetic peculiarities of the language, in order to provide a faithful orthographic representation of the language. According to the United Bible Societies records, in the fifteen-year period 1960-74 at least one biblical book has been translated for the first time into some 361 languages.

2. **Revisions and new translations.** The most important work of translation is being carried out in the some three hundred projects, involving nearly eighty per cent of the world's population, in languages already reached. These projects may consist of (1) new translations, (2) revisions of existing translations, or (3) the completion of a Testament or the whole Bible where only partial translations exist.

The need for new translations is especially urgent in countries where existing translations were made as much as a hundred years ago by missionaries, whose work is no longer adequate. For example, in Gujarati, a language spoken by over twenty million people in the state of Gujarat, India, the NT was first translated in 1820 by the Serampore missionaries; other translations appeared in 1821, 1853, and 1856, some of which were subsequently revised—all work done by Western missionaries. Only in 1968 did a fresh translation of the NT appear, done by a native Gujarat, and work on the OT is in progress. Revisions also occur where a given version has had such a wide acceptance among Bible readers that they are reluctant to accept a new one. The Almeida Version in Portuguese (completed in the mid-nineteenth century by Dutch missionaries in Batavia, Java, and Danish missionaries in Tranquebar, India) was finally completely revised in Brazil by the Brazil Bible Society in 1958. In Spanish, the Reina-Valera version of 1602 was thoroughly revised in 1960.

It is increasingly recognized that no single translation can adequately meet the needs of a large Christian community, and so more and more there are a number of different translations into major languages. New translations currently under way increasingly follow the principles of a dynamic equivalence and not of a formal equivalence to the original text. This is motivated primarily by the basic principle that a good translation should not sound like one. As Ronald Knox said, "Any translation is a good one in proportion as you can forget, while reading it, that it is a translation at all." At the same time it is recognized that a translation which may be quite clear, because familiar, to assiduous Bible readers will be quite incomprehensible to others. More and more "common language" translations are being made, which utilize that range of vocabulary and style common to all who speak the language, regardless of social class or of formal degree of schooling. In 1966 a NT in Spanish, *Dios Llega al Hombre,* appeared (at the same time that *Good News for Modern Man* was published in English). Shortly thereafter similar translations appeared in French, German, and Brazilian Portuguese. Work is going on in Thai, Finnish, European Portuguese, Korean, Japanese, Chinese, Swahili, and other languages. By the end of 1974 there were such translations of the NT in twenty-one languages.

3. **Joint translations.** One important aspect of modern translations of the Bible is the increasing degree of co-operation between Catholics and Protestants (and Greek Orthodox, where applicable) in joint translations of the Scriptures. In June 1968 a joint statement, "Guiding Principles for Interconfessional Cooperation in Translating the Bible," was drawn up by the United Bible Societies and the Vatican Secretariat for Promoting Christian Unity. The NT of the French *Traduction oecuménique de la Bible* was published in 1972, and the work is nearly complete on the OT. The joint committee of French-speaking Catholic and Protestant scholars began with Paul's letter to the Romans, on the excellent assumption that if they could succeed in a joint translation of that epistle they could do the rest of the NT. The translation of Romans was officially presented to the French-reading public at the Grand Amphitheatre of the Sorbonne on January 16, 1967, with the following declaration: "The text that divided us should be the text that draws us together." In such cases of joint work two editions or the Bible are published, one with and one without the deuterocanonical (apocryphal) books of the OT. There were some 135 joint projects under way at the end of 1974. A remarkable example of this co-operation was the translation of the NT into the five major languages of the Philippines: Tagalog, Cebuano, Ilokano, Bicol, and Hiligaynon.

New translations and revisions go forward in the main languages of Europe. A complete revision of The Luther Bible was published in 1964, when the OT revision was finally completed (the NT was given official sanction in 1956). The Herder Bible, prepared by a committee of Roman Catholic scholars, appeared in 1965; in 1968 its text was revised with reference to *La Bible de Jérusalem,* and was published with the apparatus of that Bible. *La Bible de Jérusalem* itself, perhaps the most influential of contemporary major translations, came out in a completely new edition, revised and enlarged, in 1973. This sumptuous volume, complete with introductions, notes, references, tables, appendixes, indexes, and maps, is a model for a study Bible, and its influence may be gauged by the fact that it has been translated into English, Spanish, and German, and that translations in other languages are in progress.

Interconfessional translations are being made in Spain, Italy, and Portugal. In all the Socialist countries of Eastern Europe, except Albania, there are projects under way. These total twenty, of which sixteen are new translations. In Czechoslovakia a new interconfessional translation of the NT into Czech was published in 1974, and the OT is almost finished. In Slovak a new translation of the Bible by Lutheran scholars appeared in 1974. In Hungary a new translation has been made by Protestant scholars, and a revision of the Roman Catholic Bible has appeared. In Bulgaria Roman Catholic, Orthodox, and Protestant scholars have completed a NT, and the whole Bible is to be finished in two or three years. In Poland Protestants and Orthodox co-operated on the "Millennial" Bible, the NT of which was published in 1966 to commemorate the millennium of the Polish State; the Bible is now complete. In the U.S.S.R. no work is at present under way in Russian, but there is activity in other languages. In (Eastern) Armenian (spoken by some three million) a NT was published in 1974 by the Armenian Apostolic Church; a revision of a Roman Catholic translation of the NT and Psalms was published in Latvian, and also in Lithuanian; in Estonia a new Lutheran translation of the Bible is progressing, and an Orthodox new translation of the Bible in Ukrainian is under way. In Yugoslavia, joint committees are working in Croatian, Serbian, and Slovenian. In Romania the latest Bible revision was made by the Orthodox in 1968.

In Japan an entirely new translation of the Bible (the Kogotai Version) by Japanese scholars was published in 1955. The Studium Biblicum Franciscanum is engaged in translating the whole Bible, and the Japan Bible Society is sponsoring an interconfessional translation.

4. New readers selections. One further modern development of Bible translation is the preparation of Scripture selections for new readers, using a style and vocabulary suited to their needs. Adaptations of texts from common language translations are made at three different levels. By the end of 1976 it is planned to have such selections in two hundred languages.

Bibliography. E. A. Nida, *God's Word in Man's Language* (1952); E. A. Nida, ed., *The Book of a Thousand Tongues* (rev. ed., 1972); E. A. Nida and C. R. Taber, *The Theory and Practice of Translation* (1969); W. L. Wonderly, *Bible Translations for Popular Use* (1968); United Bible Societies, *Scriptures of the World* (1975).

R. G. BRATCHER

***VIRGIN.** Biblical Hebrew uses two expressions to indicate a female who has not had sexual intercourse: (1) "[a girl] who has not known a man" (or, "whom no man has known"), and (2) the word *b^e^thûlâ* (בתולה) as used in certain contexts. However, the concept of virginity is not as significant in ancient Israel (or in the ancient Near East generally, including Greece and Rome) as it became in the postbiblical period and in Christian thought in particular.

1. *b^e^thûlâ* (Akkad. *batultu;* Northwest Semitic *btlt*). This term is attested only in the feminine, and occurs thirty-three times in the singular and seventeen times in the plural.

a. "Maiden." It most often denotes a girl who is sexually mature, of marriageable age. The element of chastity may or may not be present (or stressed), depending upon the context. For example, in Lam. 5:11-14, it is used in context with other designations of sex, age, or status: "women . . . maidens; princes . . . elders; young men . . . boys; old men . . . young men." In such a description of the society-wide effects of the destruction of Judah, the category "virgin" would be beside the point. Other contexts in which the age designations "young men" (בחורים) and "maidens" (בתולות) occur together are: Pss. 78:63 (in context with people, heritage, priests, widows); 148:12; Deut. 32:25 (in context with suckling child and gray-haired old man); Isa. 23:4; 62:5; Jer. 31:13; 51:22 (in context with a series of age and profession indicators); Ezek. 9:6; Amos 8:13; Zech. 9:17; Lam. 1:18; 2:21; II Chr. 36:17. The age designation "maiden" is also evident in Jer. 2:32; Lam. 1:4; 2:10. Especially instructive is Joel 1:8, "Lament like a בתולה girded with sackcloth for the בעל of her youth." RSV has mistranslated בתולה as "virgin" (even though she is married!), forcing בעל ("husband") to be rendered "bridegroom."

The construct form בתולת is often applied to cities, nations, or communities, again making it clear that virginity is not the issue. To render בתולת בת-ציון (II Kings 19:21) as "Fair Maiden Zion" is much more accurate than the traditional "virgin daughter of Zion." *See* ZION, DAUGHTER OF [S].

Finally, the term is applied in the Ugaritic texts to the goddess Anath (paralleled by *ǵlmt*=Heb. *'almâ,* on which *see* §3 *below*), in contexts which are quite explicit sexually. Goddess of "love" and war who passionately copulates with her brother BAAL, she is scarcely to be described as "virgin."

b. "Virgin." Although the term בתולה basically means "maiden," it is often used in contexts whose intent is to specify virginity. For example, Rebekah (Gen. 24:16) is described as a בתולה "whom no man had known"; Judg. 21:12 speaks of "four hundred young בתולה who have not known man by lying with him," to be contrasted, in the preceding verse, to "a woman [אשה] that has lain with a male." This agrees with Finkelstein's observation based upon Sumerian and Akkadian legal texts: the expression "who has not known a man" is employed when *virgo intacta* (and not *virgo* alone) is explicitly intended, i.e., the term *batultu* denotes "an age distinction . . . and only implicitly, therefore, untouched. She is then more explicitly described as not yet having been deflowered, nor taken in marriage."

Other qualifications of *b^e^thûlâ* include: "who is

not betrothed" (Exod. 22:16 [H 15]; cf. Deut. 22:23, 28); and "has no husband" (Lev. 21:3).

A transition in meaning from "maiden" to "virgin" (paralleling the semantic histories of Gr. παρθένος and Lat. *virgo*) is suggested in Lev. 21:14 and Ezek. 44:22, where a בתולה is contrasted to a "widow, or one divorced, or a woman who has been defiled, or a harlot"; II Sam. 13:2, where Amnon is tormented because Tamar "was a בתולה, and it seemed impossible to Amnon to do anything to her"; see also Judg. 19:24; I Kings 1:2-4; Esther 2:2, 3, 17, 19. Less clear are Job 31:1; II Sam. 13:18; Ps. 45:14 [H 15].

Since נעורים (often in parallel with זקונים, "old age") became the usual word for "youth, maidenhood," the masculine plural *bᵉthûlîm* came to denote "virginity" (Lev. 21:13; Deut. 22:14, 15, 17, 20; Judg. 11:37, 38). Yet, בתוליהן in Ezek. 23:3 is parallel to נעוריהן ("youth . . . maiden"), and is replaced by the latter in 23:21.

2. Parthenos (παρθένος). This word, in classical Greek—like בתולה in the ancient Near East and the Bible—meant primarily "young woman, maiden, girl," one sexually mature. Whether the παρθένος was a virgin or not was a secondary matter, to be determined, if possible, by the context. Indeed, the derived term ὁ παρθένιος denoted "the son of an unmarried woman," and ἡ παρθένος was sometimes used honorifically for the sacred prostitutes of Greek shrines (thus the name Parthenon); cf. "Virgin [*btlt*] Anath," §1*a above*.

When early Christianity developed the belief of virgin birth for Jesus (*see* VIRGIN BIRTH; VIRGIN BIRTH[S]), it was natural to point to a possible proof text in Isa. 7:14. The exclusive meaning "virgin" was assumed for παρθένος in the Septuagint, and consequently for the Hebrew term which it translated (עלמה).

3. עלמה ('almâ). This word (found four times in the singular and five times in the plural) means simply "young woman, girl, maiden"; the masculine form (found twice in the Bible), עלם, denotes "young man, boy, lad." In Gen. 24, Rebekah is referred to once as עלמה and five times as נערה (maiden) just as David in I Sam. 17 is referred to by the corresponding masculine forms עלם and נער (vss. 55-58; so also Jonathan's attendant in ch. 20). David's chastity would hardly be cited as a factor in his defeat of Goliath! In Prov. 30:19, one of the phenomena that the author found too wonderful to fathom was דרך גבר בעלמה, "the way of a man with a maiden," i.e., the way of a male with a female; virginity in the עלמה is hardly what the author had in mind, any more than in the גבר. Similarly, it is noted that Moses' sister was only an עלמה (hardly, "virgin") when she watched over him among the reeds of the Nile (Exod. 2:8).

There are five instances of the plural, עלמות: in Ps. 68:25 [H 26] where the term is used, following "singers" and "musicians," for these "playing timbrels." In Song of Solomon the עלמות who love the hero (1:3), and who with "sixty queens and eighty concubines" do not match the hero's beloved "dove" (6:8, 9), are hardly to be associated with virginity. As put by Irwin, "These alleged 'virgins' are in decidedly bad company"—a comment that is relevant to the *'lmt* in the Kition inscription (*KAI* 37B) where prostitutes (? *qdšt*) and homosexuals (*klbm*, "dogs") constitute the company. In Ps. 46:1 and I Chr. 15:20 the meaning of עלמות is uncertain.

Once the correct meaning of עלמה in Isa. 7:14 is adhered to—and the force of adjective הרה and of the participle ילדת given their natural due—it becomes clear that what the prophet Isaiah is saying to Ahaz is, "Behold, the young woman is with child and is about to give birth to a son. Let her name him Immanuel," i.e., before the baby that the pregnant woman will soon bear has grown significantly (vs. 16) the invaders will themselves be invaded. This is related to what the prophet says in the next chapter (8:1-4). As for the word order and intent of Isa. 7:14, Peters asserted bluntly: "There is a striking resemblance between this verse and Gen. 16:11. Is there any proper ground for translating the tenses differently in the two verses?" Of the newer official translations, only the Jerusalem Bible and New Jewish Version have rendered the entire Isaiah verse correctly.

Bibliography. J. P. Peters, "Miscellaneous Notes," *Hebraica*, II (1885-86), 171-75; J. J. Owens, "The Meaning of *'Almah* in the OT," *RevExp*, L (1953), 56-60; W. A. Irwin, "That Troublesome *'Almah* and Other Matters," *ibid.*, 335-60; E. R. Lachman, "Apropos of Isaiah 7:14," *JBR*, XXII (1954), 43; R. G. Bratcher, "A Study of Isaiah 7:14," *BTTr*, IX (1958), 97-126; J. J. Finkelstein, "Sex Offenses in Sumerian Laws," *JAOS*, LXXXVI (1966), 355-72, and "On Some Recent Studies in Cuneiform Law," *JAOS*, XC (1970), 243-56; R. E. Brown, "Recent Roman Catholic Translations of the Bible," *McCQ*, XIX (1966), 283-92; G. Delling, "παρθένος," *TDNT*, V (1967), 826-37.

H. M. ORLINSKY

***VIRGIN BIRTH.** As applied to the story of Jesus in Matthew and Luke, a more precise term would be "virginal conception," first, to distinguish the idea from the second-century apocryphal tradition that Mary gave *birth* miraculously, without pain and with sexual organs intact (PROTEVANGELIUM OF JAMES 19-20); and second, to make clear that the creedal doctrine, "born of the virgin Mary," may have been more concerned with the reality of the *birth* and hence of the humanity of Jesus than with the manner of his conception, which is at issue here. Some theologians use the term "virgin birth" even though they think that Jesus was or may have been conceived through sexual intercourse; for them the term is a symbol for expressing the divine element in Jesus. It is true that neither Matthew nor Luke was interested in the conception as a biological phenomenon; from the beginning the marvelous conception served as a sign of God's grace and as an idiom for the christological insight that Jesus came into the world as God's Son or the Messiah. Nevertheless, it remains a legitimate question whether the idiom is to be taken literally and whether historically Jesus was conceived without a human father. A general distrust of the miraculous scarcely excuses the modern scholar from a study of the evidence.

In terms of evidence, Isa. 7:14 (*see* VIRGIN BIRTH) currently has a less important role in the discussion: first it is widely agreed that it refers to a conception in the eighth century B.C. that somehow continued or supported the Davidic line of kings, rather than to the conception of Jesus; second, even the LXX reading, "Behold, *the virgin* will conceive and bear a son," does not necessarily envisage a virginal conception, for the future tense may mean that a woman who is now a virgin will conceive; third, granted that in his infancy narrative Matthew himself probably added the "fulfillment citations" (1:22-23; 2:5-6, 15, 17-18, 23) to existing material, the citation of Isa. 7:14 did not create the idea that Jesus was virginally conceived but was used to illustrate it.

Thus, the real biblical evidence for the virginal conception consists of Matt. 1:18-25 and Luke 1:26-38. There are six principal arguments challenging the historical value of this evidence. First, these two infancy narratives are chronologically late compositions (80s or 90s). The earlier strata of Christian tradition (Pauline letters, sermons in Acts, the synoptic accounts of the ministry) betray no knowledge of a virginal conception (*see* Mark 6:2-3; John 7:41-42). There are even sections of the infancy narratives that have no implication of it, e.g., the genealogies tracing Jesus' descent through Joseph, and Luke 2:1-6, 16, 48. Second, many points within the infancy narratives are of dubious historicity, and we do not have the same quality of witness support for the infancy material that we have for the ministry. Third, despite the weight of Christian tradition accepting the virginal conception as historical (virtually unanimous from A.D. 200), there is evidence of nonacceptance among some second-century Christians. Often such refusal stems from doctrinal or philosophical stances, e.g., a Docetism denying physical birth from a woman. But especially among Jewish Christian groups, it may represent the lack of an affirmative tradition. Fourth, most agree that a full christological evaluation of Jesus as Son of God came only gradually after his death and resurrection. If the virginal conception was historical and Mary knew from the beginning that Jesus had no human father, why was there such a gradual development in Christology? Fifth, can the absence of a human father be reconciled with an appreciation of Jesus' full humanity, as vocalized in Heb. 4:15 and the Council of Chalcedon? Sixth, can divine sonship *through* virginal conception, which seems to be the idea in Luke 1:35, be reconciled with divinity through pre-existence, as hinted in other NT works (John 1:1; 17:5; Phil. 2:6; Col. 1:15-17; Heb. 1:2, 8)?

Another set of arguments favors historicity. First, there is the long Christian tradition to that effect. Second, the two infancy narratives, which are independent of each other and agree on little else, agree on virginal conception. (For evidence that Luke does envisage a virginal conception and that 1:34-35 is not a later insert, *see* VIRGIN BIRTH.) This means that the tradition is older than either gospel. Third, it is difficult to explain how the idea arose if not from fact. Many parallels for a virginal conception have been suggested from world religions, from paganism, and from pre-Christian Judaism; but they are not really satisfactory (*see* VIRGIN BIRTH), and there is little reason to believe that most of them would have been known or acceptable to early Christians. Fourth, there was an early Jewish suspicion about Jesus' origins. The charge, explicit in later Jewish polemics, that Jesus was illegitimate seems to be foreshadowed in the NT. The reference to Jesus as "son of Mary" (Mark 6:3) has been deemed strange, for generally sons were not called by their mother's name unless paternity was uncertain or unknown. In John 8:41 an objection is addressed to Jesus: "We were not born of fornication"; is the Greek *hēmeis* ("we") emphatic by way of contrast—not us, but you? These innuendoes are uncertain, but it is difficult to think that any Christian invented the story in Matt. 1:18, which casts suspicion on Mary. More likely Matthew faced a story already in circulation. Indeed, the agreement between Matthew and Luke that Mary conceived after being espoused to Joseph but before marital intercourse suggests that Jesus was born unduly early after Joseph and Mary came to live together, a fact that would have given rise among nonbelievers to a charge of illegitimacy. Thus, it is too facile to theorize that virginal conception was invented as a symbol for a developing Christology and that previously everyone took for granted that Jesus was the natural son of Joseph and Mary. Irregularity of conception may have been rumored all along; and the virginal conception may represent not only a development in Christology but also an attempt to explain the irregularity in light of two fixed Christian attitudes, namely, a respect for the image of the blameless, pious parents (Matt. 1:19; Luke 1:35, 42) and an insistence on Jesus' freedom from sin (II Cor. 5:21; I Pet. 2:22; Heb. 4:15; John 8:46)—a freedom which may have been judged irreconcilable with sinful conception. A family tradition about the manner of Jesus' conception may have lent support to the theological solution. While there is no way of proving the existence of such a private tradition, the prominence of Jesus' relatives in the Jerusalem church—e.g., James, the brother of the Lord—should caution us about the extent to which Christians were free, at least up through the 60s, to invent family traditions about Jesus.

See also CHRISTOLOGY IN THE NT[S] §3*b*; GENEALOGY (CHRIST) and supplementary article.

Bibliography. T. Boslooper, *The Virgin Birth* (1962); H. von Campenhausen, *The Virgin Birth in the Theology of the Ancient Church* (1962); R. E. Brown, *The Virginal Conception and Bodily Resurrection of Jesus* (1973). B. M. Metzger, *A Textual Commentary on the Greek NT* (1971), pp. 2-7, discusses the various attested texts of Matt. 1:16.

R. E. BROWN

VIRGINITY, TOKENS OF. According to Deut. 22:13-21, if a husband accused his wife of not having been a virgin at the time of marriage, her parents could establish her innocence by producing her "tokens of virginity." They "spread out the garment" (vs. 17), i.e., the blood-stained cloth on which the marriage had been consummated, and which they had preserved for such an eventuality.

***VULGATE.** *See* LATIN VERSIONS[S].

W

***WAR, HOLY.** "Holy war" is a traditional designation of the religious evaluations and motivations permeating the practice and ideology of warfare in ancient Israel. The view articulated by von Rad, that holy war referred to a homogeneous and distinctive institutional and cultic matrix in Israel, is now under question. Recent research emphasizes the relative lateness and schematic shape of much of the biblical evidence, the sporadic incidence of many "typical" features of sacral war, and the widespread occurrence of similar practices and notions among Israel's neighbors (by no means confined to pastoral nomads). At the same time, scholars have traced the central role of military imagery in Israel's conception of God to an early date, and have underscored its importance in bridging and linking themes (such as Creation, kingship, and eschatology), as well as strains of religious tradition (such as covenantal, royal, prophetic, and apocalyptic "theologies").

1. Conduct of holy war. ***a. Uniformity of practice.*** The traits of holy war delineated by von Rad (*see* WAR, IDEAS OF §1 *a-d*) have been regarded as normative institutional procedures in biblical contexts, even where only one or even none are directly attested. The appropriateness of this procedure for interpreting holy-war data in terms of ideal types has been thrown into doubt by the high incidence of erratic and contradictory war practices; this strongly indicates that the entire range of traits compiled by von Rad was never normative in Israel.

Steps toward initiating holy war, for example, which von Rad viewed as serial and cumulative, may in fact have been alternative courses followed on different occasions: (1) designation of a spirit-seized person as war leader, or (2) choice of a war leader through negotiations by the initiative of the established communal leaders, or (3) choice of a war leader by consulting the accepted oracles. Even more tellingly, the different accounts of the destruction of war captives and booty, or of their reservation or setting aside for sacred use, show great variations from the schematic formulations of the later Deuteronomic program of *ḥērem* (*see* DEVOTED). It is probable that destruction or exemption of specific classes of captives and booty varied according to the specifications of an optional vow before battle (cf. Num. 21:1-3). That the *ḥērem* practice was known in Israel's environment is vividly attested by the ninth-century MOABITE STONE. What is in question, therefore, is not the existence but the frequency, scope, and degree of standardization of holy-war practices, as well as their sociopolitical basis and rationale. Deuteronomy formalized and dogmatized a range of war notions and practices that had not existed earlier in any single detectable form or within any certain all-Israelite jurisdiction.

b. Equation with Bedouin warfare. A recurrent claim is that holy war derived from pastoral nomadic military organization. To the extent that practices that were religiously taboo at MARI (e.g., failure to mobilize conscripts, unauthorized, private seizure of booty) actually parallel biblical *ḥērem,* the overlap has been attributed to the fact that both the subjects at Mari and the early Israelites were pastoral nomads. This interpretation overlooks the fact that the Mari sanctions were imposed by sedentary state officials against pastoral nomads.

Moreover, it is far from demonstrated that parallels from Arab sources are distinctive of Bedouin life in contrast to other socioeconomic influences that entered Islam. Sometimes the Islamic jihad is equated with biblical holy war, and both with pastoral nomadism. This altogether ignores the fact that jihad was, among other things, an attempt to control blood revenge among nomadic converts who did not easily assimilate to the larger Moslem brotherhood. Characteristically, jihad was directed either at the conversion of pagans or the subjection of Christians and Jews to poll and land taxes under Moslem rule. Prior to the monarchy, holy war in Israel did not function in an analogous way, and it is doubtful that it did so even during the monarchy.

Contrary to scholarly opinion, features of early Israelite warfare such as ambush, feigned flight, single combat, and ritual destruction of captives or booty are in no way specific to pastoral nomadism. It is indeed noteworthy that the great majority of holy-war parallels cited by scholars such as W. R. Smith, Schwally, von Rad, and Abel are taken either from nonnomadic tribal societies, such as Amerindian and Germanic tribes, or from ancient states such as Egypt, Assyria, Greece, and Rome. At the time of the Moabite sacral massacre of the Israelites, Moab was a monarchy with a largely sedentary populace. Weippert has pointed out that practically all the traits of holy war assembled by von Rad are as pointedly expressed in Neo-Assyrian warfare as they are in Israel.

c. War paradigms in tribes and states. If holy war was not peculiar to Israel and cannot be explained as a specifically nomadic derivative, what was its social basis and function in Israel? In tribal Israel, holy war was an activity of collaborating tribes unified by a common religion and loosely associated by covenant mechanisms that committed them to periodic pooling of troops in defense of the living space of an egalitarian independence movement. On the other hand, holy war in the time of the monarchy was a function of the state apparatus which possessed the power to enforce conscription and to declare war at the will of the ruler and his officials.

Between the tribal and state forms of holy war there were formal continuities in practice. Cultic preparations, consultation of oracles, carrying the ark into battle, battle shouts, and the like were apparently observed in both epochs. Also, while a professional officer corps and a standing army developed under the monarchy, the majority of troops in major campaigns were citizens called to arms for the occasion (*see* ARMY[S] §3). Nonetheless, there were critical differences between tribal holy war and state holy war. Tribal wars were guerrilla wars fought with the simplest of makeshift infantry weapons; they were entered upon and prosecuted by intertribal consensus. Under the monarchy wars were open pitched battles in extended campaigns fought with advanced infantry weapons and with chariotry; they were launched by state authorities and fought by drafted and mercenary troops without regard for tribal consensus.

Wars to preserve the Israelite heartland against immediate invaders gave way to wars fought on the perimeters of empire and often in alliance with foreign powers, or to defend against invasion precipitated by the obligations of shifting alliances. The earlier tribal wars had been patently "necessary" to those who fought them; tribes unconvinced of a threat chose not to fight. The state wars were far more equivocal in their contradictory benefits and losses to the people. Citizen soldiers were conscripted into battle by the state apparatus irrespective of their actual commitment and often without regard to communal or regional resistance to particular wars. It is probably accurate to say that Israel's wars under the monarchy never had the massive support of combatants and civilians that typified its earlier tribal wars. This judgment is supported by the considerable popular support given to the prophets, who frequently condemned the foreign wars of the monarchy (*see* §2*c below*).

2. Ideology of holy war. ***a. The divine warrior.*** Canaanite religious literature accents the role of the gods EL and BAAL as divine warriors who lead the assembly of the gods as an army in the battle against forces of chaos, thereby stabilizing the natural and human orders. Israelite dependence on this tradition is evident in the imagery of Yahweh as one who fights for and through his people Israel. The major transformation in Israelite appropriation of the divine-warrior imagery is that Yahweh fights less against cosmic chaos and more against oppressive historical powers such as Egypt and the Canaanite city-states. Likewise, the polytheistic assembly of gods fades into a conventional way of speaking of the plenitude of powers at Yahweh's disposal.

The most plausible explanation of the name Yahweh is that it arose from an appositional sentence-title describing El as "he who creates the [divine?] hosts" (*see* GOD, NAMES OF §§B3*b*, C1). If this be so, Yahweh from the outset was characterized as the divine warrior who absorbed the cosmic-war functions of El, while subordinating them to his sociopolitical career as Israel's deliverer and defender. Yahweh was "lord of hosts" in the double sense that he commanded both the pleroma of nonhuman powers and the citizen army of Israel in its just fight for liberation from Canaanite, Egyptian, Transjordanian, and Philistine overlords. Through this complex process of ideological differentiation and eclecticism, the theology of holy war arose conterminously with the rise of the Israelite people.

b. Cult, traditions, and holy-war ideology. Von Rad saw the cult of holy war as closely attached to the AMPHICTYONY and the central sanctuary. Recent research has departed from this perspective in two divergent directions. One line of thought sharply dissociates holy war from the amphictyony until late premonarchic times (Smend). The other line of thought suggests an even more fundamental and generative role for divine-warrior theology than von Rad envisaged (Cross, Miller). The latter view conceives the bifurcated streams of Exodus-settlement and Sinai traditions as alternate elaborations of a hypothetical epic tradition of the divine warrior first expressed in poetry (cf. Exod. 15:1-18, 21). It also suggests that the titular type of patriarchal deity identified by Alt was joined in the earliest expressions of Yahweh as divine warrior. A further implication may be that the divine-warrior imagery was integral to the central covenant-renewal cult of Israel.

In retrospect, it appears that the institutional homogeneity of holy war that von Rad proposed was a misreading of the more standardized mytho-historical language about divine warrior and fighting people. This does not mean that Israel fought no cultically activated wars, but it may mean that great variations in war practices were loosely "covered" by a more uniform and somewhat flamboyant ideology.

c. Monarchy and holy-war ideology. The basic outlines of Israel's thought about the divine warrior and his fight on Israel's behalf were well formed before Israel became a state. Early in the monarchy there developed a pronounced struggle over whose sociopolitical praxis correctly embodied the old concepts. Did the divine warrior chiefly operate through the entire Israelite people as a tribally articulated covenant community (*see* COVENANT; COVENANT, MOSAIC[S]), or did he chiefly operate through the office of his representative, the Israelite king, as commander in chief and champion of a just human order (*see* COVENANT, DAVIDIC[S])? Accordingly, forms of popular covenantal theology and forms of elitist Davidic-Zion theology struggled for mastery of the channels of religious persuasion, or were joined in various hybrids. *See* GOVERNMENT, ISRAELITE[S]; PRESENCE OF GOD, CULTIC[S].

The sociopolitical contradictions in wars that could no longer be viewed as simple necessities and undoubted gains, in contrast to the liberating tribal wars, opened deep fissures in the social body. There was growing confusion and dissent over whether the wars conducted under the conditions of political hierarchy and social stratification were in fact "wars of Yahweh." The key issue was not so much whether wars were "defensive" or "aggressive" in the legal sense; it was rather the deeper question of the constructive or destructive effects of the wars on the internal well-being of Israelite society.

Religious thought about war took a new turn with the appearance of prophets who stood holy war on its head by audaciously declaring that in the wars at hand Yahweh fought not for Israel but against Israel. Originally holy war had posited a direct correlation between an internally just society and its external self-defense. Observing the masses of domestically oppressed Israelites, some prophets argued that the axiomatic correlation between a just society and the right to self-defense and survival had been conclusively shattered. The ideology and rhetoric of holy war, formerly aimed at foreign powers, was now turned against the internal oppressors, i.e., the Israelite ruling class and state apparatus.

d. Exile, restoration, and holy-war ideology. With the independent Israelite states shattered, holy war assumed once more a hopeful prospect for those who believed that the Israelite community could be reconstituted in institutional form. A foreign power could serve Yahweh to deliver his people from Babylon, just as a foreign power had earlier served Yahweh in crushing the false political framework that had enslaved his people. Holy-war imagery could assert the prospect of Yahweh as universal divine warrior in supreme command of world history, which could likewise take the form of hope in a revived Davidic monarchy, preserving a society more just than that of the old Israelite and Judean states.

When the prospect of political independence languished, holy war could point to the divine warrior's rule over history as creator and destroyer of empires and as solace for the powerless few who trusted in him. Apocalyptic literature is replete with the language of holy war and, in large measure, the revolts against the Seleucids and against Rome proceeded on the premise that a just Jewish society worthy of independence among the nations could be restored within the framework of ongoing history. *See* APOCALYPTICISM; APOCALYPTICISM[S].

e. Jesus, the early church, and holy-war ideology. The divine warrior and religious warfare appear in early Christianity, in part through the metaphor of religious life as a battle against evil, but even more significantly as the ideology of a decisive divine intervention in impending military conflicts at the end of history.

Jesus focused on microaspects of a just society as concretized in his egalitarian company of followers. His explicit relationship to Jewish revolutionary movements, such as the Zealots (*see* ZEALOT [S]) is a matter of ongoing debate. Less often examined is the impact of Jesus and the early church on wars and revolts such as the Jewish uprising against Rome in A.D. 66-70. If for himself and his immediate followers Jesus renounced direct participation in war, he asserted war's inevitability and its indispensable role in the coming of the kingdom of God. As long as Christians expected the imminent end of history, they were deeply attentive to the correlation between just or unjust societies and the wars repeatedly fought by the political systems of which they were an inescapable part. The resolution they foresaw was an impending eruption of an overwhelming and just power that would reconstitute human societies as the single society of the divine warrior through the agency of his triumphant Son.

Bibliography. On §1: E. Tayan, "Djihād," *The Encyclopaedia of Islam,* II (new ed., 1965), 538-39; N. K. Gottwald, "'Holy War' in Deuteronomy," *RevExp,* LXI (1964), 296-310; A. Malamat, "The Ban in Mari and in the Bible," *Biblical Essays,* Die OT Werkgemeenskap in Suid-Afrika, 9th meeting (1966), pp. 40-49; F. Schwally, *Semitische Kriegsaltertuemer. I. Der heilige Krieg im alten Israel* (1901); "Djihād," in *Shorter Encyclopaedia of Islam,* ed. H. Gibb and J. Kramers (1961), p. 89; G. von Rad, *Der Heilige Krieg im alten Israel* (3rd ed., 1958); W. M. Watt, *Islam and the Integration of Society* (1961), pp. 61-67; M. Weippert, "'Heiliger Krieg' in Israel und Assyrien," *ZAW,* LXXXIV (1972), 460-93; Q. Wright, *A Study of War,* I (1942), esp. chs. VI-VII; Y. Yadin, *The Art of Warfare in Biblical Lands,* 2 vols (1963); W. R. Smith, *Lectures on the Religion of the Semites* (3rd ed., 1927), p. 641.

On §2: F. M. Cross, *Canaanite Myth and Hebrew Epic* (1973), "The Song of the Sea and Canaanite Myth," *Journal for Theology and the Church,* V (1968), 1-25, and "The Divine Warrior in Israel's Early Cult," *Biblical Motifs,* ed. A. Altmann (1966), pp. 11-30; H. Fredriksson, *Jahwe als Krieger* (1945); P. D. Miller, Jr., *The Divine Warrior in Early Israel,* Harvard Semitic Monographs, V (1973); R. Smend, *Yahweh War and Tribal Confederacy* (1970); F. Stolz, *Jahwes und Israels Kriege,* ATANT, LX (1972).

N. GOTTWALD

WAR OF THE SONS OF LIGHT AND THE SONS OF DARKNESS (1QM). A scroll from Cave 1 at Wadi Qumran, giving the plan for the final war between the forces of good and evil. Also known as the War Rule or War Scroll and sometimes identified as 1QMilh. *See* DEAD SEA SCROLLS §5*c*; DEAD SEA SCROLLS[S] §§5, 6, 7, 8, and bibliog.

***WAVE OFFERING** [תנופה, *t*e*nûphâ,* elevation offering]. The offerings subject to this ritual are: the breast of the well-being offering (שלמים, RSV "peace offering"; Lev. 7:30; 9:21; 10:14-15; Num. 6:20; 18:18), the right hind thigh and fat of the priestly consecration offering (מלאים) and its accompanying bread offering (Exod. 29:22-26; Lev. 8:25-29), the metals for the buildings of the tabernacle (Exod. 35:22; 38:24), the אשם (RSV "guilt") offering, and the oil for the purification of the healed leper (Lev. 14:12, 24), the barley sheaf (עמר; Lev. 23:11-14), the two wheat loaves (בכורים) together with two lambs of well-being (Lev. 23:17, 20), the meal offering (מנחה) of the suspected adulteress (Num. 5:25), the boiled shoulder of the Nazirite's well-being offering and its accompanying bread offering (Num. 6:20), and the Levites during their ordination (Num. 8:11, 15, 21).

When the object of the *t*e*nûphâ* is the Deity, the preposition לפני, "before," is usually used, implying a ritual within the sanctuary (as opposed to the *t*e*rûmâ* which is always ליהוה and never לפני יהוה). *See* HEAVE OFFERING[S].

The nature of the ritual is nowhere defined.

The rabbinic rendering "wave offering" (e.g., M. Men. 5.6) has been accepted by nearly all translations, dictionaries, and commentaries. The LXX exhibits total bewilderment. It renders *t^{e}nûphâ* in the purification ceremonial for the healed leper (Lev. 14) by three words: ἀφόρισμα (vs. 12), ἀφαίρεμα (vs. 21), and ἐπίθεμα (vs. 24). The Targums, on the other hand, consistently translate *t^{e}nûphâ* and its verbal forms by the root רום, "raise, elevate." This rendering is corroborated by most occurrences of הניף in the Bible (e.g., Isa. 10:15; 11:15; 13:2; 19:16), where the rendering "elevate" is clearly superior to "wave." Logical considerations buttress the philosophical evidence. Since the *t^{e}nûphâ* ritual is frequently carried out with many objects simultaneously (e.g., Exod. 29:22-24; Lev. 8:25-27), a "waving" motion would topple the entire offering, whereas their "elevation" is physically manageable. An elevation rite is indeed attested in the Egyptian cult, revealing many similar characteristics to the *t^{e}nûphâ*: (1) The Egyptian formula "elevate . . . before the face of the god" is the exact equivalent of the Hebrew formula (Exod. 29:24). (2) As depicted in the relief (Fig. W1), the offering is an aggregate, containing a sampling of all the food placed on the god's table. Correspondingly, all the objects subject to the *t^{e}nûphâ* in a single ritual must undergo the act together, never separately. (3) Like its Egyptian counterpart, the *t^{e}nûphâ* offering is placed on the palms of the hands (so explicitly for the Nazirite, Num. 6:19). A final consideration is that the allegedly parallel waving ceremonial from the ancient Near East turns out

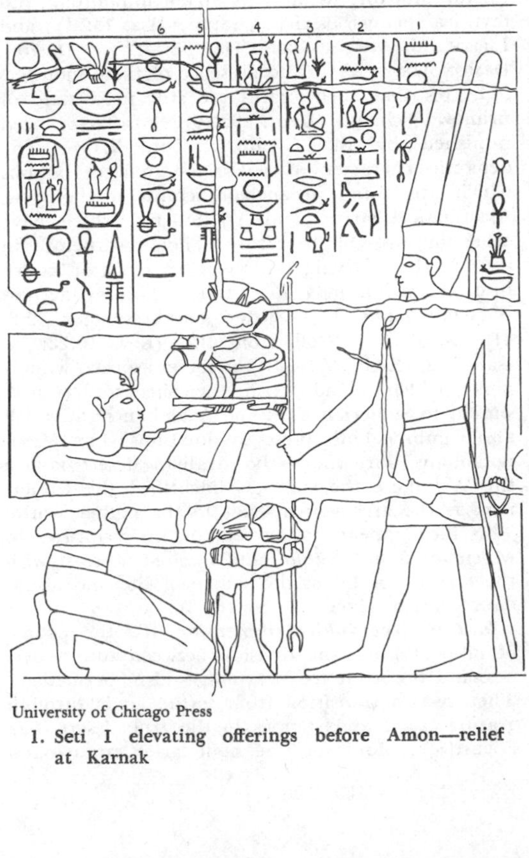

University of Chicago Press

1. Seti I elevating offerings before Amon—relief at Karnak

to be an exorcistic rite, totally unrelated to the temple cult. Thus philology, typology, and logic reinforce each other in favor of the rendering of *t^{e}nûphâ* as "elevation offering."

The *t^{e}nûphâ*-elevation is a rite of dedication governed by two postulates. The first is that any offering which still belongs to the owner when it is brought to the sanctuary requires the dedicatory rite of the *t^{e}nûphâ* (*see* SANCTIFICATION IN THE OT[S] §4*b*). Thus nearly all offerings are exempted from the *t^{e}nûphâ,* because they are dedicated before they are brought to the sanctuary. The main exception to this rule is the שלמים (RSV "peace offering") whose meat belongs to and is eaten by its owner. For the owner to benefit the clergy with the thigh and breast, he must first dedicate them to the Lord, i.e., subject them to the *t^{e}nûphâ*. The *t^{e}nûphâ* requirement for this offering is supported by the facts that it is called the offering of the people of Israel (Exod. 29:28), in contrast to the most-sacred sacrifices, called an offering to Yahweh (e.g., Lev. 10:13-14 [RSV "offerings by fire"]), and that the owner is expressly commanded to bring the dedicatory portions of the *š^{e}lāmîm* "on his hands/palms" (Exod. 29:24-25; Lev. 7:29-30; Num. 6:19-20). It also explains other anomalies of the ritual. For example, the anointment oil sprinkled on the priests (Exod. 29:7, 21; Lev. 8:12, 30) does not undergo the *t^{e}nûphâ* since it is inherently holy (Exod. 30:25, 32), but the oil for purifying the leper is profane and requires the *t^{e}nûphâ* (Lev. 14:16-17, 27-28) in order to sanctify it.

The second postulate is that the most-sacred offerings (*see* SACRIFICES AND OFFERINGS IN THE OT[S] §1*b*) whose composition, procedure, or purpose varies from the norm (i.e., Lev. 1–5) require the additional dedication of the *t^{e}nûphâ*. Thus three kinds of grain offering are subject to the *t^{e}nûphâ*: that of the suspected adulteress (Num. 5:25), and of the barley sheaf (Lev. 23:11-14) because they are made of barley and not of wheat, and the two wheat loaves (Lev. 23:17, 20) because they contain leaven; moreover, all three lack the usually required frankincense and oil. The guilt offering (אשם) brought by the healed leper differs from its genre in that its blood, being essential to the ritual, may not be commuted into silver (cf. Lev. 5:15, 18; 6:6 [H 5:25]), and in that it is the first in the sacrificial ritual (Lev. 14:12, 24) whereas normally it is last (cf. Num. 6:10-12; M. Zeb. 10.5). That the above-mentioned offerings need reinforced dedication is indicated, not only by their abnormal procedure or composition, but, more importantly, by their purpose. The barley sheaf and the wheat loaves undergo the *t^{e}nûphâ* ritual "that you may find acceptance" (Lev. 23:11), i.e., so that the Lord will grant an abundant harvest. The offering of the suspected adulteress is called "a meal offering of remembrance which recalls wrongdoing" (Num. 5:15), i.e., God is implored to intercede in this case by guaranteeing that the "water of bitterness" (vss. 23-26) will reveal the truth. Finally, on the eighth day the healed leper is daubed with the blood of the guilt offering and the oil so that he will be qualified to enter the sanctuary to complete his sacrificial rites (cf. M. Zeb. 10.5). For the distinction between *t^{e}nûphâ* and *t^{e}rûmâ, see* Heave Offering[S].

Bibliography. A. Vincent, "Les rites du balancement (tenoûphâh)," in *Melanges Syriens Offerts à Monsieur René Dussaud,* I (1939), 267-72; G. R. Driver, "Three Technical Terms," *JSS,* I (1956), 97-105; N. H. Snaith, "The Wave Offering," *ET,* LXXIV (1962-63), 127; J. Milgrom, "The Alleged Wave Offering in Israel and the ANE," *IEJ,* XXII (1972), 33-38, and "The t^{e}nûphâ," in *zer Li'gevuroth,* ed. B. Z. Luria (1972), pp. 93-110, Hebrew.

J. Milgrom

***WEALTH.** *See* Poor[S].

***WEEK.** A socially constructed unit of time whose duration is intermediate between the astronomical units of day and lunar month. In various cultures weeks of four, five, six, seven, eight, ten, or fifteen days have been known to exist. Often the length of the week is related to phases of the moon or to market-day cycles.

The seven-day week is probably of Israelite origin. At least no such week is attested prior to Israel's. Scholars disagree as to whether Israel's choice of a seven-day time unit was related to lunar phases, to a convenient market cycle, or to the ancient Near Eastern symbolism of the number Seven (wholeness, completeness, totality). Almost certainly the seven-day week did not originate in an "ancient Semitic pentecontad calendar" (*see* Week). No generally accepted evidence for such a calendar exists.

From Israel's earliest days the seven-day cycle culminating in a seventh-day sabbath ran uninterruptedly through the months and years (Exod. 34:21; 23:12). Its recurrence was independent of lunar and solar cycles, and it has remained constant in all Israelite and Jewish calendars. Even the sectarian calendar of Jub. 6:29-38, Enoch 72–75, and Qumran, which changed the length of some months and the year, left the seven-day week intact.

By the first century A.D., a seven-day week was widely known throughout the Roman Empire, probably through the influence of the large Jewish Diaspora. Although the early Gentile Christian church rejected the Jewish sabbath, it accepted the seven-day week. *See also* Sabbath[S] §1; Sabbatical Year[S].

Bibliography. *See* bibliog. under Sabbath[S].

B. E. Shafer

***WILDERNESS.** The concept is expressed by a variety of terms, but it is not always clear how they differ in meaning (*see* Schwarzenbach). The most frequently used expression is מדבר (269 times), rendered ἔρημος in the LXX and NT. The term is also found in cognate languages, e.g., Ugaritic and Aramaic, and as a Northwest Semitic loanword in Akkadian. It is often coupled with or parallel to ערבה (59 times), שמה/משמה/שממה/ישימון (116 times), ציה/ציון (18 times), and other terms. מדבר (*midhbār*) and its synonyms refer to arid or semiarid areas which are not suited for permanent settlement but in part can be utilized as pasture lands for small stock (*see* Desert; Wilderness). The noun probably derives from Aramaic *dbr,* "to bring the flock to the pasture," possibly connected with Hebrew *rbd-rbṣ,* which have a similar connotation (Isa. 13:20). *Midhbār* therefore serves in the OT also as a technical term for pasture areas adjoining a semipermanent shepherd encampment—*nāwê=nāwūm* in the Mari texts—or permanent semiurban and urban settlements.

In the majority of occurrences, "wilderness" carries negative overtones, referring to parched, inhospitable, and dangerous places. However, in reference to pasture lands it exhibits positive aspects of out-of-the-way locales, sometimes with a luxuriant growth of grass, where romance and love flourish. This results to some degree from the association of *midhbār* with the period of Israel's wandering in the wilderness, between the Exodus and the conquest of Canaan. The wide and diversified employment of wilderness language pertaining to geophysical reality and expressing various concepts affords fruitful insights into fundamental religious and social ideas which were operative in biblical Israel. They were carried over into the Qumran documents and rabbinic literature, and, with some significant conceptual variation, into the NT and early patristic writings.

1. The meanings of "wilderness." ***a. The spatial dimension.*** Wilderness terminology—ציה, מדבר, מלחה, ישימון, שממה—denotes the true desert, especially in the S of Palestine and in the Sinai Peninsula to the SW. No trees or other vegetation grow in this barren void (Num. 20:5), and no husbanded animals or civilized men live there (Jer. 2:6). Anyone who ventures into this wilderness suffers hunger and thirst (Ps. 107:4-5), and is endangered by marauders and outlaws, fearful beasts of prey, snakes, and scorpions (Deut. 8:15). In the howling wilderness roam unfamiliar and mythical beings, ostriches, satyrs, (Isa. 13:21), and Lilith, the night hag (Isa. 34:14; *see* Demon, Demonology §A4). The presence of these monsters indicates that such places are still in a state of primeval chaos (Deut. 32:10), or have been punished by the Creator (Zeph. 2:13). The demonic character of wilderness reflects notions which are found in ancient Semitic mythology—Akkadian, Ugaritic, and Arabic—and which have echos in post-OT literature. They reverberate in the ritual of driving out the *śā'îr* (goat or satyr) into the wilderness to Azazel. This wilderness is synonymous with utter darkness (Jer. 2:6, 31), a place cut off from life (Lev. 16:22; cf. Isa. 53:8; Ezek. 37:11). In these aspects wilderness-*midhbār* blends with the Sheol-underworld, similar to Sumerian *Edin* and Akkadian *ṣêru,* which also combine both these connotations. The Mesopotamians, for whom the Arabian desert lay to the W, where the sun sets, identified the wilderness as the area which leads to the nether world. This idea appears to be reflected in scriptures in which *midhbār,* *'^{a}rābhâ,* and *ś^{e}māmâ* contrast with the Garden of Eden, the source of life and abundant growth (Joel 2:3; Isa. 51:3).

b. The geographical dimension. To the people of biblical times the division between the wilderness and the sown area was not rigid or permanent. There was a transition from fertile lands through grazing tracts and steppes to the true desert (*see* Forest[S]). Moreover, the boundaries can expand as new lands are brought under cultivation, or contract through the inroads of nomads who succeed in pushing back the agricultural population (Judg. 6–7). The gradual transition from the urban and semipermanent settlements to the W and the E of the Jordan into the wilderness around the Dead Sea shows in the terminology employed in some biblical narratives. Thus, after the battle with Joab's troops, Abner's men retreat from the city of Gibeon (which lies N of Jerusalem) through the "wilderness" (מדבר) to the Arabah and from there cross the Jordan to return to Mahanaim (II Sam. 2:24-29).

The stretches of wilderness closest to the Dead Sea are sometimes appropriately termed *m^e^lēḥâ*, salty marshes (Jer. 17:6; Job 39:6). While the *m^e^lēḥâ* and the *y^e^šîmôn* are altogether unsuitable for human habitation, the parts of the nonarable wilderness designated *midhbār*, on the perimeters of settlements, are the ideal grazing ground for the flocks, predominantly goats and sheep, of the semisedentary and sedentary-agriculturist population (e.g., I Sam. 17:28; 25:4, 21; II Chr. 26:10). In this context *midhbār*, and to some degree *'^a^rābhâ*, are viewed as extensions of specific settlements, such as Beer-sheba (Gen. 21:14), Tekoa (II Chr. 20:20), or Damascus (I Kings 19:15). As a literary image this connotation is found, e.g., in Isa. 27:10, where Israel is likened to "a besieged (read *n^e^ṣûrâ* for *b^e^ṣûrâ*) city, a forsaken and desolate habitation (*nāwê*), a wilderness (*midhbār*) where cattle graze" (author's trans.). The Qumran term *midhbār y^e^rûšālayim* (1QM 1.2-3) derives from this usage.

c. The historical-temporal dimension. In a number of its occurrences in biblical literature, *midhbār* serves as a designation of the clearly circumscribed period which followed the Exodus and preceded the conquest of Canaan. During this period Israel encountered God, and these encounters decisively shaped the subsequent appreciation of the wilderness as expressed in biblical imagery and motifs. God's march through the wilderness became a prominent image in early biblical poetry (Deut. 33:2; Judg. 5:4; Hab. 3:3; Ps. 68:7-8 [H 8-9]). The movable tabernacle of the desert period was considered the forerunner of the permanent temple in Jerusalem (II Sam. 7:6).

d. The socioreligious dimension. The richness, exactitude, and diversity of the wilderness theme in the OT literature have had a far-reaching effect on modern biblical research. Buttressed by the comparison with pre-Islamic Arab culture, there emerged at the end of the nineteenth century a school of thought which presented the wilderness experience as the basis of Hebrew society and as a pivot of biblical religion. Israel was defined as a typical exponent of desert culture, her God as a desert deity, and the Yahwistic creed as an emanation of nomadism (Nyström). Not only was the wilderness viewed as the actual existential setting of the early Hebrews, but also was presented as the ultimate goal of the biblical *Heilsgeschichte* (Budde, Humbert, Meyer), and as an expression of "The Nomadic Idea and Ideal" of biblical monotheism (Flight). Most recently, one writer termed the OT "The Desert Bible" (Seale). Supposedly the most prominent promulgators of the desert ideal were the prophets, foremost among them Elijah, Hosea, and Jeremiah, whose ideas were adopted and further developed by Jesus and the early Christians (Flight). It is recognized that after the conquest of Canaan, Israel developed a predominantly agricultural and urban civilization. But some writers hold that the initial Bedouin culture still found expression in biblical mores, especially in the institution of the NAZIRITES, and was kept alive by the anticivilization clan of the Rechabites (cf. RECHAB; RECHABITES).

e. The "motif" dimension. The centrality of the wilderness in the ancient Hebrew world of thought was and is questioned by many scholars. The textual basis of the presumed desert idea and ideal is exceedingly thin (Barth). It has been argued that, in the historical experience after the Exodus, in the vicarious re-enactment of the desert theme after the Babylonian exile in Second Isaiah, and again among the Qumran covenanters, the wilderness is never presented as a goal in itself, but rather serves as the setting of an imposing rite of passage prior to Israel's reaching the Promised Land (Talmon). The recurring traditions which record the people's rebellious "murmuring in the wilderness" (Coats, Tunyogi, de Vries) tell of a wayward Israel, unthankful to the God who saved her from the Egyptian bondage and provided for the people's needs in the inhospitable desert (Deut. 32; Ps. 78; Ezek. 20). As far as mention is made of a love relationship between God and the people, it pertains to the historical-temporal dimension of wilderness, the short span of time between the Exodus and the Sinai covenant (Exod. 12–20), the only part of the desert trek predestined in the divine plan (Exod. 3:12, 18; 5:3). The love theme is altogether unconnected with the later wanderings in the desert imposed upon Israel as a consequence of the Exodus generation's lack of trust in God's ability to establish his people securely in the land of Canaan (Num. 13–14). Moreover, biblical traditions do not speak of a mutual relationship between God and the people marked by equal faithfulness on both sides; rather they highlight Israel's infidelity in the face of God's everlasting love and care. Hosea envisages a return to the desert as a new beginning which would lead to Israel's regaining the Promised Land without succumbing again to the lures of Baalism and harlotry (2:14-19 [H 16-21]). Like Miriam at the Red Sea, faithful Israel will then thank God (Hos. 2:15*b* [H 17*b*]). Reference to the positive aspect of the desert trek, namely the pre-Sinai period, reverberates in the famous Jeremiah passage which served as the main pillar of the desert ideal (Jer. 2:2-3). But these verses do not describe approvingly Israel's love for God in the desert. A textual-stylistic analysis reveals that this passage, too, extols God's unfailing love for Israel in her youth and her bridal days when he led the people through the wilderness, through a land unsown (Fox).

Nor can the Rechabites be adduced as the preservers of an all-Israelite desert culture from ancient times to Jeremiah's days, i.e., to the fall of Jerusalem at least. The biblical text simply describes the Rechabites' life-style and in no way presents it as a socioeconomic or religious ideal (*see* RECHABITES[S]).

f. The typological dimension. Notwithstanding the above strictures, traces of a positive appreciation of the wilderness period can be discerned in some strata of OT literature. However, rather than portraying wilderness life and mores as an ideal, these passages reveal the author's criticism of Israel's succumbing to pagan worship and to social corruption under the influence of settled life in Canaan. Viewed in comparison with these rejected realities of societal life, the desert period is retrospectively invested with some values which historically and existentially do not pertain to it. These appreciative aspects of "wilderness" are expressed in images that reflect the conception of the historical desert and the desert period as a place and a time of preparation before the entry into the Promised Land. Israel's renewed history after the Babylonian exile, and the Qumran covenanters' history after their "exile in Damascus," must correspondingly begin with a probationary stay in the desert. However, these new generations have already been punished for their transgression by war, destruction, and exile. Therefore, the new desert experience can be freed from the "sin-and-punishment" theme which characterizes the post-Egypt desert trek, and can become a pure and concentrated expression of the idea of "transition and preparation" (1QS 9.19-20). Unlike the hasty flight from Egyptian bondage, Israel embarks on the trek through the desert upon the return from the Babylonian exile in security and quietude, as a people already purified (Isa. 52:11-12; cf. 51:11). The desert is transformed into a land rich in water and vegetation (Isa. 43:18-19), traversable by straight paths and highways. Chaos again is subdued to become a Garden of Eden (Isa. 51:3). In these latter-day portrayals, it is not the wilderness as such or the nomadic style of life which are conceived as an idea and ideal, but rather their subjugation to cultivation and fertility, and to orderly societal life. It is only by a radical transformation that wilderness can become a prototype for an ideal time. *See also* TYPOLOGY[S].

2. Recent research. Scholars have attempted to explain the different, seemingly contradictory attitudes toward the wilderness in biblical literature as having arisen from the combination of parallel or complementary tradition strands (Noth), or from diachronic developments in the appreciation of the wilderness throughout the biblical period. This latter school holds that the early generations showed no interest in the fate and the deeds of the people, focusing their eyes exclusively on God's actions in rescuing his people (Bach, pp. 15-16). Therefore, there is no meaningful appreciation of the wilderness in relation to biblical religion and the social framework of Israel. This, then, changes completely in the time between the conquest of Canaan and the Babylonian exile. Against the background of the Canaanite pagan cult which infiltrated Israelite religion, the wilderness of the Exodus is retrospectively viewed as the locale of an ideal communion between God and Israel. With the end of the royalist first-temple period, a realistically negative or pessimistic attitude toward the wilderness takes over. It is seen in Pentateuchal accounts of the desert trek, and is mirrored in the book of Ezekiel (e.g., ch. 20) and the historiographic psalms (e.g., 78, 106, etc.).

This schematic pattern has several weaknesses. There is sufficient textual evidence upon which to base the biblical negation of the wilderness and wilderness life. But the presumed idealistic appreciation rests upon the doubtful exegesis of a few proof-texts assigned to "the middle period." Even scholars who perceive in biblical literature sure traces of an ambivalence toward the wilderness tend to agree that there never existed a tradition which viewed the wilderness altogether positively (Barth, pp. 20-23). The idealization of the desert in modern research appears to have arisen out of theological concepts and a nativist ideology which value the primitive quality of desert life as a joyfully accepted prerequisite for the attainment of spiritual bliss. In the OT world of ideas, the Promised Land lies beyond the fringes of the desert, which is the symbol of chaos and waste. The opposition between the two is conceptualized in the contrast of Jerusalem-Zion versus Sinai (Talmon, "The Biblical Concept of Jerusalem"). Only a postbiblical, predominantly Christian monastic vision conceives of the paradise to come, of celestial Jerusalem, as sprouting from the very confines of the transformed wilderness (de Vaux, p. 14).

Bibliography. On the geographical terminology: A. Schwarzenbach, *Die geographische Terminologie im Hebräischen des AT* (1954); D. O. Edzard, "Altbabylonisches *nāwūm*," *ZA*, NF XIX (1959), 168-73; A. Malamat, "Aspects of Tribal Societies in Mari and Israel," *15ème Rencontre Assyriologique Internationale* (1967), 129-38.

On the "wilderness" in Semitic cultures: J. A. Montgomery, *Arabia and the Bible* (1934); A. Haldar, "The Notion of the Desert in Sumero-Accadian and West-Semitic Religions," *Uppsala Universitets Årsskrift*, 1950: III, 1-70.

On the "nomadic ideal" in the Bible: K. Budde, "The Nomadic Ideal in the OT," *New World*, IV (1895), 726-45; E. Meyer, *Die Israeliten und ihre Nachbarstämme* (1906), pp. 129-41; P. Humbert, "Osée, le prophète bedouin," *RHPR*, I (1921), 97-118, "La logique et la perspective nomade chez Osée et l'unité d'Osée 2,4-22," in *Festschrift für K. Marti, BZAW*, XLI (1925), 158-66; J. W. Flight, "The Nomadic Idea and Ideal," *JBL*, XLII (1923), 158-226; A. Causse, *Du groupe ethnique à la communauté religieuse* (1937), pp. 15-31; S. Nyström, *Beduinentum und Jahwismus* (1946); M. Weber, *Ancient Judaism* (1952); R. de Vaux, *Ancient Israel—Its Life and Institutions* (1961), pp. 14-15, 519-520.

On the "wilderness" in biblical research: M. Noth, *Überlieferungsgeschichtliche Studien* (1943), pp. 69 ff.; R. Bach, "Die Erwählung Israels in der Wüste" (diss., Bonn, 1952); R. W. Funk, "The Wilderness," *JBL*, LXXVIII (1959), 205-14; H. H. Mallan, "Die theologische Bedeutung der Wüste im AT" (diss., Kiel, 1963); P. Riemann, "Desert and Return to the Desert in the Pre-exilic Prophets" (diss., Harvard, 1963-64); S. Talmon, "The 'Desert Motif' in the Bible and in Qumran Literature," in *Biblical Motifs—Origins and Transformations*, ed. A. Altmann (1966); C. Barth, "Zur Bedeutung der Wüstentradition," VTSup, XV

(1966), 14-23; M. V. Fox, "Jeremiah 2:2 and the 'Desert Ideal,'" *CBQ*, XXXV (1973), 441-50; V. Fritz, *Israel in der Wüste—Traditionsgeschichtliche Untersuchungen der Wüstenüberlieferung des Jahwisten* (1970); G. W. Coats, *Rebellion in the Wilderness* (1968); S. de Vries, "The Origin of the Murmuring Tradition," *JBL*, LXXXVII (1968), 51-58; A. C. Tunyogi, *The Rebellions of Israel* (1969); M. S. Seale, *The Desert Bible* (1974); S. Talmon, "The Biblical Concept of Jerusalem," *JES*, VIII (1971), 300-316.

On "wilderness" and eschatology: W. Wiebe, "Die Wüstenzeit als Typus der messianischen Heilszeit" (diss., Göttingen, 1939); G. H. Williams, *Wilderness and Paradise in Christian Thought* (1962).

S. TALMON

***WIND** [רוח, *rûaʰḥ*]. "Wind" is probably the primary meaning of the word *rûaʰḥ*, as distinct from its secondary meaning, "BREATH," and a third area of meaning, which is commonly rendered as "SPIRIT." The semantic shift from "wind" to "breath of life" (*rûaʰḥ ḥayyîm*) to "spirit" is subtle, and in some instances the context does not clearly mark the meaning.

רוח as "wind" appears frequently in the OT, e.g., in Gen. 8:1; Exod. 10:13, 19; and II Kings 3:17 (in parallel to גשם, "rain"). רוח as "direction" (Ezek. 5:10) is a logical derivation from רוח as "wind," and the inhabitants of the ancient Near East identified the winds with the four cardinal points or directions; e.g., the east wind in Gen. 41:6; Exod. 10:13; the west wind in Exod. 10:19; the north wind in Ezek. 1:4; Prov. 25:23; and Song of S. 4:16; and the south wind in Ps. 78:26; Job 37:17; and Song of S. 4:16. The four winds in the sense of the four directions appear in I Chr. 9:24 (RSV "sides"). The Greeks also identified the winds with the four primary directions from which they seemed to blow, personifying them with proper names.

The phrase *rûaʰḥ ʾaᵉlōhîm* has two quite different meanings in the OT. It is usually translated as "the spirit of God," and this is indeed its meaning in many, if not in most instances (e.g., Gen. 41:38; Exod. 31:3; Num. 11:25-29; 24:2). But the phrase can also be translated as "wind of God," and in some biblical verses it must be so understood, e.g., Gen. 1:2. E. Speiser (ABi I) translates the entire clause thus: "and only an awesome wind sweeping over the water." This is very different from JB: "and God's spirit hovered over the water." Not only is the image different, but there are theological and cosmological nuances inherent in the variant translations.

Each word and phrase in the Priestly cosmology (Gen. 1) was carefully chosen to convey a specific concept of divinity and to clarify the relationship between the Creator and the cosmology (Neiman). The cosmology stands opposed to the standard cosmologies of its time (Babylonian, Canaanite, and Greek): they postulate a universe that is polypotential, the creation of many independent forces that appear as the natural phenomena; the Hebrew cosmologist, on the contrary, insists that there is only one creative force, from whom all phenomena issue forth. Even the pre-existent state of Chaos, *tōhû* and *bōhû* (RSV "without form and void") was motivated by him.

Pre-existent CHAOS was conceived by the Babylonian and Canaanite cosmologist as primeval SEA, raging Yam or TIAMAT. The primeval sea has its own will and moves by its own power as one of the primary forces of creation. But the Hebrew cosmologist explains the existence of a pre-creation chaotic *tᵉhôm*, a depersonified raging chaos (*see* DEEP, THE), by stating that the agitation which drove the waters was a mighty wind, a wind sent by the Creator.

See also PALESTINE, CLIMATE OF; STORM; WHIRLWIND; ELIL.

Bibliography. D. Neiman, "The Polemic Language of the Gensis Cosmology," in *The Heritage of the Early Church* (1973), pp. 47-63. For wind as a primordial element in Near Eastern and other ancient cosmologies, *see* T. Gaster, *Myth, Legend, and Custom in the OT* (1969), pp. 4-5, 325-26. For worship of the seven wind-gods (*Sibittu*) by the Assyrians and Babylonians, *see* H. and J. Lewy, "The Origin of the Week and the Oldest West Asiatic Calendar," *HUCA*, XVII (1943), 1-152. For maps of the seasonal wind patterns in Palestine, *see The Israel Atlas* (1970), IV/3. D. NEIMAN

***WISDOM IN THE ANCIENT NEAR EAST.** In the OT the term WISDOM was employed to describe the attitude that proper conduct is based on knowledge—that the ability to live successfully can be imparted (*see* WISDOM IN THE OT[S]). This concept was current throughout the ancient Near East from very early times, although such works have so far been recovered only from the Nile valley and Mesopotamia. The Akkadian words usually rendered "wisdom," however, have a very different connotation from that of Hebrew חכמה, since they refer to skill in magic and ritual. Even the comparable terms in Egyptian lack the OT emphasis on reverence for the deity. Nevertheless, it is convenient to use the expression "wisdom literature" for those texts that deal with related themes in Egypt and Mesopotamia.

The literature falls into two broad categories: works designed to inculcate ethical teachings and useful advice, and those which were concerned with larger issues of life and often questioned traditional beliefs.

1. Egyptian wisdom literature. It has been maintained that Egyptian wisdom literature was basically utilitarian and pragmatic, and that only in its later stages did it manifest a religious spirit. This view has been shown to be false, because from the very beginning the Egyptian texts had a religious basis. Cf. WISDOM IN THE OT[S] §2*a*.

a. Instructions. From early times didactic treatises designated as *sbōyet* (teaching) were composed by officials for the edification of the young who attended the scribal schools and aspired to positions in government service. They were addressed by a father to his son, a practice which soon became a convention for teacher and pupil respectively. In addition to their use for instruction in the art of reading and writing, they provided models of effective speech and served to inculcate the norms of ethical conduct as well as, in the early period, the rules of court etiquette (*see* JOSEPH STORY[S] §§2*a*, 3). The style was that of formal instruction, and aphorisms do not become a feature until the demotic teachings, beginning in the Persian period. This is a characteristic also of Prov. 1–9 and 22:17–

24:34. *See* PROVERBS, BOOK OF §8; PROVERBS, BOOK OF[S] §2*b*.

Three such manuals date from the Old Kingdom and are attributed, perhaps pseudonymously, to famous figures. The only one completely preserved is ascribed to Ptah-hotep, a vizier of the Fifth Dynasty, but it was probably written late in the following dynasty (*ANET,* pp. 412-14, *see bibliog.*). Only the conclusion of the second treatise survives, addressed by an unknown vizier to his son Kagemni. Although set at the beginning of the Fourth Dynasty, it too was likely composed in the late Sixth Dynasty. Only the beginning of the third work is known, reconstructed from a number of fragmentary schoolboy exercises. The author claims to be Hardjedef, the son of Cheops of the Fourth Dynasty, but again the composition is possibly from the following dynasty.

During the centuries immediately following the fall of the Old Kingdom, the examples of this genre are all characterized by propagandist tendencies designed to serve political ends. The first purports to be the posthumous work of a Tenth-Dynasty ruler, probably Khety III, for his son and successor Merikare (*ANET,* pp. 414-18). Similarly, after the assassination of Amen-em-het I, the initiator of the Twelfth Dynasty, a document was composed for the new ruler Senwosret I and attributed to the deceased king (*ANET,* pp. 418-19). It was designed to bolster Senwosret's rightful claim to the throne. Although it is introduced as a "teaching," it hardly qualifies as a true instruction. This is also the case with a "teaching" by an unnamed author which was later incorporated into the tomb stela of an official named Sehtepibre. It was in fact a panegyric of the same Senwosret I, accompanied by exhortations to give loyal support to the ruler. Another such work is introduced anonymously as a "teaching which a man made for his son."

In the New Kingdom three didactic manuals were produced which were imbued with the personal piety characteristic of the age (*see* EGYPT §3*c*). Especially prominent was the concept of the "silent man," by which was meant the self-controlled person as opposed to the passionate or hot-tempered man. Probably from the Eighteenth Dynasty come two compositions: the fragmentary instruction of the scribe Amen-nakhte, and the more complete but carelessly copied work of the temple scribe Ani. Fortunately, the treatise of a minor official named Amen-em-opet is preserved in its entirety (*ANET,* pp. 421-25). This has been recognized by OT scholars as the source of Prov. 22:17–23:14, and its influence may also be seen in Jer. 17:5-8 and Ps. 1. The discovery of new MSS of the text compels a date for the original in the twelfth or thirteenth century, if not earlier.

This type of literature continued to be produced down to a much later time. Among the extensive hieroglyphic inscriptions on the walls of the tomb of Petosiris, high priest of Thoth at Hermopolis in the late fourth century B.C., are some didactic sections which reveal affinities with the OT, especially Ps. 128. Three works in the demotic script deserve mention. The earliest, probably from the sixth century, is a collection of maxims addressed to his son by 'Onkhsheshonqy while he was imprisoned for implication in a plot against the pharaoh's life. Slightly later is a lengthy compilation of counsels and aphorisms known as Papyrus Insinger. The beginning of a work of similar content is contained in a papyrus now in the Louvre.

b. Scribal literature. One of the most popular texts produced for the training of potential scribes has been called the Satire on the Trades (*ANET,* pp. 432-34). Written by the famous scribe Khety at the beginning of the Twelfth Dynasty, according to later Egyptian tradition, this introduced a new literary genre although it is still entitled a "teaching." In it the various professions are described in derogatory fashion and contrasted with the ideal lot of the scribe. For some reason it was attributed pseudonymously to a very minor official by the name of Dua-Khety. So great was its vogue that a spate of imitations was created during the New Kingdom. Its influence may be seen in Ecclus. 38:24–39:11.

Many anthologies of compositions offering advice and warnings to scribes as well as models for letters, hymns, eulogies, and the like began to appear in the New Kingdom. The Nineteenth-Dynasty Papyrus Anastasi I consists of a long text in the form of a letter usually known as the Scribal Controversy. It is a sarcastic quiz of an apprentice scribe by his teacher, and has been compared with Yahweh's interrogation of Job.

Another class of text devised as an aid to scribes was the "onomasticon," a list of the names of places, occupations, titles, flora and fauna, natural phenomena, and so on. These too were given the title of "teaching," so that this term had a very wide connotation for the Egyptians. Such lists are believed to lie behind the catalogue in Job 38–39 and other passages like Prov. 30:15-16, 18-20, 24-31, and even Gen. 1. They follow the order of the Egyptian lists in contradistinction to the corresponding lists prepared by Mesopotamian scribes.

c. Pessimistic literature. Four works produced in the Twelfth Dynasty all express despondency over the chaotic state of the land. Although characteristic of an earlier period, by the Twelfth Dynasty this had become merely a literary convention. The earliest is concerned with Neferti, a lector-priest who supposedly lived during the reign of Snofru in the Fourth Dynasty. His "prophecy" of the beneficent reign of Amen-em-het I, who would restore order to the land, reveals this to be a literary fiction. It is also a piece of political propaganda in support of this ruler who usurped the throne to found the Twelfth Dynasty. Somewhat later a tract appeared in which Khakheperresonbe, a priest of Heliopolis, sought for new modes of expression with which to lament over the state of the land. A long work contains the speeches of a sage named Ipuwer delivered before an unnamed king in which the latter is taken to task for his inept rule, which has resulted in anarchy (*ANET,* pp. 441-44).

To this group belongs the Dispute of a Man with his *bai,* a term rendered inadequately as "soul" (*ANET,* pp. 405-7). Its date may be slightly earlier than that of the other texts—late in the First Intermediate Period. It has been compared with the book of Job, but it does not raise the problem of theodicy. Rather does it deal with man's dissatisfaction with life and his skepticism over the value of elaborate funerary preparations.

d. Discourses. The works belonging to this category may be assigned to the Middle Kingdom. The earliest is "The Tale of the Eloquent Peasant," in which for the first time a plea for social justice is encountered (*ANET,* pp. 407-10). In the course of nine flights of rhetoric a humble peasant complains to the authorities of his mistreatment at the hands of a rapacious minor official. A long but very fragmentary papyrus contains a discourse by a certain Sisobk, who is imprisoned at the court of a prince named Inini. Its mutilated condition precludes any clear understanding of its contents. "The Song of the Harpist," which is found in several versions, is a poetic meditation on the futility of expensive mortuary arrangements and advocates a somewhat hedonistic approach to life (*ANET,* p. 467).

e. Fables and debates. Examples of this type of literature in Egypt are very rare. From the Twenty-second Dynasty comes a dispute between the heart and the stomach over their relative importance. A Twentieth-Dynasty papyrus in Turin records three poems in which different trees speak, extolling their virtues. They probably belong to the genre of love songs rather than that of contest fables. A unique allegorical tale from the Nineteenth Dynasty tells of two brothers who personify the abstract qualities of truth and falsehood. Truth is blinded by falsehood but is eventually vindicated. Animal fables first appear in written form in the demotic "Myth of the Sun's Eye." The present text is a Ptolemaic revision of an earlier form which can be shown to date back to the Ramesside period at least. Several other damaged demotic texts contain fables about animals.

2. Mesopotamian wisdom literature. Although the amount of extant cuneiform literature that may be subsumed under the heading of wisdom is less than that of Egypt, the number of genres is somewhat greater. In general, the earlier compositions were written in Sumerian and the later in Akkadian. Many of the former may have been composed as early as the beginning of the second millennium.

a. Instructions. Like the corresponding Egyptian and OT works, these were conventionally compiled by a "father" for his "son." The earliest is a Sumerian work addressed to the flood hero Ziusudra by his father Shuruppak. Most of it is still unpublished. A translation was made into Akkadian, of which only the opening lines have been preserved. In the "Counsels of Wisdom," a popular Akkadian text, a high court official instructs his son (*ANET,* pp. 426-27). It probably dates from the Kassite period, but may be as early as Old Babylonian. Most famous is that attributed to Ahikar, a royal seal-bearer during the reigns of Sennacherib and Esarhaddon in the seventh century (*see* AHIKAR, BOOK OF). Although it has not survived in the original Akkadian, an Aramaic version was discovered in Egypt among the fifth-century ELEPHANTINE PAPYRI. The work became widely diffused in many languages and recensions, and inspired such OT passages as Prov. 23:13-14 and 27:3.

Other genres were employed by Akkadian writers to transmit ethical teachings. A lengthy hymn to the god Shamash from about the tenth century contains moral precepts which led to its use as a schoolboy text. Slightly later, another work of instruction, the "Advice to a Ruler," was couched in the literary form of an omen collection.

b. Proverb collections. Unlike the Egyptians, Mesopotamian scribes drew up anthologies of proverbs, often associated by catchwords (*see* MNEMONIC DEVICES[S]). The earliest were in Sumerian and represent perhaps as many as twenty or more collections. During the following millennium, others were compiled and provided with Akkadian translations. One bilingual example is in Akkadian with a Hittite version. A few fragmentary collections are found solely in Akkadian. *See* *ANET,* pp. 425-26.

c. Scribal literature. Texts which dealt with the scribal schools, their pupils and teachers, were produced in Sumerian, to be followed later by a number of similar bilingual compositions. These were widely copied by schoolboys. As in Egypt, comprehensive lists of names of plants, animals, minerals, cities, countries, etc., were drawn up.

d. Theodicy literature. The questioning of divine justice is a theme unknown to Egypt but well attested in Mesopotamia. In a Sumerian work, "Man and His God," a sufferer finds salvation in humble submission to his deity. A long Akkadian poem entitled "I Will Praise the Lord of Wisdom" was popular as a school text (*ANET,* pp. 434-37). Composed between 1500 and 1200, it is a monologue by a nobleman in which the god Marduk is implicitly regarded as the ultimate source of all his woes. The sufferer is healed as the result of Marduk's gracious intervention. A somewhat later poem, the "Babylonian Theodicy," is a dialogue in which two friends debate the problem of the suffering of the righteous (*ANET,* pp. 438-40). As in the previous text, divine justice is declared to be incomprehensible, and deliverance is assured by unquestioning piety. *See* THEODICY[S].

e. Pessimistic literature. Only one Akkadian work falls into this category. Usually called the "Dialogue of Pessimism," it is a colloquy between a master and his slave, from the late Kassite period (*ANET,* pp. 437-38). In a satirical vein, various courses of action are proposed and rejected, and finally the only satisfactory solution is said to be death.

f. Fables and debates. A genre of texts in Sumerian from the Old Babylonian period consists of verbal contests between two antagonists. These may be animals, plants, seasons, minerals, or implements, all of which are endowed with speech. Each boasts of his own virtues and derides those of his rival, while a deity finally resolves the debate. Seven such texts are extant. Somewhat later are a few similar disputations in Akkadian. Plant and animal fables are much better represented than in Egypt. They are frequently included in proverb collections, and four occur in Ahikar, whereas one is contained in the legend of Etana.

Bibliography. Most of the texts referred to are translated in: J. B. Pritchard, ed., *ANET* (2nd ed., 1955); E. I. Gordon, *Sumerian Proverbs* (1959); W. G. Lambert, *Babylonian Wisdom Literature* (1960); E. Bresciani, *Letteratura e poesia dell'antico Egitto* (2nd ed., 1969); W. K. Simpson, ed., *The Literature of Ancient Egypt* (2nd ed., 1973); M. Lichtheim, *Ancient Egyptian Literature,* 2 vols. (1973-76).

For further reading consult: A. de Buck, "Het religieus Karakter der oudste Egyptische Wijsheid," *NTT,* XXI (1932), 322-49; J. J. A. van Dijk, *La sagesse suméro-accadienne* (1953); H. Gese, *Lehre und Wirklichkeit in der alten Weisheit* (1958); E. I. Gordon, "A New Look at the Wisdom of Sumer and Akkad," *BO,* XVII (1960), 122-52; J. Leclant *et al., Les sagesses du Proche-Orient ancien* (1963); H. H. Schmid, *Wesen und Geschichte der Weisheit, BZAW,* CI (1966).

R. J. WILLIAMS

***WISDOM IN THE OT.** An adequate definition of wisdom eludes interpreters of the OT. The many attempts to capture its essence succeed only in underscoring wisdom's enigmatic character. By analogy with Egyptian and Mesopotamian wisdom, scholars describe Israel's wisdom as humanistic, universalistic, eudaemonistic, nonhistorical. Still, differences stand out, rendering such analogy hazardous and prompting Egyptologists to avoid the word "wisdom" in favor of "wisdom literature." At least one authority in Babylonian wisdom has declared the term as applied to Israel a misnomer, because of the vast differences from Mesopotamian cultic wisdom. Though taking its stand upon human inquiry and asking above all about man's well-being, wisdom identifies human good with divine intention. Truths acquired by reason belong to no specific race, but are open to the whole of humanity. Nevertheless, Israel's wisdom functions within the context of a covenanted people and eventually embraces sacral traditions. Man's welfare is indeed the goal of wisdom; prudence, its manner of acting. Such pragmatism arises from a profound religious conviction about the order of the universe. Right behavior constitutes life itself, hence transcends mere eudaemonism. Every proverb or sentence arises within history, and the totality of wisdom literature creates a unique history of its own, both linguistic and ideological. Thus in a real sense wisdom is historical.

Recent definitions, though considerably more precise, fare little better: Wisdom is the art of succeeding in life; practical knowledge of laws governing the world, based on experience; the totality of experience transmitted by a father to his son as a spiritual testament; ability to cope; the right deed or word for the moment; an intellectual tradition. A satisfactory description of wisdom needs to face up to its complexity, for Israel's sages by no means speak with one voice.

Wisdom in the OT constitutes a body of literature, a way of thinking, and a tradition. Reaching back into the earliest stages of Israel's existence, the literature, at first oral, encapsulated lessons derived from experience. In a sense, it represented the legacy of a father to his children, embodying his authority within the extended family. In time, collections of this lore were gathered by those to whom such learning was entrusted, ostensibly for use in instruction. One such group is mentioned in superscriptions of Proverbs, namely, the "men of Hezekiah."

Each category of wisdom asks its distinctive questions and strives for its own special goals. Family or clan wisdom endeavors to master life, expresses itself in hortatory language, and makes copious use of proverbs. Courtly wisdom seeks to educate a select group of people, prefers secular vocabulary, and employs a didactic method in the pedagogic process. Scribal wisdom, more democratic than courtly, approaches a doctrinaire stance and makes full use of dialogue and admonition. Alternatively, from the perspective of the subject matter rather than of the sociological context, nature wisdom attempts to master reality for the sake of human survival and well-being. To accomplish this goal it draws up onomastica or noun lists and observes natural phenomena as they relate to man and the universe. Juridical and practical wisdom focuses upon human relationships in an ordered society, attempting to enrich life through cumulative experience. Addressing the perplexing issue of theodicy and the relationship between God and man, theological wisdom inquires about the first principle of knowledge and locates it within the religious dimension.

Out of this literature characterized by a particular type of thinking, a special tradition of the wise emerged. The sage acquired self-consciousness over against other approaches to reality, and slowly formulated his own field of discourse. Traditional lore was transmitted from father to son, teacher to student. Its contents ranged from prudential morality to radical questioning of life's meaning. The sage found no issue too trivial for his consideration, whether proper table manners or a fool's body language. Nor did he shy away from the profoundest of all questions, although painfully conscious of limitations imposed upon his knowledge. In time, wisdom honored her greatest king by making him the wise man par excellence. Dame Wisdom, it follows, became Solomon's bride and instructor in the art of living.

1. Wisdom as a corpus of literature
   a. Identification
   b. Literary forms
   c. Authorship and date
2. Wisdom as a way of thinking
   a. Anthropocentricity
   b. Radicality
   c. Humility
3. Wisdom as a tradition
   a. Clan, court, and scribe
   b. Solomon
   c. Dame Wisdom
   d. Creation

Bibliography

1. Wisdom as a corpus of literature. ***a. Identification.*** Traditionally wisdom literature comprises Proverbs, Job, Ecclesiastes, Sirach, Wisdom of Solomon, and a few Psalms. Several scholars have recently attempted to enlarge the scope of wisdom literature. Strong wisdom influence, if not actual compilation, is claimed for Gen. 1–11, 37–50; Exod. 34:6-7; Deuteronomy; II Sam. 9–20; I Kings 1–2;

Amos; Isaiah; Habakkuk; Jonah; Daniel; and Esther. Such attempts derive their impetus from a valid intuition: wisdom does not exist in a vacuum. The cumulative effect of such endeavors, however, renders wisdom diffuse beyond recognition. *See* JOSEPH STORY[S] §3; ESTHER, BOOK OF[S] §3; PROVERBS, BOOK OF[S].

Wisdom influence upon texts other than the acknowledged wisdom corpus can be established only by taking into account several factors: (1) the definition of wisdom as it can be ascertained; (2) stylistic and ideological peculiarities of wisdom literature; (3) attitudes toward wisdom and its representatives; and (4) wisdom's structural development, geographic spread, and ideologic formulation.

Two special problems merit further comment. The first concerns the circular reasoning into which scholars are forced. In short, we begin with an entity that we choose to label "wisdom," and work from it. We then exclude texts that differ essentially from that normative corpus of literature. Everything hinges upon the accuracy of our initial decision. Precisely at this point, comparison with non-Israelite wisdom literature becomes both an asset and a liability. In Israel, wisdom never acquires the cultic or divinatory quality that typifies Mesopotamian wisdom, nor does it have the aristocratic tone of Egyptian wisdom. A second difficulty is that wisdom shares a common vocabulary with prophecy, priestly discourse, and historiography. Certain words are universal, hence cannot be used to establish wisdom influence. Into this category of common linguistic stock fall such words as knowledge and intelligence, good and evil, wisdom and folly, obedience and disobedience. Impoverished indeed is the language of any group without such words. Even when an Israelite is called a wise man or woman, it does not necessarily imply a technical use of the adjective.

The presence of wisdom glosses in prophetic literature is generally acknowledged (Amos 5:13; Hos. 14:9 [H 10]). Does the matter stop there? Evidence of wisdom influence on Amos and Isaiah has been put forth with great vigor. Stylistic arguments include rhetorical questions that appeal to phenomena of nature, admonitions, calls to attention, and summary appraisal. Arguments based on a common vocabulary appeal to such words as counsel, wisdom, upright, council, understanding, father and son, hear, and keep. To these, theological issues are added, such as interest in astronomy, lack of concern for idolatry, a moralistic conception of salvation, Israel's place among the nations, attacks on luxurious living, Yahweh's plan for Israel, possession of the land, and belief in Israel's doom. Amos is thought to have moved within clan wisdom circles, while Isaiah either belonged to and turned his back upon the wisdom of the court or called sages back to their authentic faith. Isaiah thus forces representatives of a revived wisdom under King Hezekiah to recognize that true wisdom is from God, and that man possesses it only as charismatic gift. *See* ISAIAH[S] §2*c*.

Such conjectures highlight difficulties in characterizing wisdom's special qualities, whether stylistic, thematic, or theological. They also demonstrate the poverty of knowledge about clan wisdom over against courtly wisdom. Until some clarity about the distinctives of each kind of wisdom emerges, biblical interpreters need to exercise the same caution in dealing with intrabiblical influence that dominates discussions of extrabiblical parallels. Furthermore, texts such as Isa. 9:2-7 [H 1-6] and 11:1-9 do not necessarily demonstrate wisdom influence, since wisdom normally characterizes royalty.

On the other hand, prophets certainly endeavor to communicate with their audience, often entering into debate with representatives of alternative viewpoints. Use of wisdom vocabulary and ideas comes as no surprise, particularly when the argument moves *ad hominem*. Prophet and sage inevitably come to blows, for each represents a world view wholly alien to the other. Stated crassly, the extremes are revelation and reason. Given this disparity of viewpoint, the claim that Isaiah summons the wise to a true tradition long since abandoned carries little persuasive power.

b. Literary forms (*see* FORM CRITICISM; FORM CRITICISM, OT[S]). The basic unit of wisdom is the proverb, either as a statement or as instruction. Originally a sentence composed of two members in synonymous or antithetic parallelism, the proverb is a work of polished craftsmanship. Such expertise in use of literary devices excludes neither popular origin nor oral transmission. In time one-line proverbs give way to longer units linked together by particles, common letters, introductory words, numbers, themes, and rhetorical features. Pedagogy, too, enlarges the unit by threats and by appeal to motives, reasons, and consequences.

Other constitutive forms, as opposed to ornamental features such as PARONOMASIA, are riddle, fable and allegory, hymn and prayer, disputation, autobiographical narrative, lists, didactic poetry, and narrative. *See* RIDDLE[S].

Fables have disappeared from biblical wisdom, despite the tradition that Solomon spoke of animals, trees, fish, and the like, and in spite of their presence in Mesopotamian wisdom. Biblical proverbs about natural phenomena use them for didactic ends, as is the case with fables. Dialogue, however, is missing, and the form is quite distinct. Even the Solomon tradition does not necessarily imply fables, but can be understood as the gathering of noun lists. *See* FABLE.

ALLEGORY resembles fables in content if not form. Two allegories occur in Prov. 5:15-23, which characterizes a wife as a cistern, and in a related text, Eccl. 12:1-6, a profound description of old age. The connection with the allegory in Prov. 5 depends on understanding the unusual word for cistern as a *double-entendre,* which sums up the author's negative warning (remember, your grave awaits) and positive counsel (enjoy the woman you love while in the bloom of youth).

Hymnic passages abound in SIRACH and WISDOM OF SOLOMON, and strongly resemble texts throughout the OT. Unique to wisdom is the hymn about Lady Wisdom, while creation dominates other hymnic motifs. Both themes address themselves explicitly to the problem of THEODICY. A special feature of Sirach's praise of the creator is an understanding of complementary pairs ordained in the beginning to assure the principle of retribution. When pressed to defend God's justice, Sirach ultimately abandons rational argumentation in favor of a crescendo of hymnic praise.

A didactic element pervades wisdom prayer, even as early as Prov. 30:7-9. It strongly characterizes the pronounced prayer influence within Sirach (22:17–23:6; 36:1-17; 51:1-12) and Wisdom of Solomon (9:1-18; 11:21–12:27), although in the latter the form has no clear delimitation. Here is evidence that the sage has become a worshiper.

Disputation, consisting of mythological introduction, debate, and divine resolution, best characterizes the biblical JOB. Elements of lament justify the claim that Job provides a paradigm of an answered lament, but not principally so. The book also consists of a lawsuit against God, including an oath of innocence, but disputation aptly describes its total structure. Parallels within Mesopotamian culture provide the probable prototype of Job; the biblical dress differs radically because of the nature of Israel's God. Imagined discourse, a variant of disputation, appears often in contexts treating the problem of delayed retribution (Wisd. Sol. 2:1-20; 5:1-13) and false thinking in general (Prov. 1:11-14, 22-33; 3:28; 5:12-14; and *passim*). Imagined speech stimulates correct thinking and ridicules false reasoning. Its tone is often strident, the victim being consigned to destruction.

Autobiographical narrative, otherwise known as reflection or confession, derives from wisdom's experiential base. Possessing a rich heritage in Egyptian wisdom, it was spoken originally by kings, and later by lesser individuals. Two examples occur in Proverbs (4:3-9; 24:30-34), which may be compared to Ps. 37. The author of Ecclesiastes uses the autobiographical narrative most effectively (Eccl. 1:12–2:26), as do Sirach (33:16-18; 51:13-22) and Wisdom of Solomon (7–9). In the latter text, devotional confession replaces the earlier skepticism of Ecclesiastes.

Evidence for existence of onomastica in Israel is meager. The tradition about Solomon's composition of "three thousand proverbs" and "a thousand and five" songs about trees, beasts, birds, reptiles, and fish (I Kings 4:32-33 [H 5:12-13]) may allude to numerical proverbs and possibly derives from belief that prosperity demonstrates wisdom. Since Solomon was the wealthiest king in Israel, he must have been a sage par excellence. It follows that he coined proverbs and composed songs, as did all great sages of the ancient Near East. On the other hand, certain biblical texts bear striking resemblance to onomastica from Egypt (Job 38–41; Sirach 43; Wisd. Sol. 7:17-20; cf. also Sirach 38:24–39:11; Job 28; 36:27–37:13). Much of the information joined together in this fashion, however, does not necessitate a theory of encyclopedic noun lists. Differences between these lists and extrabiblical onomastica require the hypothesis of radical transformation. It can be argued that Solomon's uniqueness as a sage derives from an innovative clothing of lists in poetic dress and use in didactic settings, but no evidence for such form or usage exists.

Didactic narrative (Prov. 7:6-23), problem poetry (Ps. 49), and historical retrospect (Sirach 40–50; Wisd. Sol. 10–19), while similar to non-wisdom texts, have distinctive features justifying their inclusion as wisdom forms.

It is not possible to discover the settings of the various literary forms. With the possible exception of sentence and riddle, the forms probably had a didactic setting. Many proverbs reflect an agrarian economy, although a small number seem more at home in the earliest life of the clan, when law and wisdom go hand in hand. The language of wisdom prayers suggests that the teacher ultimately becomes a worshiper.

Wisdom literature maintains constant tension between optimism and pessimism. In so doing, it remains true to its source—experience—and to its fundamental character—applicability. Each generation tests truths acquired by previous ones, discarding whatever contradicts present experience. Ideally every claim is open to contradiction, but dogma does crystallize in the area of retribution. The result is a crisis evoking dissent literature, in which the weaknesses of optimism are subjected to close scrutiny. The profundity of Job, Ecclesiastes, and Prov. 30:1-4 derives in part from the truth resting behind more optimistic literature (Proverbs). Appropriately, Sirach displays a wedding of the two moods, abiding trust in divine goodness and anxious questioning of that same goodness.

c. Authorship and date. The sole instance in which it is possible to date a wisdom text is Sirach, the prologue of which allows us to date that book around 190 B.C. Language is a decisive factor in yet another case. Wisdom of Solomon is intelligible only against a Hellenistic setting, perhaps in the last quarter of the second century B.C. Ecclesiastes employs linguistic characteristics suggesting, if not demanding, a date in the third century. The language and content of Job accord best with a sixth-century date, although older material is certainly used. Proverbs comes from various periods, 1–9 being the latest collection, possibly postexilic. In a sense such literature is timeless, losing little by concealing its date of origin or literary formulation.

2. Wisdom as a way of thinking. *a. Anthropocentricity.* The fundamental premise of wisdom is belief in order. Implicit is a world view of reality as subject to laws established by the Creator, to governing principles discernible by use of reason. Wisdom seeks to understand these rules, to discover the appropriate deed for the moment. Asking, "What is good for man?" the sage seeks to prolong life and to assure its highest quality. Everything is subject to the sage's scrutiny, particularly human and animal behavior. Since conclusions are based on cumulative experience, they can be verified. On the basis of experience, some things are judged better than others. Although stated as advice, within the wisdom circle a saying bears the authority of its spokesman and tradition.

In time the open system hardened, approaching dogma, particularly in the realm of RETRIBUTION. The ensuing struggle led to the recognition of limits imposed upon human knowledge, especially in regard to divine inscrutability. A profound theological conviction undergirded the sage's view of reality. God has constituted the universe so as to reward virtue and punish vice, but such optimism led to a spiritual crisis when justice gave way to capricious action. The result is despair, or a faith that is held in spite of all contradictory evidence.

This process of theologizing comes about in three stages. The first introduces the fear of God as wisdom's basic principle. Much early wisdom appears secular in mood and content. Its fundamental purpose was to encapsulate precious observations about reality for the benefit of posterity. The subject matter is largely domestic: agrarian interests and natural phenomena abound. Still, this valuable insight into the way things hold together was gained by those who belonged to the people of the Lord, and thus saw themselves as a covenant community. Small wonder they came to express their faith in God and in the course of daily happenings in one and the same breath. Admonitions, motivations, and threats are soon strengthened by appeal to common faith. Such appeal links up with the ancient concept of order bestowed upon the universe by a deity who rewards goodness and punishes evil.

A second stage attempts to deal with the difficult problem of divine presence in the world of human discourse. How can truth emerge from observation of nature and culture? Can revelation take place within ordinary human decisions apart from prophetic oracle, priestly ritual, poetic vision? Representatives of wisdom are convinced that their observations about reality are congruent with ultimate truth held in trust by God alone. They express this conviction in terms of a heavenly figure, Wisdom, who enlightens sages by dwelling in their midst, thereby allowing them to salvage something of the ancient Near Eastern fertility concept, that highly desirable bride more at home in the divine than human sphere.

Sirach represents a third stage marked by the identification of wisdom and TORAH. Once this equation is made, sacred history enters wisdom circles. Sirach introduces us to the sage at worship, singing hymns, and giving voice to prayer. For the author, the actors in the divine-human drama of salvation deserve hymnic praise.

b. Radicality. Wisdom thinking combines a radical questioning of the foundations upon which knowledge rests with a conservative attitude toward tradition. Though given to simplification, particularly in distinguishing wisdom from folly, the sage realizes the incompleteness of knowledge. Appreciative of lessons learned from the past, he strives to penetrate beneath surface similarities to essential data of experience. His willingness to discard treasured values in favor of new ones more in harmony with experience comes close to blasphemy, especially where divine justice is under discussion. But even the book whose rejection of wisdom's claim to full knowledge is most radical, Ecclesiastes, summons sages to a fundamental recognition of their limitations.

c. Humility. From the outset the wise feel humble in the face of mystery, the hidden quality of human life. They express such humility in numerous ways. Perhaps best known is the assertion that "man proposes but God disposes." The Israelite sage knows the battle belongs to the Lord regardless of human preparation for conflict, and ultimately admits the race is not to the swift, for time and chance play indiscriminately. God and king are even set over against one another as if in competition: "It is the glory of God to conceal things, but the glory of kings to search things out" (Prov. 25:2). Consequently, one must be content with unanswered questions. This inability to penetrate certain mysteries prompts at least two sages to shrug their shoulders with resignation. The mysterious Agur (Prov. 30) comes close to rejecting the possibility of grasping reality, and the author of Ecclesiastes is fond of asking, "Who knows?" in such a way as to dismiss a question as unanswerable. Such humility before ultimate mystery does not mean, however, a diminution of the significance attributed to reason. By the exacting use of reason, man can know much about the nature of things and people. Reason is a gift of God and equips mankind for life, and so refusal to use it wisely constitutes an insult to Creator and creature alike. This is why the fool is considered wicked. His intractable ways and his refusal to learn endanger cosmic order, and must be offset by positive action. Sages, then, create and sustain the fabric of the universe.

3. Wisdom as a tradition. ***a. Clan, court, and scribe.*** Jer. 18:18 distinguishes three separate types of religious leadership and their essential communicative vehicle. The prophet proclaims a word; the priest dispenses Torah; and the sage gives counsel. The history of each group lies shrouded in mystery. Wisdom's development appears to concentrate upon three distinct periods: clan, court, school. Each generates its own tradition.

Clan wisdom gives birth to a world view and coins a special vocabulary. The father of a clan instructs his children, especially his sons, about mastering life. His counsel is authoritative, backed by a father's authority and an appeal to past experience. Years of observing nature and man teach the sage the predictable character of reality, instilling in him a conviction that the universe is governed by One who desires and maintains order. To communicate the means of ordering life in accord with this cosmic order, the wise man becomes an active teacher. Students receive the benefit of years' experience and acquire their fathers' vocabulary. Slowly technical terms, such as "my son," "instruction," and "fear of the Lord," emerge as wisdom's essence or first principle.

b. Solomon. In time, another quite different tradition enters the sage's world. The centrality of monarchy in Israel under David and Solomon and the necessity of good counsel in high places led to a close connection between king and wisdom. David must be content with astute advisors. Solomon, however, acquires a reputation for wisdom superior to that of any other king in the East. Whether traditions about Solomon's wisdom are grounded in actual fact or constitute a "mirage" can scarcely be answered. *See* §1*b*.

The widely held view of a Solomonic enlightenment takes seriously the tradition about a king's commitment to learning. Based primarily on analogy with Egyptian court life, it gives credence to the impetus behind such legends as that of Solomon's judgment concerning the infant, his dreams at Gibeon, and the visit by the Queen of Sheba. Such material provides little support for drawing historical conclusions, particularly since it was customary to honor a ruler by describing him as wise. Furthermore, a positive view of Solomon's connections with wisdom has too often been coupled with an assumption about a movement from a view in which everything was sacred to a kind of humanism under Solomon. No such revolution can be demonstrated; the theory errs in two directions: early Israelite thought was not thoroughly sacral, and Solomon's era was no enlightenment. If anything, it was a time of oppression, a suppressing of human dignity unsurpassed in Israel's history. Even if one were to view the JOSEPH STORY and Succession Narrative as expressions of the self-understanding of wisdom, which in itself is doubtful, the thesis of a Solomonic revolution finds minimal support.

Admittedly, these narratives share certain concerns with the wise. The Joseph story is sparing in reference to divine activity, recognizes an opposition between human intentions and divine economy, and appreciates the nature of humanity. Similarly, the Succession Narrative demonstrates the bad consequence of pride and the significance of a right word. It shows how results follow from acts, and it probes the inner life, especially that of great individuals. Even the Yahwist makes skillful use of themes found in wisdom, particularly the concern for one's name and the folly of inordinate pride. This, however, does not point to a wisdom origin for these literary traditions. Differences far outnumber similarities. Many of the supposed wisdom affinities give expression to fundamental human values. Such themes are present in Priestly Torah, prophetic word, and wise counsel. They prove nothing about dependency upon wisdom thinking.

The attempt to relate the Joseph story to wisdom by distinguishing a story within a story, namely Gen. 39–41, suffers from the same weakness of theories about glosses. The narrative as a whole has many non-wisdom themes; any theory of a wisdom kernel must reckon seriously with the larger setting. Theological interpretations of the Yahwistic narrative in light of biblical proverbs have modern religious value, but derive whatever legitimacy they have from the common life of Israel that gave birth to proverb and story. No theory of wisdom influence is necessary. Often claims of contact strike one as rather forced: the cunning of the serpent, curse upon the land and man, unfortunate results of hot anger, association of righteousness and favor, dishonoring of one's father. Nothing in this listing of supposed wisdom thought demands a sage's hand.

Recent attempts to relate wisdom and history arise from a correct premise that sages care about human history. Courtly wisdom, if such there ever was in Israel, aimed at steering the course of political events in a direction that assures well-being for the populace. In such circles the king played a decisive role, and idealized portraits became useful. Still the claim that the Yahwistic narrative serves as an apologetic work for David moves beyond such portraiture. So far no one has demonstrated that there was in wisdom a belief in a divine plan for history. Once historical data do enter wisdom's domain, emphasis falls on cultic matters, even where David and Solomon are concerned. Cf. YAHWIST[S].

c. Dame Wisdom. Traditions about royal wisdom stand over against yet another manifestation of understanding, this time in feminine form. As early as Prov. 8 and Job 28 speculation about wisdom's spokesman on earth gives voice to a tradition about Lady Wisdom. Strongly reminiscent of extrabiblical models, Maat and Ishtar, this striking figure now takes up residence on earth and extends invitations to all who seek life. Unruffled by competition, she meets her potential guests in the hustle of daily activity. In deuterocanonical wisdom literature she chooses to dwell in Israel, at Jerusalem, and assumes the form of Mosaic Torah. As such she becomes an expression of divine personality, poured out upon special individuals, to one of whom (Solomon) she gives herself in marriage.

d. Creation. An integral relationship between wisdom and creation exists. The prominence of creation in wisdom literature stems from something more than simple belief in divine ordering. Seldom does creation stand alone. Rather, it functions to buttress belief in divine justice. The Creator of the ends of the earth sees all deeds, good and evil, despite denial by vicious men that God takes note of their doings. Furthermore, he created the universe in such a way that sin is punished, virtue rewarded. Even when such reward or punishment is delayed for one reason or another, the prosperity of wicked men does not refute belief in justice. Consequently, the sage affirms trust in God by participating in a crescendo of hymnic praise.

In time alien traditions were incorporated within wisdom thought. Knowledge acquired by means of reason joined hands with the fruit of revelation. At last "instruction" utilizes examples from Israel's sacred history, paradigms both negative and positive, as well as traditional observations of nature and experience. Israel's wisdom finally parts company with that of her neighbors, and surrenders completely to a concept of an elect people.

Bibliography. Comprehensive bibliographies appear in J. L. Crenshaw, ed., *Studies in Ancient Israelite Wisdom* (1975), and "Wisdom," in *OT Form Criticism,* ed. J. H. Hayes (1974), pp. 225-64. Other recent works include: C. Bauer-Kayatz, *Einführung in die alttestamentliche Weisheit* (1969); W. Brueggemann, *In Man We Trust* (1972); H. J. Hermisson, *Studien zur israelitischen Spruchweisheit* (1968); J. Marböck, *Weisheit im Wandel* (1971); G. von Rad, *Wisdom in Israel* (1972); H. H. Schmid, *Wesen und Geschichte der Weisheit* (1966); R. B. Y. Scott, *The Way of Wisdom in the OT* (1971), and "The Study of the Wisdom Literature," *Int.,* XXIV (1970), 20-45; P. W. Skehan, *Studies in Israelite Poetry and Wisdom* (1971); R. N. Whybray, *The Intellectual Tradition in the OT* (1974).

J. L. CRENSHAW

WISDOM IN THE NT [σοφία; cf. σοφός, "wise"]. Although the word itself does not often appear in the NT, the wisdom tradition plays a significant role.

1. Introduction
  a. Overview of use of the word
  b. Influence of OT and Jewish wisdom
  c. Hymn-like passages
  d. The problem of religious backgrounds
  e. Motifs
2. Significance of wisdom in earliest Christian thought
  a. Function of wisdom in the NT
  b. Jewish doctrine of the hypostasis of wisdom
3. Wisdom material in the NT
  a. Jesus and the Synoptic gospels
  b. John
  c. Paul
  d. Deutero-Pauline letters
  e. Hebrews
  f. James
Bibliography

1. Introduction. ***a. Overview of use of the word.*** In Matt. 12:42; Luke 11:31 (cf. Acts 7:22) the word is used as a secular term to praise the wisdom of Solomon. Jesus' wisdom is extolled in a similar way (Mark 6:2; Luke 2:40, 52). The wisdom of God is referred to in Luke 11:49; Eph. 3:10, and also in doxologies (Rom. 11:33; 16:27; Rev. 7:12). The wisdom of God speaks to the world (Luke 11:49) and sends messengers (Matt. 23:34). The wisdom of the risen Christ is also praised (Rev. 5:12); in him all the treasures of wisdom and knowledge are hidden (Col. 2:3).

The faithful have received wisdom as a gift from the Spirit (Eph. 1:8; Col. 1:9); therefore, they should strive for wisdom (Eph. 5:15; Col. 4:5). There are excellent people of wisdom in the communities (Acts 6:3, 10), and wisdom should be taught in the church (Eph. 3:10; Col. 1:28; cf. Jas. 3:13).

The most important discussion of how divine and earthly wisdom contradict each other occurs in I Cor. 1–2 (with 3:18-19, cf. II Cor. 1:12; *see* §3*ci below*). *See also* Matt. 11:25; Col. 2:23; Jas. 3:13-18.

Certain stylistic elements are shared with the OT and Judaism, for instance the connection between wisdom and "Spirit," πνεῦμα (Acts 6:3, 10, etc.; cf. Wisd. Sol. 1:5-8; 7:7) or "power," δύναμις (Rev. 5:12; 7:12; cf. Job 12:13). The occurrence of "wisdom" with certain synonyms is also typical: "knowledge," γνῶσις (Col. 2:3; cf. Eccl. 1:17) or "insight," σύνεσις (Col. 1:9; cf. Dan. 2:21, LXX; Eph. 1:9; Dan 2:21, Theod.). The combination of "Spirit" and "power" especially shows that wisdom is not something to be known passively, but is an active force.

b. Influence of OT and Jewish wisdom. The literary forms and the content of OT and later Jewish wisdom literature appear much more often than does the word "wisdom" itself. These include ethical instructions in the form of aphorisms, which are put together in collections of proverbs (Proverbs; Ecclesiasticus; in the NT, the SERMON ON THE MOUNT [Matt. 5–7]; Rom. 12; Letter of James), short ethical discourses (Jas. 2–3; Heb. 3:12-19; 4:11-13; 6:1-12, etc.), lists of virtues and vices. These latter are sometimes in the tradition of the dualistic development of Jewish wisdom (Wisdom of Solomon; Philo); and are therefore double lists (Gal. 5:19-23; Col. 3:5-17; *see* LISTS, ETHICAL §5; LISTS, ETHICAL[S] §1). Certain apologetic discourses concerning the relationship of the one true God to dead idols (I Cor. 8:1-6; I Thess. 1:9-10) may be noted, as well as the allegorical and typological interpretation of scripture (I Cor. 10; Gal. 4:21-31; esp. Hebrews).

c. Hymn-like passages. Some of these (e.g., John 1:1 ff.; Col. 1:15 ff.; I Cor. 13) follow the stylistic tradition of Jewish wisdom poetry in which wisdom was personified (cf. Prov. 8; Wisd. Sol. 7:22 ff.; Ecclus. 24; Bar. 3:9 ff.; Job 28). The personifying of "wisdom," "word" (λόγος), "image" (εἰκών) developed in connection with the heightening of God's transcendence; occasionally the influence of Hellenistic mythology is recognizable (Ecclus. 24). Identification of wisdom with the law is typical (Ecclus. 24; Bar. 4:1).

d. The problem of religious backgrounds. The OT and Jewish influence in NT wisdom is fundamental. However, certain stylistic elements are reminiscent of Greek philosophy (Platonism, Stoicism), e.g., the "diatribe," the short, popular philosophical discourse. But this form had also entered into Jewish literature and penetrated into earliest Christianity from there. There are also some points of contact respecting content, e.g., with the Stoic "natural theology" in Rom. 1–2; such ideas were also transmitted by Hellenistic Judaism.

Many scholars have sought to derive the early Christian hypostases from GNOSTICISM. Sophia (wisdom) did play an exceedingly important role in the Gnostic soteriological myth, but the development of Gnosticism was later than that of earliest Christianity. The occasional relationship of motifs between the NT and Gnosticism results from their common heritage in Near Eastern and Jewish thought.

e. Motifs. "Wisdom" operates conceptually without reference to time and history. This is evident in the concepts of manifestation and hypostasis (σοφία, εἰκών, δόξα), and in Paul's antithesis of "letter" (γράμμα) and "Spirit" (πνεῦμα) (Rom. 2:29; 7:6; II Cor. 3:6). While a synthesis between wisdom and the temporal concepts of APOCALYPTICISM could occur (Enoch 42; Wisdom of Solomon), as forms of thought they are fundamentally different.

The basic theological motif of the wisdom tradition is that God is wise (Ecclus. 1:8): wisdom belongs to him (Dan. 2:20-23), befits him alone (Wisd. Sol. 9:9), and all wisdom comes from him (Ecclus. 1:1). Since God gives wisdom (Dan. 2:20), one may ask him for it (II Chr. 1:10). Since only God discloses wisdom, people must find their way to him to obtain it, and it is possible to do so (I Esd. 4:59-60). There are teachers and teachings which convey it; the beginning of wisdom is the fear of the Lord (Prov. 1:7).

There are three types of hypostatized wisdom which reappear in the NT (*see* §2 *below*): (*a*) Concealed wisdom. Only God knows the way to find her (Job 28; Bar. 3:9). (*b*) Wisdom close at hand (Prov. 8:22 ff.). She was created by God and helped with the creation of the world. This means that the world is infused with wisdom and can be spiritually illuminated and mastered by people who acquire wisdom. (*c*) Vanished wisdom. She once appeared in the world, but people rejected her and she retreated into heaven. From there she will someday appear again to a chosen few (Enoch 42).

2. Significance of wisdom in earliest Christian thought. ***a. Function of wisdom in the NT.*** Because Luther interpreted the NT in the light of Paul's doctrine of justification by faith, he moved the Letter of James, which is explicitly wisdom literature (*see* JAMES, LETTER OF[S] §§1-2) to the edge of the canon. The question is, What function can wisdom have within the framework of the proclamation of Christ's act of redemption? Both exegetes and systematic theologians must work to find criteria to determine the center of the Scripture. A historical understanding will recognize that Jewish wisdom did not invade the church from outside, but that the first Christians, as Jews, grew up with it, brought it with them into the church, and kept it as their inheritance. The God of the Christian faith is no other than the God of the wisdom of Israel, the one God, the creator. An example of this relationship is the pattern of missionary preaching in I Thess. 1:9-10: the one, true, living God is contrasted to the idols, and the christological kerygma is introduced into this framework. Wisdom thus serves as an element of continuity from the OT and Judaism to earliest Christianity.

b. Jewish doctrine of the hypostasis of wisdom. The process in Judaism by which wisdom became a hypostasis had particular importance for the development of Christology in the church. In Christianity faith in one God is connected to faith in one Lord as mediator both of creation and of salvation (I Cor. 8:6). This prevents a dualistic separation of God and the world. The doctrine of hypostasis is basic to the development of the idea of pre-existence; the uniquely Christian element in the idea is its transfer to the historical person of Jesus.

3. Wisdom material in the NT. ***a. Jesus and the Synoptic gospels.*** The history of "wisdom" in the NT begins with the preaching of Jesus and his wisdom teachings recorded in the Synoptic gospels (e.g., Matt. 6:19–7:23; cf. 7:24-27). It is probable that proverbs from other traditions (e.g., Jewish) entered the Synoptics, but it is certain that Jesus was himself a teacher of wisdom. Were this not the case, the volume of wisdom in the Christian tradition would be inexplicable. Not only is Jesus spoken of in the synoptic traditions as wise (Mark 6:2; cf. Matt. 12:42; Luke 11:31—here, Jesus is "something greater than Solomon," i.e., than his wisdom), but in some places he is also presented as the envoy of wisdom to extol her reputation (cf. Prov. 1:2-7; 8:1-36). He is even ultimately identified (by Matthew) with hypostatized wisdom.

Wisdom motifs are used in the interpretation of Jesus' preaching and his person (Matt. 11:16-19; Luke 7:31-35). Like John the Baptist, Jesus was rejected. The theme of the rejection of wisdom is bound up with the theme of the outcast and the poor. Wisdom acknowledges her "children," the tax collectors and sinners, who concede her truth. Thus, Jesus is her spokesman. When Matthew wrote the "deeds" of wisdom (11:19) instead of the "children" of wisdom (Luke 7:35), he identified Jesus with wisdom itself (cf. "the deeds of the Christ," Matt. 11:2).

The paradox of being chosen is yet more intense in Matt. 11:25 (Luke 10:21). This notion has a long history (e.g., Isa. 29:14; cf. I Cor. 1:19 below; 1QS 11.6), including the motif of the fall of the mighty and the exaltation of the lowly (Ecclus. 10:12-18; Luke 1:51-53; II Cor. 10:1 ff.). This intensification comes from relating the person of Jesus to the SON OF MAN. The same understanding of revelation is assimilated by Paul and expressed in his own way (I Cor. 1:18 ff.; *see* §3*ci below*). Finally, in Matt. 11:27 Jesus himself is defined as the content of revelation; wisdom proclaims itself. The clearest expression of this is the "I am" sayings in the Gospel of John. Matthew appends a further wisdom saying, wisdom's invitation to find rest for the soul (11:28-30; cf. Ecclus. 51:23-30 and GTh 90).

According to Luke, wisdom issued a threat (11:49-51). When Matthew attributed the threat to Jesus (23:34-36) he once more identified Jesus with wisdom; the speaker is a being beyond history. Do we have here a citation from a Jewish wisdom writing, which is now related to Jesus and his representatives (cf. the dispatch of the servants of wisdom in Prov. 9:3)? This passage shows the synthesis of wisdom and prophecy. The motif of the prophets' destiny of suffering is developed in conjunction with the Deuteronomic view of history (*see* DEUTERONOMIC HISTORY, THE [S]). The lament over Jerusalem (Matt. 23:37-39; Luke 13:34-35) is also spoken by a being beyond history; hence, Jesus as Wisdom. The motif of the disappearance of rejected wisdom and the prospect of its return is related here to Jesus' death and second coming.

b. John. The word "wisdom" is never used in the Gospel or Letters of John. John 1:1-18 praises Jesus as the pre-existent, incarnate Logos (*see* WORD, THE §5*b*), and, as a hypostasis, Logos is analogous to Sophia (*see* PHILO JUDEUS §3). The Logos hymn belongs also stylistically to the wisdom tradition; it has been conjectured that it had a pre-Christian origin. In this hymn the Logos is pre-existent and the mediator of creation; it appeared as light and was rejected, but it was accepted by a few of "its own." The new Christian element is that the historical person Jesus is proclaimed as the cosmic Logos. This includes the notion, unacceptable to Judaism, of a real incarnation and not an illusory one. The description of the power of the Logos is now identical with the story of Jesus (as interpreted by John), including his death and resurrection and the sending forth of the Spirit. This is a christological transformation of wisdom: the content of Jesus' message is Jesus himself and his having been sent from the Father ("I am . . .").

c. Paul. The word group is concentrated in I Cor. 1–2 (and Colossians, *see* §*d below*). The Jewish style of doxology is recognizable in Rom. 11:33; 16:27 (cf. style of Rev. 5:12; 7:12).

i. *The crisis of "worldly" wisdom in Corinth.* The Corinthians had been boasting of their "knowledge" (I Cor. 8:1-6) and of their consequent freedom (I Cor. 6:12; 10:23). Although they honored the exalted Lord, they neglected the historical act of salvation, the Cross. In opposition to this Paul criticized in a fundamental way all "worldly" wisdom, including the religious wisdom of the Corinthian congregation. His criticism of worldly wisdom was strictly theological; it did not refer to secular knowledge, but rather to the kind of wisdom which tries to control God and salvation, which serves the "glory" of human beings and their boasting before God. Paul did not confront an issue of intelligence and stupidity, but rather the human self-praise of the unbelieving and lost. He proclaimed the word of the Cross as the destruction of this "glorying" (for the Greeks, their wisdom; for the Jews, their demand for signs; both expected revelation to be subjected to their criteria). Thus Paul considers the topic "wisdom" as a christological one. He refers to traditional thought, explicitly to the OT (I Cor. 1:19-20), and to the doctrine of God as creator, who gave the world the possibility of knowing him "in the wisdom of God" (1:21; and honoring him, Rom. 1:21), but whose revelation of wisdom was rejected by the world. God responded to that rejection with the "foolish" wisdom of the revelation through the Cross. The motif of *disappeared* wisdom is basic here (cf. Enoch 42; John 1:1 ff.), but it is significantly transformed by the replacement of the ahistorical mythology with a Christology historically understood. This motif is especially related to Bar. 3, even in style (a series of questions which reveal the absence of wisdom, or its perversion by human beings).

Paul develops a double antithesis: (*a*) wisdom of God—wisdom of the world; (*b*) wisdom—foolishness. In contrast to the Jewish tradition, he does not say that wisdom withdrew, but rather that God turned the wisdom of the world into foolishness. Therefore, no claim to have knowledge of God is valid, except through the "word of the cross." Revelation is not only a teaching concerning the true nature of God (as the wisdom tradition understands; Wisd. Sol. 13–15), but it is also God's action to save the world for faith (cf. II Cor. 5:19). Paul has transformed the wisdom motifs by reformulating the notion of the fall of the mighty and the raising up of the lowly in accord with his "theology of the cross." Paul transforms wisdom statements about God's *being*—that God *is* wise and *makes* one wise—into statements about God's revelation in Christ—Christ is God's wisdom for us (I Cor. 1:30). A comparison with the juxtaposition of wisdom, signs, and kerygma in Q (Matt. 12:38-42; Luke 11:29-32) is especially interesting.

Reliance on the tradition is even clearer in the partially analogous discussions in Rom. 1:18-32. Although Christology is missing there, it does appear in the larger context (Rom. 1:16-17, taken with Rom. 3:19-26): Christ is the revelation of God's righteousness. Here again Paul debates the fundamental topic of revelation and rejection (cf. esp. Wisdom of Solomon) or, more exactly, perversion of revelation by people who, instead of honoring the creator, honor the creation in images of people and even of animals. The allusions to creation and fall are not made in the style of salvation history (cf. Rom. 5:12-21), but in a timeless style that is oriented to the wisdom tradition. It also had been assumed (in Wisdom of Solomon) that ethical perversion necessarily follows religious perversion. Paul radically sharpened the issues. Wisdom of Solomon endeavored to lead persons from ignorance to knowledge; Paul's presupposition was that the human race is hopelessly caught in its guilt and can only be saved by the revelation of God's righteousness (Rom. 3:21-26).

In Rom. 1:18-32 notions of Greek religious philosophy, especially of Stoic natural theology, may be recognized. But it is also especially clear in this context that Paul was acquainted with these notions as modified by Jewish thought.

I Cor. 2:6-16 is related to the notion of *hidden* wisdom (cf. the key word "secret," vs. 7). It becomes accessible to humans only by a miracle, by the Spirit (of the Lord, vs. 16).

ii. *Wisdom texts in Paul's letters* can be recognized by their style and themes. (Some of them are also present in the debate with proponents of Corinthian enthusiasm.) There is, e.g., the (timeless) typological interpretation of the exodus story in I Cor. 10:1-5, to which there are interesting parallels in Philo.

I Cor. 11:2-16 appropriates concepts of manifestation in Hellenistic-Jewish style. The relationships of God to Christ and of God to human beings are interpreted in the category of archetype and image, i.e., in the sense of ontological relationships. This is a speculative cosmology which is foreign to Paul's thought. It was originally a Platonic view of God, the world, and humanity, and was also absorbed into Judaism (Philo), where it was modified under the influence of Gen. 1:26-27. Here some of Paul's pre-Christian theological training becomes visible, especially in I Cor. 11:7 where Christ is missing in the archetype-image series (contrast vs. 3).

A key passage for Paul's hermeneutics is II Cor. 3:4-18, where serving the old covenant is interpreted as serving death. In spite of the notions of "old" and "new," the old and new covenants are not contrasted with respect to salvation history, but as "letter" and "Spirit," as mortal and immortal "splendor" (δόξα).

The motif of wisdom close at hand lies behind Rom. 10:6-13, which is an argument to support the thesis that Christ is the end of the law (vs. 4). The argument begins with the contrast between the law of Moses and justification by faith. (For the relationship between wisdom and righteousness *see* esp. the first part of Wisdom of Solomon; for that between wisdom and Law *see* Ecclus. 24.) Paul rejected christologically the notion of their identity. In this case a continuity of tradition may be seen, as Paul himself pointed out. It begins with Deut. 30:12-14, continues, among other places, in Bar. 3:9-37 (in connection with hidden wisdom), and reappears in II Esd. 4:7-12 (later than Paul). Additional traces may be found in Ps. 107:26; Prov. 30:4, etc. For the format of ascent and descent, cf. also John 1:51; 3:13; Eph. 4:8.

Paul also gave a wisdom-oriented interpretation of scripture in Rom. 7:7-25, where he referred to the story of Paradise and the Fall. But in contrast to Rom. 5:12-21, he did not place Adam and the Adamic wisdom tradition in the pattern of salvation history, but brought them into a direct relationship, by replacing "Adam" with "I," i.e., the unbeliever.

A particularly impressive wisdom text is the praise of love in I Cor. 13. The praise of truth in I Esd. 4:34-40 is a parallel in style and content. Significantly, neither God nor Christ is explicitly mentioned; love appears as an autonomous force. But that is only formally true. For Paul this wisdom discourse is Christian, since for him "love" is a christologically defined concept (Rom. 5:3-11; 8:35-39). This is shown in the eschatological perspective with which the praise of love concludes. *See* §1*b above* for the wisdom format of the PARENESIS in Rom. 12.

d. Deutero-Pauline letters. The style of wisdom literature continued, especially in Colossians and Ephesians (Col. 2:3; Eph. 3:10, here in the context of the "revelation schema"). These letters can almost be characterized as Christian wisdom literature. Colossians develops wisdom polemically against a fraudulent "philosophy" (Col. 2:8); Ephesians develops it thematically and meditatively.

In Col. 1:15-21 there is a christological hymn which refers back to the hypostasis "image" (εἰκών) (cf. Paul himself in II Cor. 4:4). The hymn was probably already extant, since there is some indication that the author of Colossians inserted new material. The original hymn is based on the correspondence between the act of creation and the act of salvation of the "image," as the first-born of creation and the first-born from the dead. The cosmological meaning culminates in the sentence: "He (Christ as the image) is the head of the body" (vs. 18). The word "body" originally meant the cosmos, but the author of Colossians relates the hymn more forcefully to the historical act of salvation, and interprets the body as the church.

e. Hebrews. A wisdom-oriented interpretation of scripture (typology) dominates the Letter to the Hebrews (*see* TYPOLOGY[S]). Its style becomes most visible when compared with Philo, whose exegesis is basically ahistorical. The exegesis in Hebrews does have a temporal dimension, because of its Christology and its christologically defined notion of the new pilgrim people of God, and because of the contrast between the first and the second covenants (8:6-13). The reflections on Melchizedek in ch. 7 are also part of the wisdom tradition, as is the listing of faithful witnesses in ch. 11.

f. James. The entire Letter of James is a wisdom document in parenetic style. Since the name of Christ appears only twice, it has been assumed that this was a Jewish writing. However, in addition to these references there is evidence of the transposition of wisdom into Christian thought patterns. In any case, the letter documents the extent to which Christianity was able to retain Jewish wisdom.

Bibliography. General: U. Wilckens, "σοφία, κτλ.," *TDNT,* VII (1964), 496 ff. (Judaism) and 514 ff. (NT), with bibliog. Literary forms: J. M. Robinson and H. Koester, *Trajectories through Early Christianity* (1971). Judaism: B. L. Mack, *Logos und Sophia,* SUNT, X (1973). Jesus and the Synoptic gospels: F. Christ, *Jesus Sophia,* ATANT, LVII (1970); M. J. Suggs, *Wisdom, Christology, and Law in Matthew's Gospel* (1970). John: R. Bultmann, *Exegetica,* ed. E. Dinkler (1967), pp. 10 ff.; F.-M. Braun, *Jean le théologien,* II (1964); R. E. Brown, *The Gospel According to John,* ABi, XXIX (1966), cxxii-cxxv. Paul: U. Wilckens, *Weisheit und Torheit,* BHTh, XXVI (1959); E. Brandenburger, *Geist und Fleisch,* WMANT, XXIX (1968).

H. CONZELMANN

WOMAN IN THE ANCIENT NEAR EAST. Despite geographical and chronological differences there existed a basic uniformity in the status of women and attitudes toward them in the societies of ancient Egypt, Mesopotamia, and Asia Minor. They were all patriarchally structured and, therefore, the woman was under the care and domination of her father before marriage and of her husband after marriage. (The earlier views that the HURRIANS recognized fratriarchy derived from a matriarchal form of family organization, and that the brother-sister marriages of the Eighteenth and Nineteenth Dynasties of Egypt reflected a transition from a matrilineal to a patrilineal succession have recently been challenged.) Nevertheless the well-to-do woman enjoyed a margin of freedom, especially with respect to her legal rights and economic independence.

1. Her status as wife. A girl was expected to marry on reaching puberty. Betrothal arrangements were usually made by the father (the mother or oldest brother would act if the father were dead), or the young man might ask for the consent of the bride's father. If the love poems of Egypt and Mesopotamia may be believed, young people had some freedom in making their own choice of a spouse. These poems also provide information about courtship practices. In Egypt the girl's parents were given presents, and in Mesopotamia they were paid "bride money." Contractual agreements were then reached and a marriage feast took place, with the bride entering the house of the bridegroom. The father of the bride gave her a dowry (Akkad. *šeriktu*), which passed to her heirs at her death.

Various art forms depict mothers nursing their children and husbands casting fond glances at their wives. These reflect, more clearly than the textual sources, the mutual warmth and love between husband and wife.

The wife was expected to take care of her husband and household, present him with children, preferably sons, and be a good mother. Most women spent their days grinding grain, baking bread, brewing beer, weaving and making clothes for their family. If her husband were a farmer, she would help when needed in the fields. The wife of the wealthy Egyptian was frequently depicted enjoy-

Courtesy Museum of Fine Arts, Boston

2. Mycerinus and his queen—Fourth Dynasty, *ca.* 2525 B.C.

ing outdoor sports with her husband or banqueting alongside him and their guests.

By and large, apart from royalty, monogamy was the rule, but a man might take a concubine. Polygamy existed among the Old Assyrian merchants, who maintained two households, and was practiced in the Old Babylonian period when the chief wife belonged to a special religious class and was prohibited from normal marital relations. The LEVIRATE marriage was found among the Assyrians, Hittites, and Hurrians of Nuzi.

The centrality of marriage and family is summed up in the advice of Siduri to the tormented Gilgamesh: "Pay heed to the little one that holds on to thy hand, Let thy spouse delight in thy bosom" (Gilgamesh Epic X.iii.12-13).

In Egypt, Isis, sister and wife of Osiris, typified the ideal wife, faithful to her husband even after death.

2. Her status as mother. The woman's main function was the bearing of children. Sterility, always assumed to be her fault (although the problem of male potency is recognized in Mesopotamia and dealt with by numerous rituals and medications), might lead to the taking of a concubine or

Courtesy The Brooklyn Museum

3. Limestone statue of Ptahiruka and his wife and son—Egypt, Fifth Dynasty, said to be from Saqqara

to divorce. Children were expected to honor their mother. If she were widowed, her sons were obligated to provide her with food and clothing; if they failed to fulfill this obligation they might be disinherited.

3. Her economic role. A woman might own property and invest the income derived from it. In the Ur III period women of high rank (queens, princesses, daughters and wives of high officials) played a significant part in buying and receiving animals, especially for temple offerings. Old Assyrian texts reveal striking instances of wives managing a home textile industry and hiring transporters to deliver goods while their husbands were in Anatolia.

Most unusual were the transactions of the *nadītu* (*see* §5 *below*) in the Old Babylonian period. They acted as creditors; they bought, sold, and leased fields and houses; and they hired out slaves at harvest time. Some of them concentrated in a given business activity.

The economic independence of the Babylonian woman continued into Neo-Babylonian times. However, to the N, by the time of the great Assyrian empires, the woman's economic power appears to have vanished, thus correlating with her greater legal disabilities in this region.

Women were employed in the food and textile industries of the palace and temple workshops, sometimes working under female supervisors. Midwifery was an occupation of women throughout the ancient Near East. Professional female mourners are attested in Egypt. The female brewer (sometimes translated "ale wife"), the *sabîtu,* prepared and sold beer, and to judge from Hammurabi Code 108, 109, 111, functioned as a creditor. Although the feminine element disappeared from this occupation at the end of the Old Babylonian period, the profession remained under the protection of a goddess. The one instance of a woman physician in the palace of Old Babylonian Larsa also deserves mention.

4. Her legal status. Rape was punishable by death when the woman was either married or betrothed, and when the man used force. In all cases the man was guilty and the woman blameless. However, the Hittite laws distinguished between rape in the city and rape in the countryside. In the former case, she also was considered guilty.

Should the husband wish a divorce for no fault of his wife, he usually had to pay a fine. According to Hammurabi Code 142, an abused but guiltless wife could deny her husband conjugal rights, and if a clean record was given her by the city authority she might divorce him. In the case of a long absent husband, a destitute wife, after a stipulated period of time, might enter another man's household.

In the case of adultery, the woman was always considered guilty. Whether she was to be put to death or pardoned was left to the discretion of her husband.

In well-to-do families, a widow was provided for by her children, but widows were often left indigent and their welfare was ideally the concern of the righteous king. In early Mesopotamia the temple provided them with their basic needs in return for labor.

Although the law codes assigned women a subordinate position, the woman of means could own and dispose of property and give testimony in lawsuits.

5. Her religious role. Except for the religious functions of royal women (*see* §6 *below*) and dream interpretation and divination, women played a minor role in cultic life. Only in the lower echelons of the "clergy" did female singers, dancers, and musicians participate in the cult. Sacred prostitution was practiced in the Sumerian Inanna temple, especially in connection with the annual sacred marriage ceremony.

Courtesy The Oriental Institute, University of Chicago

4. Stone statue of seated couple, from Nippur

Atypical was the existence of the special classes in the Old Babylonian period: *nadītu, ugbabtu, kulmašītu,* and *qadištu.* Best known is the institution of the cloister (Akkad. *gagû*) with its *nadītu* women in Sippar. Generations of families from various cities had their daughters enter a cloister to be initiated on the festival of the god, at which time the "rope of Šamaš" was placed on each girl's arm. She thereby became the "bride" of the god, living a chaste life until her death. Many of them were active in business. Some took pious names expressing special devotion to the god or his wife. Once a year, they remembered the childless dead, thus fulfilling the duty usually assumed by living progeny. Through their devout and consecrated lives these women (centuries later to be misunderstood as prostitutes) contributed to the god's continuing concern for his city.

Women were prominent as prophets (*see* Prophecy in the Ancient Near East[S]) at Mari and as mediators of oracles in the Neo-Assyrian period. In Mesopotamia and Asia Minor they were considered to be especially gifted in interpreting dreams, but functioned mainly outside official religious life.

Among the practitioners of Hittite purification rituals were the "Old Women" and the "female seer." The "Old Women" may have been organized into guilds. It is not known how they were selected and trained.

6. Her education. That women, like most men, were illiterate may be taken for granted. In Babylonia, however, some of them were scribes and therefore had received an education. Most of these scribes belonged to the cloister institution in Sippar.

The Old Akkadian princess Enheduanna, daughter of Sargon, was high priestess of the moon-god Nanna of Ur and the author of many hymns. She is the first known author in world literature and has been described as a "systematic theologian."

There is some evidence that the priestess-wife of King Šulgi of the Ur III dynasty, Šulgi-simti, was also a poet.

7. Her political status. Four princesses actually became rulers of Egypt. Best known is Hatshepsut (1504-1483 B.C.) who had magnificent monuments built in honor of Amon. Two other women of this period also achieved renown: Tiy, the commoner wife of Amen-hotep III, and the beautiful Nefertiti, her daughter-in-law. In the latter part of the Old Kingdom period greater equality between king and queen is attested by greater balance in their pictorial representations. *See* Fig. W2.

The royal princess who bore the title "God's Wife of Amon" remained a virgin for life. With the Ethiopian supremacy this appointment became an instrument of political policy. She served as her father's viceroy at Thebes, possessed great estates, with officials of her own, and had the authority to make offerings.

Ku-Baba, a low-born female tavern keeper, was the founder of the Third Dynasty of Kish, the first and only example in Mesopotamia of a woman gaining sole political power. The wife of the ruler of Lagash managed the Baba temple economy and presumably fulfilled cultic functions there. Sargon created the double office of high priestess *(entu)* of Nanna at Ur and of the god An at Uruk for his daughter Enheduanna (*see* §6 *above*) in a successful attempt to unify the Akkadian and Sumerian-speaking populations. For the next five hundred years rulers appointed their daughters high priestesses to Nanna for life. This institution served to unify the country even in times of crisis.

Other queens of Mesopotamia played political and economic roles. Šulgi-simti (probably identical with Abi-simti), mentioned above, was actively involved in business. Richly documented are the many ways in which Šiptu, wife of Zimri-Lim, king of MARI, acted as partner to her husband, coping with both administrative and political matters during his absences. Legendary was the fame of Sammuramat (Gr. Semiramis), the widow of Shamshi-Adad V, who ruled Assyria during her son Adad-narari III's reign. Her name was mentioned alongside her son's on monuments. Zakutu (Aram. Naqi'a), a wife of Sennacherib, may have been responsible for the accession of her son Esarhaddon (680-669 B.C.) to the throne. Adad-guppi (probably Gr. Nitocris), the long-lived mother of Nabonidus, and her devotion to Haran and its gods may account for her son's radical attempt to re-establish ancient rituals and institutions for the moon-god of Haran.

Hittite queens maintained even more independent positions than did those of Mesopotamia. Every queen had the title "Tawannannas," derived from the wife of King Labarnas, ancestor of all Hittite kings. They participated alongside their husbands in religious festivals. A special relationship existed between the sun goddess and the queen of Hatti. Outstanding among them was Puduhepa, wife of the great ruler Hattusilis, and daughter of a priest. She played an important role in state affairs, even corresponding with the contemporary queen of Egypt, and had her own seal for official business.

8. Attitudes toward women. It is especially the wisdom literature which reveals an ambivalent attitude toward women.

> If you are well-to-do and can maintain your household, love your wife in your home. . . . Fill her belly, clothe her back . . . make her happy while you are alive for she is land profitable to her lord. . . . Soothe her heart with what has accrued to you; it means that she will continue to dwell in your house. A vagina is what she gives for her condition; what she asks about is who will make a canal for her. (The Maxims of Ptahhotep)

Certain Sumerian proverbs display a more jaundiced view:

> He who does not support either a wife or a child, his nose has not borne a leash. (E. Gordon, *Sumerian Proverbs,* p. 120)
>
> An unseemly wife living in the house is worse than all devils. (Gordon, *Sumerian Proverbs,* p. 468)
>
> For his pleasure—married
> On his thinking it over—divorced (!?)
> (Gordon, *Sumerian Proverbs,* p. 265)

The love poems of Egypt and Mesopotamia, as well as the art of the ancient Near East, provide rich sources for expressions of the beauty and charm of women.

Bibliography. P. Grimal, ed., *Histoire Mondiale de la Femme,* "Préhistoire et Antiquité" (1965), pp. 63-266, a thorough survey of woman in the societies covered in this article, with bibliographies. For more information on priestesses and special classes of women see R. Harris, "The nadītu woman," *Studies Presented to A. Leo Oppenheim* (1964), pp. 106-35; J. Renger, "Untersuchungen zum Priestertum in der altbabylonischen Zeit," *ZA,* LVIII=NF XXIV (1967), 110-88; W. H. Ph. Römer, *AOAT,* XII (1971). R. HARRIS

***WOMAN IN THE OT.** As part of a patriarchal society, woman in the OT both mirrors and challenges that structure. In exploring this thesis, one must acknowledge the complexity and scarcity of historical data, the diversity of genres and their functions, the tensions between conflicting points of view, as well as the dynamic thrust of Hebraic faith.

1. A patriarchal culture. The activities which the OT describes are primarily those of males; its language is decidedly masculine; so far as we know, its authors and compilers were men; often its precepts address only men; and its Deity appears predominantly in andromorphic imagery (but cf. GOD, NATURE OF, IN THE OT[S].

As the basic unit of Israelite society, the family

is called בית אב (the house of one's father). This male structure extends to clans and to tribes and survives in male genealogies. In the early period, a father exercised unlimited authority as head of his family. With the transition to settled life and the development of towns, his power diminished somewhat (e.g., Deut. 21:18-21). But that change only shifted power to other male institutions, such as the elders of a city (Deut. 22:16; 25:7-10; Ruth 4:2), or a king (II Sam. 14:4-11; I Kings 3:16-28), or postexilic male assemblies (Ezra 10:1-14).

A given rather than a chosen phenomenon, patriarchy stamped the culture of ancient Israel. Within this man-centered and man-dominated world, woman made her statements.

2. Woman within patriarchal culture. ***a. Reflections.*** The female child was less desirable in the eyes of her father (and hence of her mother) than was the male child. As she grew, she stayed close to her mother, but her father controlled her life until he relinquished her to another man for marriage. If either of these male authorities permitted her to be mistreated, even abused, she had to submit without recourse (Gen. 19:8; Judg. 11:29-40; 19:1-30; II Sam. 13:1-22). As wife, her duty was to bear (male) children (Gen. 16:1-2). When a husband preceded his wife in death, his brother, or some other male relative, assumed power over her (Gen. 38). Thus from childhood to old age, the Hebrew woman belonged to the men of her family.

This sketch of the subordination of female to male is amplified in the legal corpus. The laws of Israel address only men; in this sense, women were not considered legally responsible. Indeed, one law describes them as the property of men (Exod. 20:17; Deut. 5:21). Their bodies were not their own. A man expected to marry a virgin, while there is no indication that his own virginity had to be intact. A wife who was proved guilty of fornication had violated the honor and power of both her father and her husband. Death by stoning was the penalty (Deut. 22:13-21). Likewise, adultery brought death for a woman and her accomplice, because the guilty couple had violated the exclusive right of a husband (Lev. 20:10). Only a husband (never a wife) might charge infidelity and thereby require his spouse to submit to an ordeal of testing (Num. 5:11-31; *see* Ordeal, Judicial[S] §2). If a man was found to have forced intercourse upon an unmarried woman, then he had to make a proper payment to her father and marry her. His punishment was simply denial of the right of divorce (Deut. 22:28-29). Divorce itself was never possible on a woman's initiative (Deut. 24:1-4; *see also* Divorce[S]; Marriage[S] §6). This double standard applied also to prostitution, which was a licit outlet for the male but a condemned occupation for the female.

A woman could not own property, according to most legal precepts. One exception occurred when a man had no sons. Then his daughters might inherit his estate (Num. 27:1-11), but even this decision was modified to limit the marriage of these daughters "within the family of the tribe of their father" (Num. 36:1-9, vs. 6). Although in time such laws may have become less rigid, information is scant (cf. Deut. 15:12-17).

Legislation regarding the cult illustrates further the subordination of woman to man. The people whom Moses consecrated at Mount Sinai were all men. They were instructed not to go near a woman, i.e., not to have sex for a limited time (Exod. 19:7-15). In Deut. 16:16 only males were designated to observe religious feasts. The priesthood itself was strictly a male profession. While not excluded altogether from cultic observances (Deut. 12:12; 31:12; cf. Num. 6:2), women were inferior participants, obeying rules formulated by men.

Central in these rules is the concept of ritual purity. All bodily discharges, of males or of females, were unclean; hence, they prevented a person from ritual activities (Lev. 15). But uncleanness was far more a female than a male phenomenon. When a boy was born, the mother was unclean for seven days and needed thirty-three days for purification. If the newborn child was a girl, however, the entire time doubled. At the end of her purification, the mother herself sought atonement through the male priest of the local sanctuary (Lev. 12:1-8). With his discharge of semen, a man was unclean "until the evening"; with her menstrual discharge, a woman was unclean for seven days (Lev. 15:16-24).

Leviticus placed monetary value upon persons who were dedicated to Yahweh. A male between the ages of twenty and sixty was worth fifty shekels; a female in the same category, only thirty. This monetary discrimination held for other age groups as well (Lev. 27:1-7). Furthermore, the phrase which introduces this subject indicates that it was a male (איש) who controlled these dedications; he "makes a special vow of persons to the Lord." Num. 30, which concerns the binding nature of particular vows, reinforces the inferior status of woman in cultic matters. Although she had a right to make a vow on her own initiative, her father or her husband might nullify the vow. The exception made here for widowed and divorced women speaks not of their independent status but of their precarious existence in a patriarchal world.

What the law says forcefully, certain narratives (*see above*), certain prophetic passages (e.g., Isa. 3:12; 4:1; Nah. 3:13), and certain sapiential reflections (e.g., Eccl. 7:26-28; Prov. 5:1-8; 6:24; cf. 1:8; 6:20) confirm with varying emphases and intentions. This picture requires modification, however, and that modification comes from within patriarchal culture itself. Not all who lived in it conformed to it or condoned it.

b. Challenges. i. *Exceptions.* Some individual women in ancient Israel survived as people in their own right rather than as creatures subjugated to male structures. Miriam and Deborah tower high in the premonarchic traditions. Both are called prophets (Exod. 15:20; Judg. 4:4). As a leader of the people, Miriam dared to reproach Moses for his exclusive claim to divine revelation (Num. 12). Not even her resultant punishment lessened her status in later memory (Mic. 6:4). Deborah judged Israel (Judg. 4:4), predicted the outcome of battle (Judg. 4:8-9), and actually participated as a leader in battle. From the monarchic period came the prophet HULDAH (II Kings 22:14-20), who authenticated the contents of the scroll found during the reign of Josiah. Not only did her decision effect a religious reformation, but also it inaugurated the idea of sacred scripture. From the postexilic period there is brief mention of the prophet NOADIAH, an opponent of Nehemiah (Neh. 6:14).

A litany of exceptional women might include further the midwives in the Exodus traditions, who refused to take orders from Pharaoh, a male "deity." In addition, female slaves, a mother and daughter, schemed with an Egyptian princess and her maidens to defy the oppressor. All these women acted independently, without any male presence, to bring about liberation (Exod. 1:15–2:10). Forced by the death of her husband to work out her own destiny, RUTH acted independently also. Of a different sort are the wise women of Tekoa (II Sam. 14:1-20) and of Abel (II Sam. 20:14-22). Their status in tradition is other than that of wife or mother. Perhaps such sapiential models contributed to the extraordinary portrayal of wisdom itself as a woman closely associated with Yahweh (Prov. 8).

Several foreign women deserve mention. A full-fledged monarch, the Queen of Sheba, visited Solomon to test his wisdom and to match his wealth (I Kings 10:6-13). Accustomed to rule with absolute power (cf. I Kings 21:1-16), Queen JEZEBEL was both theologian and missionary. Like Elijah, she knew that Yahwism and Baalism were incompatible. If from the viewpoint of Hebrew religion she received the death which she deserved (II Kings 9:30-37), nonetheless she met it with initiative, boldness, and independence. Indeed, adverse judgment is indirect testimony to her great ability, strength, and intellect.

Although the OT condemns harlotry by a double standard which exempts men, it has only praise for RAHAB the harlot. In order to save her own life and the lives of her family, she co-operated with the invading Israelites and thereby earned an illustrious place in the memories of Israel (Josh. 2:1-21; 6:15-25). Faithful to her own people, DELILAH fared less well in Israelite judgment. Yet she resembles a savior figure who traps the enemy (Judg. 16:4-21). Her success was exceeded by Jael the Kenite, who brought Sisera the Canaanite general to a humiliating death (Judg. 5:24-27).

Thus in a culture dominated by men, exceptional women emerged. Alone they did not alter the culture. Yet when joined with evidence which directly challenges patriarchy, these women cease to be mere tokens and become part of a dynamic remnant.

ii. *Counterculture*. The patriarchal culture of Israel knew a counterculture. Perhaps its paradigm was the Yahwist story of creation (Gen. 2–3). Special among the literature of the ancient Near East in focusing upon the creation of woman, this narrative depicts sexuality as occurring simultaneously for male and female (2:23). Moreover, the appearance of woman is the climax of the entire story (cf. Gen. 1:27). While the animals were helpers for "the man," they were inferiors. By contrast, the woman is "a helper fit for him" (2:18). This phrase connotes the equality of woman with man, an equality that is stressed in various ways. Both man and woman owe their lives solely to Yahweh. When the Lord created woman, the deity first put the man to sleep so that he did not participate at her birth. Woman herself is not the "rib" of man, for that extracted bone required the creative work of Yahweh to become woman. The rib means solidarity and equality. Out of his ecstasy man discovered a partner in woman rather than a creature to dominate.

In Gen. 2 the man remains silent while Yahweh plans his existence. He speaks only in response to the birth of woman. Then he recedes again in the narrative while woman emerges as the strong figure. In conversation with the serpent, she quotes God and adds her interpretation ("neither shall you touch it") to the divine prohibition (Gen. 3:2-3). She contemplates the forbidden fruit physically, aesthetically, and theologically (vs. 6). This primal woman is intelligent, independent, and decisive, fully aware as theologian when she takes the fruit and eats. But her husband does not struggle with the prohibition. Not a decision maker, he follows his wife without question.

The divine judgments describe (they do not prescribe) the disastrous effects of disobedience. Specifically, the rule of man over woman (Gen. 3:16) is a perversion of creation, which stands in need of grace. Thereby the culture of Israel received a formidable critique in the theology of the Yahwist.

In various ways, other theologians made similar critiques. The prophet Hosea envisions a time when Israel will no longer call Yahweh "my master" (בעלי), a term denoting the rule of one person over another (cf. Judg. 19:22-24); rather Israel will say "my husband" (אישי), a word echoing the harmony of woman and man before their corruption (Hos. 2:16 [H 18]). For this prophet the inferiority of woman is not the will of God (cf. 4:14). Nor is it for Jeremiah. In a poem replete with feminine imagery (31:15-22), Yahweh hears Rachel weeping for her lost children. God comforts her and promises her the divine restoration of Ephraim as an act of motherly compassion. Then, in the finale, Jeremiah himself proclaims the overthrow of patriarchy: "For the Lord has created a new thing on the earth: a woman protects a man" (31:22).

Yet another manifestation of the Yahwist understanding of woman is the Song of Songs. In this erotic poetry there is no tension between female and male, no male dominance, no female subordination, and no stereotyping of either sex. The woman actively seeks the man for love-making (e.g., 3:1-4). She is not hampered by laws of sexual impurity; she is not the property of the man. The poetry does not depict her as either wife or mother. An independent creature, she keeps vineyards (1:6) and she pastures flocks (1:8). The equality and harmony which she enjoys with her lover is expressed in the formula, "My beloved is mine and I am his" (2:16; 6:3). Once she says, "I am my beloved's, and his desire is for me" (7:10 [H 11]). This word "desire" recalls its use in Gen. 3:16 as divine judgment. In the Song of Songs, that description of sin is transformed into an affirmation of mutuality and delight. Both woman and man stand under grace as equal creatures of God.

3. **Woman in faith and history.** Allowing both for a constant patriarchal structure and for a variety of perspectives throughout Israel's history, one may yet discern a marked theological change between pre-exilic and postexilic understandings of woman (*see bibliog.*). Before the sixth century B.C., a depatriarchalizing principle was prominently at work in Hebrew faith. No doubt the unknown prophet of the Exile shared this vision; he employed female imagery to suggest the unfathomable love of God for a defeated people (Isa. 49:15; cf. 66:13).

Also in the exilic period, Ezekiel moved in a different direction. Reflecting his priestly heritage (1:3), he described sin at times by the category of impurity, and he specified this uncleanness by sexual metaphors demeaning to woman (22:10-11; 36:17). Zechariah, who may also have had priestly connections (Neh. 12:4; Zech. 1:1), continued the process. He identified woman with wickedness, and he saw her removed from the restored land (Zech. 5:7-11). Furthermore, the Priestly laws of the Torah, though they have a long history, received official status in the postexilic period (*see* PRIESTLY WRITERS[S]). By their increased authority, they promoted a cultic understanding of sin, with its adverse consequences for woman (*see above*). A similar attitude appeared in the regulations of Ezra, where concern for racial, ritual, and sexual purity undercut a respect for woman as human being (Ezra 10:2-3, 10-44). Gradually, then, in postexilic thinking an understanding of womanhood became dominant which moved toward misogyny: woman as an impure, subordinate, and inferior human creature.

Nevertheless, that view did not replace altogether the dynamic thrust of OT faith. Though it came to expression in a patriarchal culture, that thrust challenged, corrected, and transcended the culture. Accordingly, OT faith undercuts all man-made structures and ideas to place both woman and man *sub specie aeternitatis.*

See WOMAN; WOMAN IN THE ANCIENT NEAR EAST [S].

Bibliography. J. Pedersen, *Israel,* I-II (1926), 46-96; R. de Vaux, *Ancient Israel* (1961), pp. 19-55; W. Brueggemann, "Of the Same Flesh and Bone (Gn 2,23a)," *CBQ,* XXXII (1970), 532-42; S. Terrien, "The Omphalos Myth and Hebrew Religion," *VT,* XX (1970), 315-38 (esp. 335-37 on postexilic views); W. L. Holladay, "Jeremiah and Women's Liberation," *Andover Newton Quarterly,* XII (1972), 213-23; S. Terrien, "Toward a Biblical Theology of Womanhood," *Religion in Life,* XLII (1973), 322-33, pre-exilic and postexilic views; P. Trible, "Depatriarchalizing in Biblical Interpretation," *JAAR,* XLI (1973), 30-48; H. W. Wolff, *Anthropologie des Alten Testaments* (1973), pp. 243-58; P. Bird, "Images of Women in the OT," in *Religion and Sexism,* ed. R. Reuther (1974), pp. 41-88; C. J. Vos, *Woman in OT Worship* (1968). P. TRIBLE

***WOMAN IN THE NT.** Contrary to the position of subordination in which women generally lived in first-century Mediterranean culture, the position they discovered in the early Christian communities was one of acceptance and, particularly in the earliest decades, equality. Women were seen as equal to men and participated in every level of church activity. In the later NT church, the equality was compromised and stabilized at a point where they still received warm acceptance but were again placed in subordinate roles.

1. **The baptismal formula of equality.** Gal. 3:28, which affirms the equality of women and men, is almost surely a fragment of an early baptismal formula (cf. parallel structures in I Cor. 12:12-13; Col. 3:9-11), and thus is probably evidence for a widespread attitude in at least the early Hellenistic communities: "There is neither Jew nor Greek, there is neither slave nor free, there is neither male nor female; for you are all one in Christ Jesus." To enter the Christian community thus meant to join a society in which male-female roles and valuations based on such roles had been discarded. The community was powerless to alter role valuations in the outside culture, but within the church, behavior patterns and interrelationships were to be based on this affirmation of equality.

2. **The Pauline churches.** The new behavior patterns are clearly visible in Paul's writings, both with respect to his own views and to accepted behavior in his congregations.

a. Women's roles in the church. Paul never had to defend the right of women to evangelize or to participate in local church activity. Apparently his churches accepted female as well as male leaders (*see* Rom. 16:1, 3, 6, 12, 15). In Phil. 4:2-3 he singles out two women church leaders, then at odds with each other, and emphasizes that "they have labored side by side with me in the gospel." There is no suggestion that their labor differs from that of their male colleagues. Priscilla appears to have been at least the equal of her husband Aquila in their joint work as teachers (Acts 18:2, 18, 26; I Cor. 16:19; Rom. 16:3). *See also* AQUILA AND PRISCILLA.

The one time the leadership of women becomes an issue in the authentic Pauline correspondence (*see* PAUL THE APOSTLE §A1*a*), it is clear that both sides in the dispute agree at least that women can be worship leaders (I Cor. 11:2-16). While the reason Paul insists upon a head covering for women leaders may never be certainly explained, he does not question their right to perform the same liturgical functions as men and concludes that the sexes are now equal in the church ("in the Lord") and before God (vss. 11-12). This affirmation is, however, blatantly contradicted by a passage later in the same letter (I Cor. 14:33*b*-35), in which women are admonished not even to ask questions during the church services. While some scholars have attempted to smooth out the contradiction, the evidence seems to favor those who regard I Cor. 14:33*b*-35 as an insertion into the letter by someone later than Paul himself, perhaps by someone from the time of the writing of I Timothy (cf. I Tim. 2:11-12). *See also* CORINTHIANS, FIRST LETTER TO THE[S] §6*e*.

b. Role in the family. The authentic Pauline correspondence deals with the rights and responsibilities of women in the family only in I Cor. 7.

Here Paul asserts that the same rights and responsibilities apply to the woman as to the man. Both are called to be responsible sexual partners and to follow the same procedures with regard to marriage, divorce, and remarriage. He is sensitive to the desires of each sex to be a caring partner within the marriage bond (vss. 32-35), and there is no hint of the subordination which appears in later strata of the NT. *See* §4*b below*.

In apparent contradiction, however, to both the baptismal formula and Paul's own explicit attitude and practice is his statement in I Cor. 11:3: "The head of every man is Christ, the head of a woman is her husband, and the head of Christ is God." If the proper metaphorical meaning of "head" (κεφαλή) here is "ruler" or "superior authority," as usually assumed, then Paul indeed has assigned a subordinate rank to woman (cf. also the Deutero-Pauline Eph. 5:22-23). In that case I Cor. 11:3 would be a remnant of Paul's Jewish perspective as yet uncorrected by the baptismal formula of Gal. 3:28, and he would be involved in an irreconcilable self-contradiction. There is, however, another possible interpretation. In ordinary Greek of Paul's day, κεφαλή, when used metaphorically, signifies, not "authority" but, among other possibilities, "source," e.g., the source (origin) of a river. Since a remark in I Cor. 11:12 suggests that Paul in this passage is thinking of Gen. 2, where man is said to be the source of woman, that may also be the point in I Cor. 11:3. Belief in Christ as the agent of creation (e.g., I Cor. 8:6) would explain the associated statement that Christ is man's head (i.e., source). Such an interpretation would make I Cor. 11:3 consistent with all of Paul's other statements and actions.

3. The church of the gospels. The gospels portray Jesus dealing with women naturally and unself-consciously, both in the stories about him and and in his reported teaching (*see* WOMAN §11). The general lack of dogmatic concern suggests that, in the churches which transmitted the gospel traditions, the position and prevalency of women within the church was not a problem. Only the story of the Samaritan woman in the Gospel of John registers surprise about Jesus' freedom in relating to women (4:9, 27). While there are no hints of the baptismal formula in the gospel material, three things reflect the same new-found regard of women that is evidenced in the Pauline churches.

a. The role of the disciple. The story of Mary and Martha (Luke 10:38-42) does indeed point to a conflict over the issue of the proper place of woman in the church. Martha, busy with cooking, complains that Mary, listening to the teaching of Jesus, is not in her proper role. Jesus, however, rejects Martha's complaint and affirms that Mary is in the right place. Thus the conflict is resolved in favor of the continuing right of women to full discipleship.

b. Travel companions of Jesus. Luke 8:1-3 and Mark 15:40-41 contain two different lists of women who are said to have been traveling companions of Jesus and his male disciples. Since these women are not wives of the disciples, a picture emerges of an itinerant traveling entourage of males and females unmarried to each other—a situation which would have been scandalous to the pious Jew. Whether these lists have their origin in the actual situation of Jesus' ministry (as is inherently possible) or in the story building of the gospel writers (as is supposed by many scholars), they reflect in either case a view of women and men liberated from the strong prohibitions which the pious fear of sexual license had long before created. The tradition also honors some of these women as the first to hear the news of the Resurrection and as the first to see the resurrected Jesus (Mark 16:1-8; Matt. 28:1-10; Luke 24:1-11, 22-24; John 20:11-18).

c. Acceptance of outcasts. The attention and acceptance given in the gospel tradition to prostitutes and women with other immoral sexual histories is startling, seen against the backdrop of Jewish piety. The genealogy of Jesus' ancestry in Matt. 1, despite the fact that it is based on male descent, contains the names of four women, apart from Mary, and all of these four were involved in some form of sexual irregularity: Rahab (a prostitute, Josh. 2:1), Tamar (intercourse with her father-in-law, Gen. 38), Ruth (obtains her husband by an act of intercourse, Ruth 3:6-18), and Bathsheba (adulteress, II Sam. 11:2-5). Rahab is also mentioned positively elsewhere in the NT (Heb. 11:31; Jas. 2:25). In Matt. 21:31-32 Jesus asserts that prostitutes will enter the kingdom of God before the Jewish religious leaders, because the former rather than the latter accepted the preaching of John the Baptist. The female sinner who appears at a banquet to minister to Jesus is portrayed as a societal outcast and may have been understood to be a prostitute (Luke 7:36-50). The church obviously did not approve of any form of sexual license (cf. Matt. 5:27-28; I Cor. 6:12-20), but it did not turn away from ministry to those considered immoral by polite society.

d. Jesus' attitude. Behind this openness to women must stand the person of Jesus. Unfortunately the task of determining which gospel traditions originate with Jesus himself is so difficult as to be virtually impossible. All that can be said with assurance is that it is difficult to explain the prevalence and equality of women in the earliest church if such attitudes were not initiated by Jesus himself.

4. The later church. ***a. The Gnostic Christians.*** The movement toward liberation and equality for women in the later period seems to have found its main continuation in emerging Christian GNOSTICISM, although data about that development in the NT are sparse. At some very early point this movement made a significant step not approved by Paul. Although he affirmed the equality of male and female, Paul rejected efforts to deny the sexual distinctions themselves (I Cor. 7:1-5; 11:2-16). The more radical groups, however, attempted to deny sexual difference by denying that which most characterized the distinction, the sexual act itself. The Christians opposed by the author of I Timothy were prohibiting marriage (4:3), and in the later Gospel According to the Egyptians (*see* EGYPTIANS, GOSPEL ACCORDING TO THE) childbearing was opposed (Clem. Misc. III.ix.64). According to Irenaeus, Saturninus believed that marriage and procreation were from the devil (Iren. Her. I.xxiv.2) and in the apocryphal Acts (e.g., Acts of Thomas 12) sexual intercourse is the worst sin. In the Gospel of Thomas the overcoming of sexual differentiation is portrayed as the goal of humankind in the eschatological era (in itself a Jewish and early Jewish-Christian motif, e.g., Mark 12:25). This view perhaps rests upon a belief in the original androgynous nature of humanity, to which eschatological humanity is to return. *See* THOMAS, GOSPEL OF[S] §2.

The evidence also suggests that in some circles women continued to exercise church leadership. The author of the book of REVELATION inveighs against a Christian female prophet who is the leader of what he considers a false (and perhaps Gnostic) Christian libertinism (2:20-23). And the second-century Acts of Paul (*see* PAUL, ACTS OF, a writing which has, however, only a tenuous relationship to known Gnostic ideas) portrays Thecla as a female missionary in men's clothing with, apparently, shorn hair (25:40-43), and Tertullian suggests that she had become a model for women who wanted to teach and baptize (*On Baptism* XVII). The Gnostic endorsement of the original Christian libertarian posture must have proven attractive to women; at least the Christian opponents described in the Pastorals are begrudgingly accorded success in evangelizing women, there called pejoratively "weak women" (II Tim. 3:6-7).

b. The mainstream church. The church whose documents are the later canonical NT writings moved in the opposite direction. Appealing to the orders of creation as understood through the Hebrew Scriptures, the church (*a*) condemned sexual asceticism and the denial of the sexual role within marriage, (*b*) encouraged the marriage state, (*c*) refused women participation in the liturgical and political leadership of the church, and (*d*) concluded that women should be subordinated to men. These views represent in part a return to the cultural mores of the environment, and in part a strong reaction against those claims of Gnostic Christianity which seemed to deny the orders of creation.

The new position is clearly stated in the so-called "household rules" (*see* LISTS, ETHICAL §§1-4; LISTS, ETHICAL[S] §2), where marriage is assumed to be the normal situation of adults; elders, deacons, and bishops are known (and perhaps encouraged) to be married (cf. Tit. 1:6; I Tim. 3:1, 4, 12); younger widows are to remarry (I Tim. 5:14); child-bearing and child-raising reappear as the function of marriage (contrary to Paul) and, it is implied, as the primary function of women within marriage (I Tim. 2:15; 3:4, 12; 5:14).

Throughout this later literature women are consistently commanded to be submissive to their husbands, that is, to accept a position of complete subordination to the male (Col. 3:18; Eph. 5:22; I Tim. 2:11; Tit. 2:5; I Pet. 3:1, 5). The rules in I Tim. 2:8 ff. are the most stringent of them all, and obviously represent a reaction against emerging Gnosticism. Women are enjoined to silence in the worship, presumably in contrast to the public prayer of men (although it is possible to interpret vs. 9 as speaking about proper dress of women while they participate in public prayer). Women are also denied the office of teacher, as well as any role which would give them authority over males.

Through these rules, the mainstream church attempted to protect itself against the ascetic extremes of Christian Gnosticism and what it considered the unnatural (i.e., against the created order) equality of woman in church and home. Since these rules must have been directed against fairly widespread practice, it is impossible to judge whether, in Christian congregations at the end of the first century, women were more often accorded equality or admonished to submission. Eventually, however, the rules proved to be as successful as they were fateful for the history of Western civilization.

See also FAMILY; MARRIAGE; MARRIAGE[S]; MARRIAGE IN THE NT[S]; SEX, SEXUAL BEHAVIOR; SEX, SEXUAL BEHAVIOR[S]; ETHICS IN THE NT[S] §§1*ei*, 3*dii*, 4*a*, *b*, 5.

Bibliography. K. Stendahl, *The Bible and the Role of Women,* FBBS, XV (1966); J. Leipoldt, *Die Frau in der antiken Welt und im Urchristentum* (2nd ed., 1955); E. Kähler, *Die Frau in den paulinischen Briefen* (1960); W. Meeks, "The Image of the Androgyne: Some Uses of a Symbol in Earliest Christianity," *History of Religions,* XIII (1974), 165-208; R. Scroggs, "Paul and the Eschatological Woman," *JAAR,* XL (1972), 283-303; E. Laland, "Die Martha-Maria-Perikope Lukas 10, 38-42," *ST,* XIII (1959), 70-85; M. Hengel, "Maria Magdalena und die Frauen als Zeugen," in *Abraham Unser Vater: Festschrift für O. Michel,* Arbeiten zur Geschichte des Spätjudentums und Urchristentums, V (1963), 243-56.

R. SCROGGS

WORDPLAY IN THE OT. Paronomasia is the term employed by ancient Greek commentators when referring to rhetoric devices designed to engage the attention of an audience. The use of paronomasia promoted a certain aura of ambiguity, which was intended to excite curiosity and to invite a search for meanings that were not readily apparent. It is not surprising, therefore, that divine revelations were often couched in paronomastic forms. There were also times when Hebrew wordplays expressed a spirit of playfulness. The term is known in Latin as *adnominatio* and in Arabic as *tajnīs*. Medieval Hebraic literature called it *lāšôn nōphēl ʿal lāšôn,* literally, "language falling upon language."

To varying extents, Near Eastern literature preserves examples of wordplay. Peeters has collected examples from Egypt and Fishbane from Babylonia.

1. Visual wordplay depends on the written word, tends to be intellectual, even esoteric, and is meant for the limited circles of knowledgeable scribes. This category includes the following types.

a. Gematria. Since in Hebrew a numerical equivalent existed for every consonant, the "value" of a certain word could be calculated, and the total number is said to provide a meaning that is otherwise hidden. Talmudic rabbis (T.B. Ned. 32a) have posited that the 318 "trained men" who aided Abraham in routing the Eastern coalition (Gen. 14) stood for a *gematria* of his servant Eliezer, since the value of consonants forming that name adds up to 318. Gad, whose *gematria* is 7, is reckoned seventh in the listing of tribes in Gen. 46, a chapter where the number 7 and its multiples are repeatedly invoked. Furthermore, seven sons are ascribed to him (*see also* GENERATION, SEVENTH[S]). Some see in the census of Israel in Num. 1:46 (603, 550) a *gematria* for *bᵉnê Yiśrā'ēl kol rō'sh,* "the children of Israel, each individual."

b. Notrikon. Letters of each word are considered, acronymically, as abbreviations for a series of words. Examples often cited are *'yk,* "how," in Jer. 3:19, said to stand for '[āmēn] y[hwh] k[î], "Amen, O Lord for"; *hmh* of Jer. 7:4 which is said to be acronymic for h[am]m[āqôm] h[azzê], "this place."

c. Acrostics. A poetic form in which successive lines begin with consonants in alphabetical order. Lam. 1–4 and Pss. 111–112 offer excellent examples. A full listing is found in Gottwald.

d. Atbash. The first letter of the alphabet (*'āleph*) is used as substitute for the last (*tāw*), the second (*bêth*) for the penultimate (*šîn*), etc. Two well-known examples are *ššk* (Jer. 25:26; 51:41), which is *atbash* for *bbl* (*Babylon*), and *lb qmy* (Jer. 51:1, RSV n. "Leb-qamai"), which is to be replaced by *kśdym* (Chaldea). In an address to the Society of Biblical Literature (1973), C. H. Gordon suggested that *kbwl* of I Kings 9:13 (RSV "Cabul") be read as *atbash* for *lšpk,* referring to "worthless land."

e. Anastrophe. Usual word order is upset in order to emphasize a play on words. Thus in Gen. 6:9, the name of the patriarch Noah is purposely placed at the end of a verbal sentence in order to underscore a relationship with the admired ancestor Enoch (cf. Gen. 5:22, 24). In the clause *'eth hā'ᵉlōhîm hithhallēkh nōaḥ,* the last three consonants, read backwards, spell the name "Enoch" (*ḥanôkh*).

f. Epanastrophe. In this type of paranomasia, not strictly visual, the final syllable of one word is reproduced in the word that immediately follows, e.g., *wᵉlir'ôt šᵉhem bᵉhēmmâ lāhem* (Eccl. 3:18); *paraś rešeth lᵉraglay* (Lam. 1:13; Prov. 25:13). A variation on this genre may lie behind the grammatically troubling first words of Gen. 1:1, *bᵉrē'šîth bārā'*. Here the first two syllables, composed of three consonants, are repeated in the second word (cf. II Kings 8:12).

2. Oral wordplay. The terminology and definitions are adopted from Glück.

a. Equivocal. This type of wordplay depends on homonymy, that is, the similarity of sound among varying words, e.g., *kîmê nōaḥ zō'th lî . . . mê-nōaḥ 'ôdh 'al-hā'āreṣ:* "For this is like the days of Noah to me . . . the waters of Noah . . . over the earth" (Isa. 54:9); *wᵉhaḥēmār hāyâ lāhem laḥōmer:* "And they had . . . bitumen for mortar" (Gen. 11:3). The homonymy that allowed such punning occurred when consonants which were phonemically different in Proto-Semitic fell together in Hebrew—*ḥereb* [**ḥrb*] *'al-kaśdîm . . . ḥoreb* [**ḫrb*] *'el-mêmêhā:* "A sword upon the Chaldeans . . . a drought upon her waters" (Jer. 50:35-38; cf. Hag. 1:9-11; Ezek. 33:27).

b. Metaphonic. Changes of meaning depend on vowel mutation—*maqqēl šāqēdh 'ᵃnî rō'ê . . . kî šōqēdh 'ᵃnî:* "I see a rod of almond–[tree] . . . for I am watching" (Jer. 1:11-12; *see also* Amos 8:1-2). Metaphonic puns are facilitated by the occurrence of verbal forms in which a change in stem conjugation does not affect the consonantal root but alters, sometimes radically, the nature of the act: "If you are willing and obedient, you shall *eat* (*tō'khēlû*) the good of the land; But if you refuse and rebel, you shall be *devoured* (*tᵉ'ukkᵉlû*) by the sword" (Isa. 1:19-20, cf. Isa. 7:9; Gen. 49:19).

c. Parasonancy. Possibly the most widely attested type of wordplay, parasonancy involves the use of verbal and nominal roots which differ in one of their three consonants: "And he looked for justice (*mišpāṭ*), but behold, bloodshed (*mišpāḥ*); for righteousness (*ṣᵉdhāqâ*), but behold, a cry (*ṣᵉ'āqâ*)!" (Isa. 5:7; *see also* Judg. 5:15-16; 10:8; Ezek. 5:14; Ps. 28:1). A somewhat more sophisticated parasonant pun is the type in which consonants of one word are found in another word but in a differing order: "He delivers (*yᵉḥallēṣ*) the afflicted by their affliction, and opens their ears by adversity (*laḥaṣ*)" (Job 36:15); "All my enemies shall be ashamed (*yēbhōšû*) and sorely troubled; they shall turn back (*yāšubhû*), and be put to shame (*yēbhōšû*) in a moment" (Ps. 6:10 [H 11]).

d. Farrago. Confused, often ungrammatical wording which gains meaning only because of the context (e.g., English "hodge-podge," "helter-skelter," etc.). One characteristic of farrago is that some of the elements involved often display a tendency to rhyme. *Mahēr šālāl ḥāš baz* (Isa. 8:1, 3) affords a good example. Each word is understandable, but when they are strung together the result is awkward grammatically; yet it is quite precise in conveying the intention of the speaker. Other examples of farrago may be found in *tōhû wābhōhû* (Gen. 1:2); *'ûrîm wᵉthummîm* (Exod. 28:30); *šeṣeph qeṣeph* (Isa. 54:8); the name *Kušān riš'āthayim* (Judg. 3:8), king of Aram Naharayim; *'ûbhen-mešeq bêthî hû' dammešeq 'ᵉlî'ezer* (Gen. 15:2).

e. Assonance. Words are strung together primarily for oral effect rather than for furthering the meaning of a given phrase. Isa. 24:16-17 is ideally suited to illustrate this type: *wā'ōmar rāzî-lî rāzî-lî' ôy lî bōghᵉdhîm bāghādhû 'ûbheghedh bôghᵉdhîm bāghādhû: paḥadh wāphaḥath wāphāḥ 'alêkhā yōšēbh hā'āreṣ*—"But I say 'I pine away, I pine away. Woe is me! For the treacherous deal treacherously, the treacherous deal very treacherously.' Terror, and the pit, and the snare are upon you, O inhabitants of the earth!" Other examples are found in Isa. 22:5; 29:9; Amos 5:5; Gen. 49:19.

f. Onomatopoeia. The use of words imitative of natural sounds: "Then hammered the hooves of his horses, his chargers galloped, galloped away" (Judg. 5:22, NEB)—*middahᵃrôth dahᵃrôth 'abbîrāw*. Isa. 10:14 affords another example: "And there was none that moved a wing, or opened the mouth, or chirped (*ûphōṣê phê ûmᵉṣaphsēph*)." In Isa. 28:10, 13, the gibberish of foreign tongues is imitated, if not mocked. *See also* Isa. 47:2; Song of S. 1:2.

g. Antanaclasis. The same word, when repeated, sometimes requires different renditions: "I saw the tears of the oppressed, and I saw that there was *no one to comfort them* (*'ên lāhem menaḥēm*). Strength was on the side of their oppressors, *and there was no one to avenge them* (*'ên lāhem menaḥēm*)" (Eccl. 4:1, NEB). *See also* Eccl. 10:4 (*tannaḥ/yannîᵃḥ*); Isa. 58:10 (*naphšekhā/nepheš*); Prov. 24:10 (*ṣārâ/ṣar*); Lam. 2:6 (*mô'ᵃdhô/mô'ēdh*).

3. Extended wordplay. The attainment of rhetorical felicity was by no means the sole inspiration behind the use of wordplay. The biblical writer knew quite well how to unfold playfulness, sometimes beyond the confines of paragraphs or even chapters. To be noted here are examples of fairly long narratives from Genesis which benefited from paronomastic displays: (1) a play on *'îš* (man) and *'iššâ* (woman) explains the origin of woman (Gen. 2:23); (2) a play on *'ᵃrûmmîm* (naked) and *'ārûm* (clever) sets up the serpent as the immediate cause of the Fall (Gen. 2:25 and 3:1); (3) a possibly play on *'ēṣ* (tree) and *bēn* (son) might explain the use of the rare word *'iṣṣābhôn* (toil, pain) for the birth pangs meted out to the first partaker of the tree of knowledge (Gen. 3:16); (4) a play on *bᵉkhorâ* (status of an elder son) and *bᵉrākhâ* (blessing) underscores Jacob's triumphs against his brother Esau (Gen. 27); (5) repeated plays on derivates of the verbs *rā'â* (to see) and *yārā'* (to fear) are obvious in the narrative in Gen. 22.

A further type of extended paronomasia could be called "leitmotif." Cassuto has pointed out a good example in the biblical account of the Flood. The narrator repeatedly plays on the consonants in the name "Noah": "this one shall bring us relief" (*yᵉnaḥᵃmēnû;* 5:29); "the Lord was sorry" (*wayyināḥēm;* 6:6); "but Noah found favor" (*ḥēn;* 6:8); "the ark came to rest" (*wattānaḥ;* 8:4); "place to set her foot" (*mānōᵃḥ* 8:9); "the pleasing odor" (*nîḥōᵃḥ;* 8:21). Leitmotif paronomasia can also be found in the Isaac narratives in which all the biblical attestations of the *qal*-stem of the verb *ṣāḥaq* are embedded.

An appreciation of paronomasia allows scholars to reconstruct or interpret certain OT passages. Miller thinks Gen. 9:6*b* might originally have read *kî bidmûth 'ᵃᵉlōhîm ᵉāśâ 'eth-hā'ādhām*—"For in [divine] likeness, did Elohim create man." Such a reconstruction would allow punning on *dᵉmûth* (likeness) and *'ādhām* (man) as well as *dām* (blood).

The appearance of *'ar* in Ugaritic with a possible translation of "honey" (cognate to Arab. *'ary*) has permitted Porter to suggest that *'ᵃrî* (RSV "lion") in the answer to Samson's riddle (Judg. 14:18) is a pun on a word no longer in general use among his contemporaries.

The above typology in no way exhausts the possibilities in biblical paronomasia. Casanowicz has gathered some 502 examples, which show that paronomasia was resorted to most widely by the minor prophets Joel, Habbakuk, Micah, Zephaniah, Nahum, and Hosea, in descending order of frequency. Of the major prophets, only Isaiah (mostly First Isaiah) can be reckoned as an inveterate punster. The Writings that are best stocked with wordplays are Proverbs, Lamentations, and, to a lesser extent, Job. With the exception of Genesis, the historical books seldom indulged in this art.

Bibliography. I. M. Casanowicz, *Paronomasia in the Old Testament* (1894); H. Reckendorff, *Über Paronomasie in den Semitischen Sprachen* (1909); G. Boström, *Paronomasi i den Äldre Hebraiska Maschallitteraturen* (1928); F. de Liagre Böhl, "Wortspiele im Alten Testament," *Opera Minora* (1953), pp. 11-25; U. Cassuto, *From Adam to Noah,* I (1961), 288-89; N. Gottwald, *Studies in the Book of Lamentations* (2nd ed., 1962), pp. 23-32; J. Porter, "Samson's Riddle: Judges XIV,18," *JTS,* XIII (1962), 106-9; C. Carmichael, "Some Sayings in Genesis 49," *JBL,* LXXXVIII (1969), 438-44; J. Glück, "Paronomasia in Biblical Literature," *Semitics,* I (1970), 50-78; M. Fishbane, "Jeremiah IV.23-26 and Job III.3-13: A Recovered Use of the Creation Pattern," *VT,* XXI (1971), 161-62; L. Peeters, "Pour une interpretation du jeu de mots," *Semitics,* II (1971-72), 127-42; W. Holladay, "The Covenant with the Patriarchs Overturned," *JBL,* XCI (1972), 305-20, on Jer. 20:1-6; J. Max Miller, "In the 'Image' and 'Likeness' of God," *JBL,* XCI (1972), 289-304; J. Ouellette, "Le mur d'étain dans Amos VII.7-9," *RB,* LXXX (1973), 329-30; A. Hamori, *On the Art of Medieval Arabic Literature* (1974), ch. 5; J. Tigay, "Moses' Speech Difficulty," *Gratz College Annual,* III (1974), 31-32; M. Fishbane, "The Qumran Pesher and Traits of Ancient Hermeneutics," *Proceedings of the VIth World Congress of Jewish Studies* (forthcoming); J. Sasson, "Word-Play in Gen. 6:8-9," *CBQ,* XXXVII (1975), 165-66.

J. M. SASSON

Y

YAHWE yäh′ wə [Egyp. *Ya-h-wə*]. A Syrian place name in Egyptian records of the New Kingdom, onomastically identical with the divine name Yahweh.

The list of Asiatic places in Ramses II's temple at ʿAmārah West (Nubia) includes six names (nos. 93-98), all of them preceded by *tə šə-śu,* "Bedouin area": *Śə-ʿ-rə-r, Rə-bə-n-tu, Pi-ś-pi-ś, Śə-mə-tə, Ya-h-wə, Tu-r-bə-rə* (the last three entries are also preserved in Amen-hotep III's topographic list at Soleb, from which the ʿAmārah West list was largely copied). It is generally assumed that *Śə-ʿ-rə-r*=Seir, and thus that all six areas were located in Edom. This was compared with the OT passages in which Yahweh is associated with Edom, Seir, and Paran, and was taken as proof that this divine name was known on the S confines of Palestine *ca.* 1400 B.C., or even as confirmation of Yahweh's origins in the (hypothetical) Midianite AMPHICTYONY. However, the crucial equation *Śə-ʿ-rə-r*=Seir is dubious; it leaves unexplained the reduplication of *r*; Seir is found elsewhere in Egyptian correctly written *Śə-ʿ-r.* Three of the relevant place names, written *Rə-bə-n-ta, Tu-rə + bu-rə,* and *Yi-ha,* appear in a short topographic catalogue (Nos. 70-75 + 111-122 of Ramses III's composite Medinet Habu list), all of whose identifiable entries belong to central Syria. In particular, *Śə-ʿ-rər* corresponds to cuneiform *Šeḫlal* (N Phoenicia), *Rə-bə-n-ta* to cuneiform *Labana* (SE of Kadesh on the Orontes), *Śə-mə-tə* to modern Šamat (N Phoenicia), *Tu-rə-bu-rə* to modern Tarbul (Biqaʿ). *Ya-h-wə/Yi-ha* must also be located in the same general region, which contemporaneous Egyptian sources describe as heavily infiltrated by Shasu Bedouin. Whatever the connection between the place name and the divine name, the occurrence of the former in Egyptian records cannot be used as evidence for an early presence of the latter in Edom.

Bibliography. H. W. Fairman, "Preliminary Report on the Excavations at ʿAmārah West," *JEA,* XXV (1939), 139-44, esp. pl. XIV, 4; B. Grdseloff, "Édom, après les sources égyptiennes," *Revue d'hist. juive d'Egypte,* I (1947), 66-69; S. Herrmann, "Der Name Jhw; in den Inschriften von Soleb," *Fourth World Congress of Jewish Studies: Papers,* I (1967), 213-16; R. de Vaux, *Histoire ancienne d'Israël,* I (1971), 316-17.

M. C. ASTOUR

YAHWIST. A hypothetical figure who gave a decisive shape to parts of the literature of the PENTATEUCH. The Yahwist is variously regarded as author, editor, redactor, or circle of tradition. The hypothesis continues to receive broad support among critical scholars as the best explanation for the present form of the text. The name "Yahwist" derives from the term *Yahweh,* most often translated "Lord" in English renderings, to refer to the God of Israel, in contrast to other narrative traditions which prefer Elohim, most often translated "God" (*see* ELOHIST[S] §1). The documentary hypothesis of which the Yahwist is a part was devised primarily by German scholars who transliterated the Hebrew term *Yahweh* as *Jahweh.* Hence the author is referred to as "J" and the material assigned to him as the "J document," or better, the "J tradition." *See* SOURCE CRITICISM, OT[S]; DOCUMENTS.

1. Literary presuppositions
2. Cultural crisis of the tenth century
3. Theological affirmations
4. The prehistory
5. Blessing and curse
6. The Yahwist and Israel's normative faith
7. Wisdom resources
Bibliography

1. Literary presuppositions. The documentary hypothesis is a scholarly construct seeking to explain how the Pentateuch received its present form through a complex process of editing, redaction, and transmission. It assumes that the transmitting community of faith was actively engaged, not only in preserving the memory of the past, but in discerning its present significance for faith.

The hypothesis stems from the work of the great German literary critics of the nineteenth century, who held that there were four primary identifiable efforts at redaction or adjustment, each of which was made in response to a particular cultural crisis. The earliest of these was the Yahwist, who most decisively and enduringly shaped the tradition as it has been preserved to the present. *See* BIBLICAL CRITICISM §§1-4; BIBLICAL CRITICISM, HISTORY OF §§1*a-b,* 2.

Two significant changes have been made in the hypothesis since its articulation in the era of Wellhausen. (1) It was argued that J represented an early and primitive form of religion which was polytheistic and magical and did not express any authentic Israelite faith. Scholarly understanding has so shifted that J is seen as a mature and sophisticated theological formulation, notwithstanding its relatively early dating and its primitive form of expression. (2) The older scholars spoke of "authors" and "redactors," and presented the documentary hypothesis as a rational literary process. The process is now seen as communal and not individualistic; it is to be understood, not in terms of documents, but in terms of traditions which are linked to an ongoing community whose perceptions and understandings are related to their historical experience. Moreover, J can no longer be understood as a mere editor or redactor or transmitter, but must be seen as an active agent making bold and innovative efforts to present the tradition of Israel in ways pertinent to the pluralism and secularism of the age of monarchy.

2. Cultural crisis of the tenth century. Although older critics dated J somewhat later, it is now generally ascribed to the tenth century B.C., either the time of Solomon (962-922) or just after, in response to the crisis of culture and faith evoked by Solomon. Following Noth, it is plausible to assume that before the monarchy Israel already had a well-fixed confessional tradition, G (*Grundschrift*), which contained the major themes and components of the Pentateuch. It is in the context of that stable tradition that J worked. Moreover, tenth-century traditionists had other independent stories which permitted various interpretations and could be attached to the dominant tradition. In this view the Yahwist had the following literary and traditional elements available for use: (*a*) The credo articulating Israel's primary articles of faith, e.g., Deut. 26:5-9 (*see* CREDO, ANCIENT ISRAELITE[S]). (*b*) A relatively fixed narrative tradition which reflected the movement of the credo, but which was inventive in its use of the norms and themes of the credo; this includes expanded narratives clustering around themes of promise and Exodus. (*c*) Other traditional materials not yet attached or given a decisive confessional meaning or placement, including old folk tales, cultic etiologies, and tribal memories.

It is now generally held that the royal establishment of David and more especially of Solomon caused a decisive shift in the cultural perceptions and intellectual foundations of Israel. In two generations Israel was abruptly led from a folk culture to an urban-royal culture, from subsistance to affluence, from precariousness to security, from political insignificance to dominance. As its political and economic situation improved, it became intellectually more sophisticated. There was an effort to articulate faith and meaning in more humanistic and less theocentric terms. Historical activity was, perhaps for the first time, understood in terms of human initiative, with new appreciation for human freedom and responsibility. The older ways of speaking about a God who intervened in human affairs became increasingly problematical. The focus of life shifted so that sacral activities were less compelling; and economic planning, diplomatic shrewdness, and military calculation became increasingly important.

In such a milieu, new questions were posed for faith, and at the same time Israel came into possession of new intellectual resources. Solomonic entry into a vigorous internationalism made Israel especially open to influence by the literature and intellectual resources of myth and wisdom. *See* MYTH; WISDOM; WISDOM IN THE ANCIENT NEAR EAST[S]; WISDOM IN THE OT[S].

The Yahwist, then, was both a faithful traditionist and a creative theologian. Von Rad has made a strong case that it was J in the tenth century who did the primary shaping of the tradition, whereas Noth has argued that the early *Grundschrift* from the premonarchic period determined the shape. The issue cannot be decided, because we have no certain evidence about the extent or character of conjectured G. However, it is plausible to assume that Israel's normative confessional statement was well fixed by the tenth century, and J was free to operate only in a context which was by that time normative or canonical.

3. Theological affirmations. We may best understand the creativity of J if we formulate the questions he apparently sought to answer, questions of faith evoked by the new cultural situation of Solomon: (*a*) What does Israelite identity mean in a world of many nations? (*b*) What is the meaning of monarchy in Israel, since it is a new and not constitutive institution? (*c*) How does believing Israel relate to the royal-urban myths so central in Solomonic self understanding? (*d*) How does Israel speak of the lordship of Yahweh in a time of Solomonic dominance and of pluralism?

In coming to an answer about these questions, J used a variety of old narratives which present the patriarchs in situations of deep distress. Because of Yahweh's action or presence, they are repeatedly rescued and blessed. Thus a barren Sarah (Gen. 11:30) is unexpectedly the mother of an heir (18:1-15), and much of the narrative is preoccupied with that desperately yearned for but unlikely blessing. Repeatedly Israel is near death from famine, and because of God's leadership she survives and prospers (12:10-20; 26:1-33). The famine motif becomes the dominant theme in the Joseph narrative. In the Jacob narrative, the issue of precariousness is expressed in the giving of the promise to the younger son (27:18-29)—albeit by deception—whose life is then endangered by his brother. But he emerges prosperous and triumphant (Gen. 33). It is not likely that the Yahwist has imposed this theme on the older sagas. He has discerned in these narratives a common theme of promise in the face of precariousness, which made them a vehicle for faith in the tenth century.

A more problematic issue concerns the conclusion of the work of the Yahwist. While older scholarship thought J extended through the books of Kings, and Hölscher had discerned its ending at I Kings 12, more recent study has been reluctant to identify J materials after Numbers. Von Rad understood J as a scheme of promise-fulfillment in which the patriarchal narratives presented the promise, and the land narratives of Joshua the fulfillment. However, it is far from clear that portions of Joshua can be assigned to J. Mowinckel more recently has found the conclusion of J in Num. 32 and Judg. 1, material related to the conquest. Wolff, by contrast, has discerned the end of J in Num. 25:1-5, short of entry into the land, a suggestion which has considerable dramatic power, for it leaves Israel on the brink of the land of opportunity and temptation, confronted by hard decisions. *See* DEUTERONOMIC HISTORY, THE[S] §§1, 2; JOSHUA, BOOK OF[S] §1; ELOHIST[S] §4.

The enduring gain of such a perspective, even if the literary questions remain unresolved, is that J can in one form or another be understood in terms of promise and fulfillment. If J includes conquest narratives, the fulfillment is complete. If, as seems more likely, it does not, then the fulfillment is still uncertain, as is characteristic of the patriarchal stories.

The promise-fulfillment dynamic serves J's purposes of fidelity to tradition, and at the same time provides relevance to the cultural, theological crisis of the tenth century. The Yahwist was able to look back to show that promise is the driving power of the narratives, that the narratives state not only what is but what is to be. J subtly affirmed that the long-standing promises were now being actualized in the Israel of David and Solomon (*see* PROMISES TO THE PATRIARCHS[S]). (*a*) The ancient promise of a son and heir (Gen. 18:10) is now gloriously fulfilled in the royal son, Solomon (cf. II Sam. 12:24). (*b*) The ancient promise of the land (Gen. 12:1; 13:14-15) is now fulfilled in the empire, which controlled the land bridge of the Fertile Crescent (I Kings 4:24). (*c*) The great name (reputation) long ago promised to these nobodies (Gen. 12:2) is now fulfilled in Solomon (I Kings 1:47; 10:1-10), who became the envy of both his followers and his adversaries. (*d*) The ancient promise of blessing to other nations by means of Israel (Gen. 12:3) is affirmed. Israel now possesses resources, means, and opportunity to bring a blessing to her neighbors (cf. I Kings 4:20-21), but she also has the capacity to bring a curse (Gen. 12:10-20).

It follows that a proper reading of the old narratives, as they have been presented by J, requires a double reading. The old Israel is remembered as bearer of promise yet to be fulfilled; the new Israel as recipient of a fulfillment far exceeding the prospects of the promise.

Thus J (or perhaps G) linked together unrelated materials of patriarchs and conquest, and in so doing linked old hopes and new realities. In the process, he affirmed to his contemporaries an unpopular view, namely that Israel's present well-being was the result of Yahweh's promise and not a royal achievement. Thus the juxtaposition permits the old materials of promise to reinterpret the present circumstance of well-being.

4. The prehistory. The third element of J which warrants special attention is the "prehistory," in Gen. 2–11. The capacity to use such materials reflects the open mood of the Solomonic environment; they are not used, however, simply to preserve old materials or to deal with questions of cosmic origin. Rather, here as elsewhere J addresses questions of Israel's faith, identity, and vocation as they become problematical to his contemporaries. J's creativity is to be discerned by the ways in which these materials are arranged in a sequence of growing disillusionment and degeneration, and the way in which they are brought into tension with the patriarchal narratives. (*a*) After the initial statement of the gift of life in Gen. 2, four stories (expulsion from the garden [Gen. 3], Cain and Abel [Gen. 4], Noah and the Flood [Gen. 6–9], and the Tower of Babel [Gen. 11:1-9]) are placed in a sequence demonstrating the movement of world history toward hopelessness and death. The narrator creates a context in which the appearance of the people of promise (Abraham-David) is a welcome contrast. (*b*) The narratives present the world's history as being under a curse, in contrast to the history of blessing borne by Israel, announced in Gen. 8:22 and 12:3, and actualized in subsequent narratives. Thus the Yahwist affirms to royal Israel that she is to be in world history in a peculiar way. (*c*) By the eloquent resolution of the Flood in 8:22, J indicates that he is no parochial pleader for Israel. In royal Israel, the history of blessing continues as a counterpoint to the history of curse. But Yahweh's blessing is not conterminous with Israel, for it existed prior to and independent of Israel. (*d*) While J's prehistory is drawn from ancient Near Eastern mythical material, he ordered it as he did because he discerned in the life of the royal family in Jerusalem specific historical manifestations of mythical themes. (i) Expulsion from the Garden —David's seizure of Bathsheba and murder of Uriah (I Sam. 11–12). (ii) Cain and Abel—Amnon's murder by Absalom (II Sam. 13–14). (iii) Noah and the Flood—Absalom's rebellion against David (II Sam. 15–19). (iv) The Tower and the Scattering—Solomon's ruthless pride and assumption of power (I Kings 1–2). If such a correlation can be sustained, Gen. 2–11 would present the Davidic family as bearer of a curse, while the Abraham story affirms an alternative possibility as bearer of blessing.

5. Blessing and curse. Recent scholarship has focused on Gen. 12:1-4*a* as the key to J's theology. This text is undoubtedly formulated by J and is not borrowed from older material. The divine decree brings together the central issues. (*a*) It affirms the effective end of the history of curse. No more is heard of degeneracy and rebellion. (*b*) It announces the beginning of a new history, that a bearer of blessing and promise in the world of nations has been ordained by Yahweh. Thus he boldly asserts an enormous theological meaning for the united monarchy. (*c*) It presents Israel with a destiny of becoming a blessing, but the subsequent stories indicate that Israel also is tempted to participate in the history of curse. Israel can become part of the history of curse if she so chooses, but it need not be.

Of the other components of the J narrative, special attention should be given to the Joseph narrative, Gen. 37, 39–50 (*see* JOSEPH STORY[S]). As elsewhere in J, the Joseph narrative testifies to a direction in Israel's history that is not of her own making, but is under the rule of the One who has announced his purposes for well-being and blessing, both within and beyond Israel.

The J narrative makes good use of the old poetic Balaam cycle of Num. 22–24. On Wolff's reading this material is found at the end of the J tradition, but in any case it is crucially placed to articulate a central question about Israel. Balaam, despite royal pressure and his own inner resistance, is unable to bring a curse upon Israel. The narrative reiterates the conviction already announced in Gen. 12:1-3, that Yahweh has promised a blessing to Israel, and that he abides by that promise. He has determined it, and no one can modify it in the least. (In other traditions, the same ringing affirmation, perhaps learned from J, can be seen in Gen. 50:20; Josh. 21:43-45; 23:14.)

6. The Yahwist and Israel's normative faith. J has imposed a distinctive theological reading on the history of Israel, interpreting it in terms of blessing and promise. Since then, this interpretation has been unavoidable, and it has been followed by Israel's major historians and poets. Through this interpretation, J has provided important responses to the Solomonic situation, when Israel experienced a crisis of theological categories.

a) Solomon was tempted to be like others and to secure his own existence (cf. Gen. 11:1-9; and even 12:10-20). J makes subtle protest against any self-understanding in which Israel denied its role as a bearer of blessing. J rejects the syncretism which is content to settle for the ways of the world (the other cultures), which places no credence in the power of promise to direct life, and which makes no investment in blessing in a world seduced by curse.

b) Monarchy constituted a problem in Israel because it was an alien institution without traditional legitimization. J presents it as a way to implement Israel's peculiar identity. In depicting Abraham as a prototype of Israelite kings, J presents the royal establishment as a bearer of blessing in a world organized against blessing. Even in Israel, however, kings do not act this way and are bearers of curse, but J holds out another possibility.

c) The royal-urban myths in Solomon's time invited a royal regime to claim theological absolutism for itself (cf. Gen. 3; 4; 6–9; 11:1-9). J resisted such a temptation; when J speaks of Israel, as he finally does in Gen. 12 ff., he does not utilize ancient Near Eastern myth but instead has recourse to Israel's old traditions. As blessing answers curse, so Israel's communal memory responds to the world's myth. Clearly J defines Israel by old tribal memories which he shows to be relevant even in the new situation.

d) J affirms that the well-being of Israel and the performance of her historic mission are understood, not in terms of royal policy, enlightened though it may be, but in terms of the abiding promises of Yahweh which kings can neither invent nor void. Thus J issues a mighty protest against undue managing of history by the royal regime.

7. Wisdom resources. It is likely that the history-of-traditions approach to the J material, summarized above, has reached its full expression. One direction for future study is the way in which sapiential influences may be discerned in the material. Examples include the various elements in the prehistory which pursue characteristic wisdom themes; the narrative of Gen. 24, the Joseph narrative, and perhaps the blessing-curse issue in Num. 22–24. More important is the firm conviction that God's hidden purposes will come to fruition.

The capacity to take actions and the inevitable need to face their consequences required the royal managers of Israel to discern wisely. It may be that the J introductory narrative addresses that question: "When you eat of it your eyes will be opened, and you will be like God, knowing good and evil" (Gen. 3:5). It was the task and gift of kings to know "good and evil" (cf. II Sam. 14:17, surely from the same milieu). The Yahwist has clearly honored Israel's old confessional self-identity; but he did it in order to affirm: "Many are the plans in the mind of a man, but it is the purpose of the Lord that will be established" (Prov. 19:21). Or perhaps more subtly he recognized the tension between the inscrutable ways of Yahweh and the drive of monarchy to manage its own affairs: "It is the glory of God to conceal things, but the glory of kings is to search things out" (Prov. 25:2). J makes abundant room for royal "searching out," but he retains as the final reality the concealing activity of God, which ultimately orders Israel's life.

J's effort is based on the presupposition that the old traditions, if properly articulated, could sustain Israel in a time of theological crisis. He believed in the monarchy and affirmed it, but only under a certain reading. To both adherents and adversaries of the monarchy, he put the subtle, burdensome question: What does it mean to live in history with power, but clearly *sola gratia*? He knew that it is hard for a rich man to enter the kingdom, but he affirmed that a royal Israel, with its enormous staying power, can still be a bearer of blessings and a recipient of promises.

Bibliography. L. Alonso-Schökel, "Sapiential and Covenant Themes in Genesis 2–3," *Modern Biblical Studies,* ed. D. J. McCarthy and W. B. Callen (1967), pp. 49-61; B. W. Anderson, *The Beginning of History* (1963); J. Blenkinsopp, "Theme and Motif in the Succession History (2 Sam. XI 2 ff.) and the Yahwist Corpus," VTSup, XV (1966), 44-57; J. Bright, "Modern Study of OT Literature," *The Bible and the Ancient Near East,* ed. G. E. Wright (1961), pp. 13-31; W. Brueggemann, "David and His Theologian," *CBQ,* XXX (1968), 156-81, *In Man We Trust* (1972); W. M. Clark, "The Flood and the Structure of the Pre-Patriarchal History," *ZAW,* LXXXIII (1971), 184-211; R. Clements, *Abraham and David,* SBT, V (1967); P. F. Ellis, *The Yahwist, the Bible's First Theologian* (1968), the best summary of recent study; G. Fohrer, *Introduction to the OT* (1968), pp. 103-65; T. Fretheim, *Creation, Fall and Flood* (1969); M. L. Henry, *Jahwist und Priesterschrift* (1960); D. A. Knight, *The Traditions of Israel,* SBL Dissertation Series (1973); S. Mowinckel, *Erwägungen zur Pentateuch Quellenfrage* (1964), "Tetrateuch—Pentateuch—Hexateuch," *BZAW,* XC (1964); M. Newman, *The People of the Covenant* (1962); M. A. Noth, *History of Pentateuchal Traditions* (1972); G. von Rad, *Genesis* (1961), "The Joseph Narrative and Ancient Wisdom," *The Problem of the Hexateuch and Other Essays* (1966), *OT Theology I* (1962), most programmatic statement on the theology of the Yahwist; R. Rendtorff, "Genesis 8, 21 und die Urgeschichte des Jahwisten," *Kerygma und Dogma,* VII (1961), 69-78, "Hermeneutische Probleme der Biblischen Urgeschichte," *Festschrift für Friedrich Smend* (1963), pp. 19-29; W. Richter, "Urgeschichte und Hoftheologie," *BZ,* X (1966), 96-105; L. Ruppert, "Der Jahwist—Künder der Heilsgeschichte," *Wort und Botschaft,* ed. J. Schreiner (1967), pp. 88-107; H. S. Steck, "Genesis 12:1-3 und die Urgeschichte des Jahwisten," *Probleme biblischer Theologie,* ed. H. W. Wolff (1971), pp. 525-54, *Die Paradieserzählung* (1970); H. J. Stoebe, "Gut und Böse in der Jahwistischen Quelle des Pentateuch," *ZAW,* LXV (1953), 188-204; S. L. Terrien, "The Theological Significance of Genesis," *JBR,* XIV (1946), 29-32; N. E. Wagner, "Abraham and David," in *Studies on the Ancient Palestinian World,* ed. J. W. Wevers and D. B. Redford (1972), pp. 117-

40, a serious criticism of the Solomonic hypothesis as presented above; C. Westermann, *The Genesis Accounts of Creation,* Facet Books, VII (1964), "The Way of the Promise Through the OT," *The OT and Christian Faith,* ed. B. W. Anderson (1969), pp. 200-224; N. Whybray, "The Intellectual Tradition in the OT," *BZAW,* CXXXV (1974); H. W. Wolff, "The Kerygma of the Yahwist," *Int.,* XX (1966), 131-58, important articulation of a central motif in Yahwist's theology; W. Zimmerli, "Promise and Fulfillment," *Essays on OT Hermeneutics,* ed. C. Westermann (1963), pp. 89-122.

W. Brueggemann

YARMULKE. *See* Head Covering[S].

YA'UDI yä oo' dĭ [Zenjirli inscription יאדי; Assyr. KUR*Ia-ú-du/Ia-ú-di/Ia-u-di;* ethn. KUR*Ia-ú-da-a-a*]. יאדי appears in the inscriptions of Zenjirli (ninth-eighth centuries B.C.) as the native appellation of the NW Syrian state alternately called שמאל for its capital city (Assyrian Sam'al/Sam'alla/Samalla). The identity of Azriyau of Ya'udi, the leader of resistance to Tiglath-pileser III in northern Syria (738 B.C.) has been the subject of a long controversy. One school of thought regarded this Ya'udi as the Assyrian transcription of יאדי, and identified Azriyau with the nameless usurper whose coup and subsequent defeat by Tiglath-pileser III are described in the Zenjirli inscription of Bar-Rakib. The other school identified Azriyau with Uzziah (Azariah), king of Judah, denied that יאדי was vocalized Ya'udi, and claimed that *Ia-ú-di/du* in Assyrian sources always designated Judah. In favor of the former assumption, besides considerations of historical and geographical probability, is the comparison of two versions of Sargon II's records referring to his second year (720). The Nimrud Inscription (*ARAB,* II, §137) calls Sargon "subduer of the land of *Ia-ú-du,* which lies far away; who carried off [the people of] Hamath, whose hands captured Iau-bi'di, their king." The corresponding passage of Prism B (*ARAB,* II, §197) has "The city of Samalla . . . in the city of Hamath, Damascus . . . together with my cavalry . . . in the midst of Hamath set up." Thus Ya'udu equals here Samalla, especially so since Judah was not subdued by the Assyrians in 720 but remained a loyal vassal till 713, and was not invaded till 701.

There is no reason to speak of Ya'udi as of N Judah; the two names are onomastically unrelated, and their similarity in Assyrian transcription is because of the phonetic deficiency of the cuneiform script. Even so, the inscriptions of Zenjirli and its neighborhood, composed in the native (Ya'udic) dialect and in Old Aramaic, shed much light on the social, political, and religious life of the West Semitic world before the Assyrian conquest. *See* Hittites[S] and map.

Bibliography. Zenjirli texts: *KAI,* Nos. 24, 214-18; J. B. Prichard, ed., *ANET* (3rd ed.), pp. 654-55; S. Parpola, "Sam'al," *Neo-Assyrian Toponyms* (1970), Neo-Assyrian occurrences. On the question of Azriyau of Ya'udi, opinions are divided as follows: For his identity with Uzziah of Judah: H. M. Haydn, "Azariah of Judah and Tiglath-pileser III," *JBL,* XXVIII (1909), 182-99; D. D. Luckenbill, "Azariah of Judah," *AJSL,* XLI (1925), 217-32; E. R. Thiele, "The Chronology of the Kings of Judah and Israel," *JNES,* III (1944), 156-63; H. Tadmor, "Azriyau of Yaudi," *Scripta Hierosolymitana,* VIII (1961), 232-71. For his being a king of Sam'al: A. T. Olmstead, *History of Assyria* (1923), pp. 184-88; A. Dupont-Sommer, *Les Araméens* (1949), pp. 24, 42, 61; O. Eissfeldt, "Syrien u. Palästina. . . ." *Fischer Weltgeschichte,* IV (1967), 178, 198-99.

M. C. Astour

Z

***ZADOK THE PRIEST. 1. Origin.** In II Sam. 8:17 David's priests are listed as Zadok son of Ahitub and Ahimelech son of Abiathar (cf. I Chr. 18:16). However, it seems clear from I Sam. 22:20; 23:6; and 30:7 that Ahimelech was actually the father of Abiathar. Furthermore, Ahitub is called the father of Ahijah/Ahimelech in I Sam. 14:3 and 22:9, 11, 20. Accordingly, most scholars have concluded that MT II Sam. 8:17 is out of order and that its original form was something like, "Zadok and Abiathar, son of Ahimelech, son of Ahitub, were priests." Thus Zadok would be left entirely without genealogy. Consequently, Zadok has generally not been thought to be a descendant of Aaron as recorded in I Chr. 6:1-8 [H 5:27-34]; 6:50-53 [H 6:35-38]; and Ezra 7:2-5. Various theories have been proposed as to his origin.

a. Jerusalem. The theory that Zadok was originally a Jebusite priest probably has enjoyed the greatest popularity. It considers Zadok to have some connection with Melchizedek and Adonizedek and to have been the priest of 'Ēl 'Elyôn in Jerusalem prior to David's conquest of the city. A variation considers Zadok to be a Jebusite priest who deserted to David at Hebron.

The most elaborate attack on the "Jebusite hypothesis" is by Cross. First, to link Zadok with the tradition of Melchizedek or Adonizedek simply because of the similarity in names is without significance, because *ṣdq* is a common element in Amorite, Ugaritic, Canaanite, and Hebrew names. Further, there is no evidence in the texts (II Sam. 24:18-25 and I Chr. 21:18-30) that David pitched his tent at the Canaanite shrine of 'Ēl 'Elyôn. Next, David, an orthodox Yahwist, would hardly have invited a pagan priest to serve as one of the chief priests in his realm. Finally, if Zadok really descended from Melchizedek, why didn't the later Zadokites claim him as their ancestor instead of Aaron?

b. The Aaronite (Hebron) hypothesis. Cross has proposed taking another look at the genealogies which make Zadok the son of Ahitub (II Sam. 8:17) and the descendant of Aaron (I Chr. 6:1-15 [H 5:27-41]). Since Wellhausen, this information has been considered to have no historical value. Behind Wellhausen's skepticism was his assumption that Ahitub the father of Zadok was the same Ahitub as the grandson of Eli in I Sam. 14:3 and the grandfather of Abiathar in I Sam. 22:20. Accordingly, Wellhausen thought that the text of II Sam. 8:17 (MT *wṣdwq bn 'ḥyṭwb w'ḥymlk bn 'bytr khnym*) had been corrupted intentionally and that it originally read: *'bytr bn 'ḥymlk bn 'ḥyṭwb wṣdwq khnym.*

There is, however, no textual evidence for Wellhausen's emendation, and it does not seem likely that, if an ancient Zadokite wished to change the text, he would have put Zadok last. Furthermore, Wellhausen's reading gives no patronymic for Zadok but two generations of ancestry to Abiathar. One would expect a single patronymic in each case (cf. II Sam. 8:16).

According to Cross's reconstruction, there is no reason for removing Ahitub as Zadok's father. Also there is no *a priori* reason why there could not be two Ahitubs, one the grandfather of Abiathar and the other the father of Zadok, as the genealogies (e.g., I Sam. 22:20; I Chr. 6:1-8 [H 5:27-34]) indicate. Already on the basis of I Sam. 2:20-36, where according to most interpreters the line of Zadok is presented as a replacement for the line of Eli, Zadok would not be expected to be of the same line as Abiathar.

Cross's reconstruction of II Sam. 8:17 starts with the Syr. text: *ṣdwq bn 'ḥyṭwb w'bytr bn 'ḥymlk.* At one point in the textual tradition Abimelech stood for Ahimelech (cf. MT I Chr. 18:16), thus: *ṣdwq bn 'ḥyṭwb w'bytr bn 'bymlk.* By haplography *'bytr bn* could have dropped out, resulting in *ṣdwq bn 'ḥyṭwb w'bymlk.* Later, *'bytr* could have been reinserted, but at the wrong place, and filled out by *bn: ṣdwq bn 'ḥyṭwb w'bymlk bn 'bytr.* Finally, the MT version would have resulted by adding *w* to *ṣdwq* and changing *w'bymlk* to its variant *w'ḥymlk.*

Accepting this reconstruction would mean that Zadok was indeed an Aaronide and it would explain how Abiathar mistakenly became the father of Ahimelech.

If the Aaronides had their center in Hebron, as some scholars believe, then it is possible that Zadok originated there. I Chr. 12:26-28 [H 12:27-29] speaks of Zadok as being over the priests (=Aaronides?) in Hebron. Since David ruled Judah from Hebron (II Sam. 5:5), he could have made contact with Zadok and later brought him to his capital in Jerusalem.

2. The descendants of Zadok. The genealogy of I Chr. 6:1-15 [H 5:27-41] (cf. 9:11; Neh. 11:11; Ezra 7:1-5), which begins with Levi and includes Zadok, presents Zadok's descendants as follows (probably to be construed as a list of high priests): Zadok (I), Ahimaaz, Azariah (I), Johanan, Azariah (II), Amariah (II), Ahitub (II), Zadok (II), Shallum, Hilkiah, Azariah (III), Seraiah, Jehozadak.

Because of the apparent discrepancies between this genealogy and the narratives of Kings and Chronicles, many scholars believe that it is an artistic creation of a priestly scribe. If one allows three hundred years (twenty-five years per generation) for the twelve generations between Ahimaaz and Jehozadak and figures back from the destruction of Jerusalem in 587 B.C. (when Jehozadak lived, cf. I Chr. 6:15 [H 5:41]), one falls considerably short of 959 B.C., when the temple was begun. This can, however, be explained by assuming that the genealogy represents a list which became stylized in Zadokite circles long before the Chronicler used it. Hence, there would probably be historical gaps in the genealogy. Furthermore, the repetition of Amariah-Ahitub-Zadok, which has likewise caused scholars to doubt the genealogy's reliability, is not without its historical parallels.

It therefore appears likely that the descendants of Zadok controlled the priesthood in Jerusalem from Solomon till the Exile and that I Chr. 6:8-15 [H 5:34-41] presents a reasonably accurate listing of its main members. If the Aaronite ancestry of Zadok is sound, the terminology "sons of Aaron" for priests prior to Solomon (so in P) and "Zadokites" for those after his time (cf. Ezek. 40:46; 43:19; 44:15; 48:11) would be precisely what one would expect.

See also AARON, AARONIDES[S]; CALF, GOLDEN[S]; PRIESTS[S].

Bibliography. K. Möhlenbrink, "Die levitischen Überlieferungen des Alten Testaments," *ZAW,* LII (1934), 184-231; R. de Vaux, *Ancient Israel* (1961), pp. 372-405; C. E. Hauer, "Who Was Zadok?" *JBL,* LXXXII (1963), 89-94; A. H. J. Gunneweg, *Leviten und Priester* (1965), pp. 98-116, 188-203; J. R. Bartlett, "Zadok and His Successors at Jerusalem," *JTS,* XIX (1968), 1-18; A. Cody, *A History of Old Testament Priesthood* (1969), pp. 88-93, 141-42, 156-74; F. M. Cross, *Canaanite Myth and Hebrew Epic* (1973), pp. 195-215; J. Wellhausen, *Der Text der Bücher Samuelis* (1871), p. 177.

M. D. REHM

ZAPHON, MOUNT Zä fōn′ [צפון, from צפה, to keep watch]. The sacred mountain of the Syrian storm-god Baal-Hadad (*see* BAAL). It is to be identified with Mount Hazzi of the Hurrian texts, the classical Mount Casius, and the modern Jebel el ʿAqra, a 5,807-foot-high peak located on the Syrian coast opposite the finger of Cyprus, about thirty miles N of ancient UGARIT. The Israelites used the name of this northern mountain as their common noun for north, just as they used the word "sea" to mean west. The older English translations always translated Zaphon as "north." There are four passages where the primary meaning shows through when properly translated.

Zaphon occurs in Ps. 89:12 [H 13] with the names of three other sacred mountains. MT may be amended to read: "Zaphon and Amana you created, Tabor and Hermon shout for joy at your name" (author's trans. throughout).

Isa. 14:13-14 mentions the mountain in an old mythical motif about the revolt and subsequent fall of one of the divine beings: "You said in your heart, 'I will scale the heavens. I will exalt my throne above the stars of El. I will sit enthroned on the mount of assembly, on the heights of Zaphon.'" This passage contains a strangely confused mixture of Canaanite mythology, since it assigns Zaphon, Baal's mountain in the Ugaritic texts, to EL and identifies it with the mount where the divine council met (El's Mount *Ll* in Ugaritic texts). Such confusion seems to reflect Yahwistic appropriation of both El and Baal material.

Dewey Beegle
1. Mount Zaphon

In Ps. 48:1-2 [H 2-3], the far more lofty, majestic, and famous Zaphon is equated with Jerusalem's Mount Zion: "Great is Yahweh, and greatly to be praised. In the city of our God is his holy mountain, The most beautiful peak, the joy of all the earth. Mount Zion is the heights of Zaphon, the city of the great King." Such identification of Zaphon with a different and smaller mountain may be paralleled in Canaanite material where the cult of the original site was transferred to a secondary location, but normally the distinctive name of the smaller mountain is not preserved in those cases. The identification in this text would appear to represent Israelite glorification of Jerusalem, therefore, rather than Canaanite cultic tradition. *See* ZION TRADITION[S].

Finally, Job 26:7 refers to the mountain in striking, though seldom understood imagery: "He stretches out Zaphon over the void, He hangs the earth upon nothingness." Seen at a distance, high mountains like Zaphon often have their bases shrouded in clouds or obscured by haze, while their tops remain clearly visible. The visual impression made by such a scene is that of a mountain floating in the air, and it is precisely this impression of land hanging unsupported which the poet has captured in these two synonymous lines.

Bibliography. O. Eissfeldt, *Baal Zaphon, Zeus Kasios und der Durchzug der Israeliten durchs Meer* (1932); R. J. Clifford, *The Cosmic Mountain in Canaan and the OT* (1972); O. Mowan, "Quatuor montes sacri in Ps. 89. 13?" *VD,* XLI (1963), 11-20; J. J. M. Roberts, "*Ṣāpôn* in Job 26, 7," *Bibl.* (1976).

J. J. ROBERTS

***ZAREPHATH.** The identification of ancient Zarephath with the modern village of Sarafand, nine miles S of Sidon, was confirmed by a discovery in the village of a stone inscription which contained the phrase [θε]ῷ ἁγ[ιῷ] Σαραπτην[ῷ], "to the holy god of Sarepta." The line may be restored on the basis of other extant inscriptions with the same phrase.

In addition to the OT reference in connection with the story of Elijah's visit there (I Kings 17:8-24), and a thirteenth-century B.C. Egyptian letter, the Phoenician town is mentioned in Assyrian texts of Sennacherib, who states that it was one of the cities which submitted to him during the campaign he conducted in 701 B.C. Esarhaddon says that he turned the city over to Baʿli, king of Tyre. Classical writers comment on the wine and purple dye of Sarepta, and in the Middle Ages travelers frequently stopped there during pilgrimages.

Phoenician and Roman settlements have come to light as the result of excavations undertaken by the University of Pennsylvania Museum, beginning in 1969. A Roman port was uncovered, dating from the first to the sixth centuries A.D. It consisted of a quay with a mooring ring, a water system which ran down to an outlet at the quay after passing through four rock-cut basins, and adjoining sluice gates. The basins apparently were used to filter fresh water to be taken aboard boats moored in the harbor. Public buildings adjoined the quay.

The Phoenician settlement lies about a half-mile N of the Roman port and is situated on a rise overlooking the main harbor used by fishermen today. Excavations to bedrock revealed that the Phoenician settlement, which underlies at least one Roman stratum, was occupied during the Late Bronze Age and much of the Iron Age. Zarephath must have been an important center for the manufacture of Phoenician pottery because a large portion of the excavated area contained a series of over twenty pottery kilns, basins for the levigation of clays, and massive piles of pottery rejects.

A small shrine with an offering table and benches along the side walls, replete with votive objects, was found adjacent to the industrial area. A variety of terra-cotta figurines and a few carved ivory objects were located near the offering table. One of the deities worshiped at Zarephath was the goddess Tanit, whose symbol was recently found on a glass stamp. Sometimes identified with the goddess Astarte, she was worshiped at Carthage in conjunction with ceremonies involving child sacrifice. Fig. Z2.

At Sarafand several tombs have been discovered on a hill overlooking the Phoenician settlement; they contained Phoenician pottery dating to the sixth and fifth centuries B.C. Another burial of the Late Bronze Age, said to be from Sarafand, contained Mycenaean pottery.

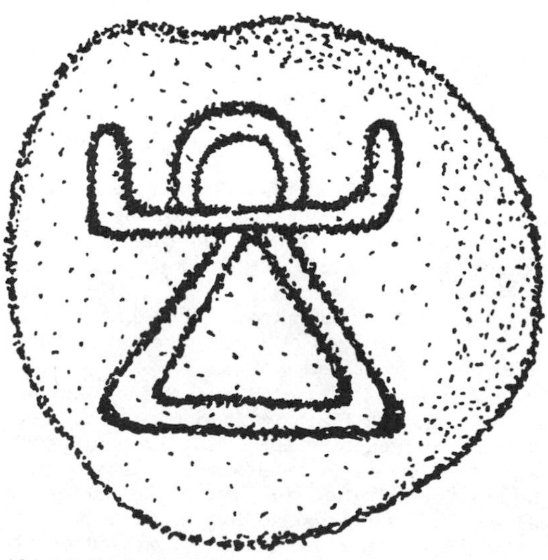

After J. B. Pritchard, *Expedition*, XIV
2. Tanit seal from Zarephath

Bibliography. D. C. Baramki, "A Late Bronze Age Tomb at Sarafand: Ancient Sarepta," *Berytus,* XII (1958), 129-42; W. Culican, "Phoenician Oil Bottles and Tripod Bowls," *Berytus,* XIX (1970), 5-18; J. B. Pritchard, "The Roman Port at Sarafand (Sarepta)," *Bulletin du Musée de Beyrouth,* XXIV (1971), 39-56, "The Phoenicians in Their Homeland," *Expedition,* XIV, 1 (1971), 14-23, "Sarepta in Tradition and History," in *Understanding the Sacred Text,* ed. John Reumann (1972), pp. 101-14, and *Sarepta: A Preliminary Report on the Iron Age* (1975); R. Saidah, "Archaeology in the Lebanon 1968-1969," *Berytus,* XVIII (1969), 134-37; C. C. Torrey, "The Exiled God of Sarepta," *Berytus,* IX (1948-49), 45-49.

T. L. McClellan

*ZARETHAN. Often identified with Tell es-Sa'idiyeh, but alternative identifications include Tell Umm Ḥamad and a site SW of Tell el-Meḳbere. Excavations at the double site of Tell es-Sa'idiyeh by the University of Pennsylvania Museum (1964-67) uncovered a cemetery on the lower mound dating from the thirteenth to the eleventh centuries B.C., and on the upper mound a domestic quarter of the ninth to seventh centuries B.C., and an area with public buildings from the Persian, Hellenistic, and Roman periods.

In the cemetery over forty burials were discovered, many of which contained bronze weapons and vessels, together with Mycenaean pottery. The richest burial, grave 101, was that of a female who wore toggle pins and breastplates of silver and a necklace with beads of carnelian and gold. Several ivory cosmetic objects and seven bronze objects were in the grave (*see* Fig. Z3).

Courtesy the University Museum
3. Bronze bowl with smaller bowl, strainer, and juglet as they were found fused together in a tomb at Zarethan

Nearby a burial of a warrior revealed an interment custom hitherto unknown in Palestine; the bones of the deceased had been wrapped in cloth and covered with a protective coating of bitumen. Grave goods with the warrior included several bronze objects, of which the most outstanding was a long bronze sword with a cast-bronze hilt. Many of the other burials contained bronzes and imported pottery and other objects, some from Egypt and Cyprus, but mostly from the Aegean area. The numerous Mycenaean vessels and distinctive burial practices suggest that the cemetery may contain burials of Sea Peoples. The PHILISTINES, one of the Sea Peoples, were distinguished for their metallurgy. Although it is often assumed that most of their tools and weapons were of iron, this metal is not specifically mentioned in the key OT reference (I Sam. 13:19-22). At the neighboring mound of Deir'alla (Succoth?) Dutch excavators have found evidence of a bronze-smelting industry during the twelfth and eleventh centuries B.C. The biblical statement that Solomon cast bronze vessels for the temple in the plain between Zarethan and Succoth (I Kings 7:46) coincides with the discovery of numerous bronzes at Tell es-Sa'idiyeh and the nearby smelting activities.

In the domestic quarter of the city there were four major Iron Age II levels. In stratum III (eighth century B.C.), one partially excavated building had a white plastered mud-brick platform containing two small depressions. One was filled with ashes which surrounded a tripod incense burner; three other incense burners were found nearby. The platform may have served a cultic purpose. A similar installation was found at ASHDOD. In a later city, stratum II, which was destroyed in the eighth century B.C., rows of houses stood back to back on parallel streets. The plans of the houses were identical, a long front room divided into two parts by a row of pillars, and a small back room for storage. In the latest Iron II level, stratum I, over seventy circular pits and several rectangular mud-brick bins had been cut into the ground for the storage of grain. An Iron Age stairway-tunnel descended to a spring. A mud-brick wall ran down the middle of the stone stairway, and probably was used to support a camouflaged roof.

In the area of the public buildings on the peak of the upper mound, a large square palace or fortress with a central courtyard had been built during the Persian period. A tower on one corner of the building near the edge of the tell provided a lookout with a view of the Jordan Valley for miles around. One of the few objects in the fortress was a small decorated limestone incense burner inscribed with the owner's name, "Belonging to Zakkūr." *See* Fig. Z4.

See also ZEREDAH §2; ZERERAH.

Bibliography. Y. Aharoni, *The Land of the Bible* (1967), pp. 31, 115, 278; M. Ottosson, *Gilead* (1969), pp. 216-17; J. B. Pritchard, "Two Tombs and a Tunnel in the Jordan Valley," *Expedition,* VI, 4 (1964), 2-9, "A Cosmopolitan Culture of the Late Bronze Age," *Expedition,* VII, 4 (1965), 26-33, "The Three Ages of Biblical Zarethan," *ILN,* CCXLIX (July 2, 1966), 25-27, "An Eighth Century Traveller," *Expedition,* X, 2 (1968), 26-29, "The Palace of Tell es-Sa'idiyeh," *Expedition,* XI, 1 (1968), 20-22, "New Evidence on the Role of the Sea Peoples," in *The Role of the Phoenicians on the Interaction of Mediterranean Civilizations,* ed. W. A. Ward (1968), pp. 99-112, "On the Use of the Tripod Cup," *Ugaritica* VI (1969), 427-34, "An Incense Burner from Tell es-Sa'idiyeh, Jordan Valley," in *Studies on the Ancient Palestinian World,* ed. J. W. Wevers and D. B. Redford (1972), pp. 3-17.

T. L. MCCLELLAN

*__ZEALOT.__ Term which Jewish resistance fighters used of themselves in their struggle against the Roman occupation. In modern research, this term has been interpreted as the party label of the entire resistance movement of the first century A.D., which began with Judas the Galilean (6 B.C.) and ended with the suicide of the defenders of the fortress Masada (A.D. 74). *See* MASADA[S].

Recently the Zealots have been discussed from two perspectives.

(1) On the basis of the somewhat unclear report in Josephus (*see* JOSEPHUS, FLAVIUS), the suggestion has been made that perhaps only one of several resistance groups claimed the name "Zealots." The term would then not apply to a unified front, and the question would be what the special concerns of the individual groups were.

(2) Starting from some traces in the synoptic tradition, an old thesis has been revived, which was first introduced by Reimarus: that Jesus was himself a Zealot, or at least was sympathetic to the political freedom fighters.

1. The Zealot resistance. Josephus gives the impression that there were at least five resistance groups:

a. The so-called Sicarii (from the Latin *sicarius,* the "Dagger-man," the assassin). They could presumably be traced back to Judas the Galilean, who led the resistance to the census of A.D. 6. After the murder of their leader Menahem at the beginning of the war, this group retreated to the fortress

After J. B. Pritchard, *Expedition,* XI
4. Limestone altar with inscription

of Masada, where their resistance ended in mass suicide (A.D. 74). However, Josephus also uses the term "Sicarii" for those Jewish refugees who fled to Egypt after the end of the war.

b. The Zealots. This was a title of honor, probably used by a group which occupied the temple precincts under the leadership of the priest Eleazar.

c. The followers of the Galilean, John of Gischala. This group united with the Zealots during the war and exercised a reign of terror in Jerusalem from time to time (Jos. War IV.v.3).

d. The followers of Simon bar Giora. They controlled S Judea (Jos. War IV.ix.5, 9) and were called on by the population of Jerusalem to help fight the Zealots (Jos. War IV.ix.11).

e. The Idumeans. This group was first affiliated with the Zealots, then partially with John of Gischala, and finally with Simon bar Giora (Jos. War IV.iv.1, ix.5, ix.11; V.vi.1).

2. Origins. It must be remembered that Josephus himself witnessed only a small part of the events he reported. Thus, in many cases he probably was following the linguistic usage of his sources. In addition, especially in *The Jewish War,* he writes as an apologist for his people, in whose interest he presented the rebellion against Rome as the work of a few insignificant circles. So it is probable that his pejorative labels "assassin" and "robber" came from his tendency to free the population at large from the accusation of rebellion.

Josephus states that the entire anti-Roman movement goes back to Judas the Galilean (Jos. Antiq. XVIII.i.6). This is confirmed by the few Talmudic and early church references to the resistance against Rome.

Thus the view of Baumbach that the Sicarii were a socially oriented Galilean lay movement and the Zealots a priestly party has no basis in the sources. The assumption by Smith that the Zealots were a special fighting group of the Jewish rural population is also contradicted by the sources.

The most probable assumption remains, therefore, that the Zealots were a relatively unified movement. It is possible that the Sicarii were an especially active group named for their guerrilla tactics. In addition, it is not surprising that rivalries between individual leaders, as well as sociological distinctions led to tensions and feuds in the Zealot camp.

The ideological background of the Zealot movement is most clearly illuminated by examining its founders. When Judea was made a Roman province in 6 B.C., Judas the Galilean and the Pharisee Zadok established the "fourth school of Jewish philosophers" (Jos. War II.viii.1). Josephus—himself a Pharisee—denies a relationship between the Pharisees and the Zealots, but there are many indications that the two groups held similar beliefs. The Zealots distinguished themselves by strict observance of the sabbath commandment (Jos. War II.xxii.8) and rigorous requirements for cleanliness. They demanded circumcision even of heathen. There was a ritual bath and a synagogue in Masada—cultic installations which prove the Pharisaic character of the resistance fighters. Judas the Galilean departed from the Pharisaic way of thinking by an uncompromising insistence on the first commandment of the Decalogue; no one except God was to be honored as "king" or "lord." Therefore, no foreigner was to rule over Israel. Paying taxes to the emperor, which would mean a recognition of the foreign rule, would be idolatry and defection from Yahweh. People and God would have to work together to bring about the liberation of Israel, and military force would be used against both heathen and Jewish lawbreakers. The models of such "zealousness" for Yahweh were Phinehas and Elijah, as well as the Maccabees. Accordingly, the self-designation "Zealots" might have been a party platform. The willingness to be martyred and the scorn of death, which not even Josephus can deny the Zealots (Jos. War II.ix.3; III.ii.1), can be understood only in the context of this kind of religious motivation. An interpretation of the resistance movement based almost exclusively on socioeconomic conditions (Kreissig) is inadequate. The exploitation in other areas of the Near East was just as bad, but comparable movements did not develop. However, the strong social component cannot be overlooked; when the Zealots conquered Jerusalem in A.D. 66, the first thing they destroyed was the city archives with the records of debt (Jos. War II.xvii.6). Two years later Simon bar Giora proclaimed a general emancipation of Jewish slaves (Jos. War IV.ix.3). So it is understandable that the simple people and the young sided with the resistance fighters.

The most profound reason for the Zealots' persistent willingness to sacrifice was probably their basic eschatological orientation. Josephus does not speak of this, just as he is consistently silent for apologetic reasons about the messianic expectations of his people. But there are signs from which one could well assume that the Zealots were hoping for the appearance of a Messiah and the establishment of his kingdom. Josephus mentions that the Zealots used "prophets" for propaganda purposes (War VI.v.2). He mentions among the main causes of the resistance "an ambiguous oracle that was also found in their sacred writings, how, 'about that time, one from their country should become governor of the habitable earth.' The Jews took this prediction to belong to themselves in particular" (Jos. War VI.v.4). This probably is a reference to Num. 24:17-19. This text is important in the Dead Sea Scrolls (4 QTest 12-13, etc.) and was later applied to Simeon bar Kochba by Rabbi Akiba (J. T. Ta'an 4:7). When Josephus says that Menahem, the son (or grandson) of Judas the Galilean (War II.xvii.9) and Simon bar Giora (War IV.ix.4) laid claim to royalty and acted as if they were kings, this means that they understood themselves to be fulfilling that prophecy.

When the Zealot movement was founded in A.D. 6-7 it could have been a Pharisaic splinter group —the radical left wing of Pharisaism, so to speak. The movement expanded rapidly, especially among the youth (Jos. War II.xii.1, xvi.4, etc.). From caves and other hiding places on the E edge of the Judean mountains they attacked smaller Roman military units and traveling officials, as well as the residences of wealthy Jewish collaborators.

Judas himself seems to have been killed in his attempt at rebellion (Acts 5:37).

In the period from A.D. 8 to the death of Herod Agrippa I (A.D. 44), Josephus does not mention any Zealot activity.

After Judea was reconverted into a Roman province, the "robber nuisance" revived. The procurator Tiberius Alexander (A.D. 46-48) had two sons of Judas the Galilean crucified, probably because they continued their father's rebellion. Under Ventidius Cumanus (A.D. 48-52) there were dangerous episodes, which led to the removal of the procurator. Under his successor Antonius Felix (*ca.* 52-58) "things grew worse and worse continually; for the country was again filled with robbers and impostors, who deluded the multitude" (Jos. Antiq. XX.viii.4). In his time the guerrilla tactics of the Sicarii seem to have prevailed. Felix had a great number of the "robbers" (i.e., Zealots) crucified (Jos. War II.xiii.2), as did also his successor, Porcius Festus (*ca.* A.D. 58-63; Jos. War II.xiv.1). During Albinus' rule (62-64), the Zealots seem to have won control over the plains. Under Gessius Florus, who, like Albinus, sought primarily his own enrichment, rebellion broke out (Jos. War II.xiv.2). First the procurator had to surrender Jerusalem; and the temple treasurer, Eleazar, abolished the daily sacrifice to the emperor. Then the fortress of Masada near the Dead Sea was taken in a surprise attack by a group under the leadership of Menahem, a son (or grandson) of Judas the Galilean. Menahem also overcame the last Roman pockets of resistance in Jerusalem. When he had the high priest Ananus murdered, Ananus' son, Eleazar, arranged for the murder of Menahem; only a few of Menahem's followers escaped to Masada (Jos. War II.xvii.9). This broke the united front of the rebels. Shortly thereafter they suffered severe defeats in Galilee, Perea, and Idumea. By contrast, in Jerusalem they were initially successful, until quarrels among themselves forced them to submit to Titus (A.D. 70). The last to fall were the Sicarii, who had fled to Masada (A.D. 74).

2. Jesus' relationship to the Zealots. ***a. Zealots and the mission of Jesus.***

i. According to Mark 3:18 and Luke 6:15, Simon, one of Jesus' disciples was a Zealot; nothing else is known of him. This fact loses its significance when one considers that Jesus also called to discipleship a tax collector, hence, a collaborator with the occupational power. The LOGIA source collection of Jesus' sayings bears witness to his acceptance of the universally despised tax collectors (Matt. 11:19; Luke 7:34). As disciples of Jesus, tax collectors and Zealots would have to have renounced their old ideals.

Peter's surname, "Bar-Jona," appears only in Matt. 16:17. Occasionally it has been interpreted as "Zealot," but this is unlikely. The upper-middle-class circumstances in which Peter probably lived negate the assumption that he was an "outlaw."

ii. The cleansing of the temple (Mark 11:15-19; cf. Matt. 21:12-17; Luke 19:45-46) has been interpreted as an attempt by Jesus to occupy the temple with an armed band. Of course, the oldest gospel report does not mention this; one would have to suppose that Mark watered down the affair, as was his tendency. But from our knowledge of similar events which Josephus reported, it is much more likely that Mark exaggerated the extent of Jesus' action. During major disorders the Jewish temple guard or the Roman cohorts, who were stationed in the fortress Antonia at the NW corner of the temple, intervened. Originally the cleansing of the temple was probably an act intended by Jesus to be a prophetic sign against the sacrificial cult.

iii. Individual sayings of Jesus, such as Luke 22:36*b*, "And let him who has no sword sell his mantle and buy one," have been interpreted as reflecting Zealot thought. This saying, which is supposed to be an instruction for the time after Jesus' death, does not have to be understood as a summons to Zealot activity. It can be understood as a paradoxically formulated allusion to the temptations and persecutions which the disciples will encounter. Also the saying in Matt. 10:34, "Do not think that I have come to bring peace on earth; I have not come to bring peace, but a sword," is not a challenge to armed action, but alludes figuratively to the schisms and conflict which the call to follow Jesus brings (cf. Luke 12:51).

iv. It would seem that the most obvious indication is Jesus' crucifixion. Without doubt, the Romans usually crucified agitators and traitors. The caption over the cross, which called Jesus "the King of the Jews," points to this political dimension. But the fact of the crucifixion does not prove that the charges against Jesus were objectively substantiated. It is equally possible that the Jewish authorities brought the political charges in order to get rid of a man who was intolerable to them for religious reasons—at least that is the way it is presented in the Synoptic gospels.

b. Was Jesus himself a Zealot? Unless individual sayings of Jesus or events of his life are taken out of context, it is impossible to regard him as a Zealot.

i. Co-operation between God and human beings to bring about the KINGDOM OF GOD was basic to the Zealot ideology. Jesus also talked about the kingdom of God, but in the parable of the seed growing secretly (Mark 4:26-29) he emphasized that God will bring about his kingdom without human help. The patience of the farmer is an example for faith, which should wait for everything to come from God.

Jesus reinterpreted the conception of the kingdom even more radically. It is no longer something which is to come, but by his deeds it has already begun (Luke 11:20; Matt. 12:28). Jesus' devoting of himself to the rejected, the poor, and the sick helped to bring about the kingdom of God.

ii. The event which led to the formation of the Zealots was the census of A.D. 6. The question to Jesus in Mark 12:14 must undoubtedly be understood against this background: "Is it lawful to pay taxes to Caesar, or not?" Jesus' answer, the authenticity of which cannot be doubted, was: "Render to Caesar the things that are Caesar's, and to God the things that are God's" (vs. 17). This is a clear renunciation of the Zealot tax evasion, without metaphysically reinterpreting the existing power structures.

iii. The decisive difference between Jesus and the Zealots comes into focus in their relation to their fellow human beings. The Zealots believed that to serve God they had rigorously to exterminate anyone who broke his law, while Jesus required love for one's neighbors, and even for one's enemies (Matt. 5:43-48; Luke 6:27-28, 32-36). This demand was just as unprecedented in late Judaism as it was in primitive Christianity, so that its authenticity cannot be doubted. At another place Jesus formulated the double commandment of love (Mark 12:29-31): "Hear, O Israel: the Lord our God, the Lord is one; and you shall love the Lord your God with all your heart, and with all your soul, and with all your mind, and with all your strength." Every Zealot would have agreed to this point, but would have drawn the conclusion: "Therefore, you should love all those who keep God's law and hate all those who break God's law." But Jesus added to the commandment to love God: "You shall love your neighbor as yourself." If the commandment to love is to be the center and norm of Christian action, then it simply cannot yield a justification for violence against one's fellow human beings. The good Samaritan serves as a prototype for this kind of love of neighbor (Luke 10:30-37). The Samaritan helped the man in need without asking about his nationality, creed, or world view and no Zealot would have approved of that.

The God of Jesus demands so much service to our fellow human beings that for their sake even the sacred order of the Mosaic law is repealed. Jesus broke the sabbath commandment repeatedly (Mark 2:23 ff.; 3:1 ff.), and gave the well-being of people a higher priority than the strict observance of the sabbath (Mark 2:27). He annulled the laws of purification (Mark 7:15), since nothing outside a person can influence one's relationship to God. He negated the permission for divorce, which in those times caused great hardship for the women involved (Mark 10:9). For Jesus, what was important was, not service to ideas or ideals, however great or sacred they might be, but service to the preservation of life (Mark 3:4). With this freedom, not only from rabbinic casuistry, but also from the letter of the OT law, Jesus stood beyond all parties of his time. Neither the Zealots nor the Pharisaic party from which they descended would have tolerated this aspect of Jesus' teaching.

There is no bridging the gap between Jesus' teaching and the ideals of the Zealots. The old and new attempts to interpret Jesus as a revolutionary must be viewed as failures. *See also* Pharisees[S.]

Bibliography. M. Hengel, *Die Zeloten* (1961); *Was Jesus a Revolutionist?* (1971), "Zeloten und Sikarier," in *Josephus-Studien,* ed. O. Betz, K. Haacker, M. Hengel (1974), pp. 175-96; G. Baumbach, *Jesus von Nazareth im Lichte der jüdischen Gruppenbildung* (1971); K. Wegenast, "Zeloten," PW, Zweite Reihe IX (1967), col. 2474 ff.; M. Smith, "Zealots and Sicarii," *HTR,* LXIV (1971), 1-19; H. Kreissig, *Die sozialen Zusammenhänge des judäischen Krieges* (1970); H. S. Reimarus, "Vom Zwecke Jesu und seiner Jünger," in *Beiträge zur Geschichte und Literatur,* ed. G. E. Lessing (1778); O. Cullmann, *Jesus und die Revolutionären seiner Zeit* (1970).

H. Merkel

***ZEBUL.** While most English translations consider this word to be a proper name, it could also be the Canaanite word "prince," "ruler," an alternative designation to the word *śar* which immediately follows in Judg. 9:30. *See* Conflate Readings[S] §6*j*.

ZECHARIAH, BOOK OF. 1. Socioreligious setting.** ***a. Chs. 1–8. While the international background described for this section requires little modification, new light can be shed on its setting within the postexilic community. Chs. 1–8 took form in several stages within the hierocratic (Zadokite) circles which supplied the impetus for the postexilic restoration (*see* Zadok the Priests[S]). The final stage involved the addition of a chronological framework embracing also the book of Haggai. Behind it lie several earlier stages of growth.

Stratum I comprises a series of seven visions or apocalypses centered in architectonic symmetry around the Menorah, then radiating out to embrace temple cult, ritual community, and finally the entire universe subject to the watchful eyes of Yahweh. The visions are accompanied by prophetic oracles relating especially to the rebuilding of the temple and the diarchy of the two messiahs (*see* Temple, Jerusalem §B). The visions and oracles seem to be authentic, having functioned in the activity of Zechariah as a prophetic endorsement of the Zadokite temple program.

Stratum II introduces later additions to the oracles. For example, the original form of the first vision (1:8-15) responds to Haggai's prophecy of an imminent cataclysm introducing the eschaton (Zech. 2:6-9): Jeremiah's seventy years had passed, and yet the earth remained under the firm control of the Persians. The original oracle explicating the vision gives assurance that Yahweh remains zealous on Israel's behalf (1:13-15). But completion of the temple did not inaugurate the eschaton. Zech. 1:16-17 was added to counteract doubt and to defend Zechariah's prophecy (2:10-17 is best interpreted in a similar way).

Zech. 4:6*a*β-10*a* also belongs to stratum II. Here the original vision related the all-seeing Yahweh of the temple to his twin messiahs. Again delay and doubts best explain the awkward addition of these words defending the charismatic authority of Zerubbabel against criticism (cf. Isa. 66:1-2).

In Zech. 3 a unit disrupts the symmetry of the original vision cycle. Standing apart from the original seven in form and content, it belongs to stratum II and adds a defense of the legitimacy of Joshua as high priest (clothed in stately rather than soiled clothing), and of the transfer to his office of a prophetic prerogative, the right of access to the Divine Council. *See* Council, Heavenly[S].

To what extent stratum II stems from Zechariah or from disciples remains an open question. Whereas the time span between strata I and II is not great, in the case of 4:6*a*β-10*a* at least it is difficult to attribute the awkward intersplice (if not the words themselves) to Zechariah. More germane, however, is the observation that, taken together, strata I and II sketch the literary history of a systematic defense of the Zadokite temple program. Alongside additions, stratum II includes tendential alterations, best illustrated by 6:9-15, where Zerubbabel is denied the crown, which comes to rest solely upon the priest Joshua. This textual alteration documents the transformation of the original Zadokite diarchy into the later priestly heirarchy.

Between the two earliest strata and the final form lie stages offering further interpretation, especially through construction of a framework provided by prophetic words in chs. 7–8 and related materials in 1:2-6.

b. Chs. 9–14. Arising in a setting distinct from Zech. 1–8, these chapters preserve oracles produced by circles opposed to the hierocratic program and its Zadokite protagonists. Only after time dimmed the memory of earlier controversies were chs. 9–11 and 12–14 appended to the eleventh minor prophetic book, and a related booklet was added as a twelfth book (MALACHI).

Because reliable historical references are lacking in these chapters, attention must turn to typological considerations. In the case of Zech. 9 and 10, genres, concepts, and prosody resemble Isa. 56–66, suggesting a sixth-century date. As in Second and Third Isaiah, archaic forms and motifs are applied to formulate a vision of divine intervention and radical transformation. For those who espoused these visions, temple builders and Zadokite leaders were not harbingers of the eschaton, but antagonists. In ch. 11 the attack on community leaders is intensified, reflecting conditions in the period of demoralization between 515 and the time of Malachi. Chs. 12–14 go even further in attacking the Jerusalem hierocracy and describing cataclysmic divine acts on behalf of the oppressed. As a whole, therefore, chs. 9–14 preserve a stream of tradition opposed to the hierocratic position seen in Ezek. 40–48, Haggai, Zech. 1–8, and Chronicles. Reflecting the feelings of those who smarted under defeat and oppression and were blindly dedicated to eradicating the Zadokite hierocracy, this section presents a vision of divine intervention and vindication, a vision which generates the main features of a universe rich in apocalyptic symbolism.

2. Relation to apocalypticism. Both Zech. 1–8 and 9–14 reflect modifications within prophetism which are characteristic of the period: heightened eschatology, recrudescence of mythic motifs, broadening universalism. A significant difference nevertheless exists.

a. Chs. 1–8 are the product of the victorious party among the groups that vied for control of the restoration cult. The seven apocalypses of stratum I arose amidst the eschatological excitement of the first years of the reign of Darius I. After the temple was completed, they were expanded and finally embedded in an interpretive framework. The result was a divine decretal authorizing the new hierocracy under the high priest. The visions, now identified with institutional realities, entered the domain of realized eschatology and gave birth to no further apocalypses. The gap between vision and reality had been closed through identification of divine decree and the hierocratic order. The need was no longer for apocalypses that announced radical transformation, but for legislation to preserve and regulate existing structures.

b. Chs. 9–14, on the other hand, stem from visionaries whose dreams were increasingly frustrated by realities. Slight modifications of earlier visions were insufficient. Experiences evoked increasingly desperate visions of judgment, as the gap widened between restoration ideal and experience. Thus while within the hierocratic party the social conditions that produced apocalypticism disappeared, they became more pronounced among the visionaries of Zech. 9–14. The history of the hierocratic party, as it can be reconstructed on the basis of Zech. 1–8, is a path from apocalypticism to a pragmatic position of community control, and, by contrast, the history discernible in Zech. 9–14 is that of an apocalyptic movement of increasing intensity and greater and greater hostility toward existing community structures.

As a result, the contributions of Zech. 1–8 to later apocalypticism are primarily in the area of individual motifs and the genre of apocalypse, whereas the oracles of Zech. 9–14, while also exerting influence on the development of genres that were later utilized in apocalyptic writings, have their primary significance in carrying a living apocalyptic movement out of the early years of Darius I into the fifth century and beyond.

See APOCALYPSE, GENRE[S]; APOCALYPTICISM[S] §3.

Bibliography. P. D. Hanson, *The Dawn of Apocalyptic* (1975); K. Seybold, *Bilder zum Templebau: Die Visionen des Propheten Sacharja,* SBS, LXX (1974), both of which provide further bibliog. P. D. HANSON

***ZEPHANIAH, BOOK OF. 1. The time of Zephaniah.** The superscription (1:1) places the prophecies at the time of Josiah, king of Judah (640-609 B.C.).

a. The Scythian invasion? Some scholars have tried to connect Zephaniah's utterances with the Scythian invasion mentioned by Herodotus. This is, however, problematic. Herodotus is the only witness to such an invasion. Furthermore, his account is colored by legendary material throughout. It is also unlikely that the invasion could have happened during the reign of Psammetichus I. Consequently the Scythian hypothesis has now been almost universally abandoned (*see* SCYTHIANS[S]). Another opinion is that the crisis mentioned by the prophet must be connected with a flare-up of Assyrian power in the first years of Josiah's reign. Other scholars have proposed that the prophecies were made during the time of Jehoiakim (609-598 B.C.). Another opinion is that Zephaniah prophesied in the time of Zedekiah (*ca.* 590 B.C.).

b. Possible date from internal evidence. It is clear that Nineveh was not yet demolished (2:13-15); a strong syncretistic religion was practiced in Jerusalem (1:4-5); the royalty abused the religion of the Lord by wearing foreign clothes (1:8); the Moabites and Ammonites showed contempt for Judah (2:8). From these passages we may deduce that the prophecies were pronounced before the fall of Nineveh (612 B.C.). The adherence to syncretistic religion suggests that the utterances were made before the religious reform of Josiah (*ca.* 621 B.C.). The rapid decline of Assyrian power after 626 B.C. might point to a date between 640 and 626, preferably in the earlier years of Josiah when he was still a child and when officials and princes were still in charge (1:8).

c. Historical background. The Assyrians, who had dominated politics in the ancient Near East since 745 B.C., were rapidly declining, and this was an incentive to other nations to rebel. Ashurbanipal's long war against Elam was successfully concluded in 639. There was also a prolonged war against the Arabs. In Babylon a rebellion flared up after 626 which ultimately led to the destruction of Nineveh. In uncertain times like these rumors could have created an atmosphere for the prophecies of Zephaniah.

2. Contents. ***a. Superscription (1:1).***

b. The coming judgment against Judah (1:2-18). i. *Introduction (1:2-6).* The Lord pronounces his judgment against idolatry. His judgment will even affect nature (1:3).

ii. *The day of the Lord (1:7-18).* Zephaniah takes up this theme found in Amos and develops it in an original way. Judgment is pronounced against Judah for the breaking of the covenant. Various scholars have proposed connecting the language of these oracles with holy war imagery. The close links with covenant curses are, however, noteworthy.

c. Exhortation by the prophet (2:1-3). There is still time to become humble and to avert the judgment.

d. Oracles against foreign nations (2:4-15). Like other prophetic writings, Zephaniah contains oracles against foreign nations. More space is allocated to the destruction of Nineveh than any other (2:13-15), which shows how important Assyria was still considered.

e. Invective against the leaders of Jerusalem (3:1-5). In Jerusalem there was no obedience to the commandments of God. In beautiful metaphorical language the princes are likened to roaring lions, the judges to wolves, and the prophets to braggarts and impostors, while the priests do violence to the Law.

f. Judgment of the nations (3:6-8). This pericope reiterates the theme of 2:4-15 and shows how the Lord will vent his anger on the nations.

g. A promise of salvation to the nations and Judah (3:9-13). The Lord will purify Judah from proud boasters and the high and mighty. Foreign nations will also be purified and will serve the Lord. It is possible that this tendency to universalism was added during postexilic times when such ideas were common.

h. Song of joy in Zion (3:14-17). The Lord will again become king in Jerusalem. He is furthermore likened to a soldier-hero who will save the obedient remnant.

i. Final message of salvation (3:18-20). The refugees will be brought back to Jerusalem. The lame and those who have gone astray will come back and their misfortune will be turned into praise.

3. Language, structure, and form. The language of the book shows close affinity with that of writings from the end of the seventh century and the beginning of the sixth, e.g., with Nahum, Habakkuk, Joel, Jeremiah, Ezekiel, and Deuteronomy. Certain difficult words, e.g., *'āsōph, 'āsēph* (1:2), can now be explained with the help of Ugaritic.

It is also clear from Zephaniah's language that he was influenced by wisdom literature, e.g., his application of the phrase *lāqaḥ mûsār* (3:2, 7). He uses various types of prophetic oracle. The prophetic threat can be subdivided into three types: a threat to individuals, like the invective with threat in 3:1-5; a threat to his own nation, in 1:7-18; and a threat against foreign nations, in 2:4-15. The positive prophetical saying is present in 3:6-20. Formerly, scholars were inclined to regard declarations of salvation as later additions, but this position has now been largely abandoned. Although it is an invective with a threat, 3:1-5 can also be classified under positive prophetical sayings. Another type of positive prophetical saying is the exhortation in 2:1-3.

Bibliography. P. C. Snijman, *De Profetie van Zefanja* (1913); M. Bič, *Trois prophètes dans un temps de ténèbres: Sophonie-Nahum-Habaquq* (1968); A. Deissler, *Sophonie* (1964); R. Vuilleumier, C. A. Keller, *Michée, Nahoum, Habacuc, Sophonie* (1971); T. Laetsch, *The Minor Prophets* (1956); P. G. Rinaldi, F. Luciani, *Sofonia* (1969); L. Sabottka, *Zephanja* (1972).

Special studies: H. Cazelles, "Sophonie, Jérémie et les Scythes en Palestine," *RB,* LXXIV (1967), 24-44; H. Donner, "Die Schwellenhüpfer: Beobachtungen zu Zephanja 1, 8f," *JSS,* XV (1970), 42-55; Th. H. Robinson, F. Horst, *HAT,* XIV (3rd. ed., 1964), 188-89; T. H. Gaster, "Zephaniah 3, 17," *ET,* LXXVIII (1966/67), 267; J. Gray, "A Metaphor from Building in Zephaniah II.1," *VT,* III (1953), 404-7; J. Heller, "Zephanjas Ahnenreihe," *VT,* XXI (1971), 102-4; B. Jongeling, "Jeux de mots en Sophonie 3:1 et 3?" *VT,* XXI (1971), 541-47; J. S. Kselman, "A Note on Jer 49, 20 and Ze 2, 6-7," *CBQ,* XXXII (1970), 579-81; M. Stenzel, "Zum Verständnis von Zeph. III 3b," *VT,* I (1951), 303-5; D. Winton Thomas, "A Pun on the Name Ashdod in Zephaniah 2.4," *ET,* LXXIV (1962/63), 63; A. S. van der Woude, "Predikte Zefanja een wereldgericht?" *Nederlands Teologish Tijdschrift,* XX (1965), 1-16.

F. C. FENSHAM

***ZIKLAG.** The location of this town is disputed. It has been suggested that the biblical name is echoed in Arabic Khirbet Zuḥeilîqah, ten miles ESE of Gaza, but the resemblance is superficial at best and the ruin is evidently Byzantine and later. The identification with Tell el-Khuweilfeh (Tel Halif), *ca.* fourteen miles N of Beer-sheba, is widely accepted, but the site stands in the midst of Judean territory. Thus it does not suit well the location of a base from which David was reputedly attacking the Negeb of Judah! A more likely candidate is Tell el-Mâliḥah (or Muleiḥah; modern Tel Milḥa), eighteen miles E of Gaza and ten miles S of modern Kiriat-Gat, or else Tell esh-Sherî'ah (Tel Sera'), *ca.* fifteen miles SE of Gaza. The excavations at this latter site have produced rich evidence of an Egyptian cult center during the Late Bronze Age, a settlement in the Philistine period (Early Iron Age) with a terrific destruction (cf. I Sam. 30:1, 3, 14), and important occupation in the later Iron Age. These finds accord well with the known history of Ziklag, but epigraphic confirmation of the site's ancient name has yet to be discovered (though Egyptian hieratic ostraca have been found).

Bibliography. Y. Aharoni, *The Land of the Bible* (1967), pp. 258-60, 298, and "Ṣiqlag," *Encyclopaedia Biblica,* VI (1971), 764-65, Hebrew; E. Oren, "Tel Sera' (Tell esh-Shari'a)," *IEJ,* XXII (1972), 167-69, XXIII (1973), 251-54; E. Oren and E. Netzer, "A Cult Building in the Excavations at Tel Sera'," *Qadmoniot,* VI (1973), 53-56, Hebrew; S. Groll, "A Note on the Hieratic Texts from Tel Sera'," *ibid.,* pp. 56-57, Hebrew.

A. F. RAINEY

***ZION, DAUGHTER OF.** A mistranslation of the Hebrew phrase בת-ציון found in most English versions, with the exception of Moffatt's translation, The New American Bible, The New Jewish Version, and Today's English Version (*see* VERSIONS, ENGLISH and supplementary article). This phrase (in order of frequency) appears in Lam. 1:6; 2:1, 4, 8, 10, 13, 18; 4:22; Isa. 1:8; 10:32; 16:1; 37:22 (=II Kings 19:21); 52:2; 62:11; Mic. 1:13; 4:8, 10, 13; Jer. 4:31; 6:2, 23; Zech. 2:10; 9:9; Zeph. 3:14; Ps. 9:14. The usual translation, "the daughter of Zion," can only mean, according to English idiom, that Zion had a daughter. But Zion did not have a daughter; Zion (by personification) *was* the daughter, though "maiden" would be a better rendering in these cases, since בת is often used as a term of affection for any girl or young woman, as when Boaz addressed Ruth (Ruth 2:8) as בתי, not meaning "my daughter," but something like "my dear."

As the prophets and poets contemplated the fate of their beloved Zion (or Jerusalem), they personified the holy city as a beautiful young maiden, ravished and wretched, or about to be so; or in the oracles of restoration as a maiden about to experience great joy. Thus they used the phrase בת-ציון or sometimes in parallelism בת-ירושלם (Lam. 2:13, 15; Isa. 37:22 [=II Kings 19:21]; Mic. 4:8; Zeph. 3:14; Zech. 9:9). In either case, the first word is in the construct state, and the following genitive is not the usual genitive of possession, but the appositional genitive. The correct translation is, therefore, not "the daughter of Zion" or "the daughter of Jerusalem," but "maiden Zion" or "maiden Jerusalem," with a meaning something like "darling Zion" or "dear Jerusalem." Most of the standard grammars (*see bibliog.*) explain this matter correctly, though the translators with few exceptions have paid no attention, preferring instead the simplistic notion that the construct state must always be followed in translation by the word "of" introducing a possessive genitive.

The idiom is also applied to Judah, and to foreign and hostile cities and countries, sometimes with sarcastic or taunting connotations. Thus we have maiden Judah (Lam. 2:2, 5), maiden Edom (Lam. 4:21, 22), maiden Egypt (Jer. 46:24), maiden Babylon or Chaldea (Isa. 47:1, 5; Jer. 50:42; 51:33; Zech. 2:7; Ps. 137:8), girl Gallim (Isa. 10:30), etc.

Attention should be called to passages that use the word בתולה, "virgin," in the same way or prefixed to בת (II Kings 19:21; Isa. 37:22; 47:1; Jer. 14:17; 18:13; 31:4, 21; 46:11; Lam. 1:15; 2:13; Amos 5:2). The proper translations are not "the virgin of Jerusalem" or "the virgin daughter of Zion," but something like "virgin Jerusalem," "the virgin girl Zion" (terms of affection), or "virgin girl Babylon" (sarcastic and ironical; Babylon is really a shameless hussy, or the like).

Another example of the idiom is the phrase בת-עמי, conventionally translated "the daughter of my people" (Isa. 22:4; Jer. 4:11; 6:26; 8:11, 19, 21, 22; 9:1 [H 8:23]; 9:7 [H 9:6]; 14:17; Lam. 2:11; 3:48; 4:3, 6, 10). The meaning is something like "my beloved people" or "my unfortunate people," with love and sorrow combined. Note also בת-פוצי (Zeph. 3:10), rendered by RSV as "the daughter of my dispersed ones." A better translation would be "my dear dispersed ones."

Bibliography. E. Kautzsch, *Gesenius' Hebrew Grammar* (1910 [repr. 1946]), §§122 *h* and *i,* 128 *k* (trans. from the 28th Ger. ed. by A. E. Cowley; the Ger. original is somewhat more precise); C. Brockelmann, *Hebräische Syntax* (1956), §§70*d,* 77*a, b* (states the case fairly well, but gives a wrong translation); R. J. Williams, *Hebrew Syntax,* §42; W. F. Stinespring, "No Daughter of Zion," *Encounter,* XXVI (1965), 133-41 (full discussion), "The Participle of the Immediate Future and Other Matters," *Translating and Interpreting the OT,* ed. H. T. Frank and W. L. Reed (1970), pp. 67-69, and "Some Remarks on the New English Bible," *Understanding the Sacred Text,* ed. J. Reumann (1972), pp. 88-90. The lexicons of Gesenius-Buhl, Brown-Driver-Briggs, and Koehler-Baumgartner offer little help.

W. F. STINESPRING

ZION TRADITION. A complex of motifs used to glorify Zion/Jerusalem as Yahweh's royal city, God's earthly abode from whence he exercises his worldwide rule (Joel 3:16-17 [H 4:16-17]; Zech. 14:8-9; Pss. 48:1-2 [H 2-3]; 76:1-2, 12 [H 2-3, 13]; cf. Matt. 5:35).

1. The motifs. Four, or sometimes five, motifs are analyzed as belonging to this complex.

a. The divine mountain. The low hill on which Jerusalem was built is regarded as an exceedingly high mountain (Isa. 2:2=Mic. 4:1; Ezek. 40:2; Zech. 14:10; cf. Rev. 21:10) or even identified with Mount Zaphon (Ps. 48:2 [H 3]; ABi), the site of the divine assembly in Israelite thought (Isa. 14:13, translating "in the heights of Zaphon" [בירכתי צפון] for RSV's "in the far north"). *See* ZAPHON, MOUNT[S].

b. The river of paradise. One of the springs in Jerusalem is seen as a mighty, paradisiacal river, bringing joy to God's city and fertility and healing to his people (Ezek. 47:1-12; Joel 3:18 [H 4:18]; Zech. 13:1; 14:8; Ps. 46:4 [H 5]; cf. Rev. 22:1-2).

c. The conquest of chaos. Because Yahweh is in his city, Zion/Jerusalem cannot be shaken by the threatening waters of chaos (Ps. 46:1-5 [H 2-6]; cf. Isa. 17:12-14). *See* CHAOS[S].

d. The defeat of the nations. Yahweh also saves the holy city by his sudden defeat of the foreign kings who had gathered their nations together against Jerusalem; the result is the abolition of war and an era of peace (Isa. 14:32; 17:12-14; 18:1-6; 29:1-8; 31:4-9; Ezek. 38–39; Joel 3:9-21 [H 4:9-21]; Zech. 12:1-9; 14:3, 12-15; Pss. 46:6-11 [H 7-12]; 48:4-8 [H 5-9]; 76:3-9 [H 4-10]).

e. The pilgrimage of the nations. Finally, the survivors among the nations acknowledge Yahweh's sovereignty and go on pilgrimage to Jerusalem to worship and pay tribute (Isa. 2:2-4=Mic. 4:1-4; Isa. 18:7; Zech. 14:16-19; Ps. 76:11-12 NAB [H 12-13]).

2. Sources. These motifs, which describe past experience, present reality, or future hope, depending on the particular text in which they occur, were originally independent of one another and may be traced to separate sources. The last two motifs appear to be rooted in some historical experience while the first three clearly derive from Canaanite mythology. Although the conception that the gods live on very high mountains is common to much of the ancient Near East, Mount Zaphon is a particular divine mountain sacred to the Canaanite god Baal. Yahweh's victory over the waters of chaos may also be traced back to a Canaanite myth about Baal's victory over prince Yamm, the Sea (*see* BAAL).

The Zion tradition does not preserve a pure Baal mythology, however. The portrayal of the divine dwelling as the source of a paradisiacal river seems to go back to the Canaanite description of El's abode at the "spring of the two rivers, the source of the two seas" (*see* EL; EL[S] §1*b*). This place is presumably located on El's Mount *Ll,* a quite distinct mountain from Baal's Zaphon.

3. Date. Such a mixture of El and Baal mythology in the Zion tradition makes it difficult to accept the popular view which attributes the formation of that tradition to the pre-Israelite inhabitants of Jerusalem. Not only is El, the pre-Israelite god of Jerusalem (Gen. 14:18, 22), assigned functions original to Baal, but the holy city itself is given a mythological topography based upon two separate mountains, sacred to two distinct deities. It is doubtful that one can attribute such confusion to the Jebusites who, whatever their ethnic background (*see* JEBUS), appear to have shared in the basically homogeneous culture of Canaan. Moreover, a Canaanite origin for the historical motifs is also problematic. Prior to David, Jerusalem had never been more than a modest city-state with marginal control over neighboring villages and a few nearby city-states (*see* JERUSALEM §3). It possessed neither the political nor the religious importance which the pretensions of world-wide rule explicit in the Zion tradition presuppose.

On the other hand, one can hardly date the formation of this tradition to the exilic or postexilic periods even if most of the passages containing it could be dated that late. None of the individual motifs fit well in that period. The mythological motifs may more naturally be seen as a theological despoilment of the pagan gods dating from a period when real theological conflict coexisted with a confident, triumphant Yahwism. Moreover, if pre-Davidic Jerusalem lacked the political and religious importance presupposed by the grandiose claims of the Zion tradition, the exilic ruins and postexilic restorations hardly fare better. How could any Israelite in that period possibly regard Jerusalem as important enough to merit a united attack by all the nations of the world unless this motif had already become a fixed part of the tradition prior to the demise of the city's significance?

The presence in the royal psalms (*see* PSALMS, BOOK OF §B2*b*) of material strikingly similar to both the defeat of the nations and the pilgrimage motifs (Pss. 2:1-3, 10-11; 18:43-45 [H 44-46]; 72:8-11) confirms this judgment, since this related material cannot be wholly disassociated from the Zion tradition, and since the royal psalms undoubtedly date to the period of the monarchy.

The ancient and extremely difficult Psalm 68 appears to contain, at least in germinal form, four of the five motifs: (*a*) the divine mountain (vss. 15-18 [H 16-19]); (*b*) the conquest of chaos (vss. 21-23 ABi [H 22-24]); (*c*) the defeat of the nations (vss. 11-14 [H 12-15]); and (*d*) the pilgrimage of the nations (vss. 29-31 [H 30-32]). The psalm may be pre-Davidic in part, and certainly some of the impetus for the formation of the Zion tradition should be attributed to the early theological conflict of the settlement period, when the fanatical Yahwistic invaders were forced to give a theological explanation for the pagan deities they encountered. The Israelites' elevation of Yahweh above the Canaanite gods, their identification of him with ELYON, and their claims for Yahweh's world rule are probably premonarchic. Nevertheless, the tradition in its present form presupposes David's imperial conquests. Two concerns fell together as a result of those conquests in which David, as Yahweh's agent, imposed Israelite rule on the surrounding nations, forcing them to recognize and pay tribute to Yahweh, the imperial god (II Sam. 8:1-12). On the one hand, David's conquests gave credibility to the theological claims made for Yahweh; on the other hand, those claims provided a theological rationale to justify and stabilize David's imperial expansion. It was probably to meet both needs, political and theological, that church and state co-operated in formulating the Zion tradition.

It is evident that the origins of the tradition of Yahweh's covenant with David and choice of Jerusalem date to the period of David's reign (*see* COVENANT, DAVIDIC[S]), but the motifs of the Zion tradition fit best there as well. The syncretism involved in attributing the mythological motifs to Jerusalem might point more to Solomon, but it meshes well enough with David's known policy of shoring up the religious authority of his new capital, as seen, for example, in his transfer of the ark (II Sam. 6). This is also the one time in Israel's existence when there would have been a constant stream of foreign vassals to the imperial capital and royal sanctuary (II Sam. 8; I Kings 8:65), which is the historical reality behind the pilgrimage motif. Moreover, since the Davidic-Solomonic era was the period when there was a real concern to maintain an actual empire, the motif of the foreign enemies, often portrayed as rebellious vassals, could very well derive from this age.

4. Later development. Following the breakup of the empire, the Zion tradition, bereft of its historical foundation, suffered the same fate as the related tradition of the choice of David. The ideology was retained as expressing what should be, but because the ideal was not realized, it began to be projected more and more onto the screen of the future. In the process what had once been seen as realizable within human history gradually assumed the transhistorical dimensions of apocalyptic (*see* Apocalypticism §1*b* and supplementary article), and this ultimately resulted in the denigration of the earthly Zion (Apocal. Bar. 4:2-7). The present city was no longer considered God's actual dwelling or the real mother of his people (Gal. 4:25-26). Those honors had been transferred to the heavenly Jerusalem, which would only be revealed at the final judgment (Rev. 21–22).

Bibliography. H. Wildberger, "Die Völkerwallfahrt zum Zion, Jes. II 1-5," *VT*, VII (1957), 62-81; W. H. Schmidt, *Königtum Gottes in Ugarit und Israel, BZAW,* LXXX (2nd ed., 1966), 57-58; G. Wanke, *Die Zionstheologie der Korachiten, BZAW,* XCVII (1966); J. J. M. Roberts, "The Davidic Origin of the Zion Tradition," *JBL,* XCII (1973), 329-44 (includes extensive additional bibliog.).

J. J. M. Roberts

***ZOAN.** *See* Hyksos[S].

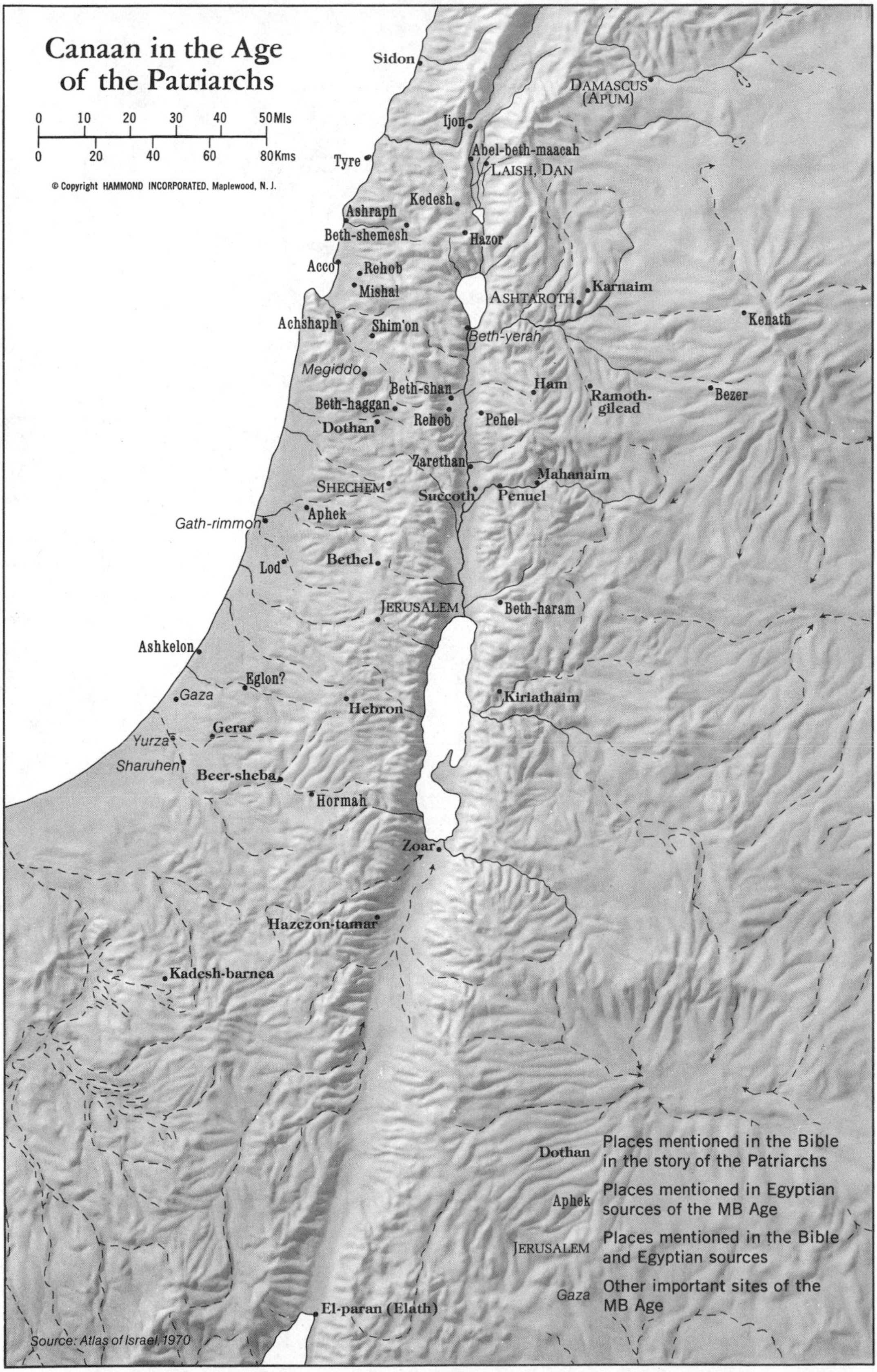

Canaan in the Age of the Patriarchs
0 10 20 30 40 50 Mls
0 20 40 60 80 Kms
© Copyright HAMMOND INCORPORATED, Maplewood, N. J.
Sidon
Damascus (Apum)
Ijon
Tyre
Abel-beth-maacah
Laish, Dan
Kedesh
Ashraph
Beth-shemesh
Hazor
Acco
Rehob
Mishal
Karnaim
Ashtaroth
Achshaph
Shim'on
Kenath
Beth-yerah
Megiddo
Beth-shan
Ham
Ramoth-gilead
Bezer
Beth-haggan
Rehob
Pehel
Dothan
Zarethan
Mahanaim
Shechem
Succoth
Penuel
Aphek
Gath-rimmon
Lod
Bethel
Jerusalem
Beth-haram
Ashkelon
Eglon?
Gaza
Kiriathaim
Hebron
Gerar
Yurza
Sharuhen
Beer-sheba
Hormah
Zoar
Hazezon-tamar
Kadesh-barnea
Dothan — Places mentioned in the Bible in the story of the Patriarchs
Aphek — Places mentioned in Egyptian sources of the MB Age
Jerusalem — Places mentioned in the Bible and Egyptian sources
Gaza — Other important sites of the MB Age
El-paran (Elath)
Source: Atlas of Israel, 1970

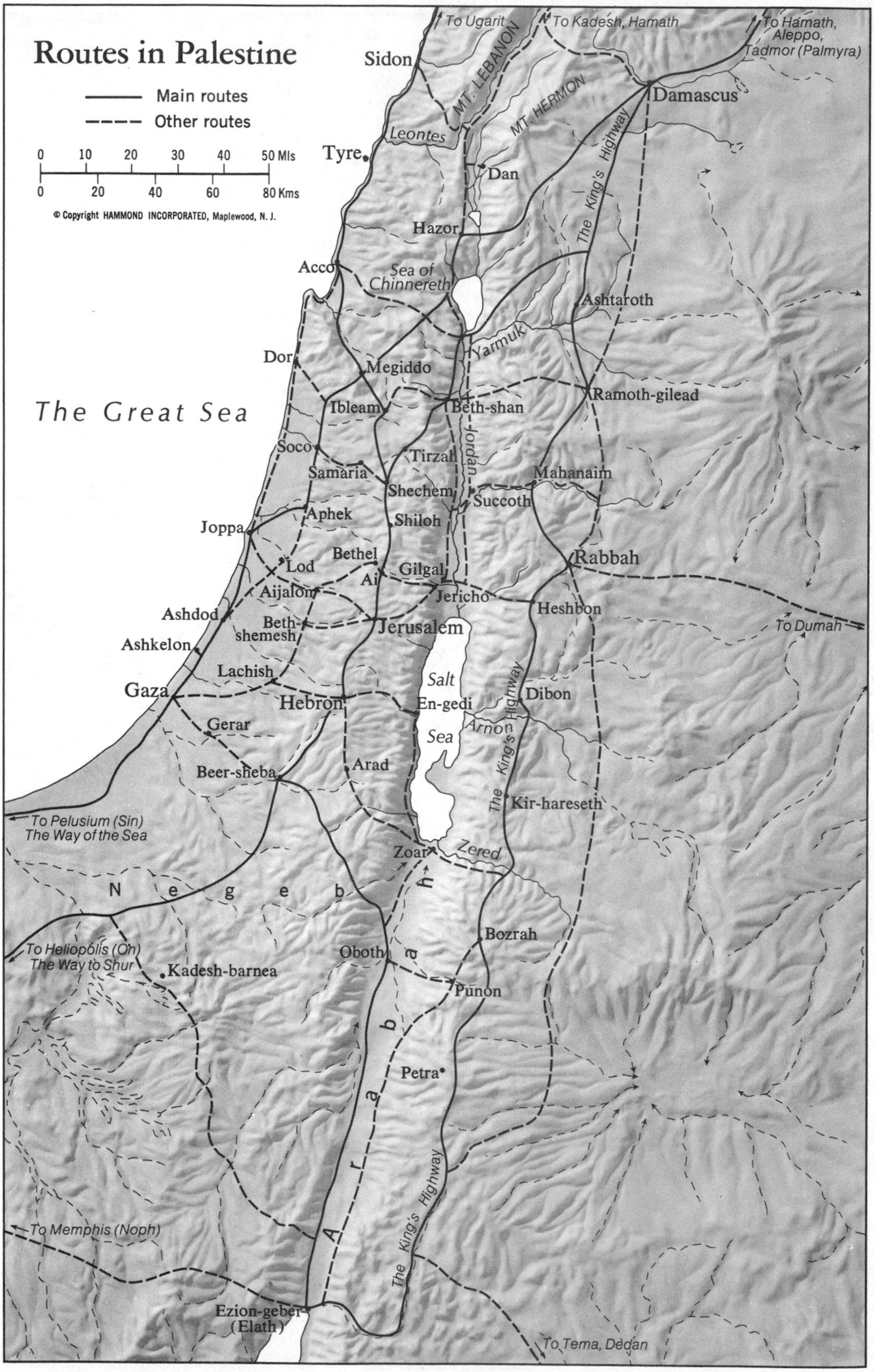
Routes in Palestine
Main routes
Other routes
0 10 20 30 40 50 Mls
0 20 40 60 80 Kms
© Copyright HAMMOND INCORPORATED, Maplewood, N. J.
The Great Sea
To Ugarit
To Kadesh, Hamath
To Hamath, Aleppo, Tadmor (Palmyra)
Sidon
MT. LEBANON
MT. HERMON
Damascus
Leontes
Tyre
Dan
The King's Highway
Hazor
Acco
Sea of Chinnereth
Ashtaroth
Yarmuk
Dor
Megiddo
Ramoth-gilead
Ibleam
Beth-shan
Soco
Tirzah
Jordan
Samaria
Mahanaim
Shechem
Succoth
Aphek
Shiloh
Joppa
Rabbah
Bethel
Lod
Gilgal
Ai
Aijalon
Jericho
Heshbon
Ashdod
Beth-shemesh
Jerusalem
To Dumah
Ashkelon
Salt
Lachish
Gaza
Dibon
Hebron
En-gedi
Gerar
Arnon
Sea
Arad
Beer-sheba
Kir-hareseth
To Pelusium (Sin)
The Way of the Sea
Zoar
Zered
N e g e b
Bozrah
To Heliopolis (On)
The Way to Shur
Oboth
Kadesh-barnea
Punon
Petra
A r a b a h
To Memphis (Noph)
Ezion-geber (Elath)
To Tema, Dedan

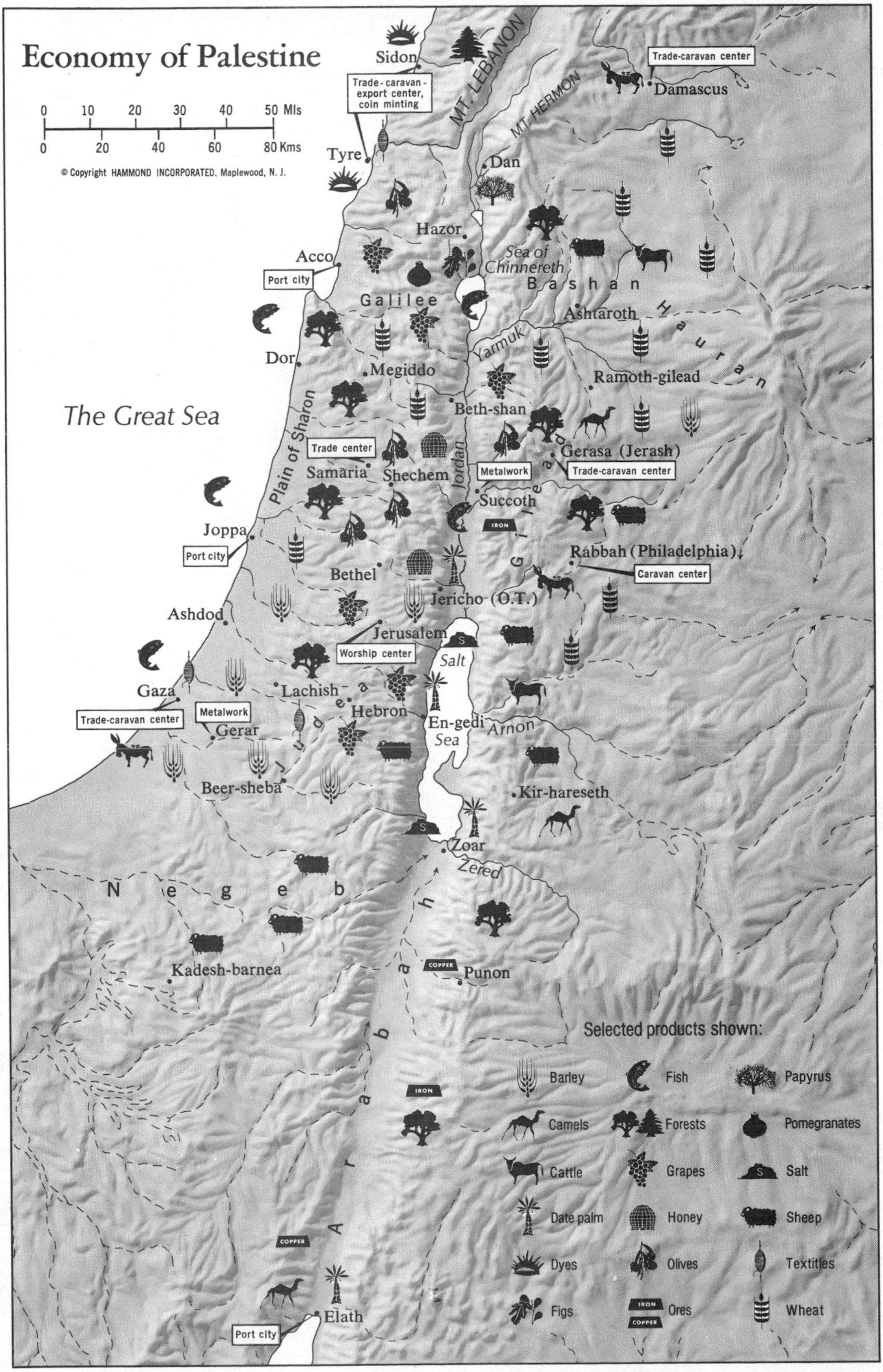
Economy of Palestine
0 10 20 30 40 50 Mls
0 20 40 60 80 Kms
© Copyright HAMMOND INCORPORATED, Maplewood, N. J.
Sidon
Trade-caravan-export center, coin minting
Tyre
MT. LEBANON
MT. HERMON
Trade-caravan center
Damascus
Dan
Hazor
Acco
Port city
Sea of Chinnereth
Bashan
Galilee
Ashtaroth
Hauran
Dor
Yarmuk
Megiddo
Ramoth-gilead
The Great Sea
Plain of Sharon
Beth-shan
Trade center
Gerasa (Jerash)
Samaria
Shechem
Jordan
Metalwork
Trade-caravan center
Succoth
Gilead
IRON
Joppa
Port city
Rabbah (Philadelphia)
Caravan center
Bethel
Jericho (O.T.)
Ashdod
Jerusalem
S
Worship center
Salt
Gaza
Lachish
Judea
Hebron
Trade-caravan center
Metalwork
Gerar
En-gedi
Sea
Arnon
Beer-sheba
Kir-hareseth
S
Zoar
Zered
Negeb
Arabah
Kadesh-barnea
COPPER
Punon
Selected products shown:
Barley
Fish
Papyrus
IRON
Camels
Forests
Pomegranates
Cattle
Grapes
Salt
Date palm
Honey
Sheep
COPPER
Dyes
Olives
Textiles
Figs
Ores
Wheat
Elath
Port city

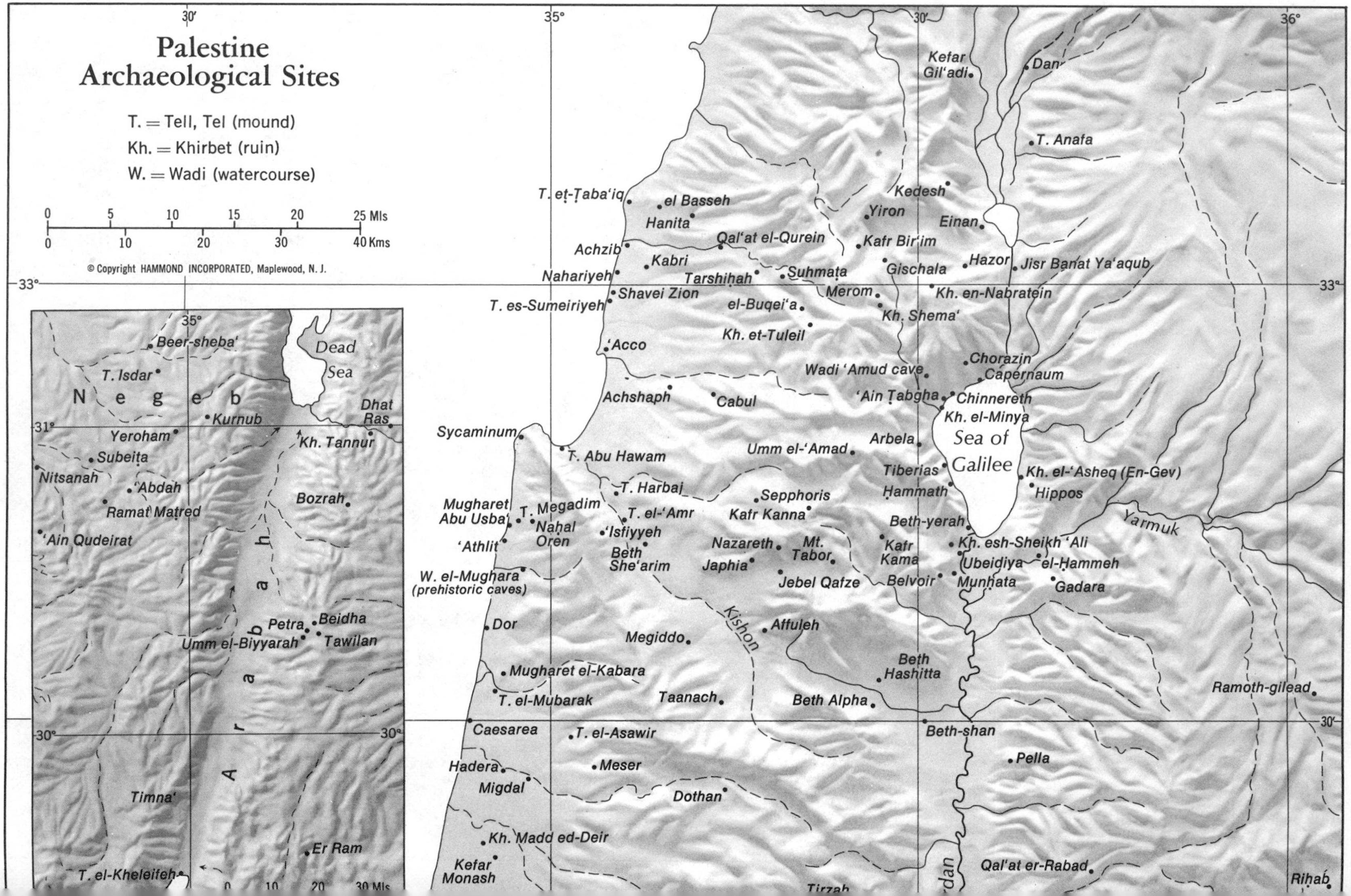
Palestine
Archaeological Sites
T. = Tell, Tel (mound)
Kh. = Khirbet (ruin)
W. = Wadi (watercourse)
0 5 10 15 20 25 Mls
0 10 20 30 40 Kms
© Copyright HAMMOND INCORPORATED, Maplewood, N. J.
Kefar Gil'adi
Dan
T. Anafa
T. et-Taba'iq
el Basseh
Hanita
Kedesh
Yiron
Einan
Qal'at el-Qurein
Kafr Bir'im
Achzib
Kabri
Hazor
Jisr Banat Ya'aqub
Nahariyeh
Tarshihah
Suhmata
Gischala
Shavei Zion
Merom
Kh. en-Nabratein
T. es-Sumeiriyeh
el-Buqei'a
Kh. Shema'
Kh. et-Tuleil
'Acco
Chorazin
Wadi 'Amud cave
Capernaum
Achshaph
Cabul
'Ain Tabgha
Chinnereth
Kh. el-Minya
Sycaminum
Arbela
Sea of Galilee
T. Abu Hawam
Umm el-'Amad
Tiberias
Kh. el-'Asheq (En-Gev)
Hippos
T. Harbaj
Sepphoris
Hammath
Mugharet Abu Usba
T. Megadim
T. el-'Amr
Kafr Kanna
Beth-yerah
Yarmuk
Nahal Oren
'Isfiyyeh
'Athlit
Beth She'arim
Nazareth
Mt. Tabor
Kafr Kama
Kh. esh-Sheikh 'Ali
Ubeidiya
el-Hammeh
W. el-Mughara
(prehistoric caves)
Japhia
Jebel Qafze
Belvoir
Munhata
Gadara
Dor
Kishon
Affuleh
Megiddo
Beth Hashitta
Mugharet el-Kabara
T. el-Mubarak
Taanach
Beth Alpha
Ramoth-gilead
Caesarea
T. el-Asawir
Beth-shan
Pella
Hadera
Meser
Migdal
Dothan
Kh. Madd ed-Deir
Kefar Monash
Jordan
Qal'at er-Rabad
Tirzah
Rihab
Beer-sheba'
Dead Sea
T. Isdar
Negeb
Kurnub
Dhat Ras
Yeroham
Kh. Tannur
Subeita
Nitsanah
'Abdah
Bozrah
Ramat Matred
'Ain Qudeirat
Arabah
Petra
Beidha
Umm el-Biyyarah
Tawilan
Timna'
Er Ram
T. el-Kheleifeh
0 10 20 30 Mls
30'
35°
36°
33°
31°
30°

T. Qudadi
T. el-Qasileh
Aphek (T. Ras el-'Ain)
Gath-rimmon
Bene Barak
Joppa
Shiloh
Mugharet Abu Shinjeh
32°
Holon
Ben Shemen
Shuqba
Dhahr Mirzbaneh
T. Abu Habil
Rabbah
Dhahrat Humraiyeh
Lod
Bethel
Mesad Hashavyahu
Minat Nebi Rubin
el-Jisr
Ramleh
Kh. Ruddana
Ai
'Araq el-Emir
'Ain ed-Duq
Gilgal
Eltekeh? (T. esh Shallaf)
Mizpah
Salbit
Deir el-Quruntul
Jericho, O.T.
Jericho
Kalandia
Deir el-Qilt
Gezer
el-Qubeibeh
Deir Mar Jiryis
Jericho, N.T.
T. Iktanu
T. el-Kheidar, T. Mor
Emmaus
Qaryat el-'Inab
Gibeon
Gibeah
Teleilat el-Ghassul
Heshbon
Azotus-Paralius
Timnah
Jerusalem
Bethany
Khan el-Ahmar
'Ain Karim
Qumran caves
Mt. Pisgah
Ashdod
Beth-shemesh
Manahath
Beth-Haccherem
Kh. Qumran
Kh. Mukhayyat
Bether
Beit Jimal
Bethlehem
Beit Sahur
Middin
En-Eglaim
Medeba
Azekah
Gath (T. es Safi)
Bethletepha
Kh. es-Siyar
Kh. el-Mird
Nibshan
Ma'in
T. Sippor
Kh. el-Hubeileh
Herodium
Ashkelon
Moresheth-gath
Kh. Asideh
Umm Qatafa (prehistoric caves)
Kh. Iskander
Beth Guvrin
Mareshah
Beth-zur
Murabba'at caves
Lachish
Kh. el-Kom
'Eglon? (T. el-Hesi)
Dead
Mamre
Khalit el-Ful
Gaza
30'
T. Najila
'Eglon? (T. 'Aitun)
'Ain el-Ma'mudiyeh
Dibon
'Aroer
Beth-eglaim
En-gedi
Arnon
T. Beit Mirsim
Debir (Kh. Rabud)
T. er-Ruqeish
Ziklag? (T. esh-Sheri'ah)
Nahal Hever caves (Cave of the Letters)
Sea
Yurza
T. Halif
Eshtemoa'
Balu'a
Nahal Mishmar caves
Masada
Sharuhen
'Arad (T. 'Arad)
Beer-sheba'
T. Abu Matar
Bab edh-Dhra'
Kh. Bitar
'Arad (T. el-Milh)
'Ader
Kh. el-Mishash
Kir-hareseth
30'
35°
Longitude East of Greenwich
36°

Hazor Provincial capital
Lod District capital
Jabneh Secondary district capital
Haipha Town
Tyre Autonomous city
Tyrian territory
Sidonian territory
Territory of independent cities
DAMASCUS
Tyre
Achzib
Hazor
Acco
Haipha
ASHTAROTH KARNAIM
Karnaim
HAURAN
GALILEE
Nazareth
Dor
Megiddo
Tower of Abdashtart
Beth Shean
Narbatah
GILEAD
Irbid
Samaria
Shechem
Rishpuna
SAMARIA
Acrabbah
Joppe
Arimathaea
Ono
Hadid
Lod
AMMON
Aphairema
Lower Beth Horon
Magdal senaa
Rabbath Ammon
Birtha
Jabneh
Upper Beth Horon
Mizpah
Gibeon
Jericho
ASHDOD
Ashdod
Beth Cerem
Jerusalem
Netophah
Zanoah
JUDAH
Adullam
Ashkelon
Mareshah
Keilah
Tekoa
Beth Zur
Gaza
Lachish
Hebron
EDOMITES
Dead Sea
NABATAEAN ARABS
N. Arnon
Beersheba
Karak
N. Zered
1:2.000.000

ARCHAEOLOGICAL SITES

The following alphabetical list contains each archaeological site shown on the preceding map, plus ancient or modern alternative designations which may be encountered in secondary literature.

Key to Spellings

Italic type: Arabic place name, e.g.. *'Abdah*
Roman type: ancient place name, e.g., Eboda
[Brackets]: modern Hebrew place name (if different from other designations), e.g., ['Avdat]
CAPITAL LETTERS: IDB [S] entry (often with phonetic symbols added, e.g., 'ACCO)
(Parentheses): nearby village by which a site is sometimes identified, e.g., (Abu Ghosh)

/: alternative spellings, e.g., 'Araq el-Emir/'Iraq el-Amir
//: alternative identifications, e.g., T. Aiṭun//T. el-Ḥesi
?: possible identification, e.g., T. Kison?

Abbreviations

T.: Tell (Arabic); Tell (Hebrew) =mound
Kh.: Kirbat (Khirbet) =ruin
Ḥ.: Ḥorvat=ruin

The spellings used here are popular ones, although variations will often be encountered in secondary literature, e.g., ḫ/ḥ/ch/kh; e/eh/a/ah; b/bh/v; f/p/ph; k/ḳ/q; ṣ/ts/z/tz; i/e; o/u; al/el; ain/ein/en.

'Abdah: Eboda; ['Avdat]
(Abu Ghosh): Qaryat el-'Inab
(Abu Shusheh): see GEZER
'ACCO: Ptolemais; Acre; *T. el-Fukhkhar;* [T. 'Akko]
ACHSHAPH: *T. Kisan;* [T. Kison]?
ACHZIB: *T. ez-Zib*
Acre: see 'ACCO
'Ader
'Affuleh: ['Afula]
'AI: *et-Tell*
'Ain ed-Duq: [Na 'aran]; Noaran; NA'ARAH?
'Ain el-Jabra
'Ain el-Ma'mudiyeh
'Ain Feshkha: 'EN-EGLAIM?
'Ain Karim: ['En Kerem]
('Ain Shems): see BETH-SHEMESH
'Ain Qudeirat: KADESH-BARNEA'?
'Ain Ṭabgha: Heptapegon; *Birkat 'Ali edh-Dhahir;* ['En-Sheva']
'Amman: see RABBAH
Ammathus: see *Ḥammam Ṭabariyeh*
'Amwas: see EMMAUS
ANTIPATRIS: see APHEḲ in Sharon
APHEḲ in Sharon: ANTIPATRIS; *Ras el-'Ain*
APHEḲ in Transjordan: *Kh. el-'Asheq;* ['En-Gev]?// *(Fiq.)*?
Appolonia: see Rishpon
'ARAD, Canaanite: *T. el-Milḥ;* [T. Malḥata]
'ARAD, Israelite: *T. 'Arad*
'Ara'ir: see 'AROER
'Araq el-Emir/'Iraq el-Amir
('Araq el-Menshiyeh): see *T. el-'Areini*
ARBELA in Galilee: *Kh. 'Irbid*
'AROER in Moab: *'Ara'ir*
ASCALON/ASHḲELON: *'Asqalan*
ASHDOD: Azotus; *Isdud/Esdud;* see also Azotus Paralius
[Ashdod-Yam]: see Azotus Paralius
'Asqalan: see ASCALON
['Atar ha-Ro'ah]
'At(h)lit
'Auja el-Ḥafir: see [Nitsanah]
['Avdat]: *'Abdah*
'AZEḲAH: *T. ez-Zakariyeh*
[Azor]: *Yazur*
Azotus: see ASHDOD
Azotus Paralius: *Minat el-Qala';* [Ashdod-Yam]; see also ASHDOD
Bab edh-Dhra'
Baca: *el-Buqei'a*
Balu'a
Bar'am: *Kafr Bir'im*
(Battir): see BETHER
BEER-SHEBA': *T. es-Saba'*
Beidha: (PETRA)
Beisan: see BETH-SHAN
Beit Alfa: [Beth Alpha]
Beit 'Arif: [Ben Shemen]
Beitin: see BETHEL
Beit Jibrin: see Beth-Guvrin
Beit Hashiṭṭa: [Beth-Hashiṭṭa]
Beit Laḥm: BETHLEḤEM
Beit Nattif: Bethletepha; [Beth-Naṭiph]
Beit Saḥur: (BETHLEḤEM)
Belvoir: [Kokhav-ha-Yarden]
BENE-BERAḲ: *Ibn Ibraq*
[Ben Shemen]: *Beit 'Arif*
[Beth-Alpha]: *Beit Alfa*
BETHANY: *el-'Azariyeh*
[Bethar]: see BETHER
BETH-AVEN: *see* BETHEL
Beth-'Eglaim: *T. el-'Ajjul*
BETHEL: LUZ; BETH-AVEN; *Beitin*
BETHER: *Kh. el-Yahud; (Battir);* [Bethar]
Beth-Guvrin: Eleutheropolis; *Beit Jibrin*
BETH-HACCHEREM: *Kh. Ṣaliḥ;* [Ramat-Raḥel]
[Beth-Hashiṭṭa]: *Beit Hashiṭṭa*
BETHLEḤEM in Judah: *Beit Laḥm;* see also *Beit Saḥur*
Bethletepha: see *Beit Nattif*
[Beth-Naṭiph]: see *Beit Nattif*
BETH-SHAN: Scythopolis; *T. el-Ḥuṣn; (Beisan)*
Beth-She'arim: *Sheikh Abreiq*
BETH-SHEMESH in Judah: *T. er-Rumeileh; ('Ain Shems)*
Bethṣura: see BETH-ZUR
[Beth-Yeraḥ]: *Kh. Kerak;* Philoteria
BETH-ZUR: Bethṣura; *Kh. Ṭubeiqah*
Birkat 'Ali edh-Dhahir: see *'Ain Ṭabgha*
(Battir): see BETHER

BOZRAH in Edom: *Buṣeira*
Buṣeira: BOZRAH

CABUL: *Kabul*
CAESAREA in Palestine: *Qeisariyeh*
CANA: *Kafr Kanna?*
CAPERNAUM: *T. Ḥum;* [Kefar Naḥum]
CHINNERETH/CHINNEROTH: *Kh. el-ʿUreimeh/ʿOreimeh;* [T. Kinrot]
CHORAZIN: *Kh. Kerazeh*

DAN: LAISH; *T. el-Qaḍi*
DEBIR in Judah: *Kh. Rabud*
Deir el-Qilt
Deir el-Quruntul
Deir Mar Jiryis
Dhahr Mirzbaneh
Dhahrat Ḥumraiyeh: [Ḥ. Ḥumra]
Dhat Ras
Dhiban: DIBON
DIBON: *Dhiban*
Diocaesarea: see *Ṣaffuriyeh*
DOR: Dora; *eṭ-Ṭanṭurah*
Dora: see DOR
DOTHAN: *T. Duthan/Dotha*

Eboda: see *ʿAbdah*
ʿEGLON: *T. ʿAiṭun // T. el-Ḥesi?*
ʿEinan/ʿEnan: *Mallaḥa*
el-ʿAzariyeh: BETHANY
el-Basseh
el-Bireh: Kh. Ruddana
el-Buqeiʿa: Baca
Eleutheropolis: see Beth-Guvrin
el-Ghazzeh: GAZA
el-Ḥammeh/Ḥamma: see Emmatha
el-Jib: GIBEON
el-Jish: see Gischala
el-Jisr
el-Kerak/Kerak: KIR-HARESETH
el-Khalaṣe: Ḥalutsa
el-Khiam
el-Malḥah: MANAḤATH
el-Mughara
el-Qubeibeh
el-Quds: JERUSALEM
ELTEḲEH: *T. esh-Shallaf;* [T. Shalaph]
Emmatha: *el-Ḥammeh/Ḥamma;* [Ḥamat Gader]; (GADARA)
EMMAUS: Nicopolis; *ʿAmwas/ʿImwas?*
ʿEN-EGLAIM: *ʿAin Feshkha?*
ʿEN-GEDI: *T. ej-Jurn;* [T. Goren]
[ʿEn-Gev]: see APHEḲ in Transjordan
[ʿEn-Kerem]: *ʿAin Karim*
en-Naṣireh: NAZARETH
[ʿEn-Shevaʿ]: *ʿAin Ṭabgha*
Esdud: see ASHDOD
ESHTEMOAʿ: *es-Samuʿ*
es-Samuʿ: ESHTEMOAʿ
es-Sebbeh: MASADA
eṭ-Ṭanṭurah: see DOR
et-Tell: ʿAI
ez-Zib: see ACHZIB

Frank Mountain: see HERODIUM

GADARA: *Umm Qeis; Muqeis;* see also Emmatha
GATH of the Philistines: *T. eṣ-Ṣafi;* [T. Zafit]?
GATH-RIMMON: *T. ej-Jerisheh;* [T. Gerisa]
GAZA: *el-Ghazzeh*
Gazara: see GEZER
Georgiopolis: see LOD
GERASA: *Jerash*
GERIZIM, MOUNT: *Jebel eṭ-Ṭur;* also *T. er-Ras*
[Gesher Benoth Yaʿaḳov]: *Jisr Banat Yaʿaqub*
GEZER: Gazara; *T. Jazer; (Abu Shusheh)*
Ghrubba
GIBEAH: *T. el-Ful*
GIBEON: *el-Jib*
GILGAL near Jericho: *Kh. el-Mafjar?*
Gischala: *el-Jish;* [Gush Ḥalav]
[Gush Ḥalav]: see Gischala

[Ḥadera]
Ḥaifa: see Sycaminium
Ḥalutsa: *el-Khalaṣe*
[Ḥamat Gader]: see Emmatha
Ḥamat-TIBERIAS: see *Ḥammam Ṭabariyeh*
[Ḥame Ṭeveriyah]: see *Ḥammam Ṭabariyeh*
Ḥammam Ṭabariyeh: Ammathus; ḤAMMATH; [Ḥame Ṭeveriyah]; also called Ḥamat-TIBERIAS
ḤAMMATH: see *Ḥammam Ṭabariyeh*
[Ḥanita]: *Kh. Ḥanuta*
[Ḥar ha-Qefiṣa]: see *Jebel Qafze*
HAROSHETH-HAGOIIM: *T. el-ʿAmr;* [T. Gevaʿ Shemen]
ḤAZOR: *T. el-Qedaḥ*
(ḤEBRON): see *Kh. el-Ḳom;* see *Khalit el-Ful;* see *Jebel Qaʿaqir*
ḤELḲATH: *T. Harbaj;* [T. Regev]?
Heptapegon: see *ʿAin Ṭabgha*
HERODIUM: *Jebel Fureidis;* Frank Mountain
Ḥeshban: ḤESHBON
ḤESHBON: *Ḥeshban*
Hippos: Susitha; *Qalʿat el-Ḥuṣn*
[Ḥolon]
[Ḥorvat ʿAmmudim]: *Umm el-ʿAmad*
[Ḥorvat Beter]: *Kh. Biṭar*
[Ḥorvat Ḥumra]: *Dhahrat Ḥumraiyeh*
[Ḥorvat Minḥa] *Munḥata*
[Ḥorvat Nevorayah]: *Kh. en-Nabratein*
Hyrcania: *Kh. el-Mird*

Ibn Ibraq: BENE-BERAḲ
ʿImwas: see EMMAUS
Isbeita: see *Subeiṭa*
Isdud: see ASHDOD
ʿIsfiyyeh

Jaffa: see JOPPA
Jalamet el-ʿAsafna
JAPHIA in Zebulon: *Yafa*
Jebel eṭ-Ṭur: see GERIZIM, MOUNT
Jebel eṭ-Ṭur: TABOR, MOUNT
Jebel Fureidis: HERODIUM
Jebel Qaʿaqir: (ḤEBRON)
Jabel Qafze: [Ḥar ha-Qefiṣa]; [Qedumim]
Jerash: GERASA
JERICHO, OT: *T. es-Sulṭan*
JERICHO, NT: *Tulul Abu el-Alayiq*
JERUSALEM: *el-Quds*
Jisr Banat Yaʿaqub: [Gesher Benoth Yaʿaḳov]
JOPPA: *Jaffa/Yafa*

[Kabri]
Kabul: CABUL
KADESH-BARNEAʿ/KADESH: *ʿAin Qudeirat?*
Kafr Birʿim: Barʿam
Kafr Kama
Kafr Kanna: CANA?
Ḳalandia/Qalandia
ḲEDESH in Naphtali: *T. Qades;* [T. Qedesh]
[Kefar Gilʿadi]
[Kefar Monash]
[Kefar Naḥum]: see CAPERNAUM
Khalit el-Ful: (ḤEBRON)
Khan el-Aḥmar
Khirbet Abu Ṭabaq: MIDDIN
Kh. Asideh
Kh. Biṭar: [Ḥ. Beter]
Kh. el-ʿAsheq: see *APHEḲ* in Transjordan
Kh. el-Hubeileh
Kh. el-Ḳom: (ḤEBRON)
Kh. el-Mafjar: GILGAL?
Kh. el-Maqari: NIBSHAN?
Kh. el-Minya
Kh. el-Mishash: [T. Masos]
Kh. el-Mird: Hyrcania
Kh. el-Ureimeh/ʿOreimeh: see CHINNERETH
Kh. el-Yahud: see BETHER
Kh. en-Nabratein: [Ḥ. Nevoraya]
Kh. es-Siyar
Kh. esh-Sheikh ʿAli: [T. ʿEli]
Kh. esh-Sheikh Meisar: [Meser]
Kh. et-Tannur
Kh. et-Tuleil: Kh. Ras es-Suq; [T. Ḥarashim]
Kh. Faḥil: see PELLA
Kh. Ḥanuta: [Ḥanita]
Kh. Irbid in Galilee: ARBELA
Kh. Iskander
Kh. Kerak: see Beth-Yeraḥ
Kh. Kerazeh: CHORAZIN
Kh. Madd ed-Deir: [Maʿavaroth]
Kh. Mukayyat: NEBO
Kh. Musheyrifa: ([Rosh ha-Niqrah]); *T. eṭ-Ṭabaʿiq*
Kh. Qumran
Kh. Rabud: DEBIR
Kh. Ras es-Suq: see *Kh. et-Tuleil*
Kh. Ruddana: el-Bireh
Kh. Ṣaliḥ: see BETH-HACCHEREM
Kh. Shemaʿ
Kh. Ṭubeiqah: see BETH-ZUR
ḲIR: see ḲIR-ḤARESETH
ḲIR-ḤARESETH=ḲIR(?): Ḳir-Heres; *el-Kerak*
[Kokhav ha-Yarden]: Belvoir
Kurnub: Mampsis; [Mamshit]

LACHISH: *T. ed-Duweir*
LAISH: see DAN
LOD: Lydda; Georgiopolis
LUZ: see BETHEL
Lydda: see LOD

[Maʿavaroth]: *Kh. Madd ed-Deir*
Madeba: MEDEBA
Maʿin
Mallaḥa: ʿEinan
Mampsis: see *Kurnub*
MAMRE: *Ramat el-Khalil*
[Mamshit]: see *Kurnub*
MANAḤATH: *el-Malḥah*
MAREṢHAH: Marisa; *T. Sandaḥannah*
Marisa: see MARESHAH
MASADA: *es-Sebbeh*
MEDEBA: *Madeba*
Meirun/Meiron: MEROM
MEGIDDO: *T. el-Mutesellim*
MEROM: *Meirun/Meiron*
[Meṣad-Ḥashavyahu]
[Meser]: *Kh. esh-Sheikh Meisar*
MIDDIN: *Kh. Abu Ṭabaq*
Migdal: *T. edh-Dhurur;* [T. Zeror]
Minat el-Qalaʿ: see Azotus Paralius
Minat Nebi Rubin: ([Yavneh-Yam])
MIZPAH: *T. en-Naṣbeh*
Montfort: *Qalʿat el-Qurein*
MORESHETH-GATH: *T. Judeideh;* [T. Goded]
Mugharet Abu Shinjeh: Wadi Daliyeh Cave
Mugharet Abu Uṣbaʿ

Mugharet el-Kebara
Munei'iye: [Timna' in the 'Arabah]
Munhata: [Ḥ. Minḥa]
Murabba'at, Wadi Caves

NA'ARAH: see *'Ain ed-Duq*
Na'aran: see *'Ain ed-Duq*
[Naḥal Ḥever]: *Wadi Ḥabra* caves
[Naḥal Mishmar]: *Wadi Maḥras* caves
[Naḥal Oren]
[Nahariyeh]
NAZARETH: *en-Naṣireh*
NEBO: *Kh. Mukayyat*
Nessana: see [Nitsanah]
NIBSHAN: *Kh. el-Magari*?
Nicopolis: see EMMAUS
[Nitsanah]: Nessana; *'Auja el-Ḥafir*
Noaran: *see 'Ain ed-Duq*

PETRA: Rekem/Raqmu; see also *Umm el-Biyyarah* and *Beidha*
Peḥel: see PELLA
PELLA: *Kh. Faḥil;* Peḥel
Philadelphia: see RABBAH
PISGAH, MOUNT: Ras Siyaghah?
Ptolemais: see 'ACCO
Philoteria: see [Beth-Yeraḥ]

Qal'at el-Ḥuṣn: see Hippos
Qal'at el-Qurein: Montfort
Qal'at er-Rabad
Qaryat el 'Inab: (Abu Ghosh)
[Qedumim]: see *Jebel Qafze*
Qeisariyeh: CAESAREA

RABBAH/RABBAT-'AMMON: Philadelphia; *'Amman*
Ramat el-Khalil: MAMRE
[Ramat-Maṭred]
[Ramat-Raḥel]: see BETH-HACCHEREM
Ramleh: [Ramlah]
RAMOTH-GILEAD: *T. Ramith*
Raqmu: see PETRA
Ras el-'Ain: see APHEḲ in Sharon
Ras Siyaghah: PISGAH, MOUNT?
Rekem: see PETRA
Riḥab
Rishpon: Appolonia; *T. Arsuf;* [T. Resheph]
([Rosh ha-Niqrah]): *T. eṭ-Ṭaba'iq; Kh. Musheyrifa*

Ṣaffuriyeh: Sepphoris; Diocaesarea
Salbiṭ: [Sha'alvim]
SAMARIA: *Sebasṭiyeh;* Sebaste; [Shomron]
Scythopolis: see BETH-SHAN
Sebaste: see SAMARIA
Sebasṭiyeh: see SAMARIA
Seilun: SHILOH
Sepphoris: see *Ṣaffuriyeh*
[Sha'alvim]: see *Salbiṭ*
[Shavei Zion]
Sharuḥen: *T. Far'ah*
SHECHEM: *T. Balaṭah*
Sheikh Abreiq: Beth-She'arim
SHILOH: *Seilun*
[Shivṭa]: see Isbeita
Shomron: see SAMARIA
Shuqba
Subeiṭa: Isbeita; [Shivṭa]
SUCCOTH: *T. Deir 'Allah*
Suḥmata
Susitha: see Hippos
Sycaminium: *T. es-Samak;* Ḥaifa; [T. Shiqmona]

TA'ANACH: *T. Ta'annak/Ti'innik*
Ṭabgha: see *'Ain Ṭabgha*
TABOR, MOUNT: *Jebel eṭ-Ṭur*
Ṭanṭurah: see DOR
[Tarshiḥah]
Tawilan
[Tel 'Akko]: see 'ACCO
[Tel Anafa]: *T. el-Akhdar*
[T. Baṭash]: see TIMNAH
[Tel 'Eli]: *Kh. esh-Sheikh 'Ali*
[Tel Esur]: *T. el-Asawir*
[Tel Gamma]: see *Tell Jemme*
[Tel "Gath"]: see *Tell el-'Areini*
[Tel Gerisa]: see GATH-RIMMON
[Tel Geva' Shemen]: see HAROSHETH-HAGOIIM
[Tell Goded]: see MORESHETH-GATH
[Tel Goren]: see 'EN-GEDI
[Tel Ḥalif]: *Tell Khuweilifa*
[Tel Ḥarashim]: see *T. et-Tuleil*
[Tel Isdar]
[Tel Kinrot]: see CHINNERETH
[Tel Kison]: see ACHSHAPH
[Tel Malḥata]: see 'ARAD, Canaanite
[Tel Masos]: *Kh. el-Mishash*
[Tel Megadim]
[Tel Mor]: *Tell el-Kheidar*
[Tel Nagila]: *T. Najila*
[Tel Poleg]
[Tel Qasile]: *T. el-Qasileh*
[Tel Qedesh]: see ḲEDESH
[Tel Regev]: see HELḲATH
[Tel Resheph]: see Rishpon
[Tel Sera']: see ZIKLAG
[Tel Shalaph]: see ELTEḲEH
[Tel Shiqmona]: see Sycaminium
[Tel Ṣippor]: *T. eṭ-Ṭuyur*
[Tel Zafit]: see GATH
[Tel Zeror]: see Migdal
Teleilat el-Ghassul
Tell Abu Ḥabil
Tell Abu Ḥawam
Tell Abu Maṭar
Tell 'Aiṭun: see 'EGLON
Tell 'Arad: see 'ARAD, Israelite
Tell Arsuf: see Rishpon
Tell Balaṭah: SHECHEM
Tell Beit Mirsim
Tell Deir 'Allah: SUCCOTH
Tell Dotha/Duthan: DOTHAN
Tell ed-Duweir: LACHISH
Tell edh-Dhurur: see Migdal
Tell ej-Jerisheh: see GATH-RIMMON
Tell ej-Jurn: see 'EN-GEDI
Tell el-'Ajjul: Beth-'Eglaim
Tell el-Akhdar: [T. Anafa]
Tell el-'Amr: see HAROSHETH-HAGOIIM
Tell el-'Areini: ('Araq el-Menshiyeh); T. Sheikh Aḥmed el-'Areini; [T. "Gath"]
Tell el-Asawir: [T. Esur]
Tell el-Baṭashi: see TIMNAH in Judah
Tell el-Fukhkhar: see 'ACCO
Tell el-Ful: GIBEAH
Tell el-Ḥesi: see 'EGLON
Tell el-Ḥuṣn: see BETH-SHAN
Tell el-Kheidar: [T. Mor]
TELL EL-KHELEIFEH
Tell el-Menshiyeh: see *T. el-'Areini*
Tell el-Milḥ: see 'ARAD, Canaanite
Tell el-Mubarak
Tell el-Mutesellim: MEGIDDO
Tell el-Qadi: see DAN
Tell el-Qasileh: [T. Qasile]
Tell el-Qedaḥ: See ḤAZOR
Tell el-'Ureimeh: see CHINNERETH
Tell en-Naṣbeh: MIZPAH
Tell er-Ras: see GERIZIM, MT.
Tell er-Rumeileh: BETH-SHEMESH
Tell er-Ruqeish
Tell esh-Shallaf: see ELTEḲEH
Tell esh-Sheri'ah: see ZIKLAG
Tell esh-Shuni: T. Qudadi
Tell eṣ-Ṣaba': BEER-SHEBA'
Tell eṣ-Ṣafi: see GATH of the Philistines
Tell es-Sa'idiyeh: see ZARETHAN
Tell es-Sulṭan: JERICHO, OT
Tell es-Samak: see Sycaminium
Tell es-Sumeiriyeh
Tell eṭ-Ṭaba'iq: ([Rosh ha-Niqrah]); *Kh. Musheyrifa*
Tell et-Tuleil: [T. Harashim]
Tell eṭ-Ṭuyur: [T. Sippor]
Tell ez-Zakariyeh: see 'AZEKAH
Tell ez-Zib: ACHZIB
Tell Far'ah/Fari'ah: TIRZAH
Tell Far'ah/Fara'ah: Sharuḥen
Tell Harbaj: see HELḲATH
Tell Ḥum: see CAPERNAUM
Tell Iktanu
Tell Jazer: see GEZER
Tell Jemme: Yurza?; [T. Gamma]
Tell Judeideh: see MORESHETH-GATH
Tell Kheidar: [T. MOR]
Tell Khuweilifa: [T. Ḥalif]
Tell Kisan: see ACHSHAPH
Tell Kudadi: see *Tell Qudadi*
Tell Makmish
Tell Najila: [T. Nagila]
Tell Qades: see ḲEDESH in Naphtali
Tell Qudadi/Kudadi: T. esh-Shuni
Tell Ras el-'Ain: see APHEḲ in Sharon
Tell Ramith: RAMOTH-GILEAD
Tell Sandaḥannah: see MARESHAH
Tell Sheikh Aḥmed el-'Areini: see *Tell el-'Areini*
Tell Ta'annak/Ti'innik: TA'ANACH
Tell Zakariyeh: see AZEḲAH
(TIBERIAS): see *Ḥammam Ṭabariyeh*
[Timna' in the 'Arabah]: *Munei'iye*
TIMNAH in Judah: *T. el-Baṭashi;* [T. Baṭash]
TIRZAH: *T. Far'ah/Fari'ah*
Tulul Abu el-Alayiq: see JERICHO, NT

'Ubeidiya
Umm el-'Amad: [Ḥ. 'Ammudim]
Umm el-Biyyarah: (PETRA)
Umm Qatafa
Umm Qeis; Muqeis: GADARA

Wadi 'Amud cave
Wadi Daliyeh cave: *Mugharet Abu Shinjeh*
Wadi Ḥabra caves: [Naḥal Ḥever]
Wadi Maḥras caves: [Naḥal Mishmar]

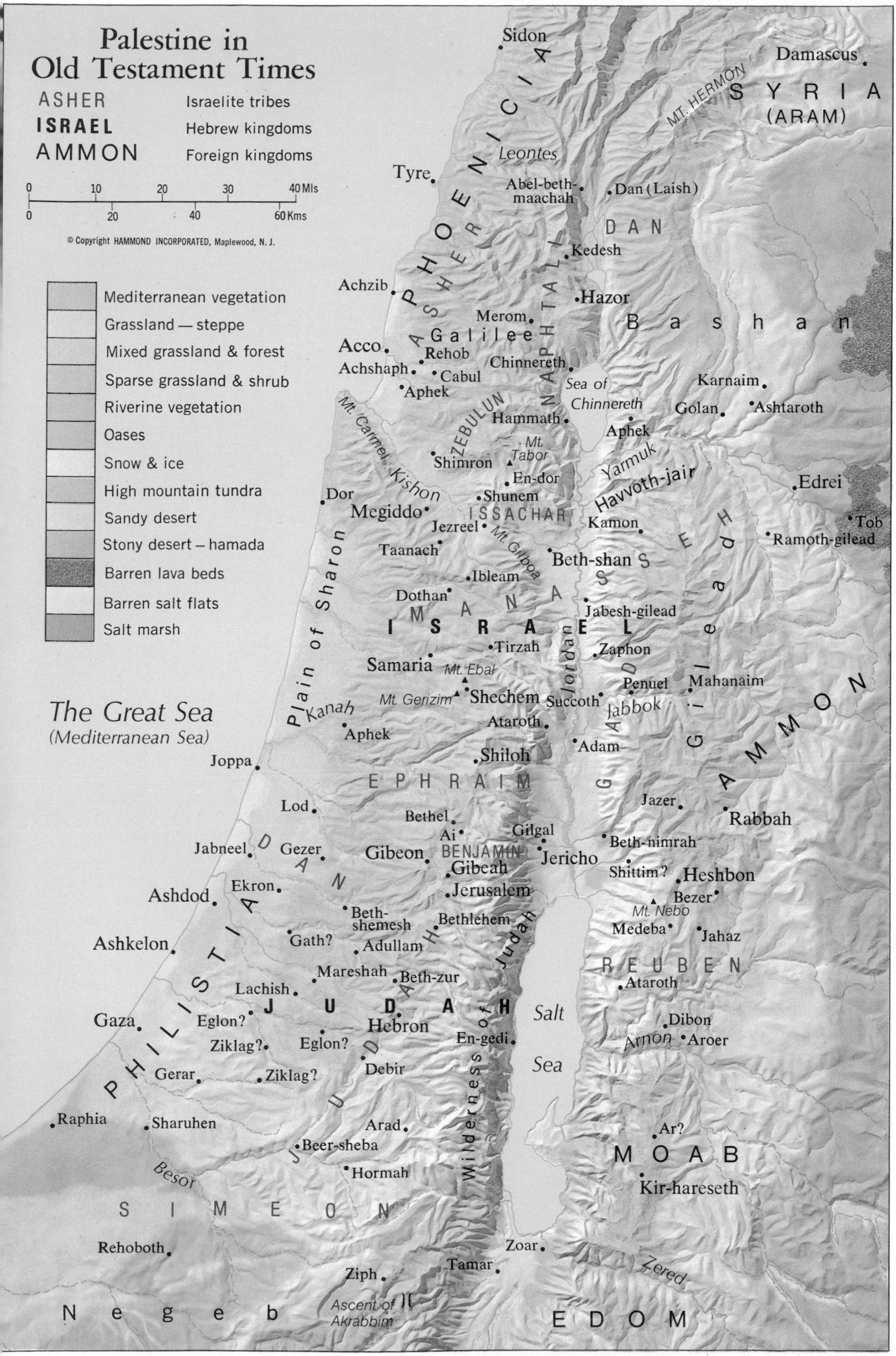
Palestine in Old Testament Times
ASHER Israelite tribes
ISRAEL Hebrew kingdoms
AMMON Foreign kingdoms
0 10 20 30 40 Mls
0 20 40 60 Kms
© Copyright HAMMOND INCORPORATED, Maplewood, N. J.
Mediterranean vegetation
Grassland — steppe
Mixed grassland & forest
Sparse grassland & shrub
Riverine vegetation
Oases
Snow & ice
High mountain tundra
Sandy desert
Stony desert – hamada
Barren lava beds
Barren salt flats
Salt marsh
The Great Sea
(Mediterranean Sea)
Sidon
Damascus
SYRIA
(ARAM)
MT. HERMON
PHOENICIA
Leontes
Tyre
Abel-beth-maachah
Dan (Laish)
DAN
ASHER
NAPHTALI
Kedesh
Achzib
Hazor
Merom
Galilee
Bashan
Acco
Rehob
Achshaph
Cabul
Chinnereth
Aphek
Sea of Chinnereth
Karnaim
Golan
Ashtaroth
Mt. Carmel
ZEBULUN
Hammath
Aphek
Mt. Tabor
Shimron
Yarmuk
En-dor
Kishon
Edrei
Dor
Shunem
Havvoth-jair
Megiddo
ISSACHAR
Tob
Jezreel
Kamon
Ramoth-gilead
Mt. Gilboa
Taanach
Beth-shan
MANASSEH
Plain of Sharon
Ibleam
Dothan
Jabesh-gilead
ISRAEL
Gilead
Tirzah
Zaphon
Jordan
Samaria
Mt. Ebal
Penuel
Mahanaim
Mt. Gerizim
Shechem
Succoth
Jabbok
Kanah
AMMON
Ataroth
GAD
Aphek
Adam
Joppa
Shiloh
EPHRAIM
Jazer
Lod
Rabbah
Bethel
Gilgal
Ai
Beth-nimrah
Jabneel
DAN
Gezer
Gibeon
BENJAMIN
Jericho
Gibeah
Shittim?
Heshbon
Ekron
Jerusalem
Ashdod
Bezer
Beth-shemesh
Mt. Nebo
Bethlehem
Medeba
Jahaz
Ashkelon
Gath?
Adullam
Judah
REUBEN
Mareshah
Beth-zur
Ataroth
Lachish
JUDAH
Salt Sea
Gaza
Eglon?
Hebron
Dibon
En-gedi
Arnon
Aroer
Ziklag?
Eglon?
PHILISTIA
Gerar
Ziklag?
Debir
Wilderness of Judah
Raphia
Sharuhen
Arad
Ar?
Beer-sheba
MOAB
Besor
Hormah
Kir-hareseth
SIMEON
Rehoboth
Zoar
Tamar
Zered
Ziph
Ascent of Akrabbim
Negeb
EDOM

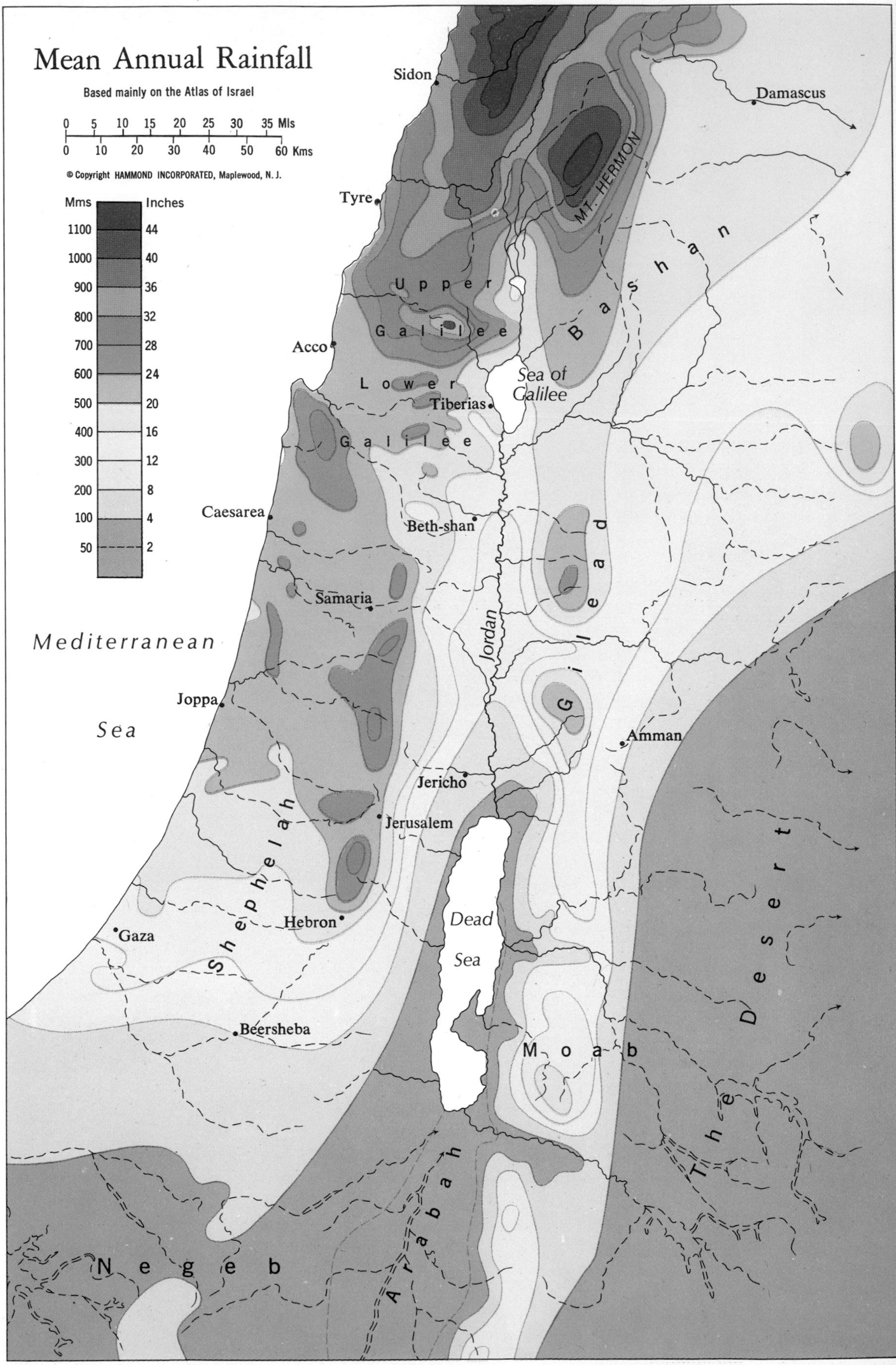

Mean Annual Rainfall
Based mainly on the Atlas of Israel
0 5 10 15 20 25 30 35 Mls
0 10 20 30 40 50 60 Kms
© Copyright HAMMOND INCORPORATED, Maplewood, N. J.
Mms
Inches
1100 44
1000 40
900 36
800 32
700 28
600 24
500 20
400 16
300 12
200 8
100 4
50 2
Sidon
Damascus
MT. HERMON
Tyre
Upper
Galilee
Acco
Bashan
Sea of Galilee
Lower
Tiberias
Galilee
Caesarea
Beth-shan
Gilead
Samaria
Mediterranean
Jordan
Joppa
Sea
Amman
Jericho
Jerusalem
Shephelah
Dead Sea
Hebron
Gaza
The Desert
Beersheba
Moab
Arabah
Negeb

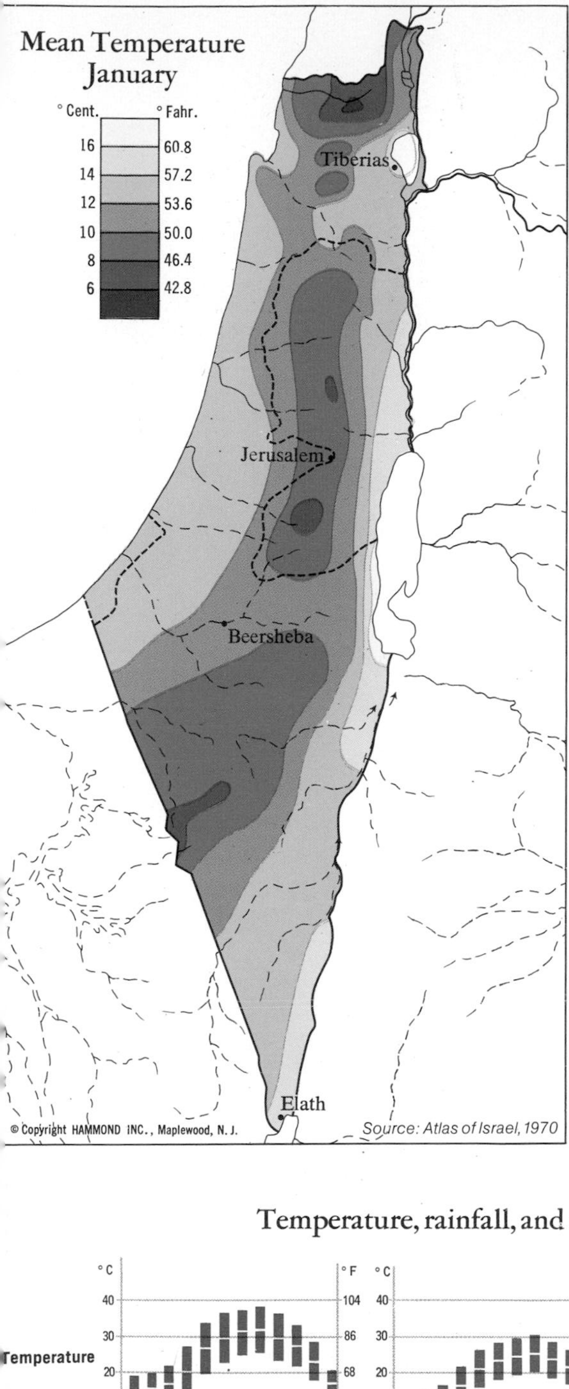

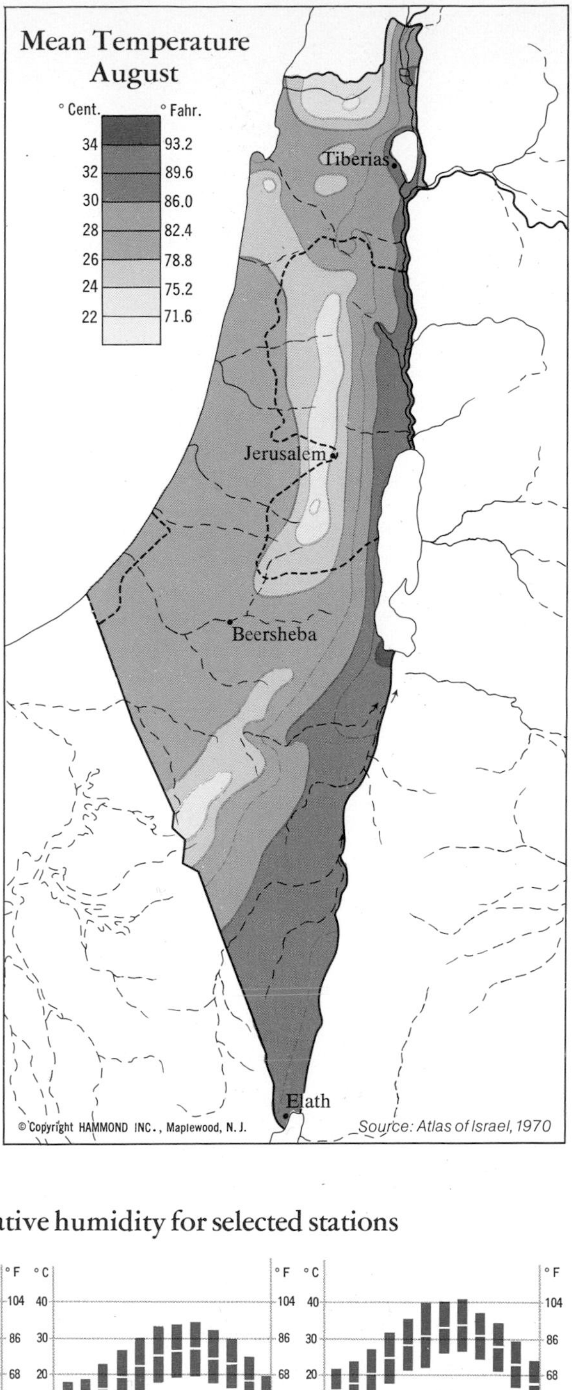

Temperature, rainfall, and relative humidity for selected stations

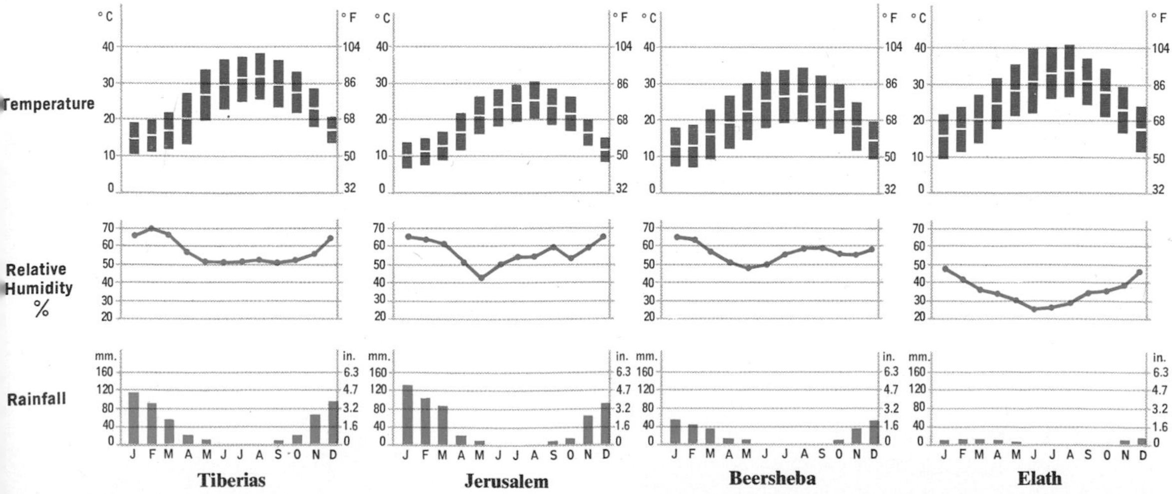

Sources: World Climatic Data, 1972; Statistical Abstract of Israel, 1969

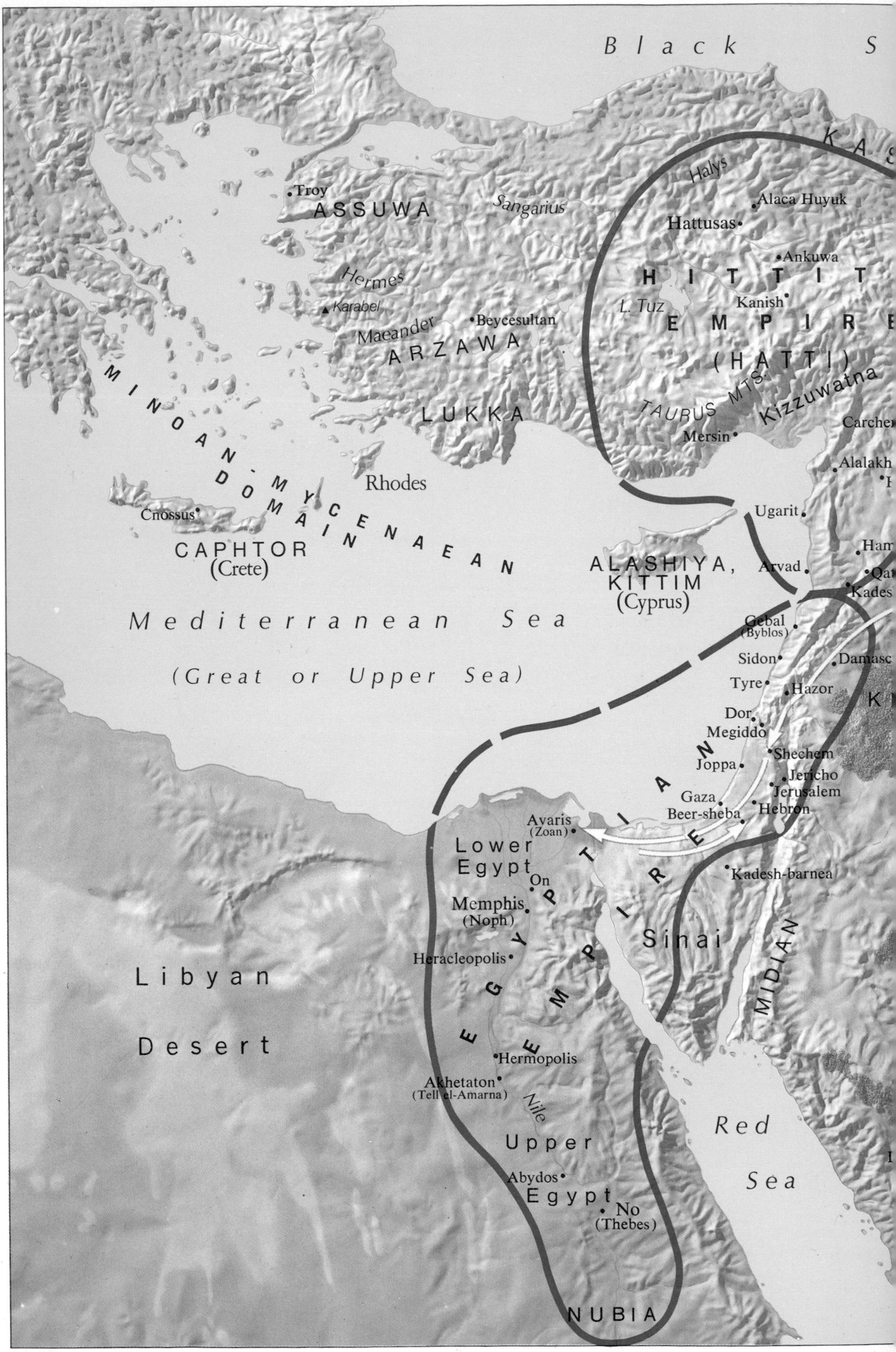
Black S
KAS
Halys
Alaca Huyuk
Hattusas
Ankuwa
HITTIT
EMPIRE
(HATTI)
L. Tuz
Kanish
Troy
ASSUWA
Sangarius
Hermes
Karabel
Maeander
Beycesultan
ARZAWA
LUKKA
TAURUS MTS.
Kizzuwatna
Carche
Mersin
Alalakh
MINOAN-MYCENAEAN
DOMAIN
Rhodes
Cnossus
CAPHTOR
(Crete)
Ugarit
ALASHIYA,
KITTIM
(Cyprus)
Arvad
Ham
Qa
Kades
Mediterranean Sea
(Great or Upper Sea)
Gebal
(Byblos)
Sidon
Damasc
Tyre
Hazor
Dor
Megiddo
Shechem
Joppa
Jericho
Jerusalem
Gaza
Beer-sheba
Hebron
Avaris
(Zoan)
Lower
Egypt
On
Kadesh-barnea
Memphis
(Noph)
Sinai
Heracleopolis
MIDIAN
Libyan
Desert
EGYPTIAN EMPIRE
Hermopolis
Akhetaton
(Tell el-Amarna)
Nile
Red
Sea
Upper
Abydos
Egypt
No
(Thebes)
NUBIA

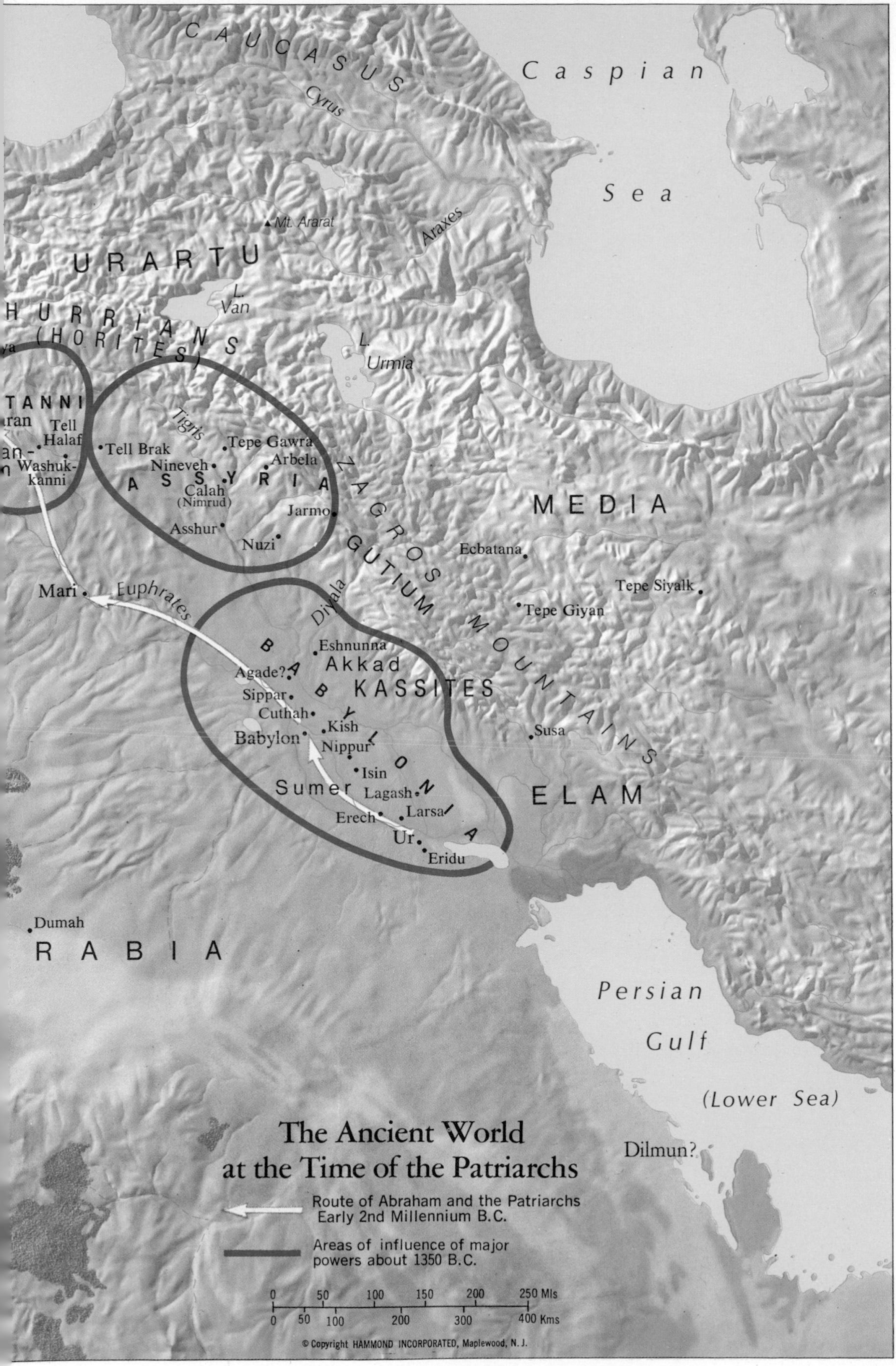
CAUCASUS
Cyrus
Caspian
Sea
Mt. Ararat
Araxes
URARTU
L. Van
HURRIANS
(HORITES)
L. Urmia
TANNI
Tell Halaf
Washuk-kanni
Tigris
Tell Brak
Tepe Gawra
Nineveh
Arbela
ASSYRIA
Calah (Nimrud)
Jarmo
Asshur
Nuzi
ZAGROS
GUTIUM
MOUNTAINS
MEDIA
Ecbatana
Tepe Siyalk
Tepe Giyan
Mari
Euphrates
Diyala
Eshnunna
Akkad
BABYLONIA
KASSITES
Agade?
Sippar
Cuthah
Kish
Babylon
Nippur
Isin
Susa
Sumer
Lagash
Larsa
ELAM
Erech
Ur
Eridu
Dumah
RABIA
Persian
Gulf
(Lower Sea)
Dilmun?
The Ancient World at the Time of the Patriarchs
Route of Abraham and the Patriarchs Early 2nd Millennium B.C.
Areas of influence of major powers about 1350 B.C.
0 50 100 150 200 250 Mls
0 50 100 200 300 400 Kms
© Copyright HAMMOND INCORPORATED, Maplewood, N. J.

Ister (Danube)
MOESIA
ILLYRICUM
Mesembria
Hebrus
Philippolis
THRACE
Dyrrhachium
MACEDONIA
Heraclea
Apollonia
Doberus
Philippi
Pella
Neapolis
Byzan
Perinthus
Cha
Beroea
Thessalonica
Amphipolis
Thasos
Doriscus
Apollonia
Chalcidice
Propontis
Epirus
Samothrace
Cyzicus
Mt. Olympus
Imbros
Abydos
Thessaly
Mysia
Lemnos
Ilium
Larisa
Troas (Alexandria)
Aegean Sea
Adramyttium
Assos
Pharsalus
Nicopolis
Actium
Mitylene
Lesbos
Pergamum
Euboea
Thyatria
Aetolia
A
Delphi
Adria
Patrae
ACHAIA
Smyrna
Sardis
Chios
Thebes
Lechaeum
Lydia
Phil
Eleusis
Sicyon
Athens
Metropolis
Corinth
Isthmia
Andros
Piraeus
Claros
Ephesus
Hi
Olympia
Cenchreae
Samos
Tralles
Panionium
Tenos
Magnesia
L
Priene
Trogyllium
Aphr
Miletus
Delos
Patmos
Didyma
Sparta
Paros
Caria
Naxos
Halicarnassus
Cos
Melos
Cnidus
Cythera
Rhod
Carpathos
Heracleon
Phoenix
Mt. Ida
Cnossus
C. Salmone
CRETE
Lasea
Cauda
(Claude)
Fair Havens
Mediterranean

Greece and Asia Minor
Mid-First Century A.D.
Provincial boundaries
Principal roads
0 50 100 150 200 Mls
0 100 200 300 Kms
© Copyright HAMMOND INCORPORATED, Maplewood, N. J.
Black Sea
Sea
Sinope
Amastris
BITHYNIA & PONTUS
Amisus
Side
Heraclea
Paphlagonia
Amasea
KINGDOM OF POLEMON
Nicomedia
Claudiopolis
Gangra
Halys
Comana Pontica
icaea
Sangarius
GALATIA
Ancyra
Tavium
rylaeum
Gordium
Cotiaeum
Pessinus
CAPPADOCIA
Appia
Nyssa
Lake Tatta
Caesarea (Mazaca)
Amorium
A
Comana Cappadociae
Arabissus
Nazianzus
rymnessus
Synnada
Archelais
Antioch
Lycaonia
COMMAGENE
rygia
Apamea
Tyana
Iconium
Pisidia
Lystra
Cilician Gates
Derbe
PAMPHYLIA
Laranda
CILICIA
Mopsuestia
Issus
&
ermessus
Perga
Aspendus
Tarsus
Attalia
Soli
Alexandria
Side
CIA
Corycus
Coracesium
Cilicia Trachea
Antioch
Seleucia
Selinus
Seleucia Pieria
Myra
Anemurium
SYRIA
Laodicea ad Mare
Apamea
Epiphania
Salamis
Tamassus
CYPRUS
Citium
Paphos
Limassol
Tripolis
Berytus
Sidon
Damascus

Palestine in New Testament Times
Political boundaries A.D. 6-34
Cities of the Decapolis
Fortresses
0 10 20 30 40 Mls
0 20 40 60 Kms
© Copyright HAMMOND INCORPORATED, Maplewood, N. J.
Phoenicia
Sidon
Sarepta
Leontes
Tyre
Ladder of Tyre
Ecdippa
Ptolemais
MT. LEBANON
MT. HERMON
Abila
ABILENE
Iturea
Damascus
SYRIA
Paneas
Caesarea Philippi
Ulatha
Gaulanitis
Batanea
Raphana
Cadasa
Gischala
Chorazin
Bethsaida-Julias
GALILEE
Capernaum
Cana
Magadan
Sea of Galilee
Asochis
Tiberias
Hippos
Sepphoris
Dion?
Yarmuk
Mt. Carmel
Nazareth
Mt. Tabor
Abila
Mediterranean Sea
Plain of Esdraelon
Nain
Gadara
Capitolias
Dora
Agrippina
Arbela
Caesarea
Scythopolis
DECAPOLIS
Narbata
Pella
Ginae
Salim
Aenon
Jordan
SAMARIA
Gerasa
Plain of Sharon
Sebaste (Samaria)
Neapolis
Mt. Ebal
Amathus
Apollonia
Mt. Gerizim
Sychar
Jabbok
Antipatris
Alexandrium
Joppa
Arimathea?
Phasaelis
Gadara
Ephraim
PEREA
Philadelphia
Lydda
Gophna
Archelais
Jamnia
Emmaus (Nicopolis)
Jericho
Betharamphtha (Livias, Julias)
Emmaus?
Cyprus
Esbus
Azotus
Jerusalem
Bethany
Qumran
Bethlehem
Hyrcania
Medeba
Ascalon
JUDEA
Herodium
Marisa
Bethsura
Callirrhoe
Machaerus
Agrippias
Gaza
Hebron
Engaddi
Arnon
Lake Asphaltitis (Dead Sea)
NABATEA
Masada
IDUMEA
Areopolis
Bersabe
Malatha
Charachmoba

THE OLD TESTAMENT

Genesis
Exodus
Leviticus
Numbers
Deuteronomy
Joshua
Judges
Ruth
I and II Samuel
I and II Kings
I and II Chronicles
Ezra
Nehemiah
Esther
Job
Psalms
Proverbs
Ecclesiastes
Song of Solomon
Isaiah
Jeremiah
Lamentations
Ezekiel
Daniel
Hosea
Joel
Amos
Obadiah
Jonah
Micah
Nahum
Habakkuk
Zephaniah
Haggai
Zechariah
Malachi

THE APOCRYPHA

I and II Esdras
Tobit
Judith
Additions to Esther
Wisdom of Solomon
Ecclesiasticus (Wisdom of Jesus the Son of Sirach)
Baruch
Letter of Jeremiah
Prayer of Azariah
Song of the Three Young Men
Susanna
Bel and the Dragon
Prayer of Manasseh
I and II Maccabees